4. European Community developments

The Draft European Union Bankruptcy Convention ("the Draft")

Purpose and problems

Although the European Union has so far failed in its attempts to establish a bankruptcy convention binding on all members, the preamble to the Draft records that "it is necessary" for strengthening the legal protection of persons established in the Community.

> "to determine the jurisdiction of [the] courts or authorities with regard to the intra-Community effects of insolvency proceedings, to create certain uniform conflict-of-laws rules for such proceedings, to ensure the recognition and enforcement of judgments given in such matters, to make provision for the possibility of opening secondary insolvency proceedings and to guarantee information for creditors and their right to lodge claims."

The Draft at present under discussion, like all its predecessors, is a long and complex document which purports to cover, in cross border circumstances, many of the eventualities which might arise in a purely domestic insolvent liquidation. In an ideal world, this would mean a single set of principles applicable throughout all the Member States for the resolution of the procedural and substantive disputes in those insolvency proceedings covered by the Convention. When it is noted that liquidation is simply a regime in which there might arise for resolution virtually any disputes that arise in solvent circumstances, it is immediately apparent how hopeless the task would be of constructing a single set of legal principles governing corporate bankruptcy and applicable throughout the territories of the European Union. Successful accomplishment of this task would require in substance no less than the unification of all the legal systems of all Member States.

The Draft recognises these limitations and does not strive towards the creation of a single set of principles, save insofar as they relate to the *fact* of the Convention. Indeed, it could be said that the Draft provides for structured disunity in the way it seeks to lay down which of the legal systems of the Member States would apply in any given circumstances.

Scope of the Draft

The Draft now under discussion covers all insolvencies except those concerning insurance undertakings, credit institutions and certain investment undertakings. It is at present largely restricted in its effect to liquidation, although further proposals are expected to widen the scope of the proposed Convention to include

EUROPEAN CORPORATE
INSOLVENCY

EUROPEAN CORPORATE INSOLVENCY

A Practical Guide

Foreword by

The Rt Hon The Lord Browne-Wilkinson

Lord of Appeal, United Kingdom

Edited by

Harry Rajak,

Professor of Law, University of Sussex

and

Peter Horrocks & Joe Bannister

Lovell White Durrant

John Wiley & Sons

Chichester • New York • Brisbane • Toronto • Singapore

This second edition published in the United Kingdom in 1995 by John Wiley & Sons Ltd,
Baffins Lane,
Chichester,
West Sussex,
PO19 1UD

National 01243 779777
International (+44) 1243 779777

First edition published in 1992 by Westminster Management Consultants Limited.

Other Wiley Editorial Offices

John Wiley & Sons Inc., 605 Third Avenue,
New York, NY 10158-0012, USA

John Wiley & Sons Inc., Editorial, Administration & Marketing,
7222 Commerce Center Drive, Suite 240,
Colorado Springs, CO 80919

Jacaranda Wiley Ltd, 33 Park Road, Milton,
Queensland 4064, Australia

John Wiley & Sons (Canada) Ltd, 22 Worcester Road,
Rexdale, Ontario M9W 1L1, Canada

John Wiley & Sons (SEA) Pte Ltd, 37 Jalan Pemimpin #05-04,
Block B, Union Industrial Building, Singapore 2057

British Library Cataloguing Publication Data

A catalogue record for this book is available from the British Library

ISBN 0471 95239 7

Typeset in 10/12pt Baskerville by Fotek, Letchworth, Hertfordshire
Printed and bound in Great Britain by Bookcraft (Bath) Ltd
This book is printed on acid-free paper responsibly manufactured from sustainable forestation, for
which at least two trees are planted for each one used for paper production.

CONTENTS

Pages

FOREWORD
The Rt Hon The Lord Browne-Wilkinson
  Lord of Appeal United Kingdom   *xi*

EDITOR'S ACKNOWLEDGEMENTS   *xiii*

Chapter 1
EUROPEAN CROSS BORDER INSOLVENCY DEVELOPMENTS
Professor Harry Rajak, University of Sussex   *1*

1.	Introduction	*3*
2.	A brief history of bankruptcy conventions	*5*
3.	The European Convention on Certain International Aspects of Bankruptcy	*6*
4.	European Community developments	*8*
5.	Conclusion	*20*

Chapter 2
CORPORATE INSOLVENCY LAW IN BELGIUM
Christian Van Buggenhout and William Nauwelaerts, Stibbe Simont
Marahan Duhot   *21*

1.	Introduction	*23*
2.	Corporations	*24*
3.	Survival of the insolvent corporation or its business: concordat judiciaire	*31*
4.	Termination of the corporation: bankruptcy and solvent liquidation	*38*
5.	Augmenting the assets of the insolvent corporation	*59*
6.	Public control over insolvent corporations	*63*

Chapter 3
CORPORATE INSOLVENCY LAW IN DENMARK
Erik Malberg and Christian Emmeluth,
Koch-Nielsen & Grønborg   *65*

1.	Introduction	*67*
2.	Corporations	*68*
3.	Survival of the insolvent corporation or its business	*75*
4.	Termination of the corporation: liquidation and dissolution	*88*
5.	Augmenting the assets of the insolvent corporation	*99*
6.	Public control over insolvent corporations	*106*

Chapter 4
CORPORATE INSOLVENCY LAW IN FRANCE
Moquet Borde & Associés, Revised by Lovell White Durrant   *111*

1.	Introduction	*113*
2.	Corporations	*115*
3.	Survival of the insolvent corporation or its business: rehabilitation in bankruptcy	*132*
4.	Termination of the corporation: liquidation	*155*
5.	Augmenting the assets of the insolvent corporation	*162*
6.	Public control over insolvent corporations	*167*

Chapter 5
CORPORATE INSOLVENCY LAW IN GERMANY
Kurt G Weil, DROSTE Rechtsanwälte and Graham J C Vincent,
Solicitor, Brussels   *171*

1.	Introduction	*173*
2.	Corporations	*178*
3.	Survival of the insolvent corporation or its business	*192*
4.	Termination of the corporation: voluntary liquidation and compulsory liquidation	*206*
5.	Augmenting the assets of the insolvent corporation	*239*
6.	Public control over insolvent corporations	*248*

Chapter 6
CORPORATE INSOLVENCY LAW IN GREECE
Costas Vainanidis, Vainanidis, Schina & Economou   *251*

1.	Introduction	*253*
2.	Corporations	*254*
3.	Survival of the insolvent corporation or its business	*271*

4.   Termination of the corporation: bankruptcy and solvent li-
     quidation   *275*
5.   Augmenting the assets of the insolvent corporation   *293*
6.   Public control over insolvent corporations   *295*

Chapter 7
CORPORATE INSOLVENCY LAW IN IRELAND
Francis E Sowman and Michael Quinn, William Fry   *299*

1.   Introduction   *301*
2.   Corporations   *302*
3.   Survival of the insolvent corporation or its business   *310*
4.   Termination of the corporation: liquidation and dissolution   *333*
5.   Augmenting the assets of the insolvent corporation   *360*
6.   Public control over insolvent corporations   *367*

Chapter 8
CORPORATE INSOLVENCY LAW IN ITALY
Giovanni Verusio, Pavia Ansaldo e Verusio Studio Legale   *369*

1.   Introduction   *371*
2.   Companies   *372*
3.   Survival of the insolvent corporation or its business   *386*
4.   Termination of the insolvent corporation: bankruptcy   *390*
5.   Augmenting the assets of the insolvent corporation   *398*
6.   Public control over insolvent corporations   *401*

Chapter 9
CORPORATE INSOLVENCY LAW IN LUXEMBOURG
René Diederich, Loesch & Wolter   *405*

1.   Introduction   *407*
2.   Corporations   *408*
3.   Survival of the insolvent corporation or its business   *415*
4.   Termination of the corporation: bankruptcy and compul-
     sory winding up   *430*
5.   Augmenting the assets of the insolvent corporation   *438*
6.   Public control over insolvent corporations   *443*

Chapter 10
CORPORATE INSOLVENCY LAW IN THE NETHERLANDS
W F Th Corpeleijn and M Herschdorfer, Stibbe Simont Monahan
Duhot   *445*

1.	Introduction	*447*
2.	Corporations	*448*
3.	Survival of the insolvent corporation or its business: mora-torium of payment	*460*
4.	Termination of the corporation: dissolution and bankruptcy	*464*
5.	Augmenting the assets of the insolvent corporation	*474*
6.	Public control over insolvent corporations	*476*

Chapter 11
CORPORATE INSOLVENCY LAW IN NORWAY
Gerhard Holm and Berit Stokke, Thommessen Krefting Greve Lund   *479*

1.	Introduction	*481*
2.	Corporations	*483*
3.	Survival of the insolvent corporation or its business	*492*
4.	Termination of the corporation: insolvent liquidation	*500*
5.	Augmenting the assets of the insolvent company	*511*
6.	Public control over insolvent corporations	*516*

Chapter 12
CORPORATE INSOLVENCY LAW IN PORTUGAL
Carlos Martins Ferreira, José Alves Pereira e Associados   *519*

1.	Introduction	*521*
2.	Companies	*522*
3.	Survival of the insolvent corporation or its business	*534*
4.	Termination of the corporation: bankruptcy and liquida-tion	*545*
5.	Augmenting the assets of the insolvent corporation	*553*
6.	Public control over insolvent corporations	*556*

Chapter 13
CORPORATE INSOLVENCY LAW IN SPAIN
Fernando Lopez-Orozco, Bufete Mullerat & Roca   *557*

1.	Introduction	*559*
2.	Corporation and other business entities	*563*
3.	Survival of the insolvent corporation or its business	*582*
4.	Termination of the corporation: bankruptcy	*599*

5.	Augmenting the assets of the insolvent corporation	*612*
6.	Public control over insolvent corporations	*614*

Chapter 14
CORPORATE INSOLVENCY LAW IN SWEDEN
Leif Baecklund, Thomas Ehrner, Thomas Sjöberg and Elisabet Fura-
Sandström, Advokatfirman Vinge   *617*

1.	Introduction	*619*
2.	Corporations	*619*
3.	Survival of the insolvent corporation or its business	*630*
4.	Termination of the corporation: liquidation and bankruptcy	*638*
5.	Augmenting the assets of the insolvent corporation	*647*
6.	Public control over insolvent corporations	*654*

Chapter 15
CORPORATE INSOLVENCY LAW IN SWITZERLAND
Tis Prager and André E Lebrecht, Prager Dreifuss & Partner   *659*

1.	Introduction	*661*
2.	Corporations	*665*
3.	Survival of the insolvent corporation or its business	*681*
4.	Termination of the corporation: bankruptcy and composition with assignments of assets	*693*
5.	Augmenting the assets of the insolvent corporation	*705*
6.	Public control over insolvent corporations	*716*
7.	Recognition of foreign bankruptcy decrees and composition proceedings in Switzerland	*719*

Chapter 16
CORPORATE INSOLVENCY LAW IN THE UNITED KINGDOM
Professor Harry Rajak, University of Sussex and Peter Horrocks and Joe
Bannister, Lovell White Durrant   *723*

1.	Introduction	*725*
2.	Companies registered under the Companies Act	*727*
3.	Survival of the insolvent corporation or its business	*743*
4.	Termination of the corporation: liquidation and dissolution	*781*
5.	Augmenting the assets of the insolvent corporation	*800*
6.	Public control over insolvent corporations	*807*
7.	Special insolvency regimes	*810*

Index   *813*

FOREWORD TO THE FIRST EDITION

Anyone familiar with the contemporary work of the Chancery Division in London will be aware of its international nature. The majority of the large cases raise transnational issues to a lesser or, usually, greater extent. This is because modern technology permits the conduct of business and the relocation of assets on a worldwide basis having little reference to the geographical areas of political sovereignty.

Whilst national boundaries no longer have much relevance to economic activity, the same is not true of the courts which have to resolve disputes arising from such activity. Political sovereignty remains the basis on which the courts of each country assert and exercise their jurisdiction. There is a mis-match between the nature of the disputes and the powers of any one court to resolve them. The rules of private international law, of course, ameliorate the position as do a number of international conventions. But in some areas the rules of private international law are far from clear and international conventions non-existent: most notably the law of international insolvency.

The BCCI case provides a striking example. A grossly insolvent Luxembourg company has businesses, subsidiaries and assets in more than 30 jurisdictions. In justice to the body of creditors as a whole, it is important that its affairs be wound up on a worldwide basis, since otherwise creditors in each country where there are substantial assets will seek to exploit that chance by obtaining preferred payment of their debt out of local assets. Yet, with the possible exception of the United States, there is no national law which effectively ensures such fair liquidation or even provides for co-operation and *de jure* recognition of foreign liquidators or administrators. To date, the only cohesive factor in the BCCI liquidations has been a purely administrative one, *viz* that the individuals appointed by each of the national courts to conduct the liquidation have all been members or associates of the same international firm of accountants.

It is this lack of any effective international law of insolvency that makes this publication so valuable. A liquidator, administrator or trustee in bankruptcy in an international insolvency is forced to discover and apply the widely differing insolvency rules of each country in which assets or creditors are to be found. For the first time, so far as I am aware, this work enables him to find in one place the relevant principles in some 15 European countries. It is a remarkable effort to have produced such a survey of the relevant law and it will, I am sure, be an essential tool for all those involved in international insolvency work.

I hope that it may also make a wider contribution. It is noteworthy that, in all the jurisdictions surveyed in this book, although the details of the procedure differ the tendency of the law is away from liquidation and towards saving the company or its business. Given so much common ground, is it not possible that the United Kingdom could at least accept that the officer appointed by a foreign court to seek to rescue a company should be afforded the same rights as an administrator appointed by the courts in this country? Better still, despite the unhappy history of attempts to reach agreement on an international insolvency convention, could not such a limited recognition of the status of a foreign administrator be adopted at least within the EC? In the modern world, such a step is a matter of considerable urgency.

Until the time when such recognition of the international nature of insolvency has taken place, this book will be indispensable.

THE RT HON THE LORD BROWNE-WILKINSON
Lord of Appeal, United Kingdom

FOREWORD TO THE SECOND EDITION

In the Foreword to the first edition of this work, I expressed the hope that its publication might provide a spur towards the international recognition in all states of the position of an administrator appointed in one of those states to oversee the insolvency of a company. This hope has not been realised: each state continues to operate its own domestic system of insolvency without regard to the international ramifications inherent in any major corporate insolvency.

In consequence, this book remains of unique importance, providing as it does a conspectus of the insolvency law of the Member States of the European Union. The deserved success of the first edition demonstrates a need for such a work. I have no doubt that his new edition, with its up-to-date account of the relevant laws of the individual states, will repeat that success. I wish it well.

THE RT HON THE LORD BROWNE-WILKINSON
Lord of Appeal, United Kingdom

EDITOR'S ACKNOWLEDGEMENTS

I was more than happy to accept Lovell White Durrant's invitation to edit the second edition of European Corporate Insolvency Law, in addition to revising the United Kingdom and European Community (Union) chapters. I have been fortunate in being able to rely on the wholehearted support of many people in Lovells, especially Peter Horrocks and Joe Bannister. Peter has again played a pivotal supervisory role in seeing the volume through to press, as well as making a major contribution to the revision of the UK chapter. As Lovells' in-house editor, Joe replaced his close colleague and friend, Gordon White, who was no longer available to work on this edition. In this role he organised the collection of the various contributions, read the first drafts (a task in which he was most ably assisted by Katherine Stones) and played a major role in the preparation of the United Kingdom chapter. I relied enormously on Joe's efficiency and analytical skill. Our European colleagues, whose labours fill so much of this volume, gave of their time and energy with great expertise. Our new publisher, David Wilson of John Wiley & Sons, always combined enthusiasm with realism and avoided the Scylla of too much pressure and the Charybdis of being too laid back.

Lord Browne-Wilkinson, whose judgments have done so much to increase our understanding and appreciation of the theory and practice of insolvency, generously agreed to write the foreword to this second edition.

The frustration felt at the failure to make real progress at the multilateral convention end of the world of international and comparative insolvency is more than compensated for by the excitement of finding so much in the principles of the legal systems of others which resembles and echoes our own. We hope that this volume has recorded these similarities and identified the differences in a way that will be helpful to those who practice, judge, teach, research, legislate and suffer in this field.

Harry Rajak
St. David's Day 1995

Contents of Chapter 1

EUROPEAN CROSS BORDER INSOLVENCY DEVELOPMENTS

1.	**Introduction**	3
2.	**A brief history of bankruptcy conventions**	5
3.	**The European Convention on Certain International Aspects of Bankruptcy**	6
4.	**European Community developments**	8
	The Draft European Union Bankruptcy Convention ("the Draft")	8
	European Community legislation	14
5.	**Conclusion**	20

Chapter 1

EUROPEAN CROSS BORDER INSOLVENCY DEVELOPMENTS

Professor Harry Rajak, University of Sussex

1. Introduction

Where legal problems extend beyond domestic borders, some form of international co-operation will often be necessary if the problem is to be solved satisfactorily. A may have a judgment for debt against B, but B may be resident in a different jurisdiction from A or may have assets in a jurisdiction different from that in which the judgment was granted. Considerable problems may, by contrast, arise where, for example, a multinational corporation registered in one country but with assets in several different jurisdictions, is placed into an insolvency regime.

Compared with international insolvency, the problem of enforcing in country B a judgment granted in country A, is a simple one. The enforcement of foreign judgments has been facilitated by judicial comity, by bilateral treaties between countries and, most recently, by multinational convention. The most notable convention is the Convention on Jurisdiction and the Enforcement of Judgments in Civil and Commercial Matters ("the Jurisdiction and Judgments Convention") entered into by the Member States of the European Community (and brought into force in the United Kingdom by the Civil Jurisdiction and Judgments Act 1982).

While, at least commercially, the enforcement of judgments is closely related to bankruptcy and insolvency, the European Community is still struggling towards a convention to deal with insolvencies or bankruptcies which cross borders within the Community. At the moment, however, the Jurisdiction and Judgments Convention does not apply to "bankruptcy, proceedings related to the winding up of insolvent companies or other legal persons, judicial arrangements, compositions and analogous proceedings" (Title 1, art 1).

There is, of course, a huge gulf between the enforcement of a foreign judgment and the recognition of foreign insolvency and bankruptcy proceedings. When asked to enforce a foreign judgment a court may, for example, be concerned with whether the defendant was given adequate protection to know the case against him, to present his defence, and so on. It may also be concerned by the principles of law under which the foreign judgment was rendered. But such reservations aside, no issues of policy arise in connection with the enforcement of a foreign judgment. In particular, enforcement will not generally be contrary to the law and public policy of the enforcing state.

The enforcement in the United Kingdom of a French judgment based on a contract entered into in France should not, in consequence, compromise English contract law principles, even if the contract would not have been enforceable under English law. Enforcement is in general a prodecural matter, with safeguards aimed principally at verifying the judgment obtained. The prodecures are generally similar in most European countries.

As the chapters in this volume reveal, where the two countries are both members of the European Community, the judgment is enforceable in the same way as a domestic judgment. If this were not the case, a fresh action on the foreign judgment would be necessary as a prelude to enforcement (for a recent example, see *Adams* v *Cape Industries* ([1990] Ch 433, [1991] 1 All ER 929, [1990] BCLC 479, [1990] BCC 786). The Jurisdiction and Judgments Convention may have required some concessions and consequent new legislation to provide procedural safeguards on the part of some Member States, but little threat was posed to the respective substantive legal principles of each country.

However, foreign insolvency does pose such a threat. A judgment of insolvency or bankruptcy by itself merely creates a regime; it looks forward to the resolution of a number of problems. Such resolution often involves the application of principles of law which, while not fundamental in the human rights sense, are part of the foundation on which a particular country's principles are built. An insolvency regime may require the application of many such fundamental private law principles and, to be meaningful, a convention on bankruptcy, may require participating states to concede that such disputes in their countries will be resolved by unified and, therefore, quite possibly different principles from those which apply in purely domestic disputes.

Insolvency thus raises many issues. These may seem straightforward and politically unproblematic (or are largely resolved) in the national context. Internationally, by contrast, their resolution may give rise to many difficult legal and political issues. This may be so even where there is general agreement. Most jurisdictions accept that, in an insolvency regime, certain creditors of a bankrupt debtor should be preferred to others. Indeed, they often agree as to the general categories of such preferential creditors (which are invariably government departments and employees of the bankrupt debtor). A convention which provides, by contrast, for a foreign revenue claim to have priority over the claims of local creditors is certain to be very unpopular in the countries where enforcement is sought to be made.

Without a multilateral or bilateral convention, the courts would lack guidance as to how to resolve problems arising from competing claims between foreign creditors and creditors local to the jurisdiction where the insolvency proceedings had been initiated. Foreign creditors might enjoy preferential status under their own legal systems, but not under the legal system of the state where insolvency proceedings were being conducted.

The court with charge of an international insolvency could apply its own law or it could apply foreign law. Alternatively, it could seek some reconciliation between the two. Given the number of possible conflicts in such circumstances, it is inevitable that the claims of different groups of creditors (and other interested parties) would be substantially influenced by which country had charge of the insolvency, unless a binding treaty or convention imposed on the courts of the states concerned either:

- identical substantive principles for the resolution of such disputes; or
- principles which dictated which country's laws would apply in given circumstances.

It goes without saying that any treaty or convention would also have to provide a means whereby its provisions could be enforced in states which had acceded to it.

2. A brief history of bankruptcy conventions

Multilteral treaties relating to bankruptcy seem to have originated in South America and first came to Europe as late as 1925. There is now only one operating European Bankruptcy Convention – that between the Nordic countries which dates from 1933. There is also one treaty – drafted for the twenty-four countries which are members of the Council of Europe – which was opened for signature on 5 June 1990 in Istanbul. To date, only seven countries have signed it and none has ratified it. This treaty is summarised below.

A committee of experts established in 1990 by the European Community is currently working on establishing a treaty (under the provisions of article 220 of the European Community treaty) acceptable to the current Member States. At the date of writing, no draft treaty has been agreed for submission to the governments of the Member States although the committee of experts is considering a working draft prepared in late 1994 and amended in 1995. An earlier draft, arising from the work which resulted in the Jurisdiction and Judgments Convention, was abandoned in 1980. Negotiations between representatives of each Member State have now been going on for several years, yet agreement on a draft to be put before the governments of the Member States seems as far away as ever. The chances of a European Union Bankruptcy Convention, at least in the short term, are very small. The present working draft is summarised below.

A further proposal by Peter Totty, (*Proposal for a Model International Insolvency Treaty*, (Fletcher (ed) *Cross Border Insolvency: Comparative Dimensions* 1990 p271) tries to achieve the best of the bilateral and multinational approaches. This approach is described as "a tentative solution" which would be "practical", "effective" and "speedy". It is, in essence, a series of bilateral treaties all based on the same model which might remove the complexity inherent in a multilateral treaty and allow for certain variations as between any two countries where special circumstances existed. There is no indication, as yet, of this approach being adopted anywhere.

3. The European Convention on Certain International Aspects of Bankruptcy

This is the treaty agreed by the negotiators under the auspices of the Council of Europe and opened for signature on 5 June 1990. It is expressed to apply to "collective insolvency proceedings which entail a disinvestment of the debtor and the appointment of a liquidator and which may entail the liquidation of the assets" (art 1). Apart from an introduction and a conclusion, this treaty comprises three chapters (II, III and IV) which deal, respectively, with the "Exercise of Certain Powers of the Liquidator", "Secondary Bankruptcies" and "Information of the Creditors and Lodgment of Their Claims". Chapters II and III apply only to final liquidation or termination proceedings and the only part of this treaty which extends to rescue procedures is chapter IV. Insurance companies and credit institutions are excluded from the Convention.

Only the courts (or other authorities) where the debtor has "the centre of his main interest" will be competent to preside over the opening of bankruptcy proceedings (unless the debtor's main interests are located outside the territories of all the party states, or the courts of the country where the main interests are located are not competent). Companies are rebuttably presumed to have their main interests in the country where their registered office is located.

"Liquidator" is defined as "any person or body whose function is to administer or liquidate the assets of the bankrupt or to supervise the activities of the debtor". The chapter on liquidators' powers covers, *inter alia*, the liquidator's capacity, his powers and duties to protect and dispose of the debtor's assets, and advertisement. The concept of the "Secondary Bankruptcy" (chapter III) allows for the opening of further bankruptcy proceedings in a different country. This is designed to enable the liquidator in the first (or primary) bankruptcy to reach property or assets belonging to the debtor in the country of the secondary bankruptcy, as well as to protect the creditors of the debtor in that country. Chapter IV requires "the competent authority" of the Member State or the liquidator to advise all known creditors residing in other Member States of the details of the proceedings and, in particular, to advise those creditors of what needs to be done for the lodging of claims.

A liquidator appointed in the country where the corporate debtor has its registered office may exercise various powers granted under the treaty in other Member States, without the need to open a secondary bankruptcy. He must, however, obtain authorisation to act and advertise the fact of his appointment.

Thus, under article 9, the liquidator may take "in accordance with the law of the Party in which he intends to act, any necessary steps to protect or preserve the value of the assets of the debtor, ... without, however, removing those assets from the territory of the Party where they are situated."

In addition to his powers for protecting the debtor's assets, the liquidator is given powers to administer, manage and dispose of the debtor's assets "including removing them from the territory of the Party where they are situated", provided that any such measures are "subject to the law of the Party in whose territory the assets are situated" (art 10). The exercise of these powers is, however, automatically suspended for two months – a period which is extended if any request is made for the bankruptcy of the debtor and at least until any such request has been dealt with.

Under article 11.2, preferential creditors in the country in which the liquidator wishes to exercise his powers and creditors "who have a public law claim" or creditors who have a claim "arising from the operation of an establishment of the debtor" or from employment, may commence or continue proceedings during the suspension period of at least two months as referred to above.

Under article 14, the liquidator may not exercise any of these powers if:

- bankruptcy proceedings (or proceedings preventing bankruptcy) are opened in the country in which the liquidator wishes to exercise his powers; or

- the liquidator's proposed action is contrary to any security held by anyone other than the debtor; or

- the proposed exercise of power by the liquidator is "manifestly contrary to the public policy" of the country in which he proposes to act.

Chapter III provides for the opening of secondary bankruptcies. These operate to assist the primary bankruptcy in that claims made by creditors in the secondary bankruptcy are transferred to the primary liquidator to be treated as claims in the primary bankruptcy. The claims transferred will include claims which arose after the opening of the primary bankruptcy. This transfer regime is, however, subject to the claims of those who enjoy "a right to preferential payment or a security over land or other property, public law claims and claims arising from the operation of an establishment of the debtor or from employment in the Party where the secondary bankruptcy is opened ... ." Such claims are to be met from the proceeds of the liquidation of the assets in the secondary bankruptcy.

compositions and other non-liquidation regimes, such as statutory rescue procedures.

Jurisdiction and applicable laws

Jurisdiction for insolvency proceedings under the Draft is conferred on the courts of the country where the debtor's principal business interests are located. This is rebuttably presumed to be the country where the debtor's registered office is located. Alternatively, the courts of a country where the debtor has an establishment may also claim jurisdiction, but only in respect of assets within that jurisdiction and only on a secondary basis if insolvency proceedings have been opened in the place where the debtor's principal business interests are located.

Leaving aside for the moment the complication of two sets of simultaneous proceedings, the law of the country where insolvency proceedings are opened will govern the entirety of the insolvency proceedings other than in relation to

- a third party's proprietary rights (rights *in rem*) exercisable in another contracting state ;
- contracts relating to the use or acquisition of immovable property
- contracts of employment ;
- rights of the debtor in immovable property, or a ship or aircraft subject to registration in a public register;
- contracts entered into after the opening of the insolvency proceedings, for the disposition for consideration of a ship, aircraft or an immovable asset. These provisions are designed for the protection of a third party purchaser who might reasonably have been unaware of the opening of the proceedings ;
- the effect of the proceedings on pending lawsuits in which the debtor has been divested of an asset. Such proceedings will be governed by the laws of the country where the suit is pending.

The principles of other jurisdictions may be invoked, together with the principles of the jurisdiction in which the proceedings were opened, on the following issues:

- set-off
- reservation of title
- proceedings to set aside contracts detrimental to creditors

The law governing insolvency proceedings will therefore be in the main the law of the Member State where the principal insolvency proceedings are initiated. The Draft Convention does not seek in this respect to unify or harmonise. It seeks instead to obtain agreement on the application of a particular set of principles. There are a few provisions, however, where it does seek to lay down uniform principles of law. Under article 12 ("Imputation and Return"), a creditor who has, after the opening of the insolvency proceedings, obtained "total or partial satisfaction of his claim on the assets belonging to the debtor situated within the territory of another contracting state, shall return what he has obtained to the liquidator ..." Furthermore, as part of the requirement for creditors of the same class to be treated in the same way, a creditor who has been paid a dividend will have to account for that dividend in any distributions subsequently made to all creditors.

A creditor is protected where, in ignorance of the opening of insolvency proceedings in another country, he has honoured an obligation to the debtor in such a way as benefits the debtor over and above other creditors. He will not be under any obligation to compensate the liquidator except that, if the creditor has made payment after the beginning of the insolvency proceedings, he will be presumed not to be ignorant of those proceedings. In secondary liquidation proceedings (p11 *infra*), the laws of the state in which the secondary proceedings are initiated will apply, although here, too, the Draft lays down the general approach to be taken in all cases. Thus, it is declared that secondary proceedings may only be sought by a creditor where he "has a specific interest in the opening of secondary proceedings" (defined as less favourable treatment *vis-a-vis* other creditors in the main proceedings than in the secondary proceedings).

Interpretation and enforcement

The Draft makes the most of a number of key features of the European Union, namely the existence of a supra-national court (the European Court of Justice) which is given the jurisdiction to interpret the Bankruptcy Convention and the Jurisdiction and Judgments Convention. The latter is to be relied upon for the recognition and enforcement of judgments in insolvency proceedings conducted under the Bankruptcy Convention, subject to a state's public policy, for example where enforcement of any judgment "would be manifestly contrary to that State's public policy, in particular its fundamental principles and the constitutional rights and liberties of the individual" (art 18).

The powers of the liquidator

The powers of the liquidator appointed in the insolvent's principal jurisdictional base (the centre of the debtor's main interests) are declared to be those conferred upon him by the laws of the country in which the proceedings are opened, but subject to any measures already undertaken in proceedings opened under the alternative jursidiction (where the debtor has an establishment). The liquidator, thus far, only has the powers of a domestic liquidator of a particular state. However, the Draft seeks to extend these powers by a principle which would, presumably, apply uniformly throughout the territories of the Member States, namely that the liquidator "may, in particular remove the debtor's assets from the territory in which they are situated, subject to articles 4 [protection of third party's proprietary rights] and 5 [rights under a reservation of title]."

A number of provisions, as preconditions to their effectiveness, require proof of the liquidator's appointment and proper publicity of the proceedings though-out the European Union. They place the liquidator under a duty to inform cred-itors as to the opening of the proceedings and their rights with regard to the lodging of their claims. Where there is a secondary liquidation, claims may be lodged in either the country of the principal liquidation or that of the secondary liquidation.

Secondary liquidations

Finally, the Draft deals with secondary insolvency proceedings. The opening of insolvency proceedings in the state where the debtor has the centre of his main interests is a sufficient ground for the opening of secondary proceedings in an-other state where the debtor has an establishment. The liquidator or any other person or authority (such as a creditor) so permitted by the laws of the other state may request the opening of secondary proceedings. As pointed out above, however, such creditor must show that he "has a specific interest in the opening of secondary proceedings" (defined as less favourable treatment *vis-a-vis* other creditors in the main proceedings). The tax authorities and the debtor's employ-ees are also presumed to have the necessary legal interest to justify the opening of secondary proceedings. To that extent, the Draft here tacitly accepts that pre-ferential creditors should have superior rights throughout the European Union.

The main proceedings are, therefore, the proceedings opened at the centre of the debtor's main interests and secondary proceedings are those opened, while main proceedings are in progress, at a place where the debtor has an establish-ment. The Draft also makes clear that, if proceedings are first opened at a place where the debtor has an establishment and, subsequently, at the place where the debtor has the centre of his main interests, the latter become the main proceed-ings and the former become the secondary proceedings.

The two liquidators are enjoined to communicate with each other about their respective proceedings and each may participate in the other's proceedings on the same basis as a creditor (including, where claims have been lodged in one li-quidation, lodging those claims in the other liquidation). At the request of the li-quidator in the main proceedings, the appropriate court must stay the secondary proceedings for up to three months, unless the request for the stay "is manifestly of no interest to the creditors in the main proceedings." The stay can be extended, but the court may require the applicant liquidator to take suitable measures to guarantee the interests of the creditors in the secondary liquidation.

The stay will be terminated if the liquidator in the main proceedings so re-quests. Also, the court may terminate the stay if so requested by a creditor in, or the liquidator of, the secondary proceedings and where the stay "no longer ap-pears justified, in particular, by the interests of creditors in the main proceedings or in the secondary proceedings." If the secondary liquidation results in the pay-ment in full of all claims lodged, any balance must be passed to the liquidator in the main proceedings.

Apart from the power to request a stay of the secondary proceedings, the liqui-

dator is the only person (other than the debtor who may only do so with the liquidator's consent) who, during a stay of the secondary proceedings, is entitled to
propose a rescue plan, composition or comparable non-liquidation discharge of
the secondary proceedings. Here, the Draft makes it clear that the liquidator's
power in this regard depends on the availability of such a rescue procedure in
the country where its use is proposed. Where there is no stay, it seems that any
proposal for termination of the secondary proceedings other than by liquidation
may be made by anyone so entitled under the applicable law. The court may only
act on such a proposal if the liquidator in the main proceedings consents, a requirement which will only be dispensed with where "the financial interests of
the creditors in the main proceedings are not affected by the measure proposed."

The liquidator in the main proceedings may request the closure of the secondary proceedings on the grounds that they are not justified, where either the creditor or the public authority, at whose instance they were opened, cannot,
respectively, substantiate the "specific legal interest" or the "public interest" on
the basis of which the secondary proceedings were opened.

The liquidator in the main proceedings can, therefore, be seen, potentially, to
have substantial control over the secondary proceedings, although much would
depend on how the local court in the secondary proceedings exercised the discretion which the Convention would confer upon it. This is a crucial question to
be left to the whim of the local courts. It is somewhat depressing to be considering an elaborate and complex Convention whose effectiveness, at the end of the
day, may still be subject to the attitude of local courts.

Levels of agreement

The proposed Convention may be viewed as an attempt to establish agreement
at three levels. In the first place there is agreement among all the states to certain
unifying principles excluding anything to the contrary in any of their domestic
laws (such as respect for the *fact* of the Convention and its provisions). We may
describe this as the "unifying level". Secondly, there is agreement that in given
circumstances, the domestic principles of one particular country should apply.
This is a partial illustration of the first level of agreement (a unifying principle
as to whose law will apply) but is then supplemented by a particular country's existing law.

This hybrid mix, despite having a unifying element, is radically different from
the first level of agreement. At the first level, every country's courts apply the
same principle (for example, that the Convention exists). At the second level,
the principles in terms of which any particular problem is eventually resolved
may well differ from occasion to occasion. The actual resolving principles which
are applied will depend on whose laws are prescribed by the unifying element.
We may describe this second level as the "Convention-prescribed domestic level".

The third and final level is that of disputes which the Convention, either expressly or by implication, does not cover. Here, a solution has to be found in the
conflict of laws principles in the domestic laws of the country by whose court

the dispute is heard. This level, which we may describe as the "conflict of laws level" must be subject to the implied limitation that it only comes into operation if neither the first nor the second level can provide a solution. It will also be noted that the third level, like the second, but unlike the first, will result in different answers being given to identical legal issues in different Member States. The difference in solution will be dictated by the many differences that exist between any two or more legal systems. It also follows that none of the principles just referred to are conducive to achieving *harmonisation* of the legal regimes governing corporate insolvency applicable to different Member States of the European Union.

Given that unification of principles, except at the most general level, is unattainable it must be asked whether a Convention of this kind is desirable. The alternative is not necessarily to dispense with the Convention. It may be a Convention similar in its approach to that taken by the United States of America to insolvency. There, the Federal Bankruptcy Code of 1978 establishes a certain degree of procedural and institutional unity, for example, in the insolvency regimes and the courts and judges involved in insolvency disputes. It also establishes a small measure of substantive unity in those areas which are specifically insolvency inspired (such as the nature of preferential creditors and the principles for setting aside pre-insolvency-regime transactions – the so-called "claw-back provisions"). By contrast, the many common law problems which may arise between parties, whether or not one or more of them is insolvent, are left to be resolved by the common law of the appropriate state.

The European Union is not yet at a stage where procedural and institutional unity can be achieved but work is proceeding on mutual recognition of each country's insolvency institutions and officers. Agreement may then be sought on the powers which such officers might have when they cross borders. The present Draft restricts such powers to those which are available in the country under whose laws the officer was appointed. Perhaps, the bold step of extending them to include those available to insolvency practitioners in the country to which the officer has gone to seek and collect further assets for the insolvent estate might be contemplated. This could have a unifying effect in the long term and would also serve to familiarise courts in all the European Union countries with the nature of insolvency institutions in other Member States.

Given that insolvency regimes in most countries have claw-back provisions, unity here might not be an unattainable goal. Such an approach is, in one sense, bolder than the present Draft. It would seek more unity and lead to the development of composite insolvency procedures made up of elements of the procedures in the two or more countries in which a particular cross-border insolvency is operated. The Convention is, by contrast, much less ambitious in approach, by avoiding any attempt to prescribe which set of legal principles in the relevant Member States would apply to a wide variety of substantive issues. As we have seen, however, the Draft contemplates some resistance to this approach by allowing for the establishment of secondary insolvencies to run alongside the primary insolvency established in the territory where the debtor's main interests are located. The major purpose of such secondary insolvencies may well be to prevent the laws of the country of primary insolvency being used to resolve certain substantive disputes.

In my view, if a Convention based on the present Draft is ultimately ratified, it would be likely to cause as much trouble as it might save. There would be an extra level of dispute, that between primary and secondary bankruptcies, which may replace, but is likely to be additional to, the present day conflict of jurisdiction. Their resolution depends on the application of domestic conflict of laws principles. The prize, offered by the more limited approach, is some unity plus the development of composite insolvency institutions which would be common to two or more countries and which could, later, be the basis of codification and consolidation by a further Convention.

European Community legislation

Aside from its activity in relation to a Bankruptcy Convention, the European Union has enacted some legislation which is relevant to bankruptcy. This legislation has been by means of Directives, a form of legislation which, under the European Community treaty, obliges all Member States to amend their domestic laws as far as necessary to ensure that such laws comply with the content of the Directive.

The Acquired Rights Directive

On 14 February 1977, the Council of the European Community enacted Council Directive 77/187 on the Approximation of the Laws of the Member States Relating to the Safeguarding of Employees' Rights in the Event of Transfers of Undertakings, Businesses or Parts of Businesses (OJ 1977, L61/26). According to its preamble, this Directive was adopted to ensure the protection of employees in circumstances where their employer changed as a result of the transfer of the undertaking by which they were employed. The thrust of the Directive is to transfer to the purchaser of a business ("the transferee"), the vendor's rights and obligations arising from a contract of employment or from an employment relationship existing on the date of transfer. Any entitlement which the employee has to accumulated benefits can thus be preserved against the new employer.

The Directive has assumed a significant role in specific insolvency circumstances, namely the sale of a business by or on behalf of an insolvent vendor. It is not uncommon for employees of the vendor to be made redundant prior to the transfer of the business, thereby giving rise to such claims as compensation for redundancy and damages for unfair dismissal. The concern here has been whether such claims can be pursued against the transferee of the business.

This issue – and others concerned with this Directive – have been considered at two levels:

- the local courts of the Member States of the European Community have made decisions in the course of litigation based on the interpretation of the legislation enacted for the purpose of implementing the Directive; and

- there have been a number of occasions on which the European Court of Justice has been asked to express its opinion as to the intrepretation of different articles of the Directive. Such requests have come from the courts of the Member States under the provisions of article 177 of the European Community Treaty and in the context of specific litigation in the state from which the request has come.

In the latter instance, the Court of Justice has provided its opinion as a guide for the interpretation of the local legislation enacted for the purpose of implementing the Directive (*Knut Wendelboe and Others* v *L.J. Music ApS, in liquidation* Case 19/83, [1985] ECR 457, 466).

The Directive does not make clear whether it is restricted to transfers of solvent undertakings or whether it applies also to transfers of insolvent undertakings. It does, however, indicate that it is designed to provide a minimum level of protection for employees and that any state is at liberty to increase the level of such protection. Roughly half of the Member States have, in their implementing legislation, extended the terms of the Directive to include transfers of undertakings by insolvent transferors by making no exclusion in this regard.

There is, however, some confusion about the meaning of "insolvent". In *Abels* v *Administrative Board of the Bedrijfsvereniging*, Case 135/83, [1985] ECR 469, the ECJ expressed the opinion that the terms of the Directive do not apply to the transfer of an undertaking where the transferor has been adjudged "insolvent" and where the undertaking forms part of the assets of the insolvent transferor. The court went on to say that the Directive *did* apply (apparently irrespective of whether or not it had been implemented with or without the extension to insolvent transfers) to a transfer which took place in the Dutch insolvency regime of "surseance van betaling" ("moratorium of payments").

Since a company in the latter regime would, under English law, be regarded as "insolvent", it is likely to be the case that the distinction drawn in the *Abels* case is one between a sale effected in liquidation – where the provisions of the Directive do not apply – and one effected during the course of a regime under which judicial leave was given to the transferor to suspend payment of debts, where the terms of the Directive do apply. This distinction had been expressed by the court in *Botzen* v *Rotterdamsche Droogdok Maatschappij*, Case 186/83, [1985] ECR 519 and *Industriebond FNV and Federatie Nederlandse Vakbeweging* v *Netherlands*, Case 179/83, [1985] ECR 511 and the *Abels* decision was followed by the European Court in *G. d'Urso* v. *Ercole Marelli Elettromeccanica*, Case 362/89, where the opinion was expressed that the terms of the Directive can apply in Italy to the special administration regime as opposed to liquidation for major companies experiencing a financial crisis.

The European Court seems to be establishing here a distinction between the transfer of a business which is a going concern and, by contrast, a piecemeal transfer of the assets of a former business. This distinction is clearly in line with the terms of the Directive and the United Kingdom's implementing Regulations. It is unfortunate, however, that the distinction has also been expressed in terms of the different regimes, namely that a transfer of a business from a company in compulsory liquidation (or its equivalent in each Member State) is not covered by the Directive as opposed to a transfer from a company under the protection of a regime which provides a moratorium against payment of debts.

In *Abels*, however, the ECJ did add that the Directive could be implemented so as to include within its coverage sales of businesses by companies in liquidation and, given the unrestricted nature of its implementing Regulations, the United Kingdom must be taken to have done so. There is an undoubted practice in the United Kingdom of selling businesses (as opposed to selling assets piecemeal) by liquidators of companies in voluntary liquidation. This may also occur, although much more rarely, in respect of companies in compulsory liquidation, and the well-founded view that the Directive and Regulations *do* cover such sales has been expressed by a leading writer on Labour Law (McMullen, *Business Transfers and Employee Rights*, 2nd ed, 1992, pp153-54, 221-22).

In *Wendelboe* (*supra*), the European Court of Justice was specifically asked whether the protection of the Directive only extended to employees employed by the transferor at the time of the transfer (*i.e.* not to former employees dismissed before the transfer). It answered this question in the affirmative, but it should be observed that, in *Wendelboe*, it seemed clear that the dismissal of the employees took place well before there was any contemplated transfer of the undertaking.

Subsequently, and building on statements made in that case, the European Court of Justice has held that the Directive extends to protect employees who, although no longer employed at the time of the transfer, were dismissed on account of the transfer (*P Bork International A/S* v *Foreningen af Arbejdsledere i Danmark*, Case 101/87, [1988] ECR 3071). In the United Kingdom, the House of Lords applied this opinion in *Litster* v *Forth Dry Dock Co Ltd* [1989] 1 All ER 1134, where the transfer of the undertaking was by a company in receivership.

The European Court of Justice has also expressed the opinion that the Directive is mandatory. Thus, it operates irrespective of the wishes of the employee (*Berg and Busschers* v *Besselson* Cases 144 & 145/87, [1988] ECR 2559) and irrespective of any purported waiver of the rights conferred by it (*Foreningen af Arbejdsledere i Danmark* v *Daddy's Dance Hall A/S*, Case 324/86, [1988] ECR 739).

It is clearly of considerable significance in assessing whether the Directive applies in any particular case to establish whether there was, in fact, a transfer of the undertaking. There may have been only a transfer of assets rather than of the business. In this regard, the European Court of Justice has expressed the view that it would be material in this connection to establish whether the operation of the business was continued by the new employer (*Spijkers* v *Gebroeders Benedik Abattoir CV*, Case 24/85, [1986] ECR 1119). It has also been held by the European Court that, where an undertaking entrusted the running of a business to another undertaking by agreement for the benefit of the transferor, this did not preclude the operation of the Directive (*Rask and Christensen* v *ISS Kantineservice A/S*, Case 209/91, [1993] CLY 4281). Nor was the Directive excluded where a commercial activity was only peripheral to the business of the transferor and employed only one employee (*Christel Schmidt* v *Spar und Leihkasse der Früheren Ämter Bordesholm, Kiel und Cronshagen*, Case 392/92, [1994] CL August, 481).

The protection of the Directive will be lost where a former employee of the transferor continues his association with the transferred undertaking, but no longer as an employee (*Foreningen af Arbejdsledere i Danmark* v *A/S Danmols Inventar, in liquidation*, Case 105/84, [1985] ECR 2639). Here, the former employee continued his association with the undertaking as a substantial shareholder. In certain circumstances, only part of the vendor's undertaking may be transferred. If so, only those employees employed in the transferred part will benefit from the Directive (*Botzen* v *Rotterdamsche Droogdok Maatschappij BV*, Case 186/83, [1985] ECR 519).

The Acquired Rights Directive also makes provision for proper consultation with employees' representatives with a view to reaching agreement in situations of mass redundancy and, in proceedings against the United Kingdom for its failure to implement the Directive properly, the European Court emphasised the importance of these provisions for consultation (*EC Commission* v *United Kingdom* Cases 382/92, 383/92, [1994] CL, November, 694). In response to these proceedings, the Transfer of Undertakings (Protection of Employment) Regulations were amended by section 33 of the Trade Union and Employment Rights Act 1993, but this amendment only addressed one of the Commission's complaints. This was in relation to the United Kingdom definition of "undertaking", which was a source of dispute in the increasing number of cases involving the contracting out of public services in the wake of the government's privatisation programme, and ignored the complaint as to the inadequacy of the consultation process.

The Transfer of Undertakings (Protection of Employment) Regulations and the Directive have been the subject of sustained criticism, especially from insolvency practitioners. This criticism arose after the *Litster* decision (*supra*) which closed a loophole in the Regulations. This had previously been exploited to enable certain transfers of businesses by insolvent companies to be made in such a way as to avoid the effects of the Regulations. Where a transfer is held to be covered by the Regulations, employees who were dismissed to facilitate the transfer of the business may pursue claims arising out of those dismissals against the transferee of the business. Thus, not only do employees achieve more favoured status as against other creditors of an insolvent company, but the purchase of the business is often made at a discounted price to take account of prospective claims by dismissed employees.

The Commission of the European Communities has accepted much of this criticism in its proposals for a new Directive to replace the present Acquired Rights Directive. Under these proposals, the Directive would only apply to transfers of an entity – which includes both private and public entities and both profit and non-profit making entities – plus its activity, not simply to an activity alone. This would serve to reverse the ruling of the ECJ in *Rask and Christensen* v *ISS Kantineservice A/S*, Case 209/91, [1993] CLY 4281 and *Christel Schmidt* v *Spar und Leihkasse der Früheren Ämter Bordesholm, Kiel und Cronshagen*, Case 392/92,

[1994] CL August, 481.

More significantly from the viewpoint of an insolvent company and its creditors, the proposed replacement Directive would assist the survival of the business by allowing insolvency practitioners and employees' representatives to agree to alterations in the terms of contracts and the dismissal of some of the employees. Such agreement would carry the presumption of having been undertaken for an economic, technical or organisational reason, which would have the effect of taking the agreement and its execution outside the terms of the Directive.

In the absence of any such agreement, however, insolvency practitioners will be greatly assisted by the following provision in the new proposals for transfers in insolvency circumstances:

> " [T]he laws of the Member States may provide that the transferor's debts – arising from a contract of employment or an employment relationship – due before the transfer or before the opening of insolvency proceedings, shall not be transferred to the transferee in cases of transfers effected in the context of insolvency proceedings ... such as administration or judicial arrangements, compositions, suspension of payments, or other analogous non-liquidation proceedings, provided that such proceedings
>
> (a) are conducted under the supervision of a competent public authority, which may be an insolvency practitioner authorised by a competent public authority, and
> (b) give rise, under the legislation of the Member State in question, to the protection laid down by its national law, ensuring a level of protection at least equivalent to that provided for by the Council Directive 80/987/EEC on the approximation of the laws of the Members States relating to the protection of employees in the event of the insolvency of their employer."

This provision, if enacted unamended, would exempt purchasers of businesses from companies in administration and administrative receivership – the two principal corporate rescue regimes in the United Kingdom (see chapter 16, s3) – from any liability arising out of the dismissal of employees, where those dismissals were effected to make the sale of the business more attractive. Administrative receivers and administrators will welcome these proposals, which should remove a current obstacle to such transfers.

The United Kingdom satisfies the requirement laid down in section (b) of the extract from the draft proposal set out above. In addition, there is a specific provision in the proposal which exempts states from any obligation to implement the Directive so as to cover transfers of businesses where the transferor is the subject of bankruptcy proceedings "instituted with a view to the liquidation of the assets of a natural or legal person and under the supervision of a competent public authority". In fact, this simply expresses a facility already available by implication under the present Directive but of which the United Kingdom did not take advantage. It would also seem that if this proposal were enacted unamended, any transfer of a *business* (as opposed to a piecemeal sale of the assets) by the liquidator of a company in voluntary or compulsory liquidation would not come within the terms of the proposed exemption.

The British Government has expressed its views on the new proposals and has made it clear that it would take advantage of this exemption when implementing a replacement Directive. In fact, the Government would prefer to exempt all transfers undertaken in insolvency circumstances from the effects of the Directive, but the new proposal, in its careful elaboration of the regime for transfers in insolvency circumstances other than the liquidation of the assets of the transferor, would seem to preclude such a blanket exemption.

Council Directive 80/987

On 20 October 1980, the Council adopted Directive 80/97 on the Approximation of the Laws of the Member States Relating to the Protection of Employees in the Event of the Insolvency of their Employer. This Directive was amended by Directive 87/164. The thrust of the Directive is to require all Member States to guarantee payments to employees of outstanding claims resulting from contracts of employment or employment relationships where these cannot be met by the employer on account of the latter's insolvency. The provisions of this Directive were implemented in United Kingdom law by the insolvency payments provisions of the Employment Protection (Consolidation) Act 1978 as amended.

An interesting point has come before the European Court of Justice in connection with the current Acquired Rights Directive. Italy had failed to implement this Directive and a claim was brought against the Italian Republic on behalf of a number of employees who were left owed substantial arrears of salary on account of the insolvency of their former employer. Had the appropriate guarantee institution as prescribed by the Directive been in place, it would have been responsible for meeting the employees' claim. The employees presented their claim on two grounds, first on the Directive itself and, secondly, for damages suffered on account of the failure of the Italian government to carry out its obligations under European Community law.

Claims under the first head could only succeed where the Directive was sufficiently certain and self-contained as to constitute a legislative instrument (the doctrine of "direct effect"). Here it was held not to. The European Court of Justice did, however, express an opinion that Member States of the European Community were obliged, under Community law, to make good any damage caused to individuals by infringements of Community law for which the States were responsible (*Francovich* v *Italian Republic*, Cases C-6/90 and C-9/90, The Times, 20 November 1991, CLY 2904/92). It has also been held that the Directive cannot be implemented so as to exclude from its provisions higher management employees and while the Directive does not have direct effect on such employees, a claim can be brought against the state for any loss resulting from the inadequate implementation of the Directive (*Wagner Miret* v *Fondo de Garantia Salarial*, Case 334/92 [1994] CL, April, 624).

5. Conclusion

The only area in which Europe has achieved some degree of unanimity in the area of corporate insolvency is in respect of the treatment of employees of insolvent corporations. Thus, where the insolvency practitioner is put into control of an insolvent corporation with assets in different jurisdictions, he or she will need advice on the relevant insolvency legislation that applies in that jurisdiction. The following chapters of this book attempt to summarise for the practitioner the key principles of that legislation.

Contents of Chapter 2

CORPORATE INSOLVENCY LAW IN BELGIUM

1.	**Introduction**	23
2.	**Corporations**	24
	Characteristics	24
	Management	25
	Available information	26
	Financing and security for creditors	27
	Attitude of the creditors to a company in financial distress	29
	Debt collection and asset recovery	30
3.	**Survival of the insolvent corporation or its business: concordat judiciaire**	31
	Purpose and effect and pre-application considerations	31
	Procedural requirements	32
	"Akkoordvoorstellen" (proposition)	34
	Conclusion	37
4.	**Termination of the corporation: bankruptcy and solvent liquidation**	38
	Bankruptcy	38
	Solvent liquidation of a company	57
5.	**Augmenting the assets of the insolvent corporation**	59
	Acts committed during the suspect period	59
	Article 445 of the Bankruptcy Law	59
	Article 446 of the Bankruptcy Law	60
	Article 447 of the Bankruptcy Law	61
	Article 448 of the Bankruptcy Law	61
	Liability case	62
6.	**Public control over insolvent corporations**	63

Chapter 2

CORPORATE INSOLVENCY LAW IN BELGIUM

Christian Van Buggenhout and William Nauwelaerts,

Stibbe Simont Monahan Duhot

1. Introduction

Belgian law still recognises the fundamental distinction between civil law and commercial law. Hence, the term "daden van koophandel" (acts of commerce) is highly important since the application of the Bankruptcy Act, which dates back to 18 April 1851, is dependent upon it.

Only merchants can go bankrupt. Belgian bankruptcy law is therefore predicated on the status of "merchant". This status also has other far reaching consequences, such as the subjection of merchants to commercial law and to the jurisdiction and case law of the commercial courts and the mandatory registration in the trade register. It also follows that neither a non-merchant nor a civil company can be declared bankrupt even though they have ceased to repay their creditors.

The Belgian Companies Act defines commercial companies as "companies that have as their object the execution of acts of commerce". These commercial companies are therefore "merchants" for the purposes of the Bankruptcy Act.

When businesses are set up, they are frequently not conducted through the medium of a legal entity separate from the individual business people involved. In such circumstances, therefore, the latter will retain personal liability in the event of the non-execution of any contractual obligation. In the case of bankruptcy these people might lose all their possessions through the seizure and liquidation proceedings and once these proceedings have been terminated, many entrepreneurs will try to survive by acquiring possessions and conducting further business in the names of others.

Where a business is conducted through the medium of an incorporated company, on the other hand, the members enjoy the advantage of not being liable to pay any debts of the company which remain due after the bankruptcy procedures have been terminated. This advantage applies not only to commercial companies set up under the Companies Act but also to the "one-man company" with limited liability now provided for by the Act of 14 July 1987. Any company set up under this Act separates the private property of the entrepreneur from that of the company and it is only the latter which is liable for the debts which it incurs. Thus, it is not surprising that the company is fast becoming the pre-eminent legal entity for the development and conduct of economic activity in Belgium.

A bill revising Belgian bankruptcy law, introduced on 10 September 1992 and currently being discussed in the Chambre Commission, provides for a bankrupt to be released from liability for debts arising prior to his bankruptcy. Its purpose is to give a bankrupt discharge from prosecution by creditors on the conclusion of the liquidation of his assets.

This provision is intended to bring Belgian law into line with other modern insolvency regimes. It is of paramount importance to creditors that a bankrupt debtor is given the opportunity of resuming his activities in financially more advantageous circumstances. Thus, if the new bill is passed, the bankrupt will be able to resume his activities without a record in cases where he was the victim of circumstances beyond his control or in cases where he is able to provide creditors with some reassurance as to his future solvency.

2. Corporations

Characteristics

Belgian law distinguishes between six types of company each of which has a legal personality separate from that of its members. These are:

(a)   de naamloze vennootschap (society anonyme – private limited liability company)
(b)   de besloten vennootschap met beperkte aansprakelijkheid (société responsabilité limité – private limited liability company)
(c)   de samenwerkende vennootschap (société co-operative – coöperative company)
(d)   de gewone commanditaire vennootschap (société en commandite simple – limited liability partnership)
(e)   de commanditaire vennootschap op aandelen (société en commandite par actions – partnership limited by shares)
(f)   de vennootschap onder firma (société en nom collectif – general partnership).

The choice of organisational structure open to incorporators is limited to this list. They may however, agree on any subject that has not been specifically regulated by law and thus change the objects of the association. Furthermore each of these types of company, the liability of the members can be limited to their agreed contribution.

The above types of company fall into two groups, partnerships and companies limited by shares. In partnerships, the identity of the partners is of the utmost importance. Hence, notwithstanding any clause to the contrary, a partnership will be wound up when a partner – for whatever reason – drops out.

With companies limited by shares, on the other hand, it is the contribution rather than the identity of the contributor which is of crucial importance. In principle, the shares are freely transferable, with the liability of the member limited to his or her agreed contribution. The société anonyme is the archetypal company limited by shares.

Some companies, like the société responsabilité limité, present characteristics of both partnerships and companies limited by shares. For example, where the appointment of a managing director is required by statute, he or she cannot be removed at the will of the members. In addition, the transferability of shares can be limited or even excluded by the company's articles. On the other hand, there is no winding up when a partner dies and the liability of the shareholders is always limited to their contribution.

An essential feature of all types of company is the element of co-operation. Hence, any agreement allocating the whole of the profit to one of the partners will be null and void. This is equally true for any stipulations exempting contributors of money or goods from bearing any part of the losses.

The obligations of the members towards third persons differs significantly according to the type of company. In commercial companies, partners may be jointly and severally liable. Alternatively, their liability may be limited to a specified sum. This depends on the role to be played in the management of the company by the respective participants. Thus, in some companies, there are two types of member – the sleeping partners whose liability is limited, and the active managing partners who guarantee the fulfilment of the company's obligations with their personal property. In addition, it should be noted that in certain instances where there are irregularities in the incorporation of the company, members may sometimes be held liable for an amount in excess of their agreed contribution.

Management

All companies have the following three functional organs:

- an organ of management and representation (roughly equivalent to the management board)
- an organ exercising control over management (roughly equivalent to the supervisory board)
- an organ having the power to appoint and to discharge the other organs (roughly equivalent to the general meeting of shareholders).

As long as these organs act within the boundaries of their mandate, their acts will bind the company. Not surprisingly, the most commonly used type of company, the société anonyme, is also the most meticulously regulated. So, the management board has day-to-day management powers, the general meeting of shareholders has residual powers and the supervisory board exercises overall strategic control.

The management board consists of at least three directors who may or may not be members. An undischarged bankrupt merchant cannot be a director.

The directors are appointed for a term that may not exceed six years. They are appointed by the general meeting and their appointment is published in the annexes of the Belgian Official Journal. They can be discharged at any time in accordance with the will of the general meeting. While directors are not personally bound by the company's obligations, they may in certain circumstances be held liable for short-comings in management (see p62 *infra*). Directors are expected to be well-informed as to the financial circumstances of the company and must, therefore, take the appropriate measures where the future of the company is threatened by inability to pay its debts. Thus it is their responsibility in such circumstances to file for the bankruptcy of the company or else to request a composition ("concordat judiciaire", see p31 *infra*).

The Bankruptcy Act also compels the directors to keep watch over the capital of the company. Thus it prohibits them from distributing profits when the net assets have decreased (or would decrease as a result of the distribution) below the share capital as augmented by the non-distributable reserve capital.

When losses have made the net assets decrease below 50% of the share capital, the general meeting must be convened to decide on the possible winding-up of the company. The board of directors is then required to justify its conduct and to submit a special report to this effect. This obligation on the directors forms part of their general duty to provide information when the company is in financial distress.

Where the net assets have fallen to less than 25% of the share capital, a quarter of the votes cast (according to the value of the shares) at the general meeting will suffice to wind up the company. Here, again, there is an obligation on the management board to convene a general meeting of shareholders. Where this obligation is ignored or neglected, any damage to third parties arising out of the financial demise of the company will be rebuttably presumed to have been caused by the failure to call this meeting.

Available information

The annual accounts provide relatively detailed information about the company's financial position and the development of its business. The accounts comprise the balance sheet, the profit and loss account and the management's commentary thereon and are drawn up in Belgian francs.

The balance sheet and the profit and loss account are based on the company's accounting records and are composed of various different headings (Roman numerals) and sub-headings (Arabic numerals). For each heading or sub-heading, an amount is given both for the current and the previous accounting year.

Two copies of the annual accounts have to be submitted to the registry of the commercial court of the location where the company has its main place of business within 30 days from the date of its approval by the general meeting.

The annual report is another important source of information. Like the annual accounts, it is filed with the registry of the commercial court; it can also be consulted at the company's place of business.

A copy of the annual accounts is sent to a special service ("balanscentrale") with the National Bank, which will provide photocopies upon request.

Many private businesses have specialised in accumulating and procuring information on companies' annual accounts, modifications to their articles, on whether any bills of exchange have been protested or whether any attachments have been effected. Banks and credit agencies also provide information as to the creditworthiness of other businesses. This is considered to be an important aspect of banking activity in Belgium.

Financing and security for creditors

Aside from shareholders who provide the share capital, a company may also obtain finance from creditors who advance money to the company by way of loan. Since a company in financial distress is likely to go into one of two statutory·insolvency regimes, either liquidation or concordat judiciaire (which are discussed in detail below), where all "unsecured" creditors are bound together and may not proceed individually in attempting to recover the amount owed by the company, creditors who loan money very often obtain "security" in the form of the "mortgage" and the "pledge" to ensure that their loans are repaid in priority to all other creditors. The mortgagee and the pledgee are described as "separatists" because, in spite of the company's bankruptcy, they have the right to sell the property which secures the loan and they are not subject to the statutory limitations that govern the rest of the creditors.

A mortgagee is a creditor whose loan to the company is secured against some real or immovable property owned by the company. A pledgee, on the other hand, is a creditor whose security is over moveable rather than immovable property belonging to the company. This moveable property may comprise tangible assets (such as furniture and tools) and intangible assets (such as, the company's clientele, its name and logo). However, a pledge may not include more than 50% of the company's moveable property.

A contract of pledge does not need any special formalities but, since the pledged goods remain in the possession of the borrower, the Act prescribes that the pledge can only be invoked against third parties if the contract of pledge has been registered with the local registrar of mortgages. Once this formality has been complied with, the pledgee has priority over all other creditors of the company by virtue of being able to seize the assets covered by the pledge and the money thus raised must first be used to repay the outstanding loan to the pledgee.

The pledgee of a registered pledge is also entitled to the right of "volgrecht" which arises where the debtor has sold the pledged assets. In such a case the volgrecht empowers the pledgee to pursue his rights both against the assets which have replaced the assets sold by the debtor and against the pledged assets themselves in the hands of a third party who had notice of the pledge. In this manner the pledgee retains his security and priority as against other creditors of the debtor. In theory, the pledged assets can only be sold with the permission from the president of the commercial tribunal. In exercising the volgrecht, therefore, the pledgee exposes a breach of the principle that the sale of pledged goods requires permission.

In recent years, there have been a large number of sophisticated developments in the area of quasi-security interests.

The following are examples of some of them.

- Personal security interests link the assets and debts of the bankrupt debtor to the assets and debts of others, so as to ensure that the beneficiary of the security interest would not be prejudiced by the concourse of creditors, receiving due compensation even if there appears to be a lack of bankruptcy dividends.

  A distinction can be drawn between traditional personal security interests, as created by law, and those that result from common practice such as guarantees on first request, irrevocable documentary credits, banking and credit cards, letters of intent, loans set-back and negative commitments).

- Also given preferential status are certain creations of Belgian contract law, like the clause on behalf of a third party and the assignment for the benefit of the creditors.

- A number of quasi-security interests may arise from the legal relationship between parties, as modified by contract. If the commodity over which security is claimed and the creditor's claim against the debtor arise out of a common business relationship between the parties (even if that relationship is documented in separate agreements), sufficient connection will exist to enable the creditor to reserve title over the asset he has supplied until paid sums owing to him. Such clause cannot stand against third parties, if the contract would engender an artificial concourse of creditors, implying a conjunction of claims.

In the case of bankruptcy, set-off provides creditors who are also indebted to the company with a form of security. They are entitled to avoid paying the debt owed to the bankrupt company and having to accept a distribution from the debtor's estate for debts owed to them. They simply deduct the debt owed by the company to them from the debt they owe to the company, with the result that they are paid in full or at least to the extent of their debt to the company.

The prohibition of set-off in bankruptcy cases does not apply as between connected transactions. Thus, for example, a clause with regard to the indivisibility in a temporary corporation shall not be considered valid since such clause does not create an artificial bond between the claims and it finds its objective mainstay in the nature of the co-operation between the parties.

A provision in a contract stating that on the bankruptcy of a contracting party the contract is automatically terminated must be respected and taken into account by the bankruptcy trustee or "curateur". The same principle applies in a case where a clause gives one party the option of terminating the agreement in the event of the other parties' bankruptcy. Furthermore any explicitly dissolving clause ("pactum commissorium") that incorporates a sanction for contractual malice and a contingency to resolve the agreement in question by one's own motion will be recognised by the bankruptcy trustee, provided that the creditor invoking the clause does so before the concourse of creditors has come into existence. As regards retention of ownership between contracting parties, the seller remains proprietor of the commodity as long as the buyer has not paid the purchase price in full. However, such a clause may not prevent a bankrupt from concluding a compromise with his creditors. If the seller invokes the clause through a notice sent to the debtor by registered post and received by the debtor before any compromise is agreed, the seller may be able to enforce his reservation of title notwithstanding the subsequent approval of a compromise between the debtor and his creditors.

Attitude of the creditors to a company in financial distress

Whereas the "separatists" – the mortgagee and the pledgee – usually exercise substantial power as against a debtor company, the social security authorities and the fiscal authorities often act rather nonchalantly towards distressed companies. This may be due to the fact that these authorities have no special priority as creditors of a bankrupt company. Indeed, employee creditors (as general preferential creditors) have priority over both these authorities and, since employees frequently take up most or all of the assets that remain after the special preferential creditors have been repaid, the fiscal and social security authorities often remain unpaid. The category of special preferential creditors includes the pledgee and the unpaid vendor of tools and equipment.

The social security authorities do however sometimes play an important role in signalling which companies are about to collapse. Indeed, these authorities are sometimes the petitioning creditors for a declaration of bankruptcy and are known for frequently putting pressure on their debtors for repayment of the debts owing to them. The fiscal authorities on the other hand take little interest in those companies against which they have claims.

It is also important to emphasise the vital role played by banks in this connection. Companies in financial distress are, by definition, in need of funds and the attitude of the banks is therefore crucial. There is a duty on the banks to supervise the development of their debtor's business to ensure that proper use is made of loans made by the bank. And while the contract under which the loan was made might appear to give great flexibility to the banks as to the steps to be taken in recovery of the loan, in reality the discretion of the banks to terminate, suspend or maintain credit is much more limited. The dilemma for banks dealing with distressed companies is often acute. If credit is maintained for too long a period, there is a substantial risk that the impression will be created as far as third parties are concerned that the company is creditworthy. On the basis of such an impression such third parties may themselves provide credit to the company. If and when the company debtor goes bankrupt, the banks which provided the credit may be liable to such third parties.

On the other hand a decision to terminate the debtor's credit facilities may also entail liability on the part of the bank. This would arise where it can be established that the company was still a viable commercial entity when the credit was terminated and that it was due to a wrongful termination of credit which brought about the company's bankruptcy. Despite this dilemma, however, the number of cases successfully brought against banks in these circumstances is remarkably low.

Another important figure in the bankruptcy scene in Belgium is the credit insurer. Its role is to insure contracts under which a company debtor undertakes liability. Where an announcement is made that a particular credit insurer will no longer insure deliveries to a particular company, this will play an important and possibly decisive role in reducing the credit rating of that company and may lead to the latter's collapse.

Debt collection and asset recovery

Contrary to the collective liquidation procedures that derive directly from statutory law, Belgian law recognises the right of individual creditors to take measures aimed at recovery of debts owed to them by the realisation of the debtor's assets. Again, the principle of equality among (non-privileged) creditors governs the distribution on the proceeds of sale of the goods.

To prevent this principle from being eroded in practice, legislation lays down a system of publicity for the seizure of both moveable and immoveable assets. Indeed, since all the debtor's goods are subject to seizure, the system of publicity prevents the creditor who acts first from appropriating all the proceeds of the sale(s) of the seized goods. This ensures that it is possible for all the other creditors to join in the procedure of seizure and in the eventual distribution of the proceeds of sale.

The publicity is limited to those measures that are taken in the particular jurisdiction in which the debtor is domiciled and, in spite of the "collective" character of the measures, they cannot lead to seizure of the whole of the debtor's estate – an event which is dependent upon a declaration of bankruptcy.

A creditor can only petition for a declaration of bankruptcy if he is in possession of both an executory title (either a judgment or an official executory deed) and proof that individual measures of seizure were unsatisfactory.

Thus, the collective character of the individual measures of seizure means that the seized assets (even if they are in the hands of the third party) cannot be disposed of by the creditor who took the initiative nor by any other creditors that joined in the procedure.

Goods present in the debtor's estate but not belonging to him (eg leased goods and goods held in trust) can be reclaimed by the true owner if he can prove title provided they are still physically present and can be sufficiently identified.

Measures of preservation and realisation taken against goods outside Belgian territory are primarily governed by international treaties such as the European Economic Community Convention of Civil Jurisdiction and the Enforcement of Judgments (Brussels' Convention of 27 September 1968) which became part of Belgian law in 1971. This treaty provides for recognition of a foreign judgment without the need for separate Belgian legal proceedings (art 28).

3. Survival of the insolvent corporation or its business: concordat judiciaire

Purpose and effect and pre-application considerations

Where the management of the company are unsuccessful in persuading the shareholders to increase the company share capital and also in attracting outside financing, they will seek to secure the continuation of the company by attempting to renegotiate agreements with the company's largest and most important creditors individually.

Such negotiations and agreements do not, strictly speaking, give rise to any legally-binding agreement among all creditors. In practice, however, a large and important creditor will agree to the partial discharge of the debt owing to it on condition that a similar agreement is reached with other large and important creditors. Thus, where one such creditor refuses to co-operate, the company debtor may be unsuccessful in its negotiations to continue in existence. Such failure is likely to have a disastrous effect on the company's creditworthiness and lead to bankruptcy and liquidation. The dangers inherent in such informal negotiations might, therefore, induce the management of the company to avoid such an approach and seek straight away to secure a binding agreement (the "concordat judiciaire") as specifically regulated by statute.

Only the management of the company may petition for a concordat judiciaire. Its purpose is to ensure the continuation of the company's existence through a plan which combines a moratorium on all claims with or without discharge or partial discharge of the claims, of a majority of the creditors. The concordat judiciaire gives rise to a binding agreement ("concursus") which will ensure the application of the principle of equality among creditors. Thus, any individual creditor will have to abstain from any act of execution against the company or against the company's property until such time as the concursus is dismissed. It should be pointed out, however, that the principle of equality among creditors is not absolute since it is undermined by various kinds of preferences which can be claimed by an ever growing number of different creditors (this is discussed further below).

The decision whether or not the business of the company should be continued is increasingly dependent upon the goodwill of these preferential creditors. They will weigh up the advantages to themselves of a reorganisation as opposed to a forced liquidation, leaving the ordinary creditors and often even the judge in a relatively powerless position.

Procedural requirements

Eligibility for petitioning the concordat judiciaire

The procedure of the concordat judiciaire is governed by the Decree of the Regent of 25 September 1946. The Decree prescribes three requirements which a debtor must fulfil in order to be eligible for a concordat judiciaire:

- the debtor must have the status of a merchant;
- the debtor must have ceased making payment of its debts and must be unable to obtain further credit; and
- the application must be made in good faith.

These conditions must be present at the time of the judge's decision, otherwise the request for the concordat judiciaire will be dismissed regardless of how bad the financial plight of the debtor is. In such circumstances, the only option remaining to the debtor will be the informal negotiations previously referred to.

The questions of whether or not the debtor has ceased payment of its debts or is still able to obtain credit are essentially issues of fact left to the discretion of the court. The requirement that the application be made in good faith is one which goes to the heart of the Belgian legal order. The concordat judiciaire is regarded as a favour bestowed upon the debtor to enable it to escape from bankruptcy and the consequent forced liquidation. It is thus essential that the debtor prove its good faith in order to be able to take advantage of this favour. As part of this requirement of good faith the debtor must show that the financial plight has arisen through circumstances beyond its primary responsibility. It must thus show that the financial difficulties are not primarily due to its fault, negligence or incompetence but that it was, simply unfortunate.

Thus, a debtor whose financial difficulties are due to disorderly management or a lack of elementary precautions will not satisfy this requirement and therefore be ineligible for the concordat judiciaire. The same would apply to a debtor which continues trading while insolvent without seeking to establish the causes of the insolvency or taking measures to rectify the position.

In order to establish its good faith, the debtor will need to prove an absence of gross negligence. This concept is established by either of two criteria namely:

- that the debtor knew or should have known that continued operations would cause damage; or
- that there has been a violation of a rule or norm which is crucial to the sur-

vival of the company. The following short-comings have, for example, been held to be incompatible with the requirement of good faith:
- the absence of regular book-keeping;
- large debts with public creditors;
- continuing to trade while insolvent.

In principle the bad faith of any individual shareholder will not be attributed to the company.

The procedure

As already mentioned, the debtor in financial distress is the only eligible petitioner for a concordat judiciaire. For companies such as the société anonyme, this procedure will be initiated by the management board. The petition is presented to the commercial tribunal which has jurisdiction in the area in which the debtor is domiciled at the time the procedure is initiated. The court will immediately appoint a judge commissioner who is required to report on the admissibility of the petition and who will subsequently report on the debtor's financial situation. No later than eight days after the presentation of the petition the court will hear the judge commissioner's report on the eligibility of the petitioner and will decide on the admissibility of the petition. If the petition is declared admissible the judge commissioner must then immediately proceed to prepare a second report on the debtor's financial position. This report must be presented no later than 15 days after the decision declaring the admissibility of the petition. Where the court dismisses the petition as being ineligible, it may declare the debtor bankrupt.

The consequences of the concordat procedure

The presentation of the petition for a concordat has two immediate and important consequences. First, any attempted disposition of the debtor's assets is void and, second, any acts of execution by creditors against the debtor or its goods are suspended. Both the creditors and the debtor therefore are rendered impotent by the presentation of this petition. Article 11 of the Decree states that:"pending the procedure of concordat judiciaire, the debtor can neither alienate nor mortgage nor contract except with the authorisation of the judge commissioner". This constraint extends to any attempted payment by the debtor. The constraints upon the creditors relate specifically to acts of execution. Thus, any seizure and attachment for the purpose of conserving the debtor's assets is not prevented by the presentation of the petition. Creditors subject to the concourse may seek the court's permission to pursue a claim against the company, although any judgment made will not be enforceable as long as the concordat is in force.

The suspension of claims is only binding on ordinary creditors whose claims arise out of debts incurred prior to the initiation of the concordat procedure. The suspension does not apply to mortgagees, pledgees or preferential creditors (generally referred to as "créanciers hors masse") nor to the creditors who have entered into contracts with the "curateur" (collectively referred to as "créanciers de la masse"). The curateur is the official appointed by the commercial court to administer and realise the assets of the company and to distribute the proceeds of realisation among creditors in accordance with their statutory rights (see pp49 and 55).

Thus, creditors who fall into the categories of either créanciers hors masse or créanciers de la masse remain entitled to take measures of execution against the debtor. The court de cassation has also ruled that the same is true for the general preferential creditors, including, the employees and the tax authorities.

Since the fundamental purpose of a concordat judiciaire is the continuation of the business it is essential to induce suppliers and other creditors to continue to trade with the company. It would thus be senseless to apply the moratorium effect of the concordat to those creditors whose claims arise after the initiation of the concordat petition.

The principle of suspension

Certain creditors, in particular lessors or depositors who retain ownership of goods which have been transferred into the possession of the debtor, are entitled to recover such goods provided they retain their physical form and remain in the debtor's possession.

Set-off ceases to apply once the petition has been presented. In certain circumstances, however, the judge commissioner may authorise the application of set-off between the company debtor and a creditor where mutual debts and credits have been incurred.

Since a current bank account is regarded as a personal contract between the banker and the customer, it will be terminated automatically as soon as the concordat procedure has been initiated. As far as interest is concerned, it is provided that this continues to run on behalf of mortgagees and preferential creditors.

"Akkoordvoorstellen" (proposition)

Here we are concerned with the plan presented by the debtor for payment or partial payment of the debts owed. In putting forward any proposition, a debtor is bound to have regard to provisions of public order and public interest and in particular to the principle of equality among creditors. Thus, it would not be acceptable for the debtor to propose a plan which favoured a non-preferential creditor as against other creditors of equal rank. In principle, the plan is concerned only with matters of financial recovery such as rescheduling of debts or reduction of debts. Most commonly debtors propose to reduce the debt by 30 to 40%, spread out over two years. Radical reconstruction of the debt is generally excluded from such plans, Although this is not excluded by statute and in certain instances, where proposed radical reconstruction alters the rights of creditors and the nature of their claims, these may be included in the plan.

Declaration of claims

In general, creditors will give notice of their claims to the judge commissioner at the first creditors' meeting called by the Court within the time limit fixed by the Court in the order upholding the petition for the concordat.

Creditors may also submit their claims and proof thereof to the registry of the court within eight days after that meeting. At this stage the submission of the claim has only one purpose, *i.e.* securing the creditors' right to vote on the plan.

The voting process

Creditors are invited to the creditors' meeting by registered letter. Foreign creditors may be sent a telex or telegram. The meeting is presided over by the judge commissioner. Both the debtor and any of the creditors may be represented by their agents. The first business will be a report by the judge commissioner as to the debtor's financial position. Thereafter the debtor's proposals will be put to the meeting to be voted upon.

For the concordat to be approved there must be a vote in favour by a majority of the number of creditors and the amount of their claims. Only participating creditors – that is creditors who attend and participate in the meeting – are taken into account in calculating these majorities. It should be mentioned that secured creditors, like mortgagees or pledgees, would normally not participate in such proceedings, because to do so would lead to the loss of the security. The concordat will be treated as accepted when 50% plus one of the creditors present at the meeting vote in favour of it and provided that the claims of these creditors represent two-thirds of the total debt. Votes can be cast at the registry of the court at any time during the eight days after the meeting.

Ratification

After the concordat has been approved by the creditors it needs to be ratified by the court before it will come into effect. The aim is to prevent any possible abuse through the principle of majority rule, as well as to avoid a concordat which might be seen as being contrary to the interest of the public or the creditors. When an unscrupulous debtor has induced the creditors to approve a proposal which the court considers either unreasonable or unrealistic, the court will refuse to ratify it. It is clearly not in the interests of the creditors to be bound by a plan proposed by an over-optimistic debtor nor to one where the preferential claims are so significant as to make any possible recovery by the ordinary creditors remote in the extreme.

When ratified, the concordat becomes binding on all ordinary creditors whose claims arose prior to the initiation of the concordat procedure. Taxes and other public debts, preferential claims, mortgages and pledges and claims which arose after the initiation of the concordat procedure do not fall within its ambit.

Termination of the concordat

Where the debtor fails to carry out the concordat, it can be terminated by the court of its own volition or on petition of a creditor, such termination being retrospective to the date of the ratification. Once the petition for the concordat has been found to be admissible and the concordat has been ratified, the latter cannot be terminated on grounds which should have been apparent at the preliminary stage. Thus, if after ratification it is established that the debtor presented the petition in bad faith, this will not be a basis on which the concordat can subsequently be terminated.

The concordat judiciaire does not permanently free the debtor from his debts. According to article 34 of the Decree, the debtor is required to repay the creditors in full as soon as the business has improved sufficiently for this to be done. This is a mandatory provision and anything in the plan to the contrary will not be ratified.

Terms of payment

"Terms of payment" is a procedure which is an alternative to the concordat judiciaire and is designed to provide a moratorium for a debtor who is encountering temporary financial difficulties. Like the concordat, it is designed to ensure the continuation of the business in the medium term. Unlike the concordat, however, there is no scope in terms of payment for any debt reduction. It simply imposes a temporary moratorium.

The procedure of term of payment presupposes the condition that the company is a viable economic entity and would normally be able to pay its debts in full, but is nevertheless forced by unpredictable and extraordinary circumstances into a state of temporary insolvency. This regime will therefore be unavailable to a merchant who has conducted his business in a disorderly fashion and has thus been the architect of his own financial difficulty.

The petition for a term of payment must be accompanied by a detailed financial statement establishing the underlying solvency of the petitioning company. The commercial tribunal to which the petition is presented will appoint experts to verify the financial statements accompanying the petition.

The court will convene a meeting of the creditors who will be asked to decide whether or not a moratorium should be granted. In no event may a term of payment order exceed two years.

Approval of this procedure requires the affirmative vote of the majority of the creditors representing 75% of all debts against the company. As with the concordat, this procedure takes effect upon ratification by the Court of Appeals. The commercial tribunal is also empowered to put into effect a temporary moratorium pending the outcome of the petition.

During the period of the moratorium the company is under the supervision of one or more judicially appointed commissioners. Apart from conservatory measures the debtor may only take on new obligations with the prior approval of the commissioners. During the period of the moratorium no ordinary creditor may take any execution proceedings against the debtor or its property and any payment of debts existing at the time of the petition may only be made proportionately. As in the case of the concordat, the moratorium granted under the term of payment procedure has no effect on claims of mortgagees and pledgees, preferential claims, fiscal claims and claims that have arisen after the petition was presented. The moratorium will be terminated in cases of fraud by the debtor or where it is established that the company is clearly insolvent and cannot be described as simply suffering from a brief cash flow crisis.

In practice, neither the concordat nor this procedure have proved to be very successful. Their scope is somewhat limited and very often they offer nothing for the ordinary creditors. It has also proved to be pointless in an open and very competitive economic system such as that in Belgium to transfer funds by means of direct or indirect subsidies from profitable companies to those on the margins of insolvency.

Conclusion

Where a company or other business entity can no longer pay its debts, bankruptcy is the most likely result, although a debtor in financial distress who has reached a ratified concordat with its creditors or which has applied for a moratorium is still considered by the court to be able to avoid bankruptcy. Granting the concordat or term of payments against the wishes of a minority of the creditors is deemed to be in the general interest as well as in the interests of both the debtor and the creditors. It should be mentioned, however, that the statute which defines and provides such procedures is considered by some to be an abuse of the rights of the minority creditors.

One of the limitations of the concordat judiciaire is that it can only be initiated by the debtor. A second drawback is thought to lie in the fact that, even after ratification, any reorganisation of the debtor will be hindered by the fact that the management remains in charge of the company's business. But the most significant obstacle to a successful concordat culture lies in the fact that the concordat is not binding on the preferential creditors who in most instances outnumber the ordinary creditors. Even on a formal level, therefore, it will in many instances be impossible for the ordinary creditors to attain a sufficient majority to approve a concordat.

As far as the term of payment is concerned, it is of little practical importance both because of the complexity of the procedure and because it is predicated on the rarely-fulfilled condition that the debtor is capable of paying its creditors in full. The most successful procedure designed to avoid bankruptcy and to ensure the continuation of the business is quite clearly the amicable arrangement between the debtor and its creditors.

The legality of any such agreement depends on its compliance with the principle of equal treatment of creditors. Of course where no such agreement can be negotiated the debtor may try to seek a term of payment arrangement with some of its creditors.

Pending legal reform

The Bill relating to the re-organisation treaty dated 19 April 1993, sets out proposals for reform of the concordat judiciaire which are widely supported by Belgian lawyers. The bill provides for a possible stay of payment which can be granted if the debtor cannot repay his creditors temporarily and the continuity of his enterprise is endangered. In contrast with the concordat judiciaire, this procedure is only available to enterprises which have some prospect of survival. If the enterprise ceases to be able to effectively and continuously service the debt the new suspension procedure can be brought to an end and a conventional bankruptcy initiated.

Third parties affected by an enterprise's financial difficulties can ask the tribunal to replace any businessman whose performance is suspect by a temporary director who could then request the implementation of a suspension of payment. If, in the tribunal's view, the enterprise has good prospects of surviving, the tribunal may order that it be allowed temporarily to suspend payment to creditors. A payment suspension may be granted for up to six months during which time the enterprise must draw up a recovery plan.

At the end of the suspension period, the creditors must decide whether or not to approve the proposed recovery plan. If a majority does consent to the plan, it can be approved by the tribunal and a further moratorium can be granted, for a maximum period of 24 months. However, there can be no deferment of the right of special preferential creditors and national fiscal authorities to payment in accordance with their pre-existing rights. The tribunal can at any time terminate the procedure on the suit of any interested party. The tribunal also has a residual discretion itself to declare the debtor bankrupt.

4. Termination of the corporation: bankruptcy and solvent liquidation

Bankruptcy

Purpose and effect

The purpose of the bankruptcy procedure is to put the assets of the bankrupt business at the disposal of its creditors. In normal circumstances a bankrupt business will cease to carry on its activities except where a post-bankruptcy agreement can be reached or where the official appointed to administer the bankruptcy ("curateur") is able to separate certain parts of the business which can be saved from the rest.

In bankruptcy, the financial risk falls most heavily on the ordinary creditors and those like the social security and fiscal authorities whose general preferential claims are outranked by creditors who have special preferential status. Employees are the best example of the latter category. To many creditors, therefore, bankruptcy is a pointless exercise offering little more than the right to enter a deductible loss or to recover the VAT on unpaid invoices.

The obligation to bring about the bankruptcy of an insolvent commercial entity falls substantially on the debtor itself. Failure to seek bankruptcy in appropriate circumstances is treated as contrary to the public interest. Thus, a debtor who fails to inform the court that it is in a state of insolvency may be subject to penal sanctions for fraudulent bankruptcy ("eenvoudige bankbreuk"). In theory, debtors who fail to pay their creditors could be prosecuted in order to seek declarations of bankruptcy against them. This would, however, only arise where such declarations were considered to be in the public interest.

Discovering financially-distressed businesses

One problem which has plagued Belgian commercial life is that of debtors operating in the grey area of reorganisation between solvency and insolvency. Here, there might be insufficient reason for the debtor to seek some form of rescue procedure and there might be nothing to be gained on the part of any creditor seeking the debtor's bankruptcy. This gap has been partially filled by the commercial tribunals which have the power to declare a business bankrupt. These tribunals have organised business enquiry services known as "diensten voor handelsonderzoeken". The purpose of such services has been to enquire as to the precise state of solvency of debtors. Recent case law, however, guided by the cour de cassation, relegates the role of these services to that of simply establishing whether or not a business is in a state of bankruptcy. However, the very existence of business enquiring services acts as a spur to the debtor to take appropriate action.

In practice an enquiry conducted by this service would work as follows. At the preliminary stage, the services try to establish what obstacles prevent the debtor from paying the debts. Although at this preliminary stage of the investigation there are no formal requirements, the judge carrying out the investigation is limited in the enquiries that he is allowed to make. For example, such questions as, the profile of the shareholders would be treated as beyond the scope of the investigation.

The enquiry at this stage is therefore dependent on the company's voluntary co-operation. It cannot be forced to appear before the court and any reluctance to co-operate cannot be punished in any way. But the importance of this first stage often rests in the fact that semi-official contacts between the debtor and its creditors are established and often yield good results without the necessity for any further proceedings or negotiations.

Where the investigating judge is satisfied that the debtor is in a state of insolvency, he will remit the file to the court. The court will then summon the debtor and continue the investigation under the provisions of the appropriate code. It will lead an enquiry, conduct a local inspection and, it appropriate, render a bankruptcy decision.

The principle of impartiality demands that the judge in charge of the preliminary enquiry is precluded from hearing the matter when it comes before the court. This is especially true in the case of a bankruptcy which is declared by the court of its own motion. In the second phase of the investigation (when the matter is brought before the court) the prosecution will be represented.

The Belgian Supreme Court has decided that, given the tribunal's ability to vary of its own accord the rights of a bankrupt debtor, such debtor is granted the protection of article 6 of the European Treaty on the Protection of Human Rights. Hence this binding caselaw requires that the "judex ordinarius" (commercial court) summons the potential bankrupt debtor, or at least hears his arguments, before rendering a decision. Only one exception is allowed to this compulsory rule, and this exception has reference to the situation in which the commercial court can deliberate on the issue of a bankruptcy without prior hearing of the potential bankrupt debtor, on condition that exceptional circumstances necessitate a swift and immediate intervention on his part, for instance if the debtor is selling out in a suspicious manner.

However, should the commercial court declare a debtor bankrupt without giving the debtor an opportunity to expound his situation, the Court of Appeal will not be able to undo such an irregularity, even if the Court has come upon circumstances proper to the debtor's case and advantageous to the debtor, as the court of Appeal has no decisive authority to effect a bankruptcy in the first place.

The new bankruptcy bill does away with the concept of bankruptcy ex officio except for the new procedure of suspension of payment (see p37 *supra*). It tries to eliminate any scope for argument by the debtor that the Court's action might be contrary to his human rights. It also recognises the fact that a debtor who is declared bankrupt unjustly will often suffer irremediable damage as a result of the inevitable and immediate withdrawal of credit with which it will be faced. The Bill recognises in consequence (and reinforces) a creditor's ability to file a petition for the debtor's bankruptcy if the debtor has not sought to protect its position in a timely manner.

The Bill also seeks to give creditors some protection against covert action on the debtor's part. It provides that a creditor may, after service of a bankruptcy petition in respect of a debtor, apply for an order restraining the debtor from dealing with his property. The maximum duration of such an order is four months.

The basic bankruptcy procedure

Article 437 of the Bankruptcy Act provides that "any merchant who ceases to repay his debts and who is unable to obtain credit is in a state of bankruptcy". Being unable to obtain credit is not treated as an independent requirement but is closely connected with the cessation of payment. Often the interpretation of this concept is influenced by the judicial policy towards troubled businesses. A substantial amount of case law has been built in this area and it is clear that for a declaration of bankruptcy to be made, more is required than that some creditors have remained unpaid. It must be shown that this failure to pay is permanent, that it cannot be solved through the obtaining of further credit and that the unpaid debts have become sufficiently important as to evidence a general state of illiquidity. There is a corresponding obligation on a debtor to notify the court when such circumstances have arisen within three days after the cessation of payment. Failure to do this is a criminal offence ("eenvoudige bankbreuk" or "fraudulent bankruptcy"). The fact that this is a criminal offence illustrates the views of the Belgian Parliament that bankruptcy is a serious disturbance which should be terminated as quickly as possible.

Bankruptcy procedure itself operates largely or exclusively for the benefit of the creditors. Where the debtor is in a state of permanent illiquidity, this justifies the transfer of its property to the creditors. This may be open to criticism as a matter of economic rationality but it is a system deeply embedded in Belgian commercial procedure. Another contradiction lies in the fact that while bankruptcy is primarily an instrument of private law, it is ill-suited to a policy aimed at saving insolvent businesses.

Where the debtor in question is a company, the requirements for bankruptcy are generally considered to be satisfied where several of the company's creditors have remained unpaid for a period of approximately six months. The fact that the company may have certain short term profit-making potential will not save it from being declared bankrupt unless it is clear that this potential will ensure the obtaining of new credit for the Company.

Once bankruptcy has been declared, the business may only be continued through

- a concordat in bankruptcy in which the creditors have agreed to release a part of the debt or have granted a moratorium; or
- the official appointed to carry out the bankruptcy procedure (the "curateur") transferring certain viable parts of the company.

The legal mechanisms for continuation of all or part of the business of a bankrupt company are therefore limited. The thrust of the procedure is on liquidation, *i.e.* a sale of the individual assets of the debtor, an approach which in the view of the legislator best meets the twin demands of putting an end to a disturbing presence in the market and promoting competition. Once it is established that the debtor has ceased to pay its debts and is in a permanent state of illiquidity, the judge before whom the petition is presented has no discretion. He is obliged to make a declaration of bankruptcy. Such a decision will be rendered by the commercial tribunal on a petition either by the debtor or by the creditors or might be a decision taken of its own motion by the court. However, in the last case, the court has a discretion and, even if circumstances are established which satisfy a finding of bankruptcy, it is not obliged to make such a declaration.

Procedural requirements

Bankruptcy procedure is only available to a person who qualifies for the description of "merchant". This description can of course be attributed either to an individual person or to an association of persons. In the case of an individual person, the description "merchant" will apply where that person is engaged in what are described as "acts of commerce" either as a principal or as part of that person's profession. In the case of an association of persons, the description "merchant" will apply where that association has as one of its objects the carrying out of acts of commerce. Thus, in practice, any legal person involved in business will be deemed to be a merchant and thus subject to the bankruptcy procedure. The Bankruptcy Act provides that a merchant who has stopped conducting acts of commerce – owing to death or some other reason – is still susceptible to the bankruptcy procedure for a period of six months after the cessation of the business activities.

Belgian law provides for the registration of civil companies as well as commercial companies. Civil companies do not in general undertake acts of commerce and are thus not governed by the Companies Act or susceptible to the bankruptcy procedure. There can, however, be circumstances where acts of commerce are conducted on behalf of a civil company and in violation of its constitution. In such circumstances, the acts in question may be imputed to the company but this will still not serve to make the company, as a whole, susceptible to the bankruptcy procedure, although they may result in the company being wound-up.

The above rules relating to civil companies may also be made in relation to the so-called "VZW's" (non-profit making associations) where these in fact conduct business.

As already pointed out the twin conditions for a judgment of bankruptcy in relation to the merchant are, first, that the merchant has ceased to make payment of his or its debts and, secondly, that the merchant is unable to obtain credit. There has been a long debate as to whether these constitute two separate autonomous conditions to be separately satisfied or whether the same evidence can be used to satisfy both conditions. It would seem from the statutory history of the Bankruptcy Act that the condition of "inability to obtain further credit" was designed to ensure that, when assessing whether or not there was a permanent cessation of payment of debts, only the commercial debts of the debtor were taken into account.

It has become clear, therefore, that any bankruptcy judge must consider each requirement but that this does not mean that they have to be considered separately. The relevant case law shows that, where a debtor has ceased to make payments and that this cessation is permanent, it will be assumed that this will create sufficient suspicion among the creditors to result in the debtor being unable to obtain further credit.

The court has also been required to sort out problems where a debtor has been able to obtain credit but where it has been established that this is either artificial or the credit was obtained by illegal means. Once it is established that a fraudulent practice has been used to obtain credit which would otherwise not have been forthcoming, or that the credit has been artificially obtained "for example, by allowing social security or certain fiscal debts to remain unpaid for a long time" the conditions for bankruptcy will be considered to have been established. Another example of fraudulent or artificial obtaining of credit is the practice known as "kite-flying". This is the practice of drawing a cheque on one bank account and depositing it in another and then doing the same thing in reverse so as to make it appear that both accounts contain the amount represented by the cheques going backwards and forwards.

In some instances the fraudulent practices may lead to the company debtor being unable to maintain its payments but will not have been responsible for the non-availability of credit. Thus, where money is transferred by a director or manager from the company to himself in breach of the law or constitution of the company, that director or manager may be liable to criminal prosecution. The company, on the other hand, may well be able to re-establish credit when the particular fraudulent practice has ceased. Similarly, other fraudulent practices (such as preparing deliberately misleading accounts) will themselves be subject to possible criminal prosecution but do not provide an automatic link with any eventual bankruptcy of the company.

It should be clear from the above that mere cash shortages, disorderly book-keeping, bad economic prospects and the temporary delay in the payment of debts do not suffice to satisfy the conditions for bankruptcy. It is necessary to wait to see whether the cessation of payments becomes permanent or whether this difficulty is resolved. Above all, it must be clear that where there are interruptions of payments anyone wishing to seek the bankruptcy of the debtor must establish that the debtor was aware of the problem.

Thus, where a petition is presented to the court for the bankruptcy of the debtor, the court will look not only to establish that the debtor is insolvent but will need to be satisfied that the insolvency is permanent and that credit cannot be obtained either by a further loan or solvency restored by the sale of assets. When such a petition is presented, the court will fix a date for the hearings, which is not advertised (at this stage it is still a private litigation between two parties). The judge will also consider the potential viability of the business and, if he declares that the business has a future, this will often be treated as evidence that the insolvency is only temporary. Even after an adjudication of bankruptcy, representations may be made by creditors to the effect that they are now willing to accord to the debtor a term of payment arrangement. Such representations would thus establish that the debtor was in a position to obtain credit and the bankruptcy order would be lifted. It has further been established that the mere fact that creditors making new deliveries of goods to the company wish to be paid in cash does not suffice as proof that the debtor has ceased making payments of its debts. Similarly, no such inference can be drawn where the only evidence is the collection of a debt by means of an enforcement procedure (for example an attachment or seizure).

On the other hand, it may be possible to infer that the conditions for bankruptcy exist even where the debtor appears not to be insolvent. Thus, although immediate payments of debts are being made, bankruptcy may be declared if, according to the debtor's balance sheet, liabilities are substantially in excess of assets. This may be treated as decisive proof of the inability of the debtor to obtain further credit. According to the commercial tribunal of Kortijk, for a cessation of payments to be treated as sufficient to lead to bankruptcy, there must be evidence of a general refusal by most of the debtor's creditors to provide further credit.

The court will generally be suspicious where the petition for bankruptcy is presented by a shareholder of the debtor. This is looked upon as an attempt by the shareholder to obtain payment in priority to the debtor company's creditors. Furthermore, where the petitioner cannot establish a definitive claim, the petition will be rejected unless it is clear from other evidence that the requirements for bankruptcy are established.

Finally, it should be stressed that the requirements for bankruptcy must be shown to be present at the time of the adjudication by the court. Similarly, where there is an appeal against an order of bankruptcy, these conditions must be shown to be present at the time of the appeal hearing. If they are no longer present the appeal will be upheld.

In an important bankruptcy case (where notice was given to the debtor), the Court of Dendermonde, division Sint-Niklaas decided after a thorough analysis of the debtor's economic situation, the depositions of the board of directors and the attitude of affected third parties, that the debtor's enterprise was undoubtedly in financial difficulty although not bankrupt. The court found that the enterprise's financial problems had arisen because of disagreement between the shareholders as to the company's policy. The court stressed in consequence that the directors could, if required, be held responsible for allowing the deadlock to arise.

The procedure: jurisdiction, appeal, opposition

The commercial court has exclusive jurisdiction over any issues arising within a bankruptcy and will seek the solution to any such problems within the special rules formulated for the governing of a bankruptcy estate. The particular commercial court will be that of the place where the bankrupt debtor has his or its main place of business and any claim in the bankruptcy will need to be referred to that court.

Where an appeal is launched against a declaration of bankruptcy, this must be done within 15 days from the date on which the bankruptcy order is published in the appropriate newspaper. The appeal may be presented by anyone whose rights are affected by the bankruptcy judgment, but where it is the bankrupt himself or itself that presents the appeal the time limit is reduced to eight days.

If the court adjudges a debtor bankrupt by its own motion, the bankrupt debtor, the curateur or interested third party can petition the Commercial Court for the rescission of the bankruptcy.

If the Commercial Court dismisses the application to rescind the bankruptcy, notice of appeal can be given to the appropriate Court of Appeal. If the Court of Appeal rescinds the bankruptcy, this generally disposes of the matter.

This means that, for physical persons, there is generally no chance of obtaining a new bankruptcy order if the debtor has suspended his commercial activities for more than six months.

Creditors' involvement and position

The ordinary and general preferential creditors

As indicated above there are at least three categories of creditors interested in the estate of the bankrupt. The special preferential creditors include any mortgagee, pledgee or lessee and they are entitled to pursue their rights against the property by which their claims are secured. They are thus unaffected by the bankruptcy procedure. The general preferential creditors include the social security and fiscal authorities whose claims must be presented in the bankruptcy together with those of the ordinary creditors (*i.e.* those who enjoy no preference at all). It is only by the presentation of these claims that the ordinary and preferential creditors may have any participation in the progress of the bankruptcy.

The curateur will send a notice to all the known creditors of the company asking them to submit proof of their debts. The date of the hearing of such proof is decided at the declaration of bankruptcy and cannot exceed 40 days, although, for foreign creditors, the judge commissioner can extend the time limit. After the limit has been passed, the claims will not be deemed to be null and void but the creditors will have to sue the curateur in court.

Since the effect of the bankruptcy order is to ensure the equal treatment of all creditors all attempts designed to recover money from the debtor on behalf of any creditor are suspended. This does not however prevent a potential creditor whose claim has not yet been established from continuing an action against the bankruptcy estate. Such a claim may be continued until judgment in order to establish whether the person pursuing the claim does in fact become a creditor in the bankruptcy estate or not.

The official appointed to administer the bankruptcy estate is known as a "curateur". In general, Belgian bankruptcy law provides strong support for decisions by the curateur and the creditors have little power to influence his policy and decisions. This is designed to speed up the liquidation process. The only real remedy available to creditors who object to the policies and decisions of a curateur is to apply to the court and to ask the judge commissioner to revoke the powers of the curateur. In general, this can only be done when the curateur has presented accounts concerning the actions taken on behalf of the bankruptcy estate.

A curateur may, in certain circumstances and with the approval of the court, continue the business or part of the business in the bankruptcy estate. The creditors, in turn, may oppose the continuation of the bankrupt business where it can be established that continuation requires the transfer of assets from the bankrupt away from the creditors themselves, or where the continuation of the business will increase the estate's liabilities. The curateur will have taken a decision to continue the business in order to try to be in a position to sell it as a going concern at a higher price than would have been possible were the assets of the bankrupt to be sold separately. Even where this is achieved, in practice it is unlikely to be of benefit to the ordinary or general preferential creditors. The increase in price for the sale of the business as a going concern is likely to benefit the special preferential creditors without improving the position of the ordinary or general preferential creditors.

From a procedural point of view, where the ordinary creditors wish to oppose a decision taken by the curateur, an "*ad hoc* curateur" must be appointed to represent the creditors.

In presenting his accounts, the curateur will have to account for any damages which result from wrongful policy decisions, for example in the continuation of the business which had resulted in an increased loss on the part of the bankruptcy estate. In such circumstances the curateur himself will be liable to make good the loss and it will also be possible to pursue a claim in respect of this loss against the bankruptcy estate itself. Any such loss is quantified by reference to the inventory of assets in the bankruptcy estate that will have been filed with the registry of the commercial court at the opening of the bankruptcy proceedings.

Special preferential creditors

Special preferential creditors such as lessors, pledgees or mortgagees are privileged in that their claims are secured on assets owned by the bankrupt. They cannot exercise any rights in relation to the secured assets until the time for all claims to be made against the bankruptcy estate has expired. Thereafter, however, such creditors may pursue their rights irrespective of the bankruptcy since the rule of equality of treatment of creditors does not apply to them.

Thus a lessor may repossess the leased premises. The lease will usually be ended by the curateur as one of the first acts in the administration of the bankruptcy estate. A mortgagee has the power to sell the assets over which the mortgage has been granted, to the exclusion of the curateur. The latter may only sell the secured assets in question where the mortgagee so consents. A pledgee derives his rights from the law of 5 May 1872 which states that "the rights granted to a pledgee are not suspended by the bankruptcy of the pledgor." The curateur is thus unable to dispose of the pledged assets against the will of the pledgee nor may he exercise any rights in the proceedings under which the pledged assets are realised.

There may be a dispute between one special preferential creditor and another where, for example, each claims security over the same assets. Here too, the curateur has no right in any proceedings except in relation to any balance remaining after the resolution of the claims between the two special preferential creditors.

However, subject to the authorisation of the judge commissioner, the curateur may pay the debt owing to the special preferential creditor and then take possession of the assets which constitute the security. This might be done if the curateur believes that the realisation of such assets will be more beneficial to the bankruptcy estate, but rarely occurs in practice. An example might be when the curateur wishes to sell the business as a going concern. To do so together with the secured asset may enable a higher price to be realised whereas the special preferential creditor may seek to realise the asset in question simply with a view to the repayment of his own debt.

The "creanciers de la masse" and the new estate

The debts payable by the bankrupt's estate are satisfied out of the assets belonging to the bankrupt and over which the curateur can exercise power. The identity of these assets may be established by reference to the inventory filed with the registry of the commercial court at the opening of the bankruptcy. However, if the curateur enters into any agreements with third parties, those third parties will have claims both against the assets of the debtor and against the curateur personally if the obligations entered into by the curateur are not met. The publication of the bankruptcy order is thus notice to such third parties that they can contract with the curateur in the knowledge that any obligations incurred by the debtor acting through the curateur are virtually certain to be met.

There has been much debate in the Belgian courts as to what makes a debt a "créance de la masse" (and thus eligible for payment in full as an expense of the bankruptcy) as against merely an ordinary claim against the bankrupt for which the creditor can expect at most to receive a dividend. A recent decision of the Supreme Court indicates that, to make that debt a "créance de la masse" a close bond must exist between the debt in issue and the administration of the bankrupt enterprise. In other words, to be eligible for payment as an expense of the bankruptcy, the debt must have been consciously incurred by the curateur. Only then will it be a créance de la masse.

The institutions within the bankruptcy proceedings

The judge commissioner

The judge commissioner is a member of the commercial court whose task is to supervise the curateur and to provide whatever assistance is necessary in the conduct of the bankruptcy. Thus, the judge commissioner will consider all steps taken by the curateur and will ensure that the liquidation process is carried out as quickly as possible. He is also required to report to the court on any disputes that arise within the bankruptcy.

The judge commissioner is able to grant permission to the curateur to sell certain assets and make decisions in relation to the custody of assets belonging to the bankruptcy estate. Any decision by the judge commissioner can be appealed against to the commercial court and such appeal can be presented either by the creditors or by the curateur himself. The decision of the commercial court in such circumstances is final.

As part of his overall remit, the judge commissioner must monitor the liquidation proceedings and prevent any needless delay in the liquidation of the bankrupt's assets.

He is entitled in the interests of creditors to question the curateur's conduct, but he does not have the power to take decisions in place of the curateur or negotiate with potential buyers, even in dialogue with the curateur. In one instance, a judge commissioner was not allowed to recover from the bankrupt's estate transportation costs he had incurred in travelling to see a potential buyer of the bankrupt's assets.

The bankruptcy bill also limits the role of the judge commissioner to supervision of the bankruptcy process and in particular, its swift conclusion. It is also the judge commissioner's duty to allow the curateur to act unhindered, when swift decision-making is of overriding importance.

Where the sale of moveables and immovables is in issue, certain matters are within the sole remit of the judge commissioner and he will have to play a full part in the bankruptcy process to carry out his functions. Although prevailing circumstances may make the need for a decision imperative, the judge commissioner alone cannot act to ensure the continuity of a business in financial difficulty. For instance, he cannot authorise the transfer of an industrial entity to a third party as a going concern without approval of the commercial court.

Once the judge commissioner has reported to the court, commenting on all suggestions and proposals that are deemed useful and to the benefit of the bankrupt's estate, and the court has determined the conditions and the way in which they may be given effect, the specific role of the judge commissioner comes to an end. He will only remain involved in a supervisory capacity. It would therefore be invidious for him to have any role in the sale process, in respect of which he is given no powers. He is also unable to sanction public or private share allotments, nor can he determine the book of charges. He is unable to insist on guarantees and has no say in the assets sold, for instance, to withdraw assets from any proposed sale. The commercial court, in contrast, is entitled to lay down a minimum sale price, to delay a sale or to demand a valuation report.

In his report to the commercial court, the judge commissioner may object to a sale by private treaty where there are a number of potential purchasers. This certainly applies to real estate, where the court will expect the judge commissioner to agree with the curateur. If there are several potential buyers, but the judge-commissioner has nonetheless deemed that sale must be by private treaty, the court can still refuse to give effect to this. This is because article 1193ter of the Belgian Judicial Code provides for an exceptional procedure and the public sale constitutes the common law; moreover there is no possibility of making a bid, nor of starting an allotment proceeding.

Consequently neither the judge commissioner, nor the commercial court can allow their decision to be influenced by the curateur's request for a favourable opinion or authorisation. This will always be the case where the curateur has chosen a buyer by means of an allotment proceeding in which potential buyers are required to submit sealed bids to the curateur.

Case law quite rightly holds that no prior agreement between the curateur and a bidder can bind the court. The court alone is empowered to act in the interests of creditors by laying down the terms on which a sale is to be allowed.

The report of the judge commissioner, who in general is a practitioner in business life, is an important element of the authorisation process.

The procedure is an authorisation rather than a homologation, which means that a curateur who signs an agreement before having received authorisation would act without proper competence and could in consequence be held liable for any loss the other party to the contract might suffer as a result of the curateur's actions.

The curateur

There is still doubt amongst Belgian scholars as to whether the curateur represents the bankrupt or the creditors. It is preferable, however, to consider him as the person whose task it is to administer the assets which belonged to the debtor at the time of the declaration of bankruptcy. Such administration is carried out through powers directly conferred upon the curateur by the law of bankruptcy. The curateur exercises those rights which might have been exercised by the bankrupt not through any theory of representation or agency but because he is so enabled by the law relating to the administration of bankruptcy estates.

If one accepts that the curator, as administrator of the estate of the bankrupt debtor, is bound by the prior rights and obligations of that estate, then one must accept in consequence that certain actions of the debtor, carried out before its bankruptcy, will remain valid as follows:

- The curateur cannot set aside a sale of immovable property agreed prior to bankruptcy but not fully documented or registered at the time the bankruptcy order was made.

- The curateur must give effect to a transfer of shares agreed before bankruptcy but not properly registered in the company's statutory records at the time the bankruptcy order is made.

- A pledge of a bankrupt debtor's assets is valid against the curateur, even if it has not been properly registered.

Where the actions at issue are capable of challenge under the bankruptcy legislation, the curateur's powers to make such a challenge stem directly from that legislation.

The legislation gives the curateur the exclusive right to institute proceedings on behalf of the bankruptcy estate to seek compensation for any loss suffered by the estate. Any benefit derived from this litigation will of course be held for the account of the estate. It is through the exercise of this power that the curateur is able to bring proceedings against a former director or former directors of the bankrupt company whose estate he is administering. Here, he is quite clearly acting not as a representative of all the creditors but for the benefit of the bankruptcy estate itself.

Such claims against a director should be distinguished from those which might be brought by each individual creditor seeking to be indemnified against the loss that might have been suffered through the wrongful act of the director causing them to agree to continue to trade with the company after it had ceased to pay its debts. A wrongful act on the part of the director may be the same in each case but the actions which can be brought in respect of that wrongful act differ depending upon whether the action is brought by the curateur on behalf of the bankruptcy estate or by the creditor seeking to be indemnified for the loss suffered. In such circumstances, the curateur will be seeking compensation equal to the reduction of the asset value of the estate caused by the wrongful act of the director. Individual creditors, on the other hand, will be seeking an indemnity in respect of a loss which will constitute the sum total of their individual claims. This amount will be reduced by what may be expected as a dividend paid out by the bankruptcy estate. The curateur has no right to act in respect of the claims by the individual creditors in these circumstances but, where the curateur acts on behalf of the bankruptcy estate in deciding whether or not proceedings should be brought, the decision is a decision for the curateur alone.

In summary, the tasks of the curateur are, first, to gain control of and manage the assets in the bankruptcy estate. Secondly, the curateur will take whatever steps are necessary to ensure that those assets are increased by the collection of assets which legitimately belong to the bankrupt. This will include the bringing of claims against persons who have caused loss to the bankrupt. Thirdly, the curateur will realise the assets and finally, he will ensure the distribution of dividends amongst the creditors in accordance with the legal rules establishing the priority of one group of creditors as against another. All these tasks will be carried out under the supervision of the commercial court and the particular judge commissioner.

The remuneration of the curateur

There are no uniform rules governing the remuneration of the curateur. It will be left to the commercial court to establish the remuneration to be paid according to a special tariff. The remuneration is treated as a first charge on the assets belonging to the bankrupt, even to the exclusion where necessary, of the claims of a pledgee or mortgagee. Although the remuneration of the curateur has this privileged status, the payment is to be made only when the bankruptcy proceedings are closed.

The tariff which determines the remuneration payable to the curateur requires an evaluation to be made of all the tasks which have been performed. These should only include the sale of assets which had been either mortgaged or pledged in order to realise sufficient assets to meet the remuneration. Under existing case law, the principle has been established that the evaluation of these tasks cannot be done simply by applying the existing tariff but must be done on a case by case basis subject to the control and approval of the commercial court. Where mortgaged or pledged assets have been sold unnecessarily for the purposes of the curateur's remuneration, no claim can be made for remuneration in relation to such sale. This is also the case where such sale was carried out by the mortgagee or pledgee himself.

On the other hand, where a mortgagee or pledgee has entrusted the sale of the assets in question to the curateur, such mortgagee or pledgee must contribute on a pro rata basis to the remuneration of the curateur. The justice of this cannot be doubted in view of the fact that in such circumstances, the curateur is largely, if not exclusively, concerned with the interests of such special preferential creditors.

If the bankruptcy judgment is revoked, or if the task of curateur comes to an end as a result of a composition or other agreement which will be administered by a trustee, the latter will be entitled to remuneration for taking care of the assets belonging to the bankrupt during the period when the composition or other agreement is carried out. The judgment by which the bankruptcy is revoked will generally state who will be responsible for the remuneration of the trustee. If not, or if the bankruptcy comes to an end as a result of an agreement in bankruptcy, the debtor itself will be responsible for such remuneration. As far as the curateur is concerned in these circumstances, it may not always be possible to apply the tariff of remuneration as established by the commercial court. In such event, the remuneration of the curateur will be fixed by reference to the actual activities which he has undertaken.

The liabilities of the curateur

The curateur is entrusted by law with the administration of the assets in the bankruptcy estate and is expected to observe due diligence and good faith in the performance of his required duties. As a person entrusted with a public service the curateur will be required to account for the way in which he has managed the assets that have been placed under his control. He will, of course, be criminally liable for any embezzlement and will be liable to indemnify anyone (that is either the creditors or the bankrupt debtor itself) for any loss suffered as a result of the administration of the bankruptcy estate. The following are examples where the actions of the curateur may damage the bankruptcy estate:

- sale of the bankrupt's real estate at an inappropriate time;
- selling goods that do not in fact belong to the bankrupt;
- distributing dividends in accordance with a hierarchy based upon an alleged privilege which was not specifically invoked;
- paying out his own remuneration in accordance with his own calculations without authorisation or supervision by the court;
- continuing a loss-making business activity to the detriment of the estate;
- failing to comply with the procedure laid down by bankruptcy law.

The above are instances where the wrongful acts of the curateur caused loss to the bankruptcy estate itself. There are also circumstances where such wrongful actions may render the curateur liable to individual creditors. Examples of this are:

- where requested by a pledgee or mortgagee to sell the assets in question, failing to remit the proceeds;
- selling equipment made available to the bankrupt by lease agreement;
- damage caused to the leased premises by the removal of furniture.

A tort committed by the curateur in the performance of his functions can be pursued against those assets in the bankrupt's estate which are no longer in the debtor's possession. These assets, as well as the curateur personally, can be pursued for damages. The debtor and individual creditors can only pursue the curateur for damages at the end of the bankruptcy proceedings, at which time the court can refuse to give the curateur his release.

Individual creditors applying to the curateur for damages can only obtain compensation for losses they have themselves suffered. They are not entitled to act on behalf of the bankrupt's estate.

Dismissal of the curateur
The commercial court has exclusive jurisdiction to decide any dispute relating to the management of the bankruptcy in general and the liability of the curateur in particular. Since the curateur is appointed by the commercial court and performs his functions under the supervision of that court, he can be dismissed and replaced by that court. In the exercise of its power to dismiss a curateur, the court will be very careful to ensure that it acts only on the basis of real and serious facts and also only after having first heard the response of the curateur to the allegations made.

Management and liquidation by the curateur

Existing agreements – general
The general principle in Belgian law is that bankruptcy does not put an end to agreements that have been entered into prior to the bankruptcy. There are certain exceptions to this general rule. Thus, agreements that had been entered into which depend on the identity of the particular parties would come to an end as a result of the bankruptcy of one of these parties. A similar result will be obtained in the case of agreements that contain explicit clauses which provide for the termination of such agreements on the bankruptcy of one of the parties. This exception to the general principle does not, however, apply in the case of labour agreements.

The special position of the curateur, however, gives him the right to determine any existing agreement unilaterally. If he were unable to do this, the principle of equality amongst creditors could not be respected. Such unilateral termination on the part of the curateur may be either explicit or implicit, although the curateur ought to act in such a way so as to ensure that there is no misunderstanding. Indeed, where he does terminate a contract unilaterally, the other party will have a claim for any resulting damages against the bankruptcy estate.

Labour agreements
Labour agreements are, of course, of major importance, especially in the circumstances where the curateur is intending to continue the activities of the bankrupt debtor. In theory, he is entitled, should he wish to do so, to continue to employ the employees, notwithstanding the bankruptcy. In practice, however, he will take steps to put an end to the acquired rights of the employees and, also, unilaterally put an end to the labour agreements. In certain instances, however, some employees will be essential where the business is to be sold as a going concern, particularly those who have knowledge and experience which will be important in the continuation of the business after its transfer. In the case of such employees, the curateur will attempt to avoid such breach of contract.

Once the curateur has acted to terminate the acquired rights of the employees, the way is open for a purchaser to make proposals for taking over the business and possibly re-employing the employees. Where the curateur does not act to terminate such labour contracts, the proposals for the purchase of the business will have to take account of the possible liability which might arise where the purchaser himself will have to act to terminate any particular labour agreements.

A curateur who wishes to continue the labour agreements will be confronted by several legal problems. In the first place, he will be required to provide employment under the same conditions, in the same place, and at the same time as was the case prior to the bankruptcy. If he attempts unilaterally to modify any of these conditions or to attach any additional duties, he runs the risk of perpetrating a breach of contract. The same would be true where the curateur seeks to relieve the employee from duties to which the latter was subject under the labour agreement, even where this remission purports to take effect during the notice period given by the employee or employer prior to the bankruptcy.

In any of the cases where a breach of contract by the curateur can be established, an indemnity may be claimed by the employee as a debt in the bankrupt's estate. This in turn might enable the other creditors to seek an indemnity against the curateur personally.

In general, the sentiment in Belgium is against the maintenance of labour contracts after a declaration of bankruptcy. This is, of course, subject to the obvious exceptions already mentioned but is in accordance with the generally held view that bankruptcy should normally mean the end of the activities of the company. Even where the curateur is given permission to continue the activities of the bankrupt debtor, such permission is rarely, if ever, given for a long period. The curateur will not have any certainty with regard to the continuation of the activities of the bankrupt debtor and thus cannot take the chance that he will be able to transfer the labour agreements with the business as a going concern. It is likely that any interested purchaser will want only some or, indeed, none of the employees. Maintaining the labour contracts, therefore, may make the business unsaleable.

Leases
The bankruptcy declaration does not automatically put an end to a lease. The curateur may decide to continue the lease agreement, terminate it, or even enter into a new agreement with the lessor. In the last hypothesis, any payments to be made under a new lease will be considered to be debts of the estate beginning from the date of the bankruptcy judgment and enjoying a preference over the debts of the ordinary creditors and the general preferential creditors. The curateur may also be able to assign a commercial lease but, in such a case, he may be jointly and severally liable for the obligations imposed by that lease. In practice, the curateur usually terminates the lease.

The continuation of the business activity

The bankruptcy of the debtor will normally result in the cessation of its operations. Only in exceptional circumstances will the curateur apply for a continuation of these business activities. As already mentioned, this will only be done with the permission of the court or by agreement with the creditors. The justification for this unusual course will usually be the fact that the assets of the bankrupt debtor consist of a large quantity of unfinished goods or partially-treated raw materials. Such goods may be worthless in their condition at the time of the declaration of bankruptcy but may yield a substantial value if turned into finished products. A limited continuation of the business activities of the bankrupt debtor will then be necessary to enable the curateur either to ensure that the work in progress is completed or to sell the products to existing clients. It may also be that maintaining the business activity in order to sell the entire business as a going concern will yield a great deal more than would an immediate cessation of the business and the piecemeal sale of the assets of the bankrupt debtor.

Once the court has granted permission for the continuation of the business or such continuation has been agreed upon by the creditors, the permission will extend to all acts that are necessarily implied by the continuation.

Realising the assets

Realising the assets is one of the most important tasks of the curateur. The procedure is linked in bankruptcy law to the possibility of an agreement between the creditors and the curateur which would enable the business or part of the business to be continued. Applications to the court for approval of such agreements are rare because the effect is to place a moratorium on the sale of the bankrupt debtor's assets. Until a meeting of creditors has been called to consider the proposal for an agreement, any real estate belonging to the bankrupt debtor cannot be sold and moveable goods can only be sold prior to this meeting if authorisation has first been obtained by the court. If, however, the goods in question are perishable or will decrease quickly in value, they can be sold with the permission of the judge commissioner.

The restrictions imposed on the sale of the company's assets by the application for an agreement may seriously inhibit the sale of the business as a going concern. Indeed, in certain instances the application may destroy whatever chance there might have been for the sale of the business as a going concern.

In principle, when it comes to the sale of real estate, a public auction is the generally accepted method. Exceptional circumstances would be required for a private sale. Where it is believed that such exceptional circumstances exist, the curateur must apply to the court for prior permission to effect the sale of the real estate by private sale rather than by public auction. If he acts without such permission, such act would not be binding on the bankruptcy estate. In the absence of exceptional circumstances, the courts will not give permission for a private sale. It has been held, for example, that the mere fact that the building would be empty for a long period of time owing to the fact that an appeal had been launched against the bankruptcy judgment and that the bankrupt was willing to give permission for the sale to be effected in order to avoid a decrease in value does not constitute exceptional circumstances such as to enable the sale to be effected by private treaty.

Distribution

Having realised the assets, the duty of the curateur will be to distribute the proceeds amongst the creditors. In effecting such distribution he must have regard to the hierarchy of categories of creditors and ensure that a superior category is paid in full before any distribution is made to creditors in the next category down.

There are four categories of privileged creditors:

(i)   creditors with a general privilege over moveable goods and real estate;
(ii) creditors with a general privilege over moveable goods;
(iii) creditors with a special privilege over moveable goods;
(iv) creditors with a special privilege over real estate.

Creditors that fall into categories (iii) and (iv), *i.e.* those with special privilege, are the mortgagee, lessee and pledgee. These creditors are characterised by having a specific link between their claim and specific goods or assets. They are not, in principle, concerned with the usual distribution process since claims are satisfied out of the sale of the specific assets. However, if, in the realisation of these specific assets, the amount received exceeds the claim of the creditor in question, the difference must be paid over to the curateur for the benefit of creditors in the lower categories. Where the amount realised from the sale of the specific goods or assets is insufficient to satisfy the claim of the mortgagee, pledgee or lessee, the latter will rank as an ordinary creditor to the extent that his claim is unsatisfied.

The creditors who fall into categories (i) and (ii) above, *i.e.* those who have general privileges over moveable goods and/or real estate, are next in the hierarchy of creditors to be paid out of the bankruptcy estate. There is no specific link between their claim and any specific goods in the estate and their claims must be fully satisfied before any distributions can be made to the ordinary creditors. These general preferential creditors include the social security and fiscal authorities.

The above categories of creditors have been listed in a simplified form. In fact the number of preferential creditors is increasing and these are listed in a wide number of legislative texts. There are, therefore, many instances where creditors fail to realise that they might enjoy certain privileges. The effect of the legislative changes is to reduce the rule of equality of treatment of creditors. It should be pointed out, however, that the court of cessation (cour de cassation) has held that claims based upon a reservation of title clause are ineffective against the bankruptcy estate.

Position of shareholders and officers

After a declaration of bankruptcy has been made against a corporate debtor, a period will still be required during which the realisation process will take place. Until this process is completed, the directors of the company remain in office but the curateur will exercise their authority and power. The directors continue to represent the company and, as the board of directors, they are able to take all decisions that do not come under the control and power of the curateur. An example of a decision which can still be taken by the board of directors after the declaration of bankruptcy is the application for an agreement between the bankrupt company and its creditors.

The shareholders generally play a passive role even prior to the declaration of bankruptcy. They do, however, have certain rights. Thus, if no auditor has been appointed by the company, the shareholders have an individual right of control which can be effected through the appointment of a certified accountant who is paid by the shareholders. The shareholders are also entitled to have an extraordinary general meeting of the company summoned. They may apply for the appointment of a temporary administrator to perform all or part of the functions of the directors. The latter request is generally granted in circumstances where the economic condition of the company is unstable and is threatening to disintegrate as a result of policy decisions or disagreements amongst the directors.

The termination of the bankruptcy

Insufficient assets

As soon as the curateur has prepared an inventory of the assets belonging to the bankruptcy estate, he must make an assessment as to whether the estate has sufficient resources to cover the cost of the administration of the bankruptcy estate. If he concludes that the resources are insufficient he must immediately apply to the commercial court to have the bankruptcy terminated owing to a lack of resources.

If, on appointment, the curateur discovers that there are no assets he will request termination of the bankruptcy immediately.

As far as the creditors are concerned the law requires that either they should receive a dividend out of the liquidated assets as soon as possible or, if there are insufficient assets to cover the bankruptcy procedure, that they should be entitled to regain their individual rights of action.

The court will grant this request of the curateur when it is clear that no dividend can be distributed to either the ordinary or different classes of preferential creditors. It will also grant this request even where there are assets where it is clear that all these assets will be consumed by the claims of the specially preferential creditors (*i.e.* lessees, pledgees and mortgagees). Applications for termination of the bankruptcy in these circumstances can be made by creditors as well as by the curateur and it is also clear that such termination can be made by the court of its own motion. Once the order for termination is granted, the curateur loses all authority and the bankruptcy comes to an end.

Termination following bankruptcy

The role of the curateur will also come to an end and the bankruptcy will be terminated when the creditors accept a draft statement of distribution accounts presented to them by the curateur at a meeting specially convened for the purpose and presided over by the judge commissioner. At the same time the curateur will be discharged of his functions.

Where the accounts are approved and the discharge granted in respect of the curateur, no further claims can be made against the curateur in respect of the performance of his functions even where it is later established that errors were made in the conduct of his office.

The binding nature of the resolutions taken at this meeting apply only to those creditors who attended or who through their own negligence were not present at the meeting. Thus, even the bankrupt himself who is not present at the meeting may still be entitled to hold the curateur accountable for the way in which the latter performed his functions. On the other hand, it is still open to the curateur to apply for a modification of the approved accounts where it is established that a material mistake has been made in their preparation.

Thus, prior to any resolution to discharge the curateur, it is possible for the creditors to seek to hold the curateur liable in respect of any alleged wrongful acts committed during the performance of his functions. Where such disputes arise they will be decided by the commercial court.

Solvent liquidation of a company

The solvent liquidation of the company will take place as a result of:

- a decision of a meeting of the shareholders; or
- a decision of a competent court; or
- operation of law.

Where this occurs, one or more liquidators will be appointed to carry out the liquidation of the company. The liquidator or liquidators will realise the assets of the company and repay the debts on a pro rata basis. Surplus assets remaining after such repayment will be distributed amongst the shareholders in accordance with their shareholding. The liquidation is then terminated.

Consequences of putting the company into liquidation

The company takes the form of a company in liquidation and all documents issued by the company must make mention of the fact that it is now in liquidation. As a result of the resolution or order liquidating the company, the only competent organs are the shareholders' meeting and the liquidator or the college of liquidators. The power to be enjoyed by the latter will be determined by the order appointing them. Any powers granted to the liquidator or college of liquidators can be invoked against third parties provided that the fact of the liquidation has been published in the appropriate official journal ("Moniteur Belge"). Within the company in liquidation, the general meeting of shareholders has the broadest of powers and the functions of the board of directors are abolished.

In these circumstances the company's sole purpose has become its liquidation. Its activities should therefore be reduced and the liquidation brought about as quickly as possible.

As in the case of the bankruptcy, the liquidation creates a suspension of all claims by creditors. The rights of creditors are determined as at the date of the resolution or order. While any creditor or potential creditor is still able to obtain a judgment in order to have his rights against the company fixed by the court, the decision or resolution which winds up the company suspends any measures of execution to be taken by a creditor in the enforcement of such rights. Any interest on debts owed by the company stops running from the date of the resolution or order unless and until it is shown that there are sufficient assets to pay both the debt in question and any interest thereon.

The liquidator(s)

The liquidator or the college of liquidators is appointed by the general meeting of shareholders or by the commercial court. Unless the articles of association contain provisions laying down the powers of the liquidator or liquidators, the general meeting of shareholders or the court will determine what they are to be. To the extent that authority has been given for this purpose, the liquidators may continue the business for a reasonable time in order to facilitate the liquidation of the company. They may take out loans to repay debts owed by the company, grant mortgages, sell both moveable and immoveable property and distribute the assets of the company in part or in whole to other companies.

The decision or resolution to wind up the company does not terminate existing agreements. The liquidator, like the curateur in the case of the bankrupt company, may act to terminate any continuing agreements where this is in the interests of the company. This may be done especially where the company had entered into agreements for an unlimited duration. In such a case, provision will have to be made for any indemnities given by a company to the other contracting parties and any compensation payments will have to be added to the debts owed by the company. Alternatively, it may be thought preferable to continue such agreements at the expense of the assets to be liquidated.

The liquidators are liable both towards the company and towards third parties for any wrongful acts committed in the performance of their duties. They are, moreover, required to prepare annual accounts and submit these for approval to the annual general meeting of shareholders.

The liquidators may pay both debts that are due and debts that are owed but are not yet due although, in the latter case, the prudent liquidator will ensure a deduction for earlier payment. Such payments should be made on a pro rata basis and in accordance with the rules as to priority.

Once six months have elapsed since the decision or resolution to wind up the company, the liquidation will proceed without any further possibility of a declaration of bankruptcy provided that it cannot be shown that, at the time of the resolution or decision for liquidation, the company had already stopped making payments.

At the termination of the liquidation, the liquidators will report to the general meeting of shareholders as to the performance of their functions and the results of the liquidation. The termination of the liquidation will be published in the "Moniteur Belge". Any money that has not been distributed will be deposited with the "caisse de dépôt et consignation").

5. Augmenting the assets of the insolvent corporation

Acts committed during the suspect period

In the bankruptcy judgment the commercial court will determine the date on which the bankrupt stopped making payments. This date cannot be earlier than six months prior to the date of the bankruptcy judgment. The period between the date on which the court establishes that payments were stopped and the declaration of bankruptcy is known as the "suspect period".

Article 445 of the Bankruptcy Law

Under article 445 of the Bankruptcy Law certain specified acts carried out by the debtor during the suspect period can be set aside on application by the curateur on the ground that they breach the fundamental rule of equal treatment of creditors. Once an act is found to come within article 445 it is presumed to be prejudicial to the bankruptcy estate in that a greater benefit was derived by the third party than by the debtor. The defendant third party can only escape the application of article 445 by establishing that the transaction which is attacked by the curateur did not in fact cause any prejudice to the bankruptcy estate. The transactions in question provided for under article 445 are:

- where the debtor makes a gift or carries out some other benevolent act;
- where the debtor transfers a lease at a price significantly lower than that prevailing in the commercial market at the time;
- where the healthy parts of a going concern are transferred to another company.
- the payment of a debt during the suspect period is voidable where it is shown that this was done in contravention of the principle of equal treatment of creditors.

This will apply where the attempt is made to disguise the fact that the repayment is made in circumstances prejudicial to the other creditors. Thus, article 445 will apply where, for example, a loan is purportedly repaid by the delivery of a quantity of wine which is disguised to appear as a sale. Another example might be found where a car purchased by way of instalments is returned to the lessor immediately prior to the declaration of bankruptcy.

Where the company debtor grants a fresh security during the suspect period this will not normally be regarded as null and void provided that the new security replaces an old security and does not grant any additional rights.

Where an agreement is found to be ineffective against the estate by virtue of the application of article 445, the situation that existed prior to the conclusion of that agreement will be restored. Thus, if goods were transferred under an agreement rendered null and void by article 445, those goods must be returned. If that is not possible, restitution must take the form of a payment of the value of the goods. Where payment in lieu of the goods is restored to the bankrupt debtor, that payment must be equal to the value of the goods at the time the claim was instituted. Even where the goods in question have been sold on by a third party and the price received is less than the value of the goods at the time the claim under article 445 is made, the bankruptcy estate is entitled to receive the full value of the goods in question. Where the goods themselves are returned, this must be done at the expense of the party returning them to the place indicated by the curateur.

Article 446 of the Bankruptcy Law

All payments other than those referred to in article 445 carried out during the suspect period can be declared null and void if it is shown that the creditor knew that the debtor satisfied the conditions for bankruptcy at the time of the payment. Thus, where the creditor knew that the debtor had stopped making payment of its debts, that it was unable to obtain further credit and that the payment made was detrimental to the debtor's other creditors, such payment can be set aside under article 446.

Such knowledge on the part of the creditor will be inferred where:

- a writ calling for the debtor to be declared bankrupt has been issued against the debtor at the request of the creditor;

- the statutory auditor has drafted a report as to the value of the assets of the debtor or has accompanied the debtor when the debtor was required to appear before the "dienst voor handelsonderzoeken" (business enquiry service); the tax authorities have derived the information from tax returns made by the debtor;

- the social security authorities have issued a summons against the debtor that it be declared bankrupt – something which is generally done as soon as such authorities believe that the debtor fulfils the conditions for bankruptcy.

Knowledge that the debtor has ceased to make payments and is unable to obtain further credit can be derived from:

- the refusal of a creditor to grant further credit to the debtor;
- the fact that that creditor made advances to the debtor to enable the latter to overcome temporary payment difficulties;
- actual knowledge of the financial difficulties of the debtor.

Article 447 of the Bankruptcy Law

Under article 447, no mortgage or other privilege may be conferred after the declaration of bankruptcy. The one exception to this rule is a legal mortgage granted to the tax authorities.

Article 448 of the Bankruptcy Law

Under article 448, any act or payment performed with the intention of harming other creditors of the debtor are null and void regardless of the date on which such acts were undertaken (*i.e.* even prior to the suspect period). This jurisdiction arises as an application of the "actio pauliana", a fundamental principle of law. The application of this principle in bankruptcy has the slightly curious effect of benefitting those creditors who became creditors of the debtor after the payment which was subsequently avoided.

Article 448 is rarely invoked in bankruptcy proceedings. This is due to the fact that most suspect acts can be brought within the provisions of article 445 which is a much simpler jurisdiction from the point of view of the curateur because the curateur does not have to prove that the third party was aware of the abnormal or prejudicial nature of the act. Nevertheless there have been a sufficient number of applications under article 448 to enable the courts to define the criteria which have to be met for a successful application. Thus a payment will be declared to have been made in a fraudulent manner (*i.e.* it will be declared to be null and void as having been to the detriment of the other creditors of the debtor) where it is found to be abnormal and where the debtor has acted with the knowledge that other creditors would be harmed.

The extent of jurisdiction conferred by article 448 can be very broad. Thus it can be used for declaring null and void:

- a sale accompanied by a loan;
- the fraudulent transformation of a blue collar employment agreement into a white collar employment agreement;
- the transfer of business assets in order to remove them from the claims of creditors;
- the repayment of advances made by way of transfer of machinery and goods to a creditor who was well aware of the debtor's untenable situation;

- the grant of a mortgage to a creditor without any consideration being given to the debtor;
- the modification of the matrimonial regime between a director of the company and his or her spouse in order to transfer the assets of the company to the director's spouse.

Liability case

The curateur has the power to institute any proceedings that might have been instituted by the debtor itself. Thus, the curateur may bring an action against any defendant alleged to have committed a tort against the company causing the latter damage. This jurisdiction is of particular importance when considering the role of the directors prior to the declaration of bankruptcy.

During its life, the company would have been entitled to bring proceedings against the directors where the latter damaged the company by reason of mistakes made in the management of the company or in violation of the company's constitution.

In addition to these generally available remedies, bankruptcy law has also conferred certain specific powers on the curateur to enable him to institute proceedings against the directors and those responsible for the company's incorporation. Under such provisions, where at the time of bankruptcy the company's debts exceed its assets, any director or former director or any other person who acted as a manager of the business of the company can be held liable for part or all of the company's debts. In order to invoke this jurisdiction, it must be shown that the defendant was guilty of clear and serious negligence in his or her management of the company. This jurisdiction may even be invoked against a shareholder who is shown to have acted as a manager of the company. This is particularly useful in circumstances where the shareholder is another company owning all or most of the shares in the bankrupt company.

Under article 35 of the Belgian Companies Act, special procedures are provided where a company is declared bankrupt within three years following its incorporation and where the registered share capital at the time of incorporation was manifestly insufficient for the normal exercise of the intended activities of that company for a period of at least two years. This provision will be satisfied where the judge finds that no normal or reasonable business man would have concluded that the registered capital was sufficient for the company's stated purpose. The incorporators may be declared jointly and severally liable in respect of any obligations of the company to the extent determined by the court.

6. Public control over insolvent corporations

The curateurs are appointed by the commercial court. Since bankruptcy proceedings invariably give rise to all kinds of legal problems they most often are lawyers. Sometimes an accountant is appointed to assist the curateur.

The general meeting predominantly appoints former directors or managers, external accountants or lawyers to become liquidators.

The curateur performs his functions under the supervision of the judge commissioner and the commercial court, while the liquidators are supervised by the general meeting.

Contents of Chapter 3

CORPORATE INSOLVENCY LAW IN DENMARK

1.	**Introduction**	67
2.	**Corporations**	68
	Characteristics	68
	Management	69
	Ownership	70
	Financing and security for creditors	71
	Available information	72
	Other business entities	72
	Debt collection and asset recovery	73
	Cross-jurisdictional procedures	74
3.	**Survival of the insolvent corporation or its business**	75
	Suspension of payments	75
	Enforced composition and enforced moratorium	81
4.	**Termination of the corporation: liquidation and dissolution**	88
	Liquidation/bankruptcy	88
	Dissolution	98
5.	**Augmenting the assets of the insolvent corporation**	99
	Transactions at risk	99
	Personal liabilities of officers	104
6.	**Public control over insolvent corporations**	106
	Licensing and control of the appointee	106
	Examinations and investigations	108
	Publicity and records	109

Chapter 3

CORPORATE INSOLVENCY LAW IN DENMARK

Erik Malberg and Christian Emmeluth,

Koch-Nielsen & Grønborg

1. Introduction

Denmark is a civil law country, and the acts passed by the Danish Parliament ("Folketinget") are the most important sources of law. As Denmark is a member of the EU, many areas of Danish law are regulated by EU directives and regulations.

Certain laws authorise various ministers to issue regulations which are binding on all Danish citizens. These ministers may also issue governmental circulars on a specific issue, which are only binding on the ministry itself and its subordinates.

The Danish court system is a three tier system consisting of trial courts, the Courts of Appeal and the Supreme Court. The trial courts are important in insolvency law as a petition for bankruptcy must be filed with the probate court division of the particular trial court. However, if a bankruptcy petition is filed against a debtor domiciled in the Copenhagen area, the petition must be filed with the probate court division of the Sea and Maritime Court in Copenhagen.

Any decisions rendered by a trial court may be brought before the two Courts of Appeal, one situated in Jutland ("Vestre Landsret") and one in Copenhagen ("Østre Landsret"). Generally, only one appeal may be made against a decision rendered by a court. However, it is possible to apply to the Ministry of Justice for permission to appeal to the Supreme Court, against a decision rendered by the Courts of Appeal on a judgment by a trial court.

Any civil law matter involving a claim exceeding DKK500,000 may be brought before the Courts of Appeal in the first instance with a right of appeal to the Supreme Court.

For insolvency law purposes the most important body of law is to be found in the Act of Bankruptcy ("Konkursloven") Act No. 215 and 363 of 1991. This Act contains provisions concerning reorganisation procedures and permanent procedures. The preliminary remedies available to a creditor are described in Act

No. 905 of 1992 as amended by Act No. 469 of 1993 on Legal Procedures ("Retsplejeloven"). Act No. 617 of 1993 as amended by Act No. 1094 of 1993 on Danish public limited companies ("Aktieselskabsloven") also contains important provisions on the liability of directors and their duty towards shareholders, and similar provisions are contained in Act No. 1094 of 1993 in regard to limited companies ("Anpartsselskabsloven").

2. Corporations

Characteristics

Under Danish corporate law two types of company may be formed:

The "A/S" or "Aktieselskab" is governed by the Act on Public Limited Companies and may be compared with the United Kingdom public limited company (plc) or the German "Aktiengesellschaft" ("AG");

The "ApS" or "Anpartsselskab" (limited company) is governed by the Act on Limited Companies (Anpartsselskabsloven) and may be compared with the United Kingdom limited company (Ltd) or the German "Gesellschaft mit beschränkter Häftung" ("GmbH").

The Act on Public Limited Companies stipulates the minimum capital of an A/S as DKK500,000 and, according to the Act on Limited Companies, the minimum capital of an ApS is DKK200,000.

All companies are registered with the commerce and companies agency in Copenhagen.

Both the A/S and ApS are formed by one or more persons (natural or legal) signing the articles of incorporation. At least one of the incorporators must be a resident of Denmark.

The articles of incorporation of an A/S must contain the following information:

- the name, occupation and address of each of the subscribers;
- subscription price for the share capital;
- time limits for subscription and payment of the shares;
- the date before which the general meeting of incorporation shall be held;
- information on whether the company is to pay any cost in relation to the formation and, if so, a specification of those costs;
- a draft of the articles of association.

The articles of association must as a minimum contain information about the following:

- the name or any auxiliary names of the company;
- the name of the municipality in Denmark in which the company will have its domicile;

- the objects of the company;
- the nominal amount of the share capital;
- the denomination of the shares and voting rights of the shareholders;
- the number or the minimum or maximum number of members of the board of directors and any board of deputies and the term of office of the members of the board.

The articles of association must also contain information about the following:

- the number or minimum and maximum number of auditors and their term of office;
- the requisite notice for the general meeting and the matters to be dealt with at the ordinary general meeting;
- the period to be covered by the company's financial year;
- whether the shares are to be registered or bearer shares and whether or not they are to be negotiable.

Under the Act on Public Limited Companies the incorporators are personally liable for any debts incurred by the company until it is registered with the commerce and companies agency. The board of directors must file for registration within six months of the date of the articles of incorporation. The registration period may last for approximately six months and the use of shelf companies is quite common in Denmark.

The minimum share capital must be paid into the company in cash or in kind upon incorporation. If the company is established with a share capital exceeding the minimum requirement, then any excess amount must also be paid in.

The liability of a shareholder is limited to the number of shares subscribed.

The formal requirements relating to the articles of incorporation and articles of association of an ApS are less comprehensive. Thus, if its share capital does not exceed DKK 300,000, no supervisory board need be established.

Management

An A/S must have a board of directors consisting of at least three members. The duties of the board include supervision of the management and the establishment of a responsible organisation to carry out the activities of the company.

The management is in charge of the day-to-day business and is under an obligation to follow the guidelines and directions issued by the board of directors.

Where an ApS is established without a board, the duties of the board of directors are vested in those who run its affairs on a day-to-day basis. In this case the manager must carry out the duties of the board.

Both the Act on Public Limited Companies and the Act on Limited Companies contain provisions concerning serious loss of capital.

As far as an A/S is concerned, the board of directors is under a duty to convene an extraordinary general meeting of the company if the net assets are less than half the amount of the company's paid-up share capital. The meeting must be convened within six months of such a loss occuring. The board is thus under a continuous obligation to supervise the capital position of the company and may not await the result of a particular financial year before any action is taken.

At the extraordinary general meeting the board shall make a statement concerning the financial position of the company, and the board is required to submit a proposal concerning the measures which should be taken to deal with the situation or a proposal for the winding-up of the A/S.

Further, the board of an A/S is required to decide whether the financial funding available to the company at any time is at a level appropriate to the business activities of the company.

Failure to comply with the relevant section renders the responsible directors liable to criminal sanctions under the Act, but the Act does not stipulate any civil consequences. However, if the extraordinary general meeting does not pass the proposal submitted by the board, and if the board finds it unacceptable to continue trading, then the board must resign.

As far as an ApS is concerned the board of management is under a duty to the company if the company has lost more than half of its paid in share capital. If a recapitalisation is not possible, the board should take the necessary steps to wind up the company. If the manager or the board fails to call the general meeting or if the general meeting fails to recommend measures to restore the capital of the company, the company may be dissolved by an order of the Commerce and Companies Agency, unless the capital is re-established within a time limit set by the Agency.

Members of the board and managers may be made personally liable under the Act for any damage caused to the company if inflicted intentionally or negligently. The Danish courts have, however, been reluctant to award damages in such cases (see pp104-5 *infra*).

Ownership

A Danish A/S or ApS is solely owned by its shareholders. Upon a liquidation of a solvent company all net assets of a company are distributed proportionately amongst the shareholders. If the shareholders in an A/S disapprove of the actions taken by the board or the managers, those shareholders owning at least 10% of the nominal share capital may call for an extraordinary general meeting. With regard to an ApS at least 25% of the shareholders must agree to call an extraordinary general meeting. The board is under an obligation to call such a meeting within a fortnight after having received written notice of the specific subject which the shareholders want the extraordinary general meeting to decide.

At the general meeting or at an extraordinary general meeting, all decisions are made by a simple majority of the votes cast, unless otherwise provided by the Acts or the articles of association. Under Danish corporate law, shares may carry one or several votes. It is thus necessary to determine the total number of votes represented at the meeting in order to establish the number of votes necessary for a majority. The election of a new board or, in case of an ApS a new management, may be made by a simple majority.

Financing and security for creditors

Bank financing

If the corporation conducts its business from its own freehold property it may grant its financing bank a legal charge over its property. The legal charge is secured by means of an "owner's mortgage" issued for a special amount. This is a mortgage issued by the freehold owner to himself and he is thus mortgagor as well as mortgagee.

The mortgage may be pledged with the financing bank as security for a credit facility. If the corporation defaults on the terms of the credit facility, the bank may foreclose on the mortgage and put the property up for auction or take possession of the property and collect any incoming amounts. The bank may exercise its rights under the owner's mortgage as an individual creditor without having to file a petition for bankruptcy.

The bank may not create a floating charge over the property, unless the borrower conducts its business from a leasehold property, in which case a floating charge may be created over the business assets except for stock, work in progress and finished goods. The floating charge is created by means of a mortgage which is registered with the trial court in the municipality where the business has its principal place of business or registered office. Registration with the court is a pre-requisite for creating a valid charge. Under the charge the bank may put the assets up for auction after obtaining judgment for its claim. A creditor who has a floating charge cannot himself sell the charged assets in case of bankruptcy but must await the sale by the trustee (see p96 *infra*). A floating charge cannot be created if the business is conducted from a freehold property.

Security interests in vehicles must always be registered with the computerised registry "Bilbogen" at the court in the municipality of Aarhus.

Factoring is also a common way to finance a business. In order to create a valid security interest in the outstanding claims of a particular corporation, it is necessary to notify the debtor that the right to receive the payments under a particular contract has been assigned to the bank. The notification may be made by the bank, but it is generally accepted that a notification stated on the invoice from the corporation to its customers will be sufficient. However, it must be clear and leave no doubt that the debtor will only be released from his obligations if the payment is made to the bank. If payment is made to the original contracting party after the debtor has been duly notified, the bank may demand that the debt is paid twice, the second time to itself.

A security interest in the shares and bonds listed on the Copenhagen Stock Exchange can only be created by registering the interest with the computerised central register ("Vardipapircentralen" – "VP") for such security interests. Registration of a security interest is made via a bank or certain brokers. Protection against other creditors is obtained from the date the bank or a broker is requested to register the interest with VP. A statement, confirming the registration, is then issued.

Security for other creditors

Creditors other than banks may also secure their interest by the means described above. However, a seller of goods may retain the title to his goods until paid in full. This does not apply to deliveries made to a seller for the purpose of being sold by his business, unless the delivery is made under a consignment contract. A retention of title must be made before physical delivery of the goods to the purchaser or his representative, for instance a transport company acting on behalf of the purchaser. Such a clause will usually be incorporated in the original purchase contract. Further, it is possible to settle an action by setting off any claims the creditor may have against a debtor in a situation where these are mutual obligations. Under Danish law it is not possible to create an interest ranking above other creditors unless it is secured under a valid security agreement.

Available information

A creditor may make a search with the local trial court to investigate whether any charges have been created over a debtor's freehold property or over his chattels. Searches with regard to vehicles must be made with the Bilbogen. Since under the Danish Companies Acts, companies are required to file their annual financial accounts with the Commerce and Companies Agency their accounts are available for public inspection, and it is possible to obtain a copy of any accounts filed. Further information may be sought with credit agencies for a fee, and information may also be obtained from banks.

Other business entities

Other business entities which exist under Danish law include:

- the sole trader
- the general partnership
- the limited partnership
- co-operative societies

The sole trader is a typical one-man business operation.

The trade or business of a general partnership ("Interessentskab"-"IS") is carried out for the joint benefit or profit of the partners, whether their contribution to the partnership is equal or not. The partners are personally, jointly and severally liable for the debts of the partnership and creditors have a preferential claim on the assets of the partnership.

A limited partnership ("Kommanditselskab" – "K/S") is an entity consisting of a general partner ("komplementar") – typically an A/S or an ApS – and a number of limited partners ("kommanditister"). A general partner is liable for all the obligations of the partnership without limitation, whereas a limited partner is not liable beyond the share of the partnership to which he subscribed.

The organisation of co-operatives is not governed by any statute. However, the constitution of a co-operative generally states that it is a society whose members' liability is limited to the amount injected. However, joint and separate liability may be provided for in the articles of association. There are no statutory requirements as to the minimum capital of a co-operative society.

The co-operative is an independent legal entity, which will only qualify for co-operative status if the objective is co-operative, for example engaging in purchasing, improving and selling products of the participating members, all of whom must be economically independent parties.

All the entities described above – sole trader, general partnership, limited partnership, and a co-operative – may create the security interests outlined on p71 *supra* and may seek protection under the Bankruptcy Act's provisions on suspension of payment. They may also be declared bankrupt under the Bankruptcy Act.

Under Act No. 123 of 1994 on Business Entities, legal entities in which none of the partners are personally liable must be registered with the commerce and companies agency within eight weeks of the date of their incorporation. Existing business entities must be registered on 1 July 1995 at the latest. Until registration, a partner is personally liable for any debts incurred by the legal entity.

A sole trader, an IS and a K/S cannot and must not be registered according to the Business Entities Act. Business entities registered under the Act must file annual accounts in accordance with the Annual Accounts Act.

Finally, foundations are governed by special legislation.

Debt collection and asset recovery

The preliminary remedies available to a creditor before the commencement of a legal action against the debtor are described in the Act on the Legal Procedure. Under this Act, a creditor may attach a debtor's assets. A petition for attachment must be submitted to the bailiff of the trial court in the jurisdiction in which the debtor has his principal place of business or registered office except for the registration of attachment of vehicles, which shall be submitted to the registry "Bilbogen". The petition for attachment will be successful, if:

- there is significant risk that by the time a judgment is given in favour of the creditor the debtor's assets may have been dissipated; and
- it is not possible to seize the property of the debtor under a judgment.

If an attachment is granted, the bailiff will usually require a deposit by the creditor equal to the amount of the attachment sought. The deposit, which may be made either in cash or by a bank guarantee, is a security against any claims the debtor may have against the creditor for any losses caused by the attachment if the court in the subsequent legal proceedings finds that the attachment was unjustified. If an attachment is granted, the creditor must initiate legal proceedings within a week of the date of the attachment.

A creditor may also seek an injunction against a debtor, but this is not likely to be the most appropriate means of debt recovery.

A creditor may also elect to seek a judgment against a debtor without trying to obtain an attachment or an injunction. In this case a writ of summons must be filed with the trial court or the Courts of Appeal, depending on the amount in dispute. The writ of summons is served on the debtor before the case may be heard by the court. If the debtor does not appear as notified, the court has the power to render a default judgment against the debtor.

Otherwise the defendant submits this written answer, the plaintiff a reply and the defendant a final rejoinder. A case is then argued orally before the court, before final judgment is given.

Any judgment rendered in favour of the plaintiff may be executed against the defendant's assets, unless there is an appeal. This must be brought within four weeks in the case of a judgment rendered by a county court and eight weeks in the case of a decision rendered by the Courts of Appeal.

The judgment is executed by the local bailiff.

Cross-jurisdictional procedures

A final judgment rendered by a court of another EU country may be executed under the EC Convention of 1986. Similarly a decision rendered by a Danish court may, under the EC Convention, be executed in other EC countries if the debtor has assets there. Conventions concerning the recognition of foreign judgments exist between the Nordic countries, between Denmark and England (1932) and between Denmark and with Germany (1938).

In the absence of a treaty, foreign judgments will usually not be recognised by Danish courts except in the family law area. Such judgments may therefore not be executed, and anyone wishing to enforce one will need to bring an action in the Danish courts on the basis of the foreign judgment. If the Danish court grants a judgment to the creditor, the creditor will, of course, be able to enforce that judgment in the manner described above.

3. Survival of the insolvent corporation or its business

Suspension of payments

Purpose of effect

The purpose of a suspension of payments ("betalingsstandsning") is to establish the necessary calm in order to conduct a close examination of the situation of the corporation, and to negotiate with the creditors in order to examine the possibility of carrying on the business maintaining existing jobs. The suspension gives reassurance to the creditors that they have no need to fear any preferential treatment of other creditors.

A suspension of payments is a means by which to achieve a settlement with the creditors, but it is not in itself a settlement. It may lead to the establishment of a legally sanctioned settlement with the creditors, an enforced composition, or an enforced moratorium (see p81 *infra*), but it could lead to a resolution of the financial problems of the corporation in any other way which may be negotiated, for example through negotiation with one or several of the main creditors who may perhaps accept a reduction of their claims or the conversion of their claims or a part thereof into share capital. Another possibility may be the injection of new capital to remedy any lack of funds which may have been the cause of the suspension of payments.

In connection with the filing of the suspension of payment with the probate court, a deadline "fristdag" is established, as far the legal consequences of the suspension of payments are concerned.

The establishment of the fristdag , has a number of consequences:

- Any debts which are paid after the fristdag will, as a general rule, be voidable in accordance with section 72 of the Bankruptcy Act if the corporation does subsequently go bankrupt or achieves an enforced composition or an enforced moratorium.

However, a payment cannot be voided if the creditor in question would in any case have received payment in full because, for instance, he holds a mortgage or pledge.

The ban on payments after the fristdag means that a creditor is not allowed to seek redress through setting off his claim against a claim which the corporation (which is now in suspension of payments) had obtained against that creditor after the fristdag (s16 of the Bankruptcy Act). For example, if, after the fristdag, the corporation sells goods on credit to a buyer who is also a creditor, the buyer cannot refuse to pay, *i.e.* he cannot set-off the purchase price against his own claim.

- The creditors cannot seize any assets even though they may have obtained judgment. This is due to the fact that, if a bankruptcy subsequently follows, such a seizure would be void, and a seizure conducted with the aim of auctioning off the seized assets would, during a suspension of payments, undermine the purpose of the suspension.

However, this does not apply to creditors who have got a non-voidable mortgage or pledge over assets of the company. Such creditors are, as a general rule, allowed to seize the mortgaged assets such as real estate with the aim of auctioning off the assets in order to obtain payment.

However, in accordance with section 16A of the Bankruptcy Act, the probate court may, on application of the debtor company, rule that a mortgagee may not after all conduct a seizure with the aim of auctioning off the assets, if the court is persuaded that such a ruling is necessary in order to achieve the overall purpose for which the suspension of payments was granted. Such a decision would be made, for instance, if a mortgagee or pledgee holds a security over one or more machines or some real estate which the corporation needs in the ordinary course of business.

To provide the mortgagee with compensation for the temporary loss which he would suffer, it is a condition that the corporation in suspension of payments, should pay all running costs on the mortgages, whenever these costs fall due. To ascertain whether this has taken place, the probate court may decide that the corporation in suspension of payments must make continuous payments of specific amount which should then be placed in a separate bank account.

If, however, the mortgage document held by a creditor is unlikely to provide full security for the value of the mortgage, the probate court may decide that such continuous payments should not be made.

- The fristdag decides the calculation of the time limits that are of relevance in relation to the rules on avoiding transactions, (see pp99-100 *infra*).

- The fristdag is also of importance in order to establish preferential status for individual creditors, since only claims for salary which have fallen due during the last six months prior to the fristdag have the right to preferential treatment in the case of a subsequent bankruptcy.

- Debt incurred after the fristdag with the acceptance of the "tilsynsførende" (administrator) is granted a preferential position in a subsequent bankruptcy.

Pre-application/appointment considerations

An alternative to a suspension of payments which is actually filed with the probate court could be an "unofficial" suspension of payments. Here, the debtor company usually reaches agreement with certain key creditors that payment will be delayed. This may be preferable in order to avoid general knowledge of the situation but will obviously only be possible for a limited period.

A suspension of payments which has not been filed is outside any legal regulation, and has none of the legal consequences described above. Thus, if a supplier should, through an error, not receive payment in cash during a suspension of payments and the corporation subsequently goes bankrupt, the claim of the supplier will not be granted preferential status in the bankruptcy estate. Since in this situation the supplier has had no knowledge about the suspension of payments, those who have been instrumental in establishing this suspension of payment – especially the debtor's lawyer – may be personally liable for any loss incurred.

Thus it is generally considered inadvisable to rely on an unofficial suspension of payments.

Procedure for suspension of payments

The suspension of payments is established through the filing of a statement to this effect with the probate court in the jurisdiction in which the corporation is domiciled.

The statement should be signed jointly by all the members of the board of directors.

A "tilsynsførende" (administrator) must be appointed on the suggestion of the corporation, and this will nearly always be a lawyer. He must sign a statement to the effect that he is willing to undertake this task and that he has no conflict of interest.

The task of the tilsynsførende is to become acquainted with the situation of the corporation as quickly as possible and, together with the auditor of the corporation, to analyse the reasons for the suspension of payments.

It should also quickly be decided whether the corporation may continue trading perhaps on a reduced basis. This will necessitate the preparation of special budgets analysing the expected results of the operation and the availability of cash in a period of, for example, three to six months.

Whether or not the corporation is to continue trading, a decision must be made as to whether the employees' contracts should be terminated and whether they should all be dismissed immediately or whether some of them should be retained. This is because the employees may have the right to a long period of notice and, if the attempt to reconstruct the corporation does not succeed, they will be a heavy burden on the future bankruptcy estate with very considerable claims which are granted a preferential position as compared to ordinary creditors.

The tilsynsførende should also make sure that all assets of the company are registered and perhaps valued, and he should also examine whether necessary insurances have been taken out on behalf of the corporation.

Obviously, it is also the task of the tilsynsførende to ascertain that no payments are made to any creditors which could be considered contrary to the purpose of the suspension of payments. In this connection it is important to note that the suspension of payments does not only apply to trade creditors and banks or other providers of finance but also to other creditors such as insurance companies, suppliers of electricity, landlords and the tax and VAT authorities. In these cases a completion statement must be prepared in order that claims relating to the period prior to the fristdag are also subject to the suspension of payments, whereas costs that are incurred after the "fristdag" are paid during the period of the suspension of payments.

Also the tilsynsførende must ensure that any goods delivered are not returned to the suppliers because of non payment unless a valid retention of ownership has been established. It is essential that the tilsynsførende forms a correct impression of the liabilities of the corporation and consequently will often ask the creditors to file and prove their claims.

The tilsynsførende should further check whether any voidable transactions have taken place or whether any claims for damages may be made against the officers of the company, as such claims would make it possible for a subsequent bankruptcy estate to increase the assets of the estate. If such possibilities do indeed exist, the creditors should be notified thereof and asked if they wish to participate in the establishment of a voluntary settlement, since claims for the voiding of transactions can only be made by a bankruptcy estate or in connection with an enforced composition or an enforced moratorium, (see pp81-83 *infra*).

The tilsynsførende is obliged to despatch a circular letter to the creditors no later than one week after the establishment of the suspension of payments. It should be sent to all creditors including mortgagees, (even if they have full security for their claim) and, under section 12 of the Bankruptcy Act, include the following:

- information about the most important assets and liabilities, and a possible list of creditors and any security held by them.
- information about the present condition of the bookkeeping of the company.
- an account of the reasons for the suspension of payment and its purposes, *i.e.*, which settlement the administrator is trying to obtain, if it is possible to specify this at such an early stage.
- A summons to the creditors to appear in the probate court at a specified time.

Creditors' involvement and position

No later than three weeks after the filing of the suspension of payments, a meeting must take place with the creditors in the probate court. The creditors will be informed about this through the circular letter sent out by the tilsynsførende.

The meeting should, above all, decide whether a suspension of payments can be sustained, and this in turn will depend on the attitude of the creditors after they have received the report of the tilsynsførende and have been granted the possibility of asking him questions. The probate court will not sustain a suspension of payments if, in exercising its discretion, it finds that there is no reasonable purpose for the suspension of payments, and creditors, representing a substantial amount of the debtor's combined liabilities, are unfavourably disposed to the continuation of the suspension of payments. Further, a creditor may at any time file a petition for bankruptcy during the course of a suspension of payments but in such a situation the probate court may postpone any ruling on the petition if it believes that there is a reasonable chance of obtaining a settlement with the creditors, through the establishment of an enforced composition or an enforced moratorium.

If the probate court decides that the suspension of payments should be sustained, the creditors may call for the appointment of different tilsynsførende or else an additional tilsynsførende. Although it is the probate court that decides this, a wish which has been supported by a majority of the creditors, based on the size of their claims, will be of decisive importance since these creditors could ask the court to declare the corporation bankrupt if their suggestion about the appointment of the tilsynsførende is not followed.

The meeting must also decide whether a committee of creditors is to be established. This committee should have no more than three creditor members and, if the corporation has more than 25 employees, a representative of the employees will also be allowed to join. Thus, the committee of creditors can have no more than four members. The task of this committee of creditors is to supervise the work of the tilsynsførende during the suspension of payments.

In general, the creditors should be informed before any specific material dispositions are made, unless these are necessary in order to keep the debtor corporation intact, or for the reasonable defence of the interests of the creditors in general. This provision means that it will often be necessary for the tilsynsførende to provide the creditors with prior information before a decision is made to sell off the business. If creditors representing no less than 15% of the known creditors in value of claims object to an intended disposition, the tilsynsførende should call a meeting of the creditors and the proposed disposition may then take place only if a majority of the creditors represented in terms of claims accept. The time limit for any objection against an intended disposition is seven days.

In general, the creditors are not directly involved in the business during the suspension of payments and they have to trust the tilsynsførende to represent their interests, as well as those of the company and the employees. Generally speaking, important decisions may only be made by the corporation in suspension of payments if the tilsynsførende approves.

As far as the employees of the corporation are concerned they may demand that security be granted for their salaries and if this security cannot be provided, they may terminate their employment without notice even if no unpaid salary is due.

The special situation of the mortgagees/pledgees is regulated as described on pp77-78 *supra*.

Powers and duties of the management and administrators

The tilsynsførende does not, like a "kurator" (trustee in a bankruptcy), have any specific independent authority to act on behalf of the corporation during a suspension of payments. The authority to act still rests with the officers of the company, *i.e.*, the board and the management. Further, the position of shareholders is not affected by the suspension of payments.

The limitation on the authority of the officers to act stems from the fact that any dispositions may only take place if the tilsynsførende agrees. For practical purposes the tilsynsførende will be a lawyer who, besides acting as tilsynsførende, will also act as lawyer for the company in connection with all the problems which may arise during the suspension of payments.

If any conflicts arise between the officers and the tilsynsførende the question arises as to whether a new tilsynsførende should be appointed. If the present tilsynsførende has got the support of the creditors, but not the officers of the company, the only option remaining for the creditors is to demand that the company be declared bankrupt.

There is a strong possibility of avoiding any dispositions which have been undertaken by a company in suspension of payments if they do not have the assent of the tilsynsførende (s72 of the Bankruptcy Act) as discussed on pp99-100 *infra*.

Clearly, then, a suspension of payments is only an appropriate means of solving the financial problems of a corporation if there is the necessary confidence that the officers of the company will act in the interests of the creditors.

If the tilsynsførende on behalf of the corporation or the creditors incurs liabilities through his conduct of the business, he may be held liable in accordance with applicable tort law.

Termination

A suspension of payments will usually continue for three months after filing, but the probate court may prolong the period for a further three monthly periods if application is made before the expiry of the first period as long as it is supported by the tilsynsførende.

A suspension of payments cannot continue for more than 1 year after the fristdag.

Usually a suspension of payments is followed by:

- adoption of an enforced composition or an enforced moratorium, or
- bankruptcy, or
- implementation of a kind of voluntary settlement which will often only apply to the major creditors.

If the suspension of payments expires without being followed in any of the ways described above at the initiative of the company or any of its creditors, the probate court will not of its own initiative take any steps and especially will not, of its own initiative, declare the company bankrupt. Such a situation will often be unsatisfactory for the creditors and they should therefore consider whether they ought to file for bankruptcy if the suspension of payments ceases without any solution being found. A bankruptcy would be necessary in order to maintain the preferential position which certain creditors have obtained during the suspension of payments.

If for example a supplier supplies goods on credit after the commencement of the suspension of payments, and the supervisor has accepted this delivery, this would mean that the supplier will obtain a preferential position. In order to maintain that preferential position it may be necessary to opt for bankruptcy (s94 of the Bankruptcy Act).

Even if a suspension of payments has not expired, the probate court may cause the suspension to be cancelled on petition of the creditors:

- if the company does not co-operate in good faith with the tilsynsførende;
- if there is no reasonable purpose for the suspension of payments;
- if no reasonable attempt is being made to obtain a complete settlement with the creditors.

Further, the company is at any time allowed to revoke the filing for a suspension of payments of its own accord.

Enforced composition and enforced moratorium

Purpose and effect

In accordance with section 157 of the Bankruptcy Act, one of the three settlements described below may be implemented by a specific majority of the creditors:

- a reduction of the debts of the company, usually to no less than 25% of their former value. In very exceptional circumstances the debt may be written down even further if the probate court agrees;
- a liquidation of the business conducted by the company which would lead to creditors receiving the dividends earned in full and final settlement of their claims – a so-called liquidation composition ("likvidationsakkord");

Such compositions apply especially to natural persons who are otherwise fully liable for their debts and who may, through a liquidation composition, obtain a reduction of the unsecured debt. A liquidation composition for a corporation with limited liability would not serve any sensible purpose since the creditors would only obtain that which they would obtain through a bankruptcy.

- a moratorium which will only lead to the corporation obtaining a specified extension as regards repayments of debt.

The first two types of settlement will often be combined, so that an enforced composition is carried through leading to a certain part of the agreed dividends being paid in cash on the adoption of the composition and a certain part being paid in instalments over a period of time.

The purpose of establishing a settlement through a reduction of debts or mor-

atorium would be to give the corporation an opportunity of carrying on in circumstances where a temporary financial crisis has erupted. It also allows the
possibility of a higher dividend for the creditors than would be the case in a bankruptcy – unless the bankruptcy estate was able to sell the activities of the bankrupt corporation as a going concern.

For a discussion of specific considerations governing the submitting of a proposal for a composition, see below.

Pre-application/appointment considerations

The alternative to an enforced composition or an enforced moratorium would be
to try to obtain a voluntary settlement with the creditors. However, it will often
be preferable to carry out an enforced composition or an enforced moratorium
owing, *inter alia*, to the following reasons.

- Experience shows that it is rarely possible to obtain full acceptance of a voluntary settlement if there are more than a few creditors.

- An enforced composition will lead to a reduction of all claims including un-
  recorded claims (*i.e.* including those which are not known). A voluntary settlement will only apply to those creditors who specifically adopt the
  settlement.

- If an enforced composition or an enforced moratorium is carried out it is
  possible to set aside transactions in accordance with section 184 of the Bankruptcy Act. This is not possible with a voluntary settlement.

- If an examination shows that it may be possible to set aside certain transactions, the creditors will usually not be satisfied with a voluntary settlement
  (which would lead to the rejection of any demand that transactions be set
  aside).

- If a transaction is set aside under an enforced composition, the consequence
  is that any funds obtained will be distributed to the creditors in addition to
  any dividend which they will have received through the composition.

Several factors should be considered when determining the dividend which
should be offered to the creditors under a composition. The corporation will try
to make the proposal as attractive as possible in order to persuade the creditors
to adopt the proposal and in order to avoid the need for a majority which applies
in the case of an involuntary composition.

On the other hand it should be borne in mind that the corporation is expected
to survive after the composition and that it will frequently be difficult to finance
a large dividend in a composition since the assets of the company – primarily
the plant, machinery and chattels – obviously cannot be sold.

The result will frequently be that the corporation obtains cash through taking
out a loan or receiving an infusion of capital which will enable it to pay a certain
part of the dividends in cash when the composition is adopted, and the corpora-

tion will then undertake an obligation to pay the rest of the dividends with the earnings which it will obtain in the immediate future.

In determining the size of the dividend which should be offered to the creditors, reference will frequently be made to the so-called "status" dividend which will appear in the balance sheet which must be prepared in connection with an enforced composition (see below). In this balance sheet the assets will be estimated on the basis of the business as a going concern. Accordingly, the balance sheet will not take into account the very considerable claims of the employees for salary in the termination period, since it is assumed that the employees will continue to be employed by the corporation.

To persuade the creditors to adopt a composition, it may be necessary to offer dividends which are higher than these status dividends. This might be possible where certain creditors who are closely connected with the corporation forego any dividends, if the composition is adopted. There are also several other ways of making a composition attractive to the creditors.

On the other hand it may be financially impossible for the company to offer a dividend which will be comparable to the "status" dividend. In this case the creditors must decide whether such a composition is acceptable.

If a majority of the creditors adopt an enforced composition despite the opposition of a minority, the latter may ask the probate court to intervene if they can prove that the dividends offered are disproportionate to the financial situation of the corporation (s180 of the Bankruptcy Act).

In cases where the dividends are paid over a period of time it will be necessary for budgets to be produced, to prove that the composition can be complied with by the corporation.

For practical purposes the amount of the dividend and the conditions under which it is to be paid should always be negotiated with the major creditors. There is no purpose in spending resources in order to work out a proposal for a composition unless there is a reasonable chance that this will be adopted.

Procedure for an enforced composition

The first step in relation to the probate court is to obtain a decision about the commencement of negotiations for an enforced composition. Such a decision may be rendered by the court when specified records have been produced and when no less than 40% of the creditors, depending on the size of the claims as well as the numbers, have accepted the commencement of negotiations.

Most of the work in bringing about an enforced composition takes place in the period between the decisions to obtain an enforced composition and the commencement of negotiations after the decision by the probate court. The major tasks will be:

- A balance sheet must be prepared after registering all the assets and liabilities. This work will be performed by two "tillidsmaend" (mandatories). One of these should be knowledgeable about accounts and the other about the specific business of the corporation (see p106 *infra*). The tillidsmaend who deals with the accounts, will often be the permanent auditor of the company.

The principles on which the valuation of the assets is based must be stated clearly. In order to make comparisons, it is also necessary that the purchase prices paid for the individual assets or the manufacturing costs be stated.

If the assets are pledged or mortgaged or are subject to a retention of ownership provision, this must be stated and such encumbrances should be deducted directly from the assets in order to make it possible to prepare a net balance.

This also applies to claims where debtors have the possibility of set-off. Thus their claims against the debt should be deducted so that only net amounts are included.

These steps are required to ensure that the balance sheet is not misleading.

- A list of creditors must be prepared, including their names, addresses, and the size of their claims and any possible security which they might have. Any claims that are rejected should be included, and the fact of rejection should be stated.

- The tillidsmaend (mandatories) must prepare a written explanation of the reasons for the enforced composition. It must include a statement about the way in which the debtor has conducted the business and his bookkeeping, and whether it will be possible to set aside specific dispositions. The written explanation must be made by the tillidsmaend assisted by the lawyer who has been appointed supervisor during the suspension of payments. If, after consulting the "tilsynsførende" (administrating lawyer), the tillidsmaend find that felonies have been committed this should also be mentioned in the statement.

  Further the tillidsmaend must make a statement as to whether the proposal for an enforced composition is deemed reasonable and whether it is sufficiently likely that the composition can actually be complied with. It should be noted that many compositions are actually a mixture of compositions, but within a stipulated timescale.

  Finally the tillidsmaend must state their view as to the likely dividend if the composition is not adopted and the corporation is declared bankrupt and the tillidsmaend should explain the basis for their estimates. The mere fact that a corporation is declared bankrupt does not necessary lead to its assets being sold off at scrap value since a bankruptcy estate may sometimes be able to sell the business as a going concern. If, however, this is not possible, the dividends in a bankruptcy will be considerably lower than the dividends in a composition due partly to the fact that the assets are sold at lower prices and partly to the claims for salary from the employees, who are granted preferential status.

When the records described above have been produced, they will be forwarded to the creditors together with the proposal for a composition prepared by the debtor, a voting card and a statement from the tilsynsførende recommending the procedure he believes the creditors should follow. There will also be a statement from the debtor declaring solemnly that it has provided information about all its assets and liabilities.

As mentioned above, the probate court may only commence negotiations about an enforced composition if there is sufficient approval from the creditors. Section 166.1, subsection 2, of the Bankruptcy Act stipulates that approval is needed from 40% of the creditors in value of claims *and* in actual numbers.

The voting cards will frequently be prepared in such a manner that the creditors are not only voting in favour of commencing negotiations for an enforced composition, but are also voting on the proposal for the composition itself. However, even though it is often already certain that the proposal will be adopted when the records are delivered to the probate court, in order for the court to render a decision about commencement of negotiations, it is necessary to conduct a "period of negotiations" as described in the Bankruptcy Act.

As a first step in this process the probate court announces in the Official Gazette that negotiations for an enforced composition have been commenced and the creditors are urged to file their claims if they have not already done so. A notice must also be sent to creditors whose claims have been rejected.

It must be emphasised that the probate court will not at this or any subsequent point in time decide whether the objections raised by the debtor against any claim are valid or not. Such disagreement must be decided in the ordinary courts where the creditor must sue the debtor. If the creditor is successful he will obtain dividends of 100% of his original claim plus *full* costs.

At the request of a creditor, the probate court may decide that the dividends in respect of a claim which has been rejected (and thus not registered), should be placed in a separate bank account until the outcome of the court proceedings is known. This also applies if the dividend cannot be paid in full immediately because the claim is conditional and the possible fulfilment of the condition has to be awaited.

If non-registered or conditional claims are large and considerable sums have to be placed in a separate account, the proposal for a composition should be designed so that the actual dividend depends on the outcome of the court proceedings or fulfilment or non-fulfilment of the relevant conditions.

Under section 171 of the Bankruptcy Act no seizure of the assets of the debtor may take place during negotiations for a composition. This provision is, however, of no practical importance, since, in most cases, the debtor will have filed for a suspension of payments prior to the composition and the creditors will already be barred from making any seizures.

The voting takes place in writing but the announcement in the Official Gazette mentioned above will call the creditors to a meeting in the probate court, and the creditors who have not voted prior to that meeting should appear in court in order to cast their vote.

The result of the vote depends not only on the number of creditors voting but also on the size of their claims. Certain claims do not confer any rights to vote on the basis that only creditors who have a vested interest in the result of the voting have the right to vote. Thus claimants who will be paid in full, regardless of the composition (such as preferential creditors), are not allowed to vote. This also applies to a creditor who has got full security for his claim through a mortgage or pledge executed by the debtor.

Frequently, creditors who are closely related to the debtor will accept a waiver of their claims in order to bring about higher dividends for the composition than the one which appears likely from the balance sheet. If this waiver is expressed to be conditional upon the composition being adopted, such a creditor will retain his right to vote.

The rules applying to the voting for the final proposal for a composition are fashioned in such a way that a larger proportion of votes in favour is necessary the lower the dividends that are offered. The votes in favour required are computed by deducting the percentage of dividends offered from 100. Thus, a dividend of 30% must be supported by 70% of the creditors' claims. However, at least 60% in value of the creditors must vote in favour of the proposal regardless of the size of the dividend.

As specified on p81 *supra*, dividends offered will usually not be less than 25%.

In the case of a moratorium at least 60% of the creditors (based on the size of their claims), must vote in favour. A 60% or greater majority is also necessary among the number of creditors participating in the voting. Thus, creditors who remain passive will have no influence on the voting.

In contrast, where the vote on the composition is concerned, all creditors are counted since the required percentage is computed on the basis of liability in accordance with the balance sheet.

Once a composition has been accepted by the creditors, it must be approved by the probate court. This approval may be refused, *inter alia*, for the following reasons:

- the proposal is illegal or procedural errors have distorted the result by denying or enhancing voting powers;
- the debtor has provided one or several creditors with preferential treatment (whether openly or in secret);
- a third party has granted preferential treatment to some creditors in order to influence the voting;
- the dividends stated are not sustainable having regard to the financial position of the debtor;
- there is no reasonable chance that the composition can be complied with, because the debtor has been acting recklessly and has thus impaired his financial position.

The probate court may, in addition, refuse to uphold an enforced composition unless a tilsynsførende is appointed for the debtor in order to ensure that the debtor complies with the conditions of the composition. However, such a tilsynsførende would have no powers comparable to those described p77-78 *supra*. Thus, if it is established that the debtor does not act in accordance with the instructions of the tilsynsførende the latter has no other option than to report this to the probate court, and this may lead to the consequences described below.

The negotiation for the composition as such cannot be regarded as finished until the probate court has upheld the composition and the two weeks allowed for appeal to the High Court have expired.

The period from the day on which the suspension of payment is filed until the probate court finally decides to uphold the composition may be between three and six months or even longer.

The result of the negotiations for a composition will be made public in the Official Gazette by the probate court.

Creditors' involvement and position

The position of the creditors is primarily as described above and includes the provision that a creditor during the negotiations for a composition cannot try to obtain payment through seizing the assets of the debtor.

When an enforced composition has been upheld by the probate court and the creditor comes to the conclusion that it has not been complied with, the composition is not necessarily invalidated. However, if payment does not take place when specified in the composition, the creditor may seek to obtain payment through an application to the bailiff.

However, section 194 of the Bankruptcy Act states that a composition may be rescinded in special cases on the demand of a creditor or at the suggestion of the tilsynsførende. This may happen in the following two situations:

- if it is determined that the debtor has been acting fraudulently or if preferential treatment has secretly been granted to a creditor;
- if the debtor grossly violates his obligations in accordance with the composition.

As mentioned above this does not apply to ordinary cases of non-fulfilment of the composition but only to situations where the debtor has been acting with wilful recklessness, for instance, by spending large sums on private consumption, making large gifts or losing considerable assets through reckless dispositions.

The powers and duties of the tilsynsførende

Although the tilsynsførende cannot act directly on behalf of the corporation, because the officers are technically still functioning, every important disposition must be discussed with him. Thus it is up to the discretion of the tilsynsførende to decide whether, for instance, a large order entailing long-term commitments may be accepted.

Management by the tilsynsførende

The tilsynsførende is obliged to notify all creditors about the suspension of payments. Further, he should supervise the transactions of the corporation and inform the probate court if he believes that a bankruptcy is necessary. This will be especially relevant if the debtor does not co-operate.

The position of the tilsynsførende during an enforced composition is not different in principle from his position during the suspension of payments, since the corporation is still in suspension of payments until the composition/moratorium has been finally agreed upon and upheld by the probate court.

The position of officers and shareholders

As indicated above, the officers remain in their positions. However, they must co-operate with the tilsynsførende. The shareholders are still able to make decisions at a general meeting, as the enforced composition does not impose any automatic limitation on their powers but, obviously, for practical purposes they are very dependent on the attitude of the tilsynsførende administrator and the creditors.

Termination of the composition

A composition may be terminated or rescinded if the probate court refuses to uphold the composition on the grounds mentioned above. Furthermore, where the composition has been adopted but payments are not made in accordance with it, any creditor may try to obtain payment of his claim by application to the bailiff. If this fails, the debtor can be declared bankrupt. In such a case, the creditor may file his entire original claim with the "kurator" (trustee in bankruptcy) but he will receive a dividend corresponding to no more than the total payment which he would have received had the composition been fulfilled as originally intended.

4. Termination of the corporation: liquidation and dissolution

Liquidation/bankruptcy

This section deals with the insolvency procedures available in Denmark. The end result of the insolvency procedure is the final dissolution of the company.

The term liquidation has a narrower connotation under Danish law than under, for example, United Kingdom insolvency law. The term is only used in the case of the dissolution of a solvent company, whereas an insolvent company can only be dissolved according to the procedures set forth in the Bankruptcy Act.

Type, purpose and effect of liquidation/bankruptcy

Type
A Danish corporation may only be liquidated if the corporation is solvent at the time the shareholders pass a resolution for the liquidation of the company. The resolution must be passed in accordance with chapter 14 of the Public Companies Act (or chapter 14 of the Limited Companies Act) and must be approved by a majority of at least two-thirds of the votes cast as well as two-thirds of the votes represented at the general meeting. Shares may carry different voting rights depending on the class to which they belong.

The commerce and companies agency may demand a compulsory liquidation of a company in circumstances where:

- no board is acting as required under the Act;
- no auditor has been elected; or
- the company has not filed its annual accounts with the commerce and companies agency in accordance with the Acts.

In addition, the Agency may demand a liquidation in circumstances where the articles of association have not been changed in order to comply with the legal requirements under the Act on Public Limited Companies and the Act on Limited Companies.

Once the liquidation procedure has been completed, the company is dissolved.

The dissolution of an insolvent company can only be made in accordance with the procedure stipulated in the Bankruptcy Act. The terms used in this connection are "a company is declared bankrupt" or "is wound up".

Purpose
The purpose of the bankruptcy proceedings is to distribute the remaining assets of the company to its creditors in accordance with the Act and to ensure that all creditors are treated equally. Chapter 10 of the Act gives a special ranking according to which the proceeds of the corporation's realised assets will be distributed. Further,

- creditors whose claims are secured by legal charges which cannot be set aside are entitled to look to the realisation of those assets for repayment. To the extent that the claim is not covered by the proceeds from the realisation of such assets, the creditor enjoys the same position as an ordinary creditor with regard to the remaining amount of the claim;
- a supplier who has retained title to his goods may be entitled to the return of those goods;
- a creditor who himself is indebted to the company may set-off the indebtedness against money owed to him by the company.

The kurator is under an obligation to investigate whether any creditors have received preferential treatment through any pre-bankruptcy transaction, and, where this is the case, whether to set aside such transactions. Further, the kurator shall report any criminal acts committed by directors and/or managers of the company to the public prosecutor.

The purpose of a liquidation, where the company is solvent, is to distribute the assets of the company to its shareholders after paying all creditors. For further detail see below.

Effect

The legal effect of a bankruptcy order is described in chapter 4 of the Act. According to section 29 the effect of the grant of a winding-up order is that the debtor loses its legal ability to transfer or give up its assets, receive payments or other services, accept terminations of contracts, receive complaints or similar statements, enter into contracts in any other way undertake any actions in relation to its assets.

The effect of a liquidation (as opposed to a bankruptcy order) is the replacement of the board and management by a liquidator who is in charge of the winding up of the affairs of the company. The company acts as a legal entity and has, the legal capacity to enter into legal obligations. The final dissolution of the company is approved by its shareholders.

The bankruptcy order is published in the Official Gazette ("Statstidende") and is effective against anybody after the end of the day in which publication took place. Before this, the bankruptcy can only be invoked against a contracting party who knows or should have known that the company was being wound up.

With regard to preferential transactions, which a kurator may want to set aside, the important date is the fristdag (see pp100-103 *infra*).

Pre-liquidation/bankruptcy considerations

In order to reorganise a company with assets of a significant magnitude with prospects of survival, the company will often seek protection against its creditors under chapter 2 of the Act – suspension of payments. A tilsynsførende will be appointed by the court in order to explore whether a reorganisation is possible. If the tilsynsførende believes that no rescue is possible or that the company has insufficient assets, a petition for bankruptcy will usually be filed without further pre-application considerations.

The unsecured creditors often take the attitude that further rescue attempts will only involve further losses and, in order to mitigate their loss, they will usually seek an order that the company be declared bankrupt.

Procedure

Voluntary liquidation
The concept of voluntary liquidation only applies with regard to solvent companies. The creditors will be paid in full and therefore have no interest in the liquidation.

In order to liquidate a solvent company a general meeting must be called at which the liquidation must be approved by two-thirds of the votes cast and by two-thirds of the votes represented at the general meeting. Different classes of shares carrying different voting rights may be created under Danish corporate law. Notification of the liquidation must be filed with the commerce and companies agency within a fortnight after the general meeting.

In order that the general public is aware that the company is in liquidation, the company must add to its company name the words "i likvidation" (in liquidation).

According to section 120 of the Companies Act the general meeting shall elect one or several likvidators. Shareholders owning 25% or more of the share capital of a company have a right to elect a likvidator together with the likvidator elected by the general meeting.

A likvidator replaces the board and the manager and is responsible for winding up the affairs of the company. He must prepare a profit and loss account and a balance sheet from the beginning of the financial year until the date that liquidation was approved by the general meeting. This financial statement must be made available to the creditors of the company at the registered office of the company and submitted to the commerce and companies agency.

The likvidator must further place a notification concerning the liquidation of the company in the Official Gazette requiring creditors to submit their claims within three months after the notification. Non-compliance does not preclude the later filing of the claim, provided filing takes place prior to the final dissolution. A copy of the notification must be forwarded to all creditors known by the likvidator. If he rejects a claim by a creditor, the creditor must be informed of this in writing. If a creditor wants to dispute the decision of the likvidator, he must initiate legal proceedings before the probate court within three months of the date of the notification.

The distribution of the assets of the company may not take place before creditors are paid in full and any litigation has been finalised.

The likvidator is required to submit to the commerce and companies agency a copy of the final financial statement at the latest a fortnight after the statement has been approved by the general meeting. The company will be de-registered by the commerce and companies agency when the final financial statement has been received.

Bankruptcy proceedings

According to section 17 of the Act, a petition for bankruptcy may be filed by the company itself or by a creditor. It must be filed with the probate court in the jurisdiction where the company conducts its business or, if this place is unknown, at its registered office.

A bankruptcy order will be granted if the company is insolvent.

- According to the Act insolvency is presumed if:
- the debtor cannot meet its obligations as they become due, unless the inability to pay is considered to be temporary;

- the debtor acknowledges that it is insolvent; or

- a suspension of payment ("betalingsstandsning") has been issued, or if the execution of a distraint order has been made in vain within the last three months before the filing of the bankruptcy petition.

If one of the above-mentioned criteria is met, the company will usually be deemed to be insolvent, and a bankruptcy order will be granted by the probate court.

According to section 20 of the Act a creditor cannot file a petition if:

- his claim is secured by a charge over the property of the debtor;

- his claim is secured by a third party and the petition is a violation of the conditions for the security; or

- if his claim is not due and a third party offers to secure his claim by a reasonable security.

A creditor filing a petition shall state the reason for the petition.

A petition filed by the creditor shall be served on the debtor by the probate court. The first meeting in the court shall take place at the latest three days after the petition is filed. The court may at the request of the company or the debtor decide to postpone the grant of the bankruptcy order if the company or the debtor is trying to seek a voluntary settlement with its creditors and the court finds there are reasonable grounds for believing that the debtor will succeed in obtaining such a settlement. The court may postpone the grant of a bankruptcy order for a period of up to three months.

If an order for winding up is not granted immediately, the probate court may at the request of a creditor deprive the debtor company of the right to dispose of its assets, provided:

- the company accepts such an order; or

- the company is absent from the first meeting in the probate court without legal excuse; or

- there is reason to believe that the company will dispose of its assets to the detriment of its creditors.

The effect of a winding-up order is that a company may no longer transfer or dispose of its assets, receive payments or other services, receive notices, complaints or similar declarations, enter into any obligations or, in any other manner, transact business. The bankruptcy order is published in the Official Gazette (Statstidende). The notice shall further stipulate the date for the first creditors' meeting, at which the trustees shall be elected. This meeting shall take place, at the latest, three weeks after the date on which the notification is published. The above-mentioned legal consequences have effect against everybody – even those without knowledge of the bankruptcy order. Prior to the publication, anybody able to demonstrate that he did not know, nor could he have known, that the company had been declared bankrupt, could rely on any agreement entered into with the company.

Immediately after granting the winding up order the probate court appoints a "midlertidig bestyrer" (interim trustee). This appointment is made only after it has been discussed with the creditors who are present at the meeting where the winding up order is granted.

In the case of a company (as opposed to an individual debtor) the probate court further notifies the commerce and companies agency about the winding up order.

All corporate books and other business papers are collected and retained by the probate court. It is the midlertidig bestyrer's responsibility to notify the land registry and "Vaerdipapirscentralen" (computer registry of shares and bonds) and "Bilbogen" (computer registry of security interests in vehicles) about bankruptcy proceedings being initiated.

After discussing the possible continuation of the business of the company with the interim trustee, the probate court decides to what extent the business shall be carried on.

The midlertidig bestyrer must follow any directions given by the court and cannot without the approval of the court make any decisions which could be said to exceed those necessary for an interim administration of the bankrupt company.

The midlertidig bestyrer must also prepare a list of all the assets and liabilities of the company.

Creditors' involvement and position

Creditors may influence the management of the bankrupt company in several ways. First, the trustee or the trustees are elected by the creditors. The creditors may elect a creditors' committee and finally, the creditors are entitled to participate in the creditors' meetings.

A "kurator" (trustee) must be elected at the first creditors' meeting. In order for this to happen, at least one-third of all known creditors must be represented and at least half of the votes cast must be in favour of the proposed kurator. In determining whether these requirements are being met the amount of the claims is decisive.

The creditors may elect a creditors' committee if one-third of the creditors represented either by number or by the number of their claims make such a demand. The maximum number of members of the creditors' committee is three. The power of a creditors' committee is fairly limited. It is entitled to supervise the administration carried out by the trustee and can require the trustee to inform it about material transactions. It can make inquiries to the kurator and any member of the committee can call for a creditors' meeting to be held. In addition, the committee can propose to the probate court that the trustee be discharged. The creditors' committee itself may be discharged at a creditors' meeting.

Only three creditors' meetings are required by Danish bankruptcy legislation. The first meeting is to elect the kurator, the second is a meeting at which the kurator reports on the claims submitted together with a recommendation whether such claims should be agreed or rejected. Finally, there is a meeting where the accounts specify the funds available for distribution amongst the creditors.

The probate court may call for additional creditors' meetings if it believes them to be necessary. They will be held in the office of the probate court. Further, a meeting may be called for by the trustee or a member of the creditors' committee. A notice of the meeting shall be placed in the Official Gazette. Resolutions at the creditors' meeting are passed by a simple majority of creditors according to the amount of their claims. All unsecured creditors are entitled to attend and vote. A secured creditor may also attend and vote on any unsecured part of his claim. In these circumstances the court will determine the extent to which the secured creditor should be permitted to vote. An unsecured creditor having a contingent claim may also vote. If the claim is disputed by other creditors the probate court decides whether or not the creditor is entitled to vote.

Powers and duties of the kurator

Powers

The kurator has the exclusive power to determine how to deal with the assets of the bankrupt company. It also has the power to initiate legal proceedings against creditors, and to decide how and whether to settle any such disputes. He has the power to sell real property both at an auction and by private treaty. Any loans secured on the real property do not become due because the company is declared bankrupt and the mortgagee cannot make a demand for acceleration of the debt unless the debtor defaulted on the loan prior to being declared bankrupt.

The Danish Bankruptcy Act does not contain an exhaustive list of all the powers of a kurator but merely states that the bankrupt corporation shall be administered by one or several trustees.

However, it is stated in the Act that:

- the kurator may call for a creditors' meeting;
- he shall make a recommendation to the probate court as to whether a claim shall be recognised;
- he may bring legal proceedings against creditors and carry on the business of the bankrupt company/sole trader.

Duties

The kurator is under a duty to represent the interests of the bankrupt company, to litigate on behalf of the company and without unjustified delay to undertake whatever action is necessary in order to bring the proceedings to an end. He must thus see that all the assets of the company are placed under his control, that no criminal offences have been committed and that the assets are sold at the best price. He must also run the business of the company (if this is continued). He is further under a duty to collect any outstanding amounts and deposit such amounts with a reliable bank at a reasonable interest rate.

The kurator must collect the information necessary to investigate creditors' claims, and, if a creditors' committee has been established, the kurator must inform the committee about all important transactions.

He must investigate and take any necessary action concerning voidable transactions (see pp99-100 *infra*) and if he believes that a criminal offence has been committed, he must inform the police. According to section 116 of the Act, the kurator must prepare a statement of affairs and submit a document to the probate court setting out the most important reasons for the winding up of the company. Together with the statement of affairs he must prepare a balance sheet including a profit and loss account for the period from the last balance sheet. However, this last requirement is usually waived by the probate court.

Every third month, he must submit a statement of affairs to the probate court and any creditors' committee. This requirement can usually be complied with by submitting a copy of a transcript from accounts which he has prepared.

As long as the kurator continues to carry on the business of the bankrupt company, a profit and loss account and a balance sheet must be submitted to the probate court, at the latest, three months after the end of each financial year. One year after the date of the bankruptcy order he must submit a statement to the probate court explaining the reasons for the fact that the company is not yet dissolved. After the first year, a similar statement must be submitted every six months.

Management by the kurator

Steps taken on appointment
The kurator is under a duty to take out an insurance policy covering any fraudulent acts he may commit. While he must estimate the total net assets of the company it is the probate court who decides the actual amount that the policy should cover. The original policy is forwarded to the probate court.

The kurator must also familiarise himself with any transaction carried out by the "midlertidig bestyrer" (interim trustee).

Administration in office
The management of the bankrupt company and the action required to be taken by the trustee is described on p94-95 above.

Contractual position
Chapter 7 of the Act empowers a trustee to adopt any of the contracts entered into by the bankrupt company, regardless of whether the other contracting party consents. An adoption presupposes that the terms of the contract have not been breached prior to the grant of the bankruptcy order. In the absence of any action

on the part of the trustee, the other contracting party can demand that the trustee decides without reasonable delay whether he proposes to adopt the agreement. If the agreement is adopted, the bankrupt company shall meet the obligations and enjoy the benefits of the contract. If the obligation of the bankrupt company is a continuing obligation, since the debtor company's period of existence is coming to an end, the contracting party's claim is usually discharged together with other claims enjoying the highest ranking ("massekrav" – see below).

If a contract is not adopted by the trustee the contracting party is entitled to terminate the contract. If the other contracting party does terminate the contract and as a result suffers an economic loss a claim for the loss may be made against the bankrupt company. However, where the contract consists of a continuing obligation, the rule as enunciated above will apply.

As far as continuing contracts are concerned, such as leases or other contracts which provide for long notice of termination or which, according to the terms of the contract, cannot be terminated, the kurator may terminate them with the usual or with reasonable notice. To determine what is usual or "reasonable notice" will be ascertained by looking at relevant legislation which provides a notice period or at professional practice which regulates the length of such notice.

Realisation of assets
The kurator is under an obligation to return to any third parties assets which do not belong to the bankrupt corporation or assets to which a third party has retained title, although it has already been noted that the kurator is entitled to adopt such a contract.

The position of other secured creditors with a valid security interest in chattels or with a charge over land secured by the means of a mortgage is dealt with in section 85 of the Act. According to this provision such creditors cannot enforce a sale of the chattels or the land for a period of six months after the date of the bankruptcy order. The fact that the company is declared bankrupt does not entitle a creditor whose loan is secured by a mortgage to accelerate payments under the mortgage. The purpose of this provision is to enable the kurator to sell the property in the free market and thus obtain a better price than that which may be obtained by a compulsory sale. After six months any creditor may put the chattel or land up for auction.

Other assets may be sold by the trustee at his discretion.

Distribution including ranking of creditors ("massekrav")
Secured creditors are required to wait for the kurator to sell the assets over which they have a charge. Even if the bankrupt company is in default, the secured creditor may not initiate a compulsory sale immediately.

Assets of the company which are subject to reservation of title claims and rights of set-off will be returned and discounted by the kurator once he is satisfied of their validity.

According to chapter 10 of the Bankruptcy Act, the first ranking claims on the assets of the company ("massekrav") are as follows (s93):

(1) costs incurred by a creditor in connection with obtaining the bankruptcy order;
(2) costs incurred in connection with the management of the bankrupt company;
(3) debts incurred by the trustee in connection with the management of the bankrupt company.

If the assets of the bankrupt company are not sufficient to cover these claims in full, a proportionate part of claims shall be paid.

The claims ranking second are as follows (s94):

(1) reasonable costs incurred in connection with an attempt to establish a total reorganisation of the financial affairs of the company, a settlement or composition with the creditors;
(2) other debts incurred during a suspension of payments procedure, where the indebtedness was contracted with the consent of the administrator;
(3) reasonable costs incurred in connection with the liquidation of the company;
(4) duty to the probate court.

The third-ranking claims are those of the preferential creditors, but limited to the following (s95):

(1) claims for salary and other remuneration for work performed for the bankrupt company which became due up to six months before the date of commencement of the winding-up order;
(2) claims on compensation for termination of an employment contract, but not claims for compensation on salary and other remuneration which would have become due prior to six months before the date of commencement;
(3) certain demands for compensation which have become due within the last six months before the date of commencement;
(4) holiday compensation.

The claims ranking fourth are certain public duties and the fifth-ranking claims are those of all other unsecured creditors. However, the sixth and last-ranking claim is interest accrued after the date of the winding-up order, but this does not apply to first and second-ranking claims. Interest on those claims must be paid together with the principal amount outstanding.

Interim dividends may be declared and paid.

Position of officers and shareholders

A likvidator appointed to a solvent liquidation will, as a general rule, replace the officers of the company. The shareholders are still in control of the solvent company and may dismiss the liquidator and appoint a new one at an extraordinary general meeting. The final distribution accounts must be approved by the shareholders.

According to section 112 of the Bankruptcy Act, in the case of an insolvent company, one or several kuratorer shall be appointed for the purposes of the winding up. The officers lose their positions the moment the company is declared bankrupt or ceases payment of its debts and a "midlertidig bestyrer" (interim trustee) is appointed. The kurator shall, as explained above, report any criminal acts committed by the former officers or shareholders.

The shareholders do not have the position of an ordinary creditor and cannot therefore influence the election of the kurator . They must await the outcome of the winding up procedure and only where all creditors have been paid in full, including claims to interest, will any distributions be made to the shareholders.

Termination

The termination procedures are described in chapter 18 of the Bankruptcy Act. When all the company's assets have been realised and all outstanding debts have been collected and any litigation has been settled or a judgment has been rendered by the court, the kurator shall prepare a draft statement and accounts for distribution to the creditors. The statement shall contain a brief explanation of the winding up procedure and the expenses incurred by the kuratorer. The kurator must also make a statutory declaration that no further assets are available for realisation and no further funds are available for distribution to the creditors.

The draft of the final statement and accounts is submitted to the probate court which summons a creditors' meeting, notice of which is published in the Official Gazette. The notice must contain information about the amount of dividend which will be paid.

At the creditors' meeting the creditors and the directors of the company may comment on the draft, which is subsequently approved by the probate court.

Creditors who are unhappy with the accounts can appeal against the decision of the probate court to the Courts of Appeal. Such an appeal must be made within four weeks after the approval of the accounts by the probate court.

If no appeal is made within the four weeks and the accounts are approved by the probate court, the dividend will be distributed. The probate court places an announcement in the Official Gazette concerning the termination of the estate, the amount of dividend for distribution and when it will be distributed. After this the dissolution process takes place.

Dissolution

Purpose and effect

When the probate court has published the final announcement in the Official Gazette concerning the termination of the winding up procedure, it notifies the commerce and companies agency where the insolvent entity is registered about the termination. The registration of the company is then deleted and the company is extinguished.

Pre-application considerations

According to section 143 of the Bankruptcy Act, the kurator may at the first creditors' meeting or at a later stage recommend an "early" dissolution of the company. The purpose behind this is to avoid wasting time and costs where there are insufficient assets to cover the expenses of the winding up.

In the notice for the first creditors' meeting it will be mentioned that the winding up procedures will be terminated in accordance with section 143 of the Act, meaning that no formal winding up procedures will be initiated. The probate court may approve this recommendation by the kurator and the procedure described on p98 above concerning termination will apply.

5. Augmenting the assets of the insolvent corporation

Transactions at risk

Introduction

The kurator has two broad powers which may be exercised to improve the position of the estate.

First, it is possible to avoid certain transactions which the debtor has entered into immediately prior to the bankruptcy, and which have diminished the assets or increased the liabilities of the estate. These provisions in the Bankruptcy Act may be regarded to some extent as the anticipation of the legal consequences of the bankruptcy. Experience shows that a corporation which expects to go bankrupt within the near future will feel motivated to grant preferential treatment to certain creditors at the expense of others, but preferential treatment of third parties may also occur. This could either be favourable treatment extended to family and friends through "making gifts" or payments made to guarantors.

In such situations it is necessary to set aside the transactions in order to enforce the basic rule that in a bankruptcy all creditors are to be treated equally.

Secondly, the kurator may, in suitable cases, apply for the former officers of the company to be held personally liable, for example where they have been acting negligently or fraudulently.

If the kurator is able to increase the assets of the estate by one of these means, it will be to the benefit of the estate in general and not only the unsecured creditor (who will, of course, only benefit if the preferential creditors are paid in full).

General conditions

The following rules apply to all cases concerning setting aside transactions:

- a bankruptcy notice must have been issued or an enforced moratorium or enforced composition must have been adopted. A suspension of payments does not in itself make it possible to set aside transactions;

- the transaction which the estate is seeking to avoid must have been harmful to the creditors. This will not be the case, for example, if payment has been made in order to satisfy a secured claim (which would have been paid in full regardless), or if payment was made with funds which could not have become a part of the bankruptcy estate.

Objective rules on avoiding transactions

The basis of the rules on the setting aside of pre-bankruptcy transactions is that the corporation was insolvent at the time the transaction was carried out and that the creditor who obtained preferential treatment was acting in bad faith.

In order to avoid a large number of lawsuits arising in which the estate would have had to prove that these conditions did in fact apply, it has been decided to define certain transactions as being objectively of an unusual nature and thus creating an irrebuttable presumption that the corporation was insolvent and that the creditor was acting in bad faith. It is thus not necessary for the "tilsynsførende" (administrator) or kurator to prove that the debtor was insolvent and that the creditor was in bad faith, if the transaction falls into one of the categories defined as being of an unusual nature for the purpose of this jurisdiction. Indeed, the transaction may be set aside even where it might have been proved beyond reasonable doubt that the corporation was solvent at the relevant time or that the creditor receiving payment was not acting in bad faith.

The nature of these transactions is discussed below. It must be pointed out, however, that the application of such rules is subject to strict and short time limits. The Bankruptcy Act prescribes three or six month time limits depending on the circumstances. A longer time limit of up to two years applies to closely related persons/entities. The concept of "closely related" is defined in section 2 of the Bankruptcy Act.

The time limits are computed from the fristdag which is defined in section 1 of the Bankruptcy Act. It will usually be the date on which a petition for bankruptcy is filed with the probate court but if prior to this a suspension of payments has been filed, and the petition for bankruptcy is filed within three weeks after the suspension of payments has ceased or during the suspension of the payments, the fristdag will be the date on which the suspension of payments was filed.

The most important categories of transactions which can be avoided under the objective rules described above are:

Gifts
In accordance with section 46 of the Bankruptcy Act, gifts which have been granted within six months prior to the fristdag may be set aside.

The term "gifts" also includes a sale of assets at prices below market value provided that such a sale is actually an expression of a gift and not just a bad business deal.

Inheritance due

In accordance with section 65 of the Bankruptcy Act, the renunciation of a claim for inheritance due may be set aside if such a renunciation has taken place less than six months prior to the fristdag.

Renunciation of a claim for inheritance which is not due cannot be set aside. This category obviously has relevance mainly for personal rather than corporate debtors.

Payment to closely related persons

It is possible, under section 66 of the Bankruptcy Act, to set aside payments of salary and other remuneration connected with employment, paid to closely related persons less than six months prior to the limit date. This remedy is available when the salary paid is clearly in excess of the amount which could be considered reasonable under the circumstances.

This provision is actually just one example of the general rule applicable to gifts set out in section 64 of the Bankruptcy Act.

Certain other payments

In accordance with section 67 of the Bankruptcy Act certain payments which have taken place less than three months prior to the limit date may be set aside.

This applies to the following different categories of payments.

- Payment which has taken place by unusual means, *i.e.* payment by goods, real estate or claims/bonds where this means has been used instead of cash in order to secure the creditor rather than for purely commercial reasons. It is assumed that the transaction may be set aside if the creditor has no actual need of the asset in question or is not trading in such goods and also if the creditor has not on previous occasions purchased such assets from the debtor.

  An example of major practical importance is payment which has taken place through handing back goods which have been sold to the debtor without retention of ownership and where the seller receives the goods back because the purchaser is unable to pay for them.

  The parties will often seek to camouflage a payment by unusual means through the corporation selling the goods to the creditor and issuing an invoice to this effect. The intention might be that the invoice should not be paid but set off, in which case this would lead to the same result as if the goods had been used directly for payment. This situation is not directly covered by section 67 but by section 42.4 of the Bankruptcy Act which deals directly with set off.

  If a set off takes place after the bankruptcy, it is invalidated by section 42.4 and if it has taken place prior to the bankruptcy but within the three month time limit, it may be declared void in accordance with section 69 of the Bankruptcy Act.

- Payment of a debt prior to its falling due for payment is an obvious example of an unusual transaction which might be undertaken by a debtor who is in financial difficulties.

- Use of all available cash. This is related to payments by ordinary means of payment and of amounts which have fallen due. From an objective point of view, therefore, these payments are not suspicious. The salient feature of this category, however, is the size of the amount paid relative to the assets of the debtor and the division of these between cash and other assets. There is no specific percentage limit to be applied in these cases. What is decisive is whether or not a court would hold the payment to this particular creditor to be suspicious. This would, for example, be the case if, prior to the bankruptcy, the debtor received payment from one of its own debtors and then applied the entire incoming amount in paying one particular creditor.

In the case of a payment of a debt falling within the third category referred to above, as an alternative to the jurisdiction provided by section 67, section 74 (described below), may be invoked. Here, however, the bankruptcy estate will have a difficult burden of proof.

Where payment has been made in circumstances apparently falling within any of the three categories described above, the creditor who received payment may avoid the application of section 67 by proving that the payment, even though apparently covered by the wording of the section, was in fact, an ordinary transaction. If he is successful, the payment will not be set aside.

Mortgaging

In accordance with section 70 of the Bankruptcy Act it is possible to set aside the granting of a mortgage, where:

- the mortgage was not been promised to the creditor when the debt was incurred, or
- the particulars relating to the mortgage were not filed in the appropriate public registry without undue delay. Where such filing takes place within three months of the fristdag, undue delay is presumed.

This is often referred to as a dealing with mortgages which have been granted to secure an old debt. It is obviously suspicious where a creditor who held no mortgage is granted such security shortly before the debtor goes bankrupt.

As an example, this section will apply if registration of a mortgage over real estate takes place immediately prior to the limit date even though the mortgage had been granted a long time before or, generally, if anything is mortgaged immediately prior to the fristdag.

This provision is one of the most frequently used, and it is usually the bank which will be subject to transactions being set aside in accordance with this provision.

If, on the other hand, the creditor already holds a mortgage, it may be validly exchanged for another of the same value even if this exchange takes place within the three months limit.

Again, section 70 does not apply where a pledge is made to secure the debt of a third party. Setting aside such a pledge should take place in accordance with other provisions such as the "gift provision" in section 64 of the Bankruptcy Act or the provision described below (s 74).

The consequences of applying section 70 to a mortgage or a security being granted may be illustrated by the following decision by the Supreme Court in UfR 1986, page 508:

> A bank was to finance the acquisition by a corporation of a stock of goods, which were intended to be resold. The purchase price was pledged to the bank on 26 August with a guarantee being issued by the bank for the purchase of the stock. The necessary precautions for the protection of the pledge in this case would have been to inform the ultimate purchaser to make payment to the bank. This took place through notice in an invoice which was sent with the goods on 2 September.

The Supreme Court ruled that this precaution had not been taken without undue delay and the pledge granted to the bank was set aside.

Seizures within the three month period prior to the "fristdag" (limit date)

In accordance with section 71 of the Bankruptcy Act, any seizure which has taken place less than three months prior to the fristdag is automatically set aside. In this case it is not even necessary for the estate to file a suit.

Payments after the fristdag

All payments which have taken place after the fristdag will automatically be set aside unless the estate has suffered no loss through the payment due to the creditor being secured and thus being in a position where he would have obtained full payment of his claim in any event. This exception also applies to payments which were necessary in order to avoid losses.

The creditor will also have a defence to an application to set aside a transaction if he can prove that he did not know nor should have known that a suspension of payments or bankruptcy had occurred.

Other transactions which have taken place after the fristdag may also be declared void unless they may be regarded as being adopted by the tilsynsførende or the kurator or if the transaction was necessary in order to keep the business intact or was made in order to secure through reasonable means the joint interests of the creditors.

Subjective rules concerning setting aside transactions

In accordance with section 74 of the Bankruptcy Act, transactions which cannot be set aside in accordance with the objective rule may be set aside if:

- the debtor was or became insolvent through the transaction; and
- the transaction may be characterised as unjustifiable; and
- the creditor who received payment was acting in bad faith as far as these conditions are concerned.

It should be emphasised that the bankruptcy estate has the burden to prove that all three conditions have been met.

No time limit applies when invoking this provision, but it is obvious that the longer a period which elapses between the transaction and the bankruptcy the more difficult it will be for the trustee to prove that the conditions have been met.

Of paramount importance will be, firstly, the point of time at which payment took place and, secondly, whether payment was by ordinary means. If so, this would rule out the use of the "objective" sections concerning avoiding transactions, and throw a heavy burden of proof on to the tilsynsførende or kurator.

It is important to note that the requirement that the transaction be "unjustifiable" contains an important particular condition which must be met before a transaction can be set aside. This implies that the payment must have taken place in circumstances where – to the knowledge of the creditor – the bankruptcy of the debtor is the only realistic possibility.

A transaction will especially be regarded as unjustifiable if it is obvious that it benefits one creditor at the expense of others. The condition of "unjustifiability" is thus entwined with the condition concerning bad faith.

Personal liabilities of officers

The Act on Public Limited Companies and the Act on Limited Companies contain provisions concerning the liability of the officers and the auditors of a corporation (ss140 and 141 Act on Public Limited Companies; s110 Act on Limited Companies, respectively).

These provisions may be regarded as a codification in this special area of the general rule on liability in Danish law (the so-called "culparegel") in accordance with which persons who cause loss to others through negligent or fraudulent behaviour may be held liable for such losses.

It is expressly stated in the provisions mentioned above that a claim may be made by the company itself if it is the company which has suffered the loss and it is also possible for the creditors to make such a claim against the officers if the creditors individually have incurred a loss.

The most frequent case in which this question arises when a corporation goes bankrupt is where the officers of the company have continued the business regardless of continuing deficits. In such a case the estate faces the question of whether a claim for damages should be made against the officers of the company – the board and the management – to obtain compensation for the loss which has been incurred owing to increased deficits which continuing the business has caused.

Such a claim will – if payment is obtained – become an asset of the estate and will thus be distributed among the creditors in accordance with the general provisions.

It will, however, often be the case that one individual creditor makes a claim for damages which he has suffered through making a delivery on credit and where the creditor does not obtain full payment of his claim due to the bankruptcy.

An example is the decision of the Supreme Court in UfR 1977, page 274:

> In this case a department store in Copenhagen was in financial difficulties. The officers of the company discussed the situation and decided on 18th February that the corporation should file for bankruptcy. On the very same day a supplier had delivered goods on credit and thus suffered a loss due to the bankruptcy.
> The supplier sued the board of directors but was unsuccessful. Although the court held that the possibility of carrying on the business at the time of the delivery was severely limited, bankruptcy was not completely unavoidable.

The decision illustrates how difficult it is to succeed in an action under this provision.

In 1982 new provisions were added to the Act on Public Limited Companies and the Act on Limited Companies which seek to urge the board to take action in good time, before bankruptcy becomes inevitable.

The provision in section 85(a) of the Act on Limited Companies which applies to corporation with a small equity is the strictest. When the board determines that the corporation has lost half its equity, it is obliged to see to it that a general assembly of the shareholders is convened and proposals adopted which will lead either to a full restoration of the share capital or, in effect, to the termination of the corporation.

The provision in section 69(a) of the Act on Public Limited Companies which applies to corporations with a relatively high equity is considerably more lenient since a board in this situation is only obliged to call a general meeting of the shareholders where discussions (as opposed to actual proposals) must take place about the situation of the corporation.

It is at present not clear to what extent these new provisions will be of importance for the decisions of the courts concerning the awarding of damages.

In situations where the creditors have been misled, for instance due to the incorrect contents of financial statements, it is considerably easier to obtain an award for damages as will appear from the decision by the Supreme Court in UfR 1982.595:

> This case concerned a financial statement which should rightly have shown a deficit but which had been altered through the addition of uninvoiced profits on work in progress to an extent which was contrary to the rules concerning the proper conduct of auditors. A creditor who suffered a loss on deliveries which had taken place after the financial statement had been made public was awarded damages against the officers of the company and the auditor.

In section 143 of the Act on Public Limited Companies and section 113 of the Act on Limited Companies provisions have been inserted in accordance with which the liability for damages may be lessened having regard to the degree of negligence, the size of the loss and other circumstances.

Sometimes the general meeting of shareholders of a corporation grants a "discharge" to negligent officers and this means that the corporation itself has no possibility of suing the officers of the corporation whilst the company is solvent. Where the corporation becomes bankrupt and the fristdag is determined as being no more than two years after a discharge was granted, the bankruptcy estate may disregard the discharge and sue for damages. However, this should then take place no less than three months after the corporation has been declared bankrupt.

6. Public control over insolvent corporations

Licensing and control of the appointee

The Bankruptcy Act does not prescribe special conditions concerning education or qualifications in order for a person to be appointed as kurator or tilsynførende, but in fact it is nearly always a lawyer who is appointed.

Auditors who take part in settling an estate should in general be authorised public accountants. In connection with bringing about an enforced composition, one of the tillidsmaend who participates should have knowledge of the business and the other about financial matter (s164 of the Bankruptcy Act).

An accountant who is an authorised public accountant may automatically participate as the tillismaend with financial knowledge.

A tillismaend with knowledge of the business can participate if he has been authorised to do so already or if in individual cases he is authorised by the probate court.

The tillimaend is authorised by the Justice Department and his name are put on a list, which will then be used as reference by the probate court when making appointments.

The right to appoint a tilsynsførende during the suspension of payments rests with the corporation which files the suspension. Even though the probate court is not bound by the suggestion of the debtor it is unusual for the probate court to appoint another administrator. This is due to the right, which the creditors have, to review the question as to who should be the tilsynsførende at the meeting which must take place no less than three weeks after the filing for suspension (*cf* s22 of the Bankruptcy Act).

A kurator is, generally speaking, elected by the creditors at a meeting of creditors where a majority based on value of claim and not by number of creditors has the right to decide.

This, however, is based on the assumption that the assembly of creditors is representative, and this will only be the case if no fewer than one-third of all creditors, counted by value of claims, is present (s120 of the Bankruptcy Act). A claim which has been wholly secured confers no vote and one which is partially secured only confers a reduced right to vote.

It is possible to appoint a committee of creditors which can supervise the work of the trustee if the creditors should so wish (s114 of the Bankruptcy Act).

If the meeting of creditors cannot be considered as representative, because fewer than one-third are present, the probate court will appoint the trustee.

In order to register and evaluate the assets the probate court will appoint one or several tillidsmaend.

Rules concerning conflict of interest have been laid down in section 238 of the Bankruptcy Act which seeks to ensure that those who participate during the settlement of the estate as tilsynsførende, kurator, auditor or tillidsmaend are impartial.

It is expressly stated that a tillidsmaend may not participate when selling off assets which he has evaluated and it is also stated that none of the persons participating in settling the estate may themselves acquire any of the assets of the estate.

Since the kurator has unlimited powers as far as the assets of the estate are concerned, the probate court will usually demand that he puts up a bond in the shape of insurance in order to protect the creditors against loss arising from unwarranted transactions.

The above does not apply to a tilsynsførende because the debtor himself continues to control the assets and no bankruptcy estate has been established.

Generally speaking, the kurator has considerable freedom during the settlement of the estate. If a creditor believes that the kurator is acting to the detriment of the estate he will have to approach the probate court which may then call a meeting of the creditors which is the supreme authority in respect of the estate. Further, the probate court may replace the kurator.

If a creditor believes that his particular rights are being unjustifiably disregarded, he may demand that the probate court avoids the kurator's material decisions (s128 of the Bankruptcy Act). He will be subject to personal liability if he commits errors leading to a loss for the estate or individual creditors.

The meetings of creditors which take place in the estate will also be summoned through the Official Gazette unless the meeting has been called by an earlier meeting which itself had already been announced in the Official Gazette.

The meeting in which the final accounts of the estate are produced will always be summoned through the Official Gazette.

As far as the examination of claims is concerned, the trustee is obliged to inform a creditor through separate notice if the claim of the creditor has not been recognised by the estate.

When a corporation has been declared bankrupt the words "in bankruptcy" ("under konkurs") should be added to the name of the company, and the Commerce and Companies Agency will register that the company is now bankrupt.

Further, the probate court records the negotiations at the meetings of creditors and those who have a vested interest may require a transcript from the records.

Examinations and investigations

In order to analyse the situation of the estate, especially its assets and liabilities, and in order to analyse the transactions which have taken place immediately prior to the bankruptcy, the trustee may ask the management, the board and the auditor – including those who have previously held these positions – to appear in the probate court where they are obliged to answer truthfully the questions put to them concerning their role in the management of the company. They may also be required to hand over documents which are in their possession.

If any person refuses to comply, various steps may be taken in order to enforce the obligations including fines, arrest by the police and even temporary custody.

The probate court may decide that one or several of the persons in question are not allowed to leave the country for a specified period and may take their passports into custody.

The court may also demand the appearance as a witness of anyone who is able to give evidence concerning circumstances that are material to the estate. However, the probate court must make sure that the kurator shows appropriate restraint when questioning someone who is likely to be sued by the estate at a later state.

If the kurator wishes to obtain documents, the probate court may demand that these be produced. However, if the kurator wishes to obtain files or other documentation that are in the possession of a third party, he will have to approach the bailiff in order to obtain these if the third party refuses to hand them over voluntarily. A tilsynsførende in a suspension of payments has none of these means at his disposal.

In accordance with section 79 of the Penal Code, it is possible to bar a person from becoming an incorporator of, manager of or member of the board of any corporation for a specific period which will be between one and five years or until further notice. In the latter case the persons in question may, after five years have expired, ask a court to review whether they should continue to be barred. Even though this rule has been inserted in order to avoid abuse by persons who have several times caused their creditors losses by conducting business through corporations that were insolvent, it is not necessary that a bankruptcy should actually take place in order to invoke section 79. On the other hand, the mere fact that a person has participated in a corporation which goes bankrupt is not, of itself, sufficient to enable these disqualification provisions to be invoked. The decisive criteria are whether the person has actually committed a crime and whether thereafter it is likely that he would abuse his position. When deciding upon this, it is obvious that barring someone from being a managing director in a corporation is only possible if an actual violation of the Penal Code has taken place, if this is connected to the business conducted by the person, and, also, if the act committed is of a serious nature or has happened several times.

It is the responsibility of the Public Prosecutor to press charges against anyone who should be barred from being an officer, and so on. In accordance with section 79 of the Penal Code. It has been considered whether to extend the provision to anyone who is in a position of influence in the corporation in order to avoid the use of front men. However after close consideration this has not been carried out in order not to violate basic civil rights.

The provisions of the Penal Code concerning violation of the rules of book-keeping have been tightened up and a person may now become subject to criminal liability not only for committing wrongful or misleading acts, but also for not keeping the books and records in a proper fashion as prescribed by the legislation, provided that the non-observance is of a serious nature.

Publicity and records

A suspension of payments which has been filed with the probate court is not made public in the Official Gazette or in any other way. Those creditors who will be subject to the suspension of payments must therefore be informed through the despatch of a circular letter.

If the suspension of payments ends with a proposal for an enforced moratorium or an enforced composition, a notice should be issued through the Official Gazette for the meetings in the probate court where voting on the proposals will take place. Further, the creditors in such situation would be urged through the Official Gazette to file their claims.

In the case of bankruptcy, the decision to declare the corporation bankrupt will be made public in the Official Gazette this publication will be also used to urge creditors to file their claims with the kurator.

Any meeting of creditors which is convened by the estate will also be called through a proclamation in the Official Gazette unless the time and place of the meeting has been agreed upon by a previous meeting of creditors which itself had been proclaimed in the Official Gazette.

The meeting where the final accounts are produced will always be convened through a proclamation in the Official Gazette.

As far as the question of approval of claims is concerned, any creditor whose claim has not been approved by the kurator should receive special notification of this by registered mail.

When a corporation has been declared bankrupt, it should use its own name with the addition "in bankruptcy" and the Commerce and Companies Agency, will register the information that the company is now in bankruptcy.

Further, the probate court will keep records of the negotiation taking place in the meetings of creditors, and anyone having a valid interest in the matter may obtain transcripts of these records.

Contents of Chapter 4

CORPORATE INSOLVENCY LAW IN FRANCE

1.	**Introduction**	113
	The former regime	113
	The new regime	114
2.	**Corporations**	115
	Introduction	115
	Sociétés Anonymes	116
	Sociétés à Responsabilité Limitée	119
	Financing and security for creditors	120
	Available information	123
	Other business entities	123
	Debt collection and asset recovery	126
	Measures to prevent bankruptcy	128
3.	**Survival of the insolvent corporation or its business: rehabilitation in bankruptcy**	132
	Purpose and effect	132
	Pre-application considerations	132
	Powers and duties of participants in the rehabilitation in bankruptcy proceedings	134
	Procedure	137
	Creditors' involvement and position	148
	Management by the administrator	152
	Position of officers and shareholders	153
	Termination	154
	Simplified procedure	154
4.	**Termination of the corporation: liquidation**	155
	Purpose and effect	155
	Preconditions	156
	Powers and duties of the liquidator	156
	Procedure	157
	Creditors' involvement and position	159

Management by the liquidator   160
Position of shareholders and officers   161
Termination ("clôture des opérations")   161
**5.   Augmenting the assets of the insolvent
       corporation**   162
Introduction   162
Transactions at risk   163
Personal liability of officers   164
Indirect means of augmenting the assets   166
6.   Public control over insolvent corporations   167
Licensing and control of the insolvency practitioner professions 167
Publicity and records   168

Chapter 4

CORPORATE INSOLVENCY LAW IN FRANCE

Moquet Borde & Associés,
Revised by Lovell White Durrant

1. Introduction

French bankruptcy law is governed by the Law of 1 March 1984 on the Prevention and Conciliation of Economic Difficulties Incurred by Enterprises and the Law of 25 January 1985 on Rehabilitation and Liquidation in Bankruptcy. This new regime has broken away from the previous objective of French bankruptcy law which was the payment of creditors. As compared to the past regime, the current procedure is simpler and certain criminal and civil sanctions applicable to the insolvent company's officers have been reduced or even eliminated. The evolution towards the principles established by the new regime had its roots in the former Law of 13 July 1967 on Bankruptcy Reorganisation and Liquidation of Assets.

The former regime

Under the former regime, economic criteria were for the first time taken into account in examining the insolvent company's potential for reorganisation. The treatment reserved for the officers was based on their behaviour prior to the commencement of the bankruptcy proceedings.

The previous regime was, however, promulgated at a time of favourable economic conditions, and was, therefore, no longer appropriate to the recessionary period of the late 1970s and early 1980s, during which the number of bankruptcy filings increased substantially. Despite the innovation of considering economic criteria in examining the company's potential for reorganisation, most bankruptcy proceedings ended with the liquidation and the resultant termination of the insolvent company since the 1967 Law focused more on paying creditors than the survival of the company.

The new regime

The three laws governing the new regime no longer have the payment of creditors as their first priority.

Law of 1 March 1984

When a legal entity, trader or artisan encounters financial and economic difficulties, a series of preventive measures may be adopted, the goal being to avoid bankruptcy through expert assistance in the management of the company. Certain persons with an interest in the enterprise might be allowed to intervene in the management of the enterprise in the event of financial default and there is provision for conciliation between the debtor and creditor.

Most provisions of this Law concern company law and modify certain articles of the Law of 24 July 1966. It became effective on 1 March 1985.

Law of 25 January 1985

The new bankruptcy legislation came into force on 1 January 1986 and applies to all bankruptcy proceedings commenced on or after that date. The goal of the new legislation is first and foremost to save the ailing enterprise and the attendant employment. Satisfaction of the creditors' claims, although still important, is no longer the primary concern. The role of the employees has increased inasmuch as they are now often consulted during the bankruptcy proceedings.

The new regime consists of a single bankruptcy procedure composed of a rehabilitation proceeding which may, in certain circumstances, be followed by a liquidation proceeding. All debtors, regardless of their economic and financial situation, start out in the rehabilitation regime ("redressement judiciaire"), which continues either until the debtor is rehabilitated, or until it is converted into a liquidation proceeding ("liquidation judiciaire").

The traditional role of the trustee in bankruptcy has been modified by the new rules. The management functions previously performed by the trustee are now carried out by a court-appointed administrator ("administrateur judiciaire"). Claims which were previously submitted to and verified by the trustee are now the responsibility of a creditors' representative ("représentant des cranciers").

An important aspect of the new legislation is the simplified procedure ("procédure simplifiée") which applies to small and medium size enterprises and which now benefits more than 90% of all debtors in France.

While the new law applies to traders, artisans and farmers, the majority of bankruptcy proceedings involve companies.

Law of 10 June 1994

New bankruptcy legislation came into force on 1 October 1994. Its main goal is the improvement of bankruptcy prevention, the simplification of its procedure, the improvement of creditors' rights and the clarification of any proposed sale plan of the business.

In practical terms, the law should enable the President of the Court in future to obtain further information more easily and to employ additional powers for investigation, for instance, of financial and welfare organisation.

It is also now possible to trigger an immediate liquidation, for instance by the court when the enterprise has ceased all activities or when there is no chance of the enterprise being saved.

The rules concerning the declaration of receivables by creditors are more flexible, especially with respect to the statute of limitations. The role of the assistant of the creditor's representative ("controleur") is emphasised and the grounds for prosecutions or other penal sanctions are also extended.

2. Corporations

Introduction

There are two principal types of company in France: commercial companies and civil companies. The distinction between these two is important when considering, *inter alia*, the liability of the shareholders for the company's debts.

A civil company is one which carries out a civil activity and on which the law does not confer a commercial character by virtue of its legal form (art 1845(2) French Civil Code). Civil activities are not listed in the Civil Code in the same way that commercial acts are listed in articles 632 and 633 of the Commercial Code. Therefore, activities are civil if they do not fall within the list of commercial acts contained in articles 632 and 633. Civil activities may be classified into the following seven categories: agriculture, extraction, intellectual activities, groups of professionals, real property, artisanal activities, and co-operatives. Anyone wishing to form a company is more likely to select a civil company because its operation is more flexible and less expensive than a commercial company and the partners have significant freedom to determine the conditions of their relationship in the by-laws.

The majority of business entities in France are commercial companies. The "société anonyme" (SA) and the "société à responsabilité limitée" (SARL) are the most frequently used structures in this category.

SAs and SARLs are governed by the provisions of the Law of 24 July 1966 ("L") and the Decree of 23 March 1967 ("D"). SAs and SARLs are always considered to be commercial companies even if they carry out a civil activity (art 1(2) L). Their legal existence is contingent upon registration with the Registry of Commerce and Companies.

Recently, the form of "société par actions simplifiée" has appeared. This is a newly introduced type of commercial company which has been specifically designed for use as a joint venture vehicle and is more flexible in many respects than the traditional forms of commercial company.

Sociétés Anonymes

Characteristics

The minimum registered capital of an SA depends on whether it is privately or publicly financed; it amounts to FF 250,000 where the SA is privately financed and FF 1,500,000 if it is publicly financed (art 71 L).

Companies which are publicly financed are those which meet the conditions of article 72 of the 1966 Law. According to the French Stock Exchange Commission's interpretation of article 72, a company is deemed to be publicly financed where more than 300 persons are solicited and no personal link exists between the company and such persons (Regulation No. 88-04 of the Stock Exchange Commission).

While SAs must have a minimum of seven shareholders, there is no specific limit as to the maximum number thereof (art 73 L). The shareholders of an SA are normally liable for the debts of the SA only up to their contributions to capital (art 73 L). A shareholder may, however, be held liable for debts exceeding his contributions in the event that bankruptcy proceedings are commenced against the SA and he is found to have acted as a *de facto* member of management and his error or omission is considered to be the cause of the bankruptcy. His liability will, of course, also exceed contributions if he has given a personal guarantee on behalf of the SA.

Management

An SA may be managed by either a board of directors and a chairman of the board ("président directeur général"), or a directorate ("directoire") and supervisory board ("conseil de surveillance"). The most common type of management organ is the board of directors.

Board of directors and chairman of the board

SAs have a minimum of three and a maximum of 24 directors, whether or not the SA is listed on an official stock exchange (art 89(1) L). The company's by-laws must state a) the number of directors for that company (*i.e.* between three and 24) and b) the length of the directors' term of office. In any event, the directors' term of office may not exceed three years for the first directors appointed in the statutes and articles of association and six years for directors appointed thereafter.

All directors must be shareholders of the company, the minimum number of shares which must be held by each being set down in the by-laws. Foreigners may be directors and need not obtain a commercial card for such purpose. A commercial card is a special identity card granting "trader" status which is delivered by the "prefet" of the "département" where the foreigner carries out his activity. This card may only be granted to individuals. Unless an exemption is granted, all foreigners exercising a professional, commercial or artisanal activity must hold this card (Decree-Law of 12 November 1938). Nationals of EEC Member States need not obtain this card. A simplified regime (short form) may apply in cases where the foreign company investing in France through a subsidiary has been in existence for more than three years and its share capital is at least FF 5 million.

The manner in which directors are appointed depends on whether such appointment is made at the time of the SA's formation or, as is more common, during the life of the company. Their appointment during the life of the company is accomplished by the shareholders acting at an ordinary general meeting (art 90(1) L). The first directors of SAs which are not publicly financed are appointed in the by-laws (art 88 L); those of publicly financed SAs are appointed by a special vote taken at the time of the incorporation meeting of the shareholders (art 79(2) L). The shareholders may, at any time in a shareholders' meeting, remove the chairman.

The board of directors has broad powers to act on behalf of the SA. The only legal limits thereon are the powers of the shareholders acting at a general meeting and the corporate purpose set out in the by-laws. Additional limits on the directors' powers may be contained in the by-laws. Decisions made by the board which do not fall within the corporate purpose or which exceed any limitations in the by-laws are nevertheless binding on the SA *vis-a-vis* third parties (art 98(2) L).

The specific powers of the board include:

- the calling of general meetings of the shareholders;
- the review and adoption of the annual financial statements;
- the preliminary authorisation of agreements between the SA and its directors; and
- the appointment and removal of the chairman and general manager(s).

The chairman of the board is appointed from among the members of the board (art 110(1) L). His term of office is fixed by the by-laws and may not exceed his term of office as director. He may be removed at any time by the board (art 110(3) L).

The chairman is also the general manager of the SA (art 113 L). He is in charge of managing the SA, represents it in its relations with third parties, and has full power to act on its behalf, subject to any limitations expressed in favour of the board and the shareholders acting at a general meeting. Limitations may also be imposed by the corporate purpose and by the by-laws.

The SA is, however, bound to third parties by decisions of the chairman which exceed the above limits, but it should be noted that the chairman may not give any guarantees on behalf of the SA without the prior authorisation of the board (art 98(4) L). Such authorisation, which is only valid for a one-year period, may be given on a case-by-case basis or through an annual blanket authorisation. In the event of a tied vote of the board, the chairman has a casting vote.

The chairman may be assisted by no more than five general managers (art 115 L) who are considered to be subordinate to the chairman. The general manager, who does not have to be a shareholder if he is not a director, is appointed by the board on the recommendation of the chairman. Subject to prior consultation with the chairman, the board fixes the general manager's term of office and may remove him from his post. The general manager may remain in office following the expiration or termination of the chairman's term of office but only until the election of a new chairman.

The general manager's powers are fixed by the board but, in his relations with third parties, the general manager has the same power to bind the SA as the chairman (art 117 L).

Directorate and supervisory board

In SAs which have a directorate and supervisory board, the actual management functions are carried out by the directorate which is under the control and supervision of the supervisory board.

The directorate may be composed of no more than five members (or seven where the SA is listed on an official stock exchange), the exact number being set out in the by-laws or determined by the supervisory board (art 119 L, art 96 D). The members of the directorate need not be shareholders and are appointed by the supervisory board. Under article 122, their term of office is four years although since 1988, a term may be included in the by-laws setting it between two and four years.

The directorate has extensive powers to act on behalf of the SA but is subject to the limits of the corporate purpose and the powers granted to the shareholders and the supervisory board. The SA is bound to third parties by all acts of the directorate, even those which exceed these limits, in the same manner as the chairman of the board and general managers. The directorate is responsible for calling meetings of the shareholders and establishing the annual financial statements, and may give guarantees on behalf of the SA but only, where such is authorised by the supervisory board. It must abide by certain reporting requirements as regards the supervisory board, for example, it must prepare a quarterly report on the company's situation, a management report, management forecast documents and the annual accounts.

The task of the supervisory board is to oversee the directorate in the performance of its functions. While the board is generally considered to be of the same status as the board of directors, its role is very different. Nevertheless, at the same time many of the rules applicable to boards of directors are applicable to the supervisory board.

The supervisory board is composed of at least three and no more than 12 members (art 129(1) L). In the case of SAs not making a public offering, the first members are appointed by the by-laws whereas, in SAs making a public offering, they are appointed by a special vote during the initial shareholders meeting. In either case, all subsequent members are appointed by the shareholders acting at an ordinary general meeting. The term of office is provided for in the by-laws and may not exceed three years for the first members and six years for subsequent members (art 134(1) L). A member of the supervisory board may not also be a member of the directorate.

In addition to generally overseeing the management conducted by the directorate, the supervisory board is responsible for verifying the annual financial statements established by the directorate, appointing the members of the directorate, authorising agreements between the SA and members of the directorate or the supervisory board, and preparing an annual report which it presents to the shareholders at ordinary general meetings. The members of the supervisory board are not authorised to participate in the management of the company. They may not, therefore, be held liable for the debts of the SA, for errors or omissions which caused any bankruptcy nor will they be subject to civil sanctions or certain prohibitions in the event that bankruptcy proceedings are commenced against the SA, unless they are found to have acted as *de facto* members of management.

Ownership

The capital of an SA is divided into shares. Several types of shares exist including ordinary and preferential shares, shares with or without voting rights and shares with double voting rights. Shareholders may transfer their shares at any time by signature of a transfer form. However, the by-laws may impose limits on such free transferability and often do so, particularly in the case of sales to third parties.

One of the most common means of restricting transferability is through an approval clause ("clause d'agrément") in the by-laws. Such a clause may, exceptionally, be contained in the by-laws of listed companies. In this latter case, the clause must be adapted to meet the requirements applicable to stock exchange sales. Article 276 of the 1966 Law sets out the terms and conditions applicable to approval clauses in the by-laws of listed companies. It should be noted, however, that the "Conseil des Bourses de Valeurs" now makes it a condition of the admission of shares to the official stock exchange that any approval clause found in the company's by-laws be deleted.

Shareholders have the right to participate in and vote at shareholders' meetings, inspect certain corporate documents, submit written questions to the board of directors or directorate, receive dividends and liquidation distributions, and exercise preferential subscription rights.

Sociétés à Responsabilité Limitée

Characteristics

SARLs are a common business vehicle for small and medium size enterprises since they are generally easier and less expensive to incorporate, manage and operate. The number of shareholders may vary from one (in which case the company is referred to as an "entreprise unipersonnelle à responsabilité limitée" ("EURL")) to 50 (arts 34(1) and 36 L). As with the shareholders of an SA, the shareholders of an SARL may be held liable for the company's debts only up to the amount of their capital contributions, except in the case of bankruptcy where they may be held liable if found to have acted as *de facto* members of management.

The minimum registered capital of an SARL is FF 50,000 (art 35(1) L). It is prevented from making public offerings and therefore may only be privately financed.

Management

The management of a SARL is carried out by one or more managing directors ("gérants"), the number being fixed by the by-laws (art 49(1) L). The managing director need not be a shareholder (art 49(2) L). The first managing director is generally appointed in the by-laws; thereafter, he is appointed by the shareholders acting at a general meeting. His term of office is generally set out in the by-laws, failing which he is appointed for the duration of the SARL (art 49(1) L). He may be removed by the shareholders at any time with cause (art 55 L).

The managing director has broad powers to act on behalf of the SARL, although these are subject to the same limitations as those which affect the management of an SA, and the SARL is bound with respect to the decisions of the managing director made in excess of such limitations in the same manner as the SA is bound.

Ownership

The capital of an SARL is divided into shares. SARLs are not permitted to issue negotiable share certificates and transfers to third parties must first be approved by the shareholders (art 45 L). The latter have rights which are comparable to those of shareholders of SAs as they may vote and participate in shareholders' meetings, consult corporate documents and submit questions to the managing directors.

Financing and security for creditors

Financing

In addition to subscriptions to capital by the shareholders and the granting of loans by banks, companies often raise capital through the issue of debentures ("obligations"). Debentures are distinguishable from shares in that, while the latter confer ownership rights in the company, the former merely represent a debt owed by the company to the debenture holder. Debenture holders are entitled to the payment of either fixed interest, the amount of which is determined by the company at the time of issue, or variable interest based on, for instance, the company's turnover or profit or the financial market. Repayment of the principal generally occurs on the expiration of the term of the debenture.

Both the interest and principal under a debenture may be secured by guarantee, mortgage or lien. For example, a bank may guarantee the company's payments or the company itself may issue a mortgage on its real property or a lien on its "fonds de commerce" for the benefit of the debenture holders.

A "fonds de commerce" is an ongoing business which corresponds to a group of tangible and intangible personal property assets that a trader uses for the operation of his business such as customer lists, the commercial name, the commercial lease, patents, trademarks, licences and other intellectual property rights, equipment, tools, and inventory.

These security interests must be approved by the shareholders acting at a meeting voting the issue of debentures or, (on delegation of the shareholders' meeting), by the board of directors and are granted before the issue of the debenture. The subscription of a debenture is then deemed to constitute approval of the security interests by the debenture holders (arts 324, 325, 326 L). It is not common practice for the repayment of debentures to be secured by a mortgage or lien.

In the event that bankruptcy proceedings are commenced against the company, debenture holders whose debt is secured by a mortgage or lien are considered to be secured creditors and are entitled to the same privileges and rights as other similarly situated secured creditors. Those debenture holders whose debt is not secured fall within the general group of unsecured creditors.

Besides ordinary debentures, other means of financing are available to companies such as debentures convertible into shares ("obligations convertibles en actions"), debentures coupled with a stock warrant ("obligations avec bons de souscription d'actions"), investment certificates ("certificats d'investissement") and participating notes ("titres participatifs").

Security for creditors

When a bank or other lender lends money to a company, there are a number of devices available to secure the repayment of the loan. The most frequently used security devices in France are the mortgage ("hypothèque") and the pledge ("gage").

A mortgage is a right in real property given by the owner of that real property to a person (the lender or "mortgagee") from whom that owner has borrowed a sum of money (the loan), for the purpose of securing repayment of the loan. The borrower ("mortgagor") always remains in possession of the real property, and may use and sell such property as it wishes without the consent of the lender due to the lender's "droit de suite". According to the "droit de suite", the lender may attach and sell the property at any time whether or not the owner is the original mortgagor. Thus, even if the original mortgagor has sold the property to a third party, the lender may recover the property irrespective of the ownership rights of the subsequent buyer who purchased after the recording of the original mortgage. The mortgage is deemed to be extinguished if the underlying debt is extinguished.

The mortgagee who is not paid may have the real property sold at a judicial sale and will be entitled to the proceeds to satisfy his debt prior to the payment of the unsecured creditors. Where there are several mortgagees, they shall be entitled to payment in the order in which the mortgages were recorded.

Pledges concern personal property and confer on the pledgee the right to satisfy the obligation owing to him by way of a lien on the pledged property which entitles him to preference with respect to such property over the other creditors of the debtor. There are two types of pledge: the pledge where possession of the pledged property is not surrendered by the pledgor ("gage sans dépossession") and that where possession of the pledged property is surrendered ("gage avec dépossession").

One of the most common types of pledge where possession is not surrendered by the pledgor is the pledge of tools and equipment ("nantissement de l'outillage et du matériel"). This pledge may be conferred on the seller of the tools and equipment or the lender of funds used to purchase such tools and equipment within a period of two months following the delivery of the tools and equipment (Law of 18 January 1951, art 3). The pledgor may not sell or transfer the pledged goods prior to reimbursing his debt. If the pledgor fails to make payment on time, the pledgee may cause the tools and equipment to be sold through a judicial sale in which case he will be paid out of the proceeds before the unsecured creditors are paid.

Another common type of pledge where possession is not surrendered is that of a company's "fonds de commerce" ("nantissement du fonds de commerce"). Only certain assets of the "fonds de commerce" may be pledged, such as the pledgor's commercial name, commercial lease and customer list. The pledgor retains the right to manage and exploit his "fonds de commerce" without any interference by the pledgee. The rules applicable to forced judicial sales in the case of the pledge of tools and equipment also apply with respect to pledges of "fonds de commerce". A pledge over the shares of a company may also be created without possession of the pledged shares being surrendered by the pledgor.

In the case of a pledge where possession is surrendered, an actual, physical transfer of the goods must be made from the pledgor to the pledgee. If the pledgor does not satisfy the debt which is secured by the pledged property, the pledgee may either take title to the property or cause it to be sold and retain the proceeds.

While not legally considered to be a security device, the most efficient means of securing a debt in the case of a sale of goods is the insertion of a "retention of title" clause in the sales agreement. Under such a clause, title to the goods sold remains with the seller until such time as the buyer tenders full payment of the purchase price. Where a retention of title clause is contained in a contract, and where other conditions are met such as the obtaining of a court order, the seller may recover the goods even if bankruptcy proceedings have been commenced against the buyer.

Available information

In France, the principal sources of information on companies are the registry of commerce and companies and the clerk of the commercial court.

At the time of the company's registration with the registry of commerce and companies, the following information must be filed with the clerk of the commercial court located within the jurisdiction in which the company's future registered office is to be located:

- the company name;
- the juridical form of the company;
- the amount of the registered capital;
- the address of the registered office;
- the duration of the company fixed by the by-laws;
- the company's fiscal year end; and
- the names and addresses of the officers with the power to manage or bind the company.

In addition, any SA or SARL must, within one month following the annual ordinary general meeting of the shareholders, file the following documents with the clerk of the commercial court located in the jurisdiction in which the company has its registered office:

- the annual financial statements (balance sheet, income statement, and the notes to the financial statements);
- the board of directors' or directorate's report;
- the supervisory board's report, if any;
- the statutory auditor's report, if any;
- the resolutions relating to the allocation of the annual profit or loss;
- the consolidated financial statements, if any; and
- an inventory of the portfolio securities held at the end of the fiscal year if the company is listed on an official stock exchange.

Pledges of tools and equipment and going concerns are recorded with the clerk of the commercial court. Mortgages for each parcel of real property are recorded with the land registry ("conservation des hypothèque") located in the place in which the real property is situated.

Other business entities

In addition to SAs and SARLs, the most popular business entities are partnerships, economic interest groups ("groupements d'intérêt économique") and civil companies. It should also be mentioned that individuals may conduct business as sole traders without a formal corporate structure. Finally, several companies may belong to a corporate group.

Partnerships

General partnership – "société en nom collectif"

The "société en nom collectif" ("SNC") is a commercial company usually chosen for small businesses and involving a limited number of partners. Each of the members of an SNC is considered to be a trader ("commerçant") and is personally jointly and severally liable for the debts of the SNC (art 10 L). Consequently, the partners are, in general, actively involved in conducting the SNC's business. The SNC is managed by one or more managing directors ("gérants") whose term of office is relatively secure in that he may only be removed by a unanimous decision of the partners. The SNC is transparent for tax purposes and therefore is appropriate for companies earning relatively small profits.

In the event that bankruptcy proceedings are commenced against the SNC, the bankruptcy court automatically commences separate bankruptcy proceedings against each of the partners of the SNC because of their unlimited liability for the SNC's debts.

Limited partnership – "société en commandite simple" – and the limited partnership with shares – "société en commandite par actions"

There are two types of limited partnership in France, the "société en commandite simple" ("SCS") and the "société en commandite par actions" ("SCPA"). Both are commercial companies, their principal characteristic being that they have two types of partner, general and limited, whose rights and obligations differ. Currently, there are relatively few SCSs and SCPAs in France. Although SCPAs have been out of favour for some time, they are once more becoming increasingly popular.

In both types of company, the general partners are traders and are personally jointly and severally liable for the debts of the company. As with the SNC, if bankruptcy proceedings are brought against either the SCS or the SCPA, the bankruptcy court automatically commences a separate bankruptcy proceeding against the general partners of the SCS or SCPA. The general partners may not normally transfer their shares without the unanimous consent of all partners.

The limited partners of both the SCS and the SCPA are not considered to be traders and their liability for the debts of the SCS or SCPA is limited to the amount of their contributions to capital unless they actively intervene in the company's management. The transferability of shares differs, however, between the limited partners of the SCS and SCPA. Specifically, while limited partners of an SCS may not transfer their shares without the unanimous consent of the partners, the limited partners of an SCPA may freely transfer their shares at any time in the same manner as the shareholders of an SA.

Both SCS and SCPA are managed by one or more managing directors who are either chosen from among the general partners or may be an outside party. In no circumstances may the limited partners be appointed managing director because they are prohibited from intervening in dealings between the SCS or the SCPA and third parties.

Economic interest group – "groupement d'intérêt économique"

The "groupement d'intérêt économique" ("GIE") is a legal entity formed by two or more individual companies whose purpose is to permit its members to develop their respective businesses more efficiently and less expensively than if they had acted separately. The GIE benefits from a legal regime which is very flexible because the members have great latitude to determine the rules of its functioning. This is the reason why the GIE is often favoured over the more complicated and restrictive joint subsidiary. GIEs are often chosen to carry out activities such as research and development, market studies, joint advertising, and import or export activities. In principle, the goal of a GIE is not to seek profits for its own account; it is not prevented from doing so, however, and if it does, the profits must be distributed to the members and are taxable in their hands.

The principal characteristics of the GIE are that:

- it is considered to be an extension of the respective activities of its members;
- it may be formed with or without any registered capital; and
- the members are jointly and severally liable for its debts.

It may be managed by one or more managers ("administrateurs").

Civil companies ("sociétés civiles")

Civil companies may only carry out civil activities. The shareholders are personally liable for the debts of the civil company in proportion to their equity interest. Civil companies are generally used in the areas of real property construction and agriculture, and by professionals such as attorneys, accountants and physicians. The civil company is managed by one or more managing directors who may, but are not required to, be shareholders.

Sole trader

It is not necessary to create a legal entity to be able to carry on business in France. In fact, there are numerous individuals who exercise their commercial activity as sole traders.

Corporate groups

A corporate group is defined as a group of companies which are legally independent of each other and subject to common economic and strategical decisions. In general, a corporate group is composed of a parent company which exercises control over and imposes a particular strategy to be followed by several companies in which it owns shares. The notion of a group is more economic than legal. The group is not considered to be a separate legal entity.

It should be noted that, except for the corporate group, each of the above business entities may be the subject of a bankruptcy proceeding governed by the Law of 25 January 1985.

Debt collection and asset recovery

Procedure within the jurisdiction

A creditor may obtain payment for a debt owed to him by attaching all or part of the debtor's assets. To do so, he must first obtain an authorisation from the président of a court having jurisdiction or produce a "titre executoire" establishing the debt which may be either a recognition by the debtor of his indebtedness or an enforceable judgment ("jugement executoire").

Prior to the bringing of any action, the creditor must verify whether the debtor is the subject of bankruptcy proceedings because, in the latter case, all individual actions against the debtor are suspended following the declaration of bankruptcy.

There are several methods of obtaining an enforceable judgment. One such method is the injunction to pay ("injonction à payer"). This is a rapid, *ex parte* proceeding under which the creditor asks the court to issue an injunction to pay against the debtor. This injunction is served on the debtor and if he does not contest the injunction within the month following service, the injunction becomes enforceable.

Another method is the summary proceeding ("référé provision"). This is a rapid proceeding brought before the president of the court where the debt may not be seriously contested. It is not an *ex parte* proceeding. The decision issued by the judge ("ordonnance de référé") is temporary pending a decision on the merits of the case; the judge rendering the decision on the merits is not bound by the decision of the summary proceedings judge, such decision being immediately enforceable. The time period between the request and the issue of a summary proceedings decision usually varies between two and four weeks. In practice, even though a decision on the merits may not be obtained through a summary proceeding, such method of obtaining an enforceable judgment is widely used in France when the debt is well proven and may not be seriously contested.

The action on the merits ("assignation au fond") lasts longer and permits the obtaining of a final judgment, *i.e.* a final "titre executoire". The final judgment may not be appealed.

The action on the merits begins with a trial before the lower civil or commercial courts ("tribunal de grande instance, tribunal d'instance, tribunal de commerce"). It takes approximately one year to obtain a judgment from these courts and, even then, it may or may not be immediately enforceable. In the event that it is enforceable, an attachment procedure may be commenced immediately. If it is not enforceable and it is urgent that certain measures be taken in furtherance of the decision, the président of the court having jurisdiction may nevertheless authorise the plaintiff to enforce the judgment and thus commence an attachment procedure. As such authorisations are considered to be an encroachment upon the right of appeal, they are not often granted. Unless an appeal is entered within one month following service of the judgment, these decisions become final enforceable judgments. The Court of Appeal's judgment is always enforceable even if it is appealed to the Supreme Court.

Once an authorisation from the président of a court having jurisdiction or a "titre executoire" is obtained, attachment proceedings may be commenced. Attachments may be made on personal and real property.

One of the two most common personal property attachment procedures is the "saisie exécution" which covers tangible personal property. Under this procedure, the property is seized by a process server from the debtor who nevertheless remains the owner. Such property is then sold through a judicial sale and the proceeds are turned over to the creditor in satisfaction of his debt.

The other type of personal property attachment is the "saisie arret" which concerns intangible personal property. It is a proceeding under which the creditor can require a third party who is indebted to the debtor, not to pay the debtor the sums due; the creditor then requests the court to require the third party to pay direct to the creditor the amount owed to the creditor by the debtor.

Real property attachments ("saisie immobilière") permit a creditor to have real property seized and sold by judicial sale; the debt is then paid out of the proceeds of the sale. As compared to the personal property attachment, it is a complex, very formal, long and expensive proceeding. It is, nevertheless, often used owing to the stability and economic value of real property. All creditors, including unsecured creditors, may obtain an authorisation from the president of a court having jurisdiction to attach real property.

Cross-jurisdictional procedures

Foreign judgments are only enforceable in France where they have been the subject of an enforcement judgment "exequatur", and a separate legal proceeding must be brought in France to obtain it. Once obtained, the exequatur renders the foreign judgment enforceable and permits the execution of the foreign judgment in conformity with French law with the result that the terms and conditions of the execution will not be subject to the influence of the foreign law or judgment.

Before issuing the exequatur, the French judge verifies that :

- the court rendering the foreign judgment had jurisdiction over the case;
- the law applied by the foreign court is not contrary to French rules of private international law;
- the foreign judgment does not violate public policy ("ordre public"); and
- the party seeking the exequatur has not attempted to use conflict of laws rules to avoid an imperative rule of French law ("fraude à la loi").

The competent court to issue the exequatur is the "tribunal de grande instance". Such judgments are appealable according to the normal procedural rules.

It should be mentioned that France is a party to the European Economic Community Convention on Civil Jurisdiction and the Enforcement of Judgments of 27 September 1968 which became effective in France on 1 February 1973.

Under Article 26, a judgment given in a contracting State shall be recognised in the other contracting States without any special procedure being required. The enforcement of an EEC foreign judgment in France is always conditional on the obtaining of an exequatur which may be obtained through a simplified procedure. With regard to the verification by the French judge, only two conditions must be met: the foreign judgment must not violate public policy and the defendant must be accorded the rights to notice and the opportunity to be heard ("droits de la defense").

As to the procedural requirements, the exequatur may be obtained ex parte.

According to Article 1, the Convention does not apply to "bankruptcy, proceedings relating to the winding-up of insolvent companies or other legal persons, judicial arrangements, compositions and analogous proceedings". Thus, the normal rules of exequatur discussed above apply to the enforcement of all foreign bankruptcy judgments in France.

Measures to prevent bankruptcy

The Law of 1 March 1984 was the first legislative measure specifically directed at the prevention of bankruptcy proceedings. The purpose of this Law was to alert the head of an enterprise to the risks of the enterprise's financial and economic difficulties as early as possible so that they could be resolved without recourse to a formal regime designed to terminate the enterprise. The 1984 Law provides for three measures to prevent bankruptcy proceedings: the improvement of the quality of available accounting and financial information, the alert procedure, and creditor-debtor conciliation ("réglement amiable"). Some of the provisions of the 1984 Law have been incorporated into the 24 July 1966 Law discussed above. The Law of 10 June 1994 has clarified certain aspects of the Law of 1 March 1984, notably the measures intended to prevent bankruptcy proceedings taking place.

Accounting and financial information

With respect to the first measure, the 1984 Law improved the requirements concerning the production of information on the enterprise's financial situation and instituted the preparation of forecast information by certain companies. Specifically, companies which have controlling interests in other enterprises must publish consolidated accounts, *i.e.* accounts which consolidate in one document the accounts of all of the enterprises in the group. Such consolidated accounts must be certified by the parent company's statutory auditor. In addition, SAs and SARLs are required to file their annual financial statements and the notes thereto and the statutory auditor's report with the clerk of the commercial court each year following their annual shareholders' meeting.

Furthermore, large companies, *i.e.* those with more than 300 employees or an annual turnover net of tax which is equal to or exceeds FF 120 million, must prepare certain forecast information. The 1984 Law requires such companies to draw up the following four documents:

- a statement setting out the current net assets of the company and its liabilities which are due and payable ("situation de l'actif réalisable et disponible et du passif exigible");
- a statement of financial position ("tableau de financement");
- a provisional operating forecast ("compte de résultat prévisionnel"); and
- a cash flow forecast ("plan de financement")

These documents are not published since they contain information which, if divulged, could harm the company's reputation. They are, however, transmitted to the workers representation committee, the statutory auditors and to the supervisory board, if any.

The alert procedure

The alert procedure was one of the significant innovations of the 1984 Law. It permits persons other than the head of an enterprise to discover and disclose the financial and economic difficulties and encourages him to take whatever action is necessary to remedy such difficulties.

Statutory auditor alert

The statutory auditor triggers an alert when, in the exercise of his duties, he becomes aware of significant facts which could compromise the continued operation of the enterprise (art 230(1) L). In practice, such an alert must be given where the anticipated income of the enterprise will not cover the payment of its debts.

It is preferable for the statutory auditor alert to remain confidential as long as possible. The statutory auditor may request the chairman of the board or the president of the directorate to provide him with all information relating to the relevant facts (art 230-1 (1) L). In the event that there is no response to such request, or if the statutory auditor deems the response to be insufficient, he may request that a meeting of the board of directors or supervisory board be called. If the situation does not improve, the statutory auditor prepares a special report for the shareholders and, in urgent situations, may call a meeting of the shareholders.

Under the Law of 10 June 1994, the statutory auditor alert will be in future communicated to the president of the court if the board, the directorate or the manager fails to ensure the ability of the business to continue.

If the statutory auditor fails to trigger this alert, he may be held liable to all those harmed by the commencement of bankruptcy proceedings in respect of the enterprise (art 234 L).

Workers representation committee alert

The purpose of the workers representation committee alert is to avoid financial difficulties or the closing down of the enterprise, which would in turn lead to dismissals of employees. Such an alert is not mandatory, unlike that of the statutory auditor. The workers representation committee may act when it discovers facts which could seriously affect the economic situation of the enterprise.

The alert is broken down into two stages: the workers representation committee first requests the employer to provide it with explanations; then, if it does not receive a satisfactory response, it may prepare a report for submission to the board of directors or supervisory board and may, if necessary, call a meeting of the shareholders.

Shareholders alert

The shareholders may submit written questions to the members of the management when they discover a number of significant facts which could compromise the continued operation of the company. The members of the management must respond to such questions within one month. Written questions may be submitted to the members of the management at the time of the holding of general shareholders meeting and must be answered during the meeting (arts 56, 162 L).

For SAs and SARLs, shareholders representing at least 10% of the share capital may ask the court to appoint an expert to prepare a report on one or more transactions which, they consider, is jeopardising the company's financial health (arts 64(2), 226 L). This is a relatively long and consequently not very efficient procedure since its effectiveness depends upon the speed with which it is carried out.

Thus, even though it is the shareholders who have the greatest risk of losing all that they have invested, it is they who are accorded the least effective alert procedure.

Commercial court alert

The commercial court alert only applies to companies which do not prepare forecast accounts (*i.e.* commercial companies which at the end of a fiscal year have at least 300 employees or whose net turnover is equal to or exceeds FF 120 million). The members of the management of these companies may, where the company has incurred losses, be called to appear before the président of the commercial court (art 34, 1984 Law). The net loss must be greater than one-third of the company's equity ("capitaux propres") for this to happen. The président neither acts as a judicial authority nor renders any decision or judgment. He questions the members of management as to the means by which they intend to restore the company's financial health.

General information of the president of the court

The representatives of private companies and enterprises can be summoned by the president of the commercial court for an interview if difficulties arise which could challenge the continuity of the business. Moreover, the president is entitled to carry out investigations with the financial and welfare organisations (Arts 3 and 4, Law of 10 June 1994).

Debtor-creditor conciliation ("réglement amiable")

The debtor-creditor conciliation procedure is governed by articles 36-39 of the 1984 Law. It is an extrajudicial method of resolving the economic and financial problems of an enterprise. Such procedure is almost always difficult to implement since it is based on a written agreement between the debtor and the creditors, and the creditors often prefer to receive partial but immediate repayment of their debt rather than participate in a continuing recovery plan – which will usually be the debtor's preferred route.

Conciliation is an optional, flexible, rapid and confidential procedure which is initiated by the head of the enterprise. The three following conditions must be met in order for an enterprise to benefit from such procedure (art 35, 1984 Law):

- the enterprise must carry out an economic activity which includes all commercial, and agricultural activities;
- it must not be able to pay its debts through normal channels of financing (it must not, however, be in a state of "cessation de paiements" (see p134 *infra*); and
- it must have the capacity to recover its financial equilibrium, that is, its goal must not be to gain additional time prior to the filing of a bankruptcy petition.

The procedure is for the debtor to contact the président of the court in writing. If the latter determines that the three conditions are met, he appoints a conciliator whose responsibility it is to invite the creditors to conclude an agreement with the debtor. If a conciliation agreement is concluded, the effects of the conciliation will be purely contractual. Although the conciliation agreement is filed with the court it is not published.

The conciliation agreement does not necessarily have to include all of the creditors but is usually entered into with the debtor's principal creditors. Creditors are under no obligation to be a party to the conciliation agreement. The effect of the agreement is to prevent any creditor that is a party thereto from bringing an action against the enterprise for the payment of a debt, or from demanding or accepting any pledge, encumbrance or security device that secures a debt which is the subject thereof.

However, since the passing of Law of 10 June 1994, the taking of security to guarantee the payment of the parties to the "règlement amiable" is no longer permissible. Also, the president of the court may impose a moratorium, legal proceedings or payments, except with regard to the employees, for a maximum period of four months.

The failure of the debtor to abide by the financial terms of a conciliation agreement triggers the commencement of bankruptcy proceedings, even though the debtor is not in a situation of a "cessation de paiements" (art 2, 1985 Law). This is an exception to the normal rules governing the commencement of bankruptcy which necessitate a prior "cessation de paiements" (see p134 *infra*). The breach of the non-financial terms permits the creditors who are party to the agreement to seek the judicial termination of the conciliation agreement under normal rules.

However, non performance of the financial terms by the debtor is no longer viewed as an event which, of itself, would trigger the commencement of bankruptcy proceedings (art 12, 1994 Law).

3. Survival of the insolvent corporation or its business: rehabilitation in bankruptcy

The survival of insolvent enterprises in France is accomplished through rehabilitation in bankruptcy proceedings ("redressement judiciaire"). Such proceedings are divided into two phases:

- a first phase consisting of an observation period which may not generally exceed six months and during which a court-appointed administrator ("administrateur judiciaire") prepares an economic and employment evaluation and establishes a draft rehabilitation plan; and
- a second phase which commences with a judgment of the court adopting the rehabilitation plan (the "plan"). The plan, which is executed during this second phase, provides for the continuation of the enterprise, or for its partial or total transfer to a purchaser.

Purpose and effect

The primary purposes of the rehabilitation in bankruptcy proceedings are the rescue of the ailing enterprise and the protection of the employees' jobs (art 1, 1985 Law). It is thus only secondary to these goals that the needs of the creditors are taken into consideration.

If the plan provides for the continuation of the enterprise, it must do so within the framework of the existing corporation, although the latter may be remodelled. This will, of course, be greatly assisted by the moratorium which is imposed on all the creditors. Where the plan orders the transfer of the enterprise, the goal is to ensure the maintenance of the activity in a new enterprise.

The most notable effect of the declaration of rehabilitation proceedings is that new creditors (*i.e.* those who became creditors after the commencement of the rehabilitation proceedings) are granted preferential rights over all other creditors whose debts arose before such date. Another important effect is the suspension of all individual lawsuits against the debtor except those brought by any of the new creditors.

Pre-application considerations

The applicability of the 1985 Law necessarily depends both on the legal structure of the debtor and on its financial situation.

Legal structure

Rehabilitation in bankruptcy proceedings applies to certain natural persons as well as to legal entities.

Such natural persons comprise traders, artisans and farmers. To fall within the definition of a trader, a person must carry out one or more of the specific commercial acts defined in article 632 *et seq* of the French Commercial Code. Thus the 1985 Law does not apply to persons engaged in professions such as doctors, lawyers and architects ("professions liberales"). The commercial acts must be conducted on an habitual basis, *i.e.* most of the person's income must derive from, and his time be spent in, carrying out the activity.

Artisans were subject to bankruptcy proceedings for the first time as the result of the 1985 Law. The artisanal enterprise is legally very similar to small commercial and industrial enterprises.

It was not until 1988 that farmers fell within the scope of the bankruptcy law. There are a number of special features governing their regime such as the rule that rehabilitation proceedings may not be commenced unless a request for conciliation has first been filed with the president of the court (art 4, 1985 Law) as amended by the Law of 30 December 1988).

Even if the 1985 Law would not ordinarily apply to a person because of the nature of his activities, it may nevertheless be invoked in certain circumstances. First, it applies to persons who are not traders but who have benefited from a debtor-creditor conciliation agreement (see pp131-132 *supra*) and who have failed to comply with its financial terms (art 2(2), 1985 Law). Additionally, bankruptcy proceedings may be commenced against certain persons who are partners or members of the management of companies which themselves are the subject of bankruptcy proceedings (see pp153 and 164-166 *infra*).

According to article 2 of the 1985 Law, rehabilitation in bankruptcy proceedings applies to all private legal entities. In order to qualify as a legal entity, full legal existence is necessary. Full legal existence is acquired, in the case of companies, on registration with the Registry of Commerce and Companies (art 842, French Civil Code); for other associations, it is obtained upon the filing of a declaration with the "préfecture" (art 2, Law of 1st July 1901). Dissolved companies and GIEs retain their legal existence for purposes of corporate liquidation (art 1844(8), French Civil Code). Bankruptcy proceedings may, therefore, be commenced against them following dissolution and during their corporate liquidation (Judgment of 12 April 1983, Cass. com.).

As the 1985 Law only applies to private legal entities, it does not apply to the State, local governmental agencies, or public establishments. Private entities engaged in the providing of public services fall within the scope of the 1985 Law. These latter entities include "sociétés d'économie mixte" and nationalised companies (banks and insurance companies).

Financial situation

Rehabilitation in bankruptcy proceedings commence when the trader, artisan, farmer or legal entity is in a situation of "cessation de paiements" which is defined as "the inability to pay one's debts as they fall due with available assets".

The debt must be certain (*i.e.* uncontested as to its existence and amount), liquid (*i.e.* a known amount) and due. The unpaid debt may be of a commercial or civil nature.

The available assets consist of sums which are at the immediate disposal of the enterprise or goods which may be quickly converted to cash.

The previous principles, developed by case law prior to the 1985 Law, whereby an enterprise had to be in a "desperate" situation or irremediably compromised, no longer apply. These principles delayed the commencement of the proceedings and rendered rehabilitation of the enterprise more difficult.

The cessation de paiements must be proved by the person or legal entity submitting the petition for the commencement of bankruptcy proceedings. There is no one particular method of proving a cessation de paiements.

Powers and duties of participants in the rehabilitation in bankruptcy proceedings

The court

The court which renders the judgment declaring the commencement of rehabilitation in bankruptcy proceedings (the "opening judgment") plays a major role in the proceedings. It designates the principal organs, in particular, the "juge commissaire", the administrator, the creditors' representative and the expert (arts 10 and 12, 1985 Law).

All important decisions relating to the proceedings are made by the court which determines the rights of the creditors, the temporary continuation of the enterprise, and whether or not personal sanctions should be imposed on the members of the management (arts 181, 187, 189, 1985 Law). Furthermore, the court adopts the plan or orders the liquidation of the enterprise (arts 8 and 64, 1985 Law). It is competent to hear all disputes and claims relating to the rehabilitation in bankruptcy (art 174, 1985 Decree).

The président of the court

The 1985 Law grants special powers to the président of the court in order to expedite the proceedings. Among such powers are those:

- to request the Court of Appeals to transfer the proceedings to another jurisdiction (art 7, 1985 Law);
- to extend the investigation period ("période d'enquête") during the simplified procedure (pp154-155 *infra*); and
- to issue orders amounting to "titre executoire" in favour of creditors to en-

able the latter, exceptionally, to bring individual actions against the debtor upon the conclusion of the liquidation in bankruptcy proceedings (art 169(3), 1985 Law). These actions may not be brought during the liquidation proceedings because all individual actions of the creditors are frozen during this period (art 47, 1985 Law).

The juge commissaire

The "juge commissaire" is one of the judges of the commercial court having jurisdiction over the bankruptcy proceedings. He is designated in the opening judgment (art 10, 1985 Law) and is considered to be the "orchestra conductor" of the bankruptcy proceedings. Only one "juge commissaire" is appointed for each proceeding, irrespective of the complexity of the affair. He constantly follows the proceedings and sees to it that they maintain momentum. He acts as the intermediary between the court and the other participants by:

- overseeing the administrator and the creditors' representative;
- participating in the elaboration of the economic and employment evaluation; in this regard, he benefits from a broad investigative power given to him by statute (art 19, 1985 Law) to ask questions of such entities as banks, the statutory auditors, the social security administration, the Treasury Department and all governmental agencies. These questions must be answered even if they could normally be refused on the basis of professional secrecy (art 19, 1985 Law);
- making numerous decisions in the areas of, *inter alia*, the acceptance of claims (arts 51, 103, 1985 Law), the management of the enterprise during the observation period (see pp140-141 *infra*) (arts 33, 37, 39, 45, 1985 Law), the realisation of the assets (art 154 *et seq*, 1985 Law), employee dismissals for economic reasons (art 45, 1985 Law), and the contracting of loans during the observation period (art 40, 1985 Law).

The administrator

The administrator is appointed in the opening judgment. His role is principally one of management, and thus is more economic than legal. During the observation period, the administrator prepares the plan and participates in the management of the enterprise in accordance with the conditions set out in the opening judgment (art 31, 1985 Law).

During the plan execution period, the administrator is in charge of implementing the plan and he plays an important role in the event that the plan orders the continuation or transfer of the enterprise. In addition, the judgment of the court adopting the plan may appoint the administrator as the "commissaire à l'exécution du plan" (art 67(1), 1985 Law) (see pp136-137 *infra*).

He is bound by an "obligation de moyens" rather than an "obligation de résultats", that is, he may be held liable for errors or omissions in the methods of conducting his administration but not for the results thereof.

The creditors' representative

The creditors' representative is appointed in the same manner and at the same time as the "juge commissaire" and the administrator. His duties as creditors' representative are carried out during the observation period. If the plan proposes the continuation or transfer of the enterprise, he may be named the "commissaire à l'exécution du plan" (art 67(1), 1985 Law). If the enterprise cannot be rehabilitated, the creditors' representative is designated as liquidator (see pp156-157 *infra*) unless the court decides otherwise.

The creditors' representative is responsible for verifying the creditors' claims. All creditors, except employees, must submit their claims to the creditors' representative (art 50(1), 1985 Law). The latter is provided by the debtor with a certified list of the creditors containing the amount of the debt owed to each (art 52, 1985 Law). Where a claim is disputed by the debtor, the creditors' representative informs the creditor. The final decision as to whether a claim will be admitted or rejected is made by the "juge commissaire" on the basis of the creditors' representative's recommendation. He also participates in the establishment of the list of employees' claims, which is then transmitted to the employees' representative (art 123, 1985 Law). The creditors' representative alone is competent to act on behalf of and in the interest of the creditors (art. 46(1), 1985 Law). All individual lawsuits brought by the creditors prior to the opening judgment, and which are suspended as a result of such judgment, are pursued by the creditors' representative. Such lawsuits, however, may not result in the payment of any sums but may only seek to establish the existence of the debt and its amount (art. 48, 1985 Law).

At the end of the observation period, the creditors' representative remains in power for a period necessary to complete the verification of the creditors' claims (art. 66(2), 1985 Law).

The experts

During the observation period, the administrator may ask the court to nominate one or more experts to assist him in the accomplishment of his duties (art 10, 1985 Law). These experts are included in a special section of the general list of court experts compiled for each of the Court of Appeals' jurisdictions.

The commissaire à l'exécution du plan

Where the plan calls for the continuation or transfer of the enterprise, the judgment adopting the plan appoints a "commissaire à l'exécution du plan" for the period during which the plan is to be executed. The 1985 Law allows for either the administrator or the creditors' representative to be appointed to such position (art 67(1)).

The "commissaire à l'exécution du plan" is in charge of overseeing the financial, economic and employment aspects of the plan. He must report to the court and the public prosecutor if the debtor, transferee or any other person fails to carry out the Plan. The "commissaire à l'exécution du plan" continues the lawsuits pursued by the creditors' representative.

The contrôleur

One to five "contrôleurs" (of whom one must be a secured creditor and one other must be an unsecured creditor "chirographaire") must be appointed from amongst the creditors by the "juge commissaire". Their appointment is mandatory by virtue of the 1994 Law. The "contrôleur" assists the creditors' representative primarily in the verification of the creditors' claims, and the "juge commissaire" in the supervision of the administration of the enterprise (art 15, 1985 Law). The "contrôleur" may review all documents transmitted to the creditors' representative and the administrator. He is not vested with any personal management or representative rights. He is not remunerated and is bound to keep the affairs of the enterprise confidential (1994 Law).

The employees' representative (représentant des salariés)

In addition to being represented by the workers representation committee or the personnel delegates, (whose task is generally to participate in the drafting of the plan), the employees of the debtor are represented by an employees' representative designated by the workers representation committee, the personnel delegates or the employees. The employees' representative is principally responsible for verifying the employees' claims and defending the specific interests of the employees before the creditors' representative (arts 44, 123, 1985 Law). He does not participate in the drafting of the plan unless there is no workers representation committee or personnel delegates (art 45, 139(2), 1985 Law).

The public prosecutor (procureur de la république)

The public prosecutor is vested with the power to oversee the rehabilitation in bankruptcy proceedings. He is kept informed of the status of the proceedings through reports submitted to him by the administrator and the creditors' representative. He may also require the production of any documents relating to the procedure (art 13(1), 1985 Law).

Furthermore, he may, *inter alia*, cause the commencement of rehabilitation proceedings, request the replacement of the administrator or creditors' representative, and ask that civil or penal sanctions be applied against the members of the management of the debtor (arts 4(2), 12, 183, 1985 Law).

Procedure

The course and nature of the rehabilitation in bankruptcy proceedings varies depending on whether the "general regime" or "simplified procedure" applies.

The general regime is discussed below; the particularities of the simplified procedure are dealt with on pp154-155.

Petition for the commencement of rehabilitation in bankruptcy proceedings

A petition for the commencement of rehabilitation in bankruptcy proceedings may be filed by or at the initiative of the debtor, a creditor, the court, the public prosecutor or the employees (art 4, 1985 Law).

The debtor

Rehabilitation in bankruptcy proceedings must be commenced by the debtor no later than 15 days following the cessation de paiements (art 3(2), 1985 Law). Such filing is commonly known as the "dépôt de bilan" or the "filing of the balance sheet". It must be made by the debtor or an authorised agent. While the form of the petition is not regulated, there are certain documents which must be annexed to it (art 6, 1985 Law):

- the annual accounts for the last fiscal year;
- the registration certificate with the appropriate registry, if any;
- the cash situation ("situation de trésorerie") dating back no more than three months;
- the number of employees and amount of the annual turnover;
- a list of creditors and the amounts owed to each;
- a list of the security interests which creditors have in the debtor's property;
- an inventory of the debtor's assets;
- for companies whose members are jointly and severally liable for its debts, a list of such members' names and addresses; and
- the names and addresses of the representatives of the workers representation committee or personnel delegates who may be heard by the court, if already designated.

The creditor

Rehabilitation in bankruptcy may be commenced at the request of a creditor, whether the debt is commercial or civil in nature, whether the creditor is a secured or unsecured creditor, and irrespective of the amount of the debt. Where debtor-creditor conciliation has been undertaken (see pp131-132 *supra*) and the financial terms of the conciliation agreement have not been complied with, only the creditor who is a party to such an agreement may file a petition for the commencement of bankruptcy proceedings (art 5, 1985 Law).

The bankruptcy petition filing procedure is the same as that applicable to the filing of a normal complaint. It is important to note that the petition must request only the commencement of rehabilitation proceedings and thus may not also contain a request, even if subsidiary, for the payment of the debt due; moreover, claims for the payment of a debt may not include a request for bankruptcy proceedings to be commenced against the debtor (art 7, 1985 Decree).

The court

The court is entitled to commence rehabilitation proceedings in cases where neither the debtor nor any of the creditors have requested this. Cases in which the court commences the proceedings are, however, infrequent. The most significant hurdle for the court to overcome is learning when an enterprise is in a situation of cessation de paiements since there is no organised way for it to obtain such information. Generally, it is acquired through the employee representatives, or an unofficial notice of the public prosecutor, or by public rumour.

The président summons the debtor to a non-public hearing prior to the issue of the judgment commencing the proceedings (which is rendered publicly).

The public prosecutor

In practice, very few proceedings are commenced on the initiative of the public prosecutor. When this does occur, the public prosecutor files a request with the court, at which point the procedure is the same as where the proceedings are commenced at the initiative of the court.

The employees

The commencement of rehabilitation proceedings by the employees is indirect; the workers representation committee, if any, or the personnel delegates may notify the court or the public prosecutor of any facts revealing a cessation de paiements. On the basis of these facts, the court or public prosecutor may undertake further investigation and, where appropriate, the court may commence rehabilitation proceedings.

The jurisdiction of the court

Jurisdiction over rehabilitation proceedings is vested in the commercial court (if the debtor is a trader, artisan or commercial corporation), or the "tribunal de grande instance" in all other cases *i.e.* those concerning farmers, civil legal entities, associations, GIEs with a civil purpose and agricultural cooperatives (art 7, 1985 Law).

As to venue, jurisdiction over rehabilitation proceedings is reserved to certain courts listed by decree (art 7(2), 1985 Law; art 2, Decree 85-1387).

Article 174 of the 1985 Decree provides that the competent court may hear all matters relating to the rehabilitation, liquidation, and imposition of civil or other sanctions provided by the 1985 Law except for actions relating to the civil professional liability of the administrator, the creditors representative, the "commissaire à l'exécution du plan" or the liquidator, which are heard only by the "tribunal de grande instance".

The judgment ordering the commencement of rehabilitation in bankruptcy proceedings

Prior to issuing its judgment, the court must determine whether or not the debtor is in a situation of "cessation de paiements". To do so, the court must summon the debtor, the workers representation committee, if any, or the personnel delegates to a non-public hearing at which the court may obtain information concerning the debtor's financial, economic and employment situation and where the debtor may evoke any defences he may have to the declaration of bankruptcy (art 6, 1985 Law). The court may also summon any other person it deems necessary to such hearing. Furthermore, the court may appoint a judge to gather information and prepare a report on the debtor to determine if a declaration of bankruptcy is warranted.

If the court decides that the debtor is in a cessation de paiements, it issues a judgment declaring the commencement of rehabilitation in bankruptcy proceedings ("opening judgment"). In this judgment, it fixes the date of the cessation de paiements and appoints the participants of the proceedings (see p134 *supra*).

The opening judgment is rendered at a public hearing (art 9, 1985 Law). It must also be published in a legal announcements newspaper and the "Bulletin Officiel des Annonces Civiles et Commerciales" ("BODAC"), and recorded in the register of commerce and companies or the directory of trades ("repertoire des métiers") (art 21, 1985 Decree).

The opening judgment may be appealed to the Court of Appeals by the debtor, the creditor filing the bankruptcy petition or the public prosecutor within ten days following its publication in the BODAC (art 171, 1985 Law; art 156, 1985 Decree). The judgment of the Court of Appeals may be appealed to the Supreme Court ("Cour de Cassation"). These two judgments are immediately enforceable regardless of whether or not an appeal has been filed.

The issuance of the opening judgment results in the commencement of the observation period (art 8, 1985 Law).

The observation period

The observation period is a phase during which the administrator prepares a report containing an economic and employment evaluation and, based on the results of such evaluation, either a proposed plan or a recommendation of liquidation (art 18, 1985 Law). During this phase, the debtor continues to operate and all lawsuits and proceedings against the debtor are stayed.

The initial duration of the observation period is fixed in the opening judgment and may not exceed six months. The observation period may be renewed by the Court for no more than six months, either on its own initiative or at the request of the debtor, the administrator or the public prosecutor. Exceptionally, it may be renewed for a third period not greater than six months at the request of the public prosecutor (art 8 (2), 1985 Law). Article 45 of the 1985 Decree provides that if the report is not submitted in the eight days preceding the end of the observation period as extended or if it appears that such report cannot be so submitted, the "juge commissaire" notifies the court which then decides on the measures to be taken. The sanction imposed by the court will consist of an order that the rehabilitation proceedings be converted to liquidation proceedings. Exceptionally, certain courts agree to examine the report even after such deadline has passed.

Since the Law of 10 June 1994, the observation period does not have to be respected insofar as the entreprise has ceased all activities or if the rehabilitation of the entreprise is definitely not possible. In such cases, the court may order an immediate liquidation.

Continuation of the enterprise's activity

Article 35 of the 1985 Law provides for the continuation of the enterprise's activity during the observation period. The court may, however, at any time and at the request of the administrator, the creditors' representative, the debtor, the public prosecutor, or upon its own initiative and based on a report of the "juge commissaire", order the partial or total cessation of the debtor's activity or the liquidation in bankruptcy of the debtor. It could be decided, for example, that certain non-profitable or loss-making activities are to be discontinued in order to restore the debtor's financial well-being.

The continuation of the operation of the debtor's enterprise often involves entering into new contracts and maintaining existing contracts. In addition, the enterprise may exceptionally be the subject of a lease agreement covering the assets and activities of the enterprise ("contrat de location-gérance").

Existing contracts

The maintaining of existing contracts between the debtor and its suppliers, bankers or clients may be indispensable to the enterprise's continuation. The maintenance of such contracts is specifically governed by Article 37 of the 1985 Law. While continuation of the contracts is presumed, it is not necessarily automatic; indeed, it is the administrator who decides whether they should be continued and he need not consult the "juge-commissaire" before making such decision. If the debtor decides to continue existing contracts contrary to the dictates of the administrator, the decision is deemed null and void. It is important to note that any provisions in the pre-bankruptcy contracts of the debtor which provide for the automatic termination on the commencement of bankruptcy proceedings by or against the debtor have no effect in France.

There is no time limit within which the administrator must inform those who entered into pre-bankruptcy contracts with the debtor of the continuation of their contracts. If a formal written request is submitted to the administrator asking whether he intends to continue the contract in question and the administrator fails to respond within one month of his receipt of the request, the administrator is deemed to have *de facto* abandoned the contract (except in the case of a moratorium ordered by the juge commissaire).

Where the administrator or the debtor elects to continue the contract, he must respect its terms and conditions and must have envisaged the method of financing. The other contracting party may request the judicial termination of the contract and damages due to the failure of the debtor to meet his contracted obligations after the date of the opening judgment.

Specific rules apply to contracts relating to sales of personal property, real property leases (art 36, Decree of 30 September 1953), insurance contracts (art 221, 1985 law) and publishing contracts (art 232, 1985 Law).

Employment contracts, which are expressly excluded from the scope of article 37 of the 1985 Law, are automatically continued during the observation period. The 1985 Law reinforces employees' rights to retain their employment by making it a condition of all dismissals that prior authorisation is obtained from the juge-commissaire (during the observation period) or from the court (during the plan execution period) (arts 321-7, 321-9, and 321-11, French Labour Code).

Lease agreement (contrat de location gérance)

The court may on the request of the public prosecutor, and after consulting the workers representation committee (or where there is none, the personnel delegates), exceptionally authorise the conclusion of a lease agreement under which the lessee manages the enterprise. The lessee may be, for example, a potential future purchaser of the business. The administrator oversees the fulfilment by the lessee of his obligations.

The lease agreement covers the assets and activities of the enterprise and may only be authorised where the disappearance of the enterprise would impose a serious hardship on the national or regional economy (art 42(1), 1985 Law). The goal of this agreement is to gain time to find a solution (which is often political) to the difficulties of what may be a very large company. The objective of this lease agreement and the attendant regime is different from that of the lease agreement included in the plan calling for a total transfer (see "Transfer Preceded by a Lease Agreement" *infra* on p147). In the latter case, for instance, the lessee is under an obligation to ultimately purchase the enterprise in accordance with the terms of the plan (art 61(3), 1985 Law), whereas such purchase obligation does not exist in the former case. Moreover, the sanctions for the lessee's failure to abide by its commitments differ in each case: whereas the lessee may have bankruptcy proceedings instituted against him in the latter case, the court may only order the termination of the lease agreement in the former.

The agreement must be concluded for a minimum of two years, in which case the observation period is extended until the expiration this period. After the expiration of the lease agreement, a plan is adopted or liquidation ordered.

Economic and employment evaluation ("bilan économique et social")

Throughout the course of the observation period, the administrator, assisted by the debtor and possibly by one or more qualified experts, prepares an economic and employment evaluation of the debtor's enterprise to determine whether it is capable of being rehabilitated.

The evaluation must present a general overview of the debtor and must include, *inter alia*, the following:

- accounting and financial information;
- the number of employees, salary levels, applicability of any collective bargaining agreements and general employment climate; and
- a review of the existing contracts and pending litigation, and an examination of the efficiency of the debtor's legal structure.

Furthermore, the evaluation must specify the cause, extent and nature of the debtor's difficulties, so that a truthful picture of the enterprise can emerge.

Contents of the proposed plan
The proposed plan covers three different facets:

- an assessment of the debtor's chances of recovery, taking into account the feasibility of its continuing to carry on its business and the means of conducting such business in view of current market conditions and available financing. In particular, it should disclose whether the enterprise is capable of properly financing the continuation and development of its business. It should also evaluate the commercial situation of the enterprise, *i.e.* the competitive value of its products or services on the market and the type and extent of its competition;.
- the terms and conditions of paying the enterprise's debts and any undertakings that the head of the enterprise must give in order to guarantee such payment;
- an explanation and justification of the employment levels and prospects and the employment conditions envisaged for carrying on the business. If the plan provides for dismissals on grounds of redundancy, it must describe the measures already adopted and define the actions to be taken to facilitate the reclassification (*i.e.* retraining or transfer to an affiliated company) and indemnification of the dismissed employees (art 18, 1985 Law).

Preparation of the proposed plan
The plan is prepared by the administrator assisted by the debtor and, if necessary, qualified experts. It may call for the transfer of the enterprise, or the continuation of the enterprise with the ensuing payment of creditors by the debtor. In order to determine the terms and conditions of the plan, the administrator must *inter alia* examine the purchase offers submitted to him, consult the creditors, and explore possible steps to be taken where the debtor is a legal entity.

Examination of purchase offers
Third parties may submit offers to the administrator which would have as their effect the maintenance of the debtor's business. These offers may concern the purchase of all or part of the enterprise or any other means of maintaining the business such as a lease agreement ("contrat de location-gerance") (art 21, 1985

Law). The form of the offer must be sufficiently specific and firm. The proponent of the offer must attach to his offer his annual accounts, if any, for the last three fiscal years. The administrator must file all offers with the clerk of the court. Offers may neither be modified nor withdrawn following the filing of the administrator's report containing the proposed plan.

Consultation with the creditors

Proposals for the payment of debts are conveyed to the creditors' representative and to the "contrôleurs" by the administrator as they are developed. They are then sent by the creditors' representative to the creditors, and the creditors' responses thereto are obtained either individually in writing, or collectively at a creditors' meeting (art 24, 1985 Law). The creditors' representative prepares a list of the creditors' responses which is sent to the administrator. Only those creditors which have declared their claims (see pp149-150 *infra*) may be consulted on the proposals.

Steps to be taken where the debtor is a legal entity

For legal entities, the preparation of the plan may lead to certain decisions, some of which may be implemented during the observation period and others which may be contained in the plan.

The plan ordering the rehabilitation of a company may contain a proposal to increase its share capital. In this case, the administrator requests the board of directors to convene an extraordinary general meeting of the shareholders to accomplish such modification.

The rehabilitation of a company may also be facilitated by the dismissal of certain of the company's officers. The court is thus empowered, at the request of the administrator, public prosecutor or upon its own initiative, to take certain action concerning such officers. In particular, it may make the adoption of the plan subject to the replacement of one or more members of management. It may also order that the voting rights attached to the shares held by certain officers be exercised by a court-appointed agent. Finally, the court may order that these shares be transferred. Such measures cannot be applied to shareholders, even majority shareholders, unless they are found to be *de facto* members of management.

Judgment adopting the plan or ordering liquidation

The observation period is concluded by a judgment which either adopts the proposed plan or orders liquidation (art 8(3), 1985 Law). The powers of the court are extensive in that it alone decides the debtor's future (art 61, 1985 Law) and the means by which the creditors are to be paid.

The court will only render its judgment after first having heard the debtor (to learn whether the latter accepts the measures contained in the plan), the administrator, the creditors' representative, the contrôleurs (to learn whether he deems the time periods within which the creditors are to be paid acceptable), and the representatives of the workers representation committee or, if there is none, the personnel delegates (to determine their reaction to the proposed Plan particularly where the latter provides for employee dismissals).

The court bases its decision on the administrator's report. If it decides that the course of action to be pursued is rehabilitation of the debtor, the judgment which adopts the plan will specify, *inter alia*:

- the duration of the plan (art 65, 1985 Law);
- the terms and conditions of rehabilitating the debtor which may be the continuation or the partial or total transfer of the enterprise (art 61, 1985 Law). As indicated above, the court may also decide to remove the members of the management or force them to transfer their shares (art 23, 1985 Law);
- those employee dismissals which are to have immediate effect (art 63, 1985 Law);
- the appointment of the commissaire à l'exécution du plan (art 67, 1985 Law);
- the postponements of payment to be imposed on the creditors (art 74, 1985 Law); and
- the adoption of the acts undertaken by the participants with a view to the debtor's rehabilitation (art 62, 1985 Law). Examples of the acts which are adopted by the court include the following: the promise by the debtor, the shareholders or the members of the management to increase the capital of the company; the creditors' acceptance of postponements in payment or the abandonment of their claims; the amount of the purchase price to be paid by the future purchaser of all or part of the enterprise or his undertaking not to dismiss any employees; and the agreement by third parties, such as bankers, to finance the rehabilitation.

If the court decides that a plan cannot be adopted, it must order the liquidation of the debtor (see p155 *et seq, infra*).

The judgment approving the plan is not always final. Where it orders continuation and the debtor fails to abide by the financial obligations of the plan, the court may retract its prior judgment and substitute a new judgment ordering either the total transfer or liquidation of the enterprise. If the unfulfilled obligations are not financial, the debtor may request that the Plan be modified. Where the judgment orders the transfer of the enterprise, and the purchaser fails to meet his obligations, the court will appoint a temporary administrator and determine what he is to do and the powers for doing this (art 90, 1985 Law).

The judgment adopting the plan or ordering liquidation may be appealed against by the debtor, the administrator, the creditors' representative, the workers' representation committee and the public prosecutor. The judgment is normally executed pending the appeal. The appealing party may, however, in a summary proceeding brought at the time he files his appeal, request the président of the Court of Appeals to suspend execution of the judgment until the court makes a decision. In the event that the judgment is suspended, the observation period is extended until such time as the Court of Appeals' decision is rendered (art 177, 1985 Law and art 155 (2), 1985 Decree).

Continuation of the enterprise

This first solution comprises the continued operation of the enterprise by the debtor.

The plan calling for such continuation provides for the payment of debts and organises the financing of the enterprise. The judgment may impose postponements of payment on the creditors but may not extinguish the debts owed to them. From this point on, the debts are no longer paid according to their originally scheduled due dates but rather according to the dates fixed by the judgment adopting the plan. The duration of the postponements of payment is fixed by the court; this applies to any type of debt and must be the same for all creditors.

In general, the plan indicates the commitments to be undertaken in order to finance the rehabilitation of the enterprise. These will most often consist of bank loans and contributions of capital by existing and/or new shareholders.

The plan may require the modification of the by-laws of the debtor (art 71, 1985 Law), in which case a shareholders' meeting is called by the administrator for this purpose. If the shareholders fail to adopt the resolutions which are necessary to carry out such modification, the plan is automatically terminated.

The plan may call for the cessation or transfer of certain branches of the business. It may impose the partial transfer of assets (art 78, 1985 Law) which permits both the disposal of certain useless assets and the increase of the debtor's cash. This partial transfer may be of either isolated assets or an autonomous branch of the business. Such transfers are governed by the same rules as those applicable to total transfers (see *infra*).

The continuation of the enterprise often leads to employee dismissals in order to reduce overhead costs. These dismissals are an integral part of the plan.

Continuation of the enterprise is not frequently adopted because the conditions necessary for its realisation, such as enough cash to pay the employees' salaries, a business generating enough profit to cover expenses and pay past liabilities, the confidence of business partners, and a favourable employment climate, are rarely met.

Total transfer of the enterprise

The purchase of the debtor's enterprise by one or more companies is often adopted because it appears the most efficient means of ensuring the continuation of the business and employment. The decision to transfer the enterprise (which may, as indicated above, be preceded by a lease agreement) is made by the court.

Transfer

In contrast to continuation, transfer simply involves the turning over of assets and thus does not include the obligation by the transferee to pay the debtor's creditors. The transferee is only obliged to reimburse loans secured by pledges (art 93 (2), 1985 Law) and continue existing employment contracts (art L.122-12,

French Labour Code). However, the judgment ordering the transfer may authorise employee dismissals under the conditions contained in article 63 of the 1985 Law. The transferee must be neither the manager, a parent nor a relative of the debtor, the only exception being farmers (1994 Law).

The decision to transfer the debtor's business will usually only be made when it is impossible for the debtor to rehabilitate its enterprise. This is only done as a last resort since such transfer extinguishes the debtor's ownership rights in the business. It is also conditional upon the enterprise being capable of transfer and the ability of the enterprise to be rehabilitated as a result of the transfer. The terms of the transfer must be reasonable in order to facilitate rehabilitation.

The court chooses the offer which it believes will best ensure the rehabilitation of the enterprise, the maintenance of employment and the payment of debts (arts 81, 85, 1985 Law). It is often difficult to unite these three factors and thus all interested parties may be called upon to make sacrifices. The court must not choose the easiest solution, *i.e.* accepting the offer containing the highest purchase price, but must conduct a general economic overview taking into account all of the debtor's business partners. When it has made its choice, the court orders the transfer, calls on the administrator to execute all documents necessary to realise the transfer and determines which contracts will be transferred with the enterprise. The transfer is carried out without the debtor's participation. If no offer appears satisfactory, the court must order liquidation.

The judgment ordering transfer may be appealed against by the public prosecutor, the transferee, and those who have subsisting contracts with the debtor (art 174, 1985 Law). So as not to delay and compromise the rehabilitation of the enterprise, the persons or entities whose bids for the enterprise were not accepted may not appeal this judgment.

Transfer preceded by a lease agreement
The transfer may be preceded by a period during which the enterprise is leased by the future transferee. The lease agreement must always be followed by the purchase of the enterprise by the lessee (art 94, 1985 Law). The lease is authorised by the judgment adopting the plan.

The Commissaire à l'exécution du plan supervises the execution of the lease and, in particular, ensures that the lessee does not sell the assets which are the subject of the lease. The failure of the lessee to comply with its lease obligations results in the court's pronouncing the termination of the lease agreement and the cancellation of the plan (art 95, 1985 Law). The lease may not exceed two years. If upon the expiration of such period, the lessee does not follow through with his purchase obligation, the Commissaire à l'exécution du plan, the public prosecutor or any interested party may request that bankruptcy proceedings be instituted against him (arts 97, 98, 1985 Law).

Creditors' involvement and position

During the observation period

During the observation period, the enterprise continues its operations, which creates a need for financing and "new" creditors. The 1985 Law distinguishes between creditors whose claims arose prior to the opening judgment (arts 47, 50) and those whose claims arose subsequent to that Judgment (art 40). These latter new creditors are granted preferential rights because their assistance is often indispensable to the survival of the enterprise.

The different treatment accorded to the creditors thus depends upon the date on which their claims arose. The employees, in their capacity as creditors, benefit from a special regime whose goal is to accord them the greatest protection with respect to the payment of their salaries.

A claim is considered to have arisen prior to the opening judgment where its source occurred prior to such date. The Law considers that, in the case of a commercial contract, the date the claim arose may be determined by any means.

Creditors whose claims arose prior to the opening judgment
The 1985 Law imposes a restriction on creditors' individual rights. In addition, there is no longer any creditors' committee and the creditors' claims must be declared and verified.

Restrictions on creditors' individual rights
Upon the issuance of the opening judgment, all individual legal actions by creditors against the debtor are prohibited or stayed (art 47, 1985 Law). This rule applies to all creditors whose claims arose prior to the Judgment, *i.e.* both unsecured and secured creditors, including the tax authorities and the social security administration. Only employees are exempted from this rule (art 124, 1985 Law).

The stay applies in effect to the following categories of action: those involving the rescission of a contract for failure to pay a sum of money and those condemning the debtor to pay a sum of money. It also applies to actions relating to the enforcement of previously obtained judgments ("voies d'exécution").

Pending actions which are stayed resume once the creditor has formally declared his claim, but this may simply result in the establishment of the claim and its amount.

Following the opening judgment, mortgages, pledges and other security interests may no longer be recorded and therefore may not serve as a binding, enforceable security for the creditor. Those which are recorded in violation of this rule are deemed to be non-binding (art 57, 1985 Law).

The opening judgment suspends the running of all interest, including contractual and late payment interest. This rule applies to all creditors. Interest due as of the opening judgment is, however, included in the total amount of the claim (art 55, 1985 Law).

Absence of a creditors' committee
Prior to the 1985 Law, creditors existing prior to the opening judgment were mandatorily and automatically grouped together in a creditors' committee whose purpose was to defend the creditors' interests. Such committee was known as the "masse des créanciers". Provision for this committee was not made in the 1985 Law (indeed, the Law contains no reference to the collective interest of the creditors) and therefore the only representative of the creditors' interests is now the creditors' representative (see p136 *supra*).

Proof of claims
Those creditors whose debts arose prior to the opening judgment may only seek payment of debts owing to them once they have presented adequate proof of the validity of their claims to the creditors' representative and such claims have been duly admitted (art 50, 1985 Law). These requirements apply regardless of whether the Judgment ultimately calls for the continuation, transfer or liquidation of the enterprise.

The declaration obligation applies to all civil or commercial claims, and both secured and unsecured creditors. However, employees do not have to declare any claims resulting from an employment contract.

There is no designated form for the creditor's declaration. It must, however, contain *inter alia*, the following information (art 51, 1985 Law; art 67, 1985 Decree):

- the amount of the claim due as of the date of the opening judgment;
- the amounts and payment dates of those portions of the claim which are due to be paid subsequent to the opening judgment;
- the nature of the "privilege" or security interest, if any, appurtenant to the claim;
- if the claim is not established by a written document, evidence of the claim's existence and its amount;
- where the amount of the claim has not yet been determined, an estimate of the same;
- the methods of calculating interest; and
- the court with jurisdiction over any on-going litigation involving the claim.

The declaration must be transmitted to the creditors' representative within two months of the publication of the opening judgment in the "Bulletin Officiel des Annonces Civiles et Commerciales". Creditors domiciled outside metropolitan France have an additional two months in which to file their declaration. Those creditors who have not submitted their claims during the requisite two-month period are barred from receiving distributions made in connection with the bankruptcy proceedings and their unasserted claims are extinguished (art

53 (1,3), 1985 Law). However, if a creditor can show that his claim was filed late for reasons beyond his control, he can petition the "juge commissaire" within one year of the opening judgment for an order accepting his claim and may also present a petition before the Court of Appeals. The Law of 10 June 1994 clearly states that a declaration can be made by proxy (art 35-II, 1994 Law).

The Debtor is required to prepare a certified list of the creditors which must be filed with the clerk of the court and transmitted to the creditors' representative within three days following the opening judgment. The latter must then, within eight days of the issue of the opening judgment, notify all known creditors that they must submit their claim to him. Creditors who hold security or who have leased assets to the enterprise cannot be prevented from submitting their claims unless they have been finally notified as to where and by whom those claims must be submitted.

The creditors' representative must verify the creditors' claims. If he contests a claim he must notify the creditor concerned who has 30 days to explain the basis of his claim.

After verification of all claims, the creditors' representative submits a list of claims, together with his recommendations and the debtor's comments to the juge commissaire who has the responsibility of admitting or rejecting the claims. Where the juge commissaire intends to reject all or part of a claim, he must summon the creditor, the debtor, the administrator and the creditors' representative to a hearing (art 101, 1985 Law); the parties are informed of the juge commissaire's decision within eight days of the hearing. Appeals against his decisions may be made to the Court of Appeals.

Third parties who have an interest in the proceedings may file objections to the juge commissaire's admission or rejection of claims. If this happens, they are summoned before the "juge commissaire" who rules on the objections. Appeal is to the Court of Appeals.

Creditors whose claims arose after the opening judgment
As mentioned above, the debtor's enterprise continues to operate during the observation period. If it is going to obtain essential financing and acquire goods and services, those creditors whose claims arose subsequent to the opening judgment ("new creditors") must be given preferential treatment over those whose debts arose prior to the opening judgment. Article 40 of the 1985 law grants the new creditors such priority status.

The scope of Article 40 is strictly limited to debts incurred for the purpose of the continuation of the enterprise's activity. Moreover, new creditors are only given priority as long as the debtor or the administrator or both (depending on who was given the power to manage the enterprise) did not exceed the general or specific powers granted to them by the opening judgment when dealing with such new creditors. The debts may be contractual, quasi-contractual, or relate to damages in tort, taxes or social security contributions.

The new creditors need not declare their claims or have them verified, they are paid when their debts are due. If they are not paid, and if the enterprise's activity is continued or there is a total transfer or liquidation of the enterprise, they are, in principle, paid before all other creditors, even secured creditors. They rank before the tax authorities but after employee wage and indemnity claims. However, since the 1994 Law, in the case of a liquidation by the court, certain secured creditors whose claims arose before the opening judgment are paid before them.

Article 40(2) ranks the new creditors in the following order:

- certain wage claims;
- legal expenses;
- loans granted by credit establishments and claims resulting from the continuation of existing contracts pursuant to article 37 of the 1985 Law (see pp141-142 *supra*);
- certain sums advanced in accordance with provisions of the Labour Code; and
- all other claims according to their rank.

During the plan execution period

During the period in which the plan is executed, the creditors are paid according to the terms set out in the plan.

In the event that the plan orders the continuation of the enterprise, the new creditors are paid when their debt is due and the creditors existing prior to the opening judgment are paid in accordance with the postponements of payment and price reductions contained in the plan. According to article 76 of the 1985 Law, employees' claims can neither be postponed nor reduced.

The postponements and reductions specified in the plan apply to secured and unsecured creditors, the tax authorities and the social security administration. Where the plan calls for the total transfer of the enterprise, the purchase price is immediately divided among the creditors in the same manner as in the case of liquidation (see pp159-160 *infra*). The payment by the debtor of his debts is not guaranteed by the transferee.

The creditors' representative will normally not proceed with the verification of any unsecured claims if, based on an evaluation of the proceeds to be divided from the sale of the debtor's assets, it appears that all of the assets of the debtor will be consumed by the costs of the bankruptcy proceedings and by the satisfaction of the debts of the preferred creditors (art 99, 1985 Law). The judgment adopting the plan renders due all debts which would otherwise be due at a later date.

Where there is only a partial transfer of the enterprise, the purchase price becomes part of the debtor's assets to be used for the operation of the enterprise.

Management by the administrator

During the observation period, the activity of the debtor continues under conditions as close as possible to those existing prior to the opening judgment. This is why the 1985 Law provided for as little judicial intervention as possible in the conducting of the debtor's business. Under article 32, the debtor does not relinquish control over his assets, but continues to have the right to dispose of and administer his property, and exercises all those powers which have not been expressly granted by the court to the Administrator.

The duties of the administrator will be those given to him by the court. Specifically, the court may order the administrator to:

- supervise the debtor's operation of the enterprise;
- assist the debtor with one or more aspects of the operation of the enterprise; or
- operate all or part of the debtor's enterprise without the debtor's participation (art 31, 1985 Law).

The administrator's powers may be modified at any time by the court at the request of the administrator, the creditors' representative, the public prosecutor or by the court upon its own initiative. Even so, regardless of any specifically defined powers, the administrator is always empowered to continue contracts existing at the time of the opening judgment. Anything done by the debtor in contravention of the powers given to the administrator will be declared void. Such acts which relate to day-to-day management, however, are valid as regards third parties acting in good faith.

It should be noted that neither the administrator nor the debtor may pay any of the debts which arose prior to the Opening Judgment (art 33, 1985 Law). Payments made in violation of this rule will be cancelled at the instance of any interested party provided that the appropriate proceedings are brought within three years of the payment.

The set-off of debts between the debtor and a creditor is, as a general rule, prohibited. However, as the result of a recent case in the Supreme Court: Cour de Cassation Commerciale 2 March 1993, the Law of 10 June 1994 authorises set-off of debts arising out of related transactions.

The powers of the administrator are limited by the requirement that certain acts should first be approved by the juge commissaire. In particular, the administrator may not pay a debt arising prior to the opening judgment in order to discharge a security interest or obtain or recover property which is validly held by a creditor unless he is authorised to do so by the juge commissaire. Additionally, all dispositions of property not made in the ordinary course of business and the granting of all mortgages and pledges must first be approved by the juge commissaire. Finally, the administrator may not compromise claims or enter into settlements without the juge commissaire's authorisation.

Position of officers and shareholders

Shareholders

Shareholders of "sociétés en nom collectif", members of GIEs, and general part-ners of limited partnerships and limited partnerships with shares have unlim-ited, joint and several liability for the company's debts. Thus, in the event that rehabilitation in bankruptcy proceedings are commenced against such compa-nies, they are also automatically commenced against each shareholder, member or general partner thereof (art 178, 1985 Law). Where a shareholder, member or general partner withdraws from the company prior to the opening judgment, re-habilitation proceedings may only be commenced against him if they occur within one year of the registration of his withdrawal in the registry of commerce and companies.

The commencement of rehabilitation proceedings has no direct effect on shareholders of SAs and SARLs and limited partners of SCSs and SCPAs, all of whom have limited liability. They must, however, pay up whatever remains un-paid in respect of their shares. Where such shareholders have intervened in the management of the company they are considered to be *de facto* members of the management, and the court may commence separate bankruptcy proceedings against them personally (see pp164-166 *infra*).

Officers

Following the opening judgment, the officers remain in office and retain all their previous powers to represent the company, subject to limitations given by the court to the administrator.

When it thinks necessary, the court may, at the request of the administrator, the public prosecutor or on its own initiative, make it a condition for the adop-tion of the plan that one or more officers be dismissed or replaced (art 23(1), 1985 Law).

During the opening judgment, the *de facto* and *de jure* officers, whether remun-erated or not, may only transfer their shares or investment certificates under the conditions fixed by the Court (art 28, 1985 Law). The shares and investment certificates are transferred to a special account opened in the officer's name by the administrator. No movements may be made from this account without the prior authorisation of the juge commissaire.

In addition, if the survival of the company is at stake, the court may, at the re-quest of the administrator, the public prosecutor or on its own initiative, freeze the transfer of the *de facto* and *de jure* officers' shares or investment certificates. It may also order that the voting rights attached to such shares be exercised by a court-appointed agent (often the administrator) for a term fixed by the court (art 23(2), 1985 Law) and order the transfer of shares for a price fixed by an ex-pert. In the latter two cases, the Court may not render its decision until it has first heard the officers and the representatives of the workers representation com-mittee, if any, or the personnel delegates.

Termination

There is no specific judgment by the court reflecting the termination of the rehabilitation in bankruptcy proceedings. Once the obligations imposed on it by the plan have been satisfied, the debtor has, by definition, returned to financial health.

Where there has been a total transfer of the debtor's enterprise, however, the court pronounces the closing of the rehabilitation proceedings ("clôture des opérations") on the completion of all necessary acts associated with the transfer (art 92, 1985 Law). After this pronouncement, the creditors may only commence individual actions against the debtor only in the specific cases listed in article 169 of the 1985 Law (see p161 *infra*).

Simplified procedure

As previously mentioned, the simplified procedure applies to debtors with no more than 50 employees and an annual turnover of less than FF 20 million (art 2(3), 1985 Law). The annual turnover is equal to the value of the goods and services sold by the debtor in the course and in furtherance of its normal activities, (as reduced by rebates and taxes), as at the end of the most recent fiscal year. Depending on who commences the bankruptcy proceedings, the number of employees may be determined as at

- the date of the debtor's declaration of the "cessation de paiements";
- the date of the creditor's petition to commence bankruptcy proceedings;
- the date of the public prosecutor's request for such proceedings; or
- the date the debtor is summoned by the court when the latter initiates bankruptcy proceedings (art 2, 1985 Law)

The Court may, in its discretion, order that the general regime apply to debtors otherwise qualified for the simplified procedure if it believes the debtor's chances of recovery are greater under the general regime than under the simplified procedure.

The provisions of the general regime apply to debtors subject to the simplified procedure where such provisions do not conflict with those of the simplified procedure. Consequently, only the special features of the simplified procedure are discussed below.

For sole traders, artisans and farmers, the competent court is that located in the jurisdiction where he has his principal place of business. For legal entities, the competent court is that of the jurisdiction where its registered office is located (or its principal establishment if its registered office is not located in France) (art 1, 1985 Decree).

The observation period consists of two phases. The first phase, called the investigation period ("période d'enquête"), is generally limited to 30 days and may, exceptionally, be renewed for 30 more days at the request of the debtor, the public prosecutor or the "juge commissaire" (art 140, 1985 law). The investigation results in a report, prepared by the juge commissaire (who may be assisted by one or more experts), evaluating the enterprise's economic and financial situation and its chances of recovery.

On the basis of this report, the court decides whether or not the proceedings should enter into a second phase during which a proposed plan is prepared while the debtor's business continues. This second phase lasts for four months and may, exceptionally, be extended for a further two months by the court (art 143, 1985 Law). In making its decision, the court obtains the opinion of the public prosecutor and consults the creditors' representative, the administrator and the debtor when it is not they who requested the commencement of the phase. The judgments relating to the duration of the observation period may only be appealed against by the public prosecutor.

If the court considers it unnecessary to appoint an administrator, the business is continued by the debtor. When an administrator is appointed, the debtor is either divested of all power to manage the assets or continues to manage them with the assistance of the administrator. Where the debtor is divested of its powers of management, the administrator represents the debtor in the administration of all the assets and has powers identical to those given to him under the general regime.

Where the debtor continues the management functions, the proposed plan calling for the continuation or transfer of the enterprise is prepared by the debtor and filed with the clerk of the court (arts 103(2), 145, 1985 Law). The plan is then submitted to the court by the juge-commissaire together with his opinion of it. The debtor decides whether or not existing contracts should be continued, and his decision must be approved by the juge-commissaire. However, if an administrator is appointed, the decision to continue the contracts falls within the administrator's powers.

At any time during the observation period, the court may order either the cessation of the debtor's activity or the commencement of liquidation proceedings (art 146, 1985 Law).

4. Termination of the corporation: liquidation

It has already been noted that liquidation in bankruptcy is not a separate, independent proceeding but stems from the rehabilitation in bankruptcy proceedings. However, the 1994 law states that, when it is considered that the rehabilitation in bankruptcy proceedings is fruitless, that the entreprise must be immediately liquidated.

Purpose and effect

The primary goal of the liquidation in bankruptcy proceedings is to pay the creditors to the greatest extent possible through the sale of the debtor's assets. It is governed by articles 148 *et seq* of the 1985 Law, which set out the procedure to be followed in carrying out such sale and the allocation of the proceeds among the various creditors.

The judgment ordering the commencement of liquidation proceedings (the "liquidation judgment") has three main effects:

- as a general rule, the enterprise's business ceases;
- the debtor is automatically divested of all power to manage the enterprise and to dispose of the assets; and
- the creditors may obtain payment of all or part of their debts and, in certain cases, recover the right to commence or continue litigation.

Preconditions

According to article 1 (2) of the 1985 Law, the plan provides for either the continuation of the enterprise or its transfer. When neither of these solutions appears possible, the court must order liquidation. In France, approximately 90% of all cases which are the subject of bankruptcy proceedings end in liquidation.

Powers and duties of the liquidator

The liquidator is the central officer in the liquidation proceedings. On liquidation, the administrator's role terminates and the court will, in most cases, use the liquidation judgment to appoint the creditors' representative as liquidator unless, at the request of the administrator, a creditor, the debtor or the public prosecutor, it concludes that someone other than the creditors' representative should be appointed (art 148(1), 1985 Law). The court may, of its own volition or at the suggestion of the juge commissaire or the public prosecutor, replace the liquidator at any time during the proceedings.

The liquidator's role is wide-ranging. First, he represents the creditors and, as such, includes any litigation commenced prior to the liquidation judgment and may commence new litigation (art 148(3), 1985 Law). The liquidator completes the verification of the creditors' claims and establishes the order in which the creditors are to be paid.

Additionally, in most cases he exercises the rights over and actions concerning the debtor's assets since the debtor has been divested of such rights and actions. In this regard, the 1985 Law permits the liquidator to proceed with any employee dismissals designated in the liquidation judgment. In addition, he may be authorised to recover property which is retained by a creditor pursuant to a security interest by paying the underlying debt.

Finally, he is in charge of undertaking all transactions necessary to sell the debtor's assets and pay its debts. He may take proceedings against the members of the debtor's management with a view to their being held liable for the debts of the company and their being made subject to penal or civil sanctions (see pp164-166 *infra*).

The liquidator must report to the juge commissaire and the public prosecutor every three months.

Procedure

The liquidation judgment

Liquidation may be ordered either during the observation period (where the General Regime is in operation) or at any time during the proceedings or investigation period (where the Simplified Procedure is in operation) (arts 36, 146, 1985 Law).

The most controversial aspect of the 1985 Law used to be the moment at which liquidation proceedings could be declared when it was obvious that the situation of the debtor was hopeless. In particular circumstances in the past, certain courts had, where specific conditions were met, declared the commencement of liquidation without first declaring the commencement of rehabilitation proceedings. Other courts, however, emphasised the importance of first declaring the commencement of rehabilitation and the ensuing observation period. To resolve this controversy the Supreme Court held that the court must declare the commencement of rehabilitation proceedings prior to declaring liquidation (Judgment of 4 November 1986, Cass. civ. com.).

Since the 1985 Law does not establish a minimum duration for the observation period, some courts pronounce liquidation in the same judgment as the rehabilitation declaration (the process was expressly approved by the Supreme Court on 29 March 1989), others pronounce liquidation the same day by a second judgment, while still others declare liquidation not less than 24 hours but not more than one week later than rehabilitation.

However, based on article 11 of the Law of 10 June 1994, if it is considered that the rehabilitation in bankruptcy proceedings is unlikely to work, the enterprise can be immediately liquidated. This provision has been implemented to circumvent the contrived situation of double judgments mentioned above.

The liquidation judgment may be appealed against by the debtor, the administrator, the creditors' representative, the workers representation committee (if any) or the personnel delegates, or the public prosecutor.

Effects of the liquidation judgment

Following the liquidation judgment, the debtor is totally divested of all rights pertaining to the management of the enterprise and the disposition of the assets (art 152, 1985 Law). Such divestment is of a general nature and applies to all assets and any administrative acts. Thus it applies to assets which existed on the date of the opening judgment, those acquired by gift or inheritance during the proceedings and those recovered by the Liquidator through, for instance, the setting aside of certain transactions made during the "periode suspecte" (see p163 *infra*). The Debtor recovers rights to any remaining assets at the end of the liquidation proceedings. The debtor does not participate in the liquidation proceedings but is represented by the liquidator who has all of the powers and responsibilities normally vested in the head of an enterprise.

The liquidation judgment automatically terminates the enterprise's business activity. Where, however, it is in the public interest or in the interest of the creditors, the business can be continued under court authorisation, but only for purposes of the liquidation and for a maximum period of three months (art 153, 1985 Law). The judgment authorising such continuation may only be appealed against by the public prosecutor.

If the debtor is a company, the liquidation leads to its dissolution (art 1844-7, Civil Code). This rule, even if not expressly provided by law, also seems to apply to GIEs and associations.

Liquidation of the assets

Under the rules for liquidation of assets the liquidator sells the debtor's assets and recovers sums due to the debtor.

Real property is usually sold at a judicial sale according to the procedure applicable to real property attachments ("saisie immobilière"). The reserve price ("mise à prix"), the material terms and conditions and the means of advertising of the judicial sale are fixed by the juge commissaire after consulting the contrôleur(s), the debtor and the liquidator. The juge commissaire may authorise the transfer of real property by tender ("adjudication amiable") or by mutual agreement ("de gré à gré") according to the terms and conditions fixed by him. He fixes the reserve price in the case of adjudication amiable and the price where the sale is made by gré à gré (art 154, 1985 Law).

Units of production may be the subject of a global transfer. They include tangible and intangible property such as commercial or industrial real property, equipment, and inventory. Offers to purchase units of production must be submitted in writing to the liquidator within the time period set by the latter and contain those elements required of offers submitted during the observation period of rehabilitation proceedings. After consulting the debtor, the workers' representation committee (if any) or the personnel delegates, and the "contrôleur(s)", the liquidator selects the offer most likely to ensure the maintenance of employment levels and the payment of creditors (art 155, 1985 Law).

With respect to all other personal property, the juge commissaire orders either sale at public auction or sale by mutual agreement. He fixes the sale conditions and price and may insist on reviewing the draft sale agreement (art 156, 1985 Law). It should be noted that the sale of a "fonds de commerce" may be conducted by means of mutual agreement (see p121 for a description of a "fonds de commerce").

Creditors' involvement and position

Effect of the liquidation judgment on the creditors

The liquidation judgment causes all amounts which were not due by the debtor at the time of the opening judgment to become due (art 160(1), 1985 Law). The conversion into French Francs of sums due in foreign currency, occurs according to the exchange rate in force on the date of the liquidation judgment.

Secured creditors such as mortgagees and pledgees and certain preferential creditors may bring individual legal proceedings following the liquidation judgment if the liquidator has not commenced proceedings to sell the corresponding assets within three months following such judgment and as long as they have properly declared their claim.

As already stated, the liquidator completes the verification of the creditors' claims. In the liquidation judgment, the court may order that the deadline for the declaration of creditors' claims be extended. The juge commissaire may decide that the verification of any unsecured claims need not be carried out if an evaluation of the purchase price suggests that all of the debtor's assets will be consumed by the costs of the bankruptcy proceedings and the satisfaction of the debts of the preferred creditors (art 99, 1985 Law).

The liquidator completes the list of claims which arose subsequent to the opening judgment which benefit from preferential treatment. All claims arising during the liquidation phase benefit from the priority status granted by article 40 of the 1985 Law (Cass. com. 20 February 1990) (see pp150-151 *supra*). The liquidator may therefore have to continue adding to the list up until the day preceding the last distribution of the sale proceeds.

Distribution of the sale proceeds among the creditors

The sums received by the liquidator are immediately deposited in an account with the "Caisse des Dépôts et Consignations" (art 151, 1985 Law). The liquidator establishes the order in which the creditors are to be paid. The allocation of the proceeds is ordered by the juge commissaire who decides whether several distributions will be made throughout the liquidation proceedings or whether one single distribution is to be made at the end of the proceedings. As soon as a distribution is ordered, the liquidator sends to the corresponding creditors cheques payable out of the Caisse des Dépôts et Consignations account.

Creditors who benefit from a retention of title clause and credit establishments to which the debtor assigned any professional debts (*i.e.* debts which arose as a result of the carrying out of the debtor's business) have exclusive and direct rights of ownership in the property or debts concerned and, therefore, fall outside the hierarchy of the creditors.

Differentiating between secured creditors is complicated since it involves both the normal rules and the specific bankruptcy rules applicable to secured creditors. Certain security interests relate only to real property, others to tangible and intangible personal property while others concern both real and personal property. This differentiation is one of the liquidator's tasks, the major principles of which are indicated below.

- The employees' "super privilege" ranks before both real and personal property security interests.

- Pledgees have first priority with respect to the pledged property even where there are tax claims, as long as they claim their retention right or exercise their right vis-à-vis the pledged property.

- Mortgagees or holders of special real property security interests ("privilèges spéciaux sur les immeubles") have priority in regard to the property secured as long as the mortgage or special security interest was properly recorded prior to the opening judgment.

- Special personal property security interests ("privilèges spéciaux mobiliers"), rank before general personal property security interests ("privilèges généraux mobiliers") except for the employees' "super privilege", judicial costs, and tax claims.

- Creditors whose claims arose subsequent to the opening judgment are ranked in the order set forth in article 40 of the 1985 Law. It should be noted that before the Law of 10 June 1994, these creditors were paid before the creditors of the third and fourth categories above and, in any case, before all claims arising prior to the opening judgment whether or not these claims were subject to security interests.

- General personal property security interests which are subordinate to the tax claims are paid in the order set out in article 2101 of the Civil Code.

- The last creditors to be paid are unsecured creditors whose claims arose prior to the opening judgment.

Management by the liquidator

Since the activity of the enterprise usually ceases on the issue of the liquidation judgment, there will be no need to manage the enterprise after this point. Where the activity has, however, been maintained, management is conducted as follows:

- in the case of the general regime, the administrator remains in office and controls the administration of the enterprise (art 153(2), 1985 Law); and

- in the case of the simplified procedure, if the court had designated an administrator, he remains in office and administers the enterprise; if none had been appointed, the administration of the enterprise is carried out by the liquidator (art 153(2), 1985 Law).

The liquidator or administrator keeps the juge commissaire and the public prosecutor informed of the results of the business activity at the end of the period during which it was maintained.

Position of shareholders and officers

The effects of the liquidation judgment on the shareholders are the same as those in the case of rehabilitation proceedings (see p153 *supra*). The officers automatically lose all powers to manage the enterprise and dispose of its assets.

Termination ("clôture des operations")

There are two types of circumstance in which the liquidation proceedings may be terminated (art 167, 1985 Law): first, where there is no longer any debt due by the enterprise or the liquidator has sufficient monies to satisfy all of the creditors ("clôture pour extinction du passif exigible") and second, where the pursuance of the liquidation proceedings is rendered impossible due to insufficient assets ("clôture pour insuffisance d'actifs").

Clôture pour extinction du passif exigible

Termination in this case applies to debts of secured and unsecured creditors. The court may pronounce the termination at any time after having heard the debtor and having received a report from the juge commissaire.

The closing judgment ends the debtor's loss of power over the enterprise and the functions of the participants. The closing judgment may be appealed against.

Clôture pour insuffisance d'actifs

In this case, the proceedings are terminated due to insufficient assets with which to pay the creditors. The conditions and effects of this judgment are the same as those applicable to clôture pour extinction du passif exigible.

The creditors who received partial or no payment of their claim may not bring or pursue legal proceedings against the debtor except in the following instances; namely where:

- the claim arose from acts not within the debtor's corporate purpose and for which the debtor was criminally convicted;

- the claim was personal in nature;

- the creditors were defrauded;

- the debtor's management was subjected to civil or penal sanctions in connection with the bankruptcy proceedings; or

- the debtor was subjected to collective clôture pour insuffisance d'actifs in connection with another bankruptcy proceeding (art 169, 1985 Law).

Except in these five cases, the termination leads to the extinction of all unpaid debts.

If it appears that the assets were concealed or the debtor or its officers committed a fraud, the liquidation procedure may be revived at the request of any interested party by a decision of the court. The expenses to be incurred in the re-opening of the liquidation must be deposited in advance in an account with the Caisse des dépôts et consignations by the interested party (art 170, 1985 Law).

Also, since the Law of 10 June 1994, after the final judgment any creditor may request the re-opening of the liquidation if it is shown that:

- some assets have not been realised; or
- certain proceedings in favour of the creditors have not been initiated.

In addition, the French Treasury would still be entitled to pursue a debtor who had been convicted of fiscal fraud and was subject to penal sanction.

Once the liquidation proceedings are terminated, the liquidator prepares his accounts which he must file with the clerk of the court and transmit to the debtor within three months. These accounts set out the details of the sale of the assets and the allocation of the sale proceeds. Any creditor may consult the accounts at the clerk's office. The liquidator must retain all documents relating to the bankruptcy proceedings for a five-year period (art 168, 1985 Law).

5. Augmenting the assets of the insolvent corporation

Introduction

The 1985 Law provides means by which the debtor's assets may be augmented. In doing so, it preserves the creditor's rights by ensuring them the best reimbursement possible.

As from the opening judgment, the debtor's assets are, for the most part, frozen. The participants in the bankruptcy proceeding must examine the past activity of the debtor with a view to setting aside certain transactions already undertaken or to recovering certain rights given away before the opening judgment. During the period between the date of the cessation de paiements and the opening judgment, the debtor may have entered into certain agreements which are fraudulent *vis-a-vis* the creditors. To ensure the equal treatment of the creditors, the legislator included provisions which permit property which was fraudulently removed from the debtor's assets to be claimed back. This is accomplished through litigation to set aside these agreements.

Augmentation of the debtor's assets may also be accomplished through holding the members of management liable for the company's debts. The 1985 Law lays down specific rules which permit the usual regime of limited liability applicable to the shareholders to be set aside in relation to the members of the management even though they are shareholders.

Finally, there is what may be considered as an indirect means of augmenting the assets through certain restrictive rules limiting a seller's right to recover goods sold to the debtor and the rights of the debtor's spouse in his or her property.

Transactions at risk

Legal acts undertaken on or after the date of the cessation de paiements may be considered to be surrounded by fraud. This is the reason why the period between that date and the opening judgment is called the "periode suspecte". The administrator, the creditors' representative, the liquidator or the "commissaire à l'exécution du plan" may have certain acts declared null and void by means of a special legal proceeding termed an "action en nullité" which is directed at having the property which is the subject of the act reincorporated into the debtor's assets.

The court which declared the opening judgment is competent to hear "actions en nullité". Certain types of legal acts which are undertaken during the "periode suspecte" must be nullified by the court while other types may be nullified at the court's discretion.

The types of acts which must be nullified by the court are those which are specifically listed in article 107 of the 1985 Law and include, *inter alia*, gifts, contracts in which the debtor's obligations outweigh those of the other parties, the payment of debts which are not due, the giving of certain security interests, and the payment of debts due by means other than cash, commercial paper, bank transfer or certain transfers of debt ("cessions de créance"). When an act falls within this list, the court need only determine that the act was conducted during the "periode suspecte" in order to pronounce its nullity. It is not necessary to prove fraud in these cases.

A court may declare an act undertaken during the "periode suspecte" void where:

- the third party dealing with the debtor was aware of the debtor being in a situation of cessation de paiements; and
- the act caused harm to the creditors and the debtor.

The court must decide if these conditions are met. Examples of acts where nullification by the court is optional include: sales, capital contributions to companies, the giving of certain security interests, payments in cash or by bank transfer, deposits in shareholder current accounts in companies other than the debtor, endorsements of commercial paper and certain leases.

In addition, a court may, exceptionally, nullify certain acts such as gifts which were made during the six months preceding the cessation de paiements. It should be noted that article 109 of the 1985 Law grants an exception to the above rules in favour of the holder of a bill of exchange ("lettre de change"), a promissory note ("billet à ordre") or a cheque which was paid by either the drawee or drawer; this payment cannot be declared null and void.

Personal liability of officers

"Action en comblement de passif"

In the event that the rehabilitation or liquidation shows that there are insufficient assets ("insuffisance d'actif") to pay the debts, the officers may be required to bear all or some of the company's debts . Payment is obtained through a legal proceeding termed "action en comblement de passif".

Payment of the company's debts may be borne by all or some of the *de jure* or *de facto* officers, whether or not they are remunerated (art 180(1), 1985 Law). *De jure* officers are deemed to be the chairman of the board, the general manager, the directors, the members of the directorate, the managing directors and the corporate liquidators, whether or not they are shareholders and irrespective of their nationality.

As to de facto officers, it is for the plaintiff in an action en comblement de passif to prove that a person, although not a *de jure* officer, may be considered a *de facto* officer. Although not defined by law, it has been held that a *de facto* officer is "any individual who or legal entity which, assuming the same functions and powers as a *de jure* officer, in fact independently exercises a management activity" (Cour d'appel de Paris, 17 March 1978).

In principle, the officers may only be subject to these proceedings if they were in office at the time of the opening judgment. In addition, they may only be obliged to pay the company's debts if there are insufficient assets at the time of the opening judgment. They are only held liable if they were guilty of mismanagement ("faute de gestion") which led to the company's having insufficient assets. The plaintiff must therefore prove :

- the existence of mismanagement; and
- a causal link between the mismanagement and the insufficiency of assets.

The action en comblement de passif may be commenced by the administrator, the creditors' representative, the "commissaire à l'exécution du plan", the liquidator, the public prosecutor or the court on its own initiative. It may be brought at any stage of the proceedings regardless of the solution chosen, *i.e.* whether continuation, total or partial transfer or liquidation has been ordered.

The court competent to hear actions en comblement de passif is that which pronounced the opening judgment. It may decide that the debts will be borne in whole or in part, whether or not jointly and severally, by some or all of the officers. The sums paid by the officers held liable become part of the company's assets and are used to pay the creditors in accordance with the terms of the plan (in the case of rehabilitation) or in the order of their established rank in (the case of liquidation). If an officer fails to pay any amounts ordered, he may be:

- made the subject of a bankruptcy proceeding;
- made subject to civil sanctions ("faillite personnelle"); and/or
- prohibited from managing or controlling any commercial business ("interdiction de gerer").

Extension of the bankruptcy proceedings to the officers

The court may extend bankruptcy proceedings to any *de jure* or *de facto* officer who:

- under the veil of such legal entity carried out personal business transactions;
- used corporate assets as his own;
- continued the operation of the legal entity in order to further his own interests, even though such continuation could only cause the bankruptcy of the legal entity;
- used corporate assets or credit for his personal benefit or for the benefit of another corporation or enterprise in which he had a direct or indirect interest;
- conducted book-keeping that was false or not in accordance with appropriate accounting procedures or caused the disappearance of the corporation's accounting books; and/or
- embezzled or cancelled all or part of the assets or fraudulently increased the legal entity's debt (art 182, 1985 Law).

Civil sanctions

In certain instances, civil sanctions may be imposed on the *de facto* and *de jure* officers (as well as upon sole traders and artisans). Such sanctions may consist of:

- a prohibition against participating in the management of or controlling directly or indirectly any commercial or artisanal enterprise;
- a prohibition against exercising the voting rights attached to the stock of the bankrupt company;
- an obligation to transfer any shares held in the bankrupt company; and/or
- a loss of certain civil rights such as the right to vote or hold elected office, the right to be a civil servant, the right to be a member of a jury in criminal proceedings, and the right to carry out certain other enumerated activities (art 186, 1985 Law).

These sanctions may be imposed on officers who, *inter alia*, concealed or destroyed the accounting books of the bankrupt company, embezzled or concealed all or part of its assets, fraudulently caused an increase in the bankrupt company's debt, and/or failed to make a declaration of cessation de paiements within the required fifteen-day period.

Penal sanctions ("banqueroute")

The *de jure* and *de facto* officers may be imprisoned for between three months and five years and/or fined from FF 10,000 to FF 100,000 if:

- in order to avoid or delay the commencement of bankruptcy proceedings they either made purchases in order to resell the goods at a loss or obtained credit at grossly expensive rates;

- they embezzled or concealed all or part of the debtor's assets;
- they fraudulently increased the debtor's liabilities; and/or
- they conducted book-keeping that was false, caused the company's accounting documents to disappear or abstained from conducting any accounting (art 197, 1985 Law).

These penal sanctions may be in addition to the civil sanctions. It should be noted that even in the absence of bankruptcy proceedings, the members of management may be subject to penal sanctions if found guilty of using the corporate assets for purposes contrary to the company's interest ("abus de biens sociaux") (art 437, 1966 Law).

Indirect means of augmenting the assets

Restrictions on seller's rights

In certain cases, French law allows a seller to recover goods sold to or deposited with the debtor. The 1985 Law, whose foremost goal is to safeguard the debtor's business, restricts the application of this right by preventing the dismantling of the enterprise.

The recovery of personal property deposited with or left on consignment with the debtor is only permissible for the three months following the opening judgment (art 115, 1985 Law). The person seeking to recover personal property must prove that he is the owner and must file the appropriate legal documents with the competent court. The goods must be tangible and their independent identity must not be lost as at the date of the opening judgment.

Under normal rules, the unpaid seller of personal property sold for cash may retain the property of the sale and bring a legal action to cancel the sales contract (arts 1184 and 1654, French Civil Code). Article 2102 of the Civil Code, furthermore, gives the seller of personal property an automatic security interest in the property sold and the right to recover the property as long as it remains in the possession of the debtor. The bankruptcy law partially sacrifices the seller's rights by imposing restrictions on the recovery rights, automatic security interest and sales contract cancellation rights (art 116, 1985 Law).

When the goods were delivered to the debtor before the opening judgment, the seller's usual right to recover the goods ceases eight days after they have been delivered. The seller also loses his automatic security interest and the right to cancel the sale for failure to pay. The seller thus becomes an unsecured creditor unless he took steps to cancel the sale prior to the opening judgment or included a retention of title clause in the sales contract.

Spouse's rights

A spouse who claims that certain of the debtor's assets are his or her property must prove his or her ownership in accordance with the rules applicable to legal matrimonial regimes (art 111, 1985 Law). By this article, the legislator sought to prevent the debtor from being able to transfer a portion of his fortune to his spouse in order to avoid being pursued by his creditors. Thus all gifts made to spouses and all matrimonial benefits ("avantages matrimoniaux") are not binding *vis-a-vis* the creditors if the debtor was a trader or artisan at the time of marriage or became a trader or artisan in the year following the marriage (art 114, 1985 Law).

6. Public control over insolvent corporations

Licensing and control of the insolvency practitioner professions

Law No. 85-99 of 25 January 1985 created two new professions to replace the former trustee ("syndic"): administrators ("administrateurs judiciaires") and liquidators ("mandataires liquidateurs"). A person may not be both an administrateur judiciaire and a mandataire liquidateur. Thus, following the publication of the 1985 Law, all former "syndics" had to choose between becoming an "administrateur judiciaire" or a "mandataire liquidateur".

Administrators

Administrators are legal agents ("mandataires de justice") in charge of formulating the plan. Their role, which is determined by the court, is either to oversee the operations, or to assist or replace the head of the enterprise in the management of his business.

As a general rule, only those persons registered on the national list established by a National Commission may be designated as an administrator. The court may, however, exceptionally appoint a qualified or experienced person as administrator for a particular bankruptcy proceeding even if he is not on this list. The national list is constantly updated by the Commission which deletes the names of administrators who are deceased or who have resigned or who were removed as a result of disciplinary proceedings.

The National Commission is composed of eleven members including upper level court judges, a professor, and administrators. In order to be entered on the list, the person must:

- be a French national;
- present guarantees of moral character such as those required for lawyers, "notaires" and court clerks; and

– pass an examination after conducting a professional internship (art 5, Law No. 85-99).

The persons enrolled on the national list may perform their duties throughout France. The list is divided into regional sections which correspond to the jurisdictions of each court of appeals, but the court is not obliged to choose an administrator from the regional section of its jurisdiction.

The National Commission is also a disciplinary body and may:

- issue warnings;
- give reprimands;
- order temporary suspensions from practice for a period which may not exceed one year; or
- permanently remove persons from the list.

The first two sanctions may last for a one year period following their imposition and be accompanied by control measures according to which the administrator must abide by certain obligations determined by the Commission. The statutory of limitation for invoking a disciplinary proceeding is ten years.

Liquidators

Law No. 85-99 set up a new category of legal agents known as liquidators ("mandataires liquidateurs") who ensure the realisation of the assets and the allocation of the sale proceeds among the creditors.

In order to be designated as a liquidator in a bankruptcy proceeding, a person must be entered on a regional list established by a commission instituted in the seat of each court of appeals. Contrary to administrators who are on a national list and may perform their duties nationally, liquidators are organised according to the jurisdiction of each court of appeals and may only exercise their profession in the jurisdiction in which they are registered. A liquidator may only be enrolled on one regional list.

The Regional Commission is the disciplinary body for liquidators and may order the same sanctions as the National Commission for Administrators.

It is composed of nine members including a judge of the court of appeals, a judge of the commercial court, a law or economics professor, and two liquidators.

To be on the regional list, a person must fulfil the requirements necessary for entry on the national list of administrators and must have his professional domicile located in the corresponding court of appeals jurisdiction.

Publicity and records

There are common publicity formalities for the opening judgment, the judgment ordering rehabilitation, the judgment pronouncing liquidation and the judgment pronouncing the termination of the liquidation proceedings (whether the latter is due to the satisfaction of all creditors or to insufficient assets). Such formalities are set out in article 21 of the 1985 Decree.

All judgments are recorded in the registry of commerce and companies for debtors which are legal entities or traders, and in the directory of trades ("répertoire des métiers") for debtors who are artisans; for persons who are not registered in either the registry or directory, registration is made in a special register kept by the clerk of the "tribunal de grande instance". Such registrations are made by the clerk of the competent court within the eight days following the date of the judgment.

Notice of the judgment is inserted in the "Bulletin Officiel des Annonces Civiles et Commerciales". This notice should indicate the name of the debtor, its registered office, its registry or directory registration number, its business activity and the date of the judgment. It must also state the name and address of the creditors' representative and the administrator or liquidator. This notice which is entered by the clerk must inform the creditors that they must submit their claims to the creditors' representative. The date of the notice is used as the reference date for calculating the time periods applicable to the bankruptcy proceeding.

A notice is also inserted in a legal announcements newspaper located in the jurisdiction in which the debtor has his principal office or a secondary establishment. It must contain the same information as that included in the Bulletin notice. The clerk is in charge of inserting the notice.

When an individual is the subject of liquidation proceedings, the judgment is mentioned in his police record ("casier judiciaire").

Contents of Chapter 5

CORPORATE INSOLVENCY LAW IN GERMANY

1.	**Introduction**	173
	Terminology	173
	Sources of law in Germany	173
	The insolvency law reform	174
	Statutory procedures	176
	The legal position after the reform; uniform proceedings in the form of an insolvency (reorganisation) plan	177
2.	**Corporations**	178
	Characteristics	179
	Management	180
	Ownership	181
	Financing and security for creditors	183
	Available information	186
	Other business entities	187
	Debt collection and asset recovery	188
3.	**Survival of the insolvent corporation or its business**	192
	Compulsory arrangements with creditors	192
	Arrangement proceedings	196
4.	**Termination of the corporation: voluntary liquidation and compulsory liquidation**	206
	Members' voluntary liquidation	210
	Compulsory liquidation	221
5.	**Augmenting the assets of the insolvent corporation**	239
	Introduction	239
	Transactions at risk (challenges under the KO)	240
	Personal liability of officers	245
6.	**Public control over insolvent corporations**	248
	Appointment and control of the Konkursverwalter	248

Examinations and investigations   249
Publicity and records   249

Chapter 5

CORPORATE INSOLVENCY LAW IN GERMANY

Kurt G Weil, DROSTE Rechtsanwälte,

and Graham J C Vincent, Solicitor, Brussels

1. Introduction

Terminology

The German law of insolvency has a detailed terminology, the English transla-
tions of which can be thoroughly misleading and fail to convey the function of
the terms as they are used in German legal practice. In this chapter, therefore,
the German term is followed by an equivalent term in English, whose purpose
is to orientate the reader to the idea behind the German term, rather than being
a strict translation. Subsequent references will use the English translation.

One particular area of confusion should be drawn to the reader's attention at
this stage – the terms "Konkurs" and "Liquidation". The latter term is, in German law, restricted solely to the case of a members' voluntary liquidation of a
corporation. All other forms of insolvency, be they the creditors' liquidation of
a corporation or the bankruptcy of a firm or individual at its own or its creditors'
initiative, are referred to as "Konkurs". In this chapter, "Konkurs" is, however,
translated in its more restricted sense, as "compulsory liquidation", with "Liquidation" translated as "members' (voluntary) liquidation".

Sources of law in Germany

German law is a codified civil law system. The vast majority of the references in
this chapter, therefore, are to the Acts and codes which regulate the law of insolvency in Germany. While case law is not unknown, and in many areas plays a
very important role in law making, the absence of a developed principle of "stare
decisis", means that its role is not as significant as in those states with the common law systems.

Virtually all German statute law has attracted academic attention, and this
has led to a long-established tradition of contemporary institutional writers.

The "Kommentare" (commentaries) to the various codes and Acts are regarded with a great deal of deference and, on occasion, with great authority by the courts. The views of the commentators on any one question of law are usually attributed to either "the minority opinion" ("Mindermeinung") or the "prevailing opinion" ("herrschende Meinung"). This nomenclature is not intended to prejudge the correctness of the views stated but simply gives an indication of the extent to which the views expressed are shared amongst the writers' academic colleagues. The major commentary in the field of insolvency law in Germany is the commentary to the "Konkursordnung" (Insolvency Act) by Kuhn and Uhlenbruck. This work will be referred to in this chapter.

The principal statutes are referred to in the text and, once explained, designated by their common German abbreviations. These are all contained in the glossary at the end of the chapter.

Insolvency Law is dealt with slightly separately as between the former Federal Republic and the former German Democratic Republic. Whilst Germany was still split, there were two independent legal systems. However, the main theme of this chapter concerns the law as it is and was in West Germany (including West Berlin). East Germany had a system of insolvency law during the socialist regime, but it was rarely, if ever, applied. Its insolvency legislation has now, to a large extent, been assimilated to that of West Germany, but a number of differences still remain. Where these are of particular note, reference is made to them in a separate paragraph at the end of the relevant section, while the more important deviating provisions of the West German and East German legislation are specifically drawn to the reader's attention.

The principal statutes governing insolvency and its related topics in West Germany are the "Konkursordnung" ("KO") and "Vergleichsordnung" ("VerglO").

In East Germany, the picture is a little more complicated. In West Germany, in 1978, a commission was set up to investigate the law of insolvency and propose a number of reforms. It reported in 1985 and again in 1986, and published a final report in 1992. As a result of the situation of flux as regards possible reforms, it was decided not to introduce the West German provisions wholesale into east Germany upon unification. Rather, the East German statutes, which, although still in existence, were rarely deployed during the communist era, have been assimilated in a number of moves to approximate the West German model. The principal statute at present is thus the "Gesamtvollstreckungsordnung" ("GesO") (originally called the "Gesamtvollstreckungsverordnung" ("GesVVO"), a statute passed by the former GDR government on 6 June 1990). Also of importance is the "Gesetz über die Unterbrechung von Gesamtvollstreckungsverfahren" ("GUG") (formerly the "Zweite Verordnung über die Gesamtvollstreckung" of 25 July 1990).

The insolvency law reform

The German legislators have begun to pave the way towards a uniform insolvency (bankruptcy) law. A draft bill was adopted by the German "Bundestag" (Parliament) on 21 April 1994. However, the "Bundesrat" (German Senate), unsatisfied with the draft insolvency law adopted by the Bundestag, therefore applied to the Mediation Committee on 20 May 1994. The Federal Ministry of Justice therefore expects the passing of the bill to be delayed and to be subject to lengthy debates within the Committee. The reform, to be incorporated in the "Insolvenzordnung" ("InsO"), will not only standardise the entirety of German bankruptcy (*i.e.* forced liquidation) law, but will also change the fundamental principles of Germany bankruptcy law which have dictated the practice of insolvency law since the "KO" became law in 1877.

The profound need for reform has been recognised as unquestionable in Germany for a long time. The fact is that in over 75% of German bankruptcy cases, the insolvency petition is dismissed because the assets of the bankrupt company are not sufficient to cover the costs of the insolvency proceedings (a situation known as "dismissal for lack of means").

The main aim of the reform is to avoid a large number of bankruptcy applications being dismissed on account of insufficient assets and to enable at least the commencement of bankruptcy proceedings. This should be made possible through a reduction in the level of preconditions necessary to commence proceedings. The right of rescission is to be improved in order to help increase the size of the bankruptcy estate. In addition, all creditors' rights existing prior to bankruptcy are to be totally removed. Property which until now has been subject to satisfaction by a preferential creditor, and therefore realisable by such creditor, shall in future remain in the bankrupt's estate to be realised by the administrator of the estate and made available for disribution to creditors less costs. In addition, it has been proposed that the labour courts be empowered to give appropriate directions where urgent changes need to be made to the bankrupt's business operations. These may include the release of outstanding debts owed by *bona fide* individual debtors.

The government's attitude, which has in the past been regarded by practitioners as hostile to bankruptcy reorganisations, will be more receptive to such reorganisations in this amended version of the statute (BR-Druks. 12/2443 of 15 April 1992).

Because of the scope of the reform, the new law will first enter into effect on 1 January, 1997, so that practitioners will have time to familiarise themselves with the changes in the law, which are quite extensive in some areas.

This chapter will, where relevant, refer to the most important areas where the Insolvenzordnung ("InsO") differs from the legal rules currently in effect.

Although there are essentially two systems of insolvency law in Germany, proceedings in one jurisdiction will extend to assets situated in the other, thus avoiding the necessity of two insolvency cases. One strange consequence of the bi-jurisdictional system is that in Berlin, although the two halves of the city-state are subject to different jurisdictions, the western "Amtsgerichte" (Lower Regional Courts) administer the East German procedures, as well as those under the West German provisions.

Statutory procedures

The principal statutory procedures in the West German law of insolvency are the "Konkursverfahren" (compulsory liquidation or bankruptcy proceedings) (in East Germany, called "Gesamtvollstreckung" (sl (4) sentence 2 GesO)) and the "Vergleichsverfahren" (proceedings for arrangement or composition with creditors). The concept of "compulsory liquidation" must be distinguished from the German concept of "Liquidation" (members' (voluntary) liquidation). The two types are governed separately in each of the two Acts regulating the two principal forms of corporation in Germany (see p178 *infra*).

Compulsory liquidation proceedings

Compulsory liquidation proceedings are regulated by the "Konkursordnung" ("KO" – Insolvency Act) in West Germany and the "Gesamtvollstreckungsordnung" ("GesO" – Full Enforcement of Judgments Act) in East Germany: in matters not governed by the "GesO", reference is made by implication to the terms of the "Zivilprozeßordnung" ("ZPO" – Code of Civil Procedure) (sl (3) "GesO" read together with the Unification Treaty ("Einigungsvertrag") (Schedule 2 III A II No. 3, Schedule I III A III No. 28b)). The aim of the procedure is the satisfaction of the claims of a debtor's creditors by means of the realisation of its entire assets. From this basic aim, the following principles emerge:

- in the event of the commercial collapse of the debtor, such that full satisfaction of the creditors is no longer possible, all creditors are satisfied on a pro rata dividend basis. There is therefore a "sharing of loss" amongst the creditors and no creditor may gain any pecuniary advantage over the others;

- basically, the compulsory liquidation encompasses the entire assets of the debtor (sl (1) KO), with the intention that the creditors should be equally and collectively satisfied out of those assets to the greatest extent possible;

- for this purpose, the creditors are represented collectively by two particular organs, namely the "Gläubigerversammlung" (meeting of creditors) and the Gläubigerausschuß" (committee of creditors). Through these organs the creditors are able to exercise a broad degree of influence over the procedure;

- the creditors may not act on their own individual initiative, but must co-operate towards the realisation of the assets, hence the term "Gemeinschuldner" (common debtor) which is applied to the insolvent. Because the entire estate of the common debtor is brought under consideration, the common debtor is much more seriously affected than by individual enforcement measures. In particular, it loses the power to manage and administer its assets, both of which functions pass to the "Konkursverwalter" (insolvency administrator);

- in the compulsory liquidation procedure itself, the Konkursverwalter must take a decision as to whether he is going to admit individual claims to be included in the official list of claims ("Konkurstabelle"). If he rejects a claim, the creditor can take legal action through normal court procedures to challenge the rejection.

The function of the compulsory liquidation procedure is merely to enforce, *inter alia*, judgments against the common debtor. It is an intervention by the state in the legal position of the common debtor, akin to confiscation of the common debtor's assets, *i.e.* it is a compulsory liquidation of the entire assets of the debtor for the satisfaction of the creditors, who themselves need have no standing to commence enforcement procedures. The Konkursverwalter is appointed to carry out the procedure in the most appropriate commercial manner, bearing in mind the overriding interests of the creditors. He is responsible above all for the realisation of the assets. The major characteristics of the compulsory liquidation proceedings are that the creditors supervise and control the actual management and realisation of the assets by the Konkursverwalter. The task of the "Konkursgericht" (insolvency court) is accordingly limited to overseeing the procedure.

The entire estate of the insolvent company is confiscated and formed into the "Konkursmasse" (insolvency assets) (sl (1) **KO**) comprising all those assets which may be subject to the individual enforcement of judgments – for example, the company's books are included, but not those items over which no security can be granted (such as trust property). The estate is realised and converted into cash, and the free proceeds distributed to the creditors. This entails the full liquidation of the insolvent company and results in its termination.

Creditors' arrangement

To avoid the drastic consequences of liquidation, the Creditors' Arrangements Act ("Vergleichsordnung") was passed in 1935, regulating the procedure in such creditors' arrangements (or compositions) ("Vergleich"). The purpose of an arrangement is to avoid having to resort to compulsory liquidation proceedings. The basic distinction between the two is that the initiative in the case of an arrangement lies with the company itself, which retains the management and control of its assets whereas, in compulsory liquidation, management and control passes to the Konkursverwalter; moreover the aim of the arrangement is the rehabilitation, rather than the liquidation, of the company.

The legal position after the reform; uniform proceedings in the form of an insolvency (reorganisation) plan

The introduction of the "InsO" in 1997 will fundamentally change the conciliation proceedings as well as the institution of forced settlements in bankruptcy proceedings (see *infra*) and the duration of the opening proceedings (Eröffnungsverfahren) in general. In the place of settlement and forced settlement, there will be an insolvency plan (akin to a Chapter 11 reorganisation plan in the United States).

These proceedings, which are to a large degree based on the American reorganisation procedure constitute the heart of the insolvency law reform. The insolvency administrator will be required to draw up a plan for reorganisation in which all interested parties co-operate. The plan will set out how the continuance of the undertaking is to be secured and how its earning capacity is to be restored. It will be necessary to conclude all relevant negotiations with creditors, potential transferees and the like before such plan is drawn up.

The plan must also indicate the amount of and time at which the claims and rights of the insolvency creditors are to be fulfilled or secured. All legal transactions necessary to carry out a successful reorganisation will have to be linked (including the renunciation of claims, increase in capital, release by affiliated companies, removal of management and exclusion of shareholders).

Creditors or groups of creditors will be able to draw up separate plans independently from the insolvency administrator and submit these to a vote. Until a decision has been made as to which plan is to be implemented, neither the administrator nor the insolvency court will be able to make provisional decisions, which might run contrary to any of the proposed plans. This means that, in fact, insolvency proceedings will be suspended from the beginning of reorganisation proceedings until a legally binding decision is made to approve one of the submitted insolvency plans.

Before a vote is taken on the proposed plan(s), all registered claims will be examined. This will determine who is entitled to vote on the various insolvency plans. The plans will be voted on in groups, with secured creditors, unsecured creditors, and employees all voting separately. For a plan to be accepted, it will have to be approved by at least 80% (of registered claims) of secured creditors, 60% (of total unsecured claims) of unsecured creditors and 80% (on a one man, one vote basis) of the employees concerned. The plan, once accepted by creditors, must be approved by the court, which can only reject it if there have been serious breaches of procedure in its implementation. Once an approved decision has taken legal effect, the legal amendments as set out in the plan will be put into effect. The plan will take effect as for and against all creditors, even if they have not participated in the proceedings or if they have voted against the plan.

2. Corporations

The most important corporations in German law are the "Aktiengesellschaft" ("AG"), governed principally by the "Aktiengesetz" (AG Act), and the "Gesellschaft mit beschränkter Haftung" ("GmbH") governed principally by the "Gesetz betreffend die Gesellschaften mit beschränkter Haftung" (GmbH Act). Also of importance is a special form of the GmbH which is the "GmbH & Co. KG", a limited partnership with a limited partner ("Kommanditist") and a general partner ("Komplementär"), where the "Komplementär" itself is a private limited company.

Characteristics

AG

The AG is a legal person which is liable for its debts only to the extent of its assets and whose capital comprises shares ("Aktien"), which can be quoted on a stock exchange if certain legal requirements are fulfilled; for instance, the minimum share capital must be DM100,000 and all shares must be issued. The organs of the AG are the "Hauptversammlung" (general meeting of shareholders), the "Aufsichtsrat" (supervisory board), and the "Vorstand" (board of management). The distinction between the board of management and the supervisory board is reflected in the UK in the distinction between executive and non-executive directors.

GmbH

The GmbH is a private body corporate, limited by shares, which may not be listed on any stock exchange. It may be incorporated with one or several members. The authorised share capital ("Stammkapital") must be at least DM50,000 and the entire authorised share capital must be issued (*i.e.* there is no distinction in German law between authorised and issued share capital). The participation of each member must amount to a multiple of DM1,000 and, in German terminology, each total participation is known as "a share" ("Geschäftsanteil"). The organs of the company are a minimum of one director ("Geschäftsführer") and the shareholders' meeting ("Gesellschafterversammlung").

In addition, the company may have a supervisory board and must have one if there are more than 500 employees (with special provisions applying in the coal and steel industries). The directors are the legal representatives of the GmbH and their authority vis-à-vis third parties cannot be limited, so long as such third parties act in good faith. The shareholders' meeting is the forum in which resolutions of the shareholders as a body are made.

The shareholders are not personally liable for the obligations of the GmbH (except in cases of fraud); it alone is liable as a legal person. Individual shareholders may, however, be liable for unpaid calls on share capital owed by their fellow-shareholders. There can, under certain circumstances, be a duty to make additional payments ("Nachschußpflicht") and further obligations may be set down in the Memorandum/articles of association ("Gesellschaftsvertrag"), which takes the form of a single document, unlike in the UK. There is a general duty of confidentiality incumbent upon the shareholders vis-à-vis the company. Amendments to the Articles require a 75% majority resolution based on numbers of shares held by those voting, whether in person or by proxy.

Management

AG

The day-to-day business operations of an AG are controlled solely by the board of management. Differences of opinion within the board are resolved by simple majority taking account of the number of members on the board. The Articles may provide that certain types of transaction shall not be entered into without the approval of the supervisory board. In general, third parties cannot be prejudiced by the absence of such approval in transactions with the AG, unless they act in bad faith, since the ostensible authority of the board of management to bind the company cannot be limited.

The board of management is required to keep the supervisory board informed of:

- future business policy;
- the profitability of the company;
- the rate of business;
- the general situation of the company and its business, in so far as such could be of substantial importance.

It is also responsible for the statutorily prescribed accounting methods, the preparation of the annual accounts and ensuring that they are properly audited.

The standard of care incumbent upon the members of the board of management is that of a "well-organised and conscientious manager", as stated in section 93(1) AG Act; should a board member breach this duty, he is liable to the company, but not to the shareholders for any damages caused thereby.

GmbH

The directors ("Geschäftsführer") are responsible for the day-to-day running of the company. In particular, they are responsible for:

- making the necessary notifications to the Commercial Register ("Handelsregister");
- the proper accounting methods of the company;
- the calling and holding of the shareholders' meetings and the making of resolutions thereat;
- the fulfilment of the company's duties of publication (e.g. in relation to the annual report and the accounts).

The duties under tax law which are incumbent upon the company also fall to be fulfilled by the directors. They are required to exercise the standard of care in the affairs of the company which would be expected of a "well-organised businessman", as stated in section 43(1) GmbH Act, and are liable for all damages caused to the company by any breach of this standard – in many cases this is a joint and several liability.

Although not usual in a GmbH, there may be a supervisory board appointed to assist in overseeing management functions. Such a board is compulsory where the size of the GmbH or its area of business fall within the terms of the Co-determination Act ("Mitbestimmungsgesetz") or the Works Councils Act ("Betriebsverfassungsgesetz").

Ownership

AG

The minimum number of founders for an AG is five: thereafter, the shares may become concentrated in the hands of one person. The minimum share capital is DM100,000, divided into shares of a minimum of DM50 or of a multiple thereof. It should be noted in this respect that the German federal government plans to reduce the minimum nominal share to DM5 in order, among other things, to make investment on the German stock exchange more attractive. This amendment is now in effect since 26 July 1994.

Shares may be issued with various nominal values. There is no "authorised" and "issued" share capital – all shares must be issued. Share certificates are in practice bearer shares: partially paid-up shares (minimum 25%) must be order shares. Shares with no par value are prohibited. The shares have the function of negotiable securities and may, if desired, be admitted for listing and trading on any number of the German stock exchanges (although in practice, relatively few are). Certain shares may be created as nominative shares ("vinkulierte Aktien"), with transfer subject to the approval of the board of management. Shares may be issued as preference or ordinary shares and the articles of association will state how many shares are to be allocated to each class. Where preference shares are denied voting rights ("Vorzugsaktien ohne Stimmrecht"), their total nominal value may not exceed 50% of the total nominal value of the company's entire shares (s139(2) AG Act). Such non-voting shares acquire voting rights in the event of two years' non-payment of full preference dividends, and are included in the requirements for majorities that may apply at such time (s140(2) AG Act). Alterations to preference rights require a two-thirds majority of the votes tendered at a special meeting of the preference shareholders, unless a higher majority is provided for in the articles of association. It is possible for the articles to provide for larger shareholders to have reduced voting rights proportional to their shareholdings, or for these to be a maximum number of votes regardless of the size of the shareholding (s134 AG Act).

Minority shareholders are granted certain rights, depending on the exact size of the minority. A minority of over 25% may veto *inter alia* the dismissal of members of the board of management and supervisory board, alterations to the articles, and increases or decreases in capital. Shareholders holding one-tenth (or in some cases a nominal amount of DM2 million) of the share capital may, *inter alia*, apply for the dismissal of members of the supervisory board, or for their exoneration (see *infra*) to be voted on individually, and demand that claims be raised against the founders; shareholders holding one-twentieth (or in some cases a nominal amount of DM1 million) of the share capital, may *inter alia* call a shareholders' meeting and specify items to be included on the agenda, apply for a special audit of the company, and challenge the application of retained profits. In some cases, the shares must have been held for at least three months.

According to the "Aktiengesetz" (the AG Act, relating to public limited companies), the shareholders' meeting is, *inter alia*, responsible for:

- the appointment of the members of the supervisory board. Since the supervisory board, in its turn, appoints the board of directors, the membership of the board of directors is indirectly dependent on the decision of the shareholders' meeting;
- the application of profits;
- the confirmation that the members of the board of management and supervisory board have properly fulfilled their duties (exoneration);
- the appointment of the auditors;
- amendments to the memorandum and articles of association ("Satzung");
- measures involving increases or reductions in the share capital;
- the appointment of experts to oversee the activities of the management.

If required by the shareholders' meeting, the board of management is obliged to furnish each shareholder with information concerning the company's affairs, in so far as such is necessary for making a substantive judgment in relation to a particular item on the agenda. Such information may only be refused under particular, individually and statutorily prescribed circumstances, when required in the interests of the company.

GmbH

The minimum share capital of a GmbH is DM50,000, 25% (or a minimum of DM25,000, whichever is the lesser) of which must be paid up either in cash or in kind, provided that a payment of cash is not in reality a payment in kind. Such is the case where a cash contribution is immediately repaid in consideration, say, for the initial plant and machinery: in the event of insolvency, such a subscriber would risk being ordered to repay the cash (decision of the Hanseat. OLG, BB 1988, p. 504). The subscribed capital must be at the free disposal of the directors and must not at any stage be paid back to the shareholders, either declared or as disguised dividends or otherwise.

Since the usual purpose of a GmbH is to provide a private business vehicle which is controlled by a small number of, traditionally, family shareholders, the varieties of the classes of privileges attaching to shares in a GmbH are limitless, depending on the articles of association. Shares may even be issued without any dividend or voting rights at all, if special circumstances happen to dictate this.

It is the level of participation in the shares of the GmbH that dictates the membership rights and obligations of each shareholder vis-à-vis the company. The amount of share capital represented by the shareholding determines the amount of any dividend received by the shareholder, his voting rights, and the right to participate in the free proceeds of any dissolution of the company. It is not usual for share certificates to be issued.

The shareholders are the ultimate decision-making organ of the company. Their rights in relation to the management are dependent upon the terms of the articles of association, so long as they accord with the Act governing GmbHs ("GmbH-Gesetz" – GmbH Act). The shareholders' meeting has greater power than the directors as far as decision-making is concerned. It is, in particular, responsible for:

- the appointment, dismissal and exoneration of the directors. (Where rules as to co-determination or works' councils apply to the company, it is the supervisory board, rather than the shareholders' meeting, that is responsible in this regard);
- the checking and overseeing of the management;
- the appointment of general fully-authorised powers of attorney ("Prokura") and trading powers of attorney ("Handlungsvollmacht") which concern the entire business operations of the company;
- the raising of claims for damages on the part of the shareholders against the directors arising from the conduct of the management of the company, and the representation of the company in court actions raised by the shareholders against the directors.

The directors are in principle obliged to provide the shareholders with information on demand and without delay concerning the company's affairs and to afford them the opportunity of inspecting the company's books and documents.

Financing and security for creditors

Persons or institutions advancing money to the corporation without participating in the share capital will often require some form of security in return for providing the finance. Depending on the type of security which the corporation has granted in favour of the creditor providing finance, the creditor can, in certain circumstances, require preferential satisfaction of his claims in any insolvency. There are many different types of security and quasi-security interests that may be created over both moveable and immoveable property under German law. As far as land is concerned, the most important are the "Grundschuld" and the "Hypothek", the former being by far the most common. The existence of the two separate instruments is more an accident of history than specifically designed. In respect of the "Hypothek", repayment of the loan automatically extinguishes the "Hypothek". The "Grundschuld", however, remains in place notwithstanding repayment of the loan until specifically released by the creditor at the request of the debtor. This makes the "Grundschuld" a much more flexible form of security, which can be used for a variety of loans in succession or for different purposes. It also avoids considerable fees by virtue of the fact that loan documentation for land requires to be notarised in Germany. In neither case must the loan be given in order to purchase the property over which the security is granted, nor must the borrower be the creator of the security. In both cases, default on the relative loan payments will entitle the security-holder to realise the security.

In respect of movables, the most important quasi-security interest is retention of title whereby the seller retains ownership of goods until the buyer has paid the full purchase price for them. This concept has been expanded under the doctrine of "extended retention of title" ("erweiterter Eigentumsvorbehalt") to cover part-ownership of goods which have been produced by mixing goods in respect of which there was a valid retention of title with other goods.

In addition, but of much less significance, there are pledges ("Pfandrechte"), which may be granted over movables as security. The contract of security must be combined with delivery of the movables which form the subject matter of the security to be retained by the creditor. Exceptions include liens created over items being, for example, repaired, and agents', carriers', storers', landlords' liens, or seizures of debts due to the debtor by third parties. Where the debtor does not have title to the movables concerned, an enforceable security may nonetheless be created if the creditor acted in good faith. Where several "Pfandrechte" are created in respect of the same goods, they rank chronologically. Creditors entitled to prior satisfaction are either segregated ("ausgesondert"), or secured ("abgesondert"). The term "segregation" ("Aussonderung") applies in the case of assets which, in law, do not actually belong to the insolvent company and which are separated from the liquidation assets as assets which are, at the point the company becomes insolvent, the property of third parties. German law initially includes these in the insolvency assets, only to segregate them out again. "Absonderung", on the other hand, is a procedure whereby creditors holding a security over an asset to which the common debtor has legal title are granted a preference in respect of the proceeds of the realisation of the secured asset. Any part of the secured creditors' claims not discharged from the proceeds of sale rank along with the rest of the non-preferred creditors.

Creditors with a right to segregation ("Aussonderung")

These creditors may lay direct claim to an asset included within the liquidation assets on the basis that the debtor has no legal title to it (ss43 *et seq* KO). Such assets include:

- an asset sold under a valid retention of title clause, whether or not the vendor has rescinded the contract. It is debatable whether the vendor also has a right of segregation in the case of extended retention of title clauses as these apply to newly-created goods following incorporation into or commixture with other assets of the company, and go beyond the parameters of the doctrine of retention of title as it has been developed in the common law jurisdictions;

- assets in respect of which a creditor has a right against the debtor company for delivery, such as in the case of rent or bailment/deposit;

- in certain circumstances, land and similar assets which are the subject of a security, where the mortgagee is insolvent but retains a right to retain or obtain possession of the assets as against the debtor. Relevant securities include the "Hypothek"and "Grundschuld". In particular, the "Grundschuld" entitles the holder to retain all proceeds of the sale of the secured assets regardless of the level of the outstanding debt (although a provision requiring repayment of surplus funds to the debtor upon realisation of the security is usually included in the security agreement and, if not expressly included in the agreement granting the "Grundschuld", will be implied: the question is often particularly relevant where the security holder is insolvent and the "Grundschuld" is enforced, leaving the debtor only ranking as an unsecured creditor for any surplus proceeds).

In the case of a "right of segregation", the claim of the creditor is judged under the terms of the Civil Code ("Bürgerliches Gesetzbuch" – BGB) and the type of claim is determined by normal civil procedure. Insolvency law is, to that degree, inapplicable. A claim lies against the Konkursverwalter for delivery where assets which he is not entitled to hold are to be segregated. In East Germany, the Konkursverwalter may satisfy the claim in cash (s12(1) GesO).

Under the new law, the reservation of a right to rescind another's ownership will be further conceded as a segregation right (Aussonderungsrecht). Above all, the InsO declares the so-called "group reservation right" inoperative. Under current law, a seller can reserve proprietary rights in goods sold by him and thus secure not only his claims to the purchase price or other claims against the buyer, but also the claims of companies related to the seller. Once the new InsO is in place, this will no longer be possible.

Secured creditors (Absonderung)

Creditors who have a secured right may require that the proceeds of certain items within the insolvency assets be paid over to them in satisfaction of their secured claims because that right of satisfaction is "insolvency-proof" (ss47 *et seq* KO). Such creditors principally include:

- creditors holding certain securities in land;

- holders of legal liens ("Pfandrechte") over movables or pecuniary claims;

- holders of an equitable lien ("Sicherungseigentum"), a legal institution whereby security is granted over movables which then remain in the possession of the debtor in a form of trust relationship in favour of the creditor;

- assignees under an assignment or assignation in security ("Sicherungsabtretung");

- holders of commercial rights of retention of goods ("kaufmännische Zurückbehaltungsrechte").

As with segregation, preferred rights are exercised in accordance with the Civil Code and enforced under normal civil procedure, outside the main liquidation proceedings. The asset concerned is realised by the preferred creditor or by the Konkursverwalter, *e.g.* in the case of a land security, by means of public auction or court administration (where the court appoints a Konkursverwalter to collect the rents from the property). The proceeds are used to satisfy the claim of the preferred creditor. If the proceeds are insufficient to satisfy the claim, the creditor ranks *pari passu* with the other unpreferred creditors for the balance.

Under the InsO, the secured creditor will suffer considerable loss of rights compared with the old regime. The legislators proceed on the assumption that the interests of the parties must be co-ordinated such that the value of the bankruptcy estate is maximised. The administrator in bankruptcy would, for example, be entitled to apply for the release of a lien if it were necessary for a sensible estate value (for the continued running of a business, for a collective bulk sale or for the reorganisation of a debtor). The administrator would be able to order the forced valuation of the land creditor's security interests, if it were shown that the interest of the bankruptcy estate outweighed the interest of the creditor in question. Moreover, secured creditors will in the future be faced with paying up to 6% of any share in the bankruptcy proceeds for the general litigation costs.

Set-off

Where a creditor had a right of set-off against the common debtor prior to the commencement of insolvency proceedings, he can enforce that right against the Konkursverwalter (s53 KO, s7(5) GesO). Creditors are not required to notify such claims in the liquidation proceedings, but both the debtor's and the creditor's claims must in principle have been subject to set-off at the time of the commencement of the liquidation. In West Germany, the possibilities for set-off may be extended or restricted in certain circumstances (ss54 and 55 KO); in East Germany, these provisions have not been expressly adopted, but would probably arise as a result of the broad interpretation of section 7(5) GesO.

For set-off to apply, there is no requirement that both debts be for a stipulated amount of money (s54(1) KO). Where set-off is to be made against items not for a stipulated amount, however, they must be given a monetary value, since, under the Civil Code, set-off is dependent upon the two claims being of the same kind (s387 BGB). However, section 55 KO contains detailed restrictions on the application of set-off, the most important of which prohibits the purchase by or assignation to debtors of the corporation of debts due by the corporation to its creditors, either after the commencement of compulsory liquidation or in knowledge of circumstances indicating that compulsory liquidation would be applied for.

Available information

Certain important information concerning corporations is contained in the Commercial Register. In the case of a GmbH, the entries in this public record include:

- the name of the company;
- the town in which its registered office is situated (its seat);
- the objects of the company;
- the amount of share capital in the company;
- the dates of certain resolutions by the shareholders;
- the names of the directors and the extent of their authority to represent the company; and
- the duration of the company if such is limited to a particular period.

Further information must be registered upon the occurrence of particular events, such as the winding-up of the GmbH (see pp206-210 *infra*) by reason of the commencement of members' liquidation or compulsory liquidation proceedings or by reason of a refusal to begin such proceedings due to a lack of assets, and the names of the liquidators or Konkursverwalter.

In the case of an AG, the following must also be registered:

- the most important incorporation procedures;
- the composition of the board of directors;
- the names of those authorised to represent the company;
- alterations to the articles of association; and
- increases in capital.

Similarly, the commencement of members' liquidation or compulsory liquidation proceedings, or the refusal to begin such proceedings by reason of a lack of assets, and the names of the liquidators or Konkursverwalter must be registered.

Most corporations (AGs and GmbHs) are obliged to publish their annual accounts, by submitting them to the local court which administers the Commercial Register for the district in which they are situated (there is no national, centralised register in Germany) and to publish them in the "Bundesanzeiger" (Federal Gazette). The existence and extent of the duty of publication are dependent on the size of the company.

Banks will provide nothing more than very general information on corporations and credit-rating agencies do not exist in Germany. However, there are the usual tracing and inquiry agents who are able to produce reports which may reveal more detail of the commercial side of a business than the Commercial Register.

Other business entities

In addition to the special forms of corporations already discussed, there are other forms of business undertaking in Germany. These are:

- the "Gesellschaft bürgerlichen Rechts" (GbR);

- the "offene Handelsgesellschaft" (oHG) (which has its own legal identity, and carries on a commercial enterprise under a firm name); and

- the "Kommanditgesellschaft" (KG) (limited partnership).

Although both the GbR and the oHG are similar in principle to the concept of partnership, there are distinct differences between the legal rights and constitution of these two business entities. The GbR is the basic form of unincorporated association and may be set up to fulfil a particular chosen purpose. The members hold all property jointly and are jointly and severally liable to an unlimited extent for the partnership debts. Court actions are not raised by and against the GbR but rather by and against all the individual partners, jointly and severally.

The oHG is a variation on the GbR. As in the case of the GbR, the liability of the members for the debts of the partnership is unlimited. The oHG differs from the GbR in that partners of an oHG intend to run a "commercial trade" (as defined in sections 1 to 3 "Handelsgesetzbuch" (HGB – Commercial Code)) under a firm name. A GbR may not undertake a "business" as so defined. The oHG can acquire rights in the name of the firm and is capable of being made insolvent as a firm while the entire membership is jointly and severally liable.

The KG is also derived from the GbR and is based on the principle of a trading company under a joint name. However, with the exception that it must have at least one unlimited general partner ("Komplementär"), the KG can have members whose liability towards the company's creditors is limited to the amount of a certain capital sum paid into the company ("Kommanditist"). The insolvency procedure which applies to the oHG also applies to the KG.

The insolvency procedures in the case of both the oHG and the KG are regulated generally in the KO, with special provisions contained in sections 209 to 212. In principle, the only ground for insolvency is the entity's inability to pay its debts (and not a deficiency of assets over liabilities, as in the case of corporations).

Debt collection and asset recovery

Compulsory enforcement of judgments

A private law claim can be satisfied by compulsory enforcement ("Zwangsvollstreckung") of a judgment obtained through a successful debt action in the court. The procedure is regulated under sections 704 *et seq* of the Civil Procedure Code ("Zivilprozeßordnung" – ZPO).

A creditor can only use the compulsory enforcement procedure if he has a title to enforce. Such title chiefly takes the form of one of the following:

- a legally enforceable judgment made by the court following a court action;

- a judicial settlement to which the court has given its authority (s794(1) No. 1 ZPO);

- an order for enforcement made in connection with a summary debt action ("Mahnverfahren");

- an attachment order or arrestment ("Arrest") whereby the creditor is empowered to seize assets belonging to the debtor and sell them to satisfy his debt;

- an injunction or interdict; or

- the confirmation of a claim in an insolvency by means of registration on the official list of claims.

Enforcement procedures may also be undertaken in respect of certain deeds executed by the court or by a notary ("Notar") (s794(1) No. 5 ZPO). The relevant deeds are those that impose an obligation on one party to undertake the payment of money or the transfer of goods and under which that party subjects itself to immediate enforcement procedures without the necessity of his opponent instituting a court action.

Since April 1991, the law has provided for the possibility of what is known as a "settlement between lawyers" ("Anwaltsvergleich") (s1044b(1) ZPO)). This form of settlement, which is executed by the parties and their lawyers, has the same status as an arbitral decision. Enforcement of the settlement is by way of writ of execution ("Vollstreckbarerklärung") which can be obtained under a special procedure either before the court, or, at the claimant's option, before a notary.

The summary debt procedure (ss688 to 703d ZPO) is a shortened civil procedure intended to aid the creditor in quickly obtaining an enforceable title. Only claims for payment of a specified sum of money couched in Deutschmarks may be the subject of such proceedings. If the debtor neither lodges a defence ("Widerspruch") nor objects to the granting of undefended judgment ("Einspruch"), then the process terminates with an order from the court containing a warrant to enforce. Only if the debtor lodges a defence or raises an objection does the procedure then continue to a normal debt action before the competent court. Otherwise, the creditor may proceed to serve the warrant on the debtor and commence enforcement procedures.

The particular enforcement procedures vary depending on the nature of the claim which is being enforced and the type of asset involved. The principal distinction lies between:

- Enforcement procedures arising from pecuniary claims undertaken against:
  - moveable assets, which can be (a) tangible property; or (b) claims and other intangible asset rights; or
  - immoveable assets.

- Enforcement procedures resulting from other claims, such as for:
  - delivery of property;
  - specific performance;

— sufferance ("Duldung") or injunction/interdict. Sufferance is where a party is ordered to allow certain enforcement measures to be undertaken (for instance, against a piece of real property owned by him) by persons holding an enforceable title, and usually takes the form of a notarial or court deed (see above).

Compulsory enforcement procedures resulting from pecuniary claims against moveable assets belonging to the debtor are executed by means of seizure ("Pfändung") undertaken by the enforcement officer ("Gerichtsvollzieher"). Seizure is effected by the enforcement officer taking the tangible property in the custody of the debtor into his official possession (ss803, 808 ZPO).

Enforcement procedures arising from pecuniary claims against moveable intangible property (such as against debts due by third parties or other asset rights belonging to the debtor) are implemented by the regional court ("Amtsgericht"). Upon application by the creditor, the court will issue a seizure and transfer order ("Pfändungs- und Überweisungsbeschluß") which prohibits the third party from making payment to the common debtor and which prohibits the debtor himself from exercising any power of disposal over the debt due. At the same time, the claim against the third party is transferred to the creditor for collection.

Enforcement procedures in respect of immoveable property are implemented by means of the registration of a security or by means of the compulsory administration of the property concerned ("Zwangsverwaltung") or compulsory auction ("Zwangsversteigerung") (ss864 to 871 ZPO, Forced Sales Act ("Zwangsversteigerungsgesetz")).

Where enforcement procedures are intended to procure delivery of particular property, the claim must be in respect of a particular piece of moveable property or to a particular quantity of generic goods. The enforcement officer undertakes the task of dispossessing the debtor of the property in question and turning it over to the creditor. Where certain property which is subject to a delivery order cannot be located, the debtor must, upon the application of the creditor, give an affirmation to the court that the whereabouts of the property are unknown to him (s883 ZPO).

In the case of the enforcement of an order for specific performance, the following cases must be differentiated:

- where the performance can also be undertaken by a third party (transferable performance), the creditor can apply to the court for an order that the performance be undertaken at the debtor's cost (known as substitute performance ("Ersatzvornahme")) (s887(1) ZPO). An example might be the transportation of goods;

- where the specific performance cannot be undertaken by a third party (non-transferable performance), and the performance is dependent upon the debtor, then the debtor is compelled by the court under threat of a fine or imprisonment to undertake the performance itself (s888 ZPO). An example of such would be where the debtor is required to submit certain information.

In the case of enforcement procedures in respect of sufferance or injunction/interdict, contravention of the terms of the order on the part of the debtor results in the levying of a fine of up to DM500,000 or imprisonment for up to six months. Such fines and terms of imprisonment are ordered under the procedures provided in German law for what can be roughly translated as minor offences ("Ordnungswidrigkeiten") which are legally (and, to an extent, morally) distinguished from more serious criminal acts ("Straftatbestände") – although the practical effect on the offender is the same. The creditor may apply for such an order against the debtor in the case of any culpable contravention of the terms of the original order on the part of the debtor (s890 ZPO).

Cross-jurisdictional procedures

The recognition and enforcement of foreign judgments is regulated in a number of treaties and conventions. The most important convention applying in legal proceedings with Member States of the European Community is the EEC Convention on Civil Jurisdiction and the Enforcement of Judgments (Brussels Convention) of 27 September 1968 (incorporated into German law by means of publication in the Bundesgesetzblatt for 1973, II., 60). Under Title III, Articles 25-49, this Convention regulates the recognition and enforcement of judgments issued by jurisdictions outside Germany within the Member States of the EEC.

Where there is no applicable international treaty, then a decision as to the recognition of a foreign judgment is made under s328 ZPO. Under this provision, the recognition of such judgments is dependent upon:

- the international jurisdiction of the foreign court;
- compatibility with the German concepts of public policy ("ordre public"); and
- the mutual recognition of German judgments in the country issuing the judgment in question.

The most important of these prerequisites is the first, which is judged in the light of the German international law of procedure.

The public policy provision is intended to ensure that only those judgments which would be justified according to the material procedural and private law principles of German law will be enforced. The concept of public policy is partly embodied in s328 ZPO.

The recognition of foreign judgments does not require any particular judicial or administrative confirmation, with the exception of family matters. For enforcement of the foreign judgment, however, there must be an enforcement order from a German court (known as an exequatur; ss722 and 723 ZPO). This also applies to decisions by foreign arbitral tribunals (s1044 ZPO).

3. Survival of the insolvent corporation or its business

The law presently provides two procedures to facilitate the commercial survival of an insolvent undertaking. These are the creditors' arrangement, already mentioned *supra* , and the compulsory creditors' arrangement, effected between the insolvent and non-preferred creditors and involving the distribution of the insolvent's assets within the framework of the compulsory liquidation proceedings themselves (see pp221-227 *infra*). The possibilities available under both procedures are somewhat limited and, in practice, unsatisfactory. Consequently, in spite of several spectacular cases in recent times, their practical importance is rather small. As a result of the InsO, the current arrangement under the "Vergleichsordnung" and the compulsory settlement in bankruptcy are being replaced with a new "insolvency plan", which should make reorganisation considerably easier to effect. The German legislators treat the goals of the proceedings – namely the liquidation, reorganisation and assignment or transfer of property – as of equal importance. Each of the participants can opt for one or the other type of valuation and liquidation according to his needs. Thus private autonomous negotiations concerning solutions to problems in insolvency are encouraged.

The equal treatment of reorganisations through assignment and the other forms of insolvency liquidation demonstrates clear progress in German insolvency law. Two ways of achieving a reorganisation by assignment are emerging: on the one hand, the sale and transfer of a company from the bankruptcy estate, which would be effected with approval of the creditors' committee; and on the other hand, the transfer or assignment of a company's assets by the use of a formal restructuring plan, which would have to fulfill all of the requirements of a formal insolvency regime. The debtor has the following two possible arrangements with the creditors: a compulsory arrangement during the liquidation proceedings or arrangement proceedings before the liquidation proceedings.

Compulsory arrangements with creditors

The compulsory arrangement with creditors ("Zwangsvergleich") is a procedure which can only be initiated during the liquidation procedure regulated by sections 173 to 201 KO. In this sense, the word "compulsory" relates not to the insolvent company, but to any minority creditors who do not agree to the arrangement proposal. The compulsory arrangement takes the form of a contract between the common debtor and the non-preferred creditors, confirmed by the court and having the effect of providing an agreed level of satisfaction for those creditors in lieu of a general distribution from the insolvent assets.

Purpose and effect

Where the assets of a company are sold hurriedly during the course of a compulsory liquidation (see p221 *infra*), there is always a danger that prospective purchasers will exploit their "buyers' market" position in order to keep the purchase price down. Since there is usually pressure to complete the procedures as quickly as possible, there is not always time to wait for better offers to come in from other interested parties. The element of time pressure can be avoided if the creditors can be persuaded to waive or grant a moratorium on their claims and to agree that the business only be liquidated over a period of time or that a rescue package be put into operation. The creditors will be encouraged to take this path in circumstances where they can thereby expect to receive a higher rateable dividend.

It will, however, be impossible in all but a few cases to win the creditors over to the idea of even partial waivers and moratoria, especially where the body of creditors comprises both economically strong and economically weak parties. Creditors with a substantial capital backing, such as banks and industrial undertakings, are more likely to be prepared to agree to the gradual liquidation of the common debtor's assets or to a rescue package, since they are more easily able to sustain a postponement of payments or a waiver of part of their claim than weaker creditors who, under certain circumstances, need to be satisfied immediately in order to preserve their cash-flow situations. It is therefore often not possible to reach an accord with all of the creditors as a body.

For this reason, the KO provides for the possibility of implementing compulsory arrangement proceedings by means of a majority decision (s182).

Pre-application considerations

Compulsory arrangement proceedings can only be initiated by the common debtor and only affect the non-preferred creditors (s173 KO). The arrangement proposal must state the manner in which satisfaction of the creditors is to be achieved and whether and how the creditors' positions are to be secured (s174 KO).

The first problem is therefore the preparation of the arrangement proposal. It must include details of the level, manner of and time period for the satisfaction of the creditors' claims. In addition, arrangements may be made for a moratorium on claims, and there may also be liquidation arrangements ("Liquidationsvergleiche") by means of which the assets are realised for the proportional satisfaction of the creditors in return for a waiver of their remaining debts.

If the position of the creditors is to be secured, the manner in which this is to be done must be shown. Common types of security include: providing a bond of guarantee/caution; the pledging of moveable property, stocks and negotiable instruments; the registration of a land/heritable security; in the case of moveable property and rights, the delivery and transfer thereof as security; and a notice of prior title to land ("Auflassungsvormerkung"). The last of these is a registrable document which precedes registration of title to land in the Land Register ("Grundbuch"). It may be granted prior to completion and prevents further dispositions over the land in question on the part of the seller/creator of the security, thereby protecting the buyer's/secured creditor's position until the deed in his favour has itself been registered.

Procedure

Compulsory arrangement proceedings are permissible only after the examination hearing ("Prüfungstermin" the court hearing at which the common debtor's state of affairs is looked into), and as long as a judgment authorising a final distribution to the creditors has not been pronounced (s173 KO).

The arrangement proposal is discussed at an arrangement hearing which, upon application, can take place simultaneously with the examination hearing. It is only at this hearing that the arrangement may be authorised.

Notice of the meeting is given by the court, by publication in one of the newspapers authorised by the court for notification within its jurisdiction. This is deemed to be adequate notice, even where additional service of notice is required by law (s76 KO). The maximum period of notice is one month. There is no minimum. Notice should also be served, subject to s76 KO, on the members of the committee of creditors, the non-preferred creditors, the debtor, and the Vergleichsverwalter.

It is the court which presides at the hearing and takes the final decision. The Vergleichsverwalter and the common debtor, upon whom there is a duty to present the arrangement proposal verbally, must be present. The non-preferred creditors then take a vote at the hearing as to whether or not to accept the compulsory arrangement, although it will not come into effect until the court, having heard each of the creditors, the Vergleichsverwalter and the committee of creditors, makes an order to confirm its terms (s184 KO). The court's task is to ensure that the legal requirements for the arrangement have been fulfilled and that no procedural errors have been made. It is not required to check whether or not the arrangement is advantageous to the creditors.

Sections 186 *et seq.* KO contain a list of situations in which the confirmation of the proposed arrangement can or must be rejected. The court will reject the arrangement:

- of its own accord, where the essential procedural requirements have not been observed (and the defects cannot be remedied) or where the creditors are not guaranteed a dividend payment of at least 20%, because of the culpable dishonesty of the common debtor;
- upon the application of one of the creditors, where agreement by the creditors to the proposed arrangement has been obtained dishonestly or where it contravenes the collective interests of the creditors. In this respect, the court also draws upon commercial considerations.

As soon as the court has pronounced its order confirming the compulsory arrangement, the compulsory liquidation proceedings themselves are dismissed. The common debtor thereby regains legal control of its assets (s192 KO). Since neither the claims legitimately arising from the administrative acts of the Konkursverwalter (Masseansprüche) (s59 KO) nor those of the preferred creditors are affected by the terms of the compulsory arrangement, the Vergleichsverwalter must ensure that they are satisfied or secured prior to the dismissal of the compulsory liquidation proceedings.

Any failure on the part of the common debtor to fulfil its obligations under the compulsory arrangement does not lead to the court's order being ineffective (s195 KO). Where, however, a clause to the effect that the compulsory arrangement shall cease to be of effect in the event of non-performance on the part of the debtor ("kassatorische Klausel") has been expressly included in the composition, then, depending on the precise terms of the clause, a creditor ceases to be bound by the restrictions imposed on his claim by the compulsory arrangement and is once again entitled to initiate compulsory liquidation proceedings. In such a case, the creditors are entitled to register their former claims to their full extent in any new compulsory liquidation.

Creditor's involvement and position

After hearing the arguments for the arrangement proposal, the committee of creditors is granted leave to state its views to the court. Following a general discussion, the non-preferred creditors tender their votes for or against the arrangement as proposed. To be accepted, the arrangement must be approved by (s182 KO):

- a simple majority of those creditors present; and
- creditors whose claims represent at least 75% of the value of the claims of those creditors affected by the compulsory arrangement procedure. In East Germany, this requirement is reduced to a 75% majority of the total pecuniary claims represented at the meeting at which the vote is taken (s16 (4) No. 3 GesO).

This procedure is intended to prevent:

- a majority of smaller creditors being outvoted by a smaller number of major creditors; and
- a major creditor being outvoted by a majority of minor ones.

The compulsory arrangement is binding and effective for and against all non-preferred creditors even if they have voted against it or did not take part either in the vote or in the compulsory liquidation proceedings (s193 KO). The confirmation of the arrangement by the court grants a right to begin enforcement procedures to a creditor comprised within the official list of creditors in the event of the debtor's default. The legally confirmed arrangement can also be enforced against any guarantors who have been involved in providing guarantees (s194 KO).

In the event that the compulsory arrangement has been entered into as a result of fraud on the part of the common debtor or a third party or the Vergleichs-

verwalter, then each individual creditor is entitled to challenge any waiver of
claim granted in the compulsory arrangement, provided that the creditor was
not aware of any grounds upon which he was entitled to challenge the order at
the time it was made (s196 KO).

The authorised and accepted compulsory arrangement effects an executory title in favour of the creditors. In effect, the court ceases to be involved and the
composition takes on the same status as any extra-judicial settlement (ss192 and
194 KO).

Arrangement proceedings

Purpose and effect

One significant disadvantage of the compulsory arrangement is that it cannot be
applied for in order to avoid compulsory liquidation proceedings. It is only an
available option once the compulsory liquidation has begun. However, by the
time compulsory liquidation proceedings have been commenced, the company
is often no longer capable of being rescued. The mere fact that compulsory liquidation proceedings have commenced has a very deleterious effect on the commercial value of the company and, in short, has the effect of ruining its credibil-
ity. There is, however, a voluntary form of arrangement proceeding which can
be entered into prior to the commencement of compulsory liquidation proceedings and whose aim is to avoid the compulsory liquidation of the common debtor
by means of a composition with the creditors of the company. The procedure is
governed by the Arrangements with Creditors Act ("Vergleichsordnung" –
"VerglO").

The debtor may also attempt to reach an accord with its creditors through an
extra-judicial arrangement ("außergerichtlicher Vergleich") which may contain
agreement as to, *inter alia*:

- pro rata payments,
- moratoria on claims or the liquidation of assets,
- differential treatment of creditors.

Such an extra-judicial arrangement can, however, easily be foiled by those creditors who are not in agreement. In the case of arrangements under the VerglO,
on the other hand, just as in the case of compulsory arrangement proceedings,
the minority is bound by the decision of the majority.

Pre-application consideration

The first consideration is whether or not an application for the commencement
of proceedings should be lodged. The application can only be initiated by the
common debtor, since the aim of the procedure is to avoid compulsory liquidation. (This is in contrast to compulsory liquidation proceedings in which the
creditors themselves lodge an arrangement application.) Once compulsory liquidation proceedings have been commenced, such an application has no effect.

The proper forum for the application is the court in which compulsory liquidation proceedings would have been commenced, *i.e.* in West Germany, the Lower Regional Court ("Amtsgericht") for the district where the corporation has its place of business (s71 KO) and, in East Germany, the "Kreisgericht" for the analogous district (sl (2) GesO). As to the special status of the state of Berlin, see p175 *supra*.

The application for an arrangement must also contain an application for the commencement of compulsory liquidation proceedings in the event that the court should refuse to commence the arrangement proceedings. In such a case, the court commences what is known as a subsequent liquidation ("Anschlußkonkurs") or pronounces an order that the proposed commencement of compulsory liquidation proceedings is rejected due to a lack of the prerequisite conditions, such as sufficient assets (see p206 *infra*). Such a decision could be prevented by the debtor, since it can retract its application at any time prior to the opening of the arrangement or subsequent liquidation proceedings.

Where a creditor lodges an application for compulsory liquidation and liquidation proceedings have not yet been commenced, the common debtor can preempt a decision thereon by lodging an application for an arrangement. The application must be accompanied by certain documentation from which the financial situation of the common debtor can be seen and by means of which that situation can be verified. This documentation must also demonstrate the trustworthiness of the common debtor. Accordingly, the arrangement application must include submissions as to whether compulsory liquidation proceedings have been commenced within the last five years or whether the debtor has given a confirmation in the course of other enforcement procedures that it has revealed all its assets and has no others which have not been disclosed (s3 VerglO). In addition, a list of creditors and debts must be included (s4 VerglO).

As in the case of compulsory arrangement proceedings, the application must include the arrangement proposal and show whether and how fulfilment of the arrangement is to be secured. The actual structure of the arrangement proposal is decisive for the success of the proceedings and, therefore, requires a great deal of care in its preparation. However, subsequent amendments are possible until the moment the court takes a vote on the arrangement. Where alterations are made prior to the commencement of the proceedings, the court must base its decision whether to allow the proceedings to begin on the latest version of the proposal.

The preparation of the material for the arrangement, the drafting of the application and its schedules, obtaining the information concerning the creditors and the other parties, the granting of the approval and the preparation of the votes are legally and factually so difficult that the debtor company often engages professional assistance, usually in the form of an accountant ("Wirtschaftsprüfer"), tax adviser ("Steuerberater") and/or lawyer ("Rechtsanwalt") experienced in this area, to ensure that the arrangement proposal must be clear and unambiguous. The arrangement takes the form of a:

- time extension arrangement ("Stundungsvergleich"),
- waiver or dividend arrangement ("Erlaßvergleich" or "Quotenvergleich"),
- liquidation arrangement ("Liquidationsvergleich"), in which case the common debtor passes its property in whole or in part to the creditors under the condition that any demands which are not met by the sale or other application of these assets will not be pursued.

It is not possible to make several alternative arrangement proposals.

Where a waiver arrangement is proposed, the level of payment must be stated in percentage terms, and this must be at least 35% of the creditors' claims, in particular where a figure has been put forward as to the degree to which a waiver should be granted. This minimum rate of satisfaction ("Mindestsatz") increases to 40% where the debtor is applying for a time period for fulfilment of more than one year following confirmation of the arrangement. The debtor may only apply for a payment period of more than 18 months for that part of its proposal exceeding 40%. Waiver arrangement proposals must offer the creditor payment in cash to the level of the respective legal minimum rate (35 or 40%) (s7 VerglO).

The liquidation arrangement is particularly suited to the situation where part of the business of the debtor is not to be continued. Such liquidation arrangements take the form of transferring some of the debtor's assets to the creditors. Where the whole of the business is to be discontinued, liquidation proceedings are more usual, although the liquidation arrangement is sometimes used. The essence of a liquidation arrangement is therefore not the total liquidation of the debtor's assets but rather that the debtor is put in a position whereby it can continue in business. The minimum rates referred to *supra* also apply in the case of liquidation arrangements.

In most cases of liquidation arrangement, that part of the assets which is to be applied for the satisfaction of the creditors is transferred to a trustee, who then undertakes the sale thereof and the distribution of the free proceeds. The court order approving the arrangement may either, itself contain the necessary trust agreement between the common debtor and the trustee or, alternatively, it may merely contain an undertaking on the part of the common debtor to conclude a trust agreement where appropriate. The conclusion of the trust agreement takes place after the acceptance and confirmation of the arrangement.

The creditors affected by the arrangement must be treated on an equal footing. Anything to the contrary will only be permitted where approved at the arrangement hearing by a majority of those arrangement creditors who are present and entitled to vote and who are deferred as a result of the proposal. The total sum of the claims of the approving creditors must then amount to at least three-quarters of the total claims of the deferred creditors entitled to vote. Any other agreements between the debtor or other persons and the individual creditors, as a result of which such creditors are preferred, are null and void (s8 VerglO). In certain cases, therefore, such approval by the deferred creditors will have to be obtained before the arrangement proposal is put forward with a view to opening the arrangement proceedings.

Procedure

Commencement of proceedings

Immediately after the lodging of the application or the commencement of arrangement proceedings, the court will appoint a provisional Vergleichsverwalter (s11 VerglO) and may also make an order to prevent any alteration in the assets which may have an unfavourable effect on the creditors (s12 VerglO).

Prior to making an order for the commencement of proceedings, the court will grant a hearing to a representative experienced in the trade or business in which the insolvent company has been operating (s14 VerglO). This is usually an official of the local chamber of commerce, to which, in Germany, all trading entities must belong and which has an advisory function in relation to such entities (ss2 and 11, Chambers of Commerce (Temporary Provisions) Act: "Gesetz zur vorläufigen Regelung des Rechts der Industrie-und Handelskammern"). This official will give evidence in particular as to whether the debtor is in a position to be able to adhere to the arrangement and whether the dividend is reasonable, as well as offering an opinion as to the security proposed in the arrangement proposal and the possibility of continuing the business after implementation of the arrangement. In East Germany, a representative of the "Treuhand" (the government agency set up by the GDR government in March 1990 to administer the privatisation of the former state-owned enterprises there) will also be heard.

There are a number of mandatory grounds provided by law upon which the application must be rejected. These are:

- the absence of any prospective ability to see the arrangement through;
- the inappropriateness of the arrangement proposal; or
- the fact "that in the event of the continuation of the company, it is not obviously to be expected that, by means of the arrangement, the company's continuance will be guaranteed" (s18(4) VerglO).

If one of these grounds is present, then the court is obliged to reject the arrangement application and to make an order for the commencement of compulsory liquidation proceedings.

When making the order beginning the arrangement proceedings, the court will nominate a Vergleichsverwalter and will fix a date for a hearing at which the arrangement proposal will be discussed. The same rules as to notice apply here as are mentioned at p194 *supra*. The creditors are required to register their claims with the Vergleichsverwalter (s20 VerglO). The commencement of proceedings is noted in the Commercial Register for the district in which the corporation is registered (s23 VerglO) and, at the same time the court will, if necessary, nominate a committee of creditors (s44 VerglO).

Arrangement hearing

The committee of creditors takes part in the arrangement hearing as a body. The common debtor and Vergleichsverwalter must also be present (s68 VerglO).

The basis of the arrangement hearing is the list of creditors, submitted by the debtor upon lodging the application. However, the pecuniary demands of creditors who are not named on the list of creditors, but whose claims are notified prior to the taking of the vote, must also be taken into consideration.

If no criteria are laid down to determine when promptly filed claims will be challenged in composition proceedings, objectionable as to cause, amount, or capacity to make allowance (Berücksichtigungsfähigkeit), then the sums in question should be held until the end of the relevant legal proceedings (German Supreme Court decision of April 8, 1992, ZIP 1992 at 708).

The debtor company must, when requested by the Vergleichsverwalter or any of the creditors, provide information concerning its financial situation, the appropriateness of the arrangement proposal, and its ability to carry it out. The court can oblige the officers of the debtor company to give an affirmation as to the submissions made by them in respect of its assets and liabilities (s69 VerglO). The creditors' claims are discussed at the arrangement hearing and a decision is taken as to whether they qualify for a vote in the proceedings (s70 VerglO). Where a pecuniary claim is not disputed by either the debtor, the Vergleichsverwalter or any of the other creditors, the creditor is entitled to a vote. Where a claim is contested and no unanimous decision can be reached, the court will decide whether that claim should confer a vote (s71 VerglO).

Minor creditors, (i.e. those who are to be fully satisfied directly after the legal confirmation of the arrangement under the arrangement proposal) have no voting rights (s72 VerglO). Such creditors are those whose claims are so minor that they will not impair the effect of the arrangement. The rationale behind this provision is to dispense with the necessity of involving creditors with virtually negligible claims in the proceedings.

The voting takes place at the hearing and, in order for the arrangement to be accepted, a double majority is required (s74 VerglO):

- the majority of those creditors present at the hearing, including those who are present in writing, must approve the arrangement proposal; and

- in West Germany, the entire sum of the claims of the approving creditors must amount to at least three-quarters of the claims of those creditors having a vote. This proportion is increased to four-fifths where the arrangement proposal does not grant the creditors a dividend of at least 50%. In East Germany, this second majority is limited to three-quarters of the claims represented at the vote (sl6 (4) sentence 3 GesO).

Confirmation of the arrangement

Once accepted, the arrangement must be confirmed by the court. The court reaches its decision after hearing the debtor, the Vergleichsverwalter and any committee of creditors (s78 VerglO). The court is obliged to refuse confirmation of the arrangement where (s79 VerglO):

- the debtor has conducted himself dishonestly;

- the procedure has not been properly complied with; or
- the arrangement does not correspond to the collective interests of the creditors.

The consequences of such refusal are referred to at pp196-198 *supra*.

Effect of the confirmed arrangement

The confirmed arrangement is legally valid in favour of and against all creditors, even if they have voted against it or did not take part in the procedure. The creditors' claims are limited to the level of payment provided for in the arrangement. This also applies for any claims against guarantors under the arrangement, *i.e.* third parties who have undertaken to make payment in the event of default on the part of the common debtor (s82 (2) VerglO).

Enforcement procedures can be initiated against the debtor on the basis of the confirmed arrangement by any creditor who is included in the authorised list of creditors (on the basis of the arrangement demand registered therein) just as with any other court judgment upon which enforcement procedures can be commenced (s85 VerglO). Creditors who are not listed must claim against the debtor according to the terms of the arrangement in the event that the debtor does not voluntarily pay up.

The arrangement does not, however, affect the rights of the creditors against joint and several debtors or guarantors of the debtor or rights arising out of:

- securities granted in respect of the claims;
- securities on land or for rent;
- notices of prior title registered as security (see pp193-194 *supra*).

These rights can still be enforced to their full extent.

Each of the creditors affected can individually challenge the arrangement where it has been brought about through misrepresentation and where the creditor through no fault of his own was not in a position to enforce his ground of challenge at the arrangement hearing (s89 VerglO). Any advantage to any particular creditor affected by the arrangement which is withheld from the other creditors would entitle the latter to challenge such advantage.

Under what is known as the "revival clause" ("Wiederauflebensklausel") (s9 VerglO), the moratorium or waiver would lapse against any creditor in respect of whom the debtor is in breach of the terms of the arrangement. This clause basically applies to all time extension and waiver arrangements where nothing is agreed to the contrary in the arrangement. In the case of the liquidation arrangement the clause has limited application because liability lies with the trustee. The debtor is only responsible for ensuring that the figure of 35% is achieved and is therefore not in breach of its duty if the trustee is in breach. The revival of the entire demand therefore does not arise in most cases of liquidation arrangements.

Creditors' involvement and position

It is mainly the creditors who are responsible for the success or failure of an application for the arrangement procedure, since they have the final say at the arrangement hearing as to whether the arrangement proposal is to be accepted or not.

The court can appoint a committee of creditors to support and supervise the Vergleichsverwalter if the size of the debtor company seems to require this. Not only individuals, but also corporate entities can be appointed as members of this committee (s44 VerglO). The court also has sole responsibility for deciding the number of members of the committee and who those members shall be. For instance, the chairman of the works council is often appointed to represent employees. The duty to support and supervise the Vergleichsverwalter is incumbent upon each member of the committee personally and is related to the entire range of duties of the Vergleichsverwalter. Where he has undertaken the collection and distribution of moneys, then the members of the committee of creditors are obliged to ensure that this is done properly.

The members of the creditors' committee are entitled to inspect the books and business documents of the debtor and of the Vergleichsverwalter and to require explanations as appropriate. They must advise the court immediately they become aware of circumstances which would entitle the court to step in, in particular justifying the waiver of limitations on the power of disposal, the closing of the arrangement procedure or the refusal to confirm the arrangement (s45 VerglO).

Powers and duties of the Vergleichsverwalter

The Vergleichsverwalter is a professional person, nominated by the court, who is independent of the creditors and the debtor (s38 VerglO). The court mostly appoints such persons from a relatively small circle of specialist insolvency and arrangement practitioners.

The Vergleichsverwalter has the duty of looking into the commercial situation of the debtor and supervising the management of the debtor company (s39 VerglO), and, for this purpose he is granted a number of rights and duties under s40 VerglO:

- he is entitled to obtain entry to the business premises of the debtor company and to undertake investigations there;
- he may demand access to the company's business books and other documentation;
- he is entitled to be issued with all necessary information.

He must keep the court informed of all important procedures undertaken in connection with the arrangement. At the arrangement hearing he must advise the court of the factual circumstances, in particular of the causes of the commercial collapse of the debtor, the appropriateness of the arrangement proposal and the prospects of the arrangement being fulfilled. In practice, the Vergleichsverwalter usually makes such a report prior to the composition hearing.

The Vergleichsverwalter is under the supervision of the court which is entitled to impose fines on him and to dismiss him from office in the event of severe breaches of his duties (s41 (2) VerglO). He is answerable to all those affected by any failure to fulfil his duties (s42 VerglO).

The issue of liability of a trustee in composition proceedings (Vergleichsverwalter) is submitted to a three-year procedure ("Verfährung") (German Civil Code (BGB) s852, see also BGH Decision of 24 September 1992, ZIP 1992 at 1646).

Management by the Vergleichsverwalter

The legal position of the Vergleichsverwalter, and of the provisional Vergleichsverwalter, is strengthened by the fact that he is responsible for the management of the corporation and is invested with the powers of the directors.

The debtor may enter into transactions which go beyond the normal day-to-day business of the company only with the approval of the Vergleichsverwalter.

Even transactions which are a part of the company's day-to-day business are not to be entered into where the Vergleichsverwalter raises an objection (s57(1) VerglO). Nevertheless, during the arrangement proceedings, the debtor retains the control of the company's assets in both the legal and the technical/ commercial sense. The Vergleichsverwalter may, however, exercise his right of objection to the entering into of transactions and the incurring of consequent obligations where such transactions appear to be incompatible with the efficient administration and the financial situation of the debtor company or with the development of and prospects of success for the arrangement.

Generally speaking, the legal provisions do not give the Vergleichsverwalter any authority to represent the debtor, although the debtor may, if it wishes, issue him with the customary power of attorney. There is one exception to this. The Vergleichsverwalter can demand that only he receive incoming moneys and pay moneys out (s57 (2) VerglO). The purpose of this provision is to avoid cash deals in bad faith on the part of the debtor and the illegal syphoning-off of funds or the taking-out of short-term credit without the approval of the Vergleichsverwalter. In the collection and payment of moneys, the Vergleichsverwalter then acts as the legal representative of the debtor.

Limitations may be imposed on the debtor's power of disposal. This can occur by the court making an order of its own accord or on the application by the Vergleichsverwalter, a member of the creditors' committee or one of the creditors affected by the arrangement (s58 VerglO). However, the commencement of arrangement proceedings itself does not affect the debtor's powers of administration and disposal. The court is deemed to have sufficient grounds for limiting the powers of disposal:

- where this is the only means by which the concurrence of the creditors can be achieved or maintained for agreeing to the arrangement in the justified interests of the creditors as a whole;

- when it is only in this manner that measures undertaken by those disagreeing with the arrangement can be countered; or
- where such is necessary in order to secure the assets in the event of a subsequent liquidation.

Position of officers and shareholders

From the foregoing, it can be seen that the legal positions of the officers and the shareholders of the debtor company are limited, in particular by the following provisions:

- the debtor cannot enter into any transactions which do not form part of the usual day-to-day business of the company without the approval of the Vergleichsverwalter;
- transactions which are a part of the day-to-day business of the company should not be entered into where the Vergleichsverwalter raises an objection thereto;
- the Vergleichsverwalter has the authority to require that he, alone, administer the company's cash transactions;
- the court can impose upon the debtor a limitation on its power of disposal. The debtor can be subjected to a general prohibition of disposal or it can be prohibited from disposing of particular individual assets.

The management of the company is subject to the supervision of the Vergleichsverwalter (see p203 *supra*).

Termination

Dismissal of proceedings

The court must dismiss the arrangement proceedings (s90 VerglO) where:

- prior to a decision being taken about the confirmation of the arrangement, the creditors at the arrangement hearing so request with the same majority as required for an acceptance of the arrangement;
- the total sum of the claims which are subject to the arrangement and which may be judicially enforced is less than DM20,000, without taking into account the waivers provided for in the arrangement;
- up until the fulfilment of the arrangement or of some condition set down therein, the debtor has subjected himself to the supervision of one or several persons stipulated in the arrangement, and who act as agent of the creditors (ss91 to 95 VerglO).

In the last case, the Vergleichsverwalter will usually be the agent referred to. He is appointed at the arrangement hearing by the creditors and the common debtor. He essentially has the rights and duties of the Vergleichsverwalter, already discussed (see p203 *supra*; s92 (1) VerglO).

Continuation by the court

If, as is usually the case, the pre-conditions for a dismissal order are not fulfilled, the arrangement proceedings continue until the Vergleichsverwalter can confirm that the debtor has fulfilled the terms of the arrangement or where the debtor applies for dismissal of the proceedings (in which case it must persuade the court that it has in fact fulfilled its terms (s96 (4) VerglO)).

In the event that the Vergleichsverwalter demonstrates to the court that the arrangement cannot be fulfilled, or should this be evident to the court for some other reason, then the court will of its own accord order the commencement of compulsory liquidation proceedings. The arrangement proceedings terminate immediately upon the making of the compulsory liquidation order (s96 (5) VerglO).

Cessation of the effect of the arrangement

Reference has been made above (p201) to the revival clause, under which the waived part of any demand revives if the debtor is in arrears with instalment payments (s9 VerglO) or in breach of some other term of the composition.

The arrangement becomes entirely ineffective as against all affected creditors if the debtor or its representatives (s14 Penal Code – StGB) are convicted of "fraud leading to bankruptcy" under the appropriate criminal law procedure or if they have deliberately perjured themselves at the arrangement proceedings (s88 VerglO).

Cessation of proceedings

The court can order that the arrangement proceedings cease in certain circumstances. These include:

- where the debtor does not comply with the limitations on its powers of disposal or on its ability to enter into transactions, and its conduct is not excusable;
- where the debtor refuses to allow the Vergleichsverwalter or a member of the committee of creditors access to its books and business documents or refuses to give information or explanations without sufficient reason;
- where at the arrangement hearing the necessary majority for an acceptance of the arrangement proposal is not reached and an application for adjourning the hearing is not lodged or is rejected.

In these circumstances, the court will simultaneously make an order for the commencement of compulsory liquidation proceedings or order that compulsory liquidation proceedings be rejected. Where the commencement of proceedings is rejected, the creditors may pursue their claims by individual enforcement measures. The situation in East Germany is somewhat different in this regard to that in West Germany. In East Germany, the debtor's "justified interests" are better protected, granting it a better chance of maintaining its economic existence.

Subsequent liquidation

Subsequent liquidation, which has already been mentioned (p197 *supra*), is defined as those compulsory liquidation proceedings which are commenced (s102 VerglO):

- where the court refuses to commence arrangement proceedings;
- where the court refuses to grant its confirmation (see pp200-201, *supra*); and
- where the court orders that arrangement proceedings cease.

The limitations on the power of disposal, ordered in the arrangement proceedings, continue to apply in favour of the liquidation creditors in the case of subsequent liquidation proceedings. The costs of the arrangement proceedings are counted as liquidation expenses in the subsequent liquidation proceedings (s105 VerglO).

East Germany

It should be noted that in East Germany the GesO does not differentiate between the concepts of dismissal of proceedings and cessation of proceedings. Instead it uses the concept of "stoppage" ("Einstellung"), a procedure regulated by section 19(1) GesO.

The possible intervention of the "Treuhand"Agency or banks is mentioned in connection with the court's refusal of the opening of proceedings later in this chapter (see p227 *infra*). Such intervention may also serve to interrupt the proceedings, at least to allow the East German undertaking to win time to implement measures designed to allow the continuation of the company and, above all, to preserve jobs. In such circumstances, the court will only countenance stoppage where the institution concerned provides a guarantee in respect of all existing and future obligations. Before reaching a decision, the court will hear the "Treuhand"Agency's views as to the prospects of rehabilitation and will require the presentation of a "rehabilitation concept". The court may order certain additional securities before permitting a stoppage of proceedings.

The involvement of the court, not only in arrangements but also in compulsory liquidation proceedings, is mostly administered by the judge, contrary to the previous situation in the GDR. However, certain tasks can be transferred to the court officer ("Rechtspfleger)"or, where there is no such person (since the office was only introduced in the early part of 1991), to the clerk of court ("Sekretär").

4. Termination of the corporation: voluntary liquidation and compulsory liquidation

The two most important forms of German corporation, the AG and the GmbH, can be terminated by:

- voluntary liquidation ("Liquidation"), regulated in the AG Act (ss264 to 274) and the GmbH Act (ss66 to 73), respectively; and

- compulsory liquidation ("Konkurs") by the court, which is regulated by the KO.

It is important to note that "winding-up" ("Auflösung") in German terminology signifies the point at which liquidation (whether members' voluntary or compulsory) commences. "Termination" is the point at which the company ceases formally to exist, whereupon the company is to be removed from the Commercial Register (Löschung), which act of removal is itself declaratory and not constitutive. The period between the winding-up and the termination is known as "Konkurs" or "Liquidation".

Further, a distinction must be drawn between the procedures under the respective company law provisions and under the compulsory liquidation (KO) provisions.

The most important reasons for winding-up in the case of the AG and the GmbH are regulated in the AG Act and the GmbH Act respectively.

Circumstances leading to winding-up: AG
The following circumstances lead to winding-up (s262 AG Act):

- the expiry of the period stipulated in the articles of association;
- resolution of the shareholders' meeting;
- the commencement of compulsory liquidation proceedings in respect of the assets of the company;
- a court order that the commencement of liquidation proceedings has been rejected due to a lack of assets; and
- an order of the court at which the company is registered to the effect that a deficiency in the articles of association has been established.

In addition, the company can be wound up for other reasons of a nature stemming from the laws affecting AGs or otherwise. Under general AG law, a reason for winding-up can also arise from a condition or conditions contained in the articles of association (see the commentary by Baumbach-Hueck: Aktiengesetz, 262, margin no. 9).

A resolution by the shareholders' meeting for the winding-up of the company requires a majority of at least three-quarters of the share capital represented at the meeting at which the resolution is taken. The articles of association can provide for a larger majority of represented capital and for further requirements (for example, regarding the voting majority or a quorum). Multiple voting rights arising out of shares carrying such rights are consequently of no importance. The sole criterion is, generally, the capital majority. The articles of association may neither limit nor hinder the shareholders' right to wind the company up to any extent greater than that provided for by statute. Therefore, a requirement of unanimity would be just as impermissible as a requirement that a quorum will only be reached when a proportion of the shares is represented which, in practice, is difficult to achieve with the type of company in question.

It is not necessary for the shareholders' resolution to have the winding-up of the company as its main object. It could, for example, also be a resolution providing for a transfer of the registered office of the company to a location abroad. A transfer of the registered office to another country would automatically entail the loss by the company of its legal powers to act and therefore would have as a natural consequence its winding-up.

A resolution to wind up which contravenes the legal provisions (for instance with regard to majority relationships) is not null and void but only voidable (s243(1) AG Act).

Winding-up is of effect upon the coming into effect of the resolution, *i.e.* upon the announcement by the chairman of the meeting. This does not apply where the resolution is effectively made by means of an alteration to the articles of association, *i.e.* an alteration to the period for which the company has been incorporated. The winding-up resolution is effective without the necessity of the one-month period for challenge having expired (s246(1) AG Act).

When winding-up is occasioned by the commencement of compulsory liquidation proceedings over the assets of the company or by the rejection of compulsory liquidation proceedings as a result of a lack of necessary assets, this must be founded on a legal ground of insolvency. In the case of an AG, such grounds are:

- the inability to meet debts arising (s102 KO), *i.e.* an inability on the part of the debtor to settle a significant portion of its short-term debts by reason of a lack of liquid funds; and

- overindebtedness (s207 KO), *i.e.* an excess of liabilities over debts receivable.

In both of the cases of winding-up by reason of the expiry of the period stipulated in the articles of association and by resolution of the shareholders' meeting, the winding-up is to be notified for registration in the Commercial Register by the board of management. Any failure to comply with this duty does not, however, render the winding-up ineffective. In the other modes of winding-up, registration takes place automatically.

AGs can be wound up under the Act Concerning the Termination and Extinction of Companies and Cooperatives of 9 October 1934 ("Löschungsgesetz": Extinction Act) if the company possesses no assets. Winding-up is also a legal consequence of deregistration, *i.e.* removal from the Commercial Register, which is an automatic consequence of an application by the Chamber of Commerce or the German Inland Revenue. The company must be deregistered if, in contravention of its legal duty, it has failed to publish its annual accounts (in a newspaper, as all German AGs are obliged to do) and submit them to the Commercial Register for three consecutive years.

Circumstances leading to winding–up: GmbH
The GmbH can be wound up (s60 GmbH Act) by:

- the expiry of the period provided for in the articles of association;
- resolution of the shareholders: to be passed, this resolution requires, to the extent that nothing to the contrary is provided for in the articles of association, a majority of three-quarters of the votes tendered;
- a successful shareholders' court action for obtaining judicial winding-up ("Auflösungsklage");
- the commencement of members' liquidation proceedings: if proceedings are dismissed after the conclusion of a compulsory arrangement or if, upon the application of the common debtor, such proceedings cease, then the shareholders may resolve upon a continuation of the company;
- order of the court at which the company is registered that it has established the existence of an illegal provision in the articles of association.›

The above legal grounds for winding-up may not be excluded, *e.g.* by the articles of association. The articles may, however, provide for further grounds for winding-up, such as the insolvency of one of the shareholders.

A resolution by the shareholders to wind the company up does not have the effect of altering the articles of association. It does not therefore require to be in a notarially-executed form and can consequently be resolved upon (either verbally or in writing) without adhering to formal requirements. By law, a majority of 75% of the votes tendered is necessary for the resolution to be passed (s60(2) GmbH Act). The articles of association may, however, stipulate that, for example a simple majority shall be sufficient or that even a minority can require winding-up as their right to give notice of their desire to cease their participation in the company ("Kündigungsrecht"). The resolution may also be made more difficult. Unanimity can even be set down as a requirement. The approval of all the shareholders is necessary if the company is incapable of being wound up under the articles.

Where legal action by the shareholders has successfully resulted in obtaining judicial winding-up, the company is wound up by virtue and on the terms of the court order. The claim is made against the GmbH itself and may only be raised by the shareholders. A minority of shareholders can also raise a claim but their shareholdings must, together, amount to at least 10% of the share capital (s61(2) GmbH Act). This percentage figure can be set at a lower figure in the articles but not at a higher figure.

The claim is deemed justified if the achievement of the objects of the company has, over a period, become impossible or when some other material reason exists for winding-up. Such a material reason could be where continuation of the business of the GmbH appears to be impossible for commercial reasons or when there are personal differences amongst the shareholders. The claim for winding-up is, however, only a last resort in such cases and particularly strict standards are laid down for this claim to be successful.

Unlike the case of the bankruptcy or compulsory/members' liquidation of one of the shareholders, which in principle does not affect the continued existence of the GmbH, the opening of compulsory liquidation proceedings over the GmbH itself will automatically wind the company up. The inability to pay debts as they become due or overindebtedness also has, as a consequence, the commencement of compulsory liquidation proceedings in the case of the GmbH.

Winding Up Proceedings under the InsO

Where winding-up occurs, the administrator must realise the bankrupt's assets as soon as possible. Continuation of the debtor's business will only be possible with court consent. The winding up is basically carried out in the manner set out in the KO.

Members' voluntary liquidation

Purpose and effect

The aim of this form of liquidation is the termination of the company coupled with its removal from the register. The procedure applies equally to AGs and GmbHs. The resolution voluntarily to liquidate the company will be made at a shareholders' meeting, which is normally called by the directors, but which can be called in any way approved by the appropriate Act. No court application is necessary. Once liquidation has been chosen, this is the sole object of the company. In the interests of third parties, termination does not take immediate effect since it is assumed that a company registered in the Commercial Register continues validly to exist up until the point at which it is removed from the Register. Thus, the identity of the company as an independent legal person continues during the liquidation process.

The board of management (AG) or directors (GmbH), the supervisory board (if applicable) and the shareholders' meeting continue to exercise their activities with this new aim of terminating the company. The shareholders retain their full rights and the company retains its capacity to be a party to court proceedings until the extinction of the company from the Commercial Register upon the conclusion of the liquidation process. The company can therefore continue to raise and defend actions in so far as this is required with regard to the liquidation. Legal relationships between the company and third parties are not affected by the liquidation. In the case of service contracts and, in particular, employment contracts, which in principle continue to exist, members' liquidation can provide a material reason for giving notice, in particular where the liquidation is carried out in conjunction with the closure of the business.

It should be noted that members' voluntary liquidation is a voluntary act on the part of the shareholders. It does not require insolvency, as such, as a prerequisite. There is no involvement on the part of the court, except in respect of questions which may arise as to the appointment of liquidators, or challenges to the acts of the liquidators. If, however, the company is insolvent, the procedure will be halted and the regular compulsory liquidation proceedings will be instituted in the normal fashion.

Pre-liquidation considerations

Members' voluntary liquidation is only possible in the absence of circumstances which would oblige the company to be wound up under a compulsory liquidation. The liquidators ("Abwickler/Liquidatoren") are normally the members of the executive (*i.e.* board of management (s265(1) AG Act) or directors (s66(1) GmbH Act)). It is, however, possible for the articles of association or the shareholders' meeting to appoint other persons (such as accountants) as liquidators or for such provision in the articles to be departed from, upon a resolution of the shareholders, passed by simple majority and resolved according to their absolute discretion. In such a case, prior to such appointment, the management must examine and verify which of the possible appointees has the best knowledge of the business in which the company is involved or has other necessary qualifications. Corporate bodies can also be liquidators. There may be one or more liquidators at any time.

The liquidators assume the position of an auditor or investigatory accountant on the basis of a business management contract. This also in principle applies to the executive unless the prior management agreement also applies to liquidations. The terms of the business management contract should be negotiated and set down prior to the commencement of the liquidation.

The members of the supervisory board (if applicable) and the shareholders should weigh up whether and how they wish to exercise their influence on the appointment of the liquidators. In the case of the AG, upon the application of the supervisory board (or of a minority of shareholders whose shares collectively amount to 5% of the issued share capital or a nominal sum of DM1 million), the court must appoint new liquidators and remove the incumbent liquidators where there are shown to be material grounds to do so (s265(3) AG Act). In the case of the GmbH, upon the application of a minority of shareholders holding at least 10% of the share capital, the Lower Regional Court ("Amtsgericht") at which the company is registered must, where there are material reasons, order the appointment of new liquidators and simultaneous removal of the incumbent liquidators (s66(2) GmbH Act). This right of application is a minority shareholders' right and cannot be excluded by the company's articles. It can, however, be reinforced, for instance, by means of a stipulation in the articles of association that a minority of shareholders holding only 5% of the issued share capital may lodge such an application.

In the interpretation of the term "material reason", each case must be looked at on its own merits. Culpability is not necessary. It may be, for example, that an existing liquidator is, by reason of the circumstances, unsuitable for the particular liquidation. The court will only make an order stipulating the allowable expenses and remuneration of the liquidators if it has been shown that the company and the liquidators appointed by the court are not able to reach agreement in that regard.

Procedure

General

Voluntary liquidation proceeds on the basis of a resolution passed by the shareholders at a meeting called by the executive. An application is then made to the court for the commencement of the procedure and appointment of the liquidators.

The implementation of the liquidation is governed by general provisions insofar as nothing to the contrary is provided for by law or required for the purpose of the liquidation. For instance, even after the resolution to terminate the company has been passed, it can change its name and, by altering its articles, undertake an increase or decrease in capital, as long as these measures are seen to be taken within the context of the liquidation.

The liquidators assume the position of the legal representatives of the company. They undertake the conversion of the assets into cash. The procedure commences by drawing up a liquidation opening balance sheet and closes with the liquidation closing balance sheet.

It is the liquidators' duty to call upon the creditors of the company to notify their claims, under reference to the members' liquidation of the company. The request must be published three times in the appropriate daily newspaper. The law does not provide for a particular period between publications but, taking into account the purpose of the regulation, such period must be reasonable. Furthermore, the liquidators must draw up an opening balance sheet and a report explaining the details of this balance sheet as at the commencement of the members' liquidation, and a set of annual accounts and a management report at the close of every year thereafter. The opening balance sheet constitutes the basis for the bookkeeping of the liquidators during their period of office up until the conclusion of the members' liquidation and the termination of the company, which is a corollary thereto. The opening balance sheet should be tailored towards the amended aims of the company, the conversion of the assets into cash, the satisfaction of the creditors and the definitive disposal of the assets. It should contain submissions in respect of the value of the company's:

- real estate;
- receivables and liabilities;
- cash in hand; and
- other individual assets.

It should contain conclusions which present the relationship between the assets and the debit items. The opening balance sheet must always be drawn up, even where annual accounts have been produced only a short time previously. The provisions relating to annual accounts and the auditing thereof (ss242 *et seq*, 264 *et seq* and 316 *et seq* HGB) apply equally to the opening balance sheet. The same applies to the provisions regarding public disclosure (ss 325 to 329 HGB).

Special provisions applying to the AG

In the case of the AG, the opening balance sheet and the individual annual accounts are not, as is normally the case, confirmed by the board of management and the supervisory board, but by the shareholders' meeting, which also passes judgment on the way in which matters have been handled by the liquidators and the supervisory board (s270(2) AG Act). The supervisory board is therefore excluded from this important area of the members' liquidation.

Any assets remaining after satisfaction of the company's obligations are distributed amongst the shareholders (s271 AG Act). Prior to this distribution, there must be a delay of one year following the third call to the creditors to submit claims (s272 AG Act). Moreover, the shareholders are all to be treated on an equal basis, proportional to their shareholdings (depending on the rights accorded, for instance to holders of preference shares or nominative shares) (s271(2) AG Act).

In the event of a members' liquidation caused by the expiry of the period specified in the articles of association or following a resolution of the shareholders' meeting, the shareholders' meeting can resolve to continue the company for as long as the distribution of the assets amongst the shareholders has not yet commenced (s274 AG Act). This resolution requires a majority comprising at least three-quarters of the issued share capital represented at the meeting at which the resolution is proposed. The liquidators must notify the continuation of the company for registration in the Commercial Register. At the time that this notification is given, it must be evident that the distribution of assets to the shareholders has not yet commenced.

Creditors' involvement and position

AG

The creditors of the company rank higher than the shareholders when the distributions are made from the assets of the company. The assets must be distributed in the following order:

1. in satisfaction of registered creditors or other creditors who are known but have not registered and whose claims cannot objectively be disputed (contingent creditors' claims being evaluated at the sum which would apply to the non-contingent claim (s154(1) KO));
2. in making deposits into court in so far as there is a right thereto under the Civil Code for creditors who are known but have not registered and who would otherwise not be satisfied;
3. in making payments under securities in the case of claims which are disputed but which are to be adjusted and in respect of which there is furthermore no entitlement or obligation to make a payment into court;
4. to the shareholders according to the number and type of shares each holds.

The creditors are offered protection first of all by the publication of the fact that the company is being voluntarily wound up. This publication takes place:

- by registration of the resolution to liquidate the company in the Commercial Register and the publication of the fact of that registration;
- the registration of the liquidators in the Commercial Register (s266 AG Act);
- the triple call to the creditors to lodge their claims (s267 AG Act).

The creditors are also protected by the prevention of any distribution of assets until certain requirements are fulfilled or complied with, for example:

- the distribution of any assets to the shareholders can only be commenced after the expiry of one year following the third call to the creditors (ss267, 272 AG Act). This preventative time period is also an exclusionary time period since, once it has expired, demands from unsatisfied or unknown creditors are held to be null and void;
- deposits into court, as mentioned above;
- payments under securities, as mentioned above.

The creditors are also entitled to challenge actions taken by the liquidators where they consider these actions to be unnecessary for the satisfaction of the creditors' claims.

GmbH

Satisfaction of creditors
The claims of the creditors must be fully and properly satisfied within the framework of the members' liquidation.

Since the creditors do not have recourse to the shareholders personally, but can only claim against the assets of the GmbH, the legislature has regulated the protection of creditors in the case of a members' liquidation of a GmbH particularly carefully. The claims are submitted to the liquidators under no particularly regulated procedure. The merits of the claim are evaluated by the liquidators and in the event of dispute it is up to the creditor to raise a court action to prove his claim.

The distribution to shareholders may not take place either before the creditors' claims are paid or secured or prior to the expiry of a period of one year following the third publication of an advertisement calling for the lodging of claims by creditors (s73 GmbH Act). During this period, there is a stop on all payments out of the company except in respect of claims made by them in their capacity as "third party creditors". The members' liquidation continues during the "stop year" ("Sperrjahr") and, during this period, the company may not be extinguished. Exceptionally, a court may permit the company to be extinguished where the liquidators can show that the assets of the company have been exhausted.

During the stop year, the liquidators must satisfy the known creditors, irrespective of whether the creditors have formally notified their debts to the liquidators or not. All undisputed payments due must, therefore, be paid even if the creditors only register following the expiry of the stop year.

Should any known creditor not register and should the legal conditions exist whereby a deposit into court can be made (ss372 *et seq* BGB), then the appropriate sum is to be deposited in favour of the creditor. As an alternative, security may be found for the sum. This must also be done if the claim is disputed or is not due or where it is not at that time possible to ascertain its amount.

There is no hierarchy of creditors. Their claims are satisfied in the order in which they are notified. There is no statutory requirement that they be dealt with on an equal footing, as in the case of insolvency proceedings.

Claims for damages

The creditors can claim damages where the liquidators have acted illegally satisfied the company's debts (s73(3) GmbH Act). This might occur where known creditors are not paid or where their claims have been ascertained but, nevertheless, following the expiry of the stop year, the company's assets have been distributed to the shareholders. Such a distribution or transfer of company's assets would be legally void. Under the mandatory legal provisions, the liquidators are under a duty towards the GmbH, but not to the creditors, to pay damages.

A claim for damages can still be made on the basis of a resolution of the shareholders' meeting, even after the assets have been distributed and the GmbH has been extinguished from the Commercial Register. The claim is for reimbursement of any sums which have been distributed contrary to law and is time-barred after five years (s43(4) GmbH Act). Where the liquidators have acted culpably, they are jointly and severally liable to the company.

The disadvantaged creditors can force the GmbH, to make a claim for damages against the liquidators since they themselves have no direct claim against the liquidators or any individual shareholders.

It is a matter of legal dispute whether the liquidators, having distributed damages to the creditors, can make a further claim against the shareholders who have been unjustly enriched as a consequence of the distribution.

Powers and duties of the liquidators

AG

The liquidators represent the company judicially and extra-judicially (s269(1) AG Act) and, to this extent, occupy the position of the board of management. The authority on the part of the liquidators to represent the company cannot be limited.

All business letters from the company to a particular addressee must state the legal form and the registered office of the company, the court at which the company is registered and the company number. In addition, attention must be drawn to the fact that the company is in members' liquidation. Instead of listing the members of the board of management, the names of the liquidators and the chairman of the supervisory board must be stated (s268(4) AG Act).

The liquidators are obliged:

- to take under their control all the assets of the company (s117 KO);
- to terminate pending transactions;
- to call in receivable debts;
- to convert all other assets into cash; and
- to satisfy the claims of the creditors (s268(1) AG Act).

The liquidators are invested with the rights and duties of the board of management within the company's area of business, and insofar as required by the members' liquidation, may enter into new transactions. Like the board of management, the liquidators are subject to the supervision of the supervisory board (s268(2) AG Act).

The liquidators' duty to draw up an opening balance sheet has already been discussed (see p212 *supra*).

GmbH

The liquidators take up the position of the legal representatives of the company. They must fulfil their functions both in their internal company relationship and towards third parties. They represent the GmbH jointly as collective representatives in the event that nothing to the contrary is provided for in the articles of association or in the terms of their appointment. The liquidators (who, in most cases, are the directors, see p217 *infra*) are therefore entitled to represent the company in the same manner as they were when entitled to represent the company as directors. Any possible deviation from the representative authority provided by law, which can also be undertaken by means of an alteration to the articles of association, must be registered in the Commercial Register.

All acts undertaken by the liquidators must be as advantageous to the implementation of the liquidation as possible. In particular, the liquidators must terminate pending transactions, fulfil obligations which have not yet been satisfied and convert the assets of the company into cash. In so doing, they are entitled to act according to their own discretion. It is also permissible for them to sell the undertaking, including its name (although the company must first change its name by means of an alteration to the articles of association).

The liquidators must notify the commencement of the winding-up of the company to the Commercial Register and publicise the winding-up three times in those publications which are provided for this purpose. At the same time, they must call upon the creditors of the company to register their claims (s65(2) GmbH Act). At the commencement of the liquidation, the liquidators must draw up a liquidation opening balance sheet and an annual balance sheet thereafter (s71 GmbH Act). The liquidators have a duty to revalue balance sheet positions (where necessary), since the liquidation balance sheets have a different function to normal annual balance sheets, not being drawn up for the purpose of showing business results but simply to show the assets and liabilities of the company. The closing balance sheet to be drawn up by the liquidators must be confirmed by the shareholders.

In implementing the members' liquidation, the liquidators must comply with statute law, the articles of association and any resolutions by the shareholders. For instance, particular sales may be prohibited or required to be undertaken by them or they may be required to carry out the liquidation in a particular manner. In cases of doubt, the liquidators must obtain the approval of the shareholders' meeting.

In the event that the liquidators are in breach of duty, the effects of that breach vary according to the person to whom the duty is owed:

- with regard to the company, the liquidators are liable as directors;
- in their relationships with third parties, it is questionable whether the company is bound by the acts of the liquidators, since there are limitations on their powers in representing the company, resulting from their appointed tasks in respect of the liquidation. On one view, all legal transactions by the liquidators with third parties must be regarded as being legally valid in so far as the third party was unaware and could not be expected to have known of the individual breaches of duty.

Management/supervision

Steps taken on appointment

The liquidators are appointed upon commencement of the winding-up, the company thereafter entering into the period known as liquidation ("Liquidation" or "Abwicklung") until finally being terminated. It is the members of the board of management who are the liquidators in the case of the AG (s265(1) AG Act) and the directors in the case of the GmbH (s66(1) GmbH Act), unless otherwise stipulated (s265(2) *et seq.* AG Act; s66 GmbH Act). The appointment of the liquidators, the extent of their authority and any changes must be notified to the Commercial Register (s266 AG Act; s67(1) GmbH Act). Upon appointment, the liquidators must publicise the winding-up of the company and invite creditors to notify their claims; this is done by advertising three times in the appointed newspapers (s267 AG Act; s65 GmbH Act).

Administration in office

The liquidators are responsible for terminating pending transactions, calling in sums receivable, converting the assets into cash and, where required in the interests of the liquidation, entering into new transactions (s268(1) AG Act; s70 GmbH Act). The liquidators assume the rights and duties of the executive and are subject to the supervision of the supervisory board, where applicable, in their administrative acts (s268(2) AG Act; ss71, 37(1) GmbH Act). This means that they are, *inter alia*, under a duty to report in respect of basic questions concerning the future management of the company, the on-going business and the situation of the company as well as other material events affecting the company. Correspondence issued by the liquidators must make sufficient reference to the liquidation of the company (s268 (4) AG Act; s71 (5) GmbH Act). The liquidators must draw up an opening balance sheet as at the date of appointment and yearly balance sheets and management reports thereafter. These do not require to be audited if the court is satisfied that the financial position of the company is clear and such is not required in the interests of the creditors and shareholders (s270(3) AG Act; s71 (3) GmbH Act).

Contractual position

The liquidators are the legal representatives of the company both in judicial causes and extra-judicially. The ostensible authority of the liquidators is unlimited as regards third parties. Thus, they have full discretion in carrying out the duties imposed upon them by s268(1) AG Act or s70 GmbH Act. These duties do not entitle the liquidators to terminate contracts which would result in the company being in breach of its obligations. All contracts legally entered into must be fulfilled in an orderly fashion. Pending court actions must be followed to their conclusion; patent or trademark applications, applications for licences and permissions, and other similar administrative procedures must also be pursued. (It is worth noting that patent applications do not take the form of a court action in Germany). Where notice of termination can be served, this should be done in a reasonable manner (as, for instance, in the case of leases). As stated above, new contracts may be entered into where these would benefit the winding-up process. Claims based on any other ground, whether in contract, tort/delict or arising from public law, must be reasonably pursued in the interests of the company.

Realisation of assets

The liquidators must turn the assets of the company into cash. The law does not state how this should be done, and the liquidators therefore have an absolute discretion. They may even sell the business as a going concern. The realisation must encompass all assets and not merely those which will be sufficient to satisfy the creditors' claims. The academic authorities are split as to whether creditors/ shareholders may be satisfied in kind. The prevailing view is that, exceptionally, this may occur. The minority view states that a unanimous resolution by all shareholders would be required, and it appears that this latter view has recently been gaining support.

Employees

Employees' contracts of employment remain intact in a liquidation until notice is served in the normal fashion, the contracts expire, or the company is terminated, in which case the contracts are brought to an end. Where termination of the company is contemplated, the works council, where there is one, must be informed and a "social plan" drawn up providing for appropriate compensation, which then ranks in the insolvency as a creditor's debt; immediate termination is an option open only to the employee.

Taxation

Under section 104 "Abgabenordnung" ("AO" – Taxation Code), the liquidator is personally liable for fulfilling the duty of payment of taxes incurred during the course of the insolvency proceedings. The liquidator must fulfil the tax liabilities in relation to the assets administered by him which would have been borne by the common debtor had the liquidation not been commenced. Tax claims arising prior to the commencement of the liquidation must be notified for inclusion on the official list of creditors by the Tax Office. The principal risk therefore relates to taxes becoming due following the commencement of proceedings.

The corporation will continue to be assessed to corporation tax after the commencement of proceedings, but only as long as the business is continued by the liquidator. During the course of the liquidation proceedings, a point will come at which the company is deemed to have ceased trading and the realisation of the assets begun and any profits realised from the sale of assets after this point will also be liable to corporation tax. The basis of the calculation of the profit is the value of the individual assets as given in the last accounts prepared for corporation tax purposes.

In the case of value added tax, this continues to be payable in the normal manner during the continuation of the company's business and is also due where the liquidator arranges for the auction of assets which are subject to the liquidation via a bailiff, a situation which would otherwise not occur in the case of sales by a bailiff under the compulsory enforcement of judgments. In the event that the entire company is sold, although the purchaser assumes liability for the land acquisition tax ("Grunderwerbsteuer"), the value added tax liability for any assets sold with the business is borne by the corporation itself, failing any agreement to the contrary. As in the case of corporation tax, it is the liquidator who is personally liable for all value added tax declarations and payments.

Pay-as-you-earn tax in respect of employees retained during the continuance of the corporation is also the personal responsibility of the liquidator.

Distribution

The distribution of the assets is undertaken by the liquidators, first and foremost, in satisfaction of the company's obligations. Thereafter, in the case of the AG, the remainder is divided amongst the shareholders such that first, the paid-up capital is repaid, and the excess distributed in relation to the nominal value of the issued shares. Where the funds are not sufficient to cover the paid-up capital, the loss is to be borne by the shareholders in proportion to the capital paid in (and not to the nominal share value) (s271 AG Act). The precise mode of distribution is not regulated by the Act; since it is highly likely in the case of an AG that the shares will be bearer shares, notices will normally be posted in the appointed newspapers publicising the distribution. Payment will in practice only be made against delivery of the share certificates, although this has no legal basis. Furthermore, a register of payments will be kept so that restitution claims may be made if it transpires that there has been some procedural or legal error made in the calculation of the distributions to be made. Shares held by the company itself are not entitled to a distribution. Additionally, the articles of association may provide for distribution rights which depart from the statutory norms.

Under the GmbH Act, the assets are to be distributed amongst the shareholders in proportion to the size of the relative shareholdings. However, it is permissible for the articles of association to stipulate some other form of distribution (s 72 GmbH Act).

Position of shareholders

AG

The assets of the company which remain after the adjustment of the obligations are distributed amongst the shareholders. Deviations from this principle may be provided for in the articles of association or by the shareholders' meeting via a corresponding provision in the articles or by all parties concerned acting collectively.

The shareholders may contest the implementation of seemingly unfavourable liquidation measures through their power, to apply for the existing liquidators to be removed by the court and for new liquidators to be appointed.

Apart from these protective measures, the shareholders' involvement is in respect of their claim to an equal pro rata distribution.

Where the distribution made to a particular shareholder has been incorrect or there has been a failure to make such distribution, the shareholder may claim against the company for payment. Since this is essentially a creditor's right being exercised by the shareholder, the liquidators and the supervisory board are liable to him as though he were a creditor. It is sometimes considered that although the claim is made against the company in the first instance, a claim may also validly be made against the other shareholders who have benefited from the incorrect distribution.

GmbH

The shareholders may both nominate and remove the liquidators (see p211 *supra*). They may also by resolution stipulate the manner in which the liquidation is to be undertaken, generally or in particular.

No further claims to profits on the part of the shareholders may be made as from the commencement of the liquidation. Claims for profits arising during the period preceding liquidation, on the other hand, remain enforceable. A distinction must be drawn between:

- claims to dividends which were confirmed prior to the commencement of the liquidation. They may be distributed prior to the expiry of the stop year (see p214 *supra*); and

- claims to profits which arose prior to the commencement of the liquidation, but which were not, at that time, confirmed. These may be taken into account only once the final distribution is made.

The shareholders have a claim against the GmbH for a distribution of the liquidation dividend to which they are entitled according to the amount of shares that they hold. The claim for a distribution becomes due as soon as the stop year has expired and the creditors have been satisfied.

The distribution is made according to the proportions which the relative shareholdings bear to one another. The articles of association may provide for a different mode of distribution (s72 GmbH Act). For instance, they may stipulate that the distribution be made not according to capital share but equally amongst all the shareholders, or that individual shareholdings shall be entitled to a higher liquidation dividend.

Such provisions must be contained in the articles of association and can be inserted after the creation of the company by means of an alteration to the articles. Since this is an inalienable membership right exercisable in the context of a legitimate dividend payment, any later alteration to the articles would require the unanimous approval of all shareholders concerned. The distribution must be made in cash, unless the articles of association stipulate some other means, or that the distribution be fully or partially made in kind.

Dissolution

The company is dissolved as a consequence of the distribution of its assets. The dissolution of the company must be registered in the Commercial Register. Such registration is only declaratory, the company being dissolved the moment all its assets have been distributed.

Where assets of the company are discovered following dissolution, then the liquidation is deemed not to have concluded and new liquidators must be appointed by the company or, if applicable, by the court if the old liquidators have resigned from office in the interim.

The liquidators are responsible for maintaining the books and documents of the company and these must be retained for a period of ten years. The shareholders and their legal successors in title have a right to inspect the books. Creditors may be empowered by the court to look into the documents of the company provided they are able to prove a legal interest.

Compulsory liquidation

The compulsory liquidation of corporations is not specifically regulated by the KO. However, in general terms, the same provisions apply to both AGs and GmbHs. In addition, the AG and GmbH Acts contain a few provisions relating to compulsory liquidation proceedings (ss262 to 263 AG Act; ss63, 64 and 84 GmbH Act). These concern the duty to apply for compulsory liquidation and breaches of duty on the part of the executive in the case of the company's becoming unable to meet its debts as they arise or overindebtedness (where the volume of the assets is less than the amount of the debts of the company whenever the debts are due).

Purpose and effect

The procedure described on pp210-211 *supra* differs from compulsory liquidation, which is a court procedure in the Lower Regional Court ("Amtsgericht"), in which the compulsory sale of the entire assets of the common debtor is designed to satisfy all the personal creditors on a pro rata basis. The purpose of compulsory liquidation is therefore to give the creditors an equal (but only partial) fulfilment of their claims.

Voluntary liquidation proceedings can become compulsory liquidation proceedings where one of the circumstances justifying such compulsory liquidation arises. The application, in such a case, must be filed by the liquidators, or can be filed by any creditor or shareholder.

The common debtor is the company as a legal person. As already discussed (see pp210-211 *supra*), the dissolution of the company is set in motion by means of the commencement of compulsory liquidation proceedings over its assets, but the dissolution does not take place immediately and there is no immediate loss of legal personality. The company continues to exist for the purpose of implementing the compulsory liquidation. The company's organs remain in position. Indeed, the position of the management is not taken by any Konkursverwalter and, accordingly, the authority of the common debtor is exercised by the management. The managers are also subject to the duties imposed upon the common debtor. Where the company is already in members' liquidation when compulsory liquidation proceedings are commenced, it is the liquidators who assume the rights and duties of the common debtor.

Pre-application considerations

An application for compulsory liquidation may be lodged by a creditor of the corporation and, where it is insolvent, must be lodged by the corporation itself. In all practical senses, the only ground upon which a creditor is able to lodge an application is in the case of the company's inability to meet debts arising (as opposed to overindebtedness), which it would evidence by means of a certificate executed by a bailiff that payment has been refused on an enforceable deed or judgment. The application must be made to the Lower Regional Court ("Amtsgericht") for the district in which the defendant company has its registered office. With respect to an application by the company itself, consideration must be given as to when the application should be made and the choice of the Konkursverwalter.

Time for lodging insolvency application; rescue packages

According to the view of the Federal Supreme Court ("Bundesgerichtshof"), the management of a company is not obliged immediately to lodge a compulsory liquidation or arrangement application upon establishing that the company is insolvent. The management must, rather, only act without culpable delay. This provides the management with the authority and, where applicable, even the duty to investigate and decide whether other less decisive measures would be preferable to compulsory liquidation proceedings to avoid any deterioration in the situation of the company, its creditors or the general interests of the community. The members of the management must, in reaching their decision, regard the position of the company objectively, having as their standard the duty of care which would be exercised by a proper and conscientious manager.

The legal duty to lodge an application for compulsory liquidation does not at the same time impose a duty on the management to attempt to implement a rescue package for the company, even if this is possible, in order to protect the interests of the creditors. This duty to rescue only exists within the internal company relationship as a part of the general duty of care owed by the management to the company itself. Having said that, the breach of such a duty can lead to the management being held liable by a court to pay damages to the company.

Where the company is insolvent, the AG and GmbH Acts stipulate that the executive or the liquidators, if applicable, must apply for the commencement of compulsory liquidation proceedings or judicial composition proceedings without culpable delay but not later than three weeks after the point in time at which the company has become unable to meet its debts arising or overindebted (s92(2) AG Act; s64(1) GmbH Act, cf. pp245-246 and 247 *infra*). Should they fail in this duty, they are personally liable under both civil and criminal law. It is a matter of dispute whether efforts to rescue the company are sufficient to justify an extension of this time limit beyond the three-week period. The Federal Supreme Court has only confirmed that the company's representatives are not prevented from investigating extra-judicial possibilities of rescuing the company within the legal period for application and, in this manner, of remedying the factors leading to the insolvency of the company (BGHZ 75, 96, 108).

There is a school of thought that a company cannot truly be said to be insolvent where rescue efforts are entered into which have the effect of stabilising the undertaking, so demonstrating that the "insolvency" was in fact only a cash flow problem or a case of temporary indebtedness. However, considerable dangers exist for creditors and third parties entering into legal transactions with the company if the company continues to trade despite the fact that it is insolvent and this, in itself, is an argument against any extension of the application period beyond the legal maximum.

In the case of the GmbH, the application to the court may be lodged by means of a writ in the appropriate form together with any appropriate evidence of insolvency, such as a bailiff's certificate of non-payment under an enforceable writ or judgment. The application may be lodged by the creditors, the directors or the liquidators (under a members' liquidation) (s63 (2) GmbH Act), but not the shareholders, even where there is only a sole shareholder who is not a director, and no application may be made by any generally authorised representative of the company acting under a power of "Prokura" (general commercial power of representation).

Choice of Konkursverwalter
Upon the commencement of compulsory liquidation proceedings, the court no-

minates the Konkursverwalter. At the meeting of creditors following the nomination of this official , the creditors can elect some other person in place of the Konkursverwalter nominated by the court. Interested creditors should therefore consider in good time whether they would prefer some other Konkursverwalter to that appointed by the court and should procure the necessary majority for the resolution. The court can, however, refuse the nomination of the elected Konkursverwalter.

Procedure

General

The KO does not contain any comprehensive regulation of the compulsory liquidation procedure for AGs or GmbHs but only provides special provisions (ss207, 208 KO read together with s63(2) GmbH Act). The general law relating to compulsory liquidation is, therefore, essentially applicable to compulsory liquidations in the case of corporations, although certain special considerations must be noted. The application may be lodged by any creditor, members of the supervisory board or liquidators under a voluntary liquidation (s208 KO).

The application for insolvency may be filed by any creditor (who would then become an insolvency creditor), employees, agents, beneficiaries of pension schemes and institutions entitled to the receipt of social security contributions under certain specific conditions (s103 KO), or even, in certain circumstances, by the company itself. The application for compulsory liquidation may be rejected, for example, where there are insufficient assets to cover the anticipated costs of procedure. Special considerations apply in the case of the rejection of compulsory liquidation in East Germany (see p227 *infra*).

The insolvency court opens the proceedings with an order as to whether the company is insolvent either through an inability to meet debts as they arise or through overindebtedness (s207 KO). Legal opinion is divided, but the prevailing view is that there is a two-step procedure for establishing overindebtedness (cf. Kuhn-Uhlenbruk, Konkursordnung, 10th Edn., §. 207, margin nos. 7 *et seq*):

- first, an arithmetical calculation of the liquid value of the corporation is made;
- secondly, the figure arrived at is adjusted by taking into consideration the company's cash-flow and its viability which justifies a valuation as a going concern.

The overindebtedness is particularised in a special balance sheet. It is the duty of the applicant to persuade the court of the justifiability of commencing the proceedings, for instance, by production of a bailiff's certificate regarding non-payment under an enforceable judgment or deed.

When it makes the order for the opening of proceedings, the insolvency court nominates a Konkursverwalter, fixes a date for the first meeting of creditors, stipulates the period within which claims must be notified and sets the date of the examination hearing (s110 KO).

As a consequence of the commencement of proceedings, the assets of the company are effectively confiscated by the court with the following effects:

- only the Konkursverwalter, and not the common debtor, may administer and dispose of the insolvency assets (s6 KO);
- any new legal transactions entered into by the common debtor in relation to the insolvency assets are null and void as against the insolvency creditors (s7 KO);
- performance under a contract undertaken by a contracting party only releases that party under the contract when the performance itself becomes incorporated within the insolvency assets (s8 KO) and it is not proved that, at the time of performance, the contracting party knew of the commencement of proceedings. The similar rule in East Germany (s7(4) GesO) does not delve so deeply into the question of the state of the contracting party's knowledge, but simply differentiates between performance completed prior to publication of the court order commencing the proceedings and those undertaken thereafter;
- rights to assets which are covered by the compulsory liquidation of the company can no longer effectively be acquired even if the acquisition does not result as a consequence of a legal transaction entered into on the part of the common debtor;
- in mutual transactions which have not yet been fulfilled, the Konkursverwalter has a choice as to whether or not he wishes to assume the debtor's obligations under the contract (s17 KO);
- individual enforcement procedures already in place cease to be effective and no such procedures may be effected (s14 KO).

The assets which are covered by the liquidation are all the assets of the corporation which may be subjected to enforcement procedures and which belong to the company as at the point at which the proceedings are opened. Included are:

- claims on the part of the company against the shareholders;
- claims against members of the management and their representatives;
- claims against members of the supervisory board;
- claims arising from the liability of the shareholders and/or the auditors for the formation of the company;
- claims arising from the exercise of undue influence over the company. In this respect, anyone who deliberately exercises his influence over the company in order to force a member of the executive or of the supervisory board or any generally authorised representative of the company to act to the detriment of the company or its shareholders is liable to the company to reimburse any damages arising from such action;
- claims against the liquidators;

- particular claims against affiliated companies, including claims against the parent company or against the legal representatives of the parent company;
- claims for the return of assets recovered as a result of the exercise of the power to set aside pre-liquidation transactions.

The assets include not only the fixed and financial assets over which a security may be granted, but also other rights, such as the name of the company, registered trademarks, life-rents and other subjective personal rights which can be disposed of together with the undertaking or business activities. If the name of the corporation is in the form of a personal name and if it contains the name of one of the shareholders, then it is still part of the assets notwithstanding the fact that no security can be granted over it.

The creditors entitled to participate in the compulsory liquidation are those who, at the commencement of the compulsory liquidation proceedings, have a claim founded in law against the assets of the common debtor (cf. pp227-228 *infra*).

There are preferences for certain compulsory liquidation claims (s61 **KO**), ranking order as follows:

- claims arising within the period of one year prior to the commencement of insolvency and due to:
- – employees, in respect of salary
- – employees, in respect of competition agreements
- – trade representatives, in respect of remuneration and commission, under certain conditions
- – beneficiaries under occupational pension schemes
- – statutory authorities charged with the administration of social security contributions
  to the extent that these are not incurred after the commencement of insolvency under the instructions of the Konkursverwalter;
- taxes and public charges becoming due in the year prior to insolvency;
- claims due to churches, schools, public associations and statutory fire insurance institutions arising during the year prior to insolvency;
- claims by members of the medical, veterinary, paramedical and pharmaceutical professions under the statutory scales, arising during the year prior to insolvency;
- claims by dependants, under certain conditions.

Thereafter, all other insolvency claims rank equally.

In order for a claim to be taken into account in the liquidation, it must be notified for inclusion in the list of liquidation claims ("Konkurstabelle"). This list shows all liquidation claims against the company, making reference to the creditor, the legal basis of the claims, the sum of the claims and any preference and proof (ss. 138 to 140 **KO**). In West Germany, the claims are notified to the court's business section, in East Germany to the Konkursverwalter (s5 **GesO**). The time for lodging claims is fixed at between two weeks and three months following the commencement of proceedings by the court.

The claims are discussed at the examination hearing and the results of these discussions are noted in the list of claims (ss141, 145 KO).

East Germany
In East Germany, the commencement of compulsory liquidation proceedings must be publicised and specifically notified to the relevant Chamber of Commerce, the debtor's credit institutions, the Commercial Register, the Land Register ("Grundbuchamt") and the Register of Trade Memberships ("Vereinigungsregister"), in order to prevent third parties dealing with the company from maintaining they acted in good faith on the basis of ignorance (s6 GesO).

The commencement of compulsory liquidation proceedings in East Germany is susceptible to rejection in a number of situations which do not apply in the west, for instance, where professional advice from an independent source is offered showing a guarantee that the circumstances otherwise warranting insolvency can be made good (s4(2), 2nd alternative, GesO). Rejection due to a lack of assets is also possible in East Germany (s4(2), 1st alternative, GesO). Even after the application has been filed and before a decision has been reached by the court, an East German company which has been formed from one of the former GDR entities has a number of rescue opportunities available to it which are not at the disposal of West German companies, including public subsidies and grants, in particular from the "Treuhand" and, in general, from banks.

The claims of workers in East Germany are somewhat stronger than in West Germany, taking a higher ranking position (s17(3) No. 1 GesO). The general ranking is (s17 GesO):

- wage claims;
- claims arising from a social plan agreed with the Konkursverwalter;
- claims for dependants;
- taxes and public charges;
- all other claims.

Creditors' involvement and position

Category of creditors
The ranking of creditors for distribution purposes is as follows:

- Segregated creditors ("Aussonderung");
- Secured creditors ("Absonderung");
- Preferred creditors;
- Non-preferred creditors;
- Shareholders.

The compulsory liquidation creditors are those who, as at the time of the commencement of the compulsory liquidation proceedings, have a personal claim against the company (s3 KO). The creditors of the shareholders are not creditors in the compulsory liquidation of the company. Even creditors of a sole share-holder are in principle not able to claim against the assets of the company (BGH NJW 1957, 1877).

The shareholders themselves are not, as such, creditors as their equity capital is the fund which is liable for the claims of the creditors. However, they can be creditors on the basis of legal transactions with the company or on the basis of their membership rights based on, *inter alia*:

- share dividends where a resolution has been passed for a distribution from profits;
- claims for remuneration for services rendered; and
- claims for payment resulting from a reduction in capital.

These shareholders' rights are the only ones which may be registered for inclusion in the list of claims, where they are justified. No shareholder can acquire any right as a creditor as a result of any agreement made with the company for amortisation of his shares, *i.e.* an obligation on or an option available to the company to buy the shares back from the shareholder for value. Such contracts are null and void.

Supervision by and involvement of the creditors

The creditors are involved in the compulsory liquidation through the meeting of creditors and the committee of creditors. The meeting of creditors is convened and chaired by the court. The meeting must be convened upon the demand of the Konkursverwalter or of the committee of creditors or five creditors whose total claims amount to one-fifth of the claims lodged in the compulsory liquidation (ss93, 94 KO). Under West German law, a simple majority is required for resolutions by the meeting of creditors. In East Germany, under section 15(4) GesO, there must be a majority of the claims of those creditors present and there must also be a per capita majority of those present, to avoid major creditors having the last word.

In the case of all but the smallest compulsory liquidations, the meeting of creditors is too cumbersome to be suited to the day-to-day administration or supervision of the Konkursverwalter. In addition, if it were to meet on a more regular basis, the creditors' dividends from the insolvency would be reduced as a result of cost of holding such meetings. The involvement of the meeting of creditors is consequently somewhat limited. It includes the following tasks:

- the choice of the Konkursverwalter where some other person is to be elected in place of the Konkursverwalter appointed by the court, a situation which is somewhat unusual (s80 KO, cf. pp223-224 *supra*);
- the definitive appointment of a committee of creditors and the choice of its members (the committee of creditors has up until this point provisionally been appointed by the court) (s87 KO);

- the receipt of reports from the Konkursverwalter, including his financial calculations (ss131, 132 KO). In this manner, the creditors should be in possession of all information relevant to the compulsory liquidation which they require to make a reasoned judgment as to the appropriateness of the steps undertaken;
- voting upon resolutions concerning particular measures of importance.

The role of the committee of creditors is to support the day-to-day management by the Konkursverwalter and to supervise him. The individual members are therefore entitled to be kept informed about the Konkursverwalter's management activities.

The tasks of the committee are:

- to receive reports from the Konkursverwalter concerning the actual material situation of the company and his management thereof (s88 (2) KO);
- to approve those transactions on the part of the Konkursverwalter which require prior approval by the committee, such as the fulfilment of legal transactions entered into by the common debtor, the initiation of court actions, the formulation of compositions and social measures, the recognition of claims to segregation (see pp184-185 *supra*), claims by secured creditors (see pp185-186 *supra*) and claims by the priority creditors (see pp230-232 *infra*), the disposition of immoveable property by private contract or of the business or stocks of the common debtor as a whole, the taking-out of credit facilities and the granting of securities over assets (ss133, 134 KO). In sum, the committee's scope of duties covers all measures of substantial commercial importance for the implementation of the compulsory liquidation;
- the authorisation of the distribution (s150 KO) and calculation of the rate of dividend which will be applied for the distribution of the free proceeds (s159 KO);
- involvement in compulsory arrangement proceedings (see p192 *supra*).

The committee of creditors is thus of more practical importance than the meeting of creditors. It is composed of members elected by the meeting of creditors, these choices are then normally rubber-stamped by the court (s87 (2) KO). Individual creditors may also make nominations for the committee, and these may be accepted or refused by the court. The possibilities of an appeal from a refusal are limited. The minimum number of members in practice is three: there is no maximum.

As a small group, the committee of creditors is entrusted to a much greater degree with decision-making powers. It therefore should be composed of experienced professional men and women who are familiar with the business in which the insolvent company has been involved. It is not necessarily entirely composed of creditors, notwithstanding its name, but may include bankers, accountants and other experts. In fact there is a danger of a conflict between the interests of the individual members themselves and those of the body of creditors as a whole where a creditor is appointed or elected as a member of the committee.

Powers and duties of the Konkursverwalter

The Konkursverwalter is not an organ or representative of the company and thus he is not subject to control by the company's supervisory organs; nor does he need the company's approval for acts undertaken by him under company law, so long as such acts are within the authority granted to him in order to administer and dispose of the assets of the company.

However, the management remains as the legal representatives and bears the role of the common debtor. According to prevailing opinion, the powers of the company's organs are limited to the formulation of proposals relating to the internal workings of the company, in addition to the administration of any assets which are not included within the compulsory liquidation. It is, however, difficult to be precise as to the exact scope of the powers of the Konkursverwalter and that of the organs of the company (Kuhn-Uhlenbruck: Konkursordnung, §. 207 introductory remark D 21).

The Konkursverwalter must ensure that undertakings on the part of shareholders to pay up share capital, which have not been or are not yet required to be fulfilled, are fulfilled. Claims to outstanding payments in respect of an increase in capital which has been resolved upon and notified to the Commercial Register can be collected by the Konkursverwalter and added to the assets, since these claims by the company are an integral part of the assets. The winding-up of the corporation, which begins with the commencement of the compulsory liquidation proceedings, does not confer upon the shareholders any right to refuse to pay up, since the subscriptions are required for the satisfaction of the creditors.

The Konkursverwalter may also make claims arising as a result of undercapitalisation. According to the principle of the maintenance of capital, the assets necessary to maintain the share capital of the company may not be paid out to the shareholders. Any payments which have in fact been made to the shareholders must be returned.

Furthermore, the Konkursverwalter is obliged to pursue claims on behalf of the company against the management which arise from any culpable breach of duty upon the foundation of the company or during the course of the management of the company. In this respect, there is no requirement for a resolution by the shareholders.

The Konkursverwalter is responsible to all parties concerned for his activities (s82 KO). He is liable for each act undertaken by him and any damages arising therefrom. This liability is based on a legal duty of care. The "parties concerned" include all those persons to whom the Konkursverwalter has an official duty as a Konkursverwalter. Included are:

- those with a claim for segregation or secured claims;
- the creditors whose claims arise by virtue of contracts with the Konkursverwalter for supplies or services (priority debtors: "Massegläubiger");

- the unsecured creditors; and
- the common debtor.

Claims against the Konkursverwalter in this regard are made in the same manner as any other claim in tort/delict.

The Konkursverwalter is entitled to remuneration, the level of which is set by the court (s85 KO).

A bankruptcy administrator does not act as the agent of the creditors. In particular, the transfer (assignment) of assets to the bankruptcy estate is not deemed to be an indirect payment for the benefit of the creditors (See BGH decision of 21 January 1993, ZIP 1993 at 208). Indeed, the administrator acts in his own capacity, independent of any other party and is obliged to observe and protect the interests of all parties to the insolvency, including those of the insolvent.

The Konkursverwalter exercises the rights of disposal and administration over the assets in the place of the common debtor (s6 KO). He consequently has the right and the duty upon appointment immediately to take the assets into his possession and under his management (s117 KO). The legal powers of the Konkursverwalter are objectively limited by the purpose of the compulsory liquidation, which is, as far as possible and in equal measure, to satisfy the creditors. Legal acts by the Konkursverwalter which are obviously contrary to this aim, such as the recognition of obviously unjustified segregation claims, are void. It is also the Konkursverwalter who undertakes the representation of the company in court actions. New court actions, which commence after the opening of the compulsory liquidation, must be instructed or defended by the Konkursverwalter. Pending legal actions which affect the assets are suspended, or frozen, by the commencement of the compulsory liquidation (s240 ZPO). The KO differentiates between active and passive court actions:

- active court actions are those involving assets covered by the compulsory liquidation. Such court actions can be assumed only by the Konkursverwalter, who must decide whether a continuation of the court action will be beneficial to the compulsory liquidation as a whole. Should the Konkursverwalter decide not to pursue the action, because he does not consider there to be any benefit in such continuation, either because the prospects of success are not good or because enforcement following any court decree will be difficult, this has the consequence of releasing the asset to the other party. In such a case, only the common debtor or the opposing party to the court action can move the court to continue the court action (s10 (2) KO). The result of the court action, however, will no longer affect the assets in the liquidation, since the asset forming the subject of dispute then forms a part of the free assets of the common debtor;

- in the case of passive court actions, the subject of dispute is a claim against the common debtor. This may have the effect of reducing the possible dividend or the assets available for realisation. Claims already involved in the compulsory liquidation may not be the subject of such court actions. The reason for this is that no creditor may conduct an individual court action alongside the compulsory liquidation procedure. Claims by creditors are registered and examined in the course of the compulsory liquidation proceedings (s12 KO). The Konkursverwalter or the opposing party may only pursue the court action to the extent that the substance of the action does not impact upon claims to segregation or secured claims or priority debts (s11 KO).

It is the Konkursverwalter's task to collect the assets and turn them into cash (s117(1) KO). For this purpose, he is granted a right of disposal over them and can stipulate the type and time of such disposal. He must obtain the approval of the committee of creditors or of the meeting of creditors for a whole series of important measures (ss133, 134 KO). However, the enforceability of transactions entered into with third parties is not dependent on that approval (s136 KO). The Konkursverwalter is only liable to the creditors for damages where he proceeds without authorisation but he can, on application, be discharged from office where he commits a serious contravention.

Finally, the Konkursverwalter also has a decisive function in confirming the total amount of the debts, *i.e.* the claims of the insolvency creditors. In order to refuse unjustified claims, he may raise objections against any registered claim and thereby incite a court action for the confirmation of such refusal (ss144(1), 146 KO).

The Konkursverwalter distributes the free proceeds of the assets sold (ss149 *et seq* KO) and is responsible for exercising his right of challenge (s36 KO) by means of which any reduction in the assets prior to the opening of the compulsory liquidation proceedings can, under certain conditions, be reversed (see p239 *et seq*, *infra*).

Supervision by the court

The Konkursverwalter is subject to the supervision of the court (s83 KO). This duty of supervision does not simply arise where the court has reason to believe that the Konkursverwalter is not worthy of trust. Supervisory measures can also appear to be necessary where there is no committee of creditors or where the compulsory liquidation procedures are taking an unduly long time. The type and extent of individual measures lie within the discretion of the court but can also be required by reason of the length and scope of the procedure.

In order to supervise the Konkursverwalter, the court has authority to demand information at any time concerning the management of the company by the Konkursverwalter and to look into the books and ledgers and the financial situation of the company.

Any party concerned may apply to the court to take action against the Konkursverwalter. According to the most recent case law, however, the parties concerned have no right to raise a complaint if the court rejects the application to take measures against the Konkursverwalter within the context of its supervisory duties.

To a large extent, the efficient implementation of the compulsory liquidation depends on the Konkursverwalter being able to carry out his activities in an independent manner. Supervision by the court therefore has its limits. Apart from certain particular statutory exceptions, the court may only take steps against obviously spurious measures involving a breach of duty by the Konkursverwalter.

The court can also discharge the Konkursverwalter from office on application by any party concerned or of its own accord. In such a case, an order is made by the court following a hearing of the Konkursverwalter.

Position of officers and shareholders

Executive

Upon the commencement of the compulsory liquidation, the board of management of the AG or the directors of a GmbH lose their authority to administer and dispose of those assets of the company covered by the liquidation. This right of administration and disposal is exercised by the Konkursverwalter (s6 KO). He takes possession and undertakes the administration of the assets belonging to the company immediately upon the commencement of the proceedings with the purpose of converting them into cash (s117 KO). However, the management do retain certain rights and duties, as do the supervisory board and the shareholders' meeting. The basis of this division of power is that the organs of the company are able to exercise their former powers where these have not been assumed by the Konkursverwalter after the commencement of the proceedings.

In particular, the management has the following rights:

- it can raise immediate objections to the order commencing the compulsory liquidation (s109 KO);
- it may demand that the Konkursverwalter provide it with information of any intention to enter into certain transactions as follows:
  - before the Konkursverwalter obtains the approval of the creditors' committee for measures he intends to undertake in relation to the sale of assets;
  - where a loss may be involved and where such sale would take place prior to the examination hearing;
  - for certain transactions involving assets worth over DM300 where such transactions involve entering into court actions, settlements or arbitration agreements or the realisation of securities or sale of accounts receivable (s135 KO);
- it may make an application to the court for an interim injunction where the creditors have not authorised such transactions;
- it can apply for the cessation of the compulsory liquidation procedure if, after the expiry of the period within which claims are to be registered, all the liquidation creditors who have lodged claims agree (s202 KO);
- it can raise objections against the final account of the Konkursverwalter (s86 KO);

- provided it complies with certain requirements as to the form thereof, it can lodge a proposal for a compulsory arrangement and, under certain conditions, enter into a compulsory arrangement with those insolvency creditors of the corporation who are not preferred (s173 KO). Such conditions include ensuring that the secured and priority creditors will not be prejudiced, and that neither the court nor the creditors have already rejected an arrangement proposal. It can also raise objections to any order by means of which any proposed compulsory arrangement is confirmed or rejected. A compulsory arrangement is not permissible in circumstances where the debtor or its representatives have absconded, have been convicted of fraud leading to bankruptcy, or where a fraud investigation is under way (s5 KO). Furthermore, the management can apply for the arrangement hearing and the examination hearing to be held at the same time and for a second vote in connection with the arrangement proposal to be taken at a new hearing where the necessary voting majority for the acceptance of the arrangement is not achieved at the first hearing (ss173 *et seq* KO). Although the statutory provisions do not appear to give the Konkursverwalter any crucial responsibilities in any compulsory arrangement proceedings, his role is in practice vital in ensuring that any such procedure has a chance of success, if only because, by this stage, it is he and not the management who is holding the reins.

The board of management also has the following particular duties:

- it must apply for the commencement of compulsory liquidation proceedings over the assets of the company without culpable delay but at the latest within three weeks following the company's becoming unable to meet its debts as they arise or of the company becoming overindebted (s92 AG Act; s62 GmbH Act);
- it must give the Konkursverwalter, the committee of creditors and, where there is a court order to this effect, the meeting of creditors, information concerning all aspects of the proceedings (s100 KO);
- the members must not leave their place of residence without the permission of the court (s101 KO) and must give an oath that all assets have been revealed upon the application of the Konkursverwalter or one of the insolvency creditors (s125 KO);
- it must state its position with regard to the claims which have been registered and discussed at the examination hearing (s141 (2) KO);
- it must call a meeting of all shareholders to confirm the contents of any compulsory arrangement proposal (ss121 AG Act, 49(2) GmbH Act, 174 KO).

Where the board of management of an AG consists of more than one person, in the absence of any provision to the contrary contained in the articles of association, the board of management is only collectively entitled to make a declaration of an intention to enter into any legal transaction (s78 AG Act). This situation is not altered in any way in the case of compulsory liquidation.

The Konkursverwalter is largely dependent on the cooperation of the board of management. Although he can terminate the service contracts of the management and liquidators (ss22 KO, 622 BGB), he cannot revoke their appointment.

In the case of the members of the board of management of an AG, the parties concerned can only claim payment of any damages arising from such termination for a period of two years following the expiry of the service contract (s87 (3) AG Act). The supervisory board is entitled to require a reasonable reduction in the total emoluments of the members of the board of management. Since termination of the contract of service does not result in the termination of the member's position within the respective company organ, this continues for as long as the company is not extinguished or the particular member concerned is not dismissed by the relevant company organ.

Further, in relation to the AG's board of management it must, prior to filing for compulsory liquidation, notify the supervisory board of the company's inability to meet its debts arising or of its overindebtedness (s90 AG Act, s207 KO).

Supervisory board

AG

The supervisory board still, theoretically, continues to exercise a supervisory function with regard to the activities of the board of management in respect of those areas of operations of the AG which are not covered by the compulsory liquidation. In practice, however, this duty of supervision falls away, since no further transactions are entered into by the board of management. The compulsory liquidation is implemented by the Konkursverwalter under his own powers and responsibilities. The supervisory board has no supervisory authority over the Konkursverwalter.

The supervisory board has the right to convene a meeting of the shareholders. It can revoke the appointment of a member of the board of management on material grounds or appoint new members to the board of management. Upon such appointment, however, there arises no automatic contract of service between the appointee and the Konkursverwalter. A strict distinction is to be made between the position of such person in the organ concerned and an employment relationship.

The members of the supervisory board cannot lay claim to any emoluments out of the insolvency assets for activities carried out by them following the commencement of the compulsory liquidation. This does not mean that the supervisory board is obliged to observe the tasks falling within its area of responsibility during the compulsory liquidation of the AG. Some writers do not, however, fully accord with this view.

GmbH

Where the company has a supervisory board, this remains in office but retains only very minor responsibilities. It has no rights to supervise the Konkursverwalter. The question of the effect on the contracts of the members of the supervisory board is a matter of some debate. According to one view, the service contract is extinguished in circumstances where the insolvency assets would be reduced by any claim to remuneration. According to another view, the contract remains in full force and effect but cannot be enforced against the assets of the company with the result that, the members of the supervisory board are accorded a right to immediate termination as a result of the loss of remuneration (cf. Scholz: GmbH-Gesetz, 6th Edn., 63 margin no. 37).

Shareholders' meeting

AG

The shareholders' meeting continues to vote on those matters expressly stipulated by law and in the articles of association as being within its jurisdiction (s119 AG Act), even after the commencement of compulsory liquidation proceedings, but only to the extent that these duties have not been restricted by such commencement or by the area of responsibility of the Konkursverwalter. The shareholders' meeting has, in particular, the following tasks:

- considering and voting on resolutions concerning the contents of compulsory composition proposals suggested by the board of management;
- considering and voting on resolutions concerning the continuation of the AG. A resolution to continue the company is only effective after registration thereof in the Commercial Register (s274(4) AG Act);
- the exoneration of the board of management and of the supervisory board (s120 AG Act), in so far as there are no claims arising against the management which would benefit the assets. Where such claims exist, it is the Konkursverwalter who is responsible for granting such discharge. He is also authorised to take action in respect of such claims on behalf of the company or its creditors against the board of management and the supervisory board. It should be noted that the "exoneration" referred to is merely a formal approval of the manner in which the company's affairs have been administered and constitutes a discharge of legal liability.

Resolutions by the shareholders' meeting for the distribution of profits (s173 AG Act) are not possible since such profits, in so far as they can ever be achieved, must be included in the assets controlled by the Konkursverwalter.

The Konkursverwalter has a right to challenge resolutions made by the shareholders' meeting if such resolutions affect the insolvency assets. In this regard, it is a right of the board of management (s245(4) AG Act) which is transferred to the Konkursverwalter on commencement of the compulsory liquidation.

GmbH

The shareholders remain the highest authority in the GmbH except that they have no power over the Konkursverwalter. They may:

- make resolutions, although these must be limited to matters aiding the implementation of the compulsory liquidation;
- nominate and remove the directors, but may not conclude service contracts which might have a negative effect on the assets;
- issue instructions to the directors (but not to the Konkursverwalter) in so far as these are limited to the powers exercisable over any assets remaining outside the liquidation assets;
- exercise their supervisory powers over the directors, but, similarly, only to the extent that the directors still have responsibility.

It is debatable whether alterations to the articles of association can still be made. Such a view is partially supported – with the reservation that the purpose of the insolvency must not be hindered – by the argument that an increase in capital should be possible if it enables money to be brought into the company to support an offer of compulsory arrangement (cf. Scholz: GmbH-Gesetz, 6th Edn., §. 63 margin no. 34).

Dissolution

The dissolution of the compulsory liquidation proceedings is effected:

- by the holding of the final hearing following distribution of the assets amongst the creditors (sl63 KO);
- by a legally confirmed compulsory arrangement (ssl73 *et seq*, 190 KO);
- upon an order being made for the cessation of proceedings on the application of the common debtor with the approval of all creditors (ss202, 203 KO);
- where the assets themselves do not cover the costs of the procedure (s204 KO).

The company is dissolved upon the final distribution of the assets unless it later transpires that it still owns certain other assets. Under these circumstances, it is deemed to have continued to exist. The continued existence is, however, only a legal technicality for the purposes of the compulsory liquidation and does not in any way enable the company to continue trading. Any such additional assets must be dealt with in the customary fashion and a distribution made by the Konkursverwalter to any creditors who have not been fully satisfied, upon the order of the court (sl66 KO).

The shareholders' meeting can pass a resolution as to the continuation of the company if the court has ordered that compulsory liquidation proceedings cease upon the application of the company or if the proceedings are dismissed following a confirmation by the court of a compulsory arrangement. If the shareholders wish to continue the operations of the company, they can eliminate the reason for the liquidation by taking suitable measures in respect of the company's capital and finances:

- either by means of a compulsory arrangement (cf. p192 *supra*), or
- by obtaining a court order stopping the compulsory liquidation proceedings on the application of the common debtor. This would succeed where:
  - after the expiry of the period for registering claims, the debtor obtained the approval of all of the liquidation creditors who had registered a claim for such a cessation, or
  - before the expiry of such period, the debtor obtained the approval of all creditors thus far registered and no other creditors are known of (s202 KO). Such may occur where sufficient finance has been arranged to allow the company to continue, for instance by the shareholders.

Instead of a continuation, the shareholders can resolve to convert the company into an unlimited commercial partnership ("offene Handelsgesellschaft") or limited partnership ("Kommanditgesellschaft") (see pp187-188 *supra*) under the terms of what is known as the Commercial Conversions Act ("Umwandlungsgesetz"), where at least one party can be found who is prepared to assume full personal liability for the company's debts.

Organisation of insolvency proceedings after the reform

The German government is preparing an insolvency law reform, which proceedings are organised in the following manner.

Preliminary Proceedings

After commencement of proceedings, the insolvency court must appoint an insolvency administrator, advisory board, and creditors' committee.

An advisory board, to which the major creditors and representatives of the works council should belong, will always be appointed if a reorganisation of the business is intended. In addition, the court should appoint a creditors' committee, which must support and supervise the insolvency administrator and approve key transactions in the insolvency. If a reorganisation of the business can be achieved, a date for a hearing will be set, at which the insolvency administrator will report on the undertaking's situation and the chances of the reorganisation being successfully carried out. After the hearing, the insolvency court will decide as to whether winding-up proceedings must be carried out, whereby the remaining assets would be broken up and realised, or whether the business should be reorganised.

Relationship between the court and the insolvency administrator

The administrator is to be subject to a greater degree of supervision by the court than previously. The court can compel the administrator to comply with his duties by threatening compulsory measures. For example, he can be compelled to carry out an existing obligation to return property by means of an enforceable complaint. The insolvency court can remove an insolvency administrator from office where it finds him to have repeatedly breached his duties.

Insolvency proceedings can start if there are sufficient assets to cover at least the costs that will be incurred up to production of the first report. In addition, anyone who has paid costs in advance to enable the proceedings to be started should be reimbursed by those who delayed submission of the petition for insolvency.

Special proceedings

The debtor can apply for self-administration under supervision of the creditors' trustee as an alternative to the appointment of an insolvency administrator, as long as this is not likely to lead to creditors being disadvantaged. It remains to be seen whether the desired advantages (use of management expertise, saving of costs) will thereby be realised. In addition, self-administration by the debtor can be ordered in small cases. The final decision as to whether special proceedings are to be applied shall rest with the first creditors' meeting.

5. Augmenting the assets of the insolvent corporation

Introduction

The principle of the equal treatment of creditors is fundamental to German insolvency law. One of the cornerstones of the procedure is the right to challenge acts undertaken by the insolvent company. It is possible retrospectively to undo legal transactions which have validly been entered into prior to the commencement of the compulsory liquidation and which have had the effect of reducing the assets and therefore have disadvantaged the creditors as a body. Since it is possible to challenge and set aside such transactions, any reduction in the assets can be made good and the disadvantage to the creditors thereby nullified. Those transactions undertaken up to the commencement of the compulsory liquidation proceedings are not, however, void, but merely voidable. There is a claim to restitution of that sum by which the assets have been reduced as a result of the challengeable transaction. This remedy exists in the interests of all the insolvency (as opposed to priority) creditors and is therefore an instance of the extension of the protection of the creditors. The practical importance of such a challenge is considerable, since it is an important instrument for increasing those assets which serve to satisfy the creditors of the insolvent company.

As an exception to the principle that liability for a company's debts is limited to the extent of its assets, in the case of compulsory liquidation a claim can be raised in certain circumstances against the members of the board of management and supervisory board of an AG and against the directors of a GmbH. These remedies are available, in particular:

- where the company organ responsible has failed to lodge an application for insolvency in time, known as "protraction of insolvency" ("Konkursverschleppung");

- where the responsible company organ has made payments after the company became unable to meet its debts as they arose or after the company became overindebted.

Transactions at risk (challenges under the KO)

Transactions liable to challenge under the compulsory liquidation procedure are regulated by sections 29 to 42 KO. The challenge must be raised by the Konkursverwalter (s36 KO). In West Germany, such challenges must be made within one year after the opening of the insolvency (s41 (1) sentence 1 KO). In East Germany, this period is extended to two years (s10(2) GesO). After the expiry of this period, the Konkursverwalter no longer has the right to commence proceedings, but he retains the right to refuse performance (s41 (2) KO). For example, he may refuse delivery of goods which the claimant has acquired under a transaction which is subject to such a challenge, even after the expiry of the time limit.

Prerequisites

The challenge is directed against any transaction which has legal effect, whether this is desired or not.

The transaction must have a disadvantageous effect on the creditors in that the possibility of satisfying the creditors has been impaired by the transaction. In this regard, it is sufficient that the ability of the creditors to claim the goods concerned has been impeded. There is, however, no disadvantage where, notwithstanding the transaction concerned, the creditors are fully satisfied from the other assets within the company. The transaction must be deemed to be causally linked to the disadvantage, and the following circumstances must be differentiated:

- certain provisions require direct disadvantage (s30 No. 1, case 1; s31 No. 2 KO). In such cases, the disadvantage must immediately occur as a result of the transaction and simultaneously therewith. Any consequential effects which only occur later are of no importance. Examples include sales for less than and purchases for more than value or taking out loans under unfavourable conditions. Such cases are always one of contract (whether unilateral or bilateral);
- in the case of other provisions, it is sufficient if there is an indirect disadvantage (s30 No. 1, case 2; s30 No. 2; s31 No. 1; s32 KO). In these cases, it is not necessary to show that the legal transaction itself has immediately and directly brought about the disadvantage. It is sufficient if this arises as a result of circumstances which only occur later. Examples include all legal dealings, be they contracts or not, such as set-off, arrestments, compulsory enforcement of judgments, assignment of rights by one creditor to another whereby a security is created for the second creditor against the common debtor.

The test of whether there is a disadvantage must be regarded from a commercial point of view. For instance, the sale of an over-charged piece of real estate (for example as a result of excessive securities granted on it) is not challengeable in the absence of any disadvantage to the creditors, since the creditors would in any case obtain no advantage from the sale and disposition of the land concerned (cf. BGHZ 90, 212). In addition to a disadvantage to the creditors, there must also be present one of the particular grounds of challenge discussed in the following paragraphs.

Particular grounds of challenge

Challenge during compulsory liquidation
The most significant transactions open to challenge fall under what are known as "particular challenges under compulsory liquidation" (s30 KO). These can be subdivided into three categories:

Transactions which are disadvantageous to the creditors and are undertaken in the knowledge of a financial crisis.
Under this category, legal transactions undertaken by the common debtor prior to the opening of insolvency proceedings are challengeable where they are directly disadvantageous to the creditors upon their being entered into and they were undertaken during a financial crisis, the other party being aware of the existence of the critical situation. The company is deemed to be in a financial crisis from the moment it stops making payments or upon its lodging an application for the commencement of compulsory liquidation proceedings until the time the compulsory liquidation actually commences. A company "stops making payments" where it is discernibly unable to pay a substantial proportion of its due and payable debts as a result of a long-term cash deficiency. Examples of this category include the sale of goods at a price much lower than their market value or the taking out of a loan under unreasonable conditions.

The granting of securities or the satisfaction of a debt in the knowledge of a financial crisis.
Legal transactions are challengeable under this category where they grant a security or are made in satisfaction of a debt due to a creditor who knew of the critical situation. It is immaterial whether the creditor was entitled to the security or satisfaction. This may appear draconian, but the reason is that the individual creditor would thereby receive full satisfaction of his claim at the last moment whereas the majority would have to make do with a correspondingly reduced sum. Examples include any payments or other performances on the part of the common debtor to the other party, granting securities over movables, transfers of securities or taking out securities over land.

Transactions granting an unjustified security or satisfaction prior to or during a financial crisis.

Those transactions challengeable under this category are those which are entered into during the last ten days prior to the coming into existence of the financial crisis or during it and by means of which the creditor procures satisfaction or a security which he would otherwise either not have been able to lay claim to or, at least, not in that manner or at that time. The creditor has thus been preferred to the other creditors. There is a presumption that the common debtor intended to prefer the creditor in these circumstances. The provisions place the party against whom the challenge is brought in a substantially worse position than in the previous category. For one thing, the right to challenge the transaction is extended to transactions entered into ten days prior to the financial crisis. For another, the burden is on the creditor to prove that he was unaware at the time of the transaction either of the crisis or the intention on the part of the common debtor to prefer him to the other creditors. The example cited in the second category also applies here, with the difference that the creditor must have been in such a position as not to have been entitled to lay claim to the performance in the manner in which it was claimed. Of particular practical importance is the judicial enforcement of a security over movables or of rights in connection with securities over land. Such transactions are rendered challengeable in order to put all the creditors in the same position for the critical period.

Loans to GmbHs in lieu of capital

The legislature has provided two particular grounds of challenge for the protection of the creditors of a GmbH (s32a KO):

- Where a shareholder has granted what is known as a loan in lieu of capital ("kapitalersetzendes Darlehen") to a GmbH and obtained a security therefor, this transaction is challengeable. Shareholder loans are deemed to be in lieu of capital where the shareholder would, at the time of granting the loan, instead have paid in equity capital. The claim to reimbursement of such a loan in the compulsory liquidation or in composition proceedings designed to avoid insolvency cannot be enforced by the shareholder who granted it (s32a GmbH Act). This may also apply in the case of loans granted by third parties, where that third party has been granted a security or guarantee by the shareholder in consideration for the loan;

- Challenges may be made against transactions which confer satisfaction on the shareholder or third party as a creditor in respect of the loan in lieu of capital, provided the transaction was undertaken during the year prior to the commencement of compulsory liquidation proceedings.

Intentional disadvantages

Furthermore, any transaction on the part of the common debtor may be challenged where it has been undertaken with the intention of disadvantaging the insolvency creditors with the knowledge of the other party (s31 No. 1 KO). Intention is defined as the dishonest wish to prejudice the position of the creditors. Since it is incumbent on the Konkursverwalter to prove the intention to prejudice the creditors and to prove the knowledge of the common debtor and the other party in the proceedings, such challenges are rarely made. The burden of proof is, however, reversed where the challenge is directed against certain persons standing in a close relationship to the common debtor as an individual (such as may be the case with a one-man company having a sole shareholder). The concept of "close relationship" is more broadly interpreted in East Germany than in the West. In such a case, such persons must prove that they did not know of the intention to prejudice the creditors (s31 No. 2 KO).

Under the East German rules, the concept of "knowledge" is expanded to include what the third party "ought to have known". As a result of the reduction of the burden of proof in this regard, there is no reversal of that burden in East Germany.

Gifts

Finally, section 32 KO provides for the challenge of all disposals by the common debtor for no consideration undertaken during the year prior to the commencement of compulsory liquidation.

Legal consequences

Those assets which are disposed of, given away or surrendered by the common debtor under a challengeable transaction must be returned and become part of the liquidation assets (s37(1) KO). Any assigned claims must be re-assigned. The return of the assets must be effected in their original form.

Only where the goods are no longer in existence or available can reimbursement take place in cash. Where the goods perish, it is the partner to the challenged contract who is liable, even in the absence of negligence.

In most cases, the contract partner will have a claim against the common debtor for breach of contract. This is a claim on the assets which ranks as a priority debt ("Masseanspruch") to the extent that the assets or their value have been increased by the actions of the third party in pursuance of the contract (s59 (1) No. 4 KO); otherwise the claim ranks along with those of the main body of creditors (s38 KO).

Extension of conditions for rescission under the InsO

Extension of conditions for rescission

The grounds for rescission set out above remain unchanged. The effectiveness of rescission, however, is to be improved through the introduction of numerous modifications. As it is often disputed from what point in time the debtor was unable to pay, or when the relevant petition for commencement was submitted, this is to be clarified in special "determining proceedings". All time periods relevant to rescission will then be determined by reference to the first admissible, justified, petition for the commencement of proceedings. In addition, the preconditions for rescission are lowered, and instead of a one year exclusion period for rescission, a two year period of limitation for the assertion of rights of rescission will be introduced. Finally, the number of affiliated individuals in respect of whom the normal burden of proof is reversed has been significantly increased. In the future, an affiliated individual in this sense will be not only the debtor's spouse and direct relatives but also, in the case of corporate bodies, members of the managing and supervisory boards, shareholders holding at least 15% of the share capital and undertakings which are dependent upon the debtor or upon whom the debtor is dependent.

The provision of security or satisfaction by the debtor in favour of a creditor ("congruent cover"), may be rescinded if:

- It was made within the three months prior to the opening of the insolvency proceedings (or after the request to open the proceedings), and
- the debtor was illiquid at the time of the transaction by which the security or satisfaction was given, and
- the creditor was aware of the debtor's illiquidity or, of not, was grossly negligent in not so knowing.

Where the creditor was an affiliated individual, he is presumed to know that the debtor was illiquid at the appropriate time.

If the transaction by which the security or satisfaction was provided took place in the month before the request to, open the insolvency proceedings or after the request, it is presumed that the creditor was not entitled to such security or satisfaction ("incongruent cover") and there is no need to establish knowledge as to the debtor's illiquidity.

On the whole, the proposed improvements to the right of rescission constitute the most effective measures for increasing the size of the bankrupt's estate. It is, at the moment, impossible to predict how far the modifications in relation to burden of proof and prima facie evidence in favour of the bankrupt's estate will go in making it easier for transactions in the period leading to insolvency to be scrutinised and where appropriate, set aside.

Cancellation of preferential claims

All established claims, in principle, rank equally. This, however, does not exclude an insolvency plan allowing for certain claims to be satisfied with a higher preference than other claims. The order of ranking, presently determined by statute, will thereby be left largely to the creditors' own discretion.

Labour law

The Draft Insolvency Act provides for particularly drastic changes in this area. In particular, if a reconciliation of interests ("Interessenausgleich") is agreed with the works' council, any redundancies made in accordance with this agreement will be presumed to have been properly implemented. If no reconciliation of interest is agreed with the works' council, special proceedings for speedy and collective clarification of the validity of all redundancies made in connection with the change in business operations will be available. This will, in practice, allow all redundancies made within the framework of a rescue transfer to be dealt with in a similar and consistent fashion.

Release from outstanding debts
The draft legislation provides that individuals, provided their bankruptcy was not a result of gross negligence, should have the opportunity to be released from all outstanding debts. At the moment it is a matter of dispute as to whether this rule should be included in the Draft Insolvency Act or whether a later amendment should take care of the issue. The rule, based on the American law of discharge, provides, in its current form, that for seven years the debtor must place any income in excess of the amount exempt from attachment at the disposal of a trustee, who shall distribute such funds equally amongst all creditors. At the end of this period, the debtor shall be released from all debts.

Personal liability of officers

The officers of an AG or of a GmbH can be held to have caused loss to the creditors of the company where the company is insolvent but compulsory liquidation proceedings have not yet been commenced, in that they:

- are late in applying for the commencement of compulsory liquidation proceedings or the commencement of judicial arrangement proceedings ("Konkursverschleppung");
- undertake contractual performances which have the effect of reducing the assets; and
- enter into new obligations.

Both the AG Act and the GmbH Act prohibit such measures being taken by the officers of the company. Breaches are subject to criminal and civil sanctions which have the effect of granting:

- indirect protection to the creditors where a claim is available to the company for payment of damages;
- direct protection to the creditors where the claim for payment of damages is available to the individually affected parties, in particular the creditors.

AG

Board of management

Failure to make an application
Where the company is unable to meet its debts as they arise or is overindebted, the board of management must apply for the commencement of compulsory liquidation proceedings or of judicial arrangement proceedings without culpable delay and at the latest within three weeks of the occurrence of the events justify-

ing such application (s92(2) AG Act).

Where there is a culpable breach of this duty on the part of the members of the board of management, they are liable for damages to the company, the creditors and the shareholders. The liability for damages to the company results from the general provision that members of the board of management who breach their duties are jointly and severally liable for any damage arising therefrom (s93(2) AG Act). The duty to pay damages to the shareholders and the creditors is a result of the fact that the provision regarding the duty to make an application is intended to protect both of these groups. Consequently, breach of the duty imposed by this "protective law" ("Schutzgesetz") makes the board liable in damages (s92(2) AG Act, read together with s823(2) BGB). In principle, there is also a liability for loss occasioned to those persons who have become creditors of the company only after that point in time at which the application for the commencement of compulsory liquidation proceedings should have been filed.

Prohibition against making payments

Once the company has become unable to meet its debts as they arise or has become overindebted, the board of management is prohibited from making any further payments out of the AG's assets. This does not apply to payments which, even after this point in time, are compatible with the duty of care of a well-organised and conscientious manager (s92 (3) AG Act) (see p180 *supra*).

The board of management is only liable as a result of a breach of this prohibition against making payments if, in fact, liquidation or arrangement proceedings have been commenced or an application has been rejected due to the fact that the assets are not sufficient to cover the costs of the proceedings. It is debatable whether liability must be based on the actual knowledge of the members of the board of management (*i.e.* whether they must have known that the company was insolvent) or whether it is sufficient that circumstances justifying compulsory liquidation had in fact occurred.

Breach of the prohibition results in a claim for damages on the part of the company in favour of the body of creditors (s93(3) No. 6 AG Act). The claim is aimed at making good the corresponding reduction in the assets without taking into consideration the damage sustained by the company. The claim is calculated by deducting the dividend which the previously satisfied creditors should have received (had payment been made to them properly) from the payments that have been made. There must also be deducted the equivalent value which has accrued and remained in the assets. The board of management may advise the Konkursverwalter to take steps to lay claim to the payments by means of a challenge under the compulsory liquidation.

This prohibition against payment is also a protective law in favour of the creditors of the company. The creditors are consequently entitled to claim damages (s92(3) AG Act read together with s823(2) BGB).

Supervisory board

The supervisory board itself is not subject either to the duty to file an application or to the prohibition on making payments. However, on the basis of its supervisory duties, it must exercise its influence over the board of management to ensure that the directors observe these duties. Failing this, any members of the supervisory board acting culpably are liable to pay damages (ss116 and 93(2) AG Act).

Directors of a GmbH

The liability of the directors for failing to apply for compulsory liquidation or breach of the prohibition on making payments is similarly regulated as in the case of the corresponding liability of the members of the board of management of an AG.

Failure to make an application

Where the company is unable to meet its debts arising or becomes overindebted, then the directors must apply for the commencement of compulsory liquidation proceedings or the commencement of judicial arrangement proceedings without culpable delay and at the latest within three weeks following the occurrence of the circumstances justifying such action (s64(1) GmbH Act).

Any breach of this provision results in a claim for damages not only on the part of the GmbH itself but also of the creditors against the directors (s64(1) GmbH Act read together with s823(2) BGB). There is also liability in principle towards those creditors who have only become creditors after the point in time at which the application for compulsory liquidation should have been lodged. According to the newest case law from the German High Court or "Bundesgerichtshof" (BGH Decision of 1 March 1993, GmbHR 1993 at 420; and BGH Decision of 20 September 1993 GmbHR at 733), the creditors whose claims were entered and substantiated before the institution of the company's insolvency suit have the sole right to the pro rata damages, *i.e.* to the mathematical difference between the hypothetical insolvency estate (as it should have been if the managing directors had filed for insolvency at the proper time) and the actual estate. The other creditors who agreed to and filed their claims against the company after the insolvency was instituted receive greater compensation in the form of money damages. In so far as payments of damages are included within the assets, individual creditors no longer have any further claim under this head.

Prohibition against making payments

The directors are liable to pay damages to the company when payments have been made after the company has become unable to meet its debts as they arise or after confirmation of the company's overindebtedness. This does not apply to payments which, although made after this point in time, are compatible with the duty of care of a proper businessman (s64(2) GmbH Act) (see pp180-181 *supra*).

This provision is a special regulation which has the effect of reimbursing the creditors by making payment to the company. In addition, the creditors may also raise a claim for damages, since the prohibition against making payments is also a protective law (s64(2) GmbH Act read together with s823(2) BGB).

Legal situation under the InsO

In the case of partnerships and associations (*i.e.* bodies which are not legal "persons" but rather a group of individuals, called "Personengesellschaften") the company's creditors can bring a claim for liability directly against the members, who are individually liable. The members are not only liable for the deficiency to the creditors, but also directly and fully liable for all of the company's debts.

It also intended that the executives of companies considered "legal persons," who have the duty to file for insolvency – especially directors of incorporated "capital" companies (*i.e.* "Kapitalgesellschaften" such as AGs and GmbHs) – will be secondarily liable for the costs of the insolvency proceedings. Creditors or other persons who preliminarily pay the court fees can have recourse to these directors for the costs. Violation by executives of their duties can be rebuttably presumed if at the time of the decision regarding the insolvency petition, the company's assets were no longer sufficient to cover the costs of the proceedings.

6. Public control over insolvent corporations

Appointment and control of the Konkursverwalter

Appointment

The Konkursverwalter is appointed by the court (s78(1) KO) although the creditors' meeting is entitled to choose some other person (see pp223-4 and p228 *supra*) where a particular Konkursverwalter is proposed by a major creditor or a class of creditors, the court is entitled to regard this only as a suggestion and can overturn the appointment of the person chosen by the creditors (s80 KO). The appointment is advertised by the court in the appointed newspapers (ss81(1) and 76 KO).

The choice of appointee lies in the limited discretion of the court. The appointee must be a professionally experienced person, independent of both the common debtor and the creditors. Such appointees are persons with the necessary professional background, such as lawyers, accountants or experienced merchants (in the sense legally defined in German law under ss1 and 2 HGB). The appointment is regarded as the most difficult of the procedural decisions to be made by the court, since the qualifications of the Konkursverwalter can often determine the fate of the procedure.

The Konkursverwalter cannot be someone who has a conflict of interests. He may not pursue only the interests of the creditors or of the common debtor. He must advise the court of any existing or possible conflicts of interests. Following on from the requirement for independence, it would be inappropriate if the Konkursverwalter had offered advice to the common debtor during the earlier stages of the financial difficulties prior to compulsory liquidation.

The legal representatives of the common debtor may not be appointed to the office of Konkursverwalter. This means, for instance, that the board of management of an AG cannot be appointed as Konkursverwalter in the compulsory liquidation of the company. The reason for this is that the office of Konkursverwalter would then have to be exercised by the legal representatives of the legal person concerned. Since these legal representatives can be dismissed by the shareholders, they cannot occupy a position from which, under the KO, they may only be dismissed by the court.

The appointment of a person not having the capacity to fulfil the office of Konkursverwalter to that office is null and void. The administrative acts of such an appointee are therefore of no legal effect. Should it become apparent that the Konkursverwalter does not have the required capacity, this is a valid ground for his or her discharge (s84 KO).

The period in office commences with acceptance of the office. Although there is no obligation to take up office, once accepted, the position of Konkursverwalter may only be renounced from for a material reason.

Control

The Konkursverwalter is subject to the supervision of the insolvency court (see pp232-233 *supra*).

Examinations and investigations

There is no particular procedure for the examination and investigation of the Konkursverwalter other than the general supervision of the court. Where the Konkursverwalter conducts himself in a criminal manner, for instance by committing fraud or breach of trust, then, naturally, criminal proceedings may be commenced against him.

Publicity and records

In order to protect the creditors, the shareholders and any other third parties, certain procedural steps in the case of a members' liquidation and virtually all important procedural steps in the case of insolvency proceedings under the KO must be publicised in the prescribed form. Registration in the Commercial Register is of particular importance. The most important notifications have been referred to in the respective passages above.

Under the KO, the following matters must in particular be publicised:

- the name of the Konkursverwalter (s81);
- the calling of a meeting of creditors (s93(2));
- any orders for the commencement of proceedings, the period within which claims must be notified and important dates, particularly the date of the examination hearing (to be notified in the Federal Gazette ("Bundesanzeiger") (s111);

- prior to the distribution: the official list of claims which are to be recognised, which may be inspected by the parties concerned at the business premises of the company concerned; the amount of the claims and the sum of the cash assets which are available to be distributed (s151);
- any dismissal of the compulsory liquidation proceedings following the final hearing (s163);
- compulsory arrangement hearings (s179);
- any application for the cessation of the compulsory liquidation proceedings with the approval of all the creditors (s203); and
- any order by the court for the cessation of proceedings (s205).

Appendix: The insolvency law reform as described in the text has now become law since 5 October 1994.

Contents of Chapter 6

CORPORATE INSOLVENCY LAW IN GREECE

1.   **Introduction**   253
The sources of law in Greece   253
Persons, insolvency and bankruptcy in Greece   253
2.   **Corporations**   254
Classification of corporations   254
Characteristics of AEs and EPEs   255
Management of corporations   257
Ownership   258
Other business entities (OE and EE partnerships, sole traders)   259
Financing and security for creditors   260
Available information   266
Debt collection and asset recovery   267
3.   **Survival of the insolvent corporation or its business**   271
Law 3562/1956   271
Law 1386/1983   273
4.   **Termination of the corporation: bankruptcy and solvent liquidation**   275
Bankruptcy   275
5.   **Augmenting the assets of the insolvent corporation**   293
Introduction   293
Transactions at risk   293
6.   **Public control over insolvent corporations**   295
Public control in general   295
Licensing and control of the appointees   296
Personal liability of officers of companies   296
Examinations and investigations   297
Publicity and records   297

Chapter 6

CORPORATE INSOLVENCY LAW IN GREECE

Costas Vainanidis,

Vainanidis, Schina & Economou

1. Introduction

The sources of law in Greece

The primary sources of Greek law consist of the written laws (*i.e.* the Greek Constitution, Acts of Parliament, Presidential Decrees, Legislative Decrees, and so on), custom, the generally recognised rules of international law, the Law of the European Union, and all international conventions which Greece has ratified. Case law is not a source of law, but the judgments of the Courts and in particular those of the highest Courts (Supreme Court, Council of State and Courts of Appeal), contribute to the interpretation of the existing legislation, and their impact on the evolution of the Law should not be underestimated.

Persons, insolvency and bankruptcy in Greece

Greek law draws a distinction between "physical persons" and "legal persons". Human beings are "physical persons" who have rights conferred on them and obligations imposed on them by the rule of law. "Legal persons" are those entities created and recognised by law which, although not human beings, are treated by law like human beings. These legal entities have "legal personality".

"Insolvency" is defined in Greek law as the inability of someone to pay his debts in full. It is not considered to be a subject on its own, but merely a stage preliminary to bankruptcy. "Bankruptcy" is the term used in respect of all types of commercial legal entities having legal personality and can even refer to deceased persons.

This chapter will cover bankruptcy as its main subject but will also refer to certain analogous procedures, although the practical importance of these is extremely limited.

Bankruptcy law in Greece provides a set of rules aiming primarily at the proportional satisfaction of creditors' claims. Bankruptcy law is part of the commercial law because only traders can be adjudicated bankrupt. Until 1878 the French Commercial Code (CC) was applicable in Greece. In 1878, the 1878 Law on bankruptcy replaced the third Section of the Code by introducing articles 525-707 CC. Further amendments were made by the 1910 Law on bankruptcy, by Compulsory Law 635/1937 and Law 1189/1938. Provisions relating to bankruptcy are also scattered in Law 2190/1920 on Anonymos Eteria (AEs), in the Civil Code, in the Code of Civil Procedure and in other laws referring to specific matters.

Alternative procedures of limited scope and practical importance are regulated by specific laws, namely, by Legislative Decree 3562/1956 to place AEs under the management and the administration of their creditors, and under special liquidation and by Law 1386/1983 on the formation of the Organisation for the Financial Restructuring of Enterprises.

2. Corporations

Classification of corporations

Commercial activity in Greece may be carried out either by sole traders, or through business organisations (companies) formed by more than one person and regulated by Greek Law. It is necessary, before we proceed any further, to outline the main types and features of such companies.

The hierarchy of the main business organisations is as follows:

- Anonymos Eteria or "AE" which is a public limited company;
- Eteria Periorismenis Efthinis or "EPE" which is a limited company; Omorithmos Eteria or "OE" which is a partnership of unlimited liability;
- Eterorithmos Eteria or "EE" which is a partnership of limited liability;

In addition to the above, specific laws provide for the operation, bankruptcy and/or liquidation of some other business entities such as banking institutions, insurance companies, co-operative societies, stock-broking companies, shipping companies and others which are beyond the scope of this chapter.

Some of the characteristic features of the above four main types of companies are discussed below:

Legal personality

All the above business entities possess legal personality and therefore they all have the ability to sue and to be sued and they can be adjudged bankrupt in the case of insolvency.

Companies of limited or unlimited liability

The title is misleading in the sense that all companies, whether limited or unlimited, are in reality fully liable through their own assets to company creditors. The liability refers to the individuals, shareholders or partners of the companies concerned. If liable, they may be forced to contribute their own assets to satisfy claims of company creditors. Court judgments against the companies may be executed directly against their personal assets. Moreover, depending on the type of company and on the capacity in which they participate in it, the bankruptcy of the company may result in their own personal bankruptcy.

In the case of partnerships, the partners play a central role in the decision-making process of the company. This is why partnerships are called "personal companies". This personal feature becomes less important as we move towards the more sophisticated and larger forms of companies.

The personal feature almost disappears in the case of AEs because, even when they are family-owned, the weight of each individual shareholder depends entirely on the number and type of the shares that he owns.

As a result, the power to decide on the company affairs derives from the share capital itself rather than from the individual shareholders.

Somewhere in the middle, one may find the EPE which retains part of the personal element, although here again capital ownership is increasingly significant, and, therefore, it is characterised as a company with prominent capital character.

Characteristics of AEs and EPEs

Public limited companies AEs

This type of company is formed by notarial deed by two or more physical or legal persons. The original deed remains with the notary but certified copies can be issued at any time. The articles of incorporation, which include the entire agreement between the founding shareholders, are approved by decision of the local Prefect. The incorporation is concluded by the registration of the company in the relevant Public Registry kept with the Prefecture and a summary of the articles and the approving decision are published in the Government Gazette.

There is a minimum capital requirement of Drs.10,000,000.

If admission of an AE to official listing on the Stock Exchange is sought, the company's capital and reserves, including profit and loss from the last financial year, must be at least Drs.500 million. Subscription for shares may be in cash or in kind. If in kind, the consideration is evaluated by an Experts' Committee set up by the Ministry of Commerce.

If the capital exceeds Drs.10 million the surplus can be paid in instalments within a maximum period of ten years. The capital is divided into shares which can be issued "to bearer" or can be "registered". Apart from ordinary shares, the issue of preferential shares (with or without voting rights) and of founders' shares is possible.

If the AE becomes insolvent the shareholders risk losing only their contribution to the share capital. Their personal property, as well as the property of the managing director and of the members of the board of directors, is not available to company creditors to meet the debts and obligations of the insolvent company.

Bankruptcy causes the dissolution of the AE company. Nevertheless, until the bankruptcy proceedings come to a formal end, the legal personality of the AE company is maintained exclusively for the continuation of the bankruptcy proceedings. For the implications of bankruptcy on the personal liability of the shareholders, of the members of the board and of the managing director(s), see page 257 below.

Limited companies EPEs

EPEs are established by notarial deed by one or more physical or legal persons. A copy of the notarial deed is registered with the Secretariat of the local Court of First Instance and a summary of the articles of incorporation is published in the Government Gazette. Presidential Decree 419/1986 (which further amended and completed basic Royal Decree 3190/1910 on EPEs) provides that a Public Registry with full files, similar to the one kept for AEs with the Prefectures, should be kept with the Court Secretariat for EPEs. Despite the provisions of the law, in view of the long-awaited amendment of the Commercial Code (which is likely to provide for a General Registry of all commercial companies), the relevant supporting ministerial decisions for the implementation of this law are still pending. Thus, at present EPEs are registered by the Court Secretariat in a Registry kept in alphabetical order. Instead of having a full separate file for each company, next to the company name reference is made to the year and number of the Court archives where copies can be found of the notarial documents establishing, amending or terminating the EPEs.

There is a minimum capital requirement of Drs. 3,000,000. The capital is divided into "company parts" and not into shares. Each "company part" has a nominal value which cannot be less than Drs. 10,000 and must be a multiple thereof. Each person or "partner" participating in the EPE may have one or more company parts depending on the amount he has contributed. Each partner, no matter how many company parts he owns, has only one participation share, *i.e.* a total of rights and obligations seen as a whole. The participation share reflects the personal element of an EPE whereas the ownership of the company parts reflects the prominent capital character of the EPE.

If the EPE becomes insolvent the liability of its partners is restricted to the amount contributed by them to the company capital. As in the case of an AE, the personal assets of the partners and officers are not available to meet claims by company creditors. In the case of bankruptcy, the situation is identical with the one outlined above for an AE.

For the implications of insolvency and bankruptcy on the personal liability of the partners and of the officers see page p258 *infra*.

Management of corporations

AEs

All important decisions of the company are taken within the framework of its two main organs, the general assembly and the board of directors.

The "general assembly" is the supreme organ of an AE and consists of the meeting of the company shareholders. Each voting share gives a right to one vote. Thus the power of each shareholder to influence the decision-making of the company through the appointment or dismissal of the directors is proportionate to the number of shares owned, unless the articles of incorporation specifically grant to individual shareholders the right to appoint a certain number of directors (see p258 *infra*). The general assembly holds an ordinary meeting once a year to approve the financial statements of the company and the report of the board of directors. It also holds extraordinary meetings whenever necessary.

The general assembly elects the directors of the board and it is solely competent to decide, among other matters, on the exoneration of the directors of any liability, on the premature dissolution of the company and under article 34 of Law 2190/1920 on AEs on the appointment of one or more "ekkatharistis" where the company goes into a solvent liquidation. It should be noted that in Greek a solvent liquidation is called "ekkatharisis" and the person who undertakes to liquidate a solvent company is called "ekkatharistis".

Unless the articles of incorporation provide otherwise, the decisions of the general assembly, are normally taken by a majority (50% + 1 share) of the voting shares which are present at the meeting. This means that one shareholder having 51% of the share capital present at the meeting prevails over 10 shareholders having the remaining 49%. The law provides that on certain important matters such as the dissolution of the company decisions can be taken only by a two-thirds majority of the voting shares present at the general assembly.

The general assembly is convened by the "board of directors". The board consists of three or more directors elected by the general assembly for a maximum period of six years. The directors can be re-elected. They are entrusted with the management of the company, the administration of its assets and the attainment of its objectives. Unless the articles of incorporation provide otherwise, decisions are taken by an absolute majority of the directors who are present or are represented by proxy at the meeting. A minimum number of three directors must be physically present, otherwise the Board may not meet and any decisions taken are invalid.

The managing director is elected by the board of directors and he is in charge of the daily management of the company. He reports to the board of directors regularly and acts within the framework of the powers given to him by the board. He is a director with increased duties and responsibilities compared to the other members of the board. In practice, normally only one managing director is appointed but it is possible for the board to appoint more than one.

EPEs

Unless the articles of incorporation provide otherwise, the sole partner in case of one-person EPEs, or all partners of all other EPEs, acting collectively, are in charge of its administration and representation.

In practice, almost without exception the partners appoint one or more officers to manage the company for a limited or unlimited period of time, either through the articles of incorporation or by resolution of the supreme organ of the company, the partners' general meeting. Both partners and third parties can be appointed as officers.

The partners' general meeting meets at least once every year and is competent to decide on all company affairs. This type of company combines capital and personal features in the sense that, unless the law provides otherwise, decisions at the general meetings are taken by dual majority, namely a majority of more than one half of the total number of the partners, representing a majority of more than one half of all company parts. This means that in order to acquire control of such a company, it is not sufficient to obtain a 51% majority of the company's capital. It is also necessary to secure the continuing consent of more than half of the total number of partners. The existing legislation also imposes higher majorities if the amendment of the articles of incorporation is contemplated (three quarters of the total number of partners representing at least three quarters of the total capital) and sometimes imposes unanimity, especially if decisions are to be taken which affect vested rights and the obligations of the partners. One person EPEs are fully controlled by the sole partner who exercises alone the powers of the partner's general meeting.

Ownership

AEs

The shares of AEs are owned by shareholders, who may be either physical or legal persons. The subscription for the company's capital may be in cash or in kind but not in the form of services or work, and an AE is not normally allowed to acquire its own shares directly or indirectly.

The majority of AEs are not listed on the Stock Exchange. Bearer shares are transferred by agreement and delivery between the seller and the buyer. Registered shares, if not listed on the Stock Exchange, are transferred by recording the transfer in a special registry of the AE, whereas, if listed, they are transferred by endorsement before a stockbroker or by notarial deed. The rights of shareholders are recorded in the articles of incorporation and are also found in the relevant legislation. Depending on the type and number of shares which they own, the shareholders may or may not influence the decisions taken by the company organs. The articles of association may give to an individual shareholder or shareholders the right to appoint up to one third of the members of the board of directors. Minority shareholders enjoy certain rights depending on the number of the shares owned by them as a percentage of the total number of the company shares. Even for a very small percentage (5%), some rights are reserved by the law for the protection of minority shareholders.

EPEs

The company parts of an EPE are owned by the partner(s). Normally they are freely transferable, but the articles of incorporation may provide that the owners of company parts have pre-emption rights in priority to third parties over other company parts offered for sale. Transfer takes place by notarial deed. EPEs cannot be listed on the Stock Exchange. The company is not allowed to buy its own company parts.

The capital can be contributed in cash or in kind. Services and personal work cannot be contributed in exchange for company parts. At least Drs.1.5 million of the company capital must be paid in cash. Contributions in kind are evaluated by the Experts' Committee provided by the law on AEs as described above.

This type of company is a convenient one for small and medium size businesses because the formalities, the amount of the necessary capital and the overall operating expenses are modest compared with those of AEs.

Other business entities (OE and EE partnerships, sole traders)

Partnerships are the most common type of companies in Greece and they suit mainly small or medium size undertakings. They are established in private – no notary public is necessary – by two or more partners, individuals or legal persons, who execute the company statutes in two or more original documents. One of the original documents is registered with the registry of companies kept with the Secretariat of the local Court of First Instance.

There is no minimum capital requirement and the founding and operating costs are very low, which is why they are very popular (although they are not recommended for risky business operations or when high turnovers or high profits are expected).

Unless the company statutes provide otherwise, all decisions must be taken unanimously. The law provides that the management of the company is entrusted to all partners acting collectively. In practice, normally one or more officers are appointed by the partners. Partnerships have legal personality and, therefore, have the ability to sue and to be sued in their own name.

As to whether the partners are liable to creditors for the debts of the partnership, it is necessary to distinguish between two types of partnerships:

The "Partnership of unlimited liability" (Omorithmos Eteria – "OE") is a partnership characterised by the unlimited, joint and several liability of each partner through his assets for all the debts and liabilities of the partnership. A court judgment ordering an OE to pay a debt may be executed forthwith against the personal property of its partners. Even partners who have retired or resigned are liable for the debts of the partnership which arose before their retirement or resignation. A court judgment adjudicating the OE bankrupt, does not dissolve the company on the day when the judgment was published (as is the case with AEs and EPEs) but, it does establish the immediate personal bankruptcy of the partners.

The "Partnership of limited liability" (Eterorithmos Eteria – "EE") is a partnership where at least one of the partners, the "unlimited partner", has unlimited, joint and several liability for all the partnership's debts and liabilities, whereas the liability of the "limited partners" is confined to their capital contributions.

As with OEs, bankruptcy does not dissolve the EE from the day of publication of the respective court judgment but, again, from the same day the "unlimited partner(s)" (but not the limited partners) become bankrupt.

OEs and EEs are dissolved by the bankruptcy unless a proposal for a compromise arrangement is agreed (Supreme Court 453/1953).

If a partner in an OE or an EE is bankrupted owing to his personal debts, the partnership itself is not bankrupted. Nor is the partnership dissolved as a result of the bankruptcy of one of its partners, unless the articles of association so provide, or if there are only two partners (Athens Court of Appeal 4185/88).

Finally, every single person who may act validly under civil law may operate his own personal business. This is the simplest form of business activity. In this case the property of the entrepreneur is the same as the property used for the operation of his business. As a result, all personal property of the individual trader becomes available to meet his liabilities to his business creditors. If a sole trader cannot meet his financial obligations, he can be adjudged bankrupt.

Financing and security for creditors

Although the ideal situation for an undertaking would be to be financed solely from funds contributed by its shareholders or its partners, this is not normally the case. Instead, the great majority of undertakings are financed by short, medium or long term loans. Normally, the lenders seek some security for the repayment of their loan and interest. The same applies to other creditors who agree to supply the undertakings concerned with materials, finished goods, machinery, equipment and other items on credit.

Security for lenders and creditors in Greece may take one of the following forms:

Charge (Civil Code art 1257–1345, "Ipothiki")
A charge is a right "in rem" registered on specific immovable property (real estate) owned either by the debtor himself or by a third party. The latter would be likely to be a guarantor for the debtor and would be offering the charge in support of the guarantee. The right to obtain a charge can be by statute (for example, the state has a right of charge recognised by law on the immovable property of citizens for taxes due), by a final court judgment (or a final award of arbitrators), or by a private contract (art 1261 Civil Code). Charges are registered at

the Land Registry (Ipothikofilakion) of the area where the immovable property is located. They take effect as from the time of their registration. If not registered they bear no legal effect. More than one charge can be registered on the same property. Priority among the respective charges is determined by reference to the chronological order of registration in the appropriate Land Registry. The registration of a charge refers always to specific immovable assets and to specific sums of money.

The asset remains under the ownership and the free disposal of the debtor, *i.e.* the debtor is entitled to sell the property but the charge continues to burden the property until the debt is settled by the owner or by any third party on his behalf. The security lies in the fact that, as soon as the secured debt becomes due and payable, the secured creditor may satisfy the whole or part of his claim through the enforced sale of the asset. The creditor who has the first charge will be satisfied first out of the proceeds of the enforced sale, the creditor who has the second charge will follow and so on until all claims secured by charges are settled. The unsecured creditors will share the balance left, if any, proportionally to their claims.

Although the general rule is that charges apply only on immovable property, certain statutes establish charges on movables such as the charge on floating naval constructions or vessels (Law 3816/1958) which are registered at the ship registry of the port of registration, and aircraft (L.D. 4536/1966 & Law 5017/1931). Moreover, under Legislative Decree 17.7/13.8.1923 on "Special privileges to certain AEs" and Law 4112/1929 on "charges on mechanical and other installations" as amended, charges registered upon the immovable property of debtors in favour of banks cover not only the immovable asset (usually the plot of land and the factory) but also the fixed heavy mechanical installations (such as heavy machinery and furnaces) of the debtor enterprise found on the plot (but not tools and constantly free-moving objects). Until the loan is repaid, the debtor cannot sell or lease any of the charged assets without the prior written approval of the lender bank.

Preliminary charge (art 1274–1280 Civil Code, "Prosimios Ipothikis")

A preliminary charge confers a right of preference for obtaining a charge. It can only be obtained by order of the court (art 1274 Civil Code) following interim proceedings. Such a judgment can be issued either with or without the consent of the debtor. The preliminary charge, when registered with the Land Registry, refers to a specified amount of money and a clearly defined asset as above. It is converted into a perfect charge when a final and irrevocable judgment is obtained against the debtor. In case of conversion, the preliminary charge is deemed retroactively to be a charge from the date when it was originally registered with the Land Registry.

Pledge (art 1209–1256 Civil Code, "Enehiron")

The pledge is a right "in rem" registered only on movables and it secures the satisfaction of the claim through the enforced sale of said movables. It can be created either by agreement or by statute.

The Civil Code in article 1211 provides that in the case of private agreement, delivery of a pledged movable from the debtor to the creditor is necessary and that the document incorporating the agreement creating a pledge must have a "certified date". If no delivery takes place the pledge is invalid.

Under article 446 of the CCP a document is of a "certified date" if

- it is certified by a notary public or other competent public servant;
- the person who signed it eventually died;
- its substantive contents are included in a public document.

Article 1214 of the Civil Code introduces an exemption to the general rule and a pledge without delivery would be valid if the agreement of the parties were registered in a public registry. Such registry, at least of a general character, has, however, never been introduced. Thus, normally, a pledge without delivery remains invalid.

Special statutes, however, provide otherwise. Certain pledges may be registered at a public registry maintained by the secretariat of the local court of first instance and any pledge registered there will be valid without delivery.

This register covers pledges on equipment for industrial use and over mining equipment under articles 5 & 6 of L.D. 1038/1949; it includes pledges in favour of banks for loans granted to industrial and other enterprises on movables under Law 1328/1949, pledges on hotel equipment under L.D.181/1946 and L.D.16/18.9.1946, and pledges on cinematographic films (under art 6 of Law 4208/1961). Other pledges may be registered at the local land registry and may also be valid without delivery (such as pledges on tourist coaches under art 11 of Law 717/1977). Furthermore, special legislation (Law 2184/1920) creates a pledge over agricultural equipment where neither delivery nor registration is necessary. Finally, article 604 of the Civil Code provides that the lessor has a pledge by law on the movable property of the lessee brought on to the leased premises, and such pledge secures arrears of rent relating to the two years preceding the attachment of the movables. In this case the law does not require either delivery or registration.

The same movable can be burdened with more than one pledge provided it is agreed between the debtor and its creditors that the pledged thing will be delivered and remain in the hands of one of the creditors or in the hands of a third party. Priority on pledges is established on the basis of the chronological order in which the agreements are concluded (hence the requirements for the date of the agreement to be certified) or of the registration in the registry, if applicable.

Assignment of claims (arts 455–477 Civil Code, "Ekhorisi")

An insolvent debtor who has a claim against a solvent third party can assign it without the consent of such third party. The assignment is concluded upon notification of the assignment, either by the assignor or by the assignee, to the third party. In view of this, claims by the debtor against his own debtors can be used as security for creditors. Provided that notification to the third party has taken place prior to the bankruptcy date, the creditor whose claim is secured on the debtor's claims may institute proceedings for the satisfaction of his full claim against the third party debtors. If, on the other hand, notification did not take place prior to the bankruptcy date, the claim remains the property of the bankrupt debtor, and the "syndikos", who is a lawyer appointed by the court to administer the bankrupt property (see *infra*), is entitled to include the above claim in the inventory of the assets of the bankrupt debtor and distribute the proceeds among all the creditors.

Letter of guarantee ("Engiitiki Epistoli")
The debtor may deliver to the creditor an unconditional letter of bank guarantee. When the debt becomes due and payable the creditor may collect the money due directly from the guarantor bank. The bank will be forced to repay the guaranteed sum regardless of the eventual insolvency or bankruptcy of its client-debtor.

Personal guarantee ("Prosopiki Engiisi")
As was mentioned earlier, normally businessmen who own or manage their companies (*i.e.* shareholders of AEs, managing directors and members of the board of directors of AEs, partners and administrators of EPEs and unlimited partners of EEs), are not liable for the debts of their companies.

Where companies have no property other than movables of doubtful value, which is very often the case, or when the immovable property owned by them is insufficient to provide security, the creditors may demand personal guarantees from the real owners of the business. The contract of guarantee must be in writing. It normally contains a clause under which the guarantor accepts joint and several liability with the debtor company. Moreover, normally the guarantor waives his right to refuse to pay until the creditor exhausts his efforts to satisfy his claim from the property of the debtor company. As a result, once the debt becomes due and payable, the creditor may satisfy his claim by attaching directly the movable or the immovable property of the guarantors. The insolvency or the bankruptcy of the debtor does not deprive the creditor of his right to demand payment by the guarantor.

Cheques
Quite often, especially if the debtor has no immovable property, cheques are given as a security for the timely payment of debts. The debtor and the creditor enter into an agreement whereby the debtor delivers to the creditor some cheques issued by the debtor for the amount due, plus interest. The date remains open. The debtor authorises the creditor in writing to fill in the dates and to present the cheques for collection if he does not pay the debt in time.

If the cheques are refused by the bank for lack of funds, not only can a court payment order be issued within a few days against the debtor company, but the public prosecutor is obliged by law to institute criminal proceedings against the individual who signed the cheque. Furthermore, the creditor may commence proceedings against the physical person who signed the uncovered cheque and demand compensation equal to the amount of the cheque.

To secure only a nominal conviction, the debtor has to prove that the cheque was eventually paid. Thus, a large number of unpaid cheques are settled later, normally a few days before the criminal court hearing.

This method works well if the debtor is merely insolvent because, normally, the satisfaction of the holder of an unpaid cheque takes priority over the settlement of other liabilities of the debtor. Nevertheless, if the debtor is adjudged bankrupt the creditor has no priority over unsecured creditors and the debtor loses the motive to pay the cheque because, at this stage, he may escape criminal conviction by pleading that he did not pay it because he would have been in breach of the law preventing him from satisfying one creditor to the detriment of the others.

Bills of exchange
Bills of exchange are usually guaranteed by a solvent guarantor, and are also extensively used as a form of security for debts. If they are not paid on time, there is no criminal sanction against the debtor or the guarantor but, again, the creditor may obtain a court payment order ("CPO") within a few days against both of them. The CPO is deemed equal to an immediately enforceable court judgment. The security lies in the fact that a CPO offers the creditor the opportunity to attach, immediately, property owned by the debtor or the guarantor (provided of course that some property exists to attach) and to proceed to an enforced sale of the same. This may lead to a speedy satisfaction of the claim in question; otherwise the creditor might wait years before an enforceable judgment is issued.

Of course, if prior to the creditor's satisfaction the debtor is adjudged bankrupt and the guarantor has insufficient property to be attached, the creditor may well find himself in the same position as the other unsecured creditors of the bankrupt debtor.

Preliminary attachment ("sintiritiki katasxesi")
Quite often, the economic situation of a formerly solvent debtor deteriorates to an extent that it becomes more or less clear that he will not be able to settle the debt when this becomes due and payable. In the meantime, since the debt is not overdue, the creditor is unable to obtain a court judgment ordering the debtor to pay. If the debtor is not prepared to offer some kind of security, the creditor may initiate interim court procedings. If the court is convinced that the debtor is "insolvent" it may order a preliminary attachment of the debtor's property. As a result, the debtor cannot sell or burden any of the movable or immovable assets which the court bailiff will eventually seize.

If the debtor is adjudged bankrupt the creditor has no priority rights over the other unsecured creditors. Thus if the debtor owns immovable property the plaintiff normally requests from the court a preliminary charge on the immovable property of the debtor (see pp260-261 *supra*), and a preliminary attachment of all the other property of the debtor.

Retention of title ("Parakratisi Kiriotitos")

To secure payment of the purchase price when movables are sold to a buyer, the seller may retain title to the goods sold until full payment is effected. The seller may enforce a retention of title clause against a bankrupt undertaking provided that:

- the default of the buyer occurred prior to the bankruptcy date; and
- the seller repudiates explicitly or tacitly the contract of sale by expressing his will to take the goods back (Supreme Court Judgment 22/1987 in Plenary Session, and Supreme Court Judgment 1581/88).

In principle, the manifest owner of easily identified movable or immovable property (but not of money) which is found in the possession of a bankrupt undertaking is entitled to claim such property back. In this case, the property which does not belong to the bankrupt undertaking must be separated and delivered to the claimant.

In addition, bankruptcy legislation (arts 668 – 673 CC) provides that the owner of movables may claim them back from the bankrupt debtor where:

- the goods remain unchanged (*i.e.* they have not been processed or changed in their substance);
- they can be identified; and
- they have been given to the debtor in order to be sold by him on the supplier's behalf and in the name of the supplier. Here, if goods have already been sold to third parties by the debtor on behalf of the supplier of the goods on credit, the supplier may recover directly from such third parties the balance due.

Cheques, bills of exchange, and other negotiable instruments can be recovered from the bankrupt undertaking if they have been handed over to it merely for collection on behalf of the owner. Moreover, the seller may repudiate the sale to a bankrupt undertaking provided that delivery of the goods at the premises of the bankrupt buyer has not taken place prior to the bankruptcy date.

Set-off (art 440 Civil Code, "Simpsifismos")

A creditor who has a claim against a bankrupt debtor may reduce his claim by the amount due from him to the bankrupt debtor, provided that the respective claim and counterclaim were in existence prior to the bankruptcy of the debtor (Supreme Court 1070/1976).

It was shown above that there exist various ways to secure collection of a debt. However, not all security interests will be valid and enforceable if the debtor becomes bankrupt. In particular, the validity and the enforceability of security interests in case of bankruptcy depend not only on whether the necessary procedural requirements were carefully respected, nor on whether the creditor is a bank or not, nor on whether the Greek state has a claim against the debtor and for what amount and reason (see p278 *infra*); and the precise time at which the security interest was established. As far as charges, preliminary charges and pledges are concerned, timing is of paramount importance both because they are satisfied in chronological order and also because they may be null and void or voidable depending on the time of their establishment or registration at the appropriate registry (below pp293-295 *infra*).

Available information

Depending on the legal form of the undertakings concerned the following sources of information are available:

The competent prefecture keeps a public registry of the AEs established in its area, which is open to public inspection (arts 7a, 7b, of Law 2190/1920 on AEs). It also keeps a file referring to each AE which contains the articles of incorporation, details of the representatives of the company, names and addresses of managing directors and of members of the board, amendments to company statutes, increases and reductions in the company's capital, annual financial statements, appointment and replacement of "ekkatharistis" and other information. From this file one can trace issues and numbers of the Government Gazette where various announcements are published. Bankruptcies should appear in the company file kept with the prefecture, but in practice, this is not always the case, because the prefecture does not carry out independent research on the whereabouts of each company. Only if the debtor or the creditor or the "syndikos", who is the official that administers the bankruptcy estate (see p285 *infra*), informs the prefecture, will the notice of the bankruptcy appear in the company file.

Copies of the articles of incorporation of EPEs, OEs and EEs including any amendments thereof, can be obtained from the registry of companies kept with the secretariat of the Court of First Instance in the place of their establishment.

It is difficult to obtain information on sole traders. Sometimes, information can be obtained from the local chamber of commerce and industry, or the local chamber of handicraft industries, provided of course that the sole trader has registered himself with any one of them. This is not always the case.

The above information refers to the normal course of company business and not to information related to bankruptcy or other similar procedures. To ascertain whether a company or a sole trader is in bankruptcy, the local registry of bankrupt undertakings which is kept with the Court of First Instance of the place where the undertaking is established, must be checked. The bankruptcy department of the Athens Court of First Instance keeps a general registry where bankruptcies from all over Greece are reported. Moreover, one may check whether a petition for bankruptcy is pending before the competent court. The court secretariat, upon request, issues certificates showing whether an undertaking is bankrupt or not, whether it is subject to special administration, and whether a petition is pending against it.

If the insolvent corporation owns real property, it is possible to find out whether the property is burdened with charges, preliminary charges and attachments by carrying out an investigation at the local Land Registry.

Lately, independent private sources of information have also appeared in the market, but there is still considerable doubt as to their reliability.

Banks often give confidential information to their clients for blacklisted companies and the Union of Greek Banks keeps a list of unpaid cheques open for public inspection, where the names of those who signed such cheques are recorded.

Debt collection and asset recovery

Debt collection

Debts are not always settled in an amicable way. Often legal proceedings are undertaken for their collection. Depending mainly on the facts, on the amount claimed, and on whether the creditor is secured or unsecured, a legal dispute for the collection of a commercial debt may last anything from a number of months to a number of years. Therefore, it is important to know what legal procedures are available to claimants for the satisfaction of such claims and how soon they may reasonably hope to collect a bad debt.

To proceed with the enforcement of a claim the creditor must obtain one of the following:

- an enforceable court judgment;
- a court payment order ("CPO");
- a final award of arbitration; or
- an enforceable notarial deed

To obtain an enforceable court judgment, if the principal sum claimed is not more than Drs.600,000 the creditor must lodge a claim before the Magistrates Court (Irinodikion – "IR"). If the principal sum claimed is greater than Drs.600,000 but not more than Drs.3 million the claim must be filed before the Single Member Court of First Instance (Monomeles Protodikio – "MP"), and, if the principal sum claimed exceeds Drs 3 million, the claim must be lodged before the Multimember Court of First Instance (Polimeles Protodikio – "PP").

The procedure before the IR and the MP is a relatively rapid one and a judgment in the first degree, unless an unforeseen event occurs (such as a strike or adjournment), can normally be obtained within about six months from the date that the claim was lodged with the court secretariat.

Consecutive amendments to the Code of Civil Procedure (in 1993 and 1994) resulted in a substantial shortening of the procedure before the PP. It is expected that normally a judgment could be issued in about a year for cases with few legal issues and within one and a half to two years for more complicated cases.

The Court has the power to declare its judgment "provisionally enforceable". This means that the plaintiff may enforce the judgment, even if the debtor files an appeal before the Appeal Court.

Normally, judgments in the first degree are not declared provisionally enforceable and, if they are, they are declared enforceable for part only of the total claim.

A judgment becomes enforceable if the defendant fails to file an appeal in time. If the defendant files an appeal, it will normally take another year until a judgment is issued by the Court of Appeal.

If the judgment of the Court of First Instance is sustained by the Court of Appeal the judgment of the Court of First Instance becomes fully enforceable.

The defendant may appeal further to the Supreme Court on questions of law.

If the defendant company proceeds with an appeal before the Supreme Court, it may seek a suspension of the execution of the enforceable judgment until the judgment of the Supreme Court is published, but such petition is normally rejected.

Even if the claimant obtains an enforceable judgment, however, satisfaction of the claim is not an easy matter. In particular, if the debtor company has no assets to be attached and in the meantime has closed down its premises, there is practically nothing that a creditor can do to enforce the judgment, unless the debtor company was an OE or EE where the personal property of the unlimited partners can also be attached.

Even if there is property to be attached, the existing legislation offers to debtors many opportunities to delay the enforced sale of their property. Thus, the creditor should estimate that it will take at least another year until he collects the proceeds of the enforced sale of such property.

It is evident from the above that an unsecured creditor who is forced to follow all three stages may spend approximately five years in Court from the commencement of the proceedings until enforcement. In the meantime his claim will be eroded by inflation. His only consolation is that the annual interest on deferred payment, when calculated in Greek drachmas, is high (it was 34% until mid May 1994 and after having increased to 37% it is now again 34%). Such interest is accumulated on the principal sum due from service of the proceedings on the defendant onwards. Of course, five years after the commencement of the proceedings, one never knows whether the debtor will still own assets or be in business.

The creditor may satisfy his claim in a much shorter time if he can obtain the court payment order (CPO) provided by articles 623 – 634 of the Code of Civil Procedure.

A CPO may be issued on the basis of duly signed bills of exchange, cheques, promissory notes, unconditional letters of guarantee, lease agreements, invoices itemising the goods sold and the price of each unit bearing the signature of the person who took delivery of the goods (provided that such person is the lawful representative of the company or the sole trader himself), simple commercial letters of apology where the representative of the debtor company acknowledges the debt and promises to settle it in future and generally on the basis of any other document signed by the person who binds the company with his signature, recognising unconditionally that a certain debt is due and payable. The CPO can be issued by the court in less than a week without any prior notice in the absence of the defendant (ex parte).

This means that a creditor may save many years of litigation and proceed immediately to execution. Moreover, CPOs offer to the creditor the opportunity of applying to the competent land registry to register immediately a "preliminary charge" on immovable assets of the debtor without the necessity of proving in court that the debtor is insolvent. A preliminary charge is converted to a "charge" as soon as the CPO becomes final and irrevocable.

The debtor is entitled to appeal against a CPO or he may apply for a delay or suspension of the execution but, generally, the creditor will hold the upper hand here far more effectively than in any ordinary proceedings.

The difficulties encountered by creditors who seek to obtain or to enforce court judgments in Greece have resulted in the filing of a substantial number of bankruptcy petitions, not because the plaintiff really wishes to have the debtor adjudicated bankrupt, but in order to exert pressure on the debtor to settle overdue debts prior to the date of the hearing.

If the debtor hopes to overcome his financial problems, he may pay part or even the whole claim in order to avoid bankruptcy. In that case, arrangements are made between the litigants so that the hearing is adjourned to a later date or the petition is withdrawn, perhaps to be followed by a new petition later on.

Arbitration as an alternative to the conventional method of debt collection avails the creditor of more chances to satisfy his claim. The procedure is less bureaucratic and formal than the ordinary court procedure, and final enforceable awards are made sooner. This is sometimes extremely important, especially when the debtor is nearly bankrupt.

Awards of arbitrators are usually final and irrevocable. They are issued in a much shorter period of time than ordinary court proceedings, but they are more expensive. The ordinary courts may have no jurisdiction to try the main dispute where, for example, there is a binding agreement between creditor and debtor to submit the claim to arbitration. If there is a fear that certain assets of the debtor may disappear during the arbitration proceedings, the creditor may seek security by instituting interim proceedings before the courts, notwithstanding that the latter lack jurisdiction.

Notarial deeds may provide that the default of the debtor to repay the whole or part of a loan or any other liability at a fixed date renders the contract immediately enforceable. In this case the creditor may proceed to the execution of the deed against the property of the debtor without any prior hearing of the case before a court.

The Code of Civil Procedure (arts 1034-1046) provides for another method of enforcement, the so called "Enforced Administration". A creditor who obtains a final and enforceable court judgment serves it on the defendants demanding payment of the amount due. If the debtor fails to pay, the creditor is entitled to request the court to appoint an administrator who undertakes the management of one or more immovable assets owned by the debtor, or even the management of the debtor's enterprise as a whole. The administration is ordered for the purpose of satisfying the creditor from the income (such as rents) collected from the use of the property belonging to the enterprise.

The Enforced Administration is terminated if the immovable assets are auctioned, or if the debtor's enterprise is adjudged bankrupt (art 1036 para 3), or by court judgment (art 1046). This method of execution is rarely used by creditors.

Finally, under article 1047 of the Code of Civil Procedure ("CCP"), in ordinary court proceedings for the satisfaction of a commercial claim, following the request of the creditor, the court is obliged to order a maximum of one year "personal detention" of the debtor as a means of enforcement of the judgment to be issued in the dispute. Thus, if the judgment is served on the debtor and he either refuses or he is unable to pay, the court bailiff may escort him to prison in order to serve the sentence.

Personal detention under article 1047icle of the CCP cannot be ordered against the lawful representatives of AEs (managing director and members of the board) or of EPEs (administrators and partners), whereas, it can be ordered against the lawful representatives of OEs and EEs.

It should be mentioned that creditors cannot attach money of debtors deposited with banks operating in Greece (Legislative Decree 1059/1971 in conjunction with the Supreme Court in Plenary Session – judgment no. 1224/1975).

Asset recovery

In the absence of any conflicting superior right of a particular debtor, certain rights, such as the absolute right of ownership or the right of possession, entitle the claimant to demand delivery of property held by the debtor. If the debtor refuses, the claimant may have recourse to court proceedings.

If the bankruptcy of the debtor occurs, this general principle continues to apply and the owner (or the person who has a lawful right to claim possession) is entitled to recover the property in question. Recovery may be based either on an appropriate contractual provision (see for example p265 *supra* – "retention of title"), or on the right of ownership and/or possession itself.

Only exceptionally will the *prima facie* right of the owner to recover his property be restricted.

Cross-jurisdictional procedures

Greece has ratified (by Law 1814/1988) the Brussels Convention of 27 September 1968 "on the International Jurisdiction and the Enforcement of Judgments in Civil and Commercial cases", with the result that the Convention became fully applicable in Greece from 1 April 1989.

Consequently, a judgment given in any of the Member States to the Convention is fully enforceable in Greece without any other procedure being required.

It should be noted, however that bankruptcies, compromise arrangements in bankruptcy and other analogous procedures fall out of the scope of the Convention (see *inter alia* for an interpretation of title 1, art 1 para 3 of the Convention, *Henri Gourdain* v *Franz Nadler*, ECJ case 133/78).

Moreover, under article 780 of the Code of Civil Procedure, judgments issued by foreign courts in cases which would have been tried in Greece under a special procedure called "voluntary procedure" – which includes bankruptcy cases – are recognised in Greece with no other procedure being required.

Judgments issued by courts of states which have not acceded to the Convention can be recognised in Greece as enforceable by decision of a Greek court, provided certain requirements are met (arts 905 and 323 of the Code of Civil Procedure). For example, such foreign judgments cannot be declared enforceable if they are contrary to Greek notions of morality or public policy, if the defendants were denied the right of defence, and if they conflict with judgments issued by Greek courts creating a "*res judicata*" between the litigants.

Greece has also ratified (by Legislative Decree 19/19.9.1961) the Convention on the Recognition and Enforcement of Foreign Arbitral Awards, New York, 10 June 1958 ("the N.Y. Convention"). Greece entered into the New York Convention on the basis of reciprocity and it applies the Convention only in relationships which are considered as commercial under Greek national law (see reservations of art 1 para 3 of the N.Y. Convention).

The recognition and enforcement of foreign arbitral awards of states who are not signatories to the N.Y. Convention is conditional upon certain conditions laid down by article 903 of the Code of Civil Procedure and these are similar to those of articles 905 and 323 of the same Code.

As far as the declaration of bankruptcy is concerned, it has been consistently found that, where a United Kingdom court has declared bankrupt a debtor whose place of establishment is in the United Kingdom, the judgment has been considered valid in Greece on the basis of article 780 of the Code of Civil Procedure, without any other procedure being required.

In bankruptcy Greece follows the principles of "unity" and "universality". This means that only the courts in the debtor's place of establishment may declare the debtor bankrupt and the bankruptcy then extends to assets located in foreign jurisdictions. Thus, under Greek law the "liquidator" of a company established and adjudicated bankrupt in the United Kingdom will be able to take possession of assets belonging to the bankrupt undertaking and found in Greece. Similarly, Greek law recognises the right of a syndikos of a Greek bankrupt undertaking to take possession of movable and immovable assets located in a foreign state.

3. Survival of the insolvent corporation or its business

Law 3562/1956

In 1956, in the middle of the decade when the Greek economy was recovering from the effects of the second world war and the civil war, special attention was focused on the debts owed to the Greek state, to state-owned banks, and to creditors in the private sector by big enterprises, especially in the spinning mill and weaving industry, which had collapsed as a result of the liberalisation of imports (1953) and the formation of modern competitive enterprises. To cope with the acute problems of those days special procedures were introduced as an alternative to traditional bankruptcy, by Legislative Decree 3562/1956 "to place AEs under the management and the administration of creditors" and under special liquidation referred to as Law 3562/1956. Since then, Law 3562/1956 has been amended on several occasions and is still applicable, but remains in practice largely unused.

The purpose of this law was to satisfy creditors by decreasing or eliminating the personal participation of the existing shareholders. To achieve its purpose, the law offered the management and the administration of the insolvent enterprise to its creditors and, as an alternative, if no proper solution was found to satisfy the legitimate interests of the creditors and the continuation of the operations of the insolvent enterprise, the law placed the insolvent debtor under a "special liquidation".

This "special liquidation" would make it possible to sell the various departments of the debtor company as separate economic units in public auctions. This enabled a higher price to be obtained for the assets of the debtor company and therefore a greater distribution to creditors.

The new procedure referred also to pure bankruptcy law, and included references to transactions at risk (see p293 *infra*) and to verification of claims (see p283 *infra*).

Under Law 3562/1956 an insolvent corporation can be placed under the management and administration of its creditors or it can be placed under special liquidation by the same court which is competent to adjudicate bankruptcy if the following cumulative requirements are present:

- A special Committee sitting with the Bank of Greece does not object to the application of Law 3562/1956 on the insolvent company, within 45 days following a petition by the company's creditors. The fulfilment of this requirement is proved by a certificate issued by the secretariat of the committee. The decision of the committee is not subject to appeal so if the committee answers in the negative, the creditors are free to follow the normal bankruptcy procedure.
- The petition is filed by one or more creditors representing in value more than 51% of the claims appearing in the official books of the insolvent company.
- The insolvent company has suspended payment of its debts.

The court judgment places the insolvent company under a provisional administration leading either to the management and administration of the company by the creditors or to the liquidation of the company under special rules different from those applicable in the ordinary liquidation provided by the legislation on AEs.

The incentive offered to the creditors, in order to file the petition necessary for the commencement of this procedure, is the opportunity to appoint the administrator of their choice (not necessarily a lawyer) and to undertake the management of the insolvent AE by participating in the "assembly of the creditors" (which replaces the general assembly of the shareholders) and the "managing committee" (which replaces the previous board of directors).

The task of the administrator is twofold: first, to preserve the property of the insolvent corporation and, second, to continue its business operations, or at least to continue the operations of its more productive sectors, if this is deemed beneficial to the corporation's affairs.

It was hoped that by participating in the company management and affairs, the creditors would be assured that the best was done for the satisfaction of their claims. Moreover, the creditors were given the opportunity to obtain shares of the debtor company, so that, if it survived they would remain shareholders.

In practice, the application of the law did not meet the expectation of its drafters. The new philosophy did not displace traditional bankruptcy procedure from creditors' minds. It appears that the idea of involvement in the management of an insolvent undertaking and the personal engagement of the creditors in the administration of the debtor, at the expense of their personal businesses, worked as a strong deterrent to the invocation by creditors of Law 3562/1956.

Instead, the opposite has happened. It is the debtor companies who try to persuade creditors having in value at least 51% of the total claims against the company (*i.e.* normally state-owned banks, the Greek state or public undertakings) to initiate the special procedure of Law 3562/1956 by filing a petition for approval to the special committee of the Bank of Greece provided by article 3 of Law 3562/1956.

This is so because, from the filing of the petition, any attachment against the company, any interim measure against its property, and any bankruptcy proceedings for debts incurred before the filing of the petition, is prohibited. Moreover, from the same date, all procedures for the enforced sale of company assets are suspended. This means that in effect, for a considerable period of time until the initial procedural requirements are satisfied (about one year), the insolvent company will remain immune from all possible actions by its creditors.

Thus, within this one year grace period the insolvent debtor will not be threatened by measures which could have been taken by its creditors. There is, furthermore, some hope that it may overcome its immediate financial problems and settle its debts or conclude some compromise arrangement with its creditors.

Law 1386/1983

In June 1983, less than two years after the general elections of 1981 which brought into power the socialist party, the Government passed Law 1386/1983 "on the Formation of the Organisation for the Financial Restructuring of Enterprises".

The law established a state-owned AE under the name "Organisation for the Financial Restructuring of Enterprises" (the "OAE").

At the same time, Law 1386/1983 was amended by Laws 1472/1984, 1882/1990 and 1892/1990, 2000/1991 and Law 2065/1992.

Under article 1 of Law 1386/1983, the OAE was established to protect the social interest under the supervision of the state exercised by the Minister of National Economy.

The main objective of the OAE was to contribute to the financial recovery of large business concerns which were insolvent. It was therefore empowered to undertake the management and the restructuring of enterprises which:

- had suspended or discontinued their operations for financial reasons; or
- had suspended payment of debts; or
- had been adjudged bankrupt or placed under the administration and management of their creditors or under provisional administration or insolvent liquidation; or
- had a total debt of five times the aggregate of its capital and overt reserves and which were evidently unable to settle their debts for financial reasons; or
- were of interest to the national defence or of vital importance for the development of national resources or which had as their main object the rendering of services to society and which were unable to settle their debts as above; and
- had petitioned to be placed under the protection of this law.

Following an opinion of a special advisory committee, the Ministry of National Economy might place any eligible company under the protection of this provision. Such a decision must be published in the Government Gazette.

This decision follows a petition filed either by the debtor company or by certain creditors and in particular, by the Greek state, by state-owned enterprises, by the lender Bank, by the syndikos (if the company is in bankruptcy), by the administrator (if the company is under administration), by the Labour Employment Organisation (OAED), or by creditors representing at least 20% of the debts overdue on the day of the filing of the petition but not less than 10% of its total debts.

In the event of a decision to place the management of a problematic company under the control of the OAE, the administration is conducted by one or more persons appointed by the OAE, usually professional managers, successful entrepreneurs, economists, or lawyers, and one representative of the company's employees.

The previous board of directors is abolished, whereas the general meeting of shareholders is maintained, but cannot revoke the appointment of the new management.

The OAE administration is given wide powers to conduct the affairs of the enterprise. It can conduct investigations and seek information from any bank or authority. It can continue the operations of sections of the company which are efficient or productive. It should prepare an inventory and a balance sheet and seek financing for the business. During this time the Minister may (and invariably does) suspend payment of debts overdue to any third party, including the Greek state, as well as all measures of individual or collective enforcement.

During this period a viability report is prepared and negotiations entered into for a compromise agreement with creditors. If a compromise agreement is reached, the administration by the OAE ceases and the company resumes operations under its former board of directors.

If no agreement is reached, the company, the OAE or any other interested party may file a petition before the Court of Appeal and request the appointment of a special liquidator. The Court of Appeal, if satisfied that the parties have exhausted all possibilities for a compromise arrangement, may order the special liquidation of the company. Such special liquidation would take place pursuant to L.D. 3562/1956.

Under article 10 of Law 1386/1983, in its original form, any increase in the capital of the company and any capitalisation of its debts to banks, credit institutions, insurance companies, the Greek state and others was decided by the Minister. Such capital increases and capitalisations have diminished the role and participation of the shareholders and most, if not all, such companies have become state-owned enterprises. Court cases have been brought before the Council of state and article 177 EEC references have been made to the European Court questioning the compatibility of such capital increases with the second EEC Company Law Directive (71/91/EEC). On 30 May, 1991, the European Court, in interpreting articles 25 and 41 para 1 of directive 71/91/EEC, found this was not compatible with a provision of national law allowing the Member State to increase by administrative decision the share capital of an AE against the free will of its shareholders. In the meantime, this article was abolished.

Many large companies with huge debts have been subjected to this regime. In July 1990 the right wing government which came to power in the previous April passed Law 1892/1990 "on Modernisation and Development" in order to facilitate the liquidation of non-viable enterprises and the transfer through the Stock Exchange of the direct sale of viable corporations to private investors. By Law 2009/1991 and article 70 of Law 2065/1992, detailed procedural rules for the special liquidation of insolvent enterprises owned either by private parties or by the Greek state were introduced in order to speed up the relevant procedures. These provisions are of a highly technical nature and therefore interested parties dealing with companies falling under them should seek local legal advice. Quite a number of corporations have been sold since then. The Socialist Party, which won the elections in 1993, appears to have accepted that it must continue the liquidation or the sale of such enterprises. Law 1386 is the first Greek law which, in contrast with traditional bankruptcy law, had as its primary object the survival of insolvent companies.

4. Termination of the corporation: bankruptcy and solvent liquidation

Bankruptcy

Purpose and effect

Bankruptcy (in Greek "ptohefsi") is the term given to the legal status of commercial undertakings including legal persons and physical persons which have been declared bankrupt by court judgment.

In order for a Court to adjudge a debtor bankrupt it must be persuaded that:

- the debtor is a "commercial undertaking" in the sense that either it is by law characterised as "commercial" or it is (or was) engaged in trading and;
- the debtor has suspended payment of its debts.

The purpose of bankruptcy is to ensure that, subject to the rights of preferential and of secured creditors, the property owned by an undertaking on the morning of the day when the judgment was published (hereinafter called the "bankruptcy date"), will be distributed equitably between all creditors.

Before we proceed any further, it is necessary to draw attention to the first major distinction between the various categories of creditors.

The creditors of a bankrupt debtor are classified in three broad, but clearly defined, categories:

- creditors whose claim against the debtor arose before the bankruptcy date. Creditors in this category are seen as a society the members of which have a common interest in trying to satisfy their claims through their involvement in the bankruptcy procedure.
- creditors whose claims have arisen after the bankruptcy date as a result of acts of the syndikos. Normally, creditors in this category are not involved in the bankruptcy procedure, but enjoy a privilege over the first category, *i.e.* their claims are satisfied in the course of the bankruptcy and the creditors of the first category share what is left.
- creditors who have claims which have arisen after the bankruptcy date as a result of acts of the debtor as opposed to the syndikos. For example, a bankrupt AE company may have used the professional services of a tax expert after the bankruptcy date without being aware that the judgment adjudicating the company bankrupt was published the day before. Although, the tax expert has a claim for fees, he cannot participate in the bankruptcy procedure. Instead, until the bankruptcy procedure comes to a formal end, he may only seek satisfaction by looking to property, if any, earned by the debtor company after the bankruptcy date.

One may wonder how a bankrupt company may acquire property after bankruptcy. Although in practice this is very unlikely to happen, it might, for instance, accept a donation after bankruptcy, or it may acquire property after it has reached a compromise agreement with its creditors and its administration has regained control of the company. Supposing that the compromise agreement is eventually annulled, the company would have acquired property after bankruptcy.

The first category of creditors – which is the only category which is addressed in this section, unless specifically stated otherwise – is further divided into secured, unsecured and preferential creditors (see p278 *infra*).

Another clarification that has to be made before we proceed is that the same rules apply on the bankruptcy of individuals and legal persons (corporations).

Some of the immediate effects of bankruptcy are described below. In order to achieve equality between unsecured creditors, claims which are not overdue at the bankruptcy date become payable from that date.

For the same reason interest ceases to accumulate on the claims of unsecured creditors. Thus, such claims will be satisfied proportionally as to the principal and the interest accrued up to the bankruptcy date. Nevertheless it should be noted that if bankruptcy ceases for any reason other than by compromise arrangement, the accumulation of interest is not suspended until the claim is fully settled.

Secured creditors are obliged to wait until the real date on which their claims become enforceable before proceeding to the enforced sale of the asset over which they have the security. Also, interest accrued on secured and preferential claims may only be recovered through what is realised by the enforced sale of the specific asset which constitutes the security.

Bankruptcy brings about serious consequences for the debtor, the most important being that from the bankruptcy date the debtor loses control of its property, and a "syndikos" nominated in the court judgment takes over its administration. Here, it should be noted that the debtor is not deprived of the administration of its post-bankruptcy property.

As was stated above, AEs and EPEs are automatically dissolved on the bankruptcy date, whereas their legal personality remains alive until the bankruptcy procedure comes to an end.

In contrast, according to the prevailing view followed by the majority of court judgments (Supreme Court 453/1953, 675/1962, 113/1965, Athens Appeal Court 178/1959, Thessaloniki PP 77/1982), OEs and EEs are not automatically dissolved on the bankruptcy date. This view is based on the fact that the Commercial Code which deals with OEs and EEs does not provide that the bankruptcy of such companies causes their dissolution whereas this is explicitly done in the case of AEs and EPEs.

This matter is not beyond dispute, however. Some scholars argue, on the basis of a few judgments (Volos PP 30/1972), that OEs and EEs are automatically dissolved on the bankruptcy date. This argument is also based on article 775 of the Civil Code which is complementary to the Commercial Code and which provides that a partnership shall be dissolved where a partner is declared bankrupt unless it has been specifically agreed that in such a case the partnership shall continue as between the other partners. This argument is also supported by analogy with the legislation on AEs and EPEs.

The true position seems to be that the personal bankruptcy of the partners of OEs and EEs does not necessarily dissolve the respective companies unless:

- there are only two partners and the bankruptcy of one of them leaves the company with only one partner; or
- it is explicitly provided by the articles of association that bankruptcy of one

of its partners causes the dissolution of the company (Athens Court of Appeal 4185/88).

Here, it should also be mentioned that under Greek law the "dissolution" of a company is a stage which precedes that of "liquidation" and "termination". The dissolution of a company can be caused by several reasons such as:

- expiry of the period of existence provided in the company statutes;
- fulfilment of the company's object;
- decision of the general assembly;
- revocation by the prefect of the licence to operate (in case of AEs);
- decision of the partners' general meeting (in case of EPEs);
- unilaterally or by common accord by one or more partners of an OE or an EE; and
- bankruptcy.

Dissolution is always followed by liquidation. There are two types of liquidation: the "ekkatharisis" (a solvent liquidation) which follows the dissolution of a company by any of the above means other than bankruptcy, and the "ptoheftiki ekkatharisi" (liquidation in bankruptcy). As soon as either of these is over, there follows the "termination" stage, by which the legal personality of the company is extinguished.

Bankruptcy also affects the legal position of creditors. Secured creditors will normally be satisfied through the proceeds of the auction of the specific assets upon which their claims are secured or through the special privilege recognised by law (including necessary expenses incurred for the preservation of a specific asset). If such proceeds are not sufficient to satisfy the claim of the secured creditor, he may participate, on equal terms with the unsecured creditors, in the pro rata distribution of the remaining property.

Unsecured creditors are deprived of their right to pursue their claims individually. Instead, they are obliged to follow the special procedure provided by bankruptcy law for the pro rata satisfaction of their claims.

Finally, preferential creditors are those enjoying a general privilege over the proceeds of the enforced sale of property owned by the bankrupt debtor. (Examples of preferential debts are the claims of employees, claims of the Greek state, claims of Social Security Funds.)

The Greek state has general preferential rights over the bankrupt's property for the repayment of debts which were due and payable prior to the bankruptcy date (arts 2, 5 and 61 of L.D. 356/1974, also Council of state judgment 1958/1989). However, the state is an unsecured creditor in respect of debts due and payable after bankruptcy. Where an asset of the company which is charged by way of security to any creditor is sold at public auction, the state is entitled to up to one third of the proceeds of sale in respect of any claim that it may have against the debtor in question. The balance realised – two thirds or more depending on the state's claim – is used to repay the secured creditor (art 61 para 2 & 5 of L.D. 356/1974).

Social Security Funds enjoy a general privilege for claims arising within six months of the bankruptcy (Supreme Court 1739/81).

From the legal and practical point of view, the present situation is very disappointing and the need for a radical amendment of the existing legal framework has been repeatedly suggested by scholars and commentators. The present legal regime with its extremely complicated, bureaucratic and protracted procedure combined with the eventual disorganisation which follows the declaration of bankruptcy, does not work in favour of the creditors (who normally receive only a small proportion of their claims) or the undertaking itself (which is always terminated).

The lawyers appointed as syndikos are not only underpaid but are also vulnerable to claims for any fault committed during the performance of their duties. This makes them reluctant to undertake the responsibility. Bankruptcies last many years and in most cases the bankrupt property hardly covers the claims of secured and preferential creditors (the Greek state and Social Security Funds included), leaving the unsecured creditors with the feeling that they have not only lost their money but wasted their time as well.

Pre-application considerations

Although the competent court is in theory entitled to adjudge a debtor bankrupt *ex-officio*, in practice it is the creditors who normally seek the bankruptcy of their debtor.

The main consideration lying behind a petition for bankruptcy is usually to press the debtor to make some payment prior to the date of the hearing. If the position of the debtor is not already hopeless, he may settle the claim of the particular plaintiff in order to avoid bankruptcy, or, if he has not already done so, he may offer one of the securities listed earlier in this book (see pp260-266 *supra*).

Petitions for bankruptcy are also lodged when all available legal means for collection have failed and the creditor wishes to write off the debt. If the debtor is adjudged bankrupt and has no property or the existing property is insignificant compared to the claims of his creditors, the tax authorities will accept that the amount due should be written off from the books of the creditor.

Desperate debtors, who find themselves under heavy financial and psychological pressure, sometimes enter into catastrophic sales which may minimise their property to the detriment of the majority of their creditors. Others try to conceal their property by committing fraudulent acts. By having the debtor adjudicated bankrupt it is likely that such transactions will be reviewed. As a result, creditors who are interested in revoking such transactions may seek the bankruptcy of the debtor.

Sometimes, but not very often, the debtor himself may declare to the court that he has suspended payment of debts. The debtor is adjudged bankrupt on the basis of this declaration.

It may happen that a debtor, who has reasons to be adjudged bankrupt, arranges his bankruptcy in collusion with one of his creditors. Obviously this is not permitted by law, but in practice it happens and often there is no way to detect it.

The petition is submitted by one creditor and heard either in default of the debtor's appearance or, if he appears, he may either himself or through a witness admit the suspension of payments. If the plaintiff is a valid creditor he may, in return for his help, collect in secret the whole or the greater part of his claim. Moreover, the same creditor will usually be a witness before the criminal court, which investigates whether the bankruptcy was a result of a fraudulent act. He may testify to the court that the bankruptcy was due to unfortunate circumstances beyond the control of the debtor. If the debtor has the necessary time to organise his bankruptcy, he may even use fictitious creditors. Judges are not experts on accounting and they pass judgment mainly on the basis of the testimony of witnesses. In a more or less stagnating economy where bankruptcies are a daily phenomenon, it is not surprising that bankruptcies are normally attributed to the overall situation of the market, the extremely high cost of borrowing money, or to the devaluation of the Greek currency which makes repayment of debts to foreign creditors extremely onerous for the debtor.

It appears that normally there are two main considerations lying behind the so-called "pre-organised bankruptcies". The first is to defraud creditors.

In particular EPEs are used to this end. They are started with the minimum capital of Drs 3 million (until very recently the minimum was Drs200,000 only) and they undertake obligations by ordering goods worth many millions of drachmas. The founding members sell the goods, pocket the money, sometimes they manipulate company books, and then the company is declared bankrupt. The personal status of the partners (who are all limited partners) is not affected by the bankruptcy of the EPE and, next morning, they may come up with a new EPE (they often employ a paper relative to shield them from their creditors' eyes). Even if it is proved that they defrauded their creditors, in practice the criminal penalties imposed on them are lenient compared with the money earned.

The second consideration usually arises when the debtor realises that his financial situation has become so desperate that only a compromise arrangement with the majority of the creditors will allow him to continue the business.

Experience has shown that in this latter case, very often, a few months prior to bankruptcy date, if the debtor owns the premises, he leases them (including any movables) to a friend or to a company formed by relatives or friends but controlled by the debtor.

As a result, the entrances and exits of the premises cannot be sealed by the magistrate (as would be the case if the premises were not leased) and the machinery and the enterprise remain in perfectly operative condition in the hands of the lessee.

The rent is negotiated to cover the running expenses for the continuation of the bankruptcy procedure (such as syndikos' fees and accountants' fees).

Even lender banks, which almost always have a security over the land and the machinery of the debtor, normally remain silent in order to avoid any depletion of the debtor's assets.

As soon as the bankruptcy is established the debtor strives to persuade the necessary majority of its creditors to accept a compromise arrangement. Very often, in order to achieve certain creditors' consent the debtor makes special secret arrangements with some of them.

Sometimes, debtors pre-organise bankruptcies in order to avoid part of the taxes and the contributions due to the Greek state and/or to Social Security Funds. Of course such evasion is limited only to the extent that the state and the Social Security Funds in question are bound by the compromise arrangement reached between the debtor and his unsecured creditors (Council of State Judgment 1958/89).

Finally, under the existing legislation personal detention for commercial debts ceases to be applicable from the date that the debtor is adjudged bankrupt.

Procedure

Petition by creditors
The petition is filed in court (which fixes a venue and the date for the hearing) and then served on the debtor by a court bailiff. At the date of the hearing the court examines the witnesses of both parties, and allows third parties to intervene in order to support either the plaintiff or the defendant. The decision is issued usually between one and two months after the hearing, by the Multimember Court of First Instance (PP). The judgment is effective from the morning of the day of its publication, and it is automatically enforceable. A summary of the decision is published in the Bulletin of the Legal Pension Fund (DTSN) and the company's name (or the name of the bankrupt debtor, if an individual) is registered in the Registry of Bankrupt Undertakings, an official book kept with the court, which is open for public inspection.

Declaration by debtor
The court will also adjudge the debtor bankrupt if the latter declares in writing to the court secretariat, on its own initiative, that it has suspended payment of its debts. If the debtor is a company the declaration must be submitted to the court by the organs or persons duly representing the company concerned. In that case the judgment is issued without examining witnesses or other evidence. The debtor is obliged to submit to the court together with the declaration that payment has been suspended, a signed balance sheet verifying its contents. Within 15 days, the business books must also be deposited with the court secretariat.

The judgment adjudicating the debtor bankrupt

The judgment adjudicating a debtor bankrupt appoints a judge rapporteur and a "provisional syndikos" and fixes a date for the election of the "definite syndikos".

The judgment is subject to appeal, and is subject, at any time, to revocation by the same court following a petition by the debtor if all creditors have been paid in full or if all known creditors declare in writing that they consent to the revocation of the judgment. In this case, the bankruptcy is revoked retroactively.

The organs of the bankruptcy

The court
The court is the supreme authority for all bankruptcy affairs. Apart from the fact that it adjudges the debtor bankrupt, it renders judgments on many occasions during bankruptcy in order to solve all relevant disputes.

The judge rapporteur
The judge rapporteur supervises the progress of all bankruptcy procedures. He submits reports to the court when required by law to do so and he issues decisions related to the bankruptcy affairs. He also convenes and presides at the meetings of the creditors. In practice, the syndikos seeks the prior approval of the judge rapporteur on almost all his actions during the performance of his duties.

The meeting of the creditors
The meeting of the creditors is not a permanent organ in the sense that it is convened only when the law so provides. It is convened by the judge rapporteur save for the first meeting which is convened by the bankruptcy judgment. All creditors (secured, unsecured and preferential) are entitled to participate in the meetings. In the early stages of the procedings all the undertakings which maintain that they are creditors of the debtor (presumptive creditors) may participate. Later, only those creditors whose claims have been provisionally or definitely accepted by the definite syndikos may participate. All creditors participate at the meetings at their own expense. They are not obliged to appear at the meeting if they do not wish to. However, decisions taken during the meeting are binding upon all creditors, including those not present.

The law makes no provision for a quorum. The meeting reaches its decisions by an absolute majority in number of the creditors present at the meeting. Exceptionally, a special greater majority both in amount of claim and in number of creditors is necessary for the conclusion or the revocation of a compromise arrangement with the bankrupt debtor company or for the continuation of its business by the syndikos.

The decisions/opinions delivered by the meeting, depending on the occasion, may have either an advisory or an obligatory character and quite often, they are subject to court ratification.

The definite syndikos
The definite syndikos plays an important role in bankruptcy proceedings because he undertakes the administration of the property of the bankrupt debtor. The powers and duties of the syndikos are outlined below.

Identification of assets and verification of debts

One of the essential elements of the procedure is the identification and the evaluation of all the assets (rights and claims against third parties included) and of all the debts of the bankrupt undertaking. On the basis of this knowledge, all interested parties (especially the various classes of creditors and the debtor) will base their further action.

One of the main duties of the definite syndikos is to prepare an inventory of the assets of the bankrupt undertaking. He is given wide powers to carry out this task, whereas the debtor is threatened with personal detention if he tries to hide his property or if he is not cooperative.

Creditors' claims can be officially notified either to the court secretariat or directly to the syndikos from the bankruptcy date onwards until the syndikos starts to verify the debts. This notification period can be extended by the judge rapporteur following a petition by the creditor and the syndikos. It is important that the debts are checked one by one in order to ensure that only real creditors participate in the bankruptcy proceedings. Thus, during a certain period of time, which is fixed by the judge rapporteur and in practice is not more than ten days, creditors present their claims to the syndikos. Depending on the number of creditors who wish to verify their debts this ten day period can be extended by the judge rapporteur. The debtor may attend the proceedings and raise objections to the admissibility of claims. The burden of proof lies on the creditor. If the bankrupt undertaking is a company with some substance, the "syndikos" may at an early stage seek the assistance of an accountant to help with the identification of the claims in the company books. Quite often the accountant will be present during the verification procedure.

Normally, the syndikos accepts most of the claims, especially those appearing in the debtor's business books. Each claim is accepted for a precise amount which is duly recorded. Of course the syndikos may refuse to accept certain claims. The dispute between the creditor and the syndikos on the admissibility of a claim is solved by the judge rapporteur, who may agree with the syndikos and reject the claim or, on the contrary, he may declare it as "provisionally acceptable", either in full or for a certain amount. Creditors with provisionally or definitely accepted claims are obliged, within eight days from the verification of their claims, to confirm them for the amount accepted on oath. For any excess amount claimed but not accepted, or for claims which have been rejected, interested creditors have the right of objection before the competent court. The same right of objection can be exercised by both the syndikos and by the debtor if claims have been accepted or rejected in a way prejudicial to their interests. Creditors who have failed to submit their claims within the stipulated period may apply to the competent Court of First Instance to have their claims admitted. Until the court judgment on the above application is issued, the creditor in question cannot participate in the distribution of the bankrupt's property. If the application proves successful the creditor will participate in future distributions, if any.

Since the syndikos cannot verify his own claims against the bankrupt undertaking, two major creditors undertake this duty when necessary.

Cessation of the bankruptcy procedings

The bankruptcy procedure cannot continue without the necessary financial support. Therefore, at any stage of the proceedings, if it becomes apparent that there is no cash available to finance the procedure, the court, either ex-officio or following a petition lodged with the court secretariat by the syndikos or one of the creditors, may issue a judgment ordering the cessation of the proceedings. The question has arisen whether the court should order the cessation when there is immovable property but no cash. Most scholars, supported by the majority of court judgments, take the view that the court may still order a cessation of the proceedings in such a case.

The judgment ordering the cessation can be reversed if the debtor or any interested third party files a petition and persuades the court that there is enough money or that he will make a payment to the syndikos of the money needed for the continuation of the proceedings.

As a result of the cessation, each creditor resumes his right to chase the debtor individually by commencing proceedings, enforcing judgments, attaching property and seeking the personal detention of the debtor for commercial debts.

Creditors' involvement and position

Creditors are heavily involved in bankruptcy proceedings, and in particular in

- filing the petition for bankruptcy;
- proposing names of syndikos;
- notifying their claims to the syndikos;
- presenting their claims to the syndikos, to the judge rapporteur and/or to the court in case of a dispute during verification;
- forming one of the organs of the bankruptcy, the meeting of the creditors;
- holding a meeting and in voting on the compromise arrangement proposed by the debtor;
- filing, either individually or by a majority, a reasoned appeal before the competent court seeking the revocation of the compromise arrangement (see *infra*);
- authorising the syndikos of the "union of creditors" (see p285 *infra*) by a special three quarters majority of creditors and values to continue the trading of the debtor;
- receiving an account from the syndikos of the union of creditors;
- issuing a reasoned advisory opinion on whether the bankruptcy was a result of certain fraudulent acts or not.

Unfortunately, 75% of the bankruptcies adjudicated by the courts are prematurely terminated for lack of funds which means that most of the creditors are unable to collect even a small fraction of their claims.

Powers and duties of the syndikos

As was mentioned above, the syndikos, whether a provisional or definite syndikos or a syndikos of the union of the creditors (see *infra*), holds a position of great responsibility. Only a lawyer practising for at least three years can be appointed as a syndikos.

The syndikos is liable to the creditors and the debtor for any loss caused during the performance of his duties. He may be brought before the disciplinary board of the competent Bar Association or even before a criminal court if he commits a serious or a minor offence during the term of his appointment.

The fees of the syndikos are normally not adequate compensation for the risk that he undertakes. Thus, lawyers are normally very reluctant to undertake this office and if the bankrupt undertaking is of medium size or small it may take many months before a syndikos is found to accept the appointment.

Only one syndikos is appointed at each time but three different types of syndikos are involved successively in the bankruptcy. There are powers and responsibilities common to all three of them but there are also powers and responsibilities pertaining to each different type of syndikos. The common feature is that they are all administrators of the bankrupt property.

The provisional syndikos is appointed by the court judgment adjudicating the debtor bankrupt. He restricts himself solely to actions having an urgent character. For example, he may prepare an inventory of the bankrupt property only in cases where this is expected within one day; he may seek interim injunctions against third parties in order to secure claims of the bankrupt debtor; he may take legal action in order to interrupt the prescription period for claims by the bankrupt undertaking, and he prepares a list of presumptive creditors.

The definite syndikos is appointed by the court following an advisory proposal of the presumptive creditors accompanied by a report of the judge rapporteur. The provisional syndikos may be appointed as the definite syndikos. His main duty is to identify, maintain and administer the property of the bankrupt undertaking. In this respect, if the premises or other properties of the bankrupt have been sealed by the magistrate the syndikos unseals them and prepares an inventory of all movable and immovable assets owned by the debtor. He registers a charge upon the immovable property of the debtor, if any, in favour of the creditors, and may challenge certain acts of the debtor which took place (during the suspected period) prior to the bankruptcy to the detriment of the creditors. He may also continue the current business of the debtor if the judge rapporteur allows it. He verifies the claims of the creditors and in general he is the person who pursues the bankruptcy procedure.

Finally, the syndikos of the union of creditors is appointed by the court following an advisory proposal of the "real" creditors submitted to the court together with a report of the judge rapporteur as above. The appointment takes place if the attempt for a compromise arrangement between the debtor and the creditors fails. He undertakes the sale of the property of the debtor and the distribution of the proceeds among the creditors.

Exceptionally, following a decision taken by a three quarters dual majority in amount of claims and in number of creditors, he may continue the business of the bankrupt debtor during liquidation in bankruptcy.

Management by the syndikos

The syndikos undertakes the management of the property of the bankrupt debtor as soon as the relevant inventory is prepared. In this respect, he is obliged to undertake all measures necessary for the preservation of the property and the collection of the debts owed to the debtor. Moreover, he represents the bankrupt debtor in all legal proceedings related to its property. He is also obliged to sell the movables which are threatened by immediate deterioration or devaluation or whose maintenance is particularly expensive. The sale is effected on the basis of permission granted by the judge rapporteur.

The continuation of the business of the bankrupt debtor by the syndikos is a provisional measure justified mainly in order to prevent the devaluation of the debtor's property, until such property is either returned to the debtor (in case a compromise arrangement is reached between the debtor and his creditors) or liquidated in bankruptcy. The syndikos may manage the property either personally or through third persons appointed by him. If third persons are used, the syndikos is responsible for their acts. He may buy and sell goods, he may lease the premises of the debtor, renew contracts and employ personnel. Nevertheless, the management must be limited only to the minimum acts required to achieve the best possible realisation of the property of the debtor. The Highest Administrative Court (Council of State) ruled that in view of the temporary character of the syndikos' management, the latter was not allowed to expand the existing activities of a bankrupt AE

Position of officers and shareholders/owners

Article 47a para 3 of codified Law 2190/1920 on AEs provides that the dissolution of an AE is always followed by an ekkatharisis (solvent liquidation). The "ekkatharisis" is carried out by one or more "ekkatharistis" (the person in charge of the ekkatharisis) appointed either by the articles of incorporation or by the general assembly (*i.e.* the shareholders' meeting).

Under article 47a para 1c of the same law an AE is dissolved as soon as it is adjudged bankrupt. This is the only case where the dissolution of an AE is not followed by the ekkatharisis of Law 2190/1920 but rather by the appointment of a syndikos and the bankruptcy procedure.

As was stated above (see pp271-275) the legal personality of a bankrupt AE remains in existence only for a limited period of time, namely, until the bankruptcy procedure is completed.

As far as the company organs of an AE – the board of directors and the general assembly – are concerned, it is generally accepted that they remain in place during bankruptcy in order to exercise the powers and carry on the duties which are not in conflict with the bankruptcy procedure. In particular, the board of directors may manage the property acquired by the company after adjudication of bankruptcy; it may submit proposals for a compromise arrangement; it may file appeals and raise objections if the law so provides or if the syndikos remains idle. Of course, the board of directors loses the power to administer the company's property.

If the bankruptcy is terminated by an official compromise arrangement (see p288 *infra*), or by settlement of all debts including the interest accrued until the bankruptcy date (see "reinstatement" p290 *infra*), the shareholders may reinstate the AE. The right of reinstatement is recognised as being available to shareholders by article 47a para 4 of Law 2190/1920, but a special quorum (two thirds of the total paid up capital) and majority (two thirds of the votes present at the meeting) is required.

By analogy with Law 2190/1920, EPEs are treated in the same way as AEs. The directors, shareholders, administrators and partners of AEs and EPEs are not, of course, adjudged bankrupt as a result of company bankruptcy.

Even if all the shares of an AE are in the hands of one shareholder, and the AE is adjudged bankrupt, the sole shareholder (or the sole partner of an EPE) is not made personally bankrupt. Also, if the sole shareholder of an AE or the sole partner of an EPE is adjudged personally bankrupt, the AE or the EPE in question is not adjudged bankrupt.

According to the prevailing view, OEs and EEs are not automatically dissolved if adjudged bankrupt, but some scholars and judgments support a different view (see p277 *supra*). The bankruptcy of an OE or an EE causes the automatic personal bankruptcy of the unlimited partners.

Finally, the personal bankruptcy of the partners of OEs or EEs does not necessarily dissolve the partnerships because OEs and EEs are only dissolved if:

- there are only two partners and the bankruptcy of one of them leaves the company with only one partner;
- it is explicitly provided by the articles of association that bankruptcy of one of its partners causes the dissolution of the partnership.

Employees

The bankruptcy of an undertaking does not terminate contracts of employment. Thus, it is usually one of the first duties of the syndikos to terminate such contracts, unless he intends to continue, temporarily, the operation of the bankrupt business.

The Manpower Employment Organisation (OAED), a public organisation, has been entrusted by Law 1172 of 3/9 July 1981, on the basis of social considerations, to pay to employees overdue salaries and/or compensation for dismissals in the case of insolvency or bankruptcy of their employer.

Moreover, by Law 1836/1989 Greece implemented EEC directive 80/987. In this respect, it introduced an "Account for the Protection of Employees from the Insolvency of their Employers". The account is held with the OAED and it is maintained by contributions paid in by both employers and the state. The purpose of the account is to cover employees' claims against bankrupt employers only in cases where the bankrupt employers have ceased their operations. It does not apply to insolvent employers or to bankrupt employers who continue their operations through the syndikos.

Finally, employees are preferential creditors superior to the claims of the Greek state for claims related to the contract of employment which occurred within two years of the bankruptcy date (art 31 of Law 1545/1985 in conjunction with art 975 of the Code of Civil Procedure).

Termination of bankruptcy

Bankruptcy is terminated by a compromise arrangement, by liquidation in bankruptcy, or by reinstatement.

Compromise arrangement

As soon as the verification of the various claims comes to an end, the accepted creditors (*i.e.* creditors whose claims have been accepted provisionally or definitely as valid), meet at a fixed date and place under the presidency of the judge rapporteur and in the presence of the syndikos and the debtor in order to explore the possibility of a compromise arrangement between the majority of the creditors and the debtor (arts 597 – 624 CC).

At least eight days before the meeting the syndikos prepares a report on his findings and the overall progress of the bankruptcy affairs and the debtor makes a proposal for a compromise arrangement in cash or in instalments.

If the bankrupt debtor makes a proposal for the settlement of at least 60% of the unsecured debt, a compromise arrangement is reached if such proposal is accepted by an absolute majority (50%+1) of creditors holding at least three quarters of the total unsecured claims. If the debtor's proposal for settlement refers to a percentage from 25% to 60% of the unsecured debt, an absolute majority of debtors holding four fifths of the unsecured claims must accept the proposal. Finally, if the debtor is prepared to pay less than 25% of the claims, creditors can accept the proposal if a dual majority votes for the arrangement, namely, two thirds of the creditors holding four fifths of the unsecured claims.

There is an alternative proposal for a settlement open to the debtor. It may propose the abandonment of the whole or part of its property to the creditors. This proposal may reach a compromise arrangement if it is approved by an absolute majority of creditors holding three quarters of the unsecured claims. If this happens, the creditors appoint an administrator who takes the abandoned property under his control and proceeds with its liquidation under the supervision of the judge rapporteur. The proceeds of said liquidation are distributed *pro rata* to the unsecured creditors. At least once a year and upon the completion of the liquidation, the administrator renders an account to the creditors.

The compromise arrangement is reduced to writing and must be signed by the debtor and the majority of the creditors during the same meeting. If the debtor is an AE or an EPE the agreement is signed by the board of directors or the company administrators respectively whereas, if it is an OE or an EE, not only the administrator but all the partners must sign it. The arrangement is sanctioned by the court.

Secured and preferential creditors may participate in the meeting, if they so wish, but their vote is deemed as a waiver of the security or of the right of preference if a compromise agreement is reached and is eventually sanctioned by the court.

As a result of a final and irrevocable judgment sanctioning the compromise arrangement, the syndikos returns to the debtor all its property and renders to it a full account. The syndikos and judge rapporteur are released from their duties and the debtor company regains the administration of its property. Finally, all unsecured creditors, regardless of whether they participated in the meeting, are bound by the compromise arrangement.

If the debtor is convicted by a criminal court of fraudulent bankruptcy, the compromise arrangement is automatically annulled. Moreover, if the debtor fails to pay the agreed percentage, the compromise arrangement may be annulled by the court.

Liquidation in bankruptcy

If no compromise settlement is reached, the bankruptcy automatically enters a stage called the "union of creditors" which leads straight to the liquidation of the company under the special rules pertaining to bankruptcy (arts 625 – 636 CC).

As seen above, a syndikos of the union of creditors is appointed by the court following an advisory opinion of the creditors' meeting. The syndikos proceeds to the liquidation of the movable (arts 660-664 CC) and immovable property (arts 665-667 CC) of the debtor.

Although the union of creditors aims at the liquidation of the debtor's property, exceptionally the syndikos can be authorised to continue the business of the debtor during liquidation in bankruptcy (art 628 CC). Such authorisation is granted by decision taken at a meeting presided over by the judge rapporteur by a three quarters dual majority in number of creditors and amount of claims.

The movable assets are sold under the supervision of the judge rapporteur, normally by public auction. A private sale is permissible provided the judge rapporteur approves the private sale. Movable assets and claims by the debtor against third parties can be sold as a whole. Immovable assets, vessels and aircrafts are sold by public auction.

If the existing property is more than enough to cover creditors' claims, the syndikos is obliged to sell only the property which is necessary for the satisfaction of creditors' claims.

From the bankruptcy date onwards, preferential and unsecured creditors are not allowed either to initiate or to continue any procedure (seizure, attachment, distraint on real property) leading to an enforced sale of the debtor's movables or immovable assets. If such procedures have already started they cease and the unsecured creditors subject their claims to the verification procedure before the syndikos (art 534 CC).

On the contrary, secured creditors are allowed to initiate and to continue such procedures provided that their claims are already due and payable and the union of creditors stage has not yet occurred (arts 647, 648, 665, 666 CC).

Preferential creditors too may initiate civil processes against the debtor to attempt to recover their debts. Again, this privilege does not extend beyond the point when the union of creditors stage is reached.

Once the union of creditors stage has occurred, only the syndikos is entitled to proceed with the sale of the immovable or movable property of the bankrupt company. Of course, the syndikos is not released from his obligation to respect the rights of secured and preferential creditors.

All cash collected during the liquidation in bankruptcy, namely, cash realised through the sale of both movable and immovable property of the bankrupt company, cash found with the bankrupt undertaking on the bankruptcy date plus cash extracted by the syndikos from other sources, is deposited by the syndikos with the Consignment and Loans Fund and the judge rapporteur may order its distribution to the company creditors under the following general rules:

The above cash is distributed to the unsecured creditors *pro rata* to their claims where these have been verified and confirmed by sworn statements or by the competent court (in the case of a dispute).

Prior to such distribution the syndikos is obliged to deduct the amounts corresponding to the following claims which take precedence over the pro rata satisfaction of unsecured creditors' claims:

-   claims for general expenses related to the administration of the debtor's property and court expenses (art 660 CC).
-   claims of preferential creditors having a general privilege (art 975 of the CCP and CC art 646 as amended by art 975 (3) of the CCP).
-   claims of preferential creditors having a special privilege and claims of secured creditors (arts 976, 977, 1007 CCP).

When liquidation comes to an end and the relevant proceeds are distributed to the creditors, the meeting of the creditors is called by the judge rapporteur and in the presence of the debtor the syndikos gives an account of the bankruptcy process. At the end of this meeting, bankruptcy is terminated.

Reinstatement

Reinstatement is governed by articles 14-18 of Compulsory Law 635/1937, and may be ordered by judgment of the court following a petition filed with the court secretariat by the persons who represent the bankrupt company.

The court may declare the company reinstated if either of the following two circumstances occurs:

-   the bankrupt company produces written evidence that it has paid off, at any time, its debts including interest accrued up to the bankruptcy date and that

as a result its creditors have no further claim against it, or
- it proves that the judgment sanctioning the compromise arrangement between itself and its creditors has become final and irrevocable.

Reinstatement becomes effective as soon as the court judgment ordering reinstatement becomes final and irrevocable. If ordered on the basis of the circumstances first mentioned under the heading "Compromise arrangement" (see p288 *supra*) above, it acts to terminate the bankruptcy, whereas reinstatement ordered on the latter basis of the heading "Liquidation in bankruptcy" (see p289 *supra*) above does not of itself put an end to the bankruptcy procedure.

The effect of reinstatement on bankrupt companies is that the disgrace attributed to it is lifted and, next to the company name in the book of bankrupt undertakings kept by the court secretariat, it is explicitly annotated that the company was reinstated. The number of the judgment ordering reinstatement is also recorded next to the company name. The above annotation is equivalent in practice to a removal of the company's name from the Register of Bankrupt Undertakings.

Reinstatement relates primarily to individuals but, on the basis of article 47a para 4 of Law 2190/1920 on AEs and article 16 of Law 635/37 which provides that companies liquidated under special laws cannot be reinstated (argument *a contrario* that in case of liquidation in bankruptcy they can be reinstated), it is generally accepted that the relevant provisions are also applicable to bankrupt AEs and to other legal entities.

Here, it should be mentioned that an AE which has been dissolved owing to bankruptcy may be revived by decision of the general shareholders' meeting (Law 2190/20, art 47a para 4) if the Court accepts its application for reinstatement. In the case of an OE or an EE, however, reinstatement does not follow the reinstatement of the formerly bankrupt unlimited partners.

Solvent liquidation

The shareholders of an AE or the partners of an EPE may decide to terminate the company if the company accumulates losses and has debts that cannot be paid in the normal course of business affairs. If the company has not been adjudged bankrupt, the termination and the "ekkatharisis" (solvent liquidation) of the company will be conducted under the relevant rules of company law (which are more or less identical for the above two types of companies), and not under the rules of bankruptcy law. Of course, even during the ekkatharisis a company can be adjudged bankrupt and, in that case, the ekkatharistis (the person appointed to conduct the ekkatharisis) will be replaced by the syndikos and the ekkatharisis will continue as a liquidation of bankruptcy law.

The remainder of this section outlines the ekkatharisis provided by company law for the two main types of corporation, namely the AEs and the EPEs and finally, the "ekkatharisis" of OEs and EEs which is governed by the Civil Code.

AEs

As we have already seen (see p286 *supra*) the dissolution of an AE for any reason other than bankruptcy is followed by an ekkatharisis.

During ekkatharisis the company name is followed by the words "in ekkatharisis". The ekkatharisis of AEs is governed by the provisions of Law 2190/1920 on AEs in conjunction with the relevant provisions of Law 3190/1955 on EPEs.

On the commencement of the "ekkatharisis" the "ekkatharistis" is obliged to prepare an inventory of the company's property and to draw up a balance sheet of the company which he causes to be published in the press and in the Government Gazette as provided by law (art 7a and art 49 para 1 & 2 of Law 2190/20). The ekkatharistis is subject to the same obligation as above at the termination of the ekkatharisis.

The powers and the duties of the ekkatharistis are, by analogy, those provided by articles 49 & 50 of Law 3190/1955 for the ekkatharistis of EPEs. In particular, he represents the company and signs on its behalf. He has to take care of all outstanding company affairs without delay, settle its debts, collect its claims, and turn the company's property into cash.

Upon termination of the ekkatharisis, provided there is a balance left after settlement of company debts, the ekkatharistis is obliged to distribute such balance to the shareholders of the company proportionally to the nominal value of their shares having regard also to the rights of preference shareholders.Once he has completed the distribution, the "ekkatharistis" must register the termination of the company in the relevant book kept with the competent prefecture.

The "ekkatharistis" is jointly and severally liable to indemnify the creditors of the corporation for any damage sustained as a result of any breach of his obligations.

The above rules cannot be set aside by private agreement because they are primarily intended to protect the creditors of the respective corporations and, therefore, they are seen as serving public policy.

EPEs

The above basic rules for the ekkatharisis of AE companies also apply to EPEs.

OEs and EEs

On the ekkatharisis of OEs and EEs for any reason other than bankruptcy, the Civil Code applies (arts 72 – 77 and arts 777 – 783). Article 780 para 1 requires that, in the first place, the debts of the company in favour of third parties must be settled. If the property of the company is not sufficient to cover its debts, each unlimited partner is liable to the creditors. As far as the internal relationships of the partners is concerned, if the assets of the company are not sufficient to cover the debts, the partners may contribute in cash to the extent that each one is obliged to do so by the company's bylaws.

5. Augmenting the assets of the insolvent corporation

Introduction

The equal treatment of unsecured creditors and their expectation of recovering the total or part of their claims could be prejudiced or even frustrated by the debtor through acts committed either before bankruptcy (*i.e.* before the administration of his property is taken over by the syndikos) or even afterwards. The debtor could discriminate in favour of certain creditors or he could act against the interests of all creditors, for instance by concealing or assigning part of the bankrupt property.

To discourage and prevent such acts, rules exist which render them void or voidable. Moreover, rules of a criminal character provide sanctions against the debtors and against third parties (the syndikos included), who attempt to frustrate the equal and just treatment of creditors.

Transactions at risk

When the court adjudges a debtor bankrupt as a result of a petition filed by a creditor, it normally fixes an anterior date on which it deems that the debtor suspended payments (suspension of payments date – "SPD"). If the Court fails to fix such a date, SPD becomes the bankruptcy date. If the debtor was adjudged bankrupt on the basis of his own petition to the court and he specifies in his petition the date on which he suspended payments, the same date is fixed by the court as the SPD. If the debtor fails to fix a date, the SPD is the date of his petition.

The period of time between the SPD and the bankruptcy date (which can be up to two years) is called the suspect period, in order to reflect the reasonable doubt as to the intentions of the debtor who transacted within this period of time.

Different rules apply depending on the timing of the transactions. Therefore, we have to distinguish between acts which have taken place:

- prior to the "suspect period";
- within the suspect period (and, occasionally, also within a ten day period prior to the suspect period); and
- after the adjudication of bankruptcy.

Acts committed prior to the suspect period
Acts committed within this period can be annulled under the general provisions of the Greek Civil Code (arts 939, 940, 941, 942, 944, 945) which do not mention the status of bankruptcy.

The relevant articles provide that a creditor who cannot recover his claim because he is unable to find sufficient property owned by the debtor may seek the annulment of any transfer of property which has taken place with the aim of frustrating the satisfaction of his claim, provided that the transferee was aware of the malicious intention of the transferor. If the asset was donated, annulment is possible even if the donee was not aware of debtor's intentions. Where the debtor paid a debt that was due and payable, this is not deemed to be a transfer within the meaning of this provision.

The syndikos, acting on behalf of the creditors, may invoke these generally applicable provisions and he may commence proceedings, seeking the annulment of any transfer effected prior to the suspect period which diminished the property of the debtor.

In practice, the above provisions are rarely used by the "syndikos" because it is he who has the onus of proof and it is not easy to prove both the fraudulent intent of the debtor and the knowledge of the transferee, especially if the transaction took place long before the bankruptcy. Only if it is shown that the asset was sold to a close relative of the debtor within one year prior to the service of proceedings seeking the annulment on the debtor, is the burden of proof reversed.

Acts committed within the suspect period (and also within a ten day period prior to the suspect period)

Under article 537 CC, transactions within the suspect period and ten days prior to it are void. This relates to all unilateral acts committed by the debtor reducing his movable or immovable property (*i.e.* all acts of assignment, or release if the debtor received nothing in return), all payments either in cash or by assignment, sale, set-off or payment of debts which have not become due and payable, all payments by other means than in cash or by drafts of debts due and payable, and all acceptances of charges or pledges by private will or by court judgment granted as a security for old debts. Preliminary charges are void if they are registered with the competent Land Registry within the above time period, whereas, in case of charges and pledges, there is no nullity if the actual charge deed was signed or the judgment was issued prior to the suspect period as above, and registration was merely effected within the above period. The nullity of article 537 CC does not apply to charges registered by banks against their debtors during the suspect period and ten days prior to it, which means that such charges or pledges remain valid and they are not affected by the eventual bankruptcy of the debtor.

Under article 538 CC, all payments made of debts due and payable, and all bilateral agreements concluded by the debtor within the suspect period can be set aside (*i.e.* they are voidable) by the court if the payee or the other contracting party knew at the time of payment or execution of the contract, that the debtor had suspended payments. Again the syndikos has the onus of proving the knowledge of the third party.

Acts committed after the adjudication of bankruptcy (*i.e.* from the morning of the bankruptcy date onwards)

Considering that the bankrupt debtor is deprived of his right to administer the bankrupt property from the bankruptcy date onwards, it is not surprising that after bankruptcy all transactions, contracts or unilateral acts of the bankrupt debtor relating to his property are void *vis-a-vis* his creditors (art 2 para 2 of Law 635/37 and art 537 CC). In particular, from the morning of the bankruptcy date onwards, the following acts are void if made by the debtor or his proxy – transfers of assets, releases of debts, acceptances of charges or pledges, recognitions of debts, frustrations or completions of contracts, assignments of claims, waiving of rights to appeal against judgments, consents to third parties' claims. At the same time, payments by third parties made directly to the debtor or his proxy, and not to the syndikos, are void and of no effect against the creditors of the bankrupt undertaking and the payer is not released from his obligation. The payer can be forced to pay the same debt for a second time, this time directly to the syndikos. The buyer of bankrupt property, who bought from the bankrupt debtor, cannot obtain a good title and the syndikos may claim it back by commencing proceedings against the buyer.

The above provisions are designed to augment the assets of the bankrupt undertaking and to achieve equality of treatment between creditors. In practice, the good intention of the legislator is undermined by the protracted procedures and the time and effort which is necessary for the recovery of the assets in question. Proceedings of this type are tried through the ordinary procedure and they normally last many years.

6. Public control over insolvent corporations

Public control in general

If a company is adjudged bankrupt it is the judge rapporteur acting on behalf of the judiciary who supervises and controls the acts of the syndikos, the creditors and the debtor, at all stages of the proceedings, and who on several occasions reports to the court. An investigation of the reasons for the bankruptcy is also carried out ex-officio by the criminal courts. As we have seen earlier in this chapter (see p274 *supra*) the management and public control over the problematic companies of Law 1386/1983 is entrusted to the Organisation for the Restructuring of Enterprises (OAE), which is under ministerial control, whereas companies under the administration of their creditors under Law 3562/1956 as amended, are subject to public control exercised on the one hand by the judiciary and on the other hand by the Special Committee of the Bank of Greece and by the Special Council under article 1 of Law 3956/1959. (Often in these cases one of the creditors is the Greek State, the Bank of Greece, the National Bank of Greece or the Social Security Fund).

Licensing and control of the appointees

The administration of bankruptcies is entrusted by the existing legislation solely to lawyers with no other licence or qualification than three years' general experience.

Any person can be appointed as an administrator of an AE under the management of its creditors since no qualifications are necessary.

The members of the board of directors of the problematic companies under Law 1386/1983 as amended, are appointed by the OAE. They are usually economists, professional managers, lawyers, or entrepreneurs. Normally, banks and other institutions participating in the company capital are represented on the board of directors by a bank director or a director of the respective institution.

Finally, among the members of the board there is always a representative of the company's employees, elected by the employees of the problematic company.

Personal liability of officers of companies

We have already seen that the personal assets of unlimited partners of OEs and EEs are subject to claims by company creditors, whereas the personal assets of the officers of AEs and EPEs are out of the reach of company creditors.

Moreover, it has been mentioned earlier in this paper that under article 1047 of the Code of Civil Procedure "personal detention" is a means of enforcement for the execution of judgments referring to commercial debts and can be ordered by the court only against representatives of OEs and EEs.

Notwithstanding the above, it would be misleading to think that the officers of AEs and EPEs take no personal risks if their company becomes insolvent or is adjudged bankrupt. In reality they may involve themselves in serious personal trouble if the Greek state is among the creditors of the insolvent corporation.

In particular, the managing directors of AEs at the time of their dissolution are jointly and severally liable with the respective companies for the payment of the relevant income tax (art 17 of Law 3843/1958 as amended).

In cases of insolvency and/or bankruptcy, managing directors of AEs, administrators of EPEs and the nominated agents and/or representatives of foreign companies can be prevented from leaving the country if the companies concerned are indebted to the Greek state for more than Drs.10 million (art 27 of Law 1882/1990 and Ministerial Decision 1106544/7010/0016/9/8/93).

Moreover, article 25 of the same Law 1882/1990 on the collection of public revenues threatens with imprisonment the managing director, chairman of the board of directors and any other person involved in the management or administration of an AE, if the company does not settle its debts to the Greek State.

For the same reason as above, the same criminal sanctions apply to the administrators of EPEs, OEs and EEs and, in case of their absence, all partners.

Article 526 of the Commercial Code provides that the representatives of a bankrupt AE must appear before the judge rapporteur and the syndikos on request and furnish all relevant information. Article 530 of the Commercial Code provides that the court which adjudges a debtor bankrupt may order the personal detention of the debtor, especially if the debtor disappeared or if it failed to present a balance sheet. However, the Supreme Court has held that this provision applies only to physical persons and not to the directors and administrators of AEs and EPEs (Supreme Court-judgment 2/88).

Finally, articles 678 to 693 of the Commercial Code are devoted to criminal sanctions for fraudulent acts related to bankruptcy. For example, article 685 provides that the administrators of companies adjudged bankrupt are liable if they fraudulently gave rise to the bankruptcy of the company, whereas article 690 provides for criminal sanctions and pecuniary penalties against both the syndikos if he acts fraudulently, and those who pretended that they were creditors with valid claims when in fact their claims were fraudulent.

Examinations and investigations

When an undertaking is declared bankrupt, an investigation is carried out by the judiciary ex-officio in order to find out whether the bankruptcy was a fraudulent act or not. Eventually a hearing takes place before a criminal court where witnesses are examined in open court and a judgment is issued on the same day.

Publicity and records

As noted earlier, press announcements and registrations in books and records open to public inspection must be made in order to keep the public informed of all developments related to the insolvency or bankruptcy of corporations and physical persons (see p266 *supra* for further information).

Contents of Chapter 7

CORPORATE INSOLVENCY LAW IN IRELAND

1.	**Introduction**	301
	Sources of Irish company law	301
2.	**Corporations**	302
	Types of company	302
	Formation of a company	305
	Constitution, by-laws and share capital	306
	Management of companies	307
	Reconstruction and liquidation	307
	Establishment of a branch	307
	Debt collection and asset recovery	308
3.	**Survival of the insolvent corporation or its business**	310
	Arrangements with creditors	310
	The appointment of an "examiner"	311
	Receivership	323
4.	**Termination of the corporation: liquidation and dissolution**	333
	Liquidation of the company	333
	Dissolution of the company	360
5.	**Augmenting the assets of the insolvent corporation**	360
	Introduction	360
	Transactions at risk	361
	Personal liability of officers	362
	Aggregation orders	366
6.	**Public control over insolvent corporations**	367
	Licensing and control of appointee	367
	Examinations and investigations	367
Appendix		
	Insolvent companies not being wound up	367

Chapter 7

CORPORATE INSOLVENCY LAW IN IRELAND

Francis E Sowman and Michael Quinn,

William Fry

1. Introduction

Sources of Irish company law

The system of company law in Ireland is closely modelled on that of England. We share both geographic proximity and common law tradition; indeed, the Parliament at Westminster legislated for Ireland from the Act of Union in 1800 to the foundation of the Irish Free State in 1921. At that date, all existing English legislation was assumed into Irish law insofar as it did not conflict with the newly-drafted Constitution. Whereas Ireland then became the sovereign independent and democratic state it is today, similarities in legislation have continued. In particular, Irish company law shares more similarities than divergences with its English counterpart. Thus, in its development, Irish company law followed England's example. However, since Ireland's accession to the EC on 1 January 1973, new company legislation has increasingly reflected the European aim of establishing safeguards to protect the interests of various parties including the members of companies, potential members, potential investors, creditors actual and potential, and employees.

The principal legislation governing companies in Ireland consists of the Companies Act 1963, the European Communities (Companies) Regulations 1973, the Companies (Amendment) Acts of 1977, 1982, 1983, 1986, 1990, the Companies Act 1990 and the European Communities (Stock Exchange) Regulations 1984. All of these are construed together as one Act. Subsidiary legislation includes the Stock Transfer Act 1963, Rules of the Superior Courts in relation to the winding-up of companies and various statutory instruments concerning forms and fees.

It is trite to say that company law is founded on statute. In reality, the system of administration and supervision is governed by an amalgam of legislative enactments and judicial decisions. Much of the case law hitherto followed in Ire-

land in company matters has been English, since most of the companies' legislation, as explained, is derived from England together with more general principles of law. But if the courts are to follow foreign authorities, they may pick and
choose among them. Therefore, it has become an increasingly perilous exercise
to rely uncritically on English commentaries, as indigenous facts have and do
mark the divergences in both systems of law.

2. Corporations

Private enterprise in a corporate form is predominantly carried out under the ae-
gis of an incorporated company limited by shares registered under the Companies Act 1963. This is the most common method of business organisation in Ireland. The attraction is understandable as the liability of the shareholders of such
a company for the debts and liabilities of the company is limited to the amount
unpaid on the shares.

Though trade is the most common activity of incorporated bodies, the corporate status of a company formed and registered under the Companies Acts can
be used for other purposes such as trade unions and building societies. This is
dealt with in more detail below. Corporate status confers on the association
(company) a legal personality, separate and distinct from the individual members. Having a legal personality means that the entity has perpetual succession,
can own property and can sue and be sued in its own name.

The legislation enables corporate bodies to be formed for a variety of reasons,
endows them with certain rights and provides a general legal framework within
which they are required to operate. On an administrative level, the Companies
Office situated at Dublin Castle was set up to co-ordinate registration and compile the public registers required under the Companies Acts under the auspices
of the Department of Enterprise and Employment. The Minister for Enterprise
and Employment ("the Minister") has responsibility, in his portfolio, for the
supervision of all company matters.

Types of company

Whereas Irish company law deals primarily with companies formed and registered under the Companies Act 1963, three other forms of company exist in the
business forum:

- Chartered companies or corporations. These are is common in Ireland but
  rarely trade for profit. They are mostly constituted by educational and professional bodies such as voluntary hospitals, Kings Inns, Royal Colleges of
  Surgeons and Physicians and the Incorporated Law Society of Ireland.
  Originally, these bodies were incorporated by charter or grant of letters patent from the British Crown.

- Companies incorporated by statute. This category originally included the
  companies established to run the first railways. These railways were pro-

moted by private enterprise and to facilitate their establishment Parliament passed legislation providing for the incorporation of such undertakings as companies. The majority of these companies have been dissolved since 1921 and their assets and functions transferred to other bodies. (The railways and canals were transferred to Coras Iompair Eireann which is not a company but a board established by statute. Its assets are now vested in three subsidiary companies, Iarnrod Eireann, Bus Eireann and Bus Atha Claith). This category now includes companies, such as Aer Lingus Teoranta (national airline), An Post (postal service) and Telecom Eireann which are intended by the Irish Legislature ("the Oireachtas") to carry out certain functions of national importance, and the shares of which are owned by the state and for administrative purposes held by the Minister. The incorporating Act will usually make special provision in relation to the constitution of the board of directors, the Minister's shareholding and authorised share capital. These companies play a significant role in the Irish economy and are of a special nature as they will primarily be governed by their enabling Act which will take precedence over the Companies Act 1963.

• Bodies with special objects. These are companies formed under statute other than the Companies Act 1963. They include industrial and provident societies, trade unions and friendly societies.

• There is one further entity operating in the Irish business forum. Such entities are commonly prefaced with "bord" or entitled "authority". Although they are not incorporated under the Companies Act 1963, they are established by statute and have a legal personality and therefore can sue and be sued, own property and enjoy perpetual succession. However, they have no share capital or shareholders: all their funds are provided by the state or by borrowing guaranteed by the state, and are the exact equivalent of the British "public corporation". Such bodies include the Electricity Supply Board and Radio Telefis Eireann (television service).

The registered company

The classification of companies in Ireland is confusing since categories overlap. Broadly speaking, the legislation distinguishes between limited and unlimited, between the methods by which the liability of members is limited, between those companies with and those without a share capital, between public and private companies and between public and public limited companies (PLCs), and between old public limited companies and PLCs. The distinctions of major practical importance are those between limited and unlimited companies and the PLCs and the remainder.

In brief, when forming a company, whether public or private, the most important question for the promoters is whether they wish to avail themselves and their successors of the benefits of limited liability and, if they do, whether the company should be limited by shares or by guarantee.

Companies limited by guarantee

In companies limited by guarantee, the liability of the members is limited by the Memorandum to the amount which each undertakes to contribute to the assets of the company in the event of its being wound up whilst he is a member, or within a year of his ceasing to be a member. The company only looks to its guarantee fund in the event of a winding up leading to a dissipation of assets. The fund cannot even be used as security for a loan. The guarantee company therefore is an unsuitable medium through which to trade and is used primarily as a form of association for professional bodies, trade associations, proprietary clubs and people who wish, in the broadest sense, to do "good works". Being a limited company, a guarantee company must bear the words "limited" or "teoranta" at the end of its title as a warning to the public that the members are not liable beyond a stated limit for its debts. The Minister, however, may exempt a limited company from this requirement if he is satisfied that it has the purpose of "promoting commerce, art, science, religion, charity or any other useful object and intends to apply its profits, if any, or other income in promoting its objects, and to prohibit the payment of any dividend to its members".

Unlimited companies

A company may be formed and registered under the Companies Acts which is limited neither by shares nor by guarantee. Such companies are frequently formed where it is intended that the company will not trade. They are used as instruments in tax planning schemes, since such schemes frequently involve the transfer of assets from individuals to companies. They, therefore, can be used as holding companies vested with property on behalf of the individual whose tax burden is being lightened. In such circumstances, the protection of limited liability is not required.

Distinction between public and private companies

The theory which has always been present in companies legislation is that the public company is the basic form of company, and that private companies are variants from the norm. In practice, and especially in Ireland, the reverse is the case; there are far more private than public companies in Ireland. A private company by definition must have a share capital and include three provisions in its articles:

- the right to transfer shares must be restricted;
- the number of members must not exceed 50;
- there must be a prohibition on any invitation to the public to subscribe for shares or debentures of the company.

A public company is defined by section 2 of the 1983 Act as being "a company which is not a private company". This was in fact the first time that the legislation defined a public company. A public company must have at least seven members. A private company may become a public company by the alteration of its articles of association, and similarly a public company may become a private company by the alteration of its articles of association.

Formation of a company

The procedural steps for the incorporation of a private company are relatively simple and may be accomplished within a short time, normally three weeks after the contents of the memorandum and articles of association of the company have been settled. The steps are as follows:

- subscription by two persons for at least one share each (or by one person in the case of a single member company; see p 306 *infra*); and

- the filing of the memorandum and articles of association with the Registrar of Companies together with:
  - a statutory declaration by the solicitor engaged in the formation of the company or by a person named in the articles as a director or secretary of the company of compliance with the requirements of the Acts in respect of registration;
  - a statement in the prescribed form containing particulars of:
    - in the case of the first directors:
      - their present and former first names and surnames;
      - their usual residential addresses;
      - their nationality, if not Irish;
      - their business occupation, if any; and
      - particulars of any other directorships of bodies incorporated in Ireland held by them;
    - in the case of the secretary or joint secretaries:
      - where he is an individual, his present and former first names and surnames and his usual residential address; and
      - where it is a body corporate, the corporate name and registered office;
    - the situation of the registered office of the company.

Following approval of the documentation, the Registrar will issue a Certificate of Incorporation. It is then necessary to hold a first meeting of directors of the company to deal with certain technical matters. Initially, it is normal for the subscribers to the memorandum and articles of association to be persons or nominee companies from the professional advisers to the company being incorporated.

The first directors of the company are normally appointed by the subscribers although it is also possible, though not usual, to appoint directors by naming them in the articles of association.

A limited company is not formed for any particular period of time. Once incorporated it will exist until it is either liquidated or dissolved.

Constitution, by-laws and share capital

The memorandum of association of a company is a formal document which sets out the objects and powers of the company. The articles of association (the by-laws) set out the rules for the internal organisation of the company. These may be framed in many different ways. It is normal to adapt the standard set of memorandum and articles contained in Table A to the First Schedule of the Companies Act 1963 to the circumstances of the particular case.

The articles of association of a company are available for public inspection in the Companies Office. Accordingly, parties to a joint venture through the medium of a private company often prefer to adopt a standard set of articles and to enter into a private shareholding/voting agreement to regulate their rights among themselves.

Share capital

An Irish company need only have two issued shares (or one issued share of if it is a single member company; see *infra*). There is no minimum requirement as to the paid-up share capital of private companies. Thus, the amount of funds contributed to a company by way of share capital does not legally have to bear any relation to the capital employed in its business.

Capital duty of 1% of the amount contributed is payable on the issue of share capital but not of loan capital. Funds contributed to a company in the form of share capital may not be returned to shareholders except on the liquidation of the company and after repayment of creditors, or by a reduction of capital (for which the consent of the High Court is required).

Shareholders

Every company must have at least two shareholders unless it has been registered as a single member company under the European Communities (Single Member Private Limited Companies) Regulations, 1994 (the enactment of the Twelfth Company Law Directive, which took effect in Ireland on 1 October 1994). There is generally no requirement that the shareholders be Irish nationals or residents *but certain restrictions apply in the case of companies purchasing non-urban land in Ireland.* The liability of any shareholder in a company limited by shares, except in exceptional circumstances, is limited to the amount (if any) unpaid on his shares.

Reporting requirements

A private company does not have to make its accounts public but does have to file an annual return giving details of its share capital, shareholders, directors, secured indebtedness and other similar matters. Changes in shareholding need only be filed on an annual basis but changes of directors and issues of new shares must be filed within a short period of each such change.

Management of companies

The management of an Irish company is vested in the board of directors. The articles of association will normally provide for the appointment of the directors by the shareholders. A company must have at least two directors. It is not possible for a body corporate to be a director. The directors need not be residents or nationals of Ireland although, if they are not resident, it is prudent to appoint "alternate directors" who are resident to act on their behalf in the execution of documents and performance of other administrative duties. Shareholders may dismiss a director by a majority vote. A company must also have a secretary, whose duties are ministerial rather than managerial. The secretary may be a director but need not be an employee.

Reconstruction and liquidation

Provisions exist for the rescue or reconstruction of ailing but potentially viable companies under the Companies (Amendment) Act 1990. The principal feature is the provision for appointment by the court of an examiner to report on its viability and the placing of the company concerned under the protection of the court for a specified period.

A company may be put into liquidation either voluntarily by its members or by its creditors or compulsorily through the process of the court. Directors can in certain circumstances be liable for the debts of the company.

Establishment of a branch

Initial requirements

Any foreign corporation is free to establish a place of business in Ireland, but is subject to the requirements of Part XI of the Companies Act 1963. The foreign corporation must, within one month of establishing a place of business in the state, deliver to the Registrar of Companies the following:

- a certified copy of the charter, statutes or memorandum and articles of the company (together with a certified translation where appropriate)
- a list of the directors and secretary of the company containing full particulars as to their names, residential addresses, nationalities (if not Irish) occupations and directorships of other bodies corporate in the state;
- the name and address of the person resident in the state who is authorised to accept service of legal processes and notices on behalf of the company;
- the address of the principal place of business of the company in the state.

Any changes from time to time in the above particulars must be notified to the Registrar of Companies.

Annual requirements

Any foreign corporation which, if it were an Irish company would be a public company, must file with the Registrar of Companies in every calendar year a balance sheet and a profit and loss account of such corporation and subsidiaries (if any). There must also be attached to these documents a report by the directors and the auditors of the company, the contents of which are prescribed by law.

Publication requirements

A foreign corporation establishing a branch must display its name on every place in the state where it carries on business and must also indicate the country in which it is incorporated. This information must be contained on all billheads and notepaper and in all notices and official publications of the branch.

Status and liabilities

In contrast to a subsidiary company the acts of a branch are regarded as the acts of the parent and the parent company will be liable for the debts and other contractual obligations of the branch and also for its tortious and criminal acts. The establishment of a place of business automatically brings the foreign company within the jurisdiction of the Irish courts. A judgment against the company can be enforced against the assets of the branch in the state, and may in certain circumstances be enforced against assets of the company elsewhere (see pp309-310 *infra*).

Debt collection and asset recovery

Unsecured creditors in Ireland

The most common procedure for an unsecured creditor in Ireland is to seek judgment from the court declaring that the amount of money claimed is owing by the debtor. However, the following provisions should be noted:

- The remedy of "distraining" or the levying of "distress" is still theoretically available to a landlord in respect of rent arrears due in Ireland. However, there are various statutory requirements as to procedure together with a possibility of unconstitutionality which do not make this a very attractive remedy. Since it involves the seizure of the goods of one person by another without any court order authorising such seizure, it is rarely invoked, except by the Irish Revenue authorities who make widespread use of this remedy without a court order to collect unpaid taxes. The authority for them to do so is contained in Irish income tax legislation.
- The District Court in Ireland often incorporates the remedy of "distress" if

a defendant fails to pay a penal fine. However, this is not so in simple debt recovery cases. In such cases, the remedy never forms part of the Order of the Court granting judgment for the debt due. The order of the Court must be forwarded by the creditor to the sheriff for execution.

- In the case of a debt due by a company, under the provisions of sections 213 and 214 of the Irish Companies Act 1963, a creditor may make a written demand for payment and, if such payment is not discharged within three weeks, then, providing the debt is for a sum of not less than IR£1,000, the creditor is entitled to petition the High Court for an order winding up the debtor company. A writ of *fieri facias* can be issued in Ireland whereby the sheriff as officer of the court is empowered to take delivery of the debtor's goods. However, obtaining an "order of garnishee" (which entitles the creditor to receive money owing to the debtor) very much depends on the judgment creditor acquiring knowledge of monies recently paid or about to be paid into the hands of the debtor.

- The provisions of the Judgment Mortgage (Ireland) Act 1850 allow a judgment creditor to register his judgment as a mortgage on lands owned in Ireland by the debtor. Although he cannot register his judgment as a charge on stocks or securities of the debtor. Once the judgment is registered as a mortgage, he may seek an order from the court that the debt is validly secured or "stands well charged" on the lands and he may also seek an order for the sale of those lands to realise the debt.

Floating charges

Any entity, whether an individual person or an incorporated or unincorporated body can create a legal mortgage or a fixed charge, which is a form of security over specific identified assets. Such a charge restricts the owner of the asset from dealing with it or disposing of it without the consent of the holder of the charge.

Irish law recognises the concept of a floating charge, which is a charge which floats over all the assets of a company from time to time falling within a general description. The creator of the charge is free to use and dispose of the charged assets in the ordinary course of its business. Such a charge can only be created by a limited liability company.

Cross-jurisdictional procedures

The EC Convention on Civil Jurisdiction and the Enforcement of Judgments 1968 became part of the domestic law of Ireland on 1 June 1988 when the Act of the Oireachtas (the Irish Parliament) enabling it to become part of the domestic law came into force.

By reason of article 26 of that Convention a judgment for monies due given in any of the Member States is recognised in Ireland without a special procedure or leave being required. Under the relevant rules of court, a judgment creditor within the EC can enforce his judgment in Ireland by means of a simple application to the Irish High Court.

This contrasts with the general principle that foreign judgments of other jurisdictions, while being recognised, will not be directly enforced in Ireland. The practical effect of this principle is to force a judgment creditor from outside the EC to institute fresh proceedings in the Irish courts by suing on the judgment obtained or to bring fresh proceedings based on the original claim.

Finally, an application for a "Mareva" type injunction may be made *ex parte* before the High Court of Ireland and will be granted if it is shown that the debtor is about to remove any of his assets out of the jurisdiction in an attempt to put these assets beyond the reach of his creditors. The assets will normally be frozen by order of the High Court pending resolution of the dispute between the parties.

3. Survival of the insolvent corporation or its business

When facing financial difficulties, there are three options open to a company which may enable it to continue. The alternative to following one of these options is for the company to be placed in liquidation, and the liquidation process under Irish law will be considered later in this chapter.

The options of survival are as follows:

- an arrangement with the creditors;
- the appointment of an "examiner" under the Companies (Amendment) Act 1990;
- the appointment of a receiver.

Arrangements with creditors

Statutory scheme of arrangement

Section 201 of the Companies Act 1963 provides a procedure whereby a company can enter into a formal scheme of arrangement with its creditors or with a particular class of creditors. In order to make use of this procedure, the company must first prepare a scheme which contains details of the manner in which the company proposes to discharge its liabilities to its creditors. Proceedings are then commenced in the High Court pursuant to which the company requests the High Court to convene meetings of the various classes of creditors of the company. In order to make this request, the company must present to the Court the scheme of arrangement which in turn is proposed to be submitted to the creditors so that the classes of creditors to be affected by the scheme can be identified, and meetings of those classes of creditors convened.

When such an application is made, the Court is given a power by section 201 (2) of the Companies Act 1963 to stay all proceedings or restrain further proceedings against the company on such terms and for such a period as the Court may decide. It is usual for this provision to apply until the Court receives a report on the meetings of creditors, by which time the success or otherwise of the scheme is likely to be evident. The protection against proceedings cannot be sought until a scheme of arrangement has been formulated by the company and an application has been made to the Court seeking orders convening meetings of the classes of creditors.

The problem with this procedure is that, in order for any scheme to be binding on a class of creditors, the proposals contained in the scheme must be approved by 75% in value of the creditors in the particular class present and voting at the meeting. As the creditors who would, by statute, have a preferential status in an insolvency will usually form a separate class and as, invariably, the Revenue Commissioners have the highest claim in this category, the practical effect is that if the Revenue Commissioners do not support the scheme, the process will not succeed. In recent times the Revenue authorities have not looked favourably on schemes of this nature, with the result that the provisions have not been used, and indeed it is some time since a formal scheme of arrangement under the Companies Act 1963 has been successfully implemented.

However, the provisions remain and if the proposals are accepted by the various categories of creditors, and subsequently sanctioned by the court, such proposals will be binding on all the creditors of the company.

Informal arrangements with creditors

There is no statutory basis for informal arrangements with creditors. However, it may be possible for a company to come to some arrangement with its major creditors whereby the quantum is reduced or the period of payment is extended, thereby enabling the company to continue to meet its liabilities on the basis that it has sufficient resources to discharge its other debts as they fall due. Such procedures have been successfully implemented from time to time on an entirely informal basis. The major creditors will normally reserve their right to revert to the original terms in the event of a winding up, but otherwise will have formed the view that agreeing to vary the terms of payment is likely to generate a greater return than forcing the debtor company into insolvency.

The appointment of an "examiner"

The Companies (Amendment) Act, 1990 provides for an alternative to liquidation and affords a company in financial difficulties a limited period of protection from its creditors for a period of three months (which the court can extend to four) while proposals for reconstruction and survival are being formulated and negotiated. The Act provides for the appointment of an "examiner" to oversee this process.

Circumstances for appointment

An examiner can only be appointed by order of the High Court, based on a petition presented to the court seeking such an appointment. The petition may be presented by the company itself, the directors of the company, a creditor of the company or members of the company holding not less than one-tenth of the paid up voting shares of the company. A petition must be supported by evidence showing that there is justification for the appointment of an examiner, and, where the petition is presented either by the company itself or by its directors, it must include a statement of the assets and liabilities of the company at the date of presentation of the petition or at a date not earlier than seven days prior to the presentation.

However, even when these requirements are met, the legislation stipulates that before an examiner can be appointed, the court must form the opinion that the company is, or is likely to become, unable to pay its debts. Furthermore, there are specific circumstances in which a court cannot exercise its discretion to appoint an examiner on presentation of a petition, namely:

- when a resolution has been passed or an order has been made for the winding-up of the company; or
- if a receiver (see pp323-324 *infra*) stands appointed to the company for a continuous period of at least three days prior to the presentation of the petition.

Section 2 of the Act provides as follows:

" (i)   Where it appears to the Court that:
       (a)   the Company is or is unlikely to be able to pay its debts;and
       (b)   no resolution subsists for the winding up of the Company;and
       (c)   no Order has been made for the winding up of the Company
      it may on application by petition presented appoint an examiner to the Company for the purpose of examining the state of the Company's Affairs and performing such duties in relation to the Company as may be imposed by or under this Act.
(ii)   Without prejudice to the general power of the Court under Sub-Section (1) it may in particular make an Order under this Section if it considers that such Order would be likely to facilitate the survival of the Company, and the whole or any part of its undertaking as a going concern."

The threshold for qualifying for protection under these sections has been regarded as relatively low. In the case of *Re Atlantic Magnetics Limited* (Supreme Court, 5 December 1991) the Court appointed an examiner in the face of opposition from secured lenders who had previously appointed a receiver. The High Court had held that before it would appoint an examiner it must be demonstrated on the hearing of the application that there was a "reasonable prospect" of survival. The Supreme Court however deleted the word "reasonable" and set out the principles to be taken into account in considering an application under Section 2:

"it is quite clear that there cannot be on a petitioner seeking an Order for the appointment of an examiner an onus of proof to establish as a matter of probability that the Company is capable of surviving as a going concern.

Having regard to the clearly preliminary stage at which a decision under section 2 has to be made and having regard to the phraseology contained in sub-section 2 of that Section, which in my view, provides a strongly persuasive obligation to make an order appointing an examiner where the Court considers such an Order is likely to facilitate a survival of the Company, I do not see any warrant for incorporating into the exercise of the power contained in section 2 of the Act of 1990 the necessity for establishment at that stage to the satisfaction of the Court 'a real prospect for survival' (Chief Justic Finlay CJ).

Consequences of appointment

When an order is made appointing an examiner to a company, there are important consequences which automatically follow. First and most important, the company is placed under the protection of the court from the date of the presentation of the petition. This protection will continue for a period of three months from the presentation of the petition, with the discretion to the court to extend this period if it requires additional time to consider the proposals of the examiner for the survival of the company. If the proposals are accepted by the court, the protection continues until a scheme of arrangement comes into effect – which must happen within 21 days of the date on which the scheme of arrangement has been approved by the court.

Once a company is placed under the protection of the court on the appointment of an examiner, the normal remedies of creditors against the company are very severely restricted. In particular,

- no proceedings for the winding-up of the company may be commenced, nor any resolution for winding up passed;
- no receiver may be appointed over the assets of the company;
- no attachment, sequestration, distress or execution may be put in force over the company's goods;
- a creditor whose claim against the company is secured by a charge over the assets of the company or any of them may not take any steps to realise that security without the consent of the examiner;
- no steps can be taken to repossess goods in the company's possession under a hire-purchase agreement, a retention of title agreement or an agreement for bailment of goods which is capable of subsisting for more than three months;
- no proceedings or enforcement proceedings may be instituted against any guarantor of the debts of the company to which the examiner has been appointed;
- no orders for relief may be made under the legislative provisions which seek to protect the interests of minority shareholders against the conduct of the

affairs of the company or the exercise of the powers of the directors prior to the presentation of the petition;

- the right of set-off between separate bank accounts will not apply except with the consent of the examiner;
- no other proceedings may be commenced against the company without leave of the court and in relation to existing proceedings the examiner may apply for such orders as the court considers fit including an order staying the proceedings.

This comprehensive schedule of restrictions provides the examiner with the opportunity to examine the affairs of the company and to formulate proposals for its survival without the fear that at any time steps may be taken to terminate the company's existence or to render any proposals unworkable.

Function of the examiner

The primary function of the examiner is to examine the state of the company's finances and to formulate proposals for its survival for consideration by the creditors and by the High Court. To enable the examiner to achieve this objective specific powers are given to him under the legislation. He is entitled to convene, set the agenda for and preside at board meetings of the company. Where the examiner is of the opinion that any actual or proposed course of action on behalf of the company is likely to be to the detriment of the company, he can take whatever steps are necessary to prevent such a course of action taking place. This is a wide-ranging power, but must be exercised subject to the rights of parties acquiring an interest in good faith and for value in the assets of the company.

The examiner can also make application to the high court under the legislation seeking an order vesting in him the powers and duties of the directors. In order for the High Court to accede to this request, it must be satisfied that it is just and equitable so to do. The court can grant the examiner all the powers which he would have had under the various statutory provisions had he been appointed "official liquidator" of the company. Furthermore, he is given wide powers to oblige officers, agents of the company and third parties who may have books, records, or other relevant documentation, to produce such items and to give the examiner all assistance in the discharge of his functions. In this regard, the legislation empowers the examiner to examine (on oath, by word of mouth or in reply to written questions) such officers, agents or third parties, and failure to comply with the requirements of the examiner may result in the individual suffering consequences similar to those applicable to a party held to be in contempt of Court.

Consequences for receivers and liquidators

An examiner may be appointed to a company by the High Court notwithstanding that a receiver has been appointed to that company, provided the receiver has not been so appointed for a continuous period of three or more days prior to the presentation of the petition for the appointment of an examiner. Consequently, if an examiner is to be appointed once a receiver has been put in place, prompt action is required. If a petition for the appointment of an examiner is presented within three days from the appointment of a receiver, the Court has power to order the receiver to cease to act, or to act only in relation to certain assets.

On the presentation of a petition for the appointment of an examiner the Court will give directions as to the hearing of the petition, which will normally take place approximately seven to ten days after the presentation of the petition. The practice has also developed of appointing an examiner on an interim basis pending the hearing of the petition.

In the case of *Re Holidair Limited and Companies, (Amendment) Act 1990* 7 March 1994 receivers had been appointed on the day before the petition for the appointment of an examiner was presented. The Court appointed an interim examiner pending the hearing of the petition and made an order to the effect that the receivers if they should so elect be permitted to continue to act. This permission was subject to an undertaking by the debenture holders which had appointed the receivers to continue to support the companies trading as a going concern, and an undertaking of the receivers not to sell or dispose or contract to sell or dispose of any of the assets of the company otherwise than in the ordinary course of trade pending the hearing of the petition. The order made in that case caused considerable practical difficulties, but represented a balance as far as the Court was concerned in terms of the respective rights of the company and the examiner on the one hand and the debenture holders and the receivers on the other hand. Ultimately at the hearing of the petition seven days later, the Court confirmed the appointment of the examiner and directed that the receivers should cease to act during the period of protection.

As regards a winding up, an examiner cannot be appointed once a resolution for the winding up of a company has been passed or, in the case of compulsory liquidation, once a winding up order has been made by the High Court.

Contractual obligations of the examiner

The business of a company does not cease on the appointment of an examiner. Indeed this would be quite contrary to the concept of the legislation. The company should continue its business and the directors remain in office and, subject to certain exceptional provisions, retain all their powers. Consequently liabilities will continue to be incurred and the first and perhaps most important issue to be determined is the extent of the responsibility of the examiner for such liabilities. Section 13(6) of the Act states that:

> "An Examiner shall be personally liable on any contract entered into by him in the performance of his functions (whether such contract is entered into by him in the name of the company or in his own name as examiner or otherwise) unless the contract provides that he is not to be personally liable on such contract, and he shall be entitled in respect of that liability to indemnity out of the assets;...."

Therefore, unless it can be shown that the examiner:

- did not enter into the contract in his own name;
- did not enter into the contract in the name of the company;
- in effect had no role in negotiating the contract or incurring the liability,

then he will be personally liable under a contract entered into by him in the performance of his functions unless personal liability is specifically excluded. The protection for the examiner in such circumstances under section 13(6) of the Act is that he is entitled to be indemnified out of the assets of the company in addition to any other indemnity to which he may be entitled under the particular contract. There are at least two important points to be stressed in relation to such indemnity:

- it is an indemnity "out of the assets" of the company consequently its worth is restricted to the value of such assets and;
- it relates to contracts entered into by the examiner "in the performance of his functions" and consequently has no application to contracts entered into without authority.

Power to deal with charged property

An important consequence of the appointment of an examiner is that, provided he can satisfy the court that to do so would facilitate the survival of the whole or any part of the company as a going concern, the examiner can be empowered to realise assets notwithstanding that such assets are subject to a security.

Where such security comprises a floating charge, the legislation states that on the sale of such assets by the examiner, the holder of the floating charge has the same priority in respect of any property of the company directly or indirectly representing the property disposed of as it would have had in respect of the property formerly subject to the floating charge.

Where the security in question is a fixed charge, somewhat more stringent provisions apply with regard to a realisation. The Act provides that the net proceeds of the disposal of such assets shall be applied towards discharging the sums secured by the fixed charge. Furthermore, where the court is satisfied that such net proceeds do not represent the open market value, the net proceeds together with such sum as may be required to make up the deficiency must be applied towards discharging the sum secured by the fixed charge. Provisions similar to those relating to a fixed charge will also apply where the asset to be realised is held subject to a hire purchase agreement, conditional sale agreement, a retention of title agreement or an agreement for the bailment of goods which is capable of subsisting for more than three months.

In the case of *Re Holidair Limited and Companies (Amendment) Act 1990* 7 March 1994 the Supreme Court held that the charge over book debts created by the debenture under which the receivers had been appointed was a floating charge, and not a fixed charge as contended for by the bank. The Court held that the floating charge had crystallised on the appointment of the receivers on 19 January 1994 and therefore, when the company came under the protection of the Court on the following day by the presentation of the petition, the charge had become a fixed charge. The Court further held that the effect of the order appointing the examiner was to "decrystalise" the charge on book debts so that it reverted to being only a floating charge and the company was entitled to use the proceeds of collections from debtors in the ordinary course of its business.

The concept of "decrystallisation" is one which is not otherwise known or recognised in this jurisdiction. However the Supreme Court judgments make it clear that it was determined to ensure that, in the circumstances of the case, practical effect was given to the legislation and that the relevant provisions of the debenture and of the Act itself be interpreted in such fashion as would achieve that objective. In the *Holidair* case the debenture holder, following the confirmation of the examiner's appointment, had sought to compel the company to lodge all sums collected from debtors in the ordinary course of business to designated bank accounts pursuant to the charge on book debts. In addition to its decision that the charge as created was only a floating charge the Court held that the direction to lodge monies to a particular designated account was an attempt to realise the assets subject to the charge and was in breach of the prohibition on enforcement against the company effected by the order granting protection.

Obligations of the examiner

The examiner's obligation is to conduct an examination into the affairs of the company to which he is appointed. The results of this examination must be reported to the court within 21 days of his appointment or such longer period as the court may allow. A copy of this report must be delivered to the company on the same day as it is delivered to the court. Section 16 of the Companies Amendment Act 1990 stipulates the information which must be included and aspects which must be covered in the report. In addition to an obligation to recite details of the officers of the company and, insofar as it is reasonably possible to do so, to incorporate a "statement of affairs", the examiner's report must make the following recommendations relating to the following concerns :

- whether in the opinion of the examiner any deficiency between the assets and liabilities of the company has been accounted for satisfactorily;
- whether in the examiner's opinion all or part of the company is capable of survival as a going concern and, if so, the conditions which he feels are necessary to ensure such survival and whether a proposal for a compromise or scheme of arrangement would facilitate such survival;
- whether in the opinion of the examiner continuation of the whole or part of the company would be more advantageous to the members and creditors than a winding up;
- what course should be taken by the company including, if appropriate, a draft proposal for a compromise or scheme of arrangement;

- whether on the basis of his findings, the examiner would be justified in making further enquiries with a view to instituting proceedings under the provisions of the Companies Act 1990 relating to fraudulent or reckless trading.

If the examiner forms the opinion that:

- the company, either in whole or in part, is not capable of survival as a going concern; or
- that the formulation, acceptance or confirmation of proposals for a compromise, or scheme of arrangement would not facilitate such survival; or
- that an attempt to continue the whole or part of the undertaking of the company would not be more advantageous to the members and creditors than a winding up; or
- there is evidence of a substantial disappearance of property that is not adequately accounted for, or of other serious irregularities in relation to the company's affairs;

the court will hold a hearing to consider the contents of the examiner's report and at this hearing, in addition to the examiner and the company itself, a member or creditor of the company together with anyone alleged to have a responsibility for any irregularities of the company, is entitled to be heard. At the conclusion of this hearing, the court is given power to make such order or orders as it deems appropriate (including an order for the winding up of the company).

Proposal for continuation

If in his report the examiner expresses the view that the whole or part of the company is capable of survival as a going concern, he shall formulate proposals for a compromise or scheme of arrangement. These proposals must:

- specify each class of members and creditors of the company;
- specify any class of members or creditors whose interests or claims will not be impaired by the proposals – which means in the case of a creditor that the creditor will still receive payment in full, and in the case of a shareholder that (i) the nominal value of the shareholding is not reduced, or (ii) the rights relating thereto are not impaired, or (iii) the percentage interest in the total issued share capital is not decreased;
- specify any class of members or creditors whose interests or claims will be impaired under the proposals;
- provide equal treatment for each claim or interest of a particular class, unless the party having such claim or interest expressly agrees to the contrary;
- provide for the implementation of the proposals.

In addition, the examiner has the discretion to incorporate in such proposals changes which he feels necessary in the management of the company or in the memorandum and articles of association. To facilitate the members and creditors in contrasting the likely outcome of the proposals as against a winding up, the report should estimate the outcome of a winding up of the company for each class of members and creditors.

Once the proposals have been formulated, the examiner must convene and preside at meetings of each of the classes of members and creditors which have been identified in the proposals, and report on the outcome of these meetings to the court within 42 days of his appointment. The court has a discretion to allow a further extension not exceeding 30 days after the expiration of the period of three months referred to above, being the period for which the examiner is initially appointed.

The report on the outcome of the meetings will, in addition to citing the proposals placed before the meetings including any modifications thereof and the outcome of the meetings, incorporate an up-to-date statement of the assets and liabilities together with a schedule of creditors. In order for the examiner's proposals to be accepted by a class of members the proposals must be supported by the majority of votes cast at the meeting whether in person or by proxy. In the case of meetings of creditors or classes of creditors the proposals must be supported by a majority in number also representing a majority in value of the creditors attending and voting at the meeting whether in person or by proxy.

This report by the examiner must be considered by the High Court as soon as possible after it has been delivered. Any creditor or member whose claim or interest would be impaired under the proposals is entitled to be heard, notwithstanding that such creditor or member may already have voiced his objection to the proposals at the relevant meetings.

The High Court is given wide discretion on the question of whether to accept the examiner's proposal. However, such discretion is not unlimited, and the legislation specifically provides that the Court shall not confirm a proposal unless at least one class of members and one class of creditors whose interests or claims would be impaired by the proposals have accepted the proposals. There is a specific provision prohibiting the Court accepting proposals whose sole or primary purpose is the avoidance of payment of tax. Furthermore, the Court must be satisfied that the proposals are fair and equitable in relation to any class of member or creditor objecting to the proposal and whose interests would be impaired. It must also be satisfied that the proposals are not unfairly prejudicial to the interests of any creditor or member of the company.

Having reviewed the examiner's report and considered the submissions of parties entitled to be heard on the issue, the Court can:

- confirm the proposals; or
- confirm the proposals subject to modifications; or
- refuse to confirm the proposals.

If the Court follows either of these options, the proposals become binding on all members and creditors or classes of members and creditors affected by the proposals. The Court may when confirming the proposals make such orders regarding the implementation of the proposals as it deems necessary, and such proposals will come into effect from a date fixed by the Court, which date must be not later than 21 days from the date of the confirmation of the proposals.

The Court may, however, decide not to confirm the proposals. This step will be inevitable if the examiner's report concludes that it has not been possible to reach agreement on the proposals at the required meetings of creditors and members.

Similarly, the Court will have no option but to refuse to confirm the proposals if it decides that they are contrary to or not in accordance with the requirements specified above.

In a number of cases which have come before the Court modifications have been sought by creditors. The Court has a discretion to impose the modification sought but one of the significant features of hearings to confirm proposals has been a consideration by the Court as to whether the modifications are such that they could not properly be made without convening further meetings of the members and creditors for the purposes of considering those modifications. In practice the Court has been reluctant to set about convening such further meetings where this would have the effect of delaying the procedure further and putting at risk the successful outcome of the examinership (*Re Holidair Limited*).

In the case of *Re Goodman International Limited* 28 January 1991, following meetings of creditors held to consider the examiner's proposals, a number of creditors made submissions on the subsequent hearing before the High Court and proposed that the Court should consider and accept modifications to the proposals which proposals had already been considered at the meetings of creditors and members. The right of the Court to consider modifications, notwithstanding that proposals have already been considered by creditors at the respective statutory meetings, poses a potential dilemma for the Court which the then President of the High Court, Mr Justice Hamilton, addressed as follows in his judgment delivered on 28 January 1991:

"The only serious question which arose in connection with these modifications was whether it was necessary to convene a further meeting of the members and creditors of the companies to consider and approve of the proposals as modified.
Section 24, sub-section 3 of the Act provides that:
"At a hearing under sub-section 1, the Court may, as it thinks proper, subject to the provisions of this section and section 25, confirm, confirm subject to modifications, or refuse to confirm the proposals."
This section appears to me to give absolute discretion to the Court in this regard. It is of course a discretion that must be exercised judicially and if the modifications suggested were to fundamentally alter the proposals which had been considered by the members and creditors of the companies, then a Court would be slow to modify the scheme in a fundamental manner without having the modifications considered by the members and creditors. I am however satisfied that the modifications to the Scheme do not fundamentally alter the proposals" Hamilton P.

Where the proposals have been rejected, the Court has authority to make an order for the winding-up of the company or any other order it deems fit.

Costs and remuneration of the examiner

Under section 29(1) of the Act, the Court can make orders from time to time "as it thinks proper for the payment of the remuneration and costs of and reasonable expenses incurred by an examiner". The determination of the quantum of remuneration fees and expenses is a matter for the Court. These payments cannot be discharged from the assets of the company without the approval of the Court even in circumstances where the quantum has been fully agreed by the examiner and the company over which he is appointed.

Having obtained the approval of the Court the next point is how the remuneration, costs and expenses can be paid. Section 29(2) provides for payment either:

- out of the revenue of the business; or
- out of the proceeds of realisation of assets of the company to which the examiner has been appointed.

Once again it is important to evaluate at an early stage whether these two sources are likely to be sufficient to meet the anticipated requirements.

One cannot presume that the liabilities incurred by the examiner together with his remuneration, costs and expenses will necessarily be discharged during the examiner's term of office. By the passage of time or for other reasons an examiner may cease to act before these payments have been made. In these circumstances, the examiner is protected by section 29(3) of the Act which provides that the remuneration, costs and expenses of the Examiner will rank in priority to any other claim, secured or unsecured which arises:

- under any compromise or scheme of arrangement; or
- in a receivership; or
- in any winding up

of the company to which the examiner has been appointed. Section 10 provides that the liabilities of the company certified by the examiner as necessarily incurred to enable the company to survive as a going concern shall be treated as expenses properly incurred by the examiner. Consequently, such liabilities shall be afforded the priority granted by section 29(3).

Since the introduction of the Companies (Amendment) Act, 1990 there had been some speculation as to whether it could be argued that the assets of a company available to meet liabilities and expenses under section 29 could only mean unencumbered assets of the company and would not include assets which are the subject of a mortgage or fixed charge. In *Re Holidair Limited and Companies (Amendment) Act 1990* 7 March 1994 the Supreme Court held that the assets subject to such charges do form part of the assets available to meet expenses under section 29 and gave the following clear statement on this issue:

"The true interpretation of section 29(3) is that the remuneration, costs and expenses as defined in that section of an examiner which had been sanctioned by Order of the Court shall be paid in actual priority to the claims of any secured or unsecured creditor and under the provisions of Section 29(2) the Court may if necessary and must if it has sanctioned such remuneration, costs and expenses in a case where unsecured assets are insufficient to pay the total of the amounts involved direct their payments out of secured assets" (Chief Justice, Finlay CJ).

This judgment is treated as a direction to the effect that the assets which are the subject matter of security should only be applied in discharge of fees, costs and remuneration to the extent that the unsecured assets are insufficient for that purpose.

Additional provisions

Certain of the provisions relating to the winding up of companies are also applicable in situations where an examiner has been appointed to a company. The provisions of particular importance are:

- the prohibition against withholding possession of, or obtaining a lien over, documents belonging to the company or the documents or papers relating to the accounts or trade, dealings or business of the company as against the examiner;
- the right of the examiner to apply to court for an order holding a person who, while an officer of the company, was knowingly a party to the carrying on of any business of the company in a reckless manner, personally responsible for all or any parts of the debts or the liabilities of the company.

These provisions are considered in more detail in the section of this chapter relating to the winding up of companies. The provisions in relation to fraudulent trading contained in section 297 of the Companies Act 1963 are also made applicable to companies to which an examiner has been appointed.

Conclusions

The Companies (Amendment) Act 1990 came into effect in August 1990. Whilst the procedure has been successfully implemented in a number of major companies, the strict procedures which must be followed and the frequency with which applications to court are necessary have had the effect of restricting the operation of the legislation to larger companies which have available to them the resources necessary to discharge the inevitable expenses of such an exercise. Furthermore, the legislation has been the subject matter of considerable opposition, most notably from financial institutions which regard the potential for erosion of the value of their security as fundamentally objectionable. As a consequence the Minister for Enterprise and Employment has established a working group charged with the function of reviewing the operation of this legislation and considering the possibilities of reform.

Receivership

The concept of receivership in Irish law has its origins in law relating to receivership applicable in England and Wales. Indeed, it was not until the introduction of the Companies Act, 1963 that specific legislation was enacted in this jurisdiction relating to receiverships. The Companies Act 1990 makes certain modifications in the law relating to receivership.

There are three basic ways in which a receiver may be appointed, namely:

- by order of the court. Under its equitable jurisdiction, the court may appoint a receiver. This may arise either where a debenture which creates the security does not contain provisions for the appointment of a receiver, or where the event placing the security in jeopardy is not one of the events recited in the debenture as authorising the appointment of a receiver. Furthermore, the court can appoint a receiver for the purpose of discharging a particular function, such as the appointment of a receiver by way of equitable execution. Such an appointment is authorised under Order 45 rule 9 of the Rules of the Superior Courts and it provides for the appointment of a receiver over specific assets of the debtor company on the application of a judgment creditor. This procedure enables the receiver to realise these specific assets of the debtor company to discharge the indebtedness to the judgment creditor. However, the appointment of a receiver by the court is a very rare event in Irish law and would now only arise in very exceptional circumstances:

- by operation of statute. The specific power to appoint a receiver is granted to a mortgagee where the mortgage is made by deed by reason of section 11 (iii) of the Conveyancing and Law of Property Act 1881. This power arises when the mortgage money has become due, and applies as if the power had been contained in the mortgage deed. However, the power applies only if and as far as a contrary intention is not expressed in the mortgage deed and shall have effect subject to the terms of the mortgage deed. Section 24 of the 1881 Act details the statutory powers of receivers so appointed and the manner in which such receiver shall apply all monies received. Once again, the appointment of a receiver in this manner is now relatively rare in Ireland as most mortgage debentures will contain specific and detailed provisions relating to the appointment of a receiver. However, these statutory provisions can from time to time still be of benefit to mortgagees and it is important that a mortgagee should be aware of the statutory rights which are automatically afforded to them by reason of these provisions. Section 17 (4) (d) of the Companies (Amendment) Act, 1990 empowers the High Court having considered the report of an examiner filed in accordance with this legislation, to appoint a receiver for the purpose of the sale of the whole or part of the undertaking concerned if it deems it appropriate so to do.

- pursuant to the provisions of a debenture. In recent Irish legal history the vast majority of situations in which a receiver has been appointed have arisen from the provisions of the debenture deed by which the security is created. This chapter hereafter considers the law relating to receivers appointed pursuant to the terms of a debenture.

Circumstances of appointment

The debenture deed will detail the situations in which the debenture holder is entitled to appoint a receiver and, in addition to the statutory power applicable in the case of a mortgage which we have already considered, most modern debentures will contain a comprehensive list of circumstances in which the appointment of a receiver is justified. Nevertheless, any potential receiver would be well advised to ensure that circumstances have arisen which justify the appointment under the terms of the debenture. Furthermore, care should be taken to verify that the security under which a receiver is proposed to be appointed has been registered in the Companies Registration Office in accordance with the provisions of section 99 of the Companies Act 1963. That section details the forms of security which must be registered in the Companies Registration Office in order to provide notification to all parties interested in the company (and particularly to its creditors) of the existence of a charge. The requirement of this section will apply to virtually all categories of security pursuant to which a receiver is likely to be appointed.

The nature and extent of the security

A priority for any receiver appointed by a debenture deed is to identify the precise nature of the security under which he has been appointed and the extent of the borrowings from the debenture holder to which the security relates. In considering the nature of the security, the fundamental question to be answered is whether the debenture creates a fixed or floating charge or both. Due to the fact that the wide and apparently ever increasing categories of statutory preferential claims rank in priority for distribution to creditors secured by a floating charge, it is clearly imperative for a receiver to be satisfied as to the identity of the security.

The debenture deed itself will usually stipulate whether it is intended to create a fixed or floating charge over specific assets of the borrowing company. However, the mere fact that a security is described either specifically or by implication as a "fixed" charge does not automatically mean that it will be so determined at law. This point is well illustrated in the judgment of Mr. Justice Costello in the case of *Lakeglen Construction Limited (In Liquidation)* delivered in December 1978. In that case the borrowing companies charged "in favour of the major creditors all their respective book debts and all rights and powers of recovery in respect thereof to hold the same unto the Major Creditors absolutely".

Was it the intention of the parties that the company should be free to receive the proceeds of its book debts and bring new ones into existence as if the debenture had not been created? The judge concluded that, in the absence of provisions to the contrary, when permission to trade is given in a debenture, permission to receive book debts is more readily to be inferred than is an arrangement by which the company is required to hand them over to a debenture holder, and nothing in the debenture itself displaced that inference. This case was decided when the concept of fixed charges on book debts was in its relative infancy. Clauses in subsequent debentures became somewhat more sophisticated and have been upheld as creating valid fixed charges on book debts (see, for example, *Re Keenan Brothers Limited* [1985] 1 IRLM).

For a relatively short period of time the practice of incorporating a fixed charge on book debts in securities became very popular in Ireland, encouraged by a line of authorities both in Ireland and in the United Kingdom, suggesting the validity and enforceability of this concept. However, the success of this idea, culminating in *Re Keenan Brothers Limited (supra)*, was viewed with serious concern by the revenue commissioners who saw their very considerable preferential entitlements, granted initially under section 285 of the Companies Act 1963 and extended by subsequent legislation, being seriously eroded.

Consequently, in response to this development, section 115 of the Finance Act 1986 contains a rather severe provision to the effect that if:

- a bank or other party holds a fixed charge over a company's book debts created on or after the passing of the Finance Act 1986; and
- the company fails to pay the Revenue Commissioners any amount of PAYE deductions, including interest for late payment, and VAT; and
- the Revenue Commissioners serve notice on the bank of that default on the part of the company; and
- after receipt of such notice, and assuming that the bank continues to hold the fixed charge on book debts, the bank receives any payment, directly or indirectly, from the company in respect of any debt due by the company to the bank;

then the bank is obliged to pay to the Revenue Commissioners, up to the amount of any payments so received by the bank from the company, the full amount demanded by the Revenue Commissioners in respect of unpaid PAYE, interest and VAT liability of the company.

By virtue of section 174 of the Finance Act 1995, where the fixed charge holder notifies the Revenue Commissioners of the existence or creation of the fixed charge over book debts his liability under the section is confined to the amount which the company failed to pay after the holder of the charge has been notified by the Revenue Commissioner of any potential liability under the section.

It should be noted that this section is operative while the company remains a going concern, as well as in a situation where the company is in liquidation or receivership. Not surprisingly, financial institutions and other lenders became most reluctant to risk finding themselves in a position of having responsibility for the tax liabilities of their borrowers, and consequently very few securities created since the provisions of section 115 of the Finance Act came into force contain a fixed charge on book debts.

It is also important to remember that a mortgage or debenture is to be construed, in the case of ambiguity, against the lender by whom it has normally been prepared. Therefore if a debenture is silent on whether a particular security is to be fixed or floating it will be treated as the latter unless the terms of the debenture are such as to establish beyond doubt the intention of the parties to create a fixed charge.

A debenture can either be for a specified quantum of borrowing or for all borrowings and indebtedness. If the former is the case then a receiver can only pay the secured creditor the amount specified and secured by the debenture together with any interest properly payable. On the question of the entitlement of a secured creditor to interest where the borrowing company has been placed in liquidation, see the section on winding up (p333 *et seq infra*).

It is important to check precisely what forms of liabilities are covered by the wording. A well-worded debenture will ensure that every conceivable form of indebtedness, whether by direct borrowing or by guarantee and whether jointly or severally, will be covered by the security. However, this is not always the case. One often comes across situations in which certain of the transactions between the debenture holder and the company will not come within the definition of the liabilities secured under the debenture. A careful examination of this aspect of the security document is therefore essential before distribution.

Eligibility to act

Under the Companies Act 1963 a body corporate or an undischarged bankrupt could not act as a receiver. Section 170 of the Companies Act 1990 extended the categories of persons disqualified from acting as receivers by excluding the following parties:

- a person who is, or who has within 12 months of the commencement of the receivership been an officer or servant (which includes an auditor) of the company;
- a parent, spouse, brother, sister or child of an officer of the company;
- a person who is a partner of or in the employment of an officer or servant of the company;
- anyone disqualified under one of these headings in relation to the subsidiary or holding company or a subsidiary of the holding company of the company in question;
- anyone convicted of an indictable offence in relation to a company for a period of at least five years from date of conviction.

Consequences of appointment

On appointment the receiver must send notice to the company of his appointment. The party making the appointment must also, within seven days after the date of the appointment publish notice of his appointment in both *Iris Oifiguil* (which is the Official Gazette in Ireland) and in at least one daily newspaper circulating in the district where the registered office of the company is situated. Furthermore, notification of the appointment of a receiver must likewise be given by the debenture holder to the Registrar of Companies.

Once a receiver has been appointed every invoice or business letter or similar document bearing the name of the company which is issued by the company or the receiver must state that the company is in receivership.

Following the appointment of a receiver there is a statutory obligation on one or more of the directors, together with the secretary of the company, to submit on affidavit a statement of affairs giving full details of the company's assets, debts and liabilities as at the date of the appointment of the receiver.

On receipt of this statement of affairs, the receiver has an obligation to send copies of the document (among other things) to the Registrar of Companies accompanied by any comments he sees fit to make on the contents.

A further statutory obligation which applies throughout the receivership is the duty of the receiver to deliver to the Registrar of Companies at six monthly intervals an abstract showing the receipts and payments in the receivership. Every receiver must also bear in mind, as already discussed above, the fact that for a period of three days after the appointment a receiver may be removed from office by order of the High Court in the event of the company being placed under the protection of the High Court and an examiner appointed to the company under the provisions of that legislation.

Powers and duties of a receiver

General

The powers of a receiver are detailed in the debenture document under which the appointment has been made. These powers are normally very comprehensive and will enlarge considerably on the powers given to a receiver appointed under a mortgage pursuant to the provisions of the Conveyancing Act 1881. In particular, the receiver will be given extensive powers of management so that, if he deems it appropriate so to do, he can continue to trade in an endeavour to sell the business as a going concern or alternatively (and much more infrequently) to return the company as a going concern to its directors having raised sufficient funds or made satisfactory arrangements to discharge the demands of the debenture holder together with those of any party ranking in priority.

The Companies Act 1963 as amended by the Companies Act 1990 gives a receiver the entitlement to apply to the court for directions in relation to any matter arising in connection with the performance of his functions. This provision is utilised by receivers from time to time when issues of law arise in relation to the terms of the debenture, the priority of securities or other similar matters.

In virtually every debenture the receiver will be appointed the agent of the company and this agency will continue throughout the receivership unless or until a liquidator is appointed. Furthermore, most debentures will specifically appoint the receiver as attorney of the company for the purpose of completing any agreement, deed or other document required to enable the receiver to discharge his functions. This power of attorney has been included in debentures in order to overcome the difficulties encountered by receivers in situations where the directors refused to comply with requests to execute deeds in the manner required under the articles of association. The effectiveness of such a provision for the purpose of conveying an interest in land was upheld by the Supreme Court in *Re Cork Shoe Company Limited, IDA* v *Moran* 29 November 1978.

Realisation of assets

It has been established for some time, through a series of decided cases, that a receiver's obligation is not restricted to realising sufficient monies from the assets of the company to enable the receiver to discharge the indebtedness to the debenture holder. The receiver has an obligation to take all reasonable steps to ensure that proper consideration is received for the assets disposed. This obligation is stipulated by statute, and section 172 of the Companies Act 1990 places an obligation on a receiver to take all reasonable care to obtain the best price reasonably obtainable at the time of sale of the assets of the company over which he is appointed. If a receiver is challenged under this provision he cannot raise the defence that he was acting as agent of the company or under a power of attorney given by the company and he is not entitled to be indemnified by the company in respect of any liability which may be incurred under this provision.

It has frequently been the case that when a receiver is selling the assets or business of the company over which he is appointed, such sale has been to a party who, prior to the receivership, had an interest in or who was involved in the running of the company. In the vast majority of cases this has arisen simply because such parties were prepared to pay a sum for such assets or business in excess of that obtainable from any other source. However, such a sale was always a source of concern to the creditors of the company and the Companies Act 1990 reflects this concern by providing that a receiver cannot sell a non-cash asset by private contract to anyone who is, or who has been within three years prior to the date of the appointment of the receiver, an officer of the company unless the receiver gives at least 14 days' prior notice in writing to all known creditors of the company of his intention so to do.

Contracts

A receiver will normally be appointed the agent of the company and consequently he is not liable for the contractual obligations of the company undertaken prior to his appointment. Consequently, if a receiver is of the opinion that a particular contract no longer benefits the company, he can refuse to perform that contract and the injured party will rank as an unsecured creditor of the company in respect of any damages incurred by such breach. However, as agent of the company the receiver has no greater rights in respect of any contract than that which attaches to the company itself. Consequently, in *W & L Crowe & Another* v *Electricity Supply Board* 9 May 1993 it was held that the Electricity Supply

Board was entitled to refuse to furnish a supply contract to a receiver until the account due by the company had been paid. The court so decided notwithstanding the fact that the receiver had undertaken to be personally responsible for payments for electricity supplied from the date of his appointment.

Although a receiver does not have a personal liability for contracts of the company entered into prior to his appointment, it is provided in section 316 of the Companies Act 1963 that a receiver shall be personally liable on any contract entered into by him in the performance of his functions unless the contract provides to the contrary. Insofar as a receiver is personally liable on such contracts, he is entitled to be indemnified in respect of such liability out of the assets of the company. However, such a right of indemnity will not apply if the contract exceeds the receiver's authority or if he has failed to discharge his statutory obligations, such as that to acquire the best obtainable price for the assets.

Employees

The appointment of a receiver by order of the court terminates the contracts of employees. However, this is not the case where the appointment is made pursuant to the powers contained in a debenture, which is the basis of appointment in the vast majority of cases. The provisions of section 285 of the Companies Act 1963 (as extended by subsequent legislation), grant preferential status to employees in respect of many of the payments to which they are entitled on the termination of their employment by reason of the employer being placed in receivership or insolvent liquidation. However, prior to 1983 the question of whether employees would actually receive payment in respect of these entitlements was dependent on there being sufficient assets in the company to enable preferential creditors to be paid. In a receivership, if all the assets were secured by a fixed charge and were necessary to pay in full or in part the indebtedness to the debenture holder, then there were no resources from which the preferential debts due to employees could be paid.

The Protection of Employees (Employers Insolvency) Act, 1984 changed this. It applies to all insolvencies commencing after 22 October 1983, and operates by establishing an insolvency fund financed by the state from which virtually all preferential entitlements of employees are funded irrespective of the ability of the insolvent company to meet its preferential liabilities. Under the legislation where monies are provided by the insolvency fund the Minister for Labour is given subrogation rights in respect of the claims which would otherwise have been provable by the employees. Prior to the introduction of this legislation, under the Redundancy Payments Acts 1967 to 1979, a redundancy fund had been established which specifically ensured that there were monies available, independent of the insolvent company, to meet only the redundancy entitlement of employees.

Where a receiver continues to trade and the contracts of employment have not been terminated, the employees remain in the employment of the company. The question of whether such employees have any greater rights than any other contract creditors in respect of remuneration or any other entitlements arising subsequent to the commencement of the receivership has not been specifically decided but, in practice, no receiver can expect the co-operation of the employees unless they have been assured by the receiver that he will be personally responsible for their remuneration and other entitlements. It is usual for a receiver to give this form of commitment at the commencement of the receivership.

Statutory Instrument No. 306 of 1980 implements the European Communities (Safeguarding of Employees Rights on Transfer of Undertakings) Directive, designed to harmonise the applicable principles throughout the EC where there has been a transfer of an undertaking, business, or part of a business. Under these regulations the rights and obligations of the transferor arising from employment contracts are transferred to the transferee of the business.

It was held in *Mythen* v *Employment Appeals Tribunal* 29 June 1989 that the Directive applies where the business assets are sold by a receiver appointed by a debenture holder and that, where the business is sold as a going concern, the purchaser assumes the company's obligations to its employees. Some uncertainty has developed as to whether this applies in cases where the employees are dismissed by the receiver before the sale takes place and this has resulted in considerable concern for receivers. The precise circumstances in which the purchaser of a business from the receiver would be held responsible for employee contracts has still not been defined. This uncertainty can unsettle a potential purchaser and cause difficulties to a receiver in his endeavour to sell the business and thereby generate or maintain employment.

Tax

Under the provisions of section 56 of the Finance Act 1983 a receiver is an accountable person in respect of any corporation tax or capital gains tax payable in connection with a chargeable gain. Under section 11 (3) of the Capital Gains Tax Act 1975 every gain is a chargeable gain except so far as otherwise expressly provided by that Act. Consequently, if in the course of the realisation of assets in a receivership a chargeable gain arises, then the receiver has a legal responsibility to ensure that the corporation tax or capital gains tax arising from such a gain is discharged. This is the case notwithstanding that the receiver is the agent of the company under the debenture and that the asset in question may have been realised by means of a power of attorney granted to the receiver in the debenture.

However, in contrast to the situation relating to a chargeable gain, it has been held that a receiver appointed by a debenture holder over the assets of a company is not liable to discharge corporation tax payable under the Corporation Tax Act, 1976 on "profits" arising during the receivership. (In *Wayte Holdings Limited (In Receivership)* 9 October 1986), the receiver was appointed agent of the company and he realised assets of the company and placed the proceeds on deposit. Interest accumulated on the sums deposited and the Inspector of Taxes failed in his claim that the receiver was liable to pay corporation tax on the interest which the money earned. The effect of the decision is that the corporation tax accrued is a liability of the company but not of the receiver.

Distribution of assets

The primary objective of a receiver is to realise the assets procured by the debenture, hopefully by means of a sale as a going concern, so that he is in a position to discharge the indebtedness to the debenture holder by whom he was appointed. However, in making a distribution there are certain factors which must be taken into consideration.

Trust claims

As a company can only give security over its assets, it follows that such security cannot extend to any monies or other items deemed at law to be held on trust by the company. Therefore, particularly in the case of a distribution of the proceeds of a debtor, it is necessary to be satisfied that such proceeds form part of the assets of the company and are thus covered by the charge. There are a number of precedent cases to illustrate situations in which the proceeds of debtors will be held on trust for third parties, as for example where a travel agency collects money for airline tickets (In *Re Shannon Travel Limited (In Liquidation)* [1972]), or where a company acting as an agent for a shipping line collects freights from consignees for the carriage of goods (In *Re Palgrave Murphy Limited (In Liquidation)* [1979]).

Retention of title

A receiver has no greater rights to the assets over which he has been appointed than those formerly enjoyed by the company. Consequently, the concept of retention of title which has been recognised in Ireland in a series of court decisions will apply in a receivership. A receiver will have to adjudicate such claims and be satisfied that the proceeds of the sale of the assets and particularly the sale of stock are free from claims of this nature and available for distribution. The extent to which retention of title is likely to be relevant in a receivership will depend largely on the nature of the business. For example it has an obvious significance in companies in the retail and construction sectors.

Prior secured creditor

It goes without saying that a receiver must be satisfied that there is no other secured creditor with a claim ranking in priority to the secured creditor by whom he was appointed. In addition to identifying any prior secured creditor, the receiver should ensure that such security is valid and enforceable before making a distribution.

Preferential creditors

The category of creditors having a statutory right to preference has expanded considerably from those detailed in the Companies Act 1963. Under Irish law, preferential creditors are entitled to rank in priority to creditors secured by a floating charge. The categories of preferential creditors are considered in more detail at pp355-356 *infra*. In some receiverships, it proves possible to discharge the indebtedness to the debenture holder out of the proceeds of sale of assets secured by a fixed charge. In *Re United Bars Limited (In Receivership)* [1991], following a decision in England in *GL Saunders Limited* [1986], it was held that a surplus from assets secured by a fixed charge must be paid to the company and not to the preferential creditors.

A further issue arising, in a situation where a receiver appointed under a debenture containing a fixed and floating charge is followed by a liquidator, is whether the receiver or the liquidator has the responsibility to discharge the preferential claims. In the normal course it is clear that, if the receiver has to have recourse to the assets secured by the floating charge to enable him to pay the debenture holder, he must discharge the claims of the preferential creditors at the date of his appointment before doing so. However, in the case in question, (*In Re Eisc Teoranta* 2 March 1989), the receiver was in a position to pay the debenture holder in full out of the proceeds of the realisation of assets subject to the fixed charge. Nevertheless, it was held that once a receiver was appointed under a debenture containing a floating charge, he thereby became responsible for discharging the claims of the preferential creditors and the realisation of assets subject to that charge and was therefore obliged so to do before accounting to the liquidator for the surplus in the receivership.

Consequences of liquidation

It is established in Irish law that the agency between the company and the receiver is terminated on liquidation. However, to avoid the implication that the receiver thereby becomes the agent of the debenture holder, there is usually an express provision to the contrary in the debenture document.

Termination of receivership

A receivership will normally be terminated by means of a "deed of discharge" when the receiver has realised all or so much as may be necessary of the assets of the company and accounted to the debenture holder. There is a statutory obligation on a receiver, on ceasing to act to deliver notice of such cessation to the Registrar of Companies. In addition to the normal means of termination of a receivership, section 175 of the Companies Act 1990 contains a power enabling the court on cause shown to remove a receiver and appoint another receiver. A receiver must be given not less than seven days' notice of such an application, and the receiver and the debenture holder are both specifically given the right of audience on the hearing of an application under this section.

Furthermore, an important provision is contained in section 176 of the Companies Act 1990 which allows a liquidator of a company being wound up and over which a receiver has also been appointed, to apply for an order that the court either directs the receiver to cease acting from a specified date or alternatively that he should act only in respect of certain assets as specified by the court. Although it is specifically stated that no order under this section shall otherwise effect the validity of any security or charge over the assets of the property in question, this is a radical new provision and it remains to be seen how it will be applied and the circumstances in which the court will be prepared either to restrict or terminate the powers of a receiver.

4. Termination of the corporation: liquidation and dissolution

The legal existence of a limited liability company comes to an end when it has been dissolved. Dissolution usually takes place after the completion of a winding-up by a liquidator. However, dissolution is also possible in circumstances where a company has been struck off the Register by the Registrar of Companies. This usually occurs in cases where the company has failed to file statutory returns to the Registrar, causing him to believe that the company is no longer carrying on business. (s311 Companies Act 1963). (Dissolution will be dealt with in more detail at p360 *infra*.)

The law and practice relating to the liquidation of companies in Ireland is governed principally by the Companies Act 1963. There have been a number of amendments to the provisions of that Act, most notably a variety of legislative provisions extending the categories of creditors entitled to preferential status, and the Companies Act 1990 which contains a number of substantial amendments to the Act of 1963. References to sections of the Act should be taken as references to the Companies Act 1963 unless otherwise stated.

Many of the procedural aspects of liquidations are governed by Order 74 of the Rules of the Superior Courts 1986. Although the majority of the rules contained in Order 74 apply only in a compulsory winding up, a number of these rules apply also to the conduct of voluntary liquidations. References to rules should be taken as references to rules comprised within Order 74. The High Court has exclusive jurisdiction to determine all issues arising under the Companies Acts and the Rules.

Liquidation of the company

Liquidation is the means whereby the rights of all creditors are in effect enforced collectively. The liquidator's function is to realise the assets of the company, identify its liabilities and distribute the proceeds of the assets amongst the creditors in accordance with their lawful priority. In order to facilitate this exercise, the rights of individual creditors to enforce their claims against assets of the company are suspended and the liquidator acts for their collective benefit.

Types of liquidation

There are three types of liquidation. First, a compulsory liquidation which is a winding-up pursuant to an order of the High Court which directs that the company be wound up and a liquidator be appointed. The winding up is then conducted under the supervision of the High Court and the liquidator is known as an "official liquidator". Second, there is a creditors' voluntary winding-up and third, a members' voluntary winding-up (described more fully at pp337-339 *in-fra*).

The following are the circumstances in which the court may make a winding up order (s213):

- Where the company itself has by special resolution resolved that it be wound up by the court. A small number of compulsory liquidations are initiated this way. It has in a number of cases been applied where a company considers of its own initiative that it cannot by reason of its liabilities continue to trade, and also considers that there are circumstances which would justify an application for the appointment of a "provisional liquidator" (see *infra*).
- where the company does not commence business within a year from its incorporation or suspends its business for a whole year.
- where the number of members is reduced in the case of a private company below two (except where that company has been registered as a single-member company) or, in the case of any other company, below seven.
- where the company is unable to pay its debts. This is the most frequently adopted ground for a winding up order.
- where the court is of the opinion that it is just and equitable that the company be wound up. This is infrequently used but has been invoked in cases where there is deadlock amongst the shareholders. If the company is in effect a quasi partnership, which if it were a partnership ought to have been dissolved, the court may in such circumstances grant a winding up order on the petition of one or other of the "partners".
- where the court is satisfied that the company's affairs are being conducted in a manner oppressive to any member or in disregard of his interests as a member.

A creditors' voluntary winding up arises where the directors of the company consider that the company is insolvent and ought to be wound up. They take the initiative by summoning a meeting of members for the purpose of passing a resolution to wind up the company, and subsequently a meeting of creditors to inform them of the circumstances and afford to them the opportunity to confirm the appointment of the company's nominee as liquidator or substitute their own liquidator.

A members' voluntary winding-up arises where the company is solvent. The members may resolve that the company ought to be wound up either because it has ceased trading or as part of an amalgamation or reconstruction. In such circumstances, the members themselves may pass the necessary resolution appointing a liquidator, thereby effectively placing the company in liquidation. Provided certain requirements as to solvency are satisfied there is no obligation to summon a meeting of creditors for the purpose of initiating the procedure.

Effect of liquidation

Effect on the company
The effect of the appointment of a liquidator is that the company's business immediately ceases except insofar as may be necessary for the beneficial winding up of the company. The liquidator assumes the functions of the board of directors insofar as may be necessary.

Effect on creditors
The effect of liquidation on creditors is that all actions taken by them to enforce claims against the assets of the company are effectively suspended. In a compulsory liquidation the prior approval of the High Court is necessary if a creditor wishes to institute proceedings against the company in liquidation or to maintain an action which is in being before the liquidator is appointed (s222).

By obtaining judgment against the company in liquidation a creditor gains no priority over other creditors by virtue only of that judgment, unless one of the following conditions applies:

- he has registered the judgment as a "judgment mortgage" not less than three months prior to the commencement of the winding up, thereby becoming a secured creditor, or;

- he has enforced the judgment and completed the execution of that judgment before the commencement of the winding up. Even where the sheriff has enforced an execution order by sale of the debtor company's goods, the sheriff will hold such monies for a period of 14 days before releasing them to the judgment creditor. If notification of the commencement of a winding up is served on the sheriff at any time within 14 days prior to the commencement of the winding up or thereafter, he is obliged to remit the net proceeds of the execution to the liquidator for the benefit of the winding up (ss291 and 292).

In a compulsory liquidation where any payment is made to a creditor after the commencement of the winding up, *i.e.* the presentation of a winding-up petition, that payment will be void and the liquidator may seek repayment (s.218). There have been a number of decided cases which have established the principle that where it can be shown that a payment or other disposition to which section 218 applies has been made bona fide and in the ordinary course of business and that it is for the benefit of the creditors as a whole such a payment may be validated (*Re Pat Ruth Limited* [1981] ILRM 51; *Re Ashmark [No.2]* [1990] ILRM 455).

Effect on employees
A winding up order made by the court will have the effect of automatically terminating the contracts of employment and is regarded as notice to the employees of the immediate termination of their employment (*Donnelly v Gleeson*, Hamilton J. unreported 1978; *Irish Shipping Limited, (In Liquidation) v Byrne*, unreported

Lardner J, 8 July 1986.)

The passing of a resolution for a voluntary winding up is not regarded as automatic termination of the contracts of employment, and a liquidator so appointed will be obliged to consider whether he wishes to retain employees or dismiss them.

In the context of a compulsory winding up where the liquidator offers employment to employees after the date of his appointment, that subsequent employment is regarded as a new contract of employment entered into with the official liquidator.

Effect on contracts

Section 290 empowers a liquidator to disclaim onerous properties or contracts, notwithstanding the fact that he may, following his appointment, have endeavoured to assert the company's title to such assets. He may at any time within 12 months after the commencement of the winding up apply to the court to disclaim the property or contract concerned. Where this power is exercised, the other party to the appropriate contract may still maintain a claim for damages for breach of the contract against the company (*Ranks Ireland Limited (In Liquidation)* [1988] IRLM).

An important aspect of the provisions of section 290 is that a creditor may apply to the liquidator and require him to decide whether he wishes to disclaim. If the liquidator fails to give notice within 28 days of such application of his intention to apply to the court for leave to disclaim, he will thereafter be precluded from disclaiming. This time period may be extended by application to the court.

Pre-liquidation considerations

From the point of view of officers of a company which has become insolvent, the most important consideration is that they act responsibly in the interests of their creditors. If it can subsequently be established that officers of the company acted either fraudulently or recklessly causing loss to the creditors, they may be held personally liable in respect of the debts of the company (s297). (See also pp362-363 *infra*). Therefore, the principal obligation of officers in such circumstances is to take immediate measures to avoid further deterioration of the overall position or any increase in the deficiency. The directors should first consider whether there is any alternative to liquidation which may be preferable in the interests of its creditors and any other parties concerned, such as the appointment of an examiner who will formulate a scheme of arrangement which might facilitate the survival of the company for the benefit of all concerned including the creditors (Companies (Amendment) Act 1990). Where a creditor considers initiating a winding up by way of petition to the High Court, the paramount consideration will be whether the dividend which the creditor is likely to receive in the winding up is the best possible outcome, or whether their interests would be better served by refraining from forcing a liquidation and permitting the company to continue trading in the hope that it will trade out of its difficulties and subsequently be in a position to repay the outstanding debts. A creditor owed an undisputed amount exceeding £1,000 is entitled to a winding up order subject to the discretion of the court (see p340 *infra*).

Section 140 of the Companies Act 1990 provides that in certain circumstances a court may order that a company which is related to the company in liquidation should pay in whole or in part all or any of the debts of the insolvent company. Therefore, related companies and their officers should consider whether there are any steps which they should be taking in order to avoid a deterioration in the deficiency insofar as the creditors of the insolvent company are concerned.

Procedure

Members' voluntary winding up

This procedure is usually adopted in cases where a company is solvent and the members form the view that it should be wound up either following a cessation of trade or for the purposes of an amalgamation or reconstruction. The resolution initiating the procedure must be a special resolution, *i.e.* passed by not less than three-quarters of the members present either in person or by proxy at a meeting specially called for the purpose, with no less than 21 days' notice having been given to all the members (s141).

In order for a liquidation to proceed as a members' voluntary winding-up, the directors, or where there are more than two directors, the majority of the directors, must make a statutory "declaration of solvency" (s256 as amended by s128 1990). The following are the essential features of a declaration of solvency complying with the section:

- The directors must swear that they have formed the opinion that the company will be able to pay its debts in full within such period as may be specified in the declaration, being a period not exceeding twelve months from the commencement of the winding up

- The declaration must be made within 28 days immediately before the passing of the resolution for winding up and delivered to the Registrar of Companies within 15 days thereafter.

- The declaration must contain a statement of the company's assets and liabilities at the latest practicable date, not being a date more than three months before the making of the declaration.

- There should be attached to the declaration a report by an independent person stating whether he thought reasonable the opinion of the directors that the company was able to pay its debts in full and the statement of the company's assets and liabilities embodied in the declaration of solvency. An independent person for the purpose of this requirement is a person qualified at the time of the report to be appointed an auditor (s187, 1990 Act, prescribes the persons who may act as auditor of a company to include members of a recognised body of accountants within or outside the state, but specifically excludes officers of the company, close relatives, partners or employees of officers and body corporates).

The notice convening the meeting of members at which the special resolution will be proposed must be accompanied by a copy of the declaration of solvency. A director making a declaration of solvency who is subsequently shown to have made such a declaration without having reasonable grounds for his opinion may be held personally liable for the debts of the company (s256 (8)). Where a liquidator appointed in a members' voluntary winding up forms the opinion that the company will be unable to pay its debts within the time mentioned in the declaration of solvency, he must hold a meeting of creditors within 14 days of forming this opinion, (s261, amended by s129, 1990 Act). Notice of this meeting must be issued within seven days of the liquidator forming the required opinion, and must also be published at least ten days before the date of the meeting in *Iris Oifiguil* (the Official Gazette) and once at least in two daily newspapers circulating in the locality in which the company's principal place of business was situated.

During the period before the creditors' meeting is held, the liquidator is required to make available to creditors free of charge any such information as they require regarding the affairs of the company.

At the creditors' meeting, the liquidator will present a statement of the company's assets and liabilities and the winding up will thereafter be conducted as a creditors' voluntary winding up.

Where creditors believe that the company is unlikely to be able to pay its debts within the period specified in the declaration they may apply to court for an order directing the winding-up to be conducted as a creditors' voluntary winding-up. In such circumstances, the creditors, who must represent one-fifth at least in number or value of the creditors, must satisfy the court that the company is unlikely to pay its debts within the specified time (s256(5) as inserted by s129, 1990 Act).

Creditors' voluntary winding-up

This form of voluntary winding-up is initiated by the summoning of a meeting of members for the purpose of passing an ordinary resolution to the effect that the company cannot by reason of its liabilities continue its business and that it should be wound up voluntarily. The same resolution will appoint a liquidator (s251). The company must summon a meeting of creditors to be held on the same day on which there is to be held the meeting of members, or on the following day (s266). Notice of such meeting must be given at least ten days before the holding of the meeting both by notification to each individual creditor, and by publication once at least in two daily newspapers circulating in the district where the registered office or principal place of the business of the company is located.

Section 266 requires the directors to prepare a statement of affairs of the company to be submitted to the creditors at the meeting, and requires that the directors appoint one of their number to attend at the creditors' meeting and preside thereat.

If the creditors nominate a liquidator different to the liquidator nominated by the company, the person nominated by the creditors shall be liquidator. In order for the creditors to pass a resolution valid for this or any other purpose, there must be cast in favour of the resolution a majority of votes both in number and value of the creditors present personally or by proxy (rule 62). Any creditor participating in this vote who has a connection with the proposed liquidator must disclose that fact to the meeting of creditors (s301A, inserted by s147, 1990 Act).

The creditors may as they think fit appoint a committee of inspection consisting of not more than five persons. The company may, if it considers it appropriate, appoint three persons to act on the committee of inspection (s268).

There have been cases where creditors aggrieved by the outcome of a creditors' meeting, have successfully applied to court for the appointment of their nominee as liquidator. In *Re M & R Electrical Limited* August 1985, the main body of creditors attending the meeting had their votes disallowed because they did not have with them the special resolution from their various company boards of directors apointing them official representatives for their companies. The court ruled that although the strict letter of the law and the rules had been adhered to at the creditors' meeting, the spirit of the law had not been complied with. Barrington J. held that the liquidator who was the choice of the creditors should be appointed in place of the company's nominee.

It is usual practice to hold meetings of creditors immediately after the members' meeting at which the resolution for a voluntary winding up is passed. However, it is open to the company to hold the creditors' meeting a day later if it so wishes. If this occurs there are certain restrictions on the exercise of the liquidator's powers during the period between the two meetings. He is confined to exercising only those powers necessary to preserve and protect the assets and may dispose only of perishable goods and goods whose value is likely to be diminished if they are not immediately disposed of. He must then report to the creditors' meeting on any exercise by him of these powers (s131, 1990 Act).

The commencement of a winding-up as a members' or creditors' voluntary winding-up does not limit or impair the right of any creditor to initiate a compulsory winding-up in appropriate circumstances.

Compulsory winding up

The most frequent ground for the making of a winding up order is the inability of a company to pay its debts. Although there have been cases in which petitions have been presented by debtor companies, the most frequent method by which compulsory liquidations are initiated is by creditor petition invoking the provisions of section 214 which are discussed below. Whereas the most desirable method from the point of view of a creditor is first to obtain a judgment, the statutory demand procedure whereby the debtor is given 21 days to pay a liquidated amount is frequently invoked by the Revenue Commissioners in order to ground winding up petitions.

A petition may be presented by any of the following parties (s215):

- the company itself. The shareholders must first resolve by special resolution that the company should be wound up by the court and they will in that resolution authorise the directors to take the necessary steps for that purpose.
- any one or more of the company's creditors.
- any one or more of the company's shareholders. A shareholder may only present a petition where the number of members is reduced below two in the case of a private company, or below seven in any other case; or provided he meets certain qualifications as to the duration of his shareholding (s215(9)).
- the Minister for Industry and Commerce in certain circumstances.
- in cases where the basis for the petition is oppressive conduct, any party who complains that his interests are being disregarded by such oppressive conduct.

The most frequent ground for the making of a winding up order is that the company is unable to pay its debts. Where a creditor invokes this ground it will usually rely on the deeming provisions of section 214 which provides that a company will be deemed unable to pay its debts in any one of the following circumstances:

- where a creditor owed not less than £1,000 makes demand in writing for payment and the company fails to pay the sum due within three weeks.
- where a judgment against the company is unsatisfied.
- where it can be proved to the satisfaction of the court that the company is unable to pay its debts taking into account its contingent and prospective liabilities.

It is usually impossible for a creditor to be in possession of sufficient information to satisfy the court under the third of these headings. Creditors frequently invoke the first of these grounds, known as the "statutory demand" and winding-up orders are often made pursuant to such demands. However, if the debtor company seeks to persuade the court that there is a *bona fide* dispute as to the existence or extent of the debt, the court will generally decline to make a winding up order. By obtaining judgment first, the creditor will usually ensure that no dispute can arise on the debt, because the High Court hearing the petition will be reluctant to reopen an issue which has already been determined by another court.

The statutory demand must be made in writing and delivered by hand to the registered office of the company. If the company has not delivered to the Registrar of Companies particulars of its registered office, the demand may be served on the Registrar of Companies.

If payment is not made within the period of 21 days, or if the debtor fails to secure or compound the debt to the reasonable satisfaction of the creditor within that time, the creditor may present a winding up petition. The petition is an originating High Court document which contains a recital of basic information as to the debtor company including particulars of its registered office, date of incorporation, trading address, nominal capital, issued share capital and a recital of the objects contained in the memorandum of association. The petition will then recite that the debtor company is indebted to the petitioner and will recite that the statutory demand has been served and that the debtor company has failed to pay or compound the amount due to the satisfaction of the creditor.

The petition will contain a prayer to the court that the company be wound up. When the petition is presented in the central office the Registrar allocates a return date, usually being a date approximately three weeks away, in order to allow time for the service and advertisement of the petition.

The petition must be advertised seven clear days before the hearing date, once in *Iris Oifiguil* and once at least in two Dublin daily morning newspapers, or in such other newspapers as the Registrar may direct (rule 10).

Unless it has been presented by the company itself, every petition must be served on the company at its registered office or, if there is no registered office then at the last known principal place of business of the company (rule 11).

The petition itself is not a sworn document, and therefore the petitioner must within four days after the presentation of the petition file in the Central Office of the High Court an affidavit sworn by some person duly authorised on behalf of the petitioner verifying the facts recited in the petition itself (rule 12).

Any party who intends to appear and wishes to be heard at the hearing of the petition serves notice to that effect on the petitioner or his solicitor (rule 15). Any party opposing the petition may file an affidavit in opposition within seven days after the publication of the advertisement of the forthcoming hearing (rule 17).

Where a petition is contested, the dispute will be heard on affidavit. If the court forms the view having heard the parties that there is a bona fide dispute as to the existence of the debt, it will usually strike out the petition and order costs against the petitioner. Where the court is satisfied that there is no bona fide dispute as to the existence of the debt grounding the petition, it will make a winding up order and appoint an official liquidator. The order usually contains the following directions in addition to ordering the windingup of the company:

- an order appointing an official liquidator. (The term official liquidator is the correct title of a liquidator appointed by the court, and distinguishes him from a liquidator appointed in a voluntary winding up.);

- an order granting to the official liquidator liberty to act prior to giving security (*i.e.* before entering into a bond; see pp348-349 *infra*) (s228(a));

- an order directing the examiner of the high court to fix the amount of the security to be given by the official liquidator;

- an order directing the filing of a statement of affairs (s224);

- an order providing for the costs of the petition. The petitioner will usually be awarded his costs to be discharged out of the assets of the company in priority to all other expenses, and it is common for an order for costs to be made in favour of any creditors who appear at the hearing of the petition.

- in certain cases, the court may order that the official liquidator summon a meeting of creditors and contributories/shareholders for the purpose of determining whether or not an application be made to the court for the appointment of a "committee of inspection" (s232).

Any party to the making of a winding up order may appeal to the Supreme Court. If the Supreme Court is satisfied that the presentation of the petition, although grounded on a valid and undisputed debt, is an abuse of the process, it may exercise its discretion to refuse a winding up order. In the case of *Bula Limited* (Supreme Court, unreported 13 May 1988), the Supreme Court discharged a winding up order which had been made by the High Court in circumstances where it was the admitted object of the petitioning creditor which itself was a secured creditor to prevent another judgment creditor from obtaining priority by registering its judgment as a judgment mortgage.

At any time after the presentation of the petition and the making of the winding up order a provisional liquidator may be appointed. (s226: rule 14). An application for the appointment of a provisional liquidator will usually be made by the company itself. The court will only make such appointment where it is satisfied that the assets are in jeopardy and that it is necessary that a provisional liquidator be appointed for the purpose of preserving and securing the assets before the winding-up order is made. Such an appointment is usually made without prior advertisement.

After the court has made a winding up order, the petitioner is obliged to take certain formal steps which may be summarised as follows:

- service the winding up order on the Registrar of Companies (s221, 227).
- publish the making of the order in the same publications in which the petition was published (rule 20).
- lodge the order with the examiner of the High Court (rule 21).
- serve the order on the company (rule 22).
- notify the local sheriff of the making of the order (rule 23, and see also ss291 and 292).

Creditors' involvement and position

Secured creditors

Assets which are the subject matter of a fixed charge are not assets of the company falling to be realised and distributed within the liquidation. However, in circumstances where the holder of such a fixed charge does not take other steps to realise his security, (for instance, by appointing a receiver where possible or by seizing possession of the assets concerned if so empowered by the terms of his security), he will be entitled to the net proceeds of those assets realised by the liquidator up to the amount of his debt.

Where there is a shortfall after the proceeds of assets subject to a fixed charge are paid to the holder of that charge, the balance of the creditor's claim will rank along with the other unsecured creditors (subject to any claim he might have under a floating charge).

For the purpose of voting on any matters arising in the liquidation the secured creditor must either surrender his security, or value it and vote only in respect of the balance due after deducting the value of the security. If he votes in respect of the entire debt, he will be deemed to have surrendered his security (rule 69).

Unsecured creditors
In a members' voluntary winding-up, unless the liquidator forms the view that the company will be unable to pay its debts within 12 months, the creditors have no formal role in the conduct of the winding up. As the passing of the winding-up resolution must be advertised in *Iris Oifiguil* within 14 days, creditors have the opportunity to apply to the court to convert the liquidation into a creditors' voluntary liquidation if creditors representing one-fifth at least in number or value of the creditors believe that the company is unlikely to be able to pay its debts within the period specified in the declaration of solvency. Other than publication in the Official Gazette, the only other protection available to creditors is that the final meeting of members required at the conclusion of a members' voluntary winding-up must be advertised in two daily newspapers circulating in the district where the registered office of the company is situate (s263). The court may on the application of the liquidator "or of any other person who appears to the court to be interested make an order deferring the date of the dissolution of the company".

Where a liquidator in a members' voluntary winding up forms the opinion that the company will be unable to pay its debts in full, he is required to convene a meeting of creditors (s261 as inserted by s129 of the Act of 1990). In such event, the liquidation will continue as a creditors' voluntary winding up.

In a creditors' voluntary winding-up, certain involvement by the creditors has already been discussed (pp338-339 *supra*). In addition, the creditors in a creditors' voluntary winding up will have the following continuing involvement in monitoring the liquidation:

- the remuneration of a liquidator is fixed either by the committee of inspection, or if there is no such committee by the creditors (s269). If a creditor alleges that the remuneration fixed by the committee of inspection or the creditors generally is excessive, he may apply to the court to have the remuneration determined.

- where the winding up continues for more than one year, the liquidator is obliged to summon a meeting of creditors at the end of each year and lay before the meeting an account of his acts and dealings (s272). On completion of the winding up the liquidator is obliged to call a meeting of creditors for the purpose of laying before the meeting an account of how the winding-up has been conducted and giving any explanation of that account which may be required (s273). By virtue of the right to be summoned to these meetings, the creditors have an entitlement to be provided with information necessary for them to assess whether the remuneration sought by a liquidator is reasonable, and in this manner they are afforded some element

of protection and participate in the supervision of the conduct of the liquidation. Similarly, the power of a liquidator to pay certain classes of creditors, to make any compromise or arrangement with creditors, or to compromise debts due to the company may only be exercised either with the
sanction of the committee of inspection or in the absence of such a committee, a meeting of the creditors (s276).

In a compulsory liquidation creditors have the right to appear and be heard on
the hearing of the petition itself. Although the debt upon which the petition is
grounded may be undisputed, creditors have the right to submit to the court that
it is not in the interests of the general body of creditors that a winding up proceed. If the court makes a winding up order it may direct that a meeting of creditors and contributories be convened for the purpose of determining whether a
committee of inspection be appointed (s232). This is relatively unusual, although
in the case of *Re SEAL Limited, Trading As Solicitors Property Service* (Lardner J 15
April 1991), the Court directed the summoning of such a meeting, having heard
submissions from creditors who expressed concern as to the identity of the liquidator being appointed.

Any creditor is entitled to inspect and be given a copy of the statement of affairs sworn by the directors (s224).

During the course of a compulsory liquidation, there is no requirement for the
liquidator to summon annual meetings of creditors. However, it is usual for the
official liquidator to report to the court, at least on an annual basis, when he is
seeking remuneration out of the assets for his services. On the hearing of applications for payments on account or determination of remuneration, the court as a
matter of practice requires to hear the views of the creditor most affected by the
outcome of the liquidation. The development of this practice on the part of the
court affords further opportunity for the creditors' interests to be represented
on an ongoing basis during the course of a compulsory liquidation. Similarly,
on the hearing of the official liquidator's final application following the completion of the liquidation, the creditor or creditors most affected by the outcome of
the liquidation will be heard by the court.

The procedure whereby the claims of creditors are adjudicated upon is described in the context of distribution (see pp352-353 *infra*).

Powers of liquidator

An official liquidator will have the following powers (s231):

- to bring or defend any action or legal proceedings on behalf of the company;
- to carry on the business of the company;
- to employ a solicitor;
- to pay any class of creditors in full;
- to settle or compromise any claim against the company or any call on contributories or debt otherwise due to the company.

The above powers may be exercised only with prior approval of the court. The following powers may be exercised without prior approval of the court, although at all times subject to the overall control of the court:

- to sell any property of the company;
- to prove in the bankruptcy of a contributory where necessary;
- to raise money for the purpose of the winding up by giving security over the assets of the company;
- to give security for costs in any proceedings commenced by the company or by him on behalf of the company;
- to appoint an agent (such as an auctioneer) to assist him in connection with any aspect of the winding up for which he himself may not be qualified.

The powers described above are essentially for the purpose of enabling the liquidator to realise the assets and identify the liabilities. A number of additional powers are conferred on him to enforce his position *viz-a-viz* third parties:

- He may apply to court for an order directing that any money, property or books and papers in the hands of any third party be delivered to him forthwith (s236).
- He may summon for examination before the court any officer of the company or other person known to be in possession of property of the company or who may be capable of assisting with information as to the affairs of the company (s245).
- He may apply to the court for directions on any matter arising in the course of a winding up (s280).
- The liquidator has power to disclaim onerous property of the company (s290).
- A liquidator may apply to the court for directions in relation to any matter relating to the performance by a receiver of the company of his functions (s171 1990 Act). Under this provision, an application must be grounded by evidence that the liquidator, or the conduct of the liquidation, is being unfairly prejudiced by any action or proposed action on the part of the receiver.
- Section 322(b), (inserted by s176 1990 Act) provides that where a receiver has been appointed, whether before or after the appointment of the liquidator, the latter may apply to the court for an order, either:
  - that the receiver shall cease to act and prohibiting the appointment of any other receiver; or
  - that the receiver shall act only in relation to certain specified assets.
- Section 322(a) (inserted by s175 1990 Act) provides that the court may "on cause shown" remove a receiver and appoint another receiver. This is also a new provision, although the Act does not identify who may be entitled to bring an application to the court for removal of a receiver, it is likely that a liquidator is one of the persons who might have the *locus standi* to bring

such an application.

- Later in this chapter we summarise the provisions of the Companies Acts for augmenting the assets of insolvent companies, including certain provisions which may impose personal liability on the officers of a company. A liquidator has power to invoke any of the provisions described in that section. These include not only the power to initiate actions against third parties or against officers, but also powers of investigation into the affairs of the company including such powers as are necessary for him to obtain access to the books, records and other documents relating to the affairs of the company.

In a voluntary liquidation, the liquidator may exercise the same powers as an official liquidator subject to the supervision of the committee of inspection if there is one appointed and otherwise the creditors generally.

In a voluntary liquidation, the liquidator has power to transfer the assets of the company to another company in exchange for shares in the other company. This power may only be exercised in a members' voluntary liquidation with the sanction of a special resolution of the company, and in a creditors' voluntary liquidation with the sanction of either the committee of inspection or the court (ss260 and 271). The shares issued to the company in liquidation will be distributed in a members' voluntary liquidation amongst the members of that company and this procedure is generally used for the purpose of effecting a transfer of business or an amalgamation of businesses. A shareholder who voted against the special resolution may insist that the liquidator either abstain from carrying the scheme into effect or purchase his shares at a price to be determined by arbitration. Although in theory the Act permits such a scheme even in a creditors' voluntary winding-up, the liquidator requires the consent of the creditors in such a case. The interests of the creditors in an insolvent creditors' winding-up are not usually served by such a scheme.

Duties of liquidator

The duties of the liquidator following his appointment may be summarised as follows:

- to take possession of all property and assets of the company (ss229, 235 and 236);
- to realise the assets. The liquidator is given power by section 231 to dispose of the assets of the company. That is a power which may be exercised without the sanction of the court in a compulsory liquidation or of the creditors in a creditors' voluntary liquidation. However, in a compulsory liquidation it is common practice for the official liquidator to apply to the court for approval of contracts for the disposal of assets. In support of any such application, he will exhibit to the court evidence of the efforts which he has made to ensure that he is obtaining the best price available.
- the liquidator is responsible for identifying and settling a list of contribu-

tories and identifying the liabilities of the company. In this regard he is responsible for contesting on behalf of the company any claims which he believes may be invalid. In a compulsory liquidation he may refer such disputed claims to the court, and in a voluntary liquidation he may either apply to the court for directions, or merely reject the claim, leaving the creditor with the option of instituting proceedings.

- having realised the assets and identified the liabilities the liquidator must distribute the proceeds of the assets in accordance with their lawful priorities.

- if there is a surplus available after discharging the fees, costs and expenses of the liquidation and the claims of creditors, it is the liquidator's function to distribute that surplus amongst the contributories.

- the liquidator will be responsible for carrying out such examinations and investigations as he considers necessary in order to ascertain whether any measures may be taken by him to augment the assets available for the benefit of the creditors, either by endeavouring to restore dissipated assets to the company or to pursue officers of the company personally.

- the official liquidator is responsible for summoning meetings and reporting to the members in a members' voluntary winding up, the creditors in a creditors' voluntary winding up, and to the court in a compulsory winding up.

- the liquidator is obliged to include in periodic returns to the Registrar of Companies a statement as to whether any officer of the company is subject to a disqualification order, or has been the subject of a declaration of personal liability (s144, 1990 Act).

- the liquidator has ultimate responsibility for ensuring that following the conclusion of the liquidation and holding of the necessary final meetings, the company is dissolved (ss263, 273, 249).

- in a members' voluntary winding up which continues for more than one year, and in any creditors' voluntary winding up the liquidator is obliged to summon at the end of each year a meeting of members and creditors. His function is to produce an account of his dealings and the conduct of the winding up during the year and lay this before the meeting. (ss262 and 272). He is also obliged to file within seven days from the holding of that meeting a copy of the account laid before the meeting with the Registrar of Companies.

- where the winding up of a company is not concluded within two years after its commencement, the liquidator is required to lodge with the Registrar of Companies within 30 days of the end of the second year a detailed account of all realisations and disbursements in respect of the company. This is a detailed statement containing a record of all receipts derived from assets existing at the date of his appointment and must contain particulars of the gross proceeds of such realisations showing also the expenses incidental to the realisations. In a compulsory liquidation which continues after the expiry of two years the liquidator is obliged to file such a return on an annual basis after the expiry of the second year, and in a voluntary liquidation such return must be filed on a six monthly basis (s306: rule 130).

- during the course of a compulsory liquidation, applications are brought before the court in relation to certain aspects of the conduct of the liquidation. The examiner of the High Court, who is a High Court official with quasijudicial powers, exercises a supervisory and administrative role in the conduct of a compulsory liquidation. The official liquidator is obliged in a compulsory liquidation to lodge with the court examiner particulars of all receipts and payments made by him in the course of each year. Having lodged particulars of these receipts and payments he subsequently attends before the examiner for the purpose of vouching all such transactions to the satisfaction of the examiner (rules 117 – 123).

Management by liquidator/supervision

Steps taken on appointment

The following description refers not only to those steps which the liquidator is obliged to take by statute or by the rules, but also additional steps which a prudent liquidator will adopt in order to ensure that he complies with his general obligation to identify and preserve and realise the assets as quickly as possible. In compulsory liquidations a number of additional requirements arise from the provisions of Order 74 and these have been classified separately.

- Steps taken by liquidator in voluntary liquidation:
  - The liquidator must notify the Registrar of Companies of his appointment (s278).
  - The company is obliged to notify the Registrar of Companies of the passing of a special resolution for a winding up (s252). It is prudent for a liquidator to ensure that this requirement has been complied with by the company.

- Steps taken by an official liquidator:
  - The petitioner will publish notification of the making of the winding up order in *Iris Oifiguil*, serve a copy of the order on the examiner of the high court, the Registrar of Companies, and on the company and notify the sheriff for the purpose of section 292 (rules 20-23). It is prudent for the official liquidator to ensure that these steps have been complied with, failing which he himself may arrange compliance.
  - Section 228 provides that the court may determine what security must be given by a liquidator on his appointment. This security takes the form of a bond taken out by the official liquidator with an insurance company recognised by the court, the amount of which will be assessed by the examiner of the court having heard the official liquidator as to

the estimated value of the assets coming into his possession (rule 31).
- The winding up order will usually direct that the official liquidator lodge all monies received by him in an account in the joint name of the official liquidator and the examiner of the high court. Rules 117 to 123 contain provisions giving effect to this requirement and provide that all payments made out of the account of the official liquidator require the counter-signature of the court examiner. It is usual practice for the official liquidator to prepare for signature by the court examiner a direction to the bank to open an account in the name of the official liquidator of the company. All such accounts are maintained at one Dublin branch of the bank of Ireland.
- The appointment of a solicitor to assist the official liquidator is one of the powers which may be exercised only with the sanction of the court (s231). The official liquidator will usually therefore cause to be prepared a form of "appointment of solicitor" for the counter-signature of the court examiner.

- Steps taken by liquidators in all forms of winding up:
  - The liquidator should notify the local sheriff of his appointment for the purpose of sections 291 and 292, which provide that the sheriff must hold the proceeds of any disposal of goods seized by him in the execution process for a period of 14 days before releasing them to the judgment creditor. Where a liquidator is appointed within the period of 14 days, the sheriff must pay the net proceeds of any such disposal to the liquidator.
  - Where a company is being wound up, every invoice, order for goods or business letter issued by or on behalf of the company or its liquidator on which the name of the company appears should contain a statement that the company is being wound up. This requirement is complied with by inserting the words "In liquidation" after the name of the company on all such invoices, orders or letters (s303).
  - The liquidator will immediately take possession of all assets of the company. The most urgent of such steps will be directed to taking physical possession of all land and buildings in the company's name, plant and equipment, motor vehicles, stocks and debtors. His obligations in this regard will extend not merely to taking possession of assets which are readily identifiable in the possession or name of the company, but also any such assets as he may discover are in the hands of third parties such as carriers, warehouses or repairers. His rights to take possession of such assets may in some circumstances be subject to the rights of such third parties to retain liens, and there are many well-established and recognised forms of liens. A lien is essentially the right to retain possession of property and in certain circumstances to sell it in order to enforce payment of money owed by the owner of the property to the party who is in possession of it. Section 244(A), (inserted by s125, 1990 Act) abolishes liens over documents or other papers which are the property

of a company in liquidation, but subject to that exception the lien is a recognised right of third parties which will often impair the liquidator's power to repossess such assets.

- The liquidator will immediately notify his appointment to the directors, whose functions in regard to management of the company's affairs have been assumed by him (ss231 and 254).
- The liquidator will always inform employees of his appointment. In the context of a voluntary liquidation, the passing of a resolution for a winding up does not automatically terminate contracts of employment. The liquidator must therefore take a decision as to whether he wishes to continue those contracts or terminate them.
- For the purpose of realising debts, it is essential that the liquidator obtain immediate access to the debtors ledger of the company, thereby enabling him formally to notify all debtors that he has been appointed liquidator and that payment should be made only to him.
- The liquidator will notify the company's bank of the fact of his appointment. From the date of his appointment, he should direct the bank that only withdrawals or other transactions authorised by him may be made. Similarly, payments which are made to the account of the company at the bank after the date of the commencement of the winding up must be remitted to the liquidator and may not be applied to the company's general bank accounts.
- The liquidator will make immediate arrangements relating to insurance cover on the assets. It is generally a condition of policies of insurance that the policy will terminate on the passing of a resolution for a winding up or the making of a winding-up order, and in such circumstances liability may be repudiated by the insurer. It is therefore essential that the liquidator either make arrangements with such insurers for the continuance of the policy in force by agreement, or alternatively make his own arrangements for the cover on the assets. There are available, and used by many insolvency practitioners, policies which automatically apply to the assets of companies of which they are appointed liquidator.
- Where a committee of inspection has been appointed, the liquidator should arrange the earliest possible meeting of that committee in order to ascertain the wishes of the creditors.

Contractual position

Reference has been made above (see pp344-346) to the powers of a liquidator under section 290 to disclaim onerous property by order of the court. If a liquidator causes a breach of the company's contracts with third parties, such parties may maintain a claim for damages for breach of contract, and these damages will rank as an unsecured liability of the company.

Where a liquidator seeks to continue existing contracts with the agreement of third parties, or enter into new contracts where he is carrying on the business of the company for the beneficial winding up thereof, he will enter into such contracts for and on behalf of the company, and obligations under such contracts will be discharged as an expense of the winding up. A liquidator will be personally liable if such contracts were not necessary for the winding up of the company.

Certain contractual arrangements between the company and third parties cannot be disregarded by a liquidator in the realisation and disposal of assets. In particular, where a contract for the supply of goods to the company includes provision that ownership of the goods concerned remain with the supplier until such time as they had been paid for, and if there are in the possession of the company as at the date of the liquidator's appointment goods which are the subject of such a condition, they will not be assets of the company and can therefore only be disposed of by the liquidator with the prior agreement of their owner.

Where assets are held by the company in trust for third parties, again these are not assets of the company properly so called and the liquidator is unable in law to dispose of them within the liquidation. As trustee, he must account to the beneficiary of any such assets for their full value or procure agreement from the beneficiary as to the disposal of such assets.

A liquidator cannot disregard the provisions of any contract with third parties which confer on such parties a valid fixed charge.

Assets subject to a fixed charge are at law the property of the holder of the charge, subject to the right of the company itself to redeem the security. The liquidator may only deal with or dispose of such assets by agreement with the holder of the charge.

Realisation of assets
A principal function of a liquidator is to sell the property and assets of the company, and he may exercise this function by public auction or private contract (s231(2)(a)).

A liquidator may not sell a non-cash asset by private contract to a person who is or has been an officer of the company within three years prior to the date of the commencement of the winding up unless 14 days' notice at least of the intention to do so is given to all creditors of the company known to the liquidator. This restriction only applies to the sale of non-cash assets worth more than £50,000 or 10% of the company's net assets at the time of the transaction (s124 1990 Act).

In addition to the liquidator's function of realising assets which are readily identifiable on his appointment, reference should be made to the powers of the liquidator to improve the value of the assets available for creditors by invoking a number of the provisions facilitating the augmentation of the assets of an insolvent company, discussed in more detail at pp360-366 below.

Taxation
As a result of the introduction of section 56 of the Finance Act 1983, a liquidator is responsible for discharging any capital gains tax that may be incurred as a result

of his realisation of the assets in the course of the winding up. This legislation was introduced following the decision of the Supreme Court in the case of *Van Hool McArdle Limited* [1983] which held that tax arising from a capital gain was not "a necessary disbursement" within rule 129 as it was held that this rule was intended to deal with costs and expenses and not with the liabilities of the company, and could not therefore include a liability in respect of such tax.

However, although amending legislation was introduced to deal with tax payable as a result of a capital gain arising in the course of a winding up, such legislation did not extend to corporation tax payable in respect of income earned during a winding up. Consequently, in the case of *Hibernian Transport Companies Limited (In Liquidation)* [1983] the High Court held that a liquidator in a compulsory liquidation was not obliged to pay, as a disbursement incurred in the winding up, corporation tax on deposit interest earned during the liquidation. The effect of this decision is that although such corporation tax is a liability of the company, there is no source from which this liability can be discharged as it is a liability incurred subsequent to the commencement of the winding up.

Rule 129, however, is only applicable in the case of a compulsory liquidation and it has been held that in a voluntary liquidation a liquidator is obliged to discharge corporation tax on interest earned during the liquidation. This falls within the definition of "all costs charges and expenses properly incurred in the winding-up" as stated in section 281 of the 1963 Act (see *A. Noyek & Sons* 25 July 1988).

Thus, the liability of a liquidator to discharge corporation tax on income arising during the liquidation will be dependent on whether the liquidation is compulsory or voluntary.

Where a liquidator trades in the winding up, he may be required to register for VAT in which case he will be an accountable person for the purpose of the VAT legislation and will be required to make VAT returns in accordance with the regulations under this legislation.

Distribution

The Act and the rules of the Superior Courts contain detailed provisions as to the priority of payments in a windingup. The order of priority may be summarised as follows:

Secured creditors

Where assets are subject to a valid fixed charge, the only interest of the company in those assets is the extent to which the realised value exceeds the indebtedness to the holder of the charge. In a liquidation, it is commonly the practice that the assets subject to a fixed charge will be realised by the liquidator in consultation with the holder of the fixed charge and the liquidator will then account for the net proceeds of sale. For the purpose of identifying the assets available for distribution, assets subject to the fixed charge should not be regarded as assets available in the winding up generally. In a compulsory liquidation, the court discourages official liquidators from realising properties on behalf of the holders of a fixed charge unless the realisation is likely to exceed the indebtedness to the holder of the fixed charges. Unless there is such a surplus available, the costs, fees and expenses in connection with the realisation of the property subject to the fixed charge must be deducted from the assets subject to that charge. A liquidator must satisfy himself as to the validity of a fixed charge, and in particular that it does not contravene the provisions of section 286 relating to fraudulent preference. Once a liquidator is satisfied as to the validity of the fixed charge, then the proceeds of the sale of the assets subject to such a charge will be paid to the holder of the charge subject to deduction of the costs, fees and expenses relating to the realisation thereof. The holder of the charge will be entitled to payment of interest up to the date of repayment, provided the proceeds of sale of the assets subject to the charge are sufficient for this purpose (*Re McCairns PMPA Limited* 18 July 1991).

A fixed charge may apply not only to land and buildings, but also to book debts (*Re Keenan Brothers Ltd (In Liquidation)* Supreme Court [1985] IR p401).

It is also possible to create a valid fixed charge on plant machinery and other fixtures. However, the terms of such a charge must be carefully scrutinised and the charged items clearly identified by reference to the text of the instrument concerned before making any distribution to its holder.

Costs and expenses of getting in, preserving and realising the assets

In Ireland there is no scheme for the central funding of liquidations and consequently the costs, fees and expenses of a liquidation, including the remuneration of the liquidator, fall to be discharged out of the assets of the company in question. In circumstances where the assets of the company are insufficient to meet the costs, fees and expenses, the risk of the shortfall will lie with the liquidator unless he has reached some prior agreement to be indemnified by a creditor or other interested third party. As such, these fees, costs and expenses represent the first claim on the assets of an insolvent company. The following are the provisions governing the payment of such fees, costs and expenses.

Members' voluntary liquidation

Section 281 of the Act provides that all costs, charges and expenses properly incurred in the winding up, including the remuneration of the liquidator, shall be payable out of the assets of the company in priority to all other claims. Section 258 of the Act provides that in a members' voluntary liquidation the remuneration of the liquidator may be determined by the resolution appointing him.

Creditors' voluntary liquidation

The remuneration of the liquidator will be determined by the committee of inspection, or where no such committee has been appointed, the creditors (s269). Any creditor who alleges that such remuneration is excessive may apply to the court to have the remuneration determined. These provisions are implemented either when the liquidator is reporting to meetings of the committee of inspection, or at the annual meeting of creditors, where he will seek approval of the fees incurred to date. The costs and expenses which he has incurred will be shown as items of outlay in the annual accounts of which he seeks approval at the meeting.

Compulsory liquidation

The Act provides (s228) that an official liquidator shall receive such salary or remuneration as the court may direct. The court may allow such remuneration on an application made by the official liquidator on notice to such parties and supported by such evidence as the court may require. The court may from time to time direct that an enquiry be held by the examiner or the Master of the High Court as to the remuneration of the official liquidator (rules 46-48). The practice has developed that the official liquidator through his solicitors will apply to the High Court at regular intervals for a payment on account of his remuneration. This application is usually made on notice to the largest creditor, or the creditor most materially affected by the outcome of the liquidation, and is accompanied by a report prepared by the official liquidator giving details of the current position in the winding up to include a financial summary, full details of the fees sought and an estimate of the time to completion and the likely outcome of the liquidation.

If there are no objections raised by the representative creditor, and if the court is satisfied with the contents of the official liquidator's report, it will usually grant the official liquidator a payment on account, which will be conditional upon the official liquidator undertaking to make a repayment in the event of any portion of such payment being disallowed when the quantum of the official liquidator's remuneration in the case is ultimately determined. When the winding up has been completed or from time to time in protracted cases, the official liquidator will apply for an order determining the amount of his remuneration for the entire liquidation or for a specified period, and an order directing the payment of that sum after giving credit for such payments on account as may previously have been allowed by the court at intervals during the course of the liquidation.

As between the fees, costs and expenses which might be payable, rule 128 specifies in more detail the priority as follows:

- fees and expenses properly incurred in preserving, realising or getting in the assets, including where the company has previously commenced to be wound up voluntarily, such remuneration, costs and expenses as the court may allow to the liquidator appointed in the voluntary winding up;
- the costs of the petitioner, and the costs awarded to any party who appeared on the hearing of the petition and whose costs were allowed;
- the costs and expenses of any person who makes or assists in the making of the company's statement of affairs;
- the necessary disbursements of the official liquidator other than expenses relating to the preservation, realisation or getting in of the assets;
- costs payable to the solicitor for the official liquidator. These must be taxed by a Taxing Master of the High Court (rule 128(2));

- remuneration of the official liquidator;
- out-of-pocket expenses incurred by members of the committee of inspection.

The claims of creditors

Super preferential claims
Section 120 of the Social Welfare (Consolidation) Act 1981 provides that any sum which has been deducted by the employer from the remuneration of an employee in respect of pay-related Social Insurance contributions and unpaid by the employer in respect of those contributions shall not form part of the assets of the company in a winding up. In this case a sum equal to the amount so deducted shall be paid to the social insurance fund in priority to the debts specified in section 285 of that Act (*i.e.* the preferential debts). The effect of this section is that the liquidator must calculate the amount of deductions made by the company from employee wages and salaries in respect of employment contributions which have not been paid over by the employer to the social insurance fund and then set aside an equivalent sum of money out of the general assets to be paid in priority to the preferential claims.

Preferential claims
This is a category of claim which, whether for social or fiscal reasons, have been given priority by statute over the claims of both creditors secured by a floating charge and unsecured creditors. The basic source of these claims is section 285 of the 1963 Act, but in the years following the passing of that Act, more than 15 statutory provisions have extended the category of preferential claims. These may be summarised as follows:

- local rates;
- taxes assessed on the company up to 5 April before the appointment of the liquidator;
- VAT due within the period of 12 months before the appointment of the liquidator;
- amounts deducted by the company for taxation purposes from payments to employees or sub-contractors;
- arrears of wages and salaries due within four months prior to the appointment of the liquidator and subject of a maximum of £2,500 per person;
- arrears of holiday remuneration;
- social welfare contributions;
- compensation due to employees in respect of any accidents which are not indemnified by insurance;
- arrears of pension contributions;
- entitlements of employees under legislation relating to the Unfair Dismis-

sal, Minimum Notice and Redundancy Payments Acts;

- the Minister for Labour where he has made payments to employees out of the insolvency payments fund. The Protection of Employees (Employers Insolvency) Act 1984 provides that payment of certain debts to employees are guaranteed out of the redundancy and employers insolvency fund maintained by the Department of Labour. On the occurrence of a liquidation the Department will make immediate payment to employees in respect of arrears of wages and holiday pay, and their entitlement under the legislation relating to unfair dismissals, redundancies and minimum notice entitlements. Having made such payment, the Minister has the right to maintain a subrogated claim in respect of such entitlements, and to the extent that these entitlements may be preferential that status will attach to the claim of the Minister.

  In the event that the realisable value of the assets is insufficient to discharge in full the liabilities to the preferential creditors, then such claims will abate *pro rata*.

  Section 285 (amended by s134 1990 Act) provides that a person claiming to be a preferential creditor will only have that status if he has notified the liquidator of this claim within six months after the advertisement for claims in the daily newspapers.

Debts secured by floating charges

Most debentures, in addition to creating a fixed charge on certain assets of the borrowing company, create a floating charge over all other assets. Such a charge entitles the debenture holder to seek payment out of the proceeds of the assets subject to the floating charge in priority to the unsecured creditors and after payment of any preferential liabilities. Furthermore, in a liquidation, the general costs, fees and expenses incurred in the winding up and not merely those relating to the realisation of the assets secured by the floating charge can be paid before distribution to the holder of the floating charge.

Where there are funds in the hands of the liquidator for distribution to the holder of a floating charge he should satisfy himself that the floating charge complies with the provisions of section 288 before making any payment. This section provides that any floating charge created within 12 months of the commencement of a winding up shall be invalid except in the amount of any cash advanced to the company at the time of, or subsequent to, the creation of and in consideration for the charge and interest on such advances subject to a maximum rate of 5% per annum. Similarly the charge will be valid in respect of goods or services supplied to the company at the time of or subsequent to the creation of the charge and in consideration for the execution of the charge.

Where the floating charge has been created in favour of a party connected to the company, it will come under scrutiny if it has been made within two years prior to the commencement of the winding up. If the holder of the charge can prove that at the time the charge was created the borrower company was solvent, then the provisions of this section will not apply.

Unsecured claims

Once the liquidator is satisfied with payment of all the prior expenses and the entitlements of secured and preferential creditors, he will advertise for the claims of unsecured creditors and embark on the process of adjudicating them. In a voluntary liquidation, the liquidator has sole responsibility for the adjudication of claims and distributions to creditors, and it will be a matter for himself to ensure that before he makes any such distribution all claims have been adjudicated and quantified. In a compulsory liquidation, the process of advertising for and adjudicating the claims of creditors is carried out under the supervision of the examiner of the High Court and admission of claims must be ruled formally by the examiner (rules 95-101).

Claims in respect of a tort which as at the commencement of the winding up is unquantified or unascertained may be converted into liquidated claims by the creditor continuing or bringing proceedings against the company and proving as an unsecured creditor in the winding up. Where a creditor chooses to adopt such a course of action, it will be a matter for the liquidator to consider the merits of the claim and the wisdom of incurring the expense of defending the action.

Debts barred by the Statute of Limitations before the commencement of the winding-up cannot be proved in a liquidation. However, the statute does not continue to run against creditors after the date of the commencement of the winding up.

In circumstances where the liquidator is unable to trace certain creditors, section 307 and rule 131 provide that unclaimed dividends may be lodged to the company's liquidation account at the High Court.

Completion of the liquidation

Section 309 provides that where a company has been wound-up and is about to be dissolved, the books, records and other papers of the company may be disposed of, in a members' voluntary winding up in such manner as the company may by special resolution direct, in a creditors' voluntary winding up in such manner as may be directed by the committee of inspection or, in the absence of such committee having been appointed, the creditors. In a compulsory winding up the court will give directions as to how the books and records may be disposed of.

Position of officers and shareholders

Position of officers

Under section 150 of the 1990 Act, a director who has been at any time within 12 months preceding the commencement of a winding up an officer of a company which is insolvent will be liable to a "restriction order". This is an order declaring that for a period of five years he may not act in any way directly or indirectly or be concerned or take part in the promotion or formation of any company unless it meets certain minimum capital requirements. These are a requirement that the nominal value of the allotted share capital be £20,000 (£100,000 in the case of a public limited liability company) and that all such shares be fully paid up in cash.

Section 160 provides that a person who has been guilty of certain categories of conduct in relation to the affairs of a company may be disqualified from acting as auditor, director or other officer, or receiver, liquidator or examiner of any company or take part in the promotion, formation or management of any company for a period of five years, or such further or longer period as the court may decide. The categories of conduct which may give rise to a disqualification order include convictions in relation to companies or involving fraud or dishonesty, conduct which has resulted in a declaration of personal liability on the grounds of fraudulent trading, conduct which the court considers renders a person unfit to be concerned in the management of a company, or persistent default in relation to compliance with Companies Office filing requirements. Persistent default is defined as three convictions within five years on such matters.

In a compulsory liquidation the directors must swear a statement of affairs on oath and file this in the High Court (s224: rules 24-28). In a voluntary winding up, they are principally responsible for ensuring that the winding up resolution is published in *Iris Oifiguil* within 14 days of its passing (s252).

Officers of the company are obliged to co-operate with the liquidator in his investigation and management of the winding up. Failure to co-operate is an offence punishable by a fine or term of imprisonment (ss293, 294, 295 and 296).

There are a wide range of circumstances in which officers may be held personally liable for the debts of a company, including fraudulent trading, reckless trading, failure to keep proper books of account contributing to the insolvency, acting in breach of a restriction or disqualification order and making a statutory declaration of solvency without reasonable grounds (see pp362-365 *infra*).

Misfeasance proceedings
Section 298 provides that an officer of the company may be examined as to his conduct and, where it appears that he has misapplied or retained any assets of the company or has been guilty of misfeasance or breach of trust in relation to the company, he may be ordered to compensate the company for such misfeasance or breach of trust. This provision may apply also to the directors of a company's holding company (s148 1990 Act).

Position of shareholders
In a voluntary liquidation, the initiative to place the company in liquidation is taken by the shareholders by the passing of the necessary resolution of the company. A compulsory liquidation may only be initiated by petition of the shareholders in circumstances where the number of members is reduced, in the case of a private company below two (unless it has been registered as a single member company) or, in the case of any other company, below seven, or where the winding up is just and equitable (for instance, where it is a small company and winding up is the means of ending internal strife). In the latter case, the petitioner

must have owned his shares for a period of at least six months during the 18 months before the commencement of the winding up, or the shares must have devolved on him through the death of a former holder whose shareholding met this qualification (s215).

In theory every past and present member is liable to contribute to the assets of a company to the extent of the amount of any uncalled liability on his shares in the company. In a limited liability company, the liability of a member will be limited to the amount unpaid on his shares. In the case of a company limited by guarantee, the liability of members will be limited to the specific amount undertaken by them to contribute in the event of a winding up (s207). In a compulsory liquidation, the court has power to settle a list of contributories (s235) and to direct any contributory to make any such payment as may be required in order to meet his liability (s237).

The court also has power to make an order directing the arrest of a contributory who is believed to be absconding in order to avoid payment of a call or his examination (s247).

If a contributory, being itself a company, is sufficiently closely connected with the business of the company being wound up, there may be circumstances in which as a related company it may be ordered to contribute to the debts of that insolvent company (s141 1990 Act).

The outcome of an insolvent liquidation is most commonly of concern only to its creditors. It is usually only in a members' voluntary liquidation that the outcome will be of concern to the shareholders. In *Re Hibernian Transport Companies Limited* 13 May 1993, however, the company was insolvent at the date of the commencement of the winding up, but a surplus arose in the liquidation by reason of the fact that corporation tax did not have to be paid on the substantial interest earned on the assets over the period of the liquidation. An issue therefore arose as to whether all the creditors should be paid interest on their debts during the liquidation period, or whether the surplus should be distributed immediately to the shareholders. The High Court held that interest should be paid to all creditors and that the surplus would not in fact materialise until such time as such interest had been discharged. On appeal to the Supreme Court the Court held that only creditors with a contractual right to interest were entitled to interest. The shareholders were entitled to any balance remaining after repayment of contractual interest, all outstanding debts, liabilities and all fees, costs and expenses of the liquidator.

Termination of the liquidation

In a voluntary liquidation, the winding up will be completed when the liquidator, having realised all available assets and discharged the claims of creditors in accordance with their lawful priority, convenes a final meeting of members (s263) or, where appropriate, of creditors (s273).

In a compulsory winding up, the liquidator will prepare a final report for submission to the court in connection with a final application (s249) in which the reliefs sought will include an order for the distribution of any funds remaining in the winding up, and an order dissolving the company (rule 137).

Dissolution of the company

In a voluntary winding-up, the company is deemed to be dissolved on the expiration of three months from the registration with the Registrar of Companies of the liquidator's final account of his acts and dealings in the winding up and the return of the holding of the final meeting (ss263(4), 273(4)).

In a compulsory winding up the company will be dissolved from the date of the final winding up order, or such later date as the court might direct (s249).

At any time within two years from the date of the dissolution, the liquidator or any other person interested may apply to the court for an order declaring the dissolution to have been void, and thereupon be at liberty to take further proceedings as if the company had not been dissolved (s310).

Section 311 empowers the Registrar of Companies to strike a company off the Register where he believes that it is not carrying on business. He is obliged to notify the company of his intention to do so and to publish notice of his intention in *Iris Oifigiul*. Unless cause is shown to the contrary by the company, the Registrar will, after giving the required notices, strike the company off the Register and on publication of a further notice to that effect in *Irish Oifigiul*, the company will be dissolved. The Registrar has a similar power to strike the company off the Register in cases where a company is being wound up and the Registrar has reasonable cause to believe that no liquidator is acting or that the affairs of the company have been fully wound up and the returns required to be made by the liquidator have not been made for a period of six consecutive months.

Where a company is dissolved under this procedure the liabilities of directors, officers and members continue as if the company had not been dissolved.

The court has power to order that the name of the company be restored to the Register at any time within 20 years if on application by the company or member or creditor it is satisfied that the company was at the time it was struck off carrying on business or if it is otherwise satisfied that it is just that the company be restored. In such cases the company will be deemed to have continued in existence as if it had never been struck off.

5. Augmenting the assets of the insolvent corporation

Introduction

The Companies Acts empower a liquidator to take a variety of measures for the purpose of augmenting the assets available for the benefit of its creditors. The remedies available in this regard may be classified as follows:

- transactions at risk;
- personal liability of officers.

Transactions at risk

Fraudulent preference

Any transaction relating to the assets of the company made within six months of the commencement of the winding up at a time when the company is insolvent and in favour of any creditor with a view to giving such creditor or any guarantor for the debt due to such creditor a preference over other creditors shall be deemed fraudulent and void against the liquidator (s286). This will apply where the company is unable to pay its debts at the commencement of the winding up and it must be proved that the transaction was entered into with a view to giving the creditor concerned a preference over the other creditors. The burden will be on the liquidator to establish that the dominant intention of the company when entering into the transaction concerned was to prefer the creditor concerned. However, in the absence of direct evidence of intention on the part of the officers of the company, the Court may draw an inference of such an intention where no other explanation for the transactions concerned can be acceptable (*Re Station Motors Limited*, unreported). The intended beneficiary may be the guarantor, rather than the creditor. A director, for example, may have personally guaranteed the company's borrowings, and procured the repayment of these borrowings with a view to eliminating his personal liability. Here the court will infer the necessary intention on the part of the directors to bring this payment within the section (*Station Motors Limited*; *Eddison v Allied Irish Banks*; *Re Northside Motors Limited*).

The scope of this provision has been extended by section 135 of the 1990 Act which provides that in cases where the transaction is in favour of a connected person, the period of six months will be extended to two years, and there will be a presumption that the transaction was made with a view to giving the connected person a preference over the other creditors and that it was therefore a fraudulent preference. In such cases, the onus will shift to the creditor concerned to disprove that the dominant intention was to give a preference. A floating charge created within 12 months before the commencement of a winding up will be invalid except to the extent of any cash or goods and services supplied in consideration for the execution of the charge (s288). Where the floating charge has been created in favour of a person connected with the company, the period of 12 months is extended to two years (s136 1990 Act).

Any transaction made after the commencement of a winding up may be set aside, although the court may exercise its discretion to validate such a transaction in certain circumstances.

Related companies

A court may order that a related company pay in whole or in part all or any of the debts of the company in liquidation, where it considers that it is "just and equitable to do so" (s140 1990 Act). In considering whether it is just and equitable to make such an order, the court will have regard to all the circumstances including in particular the following:

- the extent to which the related company took part in the management of the company being wound up;
- the conduct of the related company towards the creditors of the company being wound up;
- the effect which such an order would be likely to have on the creditors of the related company.

The court may not make an order unless it is satisfied that the circumstances which gave rise to the winding up of the company are attributable to the acts or omissions of the related company, or in circumstances where the only ground for making such an order is the fact that there is a relationship between the companies. In identifying when a company is related to another for the purpose of this new provision, the criteria to be taken into account will be whether there is a substantial shareholding relationship between the two companies *i.e.* one may be a subsidiary or holding company of the other, or whether the businesses of the companies have been carried on in such a manner as to prevent them from being readily identifiable separate businesses.

Assets improperly transferred

Where it can be shown to the satisfaction of the court that any property of the company has been disposed of fraudulently, the court may if it deems it just and equitable to do so order that any person who has come into possession of such property or its proceeds return them to the liquidator (s139 1990 Act). In considering whether to make such an order, the court will have regard to the rights of persons who have in good faith and for value acquired an interest in the property concerned. The effect of such an order will be not to invalidate the transaction but to require any person benefiting from the fraud to return the assets or to compensate the company for their value.

Personal liability of officers

Fraudulent and reckless trading

Under the 1963 Act the only circumstances in which officers could be held personally liable for the debts of the company without limitation of liability were where such officers were found to be knowingly a party to the carrying on of the business with intent to defraud the creditors (s297). Since the enactment of the 1963 Act, only four successful cases have been brought under this section, partly because, in order for a declaration to be made under section 297 it was necessary to show a conscious intention on the part of the officers concerned to defraud the creditors. Section 297 has now been extended by section 138 of the 1990 Act which provides that the civil sanction of personal liability for the debts of a company may apply in either of the following circumstances:

- where a party was knowingly a party to fraudulent trading on the part of the company; or
- where it is established that the person, while an officer of the company, was knowingly a party to the carrying on of any business of the company in a reckless manner.

Although even under the latter provision, a certain state of mind on the part of the officer concerned must be proved, the Act provides that an officer of the company shall be deemed to have been knowingly a party to the carrying on of any business of the company in a reckless manner in either of the following two situations, namely:

- he was a party to the carrying on of such business and having regard to the general knowledge, skill and experience that may reasonably be expected of a person in his position, he ought to have known that his actions, or those of the company, would cause loss to the creditors of the company or any of them. This is an objective test and reference will be made to the experience and skill of the officer concerned.
- he was a party to the contracting of a debt by the company and did not honestly believe on reasonable grounds that the company would be able to pay the debt when it fell due for payment as well as its other debts.

While the Act instances these two deeming provisions, it does not limit the definition of reckless trading and the court may hold that any particular set of circumstances or conduct amounts to reckless trading. The provisions relating to fraudulent and reckless trading are not retrospective in their operation. (*Hefferon Hefferon Kearns Ltd (No. 1)* [1993] 3 I.R. 177, and *Hefferon Kearns (No. 2)* 3 I.R. 191).

In order to maintain a claim for reckless trading, it must be established that the company is insolvent, that the creditor or contributory who initiates the application has suffered loss or damage as a result of the alleged reckless trading, and that the party against whom a declaration is sought is an officer of the company. For this purpose an officer will include an auditor, liquidator, receiver or a shadow director, *i.e.* a party in accordance with whose instructions the officers are accustomed to act. An examiner under the 1990 Act cannot be liable because trading during a period when the company was under the protection of the court is specifically excluded.

Where the party concerned can establish that he acted honestly and responsibly in relation to the conduct of the affairs of the company, the court may relieve him of liability for a particular debt or all of the debts of the company.

There has been one decided case in relation to this Section since its enactment, namely the case of *Dublin Heating Company Limited v Hefferon Kearns and Others*. In that case the High Court held that the directors were party to the contracting of debts by the company at a time when they knew that those debts, together with all the other debts of the company, including contingent and respective liabilities, could not be paid by the company as they fell due for payment but that they acted honestly and responsibly and bona fide in what they considered to be the best interests of the creditors. The court held that whilst the conduct of the officers of the company therefore fell within the ambit of section 297 they should be relieved from liability on the grounds that they acted honestly and responsibly. The court held as follows:

"Paragraph (b) of Sub-Section 2 appears to be a very wide ranging and indeed draconian measure and could apply in the case of virtually every company which becomes insolvent and has to cease trading for that reason. If for example a company became insolvent because of the domino effect of the insolvency of a large debtor, it would be reasonable for the directors to continue trading for a time thereafter to assess the situation and almost inevitably they will incur some debts which would fall within paragraph (b) before finally closing down. It would not be in the interest of the community that whenever there might appear to be any significant danger that a company was going to become insolvent the directors should immediately cease trading and close down the business. Many businesses which might well have survived by continuing to trade coupled with remedial measures could be lost to the community. I think that it is because sub-section 2 and especially paragraph (b) is so wide ranging that sub-section (c) (the provision for relief in circumstances where the officers have acted honestly and responsibly) was included in Section 33 of the Act. I am satisfied that the first defendant acted honestly and responsibly in relation to the conduct of the affairs of the company to such an extent that having regard to all the circumstances of the case I relieve him wholly from any personal liability without imposing any terms."

In the circumstances of that particular case the court found that there was an increase to the extent of £11,760 in the debts of the company from the date upon which the directors could first be said to be aware of the risk that the creditors would not be paid in full to the date upon which they ceased trading. The court held that this caused a diminution of about 2% in the dividend available to creditors, which in the case of the plaintiffs in that case resulted in a diminution of £90 only. The court held that such a trivial amount was not within the meaning of "loss or damage" as contemplated by the section.

The court also made the observation that the section does not impose a collective responsibility on a board of directors as such in respect of the manner in which a company has been run. Mr Justice Lynch held:

"Section 33 operates individually and personally against the Officers (which includes the directors) of a company and the onus rests on the Plaintiffs to prove in relation to each of the Defendants in this case that his conduct falls within the ambit of conduct prohibited or liable to be penalised by Section 33."

Whilst every case is decided on its own facts, the decision in *Dublin Heating Company v Hefferon Kearns* appears to be somewhat lenient and it remains to be seen the extent to which it will be applied generally.

The court has a discretion as to how monies paid under a declaration of personal liability shall be applied. It may therefore consider it appropriate to direct payment, not into the general fund to be discharged in accordance with the priorities already described, but to a particular creditor or creditors.

Failure to keep proper books of account

If a company fails to keep proper books of account and the failure is regarded by the court as having contributed to its inability to pay its debts or as having resulted in substantial uncertainty as to the assets and liabilities of the company or as having impeded the winding up, any officers or former officers responsible for the default shall be guilty of an offence and liable to a fine or a term of imprisonment, and also may be held personally liable without limitation of liability for the debts of the company. It will be a defence to such a claim if the officer can show that he took reasonable steps to secure that the company complied with its obligations or that he believed on reasonable grounds that responsibility for complying had been properly and formally delegated (ss202, 203 1990 Act).

Acting in breach of restriction or disqualification order

Where an officer has acted in breach of a restriction or disqualification order, or a company has carried on business having on its board a party who is restricted without the capital requirements in such circumstances being met, the officers of the company may be held personally liable for debts.

Liability for loans to directors

Section 31 of the Companies Act 1990 prohibits a company from making any of the following:

- loans or quasi-loans to any director of the company or of its holding company or to any persons connected with such Director or;
- entering into credit transactions for the benefit of any such director or connected person or;
- providing a guarantee (including an indemnity) or other security in connection with any loan, quasi-loan or credit transaction made by a third party to any such director or connected person.

There are certain exclusions from this rule as follows:

- The restriction will not apply where the value of the arrangement (together with the total amount outstanding under any other similar arrangement between the company and the director or a person connected with the director of the company is less than 10% of the net asset value of the company). This exception applies to loans, quasi-loans and credit transactions, but not to guarantees.

- Loans, quasi-loans, guarantees and credit transactions made to or for the benefit of a holding company are exempt from the restrictions contained in section 31.

Section 39 provides that where a company is being wound up and is unable to pay its debts and the court considers that any loan, quasi-loan or credit transaction with a director or person connected with a director which is below the 10% limit prescribed, has contributed materially to the company's inability to pay its debts or has substantially impeded the orderly winding up, it may if it thinks proper to do so, declare that any person who benefits from such an arrangement shall be personally liable for the debts and other liabilities of the company.

Aggregation orders

Section 141 of the Companies Act 1990 provides that where two or more related companies are being wound up and the court is satisfied that it is just and equitable to do so, it may order that the companies be wound up together as if they were one company. In making such an order the section requires the court to have specific regard to the interests of any persons who are members of some but not all of the companies concerned.

The section expressly provides that the rights of secured creditors of the individual companies will be preserved in each of those companies.

In general the claims of preferential creditors enjoy priority over the holder of a floating charge. However, where an aggregation order is made there is a specific provision to the effect that where the preferential creditors of one company are not paid in full from the assets of that company, their claim on the assets of another company affected by the aggregation order will rank after the claim of the floating charge holder in that second company and before the unsecured non-preferential creditors. Unsecured creditors will rank equally amongst themselves. The order of priority in each company will, therefore, be as follows:

- fixed charges;
- preferential creditors of that company;
- floating charges;
- preferential creditors of other company in "pool" not discharged out of assets of those other companies;
- unsecured creditors.

6. Public control over insolvent corporations

Licensing and control of appointee

There are no laws regarding qualification or eligibility for the acceptance of an appointment as a liquidator. However, section 300 of the Act (as amended by s146 1990 Act) provides that none of the following persons may act as liquidator of a company:

- a body corporate;
- a person who has been an officer (including an auditor) of the company within 12 months of the commencement of the winding up, or any close relative or partner of such an officer or servant;
- any person who is by virtue of the above provisions disqualified from being liquidator of the company's holding or subsidiary company;
- an undischarged bankrupt (s169 1990 Act).

The Minister for Industry and Commerce has power to add at any time to the list of disqualified persons by making regulations (s237).

Examinations and investigations

Section 245 of the Act 1963 (amended by ss126 and 127 1990 Act) establishes a procedure whereby any officer of the company or person known or suspected of being in possession of assets of the company or indebted to the company, or any person considered capable of giving information relating to the affairs of the company, may be summoned for examination before the court. On the hearing of such an application, if it appears to the court that a person being examined is indebted to the company or is in possession or control of assets of the company, the court may order such person to repay the debt or return the assets concerned.

Appendix

Insolvent companies not being wound up

Section 251 of the 1990 Act provides that a number of the provisions of the Companies Acts which previously only applied where a company was being wound up, may now apply where a company is not being wound up and the principal reason why it is not being wound up is the insufficiency of its assets. The provisions which will have application in such circumstances may be summarised as follows:

- The power of the court to order the return of assets improperly or fraudulently transferred (s139 1990 Act);
- The power of the court to order a company to contribute to the debts of related companies (s140 1990 Act);
- Criminal and civil liability of officers where the company's failure to keep proper books of account contributes to the inability of the company to pay its debts (ss203, 204 1990 Act);
- The power of the court to order inspection of books and papers by creditors and contributories (s243);
- The power of the court to summon persons for examination before the court and make orders for return of assets (s245, as amended by ss126, 127 1990 Act);
- Power to arrest an absconding contributory (s247);
- Liability for fraudulent and reckless trading (s297 as amended by the 1990 Act and s295);
- Liability of officers for misfeasance (s298, amended by the 1990 Act);

In order for such provisions to be invoked in the absence of a winding up, it will be essential for the party seeking to invoke the provisions to establish that the principal reason why the company is not being wound up is the insufficiency of its assets. This is a far-reaching new provision, the scope of which has not yet been the subject of any judicial decisions.

Contents of Chapter 8

CORPORATE INSOLVENCY LAW IN ITALY

1.	**Introduction**	371
2.	**Companies**	372
	"Società di persone" ("partnerships")	372
	"Società di capitali" ("corporations")	373
	Financing and security for creditors	377
	Available information	380
	Debt collection and asset recovery	381
	Transnational insolvency – conflict rules	383
3.	**Survival of the insolvent corporation or its business**	386
	Composition with creditors	386
	Controlled administration	388
4.	**Termination of the insolvent corporation: bankruptcy**	390
	Introduction	390
	Effects of bankruptcy	391
	Procedure	394
	Termination of the proceedings	396
	Summary bankruptcy procedure	397
5.	**Augmenting the assets of the insolvent corporation**	398
	Proceedings brought by the curatore	398
	Personal liability of directors, liquidators and managing partners	399
6.	**Public control over insolvent corporations**	401
	Forced administrative liquidation	401
	Extraordinary administration of large enterprises in crisis	402

Chapter 8

CORPORATE INSOLVENCY LAW IN ITALY

Giovanni Verusio,

Pavia Ansaldo e Verusio Studio Legale

1. Introduction

The material in this chapter relating to types of company, how they are financed and so on – is almost exclusively drawn from the fifth book of the Italian Civil Code ("CC") which, with some amendments, has applied since the date of its publication on 16 March 1942 (Royal Decree 262/1942). The material dealing with debt collection and asset recovery is based on the provisions as amended of the Code of Civil Procedure ("CPC") in force with several amendments (lately Law 477/1992) since 28 October 1940 (Royal Decree 1443/1940).

Section 3 deals with two procedures which are aimed at salvaging insolvent or shaky undertakings, while section 4 concerns the provisions of the Bankruptcy Act (Royal Decree 267/1942) which, like the Civil Code, dates from October 1940.

The statutory sources for a description of how public control over insolvent corporations is exercised forms the subject of Section 6. The sources therefore are in part much more recent (Law 26/1979 as amended by Legislative Decree 17/1993).

Until the late 1970s, the legislation was primarily concerned to protect the position of creditors. The satisfaction of their claims seemed to afford the best basis on which to build for the orderly development of trade. More recently however, there has been a shift in attitude. The legislator now seems to place the preservation of an economic undertaking, its know-how, market and manpower ahead of the satisfaction of the claims of its creditors. The loss of wealth and the resulting mounting unemployment has become intolerable and legal methods have been developed to try to conciliate the claims of the creditors with the survival of the debtor.

2. Companies

Under Italian law, companies are incorporated by a contract described in article 2247 CC which states as follows:

> "By a company contract, two or more persons contribute property or services for the exercise in common of an economic activity for the purpose of sharing in the resulting profits".

"Società di persone" ("partnerships")

This term "società di persone" indicates those partnerships which do not have autonomous legal and financial status with respect to their partners. This category includes three types of undertakings:

- the "società semplice";
- the "società in nome collettivo";
- the "società in accomandita semplice".

Società semplice

This is a "residual" form of undertaking in the sense that it is the form deemed to have been adopted by the partners unless a different kind of company is expressly selected. It is, generally, the form of association for the carrying out of craft and agricultural activities or those concerned with professional or intellectual services.

Società in nome collettivo

This form of organisation is generally adopted for the performance of commercial activities. The law provides that all partners of either società semplice or società in nome collettivo are liable "in solido" (*i.e.* jointly) to an unlimited amount for the company's obligations, but creditors must first exhaust the company's assets in satisfaction of their claims.

Società in accomandita semplice

This form of organisation is adopted for the same purpose as the società in nome collettivo. There is, however, one main difference. In this type of partnership, there are two categories of partner:

- general partners who are liable "in solido" and without limit for the partnership's obligations; and
- special partners who are liable to the extent of the capital contributed by them, provided they take no part in the management of the partnership.

"Società di capitali" ("corporations")

This term indicates entities having an autonomous legal and financial status with respect to their members or shareholders. Thus the entity alone (ie. not the members) is answerable for obligations undertaken by it.

Under this category, Italian law provides the following types of company:

- "società cooperativa";
- "società a responsabilità limitata";
- "società per azioni";
- "società in accomandita per azioni".

The Società cooperativa is the entity usually used for non-profit-making undertakings. We shall, therefore, confine our attention to the other three entities in this group.

Società per Azioni ("Spa")

General provisions
As pointed out above, the entity alone is answerable for all obligations which it undertakes. The liability of members (ie. shareholders) is limited to the capital respectively subscribed. If, however, the number of shareholders falls to one when the company is insolvent, the shareholder is subordinately liable without limitation for the company's obligations undertaken while he held 100% of the shares.

Incorporation
An Spa's minimum share capital requirement is Lire 200 million, at least 30% of which must actually be paid upon incorporation. For the validity of the incorporation procedure, the entire share capital must be subscribed, either in cash or by way of contribution in kind. Incorporation is by act of a notary public (deed of incorporation).

An alternative method of incorporation and of raising capital for a new Spa is by public subscription for shares. The subscription is made on the basis of a prospectus, filed with a notary, which sets out the purposes of the company, the capital stock and the main provisions contained in the by-laws. A meeting of the subscribers is then held at which the deed of incorporation is executed. Irrespective of the method of incorporation and raising of capital, a meeting of the subscribers then approves the contents of the by-laws which will govern the internal administration of the Spa (the holding of the shareholders' meeting, the appointment of the directors, of the auditors, and so on).

The share capital is generally divided into shares of the same par value conferring equal rights on their holders, but it is possible to provide in the by-laws for categories of shares carrying different rights. Shares are indivisible and, in the case of common ownership, the rights of the co-owners are exercised by a joint representative. Subject to this, each share gives its holder the right to one vote at shareholders' meetings.

Management

An Spa is governed by three different organs, namely:

- the shareholders' meeting,
- the board of directors, and
- the board of auditors.

Shareholders' meeting

A shareholders' meeting can be either ordinary or extraordinary. The ordinary shareholders' meeting approves the balance sheet, appoints the directors and the auditors and, in general, resolves other matters pertaining to the management of the company which are reserved to its jurisdiction by the by-laws or submitted to its consideration by the directors.

The ordinary shareholders' meeting is called at least once a year within four months from the closing of the company's financial year or within six months when particular reasons require it.

The extraordinary shareholders' meeting resolves amendments to the by-laws, the issue of debentures, and the appointment of liquidators.

Meetings must be convened by a notice published in the Official Gazette at least 15 days prior to the meeting.

The notice must indicate the place, date and hour on which the meeting will be held and the items on the agenda. The notice may also indicate a second date on which the meeting will be held should no quorum be in attendance on the first call. An ordinary meeting on first call is considered quorate with members present holding as represent at least on-half of the company's share capital, not counting the shares with limited voting rights, and on second call by whatever percentage of share capital is represented. Votes are counted according to the number of shares held.

The ordinary meeting adopts resolutions by an absolute majority of the attending shareholders unless a higher quorum is required in the by-laws. Qualified majorities for resolutions adopted by ordinary meetings on second call are usually not admitted by supervising courts.

The extraordinary meeting adopts resolutions by the concurring votes of as many shareholders as represent more than one-half of the share capital of the company on first call and more than one third on second call, unless in either case a higher quorum is required in the by-laws.

Board of directors

The management of an Spa is entrusted to a sole director or to a board of directors, whose members do not need to be shareholders.

If permitted by the by-laws or by the ordinary shareholders' meeting, the board of directors can delegate its functions to an executive committee composed of some of its members, or to one or more managing directors, specifying the limits of such delegation.

Directors, as noted above, are appointed by the shareholders' meeting for a period not exceeding three years and may be re-appointed unless otherwise provided by the by-laws. The shareholders' meeting may however revoke the appointment of any member of the board at any time.

Directors are jointly liable to the company for damages arising from the nonobservance of their duties, except for functions vested solely in the executive committee or in one or more directors in which case only the directors concerned are liable.

Unless their dissent was recorded in the minutes of the relevant board meeting, directors are jointly liable if they fail to supervise the general conduct of the company's affairs or if, being aware of acts prejudicial to the corporation, they do not do whatever they can to prevent the performance of those acts or to eliminate or reduce their harmful consequences.

Board of auditors

The board of auditors consists of three to five members and two alternates elected by the shareholders' meeting for a term of three years. This term may be renewed, but, once the appointment is made, it is not revocable as is the case with the appointment of directors. The board of auditors supervises the management of the corporation, sees to the observance of the law and the by-laws, and verifies that the company's accounts are regularly kept, that the balance sheet and profit and loss statement accord with the company's books and accounting records, and that the rules concerning the evaluation of the company's assets are observed.

The auditors (who must all be registered chartered accountants) are responsible for the accuracy of their reports and must keep confidential the facts and the documents of which they have knowledge by reason of their office.

Article 2407 CC provides that:

"Auditors are jointly liable with directors for acts or omissions of the latter when the injury would not have occurred if they (the auditors) had exercised vigilance in conformity with the duties of their office".

Società a responsabilità limitata ("Srl")

As mentioned above in relation to the other corporations, the Srl alone is liable for its obligations.

If, however, the number of quotaholders falls to one when the company is insolvent, the quotaholder is subordinately liable without limitation for the company's obligations undertaken while he held 100% of the quotas whenever:

- the sole quotaholder is another company or the sole quotaholder of another company; or

- contributions in kind to capital have not been made as prescribed by law

until his status of sole quotaholder has been recorded in court (Art 2497 CC). Besides the lower minimum capital required (Lire 20 million as opposed to Lire 200 million in the case of an Spa), the differences between an Srl and an Spa as follows:

- while an Spa needs at least two founders, one is sufficient for an Srl;
- while only three-tenths of the initial share capital need be paid in for an Spa, the entire share capital must be paid in for an Srl with only one founder;
- the capital of an Spa is divided into shares all having the same par value and represented by stock certificates which are negotiable instruments, whereas the capital of the Srl is divided into quotas (of which there are as many as there are quotaholders of the company) which are not represented by stock certificates, but are merely registered as an entry in the shareholders' book and which might be of different par value. Each quotaholder has the right to at least one vote in quotaholders' meetings. If his quota is a multiple of one thousand lire, the quotaholder is entitled to one vote for each thousand lire;
- an Srl cannot issue bonds or debentures, as an Spa may. It can, however raise money in addition to that subscribed by quotaholders, by borrowing. Such borrowing is generally from a bank or other financial institution;
- the procedure for convening and holding a quotaholder's meeting of an Srl is shorter and less formal than that for the Spa;
- whereas the term of office for directors of an Spa cannot exceed three years (but re-appointment is permitted), directors of an Srl may be appointed for an indefinite term (*i.e.* until resignation or removal);
- for an Srl, the appointment of statutory auditors is not mandatory (as it is for Spas), unless the stated capital of the company is Lire 200 million or greater or unless auditors are required by the by-laws; and
- if an Srl has only one quotaholder, mention thereof must be made in the letter heading.

Partnership limited by shares (Società in accomandita per azioni) ("SAA")

Under Italian law, the società in accomandita per azioni is a partnership which has legal personality and which provides for two different kinds of member:

- members who are jointly liable without limitation for the partnership's obligations ("general partners"). These members manage the partnership; and

- members who are liable within the stated limit of their participation, represented by shares, in the partnership.

Similar rules apply to these SAAs as apply to the Spas. In particular, they may raise money through the issue of bonds or debentures.

Financing and security for creditors

Corporations may in general obtain financing by one of the following means:

Capital subscription by the shareholders

Corporations obtain the initial funds for carrying out their business by subscription for the shares into which the share capital is divided.

Increasing the share capital involves an amendment to the by-laws, and thus needs to be resolved upon by the extraordinary shareholders' meeting. This enables the corporation to obtain further financing by subscription for new shares. New shares cannot be issued until those already outstanding are fully paid up.

A capital increase does not necessarily require contribution of fresh funds by the shareholders. The extraordinary shareholders' meeting may, for example, increase the share capital by capitalising disposable reserves shown in the balance sheet.

Debentures

Corporations may obtain financing by issuing debentures which represent a loan by the holder to the corporation. As noted earlier, only the Spa and the SAA may issue debentures. To issue debentures, a resolution to this effect must be passed by the extraordinary shareholders' meeting.

Article 2410 CC states that a "company can issue bearer or registered debentures for an amount not exceeding the paid-up and existing capital according to the last approved balance sheet". "Paid-up" refers to the capital that has not only been subscribed but in respect of which the cash or assets have also been paid or contributed to the company's treasury. In particular circumstances, however, debentures may be issued in excess of the amount of paid-up and existing capital. These are:

- when the debentures are secured by mortgage upon immoveable property, or
- when the amount by which the debentures exceed the paid-up capital is secured by registered securities issued or guaranteed by the state, or
- when a government authorisation is granted.

Debenture holders are entitled to the agreed interest rate accrued and to the repayment of the amount loaned at the expiry date.

Italian law provides for two kinds of debentures:

- "simple debentures", giving the holder the right to be reimbursed at maturity and to a fixed or indexed interest during the time the loan is outstanding;
- "convertible debentures", giving the holder a right to convert the debentures into shares on certain pre-set conditions.

Loans (financing agreements)

Corporations may also obtain financing by entering into loan contracts. The Italian Civil Code outlines the structure of the loan agreement ("mutuo") as follows:

"A loan is a Contract by which one party delivers to another a certain quantity of money or of other tangible things, and the other undertakes to return an equal amount of things of the same kind and quality".

Such loans to a corporation may be secured by personal warranties by the directors (such as guarantees, performance bonds) or by real securities.

Italian law provides for the following basic types of securities which are called "real" because they are effected over the guarantor's assets:

Liens

According to article 2745 of the Italian Civil Code "the law grants liens depending on the source of the credit". There are two kinds of lien:

- general liens that can be exercised upon all moveable property of the debtor; and
- special liens that can be exercised upon specific moveable or immoveable assets of the debtor.

This form of security corresponds to the floating and fixed charges, respectively, of United Kingdom security provision.

Italy does not provide for a class such as governmental entities, which are entitled to be paid before ordinary or unsecured creditors. Certain claims, however, such as those of the tax authorities for tax claims, of personnel for unpaid salaries and wages, and of welfare agencies for uncollected social contributions do have a preference over other creditors. The law (art 2778 CC) actually sets out the order in which these preferential creditors – 18 in all – are to be paid.

Pledge

A pledge is a security over chattels and is governed by articles 2784 to 2807 of the Civil Code. Only moveable property, claims, and other rights over moveables can be pledged (art 2786 CC).

In order to be effective as against third parties, the pledged assets must be phy-

sically delivered to the pledgee and such delivery must be based on a written instrument having a certain date.

The assets subject to pledge may also include receivables, in which case the
document evidencing the receivable is delivered to the pledgee.

Equity participation may also be pledged. A pledge of shares in Italian companies is recorded, in the same way as a transfer, by an appropriate entry in the
shareholders' book kept by the company in question and, if stock certificates exist, by an appropriate endorsement thereon and delivery to pledgee. Debentures
may also be pledged in a similar way.

Under article 2787 of the Civil Code "A pledgee has the right to be paid in preference out of the proceeds of the sale of the pledged asset".

In order to obtain payment of what is due to him, the pledgee may in fact effect
the sale of the pledged asset (art 2796 CC). Before proceeding with the sale, the
pledgee must serve on the pledgor a notice to the effect that if the latter fails to
pay the debt, the pledged assets will be sold.

If no payment is made, or no objection is raised by the pledgor within five days
of the notice, or if any objection made is overruled by the court, the pledged assets are sold at public auction or, if they have a market price, at current prices.
The pledgee can then satisfy his claim out of the proceeds up to the claimed
amount, any balance being held for the pledgor's account.

The pledgee may, however, petition the judge for the assets to be awarded to
him in payment of the claimed amount upon an appraisal of their value made
by an expert appraiser or at market price, if there is one.

Mortgage

A mortgage is a form of security over real estate and certain specific chattels.

Article 2810 of the Civil Code specifically lists the real estates and chattels that
can be mortgaged, namely:

- immoveable property, with their appurtenances;
- the usufruct of (*i.e.* the rights in) such immoveable property;
- the right of superficie (*i.e.* the right to erect and maintain a structure above
  the soil belonging to a third party);
- the rights of the emphyteutic tenant and of the grantor in the emphyteutic
  land. Under the principle of emphyteusis, perpetual rights can be granted
  by the owner of land ("the grantor") in that land to another (the "emphyteutic tenant");
- government rentals, vessels, aircraft and motor vehicles.

The mortgage gives the creditor rights over the mortgaged property, even as
against third party transferees. These are rights of payment of the debt due out
of the proceeds of the sale or, in certain circumstances, the transfer to the mortgagee of the mortgaged assets.

The mortgage may be granted by the debtor by unilateral deed or may arise
out of a bilateral agreement. The deed must then be entered in the public land

register of the district where the asset is located.

In order to obtain payment of what is due to him, the creditor may effect the sale of the mortgaged asset. To do this, he must first serve a notice on the mortgagor indicating what assets are to be sold. At any time before the sale of the mortgaged asset, the mortgagor may offer a sum in payment of what is due in order to avoid the expropriation. Failing this, however, the mortgaged asset is sold at public auction or by private contract on order of the judge.

Once the asset has been sold, the creditor will satisfy his claim out of the proceeds of the sale and any balance will be held for the mortgagor's account. The creditor may, however, ask the judge for the asset to be awarded to him in payment up to the claimed amount.

Where the mortgagor has transferred the mortgaged assets to a third party, the mortgagee will be entitled to enforce his rights – including expropriation of the mortgaged assets – against the third party to whom those assets have been transferred. This is, of course, subject to proper filing of the mortgage particulars.

Retention of title
Retention of title is only available in instalment sales in which ownership is retained by the seller. The buyer acquires ownership upon payment of the last instalment and bears the risk of damage or loss of the assets during the period between delivery and payment of such last instalment (art 1523 CC).

Set-off
Article 1241 of the Civil Code ("extinction by compensation") provides as follows: "When two persons are obliged to each other, both debts are extinguished to the extent of their corresponding amounts". Set-off is only permissible if the two claims are both outstanding and for money payments.

Available information

Information regarding companies may be obtained through the several registration systems:

- *Register of enterprises*: this register is kept by the chancery of the tribunal where the company is located. The register of enterprises contains the deed of incorporation, from which the names of the directors, the auditors and the legal representatives may be obtained. Also available are the by-laws, and, in the case of corporations, copies of the minutes of all shareholders' meetings and of all meetings of the board of directors with related annexes and exhibits. The file of each corporation contains all balance sheets and enables verification of the actual powers of each director or agent of the corporation;
- *Register of business names*: this register is kept by the chamber of commerce and contains the same information as above;

- *BUSA and BURSAL*: these are official bulletins in which the deed of incorporation, the by-laws and any modification thereof, as well as the balance sheets of corporations are published. The publication of this information is mandatory.

As a general rule banks and credit agencies are not available as sources of information. The law in fact imposes a requirement of secrecy on bank officers in relation to their professional operations. Thus, information on clients from this source is not available to the public unless authorised by the client himself.

In practice, however, even in the absence of a client's authorisation, banks do give information as to the solvency of the client and whether he is late with payments although, generally, without reference to specific operations. During a trial the judge may, upon petition by the counterparty, order a party to exhibit his accounting books if this is required for the proof of a specific fact.

Bank officers may be called by the judge as witnesses in criminal trials and, if requested by him, cannot refuse to answer on the grounds of client privilege.

Debt collection and asset recovery

Under Italian law debt collection procedures are divided into two categories:

- satisfaction of claims by execution on identified assets of the debtor by individual creditors, enforceable against all debtors, whether businesses or not; and

- bankruptcy and similar procedures which are applicable only to businesses and which involve all the debtor's assets and all the creditors at the same time. The main purpose of bankruptcy procedures is to guarantee the equal treatment of all creditors ("par condicio creditorum"). This section deals only with individual debt collection where the procedures are the same whether the debtor is an individual or a corporation.

In order to start a collection procedure, the creditor must be equipped with an "execution title". There are two types of such titles:

- judgments not subject to further appeal ("res judicata") and court orders;

- contractual documents or securities to which the law accords the status of execution title, for example, bills of exchange, notarial deeds, invoices and cheques.

Any collection proceedings which use any of the above documents must be complemented by the "execution legend" (a particular form of wording signed by the clerk of court, the notary or other public officer ordering all bailiffs to enforce the title) which is served upon the debtor together with a court order addressed to the debtor to pay the sums indicated therein within a term of at least ten days. A warning that failure to pay will result in expropriation of the debtor's assets must be included.

Only if that term expires without any payment being made may the actual execution begin. The court before which the execution proceedings are brought will depend on the property which is to be expropriated. The Magistrates Court ("Pretore") has jurisdiction in relation to the expropriation of chattels; the order of the Pretore can be executed as against:

- the debtor – in which case the bailiff is empowered to seize assets of a value corresponding to the claim and costs, draft minutes of his action and appoint a ward of court responsible for the protection of the assets;
- third parties – in which case, the third party is ordered not to pay to the debtor a debt owed by that third party to the debtor nor to hand back to the debtor assets of the debtor deposited with that third party. The seizure occurs by serving the court order upon both the debtor and the third party and ordering both to abstain from any act of disposal of such chattels.

The Tribunal has jurisdiction to act in the expropriation of real estate. This expropriation procedure begins by serving upon the debtor the court order listing the real estate subject to seizure or the rights (such as usufruct, emphyteusis, uses and servitudes) therein and ordering the debtor to abstain from any act of disposal in relation to that real estate. The seizure is effective as against third parties from the date it is entered into the appropriate land registry.

Once chattels have been seized, other creditors may request that their claims be satisfied, provided that such claims are certain, liquid and immediately due. These claims can be made even if not based on execution titles. The same applies in the case of the execution upon real estate except that the intervention of other creditors is admitted even if a claim is subject to a condition precedent or the time for the payment has not yet expired.

If the time set by the judge for payment of the claim in the execution title elapses without the claim being settled, any of the creditors taking part in the procedure may ask the judge to:

- sell any or all of the seized assets;
- assign to them any or all of the seized assets in lieu of their value in money.

The second request is extremely rare in the case of execution on real estate and is admitted only in cases where a sale has proved impossible.

The sale of chattels is made either:

- through a sales commissioner who sells the assets for cash at a price not lower than that indicated by the judge; or
- by public auction.

The sale of real estate is made:

- on the basis of tender offers deposited with the chancery of the Tribunal in whose district the real estate is located. If more than one offer is tendered, the judge calls individually on all the offerors inviting them to bid separately. If such invitation is refused, the judge decides either to assign the assets to the party who, in his opinion, has submitted the most attractive offer or calls for an auction;

- by auction; through a public bidding which takes place before the judge.

A successful bid will not, however, always be final since the judge may renew the auction if, within the following ten days, he receives one or more bids exceeding by more than one-sixth the highest prior bid.

If the auction is unsuccessful and the real estate is not sold, the creditors may ask for it to be assigned to them (as noted above). Alternatively, the real estate may be managed for no more than three years by a commissioner appointed by the court. The revenue from the asset is distributed among the creditors. Thereafter, the asset is again put on auction subject to a reserve price which is calculated as four-fifths of the price previously determined in the earlier attempted sale.

Once the sale is completed, the price received is distributed among the creditors in full satisfaction of their claims and the balance, if any, is paid to the debtor. Only creditors having an execution title are sure to take part in this distribution, while those who do not are allowed to take part only if their claims are uncontested by the others.

Italy is a signatory to the Brussels Convention of 27 June 1968 concerning the enforcement of foreign judgments in commercial and civil matters. Italian judgments may therefore be enforced in other signatory states pursuant to articles 31 to 45 of the Convention. Likewise, the judgments of other signatory states are enforceable in Italy.

Transnational insolvency – conflict rules

Transnational insolvency seems to pose rather complex problems in most jurisdictions, and Italy is no exception. This is probably due to the absence of specific statutory provisions in domestic legislation and to the scarcity of cases which the courts have been called upon to decide, a fact resulting from considering that the prevalent practice for a company intending to expand its operations in a foreign country has so far been through the creation of a subsidiary rather than through a branch.

Italian law, which normally sets out very clear rules to resolve conflicts of law and jurisdiction, is practically silent on choice of law in matters of insolvency. The only indirect legislative clues available are section 9 of the Bankruptcy Act and article 4 of the CPC.

Section 9 of the Bankruptcy Act provides that "Bankruptcy is adjudicated by the tribunal in whose jurisdiction the debtor has its main place of business. A debtor which has its main place of business abroad may be adjudicated bankrupt in Italy even if an adjudication in bankruptcy has been handed down abroad. International treaties are unaffected."

In laying down general rules on jurisdiction vis-à-vis foreigners, article 4 of the CPC provides, *inter alia*, that non-resident foreigners can be summoned to appear as defendants in the Italian courts if they are domiciled in Italy or if the claim relates to property situated in Italy or to obligations which arose in or are to be performed in Italy.

Thus, aside from international treaties to which we shall devote a few lines later on, Italian courts and legal literature have, with reference to section 9 of the Bankruptcy Act and article 4 of the CPC, developed two main trends of thought on the application of Italian jurisdiction to the insolvency of non-resident foreigners.

Under the first theory, which has been followed by a number of decisions of lower courts, a foreign trader can be adjudicated bankrupt in Italy even on the simple grounds of default in respect of an obligation undertaken or to be performed in Italy.

This rather direct approach to the problem is mitigated by some courts and authors by the requirement that the non-resident debtor should, in order to be adjudicated in bankruptcy, at least own some assets in Italy which may be apprehended and liquidated for the benefit of the Italian creditors.

The second theory, which has been advanced by other authors and followed by the present trend of recent decisions of the "Corte di Cassazione" (the Supreme Court), postulates that the simple non-performance of an obligation by a debtor is not sufficient to justify an adjudication of bankruptcy in Italy. Instead, this can be decided only in respect of debtors engaging in business in Italy in a continuing and organised business undertaking, a concept that implies the presence in Italy of either the main location or a permanent branch or office of the business.

An Italian court will, of course apply Italian law (*i.e.* the Bankruptcy Act), in adjudicating a debtor bankrupt in Italy. However, foreign law may have to be applied pursuant to the relevant rule on conflicts in respect of specific issues arising in the general context of the bankruptcy proceedings, such as, for example, issues on the validity of a claim under a contract governed by foreign law or of security granted on property located outside Italy.

Needless to say, the enforceability of an Italian judgment on the entrepreneur's business and assets abroad will largely depend on the rules governing the acknowledgement of foreign (in this case, Italian) judgments and the granting of enabling judgments prevailing in the country where enforcement is sought.

In the absence of specific treaty provisions, the enforceability in Italy of foreign judgments (including those making an adjudication of bankruptcy) is subject to a special procedure.

This procedure must be instituted in the Court of Appeal having jurisdiction over the location where the foreign judgment is to be enforced. The enabling judgment or "order of exequatur" is conditional upon the verification by the court of the existence of certain prerequisites listed in article 797 CPC, namely:

- the court of the state where the foreign judgment was handed down was competent to try the matter according to Italian provisions on jurisdiction;
- the writ of summons was served on the debtor pursuant to the law of the country where the litigation took place and an adequate period of time for appearance was provided;
- the parties appeared in court or their absence was taken into account in

reaching a decision pursuant to the law of the country where the litigation took place;

- the judgment is considered by the law(s) of the country where it was handed down as final (or non-appealable);
- the foreign judgment does not conflict with any other judgment handed down by an Italian court;
- litigation on the same matter as that considered by the foreign judgment is not pending before an Italian court between the same parties;
- the foreign judgment does not contain provisions conflicting with Italian rules on public order and policy.

The reference in section 9 of the Bankruptcy Act to the applicability of international treaties is not of great avail, considering that bankruptcy and the related proceedings are expressly excluded from the scope of most of the treaties on the recognition and enforcement of foreign judgments to which Italy is a party. See, in this context, the Rome Convention between Italy and Switzerland of 3 January 1933 and the EC Brussels Convention of 27 September 1968. Other conventions, such as that between Italy and the Republic of San Marino of 31 March 1939, are silent on the bankruptcy issue. It follows that a San Marino judgment of adjudication in bankruptcy should be supplemented with an enabling judgment of an Italian court in order to become enforceable in Italy.

The only two treaties touching specifically on the subject matter of insolvency are the Rome Treaty between the United Kingdom and Italy of 7 February 1964 and the Rome Treaty between France and Italy of 3 June 1930. The United Kingdom/Italian Treaty (which must in that limited context be deemed to be still in force even though both countries have since ratified the 1968 Brussels EC Convention) confines its provisions on insolvency to stating that a determination of the jurisdictional venue shall be made pursuant to the procedural rules of the country where the enforcement is sought.

The Italian/French Treaty is more direct in providing that:

- an adjudication in bankruptcy handed down in one of the contracting states shall have the effect of a final judgment in the other state;
- before being enforced in such other state, an enabling judgment must be obtained on the judgment;
- jurisdiction, in connection with bankruptcy-related actions, lies with the court within whose district the debtor had his principal business address (if an individual entrepreneur) or its legal address (if a partnership or company), except that claims concerning rights in immoveable property are to be instituted in the courts of the country where the property is located; and
- the trustee ("curatore") appointed in accordance with, and vested with the powers provided by, the law of the country in which the bankruptcy was adjudicated, which law shall also govern the allowance of claims, possible compositions and the trustee's actions to set aside the debtor's acts detrimental to the creditors.

A draft EC convention on bankruptcy and similar procedures was submitted to the Member States in 1980. The draft met with lively opposition from several members and in spite of recent efforts no great progress appears to have been made in the relevant negotiations. The eventual execution and ratification by the countries concerned of a convention which regulates conflicts of law and procedure in matters of insolvency will mark a significant step towards the solution of problems which are destined to become more and more frequent in the light of the ever increasing unification of the European Union.

3. Survival of the insolvent corporation or its business

The insolvency procedures which provide for the survival of the business of the insolvent debtor are:

- composition with creditors ("concordato preventivo") and
- controlled administration ("amministrazione controllata").

Two other procedures, which may lead to the survival of the insolvent company or its business, are discussed at pp401-403. They are :

- forced administrative liquidation ("liquidazione coatta amministrativa"); and
- extraordinary administration of large enterprises in crisis ("amministrazione straordinaria delle grandi imprese in crisi")

Composition with creditors

Purpose and effect

Composition with creditors (ss160-186, Bankruptcy Act) is a procedure whereby a debtor, with the creditors' prior consent, seeks to avoid bankruptcy (see p390 *infra*). This process may be used whether the debtor is incorporated or unincorporated and is generally employed in the case of debtors engaged in commercial and industrial operations.

Procedure

An insolvent debtor who has a clear record and has kept regular accounts may, prior to being adjudicated bankrupt, submit to the tribunal of the place where he has his principal place of business a petition for composition with creditors, offering either:

- to provide adequate security or personal guarantees for the payment of the full amount of preferred claims and no less than 40% of common or unprivileged claims or;

- to assign all of his assets to his creditors for their benefit, provided that the valuation thereof leads to a reasonable assurance that the creditors' claims will be satisfied at least to the same extent as above.

The petition must be accompanied by the debtor's accounting books, by a list of the assets, their estimated value and by a list of all the creditors.

If the tribunal decides that the petition has not satisfied the required conditions, it rejects the petition and hands down a judgment adjudicating the debtor bankrupt (see p390 *infra*)

Under Italian law the term "privilege" implies the right to be paid ahead of other creditors whose claims are not privileged. Italian law does not provide for any other right for a creditor holding a privileged claim. The terms "privileged" and "preferred" are synonymous, and article 2741 of the Italian Civil Code in fact provides that: "Creditors have equal rights to be paid out of the property of the debtor". The three causes of preference are (as we have seen above) liens, pledges and mortgages.

If the tribunal considers the offer worthy of further consideration, it opens the composition proceedings through issuing a decree whereby it designates a judge, orders the calling of a meeting of the creditors within 30 days from the date of the decree, appoints a judicial commissioner and sets a time limit of no more than eight days for the applicant to deposit the amount required to meet the costs of the proceedings.

Throughout the proceedings the debtor retains control of the assets and the management of the business under the supervision of the judicial commissioner and the direction of the judge.

No transactions other than those in the ordinary course of business can be validly performed without the consent of the judge. No levying of execution on the debtor's assets may be initiated or continued until the judgment ratifying the composition has become final.

The judicial commissioner, after checking the list of claims, calls a creditors' meeting for the day set by the tribunal, outlining in the notice the debtor's proposals. He then proceeds to draw up an inventory of the debtor's assets and a detailed report setting out the reasons for the insolvency, the debtor's past conduct, the proposals for composition, and the security or guarantees offered by the debtor. The inventory and report must be placed with the court clerk's office for no less than three days prior to the meeting.

The meeting called to resolve upon the approval of the composition is chaired by the judge.

Privileged or preferential creditors cannot participate in the voting unless they waive their priority. A resolution approving the composition must be passed with the favourable vote of as many creditors as represent a majority of those casting their vote and two-thirds of the total amount of all the claims of creditors eligible to vote.

The proposal for composition, if approved by the creditors' meeting, must be ratified by judgment of the tribunal. The tribunal, having verified the concurrence of all legal requirements and the favourable vote of the creditors as required by law, approves the preliminary settlement by issuing a judgment establishing the sums to be paid and the deadlines for such payments.

During the settlement procedure, the debtor maintains the management of his enterprise under the surveillance of the judicial commissioner.

If the tribunal denies approval or if at any time during the proceedings it becomes apparent that the conditions for the composition no longer exist, or the opposition of a dissenting creditor is upheld, the tribunal must render a judgment adjudicating the debtor bankrupt.

If the composition is based on an assignment of the assets for the benefit of the creditors, the tribunal appoints one or more officials ("liquidatori") to proceed with their sale and with the distribution of the proceeds among the creditors *pro rata* to their respective claims. The officials are assisted by a committee of three to five creditors.

If the debtor fails for any reason to comply with the terms of the composition, the tribunal hands down a judgment providing for the cancellation of the composition and the adjudication of bankruptcy.

In the case of an assignment for the benefit of creditors, as long as preferred claims are fully satisfied, the composition will be upheld even if the balance of the proceeds from the liquidation of the debtor's assets is ultimately insufficient to cover 40% of the total of common claims.

Controlled administration

Purpose and effect

Controlled administration ("amministrazione controllata") (ss187-193 Bankruptcy Act) is available in cases where the debtor, without being in an actual state of insolvency, is in temporary financial difficulties. It consists of a moratorium to enable a reorganisation of the undertaking.

A procedure for judicial moratorium or controlled administration is available to a debtor which does not have a deficiency of assets but, nevertheless, has liquidity problems expected to be solved in the short term. The bankruptcy law provides for a moratorium of up to 24 months on debts incurred before the debtor's petition. The debtor's undertaking becomes subject to court supervision, but the debtor retains responsibility for its day-to-day management.

This procedure is frequently proposed but is seldom successful. An unsuccessful petition can result in a proposal for composition, but very often the damage already done to the debtor's undertaking is such that bankruptcy inevitably follows.

Procedure

The basic condition for a debtor to have his business admitted to the controlled administration procedure is the existence of a real possibility of a return to financial stability by re-financing or re-structuring the business over a period of two years during which no claims relating to prior debts can be enforced.

The remedy comprises:

- the submission of the management and the administration of the company to judicial control and, as noted above,
- the prohibition on those creditors whose claims arose prior to the date of the court's writ establishing controlled administration, from attaching the assets of the company for a period not exceeding two years.

A debtor seeking the benefit of controlled administration must file a petition with the tribunal in whose jurisdiction the business has its principal address.

The tribunal will issue a decree provided that:

- the petition has been approved by the majority of the creditors representing the majority of the claims;
- the conditions set forth in the law are fulfilled; and
- the tribunal believes that the debtor deserves the benefit of the controlled administration

Once it has authorised the controlled administration, the tribunal designates a judge to oversee the administration, orders the calling of a meeting of the creditors, appoints a judicial commissioner and sets a deadline not exceeding eight days for the debtor to deposit with the tribunal the anticipated costs of the proceedings.

A procedure similar to that contemplated in respect of the creditors' meeting in composition proceedings applies, except that the resolution approving controlled administration is validly passed by a vote in favour of a majority of the creditors representing the simple majority of unsecured claims.

Administration of the assets and management of the business during the controlled administration are retained by the debtor, provided that any act which is not in the ordinary course of business is approved by the judge. The court may, however, at the request of any creditor or of its own motion entrust the management and the administration of the whole or part of the company to a judicial commissioner. Settlement of pre-existing debts, and the institution or continuation of execution processes in connection with such debts, are suspended throughout the duration of the proceedings.

The judicial commissioner reports to the judge on the operation of the business. If at any time it becomes apparent that the controlled administration cannot be effectively continued or if, at the end of the two-year period, it becomes evident that the undertaking is unable to meet its obligations, the judge initiates proceedings for an adjudication of bankruptcy unless a petition for composition with creditors is warranted.

4. Termination of the insolvent corporation: bankruptcy

Introduction

Bankruptcy ("Fallimento") is governed by sections 1-159 of the Bankruptcy Act and has two main aims: (i) the exclusion from the market of those businesses that are not self-sustaining; and (ii) the protection of the principle that the creditors of the insolvent trader should be treated equally (the so-called "par condicium creditorum").

The main prerequisites for an adjudication of bankruptcy are that:

- the debtor must be insolvent, *i.e.* unable to pay the debts of the undertaking (s5 Bankruptcy Act). This condition is met when the debtor is no longer capable of performing regularly, in a timely fashion and in the normal course of business, the obligations undertaken. Insolvency is defined not as a simple default, but as a structural and continuing inability to discharge one's obligations in business operations;

- the debtor must be engaged in business operations. Agricultural business (art 2195 CC), public bodies (art 2201 CC) and small businesses *i.e.* farmers who personally cultivate the land, artisans, small tradesmen and those who engage professionally in an activity organised mainly with their own work and that of the members of their families (art 2083 CC) are excluded from the scope of bankruptcy, composition with creditors or controlled administration.

The debtor may, however, be an individual, partnership, company, foundation, co-operative society (when mostly engaged in trading) or a consortium "syndicate contract". A "syndicate contract" (or joint venture vehicle) arises where two or more entrepreneurs establish a joint organisation for the regulation or the carrying out of certain phases of their respective activities. A syndicate contract may also be incorporated in any of the above-mentioned forms. The public authority may in certain cases order the formation of consortia among businesses operating in the same or in similar fields within a certain area.

Bankruptcy proceedings commence pursuant to a petition filed by the debtor itself, by one or more creditors or by the public prosecutor, or else may be instituted by the tribunal of its own motion (when knowledge of the insolvency is acquired in the context of other proceedings).

An adjudication of bankruptcy is pronounced by a judgment issued by the tribunal in whose territorial jurisdiction the debtor has established its main place of business ("sede principale") (s9 Bankruptcy Act).

The tribunal consists of a panel of three career judges. Before handing down the judgment, the tribunal must interview the debtor and determine the existence of the conditions for the adjudication. The judgment provides also for the appointment of one of the panel's members as the judge delegate ("the judge") and of a trustee or receiver in bankruptcy ("curatore").

The judge directs the proceedings and supervises the actions of the curatore. The curatore is not only the administrator and custodian of the bankruptcy assets under the supervision of the judge; he also performs a leading role in the bankruptcy procedure. His office is compensated with a fee assessed by the tribunal. The curatore must accept his appointment within two days. If he does not do so the tribunal appoints another curatore.

In exercising his functions the curatore is a public official. Relatives of the bankrupt and bankrupted and unrehabilitated individuals cannot act as curatori who, as a rule, are chosen from the registers of lawyers, accountants or bookkeepers. The curatore cannot sue or accept service of summons on behalf of the bankruptcy without the judge's consent and cannot act as solicitor in lawsuits concerning the bankruptcy. He must exercise his functions personally, but may be authorised to avail himself of the help of experts and professionals. The curatore may, if authorised by the judge, reduce claims against the bankruptcy estate, make settlements, withdraw from lawsuits, lift mortgages, return pledged chattels and accept donations. The curatore reports to the judge on the causes of the bankruptcy, on the diligence exercised by the bankrupt or its officers in managing the business, on the standard of living of the bankrupt and of his family, on the responsibilities of the bankrupt and on those acts which have been opposed by the creditors or will be opposed by him. All sums collected by the curatore are deposited within five days in a special account. A creditors' committee of three to five members is appointed by the judge with advisory and supervisory duties (ss40, 41 Bankruptcy Act).

The adjudication of bankruptcy is given ample publicity by, *inter alia*, posting the ruling at the gate of the tribunal, publication in the District Bulletin of Legal Notices and the entry in the register of bankrupts kept by the clerk of the tribunal (ss 17, 50 Bankruptcy Act).

The debtor and any interested third party are entitled to file an opposition within 15 days from the posting, by serving a deed of summons on the curatore and the creditor who petitioned for the declaration of bankruptcy. The opposition, however, does not result in a stay of the execution of the judgment; this must be done through normal lawsuit. If the plaintiff wins, the bankruptcy is revoked.

Effects of bankruptcy

General

The main consequence of the opening of bankruptcy proceedings for the bankrupt is "dispossession", that is the transfer to the trustee ("curatore") of the administration of and the right of disposal of present and future assets excluding, in the case of an individual, those that are necessary for the bankrupt's own and his family's sustenance (ss45-46 Bankruptcy Act).

The curatore can demand that any transaction performed by the bankrupt relating to the assets of the bankrupt debtor conflicting with the dispossession provisions (such as contracts of sale, donations, leases and grant of use) and which, if valid, would have the effect of reducing the debtor's estate and thus affect the creditors' claim, be declared ineffective *vis-à-vis* the creditor.

Nevertheless, the bankrupt is entitled to perform urgent acts to safeguard his and the creditors' interests and any other act not performed by the curatore, owing to the latter's negligence. Dispossession implies the vesting in the curatore of the capacity to appear, as noted above, in judicial proceedings as plaintiff or defendant in the interest of the majority of creditors.

Entry in the register of bankrupts carries for the bankrupt (but not automatically the directors of a company adjudicated bankrupt) a number of restrictions set out in the Civil Code or other statutes, including:

- the loss of the right to participate in political contests either as a voter or a candidate until the closing of the bankruptcy proceedings, but for no more than five years from the adjudication in bankruptcy;
- non-eligibility to be appointed as a justice of peace, as a tax collector, as a director, liquidator or statutory auditor of a company or as a guardian of infants or to engage in certain professions such as a lawyer, stock exchange broker or pharmacist;
- exclusion from admission to the premises of the stock and commodities exchanges where business is transacted, and non-eligibility as an affiliant in "affiliation" proceedings. (Minors kept by public assistance institutions may be entrusted to the ward of trusted persons. After three years that person may ask to affiliate the minor. The affiliation results in the affiliant acquiring parental authority over the minor and, upon his request, in the granting of his family name).

These disabilities cease as soon as the judgment of adjudication in bankruptcy is revoked or the bankrupt is rehabilitated.

Rehabilitation is granted by a judgment of the tribunal in any of the following circumstances (ss142-144 Bankruptcy Act):

- when the bankrupt has fully paid all of the claims admitted in the proceedings, including interest and costs;
- when the bankrupt has performed his obligations under a settlement agreement ("concordato fallimentare") entered into with the creditors pursuant to which he paid all preferred claims and a minimum of 25% of the aggregate amount of unsecured claims; and
- when the bankrupt offers actual and constant evidence of good behaviour for a period of five years after the closing of the bankruptcy proceedings.

As a result of the adjudication, companies and partnerships cease operations and, once the liquidation has been completed, the company is dissolved.

Effects on creditors

An adjudication of bankruptcy prevents any creditor from instituting or continuing individual proceedings for the levying of execution on the bankrupt's assets. Secured creditors, *i.e.* those whose claims are secured by a mortgage, pledge or supported by a lien, have priority in payment from the proceeds of the sale of the bankrupt's assets and, to the extent they are not fully satisfied, may participate with unsecured creditors in the distribution of the remaining assets.

Pecuniary debts become automatically payable upon the adjudication of bankruptcy.

In addition, creditors are entitled to set-off debts owed to the bankrupt against their claims on the bankrupt, even though the claims had not become payable prior to the adjudication.

Effects on existing contracts

The Bankruptcy Act contains a number of provisions regarding the effects of the bankruptcy on certain existing contracts (ss72-83). For example:

Sale
If performance of a sale contract is not yet completed when the bankruptcy of the purchaser is adjudicated, the seller is entitled to enforce the contract against the bankrupt purchaser and to file proof of his claim for payment of the price. If the seller does not exercise this right, the contract is suspended until the curatore declares whether he intends to maintain the contract, in which case he thereby undertakes all the relevant obligations. Otherwise the contract is abandoned without any liability on the part of the bankrupt debtor.

If it is the seller who is adjudicated bankrupt and the property has already been delivered to the purchaser, the contract does not lose its effect. If the property has not been delivered, the curatore may choose either to perform or dissolve the contract.

Mandate, current account, commission agency
These contracts are terminated as a result of the bankruptcy of either party.

Lease of immoveable property
Unless otherwise agreed, the lessor's bankruptcy does not terminate the contract. If the lessee is adjudicated bankrupt, the curatore can terminate the contract at any time by paying fair compensation to the lessor. The lessor's claim for compensation has priority over common claims.

Building or service contract
A building or a service contract is terminated by the bankruptcy of either party unless the curatore declares, within 20 days from the adjudication, his intent to carry out the contract, offering adequate guarantees.

Insurance

The bankruptcy of the insured does not terminate property and casualty insurance policies unless otherwise agreed in the contract. If the contract continues, the insurer is entitled to the full payment of premiums, even if these fell due prior to the adjudication of bankruptcy.

Because of the stringent administrative control exercised on insurance companies and of public policy aspects involved therein, the insolvency of the insurer is governed by a different procedure – forced administrative liquidation (see pp401-403 *infra*). In the event, the effect on existing policies is as follows:

- all existing policies continue to cover the insured risks for a period of up to 60 days as from the date on which the judgment commencing this procedure is published in the Official Gazette;

- assureds even prior to expiration of this 60 day term, have the right to terminate their policies and enter new ones with other insurers. They must give notice to the judicial commissioner;

- from the day following the notice of termination, if any, the effects of the earlier policies cease; assureds who have a claim against the insurer will participate in the distribution of the proceeds resulting from the liquidation of the bankrupt insurer's assets.

The law provides that, upon expiration of the above 60 day term or upon notice of termination of the policy given by the assured, life insurance policies are transferred ex-lege to the National Insurance Institute (INA).

There is also a procedure known as extraordinary administration of large enterprises in crisis (see pp401-403 *infra*). There is some debate as to whether bankrupt insurance companies can be made subject to this procedure. The law is silent on this point: in the absence of any prohibition to this effect, most Italian authors consider that forced administrative liquidation and extraordinary administration of large enterprises in crisis are both applicable to insurance companies.

Procedure

Once bankruptcy is adjudicated, the proceedings encompass three main stages: augmenting the assets of the insolvent corporation, establishing the claims against the bankrupt organisation, and liquidation and distribution of assets.

Augmenting the assets of the insolvent corporation

As an immediate preliminary measure, all assets of the bankrupt enterprise are placed under seal by the judge. Thereafter, the curatore applies to the judge for removal of the seals and draws up an inventory of the assets, taking them into his custody. The curatore also institutes or continues actions for the collection of the bankrupt's claims or receivables and has the authority to set aside a number of acts performed by the debtor which are regarded by law as being detrimental to the creditors' claims. These court actions are dealt with in more detail below at pp398-401.

Establishing the claims against the bankrupt corporation

Any claim, even if secured, is admitted through a detailed procedure set forth in the Bankruptcy Act (ss92 *et seq*).

The judge evaluates the application submitted by the creditors within the time period set by the judgment of adjudication in bankruptcy and notified to them by the curatore by registered mail ("insinuazione nel passivo del fallimento"). The judge either (a) allows the claim, totally or with a reservation (if for example the claim is subject to a condition or is not adequately supported by documentary evidence), or (b) refuses to admit it in whole or in part on the strength of the documents submitted. The rejection must be justified and, if the claim has already been assessed in a judgment not subject to further appeals, the claim cannot be rejected (s95 Bankruptcy Act).

The list of claims is reviewed at a meeting before the judge, in the presence of the curatore, the debtor and the creditors. It is then approved by the judge by a decree having the force of an enforceable judgment. The decree can be appealed by creditors whose claims were totally or partially disallowed and all such appeals are resolved by the tribunal in a single judgment.

Liquidation and distribution of assets

After the issue of the decree determining the amount of the claims (and the settlement of any appeals), the curatore proceeds with the liquidation of the assets under the supervision of the judge. To the extent that they are compatible with the Bankruptcy Act, the provisions of the Code of Civil Procedure ("CPC") governing the forced sale of moveable or immoveable property apply.

The proceeds from the liquidation of assets are distributed in the following order of priority:

1. defraying the costs of the procedure;
2. paying the secured claims, in the order contemplated by law;
3. paying unsecured claims *pro rata* to the portion of the claim allowed for each of them, including those secured claims whose security was not enforced or to the extent that it proved insufficient to cover the claim.

Partial distributions may be made during the course of the proceedings but these cannot exceed 90% of the sums available.

On completing the liquidation of assets and prior to the final distribution, the curatore submits to the judge an account of the operations completed.

The judge orders that the account be deposited with the clerk and sets a date for a hearing at which any interested party (*i.e.* all the creditors who have submitted claims – both those whose claims have been admitted and those whose claims have been rejected) may submit their comments. The deposit of the final accounting and the date for a hearing are immediately notified to the bankrupt and to each creditor. There is no statutory advance notice period. If no objections are submitted at the hearing, the judge approves the final account, failing which the disputes are resolved by a full sitting of the court.

Termination of the proceedings

Termination of the bankruptcy procedure

Article 118 of the Bankruptcy Act provides for termination of the bankruptcy procedure. According to this provision, a bankruptcy will terminate:

- when no claims are filed within the terms set out by the adjudication of bankruptcy;
- when, even prior to the final distribution of the proceeds resulting from the liquidation of the bankrupt's assets, creditors have been paid in full and the curatore's fees and procedural costs have been settled in full;
- when both liquidation and distribution of the bankrupt's assets have been completed;
- when, because of the insufficiency of the bankrupt's assets, the procedure cannot be profitably continued.

The termination of bankruptcy is declared by decree handed down by the tribunal of its own initiative or upon petition filed by the curatore or by the bankrupt himself or itself and may be challenged within 15 days of its issue.

Following the decree of termination of bankruptcy, the creditors regain their right to proceed against the debtor for any unsatisfied balance of their claims, together with interest thereon. However, there is rarely any practical value in doing so, especially if the debtor is an incorporated entity. Alternatively, bankruptcy can be terminated on the acceptance by creditors of a composition as described below.

Composition to terminate bankruptcy

The debtor may offer his creditors a composition. This may be proposed by the debtor at any time after the judge as issued the list of enforceable claims. In order to be acceptable, the composition must offer creditors either a greater or a quicker return than would be possible under bankruptcy proceedings.

The procedure for this form of composition, ("concordato fallimentare") which implies that an adjudication in bankruptcy has occurred already, is briefly as follows:

- the bankrupt notifies the judge of the proposal. If the judge feels that it is in the creditors' interests, he issues an order for the curatore to notify creditors of the proposal by registered mail, fixing a term of no less than 20 and no more than 30 days within which the creditors must inform the chancery of the tribunal of their dissent.

- the tribunal convenes a meeting of creditors to receive details of the proposals. The composition must be approved by a majority of unsecured creditors representing, in aggregate, at least two-thirds of the amount of all unsecured claims. Creditors who do not vote are assumed to accept the proposal. Voting may also be by proxy or by written notice to the tribunal within the time limit given in the notice convening the meeting;

- the tribunal considers the creditors' answers and the adequacy of the security, if any, offered by the debtor in respect of his undertakings in the composition. If appropriate, the tribunal approves the composition by handing down a judgment and may impose certain conditions for its enforcement.

Dissenting creditors and the bankrupt may appeal against the judgment approving or rejecting the composition, within 15 days from its publication. The appeal must be notified to the curatore and to the bankrupt (unless, obviously, the bankrupt is the appellant). The judgment on appeal may itself be appealed against by the same parties to the Supreme Court within 30 days from the publication of the judgment on appeal. When the judgment approving the composition has become final, the bankruptcy is closed.

The judge, the curatore, and the creditors' committee remain in office until the completion of the composition. If the bankruptcy proceedings are re-opened, these officers resume their duties.

If the debtor does not grant the promised securities, the curatore must report this to the tribunal which then hands down a judgment cancelling the composition, the effect of which is the re-opening of the bankruptcy procedure.

Re-opening of the procedure

In addition to the above case, the bankruptcy procedure may be re-opened within five years from the decree of termination, upon petition of the debtor or of any creditor, provided that the bankruptcy procedure was terminated:

- because the distribution of assets was completed; or
- because it appeared useless to continue the proceedings owing to lack of assets.

In either case one of the following conditions applies:

- the debtor has sufficient assets to render profitable the re-opening of the procedure; or
- the debtor offers to pay at least 10% of old and new claims.

The re-opening of the bankruptcy procedure is declared by a judgment of the tribunal which cannot be appealed. The procedure for the re-opened bankruptcy is the same as that outlined in the preceding paragraphs.

Summary bankruptcy procedure

In cases where it appears that the debtor's liabilities do not exceed Lire 1,500,000, the tribunal hands down a judgment declaring that summary bankruptcy procedure shall be adopted. This implies a simplified procedure whose stages may be summarised as follows:

- the functions of the judge can be exercised by the local magistrate (pretore);
- the curatore may dispense with physical custody of the debtor's tangible assets;
- the statement of outstanding claims is prepared from the debtor's accounting records, statements made by the debtor and information received from the curatore. The curatore must notify all creditors, within three days of the lodging of this statement, that the summary procedure has been adopted. Creditors can object to the amount for which their claim has been entered, within 15 days of the lodging of the statement. In such a case, a court hearing will be granted so that disputes will be resolved. In the absence of any protest, creditors' claims are taken as accepted;
- the debtor may propose a composition which, if approved by creditors representing a majority both by number and by value of the claims, will be sanctioned by the tribunal without any right of appeal by dissenting creditors.

This summary procedure is actually seldom adopted since the threshold of Lire 1,500,000 presently provided by the Bankruptcy Act has never been updated, thus drastically limiting the number of cases in which this procedure can be used.

5. Augmenting the assets of the insolvent corporation

Proceedings brought by the curatore

Once a corporation has been adjudicated bankrupt, the curatore can bring proceedings to set aside a number of acts performed by the debtor prior to the adjudication which are regarded by the law as being detrimental to the creditors' claims. If successful, these proceedings result in an increase in the assets available for distribution to creditors. The transactions that can be the subject of these proceedings are as follows:

- all disposals by the bankrupt of any of its assets for no consideration, except customary or charitable gifts, made in the two years preceding the bankruptcy;
- payment of claims due on or after the date of adjudication of bankruptcy, but made at any time in the two years preceding the bankruptcy;

The curatore may in addition request the tribunal to declare void all acts of the bankrupt prejudicial to the rights of the creditors. "Prejudicial acts" are acts of disposal by the debtor of his assets resulting in a prejudice to the position of the creditor, provided:

- the debtor knew that this action created such prejudice or, if performed before the indebtedness was incurred, would create such prejudice in the future; and
- in case of disposals for consideration, the third party was aware of the prejudice or, if the deed was prior to the date on which the indebtedness was incurred, was aware of the prospect of the prejudice to the creditors in the future.

This action is called "revocatoria ordinaria".

Transactions will also be revoked where the third party fails to prove that he or it was not aware of the state of insolvency of the debtor, and the transaction was entered into during the two years preceding the bankruptcy (one year in the case of mortgages and pledges granted as security for mature debts); and

- where, although they were entered into for consideration, the performance given or the obligations undertaken by the bankrupt exceeded significantly the consideration paid or promised; or
- where due and collectible pecuniary debts in favour of the bankrupt debtor were released without payment of money or by other normal means of settlement; or
- where pledges and mortgages were granted as security for pre-existing non-matured debts; or
- where pledges and mortgages were granted as security for matured debts;

Finally transactions will be revoked where the curatore proves that the other party was aware of the debtor's state of insolvency and the transaction was entered into during the year preceding the bankruptcy. Such transactions include payments of debts due and collectable, transactions for consideration, and transactions resulting in a right of priority with respect to debts concurrently created.

This action is called: "revocatoria fallimentare".

Personal liability of directors, liquidators and managing partners

Extent of liability

Another way in which the assets of the insolvent corporation may be augmented (or, at least, preserved) is via proceedings alleging some personal liability on the part of directors, liquidators and managing partners. Consequently, as with a bankrupt individual, the directors, liquidators and managing partners of a bankrupt company or partnership cannot leave their place of residence without the judge's permission. Furthermore, they are bound to appear before the judge, curatore and creditor's committee, to be personally interviewed whenever requested to do so (ss49 and 146 Bankruptcy Act).

Under section 146, para 2 of the Bankruptcy Act, the curatore may, if authorised by the judge and after consultation with the creditors' committee, institute an action for damages against directors, statutory auditors, general managers and liquidators of bankrupt companies for having negligently or wilfully caused damage to the company or for having dissipated its assets to the detriment of its creditors.

The Bankruptcy Act provides for different consequences for shareholders and partners, depending on the specific structure of the relevant concerns.

In the case of limited liability companies (including joint-stock companies and partnerships limited by shares), since the liability of shareholders is limited to the amount of capital subscribed by them, the company's adjudication in bankruptcy will not, in principle, affect the shareholders. Nevertheless, the normal protection afforded to shareholders might be reduced or even eliminated. Thus, shareholders might be ordered by the judge to make the payment of the capital subscribed and not yet paid-up, even if the time limit to satisfy this obligation has not yet expired.

In spite of the rule concerning the unlimited liability of the sole shareholder of an insolvent company (see p373 *supra*), it is the opinion of the courts and legal authorities that the bankruptcy of a company does not automatically extend to its sole shareholder. Nevertheless, that sole shareholder may suffer subsequent bankruptcy proceedings, provided that a petition to this effect is presented by an individual creditor of the insolvent company and provided always that the shareholder is eligible for bankruptcy within the meaning of the Bankruptcy Act.

Section 147 of the Bankruptcy Act provides that "the adjudication of bankruptcy of a partnership with partners who are liable without limit results in the bankruptcy of such partners". It follows that the adjudication in bankruptcy of a general partnership (either registered or not) leads to the bankruptcy of all partners (arts 2291, 2297 CC) and the adjudication in bankruptcy of a limited partnership involves the bankruptcy of all general partners and of those special partners who:

- performed acts of management, negotiated or transacted business in the name of the partnership, except by virtue of a special power of attorney for a single transaction (art 2320 CC); or
- consented to their names being included in the name of the partnership (art 2314 CC) even though they took little or no part in the management.

Penal provisions

Although they do not lead to any increase in the assets available to creditors, it is worth noting that fraud and negligence may also involve the directors in criminal liability, the penalties for which can be severe. In fact, sections 216-241 of the Bankruptcy Act contain penal sanctions for several acts related to bankruptcy.

A peculiar feature of these provisions is that some of the relevant acts have no criminal connotation in themselves but acquire it retroactively, pursuant to an adjudication in bankruptcy. Thus, a director of a company who failed to keep regular accounting books and records would, in normal circumstances, be exposed simply to certain tax consequences, but if his company is adjudicated bankrupt he may be prosecuted and eventually sentenced to imprisonment for between six months and two years.

The same applies to a debtor who failed to meet the obligations undertaken in a prior composition with creditors, or, in the case of an individual, who incurred personal or family expenses greater than his financial conditions warranted.

All the above acts fall within the category of "bancarotta semplice".

Much more serious are the consequences of acts classified as "bancarotta fraudolenta" such as removal, concealment, destruction or dissipation of assets, forgery or destruction of accounting records, insertion of false entries in the balance sheets of the company, unlawful distribution of profits and payments made to some creditors with the aim of favouring them to the detriment of others. All these acts entail imprisonment from three to ten years.

6. Public control over insolvent corporations

As noted in the earlier sections, the insolvency procedures available in Italy are conducted under the supervision of the relevant tribunal which appoints the relevant individual officials. In the remainder of this section, we shall deal with two procedures which may lead to the survival of the insolvent corporation or its business and which are subject to stringent administrative control.

Forced administrative liquidation

Forced administrative liquidation ("Liquidazione coatta amministrativa") (ss194-215 Bankruptcy Act) applies to concerns whose functions or structure are of particular interest to the public, such as banks, insurance companies, institutes for popular housing and co-operative societies.

In the case of banks, the law provides only for forced administrative liquidation whereas, in other cases, provision is made for either forced administrative liquidation or bankruptcy.

The procedure is designed to provide, if at all possible, for the reorganisation of the business by way of a composition. In practice, however, this seldom happens, and the company normally ceases trading.

The liquidation must be preceded by a declaration of insolvency of the enterprise issued by the tribunal upon the petition of any creditor or by the tribunal of its own motion whenever (during composition or controlled administration proceedings) conditions prevail which in normal circumstances would necessitate an adjudication in bankruptcy.

This procedure is administrative rather than judicial. In fact, the liquidation is steered by the government authority under whose supervisory jurisdiction the insolvent business falls.

Thus, the ruling ordering the liquidation is made by the Minister of Industry, Commerce and Handicrafts with respect to insurance companies; by the Minister of Public Works in respect of institutes for public housing; and so forth.

By the same or a subsequent ruling one or three liquidating commissioners and a supervisory committee ("the committee") are appointed. The committee consists of three or five members chosen from among persons who are experienced in the debtor's business. Such individuals need not be creditors.

The liquidation is carried into effect by the liquidating commissioner under the supervision of the committee and the directives of the government authority. Specific rules govern the procedure by which the commissioner agrees the creditors' claims.

The powers of the liquidating commissioner are based on those of the curatore in ordinary bankruptcy proceedings and the effects of the opening of forced administration procedure are similar to those of the opening of a bankruptcy procedure.

Several provisions set down in the Bankruptcy Act with regard to bankruptcy proceedings are incorporated by reference in those governing forced administrative liquidation; unlike bankruptcy and the other reorganisation procedures, however, the procedure here is purely administrative. There is no judge or judicial commissioner in charge. The liquidating commissioner's duties are to agree to the claims of creditors and to establish whether a composition is feasible. If it is, the commissioner will develop, together with the directors of the company subject to the procedure, a scheme upon which the creditors must vote.

However, the commencement of the procedure for a compulsory administrative liquidation often causes irretrievable damage to the goodwill of the business concerned and it may not be feasible to consider a composition. In this case, the debtor's assets are sold and the funds distributed to creditors in the same order as in any bankruptcy proceedings.

Extraordinary administration of large enterprises in crisis

A further administrative procedure is the extraordinary administration of large enterprises in crisis ("amministrazione stroardinaria delle grandi imprese in crisi") that was introduced into the Italian system by Decree Law No. 26 of 30 January 1979 to enable large enterprises in a critical financial situation to avoid bankruptcy.

To qualify as a "large enterprise in crisis", a company must employ at least 300 units and either:

(a) have medium or long-term indebtedness of no less than Lire 71,382 million (or such amount as may be established by the Minister of Industry from time to time), or such as exceeds by more than five times the paid up capital as shown in the last approved balance sheet, or

(b) be made insolvent as a result of an obligation to pay back to the state, public agencies or state owned companies a sum exceeding 51% of their own share capital and exceeding Lire 50 billion. Furthermore, the insolvency of the large enterprise must have been judicially ascertained, for instance, by judgment on a bankruptcy petition.

If the aforesaid conditions occur, the enterprise is admitted to extraordinary administration by a decree of the Minister of the Treasury in agreement with the Minister of Industry, Trade and Handicrafts. The decree prevents an adjudication in bankruptcy, and any such adjudication previously made will be revoked by a judgment of the relevant tribunal.

The following authorities are in charge of the procedure:

- one or three commissioners;
- a supervisory committee;
- the Minister of Industry, Trade and Handicrafts, as lead supervising authority;
- the Interministerial Committee for Industrial Policy Co-ordination ("CIPI").

The commissioners and the supervisory committee are appointed in the same manner as their equivalent in forced administrative liquidation.

Unlike forced administrative liquidation and composition with creditors, which ordinarily lead to the winding up of the enterprise, the statutory objective of extraordinary administration is a reorganisation aimed at a continuation of the business.

The commissioners, who are public officials, are appointed by the Minister of Industry, Trade and Handicrafts to supervise the affairs of the company, for a period which must not exceed three years.

The commissioners draw up a rehabilitation programme, whose implementation is subject to the approval of the supervisory committee once it has been recommended by the CIPI. Special financial facilities may be granted in support of the programme.

The freezing of execution proceedings, the removal of the debtor's power to dispose of and to manage the assets, the suspension of all the functions and powers of the directors and of the shareholders' meeting of the insolvent companies, are provisions of the Bankruptcy Act which also apply to extraordinary administration.

Contents of Chapter 9

CORPORATE INSOLVENCY LAW IN LUXEMBOURG

1.	**Introduction**	407
	The sources of law in the Grand Duchy of Luxembourg	407
	Persons, insolvency and bankruptcy	407
2.	**Corporations**	408
	Characteristics	408
	Management	409
	Ownership	411
	Financing and security for creditors	412
	Available information	412
	Other business entities	412
	Debt collection and asset recovery	414
3.	**Survival of the insolvent corporation or its business**	415
	The reprieve from payment ("sursis de paiement")	416
	Composition in order to avoid bankruptcy ("concordat préventif de faillite")	419
	The controlled management ("gestion contrôlée")	424
	Creditors' involvement and position	427
	Powers and duties of the designated judge and of the commissioners	428
	Termination and cancellation of the plan which has been approved	429
	Procedure applicable to credit institutions	429
4.	**Termination of the corporation: bankruptcy and compulsory winding up**	430
	Bankruptcy	430
	Compulsory winding up	437
5.	**Augmenting the assets of the insolvent corporation**	438
	Introduction	438

Transactions at risk   438
Personal liability of officers   440
6.   Public control over insolvent corporations   443
Licensing and control of the appointee   443
Examinations and investigations   443
Publicity and records   444

Chapter 9

CORPORATE INSOLVENCY LAW IN LUXEMBOURG

René Diederich,
Loesch & Wolter

1. Introduction

The sources of law in the Grand Duchy of Luxembourg

The main provisions governing corporate insolvency are contained in the Luxembourg commercial code ("code de commerce") laid down in the law of 15 September 1807 as amended. There are also a certain number of specific laws and regulations which will be mentioned in this chapter dealing with the survival of the insolvent corporation or its business such as:

- the Law of 14 April 1886 as amended concerning compositions in order to avoid bankruptcy;
- the Grand Ducal Decree of 24 May 1935 concerning controlled management;
- articles 38 to 46 of the Law of 27 November 1984, as amended, on access to the financial sector and its supervision, dealing with the reprieve from payment, controlled management and the winding up of credit institutions.

Reference will also be made throughout this chapter to the Law of 10 August 1915, as amended, on trading companies.

Persons, insolvency and bankruptcy

The Luxembourg Civil Code draws a distinction both between individual and legal entities, and between civil entities and business entities. This latter distinction is of importance to the extent that only business entities may be subject to insolvency and bankruptcy proceedings as provided for in the commercial code.

Obviously civil entities may also come into a situation where they fail to meet their liabilities. This failure ("déconfiture") will, however, not be acknowledged by a judgment which has effect as against third parties.

The Civil Code does not give a clear-cut definition of what amounts to déconfiture. The main consequence of a failure to meet liabilities will be that all the money borrowed by the company will become immediately repayable. This chapter deals almost exclusively with the failure of corporate business entities.

Article 1 of the Luxembourg Commercial Code defines "business entities" as those entities performing a business activity on a regular professional basis. The code does not, however, contain any clear-cut definition of "business activity", containing instead a non-exhaustive list of activities which are deemed to be business activities. Article 1 of the law of 10 August 1915 on trading companies defines corporate business entities as entities whose purpose it is to perform business activity.

This chapter deals principally with the procedures applying in the case of insolvency of corporate business entities. It should be remembered, however, that the same procedures also apply to individuals performing a business activity on a regular professional basis (*i.e.*"commerçants").

2. Corporations

Luxembourg company law is very similar to Belgian company law and the reader is therefore referred, for comparative purposes, to the Belgian chapter of this book.

Luxembourg law recognises the following companies:

- the civil company ("société civile");
- the general partnership ("société en nom collectif");
- the limited partnership ("société en commandite simple");
- the partnership limited by shares ("société en commandite par actions");
- the co-operative company ("société co-opérative");
- the private limited company ("société à responsabilité limitée");
- the public limited company ("société anonyme").

As the most commonly used business associations in Luxembourg are the private limited company ("société à responsabilité limitée") and the public limited company ("société anonyme"), these two types of business associations will be examined in detail in this section, while the main characteristics of the other business entities will be covered more briefly.

Characteristics

The private limited company ("société à responsabilité limitée" – "sàrl")

This is incorporated by deed, containing the statutes (*i.e.* the constitution), which must be executed before a notary public. The company is formed for a limited or an unlimited duration. In the latter case, it is generally accepted that any member has the right to give notice of cessation of membership at any time, cessation taking effect after a prescribed period.

There must be a minimum of two members and a maximum of 40. Both individuals and legal entities may be members.

The constitution must be published in full in the Official Gazette (the "Mémorial") and lodged with the companies' registrar of the district court in whose jurisdiction the company's principal place of business is located.

The minimum capital is LUF500,000,– or its equivalent in a foreign currency. The company's capital must be fully subscribed and paid up in all cases. No sàrl may have any unpaid share capital.

The public limited company ("société anonyme" – "SA")

The establishment of a public limited company requires the fulfillment of the following four conditions:

- There must be at least two shareholders who may be individuals or legal entities.
- The minimum capital is LUF1,250,000, or its equivalent in foreign currency.
- The company's capital must be fully subscribed.
- At least one-fourth of each share must be paid up in cash or in kind. In case of a capital contribution in kind, the shares must be paid up within five years from the date of the incorporation of the company. The assets contributed in kind need to be valued by independent auditors and their conclusions must be summarised in the official deed of formation of the company (or in the deed of increase of its share capital if appropriate). If shares are paid up in kind, the assets contributed must be described in full in the corporate constitution. Full details must be published in the Official Gazette and filed in the companies' register.

Management

The private limited company

The company is administered by one or more managing directors ("gérants"), who need not be members of the company.

Sometimes they are designated in the constitution; if not they are elected by the members by simple majority, or such larger majority as the constitution may provide.

The appointment of a managing director may be for a limited or unlimited period and must be publicised in the same way as the constitution.

Managing directors designated in the constitution may not be removed unless the constitution provides for their removal or is suitably amended to incorporate the names of their replacements. Moreover, unless the constitution provides to the contrary, no managing director may be removed without cause.

Every managing director has the power to perform any acts necessary or useful for the accomplishment of the objects and the purposes of the company. This power covers all acts that are not expressly assigned by law to be decided by the members. The constitution may restrict the powers of the managing directors, but such restrictions are of no concern to third parties, even if published. The only exception is if there are two or more managing directors, who are required by the constitution to act jointly. In this case, the restriction is binding on third parties.

The public limited company

The public limited company is administered by a board of directors ("conseil d'administration"), consisting of at least three members. The law does not fix a maximum number. The directors may (but need not) be shareholders.

Board members are appointed by the general meeting of shareholders for a period which may not exceed six years. They may be re-elected or removed by the general meeting at any time, with or without cause. Their appointment must be publicised in the same way as the constitution. Legal entities may also be appointed directors of public limited companies.

The board of directors as a body has the widest powers to perform all acts necessary or useful for the accomplishment of the company's objects. All powers not expressly assigned to the general meeting of shareholders by the principles of company law, or by the constitution, fall within the competence of the board of directors. The board represents the company in its dealings with third parties.

The board of directors may not delegate its discretionary powers, whether it be to its own members, third parties, a committee or sub-committee. It may only delegate the day-to-day management. Whether a given act or transaction falls within day-to-day management depends on its precise circumstances. The position may differ from one case or company to another.

Delegation by the board of directors of the day-to-day management to one or more of its own members is subject to the prior authorisation by the company's shareholders in general meeting. The board must account annually to shareholders for the remuneration granted to the delegate(s). Any such delegation is of no concern to third parties.

A specific delegation applies only to specific acts or transactions or to a series of acts or transactions. Any third party who relies on a delegate's authority must take care to ensure that the delegate is at all times acting within his mandate.

The ability of the board and managing director to bind the company in transactions with third parties cannot generally be restricted by the company's constitution. An exception is a provision in the constitution requiring documents to be signed by two or more people. Such a provision is enforceable against third parties.

A properly constituted general meeting of shareholders represents the company's entire body of shareholders. A general meeting must be held at least once a year. Other general meetings may be convened at any time by the board of directors or by the auditors, and must be convened upon the request by shareholders representing one-fifth of all shares issued by the company. The powers of the general meeting are those which the company law and the constitution entrust to it.

Ownership

The private limited company

The capital of a private limited company is divided into shares. All the shares must have the same par value, which must be of LUF1,000, or multiples thereof or a corresponding amount in foreign currency. Shares confer equal rights as to voting and as to allocation of profits during the life of the company and on its liquidation.

All shares must be in registered form and are recorded in the register of members. The company may issue debentures or other similar debt instruments, but purely on a private basis.

Shares are not freely transferable. The law imposes certain minimum restrictions, which may be strengthened by the constitution. Transfer of shares "inter vivos" or upon the death of a shareholder to a non member requires the approval of members representing at least three quarters – of all the shares. However, no agreement is required (unless the constitution provides otherwise) in the case of transfer to members, to spouses and to certain heirs.

To be valid, a transfer between the company and third parties must be accepted by the company in a notarial deed or, if made by private deed, must be notified to the company by a bailiff. It must also be publicised in the same way as the constitution.

The public limited company

The share capital of public limited companies is divided into shares, which may have a par value or no par value. The company may also issue shares which do not form part of its capital. The rights and privileges of these latter shares must be defined by the constitution. The constitution may also provide for several categories of shares with different financial rights and privileges.

Shares in the company are either registered or bearer shares. The name of the owner of registered shares is entered into a shareholders' register kept at the registered office of the company. A registered share is transferred by the corresponding entry into the register of the transferee's name pursuant to an agreement between transferor and transferee. Holders of bearer shares can always request the conversion of their shares into registered shares, and vice versa, unless this is prohibited by the company's constitution. Bearer shares are transferred by delivery.

The shares are freely transferable unless the law, the constitution or an agreement among shareholders restricts transferability.

Financing and security for creditors

The private limited company

The private limited company may issue debentures and other similar debt instruments, but not to members of the public at large.

The public limited company

The public limited company may issue, privately or publicly, any debentures or similar debt instruments. The criteria for the issue of debentures or similar debt instruments are statutorily prescribed.

Available information

All business entities have to be registered with the companies' registry and they must indicate in the companies' register all the particulars concerning their business, namely:

- in the case of an individual, his name, the name of the business, address, object of the business, date of creation and, if applicable, names of the managers and proxies;

- in the case of a legal entity, the kind of corporation, name, its objects, registered office, share capital, members' names and, if applicable, names of the managers, directors and proxies.

All changes in a company's particulars must be recorded in the companies' register within one month of the occurrence of the change.

The annual accounts of companies, whether public or private, must be prepared in accordance with a certain format and deposited at the district court with the companies' registry.

Other business entities

The general partnership ("société en nom collectif")

A general partnership consists of two or more persons who wish to carry on business as a firm ("raison sociale"). It is established by private deed, "the deed of establishment" which has to be published, by way of extract only, in the Official Gazette and filed at the companies' registry. The partnership's name may only comprise the names of the individual partners. All partners are jointly and severally liable without limitation for all obligations entered into by the partnership.

The limited partnership ("société en commandite simple")

A limited partnership is formed between one or more partners without limited liability ("general partners" – "associés commandités") and one or more partners with limited liability ("limited, silent partners" – "associés commanditaires") whose liability is limited to the amount of the funds contributed by them to the partnership.

The name of the partnership may contain the name or names of one or more of the general partners only, and may not contain the name of any limited partner.

A limited partnership is managed solely by one or more of its general partners. A limited partner is not allowed, in any way, to participate in the management, whether by way of proxy or otherwise. He may only advise and supervise management.

The rules concerned for establishment and publication are the same as those applicable to a general partnership.

The partnership limited by shares ("société en commandite par actions")

A partnership limited by shares consists of one or more general partners ("associés commandités") and of shareholders with limited liability ("actionnaires"), whose liability is limited to the amount of capital contributed by them to the partnership. It is thus a combination of a limited partnership and of a public limited company.

The name of the partnership may contain only the name or names of one or more general partners and may not contain the name of any limited partner.

A limited partnership can be managed solely by one or more of the general partners, to the exclusion of any shareholder. The rights and duties of the shareholders are the same as those of shareholders in a public limited company.

There must be a supervisory board ("conseil de surveillance") of at least three members, and the rules concerning establishment and publication are the same as those applicable to public limited companies.

The co-operative association ("société coopérative")

The co-operative association consists of associates (members) whose number and contribution are variable. Members' liability is either limited or unlimited. Members' rights to transfer their shares to non members is restricted.

The non commercial company ("société civile")

The non commercial company is also a separate legal entity under Luxembourg law. However, it is not a commercial company, since its activities are limited to non commercial transactions, such as owning and administering real estate or mines, or performing non commercial professional activity. Its liabilities are divided among its members proportionately to their number, irrespective of the percentage of interest held by each one of them.

Debt collection and asset recovery

Commercial claims arising out of contracts may either be in respect of an obligation to pay a certain sum of money or for specific performance by the contracting party. Generally under Luxembourg law, the non performance of a contractual obligation entitles the beneficiary of the contractual obligation (almost invariably the other or another contracting party) to claim damages for breach of contract.

It should be noted in this context that, according to article 1150 of the Civil Code, contractual compensation is only due in cases of foreseeable damages, *i.e.* for damages which were or could be foreseen when the contract was concluded. This is not the case if the non performance of the contractual obligation is a consequence of fraud or wilful misrepresentation on the part of the party in breach.

Commercial claims may also be made for asset recovery (as opposed to debt recovery). In most cases this implies that the claimant is the owner of the asset concerned. A supplier of goods may, for example, have incorporated a retention of title clause in his contract with the debtor, thereby retaining ownership of the goods until paid in full. Reservation of title clauses cannot be relied upon against third parties, except in very specific cases. Even then the supplier can only use the clause for two years starting from the date of the delivery. This is of considerable importance if the purchaser becomes bankrupt.

Categories of creditor

Creditors who wish to recover money owing to them fall into two categories, secured and unsecured.

Unsecured creditors

The most common procedure is for the creditor to seek judgment from the court that the money is owing and thereafter to enforce that judgment.

If the creditor can supply evidence that he has a claim which is certain as to its amount and which has fallen due, he may also file an application with the president of the commercial court for an order authorising the provisional attachment of all the assets belonging to the debtor ("saisie conservatoire").

In the same way, the creditor may obtain from the president of the civil court an order authorising a third party attachment ("saisie-arrêt"), *i.e.* an attachment of goods or money to which the debtor is entitled but which at the time is in the possession of a third party.

In neither case does the attachment order give any right of priority or privilege to the creditor over the assets which have been seized.

The creditor will always have to start proceedings either before the commercial court or before the civil court in order to obtain a final judgment ordering the debtor to pay the amounts outstanding. To the extent that the creditor can show that the debtor's obligation is to pay a sum of money which is certain and not substantially disputed, the creditor may also start summary proceedings in order to obtain a provisional order that the debtor pay the amount in question.

Secured creditors

The debtor's obligations may be secured by mortgages, pledges and guarantees issued by third parties. Certain claims are also secured by a right of priority ("priviléges"), examples including tax claims, claims relating to contributions to the social security schemes and the right of priority in favour of the landlord for the recovery of the rentals on the leased premises.

Asset Recovery

As indicated above, in most of the cases, the claimant attempts to recover particular property on the basis of his ownership. He may be also have to start court proceedings either before the commercial court or before the civil court in order to recover the assets belonging to him. He will of course have to give full evidence that he is the legal owner of the assets concerned.

Cross-jurisdictional procedures

The Grand Duchy of Luxembourg is a party to the EEC Convention on Civil Jurisdiction and the Enforcement of Judgments of 27 September 1968.

Under article 26 of this Convention, any judgment given in any of the Member States is recognised in all other Member States without any special procedure or leave being required. Under article 31 of the Convention such a judgment is enforceable in any of the Member States after an order for its enforcement is made on the application of any interested party.

Aside from this Convention, the general principle is that a foreign judgment may only be recognised and enforced in Luxembourg by exequatur proceedings taken before the civil court.

The court will then have to satisfy itself that:

- the judgment submitted to it has been rendered by a competent court;
- it has been obtained in a procedurally correct manner;
- the foreign court has applied the law which is applicable according to Luxembourg conflict of law rules; and
- the foreign judgment does not contravene Luxembourg public policy ("order public") including the principle that there has not been any fraud of the law ("fraude à la loi").

3. Survival of the insolvent corporation or its business

Corporations experiencing difficulties in getting the necessary funds to run their businesses may obtain by means of agreement with their creditors either an extension of the terms of payment of their debts or the remittance of their debts. Such agreements are subject to the normal rules applicable to the law of contracts and are only binding on the parties to the agreements. As a consequence these agreements may only succeed if and to the extent that they are accepted by all the creditors of a given debtor.

Concerned to protect small growing businesses at the beginning of this century, the Luxembourg legislator was driven to set up three types of judicial procedure with the purpose of putting in concrete form the agreements which had been reached between debtors and their creditors.

These procedures are:

- the reprieve from payment ("sursis de paiement");
- the composition in order to avoid bankruptcy ("concordat préventif de faillite");
- the controlled management ("gestion contrôlée").

The procedures of reprieve from payment and composition in order to avoid bankruptcy, although never abolished, have scarcely been used, since it appears to be difficult for a debtor to meet the conditions necessary for implementing the procedures.

Although the controlled management procedure is not used very frequently, it remains the procedure preferred by corporations contemplating an orderly reorganisation of their business or liquidation of their assets.

A recently enacted regime, applicable only to credit institutions experiencing financial difficulties, has its origins in these procedures.

The reprieve from payment ("sursis de paiement")

This procedure was established by a Grand Ducal decree of 4 October 1934 and was inserted in the Luxembourg Commercial Code under articles 593 *et seq*.

Purpose and effect

The purpose of the reprieve from payment is to allow a corporation experiencing financial difficulties to suspend its payments for a limited time. Reprieve from payment acknowledges and ratifies, by means of court judgment, an agreement which has been reached with the creditors of a company.

The reprieve from payment is, however, not of general application – one of the main reasons why it has lost its appeal. It only applies to those commitments which have been assumed by the debtor prior to obtaining the reprieve from payment and has no effect as far as taxes and other public charges or secured claims (by right of priority, a mortgage or a pledge) are concerned.

During the time for which a reprieve from payment is in force, the beneficiary of the reprieve loses the right to administer his assets and is only allowed to manage his business under the control of commissioners.

Pre-application considerations

Under article 593 of the Commercial Code, the reprieve from payment may only be granted to a businessman or a business entity forced by extraordinary and unforeseeable events to cease their payments temporarily and who, according to the duly verified balance sheet of the business, has sufficient assets and funds in order to satisfy all creditors, both as to principal and interest.

Reprieve from payment may also be granted if the situation of the businessman or of the business entity concerned, although currently in deficit, shows strong potential which could allow a restoration of a balanced financial situation.

The reprieve from payment may only be granted if the application has been approved by a majority of the creditors representing, by the amount of their claims, three-quarters of all of the outstanding amounts. This majority must be achieved at a meeting which has been convened by the court and is only of those of the creditors against whom the reprieve from payment applies. This means that for the purpose of calculating the requisite majority, the claims which are secured by rights of priority, mortgages or pledges, as well as the tax claims and other public charges, are not taken into consideration.

Creditors are required to attend the meeting to approve the proposals, before they can take effect. This requirement may also be one of the reasons which renders this procedure unattractive and difficult.

Procedure

The corporation has to file an application simultaneously with the commercial court of the district where the corporation has its registered office and with the Court of Appeal. The president of the commercial court determines the place where and the date and hour when, within two weeks, the creditors' meeting will be convened. The court may appoint experts in order to verify the current situation of the debtor's business and may appoint a judge who will supervise this verification process.

From the date of the filing of the application, or in the course of its investigation, the court may grant to the debtor a provisional reprieve from payment. If this happens, the court will appoint one or more commissioners who will be entrusted with the supervision and the control of the debtors' activities during the period of the reprieve.

The law does not contain any indication with respect to the duration of the reprieve and an extension may be granted to the debtor on the basis of an application to be filed with the Court of Appeal. Rejection of such an application will automatically mean a revocation of the provisional reprieve.

Creditors' involvement and position

It is necessary to make a distinction between two categories of creditors:

- those having claims secured by rights of priority, mortgages or pledges; and

- those having unsecured claims.

Creditors who have claims secured by rights of priority, mortgages or pledges do not intervene in the reprieve from payment procedure. Even if the reprieve from payment is granted, it will not affect them and they may continue to act against the debtor for payment of their claims.

Their actions may, therefore, have an adverse effect on the situation of the beneficiary of the reprieve because they may create new and additional financial difficulties for the debtor by placing it in a situation where it will no longer be able to have regard to the commitments to the other creditors against whom the reprieve from payment applies.

Secured creditors may also seize and sell secured assets of the company or business for their benefit, subject to article 606 of the Commercial Code which provides that creditors having claims secured by mortgage or pledge may not, for the duration of the reprieve, obtain the seizure or sale of real estate and other property needed for the performance of the profession or the business of the debtor, provided that accruing interest on the secured claims is paid in accordance with the terms of the loan.

Creditors having unsecured claims arising from contracts concluded after the date on which the reprieve from payment was granted will not be bound by the reprieve. They may insist on payment in full of their claims even to the extent of enforcing a judgment rendered against the debtor. Unsecured claims existing at the date when the application for a reprieve from payment was filed, however, may only be enforced during the reprieve to the extent to which all such creditors are entitled under the terms of the reprieve.

Management of the corporation

When granting a reprieve from payment, the Court of Appeal will designate one or more commissioners who will be entrusted with the supervision and the control of the activities of the debtor during the whole period of the reprieve from payment.

The Court of Appeal is the only court with jurisdiction to grant the order for reprieve from payment. The commercial court undertakes the preparatory work and will issue an opinion which will be forwarded (within three days) to the public prosecutor (the "Procureur General") at the Court of Appeal. The latter submits this opinion together with his comments to the President of the Court of Appeal, who, through another magistrate, will prepare a report and render his decision within eight days of the receipt of the documents.

The commissioners will be chosen from among those qualified persons resident in the district of the debtor's residence or place of registration. The law is not specific as to who is a qualified person, although invariably the persons chosen will be lawyers or accountants.

During the reprieve, the debtor may not sell or grant security over any of its movable property or real estate, nor may it plead, compromise, take loans, receive funds, make payments or perform any management activity, without the authorisation of the commissioners. This authorisation is not subject to any specific formality.

The supervising commissioners will, however, only have overall control of the business as opposed to the power of active management. This control rests in granting or in refusing to the debtor the authorisation to enter into transactions. If the commissioners refuse the authorisation, and the debtor persists, the final decision will have to be taken by the commercial court.

Termination

Under article 608 of the Commercial Code, a debtor may decide to withdraw his application for a reprieve even prior to the court decision granting him the reprieve from payment.

Under article 607 of the Commercial Code, revocation of a reprieve may be requested by one or more creditors or by the supervising commissioners if it appears that the beneficiary of the reprieve committed a fraud, acted in bad faith, violated the rules regulating his incapacity, or if it appears that the debtor refuses to dispose of sufficient assets to repay all its debts in full. A request for revocation has to be filed with the commercial court, which will, after having heard the arguments of the debtor beneficiary of the reprieve, either take a decision where the reprieve had been granted provisionally, or issue an opinion where the reprieve was final. In the latter case, the commercial court will defer to the Court of Appeal which will have to render a final decision. Once a reprieve from payment has been revoked, creditors' ability to enforce their claims against the debtor is restored.

Composition in order to avoid bankruptcy ("concordat préventif de faillite")

The composition in order to avoid bankruptcy ("concordat préventif de faillite" – hereinafter referred to as the "composition" is governed by the law of 14 April 1886 (the "1886 Law"), which has been amended successively by a law of 1 February 1911 and a Grand Ducal decree of 4 October 1934, and, most recently by a Grand Ducal decree of 24 May 1935.

Purpose and effect

A composition is defined as an agreement between a corporation experiencing financial difficulties and its creditors. The agreement is made under the control and with the approval of the court in order to avoid bankruptcy.

The agreement (which will be negotiated by the debtor with his or its creditors) may take various forms. It may consist of extension of the time for payment of the debts, reimbursement of part of the claims by means of a lump sum payment, the partial reimbursement by instalments of the debts, and similar devices.

After ratification by the court, the composition will be binding on all unsecured creditors and on all creditors who have waived their rights of priority or mortgages.

While a composition is under negotiation, the debtor will be unable to alienate or grant mortgages over real estate without the supervision of a judge. After ratification of the composition, the debtor can again conduct its business without any restrictions, save for those restrictions provided for in the composition treaty. The "liquidateur" (see p423 *infra*) appointed to assist the debtor in the event that the composition results in the debtor renouncing all his assets, will only be called upon to convert the assets into cash and to distribute them between the creditors. After ratification of the composition, the court will continue to supervise the activities of the beneficiary of the composition.

A composition ratified by the court may be challenged if the financial situation of the debtor appears to improve. In this event, it or he will have to repay all the creditors.

Pre-application/appointment considerations

A composition may only be applied for by an individual businessman or a business corporation wishing to avoid a bankruptcy procedure and having become insolvent or having lost all creditworthiness. The applicant must be deemed "unfortunate" and acting in good faith ("bonne foi"), *i.e.* the remedy is discretionary and will only be available in deserving cases.

The discretion of determining whether, given the facts and circumstances submitted to them, the applicant is acting in good faith or not rests with the courts (Cour Supérieure de Justice du Grand-Duché de Luxembourg, 23 December 1887, Pasicrisie 2, p555). The applicant will therefore have to prove that he deserves this procedure.

In practice, this proof may be given by the applicant showing that it is not possible to demonstrate that he committed any gross mistake or irregularity and that the situation of the applicant's business cannot clearly be attributed to negligence or imprudence on his or its behalf.

In a decision of 19 February 1899, the Court of Appeal expressed its view as follows:

> ""Persisting over years in raising credit facilities on conditions unknown in normal business practice, and where disastrous results of successive business accounts could not leave the applicant for a composition with the faintest illusion with regard to the final outcome of these business activities, does not allow the judge to decide that the applicant may be considered as an unfortunate debtor and a debtor acting in good faith who, alone, is entitled to claim the benefit of the favourable provisions of the law of 14 April 1886".

A composition may only be obtained if a majority in number of the creditors representing three-quarters of those amounts outstanding which are not challenged or which are accepted provisionally, support the application. The composition will only take effect after being ratified by the commercial court.

These majorities in the amount of the claims and of the creditors are determined by including creditors who have abstained from voting and who are, therefore, deemed to have approved the composition. Creditors who have secured or privileged claims will not be taken into consideration. In this particular procedure (as opposed to the procedure for the reprieve from payment), creditors may express their votes in writing, and are not obliged to be present at the meeting at which the vote is counted.

Procedure

The corporation has to file an application with the court of the district where the corporation has its registered office and has to enclose, with its application, a report on the events justifying its application as well as a detailed statement of its assets, a list of its creditors (whether recognised or presumed) with an indication of their domicile and the amount of their claims and the proposals made for the composition.

Prior to examining the merits of the application, the court will appoint one of its judges to verify the situation of the debtor and to make a report within a short time so that the court may take a final decision within eight days of the application being made. The court's decision to appoint one of the judges will automatically result in a provisional stay on all further acts of enforcement against the applicant. The stay will not, however, benefit co-debtors or guarantors who have waived the right to insist that creditors proceed first against the principal debtor.

The judge appointed by the commercial court may appoint one or more experts to assist him in the performance of his task. This might be done at any time during the investigation of the matter until the judgment ratifying the composition.

The court will decide, on the basis of the judge's report, whether the procedure should continue or whether to declare the applicant bankrupt.

If the court is of the opinion that the procedure should continue to composition, it will determine the place where and the day and the time when the creditors will be convened. The notice convening the meeting will contain the proposals for the composition, and the meeting will be presided over by the appointed judge. The applicant has to explain the proposals. The creditors who have to declare in writing the amount of their outstanding claims must then indicate whether they approve the proposal. These declarations and votes may be sent by the creditors to the court prior to the creditors' meeting.

The proposal must have the support of a majority of the creditors representing, by way of unchallenged or provisionally accepted claims, three-quarters of all of the outstanding amount. Creditors having claims secured by rights of priority, mortgages or pledges may only express their votes if they waive such rights.

When calculating votes at the creditors' meeting, creditors with secured claims automatically waive their rights of priority, mortgages or pledges. They may, however, vote at the creditors' meeting while waiving such rights only for

part of their claims, provided this waiver amounts to at least one-half of their total claim. Only that part of the claim in respect of which the creditor's security
or privilege has been waived will be taken into account in evaluating the level
of support for the composition proposal.

After the creditors' meeting, the court will decide whether or not to sanction
the composition, basing its decision on a report presented to it by the appointed
judge. The court will then verify whether the applicant is unfortunate and acting
in good faith, whether the proposals for the composition are serious and appear
to be realistic and whether the majorities in number and in claims have been
reached.

If all these conditions are met the court will ratify the composition.

The judgment ratifying the composition has immediate effect against all creditors who attended the meeting and who had notice of the meeting whether they
attended or not. Evidence of any opposition to the composition order will not
suspend the order. If there is any opposition, the court will only withdraw the
judgment ratifying the composition if it appears that the applicant acted in bad
faith.

Any applicant and creditors who had no notice of the creditors' meeting or
who voted against the composition may appeal against the judgment which ratified the composition.

Creditors' involvement and position

Here, it is important to distinguish between two categories of creditors – on the
one hand those having claims secured by rights of priority, mortgages or pledges
and, on the other hand, creditors having unsecured claims.

Ratification of the composition will have no effect on creditors who, having secured claims, did not participate in the composition proceedings and did not,
therefore, waive their rights of priority, mortgages or pledges. These creditors
may continue to act against the debtor in order to obtain payment of their claims
and they may enforce their rights, obtain attachments and obtain the sale of the
assets securing their claims.

The creditors who, having claims secured by rights of priority, mortgages or
pledges, did vote at the creditors' meeting and who in doing this did waive their
mortgages or their pledges, are bound by the terms of the composition and are
no longer able to obtain any enforcement of the debtor's obligations through the
enforcement of the proprietary rights which they have waived. If these creditors
only participated in the voting procedure for a certain part of their claim and
right of priority, they will only be bound by the composition reached to the extent that their claim is deemed to be an unsecured claim.

Thus, all creditors with unsecured claims (including creditors who have
waived their rights of priority and security) will be bound by the composition
after it has been ratified by the court.

It is, however, important to stress that a ratified composition is only binding
on creditors existing at the date of the composition. Creditors who did not de-

clare their claim in the course of the composition proceedings do not lose their rights. They may only enforce them subject to and in accordance with the terms of the composition.

The composition does not benefit co-debtors or any guarantors who have waived their right to insist on creditors proceeding solely against the principal debtor.

Creditors who are bound by the composition may only enforce their rights in accordance with the terms and subject to the conditions of the composition agreement. Thus, if this agreement provides for the creditors to receive a lump sum payment, no creditor may act against the debtor in order to obtain the payment of his entire claim. If the composition agreement provides for liquidation by way of the debtor's renunciation of his assets, no creditor may question this method of liquidation.

The debtor may only be forced to repay his creditors in full if it appears that his financial situation has improved.

Management

During the proceedings and up to the date of the ratification of the composition, the applicant is, pursuant to article 6 of the 1886 Law, incapable of performing certain activities. For instance, he may not alienate or grant mortgages over any of his property or take on any commitments without the authorisation of the judge appointed by the court. If any activities have been authorised by the judge, the applicant may perform them without the latter's assistance.

As a result of the ratification of the composition, the applicant is relieved of the incapacity provided for by article 6 of the 1886 Law. Subject to the restrictions existing under the composition agreement, the applicant is restored to his former position with full power to exercise his rights and to dispose of his assets.

The applicant's activity will, however, be supervised by the appointed judge who will have to examine the status of the applicant's business every three months with the assistance of one or more experts. If it appears that the beneficiary of the composition has not complied with the terms and conditions of the composition agreement, or if it appears that the conditions under which the composition was established can no longer be fulfilled, the court may, on the basis of a report made by the judge, open bankruptcy proceedings and cancel the composition.

In case of a composition by way of renunciation of all or part of the assets, the applicant and the creditors have to appoint, in the composition agreement, one or more persons who will be entrusted with the conversion into cash of the applicant's assets under the supervision of the appointed judge. Such person or persons is known as the "liquidateur".

The liquidateur may, subject to authorisation by the judge, and in the name of the debtor and of the creditors, start court proceedings, compromise, tender conclusive oath (*i.e.* an oath which gives conclusive evidence and terminates the proceedings) and sell the real estate belonging to the applicant.

The creditors may also appoint the persons who will be entrusted with obtaining the cancellation of all the actions performed prior to the composition proceedings by the debtor in fraud of their rights ("action paulienne") (see pp438-443 *infra*).

If they have not been designated in the composition agreement, the liquidateurs will be appointed by the commercial court either in the ratification judgment or in a subsequent judgment. In case of composition by way of renunciation of assets, the liquidation will follow the same procedure as in the case of a bankruptcy (see p438 *infra*)

Cancellation and termination of the composition

The guarantors and all the creditors bound by the composition may request its cancellation either if the debtor has been convicted of fraudulent bankruptcy ("banqueroute simple" or "banqueroute frauduleuse") after the ratification judgment, or if it appears after this ratification judgment that the debtor has fraudulently dissimulated or exaggerated the assets. In these two latter cases, the court may, of its own volition, cancel the composition and open bankruptcy proceedings.

If the debtor does not comply with the terms and conditions of the composition, the creditors may start court proceedings in order to obtain the termination of the composition. Such proceedings will take place in the presence of the persons who have guaranteed the total or partial performance of the composition by the debtor. Termination of the composition agreement in these circumstances will not release any guarantors from their obligations.

The controlled management ("gestion contrôlée")

Controlled management ("gestion contrôlée") is governed by the Grand Ducal Decree of 24 May 1935 (the "1935 Decree").

Purpose and effect

It is obvious from what has been said so far that the procedures of the reprieve from payment and of the composition in order to avoid bankruptcy are not suitable for the purpose of obtaining the reorganisation of an undertaking in financial difficulties. Indeed, practice has shown that they are complicated and have the major defect of having no effect on secured and privileged creditors.

Controlled management is a remedy granted by the court to protect a company which has lost its creditworthiness or which has difficulties in meeting all of its commitments. Controlled management should help such a company either to reorganise its business or to convert its assets into cash under the supervision of the court and of commissioners appointed by the court with the approval of the creditors. To liquidate its assets under such circumstances is likely to be far more satisfactory from the point of view of the company and its creditors than if the liquidation were forced upon the company by a terminal bankruptcy.

In the controlled management procedure the company will be placed under the control of the court and the commissioners. It will keep the power to manage its assets but is no longer allowed to act without the authorisation of the commissioners. The latter also have the power to force the company to act.

The commissioners are entrusted with the preparation of a plan for the reorganisation of the undertaking or for the realisation of the assets. This plan is submitted to the creditors who will vote on it. If approved by a majority of more than 50% of the votes, counted by reference to the undisputed amount of the claim, the plan will be presented to the court for approval.

During the gestion contrôlée procedure, the right of the creditors to enforce a court order, notarial deed or any claim (even if secured) against the debtor, is suspended.

If the plan is approved by the requisite majority of creditors and by the court, it is binding on all the creditors.

Pre-application/appointment considerations

Pursuant to the provisions contained in article 1 of the 1935 Decree, the benefit of controlled management is available either to individual businessmen who (or to corporate business entities which) have lost their creditworthiness or are having difficulties meeting all their commitments. Controlled management is not available, however, if the applicant has already been declared bankrupt by final judgment. Loss of creditworthiness is established by the fact that no creditor or other unrelated party is willing to grant any further credit to the debtor, whether in the form of a loan, guarantee or in the rescheduling of debts.

Although the legal provisions governing controlled management do not require as a condition precedent the debtor to act in good faith, the courts give much importance to the motive of the debtor in applying for controlled management. Any applicant who appears to have committed fraud or gross mistakes or irregularities in the management of the business will not be entitled to the benefit of controlled management.

The application for a controlled management order must either envisage a reorganisation of the business or a better realisation of the assets of the applicant than would be the case in bankruptcy. An order of controlled management will not be granted if it appears that the applicant only wishes to reschedule or cancel in part the existing debts.

Procedure

The applicant must file a formal application with the commercial court of the district of his domicile or its registered office. This application must set out the reasons justifying a controlled management order. At the same time the applicant must list all the creditors and must attach to the application all documents justifying the request. At this stage the procedure is not open to the public. The court will schedule a preliminary hearing at which the applicant presents the arguments in favour of an order for controlled management.

If the court thinks that the arguments and documents produced by the applicant are not sufficient to justify a controlled management order – where for example it cannot be established that controlled management would provide for an improvement of the financial situation of the applicant and allow normal business activity or improve the conditions for realising the assets of the undertaking – the court will reject the application.

If the court finds that the applicant has already ceased the payment of debts, it can immediately open bankruptcy proceedings.

If, however, the court does not dismiss the application, it will designate one of the judges of the commercial court as responsible for the preparation of a report on the financial situation of the applicant's business. The designated judge may obtain the assistance of an expert in order to verify the business situation of the applicant. It is normal practice for the judge to be assisted by an accountant.

The court's order designating the judge does not prevent creditors from starting or continuing court proceedings against the applicant, but the creditors are now no longer allowed to enforce any court decisions against the applicant. On the other hand, the applicant no longer has the right to dispose of or to pledge or mortgage any assets without the authorisation of the designated judge.

Once the report of the judge has been filed, the court will schedule a further hearing for the pleadings and decide whether the controlled management should continue. At this stage the court may either dismiss the application for a controlled management order or decide to place the assets of the applicant under the control of one or more commissioners.

If the court decides to dismiss the application, it may open bankruptcy proceedings if the conditions for a bankruptcy order are met. If the court accepts the application and makes an order for controlled management, it will place the assets of the applicant under the control of one or more commissioners who will be entrusted with the preparation of a plan for the reorganisation or the liquidation of the assets within a certain time.

The decision of the court ends the role of the judge designated to review the matter. This decision will be published in the Official Gazette.

It is normal practice for the expert who has assisted the designated judge in the preliminary proceedings to be designated as one of the commissioners. Very often the court also designates a member of the Bar who is experienced in issues of insolvency as one of the Commissioners.

From the date of the court's decision placing the undertaking concerned under controlled management, the undertaking will be supervised by the commissioners. The business entity may not alienate, pledge or mortgage any of its assets, plead, compromise, borrow or receive any amounts of money, make any payment or perform any management activity including committing itself under any agreement, without the formal authorisation of the commissioners.

The commissioners also have the power to cause the debtor to act positively and to refrain from acting.

They will draw up an inventory of all the assets which are under controlled management and they will make an inventory of the assets and liabilities of the business entity. They will also prepare a balance sheet and profit and loss account in accordance with the law and the debtor's articles of incorporation.

They must prepare, within a time fixed by the court, either a plan for the reorganisation of the business of the applicant or a plan for the realisation of the debtor's assets and the distribution of the proceeds. They will communicate this plan to all the creditors irrespective of whether they have secured or unsecured claims or deferred or conditional claims. The plan will also be communicated to the co-debtors who are jointly and severally liable with the applicant and to the guarantors known to the commissioners. This plan will be published in the Official Gazette and will be submitted for approval by the court.

Within 15 days of the date of the communication and publication of the plan, the creditors must inform the court whether they accept or refuse the proposals made by the commissioners. There is no requirement in this procedure for creditors to attend a meeting. They vote in writing and may – just like others having any interest (the applicant, the shareholders, the co-debtors and guarantors) – address any written comments to the court.

The court may only approve the commissioners' plan if it has been accepted by a majority of more than 50% of the creditors calculated by reference to their unchallenged claims (ie. more than half of the liabilities of the business entity). Any creditors who abstain from voting are deemed to have accepted the plan.

The court retains a residual discretion to reject a commissioner's plan approved by creditors and will verify whether or not the legal provisions have been complied with, whether the proposals made by the commissioners take into account the ranking of the existing rights of priority, and whether there is any other reason which could stand in the way of the approval of the plan.

If the court considers it is not possible to approve the commissioners' plan, the application for controlled management will be dismissed or the court may decide to order the commissioners to prepare a new plan within a specified time. The court may even appoint new commissioners.

If and when approved by the court, the plan becomes mandatory for the business entity, for all its creditors (even for those who abstained from voting or who voted against) and for all the co-debtors and guarantors.

The court decisions rendered in this controlled management procedure are immediately enforceable, save when the application is dismissed. The applicant, or any of the creditors may, within eight days or the order, appeal against the decision dismissing the application for a controlled management order.

The court can neither interfere in the execution of the plan which has been approved nor supervise its execution. Finally, after the commissioners' plan has been approved by the court, the latter are relieved of their functions.

Creditors' involvement and position

As has been explained above, the creditors do not participate in any way in the preliminary procedure. They may, however, appeal against the court decision which has placed their debtor under controlled management. This is, however, often only a theoretical right as the appeal has to be filed within quite a short time and the judgment placing the debtor under controlled management is not published. As a result, the creditors may well only be informed of the court's decision after the time for the appeal has expired.

The creditors begin to participate in the controlled management when they have to make the declaration of their claims and when they are entitled to vote on the plan which has been submitted to them by the commissioners.

As has already been mentioned, during the entire court procedure, *i.e.* from the date when the application for a controlled management order is filed up to the very last procedural step, when the commissioners' plan is approved by the court, the creditors – whether secured or unsecured – cannot enforce any court decisions or notarial deeds against the debtor. This moratorium continues up to the date on which the plan is approved. Thereafter they are bound by the terms and conditions of the approved plan, subject to their right to take proceedings for the termination of the plan.

If the company defaults on the commissioner's plan, it may be opposed by any creditor (whether he has voted in favour of the plan or not) by starting court proceedings against the debtor in order to obtain the cancellation of the plan.

Powers and duties of the designated judge and of the commissioners

During the preliminary procedure and up to the date the company is placed under controlled management, its activities will be supervised by the judge who has been designated by the court to make a report on its financial situation. The company may not perform any act without the authorisation of the designated judge; if it does so, the acts will be null and void. The judge will only give his authorisation if the contemplated act does not cause any harm to the interests of the creditors and does not have an adverse effect on the pursuit of the controlled management procedure.

The commissioners appointed when the debtor is placed under controlled management are entrusted to look after the interests both of the creditors and of the debtor.

The duties of the commissioners may be summarised as follows:

- to draw up an inventory of all the assets which are under controlled management, and to draw up an inventory of the assets and of the liabilities of the debtor;
- to verify the claims which have been filed;
- to prepare a plan for the reorganisation or for the realisation of the assets;
- to supervise the company, which has been placed under controlled management, and to give the authorisation which is necessary for those acts which the company is no longer free to perform due to the controlled management.

The commissioners are authorised agents appointed by the court and their powers are regulated by law. The fees which they receive are fixed by the court and will depend on the importance and duration of the appointment and the difficulty of the duties they have performed. The fees are payable by the company and the commissioners have a right of priority over other creditors.

The functions of the commissioners cease upon approval by the court of the plan submitted to the creditors.

Termination and cancellation of the plan which has been approved

Once approved, the commissioners' plan is deemed to be a binding agreement between the company and its creditors. If the company does not then perform its obligations, any creditor may institute court proceedings for the cancellation of the plan. If unsuccessful, the court may terminate the plan and declare the company bankrupt.

Procedure applicable to credit institutions

The law of 5 April 1993 (the "1993 Law") applies to institutions whose activities consist of managing funds belonging to third parties and who are supervised by the Institut Monétaire Luxembourgeois ("IML") – the supervisory authority for credit institutions. In particular, articles 60-62 dealing with reprieve from payment, controlled management and winding-up of credit institutions.

Reprieve from payment and controlled management

The reprieve from payment may be granted to a credit institution if:

- the credit of the institution is exhausted;
- the institution has no available liquid funds, regardless of whether the institution has or has not ceased its payments;
- the entire performance of the institution's obligations is endangered;
- the licence to do business has been withdrawn, even if this decision is not yet final.

Either the credit institution or the management of the IML may apply to the court for a grant for a reprieve from payment for the credit institution concerned.

The court will determine the terms and conditions of the reprieve from payment for a period which may not exceed six months. It will also appoint one or more supervising commissioners.

The commissioners' authorisation in writing will be required for all acts and decisions of the institution and those acts which have not been duly authorised are deemed to be null and void.

The commissioners may submit to the company (either to the shareholders' meeting or to the board of directors, depending on the kind of decision which has to be taken) every proposal they think appropriate. They may also attend any meeting of the shareholders, of the board of directors or of any other managing or supervising body.

Any conflict between the bodies of the corporation and the commissioners will be settled finally by the court. The decision is not subject to appeal.

Liquidation of the institutions of the financial sector

If it appears that the reprieve from payment has not, in fact, led to an improvement of the initial situation, or if the institution experiences such financial difficulties that it cannot meet its commitments, or if the licence to do business has been withdrawn and this decision has become final, the commercial court may, at the public prosecutor's or the IML management's request, decide to order the liquidation of the credit institution. If it does so, the court will, at the same time, commission a judge to supervise the liquidation and appoint one or more liquidateurs.

The court will also determine the course to be followed in the liquidation. It might, for example, decide that certain rules applicable in bankruptcy proceedings will apply in whole or in part.

From the date of this judgment, all personal actions or actions based on title to real property, and all kinds of enforcement procedures on movables and immovables must be exercised against the liquidateurs.

4. Termination of the corporation: bankruptcy and compulsory winding up

Apart from the cases where the company itself resolves to be wound up or where the period for which it has been incorporated has expired, a company may cease its activities in the following cases:

- when it is declared bankrupt by the court;
- when the court decides that it must be wound up.

The two court procedures are different to the extent that a company may only be declared bankrupt if it is unable to meet its commitments whereas a court may decide to wind up a company even though the company is still solvent, but where it is in breach of the governing rules of company law.

Bankruptcy

The bankruptcy procedure is governed by provisions which were introduced into the Luxembourg Commercial Code (art 437-592) by the law of 2 July 1870.

Purpose and effect

The purpose of the bankruptcy procedure is to realise the assets of the debtor and to distribute the proceeds to its creditors.

A company which has been adjudicated bankrupt does not inevitably disappear as a result of the bankruptcy. The bankruptcy does not, indeed, necessarily entail the winding up of the company. However a company whose assets have been liquidated and distributed to the creditors does, to all intents and purposes, disappear.

From the date of the bankruptcy order up to the date of the closing of the bankruptcy proceedings, the bankrupt company is relieved of the administration and disposal of its assets. From the date a company is adjudicated bankrupt, the creditors are no longer entitled to obtain individual enforcement of their rights against the debtor.

Conditions for the adjudication in bankruptcy

Under article 437 of the Commercial Code, a company is bankrupt when, having a commercial object, it has ceased its payments and is unable to meet its commitments, and when its credit is exhausted. A bankrupt company is, however, only subject to the legal provisions of bankruptcy when it has been adjudicated bankrupt by the court.

The bankruptcy of a company is declared by the commercial court of the district where the company has its registered office either at the request of a creditor or by the court of its own motion. In the former case, an application is filed with the commercial court but this does not automatically entail an adjudication in bankruptcy as creditors frequently use this means of pressure on the company to get payment of their claims. Thus, if the debtor pays, the creditor will withdraw his application, but if the application has already come before the court, the court may declare the debtor bankrupt if it considers that there is sufficient evidence that the debtor is insolvent and has lost its creditworthiness.

Bankruptcy is declared by the court of its own motion where the court, by virtue of its own personal knowledge gained in the course of actions brought against the company, considers that the company is bankrupt. The court may also declare a company bankrupt of its own motion if an application for a controlled management order or for reprieve from payments has been dismissed on the basis of the documents which were submitted to the court in support of the application.

Bankruptcy may also arise on the basis of an admission to this effect by the company.

Under article 440 of the Commercial Code, a business or a business corporation experiencing insolvency and loss of creditworthiness must acknowledge the suspension of payments at the clerk's office of the commercial court of its residence or in the case of a company, place of registration, within three days from the suspension of payments.

Thus, any company which is unable to meet its commitments and which is admitted neither to the benefit of a reprieve of payment proceedings nor to controlled management, may file a statement of affairs and admit its bankruptcy, in order to avoid pursuit by its creditors.

Only companies which pursue a commercial purpose and traders who have traded during the six months preceding the adjudication in bankruptcy may be adjudicated bankrupt.

There is only one exception to this rule: a dissolved trading company is considered as continuing to exist so long as the winding up procedure is not closed and may therefore be adjudicated bankrupt even though the liquidateurs have been inactive for more than six months. This can occur whether or not the company still has assets. Creditors might, therefore, wish to try to recover payment. On the other hand, the public prosecutor and the commercial court may have an interest in obtaining the bankruptcy of such a company so as to ensure that all creditors are treated equally.

The company must have suspended payment of its debts

A prerequisite of bankruptcy is that the debtor cannot meet its liabilities. This might be established in a number of ways, for example:

- existence of protests on bills of exchange;
- numerous summonses for debts;
- it appears that a judgment ordering the company to pay a given amount of money cannot be enforced;
- the company's property is seized;
- the registered office is closed.

The credit of the company has to be exhausted

This is another condition which must be met for an adjudication in bankruptcy. The credit of a company is considered exhausted if the suspension of payments is such that the state of the debtor's business does not inspire any confidence. Thus, if the debtor has obtained a rescheduling of the repayment of its debts or if it has obtained a bank loan, this condition is not fulfilled.

These conditions must be present at the date of the bankruptcy order.

Procedure

As mentioned above, the commercial court of the place where the company has its registered office will declare the company bankrupt either at the request of a creditor or of its own motion or upon the admission of the company that it is insolvent and has lost its creditworthiness.

If the court declares the company bankrupt of its own motion the company will not be heard in its defence. Further, if a petition for a bankruptcy order has been filed with the court on the initiative of a creditor and the company does not attend the court proceedings, a default judgment will be rendered against it. If the company decides to admit its insolvency and loss of creditworthiness and thus its bankruptcy, it will, of course, explain its situation to the court.

The period of time between the company admitting its bankruptcy in court and the bankruptcy order being made is only a few days.

If a petition for a bankruptcy order has been filed with the court and the court deems that it has sufficient evidence with regard to the financial situation of the company, it may open the bankruptcy proceedings within a very short time. If however, it appears that the court does not have sufficient evidence (for instance if the company does not appear on the list of the persons having protested bills of exchange, or if there are no or only very few court proceedings initiated against the company), the court may decide to seek information on the solvency of the company from the financial division of the police.

If it appears from the report of the police that there is sufficient evidence that the conditions of a bankruptcy have been fulfilled, the court will then immediately adjudicate the company bankrupt.

At the same time the court will appoint a judge to supervise the bankruptcy proceedings and appoint one or more bankruptcy officials ("curateurs"), depending on the importance of the company concerned. The provisions of articles 455 to 460 of the Commercial Code deal with the appointment of liquidateurs from among whom the curateurs are appointed. In practice, the curateurs are also usually members of the bar skilled and experienced in solvency practice. If, as is usually the case, they are not sworn liquidateurs the curateurs in bankruptcy will take an oath before the appointed judge.

The bankruptcy judgment orders creditors to file and prove their claims within a period not exceeding 20 days from the date of the bankruptcy judgment. The judgment also fixes a closing date for the verification of claims and a date for a hearing at which the challenged claims will be examined by the court. The two dates must be between five and twenty days apart.

The court will fix a similar period between the time when the claims are recorded and the time when the hearing dealing with the claims which have been challenged is to take place.

This means that only the claims filed with the court clerk prior to the date on which the claims are recorded will be examined at the court hearing dealing with the challenged claims. Creditors may still file their claims later on. This does not have any adverse effect on the legal situation of the creditors who have filed their claims at a later stage of the proceedings.

The curateurs are under an obligation to publish the bankruptcy judgment immediately after having been appointed and excerpts from the judgment have to be published within three days in newspapers specified by the court so that the creditors will be made aware that they may present their claims.

Within three days of their appointment, the curateurs have to draw up the inventory of the assets belonging to the bankrupt company in the presence of a court clerk. They must go to the registered office of the company, to its place of business and to all other places where assets belonging to the bankrupt company may be found. The inventory must be signed by the clerk and by the curateurs and a copy deposited with the court.

The bankruptcy judgment is immediately enforceable notwithstanding any right or recourse. Any interested parties who have not been parties to the lawsuit may appeal against the judgment within eight days of its having been made. The company declared bankrupt has 15 days to appeal, starting from the date when the bankruptcy judgment is published in the newspapers. The company may also appeal within 15 days if it was a party to the court proceedings which led to the bankruptcy judgment. The company may not, however, appeal against a bankruptcy judgment if the court has declared the company bankrupt of its own motion or in proceedings initiated by a creditor leading to a default judgment against the company.

As soon as the inventory of the bankruptcy has been completed, the bankrupt company must transfer all accounting books and documents to the curateurs for examination and the preparation of a balance sheet.

The clerk of the court will inform the post office of the appointment of the curateurs so that all correspondence addressed to the bankrupt company can be directed to the curateurs.

After having established an inventory of assets belonging to the bankrupt company, the curateurs will agree with the company to sell all the movable assets belonging to the bankruptcy. The court will then authorise the curateurs, upon their request, to sell the assets mentioned in the inventory subject to certain conditions (wholesale or retail sale, private treaty or a public auction).

The curateurs will also have to pursue claims which the bankrupt company may have against its debtors.

After having converted into cash all assets belonging to the bankrupt company and having finally determined all its liabilities, the curateurs will distribute the money which has been realised from the sale to the creditors after deduction of the curateurs' fees and the administration costs of the bankruptcy. The commercial court will fix the fees and also check the costs of the bankruptcy on the basis of the records which the curateurs have to file with the court. The fees depend on the value of the assets which have been sold, and are determined in accordance with the provisions of a Grand Ducal Decree of 22 October 1979 which reformed the schedule of fees in bankruptcy matters.

Once the fees and the costs have been fixed, the court will arrange a hearing where the curateurs will have to render the accounts of the bankruptcy. They must invite both the bankrupt company and all the creditors whose claims have been accepted to attend the hearing and present their comments. A notice outlining the plan for the distribution of the remaining funds must be attached to the invitation. The curateurs must give evidence to the court that they have notified the creditors and the bankrupt company in respect of the hearing on the rendering of the accounts.

At the hearing, the curateurs will present their plan for the distribution of the remaining funds and if it is not questioned, the curateurs, the appointed judge and the clerk of the court will sign it. The curateurs may then pay the creditors in accordance with the plan.

Once all the funds have been paid, the curateurs will file an application with the commercial court for the termination of the bankruptcy proceedings. In support of their application they have to give evidence that they have made all payments they were bound to make. The court will declare the bankruptcy proceedings closed by ordering the winding up of the company.

This judgment terminates the duties of the curateurs in bankruptcy and of the appointed judge.

Creditors' involvement and position

Apart from filing a petition for a bankruptcy order against the company, the creditors have no right of intervention in the procedure leading to the making of the bankruptcy order. After the order has been made, creditors will present their claims as secured or unsecured creditors of the bankrupt company.

Although articles 508 and 525 of the Commercial Code provide that creditors whose claims have been definitely or provisionally admitted, may, pending the bankruptcy proceedings, enter into a composition with the bankrupt company, these provisions are not used in practice.

The creditors may question the curateurs as to the rendering of their accounts and, if this leads to a dispute (which must be mentioned in the minutes of the rendering of account) the commercial court will give judgment on the point.

As a rule once a judgment declaring bankruptcy has been given, creditors are no longer allowed to take any individual action against the bankrupt company.

Any form of proceeding, whether a personal action or proceedings based on title to real property and all means of compulsory enforcement on movables or immovables may now only be taken, or exercised, against the curateurs. The making of a bankruptcy order stops every seizure or attachment made at the request of any unsecured creditors on movable or real estate. Bankruptcy removes third parties' rights to take enforcement action against the bankrupt's assets. If, prior to the bankruptcy judgment, a sale of seized movable assets or real estate through a public auction had been scheduled, the sale will take place for the account and benefit of the bankruptcy.

From the date of the bankruptcy order interest on any unsecured claim will cease although, if at the end of the bankruptcy there is a surplus after all creditors have been paid in full, interest will be paid to creditors for the period between the bankruptcy order and payment of their claims.

Creditors may, notwithstanding bankruptcy, initiate proceedings against co-debtors of a bankrupt person or company.

If the curateurs sell real estate belonging to the bankrupt company, they are authorised to distribute the proceeds of the sale to those creditors with either mortgages or liens on this real estate. If the proceeds of the sale are not sufficient to reimburse secured creditors, these creditors will be treated as unsecured creditors for the balance of their claims.

Once all the assets in the bankruptcy have been converted into cash, the funds remaining after deduction of the costs and charges linked to the administration of the bankruptcy will be distributed first to secured creditors in order of priority. Any balance remaining will then be distributed to unsecured creditors in proportion to their claims.

Powers and duties of the curateurs

As already mentioned, administration of a Luxembourg bankruptcy is carried out by one or more curateurs under the supervision of a judge appointed by the court. The curateurs have to defend the interests both of the creditors and of the bankrupt company.

As the bankruptcy judgment relieves the bankrupt company of the administration, management and disposal of its assets, the curateurs will represent the company in any proceedings and in any relationship with third parties. They also represent the creditors insofar as they act for their benefit.

The appointed judge has to supervise the transactions, the management and the winding up of the bankruptcy. It is also his duty to speed up the bankruptcy proceedings.

If and to the extent that a decision has to be taken by the commercial court in connection with the bankruptcy proceedings (for instance, the grant of the licence to sell the movable assets, authorisation of certain transactions, disputes and court actions connected with the bankruptcy proceedings, application for the closing of the bankruptcy proceedings), the appointed judge must present a report to the commercial court.

Closing of the bankruptcy proceedings

The commercial court of the district where the corporation had its registered office will decide on the closing of the bankruptcy proceedings. This may occur immediately if the curateurs come to the conclusion that there are no assets belonging to the bankrupt company which could be converted into cash. The bankrupt company proceedings may then be closed on the basis of a complete absence of assets.

The bankruptcy proceedings may also be closed if it appears that the existing assets will be insufficient to cover the administration costs and the fees of the curateurs.

In this case, the cost of the bankruptcy proceedings will be paid partly out of the existing assets which will have been converted into cash and the balance of the costs and fees will be chargeable to the State. The bankruptcy proceedings will then be closed by reason of an insufficiency of assets.

However, if it appears that the assets will suffice in order to pay at least a dividend to the creditors, the curateur will act according to the rules for declaring the company bankrupt.

The judgment relating to the bankruptcy proceedings will also order the termination of the winding up.

Compulsory winding up

Compulsory winding up is governed by article 203 of the law of 10 August 1915 on trading companies. This article has been inserted into the Law of 1915 by the more recent Law of 19 May 1978.

Purpose and effect

The purpose of a compulsory winding up is to terminate a company which pursues activities infringing the criminal law or which seriously contravenes the provisions of the law on trading companies. During the entire winding up procedure, and as long as the company has not been completely wound up, the company will continue to exist.

Conditions of the compulsory winding up

The circumstances in which the procedure might be invoked are as follows:

- the company has denied that it occupies its registered office and has no known new registered office;
- the directors of the company have resigned and no new directors have been appointed;
- the share capital is insufficient, *i.e.* it is less than the required legal minimum;
- the annual accounts of the company have not been prepared and published in accordance with the legal provisions.

Procedure

In order to obtain the compulsory winding up of a company, the public prosecutor files an application with the commercial court. If the court decides to liquidate the company, it will at the same time and in the same judgment commission a supervising judge and appoint one or more liquidateurs. The court will also determine the way in which the liquidation is to proceed, and the extent to which, if at all, the rules governing bankruptcy proceedings should be made applicable.

This judgment of the commercial court only becomes enforceable if there is no opposition to the proceedings or no appeal has been lodged within the time provided for by law.

The liquidateur will have to publish excerpts of the court decision ordering the compulsory winding up and liquidation of the company in the Official Gazette and in newspapers specified by the commercial court.

The Statute of Limitation for actions against liquidateurs provides for a five year period starting from the date of the close of the liquidation proceedings. This follows the rules which apply to the closing of bankruptcy proceedings.

5. Augmenting the assets of the insolvent corporation

Introduction

It is a fundamental rule that the creditors have to be treated equally. Apart from the exceptions regarding secured and preferential creditors, the courts are very strict in their enforcement of this equality principle and any attempt to contract out of it will be invalid.

If, immediately prior to the commencement of the bankruptcy proceedings, the company paid certain unsecured creditors in full or in part, such creditors would indeed have been preferred to those who had received no payment. It is, therefore, essential to the equal treatment of creditors that certain pre-bankruptcy transactions may be set aside so that the company's assets will be augmented.

The company's assets may also be augmented in obtaining a contribution from those who were in charge of the company's management before the company was declared bankrupt.

Transactions at risk

At the time of making of the bankruptcy order, the court will fix the date of the debtor's cessation of payments, which is assumed to be the date after which the debtor was unable to meet his commitments. In the absence of evidence to the contrary, this date is normally assumed by the court to be six months and ten days before the making of the bankruptcy order.

The period between the cessation of payments and the date of the bankruptcy order is known as the suspect period – "période suspecte". Certain transactions which were undertaken during the suspect period must be declared null and void (art 445 of the Commercial Code) whereas other transactions undertaken during this period may be declared null and void, in each case at the request of the curateur, by the commercial court, (arts 446-449 of the Commercial Code).

Article 445

The following transactions must be declared void if undertaken during the suspect period:

- disposition of assets without consideration or for materially inadequate consideration;
- payments of debts which had not fallen due, whether the payment was in cash or by way of assignment, sale, set-off, or by any other means;
- payments of debts which had fallen due, by any other means than in cash or by bills of exchange; and

- mortgages or pledges granted to secure pre-existing debts.

It may be interesting to note, in this context, that the courts have decided that the cancellation of a sale and the restitution to the vendor of the sold goods which had been delivered may be declared null and void in accordance with article 445 of the Commercial Code unless the vendor has obtained the cancellation of the sale on the basis of a provision contained in the sale agreement.

Set-off is permitted only if the reciprocal claims satisfy the conditions of independent set-off prior to the relevant insolvency date (*i.e.* they must be mutual), they are liquidated and they have matured. If the claims do not satisfy these requirements by the relevant date (*i.e.* prior to the suspect period), there can be no set-off and the creditor must pay the cross-claim into the insolvent estate and prove for his primary claim.

Article 446

Any other payments made by the debtor of debts which had fallen due and any other transactions entered into during the suspect period may be declared null and void if the curateur can establish that the persons who received payment from the debtor or the persons who entered into a transaction with the debtor knew at that time of the cessation of the debtor's payments.

Article 447

Mortgages and rights of priority which have been acquired on a regular basis may be recorded on a register held by the Conservation des Hypotheques up to the day of the bankruptcy order. However, any registration made within the period between ten days prior to the date of the cessation of payments and the date of the bankruptcy order may be declared null and void if more than 15 days have passed between the date of the deed granting the mortgage or the right of priority and the date of the registration.

Article 448

This article sets out the general principle that all acts or payments made to defraud the creditors will be declared null and void regardless of the date when they were made.

Article 449

This article provides that, where bills of exchange have been paid during the suspect period, the curateur may only obtain the restitution of the amounts paid under such bills of exchange from the initial beneficiaries of the bills of exchange (*i.e.* the initial creditors). Even here, however, the curateur will only succeed against the original creditor if he can establish that the latter was aware of the fact that debtor had ceased its payments. Article 449 thus protects the interests of third party holders of bills of exchange.

Personal liability of officers

Apart from the case of the manager who is a partner in a general partnership or a general partner in a limited partnership, Luxembourg law did not until recently have any specific provisions dealing with the personal liability of the officers who manage a company which becomes insolvent or is declared bankrupt. In principle, the directors do not incur any personal liability deriving from the liabilities of the company. This is an application of the general rules relating to mandates that the proxy does not bind himself and that the person (in this case the company) represented must execute the obligations undertaken in its name by the proxy.

Directors are, however, responsible for damage caused by their fault. This responsibility may exist towards the company, the shareholders and third parties.

A law of 21 July 1992 has been introduced into the Commercial Code articles 444-1, 495 and 495-1 which deal with the liability of the directors and managers of a company which has been declared bankrupt.

The principle of the personal liability of the directors of a public limited company

Article 59 of the company law of 10 August 1915 ("the 1915 Law") deals with the personal liability of directors of a public limited company.

The wording of this article is as follows:

> ""The directors are responsible towards the company, in accordance with common law, for the execution of the mandate which has been conferred upon them and for the faults committed during their management. They are jointly responsible either towards the company or towards third parties for all damages resulting from any infringements of the provisions of company law or of the articles of incorporation. They shall be discharged of this responsibility in respect of infringements in which they did not take part, only if no fault is imputable to them and if they have denounced the infringements to the next general meeting of shareholders after the date on which they became aware thereof".

In the provisions of article 59, two different cases may be distinguished:

- acts which simply relate to the execution of the mandate and which do not constitute a violation of the law or of the articles of incorporation;
- acts which constitute a violation of legal or statutory provisions.

In the first case, the responsibility is of a contractual nature and in the second case it is extra-contractual. This distinction is important since the persons who may claim damages from the directors differ in each case.

Ordinary faults committed by directors

Where faults which do not constitute a violation of the law or of the articles of incorporation are committed by one or more directors, the general principles of the Civil Code relating to the mandate apply.

The director or the directors will be liable for the resultant loss if he has or they have not executed the mandate with all the normal care of a *pater familias*, *i.e.* a person acting with normal care and prudence. In such a case, there will be no joint liability of all the directors but only those who fail to attain the required standard of care. Any such responsibility will exist only *vis-à-vis* the company since the claim for damages arises out of the mandate and the "actio mandati" (the appropriate action) only belongs to the company. As long as the company is in good standing, the general shareholders' meeting can decide whether or not an action should be commenced against the appropriate directors.

Article 63 of the 1915 Law provides for the meeting to delegate decisions to one or more persons.

Acts constituting a violation of legal or statutory provisions

In this case the responsibility of the directors is viewed much more strictly and they will be jointly responsible not only towards the company but also towards third parties for all damages arising from their wrongful act or omission.

The loss, for which an indemnity may be claimed, must result from a specific fault. The infringement of the legal and statutory provisions must be clear. Thus, if a director had incorrectly interpreted a provision, the sense of which is controversial, he will not be regarded as having been at fault for the purpose of this liability.

Both the company and third parties may institute proceedings against the directors. The basis of the company's action would be the actio mandati and the general meeting of shareholders has to decide whether or not to start such proceedings. If the company is bankrupt, the curateur may take this decision.

Third parties may start proceedings against the director or against the company or both on the basis of article 59 of the 1915 Law. This action is independent of the right of the company to sue the directors. If the shareholders decide not to institute proceedings, this waiver does not bind creditors or other third parties.

Shareholders individually have no particular right to act against the directors, except in the same circumstances and on the same basis as any other third parties.

The consequences of the directors' liability

If the directors' responsibility is established in court, they are bound to indemnify the person or persons who initiated the proceedings for the entire loss, *i.e.* not only the direct loss, but also the lost profit. Under article 1150 of the Civil Code, the directors would only be liable for such damages as would have been foreseen or foreseeable.

Where the action against the directors arises out of ordinary fault (p441 *supra*), that is, without violation of the law or of the articles, each director is individually liable only for damage arising from his own action. The responsibility deriving from the second case (implying a violation of the law or of the articles) is joint responsibility (*i.e.* each director is jointly liable with anyone else responsible for the loss caused. Each director is thus liable in full to the party suffering loss or damage).

Under article 59, paragraph 2 of the 1915 Law, the directors can only escape liability if they can demonstrate that they have not committed any fault, that they have not participated in the infringement and that they have denounced it at the next general meeting of shareholders. Resignation does not release them from responsibility.

Personal liability of the directors in bankruptcy

Brief mention must be made of the fact that the Luxembourg courts may in certain circumstances pierce the corporate veil and "extend" a company's bankruptcy to its manager(s) or director(s), thus rendering them personally liable for the company's debts. This occurs when the director or manager in question has confused the assets of the company with his own property and has treated company property as if it were his own. This extension obviously occurs mostly in the case of small privately owned companies and is normally not relevant to multinational subsidiaries.

Under article 444-1 of the Commercial Code, where the bankrupt person or the *de iure* or *de facto* directors of a company have contributed by a gross and indisputable mistake to the bankruptcy, the commercial court which ordered the bankruptcy (or, in case of a bankruptcy declared by a foreign court, the commercial court in Luxembourg) may order at the request of the bankruptcy receiver or the public prosecutor that those persons are prohibited from performing directly or through an intermediary a business activity. Such activity includes the position of director, manager, statutory auditor, independent auditor or any other activity that binds the company. This prohibition may be for a period of between one and twenty years and mandatorily applies to anyone who has been sentenced for fraudulent bankruptcy. It applies to all directors, whether or not they are partners and whether they are apparent or covert, remunerated or not and whether or not they are in office at the time of the bankruptcy.

Article 495 of the Commercial Code provides that the *de iure* or *de facto* directors of a bankrupt company who have conducted company business or disposed of the company's assets in their own personal interest or continued the business at loss may themselves be declared bankrupt if it is obvious that the company would have to cease its payments at the end of the day.

Furthermore article 495-1 of the Commercial Code provides that, when in the course of the bankruptcy it becomes apparent that the assets of the bankrupt entity are insufficient to pay all the claims, the commercial court may at the request of the bankruptcy receiver decide that the company's debts must be met totally or partly by the *de iure* or *de facto* directors if they have committed material and self-evident mistakes which contributed to the bankruptcy. Such an action has to be brought within three years from the date on which the final account of creditors' claims has been presented in the bankruptcy procedure.

6. Public control over insolvent corporations

Licensing and control of the appointee

The Commercial Code provides that the government may establish a profession of licensed insolvency practitioners for the administration of bankruptcies. However, this has never been done and the commercial courts have the choice, when appointing curateurs, to select such persons as they think fit and who have the knowledge, skill and experience required for the job.

In fact the commercial courts normally appoint as curateurs advocates who are skilled and experienced in matters of insolvency. The curateurs perform their duties under the control and the supervision of the commercial courts which may at any time replace both the appointed judge and the curateurs.

The particular role of the judge is to accelerate the proceedings and to control the administration and the implementation of the bankrupt entity.

Examinations and investigations

As has already been indicated, the curateur must, on appointment, establish an inventory of the assets belonging to the bankrupt entity. The Commercial Code also requires curateurs to draw up a balance sheet of the bankrupt entity on the basis of the existing accounting documents and all other available information. This must be done in the presence of the bankrupt person. The balance sheet will then have to be deposited with the commercial court and the commissioned judge has the right to hear an explanation from the bankrupt person, the officers and employees of the bankrupt entity, and any other involved person as to the exact circumstances which led to the bankruptcy.

The curateur may also employ the bankrupt person in order to facilitate the conduct of the bankruptcy. The appointed judge will determine the working conditions of the bankrupt person.

The Commercial Code furthermore provides that the curateurs have to remit to the appointed judge, within 15 days of their appointment, a memorandum on the apparent situation of the bankruptcy, the main reasons for it and the circumstances and characteristics of the bankruptcy. The judge will then transmit the memorandum with his comments to the public prosecutor.

On the basis of a complaint made by the curateur or by any interested person, the public prosecutor may make such other and further investigations as he thinks appropriate and criminal proceedings may be initiated against the individual person who has been declared bankrupt or against the officers of the corporate entity which has been declared bankrupt if it appears that they acted in a fraudulent way.

Publicity and records

As already mentioned above, most of the court decisions rendered in the various insolvency procedures have to be publicised either in the Official Gazette or in several newspapers designated by the relevant court decisions. We have also seen that the same publicity must be given to a compulsory winding up of a company.

All these decisions have to be notified in the companies' register, which is open to public inspection. Records must also be kept of the proceedings of all meetings held during the company's insolvency.

All the persons appointed by the court, including the commissioners to a controlled management, the curateurs, the liquidateurs in a compulsory winding up and other appointees are all subject to the rules contained in the mandate granted to them by the court. They are required to report on their administration and maintain accurate accounts of receipts and payments.

The public has the right of inspection of any company's file at the companies registry kept at either Luxembourg or the Diekirch district court. Copies of entries may be obtained at a small charge.

A register of mortgages and charges is kept at the mortgage registration office ("Bureau des Hypothèques"). Mortgages are required to be registered to establish their rank or relative rights of priority. The details recorded in the register include the assets charged, the amount secured and the name of the creditor holding the charge.

Every company's letter-head must disclose its name, registered number, registered office or head office, corporate status and VAT number.

Depending on the circumstances, banks and credit agencies may be further sources of information.

Contents of Chapter 10

CORPORATE INSOLVENCY LAW IN THE NETHERLANDS

1.	**Introduction**	447
	Sources of law	447
	Constituent parts of the Kingdom of the Netherlands	448
2.	**Corporations**	448
	Introduction	448
	The association ("vereniging")	449
	The co-operative ("coöperatieve vereniging") and the mutual insurance society ("onderlinge waarborgmaatschappij")	450
	The foundation ("stichting")	451
	Companies	451
	Contractual partnerships	455
	Security for creditors, debt collection and asset recovery	456
3.	**Survival of the insolvent corporation or its business: moratorium of payment**	460
	Considerations and initiation of the moratorium proceedings	460
	The provisional order, "bewindvoerder" and supervising judge	461
	The meeting of creditors	462
	The final moratorium order	462
	Termination of the moratorium	463
4.	**Termination of the corporation: dissolution and bankruptcy**	464
	Dissolution	464
	Bankruptcy	466
5.	**Augmenting the assets of the insolvent corporation**	474
	Transactions at risk	474
	Set-off ("schuldvergelijking")	476
	Liability of officers	476
6.	**Public control over insolvent corporations**	476

Chapter 10

CORPORATE INSOLVENCY LAW IN THE NETHERLANDS

W F Th Corpeleijn and M Herschdorfer,

Stibbe Simont Monahan Duhot

1. Introduction

Sources of law

In this chapter we will be discussing – in basic outline – corporations, securities law, and bankruptcy in the Netherlands. These subjects are codified by statute. The legislation we shall be dealing with is enacted in the following statutes:

- The Civil Code (Burgerlijk Wetboek – BW)
- Commercial Code (Wetboek van Koophandel – "K");
- Bankruptcy Act (Faillissementswet – "F"); and
- Act on Litigation (Wetboek van Rechtsvordering- "L Rv").

The Netherlands does not have the Anglo-Saxon system of legally-binding court precedents, but the interpretation of provisions in statutes by the Supreme Court of the Netherlands ("de Hoge Raad der Nederlanden") is usually followed by lower courts. Thus, where necessary, we have referred to the case law of the Netherlands Supreme Court.

Some cautionary notes must be made here. The first note regards the Civil Code. As from 1 January 1992 the Civil Code has been changed in the Netherlands. For practical purposes we have written this section on the basis of the new legislation. We have not dealt with the transitional provisions ("overgangsrecht"). The second cautionary note relates to terminology. As shall be seen at pp474-475 below in the Netherlands "bankruptcy" ("faillissement") is not synonymous with "insolvency" ("insolventie"). Bankruptcy is a general attachment procedure, whereas insolvency is a qualification as to the financial state of a company and implies that the company cannot pay its debts in full as they fall due. Although a bankrupt company can be insolvent, it is not a constituent requirement for the company to be bankrupted. Furthermore, in order to avoid confusion regarding the terminology for the persons involved in the various procedures to be described, their Dutch names have been used.

Constituent parts of the Kingdom of the Netherlands

Since 1 January 1986 the island of Aruba has been a separate country within the Kingdom of the Netherlands, although there have been few significant changes in its Commercial Code or practice.

The current Kingdom of the Netherlands includes the Netherlands Antilles (Curaçao, Bonaire, Sint Maarten (half), Saba en Sint Eustatius). A bankruptcy order against a company in the Netherlands also applies against assets in these overseas territories.

2. Corporations

Introduction

Dutch Civil law distinguishes three main types of legal person in addition to national persons. These are:

- public legal persons such as government and municipalities;
- religious bodies;
- private legal persons *i.e.* associations, companies and foundations.

For the purposes of this section, we shall deal solely with private legal persons and in particular with companies.

Two main characteristics distinguish a legal person from a natural person; namely:

- the capital of a legal person is separate from its incorporators or members and
- a legal person has an objective which is independent from its shareholders or corporate bodies.

However, the Civil Code (BW) only contains two provisions which actually regulate the essence of a legal person. Under section 2:5 BW, a legal person is equated with a natural person in matters of property law and, under section 2:8 BW, it is laid down that the legal person and those involved in its organisation must conduct themselves towards each other in accordance with reasonableness and fairness. In legal literature these rules are interpreted as showing that a legal person is not so much a contractual entity as an institution separate from its shareholders or members with its own rights and obligations.

A legal person – aside from the two forms of association discussed below is created by a "legal act" in the form of a deed of incorporation drawn up by a notary public.

A legal person is obliged to register its undertaking with the chamber of commerce in either the Trade Register or the Register of Associations and Foundations of the district where it has its statutory seat. The information that the legal person must register with the chamber of commerce is its (trade) name and address, the names and addresses of its management together with any restrictions on their representational powers, and its corporate objectives. The legal person must also deposit its articles of association and under certain circumstances its annual accounts. The registers of the chamber of commerce are publicly accessible.

All legal persons have corporate "organs" which means a functional unity of one or more (legal) persons with decision-making powers given by law or provided for in the articles of association. Such organs of the legal person are the board of management ("bestuur") – *i.e.* a board of directors and occasionally a supervisory board (see p451 *infra*) – and the general meeting of shareholders ("algemene vergadering van aandeelhouders") in the case of a company, or general meeting of members ("algemene vergadering van leden") in the case of an association (see below). The articles of association must regulate – *inter alia* – the internal organisation of the representational powers of the corporate bodies within the legal person, and the corporate objective.

The next part of this Section reviews the various legal persons in the Netherlands, and deals briefly with contractual partnerships which – as yet – do not qualify as legal persons.

The association ("vereniging")

Introduction

An association ("vereniging") is established by an act of two or more (legal) persons for any legal objective other than the fulfilment of the material needs of the members and the insurance of its members (for both of which there are separate types of association discussed below). An association is not entitled to distribute profits amongst its members. Typically an association will be used as the form of legal person for mutual interest groups (such as the rather obvious cases of persons pursuing a hobby (such as philatelists) and football clubs but also other types of activity such as banks, and members of the Stock Exchange).

Establishment

Dutch civil law distinguishes between "formal" and "informal" associations.

As a rule, an association will be established by notarial deed of incorporation, which also encompasses the articles of association. However, the general meeting of members of the association may decide to have the articles of association drawn up in notarial form without an actual deed of incorporation (s2:28 BW). In both cases the association is deemed to be a "formal association" and all provisions regarding associations are equally applicable.

An "informal association", on the other hand, is not incorporated by a notarial deed, nor are its articles of association laid down in a notarial deed. An informal association has only limited legal capacity although it has the status of a legal person (s2:30 BW). The informal association cannot acquire registered property (for instance real property, and registered ships and patents), nor inherit. Furthermore, a manager who binds an informal association by an act intended to have legal consequences is jointly and severally liable with the association for performance or damages unless the association is registered with the chamber of commerce. In the latter case, there is only joint and several liability of the manager insofar as the contracting third party can show that it is unlikely that the association will perform the obligation (s2:30(4) BW). A manager of an informal association is also liable for debts incurred during his office if, having retired from office, there is no successor. He may however escape liability if he can show that he was not consulted about the transaction in question and that, having become aware of the transaction, he refused to accept responsibility.

Management

All the powers of an association are vested in the general meeting of members unless otherwise provided for by law, or by the articles of association. Unless the articles of association provide otherwise, appointed managers ("bestuur") are charged with the management of the association.

In principle, the management is appointed from and by the general meeting of members. However, section 2:37 (1) and (2) BW allow non-members to be appointed to the management, even without a vote in the general meeting of members, provided that each member can, in some way, participate in the vote. Furthermore, the appointment may be made by persons other than the members but, in such a case, the majority of the board of management must have been appointed by the members (s2:37(3) BW). Removal or suspension of a manager is effected by the appointing corporate organ. The management submits its annual report to the general meeting for approval (s2:48 BW).

Unless the articles of association provide otherwise, under section 2:44 BW, there is a basic restriction prohibiting the management from entering into contracts for the acquisition, sale or encumbrance of real property and registered ships, contracts for security, or contracts which involve the association accepting or providing liability for third parties.

The co-operative ("coöperatieve vereniging") and the mutual insurance society ("onderlinge waarborg-maatschappij")

A co-operative ("coöperatieve vereniging") and a mutual insurance society ("onderlinge waarborg maatschappij") are associations, to which the provisions regarding associations apply with the notable exception that these two specific forms of association have, as their objective, the fulfilment of material needs of their members. Furthermore, they do not suffer the same basic restriction imposed by section 2:44 BW on the management of an ordinary association against entering into certain contracts.

A co-operative has as its objective the fulfilment of material needs of its members by agreements (other than insurance agreements) entered into with them. A mutual insurance society, on the other hand has, as its objective, entering into insurance agreements with its members or, keeping third parties insured.

Both co-operatives and mutual insurance societies are established by a notarial deed of incorporation and are obliged to be registered in the chamber of commerce of the district where they have their statutory seat.

For so called "large" co-operatives and mutual insurance societies specific regulations apply, similar to those applicable with large NVs and BVs (see below).

The foundation ("stichting")

A foundation is a legal person without members, its aim being the achievement of objectives as set out in the articles of association – by means of its capital (s2:285(1) BW). Foundations are used both for charitable and idealistic purposes, but are also used as the holders of (priority) shares of companies. The distributions made by a foundation must, however, have either an idealistic or social purpose. The establishment of a foundation is very straightforward as it only requires a notarial deed (s2:286 BW) and no minimum capital. The foundation must be registered in the register of foundations held at the chamber of commerce and must have a board of managers. The management is prohibited from entering into certain types of agreements – unless its articles of association provide otherwise – such as the purchase, disposal or encumbrance of real property or registered ships, and agreements which involve the foundation accepting or providing liability for third parties.

Companies

The Netherlands has two types of limited companies, namely the public limited company ("naamloze vennootschap" – "NV") and the private limited company ("besloten vennootschap" – "BV"). The latter was introduced in 1971 in order to bring the Netherlands into line with other European countries, as the Netherlands only had one basic form of capital company at the time and the first EC company directive (9 March 1968) provided for two types of capital companies. These two types of company are regulated by the provisions in the Civil Code. Many of the provisions apply equally to the two, but there are prominent differences relating to transferability of shares, minimum capital requirements and the scope of purchase by the company of its own shares.

The BV is the more popular of the two (approximately 170,000 to 180,000 currently in existence, as against approximately 3,000 to 4,000 NVs). Consequently, this chapter will deal with the two types of companies separately. As most provisions for the NV also apply to the BV, only the most important differences between them will be mentioned.

Finally, a general comment, applicable to both the NV and the BV, about the so called "large" NV's or BV's (the so-called "structuur vennootschap"). A company is "large" when its capital and reserves exceed Dfl.25 million and if it usually has 100 employees or more and an obligatory works council. If a company fulfils these criteria, then it must register itself with the chamber of commerce as a "large company". A consequence of being "large" for three years is that such a company must have a supervisory board – in addition to the managing directors – consisting of at least three members. The first members of the supervisory board are appointed by shareholders' resolution. Any subsequent member is appointed by the members of the supervisory board themselves ("coöptatie" s2:158/268 BW). The articles of association may provide for one or more members of the supervisory board to be nominated by the Dutch Government.

The supervisory board of a "large" company appoints and dismisses members of the management board, adopts the annual accounts and approves important management decisions. Not all large companies are fully subject to the obligation to establish a supervisory board with such far reaching powers. Some companies have a "mitigated regime" according to which the powers of the supervisory board are restricted, and the general meeting of shareholders, rather than the supervisory board, appoints managing directors and adopts the annual accounts. To qualify for a mitigated regime, the company must have more than half its workforce outside the Netherlands. Other large companies are completely exempt from having a supervisory board at all. An example would be a subsidiary of a large company which has a mandatory supervisory board.

The public limited company ("naamloze vennootschap" – "NV")

Characteristics

> "A company limited by shares is a legal person with an authorised capital divided into transferable shares. The shareholders are not personally liable for acts performed in the name of the company and are not liable to contribute to losses of the company in excess of the amount which must be paid upon these shares" (s2:64 BW).

This definition shows one of the distinctive characteristics of the "NV" as opposed to the "BV", namely the free transferability of shares. The shares of an NV may be registered and their transferability may be restricted by the articles of association, but section 2:87 BW stipulates that any such restriction may not render transfer impossible or exceedingly onerous.

Establishment

The NV is incorporated – by one or more incorporators – by notarial deed of incorporation, for which a "certificate of no objection" has been acquired from the Ministry of Justice. A certificate of no objection will only be refused on very limited grounds. The deed of incorporation contains the articles of association, which must state: the company's name, registered office and corporate objectives, as well as the amount of authorised share capital and denomination of the shares. Upon incorporation, the managing directors must have the company registered and must deposit an authentic copy of its deed of incorporation with the Trade Register. The managing directors are jointly and severally liable for each legal act binding on the company until the registration is complete and until that part of the capital prescribed to be paid up on incorporation (at least 25% of the nominal value of the capital issued upon incorporation) has been paid (s2:69 BW).

Shares
Shares can be bearer shares or registered shares and are, in principle, freely transferable. At least 25% of the nominal value of registered shares must be paid up (s2:80(1) BW). If the shares are registered shares, the company must keep a register in which the names and addresses of each holder of the shares are recorded together with the amount paid up and details of any charges which have been placed on the shares. The Dutch Civil Code both allows ordinary shares, and the articles of association to provide indirectly for priority shares. The articles of association may confer some powers of shareholders in general meeting on the priority shareholders. Such priority shares are usually held by members of the supervisory board and by members of the management board, either personally or through a legal person such as a foundation which is controlled by them. Thus, for example, it may be that appointments to the management board can only be made from candidates selected by priority shareholders, or that changes in the articles of association can only be initiated if proposed by the priority shareholders.

Under Dutch law, the shareholders alone have voting rights. They also have a right to receive cash dividends and, under certain conditions, interim dividends. In general, the payment of a dividend will be recommended by the management board, after an approving resolution has been passed by the shareholders. A dividend may be distributed in the form of stock or option rights on the issue of new shares.

There is one general meeting of shareholders per year which adopts the annual accounts (unless the company is a so called large company, in which case the adoption of the annual accounts is then the prerogative of the supervisory board). Subject to the rights of the priority shareholders, any amendment to be made to the articles of association is the prerogative of the general meeting of shareholders and although amendments do not require specific majorities by law, the articles will usually require a qualified majority.

Management board
The management of the company is a matter for the board of managing directors, unless there are specific restrictions in the articles of association. The articles of association will also determine whether or not a managing director is entitled to represent the company severally, or whether that representation may only be joint with another director or directors. Any restrictions on the represen-

tational powers of the directors has to be registered with the chamber of commerce.

Although a supervisory board is obligatory for a large NV, any NV can opt to have a voluntary supervisory board to supervise and assist the board of managing directors through regular meetings. The members of the supervisory board are usually appointed from nominations made by the general meeting, unless the company is large, in which case the supervisory board appoints its own members. The obligations of the supervisory board relate to the interests of the company as a whole and not specifically to the interests of its shareholders. The supervisory board may thus represent the company where there is a conflict of interest between the management and the company.

The private limited company ("besloten vennootschap" – "BV")

"A private company with limited liability is a legal person with an authorissed capital divided into shares. No share certificates shall be issued. The shares are not freely transferable. The shareholders are not personally liable for acts performed in the name of the company and are not liable to contribute to losses of the company in excess of the amount which must be paid upon their shares" (s2:175 BW).

As was noted above, the BV is the most popular form of company, with a minimum capital requirement which is lower than that of an NV (Dfl.40,000 as opposed to Dfl.100,000). The most important difference between the two types of companies is the transferability of the shares. The shares of a BV are not freely transferable, being restricted by a "blocking clause" which must be included in the articles of association. Section 2:195 BW requires such blocking clauses to consist either of a requirement for the approval of the transfer by a corporate organ of the BV (for example the board of managing directors), or an obligation first to offer the shares to the existing shareholders. There is, however, an exception to the blocking clause, in that the articles of association may provide for an unrestricted transfer of shares to a relative or spouse. Another important difference between the NV and the BV is that a BV may not issue share certificates or bearer shares.

The shareholders of a BV are registered in a shareholders' register kept by the company (s2:194 BW). It also records any charges to which the shares may be subject. The register is not a publicly accessible document, although shareholders and those who have a real right to particular shares of the company are entitled to inspect it.

The management provisions of the BV are the same as those applying to the NV.

Contractual partnerships

Introduction

Finally, we deal with companies based on contract, which are not legal persons. Such contractual partnerships occur in a large variety of forms, the three most basic of them being:

- contractual partnerships: the (basic) partnership ("maatschap");
- the company of partners ("vennootschap onder firma" – "vof"); and
- the limited partnership ("commanditaire vennootschap" – "cv").

The basis for all these partnerships is a contract of co-operation between the partners, founded on mutual trust. Indeed a partnership is sometimes referred to as a contract of the utmost good faith.

The agreement which forms the basis for the (basic) partnership is regulated by the Civil Code. The company of partners, and the limited partnership are further regulated by the Commercial Code ("Wetboek van Koophandel").

A basic partnership as such cannot be declared bankrupt (but its partners can) whereas a company of partners and a limited partnership can be declared bankrupt.

The basic partnership ("maatschap")

The contract which establishes a basic partnership is distinguished by the fact that its objective is co-operation between the partners for a common goal, *i.e.* the partnership requires a contribution from each partner so that the common goal can be achieved. In this sense it is not a legal person. It cannot sue or be sued in court although there are cases in which, where a partnership clearly operated under one name (the "public partnership"), it has been held that a writ can be issued in the name of the partnership itself (H.R. 5 November 1976, N.J. 1977, 586).

In principle, as the partnership is based on contract, there are no formalities, although, for obvious reasons of proof, a written contract is usually drawn up. It is not obligatory to register the partnership with the chamber of commerce, and there are no other formalities.

Unless agreed otherwise, each partner is entitled to perform acts related to the day to day running of the business ("beheersbevoegdheid", s7A:1676(1) BW), and other acts ("beschikkingsbevoegdheid") must be decided collectively.

The company of partners ("vennootschap onder firma" – "vof")

This type of undertaking is a partnership which carries on business under a joint name and is, again, contractual in nature. Although section 22 of the Commercial Code provides that a company of partners to be established by a deed (which may or may not be drawn up by a notary public), this is not a constituent requirement, and is only of evidential significance.

Although the company of partners is not currently viewed as a legal person, legislation is pending which will change this position. It is, however, uncertain when this legislation will be enacted.

The company of partners has assets which are separate from the assets of the partners. Furthermore, there is an obligation both on the partnership and on the individual partners to keep accounts.

The partners of the company of partners must be registered with the chamber of commerce. In principle, they all have full representational powers unless the partnership agreement provides otherwise, in which case the restriction on representational powers of any individual partner must be registered with the chamber of commerce for third party protection.

Internally, the liability of the partners towards each other can be freely arranged in contract. Externally there is joint and several liability of each individual partner towards third parties, for obligations entered into by one or more partners on behalf of the company of partners.

The limited partnerships ("commanditaire vennootschap" – "cv")

Finally, a limited partnership is a company of partners which has one or more partners ("silent partners" or "partners en commanditaire") whose external liability is limited to the amount of their contribution. A silent partner may not in any way act on behalf of the partnership, but, if he does, he becomes externally liable as if he were a normal partner. This limitation on the liability of one or more partners in the partnership must be registered with the chamber of commerce.

Security for creditors, debt collection and asset recovery

In Dutch law there are various securities created by contract and other institutions with an effect similar to that of contractually-created securities, which place the creditor in a stronger position *vis-a-vis* the debtor's other creditors. This arises because the creditor is able to assert a right against some property owned by, or in the possession of, the debtor. Basically, debt recovery can only be effected by a creditor who has ownership, real rights or an enforceable judgement. These will be discussed below.

Securing debts in contract

Retention of ownership
The Dutch Civil Code affords an unpaid and unsecured seller of goods or rights/securities, three possible remedies against default by the purchaser.

The first remedy is rescission ("ontbinding") of the purchase agreement due to default. Under the Civil Code, rescission does not have retroactive effect (s6:269 BW). In principle, the vendor will only be able to sue for damages due to default. Thus, upon the bankruptcy of the purchaser the vendor will become an ordinary unsecured creditor, and usually will only be able to retrieve a small part of its debt.

A second legal remedy is the right of reclaim ("recht van reclame") provided for in section 7:39 BW. This right enables a vendor of movable goods to demand the return of the goods, by written notice, within six weeks after the debt has become due and payable or 60 days after delivery. The purchaser is then obliged to return the goods and, on issue of the written notice, ownership of the goods reverts to the vendor. The right of reclaim may also be enforced if the debtor goes bankrupt. This remedy is certainly a powerful right in bankruptcy, but the disadvantage is that it is limited in time.

The third remedy is that the vendor of movable goods sells and delivers the goods, whilst retaining ownership until the goods have been paid for (s3:92 BW). Such a sale is basically a delivery of the goods, subject to the suspended condition of payment. Retention of ownership is not restricted to the debt arising from the delivery of goods, but can also be used where there is default in the payment for (connected) services.

Real rights
A "real right" ("beperkt zakelijk recht") can be described as a right which attaches to property and which can, in principle at least, be pursued by its holder against all others, including the owner of the property to which it attaches. Real rights are conferred by contract, and the real rights dealt with below – pledge and mortgage – are used as security and thus particularly suitable for ordinary commercial transactions. There are other real rights – such as usufruct – but these have little relevance for ordinary commercial transactions.

Pledge
A creditor can contract for a right of pledge on future movable goods, future receivables, money, shares or depositary receipts (s3:236 BW). The pledge on movable goods is established by the debtor ("pledgor") transferring the pledged asset into the physical possession of the creditor ("pledgee"), or to a third party agreed between the pledgee and pledgor. Obviously, in ordinary commercial transactions, it is impractical for every pledged asset to be transferred in this way. Thus the Civil Code allows the so-called "silent pledge" on movable goods (art 3:237 BW), which does not require physical transfer of the asset. The silent pledge is established either by an "authentic" deed (*i.e.* a deed drawn up by a notary public) or by registration of a non-authentic deed. The advantage of the silent pledge is that the debtor can continue to use the pledged asset. If the pledge is for a receivable, the pledgee is entitled to demand and to receive the payment directly from the third party provided that latter has been informed of the pledge. If the pledge of the receivable was "silent", notice of the pledge to the third party debtor is not required (s3:239 BW).

Enforcement by the pledgee in respect of the pledged asset occurs upon default by the pledgor. If possession of the pledged asset was transferred to the pledgee, the latter then has a lien on the asset, *i.e.* the pledgee retains the asset until his claim (increased by any interest and costs) has been paid. If payment is not received the pledgee is entitled to sell the pledged asset (other than a receivable) at public auction, and to recover his debt from the proceeds. If the pledged asset is goods or a receivable which is commonly sold in the market, or on the stock exchange, then the pledgee may sell the pledged object or receivable there. With the consent of the pledgor or the court, the pledged asset may also be sold privately (s3:251 BW). Any surplus in the proceeds is paid to the pledgor. The first significant advantage of the pledge is that the pledgee does not require a judgement of the court to authorise the execution of his rights against the pledged object (the so-called "parate executie").

The second advantage of the right of pledge is that in the event of the bankruptcy of the pledgor, section 57 of the Bankruptcy Act provides that the pledgee can enforce his right against the pledged object as if there were no bankruptcy. Where the pledgor becomes bankrupt, execution of the pledge against pledged assets is again by public auction, unless the "curator" (see p469 *infra*) and the pledgee agree to a private sale (HR 8th April 1983, NJ 1984, 434). The pledgee can recover his debt from the proceeds and any surplus is paid to the curator. If there are other interested third parties (such as other pledgees) who have claims which are secured by the assets which have been sold, the surplus of the proceeds is divided amongst them.

Mortgage

A mortgage is a real right created by contract to grant security over "registered goods" (such as real property, and registered ships), in favour of a creditor ("the mortgagee") by the debtor ("the mortgagor"). The mortgage is drawn up in the form of a notarial deed and registered in the real property register ("hypotheek register"). A mortgage deed must include a description of the debt, the exact amount of the debt for which the mortgage has been established and the property over which the mortgage is established (s3:260 BW).

The execution of a mortgage is a public sale of the mortgaged property by a notary, or a private sale with the permission of the court (s3:268 BW) or of the mortgagor (or, if the mortgagor is bankrupt, of his curator).

Again, as in the case of a pledgee, the mortgagee can sell the mortgaged property and recover his debt from the proceeds in bankruptcy as if there were no bankruptcy. Furthermore, the curator can, in agreement of the mortgagee, sell the mortgaged property privately (s176 F), in which case the mortgagee is not liable for bankruptcy costs either (HR 28 June 1985, NJ 1985, 887). The proceeds of the sale of the mortgaged property are deposited with a notary (s3:270 BW) and, after the expenses have been met, are paid to the mortgagee.

Securing debts after default and recovery

Unless a creditor has a right to recover his debt based on ownership or other real right as explained above, the recovery of his debt from a defaulting debtor in the Netherlands may only be achieved by way of "legal enforcement" ensuring compliance with a judgment given against the debtor. This is known as a "title for enforcement".

The Dutch term "title", in this context, means "written proof of a right". The most commonly enforceable titles are court and arbitral judgments and foreign court judgments as well as certain notarial deeds. It must, however, be noted that not all such "titles" are directly enforceable. Foreign judgments are enforceable if there is a convention or the law so provides. Enforcement of a foreign judgment will be possible after a court has given leave to enforce the judgment in an exequatur procedure (see for example article 32 of the EEC Convention of Jurisdiction and the Enforcement of Judgments in Civil and Commercial Matters 1968 ("EEX"), to which the Netherlands is a contracting nation).

Enforcement attachment ("executoriaal beslag")

A creditor with an enforceable title can enforce the judgment by attaching the assets of the debtor and selling them at public auction. The debt is then recovered from the proceeds of the sale. However, some assets of the debtor cannot be attached – such as goods intended for public service, basic goods required for life and a certain proportion of the debtor's income. Enforcement attachment and the execution of the attachment can also be performed against the debtor's assets (such as receivables or goods) in the physical possession of a third party. The third party must declare what assets are held by him on behalf of the debtor. In the event his declaration is not accepted as correct by the creditor, special proceedings ("verklarings procedure") may be initiated by the creditor against the third party, leading to a judgment on the extent of the obligations of the third party towards the debtor. Any amount held by the third party (typically a bank) for the debtor has to be paid to the creditor. Any movable goods held by the third party have to be delivered to the creditor for an enforcement sale. Finally, a creditor can attach assets which belong to the debtor but which are in his own (the creditor's) possession.

If the judgment is not for the payment of money but for delivery of goods, there is a specific attachment which a creditor can use called the "attachment for delivery of goods" (s730 L Rv) which is based on the right to delivery. In bankruptcy, there is an important distinction between a claim based on ownership and a claim based on a right of delivery. Ownership is an absolute right and on bankruptcy the curator cannot prevent this kind of attachment, whereas a contractual right of delivery (such as a purchaser has) – even though based on a court judgment – is a personal right which in bankruptcy will be converted into an ordinary unsecured claim for which no attachment can be made.

Restraining attachment ("conservatoir beslag")

Pending the acquisition of an enforceable judgment against the debtor, a creditor may wish to secure assets of the debtor against which the creditor may wish, at a later date, to execute his title. Dutch law provides that, pending the acquisition of an enforceable title, a creditor can request the court to place a "restraining attachment" on assets of the debtor, which will then remain attached until the enforceable title is acquired. In the event of the bankruptcy of the debtor, this attachment lapses in favour of the general bankruptcy attachment and does not lead to any preferential position of the creditor that made the attachment.

3. Survival of the insolvent corporation or its business: moratorium of payment

Whilst bankruptcy can be described as a general attachment on all the assets of a debtor on behalf of all creditors, "moratorium of payment" ("surseance van betaling") is characterised by a general suspension of payments for ordinary unsecured creditors for a specified period of time in order to give the debtor the opportunity to propose some form of composition with its creditors.

Generally, moratorium of payment is used by the debtor to reorganise its business, and thus to stave off bankruptcy proceedings. Due to the far reaching consequences a bankruptcy can have, the Bankruptcy Act provides that if there are contemporaneous petitions for bankruptcy and moratorium, the moratorium petition will be dealt with first (s218 F). It must, however, be noted that, in practice, moratorium of payment is usually followed by bankruptcy.

Under a moratorium, the consequences are far less drastic than under bankruptcy, although the debtor does lose control over its assets and, in particular, the right to dispose of them. Control and disposal of assets by the debtor requires the co-operation of the "administrator or bewindvoerder" (see p461 *infra*) and vice versa.

Moratorium of payment does not affect the rights of secured creditors (such as a pledgee or mortgagee who can proceed with the attachment and sale of secured assets upon default by the debtor company) or preferential creditors (such as tax authorities and some specific auditors, such as alimony, or hire-purchase), although these creditors cannot petition for the debtor's bankruptcy during the period of moratorium. Only unsecured creditors may vote at meetings.

Considerations and initiation of the moratorium proceedings

If a debtor company foresees that it will not be able to pay its debts, but that there is a realistic chance that upon reorganisation it may become profitable, a petition can be presented to the court for a moratorium on all claims and proceedings against it. Only the debtor company itself can petition for a moratorium.

The company petitions the district court ("Arrondissementsrechtbank") in the district where it is registered for the proceedings to start. The petition is signed by the directors of the company (unless the articles of association specify another corporate organ) and an attorney. The application must contain the following information:

- a schedule of creditors' names, addresses and claims;
- the latest available financial statements, or a summary of the debtor's asset and liabilities; and
- a statement that the company will not be able to pay all debts due, although it foresees that creditors' claims will be satisfied eventually, either in full or partially by composition.

The application may also contain a composition proposal.

The provisional order, "bewindvoerder" and supervising judge

Unless the formalities for the application of moratorium have not been complied with, or the company has already been declared bankrupt, the court will grant a provisional order of moratorium. The reason for this is that the court cannot decide immediately to grant the moratorium because the creditors need to be heard. The provisional moratorium order will include the following:

- the appointment of a "bewindvoerder", who will from that moment on control the assets of the business and oversee the management of the debtor (see p460 *supra*). Usually, a bewindvoerder is an attorney practising at the local bar;
- (usually) the appointment of a supervisory judge;
- the determination of a date for the creditors' meeting which will vote on the debtor's application for a moratorium;
- the determination of the latest date on which the creditors may submit their claims to the bewindvoerder in order to vote at the meeting of creditors;
- suspension of all litigation by ordinary and unsecured creditors against the debtor and the enforcement of judgments by such creditors against the debtor.

The bewindvoerder is appointed by the court to administer the debtor's affairs during the moratorium. This can sometimes create problems. As was mentioned above, all control and disposal of the assets of the debtor requires a joint decision of the debtor and the bewindvoerder. If the debtor refuses to co-operate with the bewindvoerder, the latter can request the court to end the moratorium, and the court will generally declare the debtor bankrupt and appoint the bewindvoerder as curator, enabling him to act independently of the debtor (see s242 F). If the debtor co-operates, the bewindvoerder receives the creditors' claims and draws up a list of them for the creditors' meeting.

In almost all cases, a supervising judge will be appointed by the court, although this is not a prerequisite for a moratorium. If a supervisory judge is appointed, his duties are to advise and supervise the bewindvoerder to hear witnesses under oath on any matters concerning the circumstances leading to the suspension of payments.

Under section 24la F the court may grant a "cooling-off period" of up to one month (which can be extended to two months), during which creditors are not allowed to enforce their rights (such as taking possession of goods) towards the debtor.

The meeting of creditors

Once the provisional order of moratorium has been made, a meeting is convened for the creditors to vote on whether or not the moratorium should be made final. The court sets the date for the meeting at which the creditors, the management of the debtor and the bewindvoerder will be heard. Usually this meeting will be convened between one and three months after the provisional order, the creditors are informed of the date by post from the court, and the date is also published in a daily newspaper and in the Netherlands Official Gazette ("Staatscourant").

The unsecured and non-preferential creditors will be allowed to vote on whether or not the moratorium should be made final. The debtor's application for a final moratorium must be approved by 75% in value and two-thirds in number of the creditors affected by the moratorium present or represented at the meeting. The court is obliged to refuse to continue the moratorium in the following circumstances:

- if the required majority was not reached;
- if there are valid reasons to believe that the debtor will try to prejudice the creditors' rights during the moratorium;
- if there is no realistic prospect that the debtor will be able to satisfy the creditors.

The moratorium may last up to 18 months (as from the date of the provisional order). During that time an extension can be applied for which will be decided by the court via a similar procedure as for the finalisation of the moratorium. Further extensions can be granted in the same way.

If the continuation of the moratorium is refused, the court can (but is not obliged to) declare the debtor bankrupt.

The final moratorium order

If the moratorium is continued, the debtor company loses control over its assets and is obliged to co-operate with the bewindvoerder. Any unilateral acts performed by the debtor company are avoidable by the bewindvoerder, and can be penalised as follows:

- the moratorium can be withdrawn (s242 F);

- the bewindvoerder may act to do anything necessary to protect the estate (s228 F);
- the debtor can be prosecuted under the criminal law (s442 Criminal Code).

As was stated above, the moratorium only affects ordinary unsecured creditors. Thus, the debtor can be forced to pay its debts to pledgees or mortgagees, and to preferential creditors. Although, during the moratorium, the debtor cannot be forced to pay other debts, as payment is suspended, it is entitled to pay them if permitted to do so by the bewindvoerder. However, such payment should be made to all ordinary unsecured creditors and be proportional to their claims. This relates to the principle of "paritas creditorum" in the Netherlands under which all unsecured and non-preferential creditors are treated equally.

In line with the principle of the moratorium, any pending enforcement proceedings with ordinary unsecured creditors are suspended, and any restraining attachments lapse. Litigation against or by the company is, by contrast, continued. The moratorium does not prevent the initiation of litigation. However, for the company to act as plaintiff in litigation, the bewindvoerder is required to co-operate (s231 F).

Termination of the moratorium

The moratorium can be terminated by the agreement of a composition with the creditors. The debtor can offer a composition at the beginning of the proceeding upon application, or at any time during the moratorium.

A composition is an agreement between the creditors and the debtor, and which requires a majority vote (see *infra*) by the creditors (according to the value of their claims) for approval. In order to be entitled to vote on the composition proposal, the creditors will need to submit their claims for verification. However, if a secured or preferential creditor does this and then votes on the composition, he loses his security or preference (s257 F).

Once the composition proposal has been submitted, the creditors' meeting is convened by the court. At the meeting, the bewindvoerder reports on the debtor's proposals and on the claims which have been accepted. The proposed composition must be approved by 75% in value and two-thirds in number of the unsecured creditors present or represented. However, even if these majorities are obtained, the court is not obliged to give its consent to the proposed composition.

An appeal against the court's decision can be lodged by creditors who voted against the composition proposal and who can show that their interests are being prejudiced. An appeal can also be lodged against a court decision rejecting the composition by the debtor or any creditors who voted in favour of the composition. The appeal must be lodged within eight days of the court order.

Upon agreement, the composition is formalised in a "court order of the composition" ("homologatie van het accoord") which, after the term for appeal has lapsed, becomes binding and ends the moratorium. If the debtor does not perform under the court order for composition, the composition can be rescinded and the court will declare the debtor bankrupt (s280 F).

Finally, the period of moratorium will end either on the date specified in the moratorium order itself, by being withdrawn on the application of the debtor, the bewindvoerder or of a creditor. In this latter case, the court will usually declare the debtor bankrupt.

4. Termination of the corporation: dissolution and bankruptcy

A company terminates through its dissolution ("ontbinding"). Section 2:19 BW provides that a company is dissolved:

- upon expiry of the duration of the corporation, or through an act stipulated in the articles of association to result in dissolution;
- by court order;
- by shareholders' resolution;
- if, after it has been declared bankrupt, the debts exceed the assets and this has been formally established.

This work deals only with the last two bases for dissolution.

Dissolution

A company can be terminated voluntarily by a shareholders' resolution for dissolution. It is a prerogative of the shareholders to be entitled to terminate the company, and the articles of association cannot exclude this prerogative. The articles of association however can (and usually do) determine the size of the majority vote required to effect termination, and under somewhat exceptional circumstances the shareholders resolution for termination may be either void (s2:14 BW) or voidable (s2:15 BW).

On the passing of the shareholders' resolution for dissolution, the managing director of the company becomes the official liquidator ("vereffenaar") of the company unless the articles of association determine otherwise or the shareholders' resolution appoints an alternative. If there is more than one managing director, they act jointly. Unless the articles of association determine otherwise, a vereffenaar has the same rights, entitlements and liabilities as the board of managing directors in so far as these are in accordance with his task as vereffenaar (s2:23a BW). The vereffenaar has independent rights and entitlements and no corporate organ, including the shareholders, can give him instructions as to the way he is to fulfil his obligations, although he can be dismissed by the general meeting of shareholders. The vereffenaar can call a general meeting of shareholders. If there is a board of supervisory directors, its supervisory tasks remain intact, even if the supervisory tasks are related solely to the purpose of liquidation. No public authorities control or regulate the actions of the vereffenaar, but he is responsible to the company, the shareholders and the creditors to perform his task. If negligent, he is liable for damages.

Since third parties could be damaged if they were unaware of the resolution terminating the company and of the ensuing liquidation, section 2:19(3) BW stipulates that the vereffenaar must ensure that the chamber of commerce is notified of the dissolution and, furthermore, that in all correspondence and notices from the company, the words "in liquidation" are added to the company name.

From the moment of the shareholders' resolution for dissolution, the company merely exists in order to liquidate all its assets and pay off all debts. If the vereffenaar finds that the company is insolvent (its debts outweighing its assets), he is obliged to file for the bankruptcy of the company, unless the creditors agree to a continuation of the liquidation – and thus agree to only partial recovery of their debt (s2:23a(4) BW).

In order to liquidate the company, all the assets must be sold, and it is the task of the vereffenaar to obtain the highest possible price. He is free to determine in which way he will go about his task. It may be necessary to continue the operations of the company for some time in order to realise a higher yield for the assets. These can be sold individually (either privately or at public auction) or together, and sometimes the whole business is sold in its entirety. Creditors may also accept payment in kind. The vereffenaar is legally entitled to oblige shareholders to pay up any outstanding amount on their shares and they are not entitled to set this amount off against a debt owed to them by the company.

The Civil Code has no specific provisions regarding the payment of debts to creditors, and the vereffenaar will try to redeem all debts in accordance with agreements made with the creditors.

The vereffenaar also draws up a liquidation account ("rekening en verantwoording"). If, after payment of the creditors, some proceeds still remain, the vereffenaar draws up a distribution plan ("plan van uitkering"), which sets out his proposals for dividing the proceeds amongst the shareholders or other persons nominated by the articles of associations, in accordance with their respective rights. Both the liquidation account and the plan for distribution are registered at the chamber of commerce and must be available for inspection at the offices of the company. The registration is also advertised in a national newspaper. These documents must be available for inspection for two months, during which time any creditor can oppose the plan of distribution. After the two month period has expired, the distribution plan becomes final and those entitled to payment are paid. This brings the liquidation to an end.

The liquidation can be reopened by the court if, after it has been completed, a creditor claims any part of the liquidation proceeds which were paid out either to the shareholders or to any other persons entitled thereto pursuant to the articles of association. A creditor must petition the court to re-open the liquidation, and to appoint a new vereffenaar. In that case, the company "revives", although only in order to finalise the re-opened liquidation. The vereffenaar is, in that case, entitled to demand reimbursement from any of the shareholders (or other persons) who have received proceeds under the plan of distribution (s2:23c BW).

Finally, all accounts and documents of the dissolved corporation must be kept for ten years after the liquidation.

Bankruptcy

The principle of bankruptcy ("faillissement") as laid down in the Bankruptcy Law, is that, by court order, a general attachment is laid on all current and future assets of a debtor on behalf of all the debtor's creditors. This means that the debtor can no longer control or dispose of any of its assets nor acquire any assets. Furthermore, any payments made by third parties to the debtor itself do not relieve the third party of its obligation to pay to the debtor, as payment must be made to the curator (see p469 *infra*). If an order of bankruptcy is made by the court, the assets of the debtor become an "attached estate" ("boedel") for the purpose of distribution to the creditors. One of the notable effects of the bankruptcy order is that any attachments (see p458-459 *supra*) which rested on assets of the bankrupt company automatically lapse in favour of the general bankruptcy attachment.

It is most important again to note here that bankruptcy, in the Netherlands, is not synonymous with insolvency, although the bankrupt debtor may actually be insolvent. Bankruptcy is first and foremost an attachment procedure, and may terminate without liquidation of the company through a composition with the creditors, although in practice bankruptcy will usually lead to liquidation.

Persons who can be declared bankrupt

All legal and natural persons can be declared bankrupt. Indeed, even though a "company of partners" is not a legal person (see p455 *supra*), it can be declared bankrupt, as its assets which are separate from those of the partners. On the other hand, the " basic partnership" (see p455 *supra*) cannot be declared bankrupt, although it will terminate with the bankruptcy of one of its partners.

The basic requirement for bankruptcy is that the debtor "is in the situation that it has ceased payments" (see p467 *infra*).

The applicants

The debtor
A debtor can apply for its own bankruptcy (sl F). If it is a company, a resolution for such an application is required from the general meeting of shareholders. The directors of the company must sign a statement at court that the company is "in a situation that it has ceased payments" and, therefore, requests bankruptcy. In practice, the court will immediately declare the company bankrupt without further investigation.

The debtor itself may apply for a declaration of bankruptcy for a variety of reasons, although the most usual is that it is seeking a bankruptcy as the only way in which to arrange matters with its creditors.

The public prosecutor

Section 1 of the Bankruptcy Act provides that the public prosecutor ("Openbaar Ministerie") can – in the public interest – petition the court for the bankruptcy of a (legal) person. The public prosecutor only makes use of these powers in exceptional cases, such as public functionaries like bailiffs and notaries. However there is case law (*e.g.* H.R. 20 September 1957, N.J. 1957, 568) in which an NV was declared bankrupt for reasons of public interest. In that case, the management was detained in prison on suspicion of widespread fraud as one of the directors had tortiously procured Dfl. 40,000 from the company. As there was no chance of future bank credit, or of any of the contracts being performed, the petition was granted.

The court

The Bankruptcy Act provides a number of circumstances in which the court can declare a debtor bankrupt without a petition. These relate predominantly to the moratorium (see pp460-464 *supra*). If the court declares a debtor bankrupt of its own volition, this is for the purpose of liquidation.

Tax authorities and social security authorities

Under new legislation, the tax authorities can petition the court for bankruptcy of a debtor (s3,"Invorderingswet") and the social security authorities ("Bedrijfsverenigingen") can petition the court under the same conditions as those required for ordinary creditors described below.

Creditors

By far the majority of bankruptcies are the result of an application to the court by an unsatisfied creditor. In principle, any unpaid creditor can initiate bankruptcy proceedings. It is important to note again that the actual petitioning of the court for a bankruptcy order does not necessarily have anything to do with insolvency of a debtor. Indeed, the petitioning is quite often used by a creditor as a way of exerting pressure on the debtor to pay the debt. A creditor can withdraw the petition at any time up to the moment of the debtor being declared bankrupt by the court.

A creditor can only petition the court in writing through an attorney, and the petition must state the facts which justify an order declaring the debtor bankrupt.

Requirements for bankruptcy

Irrespective of who has petitioned the court, the Bankruptcy Act requires that, for an order of bankruptcy to be made, a debtor should be "in the situation that it has ceased payments". As this criterion is very broad, the Supreme Court requires two conditions to be met:

- the debtor must have two or more unpaid creditors (the so-called "plurality of creditors" criterion); and

- this must have led to a situation of default.

A creditor petitioning the court for the bankruptcy of his debtor must fulfil four basic requirements:

- a debt is owed by the creditor
- default by the debtor
- plurality of creditors
- the debtor has ceased payments

Each of these is discussed below.

A debt is owed by the debtor to the creditor
The applicant must have a claim against the debtor but need not prove the claim. The court need only be shown that the claim is "plausible". Indeed, the Bankruptcy Act specifically states that the court need only be convinced that the debtor is "in the situation" (see *infra*) that it has ceased payments (s6(3) F). The creditor does not even need to prove the exact amount of the debt. It is sufficient if only part of the debt is "plausible". Dispensing with proof of the amount of the debt is particularly important in the case of a creditor with a claim part of which is disputed by the debtor.

Default of the debtor
In practice, a creditor must show that the debt is due and payable and that, despite demands by the creditor, the debtor has failed to pay all or part of the debt. However, it must be noted that this is not a strict requirement for the bankruptcy to be declared. The Supreme Court has held (H.R. 19 April 1974, N.J. 1974, 440) that the applicant's claim does not have to be due and payable, but in such a case the creditor will have to show – although not in great detail – that one or more other debts are due and payable.

Plurality of creditors
Although the applicant may have more than one outstanding debt with the debtor, this does not suffice to show that the debtor is "in the situation" of having ceased payments. Thus, the creditor must show that there is at least one other creditor. Nevertheless, the Supreme Court has held more than once (*e.g.* H.R. 18 March 1983, N.J. 1983, 568), that the second debt need not be due and payable. As was mentioned above, if the applicant does not have a due and payable claim, this other debt must be due and payable.

The debtor has ceased payments
Obviously, every company will at any given time have unpaid debts. The Supreme Court has thus held that those debts must have remained unpaid for longer than would be usual (H.R. 23 June 1922, N.J. 1922, 1031).

The court order, appeal

The bankruptcy order

A declaration of bankruptcy is applied for at the district court ("Arrondisse-mentsrechtbank") of area in which the debtor company is registered (s2 F). Under the Bankruptcy Act there is also a forum in the case of a company without a statutory seat in the Netherlands – such as a branch of a foreign company – namely the district court where the company carries on its business, or where it previously carried on its business if the branch has since ceased trading in the Netherlands.

The court will summon the debtor as soon as possible after receiving the application for its bankruptcy. The court hearing is not in public. The court will decide if the requirements for bankruptcy (see p467 *supra*) have been fulfilled. Often, however, a debtor will try to stave off bankruptcy by offering payment to the applicant. In this case, if negotiations are not successful, and the creditor does not immediately accept the offer, the court will often adjourn the proceedings for some time to give the parties the chance to negotiate a settlement. If an agreement is then reached, the creditor can withdraw the petition; if not, the bankruptcy may be declared.

In the bankruptcy order, the court will appoint a supervising judge, and one or more curators (see *infra*).

The bankruptcy order is made in public and published in the Netherlands Official Gazette and in one or more daily newspapers (s14 F).

Under section 63a of the Bankruptcy Act the supervising judge may grant a cooling-off period of one month (which can be extended by one more month), during which specific categories of creditors such as estate creditors, separatists and preferential creditors (see p470-472 *infra*) are allowed to enforce their rights.

Appeal

The bankruptcy order can be objected against ("verzet") within 14 days after the order was granted if the debtor was not present at the court hearing or within one month if the debtor – or the managing directors of the debtor company – were abroad at the time. The objection is made before the court who granted the order. If the debtor was present at the hearing, or the aforementioned objections were denied, the order can be appealed within eight days by the Court of Appeal. Any interested parties are also entitled to appeal against the order. The order is effective from the moment of pronouncement, and is not suspended by the objection or appeal proceedings. In the appeal proceedings, the Court of Appeal will reconsider fully the question as to whether all the requirements for bankruptcy have been met at the time the appeal is heard.

The curator

When the bankruptcy of a debtor is declared, the court appoints a person (a "curator") to administer the bankruptcy estate and, if need be, to liquidate it. It is common practice in the Netherlands for an attorney practising at the local Bar to be appointed as curator. In complicated bankruptcies such as large corporations, more than one curator will be appointed.

The curator has all the powers of the board of management and is fully empowered to represent the estate, being entitled to open post, dispose of assets, terminate agreements, and so on. The curator is paid a salary determined by the court, and reports to the supervising judge (see *infra*).

The supervising judge

The supervising judge ("rechter commissaris") is appointed by the court in its bankruptcy order, and has the following duties:

- authorisation of the continuation of the debtor's business after the bankruptcy;
- supervision of the administration and liquidation of the assets by the curator;
- where necessary, calling of witnesses to give evidence under oath;
- where necessary, the ordering of investigations by experts to establish the cause of failure of the company;
- presiding over meetings of creditors;
- authorisation of the curator to enter into specific transactions such as the sale of assets, litigation or compromises for the benefit of the estate;
- cancellation of mortgages and attachments on the debtor's real property, where the mortgage debt has been repaid or the attachment has become void by reason of the bankruptcy.

The creditors ("crediteuren")

Each creditor in the bankruptcy of the debtor will be in doubt as to whether or not he will be paid. As was mentioned earlier, Netherlands law has the principle of the equal treatment of creditors or "paritas creditorum" although there is an exception in the case of preference creditors (s3:277 BW). A distinction must be made, however, between "estate" creditors (boedelcrediteuren), "separatists" (pledgees and mortgagees), "preferential" creditors and ordinary unsecured creditors.

Estate creditors ("boedelcrediteuren")

This category of creditors consists of creditors whose debt came into existence by reason of, or after the bankruptcy (H.R. 28 November 1930, N.J. 1931, 253 "Teixeira de Mattos"). Examples include the costs/salary of the curator, rent and the salaries of employees due after the bankruptcy. These "estate costs" have preference over all other creditors.

"Separatists" ("separatisten")

On p456 above, we dealt with the real rights of the pledgee and mortgagee. We saw that, in principle, these "separatists" can enforce their right as if there were no bankruptcy (s57 F).

Section 58 of the Bankruptcy Act provides that the curator should give the pledgee/mortgagee a reasonable period of time within which to exercise his rights. If this period is allowed to lapse, the curator may sell the assets. In that case, the pledgee/mortgagee is entitled to the net proceeds (F 182). Furthermore, the curator can pay off the debt of the pledgee/mortgagee, and thus release the real right attaching to the asset.

Preferential creditors ("bevoorzechte crediteuren")

Dutch law distinguishes between:

- exceptional preferential creditors (s3:283 BW)
  – where the preference of the creditor attaches to a certain asset (for example, on funds to be paid to the debtor by an insurance company for damages caused to the creditor, in which case the creditor has a preference on those funds); and
- general preferential creditors (s3:288 BW)
  – where the creditors have a preference over all assets (for example, pensions and wages of employees).

As a rule, exceptional preferences have precedence over general preferences.

A very high general preference is accorded to the tax and social security authorities, who will receive distributions after the payment of bankruptcy costs and any mortgagee. Furthermore, the tax authorities have a unique preference on movable goods on the premises of the debtor which are intended for permanent use, such as office equipment, paintings and computers, irrespective of whether they are owned by the debtor. This right constitutes a clear risk, for example, for a company which leases equipment.

In addition, there are the "factual preferential creditors" who are preferential owing to the particular circumstances of their claim. A vendor, having sold under "retention of title" or being able to claim "recht van reclame" (see p456 *supra*), will fall into this category. The Bankruptcy Act, furthermore, specifically provides for right of "set-off" in bankruptcy (s53 F). A creditor is entitled to set-off its debt to the company against its claim against the company if both debts came into existence before the bankruptcy, or resulted from acts prior to the bankruptcy (H.R. 27 January 1989, N.J. 1989, 422).

Furthermore, there is a specific provision (ss3:290 and 6:52 BW and s60 F) regarding the rights of so-called "retentors". This right of retention ("retentierecht") is the right a creditor has not to fulfil his delivery obligations (thus "retaining" goods which are owned by the debtor), pending full payment of the debt. An example of this is a mechanic, who, having repaired a car owned by the debtor, is not obliged to deliver the car to the owner until he has been paid. The curator is entitled to pay the retentor and reclaim the asset for the estate. The curator is also entitled to demand delivery of the asset for the purpose of selling it. If the curator follows this latter course, he must ensure that the retentor is paid first out of the proceeds of the sale.

Unsecured and non-preferential creditors ("gewone crediteuren")
Finally, there are the unsecured and non-preferential creditors. These will receive a pro rata dividend from the estate after all secured and preferential creditors have been paid. In general, however, the unsecured and non-preferential creditors will not recover any substantial part of their debts.

Termination of bankruptcy for lack of assets

The supervising judge can advise the court to terminate ("opheffen") the bankruptcy if the estate does not contain enough assets to pay anything to creditors after disbursement of the bankruptcy costs and tax debts (sl6 F). For legal persons this automatically initiates their "dissolution" and liquidation of a company (s2:19 BW) along the lines discussed above.

The termination ("opeheffing") is published in a daily newspaper and in the Netherlands Official Gazette.

Result of the bankruptcy

Attachment of assets
As mentioned above, bankruptcy is an attachment procedure on all the assets of the debtor on behalf of all creditors. Primarily, it is a restraining attachment which can become an enforcing attachment when followed by liquidation.

Once bankrupt, the bankrupt company loses its entitlement to dispose of, or otherwise control, its estate. All powers and entitlements are vested, from that moment onwards, in the curator. The management and, if applicable, the supervisory board are obliged to co-operate fully with the curator and to give all requested information (sl06 F). If the curator or the supervisory judge is wilfully misled, this constitutes a criminal offence punishable with one year of imprisonment. Furthermore, the directors are not entitled to leave their places of residence without explicit permission from the supervisory judge (s91 F).

Litigation
If the company is involved in litigation at the time of bankruptcy, where the purpose of the litigation is something other than payment from the bankruptcy estate (s28 F), the suit may be taken over by the curator.

If, on the other hand, the suit has as its objective some payment or performance out of the estate, the proceedings will be adjourned to enable the creditor to submit his claim for verification (see *infra*). If verification of the claim is disputed then the suit may be resumed, either against the curator or against a third party creditor who disputed the claim in the verification procedure (H.R. 16 January 1981, N.J. 1981, 155).

Meeting of creditors and verification

A meeting of creditors is convened in court to agree the creditors' claims. The objectives of the meeting are as follows:

- to receive the curator's report on the debtor's assets and liabilities;
- to agree the creditors' claims;
- to consider any composition proposal made by the debtor;
- to nominate a creditors' committee. The creditors' committee will advise the curator and will supervise the administration of the liquidation of the estate; it may examine any documents of the debtor, approve any settlement of litigation, and will, if necessary, approve the continuation of the debtor's business.

All creditors, apart from the "separatists" and estate creditors, must submit their claims for verification. The court will determine in the verification meeting whether or not the claim is valid and if so, for what amount.

Termination of the bankruptcy

Composition

A bankruptcy can terminate through composition (s161 F) without liquidation of the company. If the creditors agree to the composition, the court will incorporate the composition in a court order which will bind all competing creditors.

Liquidation

The bankruptcy can also terminate through liquidation (ss173-194 F). Here, the curator liquidates the assets and pays the creditors out of the proceeds. If no composition is reached in the meeting of creditors, the curator will start liquidating the company immediately. This phase is the "insolvency phase" of the company. The curator will sell the assets, by public auction or privately, if he has permission from the supervising judge to do so (s176 F). He is also entitled to dismiss employees, even if the business of the company is sold as a going concern (E.C. Court of Justice 7 February 1985, N.J. 1985, 900 and H.R. 30 October 1987, N.J. 1988, 191).

On completion of the final distribution of the liquidated assets to creditors the company is dissolved ("ontbonden") and thus ceases to exist for all intents and purposes unless necessary for the completion of the bankruptcy.

International aspects of bankruptcy

It is not uncommon for a Netherlands company to have assets located outside the Netherlands. In this section we shall give a summary of the effect of a Netherlands bankruptcy on those foreign assets.

Basically the Netherlands holds to the principle of the territorial effect of a bankruptcy order, *i.e.* that a bankruptcy (especially the general attachment of the debtor's assets) only affects assets in the country where the bankruptcy was declared, unless there is an international convention providing otherwise. Currently, the Netherlands only has such an international convention with the Kingdom of Belgium. Indeed, the EEC Convention on Jurisdiction and the Enforcement of Judgments in Civil and Commercial Matters 1968 ("EEX") explicitly excludes bankruptcy. A bankruptcy judgment order in the Netherlands is also effective against the debtor's assets located in the overseas territories of the Kingdom.

The result of this territorial effect of Netherlands bankruptcy is that, in principle, creditors are free to seek recovery of their debts individually out of the foreign assets of a bankrupt debtor. However, due to the nature of the bankruptcy order (an attachment on all the assets of a debtor on behalf of all the creditors), section 203 of the Bankruptcy Act provides that, if a creditor has recovered his debt from foreign assets, he must recompense the bankruptcy estate for the recovered amount. Thus, all creditors will profit.

5. Augmenting the assets of the insolvent corporation

Under Netherlands law everybody is free to dispose of his assets in any way he chooses. Thus, in principle, a company may pay one creditor, whilst leaving another creditor unpaid. Under certain circumstances, however, Netherlands law affords an unpaid creditor relief if the debtor has withdrawn assets from its estate, thus prejudicing the rights of the creditor. This relief is called the "Actio Pauliana" (fraudulent conveyance) and is provided for in section 3:45-48 BW outside bankruptcy and in sections 42-49 F for bankruptcy situations. For our purposes here however, we shall deal solely with the bankruptcy situation.

Transactions at risk

As already mentioned, in bankruptcy all rights of control and disposal of the estate are vested in the curator. As his primary task is to satisfy creditors, he can initiate any actions in order to avoid transactions prior to the bankruptcy and which allegedly prejudiced the estate. Section 42 F provides that if certain conditions have been met the curator can claim that a transaction between the debtor and a third party is void on the basis of the Actio Pauliana. The curator will need to prove three requirements:

- the transaction was a voluntary act
- the transaction prejudiced the creditor's rights
- the debtor knew of ought to have known that the transaction would prejudice the creditor's rights

The transaction was a voluntary act

In Dutch case law, it has been held that the act which was intended to effect legal consequences ("rechtshandeling") upon which the transaction was based must have been voluntary, *i.e.* there must have been no legal obligation to enter into the transaction (H.R. 10 December 1976, N.J. 1977, 617). A requirement by law to act, or a contractual obligation to perform, is deemed to be an involuntary transaction. Thus, in principle, if a debtor paid a debt which was due and payable before bankruptcy, this payment cannot be avoided. However there is one exception. The curator can avoid the payment if it can be shown that the payee knew that the bankruptcy of the debtor had been applied for, or that there was collusion between the debtor and the creditor to the prejudice of other creditors (s47 F).

The transaction prejudiced the creditors' rights

In order to determine whether or not the act has prejudiced the rights of the creditors, a comparison must be made between the estate after the transaction took place and what it would have been if the transaction had not taken place. This requirement is fulfilled if the comparison shows that the estate is worse off for the transaction having been undertaken. It is not necessary to show that all creditors have been prejudiced by the transaction.

The debtor knew or ought to have known that the transaction would prejudice the creditors' rights

This is one of the most difficult requirements for a curator to meet. However, section 43 F does provide a legal presumption of knowledge of prejudice. The presumption will arise in any of the following cases for transactions that took place within one year before the bankruptcy:

- when the value of the performance by the debtor substantially outweighs the value of the performance by the creditor; or
- when a debt which was not due and payable was paid or security was provided therefor; or
- when the creditor is either a member of the family of the debtor or his spouse, or the creditor is a managing director, member of the supervisory board or shareholder of the debtor; or
- when the transaction was for no for consideration.

If the transaction is avoided, the creditor must return the asset to the curator. This can either be the actual return of a tangible asset or the payment of damages. If the creditor has disposed of the asset prior to the avoidance, the curator can oblige a third party to return the asset unless the third party acquired the asset in good faith (s51 (2) F).

Set-off ("schuldvergelijking")

Under Dutch law if two persons have mutual debts one to the other, these debts can be set-off ("verrekening" s6:127 BW).

The right of set-off is also applicable in bankruptcy albeit that the Bankruptcy Act requires that both the claim and the debt on the bankrupt company are to have either existed before bankruptcy or to have resulted from acts by the bankrupt company before bankruptcy (s53 F). Importantly, this means that neither debt need have been due and payable at the time of bankruptcy (H.R. 21 January 1983, N.J. 1983, 513). A shareholder is, however, not entitled to set-off an amount still payable upon his shares against a debt owed to the shareholder by the company (s2:80 BW).

Liability of officers

One final remark must be made about the liability of each director of a company that has become bankrupt. If the management ("bestuur") has clearly performed its duties improperly and if it is clear that the failure to manage properly has led to, or been a cause of, the bankruptcy, then the directors are jointly and severally liable for the deficit upon liquidation of the company. If a director can show that the management's improper performance is not attributable to him personally, and that he has not been negligent in taking measures to prevent the consequences, he is not liable. It is also important to note that a court may reduce the amount for which the director is liable if it considers it to be excessive, having regard to the nature and seriousness of the improper performance of the duties as director, as well as taking into account other causes of the liquidation and the manner in which the company is liquidated. Furthermore, the court can reduce the amount of liability of an individual director if, given the amount of time that the director was in office during which the improper performance took place, appears excessively harsh to impose liability on that director. There is a legal presumption that the above conditions are met, for example, if there is no proper bookkeeping or if the annual accounts have not been registered in time with the chamber of commerce. A specific regulation applies to claims of the tax and social security authorities. The managing directors are obliged by law to notify these authorities if and when they foresee that the debtor will not be able to fulfil its obligations towards them. If the managing directors fail to do so, they become in consequence personally liable for these obligations.

6. Public control over insolvent corporations

In the Netherlands, the only public control over the bewindvoerders or curators appointed is exercised by the court and, specifically, by the supervisory judge who is usually appointed. The court will adjudicate where any complaint is made by the creditors, officers or shareholders in respect of the conduct of the above officials or where there is a dispute between those officials and the supervisory judge. The bewindvoerders and curators are normally appointed from lawyers in private practice working in the insolvency field.

Contents of Chapter 11

CORPORATE INSOLVENCY LAW IN NORWAY

1.	**Introduction**	481
	Sources of law	481
2.	**Corporations**	483
	Characteristics	483
	Management	484
	Ownership – capital	486
	New legislation	487
	Financing and security for creditors	487
	Available information	488
	Other business entities	489
	Debt collection and asset recovery	490
3.	**Survival of the insolvent corporation or its business**	492
	Debt arrangements – purpose and effect	492
	Procedure	493
	Powers and duties of the debtor	498
	Position of officers and shareholders/owners	499
	Termination	499
4.	**Termination of the corporation: insolvent liquidation**	500
	Liquidation	500
5.	**Augmenting the assets of the insolvent company**	511
	Introduction	511
	Transactions at risk	511
	Personal liability of officers	515
6.	**Public control over insolvent corporations**	516
	Licensing and control of the appointee	516
	Examinations and investigations	516
	Publicity and records	517

Chapter 11

CORPORATE INSOLVENCY LAW IN NORWAY

Gerhard Holm and Berit Stokke,

Thommessen Krefting Greve Lund

1. Introduction

Sources of law

The law in Norway is based on a system of codified law and the principal source in any particular area of law will be the relevant Statute. A second important source of law will be found in decisions of the courts on the application of the statute law. The main source of Norwegian insolvency law is the Act on Debt Arrangements and Corporate Insolvency of 8 June 1984 (the "Insolvency Act") in force in Norway since 1 January 1986. The Insolvency Act is divided into two main parts: the first concerns debt arrangements (arrangements between the creditor and debtor) conducted through a court appointed administrator (where the purpose and outcome is not necessarily liquidation of the company); the second concerns corporate insolvency or bankruptcy, *i.e.* insolvent liquidation of the assets and debts of a company or individual with the help of a liquidator appointed by the court.

The rules for debt arrangements, insolvent liquidation and bankruptcy apply to individuals and companies which are in a critical financial situation or insolvent. In this chapter, the term "corporate insolvency" or "insolvent liquidation" is used for the compulsory liquidation of a company which is insolvent. The Insolvency Act sets out the procedure to follow but also contains provisions of substantive law. However, the main source on substantive insolvency law is the Act on Debt Recovery dated 8 June 1984 in force from 1 January 1986 ("the Recovery Act"). The Recovery Act sets out:

- which of a debtor's assets are protected from debt recovery;
- the criteria for establishing the invalidity of certain of the debtor's dispositions made within a certain period of time prior to the appointment of an administrator or liquidator;

- provisions relevant to preferred creditors; and
- provisions on the consequences of liquidation for the continuation of the business of the company.

The Insolvency Act and the Recovery Act were passed to codify the old Insolvency Act 1863 and the court practice that developed around it. To date there are not too many decisions made by the Supreme Court of Norway relevant to interpretation of the Insolvency Act and the Recovery Act, because they are relatively "young".

A third source of law is contained in the regulations issued by the Ministry of Justice under the Insolvency Act and the Recovery Act, and the preparatory works, (in particular a Norwegian Official Report from 1972) which preceded the Acts.

The Insolvency Act deals with corporate insolvency and several creditors' joint efforts to recover debts. The relevant source of law in connection with a single creditor's recovery of a debt is the Enforcement Act of 26 June 1992 which has provisions on the establishment of legal charges, enforced sale of assets, and so on.

The "insolvency court" in Norway is the local city or country court. When dealing with bankruptcies, insolvent liquidation of companies and debt arrangements, these courts operate as *skifterett*. There is no similar court in England and for translation purposes it will be called the "insolvency court" in this Chapter. The most common form of debt recovery against a company is insolvent liquidation. The Insolvency Court in Oslo dealt with only 19 new debt arrangements in 1993 whereas there were 959 companies which went into insolvent liquidation.

In Norway during recent years there have been a considerable number of so-called "black corporate insolvencies" where companies have ceased operating and have entered into members' voluntary liquidation because of financial difficulties and then been deleted from the Company Registry before the creditors have had time to consider a recovery action. The effect of such "black corporate insolvencies" is, of course, that the debtor uses "financial difficulties" and lack of funds as an easy way out of its debts. Larger corporations with substantial financial creditors often use private (as opposed to public) debt arrangements as a more appropriate way out of difficulties. Such arrangements are based on private agreements with creditors and often include the payment of current trade creditors or large "difficult" creditors and the postponement or rescheduling or even liquidation of the large financial creditors' claims. This way out of a financial crisis has in the past been used with success by the bigger shipowning companies in Norway, because a private debt arrangement very often turns out cheaper and more effective than a public debt arrangement. The rules relevant to a public debt arrangement are frequently applied in a private arrangement.

A members' voluntary liquidation of a company limited by shares will follow the rules set out in chapter 13 of the Joint Stock Companies Act of 4 June 1976 ("the Joint Stock Companies Act"). The rules for other companies are set out in the Companies Act of 21 June 1985 ("the Companies Act").

Norwegian law distinguishes between entities with legal personality ("legal subjects") and those without. Adult individuals and incorporated associations are legal subjects. In Norwegian insolvency law, individuals and certain incorporated associations may be declared bankrupt or insolvent. However in this chapter we will be concerned exclusively with incorporated associations which are incorporated by registration under the provisions of the Act on Registration of Business Corporations of 21 June 1985 ("the Registration Act") with specific emphasis on joint stock companies.

2. Corporations

Characteristics

All entities conducting business in Norway must be entered in the Company Register. The procedure is laid down in the Registration Act and is concluded by the Registrar's issue of a Certificate of Incorporation ("firmaattest"). Anybody can ask for a firmaattest from the Registry and this document contains crucial information about the relevant corporation, such as name, form of liability, capital, directors, managing director, auditors and rights of signature on behalf of the company. The firmaattest is issued on the basis of the documents which are required to be filed with the Registry, and these requirements vary depending on the form of the subject company. However, all companies must notify their name, form of liability, objects, business address, restrictions on transfer of shares or parts and rights of signature.

Norwegian law distinguishes between companies with limited liability and companies where the members have unlimited joint and several liability for the company's debts. The typical limited liability company is a joint stock company, where the liability is limited by shares. These companies are regulated by the Joint Stock Companies Act and are recognised by the abbreviation AS (or A/S) after the company name. The joint stock company can be a listed or private company, but this cannot be deduced from the name. In Norway a joint stock company may have one or several shareholders. There are relatively few listed companies, less than 150 on the Oslo Stock Exchange, and some of the more important Norwegian industrial entities are in fact "closed" joint stock companies owned by one or two families.

The Companies Act regulates unlimited companies and limited partnerships and applies where commercial activity is conducted for the account and risk of one or more participants and where one of the participants has unlimited personal liability for the obligations of the business. In unlimited liability companies all the members have direct unlimited, joint and several liability for the obligations of the company. Such companies are recognised by the abbreviation "ANS" after the company name.

Another form of unlimited liability company is a company with pro rata unlimited liability, *i.e.* the members have direct unlimited and joint liability for the debts of the company, but so that each member can only be claimed pro rata, *i.e.* for a certain percentage of the total debt of the company (the percentage being equal to the members' share of the company). Such companies will have the abbreviation "DA" ("split liability") after the company name. This form of company is frequently used for shipowning businesses.

In addition there are companies with mixed liability, namely silent partnerships and limited partnerships. The limited partnership will have one general partner who has unlimited liability for the company's obligations and one or more limited partners who are only liable to the extent of their called and uncalled capital contribution. Very often the general partner is itself a joint stock company. The Companies Act requires that the general partner's capital contribution be at least 10% of the total registered capital of the limited partnership (see p486 *infra*). The limited partnership will be recognised by the abbreviation KS (or K/S) in its corporate name.

The silent partnership consists of one general partner and one limited partner who is a "silent" partner responsible for a fixed amount of the partnership's debt and whose participation is invisible to third parties or creditors (hence the name "silent partnership"). If the general partner is a sole trader; the silent partnership will appear as a sole trader to the outside world; if the general partner is a joint stock company, the silent partnership appears as a joint stock company.

All the above forms of company, except for the silent partnership, can be the subject of debt arrangements or corporate insolvency (Chapter 4 of the Recovery Act). Creditors of a silent partnership can pursue their claim against the general partner only.

The joint stock company is the most common form of company in Norwegian business life. As at 7 July 1994 there were 116,687 registered joint stock companies, 2,387 registered companies with pro rata liability, 12,836 registered unlimited liability companies and 1,708 registered limited partnerships. The Company Register has advised that between 1 January 1994 and 7 July 1994 1,203 joint stock companies, one limited partnership, two companies with pro rata joint liability and 18 companies with joint several liability went into insolvent liquidation. In this chapter our description of the regulations relevant to corporate insolvency will concentrate on joint stock companies.

Management

The Joint Stock Companies Act contains detailed provisions on the structure and management of a joint stock company.

The highest authority is vested in the shareholders who are required to hold an annual shareholders' meeting. The shareholders' meeting elects and removes directors and auditors, fixes their remuneration, approves the accounts and decides on allocation of profits and losses, including the distribution of dividends. A shareholders' meeting is required in order to change the company's articles of association. The shareholders act in general by majority vote although certain decisions require a qualified majority. For example, a change in the articles of association requires the consent of two-thirds of the votes and the share capital present at the shareholders' meeting. Abolition of the shareholders' right to dividends, increase of the shareholders' commitments towards the company, redemption of shares and differentiating between shares, requires the consent of all the shareholders or the shareholders affected by the decision, as well as consent from two-thirds of the votes and capital present at the meeting.

Immediately below the body of shareholders is the board of directors. Companies with less than NOK 1 million share capital may have only one director whereas the minimum requirement for companies with more than NOK 1 million share capital is three directors. However, it is up to the shareholders to decide how many directors the company should have, provided the minimum requirement is met. The directors must elect a chairman who may be (but is not required to be) an executive director. The articles of association may determine that the shareholders' meeting shall elect the chairman.

The board is elected for two years. There is a quorum when more than half of the directors are present. A valid decision is made by simple majority of those present. The board of directors in companies with more than NOK 1 million share capital must employ a managing director. He is responsible for the daily operations of the company and is under the control of the board of directors. He may, but is not required, to be a member of the board of directors. The board of directors represents the company towards third parties. Often, the shareholders authorise one or two directors jointly to sign on behalf of the company. Such general authorisation will be noted on the firmaattest (corporate certificate issued by the Registrar). While it is common in Norway to have non-executive directors, the Joint Stock Companies Act does not distinguish between executive and non-executive directors. Directors of companies which go into insolvent liquidation may be personally liable to contribute to the company's assets if the insolvency can be ascribed to their fault or incompetence (see pp515-516 *infra*).

Large industrial companies with more than 200 employees also have an employees' or workers' council, a third of those members must be employees. Two-thirds of the members arc elected by the shareholders and one-third from among and by the employees. In companies with a workers' council, it is the workers' council which will elect the directors and the chairman of the board. Under sections 8-20 of the Joint Stock Companies Act, one-third of the members of the workers' council can request that up to one-third (at least two) of the directors should be appointed from among and by the employees of the company. The workers' council is competent to elect the board of directors and will do so in place of the shareholders meeting.

The structure and management of companies governed by the Companies Act (*i.e.* unlimited companies and limited partnerships), will normally depend on the provisions set out in each individual partnership or company agreement. The highest corporate body is the partnership meeting which consists of all the partners. The partnership meeting can agree to appoint a board of directors which will be responsible for running the business of the partnership and which will represent the company and sign on behalf of the company. If there is no board of directors, each partner in an unlimited liability company is entitled to sign on behalf of the company, although alternative arrangements as to how the company or partnership is to be run can be agreed by the partners. The board of directors can employ a managing director who will have to follow instructions issued by the board.

The Companies Act has certain specific provisions relevant to limited partnerships. The highest corporate body is the limited partnership meeting and the general partner will normally be responsible for the organisation of the company. If the limited partnership meeting has decided to appoint a specific board of directors, this board will have the second highest authority in the company. However, the daily conduct of the business of the company is carried on by the general partner. A managing director can be employed either by the general partner or, if there is a board of directors, by the board of directors. The duties of the managing director are defined in the employment contract which will have been agreed either with the board of directors or with the general partner. The general partner is entitled to sign on behalf of the limited partnership. The limited partnership meeting can decide that one or several general partners jointly shall be entitled to sign on behalf of the partnership. However, if the representative body of the partnership is a board of directors, this board can sign on behalf of the partnership, but the general partner will still be able to sign and represent the partnership in the day-to-day conduct of its business. In order to avoid having to have the signatures of all directors, one or several of the directors jointly can be vested with the authority to sign on behalf of the limited partnership.

Norwegian companies do not have a company secretary. The fact that most Norwegian companies are small private companies (often with only one shareholder) means that, although a company has the organs discussed above, there will be overlap between the functions of the shareholders, directors and the managing director.

Ownership – capital

The minimum share capital of a company limited by shares is NOK 50,000 of which 50% must be paid up on registration of the company and the rest within one year after registration. There may be two or more classes of shares, "A" and "B", and so on. Where there are two or more classes of shares, it is permissible to confer voting rights on the holders of only one of the classes of shares. Rights to dividends may also vary between one class and another.

A limited partnership is required to have a fixed company capital. Twenty per cent must be paid upon registration and another 20% within two years thereafter. The general partner must contribute at least 10% of the capital. When a limited partnership is in financial difficulties the first step will be to call for payment of the unpaid capital. Before giving a loan, lenders will normally require that there be a certain ratio between debt and equity including, in a limited partnership, uncalled capital.

When a joint stock company goes into liquidation the company's creditors must be paid off before the shareholders receive anything. The limited partners in a limited partnership are only responsible for the amount of their investment as represented by the nominal value of their parts, in practice the uncalled part of their capital contribution, whereas the general partner can be sued without limit.

New legislation

As a consequence of the European Economic Area (EEA) Agreement between the EFTA and EU countries the Norwegian authorities have started to revise the Norwegian Joint Stock Companies Act. The proposed changes will problably not be passed until next year, and it is therefore impossible to give a detailed description of the changes that will be adopted. However, it is reasonable to expect that the new Joint Stock Companies Act will be in accordance with various EC Directives on company law.

Financing and security for creditors

Shareholders and partners in limited partnerships advance money to the company by paying for shares or by contributing to the company capital, whereas any other "investor" advances money by way of a short or long term loan, very often in exchange for a promissory note evidencing the debt. Under Norwegian law certain promissory notes can be used as a basis for recovery without first obtaining a judgment evidencing the debt (see p490 *infra*).

The creditors' interest in the company comprises repayment of the money advanced with interest. In the case of some loans it is stipulated that, in certain circumstances, the outstanding loan will or can be converted into share capital.

It is common to distinguish between financial and trade creditors. Financial creditors will normally require security over one or more of the company's assets as a condition for advancing money to the company. Trade creditors, on the other hand, will often require that the title to the goods supplied remain with the supplier until the goods have been paid for. The most common form of security for a financial creditor is, of course, a registered charge over the company's title to real property or a long term leasehold, often a factory or warehouse. If the mortgage is registered in the local "property registry" where the property is situated the company cannot dispose of or recharge the property without the consent of the mortgagee. A charge over a business property can include a charge over the company's operational assets such as machinery, inventory, tools, trade-marks, patents, patterns, acquired intellectual property rights, and so on, which often are the most valuable security. Such charges will then have to be registered in the local property registry, together with the charge over the property itself (the title or a long term transferable lease) in order to obtain protection from creditors. Separate charges can be established in stock in trade, cars, lorries, and moveable machinery, and all these charges must be registered in the centralised Moveable Property Registry in order to obtain protection.

In addition a company can create security over all or part of its present and outstanding claims. Such a charge should also be registered in the Moveable Property Registry in order to obtain protection.

Some of the charges referred to above share the attribute that it is impossible to identify the charged assets except in general terms, *i.e.*"operational assets such as machinery ....," and "all present and future outstanding claims", and so on. The giving of such charges is intended to enable the debtor to carry on business as usual until a default situation arises or until the company becomes insolvent. Business as usual implies the power to transfer any of these charged assets.

A consequence of the provisions described above is that most of a company's assets can be used as security. However it is worth noting that these various forms of charges obtain protection by registration in various registries (local property registries, ship registries and the centralised Moveable Property Registry), but that none of them is registered in the Central Company Registry. A general charge over all of a company's assets as such is not recognised under Norwegian law.

In order to be valid, trade creditors' retention of title clauses must be agreed, at the latest, on delivery of the goods or immediately thereafter in writing. A supplier's retention claim will rank before a creditor who has a registered charge over stock in trade. Retention of title clauses can only be validly created in goods not registrable in the Moveable Property Registry, (i.e not in relation to the supply of cars, lorries, or moveable machinery) and in goods that are not intended to be sold on.

Another very efficient security for a creditor is the right of set-off which applies to creditors who owe money to the company. These creditors can set off their own debt to the company in their claim against the company and thereby, depending upon how much they owe the company, be paid in full.

Available information

Under the Registration Act, almost all business entities with a commercial purpose must be registered in the centralised Company Registry. Sole traders engaged in buying and selling goods or sole traders who employ more than five principal employees must also be registered.

The documentation that the Registrar requires in order to register the business entity will, as already stated, vary depending on which form of company is being registered. The specific filing requirements have also been mentioned above. All documents filed are available to the public.

Any termination of a business by voluntary or insolvent liquidation must be notified to the Registrar.

As mentioned above, charges over a company's assets are registered in the various registries and these must all be checked for relevant entries.

All companies conducting commercial business must file their annual accounts in the Accounts Registry within a specified time after the end of their accounting year . The annual accounts will contain the balance sheet, the profit and loss account, the report from the directors of the board of the company and a declaration from the company's auditor. Documents which are filed in the Accounts Registry are public and can be inspected by any member of the public.

Information about the creditworthiness of companies can be obtained from credit information agencies. They can assist in obtaining financial information about the company but their information is normally based on information from the various public registries. With the consent of a company it is possible to obtain financial information from the company's bankers.

None of the public registries referred to above will reveal the identity of the shareholders. All they will reveal is what follows from the company's constitutional document, *i.e.* for joint stock companies, the initial shareholders. Joint stock companies however have shareholders' registries which list the beneficial shareholders of shares . They are public and can be inspected at the company's registered office. Registration of nominee shareholders is only permitted subject to consent from the Ministry of Finance. When a joint stock company is listed on the Stock Exchange, information about the shareholders can be obtained through Stock Exchange.

Other business entities

As the 1994 statistics show, the joint stock company is by far the most popular form of organisation for the conduct of business in Norway. The other common corporate forms such as limited partnerships, unlimited liability companies and pro rata liability companies, have already been described. Banks and insurance companies are also incorporated but are subject to requirements set out in the special legislation relevant to these types of businesses (such as the Commercial Bank Act, the Savings Bank Act, the Insurance Companies Act, the Act on Financial Institutions, and so on). In general these business entities cannot be put into insolvent liquidation but can be put under so-called "public administration". Several of the provisions of the Insolvency Act do apply, however, for corporations under public administration. Individuals conducting business as sole traders may be declared bankrupt.

The provisions relevant to the winding up of companies vary depending on the type of company in question and whether it is a voluntary or compulsory liquidation. However, as stated above, joint stock companies and companies subject to the Companies Act must, in the case of an insolvent liquidation, follow the winding up procedure set out in the Insolvency Act. The voluntary liquidation of these companies must follow the provisions of either the Joint Stock Companies Act or the Companies Act. It should be noted that a creditor cannot request the voluntary liquidation of such companies. The term "voluntary liquidation" is defined in this chapter as the ordinary winding up procedure directed by the company itself. The board of directors of a company may decide to put the company into voluntary liquidation because of financial difficulties or lack of funds and will avoid insolvent liquidation pursuant to the Insolvency Act if none of the creditors take action. If there are no assets in the company, there is no inducement for a creditor to take action.

The obvious advantage of carrying on business through the form of a joint stock company is that the participants will be able to limit their liability, *i.e.* if the company incurs debt beyond its assets the losers are the creditors and not the shareholders. Another obvious advantage is that the company is a legal subject and can as such enter into contracts. Further, the shareholders can get out of the business by transferring their shares.

Debt collection and asset recovery

Claims arising out of commercial contracts fall into two categories: personal claims and secured claims. Personal claims are those against the individual or the debtor company whereas secured claims will be personal claims which are secured by a charge over one or more of the company's assets. The secured creditor has in fact two options; he can either pursue his personal claim or he can seek recovery by way of sale of the secured asset and thereby recover his claim from the sale proceeds. Obviously if the company is in a bad financial situation the secured creditor will always seek recovery through disposal of the actual charged assets and it is only when the proceeds from this sale do not cover fully his claim that he will fall back on his personal claim on the company and use that as a basis for claiming the remaining part of the outstanding debt.

Personal creditors

The most common procedure for the personal creditor is to seek judgment from the court in order to establish that the money is owing and thereafter seek to enforce this judgment through the courts and thereby obtain payment.

Some creditors can enforce payment of their claim without first obtaining a judgment establishing the debt, namely in cases where the debtor has issued a promissory note as evidence for the debt and acknowledged in writing that the payment can be enforced without prior judgment. In order to be enforcible without prior judgment such document has to be witnessed by two witnesses. Most mortgage documents will be a combined document, *i.e.* a mortgage document and also a promissory note allowing the creditor to use the mortgage deed itself directly for enforcement purposes.

A creditor who has obtained judgment that he is owed a certain sum of money will then have to apply to the local sheriff or bailiff at the place where the company is domiciled and request a legal charge over any of the debtor's assets. This "enforcement charge" will then be registered and will have the same effect as a fixed contractual charge although it will, of course, rank after any prior registered fixed contractual charges. After a certain time the creditor can require a sale of the charged goods and thereby obtain payment of his outstanding debts from the sale proceeds. (Whether or not the creditor obtains payment depends, of course, on the value of the actual assets and the number of other charges registered over these assets.)

Secured creditors

The normal procedure followed by a creditor with a charge over any of the company's fixed or moveable assets is to request a sale of the actual subject asset and thereby obtain payment of the debt out of the proceeds (similar to the procedure to be followed for an enforcement charge (see above)). Any surplus money which derives from the sale must be accounted for to the debtor.

The sale will normally take place upon the request from the creditor to the courts. Certain charges may also entitle the creditor to take control of the actual asset and use it or operate it and then seek recovery of the outstanding debt by using the operational income. This method of debt recovery is particularly practical for vessels and real estate. In cases where the creditor has secured his claim by a charge over the debtor company's outstanding claims, the creditor can obtain recovery through collection of the money owing under the outstanding claims. This latter form of recovery does not involve the court at all.

A creditor who has delivered goods to the debtor company on condition that the title to the sold goods remains with the creditor until full payment has been made may, as long as the retention of title clause has been validly entered into, seek a judgment through the courts which entitles him to have the goods redelivered to him. In consumer relations, *i.e.* when a consumer has purchased goods on credit, the creditor may request return of the goods without going through the courts. The conditions are that a written agreement on retention of goods has been entered into, that at least 20% of the purchase price has been paid in cash (for goods valued at more than 10% of NOK 34,000) and that the agreement contains information on the cash price of the item, minimum cash payment, credit costs, (*i.e.* costs of interest), credit price, (*i.e.* the aggregate of the cash price and the credit costs) and credit period.

In cases where the creditor has obtained security by way of money deposited with him, he can seek recovery of the deposited money without assistance from the courts.

Cross jurisdictional procedures

Norway has acceded to various conventions with other western European countries regarding recognition and enforcement of foreign judgments. However, the most important of them is the Lugano Convention between all the EU and EFTA countries, as it supersedes most provisions in the other conventions that Norway has with other western European countries.

The rule is that any judgment for an outstanding debt made in a convention country can be enforced in Norway without any special procedure or leave being required. If no convention applies, and the parties have not entered into any valid agreement regarding venue, the rule is that a foreign judgment is not automatically enforceable in Norway.

A foreign creditor who wants to pursue a claim in Norway based on a judgment from a non-convention country will have to bring a claim in Norway based on the original cause of action. The foreign judgment will, of course, have great evidentiary effect unless the judgment was obtained in circumstances which, according to Norwegian law, make it contrary to public policy.

Norwegian enforcement authorities such as the Insolvency Court and the local bailiff only have jurisdiction over assets situated in Norway. Furthermore, only companies registered in the Company Registry which have their principal place of business in Norway can be put into insolvent liquidation in Norway.

Whether or not the liquidator can attack the company's assets situated abroad will depend on the legislation in the actual country where the assets are and whether there is a convention between Norway and that country. At present Norway is a party to only one convention on insolvent liquidation, namely a convention dated 7 November 1933 between Norway, Denmark, Iceland, Finland and Sweden. Under this convention, a liquidator of a company in insolvent liquidation in Norway can freeze all the company's assets in all the Nordic countries (i.e the parties to this convention). In cases where there is no convention, the liquidator is still obliged to try to recover all the assets of the company regardless of where the assets are situated, whether in Norway or abroad. Whether the liquidator will actually be in a position to seize assets abroad will then depend on the rules and regulations and, perhaps, the cooperative spirit in the country where the asset is situated.

If a foreign company which has assets in Norway is put into insolvent liquidation abroad, it does not lose its right of disposal over assets in Norway and it may be possible for individual creditors to seek recovery via assets in Norway. A foreign liquidator will, however, probably be recognised as entitled to sue in Norway as a representative for the creditors and thereby to enforce charges over the debtor company's Norwegian assets.

3. Survival of the insolvent corporation or its business

Debt arrangements – purpose and effect

The purpose of debt arrangements is normally to prevent liquidation of the debtor company. Through a debt arrangement the company may have a chance to overcome its financial difficulties and become a healthy enterprise again.

There are several reasons why unnecessary liquidation should be avoided. First, when a company is put into insolvent liquidation and all the assets are sold piecemeal, value such as know-how, goodwill and the composition of the factors of production is lost in the process.

Secondly, insolvent liquidation of a company is a time-consuming and costly process and the creditors, or at least those without preference of security, will usually gain little or no financial return.

Thirdly, the liquidation of a company is, from a social viewpoint, hard for the people involved – including employees who become unemployed and other companies who may suffer financial problems as a result. Hence, in situations where the company in debt has a fair chance of survival, a liquidation should be avoided if at all possible.

As already mentioned, two options are available to a company which wants a debt arrangement. One option is to try to reach a private arrangement with the creditors. Alternatively the company can try to obtain a debt arrangement under Part I of the Insolvency Act.

The purpose of Part I is to protect the company and to assist it in reaching a permanent arrangement with its creditors. To benefit from this regime, the company itself must apply to the Insolvency Court, follow the requisite procedure and satisfy the various conditions (see *infra*).

The main effect of the debt arrangement proceedings under the provisions of the Insolvency Act is that the company will be in a better bargaining position in relation to its creditors than under a private arrangement. These provisions give the company, together with the majority of its creditors, power to impose a debt arrangement on other dissenting creditors.

These provisions also give the company protection against its creditors since during the debt arrangement proceedings, the creditors can neither individually nor collectively enforce their claims against the company through the courts.

Another important effect of the debt arrangement proceedings is that the application to the Insolvency Court for such proceedings settles the cut-off date, which is crucial for revoking certain dispositions in a subsequent insolvent liquidation of the company (see pp511-516 *infra*).

To sum up, therefore, a debt arrangement order made under Part I of the Insolvency Act, gives an insolvent company:

- the power to impose an agreement on dissenting creditors;
- a moratorium on claims against it; and
- the basis on which certain unfair pre-liquidation transactions can be set aside.

None of these advantages arise under a private debt arrangement.

However, private debt arrangements are used much more frequently than debt arrangement proceedings, partly because a debt arrangement under supervision by the Insolvency Court can be costly. The court can require the company to make an advance payment to the court to cover costs which are not covered by ordinary court fees or, alternatively, to put up security to cover these costs. However the party primarily responsible for the costs is the debtor company and, if it cannot pay, the government will pay the expenses. The reasoning behind this is that a debtor's lack of funds should not hinder debt arrangement proceedings.

Procedure

Introduction

Debt arrangement proceedings under the Insolvency Act consist of three steps:

1. a non-public phase during which the company's financial position is assessed and where the company prepares a proposal for settling the debts with the court-appointed supervisory committee.
2. still a non-public phase – where the company and the creditors negotiate a voluntary debt arrangement. In order to reach such an arrangement, all the creditors must agree.
3. if the parties do not reach an agreement – a public phase during which the company and the creditors negotiate a compulsory debt arrangement or re-scheduling of the debt. If this third phase does not succeed, the company goes into insolvent liquidation.

Pre-conditions

To start debt arrangement proceedings the company must apply to the Insolvency Court (s2 of the Insolvency Act). The application must contain :

- a short statement concerning the cause of the financial problems and a proposal for the settlement of the debts;
- a list of the company's assets and debts, including the names of all creditors (secured and unsecured); and
- a statement as to how the company's accounts are arranged. The Insolvency Court can request further information from the company and the creditors.

Two substantial conditions must be fulfilled before the Insolvency Court can consent to debt arrangement proceedings. First, the company seeking an arrangement must be "illikvid", *i.e.* not able to pay its debts as they fall due. Second, there must be an expectancy or a fair chance that the company may obtain debt re-scheduling arrangements with its creditors.

The company need to be solvent in order for debt arrangement proceedings to apply.

The Insolvency Court's decision to reject an application for debt arrangement proceedings can be appealed against by the debtor company. On the other hand creditors cannot appeal against the Court's consent to debt arrangement proceedings.

Creditors' involvement – the "supervisory committee"

When the Insolvency Court has consented to the debt arrangement proceedings, it must appoint a "supervisory committee" immediately. It may however, wish to consult informally various creditors or groups of creditors about the composition of the supervisory committee prior to the appointment. On the recommendation of the supervisory committee, the Insolvency Court must appoint an auditor unless the Insolvency Court decides that one of the members of the supervisory committee can act as auditor. The auditor is required to audit the company's accounts and business and make a report.

The supervisory committee's main tasks are to:

- assist the company in the efforts to reach an agreement; and
- to represent and protect the creditors' interests.

The supervisory committee must analyse and report on the company's financial position (s21 Insolvency Act). This report is an important document in the debt arrangement proceedings. The supervisory committee must also co-operate with the authorities in order to ensure that the interests of the employees and the public (*i.e.* claims for tax, VAT, etc) are protected.

Upon appointment, the supervisory committee contacts all known creditors and

- informs them of the debt arrangement proceedings, and of the committee's appointment; and
- asks the creditors to register their claims.

The supervisory committee consists of a chairman, (normally a lawyer) and between one and three members appointed from among the creditors. If the majority of the employees of a larger company or the trade union demands to be represented on the supervisory committee, the Insolvency Court is obliged to appoint one representative from among the employees. One of the members of the supervisory committee should as far as is possible have professional knowledge of the business of the company.

Decisions by the supervisory committee require a majority vote of its members. If there is no majority, the chairman has the casting vote. The supervisory committee can also, at its own discretion, authorise the chairman to make decisions on matters that are not of major importance for the company.

The company, the creditors or a member of the supervisory committee can challenge a decision made by the supervisory committee and the Insolvency Court.

Result of debt arrangement proceedings

If the company and the supervisory committee believe that a scheme for setting the debts might be approved, they must propose such a scheme. There are no formal requirements for the proposal other than that it must be in writing; the Insolvency Act only lists what the scheme may include, such as postponement on repayment of debts, disposal or liquidation of all or part of the company's assets without the release of the debtor's commitments which are not liquidated, or a combination of the two. It is possible to keep secured and legally preferred claims outside the scheme. The proposal is then sent to the creditors who must be given at least two weeks within which to respond.

If all the creditors accept the scheme, or if three-quarters of the aggregate value of the claims and no creditor objects, the supervisory committee notifies the Insolvency Court and the debt arrangement proceedings are then formally terminated. If only some of the creditors agree, the company may make a new proposal with the approval of the supervisory committee (s25 Insolvency Act).

If the company fails to obtain the consent of all the creditors , it may try to obtain a compulsory settlement of the debts through the provisions on compulsory debt arrangements contained in Chapter 6 of the Insolvency Act.

Compulsory debt arrangements

Procedure

The company must apply to the Insolvency Court for consent to start negotiations with the creditors on a compulsory arrangement. The company must show that it has the support of at least two-fifths of the known creditors with voting rights representing at least two-fifths of the aggregate amount of outstanding claims entitled to vote on a proposal for settling its debts.

If the Insolvency Court consents to the request for a compulsory debt arrangement, the supervisory committee must immediately publicise the opening of such proceedings and ask the creditors again to notify it and specify their claims. At the same time a date must be given for a meeting of the creditors for the purpose of voting on the debtor company's arrangement proposal. The opening of the proceedings must be published in the Norwegian Gazette and be registered in the various registries mentioned above. The supervisory committee can seek to revoke certain of the debtor company's dispositions made prior to the cut-off date, *i.e.* the date the court received the application for debt arrangements. The time limit and a specification of which dispositions can be revoked are discussed at pp511-516 below.

Majority voting requirements

To become binding the proposal must be approved by a majority in value and number of the creditors. The majority required varies, depending on the amount of the debt which the proposal would offer to repay. The proposal must offer a minimum 25% payment to each creditor (s30 Insolvency Act). If a minimum 50% payment to the creditors is proposed, the proposal requires approval by at least three-fifths of the voting creditors representing at least three-fifths of the aggregate outstanding debt held by creditors having voting rights. If less than 50% payment is proposed, a 75% majority of voting creditors representing at least 75% of the aggregate outstanding debt is required. If the proposal contains a suggestion to liquidate part of the business, a 75% majority is required.

All known claims are considered for voting purposes even if they are not registered with the supervisory committee. Certain claims, however, do not confer voting rights. These include : secured claims (claims secured by charges over assets, retention of title clauses); preferential claims; claims that will be satisfied through set-off and conditional claims; claims acquired after the opening of the debt arrangement proceedings; and claims that will be fully satisfied by the proposed arrangement. (The compulsory debt arrangement is not binding on these claims anyway.) Any dispute as to voting power is decided by the Insolvency Court.

Result

The supervisory committee shall within a week after the meeting held for the purpose of voting on a compulsory debt arrangement scheme, send a report of the meeting with, if possible, a recommendation to the Insolvency Court to confirm the compulsory debt arrangement that has been approved. The supervisory committee must enclose :

- proof that the compulsory debt arrangements proceedings has been made public and that the creditors have been called in accordance with the legal provisions
- the supervisory committee's minute book;
- lists of registered claims presented to the meeting and documentation in support of disputed claims;
- the final debt arrangement proposal from the debtor and the creditors's approval of it;
- other documents presented to the meeting and all objections made against the debt arrangement proposal.

Within three weeks of the receipt of the report from the supervisory committee, the Insolvency Court must hold a meeting to confirm the approved proposal. The debtor and the supervisory committee are invited to attend and, if it is uncertain whether the creditors have approved the proposal, they are also invited to the meeting.

At the meeting the Insolvency Court will resolve any dispute regarding the creditors' voting rights. The Court must reject the proposal (s48 Insolvency Act) if :

- the prescribed procedure has not been followed and it is likely that this failure has influenced the voting result;
- the proposal offers payment of less than minimum dividend or has not been approved by the required majority;
- the proposal does not give equal rights to unsecured creditors who have not consented to subordinate their claims;
- certain creditors have been favoured in the proposal by a promise from the debtor or a third party or if there is evidence that the proposal is not in accordance with the common interests of the creditors.

The Insolvency Court may reject the proposal if the debtor is without good reason absent from the meeting held to vote on the proposal or the meeting held to confirm the proposal, or if the debtor is unwilling to give the court the required information in order to confirm the proposal. The Court can also reject the proposal if, during the last three years prior to the opening of the debt arrangement proceedings, the debtor has violated certain provisions of the Penal Code of 1902 (s281-286) (*i.e.* fraudulent behavior vis-à-vis creditors).

If the Insolvency Court decides to reject the proposal, it must terminate the debt arrangement proceedings and commence compulsory liquidation proceedings. If it decides to confirm the proposal, the confirmation must be given within a week of the meeting held for that purpose. Any creditor affected by the confirmation or the debtor may file an appeal, the time limit for such appeal being two weeks.

The supervisory committee must inform all creditors about the Insolvency Court's confirmation and thereafter publicise the decision.

Powers and duties of the debtor

The commencement of debt arrangement proceedings has a significant impact on the debtor's legal position. The proceedings limit the company's power to continue the business and place it under certain additional duties. For instance , although the company is still in charge of the business, it is now under the supervision of the supervisory committee, and some significant dispositions, such as borrowings, sale and lease of real estate and other assets of significant value, are unlawful without prior consent from the committee (s14(2) Insolvency Act).

Further, the supervisory committee has unlimited authority to impose restrictions and instructions on the company, including rejecting new employment contracts and purchase contracts for new equipment, and ordering the payment of crucial bills, such as telephone, and electricity. However, if the debtor refuses to follow a restriction or an instruction from the supervisory committee, the only available sanction available to the committee is to request the Insolvency Court to terminate the debt arrangement proceedings and commence compulsory liquidation of the company.

If the company acts beyond its powers, any transaction is valid if the third party has acted in good faith. If the third party had knowledge about the debt arrangement proceedings the transaction can still be enforced by law, but a third party in this situation must wait for the completion of debt arrangements before being able to enforce the obligations against the company.

The company must co-operate with the Insolvency Court and the supervisory committee and provide all relevant information about its financial situation and its business. The Court can, if required, order the company to reveal confidential information to the extent that such information is material to the operation of the debt arrangement.

The debtor is obliged to be present at the meeting of creditors when the vote is taken on the proposal for a compulsory debt arrangement. When the debtor is a company it is the board of directors or the representative body of the company who must be present. In practice however, the board of directors may authorise one or more directors or the managing director to represent the board at the meeting.

If the debtor company obtains the approval of the supervisory committee for an amendment to the proposal, a new meeting must be held to vote on the amended proposal. A new meeting must be held within three weeks.

Once the Insolvency Court has confirmed a compulsory arrangement, it may, on request of a creditor, decide that the debtor company shall be under its control until the company has complied with the confirmed arrangement.

Position of officers and shareholders/owners

Unless the debt arrangement proceedings are compulsory (see p496 *supra*) they are not made public, *i.e.* they are not published anywhere. The company must carry on its day-to-day business. For the staff, the officers and labour in general, it is "business as usual" under the proceedings. However, the executive officers of a company inevitably will be involved in the debt arrangement proceedings, for example in providing financial information about the company.

In a company with unlimited responsibility it is the partners' meeting which decides if the company should file a petition for debt arrangements. This decision requires the consent of all the partners unless the partnership agreement provides otherwise. Debt arrangement proceedings in joint stock companies can be decided by the board of directors, through a decision made by simple majority. If this decision is in favour of a compulsory debt arrangement, the board of directors will present the petition to the court. The procedure as to the proposed debt arrangement scheme is the same as that set out above (p496).

Termination

The debt arrangement proceedings can be terminated by the Insolvency Court on request of the debtor company if all the unsecured creditors have consented. The usual reason for such a request is that the debtor's financial position has improved. If the Court grants the request, the owners resume full unrestricted control over the company. The Court can also terminate the proceedings if:

- it is unlikely that a settlement will be agreed;
- the debtor has not, within a reasonable time, filed a proposal for settlement;
- the court rejects an application for a compulsory settlement or refuses to confirm a compulsory settlement agreement; the supervisory committee has requested a termination because the debtor company has breached its duties in the course of the proceedings under the Insolvency Act.

Upon termination of the proceedings, the Insolvency Court will at the same time order the company into insolvent liquidation. The debt arrangement proceedings are final when either a voluntary or compulsory settlement of the debts has respectively been agreed or ordered pursuant to the provisions described earlier in this chapter.

4. Termination of the corporation: insolvent liquidation

Liquidation

This section deals with the insolvency procedure in Norway which leads to the termination of a corporation. Once the liquidation is complete, the corporation's legal personality is lost. Until then, however, during the process of liquidation, the company in insolvent liquidation ("the insolvent company") has its own legal personality which, is different from that of the corporation prior to the commencement of the liquidation process.

The term "liquidation" is used to describe the process by which the company's existence is brought to an end and the company's assets converted to cash and paid to the unsecured creditors.

Types, purpose and effect of liquidation

Types of liquidation
Section 3 described how the total or partial liquidation of a company can be the result of debt arrangement proceedings. It has also been mentioned that a company can be liquidated or cease to exist voluntarily, *i.e.* through a decision by its members. A voluntary liquidation can be motivated by the company's financial difficulties, but can also be caused by a number of other factors. These are described below.

A voluntary liquidation of a company will follow the provisions in the Joint Stock Companies Act or the Companies Act, depending on the form of company in question. If a joint stock company is insolvent, its board of directors may be obliged to request a compulsory liquidation (s13-17 Joint Stock Companies Act; s283a Penal Code) if the creditors are likely to be treated unequally and thereby suffer loss in voluntary winding up proceedings. There are no provisions in Norwegian law which entitle the *creditors* to request a voluntary liquidation of a company based on insolvency.

The shareholders' meeting may, with a two-thirds majority resolve to liquidate the company. In certain circumstances the Insolvency Court must order the liquidation of the company, *i.e.* if the company should be dissolved pursuant to the articles of association and the shareholders have not made the required resolution to dissolve; if the requirement for filing of accounts or board of directors are not complied with; or if no auditor is willing to audit the company's accounts.

When the shareholders resolve to dissolve the company, they must appoint a board of directors to liquidate it. The board of directors must register the company's assets and debts and notify to the Companies Registry the intention to liquidate. All creditors are asked to register their claims on the company within six months and, and during this period, the company may continue its business to the extent that it is required for the purpose of terminating the business. In order to cover the debt the company's assets must be liquidated.

Where the Insolvency Court has ordered the liquidation, the Court replaces the board of directors and deals with the notification, registration of claims and liquidation of assets.

Purpose of insolvent liquidation

The insolvent liquidation has a number of purposes. These are:

- to look after all the creditors' rights and to protect the creditors' common interest from the specific interest of one creditor or other persons. This may include the revocation of certain of the company's transactions undertaken shortly before the liquidation, such as insolvency motivated dispositions, the giving of gifts, extraordinary payments of debts or the granting of security for existing debt during the period (generally three months) prior to the cut-off date (see pp511-516 *infra*).
- to pay off the company's debts and obtain as high a distribution to the creditors as possible.
- to consider the interests of the employees.
- to examine the corporation and the accounting practices.

The fundamental aim of the equal treatment of creditors is subject to the following exceptions :

- A creditor who himself is indebted to the company may normally set off that indebtedness against the money owed to him by the company (ss8-1 to 8-6 Recovery Act).
- A creditor may have claims that are secured by a charge over one or more of the company's assets or by a retention of title clause. Secured creditors are entitled to recover their claims out of the proceeds from the sale of the asset or by ordering the return of the unpaid asset.
- Some creditors may have claims which are preferential under the law (such as salary, tax and claims for VAT) and as such are payable before other claims. Other creditors may have subordinated claims (*i.e.* claims that rank behind other claims, for example, certain lenders).

Effect of liquidation

The source of an insolvent liquidation is an order of the Insolvency Court. The effect of the order is, in general terms, the "confiscation" or "seizure" of all assets of the company and the placing of these under the control of the liquidator (see pp506-506 *infra*). This confiscation lasts until the liquidation is complete. As a result of the court order, the directors of the company lose all power of management of the company, as well as all authority to bind the company (ss100 and 108 Insolvency Act). The directors are obliged to assist the Court and the liquidator in the proceedings.

The winding up order has retrospective effect. The date on which the petition for winding up was presented to the Court is the cut-off date in relation to the time limits relevant to setting aside transactions, etc (s1-2 Recovery Act and pp511-516 *infra*). If the commencement of the insolvent liquidation is the consequence of unsuccessful debt arrangement proceedings, the cut off date is the day the petition for debt arrangement proceedings was presented to the Insolvency Court. However, the company retains its authority over its assets until the Insolvency Court has made an order to commence the liquidation of the company. The Insolvency Court may in certain circumstances order that the debtor's authority over the company shall be frozen until the Court's order has been made. This is in many ways a temporary injunction that will freeze the assets of the company pending the Insolvency Court's decision. Such an injunction may be requested by the creditors or can be made at the Court's discretion. However the Court may only make an order to this effect if it is likely that the debtor will dispose of the assets to the detriment of the creditors. This order will be registered and will normally be void if the Insolvency Court rejects the petition for insolvent liquidation (s75 Insolvency Act).

The insolvent company is bound by dealings by the directors and third parties made in good faith on the third day (at the latest) after the commencement of the liquidation was announced in the Norwegian Gazette. This rule applies for a maximum of ten days (which is the maximum number of days allowed to elapse before the announcement of the liquidation) after the commencement of the liquidation.

Procedure of liquidation

Commencement of insolvent liquidation

Chapter 8 of the Insolvency Act lists the conditions which must be fulfilled before the court can order the company to be put into liquidation.

A winding up petition can be filed by the debtor or by a wholly or partly unsecured creditor (s60 Insolvency Act).

In the petition, the petitioner must allege and offer evidence for the allegation that the company is insolvent. In Norwegian law, the company is insolvent when it is both "illikvid" and "insuffisient". The term "illikvid" is defined as the company's continuing (*i.e.* not merely temporary) inability to pay debts as they fall due. A company is "insuffisient" if the liabilities exceed assets.

According to sections 62 and 63 of the Insolvency Act there is a legal presumption of insolvency if

- the company acknowledges that it is insolvent;
- a creditor has served an insolvency notice on the company asking for payment of an overdue, undisputed claim; or
- according to section 62, unsuccessful individual debt recovery actions over the last three months prior to the presentation of the request for a compulsory liquidation have been undertaken, regardless of the size or number of claims.

Creditors whose claims are :

- fully secured by the debtor company's assets;
- fully secured by a third party and a petition for a winding up order will be contrary to the terms of that security,
- not due for payment *and* secured by a third party, cannot file a petition for a compulsory winding up order (s64 Insolvency Act).

The company itself or the creditor requesting the order has to make a cash payment to the court as security for the costs of the proceedings. Currently the amount is NOK 20,000. In many cases insolvency proceedings are never initiated because nobody wants to pay this amount. In practice, the majority of the liquidation proceedings are initiated by employees, because they do not have to pay the NOK 20,000 fee, or by the tax or excise authorities.

Liquidation proceedings are initiated by an application to the Insolvency Court. The application has to be in writing and must state the circumstances on which the application is based (s66 Insolvency Act). If the debtor company is initiating the proceedings, a statement of assets and liabilities, the names and addresses and a description of the creditors, (including the exact date of creation of the debts) and any charges must be included in the application.

The Insolvency Court must call a hearing regarding the opening of an insolvent liquidation as soon as possible and, preferably within a week of receipt of the petition. If the debtor has initiated the order, he must be called to the hearing. If a creditor has started the process, the creditor and the debtor will be called.

According to section 72 of the Insolvency Act, the Insolvency Court shall as soon as possible after this hearing resolve whether liquidation proceedings shall commence or not. If the debtor company has initiated the proceedings, the Insolvency Court will resolve the question on the day of the hearing. The Court may also make the order on the day of the hearing when a creditor has initiated the proceedings, except in cases where strong objections against insolvent liquidation have been made. In this case the Court might need a few days to consider the application. If the Insolvency Court grants an order, the winding up proceedings are deemed to have commenced on the date of that order.

The order is made public by being registered in the Company Registry, the Moveable Property Registry, the Property Registry and in other relevant registries, such as the Ship Registry if the company owns ships. It is also advertised in appropriate newspapers, in the Norwegian Gazette and in a newly established Bankruptcy Register (ss78, 79 and 144 Insolvency Act). The winding up proceedings take place under the supervision of the Insolvency Court and under the management of various appointed entities strongly influenced by the creditors.

Organisation of the liquidation process

In practice the liquidator is the essential figure in the liquidation proceedings. He will co-operate with the creditors and report to the Insolvency Court. The

Court can in turn instruct the liquidator to present certain matters to the creditors' meeting. This is a meeting of all creditors held under the guidance of the Court. The resolutions adopted by the creditors' meeting are binding on the other bodies in the proceedings, unless the resolutions are changed or abolished by the Court. All creditors are qualified to vote at the creditors' meeting to the extent that their claims are unsecured and not preferential (see *infra*).

The practical management of the liquidation proceedings is carried out by the liquidator, who normally is a lawyer (see pp505-506 *infra*). Immediately after the commencement order the Insolvency Court will appoint a temporary liquidator. He is appointed at the discretion of the Court but the Court will often consult with the creditors, in practical terms, the creditor who has initiated the proceedings. After the first meeting of all the creditors the permanent liquidator must be appointed (normally the temporary appointed liquidator will be appointed permanently).

The creditors' committee consists of one, two or three individuals elected by the creditors and, if requested by unions representing the company's employees, a representative of the employees nominated by the Insolvency Court (s84 Insolvency Act).

The creditors' committee takes care of much the same interests as the liquidator. The liquidator and the creditors' committee form the board of the insolvent company and as such take decisions on all questions of material significance for the liquidation. (However, in practice the liquidator makes most of the decisions and only consults with members of the board when he finds it necessary). The interests to be protected are the common interests of the creditors, the employees and the public interest.

A separate auditor is appointed to audit both the company's business prior to the liquidation and the business of the insolvent company. He is appointed after the first meeting of all the creditors (s90 Insolvency Act). Often a temporary auditor is appointed at the same time as the temporary liquidator. In addition to the financial audit, the auditor shall make an audit report to the creditors.

Creditors' involvement and position

The type and size of each creditor's claim will influence that creditor's involvement and position in the liquidation proceedings.

Once the commencement order has been made, the Insolvency Court will immediately request all creditors to notify their claims within a period of between three and six weeks of receiving the request, and give them notice of the first creditors' meeting which should be held within three weeks of the announcement of the commencement order in the Norwegian Gazette. Creditors who do not give notice run the risk that their claims will not be examined at the first creditors' meeting and consequently of any extra costs incurred by a later examination being charged to them. The late creditor also takes the risk that he will not be able to participate in the possible preliminary distribution of the insolvent company's assets. Further, a creditor's claim will be lost if notice of the claim is not given until after the final distribution of the insolvent company's assets.

The creditors participate in the liquidation proceedings by attending the creditors' meeting and the creditors' committee (see p504 *supra*). Each creditor's voting power and position will depend on the size of the claim and whether the claim is secured or preferential.

There are five main types of claim: secured, preferential, ordinary, subordinated and claims on the insolvent company as such (*i.e.* those incurred during the liquidation process).

The secured creditors can recover payment out of the proceeds of the sale of the secured asset. Alternatively, the liquidator may decide to abandon the actual asset to the benefit of the creditor. Where, however, the secured creditor's claim exceeds the value of the secured assets, that creditor is considered as unsecured for the excess amount.

Debts established by the insolvent company during the liquidation have priority over all claims with the exception of those made by the secured creditors (s9-2 Recovery Act).

Preferential claims consist of certain pension and salary related claims due for a period of up to three months before the cut off date, as well as claims for income tax, VAT and other government department claims due for a period of up to six months before the cut-off date (s9-3 and 9-4 Recovery Act).

Subordinate claims are claims for interest incurred after the cut off date, penal taxes and fines, gifts promised but not fulfilled, etc (s9-7 Recovery Act). Such claims are subordinate to those of the ordinary creditors.

All claims other than those described above are ordinary claims (s9-6 Recovery Act).

Only claims which can expect dividend are entitled to vote. Creditors who can expect full payment or nothing will therefore not be able to vote at the creditors' meeting. Secured creditors can vote for the amount that is anticipated not to be covered by the security (this will, of course, depend on the market value of the security and the size of the claim). Preferential creditors cannot vote if it is clear that they will receive payment in full. If it is clear that the legally preferential claims are the only claims that will receive dividend, only these claims are entitled to vote. It is the Insolvency Court which resolves any dispute on voting rights (s97 Insolvency Act).

At the creditors' meeting a decision is made by simple majority of those present based on the amount of the claims, but so that that majority must represent at least one-fifth of the total aggregate amount entitled to vote. If, as a result, there is no majority, the number of creditors will be decisive.

At the board of the insolvent company, decisions are made by simple majority, and if there is no majority, the liquidator's vote will be binding.

Powers and duties of the liquidator

The liquidator is the person who in practical terms is most important in the liquidation proceedings. He has a responsibility to co-operate with the former management of the debtor company and secure the equal treatment of all claims (s85 Insolvency Act). As far as it is consistent with the common interests of the creditors, he must co-operate with the authorities to protect the interests of the employees and of the public during the liquidation.

As part of the process of liquidation the liquidator must :

- assess the assets of the insolvent company, secure these and protect them against other claimants;
- collect outstanding debts due to the company;
- preserve, enhance and dispose of the assets in the best possible manner;
- compile, assess and rank the claims;
- propose dividend distributions to be approved by the court (s85 Insolvency Act).

In conjunction with the creditors' committee the liquidator must prepare a report containing information on the debtor company's business, accounting principles and the reason for the insolvent liquidation, a statement of the assets and debts of the insolvent company (including guarantee obligations, securities and assets evaluation), a statement as to whether any transactions prior to the cut-off date are voidable and information on whether the company should be prosecuted for any criminal offence due to the business methods it used. The report must also make a recommendation as to whether the debtor should be disqualified from establishing a new company or from acting as executive, non-executive or managing director in a new business for a period of two years (s120 Insolvency Act).

The report must be distributed to the creditors and the company, and a copy must also be sent to the prosecuting authorities if the liquidator and the creditors' committee conclude that a criminal investigation should be made.

The liquidator decides whether or not the board of directors or the managing director of the company shall be present at the creditors' meeting (ss103 and 108 Insolvency Act) and the liquidator can demand to be in charge of all post coming in to the insolvent company (s104 Insolvency Act). If the liquidation proceedings are not completed within one year, the liquidator will account to the Insolvency Court for the course of the liquidation proceedings and file accounts of the insolvent company (s121 Insolvency Act). When the liquidation is complete, final accounts are filed by the liquidator. These accounts are, together with the auditors' report, sent to the Insolvency Court and to the directors of the company. Once the accounts have been approved, the liquidator sends them to all the creditors (s122 Insolvency Act).

The liquidator is entitled to act on behalf of the insolvent company. It cannot be claimed against a third party in good faith that the liquidator has acted contrary to decisions made by the creditors' committee, the creditors' meeting or the Insolvency Court. Neither can it be claimed against a third party in good faith that the liquidator has exceeded his authority in other ways. However, on questions of great importance, the liquidator must consult with the members of the board and the creditors' committee.

Management of the insolvent company

As stated above the bulk of the liquidation proceedings are carried out by the liquidator.

Steps taken on appointment

Once the Insolvency Court has made the winding up order, temporary liquidator will be appointed .

The Insolvency Court must then arrange for a notification of the insolvent liquidation proceedings to be entered in the Bankruptcy Register. Either the Court or the liquidator must ensure that the notification is registered in the various registries and published in the Norwegian Gazette.

The Insolvency Court must as soon as possible register the insolvent company's assets and seize further assets if necessary. The liquidator must take money, valuable papers, etc, into his possession (s80 Insolvency Act) and make all the necessary decisions as to the level at which the business of the insolvent company can continue to operate.

Administration in office

The duties of the liquidator have been described before.

His purpose is to terminate the company's trade or business, but the liquidator may wish to continue certain parts of the business in order to accumulate income for the benefit of the creditors.

According to Norwegian law, the liquidator may be personally liable if he behaves negligently or is in breach of the trust imposed on him as trustee of the insolvent company's assets. He must avoid any conflict between his personal interest and the duty imposed on him as liquidator.

Contractual position

The liquidation proceedings do not *per se* give a party that has entered into a contract with the company prior to the liquidation an immediate right to terminate the contract. If the liquidator finds that a contract is a benefit to the creditors, the insolvent company can elect to continue the contract. However, certain contracts are of such a nature that they cannot be continued, typically certain licensing agreements or partnership agreements. The solvent party may however force the liquidator to declare his position as soon as possible. If there is no benefit in the contract, the liquidator will terminate it, leaving the other party with an unsecured claim against the company.

Contracts for the lease of real property occupied by the insolvent company can be continued without a specific declaration from the liquidator.

As previously stated, the liquidator can enter into contracts after his appointment for and on behalf of the company provided that this is necessary for the purpose of winding up the company.

Realisation of assets

Those assets of the insolvent company which are under the company's control (*i.e.* excluding those which constitute the security of any secured creditors or which can be recovered by claimants who may assert rights under a retention of title provision) are sold to enable the company to distribute the proceeds among the creditors.

Often the liquidator tries try to sell the whole business of the insolvent company as a going concern and obviously this is beneficial to the employees. Normally, the assets are sold by private sale, unless there is reason to believe that a better price can be obtained at public auction.

Employees

Employment contracts

Employment contracts follow the rules relating to creditor contracts described above. The insolvent company has the right to decide whether it wants to continue the contracts with the employees or not.

If the company continues a contract, no default arises simply as a result of the opening of liquidation proceedings. If an employee wants to terminate his contract he must give notice pursuant to the provisions of the Act on Worker's Protection and Working Environment of 1977 ("the Working Environment Act"). The period of notice to be given will depend on the duration of the employment contract and normally varies from one to six months for each party (s58 Working Environment Act).

If the company decides not to continue the contracts, the period of notice which must be given to each employee is not reduced by the liquidation (s59 Working Environment Act).

The company may choose to terminate some contracts and continue others. In this event, the notice given to those employees whose contracts are terminated must explain that the business is being terminated or rationalised and that no alternative employment can be offered (s60 Working Environment Act).

Salary payments

If the insolvent company continues the contracts, the employees' salary claims for the period after the cut-off date are debts established by the company (s7-4 Recovery Act) and will have priority over all other claims with the exception of secured claims (s9-2 Recovery Act).

The preferential nature of employees' pre-liquidation salary claims against the company is subject to certain limitations (s9-3 Recovery Act). To be preferential a claim has to be for salary due within the last three months before the cut-off date. Claims for salary which was due more than three months before the cut-off date are not preferential. Claims other than for salary (such as claims for expenses in connection with the work) are preferential if the claim is for less than six times the average of the amount the employee has earned over the last six months before the cut-off date. Salary claims for the period after the cut-off date are only preferential as far as the claim exceeds other payments the employee has had in the period from the insolvent company.

Claims by the directors of the company and by employees with material influence on the company's business conduct or ownership interests in the company (in practical terms, the managing director), are not preferential.

The Government has, by an Act of 1973, guaranteed the payment of preferential salary claims, but this guarantee is limited to three times the National Insurance Basic Amount, which on 1 May 1994 was NOK 38,080.

Taxation

Tax claims
Tax claims are preferred but rank after salary claims (s9-4 Recovery Act). In general, tax claims are only preferred insofar as they are due within a period of six months before the cut-off date. Additional (penalty) tax claims are subordinated.

Taxation of the insolvent company
In accordance with section 15 of the Tax Act of 1911, the insolvent company is liable to pay tax, but is not liable to pay tax on income or capital gains in relation to the liquidation (s2 Tax Act). Tax shall only be paid on income or capital gains in connection with commercial and industrial activities. The insolvent company continues the debtor's obligation to pay VAT on any sale of assets. When an asset is abandoned to the creditor whose claim is secured in that asset VAT may be avoided.

Distribution
As stated earlier, there are six main types of creditors who will be paid according to the following priority :

1. secured creditors (whose claims will be settled from the assets over which they have security);
2. creditors whose claims arose during the insolvent liquidation;
3. creditors with first-class preferential claims;
4. creditors with second-class preferential claims;
5. creditors with ordinary claims, and
6. creditors with subordinated claims .

If the proceeds from the sale of secured assets exceed the secured claim, the balance will be paid over to the insolvent company. If the proceeds are insufficient to meet the claim, the balance can be treated as an ordinary unsecured claim. However, that asset will normally be abandoned to the creditor and the liquidator and the creditor will have to agree on the size of the uncovered amount. Assets of the company which are subject to retention of title claims and rights of set-off will be returned or discounted by the liquidator once the validity of the claim is established.

The first claim on the assets of the insolvent company is expenses incurred in the liquidation (s9-2 Recovery Act). These have priority over salary claims and tax claims.

Position of shareholders and partners

In unlimited companies and limited partnerships it is the partners' meeting which decides whether or not to put the company into insolvent liquidation. In joint stock companies, it is the shareholders' meeting which makes the decision The board of directors files the application to the Insolvency Court (Joint Stock Companies Act, s13-17).

In a compulsory liquidation the shareholders or the partners only receive repayment of the share capital or company capital if all the creditors have been paid. Repayment of contributed capital is unlikely because that would imply that the company is, in fact, solvent.

Termination

The insolvent liquidation of a company is complete when the Insolvency Court has rendered its final decision on distribution of dividends (s128 Insolvency Act). Such decision is given in a court hearing on the basis of the proposal from the liquidator. The creditors have two weeks in which to appeal against the Court's final decision. If no appeal is filed, the decision is final and subsequent claims will not be considered (s133 Insolvency Act).On recommendation of the liquidator or the board of the insolvent company the Insolvency Court may decide to suspend or discontinue the liquidation proceedings long before they are completed if there are insufficient assets in the insolvent company to cover the costs of liquidation (s135 Insolvency Act).

The liquidator must inform the Company Register when the liquidation is terminated. If the liquidation is suspended or terminated (s128 or 135 Insolvency Act), he must request the Company Registrar to delete the company from the Register. The creditors' committee shall make a proposal to the insolvency court about compensation by way of fee to the members of the creditors' committee.

The insolvent company can be delivered back to the debtor (*i.e.* the directors) if all unsecured creditors consent thereto in writing or of it is proven that all unsecured creditors have been paid in full. The Insolvency Court must make a public decision to give the insolvent company back to its owners. The reason for this termination of the winding up procedure is of course that the winding up procedure has showed that the company in fact is solvent (s136 Insolvency Act).

5. Augmenting the assets of the insolvent company

Introduction

It is a fundamental principle in the insolvent liquidation of any company that all creditors should be treated equally. Apart from obvious exceptions established by the principles which provide for, *inter alia*, secured and preferential creditors, insolvency law is strict in its enforcement of this equality principle and has provided a number of rules for invalidating transactions not compatible with that principle. These rules are contained in Chapter 5 of the Recovery Act which comprises a number of sections designed to regulate all questions relevant to this type of jurisdiction.

The transactions which fall within the scope of these rules can be divided into three groups:

1. gifts and other unilateral dispositions made when a company is or is virtually insolvent;
2. payment of or security arrangements for debts at a time when the company is or is virtually insolvent; and
3. transactions endangering the company's financial situation and where the counterparty is not in good faith in this respect.

These rules aim to protect creditors and, when applicable, empower the liquidator to set aside such pre-liquidation transactions. The effect of the rules is, consequently, to augment the company's assets (see *infra*).

Another way of augmenting the company's assets is to invoke the jurisdiction in company law concerning personal liability of those officers and directors who took part in decisions and transactions to the detriment of the company prior to liquidation . The rules dealing with this issue are largely contained in the Joint Stock Companies Act and are discussed at pp515-516 *infra*.

Transactions at risk

The Act contains three groups of sections which are designed to enable certain pre-liquidation transactions to be set aside: sections 5-2 and 5-4; sections 5-5, 5-6, 5-7 and 5-8; and finally section 5-9. The first two groups are distinguished from each other by the different kinds of transaction they comprise. Section 5-9 is separated from the other two by reason of the standard of proof required. The two first groups do not require evidence as to the counterparty's knowledge of the company's difficult financial situation, but are mainly based on objective criteria. Section 5-9, by contrast, does require such evidence to be produced by the liquidator.

Sections 5-2 and 5-4

The first paragraph of section 5-2 comprises transactions which represent a gift. Any unilateral transaction by the company which cannot be treated as an expenditure (leaving aside relatively small celebration gifts, social contributions and donations of a reasonable amount at the time of donation) will be deemed a gift within the meaning of section 5-2. In addition, transactions which are given in exchange for something fall within the scope of section 5-2 to the extent that the transaction represents a significant undervalue to the company's disadvantage, subject to the qualifications referred to above. If a transaction is held to be a gift within the meaning of section 5-2, the transaction can be set aside if it has taken place within one year of the cut-off date.

The second paragraph of section 5-2 provides for the setting aside of gifts given to a person who (or a company which) has a major ownership interest in the company or takes a major part of its income or has substantial influence on the company by virtue of being its managing director. The time limit here is two years from the cut-off date.

Paragraph 2 of section 5-2 applies to any gift transaction within two years of the cut-off date (as defined above), but only as far as the person or company receiving the gift is not able to prove beyond doubt that the company remained solvent at the time the gift was given. Even though paragraph 2 only establishes a presumption in favour of the liquidator, the shifting of the onus of proof in this way makes it a great deal easier to apply this section.

Section 5-4 is concerned with unreasonable salary payments, *i.e.* payment of salaries and other work remuneration which obviously exceed the commensurate consideration from the company taking into account the work performed and the company's turnover. The amount deemed to be in excess of a commensurate remuneration can be set aside if the conditions set out in the second paragraph of section 5-2 are met. Thus this section only applies to excessive payment to a person related to the company as outlined above in connection with the second paragraph of section 5-2.

Sections 5-5, 5-6, 5-7 and 5-8

Section 5-5 concerns transactions which amount to "extraordinary payments". Payment or part-payment of debts made by the company within three months of the cut-off date can be set aside if the payment was made by unusual means or prior to the due date, or the payment substantially reduced the company's ability to pay its other debts and provided that the payment did not, in all the circumstances, appear ordinary. If such a transaction is made to a person or a company related to the company, as described above in relation to section 5-2, it can be set aside within two years of the cut-off date, provided that it is not proved beyond doubt that the company remained solvent at the time the payment took place. According to the fourth paragraph to section 5-5, pledges or assignments of claims made by the company are to be treated as a kind of payment by the pledgor within this section.

Under the first paragraph of section 5-6, a set-off against a claim of the company created by the acquisition (from a third party) of a counterclaim against the company within three months of the cut-off date, can be set aside. No time restriction applies if the acquisition took place at the time the company was insolvent and the acquirer was not in good faith. According to the second paragraph of section 5-6, a counterclaim that, because of its nature or due date could not have been used for set-off after the cut-off date (*i.e.* in the liquidation proceedings), but which has during the last three months prior to the cut-off date been set-off, can be revoked and if the claimant ought to have had knowledge of the insolvency of the company. No time restriction applies.

The first paragraph of section 5-7 comprises mortgages and other security arrangements made by the company within three months of the cut-off date. Such arrangements can be set aside if:

- the security is created later than the debt which it secures; or
- if the relevant act of protecting the mortgagee against third parties and a liquidator and the establishing of priority, normally by recording the security, did not take place within due time after the requisite debt was incurred or established.

According to the second paragraph of section 5-7 such transactions can be set aside within two years of the cut-off date if the security is created in favour of a related person or company as described above, unless it can be proved that the company was solvent at the time the security was created.

The first paragraph of section 5-8 enables the liquidator to set aside any enforcement charges on the company's assets created within three months of the cut-off date. According to the second paragraph of section 5-8, such enforcement charge created in favour of a person or company related to the company as described above can be set aside if it was made within two years of the cut-off date, unless it is proved beyond doubt that the company remained solvent at the time the enforcement charge was created.

Section 5-9

Section 5-9 comprises transactions which were made at a time when the company's financial situation was weak or became severely impaired by the transaction, combined with the lack of good faith in this respect by the counterparty to the transaction. The transactions in question are divided into three groups:

- a transaction favouring one creditor at the expense of the others;
- a transaction which withdraws the company's assets from the liquidation; or
- a transaction which increases the company's debts to the detriment of the other creditors.

If it can be proved that the counterparty knew or ought to have known of the company's troubled financial situation and that the transaction was made under such circumstances as outlined, the transaction can be set aside. This will apply for all such transactions being carried out within ten years from the cut-off date.

Effect

The amount which the insolvent company can retrieve from the other party if the conditions laid down in sections 5-2 to 5-8 are met is governed by section 5-11. Under this section the retrievable amount is limited to the gains obtained by the other party, who is thus not liable to make good the total loss suffered by the insolvent company. This distinction will not always be of any significance in practical terms. The limitation may have practical implications, for example, if the goods, at the time of action to revoke the transaction, have been sold on, spent or consumed. The amount to be recovered is then limited to what is left in the other party's hands. Income derived from the goods after being transferred to the other party, (such as dividends on shares), and up to the time when an action is commenced in order to revoke the transaction, remain the property of the counterparty even if the relevant goods are recovered by the insolvent company later. This principle applies to income earned up to the time the transaction is revoked. This rule applies only if the other party was in good faith. If that is not the case, the liquidator can retrieve the income as well.

If the other party has sold the goods on to a third party, but this party ought to have known the circumstances under which the initial transaction took place, the liquidator can claim back the goods from this third party.

A recovery action as described above can be satisfied either by restitution of the goods in question or, alternatively, by the other party paying cash. If a charge over an asset is revoked, the insolvent company and all creditors will benefit from it equally.

If a transaction is set aside under section 5-9, the liquidator is entitled to demand full compensation for the loss suffered by the company due to the transaction (s5-12 Insolvency Act). The option to choose between recovery in kind or equivalent cash value under this section is vested in the liquidator. If the other party to the transaction has merely been negligent (in failing to know about the company's financial situation when he ought to have known), his liability can be reduced or eliminated if payment of full compensation is unreasonably burdensome in economic terms or if other specific reasons make it justifiable. A third party who derives his ownership from the other party will be subject to the same rules for payment of compensation.

Assets or funds recovered under sections 5-11 and 5-12, are subject to the usual hierarchy of payments to creditors. If for example the assets of the insolvent company prior to any augmentation are not sufficient to cover preferential creditors, later recaptured assets or funds will first be used to cover all remaining preferential claims before non-preferential creditors are able to take any advantage of the new funds.

Section 5-15 sets out time limits for taking steps to set aside transactions under

Chapter 5 of the Recovery Act. The general time limit is one year from the cut-off date. If however the creditors only became aware of the circumstances on which the action to set aside was based at a later stage in the insolvency proceedings, time will not start to run until six months after the time when the creditors became aware or ought to have become aware of the circumstances. This extension of the time limit is subject to an absolute limit of ten years from the cut-off date. The time limit does not apply if the liquidator claims that a transaction should be set aside as a defence to a claim made against the insolvent company (s5-15).

There are provisions in the Joint Stock Companies Act that may also lead to the augmentation of the insolvent company's assets by revoking certain pre-liquidation transactions. If the company prior to the cut-off date had made dividend distributions contrary to the provisions of section 12-8 of the Joint Stock Companies Act, a shareholder who ought to have understood that the distribution was illegal must repay any amount received to the company. Loans to officers and shareholders of a joint stock company are subject to restrictions regarding equity, ratio and adequate security (s12-10 Joint Stock Companies Act) and if the company has made any loans which do not comply with the restrictions, the loan arrangements are not valid and any amount drawn must be paid back to the insolvent company.

Personal liability of officers

Both the Joint Stock Companies Act and the Companies Act have provisions on liability for officers of a joint stock company or a limited partnership. These provisions repeat the general principle set out in general tort law, namely that an officer is liable for any damage intentionally or negligently caused by him during the conduct of his task as an officer of the company. The Joint Stock Companies Act has detailed regulations as to which persons or officers of a company this rule applies to, extending it to a promoter, director of the board, member of the workers' council, the managing director, the auditors and the shareholders of a company. The provisions of the Companies Act include liability for part owners, members of the partnership meeting, directors of the board, a managing director and a member of the board in voluntary winding up proceedings. The rules establish individual liability for the actual officer and not collective or joint responsibility for the body that he actually represents. Whether or not joint liability can be established will depend on general tort law and whether the officer in question acted as a representative of the relevant corporate body or whether he acted jointly with the rest of the board.

The effect of the rules is that any creditor or third party (and even the company) may sue any officer of the company for compensation if the officer has committed a tortious act with intent or negligence. A joint stock company's liquidator may sue the relevant officer but only if the company has incurred a loss through the officer's fault. If only *one* creditor has suffered a loss, this creditor must sue the officer individually (for instance a creditor may have supplied goods to the company at a time when the company was insolvent).

An act or omission by a relevant officer will normally be tortious, if, for instance, he has exceeded his powers under the Joint Stock Companies Act or the Companies Act or the powers set out in his employment contract. If a shareholders' meeting of a joint stock company has decided by majority vote not to pursue a claim for compensation against an officer of the company, the liquidator is not bound if this decision was made when the company was insolvent and the company went into insolvent liquidation within one year of the shareholders' resolution. It is sufficient for this purpose if it is shown that it was considerably likely that the company was insolvent at the time of the decision.

6. Public control over insolvent corporations

Licensing and control of the appointee

An administrator/liquidator under to the Insolvency Act should preferably be an "advokat". An "advokat" is a law graduate who is licensed by the Ministry of Justice to sell his services as a legal advisor and to plead before the Norwegian courts. The licence can be obtained by a person holding a specific Norwegian law degree and the normal additional requirement is more than two years' qualified work experience which includes a certain number of court appearances according to specific rules. Thus, this licence is a general permission to act as a legal advisor in all circumstances and there are no other particular licensing requirements for an administrator or liquidator of an insolvent company.

The administrator or liquidator acts in accordance with instructions from the supervisory committee or the creditors' commitee under the supervision of the Insolvency Court.

There are no other ways of controlling an administrator or liquidator.

Examinations and investigations

The Insolvency Act has no specific provisions giving the administrator or liquidator a right to carry out investigations or examinations of any of the officers of the company, other than the right to request the presence of the officers of the company at creditors' meetings and the auditor's duty to audit the insolvent company's affairs. Under sections 18 and 101 of the Insolvency Act, the directors of the company have an obligation to reveal all information about the financial situation and conduct of the business before or after the liquidation. This duty applies to all the relevant liquidation bodies. Moreover the directors are obliged to co-operate with the relevant bodies and to use their best endeavours to assist in augmenting the assets of the company and to ascertain its obligations.

Under section 149 of the Insolvency Act, the insolvency proceedings must follow the rules contained in the Civil Procedure Act of 1915. This Act comprises rules regarding production of evidence, court explanations and hearing of witnesses. The full effect of the reference to the Civil Procedure Act is realised in "Probate disputes", which are subject to the rules of the Civil Procedure Act, the implication being implied that the Insolvency Court will hear the dispute under ordinary civil procedure.

Publicity and records

The Insolvency Act distinguishes between debt arrangement proceedings and the compulsory liquidation of an insolvent company. The debt arrangement proceedings are unofficial up to a certain stage. If the debt arrangement proceedings reach the stage of a compulsory debt arrangement, they must be publicised (s35 Insolvency Act and p496 *supra*). The insolvent liquidation proceedings are public. The various steps are advertised in the Norwegian Gazette, in a local newspaper and in the Bankruptcy Register. As mentioned before, compulsory debt arrangements and liquidation proceedings must be registered in the Company Registry, the Property Registry, the Immoveable Property Registry and in other relevant Registries. The completion of the liquidation must also be publicised. When the liquidator acts on behalf of the insolvent company, he must disclose to third parties that he acts in the capacity of liquidator to "Company X under liquidation".

Contents of Chapter 12

CORPORATE INSOLVENCY LAW IN PORTUGAL

1.	**Introduction**	521
	Sources of law	521
	Entities not subject to recovery or bankruptcy proceedings	522
	Important notes	522
2.	**Companies**	522
	Introduction	522
	Characteristics	523
	Management/internal structure	524
	Ownership	527
	Financing and security for creditors	528
	Available information/Commercial Registry	531
	Other businesses	532
	Debt collection and asset recovery	532
3.	**Survival of the insolvent undertaking or its business**	534
	Recovery procedures	534
	The composition with creditors ("concordata")	540
	The creditors' agreement	542
	Financial restructuring	543
	Controlled administration	544
4.	**Termination of the corporation: bankruptcy and liquidation**	545
	The initial procedure	546
	The making and challenging of bankruptcy orders	547
	The judicial liquidator	548
	The committee of creditors	549
	Effect of the bankruptcy order	549
	Seizure of goods and assets	550
	Liquidation of the assets	551
	Verification of claims against the bankrupt	552

Termination of liquidation   552
Rehabilitation of the bankrupt   552
"Extraordinary agreement"   553
**5.   Augmenting the assets of the insolvent
        corporation**   553
Recovering the assets   553
Shareholders' and managers' liability to creditors   555
6.   Public control over insolvent corporations   556

Chapter 12

CORPORATE INSOLVENCY LAW IN PORTUGAL

Carlos Martins Ferreira,

José Alves Pereira e Associados

1. Introduction

Sources of law

Insolvency and survival of insolvent "undertakings" ("Empresas") is presently regulated by Decree-Law No. 16/92 of 6 August 1992 which instituted the "Code of Special Procedures of Bankruptcy and Recovery of Undertakings" ("CSPIRU").

Decree-Law No 16/92 introduces a new legal regime which revokes the former one contained in articles 1135 to 1312 of the "Civil Procedure Code" ("CPC") and in Decree-Law No 177/86 of 2 July 1986.

The new law has greatly changed the terminology previously used by the Portuguese legislature. Traditionally, Portuguese scholars distinguished, in accordance with the legal regime, "falência", as the condition of a trader or other business entity who could not meet his liabilities, from "insolvência", being the similar condition applying to non-traders. Therefore, the trader was considered "falido" while the non-trader was considered "insolvente". In accordance with such distinction, the previous law subjected non-traders to a specific regime regulated by articles 1313 *et seq* of the CPC different in procedure and effect from the one applicable to traders.

Article 1 No 1 of CSPIRU envisages that any undertaking in a condition of "insolvência" may be subject to one or more recovery procedures or declared in a regime of "falência".

The term "undertaking" applies both to traders and non-traders and is defined as any sort of organisation of the factors of production aimed at the exercise of any agricultural, commercial, industrial or services activity (art 2 CSPIRU).

Insolvência is now considered to be the condition of an undertaking which, due to lack of resources or credit, cannot meet its liabilities (art 3 CSPIRU), Falência being the specific liquidation procedure for the assets of an undertaking which is not in a position to make a financial recovery.

An insolvent debtor who is not an undertaking may be declared to be in a condition of falência, but he will not be able to take advantage of the procedure for recovery applicable to undertakings, although he may subject himself to a court-approved composition with creditors.

The criteria of insolvency on which any creditor or the district attorney may require the adoption of recovery procedures or the declaration of falência, will be dealt with below.

Finally, it is important to stress the duty of the administrative organs of an undertaking to apply for recovery or a declaration of bankruptcy within 60 days from the non-fulfilment of one of the obligations of the undertaking. The non-fulfilled obligation must be one which, whether in amount or the circumstances of non-payment, infers the debtor's inability to discharge its debts in a timely manner (arts 6, 7, 8/1 (a) CSPIRU).

Entities not subject to recovery or bankruptcy proceedings

The legal regime of recovery of undertakings and bankruptcy is not applicable to entities subject to state or public control ("pessoas colectivas públicas"). It has no bearing on the specific legislation relating to State undertakings ("empresas públicas"), credit or financial institutions and insurance companies (Decree-Law No 16/92 art 2).

Important notes

- For the remainder of this chapter, the term "insolvency" is used as a synonym for "insolvência" and the term "bankruptcy" as a synonym for "falência". We use the term "undertaking" as a synonym for "empresa".
- The scope of this work is limited in two respects: first, it deals with insolvency and bankruptcy as it applies to undertakings; second it only considers undertakings incorporated as trading companies under Portuguese Law.

2. Companies

Introduction

Under the Portuguese commercial law, Code of Commercial Companies – "CCC", commercial companies can be incorporated by a decision or the agreement of the prospective shareholders, recorded by means of a formal "act" (a public notarial deed) duly registered in the Commercial Registry.

The existence of an association agreement is not in itself sufficient to create a new legal person: the agreement must fulfil a number of essential requirements.

In particular, it must identify:

- the partners or shareholders;
- the type of company being created;
- its name;
- its head office;
- its share capital;
- the contributions of each of the partners or shareholders to the share capital and the nature of these contributions;
- the subscription of capital and the amount of capital initially paid up or deferred.

Further formal requirements for the incorporation of a company include the drawing up of a notarial deed of incorporation (containing the agreement and the articles of association), its definitive registration in the competent Commercial Registry Office and the publication of a notice of incorporation (containing the text of the agreement and the articles of association) in the Official Gazette ("Diário da República") and in a daily newspaper.

To summarise, the usual procedure for the incorporation of commercial companies involves:

- a public deed of incorporation (articles of association);
- registration (in the Commercial Registry Office);
- obligatory publication (in the Official Gazette and in a daily newspaper).

An alternative procedure exists, which consists of:

- prior (provisional) registration at the Commercial Registry of the proposed articles of association;
- public deed of incorporation;
- definitive registration at the Commercial Registry;
- obligatory publication.

Characteristics

The CCC provides that different types of companies are to be divided into two major groups, depending on the personal nature of the business and on the degree of liability of the partners or shareholders: The groups are:

- personal companies – "sociedades de pessoas" which are:
    - "Sociedades em Nome Colectivo" ("SeNC"s) – non-limited liability companies or partnerships;
    - "Sociedades em comandita simples ("Secs") – a mixed type of limited and non-limited liability company.
- capital companies "sociedades de capital".
    These are:

- "Sociedades por Quotas" ("SpQ"s) – private companies whose liability is limited by shares ("Quotas");
- "Sociedades Anonimas" ("SAs") – larger corporations whose liability is limited by shares;
- "Sociedades em comandita por acçoes" ("Secpas") – a mixed-type of sociedades Anonimas and sociedades por Quotas.

For the purpose of this practical guide, the major distinction to be drawn is between SeNCs on the one hand and SpQs and SAs on the other.

In the case of SeNCs, the partners are personally liable for the company's debts. In this type of business, personal trust and credit are of major importance.

Usually the number of partners is small. In the case of SpQs and SAs, as a general principle, each shareholder is only liable for the value of his participation. There are cases, however, in which these general rules do not apply.

In the case of SpQs it should be noted that "quotas" are simply a record in the articles of association of the company and in the Commercial Registry of participations in the share capital which are not materially represented by any "title" or "paper". This contrasts with shares in an SA which are physical documents. In an SpQ, if the capital is not entirely paid-up, each shareholder, in addition to being liable for any amount unpaid on his own shares, is also liable for the total amount outstanding on all the shares. In the latter case where a shareholder has made payment in respect of amounts outstanding on the shares of other shareholders, he will, of course, have a right of recourse against those other shareholders. The minimum share capital prescribed by law is Pte 400,000. The minimum number of shareholders is two.

Once the share capital of both SpQ and SA is paid in full, only the assets of the company are available to meet any obligations to creditors; thus, the shareholders are liable only to the extent of the value of the shares they own.

For SAs, the minimum share capital prescribed by law is Pte 5 million and the minimum number of shareholders is five.

However, wholly-owned subsidiaries of SAs or SpQs, constituted under the form of SAs, may have a sole shareholder who will have unlimited liability in respect of the subsidiary company's liabilities (arts 488-490 CCC). The same applies whenever a certain company (director company) controls another company (subordinated company) by means of a "subordination agreement".

On the other hand, if a company with a sole member is declared bankrupt, this member will be liable without limit for the obligations of the company entered into during the period after he became the sole member as long as it is proved that the provisions of the Law aimed at ensuring that the assets of the company may answer for its own debts have been disregarded (art 84 CCC).

Management/internal structure

The internal management structure of commercial companies varies according to the type of company. However, all companies have administrative organs with decision-making, administrative, overseeing and deliberative functions.

Shareholders' general meetings

The shareholders' general meeting is the organ where the partners or shareholders decide the most important matters relating to the company's activity (without prejudice to the possibility of the adoption of unanimous decisions in writing under article 54 of the CCC, although prior conditions laid down by the law must be fulfilled if decisions are adopted under that procedure).

The shareholders' meeting has sole competence to:

- remove partners;
- appoint and remove managers and directors;
- approve the annual management report;
- approve the annual accounts;
- distribute profits;
- amend or vary the articles of association, and so on.

Decisions at shareholders' meetings are usually taken by a simple majority of the partners or shareholders. Qualified majority voting may be imposed by law or by the articles of association in certain cases (for example, to decide on an amendment to the articles of association or on the dissolution of the company, the law requires a majority of two- thirds of the votes cast).

In the case of SeNCs, each partner has one vote. In the case of SAs and SpQs, each shareholder will have a number of votes which are proportionate to the number of shares he owns or to the value of his shareholding.

Management and control

SeNCs
Usually, all partners (and only the partners) are managers, and every one of them controls the company.

SpQs
These are managed and represented by one or more managers who do not need to be shareholders (as laid down in the articles of association).

The managers can be appointed in the articles of association or by shareholders at a shareholders' meeting.

SpQs under a certain size need not have a specific controlling board (art 262 CCC).

SAs
SAs are, without any doubt, the companies with the most complex management and control structure. They can have one of the following two structures:

- Structure A : a board of directors (or sole director) and board of auditors (or sole auditor); or
- Structure B : a general council, management board and qualified auditor

("Revisor Oficial de Contas").

Structure A

This is the more common structure. The board of directors is made up of an odd number of members elected by the shareholders' general meeting or appointed under the articles of association. A president is chosen from among the members of the board.

Provided that it is expressly permitted under the articles of association, and that the share capital does not exceed Pte 20 million, the company can have a single director.

The board of directors has very wide competence. It adopts decisions by simple majority.

The monitoring of the company falls to the board or auditors or to a single auditor. One executive member of the board of auditors, a substitute member of the board of auditors and the single auditor must be qualified auditors ("revisores oficiais de contas").

It is incumbent on the board of auditors *inter alia* to monitor the company's management and to verify that the books and records are in order and that the balance sheet is accurate.

Structure B

The general council is composed of an odd number of members either as declared in the articles of association or as elected by the shareholders' general meeting.

The number of members of the general council must exceed the number of the directors by any amount up to a maximum of 15 and must own at least that number of shares which is set down in the articles of association. They are appointed for the period stated in the articles of association, although never for more than four calendar years.

The powers of the general council are as follows:

- to appoint and remove the directors, including the chairman;
- to supervise the activity of the board of directors;
- to represent the company in its relationship with the directors;
- to verify the information contained in the books, records and accounts;
- to consider and, if appropriate, approve the report of the board of directors and the company accounts;
- to submit an annual report as to its activity to the shareholders' general meeting.

The general council does not have the power to manage the company's activities (art 442 CSC). However, the law, the articles of association, or the general council itself may require the assent of this council in respect of certain categories of acts undertaken by the board of directors.

The management board is composed of an odd number of members as designated by the articles of association up to a maximum of five for a period not exceeding four calendar years.

The company may have one manager provided the share capital is Pte 20 million or less and two or more managers if the share capital is over Pte 20 million. The ability to appoint managers must be stated in the articles of association. The general council appoints and removes the chairman of the management board. It is the management board which manages the company and which represents the company against third parties.

As far as the qualified auditor is concerned, the general council must appoint a qualified auditor or a partnership of auditors for a period not exceeding three years to audit the company's accounts. Those so appointed have the same powers and prerogatives as the board of auditors appointed to a company established under structure A. In addition to this appointment, the general council must appoint a substitute qualified auditor to continue the auditing in the event of the appointed auditor being unable to carry out his functions.

Secs and Secpas

There is no need for an auditing organ for Secs and Secpas. In principle, only mandated partners ("comanditados") can be managers of this type of company.

Ownership

There are many different categories of partners/shareholders depending upon the type of company involved.

Thus, the situation and status of a partner of an SeNC is quite different from that of a shareholder in a limited liability company.

The situation of a shareholder of an SpQ (who until the payment of the share capital is liable for the other shareholders' quotas – see above) also differs from the situation of a shareholder of an SA who is liable only for the value of the shares he owns.

There may be many different categories of shareholders in any one company depending upon the rights attaching to or liabilities connected with the shares that they own. This is particularly true of SAs. Types of shares include:

- unpaid, partly paid or fully paid, depending upon whether (and to what extent) the nominal value of the shares has been paid;
- nominative and bearer shares, depending upon whether the name of the shareholders is recorded on the share certificates
- nominative and bearer shares, depending upon whether the names of the shareholders are recorded on the share certificates;
- preference and ordinary shares. Preference shares may be issued as an incentive to investors and may confer privileges as to dividends and return of capital on a winding up. Preference shares often confer no voting rights and may be issued as redeemable at a fixed future rate.

Financing and security for creditors

Companies (hereinafter we will only examine SpQs and SAs and shall use the term "companies" to apply to both) can be financed either by the shareholders or by third parties.

In addition to their contributions to capital, shareholders can be called upon to make additional accessory contributions ("Prestações Acessórias"). Shareholders of SPQs can also be asked to make either supplementary contributions (Prestações Suplementares") or loans ("suprimentos").

Provision for additional contributions can be made in the articles of association setting up any type of company. The rules governing these contributions will depend on the terms of the articles of association. Additional contributions may (but need not) be interest-bearing.

No interest is payable on supplementary contributions. These are compulsory and can be imposed by decision of the shareholders provided that the power to require them is included in the articles of association. Supplementary contributions cannot be returned to the shareholders who have made them once insolvency is declared.

"Suprimentos" are loans from the shareholders to the company, on which interest may be paid. However, they can only be made if specifically provided for under the articles of association, and if the company is declared insolvent, they cannot be reimbursed unless the liabilities of the company are completely paid off. They therefore rank after all other creditors of the company.

Third parties other than the shareholders may invest in commercial companies through loans or through the issue of bonds, and other instruments.

In case of insolvency third party lenders rank above shareholders in priority.

Loans from non-shareholders may be secured by pledge or mortgage. The pledge is a charge over movable assets or chattels and the mortgage is a charge over the immovable assets or real property of the company. Where the company becomes insolvent, both categories of secured creditors have priority over all other creditors of the company.

Pledges and mortgages are without doubt the most common collateral used by creditors to secure their debts, and the following aspects of these securities must be taken into consideration in any insolvency situation. Whenever pledges and mortgages are imposed on assets subject to registration, they are only effective against third parties after the registration.

Sale prior to maturity of loan

According to Portuguese civil law, before maturity of the secured amount, assets subject to pledge or mortgage can be sold without the consent of the holder of the security. However, in this case it is usual to agree that the secured amount will fall due as soon as the pledged assets are sold.

Consequently, in such a case, the debtor has to discharge the secured amount either prior to or at the time of the sale.

Pledges

Upon the maturity of the secured amount, if the obligation to pay is not voluntarily fulfilled by the debtor, the creditor may request the court to enforce the existing pledges, by means of:

Judicial sale
The creditor may request that the court proceeds with a "judicial sale" of the secured asset, so that he may satisfy the secured amount with the proceeds of such sale. The sale can be effected by public auction or by private sale.

Judicial awards (adjudication)
The parties may expressly determine in the pledge agreement that, if the debtor fails to fulfil its obligations, the secured asset will be awarded directly to the creditor after being valued by the court.

Sale by a third party appointed by the court
The parties may determine in the security agreement that an eventual sale of the pledged asset will be made not directly by the court, but by a third party appointed by the court. In this case, however, the process must similarly commence with the introduction of a court action, and will follow the normal procedure, of a judicial sale, the only difference being that it is not the court which will sell the asset directly, but someone else acting as its agent.

Mortgages

Mortgages give to secured creditors the right to be paid out of the proceeds of a judicial sale of immovable assets and this will normally occur in the course of collection proceedings brought before the courts.

If a debt is secured by a mortgage, the creditor must be paid out of the proceeds of the judicial sale and he will not be able to cause other assets of the debtor to be seized and sold in order to satisfy his debt provided the value of the mortgaged asset is sufficient for the purpose of repaying the secured debt. Judicial sale can be effected by public auction or private sale.

Aside from these forms of security which in principle give to creditors a considerable guarantee as regards the repayment of their debts, there are several other ways by which creditors can ensure that if the company (or other business entity) becomes insolvent, they will at least recover something.

The following are the most common:

Retention of title ("Reserva de propriedade")

Civil law (art 409 CC) provides that, in agreements which relate to the sale or general alienation or supply of goods, either movable or immovable, the parties may include a clause or provision establishing that the ownership of goods will remain with the seller (or supplier) until full payment for those goods has been received or until any other conditions stipulated in the contract have been fulfilled. In the case of immovable assets or movable goods subject to registration, the retention of title clause, in order to be effective against third parties, must be duly registered.

Right of retention ("Direito de retenção")

This is different from "retention of title" in that it provides that a creditor may retain some goods (movable or immovable) in his possession in spite of the fact that those goods do not belong to him but to the debtor. The right of retention is dealt with in articles 754 to 761 CC. The basic rule is that anyone who is obliged to deliver goods to their true owner may retain such goods as long as he had a debt owed to him by the owner and that debt is in some way related to expenses or damages caused by those goods.

The right of retention is not enforceable *inter alia* in the following cases:

- if possession of the goods was obtained illegally;
- if the goods in question fall into a category of goods which cannot be pledged;
- if the owner provides enough security.

Specific legislation also provides for specific rights of retention, for example:

- the transporter's right of retention in relation to goods carried, as a guarantee for debts which result from the transportation;
- the promissor-purchaser's right of retention in relation to the goods that the vendor has promised to sell, if the purchaser is already in possession of the goods and the vendor refuses to sell.

If a right of retention attaches to immovable assets, the holder of the right may enforce his debts and be paid out of the proceeds of the judicial sale of the immovable assets in preference to other creditors, including those whose claims are secured by mortgages.

Set-off ("Compensação")

When two parties are simultaneously and reciprocally debtor and creditor, either of them may compensate or reduce his debt by the amount to which he is entitled from the other (art 847 CC). Thus, the creditor of the insolvent company (or other insolvent entity) may reduce his debt by any amount he owes to the company. However, this general rule only applies if the obligations of the two parties are of the same nature.

Types of creditor

At this stage it is useful to draw a distinction between the three categories of creditors and the priorities between them. The three categories are:

- secured creditors;
- preferential creditors ("credores com privilégio creditório");
- common creditors.

The first two categories of creditors can be grouped under the general title of "preferential creditors".

Secured creditors

Secured creditors are those secured by what are, at least theoretically, guarantees of repayment such as mortgages ("hipotecas") or pledges ("penhoras"). In the event of breach of payment by the debtor, secured creditors are paid in priority to the common creditors out of the sale proceeds of certain assets (the subject of this security) such as real estate (in the case of mortgages) and movable assets (in the case of pledges).

Preferential creditors

Preferential creditors are those who benefit from a special privilege ("privilégio creditório") conferred on them by statute which entitles them to payment. Examples are debts owed to government departments, taxes and arrears in wages. Where a declaration of insolvency is made in relation to the undertaking, the preferential status of tax, social security, government and local authorities' claims ceases. Those entities become common creditors.

Common creditors

Common creditors are, under Portuguese law, the non-secured debts and the non-preferential debts (*i.e.* those which are not secured by any real guarantees of repayment or those which are not to be paid in advance of other debts by statute).

Available information/Commercial Registry

Portuguese commercial law requires certain information on the company to be registered in the Commercial Registry (which can be inspected by any third party). The following information must be registered:

- the articles of association;
- the merging, division and transfer of shareholdings;
- the constitution of any charge, pledge, attachment, garnishee order;
- the removal of shareholders of private limited liability companies;
- the annual accounts;

- the appointment and removal of managers and auditors of the company;
- the change of the head office;
- the merger, demerger and transformation of companies;
- the increase of share capital;
- any alteration to the articles of association.

Some of the above may also be subject to publication in the Official Gazette ("Diário da República") and in one of the most widely read daily newspapers of the area in which the head office of the company is situated.

Other businesses

In addition to trading or commercial companies, other forms of business to which the "CSPIRU" is also applicable are:

- sole traders, acting by themselves or through unincorporated associations or a group;
- the limited liability single shareholder company ("Estabelecimento Individual de Responsabilidade Limitada -EIRL"). EIRL is a scheme to limit the liability of the sole trader. It involves the designation of the assets used in the course of business: only the designated assets will be seized to pay debts arising in the course of the trading activity of the business. A minimum capital of Pte 400,000 is required to set up an EIRL;
- "ACE" ("Agrupamentos Complementares de Empresas") consisting of various companies grouping together to form a new corporate entity, without each of them losing its own legal personality.

Debt collection and asset recovery

Collection proceedings for commercial debts

Under Portuguese law, the same rules apply to the collection of commercial debts as to other types of debts.

Under the CPC, there are three types of collection proceedings:

- action for debt collection;
- action for asset recovery;
- action for specific performance by the debtor.

In the action for debt collection, the creditor makes an application to the court to recover a pecuniary debt by levying execution on the debtor's property (art 817 CC).

If the application is successful, the court seizes such of the debtor's goods as are sufficient to cover the debts and the creditor will be paid with the proceeds of the sale of those goods.

The creditor who has a fixed charge over real property ("garantia especial") ranks in priority over any other creditor, and he can apply to be joined as a party to any action for debt recovery whether or not he initiated the proceedings.

If various creditors have fixed charges in respect of sums due to them, the court will establish an order of priorities according to which they will be paid.

The action for asset recovery is based on a right *in rem* upon certain goods, which will be seized by the court and delivered to the petitioner.

If the goods on which the indebtedness is secured cannot be found, the action for asset recovery can be converted into an action for debt collection.

A claim for specific performance is based on a special obligation of the debtor to perform a particular obligation within a specified period of time. This action can also be converted into an action for debt collection for damages.

Cross-jurisdictional procedures

General regime

In Portugal the execution of collection proceedings based on foreign judgments, depends upon prior review and confirmation of the foreign judgment by the Portuguese High Court.

The proceedings for review and confirmation of foreign judgments must be brought in the Court of Appeal. Proceedings can only be started if a number of essential prerequisites are fulfilled, the most important of which is that the defendant must have been given notice to appear in the proceedings in which he was found liable.

Other prerequisites are:

- the exhaustion of all appeals in the jurisdiction in which the judgment was given;
- that the decision adopted by the foreign court does not contradict fundamental principles of the Portuguese law ("public order");
- that the foreign court is competent according to the Portuguese rules of jurisdiction.

The Brussels Convention on Jurisdiction and Judgments in Civil and Commercial Matters

The Brussels convention provides a scheme of jurisdiction rules and recognition of judgments for EU Member States. The Lugano Convention of 16 September 1988 has extended the Brussels convention scheme to the EFTA group of countries.

The Brussels convention on jurisdiction and judgments in civil and commercial matters was ratified by Portugal on 30 October 1991.

The convention applies to all judgments in civil and commercial matters other than:

- status and capacity of individuals, the status of the parties as married persons, wills and inheritance;

- bankruptcy, composition with creditors and similar proceedings;
- social security;
- arbitration.

Under the convention, judgments from EC countries are entitled to automatic recognition, without the need for any special procedure or formality. The convention provides for some potential defence to recognition (art 27) mainly coincident to those referred to above as prerequisites in the general rules.

A foreign judgment may be enforced in Portugal when an order to that effect has been made by the competent district judicial court (Tribunal Judicial de Círculo).

3. Survival of the insolvent under-taking or its business

Recovery procedures

The initiative

Recovery procedures may be commenced either by initiative of the debtor or by initiative of the creditor. The public prosecutor may also request the adoption of recovery procedures provided that some requisites are met.

Debtor

Any undertaking must apply for reorganisation or a declaration of bankruptcy within 60 days from the non-fulfilment of one of its obligations. The non-fulfilled obligation must be one which, whether in amount or in the circumstances of non-payment, implies the inability of the debtor to pay the generality of its debts in a timely manner (arts 6, 7 8/1 (a) CSPIRU)

Creditor

Any class of creditor may require, in respect of an undertaking he regards as financially viable, the adoption of an appropriate recovery plan. His ability to do so will depend on one of the following pointers to insolvency applying:

- non-fulfilment of one or more of the undertaking's obligations, the amount or circumstances of non-payment of which reveals the incapacity of the debtor to fulfil its obligations in a timely manner;
- cessation of the undertaking's shareholders or officers performing their functions in consequence of the undertaking's lack of liquid assets or its abandonment of its principal place of business;
- dissipation or loss of assets, creation of fictitious credits or any other anomalous behaviour which reveals the intention of the debtor to put itself in a position where it will be unable to fulfil its obligations in a timely manner.

Public Prosecutor

The Public Prosecutor may also request the adoption of recovery procedures if the undertaking, although declared to be in financial difficulties, is one the survival of which is economically and socially desirable.

Importance of recovery and bankruptcy proceedings

Reorganisation and bankruptcy proceedings in relation to an undertaking, including interplea ("Embargos") and appeals, are considered to be urgent. In court, they are given priority status.

Types and regimes for recovery procedures

Recovery may be achieved by one of the following four alternative procedures:

- "Concordata" (composition with creditors)
- "Acordo de Credores" (creditor's agreement)
- "Gestão Controlada" (controlled administration)
- "Reestruturação Financeira" (financial restructuring)

In the next pages we will examine some aspects common to these recovery procedures, and, in particular :

- applications and initial common procedure;
- the judicial administrator;
- commission of creditors, meeting of creditors and related acts.

Applications and initial common procedure

Applications

In his petition for recovery procedures, the petitioner will set out the reasons for the undertaking's state of insolvency and the matters in support of his application. The petitioner must also identify the administrative organs of the undertaking or, in the case of a named individual, the name of his or her respective husband or wife and their matrimonial status. If the petition is filed by the debtor it must include the following documents:

- a list of creditors, including their addresses, value of their claims, dates of maturity and any security held in respect of them;
- a list of all pending actions against the undertaking;
- where the undertaking has organised accounts:
  - copies of the last balance sheet and the profit and loss account
  - the books for the last three complete financial years. These will be returned to the petitioner after being closed by the judge.
- where the undertaking has no organised accounts, a complete list of the as-

sets of the undertaking indicating their respective values;

- if the undertaking is a judicial person or a company, minutes of the meeting at which the decision to petition for recovery was taken;
- if the undertaking is an individual, that individual's marriage certificate.

The petitioner must file with his petition the evidence on which he relies in support of it.

If the petition is filed by a creditor or by the Public Prosecutor, the petitioner must indicate the source, nature and amount of his claim, offer any information he may have concerning the assets and liabilities of the debtor and set out his reasons for requiring the implementation of a particular recovery procedure.

Summoning of creditors
If there are no grounds for the judge to refuse the petition he must summon:

- the debtor and the other creditors if the petition has been filed by one or more creditors;
- where the debtor is the petitioner, all the appointed creditors;
- where the petition has been filed by the Public Prosecutor, the debtor and all his appointed creditors.

The debtor and his ten largest known creditors will be summoned by name. Other creditors will be summoned by advertisement in the Official Gazette and one of the country's most widely-read daily newspapers.

Challenge of petition or substantiation of claims ("Justificação de créditos")
Within 14 days, the parties summoned may challenge the petition or substantiate their claims. The amount of substantiated claims and interest on them must be calculated as at the date of presentation of the petition. The parties may also suggest the use of a recovery procedure different to that sought in the petition. Their response must be fully substantiated.

If, before the judge's preliminary ruling, creditors representing at least 75% in value of known claims have opposed the recovery of the undertaking alleging this to be impossible, the judge must declare the undertaking bankrupt. He will do so subject to hearing the legal representatives (managers, administrators etc) and verifying the basis on which the application is made to him. If creditors representing at least 30% of known claims against the company oppose reorganisation, the judge has a discretion as to whether to make the undertaking bankrupt or to order its recovery.

Conversely, if creditors representing at least 75% in value of known claims against the undertaking oppose bankruptcy (when this is sought by the debtor, another creditor or the Public Prosecutor) alleging its feasibility, the judge after hearing the petitioner must make an order for the recovery of the undertaking. Again, he will do so subject to satisfying himself that the creditors' opposition to bankruptcy is well-founded.

If creditors representing at least 30% of the known claims against the undertaking oppose bankruptcy, the judge has a discretion as to whether to make the undertaking bankrupt or to order its recovery.

Continuation of reorganisation proceedings

Within 28 days of the end of the 14 day period which creditors have to object to proceedings, the judge will make a final order.

The orders for the continuation of the petition for recovery proceedings will generally include orders to:

- appoint a judicial administrator;
- appoint a creditors' committee;
- prescribe a 90-day period for study and observation;
- convene a meeting of creditors to take place at the end of the period for study and observation.

The principal effect of the continuation of recovery proceedings will be a stay of all enforcement or other proceedings against the debtor.

Any agreement entered into after a final order for the continuation of the recovery proceedings charging the company's shares or other assets will be null and void unless it has been previously authorised or ratified by the judge after the approval of the committee of creditors and the judicial administrator.

The judicial administrator

The judicial administrator is appointed by the judge who will take into account nominees proposed by the creditors and the undertaking. If the judge does not deem it appropriate to appoint the judicial administrator suggested by the creditors or by the undertaking, he will choose one from the appropriate offical list of individuals approved to act as judicial administrators.

The criteria on which an individual may be included on the list of individuals approved to act as judicial administrators is prescribed by Decree-Law No. 254/93 of 15 July 1993.

It is important to stress that the judicial administrator is not a civil servant of any kind, nor is he in any other way employed by or on behalf of the state. He may carry out other activities as well as serving as judicial administrator.

Judicial administrator's functions

The judicial administrator must co-ordinate the administration of the undertaking and implement measures most likely to achieve its survival. In certain cases the judge, if he deems it necessary to protect creditors' interests, may give the judicial administrator power to bind the company and suspend the power of the company's administrative organs to do so.

The judicial administrator has the following powers:

- to draft a provisional list of the liabilities of the undertaking and to give a reasoned view as to creditors' claims;
- to draft a report proposing the most appropriate recovery procedure in his

view to be presented to the meeting of creditors held at the end of the period
for study and observation;

- to take or propose to the court any urgent action which he may feel expedient in order to protect the assets of the undertaking against third parties, including the creditors, even against the undertaking's will;
- to inform the committee of creditors as to management's actions during the period of study and observation. The judicial administrator must also inform the committee of creditors of facts or documents which may have a material bearing on the choice of the appropriate recovery procedure;.
- to ensure that the legal rights of the undertaking's committee of employees are protected.

The court may, at any time, on the request of the committee of creditors or after hearing its advice, replace the judicial administrator or change his powers.

In general, the role of the judicial administrator ceases when the judge accepts or rejects any recovery proposals approved by the creditors. In the case of a financial restructuring, the judicial administrator's role ceases when the recovery proceedings come to an end.

The committee of creditors

The committee of creditors is appointed by the judge, and is composed of three or five members. In principle it must include the most representative creditors, the largest creditor being appointed chairman. One or two *ex officio* members may also be appointed. The judicial administrator must ensure that all different classes of creditors are properly represented. Where any employee creditors claim in respect of arrears of salary or wages, one of the members of the committee must be a representative of the employees.

The committee can only act through meetings of the majority of its members. Decisions are taken by majority vote of the members present. The chairman has a casting vote for use in the event that no majority decision is reached.

Committee of creditors' functions

The major functions of the committee of creditors are to:

- monitor the company's performance and assist the judicial administrator;
- to approve, together with the judicial administrator an agreement in order to allow the judge to authorise or to ratify that agreement, where it has been entered into after the order continuing the proceedings for recovery, where the agreement involves sale or encumbrance of shares or equity of the company, as well as the sale, encumbrance or rental of immovable assets of the company and the sale or rental of any establishment of the company;
- require (or recommend to the judge) the replacement of the judicial administrator, or propose any variation of his powers or the powers of the officers and other bodies of the company;
- to give an opinion about creditors' claims and to adjudicate on any dispute

between creditors as to their respective claims;

- participate in the meeting of creditors held at the end of the period of controlled management.

The creditors' meeting and the method of voting at that meeting
An interim creditors' meeting takes place under the chairmanship of the judge on a day prescribed by him. The purpose of this meeting is to verify the claims reported to it by the judicial administrator. The meeting will decide to approve or reject the claims made. The decision of the meeting of creditors can be challenged but the judge's ruling on any such challenge cannot be appealed against.

To participate in the meeting of creditors, creditors must submit their claims (if they have not already done so) within 14 days counting from the publication of an advertisement in the Official Gazette convening and giving notice to creditors of the meeting.

Claims, either made by the creditors or as reported by the debtor undertaking, may be challenged by the other creditors within 14 days after the day on which claims should have been submitted. The debtor may also, within that 14 day period, challenge the claims made.

With the advice of the committee of creditors, the judicial administrator prepares a provisional list of claims either as reported by the debtor or submitted by the creditors. The list will be prepared under the following headings:

- claims not challenged and accepted by the judicial administrator;
- claims challenged by the creditors, by the debtor undertaking or by the commission of creditors but accepted by the judicial administrator;
- claims not accepted by the judicial administrator, whether challenged or not;
- claims falling into one of the categories above but where creditors hold security over the assets of the undertaking;
- claims falling into one of the categories above but where creditors hold security over the assets of a third party or a personal guarantee given by a third party.

Claims will be voted on by the interim meeting of creditors in the order set out above and all the creditors shown on the provisional list are allowed to vote. Even if his claim is not shown on the provisional list, once his claim is approved, a creditor will be entitled to vote on those claims falling for consideration after his own claim has been voted upon.

A creditor's vote is determined by the size of his claim against the company. Claims will be approved by simple majority of those present at the meeting. No creditor may vote in favour of his own claim unless the judicial administrator has already accepted it.

After the creditors' claims have been discussed and voted on at the interim meeting, the judge will prescribe the date for the final meeting of creditors, which will discuss the report of the judicial administrator setting out his reasons for recommending a particular recovery procedure. The creditors and the undertaking may propose alternative schemes.

As a general rule, a final decision as to the appropriate recovery procedure must be approved by at least 75% of the creditors entitled to vote at the meeting. The proposed recovery does not have to be approved by the undertaking, except in case of "concordata" (see *infra*).

The decision of the meeting of creditors as to the method of recovery must be approved by the judge.

If he fails to do so, or if creditors, representing at least 75% of the claims against the company, refuse to support any proposed reorganisation, the judge will declare the undertaking bankrupt.

The reorganisation order, decision of the meeting of creditors and the judge's approval or rejection of the meeting's decision must be registered at the Commercial Registry Office.

The four alternative recovery regimes are examined in detail below.

The composition with creditors ("concordata")

Purpose and effect

The composition with creditors ("concordata") consists of the reduction or variation of ordinary, non-preferential and unsecured claims. The composition with creditors may also consist of the reduction or variation of claims secured only by third parties. In such cases, the concordata only affects the debtor undertaking. The creditor's rights against the third party remain unchanged unless he has approved the concordata. A composition may only defer payments, as against both deferring the debtor's payment obligations and reducing his liability to his creditors.

The concordata cannot alter the rights of secured or preferential creditors.

Clause "salvo regresso de melhor fortuna"

The concordata, unless otherwise decided by the meeting of creditors, is subject to the so-called clause "salvo regresso de melhor fortuna" for a period of ten years. This clause means that within that period the undertaking is required to pay creditors who have approved the concordata the full amount of their claims, as soon as its economic situation improves. However, in this case, creditors whose claims arose after the concordata rank in priority to those creditors whose claims arose before it.

Administration of the undertaking

During the implementation of the concordata, the powers of the undertaking's administrators or managers may be reduced or altered.

The committee of creditors , or one or more individual creditors, will monitor the implementation of the concordata.

Any bilateral agreements between the undertaking and those of its creditors subject to the concordata which are contrary to its terms become null and void.

Payments to creditors

Preferential or secured creditors who have not renounced their preferential status are excluded from the concordata and may recover their claims by taking enforcement proceedings in the usual way. Common creditors and those preferential or secured creditors who have renounced their preferential rights will be paid according to the terms of the concordata they have accepted.

Creditors subject to the concordata may issue "livranças" (promissory notes) and "letras" (bills of exchange) in the amount of their claims (as reduced or altered under the terms of the concordata) and present them for acceptance by the debtor.

Annulment

The concordata can be annulled:

- at the request of a creditor who obtains a judgment showing that he had a claim prior to the concordata, which, had it been accepted then, would have had a bearing on the vote to approve the concordata, if that claim could have had an effect on the majority vote needed for approval of the concordata.

  Any request for annulment of the "concordata" must be presented within 30 days after the relevant judgment becomes unappealable.

- at the request of any creditor if approval of the concordata was obtained by fraud or misfeasance on the part of the debtor or other third parties. The request must be presented within six months after the approval of the concordata by the judge becomes unappealable.

If the concordata is annulled, the judge must summon a new meeting of creditors to take place within 45 days of its annulment.

Bankruptcy

After the confirmation of the concordata, a declaration of bankruptcy can be requested by creditors with claims arising prior to the concordata if:

- the debtor's management (or the debtor in the case of individual undertakings) abandons or otherwise leaves the undertaking;
- the goods are dissipated or lost in circumstances which reveal an intention on the part of the debtor to prejudice his creditors;
- the obligations stipulated in the concordata are not fulfilled. (In this latter case the debtor may avoid bankruptcy by honouring his obligations.)

The creditors' agreement

Purpose and effect

The creditors' agreement consists of the incorporation of one or more new companies which will continue to carry on the commercial activity of the debtor or one or more of his establishments as long as the creditors (or some of the creditors) of the undertaking assume in consequence responsibility for the management of the relevant commercial activity.

Any such agreement must be signed by the creditors supporting the use of this type of recovery procedure. Other creditors may accede to the agreement subsequently until the judge has formally confirmed the result of the creditors meeting.

Creditors who want to participate in the incorporation of the new company will also sign its constitution and respective by-laws.

Subject to being authorised to do so by the meeting of creditors, creditors who have, from the outset and subsequently, subscribed to the creditors' agreement may participate in its implementation.

The percentage shareholding of each creditor in the new company is that which his claim bears to total claims against the company. Third parties who are not creditors may also acquire shares in the new company.

The bye-laws of the new company will be discussed and voted on at the meeting of creditors called to approve the agreement with creditors.

Once the creditors' agreement is approved, the debtor's interest in the business ceases, the debtor undertaking ceases to operate (and is considered dissolved) and its former business will be carried on by the new vehicle.

Payment to creditors

Creditors who have signed the creditors' agreement will, as shareholders in the new company incorporated pursuant to that agreement, be entitled to dividends on profits in the normal way.

Creditors who do not subscribe to the creditors' agreement may receive, within seven years of its execution, part payment of their claims in the manner prescribed by the agreement.

Preferential or secured creditors may recover their claims against the debtor undertaking in the normal way.

Bankruptcy

If those creditors who have signed the creditors' agreement do not perform their obligations under it, the new company can be declared bankrupt.

To avoid this, the new company will have to pay all its creditors in full.

Bankruptcy may also be declared at the request of creditors who have not accepted the agreement.

The grounds for bankruptcy are any of the following:

- the debtor's management (or the debtor in case of individual undertakings) who have not accepted the agreement;
- goods of the new company being dissipated or lost in circumstances which reveal an intention on the part of the debtor to prejudice creditors.

Annulment

An explanation of the grounds on which the concordata may be annulled is set out above (p540). Either those creditors who have signed the creditors' agreement or the new company may avoid insolvency by paying the creditor who requested the insolvency declaration.

The annulment of the creditors' agreement will result in the dissolution of the new company and the reacquisition by the creditors of their former rights against the original debtor undertaking.

Financial restructuring

Purpose and effect

A financial restructuring entails the adoption by the creditors of one or more measures with the purpose of modifying the liabilities or the share capital of the debtor company in such a way as to guarantee that the company's assets cover its liabilities and provide a positive balance working capital.

Within a financial restructuring, the following measures may be adopted in respect of the insolvent company's liabilities:

- reduction of the value of the claims against the company (both capital and interest);
- deferred or modified repayment terms in respect of claims;
- repayment by distributing assets of the debtor to creditors;
- transfer of the debtor's assets to the creditors.

The following measures may be adopted in respect of the insolvent company's share capital:

- increase the debtor company's share capital having regard to shareholders' preferential rights;
- debt for equity swaps;
- reserve to third parties the subscription of shares in the debtor company which were not subscribed for by the shareholders;
- reduction of the company's share capital to cover its losses.

Effect of approval

Implementation of one or several of the measures referred to above must be approved by a meeting of creditors and confirmed by the judge. The meeting's outcome must be advertised and registered at the Commercial Registry.

The judge's ruling is binding on third parties.

Clause "salvo regresso de melhor fortuna"

The decision of the meeting of creditors which may involve the reduction or extinction of any claims is subject to the above mentioned clause "salvo regresso de mellior fortuna" (p540 *supra*).

Annulment

Annulment of a restructuring is similar to the annulment of a concordata (p541 *supra*)

End of proceedings

As soon as the agreed strategy has been implemented – which should be no more than 60 days after confirmation of the decision of the meeting of creditors, the judge will declare the financial restructuring to have been implemented. This will enable creditors to enforce the obligations undertaken by the debtor company as part of the resulting financial restructuring.

Controlled administration

Purpose and effect

Controlled administration involves the implementation of a global plan approved by creditors and performed by a newly appointed management of the debtor who will be subject to statutorily prescribed supervision and control.

The global plan may include the following measures:

- reduction in value of claims;
- deferred or modified repayment terms in respect of claims;
- repayment by distributing assets of the debtor to creditors;
- transfer of the debtor's assets to the creditors;
- increase of the debtor's share capital;
- debt for equity swaps;
- reduction of the debtor's share capital to cover losses.

The creditors' meeting may resolve upon any means for implementing the plan, including:

- commencing a new business which, under its constitution, the company is empowered to undertake;

- obtaining funding in return for giving security over the debtor's assets;
- the sale, exchange or transfer of assets of the company;
- cancellation of contracts and agreements executed by the company.

Effect of the approval

Approval of a restructuring plan will make that plan binding upon third parties.

New management

The creditors, when the plan is approved, must immediately appoint the new management who will be responsible for implementing the plan. Former managers may be included in the new management team if this is deemed likely to assist the management of the company. The judicial administrator may also be a member of the new management team.

The approved plan may require the management of the debtor company to be performed by a specific entity, under the terms of a management agreement which would, in that case, come into force between the debtor company and such entity.

Suspension of the role of the company's usual management organs – corporate bodies

During the plan's implementation, the role of the activity of the corporate company's usual management organs, such as the shareholders in general meeting or its fiscal council, will be suspended. While the plan is being implemented, the creditors' meeting will have equivalent functions to those of the shareholders in general meeting. In principle, all decisions of the general meeting of creditors must be taken by a majority of 75% in value of approved claims.

Monitoring

The creditors in general meeting will also appoint a supervision committee which will control implementation of the plan.

4. Termination of the corporation: bankruptcy and liquidation

Bankruptcy proceedings are afforded priority treatment by the court (see p535 *supra*).

The initial procedure

Commencement

Debtor initiated

Any undertaking which is not financially viable must apply for a declaration of bankruptcy within 60 days from the non-payment of one of its debts, the amount or circumstances of non-fulfilment of which may reveal that the undertaking is unable to discharge the generality of its debts in a timely manner (arts 6, 7, 8/1(a) CSPIRU).

Creditor initiated

Any creditor, whatever the nature of his claim, may require, in respect of an undertaking he does not regard as financially viable, the adoption of appropriate recovery procedures, provided that one of the following criteria for insolvency is satisfied:

- non-fulfilment of one more of the undertaking's debts, the amount or circumstances of the non-fulfilment of which reveals the inability of the undertaking to fulfil the generality of its obligations in a timely way;

- the owner of the undertaking or the administrative organs of the undertaking have run away to the undertaking's lack of funds to function without having appointed a proper successor. An alternative ground is the abandonment by the undertaking of its principal place of business.

- dissipation or loss of the undertaking's assets, creation of fictitious claims or any other anomalous behaviour which reveals the intention of the debtor to place himself in such a condition that he will not be able to fulfil his obligations in a timely way.

The Public Prosecutor ("Ministério Público") has the same rights as any other creditor to require the bankruptcy of the undertaking on behalf of parties he may represent under the law.

Applications

In his bankruptcy petition, the petitioner will set out the reasons for the undertaking's insolvency and the facts in support of his petition. The petitioner must also identify the administrative organs of the undertaking or, in case of an individual undertaking, if its owner is married, the name of the individual's husband or wife and their matrimonial status – *i.e.* married or divorced. If the petition is filed by the debtor, it must also include the information referred to in this paragraph.

The petitioner must file in court, along with his petition, all evidence in support of it.

If the petition is filed by a creditor or by the Public Prosecutor, it must indicate the source, nature and amount of the claim on which is founded and set out the reasons why bankruptcy is regarded as the appropriate remedy.

Summoning of creditors, challenge of the petition and substantiation of claims

The procedure for summoning the creditors, challenging the petition and substantiation of claims is similar to that for recovery (p535 *supra*)

The debtor will not be summoned at the beginning of the procedings, in the event that his immediate attendance is not deemed appropriate.

Continuation of the proceedings

Within 28 days of the period within which a petition may be opposed (*i.e.* 14 days from its issue) the judge will decide whether the bankruptcy proceedings are to be continued or stayed.

Immediate declaration of bankruptcy

If the petition is unopposed, the judge will declare the debtor bankrupt.

Court hearings and judgment

If the bankruptcy petition has been challenged and the situations foreseen in articles 23/2 and 25/3 of the CSPIRU do not occur. Article 23/2 establishes that if creditors representing at least 75% in the value of known claims against the company have opposed the declaration of bankruptcy (when applied for by the debror, by another creditor or by the Public Prosecutor) alleging the undertaking's ability to continue, the judge, as long as he recognises the petition is well-founded, and after hearing the petitioner must order the continuation of the proceedings as recovery proceedings. Article 25/3 establishes that if, in the same circumstances, creditors representing at least 30% of known claims against the company oppose the bankruptcy, the judge may order the continuation of the proceedings as recovery proceedings. The judge will immediately determine a date on which the proceedings can be fully heard.

At the court hearings, the debtor, the petitioners and other interested partics will have an opportunity to present all the evidence in support of their respective claims.

After hearing the parties, the judge will rule upon whether or not the debtor should be adjudicated bankrupt. His decision not to make a bankruptcy may be appealed against.

The bankruptcy of a non-limited liability company (*supra*) creates a presumption that its shareholders are also bankrupt.

The same may occur in respect of the shareholders of companies in "commandila" (*supra*).

The making and challenging of bankruptcy orders

When adjudging a debtor bankrupt, the court will also:

• confirm his place of residence for jurisdictional purposes;

- appoint a judicial liquidator;
- appoint the creditors' committee unless it has already been appointed;
- recover and deliver to the judicial liquidator all books and records of the business together with all its goods and assets, whether or not seized or pledged in some way;
- deliver to the public prosecutor all information suggesting that criminal offences may have been committed;
- fix a length of time between 20 and 60 days in which claims are to be submitted.

The judgment declaring the bankruptcy must be registered in the Commercial Registry and published in the Official Gazette.

The judgment may be opposed, within seven days of it being given, by means of "embargos" (interpleading). This may be done by the debtor, creditors or the public prosecutor. Embargos may be heard by the same judge who made the bankruptcy order.

Any decision in relation to "Embargos" may be appealed against.

Other persons (relatives) may oppose the making of a bankruptcy order in relation to individuals.

The judicial liquidator

The judicial liquidator is appointed by the judge who will take into account nominations made by the creditors and the undertaking. If the judge does not deem it appropriate to appoint a liquidator proposed by the creditors or by the undertaking, he will choose one from the appropriate official list. Both the procedure whereby a judicial liquidator may be included in the official list and his powers are prescribed by Decree-Law No 254/93 of 15 July 1993.

It is important to stress that the judicial liquidator is not a civil servant of any kind, nor is he in any other way employed by or on behalf of the state. He may carry out other functions apart from acting as judicial liquidator.

Judicial liquidator's functions

The judicial liquidator, with the assistance and supervision of the creditors' committee, is mainly entrusted with the administration and winding up of the assets or rights which constitute the bankruptcy estate and the repayment of creditors.

The judicial liquidator is also empowered:

- to represent the bankruptcy estate in court, both as plaintiff and defendant;
- to inform the court and the committee of creditors promptly of all matters relating to the management and liquidation of the bankruptcy estate;
- to terminate under the terms of the labour law contracts entered into between the undertaking and its employees;
- to collect debts owed to the bankrupt;

The acts of the judicial liquidator may be challenged either by the committee of creditors or by the bankrupt, and the court may, at any time, at the request of the committee of creditors or on its recommendations, replace him.

The functions of the judicial liquidator cease after the judgment approving the accounts of the bankrupt becomes unappealable.

The committee of creditors

The committee of creditors is appointed by the judge. It has three or five members, and in principle, must include the most representative creditors, with the largest creditor generally being appointed chairman. One or two additional members will also be appointed.

Where there are any employee creditors claiming in respect of salary or wage arrears, one of the members of the committee must be a representative of the employees and ensure that all classes are properly represented.

The committee can only act through meetings attended by a majority of its members. Decisions are taken by majority vote. The chairman has a casting vote in the event a majority decision is not reached.

The principal functions of the committee of creditors are:

- to monitor the performance of the judicial liquidator and assist him in the performance of his function;
- to sanction, as required by law, certain actions of the liquidator

Effect of the bankruptcy order

Effect on the bankrupt

The effects of the bankruptcy order on the bankrupt are as follows:

- The goods and assets of the bankrupt are seized and handed over to the liquidator.
- The bankrupt or (in case of corporations) its organs cannot deal with or dispose of its assets.
- Both the bankrupt and the management of a bankrupt corporation will be unable to carry out any trading activities. They will aso be unable to take any part in the management of any other corporation's or individual's affairs.
- If the bankrupt is a company, its insolvency can lead to its immediate dissolution (art 141 CCC – p551 *infra*).

Effect on debts, agreements and pending actions

The effect of bankruptcy on debts, agreements and pending actions is as follows:

- The bankruptcy order freezes the debtor's current accounts and makes all his debts to creditors immediately payable, thus assisting the judicial liquidator in obtaining a clear picture of the debtor's assets and liabilities.

- Interest ceases to run on claims against the bankrupt.
- Bankruptcy extinguishes the preferential status of tax, social security, government and local authorities' claims, the relevant governmental entities becoming common creditors.
- After bankruptcy, creditors of the bankrupt cannot reduce their debts by set-off.
- Pending actions to which the bankrupt is a party must be dealt with under the statutory insolvency regime.
- The bankrupt cannot take any action in relation to its estate unless that action is first approved by the judicial liquidator.
- There are also restrictions on sale and purchase agreements into which the bankrupt can enter with its creditors.
- The judicial liquidator can in certain circumstances set aside transactions entered into by the bankrupt prior to bankruptcy. The transactions open to challenge are those which may adversely affect the assets of the bankrupt. Examples include gifts made by the debtor, preferences, and any agreements between the debtor and parties controlled by him or which control him.
- All transactions defrauding creditors may be challenged by the specific action of "impugnação pauliana" under the terms of article 610 of the Civil Code.
- Where a transaction is successfully challenged, the party who is benefiting from it must ensure that he reimburses the company in full. The third party will then become an unsecured creditor in respect of the amount that he has paid to the company. For further information see Section 5 below "Augmenting the assets of the insolvent undertaking".

Effect of bankruptcy on the bankrupt's employees

A major consequence of bankruptcy is the termination of employees' contracts of employment.

Seizure of goods and assets

After the making of a bankruptcy order, the debtor's ability to dispose of its assets is restricted. Legal and factual possession of the assets passes to the judicial liquidator in consequence of the bankruptcy order.

A sequestration order extends to the company's assets, rights and records, whether or not they were the subject of a prior order.

Procedure

Seizure may be effected in two different ways to those set out above:

- "Balanço ou entrega directa": having been duly authorised by the judge, the liquidator will compile a list of all the assets (indicating their value) in co-operation with the bankrupt.
- "Arrolamento": the "arrolamento" will be executed by the court clerk with assistance from the "judicial liquidator". There are three different stages: identification, valuation and deposit of goods.

If the goods and assets seized can be pledged, notice of seizure must be given to the registries in which pledges could be registered.

Liquidation of the assets

Dissolution and liquidation of the assets of corporations

In Portugal, as opposed to many other European countries, the dissolution of a company always precedes its winding up or liquidation. However, dissolution prior to liquidation is more conceptual and theoretical than substantive in its effect.

The dissolution of a company can be voluntary ("contractual") or statutory. Statutory dissolution will occur if certain preconditions are met. Voluntary dissolution can be initiated by a decision of the company itself (*i.e.* if the company's shareholders resolve to dissolve it). It is also possible to draw a distinction between cases of automatic dissolution and dissolution by court order or shareholders' resolution. A bankruptcy order causes statutory and automatic dissolution (art 141 CCC).

After dissolution (which results from a bankruptcy order), the company will enter the period of liquidation, during which it retains its legal personality. This will only be lost at the end of the liquidation.

In general, liquidations follow the rules and procedures laid down in the Commercial Companies Code. In cases of insolvency and judicial liquidation, the rules of the CSPIRU apply.

Liquidation

After a bankruptcy order has been made, the liquidator attempts to sell the bankrupt's assets in consultation and, in some cases, subject to the approval of the committee of creditors .

Sales of assets can be effected under one of the following procedures:

- Judicial sale (through sealed bids or public auction).
- Extra-judicial sale (through sale on a stock exchange or commodity exchange, direct sale to entities which have the right to acquire certain goods, sale by private negotiation, or sale at auction.

Liquidation must be completed within six months.

Verification of claims against the bankrupt

The purpose of the verification phase of bankruptcy proceedings is to quantify the bankrupt's precise liabilities as against the assets available to discharge them.

Within the period of time specified in the bankruptcy order, (between 20 and 60 days) the creditors must submit their claims in the bankruptcy. This includes those creditors who had submitted claims prior to the commemcement of bankruptcy proceedings.

Within 14 days of the expiry of the period within which claims have been lodged, the liquidator must present a list of all amounts claimed, together with a list of debts for which no claim has been submitted but which he considers to exist.

All claims can be challenged either by the bankrupt or by creditors within seven days of the presentation by the judicial liquidator of the list of claims submitted to him.

Within 14 days of the end of this "challenge" period, the liquidator and the committee of creditors will give their final view of the claims submitted.

Within 15 days of this, the judge will issue a declaration ("despacho saneador"), listing:

- claims considered to have been proved (*bona fide* existing claims); and
- claims which are to be the object of further investigation.

After the court hearing and the judgment, the judge will rule on the validity of claims and on the order in which creditors are to be paid. The assets of the company will be divided into two parts; one available for the satisfaction of all unsecured claims, and the other consisting of all assets over which secured creditors hold valid charges. The judge's ruling may be appealed against.

Termination of liquidation

Creditors will be paid in the order established by the judge (*supra*) and subject to the costs of the insolvency proceedings first being paid in full.

The liquidator must, within 14 days of the end of the liquidation, prepare accounts of the liquidation. Both the creditors and the insolvent company are entitled to make representations about these accounts. They will, subject to such representations, then be approved by the judge.

The termination of the liquidation of a company must be duly registered in the Commercial Registry.

Rehabilitation of the bankrupt

Rehabilitation of the bankrupt and its officers may occur in the following cases upon the request of an interested party and subject to an appropriate judicial order being made :

- after an "extraordinary agreement" (*infra*);

- after the payment to creditors;
- when more than five years have passed since the final judgment on the liquidator's accounts;
- if no criminal procedures have been introduced and the judge finds that the bankrupt or its administrators or managers (in the case of corporations) have exercised their activities and functions with proper diligence.

"Extraordinary agreement"

Both creditors whose claims have been agreed and the bankrupt may terminate the bankruptcy procedure by "extraordinary agreement" between themselves, such agreement to be approved by the judge.

5. Augmenting the assets of the insolvent corporation

Recovering the assets

Throughout Portuguese law, there is a general principle that a debtor's assets should be used for the benefit of the creditors. The debtor may act to prejudice his creditors by any of the following means:

- diminishing his assets (through alienation, creating preferences, selective payment of debts);
- increasing his debts (by contracting new obligations);
- failing to augment his assets or reduce his debts, when either of such courses is possible.

In such circumstances, the law will enable a creditor or someone acting on behalf of a creditor to take action to:

- declare a contract void under article 605 CC;
- subrogate a creditor to the debtor's own claims under articles 606 to 609 CC;
- declare a contract whose only purpose was to defraud creditors by diminishing the assets void under article 610 CC;
- seize the debtor's assets under article 619 CC.

Action for a declaration avoiding a contract under article 605 CC

A creditor may invoke this provision either before or after he has actually become a creditor, as long as he is interested in the declaration of avoidance. It must be established that the debtor's act (of which the avoidance is sought) either created or exacerbated the debtor's insolvency. The declaration of avoidance is retroactive, requiring restitution of the situation prior to the conclusion of the contract which is avoided.

Subrogatory action under article 606 CC

Where the debtor fails to take appropriate action to recover either property, or damages or compensation to which it is entitled, a creditor may exercise such rights on the debtor's behalf except in the case of those rights which by law or by their own nature may normally only be exercised by the claimant itself.

Such action is only available when essential to the satisfaction or guarantee of the creditor's rights. Nevertheless, it is not necessary to show that the omission on the part of the debtor has provoked the latter's insolvency. Although by this means the creditor may act directly against the third party, the debtor must be made a party to the action.

Acting for a declaration avoiding a contract defrauding creditors under article 610 CC

This allows a creditor to challenge certain acts on the part of the debtor, where such acts are bound to jeopardise the debtor's creditworthiness. Certain factors must be shown to be present for the proper exercise of this action:

- the challenged act must not be personal in nature;
- the act must be the cause of the creditor's inability to receive payment in full. Thus this action can only be brought to challenge an act which has caused or worsened the debtor's insolvency;
- the third party must be a volunteer (*i.e.* one who has conferred no benefit on the debtor) or in bad faith (*i.e.* has connived with the debtor to defraud the creditor);
- the creditor's claim must pre-date the challenged act or, if it does not, the challenged act must have been done knowingly for the purpose of preventing the satisfaction of the future creditor's rights.

The burden of proof in relation to the amount of the debt lies with the creditor. The debtor or the third party seeking to prevent the challenged act from being declared void bears the burden of proving the debtor's solvency. This action can also be used to challenge subsequent transfers by the original transferee to third parties provided that:

- the general requirements set out above apply to the first transfer;
- the second transfer was not made for value or, if made for value, the parties to the transfer were acting in bad faith.

If the creditor is successful, he may be entitled to the restitution of the assets to the extent of his interest and may be entitled to enforce his debt against the assets of the third party.

Seizure under article 619 CC

Any creditor who justifiably fears that the debtor's assets will be so diminished as to jeopardise the repayment of his debt may request the seizure of the debtor's assets. If these requirements (*i.e.* the existence of the debt and a justifiable fear of diminution of the debtor's assets) are proved, the seizure may be ordered without hearing the opposite party. The creditor may be obliged to give security for damages (if that is demanded by the court) in case the seizure is found to be inappropriate.

The seizure is only the first step towards ensuring that the debtor's assets are made available to satisfy the debt. Thus, it may still be necessary to take further legal action to ensure this satisfaction.

The seizure expires if the creditor does not begin the subsequent legal action within 30 days of the order of seizure or if, having commenced the proceedings, the proceedings are interrupted during the 30 day period because of the creditor's negligence.

Shareholders' and managers' liability to creditors

Single shareholders and wholly-owned subsidiaries

If a company reduced to a single shareholder is declared bankrupt, the shareholder will be considered liable for the company's obligations which have emerged after all the "quotas" or "shares" were vested in such shareholder provided the shareholder's own assets have been intermingled with the company's assets *i.e.*, if the separation of assets between shareholder and company has not been duly observed (art 84 CCC). On the other hand it seems that, even if the separation has been duly observed, the shareholder and the company will be jointly responsible to the company's creditors, and the shareholder will be liable even if company's assets are sufficient to meet its obligations.

Articles 488 and 491 of CCC establish that, in the case of wholly-owned subsidiaries of SpQs or SAs, constituted under the form of SAs, the sole shareholder will have unlimited liability in respect of the subsidiary company's obligations.

Similar rules exist for other kinds of associations of companies (or groups of companies) whereby one of the companies is somehow subordinated to the other company (known as the "leader company of the group").

Managers and directors

Managers and directors of the company will be liable to the creditors of the company if, due to their fault or negligence, the company's assets are not sufficient to cover liabilities (for example, if they have misapplied or given away assets to the detriment of creditors) (art 78/1 CCC).

Managers and directors are also liable to the company and its shareholders for any damages resulting from breaches of legislation or the company's byelaws. Shareholders who, according to the company's articles of association, are able by themselves or with others to whom they are related due to "acordos parasociais" ("quasi social arrangements"), to appoint or remove managers or directors, will be jointly liable with such managers and directors for damages caused to the company (art 83 CCC).

If the company fails to take appropriate action to recover damages or compensation to which it is entitled, the creditors may exercise such rights under the terms of article 606 referred to above. In the case of insolvency, this prerogative may be exercised by the judicial administrator.

In the case of deliberate insolvency ("insolvência dolosa") or negligent insolvency ("falência não intencional"), the managers or directors of the company who are found guilty of fraudulent or negligent acts leading to the company's insolvency may be punished with imprisonment for up to five years if the officer acted fraudulently and bankruptcy has been declared, or with imprisonment for up to a year or a fine if the officer acted negligently and bankruptcy has been declared (arts 325, 326 Portuguese Criminal Code).

6. Public control over insolvent corporations

Article 82/1, CPC provides that jurisdiction to make a declaration of insolvency or to initiate preventive measures belongs to the district court where the company's main establishment is located, or if no such district court exists, to the court where the residence of the debtor is situated.

In the case of branches (or other forms of representation incorporated in Portugal) of a foreign company, jurisdiction belongs to the district court where such branch or office is located. That court is only competent to rule on the assets within Portuguese territory (art 82/2 CPC).

The new code (CSPIRU), together with other supplementary legislation, has privatised the functions of the judicial administrator and of the judicial liquidator, through the elimination of the sindico who, under the previous regime, had some public functions.

Neither both the judicial administrator nor the judicial liquidator are civil servants of any kind, nor are they in any other way employed by or on behalf of the state. With some limitations, they may exercise other functions along with those they undertake as judicial administrator and liquidator.

Insolvent entities remain subject to the control of the court, the judicial liquidator, the public prosecutor and their creditors.

Contents of Chapter 13

CORPORATE INSOLVENCY LAW IN SPAIN

1.	**Introduction**	559
	Sources of law	559
	The Spanish state as an autonomous state	561
	Bankruptcy law and persons	562
	Applicable bankruptcy law	563
2.	**Corporation and other business entities**	563
	Introduction	563
	Types of business entity	564
	Management	567
	Owners and holdings of interests, participations and shares	570
	Financing and security for creditors	573
	Available information relating to companies	575
	Other business entities	577
	Debt collection and asset recovery	578
3.	**Survival of the insolvent corporation or its business**	582
	Introduction	582
	Agreement with the creditors	582
	Suspension of payments	584
	Other procedures to resolve corporate crises	598
4.	**Termination of the corporation: bankruptcy**	599
	Purpose and effect	599
	Considerations prior to the submission of the application for bankruptcy	600
	The proceedings	601
	Proceedings post-declaration	605
5.	**Augmenting the assets of the insolvent corporation**	612
	Restitution	612
	Action against the management of the debtor	614

6.   Public control over insolvent corporations   614
  Interventores   614
  Comisarios   614
  Sindicos   615
  General comments   615

Chapter 13

CORPORATE INSOLVENCY LAW IN SPAIN

Fernando Lopez-Orozco,
Bufete Mullerat & Roca

1. Introduction

Sources of law

Spanish law conforms to the civil or continental system which can be outlined as follows:

Legislation

The principal legislation is the Constitution of 1978 which governs the process of law making and its effect. The Spanish Constitution was passed by the "Cortes Constituyentes" – the Parliament elected specially to pass the Constitution – and was ratified by a referendum of the Spanish people.

Legislation is drafted according to a specially established procedure which is published in Official State Gazettes or the Official Gazettes of the Autonomous Communities. The Parliamentary powers and jurisdiction of the Autonomous Communities are derived directly from the Constitution and its surbordinate statutes. Certain matters are the exclusive responsibility of the State, others of the Autonomous Communities, while some are the responsibility of both.

International Treaties and judgments of the Constitutional Court may be included within the category of legislation. All the treaties and some of the judgments, are also published in the Official Gazettes described above.

Practice

The law is implemented according to unwritten rules which are invariably observed in legal business circles and which are considered obligatory. This applies in the absence of any appropriate legislation.

The general principles of law

The general principles of law are derived from the application of legislation to resolve disputes in circumstances where those disputes are not directly resolved by any existing law. Such principles are derived by a process of logic starting from those enacted provisions which are closest to providing a resolution of the problem. Principles created in this way may themselves, in suitable cases, be extended and applied through the same logical process. In other words, when there is no express legal provision, one is created through the logical extension of existing provisions. Some of these principles have even been included in the Constitution.

Case law

Case law is not formally considered as a source of law. The Spanish Civil Code does provide, however, that the "accepted legal doctrine" repeatedly established by the Supreme Court when interpreting or applying the law will supplement the body of laws.

Although case law may in practice be consulted as a guide, it does not have the same binding nature as in Anglo Saxon countries. The Spanish system is an heir to the system described by Montesquieu in which the judge is "la voi de la loi". In this system the judge only declares a prior will assumed to be adequately stated in the Code. In practice, however, the function of the judge is of great importance, and judicial pronouncements should be considered as a source of law.

In contrast to the sources described above, procedure is not presumed to be known by the courts and it is necessary to prove it. This makes it a difficult and uncertain area within the Spanish system, even though it is relevant in areas of public life where tradition prevails.

Concepts

Public and private law

Legislation in Spain falls into the categories of both private and public law. The former relates to the laws which govern the individual and his property, including questions of ownership, contracts and other obligations. The latter governs the relationship between the administration and the citizen.

The nineteenth century liberal tradition inhibited public intervention in what was seen to be an area of private legal relations. In recent years, however, the state has not only increased the depth of its penetration into public life, it has also invaded areas which were formerly reserved for private law.

Administrative law has, therefore, been gaining in importance both generally and in the area of insolvency law, with developments such as the creation of special bodies to intervene in cases of insolvency in such strategic sectors as banking or insurance sectors. There has also been considerable development of special policies for particularly sensitive areas, such as industrial reorganisation and permanent intervention in the labour market.

The status of the debtor

This may be civil or commercial and its importance lies in the fact that the category into which the debtor falls will dictate the applicable body of laws, *i.e.* civil or mercantile law.

Mercantile law was drafted as an independent system in the Commercial Code, first in 1829, and then later in 1885. Spain has also inherited from French tradition the "Trader's Statute" and the concept of the "Commercial Act" (commercial contracts and so on). This area of law often is not very clear and gives rise to much controversy.

Relevant legislation for the purposes of this chapter

The following legal texts are particularly relevant to insolvency:

- the Commercial Code 1985;
- the Civil Procedural Law 1881;
- the Old Commercial Code 1829, to which the Civil Procedural Law refers by default;
- the Law of Suspension of Payments 1922.

As far as companies are concerned, the following are also applicable:

- The Commercial Code 1985;
- The Civil Code 1889;
- The Business Corporations Law and the Limited Companies Law, revised by the 1989 Royal Decree-Act relating to reform and adaptation to the body of laws of the European Community.

In addition to the above, there are special administrative, fiscal, labour and mercantile laws which are applicable to certain aspects of insolvency.

It must be borne in mind, however, that although there has been incessant legislative activity in the last decade leading to profound changes, Spanish legislation, and in particular that legislation which affects bankruptcy or insolvency law, may be classified not only as old, but also as antiquated, and it is common among authors to criticise its partiality, the fact that it is widely dispersed, and its lack of contact with reality.

The Spanish state as an autonomous state

The Spanish Constitution regards the Spanish state as divided up into territorial entities, with political autonomy (art 143 of the Spanish Constitution). Each Autonomous Community has an Assembly and a Government and within the scope of their competence, have their own legislative power, publishing their legislation in the appropriate official gazette.

However, autonomous bodies have little influence over mercantile law as this is considered by article 149.6 of the Constitution as the exclusive competence of the central State.

Bankruptcy law and persons

Spanish law acknowledges the existence of "juristic" persons in addition to individuals or physical persons. Juristic persons (or corporate bodies) are legal entities to which the law grants the power to act as though they were persons. They may therefore own net worth and be subject to rights and obligations with all the powers that this entails to make contracts, act in court, and so on.

According to article 35 of the Civil Code, there are three basic categories of juristic person:

- corporations;
- foundations; and
- associations.

Corporations are of a public nature and are created by public authority usually by the enactment of a law or under powers granted by a previously enacted law.

Foundations are "patrimonies" linked to the fulfilment of a particular purpose of a charitable nature. Like corporations, they are under the jurisdiction of the public powers.

Associations are voluntary groupings of persons formed by a decision taken by their members. They may be for public or private purposes. They serve as a channel for the exercise of public or political rights and include associations in general, political parties, trade unions, groups of companies and religious associations. Their basic regulations are contained in the 1964 Associations Law, although there are special laws which govern certain specific types of association.

There are various types of private association, including companies, co-operatives and mutual aid societies. Companies – the prime subject-matter of this book – may be of a civil or mercantile nature, a distinction which, as already pointed out, dictates whether the company is governed by civil or mercantile law.

Both civil and mercantile companies are voluntary groupings of persons who contribute assets, labour and/or money in common in order to share profits.

This distinction has given rise to a significant debate between numerous contradictory schools of opinion regarding the interpretation of legal texts. In principle the distinction is based on the purpose for which the company is established, some purposes being designated as civil and others as commercial. Here, however, it is sufficient to observe that the types of company which are the most common in practice, the business corporation and the limited liability company, are considered as mercantile companies simply by reason of adopting these forms.

The following are the categories of company:

- civil companies;
- companies with a mercantile form and a civil purpose (which are governed by the Civil Code and the Commercial Code, insofar as they are not contradictory);

- mercantile companies (whether characterised by their purpose, or their form).

Applicable bankruptcy law

Civil subjects and civil companies in a state of insolvency must follow the procedural channels of "quita y espera" (reduction of amount and extension of time) and "concurso de acreedores" (creditors' meeting), provided in the Civil Procedural Law.

On the other hand in the event that mercantile companies and individual traders are unable to meet their acquired debts with their assets, they must make use of the procedures of "suspension de pagos" (suspension of payments) and "quiebra" (bankruptcy) which are established in the Commercial Code, civil procedural laws and certain special laws such as the 1992 Suspension of Payments Act.

However, certain regulations are applicable to both civil and mercantile institutions.

2. Corporation and other business entities

Introduction

The origin of a company is contained in a contract (the Commercial Code calls it "the company charter") whereby two or more persons agree to contribute assets or labour to a communal fund in order to obtain a profit. However, in order for an entity to exist separately and independently from the partners (*i.e.* with its own legal status), it is necessary for it to be "legally incorporated". Thus, to attain legal status the company's charter and bye laws must be recorded in a public deed, and that deed must be entered at the Commercial Registry.

The charter includes the declarations of the parties of their wish to incorporate a company, together with the form or corporate type which they wish to adopt from among those contained in the Commercial Code.

In addition, the charter contains a statement as to what contributions are made by the partners and the participation and interest of each in the company. The system of administration, including the establishment of governing bodies, appointment to offices and acceptances and statements regarding inability to act, are frequently included in the contents of the charter.

The bye laws, which are subsidiary to the charter, contain the following information:

- the name of the company;
- its purpose or purposes;

- the date on which the operations of the company commence and, where appropriate, the duration of life of the company;
- the domicile of the company;
- rules regarding capital and other financial aspects of ownership;
- the governing bodies and methods of making decisions;
- rules on the extent of members' liability for the debts of the company and the distribution of profits, as appropriate;
- rules regarding dissolution and liquidation.

Any company incorporated under the Commercial Code and other special laws as a partnership, general partnership, general partnership by shares, limited liability company or business corporation, is a mercantile company for the purpose of the applicable bankruptcy provisions.

The main framework for each type of company is established by statute, but there is substantial flexibility as to the terms and covenants that may be contained within its constitution.

There are certain fundamental distinctions between the different types of companies to meet the requirements of those who establish the company. Thus it may be important to stress the special qualities of particular participators rather than purely financial considerations. This distinction may be expressed as personal companies as opposed to capitalist companies. Another fundamental distinction is whether the liability of the members of the company for the debts of the company is limited (to the amount agreed to be invested) or is unlimited.

Types of business entity

Partnerships

The partnership is the basic type of association in the Commercial Code. In view of its system of unlimited liability it is less common than previously, but it continues to be of importance in that its rules govern many disputes in cases where business is conducted by an association which has not been incorporated or has not been registered. It is characterised by the Spanish Commercial Code as one in which several traders use a "collective name". The members are liable jointly and severally for the debts of the limited partnership, but can only be called upon if and when the latter is unable to pay its debts. Although there are exceptions, all the members normally take part in the management and administration of the limited partnership.

The personal status of the partner is important. This is illustrated by strict control of the transferability of participation rights, equality of power and mutual consent for certain changes (although, there may be agreement to function by majority in certain instances). The bankruptcy of the company leads to the bankruptcy of the partners unless they satisfactorily discharge in full the debts of the partnership.

General partnerships

General partnerships are rare in practice. Their roots are in the medieval institution of the "comenda" and in the maritime world. Article 122 of the Commercial Code defines this type of company as one in which several subjects contribute a certain amount of capital to a communal fund, with corporate operations being directed exclusively by others under a collective name.

The legal regime governing these associations is strongly influenced by the limited partnership, whose regulations, are according to the Commercial Code, apply to general partnerships.

There are thus two types of members – those who direct the affairs of the partnership ("collective partners") and those who simply contribute to the assets of the partnership ("general partners"). The liability of the former for the debts of the partnership is unlimited, but the latters' liability is limited to their contribution.

General partnerships by shares

The general partnerships by share is a sub-category of the general partnership and was developed in order to avoid the "concesion" (a kind of government authorisation, not required for partnerships) which was necessary at a given moment in order to found a "business corporation". This endows it with certain special features but it has a great deal in common with the General Partnership.

Limited liability companies

A limited liability company has a unique feature in that the other partners normally have pre-emption rights and all the partners usually participate in the decision-making process. Although this may be reduced to a minimum by appropriate provisions in the bye laws. This type of company is therefore a hybrid, and has been reformed for the purposes of making it a channel for small or family businesses which hitherto had to resort to the form of business corporation to enable the members to enjoy the privilege of limited liability.

The minimum capital stock is Ptas 500,000 divided into equal parts called "participaciones". The legal maximum of 50 million participaciones has now disappeared though there is a still a legal maximum of 50 for the number of shareholders. The capital must be specific, determined and established in the bye laws. The participaciones are not divisible, nor are they negotiable.

It is not now necessary to enter the fact of ownership or transfer of these participaciones at the Commercial Registry. This ensures a certain measure of confidentially as to the holders, but such information must be stated in a book (known as the "libro registro de socios") which the company is obliged to keep. The partners' liability is limited to the amount of the participation that they have assumed. The capital must be fully paid on the creation of the company, either in cash or in kind.

Business corporations

The business corporation is the star of the Spanish corporate firmament, both in terms of numbers and of importance. Article 1 of the revised text of the Business Corporations Law, published through Legislative Royal Decree 1564/1989 of 22 December establishes that, "in a joint stock company the capital shall be divided into shares, and shall be paid in by means of contributions by the shareholders, who shall not be personally liable for corporate debts".

Whatever its purpose, this type of company will be of a mercantile nature and must have minimum capital of Ptas 10 million.

In the latest reform this type of company has been subject to a profound change in order to adapt it to European company law, with important provisions being introduced relating to the protection of third parties and shareholders.

Special business corporations

The business corporation has become a channel for some of the modern trends in state intervention which is manifested in two ways. First, business corporations with specially adapted regulations are established in order to control the labour market in which they are engaged. The main examples of such specially governed business corporations include real estate investment companies, companies managing funds for real estate investment, banking companies, insurance companies, groups of companies, finance companies for hire-purchase sales, journalistic or publishing companies and leasing companies.

Second, business corporations with state capital are frequently established to organise certain state controlled operations. This, in fact, is the only case in which the Business Corporations Law allows the foundation of business corporations with one shareholder.

Public capital companies (companies with finance on public markets)

Companies in Spain that wish to have access to the public securities markets must fulfil certain requirements and conditions, though this does not mean that they constitute a separate type of company. Such companies are, in fact, business corporations subject to additional requirements. These relate to the foundation and description of the corporation, savings, the system of annual accounts, the system of shares and bonds, voting rights attached to shares, the convertibility of securities, audited accounts, the system of groups of companies, and so on. The government of the securities market has undergone important developments in the last few years in Spain. Many of these developments are enshrined in the Securities Market Law 24/1988 which governs the basic institutions.

Management

Each type of company has its particular type of administration:

Partnerships

If there is no specific covenant contained in the bye laws to provide for the appointment of a specific person as administrator, or for decision-making by majority resolution, the administration is carried out by all of the partners jointly and severally, *i.e.* each one may make decisions provided that there is no opposition from any of the other partners. Any administrator appointed in the bye laws may not be removed, although it is possible to apply for the appointment of a co-administrator if the former is causing serious loss or damage to the partnership.

Administrators have the same system of liability as the partners and are therefore liable for malicious acts, abuse of powers or gross negligence. Partners who are not administrators do not participate in daily management but do have duties in the general supervision of the business.

As far as external legal relationships are concerned a corporate signature is effective if agreement is contained in the deed of incorporation or in an agreement between all the partners. In the absence of such agreement the corporate signature is held by all the partners *i.e.* any partner may use it in circumstances expressly or impliedly accepted by the other partners. Its scope extends to the whole corporate purpose.

General partnerships

The partners follow the same system as above in that they are the only ones who may participate in the administration of the company. The general partners may participate in internal management at the general meeting, where they are also empowered to appoint and remove the collective partners, but they are not allowed to carry out any act of administration.

Again, as for partnerships, dealings with external legal bodies may only be carried out by collective partners. A general partner who carries out any act of administration will immediately become collective and will incur unlimited liability.

Where the entity is a general partnership by shares, the procedure is the same with one variation – the collective partners are the managers and do not depend for their appointment and removal upon the shareholders' meeting. The shareholders function in a meeting in a similar way to the shareholders of a business corporation.

Limited liability companies

With the exception of specific aspects of lack of competence, terms of office, or removal of directors, the administration of limited liability companies is governed by the provisions contained in the Business Corporations Act.

The Shareholders may make decisions without assembling in general meeting provided that there are no more than 15 shareholders and that there is postal or telegraphic proof of the agreement by all the shareholders to any decision reached.

The personal nature of this company, as opposed to the business corporation, is reflected in the fact that, when meetings are held, the quorum must be satisfied both as to a minimum amount of capital and a minimum number of members.

The formal requirements for convening the meeting are less strict, although the system for protesting resolutions is the same as in the Business Corporations Act.

Business corporations

Corporate and government bodies

Directors are appointed by the general shareholders' meeting, which also determines their number if the bye laws only establish a maximum and a minimum number. The general shareholders' meeting may appoint and remove directors at any time, even when this is not stated as business on the agenda.

The government of a business corporation allows for several forms of administration which may consist of one or more sole administrators, with either joint and several or joint powers, or of a board of directors, which must be created whenever there are more than two persons responsible for administration jointly and when there are more than two sole administrators with joint, as opposed to joint and several, powers.

The board of directors governs daily matters, both with regard to internal management and to the external representation of the company. This latter function extends to everything related to the company's trade within the limits laid down in the corporate purpose.

Directors also have special obligations expressly imposed by company law, such as that reviewing the valuation of contributions in kind, calling general shareholders' meetings and submitting the accounts.

Directors need not necessarily be shareholders, although they must be generally authorised to carry on business and they must not be affected by any incompatibility or prohibition whatsoever. Bankrupts and those who are subject to insolvency proceedings and who are not subsequently absolved, may not be directors.

They are appointed by the general meeting for a term of office which may not exceed five years, although they may be re-elected. They may be removed at any time by the general shareholders' meeting under article 131 of the Business Corporations Law.

Directors are liable for damage caused by malicious acts and abuse of powers (even without gross negligence), though they are exempt from the effects of minor negligence. Liability actions may be brought by the company itself, by the shareholders and by the creditors as well as by individuals (either shareholders or third parties) suffering damage, or third parties who consider themselves individually damaged by any act carried out by the director.

The board of directors makes decisions by a majority when half plus one of the members are assembled, although a postal vote is possible for an individual meeting, provided that none of the directors oppose this.

Under article 141, in the absence of any resolution or provision in the bye laws, the directors may appoint the chairman. They may also exercise powers of delegation by appointing from among their members one or more managing directors or one or more delegate or executive committees. While managing directors are extremely common due to the need for day-to-day flexible management, delegate committees exist mainly in large companies.

The "delegation" of powers, to either an individual director or a committee, does not have any pre-established legal structure. It depends on the specific scope granted in each individual case by the delegating body.

Certain powers and duties may not be delegated. These include the submission of accounts and balance sheets to the general shareholders' meeting and powers received from the general shareholders' meeting unless specific authorisation to delegate has been given. There must be a two-thirds majority of the board of directors for any delegation of their powers and no delegation will be effective until it is entered at the Commercial Registry.

In the same way as is provided for general shareholders' meetings, a minute book will be kept in which resolutions will be recorded. Minutes must be signed by the chairman and the secretary. Null and void resolutions, or those which can be annulled, may be protested by the directors or shareholders representing 5% of the capital stock within 30 days from the time when they received knowledge of the resolution, provided that less than one year has passed since its adoption.

Relationships between bodies

In Spain the separation between professional managers and shareholders investing in companies – control groups and management groups – is widespread, although not where the business corporation form is used for smaller, family orientated businesses and where there is a close identification between the owners, the shareholders and the managers.

The general manager

Although not referred to in the relevant legislation, the position of general manager is frequently provided for in the bye laws. He is highly significant in the day-to-day life of the company and there has been considerable difficulty in arriving at a satisfactory conclusion as to the extent to which his powers should be limited. As a top executive, the general manager of a business corporation is treated as a "special employee" and has, since 1985, been subject to a special labour relationship. When general managers are "consejeros delegados" (*i.e.* they have been delegated wide powers of attorney from the board of directors), they are deemed to be a body of the company and the special labour laws do not apply to them.

This provides for unilateral termination of the contract with the company with advance notice of three or six months, depending on whether the duration of the contract is of more or less than five years, with compensation of seven days' salary per year worked, unless there is specific agreement setting out different compensation provisions. Over the last few years compensation agreements ("parachute clauses"), which provide a fairer level of compensation, have come into general use.

Secretary and legal consultant

The Secretary carries out the strictly administrative functions of preparing and certifying minutes of meetings of the board of directors. In addition, the office of legal consultant was established in 1975 for companies over a certain size.

Companies domiciled in Spain with a capital of at least 50 million pesetas, a turnover of over 100 million pesetas or a work force of over 50 employees – or the latter two circumstances only for those foreign companies which carry on activities in Spain – must appoint a legal consultant. The legal consultant supervises, among other things, the convening of the general shareholders' meeting, the execution of resolutions of the general meeting and certifying such resolutions which may be registered (Royal Decree 2288/1977 of 5 August).

Owners and holdings of interests, participations and shares

Partnerships

The partners in a limited partnership normally participate directly in the management unless administrators have been appointed in the deed of incorporation.

They have the right to all profits and incur all losses, normally in proportion to the interests or participation contained in the charter, unless there is express provision for equal distribution.

Partners may not carry on activities which compete with those of the partnership unless they have authorisation from the partnership to do so. If they carry out such activities they may be removed from the partnership, and any profits derived from the operations will be attributed to the company. If there are losses, these will be attributed solely to the removed partner.

General partnerships

Collective partners are subject to the same system as described in the preceding section. The law specifically forbids general partners from involving themselves in administration to the extent that they may not even act as attorneys. If they do so they become collective partners and thus liable for partnership debts.

Otherwise, the liability of a general partner is limited to the amount he has agreed to contribute or the sum mentioned in the guarantee, dependant on what is entered at the Commercial Registry.

General partners are not subject to such strict obligations regarding non-competition as collective partners are, but they must respect obligations arising from loyalty and co-operation.

General partners have a limited right to information, which is dependant on what is provided in the company charter.

The same principles apply to a general partnership by shares.

Limited liability companies

The ownership of participation rights confers on the owner membership rights to participate actively in corporate life, form part of the board, appoint administrators, receive dividends and transfer their participation rights.

The personal nature of the company is reflected in the pre-emptive right of first refusal given to the other partners or to the company itself in the event of a proposed transfer of participation rights by a living person (save in the case of a transfer arising on the death of a partner). The value is determined either by the bye laws or by a considered opinion by experts appointed by each of the parties, plus one expert duly appointed by the judge. It is not necessary to enter the transfer at the Commercial Registry, but it is necessary to inform the administrators so that the acquisition of a participation by a third party may be recorded in the ledger – a prerequisite for the exercise of corporate rights. A transfer arising on the death of a member may also be subject to pre-emptive rights in favour of the other members.

Minority members are protected by the fact that a special majority is required to amend the bye laws (a majority of members plus two-thirds of the capital at first call and two-thirds of the capital only at second call). Even where decisions are made with the required majority, protests may be made where such decisions are considered to be detrimental to the interests of the company.

Meetings of members are called by the administrators with the necessary advance notice and agenda. The meeting must also be called at the request of 10% of the members or of any lower percentage laid down by the bye laws. A quorum is not necessary, since any decision taken must be agreed to by a majority of the total capital stock (*i.e.* not simply of those present). Members may attend the general meeting in person or by proxy, provided that such representation is confirmed in writing.

Business corporations

Apart from his right to participate at the shareholders' meeting – where, *inter alia*, he may vote to appoint or remove the directors – a shareholder has no further participation in the management, and has no liability other than up to the par value of the shares for which he subscribes.

Shares confer the following minimum rights:

- to share in the profits (and the net worth resulting from liquidation);
- pre-emptive subscription for new shares or securities which may be converted into shares;
- to attend and vote at general shareholders' meetings and protest resolutions; and
- to prescribed information.

There may be several types of shares, each type with their own rights or the same rights and the same par value.

In order to create privileged shares, strict requirements of quorum and a special majority are imposed – similar to that for amendment of the bye laws. It is not permitted to create shares which, in one way or another, guarantee the payment of interest or shares which confer greater voting power than that reflected in the capital stock for which such shares were issued. Shares are represented by transferable certificates.

Under article 90 of the new Business Corporations Law, it is now possible to issue shares without the right to vote, although the number of such shares may not exceed one half of the capital paid in. They carry a right to a minimum dividend which may, in the absence of sufficient profit, have to be accumulated and paid in future years.

The holders of these shares take preference over the others and any attempt to alter the rights attached to them must be agreed to by a majority of those who hold them.

General shareholders' meetings are either ordinary or special meetings.

The ordinary meeting is obligatory and must be held during the first six months of each financial year in order to:

- approve the management's conduct of the company's affairs;
- approve, as appropriate, the accounts submitted by the directors; and
- adopt resolutions regarding the application of the profits. Any other general shareholders' meeting is a special meeting.

The general shareholders' meeting adopts resolutions which are binding on all shareholders whether or not present and whether or not opposed to the resolution and therefore, in order to protect shareholders against the possibility of a material decision being taken without their knowledge, certain requirements for calling and conducting the meeting must be observed.

The agenda must be published in the Official Gazette of the Commercial Registry and in the daily newspaper of largest circulation in the province where the company has its domicile at least 15 days prior to the date fixed for the meeting. The call is issued by the directors. They must do so when the holders of at least 5% of the capital stock request them to do so.

If all the shareholders are present and are unanimous, they may assemble as a "general shareholders' consent meeting". This enables the meeting to discuss any matter for which it is responsible irrespective of the published agenda.

The "general shareholders' consent meeting" has been and continues to be a frequent resort of small business corporations for the purpose of avoiding the complex system for convening described above.

There is a complex set of quorum provisions. The statute sets down a minimum quorum which may be increased by the company's bye laws. Special quorums are required in relation to certain basic issues such as the issue of securities, increase or reduction of capital, and mergers or amendment to the bye laws. Finally, where the company has issued registrable securities, the shareholder must have entered his title in the registered shares ledger of the company five days in advance of the date for the meeting in order to be entitled to attend. The holder of bearer shares must deposit his title or the deposit counterfoils with the company five days in advance of the meeting.

Attendance by proxy is permitted and shareholders may request information, although the Directors may validly refuse such a request where the consequence would be damage to the company.

Financing and security for creditors

Introduction

The main source of finance for companies is its capital but it also frequently resorts to outside sources of finance. This may consist of credits, loans or long, medium, or short-term credit facilities. It might issue promissory notes, bonds, debentures, and might take advantage of the reciprocal granting of commercial credit in economic life.

Under article 1911 of the Civil Code, the present and future assets of the company are charged with payment of its debts. However, to guard against the possibility of the company's liabilities exceeding its assets, lenders have sought some privileges or preferences or such guarantees as would place them in a superior position *vis-a-vis* the company and other creditors.

Guarantees

Under a personal guarantee a third party undertakes liability for all or part of a debt if the debtor does not repay the debt. In Spanish law this is referred to as a "surety" or "guarantee" and is specifically included in article 1922 of the Civil Code. Under article 439 of the Commercial Code such guarantee is a commercial contract when it insures the fulfilment of a commercial contract, even if the guarantor is not a trader.

A surety is ancillary to the main obligation. Thus, if the main obligation is annulled, then the surety's obligation will also be annulled.

In the case of a joint and several guarantee, on the other hand, the creditor may proceed against the guarantor directly without having first to recover whatever is possible from the principal debtor. And where there are two or more joint and several guarantors, each is liable in full for the whole of the principal debt, subject to a right of recourse against the principal debtor and any other guarantor.

Pledge and mortgage

This confers a right on the creditor to seek payment of the debt out of the proceeds of sale of certain specified moveable assets belonging to the debtor. In general, the asset or thing is delivered to the creditor (pledgee). The date of delivery must be recorded in a public deed.

Certain moveable assets are of great importance, may be identified individually and may be essential to the debtor as a means of production. To enable security to be given over such assets, "chattel mortgage" and "pledge without transfer" were created by legislation in 1964. Only a limited, fixed number of assets may be subject to such pledges, and they must be recorded in a public instrument by means of an entry on a special register. In this way it is possible to use commercial establishments, automobiles, aircraft, industrial machinery and intellectual or industrial rights as security.

Under this legislation it is possible to mortgage a commercial establishment "as a whole". This is governed by articles 19,20 and 28 of the Chattel Mortgage Law of 1964, although it is only possible when the person creating the mortgage is the owner or lessee of the business premises. The following are included in the mortgage: leases, commercial names, commercial signs, distinguishing marks, intellectual or industrial property, machinery, moveables and other items of equipment. In addition, it is possible to include merchandise and raw materials, but only by express agreement. During the existence of such a mortgage, the debtor company may use those assets without restriction in the ordinary course of its business. The mortgagee is not permitted to seek the sale or expropriation of any of the assets as long as the debtor is not in breach of any of its obligations to the mortgagee. In order to protect the mortgagee however, the mortgage crystallises in the case of termination of the lease agreement or if there is a loss of 25% in the value of the mortgaged assets.

As far as immoveable property is concerned, Spanish law contains the concepts of mortgage and "antichresis". The latter is a formula for the transfer of possession and administration to the creditor to enable him to pay the claim out of the proceeds.

The regulations governing mortgages are contained in the Mortgage Act 1946 and its Regulations which came into force in 1947, although both have undergone subsequent revision.

They are similar to those of the pledge and mortgage over moveable property and consist in the power of the mortgagee to sell the mortgaged asset in the event of default and to apply the proceeds to pay the debt. These powers arise by virtue of the mortgage and are exercisable independently of the current registered owner of the asset.

In addition to the mortgage on real estate, there is the floating charge up to a fixed amount to guarantee a current account (art 153 of the Mortgage Act) or to guarantee payment of endorsable or bearer securities (arts 154-156 of the Mortgage Act).

Mortgages and pledges may be enforced by judicial proceedings or by a non-judicial procedure. In the former case this is by means of accelerated proceedings. In the latter case, this is done by means of a special provision in the mortgage or pledge, with the execution of the document being carried out via the public notary certification procedure. It is also necessary to agree on certain aspects of the proceedings such as, for example, the value to be placed on the assets at auction and the addresses of the parties to be notified.

The judicial procedure takes approximately two years, but there has recently been a move to reduce this to six months by a more dynamic enforcement process, possibly through the notaries public. For the moment, however, this is only a proposal, although legislation has recently been enacted to facilitate the extra-judicial enforcement of mortgages through public notary proceedings.

Reservation of title

Here the supplier of goods reserves to himself the ownership of the goods transferred until the price of the goods has been paid in full.

Where this arises in the case of sale of moveable assets by instalments, entry in the Commercial Registry of the reservation of title provision is required.

Set-off

Provided set-off is specifically pleaded, article 1196 of the Civil Code allows mutual, matured, liquid and enforceable debts as between the same parties to be set off against each other prior to the debtor becoming bankrupt. However, although the matter is not free from doubt, the generally accepted view is that set-off is not available where the debtor becomes bankrupt except in the following cases:

- article 926 of the Commercial Code provides that a creditor who is also a shareholder/partner in the organisation and has some or all of his contribution due to the organisation outstanding is only a creditor for the balance;
- if a party is both owed and owes a debt under the same contract, only the balance is taken into account;
- set-off will apply where special provision is made for it in contractual relationships with banks that are running current accounts for the organisation.

Available information relating to companies

The Spanish corporate world does not provide abundant and clear information on the various aspects of legal business. Companies have retained a great deal of privacy.

Information on companies in Spain is obtained:

- through commercial reports by third parties, frequently from the banking system (RAI or Register of Debtors);

- through the commercial network itself (including reports by clients or suppliers); and

- by consulting the various official registers, in particular the Commercial Register and the Property Register. The latter provides information regarding ownership or rights of third parties as to the real estate that a person may hold.

The Commercial Registry publishes certain information on the corporate and financial life of companies, the function of which differs according to the type of company. However, the following details are included for all companies :

- the incorporation of the company, any amendments of the charter and of the corporate bye laws, along with increases and reductions in capital;

- the appointment and removal of directors, sindicos and auditors, and of secretaries and vice-secretaries of the corporate governing bodies;

- general powers of attorney and delegation of duties, together with any amendments, revocations and replacements;

- any transformation or merger;

- the dissolution and liquidation of the company;

- the issue of negotiable debentures and the acts and circumstances relating to them;

- the acceptance of shares for listing on an official secondary securities market, along with any exclusion therefrom;

- any suspension of payments and bankruptcy.

Some companies, such as business corporations, limited liability companies, general partnerships by shares and reciprocal guarantee companies are obliged to submit annual accounts at the commercial registry of their domicile within one month from approval, together with the certificate of agreement of the corporate body responsible, (the signatures of which must be endorsed by a notary public) and one copy of the annual accounts duly identified in the certificate referred to above. To these accounts must be attached a management report, the auditors're-port and the certificate stating that the accounts deposited correspond with those audited.

The annual accounts and the management report must be signed by all the directors and the auditors' report must be signed by them.

Information on companies may also be found in certain publications such as the Gazette of the Commercial Registry itself and the Official State Gazette or the Official Gazettes of the Autonomous Communities or in newspapers of large circulation according to provinces, since in some cases it is necessary by law to publish in them certain information, such as calls for general shareholders' meetings, increases and reductions in capital, transfer of domicile and merger projects.

Certain private agencies function unofficially, reporting and providing information on companies which suspend payments and which are declared bankrupt.

Certain private agencies co-operate by monitoring official or private journals for the announcements that companies must publish.

Other business entities

Special corporations deserving mention

The special corporations mentioned on p566 above are subject to a number of special provisions basically aimed at enabling the state to intervene. In principle, in the event of insolvency, the general system applies, but in practice the existence of public interests of enormous importance has given rise to the creation of a special regime for these circumstances.

These companies include banking and insurance institutions which have special bodies such as the Bank Deposit Guarantee Fund and the Liquidating Commission for Insurance Companies (CLEA), which act as management bodies for companies in financial difficulty.

Public or state companies

State institutions, including all their agencies, local government bodies, autonomous regional bodies or autonomous state bodies, may not be declared bankrupt (art 1 of the Litigious-Administrative Jurisdiction Law and the Spanish Constitution).

However, cases frequently arise of limited liability companies or business corporations with public capital, possibly incorporated by the administration, or with mixed capital, which are subject to private law in their relationships. These are public companies and are among the autonomous entities which are particularly intended to be governed by norms of private law in view of their commercial, financial or industrial nature (art 4.1.b of the Autonomous state Entities Act). These entities may be declared bankrupt.

Companies providing public services

Companies providing public services have a system which is specially governed in articles 930 *et seq* of the Commercial Code together with special legislation which governs their development. The special features of this are based on the need to ensure continuity of the service. It is decreed that the services must not be interrupted by any judicial or administrative action, and that a requisition committee must be created in order to ensure the organisation of the service. It is also decreed that the government must be notified of any possible bankruptcy so that it can take the appropriate measures.

Debt collection and asset recovery

Rights and actions

Spanish jurisprudence distinguishes between rights in rem and rights in personam. Rights in rem confer upon their holder a right which acknowledges either ownership or power over a specific thing against anyone who may be the holder of that thing, whereas personal rights are created upon obligations of a debtor who is liable for the fulfilment of such with all his net worth. The Spanish legal system also distinguishes between the following orders each of which has its own judicial bodies and procedures:

- civil and mercantile orders
- labour orders
- penal orders
- administrative orders

Procedure

In all orders there is a court of first instance, in most there is an appeal body, and occasionally there is a body of reversal on the model of the French cour de cassation, whose task is to review the application of the law.

If it appears that one of the rights or freedoms set out in Chapter II of Section 1 of the Constitution has been violated, there is the possibility of an appeal to the Constitutional Court. This procedure is known as a "recurso de amparo" (support appeal).

Issues of debt recovery and execution against assets and property may arise in procedures under any of the four orders. The administrative order is obligatory when the litigation is against the public administration. The labour order is applicable in litigation between employees and employers. The penal order is applicable not only in the commission of offences which have given rise to the debt or which have resulted in the removal of assets in which the creditor has rights, but also in the enforcement of damages awarded in a civil action, where damages arise as a consequence of criminal offences.

In the main, however, issues of debt enforcement and insolvency are dealt with in the civil order, although it is advisable to bear in mind the other orders as insolvency does encompass labour, administrative or penal matters and the jurisdiction and procedures of those orders may be involved.

Types of proceedings

These are three types of proceedings:

- ordinary declaratory proceedings;
- enforcement proceedings;
- special proceedings depending on their purpose.

Ordinary declaratory proceedings are those matters in which a judgment of indebtedness is sought. These are organised on the basis of the amount claimed:

- up to Ptas 80,000 – where the process is known as a verbal hearing.
- Claims for amount between Ptas 80,000 and Ptas 800,000 – known as a cognitive hearing.
- Claims for amounts between Ptas 800,000 and Ptas 160 million.
- Claims for over Ptas 160 million.

Although all these proceedings have their special features, they all consist of three stages: pleadings, evidence and decision. The pleadings stage may include preliminary hearings and rulings to correct procedural defects or to dispose of some issues.

The evidence stage is divided into the presentation of evidence followed by an intermediate stage of conclusions or summarising of evidence. The ruling stage terminates the proceedings with a judicial ruling or judgment.

In claims for more than Ptas 800,000, the parties must be represented jointly by a court solicitor who is a person whose practice differs from that of a lawyer in that he represents the parties before the court, and receives most of the notices personally. He acts in addition to each client's own lawyer and attorney. For claims of less than Ptas 800,000, only the client's own lawyer or attorney is necessary.

The average time for the duration of each of the stages varies greatly – not only according to where in Spain it takes place, but also according to the nature of the judicial body and the size of its backlog of work. It is not uncommon for proceedings at first instance to last up to two years, at second instance for two years, with a further two years in the court of appeal.

Enforcement proceedings

If the judgment is in favour of the creditor, the latter must undertake another enforcement proceeding involving the search, assessment and sale in a public auction of any assets that are owned by the debtor. Out of the proceeds the judgment creditor will be paid either the amount claimed or the amount which is set as compensation for the debtor's obligations.

Naturally, in actions claiming delivery of a particular thing, the enforcement stage is aimed at recovering the same for the creditor. It is not uncommon for enforcement proceedings to be as long as the proceedings leading to the enforceable judgement.

Occasionally a creditor may invoke summary proceedings which are "abbreviated" procedures applicable in the following circumstances:

- possession proceedings in order to retain or recover the possession of a new work and a work in a state of disrepair;
- proceedings for protection by registration of rights in rem (proprietary rights) under article 41 of the Mortgage Law;

- "Alimentos Provisionales" (preventative measures granted in Family Law cases); and
- "Procedimento Ejective" (a process available for a creditor who has a title that receives special consideration, such as public notarial deeds or bills of exchange).

Ordinary enforcement proceedings ("juicio ejecutivo") are of great practical importance. A basic premise is the existence of a debt which complies with certain formal requirements. In these circumstances, once payment has been demanded from the debtor, if he does not pay the debt immediately his assets are seized.

The declaratory stage of the proceedings is reduced to a discussion of certain formal matters and if the debtor attempts to use any other defence, he must do so in the ordinary declaratory proceedings without prejudice to the processing of the ordinary enforcement proceedings.

Article 1421 of the Civil Procedural Law contemplates "ordinary enforcement action" for those claims which are:

- recorded in a public deed;
- contained in a private document which has been endorsed by a sworn statement made before a competent judge;
- based on bills of exchange, promissory notes, cheques and other bearer securities under certain conditions; and
- based on original copies of commercial contracts signed by the parties and by registered stockbrokers.

Strictly speaking, the great advantage in ordinary enforcement proceedings lies in the preventive attachment which is automatically granted and which is difficult to obtain in proceedings of any other type.

Other civil proceedings of interest to a debtor are:

- those of the Industrial Property Law;
- those deriving from the Horizontal Property Law;
- special proceedings for protesting resolutions adopted by business corporations and co-operatives;
- special proceedings for declaration of annulment of honorary loans;
- eviction proceedings, both under ordinary legislation and with the special Urban Leases Law and the Rural Leases Law;
- certain insolvency proceedings, suspensions of payments or bankruptcy, reductions of amount or extensions of time and creditors' meeting; and
- succession proceedings.

In addition to this, there are certain proceedings, known as "voluntary jurisdiction", which may be of importance in commercial or mercantile law, for:

- production of books and documents to a shareholder;

- requirements in connection with a freight contract;
- provisional attachment and deposit of the value of a bill of exchange;
- auditing and deposits of commercial drafts;
- insurance of the value of a cargo;
- proof of causes of breakdown of a vessel;
- appointment of a co-director in community and collective companies;
- appointment of experts in insurance agreements;
- the call to hold a general shareholders' meeting under the Business Corporations Act;
- the creation of a syndicate of bond-holders in certain cases of collective companies, general partnerships, limited liability companies or associations and other corporate bodies;
- the denunciation of robbery, burglary or embezzlement of credit documents and bearer drafts;
- robbery or embezzlement of instruction of a bill of exchange;
- the liquidation of the bankrupt's total estate;
- abandonment of goods for transport payments;
- review of non-monetary contributions to a business corporation;
- appointment of an "interventor" in liquidation operations.

Finally, there is the Arbitration Law, which has recently been subject to new regulations replacing those contained in the 1953 Law.

Acknowledgement and enforcement of foreign judgments in Spain

For a foreign judicial ruling or award to be valid in Spain, two procedures must be fulfilled:

- acknowledgement (known as "exequatur") for which the competent body is the Supreme Court, and
- "enforcement" before the pertinent Court of First Instance.

The system is governed by articles 951 to 958 of the Civil Procedural Act.

A foreign judgment will be enforceable in Spain under any of the following regimes:

- under an International Treaty to which Spain is a party;
- under a principle of reciprocity; and
- in the absence of a treaty or reciprocity and provided that there is no prohibition, in accordance with general principles of Spanish law.

Where reciprocity on general principles are relied upon, it must be that the foreign judgment:

- was delivered at the end of a personal action;
- was not handed down in contempt of court;
- was based on an obligation enforceable in Spain;
- fulfils the requirements to be considered as valid in Spain.

The procedure is simple and informal, with a report to the Finance Ministry and the court declaring whether or not the enforcement order should be fulfilled.

Once the declaratory stage of the exequatur is completed, those responsible for enforcement are the competent judges at the first grade or at first instance.

Spain, is in addition, a party to several multilateral treaties of acknowledgement and enforcement of foreign awards such as the Geneva Convention and the New York Convention. The 1968 Brussels Convention has recently been ratified, along with its subsequent extensions and versions. This has resulted in major changes; for example, the first instance court is now competent to hold "exequatur" proceedings.

3. Survival of the insolvent corporation or its business

Introduction

In Spain the typical procedure for the debtor to obtain an agreement with his creditors in order to allow the company to survive is "suspension of payments" governed by the 1922 Law. The procedure typically aimed at liquidation of the company is "bankruptcy", which is governed by the Commercial Code and by supplementary procedural laws. Both the procedures may, however, lead to either outcome (agreement and survival of the company and/or liquidation of the company). Liquidation of the company may thus ensue from suspension of payments and in bankruptcy proceedings, the company may survive by means of an agreement with its creditors. This may even be the case in situations of final insolvency which, in principle, are reserved for bankruptcy proceedings.

Recent cases show the increased readiness of the regulatory authorities to take criminal proceedings against individuals found to have been in breach of their fiduciary duties in the period leading up to a company's insolvency.

Under Law 22/1993 of 29 December, creditors may now recover value added tax in respect of bad debts they incur in consequence of final insolvency proceedings in relation to a company.

Agreement with the creditors

It is possible for a debtor to reach agreements out of court with his creditors, under the principle of freedom of agreement, provided that this does not infringe a number of general limits given in articles 1255 and 1257 of the Civil Code.

Indeed, the Spanish insolvency system offers as little to the debtor as it does to the creditors, and it is therefore no surprise that there is frequent recourse to out of the court agreements.

General agreements with all the creditors using this procedure are somewhat less frequent, since it is difficult to assemble all creditors in one place and to unite their wishes. The nature of these agreements is therefore designed to prevent bankruptcy at the suit of particular creditors.

The debtor and the creditors are free to make this agreement at any time before the debtor is obliged to go to court to request the institution of insolvency proceedings (where the imbalance between assets and liabilities is so great as to indicate a situation of insolvency). Apart from this, the debtor is only under an obligation that, while the agreement is being made, "he must not default in general" from the settlement of his obligations or incur any other "act of Bankruptcy" (as specified below). Inevitably, however, the problem is practical rather than legal since, besides the difficulty of informal negotiation, other court proceedings are often in existence when the agreement is being negotiated, which may seriously endanger the feasibility of any agreement.

If an agreement is reached, it will entail a commitment on the part of the creditors to grant certain concessions to the debtor in delaying or reducing the amount owed. Such agreements must be respected by the creditors since, as the courts have stated, they have the value of a compromise under article 1809 of the Civil Code (Barcelona Territorial Court, Chamber 1, 20 May 1971). It is clear that the compromise is only binding upon the signatories, and that the other creditors, even though they are a minority, may request that the relevant insolvency proceedings be instituted (Valencia Territorial Court, Chamber 1, 10 December 1965).

One type of agreement between the creditors is the agreement with assignment of assets which may in turn act as a payment of debts up to the value of these assets, or as a "cessio pro soluto" or assignment in payment. This latter procedure is a special legal procedure whereby the creditors, when receiving such assets, are considered as finally paid, whatever the amount of the debt. The creditors will thus not have a right to request subsequent compensation ("a contrariu sensu" under art 1175 of the Civil Code). Naturally, if it affects all the debtor's assets, this type of payment is only feasible when it takes place within the appropriate procedural framework, or when all the creditors join together in making it.

One important stumbling block in such negotiations is that it is normal to require personal guarantees which directors and members or shareholders are often reluctant to give. Another is the matter of debts owed to employees, which might be resolved by means of negotiation with the significant help of the Salary Guarantee Fund (a public insurance institution which acts in favour of employees with regard to salary and compensation due to the termination of employment contracts up to certain limits). Once these hurdles are overcome, it becomes possible to save some net worth offering the creditors relatively quick, though still partial, collection of debts that otherwise might have been considered extremely doubtful.

In this way costs and complications that would otherwise result from the insolvency procedures are avoided. However, quite often costs and complications, professional fees and the time taken to reach an informal agreement themselves make an informal solution impossible.

Suspension of payments

Purpose and effect

The suspension of payments procedure may be used by a trader or mercantile company experiencing difficulties which are temporary (in principle at least),and where, in theory, the debtor's net worth is able to meet the debts.

Basically, this is a "proposal for negotiation" through court proceedings, aimed at obtaining the consent of a sufficient majority of creditors in order to approve a creditors' agreement, or an agreement for payment.

Typical agreements for payment would be either deferred payment to creditors or the reduction of amounts due to them; or a combination of both.

In order to enable the company to function with reasonable profitability during this period, the general enforcement of claims against on the total assets of the company is prohibited, attachments are lifted and the debtor and creditors are encouraged to reach an agreement for payment which will be binding on all creditors.

However, the exact nature of a suspension of payments is something which is subject to debate in Spain. The debate has affected the practical application of the law and many of the paradoxes and peculiarities of the Spanish insolvency system are explained by the tension generated by these deeply held opposing views. One such view is that a suspension of payments may operate as a means of escape from a company's legitimate obligations. To cover this, the legislation lays down certain requirements which must be met where the suspension is requested by the debtor. These may vary depending upon whether the insolvency is to be considered as provisional or whether liabilities so clearly outweigh the assets that the process should be treated as one of definite bankruptcy.

Suspension of payments has not always had the same significance and scope.

In the first Spanish Code in 1829, it was considered simply as a situation or type of bankruptcy. In the 1855 Code, due to the strictness of the application of the bankruptcy procedure to traders in this situation, suspension of payments was treated as a procedure to replace bankruptcy.

Its benefits were granted to traders who applied for it promptly, regardless of their real financial situation. It was thought of as being a prize for diligence and it could conceal situations where the creditors were being defrauded.

The system gave rise to enormous abuses and, in order to correct these, the Law of 10 June 1897 revised the regulations contained in the Code, requiring that the debtor should possess sufficient assets in order to pay his debts in full. This re-established the idea that suspension of payments was only applicable where the debtor was experiencing a temporary lack of liquidity.

Finally, the Suspension of Payments Law of 26 July 1922 once again gave rise to considerable confusion with regard to the circumstances in which a debtor could resort to the procedure for suspension of payments. These changes in policy have been complicated further by a procedure which has allowed for the possibility of processing the situations as either temporary or definite insolvency.

Despite this confusion, it must be said that it is precisely the ambiguous nature of the institution which has allowed it to play an important role. It serves as a channel for social concerns such as loss of employment if a company fails and is allied to the modern tendency to attempt to preserve the company. It also avoids any criticism falling on businessmen for lack of diligence in their business operations. The debtor faces reduced creditor pressure in consequence.

This procedure has enabled the Spanish system largely to avoid the transfer of the system of personal liability – with the application of bankruptcy proceedings including the personal arrest of the bankrupt person – to many companies which have merely suffered from a general economic crisis.

To sum up, suspension of payments allows a period of respite against those creditors who do not have a right to separate enforcement. This facilitates negotiations to obtain an agreement to reduce the amount owing and/or for an extension of time for payment.

It should also be borne in mind that the particular characteristics of the procedure – especially the fact that formal insolvency and perhaps even liquidation may follow – has transformed it into a general insolvency procedure which may be used for many different practical purposes, and which is frequently used both to refloat companies and to bury them in a discreet or uncomplicated manner.

Finally, it should be added that during a suspension of payments, no creditors may apply for the debtor's bankruptcy. There is a clear legislative priority in favour of suspension of payments for the purpose of avoiding the unsatisfactory effects which accompany liquidations of companies.

Under the judgement of 26 November 1976, once suspension of payments is accepted, bankruptcy cannot be applied for; but once bankruptcy has been declared, then the debtor cannot apply for the procedure of suspension of payments unless the declaration of bankruptcy is opposed for sound legal reasons. The principle of favouring the procedure of suspension has in fact led to its implementation after a bankruptcy, when the bankruptcy proceedings have not yet been subject to sworn testimony that payments have ceased generally (judgment of the Supreme Court, 3 July 1933). On the other hand, in a clear case of fraud, priority has been given to bankruptcy proceedings (judgment of the Territorial Court of Barcelona, 23 March 1977, chamber 2).

Prior considerations

A debtor who is experiencing considerable, but not terminal financial difficulties may well not consider making an application for suspension of payments. A cessation of operations may be perfectly appropriate where, for example, upon closure of a company, there are no further consequences than the disappointment of certain creditors, the formal procedures before the social court necessary for seeking compensation from the Salary Guarantee Fund and the processing of payment of employees and payments corresponding to provisions made in the debtor's books. In Spain, for various reasons, it is quite likely that the business of the trader or company may become dormant without any further consequences than a considerable number of unsatisfied creditors. In such circumstances there may well be no forces pressing for a suspension of payments. However, it may be that the recent law on "Sociedad Anonima" (which makes the directors jointly and severally liable for the debts of the company if they fail to call a creditors' meeting when the company has fulfilled a legal requirement enabling a declaration of bankruptcy to be made) will encourage directors themselves to place companies into some form of insolvency procedure rather than allowing them simply to become dormant.

The position is different when there is a particular social implication to the problem or because the company has considerable assets, or because the company is really viable despite its transitory difficulties. Then, both debtors and creditors have certain interests which are channelled through insolvency proceedings. The debtor will wish to avoid public pressure or to save some net-worth, and thus attempt a reorganisation which allows him to restructure the company, or simply to avoid the detriment and damage that he personally or his net-worth may suffer from the application of bankruptcy proceedings.

The debtor's prior considerations will depend to a great extent on the specific ends that he hopes to achieve and the circumstances in which his decision must be made. Certain common questions are frequently faced in practice.

The first problem consists of being able to comply with the requirements imposed to submit an application for suspension of payments. In particular, the debtor is required to submit accounts, a list of creditors, the balance sheet, a report and a proposal for agreement. In many cases, the keeping of accounts has not been a virtue much practised by small and medium-sized companies which lack a proper management apparatus. Thus, it is sometimes an impossible or extremely difficult task to write up and/or reconstruct accounts.

The application for suspension of payments requires an indication that the assets exceed the liabilities. The valuation of assets or of goodwill is, therefore, frequently crucial.

Another circumstance which must be considered is the effect of an application for suspension of payments on the company's commercial relationships, particularly when there is a real interest in safeguarding such future possibilities as the company may have. It will thus be necessary to consider the reaction of creditors or of "key" suppliers. These reactions are always important since they may mean that the business will come to an end in any event due to lack of commercial credit or finances. Special attention should be paid to institutional financial creditors which frequently hold personal guarantees.

Avoidance of bankruptcy proceedings, which could be on the point of being applied for by the creditors, and also the corresponding liabilities which may ensue for managers and directors, are also questions to be taken into account when deciding whether or not to submit an application for the suspension of payments.

Likewise, it will be necessary to consider the composition of the creditors as a whole in order to assess the likelihood of possible agreements. The structure of these creditors, the amount of their claims and their specific interest in recovery are all crucial factors.

Finally, it should be emphasised that substantial costs will be incurred in an application for suspension of payments. The debtor must, therefore, calculate whether the costs will be off-set by the benefits he anticipates will be achieved by such a suspension.

Recent case law dealing with the liability of directors of limited stockholder companies indicates that such directors will be personally liable for debts of the company if creditors have suffered any loss, damage (*i.e.* non-payment in whole or in part) as a consequence of wilfully wrong conduct or negligence on the part of the directors. For example, it would be negligence were the directors not to seek an order for suspension of payments or bankruptcy.

Procedure

An application for suspension of payments may only be made by a trader who is in debt.

As a general rule the court of the debtor's domicile is competent to hear the proceedings although, in practice, at the request of the creditors or the State Prosecutor the proceedings may be transferred to a more convenient venue.

Along with the application, the debtor must include the following documents (art 2 of the Suspension of Payments Law – "SPL"):

- the balance sheet or statement of accounts;

- a list of the creditors' names or an approximate indication if there are more than 1,000;

- a report explaining the causes for the suspension and the resources that the debtor has in order to meet his debts;

- a proposal for payment of his debts;

- in the case of a business corporation, a certificate of the resolution of the board of directors to apply for the suspension, together with the call for a general shareholders' meeting which must ratify the application for suspension of payments;

- a list of all the applicant's branches, agencies and representative offices as well as the real estate of which it is the owner or lessee or to which it is otherwise entitled.

The books of accounts must also be submitted so that they can be duly audited.

On the same day that the application is submitted or on the following working day the judge will consider the application for temporary suspension of payments, provided that the requirements laid down for the application are met. Since judges normally merely carry out a formal analysis of the proposal, it is sufficient to attach a balance sheet from which it can be inferred that the assets of the company exceed the liabilities.

The procedure is initiated by means of a "judgment of acceptance for processing", which is still not a declaration of suspension of payments, (this will take place much later), but does have important effects. This judgment must be notified by telegraph to all the courts where the applicant has branches. It will be entered

- in a register of suspension of payments kept by each court,
- at the Commercial Registry, and
- at the property registry where the real estate of the company in suspension is entered.

The "interventores" will be appointed by this ruling. They are the judicial auxiliaries responsible for everything connected with the control of the suspension and of the business of the company in suspension and its administration while the proceedings are being processed.

The "declaration of suspension of payments" is a ruling handed down by the court only after several months, once certain details have been verified. In the meantime, however, the judgment of acceptance for processing will carry important consequences:

- Insolvency proceedings are now deemed to have commenced, making important modifications to the rights of the creditors of the company;

- Joint proceedings will now take place involving all the creditors of the applicant except those who have a right to separate enforcement or abstention;

- Those in charge of the suspension start work – the judge, the state prosecutor, the interventores and the creditors' committee. Their functions and composition are set out below.

- The fact of the judgment is recorded in the register relating to suspensions of payments and bankruptcies which is held in every court. It is also recorded in the commercial registry and at any property registry where the debtor has real estate or related rights. Where individuals are concerned, the judgment is also recorded at the civil registry.

- In certain cases it is possible for the debtor in suspension to be removed from the administration of his or its assets and even to be replaced. This is allowed by article 6 of the Law, which requires a prior report by the interventores. A similar effect can be achieved through the procedural channel of the Royal Decree-Law of Attachment of Administration of Companies of 20 October 1969, which allows directors to be appointed in the case of attachment to companies.

- It is not possible to bring individual ordinary and enforcement actions, although enforcement actions guaranteed by specific assets (either mortgage or pledge) are an exception to this rule.

- Any attachment carried out in order to enforce an adverse judgment is lifted. From this moment, the debtor can make no payment or create any obligation or even enter into any contract without the approval of the interventores. If the debtor so acts without their approval, he is guilty of a criminal offence.

- Any ordinary and enforcement proceedings already instituted before the application for suspension of payments has been accepted are continued until after judgment has been obtained. The enforcement will, however, be suspended.

- Any application for a declaration of bankruptcy of the company in suspension is disqualified. The processing of the proceedings is specially protected so that neither ordinary appeals issues, nor requests for the instituting of penal proceedings are permitted.

The interventores, in the time allowed by the court, will analyse the documents and accounting background information of the company in suspension and will issue a report on the company's net assets situation, the feasibility of the company surviving, the causes of the suspension of payments and the agreement submitted. In addition, they will advise on the list of creditors which has been submitted by the company in suspension, drawing up a final list which they will submit to the judge for approval. The interventores frequently request an extension of time from the court in order to submit the report.

Once the interventores have completed their work, the suspension continues with the administration of the company's business now subject to the supervision of the interventores. For their part, the creditors supply documents as required by the interventores, requesting – although this is not obligatory – inclusion in the list of claims and, where appropriate, opposing the acknowledgement of the claims of others.

When the interventores' report has been received by the court, and after the debtor has being given three days in which to examine it, the court hands down a ruling declaring a suspension of payments, if appropriate. Different procedural steps are laid down depending upon whether the insolvency is declared to be temporary or definite, and whether or not the assets exceed the liabilities.

If the ruling declares the insolvency to be definite, it establishes the amount by which the liabilities exceed the assets and grants a term of 15 days to enable the shortfall to be suitably guaranteed. If this shortfall is guaranteed, the matter reverts to being one of temporary insolvency.

If the 15 day term has elapsed and the deficit has not been made up or guaranteed, a "classification stage" is ordered to establish the liabilities which the company in suspension may have incurred and the conditions on which it can continue to operate.

For their part, 40% or more in value of the creditors may request the cancellation of the proceedings, in order to institute bankruptcy proceedings. Otherwise the judge will convene the creditors' committee.

If the insolvency is considered to be temporary, the judge, uses the same ruling, to convene the creditors' committee, giving at least 30 days' notice. This notice ruling is enforceable immediately and may not be directly opposed, although it may be opposed as a premise for opposing the creditors' committee.

Finally, it should be mentioned that if there are more than 200 creditors, it is possible to apply for "written proceedings" to replace the meeting of the creditors' committee by an assent in writing to the agreement proposed or which may be proposed.

Position of the creditors

Creditors' actions against the company are halted, together with their right to institute proceedings or enforce judgments. Certain creditors have preferential status. In accordance with article 15 of the Suspension of Payments Law, the following enjoy such status: employee's salary arrears, social security payments, capital and interest on debts secured by a mortgage or a pledge, claims by way of pledge, credits and tax liabilities from the preceding year. This also applies to the circumstances included in sections 1 to 3 of article 913 of the Commercial Code (see Bankruptcy).

One of the three interventores will be appointed by the judge from among the first third of the list of creditors, ranked according to the amount owed to them.

In general, the creditors have a limited role. They may, however, be engaged in attending to the requirements for documents issued by the interventores in order to reconstruct the company or they may be engaged in considering the truth of the data furnished by the company in suspension. They may also be engaged in applying for acknowledgement of their claims if the applicant has not included them in the first list of creditors to be attached when instituting the proceedings or in opposing the acknowledgement of claims of third parties. These steps are taken under the supervision of the interventores without any need for a lawyer or court solicitor.

The creditors may oppose the acknowledgement of some debts at any time within 15 days before the meeting of the creditors' committee is held. If their claims have not been acknowledged, they may also apply for judicial acknowledgement of such claims by means of the same procedure.

If the written procedure is sanctioned by the Court, the creditors will have the right to attend the meeting and vote or send their vote in writing. Finally, at the appropriate time, they may record their agreement and approve the suspension of payments.

In addition, creditors with two-fifths of total claims against the company may request the cancellation of the proceedings where the insolvency is considered to be definite and if the debtor or a third person does not guarantee the shortfall that the court has established between the liabilities and the assets.

By refusing to attend the meeting or to accept the agreement, the creditors may obtain the cancellation of the agreement and become entitled to apply for bankruptcy. They will have the same opportunity if opposition to the agreement is successfully mounted or if the debtor defaults in its performance.

Organs of the suspension of payments: powers and functions

The organs of the suspension are as follows:

- The judge controls the proceedings. He performs judicial and administrative functions by directing the suspension of payment proceedings, adopting the appropriate resolutions, and resolving disputes brought before him. At the same time, he has responsibilities of an administrative nature with regard to the interventores and to certain decisions of the company. The interventores themselves are court officers. In general terms, the judge actually plays a more important part, personally, than in bankruptcy proceedings, in which he acts through a "delegate comisario".

- The state prosecutor, who plays a part from the beginning and who represents the public interest. He is particularly concerned with the classification of the liabilities of the debtor in the case of definite insolvency.

- The interventores, who are appointed by the order sanctioning a suspension of payments is accepted for processing. Two of them are appointed from a list of commercial or practical experts, authorised by the chamber of commerce and by the regional banking association. However, in practice, judges frequently appoint the same experts (whom they trust) time and again. A creditor from among those appearing in the first third of the list of creditors, ranked according to the amount owed to them, is appointed as a third interventor.

  The interventores assess the capacity of the company in suspension to assume any liabilities.

  The judge, may reduce the number of interventores to one, depending upon the relative importance of the company in suspension of payments.

- The Creditors' Committee, which has the sole duty of approving or rejecting the agreement submitted by the company in suspension.

Role and powers of the interventores

The interventores deserve special attention. They have the following obligations and powers (art 5 of the Suspension of Payments Law):

- they intervene in the business of the debtor from the first day of their appointment, after taking the appropriate oath to accept office (art 4 of the Suspension of Payments Law). Until they are appointed, their functions are carried out by the judge, if necessary;

- they inspect the books of the company in suspension and ensure that, after the "note of submission" made after the last entry in the books when they are submitted to the court by the applicant, all operations that are carried out in the future are entered in due legal form;

- they audit the operations of the company in suspension in accordance with the law, requiring that the funding balance be verified daily;

- they inform the judge of any important events relating to the company in suspension and its business, so that any necessary resolutions can be drafted, and to protect the creditors' interests;

- they inform the judge of any claims that the company in suspension may attempt to file in defence or reclamation of its rights;

- they propose action which should be taken in the interest of the company in suspension, either on their own initiative or on the initiative of any creditor, and they may also be authorised by the judge to carry out such actions by themselves in the interests of the debtor's total estate;

- in accordance with article 6 of the Suspension of Payments Law, they issue a special report with regard to the restrictions which it is advisable to adopt in connection with the management of the company in suspension;

- they verify all collections of any amount and origin, together with acceptance, endorsement, or rejection of commercial drafts;

- they authorise all the actions of the management in assuming obligations or entering into contracts or making payments, since without such approval, any purported acts by the debtor are null and void and constitute a criminal offence;

- they audit the sale of assets and merchandise belonging to the debtor.

The interventores, in accordance with article 18 of the Suspension of Payments Law and within the terms established by the judge, draw up (co-opting experts when necessary) a report dealing with the following matters:

- the accuracy of the assets and liabilities on the balance sheet, giving a statement of the nature of the claims included therein;

- a statement of the accounts of the company in suspension and any inaccuracies or other errors observed;

- the situation and accuracy of the causes for the suspension of payments stated in the report;

- a final balance sheet and list of creditors and a list of claims according to their legal classification, naming those creditors who have a right to abstain because they are privileged.

If the interventores do not submit a report within the stipulated period, they may incur some liability, and the intervenor creditor will often be penalised by the loss of his claim.

The interventores must also attend the meeting of the creditors' committee. They may speak at this meeting and they must sign the minutes of the meeting. They may be appointed as representative of the meeting to carry out actions representing the debtor's total estate, and in accordance with article 19, will issue a written report on the following:

- any request that the meeting be replaced by a written procedure; and

- any proposals for agreements and modifications of the agreements proposed by the company in suspension.

The interventores may but are not obliged to file any accusation of liability against managers in accordance with the procedure established in article 20. Furthermore, in accordance with article 21, they may intervene in the separate procedures in order to recover the debtor's assets available in the case of definite insolvency.

Administration of the business during the processing of the application for suspension of payments

It has already been stated that the company in suspension does not have its powers removed and that it retains the administration of its assets under the supervision of the interventores.

Nevertheless, in certain cases it is possible to limit the capacity of the company to manage its own affairs even further, after a report by the interventores. This is the case when the insolvency is declared to be definite. The consequences are as follows.

The employees

The employees' claims are not included in the overall proceedings. It is possible for them to be paid in full or in part by the social courts, or by the Salary Guarantee Funds which, in cases of insolvency, cover certain financial rights of the employees. However, these claims can also be included with the company's liabilities.

In principle, continuity of employment is maintained without prejudice to the fact that the directors may submit measures for "redundancy proceedings" for financial or technological reasons in order to obtain a suspension or termination of the employees' contracts. If employees are made redundant, the compensation provided in the Workers' Statute will be available.

Employee creditors are set out in a separate list drawn up by the court in order to certify those entitled for the purposes of the Salary Guarantee Funds.

It is very likely that steps will be taken by negotiation to reduce the workforce through voluntary or compulsory redundancies. It is important that agreement be reached with the employees as soon as possible so as to reduce the number and size of employee claims since these will be considerably increased by claims for actual or constructive dismissal. Substantial employee claims may make it financially impossible for the company to obtain a suspension of payments.

Legislation passed in May 1994 has reinforced the preferential status of salary arrears.

The Salary Guarantee Fund covers salary arrears for up to four months in respect of outstanding salaries and for up to one year in respect of compensation for termination of contract, which is granted either judicially or administratively. The fund is subrogated to the rights of the specially privileged employees in suspensions of payments with the same rights.

Only in a very general sense is there an obligation to inform the employees' representatives or Workers' Committee of the impending application for suspension of payments. In practice, this obligation is affected by the need for secrecy so as to prevent a run on the company by its creditors.

Contracts and enforcement

Contracts where the company is under continuing obligations may be terminated due to its default, though if debts continue to arise after the declaration of suspension of payments, they must be considered as debts of the post-bankruptcy estate and may be collected preferentially rather than being excluded or made subject to the insolvency procedures. Where the company in suspension of payments is the lessee of business premises, it is necessary to continue paying rents because eviction proceedings are not halted by the insolvency proceedings. In the case of debts being claimed by the company, set-off can be applied only if, prior to the application being filed, the debt against the company was due, enforceable, and liquid. Proceedings in connection with the collection of the debt must already have been begun by the company and the creditor must have pleaded a set-off.

Proceedings relating to assets which are especially mortgaged or pledged may be continued despite the fact that the company against which they are being pursued is in suspension of payments. Apart from this, enforcement proceedings in progress are halted prior to execution. It is not possible to institute new enforcement proceedings after the application for suspension of payments.

Executives and shareholders

The suspension of payments does not give rise to a removal of powers or to a change of executives unless, after a prior special report by the interventores, it is so decided by the judge, who might impose serious restrictions on the directors of the company, or even the removal and replacement of some or all of them. However, such measures are very unusual.

In principle, those executives who are not directors must continue, in accordance with the general principle, with their special employment relationship. Even so as they are executives, they may be dismissed by whoever carries on the administration of the company.

The shareholders play a passive role once they have ratified the application for the suspension of payments at a general shareholders' meeting especially convened for the purpose, and to which a certificate from the board of directors must have been submitted together with the application for suspension of payments.

Creditors' committee: written procedure and agreement

After the interventores have submitted to the court a final list of creditors and possible claims by the parties, the final list of creditors must be formally drawn up eight days prior to the holding of the meeting and this list may include several different sections, in accordance with article 12, namely:

- creditors included by the debtor whose claims have not been opposed;
- creditors included by the debtor who argue an increase in the amount assigned;
- creditors omitted by the debtor who have applied to be included in the list;
- creditors included by the debtor whose claims have been opposed on the basis they are regarded as being overstated;
- creditors who hold a right to abstain because of their privileged status under clauses 15 and 22 of the Suspension of Payments Law.

A creditor whose claim is not acknowledged must resort to the appropriate declaratory proceedings. Both the right of unpaid creditors and that of the debtor's estate are reserved for enforcement in normal proceedings. A creditor with the right to abstain because he has a privileged claim but whose right has not been acknowledged must commence proceedings to have his right acknowledged.

The meetings are held on the day, and at the time and place, stated in the notice and, if necessary, continue on successive days.

The meeting is presided over by the judge. The creditors may appear in person or by representatives with a power of attorney. The debtor (or in the case of a company, the board of directors) has an obligation to attend the meeting, as have the interventores. The debtor may be assisted by a lawyer to defend him or it and speak on his or its behalf.

If the debtor does not attend the meeting, the application for the suspension of payments is cancelled. It will also be cancelled in if it is impossible to hold the meeting due to a failure to attract a quorum of creditors. In order for the meeting to be considered quorate, it must be attended by creditors owed three-fifths of the debtors' total liabilities with the exception of creditors with the right to abstain.

Once the meeting commences, the debtor's application is read out along with the proposal for agreement, figures for the assets and liabilities and the interventores report. This is followed by discussion. The debtor and interventores may speak as often as they wish. It is possible for the proposal to be amended at the suggestion of either the creditors or the debtor.

The vote is taken by a show of hands and the agreement is approved if 50 % plus one of the creditors attending vote in favour, provided that the amount of their claims represents 60 % of the debtor's total liabilities, subtracting the amount of claims of creditors that have made use of the right to abstain, and provided that, if the agreement includes an extension of time for payment, that extension does not exceed three years.

If the agreement is not subject to a time limit of 3 years (or any limit) and the company is in definite insolvency, the votes of 50 % plus one of the creditors attending and of 75 % of the liabilities will be necessary to approve the agreement.

If such majorities are not obtained at the meeting, the judge calls the creditors to a new meeting at which an agreement is approved if 66.6 % of the liabilities vote in favour.

If the proceedings have been in writing, either of these types of majority will be sufficient to approve the proposal. Certain persons can, however, file an appeal opposing the agreement at any time up to eight days after the meeting. These are listed below.

In any case, the agreement is classified as a legal agreement or as legal business, *sui generis*, which basically has the effect of a compromise, but with the characteristics of being in a public procedure and therefore having wider effectiveness (judgments of the Supreme Court of 30 May 1959 and 4 July 1966).

The right to abstain is crucial. The specially-privileged creditors, mortgage creditors and those provided in sections 1, 2, and 3 of article 913 of the Commercial Code and in article 22 of the Suspension of Payments Law, along with those who invoke the rights contained in articles 908 to 910 of the Commercial Code, have the right to abstain in accordance with article 15 of the Suspension of Payments Law.

If the required majorities are not obtained for approval of the proposal, the application is closed and each creditor is then free to bring action against the company to apply for bankruptcy or to enforce his own individual claim.

As we have stated above, if there are more than 200 creditors, a judge may choose to suspend a meeting and replace it by a written procedure after a prior report from the interventores. In this case, the court grants a term of between one and four months for the creditors who assent to the agreement to appear before the clerk either in person or by means of a notarised record, or to appear, in special cases, before the clerk of the municipal court where they live. The judge will hear any proposed amendments and a report by the interventores. If there are amendments, they will be conveyed to the debtor in order for him to grant or withhold his consent.

Opposing the creditors' agreement

Within eight days of approval by the creditors, the agreement may be opposed by the following persons :

- creditors on the approved list of creditors who did not attend the meeting;
- creditors who attended and who voted against the majority;
- creditors with valid claims who were not included in the approved list of creditors;
- creditors who were in the provisional list of creditors but who were excluded from the approved list.

Such opposition may be based on any of the following grounds:

- a defect in the forms established for the adoption of agreements at the meeting. These defects may be in the notice, assembly, debate or resolutions;

- a defect in the status or representation of any of the voters where this has a decisive effect on the formation of the majority; a fraudulent misrepresentation regarding the debtor or one or more creditors in order to induce a vote in favour of the agreement;
- a fraudulent exaggeration of claims to achieve the majority relating to amount;
- an error in the estimate of liabilities, provided that this affects the classification of the insolvency;
- an illicit declaration of a right to abstain when the amount of the claims abstained affects the calculation of the necessary majority for the approval of the agreement;
- inaccuracy in the general balance sheet.

Such opposition will be filed by the procedure relating to "incidentes", and the judicial ruling handed down is subject to appeal.

If the debtor fails to fulfil the agreement, any of the creditors may request its cancellation and a declaration of bankruptcy before the judge who heard the suspension of payments application.

Definite insolvency

There is a special procedure for suspension of payments proceedings in which "final insolvency" is declared. This will occur where the report of the interventores reveals that the debtor is hopelessly insolvent and the debtor or a third party is unable to provide some form of security for the difference within 15 days. In the event of a declaration of final insolvency, the following different procedures are available:

- Restitution of the bankrupt's total estate: this is carried out exclusively by means of protest actions commenced under the provisions of articles 879, 880, 881 and 882 of the Commercial Code. They are designed to restore to the debtor's estate any assets that the debtor has attempted to remove from the estate to avoid the creditors' claims being satisfied therefrom (see pp612-614 *infra* for further details). They are processed by means of a separate procedure, to which articles 1336 and 1337 of the Law are applicable, although the interventores will carry out the duties of the comisario and the sindicos (see pp603, 614 and 615 *infra*).
- If they so wish and at their own expense, the State prosecutor, the interventores, the creditors, or any of them may commence a separate procedure by which the activities of the management of the debtor can be examined and compensation sought if there has been negligence or fraud. These proceedings are much less important than bankruptcy proceedings, since they do not have the effects of disqualification, although they may give rise to civil liability.

From the penal point of view, accepted case law states that the penalties of fraudulent and wilful insolvency contained in articles 520 and 529 of the Penal Code are not applicable (judgment of the Supreme Court of 13 February 1957). However, if the company in suspension continues in business, it may incur other typical offences such as embezzlement of assets or fraud. If the conduct of the person in suspension is declared to be criminal, this declaration will not affect the validity of the agreement provided that the agreement is clearly separable from the offence.

In the case of definite insolvency, the normal contents of the agreement may, in addition to the reduction of amount and extension of time, include an assignment on sale of the net worth to third parties or an assignment to a committee appointed by or among the creditors in order to enable a sale of the assets to take place with payment of the creditors out of the proceeds.

For this purpose, a "liquidating committee" is frequently appointed, made up of various creditors.

Termination

The suspension of payments may terminate through agreement between the debtor and its creditors.

Other grounds on which the suspension of payments may be terminated are:

- failure by the debtor to take part in the proceedings at any stage;
- non-ratification of the agreement by the creditors;
- a demand by two-fifths of the creditors (according to value of claim) to cancel the application in the event that the insolvency is classified as definite;
- failure by the debtor to attend the creditors' meeting;
- failure to secure the necessary quorum for the creditors' meeting;
- failure to secure the required majorities at the meetings;
- failure on the part of the debtor to fulfil the agreement.

Other procedures to resolve corporate crises

In Spain the end of the 1970s and the beginning of the 1980s saw the consequences of a worldwide economic crisis which had a great impact on all sectors of economic life. The State, which had marked interventionist tendencies and was responsible for the productive capacity of the country and for maintaining the level of employment, found it necessary to develop certain instruments in order to supplement or replace the classic insolvency proceedings which comprise the major sections of this chapter.

This power on the part of the state in the event of crisis has its root in the seizure of companies providing public services (articles 939 *et seq* of the Commercial Code). This law was used in 1979 and again in 1980 when, by means of respective decrees, cotton companies were seized. In fact, the cotton textile association filed an appeal and the Supreme Court, in a judgment of 17 December 1986, declared such seizure to be compatible with the Constitution.

Another example of this tendency may be observed in the precautionary measure taken by the Decree-Law of 29 October 1969 which was passed as a result of the famous "MATESA" case, whereby the possibility was opened up of granting the administration of a company to the employees or creditors. However, this is not an appropriate method to deal with insolvency and is simply a precautionary measure. It can be of considerable importance, however, if used appropriately since it allows for the possibility of agreements which avoid the liquidation of the company.

A further example is the special legislation which has been passed with regard to financial and insurance institutions. The purpose of this legislation was to re-float the respective sectors. Deposit guarantee funds have been created with their own legal status to guarantee bank clients' deposits at the same time as providing certain measures which help to preserve the institution. The fund, with mixed public and private capital, generates resources and supports the management.

Measures of the same exceptional nature, with the intention of re-floating the sector, are contained in Royal Decree-Law of 10/11 July 1984 which provides urgent measures for the insurance sector. It creates the liquidating committee for insurance institutions which will act as the instrument for liquidation plans which are then approved by the Directorate General for Insurance, replacing the procedures for suspension of payments and bankruptcy for which they are not obliged to apply. If the institution is declared in suspension of payments or in bankruptcy proceedings, then the liquidating committee takes on the same functions as the interventores and the comisario and sindicos, as appropriate.

These measures provide something of a milestone in certain sectors. They have provided a negotiating channel for resolving situations of crisis or insolvency which otherwise would have been dealt with by legislation which is not adapted to the needs of support and reorganisation which the continuation of these companies requires.

4. Termination of the corporation: bankruptcy

Purpose and effect

Bankruptcy proceedings consist of collective enforcement proceedings aimed at obtaining payments of creditors on a pro-rata basis according to their rights, and of observing a system of privileges and priorities once a trader has actually ceased to meet his obligations.

The proceedings may be commenced for various intermediary purposes. If they are instituted by the trader himself it is likely that he is seeking bankruptcy as a means of obtaining more or less honourable termination or liquidation of his company. If the proceedings are instituted by a creditor, it is possible that, besides enforcing his debts, he is attempting to salvage some of the debtor's net worth.

To a certain extent the effects of bankruptcy depend upon its classification. There are at least three types of bankruptcy:

- fortuitous bankruptcy occurs when, due to chance, the company loses its capital so that it cannot meet the payment of its obligations;

- negligent bankruptcy involves lack of diligence in the administration of the company; and

- fraudulent bankruptcy occurs as a result of certain manoeuvres by act or omission by the debtor, such as agreements to conceal assets, absence of accounts, fraudulent advance payments to creditors, and so on.

With the exception of fraudulent bankruptcy, the other types allow the bankrupt to make an agreement with his or its creditors. Fortuitous or negligent bankruptcy may thus also serve as a channel for a composition with creditors and, if appropriate, the survival of the company. It is, however, a more costly, slow and complicated process than suspension of payments, and therefore in principle the purpose must be more than merely circumstantial in order for this procedure to be adopted.

Considerations prior to the submission of the application for bankruptcy

Bankruptcy proceedings consist of legal proceedings which involve an important number of operations and at substantial cost. Thus, in the case of an application by the creditors, it is assumed that there will be assets whose net worth will compensate the creditors for the institution of the procedure. Where the application is made by the debtor, it is likely that he or it will be obliged to meet the cost.

One of the matters under consideration will be whether the application should be for the bankruptcy of the debtor or for a suspension of payments. From the pragmatic point of view, this has meant an important shift towards the insolvency procedure of suspension of payments, especially since even in such proceedings bankruptcy orders can be made. Considerations other than the mere position of the creditor (such as the need to consider the company as a manifestation of social wealth) have helped to devalue the bankruptcy procedure in favour of that of suspension of payments.

The system of imposing personal liability on the bankrupt is another factor to be taken into account when deciding whether or not to institute the proceedings. This might, for example, induce the creditors to make the application and might discourage the debtor from doing so. Finally, the possible retroactive effect of bankruptcy proceedings (if so decided upon by the judge) is of crucial importance in relation to certain purposes of the proceedings and may well be the major factor when the creditors make the decision to institute the procedure.

The proceedings

Institution of bankruptcy proceedings

Bankruptcy proceedings can be applied for by the individual trader or company or by a creditor, in the circumstances provided in the Commercial Code, (known as "objectives circumstances"). There are many different theories as to what constitutes the objective circumstances which justify bankruptcy. They range from considering insolvency as sufficient for bankruptcy to requiring, in addition to insolvency, that there should be a certain definitive impossibility or non-redeemable situation in meeting future liabilities. From a technical point of view, the legal system prescribes certain situations ("acts of bankruptcy") on the basis of which bankruptcy proceedings may be issued. However, possibility of applying for the reversal of a declaration of bankruptcy remains in the hands of the debtor and this reveals some of the uncertainty in the system.

The acts of bankruptcy are as follows:

- attachment of assets in an individual enforcement action has taken place without the creditor's debt having been satisfied due to a lack of assets (art 876, number 1 of the Commercial Code);

- the cessation or general discontinuance of payments (art 774, 876-2 of the Commercial Code). This assumes something more than simple non-payment – even though it may consist of this. It must be general inability to pay debts as they fall due and is considered by the courts as a question of fact which must be dealt with in accordance with the evidence submitted, as has been clearly established in the judgment of the Supreme Court of 26 October 1987;

- the fact that the trader has absconded, leaving no one controlling the business (art 877 of the Commercial Code);

- where the resolution of the problem by other means has failed, such as an application for suspension of payments. This would arise, for example, on failure to submit the agreement or on discontinuance of suspension of payments due to failure to ratify the proposal submitted by the debtor (see above).

In general terms, case law upholds the need for "general discontinuance of payment" as a basic criterion in order to establish a situation of bankruptcy.

The application

The application may be presented either by the debtor or by a legitimate creditor submitting sufficient evidence that the debtor is in one of the situations described above.

There are some questions as to who is a "legitimate creditor", *i.e.* one who may apply for bankruptcy proceedings against the debtor. The literal interpretation of articles 876 and 877 of the Commercial Code refer to enforcement of a claim as being a necessary basis and also refer to the requirements contained in the provisions of the Civil Procedural Law which are also to be understood as referring to enforcement. Nevertheless, the Supreme Court has accepted applications which are not based on enforcement (Judgment of 23 June 1961).

With regard to the obligation on the debtor to submit an application for bankruptcy, it is considered that the Law of 10 October 1897 repeals article 879 of the Commercial Code, which states the duty to declare the bankruptcy within three days from the general cessation of payments, unless suspension of payments has been requested. This opens up a serious problem of interpretation since article 889-2 contains the penalty of culpable bankruptcy for failure to fulfil such an obligation. In general terms, and with many variations, legal doctrine now accepts the existence of the obligation to apply within 48 hours for suspension of payments in the event of ceasing payments, though this does not apply to bankruptcy.

Declaration of bankruptcy

Declaration of bankruptcy is a decision by a judicial body, with stated reasons, which is adopted by means of a documentary record without any need to summon or hear the debtor who is to be declared bankrupt. This has been subject to the criticism that it could infringe the right of effective judicial control contained in article 24 of the Constitution. The Supreme Court, in its Judgment of 12 February 1982, considered the procedure to be constitutional in view of the fact that the declaration is provisional, and that it is possible to file an immediate appeal against it.

If the bankruptcy application has been made with malicious intent, falsehood or clear injustice, the applicant may be guilty of an offence in accordance with article 885 of the Commercial Code.

Effects of the declaration of bankruptcy

A distinction is normally drawn between the procedural and substantive effects of the declaration and the effects on the bankrupt, on his assets, on the creditors and, on the claims and certain contracts.

Procedural effects
The main procedural effects are as follows:

- A collective court procedure is generated which is binding on all the creditors, with the exception of those who hold a separate power of enforcement (for example, creditors who have mortgages or pledges).

- All proceedings that have been commenced against the debtor can henceforth only be continued in the same court (although once again creditors who hold mortgages and pledges are excepted from this requirement). This is provided for under articles 161-3 and 1186 of the Civil Procedure Act.

- Those administering the bankruptcy take up their roles. They are as follows:
  - The judge – his functions include decisions in the procedure beginning with the "declaration of bankruptcy", together with the appointment and control of the other organs.
  - The "depositario" (depositary) – a person who, with the support of the judge, immediately takes possession of the assets of the bankrupt. He also exercises powers of recovery of the debtor's property until the sindicos (see below) are appointed.
  - The "comisario" (commissioner) is also appointed by the judge. He becomes the delegate of the judge and supervises the functions of the sindicos, although he carried out some quasi-judicial activities by delegation (arts 1333 and 1363 of the Civil Procedural Act).
  - The "junta de acreedores" (creditor's meeting) which appoints the sindicos, approves the classification and the ranking of claims and votes on the proposal for agreement, if such is submitted by the debtor.
  - The "sindicos" (trustees) are responsible for the administration of the debtor's assets representing the creditors, and are authorised to carry out judicial and extra-judicial activities connected with the bankruptcy proceedings. There are three sindicos.

Substantive effects

The declaration of bankruptcy entails the arrest of the debtor, either in a penal institution or under house arrest if he provides bail. A judgment of the Constitutional Court of 19th December 1985, number 178, declares that the measure is constitutional provided that it is a question of house arrest, for a strictly limited length of time and giving due reasons.

The debtor is also disqualified from carrying on business and discharging public duties. This gives rise to a lack of capacity to carry out acts of control and administration from the moment he is declared bankrupt and, as appropriate, from the date to which such declaration is retroactive in accordance with article 878 of the Commercial Code.

The debtor is dispossessed of all his assets, together with his correspondence and documents (art 1044-3 of the Commercial Code) during the bankruptcy procedure until his debts have been paid or the agreement fulfilled.

The application for bankruptcy must be made public, either by means of declaration or by means of annotation at the commercial registry, the property registry and the civil registry.

In the case of a company debtor, the Directors have personal liability inasmuch as they have joint and several liability in the discharge of corporate operations.

One special principle is that, under article 923 of the Commercial Code, an order declaring the bankruptcy of partnerships and general partnerships is simultaneously an order declaring the bankruptcy of its members.

Effects on the debtor's assets

Possession of all the debtor's belongings including books, paper and trade documents passes to the depositario, as a person with the confidence of the court whose basic purpose is to conserve the assets until the sindicos are appointed.

A process of establishing the bankruptcy estate is commenced. It entails a separation of those assets which either cannot be the subject of attachment proceedings or which belong to third parties and includes the exercise of those powers under which the debtor's assets which are in the possession of third parties may be recovered.

Effects on creditors

A total list of liabilities is drawn up as part of the collective procedures to which all creditors must be subject. The creditors are then involved in a procedure of classification, which distinguishes between creditors "of the post-bankruptcy estate" and creditors "of the pre-bankruptcy estate".

The latter are subject to the bankruptcy procedure. They are creditors whose claims arose prior to the declaration of the bankruptcy. The claims of the former arose subsequent to the bankruptcy and they therefore enjoy the substantive privilege of not being part of the collective bankruptcy proceeding. They must be paid in full when their claims become enforceable.

All creditors, whether their claims arose before or after the bankruptcy, must register their claims. Creditors who fail to do this in good time may suffer substantial penalties. For instance, a creditor who fails to register his claim in time and whose claim arose after the bankruptcy may find that the delay means that he receives only part of his claim – the same part that corresponds to other creditors whose claims arose before the bankruptcy. In addition, such creditors who have delayed will have to register their claims at their own expense. They are also prohibited from making any claim against any of the other creditors who have registered their claim in good time.

Creditors whose claims arose before the bankruptcy are divided into three groups, namely:

- the ordinary creditors whose claims will be reduced in accordance with what is available pursuant to the law of dividend (mercantile law claims are preferred to those of civil law);

- those with a right of priority. Although they do not enjoy abstention (*i.e.* the right to be free of the collective procedure) they do receive payment before the ordinary creditors; and

- the privileged creditors.

Effects on claims against the debtor

The claims against the debtor will include contingent claims as well as those which are already due and those which become due automatically upon the declaration of bankruptcy. A discount is applicable if claims are settled in advance of their maturity date. In addition, the accrual of interest is halted, except in the case of claims based on a mortgage or pledge. Finally, claims automatically convert into monetary debts.

Claims by the bankrupt will, of course, be collected in the usual way and included in the bankruptcy estate.

It is generally accepted legal doctrine in Spain that set-off is not possible although, as noted earlier, it is possible in special circumstances such as:

- those of article 926 of the Commercial Code where the creditor is also a shareholder who owes some or all of his participation to the debtor; or

- those which involve mutual claims arising from the same contract and in respect of current accounts; or

- special agreements such as those stipulated in article 1202 of the Commercial Code.

The specific case law in a judgment of 17 March 1977 has adjudged against allowing set-off generally.

Effects on contracts

A distinction is made between various types of contract. Those contracts with a fixed time for termination are generally held to be extinguished by the declaration of bankruptcy. It is, of course, possible for them to be extended by agreement between the sindicos and the other party to the contract, since in this case the latter's future claims will be preferential debts of the bankrupt's total estate (*i.e.* they will not be subject to insolvency proceedings).

In the case of periodic contracts however (each of which may be analysed as a series of separate contracts), once a defined section has been performed, the creditor must prove for any amount owed to him in the bankruptcy. There are possible exceptions such as those contained in sections 8 and 9 of article 909 of the Commercial Code. Under these provisions

- where merchandise which has been supplied to the bankrupt on the basis of payment on delivery has not been paid for and the merchandise is still packaged and distinguishable in the bankrupt's warehouse, it may be recovered; and

- where delivery of merchandise contracted for has not yet taken place, the vendor may keep the merchandise.

Proceedings post-declaration

The post-declaration procedural steps involved in bankruptcy can be separated into four stages:

1. classifying the insolvency;
2. establishing and realising the bankruptcy estate;

3. acknowledging and ranking the claims of creditors;
4. termination of the bankruptcy procedure.

Classification of the insolvency

The basic purpose of this stage is to determine whether the bankruptcy may be considered as fraudulent or not fraudulent. If the former, the debtor is not allowed to make agreements with his creditors in the bankruptcy proceedings (art 898.2 of the Commercial Code); nor will he be granted rehabilitation, even in the event that he pays all his debts (article 920 of the Commercial Code). This classification of the insolvency as fraudulent is, similarly, the preliminary stage in the assessment as to whether any of the directors may be judged to be criminally liable.

The absence of books of account or of evidence of debts, entries and data which would enable the real financial status of the bankrupt entity to be ascertained is of special practical importance when assessing whether the insolvency is to be classified as fraudulent (judgment of 7 February 1980).

The classification of insolvency is intended to determine not only the persons who are directly implicated, such as the individual trader or directors of the mercantile company, but also all their accomplices. Creditors who are found to be accomplices will lose any right to collect any dividend from the bankruptcy estate and, in addition, must refund, with interest and compensation, what they removed from the estate.

The classification is subject to a report by the comisario and ends with the possible rehabilitation of the bankrupt in the event that the bankruptcy is not fraudulent and provided that he has paid all his debts or fulfilled the agreement.

Establishing and realising the bankruptcy estate

Two operations are carried out simultaneously. First, the date of the bankruptcy is fixed to take effect from a date prior to the declaration of bankruptcy. This causes the bankruptcy to have retroactive effect and causes any actions or enforcement against the bankrupt which have taken place prior to the declaration but after the date fixed from which the bankruptcy is to take effect, to be annulled.

Secondly, the bankrupt's total estate must be divided between those assets which must be returned to third parties and those which belong to the bankrupt. The latter are then realised.

As far as the retroactive effect of the bankruptcy is concerned, article 878.2 establishes that all acts in relation to the bankruptcy estate subsequent to the time when the bankruptcy takes effect, will be null and void. This annulment is automatic and immediate, reversing any third party ownership which might have been acquired during this period without any need for declaratory action. However, if the third party refuses to return the assets claimed, it is necessary to institute the relevant declaratory proceedings for which only the sindicos are qualified.

The annulment is inapplicable to those assets which cannot be the subject of attachment proceedings nor those which cannot be considered as part of the bankruptcy estate.

Contracts entered into during the vulnerable period may be validated since this may lead to an increase in the estate in favour of the creditors. In addition, the judgment of 11 December 1985 accepted that mortgages created during this period may be validated under certain circumstances.

A declaration of annulment leads to the restitution of payment made or goods delivered. However, as far as payment having to be restored to third parties is concerned, a debt for the appropriete amount is entered in the total liabilities of the bankruptcy. This is subject to considerable criticism as being unfair to the third party.

The declaration of the annulment extends as far as setting aside third party purchases in good faith although, by article 34 of the Mortgage Law, protection of third parties by public entry on the registry is respected on certain occasions. Any property acquired by third parties in a commercial establishment (such as a shop) is also protected (article 85 of the Commercial Code). This also applies to the acquisition of property under a judicial award.

Within the sphere of matrimony, article 1442 of the Civil Code, revised in 1981, establishes a system with identical effect to that of "presanction muciana". Where the spouses are not legally separated and have been married without community of property, it is to be presumed, unless otherwise proved, that half of the assets acquired by the non-bankrupt spouse were donated by the bankrupt spouse. That half must then be restored to the bankruptcy estate.

Under articles 879 to 882 of the Commercial Code, the sindicos may take action for restitution to the bankrupt's estate of property alleged to belong to the bankrupt, including:

- any payments made by the debtor in respect of bills due later than 15 days prior to the declaration of bankruptcy;
- contracts made in the 30 day period prior to the declaration of bankruptcy or made in the longer period if the declaration of bankruptcy is made retroactive to an earlier day, if such contacts contain any form of release such as the transfer of real estate by the bankrupt free of charge, the grant of a mortgage in connection with obligations which did not have such security, or donations made after the drawing up of the last balance sheet;
- a number of cases, such as those contained in article 881, which require proof of the intention to defraud the creditors.

All the dates mentioned immediately above are calculated from the date of the recording of the declaration of bankruptcy and, as appropriate, from the date of this declaration as back dated by the judge (if this has taken place).

There are various procedures, both special and abbreviated, including injunctive relief, for actions to set aside these aforementioned transactions listed above for further details, see pp612-614 below.

The second part of this stage is the realisation of the estate. Certain assets are excluded, namely:

- those which may not be attached;
- those which must be delivered under an obligation validated by the sindicos; and
- those which must be separated from the estate and returned to third parties where the latter have valid rights of ownership.

Finally, there are creditor's rights under a mortgage or pledge which affect specific assets and on which a right of separate enforcement may be brought.

A creditor who has a right to "separation ex iure crediti" (right to separate enforcement) may choose one of the following methods:

- being paid by the sindicos the total amount of the claim thus releasing the assets mortgaged or pledged;
- making a claim in the bankruptcy proceedings as a creditor with a preferential right;
- exercising the power of sale over the asset or assets which constitute the security as well as making a claim in the bankruptcy for the difference between the amount realised on the sale and the amount of the claim.

The accepted legal view is that mortgage creditors do not have an obligation to participate in the bankruptcy proceedings.

Where goods have been sold to the company, but remain to be delivered and the price has not yet been paid, the bankruptcy ends the respective obligations of delivery and payment.

Acknowledgement and ranking of creditors' claims

First, the claims are examined in order to ascertain that they are genuine. They are then ranked in the prescribed order. For both these operations, the sindicos draw up a proposal which is discussed by the creditors' committee. It will then be approved and submitted to the judge. His ruling on the list is subject to appeal.

The ranking of claims is carried out by dividing them into two blocks according to whether they must be paid with the proceeds from the sale of moveable assets or with proceeds from real estate in accordance with article 919 of the Commercial Code. This is an original and rather impractical system which is based on concepts which are already obsolete. Articles 913 to 916 of the Commercial Code, together with certain provisions such as article 32 *et seq* of the Workers' Statute, provide the following hierarchy of creditors.

Claims of the first section (*i.e.* for payment out of the proceeds of the sale of moveable assets)

Creditors of the post-bankruptcy estate
Although these claims are not specially mentioned in the Commercial Code, they must be paid without being subject to insolvency proceedings. They include costs such as court costs and those of the administration of the bankruptcy, feeding the debtor (if necessary), liabilities of public bodies in the exercise of their functions and contractual obligations authorised by the sindicos or assumed subsequently by them.

Creditors of the pre-bankruptcy estate
1. Claims in respect of salary for the last 30 days of work at an amount which must not be more than double the minimum interprofessional salary (which is a minimum amount established each year by the government). This claim has preference over any other claims, including those guaranteed by a pledge or mortgage (article 32.1 of the Workers' Statute). Even though this privilege is subject to a statute of limitation of one year, it may be instituted with the privilege of separate enforcement.
2. Claims in accordance with article 916 of the Commercial Code, namely for the salaries for the last 30 days, with no upper limit. The objects manufactured by the employees while they are owned by or are in the possession of the employer are security for these claims. Also in this case the workers have a right to separate enforcement, aside from the bankruptcy proceedings.
3. Taxes due on real estate in respect of which the particular real estate is a security.
4. Salary claims not already mentioned. These take preference over any other claims, except as against mortgagees' rights. This category includes compensation for dismissal – considered as deferred salary in accordance with the judgment of the Supreme Court of 27 March 1971.

Legislation passed in May 1994 has reinforced the preferential status of salary arrears.

It is important to note at this point that the Salary Guarantee Fund is a public agency which pays employees the amount of their salaries up to a maximum of four months as compensation for dismissal due to termination of the employment contract and up to a maximum limit of one year's salary plus supplementary compensation which is calculated within those four months. The Salary Guarantee Fund is subrogated to the privileged position of the employees in the bankruptcy.

5. Those claims referred to in article 913 of the Commercial Code which include claims for costs of burial, funeral and the making of wills; creditors who have supplied food to the debtor or his family and creditors for personal work in the last six months prior to the bankruptcy.

6. Other creditors who hold a preferential right as set out in the Code. These creditors have the following claims under the Code of Commerce:

- Article 98: Public commercial notaries are obliged to hold securities for damages arising from improper performance of their functions. Creditors owed such liabilities are privileged to the extent that their claims will be satisfied from those securities;

- Article 198: Creditors that hold pledges over wharehouse receipts can enforce them;

- Article 208: Creditors that hold titles representing shares in mortgages are privileged against the banks who created such titles;

- Article 276: The fees and expenses of any "comisionista" (a kind of trader's agent) who has been acting for the debtor are paid out of the goods which are the subject of his commission;

- Article 320: Creditors that hold pledges on equity provided a Public Commercial Notary has certified the rights pledged can claim the amounts secured by the pledge;

- Article 340: Vendors for the price of goods as against the goods since, if they are still in the possession of the vendor, he simply retains them;

- Article 372 and 376: Creditors who hold liens under contract for the carriage of goods;

- Article 580, 581, 701 and 730: Creditors who hold special privileges under maritime law, such as the right to be paid by means of the auction of a vessel and fees and expenses in respect of goods being transported.

7. Those creditors whose claims are privileged according to the common law (now set out in article 1922 *et seq* of the Civil Code). Article 1922 of the Civil Code provides that the following debts have privileges in that they are, so far as possible, to be satisfied from the goods mentioned:

- debts arising from building, repairing, maintaining or selling of moveable goods in the debtor's hands, are to be satisfied from those goods;

- debts secured by a pledge on equity are to be satisfied from such equity;

- fees and expenses of transportation and conservation of merchandise (for 30 days after the delivery of the merchandise) are to be satisfied from the merchandise;

- debts arising from time spent at hotels, inns, etc. are secured on the personal belongings remaining in the hotel or inn;

- debts arising from the delivery of seeds and from harvesting expenses incurred are to be satisfied from the harvest resulting;

- rent payments due for up to one year prior to the bankruptcy are to be satisfied from the moveables on the land and the fruits of the land. Other mortgage creditors (should any exist) will be paid in accordance with a scale of moveable assets (article 169 of the Mortgage Act).

8. Those creditors whose claims arise from a public deed, jointly with those who are creditors in accordance with titles or commercial contracts, including those in which special types of public notary officials (such as public faith agents and brokers) have been involved.
9. Common or ordinary claims for commercial operations.
10. Ordinary creditors in civil law.

Claims of the second section (*i.e.* for payment out of the proceeds of sale of real estate)

After the payment of employee claims (as described above), creditors in this category are paid in accordance with the following hierarchy:

1. Creditors with a right *in rem*, in accordance with that established in articles 25, 50 and 61 of the Mortgage Act.
2. Creditors of the post-bankruptcy estate as described above.
3. Specially privileged creditors and other creditors listed in the first section, in the order established therein.

If privileged creditors are not fully satisfied from the proceeds of the assets to which their privilege attaches or by the assets available to their particular class of privilege, they may fall into a separately privileged class (for example, a mortgagee who is not fully satisfied by the proceeds from the sale of the mortgaged asset will fall into the class of those whose claims arise from a public deed or commercial contract).

Termination of the bankruptcy procedure

The normal method by which the bankruptcy is terminated is insolvent liquidation, followed by the payment of creditors as set out above.

Liquidation of particular assets is proposed by the sindicos whenever they consider this most appropriate and it must be approved by the judge who, in turn, establishes a minimum price which must be realised. The sale must be carried out by public auction or through a qualified agent.

The proceedings may also be terminated in any of the following ways:

- the dismissal of the bankruptcy petition or the expiry of the discharge of the bankruptcy (as may happen where, because the debtor has little or no assets, no further actions are taken by any creditors);

- non-existence of creditors and, thus, the inability to create the organs of the bankruptcy;

- non-existence of assets to be realised;

- a creditors' agreement with the debtor which provides for a termination of the bankruptcy in circumstances other than the payment of the creditors. This is described more fully below.

Once the document containing the agreement of the creditors' committee is signed, the claims are paid and the creditors are given a note of the amount paid.

As stated above, the bankruptcy procedure may also be terminated by an agreement between the debtor and the creditors if this is approved by the committee and endorsed by the judge.

Once the acknowledgement of claims is completed and provided that the debtor has not been classified as a fraudulent bankrupt and has not absconded, the agreement may be proposed. Commercial companies may carry this out at any stage of the bankruptcy.

The proposal for an agreement must be approved by the creditors' committee without any special requirements for quorum although, if there is to be an extension of time and a reduction of the amount of the debt, a quorum of three-fifths in value of the liabilities is required. The agreement must be approved by 50 % plus one of the creditors attending, provided that they represent three-fifths of the total liabilities.

In addition to this, it is necessary for the creditors to be divided into three groups and a majority vote to be achieved in each group.

In addition to a reduction of the amount, or an extension of the time for payment, it is possible to agree to the continuation or the transfer of the business of the company in accordance with article 928. In the same way a bankrupt may make a complete assignment of all his assets for the payment of the debts.

Although the letter of the law appears to order the judge to approve the agreement, providing that there has not been any opposition within eight days, the judge must establish that the agreement is favourable to the creditors, that the forms of proceedings have not been infringed and that the debtor has not been fraudulent.

The agreement can be contested on the grounds that it has been reached by fraud or due to default in any of its terms. In the latter case, however, the judge will make the final decision.

The effects of the agreement include the extinguishing of all the debts, both of those creditors who attend and those who do not attend, except for those creditors who have exercised the right to abstain, although an express agreement is necessary for this purpose. If not so expressly stated, the right to collect the claim in full, when the bankrupt is in a better position to pay, is reserved.

5. Augmenting the assets of the insolvent corporation

Restitution

Apart from the automatic annulment of all the actions of the debtor after the bankruptcy has come into effect and the possible augmenting of the debtors' assets thereby (see p606 *supra*), under articles 879 to 882 of the Commercial Code, the sindicos may take action to restore property that has been removed from the debtor's estate by making an application to the court.

Article 879
Under article 879, the judge can order the return by the payee of any amount paid in respect of debts yet to fall due by the debtor within 15 days before the bankruptcy order.

Article 880
Under article 880, the following contracts are deemed to be void if they have been effected within 30 days before the bankruptcy order:

- transfers of real estate without consideration;
- gifts to daughters of the debtor of assets belonging to the debtor;
- transfers of rights to and title in real estate to settle debts that have not matured at that time;
- creation of voluntary mortgages in respect of debts not previously secured;
- loans and purchases of merchandise when the delivery of the monies and goods have not taken place in circumstances of what is known as a "notary public faith";
- gifts made after the last balance sheet of the debtor revealed that the debtor was insolvent.

Article 881
Article 881 provides that creditors can obtain a declaration that contracts are void if they are successful in presenting evidence that the debtor acted with a fraudulent intention in relation to:

- sales of real estate performed within one month before the bankruptcy order;
- gifts, within one month before the bankruptcy order, in favour of daughters of the debtor with assets belonging to the "sociedad conyugal", or any transfer of those assets without consideration;
- gifts and creation of debts between a married couple within six months before the bankruptcy order where they were not assets already belonging to or possessed by the other partner;
- any debt created or acknowledgement of a loan made within six months before the bankruptcy order, without the document having been executed in front of a notary public, or without uniformity in the accounting records of the two parties;
- any contract or obligation entered into within ten days before the declaration.

Article 882

Under article 882, any donation made or contract entered into within two years before the bankruptcy order can be challenged by the creditors if they have any evidence of misrepresentation or fraud.

Action against the management of the debtor

This action is for a declaration as to the liabilities of the management to contribute to the assets of the debtor because of management's contribution to the insolvency of the debtor by its own negligent or fraudulent acts. The action can be commenced by the public prosecutor, the sindicos or individual creditors but is at their own expense.

If the proceedings are successful, the court will quantify the damages the relevant member of the management must pay to the debtor's estate. A declaration of civil liability will not of itself impose criminal liability on the management.

6. Public control over insolvent corporations

Persons appointed to bankruptcy offices are appointed by the judge or by the creditors. Judges usually have a certain number of experts in their confidence whom they appoint repeatedly. Except in limited cases where the offices are filled in accordance with special legal provisions (insurance companies or certain banking situations), the applicable rules are as follows:

Interventores

Interventores for the suspension of payments are:

- chartered accountants, as recently provided for in the Auditors Act;
- persons that have been acting as interventores for more than five years before the date that the legislation relating to auditors came into force and who have to be certified by the secretary of the court. These have to be expert practitioners but do not necessarily have to have professional qualifications;
- creditors who are listed in the first third of the list presented by the debtor, ranked according to the amount of their claim. These do not need to have any qualifications at all.

Comisarios

Comisarios in bankruptcy can be any persons registered as merchants in the commercial registry, but it is a usual practice for judges to appoint persons in whom they have confidence.

Sindicos

Sindicos are creditors appointed by the creditors' meeting.

General comments

Representatives of the larger creditors, such as banks, insurance credit companies, and "fondo de garantia salarial" (a public agency that secures to certain limits salaries and compensation to be paid to employees upon termination of the employment contract due to insolvency), are usually appointed as interventores and sindicos.

In suspension of payments proceedings, the interventores review the economic position of the debtor through the accounts books and documentation and direct knowledge they acquire dealing with the preparation of their report. Nevertheless, there is no power to enable them to require the production of documents or to cross-examine witnesses. If the insolvency is considered definitive certain procedures are available to augment the assets of the company (see pp612-614 *supra*).

In bankruptcy proceedings, the comisario is in charge of conducting a separate report on the reasons for the bankruptcy, which may find that the bankruptcy was caused by fortuitous causes, by negligence or by fraudulent behaviour on the part of the debtor. If fraud is declared, further investigation will be carried out through the criminal courts.

Contents of Chapter 14

CORPORATE INSOLVENCY LAW IN SWEDEN

1.	**Introduction**	619
2.	**Corporations**	619
	The limited company "aktiebolag" – "AB"	619
	Financing and security for creditors	623
	Available information	626
	Other business entities	627
	Debt collection and asset recovery	628
	Cross-jurisdictional procedures	630
3.	**Survival of the insolvent corporation or its business**	630
	Composition	630
	Pre-application/appointment considerations	632
	Procedure	633
	Creditors' involvement and position	634
	Powers and duties of the god man (assignee)	635
	Management and supervision by the god man	635
	Position of officers and shareholders/owners	635
4.	**Termination of the insolvent corporation: liquidation and bankruptcy**	638
	Liquidation	638
	Bankruptcy proceedings	643
5.	**Augmenting the assets of the insolvent corporation**	647
	Introduction	647
	Recovery	648
	Liability to pay damages incurred by officers of a limited liability company	651
	Repayment of an improper distribution of profit	652
	Liability in the case of a compulsory winding up	653
	Liability for failing to file the company's annual report with	

the Patent and Registration Office.   654
6.   Public control over insolvent corporations   654
Persons who may be appointed konkursförvaltare (trustee)   654
Public control   654
The supervisory authority   656
Publicity and records   656

Chapter 14

CORPORATE INSOLVENCY LAW IN SWEDEN

Leif Baecklund, Thomas Ehrner, Thomas Sjöberg and
Elisabet Fura-Sandström,
Advokatfirman Vinge

1. Introduction

Swedish law mainly exists in the form of written statutes. However, these are as a rule fairly generally framed, for which reason precedents formed as a result of judgments must also be taken into consideration when assessing the legal position. The judgments of the Supreme Court carry particular weight.

Bankruptcy proceedings are primarily governed by the Bankruptcy Act 1987:672. Proceedings are the same for companies and private individuals.

2. Corporations

In Sweden there are several forms in which business may be carried on. They differ from each other, *inter alia,* in respect of the degree of liability which the owners bear for the obligations of the organisation. The most important business form is the limited company ("aktiebolag"), used for business activities of varying types and size. There are also partnerships ("handelsbolag"), limited partnerships ("kommanditbolag") and co-operatives ("ekonomiska föreningar"). It should also be mentioned that many people carry on business as sole traders ("enskilda näringsidkare").

The limited company "aktiebolag" – "AB"

The limited company is the most common form of business entity. It is used for both small family businesses and large public companies, not just in private ownership, but also within the public sector.

Characteristics

The regulations governing limited companies are set out in the Companies Act

1975 ("the Companies Act").

The chief characteristic of limited companies is that the owners (*i.e.* the shareholders) are not personally liable for the obligations or debts of the company. The share capital must be paid in to the company. Since a limited company is a legal person, *i.e.* it may sign contracts and be a party in legal proceedings.

As stated above, both large and small businesses may be in the form of a limited company. There are a number of specific provisions regarding larger companies. If the share capital is SEK 1 million or more, the company must have a board of directors consisting of at least three people. In addition, there must be a managing director (chief executive officer). Larger companies must also have an authorised public accountant as auditor. Smaller companies may have a board comprising only one person and the auditor need not be an authorised public accountant.

A limited company may not purchase its own shares or accept them as a pledge. The same applies to subsidiaries in relation to their parent company. Exceptions to this rule apply in the case of takeovers of businesses, but shares acquired in this manner must be sold as soon as possible and no later than three years after the acquisition. If the shares have not been disposed of within three years the shares are null and void.

The Companies Act also contains other provisions protecting the company's equity. Thus, the payment of dividends to the shareholders may not exceed what has been recorded in the adopted balance sheet as profit, following deduction of any losses, allocations to statutory reserves and other deductions required by law. Dividends declared may not be greater than is prudent in the light of the company's financial position, having regard to good commercial practice.

Decisions regarding the payment of dividends are taken at the annual general meeting of the shareholders.

A distribution of corporate funds which has taken place in contravention of the above provisions and which has no commercial purpose is not permitted. If such a distribution occurs, repayment must be made and those responsible for the distribution may be ordered to compensate the company for any shortfall. The same applies if the company sells property for no good commercial reason at an undervalue or purchases at an overvalue or takes similar action.

In the same way a limited company may not grant a loan to anyone owning shares in or belonging to the board of the company or to the managing director of the company or another company in the same group. The same applies to loans to associated individuals or companies. However, there are certain exceptions to these provisions.

The Companies Act has recently been amended. The amendments, which came into force on 1 January 1995, divide limited companies into two categories, public limited and private limited companies. The main difference between public and private limited companies is that public limited companies are required to have a share capital of at least SEK 500,000 compared with private limited companies which are only required to have a share of SEK 100,000. Private limited companies may not finance their business by offering their shares, subscriptions, rights, debt instruments or warrants to the general public. Instruments which have been issued by a private limited company cannot be traded on the Stock Exchange or any other similar market place.

Management

As stated above, a limited company must have a board of at least three directors. If the share capital is less than SEK 1 million, however, the board may consist of one or two directors, provided that there is at least one deputy. The board is elected at the annual general meeting but, in accordance with special legislation, the employees are entitled to appoint two directors and two deputies for such directors if the company has at least 25 employees. In companies with at least 1,000 employees the employees are entitled to three employee representatives and three deputies for them. Such board members are appointed by the local unions. In principle, the same rules apply to employee representatives as to other directors. A director is elected for a certain period, as a rule until the end of the next annual general meeting, *i.e.* for one year. An appointment as director may terminate earlier, however, if the director or those appointing him so request. In companies having a share capital amounting to at least SEK 1 million, the board must appoint a managing director. In smaller companies such officer may be appointed by the board if it so wishes. The managing director and at least half of the directors must be resident within the EEA unless the appropriate authority (the Patent and Registration Office or the government) otherwise allows. The board is responsible for the organisation and administration of the affairs of the company. If there is a managing director, he is responsible for the day-to-day management in accordance with the guidelines and instructions he receives from the board. However, a managing director may not take action of major importance or of an unusual nature without authorisation from the board, unless the delay involved in obtaining such authorisation would cause considerable inconvenience to the business of the company. In such case the board shall be notified as soon as possible.

The board must ensure that book-keeping and administration of funds are subject to satisfactory control. The managing director is responsible for ensuring that the company's book-keeping is properly carried out and that funds are administered correctly.

The chairman of the board must be one of the directors. He must ensure that meetings are held when necessary. Meetings of the board are quorate when more than half of the total number of directors, or a higher proportion if the articles of association so prescribe, are present. A resolution voted for by more than half of those present represents a decision of the board, unless the articles of association prescribe a specific voting majority. In the event of an equality of votes, the chairman shall have the casting vote.

A director or the managing director may not be involved in the consideration of matters concerning contracts if he or she has a substantial interest in the contract under consideration.

In principle, the board represents the company and signs on its behalf. The board may authorise a director, the managing director or another person to represent the company and sign on its behalf. At least one of the authorised persons must be resident within the EEA unless the appropriate authority (the Board of Trade) or the Government otherwise allows in individual cases. The managing director is always entitled to represent the company and sign on its behalf in respect of actions within the ambit of his authority, *i.e.* the day-to-day running of the company. The board or other representative of the company may not take action intended to improperly favour a shareholder or other party in relation to the company or other shareholder.

If a representative who has undertaken a transaction on behalf of the company has exceeded his authority, the transaction is not binding upon the company, provided that the other party to the transaction realised or ought to have realised that the representative had exceeded his authority. This also applies to actions taken by the managing director outside the ambit of his authority.

Ownership

The shares in a limited company are owned by one or more shareholders, who may be private individuals or legal persons. The power of the shareholders as against the officers of the company primarily comprises the right to appoint and dismiss directors and to adopt or not adopt the annual report. If a company owns so many shares in another company that it has more than half of the votes in that other company, there is a group relationship, which brings into play certain rules concerning accounting and other matters.

A list of shareholders must be kept. This is called the share register. The right of the shareholders to take decisions with regard to the affairs of the company is exercised at the shareholders' meeting.

The annual general meeting must be held within six months of the end of each financial year. The meeting must take decisions regarding adoption of the annual reports, allocation of profit or loss and discharge from liability of the board and the managing director. Other issues may also arise.

An extraordinary meeting of the shareholders must be held when the board considers that there is a reason for such a meeting to be held. An auditor or at least 10% of the shareholders may also call for such a meeting.

A shareholder is entitled to raise a matter at a shareholders' meeting provided that he makes a written request sufficiently far in advance that the matter may be included in the notice of the meeting.

The board convenes shareholders' meetings. Notice must be issued no earlier than four weeks and, as a rule, no later than two weeks before the meeting. The notice must clearly specify the matters to be dealt with at the meeting.

A resolution adopted by a shareholders' meeting is a proposal for which more than half of the votes according to the voting list have been cast or, in the event of a tied vote, reflects the view of the chairman, who has a casting vote. In the case of an election, the person receiving most votes is deemed to have been elected. In the event of a tie the vote is decided by the drawing of lots.

Certain decisions of importance to the shareholders concerning changes in the articles of association require more than a simple majority, normally two-thirds of the votes cast and the shares represented at the meeting. An amendment to the articles of association involving a reduction of the shareholders' entitlement to company profits or other assets, on the grounds that the object of the company is no longer to be the generation of profit for the shareholders, requires the support of all the shareholders present at the meeting, representing at least nine-tenths of all the shares. The same applies to a change made in the legal relationship between the shares. Certain other changes in the articles of association also require more than a simple majority.

If a decision of a meeting of the shareholders has not been properly taken or is otherwise contrary to the Companies Act or the articles of association, legal proceedings may be instituted in a court of law by a shareholder, a director or the managing director against such a decision.

The Companies Act also contains certain rules protecting minority shareholders. Among other things, 10% or more of the shareholders may request a separate auditor (a "minority auditor").

Financing and security for creditors

Persons or institutions advancing money to the corporation without participating in the share capital will often require some form of security in return for providing the finance. Clearly it is where the corporation becomes bankrupt that this security becomes most important, allowing the secured creditor to obtain repayment or settlement of his debt in priority to the general unsecured creditors from the asset over which he has security.

In the event of bankruptcy the rights of certain creditors ("preferential and secured creditors") as compared with other creditors are governed by specific legislation, the Preferential Rights of Creditors Act 1970:979. There are two types of preferential rights, specific and general preferential rights. Specific preferential rights apply to certain specific property. General preferential rights cover all property belonging to the insolvent corporation's estate in bankruptcy which is not covered by specific preferential rights. This difference in many ways also corresponds to the difference in the United Kingdom between secured and preferential creditors, the former corresponding to creditors with specific preferential rights and the latter to creditors with general preferential rights.

Specific preferential rights

Specific preferential rights apply to specific property of the debtor company and (with one minor exception) rank in priority over general preferential rights (p625 *infra*). The most important specific preferential rights are as follows:

Security interests, pledges, mortgages and liens
There are various types of security interests. These may be divided into statutory security interests (security interests arising under specific statutory provisions) and contractual security interests. Mortgages in real property, ships or aircraft

confer a security interest in the mortgaged property. Such security interests only apply in respect of specific determined property. Floating charges, on the other hand, apply with respect to the debtor's business assets (with certain exceptions), which are continuously entering and leaving the business.

One example of a statutory security interest is a repairer's lien, under which a repairer is entitled to retain possession of property on which he has carried out work if he does not receive payment. He is entitled to sell an item he has worked on, provided that:

- the work has been concluded;
- the customer has been requested to collect the item and informed that failure to do so will result in the item being sold after a certain time (no less than three months after the request to collect);
- the time limit specified in such request has expired.

The item may be sold without the customer having been requested to collect it if one year has elapsed from the conclusion of the work and the resale value of the item is negligible. If the sale generates a surplus, such surplus must be paid to the customer. Any surplus not exceeding SEK 50 may be retained by the repairer. If the customer is declared bankrupt, a repairer's lien will mean that the repairer has a specific preferential right in the property on which he has worked. A security interest is also created where property is physically transferred to a lender as security for a loan. Most chattels may be pledged in this way, but pledges are usually of securities (*i.e.* shares or debentures), as well as valuable items such as art and jewellery. Bank deposits and other claims may also be pledged. This is effected by notifying the bank or the party in debt to the pledgor. Negotiable debt instruments are pledged by means of physical transfer to the lender.

It is often agreed at the time of pledging that the lender will be entitled to sell the property if the loan is not repaid. Any surplus arising is payable to the owner of the property.

Specific statutory rules apply to maritime liens which govern: claims against the shipowner which are attributable to the vessel and which concern salaries to crew and personnel; damage to property or personal injuries arising in immediate connection with the operation of the ship; salvage fees and similar liabilities. A maritime lien expires one year after the claim arises unless the vessel is distrained upon or arrested prior to expiry of this period and subsequently sold by compulsory auction.

Liens in aircraft primarily arise in respect of salvage costs.

Mortgages in real property, ships and aircraft must be registered. A security interest arises by virtue of the fact that the mortgage is transferred to a lender as security for a loan. The lender is entitled to demand that the mortgaged property be sold by compulsory auction if the loan is not repaid. Priority as between mortgages is determined by the order in which they are registered. Registration procedures are strictly governed by statute.

Rent

A claim for rent for premises used for business purposes confers a preferential right in chattels belonging to the business (see *infra*). The preferential right only extends to a sum corresponding to three months' rent, however. Thus, a landlord always has a clear preferential right for rent in respect of a short period.

Floating charges

An enterprise may register charges on its business. The charge may cover all the company's property intended to be generally traded except cash and bank deposits and shares and debentures. Real property, vessels and aircraft are not included either, since special mortgage rules apply to such property. In reality, floating charges generally relate to the company's machinery and equipment, stock-in-trade and outstanding claims.

Where the landlord has a preferential right over the same assets as a holder of a floating charge, the landlord has priority before the charge-holder up to an amount not exceeding three months' rent.

The normal state of affairs in Sweden is that a floating charge is provided as security for credit of a more long-term nature obtained from banks or other credit institutions. It sometimes also happens that an important supplier has a floating charge on its customer's property. The value of such a change is that it confers preferential status on insolvency.

General preferential rights

The most important general preferential rights rank in priority as follows:

Cost of having the insolvent corporation declared bankrupt

A creditor lodging a petition in bankruptcy in a court of law is entitled to compensation for the cost of such petition from the bankruptcy estate. The same applies to a number of other special claims, of which the most important is probably payment of a god man (assignee) pursuant to the Composition Act 1970:847.

Auditors' and accountants' claims

The next general preferential right concerns the cost of the statutory audit and book-keeping, provided that the work has been done during the six months immediately prior to the petition in bankruptcy.

Taxes and general charges

Claims by the state for taxes and social security charges are preferred. It may also be mentioned here that the board and/or managing director can be personally liable for company taxes and charges which are not paid in due time.

Claims of the employees

Next in order of preference come the claims of employees in respect of salaries and other payments arising in connection with employment. Since personnel may be entitled to between one and six months' notice, depending on age, and holiday pay of 12% to 13% of salary, the sums given preference pursuant to this provision may be very large. It is worth noting that the employees' claims up to SEK100,000 are generally paid out of a special state fund, financed by social security charges. The state then takes over the claims of the employees in the bankruptcy and has the same preferential right.

Non-preferential claims

Claims which do not carry any of the above preferential rights are non-preferential and are of equal standing as against each other. The usual state of affairs in Sweden is that non-preferential creditors (also called "ordinary" or "general creditors") unfortunately do not receive any dividend in the bankruptcy of the insolvent corporation.

Reservation of title

A fairly common form of security in commercial relationships is for a supplier to retain title to the property supplied until such time as full payment for the property has been received. Under Swedish law, this is not permitted in respect of goods intended to be resold. Reservation of title is common with regard to machinery, vehicles and other equipment of major value intended to be used for a considerable length of time by the purchaser. One prerequisite is that the reservation was made right from the start; it may not be created retroactively. The effect of the reservation is that the vendor is entitled to repossess the property if he does not receive payment. When the property is repossessed it is valued and its value is then set off against the purchaser's debt to the seller. If the value is less than the debt, the seller will have a residual non-preferential claim against the purchaser. If the value of the repossessed property is greater than the debt, the seller must pay the difference to the purchaser. A reservation of title clause may be inserted in agreements with consumers as well as various forms of enterprise.

Finally, it is worth mentioning that the provisions of the Commission Agency Act 1914:451 mean, for example, that a commission agent undertakes to sell goods on behalf of another but in his own name. Goods may be delivered to the commission agent which are owned by the principal until the moment of resale. This procedure may thus afford a supplier security which would normally not be available because of the prohibition on reservation of title relating to goods intended for resale.

Available information

Limited companies are registered at the Patent and Registration Office, which issues a ten-digit company registration number which the company retains for all time. The company is identified by this number even if it changes its name. The Register contains information on the objects of the company, the board, auditor(s), share capital and other matters. The Patent and Registration Office must be notified of any changes in this information.

Limited companies are under a duty to draw up for each financial year (which need not necessarily be the calendar year) annual accounts, including a profit and loss account, balance sheet and management report. Copies of these are to be filed with the Patent and Registration Office. Should a company not file its annual report within 15 months from the expiry of the financial year, its officers are personally liable for debts occuring thereafter. Larger companies are also under a duty to submit interim reports.

The Companies Register is accessible to the public, and for a small charge anyone may request a print-out from the Register, showing the above-mentioned information. It is also possible to ask the Patent and Registration Office for copies of annual reports and other documents relating to limited companies, such as the articles of association.

Limited companies which do not fulfil their obligations in certain respects may be compulsorily wound up. This applies if, according to the Register, the company does not have a proper board of directors, managing director or auditor as required by the Companies Act and also if the company has not filed an annual report within 11 months from the expiry of the financial year.

It is possible to obtain information from the land registration authority ("inskrivningsmyndighet") at Malmö District Court as to whether the company has registered any floating charges. Similar information regarding mortgages may be obtained from the land registration authority at the appropriate District Court. Ship mortgages are registered in the shipping register and aircraft mortgages in the civil aviation register at Stockholm District Court.

The State authority for execution of judgments in respect of financial obligations (the "enforcement service"), provides information concerning companies' unpaid debts to the state. It is possible to purchase information from several private credit reference agencies with regard to late payers and non-payers. However, banks and finance companies are not obliged to release information about their customers.

Bankruptcies and public cancellations of payments are announced in the daily press and in the official publication, the Swedish Official Gazette.

Other business entities

Apart from limited companies, which are the most common business form, other business entities are principally as set out below. The rules applying to limited companies also generally apply to these other business forms with regard to security and preferential rights, and to some extent with regard to information.

Partnerships (handelsbolag – "HB") and limited partnerships (kommanditbolag – "KB")

Partnerships and limited partnerships are forms frequently adopted by small businesses. They have two or more partners and are legal persons. They are registered in a separate register, kept by the individual counties. The partners are personally liable for the debts of a partnership. In the case of limited partnerships, however, only one partner need be fully liable for the debts of the partnership, while the other partners are only liable to the extent of the sum which they have invested in the partnership. A limited partner may only participate in the management of the partnership's affairs if this has been expressly agreed.

Co-operatives

Co-operatives are common in the agricultural sector, the consumer co-operative movement and the housing sector. Co-operatives are independent legal persons and are owned by their members, who do not have any personal liability for the debts of the co-operative. The idea of co-operatives is to promote the financial interests of the members by business activities in which the members are expected to participate, usually as consumers. Co-operatives are registered in a separate co-operatives register.

Co-operatives are governed by specific legislation, similar in many respects to the Companies Act.

Sole traders

It is common for small businesses to be run by a sole trader. In such cases the business is conducted by a private individual under his own name and possibly also under a company name. The business is entered in the register kept by the individual counties. Thus, the business does not have a separate legal identity. Naturally, the sole trader has full personal liability for the obligations he assumes in his business.

Debt collection and asset recovery

It is possible to divide debt collection into two main categories. The first concerns special claims linked to some form of security, while the second relates to more general claims where there is no security attached. A creditor with a reservation of title claim to property supplied belongs in the first category.

Unsecured claims

The procedure is the same for enterprises and private individuals. After the claim has fallen due for payment the creditor, who is perhaps a supplier of goods (but without a reservation of title provision) or services, sends a reminder regarding the unpaid claim. A week or so later he sends another reminder, often containing a threat to the effect that the claim will be put in the hands of a debt collection agency if payment is not made swiftly. Thereafter the unpaid claim is passed over to a debt collection agency.

There are a number of such agencies to choose from, with a relatively small number dominating the market. Debt collection is governed by specific legislation, the Debt Collection Act 1974:182, which provides, *inter alia*, that the business of debt collection may only be carried on by those in possession of a permit granted by the appropriate authority. The Act further states that debt collection is to be conducted in accordance with "accepted debt collection practice". The debtor may not be subjected to unnecessary nuisance, and undue pressure must be avoided.

The debt collection agency sends a demand in which the principal sum owing is claimed, together with interest on late payment and debt collection charges. A further demand may also be sent later.

If payment has still not been made, the debt collection agency lodges a claim at the enforcement service in the debtor's place of residence, to the effect that the enforcement service should make a ruling establishing the debtor's liability to pay. The debtor is notified of the claim and is given a short period in which to raise objections. If such objections are raised, the claim will be referred to trial at the district court in the debtor's place of residence. Otherwise, the creditor's claim is established by means of a declaratory judgment by the enforcement service. At such time the creditor is also allowed minor compensation for costs.

This judgment will be enforced automatically by the same authority. The enforcement service then informs the debtor that action will be taken to enforce the debt unless payment is made within a certain limited period. The enforcement service sets a deadline for execution of the judgment upon the debtor, *i.e.* on the company or at the home of a private individual. The enforcement will take the form of seizure of goods belonging to the debtor ("distraint") and sale of these goods, with the proceeds of sale, less costs incurred, being used to pay the creditor's claim. Items which may be distrained upon may in theory be anything of value belonging to the debtor, including real property, claims, vehicles, machinery, bank deposits. There are limits regarding distraint upon the possessions of private individuals. Furniture and private household goods needed in a normal home may not be distrained upon. On the other hand, salary may be taken in satisfaction of the debt, although only to the extent that such salary obviously exceeds what is needed for the day-to-day living expenses of the debtor and his family. Salary may not in any event be taken in satisfaction of a debt for a total of more than six months in any one calendar year.

When distraint has been carried out, the items distrained upon are sold and the creditor's account is settled. If nothing which may be distrained upon is found, the enforcement service's involvement comes to an end. The remedy then available to the creditor is to seek to have the debtor declared bankrupt.

The above account is an outline only. The individual circumstances are often complicated by difficulties in notifying the debtor and a backlog of cases at the courts and the enforcement service, particularly in the major cities.

Secured claims

The procedure for enforcing secured claims varies according to the type of security in question. The initial procedure, involving reminders and letters threatening referral to a debt collection agency naturally also applies in respect of secured claims. As a rule, this is followed by a simplified written proceeding in accordance with what is stated above, leading to a ruling establishing the debtor's liability to pay. At the same time the court will also order that the claim is to be paid with a preferential right out of the mortgaged property (in the case of real property, vessels or aircraft). The creditor may then request that the enforcement service effect a compulsory sale of the property. A similar procedure is followed in the case of claims to which there is attached a lien or other security interest in chattels. However, in such cases it may be agreed that the creditor/pledgee will himself be entitled to realise the pledge without the property first being distrained upon, at which time any surplus arising must be paid to the debtor.

Repossession on the grounds of a reservation of title in goods sold is normally effected by means of an application to the enforcement service. Provided that the sale documents meets certain requirements, a court judgment is not necessary. The items are valued when they are repossessed. If they are worth more than the outstanding debt plus interest and expenses, the creditor must pay the balance to the debtor. If the contrary applies, the creditor will have a non-preferential outstanding claim on the debtor. The actual proceeds of sale thereafter obtained by the creditor are not taken into account for the purpose of settling the creditor's claim.

Repossession of other property hired or borrowed is also effected on behalf of the lessor or lender by way of a simplified proceeding of the same type as that described above, after which an application for enforcement may be made to the enforcement service.

Cross-jurisdictional procedures

There has for many years been a scheme of co-operation between the Nordic countries (Sweden, Norway, Denmark, Finland and Iceland) in respect of acknowledgement and enforcement of judgments issued in any of these countries, including judgments relating to bankruptcy law.

Agreements with non-Nordic countries in the area of civil law are more sporadic. In general, anyone wishing to enforce a claim on a debtor in Sweden must turn to a Swedish court.

3. Survival of the insolvent corporation or its business

Composition

Purpose and effect

All insolvency procedures in Sweden apply equally to incorporated and unincorporated entities, whether trading or not.

The legal definition of a composition is a financial arrangement between a debtor who is insolvent and his/its creditors.

The purpose of a composition is to relieve the insolvent company of part of its aggregated debt and thus ensure the continuation of the business. The debts written off as a result of the composition will no longer be enforceable and the debtor will no longer be regarded as insolvent.

A composition should only be considered when there is a strong belief that the business has a future. If this is not so, bankruptcy is the only solution. Generally speaking, bankruptcy will give the creditors less than a composition since bankruptcy proceedings are regarded as the least advantageous form of attempted debt recovery. Thus, if there is a chance that the business may survive, this is likely to attract the support of many of the debtor's creditors in the hope of greater recovery of outstanding claims.

Three different forms of composition can be distinguished under Swedish law, namely:

- composition within the scope of bankruptcy proceedings;
- public composition ("offentligt ackord");
- informal compromise ("underhandsackord").

Since a composition within the scope of bankruptcy proceedings is highly unusual and the informal composition is rare, the following discussion is confined to public composition, referred to as "the composition". The following text is also confined to corporate insolvencies and consequently the text refers to "company" or "debtor" when dealing with the insolvent party.

The composition must ensure the equal treatment of all non-preferential creditors and the proposal must include the payment of at least 25% of the claims made by non-preferential creditors and payment in full to preferential creditors. If the percentage of repayment is any lower, the proposal for a composition must either be agreed by all known creditors who would be affected or there must be specific reasons for accepting a lower figure. The law does not elaborate on what these specific reasons might be but leaves this matter to the discretion of the court. If a composition with a lower percentage is the only viable solution for the insolvent company and the alternatives hardly seem realistic, then the court may regard this as sufficient reason for accepting a lower figure. Payment should normally be made within a year of the day the composition was approved. It should be noted that if the company is significant to the local labour market, the government may refrain from asserting its preferential claim for taxes, in which case the claim will be treated as a non-preferential one.

A composition can also prescribe that its only effect is to allow the debtor to pay in full at a later stage. The exact date applying must be stipulated.

The proceedings begin with the appointment of a god man (assignee). Once this appointment has been made the officers of the insolvent company must exercise due care when administering the property and must not make any decisions without consulting the god man, who must ensure that the rights of the creditors are duly taken into consideration and protected.

Another important effect of the appointment of a god man is that a petition in bankruptcy filed by an unsecured creditor after the appointment will be suspended on the request of the god man pending the conclusion of the composition negotiations unless there are specific reasons to believe that the granting of such a request will endanger the creditors' rights. Such reasons might be suspicion of fraudulent behaviour by officers of the company or if the court is convinced that there is no realistic hope of reaching a scheme of composition. Legal proceedings against the debtor, such as actions for the sequestration of assets, are likewise suspended.

Once the court has decided that negotiations to finalise a composition should be commenced, the provisions on recovery in the Bankruptcy Act are applicable. The rules are described on page 627 *et seq.*

Pre-application/appointment considerations

The basic consideration before filing an application for appointment of a god man is to make sure that it is likely that a composition can be concluded within the time limits set out in the Composition Act. An application for composition negotiations must be filed within two months of the date of appointment of the god man. If no application is made before the expiry of the time limit, the procedure terminates automatically. The composition payments must be made within 12 months of the acceptance of the composition unless the creditors unanimously accept a longer term of payment. In practice, a popular formula for payment is 25% after one month, 25% after six months and the remainder after 12 months. Once it has been established that the creditors would be willing to accept a composition or at least that they are not unwilling to negotiate such a scheme, the next consideration will be how to finance a composition. The insolvent company would normally need new capital to finance the composition and secure the continued operation of its business.

Only the insolvent company is entitled to file an application with the appropriate district court regarding the appointment of a god man. The latter's functions are to investigate and negotiate with the creditors in order to conclude a composition. The court will appoint such a person upon receipt of the application unless there is reason to believe that a composition will not be possible.

The application must be in writing and should include a comprehensive report on the applicant's financial status, the reasons for the insolvency and in what way the applicant intends to satisfy the creditors once a composition has been concluded.

The application may also propose a god man, although this is not compulsory. In the absence of such a proposal the court will decide who is to be appointed by choosing from a list of approved individuals. The law requires that the god man should be a practising lawyer, with the specific knowledge and experience required in the light of the nature of the particular business operated by the debtor. In addition, the god man should be selected with a view to enjoying the confidence of the creditors.

Normally the god man will be a person who is a member of the Swedish Bar Association ("advokat") or employed by the "Ackordscentralen" a commercial organisation specialising in insolvency work with offices in several cities in Sweden.

Procedure

To initiate negotiations with the creditors the insolvent company must file a second application with the same court which has appointed the god man. The application must be filed no later than two months after the appointment, otherwise the appointment will be null and void.

The application must be accompanied by a number of documents:

- a proposal for a composition;
- an inventory showing the assets and the liabilities;
- a balance sheet;
- a report prepared by the god man;
- a statement by the god man supporting the proposed composition;
- a statement issued by the god man verifying that at least two fifths of the creditors listed in the inventory whose claims would be affected by the composition and who together hold at least two-fifths of the aggregate of these claims have stated that they are ready to accept the composition;
- proof that the proposed composition along with the report and statement has been sent to all the creditors listed in the inventory; and
- advance payment equalling a sum decided by the Government (at present SEK 3,000) for the cost of the composition proceedings in court and in addition thereto security for costs not covered by the advance payment. The security must be approved by the court.

The inventory showing assets and liabilities must be prepared by the god man (assignee).

The court will order someone duly authorised to represent the insolvent company to affirm the correctness of the statement of affairs (*i.e.* the inventory showing the assets and liabilities as mentioned *supra*).

This is a condition for the court to announce that proceedings have commenced. The court's decision will be publicised in the Swedish Official Gazette and at least one daily newspaper.

The liabilities listed in the inventory may be contested by creditors or the debtor. This must be done in writing prior to the creditors' meeting (see *infra*) and submitted to the god man.

A creditors' meeting will be convened no earlier than three weeks and no later than five weeks after the decision to institute proceedings was taken by the court. The purpose of the creditors' meeting (at which the debtor must be present) is to vote on the proposed composition. The creditors will normally grant a power of attorney to the god man to represent them at the meeting.

If the creditors' meeting decides to support the suggested composition, the court will ratify the proposed composition unless one of the provisions listed in section 36 of the Composition Act applies, namely:

- the proceedings have not been conducted in accordance with the law and the irregularities may have affected the outcome of the proceedings;
- the composition is not in compliance with the rules set out in sections 11.2-4, *i.e.* equal treatment of all creditors;
- there is reason to believe that the debtor has secretly given one or more creditors priority and thus substantially influenced the composition or otherwise fraudulently influenced the proceedings; or
- the proposed composition is clearly contrary to the interest of the creditors.

A composition may be set aside upon the application of a creditor whose rights are affected if it is proved that the debtor has behaved fraudulently in any of the ways described in the Composition Act.

Creditors' involvement and position

Creditors may be divided into two categories:

- creditors whose rights will be affected by the composition (and who are entitled to vote at the creditors' meeting); and
- creditors who are not entitled to vote, since their rights are not prejudiced by the composition. This category includes preferential and secured creditors and creditors who will be paid by reason of being able to set off their claims against payments due by them to the company. Where only a partial set-off applies, such creditors may vote to the extent that their claims are not covered by payments due to the debtor.

Participation in the proceedings is limited to those creditors whose claims arose prior to the decision to institute the proceedings. Those whose claims arise after such a decision have an automatic priority over all "pre-decision" creditors and must be paid in cash.

A creditor is entitled to participate in the proceedings even though his claim has not yet fallen due.

A composition accepted and ratified by a court ruling as described above is legally binding on all creditors, known and unknown, who were entitled to participate in the proceedings, regardless of whether they actually did or not.

The law includes special provisions regarding the right to set off. These include:

- assignment of claims;
- the possibility of allowing minor creditors to be paid in full;
- the announcement of the creditors' meeting in the Swedish Official Gazette and at least one local newspaper; and
- the automatic stay of all proceedings against a debtor, including actions for the seizure of the debtor's assets, as well as bankruptcy proceedings.

Accepting the composition does not bar the creditors from claiming payment in full from any third party who guaranteed payment, although of course if such payment is made in the course of the proceedings, that creditor drops out but may be replaced by the guarantor who discharged the debt. A composition proposal giving a dividend of more than 50% of the claims will be regarded as accepted by the creditors if 60% of the votes cast have accepted the proposal and their claims equal at least 60% of the total claims carrying a right to vote.

Should the proposed composition suggest a lower percentage, 75% of the voters must give their approval, representing 75% of the total claims.

Powers and duties of the god man (assignee)

No specific powers are given to the god man. His main duties are to investigate the possibility of coming to an agreement with the creditors and to find a basis for a composition by following the procedures described above. In doing so the god man has to ensure that the creditors' rights are always safeguarded.

Upon demand by a creditor whose rights are affected, the court may, if it deems it necessary, appoint the god man or other suitable person to supervise the debtor and ensure that he fulfils his duties as set out in the composition. In any event, the debtor is obliged to give the god man all relevant information and to follow his instructions.

Management and supervision by the god man

The god man's functions are to administer the debtor's property jointly with the debtor and to supervise the debtor's business in the interests of the creditors. The god man has no special powers and is unable to exercise the powers of the board. He cannot sell property or employ or dismiss personnel, but he may settle certain minor claims if this is deemed necessary in order to reach a general scheme of composition.

In addition, the god man is under a duty to advise the creditors in writing of the composition proposal arrived at jointly with the debtor and to invite them to agree to the composition, in practice by returning a signed form of acceptance.

Position of officers and shareholders/owners

In almost every case of insolvency leading to composition proceedings the starting point is a decision by the board to suspend payments. Sometimes the officers of the company are instructed by the owners that the board must pass a resolution to that effect and advise clients and customers thereof. The law does not define the concept of a resolution to suspend payment. Such resolution is purely informal. However, it is general practice to make such an announcement in order to create the breathing space necessary to consider the conditions for a composition and to avoid making payments that will lead to recovery claims. The breathing space comes into operation as soon as a resolution is passed, provided that it is combined with effective steps to reorganise the company. One such step might be to look into the possibility of reaching a scheme of composition or to negotiate with the tax authorities in order to obtain deferral of tax payments. In short, the steps taken should be designed to take a firm grip of the company's finances and not to incur any more debts, while at the same time protecting the interests of the creditors. Because of the informality of these steps, there are no statutory provisions regarding them. However, there is some case law on the subject suggesting that the breathing space must not be too long and that the officers of the company must show proof of firm action. If this does not happen, both claims for damages and criminal proceedings may ensue against the members of the board, who may also become personally liable for tax claims.

It is important to note, however, that suspending payments may backfire unless the debtor is convinced that a scheme of composition can be reached. For instance, the insolvent party may become even more insolvent after a period of time has elapsed. Creditors thereby suffering may then bring an action for damages against the company and/or its officers. Criminal proceedings instituted by the state prosecutor may also ensue if the directors have not acted in good faith. During the proceedings the officers and the shareholders bear the same responsibilities as they did prior to the commencement of the proceedings. Thus, in general, the shareholders bear no responsibility for the debts of the company, whereas the officers will in certain circumstances run the risk of personal liability as indicated above. However, the shareholders would also run a risk if they took active part in certain decisions concerning the continuation of the business, thereby causing loss or damage to the creditors.

If it is suspected that the equity of the company has fallen below half of the registered share capital, certain specific measures must be taken by the directors and/or shareholders jointly in order to safeguard the interests of the creditors. If the directors and/or shareholders fail so to act, they may be personally liable for the debts incurred after the date when they ought to have taken such action. A shareholder or director acting fraudulently may also be prosecuted and held liable for debts incurred. In addition, the insolvent company through its officers has a duty to consult the god man for the purposes of administering the property. If the debtor does not comply with these regulations, the court will withdraw the appointment of the god man and thus nullify the effects of the appointment with immediate effect.

Termination

Commonly, the composition proceedings are terminated because the financial status of the company makes it impossible to continue, leaving a petition in bankruptcy as the only alternative. Sometimes, however, the composition is successful and the company returns to financial health. The composition is regarded as terminated in any of the following circumstances:

- the composition proposal has been accepted and ratified by the court and the distribution completed in accordance with the proposal;
- the proposed composition is rejected by the court;
- the debtor has been allowed to withdraw the proposed composition or the proposed composition has never been accepted.

The proceedings will also be terminated when and if the debtor fails to fulfil his obligations or the court decides that for any other reason it is highly unlikely that a scheme of composition can be reached and therefore withdraws the appointment of the god man. The creditors' claims will revive in full as a result of this. The proceedings are automatically terminated if no application is lodged with the court within two months of the appointment of the god man. If the court withdraws the appointment, this also means that the creditors are no longer bound by any concessions they might have made.

A commission appointed by the Swedish Government with the task of reviewing the reorganisation procedure for insolvent business ("The Insolvency Commission") has put forward a proposal (SOU 1992:113) whereby the Composition Act would be replaced by the Reorganisation of Business Act, applicable to all economic operators. The main point in the Commission's report and recommendations is that a new business reorganisation procedure is needed as an alternative to bankruptcy in certain cases, *i.e.* the kind of businesses that are considered viable or whose activities can be continued, in whole or in part, in some form. Under the business reorganisation procedure a debtor who is engaged in business will, following suspension of payments and with the assistance of an administrator appointed by the court, attempt to reorganise his activities and make an economic settlement with his creditors without bankruptcy.

It is furthermore proposed in connection with business failures, that so called "productive labour costs" (salaries, wages and the amount which the employer is liable to pay the employee for the period of notice – as long as the business continues its activities, for a maximum period of two months) should take priority over floating charges. The purpose of this is to promote the reorganisation of businesses as an alternative to bankruptcy.

Debts incurred with the consent of the administrator during the reorganisation process prior to failure of the business should also take priority over floating charges.

It is proposed that the preferred status of taxes and rates should be abolished. One important purpose of this measure is to improve the status of ordinary creditors (suppliers, subcontractors etc.).

The proposal is modelled on the American Chapter 11 and other foreign reorganisation proceedings. No proposed legislation has yet been given to Parliament. A bill is expected to be put forward based on the Commission's report and new legislation is expected to be enacted in 1996.

4. Termination of the corporation: liquidation and bankruptcy

Limited liability companies may be wound up in a number of different ways. Liquidation is one method but companies may also be wound up by merger, whereby the company's assets and liabilities are taken over by another company, and by bankruptcy proceedings. The company is deemed to have been wound up when the bankruptcy proceedings are terminated. The company may also be wound up be means of deregistration by the Patent and Registration Office where there is reason to believe that the company has ceased trading. It is not uncommon for a limited company to cease trading without having observed the provisions of the Companies Act regarding deregistration. In such a case the company remains in the companies register despite the fact that it is no longer trading. If the Patent and Registration Office has not received any formal information regarding the company for a period of ten years, the Office is under a duty to make appropriate enquiries to determine whether or not the company is still in existence. This means that the Office must take steps which are appropriate in the light of the circumstances. This may involve issuing written requests for information as to whether or not the company still exists. If it is not possible to so determine, the company will be removed from the Register and is thereby deemed to have been wound up. The following section deals with liquidation and bankruptcy proceedings.

Liquidation

Purpose and effect

The purpose of liquidation proceedings is to terminate the activities of the company in such a way that all the company's creditors receive full payment of their claims and the assets of the company are distributed so that the shareholders get back as much as possible of the capital they have invested. A fundamental premise of liquidation proceedings is thus that all creditors receive full payment of their claims.

Pre-application/appointment considerations

Before an application is made for voluntary liquidation of a company, a balance sheet for liquidation purposes should be drawn up. This will reveal the size of the company's assets in terms of their current market value, minus the costs of sale. If this balance sheet shows that the assets are probably sufficient to cover all the company's liabilities, including the cost of liquidation proceedings, an application may be submitted for the company to go into liquidation. However, if it is concluded that the company's assets are insufficient to cover all its liabilities, a petition in bankruptcy should be lodged.

Procedure

A limited company may go into liquidation purely voluntarily if the shareholders no longer wish to continue the business. There may also be an obligation to go into liquidation whether or not the shareholders wish to do so. One such case is where the equity of the company has fallen below half the registered share capital. Another instance is where the court finds that the company must go into liquidation because a majority of the shareholders have abused their position of influence in the company. There are other examples of compulsory liquidation which will be dealt with below.

Voluntary liquidation

A meeting of the shareholders may pass a resolution to the effect that the company is to go into liquidation. When such resolution has been passed an application must be submitted to the Patent and Registration Office, which will then declare the company in liquidation. It is thus within the power of a meeting of the shareholders to decide to liquidate the company. This applies both where the company, without being under any obligation to go into liquidation, nevertheless wishes to do so, and where the company is to be compulsorily liquidated for one of the reasons stipulated in the Companies Act or the articles of association. Where there is a reason for compulsory liquidation but a meeting of the shareholders has not passed a resolution to that effect, it is the duty of the district court to order whether the company should be liquidated.

Compulsory liquidation

The board of directors is under a duty to draw up a balance sheet for liquidation purposes without delay as soon as there is reason to believe that the company's equity has fallen below half of the registered share capital. If the balance sheet for liquidation purposes confirms that this is so, the board must refer the question of whether or not the company should go into liquidation to a meeting of the shareholders as soon as possible. Unless a meeting of the shareholders held within eight months of such referral approves a balance sheet in respect of the position at the time of the meeting showing that the equity corresponds to the registered share capital, the board must lodge an application for liquidation in a court of law, unless a resolution to lodge such application has already been passed at the meeting of the shareholders. Such petition may also be lodged by a director, the managing director, an auditor or any shareholder. Failure to lodge such an application may result in the board or the shareholder being personally liable for the obligations of the company arising thereafter.

When calculating the equity of the company, the assets side must include an item showing the estimated sale value of the assets minus estimated costs of sale, if the sale value exceeds the book value. The reason for this is to avoid compulsory liquidation of companies which have hidden assets in the books which are worth more than the equity. It is not necessary to book certain types of liabilities regarding conditional loans from the state.

Another ground for compulsory liquidation is if a shareholder, by virtue of his influence in the company, has deliberately been a party to a breach of the Companies Act or the articles of association. The court may order liquidation in such a case if at least one-tenth of the shareholders agree to apply for such an order. In such a case, on request by the company, the court may instead order the company to redeem the applicants' minority shareholding within a certain time. If the company fails to redeem the shares within that time, the court must order that the company be put into liquidation if those whose shares were to have been redeemed apply for such an order. When considering this matter, the court must take particular account of the interests of the employees and creditors of the company. Redemption may not take place if the company's equity after redemption would be less than half the registered share capital.

The court, or in some cases the Patent and Registration Office, will order that the company be put into liquidation if:

- there is an obligation pursuant to the articles of association for the company to go into liquidation;

- the company is subject to bankruptcy proceedings as a result of which a surplus is achieved and a meeting of the shareholders fails to pass a resolution that the company shall go into liquidation within the prescribed time;

- according to the companies register at the Patent and Registration Office, the company has no auditor, board of directors or managing director, contrary to the provisions of the Companies Act; or

- the company has not submitted an annual report to the Patent and Registration Office within 11 months from the expiry of the financial year.

There are a number of other instances where compulsory liquidation may be ordered.

In cases where the Patent and Registration Office is not competent to decide the question of liquidation may be referred to the court by the Patent and Registration Office, or an application for a court ruling on the matter may be made by the board, a director, the managing director or any shareholder. If such an application is made, the court must immediately issue a summons to the company, shareholders and creditors to the effect that any of them wishing to be heard in the matter should attend a hearing on a certain day, when the issue of the company's obligation to go into liquidation will be considered. The summons is to be sent to the company and will be published in the Swedish Official Gazette at least two months and no more than four months before the date of the hearing.

Appointment of the "likvidator" (liquidator)

When a meeting of the shareholders has decided that the company is to go into liquidation, the Patent and Registration Office shall appoint one or more likvidators. An "advokat" (member of the Swedish Bar Association) is usually appointed as likvidator. Anyone who has been appointed as the company's auditor is not affected as a result of the company going into liquidation, and continues to act as the company's auditor.

When the company has gone into liquidation the board and managing director must immediately submit reports on their management of the company's affairs for the period not covered by previous reports and accounts presented to a meeting of the shareholders. Reports are to be put before a meeting of the shareholders as soon as possible. The same applies to the provisions regarding annual reports and the auditor's report. The annual report must thus cover the time from the preceding annual report to the point when the company went into liquidation. As a rule, the report will thus cover a period of less than a year, but in exceptional cases may relate to a whole financial year or longer. The reports are to be submitted to the annual general meeting if such meeting is to be held at a suitable time or to an extraordinary general meeting.

The likvidator or likvidators are under a duty to commence a special procedure, whereby the district court publishes an announcement notifying all the creditors. This is designed to ensure notification of the liquidation to those creditors who do not appear as such in the company's books and records. These creditors have six months within which to notify the district court of any claims they may have. Thereafter the likvidator (liquidator) must sell the company's property by public auction or other appropriate means as soon as he can. The company may continue trading if this is expedient for the winding up of the company or in order to provide the employees with a reasonable opportunity to find new employment.

The likvidator must submit an annual report for each financial year, to be put before the annual general meeting for approval. The balance sheet is to include the company's equity as a separate item, where the share capital is entered as a memorandum divided, where applicable, into different categories of shares.

Assets may not be entered at a higher value than they are expected to fetch on sale after deduction of sale costs. If an asset may be expected to fetch a substantially higher sale price than the value entered in the balance sheet, or if a liability or liquidation cost may be expected to be substantially greater than the book liability, the estimated sum of the additional asset or liability must be entered as a memorandum to the balance sheet.

Distribution of the assets of the company

When the six-month period has elapsed and all known liabilities have been paid, the likvidator is to distribute the remaining assets of the company. If any liability is disputed or has not fallen due for payment, or for any other reason cannot be paid, necessary funds are to be retained and the remainder may be distributed.

A shareholder wishing to challenge the distribution must institute legal proceedings against the company no later than three months after the final accounts for the company have been put before a meeting of the shareholders.

If a shareholder has not notified the company in respect of his entitlement pursuant to the distribution of the company's assets within five years of the final accounts being put before a meeting of the shareholders, he loses his right to his share of the distribution. If the sum in question may be regarded as negligible in relation to the assets distributed, the likvidator may notify the court that the sum is to be donated to the National Inheritance Fund.

As soon as possible after he has completed his assignment the likvidator must submit a final report on his administration of the entire liquidation. This report must also include details of the distribution of the company's assets. The report must be accompanied by detailed accounts covering the whole period of the liquidation. The report and accounts are to be submitted to auditors for examination. The auditors submit an auditor's report on the final accounts and administration no later than one month thereafter.

After the auditor's report has been submitted to the likvidator he must immediately convene a meeting of the shareholders so that the final accounts may be examined. The final report with accompanying accounts and auditor's report must be kept available for the shareholders. Copies of such reports and accounts are also to be sent to the shareholders.

When the likvidator has presented his final report the company is regarded as having been wound up. The Patent and Registration Office must immediately be notified of this for deregistration purposes. If the likvidator finds that the company is insolvent and is unable to pay the costs of liquidation, he must apply for the company to be declared bankrupt.

Creditors' involvement and position

As mentioned earlier in connection with liquidation, the creditors of the company are entitled to full payment of their claims. Most creditors will normally be known to the company, but in order for all creditors to be able to prove their debts, the district court issues a notice to unknown creditors, as described above. The creditors then have six months within which to prove their debts, thus ensuring that their rights will be taken into consideration during the liquidation proceedings.

Powers and duties of the likvidator

The court which decides that the company is to go into liquidation must also appoint one or more likvidators who will then assume the powers and duties of the board of directors and managing director and will have the task of carrying out the liquidation. The provisions of the Companies Act regarding the board and directors also apply to the likvidator of a company in liquidation (see p639 *supra*).

Management by the likvidator

The likvidator is under a duty to sell as expeditiously as possible the company's property by public auction or otherwise transform such property into money and pay off the company's debts. His task thereafter is to distribute the remaining assets of the company (p641 *supra*).

Position of officers and shareholders/owners

As mentioned on p641 above, when the company has gone into liquidation the board of directors and managing director must immediately submit a report on their management of the company's affairs during the period for which accounts have not been submitted to a meeting of the shareholders (who have the right to attend both ordinary meetings and the final shareholders' meeting held to consider the likvidator's final report). When the likvidator has submitted his final report, the company is deemed to have been wound up. The Patent and Registration Office must be notified of this fact so that the company may be removed from the register.

Even after the likvidator's final report has been submitted, shareholders representing at least one-tenth of all the shares may require the likvidator to call a new meeting of the shareholders to consider the question of a claim for damages against a director or the managing director of the company.

Termination

As a rule liquidation proceedings are terminated when the likvidator submits his final report and notifies the Patent and Registration Office for deregistration purposes. If he finds that the company is insolvent and is unable to pay the costs of liquidation, he must lodge a petition in bankruptcy.

Bankruptcy proceedings

Unlike liquidation proceedings, bankruptcy proceedings take place because the company is unable to pay all its debts and must therefore be declared bankrupt. In this case a "konkursförvaltare" (trustee in bankruptcy) is appointed for the purpose of realising and settling the assets of the company.

Purpose and effect

The purpose of bankruptcy proceedings is to wind up the company in such a way that the company's creditors receive as great a proportion of their claims as possible. The konkursförvaltare is also under a duty to investigate any possibilities of recovery and must determine whether the officers or shareholders of the company have committed any criminal acts.

Pre-application considerations

A company must be declared bankrupt if it is insolvent. If a company is unable to pay its debts as they fall due and such inability is not merely temporary, the company is deemed to be insolvent. In this situation it is not permitted for the company's board to continue trading. Instead, payments must be suspended and the company must either endeavour to reach a scheme of composition or lodge a petition in bankruptcy. Thus, the company must ascertain what prospects it has of improving its liquidity and see whether there is any possibility of paying its debts. This may be achieved by means of a shareholders' contribution or by borrowing. If these efforts fail, the company must either reach a scheme of composition or lodge a petition in bankruptcy.

Procedure

If the board of the company realises that the company is insolvent, the company must itself lodge a petition in bankruptcy with the court. As a rule, such a petition will mean that the company is declared bankrupt the same day. The court will appoint a konkursförvaltare whose main task will be to realise the assets of the company and pay the debts of the estate in bankruptcy in accordance with specific priorities regarding claims.

A creditor may also lodge a petition in bankruptcy. He must be able to show that the company is insolvent. The Bankruptcy Act stipulates a number of situations in which a debtor is regarded as insolvent:

- where distress has been attempted at any time during the six months prior to the lodging of the petition in bankruptcy and the debtor has been found to lack assets capable of being distrained upon;

- where a debtor carrying on business subject to a requirement that books of accounts be kept has received a demand for payment accompanied by a threat on the part of the creditor to lodge a petition in bankruptcy and payment has not been made within a week of receipt of such demand; and

- where the company has suspended payments and informed a substantial number of creditors of such suspension, for example, by means of a circular letter.

When the court has declared the company bankrupt and appointed a konkursförvaltare, he must draw up a statement of affairs as soon as possible. This must show the company's assets and liabilities as at the date the company was declared bankrupt. The statement of affairs is to be submitted to the district court and the supervisory authority.

The board of directors of the bankrupt company must swear an oath at the district court to the effect that the statement of affairs is an accurate reflection of the company's position.

The konkursförvaltare then sells the assets of the estate in bankruptcy in an appropriate manner and collects the estate's debts.

The konkursförvaltare is also under a duty to draw up a konkursförvaltare's report. This should contain information on the reasons for the company's insolvency, a summary of the company's assets and liabilities, particulars on any transactions regarding assets which may be recoverable, the date when the company became insolvent, the date when the board became liable to draw up a balance sheet for liquidation purposes, information regarding whether or not there is reason to suspect that any of the directors or shareholders may be liable to repay sums of money to the company, details of the company's accounting system and the manner in which the books have been kept, and finally, whether the konkursförvaltare has reported any criminal actions to the prosecution service. The report of the konkursförvaltare must be submitted no later than six months after the company has been declared bankrupt.

In addition, every six months the konkursförvaltare must report to the court and the supervisory authority on the steps which have been taken to terminate the bankruptcy. This report is to be accompanied by a statement of the accounts.

When the konkursförvaltare has realised the assets of the estate in bankruptcy he must draw up a dividend proposal including details of the creditors entitled to receive a dividend. He must then follow the provisions of the Preferential Rights of Creditors Act described at pp619-630. Finally, he must submit a final report on his trusteeship to the court and the supervisory authority.

If the konkursförvaltare believes that there is a likelihood that non-preferential creditors will receive a dividend, he must inform the district court that creditors are to be given notice that proofs of debt should be lodged. As a rule, the district court will then announce in the Swedish Official Gazette that all creditors in the bankruptcy must lodge proofs of debt with the district court within a certain time limit in order to qualify for dividend in the bankruptcy. When the time limit has expired the district court sends all proofs of debt to the konkursförvaltare for scrutiny. If he finds reason to object to any of the proofs, he must do so within a certain time limit. The court then arranges a meeting between the creditors and the konkursförvaltare at which the two sides endeavour to reach a settlement. If no such settlement is reached, the court will decide the matter.

Creditors' involvement and position

Unless the court announces that creditors must lodge proof of debt as described above, they do not have to act in a special way to qualify for dividend. To be on the safe side however, they often write to the konkursförvaltare and inform him of their claims. They may also obtain particulars from the konkursförvaltare about the estate and its administration. The konkursförvaltare is under a duty to contact creditors whose claims have been particularly affected by specific actions or omissions of the trustee.

Powers and duties of the bankrupt company and its officers

A company which is declared bankrupt thereby incurs a number of duties. It must provide the konkursförvaltare with information on its assets and liabilities. It is no longer freely able to dispose of its property. The officers of the company are also under a duty to swear an oath at the district court as to the rectitude of the statement of affairs.

If officers of the company do not provide the konkursförvaltare with the information he requires or fail to swear an oath at the district court, they may be forcibly brought to account with the help of the police or remanded in custody by order of the district court. Nobody may be remanded in custody for more than three months.

Management by the konkursförvaltare

Those who may be appointed konkursförvaltare are specified at pp654-657. His duties are as follows:

- The konkursförvaltare must immediately take over the affairs of the bankruptcy estate, including the books and other documentation concerning such estate. He must then draw up a statement of affairs specifying the assets and liabilities of the estate. This statement must be submitted to the district court and the supervisory authority no later than one week prior to the swearing of oaths at the district court. He must also draw up a report as described on p644 above as soon as possible.

- If the konkursförvaltare finds that there are grounds for suspecting that a bankrupt individual has committed fraud, he must immediately inform the state prosecutor. He must also state whether he suspects that the bankrupt individual has acted in a manner likely to render him subject to a ban on carrying on business.

- The konkursförvaltare is under a duty to ensure without delay that money received by the estate in bankruptcy earns interest. He must book payments made and received. Books and accounts must be retained for at least ten years from the end of the year during which the bankruptcy was terminated.

- His next duty is to sell the assets of the estate as quickly as possible. If the bankrupt has been trading, the konkursförvaltare may continue trading on behalf of the estate if it is expedient to do so. However, the main rule is that trading may not continue more than one year after the swearing of oaths. The konkursförvaltare should also determine whether any transactions have taken place in respect of assets which may thereby be recovered (see pp648-654 – Recovery).

Under the provisions of the Bankruptcy Act, the konkursförvaltare must pay compensation in respect of any loss which he deliberately or negligently causes to the estate, a creditor or a bankrupt company or individual in the course of his trusteeship. An action for compensation of this type is brought in the form of a protest action regarding the konkursförvaltare's final report.

Position of officers and shareholders/owners

Company directors and shareholders in a company which has been declared bankrupt are no longer entitled freely to dispose of the company's assets. They have a duty to provide the konkursförvaltare with all particulars required by him. They must also swear an oath at the district court if so required by the konkursförvaltare. Directors of a company which has been declared bankrupt may not without the court's permission travel abroad before having sworn an oath as to the rectitude of the statement of affairs.

Termination

A bankruptcy is terminated when the konkursförvaltare submits his final report and his dividend proposal to the district court and the supervisory authority. A bankruptcy in which there are no assets is terminated when the bankruptcy is removed from the court's cause list on application of the konkursförvaltare. The court must inform the Patent and Registration office which then deregisters the company.

5. Augmenting the assets of the insolvent corporation

Introduction

Swedish law has several systems for dealing with the various types of improper transactions carried out by an insolvent corporation. Apart from the criminal liability which officers of an insolvent corporation may incur if it unfairly favours certain creditors, there are three different systems by which the assets of the estate may be increased. In addition, there is a further system under which certain officers of a limited liability company may be held directly liable to the company's creditors.

The first regulatory system is recovery in bankruptcy, the rules of which also apply to public composition proceedings. The second system concerns liability for damages for representatives of limited liability companies and the third covers the duty to repay monies paid out from limited liability companies in the form of dividend, where such payment is contrary to the rules governing distribution of profit. The fourth regulatory system, which does not directly increase the financial assets of the insolvent corporation, relates to the liability of various officers of limited liability companies who have not observed certain rules concerning the maintenance of the company's equity. Liability may also attach to these officers if they do not fulfil their obligations to file the company's annual report with the Patent and Registration Office.

As seen in previous sections, aside from limited liability companies, there are a number of legal entities which may conduct business activities. Private individuals may also carry on business. The following account deals principally with limited liability companies.

In general, the regulatory systems listed above rely on concepts which at first sight appear to be easy to interpret. However, the material is extremely complex and there are a large number of judicial precedents and comment. This means that the following description of the regulatory systems is very broadly framed and thus only provides a general picture of how the rules are constructed. In order to be properly able to apply the rules to a particular set of facts, such facts must be precisely ascertained and expert advice should be sought.

Recovery

Introduction

A fundamental principle in Swedish bankruptcy proceedings is that the company's creditors must be treated equally, aside from the statutory provisions concerning the preferential rights of certain creditors. To avoid a race between the creditors for the insolvent corporation's assets and to ensure that the creditors receive as equitable a distribution of the assets as possible, the Swedish Bankruptcy Act contains a chapter on recovery. The 1975 amendment to the Act resulted in a considerable tightening of the rules. One consequence of this reform was the introduction of a number of recovery rules involving purely objective prerequisites.

The recovery rules are aimed at rendering null and void a legal act carried out during a certain period leading up to the bankruptcy. The calculation of the relevant period is based on a certain "limit date" which, for practical purposes, is nearly always the date when the petition in bankruptcy is lodged with the court. The calculation may be based on other criteria, however.

Several recovery rules involve stricter time limits, as well as rules to deal with the circumstances where the other party to the transaction is an "associated person". Chapter 4, section 3 of the Bankruptcy Act contains a list of persons and companies who are deemed to be associated with the insolvent corporation and who thus fall into the category of those whose transactions with the insolvent corporation are even more closely scrutinised as potentially damaging to the interests of creditors in general.

Recovery may be sought on several occasions and in several contexts during the bankruptcy proceedings. However, the most common procedure is probably that by which the konkursförvaltare institutes legal proceedings in a court of law.

The main rule is that such proceedings must be instituted within a year of the declaration in bankruptcy. There are exceptions where a transaction for which recovery is available only becomes known at a later date. Here, proceedings must be instituted within six months of the circumstances becoming known. If the konkursförvaltare does not wish to seek recovery or to enter into negotiations with respect to the transaction, a creditor may seek recovery on behalf of the bankruptcy estate by instituting legal proceedings in a court of law. In the case of public composition proceedings, an action for recovery may be brought by any creditor whose claim is covered by the composition.

The Supreme Court ruled in the *Minitube* case (NJA 1982, p 900) that preferential rights are retained in respect of property recovered by the estate. This means that if property subject to a floating charge is recovered by the estate, the value of such property accrues to the holder of the floating charge.

By virtue of specific legislation regarding bankruptcies occurring in other Scandinavian countries, the recovery provisions in such countries may be applied to property in Sweden. The converse is true of property belonging to a Swedish insolvent corporation but which is situated in another Scandinavian country.

As mentioned above, a number of recovery rules involving purely objective criteria were introduced in 1975. The reason behind this was a desire to facilitate recovery by the estate in respect of legal acts of an unfair or improper nature. This may result in consequences which may seem to be totally unreasonable from the point of view of those who are obliged to return property. However, the Bankruptcy Act allows for flexibility regarding such obligation where there are particular grounds for doing so.

The most important recovery rules, primarily concerning companies, are described below. A number of provisions applying to more unusual situations have been omitted.

Recovery pursuant to chapter 4, section 5 of the Bankruptcy Act

This is the prime recovery provision in Swedish bankruptcy law. The section is very loosely worded and is therefore usually invoked in parallel with the specific provisions outlined below. The provision is often cited as subordinate to other more specific provisions when recovery proceedings are instituted.

According to this provision, recovery is possible in respect of a legal act which has taken place less than five years before the "limit date" (usually the date the petition in bankruptcy is lodged) if:

- such act has improperly favoured a creditor; or
- property of the insolvent corporation has been put beyond the reach of the creditors; or
- the insolvent corporation's debts have been increased.

A further requirement for recovery under this provision is that the insolvent corporation was insolvent at the time of the act or became insolvent due to such act, either alone or in conjunction with other circumstances, and the other party to the act knew or ought to have known of the insolvency and the circumstances which rendered the act improper.

The party seeking recovery bears the burden of proof in relation to all the above circumstances. An exception to this is where proceedings are instituted against someone associated with the insolvent corporation. Such person is deemed under this section to have the necessary knowledge unless he is able to show that he neither had nor ought to have had such knowledge. Moreover, recovery is also possible in respect of transactions with such associated persons more than five years prior to the limit date.

Recovery pursuant to chapter 4, section 6 of the Bankruptcy Act

Under this provision, a gift may be recovered if it is made less than six months before the limit date. Gifts here include items acquired by purchase, exchange or other agreement where, having regard to the consideration received by the company, it is obvious that the item in question was partly in the nature of a gift. Recovery here does not require that the person seeking to set aside the transaction establish that the insolvent corporation was insolvent when the gift was made or that the recipient did not receive the gift in good faith.

Under certain circumstances, recovery is also possible for gifts made more than six months prior to the limit date. In these cases, for which the time limits vary depending on whether the recipient is an associate or not, such recipient may avoid having to return the property by showing that the insolvent corporation still had assets equal to or exceeding its liabilities even after having made the gift.

Recovery pursuant to chapter 4, section 8 of the Bankruptcy Act

Payment of salary or for services made less than six months before the limit date may be recovered if such payment clearly exceeded what could be regarded as reasonable in the light of the work done and the profitability of the business. In such a case, that part of the payment exceeding what may be regarded as reasonable may be recovered.

This section also contains a provision resembling that in chapter 4, section 6 above, regarding payments made more than six months prior to the limit date and here too the recipient may adduce evidence in the manner described above, so as to avoid making the repayment enjoined by the section.

Recovery pursuant to chapter 4, section 10 of the Bankruptcy Act

This is one of the most frequently used sections in recovery proceedings because it is relatively simple to apply.

Under this provision, payment of a debt made less than three months before the limit date may be recovered if:

- payment has been made using non-customary means of payment;
- payment has been made prematurely; or
- the payment has resulted in a substantial deterioration of the insolvent corporation's financial position.

The term "premature payment" principally relates to payments made before the due date. Payments made a short time before the bankruptcy are typically regarded as improper. The term "non-customary means of payment" refers, *inter alia,* to situations where the insolvent corporation pays with property instead of money, something which is characteristic of debtor insolvency. Payments which have "resulted in a substantial deterioration of the insolvent corporation's financial position" probably represent the most common grounds for recovery. The phrase is somewhat confusing, since a payment does not result in a deterioration of the position from an accounting point of view. However, this category is intended to cover sums which are substantial in relation to the payer's assets. As a rule of thumb, payments representing around 10% of the insolvent corporation's assets at the time of payment are in practice deemed to have resulted in a substantial deterioration in its financial position.

A payment made to an associate may be recovered in such circumstances if it was made less than two years before the limit date, although the associate may here avoid recovery if he can show that the insolvent corporation was neither insolvent at the time of the payment nor became insolvent as a result of the payment.

Under this section, the set-off of one debt against another which has taken place within the prescribed time limits may be recovered if such setting-off has been such that it could not have been carried out in the bankruptcy.

The section is relatively simple to construe and covers a large number of payments occurring before the bankruptcy. However, in order to avoid unreasonable consequences, it is possible for the defendant in recovery proceedings to avoid recovery if he can show that the payment was ordinary. The meaning of the term "ordinary" is not fully clear and has to some extent blunted the efficacy of the provision. The possibility of avoiding recovery owing to the "ordinariness" of a payment has in any case led to more litigation than had been intended.

An example of an "ordinary payment" may be where payments have been made which have caused a substantial deterioration in the insolvent corporation's financial position but where they have been made on the due date or where they are of a regular nature, such as rent.

Recovery pursuant to chapter 4, section 12 of the Bankruptcy Act

Under this section, security granted and any property transferred by way of security by the insolvent corporation less than three months before the limit date may be recovered if:

- such security was not stipulated at the time the debt arose; or
- it was not transferred without delay after the debt arose.

Security granted or property transferred by way of security to associates may be recovered if it has been granted or transferred less than two years before the limit date. The associate may successfully defend the proceedings if he is able to show that the insolvent corporation neither was nor became insolvent as a result of the grant or transfer.

This section includes other actions taken by the insolvent corporation or creditor which are intended to secure the rights of the creditor.

Where the security must be registered, the delay shall be deemed to occur if an application for registration is made more than two weeks after the debt arose. For example, floating charges require official registration in Sweden and such registration must take place within two weeks of the debt arising. This rule is very rigid and may have major consequences for a lender.

Liability to pay damages incurred by officers of a limited liability company

Chapter 15 of the Swedish Companies Act contains provisions concerning the liability of various officers of a limited liability company to pay damages.

Founders, directors, the managing director and auditors who in the course of their duties deliberately or negligently cause loss or damage to the company are liable to pay damages. Such liability may also arise if loss or damage is caused to shareholders or other parties. "Other parties" here means the company's creditors, among others. This form of liability to pay damages is not dealt with here.

A shareholder is liable to pay compensation for loss or damage which he deliberately or by gross negligence causes to the company, a shareholder or other party by virtue of his involvement in an act contrary to the Companies Act or the company's articles of association.

Liability to pay damages pursuant to the above may be moderated in accordance with what is reasonable in the light of the nature of the act, the size of the loss or damage and other circumstances. The main rule is that proceedings instituted on behalf of the company against a director or the managing director as a result of a decision or act during a financial year must be instituted no later than one year from the submission of the annual accounts and auditor's report to the annual general meeting of the shareholders.

In addition, there are rules governing protection for minority shareholders. Parties representing a minority holding of at least 10% of all shares may generally bring an action for damages on behalf of the company.

The Companies Act contains an absolute time limit for actions for damages against officers of the company. This limit is normally three years, although the date on which the period starts to run varies. Where a company is declared bankrupt as a result of a petition lodged before the period has expired, the konkursförvaltare is allowed time to bring an action notwithstanding the fact that the period expired before the company was actually declared bankrupt.

Repayment of an improper distribution of profit

Chapter 12 of the Companies Act governs the distribution of dividends to shareholders. Generally speaking, dividends may only be distributed from net profit and certain unrestricted reserves minus losses, compulsory allocations and other statutory deductions.

If a distribution is made contrary to the provisions of the Companies Act, the recipient is liable to repay what he has received, irrespective of whether or not he is a shareholder, provided that he did not have reasonable cause to assume that the payment constituted a lawful distribution of profit.

The company, as a prerequisite to the establishment of liability, is required to prove that the recipient understood or should have understood that the particular distribution was made in breach of the Companies Act.

If the recipient is not able to repay the sum unlawfully received as a profit distribution, certain officers of the company may be liable to make good the shortfall if they were involved in the decision to make the distribution or in distribution itself.

These provisions have to some extent been used to deal with asset-stripping of companies. The regulatory system has taken shape as a result of a number of Supreme Court rulings in recent decades. These cases have not infrequently concerned so-called "hidden dividends", where, for example, assets have been taken out of a company without being booked as dividends. According to the Companies Act, hidden dividends need not be unlawful. They are only unlawful to the extent that the value of the property distributed exceeds the funds properly available for distribution. The rules are particularly complicated and not uncontroversial. They are also very far-reaching, since it is suggested that it is not only the recipient who may be liable to repay sums unlawfully received, but also banks involved in the transfer of the shares of limited liability companies. In the light of the extensive scope of the rules, they are of particular importance, especially in the case of transactions of the type under discussion.

Liability in the case of a compulsory winding up

The rules do not really concern the possibility of increasing the company's assets but, owing to the liability they place upon officers of limited liability companies, their character renders them appropriate for inclusion in this chapter.

The fundamental principle of the Swedish Companies Act is that shareholders are not personally liable for the obligations of the company. Rules on protection of the company's equity have been introduced in order to reduce the risk of abuse of this principle. These rules are to be found in Chapter 13 of the Companies Act.

The rules place a duty on the board of a limited liability company to draw up a balance sheet for liquidation purposes as soon as there is reason to suppose that the company's equity has fallen below half of the registered share capital.

If the balance sheet thus drawn up for liquidation purposes shows that the equity is indeed less than half of the share capital, the board must refer the question of whether the company should be wound up to a meeting of the shareholders at the earliest opportunity.

Unless a meeting of the shareholders is held within eight months of such referral, and a balance sheet in respect of the position at the time of the meeting showing that the equity corresponds to the registered share capital is adopted, the board must lodge a petition for liquidation in a court of law, unless a resolution to lodge such petition has already been passed at the meeting of the shareholders. Such petition may also be lodged by a director, the managing director, an auditor or a shareholder.

If the directors fail to carry out their duties pursuant to the above, they will be jointly and severally liable for the then arising obligations of the company with others who act on behalf of the company in the knowledge of such failure. A director may avoid liability if he is able to show that the failure was not due to negligence on his part. A shareholder may also be jointly and severally liable for the company's obligations if, at the time a duty to wind up the company arises pursuant to the above, he participates in a decision to continue the business of the company while being aware that such duty exists.

These rules are very rigidly framed and it is essential that they are observed by the officers of the company.

Liability for failing to file the company's annual report with the Patent and Registration Office.

A limited company is obliged to file a copy of its annual report and audit report with the Patent and Registration Office within one month after it has been adopted by the annual shareholders' meeting.

If a company does not comply with this obligation and filing has not been made within 15 months of the end of the fiscal year in question, the members of the board of directors and the managing director will be jointly and severally liable for any debts falling on the company thereafter. A director can escape liability by showing that he was not himself negligent. Once the documents are filed, the directors' liability ceases from the date of filing.

6. Public control over insolvent corporations

Persons who may be appointed konkursförvaltare (trustee)

The Swedish Bankruptcy Act has been amended on a number of occasions. The current Act came into force on 1 January 1988. The Act states that a konkursförvaltare must have the special insight and experience demanded by the task, have the confidence of the creditors and the supervisory authority and also be suitable in other respects. A court employee may not be a konkursförvaltare.

- Konkursförvaltares are appointed by the court. However, the konkursförvaltare must be approved by an authority called "the supervisory authority", which came into existence in 1980. In practice, there are a number of people who are approved for appointment as konkursförvaltare. The district courts have a list of these people and appoint one of them as konkursförvaltare without referring to the supervisory authority in each individual case.

Konkursförvaltare are usually "advokater" (members of the Swedish Bar Association).

Public control

General

In Swedish bankruptcies, the konkursförvaltare is appointed by the district court. The court also fixes the dividend to be paid to the creditors and the costs of the bankruptcy, particularly the konkursförvaltare's fee.

Since 1980, the task of supervising the bankruptcy procedure has been the responsibility of the country's supervisory authorities which comprise a department of the debt enforcement services.

In composition proceedings there is no public control corresponding to the supervisory authority described here for bankruptcy proceedings.

However, the konkursförvaltare carries out his administration independently. The supervisory authority must ensure by means of regular supervision that the administration is conducted in a proper manner and in accordance with the law. Supervision is mainly in the form of subsequent checking that the actions taken by the konkursförvaltare are in accordance with the Bankruptcy Act and other statutes. Such actions should further the main purpose of the bankruptcy, which is to convert assets into money in a manner which provides the creditors with the best possible dividend. However, the konkursförvaltare may to some extent take into consideration employment issues, provided that this does not significantly prejudice the rights of the creditors. The supervisory authority must particularly observe that the administration is carried out with expediency, economy, efficiency and consistency.

An important task of the supervisory authority is to see that the winding up of the bankruptcy estate is not unnecessarily delayed. The bankruptcy must be terminated when all administrative actions have been taken. The supervisory authority sees that the konkursförvaltare duly submits a statement of affairs ("estate inventory"), konkursförvaltare's report, half-yearly report and other documentation pursuant to the provisions of the Bankruptcy Act.

Another important duty of the supervisory authority is to scrutinise the final accounts drawn up by the konkursförvaltare and issue a statement with regard to them. The supervisory authority is also responsible for ensuring that costs incurred in connection with the bankruptcy are kept at a reasonable level. For this reason, the supervisory authority examines the fee submitted by the konkursförvaltare and comments thereon in a statement to the district court before a final decision is made. The supervisory authority's statement carries considerable weight when the court is reaching this decision.

The duties of the konkursförvaltare towards the district court and the supervisory authority

As mentioned above, the konkursförvaltare is under a duty to draw up a statement of affairs following the bankruptcy. This must include a record of the estate's assets and liabilities, as far as this is possible. The statement of affairs must also contain the name and postal address of all creditors and details of the books of account and other financial documentation which has been received. The statement of affairs must be submitted to the district court and the supervisory authority as soon as possible, and no later than one week prior to the meeting for administration of oaths, where the board must swear an oath to the effect that the statement of affairs is an accurate reflection of the company's position.

The meeting for administration of oaths takes place at the district court, as a rule around six or seven weeks after the commencement of the bankruptcy.

Under the provisions of the Bankruptcy Act, the konkursförvaltare must consult the supervisory authority and creditors particularly affected with regard to matters of importance, unless there is some obstacle to doing so. One example of such a matter is the sale of a business belonging to the estate. The institution of legal proceedings where the estate is plaintiff may also constitute a matter where there should be consultation with the supervisory authority.

As soon as possible the konkursförvaltare must draw up a written report, described at pp644-645. The report is to be submitted to the district court and the supervisory authority no later than six months from the declaration in bankruptcy.

All documents submitted to the district court are a matter of public record and the creditors in the bankruptcy may gain access to them without difficulty.

If the bankruptcy is not terminated within a period of six months of the meeting for the administration of oaths, the konkursförvaltare (trustee) must submit a report to the supervisory authority containing precise details of all actions taken to terminate the bankruptcy, such report to be submitted within one month of the end of the six-month period mentioned above. If the bankruptcy continues, the konkursförvaltare (trustee) must submit a similar report within one month of the end of each six-month period. Such report must also contain full details of the reasons why the bankruptcy has not been terminated. A copy of this report must be sent to the district court.

The supervisory authority

The Government appoints certain debt enforcement services as supervisory authorities. The supervisory authority may, if it deems it to be appropriate, make an inventory of the bankruptcy estate's cash funds and other assets and request a financial report from the konkursförvaltare. In special circumstances, the authority may appoint one or more auditors to scrutinise the estate's accounts and other aspects of the administration.

The supervisory authority must have access to the books and other documents concerning the estate. It is under a duty to provide information on the estate and its administration to the court, creditors, auditors or the insolvent corporation if requested to do so.

When the konkursförvaltare has drawn up a dividend proposal he must send such proposal immediately to the court and the supervisory authority. When the bankruptcy is concluded the final accounts must be submitted to the supervisory authority accompanied by the documents necessary to check the accounts. A copy of the accounts is to be submitted to the district court.

Publicity and records

Under Swedish law, a number of items must be published in the Swedish Official Gazette and a local newspaper. These include a declaration in bankruptcy by the district court, information regarding the procedure for lodging proofs of debt, proofs of debt lodged late and dividend proposals.

Contents of Chapter 15

CORPORATE INSOLVENCY LAW IN SWITZERLAND

1.	**Introduction**	661
	Receiving information	661
	Privileges	662
	Action for avoidance (actio pauliana)	662
	Reorganisation proceeding	663
	Miscellaneous amendments	664
	Other sources of law	664
2.	**Corporations**	665
	Characteristics	665
	Management	668
	Ownership	670
	Financing and security for creditors	673
	Available information	675
	Other business entities	676
	Debt collection and asset recovery	679
3.	**Survival of the insolvent corporation or its business**	681
	Composition	681
	Stay of bankruptcy	688
4.	**Termination of the corporation: bankruptcy and composition with assignments of assets**	693
	Bankruptcy	693
	Composition with assignment of assets ("liquidation composition")	703
5.	**Augmenting the assets of the insolvent corporation**	705
	Introduction	705
	Transactions at risk	706
	Personal liability of officers, directors and auditors – the "personal liability action"	711

6.   Public control over insolvent corporations   716
Licensing and control of the appointee   716
Examinations and investigations   717
Publicity and records   718
**7.   Recognition of foreign bankruptcy decrees
         and composition proceedings in Switzerland**   719
Requirements for recognition   719
Procedure for recognition   720
Consequences of a recognition in Switzerland   721

Chapter 15

CORPORATE INSOLVENCY LAW IN SWITZERLAND

Tis Prager and André E Lebrecht,

Prager Dreifuss & Partner

1. Introduction

Since the Federal Debt Collection and Bankruptcy Act of 11 April 1889 ("Bundesgesetz über Schudbetreibung und Konkurs vom 11 April 1889" – "SchKG") came into effect more than 100 years ago, it has now for the first time been subject to a general, entire and thorough revision. In the course of this revision, which was initiated almost 20 years ago, it was decided that, despite its considerable age and despite the economical and social changes in the 100 years since its enactment, the system of the SchKG should not be changed. Therefore, only a partial revision of the Debt Collection and Bankruptcy Act together with various amendments were being proposed by the Swiss Federal Council to the Swiss Parliament in 1991. After considerable delays, due to some additional amendments (including a proposal for a new reorganisation proceeding for insolvent companies and individuals and in connection with the enactment of the "Lugano-Convention" on jurisdiction, and the enforcement of judgments in civil and commercial matters of 16 September 1988), the bill passed the Swiss Parliament in the winter session of 1994. The revised and amended SchKG will probably enter into force on 1 January 1997.

Because of the nature of the SchKG, and since the bill introduced only a partial revision and some amendments to the existing legislation, only the most important amendments relating to the field of "corporate insolvency" will be highlighted in this introduction.

Receiving information

The files of the debt collection and bankruptcy agencies are not public records. Nonetheless, parties able to show proper interest (particularly actual or future creditors) always had a right to obtain transcripts of the dockets and of the minutes of the agencies with respect to a particular debtor. The bill now lowers the standard of showing a proper interest to a level where less than a strict proof will be required (art 8a new SchKG).

Privileges

The current law provides for a wide variety of privileges – priorities – among unsecured creditors who are divided into five classes. The bill proposes to tighten radically the statutory privileges to favour only claims of unsecured creditors who need special protection (for example wages of employees for the six months prior to bankruptcy, claims of pension funds, accident-insurance claims, claims for alimonies for the six months prior to bankruptcy, and claims of infants for their assets) and to divide the unsecured creditors into only three classes, the third and last class being for claims of the general unsecured creditors. The aim of the bill is clear: the position of unsecured, non-privileged creditors should be strengthened to achieve a more equal treatment, but the problem will remain that, too often, the secured creditors erode the bankruptcy estate.

However, the current revision is not as consistent as it appears. A new article 37a of the Swiss Banking Law (Bundesgesetz über die Banken und Sparkassen vom 8 November 1934) introduces, in connection with the failure of banks, a fourth class of creditors, located between the second class of creditors and the general unsecured (third class) creditors. Claims out of an account relationship with the bank, up to an amount of Sfr 30,000, will have priority against the general unsecured creditors (the third class of creditors) of the bank. This privilege is not cumulative. Thus, every creditor of the bank can claim only one such special privilege. For all other claims out of an account relationship that are beyond the privileged Sfr 30,000, every creditor will be a third class creditor. The bill also proposes an exemption from the bankruptcy estate with respect to assets held by the bank on a fiduciary basis for its clients (new art 16 and 37b Swiss Banking law).

Action for avoidance (actio pauliana)

The bill upgrades the three different types of "action for avoidance" (action to set aside) by the following amendments:

It provides for two types of action for avoidance, namely for the action (i) to set aside gifts and (ii) to avoid preferential treatments of creditors by an insolvent debtor, a one year, instead of a six months vulnerable period prior to bankruptcy (or a preceding moratorium), *i.e.* the action allows a transfer to be set aside if it took place within the vulnerable period and if it satisfies the other requirements under to the articles 286 and 287 SchKG (*i.e.*, if it was a gift, a gratuitous disposition, a transfer for much less than a reasonable equivalent value in exchange, or if it was a preference).

Furthermore, the bill introduces a five year vulnerable period for the third type of the action for avoidance, *i.e.* for the action to set aside transfers that apparently discriminate against individual creditors according to article 288

SchKG.

The bill also introduces a two year statute of limitations for the action for avoidance itself that starts to run from the time when bankruptcy was adjudicated (the current law provides for a five year statute of limitation from the time the avoidable transfer took place). Thus, creditors can wait between three years (for the actions under arts 286, 287 SchKG) and seven years (for the actions under art 288 SchKG) from the date a transfer took place until they have to bring an action for avoidance.

Finally, the bill provides for a special place of jurisdiction for the *actio pauliana* at the place where bankruptcy was declared if the defendant, *i.e.* the party who received the particular transfer to be avoided, has no domicile in Switzerland. Swiss defendants have to be sued at their Swiss domicile.

Reorganisation proceeding

In the course of the discussion of the bill in the Swiss Parliament, a new, more liberal composition proceeding for corporate debtors (and for individual debtors under arts 332a *et seq*) has been introduced. The amended bill proposes that not only the debtor (as under the current law) but also any creditor that could petition to the bankruptcy court for an adjudication of bankruptcy can move instead for a composition proceeding. The court would then have to examine whether a reorganisation proceeding (with a view to a composition agreement) could be instituted (art 293 new SchKG). In addition the bankruptcy court itself could, on its own initiative, instead of granting a motion for involuntary bankruptcy, stay the proceeding and refer the matter to the court for composition proceedings to see whether a composition proceeding could be instituted or whether the matter should be referred back to the bankruptcy court. If the case is referred back, bankruptcy has to be declared (art 173a new SchKG).

After a request for a reorganisation proceeding has been lodged, the court has to order the necessary provisional measures, *i.e.* appointment of a provisional "Sachwalter" (administrator) or declaration of a provisional moratorium for two months (art 293 new SchKG). After a hearing with the debtor and the moving creditors (or other creditors if necessary), the court for composition proceedings has to decide whether or not to grant a regular moratorium of four to six months (in addition to the prior two months' provisional moratorium). The court has to consider the chances (on the basis of the balance sheet, the profit and loss statement and the budget) that a composition agreement may be successfully achieved. If necessary, the moratorium can be prolonged up to a maximum of 24 months (arts 294, 295 new SchKG) If the extension is for more than 12 months, creditors have a right to a hearing. The moratorium can be revoked if it becomes obvious in the course of the reorganisation that a composition agreement cannot be achieved (art 295 new SchKG).

During the moratorium, the debtor can in general continue to do business under the supervision of the Sachwalter (unless of course the court for composition proceedings ordered the contrary), but the debtor has no independent control over its assets. Dispositions of fixed capital, pledging of assets, incurring guarantees and gratuitous dispositions are only possible with court approval (art 298 new SchKG).

The composition agreement needs approval both by a majority of the creditors (art 305 new SchKG) and by the court (art 306 new SchKG); As regards approval by the creditors, the bill introduces a new, alternative quorum: either over 50% of the creditors representing two-thirds of the claims, or at least 25% of the creditors representing 75% of the claims have to approve the agreement.

The court's approval depends on its perception of the reorganisation's prospects of success.

The amended bill expressly provides for a super-priority for new debts that have been incurred by the debtor with the consent of the Sachwalter during the moratorium. In a composition agreement with assignment of assets or in a later bankruptcy, these claims will be paid out of the assets of the bankruptcy estate first, *i.e.* they are considered debts of the bankruptcy estate (art 310 new SchKG).

Miscellaneous amendments

Finally, the following amendments are noteworthy. In the course of the reorganisation of the debt collection and bankruptcy authorities, the bill introduces a primary (direct) liability of the cantons (Switzerland is divided into 26 cantons) for acts of their officers who are involved in debt collection and bankruptcy proceedings (art 5 new SchKG). In addition, the proceedings will be accelerated by abbreviating the "closed times" (recess) during which no official debt collection or bankruptcy actions may be taken (art 56 new SchKG). Furthermore, foundation in the sense of article 80 of the Swiss Civil Code of 10 December 1907 ("Schweizerisches Zivilgesetzbuch" – "ZGB"), may now also be subject to involuntary bankruptcy (art 39 Sec 1 No 12 new SchKG).

Other sources of law

The current SchKG has to a large extent been moulded by judicial interpretation of the Swiss Federal Court. One finds numerous early judgments of the Court concerning the application of the SchKG which are still valid today.

The role of supervising the entire process of debt collection and bankruptcy was assigned to the Swiss Federal Court. In order to enable it to fulfil that role, the court was granted the power to issue regulations enforcing the statute. This is an exception to the constitutional separation of powers, as here the judiciary was being authorised to perform a legislative function. The Swiss Federal Court has exercised this function on numerous occasions and has issued a number of regulations on the law of insolvency.

A further important source of law is the Swiss Code of Obligations of 30 March, 1911 ("Schweizerisches Obligationenrecht" – "OR"). The third chapter of the OR, which deals with commercial enterprises and associations, contains various provisions that are of importance for the law of insolvency.

2. Corporations

Characteristics

General

The joint-stock company is by far the most common corporate form in Switzerland. The reasons for its popularity are evident. The minimum nominal capital is Sfr 100,000 following the recent reform of the Swiss company law which came into effect on 1 July 1992. The attractiveness of the joint-stock company is also due to the fact that the stockholders cannot be held personally liable for the debts incurred by the company. As a "société anonyme" it provides a high degree of anonymity for the stockholders. Further, this legal form provides for simple investment and disinvestment by enabling shareholders to convert their capital investments at any time into liquid form. On the other hand, it is possible to secure a long-term commitment of the members of a joint-stock company by means of contractual restrictions on the transferability of stock. The joint-stock company is so flexible that it may be used for practically any size of company – from the single-member company to companies with several thousands of members. In view of its paramount importance in practice, we shall limit our discussion mainly to the joint-stock company, with only a brief discussion of the other legal forms (see pp676-679 *infra*).

The most important legal characteristics of the joint-stock company are that:

- it has its own name;
- its nominal capital is divided into shares, and
- its liabilities may only be met from its own assets.

The minimum capital required is Sfr 100,000, of which at least Sfr 50,000 must be paid in cash or in kind upon creation of the company. If the minimum capital is fully paid-up, shares may be issued either as bearer or as registered shares. However, until it is fully paid-up, only registered shares may be issued. The par value of the shares must be at least Sfr 10 each. Swiss law does not provide for shares of no par value (see arts 621, 622 OR). These characteristics will be discussed in detail below.

Capital-oriented organisation

The joint-stock company is a capital-oriented organisational form. Whereas in a general or a limited partnership (see p678 *infra*), the partners as individuals are at the forefront, in a joint-stock company it is the capital contribution of the members which characterises the company. The composition of the membership will be influenced to a great extent by this orientation towards capital rather than towards individuals.

Separate legal personality

The joint-stock company has separate legal personality, *i.e.* it may act in its own name, it may undertake legal acts and it may be held liable for tortious acts on the part of its officers. It may sue and be sued and be the subject of debt collection proceedings. Its place of domicile is independent from the place of residence of its members (art 643 OR).

Although general and limited partnerships have no legal personality under Swiss law, they may act in their own name, as may the joint-stock company. However, the joint-stock company is also a separate legal person in its internal relations, *i.e.* it is independent from its members. Thus, the company itself has legal title to the assets. Further, the company is not affected by changes in its membership. Finally, the members are not automatically officers of the company.

As it is a corporation, there must be a plurality of persons behind the joint-stock company, and at least three shareholders upon creation of the company (art 625 para 1 OR). Nonetheless, the so-called single-member company is also recognised. It is true that under article 625 para 2 OR a company must be dissolved if the number of members falls below three. However, the court may only act upon application from a member or a creditor and not of its own volition. Further, the court is not bound in every case to order the dissolution of the company. In practice this right to have the company dissolved is seldom used, with the result that single-member companies are relatively common.

In certain cases, principles of good faith will require that there be deemed to be a commercial identity between the sole shareholder and the single-member company, in other words there may be a need to pierce the corporate veil.

Commercial aims

Although a joint-stock company will normally pursue commercial aims it may also be used for "idealistic" goals be they cultural, charitable, political or social. However, this is rarely the case in practice.

Nominal capital

A joint-stock company must have determined capital at its disposal, *i.e.* a capital amount which is fixed in advance and which determines the company's net worth (the issued capital). The company must procure the issued capital from its members, although this can be left outstanding or partly outstanding until called at a later stage. Thereafter it is under an obligation to ensure the maintenance of its issued capital.

The obligation to procure the issued capital cannot be avoided because the company only acquires existence when:

- the entire issued capital has been subscribed for by the future shareholders, *i.e.* when they have undertaken to acquire shares in the aggregate amount of the issued capital; and

- the issued capital has actually been provided, *i.e.* each shareholder has either paid his participation in full or at least up to a statutory minimum, with a corresponding promise in respect of the remainder.

Payment may be in kind or in cash.

The only means provided by statute of monitoring whether or not the issued capital is being maintained is in the form of the obligation on the company to provide information about its financial position in its audited balance sheet.

Because the shareholders cannot be made personally liable for debts incurred by the company, it follows that the creditworthiness of the company depends entirely on its own net worth. The company's net worth thus represents a kind of liability pool as far as creditors are concerned.

For the shareholders, the issued capital represents a capital contribution. They must make contributions to the aggregate amount of the issued capital. If they only pay in a part of the proportion which they subscribed for at the time of the company's creation, they have an obligation to pay in the remainder. Often a security – a share – is issued in respect of the amount of each participation, though this is not compulsory. If issued, the share provides documentary proof of the entitlement to exercise membership rights. It furthermore facilitates changes or transfers of membership. The company may itself determine the amount of its issued capital. There is, however, a minimum capital requirement of Sfr 100,000.

"Authorised capital" was introduced into Swiss law as part of the recent company law reform. By modifying the memorandum and articles of association, the general meeting of shareholders may now authorise the board of directors to increase the capital up to the amount specified by the general meeting. A time limit of two years was set within which the company meeting must effect the increase in capital (art 651 OR). The purpose of this procedure is to enable the board of directors to react quickly to favourable market conditions, for instance, in preparation for acquiring a participation in another company or for a merger where the consideration to the shareholders of the other company consists of shares.

"Conditional capital" was also embodied in the revised law (art 653 OR). This enables companies to issue new shares continuously as and when there is a conversion of convertible debt or an exercise of warrants or whenever an employee share ownership scheme so requires. Only the general meeting may decide on a conditional capital increase in such circumstances . As is the case for authorised capital, conditional capital may not exceed one half of the existing share capital, and must be reflected in the memorandum and articles of association. The capital increase is effective as soon as the conversion notice or purchaser notice, having the same effect as a subscription to the shares, is exercised and the shares are paid-up in cash or in kind.

There are certain statutory safeguards to ensure the maintenance of the issued capital of companies. First, the assets of the company may not be reduced below the amount of the issued capital stipulated in the memorandum and articles of association. Thus, consideration paid by the shareholders may not be returned to them. Secondly, except in certain circumstances, the company may not purchase its own shares (art 659 OR). Thirdly, no dividends may be paid whilst the net assets of the company are less than its issued capital. Finally, no interest may be paid in respect of members' contributions to capital.

In accordance with article 725 OR, the board of directors is obliged to call an extraordinary general meeting if the amount of the net assets falls below one-half of the issued capital. The same article provides further that the court must be notified if the company is insolvent. Generally, the latter event will lead to an adjudication of bankruptcy (see pp688-689 *infra*).

Furthermore, companies are subject to stringent accounting and valuation requirements. These are intended to prevent the financial status from being wrongly presented in a favourable light in order to be able to show and distribute profits which have not actually been realised (arts 662-670 OR).

Specific provisions apply to non-cash consideration for shares. These seek to ensure that the other shareholders and future creditors are adequately informed of the nature of the contribution (arts 634, 634a, 635, 635a OR).

A final safeguard to ensure the maintenance of the issued capital is provided by the statutory reserve requirements. These require companies to allocate a certain percentage of their profits to a general reserve fund (art 671 OR). This fund may not be voluntarily reduced below the specified minimum except in certain circumstances such as to cover losses, support the company through difficult trading periods, or relieve unemployment or mitigate its consequences (art 671 para 3 OR).

Company name

The company may choose its own name within the limits of the general rules (art 950 para 1 OR). It may choose names of objects, or fantasy names or names of persons. If a name is made up only of names of objects or fantasy names, the legal form of the company need not be indicated. However, if names of persons are used, the designation of the legal form ("AG") must be included as well (art 950 para 2 OR).

Management

The executive organ of the company comprises the directors who are charged with the actual management of the company (the board of directors). One or more physical persons may be appointed as directors (art 707 paras 1, 3 OR). The board elects a chairman and a secretary.

The board of directors is elected by the general meeting of shareholders. There is an agency relationship (or a quasi-mandate relationship) between the board of directors and the company, the scope of which is, however, largely determined by company law and agreements between the parties are therefore bound to its restrictions.

Only shareholders may be appointed as directors. If non-shareholders are

elected by the general meeting, they may only take up office after they have become shareholders (art 707 paras 1, 2 OR).

If a legal entity or a (general or limited) partnership is a shareholder of a company, it may not be elected as director. However, its legal "representatives" may
be elected (art 707 para 3 OR). In such event the physical person who is actually
elected by the general meeting, and not the company or legal entity he "represents", will become the board member of the company. The representative may
promote the special interests of the entity he represents, provided they do not
conflict with the interests of the company of which he has been elected a director.

Eligibility for election as a director is subject to certain restrictions as to nationality and place of residence. In particular, the majority of the directors must
be Swiss nationals and be domiciled in Switzerland.

The general meeting of shareholders may terminate the appointment of any
director at any time and for any reason whatsoever (art 705 para 1 OR). This
right is justified by the relationship of trust that exists between the directors
and the shareholders.

The representation function of the directors is not governed by the rules relating to ordinary representation (agency). Rather, the directors are "executive organs" of the company, and as such, are deemed to be authorised to perform all legal acts that are within the scope of the objects of the company (arts 716, 716a
OR). Any other acts which they may undertake, including any tortious acts, are
binding on the company as well (art 722 OR).

The board of directors has certain duties which may not be delegated or assigned and which may not be withdrawn (art 716a OR). These are:

- the overall management of the company and the issuing of the necessary instructions;
- determining the organisation of the company;
- establishing proper accounting, financial controls and financial planning
  services, in so far as these are essential for the company's operations;
- appointing and dismissing persons responsible for the management of the
  company and other authorised representatives;
- supervising persons responsible for the management of the company, particularly as regards compliance with the laws, memorandum and articles of
  association, regulations and instructions;
- preparing the company's annual report;
- preparing general meetings of shareholders and ensuring resolutions are
  carried out;
- notifying the court in the event of insolvency.

The board of directors may delegate the preparation and execution of its decisions or the supervision of business to committees or individual members. It
may also delegate certain of its functions to management, up to the extent provided by the memorandum and articles of association (art 716b OR). However,

the functions mentioned above as being non-delegable are excluded. Further, the reform of the company law expressly limits the liability of the board of directors in respect of functions which it has so delegated. The rules governing its responsibility now require only that the directors exercise, and if necessary prove that they have exercised, "the care required under the circumstances" in the selection, instruction and supervision of the management.

The duties of the board of directors in the event of insufficiency of capital or insolvency are of particular importance (art 725 OR). If the last annual balance sheet shows that one-half of the share capital and statutory reserves is no longer covered, the board must immediately convene a general meeting of shareholders and request measures for the reorganisation of the company. If there are reasonable grounds for assuming that the company might be insolvent, the board is obliged to prepare an interim balance sheet and submit it to the auditors. If the interim balance sheet shows that the company's liabilities to its creditors are no longer covered, either on the basis of going-concern values or liquidation values, the board of directors must notify the court. However, the court need not be notified if creditors representing an amount equal to the shortfall agree to a waiver of priority behind all other creditors.

There is a general statutory presumption that the board of directors may decide on all matters which are not expressly reserved or delegated to the general meeting of shareholders or to other officers or organs of the company (art 716 OR).

Ownership

The "owners" of a company are its shareholders. Their rights may be divided into two categories: participation rights and property rights.

Participation rights

The participation rights include first of all the right to transfer shares. Bearer shares, as the name implies, are always transferable. Generally, so too are registered shares. As regards registered shares, the reform of the company law provides strict limitations on the imposition of restrictions on transferability. The result for small family owned companies is as follows: if shares are purportedly transferred under an inheritance, or under matrimonial law, or as result of compulsory execution then, as previously, the company may still only refuse to register the new shareholder in the shareholders' register if it offers to purchase the shares at their real value (art 685b, para 4 OR). However, the company must bear in mind that the newly registered heir might subsequently wish to sell his shares. In such a case, the redrafted rules apply according to which restrictions on transferability are severely limited. Under the new law, the company may only refuse the transfer if there are material grounds and such grounds are specified in the memorandum and articles of association, or if the company offers to purchase the shares at their real value (art 685b, para 1 OR). Article 685b paragraph 2 OR provides that "terms as to the composition on the membership which justify a refusal of registration on the basis of the objects or the economic independence of the company" would constitute "material grounds". The following are accepted as being valid reasons for refusal:

- to prevent competitors from acquiring a participation in the company;
- to maintain certain entrepreneurial standards;
- to preserve regional roots.

The right to vote is the most important of the participation rights. It arises by operation of law as soon as the shareholder owns shares in the corporation, whether or not he has paid fully or partly the consideration for each share fixed by statute or by the memorandum and articles of association. Unless the memorandum and articles of association provide otherwise, each shareholder's right to vote is determined by the "aggregate par value of shares owned by him" (*i.e.* one vote per share in contrast to the *per capita* voting rights in partnerships and associations).

The memorandum and articles of association may provide for a separate category of shares with special voting rights in order to ensure that a particular group of shareholders may retain control. For instance, a family owned company may provide for such a share category in order to keep control of the company within the family. Further, a company may provide for such shares in order to avoid foreign control. In the case of special voting shares, the right to vote is determined by the actual number of shares owned and not by their aggregate par value.

Similar aims can be achieved by means of shareholder voting agreements, where a group of shareholders will agree amongst themselves to exercise their voting rights as one, in order thereby to obtain a decisive influence. Such agreements may be in various forms, from a mere "gentleman's agreement" to formal, legally binding contracts whose performance is secured by penalty clauses. However, if a shareholder exercises his vote in a manner contrary to such an agreement, then his vote will be legally valid under company law, irrespective of the form of the agreement.

The shareholder has a right of control in respect of the management of the company in general, and the calculation and utilisation of the net profits of the company in particular (art 696 OR). Accordingly, each shareholder has the right to see the profit and loss account, the balance sheet, the annual report and the proposals of the board of directors for the utilisation of the net profits. In practice, the right of control depends to a large extent on the quality of the information contained in the balance sheet in the annual report of the company. In this connection it must be noted that the directors are able to create hidden reserves (which are not shown in the balance sheet). However, the new company law limits their right to create and dissolve such reserves. Further, since they determine the content of the annual report, the shareholder might not have access to the necessary information and documentation to exercise his right of control.

It is even more difficult for shareholders to gain an insight into the activities of the directors and the management. Article 697 paragraph 3 OR provides that a shareholder may only obtain relevant information if expressly so authorised by a resolution of the board of directors or the general meeting of shareholders. The scope of such authorisation will, however, always be limited by the duty of confidentiality owed by the board of directors. If the board and the general meeting of shareholders both deny him the requested authorisation, the shareholder may apply to the court for an order that the company provide him with adequate information, such as notarised copies of the company's books or correspondence, to enable him to exercise his right of control. The court may not, however, jeopardise the interests of the company (art 697 para 2 OR). Furthermore, each shareholder has the right to request at a general meeting of shareholders that certain matters be clarified in a special audit, provided that this is necessary for the exercise of his rights as shareholder and that he had already exercised his right to inspect the financial statements of the company and his right to look into the activities of the directors and the management. If the general meeting of shareholders does not accept his request, the shareholder may, provided he holds at least 10% of the voting capital or at least Sfr 2 mio. of the company's share capital, request the court to appoint a special auditor (arts 697a and 697b).

Property rights

The shareholders' property rights include the right to:

- receive a dividend;
- subscribe for new shares; and
- receive a proportion of the proceeds of liquidation.

The general meeting of shareholders may only suspend the right to subscribe for new shares if there are material grounds for doing so (art 652b para 2 OR).

The right to receive a dividend is a right to participate in the net profits of the company. Accordingly, dividends may only be paid from the net profits at the end of the financial year or from reserves ("dividend reserves") which have been created specifically for that purpose (art 675 para 2 OR). The company may not pay or promise to pay interest in lieu of a dividend. However, an exception is made for enterprises which have a long start-up period or "construction phase" before they attain full operating capacity. Here, the memorandum and articles of association may provide for the payment of interest during a specified period (arts 675 para 1 and 676 para 1 OR).

The right to subscribe for new shares entitles the shareholders to demand that in the event of an increase of the share capital a proportion corresponding to their actual shareholdings be allocated to them. Thus, the shareholders are able to maintain their proportion of the overall issued capital of the company despite any subsequent increases (art 652b OR).

Finally, the shareholders have the right to receive a proportion of the proceeds of liquidation of the company, unless the memorandum and articles of association provide for a different utilisation of any surplus achieved thereby (art 660 para 2 OR).

Financing and security for creditors

Apart from the share capital and reserves, the joint-stock company may use debt financing to finance its operations.

Types of security

The company may provide its creditors with all customary forms of security and quasi-security interests as follows:

Charges on real property
All charges (mortgages etc.) on real property have the following in common:

- the subject matter of the security is real property within the meaning of arts 655/943 ZGB, *i.e.* real estate, a mine, or an independent, permanent right or co-ownership right to real property;
- it involves a claim (*i.e.* a contractual relationship) which is incapable of becoming time-barred as long as it is secured by the charge;
- the subject matter itself is liable in respect of the claim.

Both the subject matter of the security and the claim must be individually determined. As far as the claim is concerned, this means that it must be quantified. The security must be registered in the Land Register.

The publication principle applies with the result that a charge only arises when the object is registered in the Land Register, with the exception of statutory charges such as for taxes or other public levies. A statutory charge also arises in favour of craftsmen or entrepreneurs who supply a building with materials and labour, or with labour only.

Certain types of charge (certificates of indebtedness, "Gült") are issued in the form of a security. Under a mortgage and a certificate of indebtedness, in addition to the real property, the debtor has a secondary liability with his entire estate. Under a Gült (seldom used in practice) the property alone is liable.

Charges on movable property
The charge on movable property also serves as security for a claim and gives the creditor the right to obtain payment of the claim. The creditor may not, however, demand more than that. The so-called forfeiture clause is excluded for both charges on real and movable property.

The charge must be notified to or identifiable by third parties: thus the charge on movable property is based upon possession of the subject matter of the charge.

The charge arises pursuant to a contract and following transfer of possession. It must always refer to single, individually ascertained items and may not be expressed in respect of all or parts of the debtor's fortune.

Realisation is effected under to the laws governing debt collection and bankruptcy. The parties may, however, agree that the creditor may realise the charge privately.

Rights of retention or "liens" and pledges

A right of retention or "lien" is a right which enables a creditor to retain and sell movable property or securities which are in his possession and which he would otherwise be obliged to surrender, in order to satisfy a claim.

The right of retention has much in common with the right of pledge. The creation and continuation of both rights is dependent upon possession of the movables; the purpose of both rights is to provide security for a claim; they both permit the creditor to hold the property until full satisfaction is obtained or, if full satisfaction is not obtained, to sell the property and take payment from the proceeds of sale. Further, both rights can only exist in respect of things which by their nature are capable of realisation, *i.e.* of being sold.

The distinction between the two rights is primarily that the right of pledge is usually based on a contract whereas the right of retention is a statutory right. The right of retention may be excluded contractually but may not be granted by contract.

Reservation of title

In respect of movables, it is also possible for a seller to retain ownership of goods until the buyer has paid the full purchase price. This is known as reservation of title ("Eigentumsvorbehalt"). For a reservation of title to be valid, it has to be entered in the public register at the buyer's domicile, which is kept for this purpose by the bankruptcy office (art 715 ZGB). Here, if the buyer becomes insolvent before payment has been made for the movables and the seller can identify those goods, then the seller can demand that the goods be returned.

Set-off

Although not strictly a security or even quasi-security interest, a creditor may reduce his claim against a company and thereby obtain a return greater than that available to other unsecured creditors by setting off against his claim any amount which he owes to the company, provided that both claims are due. Thus, a creditor who owes the company as much as he is owed will, in effect, recover his claim in full.

Financing by bonds

Bondholders of a corporation form by law an association which enables them to represent their common interest vis-à-vis the sole debtor in case of an infringement of their creditor rights. This association exists by law (1157, para 1 OR) and is convened by the debtor or, if necessary, by the judge. The convocation of the bondholders' meeting has the effect that respite is granted to the due claims of the bondholders (1166 OR).

In case of bankruptcy the Konkursverwalter (trustee in bankruptcy) immediately summons the meeting of bondholders who designate their representative in the bankruptcy proceedings (1183 OR).

Subordinated loans and low-priority loans

In Swiss legal practice subordinated loans and low-priority loans are common.

In a low-priority loan, the creditor undertakes to defer claiming repayment of his loan unless it is certain that the remaining creditors of the company will not suffer any loss thereby. In bankruptcy proceedings this cannot be established until immediately prior to the issue of certificates of loss. If at this point it is evident that loss will be suffered by other creditors, the creditor must waive his claim. Thus, in the worst case, a low-priority loan entails a waiver of the entire claim. The creditor under a low-priority loan may if he wishes agree that his claim shall rank after all other creditors. He will then appear in the collocation plan (list of claims) after the last category of creditors. In such event the repayment of the loan at final maturity and all rights to claim reimbursement prior to maturity are effectively excluded. However, in no case do such agreements actually result in a reduction of the level of indebtedness. Thus, they will not have the effect of avoiding or even postponing the statutory duty to notify the court in the event of insolvency, except as provided for by article 725 para 2 OR.

Whereas there is no statutory provision dealing specifically with low-priority loans, there is a provision relating to subordinated loans in the implementing order to the Swiss Banking Act. However, this provision only applies to banks and other financial institutions which fall within the scope of application of the Act. The provision stipulates that subordinated loans must be irrevocable, that they may not be set off against other claims, that no security may be provided in respect thereof and that they must be for a period of not less than seven years.

Although only subordinated loans and other institutions are subject to the Banking Act, this form of debt financing is also common in other sectors of commerce.

Available information

The official source of information about companies domiciled in Switzerland is the register of commerce.

The register of commerce

The register of commerce is a public, officially maintained register of all legally essential facts concerning commercial enterprises. An entry in the register of commerce will specify the founders of the company, its objects and its registered office and the names of both the persons who are entitled to represent the company and those who are liable as officers. The most important elements of each entry are published in the Swiss Official Commercial Gazette. Legally, joint-stock companies, all other forms of capital-based enterprises and co-operative societies only acquire their existence following their registration in the register of commerce (arts 643, 838 OR).

The principal place of business and any branches may also be registered in the register of commerce. Branches, however, may only be registered if they have a certain economic and organisational independence. The registration of a branch creates jurisdiction of the courts at the place of the register of commerce in which it is registered (art 642 para 3 OR). The representation powers granted to individuals may be restricted to the activities of the branch.

The register of commerce must indicate which individuals have representation powers and in what manner individually or collectively they are authorised to sign (art 720 OR).

Because of their importance to creditors, bankruptcies and compositions with assignment of assets must be entered in the register of commerce. If a company is adjudicated bankrupt, the court must notify the competent register of commerce (art 176 SchKG). In the case of companies and co-operative societies an adjudication of bankruptcy will lead to their dissolution, but not necessarily to their termination. Thus, they are not removed from the register of commerce. Rather their dissolution is indicated by means of an addendum to the existing entry to the effect that the company has been adjudicated bankrupt. If applicable, the name of the private Konkursverwalter is mentioned as well.

The register of commerce provides both active and passive notice of facts to the public. Further, the very fact of being entered in the register of commerce means that the facts entered have "official authentication". There is active notice in that third parties are deemed to have knowledge of whatever is entered in the register, and passive notice in that they are not deemed to have knowledge of facts which are not entered therein. "Official authentication" means that third parties may rely on the authenticity of the facts stated in the register of commerce. This does not, however, apply to third parties acting in bad faith, *i.e.* who have knowledge of the incorrectness of the entries made.

Other sources of information

Further information about companies may be obtained from banks and information agencies. As far as banks are concerned, however, they are bound by the banking secrecy laws (art 47 Swiss Banking Law) in respect of any information which is not publicly available, for example, from the specialist press. Thus, they may not divulge any information obtained as a result of their client relationship except with the express (or implied) permission of the client.

Other business entities

Other forms of companies

As already mentioned, the joint-stock company is the most frequently used company form in Switzerland. The limited liability company (the "Gesellschaft mit beschränkter Haftung, GmbH"), which originated in Germany, has until most recently not really found a place in Swiss commercial life. The ratio of joint-stock companies to limited liability companies was until 1992 approximately 40:1. This lack of popularity was due among other things to the extensive publicity requirements applicable to limited liability companies. In particular, the names of the members and the amounts of their capital contributions must be entered in the register of commerce. Further, a change of membership is more difficult than the joint-stock company as shares are more widely and easily traded than are the investments (described as "parts") in a limited liability company. Finally, it is usually easier for a joint-stock company to raise fresh capital by way of a capital increase. As a result of the recent reform of the Swiss company law, limited liability companies are becoming more popular now.

The limited liability company is an incorporated legal person with an issued capital which is determined in advance at the time of its creation. Each member must make a capital contribution to the issued capital. The members are jointly and severally liable for the debts of the company up to the amount of the issued capital (art 772 OR). This joint and several liability applies to any limited liability company.

The issued capital of the limited liability company is stipulated in the memorandum and articles of association. It must be at least Sfr 20,000 and not more than Sfr 2 million (art 773 OR). At least one-half of the issued capital must be paid-up.

Each member must make capital contributions of Sfr 1,000 or multiples thereof (art 774 OR). The capital contributions together constitute the issued capital. In contrast to shares, the certificates which are issued in respect of the capital contributions are not securities, but merely evidence of title. Each member owns "parts" in the company in the same proportion as his capital contribution is to the issued capital (art 789 OR).

The liability of each individual member is not limited to the amount of his capital contribution, but to the aggregate amount of the issued capital as entered in the register of commerce. Thus the limited liability company is itself liable for its debts with its entire assets. In addition, the members are jointly and severally liable for the debts of the company up to an amount corresponding to its issued capital if the issued capital is not fully paid up or if it has been reduced by repayment or by payment of interest or unjustified dividends (art 802 OR). The limited liability company is obliged to indicate the amounts of the individual contributions in the memorandum and articles of association and to keep a register of members. Further, the management is obliged to provide the register of commerce each year with a list of members, their capital contributions and the amounts that are actually paid-up (art 790 OR).

By law, the members of the limited liability company have wide discretion to determine the management and the powers of representation. Thus, they may perform the management and representation functions themselves, or they may appoint one or more of their members to perform them, or they may delegate them to non-members (directors, managing directors, managers; arts 811 and 812 OR).

Partnerships

A general partnership is a contractual agreement between two or more physical persons who wish to pursue a commercial trade together under a common name and without limitation of their liability for the debts incurred (art 552 para 1 OR). Thus the general partnership is contractual in nature, resulting in contractual rights and obligations for the partners as amongst themselves. Externally, however, the general partnership is similar to an independent entity (art 562 OR). It has legal capacity to sue and be sued under its own name, as does a legal entity. Thus, it may acquire rights and obligations. Accordingly, it has its own separate assets.

The general partnership has officers through whom it conducts business with third parties. If a partner has been authorised to represent the partnership, any legal acts performed by him do not directly bind him nor the other partners. Rather, they bind the partnership itself. The partnership will be bound not just by lawful acts, but also by tortious acts on the part of such partner if performed during the course of his duties. In addition, such partner will be personally liable for his tortious acts (art 567 para 3 OR).

The partners are jointly and severally liable for the debts of the partnership, to the extent of their entire personal fortunes (art 568 OR).

There are no requirements as to the form of the contractual agreement creating a general partnership. However, general partnerships must be registered in the register of commerce, as they usually perform commercial activities. The entry is only declaratory *i.e.* the partnership acquires its existence before registration. The purpose of registration is thus primarily to notify the public. Partnerships created for purposes other than commercial trade, however, only come into existence upon being registered in the register of commerce. However, the firm name is only protected when the partnership is registered. Furthermore, only a registered partnership is subject to bankruptcy proceedings. Therefore the partners are obliged to register the partnership, otherwise it may be registered *ex officio* by the competent registration authority.

In the event of the bankruptcy of a general partnership, bankruptcy proceedings relate to the assets of the partnership only. There can be no distraint against the private fortunes of the partners although claims in bankruptcy may be filed against partners in respect of any shortfall suffered by the creditors. The assets in bankruptcy are made up of the contributions of the partners, if still available, any other assets acquired by the partnership and any claims against third parties. The liabilities consist of all claims of the creditors of the partnership (art 570 OR).

In contrast to this, if a partner of a general partnership becomes bankrupt, his assets in bankruptcy include the whole of his private fortune and his claims against the partnership in respect of fees, interest of his share in the distribution of the net profits or of the proceeds of liquidation (art 572 OR). The liabilities consist of all claims against him whether by his own private creditors or by creditors of the partnership (art 571 para 3 OR). The two groups of creditors are thus in competition with each other, but neither is given priority in the bankruptcy proceedings. However, the creditors of the partnership may file claims in bankruptcy against each of the partners individually if their claims are not satisfied in the bankruptcy proceedings against the partnership (art 218 para 1 SchKG). Thus, the creditors of a partnership are likely to obtain a higher degree of satisfaction of their claims than creditors of an individual partner.

Bankruptcy proceedings against the partnership are conducted separately from the proceedings against the partners. However, there is a certain chronological link in that the creditors of the partnership may only claim in the bankruptcy proceedings against a partner if and to the extent that their claims have not been satisfied in the proceedings against the partnership. This can only be established on the conclusion of the proceedings against the partnership. Only then will the amount of the claim which is left unsatisfied be formally included in the collocation plan in the bankruptcy proceedings against the partner (art 218 SchKG).

A limited partnership is in essence a general partnership with different liability relationships. At least one of the partners (the general partner), has unlimited liability for the debts of the partnership, and at least one partner (the limited partner) has liability limited to a fixed maximum amount (art 594 para 1 OR). The general partner must be a physical person, whereas the limited partner may also be a general or a limited partnership or a legal entity (art 594 para 2 OR).

Bankruptcy proceedings may not only be brought against the partnership and the partners, but also against the limited partner if the latter is an entity which is subject to bankruptcy. The bankruptcy proceedings themselves are governed by the same principles as for general partnerships.

Debt collection and asset recovery

The procedure for debt collection against enterprises or private individuals is different depending upon whether or not the claim is a pecuniary claim.

In Switzerland, the exclusive procedure for debt collection in respect of pecuniary claims is provided for in the SchKG (*i.e.* it is a matter of federal jurisdiction). The debt enforcement procedure for types of claims other than pecuniary claims (for example, claims for the return of securities, or the process of sequestration of assets) is the responsibility of the cantons. It is governed by the Cantonal Civil Procedure Codes.

In most cantons this enforcement procedure is handled by a judge. The defendant must have an opportunity to make objections against the enforcement measure before the competent authority. The authority issues an order that the debtor transfer the asset concerned to the plaintiff. If the debtor does not comply with the order, the authority may impose a fine or refer the case to a criminal court, or the judge may empower a third party or the plaintiff to discharge such duties, or he may order the use of force against the liable party or the assets in its custody.

In the case of a pecuniary claim the debt collection procedure is instituted by filing an application with the public debt collection office at the debtor's domicile (place of residence) or the place of the debtor's registered office. The public debt collection office will then issue a so called payment order ("Zahlungsbefehl") against the debtor, but it will not undertake any assessment of the merits or validity of the claim. The debtor may stop the proceedings with similar rapidity merely by filing an objection ("Rechtsvorschlag") with the public debt collection office within ten days (art 74 SchKG). The filing of an objection by the debtor does in general not require prior court approval.

If the claim is based on a bill of exchange or a cheque, the debtor has to file its objection within five days and the court has a further five days to approve the debtor's objection provided that a prescribed number of criteria are met. If approval of the objection is denied, the court can grant interim relief (arts 178 *et seq* SchKG).

If the creditor holds a binding judgment in his favour by a Swiss or foreign court, he may apply for the objection to be set aside. The procedure for setting aside an objection is a summary procedure. If successful, the creditor obtains the right to request that distraint be levied against the debtor or, in the case of a corporation, the right to file a bankruptcy petition.

The debtor has the right to be heard in the summary procedure and may dispute both the claim and the judgment.

For instance, the debtor has a valid defence if he can prove that the claim has been waived, or been paid or deferred since the date of the judgment, or that it has become time-barred (art 81 para 1 SchKG).

The debtor may not dispute a final, legally binding judgment of a Swiss court.

However, if the judgment was rendered by a court of a different canton than that which has jurisdiction over the debt collection, he may contest the competence of the former court or, if applicable, he may argue that he was not properly summoned or represented (art 81 para 2 SchKG).

A judgment rendered by a foreign court will be treated in the same manner as a judgment by a court of a different canton. However, the debtor has an additional defence if the foreign judgment is contrary to the provisions of a treaty between Switzerland and that country (see arts 25 *et seq* of the Lugano Convention on Jurisdiction and the Enforcement of Judgements in Civil and Commercial Matters concluded at Lugano on 16 September 1988) or, if there are grounds for non-recognition according to Switzerland's International Private Law Statute ("Bundesgesetz über das Internationale Privatrecht vom 18 Dezember 1987" – the "PILS"; see in particular arts 25 *et seq* PILS and art 81 para 3 SchKG).

If the creditor has a security interest (a pledge, mortgage or charge) over assets, the charged assets will be realised by a special debt collection procedure that is limited to the charged assets (art 151 SchKG). In the case of debtors who are subject to the bankruptcy proceedings (*i.e.* corporations or physical persons registered in the register of commerce), creditors who hold security interests in the form of a charge, pledge or mortgage will rank as privileged creditors in respect of the proceeds realised from the charged assets in the subsequent bankruptcy proceedings (art 219 para 1 SchKG). The debtor may not dispose of the subject matter of the security interest. The charge has priority to the rights of ownership and restricts their exercise.

3. Survival of the insolvent corporation or its business

When a corporation is in a crisis which threatens its very existence, the initial question is always whether it can be reorganised and its operations continued.

The corporation might attempt a reorganisation, but if this proves unsuccessful it will have to be adjudicated bankrupt. This would normally lead to the termination of the corporation.

Conversely, under Swiss law it is not impossible for a corporation to be reorganised at the last minute, even though it is already close to cessation of operations and to termination.

The various possibilities for reorganisation will be discussed below. However, not all methods of reorganisation will be dealt with as some are purely practical (such as replacement of incompetent management) or purely financial in nature. Here we will describe only the two most important procedural means of reorganisation under Swiss law, composition and stay of bankruptcy.

Composition

Purpose and effect

A composition in the broadest sense of the term can be described as a measure whose purpose is to protect the debtor from the consequences of bankruptcy. If a corporation has already been adjudicated bankrupt, it may be able to achieve a revocation of the bankruptcy by means of a composition. Thus a composition may be sought even during bankruptcy proceedings.

The composition by order of court, which we will discuss here, must be distinguished from the out-of-court composition. The latter is a contract under "private law" and thus governed by the provisions of the OR and not by the SchKG. In a private law composition the debtor concludes a separate composition agreement with each individual creditor; however, the acceptance of all the creditors is required for the entire arrangement to stand.

The composition by order of court is a measure provided for by the SchKG. This statute forms part of "public law".

The composition by order of court is actually a compulsory settlement. It is reached under official supervision and with official confirmation and is based upon a proposal by the debtor which must have obtained the approval of a qualified majority of the creditors. It is also binding on any dissenting creditors. The decisive element is therefore that a public authority supervises the composition procedure and that approval of the composition is required.

In general there are three different types of composition:

- moratorium;
- dividend (or percentage) composition;
- composition with assignment of assets (or liquidation composition).

There may also be combinations of the above.

Moratorium

Moratorium is the mildest form of composition. Here, the debtor continues to promise to pay its creditors in full. However, it is granted time limits within which to pay. The debtor will normally have liquidity problems and will hope to be able to avoid distraint by means of a moratorium. As a rule, the moratorium enables the debtor to reorganise by re-establishing liquidity.

Dividend (or percentage) composition

Under dividend (or percentage) composition the debtor corporation usually aims to achieve an actual reorganisation. It offers all its creditors only a fixed dividend on (or a percentage of) their claims. The creditors waive the remainder.

In contrast to bankruptcy proceedings the creditors in composition proceedings receive no certificate of loss, *i.e.* a certificate which entitles the creditors to revive their claims against the debtor if the latter acquires new assets. The statute describes it as a "legal charitable deed" (art 293 SchKG). On the other hand, it is possible for the creditors to stipulate in the composition that they are reserving the right to revive their claims in future.

In item I of Title 11 of the SchKG both the moratorium and the dividend composition are referred to as the "ordinary composition"

Composition with assignment of assets

Composition with assignment of assets (or liquidation composition) is governed by articles 316a *et seq* SchKG (item II of Title 11). This form of composition gives the creditors the right of disposal over part of the entire assets of the debtor corporation. However, they may only exercise this right through the liquidators. As in the case of bankruptcy proceedings, the debtor continues to be the legal owner until the assets are realised. The realisation of assets and the distribution of the proceeds is the responsibility of the liquidators acting under the supervision of a creditors' committee. Thus, this form of composition to a large extent represents a form of "private" bankruptcy.

It is possible to achieve a reorganisation of the corporation by means of a composition with assignment of assets if the corporation as such can be maintained and sold as a whole or in part out of the assets in liquidation.

Upon such a sale the ownership of the corporation would change, often to a new company created by one or more of the creditors.

The result of composition proceedings is usually that the debtor corporation will survive, be reorganised and be able to continue operations. The intention of the debtor in filing for a composition might also be to achieve a best possible realisation of assets. This is often the intention in filing for a composition with assignment of assets. However, in most cases the composition with assignment of assets leads to liquidation and thus to the termination of the corporation. This form of composition will be dealt with in more detail at pp706-717 below.

The forms of composition which normally would not result in termination are the moratorium and the dividend composition. These are the most important means of reorganisation available to insolvent corporations in Switzerland.

As stated above, the debtor may file for a composition even after having been adjudicated bankrupt. To do this, it would submit a proposal for a composition to the creditors during the bankruptcy proceedings. If a qualified majority of the creditors accepts the proposal, the Konkursverwalter can move for its approval by the court (art 304 Sch KG). If the court approves the proposed composition the Konkursverwalter may ask the court to discharge the bankruptcy (arts 195, 317 SchKG).

The composition is binding on all non-secured creditors and on all secured creditors for their claims not covered by the value of the security (art 311 SchKG). Any distraints effected against assets of the debtor become void upon confirmation of the composition (art 312 SchKG).

Pre-application considerations

When an application for a composition is filed, the public composition office, usually the district court (although it varies from canton to canton) upon granting it appoints a "Sachwalter" (administrator). Any individual or entity who is capable of ensuring an impartial representation of the interests of both the creditors and the debtor may be appointed as Sachwalter. Most often auditors, auditing companies, lawyers or notaries who have the necessary experience and requisite specialist knowledge, such as book-keeping or valuation, are appointed. In some cantons in Switzerland there is actually a profession of Sachwalter. In practice civil servants, particularly debt collection or bankruptcy officials, are also appointed.

The debtor may propose a Sachwalter to the composition office, but the office is not bound to accept this proposal. As the creditors are not involved in the application procedure, they have no right of proposal. However, the debtor and the creditors may challenge the appointment of the Sachwalter before the higher public composition authority (see BGE 103 Ia 79, 80).

The Sachwalter is a public official, responsible for directing the composition proceedings. Accordingly he must protect the interests of the debtor and the creditors equally.

The Sachwalter's fee is for the account of the debtor. Although the public composition office fixes the Sachwalter's fee on a lump-sum basis, it normally refers to the fee schedule of the professional body from which the Sachwalter was selected. Thus, the composition office refers to the fee schedule of the legal profession to assess the fee payable when a lawyer is appointed as Sachwalter. Clearly the fee payable for an auditing company or a lawyer will usually be higher than for an official authority such as the Konkursverwalter. In practice, therefore, the person appointed as Sachwalter will only accept the mandate once the fee has been agreed with the public composition office.

Once it is made known, the level of the Sachwalter's fee may well cause individual creditors to challenge the appointment before the higher public composition authority (usually the supreme court of the canton). The Sachwalter himself will normally demand an advance or some form of security for his fee. If necessary, he can demand that the security be increased during the proceedings.

Procedure

The procedure for the ordinary composition may be divided into three procedural stages:

- the preliminary procedure
- the approval procedure
- the confirmation procedure.

The preliminary procedure

The preliminary procedure is initiated by the debtor when it files an application for a moratorium (which must be distinguished from the moratorium as one type of composition) with the competent public composition office. Together with the application the debtor must submit a balance sheet, a list of the business records and books and a draft for a moratorium or a dividend composition. The draft must show how the debtor intends to meet its obligations towards its creditors, although in this stage of the proceedings, it is sufficient for the debtor to show generally the manner in which its obligations might be met; a concrete plan will often only become possible during the later proceedings (see generally arts 293 *et seq* SchKG).

The public composition office examines whether a moratorium may be granted and whether composition proceedings should be continued. Factors on which the public composition office will place particular emphasis are whether the debtor is worthy of a composition (*i.e.* whether he has acted in bad faith or recklessly), and whether the proposed dividend is in the right proportion to the assets of the debtor (art 306 SchKG).

If the public composition office rejects the application the debtor may challenge its decision before the higher cantonal composition authority within ten days (art 294 SchKG). If it accepts the composition application it will grant the debtor a moratorium of up to four months, extendable by up to a further two months (art 295 paras 1, 4 SchKG).

The approval procedure

It is in the approval procedure that the creditors have their first say. The Sachwalter convenes a meeting of creditors at the earliest one month after he has made all preparations (such as drawing up an inventory and valuing the assets) and after publishing a notice to creditors ("creditors' call"). In the meeting, which is chaired by the Sachwalter, the creditors discuss the composition application. However, decisions are not actually taken at this meeting. Rather each creditor has ten days in which to file a written approval of the composition (arts 299 *et seq* SchKG). In practice this time limit is often extended and approvals will also be accepted subsequently. The composition is deemed to be accepted if a majority of creditors approves it and if such majority represents at least two-thirds of the aggregate amount of the claims that are taken into consideration. Preferential creditors are excluded from this vote.

There are five classes of unsecured creditors under Swiss insolvency law. In general, only three of the classes are relevant to corporations:

- the first class ("preferential creditors"), which includes claims by employees of a corporation for salary and other benefits and certain claims by the government for tax;
- the second class, which includes claims for various social security payments and insurance; and ,
- the fifth class, which is the class into which all other unsecured creditors fall.

The other classes are only relevant to individual debtors. Payments to creditors of a particular class will only be made if creditors of all preceding classes have been fully satisfied. Within a class all creditors will be satisfied equally in proportion to their claims.

Claims secured by charges are included in the vote at the meeting, but only in respect of amounts which, according to the valuation by the Sachwalter, are not covered by the assets charged (art 305 para 2 SchKG).

The confirmation procedure

In the confirmation procedure the public composition office decides whether the composition shall be confirmed or rejected. The public composition office examines whether the requisite qualified majority of creditors has approved the composition and whether the procedural rules have been fully complied with. It will confirm the composition if the dividend offered is in the right proportion to the assets of the debtor and if the performance of the composition and the full satisfaction of all privileged creditors are ensured. The public composition office can reject the composition if the debtor is unworthy of acceptance (art 306 SchKG).

Creditors' involvement and position

As stated above the composition requires approval of a qualified majority of the creditors.

Although creditors who filed their claims following the notice to creditors are taken into consideration first, creditors may submit their written approval at any time until the public composition office's decision on confirmation or rejection of the composition. On confirmation by the public composition office the composition is binding on all creditors, whether they are known or not (art 311 SchKG). As regards the creditors' rights against joint debtors, guarantors and warrantors, the statute distinguishes as follows:

- those creditors who did not approve the composition do not lose these rights (art 303 para 1 SchKG); and

- those creditors who approved the composition lose the rights unless at least ten days prior to the meeting of creditors they notify such joint-debtors, sureties, and so on of the time and place of the meeting and offer to assign their claims to them for consideration (art 303 para 2 SchKG).

Preferential creditors (as stated above) are given precedence in composition proceedings unless they waive such treatment and their claims must be secured and paid in full. Accordingly, they have no vote in respect of the composition (arts 305 para 2, 306 para 2(2) SchKG).

Each creditor has the right to challenge all actions and decisions of the Sachwalter including any alleged infringement of statute, unreasonableness or a denial or delay of due process of law. Such challenge must be made before the public composition office within ten days after the date on which the creditor obtained knowledge of the decision or omission (art 295 para 3, art 17 SchKG). Each creditor may also challenge the decision of the public composition office confirming or rejecting the composition before the higher cantonal composition authority within ten days after publication (art 307 SchKG).

Once the composition is confirmed the creditors are entitled to two further legal remedies: if the conditions of the composition are not fulfilled in respect of a particular creditor he may, without prejudice to his rights under the composition, request the public composition office to rescind the composition to the extent that it concerns his claim. Further, he may even request that the composition be rescinded in its entirety if it came into being in an improper manner (arts 315, 316 SchKG).

If the composition is rejected by the public composition office each creditor is entitled, within ten days of publication, to request that the debtor be adjudicated bankrupt (art 309 SchKG).

Powers and duties of the Sachwalter

The primary duty of the Sachwalter is the supervision of the debtor (arts 295 para 2, 298 para 1 SchKG). Although he has the right to give instructions to the debtor he may not act in lieu of the debtor, as his right of disposal over the assets of the debtor is limited by statute. The Sachwalter may, for example, prohibit certain actions, require that the debtor undertake payments only after consultation with him, or require that specific contracts be terminated or performed.

The Sachwalter must take various protective measures, such as making an inventory of the entire assets of the debtor corporation and estimating their individual value (art 299 SchKG).

As mentioned above he issues a notice to creditors, convenes a meeting of creditors and procures a declaration from the debtor corporation on all claims filed.

The Sachwalter also has a liaison role between the meeting of creditors and the public composition office. In that he submits an opinion to the latter about the assets and about the composition achieved (art 304 SchKG).

The Sachwalter is required to keep minutes of his actions and decisions, and both the creditors and the debtor have access to such minutes.

By contrast to the bankruptcy office, the Sachwalter's liability for his actions and omissions is not founded in the SchKG. Rather he is liable under the general rules of the OR (arts 41 *et seq* OR).

Management of the insolvent corporation

As can be seen from the above description of the limited competence of the Sachwalter, the actual management of the corporation rests with the debtor.

The directors are thus authorised to continue to manage the corporation, albeit under the supervision of the Sachwalter. Legal acts undertaken by the corporation against the instructions of the Sachwalter are not invalid. However, the Sachwalter is obliged to report such breach of instructions to the public composition office which may revoke the moratorium granted in the permission procedure (art 298 para 2 SchKG).

The purpose of the moratorium is to ensure continuity in the debtor corporation's business operations and to enable it to "recover" without being subject to debt collection or other action from the creditors. The economic survival of the corporation is thereby ensured, for the time being at least. This entrepreneurial freedom of action is not unlimited, however. The right of disposal over the assets is limited by statute in so far as it requires a consistent satisfaction of the creditors despite the preservation of commercial values.

A variety of transactions is thus removed entirely from the competence of the management and, if they are nonetheless entered into, they are void. Such transactions include encumbering real property, pledging assets, granting guarantees and all gratuitous dispositions such as gifts. If the management infringes against this prohibition the public composition office may revoke the moratorium (art 298 paras 1 and 2 SchKG).

In general, management must act in the interests of the creditors as well as in the interests of a continued existence of the corporation. This means that debts may not be paid or paid in full unless the same have to be satisfied pursuant to the composition anyway.

Legal acts or transactions which only marginally affect the assets or obligations of the debtor may be undertaken as normal. Thus, for instance, purchase contracts for the sale of products or contracts for the performance of works may be performed and payments agreed therein may be made. It would however be unreasonable to enter into long-term commitments, leasing agreements, co-operation agreements, and so on.

Activities or transactions which are in the nature of a liquidation, such as the sale of movable assets, are inadmissible, as the very purpose of the composition is to secure the existence and continued operations of the corporation.

Assets which have been distrained prior to the publication of the moratorium may not be freely disposed of by the owner. The distraint only becomes void upon confirmation (art 312 SchKG).

Position of officers and shareholders/owners

Executive directors (the management) remain in office even after permission has been granted in the preliminary procedure. The Sachwalter is not empowered to dismiss directors or replace the management. Thus, the insolvent corporation may itself decide on the constitution and competence of its "crisis-management".

Depending on the size of the corporation, it may in practice be necessary for management to form a committee which stays in close contact with the Sachwalter. This is the most effective way of ensuring that a composition can be reached and, finally, the corporation reorganised.

The shareholders or owners of the corporation have no special legal status in composition proceedings and they retain their rights. In principle, a shareholder may sell his shares but, of course, in such circumstances it may be difficult to find a buyer.

Termination

Composition proceedings end when the confirmation of the composition by the public composition office acquires the force of law. All influence of the Sachwalter and of the public composition office terminates upon such confirmation, except if the composition itself determines the way in which it is to be executed by the Sachwalter.

The execution of the composition is not regulated by statute. In practice, however, the composition authorities have some influence over the execution. Very often the Sachwalter is given the function of executory authority.

Stay of bankruptcy

Purpose and effect

The stay of bankruptcy ("postponement" is the term used by art 725a OR) is another means whereby a debtor corporation may, under certain circumstances, avoid an adjudication of bankruptcy, or more precisely, whereby the court will postpone an adjudication of bankruptcy.

In contrast to the moratorium in connection with a composition proceeding, which may be obtained by all enterprises irrespective of their legal form, the stay of bankruptcy is only available to corporations (joint-stock companies, limited liability companies and co-operative societies). Accordingly, the stay of bankruptcy is not regulated in the SchKG but in the third chapter of the OR which deals with the various forms of companies. This paragraph only considers the postponement of bankruptcy in connection with a joint-stock company, *i.e.* the rules set out in articles 725 and 725a OR.

Article 725 OR provides that, if the last annual balance sheet of the company shows that half of the share capital and the legal reserves are no longer covered by the assets of the joint stock company, the board of directors shall without delay call an extraordinary meeting of shareholders (arts 698 *et seq*) and propose a financial reorganisation (art 725 para 1 OR).

If there are reasons for believing that the company is in imminent danger of insolvency ("overindebtedness" is the term used by art 725 OR), an interim balance sheet must be prepared and submitted to the auditors for examination. The Swiss definition of solvency is based on a balance sheet test *i.e.* a company is insolvent if its assets do not exceed its liabilities based both on a going concern basis and on a liquidation basis. Thus, if the company's interim balance sheet shows that it is insolvent, based on an appraisal of its assets under both standards, the board of directors shall notify the court unless some creditors can be persuaded to subordinate their claims to the extent of any shortfall (art 725 para 2 OR).

If it is obvious that the liabilities of the company exceed its assets, and if the board of directors fails to report this fact to the court, the auditors of the company must notify the court instead (art 729b Abs 2 OR). If the corporation is already in voluntary liquidation, it is the liquidator who must give notice of the insolvency to the court (art 743 para 2 OR).

After having been notified that the company is insolvent, the court has to adjudicate bankruptcy unless the board of directors or a creditor (but not the shareholders) moves for a postponement. The court cannot stay bankruptcy of its own volition.

The rationale behind this provision is to enable liquidation to commence at a time when there are still sufficient assets to satisfy the creditors. However, very often the ensuing adjudication of bankruptcy is not the best outcome for the company as it will adversely affect the value of its assets. To avoid this, it is, as explained above, possible to petition for the postponement of bankruptcy under article 725a OR.

A successful reorganisation is thus likely to be in the best interests of both the debtor corporation, the creditors and third parties. A stay of bankruptcy enables a corporation which is insolvent but still capable of reorganisation to be restructured and to continue operations. The court has merely a supervisory role in this procedure. It may only grant a stay for as long as there is a prospect of reorganisation producing a better return to creditors. The entire reorganisation procedure is primarily the responsibility of the debtor corporation.

The only immediate result of a stay of bankruptcy for the debtor corporation is that it may, during a limited period of time, be protected from action by its creditors so that it has time to try to achieve a financial recovery.

During the stay of bankruptcy, the corporation must try to achieve financial rehabilitation or reorganisation. If the corporation concludes that a composition (see p681 *supra*) would represent the best means of reorganisation, it may also, during the stay of bankruptcy, file an application for a moratorium with the public composition office and seek to achieve a composition. If a moratorium is granted, the stay of bankruptcy ceases to be of effect. Nonetheless, under certain circumstances it is possible that the public composition office might allow the stay to remain in effect even after a composition has been achieved.

Pre-application considerations

The court may appoint a Sachwalter (administrator) either to supervise the management or actually to take over the management of the debtor corporation.

The court determines the Sachwalter's fees which may be calculated in accordance with the fee schedule of the SchKG even though that statute is not directly applicable. The fees are for the account of the debtor company. Here, too, the Sachwalter will usually negotiate his fees with the court and require some form of security before taking up office. The court can order the company to advance the costs.

Procedure

The procedure for a stay of bankruptcy is not strictly divided into separate stages and is provided for in only one article of the OR. However, it is possible to divide the procedure broadly as follows:

1. Stays of bankruptcy proceedings are either instituted by the debtor corporation or, if the board of directors fails to do so, by the creditors of the company (art 725a OR). The auditors of the company have no standing to move for a postponement of bankruptcy.
2. On the basis of the business records and books deposited with it, the court will examine whether the debtor corporation is in fact insolvent.
3. If the court finds that the corporation is insolvent (*i.e.* its assets do not exceed its liabilities based both on a going concern basis and on a liquidation basis), it must in principle declare the corporation bankrupt. This consequence can – as already mentioned – be avoided by filing an application for a stay of bankruptcy. Both creditors and directors are entitled to file such an application (art 725a para 1 OR).
4. The court may grant the stay if it considers that there is a likelihood of the corporation successfully reorganising its finances. There must be a high degree of probability that the creditors will be paid a higher proportion of their claims as a result of the stay, or at least that they will not be in a worse position than if the corporation were adjudged bankrupt immediately. The court has considerable discretion in determining whether or not to grant a stay. Above all, it will take into account the interests of the creditors.
5. If the court gives its permission for the stay, it will grant the debtor corpora-

tion a moratorium for such period as it deems fit. The stay of bankruptcy (postponement) granted by the judge according to article 725a OR need only be published if this is necessary for the protection of third parties (art 725a OR).

6. The court has to order the appropriate provisional measures to safeguard the value of the assets at the same time as it grants permission for a stay. In particular, it may appoint a Sachwalter to supervise the commercial operations or actually to take over the management of the corporation. The court will have to define the duties of the appointed Sachwalter. Finally, the court can either deprive the board of directors of its power to act for the company, or make the resolutions of the board subject to the approval of the Sachwalter (art 725a paras 1 and 2 OR).

Both the corporation and the creditors may appeal against all decisions of the court. The time limit for appeal is ten days from the date of notification or publication.

If the court rejects the application for a stay, it must at the same time adjudge the corporation bankrupt.

Creditors' involvement and position

While the creditors are entitled to file an application for a stay of bankruptcy and to appeal against the decisions of the court, they do not participate in the decision-making process in relation to any stay of bankruptcy proceedings. If necessary, the court could take its decisions, including those concerning protective measures, without hearing the creditors.

Powers and duties of the Sachwalter

If, at the time of granting a stay of bankruptcy, the court also appoints a Sachwalter, then the court itself will also have to determine the latter's powers and duties.

It is therefore possible to appoint a Sachwalter to supervise the management of the debtor corporation, with perhaps certain transactions being subject to his approval. However, it may well be that he is entrusted with the entire management of the corporation.

If the court appoints the Sachwalter in a management role, he does not actually replace the board of directors or other officers of the company. Rather he limits their powers to the extent specified by the court. The result may in practice be that the board of directors is left without any powers. It is, furthermore, possible for the court or the Sachwalter to exclude specific persons from the management or the administration of the corporation, or to appoint new persons to those functions.

Management of the insolvent corporation by the Sachwalter; supervision by the court

There is no statutory provision as a result of which specific transactions undertaken by the debtor during a stay of bankruptcy are void. Thus, even the sale and mortgaging of real property are permitted in principle, unless they are specifically prohibited by the court or the approval of the Sachwalter is required but not obtained.

As in the case of the moratorium, however, the Sachwalter will always ensure that the corporation is managed in such a way that the interests of the creditors are respected while at the same time the continued existence and operations of the corporation are secured.

The Sachwalter is responsible only to the court which appointed him. Both the creditors and the corporation may challenge the decisions of the Sachwalter to that court.

Position of officers and shareholders/owners

The extent of the powers and duties of the Sachwalter therefore determines the limits placed on the power of the board of directors and managing director of the debtor corporation. If the court appoints the Sachwalter in a supervisory role, with or without an approval requirement for certain transactions, the board of directors and managing director remain in office. Prior to the institution of stay of bankruptcy proceedings the shareholders or partners must be informed about the financial situation of the corporation in an extraordinary general meeting if the latest annual balance sheet shows that at least half of the issued capital is no longer covered (for joint-stock companies see art 725 para 1 OR).

In all other respects the legal position of the shareholders is unchanged by a stay of bankruptcy, unless the court orders the contrary for the protection of the assets or third parties (art 725a).

Termination

The stay of bankruptcy proceedings will end differently depending on the effect which the stay has on the corporation and the economic situation:

- If the corporation is able to be financially reorganised during the stay, the court will order the precautionary measures to be terminated and will confirm the reorganisation in a declaratory decree.

- It is conceivable that the debtor corporation might be granted a moratorium by the public composition office during the stay of bankruptcy proceedings, in which case the stay would usually cease to be of effect and proceedings would be terminated (see p688 *supra*).

- The court may revoke the stay of bankruptcy and at the same time adjudge the corporation bankrupt if, for instance, it becomes apparent that a reorganisation will not be possible, or if an application for a moratorium is denied (see p684 *supra*.) Adjudication of bankruptcy may also be declared if directors enter into transactions against the instructions of the Sachwalter or the orders of the court.

4. Termination of the corporation: bankruptcy and composition with assignments of assets

We have shown above that attempts to save the corporation may be made even at the last moment. However, often a corporation which is in a financial crisis cannot be saved, with the result that it must be closed down and its workforce laid off.

Usually, though, an insolvent corporation which is no longer capable of reorganisation becomes bankrupt. The bankruptcy procedure is radical in nature and is thus often destructive of the value of assets. Parallel to that process the debtor has the possibility of a "private" bankruptcy, *i.e.* the composition with assignment of assets (liquidation composition).

In the following pages we describe the most important procedures for the termination of a corporation;

- bankruptcy;
- composition with assignment of assets.

Bankruptcy

Purpose and effect

The overall aim of the bankruptcy procedure is to realise all the assets of the corporation in order to satisfy the claims of the creditors out of the proceeds.

Thus, for the insolvent corporation, the bankruptcy procedure means the end of its commercial activities and the shattering of the value of its assets. However, the procedural rules leave some possibilities open for the corporation to be saved:

- The bankruptcy court may revoke the bankruptcy (art 195 SchKG) and put the corporation back in control of its assets if either all the creditors withdraw their bankruptcy petitions or if a composition is achieved (see p682 *supra* on composition).
- Within the framework of liquidation by the bankruptcy office, the insolvent corporation may be preserved and sold either as a whole or in part, in which case it will survive and continue operations.

The latter possibility is rare in practice and will not be discussed further here.

Thus, in the following discussion we assume that the bankruptcy follows its usual course, resulting in the termination of the corporation.

Pre-application considerations

After the corporation has been adjudicated bankrupt by the bankruptcy court, the public Konkursverwalter (bankruptcy office) is for the time being the sole institution to be in contact with the insolvent corporation (arts 221 *et seq* SchKG). Ten days after the date of publication of the bankruptcy a meeting of creditors is convened which may decide whether to replace the bankruptcy office with a private Konkursverwalter (art 237 para 2 SchKG). A private Konkursverwalter would be especially suitable in the case of large corporation, because qualified private persons will often have greater specialist knowledge than the bankruptcy office. Usually lawyers, auditors or auditing companies will be appointed as a private Konkursverwalter. The private Konkursverwalter is to a large extent subject to the same statutory rules (with respect to rights, duties and liabilities) as the public bankruptcy office (art 241 SchKG).

The creditors are likely to bear in mind the high costs of a private Konkursverwalter. These must be paid from the assets of the bankrupt corporation and some form of security will normally be required.

Procedure

In this section we distinguish between:

- the institution of proceedings, including the bankruptcy debt collection procedure up to the adjudication of bankruptcy; and
- the actual bankruptcy proceedings which continue through to the termination of the bankruptcy.

Institution of proceedings

A bankruptcy order may only be made as the result of a judgment of the bankruptcy court. Specific circumstances determined by statute must prevail before there can be an adjudication of bankruptcy, *i.e.* there must be a ground for declaration of bankruptcy.

In general, the SchKG distinguishes between bankruptcy proceedings and ordinary debt collection proceedings. A debtor in bankruptcy may be any debtor registered in the commercial register with, *inter alia*, the following defined status: a businessman with a registered business firm, partners of a partnership, the different forms of partnership, the limited liability company, the joint stock company, the co-operative society, a club, and so on (art 39 SchKG). There are two routes that lead to bankruptcy. One is by executing the ordinary debt collection bankruptcy proceedings, initiated by a creditor, and the other is upon direct application by either the debtor or, under certain circumstances, a creditor.

Procedural grounds

Once the creditor has terminated the debt collection bankruptcy proceedings, he may file a bankruptcy petition with the bankruptcy court. As mentioned above, this form of debt collection may only be instituted against debtors who are capable of being adjudicated bankrupt (art 39 SchKG).

Bankruptcy debt collection is only one form of debt collection proceeding. As in the case of the other forms, this procedure is instituted by service of a payment order ("Zahlungsbefehl") on the debtor. This debt collection procedure is a peculiarity of Swiss law.

If the debtor opposes the payment order the creditor may defeat (set aside) the opposition if he can show to the court a valid legal title such as a court judgment, settlement agreement or contract in his favour and if the court upholds it (see arts 64 – 87 SchKG on the procedure).

If the creditor succeeds with his claim thus far, there are two possible further courses of action, depending on whether the claim is founded on a bill of exchange or a cheque or upon some other cause of action.

If the claim is not founded on a bill of exchange or a cheque, the further collection proceedings are divided into three phases:

- bankruptcy warning
- drawing up of a register of goods (optional)
- adjudication of bankruptcy.

The creditor may request the public debt collection office to issue a bankruptcy warning (art 159 SchKG). The purposes of the bankruptcy warning are to establish whether the debtor has the proper capacity for a bankruptcy debt collection, whether he is subject to Swiss debt collection jurisdiction generally and to establish which court has jurisdiction over him.

In the bankruptcy warning the debtor is also notified that he is entitled to propose a composition by filing an application for a moratorium with the public composition office (art 160 para 2 SchKG).

The drawing up of a register of goods is optional and is merely a provisional protective measure for the benefit of creditors (arts 162-165 SchKG). The register takes the same form as an official inventory of debtor's assets. It serves to establish which items might constitute assets in bankruptcy. The register is thus a kind of preliminary bankruptcy inventory and, in any later adjudication of bankruptcy it forms the basis of the bankruptcy inventory. For this reason the register is drawn up by order of the competent bankruptcy court, albeit upon application from the creditors.

The adjudication of bankruptcy marks the conclusion of the bankruptcy debt collection proceedings and results in bankruptcy, *i.e.* the general compulsory execution with all its "civil" and "procedural law" consequences.

A bankruptcy petition must be filed with the bankruptcy court by the creditor upon whose application the bankruptcy warning was issued.

Bankruptcy adjudication proceedings are court proceedings, during which both the creditors and the debtor are heard although neither party is obliged to appear before the court (art 171 SchKG).

The court's decision is communicated to the parties together with an instruction as to their rights of appeal. The decision may be appealed against to the higher cantonal court (art 174 SchKG). However, the right of appeal is only available to those creditors who actually participated in the proceedings.

The bankruptcy court may accept, reject or suspend the bankruptcy petition. A suspension would be appropriate mainly if the debtor shows that he has filed an application for a moratorium (art 173a SchKG).

A bill of exchange or cheque collection is a specific form of bankruptcy collection for claims which are founded on bills of exchange or cheques. The procedure is notable for its speed, which is appropriate considering the negotiability of these instruments.

We do not propose here to describe the particularities of this procedure further. By way of comparison to the ordinary bankruptcy collection, the following characteristics should be mentioned: shorter time limits, no bankruptcy warning, and no examination of the bankruptcy petition in a higher court (see arts 177-189 SchKG for further details).

Substantive grounds

If proceedings have not been instituted as described above with a bankruptcy debt collection, a debtor may only be adjudicated bankrupt in exceptional circumstances. There must be a very specific set of circumstances as determined by statute – a so-called substantive ground of bankruptcy. Such grounds are normally specific financial situations or specific actions of the debtor as a result of which the full satisfaction of the creditors appears doubtful or endangered. Under such circumstances even debtors who are not formally subject to bankruptcy, *i.e.* who are not registered in the register of commerce, may be adjudicated bankrupt. The justification for this is that in such cases the creditors must have the possibility of obtaining compulsory execution without delay.

The substantive grounds for bankruptcy may be distinguished as follows:

- a bankruptcy order may be obtained upon direct application (without a prior bankruptcy debt collection proceeding) upon either a creditor's or a debtor's petition (art 190 SchKG);

- against any debtor whose whereabouts are unknown or who has absconded in order to avoid his obligations;

- against any debtor who has acted or attempted to act fraudulently to the detriment of his creditors (or who during a collection resulting in distraint has failed to disclose assets or parts of his property);

- against a debtor who fulfils the legal criteria for bankruptcy debt collection proceedings (*i.e.* who is registered in the register of commerce) and who has ceased making payments;

- against a debtor in respect of whom a moratorium has been revoked or approval for a composition has been refused;

- against the Swiss assets of a debtor who is in foreign bankruptcy upon recognition of the foreign bankruptcy decree in Switzerland (see p719 *infra*).

- The debtor himself (regardless of whether he is capable of being adjudicated bankrupt according to art 39 SchKG) may file a petition for voluntary bankruptcy (art 191 SchKG). If the debtor is a corporation, upon being notified by the board of directors the judge adjudicates the bankruptcy in the case of overindebtedness (art 192 SchKG).

The SchKG in articles 190-192 lists conclusively the various possible substantive grounds of bankruptcy.

Bankruptcy procedure
Once the Konkursverwalter has drawn up an inventory of the assets, then depending on the values found, the further proceedings will take one of the following forms:

- suspension of bankruptcy
- summary bankruptcy procedure
- ordinary bankruptcy procedure

A suspension of bankruptcy will occur if the Konkursverwalter is not able to discover assets of the debtor which are capable of being realised. After notification to the creditors, the bankruptcy procedure will then be closed, unless a creditor posts a bond for the costs of the procedure (art 230 SchKG).

If it appears that the assets will be insufficient to cover the costs of an ordinary bankruptcy procedure the public bankruptcy office must follow the summary bankruptcy procedure (art 231 para 3 SchKG). In such event it will publish a creditors' call, realise the assets and distribute the proceeds amongst the creditors without a creditors' committee being formed or a creditors' meeting being held.

Any creditor may make a payment into court and request an ordinary bankruptcy procedure. Further, the ordinary bankruptcy procedure will always be followed if the other two forms of procedure are not compulsory under the circumstances.

Both ordinary bankruptcy procedure and the summary bankruptcy procedure may be sub-divided into the following stages:

- ascertainment of the assets in bankruptcy;
- administration of the assets in bankruptcy and ascertainment of creditors' claims;
- realisation of assets in bankruptcy and distribution of proceeds;
- termination of bankruptcy procedure.

Ascertainment of the assets in bankruptcy
Upon its being adjudicated bankrupt, the entire assets of the insolvent corpora-

tion come under the sequestration of the bankruptcy court. Thus, the corporation ceases to have any right of disposal over its assets (art 204 SchKG).

In order to be able to ascertain the assets in bankruptcy, the Konkursverwalter must draw up an inventory and secure all assets of the insolvent corporation (art 221 SchKG). If the corporation is still active, the Konkursverwalter will terminate all the corporation's operations unless it appears preferable to perform certain contracts in order to avoid claims for damages from the contract counterparties.

The Konkursverwalter keeps in safe custody the assets of the corporation, in particular cash in banks, marketable securities and so on and also the business records and books.

Administration of the assets in bankruptcy and ascertainment of creditors' claims

The Konkursverwalter is responsible for the administration of the assets in bankruptcy. However, the creditors have certain rights in the decision-making process which they exercise through the meeting of creditors and, in some cases, through a creditors' committee. These institutions are described further on pages 700-701 below.

The Konkursverwalter, whether represented by the public bankruptcy office (*i.e.* civil servants) or a private Konkursverwalter (usually a lawyer or an auditor) appointed at the first meeting of creditors, is a public institution subject to administrative control and supervision by the state. It is the executive organ in bankruptcy proceedings, responsible for the implementation of the bankruptcy in detail.

The Konkursverwalter conducts all business relating to the assets in bankruptcy and represents the assets before the court (art 240 SchKG). The Konkursverwalter must implement any administrative measures which may be decided by the meeting of creditors.

The Konkursverwalter is authorised to collect undisputed claims (receivables) that are due (art 243 s1 SchKG) and to sell all assets that have a market price or that are quoted on an exchange (art 243 s2 SchKG). If there are receivables which can be collected only with difficulty (for example, disputed claims such as liability claims against officers, directors or auditors of a corporation in bankruptcy) the Konkursverwalter may pursue these claims on behalf of the bankruptcy estate or, with the consent of the creditors, assign them to a creditor (art 260 SchKG) or even sell them to third parties. If there is a risk of a decrease in the value of specific assets, the Konkursverwalter may carry out emergency sales. The same applies if the maintenance of specific assets is likely to be unduly costly. (art 243 s2 SchKG). In principle, however, the Konkursverwalter is obliged to preserve the assets in anticipation of the liquidation itself to avoid any loss.

During this stage of the procedure the creditors' claims are ascertained and listed in the "collocation plan" (list of claims) by order of ranking in accordance with artcle 219 SchKG, which provides for five classes of creditors for the distribution of the net proceeds of the liquidation (see p685-686 above for the relevance of these classes to a corporation).

All creditors with claims against the bankrupt may participate in the bankruptcy proceedings. There are no restrictions as to territory or nationality. All claims become due on the date of the adjudication of bankruptcy and interest ceases to accrue from such date except for claims secured by a mortgage (arts 208 and 209 SchKG).

Each claim must be presented to the debtor prior to being listed in the collocation plan. However, the Konkursverwalter is not bound by the debtor's declaration as to whether he accepts the claim. Rather, he may decide at his own discretion whether to accept or reject each claim (art 245 SchKG).

The collocation plan provides information about how the individual claims are to be treated in the proceedings as regards their substance, amount and ranking. It indicates whether the Konkursverwalter has accepted or rejected the claim. Each creditor may challenge the collocation plan both in respect of his own claim and in respect of the claim of any other creditor.

Realisation of assets in bankruptcy and distribution of proceeds

Except for emergency sales effected on instruction from the meeting of creditors or by the Konkursverwalter himself (arts 238 and 243 SchKG), the assets may only be realised once a second meeting of creditors has been held at which the method of realisation of assets is determined.

The actual realisation of assets is the responsibility of the Konkursverwalter.

Realisation can be either by way of public auction or, if the second meeting of creditors so decides, by sale (art 256 SchKG). Receivables may be realised by assignment either to creditors (art 260 SchKG) or to third parties.

Just as the realisation of assets is the responsibility of the Konkursverwalter, so too is the distribution of the proceeds.

Obligations properly incurred in respect of the administration of the bankruptcy (including, in particular, the costs for the proceedings) must be satisfied first out of the proceeds of realisation (art 262 SchKG). The remainder represents the net proceeds available for distribution to the creditors. The distribution list is based on the collocation plan in the latter's final legally binding form, *i.e.* once any amendments have been made following challenges by the creditors.

Secured creditors have a preferential right to be paid out of the proceeds of the collateral which has been realised. To the extent their claims exceed the amount realised, secured creditors participate as unsecured creditors.

The distribution list and the final statement of account are available for inspection at the public bankruptcy office for ten days (arts 261, 263 SchKG).

Each creditor receives a certificate of loss in respect of the unsatisfied amount, if any, of his claim. This is an official certification of the loss incurred by the creditor during the compulsory distraint procedure.

The certificate of loss provides certain formal and procedural advantages which will not be discussed further here (see art 265 SchKG).

Termination of bankruptcy proceedings

All bankruptcy proceedings, whether ordinary or summary, must be formally declared terminated in a judgment of the bankruptcy court. This "final declaration" is based on a final report on the liquidation of the debtor corporation which is submitted to the court by the Konkursverwalter after distribution of the proceeds of realisation. The termination of the bankruptcy proceedings is published and notified to all registers of commerce (art 268 SchKG).

Creditors' involvement and position

The creditors play a decisive role in bankruptcy proceedings, each having the right to challenge the decisions and orders of the Konkursverwalter before the supervisory authority. We have already mentioned that each creditor has the right to challenge the extent to which his claim or the claims of other creditors have been recognised in the "collocation plan".

The creditors also exercise their rights collectively through various bodies, the most important of these being the meeting of creditors. The first meeting of creditors must be held not later than ten days after publication of the bankruptcy by the Konkursverwalter. This meeting may be attended by anyone whom the debtors' business records show to be a creditor or who otherwise identifies himself as a creditor a co-debtor, surety or guarantor.

For there to be a quorum, at least a quarter of all known creditors must be present personally or by proxy. If fewer than five persons are present, they must represent at least one half of the known creditors (art 235 para 3 SchKG). One person may represent other creditors by power of attorney.

Decisions are taken by simple majority vote. In practice, decisions by circular are admissible. Each creditor has one vote irrespective of the number of claims he has filed and their aggregate amount.

The meeting of creditors has, *inter alia*, the following functions (arts 237, 238 SchKG):

- to receive the report of the Konkursverwalter on the drawing up of the inventory;
- to take organisational decisions (such as the appointment of a private Konkursverwalter if deemed appropriate);
- to decide on urgent administrative measures such as emergency sales, or whether to continue or terminate the corporation's operations or court proceedings.

If during this stage of the proceedings the debtor proposes a composition, as he is entitled to do (art 238 para 2 SchKG), the first meeting of creditors may discontinue the realisation of assets.

All decisions of the first meeting of creditors may be challenged before the supervisory authority by means of administrative complaint. The statute specifically provides this right to the creditors, but in practice it is also available to the debtor and third parties.

The second meeting of creditors is summoned after the Konkursverwalter has examined the claims and drawn up the collocation plan. Only those creditors whose claims have been accepted as a whole or in part by the Konkursverwalter may participate. The second meeting of creditors has the responsibility of deciding all other matters which the Konkursverwalter cannot decide alone. These may include the sale of assets otherwise than by public auction and the assignment of receivables to creditors. If the debtor has proposed a composition it is the second meeting of creditors which decides its acceptance or rejection (art 253 SchKG).

If the Konkursverwalter deems it necessary or if required by the majority of the creditors, further meetings of the creditors may be summoned (art 255 SchKG).

In conclusion, therefore, it may be said that the meeting of creditors has decision-making powers in respect of important matters. If it is unable to achieve a quorum the Konkursverwalter is authorised as a matter of principle to take decisions concerning the management of the corporation and the administration of the assets in bankruptcy in its stead.

The creditors' committee is an optional institution which the meeting of creditors may at its discretion appoint to act with the Konkursverwalter. It derives its competence in part from the meeting of creditors and in part from the Konkursverwalter. In general the creditors' committee may be described as a controlling body with decision-making competence for certain important issues (see art 237 para 3 SchKG).

Powers and duties of the Konkursverwalter

The individual powers and duties and particularly the areas of responsibility of the Konkursverwalter have already been described in detail (see p698-700 *supra*).

Management by the Konkursverwalter and supervision by the supervisory authority

The Konkursverwalter is the body which actually manages the bankrupt corporation. The directors, managing directors, and management have a subordinated role.

The Konkursverwalter must first and foremost endeavour to preserve the assets. He can make minor investments if necessary to increase the value of the assets or to reduce the liabilities, particularly liabilities which consist of claims for damages.

The Konkursverwalter may in some cases be likened to an "entrepreneur" if at the time of the adjudication of bankruptcy the corporation is still active and its activities are continued for the time being. If so, the business records and books of the debtor corporation continue to be kept, but now for the account of the "bankruptcy estate" (which has a certain legal status of a separate entity). The Konkursverwalter will have to decide whether or not to fulfil existing contracts.

However, he may also enter into new contracts, provided these are directly or indirectly in the interests of a temporary continuation of the corporation's operations.

The creditors and the debtor may appeal against decisions and omissions of the Konkursverwalter to the supervisory authority which is in most cantons the district court. Additional functions of the supervisory authority with regard to the management of the Konkursverwalter are described on pages 716-717 below.

Position of officers and shareholders/owners

The officers and directors, as representatives of the debtor corporation, are obliged under penalty (fine or imprisonment for up to 14 days) to make themselves available to the Konkursverwalter (art 229 para 1 SchKG) and are under a general obligation to provide information. This is to enable the Konkursverwalter to obtain the necessary information about the assets, but also about the internal situation within the corporation. The Konkursverwalter is authorised to assign certain tasks, particularly the interim management of the corporation, to the officers and directors. However, this would only be appropriate in rare cases; for instance if there is a real prospect that all or part of the corporation can be sold. It is possible for the Konkursverwalter to request securities for the proper performance of any tasks so assigned, but these may prove difficult for the bankrupt corporation to provide.

The debtor corporation may challenge decisions of the Konkursverwalter before the supervisory authority, including, for example, the decision to terminate the corporation's operations.

The owners of the corporation, particularly shareholders, have no special legal status during the bankruptcy proceedings. Indeed, the Konkursverwalter may process any claims for damages which the shareholders may have against the debtor corporation. If the Konkursverwalter declines to do so, these claims may be assigned to the shareholders under the conditions described below.

If the bankruptcy proceedings are pursued to the end, the corporation is removed from the register of commerce. At that time at the very latest, its shares will become worthless.

Termination

Bankruptcy proceedings can be terminated in many different ways. In principle they end with a judgment of the bankruptcy court after all the assets have been realised and the proceeds distributed to the creditors. If there are no assets, the bankruptcy proceedings will end at this early stage (see p697 *supra*).

If during the bankruptcy proceedings the debtor corporation succeeds in achieving a composition or in persuading the creditors to withdraw their claims, the proceedings will end with the revocation of the bankruptcy by the bankruptcy court (art 195 SchKG).

Composition with assignment of assets ("liquidation composition")

On pages 681-682 above we described the various possible types of composition, however we will discuss below only the composition with assignment of assets (or "liquidation composition").

Purpose and effect

As already mentioned, the debtor corporation effectively liquidates itself in that it places all its assets at the disposal of its creditors. The debtor corporation is thereby released from its debts. By way of contrast to bankruptcy proceedings this release is full and final, as no certificates of loss are issued.

On confirmation of the composition the right of disposal over the assets passes to the creditors, or more precisely to the liquidators, as they actually exercise the right of disposal (art 316a SchKG). From this point on, the name of the corporation must include the words "in liquidation by composition" (art 316d para 2 SchKG).

Pre-application considerations

The public composition office appoints a Sachwalter for the period up to the confirmation of the composition. This has been discussed above (see p684).

The details of the composition with assignment of assets as compared to the ordinary composition procedure become apparent only upon execution. Here the statute provides for special liquidators who are charged with the entire implementation of the liquidation in accordance with the terms of the composition. The statute merely provides that creditors may also be appointed as liquidators, but without going into further detail (art 316a para 1 SchKG). Third parties, particularly lawyers and auditing companies, may thus also be appointed. The liquidators must be named in the composition. Normally, therefore, their fee will have been agreed in advance and will be paid first as an obligation properly incurred in respect of the administration of the assets in liquidation.

Procedure

The procedure up to the confirmation of the composition by the public composition office is analogous to the ordinary composition procedure.

The composition itself determines the procedure to be followed for the execution of the composition, except in so far as this is specifically provided for by the statute (arts 316a-316t SchKG). If the facts of the case so permit, provisions of the law governing bankruptcy may be applied by analogy to the composition with assignment of assets as the two are similar in many respects (BGE 105 III 31).

To begin with, a collocation plan is drawn up on the basis of the business records and books of the debtor and the claims filed by the creditors in the preceding moratorium procedure or bankruptcy procedure as the case may be (art 316g SchKG)..

The advantages of this form of composition become apparent during realisation of the assets. Here, the liquidators, with the consent of the creditors' committee, are largely free to determine the method and timing of the realisation. In particular, it is possible to transfer all or part of the assigned assets to a newly created company (art 316h SchKG).

As in bankruptcy proceedings the liquidators may also assign receivables to third parties or to creditors (art 316l SchKG).

Distribution and the final statement of account broadly follow the law governing bankruptcy.

Creditors' involvement and position

Upon confirmation of the composition the entire assets are assigned to the creditors and the Sachwalter's appointment is terminated. Thus the creditors, though represented by the liquidators, have sole decision-making competence for the further proceedings.

In principle, the organisational structures are determined in the composition itself. First, there is a meeting of creditors which then selects a creditors' committee. The liquidators are under the supervision of the committee.

The decisions of the liquidators and the creditors' committee may be challenged before the public composition office by means of administrative complaint but the debtor only has a right of challenge in respect of measures taken to realise the assets (BGE 102 III 34).

The liquidators and the members of the creditors' committee are liable to the creditors for loss caused by their negligence in the same way as are the state executive authorities (art 316f SchKG).

Powers and duties of the liquidator

The liquidators represent the estate in liquidation before the court (art 316d para 3 SchKG). They have the duty to conduct all transactions and business necessary to preserve and administer the assets in liquidation and conduct all business in connection with the realisation of the assets in liquidation.

The only restrictions on the powers of the liquidators are those specifically provided for by the statute or in the composition.

Management by the liquidator and supervision by creditors

As mentioned above the scope of the liquidators' management functions is in principle limited to the activities necessary for the liquidation of the corporation. The aim is, after all, to secure the highest possible proceeds of realisation for the creditors. However, if the corporation is still active the liquidators may continue its operations or parts thereof so long as this is in the interests of preserving or increasing the value of the assets.

If a new company has been created by the creditors or by third parties, either before or after the confirmation of the composition, the liquidators are responsible for the proper transfer and assignment of the assets to that company. Here, too, all transactions and activities undertaken by the liquidators must seek to achieve the highest possible return to all creditors.

Position of officers and shareholders/owners

After the composition has been confirmed the officers, directors and management will retain their functions only to such extent as the liquidators deem necessary. If a new company has been created, it may be conceivable that it may employ some of the officers, directors or managers to continue the management of the corporation.

Shares and participation rights become practically worthless because the old debtor transfers the assets in liquidation to the liquidators for realisation.

Following liquidation the liquidators must apply for the removal of the corporation from the register of commerce.

Termination

In principle, the proceedings for a composition with assignment of assets are concluded when the confirmation by the public composition office acquires force of law.

However, since the execution of the composition (*i.e.* the liquidation of the assets for the highest possible return) is of such importance, the proceedings actually terminate only when the assets have been realised and the proceeds distributed. After distribution the liquidators draw up a final statement of account which must be made available for inspection (art 3l6p SchKG). After the liquidation procedure is concluded, the debtor corporation must be removed from the register of commerce.

5. Augmenting the assets of the insolvent corporation

Introduction

We have described above the legal options which are open to the Konkursverwalter, the Sachwalter and the liquidator when endeavouring to secure the assets of the debtor corporation.

However, the individual measures taken are not merely intended to preserve, but also to increase the value of the assets of the corporation. If the goal of a particular procedure is to ensure the survival of the insolvent corporation, the Sachwalter may even be obliged to use every effort to maximise the value of the assets. To achieve this, he may conclude new contracts, employ new personnel, and so forth. We have already discussed such measures above (see pp687-688 and 692).

In cases where the operations of the corporation are to be terminated as a consequence of the proceedings, as will often be the case in bankruptcy proceedings, the Konkursverwalter or the liquidator will be obliged to look primarily to preserving the assets. They are unlikely to conclude new contracts or undertake new investments even if the same might serve to augment the assets. Rather, the preservation and realisation of the assets are of paramount importance.

In the following pages we shall discuss two legal institutions by means of which the assets of an insolvent corporation may be augmented. These are:

- action for avoidance (action to set aside or *actio pauliana*)

- personal liability action against officers of the insolvent corporation.

In bankruptcy proceedings, the Konkursverwalter is the only person entitled to bring an action for avoidance (an *actio pauliana* according to arts 285 *et seq* SchKG) or a personal liability action (art 757 OR), he may assign these rights to individual creditors or shareholders (art 757 OR, arts 260 and 285 SchKG). Similarly, in liquidation composition proceedings, only the liquidators are entitled to bring such actions, although they may assign them to creditors or shareholders (art 316s, art 316s SchKG).

Where an action for avoidance or a personal liability action is brought by the Konkursverwalter or the liquidator, any assets or property thereby obtained will go into the overall assets (bankruptcy estate or debtor's estate), and be distributed according to the general order of ranking of claims established under to art 219 SchKG.

Where, on the other hand, these remedies are assigned to individual creditors, any assets or property obtained by them go first towards satisfying their specific claims, with the remainder, if any, going into the overall assets.

Transactions at risk

The action for avoidance already existed under Roman law and is still known today as the *actio pauliana*.

The aim of the action for avoidance is to set aside, for reasons defined by statute, (arts 286 to 288 SchKG) contracts or other legal acts otherwise permitted under "civil law". The action's purpose is the recovery of assets for the benefit of the bankruptcy estate which have been removed from the debtor's estate prior to the adjudication of bankruptcy. The action is a means of augmenting the assets of the bankruptcy estate.

In keeping with its purpose of enabling debt collection, the action for avoidance is purely a "public law" remedy. Nonetheless, it also has indirect consequences in "private law", for instance, with regard to contracts.

Acts detrimental to the bankruptcy estate are only set aside to the extent necessary to reverse the consequential disadvantage suffered by creditors. As against third parties, the legal effect of transactions and transfers with the debtor remains unchanged until successfully challenged by the Konkursverwalter, the liquidator or assignor (usually a creditor) (arts 285, 316l and s316s SchKG). Thus, a third party will retain legal title to any movable or immovable property, or to receivables or to other rights acquired from the debtor until the final conclusion of the action to set aside. If the Konkursverwalter or the liquidator succeeds in an action for avoidance, he merely obtains a claim or the right to realise the property or other asset for the benefit of the bankruptcy estate (see art 291 SchKG).

General prerequisites

The general prerequisites for an action for avoidance are as follows:

- the contested acts must have been performed before an adjudication of bankruptcy, when the debtor corporation still had the right to dispose of its assets. Once the corporation is adjudicated bankrupt, its assets are sequestered and the debtor ceases to be able to dispose legally of title thereto (art 204 SchKG). After an adjudication of bankruptcy and its publication it is thus impossible for the debtor corporation to perform any legally binding acts which might be detrimental to the bankruptcy estate and thus to creditors' interests;

- in liquidation composition proceedings the contested acts must have been performed prior to the granting of a moratorium;

- there must have been an adjudication of bankruptcy, or as the case may be, a moratorium must have been granted. Prior to that there is no need to recover assets that have been alienated;

- the assets must have been alienated within specific time-periods. In order to be actionable, there must be a chronological link between the contested acts and the adjudication of bankruptcy or the granting of a moratorium.

Where a moratorium has been preceded by a stay of bankruptcy (see pp688-689 *supra*), valid legal acts undertaken during the period of the stay, and under certain circumstances even during the preceeding six months, may also be challenged in an action for avoidance (art 316s para 2 SchKG).

The circumstances which may form the subject of an action for avoidance are defined by statute. They are as follows:

Gifts (art 286 SchKG)

Gifts and other gratuitous dispositions which have already been effected by the debtor may be challenged by way of an action for avoidance (art 286 para 1 SchKG). Gifts which have not been fully effected do not require to be challenged in this way, as any promise to make a gift becomes void by application of law once there has been an adjudication of bankruptcy (art 250 para 2 OR). Customary gifts on special occasions, such as weddings, and birthdays, are outside the scope of the action for avoidance (art 286 para 1 SchKG), provided the occasion and the size of the gift are usual in view of the financial status of the donor.

An action for avoidance will also lie against "quasi-gifts", *i.e.* transactions in which the consideration received by the debtor corporation is notably inferior to the value of its own obligations. The action is then for restitution of the difference in value (art 286 para 2(1) SchKG).

Transactions in which the debtor corporation creates for itself or for third parties an annuity or a right to enjoy the asset in the future, or in other words in which it creates a future benefit, are treated in the same manner as gifts. Although such transactions do not strictly speaking constitute gifts, the intention is to prevent the debtor from thereby diminishing its assets to the detriment of the creditors.

The above transfers of property may only be contested, however, if they were performed within a period of six months prior to the adjudication of bankruptcy or the granting of a moratorium. Aside from the gift, this is the only additional fact which the creditors must prove.

The motives of the parties to the contested act are irrelevant in an action for avoidance. Thus, in the case of "quasi-gifts" it is not necessary for there to be an intention to incur a gratuitous obligation. Nor is it necessary that the parties knew or should have known of the disproportion between the obligations incurred and the consideration therefor. If the objective prerequisites of a gift are not fulfilled, one of the other causes of action might apply. However, these are subject to more stringent prerequisites.

Preferential treatment of individual creditors by an insolvent debtor (art 287 SchKG)

The action for avoidance under article 287 SchKG is aimed at legal acts undertaken by a debtor in order to favour specific creditors, where at the time of such acts it is established that the debtor was already insolvent. The preferential treatment will normally consist of security or even a payment to which the creditor is not entitled at all, or not in the manner chosen (at least not at that point in time).

The specific transactions which may be contested by way of an action for avoidance are enumerated in article 287 para 1 SchKG. The list is comprehensive. They are:

- creation of a charge over a tangible asset or a receivable as security for a pre-existing obligation of the debtor, where the debtor was not legally obliged to provide any security (art 287 para 1(1) SchKG). Thus if the debtor is legally obliged to create a charge in favour of a creditor, such charge when created may not be contested by way of an action for avoidance. The same applies to the provision of security by the debtor for a debt owed by a third party. However, in the latter case, if there is a lack of consideration or counter-obligation from the third party, an action for avoidance of a gift will lie in accordance with article 286 SchKG;

- repayment of a pecuniary debt in a non-customary manner, *i.e.* if, instead of making payment in cash or in some other customary mode, the debtor transfers a tangible asset or assigns a receivable in lieu of payment, or assumes a debt owed by the creditor so that the latter may balance his accounts (art 287 para 1 (1) SchKG). Regional or trade custom may be taken into consideration in determining whether a particular mode of payment is "customary". This may also include issuing a bill of exchange;

- payment of a debt which has not yet become due (art 287 para 1 (3) SchKG).

As in the case of an action for avoidance of a gift, the contested act must have taken place during a period of six months prior to the adjudication of bankruptcy or the granting of a moratorium. Furthermore, the corporation must already have been insolvent at the time, *i.e.* its liabilities must have exceeded its assets. The claimant must prove these objective facts.

The creditor who benefited from the contested act has a valid defence if he proves that he had no knowledge of the critical financial condition (insolvency) of the debtor corporation. If that is the case, the presumption to the contrary will be rebutted and the action for avoidance defeated (art 287 para 2 SchKG).

Apparent discrimination against individual creditors (art 288 SchKG)

This form of action for avoidance has the widest scope of application, but is subject to the most stringent requirements and is thus the most difficult to pursue successfully. Any act, whenever undertaken, may be challenged if it was undertaken by the debtor with the apparent intention of discriminating against or creating a preference for individual creditors.

The essential element is the intention on the part of the debtor to discriminate or to create a preference. However, it will suffice if it can be shown that the debtor could or should have known of the prejudicial consequences of the act.

Further, it will even suffice if the debtor was pursuing a different, legitimate goal and in doing so accepted that creditors would suffer damage.

An action for avoidance will, however, only be possible if the discriminatory intention was apparent to the party benefiting from the act. It is not absolutely necessary for the latter to have had actual knowledge of the debtor's intention. Rather, it will suffice if, with the exercise of due diligence, he could or should have ascertained the intention to discriminate, *i.e.* if the consequences were foreseeable to him. The duty of diligence is subject to limitations so as to avoid hampering the normal conduct of business. Nonetheless, good faith alone will not suffice to protect the debtor's contract counter-parties.

The claimant must prove all the constituent elements: the infringement of his rights as creditor, the causative legal act on the part of the debtor, and the fact that the latter was foreseeable to the benefiting party. There are no presumptions operating against the debtor and it need not provide any exonerating proof.

An action for avoidance under article 288 SchKG will normally be brought if the prerequisites for the less onerous challenge procedures under articles 286 and 287 SchKG are not fulfilled. This might be the case if, for instance, too much time has elapsed since the contested act took place. The following are examples of the types of act which might be challenged under article 288 SchKG:

- the assignment of a receivable as a security or collateral which took place prior to the commencement of the six months time limit under article 287 SchKG;

- the sale by the debtor of tangible property to a lender in order that the latter may offset the purchase price against the debt;

- an undertaking by the debtor to provide security after the event where it is foreseeable from the outset that such security will result in a unilateral benefit.

Procedure

As already mentioned, in the case of bankruptcy the right of challenge vests in the bankruptcy estate as represented by the Konkursverwalter (arts 200, 285 SchKG). Thus, only he may appear as claimant. A bankruptcy creditor will only be entitled to bring an action if the claim has been assigned to him in accordance with article 260 SchKG. The same applies in the case of a liquidation composition (arts 316l, 316s SchKG).

The action lies first and foremost against the party with whom the contested legal act was concluded, *i.e.* the contract counter-party of the debtor. However, that party's successors in title, particularly his heirs, may also be sued, regardless of whether or not they acted in good faith. Furthermore, subsequent purchasers of tangible property or subsequent assignees of receivables may be sued provided they acted in bad faith (art 290 SchKG).

The right to challenge transactions of the debtor may not only be exercised by way of an action for avoidance. It may also be raised by the bankruptcy estate as a defence plea in an action by a third party trying to enforce against the bankruptcy estate rights arising in relation to a transaction (a contract or other legal act) with the debtor.

An action for avoidance must be instituted within five years of the contested legal act. After such period the claim becomes time-barred (art 292 SchKG). The action must generally be brought at the place of residence of the defendant.

The proceedings are governed by cantonal law. Federal law merely provides for the free evaluation of the evidence.

Consequences of the judgment

If the action for avoidance is successful, its consequences are restricted to the debt collection process. In other words, the "invalidity" declared by the court in respect of a legal act applies only to the extent necessary for the purposes of debt collection. An action for avoidance provides the bankruptcy estate, or the bankruptcy creditors as the case may be, with two rights:

- the right to require that the property which the debtor had alienated be realised by the competent authorities; and

- the right to obtain satisfaction out of the proceeds.

The consequence is thus to restore the assets which may be subject to debt collection to a level which would have prevailed if the "invalid" legal act had not taken place. However, this only applies to such extent as is necessary to satisfy all the bankruptcy creditors.

If the action for avoidance is successful, the defendant is obliged to return the property to the creditors. Any value which has been removed from the debtor's property must be restored to the assets in bankruptcy and thus made available to the creditors. However, the obligation is only to restore such part of the property as is necessary to satisfy the creditors in the pending proceedings. Nothing is actually returned to the debtor.

Where possible, property must be restored together with all yield or other earnings (such as interest).

In principle, property must be restored in its original form. Restored property goes into the bankruptcy estate. Restitution does not require a re-transfer of ownership to the claimant, nor in the case of land an entry in the land register. The defendant is liable for a decrease in the value of the property if it is caused by him, but not if it is purely coincidental. On the other hand, he does not take the benefit of any coincidental increase in value.

If restitution is impossible because the property has been destroyed or sold to a subsequent purchaser in good faith, the defendant is liable to pay damages according to the general rules governing unjust enrichment.

The obligation to restore property applies only partially to a donee in good faith of a gift. The latter is only bound to restore such part of the property or the resulting enrichment as is still available to him (art 291 para 3 SchKG).

If the action for avoidance is in respect of a bilateral legal transaction, the defendant has the right to demand restitution of the consideration paid, if and to the extent that the debtor is still in possession thereof and enriched thereby. In bankruptcy that consideration will have gone into the bankrupt's estate and it is for the Konkursverwalter to ensure its restitution. The defendant may require the restitution of property transferred to the debtor as consideration in kind. If he is claiming for restitution of an enrichment, then because in bankruptcy this is an obligation owed by the bankruptcy estate, the defendant may offset the claim against his own obligation of restitution towards it. If the property or enrichment is no longer available, the only course of action available to the defendant is to file a claim for damages in the bankruptcy proceedings (art 291 para 1 SchKG).

If the repayment of a debt is successfully challenged and declared void, the debt once again becomes due when the property is restored (art 291 para 2 SchKG). The debt is included in the bankruptcy and listed in the official collocation plan.

Personal liability of officers, directors and auditors – the "personal liability action"

The personal liability action against the officers, directors, auditors and founders

of a company represents another important means by which the assets of an insolvent company may be augmented. The "personal liability" action has taken
on great importance in practice, especially as the majority of bankruptcy proceedings are discontinued for want of sufficient assets. Often the personal liability action against the managing directors, officers and auditors represents the
only or at least the most valuable source of additional assets for the creditors.

Since the members of a partnership (both general partnership and limited
partnership) are in general personally liable, a personal liability action will only
be necessary against the officers, directors and auditors of corporations; *i.e.*
joint-stock corporations, limited liability corporations or co-operative societies
(arts 753, 754, 755, 764 para 2, arts 827, 916 OR).

The following discussion, however, only refers to the respective regulations of
the most important form of company in practice, the joint-stock corporation.

The scope of the personal liability action

The founders of the company, the members of the board of directors and all persons engaged in the management or the liquidation of a joint-stock corporation
as well as the auditors are liable to the company, the company's creditors and
each individual shareholder for the damage caused by any intentional or negligent violation of their duties (arts 753 *et seq* OR). Other persons may incur such
liability depending upon the functions they actually perform, regardless of the
functions they are formally given by the by-laws. In particular, if a person exercises independent powers of administration and representation and participates
in the formation of a joint-stock company as a legal entity, as is normally the case
with "directors", then he is deemed to be considered an officer and is liable as an
officer, even if the by-laws of the company expressly deny him such status.

Thus, independence and freedom of decision-making, or at least the appearance thereof, are the decisive elements in determining which individuals are officers of a company. These elements form the legal basis for treating the actions
of individuals as the expression of intent of the company itself, and form the legal
grounds for their personal liability.

Naturally, there must be an intentional or negligent breach of duty before a
personal liability action may be brought successfully. Generally speaking, the
members of the board of directors and all other persons engaged in the management of the company are expected to carry out their duties with due care and
duly to safeguard the interests of the company (art 717 OR). The exact scope of
the duties of an individual charged with the management or administration of
a company will depend on a variety of factors, such as the status of that individual in the organisational hierarchy of the company or the financial situation of
the company. It is thus impossible to draw up a generally applicable catalogue
of duties. As far as the duties of the board of directors are concerned, they have
to pass resolutions on all matters which by law or by the articles of association
are not allocated to the shareholders in general meeting. Of particular importance are the nontransferable (nondelegable and inalienable) duties of the board

of directors listed on p669 above. The board of directors must also manage the day to day business of the company, in so far as it has not been validly delegated, in whole or in part, to individual directors or to third parties in accordance with the by-laws (arts 698, 716 *et seq* OR).

Whoever lawfully delegates the fulfilment of any of his duties to another person is personally liable for any loss caused by that other person unless he is able to prove that he applied all the necessary care in the selection, instruction and supervision feasible in the circumstances (art 754 para 2 OR).

The auditors of the company, must generally be qualified to fulfil their duties (art 727a OR). Under certain circumstances, they must meet special professional qualifications (for instance, if the company has an outstanding bond issue, its shares are listed on the stock exchange, or if it has a defined size (art 727b OR). Auditors must also be independent from the board of directors and from any shareholder who has a majority interest (art 727c OR). Their most important duties are the express statutory duties of examination and reporting (arts 728 *et seq* OR), and they are under an express statutory duty of confidentiality (art 730 OR).

In general, simple negligence will be sufficient to form the basis of liability, irrespective of whether the action is brought by the company, or by a shareholder or creditor of the company and irrespective of whether the action is brought against a founder, officer, director or auditor (arts 753 *et seq* OR). Founders, officers, directors and/or auditors may be jointly and severally liable, but only to the extent that any loss can be attributed to their intentional or negligent conduct (art 759 OR).

A Sachwalter appointed by the court at the time of granting a stay of bankruptcy under article 725a paragraphs 1 and 2 OR is also subject to personal liability in respect of any breach of duty.

Loss

As a rule, three separate groups of persons may bring an action against the founders, directors, officers and auditors of a company. These are the company itself, the shareholders and the creditors of the company (arts 753 *et seq* OR).

As far as the shareholders and the creditors are concerned, one must distinguish as to whether they have suffered loss directly or whether the loss has been suffered directly by the company and only indirectly by them, *i.e.* as a result of a decrease in the intrinsic value of the company. The procedure for bringing a claim for indirect loss is different from the procedure for bringing a claim for direct loss.

Any creditor or shareholder who suffered direct loss due to a breach of duty by a founder, officer, director or auditor of a company may bring an action on its own behalf against the liable person, as is the case with any other tort action (art 41 OR).

The procedure for bringing an action for indirect loss differs, depending upon whether the company is solvent or has been adjudicated bankrupt. The creditors can only bring an action for indirect loss, if the company has gone into bankruptcy (art 757 para 1 OR).

Direct loss

Shareholders will suffer direct loss if, for example, they are deprived of subscription rights to shares granted by statute or by the articles of association. A person will suffer direct loss if he incurs a loss as a result of acquiring shares in reliance on a balance sheet which was improperly prepared by the board of directors, or in reliance on company publications in which the board made incorrect statements. If, however, a person was already a shareholder or creditor before the board of directors committed the breach of duty, it will usually be impossible for him to prove the loss or causation between the breach of duty and the loss he suffers. Especially in the case of window dressing in financial statements, an existing shareholder will not be able to rely on the fact that the shares of the company were quoted at a higher price on the stock exchange at the time of the breach. This is because, if there had been no breach of the financial reporting requirements, the shares would already have been trading at a lower price and the shareholder would not have been able to avoid damage by selling his shares. Thus there would be a lack of causation. The same applies by analogy to existing creditors: if there had been no breach, loans would already then have been endangered, and creditors would not have been able to avoid loss by terminating them at that time.

Indirect damage

Where the company suffers a direct loss, the shareholders and creditors can suffer indirect loss. This is because their stake in the company will lose some or all of its value or they will receive a reduced dividend or no dividend at all. If the company were liquidated, they would only receive a reduced net distribution value, and might even go empty-handed. The creditors of the company, too, might suffer indirect loss in that their claims are no longer fully covered by the assets of the company.

Pursuing the claim

The plaintiff

If the company has been adjudicated bankrupt, the Konkursverwalter will decide, at its sole discretion, whether or not the responsible founders, directors, officers or auditors are to be held liable or not. Any recovery would fall into the bankruptcy estate. Only if the Konkursverwalter decided not to bring a personal liability action could the individual shareholders and creditors demand that such right be assigned to them (art 260 SchKG, art 757 paras 2, 3 OR). The proceeds of a lawsuit must first be used to satisfy the claims of the suing creditors. Any surplus must thereafter be distributed among the suing shareholders up to the amount of their interest in the company. If the shareholders sue out of bankruptcy, any damages go to the company only (art 756 OR). The remaining recovery must be transferred to the bankruptcy estate (art 757 para 2 OR).

The effect of releases (discharges)
Considering the effect of releases, it is important to take into account resolutions adopted by the general assembly (meeting) of shareholders relieving the responsible persons from liability.

Outside bankruptcy: If the general meeting released (discharges) the directors and officers, such release is effective only as to the company itself and those shareholders who have approved such a resolution or have acquired their shares knowing of such a resolution (arts 695, 698 para 2(5) OR). If such a resolution is passed by the ordinary general meeting in reliance on financial statements prepared and presented to it in accordance with statutory requirements, it will constitute a valid defence to a personal liability action brought by the company or by shareholders. Shareholders' resolutions will, however, only be effective to relieve directors and officers from liability in respect of circumstances and facts which are apparent from the statements provided to the general meeting. They will be ineffective in respect of matters which are not brought to the attention of, or which are concealed from the general meeting, nor in respect of matters of which the general meeting otherwise had no knowledge. Thus, shareholders who voted in favour of a resolution have no need to challenge it if they subsequently learn of any incorrectness in the documents which were presented to them. Instead, the resolution will be ineffective. In particular it will not constitute a valid defence in a personal liability action (art 758 OR).

During bankruptcy: Resolutions relieving officers and directors from liability are of no significance as far as claims of creditors of the company are concerned, their rights are not affected. Thus, once the company is in bankruptcy, and assuming there are still unpaid creditors, resolutions relieving officers and directors from liability are no longer a valid defence.

Costs of litigation
Outside bankruptcy, each shareholder is entitled to file a lawsuit for damages caused by officers, directors or auditors to the company. Even if the shareholder's claim is successful, any recovery goes to the company and not to the shareholder directly. If a shareholder had legitimate reasons for bringing an action for personal liability, but was not successful, the court is entitled at its discretion to allocate the costs between the plaintiff and the company. This is contrary to the general rule that an unsuccessful party to litigation should bear the costs (court costs and the opponent's attorney's fees) of that litigation. This is explicable since the shareholder is suing on behalf of the company and would not derive any direct benefit from such a lawsuit (art 756 para 2 OR).

Multiple defendants
If more than one person is responsible for losses suffered by the company, then they will be jointly and severally (arts 143 *et seq* OR) liable to the extent the losses can be attributed to such persons on the basis of their own fault and under the

particular circumstances. The plaintiff may join several defendants in the same action for the aggregate amount of damages and may move that the court shall determine the liability of each individual defendant in the same proceedings. The court will also determine the position as between the parties, in particular the order of recourse amongst them, taking into account all relevant circumstances, in particular the degree of fault of each individual, the contributory negligence and the intervening events (art 759 OR).

Basis of the company's claim

Where a company brings an action against members of the board of directors, the auditors or other persons who have a *de facto* status as officers, then the company may base its claim on its contractual (or at least quasi-contractual) relationship with the defendant. Under the general rules applicable to contracts the company need prove only loss, the breach of duty and causation. If the company successfully proves its claim, the officers must then in turn prove that they were not at fault (art 97 OR).

Statute of limitations

Under the "relative" statute of limitations a personal liability action will become time-barred five years after the date on which the party suffering damage obtains knowledge of the damage and of the identity of the person or persons responsible. However, under the "absolute" statute of limitations it will become time-barred at the latest ten years following the breach of duty which caused the damage. If the breach of duty constitutes a criminal offence, any longer limitation periods provided for by criminal law will apply to the civil action as well (art 760 OR).

The limitation periods only begin against the creditors of the company from the date of bankruptcy.

Place of jurisdiction

Personal liability actions may be brought before the courts either at the defendant's place of residence or at the place of the registered office of the company. This alternative basis of jurisdiction applies to all potential defendants (art 761 OR).

6. Public control over insolvent corporations

Licensing and control of the appointee

There are no specific statutory prerequisites as to the personal or professional qualifications of persons who may be appointed as Konkursverwalter, Sachwalter or liquidator.

The private Konkursverwalter appointed at the first meeting of the creditors (usually a lawyer or an auditor) may be either a private individual or a corporation, and their eligibility is not defined by statute.

Public bankruptcy offices and public debt collection offices are state institutions run by civil servants and, as such, are remunerated by the state. In some cantons the two offices are linked together organisationally whereas in others the public bankruptcy office is linked with the Land Registry Office, an example being the canton of Zurich. In the latter event, the public Konkursverwalter is often also the public notary.

Both the public bankruptcy office and the private Konkursverwalter are personally liable for any damage or loss arising out of their negligence (arts 5, 241 SchKG). In the case of the public bankruptcy office, the canton is liable only in respect of that portion of a claim which the bankruptcy officials are unable to meet themselves (art 6 SchKG).

The liquidators in a composition with assignment of assets are also personally liable in accordance with article 5 SchKG for any loss or damage caused (art 316f SchKG).

The Sachwalter's liability for loss or damage caused by his negligence is governed by the general rules on tort of the Code of Obligations (art 41 *et seq* OR). Claims for damages become time-barred after one year from the date when the plaintiff had knowledge of all the circumstances relating to the loss he suffered, but after ten years from the date the act which caused the damage (arts 7 SchKG and 60 OR).

In our discussion of the various insolvency procedures (see pp681-705 *supra*), we have seen that both the Konkursverwalter and the Sachwalter are under the supervision of the higher authorities (usually the competent district court). On the other hand, the liquidator is under the supervision of the creditors' committee. The decisions of the latter may, however, be challenged before the supervisory authority (art 316e SchKG).

Disciplinary action is possible against any person involved in the bankruptcy proceeding. In particular, the supervisory authority may issue warnings against them, impose fines up to Sfr 200, suspend them from duty for a period of up to six months, or order their dismissal (art 14 SchKG).

Examinations and investigations

The various insolvency procedures dicussed so far have mentioned certain opportunities which the Konkursverwalter, Sachwalter and liquidator have to obtain the necessary information and documents from the insolvent corporation. It is useful to consider them in greater detail, however. They include the following :

- The officers and "executive" organs of the insolvent corporation are under a general obligation to place themselves at the disposal of the Konkursverwalter. In particular, they are obliged to provide him with access to all necessary information and documents. A breach of this obligation constitutes a criminal offence (art 323 Penal Code, punishable by fine or imprisonment for up to 14 days). If necessary, the Konkursverwalter may request assistance from the police and may remove and keep custody of the corporation's books and records and other relevant documentation.

- Upon adjudication of bankruptcy, the responsible officers of the insolvent corporation cease to have any right to dispose of or deal with the assets of the corporation (art 204 SchKG). Thus, there is no need for the Konkursverwalter to issue special orders in that respect. The entire assets are under public sequestration from the time of the adjudication of bankruptcy. One must, furthermore, bear in mind article 169 of the Penal Code, which provides that the debtor will be guilty of a criminal offence (punishable by imprisonment for up to 3 years) if he disposes of any sequestered assets to the detriment of his creditors.

- In composition proceedings and stay of bankruptcy proceedings the Sachwalter may not undertake any measures to levy distraint against the debtor. This is because one of the main purposes of these forms of proceedings is to enable the responsible officers to continue to manage the operations of the insolvent corporation. The Sachwalter's role is thus mainly supervisory. However, if the Sachwalter discovers any irregularities or if the debtor violates any of the instructions given by the Sachwalter or the public composition office (or bankruptcy court as the case may be), then the proceedings in question may be revoked forthwith. Thus, there is an element of compulsion which is likely to convince the debtor to co-operate with the Sachwalter and in particular to provide him with all information and documents.

Publicity and records

The importance and effects of the register of commerce and of the entries therein have already been discussed on p676 above.

The commencement, revocation, discontinuation and termination of bankruptcy proceedings are all entered in the register of commerce (arts 64 to 66 of the Register of Commerce Ordinance).

On the other hand, the commencement of composition proceedings or stay of bankruptcy proceedings are not entered in the register of commerce. However, if a liquidation composition is achieved, the liquidation commission must register it in the register of commerce, giving details of the powers of representation of the liquidators and the manner in which they are authorised to sign. Once the liquidation procedure is concluded, the register of commerce must be notified of the termination of the corporation.

An adjudication of bankruptcy and a revocation or termination of bankruptcy proceedings must also be notified to the Land Registry Office (art 176 SchKG) and published in the Swiss Official Commercial Gazette.

The public bankruptcy office is subject to further publication requirements in respect of the exercise of its functions. Thus, a record must be kept of its activities and of the petitions and legal arguments filed or brought forward by the parties. These records are open for inspection by anyone who can show that he has a valid interest (art 8 SchKG).

The public bankruptcy office must keep the books and records of the insolvent corporation in a safe place for a period of ten years. However, in the case of the bankruptcy of a sole proprietorship or a general or limited partnership, the books and records are returned to the proprietor or the partners.

If during bankruptcy proceedings the enterprise is able to be sold in its entirety to a third party, the books and records must be handed over to the purchaser on demand (art 15 of the Regulations Governing the Activities of the Public Bankruptcy Office).

7. Recognition of foreign bankruptcy decrees and composition proceedings in Switzerland

Chapter 11 (arts 166 to 175) of Switzerland's Private International Law Statute ("Bundesgesetz über das Internationale Privatrecht vom 18 Dezember 1987" – the "PILS") lays down the criteria for recognition (art 166 PILS), the procedure (arts 167 to 169 PILS) and the consequences (arts 170 to 174 PILS) of the recognition of foreign bankruptcy decrees, composition agreements and similar proceedings in Switzerland (art 175 PILS). While the rules on recognition of foreign bankruptcy decrees are laid out in some detail in the PILS, the rules on recognition of foreign composition agreements or similar proceedings (such as a voluntary winding up, administration or reorganisation orders, schemes of arrangement, and the like) are limited to one article stating that any such agreement or proceeding may be recognised in Switzerland by applying some of the rules (arts 166 to 170 PILS) on recognition of foreign bankruptcy decrees by analogy (art 175 PILS).

Requirements for recognition

A foreign bankruptcy decree or composition agreement shall be recognised in Switzerland upon an application by the foreign trustee in bankruptcy ("Konkursverwaltung"), by a liquidator, receiver, administrator ("Sachwalter") or by one of the creditors if:

- the foreign bankruptcy decree or the composition agreement was issued in the country of the debtor's domicile;
- the foreign bankruptcy decree or the composition agreement is enforceable in the country where the decree was issued or the agreement was entered into (*i.e.* in the country of the debtor's domicile);

- the country where the decree was issued or where the agreement was concluded (*i.e.* the country of the debtor's domicile) grants reciprocity; and

- no grounds for denial recognition according to article 27 PILS exist.

Switzerland follows a strict domicile principle and does not recognise bankruptcy decrees issued or composition agreements concluded at the place of business of a debtor that is not also the debtor's domicile (denying recognition for a decree based on "quasi in rem" jurisdiction) or a bankruptcy decree issued or a composition agreement concluded at the place where only assets of the debtor are located (denying recognition based on "in rem" jurisdiction).

In addition, with respect to composition agreements, the PILS explicitly requires that a foreign official authority with jurisdiction has recognised the agreement. Thus, strictly private agreements between the debtor and its creditors which have been concluded without official involvement will not be recognised.

It seems that to date only the following countries grant reciprocity: Belgium, Germany, France, Liechtenstein, and Luxembourg. Reciprocity in most matters appears to exist with Greece, Italy, Spain, the United Kingdom, Canada, the United States and Australia. Finally there is probably no reciprocity to date with the Netherlands, Portugal, Japan, Denmark, Finland, Sweden, Norway, Austria and the Latin American countries. Even though there is as yet no authority, it also appears that there is no reciprocity with the various off-shore centres (such as Jersey, Guernsey, the Isle of Man, and the Cayman Islands).

There are only a few other grounds on which recognition may be refused based on the bankruptcy decree or composition agreement itself. A foreign bankruptcy decree or composition agreement cannot be recognised in Switzerland according to article 27 PILS if such a recognition would clearly be incompatible with Swiss public policy (substantive "ordre public") or if the proceedings leading to the bankruptcy decree or the composition agreement violated the Swiss notion of a fair trial (procedural "ordre public") such as:

- no proper service of process or, in the alternative, no unconditional appearance;

- violation of the right to be heard; and finally

- a violation of the procedural exclusion of a prior decree, *i.e. res judicata* or the procedural priority of an already pending proceeding, *i.e.* lis pendens.

Procedure for recognition

Jurisdiction for the recognition procedure lies with the Swiss court at the place where assets of the debtor are located. (Claims of the debtor in bankruptcy are deemed to be located at the place of domicile of the bankrupt's debtor.) If assets of the debtor are located in different jurisdictions in Switzerland, the court first seized with an application for recognition has jurisdiction over all other assets. This rule allows a limited "forum shopping" that might be of some importance, since not all jurisdictions in Switzerland have the same expertise in handling such applications. Furthermore, it is well known that some Swiss jurisdictions have a more efficient court system than others.

An application for recognition may be opposed by both the debtor itself and any creditor of the bankrupt. Thus, a creditor can oppose recognition to protect its interest in the Swiss assets of the debtor (arts 29, 167 PILS).

After an application for recognition has been lodged with the court having jurisdiction, provisional or conservatory measures necessary to protect the creditors' interests can be ordered by the court upon a motion by any applicant (*i.e.* the trustee in bankruptcy, the receiver, the administrator or a creditor). In respect of provisional or conservatory measures, the court must follow the rules that apply in bankruptcy proceedings (art 168 PILS referring to the arts 162 to 165 and 170 SchKG). Upon termination of the recognition proceeding, the decision on recognition (but not a decision refusing recognition) has to be published and communicated to various offices (such as the Debt Collection and Bankruptcy Office) and registers (such as the Land Register and the Register of Commerce) at the location of the assets of the debtor that are subject to the proceedings (art 168 PILS).

Consequences of a recognition in Switzerland

The effect of recognition in Switzerland differs as between a foreign bankruptcy decree and a foreign composition agreement. The recognition of a foreign bankruptcy decree has the following consequences:

- All of the debtor's assets in Switzerland will be subject to a so called mini-bankruptcy ("Mini-Konkurs").

- The rules on the bankruptcy proceeding according to the SchKG apply also to the mini-bankruptcy, insofar as appropriate. The procedure has, however, less stages than a normal Swiss bankruptcy, with no creditors' meeting or creditors' committee (art 173 s3 PILS).

- A trustee in bankruptcy ("Konkursverwaltung") takes control of the debtor's assets in Switzerland. These will be listed in an inventory and subsequently comprise the mini-bankruptcy estate. The debtor loses its right to dispose of the assets of the estate, and litigation involving the debtor will be suspended. Creditors will be formally notified and invited to file claims (through a creditors' call).

- An action to avoid transactions prior to bankruptcy, *i.e.* an action to set aside a preference or the like according to the *actio pauliana* may be brought by the Swiss creditors or trustee in bankruptcy and in addition by the foreign trustee in bankruptcy or by one of the creditors in the foreign bankruptcy (art 171 PILS).

- Based on the result of the creditors' call, a schedule of claims will be prepared. This will contain claims secured by pledge and claims of privileged creditors domiciled in Switzerland (art 172 PILS). Any foreign creditor not secured by pledge (regardless of whether there is a "privilege") and unsecured, non-privileged Swiss creditors will not be listed and thus will be ineligible to take part in the distribution of assets of the mini-bankruptcy estate.

- The surplus, if any, will be made available to the foreign trustee in bankruptcy or foreign creditors in bankruptcy empowered to receive the balance but only after the foreign schedule of claims has been recognised in Switzerland (art 173). Upon non-recognition or if the foreign schedule of claims has not been submitted for recognition, the surplus will be distributed to the unsecured, non-privileged Swiss creditors (art 174 **PILS**).

Where foreign composition agreement is recognised in Switzerland, the principal effect is to prevent creditors from enforcing their claim against the debtor's Swiss assets in breach of the composition agreement.

Contents of Chapter 16

CORPORATE INSOLVENCY LAW IN THE UNITED KINGDOM

1.	**Introduction**	725
	The sources of law	725
	The constituent parts of the United Kingdom	726
	Persons, insolvency and bankruptcy	726
2.	**Companies registered under the Companies Act**	727
	Characteristics	728
	Management	730
	Ownership	733
	Financing and security for creditors	734
	Available information	737
	Other business entities	738
	Debt collection and asset recovery	740
3.	**Survival of the insolvent corporation or its business**	743
	Arrangements with creditors	743
	Administration	750
	Receivership	767
4.	**Termination of the corporation: liquidation and dissolution**	781
	Liquidation	781
	Dissolution	799
5.	**Augmenting the assets of the insolvent corporation**	800
	Introduction	800
	Transactions at risk	801
	Personal liability of officers	804
6.	**Public control over insolvent corporations**	807
	Licensing and control of the appointee	807
	Examinations and investigations	808

Publicity and records   809
7.   **Special insolvency regimes**   810
Introduction   810
Insolvency and financial markets   810
The water and railways industries   812

Chapter 16

CORPORATE INSOLVENCY LAW IN THE UNITED KINGDOM

Professor Harry Rajak, University of Sussex

and Peter Harrocks and Joe Bannister,

Lovell White Durrant

1. Introduction

The sources of law

The law of the United Kingdom falls into two main groups – common law and statute. Common law is the system built up by the decisions of the courts in the application, variation and extension of principles of previous court decisions. Statute consists of the laws enacted by the United Kingdom Parliament (which sits in Westminster, in London). These laws are described as Acts of Parliament and an individual law is usually known as an Act, with a word or words preceding the word "Act" so as to describe its content, for instance Companies Act, Insolvency Act, and so on.

The common law principles include those in accordance with which the courts interpret and apply provisions of Acts of Parliament. Reference is made throughout this chapter to:

- the names of cases which have established important principles; and
- various statutes.

The main statutes referred to this chapter are:

- The Companies Act 1985 ("CA")
- The Insolvency Act 1986 ("IA")
- The Insolvency Rules 1986 ("IR")

Thus it will be common to refer to the appropriate Act, followed by a section number, with the abbreviation where applicable. Where a section number is given without any reference to an Act or abbreviation, that section is taken from the Insolvency Act 1986.

The constituent parts of the United Kingdom

It is important to note that the United Kingdom consists principally of four constituent parts – England, Wales, Scotland and Northern Ireland. Each was once independent of the others with its own legal system, but the strongly unifying forces of the United Kingdom have eliminated much of this diversity. Some individual traditions and different principles, do, however, remain. England and Wales constitute a single legal system with only language as the occasional dividing factor (see for example s25 CA which provides English and Welsh language alternatives for the words which must be included at the end of the name of a registered company). It is now common to talk of this system as "English Law" or, more specifically as, "English Common Law".

Scotland, on the other hand, maintains a strong civil law tradition, something which occasionally results in even its fundamental principles differing from those of England and Wales. In English Law, for example, the institutions of the floating charge and receivership (see pp734-735 *infra*) grew out of the common law principles of contract and property. These institutions, however, were never part of the common law of Scotland which, therefore, did not have the floating charge or receivership until they were introduced by statute in 1961. Furthermore, in the Insolvency Act, a number of provisions are expressed to apply to Scotland only (for example ss50-71, 242-243) and a separate body of Insolvency Rules (the Insolvency (Scotland) Rules 1986, No 1915 (s139)) reflect the differences in insolvency proceedings between Scotland on the one hand and England and Wales, on the other. In Northern Ireland, English common law is the basis of the legal system (as it is in the Republic of Ireland) although Northern Ireland has, in addition, its own body of case law.

Any statute will apply – either in whole or in part – to any or all of these four constituent parts of the United Kingdom in accordance with the statute's particular provisions. It may, for example, declare that it is to be applicable only to England and Wales, or that certain identified sections are to be applied only to Scotland, and so on. The statutes with which we are principally concerned are generally in force in all material respects in England, Wales and Scotland ("Great Britain"), with some variations for Scotland. As far as Northern Ireland is concerned, the pattern is to make separate parts of each of these statutes applicable within Northern Ireland by subsequent legislative instruments.

Persons, insolvency and bankruptcy

The English common law has always drawn a clear theoretical distinction between incorporated and unincorporated organisations. In principle, only the former have legal personality and are thus able to enforce legal rights or to suffer the enforcement of legal duties. Unincorporated organisations are, in principle, not recognised by the law and, thus, cannot *themselves* enjoy legal rights and suffer legal duties although their members (usually human beings) may, either individually or collectively, enforce rights or suffer the enforcement of duties. Given the context of this chapter and the subject matter of this book, the rights and duties referred to will, in the main, be those common to commercial dealings by companies incorporated in Great Britain. Examples are:

- the right to own property and to take such steps as are necessary for the protection of such ownership;

- the right to enter into and enforce contracts; a corresponding duty of having to carry out the terms of any contract entered into; and finally

- the right to act as a litigant in any legal proceedings.

Incorporated status is generally acquired through Act of Parliament by organisations whose founders follow the procedure laid down by the relevant Act. The principal scope of this work will be companies incorporated under the CA – henceforth referred to as "companies".

Partnerships – the other major form of organisation for commercial enterprise – are unincorporated associations and, therefore, in theory, exist only through the recognition by the law of the individual partners. However, certain statutes (especially taxing statutes, but even the Partnership Act of 1890 itself) speak of "the partnership" and contemplate a separate identity for the partnership. In addition, the IA enables some unincorporated organisations (including partnerships) to undergo certain insolvency procedures apparently reserved for companies. Thus, for example, while the winding up (liquidation) provisions of the IA relate to "companies" as defined by CA section 735, ("a company formed and registered under [the Companies] Act"), IA section 420, provides for the extension of the IA to insolvent partnerships. The Insolvent Partnerships Order 1994 (enacted under the provisions of s420) extends, with certain modifications, the operation of Corporate Voluntary Arrangements (IA Part I), Administrations (IA Part II) and Winding Up (IA Part IV) to insolvent partnerships.

In this volume we are primarily concerned with the situation of a debtor who cannot pay, in full, the debts owed to third parties. More specifically we are concerned with one kind of debtor, namely companies. A company unable to pay its debts in full is usually described as "insolvent" and the entire subject as "corporate insolvency". In general, English Law uses the terms "bankrupt" and "bankruptcy" to describe human beings who cannot pay their debts, but bankruptcy and insolvency have, in substance, the same ultimate legal consequences.

2. Companies registered under the Companies Act

A company is registered by following the procedure laid down in the CA which ends with the issue by the Registrar of Companies ("the Registrar") of a Certificate of Incorporation, which has been likened to the company's birth certificate. Among other documents which have to be filed with the Registrar as pre-requisites to registration are the company's constitution which is made up of two documents, the memorandum of association ("the memorandum") and the articles of association ("the articles"). The memorandum must contain:

- the company's name;
- a statement as to whether the company's registered office is in England and Wales or in Scotland;
- the objects of the company;
- where the company is limited by shares or guarantee (see *infra*), the fact that the liability of the members is limited;
- in the case of a company limited by guarantee, the amount of the guarantee;
- in the case of a company limited by shares, the total share capital that can be issued ("the nominal capital") and how it is divided into separate shares. (Each share will thus have a nominal capital value – sometimes referred to as the "par value").

The articles contain the remainder of the regulations which govern the company's dealings with the outside world together with the regulations which govern its internal structure. A statutory instrument (delegated legislation enacted under the provisions of an Act of Parliament – in this case the CA), entitled the Companies (Tables A – F) Regulations 1985 (SI 1985, No 805), contains a model set of articles ("Table A") which is generally adopted, with appropriate changes, by most companies limited by shares.

Characteristics

Limited and unlimited companies

Companies may be registered as limited or unlimited. The distinction is based on the liability of the members to contribute to the assets of the company in the event that when liquidated, it is unable to pay its debts. Unlimited companies – which not surprisingly are rare – are those whose members are liable in full for (and, who are, in effect, guarantors of) the company's debts. A limited company, by contrast, is one whose members' liability in respect of the company's debts is limited, either by reference to the nominal value of the shares held or by reference to the amount of the guarantee stated in the company's constitution.

Companies limited by guarantee are designed for non-profit making associations whose members support the (usually public spirited) aims of the association. Since 1980, no shares can be issued by such a company and it usually acquires the money it needs through the collection of an annual subscription fee from its members, in seeking awards from public and charitable bodies and other fund raising activities.

If and when a company limited by guarantee goes into insolvent liquidation, those who are members at the time are liable to contribute to the assets of the company. This contribution will be limited to the amount of the guarantee provided for in the company's constitution. Companies limited by guarantee represent only a small proportion of registered companies and, being essentially non-commercial, they are of little significance in the world of corporate insolvency.

In the case of companies limited by shares – by far the commonest kind – a member is required to contribute to the assets of the company (if the latter is in insolvent liquidation) only to the extent that any part of the nominal value of his or her shares is unpaid. There is a fundamental link between limited liability companies and corporate insolvency. When the company is unable to pay its debts, one remedy of the creditors is to put it into liquidation. The creditors have no common law recourse against the shareholders. In recent years, however, there have been moves by both judges and the legislature to make some of those closely involved with the management of the company – the directors and those who manipulate the directors ("shadow directors") – personally liable for the company's debts in certain circumstances (p804 *infra*).

There is no minimum to the amount of share capital that must be subscribed beyond the requirement that there must be at least one or two shareholders for private and public companies respectively. It is, therefore, permissible for a company to issue as few as one or two shares of one penny each.

Public and private companies

Companies may be registered under the CA as either "public" or "private" limited companies. Public companies are usually large and draw their working capital from the public (both as investing shareholders and as debenture holding creditors). Private companies vary greatly in size and usually depend on bank overdraft financing and/or on a small group of shareholders (often family dominated). The distinction does not, however, always hold good and the CA's requirements, considered in the next paragraph, are relatively modest.

Public companies must end with the words "public limited company" (or the abbreviation "plc") and a private company's name must end with the word "limited" (or the abbreviation "ltd") – or their equivalent in Welsh if the company's registered office is in Wales – (s25 CA). Only public companies can apply for listing by the International Stock Exchange or for quotation by the Alternative Investment Market and public limited companies must have an issued share capital of at least £50,000 (s118 CA).

The CA lays down a requirement for a minimum of two members for a public limited company or a company limited by guarantee but since the coming into force of the Companies (Single Member Private Limited Companies) Regulations 1992 (SI 1992 No. 1699) on 15 July 1992, private limited companies may have only one member. Where a public limited company has had only one member for more than six months, the sole member will be jointly and severally liable (with the company) for all the company's debts contracted after the conclusion of the first six month of his sole membership (s24 CA). Section 24 does not apply to companies limited by guarantee.

Management

The common internal structure of a company consists of the shareholders (often also referred to as "members") who elect the directors. The directors, in turn, may elect or appoint a managing director (increasingly referred to as the "Chief Executive"). These three elements are sometimes referred to as the company's organs and, in theory, each has a separate and vital role in the management of the company. In practice, the picture is often more complicated. It should also be noted that a company may sometimes operate without the appointment or election of a managing director or even directors, although it is highly likely that certain prominent shareholders will, in such circumstances, assume such roles in the course of the company's business at least for an interim period until new directors are appointed. Any third party (*i.e.* those dealing with a company) led reasonably to believe that such shareholders have been elected to office as directors or as managing director, will be protected by the court deeming such shareholders to have been properly appointed to the office in question.

The shareholders

The CA contains detailed provisions laying down how shareholders' votes are to be cast. They must be given the opportunity to meet at least once a year (at the annual general meeting) to decide, among other things, whether the existing directors and auditors should be re-appointed. They also have the power to summon other general meetings (described as extraordinary general meetings) and to resolve, for example, to remove some or all of the directors from the board (s303 CA). In theory, the directors might be required to consult the shareholders before undertaking specific operations (there may, for example, be a provision to this effect in the company's articles). In practice, however, the authority to carry out most of the company's operations is delegated to the directors by the articles (Table A reg 70).

In general, shareholders act by majority vote – over 50% – to pass an ordinary resolution and 75% or greater to pass a special or an extraordinary resolution. The CA or IA dictates when a special or extraordinary resolution is required, for example, alteration to the articles of association (s9 CA) or putting the company into creditors' voluntary liquidation (s84 IA); otherwise an ordinary resolution will suffice. The vote will, initially, be on a show of hands, that is, one vote per shareholder. However, the articles of association will, almost invariably, include a provision empowering any shareholder to call for a poll, which requires that the vote be based on the number of shares held by each shareholder, rather than on the number of shareholders. The common law protects shareholders by requiring that when any shareholders' meeting is called, sufficient notice of all the business to be transacted at the meeting must be given to all those eligible to attend.

The directors

The proceedings of a company's directors, by contrast, are little regulated by the CA. The articles, do not commonly provide formal regulations governing the proceedings of the directors and it is usually left to the directors to establish their own proceedings – how often they will meet, how much notice will be given for any meeting, and so on. Decisions are normally taken by a majority of directors. It is assumed that directors will attend directors' meetings. Thus, even if the notice which summons the meeting fails to disclose what business is to be transacted at the meeting, the proceedings will not be invalidated (contrast the position with shareholders' meetings, above).

In large public companies there is, commonly, an important distinction between executive and non-executive directors. The former are usually engaged full-time on the activities of the company, whereas the role of the latter usually consists of attending board meetings, giving advice in areas where they have expertise and furthering the company's external contacts. This distinction derives from practice and the terms of appointment, but is nowhere recognised by the CA with the effect that, where "directors" are referred to in this Act, this reference must be taken to include executive and non-executive directors.

This is of special significance when bearing in mind that the directors of a company which goes into insolvent liquidation may themselves be personally liable to contribute to the assets of the company if the insolvency can be ascribed to their default (see p804 *infra*). This potential liability may, therefore, attach as much to non-executive directors as to full-time directors.

Indeed, it is also worth noting that liability might attach to people who are not directors at all in that they have not been elected or appointed to the board. This will occur when the elected directors generally act in accordance with the instructions or directions of someone who is not a member of the board. The latter is described as a "shadow director" (for example, ss213, 214 IA p804 *infra*).

The managing director

The position of the managing director is not enshrined in statute, but the directors are usually given power by the articles (for example Table A reg 84) to elect one or more of their number to hold such a position. This office first emerged in United Kingdom companies at the beginning of this century and was clearly established by the time the important case of *Lennard's Carrying Company Ltd* v *Asiatic Petroleum Company Ltd* [1915] AC 705 decided that the managing director might be so central to the affairs of the company as to be treated as the company itself in certain circumstances.

At the same time, the power of a particular managing director vis-a-vis the board and the extent of his or her authority to act on behalf of the company depends on the terms of his or her appointment and the surrounding circumstances. Thus, it is quite possible for a managing director's position to be stronger in some companies than in others (see for example *H. Holdsworth & Co Ltd* v *Caddies* [1955] 1 WLR 352 and *Read* v *Astoria Garage (Streatham) Ltd* [1952] Ch 637).

The secretary

All companies are required to have a secretary (s283 CA), who has a largely administrative role, namely to ensure that the company complies with all the administrative requirements of the CA – completing the requisite forms, sending them to the Registrar of Companies, and so on. The secretary attends all meetings of the company and (usually) its directors, takes minutes of the proceedings and maintains the minute book.

Despite this emphasis on administrative responsibilities, it seems clear that the managerial role of the secretary has increased in recent years (see for example *Panorama Developments (Guildford) Ltd* v *Fidelis Furnishing Fabrics Ltd* [1971] 2 QB 711, [1971] 3 All ER 16) and it may not be much longer before a secretary is, in particular circumstances, treated as the company itself, as the managing director was in *Lennard's Carrying Company Ltd* v *Asiatic Petroleum Company Ltd* (*supra*).

The relationship between the company's organs

Although most companies will consist of the three distinct organs discussed above together with a company secretary, in the case of small, private companies there is usually a considerable overlap between the shareholders and directors, with most, if not all, of the shareholders also being directors. The management of such companies is directly influenced by the shareholders, and disputes as to how the company is managed are likely to take the form of the minority shareholders seeking relief against the majority (under the provisions of s459 CA and s122(1)(g) IA).

Such companies are sometimes described as "quasi-partnerships" to indicate the closely integrated structure of investors and managers which usually exists in partnerships. Here, too, there may be no managing director, or, if there is, he or she is likely to be closely identified with the board of directors.

As a company increases in size, however, the management functions of the company are undertaken by a small class – the executive directors and management employees – and the shareholders assume more and more the role of passive investors. From time to time, however, a dispute may arise between two organs with each claiming the exclusive right to take a particular decision in the management of the company's affairs. One organ decides the issue one way, while the other organ wants a contrary decision and the battleground becomes the extent of each organ's jurisdiction.

The relevant provisions in the company's articles of association and in any contract between the company and the managing director will most often be the basis on which such disputes are resolved. Regulation 70 of Table A, which is the basis for a similar provision in the articles of most companies, effectively gives all management functions to the board of directors. This codifies the common law which, since the beginning of this century, has seen an increase in the power of the directors at the expense of the shareholders.

Regulation 84 empowers the board to appoint a managing director, but this leaves open the extent of the latter's power. Here the terms of the appointment and, if separate, the contract between the company and the managing director may well be important in deciding a dispute where there are competing claims of management between the board and the managing director.

Ownership

It is common, though technically wrong, to talk of the ownership of the company. The metaphor of the company as a person is maintained and, like any natural person, the company is incapable of being owned. The company is, of course, itself the owner of the company's assets. When people speak of the ownership of a company, they are referring to ownership of the shares in the company, which are usually owned by those who have invested money in the company. Shares can also be issued in exchange for assets or labour.

Shareholders may fall into different categories, and will do so where the company has issued different classes of shares. Nowadays, it is relatively unusual for a company to have more than two classes of shareholders – ordinary and preference – and it will very often have only one. Preference shareholders are so called because their shares carry some preference – usually a fixed annual dividend to be paid before any other shareholders receive a dividend, and priority in the recovery of the amount invested when the company either reduces its capital or goes into solvent liquidation.

When the company goes into liquidation, the general rule is that debts are to be paid before any money is returned to the shareholders. In the case of an insolvent liquidation, since, by definition, nothing will be returned to the shareholders, it makes no difference whether they own ordinary or preference shares. In the case of a solvent liquidation, however, where all debts will be paid in full and something is over for the shareholders, the distinction between ordinary and preference shareholders will be of great significance where the preference shares carry a right for prior repayment of capital and there is insufficient money, after the payment of all the debts, to repay all shareholders the full amount of the issued capital. In such a case, the preferential shareholders may receive the full amount of the issued share capital, with ordinary shareholders receiving nothing or, at least, less than the nominal value of their investment.

It will also make a difference whether a shareholder owns fully paid, partly paid, or unpaid shares. This distinction turns on the amount of money paid to the company in relation to the particular shares and only where the shares are fully paid is the shareholder's liability in respect of the company's debts at an end. Thus, if a shareholder owns either partly paid or unpaid shares when the company goes into insolvent liquidation, that shareholder will be called upon to contribute the balance owing on the nominal value of the shares to the assets of the company. For this reason, shareholders in this position are referred to in the legislation provisions (ss 74-83 IA) as "contributories".

The category of contributory includes non-members in certain circumstances, in particular:

- those who have acquired shares but in whose names the shares have not yet been registered; and

- past members, where less than a year has elapsed between the cessation of their membership and the commencement of the company's liquidation.

Financing and security for creditors

Aside from shareholders who own the shares issued by the company, others (also sometimes described as "investors") advance money to the company by way of loan. Where a long term loan is anticipated, this form of investment is commonly effected in exchange for an instrument called a "debenture", which is simply the document that evidences the debt. Debenture-holders are, however, creditors as opposed to shareholders. They do not own any shares and as such are not entitled to any money from the company beyond the money advanced and interest at the agreed rate. As creditors, however, debenture-holders enjoy a priority over shareholders in the repayment of the investment if the company goes into liquidation, a priority which is obviously of crucial importance where the company is insolvent.

Apart from this priority over the shareholders, debenture-holders may also enjoy priority over other creditors. The company's indebtedness to its debenture-holders may be secured against the company's property and enforced if the company is unable to pay interest or repay the loan when it falls due. Such security confers on the debentureholders a right to seize and sell the company's property which constitutes the security and to claim what is due by looking to the proceeds of such sale. This confers a priority over those creditors of the company whose claims are not secured and who can rely only on personal claims against the company.

The debenture itself usually contains the provisions which grant the security. In the case of an insolvent liquidation, therefore, the company's property will first be used to satisfy the claims of secured creditors leaving the unsecured creditors with often useless claims to be satisfied out of what remains.

The most obvious form of security is that taken over the company's freehold or leasehold interest in its fixed (immovable) property, for example its factory or warehouse. As long as the secured creditor registers his security interest in the appropriate register (see p735 *infra*), the company will be unable to deal with the property which constitutes the creditor's security without the latter's consent. This form of security is known as a "fixed charge" or "mortgage".

English law has also developed the "floating charge", which is a form of security usually taken over all the company's assets thus embracing the company's everyday movable assets. This commonly includes stock in trade, manufactured articles before sale, cash and book debts. The latter – usually an important asset – are the debts owing to the company by its customers, and latterly have increasingly been the subject of a fixed rather than a floating charge (see *infra*.)

There are two significant and inter-related ways in which a floating charge differs from a fixed charge. In the first place, it is not possible to identify the charged property in a floating charge, except in general terms ("all the company's assets and undertaking" as contrasted with a typical fixed charge clause such as "the freehold/leasehold property known as .... "). Secondly, although a floating charge is registrable like a fixed charge, the company can use and dispose of the charged property without the consent of the secured creditor. It would cripple the company if it had to seek such consent every time it wished to sell, say, any of its manufactured products and this would hardly assist the company in repaying the loan. Thus, in simple terms, the distinction is that the holder of a fixed charge can identify and control the assets which are subject to the charge, whereas the holder of a floating charge cannot. Registration may have the effect of preventing the company from entering into subsequent secured borrowing transactions as potential lenders' rights would be subject to the previously created and registered security of earlier lenders.

The floating charge becomes a fixed charge (a process known as "crystallisation") either by operation of law (on liquidation or the appointment of an administrative receiver to the company) or by contract, on the happening of any of the events expressed by the floating charge to have this effect. Such an event might be the giving of notice crystallising the charge; there is controversy as to the validity of a provision to the effect that a floating charge should crystallise automatically (for example on the service of a writ against the company).

In some cases, it may not be possible to tell before the outcome of appropriate litigation whether a charge is fixed or floating. Since fixed (but not floating) charges confer a priority for the chargee over preferential creditors (p771 *infra*), attempts have been made to draft fixed charges over certain non-permanent assets (especially the company's book debts). In principle, these have been successful where provision is made for the creditor to monitor the receipts and control what may be done with them (*Siebe Gorman* v *Barclays Bank Ltd* [1979] 2 Ll Rep 142, *Barclays Bank plc* v *Willowbrook International Ltd* [1986] BCLC 45). If such monitoring is absent, the charge, however expressed, will be treated as a floating charge (*Re Brightlife Ltd* [1987] Ch 200, (1986) 2 BCC 99, 359, [1986] 3 All ER 673, *Re G E Tunbridge Ltd* [1994] BCC 563) although, where the functions of collecting the debts and monitoring the withdrawal was split between two different persons, this did not reduce the fixed charge to a floating charge (*William Gaskell Group Ltd* v *Highly* [1993] BCC 200, [1994] 1 BCLC 197).

In *Re New Bullas Trading Ltd*, [1994] BCC 36, [1994] 1 BCLC 485 the Court of Appeal held as valid a charge instrument under which the debtor company's book debts were subject to a fixed charge while uncollected, but under which the proceeds of collected book debts were left unmonitored (*i.e.* for the debtor to use as it wished) and subject to a floating charge in favour of the same creditor. Thus, should the debtor go into receivership or liquidation, the charge so drawn gives the creditor priority over the preferential creditors in respect of what is owing to the company. Such a charge also frees the creditor from having to monitor the receipts and thus provides a responsible debtor with the freedom necessary to run its business effectively.

Recent years have witnessed other sophisticated developments in creditors' security. The combined effect of the fixed and floating charges is to favour loan creditors as against trade creditors. The latter deal with the company in the ordinary course of business, supplying goods and services to the company. If, on insolvent liquidation, all the company's assets are applied in discharge of the company's secured obligations, nothing remains for the company's other ("unsecured") creditors. Trade creditors, therefore, now frequently require that the terms on which goods are supplied should include a provision in terms of which the ownership of those goods should remain with the supplier until those goods have been paid for (a retention of title clause).

In this simple form, the clause ensures that if the company goes into either liquidation or receivership, and the supplier can identify the goods supplied under a contract incorporating the reservation of title clauses, those goods *themselves* can be recovered by the supplier (who under the contract has remained the owner). The case of *Aluminium Industrie Vaassen BV* v *Romalpa Aluminium Ltd* [1976] 1 WLR 676, [1976] 2 All ER 552 first established that retention of title clauses were effective and this form of protection has been successfully extended to cover outstanding debts in respect of other goods supplied.

However, further attempts to extend this form of protection (a) to the proceeds received by the company for sub-sales of the goods, and (b) over composite goods manufactured by the company debtor out of materials supplied by several different suppliers, have been held to be unenforceable as a means of retention by the supplier of ownership of the goods supplied. The courts have stressed that such clauses may amount to a floating charge thus conferring on the relevant vendor secured creditor status, if not the protection of ownership, but this is rarely of any value. Floating charges must be registered to be valid and this is wholly impractical in relation to each supply of goods. The substance of such attempts at retention of ownership is to give security for payment of outstanding debts, hence their increasing categorisation as floating charges (see *Modelboard Ltd* v *Outer Box Ltd* [1992] BCC 945, [1993] BCLC 623)

The conceptual problem for a supplier attempting to retain ownership in such extended circumstances as suggested in the paragraph above is that the goods supplied have disappeared, being replaced either by the proceeds of their sale or by a product which is wholly different in nature.

Unless the purchaser can properly be described as the supplier's agent, the latter cannot lay claim to the actual proceeds of any sub-sale. This form of protection was, however, achieved in *Welsh Development Agency* v *Export Finance Co Ltd* [1992] BCC 270. The WDA had lent money to a company ("Parrot") and the loan was secured by a floating charge under which the WDA appointed an administrative receiver. The WDA asserted the right under its floating charge to all debts owing to Parrot.

The Court of Appeal, however, upheld an agreement between Parrot and the Export Finance Company ("Exfinco"), who also lent money to Parrot, under which Parrot agreed that all sales made by it to certain purchasers would be as undisclosed agent for Exfinco. Under this agreement, ownership in goods sold in this way vested in Exfinco, which was thus entitled to the payment for such goods. Since the title to the goods and the payment for them were vested in Exfinco, they were never part of Parrot's assets charged to the WDA under its floating charge. They were, in consequence, not subject to control by the administrative receivers appointed by the WDA.

Two other legal principles may confer security on a person owed money by the company without his having to take a charge over the company's assets. In the first place, someone who has advanced money to a company for a particular purpose may claim return of that money if the purpose cannot be fulfilled and the money can still be identified or traced. The leading example is *Barclays Bank Ltd* v *Quistclose Investments Ltd* [1970] AC 567, where Quistclose advanced £220,000 to Rolls Razor Ltd to enable the latter company to pay a dividend which had been declared. The funds were held in a separate account with Barclays Bank, Rolls Razor's bankers. Before the dividend could be paid, Rolls Razor went into insolvent liquidation. The liquidator argued that Quistclose was, in consequence, an unsecured creditor of Rolls Razor for the amount of the advance.

The claim by Quistclose to the full sum of money advanced – as opposed to the small dividend which it might have received out of the liquidated Rolls Razor's insolvent estate as an unsecured creditor – was upheld. The precise legal principle under which this decision was reached was within the body of trust law. The money advanced could only be used for a particular purpose. When this failed, the entitlement of Rolls Razor to keep the money ceased. Rolls Razor, therefore, held that money in trust for Quistclose. Alternatively, Quistclose was the beneficial owner of the money and, as such, in a superior position to any creditor with claims against Rolls Razor including the bank which had notice of the purpose for which Quistclose had made the advance.

Secondly, a creditor who is himself also indebted to a company can reduce his claim against the company by any amount which he owes to the company. This is the principle of set-off and is of particular value against an insolvent company. Whereas a creditor without any right of set-off will generally only recover part (or nothing) of what he is owed by way of dividend, a creditor who owes the company as much as he is owed will, in effect, recover his claim in full.

Available information

English Company Law has for a long while prided itself on its extensive disclosure provisions which ensure that as much commercial information about a company as possible is publicly available without jeopardising the secrecy and security necessary to maintain the company's commercial performance as against its rivals.

Among other things, the following documents are required by the CA to be filed in the company's file at the Registry of Companies and are, therefore, available for public inspection:

- the company's constitution *i.e.* the memorandum of association and the articles of association (ss10,12 CA); and
- the company's annual accounts (s241(3)(a) CA) which comprise (ss239 CA):
  - the company's profit and loss account and balance sheet (ss228,231 CA);
  - the directors' report (ss235 CA);
  - the auditors' report (ss236 CA); and
  - if there are subsidiaries, group accounts (ss230,232-4 CA).

- the company's annual return (ss363-4A CA) comprising, *inter alia*, the following information:
  - the address of the company's registered office;
  - the type of company and its principal business activities;
  - the name and address of the company secretary;
  - the name and address of each director;
  - the total number of issued shares;
  - the names and addresses of all members of the company (and the names and addresses of all people who have ceased to be members since the last return filed was made up).
- the registration of any charge created by the company (Part XII CA);
- the appointment of any administrator to the company (s21(3) IA);
- notice of appointment of a liquidator of a company in voluntary liquidation (s109 IA).

Other business entities

The registered company is by far the most popular form of organisation for the conduct of business in the United Kingdom. Other incorporated forms of organisation include industrial and provident societies (registered under the Industrial and Provident Societies Act 1965) and Building Societies (registered under the Building Societies Act 1986). The winding up legislation which applies to registered companies is applied in both these cases (Industrial and Provident Societies Act s55 and Building Societies Act ss88-90 respectively), but the definition of "company" as "a company formed and registered under the Companies Act 1985 or any of its predecessors" (see s735 CA as applied by s251 IA) excludes the application to such bodies of the major court-based corporate rescue procedure for insolvent companies *i.e.* administration.

In addition to such incorporated associations, others may be incorporated by special Act of Parliament. This is sometimes combined with the exercise of the power by the Crown to create corporations by Royal Charter. This method of creating corporations is reserved nowadays for associations of a public or charitable rather than a profitable nature (such as universities). The provisions of the IA are applied in part to such associations (the compulsory, but not the voluntary winding up provisions – section 220, and excluding the administration jurisdiction).

Partnership is the principal form of unincorporated association for commercial operations by two or more people. As a legal institution, partnership combines elements of contract and trust. The contract represents the agreement by the partners as to what business is to be transacted and how it is to be done. The trust component relates to the requirements that no partner should compete against the other partners and that any profit made in pursuit of the partnership business should be shared by all partners in accordance with their agreement.

Partnerships are, thus, created and maintained by the principles of the common law. There is, in fact, a statute, the Partnership Act 1890, but this is a codifying Act, one which reduces to simple statutory form the major relevant principles of the common law. As for the dissolution and winding up of partnerships, the grounds on which this might be effected are recorded in section 32 of the Partnership Act. In the main, these fall into two categories, namely, those which arise from the agreement between the partners and those which arise through the permanent or likely permanent frustration of the aims of the partnership.

The winding up procedure for partnerships is that laid down by Part V of the Insolvency Act for unregistered companies (see Insolvent Partnerships Order 1994, SI 1994 No 2421, paras 7, 8). Paragraphs 4 and 6 of the Insolvent Partnerships Order 1994, which came into force on 1 December 1994, also provide, respectively, for voluntary arrangements (p748 *et seq infra*) and administration orders (p750 *et seq infra*) for partnerships.

It is worth noting one further connection between partnerships and registered companies. There evolved through the common law a principle that a partnership would be wound up where this was "just and equitable". This would apply, for example, where the partners could no longer co-operate, but no provision existed in the agreement for dissolution of the partnership. This ground was included in the early legislation providing for the registration of limited companies and can now be found in section 122(1)(g) IA. By its very nature, its use is limited to the cases of small private companies (sometimes described as "quasi-partnerships").

Finally, it should be mentioned that commercial activity can, of course, be conducted by a single individual as opposed to a group of individuals. In the United Kingdom such a person is described as a "sole trader". He or she enters into contracts and holds property for the purpose of carrying on the business. As with partners in a partnership, he or she is personally liable for the debts incurred.

There are two obvious advantages of carrying on business through a company registered under the Companies Act as against a partnership or as a sole trader. First, the company has legal personality and thus itself enters into contracts and holds property. If, at some future stage, one participant wants to drop out and is to be replaced by another, this is done by a transfer of shares without affecting the company's operations.

Secondly, shareholders of limited companies registered under the Companies Act are liable only for the nominal value of the shares issued to them plus any premium. If, therefore, the company incurs debts beyond its assets, it is the creditors and not the shareholders who will suffer the loss. Where those who have managed the company have behaved fraudulently or incompetently, however, they can be made to contribute to the assets of the company if it is liquidated and cannot pay all its debts (see p804 *infra*). Also it is common for certain creditors, particularly banks and landlords, to insist upon personal guarantees from the directors and/or shareholders.

Debt collection and asset recovery

Introduction

Commercial claims arising out of contracts fall into two broad categories, those by creditors for money owing ("debt collection") and those by persons – entitled by ownership or other right to some specific property – for recovery of that property ("asset recovery"). Some claimants may fall into both categories, for example, a landlord who may have a claim for unpaid rent as well as a claim for recovery of the leased property (forfeiture of the lease).

In other cases, a claim for asset recovery (as opposed to debt collection) will arise only where the debtor is insolvent and, therefore, unable to pay the debt in full. As noted earlier, a supplier of goods may have incorporated a retention of title clause in his contract with the debtor, thereby retaining ownership of the goods until paid in full and will invoke this retention of title provision if the buyer is insolvent. Alternatively, this party may claim to be beneficial owner of particular money, held apparently to the order of the company (all of which would be recoverable if the claim were established) rather than a claim for money owed (p737 *supra*).

Debt collection

Creditors who wish to recover money owing to them fall into two categories, secured and unsecured.

Unsecured creditors

The most common procedure is for the creditor to seek judgment from the court that the money is owing and thereafter to act on that judgment in one or more of the ways detailed below. In certain cases, however, a creditor may be able to collect the debt without first getting a judgment. Certain creditors have the right to seize goods which belong to the debtor or which are found on the debtor's premises and arrange for these to be sold with proceeds used in payment of the debt. This remedy – "distraining" or "the levying of distress"- is available, without court approval, to a landlord in respect of rent arrears and to the revenue authorities in respect of unpaid taxes. It is also available in certain other circumstances (for instance, to those responsible for the collection of fines imposed by the Magistrates' Courts), with court approval.

Where the debtor is a company, any creditor may rely on the provisions of sections 122(1)(f) and 123(1)(a) IA, to make a written demand for the sum owing (minimum £750) and, if that remains unpaid for at least a further three weeks, to petition for the winding up of the company. Some creditors are prepared to take the risk of petitioning for winding up without first serving a statutory demand, but it is common for the petitioning creditor to obtain a court judgment first. United Kingdom courts have often declared that the compulsory company winding up process should not be used as a means of attempting to recover debts which are genuinely disputed.

Thus, a judgment creditor may petition for the winding up of the company. He may also take any of the following steps in the hope of recovering the money without the expense, delay and likely lack of satisfaction of liquidation:

- issue a writ of *fieri facias* which is addressed to the sheriff (an officer of the court) and which instructs him to take delivery of the debtor's goods, sell them and account to the creditor for the amount owing;

- apply to court for a garnishee order, which entitles the creditor to receive money owing to the debtor (for example, money belonging to the debtor in the debtor's bank account, in which case the garnishee order will be made against the bank);

- apply for a charging order under the Charging Orders Act 1979. When this order is made absolute, the creditor has a security over the property in respect of which the order was made.

The creditor can then recover the money owing to him in the same manner as can any creditor whose claim is secured by a fixed charge (see *infra*). This enforcement remedy can be used in relation to the debtor's land, government stock, company securities, units of a unit trust and funds paid into court. The charging order must be registered in the manner appropriate to the property over which it is obtained.

Secured creditors

Where the debtor is a company, a creditor may be secured by a fixed and/or a floating charge (see p734 *supra*). Also, as we have seen, a third party may have acquired fixed security without the debtor's consent by enforcement action. In the case of either form of security, the creditor's aim is to have the subject matter of the security sold and the debt paid out of the proceeds. The creditor is liable to account to the debtor for any surplus.

A floating charge is almost invariably enforced by the appointment of a receiver pursuant to the charge. Where the floating charge covers all or substantially all of the company's property, the receiver is classified as an "administrative receiver" under the provisions of IA Part III. In rare cases, for example, where the charge fails to provide for the appointment of a receiver or to give him adequate powers, an application can be made to court for the appointment of a receiver with appropriate powers. The powers and duties of receivers are discussed below.

A fixed charge can also be enforced by the appointment of a receiver under the provisions of the Law of Property Act 1925 (as opposed to by the appointment of an administrative receiver). If the creditor simply wishes the property to be sold, however, it may be sufficient for him to exercise the statutory power of sale, though he may have first to obtain a court order for possession. A receiver is unnecessary for this. The creditor may wish to manage the property, where, for example, it is a block of flats with incoming rents, or he may be concerned about protecting the property until sale. A receiver may be appointed for either of these purposes.

Asset recovery

In the case of asset recovery the claimant attempts to recover particular property rather than payment of a debt. The claimant is, thus, not strictly speaking a creditor, but has a claim based on some other right – most probably ownership. We have already seen the value of such a claim where the debtor is insolvent (p736-737 *supra*). The plaintiff's claim will be based either on ownership or on some lesser right of possession superior to that of the debtor. The claimant may, for example, be the debtor's landlord while at the same time being a tenant of a superior landlord.

Cross-jurisdictional procedures

The United Kingdom acceded to the European Community Convention on Civil Jurisdiction and the Enforcement of Judgments in 1978. This Convention became part of the law of the United Kingdom with the enactment of the Civil Jurisdiction and Judgments Act 1982. Under Article 26 of the Convention, any judgment given in any of the European Union Member States is recognised in all other Member States without any special procedure or leave being required. Under Article 31 such a judgment is enforceable in any of the Member States after an order for its enforcement has been made on the application of any interested party.

Aside from this Convention, the general principle is that a foreign judgment obtained according to the merits of the case will be recognised in the United Kingdom, but not directly enforced. Rather, it will be recognised as creating a debt between parties. The plaintiff may enforce his right either by suing on the foreign judgment or by bringing a claim based on the original cause of action.

Finally, reference should be made to the domestic and cross-border enforcement procedure known as the "Mareva injunction". In the case from which this term comes (*The Mareva* [1980] 1 All ER 213), the Court of Appeal developed the principle which enables the plaintiff to restrain the defendant from removing assets (money or goods) pending the decision in the trial. It was originally developed in relation to a defendant who was outside the jurisdiction of the court, but has been extended to include defendants within the jurisdiction as well as to goods or money outside the jurisdiction. What makes this a particularly powerful weapon is that it can be, and usually is, applied for *ex parte*, that is in the absence of and in the ignorance of the defendant.

This concludes our discussion of the general principles governing the creation and management of corporations in the United Kingdom as well as the most common remedies by which claims can be enforced against them. We now turn to the principles and institutions which govern the treatment of insolvent companies and the many different interests with which they are connected.

3. Survival of the insolvent corporation or its business

Arrangements with creditors

It is, of course, possible for a debtor company to reach an informal arrangement with all creditors in which the latter agree not to press their demands and the company undertakes to pay its debts at an agreed rate. Such agreements are enforceable in English Law. The problem, however, is practical rather than legal: how to secure the adherence of all the creditors. If one creditor alone refuses, the company might be put into liquidation and the agreement of all the rest not to pursue their claims would be to no avail.

It is, therefore, desirable to provide a legal regime to ensure that all creditors are bound by an agreement reached between the company and the majority of its creditors. In the United Kingdom there are two such regimes, the older being the scheme of arrangement ("scheme") under section 425 CA, and the newer being the corporate voluntary arrangement ("CVA") under IA Part I. The scheme is more formal and requires at least two months from the time the plan is formulated until its approval by the court. Under section 425 CA, the court has the discretion to approve a "compromise or arrangement" and it is under this jurisdiction that a scheme for an insolvent company is approved. Only when it has been so approved does it have binding effect.

The CVA is less formal and takes effect from approval at the meeting of creditors. This process could be completed in less than three weeks although it is rare for it to take so short a time in practice since the proposed arrangement will need to be formulated prior to the convening of the statutory meetings. This is likely to involve some discussion with major creditors as well as company officers. Unless it has been possible for preparatory work to be done in this area, it will invariably prove difficult for the necessary decisions to have been taken with the speed which a three-week "start to finish" CVA would require.

Purpose and effect

The scheme and CVA regimes enable an insolvent company to be restructured and given an opportunity to survive in whole or in part. Each requires the acceptance of a plan which may involve alterations to the company's obligations to its creditors and/or shareholders. The purpose of these regimes is to ensure a permanent solution to the company's problems, although it would be quite permissible for any plan to contain temporary elements, for example, a moratorium on claims against the company for a limited period. Indeed many are brought into being when the company is already in liquidation for the purpose of facilitating the burial rather than ensuring a longer life.

Both the scheme and the CVA are recognised as permanent solutions for companies placed in administration (see p751 *infra*) and are of increasing importance in this regard. One of the shortcomings of the administration regime is the limitation placed on an administrator in making distributions to creditors (*Re St Ives Windings Ltd* (1987) 3 BCC 634. Such distributions can, however, be made in a scheme or a CVA. Distributions might also be effected when the company is in liquidation, but liquidation alone may not be appropriate where, for example, it is intended to rescue the company. Furthermore, in liquidation, the company's funds must be placed in a government deposit (the Insolvency Services Account) which charges high fees and pays little interest.

Pre-application considerations

Neither the scheme nor the CVA provides any moratorium restraining the enforcement of claims against the company while its terms are being formulated. The major preliminary problem for the company and its supporting creditors is, therefore, to prevent liquidation and other enforcement procedures being taken before the plan is approved. This is one of the reasons why the scheme had largely ceased to be useful as a rescue regime for insolvent companies. The length of time required for putting a scheme in place successfully gives ample scope to a creditor opposed to the plan to petition for the winding up of the company.

This may, perhaps, have been, in part, the reason for the enactment of IA Part I, which establishes the CVA procedure. Even in the latter regime, however, which is much quicker and simpler than the scheme, the absence of a moratorium is a serious defect. In fact, as we shall see (p756 *infra*), the new administration procedure does effect a moratorium and this enables either a CVA, or a scheme to be formulated and approved for the company during a period when the company is protected from actions against it by its creditors.

A solution which has proved workable in the case of a company encountering difficulty at the start of the English court's long vacation was for an administration petition to be presented to the court giving the company a moratorium against creditor action while a CVA was prepared and put to the creditors. After the approval of the CVA, the court gave leave for the administration petition to be withdrawn. It has now been suggested that this procedure could work outside the long vacation, even though administration petitions are generally treated as urgent business and given early hearing dates. Conflicting opinions have, however, been expressed as to whether the use of administration petitions as a shield for the formulation of CVAs would be open to attack as an abuse of the court process.

At the end of 1993, the Government prepared a consultative document on the CVA procedure. One of its suggestions was the introduction of a moratorium period similar to that available when individual voluntary arrangements are proposed. Such a moratorium would provide a shield against creditor action for a limited period of time. The consultative document contained a number of other far-reaching recommendations, but it is unclear when or whether any of these recommendations, and therefore the moratorium described above, will be introduced. A further consultation document, containing broadly similar proposals, was published in the spring of 1995.

The absence of the moratorium even after the approval of the plan may cause further problems in the case of a CVA. Creditors who were not given notice of the meeting which is required to be held to approve the plan for the CVA will not be bound by it. Nor will creditors who come into existence after the approval of the plan be bound by it. Any of these creditors could, if not paid, attempt to wind up the company and thus defeat the plan. In the case of a scheme under section 425 CA, the order of the court bringing the scheme into effect is binding on all creditors, whether or not they have been given notice of the meetings to consider its terms.

In recent years, the scheme has seen something of a renaissance, being used by practitioners dealing with insolvent insurance companies and other complex corporate insolvencies as a potential means of maximising returns to creditors in the light of the particular difficulties (for example, claims quantification and reinsurance collection) facing this type of company when it encounters financial problems. The advantages of the scheme are often cited as being its flexibility in investment of assets and payment of claims, avoidance of the Insolvency Service Account charges (p784 *infra*) and, supposedly, a swifter distribution of assets than would be possible in a liquidation.

Protection against creditor action while the scheme is being prepared has, in the case of insolvent insurance companies, been secured by placing the company into provisional liquidation under section 135 IA and obtaining court orders to adjourn the winding up petition until after the meetings of members and shareholders held to consider the terms of the scheme. Provisional liquidation operates to prevent the commencement or prosecution of any action or proceeding against the company or its property in respect of any debt of the company except with the leave of the court and on such terms as the court may impose (s130(2) IA)

In the case of other complex insolvencies where schemes have been the chosen insolvency procedure, the protection of the company against creditor action has been secured by formulating the scheme while the company is in administration (*Re British and Commonwealth Holdings plc (No 3)* [1992] BCC 58, *Re Maxwell Communications Corporation plc (No 3)* [1993] BCC 369).

Procedure

The scheme of arrangement
The scheme requires two applications to the court. On the first application, the court will be asked to order the holding of meetings of creditors and/or shareholders to vote on the proposed compromise or arrangement. Important princi-

ples have been developed by the courts in the implementation of this procedure. First, creditors or shareholders with particular interests (as opposed to the interests, in general, of all the creditors or shareholders) must be summoned to separate meetings. Thus secured creditors will attend and vote on the proposed compromise or arrangement at a separate meeting from that held for the unsecured creditors. The same would apply to different classes of shareholders (such as preference and ordinary). In certain circumstances, different creditors or shareholders within the same class, for example secured or unsecured creditors or preference shareholders, may have different interests in relation to the proposed plan (see *Sovereign Life Assurance Co* v *Dodd* [1892] 2 QB 573; *Re Hellenic & General Trust Ltd* [1975] 3 All ER 382, [1976] 1 WLR 123; cf. *Re Holders' Investment Trust Ltd* [1972] 1 WLR 583), in which case they must vote on the plan at different meetings.

Secondly, the jurisdiction of the court to approve a "compromise or arrangement" under section 425 CA, is very wide. A rescue plan altering the company's obligations to its creditors and shareholders would certainly come within the phrase "compromise or arrangement". Thirdly, where the interests of a particular class are unaffected by the proposal, the court may dispense with the need to hold a meeting of that class. Thus, where the class has no interest to start with because the company is hopelessly insolvent and the plan proposes to eliminate that class, the court can dispense with the need for that class's consent to the proposal (*Re Tea Corporation Ltd* [1904] 1 Ch 12; *Re Oceanic Steam Navigation Co Ltd* [1939] 1 Ch 41; *Re British and Commonwealth Holdings plc (No 3)* [1992] BCC 58, *Re Maxwell Communications Corporation plc (No 3)* [1993] BCC 369). This is obviously desirable to avoid the possibility of such a class abusing the requirement that the approval of each separate interest group is necessary for the scheme's approval.

Finally, a high standard of disclosure is required in the statement which, under section 426 CA, must accompany the notices sent out convening the meetings. This statement must explain

"the effect of the compromise or arrangement and in particular [state] any material interests of the directors of the company (whether as directors or as members or as creditors of the company or otherwise) and the effect on those interests of the compromise or arrangement, insofar as it is different from the effect on the like interests of other persons."

If the proposal is approved by a majority in number representing three-fourths in value of each class of creditors or shareholders present and voting (either in person or by proxy), the second application may be made to the court to sanction the compromise or arrangement. The court has wide powers in sanctioning a compromise or arrangement including the transfer of all or part of the undertaking of one company to another company (s427 CA). The court will scrutinise any evidence which suggests that those voting were misled by insufficient or inaccurate information in the statement sent out with the notice convening the meetings. The court will also refuse to sanction a compromise or arrangement where it appears that unnecessary obstacles have hindered those entitled to vote at the meetings (*Re Dorman Long Ltd* [1934] Ch 635).

Corporate voluntary arrangements

Part I of the Insolvency Act contemplates a proposal for a CVA being made by the directors unless the company is in administration or liquidation in which case the proposal will be made by the administrator or liquidator. The proposal provides for a person – "the nominee" (who must be a qualified insolvency practitioner) – to act in supervising the proposed voluntary arrangement. The nominee might already be the administrator or liquidator himself (if there is one) or a different insolvency practitioner. If the latter, a report must be made to the court within 28 days of the proposal having been made. This must express the nominee's opinion as to whether meetings of the creditors and shareholders should be called to consider the proposal and, if so, when the meetings should be held. If the nominee is the administrator or liquidator, no such report need be made.

If the report is in favour of convening the meetings or the proposal was made by the administrator or liquidator, the meetings are summoned on at least 14 days' notice. Only two meetings are provided for – of the creditors ("every creditor of the company of whose claim and address the person summoning the meeting is aware", s3(3)) and of the members. The Insolvency Rules ("IR") prescribe that the meetings are to be held on the same day but the creditors' meeting must be fixed to take place in advance of the members' meeting. The meetings may be adjourned from time to time and may even be held together, where the chairman thinks that it is right to secure simultaneous agreement to the proposals.

Creditors' votes are calculated in accordance with the value of their claim against the company and there must be a majority of more than 75% in value (Rule 1.19 IR) more than half of whom are not connected with the company. Members' votes are prescribed by the articles of association and the requisite majority for passing a resolution at the members' meeting is anything over one half in value of the members present in person or by proxy and voting on the resolution. The value of the members' votes is determined by reference to the number of votes conferred on each member by the articles of association (Rule 1.20 IR).

Creditors' involvement and position

Scheme of arrangement

Each creditor will have an opportunity to support or oppose the scheme at the appropriate meeting. If a creditor objects, but is outvoted by more than three to one and all other meetings held also approve the scheme, his only recourse is to oppose the application to court for the sanctioning of the scheme. He will succeed if he can show some material irregularity in the procedure by which the scheme was "approved" – where, for example, he was denied a proper proxy vote, which, presumably, would have altered the result or where there were omissions, or inaccuracies in the statutory statement accompanying the proposed scheme, or where one creditor with substantial voting power really had a different interest from the interest of the smaller out-voted minority (see *Re Dorman Long Ltd* [1934] Ch 635; *Re Hellenic & General Trust Ltd* [1975] 3 All ER 382, [1976] 1 WLR 123). If he simply has a different commercial view as to the efficacy of the scheme, he will not persuade the court to reject the application for sanctioning the scheme.

Corporate voluntary arrangement

The notice summoning the meetings must state that for the creditors' meeting, 75% in value of creditors present in person or by proxy and voting on the resolution is required to pass any resolution approving the proposed plan or any modification of it. The notice must also state which votes are to be left out of account (for example, where the creditor has failed to give written notice of his or her claim or where the claim is secured) in calculating the majority and also the circumstances in which the resolution will be invalid (Rule 1.11 (2) IR, incorporating 1.19 (1), (3), (4)). The notice must also be accompanied by a copy of the proposal and a copy of the statement of affairs (or a summary) which will have been made in respect of the company by its directors.

The problem of creditors' claims which are unascertained at the time of the CVA meetings was recently considered in *Re Cranley Mansions Ltd: Saigol v Goldstein* [1994] BCC 576. The nominee followed a growing practice of attributing, without the creditor's agreement, a value of £1 to an unliquidated claim (estimated by the creditor at more than £900,000). The court held that this denied the creditor her vote and held her not bound by the proposals approved at the meeting. For the creditor to be bound, she would have had to agree the value put on her claim by the chairman.

The *Cranley* decision has been widely criticised by practitioners, since its effect is to give creditors with potentially large unascertained claims a means of holding the company to ransom, unless their claims are agreed for voting purposes at a level acceptable to them. In *Doorbar v Alltime Securities Ltd* [1994] BCC 994, Knox J, in deciding the same question but in relation to an individual voluntary arrangement (the relevant rule, 5.17 IR being in all respects virtually the same as the corresponding Rule – 1.17 IR – for CVA's) did not follow the *Cranley* decision and held that, if the chairman of the meeting considering a CVA was prepared to put a value on the creditor's claim, the creditor should be able to vote for that amount and would be bound by the CVA if it were approved.

Nothing may be done at the meetings which affects the rights of secured or preferential creditors without their consent. The results of the meetings must be reported to the court. If both meetings have approved the proposed voluntary arrangement, it takes effect as though made by the company at the creditors' meeting.

Everyone with notice of the meetings and entitled to vote is bound by the terms of the voluntary arrangement. It has been held in relation to an individual voluntary arrangement under an equivalent provision that, where the notice convening the meeting was sent to the wrong address, the creditor did not have the requisite notice and could pursue its claim against the debtor, (*Re A Debtor, No 64 of 1992* [1994] BCC 56). It has also recently been held that a landlord creditor whose claim had been assessed for the purpose of the meeting approving the proposed CVA was not bound in relation to the company's liability for future rent (*Burford Midland Properties Ltd* v *Marley Extrusions Ltd* [1994] BCC 604). Whether this will be the case in any particular CVA, however, will depend upon whether the CVA, on its construction, encompasses future liabilities (*Doorbar* v *Alltime Securities Ltd* [1994] BCC 994)

Either the nominee or some other insolvency practitioner will have been approved to supervise the voluntary arrangement and is thenceforth known as the supervisor.

If the company had been in administration or liquidation prior to the approval of the voluntary arrangement, the court may discharge the administration order or stay the winding up proceedings. Any creditor may apply to the court if he believes that the voluntary arrangement, as approved, is unfairly prejudicial to his interests. A similar right is available to a member, to the nominee, or where appropriate, to the liquidator or administrator. A similar right of objection exists where any of the company's creditors is dissatisfied by any act, omission or decision of the supervisor (s6 IA).

Post-approval management and termination

Scheme of arrangement
The statute makes no special provision for the implementation and completion of the scheme. The scheme itself will very often have made provision for how it is to be carried out. Thus, scheme administrators (who may be licensed insolvency practitioners) are likely to be appointed to evaluate and pay claims. Their management powers will be set out in the scheme and will vary from complete control to, in cases where the directors' identity is central to a rescue plan, a more supervisory function. In some instances, provision will be made for a committee of scheme creditors to be appointed to assist in the implementation of the scheme. Ultimately, if the scheme fails, the company can be put into administration or liquidation or a new scheme or CVA attempted.

Corporate voluntary arrangement
It is the supervisor's function to implement a CVA after its approval. He is empowered to seek directions from the court and may petition for the company to be placed into administration or liquidation. It is the duty of the directors of the company or, if the company had been in administration or liquidation prior to the approval of the voluntary arrangement, of the administrator or liquidator, to ensure that the supervisor gains full control over the company's assets or those included in the CVA. The supervisor is required to prepare an abstract of his receipts and payments every 12 months. If the arrangement requires him to continue the trading activities of the company, to dispose of its assets or otherwise

to administer or dispose of its funds, he must ensure that proper accounts are kept of all his dealings.

The CVA will terminate either by being revoked by the court (where, for example, there has been a successful objection) or on its successful completion. If it is revoked, the court may make some consequential order (perhaps for the company to go into liquidation). In the unlikely event of no consequential order being made and the company not being in administration or liquidation, the directors at the time the CVA was approved will resume control, or the members will elect new directors. If the company's liabilities at that time exceed its assets it is likely to be only a matter of time before it is placed, whether by its creditors or directors, into some kind of insolvency regime. When the CVA has been completed, the supervisor must advise all creditors and members of that fact.

Administration

Purpose and effect

Prior to the IA, aside from the scheme described above, there was no statutory facility in the United Kingdom for the attempted rescue of an insolvent company or its business. The scheme, as we have seen, was often unsuitable as a regime for the carrying out of such a rescue and, in the main, companies and creditors in the United Kingdom have relied on the partly statutory, partly contractual administration receivership regime (see p767 *infra*) for this purpose. That regime also has defects, including the fact that it is available only to creditors whose claims against the company are secured by a floating charge over the whole or substantially the whole of the company's business and undertaking.

The administration procedure was created on the strong recommendation of the influential Review Committee on Insolvency Law and Practice, which reported in 1982 (Cmnd 8558). It is now contained in IA Part II. The most striking effect of a company going into administration is the "moratorium" restraining any enforcement procedures against the company. This can be compared to the "temporary restraining order" effected in relation to bankrupt American corporations which seek the protection of the regime created by Chapter XI of the United States Bankruptcy Code of 1978. This moratorium is examined below.

Pre-application considerations

By the time a company is considering administration (or administration is being considered for the company), it is likely to be in serious financial trouble. It may well already have suffered the indignity of having its bank (with whom it is likely to have a large overdraft well beyond the agreed limit) commission an accountants' investigation of its affairs (for which it will have had to pay). Creditors will be threatening to take legal proceedings for the payment of their claims; some may already have done so. Suppliers of much needed goods may be refusing to continue to supply until debts are paid.

The company's own board of directors might well have become concerned that the trading by the company while insolvent is increasing potential loss to the company's creditors for which they may be personally liable under the "wrongful trading" provisions (p804 *infra*). At this juncture, the board of the company or, more rarely, one or more of its creditors might then wish to present a petition for the administration of the company. In addition, the Act allows a petition to be presented by the company (as opposed to by the directors). This is designed to deal with the occasional problem which arises where the board and the shareholders disagree on the appropriate action for the company (p732 *supra*). A recent threat to director-presented petitions (that the directors would be required personally to pay the costs of an unsuccessful petition) was removed by the Court of Appeal overruling the court below and holding that the directors, who had followed the procedure carefully, and had at all times acted in good faith and on the advice of experienced insolvency practitioners, were not personally liable for the costs of the procedure (*Re Land and Property Trust Co plc (No 2)* [1993] BCC 462).

Section 8 IA lays down that, to make an order for administration, the court must be satisfied that:

- the company is, or is likely to become, unable to pay its debts; and
- the making of the order will be likely to achieve one or more of the following four stated purposes:
  - the survival of the company and the whole or any part of its undertaking as a going concern;
  - the approval of a voluntary arrangement under Part I IA;
  - the sanctioning of a compromise or arrangement under s425 CA;
  - a more advantageous realisation of the company's assets than would be effected on a winding up.

Administration is thus most unlikely where the condition of the company is hopeless, except if the fourth stated purpose is the one alleged to be likely to be achieved.

The allegation that a company is unable to pay its debts is the commonest ground for compulsory liquidation and in relation to compulsory liquidation section 123 IA lists a number of cases from which this condition can be deduced (p786-787 *infra*). On a petition for administration the court is required to adopt the same approach.

Under the IA, an administration order cannot be sought for a company that is already in liquidation or for an insurance company within the meaning of the Insurance Companies Act 1982. By virtue of the Banks (Administration Proceedings) Order 1989 (SI 1989 No 1276) an authorised institution or a former authorised institution within the meaning of the Banking Act 1987 (s8(4) IA) and similar bodies may be the subject of an administration order as long as they are companies within the Companies Act 1985 definition (s735 CA).

The directors might also seek the company's administration to enable them to plead as a defence against "wrongful trading" proceedings under section 214 (below) that they took "every step with a view to minimising the potential loss to the company's creditors" (s214(3), see p804 *infra*). Any creditor or group of creditors might seek the company's administration because he or they might believe that the company would, in consequence, be able to pay more or all of its indebtedness. Other creditors might believe that if the company's life were prolonged, this would simply increase its indebtedness. Their decision to support or oppose administration is likely to be influenced by whether they are secured, preferential or unsecured (pp771, 790 *infra*).

A further complication must be mentioned. A secured creditor whose security consists of a floating charge or a fixed and floating charge and who has the power to appoint a receiver over the whole or substantially the whole of the company's property (an appointee who will be classified as an "administrative receiver" – s29(2) IA) can frustrate use of the administration procedure by making such an appointment. Section 9(3) makes it clear that no administrator can be appointed where an administrative receiver is validly in post and intends to remain so.

Administrative receivership does provide an opportunity for the partial or total rescue of a company, but the primary responsibility of the administrative receiver is to the secured creditor who appointed him rather than to the company. In any insolvent company, there may well be both strong support for administration and a secured creditor able to appoint an administrative receiver.

An administration order imposes a moratorium on all claims against the company and, therefore, an opportunity to take appropriate steps to restore the company to financial health. An independent insolvency practitioner (or two or occasionally even three), is appointed to prepare proposals for the restructuring of the company so as to enable it to repay its creditors in full or at least to a greater extent then would have been possible on liquidation. Thus, other creditors are prevented from putting the company into liquidation in circumstances where the company is potentially rescuable and creditors with superior rights (under a hire purchase agreement or with the benefit of a retention of title clause) cannot without permission enforce those rights to the detriment of the company and its other creditors (s10 IA).

Despite possessing the power to appoint an administrative receiver, a secured creditor may agree to forgo this power and agree to the appointment of an administrator. The following factors may influence the secured creditor's decision in this regard:

- the presence in administration, but not administrative receivership, of a moratorium (although see pp769-770 *infra*);
- the secured creditor will not be seen as the initiator of the company's insolvency and, therefore, responsible for any hardship occurring as a result;
- there will be no loss of priority in any subsequent distribution since any money received by the administrator in the sale of assets which constituted the security must be appropriated to the secured creditor's debt (ss15(5), 19(5));
- the court-appointed status of the administrator may help with realisations of the company's property abroad (many jurisdictions may refuse to accept

the authority of an administrative receiver on account of the relative informality of the latter's appointment);

- the administrator (but not the administrative receiver) has the benefit of those provisions (ss238,239, see pp800-803 *infra*) which enable certain pre-administration transactions to be set aside.

It is true, on the other hand, that the secured creditor loses control over the assets which constitute his security and may, for example, be unable to effect the sale of part or all of those assets when the company is in administration (see *Re Meesan Investments Ltd* (1988) 4 BCC 788, also known as *Royal Trust Insurance* v *Buchler* [1989] BCLC 130). In addition, the secured creditor cannot dismiss the administrator, but this is not a disadvantage peculiar to administration since it is also no longer possible to dismiss an administrative receiver without the approval of the court (s45(1) IA).

Other factors favouring the appointment of an administrative receiver as opposed to acquiescing in the administration petition are:

- the secured creditor has the choice of, and greater control over, the insolvency practitioner appointed;

- administrative receivership is quicker and cheaper;

- the administrative receiver (but not the administrator) can distribute floating charge assets (although subject to the claims of the preferential creditors).

One other question is likely to be greatly influential in the decision as to the course which the insolvent company will take, namely how any administration is to be financed. Unless the company can rely on being in funds during the attempted rescue, it is doomed from the start. An administrative receivership other than one where the debtor's business and/or assets are to be sold immediately may also require further finance. This often comes from a secured creditor who has the power to appoint an administrative receiver. If that secured creditor can be convinced that administration is a more commercially attractive option from both the debtor's and his own point of view, that secured creditor's assistance will generally be forthcoming.

Procedure

Serving and filing the petition

The application for administration is by petition supported by an affidavit giving full details of the company, explaining why administration is desirable, and setting out which of the four possible purposes is expected to be achieved (p751 *supra*). Invariably in practice (although not required by law), a report is prepared by an independent person to the effect that it would be expedient to appoint an administrator (Rule 2.2 IR). A suitably qualified insolvency practitioner must be named as the prospective administrator and that may be, and usually is, the same person who drafted the independent report. This independent report has tended to become long, complicated and, therefore, expensive. The courts, while in need of evidence that the company will benefit from administration, are conscious of the disincentive of such expense. A recent *Practice Note* ([1994] BCC 35, [1994] BCLC 347) attempts to steer petitioners towards drawing the right balance on this issue by pointing out that Rule 2.2 reports can be kept simple and stressing that they are not a legal requirement of the procedure.

The petition and affidavit must be filed in court, which then fixes a venue for the hearing. The petition must be served on anyone who has appointed or who is entitled to appoint an administrative receiver, on any administrative receiver already appointed and on the nominated administrator. If there is a pending winding up petition the administration petition should be served on that petitioner and, if one has been appointed, on the provisional liquidator (Rule 2.6(2) IR). Notice must also be given to any sheriff who has seized goods in execution of a judgment, and to anyone who might have distrained against the company or its property.

When the petition comes on for hearing, the following may be heard or represented at the hearing:

- the petitioner;
- the company;
- any creditor with power to appoint an administrative receiver (whether one has been appointed or not);
- any administrative receiver already appointed;
- anyone who has petitioned for the winding up of the company;
- if appointed, the provisional liquidator;
- the proposed administrator;
- anyone else who can justify his appearance (for instance, opposing creditors or perhaps even the company's employees).

The effect of the application

During the period from the presentation of the petition to the making of the administration order or the dismissal of the petition, there is a virtual freeze on any enforcement proceedings against the company (s10(1)). As noted above, the only clear exception to this moratorium is the exercise of the right by a creditor whose claim is secured by a floating charge with power to appoint an administrative receiver, to make that appointment. The court, too, is able to grant leave to a creditor to repossess goods or to take other enforcement proceedings.

The order and its effect

If an administration order is made, it will direct the administrator to manage "the affairs, business and property of the company" during the period for which the order is in force. The order must also specify the purpose or purposes for which it was granted. While the court does have a wide discretion, it can only grant an order for one or more of the purposes for which the petition was presented and it does not have the power to make an interim appointment (*Re A Company, No 00175/87* (1987) 3 BCC 124 [1987] BCLC 467).

In Scotland, however, the courts have accepted that they do have the power to make an interim appointment of an administrator until the hearing of the petition. Although taking a different view the English courts have achieved a similar result through the appointment of an interim manager or by some other form of restraining order (see *Re Gallidoro Trawlers Ltd* [1991] BCLC 411, [1991] BCC 691.

Notification of the order must be given in several ways. First, any invoice, order for goods or business letter which contains the company's name must specify that the company is in administration. Secondly, the administrator must send a copy of the order to the Registrar of Companies. Thirdly, the administrator must give notice of the order to a wide variety of people and officers who might be interested in the grant of the order (Rule 2.10(2),(3) IR). Fourthly, the administrator must advertise the order in a newspaper likely to come to the notice of the company's creditors.

The Act also provides for the variation and discharge of the order (s18) and the administrator and even the directors can apply for the order to be extended (*Re Newport County Association Football Club Ltd* (1987) 3 BCC 635, [1987] BCLC 582). It is also now clear that a creditor can apply for the discharge of an administration order either because he is unfairly prejudiced thereby or because there was material non-disclosure to the court in an *ex parte* hearing when the order was granted (*Cornhill Insurance plc* v *Cornhill Financial Services Ltd* [1992] BCC 818, [1993] BCLC 914).

If the order is granted, the moratorium is continued and extended in that it now also restrains the appointment of an administrative receiver (s11(3)(b)). Indeed, if an administrative receiver had been appointed, he must now vacate office (s11(1)). One further change occurs on the grant of the order – the administrator, as well as the court, can give permission to any creditor to continue proceedings against the company (s11(3)(c), (d)).

Creditors' involvement and position

Creditors are involved in several ways in an administration. First, it is up to the creditors to decide whether the administrator's proposals for achieving the purposes specified in the administration order (which the administrator must lay before the creditors within three months or such longer period as the court may allow) are to be put into effect. Secondly, they are entitled to form a committee which can request information as to the progress of the administration from the administrator. Thirdly, any one creditor may seek leave to continue proceedings against the company. Fourthly, any secured creditor may object to a proposal by the administrator to dispose of assets belonging to the company but which constitute part or all of a secured creditor's security. Fifthly, any creditor may apply to court for relief if he believes that the administrator has acted in an unfairly prejudicial way towards him.

Finally, it should be pointed out that where administrators refused leave to creditors to repossess goods held under leases and hire purchase agreements, the court held that they ran the risk of being liable for conversion. The court refused to grant the administrators their release until the outstanding claim against them for their use of the creditors' property was resolved (*Re Sibec Developments Ltd* [1993] BCC 148, [1993] BCLC 1077).

Considering the administrator's proposals

When the administrator has formulated his proposals for the course of action by which the company is to achieve the statutory purpose or purposes for which the order was granted, these proposals are put to a meeting of creditors. The meeting must be summoned on 14 days' notice not later than three months (or such longer period as the court may allow) after the order was granted. Notice must be given to each known creditor and advertised in the newspaper in which the order was advertised (Rule 2.17 IR). A resolution approving the proposals or any modification to which the administrator is prepared to agree, is passed if approved by "more than half in value of the creditors to whom notice of the meeting was sent and who are not, to the best of the chairman's (the administrator or someone nominated by him) belief, persons connected with the company" (Rule 2.28 (1A) IR). Secured creditors may only vote in respect of any balance owing after deducting the value of the security as estimated by that secured creditor (Rule 2.24 IR).

The administrator is required to report the outcome of this meeting to the court, the Registrar of Companies and each creditor who was entitled to attend the meeting. If the proposals are approved, the business of the company will be conducted by the administrator in accordance with them. If not, the court has a wide discretion, but the most likely outcome is the liquidation of the company (although a petition to this effect will have to be presented).

Where one is dealing with the administration of a substantial company, three months may be too short a period in which to formulate definitive proposals for achieving the statutory purpose or purposes for which an administrator has been appointed. A practice (with which creditors have generally concurred) has developed of holding the approval meeting early in the three month period and phrasing the proposals in broad terms so as to give the administrator maximum flexibility to deal with developments in the company's position as they unfold.

The creditors' committee

Once the proposals have been approved, the creditors may resolve to form a committee. This is designed to assist the administrator and also to enable the creditors to obtain information on the progress of the administration. There are a number of formalities (Rules 2.32-2.46 IR) and, when all have been complied with, the administrator may issue a certificate of due constitution.

Leave to continue proceedings against the company
Under section 11 (3), the following actions against the company are restrained without the permission either of the administrators or the court:

- petitions for winding up or winding up orders;
- the appointment of an administrative receiver;
- any steps to enforce any security over the company's property or to re-possess goods in the company's possession under any hire purchase agreement, conditional sale agreement, chattel leasing agreement or retention of title agreement;
- the commencement or continuation of any other proceedings or execution or other legal process or distress against the company or its property.

As far as proceedings are concerned, it seems that what are restrained are adversarial proceedings to which the company is a party as defendant or respondent. Thus, where the dispute was as to which of two applicants was to be entitled to a government contract or other privilege by way of grant, and one of the companies was in administration, the relevant proceedings did not come within the moratorium (*Air Ecosse Ltd* v *Civil Aviation Authority* (1987) 3 BCC 492). On the other hand legal proceedings before a tribunal rather than a court do fall within the section (*Carr* v *British International Helicopters Ltd* [1993] BCC 855).

As far as restraints on proceedings against the company's property are concerned, it is clear that not only hire purchase and retention of title recoveries are restrained by the order, but also claims under right of ownership, for instance, by a landlord for recovery of property of which the company is a tenant (*Exchange Travel Agency Ltd.* v *Triton Property Trust plc* [1991] BCC 341, [1991] BCLC 396). The courts have now made it clear that where a secured creditor resists the demand by the administrators for return of the property which constitutes the security, but which he has received without the leave of the court, the secured creditor is in contempt of court (*Re Sabre International Products Ltd* [1991] BCC 694, [1991] BCLC 470).

It has recently been held that the service of a contractual notice on the company was a process not requiring the assistance of the court and, thus, did not fall within the category of "other legal process" in section 11 (3) (d) and so was not restrained by the administration order (*Re Olympia and York Canary Wharf Ltd* [1993] BCC 154, [1993] BCLC 453, *Scottish Exhibition Centre Ltd* v *Mirestop Ltd* [1994] BCC 845, [1993] BCLC 1459).

In the main, it will be secured rather than unsecured creditors who will be prejudiced by the moratorium and the several reported applications for leave to take or continue proceedings against a company in administration have been made largely by secured creditors. In *Re Meesan Investments* (1988) 4 BCC 788 (also reported as *Royal Trust Bank* v *Buchler* [1989] BCLC 130) leave was refused to a secured creditor seeking to enforce its security over fixed property belonging to the company, but the administrator was required to return to the court two months later if he failed to achieve the plan of refurbishing and selling the property. He did, in fact, fail and the creditor was given permission to proceed.

In *Re Paramount Airways Ltd* [1990] BCC 130, [1990] BCLC 585, Bristol and Birmingham Airports were unsecured creditors of Paramount Airways, although in common with all other airports they had a statutory lien allowing them to detain aircraft of airlines which were in arrears with airport dues. Administrators were appointed to Paramount and trading was continued – as a result of which both airport creditors benefited. A few months later, when aeroplanes leased to Paramount were parked at their respective airports, Bristol and Birmingham applied for leave to detain them. Leave was refused: first, because to grant it would have been to promote those two creditors over other unsecured creditors; secondly, because detention of the aircraft would have frustrated the purpose of the administration; and thirdly, because the airports had enjoyed the benefit of the administration for several months and had agreed to the administrator's proposal of continuing to trade.

In *Re Atlantic Computer Systems Plc* ([1990] BCC 859, [1991] BCLC 606) – the administrators of Atlantic refused consent to several companies to repossess computer equipment let to Atlantic under hire purchase agreements and leases. The equipment had been sub-let by Atlantic and the rent was being paid to Atlantic; no payments were being made by the administrators. The Court of Appeal, although granting leave to the lessors in this case, was anxious to enable decisions as to leave to be made by administrators wherever possible and gave the following guidance for future administrators who would be asked to grant leave to creditors wishing to pursue claims against the company in administration:

- the onus is on the person seeking leave to make out the case for leave;
- leave should be given where to do so is unlikely to impede the administration;
- if leave would impede the administration, the court must balance the conflicting interests giving great weight to the proprietary interests of (in this case) the lessor;
- the court's view is that so far as possible, the administration procedure should not be used to prejudice those who were secured creditors of a company going into administration as against liquidation;
- where to grant leave would cause substantially greater loss to others out of all proportion to the benefit conferred on the lessor by the grant of leave;
- it may be material to inquire what is/are the purpose(s) of the administration, how long it has been in progress and is likely to remain in force, the prospects for success, the financial position of the company, and the respective effects on lessor and company of refusing or granting leave are all relevant criteria in the decision;
- consideration should be given to the likelihood of the applicant suffering loss;
- the conduct of the parties must be taken into account, (for instance, in *Paramount Airways*, where the airports authorities agreed to the continua-

tion of trading and then used this to try to improve their pre-insolvency claims).

Recently, in *Re David Meek Access Ltd.* ([1993] BCC 175, [1994] BCLC 680), the court refused leave to finance house creditors to repossess goods let and sold to the company under leases and hire purchase agreements. The court held that the creditors had failed to satisfy the court that they would suffer a significant loss compared to the position in which they would have been if allowed to repossess their goods. The court was also satisfied with the administrators' submission that to allow repossession would have significantly reduced the company's chances of achieving the purposes for which the administration order had been granted.

Objecting to the disposal of company property

Section 15 gives the administrator power to dispose of the company's charged property, but where the charge is fixed (and the chargee objects), an application must be made to persuade the court that the disposal "... would be likely to promote the purpose or one or more of the purposes specified in the administration order..." (s15(2)). Any money realised by the sale must be applied to discharging the debt secured, topped up where necessary by an amount equal to the difference between what was realised and what would have been realised had that disposal taken place on the open market by a willing vendor (s15(5)). In *ARV Aviation Ltd* (1988) 4 BCC 708, [1989] BCLC 664, the secured creditor objected but the joint administrators' application was successful. The secured creditor was concerned that there was insufficient evidence as to the valuation of the security; on the other hand, the administrators had to act quickly to effect the sale.

Seeking relief against unfairly prejudicial conduct

If it can be established that "the company's affairs, business and property are being or have been managed by the administrator in a manner which is unfairly prejudicial to the interests of its creditors and members generally, or of some part of its creditors or members", including the applicant (s27(1)), the court has wide powers to:

- "regulate the future management by the administrator of the company's affairs, business and property;
- require the administrator to refrain from doing or continuing an act complained of by the petitioner or to do an act which the petitioner has complained he has omitted to do;
- require the summoning of a meeting of creditors or members for the purpose of considering such matters as the court may direct;
- discharge the administration order and make such consequential provision as [it] thinks fit" (s27(4)).

One application heard and resolved under this provision which has been reported is *Re Charnley Davies Ltd* [1990] BCC 605, [1990] BCLC 760. The application charged the administrator with having sold the company's assets too quickly and, therefore, too cheaply. The application failed. The court considered that the application was not one alleging unfairly prejudicial conduct, but one alleging professional negligence. It was, therefore, not strictly within section 27. It was also made clear that to be successful against the administrator, the facts would have to be strong; the court would not be prepared to give the applicant the benefit of hindsight.

Powers and duties of the administrator

Powers
Some of the administrator's powers have already been referred to, namely, the power to:

- sell the company's assets subject to rights of objection by secured creditors whose security is threatened (p759 *supra*); and
- grant consent to creditors to commence or continue proceedings against the company (p755 *supra*).

In addition, the administrator is given very wide powers to manage the company. These powers fall into four groups, namely:

- powers given by Schedule 1 to do all that is necessary in the general management of the company (ss14, 42);
- specific management power to dismiss any of the directors, appoint other directors, call any meetings of the company or its creditors, apply to the court for directions and ignore any inhibiting provisions in the memorandum and articles of association (s14);
- powers to set aside any transaction between the company and certain of its creditors undertaken within a certain period prior to the administration at a time when the company was insolvent and which places those creditors in a better position than they would otherwise have been in (ss238-246);
- powers given by sections 22 and 233-236 to enable utilities to be maintained and investigations to be undertaken as to what happened to the company prior to the administration and to recover the company's books, papers and other property.

Duties
We have already noted the administrator's duties, namely to:

- prepare proposals for carrying out the administration and submit these to a meeting of creditors within three months of the order;
- notify a variety of people and officers as to the grant of the order;
- publicise the proposals and the outcome of the meeting which considered the proposals;

- facilitate the establishment of the creditors' committee;
- give information to the creditors' committee (s26(2), Rule 2.44 IR);
- apply for a discharge or variation of the order where it appears that the purposes for which it was granted are incapable of achievement, or where he is so instructed by the creditors' committee (s18(2)).

In addition, the administrator is required to

- take into his custody or control, the company's property (s17(1));
- manage the affairs, business and property of the company until the proposals are approved, and if approved, then in accordance with the proposals (s17(2));
- summon meetings if directed by the court or if required by creditors who constitute at least one-tenth of the claims against the company (s17(3));
- give creditors a progress report every six months (Rule 2.30(2) IR) and on vacating office (Rule 2.30(3) IR);
- every six months and on ceasing to be administrator, give to the court, the Registrar of Companies and each member of the creditors' committee accounts of receipts and payments (Rule 2.52(1) IR).

It is also important to remember that powers such as the power to set aside transactions and bring the company's property within his custody and control (p760 *supra*) are also duties. If the administrator fails to exercise such powers in appropriate cases, he may be called to account after the administration for any loss which the company might have suffered as a result.

Management by the administrator

As we have seen, the administrator has wide powers to manage the company. He will also be assisted by the provisions of section 19(4), (5). Under section 19 (4), the administrator's remuneration and properly incurred expenses are to be charged on and paid out of the company's property under his custody and control in priority to any creditor whose claim is secured by a floating charge. Section 19(5) confers the same priority and security on any sums which are payable in respect of debts or liabilities incurred during the administration. Section 19, however, draws a distinction in relation to such sums as are payable by reason of contracts entered into by the administrator and sums payable by reason of contracts of employment adopted by the administrator.

There is, in consequence, a significant distinction between employment contracts and other contracts. If the administrator is found to have adopted a contract of employment (and s19(5) adds that he is not deemed to have done so by anything done or not done within the first 14 days of the administration), the expenses arising in connection with such contracts are payable with the priority and security already mentioned. This priority and security only arises in connection with non-employment contracts if the administrator himself enters into such a contract in the performance of his duties. If he simply acts on a non-employment contract which the company itself had entered into prior to the administration, any sums which become payable will not enjoy the benefit of the priority and security conferred by section 19(5).

The problem of employment contracts is one to which administrators and administrative receivers have given much attention in order to ensure that sufficient employment is maintained (to keep the company operating so as to facilitate a rescue) but at the same time avoiding the security and priority conferred by section 19(5). Obviously current wages have to be paid, but the problem lies in the additional claims which might arise under employment contracts of an insolvent company, such as claims for unfair dismissal, holiday pay and so on. If these attract the priority and security conferred by section 19(5), this jeopardises the repayment of the creditor whose claim is secured by a floating charge and even the administrator's own remuneration and recovery of expenses incurred in the course of the administration. The formula employed to try to achieve this was one apparently used successfully in *Re Specialised Mouldings Ltd* (unreported, but referred to in Stewart, *Administrative Receivers and Administrators* (1987) para 512) in terms of which a letter, sent to all employees offering continuing employment and continuing remuneration, specifically declared that the employment contracts were not being adopted.

This decision, however, attracted some criticism (see, for example, Goode, *Principles of Corporate Insolvency Law* (1990) pp101-102) and it was overruled in relation to administration in *Re Paramount Airways Ltd (No 3)* ([1994] BCC 172, [1994] 2 BCLC 118), in which the Court of Appeal held that such an attempted disclaimer of adopting employment contracts was of no effect where employees were retained beyond the first 14 days of the administration. As a result employees were entitled to the priority and security conferred by section 19(4), (5) IA 1986 in respect of all claims arising out of their contracts, namely pay in lieu of notice (it is common in the case of insolvent companies for employees to have to have been dismissed at various stages throughout the administration and, often, without the notice period provided under the contract), pension contributions and holiday pay, with interest. The employees were not, however, entitled to the sums by way of the bonus agreement since this did not arise out of the contract of employment.

This decision has, to a large extent, been upheld by the House of Lords, in a judgment delivered on 16 March 1995 by Lord Browne-Wilkinson (with whose judgment all the other four Law Lords concurred). "Adoption" of a contract of employment was construed as arising after an employee of the company was retained in employment for more than 14 days. Thereafter, he was treated as retained in accordance with his contract of employment, including, for example, his entitlement of notice of termination of that contract or damages in place of such notice. The House of Lords decided that the employee's entitlement under section 19(5), *i.e.* those claims which enjoyed priority over the administrators' fees and expenses, were restricted to liabilities which arose *in the administration*, namely:

- wages accruing due during the administration;
- damages for failure to give the required notice under the contract;
- the employer's pension contributions during the period of the administration;
- the proportion of holiday pay for that period of the employment, by reference to which holiday pay is to be calculated, which falls within the administration.

As a direct response to the decision of the Court of Appeal in the *Paramount* case, the Government quickly enacted the Insolvency Act 1994 which has the effect of limiting to "qualifying liabilities" the security and priority to which employees would otherwise be entitled. "Qualifying Liabilities" are defined in the Act, as:

- a liability to pay a sum by way of wages or salary or contribution to an occupational pension fund;
- a payment in respect of services rendered wholly or partly after the adoption of the contract.

These amendments also apply in the case of administrative receivership (pp776-777 *infra*), but it should be pointed out that these amendments only came into force with effect from 15 March 1994 and do not apply retrospectively to contracts of employment adopted by administrators or administrative receivers before that time. The approach to be taken to these cases, as now confirmed by the decision of the House of Lords, opens the way for substantial claims by employees employed in administrations between 1987 and 15 March 1994 and whose contracts of employment were treated as unadopted by the administrator.

Action on appointment

On appointment, the administrator must ensure that he takes control of all the company's business, affairs and property. He must review the company's prospects and prepare the proposals (which will be submitted to the meeting of creditors) as to how the company's business is to be conducted to achieve the purposes for which the administration order was granted. He will have to review the company's existing contractual commitments and, where necessary, terminate these, even at the expense of potential damages claims against the company.

The legal status of the administrator

Fundamental to the ability of the administrator to carry out such tasks of managing the company so as to restore it to financial health, is the protection afforded by section 14(4), by which the administrator is deemed to be acting as the company's agent. It is this provision which ensures that any liability which arises in connection with any breach of contract will fall on the company.

The power to break contracts

An important question arises as to the powers of an administrator to disregard contracts entered into by the company prior to the administration. As we shall see in relation to administrative receivership, the exercise of this power – which leaves the administrative receiver and his appointor free of taint or liability but creates a further unsecured liability for the company – is one of the cornerstones of the operation of that insolvency regime (p774 *infra*). In the case of administration, however, while the administrator has very wide powers of management, it is unlikely that he can avoid contracts quite so readily as can an administrative receiver.

Like an administrative receiver, an administrator will have to honour contracts under which the other contracting party has already acquired a proprietary interest (for example, a contract for the sale of land where beneficial title has passed and only the transfer or conveyance of legal title remains to be completed). He may, of course, delay the completion of such contracts just as he may prevent suppliers and hire purchase creditors from repossessing their goods by refusing leave under section 11(3)(c), (d). There is also authority to the effect that an administrator may have to honour other contracts which administrative receivers were held entitled to ignore, despite the resultant claim for damages (see *Astor Chemicals Ltd* v *Synthetic Technology Ltd* [1990] BCC 97, [1990] BCLC 1). A separate regime applies in the case of employment contracts (pp762-763 *supra*).

While an administrator's management powers are extensive, he would not, for example be able to use these to weaken a creditor's status. If an administrator insists on the delivery to him of the company's property by a creditor entitled to a lien over that property, he would be expected to negotiate with that creditor so as to ensure that the latter retained the benefit of his lien (see *Re Sabre International Products Ltd* 1991] BCC 694, [1991] BCLC 470). Even where the administrator exercises his power to dispose of the company's charged assets free of the charge, he is required to follow the provisions of section 15 so as to ensure that the affected secured creditor is not prejudiced by the exercise of this power. The section contains a formula designed to ensure that the secured creditor's position is protected *vis-a-vis* creditors in an inferior position (s15(4), (5)).

Liabilities such as redundancy payments and damages for unfair dismissal arising on the dismissal of employees would also, in principle, fall on the company. However, the provision of the Transfer of Undertakings (Protection of Employment) Regulations 1981 shift this liability in certain circumstances to the transferee of any business sold by the administrator in the course of his duties. This is, as yet, an unsettled area of law and one in which the European Union is attempting to establish uniformity among all Member States. The Transfer of Undertakings (Protection of Employment) Regulations 1981 are the means through which the United Kingdom implemented EC Directive 77/189 ("the Acquired Rights Directive") and work is now proceeding to replace this with a fresh Directive.

Broadly speaking, the present Directive and the implementing Regulations provide that if the administrator dismisses employees in order to make the business of the company (or part of the business) more saleable to a particular purchaser, the liability for that dismissal shifts to that purchaser. If, on the other hand, it can be shown that the dismissal was for economic, technical or organisational reasons (rather than on grounds of redundancy), liability will remain with the transferring company.

The precise mechanism is as follows: under Regulation 5(1), a transfer of an undertaking from one person to another,

> "shall not operate so as to terminate the contract of employment of any person employed by the transferor in the undertaking ... transferred but any such contract which would otherwise have been terminated by the transfer shall have effect, after the transfer, as if originally made between the person so employed and the transferee".

The Regulation goes on to provide that "the transferor's rights, powers, duties and liabilities under or in connection with any such contract, shall be transferred ... to the transferee". Thus any claims the employee might have under his contract (including, for example, any claim for unfair dismissal) will, following the transfer, lie against the transferee. However, this transfer of rights and duties is only to have effect in the case of an employee employed by the undertaking transferred "immediately before the transfer" (Regulation 5(3)).

This last condition – that the employee be employed by the transferor *immediately* before the transfer – led the Court of Appeal in *Secretary of State* v *Spence* ([1987] QB 179, [1986] 3 All ER 616) to hold that where an employee was dismissed three hours before the transfer, the employee was not employed immediately before the transfer and that his claim for unfair dismissal did not, therefore, lie against the transferee (but, in fact, against the Secretary of State for Employment who has a statutory duty to step into the shoes of an insolvent employer in such circumstances).

However, in *Litster* v *Forth Dry Dock and Engineering Co Ltd* ([1990] 1 AC 546, [1989] All ER 1134) the House of Lords, without overruling *Spence*, held that the Regulations did apply to effect a transfer of the employee's rights to the transferee where the employee was dismissed an hour before the transfer. The facts of the two cases were materially different in that in *Spence*, it would appear that when the dismissal took place, there was no certainty that the undertaking would be transferred. In *Litster*, on the other hand, the proposed transfer was agreed well in advance of the actual transfer and certainly well before the dismissal was effected.

Drawing on decisions of courts in the European Court of Justice on the effect of the Acquired Rights Directive, the House of Lords gave a purposive interpretation to Regulation 5(3) so as to conform to corresponding developments in other European Community jurisdictions. Thus the requirement that the employee was employed by the transferor *immediately* before the transfer, was interpreted in *Litster* to include the case of an employee who would have been so employed but for his unfair dismissal within the meaning of Regulation 8(1). Under the latter, the dismissal of an employee of the transferor company for a reason connected with the transfer of the transferor's business, is an unfair dismissal within the meaning of Part V of the Employment Protection (Consolidation) Act 1978, unless the dismissal can be shown to have been for an economic, technical or organisational reason (Regulation 8(2)).

Distribution

The administrator has no power to make distributions of money to the creditors as and when this is possible. Any partial distribution (*i.e.* when the company is not yet solvent) will have to take place through the form of a CVA or a scheme or, failing that, by way of liquidation (p743 *et seq supra*).

Position of officers and shareholders

The administrator will need all the help he can obtain in the discharge of his functions and he will hope for co-operation from the directors of the company. In an ideal administration, the administrator will not need to exercise his power to dismiss any of those who were directors at the time the order was granted, nor to appoint any other directors. Indeed, if he does dismiss any director, he may render the company liable in damages if the exercise of this power constitutes a breach of the contract between the company and the dismissed director. The administrator does, however, have a large number of powers (p760 *supra*) and may well be able to carry out the administration without having to exercise this power of dismissal.

The management structure – at least in law – is quite clear. The administrator has all the powers of management and the directors have none. Third parties who deal with the administrator in good faith and for value are entitled to assume that the administrator was acting within his powers (s14(6)) but, if they deal with the directors, it is unlikely that they can rely on the similar protection (available before administration) where directors act without power. It may be different where there has been a failure to publicise properly the fact of the administration.

There is nothing to indicate that the normal management duties *vis-a-vis* shareholders cease. Thus, there is still an obligation on the directors to call and hold an annual general meeting, although there is nothing much that can be transacted at such meeting. It also appears that the obligation on every registered company to have a secretary and at least one or two directors (private and public companies respectively, ss282, 283 CA) also continues. Thus, if the administrator does exercise his power to dismiss all the directors of any company or all but one of the directors of a public company, he must, in theory, appoint at least the statutory minimum replacements.

Experience in practice is that Companies House recognises that the officers of a company in administration have no real power. The Registrar of Companies, therefore, tends to focus closely on the performance by the administrator of his statutory duties, taking no enforcement action against the directors.

Termination

As already indicated, the administrator can apply to the court under section 18 for discharge of the administration order. He must do this either where the administration has been successful in achieving the purposes for which the order was granted or where the purpose or purposes for which he was appointed have become incapable of fulfilment. Only the administrator can make this application, but he can be instructed to do so by the creditors' committee. If he refuses, the court would be prepared to consider such an application on behalf of the creditors, but it may need to be done as an unfair prejudice petition under section 27.

If the administration has been successful, in that the company has returned to solvency, the administrator would normally hand the management of the company back to the directors. If the administration order was granted for the more advantageous realisation of the company's assets than would be achieved on a winding up, the administration would most likely be followed by liquidation. Even in this case if it becomes clear that realisation of assets will result in a surplus of assets over liabilities, there seems nothing to prevent the previous management resuming control and keeping the company in existence. The administration order would first have to be discharged to enable this to be done.

On the discharge of the administration order, the administrator vacates office (s19(2)(b)). His remuneration and any properly incurred expenses are a charge on the company's property which was under his control in priority to the rights of any floating charge holder (s19(4)). The administrator is entitled to ask the court for his release on ceasing to be administrator (s20(1)(b), the effect of which discharges him as from the moment of release from all liabilities in respect of his conduct as administrator (s20(3)) other than liabilities for misfeasance or breach of duty under section 212 IA.

Receivership

Types, purposes and effect

Contractual receivers
Receivership is an old remedy in English Law which has its roots in the enforcement of rights by a charge-holder ("chargee") of "real" (immovable) property. One of the chargee's remedies where the debtor fails to repay the secured debt is to take possession of the property which constitutes the security and either sell it or collect the rents and use the money thereby derived to repay that debt. English law does, however, place severe burdens on a chargee who takes possession of the debtor's property, with the result that, in the past, chargees often gained possession through appointing someone else (called a "receiver" because one of the latter's main functions has been to receive the rents). Since the chargee would continue to be liable for the acts of the receiver (who acted as his agent), this form of remedy could only achieve its purpose of freeing the chargee from liability if

the receiver could be classified as the debtor's (or mortgagor's) agent. This is usually provided for in the original contract between the chargee and debtor (usually the charge or mortgage) and the courts have upheld this provision.

Late in the nineteenth century and in conjunction with the development of the floating charge (p734 *supra*), where the debtor (mortgagor) was a registered company, the idea of the receiver running the business of the company emerged. This was important in allowing the company to earn profits, which could be used for the repayment of the loan where it was estimated that sale of the assets would provide insufficient funds for this purpose. A receiver was thus given powers by the charge or appointment document appointed to run the business as well as powers to collect the rents and to sell the assets and, thus came to be called a receiver and manager.

The regime of receiver and manager is, thus, a creation of contract with little statutory addition. Some statutory structure was given to this regime by the IA and a distinction created between the old style receiver and manager and the new "administrative receiver". As has been noted earlier, an administrative receiver is defined by s29(2) as being "a receiver and manager of the whole (or substantially the whole) of a company's property appointed by or on behalf of the holders of any debentures of the company secured by a charge which, as created, was a floating charge, or by such a charge and one or more other securities ...".

This is a wide definition, which ensures that the new regime virtually swallows up the old one. Included in this statutory structure is the conferment on an administrative receiver of the same wide general powers of management given to an administrator (s42, Schedule 1). This will not make much difference to the regime of receivership since, prior to the coming into force of the Insolvency Act, contractually appointed receivers were usually given similar wide powers by the charge. In this section, the term "receiver" is used to denote both the old regime of receiver and manager and the new one of administrative receiver.

Three differences between the old and new regimes should be noted at this stage. First, an administrative receiver cannot be removed once appointed, except with the leave of the court (s45(1)). Secondly, an administrative receiver – but not a receiver and manager – must be a licensed insolvency practitioner (p807 *infra*). Thirdly, only the appointment of an administrative receiver (not a receiver and manager) can bring a premature end to a petition for the appointment of an administrator (ss9 (3), 10(2)).

Attention should also be drawn to the regime of receiver of fixed property only. Known as a Law of Property Act (or "LPA") receiver (from the name of the statute which codified this institution), he can be appointed by the holder of a fixed charge and has power (conferred by the Law of Property Act and usually also by the charge) to receive the rents from, and to sell, the secured property. An LPA receiver is usually only appointed to the fixed property of an insolvent company debtor either where the chargee does not have a floating charge (and thus no power to appoint an administrative receiver) or where the corporate debtor is a property owning company with few or any assets other than its "real" or immovable property.

Court appointed receivers

The court has always had a jurisdiction to appoint a receiver as an exceptional remedy. This was exercised, *inter alia*, where a mortgagee was able to establish that his security was in jeopardy. A court appointed receiver, unlike one appointed by the chargee, is an officer of the court, responsible to the court and empowered to do only that which the court has ordered. It became increasingly clear that the contractually appointed receiver had immense advantages over court appointed receivers from the point of view of the chargee. The contractual receiverships are cheaper and quicker, not requiring any application to the court, and unrestricted except by the terms of the charge. Furthermore, the chargee can be sure of the appointment of his chosen person as receiver.

The result has been that nowadays secured creditors rarely seek to enforce their rights against a company debtor by way of court appointed receivers. Nevertheless, it must be remembered that only the creditor whose claim is secured by what was, when created, a floating charge can appoint an administrative receiver and then only if the charge gives him the right to do so. Court appointed receivers are rare nowadays, and this chapter concentrates on contractually appointed receivers.

The purpose and effect of receivership

The receiver's primary responsibility is to the chargee who appointed him. Thus, the receiver will consider carefully the financial status of the corporate debtor and decide how to proceed in order to ensure the best means for payment of the debt owed to the chargee. Occasionally, the receiver will simply need to collect the debts owed to the company but it is much more common for him to have to sell the assets of the company in order to repay the chargee. Except in the most difficult cases, the receiver will continue to trade at least for a short period in the hope that he will be able to find a purchaser for the company's business as a going concern as this is most likely to achieve the maximum return. This may necessitate a restructuring of the company but will often result in the business of the company and, consequently, the jobs of some or all of its employees being saved.

Sometimes, the chargee's aim of recovering his money cannot be combined with a rescue plan and the receivership leads straight into an insolvent liquidation. Receivership may then be criticised by unsecured creditors and employees who may feel that if the company had been allowed an opportunity for restructuring, more debts would have been paid and more jobs preserved. Indeed, the receiver has a duty not to prejudice the unsecured creditors' position and, accordingly, must act reasonably in achieving the satisfaction of the chargee's debt (pp773-774 *infra*).

Pre-appointment considerations

The period prior to the appointment of a receiver is similar to that prior to the appointment of an administrator (p750 *supra*). The company's largest creditor is most often its bank, which is likely to have some form of charge over the company's assets and to have monitored the growing size of the company's overdraft for some time before the appointment of the receiver. When the borrowing exceeds the agreed limit and shows little prospect of being reduced, the bank may commission an investigation which is usually carried out by accountants who specialise in corporate insolvency.

If the report of the investigating accountants shows that there is little prospect of the company becoming solvent in the near future, the bank will weigh up the various possibilities which are open to it. If the situation is truly hopeless, the bank might initiate liquidation proceedings (p786 *infra*), but is much more likely to appoint a receiver. The report may, however, reveal the possibility of salvaging something from the wreckage and the bank may be prepared to put fresh finance into the company on certain conditions. In doing so, it will, of course, weigh up the likelihood of such a re-financing package being successful. While it may be tempting to impose strict conditions under which the company would have to operate thereafter, the bank must take care not to take such an active a role in the company's management as to be held to be a "shadow director" if and when the company subsequently slides into insolvent liquidation (p805 *infra*).

The advantages for the chargee of receivership over administration are as follows:

- the speed and cheapness arising from the fact that no application to court is necessary for the appointment;
- the appointment takes effect on acceptance by the receiver;
- the form of appointment need only follow the procedure laid down by the charge (which may not even require writing, although most often it does);
- the chargee has control over who is appointed and control over when the secured property is sold.

Furthermore, even though there is no formal moratorium on claims against a company in receivership, an application can be made to court for relief against creditors in certain circumstances (*Transag Haulage Ltd* v *Leyland DAF Finance plc* [1994] BCC 356, [1994] 2 BCLC 88).

Where, as is often the case, the security consists of a fixed charge over the company's fixed (immovable) assets and a floating charge over the rest, the appointment of a receiver gives the secured creditor the greatest possible measure of control. A creditor empowered to appoint a receiver is thus unlikely to consider putting the company into liquidation rather than appoint a receiver. If the company goes into liquidation when a receiver is in post, the liquidator must defer to the receiver in relation to the secured property. Indeed, it is not uncommon for a receiver to be appointed after the company goes into liquidation and the court has ruled that this does not prejudice the receiver's right to remuneration as laid down in the charge (*Re Potter's Oils (No 2)* (1985) 1 BCC 99,593, [1986] BCLC 98.)

The appointing chargee will usually need to fund the company during the period that trading continues and this will often dictate how long the receivership continues. Apart from the receiver's costs and such expenses and payments as he will need to incur to maximise the success of the receivership, no creditor will have any priority over the secured creditor (generally the appointer) in relation to the fixed assets which are subject to the secured creditor's fixed charge. By statute, the receiver is obliged to ensure payment of preferential creditors first out of the realisation of any assets which were subject to the charge which, as created, was a floating charge before distributing any proceeds to the secured creditor (s40).

Procedure

As indicated above, a minimum of formality is required for the appointment of a receiver out of court, the charge itself setting out the procedure. Where the receiver is appointed by the court, the formality and expense of an application to court is necessary. In the latter case, the creditor will need to indicate (in the form of an affidavit in support of the application) why he believes that it is proper for a receiver to be appointed. In connection with insolvent companies, the most common ground will be that the security is in jeopardy and should, therefore, be placed under the control of a receiver. As explained above such an application is rare, only being required where the charge does not confer adequate powers for the appointment of a receiver.

Creditors' involvement and position

In receivership, there are three main types of creditor: secured, preferential and unsecured. As noted earlier, in broad terms the secured creditor is one who has a charge, either fixed or floating, over some or all of the company's property (which property can be realised to settle the debt owed). The unsecured creditors, by contrast, are simply seeking money which they are owed, or the delivery of goods or the performance of services undertaken by the company. The preferential creditors are unsecured creditors given special treatment by the IA on the insolvency of the debtor (ss40,586). The United Kingdom government is the main preferential creditor (in respect of various taxes owed by the company), and other preferential claims include employees' unpaid wages up to a certain limit.

The receiver also has a common law duty to ensure that if and when the company's property is sold, it realises at least the market value (p773 *infra*). Aside from these duties and the duty not to prejudice unsecured creditors, a receiver appointed before 29 December 1986 (the date on which the IA came into force) is subject to little in the way of statutory regulation.

The IA does place certain additional obligations on the receiver *vis-a-vis* creditors. Under section 48, he is required to prepare a report within three months of appointment on the events leading up to his appointment, the disposal or proposed disposal of any of the company's property, the amount of money (by way of principal and interest) paid to the preferential creditors and to the secured creditor by whom he was appointed, and the amount (if any) likely to be available for other creditors.

The receiver is required to send this report to all unsecured creditors or to make it available at an address of which they are advised and to table a copy of this report at a meeting of the creditors called for this purpose. The report must also be sent to the Registrar of Companies, to any trustees for secured creditors and, if the company has gone into liquidation, to the liquidator. The meeting of creditors referred to may also decide to form a committee of creditors and the receiver can be called upon to attend any meeting of this committee and to furnish it with "such information relating to the carrying out by him of his functions as it may reasonably require" (s49).

Powers and duties of the receiver

Powers

Some of the receiver's powers have already been referred to, namely (if he is an administrative receiver):

- to prevent an order for the administration of the company (p752 *supra*);
- wide powers of management (s42(1), Schedule 1);
- wide powers to insist on the maintenance of utility supplies to the company (s233);
- to get in the company's property, books, papers and records (s234);
- to insist on the co-operation of those who were officers of the company or who, within the year prior to his appointment, took part in the formation of the company or were employed by the company or another company which was an officer of the company (s235);
- to summon before the court for investigation anyone who was an officer of the company or anyone known or suspected of having any of the company's property, or anyone thought capable of providing "information concerning the promotion, formation, business, dealings, affairs or property of the company" (s236).

In addition, at common law, a receiver and manager had the power to apply for directions from the court – a most desirable power since to act in accordance with the court's directions provides a protection for the receiver against anyone challenging such action (*Re Quaest CAE Ltd* (1985) 1 BCC 99,389, [1985] BCLC 266; *Re Tudor Glass Holdings Ltd.* (1985) 1 BCC 98,982. This power is now codified (s35) and would certainly come within the administrative receiver's general management powers (Schedule 1, para 23 IA).

An administrative receiver may on application to the court dispose of the company's property subject to a fixed charge other than one held by his appointor, free of that charge (s43), provided that all the net proceeds are paid to the fixed chargee, plus any shortfall between what was realised and what would have been realised on the open market, if offered for sale by a willing vendor.

An administrative receiver may require a statement of the company's affairs (its assets, debts and liabilities; its creditors and any securities held by them; the dates on which such securities were given) from those obliged to co-operate under section 235.

Duties

All receivers must ensure that any invoice, order for goods or business letter issued by or on behalf of the company and of which they are aware, states that a receiver has been appointed (s39). In addition, they must ensure that preferential creditors are paid before those entitled under the floating charge (s40) and must send to the Registrar of Companies, accounts of their receipts and payments as receiver (s38, Rule 3.32 IR). Administrative receivers must also send these accounts to the company, to the person by whom he was appointed and to each member of the creditors' committee if one exists (Rule 3.32 IR). In addition, administrative receivers must prepare a report on the receivership for the creditors (s48), furnish information to the creditors' committee (s49) and, on appointment, notify the company and publish a similar notice in the Official Government newspaper, "the Gazette" s46, Rule 3.2 IR).

At common law, all receivers are under a duty to exercise their powers properly. This principle was accepted in *Watts* v *Midland Bank plc* (1986) 1 BCLC 15 although, as the judge there pointed out, "remarkably there appears to be no direct authority on the point". Perhaps this principle is best illustrated by those cases which place a duty on the receiver to ensure that where any of the company's property is sold, the receiver has a duty of care to the company borrower and to anyone who has guaranteed the debt. The authority for this stems from *Cuckmere Brick Co Ltd* v *Mutual Finance Ltd* [1971] Ch 949 which established that a mortgagee has a duty to the mortgagor in the exercise of the power of sale. This duty was extended to the guarantor of a company's debt in *Standard Chartered Bank Ltd* v *Walker* [1982] 3 All ER 938 where the sale took place in very poor conditions and realised much less than if it had been held at a different time and been properly advertised.

The receiver's duty extends to ascertaining the proper market price for the property being sold, as well as consulting appropriate experts as to how to obtain that price (*Tse Kwong Lam* v *Wong Chit Sen* [1983] 3 All ER 54, *American Express International Banking Corp* v *Hurley* [1985] 3 All ER 564. Recently, in *Downsview Nominees & Another* v *First City Corporation & Another* ([1993] BCC 46 an appeal from the New Zealand Court of Appeal) the receiver, appointed by the first debentureholder, was found to have exercised his management powers for improper purposes and was held liable in damages for breach of duty to the second debentureholder.

The Privy Council, which heard this appeal, specifically described this duty as a duty to act in good faith for proper purposes and not a general duty of care in dealing with the company's assets. This distinction had not been clearly drawn in the past and in the English case which may be regarded as the origin of this jurisdiction, *Cuckmere Brick Co Ltd* v *Mutual Finance Ltd* (*supra*) Salmon LJ held that a receiver (there a Law of Property Act receiver) was subject to both a duty of care and a duty to act in good faith. Given that decisions of the Privy Council are persuasive but not binding on English courts and that there was no criticism in *Downsview* of either *Cuckmere* itself or *Standard Chartered Bank Ltd* v *Walker* in which the Cuckmere principle was applied, it is unlikely that in *Downsview*, the Privy Council wanted to do more than ensure that the duty of care was not allowed to develop too far in this area. There is still strong support for the view that a receiver is subject to both duties.

These duties must be reconciled with the complete control over the company's property which the appointment of a receiver gives to the secured creditor. Thus in *Bank of Cyprus* v *Gill* [1980] 2 Lloyd's Rep 51, it was held that there is no duty on the receiver to wait for a more favourable time before selling the debtor's property, and in *Parker-Tweedale* v *Dunbar Bank plc* ([1990] 3 WLR 767, [1991] Ch 26, [[1990] 2 All ER 577) the Court of Appeal ruled that the mortgagee's duty of care did not extend to anyone who had a beneficial interest in the property sold, (*i.e.* an interest derived under a trust of which, in this case, the mortgagor was the trustee).

Management by the receiver

Steps taken on appointment

Reference has already been made to the obligations placed on the receiver to notify the Registrar of Companies and the company of his appointment and to place a suitable advertisement in the Gazette (p772 *supra*). The receiver will then use his powers to ensure that he brings all the company's property into his custody and control. When he has done so he will be in a position to make better judgments as to the best way to maximise realisation of the assets he has been appointed to realise.

Management by the receiver and his contractual position

Reference has already been made to the receiver's general duty to act properly. If he fails to do so, he will be held liable to the debenture holder who appointed him to the company (*American Express International Banking Corp* v *Hurley* (*supra*)) and any guarantors of the company's debt. The receiver will, however, be greatly assisted while in office by the almost invariable provision in charge documents making the receiver the company's agent. This is now enshrined in statute as far as an administrative receiver is concerned, his agency lasting until the company goes into liquidation (s44). Such agency enables the receiver to make a commercial judgment as to whether contracts entered into by the company prior to receivership should be adhered to. If adherence offers no benefit to the company but only a potential liability, and the contract is broken at the instance of the receiver, any liability for damages will fall on the company as an unsecured claim. The effect will be to increase the number and amount of unsecured claims against the company.

As an increase in unsecured claims will be irrelevant to the fortunes of secured creditors (including the one by whom the receiver was appointed) the latter will benefit from the exercise by the receiver of his power to break contracts from which the company cannot benefit and from which it may well suffer.

The power of the receiver to cause a company to act in breach of contracts concluded before receivership was affirmed in the important case of *Airline Airspares Ltd* v *Handley Page Ltd* [1970] Ch 193, where the court refused to grant a permanent injunction to the plaintiff which sought to prevent the company from disposing of certain assets and where so to dispose of these assets would have put it beyond the company's powers to fulfil its obligations under the contract with the plaintiff. Contrast the more restricted power of an administrator to cause a company to breach a contract (pp763-764 *supra*). As we shall see shortly the receiver's powers in this regard are limited where the company had, prior to the receivership, entered into a contract under which the third party acquired a proprietary interest in some part of the company's assets.

The Insolvency Act 1986 has clarified the position in relation to contracts entered into by the receiver himself in the performance of his functions. It declares the receiver to be personally liable, except to the extent that this personal liability has been excluded (ss37(1)(a), 44(1)(b)). The receiver is entitled to an indemnity out of the assets of the company which are under his control. This is an important safeguard in enabling the receiver to carry out his functions. The receiver will, however, be mindful that his statutory indemnity will only be worth anything if the company has substantial assets. If not, he may seek a specific indemnity from his appointor.

Third parties who enter into such contracts with a company at the instance of its receiver may insist on immediate payment in cash or rely on an undertaking from the receiver. In the latter case, the receiver would be incurring personal liability but with the protection of the indemnity against the debtor' assets. In *Lipe* v *Leyland DAF* [1993] BCC 385, [1994] BCLC 84, the Court of Appeal confirmed this approach, holding that a receiver's personal undertaking generally provided a creditor entering into a contract with a company acting by its administrative receiver with an appropriate level of protection. In the case of employee contracts, we will shortly observe that a different regime prevails (p776 *infra*)

The ability of the receiver to ignore pre-receivership contracts does not extend to contracts where a supplier of goods to the company has incorporated an effective reservation of title clause (p736 *supra*). This is because the receiver's appointment is over the assets of the company. Assets supplied pursuant to a valid reservation of title clause do not belong to the company. The receiver must also complete any contract which has been entered into by the company prior to the receivership and by which the other contracting party has acquired a right to call for the transfer of specific property (*Freevale Ltd* v *Metro Store Holdings* [1984] BCLC 72,[1984] Ch 199, [1984] 1 All ER 495).

Other examples of the receiver being bound by pre-receivership transactions also illustrate the general principle that a third party who, prior to receivership, has acquired or always possessed a proprietary right will generally be entitled to enforce that right. In *Re EVTR Ltd* (1987) 3 BCC 389, [1987] BCLC 646, a person who advanced money to the company was held entitled to recover it when the company went into receivership and was no longer able to spend the money for the purposes for which it was advanced.

The holder of a lien (a right to retain property until paid for services relating thereto), will be able to assert his lien against the receiver (*George Barker Ltd* v *Eynon* [1974] 1 All ER 900, [1974] 1 WLR 462; *Boodle Hatfield & Co* v *British Films Ltd* (1986) 2 BCC 99,221). A creditor who has acquired rights of set-off prior to the receivership will be able to assert these against the receiver (*Biggerstaff* v *Rowatt's Wharf Ltd* [1896] 2 Ch 93; *Rother Iron Works Ltd* v *Canterbury Precision Engineers Ltd* [1974] QB 1, [1973] 1 All ER 394). However, where the third party's right of set-off arose after the appointment of the receiver, he will not be able to assert that right against any claim which the company had against him before receivership (*Business Computers Ltd* v *Anglo-African Leasing Ltd* [1977] 2 All ER 741, [1977] 1 WLR 578). This will even be the case where the claim against the company was in existence before the receivership but was only assigned to the particular company debtor after the appointment of the receiver (*N W Robbie & Co Ltd* v *Witney Warehouse Co Ltd* [1963] 3 All ER 613, [1963] 1 WLR 1324).

The explanation for this distinction lies in the principle which is central to set-off, namely mutuality – the debts to be set-off must arise between the parties acting in the same capacity. If A owes money to the company, the right to claim that money is an asset which is assigned to the chargee on the appointment of the receiver. But if the company owes A money, that liability is not similarly assigned. If there are mutual dealings between the company and the third party prior to the appointment of a receiver, what is assigned to the chargee is the right to collect the debt from A subject to the right of set-off. If A's right of set-off arose after appointment of the receiver, that right is against the company, whereas the claim against the third party is by the chargee. Mutuality is thus absent and the respective debts cannot be set off against each other.

Although it might depend on the facts in each case, it seems that in general a receiver will not be regarded as being in occupation of the company's premises for the purpose of liability for council rates (*Ratford* v *Northavon District Council* (1986) 2 BCC 99,242, [1986] BCLC 397, *McKillop & Another, Petitioners* [1994] BCC 677, [1994] 2 BCLC 550, contrast *Lord Advocate* v *Aero Technologies Ltd* [1991] SLT 134). Payment of rates will therefore remain an unsecured liability of the company and not qualify for the priority status of being a receivership expense. The only exception will be if in a particular case the receiver is found to have occupied the relevant premises in his personal capacity.

Employees' contracts

The general rule is that the appointment of the receiver under the charge does not terminate contracts of employment unless continuation of the contract of employment is incompatible with the receivership (this may happen where the employee is the company's managing director, see *Griffiths* v *Secretary of State for Social Services* [1974] 1 QB 468). Prior to the coming into force of the IA, contracts adopted by the receiver were treated as contracts entered into by the company prior to the receivership and for which the company was therefore responsible. This meant that an employee was in the same unprotected position as other contracting parties who had entered into contracts prior to the receivership (*Nicoll v Cutts* (1985) 1 BCC 99,427, [1985] BCLC 322). The effect of ss37(1) and 44(1)(b) was to reverse the rule in this case and make the receiver personally liable in respect of contracts of employment adopted by him. He is given a 14 day period within which to decide whether to adopt any existing contracts of employment.

To achieve the twin contradictory goals of maintaining employment contracts (where necessary to keep the company operating) without suffering the personal liability of being held to have adopted such contracts, receivers adopted the formula which was successful in the unreported decision of *Re Specialised Mouldings Ltd* (p762 *supra*). While receivers are entitled to a statutory indemnity against the company's property under their control, the problem is really one of priority as between employees and the claims of the secured creditor by whom the receivers are appointed.

In a parallel and almost simultaneous development to that in the case of administration and the decision of *Re Paramount Airways Ltd (No 3)* (p762 *supra*), the *Specialised Mouldings* formula was rejected as regards administrative receivers (*Re Leyland Daf Ltd; Re Ferranti International plc* [1994] BCC 658, [1994] 2 BCLC 760). The provisions of the Insolvency Act 1994 (p763 *supra*) apply to contracts of employment adopted by administrative receivers on or after 15th March 1994 but non-administrative receivers are excluded from its scope.

The position of non-administrative receivers and administrative receivers in relation to contracts of employment adopted prior to 15th March 1994 is governed by the House of Lords ruling in *Re Paramount Airways Ltd (No 3)* (p762, *supra*) The House of Lords judgment confirmed the decision of Lightmann J in *Re Leyland Daf Ltd; Re Ferranti International plc* [1994] BCC 658, [1994] 2 BCLC 760, insofar as the liabilities in question were incurred by the receiver "during his tenure of office". The amounts for which the receiver could face personal liability are therefore

- wages accruing during the receivership
- damages for failure to give notice as required by the employee's contract
- the employer's pension contributions due in the period of the receivership
- holiday pay in respect of employment during the receivership

The *Paramount* ruling and the inapplicability of the Insolvency Act 1994 to non-administrative receivers have caused great concern to the insolvency profession. Attempts are currently being made to persuade the Government to pass legislation making the Insolvency Act 1994 apply retrospectively to administrative receivers appointed prior to 15th March 1994 – and to extend its provisions to non-administrative receivers.

It remains to be seen whether the professionals' concerns will be answered; at present this appears unlikely.

Reference has already been made to the effect of the Transfer of Undertakings (Protection of Employment) Regulations 1981 (p764 *supra*) which apply equally to sales of businesses by administrative receivers as they do to sales by administrators.

Realisation of assets

Two points already made need to be stressed. First, the receiver is under a duty of care to ensure that he obtains the market price for the goods sold (p773 *supra*). Secondly, an administrative receiver is now empowered with the leave of the court to sell property subject to a fixed charge, other than that of his appointor, free of that charge even without the other chargee's consent (p772 *supra*).

Distribution

The primary duty of the receiver is to ensure that the company repays the debt of the chargee who appointed him. In an administrative receivership in England and Wales, the receiver must, however, observe the statutory provision (s40 IA) under which preferential creditors must be paid out of the process of realisation of a charge which, as created, was a floating charge, after the expenses of realisation but in priority to the chargeholder. Preferential creditors' rights to payment in priority to the chargeholder do not extend to fixed charge realisations (*Re G L Saunders Ltd* [1986] BCLC 40).

Priority over the claims of the debentureholders is also given to those creditors whose claims arise in the receivership, including the claims of the receiver himself in respect of remuneration (ss44(1)(b) and 45(3)). Creditors whose claims are secured from inception by a fixed charge retain, throughout the receivership the right to receive, less costs, the proceeds of sale of the assets which constitute the fixed charge, whether such a sale is effected by the fixed chargees themselves or by the receiver with or without the consent of the fixed chargees (s43(3)).

Any assets remaining after discharging these claims are applied in the payment of the debt due to the floating chargeholders and, thereafter transferred to the person next entitled (who may be a receiver appointed under a subordinate charge or a liquidator if the company is in liquidation, or the board of directors if the company survives).

If the receiver has been appointed under a fixed charge under the provisions of the Law of Property Act 1925, the terms of section 109(8) must be observed in relation to any distributions made. Here the order is as follows:

- in discharge of all rents, taxes, rates and outgoings affecting the mortgaged property;
- in keeping down all annual sums and interest on all principal sums having priority over the mortgage;
- in payment of the receiver's commission, premiums for fire, life, other insurance and the cost of necessary repairs;
- in the payment of interest on the principal sum owing under the mortgage under which the receiver was appointed;
- in discharge of the principal sum owing to the mortgagee, if the latter so directs in writing;

- any residue to the person who but for the receiver would have been entitled to the income, or to the person otherwise entitled to the property.

For Scotland, however, where the floating charge and the institution of receivership were only introduced by statute in 1961, there is a comprehensive statutory provision as to the order of distribution (s60 IA) subject to the rights of a fixed chargee whose property is realised by the receiver free of the security. In these circumstances, the proceeds must be applied in reduction of the debt which was secured by the fixed charge. The priority which the fixed chargee thereby enjoys extends – where the amount realised is insufficient to discharge the debt – to the difference between the price realised and the amount which would have been realised in a sale on the open market by a willing vendor (s61 IA).

Thereafter proceeds are distributed, in order of priority, to:

- creditors whose claims are secured by a fixed charge over property also covered by the floating charge and ranking in priority to or *pari passu* with the floating charge;
- creditors who have effectually executed diligence on any property subject to the floating charge (this is where the creditor has enforced a court judgment against the debtor and the proceeds effectively belong to the creditor);
- creditors whose debts were incurred on behalf of the receiver;
- the receiver in respect of his liabilities, expenses and remuneration;
- preferential creditors;
- any other receiver;
- the holder of a fixed security over property subject to the floating charge;
- the company or the liquidator.

The effect of liquidation
Liquidation terminates the agency between the company and the receiver. Whether the receiver then becomes the agent of the chargee who appointed him depends upon the facts (*Gosling* v *Gaskell & Grocott* [1897] AC 575). In *American Express Banking Corp* v *Hurley* [1985] 3 All ER 564, (1986) 2 BCC 98,993, [1986] BCLC 52, the debenture holder did appoint the receiver its agent. Despite this principle, it is clear that the receiver retains certain powers to act on behalf of the company after liquidation has supervened. He has power to dispose of the company's property which was subject to the floating charge (*Sowman* v *David Samuel Trust Ltd* [1978] 1 WLR 22) and to continue litigation on behalf of the company, even though at the peril of personal liability for costs, in the event of these costs being successfully challenged by the liquidator (*Bacal Contracting Ltd* v *Modern Engineering (Bristol) Ltd* [1980] 2 All ER 655). A well advised receiver would seek to minimise the chance of this happening by obtaining the liquidator's agreement to all items of major expenditure.

The position of the officers and shareholders

A receiver appointed under a fixed charge over all the fixed property of a company and a floating charge over all the movable property of that company has complete control. Although the contracts of employment of the directors are not automatically terminated upon the appointment of a receiver, all powers of control and management exercisable by the directors are automatically suspended (*Griffiths* v *Secretary of State for Social Services* [1974] 1 QB 468). The directors can be excluded entirely from the management of the company during the receivership, although the receiver may well try to ensure that they co-operate with him. Furthermore, it has recently been held that directors are entitled to an injunction against the receiver to prevent further disposal of the company's property until the resolution of a dispute about the remuneration to which the receiver was entitled (*Rottenberg* v *Monjack* [1992] BCC 688, [1993] BCLC 374).

The statutory obligations on the directors and the company, for instance, to submit an annual return, (s363 CA), and to hold the annual general meeting, (s366(1) CA) continue, although our experience is that Companies House, in practice, recognises the lack of control directors have over the company's affairs and concentrates its regulatory work instead on enforcing the receivers' filing obligations. As far as the shareholders are concerned, their interest is nil. Their only hope is for a successful receivership which restores the company to solvency.

Termination of the receivership

When the receiver vacates office, he must notify the Registrar of Companies (s45 (4)). This happens if he resigns or is removed or where an administrator is appointed with the consent of the receiver's appointor (s11(1)(b)), or where, if he was an administrative receiver, he ceases to be licensed as an insolvency practitioner under Part XIII of the Act (p807 *infra*). On vacating office, the receiver must also notify the members of the creditors' committee (if there is one) and the company or, if appropriate, the liquidator (IR 3.35(1)).

Accounts of receipts and payments must be sent by an administrative receiver to the Registrar of Companies, the company, his appointor and each member of the creditors' committee (if one exists (Rule 3.32 IR). An administrative receiver can resign, but can only be removed against his will by order of the court. Old-style receivers and managers cannot resign but will usually be removable by their appointors under the terms of the charge. LPA receivers, similarly, cannot resign (unless empowered by the charge) but can be removed by their appointors by notice in writing (Law of Property Act 1925) section 109.

Once the receivership is terminated, any surplus is returned to the company (generally against an indemnity). If, as is most likely, the company is in liquidation, the surplus will pass to the liquidator who will deal with it in accordance with his duties. If (again, as is likely) there is no surplus, there will be no money for any liquidation process and the company is likely to remain as a shell until struck off the register by the Registrar of Companies.

4. Termination of the corporation: liquidation and dissolution

This section deals with the insolvency procedures available in the United Kingdom which inevitably lead to the termination of the corporation. This does not necessarily mean that the corporation's business ceases (although it will, for example, where it is sold to a purchaser), but it is likely that it will not survive. The corporation retains its legal personality throughout the liquidation process and only loses it on dissolution (p799 *et seq infra*).

Liquidation

The terms "liquidation" and "winding up" are used interchangeably to describe the process by which the company's existence is brought to an end.

Types, purpose and effect

Types
The liquidation of a company in the United Kingdom can be voluntary or compulsory. A voluntary liquidation occurs where the company itself resolves (by special or extraordinary resolution – for either of which a 75% majority is required) that it be wound up. The source of a compulsory liquidation is an order of the court, generally known as a "winding up order", granting a petition for the liquidation of the company. The vast majority of liquidations arise in the case of insolvent companies either compulsorily on a petition by one of the creditors, or voluntarily when the company realises that its financial position is hopeless. Nevertheless, it should be noted that solvent companies, too, may undergo the winding up process, either voluntarily or compulsorily.

The voluntary winding up of a solvent company might arise where the members wish to cease carrying on business together and to distribute the assets among themselves. In such a case the winding up is called a "members' voluntary winding up", as opposed to a "creditors' voluntary winding up", which occurs where the company is insolvent.

The compulsory winding up of a solvent company may occur in the case of small private companies where the relationship between the members (who are usually also the directors) has broken down, perhaps because of deadlock in the management of the company. In these circumstances, one of the members might present a petition for the winding up of the company as a means of bringing the commercial relationship between the members to an end. The court's jurisdiction is based on the ground that it is "just and equitable" to wind up the company (s122(1)(g) IA). Only a member may present a winding up petition on this ground and only in the case of a company which is solvent.

In this chapter, we are only concerned with the liquidation of insolvent companies. In general, the members have little or no interest in the winding up of an insolvent company. Nevertheless, the Act does provide a role for them from time to time (such as in permitting the appointment of member representatives to the liquidation committee). But the term "members" is rarely used in this context. Instead, the term "contributories" is used. This is defined by section 79(1) as "every person liable to contribute to the assets of a company in the event of its being wound up". This definition taken together with the provision in section 74(1):

> "when a company is wound up, every present and past member is liable to contribute to its assets to any amount sufficient for payment for its debts and liabilities and the expenses of winding up, and for the adjustments of the rights of the contributories among themselves"

makes the class of contributories much wider than the class of members at the time the company is placed in liquidation, although a further provision (s74(2),(3)) restricts greatly the group within the class of contributories who might actually be called upon to contribute (in effect to those who hold shares on which the full nominal value has not yet been paid).

Purpose

The liquidation brings to an end an unsuccessful business. It ensures that such assets as the company has will be applied in paying off the company's debts (although it does, of course, incur the additional costs of the liquidation process) and that all creditors will be treated as equally as possible, subject to the following exceptions:

- Creditors whose claims are secured by fixed or floating charges are entitled to look first to the realisation of those assets for repayment

- Someone who has supplied goods to the company but has effectively retained title to the goods may be entitled to the return of those goods (p736 *supra*)

- Someone who has supplied money to the company for a specific purpose which turned out to be incapable of fulfilment, is entitled to the return of the money, if it is still in existence (p737 *supra*).

- A creditor who is himself indebted to the company may set off that indebtedness against money owed to him by the company. Thus where, for example, he owes the company as much as is owed to him, the effect of set-off is that he is paid the full amount of his claim.

- Some creditors are declared by statute to be preferential and therefore fall to be paid before the other creditors. If the company has sufficient funds to pay only the preferential creditors in full, the latter will be paid in full and the rest of the unsecured creditors and those secured creditors whose security consists of a floating charge (to whom preferential creditors are preferred by statute, ss40, 175) will receive nothing.

Liquidation also provides an opportunity to examine and, where appropriate, set aside transactions undertaken by the company shortly before liquidation. If, for example, shortly before going into insolvent liquidation, the company paid one creditor in full, that creditor will have benefited at the expense of the other, unpaid, creditors. A procedure enabling the liquidator to apply to have such transactions set aside is thus important in ensuring the equal treatment of all creditors in liquidation (p800 *infra*). Where the company was managed fraudulently or incompetently, the liquidator will be able to seek a contribution to the assets of the company from those responsible (p804 *infra*).

Effect

In general terms, on liquidation, the directors of the company lose all powers of management and any transactions undertaken by the company after the commencement of liquidation by the court are void (although some can be validated by the court under the provisions of s127 IA). A liquidator is appointed to collect in the company's assets, realise them and distribute the proceeds among the creditors. He is permitted very limited powers of continuing the business – and may do so only insofar as this is necessary for the winding up process.

A voluntary liquidation takes effect from the date on which the winding up resolution is passed (s86). A compulsory liquidation order takes effect from the date on which the winding up petition is presented to the court (s129(2)), even though the order will generally have been made subsequently. The effect will be to invalidate any transactions undertaken by the company between the presentation of the petition and the grant of the winding up order unless the transaction is validated by the court under section 127.

Pre-liquidation considerations

The most likely question for the majority of creditors faced with a company debtor unable to pay its debts in full is whether the company should be given an opportunity to try to trade back into solvency. A secured creditor may be able to appoint a receiver and this, while not strictly an alternative to liquidation, may serve to bring all the company's assets under the secured creditor's control. Unsecured creditors who support the idea of giving the company a breathing space may either themselves petition for the administration of the company (p750 *et seq supra*) or else support an administration petition by the directors. It is equally likely, however, that some unsecured creditors will take the view that administration will simply delay the inevitable insolvent liquidation and they will then seek to have the company wound up and will, of course, oppose a petition for the company's administration. The court may well be faced with an administration petition when a winding up petition has already been presented and the effect of granting the administration petition is the dismissal of the winding up petition (s11(1)(a)). In general the practical advice to clients with unsecured claims is to petition for liquidation if they believe that some aspect of the company's conduct needs independent investigation or if they believe that sufficient assets remain to enable their claims to be paid, at least in part after the payment of costs and secured and preferential creditors.

The choice of liquidator is generally a matter for the creditors, although the procedure differs depending upon whether the liquidation is voluntary or compulsory. The creditors may also be dissatisfied with a voluntary liquidation. While, in theory (and most often in practice), the creditors can control a voluntary liquidation through the liquidator, it is possible for an inside creditor (a director, for example) to solicit proxy votes from outside creditors and thereby obtain majority voting power at the creditors' meeting which decides on the choice of liquidator. This may result in the choice of someone suspected by some creditors of being insufficiently vigorous in the investigation of the circumstances leading to the company's insolvency. If this is the case, the dissatisfied creditors may petition for a winding up order so as to replace the voluntary liquidation with a compulsory one. This problem may now be said to have been reduced by virtue of the requirement of the Insolvency Act that all liquidators must be licensed insolvency practitioners (p807 *infra*).

Where a compulsory winding up order is made, the official receiver will first be appointed as the company's liquidator, although at a subsequently convened meeting, the creditors can vote to replace him with someone of their choice (IA ss136). It is possible for such choice to be manipulated by an insider, but this is less likely as the court is much more closely involved with a compulsory than a voluntary liquidation. The Secretary of State also has a discretion, at the request of the official receiver under section 137 IA, to appoint a private insolvency practitioner as liquidator of a company in place of the official receiver.

Attention should also be drawn to the fact that all money collected by the liquidator, whether in a creditors' voluntary or a compulsory liquidation, must be paid into the special account (the insolvency services account – "ISA") maintained by the Department of Trade and Industry for this purpose. This is a disincentive for liquidation (where liquidation can possibly be avoided) because an uncommercial rate of interest is paid in respect of all money deposited in the ISA. Other disadvantages arising out of this requirement are the high fees – between 10% and 15% – which are payable to the DTI for withdrawals and deposits, as well as the fact that withdrawals for the purposes of payment of accounts and distributions tend to be slow.

The Insolvency Regulations under which the provisions relating to the ISA are enacted prescribe a different regime for compulsory and voluntary liquidations. In the latter case, the liquidator must make deposits within 14 days of the expiry of every six month period during which the liquidation is in progress. In the case of a compulsory liquidation, by contrast, deposits must be made once every 14 days, or forthwith if £5,000 or more is received (reg 5(1), (2), Insolvency Regulations, SI 1994, No 2507).

These regulations came into force on 24 October 1994 and will, therefore, govern every liquidation which commences after this date. There is an important concession in the case of compulsory liquidations. Under regulation 6, the liquidator may apply to the Secretary of State for authorisation to open a local bank account for receipts of cash for the company in liquidation. This can be done where the liquidator intends to exercise his powers to carry on the company's business. Permission may then be granted for deposits and withdrawals to be made from this local bank account and to the extent that this permission is granted, the ISA is bypassed.

Procedure

Members' voluntary liquidation

As indicated above, the significant difference between the members' and creditors' winding up is that the former is of a solvent company. The creditors will be paid in full and, therefore, have no interest in the liquidation. The company decides who will be appointed as the liquidator (ss91-92) and it is the company which must approve the liquidator's annual and final accounts of everything done in the liquidation. The directors must make a statutory declaration to the effect that, after making a full inquiry, they have formed the opinion that the company will be able to pay all its debts plus interest and the expenses of winding up in full within 12 months of the commencement of the winding up (*i.e.* the passing of the winding up resolution) or such shorter time as is specified in the declaration. The purpose of this declaration is to restrict this mode of winding up to solvent companies and to prevent its illegitimate use by directors wishing to retain control of the liquidation so as, for example, to minimise the opportunities for investigating their conduct in the management of the company.

The statutory declaration must be made not more than five weeks before the winding up resolution is passed, it must be delivered to the Registrar of Companies and must embody a statement of the company's assets and liabilities up to the latest practical date (s89). A statutory declaration which contains inaccurate information renders the maker or makers liable for criminal prosecution for an offence which is taken as seriously as perjury. Reasonable belief for the directors' opinion as to the solvency of the company is a defence, but directors will have to rebut the presumption that they did not have reasonable grounds for the opinion expressed if it subsequently transpires that the company was insolvent (s89(4)(5)).

The winding up resolution may be an ordinary or a special resolution, depending upon the circumstances in which it is passed. An ordinary resolution is only appropriate where the period for the duration of the company was fixed by the articles (s84(1)). This is very rare. Otherwise, voluntary winding up is by special resolution, necessitating 21 days' notice of a general meeting of the company specifying the intention to propose and pass that resolution. (s378(2) CA). The period of notice can be shortened if this is agreed to by members holding at least 95% in nominal value of shares which carry voting rights.

To pass the special resolution requires a majority of 75% of those members who are entitled to vote and who, in fact do vote, whether in person or by proxy (s378(1), (2) CA). Within 14 days' of it having been passed, the winding up resolution (whether special or ordinary) must be advertised in the Official Gazette and within 15 days delivered to the Registrar of Companies (s380(1), (4)(a)(j), ss84(3), 85 CA).

The liquidator is appointed by the general meeting of members (s91), although in rare cases (such as deadlock) where this is not possible, the court can make the appointment (s108). Where the company turns out to be insolvent, the process has to be converted into a creditors' voluntary winding up. The liquidator must summon a meeting of creditors on not less than seven days' notice for this purpose and this meeting must be summoned not more than 28 days from the day on which the liquidator first realised that the company was insolvent (s95(1), (2)). This meeting is deemed to be the first creditors' meeting which is required at the start of a creditors' voluntary winding up (s95(2), (5), (6)).

The calling of this meeting and the provision of proper notice and such information concerning the affairs of the company as the creditors may reasonably require are obligations which, in a creditors' voluntary liquidation which begins as such, fall on the directors of the company. In this case (beginning as a members' voluntary liquidation), these obligations fall on the liquidator (ss95, 98, 99, Rule 4.51 IR).

Creditors' voluntary liquidation

In a creditor's voluntary liquidation the winding up can be by extraordinary as well as by special resolution. An extraordinary resolution is similar to a special resolution (p781 *supra*), in requiring a 75% majority in favour and there must be notice of the intention to propose the particular resolution. Fourteen day's notice is required but it, too, can be shortened if that is approved by those holding of 95% of the nominal value of the shares entitled to vote (s369 CA). An extraordinary resolution must be advertised in the same way as a special resolution.

As this is an insolvent liquidation, the creditors will have a major interest in the process. Although a liquidator will almost certainly be appointed by the members (shareholders) at the meeting at which the winding up resolution is passed, that liquidator is virtually powerless unless confirmed in office by the meeting of creditors which must be called on at least 7 days' notice, within 14 days of the passing of the company's resolution(ss98(1)(a), 166).

At this first meeting of creditors, the directors present the company's statement of affairs (s95(3), Rule 4.34 IR). This will state the company's assets, debts and liabilities, the names and addresses of its creditors, what securities have been given and on what dates, and the book value and estimated realisable value of the assets. Resolutions may be proposed on the following matters (Rule 4.52, 4.53 IR):

- the appointment of the liquidator or liquidators (who may be different from, and therefore replace, the person elected at the meeting of members, s100(2), Rule 4.63(2)(c) IR);
- the establishment of a liquidation committee (which, if established, must consist of a maximum of five, and a minimum of three persons (s101 (1), Rule 4.152(2) IR) whose debts are not fully secured and whose proof of debt has

not been rejected by the liquidator. The committee can call for information from the liquidator as to the progress of the liquidation (Rule 4.155(1) IR) and can, as an alternative to the court, give consent to the exercise by the liquidator of certain powers (s165(2)(b), Schedule 4, Part I);

- the remuneration of the liquidator;
- if two or more liquidators have been appointed, to specify which acts are to be done by one or more of them;
- adjourning the meeting for not more than three weeks;
- such other things which the chairman thinks right to allow for special reasons.

Compulsory liquidation

A petition for the winding up of a company may be presented on any of the seven grounds enumerated in section 122(1) IA. Only two are of any significance and one, that it is just and equitable that the company be wound up, has already been referred to (p781 *supra*). Inability to pay debts accounts for the vast majority of compulsory liquidations and is the only ground relevant to corporate insolvency. The IA defines what is meant by a company being unable to pay its debts by describing several cases any one of which illustrates this condition. They are:

- the failure by the company to meet a claim against it, if, for three weeks following a written demand (known as a "statutory demand"), for payment of a debt in excess of £750 the company neglects to pay, secure or compound (*i.e.* settle) the debt, the company is deemed to be unable to pay its debts (s123(1)(a)).

This ground can be relied upon even where there is clear evidence of solvency (*Cornhill Insurance plc* v *Improvement Services Ltd* (1986) 2 BCC 98,942, [1986] BCLC 26). It must, nevertheless, be clear that the debt is due. If there is any dispute as to whether it is owing, it cannot be said that the company has neglected to pay it (*Re A Company* (1983) 1 BCC 98,901, *Re A Company* [1984] BCLC 322, *Re A Company* [1985] BCLC 37, *Re Fitness Centre (South East) Ltd* (1986) 2 BCC 99,535, [1986] BCLC 518, *Re Selectmove Ltd* [1994] BCC 349. Contrast *Re A Company No 1913 of 1983* (1983) 1 BCC 98,941, *Re Dunsmure Developments Ltd* (1985) 1 BCC 98,948. In the latter two cases, the court held that there was no bona fide dispute and granted the winding up order. Likewise in *Re A Company (No 6273 of 1992)* ([1992] BCC 794, [1993] BCLC 131), where the petition was based on an undisputed debt, and where the company claimed that it had a cross claim for a greater amount but which could only, if at all, be established after litigation.

- the failure by the company to satisfy an attempt by the creditor to execute a judgment (s123(1)(b), (c), (d));
- if it is proved to the satisfaction of the court that the company is unable to pay its debts as they fall due (s123(1)(e)).

This ground will be satisfied, despite the fact that the company appears to have ample assets, if these are not in liquid form and a particular debt cannot be paid ("a company may be at the same time insolvent and wealthy", quoted in *Re Camburn Petroleum Products Ltd* [1979] 3 All ER 297, 302, [1980] 1 WLR 86, 92). Conversely, where the company does not appear to have sufficient assets to pay all its liabilities, but sufficient to pay those which are demanded, this ground of inability to pay debts will not apply (*Re Capital Annuities Ltd* [1978] 3 All ER 704, 717-19)

- if, on an analysis of the company's balance sheet, taking account of its contingent and prospective liabilities, the value of the company's assets is less than its liabilities (s123(2)).

The petition – which in almost all relevant instances will be presented by an unpaid creditor of the company – must be verified by an affidavit testifying to the debt owed, sealed by the court and served on the company (at its registered office, Rule 4.8(2)-(3) IR) and, if appropriate, on any administrator, administrative receiver, liquidator (where the company is already in voluntary winding up) or supervisor of a voluntary arrangement. The service of the petition must also be advertised before the court hearing in the Gazette, which is designed to ensure that anyone interested in the prospective winding up may appear either in support of or in opposition to the petition (Rule 4.11(4) IR). The petition can be withdrawn on the ex parte application of the petitioner as long as the application for withdrawal is made at least five days before the date set for the hearing of the petition, and the petition has not been advertised, and no notices have been received in support of or in opposition to the petition, and the company consents (Rule 4.15 IR)

If the company intends to oppose the petition, it must file an affidavit setting out its opposition at least seven days before the date set for the hearing (Rule 4.18 IR). The court has a wide discretion to substitute another creditor for the petitioner, where for some reason or another (for instance, he has been paid or is found to have been not entitled to present the petition in the first place) the latter wishes or is required to drop out of the proceedings (Rule 4.17, 4.19 IR).

The presentation of the petition has a dramatic effect on the company's commercial activities. As was pointed out above, the order, if made, is backdated to the date on which the petition was presented (s129(2)), thus invalidating any transaction undertaken between those two dates. Thus, the presentation of a petition is likely to paralyse the company, with third parties afraid that any transaction with the company in the vulnerable period will be rendered void. It is not surprising, therefore, that the presentation of a petition evokes a strong reaction by the company on occasions when it believes that it has a defence. In such circumstances, the company may well take immediate action to restrain the presentation of the petition (*i.e.* not wait until the hearing of the petition and the company's defence), so as to avoid any continuation of the crippling effects that the presentation would otherwise have.

The court's jurisdiction in this regard is founded on restraining any process which is an abuse of the process of the court and the court can restrain either the presentation or the advertisement of the petition. This jurisdiction will be exercised where, for example, the petitioner appears to be using the winding up process for an ulterior purpose (like embarrassing the company, *Re A Company* [1894] 2 Ch 349; *Re Bellador Silk* [1965] 1 All ER 667; *Charles Forte Investments Ltd* v *Amanda* [1964] Ch 240; *Re A Company* (1983) 1 BCC 98,937, [1983] BCLC 492). Another basis for the exercise of this jurisdiction would be where there is a genuine dispute as to whether the debt is owing (*Mann* v *Goldstein* [1968] 2 All ER 769; *Stonegate Securities Ltd* v *Gregory* [1980] Ch 576; *Re A Company* [1984] BCLC 322, contrast *Re R.A.Foulds Ltd* (1986) 2 BCC 99,269 where the court refused to restrain the petition despite a dispute as to a substantial part of the debt because a sufficient part of the debt – *i.e.* £750 – was undisputed).

After the presentation of the petition, and before the hearing, a provisional liquidator may be appointed (s135). This is designed to protect the company's property pending the hearing of the petition and an application for the appointment of a provisional liquidator (who must be a licensed insolvency practitioner) can be made by anyone who would have been entitled to present the petition (Rule 4.25(1) IR). As explained above, provisional liquidation is frequently used in insurance insolvencies to provide the company with protection against hostile creditor action while a scheme of arrangement is prepared.

When the petition comes on for hearing, the court may:

- dismiss the petition;
- adjourn the hearing conditionally or unconditionally;
- make an interim order;
- make any other order which it thinks fit (s125(1)).

There is a principle according to which an unpaid creditor is entitled to a winding up order (provided the petition has met all the procedural requirements) *ex debito iustitiae* ("as of right"). Yet there is a potentially conflicting principle which confers a discretion on the court to take account of the wishes of those who are opposed to the petition (s195), although even where a substantial majority of the creditors oppose the granting of a winding up order, they must show good cause for their opposition (*Re P & J Macrae* [1961] 1 All ER 302; *Re Brendacott Ltd* (1986) 2 BCC 99,164; *Re Leigh Estates (United Kingdom) Ltd.* [1994] BCC 292).

Where a voluntary winding up is already under way, the court used to be much more disposed to refuse a winding up order on the ground that the petitioning creditor had already achieved the class remedy which liquidation conferred (*Re J D Swain Ltd* [1965] 2 All ER 761, [1965] 1 WLR 909). However, this has changed substantially in the last few years with what seems to be a growing phenomenon of "inside creditors" – directors and their family and friends – who may prefer a voluntary liquidation because they may believe that it will subject them to less close scrutiny than would a compulsory liquidation. Now the courts are much readier to grant petitions at the instance of an "outside creditor" which convert a voluntary into a compulsory liquidation (for the latest of a long line of recent examples, see *Re Gordon & Breach Science Publishers Ltd* British Company

Law and Practice, Volume 2, para 96-056).

If a winding up order is granted, a copy must be sent to the Registrar of Companies by the company (s130) and the "official receiver" assumes control until he has discharged the duties imposed on him by the Act to decide whether to call the meetings that are necessary to ensure that someone else is appointed liquidator of the company (s136). In addition, during the period when he is the liquidator, the official receiver may:

- require specified people to submit a statement of affairs for the company (s131, Rule 4.32 IR);
- apply to the court for the public examination of certain persons (s133).

He is also required to:

- investigate why the company has failed (s132(1)(a));
- investigate "generally, the promotion, formation, business dealings and affairs of the company" (s132(1)(b);
- report to the creditors and contributories (Rules 4.43(1), 4.45, 4.46(2) IR).

The official receiver has both a power and duty to decide whether to summon meetings of the creditors and contributories (Rule 4.50 IR) and, at the first such meeting with each group, only those resolutions may be taken (including a resolution for the appointment of a liquidator of the creditors' choice) as at the same stage in a creditors' voluntary liquidation (Rule 4.52 IR, p786 *supra*).

From here on, the liquidation will be conducted in the same way, whether it is compulsory or voluntary. In the main, the respective liquidators will have identical powers, the one exception being in regard to the powers of the official receiver to initiate a public investigation of those who were connected with the management of the company prior to the insolvent liquidation (p808 *infra*). For this, the company must be in compulsory liquidation.

In practice, creditors' meetings take place when the company has sufficient assets to fund a liquidation by a private insolvency practitioner. The official receiver is generally the liquidator of last resort acting where there are insufficient assets or creditor interest for a private appointment to be made.

Creditors' involvement and position

As with receivership, there are three main types of creditor: secured, unsecured and preferential. A secured creditor empowered to appoint a receiver will almost always do so rather than rely on liquidation to settle his debt, since, as noted earlier, the receiver is appointed by the secured creditor and has, as his prime consideration, the repayment of the appointor's debt. The liquidator, by contrast, is appointed by all the creditors or by the members or by the court and must look to the interest of all the creditors. Liquidation is, indeed, often referred to as a "class remedy".

If the secured creditor is not able to appoint a receiver (if, for example, the charge failed to confer that power and the court does not accept that the security is in jeopardy), the priority of the secured creditor is at least protected in a liquidation since he is entitled to the net proceeds realised out of the sale of the property securing his debt up to the amount of the debt. The secured creditor may still appoint a receiver if his security entitles him to do so and he considers this to be in his interests (*Re Potter's Oils (No 2)* (1985) 1 BCC 99,593, [1986] BCLC 98).

Occasionally secured creditors who only have fixed charges over specific assets may be in a position where the value of those assets is less than the amount of the debt. That creditor will be unsecured as regards the shortfall. The position of preferential creditors and unsecured creditors is essentially the same as in receivership (p778 *supra*). Involvement by creditors in the conduct of the liquidation will come either through the liquidation committee (if there is one) or through the creditors generally by resolution at meetings summoned by the liquidator. The major role of the creditors in the liquidation will be to give or withhold approval for particular actions of the liquidator which can only be undertaken with the approval of the creditors or the court (ss165, 167, Schedule 4). It will also be for the liquidation committee (or, if there is no such committee, the creditors as a body) to fix the liquidator's remuneration (Rules 4.127-4.129 IR).

The voting power of each creditor at the initial meeting and all subsequent meetings is based on the amount of his claim, but there are certain restrictions (Rule 4.67 IR). In principle, a proof of debt (and any requisite proxy) has to have been submitted and accepted by the liquidator. However, the court might in appropriate circumstances permit a whole class of creditors to vote without being required to prove their debts and, in a creditors' voluntary liquidation, the chairman of the meeting has a discretion to allow a creditor to vote where the creditor has failed to submit a proof of debt (Rule 4.68 IR). Where the claim is for an unascertained or unliquidated amount, the creditor may only vote to the extent that a minimum value has been estimated for the claim by the chairman of the meeting. Secured creditors may vote only to the extent that the claim is unsecured (on the basis of an estimate by the creditor of the value of the assets secured). If the claim is based on a bill of exchange (such as a cheque), the creditor may not vote unless he treats the bill as security based on the number of people who might be liable on that bill and deducts the estimated value of his security. Whether a claim is admitted or rejected is initially a matter for the chairman of the meeting, but his decision is subject to appeal to the court (Rule 4.70 IR). It should be remembered that agreement of a claim for voting purposes is not agreement for dividend purposes.

The liquidation committee, if established, must consist of not more than five and, in the case of a compulsory liquidation, at least three creditors (ss101, 141) appointed by the creditors. If approved by the members of the committee, representatives of the shareholders may be appointed to the liquidation committee. The constitution and activities of the committee are governed by Chapter 12 of Part 4 of the Insolvency Rules (Rule 4.151-4.172 IR) which includes formalities as to the establishment of the committee, how meetings are to be conducted, voting rights and the obligation of the liquidator to report to the committee.

Powers and duties of the liquidator

Powers

Extensive powers have been given to the liquidator to carry out his functions in the liquidation, although it is worth noting at the outset that the power of the liquidator to carry on the trading or other activities of the company are strictly limited to that which is necessary for the purpose of winding up the company. If the liquidator goes beyond what is necessary, he will be personally liable to make good any loss the company incurs as a result.

The liquidator's powers are now largely codified by Schedule 4, IA. This schedule is divided into three Parts, each of which consists of different powers. The rationale for this division lies in the distinction between powers which are essentially impartial aids to efficient administration (Parts II and III) and powers which, although also aids for an efficient administration, may have the effect of preferring some interests to others (Part I).

Part I powers (for instance, to pay certain creditors in full and not others or to compromise creditors' claims) require approval in any winding up, whereas those set out in Part II (such as to carry on the business of the company and being involved in legal proceedings) require approval only in the case of a compulsory winding up. Part III powers can be exercised without creditor sanction, irrespective of the nature of the winding up.

The nature of the approval required depends on the circumstances. In a members' voluntary winding up, approval can be given by an extraordinary resolution of the members of the company. In a creditors' voluntary winding up, approval must come from the liquidation committee or a meeting of the creditors or the court. In a compulsory winding up, approval must come either from the court or the liquidation committee (ss165(2), 167(1)).

The liquidator has power, without approval, to appoint solicitors or other legal advisers to assist him in the performance of his duties (as being the appointment of agents to do business which he cannot do himself or as falling into the final catch-all category in Schedule 4 to do "all such other things as may be necessary for winding up the company's affairs and distributing its assets". Prior to the Insolvency Act 1986, the exercise of this power in a compulsory liquidation required approval.

In addition to the powers set out in Schedule 4, the Act enables the liquidator:

- to apply to the court for directions concerning any matter arising in the winding up (ss112(1),168(3));
- to apply to have the winding up stayed (s147);
- to call meetings (s168(2));
- to make payments to the employees either where, prior to the liquidation, the company had previously resolved to make payments on liquidation or cessation of business under the provisions of section 719 CA, (s187(1)) or where sanction is given after the commencement of the winding up (s187(2));

- to transfer the whole or part of the assets of the company to another company in exchange for "shares, policies or other like interests" or a share of the profits of that other company (s110). This power requires authorisation by a special resolution of the company or the liquidation committee if the company is in a creditors' voluntary winding up. Members who dissent have the right to have their interest in the company in liquidation bought by the liquidator at an agreed or arbitrated price;
- to take proceedings against anyone for fraudulent trading and against directors or shadow directors in respect of alleged wrongful trading (p804 *infra*);
- to insist on the continuation of utility services (s233);
- to demand the return of the company's books, papers, records or other property from anyone suspected of having them (s234);
- to obtain information from a wide variety of people as to the activities of the company prior to the liquidation (s235);
- to apply to have summoned before the court those who are known or suspected of having the company's property, being indebted to the company, or thought capable of giving information about the promotion, formation, business dealings, affairs or property of the company (s236);
- to have certain pre-liquidation transactions set aside (p800 *infra*);
- to disclaim "onerous property" (s178, p795 *infra*).

Duties
The duties imposed on the liquidator can be conveniently categorised as follows:

- to get in and realise all the company's property and distribute the proceeds in accordance with respective creditors' entitlement;
- to give notice of his appointment in a voluntary liquidation by publication in the Gazette and to the Registrar of Companies (s108);
- to ensure that the fact that the company is in liquidation appears on any invoice, order for goods or business letter issued on behalf of the company (s188);
- to hold certain meetings of members and creditors, namely:
  - those required at the start of the liquidation;
  - in a voluntary liquidation which lasts more than one year, meetings of the company and its creditors at the end of the first year and, thereafter at the end of each successive year (s105);
  - in a voluntary winding up, a general meeting of the company and its creditors when the affairs of the company are fully wound up (s196);
  - in a compulsory liquidation, a final general meeting of the company's creditors when it appears that for all practical purposes, the winding up is complete (s146);

- when requisitioned by the creditors or contributories in a compulsory winding up (s168(2), or generally, whenever ordered by the court (s195(1)(b)));
- to provide information to the liquidation committee (Rules 4.155, 4.168 IR).

Management by the liquidator

Steps taken on appointment
Reference has already been made to the duty on the liquidator, within 14 days of appointment to publish the fact of his appointment in the Gazette as well as notifying the Registrar of Companies. The liquidator is also required to acquire from his insurer a certificate of insurance covering the value of the assets under his control and to deliver this to the Registrar of Companies. He must attend the meeting of creditors called at the start of a creditors' voluntary liquidation (s98) and report on any steps taken in relation to the company's property before being confirmed as the liquidator (s166(4)).

On being confirmed or appointed by the creditors in a creditors' voluntary liquidation or on being appointed in a compulsory liquidation, the liquidator must take immediate steps to ensure that all the company's property is brought under his custody or control. He has ample powers for this (p792 *supra*). He must seek advice where necessary on whether to take legal action to set aside pre-liquidation transactions (p800 *infra*) or to bring proceedings against directors and other officers for a contribution to the assets of the company by reason of alleged fraudulent or wrongful trading (p804 *infra*). Finally, in a compulsory liquidation, the liquidator must send out forms of proof to every creditor of the company who is known to him or who has been identified in the company's statement of affairs (IR 4.74).

Administration in office
It is well established that the liquidator acts as the agent of the company and as such is not personally liable on contracts which he makes as liquidator, nor for the cost of legal advice and fees necessarily incurred in the course of the liquidation. These costs will be met as expenses of the winding up prior to any distribution to creditors. If the liquidator behaves negligently or in breach of the trust imposed on him by reason of his control of the company's assets, he will be personally liable. Under section 212 the liquidator's conduct can be examined on the application of the official receiver, a subsequent liquidator or a creditor or contributory and he may be compelled:

"(a) to repay, restore or account for the money or property or any part of it, with interest at such rate as the court thinks just, or
(b) to contribute such sum to the company's assets by way of compensation in respect of the misfeasance or breach of fiduciary or other duty as the court thinks just".

In many ways, the role of the liquidator resembles that of the board of the directors and, like them, the liquidator has to avoid any conflict between his personal interest and the duty imposed on him as liquidator. In the discharge of his following functions, the liquidator acts as a delegate of the court (s160) and as such is an officer of the court (which requires that he act in a high-minded and ethical way). His functions are as follows:

- "the holding and conducting of certain meetings to ascertain the wishes of the creditors and contributories;

- the settling of the lists of contributories and the rectifying of the register of members where required and the collection and application of assets;

- the payment, delivery, conveyance, surrender or transfer of money, property, books or papers to himself;

- the making of calls on members in respect of any part of the nominal value outstanding on shares held;

- the fixing of a time within which debts and claims must be proved".

Contractual position

The liquidator will only fulfil contracts entered into prior to his appointment by the company if there is a clear benefit to the company. If there is no benefit, he will break the contract, leaving the other party to make an unsecured claim against the company. As in the case of receivership, some third parties may have contractual or other rights that cannot be broken by the liquidator, such as reservation of title claims, liens, proprietary rights and rights of set-off.

The liquidator has express powers to disclaim "onerous property" (which means any unprofitable contract or property which is not readily saleable) even if he has taken possession of or tried to sell it (s178). He must file a notice of disclaimer containing particulars of the property at court and give notice to any person whom he knows has an interest in it. If anyone complains, the court will hear submissions on behalf of the interested parties and make a decision as to the property in question (ss179, 181). The court has ruled that it will only interfere with the decision of the liquidator to disclaim on the same basis as applies in relation to the liquidator's other powers, namely if it can be established that his decision was perverse (*Re Hans Place Ltd* [1992] BCC 737, [1993] BCLC 768). A valid disclaimer of a lease by the liquidator does not relieve any of the company's predecessors from liability under that lease (*W H Smith Ltd* v *Wyndham Investments Ltd* [1994] BCC 699, [1994] 2 BCLC 571, *Hindcastle Ltd* v *Barbara Attenborough Associates Ltd* [1994] BCC 705, [1994] 2 BCLC 728).

However, as already indicated, the liquidator can enter into contracts after his appointment, as agent for and on behalf of the company and, so long as this is necessary for the purposes of the winding up, he will incur no personal liability. Certain assets which, by reason of security or otherwise are attributable to the claims of particular creditors, are not available for sale by the liquidator.

Realisation of assets

Those of the company's assets which do fall under the liquidator's control will in normal circumstances be sold to enable him to distribute the proceeds to the creditors. In rare circumstances, the property itself might be distributed direct to the creditors according to its valuation. Secured creditors will have placed a value on their security for the purpose of submitting a proof of debt (Rule 4.75(1)(g) IR). This may be altered by agreement with the liquidator or with the leave of the court (Rule 4.95(1) IR), unless the secured creditor was the petitioner and that value was included in the petition, or that creditor has already voted in respect of the unsecured balance. In either of these last two cases, the value placed on the security can only be altered by leave of the court.

The liquidator is empowered to redeem the security at the value placed on it (Rule 4.97(1) IR) and, if he exercises this right, the creditor may exercise a corresponding right to revalue the security (Rule 4.97(2) IR). The creditor also has the right to call on the liquidator to elect whether he wishes to redeem the security or not. The liquidator has six months within which to make his election (Rule 4.97(4) IR). If the liquidator is dissatisfied by the valuation placed on the secured property, he may require the property to be offered for sale (Rule 4.98 IR).

Employees

The winding up order in a compulsory liquidation has the effect of terminating all contracts of employment. A winding up order can thus bring about a breach of contract giving rise to a claim for damages which may be proved in the winding up. A voluntary winding up, by contrast, does not necessarily result in the termination of contracts of employment. Here the principle seems to be that the winding up resolution only acts to terminate these contracts "if the surrounding circumstances are such that an employee is justified in regarding it as indicating the intention of the company to repudiate its obligations under the contract (McPherson *The Law of Company Liquidation* 3rd ed, 1987, p175).

Distribution

Secured creditors will, in general, realise their security themselves and use the proceeds of sale to satisfy their debt. If the proceeds exceed their claim, the balance will be paid over to the liquidator. If the proceeds are insufficient to meet the claim in full, the balance can be claimed by the creditor as an ordinary unsecured claim. Assets of the company which are subject to reservation of title claims, liens, proprietary rights and rights of set-off will be returned or discounted by the liquidator once he is satisfied of the validity of the particular right claimed.

The first claim on the assets of the company in liquidation are the expenses incurred in the winding up (ss115, 156) and within this class is an elaborate hierarchy established by the Rules (Rule 4.218 IR). This order can be altered by the court (s156, Rule 4.220(1) IR). The second claim is that of the preferential creditors which, as stated earlier, consists mainly of debts due to the government and for remuneration and accrued holiday pay due to employees. Where there are insufficient funds, preferential creditors have priority over secured creditors in respect of proceeds from the sale of assets over which the secured creditors had a floating charge (s175(2)(b)). Recently it was held that this priority of preferential creditors is maintained even in the face of an agreement between the floating chargeholder and a prior fixed chargee under which the claim of the latter was subordinated to that of the former. The preferential creditors and liquidation expenses, therefore, enjoyed priority over the claim of the fixed chargee (*Re Portbase (Clothing) Ltd* [1993] BCC 96, [1993] BCLC 796).

The third claim is that of "distress creditors" (who have seized goods belonging to the company under statutory or contractual right). Where such goods have been seized within three months of the making of the winding up order, preferential creditors will have priority over distress creditors in respect of the goods seized or their proceeds of sale. Insofar as this results in a shortfall for the distress creditors, the latter have priority over the next in line – the unsecured creditors (s176 IA).

The fourth claim is that of the ordinary unsecured creditors. There is usually very little, if anything, left at this stage. The liquidator must distribute any surplus equally among all the unsecured creditors according to the size of their claim. This distribution is known as a "dividend" and, before making it, the liquidator must give notice to all creditors who have not yet given him written proof of their debts. These creditors then have 21 days in which to provide proof of their debts, otherwise they can be ignored by the liquidator in making the distribution. Depending on how successful the liquidator has been in realising the company's assets and establishing the validity of claims, he may decide to make either an "interim" or a "final" dividend. However, in practice, it is only when the liquidator is confident that the liquidation has been completed, that a final dividend is made.

If there are any claims against the company which are based on rights of membership, such as unpaid dividends declared before the company went into liquidation, they will only be paid after all other unsecured creditors have been paid in full.

Position of officers and shareholders

When the liquidator is appointed in a voluntary winding up – whether members' or creditors' – the general rule is that the power of the directors comes to an end, except in so far as the continuation of that power is sanctioned by the relevant authority. In a members' winding up, that authority is the company in general meeting or the liquidator (s91(2)) whereas, in a creditors' winding up, it is the liquidation committee, or if there is none, the creditors (s103).

In the creditors' winding up there is what might be a troublesome hiatus between the passing of the winding up resolution and the appointment by the creditors of their nominee for liquidator. Before the enactment of the 1986 Insolvency Act, the solution was to insist that the meetings of the company (to pass the winding up resolution) and of the creditors (to ensure the appointment of their nominee as liquidator) should be on the same day. This solution was ineffective where, in breach of this requirement, the creditors' meeting was held days or even weeks later. There might be no liquidator for this intervening period or the liquidator would be the company's nominee. Although this was a criminal offence, the courts upheld the validity of the company meeting and their appointment of the liquidator (*Re Centrebind Ltd* [1966] 3 All ER 889, [1967] 1 WLR 377).

The Insolvency Act deals with the situation in which no liquidator is appointed by the company by greatly limiting the powers of the directors (s114). They can only act if:

- their action is sanctioned by the court;
- the liquidator is carrying out obligations imposed where a liquidation which started as a members' winding up has to be converted into a creditors' winding up (ss98, 99, p785 *supra*);
- the action is to dispose of perishable goods or other goods whose value is likely to diminish unless disposed of;
- the action is necessary to protect the company's assets.

Prior to the meeting of creditors, a liquidator appointed by the company can only exercise any power:

- to take into his custody or control, property to which the company is entitled;
- to dispose of perishable goods and other goods whose value will diminish;
- to do whatever is necessary to protect the company's assets (s166).

With a compulsory winding up, there is no hiatus between the winding up and the appointment of an independent liquidator. The official receiver becomes the liquidator until an independent liquidator is elected (s136(2)). It is clear that the powers of the directors cease on the making of the winding up order.

A provisional liquidator may be appointed between the presentation of the winding up petition and the making of the winding up order, where it is felt necessary to protect the assets and property of the company before a liquidator can be appointed. Where a provisional liquidator is appointed, the position as to the powers of the directors is more complicated. Here it is clear that some power is retained by the board of directors at least to instruct solicitors to oppose the winding up proceedings including the taking of any necessary interlocutory proceedings (*Re Union Accident Insurance Co Ltd* [1972] 1 All ER 1105, [1972] 1 WLR 640)

As far as the shareholders are concerned, as contributories (p781 *supra*) they are permitted to appoint representatives to the liquidation committee established in a creditors' voluntary liquidation, although these appointees have to be acceptable to the creditors (s 101(3)). In a compulsory liquidation the contributories can be represented on the liquidation committee only where it is a solvent winding up (Rule 4.152(1)(b) IR) or where the creditors decide against establishing a liquidation committee or decide that such a committee should not be established (s141, Rule 4.154 IR). Under Rule 4.161 (3) IR, the membership of a creditor member is automatically terminated if he ceases to be, or is found never to have been, a creditor (*Re W & A Glaser Ltd* [1994] BCC 199).

Termination

When all the company's assets have been distributed, the liquidator should take steps to bring the liquidation to an end. At that stage he must decide whether any further and final dividend can be paid. If so, he must give notice as he was required to do when making previous distributions (Rule 11.2 IR). If no final dividend is to be paid, the liquidator must give notice to this effect, stating either that no funds have been realised or those amounts been realised have already been distributed or, as the case may be, used to pay the expenses of the winding up (Rules 4.186, 11.7 IR).

Dissolution

Purpose and effect

Dissolution extinguishes the personality of the company, although there are powers (s651 CA) by which the company can be reinstated. Reinstatement would be necessary where, for example, further assets were discovered and a further dividend could be distributed. Alternatively, the company might have failed to pursue a legal action and might have failed to assign that action to anyone else before dissolution. Unless the company is reinstated, the action cannot be brought (*M H Smith (Plant Hire) Ltd* v *Mainwaring* (1986) 2 BCC 99,262, [1986] BCLC 342).

In *Re Forte's Manufacturing Ltd: Stanhope Pension Trust Ltd* v *Registrar of Companies* ([1994] BCC 84), the Court of Appeal agreed to the restoration to the register of a dissolved company where the possibility of further liability against that company had arisen. The dissolved company had been a tenant under a lease which had been assigned through several assignees to BCCI, which was wound up as insolvent and thus unable to meet its obligations under the lease. The landlord wished to pursue these claims against the dissolved company (which it was entitled to do under the lease).

Pre-application considerations

Where the company is in compulsory liquidation and the official receiver is the liquidator, it is possible to apply for "early" dissolution of the company. This is designed to avoid time and cost where there are insufficient assets to cover the expenses of winding up and it appears to the official receiver that no investigations into the company's operations prior to liquidation are necessary (s202(2)).

Procedure

In the case of early dissolution, the official receiver gives 28 days' notice of his intention to apply to the Registrar of Companies for early dissolution. The company is then deemed to be dissolved at the end of a three month period starting from the registration of the official receiver's application for early dissolution (s202(5)). It is open to the Secretary of State, a creditor, a contributory or an administrative receiver to apply to halt the early dissolution if:

- there are sufficient assets
- an investigation is necessary
- early dissolution is otherwise inappropriate.

In other cases, final meetings of the creditors must be called by the liquidator (where it was a compulsory liquidation, s146(1)) and of the creditors and the company (where it was a voluntary liquidation s106(1)). The liquidator lays an account before the meetings and it is the function of the meetings to approve or disapprove the account and to decide whether the liquidator should be released from any liability in connection with his role as liquidator. The liquidator then makes a report to the Registrar of Companies and, in the case of a compulsory liquidation, also to the court (ss106(3), 172(8)).

If the account has been approved and the release given, the company is deemed dissolved three months from the day on which the liquidator's return to the Registrar of Companies was registered (ss201(2), 205(2)).

5. Augmenting the assets of the insolvent corporation

Introduction

It is a fundamental principle of English insolvency law that creditors should be treated equally in accordance with their respective rights prior to insolvency. Apart from the exceptions applying to secured and preferential creditors', right of set-off, retention of title and recovery of money advanced for a special payment (pp734-737 *supra*), the courts are strict in their enforcement of this equality rule and any attempt to contract out of it will be held to be invalid (*British Eagle International Airlines Ltd* v *Compagnie Air France* [1975] 2 All ER 390, [1975] 1 WLR 758).

If, immediately prior to the commencement of an insolvent winding up, the company were to pay certain creditors (for example, those in whom the corporate debtor's directors had a direct interest) in full, the latter would have been preferred to those not paid. It is, therefore, essential to the equal treatment of creditors that there exists a jurisdiction to enable the courts to set aside certain pre-liquidation transactions. The effect of such a jurisdiction is to augment the company's assets and this is discussed below.

Another means by which the company's assets can be augmented is in seeking a contribution from those who were involved in the company's management before the insolvent liquidation. In principle, such a jurisdiction is contrary to a regime of limited liability and needs to exist within clearly defined limits. This jurisdiction is discussed below.

Transactions at risk

There are two groups of sections designed to enable certain pre-liquidation transactions to be set aside, the first being sections 238-245 and the second, sections 423-425.

Sections 238-245

Under section 241, the court is given wide powers to set aside or remedy in some other way transactions defined by sections 238 and 239. Section 238 concerns "Transactions at undervalue" in England and Wales (s242 sets out a similar provision for Scotland) and section 239 concerns "Preferences" in England and Wales (with s243 for the Scottish equivalent). In England and Wales, this jurisdiction can be invoked by a liquidator or an administrator. In Scotland, the liquidator, administrator and any creditor whose debt was incurred before the commencement of the winding up may invoke the jurisdiction.

A transaction at an undervalue occurs either:

- where the company makes a gift to someone; or
- where the benefit to the company under the transaction is significantly less than the benefit to the other party.

The third party may be successful in upholding the validity of a transaction which satisfies either of these requirements, where it can be established that the company entered into the transaction in good faith, for the purpose of carrying on its business and where there were reasonable grounds for believing that the transaction would benefit the company.

A preference arises where the company does something or allows something to be done which, were the company to go into insolvent liquidation, would have the effect of putting someone else (one of the company's creditors or a guarantor of any of the company's debts) in a better position than he would otherwise be in. That other person is said to be "preferred".

To invoke this jurisdiction, it has to be shown that the company "was influenced in deciding to give [the preference] by a desire to place the preferee in a better position than that in which he would have been, had the preference not been given. It will be up to whoever brings the proceedings to prove that the company was so influenced but this desire is presumed when the preference is given to someone "connected with the company (otherwise than by reason only of being its employee)". The presumption is rebuttable but shifting the onus of proof in this way makes it a great deal easier to establish the application of this section.

"Connected with a company" is very widely defined (ss249, 435) and includes relatives and cases where preferor and preferee have common directorships and common shareholdings.

Sections 238 and 239 share the following characteristics:

- Each can be invoked only by a liquidator or administrator.
- Each has strict time limits: in the case of a transaction at an undervalue, or of a preference given to a person connected with the company, the transaction must be shown to have taken place within two years of the onset of insolvency (either the commencement of liquidation or the presentation of the administration petition, whichever is the earlier); in the case of a preference given to someone unconnected with the company, the transaction must be shown to have taken place within six months of that date.
- The company in each case must be shown to have been unable to pay its debts at the time of the transaction or to have been rendered incapable of paying its debts by the transaction.
- The court has the same wide powers to deal with either transaction (s241) namely:
  - to require any property transferred to be restored to the company;
  - if property was transferred and sold or if money was transferred and in either case the money was used to buy property, to require that property to be transferred to the company;
  - to release or discharge any security given by the company;
  - to require payment to the liquidator or administrator of a sum of money in respect of benefits received;
  - to require any surety or guarantee which had been released to be reinstated;
  - to require any obligation imposed to be secured;
  - to decide to what extent anyone on whom obligations have been imposed may prove a debt in the liquidation.

It is important to draw attention to a principle established in the case of *Re Yagerphone Ltd* [1935] Ch 392. According to this principle, anything recovered by the liquidator invoking the jurisdiction to have a preference set aside, is to be applied for the benefit of the unsecured creditors, rather than (as in *Yagerphone* itself) the chargees who were secured by a floating charge. This principle has been the subject of criticism from time to time and it remains to be seen whether it will be extended to proceeds of the successful application of sections 238 and 244 as well.

Sections 244 and 245 are also available only to an administrator or a liquidator. Section 244 relates to "extortionate credit transactions".

"[A] transaction is extortionate if, having regard to the risk accepted by the person providing the credit:
(a) the terms of it are or were such as to require grossly exorbitant payments to be made (whether unconditionally or in certain contingencies) in respect of the provision of the credit, or

(b) it otherwise grossly contravened ordinary principles of fair dealing;"

There is a presumption that a transaction which is the subject of an application under this section is extortionate, and the section applies to any transaction within three years of the day on which the administration order was made or the company went into liquidation. Again, the court has wide powers to deal with what is established to be an extortionate credit transaction.

Section 245 has been in United Kingdom corporate insolvency law since 1908 (s239 – the preference provision discussed above – goes back to 1862). It recognises that a specific means by which a creditor can be favoured over other creditors is in being granted a floating charge shortly before the commencement of an insolvent liquidation. This jurisdiction, which also applies in Scotland, operates to invalidate any floating charge given by the company to the extent that the company receives nothing in return, in the following circumstances:

- it was given within two years of the onset of insolvency if given to a connected person, or one year of the onset of insolvency if given to an unconnected person; and

- if given to an unconnected person, the company was insolvent at the time, or was rendered insolvent by the transaction under which the charge was granted (if the charge was given to a connected person, this does not have to be established in order to invalidate the charge).

The period of one year or two years is calculated back from the "onset of insolvency" which, where the company goes into liquidation, is the date of the commencement of the winding up (p783 *supra*). Where the company goes into administration, it is the date of the presentation of the petition on which the order is made. It is also provided that a charge granted either to a connected or an unconnected person between the presentation of an administration order and the order granted thereon may also be invalidated under this section.

To the extent that the company receives consideration for the charge, the charge is valid. To qualify, the money must be paid at the same time as the charge is granted or thereafter and recently the Court of Appeal has stressed that this requirement will not be satisfied if "the making of the advance precedes the formal execution of the debenture by any time whatsoever, unless the interval is so short that it can be regarded as *de minimis* – for example a coffee break" (*Re Shoe Lace Ltd* [1993] BCC 609 at 619, [1994] 1 BCLC 111 p123).

Sections 423-425

These sections prevent a person from disposing of his property in order to avoid payment of his debts and thereby defrauding certain creditors. It has generally been applied as against individuals, but is sufficiently widely drafted to be capable of use against a corporation. Should an order be made under section 423 to the effect that the transaction in question was one defrauding creditors, the court has powers under section 425, which are very similar to those conferred by section 241 above. It has recently been decided that, in making an order under this section, the court must respect the accrued rights of innocent third parties and that an order can be made under section 423 (2)(a) even if it is not possible completely to restore the position to what it would have been if the transaction had not been entered into (*Chohan* v *Saggar* [1994] BCC 134, [1994] 1 BCLC 706).

Unlike section 238 – to which it is most closely related – a successful application under section 423 does not depend on the company being in liquidation or administration. Another difference lies in the fact that sections 423-425 can be invoked by a victim (such as a creditor of the company) of the transaction as well as by an administrator or liquidator. However, the standard of proof is higher than that required under sections 238 or 239 as the court must be satisfied that the debtor was essentially dishonest. Furthermore, there is no presumption that this was the case. Recently, the Court of Appeal, in dismissing an application by a creditor under section 423 as hopeless, also expressed the view that the creditor's application was based on an alleged preference of the bank by the company and that such an application could only be made by the liquidator under section 239 (*Menzies* v *National Bank of Kuwait SAK* [1994] BCC 119; as to hopeless applications, see *Pinewood Joinery* v *Starelm Properties Ltd* [1994] BCC 569, [1994] 2 BCLC 412)

Personal liability of officers

The fundamental principle of limited liability for investors in registered companies, coupled with the relative ease in the creation of such corporations, has given a freedom of entrepreneurial action to those who wish to engage in commercial activity in the United Kingdom. The courts have, however, been alive to the possibilities of defrauding creditors which are offered by trading activities through registered companies (for example, the directors and shareholders might incur large debts which they know the company will not be able to meet, whilst at the same time paying themselves large amounts by way of salary or dividend in the knowledge that the principle of limited liability will protect them).

To combat this risk, since 1929, United Kingdom Company Law has enabled action to be taken in the course of the liquidation of an insolvent company against anyone who has caused the business of the company to be carried on "with intent to defraud creditors of the company or creditors of any other person, or for any fraudulent purpose". This provision is now section 213 and the court is empowered under the section to make an order requiring that persons so responsible shall make such contribution to the assets of the company as the court decides. Such persons may also be prosecuted under section 458 CA and, if found guilty, sent to prison or fined or both fined and imprisoned.

In practice, this section has been of little use. It is restricted to circumstances where it can be established that the persons against whom it is used were actually dishonest and not simply reckless or incompetent (for example, they actually knew when taking credit that the company would be going into insolvent liquidation and would, therefore, be unable to repay the credit incurred). Successful proceedings were however brought under the predecessor of section 213 IA in *Re Gerald Cooper Chemicals Ltd* [1978] Ch 262 and again in *Re L Todd (Swanscombe) Ltd* [1990] BCC 125, [1990] BCLC 454 and *Re A Company (1418 of 1988)* [1990] BCC 526, [1991] BCLC 197.

The step of extending this liability to cases where the business of the company was conducted incompetently rather than fraudulently only entered United Kingdom insolvency law with the coming into force of the IA in December 1986. The relevant provision is section 214 under which a liquidator of an insolvent company can issue a summons against someone who was a director of the company before it went into liquidation and whose incompetence (as defined by the section) is alleged to have resulted in loss to the creditor. "Director" in this section is defined to include a "shadow director", that is, "a person in accordance with whose directions or instructions the directors of the company are accustomed to act (but so that a person is not deemed a shadow director by reason only that the directors act on advice given by him in a professional capacity)" (s251).

This section may thus apply to controlling shareholders and it has even been alleged that a company's bank could be a shadow director because of its direct intervention in the running of its business (*Re A Company No 5009 of 1987* (1988) 4 BCC 424, [1989] BCLC 13) but this claim was not established at the trial of the action, (*Re MC Bacon Ltd* [1990] BCC 78, [1990] BCLC 324). Subsequent academic and practical comment has questioned the extent to which a bank, in the exercise of its day to day credit control functions in relation to a particular borrower, could ever properly be held to be a shadow director of that borrower.

This jurisdiction is often described by the term "wrongful trading" (as opposed to "fraudulent trading" under s213). Although the term "wrongful trading" appears as the heading of the section, it does not appear anywhere in the text of the section. This term must therefore be taken as the shorthand for the compendious statement in the section for when liability will arise. This involves two stages:

- the establishment of a date prior to liquidation when the director "knew or ought to have concluded that there was no reasonable prospect that the company would avoid going into insolvent liquidation" (s214(2)(b)); and,

- that the director is not able to satisfy the court that as from that date he "took every step with a view to minimising the potential loss to the company's creditors as he ought to have taken" (s214(3)).

The test to be adopted when assessing the director's liability contains both a subjective element (the actual knowledge skill and experience of that director) and an objective element (the knowledge, skill and experience that might be expected of him). There are now four reported cases in which the substance of this section – *i.e.* what actually constitutes wrongful trading – is examined, see *Re Produce Marketing Consortium Ltd (No 2)* [1989] 1 WLR 745 [1989] BCC 569, [1989] BCLC 520, *Re Purpoint* [1991] BCC 121, [1991] BCLC 491, *DKG Contractors Ltd* [1990] BCC 903 and *Re Sherborne Associates Ltd* [1995] BCC 40.

In the first three of these four cases orders were made by the court for contributions by the respective respondents. In *Re Produce Marketing Consortium Ltd* and *Re DKG Contractors*, however, the order under section 214 simply duplicated a liability which arose under some other statutory or contractual provision. It is clear from the analysis in these cases that the facts of each case will be decisive. The necessary careful examination of these facts requires painstaking preparation. Given that applications under this section are time-consuming and expensive, invariably undertaken in circumstances where money is short and where it is quite possible that the prospective respondents will themselves have little money to satisfy any order that might be made, the efficacy of this provision is still in doubt as a matter of theory. It is understood that, in practice, liquidators and directors often reach out-of-court settlements, driven in part by the uncertainty of the outcome of any litigation. As a catalyst for settlement, the section is a useful tool in the armoury of practitioners.

The crucial distinction between sections 213 and 214 is that there is no need to prove dishonesty under section 214. Recklessness and pure incompetence are sufficient. It is just possible, however, that with this new jurisdiction the courts may be prepared to place less stringent controls on the use of section 213 (where, hitherto, proof of actual dishonesty has been required despite the fact that these are civil proceedings). This may just be discernible from the court's approach in *Re A Company (1418 of 1988)* [1990] BCC 526, [1991] BCLC 197. The widening of section 213 may be of much benefit to future liquidators, despite the view that section 214 may provide greater scope for successful applications against errant directors. Unlike section 214, section 213 is not restricted to use against former directors or shadow directors. (see *Re Gerald Cooper Chemicals Ltd* [1978] Ch 262 which is a case of a successful application against a creditor).

As with a finding of fraudulent trading, the court can, if wrongful trading is established, make a declaration that the respondent to the summons is liable to make such contribution (if any) to the company's assets as the court thinks fit. The court also has powers under section 215 to give further directions charging any contribution which the respondent is ordered to make (s215(2)). It is also the case with both sections, that only the liquidator may take proceedings. This was not the case in the section which preceded section 213 and it is distinctly possible that there might be disagreement between the liquidator and some creditors as to whether proceedings under section 213 or 214 should be taken. The creditors may have to accept the liquidator's decision, unless it is clearly perverse – in which case the court might be asked to replace the liquidator or might order the liquidator, as a public official, to take the appropriate proceedings.

Sections 213 and 214 can be seen to provide additional jurisdictions under which past officers and others connected with a company in liquidation might be held liable to contribute to the fund to be distributed among the creditors. It should also be noted that section 212 consolidates the previous jurisdiction under which the liquidator may bring proceedings by way of summons (generally quicker than proceedings begun by writ) against a variety of defendants. Section 212 does not, however, provide any substantive cause of action; it is simply procedural and any summons presented under it must be based on some cause of action such as the alleged negligence or other breach of duty of the respondent. Those against whom this procedure may be used are:

- an officer or former officer of the company;
- a liquidator, administrator or administrative receiver of the company;
- someone who, not falling within either of the above categories, is or was concerned or has taken part in the promotion, formation or management of the company.

6. Public control over insolvent corporations

Licensing and control of the appointee

Since the passing of the Insolvency legislation in 1986, the United Kingdom has had the new profession of "insolvency practitioners". Prior to this no qualifications were required of anyone acting as a receiver, liquidator or provisional liquidator to a company. Now the IA lays down that anyone who does anything as a liquidator, provisional liquidator, administrator, administrative receiver or as the supervisor of a voluntary arrangement is automatically labelled as someone who "acts as an insolvency practitioner in relation to a company" (s388(1)). It is also provided in section 1(2), IA, that the nominee appointed to act in relation to a CVA must be a qualified insolvency practitioner. A person acting as an insolvency practitioner without a licence commits a criminal offence (s389).

There are two routes to obtaining a licence: first, by direct application to the Secretary of State for Trade and Industry (s392), secondly, by membership of a professional body recognised by the Secretary of State as one which regulates the practice of a profession, and maintains and enforces rules (and sets or co-operates in the setting of examinations) for securing that those of its members who are permitted to act as insolvency practitioners are fit and proper persons so to act and meet acceptable requirements as to education, practical training and experience (s391).

Under delegated legislation, seven organisations have to date been recognised for the purpose of licensing under section 391 (Insolvency Practitioners (Recognised Professional Bodies) Order 1986 (SI 1986 No 1764)). For the most part, however, licensed insolvency practitioners are either accountants or lawyers, with the vast majority being accountants. Other delegated legislation lays down detailed provision as to what is to be taken into account in deciding who is a fit and proper person to carry on the profession of insolvency practitioner, the educational and training requirements and the extent to which insolvency practitioners are required to carry insurance for their work (Insolvency Practitioners Regulations 1990 (SI 1990 No 439), as amended by the Insolvency Practitioners (Amendment) Regulations 1993 (SI 1993 No 221)).

In addition, there are provisions which lay down that an insolvency practitioner must be an individual (s390(1)) and must not be a bankrupt, disqualified under the provisions of the Company Directors' Disqualification Act 1986 or be a patient within the meaning of the Mental Health Act 1983 (s390(4)). Finally, it should be pointed out that there is in existence an Insolvency Practitioners Tribunal to which anyone who has been refused a licence on direct application or membership of a recognised body can appeal (ss395-6, Schedule 7).

Examinations and investigations

Public examinations

A public examination can be initiated only by the official receiver in relation to a company in compulsory liquidation. Under section 133, the examination of any of the following can be applied for:

- anyone who is or has been an officer of the company;
- anyone who has acted as liquidator or administrator of the company or as a receiver or manager;
- anyone who has been concerned with, or who has taken part in the promotion, formation or management of the company.

The application is made either by the official receiver at his own instance or where requested to do so by one half in value of the company's creditors or three-quarters in value of the company's contributories (s133(2)). The court has a discretion as to whether to grant the order for examination and will be concerned to ensure that the potential examinee falls into one of the specified categories.

The public examination is a rarely used procedure.

Private examinations

We have already discussed section 236 under which a liquidator, provisional liquidator, administrator or administrative receiver can apply to the court for permission to examine:

- any officer of the company;
- any person known or suspected of having in his possession any of the company's property or known or suspected of being indebted to the company;
- anyone whom the court thinks capable of giving information concerning the promotion, formation, business, dealings, affairs or property of the company.

The major issue in deciding upon whether to grant this application is to distinguish between what is oppressive to the person summoned and what is helpful to the liquidator in the performing of his functions in the insolvent company. There are at least two ways in which this process may be seen as oppressive. In the first place, the person summoned may be required to answer questions under oath and the answers given may provide the basis or the evidence necessary for a successful prosecution in subsequent criminal proceedings. Thus, the process might deprive the respondent of certain rights against self-incrimination which have long been part of the criminal law of the United Kingdom. Secondly, the answers may assist the insolvency practitioner in formulating subsequent civil proceedings against the respondent and may, thus, be said to have given an advantage to the insolvency practitioner in those proceedings.

The court has attempted to distinguish between examinations which are sought when the liquidator has already decided to take legal action against the person he would want to examine and those where no such decision has been taken. It was thought in a series of court decisions (such as *Re Castle New Homes Ltd* [1979] 1 WLR 1075) that it would be unfair to a potential examinee to allow him to be examined when the decision had already been taken, since the answers to questions would assist the liquidator in the subsequent litigation.

This distinction has now been rejected as unworkable (*Re Cloverbay Ltd (No 2)* [1990] BCC 414, [1991] BCLC 135 (under the name of *Cloverbay Ltd* v *BCCI*) where an alternative test was laid down. This was that the insolvency practitioner would be entitled to carry out such investigation as enabled him to reconstitute the company's knowledge, so as to put the company back in the position in which it would have been when managed by its board of directors. This test somewhat limited the powers of the insolvency practitioner under section 236, but in the latest cases the scope of section 236 again seems to have been widened. In *Re British and Commonwealth Holdings plc (No 2)* [1992] BCC 977, [1993] BCLC 168 the House of Lords rejected the suggestion that the section should be read in this limiting way. In the words of Lord Slynn who gave the judgment of the whole court:

> "... it is plain that this is an extraordinary power and that the discretion must be exercised after a careful balancing of the factors involved – on the one hand the reasonable requirements of the administrator to carry out his task, on the other the need to avoid making an order which is wholly unreasonable, unnecessary or "oppressive" to the person concerned ([1992] BCC at 984E, [1993] BCLC at 177F).

Further, in *Re Arrows (No 4)* [1994] BCC 641, [1994] 2 BCLC 738, the House of Lords decided that there was no basis to an insolvency practitioner's refusal to a request by public authorities to hand over the information obtained from a respondent examined under section 236 for the purpose of bringing a prosecution against the respondent. The court did say, however, that the court before which the prosecution proposed to lead such evidence had a discretion in appropriate circumstances to refuse permission for such evidence to be used.

Publicity and records

Throughout this chapter we have seen many instances of the requirement that those active on behalf of an insolvent company publicise the company's insolvency, formal insolvency appointments and other events occurring in the course of the insolvency. It is, therefore, a requirement in an administration, an administrative receivership and a liquidation, that every invoice, order for goods or business letter issued on behalf of the company should indicate the insolvency regime in operation (ss12, 39, 64, 188).

Other examples of the publicity of proceedings required include the fact that the petition in any compulsory liquidation must be advertised in the Gazette (Rule 4.11 IR). The appointment of administrative receivers, administrators or liquidators must also be publicised in the Gazette (s21(2), Rules 2.10, 4.106 IR) and notified to the Companies Registry which, as noted above, is open to public inspection. Records must be kept of the proceedings of all meetings held during the company's insolvency (Rules 2.42, 3.15, 3.26, 4.71 IR).

Finally, it will be noted that insolvency practitioners are required to maintain accurate accounts of receipts and payments (Rules 2.52, 3.32, 4.125(2) IR). The public has rights of inspection of any company's file held by the Registrar of Companies (for England and Wales, the address is Crown Way, Maindy, Cardiff, CF4 3UZ, although copies of the registers are kept at Companies House, City Road, London EC1Y 1BG. For Scotland, the relevant address is 102 George Street, Edinburgh, EH2 3DJ). Copies of documents may be obtained at a small charge.

The Gazette may also be referred to; there are separate editions for London, Edinburgh and Belfast. Credit reference agencies and banks give information about particular companies.

7. Special insolvency regimes

Introduction

Certain privately financed commercial undertakings in the United Kingdom have significant public duties and are considered to merit protection against the normal consequences of commercial insolvency. They are thus made subject to modified insolvency regimes on account of the serious social, political and economic consequences which might follow the liquidation of any company or companies connected with such undertakings. Falling into this category are financial markets and the recently privatised railways and water industries.

Insolvency and financial markets

Part VII of the Companies Act 1989 has introduced a separate insolvency regime to deal with default in "market contracts" as defined by this Act. A "market contract" is:

- a contract entered into by a member of an exchange or a designated non-member where the contract is made on the exchange; or
- a contract entered into by a member of an exchange or a designated non-member where the contract is made subject to the rules of the exchange; or

- contract entered into by an exchange subject to its own rules and in connection with its clearing services.

The purpose of this special regime suspending normal insolvency rules and substituting for them the special rules laid down by each recognised investment exchange and each recognised clearing house, is to prevent one default and insolvency setting off a series of other defaults and insolvencies in the market, with a resultant 'domino effect' leading to a rapid escalation of collapses and insolvencies.

It is not possible here to do more than draw attention to this alternative regime and to identify the bodies which, with their members and certain categories of designated non-members, fall under it. The present list of recognised investment exchanges and recognised clearing houses is as follows:

United Kingdom
The International Petroleum Exchange
The London Stock Exchange
London FOX
London International Financial Futures Exchange
London Traded Options Market
London Metal Exchange
OM London
International Commodities Clearing House
Gafta Clearing House

United States
NASDAQ
Chicago Mercantile Exchange

Australia
Sydney Futures Exchange

There is power for bodies to be added to or removed from this list. The concept of the "designated non-member" is designed to deal with the situation where a default arises out of a market contract entered into by someone who is not a member of a recognised exchange but where the default might have the very consequences which this regime is designed to avoid. In the absence of special provision, such a person would not be subject to the rules of any recognised exchange and thus susceptible to the normal insolvency rules. Thus, not only must each recognised exchange have special rules for dealing with such defaults and their consequences, but they must ensure that such rules extend, where necessary, to designated non-members.

Where an insolvency practitioner is appointed as a liquidator, administrator or administrative receiver of any company, he must enquire whether the company placed in that particular insolvency regime falls under the special regime established by Part VII of the Companies Act 1989. If so, he must ensure that he deals with the assets of such company in accordance with that regime.

The water and railways industries

Very similar modifications to the normal corporate insolvency regimes are made
in relation to any company which, in the case of water, is appointed under section
6(1) of the Water Industry Act 1991 ("WIA") to be a water or sewerage undertaker
in England and Wales ("a water company"), and, in the case of the railways ("a
railway company"), is licensed to carry passengers, to manage a network, station
or light maintenance depot (s59(6), Railways Act 1993, – "RA"). Where such a
company is or is likely to become unable to pay its debts, provision is made for
the grant by the court of a special administration order (under s23 WIA) and a
railway administration order (under s59 RA) (here described as "a special administration order" or "SAO"). An SAO functions like an administration order
under Part II of the IA, with the following modifications:

- the purposes for which an SAO can be made are:
  - The transfer to another company or companies as a going concern as
    much as possible of the undertaking of the company subject to the
    SAO, in order to ensure the carrying out of the functions vested in that
    company are properly carried out; and
  - the carrying out of those functions pending the transfer (s23 WIA,
    s59(2) RA)
- Only the Secretary of State or, with the latter's consent, the Director General of Water Services or the Director of Passenger Rail Franchising may
  petition for an SAO;
- No petition for the winding up of the company may be presented, nor may
  an administrative receiver be appointed without the leave of the court
  (s24(5)(b) WIA, s60(5)(b) RA; contrast s10(2) IA).
- The court may not make a winding up order in the case of a water company
  (s25(a) WIA).
- The court may not make a winding up order in the case of a railway company, on a petition presented by someone other than the Secretary of State,
  unless:
  - notice of the petition has been given to the Secretary of State and the
    Franchising Director; and
  - fourteen days have elapsed since the service of the notice (to enable an
    application to be made for the making of an SAO, s61, RA).
- No voluntary winding up resolution may be passed and no administration
  order under the IA may be made in relation to a water company (s26,
  WIA).
- No voluntary winding up resolution may be passed nor administration order under the IA made in relation to a railway company, except with the
  leave of the court, which leave may only be granted after notice of the application for the court's leave has been served on the Secretary of State and
  the Franchise Director and 14 days allowed to elapse (s62(1), (5) RA).

INDEX

	EUROPE	BELGIUM	DENMARK	FRANCE	GERMANY	GREECE	IRELAND	ITALY
Abuse of process								
liquidation as,							341	
Accounts								
appeals on,			98					
balance sheets and,		26						
bankruptcies and,								
boards of management and,								
composition of,		26						
consolidated,				128				
controlled management and,								
creditors and,								
distribution,		57	98					
failure to publish,					208		365	
filing of,		26-27	89					
information on,				128-129			306-307	
liquidation and,								
management and,					180			
meetings on,			107, 109					
officers and,								
profit and loss,			91, 95					
public control of,								
publicity of,					187			
receivership and,								
registration of,								
shareholders' meetings and,					213			
suspension of payments and,								
Acquired Rights Directive, *see*	14-19							
also **Transfers of Undertakings**								
direct effect of,	19							
Actions, *see also* , **Stay of proceedings**								
administrators and,		62			231, 232			
auditors and,								
bankruptcies and,								
compositions and,								
creditors and,			94	161				
directors by,								
liquidators and,					214			
mortgagees and,				159				
multiple defendants and,				159				
officers and,								
pledgees and,				159				
preferential creditors and,				159				
subrogation of,								
summary proceedings and,				126				
time limits and,								
transfer of,				134				
Administration, *see also* ,								
Administrative receivers,								
Compositions, Management								
Settlements						271-275		
advertisements and,								
applications for,								
bankruptcies and,		51	94					
contracts and,		56						
controlled,								388-389
costs and,								

LUXEMBOURG	NETHERLANDS	NORWAY	PORTUGAL	SPAIN	SWEDEN	SWITZERLAND	UNITED KINGDOM	
								Abuse of process
								liquidation as,
								Accounts
								appeals on,
								balance sheets and,
434	452							bankruptcies and,
								boards of management and,
								composition of,
								consolidated,
427								controlled management and,
								creditors and,
								distribution,
								failure to publish,
								filing of,
								information on,
			552		642		784	liquidation and,
								management and,
								meetings on,
	476							officers and,
								profit and loss,
					654-655			public control of,
412					656-657			publicity of,
							772-773	receivership and,
	453			576				registration of,
								shareholders' meetings and,
				586, 587, 592				suspension of payments and,
								Acquired Rights Directive, *see*
								also **Transfers of Undertakings**
								direct effect of,
								Actions, *see also* , **Stay of proceedings**
						713-716		administrators and,
	474							auditors and,
	472					713-714		bankruptcies and,
423-424			549-550	603	636			compositions and,
				590		713-714		creditors and,
						713-714		directors by,
								liquidators and,
								mortgagees and,
						715-716		multiple defendants and,
						713-714		officers and,
								pledgees and,
								preferential creditors and,
			554					subrogation of,
								summary proceedings and,
						716		time limits and,
								transfer of,
								Administration, *see also* ,
								Administrative receivers,
								Compositions, Management
							750-767	**Settlements**
							756	advertisements and,
							754, 759	applications for,
								bankruptcies and,
							763-764	contracts and,
								controlled,
								costs and,

	EUROPE	BELGIUM	DENMARK	FRANCE	GERMANY	GREECE	IRELAND	ITALY
creditors and,								
creditors' committees and,								
creditors' meetings and,								389
discharge of,								
distribution of assets and,								
effect of,								
employees and,								
extraordinary,								402-403
financing,								
hearing of,								
insolvency practitioners and,								
interim,			93					
intervention in,								
large companies and,								402-403
leases and,		46, 53-54						
management of,								
moratoriums and,								
negligence and,								
officers and,								
opposition to,								
orders,								
petitions for,								
plan of,								
prejudice and,								
procedure on,								
proposals for,								388-389
publicity on,								
purpose of,								
reform of,								
reports on,								389
resolutions on,								389
retention of title and,								
set off and,								
shareholders and,								
supervision of,								
termination of,								
transfer of undertakings and,								
Administrative receivers								
accounts and,								
appointment of,								
restraint of,								
definition of,								
duties of,								
insolvency practitioners and,								
removal of,								
sale of property and,								
statement of affairs and,								
Administrators		62-63						
actions and,					231, 232			
agreements and,		38						

LUXEMBOURG	NETHERLANDS	NORWAY	PORTUGAL	SPAIN	SWEDEN	SWITZERLAND	UNITED KINGDOM	
							751-752, 755-756	creditors and,
							755, 760-761	creditors' committees and,
							756, 761	creditors' meetings and,
			545				755	discharge of,
							765	distribution of assets and,
			544-545				750, 754, 760	effect of,
							761-764	employees and,
								extraordinary,
							753	financing,
							754	hearing of,
							752	insolvency practitioners and,
								interim,
			556					intervention in,
								large companies and,
							758-759	leases and,
			545				761-763	management of,
							750, 752, 754, 757	moratoriums and,
								negligence and,
							766	officers and,
							755, 759	opposition to,
						751-752, 754-755		orders,
							751, 753-756	petitions for,
			544-545					plan of,
							759	prejudice and,
							753-755	procedure on,
							752, 756	proposals for,
							755	publicity on,
			544-545				750	purpose of,
								reform of,
								reports on,
							756	resolutions on,
							757	retention of title and,
								set off and,
							766	shareholders and,
	470							supervision of,
							767	termination of,
							764-765	transfer of undertakings and,
							752	**Administrative receivers**
							772-773	accounts and,
							752-753, 769	appointment of,
								restraint of,
							768	definition of,
							752, 755	duties of,
							768	insolvency practitioners and,
							768	removal of,
							772, 778	sale of property and,
							772-773	statement of affairs and,
								Administrators
	474							actions and,
								agreements and,

	EUROPE	BELGIUM	DENMARK	FRANCE	GERMANY	GREECE	IRELAND	ITALY
appointment of,			106-107	135-136, 155	238, 248-249	285, 296		
assets and,		50, 54-55			225, 231-232			391
distribution of,					232			
assistance to,		63						
auditors as,			106					
authorisation of,		49						
balance sheets and,								
bankruptcies and,						282		
boards of management and,					235, 248-249			
choice of,					223-224, 228			
claims against,					230-231			
compensation and,								
conflicts of interest and,					248			
contracts and,								
contracts of employment and,		52-53						
control of,					249			
court and,					238-239			
creditors and,					231-232			
creditors' committees and,								
creditors' meetings and,								
damages and,					232			
debts and,					232			
directors and,		56						
discharge of,					233			
discipline and,				168				
dismissal of,		52, 57						
due diligence and,		51						
duties of,			80			283		
East Germany and,					226			
elections of,								
eligibility of,								
employees and,								
examinations of,					249			
fees for,					285			
forms of,								
functions of,					177			391
good faith and,		51						
independence of,					231			
information and,								
investigations and,					249			
leases and,		46, 53-54						
legal status of,								
liabilities of,		51-52, 57			230	285		
licensing of,						296		
liquidators and,		52-55						
list of,			167					
management and,		52-55		152		286		
meetings and,								
negligence and,								392
powers of,		49, 62	79-80	152	230			
prejudicial conduct of,								

LUXEMBOURG	NETHERLANDS	NORWAY	PORTUGAL	SPAIN	SWEDEN	SWITZERLAND	UNITED KINGDOM	
	461, 469	516	537	567	631, 632	683, 716	755, 763	appointment of,
								assets and,
								distribution of,
								assistance to,
								auditors as,
								authorisation of,
								balance sheets and,
								bankruptcies and,
								boards of management and,
								choice of,
								claims against,
					646			compensation and,
								conflicts of interest and,
								contracts and,
								contracts of employment and,
	470							control of,
								court and,
			538					creditors and,
			539					creditors' committees and,
	462							creditors' meetings and,
								damages and,
								debts and,
								directors and,
								discharge of,
								discipline and,
								dismissal of,
								due diligence and,
				644-645	635, 691	686-687,	760-761	duties of,
								East Germany and,
					632			elections of,
	470	516	537 538					eligibility of,
								employees and,
								examinations of,
				568				fees for,
			537-538					forms of,
								functions of,
								good faith and,
	472							independence of,
								information and,
								investigations and,
							763	leases and,
				567-568		717-718		legal status of,
						717-718		liabilities of,
								licensing of,
								liquidators and,
				571	646	692	761-766	list of,
				567				management and,
								meetings and,
	470				635	686-687, 691	760	negligence and,
							759	powers of,
								prejudicial conduct of,

	EUROPE	BELGIUM	DENMARK	FRANCE	GERMANY	GREECE	IRELAND	ITALY
proposals of,								
registration of,				167				
removal of,					238			
remuneration of,		50-51			231			
replacement of,								
report of,				145	229			
retirement of,								
role of,	49, 50		167					
sale of assets and,		48						391
sanctions against,				168				
segregation and,					231			
shareholders' meetings and,					236			
supervision and,					232-233			
voidable transactions and,								
Advances								
Advertisements								
creditors' meetings and,								
financial restructuring of,								
liquidation and,								
receivership and,								
reorganisations and,								
resolutions of,								
sale of property and,				158				
winding up and,							341	
Agreements, *see also* **Contracts, Creditors agreements**								
bankruptcies and								
boards of directors and,				117				
creditors and,		31-38						
effect on,		52-53						
liquidations and,		58						
termination of,		58						
Aircraft								
Draft European Union Bankruptcy Convention and,	9							
liens over								
registration of,						261		
Alert procedure				129-130				
auditors and,				129				
courts and,				130				
liquidations on,				157				
shareholders and,				129				
worker representation committees and,				129-130				
Annual reports								
filing of,		27						
shareholders and,								
Appeals								
accounts on,			97					
bankruptcy against		44						
liquidations and,								
rehabilitation plans on,				145				
winding up and,								
Applicable law,	5							384
draft European Union Bankruptcy								

LUXEMBOURG	NETHERLANDS	NORWAY	PORTUGAL	SPAIN	SWEDEN	SWITZERLAND	UNITED KINGDOM	
							756	proposals of,
								registration of,
								removal of,
	470				690	683-684,	761-767	remuneration of,
			538					replacement of,
								report of,
							767	retirement of,
			632					role of,
								sale of assets and,
								sanctions against,
								segregation and,
								shareholders' meetings and,
								supervision and,
								voidable transactions and,
							809-810	**Advances**
							756	**Advertisements**
					634-635			creditors' meetings and,
								financial restructuring of,
			544				788-789 809-810	liquidation and,
							774	receivership and,
			536					reorganisations and,
							786	resolutions of,
								sale of property and,
		503						winding up and,
								Agreements, *see also* **Contracts, Creditors agreements**
								bankruptcies and
			549					boards of directors and,
								creditors and,
								effect on,
								liquidations and,
								termination of,
								Aircraft
								Draft European Union Bankruptcy Convention and,
					624			liens over
								registration of,
								Alert procedure
								auditors and,
								courts and,
								liquidations on,
								shareholders and,
								worker representation committees and,
								Annual reports
					654			filing of,
					622			shareholders and,
								Appeals
								accounts on,
434	469		547			696		bankruptcy against
		510						liquidations and,
								rehabilitation plans on,
437								winding up and,
				563				**Applicable law,**
								draft European Union Bankruptcy

	EUROPE	BELGIUM	DENMARK	FRANCE	GERMANY	GREECE	IRELAND	ITALY
Convention and,	9-10							
Arbitration								
Convention on,						271		
debts and,						269		
Arrangements, *see also* ,								
Compulsory arrangements,								
Voluntary arrangements								
acceptance of,								
applications for,								
auditors and,								
board of directors and,								
compulsory,								
conditions for,								
confidentiality and,								
costs and,								
courts and,								
creditors and,								
creditors' meetings and,								
debtors and,								
effect of,								
employees and,								
equality of creditors and,								
examinations and,								
moratoriums and,								
negotiations on,								
officers and,								
procedure and,								
proposals for,								
publicity on,								
purpose of,								
rejection of,								
sale of assets and,								
shareholders and,								
supervisory committees and,								
tax and,								
termination of,								
time limits and,								
voting on,								
Arrest							359, 368	
bankruptcies and,								
Arrestments					189			
Articles of association			68-69					
boards of management and,								
decision-making powers and,								
distribution of, assets and,					220-221			
inspection of,							306	
meetings and,								
Articles of incorporation			68					
Assets, *see also* **Distribution**								
of assets, Sale of assets								
administrators and		50, 54-55			225, 231			
alteration of,					199			
ascertainment of,								
assignment of,								

LUXEMBOURG	NETHERLANDS	NORWAY	PORTUGAL	SPAIN	SWEDEN	SWITZERLAND	UNITED KINGDOM	
								Convention and,
								Arbitration
				581				Convention on,
				582				debts and,
								Arrangements, *see also* **,**
								Compulsory arrangements,
								Voluntary arrangements
		495-497						acceptance of,
		493						applications for,
		494						auditors and,
		499						board of directors and,
		496-498						compulsory,
		494						conditions for,
		498						confidentiality and,
		493						costs and,
		493, 497-499						courts and,
		493						creditors and,
		496, 498						creditors' meetings and
		498-499						debtors and,
		493						effect of,
		495						employees and,
		497						equality of creditors and,
		516-517						examinations and,
		493						moratoriums and,
		494, 496						negotiations on,
		499						officers and,
		493-498						procedure and,
		494, 495						proposals for,
		496-497, 516-517						publicity on,
		492						purpose of,
		497						rejection of,
		492						sale of assets and,
		499						shareholders and,
		494-498						supervisory committees and,
		495						tax and,
		495, 497-499						termination of,
		496						time limits and,
		496-497						voting on,
								Arrest
				603				bankruptcies and,
								Arrestments
								Articles of association
	453-454							boards of management and,
	449							decision-making powers and,
								distribution of, assets and,
								inspection of,
	453	484-485						meetings and,
								Articles of incorporation
								Assets, *see also* **Distribution**
								of assets, Sale of assets
								administrators and
								alteration of,
						697-698		ascertainment of,
				583		682-683		assignment of,

	EUROPE	BELGIUM	DENMARK	FRANCE	GERMANY	GREECE	IRELAND	ITALY
attachment of,								
auctions of,			76			289	351	
augmenting,		59-63		162-167	239-248	293-295	346, 360-362	394, 398-401
bankruptcies on,								391
cash into,					232			
charges and,			89					
compositions and,								387
confiscation of,					225			
conservation of,								
disposals of,			92		232			
equality among creditors and,					176			
exhaustion of,					214			
foreign,								
fraud and,							362-363, 368	
freezing of,							309-310	
identification of,		46-47				283-284	352	
information on,			78					
insufficient,		56-57					367-368	
inventory of,								394
liquidation and,				158				
liquidators and,							349	
list of,		93						
management of,								
moratoriums and,								
mortgages of,			84					
partnerships and,								
pledges of,			84					
possession of,							349	
preferential creditors and,					186			
realisation of,		54-55	96	135	176, 177, 210, 218		316, 328, 346, 350-352	
recovery of,			73-74 77	126-127		270-271		381-383
registration and,								
rehabilitation of,				134				
retention of title and,			84		184-185 226, 243			
return of,					289		368	
sale of,								
secured,								
seizure of,		30	76, 85, 87					
statement of,							312	
stripping,								
surplus,	57, 59					359		
third parties of,			96		184			
title to,				184-186				
transfer of spouses to,,				167	198, 231			
trustees and,		62						
valuation of,			96					
verification of,		60	77, 84					
Assignment								
claims of,						283-284		
creditors and,						262-263		
debts of,		28						

LUXEMBOURG	NETHERLANDS	NORWAY	PORTUGAL	SPAIN	SWEDEN	SWITZERLAND	UNITED KINGDOM	
414								attachment of,
	459					699		auctions of,
438-443	474-476	511-516	553-556	612-614	647-654	705-716	800-807	augmenting,
								bankruptcies on,
434								cash into,
		490						charges and,
423								compositions and,
								confiscation of,
				604				conservation of,
								disposals of,
								equality among creditors and,
								exhaustion of,
473-474								foreign,
								fraud and,
		492, 502						freezing of,
		488						identification of,
								information on,
								insufficient,
	426-427, 433-434				633	697		inventory of,
								liquidation and,
		494						liquidators and,
								list of,
425								management of,
	460							moratoriums and,
				574				mortgages of,
	456							partnerships and,
				574				pledges of,
								possession of,
								preferential creditors and,
425, 431		508		608		682, 699 704	778, 796	realisation of,
414-415	456-459	490-492	532-533	578-582	628-630	679-680	742	recovery of,
444								registration and,
								rehabilitation of,
								retention of title and,
								return of,
	491							sale of,
		505						secured,
		492, 501	532, 555	580				seizure of,
								statement of,
					653			stripping,
								surplus,
								third parties of,
								title to,
								transfer of spouses to,,
								trustees and,
								valuation of,
								verification of,
								Assignment
								claims of,
								creditors and,
								debts of,

	EUROPE	BELGIUM	DENMARK	FRANCE	GERMANY	GREECE	IRELAND	ITALY
reorganisation and,				159				
security over,					192			
Associations								
annual reports of,								
formation of,								
legal capacity of,								
management of,								
purpose of,								
property and,								
registration and,								
Attachment				126-127				
bailiffs and,			73-74					
bankruptcies and,								
cancellation of,								
debt collection and,			73-74					
enforcement of,					189			
ownership and,								
personal property and,				127				
preliminary,						264		
property over,				127, 158		284		
restraining,								
suspension of payments and,								
third parties and,								
vehicles of,			73					
Auctions								
assets of,			76			289	351	
pledges of,								379
sale of assets and,								
sale of property and,	54		94, 96		186			382-383
ships and,								
Auditors								
administrators and,			106					
alert procedure and,				129				
appointment of,			89					
board of,								375
damages and,								
liabilities of,								
liquidations and,								
minority shareholders and,								
negligence and,								
reports of,				128				375
role of,								375
shareholders and,		56						
statutory,		60						376
stay of bankruptcies and,								
Bailiffs								381-382
attachment and,			73-74					
investigations and,			108					
judgments and,			74					
jurisdiction of,								
Balance sheets	26					281		
administrators and,			95					
auditing,					218			
bankruptcies and,								
stay of,								

LUXEMBOURG	NETHERLANDS	NORWAY	PORTUGAL	SPAIN	SWEDEN	SWITZERLAND	UNITED KINGDOM	
								reorganisation and,
								security over,
								Associations
	449-451							annual reports of,
	450							formation of,
	449-450			562				legal capacity of,
	450							management of,
	450							purpose of,
	449							property and,
	450							registration and,
	472			608				**Attachment**
								bailiffs and,
435	466			604, 607				bankruptcies and,
	470							cancellation of,
								debt collection and,
	459							enforcement of,
	459							ownership and,
								personal property and,
								preliminary,
	457							property over,
	459-460							restraining,
				589				suspension of payments and,
	459							third parties and,
								vehicles of,
								Auctions
	459					699-700		assets of,
								pledges of,
				611				sale of assets and,
			528-529, 549		642-643			sale of property and,
				610				ships and,
								Auditors
								administrators and,
								alert procedure and,
		494	527		620			appointment of,
			526, 527					board of,
					652			damages and,
						712-717		liabilities of,
		504			641, 642			liquidations and,
					623			minority shareholders and,
					652			negligence and,
								reports of,
								role of,
								shareholders and,
								statutory,
						689, 691		stay of bankruptcies and,
								Bailiffs
								attachment and,
								investigations and,
								judgments and,
		492						jurisdiction of,
								Balance sheets
								administrators and,
								auditing,
434, 443								bankruptcies and,
						692		stay of,

	EUROPE	BELGIUM	DENMARK	FRANCE	GERMANY	GREECE	IRELAND	ITALY
compositions and,		83-84						
controlled management and,								
dividends and,								
going concerns and,		83						
inaccuracies and,								
information and,								
liquidations and,								
liquidators and,					216-217			
salaries and,			83					
shareholders' meetings and,					213			
voluntary liquidations and,					212-213			
Bankruptcies, *see also*,								
Stay of bankruptcies						275-292		390-398
accounts and,								
actions and,								
adjournments and,								
administration and,								
administrators and,		38				282		
appeals and,		44						
applications for,								
arrest and,								
assets and,								
attachments and,								
bad faith and,								
balance sheets and,								
bank accounts and,								
bankruptcy office and,								
bills of exchange and,								
board of directors and,								
branches of,								
building contracts and,								393
compensation and,								
compositions and,								396-398
conditions for,		42-43						
consideration and,						279-281		
contracts and,								393-394
controlled management and,								
costs of,								
courts and,						282		
creditors and,								
creditors committees and,								391, 397
creditors' meetings and,						282		396
debtors and,								
debts and,								
declaration of,								
delivery and,								
directors and,								
distress and,								
distribution of assets and,								395, 396
dividends and,								
duties following,								
effect of,		38-39				275-279		391-394

LUXEMBOURG	NETHERLANDS	NORWAY	PORTUGAL	SPAIN	SWEDEN	SWITZERLAND	UNITED KINGDOM	
						684-685		compositions and,
427								controlled management and,
					620			dividends and,
								going concerns and,
				597				inaccuracies and,
						667		information and,
					638			liquidations and,
								liquidators and,
								salaries and,
								shareholders' meetings and,
								voluntary liquidations and,
								Bankruptcies, *see also* , **Stay of bankruptcies**
430-436	466-474		545-553		643-647	688-702, 693-702		
434								accounts and,
435	472		549-550	602-603				actions and,
	469							adjournments and,
								administration and,
								administrators and,
434	469		517-548			696		appeals and,
	466-467		545-546	600-603	643	693-694, 697		applications for,
				603				arrest and,
433-434	473			604		697-699		assets and,
435	466, 472, 473-474			604, 607-608				attachments and,
				602				bad faith and,
434, 443				602				balance sheets and,
			549					bank accounts and,
						701-702		bankruptcy office and,
432								bills of exchange and,
					644			board of directors and,
	469							branches of,
								building contracts and,
					646			compensation and,
435	473		541		631	696, 700		compositions and,
431-432	467-468							conditions for,
				600-601				consideration and,
			549	605, 607				contracts and,
432				610				controlled management and,
436								costs of,
431-436	467-469							courts and,
435-436	467-468		542-543, 546-547	602, 604	645	700-701		creditors and,
	473		546, 551	611-612		698, 701		creditors committees and,
	473		547			698, 700-701		creditors' meetings and,
	466- 468			605				debtors and,
432			549-550		645			debts and,
				602		663		declaration of,
				608				delivery and,
				603, 606	646-647			directors and,
					644			distress and,
434	473					699-700		distribution of assets and,
				606	645			dividends and,
					645-646			duties following,
431			549-550	599-600,	643	694		effect of,

	EUROPE	BELGIUM	DENMARK	FRANCE	GERMANY	GREECE	IRELAND	ITALY
embargoes and,								
employees and,								
equality of creditors and,								390
evidence on,								
examinations and,								
exhaustion of, credit and,								
experts and								
fees for,								434
foreign,								
fraud and,		39, 40	90			280 , 294, 297		400
grounds for,								
hearings on,								
injunctions and,								
institutions on,		47-52						
insurance and,								
interest and,								394
judge commissioners and,		47-50						
judgments and,						275-279		390, 392, 395, 397
jurisdiction and,								
leases and,								393
liability for debts and,		23-24						
liens and,								
liquidation in,						289-290		
loans and,								
management and,								
misrepresentation and,								
moratoriums and,								
mortgages and,								
negligence and,								392
officers and,						286-287		
opposition to,				165				391
orders,		92-93						
costs of,			97					
partnerships and,								
petitions,			91			279-281		
pledges and,								
preferential creditors and,								
prevention of,				128-130				
primary,	7							
procedure on,		40-44				281		394-398
property and,						276, 284		
seizure of,								
public prosecutors and,								
publicity of,			90					391
purpose of,		38-39	89-90			275-279		
ranking of claims and,								
realisation of assets and,								
reciprocity and,								
register of goods and,								
registration and,								
rehabilitation and,								392
rent and,								

LUXEMBOURG	NETHERLANDS	NORWAY	PORTUGAL	SPAIN	SWEDEN	SWITZERLAND	UNITED KINGDOM	
				602-605				embargoes and,
			547					employees and,
	473		550					equality of creditors and,
433, 435	470							evidence on,
434								examinations and,
432								exhaustion of, credit and,
	470							experts and
								fees for,
					697, 719-722			foreign,
424, 442	467		550	606, 612, 613-614	646	696		fraud and,
						695-697		grounds for,
434-435								hearings on,
				608				injunctions and,
								institutions on,
								insurance and,
			550	605	646			interest and,
								judge commissioners and,
432-436	474		547-548			694		judgments and,
	473							jurisdiction and,
								leases and,
				600				liability for debts and,
435-436	473							liens and,
432								liquidation in,
				613				loans and,
					646	701-702		management and,
				614				misrepresentation and,
	467					696-697		moratoriums and,
435				607-608, 610		699		mortgages and,
								negligence and,
					645-647	702		officers and,
						695		opposition to,
469-470		547-548						orders,
								costs of,
	466					679		partnerships and,
432-433, 435					644	695		petitions,
			546-547	608, 610				pledges and,
			549-550	604, 609				preferential creditors and,
								prevention of,
								primary,
432-435				601-605	644-645	695-696		procedure on,
435				611				property and,
432								seizure of,
	467		546					public prosecutors and,
444	469, 472							publicity of,
431				599-600		693-694		purpose of,
				608-611				ranking of claims and,
431			548	608				realisation of assets and,
						719-722		reciprocity and,
						695		register of goods and,
			548	604		718		registration and,
								rehabilitation and,
				610				rent and,

	EUROPE	BELGIUM	DENMARK	FRANCE	GERMANY	GREECE	IRELAND	ITALY
re-opening,								
summary,								
report on,								
reprieve from payments and,								
resolutions on,								
restrictions following,								392
retrospectivity and,								
reversal of,								
rights in rem and,								
salaries and,								
sale of assets and,								
sales and,								393
secondary,	6-7							
seizure and,								
set off and,								393
setting aside transactions and,		59-60						
settlements and,								
shareholders of,						286-287		
ships and,								
social security authorities and,								
spouses and,								
surpluses and,								
suspect acts and,		59-62						
suspect periods and,		59, 60				293-294		
suspension of payments and,								
taxation and,						279		
termination of,		56-57				284, 288-291		396-397
third parties and,						281		
time limits and,								
transactions and,								
verification of claims and,								
Banks								
accounts and,							349	
charges over,			71					
freezing,								
confidentiality and,								381
controlled management and,								
guarantees of,						263		
information provided by,					187	267		381
insolvency of,								
liquidators and,							349	
loans,	29-30							
third parties and,								
Bearer shares					181	255		
Bewindvoerders, *see,*								
Administrators								
Bills of exchange				163		264		
Boards of Directors, *see also*								
Chairman of the Board								
agreements and,				117				
appointment of,					182			374-375
bankruptcies and,								
stay of,								
book-keeping and,								

LUXEMBOURG	NETHERLANDS	NORWAY	PORTUGAL	SPAIN	SWEDEN	SWITZERLAND	UNITED KINGDOM	
								re-opening,
								summary,
					644			report on,
431-432								reprieve from payments and,
								resolutions on,
	466							restrictions following,
								retrospectivity and,
				600, 606-607				reversal of,
				601				rights in rem and,
				611				salaries and,
				609				sale of assets and,
				611	646			sales and,
								secondary,
435			550-553					seizure and,
			550	605				set off and,
								setting aside transactions and,
	468							settlements and,
					646-647	702		shareholders of,
				610				ships and,
	467		550					social security authorities and,
				607				spouses and,
435								surpluses and,
								suspect acts and,
438								suspect periods and,
				589, 600	644	697		suspension of payments and,
	467		550	609				taxation and,
435, 436	472-473			611-612	647	700, 702		termination of,
435-436				606-607				third parties and,
433				609	645			time limits and,
			550					transactions and,
			552					verification of claims and,
				566				**Banks** accounts and,
			549					charges over,
				574				freezing,
			549					confidentiality and,
						677		controlled management and,
429								guarantees of,
								information provided by,
						677		insolvency of,
		489						liquidators and,
								loans,
				604				third parties and,
411	453		528	574				**Bearer shares**
								Bewindvoerders, *see,*
								Administrators
432, 439-440			541	580-581		680, 696		**Bills of exchange**
								Boards of Directors, *see also*
								Chairman of the Board
								agreements and,
410		486	526		621			appointment of,
					644			bankruptcies and,
						689, 690		stay of,
					621			book-keeping and,

	EUROPE	BELGIUM	DENMARK	FRANCE	GERMANY	GREECE	IRELAND	ITALY
debt arrangements and,								
decisions by,		56						
delegation by,								
duties of,								
election of,			69					
employees and,								
financial statements and,				117				
foreigners on,				116				
liquidations and,								
management and,								
meetings and,								
members of,			69	116-117				
power of,				117				
quorum and,								
remuneration and,								
resolutions and,								
share capital and,								
shareholders and,						257		
shareholders' meetings and,				117				
term of office and,				116				
third parties and,								
voluntary liquidation and,								
Boards of management	26				180			
accounts and,					180			
administrators and,					235, 248-249			
articles of associations and,								
claims against,					239			
duties of,					234-235			
liability of,					180			
liquidators and,					215-217			
members of,								
payments and,					246			
priority shares and,								
voluntary liquidations and,					210			
Bonds								
Book debts								
charges over							316, 325, 353	
Book-keeping								
criminal liability for,			109					
directors and,								
false,			163, 166					
information on,			78					
officers and,								
Branches								
bankruptcies and,								
establishment of,							307-308	
publicity of,							308	
foreign,								
registration of,								
Brussels Convention 1968, *see also,* **Conventions on Civil Jurisdiction and Judgments**								
Building contracts								393
Businesses, *see also,* **Companies**								
continuation of,		54						

LUXEMBOURG	NETHERLANDS	NORWAY	PORTUGAL	SPAIN	SWEDEN	SWITZERLAND	UNITED KINGDOM	
		499						debt arrangements and,
				569				decisions by,
410				569		669-670		delegation by,
			526-527			668-670		duties of,
		485			621			election of,
					621			employees and,
								financial statements and,
								foreigners on,
		500						liquidations and,
				568				management and,
					621	668-669		meetings and,
		485	526		620			members of,
		485					732-733	power of,
					621			quorum and,
410								remuneration and,
				569	621			resolutions and,
					620	667		share capital and,
								shareholders and,
410-411		485						shareholders' meetings and,
410								term of office and,
								third parties and,
		489						voluntary liquidation and,
								Boards of management
	452							accounts and,
								administrators and,
	453-454							articles of associations and,
								claims against,
								duties of,
								liability of,
			527					liquidators and,
								members of,
								payments and,
	453							priority shares and,
								voluntary liquidations and,
						674-675		**Bonds**
								Book debts
							735	charges over
								Book-keeping
								criminal liability for,
					621			directors and,
								false,
								information on,
								officers and,
								Branches
	476							bankruptcies and,
	469							establishment of,
								publicity of,
		556						foreign,
						675-676		registration of,
								Brussels Convention 1968, see also,
								Conventions on Civil
								Jurisdiction and Judgments
								Building contracts
								Businesses, see also, **Companies**
	470				630-632			continuation of,

	EUROPE	BELGIUM	DENMARK	FRANCE	GERMANY	GREECE	IRELAND	ITALY
corporations,								
investigations into,		39-40						
small,			124					
survival of,			75-88					
types of,			72-73					
Cautions					193			
Chairmen of the Board				116-119				
appointment of,				117				
powers of,				117				
removal of,				117				
term of office of,				117				
Charges						260-261		
assets over,			89					
bank accounts and,								
banks and,			71					
book debts and,							316, 325, 353	
creditors and,			92					
debentures and,							324-325, 356	
debts and,							356	
enforcement of,								
fixed,		71					316, 324-325, 342	378
floating,							316-317, 324-325, 342	378
forfeiture clauses and,								
liquidation								
preliminary,						261, 266		
property over,			71, 92, 96					
realisation of,								
receivership and,								
recovery of,								
registration of,			71			260-261		
searches for,			72					
third parties and,								
Charging orders								
Charities								
Chattels								
security in,			96					
Cheques						263-264		
unpaid,		163			267			
Claims								
approval of,			109					
declaration of,		34						
notice of,		34						
time limits on,		34-35						
Commentaries								
Commercial cards				116-117				
Commercial paper				163				
Companies, *see also*								
Branches, Businesses,								
Directors, Management,								
Officers, Registered offices								

LUXEMBOURG	NETHERLANDS	NORWAY	PORTUGAL	SPAIN	SWEDEN	SWITZERLAND	UNITED KINGDOM	
				566				corporations,
								investigations into,
								small,
								survival of,
								types of,
								Cautions
								Chairmen of the Board
		485		569				appointment of,
					621			powers of,
								removal of,
								term of office of,
								Charges
		490						assets over,
								bank accounts and,
				574				banks and,
							735	book debts and,
								creditors and,
								debentures and,
								debts and,
						680-681	741-742	enforcement of,
						734-436		fixed,
					625, 649	741-742, 754, 768, 769	734-736,	floating,
						673		forfeiture clauses and,
							791-797	liquidation
								preliminary,
			533			673		property over,
						673		realisation of,
							768	receivership and,
					649			recovery of,
444		487			651		735	registration of,
								searches for,
						673		third parties and,
							741	**Charging orders**
	451			562				**Charities**
								Chattels
								security in,
								Cheques
								unpaid,
								Claims
								approval of,
								declaration of,
								notice of,
								time limits on,
								Commentaries
								Commercial cards
								Commercial paper
								Companies, *see also*
								Branches, Businesses, Directors, Management, Officers, Registered offices

	EUROPE	BELGIUM	DENMARK	FRANCE	GERMANY	GREECE	IRELAND	ITALY
articles of association and,			68-69					
articles of incorporation of,			68					
boards of management and,								
business,								
capital contributions to,				163				
capital-oriented organisation and,								
characteristics of,								
charities and,								
chartered,							302	
civil,			115, 123, 125					
commercial,		23-24		115, 124				
constitution of,							306-307	
continuation of,		41, 45, 46		141, 146	213, 237-238		318-320	
conversion of,					238			
Council of Europe Convention and,	6							
damages and,								
directorates of,								
dissolution of,								
foreign,					296	307-308	383-386	
formation of,							305-306	372
foundations and,								
guarantee,							304	
information on,					186-187, 215	266-267		
joint stock,								
judgments against,					255			
legal personality,					254		302	
liability of,								
limited,				254-255	256	303, 359		408-409
guarantee by,							304	
shares by,							304	
liquidators and,								
loans to,								
management of,		25-26				257-258	307	
mixed liability,								
names,				226				
nationalised,				133				
non-commercial,								
offers to buy,				143-144				
organs of,								
ownership of,								
parent,				226				
pre-emption rights and,								
private,							304-305	408-409
privatisation of,					199			
property and,								
public,						303-305		
public limited,					255-256		303	
public service,								
registration of,		42	69	123		266	303-304	380-381
bankrupt as,			108, 109		208			
deletion of,			98-99					

LUXEMBOURG	NETHERLANDS	NORWAY	PORTUGAL	SPAIN	SWEDEN	SWITZERLAND	UNITED KINGDOM	
	449-450, 452							articles of association and,
								articles of incorporation of,
								boards of management and,
			566					business,
								capital contributions to,
						665		capital-oriented organisation and,
								characteristics of,
	451							charities and,
								chartered,
								civil,
								commercial,
	470							constitution of,
								continuation of,
								conversion of,
	450							Council of Europe Convention and,
								damages and,
								directorates of,
								dissolution of,
	492	556	570					foreign,
	449-450, 452		522-523	563-564				formation of,
	451			562				foundations and,
								guarantee,
	449	483	531-532	575-577	626-627	676-678		information on,
		484						joint stock,
								judgments against,
					620	666	739	legal personality,
					620			liability of,
451	483	524	564-568	619	676-678	728-729		limited,
							728-729	guarantee by,
								shares by,
								liquidators and,
					620			loans to,
409-411	450-454	484-486	524-527	567-570	621-622	668-670	730-733	management of,
		484						mixed liability,
						668-669		names,
								nationalised,
413	449-450							non-commercial,
								offers to buy,
								organs of,
				571-572		670-673	733-734	ownership of,
								parent,
				565				pre-emption rights and,
451						729-730		private,
								privatisation of,
	450					729-730		property and,
			566, 577					public,
409	449, 451-454							public limited,
				577, 599				public service,
	453	483		565	626-627	675-676	727-728	registration of,
								bankrupt as,
					643	676		deletion of,

	EUROPE	BELGIUM	DENMARK	FRANCE	GERMANY	GREECE	IRELAND	ITALY
reinstatement of,								
related,						362, 368		
share capital and,								
shareholders and,								
shareholders' meetings and,								
single member,		24						
small and medium-sized								
enterprises and,				114, 119		259		
special object,							303	
state-owned,						274-275	303	
statutory,							302-303	
subsidiaries of,								
survival of,		31-37	75-88					
takeovers of,								
termination of,					237-238			
transfer of,				146-147, 151				
types of,		24-25	68	115-125	178-183		302-305	372-377
unlimited,						254-255	304	
Company secretaries								
Compensation, *see also* **Damages**								
administrators and,								
costs and,								
employees and,					218		356	
losses for,		49, 52	76					
managers and,								
negligence for,								
preferential creditors and,								
recovery of,							355-356	
termination of employment for,			97			287		
Compositions, *see also* **, Liquidation,**								386-389
acceptance of,			86-87					387-388
actions for,								
annulment of,								
applications for,								
assets and,								387
balance sheets and,			83-84					
bankruptcies and,								396
co-operatives and,								
costs and,								
courts and,								
creditors and,								
creditors' committees and,								397-398
creditors' meetings and,								387
dividends and,			82-83, 84, 88					
effect of,								386
enforced,			81-88, 109					
procedure for,			83-87					
enforcement of,								
equality between creditors								387
fraud and,								
good faith and,								
guarantees and,								386
judgments and,								387-388, 397

LUXEMBOURG	NETHERLANDS	NORWAY	PORTUGAL	SPAIN	SWEDEN	SWITZERLAND	UNITED KINGDOM	
							799	reinstatement of,
								related,
				565	620			share capital and,
								shareholders and,
								shareholders' meetings and,
						665, 666	729	single member,
								small and medium-sized enterprises and,
				577				special object,
			522	577				state-owned,
				566				statutory,
			524, 555		620			subsidiaries of,
								survival of,
					620			takeovers of,
								termination of,
								transfer of,
408-413	448-456	483-484	523-524	562-570	619-620, 627-628	665-668, 676-679	738-740	types of,
		483-484					728-729	unlimited,
				570			732	**Company secretaries**
								Compensation, *see also* **Damages**
					647			administrators and,
					629, 637			costs and,
								employees and,
				583				losses for,
				570				managers and,
		515-516						negligence for,
								preferential creditors and,
			556					recovery of,
			556	593, 694		663-664, 682-693		termination of employment for,
								Compositions, *see also* , **Liquidation,**
420-422						664, 685-686		acceptance of,
423-424					636			actions for,
			541					annulment of,
420-421						683-684		applications for,
423					633	682-683		assets and,
						684		balance sheets and,
435	473		541		631	695, 700		bankruptcies and,
						687-688		co-operatives and,
					637			costs and,
420-421						683		courts and,
						685-686		creditors and,
			541					creditors' committees and,
421-422	463		540-541		633-634	685-686		creditors' meetings and,
						682		dividends and,
419-420			540		630-631	681-682		effect of,
								enforced,
								procedure for,
						688		enforcement of,
					631			equality between creditors and,
424					634, 636			fraud and,
420								good faith and,
								guarantees and,
420								judgments and,

	EUROPE	BELGIUM	DENMARK	FRANCE	GERMANY	GREECE	IRELAND	ITALY
leases and,								
liquidations,			81					401-402
management of,			88					
moratoriums and,								
mortgages and,								
negligence and,								
negotiations on,			83, 85, 87					
officers and,			88					
pledges and,								
preferential creditors								387
procedure for,								386-388
property and,								
proposals for,			85					
public control and,								
publicity of,			85, 109					
purpose of,								386
reasonableness of,			84					
recovery of,								
rejection of,								387-388
resolutions on,								
secured claims and,								
security and,								386
set off and,								
share capital and,								
shareholders of,			88					
suspension of payments and,								
tax and,								
termination of,			88					
time limits and,								
voting on,			85-86					
written explanation for,			84					
Compromise						281, 287, 288-289		
annulment of,						289		
courts and,						289		
creditors and,		29						
fraud and,						289		
judgment and,						289		
reservation of title and,		29						
Compulsory arrangements								
applications for,					196-197			
avoidance of,					196			
confirmation of,					194			
contracts and,					192			
creditors' committees and,					195			
effect of,					195			
examinations and,					194			
form of,					192			
fraud and,					195			
management and,					234			
meetings and,					194			
minority shareholders and,					192			
procedure for,					194-196			
proposals for,					193			
purpose of,					193			
rejection of,					194			
security and,					193-194			

LUXEMBOURG	NETHERLANDS	NORWAY	PORTUGAL	SPAIN	SWEDEN	SWITZERLAND	UNITED KINGDOM	
						688		leases and,
								liquidations,
423-424						687-688		management of,
	463					682		moratoriums and,
420-422								mortgages and,
420								negligence and,
								negotiations on,
					635-636	688		officers and,
420-422			540-541					pledges and,
420-422					634			preferential creditors and,
421-422					633-634	684-686		procedure for,
424								property and,
								proposals for,
					654-655			public control and,
					633			publicity of,
419-420					630-631	681-682		purpose of,
								reasonableness of,
					648			recovery of,
								rejection of,
					636			resolutions on,
421			540					secured claims and,
								security and,
					634-635			set off and,
					636			share capital and,
					635-636	688		shareholders of,
				587	636, 637			suspension of payments and,
					636			tax and,
424					636-637	688		termination of,
					632	682, 685		time limits and,
421-422					635	685		voting on,
								written explanation for,

Compromise

annulment of,
courts and,
creditors and,
fraud and,
judgment and,
reservation of title and,

Compulsory arrangements
applications for,
avoidance of,
confirmation of,
contracts and,
creditors' committees and,
effect of,
examinations and,
form of,
fraud and,
management and,
meetings and,
minority shareholders and,
procedure for,
proposals for,
purpose of,
rejection of,
security and,

	EUROPE	BELGIUM	DENMARK	FRANCE	GERMANY	GREECE	IRELAND	ITALY
settlements and,					196			
shareholders' meetings and,					234			
termination and,					237			
voting on,					194-195			
Compulsory liquidations					207-208, 221-227			
applications for,					222-223			
failure to make,					245-246			
approval for,								
assets and,								
charges and,								
considerations for,					222			
contracts and,					225			
courts and,								
creditors and,					224, 227-239			
meetings and,					224			
damages and,					245-246			
delay and,					223, 234, 245			
disputed debts and,								
East Germany and,					227			
effect of,					222			
equality between creditors and,					221			
examinations and,								
insolvency practitioners and,								
investigations and,								
judgments and,					223			
jurisdiction on,								
management and,					222, 233-239			
notification of claims and,					224-225			
officers and,					233-237			
opposition to,								
overindebtedness and,					221			
petitions for,								
preferential creditors and,								
procedure and					224-227			
purpose of,					222			
receivers and,								
shareholders and,					233-237			
supervision of,					228-239			
supervisory boards and,					246-247			
taxes and,								
third parties and,					223			
time limits and,					222-223			
transactions and,								
Treuhand and,								
Conciliation				114, 131-132				
Confidentiality								
banks of,								381
debt arrangements and,								
shareholders of,					179			

LUXEMBOURG	NETHERLANDS	NORWAY	PORTUGAL	SPAIN	SWEDEN	SWITZERLAND	UNITED KINGDOM	
								settlements and,
								shareholders' meetings and,
								termination and,
					639-640			voting on,
								Compulsory liquidations
								applications for,
								failure to make,
							792	approval for,
								assets and,
								charges and,
								considerations for,
								contracts and,
							788-789	courts and,
								creditors and,
							790	meetings and,
								damages and,
								delay and,
							787	disputed debts and,
								East Germany and,
								effect of,
								equality between creditors and,
								examinations and,
							790	insolvency practitioners and,
							790	investigations and,
							781, 788-789	judgments and,
								jurisdiction on,
								management and,
								notification of claims and,
								officers and,
							789	opposition to,
								overindebtedness and,
							783-784, 787-790	petitions for,
								preferential creditors and,
								procedure and
								purpose of,
							784, 789-790	receivers and,
								shareholders and,
								supervision of,
								supervisory boards and,
								taxes and,
								third parties and,
								time limits and,
							788	transactions and,
								Treuhand and,
								Conciliation
								Confidentiality
						676		banks of,
	498							debt arrangements and,
								shareholders of,

	EUROPE	BELGIUM	DENMARK	FRANCE	GERMANY	GREECE	IRELAND	ITALY
Confiscation								
assets of,					225			
Conflict of interests								
administrators and,					248			
creditors' committees and,					230			
liquidators and,								
settlements and,			107					
Conflict of laws	5			127				383-386
European Union Draft Bankruptcy								
Convention and,	14							
Consultation								
creditors by,				144				
employees with,				114				
transfer on undertakings on,	17							
Contracts, *see also,* **Contracts of**								
Employment								
administration and,								
adoption of,			95-96					
avoidance of,								
bankruptcies and,								393
breaches of,							350	
building,								393
cancellation and,				166				
compulsory arrangements and,					192			
compulsory liquidations and,					225			
damages and,							350	
debts and,								
directors and,								
enforcement of,								
examiners and,							315-316	
financial markets in,								
fraud and,								
insurance,				142				
leases of,				142				
liability for,								
liquidators and,					218		335-336, 350	
maintenance of,				141-142				
managers of,								
misrepresentation and,								
partnerships and,								
personal property and,				142				
pledges and,								
publishing,				142				
receivership and,							328-329	
reprieve from payments and,								
reservation of title and,								
security and,								
setting aside,	9							
supply of goods for,							351	
termination of,		28-29	77					
third parties and,							350	
time limits on,				141				
transfers of,				147				
trustees and,			95-96					

LUXEMBOURG	NETHERLANDS	NORWAY	PORTUGAL	SPAIN	SWEDEN	SWITZERLAND	UNITED KINGDOM	
								Confiscation
								assets of,
								Conflict of interests
								administrators and,
								creditors' committees and,
							795	liquidators and,
								settlements and,
								Conflict of laws
415								European Union Draft Bankruptcy Convention and,
								Consultation
								creditors by,
								employees with,
								transfer on undertakings on,
								Contracts, *see also*, **Contracts of Employment**
							763-764	administration and,
								adoption of,
			553-554					avoidance of,
				605, 607, 613				bankruptcies and,
414								breaches of,
								building,
								cancellation and,
								compulsory arrangements and,
414								compulsory liquidations and,
416								damages and,
								debts and,
			580		621			directors and,
								enforcement of,
								examiners and,
							810-811	financial markets in,
414			554					fraud and,
								insurance,
								leases of,
440-441							794	liability for,
							795	liquidators and,
								maintenance of,
			570					managers of,
414								misrepresentation and,
	455-456							partnerships and,
								personal property and,
	457-458							pledges and,
								publishing,
							774-777	receivership and,
418								reprieve from payments and,
414	456-458							reservation of title and,
								security and,
								setting aside,
								supply of goods for,
		507	550				763-764, 795	termination of,
								third parties and,
								time limits on,
								transfers of,
								trustees and,

	EUROPE	BELGIUM	DENMARK	FRANCE	GERMANY	GREECE	IRELAND	ITALY
winding up and,					218			
Contracts of employment								
administration and,								
administrators and,		52-53						
breaches of,		53						
Draft European Union Bankruptcy Convention and,	9							
fraud and,		61						
liquidation and,							335	
modification of conditions in,		53						
notice and,								
receivership and,							329	
rehabilitation and,				142				
suspension of payments and,								
termination of,						287	335, 350	
transfers of undertaking and,	14							
voluntary liquidations and,					210			
Controleurs								
Controlled administration, see, **Administration**								
Controlled management								
accounts and,								
applications for,								
approval of,								
assets and,								
balance sheets and,								
bankruptcies and,								
cancellation of,								
commissioners and,								
courts and,								
credit institutions and,								
dismissal of,								
effect of,								
experts and,								
financial services industry and,								
fraud and,								
guarantees and,								
judges and,								
judgments and,								
loans for,								
moratoriums and,								
mortgages and,								
pledges and,								
procedure for,								
property and,								
publicity and,								
purpose of,								
remuneration and,								
reports and,								
reprieves from payment and,								
termination								
Conventions on Jurisdiction and Enforcement of Judgments	3-4, 10	31		127-128	191	270	309	383, 385
Conventions	4							
bilateral,	4-6							385
Council of Europe,	5							

LUXEMBOURG	NETHERLANDS	NORWAY	PORTUGAL	SPAIN	SWEDEN	SWITZERLAND	UNITED KINGDOM	
								winding up and,
								Contracts of employment
							761-763	administration and,
								administrators and,
								breaches of,
								Draft European Union Bankruptcy Convention and,
								fraud and,
								liquidation and,
								modification of conditions in,
		508						notice and,
							776-777	receivership and,
								rehabilitation and,
				593				suspension of payments and,
		508	547	583, 593-594			776-777, 796	termination of,
								transfers of undertaking and,
								voluntary liquidations and,
								Controleurs
								Controlled administration, see, **Administration**
424-427								**Controlled management**
427								accounts and,
425-426								applications for,
425								approval of,
424-427								assets and,
427								balance sheets and,
431								bankruptcies and,
429-430								cancellation of,
428-430								commissioners and,
424-428								courts and,
429-430								credit institutions and,
426								dismissal of,
424								effect of,
426								experts and,
430								financial services industry and,
425								fraud and,
424								guarantees and,
428-429								judges and,
428								judgments and,
424								loans for,
428								moratoriums and,
426								mortgages and,
426								pledges and,
425-427								procedure for,
430								property and,
426-427								publicity and,
424								purpose of,
429								remuneration and,
426								reports and,
429-430								reprieves from payment and,
429-430								termination
415	459, 474		533-534	582		680	742	**Conventions on Jurisdiction and Enforcement of Judgments**
								Conventions
	474					680		bilateral,
								Council of Europe,

	EUROPE	BELGIUM	DENMARK	FRANCE	GERMANY	GREECE	IRELAND	ITALY
history of,	5-6							
enforcement of,	5							
multilateral,	4-6							
Co-operatives			72					
Corporate voluntary arrangements,								
see, **Creditors agreements**								
Costs								
administration of,		56						
bankruptcy orders of,			97					
compensation for,								
compositions and,								
creditors' arrangements and,								
debt arrangements of,								
distribution of assets and,							353	
examiners and,							321-322	
liquidations and,							353-354	
litigation of,								
management of,			97					
reorganisation of,			97					
settlements of,			97					
suspension of payments and,								
Council of Europe								
European Convention on Certain								
International Aspects of								
Bankruptcy 1990	5, 6-7							
companies and,	6							
credit institutions and,	6							
creditors and,	6							
insurance companies and,	6							
liquidators and,	6							
rescue procedures and,	6							
secondary bankruptcies and,	6-7		67					
Courts								
administrators and,					238			
alert procedure and,				130				
bankruptcies and,						282		
compromise and,						289		
controlled management and,								
debts and,								
dividends and,								
examinations before,			108-109					
investigations by,				130				
jurisdiction of the,				139				
liquidation and,								
rehabilitation and,				134-135, 139				
reprieve from payments and,								
supervision and,					232-233			
Credit								
fraudulently obtaining,		42-43						
Credit establishments				151				
Credit institutions								
controlled management and,								
Council of Europe Convention and,	6							
draft European Convention and,	8							
Credit insurance	30							
Creditors, *see also*, **Claims,**								

LUXEMBOURG	NETHERLANDS	NORWAY	PORTUGAL	SPAIN	SWEDEN	SWITZERLAND	UNITED KINGDOM	
								history of,
								enforcement of,
								multilateral,
413	450-451			619, 628	676			**Co-operatives**
								Corporate voluntary arrangements,
								see, **Creditors agreements**
								Costs
436								administration of,
								bankruptcy orders of,
					629			compensation for,
					637			compositions and,
				584				creditors' arrangements and,
		493						debt arrangements of,
								distribution of assets and,
								examiners and,
							794	liquidations and,
						715		litigation of,
								management of,
								reorganisation of,
								settlements of,
				587				suspension of payments and,
								Council of Europe
								European Convention on Certain
								International Aspects of
								Bankruptcy 1990
								companies and,
								credit institutions and,
								creditors and,
								insurance companies and,
								liquidators and,
								rescue procedures and,
								secondary bankruptcies and,
								Courts
								administrators and,
								alert procedure and,
431-436	467, 470							bankruptcies and,
424-427								compromise and,
		482			629			controlled management and,
					655			debts and,
								dividends and,
								examinations before,
								investigations by,
								jurisdiction of the,
					640		788-789	liquidation and,
								rehabilitation and,
418-419								reprieve from payments and,
						664		supervision and,
								Credit
								fraudulently obtaining,
								Credit establishments
			522					**Credit institutions**
429								controlled management and,
								Council of Europe Convention and,
								draft European Convention and,
	489							**Credit insurance**
								Creditors, *see also*, **Claims,**

	EUROPE	BELGIUM	DENMARK	FRANCE	GERMANY	GREECE	IRELAND	ITALY
Creditors' agreements, Creditors' committees, Creditors' meetings, Equality between creditors, Preferential creditors								
actions and,			94	161				
administrators and,					231			
agreements with,		31-33						
assignment of the benefit of,		28						
bankruptcies and,								393
categories of,		44-45			227-228			
charges and,			92					
claims and,							355-357	
enforcement of,								
proof of,								
registration of,				149	199, 216			
verification of,				159				
common,								
competing claims and,	4							
compromise with,		29						
compulsory liquidations and,					224, 227-239			
consultation with,				144				
declarations,				149, 159				
differential treatment and,					196			
dividends and,	10	47, 56	81-86		194, 228			
employees and,		29						
estate,								
filing of claims and,			104					
financial,								
financing,		27-29		120-121				
foreign,5			149					
fraud and,				162				
human rights and,		40						
informal arrangements and,							311	
information and,	6		78			260-266		
insurance companies as,			77-78					
involvement of,						284		
judgments and,		58		150-151				
legitimate,								
liquidations and,								
liquidators and,					214			
list of,		84	150	200, 201			387	
management of,			93-94					
minors and,					200			
mortgages and,		27, 45						
partnership and,								
payments and,				151				
suspension of,		38						
personal,								
pledges and,		27, 45						
plurality of,								
prejudicing,								
protected,	10				214			
protection against,			90				311-322	
ranking of,			89, 96-97	151	184, 213, 215,			

LUXEMBOURG	NETHERLANDS	NORWAY	PORTUGAL	SPAIN	SWEDEN	SWITZERLAND	UNITED KINGDOM	
								Creditors' agreements, **Creditors' committees,** **Creditors' meetings,** **Equality between creditors,** **Preferential creditors**
								actions and,
								administrators and,
								agreements with,
								assignment of the benefit of,
	467		546		645			bankruptcies and,
								categories of,
								charges and,
423								claims and,
414-415								enforcement of,
								proof of,
								registration of,
								verification of,
			531					common,
								competing claims and,
								compromise with,
								compulsory liquidations and,
								consultation with,
								declarations,
	472							differential treatment and,
								dividends and,
470								employees and,
414, 433								estate,
								filing of claims and,
		487						financial,
		487-488						financing,
								foreign,
								fraud and,
								human rights and,
								informal arrangements and,
								information and,
								insurance companies as,
414-415								involvement of,
				602				judgments and,
		500						legitimate,
								liquidations and,
								liquidators and,
								list of,
								management of,
	471							minors and,
		484						mortgages and,
			541					partnership and,
		490						payments and,
	471							suspension of,
	468							personal,
	474-475		553					pledges and,
		493						plurality of,
								prejudicing,
								protected,
								protection against,
				608-611		698-699		ranking of,

	EUROPE	BELGIUM	DENMARK	FRANCE	GERMANY	GREECE	IRELAND	ITALY
receivership and,					226-228			
registered,					213 , 215			
rehabilitation and,				138-139				
representation of,		45		115, 137, 144, 150	176			
liquidators as,				156				
names and addresses of,				169				
reprieves from payments and,								
restrictions on,							313	
rights of action,			56					
enforcement of,		58						
restrictions on,				148				
satisfaction of,					214			
secured,				151, 159	185-186		331, 342, 352-353	
security for,	27-29		71-72	121-122		260-266		
set off and,			89					
shareholders and,					228			
summons to,			78					
supervision by,								
trade and,								
trustees and,			93					
types of,						276		
union of,						284, 285, 289-290		
unsecured,			90			278-279	308-309, 343-344, 357	
voluntary arrangements and,					202			
voluntary liquidations and,								
winding up and,							343-344	
Creditors' agreements		31-38						
annulment of,								
applications for,								
approval of,								
assignment of assets and,								
bad management of,		31-38						
bankruptcies and,								
costs and,								
creditors and,								
creditors' meetings and,								
distribution of assets and,								
dividends and,								
effect of,								
employees and,								
enforcement of,								
guarantees and,								
insurance companies and,								
management and,								
moratoriums and,								
negligence and,		32-33						
opposition to,								
payments and,								
petitions for,		33-34						
procedure for,								

LUXEMBOURG	NETHERLANDS	NORWAY	PORTUGAL	SPAIN	SWEDEN	SWITZERLAND	UNITED KINGDOM	
							771-772	receiversip and,
								registered,
								rehabilitation and,
								representation of,
								liquidators as,
								names and addresses of,
417-418								reprieves from payments and,
								restrictions on,
								rights of action,
								enforcement of,
								restrictions on,
								satisfaction of,
415, 417-418, 422, 435		490-491	531, 540		629-630		790-791	secured,
	456-460	487-488		573-575	623-626	673-675	734-737, 741-742	security for,
	471	488						set off and,
								shareholders and,
			536, 547					summons to,
		487				704-705		supervision by,
								trade and,
								trustees and,
			531					types of,
								union of,
414-415	472						740-741, 790-791	unsecured,
								voluntary arrangements and,
							783	voluntary liquidations and,
								winding up and,
			542-543	582-584 597			743-750	**Creditors' agreements**
								annulment of,
			542				744-745	applications for,
				583				approval of,
								assignment of assets and,
			542-543					bad management of,
				584				bankruptcies and,
								costs and,
							747-749	creditors and,
							743, 748	creditors' meetings and,
							744-745	distribution of assets and,
			542					dividends and,
			542				743-744	effect of,
				583				employees and,
							743	enforcement of,
				583				guarantees and,
							745	insurance companies and,
							749	management and,
							743-745	moratoriums and,
								negligence and,
				596-597			744, 747	opposition to,
			542					payments and,
								petitions for,
							745-756	procedure for,

	EUROPE	BELGIUM	DENMARK	FRANCE	GERMANY	GREECE	IRELAND	ITALY
proposals for,		32-34						
purpose of,								
reform of,								
registration and,								
remuneration and,								
reports and,								
schemes of arrangement and,								
set off and,		34						
supervision on,								
termination of,								
time limits and,								
voting on,								
Creditors' arrangements, *see,*								
Creditors agreements								
Creditors' committee			79					
absence of,				149				
administrators and								
appointment of,			107		202, 228-229, 238			
bankruptcies and,								391, 397
compositions and,								
compulsory arrangements and,					195, 228			
conflicts of interest and,					229-230			
creditors' meetings and,								
discharge of,			93-94					
election of,			93					
employees and,								
liquidators and,								
members of,			93		202, 229-230			
nomination of,					199			
notice of,								
powers of,			93-94					
role of,				229-230				
statement of affairs and,			95, 98					
suspension of payments and,								
voluntary arrangements and,					199-200			
voting and,								
Creditors' meetings						284		
accounts and,			107, 109					
administration and,								389
administrators and,								
advertisement of,								
bankruptcies and,						282		
compositions and,								387, 396
compulsory liquidation and,					224, 228-229			
creditors' agreements and,								
creditors' committees and,								
debt arrangements and,								
debtor's propositions and,		35						
decisions made at,						282		
dissolution and,								
invitations to,		35						
liquidations and,							344	

LUXEMBOURG	NETHERLANDS	NORWAY	PORTUGAL	SPAIN	SWEDEN	SWITZERLAND	UNITED KINGDOM	
			542				747	proposals for,
							743-744	purpose of,
								reform of,
				583				registration and,
				584				remuneration and,
							747	reports and,
							743,745-746	schemes of arrangement and,
								set off and,
							749	supervision on,
							749-750	termination of,
				596				time limits and,
							747, 748	voting on,
								Creditors' arrangements, *see,* **Creditors agreements**
								Creditors' committee
								absence of,
			537-538				755, 756	administrators and,
			537, 549					appointment of,
	473		548, 552	608, 611		698		bankruptcies and,
			540-541					compositions and,
								compulsory arrangements and,
			539					conflicts of interest and,
								creditors' meetings and,
								discharge of,
		504	538, 549					election of,
			548					employees and,
			549					liquidators and,
								members of,
								nomination of,
				590				notice of,
								powers of,
			538, 549					role of,
								statement of affairs and,
				590-596				suspension of payments and,
								voluntary arrangements and,
			549	595				voting and,
								Creditors' meetings
								accounts and,
			544-545				760	administration and,
	462					687	756	administrators and,
					634-635		756	advertisement of,
	470, 473		539			700		bankruptcies and,
422	463		540		633	685		compositions and,
								compulsory liquidation and,
							743, 745-746	creditors' agreements and,
			539					creditors' committees and,
		496, 498						debt arrangements and,
								debtor's propositions and,
								decisions made at,
							800	dissolution and,
								invitations to,
		504					791, 794,	liquidations and,

	EUROPE	BELGIUM	DENMARK	FRANCE	GERMANY	GREECE	IRELAND	ITALY
moratoriums and,								
negotiations during,			109					
notices of,			94				338	
number of,			94					
quorum at,						282		
recommendations at,			99					
resolutions taken at,		57	94				339	
role of,								
summoning of,			107					
suspension of payments and,			78					
termination of bankruptcy and,		57						
voluntary liquidations and,								
voting in,		35						
winding up and,							337-338	
Curateurs, *see,* **Administrators**								
Curatores, *see,* **Administrators**								
Curators, *see,* **Administrators**								
Damages			70					
administrators and,					232			
auditors and,								
bankruptcies and,								399
compulsory liquidations and,					245-246			
contracts and,							350	
directors and,								
distribution and,					215			
liquidators and,					215			
management and,					223			
minority shareholders and,								
officers and,								
recovery and,								
time limits and,								
voluntary liquidations and,					215			
wrongful trading and,			105-106					
Debentures								
charges and,				120-121			324-325, 356	
guarantees and,				121				
issue of							377	
liabilities under,							326	
liens and,				121				
loans and,								377
mortgages and,				121				377
pledges of,								379
receiverships and,							323-326	
resolutions on,								377
security and,							323	
types of,								377-378
Debtors, *see also,* **Debts**								
bankruptcies and,								
declarations of,						281		
detention of,						281, 284		
duties of,								
good faith of,	32							
information on,				140				
liquidations and,						350		

LUXEMBOURG	NETHERLANDS	NORWAY	PORTUGAL	SPAIN	SWEDEN	SWITZERLAND	UNITED KINGDOM	
	461-462						797-798	moratoriums and,
								negotiations during,
						685	756	notices of,
								number of,
								quorum at,
	504							recommendations at,
							756	resolutions taken at,
						700-701		role of,
								summoning of,
				595-596				suspension of payments and,
							784	termination of bankruptcy and,
								voluntary liquidations and,
			539			686	791	voting in,
								winding up and,
								Curateurs, *see*, **Administrators**
								Curatores, *see*, **Administrators**
								Curators, *see*, **Administrators**
								Damages
								administrators and,
					652			auditors and,
								bankruptcies and,
								compulsory liquidations and,
414							796	contracts and,
					652			directors and,
								distribution and,
								liquidators and,
				614				management and,
					652			minority shareholders and,
					652			officers and,
			556					recovery and,
					652			time limits and,
								voluntary liquidations and,
								wrongful trading and,
410-411								**Debentures**
								charges and,
								guarantees and,
								issue of
								liabilities under,
								liens and,
								loans and,
								mortgages and,
								pledges of,
								receiverships and,
								resolutions on,
								security and,
								types of,
								Debtors, *see also*, **Debts**
	466							bankruptcies and,
		498-499						declarations of,
								detention of,
								duties of,
								good faith of,
								information on,
								liquidations and,

	EUROPE	BELGIUM	DENMARK	FRANCE	GERMANY	GREECE	IRELAND	ITALY
powers of,								
propositions of,		34-35						
rehabilitation proceedings and,				138				
shareholders of,		43-44						
status of,								
summonses of,								
Debts, *see also*, **Debtors, Factoring**								
acknowledgement of,								
administrators and,					232			
arbitration and,						269		
arrangements,								
assignment of,								
bankruptcies and,				159				
cancellation and,								
contracts and,								
courts and,				152				
default and,								
directors and,							307	
disputed,								
enforcement of,								
evidence on,								
floating charges and,							356	
injunctions and,			74	126				
judgments on,						267-270, 296		
liquidators and,		58-59						
list of,								
management of,			97					
ownership of,				159				
payment of,				163-164				
proof of,	45							
time limits on,	45							
reconstruction of,	34							
recovery,			73-74			267-270	308-309	381-383
agencies for,								
reduction of,			81	126-127				
release from,					245			
repayment of,		57						
rescheduling,								
set off and,			84	152				
summonses for,								380
time limits on,							357	
Decisions								
articles of association and,								
board of directors and,								
debt arrangements and,								
liquidation compositions and,								
partners and,						255		
shareholders' meetings and,								
Delay								
Delivery					185, 190			
bankruptcies and,								393
judgments on,								
mortgages and,								
pledges of,								

LUXEMBOURG	NETHERLANDS	NORWAY	PORTUGAL	SPAIN	SWEDEN	SWITZERLAND	UNITED KINGDOM	
		498-499						powers of,
								propositions of,
								rehabilitation proceedings and,
								shareholders of,
				561				status of,
	469							summonses of,
								Debts, *see also*, **Debtors, Factoring**
				590				acknowledgement of,
								administrators and,
								arbitration and,
		492-493						arrangements,
								assignment of,
			549		645			bankruptcies and,
425								cancellation and,
415								contracts and,
					629			courts and,
	468							default and,
								directors and,
							741, 787-788	disputed,
					629	679-680		enforcement of,
		490						evidence on,
								floating charges and,
								injunctions and,
		490			629	679-681		judgments on,
								liquidators and,
	494							list of,
								management of,
								ownership of,
	468		554		642, 657		791, 796	payment of,
								proof of,
								time limits on,
								reconstruction of,
414-415	456-460, 474	490-492	533	578-582	628-630	679-681	740-742	recovery,
					628-629	661		agencies for,
								reduction of,
						711		release from,
425								repayment of,
	476							rescheduling,
								set off and,
432								summonses for,
								time limits on,
								Decisions
	449							articles of association and,
				569				board of directors and,
		495						debt arrangements and,
						703-704		liquidation compositions and,
								partners and,
			525					shareholders' meetings and,
								Delay
								Delivery
				608				bankruptcies and,
	459							judgments on,
				574				mortgages and,
				574				pledges of,

	EUROPE	BELGIUM	DENMARK	FRANCE	GERMANY	GREECE	IRELAND	ITALY
reservation of title and,								
Deposits					185			
Detention								
debtors and,						281, 284		
Direct effect								
Directives of,	19							
Directives								
direct effect of,	19							
Directorates								
term of office of,				118-119				
				119				
Directors, *see also,* **Board of Directors**								
administrators and,		56						
appointment of,		26					305, 307	375
bankruptcies and,								
banned from being,				108-109				
breaches of trust and,							358	
compositions and,								
contracts and,								
criminal sanctions against,		70						
damages and,								
debts and,							307	
dismissal of,							307	
disqualification of,							358, 365	
executive,								
foreign,								
fraud by,							358	
information and,		26						
liability of,								375, 399-401
criminal,								400-401
liquidations and,								
liquidators and,							349	
loans to,							365-366	
managing,				120				
misfeasance,							358, 368	
negligence of,								
non-executive,								
personal liability of,		26			179	296		
profit distribution and,		26						
removal of,								
role of,								
sanctions against,							357-358	
shadow,								
share capital and,		26						
shareholders as,				116				
shareholders' meetings and,								
standard of care and,					180-181			
statutory declarations and,								
tax and,					180			
term of office of,								376
third parties and,								
voluntary liquidations and,					210			
winding up and,							337, 357-358	
wrongful acts of,		49						

LUXEMBOURG	NETHERLANDS	NORWAY	PORTUGAL	SPAIN	SWEDEN	SWITZERLAND	UNITED KINGDOM	
		488, 491						reservation of title and,
		491						**Deposits**
								Detention
								debtors and,
								Direct effect
								Directives of,
								Directives
								direct effect of,
								Directorates
								term of office of,
								Directors, *see also,* **Board of Directors**
							760-761	administrators and,
409				568				appointment of,
				603	646			bankruptcies and,
								banned from being,
						687		breaches of trust and,
					621			compositions and,
				606				contracts and,
					651-652			criminal sanctions against,
								damages and,
							760	debts and,
								dismissal of,
							731	disqualification of,
					669			executive,
							804-807	foreign,
								fraud by,
								information and,
440-443	453, 476		555-556 587, 603, 606	568-569,	654	711-716 804-807	731,	liability of,
							783	criminal,
		501						liquidations and,
								liquidators and,
								loans to,
								managing,
				568	652			misfeasance,
		485					731	negligence of,
								non-executive,
								personal liability of,
409				568		669		profit distribution and,
			568			731		removal of,
								role of,
							729, 805	sanctions against,
								shadow,
		485			622	668-669		share capital and,
				568				shareholders as,
								shareholders' meetings and,
								standard of care and,
							785	statutory declarations and,
								tax and,
								term of office of,
441								third parties and,
							785	voluntary liquidations and,
437		502						winding up and,
								wrongful acts of,

	EUROPE	BELGIUM	DENMARK	FRANCE	GERMANY	GREECE	IRELAND	ITALY
Discipline								
administrators of,				168				
liquidators of,				169				
Dissolution, *see also,* **Liquidators**							333	
creditors' meetings and,								
early,								
effect of,								
procedures for,								
purpose of,								
Distrain							308-309	
Distress							308-309	
Distribution of assets	30		70	159-160	192		352-357	383
accounts of,	57		98					
administrators and,					232			
articles of association and,					220-221			
authorisation and,					229			
bankruptcies and,								395, 396
challenging,								
costs and,							353	
creditors' agreements and,								
equality of creditors and,								
expenses and,							353	
fees for,								434
final,					237			
liquidations and,			90					
methods of,					219-220			
notice of,					219			
order of,					213			
preferential creditors and,		56					331-332	
prevention of,					214			
privileged creditors and,		55						
receivership and,							331-332	
registered creditors and,					213			
reimbursement of,					215			
repayment of,								
reservation of title and,							331	
secured claims and,							331	
securities and,					213			
shareholders and,					213			
shares and,					219			
taxation and,					219			
termination and,					221			
time limits and,					214			
trusts claims and,							331	
voluntary liquidation and,								
Dividends								
balance sheets and,								
bankruptcies and,								
compositions and,			82-86, 87-88					
courts and,								
creditors and,	10	47, 56	81-83		194, 228			
distribution of,								
interim,			97					
liquidation and,								
preferential claims and,								
share capital and,					182-183			

LUXEMBOURG	NETHERLANDS	NORWAY	PORTUGAL	SPAIN	SWEDEN	SWITZERLAND	UNITED KINGDOM	
								Discipline
								administrators of,
								liquidators of,
							799-800	**Dissolution,** *see also,* **Liquidators**
							800	creditors' meetings and,
						799		early,
							799	effect of,
							800	procedures for,
							799	purpose of,
					630		740, 754	**Distrain**
					644		740, 797	**Distress**
473	509-510						796-797	**Distribution of assets**
								accounts of,
							766	administrators and,
								articles of association and,
								authorisation and,
								bankruptcies and,
					641			challenging,
								costs and,
							745	creditors' agreements and,
					648			equality of creditors and,
								expenses and,
								fees for,
								final,
		504			638		783, 799	liquidations and,
								methods of,
								notice of,
								order of,
								preferential creditors and,
								prevention of,
								privileged creditors and,
							778-779	receivership and,
								registered creditors and,
								reimbursement of,
					652-653			repayment of,
								reservation of title and,
								secured claims and,
								securities and,
								shareholders and,
								shares and,
								taxation and,
								termination and,
								time limits and,
								trusts claims and,
							781	voluntary liquidation and,
						672		**Dividends**
					620			balance sheets and,
			606		645			bankruptcies and,
						684		compositions and,
					654			courts and,
472		510, 515	542					creditors and,
					652-653			distribution of,
								interim,
		506					797, 799	liquidation and,
		505						preferential claims and,
						668		share capital and,

	EUROPE	BELGIUM	DENMARK	FRANCE	GERMANY	GREECE	IRELAND	ITALY
shareholders and,								
size of,		83						
Documents								
liens over,							322	
Draft European Union								
Bankruptcy Convention,	5, 8-14							
aircraft and,	9							
applicable law and,	9-10							
conflict of laws and,	14							
contracts and,								
setting aside,	9							
credit institutions and,	8							
employment contracts and,	9							
European Court of Justice and,	10							
immovable property and,	9							
insurance companies and,	8							
investment companies and,	8							
jurisdiction and,	9-10							
preferential creditors and,	11							
purpose of,	8							
registered offices and,	9							
rescues and,	9							
reservation of title and,	9							
rights in rem and,	9							
ships and,	9							
scope of the,	8-9							
secondary liquidations and,	10-12							
set off and,	9							
third parties and,	9							
Due diligence		51						
East Germany					174, 176, 196			
compulsory liquidations and,					225-226			
employees and,					227			
Treuhand in,					199, 205-206			
Economic interest groupings				123, 125				
Embargos								
Employees, *see also,*								
Contracts of employment,								
Salaries								
alert procedure and,				129-130				
bankruptcies and,								
boards of directors and,								
compensation and,					218	287		
consultation of,				114				
creditors and,		29, 38						
creditors agreements and,								
creditors' committees and,								
debt arrangements and,								
Directive on protection of,	19							
dismissals of,				135, 143, 146, 147				
liquidation and,				156		349-350	335-336	
preferential creditors as,			76, 77, 84	148, 159	226	278, 287	329	

LUXEMBOURG	NETHERLANDS	NORWAY	PORTUGAL	SPAIN	SWEDEN	SWITZERLAND	UNITED KINGDOM	
	453				620			shareholders and,
								size of,
								Documents
								liens over,
								Draft European Union Bankruptcy Convention,
								aircraft and,
								applicable law and,
								conflict of laws and,
								contracts and,
								setting aside,
								credit institutions and,
								employment contracts and,
								European Court of Justice and,
								immovable property and,
								insurance companies and,
								investment companies and,
								jurisdiction and,
								preferential creditors and,
								purpose of,
								registered offices and,
								rescues and,
								reservation of title and,
								rights in rem and,
								ships and,
								scope of the,
								secondary liquidations and,
								set off and,
								third parties and,
								Due diligence
								East Germany
								compulsory liquidations and,
								employees and,
								Treuhand in,
								Economic interest groupings
			548					**Embargos**
								Employees, *see also,*
								Contracts of employment,
								Salaries
								alert procedure and,
	473							bankruptcies and,
					621			boards of directors and,
				583				compensation and,
								consultation of,
				583				creditors and,
		504	538, 549					creditors agreements and, / creditors' committees and,
		495						debt arrangements and,
								Directive on protection of,
	473							dismissals of,
	508	501, 503,			641		792	liquidation and,
	470				625-626	685		preferential creditors as,

	EUROPE	BELGIUM	DENMARK	FRANCE	GERMANY	GREECE	IRELAND	ITALY
protection of,				132		287		
receivership and,							329-330	
redundancies of,					244			
re-employment of,		53						
rehabilitation and,				139				
representative committees of,				129, 137, 139, 144	244			
representatives of,				137	202	296		
salaries of,			79, 83, 84					
share ownership schemes and,								
social plan and,					218			
taxation and,					219			
transfer of undertakings and,								
winding up and,							335-336	
Employment, *see also* **Contracts of employment, Employees, Transfer of undertakings**								
compensation for termination of,			97					
continuation of,			83					
Draft European Union Bankruptcy Convention and,	9							
evaluation of,				142-143				
Enforcement, *see also,* **Seizure**								
arbitration and,								
attachment and,								
bankruptcies on,								393
compulsory liquidations and,					225			
bills of exchange and,								
charges and,								
contracts and,								
creditors' agreements and,								
creditors' rights and,		58						
debts and,								
delivery and,								
eviction and,								
freezing of,								403
insurance and,								
judgments of,	3-4	31				281	309	384-385
liquidation compositions and,								
mortgages and,								
pledges and,								
registration and,								
resolutions and,								
stay of,								
succession and,								
third parties and,								382
title to,							381	
voluntary arrangements and,					201			
Equality among creditors		31, 34			239	276, 277		
assets and,					176			
bankruptcies and,								390
compositions and,								
compulsory liquidations and,					222			
contracting out,								
debt arrangements and,								
discrimination and,						293		
employees and,								

LUXEMBOURG	NETHERLANDS	NORWAY	PORTUGAL	SPAIN	SWEDEN	SWITZERLAND	UNITED KINGDOM	
			538					protection of,
								receivership and,
								redundancies of,
								re-employment of,
		485						rehabilitation and,
								representative committees of,
		495						representatives of,
								salaries of,
						667		share ownership schemes and,
								social plan and,
								taxation and,
								transfer of undertakings and,
								winding up and,
								Employment, *see also* **Contracts of employment, Employees, Transfer of undertakings**
								compensation for termination of,
								continuation of,
								Draft European Union Bankruptcy Convention and,
								evaluation of,
				579-581				**Enforcement,** *see also* **, Seizure**
				581				arbitration and,
				580				attachment and,
	459							bankruptcies on,
								compulsory liquidations and,
				580-581				bills of exchange and,
							741	charges and,
				580				contracts and,
							743	creditors' agreements and,
								creditors' rights and,
					629	679		debts and,
				579				delivery and,
				580				eviction and,
								freezing of,
				581				insurance and,
414-415	459	491-492	533-534	581-582	630			judgments of,
						704-705		liquidation compositions and,
		490	529-530	575				mortgages and,
			529	575				pledges and,
				579				registration and,
				580				resolutions and,
		537						stay of,
				580				succession and,
								third parties and,
								title to,
		511						voluntary arrangements and,
438							800	**Equality among creditors**
								assets and,
	470							bankruptcies and,
					631		800	compositions and,
								compulsory liquidations and,
								contracting out,
		497						debt arrangements and,
								discrimination and,
		506						employees and,

	EUROPE	BELGIUM	DENMARK	FRANCE	GERMANY	GREECE	IRELAND	ITALY
fraud and,				162				
liquidation and,								
preferential creditors and,		55						
prejudice and,		60						
recovery and,								
voluntary arrangements and,					198			
voluntary liquidations and,					215			
European Bankruptcy Convention 1933	5							
European Court of Justice								
Draft European Union Bankruptcy Convention and,	10							
transfer of undertakings and,	15-16, 19							
European Economic Area								
European Union, *see,* **Draft European Union Bankruptcy Convention**								
Evidence								
bankruptcies and,								
debts and,								
liquidation on,								
recovery and,								
Examinations, *see also,* **Examiners**			108-109		194		367	
administrators and,					249			
bankruptcies and,								399
stay of,								
compositions and,								
compulsory,								
fraud and,						297		
information obtained during,								
liquidations and,					227		345	
oppressive,								
private,								
public,								
self-incrimination and,								
Examiners, *see also,* **Examinations**							311-322	
appointment of,							311-314, 336	
assets and,								
realisation of,							316-317	
contracts and,							315-316	
costs and,							321-322	
creditors' remedies and,								
restrictions on,							314	
duties of,							317-318	
function of,							314	
liquidators and,							314-315, 347	
petitions and,							312-314	
powers of,							314	
receivers and,							314-315	
remuneration and,							321-322	
reports of,							317-320	
time limits and,							318	
Exchange rates				159				
Execution, *see,* **Enforcement**								
Experts				136-137				

LUXEMBOURG	NETHERLANDS	NORWAY	PORTUGAL	SPAIN	SWEDEN	SWITZERLAND	UNITED KINGDOM	
								fraud and,
		501					782	liquidation and,
								preferential creditors and,
								prejudice and,
					648-652			recovery and,
								voluntary arrangements and,
								voluntary liquidations and,
								European Bankruptcy Convention 1933
								European Court of Justice
								Draft European Union Bankruptcy Convention and,
								transfer of undertakings and,
		487						**European Economic Area**
								European Union, *see,* **Draft European Union Bankruptcy Convention**
								Evidence
433	470							bankruptcies and,
		490						debts and,
		502						liquidation on,
								recovery and,
						717-718		**Examinations,** *see also,* **Examiners**
443-444		516						administrators and,
						717-718		bankruptcies and,
						717-718		stay of,
						717-718		compositions and,
								compulsory,
							809	fraud and,
								information obtained during,
							808-809	liquidations and,
							808-809	oppressive,
							808-809	private,
							808	public,
							808-809	self-incrimination and,
								Examiners, *see also,* **Examinations**
								appointment of,
								assets and,
								realisation of,
								contracts and,
								costs and,
								creditors' remedies and,
								restrictions on,
								duties of,
								function of,
								liquidators and,
								petitions and,
								powers of,
								receivers and,
								remuneration and,
								reports of,
								time limits and,
								Exchange rates
								Execution, *see,* **Enforcement**
426								**Experts**

	EUROPE	BELGIUM	DENMARK	FRANCE	GERMANY	GREECE	IRELAND	ITALY
bankruptcies and,			142					
Expenses								
administrators of,								
distribution of assets and,							353	
legal,			151					
liquidations of,							353-354	
Factoring			71-72					
Fieri facias, writ of							309	
Financial markets								
Financial restructuring								
advertisement of,								
annulment of,								
approval of,								
creditors' meetings and,								
effect of,								
purpose of,								
registration of,								
termination of,								
third parties and,								
Financial services sector								
controlled management and,								
Financial statements			91					
Board of directors and,				117				
filing,				128				
incorrect,			105	120-121				
Financing								
Floating charges			71					
Foreign investment				117				
Foreign judgments,	4			127-128				
recognition of,		31	74					
Foundations								
Fraud		39, 40, 61					308	
assets and,							362, 368	
bankruptcies and,						280, 294, 297		400
compositions and,								
compulsory arrangements and,					195			
contracts and,								
contracts of employments and,		61						
controlled management and,				162				
creditors of,								
debtors of,			87					
directors and,							358	
examinations for,						297		
foreign judgments and,								
insolvency and,								
insurance and,			95					
liquidation and,							336	
management of,								
officers of,								
opinions on,			104			284		
preferential creditors and,							361	
sanctions and,				165				
transactions and,								
voluntary arrangements and,					205			

LUXEMBOURG	NETHERLANDS	NORWAY	PORTUGAL	SPAIN	SWEDEN	SWITZERLAND	UNITED KINGDOM	
	470							bankruptcies and,
								Expenses
							761	administrators of,
								distribution of assets and,
								legal,
							785, 796	liquidations of,
								Factoring
			#			741		**Fieri facias, writ of**
							810-811	**Financial markets**
			543					**Financial restructuring**
			544					advertisement of,
			544					annulment of,
			543					approval of,
			544					creditors' meetings and,
			543					effect of,
			543					purpose of,
			544					registration of,
			544					termination of,
			544					third parties and,
			522	566, 599				**Financial services sector**
430								controlled management and,
								Financial statements
								Board of directors and,
								filing,
								incorrect,
								Financing
								Floating charges
								Foreign investment
								Foreign judgments,
								recognition of,
	451			562				**Foundations**
								Fraud
								assets and,
442	467		550	606, 612, 613	646	696		bankruptcies and,
424					634, 636			compositions and,
								compulsory arrangements and,
414			554					contracts and,
								contracts of employments and,
425								controlled management and,
439	474							creditors of,
								debtors of,
							804-807	directors and,
								examinations for,
415								foreign judgments and,
				597-598				insolvency and,
								insurance and,
							783	liquidation and,
				614			740	management of,
							804-807	officers of,
								opinions on,
								preferential creditors and,
								sanctions and,
							803	transactions and,
								voluntary arrangements and,

	EUROPE	BELGIUM	DENMARK	FRANCE	GERMANY	GREECE	IRELAND	ITALY
Fraudulent conveyances								
Fraudulent trading							358, 362-365 368	
Garnishees							309	
General managers				118				
Gifts					243			
bankruptcies and,								
recovery of,								
setting aside,			100-101	163				
spouses to,				167				
transactions at risk and,								
Going concerns							316, 317-318	
assets and,								
balance sheets and,			83					
expenses and,							321	
liquidations and,								
receiverships and,							327	
records of,				123				
sale of assets and,		54	84					
sale of businesses and,					218			
transfer of,		59					329	
Good faith		51						
Goods, *see also,* **Assets**								
foreign territories on,		30-31						
leased,	29, 30							
register of,								
return of,			101					
supply of,				123, 125			351	
Group of companies								
Guarantees					193			
banks of,						263		
compositions and,								386
controlled management and,								
creditors' agreements and,								
debentures and,				121				
personal,						263		
security and,								
Human rights								
creditors and,		40						
officers and,			109					
Information				123				
accounting,				128-129			306-307	
administrators and,								
assets of,			78					
balance sheets and,								
banks and,					187	267		
bookkeeping on,			78					
companies on,					187, 200, 215	266-267		380-381
creditors and,	6		78					

LUXEMBOURG	NETHERLANDS	NORWAY	PORTUGAL	SPAIN	SWEDEN	SWITZERLAND	UNITED KINGDOM	
	474							**Fraudulent conveyances**
							793, 805-806	**Fraudulent trading**
							741	**Garnishees**
								General managers
								Gifts
				613		707-708		bankruptcies and,
					650			recovery of,
								setting aside,
								spouses to,
		512				707-708, 711		transactions at risk and,
								Going concerns
								assets and,
								balance sheets and,
								expenses and,
		508						liquidations and,
								receiverships and,
								records of,
								sale of assets and,
								sale of businesses and,
								transfer of,
								Good faith
								Goods, *see also,* **Assets**
								foreign territories on,
						695		leased,
								register of,
								return of,
			532-533, 555					supply of,
				566				**Group of companies**
				573-574				**Guarantees**
								banks of,
								compositions and,
425								controlled management and,
				583				creditors' agreements and,
								debentures and,
				573				personal,
415								security and,
								Human rights
								creditors and,
								officers and,
						661-662, 675-676	737-738, 809-810	**Information**
								accounting,
	472							administrators and,
								assets of,
						667		balance sheets and,
						676		banks and,
								bookkeeping on,
412	449	488-489	531-532	575-577	626-627			companies on,
								creditors and,

	EUROPE	BELGIUM	DENMARK	FRANCE	GERMANY	GREECE	IRELAND	ITALY
debt arrangements and,								
debtors on,				140				
directors and,		26						
examinations and,								
financial,				128-129				
forecast,				128				
liquidations and,								
management of,					232			
property on,						266-267		
registration on,								380-381
shareholders of,					182			
sole traders and,						266		
Inheritance								
renunciation of claims for,			101					
shares of,								
Injunctions					190, 191			
asset freezing and,								
bankruptcies and,								
debts and,			74	123				
interim,					233	285		
mareva,							309	
Inquiry agents					187			
Insolvency								
fraud and,								
negligence and,								
presumption of,			91-92					
procedure on,								
Insolvency practitioners								
administrative receivers and,								
independent,								
insurance of,								
liability of,								
licensing of,				167-168				
liquidators and,								
records of,								
Instalments								380
Insurance, see also,			77					
Insurance companies								
bankruptcies and,								394
contracts,				142				
credit,	30	107						
fraud of,			95					
insolvency practitioners of,								
liquidators and,							350	
mutual associations and,								
security and,							348	
Insurance companies								
Council of Europe Convention and,	6							
creditors as,			77-78					
creditors agreements and,								
draft European Union								
Convention and,	8							
insolvency and,								
Interest								
bankruptcies and,								
judgments and,				148				

LUXEMBOURG	NETHERLANDS	NORWAY	PORTUGAL	SPAIN	SWEDEN	SWITZERLAND	UNITED KINGDOM	
		498						debt arrangements and
								debtors on,
							809	directors and,
								examinations and,
								financial,
								forecast,
		506						liquidations and,
								management of,
								property on,
				576				registration on,
								shareholders of,
								sole traders and,
								Inheritance
								renunciation of claims for,
						670		shares of,
								Injunctions
		502						asset freezing and,
				608				bankruptcies and,
								debts and,
								interim,
							742	mareva,
								Inquiry agents
								Insolvency
				597-598				fraud and,
				597-598				negligence and,
								presumption of,
				597-598				procedure on,
								Insolvency practitioners
							768	administrative receivers and,
							752	independent,
							807	insurance of,
							751	liability of,
							807	licensing of,
							784, 790	liquidators and,
							810	records of,
								Instalments
								Insurance, *see also,*
								Insurance companies
								bankruptcies and
								contracts,
								credit,
								fraud of,
							807	insolvency practitioners of,
							793	liquidators and,
								mutual associations and,
	450-451			566, 577, 599				security and,
			522					**Insurance companies**
								Council of Europe Convention and,
								creditors as,
							745	creditors agreements and,
								draft European Union Convention and,
		489						insolvency and,
								Interest
			550	605				bankruptcies and,
								judgments and,

	EUROPE	BELGIUM	DENMARK	FRANCE	GERMANY	GREECE	IRELAND	ITALY
liquidation and,								
loans on,								
mortgages and,		34						
preferential creditors and,		34						
Inventories								
assets of,						285		394
Investigations				115			367	
administrators and,			95		249			
bailiffs and,			108					
bankruptcy and,								
stay of,								
businesses into,		39-41	108-109					
companies into,					202			
compositions and,								
courts and,				130				
fraud and,					297			
judge commissaire and,				135				
liquidations and,								
preferential credits and,			89-90					
rehabilitations and,				154				
Investment companies								
draft European Union								
Convention and,	8							
Invoices								
set off of,			101					
Joint ventures				115				
Judge commissioners								
decisions of the,		47-48						
investigations of,				135				
limitations on the,		48						
role of,	47-50		135, 150					
Judicial intervention				151-152				
Judgments								
bailiffs and,			74					
bankruptcies and,						275-292		390, 395
companies against,						255		
compositions and,								387-388, 397
compromise on,						289		
controlled management and,								
creditors and,		58		150-151				
debts and,						267-270, 296		
declaratory proceedings and,								
default in,								
delivery on,								
enforcement of,	3-4	31	74	126-127	177, 188-191	269, 281	308, 309, 335	384-385
equality between creditors and,								390
foreign,			127-128	191	270-271	308	384-385	415
interest and,				148-149				
liquidation on,				144-146, 156-162			335	
moratoriums and,								
mortgages and,				148			342	
notice of,				169				

LUXEMBOURG	NETHERLANDS	NORWAY	PORTUGAL	SPAIN	SWEDEN	SWITZERLAND	UNITED KINGDOM	
							784	liquidation and,
			528					loans on,
								mortgages and,
								preferential creditors and,
								Inventories
426-427, 433-434					633	697		assets of,
								Investigations
	462	516				717-718		administrators and,
								bailiffs and,
						718		bankruptcy and,
						718		stay of,
								businesses into,
								companies into,
						718		compositions and,
								courts and,
								fraud and,
								judge commissaire and,
							790	liquidations and,
								preferential credits and,
								rehabilitations and,
								Investment companies
								draft European Union Convention and,
								Invoices
								set off of,
								Joint ventures
								Judge commissioners
								decisions of the,
								investigations of,
								limitations on the,
								role of,
								Judicial intervention
								Judgments
435	474		547					bailiffs and,
								bankruptcies and,
								companies against,
428								compositions and,
								compromise on,
								controlled management and,
								creditors and,
		490			629	680-681	740-741	debts and,
				578-580	630			declaratory proceedings and,
433								default in,
	459							delivery on,
415	459	491-492	533-534	581-582	630		742	enforcement of,
								equality between creditors and,
459	491-492	533-534	581-582	630	680	742		foreign,
								interest and,
								liquidation on,
								moratoriums and,
	461							mortgages and,
								notice of,

	EUROPE	BELGIUM	DENMARK	FRANCE	GERMANY	GREECE	IRELAND	ITALY
opposition to,								
pledges and,				148				
publication of,				149, 168		260		
recognition of,					191			
registration of,							309, 335	
rehabilitations on,				140, 144-146				392
security interest and,				148				
suspension of payments and,								
transactions and,								
winding up and,								
Jurisdiction								
bailiffs and,								
compulsory liquidations and,								
courts and,				139				384-385
draft European Union Bankruptcy Convention and,	9-10							
foreign bankruptcies and,								
liquidators of,	10-11							

Kurators, *see* **Compulsory liquidations**
Konkursverwalter, *see,* **Administrators**
Kurators, *see,* **Administrators**

	EUROPE	BELGIUM	DENMARK	FRANCE	GERMANY	GREECE	IRELAND	ITALY
Law of Property Act receivers								
Lawyers								
administrators as,			106					
insolvency practitioners as,								
liquidators and,							349	
Leases								
administration and,		46, 53						
administrators and,								
assignment of,		53						
bankruptcies and,								
compositions and,								393
continuation of,				141				
contracts for,				142				
goods of,		30, 34						
liquidation and,								
lower prices and,		59						
mortgages and,								
notice of,			96					
preferential creditors and,		45						
repossession of,		46						
security as,								
setting aside,				163				
termination of,			96	147				
time limits on,				147				
transfer of companies and,				147				
Legal expenses				151				
Liability								
administrators of,		51-52				230	285	
auditors of,								
board of directors and,					180			

LUXEMBOURG	NETHERLANDS	NORWAY	PORTUGAL	SPAIN	SWEDEN	SWITZERLAND	UNITED KINGDOM	
			548					opposition to,
								pledges and,
								publication of,
		491-492	533	581-582		680-681	742	recognition of,
			548					registration of,
			552					rehabilitations on,
								security interest and,
				588				suspension of payments and,
								transactions and,
437						711		winding up and,
								Jurisdiction
		492				716		bailiffs and,
							781, 788-789	compulsory liquidations and,
								courts and,
								draft European Union Bankruptcy Convention and,
						719-722		foreign bankruptcies and,
								liquidators of,
								Kurators, see Compulsory liquidations
								Konkursverwalter, see, Administrators
								Kurators, see, Administrators
							768	**Law of Property Act receivers**
							792	**Lawyers**
					632-633			administrators as,
							807	insolvency practitioners as,
		516						liquidators and,
							740	**Leases**
							758	administration and,
								administrators and,
								assignment of,
								bankruptcies and,
								compositions and,
						687-688		continuation of,
								contracts for,
								goods of,
		507						liquidation and,
								lower prices and,
				574				mortgages and,
								notice of,
								preferential creditors and,
	471							repossession of,
							734	security as,
								setting aside,
								termination of,
								time limits on,
								transfer of companies and,
								Legal expenses
								Liability
				567, 568				administrators of,
						711-716		auditors of,
								board of directors and,

	EUROPE	BELGIUM	DENMARK	FRANCE	GERMANY	GREECE	IRELAND	ITALY
companies and,								
contracts and,								
directors of,			70			296		375, 399-401
insolvency practitioners of,								
joint,								
liquidators of,		58						399-401
managers of,			70					399-401
officers of,			104-106	164-166	245	296-297	362-366	
partners of,								
resolutions on,								
shareholders of,				116	179		306	373
trustees of,					203			
winding up and,								
Licensing								
insolvency practitioners of,								
Liens								
aircraft,								
debentures and,				121				
documents and,							322	
holders of,					185			
maritime,								
receivership and,								
release of,					186			
reservation of title and,								
repairers',								
security and,					184		349	378
Liquidation compositions								
applications for,								
creditors and,								
decision-making and,								
distribution of assets and,								
effect of,								
enforcement of,								
management of,								
officers and,								
procedure for,								
purpose of,								
realisation of assets and,								
shareholders and,								
termination of,								
Liquidations, *see also,*								
Compulsory liquidations,								
Liquidation compositions,								
Voluntary liquidations				155-162			307, 333-359 341	
abuse of process and,								
accounts and,								
actions and,					214			
administrators and,		52-55						
advertisement of,								
agreements and,		58						
appeals on,				157				
arrangements and,					197-198			

LUXEMBOURG	NETHERLANDS	NORWAY	PORTUGAL	SPAIN	SWEDEN	SWITZERLAND	UNITED KINGDOM	
			524					companies and,
440-441								contracts and,
440-443	453, 476		555-556	568-569, 587, 606	654	711-716	804-807	directors of,
							751	insolvency practitioners of,
		515						joint,
							792, 794	liquidators of,
	453, 476		555-556	614	620			managers of,
440-443	476	515-516				664, 711-716	804-807	officers of,
				570		678-679, 711-712	739	partners of,
						715		resolutions on,
	454		524, 527, 555-556		636, 653-654	667	739-740	shareholders of,
		507						trustees of,
					653-654			winding up and,
								Licensing
		507				716-717	807	insolvency practitioners of,
								Liens
					624			aircraft,
								debentures and,
								documents and,
								holders of,
					624			maritime,
							776	receivership and,
								release of,
						674		reservation of title and,
					623-624			repairers',
					623-624			security and,
								Liquidation compositions
						703		applications for,
						704		creditors and,
						704		decision-making and,
						705		distribution of assets and,
						703		effect of,
						705		enforcement of,
						704-705		management of,
						705		officers and,
						703-704		procedure for,
						703		purpose of,
						705		realisation of assets and,
						705		shareholders and,
						705		termination of,
								Liquidations, *see also*,
								Compulsory liquidations,
								Liquidation compositions,
					638-643			**Voluntary liquidations**
	465		552					abuse of process and,
								accounts and,
								actions and,
								administrators and,
		503						advertisement of,
		510						agreements and,
								appeals on,
								arrangements and,

	EUROPE	BELGIUM	DENMARK	FRANCE	GERMANY	GREECE	IRELAND	ITALY
assets of,				158				
auditors and,								
balance sheets and,								
bankruptcies and,						289-290		
board of directors and,								
charges and,								
completion of,							357	
compositions and,			81					401-402
conditions for,								
consequences of,							332	
continuation of businesses and,				158				
contracts and,							336	
contributories and,								
costs and,							353-354	
courts and,								
creditors and,								
creditors' committees and,								
creditors' meetings and,							344	
debtors and,							350	
declaration of claims and,				159				
definition of,			88					
directors and,							349	
distribution of assets and,			90					
dividends and,								
effect of,				157-158			335-336	
employees and,							349-350	
equal treatment of creditors and,								
examinations and,							345, 347	
expenses of,							353-354	
forced administrative,								401-402
fraud and,							336	
gifts and,								
information on,								
insolvent,							359	
insurance and,							350	
interest and,								
intervention in,								
judgments on,				144-146, 156-162			335	
legal personality following,								
liquidators and,					218			
notification of,								
officers and,				161			357-358	
partners and,								
pensions and,								
preferential creditors and,								
procedure on,			90-93	157-158				
publication of,		58, 59		168				
purpose of,				155-156				
receivership and,								
registration of,								
re-opening of,				161-162				
resolutions on,			89					
retention of title and,			89					

LUXEMBOURG	NETHERLANDS	NORWAY	PORTUGAL	SPAIN	SWEDEN	SWITZERLAND	UNITED KINGDOM	
	465							assets of,
		504						auditors and,
					638			balance sheets and,
	473							bankruptcies and,
		500						board of directors and,
		501					791, 797	charges and,
								completion of,
								compositions and,
		502-503						conditions for,
								consequences of,
								continuation of businesses and,
							782, 798	contracts and,
								contributories and,
								costs and,
					640			courts and,
		504-505						creditors and,
			551					creditors' committees and,
		504-505						creditors' meetings and,
								debtors and,
								declaration of claims and,
								definition of,
		501-502			638		783	directors and,
		504, 509-510						distribution of assets and,
		505, 510					797	dividends and,
		501-502			638		783	effect of,
		501, 503, 504						employees and,
		501					782	equal treatment of creditors and,
								examinations and,
								expenses of,
								forced administrative,
							783	fraud and,
		505						gifts and,
	465							information on,
		500-512		611				insolvent,
								insurance and,
							784	interest and,
			556					intervention in,
								judgments on,
		500						legal personality following,
								liquidators and,
		507						notification of,
								officers and,
		510			643			partners and,
		505						pensions and,
		501, 505, 509					796-797	preferential creditors and,
		502-504			639-640		785-790	procedure on,
	465	503, 507						publication of,
		501			638		782	purpose of,
							779	receivership and,
			552		643			registration of,
	465							re-opening of,
	464-465	500			639			resolutions on,
		501, 510						retention of title and,

	EUROPE	BELGIUM	DENMARK	FRANCE	GERMANY	GREECE	IRELAND	ITALY
salaries and,								
sale of assets and,								
set off and,								
share capital and,								
shareholders and,				161			357-358	
shareholders' meetings and,		57-58						
solvent,					291-292			
subsequent,					197			
supervisory boards and,								
suspect acts and,				163				
tax and,					219-220		351-352	
termination of,		59		161-162			359-360	
third parties and,								
transactions and,								
types of,			89					
voting of,			89, 91				333-334	
winding up and,								
Liquidators, *see also,* **Liquidation**								
accounts and,								
appointment of,		57, 58, 63			217		344, 348-352	
assets and,								
assistance and,								
auditors and,								
authorisation of,	6							
balance of sheets and,					216-217			
bank accounts and,							349	
boards of directors and,					215-216			
boards of management and,					217			
breaches of duty by,					217			
challenges to,								
claims and,					225			
company representatives and,					216			
conflicts of interest and,								
contracts and,								
costs and,							350	
Council of Europe Convention and,	6							
creditors' committees and,								
creditors' meetings and,								
damages and,					215			
debts and,		58-59						
definition of,	6							
discipline of,				168				
distribution of assets and,								
dividends and,								
duties of,				156-157			346-348	
eligibility for,							367	
employees and,				156-157			335-336	
equality of creditors and,								
examiners and,							314-315	
expenses and,								
information and,								
insolvency practitioners as,								
insurance and,								

LUXEMBOURG	NETHERLANDS	NORWAY	PORTUGAL	SPAIN	SWEDEN	SWITZERLAND	UNITED KINGDOM	
		505, 510						salaries and,
			551					sale of assets and,
	465	501, 510						set off and,
					639			share capital and,
		510			643			shareholders and,
	464	500, 510			639, 643			shareholders' meetings and,
								solvent,
								subsequent,
	464							supervisory boards and,
								suspect acts and,
		503, 505, 510						tax and,
		510	552		643		799	termination of,
		502						third parties and,
							783	transactions and,
							781-782	types of,
		500-501						voting of,
		502						winding up and,
								Liquidators, *see also,* **Liquidation**
					642		784-785	accounts and,
		504, 507, 516	548		640-641	716-717	783, 786, 786, 794	appointment of,
		506			641			assets and,
							792	assistance and,
					640-642			auditors and,
								authorisation of,
								balance of sheets and,
								bank accounts and,
								boards of directors and,
								boards of management and,
			548-549					breaches of duty by,
								challenges to,
								claims and,
								company representatives and,
							795	conflicts of interest and,
		507					795	contracts and,
							794	costs and,
								Council of Europe Convention and,
		504, 506-507	548-549					creditors' committees and,
		504					784, 793	creditors' meetings and,
							796	damages and,
								debts and,
								definition of,
								discipline of,
								distribution of assets and,
		506			641-642		796-797	dividends and,
					640-642	704	797-798	duties of,
		516						eligibility for,
		506, 508-509	548		641		792, 796	employees and,
		506						equality of creditors and,
		516						examiners and,
							796	expenses and,
		506						information and,
							784	insolvency practitioners as,
							794	insurance and,

	EUROPE	BELGIUM	DENMARK	FRANCE	GERMANY	GREECE	IRELAND	ITALY
investigations by,								
jurisdiction of,	10-11							
leases and,								
legal representatives as,					212, 215			
liabilities of,		58						399-401
licensing and,								
list of,				168				
management of,				160				
negligence of,								
officers, replacing,			97-98					
official,						333, 341, 347		
partnerships and,								
powers of,	6-7, 10-11	58		156-157	216		344-346	
professional,								
property and,								
publicity and,								
realisation of assets and,								
registration of,								
remuneration of,							343, 354-355	
replacement of,								
reports of,	59			156				
rescues and,								
role of				216-218				
sale of assets and,								
sale of property and,								
secondary,	10-14							
security and,							348	
shareholders dismissing,			97-98					
shareholders' meetings and,								
solicitors and,							349	
solvent,			57-59					
stay of proceedings and,	11							
supervision of,			83					
supervisory boards and,					216			
suspension of,								
taxation and,								
third parties and,								
winding up and,					216		349-350	
Litigation, *see,* **Actions**								
Loans								376, 378-380
bankruptcies and,								
banks and,		29-30						
capital in lieu of,					242			
companies to,								
contracting of,								
controlled management and,				135				
credit establishments and,				151				
debentures and,								377
directors to,							365-366	
interest on,								
liens on,								378
low priority,								
mortgages and,								379-380
pledges and,								378-379
property on,			94	121				

LUXEMBOURG	NETHERLANDS	NORWAY	PORTUGAL	SPAIN	SWEDEN	SWITZERLAND	UNITED KINGDOM	
		516						investigations by,
								jurisdiction of,
		507						leases and,
								legal representatives as,
		507				717	792, 794	liabilities of,
		507				716-717		licensing and,
			548					list of,
	465	507-510			642-643	704-705	794-797	management of,
							794	negligence of,
								officers, replacing,
								official,
		506-507						partnerships and,
					642	704	792-797	powers of,
						796		professional,
		516-517				793		property and,
						796		publicity and,
								realisation of assets and,
								registration of,
						703-704	787, 791	remuneration of,
								replacement of,
		506	547		642			reports of,
								rescues and,
		503-504	548-549					role of,
		508						sale of assets and,
					642-643			sale of property and,
								secondary,
								security and,
								shareholders dismissing,
					640-642			shareholders' meetings and,
								solicitors and,
								solvent,
								stay of proceedings and,
								supervision of,
								supervisory boards and,
								suspension of,
		509-510						taxation and,
		506						third parties and,
								winding up and,

Litigation, *see,* **Actions**
Loans

LUXEMBOURG	NETHERLANDS	NORWAY	PORTUGAL	SPAIN	SWEDEN	SWITZERLAND	UNITED KINGDOM	
				613				bankruptcies and,
								banks and,
								capital in lieu of,
					620			companies to,
								contracting of,
425								controlled management and,
								credit establishments and,
							734	debentures and,
								directors to,
			528					interest on,
								liens on,
						675		low priority,
								mortgages and,
								pledges and,
								property on,

	EUROPE	BELGIUM	DENMARK	FRANCE	GERMANY	GREECE	IRELAND	ITALY
repayment of,					183-184			
reservation of title and,								380
restrictions on,								
sale of assets and,								
sales and,		61						
security for,		27			184	260		
set off and,								380
share capital and,								
shareholders and,								
subordinated,								
Losses								
competition for,		50, 52	76					
mitigation of,			90					
Lugano Convention 1988, *see,*								
Conventions on Jurisdiction and Enforcement of Judgments								
Management, *see also,*								
Board of management, Controlled management, Directors, Officers, Supervisory Boards								
administrators of,		52-55	95-98	152		286		
appointment of,								
asset,								425
assistance in,				114				
associations of,								
bad,	32							
board of directors and,								
breaches of duty and,					223, 230			
companies of,		25-26						374
compositions of,			88					
compulsory arrangements and,					234			
compulsory liquidations and,					222-223			
contracts and,								
costs of,			97					
creditors and,			93-94					
damages and,								
debts and,			97					
fraud of,								
general manager of,								
grant of,		62						
information on,					232			
liability of,								399-401
liquidators by,				160				
negligence of,		62						
personal liability of,			70					
powers of the,			79-80					
receivership and,								
removal of,								
reprieve from payments and,								
seizure and,			76					
shareholders and,				153			307	
standard of care and,					223			
supervision of,				153				
suspension of,								

LUXEMBOURG	NETHERLANDS	NORWAY	PORTUGAL	SPAIN	SWEDEN	SWITZERLAND	UNITED KINGDOM	
								repayment of,
								reservation of title and,
		515						restrictions on,
			528					sale of assets and,
								sales and,
								security for,
								set off and,
		487						share capital and,
								shareholders and,
			528			675		subordinated,
								Losses
								competition for,
								mitigation of,
								Lugano Convention 1988, *see,*
								Conventions on Jurisdiction
								and Enforcement of
								Judgments
								Management, *see also,*
								Board of management,
								Controlled management,
								Directors, Officers,
								Supervisory Boards
			545				761-765	administrators of,
	450		525, 527					appointment of,
								asset,
	450							assistance in,
								associations of,
								bad,
				568				board of directors and,
								breaches of duty and,
			524-527	567-570				companies of,
423-424								compositions of,
								compulsory arrangements and,
								compulsory liquidations and,
				570				contracts and,
								costs of,
								creditors and,
				614				damages and,
								debts and,
				614			740	fraud of,
				569-570				general manager of,
								grant of,
								information on,
	453, 476		555-556	614				liability of,
		507-510			642-643	704-705	794-797	liquidators by,
				614				negligence of,
								personal liability of,
								powers of the,
							774-779	receivership and,
	450							removal of,
418								reprieve from payments and,
								seizure and,
				569				shareholders and,
								standard of care and,
								supervision of,
	450							suspension of,

	EUROPE	BELGIUM	DENMARK	FRANCE	GERMANY	GREECE	IRELAND	ITALY
transfer of undertakings and,	18							
trustees and,			108					
voluntary arrangements and,					203-204			
Mareva injunctions							309	
Meetings, *see also*								
Creditors' meetings,								
Shareholders' meetings								
administrators and,								
articles of association and,								
associations and,								
boards of directors and,								
compulsory arrangements and,					194			
extraordinary general,		56	70					
general,								
notice of,					194			
quorum of,								
partners of,						258		
records of,								
shareholders of,		26						
winding up and,							347	
Members' voluntary liquidations,								
see, **Voluntary liquidations**								
Merchant status		23, 41-42						
Minority shareholders								
auditors and,								
compulsory arrangements and,					192			
protection of,								
rights of,					181-182	258-259		
Misfeasance proceedings							358, 368	
Misrepresentation								
bankruptcies and,								
contracts and,								
voluntary arrangements and,					201			
Moratoriums					193, 196			
accounts and,								
actions for,								
administration and,								
administrators and,								
applications for,								
assets and,								
attachments and,								
bankruptcies and,								
cancellation of,								
compositions and,								
contracts and,								
controlled management and,								
costs and,								
courts and,								
creditors' agreements and,								
creditors' committees and,								
creditors' meetings and,								
directors and,								
duration of,								
effect of,								

LUXEMBOURG	NETHERLANDS	NORWAY	PORTUGAL	SPAIN	SWEDEN	SWITZERLAND	UNITED KINGDOM	
								transfer of undertakings and,
								trustees and,
								voluntary arrangements and,
							742	**Mareva injunctions**
								Meetings, *see also,*
								Creditors' meetings,
					622	668		**Shareholders' meetings**
				571				administrators and,
								articles of association and,
	453							associations and,
	450							boards of directors and,
					621	668-669		compulsory arrangements and,
								extraordinary general,
410-411	450							general,
								notice of,
				571				quorum of,
				567-568				partners of,
							810	records of,
								shareholders of,
								winding up and,
								Members' voluntary liquidations,
								see, **Voluntary liquidations**
								Merchant status
								Minority shareholders
					623			auditors and,
								compulsory arrangements and,
				571	652		732	protection of,
								rights of,
								Misfeasance proceedings
								Misrepresentation
				614				bankruptcies and,
414								contracts and,
								voluntary arrangements and,
428	460-464	493		582-589				**Moratoriums**
				586, 587, 592, 590				accounts and,
								actions for,
							752, 757	administration and,
	461-462			586-588		692		administrators and,
	460					684		applications for,
				589				assets and,
	467			589		696-697		attachments and,
				590-591, 596, 597		692-693, 707-708		bankruptcies and,
	463			587		682, 687		cancellation of,
				594				compositions and,
								contracts and,
				587				controlled management and,
								costs and,
							743-744	courts and,
				590-596				creditors' agreements and,
	461-463			595				creditors' committees and,
				587, 594-595				creditors' meetings and,
								directors and,
				584-585,				duration of,
								effect of,

	EUROPE	BELGIUM	DENMARK	FRANCE	GERMANY	GREECE	IRELAND	ITALY
employees and,								
enforcement and,								
enhanced,			81-88, 109					
filing of,								
final orders and,								
floating charges and,								
fraud and,								
goodwill and,								
information in,								
interventores and,								
judges and,								
judgments and,								
judicial,								388
management and,								
mortgages and,								
negligence and,								
officers and,								
opposition to,								
payments and,								
petitions for,								
pledges and,								
preferential creditors and,								
procedure for,								
property and,								
proposals for,								
provisional orders and,								
public prosecutors and,								
purpose of,								
ranking of creditors and,								
register of,								
rent and,								
reorganisation and,								
report on,								
resolutions on,								
secured claims and,								
set off and,								
setting aside transactions and,								
shareholders and,								
termination of,								
time limits and,								
voting on,								
Mortgages								
actions and,				159				
assets and,			84					
bankruptcies and,								
cancellation of,								
controlled management and,								
creditors and,	27, 45							
debentures and,				121				377
definition of,				121				
delivery and,								
enforcement of,								
filing of,			102					

LUXEMBOURG	NETHERLANDS	NORWAY	PORTUGAL	SPAIN	SWEDEN	SWITZERLAND	UNITED KINGDOM	
				588				
				593-594				employees and,
				589				enforcement and,
								enhanced,
								filing of,
	462-463							final orders and,
								floating charges and,
				597-598			754	fraud and,
				586				goodwill and,
	461							information in,
				591-593, 615				interventores and,
				591-592				judges and,
	461, 463			588				judgments and,
								judicial,
								management and,
								mortgages and,
				587				negligence and,
				594				officers and,
				590				opposition to,
	460-464							payments and,
	460-461							petitions for,
								pledges and,
	463			593				preferential creditors and,
				587-590				procedure for,
								property and,
				586, 587				proposals for,
	461-462					663		provisional orders and,
				591				public prosecutors and,
				584-585				purpose of,
								ranking of creditors and,
				588				register of,
				594				rent and,
	460, 462							reorganisation and,
				587, 588, 592				report on,
								resolutions on,
								secured claims and,
				587				set off and,
								setting aside transactions and,
				594				shareholders and,
	461, 463-464			598		682		termination of,
	461-462							time limits and,
	462-464			595				voting on,
				574-575				**Mortgages**
								actions and,
439				574				assets and,
				607, 608		699		bankruptcies and,
	470							cancellation of,
426								controlled management and,
								creditors and,
								debentures and,
								definition of,
				574				delivery and,
			529-530	575		680-681		enforcement of,
								filing of,

	EUROPE	BELGIUM	DENMARK	FRANCE	GERMANY	GREECE	IRELAND	ITALY
foreclosure of,			71					
interest and,		34						
judgments on,				148			342	
leases and,								
legal,	61							
preferential creditors and,								
records of,				122				
receivership and,							323-324	
registration of,			102				309	
reprieve from payments and,								
sale of assets and,		46						
security as,			71	160				379-380
setting aside,			102-103					
third parties and,								379
transfer of,								
voluntary,								
Negligence								
administrators and,								
auditors and,								
bankruptcies and,								392
compensation and,								
concordat judicaire and,		32-33						
directors and,								
insolvency and,								
liquidators and,								
management and,		62						
officers and,			104					
Negotiable instruments					193			
Negotiations								
compositions and,			83, 85, 87					
publication of,			87					
creditors' meetings and,			109					
debt arrangements and,								
private,				192				
reorganisations and,					178			
Notice								
claims of,					224-225			
creditors' committees and,								
creditors' meetings of,								
distribution of assets and,					219			
employment contracts and,								
judgments of,				169				
leases and,			87					
liquidation of,								
meetings and,					194			
reasonable,			87					
resolutions of,								
seizure of,								
shareholders' meetings of,								
title of,				201				
Observation period				140-141, 148-151, 154-155				
Officers, *see also,* **Directors**								
accounts and,								

LUXEMBOURG	NETHERLANDS	NORWAY	PORTUGAL	SPAIN	SWEDEN	SWITZERLAND	UNITED KINGDOM	
								foreclosure of,
								interest and,
		490						judgments on,
				574				leases and,
								legal,
422	471				623-624			preferential creditors and,
								records of,
								receivership and,
444	458	487			627			registration of,
417								reprieve from payments and,
			529	574				sale of assets and,
415								security as,
		513						setting aside,
								third parties and,
				574				transfer of,
				613				voluntary,

Negligence
administrators and,
auditors and,
bankruptcies and,
compensation and,
concordat judiciaire and,
directors and,
insolvency and,
liquidators and,
management and,
officers and,
Negotiable instruments
Negotiations
compositions and,
  publication of,
creditors' meetings and,
debt arrangements and,
private,
reorganisations and,
Notice
claims of,
creditors' committees and,
creditors' meetings of,
distribution of assets and,
employment contracts and,
judgments of,
leases and,
liquidation of,
meetings and,
reasonable,
resolutions of,
seizure of,
shareholders' meetings of,
title of,

Observation period

Officers, *see also*, **Directors**
accounts and,

LUXEMBOURG	NETHERLANDS	NORWAY	PORTUGAL	SPAIN	SWEDEN	SWITZERLAND	UNITED KINGDOM	
				567				administrators and,
					652	713		auditors and,
		515-516						compensation and,
				568, 587	652	712		directors and,
				597-598				insolvency and,
							794	liquidators and,
				614				management and,
					652	712		officers and,
		494, 496						debt arrangements and,
				590			756	creditors' committees and,
		508						employment contracts and,
		507						leases and,
							786	resolutions of,
					622			shareholders' meetings of,
	476							accounts and,

	EUROPE	BELGIUM	DENMARK	FRANCE	GERMANY	GREECE	IRELAND	ITALY
administration and,								
bankruptcy proceedings and,				165		286-287		
stay of,								
bans from being,			108-109					
bookkeeping and,								
compositions and,			88					
de facto,				164				
debt arrangements and,								
dismissal of,			144					
fraud of,			104					
liabilities of,			104-106	164-166	245	296-297	362-365	
liquidation and,				161			357-358	
liquidation compositions and,								
liquidators and,			97-98					
negligence of,			104					
receivership and,								
rehabilitation and,				152				
sanctions against,				165-166				
suspension of payments and,								
voluntary arrangements and,					204	284		
Ownership								
attachment of,								
companies of,								
debts of,				159				
partnerships of,								
rescission of,					185			
shareholders and,								
shares of,						258-259		
Participation rights								
voting and,								
Partnerships				123-124	188			
administrators and,								
assets of,								
bankruptcies of,								
contractual,								
creditors and,								
decision-making and,						255		
dissolution of,						287		
general,				124				
good faith and,								
joint and several liability of,	25		72-73		188	259-260		
liability of,								
limited,			124	188				412-413
management of,								
meetings of,						258		
ownership of,								
preferential creditors and,			72-73					
registration of,								
share capital and,								
shares, limited by,								376-377
silent,								
termination of,								
unlimited commercial,					238			

LUXEMBOURG	NETHERLANDS	NORWAY	PORTUGAL	SPAIN	SWEDEN	SWITZERLAND	UNITED KINGDOM	
							766	administration and,
						702		bankruptcy proceedings and,
						692		stay of,
								bans from being,
	476							bookkeeping and,
						688		compositions and,
								de facto,
		499						debt arrangements and,
								dismissal of,
								fraud of,
440-443	476	515-516				664, 712-716	804-807	liabilities of,
						705		liquidation and,
								liquidation compositions and,
							797-799	liquidators and,
					652			negligence of,
							779-780	receivership and,
								rehabilitation and,
								sanctions against,
				594				suspension of payments and,
								voluntary arrangements and,
411			527-529	570-573				**Ownership**
	459							attachment of,
				571-573	622-623	670-673		companies of,
								debts of,
				570-571				partnerships of,
								rescission of,
						676-678		shareholders and,
		486-487						shares of,
						670-672		**Participation rights**
						671		voting and,
					619			**Partnerships**
				567				administrators and,
	456							assets of,
	466			564				bankruptcies of,
	455-456					678-679		contractual,
		484						creditors and,
								decision-making and,
412				564, 567, 570, 571		678-679		dissolution of, / general,
	455			567				good faith and, / joint and several liability of,
	456			570		678-679, 712		liability of,
456 413	484, 486		564	627	679			limited, / management of,
				567-568 570-571				meetings of, / ownership of,
								preferential creditors and,
	455-456				627	678		registration of,
		486						share capital and,
								shares, limited by,
	484							silent,
		507						termination of,
								unlimited commercial,

	EUROPE	BELGIUM	DENMARK	FRANCE	GERMANY	GREECE	IRELAND	ITALY
winding up of,		25						
Payments, *see also,* **Moratoriums**								
bank transfer by,				163				
cash,			163	182				
debts and,								
demands for,				164			309	
extraordinary,								
postponement of,				145, 146	193			
priority of,							352-357	
pro rata and,					196			
protection against,					246			
register of,					219			
suspect period and,								
unusual means by,			101-102					
Pension schemes					226			
preferential creditors and,							355	
receivership and,								
Personal property				127				
contracts and,				142				
recovery of,				166				
sale of,			158					
security and,				159-160				
Petitions								
administration and,								
bankruptcy and,			91					
compulsory liquidations for,								
contested,							341	
filing,		91						
moratoriums and,								
opposition to,								
reasons for,			92					
recovery and,								
service of,			92					
winding up and,							339-341	
Pledges								
actions and,				159				
assets of,			84					
auctions and,								379
bankruptcies and,								
contract of,		27						
controlled management of,								
creditors and,		27						
debentures of,								379
definition of,								
delivery and,				122				
disposal of assets and,		46						
enforcement of,								
equity participation and,								379
execution of,								
judgments on,				148				
preferential creditors and,				159				
preliminary,						266		
realisation of,								
records of,				123				

LUXEMBOURG	NETHERLANDS	NORWAY	PORTUGAL	SPAIN	SWEDEN	SWITZERLAND	UNITED KINGDOM	
							739	winding up of,
								Payments, *see also,* **Moratoriums**
								bank transfer by,
								cash,
								debts and,
								demands for,
		512						extraordinary,
								postponement of,
								priority of,
								pro rata and,
								protection against,
439								register of,
								suspect period and,
								unusual means by,
		505						**Pension schemes**
								preferential creditors and,
							777	receivership and,
								Personal property
								contracts and,
								recovery of,
								sale of,
								security and,
								Petitions
							751	administration and,
			546		644	695		bankruptcy and,
							783, 787-790	compulsory liquidations for,
						753		contested,
								filing,
	460							moratoriums and,
							788	opposition to,
								reasons for,
			535-537					recovery and,
							753-754, 788	service of,
		502					783, 787-790	winding up and,
				574-575				**Pledges**
								actions and,
439	458			574				assets of,
								auctions and,
				607, 608				bankruptcies and,
	457-458							contract of,
426								controlled management of,
								creditors and,
								debentures of,
				574				definition of,
								delivery and,
								disposal of assets and,
			529	575		680-681		enforcement of,
								equity participation and,
	458							execution of,
								judgments on,
422	471							preferential creditors and,
								preliminary,
					630			realisation of,
								records of,

	EUROPE	BELGIUM	DENMARK	FRANCE	GERMANY	GREECE	IRELAND	ITALY
registration of,		27-28				261		
reprieve from payments and,								
rights in rem and,						261-262		
rights of retention and,								
security and,					184			378-379
setting aside,			103					
shares and,								
silent,								
third parties and,		28	103					
tools and equipment and,				122, 123				378
types of,				122				
Police records				169				
Powers of attorney							327	
Powers of sale								
Pre-emption rights						259		
Preferential creditors,	4, 11	28					355-356	
actions by,				159				
assets and,					186			
avoidance of,								
bad faith and,								
bank creditors and,			100					
cancellation of,								
claims and,					244			
compositions and,								
costs and,								
creditors' arrangements and,								
creditors' meetings and,								387
date of claims and,				148				
debentures and,								
discrimination against,								
disputes between,		46						
distribution of assets and,		56					331-332	
dividends and,								
employees and,		31	71, 77, 84	148, 160	226	278, 287	356	378
compensation to,							356	
equality of creditors and,		55						
fraud and,							361	
goodwill of,		31						
guarantees and,								
interest on,		34						
investigations of,			89-90					
leases and,								
legal expenses and,				151				
liens and,								
liquidations and,								
loans and,				151				
mortgages and,		45						
partnerships and,			72-73					
pensions and,							355	
pledges and,				159				
proceedings by,						290		
ranking of,								
receivership and,							329, 331-332	
recovery of,								
rehabilitation and,				132				

LUXEMBOURG	NETHERLANDS	NORWAY	PORTUGAL	SPAIN	SWEDEN	SWITZERLAND	UNITED KINGDOM	
				574				registration of,
417-418								reprieve from payments and,
						674		rights in rem and,
								rights of retention and,
								security and,
					620			setting aside,
457								shares and,
415								silent,
								third parties and,
								tools and equipment and,
								types of,
								Police records
								Powers of attorney
							742	**Powers of sale**
				565, 571				**Pre-emption rights**
						662-664	733, 790-791	**Preferential creditors,**
					623-626			actions by,
414								assets and,
						662-663		avoidance of,
								bad faith and,
						662		bank creditors and,
								cancellation of,
								claims and,
			540		634	685-686		compositions and,
					625			costs and,
			542-543					creditors' arrangement and,
								creditors' meetings and,
								date of claims and,
							734	debentures and,
						709-710		discrimination against,
								disputes between,
								distribution of assets and,
		505						dividends and,
					625-626	662, 685		employees and,
								compensation to,
								equality of creditors and,
								fraud and,
								goodwill of,
415								guarantees and,
								interest on,
								investigations of,
415	471							leases and,
								legal expenses and,
					623-624			liens and,
		501, 505					796-797	liquidations and,
								loans and,
415, 417-418	471				623-624			mortgages and,
								partnerships and,
		505				662		pensions and,
415, 417-418	471				623-624			pledges and,
								proceedings by,
		514						ranking of,
							771, 778	receivership and,
					649			recovery of,
								rehabilitation and,

	EUROPE	BELGIUM	DENMARK	FRANCE	GERMANY	GREECE	IRELAND	ITALY
rent and,								
repairs and,								
reprieves from payments and,								
reservation of title and,								
revenue authorities and,		38, 45		151				
salaries of,			97				329, 355	378
set off and,								
social security authorities of,		38, 45		151		278-279	355	378
special,		46						
suspension of payments and,			81					
taxes and,					226		355	378
time limits and,								
wages and,				151				
Priorities, *see also,*								
Preferential creditors								
Privatisation								
transfers of undertakings and,	17							
voluntary arrangements and,					199			
Proceedings, *see,* **Actions**								
Profit distribution		26			220-221			
Promissory notes								
Property. *See also* **Personal property,**								
Sale of property								
associations and,								
attachment proceedings and,				127, 158		284		
auctions of,								382-383
bankruptcies and,						276, 284		
charges over,			71, 92, 96					
compositions and,								
disposal of,								
draft European Union Bankruptcy								
Convention and,	9							
execution against,								381-383
immovable,	9							
information on,						266-267		
inventories of,						285		
loans on,				94				
mortgages on,		27						
onerous,							350	
registration of,					193-194			
rights,								
security and,				159-160	185			
seizure of,								
transfer of,		41						
undervalue, at an,								
Propositions								
creditors' meetings and,		35						
debtors of,		34-35						
Public control			106-109	167-169		295-297	367	401-403
Public prosecutors				137, 139				
Publicity			109		249-250	297		
accounts of,					187			
administration and,								
bankruptcies of,			90					391
branches of,							308	

LUXEMBOURG	NETHERLANDS	NORWAY	PORTUGAL	SPAIN	SWEDEN	SWITZERLAND	UNITED KINGDOM	
					625			rent and,
					623-624			repairs and,
417-418								reprieves from payments and,
	471							reservation of title and,
417								revenue authorities and,
		505, 508, 510	531	593-594, 609	625-626	685		salaries of,
								set off and,
	471							
415	471		531, 550		625-626	685		social security authorities of,
								special,
								suspension of payments and,
415, 417	471	505, 509, 510	531, 550		625			taxes and,
						663		time limits and,
								wages and,
								Priorities, *see also*,
								Preferential creditors
								Privatisation
								transfers of undertakings and,
								voluntary arrangements and,
								Proceedings, *see*, **Actions**
								Profit distribution
								Promissory notes
								Property. *See also* **Personal property, Sale of property**
	450							associations and,
	457							attachment proceedings and,
								auctions of,
			532	611				bankruptcies and,
						673-674		charges over,
424								compositions and,
							759	disposal of,
								draft European Union Bankruptcy Convention and,
								execution against,
								immovable,
								information on,
								inventories of
								loans on,
							793, 795	mortgages on,
								onerous,
						672-673		registration of,
							734	rights,
432, 435								security and,
								seizure of,
				613				transfer of,
					620			undervalue, at an,
								Propositions
								creditors' meetings and,
								debtors of,
443-444	476-477	516-517	556	614-615	654-657	716-719		**Public control**
	467		546					**Public prosecutors**
					656-657	718-719	809-810	**Publicity**
412								accounts of,
							755	administration and,
444	469, 472							bankruptcies of,
								branches of,

	EUROPE	BELGIUM	DENMARK	FRANCE	GERMANY	GREECE	IRELAND	ITALY
compositions of,			85					
negotiations of,			87					
constitutions of,								
controlled management of,								
debt arrangements and,								
judgments of,				149, 168		260		
liquidations of,				168	212			
liquidators and,								
receivership and,							326-327	
rehabilitation and,				168				
seizure and,	30							
share register and,								
shareholders' meetings and,								
winding up,					213, 216-217		343, 348, 358	
Publishing contracts				142				
Purchase offers				143-144				
Real rights								
Receivers, *see also*, **Receivership**								
appointment of,							323-324, 326-327	
compulsory liquidations and,								
contracts and,							328-329	
duties of,								
eligibility to act as,							326	
examiners and,							314-315	
Law of Property Act,								
liquidations and,								
powers of,							327-330	
publicity and,							326-327	
removal of,							327	
remuneration of,								
reports of,								
taxation and,							325	
Receivership, *see also* **Receivers**							323-333	
advantages and,								
charges and,								
consideration on,								
contractual,								
court appointed,								
creditors and,								
debentures and,							323-324, 327-328	
distribution of assets and,							331-332	
effect of,								
employees and,							329-330	
liens over,								
liquidation and,								
management and,								
mortgages and,							323-324	
officers and,								
powers of attorney and,							328	
preferential creditors and,							331-332	

LUXEMBOURG	NETHERLANDS	NORWAY	PORTUGAL	SPAIN	SWEDEN	SWITZERLAND	UNITED KINGDOM	
					633			compositions of,
								negotiations of,
409								constitutions of,
426		496-497, 517						controlled management of,
								debt arrangements and,
								judgments of,
		517						liquidations of,
							794	liquidators and,
								receivership and,
								rehabilitation and,
								seizure and,
	454							share register and,
				572				shareholders' meetings and,
								winding up,
								Publishing contracts
								Purchase offers
	457							**Real rights**
								Receivers, *see also,* **Receivership**
							767, 769, 774, 790	appointment of,
							784	compulsory liquidations and,
							774-776	contracts and,
							773	duties of,
								eligibility to act as,
								examiners and,
							768, 778	Law of Property Act,
							789	liquidations and,
							767, 772	powers of,
							774	publicity and,
								removal of,
							770, 778, 779	remuneration of,
							771, 773	reports of,
								taxation and,
							767-780	**Receivership,** *see also* **Receivers**
							770	advantages and,
							769, 770, 772, 778	charges and,
							769-771	consideration on,
							767-768	contractual,
							789	court appointed,
							771	creditors and,
								debentures and,
							778-779	distribution of assets and,
							767-769	effect of,
							776-777	employees and,
							776	liens over,
							779	liquidation and,
							774-776	management and,
								mortgages and,
							779	officers and,
								powers of attorney and,
							771	preferential creditors and,

	EUROPE	BELGIUM	DENMARK	FRANCE	GERMANY	GREECE	IRELAND	ITALY
procedure on,								
purpose of,								
realisation of assets and,								
relief against creditors and,								
retention of title and,							331	
sale of property and,								
secured creditors and,							331	
set off and,								
tax and,							330	
termination of,							332-333	
third parties and,								
transfer of undertakings of,							329-330	
trust claims and,							331	
types of,								
Reckless trading							358, 362-365, 368	
Reclaim								
Recognition								
foreign judgments and,		31	74					
foreign proceedings and,	3							
insolvency regimes and,	13							
Reconstruction							307	
Records					249-250	297		
inspection of,								
transcript of,								
Recovery								
actions and,								
compositions and,								
distribution of assets and,			109					
floating charges and,								
gifts and,								
objection to,								
preferential creditors and,								
premature payments and,								
procedure on,								
proof on,								
salaries of,								
set off and,								
time limits and,								
Redundancies					244			
Registered offices	6							
closure of,								
draft European Union Bankruptcy Conventions and,	9							
financial statements at,			91					
foreign,	4							
transfer of,					208			
winding up and,					186-187			
Registration								
accounts of,						261		
aircraft of,			77			261		
assets of,								
bankruptcies and,								
branches of,			71					
charges of,					189, 216			
claims of,								

LUXEMBOURG	NETHERLANDS	NORWAY	PORTUGAL	SPAIN	SWEDEN	SWITZERLAND	UNITED KINGDOM	
							771, 778	procedure on,
							767-769	purpose of,
							778	realisation of assets and,
							770	relief against creditors and,
								retention of title and,
							771, 773	sale of property and,
								secured creditors and,
							776	set off and,
								tax and,
							780	termination of,
							775	third parties and,
							777	transfer of undertakings of,
								trust claims and,
							767-769	types of,
	457							**Reckless trading**
								Reclaim
								Recognition
								foreign judgments and,
								foreign proceedings and,
								insolvency regimes and,
		517				718-719	810	**Reconstruction**
444					656		810	**Records**
								inspection of,
								transcript of,
								Recovery
					648			actions and,
					648			compositions and,
					648			distribution of assets and,
					649			floating charges and,
					650			gifts and,
						680		objection to,
					649			preferential creditors and,
					650			premature payments and,
					648			procedure on,
					649			proof on,
					650			salaries of,
					651			set off and,
					648-651			time limits and,
							764	**Redundancies**
								Registered offices
432								closure of,
								draft European Union Bankruptcy Conventions and,
								financial statements at,
								foreign,
								transfer of,
437								winding up and,
							737-738	**Registration**
			565					accounts of,
								aircraft of,
444								assets of,
						718		bankruptcies and,
						676		branches of,
444		487-488			652		735	charges of,
		495, 497,	604					claims of,

	EUROPE	BELGIUM	DENMARK	FRANCE	GERMANY	GREECE	IRELAND	ITALY
companies of,				123		266		
continuation of,					213			
deletion of,			98-99, 109		208			
creditors' agreements and,								
financial restructuring and,								
goods and,								
information and,								
judgments of,								
liquidations and,							309	
liquidators of,					214			
mortgages of,			102				309	
partnerships of,								
pledges of,						262		
property and,					193			
reservation of title and,								
resolutions of,					214			
security of,			71-72				324	
share capital and,								
shares of,								
ships of,					261			
sole traders of,								
suspension of payments and,								
third parties and,								
winding up of,					208			
Rehabilitations				114, 132-155				403
agreements on,								
appeals and,				145-146				
assets and,				134				
courts and,				134-135, 139				
debtors and,				138				
declarations on,				157				
employees and,				139				
investigations and,				154-155				
judgments over,				140				392
jurisdiction over,				139				
leases and,				142				
legal structure of,				133				
officers and,				153				
petitions for,				138-139				
plan for,				143-145				
preferential creditors and,				132				
public prosecutor and,				139				
publicity of,				168				
purpose of,				132				
shareholders and,				152-153				
simplified procedure and,				154-155				
suspension of actions during,				132				
termination of,				154				
transfer of companies and,				147				
Reinstatement						290-291		
Releases								
liability from,								

LUXEMBOURG	NETHERLANDS	NORWAY	PORTUGAL	SPAIN	SWEDEN	SWITZERLAND	UNITED KINGDOM	
	452, 453	500 483		565	626-627	675-676	727-728	companies of,
					643			continuation of,
								deletion of,
				583				creditors' agreements and,
			544					financial restructuring and,
						695		goods and,
				576				information and,
								judgments of,
			548, 552					liquidations and,
								liquidators of,
444	458	487			627			mortgages of,
	456				627	678		partnerships of,
				574				pledges of,
								property and,
			529-530	575				reservation of title and,
								resolutions of,
					624			security of,
					639			share capital and,
411	452, 453, 454				622	670-671		shares of,
								ships of,
		488						sole traders of,
403				588				suspension of payments and,
						676-677		third parties and,
		502, 503						winding up of,
								Rehabilitations
			552					agreements on,
								appeals and,
								assets and,
								courts and,
								debtors and,
								declarations on,
								employees and,
								investigations and,
			552					judgments over,
								jurisdiction over,
								leases and,
								legal structure of,
								officers and,
								petitions for,
								plan for,
								preferential creditors and,
								public prosecutor and,
								publicity of,
								purpose of,
								shareholders and,
								simplified procedure and,
								suspension of actions during,
								termination of,
								transfer of companies and,
								Reinstatement
								Releases
						715		liability from,

	EUROPE	BELGIUM	DENMARK	FRANCE	GERMANY	GREECE	IRELAND	ITALY
Remuneration, *see also,* **Salaries**								
administrators of,		50-51			231			
compulsory liquidation and,					228			
contributions to,		50						
controlled management and,								
creditors' arrangements and,								
directors and,								
examiners of,							321-322	
excessive,								
liquidators of,							343, 354	
receivership and,								
tariffs on,		50-51						
Rent					185, 201	280		
bankruptcies and,								
distress for,							308	
preferential creditors and,								
receivership and,								
unpaid,								
Reorganisations, *see also,*								
Controlled management			90	113	175, 238			388, 401
administrators and,								
advertisements and,								
applications for,								
assignment and,					192			
challenges to,								
continuation of,								
costs of,			97					
creditors and,								
debtors and,								
moratoriums and,								
negotiations and,					178			
petitions on,								
plan of,				177-178				
procedure on,								
voting on,					178			
Reporting requirements, *see,*								
Information, Publicity								
Reprieve from payments, *see,*								
Moratoriums								
Reputation				129				
Rescission					243-244			
contracts and,								
time limits on,					243-244			
Rescues								
Council of Europe								
Convention and,	6							
draft European Union								
Bankruptcy Convention and,	9							
liquidators and,	12							
time limits and,					222-223			
transfers of undertakings and,	18							
Reservation of title		55	72, 78	166				
administration and,								
assets and,			84, 96-97	159	184-185			
compromise and,		29						

LUXEMBOURG	NETHERLANDS	NORWAY	PORTUGAL	SPAIN	SWEDEN	SWITZERLAND	UNITED KINGDOM	
	470					683-684, 690	761, 767	**Remuneration,** *see also,* **Salaries** administrators of,
								compulsory liquidation and,
429								contributions to,
				584				controlled management and,
410								creditors' arrangements and,
								directors and,
		512						examiners of,
								excessive,
							787, 791	liquidators of,
							770	receivership and,
	470			594			740	tariffs on,
				594			740	**Rent**
				610				bankruptcies and,
					625			distress for,
							768	preferential creditors and,
						740		receivership and,
				586	637			unpaid,
					670, 690			**Reorganisations,** *see also,* **Controlled management**
						663-664		
			537-538			663-664		administrators and,
			536					advertisements and,
			535-538					applications for,
			536-537					assignment and,
			537					challenges to,
								continuation of,
			534					costs of,
			534					creditors and,
	460							debtors and,
								moratoriums and,
			535-537					negotiations and,
								petitions on,
			534-535					plan of,
			539					procedure on,
								voting on,
								Reporting requirements, *see,* **Information, Publicity**
								Reprieve from payments, *see,* **Moratoriums**
								Reputation
								Rescission
	456-457							contracts and,
								time limits on,
								Rescues
								Council of Europe Convention and,
								draft European Union Bankruptcy Convention and,
								liquidators and,
								time limits and,
	457							transfers of undertakings and,
								Reservation of title
							757	administration and,
								assets and,
								compromise and,

	EUROPE	BELGIUM	DENMARK	FRANCE	GERMANY	GREECE	IRELAND	ITALY
delivery and,								
draft European Union Bankruptcy Convention and,	9							
holders of,					186			
instalments and,								380
liens and,								
liquidation of,			89					
pledges and,								
preferential creditors and,								
registration of,								
repossession and,								
security as,				122	184	265	316	
third parties and,								
Resolutions								
administration on,								389
advertisements of,								
bankruptcies and,								
board of directors of,								
creditors' meetings at,		57	94					
damages and,					215			
debentures on,								377
debt collection and,								
liability on,								
liquidations on,			89					
notice of,								
registration of,					214			
shareholders',							358	
shareholders meetings and,					179, 180, 236			374
suspension of payments and,								
voluntary liquidations and,					210-211			
voting on,								
winding up on,					207-209		337-338, 348	
Restitution		60			219, 239			
Retention of title, *see,* **Reservation of title**								
Revenue authorities	4							
preferential creditors and,		29, 45		151				
Rights in rem						260		
bankruptcies and,								
debt collection and,								
draft European Union Bankruptcy Convention and,	9							
pledges and,						261-262		
Rights of retention								
Romalpa clauses, *see,* **Reservation of title**								
Sachwalters, *see,* **Administrators**								
Salaries			79, 83, 84					
balance sheets and,			83					
preferential creditors and,			97	151	226		329	378
receivership and,								

LUXEMBOURG	NETHERLANDS	NORWAY	PORTUGAL	SPAIN	SWEDEN	SWITZERLAND	UNITED KINGDOM	
		488, 491						delivery and,
								draft European Union Bankruptcy Convention and,
								holders of,
								instalments and,
		501, 510						liens and,
								liquidation of,
	471							pledges and,
			529	575		674		preferential creditors and, registration of,
					630			repossession and,
	491			575	626		736	security as,
414								third parties and,
								Resolutions
							756	administration on,
							786	advertisements of,
	466							bankruptcies and,
					621			board of directors of,
		504						creditors' meetings at,
								damages and,
				580				debentures on,
						715		debt collection and, liability on,
		500					790	liquidations on,
							786	notice of,
	452							registration of, shareholders',
			569, 572	622				shareholders meetings and,
					636			suspension of payments and,
							781, 783, 786	voluntary liquidations and,
					622			voting on,
							785, 792	winding up on,
			554	597, 607, 612		711		**Restitution**
								Retention of title, *see,* **Reservation of title**
								Revenue authorities
								preferential creditors and,
								Rights in rem
			533	578				bankruptcies and,
				611				debt collection and,
				579				draft European Union Bankruptcy Convention and, pledges and,
			530			674		**Rights of retention**
								Romalpa clauses, *see,* **Reservation of title**
								Sachwalters, *see,* **Administrators**
				609	625-626			**Salaries** balance sheets and,
	470	505, 508, 510	531, 549	593-594, 609				preferential creditors and,
							777	receivership and,

	EUROPE	BELGIUM	DENMARK	FRANCE	GERMANY	GREECE	IRELAND	ITALY
recovery of,								
setting aside,			101					
unreasonable,								
Sale of assets								
administrators and,		48						
advertisement of,				158				
auction by,								
bankruptcies and,								
below market value,			100-101					
going concern and,		54						
judicial,								
loans and,								
mortgages and,								
personal property and,				158				
pledges and,								
third parties and,								
Sale of companies					192			
Sale of property			94	158				
administrative receivers and,								
auctions by,		54	94		186			
compulsory,			96					
free market in,			96					
judicial sales and,				122				
receivership and,								
Sales								
assets of,						289		
bankruptcies and,								393
enforced,						289		
loans and,		61						
prohibition of,					217			
Schemes of arrangement							310-311, 336	
Revenue Commissioners and,							311	
Searches			72					
charges for,								
Secrecy, *see,* **Confidentiality**								
Security, *see also,* **Charges**								
assignment of,					185			
auditors and,								
chattels and,			96					
compositions and,								386
compulsory arrangements and,					193			
contracts and,								
costs and,								
creditors for,			71-72	121-122				
deposits as,								
employees and,								
guarantees and,								
insurance and,							348	
leases and,								
liens and					184		349	378
liquidators and,							348	
loans for,					184	260		
mortgages as,			71					379-380
personal,		28						
pledges and,					184			378-379
pledges and,					184			378-379

LUXEMBOURG	NETHERLANDS	NORWAY	PORTUGAL	SPAIN	SWEDEN	SWITZERLAND	UNITED KINGDOM	
					650			recovery of,
								setting aside,
		512						unreasonable,
			527-530					**Sale of assets**
								administrators and,
								advertisement of,
		508	529, 551	611		699		auction by,
					646	699		bankruptcies and,
								below market value,
			529, 551					going concern and,
			528					judicial,
			529-530					loans and,
								mortgages and,
			529					personal property and,
			529					pledges and,
								third parties and,
								Sale of companies
								Sale of property
							778	administrative receivers and,
					643-644			auctions by,
					629			compulsory,
								free market in,
435								judicial sales and,
							771, 773	receivership and,
								Sales
								assets of,
								bankruptcies and,
								enforced,
								loans and,
								prohibition of,
							743, 745-746	**Schemes of arrangement**
								Revenue Commissioners and,
								Searches
								charges for,
								Secrecy, see, Confidentiality
								Security, see also, Charges
					625			assignment of,
								auditors and,
								chattels and,
								compositions and,
	456-460							compulsory arrangements and,
					625			contracts and,
								costs and,
		491		573-575	623-626	673-675	734-737	creditors for,
								deposits as,
415					625-626			employees and,
								guarantees and,
								insurance and,
						673		leases and,
					623-624			liens and,
								liquidators and,
								loans for,
415					623			mortgages as,
								personal,
415								pledges and,
								pledges and,

	EUROPE	BELGIUM	DENMARK	FRANCE	GERMANY	GREECE	IRELAND	ITALY
property over				159-160	183-185			
registration of,			71-72				324	
rehabilitation and,				148				
rent and,								
replacement of,		60						380
reservation of title and,				122	184			380
set off and,		28						380
setting aside,								
social security authorities and,								
taxes and,								
types of,								378-380
vehicles over,			71, 93					
voluntary arrangements and,					201			
Segregation					184-186			
administrators and,					230, 231			
Seizure								
assets of,		30	76, 85, 87		190		308	
goods and,								
mortgages and,			76					
notice of,								
property and,								
publicity of,		30						
taxation and,							308	
time limits and,			103					
Sellers' right				166				
Service								
petitions of,			92					
Set off			71			265-266		
assets and,			97					
bankruptcies and,								393
compositions and,								
creditors and,			89					
debts and,			84	152				380
draft European Union Bankruptcy Convention and,	9							
invoices of,			101					
liquidations and,								
preferential creditors and,								
receivership and,								
recovery of,								
right of,					186			
security as,		28						
setting aside,								
suspension of payments and,								
time limits and,			101-102					
Settlements, *see also,* **Compositions**					189			
authorisation of,				152				
bankruptcies and,								
compulsory arrangements and,					196			
conflict of interest and,			107					
costs of,			97					
debt reduction and,			81-82					
enforcement of,					189			
liquidation of,			81					
moratoriums and,			82					
voluntary,			80, 82					
Share capital						255-256	306	373, 376

LUXEMBOURG	NETHERLANDS	NORWAY	PORTUGAL	SPAIN	SWEDEN	SWITZERLAND	UNITED KINGDOM	
						673		property over
					624			registration of,
								rehabilitation and,
								rent and,
								replacement of,
				575	626		736	reservation of title and,
				575		674	737	set off and,
		513						setting aside,
					625-626			social security authorities and,
					625			taxes and,
						673		types of,
								vehicles over,
								voluntary arrangements and,
								Segregation
								administrators and,
			550-551					**Seizure**
414		501	532, 555	580				assets of,
							740	goods and,
								mortgages and,
435			551				754	notice of,
								property and,
								publicity of,
								taxation and,
								time limits and,
								Sellers' right
								Service
			530					petitions of,
								Set off
439			550	605				assets and,
					634-635			bankruptcies and,
								compositions and,
		488						creditors and,
	476							debts and,
								draft European Union Bankruptcy Convention and,
								invoices of,
		501, 510						liquidations and,
	471							preferential creditors and,
							776	receivership and,
					651			recovery of,
								right of,
				575		674	737	security as,
		513						setting aside,
				587				suspension of payments and,
								time limits and,
								Settlements, *see also,* **Compositions**
								authorisation of,
	469							bankruptcies and,
								compulsory arrangements and,
								conflict of interest and,
								costs of,
								debt reduction and,
								enforcement of,
								liquidation of,
								moratoriums and,
								voluntary,
								Share capital

	EUROPE	BELGIUM	DENMARK	FRANCE	GERMANY	GREECE	IRELAND	ITALY
authorised,								
board of directors and,								
directors and,		26						
dividends and,					182-183			
increase in,				144	182			377
insufficient,		62						
loans of,								
loss of,		69-70						
maintenance of,					230			
minimum,			69					
nominal,								
ownership and,								
partnerships of,								
reductions in,					182, 228			
registration and,								
shareholders' meetings and,								377
supervisory boards and,			69					
undercapitalisation and,					230			
winding up and,								
Shareholders, *see also*								
Minority shareholders,								
Shareholders meetings								
accounts and,					213			
administration and,								
alert procedure and,				130				
annual reports and,								
auditors and,		56						
balance sheets and,					213			
bankruptcies and,						286-287		
stay of,								
changes in,							307	
compositions and,			88					
confidentiality of,					179			
creditors and,					228			
debt arrangements and,								
debtors of,		43-44						
directors as,				116				
dividends and,								
extraordinary general,		56						
information and,					182			
liabilities of,				116	179		306	373
limited liability of,				162				
liquidation compositions and,							357-358	
liquidations and,				161				
liquidators, dismissed by,			97-98					
loans by,								
management and,				153				
meetings of,		26						
number of,				119-120				
ownership and,								
profits and,					220			
protection of,								400
receivership and,								
rehabilitations and,				153				
resolutions of,							358	
rights of,					183			

LUXEMBOURG	NETHERLANDS	NORWAY	PORTUGAL	SPAIN	SWEDEN	SWITZERLAND	UNITED KINGDOM	
						667		authorised,
					620	667		board of directors and,
								directors and,
						668		dividends and,
						667		increase in,
								insufficient,
		487						loans of,
								loss of,
						668		maintenance of,
			524			667	729	minimum,
						666-667		nominal,
		486-487						ownership and,
		486						partnerships of,
					636			reductions in,
					639			registration and,
								shareholders' meetings and,
								supervisory boards and,
								undercapitalisation and,
437								winding up and,

Shareholders, *see also*
    Minority shareholders,
    Shareholders meetings

LUXEMBOURG	NETHERLANDS	NORWAY	PORTUGAL	SPAIN	SWEDEN	SWITZERLAND	UNITED KINGDOM	
								accounts and,
						766		administration and,
								alert procedure and,
					622			annual reports and,
								auditors and,
								balance sheets and,
						702		bankruptcies and,
						692		stay of,
								changes in,
						688		compositions and,
								confidentiality of,
								creditors and,
		499						debt arrangements and,
								debtors of,
410-411					622	668-669		directors as,
	453				620			dividends and,
								extraordinary general,
								information and,
	454		524, 527, 555-556		636, 653-654	667	739-740	liabilities of,
								limited liability of,
						705		liquidation compositions and,
					641		797-799	liquidations and,
								liquidators, dismissed by,
			528					loans by,
				569				management and,
								meetings of,
								number of,
						676-678		ownership and,
								profits and,
								protection of,
							779	receivership and,
								rehabilitations and,
								resolutions of,
	452							rights of,

	EUROPE	BELGIUM	DENMARK	FRANCE	GERMANY	GREECE	IRELAND	ITALY
rights of,				119, 120	183			
role of,	56							
supervisory boards and,					213			
suspension of payments and,								
types of,								
voluntary arrangements and,					204			
voting and,								
winding up and,					209-210			
Shareholders' meetings			70					
accounts and,								
administrators and,					236			
articles of association and,								
bankruptcies and,								
stay of,								
board of directors and,				117		257		
calling,					182			
compulsory arrangements and,					234			
damages and,					215			
decisions of,								
directors and,								
liquidation and,		57-58						
notice of,								
powers of,					183			374
publicity and,								
quorum and,								
resolutions on,					179, 180, 236			374
responsibilities of,					182			
share capital and,								377
supervisory boards and,								
voluntary liquidations and,					210, 213			
voting in,			70-71					314
winding up on,					207-208			
Shares, *see also*, **Share capital, Shareholders**								
bearer,								411
certificates,					181			
distribution of assets and,					213, 219			
inheritance and,								
ownership of,						258-259		
paid up,								
pledges as,								
preference,					181			
priority,								
purchase of own,								
registration of,								377
subscription to,								
title to,								
transfer of,		25		119, 120, 144, 153, 165		258	346	
types of,								
unpaid,								
voting rights and,				153				
Ships								

LUXEMBOURG	NETHERLANDS	NORWAY	PORTUGAL	SPAIN	SWEDEN	SWITZERLAND	UNITED KINGDOM	
				571-572				rights of,
					622			role of,
								supervisory boards and,
				594				suspension of payments and,
							733	types of,
								voluntary arrangements and,
	453							voting and,
								winding up and,
	453			572-573				**Shareholders' meetings**
								accounts and,
		484-485						administrators and,
	466							articles of association and,
						688		bankruptcies and,
								stay of,
								board of directors and,
								calling,
								compulsory arrangements and,
			525					damages and,
				568				decisions of,
		500, 510						directors and,
								liquidation and,
		484-485	525		622			notice of,
				572			730	powers of,
				573				publicity and,
		500		569, 572	622			quorum and,
								resolutions on,
								responsibilities of,
	452							share capital and,
								supervisory boards and,
								voluntary
		484-485	525				730	liquidations and,
								voting in,
								winding up on,
453		527	573, 574					**Shares,** see also, **Share capital, Shareholders**
				572				bearer,
						670		certificates,
								distribution of assets and,
	453							inheritance and,
					620			ownership of,
	453							paid up,
					620	668		pledges as,
411	452, 453, 454				622	670-671		preference,
								priority,
								purchase of own,
			573					registration of,
411, 413	452	490				670-671		subscription to,
								title to,
								transfer of,
			527					types of,
		527						unpaid,
411								voting rights and,
								Ships

	EUROPE	BELGIUM	DENMARK	FRANCE	GERMANY	GREECE	IRELAND	ITALY
auction of,								
draft European Union								
Bankruptcy Convention and,	9							
registration of,						261		
Small and medium-sized								
enterprises				114, 119		259		
Social security authorities								
bankruptcies and,								
preferential creditors and,		29, 38, 45		151	226	278-279	355	378
summons issued by,		60-61						
Sole traders			72-73	123, 125				
information on,						266		
liability of,								
registration of,								
Solicitors, *see,* **Lawyers**								
Sources of law			67-68	113-115	173-174	253	302-303, 333	372
Specific performance					190-191			
Spouses								
bankruptcies and,								
gifts to,				167				
rights of,				167				
transfer of assets to,		62						
Statutory demands							339-340	
Stay of bankruptcies								
applications for,								
auditors and,								
balance sheets and,								
board of directors and,								
creditors and,								
effect of,				148				
moratoriums and,								
officers and,								
procedure for,								
purpose of,								
rejection for,								
reorganisation and,								
shareholders and,								
shareholders' meetings and,								
termination of,								
Stay of proceedings								
creditors and,								
rehabilitations and,				140				
schemes of arrangements and,							310	
secondary liquidations and,	11							
Striking out							360	
Subordination agreements								
Subrogation								
Subsidiaries								
Subsidies								
Sufferance					190			
Summons								
creditors to,			78					
Supervision								
administration of,					232-233			
board of directors and,			69-70					

LUXEMBOURG	NETHERLANDS	NORWAY	PORTUGAL	SPAIN	SWEDEN	SWITZERLAND	UNITED KINGDOM	
				610				auction of,
								draft European Union
								Bankruptcy Convention and,
								registration of,
								Small and medium-sized
				586				**enterprises**
								Social security authorities
	467							bankruptcies and,
415	471		531, 550		625	685		preferential creditors and,
		484	532		619, 628			summons issued by,
								Sole traders
								information on,
							739	liability of,
		488						registration of,
								Solicitors, *see,* **Lawyers**
407	447-448	481-483	521-522	560-561	619	662	725	**Sources of law**
			532					**Specific performance**
								Spouses
				607				bankruptcies and,
								gifts to,
								rights of,
								transfer of assets to,
							741	**Statutory demands**
						688-693		**Stay of bankruptcies**
						690		applications for,
						689, 690		auditors and,
						689, 692		balance sheets and,
						689, 690		board of directors and,
						691		creditors and,
						688-690		effect of,
						708		moratoriums and,
						692		officers and,
						690-691		procedure for,
						688-690		purpose of,
						691		rejection for,
						689, 682-690		reorganisation and,
						692		shareholders and,
						689		shareholders' meetings and,
						692-693		termination of,
								Stay of proceedings
								creditors and,
								rehabilitations and,
								schemes of arrangements and,
								secondary liquidations and,
								Striking out
			524					**Subordination agreements**
			553-554					**Subrogation**
			524-555		620			**Subsidiaries**
								Subsidies
								Sufferance
								Summons
								creditors to,
								Supervision
								administration of,
								board of directors and,

	EUROPE	BELGIUM	DENMARK	FRANCE	GERMANY	GREECE	IRELAND	ITALY
court by,					232-233			
liquidators of,		63						
self-administration of,					239			
Supervisory boards					179			
appointment of,					182			
claims against,					239			
compulsory liquidations and,					246-247			
debt arrangements and,								
dismissals of,					182			
liquidators and,					216			
members of,				118				
powers of,				118-119	235			
priority shares and,								
shareholders' meetings and,					213			
term of office of,				118-119				
voluntary,								
voluntary liquidation and,					210, 211			
Sureties, *see*, **Guarantees**								
Survival	31-38		75-88	132-155	192-206	271-275	310-333	386-390
Suspension of payments, *see*, **Moratoriums**								
Syndikos, *see*, **Administrators**								
Takeovers								
Tax								
bankruptcies and,						279		
compositions and,								
debt arrangements and,								
directors and,					180			
distribution of assets and,					219			
employees and,					219			
liquidators and.					219-220		351-352	
preferential creditors and,					226		355	378
receivership and,							325, 330	
reprieves from payment and,								
seizure of goods and,							308	
VAT and,					219		352	
Terms of payment		36-37						
Third parties								
assets of,				96	184			
attachment of,								
bankruptcies and,								
charges and,								
contracts and,							350	
directors and,								
Draft European Union Bankruptcy Convention and,	9							
enforcement and,								382
financial restructuring and,								
intervention,						281		
liquidation and,								
mortgages of,								379
pledges and,		28	103					378
preferential interests and,		28	99					
receivership and,								
registration and,								

LUXEMBOURG	NETHERLANDS	NORWAY	PORTUGAL	SPAIN	SWEDEN	SWITZERLAND	UNITED KINGDOM	
						664		court by,
								liquidators of,
								self-administration of,
								Supervisory boards
	452							appointment of,
								claims against,
		494-495						compulsory liquidations and,
								debt arrangements and,
								dismissals of,
								liquidators and,
								members of,
								powers of,
	453							priority shares and,
	452							shareholders' meetings and,
								term of office of,
	454							voluntary,
								voluntary liquidation and,
								Sureties, *see,* **Guarantees**
415-430	460-464	492-499	534-545	582-589	630-638	681-705	743-780	**Survival**
								Suspension of payments, *see,*
								Moratoriums
								Syndikos, *see,* **Administrators**
					620			**Takeovers**
								Tax
	467							bankruptcies and,
					636			compositions and,
		495						debt arrangements and,
								directors and,
								distribution of assets and,
		503						employees and,
								liquidators and.
								preferential
415	471	505, 510	531, 550					creditors and,
								receivership and,
417								reprieves from payment and,
							750	seizure of goods and,
		509						VAT and,
								Terms of payment
								Third parties
			607					assets of,
	459							attachment of,
434			604					bankruptcies and,
						673		charges and,
								contracts and,
410, 441								directors and,
								Draft European Union Bankruptcy
								Convention and,
								enforcement and,
			543					financial restructuring and,
								intervention,
		506						liquidation and,
								mortgages of,
								pledges and,
								preferential interests and,
							775	receivership and,
						675-676		registration and,

	EUROPE	BELGIUM	DENMARK	FRANCE	GERMANY	GREECE	IRELAND	ITALY
reservation of title and,								
sale of assets and,								
suspension of payments and,		38						
transactions of,					232			399
winding up and,								
Time limits								
actions on,								
bankruptcies and,								
claims on,		34-35						
compositions and,								
compulsory liquidations and,					222-223			
contracts and,				141				
damages and,								
debts and,							357	
distribution of assets and,					214			
examiners and,					318-319			
leases and,								
moratoriums and,				147				
proof of debts and,		45						
recovery and,								
rescission and,					243-244			
seizure and,			103					
set off and,			101-102					
setting aside transactions and,			100-104					
share capital and,								
suspension of payments and,			100					
transactions at risk and,								
voiding transactions on,			76					
waiver arrangements and,					198			
winding up and,								
Transactions								
avoidance of,			99, 100					
challenging,					240-246			
disadvantageous,								
effects of,					240-246			
extortionate credit and,								
fraud and,								
judgments on,								
liquidations and,								
performance of,					225			
risk at,					240-246	293-295	360-362	398-399
setting aside,			99-104	162				
time limits and,			100					
third parties of,					232			399
undervalue, at,								
Transfers of undertakings	14-19							
administration and,								
consultation of employees and,	17							
contracts of employment and,	14							
employees and,		52						
European Court of Justice's opinions on,	15-16, 19							
going concerns and,							331	
insolvent companies and,	15							

LUXEMBOURG	NETHERLANDS	NORWAY	PORTUGAL	SPAIN	SWEDEN	SWITZERLAND	UNITED KINGDOM	
								reservation of title and,
		514	529					sale of assets and,
								suspension of payments and,
		502						transactions of,
								winding up and,
								Time limits
						716		actions on,
				609	645			bankruptcies and,
								claims on,
					632	682, 684		compositions and,
								compulsory liquidations and,
								contracts and,
								damages and,
								debts and,
					651-652			distribution of assets and,
								examiners and,
								leases and,
						682		moratoriums and,
								proof of debts and,
					649-650			recovery and,
								rescission and,
								seizure and,
								set off and,
								setting aside transactions and,
						667		share capital and,
		512, 514-515					801	suspension of payments and,
								transactions at risk and,
437								voiding transactions on,
								waiver arrangements and,
								winding up and,
								Transactions
						710-711		avoidance of,
								challenging,
								disadvantageous,
								effects of,
							802	extortionate credit and,
							803	fraud and,
						710-711		judgments on,
							783, 788	liquidations and,
								performance of,
438-440	474-476	511-516			647-654	706-711	801-804	risk at,
		512, 514	550				783, 801-804	setting aside,
		512, 514-515					802	time limits and,
		514						third parties of,
		512					801	undervalue, at,
								Transfers of undertakings
							764-765	administration and,
								consultation of employees and,
								contracts of employment and,
								employees and,
								European Court of Justice's opinions on,
								going concerns and,
								insolvent companies and,

	EUROPE	BELGIUM	DENMARK	FRANCE	GERMANY	GREECE	IRELAND	ITALY
management and,	19							
privatisation and,	17							
public entities and,	17-18							
receivership and,							329-330	
rescues and,	18							
Treuhand					199, 205-206			
Trustees, *see also,* **Trusts**								
appointment of,								
courts and,								
duties of,								
reports of,								
supervisory authorities and,								
Trusts, *see also,* **Trustees**								
assets and,			96		198			
breaches of,							358	
contracts and,			95-96					
creditors and,			93					
discharge of,			93-94					
distribution of assets and,							331	
liability and,					203			
management of,			107					
receivership and							331	
role of,		109						
winding up and,			93					
Undue influence					225			
Unincorporated associations								
United States								
Chapter 11 and,					177-178			
Federal Bankruptcy Code 1978,	13							
Unjust enrichment					215			
Utilities								
Valuation								
assets of,			77, 84					
VAT					219			
Vehicles								
attachment of,			73					
security over,			71, 93					
Vereffenaars, *see,* **Liquidators**								
Voidable transactions			78					
administrators and,			95					
time limits and,			76					
Voluntary arrangements								
actions and,					210			
applications for,					196-197, 202			
board of management and,					210			
commencement of proceedings and,					199			
confirmation of,					200-201			
considerations for,					196, 211			
creditors' committees and,					199-200, 202			
directors and,					210			
dividends and,					197			

LUXEMBOURG	NETHERLANDS	NORWAY	PORTUGAL	SPAIN	SWEDEN	SWITZERLAND	UNITED KINGDOM	
								management and,
								privatisation and,
								public entities and,
								receivership and,
								rescues and,
								Treuhand
								Trustees, *see also,* **Trusts**
					654			appointment of,
					654-655			courts and,
					655-656			duties of,
					656			reports of,
					654-657			supervisory authorities and,
								Trusts, *see also,* **Trustees**
								assets and,
								breaches of,
								contracts and,
								creditors and,
								discharge of,
								distribution of assets and,
	507							liability and,
								management of,
								receivership and
								role of,
								winding up and,
								Undue influence
							726,	**Unincorporated associations**
							738-839	
								United States
					637		750	Chapter 11 and,
								Federal Bankruptcy Code 1978,
						711		**Unjust enrichment**
							812	**Utilities**
								Valuation
								assets of,
								VAT
								Vehicles
								attachment of,
								security over,
								Vereffenaars, *see,* **Liquidators**
								Voidable transactions
								administrators and,
								time limits and,
								Voluntary arrangements
								actions and,
								applications for,
								board of management and,
								commencement of proceedings and,
								confirmation of,
								considerations for,
								creditors' committees and,
								directors and,
								dividends and,

	EUROPE	BELGIUM	DENMARK	FRANCE	GERMANY	GREECE	IRELAND	ITALY
effect of,					196			
employment contracts and,					210			
enforcement of,					201			
fraud and,					205			
hearings on,					199, 200			
liquidation,					197-198			
management of,					203-204			
misrepresentation and,					201			
officers and,					204			
procedure on,					199-202			
professional assistance on,					197			
purpose and,					196			
rejection of,					199			
revival clause and,					201, 205			
security and,					201			
shareholders and,					204			
meetings and,					210			
termination of,					204-206			
time extension and,					197			
voting on,					200			
waiver of,					197-198, 201, 204			
Voluntary liquidations								
board of directors and,								
causes of,								
creditors and,								
committees on,								
resolutions on,								
statement of affairs and,								
creditors' meetings and,								
definition of,								
distribution of assets and,								
liquidators and,							346-348	
management of,								
members,								
balance sheets and,					212-213			
damages and,					215			
effect of,					210-211			
expenses of,								
procedure on,								
publication of,					212			
purpose of,					210-211			
resolutions on,					210			
shareholders' meetings and,					213			
statutory declarations on,								
supervisory boards and,					210, 211			
management of,							348-350	
resolutions on,								
termination of,					221			
transfer of shares and,							346	
Voting								
compositions on,			85-86					
compulsory arrangements and,					194-195			
creditors' committees and,								
creditors' meetings and,								

LUXEMBOURG	NETHERLANDS	NORWAY	PORTUGAL	SPAIN	SWEDEN	SWITZERLAND	UNITED KINGDOM	
								effect of,
								employment contracts and,
								enforcement of,
								fraud and,
								hearings on,
								liquidation,
								management of,
								misrepresentation and,
								officers and,
								procedure on,
								professional assistance on,
								purpose and,
								rejection of,
								revival clause and,
								security and,
								shareholders and,
								meetings and,
								termination of,
								time extension and,
								voting on,
								waiver of,
								Voluntary liquidations
		489						board of directors and,
		500						causes of,
		500					784	creditors and,
							786-787	committees on,
							786	resolutions on,
							786	statement of affairs and,
							784, 785-786	creditors' meetings and,
		489						definition of,
							781	distribution of assets and,
								liquidators and,
								management of,
								members,
								balance sheets and,
								damages and,
								effect of,
							785	expenses of,
							785-786	procedure on,
								publication of,
								purpose of,
							785	resolutions on,
								shareholders' meetings and,
							785	statutory declarations on,
								supervisory boards and,
								management of,
							781, 783, 793	resolutions on,
								termination of,
								transfer of shares and,
								Voting
	463				635			compositions on,
								compulsory arrangements and,
			549					creditors' committees and,
			539				791	creditors' meetings and,

	EUROPE	BELGIUM	DENMARK	FRANCE	GERMANY	GREECE	IRELAND	ITALY
debt arrangement and,								
liquidations on,			89, 91					
moratoriums and,								
participation rights and,								
resolutions on,								
shareholders and,								
shareholders' meetings in,			70-71					374
shares and,				153				
suspension of								
payments on,								
voluntary arrangements on,					200			
Wages, *see,* **Salaries**								
Winding up			89, 92		207-210			
account of							347	
advertising of,							340	
appeals and,								
assets and,								
realisation of,					210			
compulsory,								
conditions for,								
contracts and,					218			
creditors of,							343-344	
creditors' meetings and,							337-339	
delay and,								
directors and,							337, 357-358	
disputed debts and,								
effect of,								
employees and,							335-336	
judgments and,								
liquidations and,					216		333	
liquidators and,							349-350	
meetings and,							347	
partnerships and,								
petitions for,							339-341	
procedure on,							337-342	
publication of,					213, 216-217		343, 348, 358	
purpose of,								
reasons for,							333-334	
refusal of,								
registration of,					208			
reports on,							359	
resolutions on,					207-208		338, 348	
retrospectivity and,								
service of order of,							342	
share capital and,								
statement on,							337	
statutory demands and,							339-340	
stay of,								
third parties and,								
time limits and,								
trustees of,			93					
voluntary,							333-334, 337-339	
Writs		60	74					

LUXEMBOURG	NETHERLANDS	NORWAY	PORTUGAL	SPAIN	SWEDEN	SWITZERLAND	UNITED KINGDOM	
		496						debt arrangement and,
								liquidations on,
	462							moratoriums and,
						671-672		participation rights and,
					622			resolutions on,
	453							shareholders and,
		484-485	525				730	shareholders' meetings in,
								shares and,
								suspension of
				595				payments on,
								voluntary arrangements on,
								Wages, *see,* **Salaries**
		489						**Winding up**
437								account of
		503						advertising of,
437								appeals and,
								assets and,
								realisation of,
437								compulsory,
437								conditions for,
								contracts and,
								creditors of,
					654-655			creditors' meetings and,
								delay and,
437		502						directors and,
							741	disputed debts and,
437								effect of,
								employees and,
437								judgments and,
								liquidations and,
		507						liquidators and,
								meetings and,
							739	partnerships and,
		502						petitions for,
								procedure on,
437								publication of,
437								purpose of,
								reasons for,
							789	refusal of,
		502, 503						registration of,
								reports on,
								resolutions on,
		502						retrospectivity and,
								service of order of,
437								share capital and,
								statement on,
								statutory demands and,
						792		stay of,
		502						third parties and,
437								time limits and,
								trustees of,
								voluntary,
								Writs

	EUROPE	BELGIUM	DENMARK	FRANCE	GERMANY	GREECE	IRELAND	ITALY
Wrongful trading,			104					
damages for,								
Zwangsvergleichs, *see,* **Compulsory arrangements**			105-106					

LUXEMBOURG	NETHERLANDS	NORWAY	PORTUGAL	SPAIN	SWEDEN	SWITZERLAND	UNITED KINGDOM	
							750-751, 805-806	**Wrongful trading,**
								damages for,
								Zwangsvergleichs, *see,* **Compulsory arrangements**

Marc Pansu
Jacques Gautheyrou
Handbook of Soil Analysis
Mineralogical, Organic and Inorganic Methods

Marc Pansu
Jacques Gautheyrou

Handbook
of Soil Analysis

Mineralogical, Organic
and Inorganic Methods

with 183 Figures and 84 Tables

 Springer

Dr Marc Pansu
Centre IRD BP 64501
Avenue Agropolis 911
34394 Montpellier Cedex 5
France

E-mail : pansu@mpl.ird.fr

Jacques Gautheyrou
Avenue de Marinville 6
94100 St. Maur des Fossés
France

Updated English version, corrected by Daphne Goodfellow. The original French book "L'analyse du sol, minéralogique et minérale" by Marc Pansu and Jacques Gautheyrou, was published in 2003 by Springer-Verlag , Berlin Heidelberg New York.

Library of Congress Control Number: 2005938390

ISBN-10 3-540-31210-2 Springer Berlin Heidelberg New York
ISBN-13   978-3-540-31210-9 Springer Berlin Heidelberg New York

Springer is a part of Springer Science+Business Media
springer.com
© Springer-Verlag Berlin Heidelberg 2006
Printed in The Netherlands

Cover design: E. Kirchner, Heidelberg
Production: Almas Schimmel
Typesetting: SPI Publisher Services
Printing: Krips bv, Meppel
Binding: Stürtz AG, Würzburg

Printed on acid-free paper   30/3180/as 5 4 3 2 1   SPIN 12038787

FOREWORD

This new book by Marc Pansu and Jacques Gautheyrou provides a synopsis of the analytical procedures for the physicochemical analysis of soils. It is written to conform to analytical standards and quality control. It focuses on mineralogical, organic and inorganic analyses, but also describes physical methods when these are a precondition for analysis. It will help a range of different users to choose the most appropriate method for the type of material and the particular problems they have to face. The compiled work is the product of the experience gained by the authors in the laboratories of the Institute of Research for Development (IRD) in France and in tropical countries, and includes an extensive review of the literature. The reference section at the end of each chapter lists source data from pioneer studies right up to current works, such as, proposals for structural models of humic molecules, and itself represents a valuable source of information.

IRD soil scientists collected data on Mediterranean and tropical soils in the field from West and North Africa, Madagascar, Latin America, and South East Asia. Soil materials from these regions are often different from those found in temperate zones. As their analysis brought new problems to light, it was essential to develop powerful and specific physicochemical methods. Physicists, chemists and biologists joined forces with IRD soil scientists to contribute knowledge from their own disciplines thereby widening its scope considerably. This work is the fruit of these experiments as applied to complex systems, involving soils and the environment.

The methodological range is particularly wide and each chapter presents both simple analyses and analyses that may require sophisticated equipment, as well as specific skills. It is aimed both at teams involved in practical field work and at researchers involved in fundamental and applied research. It describes the principles, the physical and chemical basis of each method, the corresponding analytical procedures, and the constraints and limits of each. The descriptions are practical, easy to understand and implement. Summary tables enable a rapid overview of the data. Complex techniques are explained under the heading 'Principle' and concrete examples of methods include: spectra (near and far IR, UV-visible, ^{1}H-NMR, ^{13}C-NMR, ESR, ICP-AES, ICP-MS, X-ray fluorescence, EDX or WDX microprobe, neutron activation analysis), diffractograms (XRD, electron microdiffraction), thermograms (DTA, DTG, TGA), chromatograms (GPC, HPLC, ionic chromatography, exclusion chromatography), electrophoregrams, ion exchange methods, electrochemistry, biology, different physical separation techniques, selective dissolutions, and imagery.

The book will be valuable not only for researchers, engineers, technicians and students in soil science, but also for agronomists and ecologists and others in related disciplines, such as, analytical physical chemistry, geology, climatology, civil engineering and industries associated with soil. It is a basic work whose goal is to contribute to the scientific analysis of the environment. The methodologies it describes apply to a wide range of bioclimatic zones: temperate, arid, subtropical and tropical. As with the previous books by the same authors (Pansu, Gautheyrou and Loyer, 1998, Masson, Paris, Milan, Barcelona; Pansu, Gautheyrou and Loyer, 2001, Balkema, Lisse, Abington, Exton, Tokyo), this new book represents a reference work for our laboratories. We are confident its originality and ease of use will ensure its success.

Alain Aventurier, Director of Analytical Laboratories of CIRAD[1]
Christian Feller, Director of Research at IRD[2]
Pierre Bottner, Director of Research at CNRS[3]

---

[1] CIRAD, *Centre International pour la Recherche Agronomique et le Développement* (France).
[2] IRD, *Institut de Recherche pour le Développement (ex ORSTOM*, France).
[3] CNRS, *Centre National de la Recherche Scientifique* (France).

CONTENTS

PART 1 - MINERALOGICAL ANALYSIS

CHAPTER 1 **Water Content and Loss on Ignition**

1.1 Introduction 3
1.2 Water Content at 105°C (H_2O^-) 6
    1.2.1 Principle...6
    1.2.2 Materials..6
    1.2.3 Sample..6
    1.2.4 Procedure 7
    1.2.5 Remarks 7
1.3 Loss on Ignition at 1,000°C (H_2O^+) 8
    1.3.1 Introduction 8
    1.3.2 Principle...11
    1.3.3 Equipment..11
    1.3.4 Procedure 11
    1.3.5 Calculations 12
    1.3.6 Remarks 12
Bibliography 12

CHAPTER 2 **Particle Size Analysis**

2.1 Introduction 15
    2.1.1 Particle Size in Soil Science 15
    2.1.2 Principle...17
    2.1.3 Law of Sedimentation 18
    2.1.4 Conditions for Application of Stokes Law................................24
2.2 Standard Methods 26
    2.2.1 Pretreatment of the Sample 26
    2.2.2 Particle Suspension and Dispersion 31
    2.2.3 Pipette Method after Robinson-Köhn or Andreasen 35
    2.2.4 Density Method with Variable Depth..42
    2.2.5 Density Method with Constant Depth.......................................47
    2.2.6 Particle Size Analysis of Sands Only 48
2.3 Automated Equipment 50
    2.3.1 Introduction 50
    2.3.2 Method Using Sedimentation by Simple Gravity.....................51
    2.3.3 Methods Using Accelerated Sedimentation 53
    2.3.4 Methods Using Laser Scattering and Diffraction.....................54
    2.3.5 Methods Using Optical and Electric Properties.......................55
    2.3.6 Methods Allowing Direct Observations of the Particles...........55
    2.3.7 Methods Using Conductivity 56
References 56
Bibliography 58
    Generality 58

Pre-treatment...58
Pipette Method..61
Hydrometer Method 62
Instrumental Methods 62

CHAPTER 3 Fractionation of the Colloidal Systems

3.1 Introduction...65
3.2 Fractionation by Continuous Centrifugation..........................66
    3.2.1 Principle..66
    3.2.2 Theory 69
    3.2.3 Equipment and reagents 73
    3.2.4 Procedure..75
3.3 Pretreatment of the Extracted Phases 79
References..81
Bibliography 81

CHAPTER 4 Mineralogical Characterisations by X-Ray Diffractometry

4.1 Introduction...83
    4.1.1 X-Ray Diffraction and Mineralogy....................................83
    4.1.2 Principle...86
    4.1.3 XRD Instrumentation 87
4.2 Qualitative Diffractometry...90
    4.2.1 Overview of Preparation of the Samples 90
    4.2.2 Preparation for Powder Diagrams 90
    4.2.3 Preparation for Oriented Diagrams.................................94
    4.2.4 Pretreatment of Clays..99
    4.2.5 Qualitative Diffractometry 113
4.3 Quantitative Mineralogical Analysis 118
    4.3.1 Interest 118
    4.3.2 Quantitative Mineralogical Analysis by XRD..................118
    4.3.3 Multi-Instrumental Quantitative Mineralogical Analysis....124
References..126
Bibliography 127
    General...127
    Preparation of Oriented Aggregates on Porous Ceramic Plate 128
    Saturation of Clays by Cations 129
    Saturation, Solvation, Intercalation Complex, Dissolution 129
    Preparation of Iron Oxides...130
    Quantitative XRD...130

CHAPTER 5 Mineralogical Analysis by Infra-Red Spectrometry

5.1 Introduction 133
    5.1.1 Principle...133
    5.1.2 IR Instrumentation 135
5.2 IR Spectrometry in Mineralogy...138
    5.2.1 Equipment and Products 138
    5.2.2 Preparation of the Samples 139
    5.2.3 Brief Guide to Interpretation of the Spectra....................146
    5.2.4 Quantitative Analysis 152

5.3 Other IR Techniques 156
    5.3.1 Near-infrared Spectrometry (NIRS).. 156
    5.3.2 Coupling Thermal Measurements and FTIR Spectrometry of Volatile
        Products 158
    5.3.3 Infrared Microscopy 159
    5.3.4 Raman Scattering Spectroscopy 159
References...161
Chronobibliography 162

CHAPTER 6 **Mineralogical Separation by Selective Dissolution**

6.1 Introduction 167
    6.1.1 Crystallinity of Clay Minerals... 167
    6.1.2 Instrumental and Chemical Methods 169
    6.1.3 Selective Dissolution Methods 172
    6.1.4 Reagents and Synthetic Standards 174
6.2 Main Selective Dissolution Methods.. 180
    6.2.1 Acid Oxalate Method Under Darkness (AOD).......................... 180
    6.2.2 Dithionite-Citrate-Bicarbonate Method (DCB) 187
    6.2.3 EDTA Method 192
    6.2.4 Pyrophosphate Method.. 196
    6.2.5 Extraction in Strongly Alkaline Mediums 201
6.3 Other Methods, Improvements and Choices 206
    6.3.1 Differential Sequential Methods 206
    6.3.2 Selective Methods for Amorphous Products............................. 210
    6.3.3 Brief Overview to the Use of the Differential Methods 214
References 215

CHAPTER 7 **Thermal Analysis**

7.1 Introduction 221
    7.1.1 Definition... 221
    7.1.2 Interest.. 223
7.2 Classical Methods 226
    7.2.1 Thermogravimetric Analysis... 226
    7.2.2 Differential Thermal Analysis and Differential Scanning Calorimetry 235
7.3 Multi-component Apparatuses for Thermal Analysis.......................246
    7.3.1 Concepts... 246
    7.3.2 Coupling Thermal Analysis and Evolved Gas Analysis.................247
References 249
Chronobibliography 250

CHAPTER 8 **Microscopic Analysis**

8.1 Introduction 253
8.2 Preparation of the Samples 254
    8.2.1 Interest.. 254
    8.2.2 Coating and Impregnation, Thin Sections 255
    8.2.3 Grids and Replicas for Transmission Electron Microscopy 261
    8.2.4 Mounting the Samples for Scanning Electron Microscopy 263
    8.2.5 Surface Treatment (Shadowing, Flash-carbon, Metallization) 265

8.3 Microscope Studies.. 267
  8.3.1 Optical Microscopy 267
  8.3.2 Electron Microscopy, General Information 270
  8.3.3 Transmission Electron Microscopy, Micro-diffraction....................... 271
  8.3.4 Scanning Electron Microscopy... 279
  8.3.5 Ultimate Micro-analysis by X-Ray Spectrometry............................. 282
References 283
Chronobibliography 284

PART 2 - ORGANIC ANALYSIS

CHAPTER 9 **Physical Fractionation of Organic Matter**

9.1 Principle and Limitations 289
  9.1.1 Forms of Organic Matter in Soil...289
  9.1.2 Principle...289
  9.1.3 Difficulties 291
9.2 Methods 293
  9.2.1 Classification 293
  9.2.2 Extraction of Plant Roots 293
  9.2.3 Dispersion of the Particles..296
  9.2.4 Separation by Density. 309
  9.2.5 Particle Size Fractionations 314
  9.2.6 Precision of the Fractionation Methods 320
9.3 Conclusion and Outlook...321
References..322

CHAPTER 10 **Organic and Total C, N (H, O, S) Analysis**

10.1 Introduction 327
  10.1.1 Soil Organic Matter...327
  10.1.2 Sampling, Preparation of the Samples, Analytical Significance.......330
10.2 Wet Methods..333
  10.2.1 Total Carbon: General Information 333
  10.2.2 Organic Carbon by Wet Oxidation at the Temperature
        of Reaction 335
  10.2.3 Organic Carbon by Wet Oxidation at Controlled Temperature 340
  10.2.4 Organic Carbon by Wet Oxidation and Spectrocolorimetry.............342
  10.2.5 Total Nitrogen by Wet Method: Introduction 342
  10.2.6 Total Nitrogen by Kjeldahl Method and Titrimetry 344
  10.2.7 Kjeldahl N, Titration by Spectrocolorimetry....................................349
  10.2.8 Kjeldahl N, Titration by Selective Electrode 351
  10.2.9 Mechanization and Automation of the Kjeldahl Method..................353
  10.2.10 Modified Procedures for NO_3^-, NO_2^- and Fixed N 354
10.3 Dry Methods 355
  10.3.1 Total Carbon by Simple Volatilization..355
  10.3.2 Simultaneous Instrumental Analysis by Dry Combustion: CHN(OS)356
  10.3.3 CHNOS by Thermal Analysis 362

10.3.4 C and N Non-Destructive Instrumental Analysis 363
10.3.5 Simultaneous Analysis of the Different C and N Isotopes 364
References 365
Bibliography 367

CHAPTER 11 Quantification of Humic Compounds

11.1 Humus in Soils 371
11.1.1 Definitions 371
11.1.2 Role in the Soil and Environment 373
11.1.3 Extractions 374
11.2 Main Techniques 375
11.2.1 Extraction 375
11.2.2 Quantification of the Extracts 379
11.2.3 Precision and Correspondence of the Extraction Methods 383
11.2.4 Purification of Humic Materials 389
11.3 Further Alternatives and Complements Methods 392
11.3.1 Alternative Method of Extraction 392
11.3.2 Fractionation of the Humin Residue 392
References 395
Humic Materials 395
Extraction, Titration, Purification and Fractionation of Humic Materials 396

CHAPTER 12 Characterization of Humic Compounds

12.1 Introduction 399
12.1.1 Mechanisms of Formation 399
12.1.2 Molecular Structure 400
12.2. Classical Techniques 401
12.2.1 Fractionation of Humic Compounds 401
12.2.2 Titration of the Main Functional Groups 408
12.2.3 UV–Visible Spectrometry 410
12.2.4 Infra-Red Spectrography 413
12.3 Complementary Techniques 415
12.3.1 Improvements in Fractionation Technologies 415
12.3.2 Titration of Functional Groups 418
12.3.3 Characterization by Fragmentation 419
12.3.4 Nuclear Magnetic Resonance (NMR) 424
12.3.5 Fluorescence Spectroscopy 433
12.3.6 Electron Spin Resonance (ESR) Spectroscopy 435
12.3.7 Measurement of Molecular Weight and Molecular Size 437
12.3.8 Microscopic Observations 440
12.3.9 Other Techniques 441
References 442
Molecular Models 442
Fractionation, Determination of Molecular Weights and Molecular Sizes .. 443
Functional Group of Humic Compounds 445
Spectrometric Characterizations 446
UV–Visible, IR, Fluorescence, ESR Spectrometries 446
Nuclear Magnetic Resonance 447

Methods of Characterization by Fragmentation 449
Other Methods (Microscopy, X-ray, Electrochemistry, etc.) 451

CHAPTER 13 **Measurement of Non-Humic Molecules**

13.1 Introduction 453
13.1.1 Non-Humic Molecules.. 453
13.1.2 Soil Carbohydrates 453
13.1.3 Soil Lipids 456
13.1.4 Pesticides and Pollutants.. 457
13.2 Classical Techniques.. 458
13.2.1 Acid Hydrolysis of Polysaccharides 458
13.2.2 Purification of Acid Hydrolysates 462
13.2.3 Colorimetric Titration of Sugars 464
13.2.4 Titration of Sugars by Gas Chromatography.................................. 467
13.2.5 Quantification of Total Lipids.. 472
13.2.6 Quantification of the Water-Soluble Organics 474
13.3 Complementary Techniques 475
13.3.1 Carbohydrates by Gas Chromatography...475
13.3.2 Carbohydrates by Liquid Chromatography 475
13.3.3 Fractionation and Study of the Soil Lipid Fraction 478
13.3.4 Measurement of Pesticide Residues and Pollutants 483
References..492
Soil Carbohydrates...492
Soil Lipids 494
Aqueous Extract 495
Pesticides and Pollutants.. 495

CHAPTER 14 **Organic Forms of Nitrogen, Mineralizable Nitrogen
                        (and Carbon)**

14.1 Introduction 497
14.1.1 The Nitrogen Cycle..497
14.1.2 Types of Methods 499
14.2 Classical Methods..500
14.2.1 Forms of Organic Nitrogen Released by Acid Hydrolysis 500
14.2.2 Organic Forms of Nitrogen: Simplified Method 509
14.2.3 Urea Titration 511
14.2.4 Potentially Available Nitrogen: Biological Methods.........................513
14.2.5 Potentially Mineralizable Nitrogen: Chemical Methods...................521
14.2.6 Kinetics of Mineralization..526
14.3 Complementary Methods 531
14.3.1 Alternative Procedures for Acid Hydrolysis....................................531
14.3.2 Determination of Amino Acids 532
14.3.3 Determination of Amino Sugars..535
14.3.4 Proteins and Glycoproteins (glomalin)...538
14.3.5 Potentially Mineralizable Nitrogen by EUF 538

References 540
  Organic Nitrogen Forms: General Articles 540
  Nitrogen Forms by Acid Hydrolysis and Distillation 541
  Improvement of Acid Hydrolysis 541
  Determination of Amino Acids 541
  Determination of Amino Sugars..542
  Glomalin...542
  Urea Titration...543
  Potentially Mineralizable Nitrogen: General Papers 543
  Potentially Mineralizable Nitrogen: Biological Methods 544
  Potentially Mineralizable Nitrogen: Chemical Methods..............................545
  Potentially Mineralizable Nitrogen by EUF 545
  Mineralization Kinetics 546

PART 3 - INORGANIC ANALYSIS – Exchangeable and Total Elements

CHAPTER 15 **pH Measurement**

15.1 Introduction 551
  15.1.1 Soil pH 551
  15.1.2 Difficulties 553
  15.1.3 Theoretical Aspects 554
15.2 Classical Measurements.. 556
  15.2.1 Methods... 556
  15.2.2 Colorimetric Method... 557
  15.2.3 Electrometric Method 560
  15.2.4 Electrometric Checking and Calibration...................................... 564
  15.2.5 Measurement on Aqueous Soil Suspensions 565
  15.2.6 Determination of the pH-K and pH-Ca 567
  15.2.7 Measurement on Saturated Pastes 567
  15.2.8 Measurement on the Saturation Extract....................................... 568
  15.2.9 Measurement of the pH-NaF 569
15.3 In Situ Measurements 570
  15.3.1 Equipment.. 570
  15.3.2 Installation in the Field 570
  15.3.3 Measurement on Soil Monoliths... 572
References 574
Bibliography 575
Appendix.. 576
  Appendix 1: Table of Electrode Potentials 576
  Appendix 2: Constants of Dissociation of Certain Equilibriums.................. 577
  Appendix 3: Buffer Solutions... 577
  Appendix 4: Coloured Indicators.. 579

CHAPTER 16 **Redox Potential**

16.1 Definitions and Principle 581
16.2 Equipment and Reagents 583
  16.2.1 Electrodes... 583
  16.2.2 Salt Bridge for Connection 584
  16.2.3 System of Measurement 584
  16.2.4 Calibration Solutions.. 585

16.3 Procedure.. 585
   16.3.1 Pretreatment of the Electrode 585
   16.3.2 Measurement on Soil Sample....................................... 586
   16.3.3 Measurement on Soil Monolith 586
   16.3.4 In Situ Measurements... 587
   16.3.5 Measurement of Oxygen Diffusion Rate 588
   16.3.6 Colorimetric Test of Eh 589
References 589
Bibliography 590

CHAPTER 17 **Carbonates**

17.1 Introduction 593
17.2 Measurement of Total Carbonates............................... 595
   17.2.1 Introduction 595
   17.2.2 Volumetric Measurement by Calcimetry 596
   17.2.3 Acidimetry... 599
17.3 Titration of Active Carbonate 601
   17.3.1 Principle... 601
   17.3.2 Implementation.. 601
   17.3.3 Index of Chlorosis Potential 603
References.. 604

CHAPTER 18 **Soluble Salts**

18.1 Introduction 605
18.2 Extraction 606
   18.2.1 Soil/solution Ratio... 606
   18.2.2 Extraction of Saturated Paste 607
   18.2.3 Diluted Extracts 608
   18.2.4 In Situ Sampling of the Soil Water................................ 609
   18.2.5 Extracts with Hot Water 610
18.3 Measurement and Titration 610
   18.3.1 Electrical Conductivity of Extracts................................ 610
   18.3.2 In Situ Conductivity.. 613
   18.3.3 Total Dissolved Solid Material 614
   18.3.4 Soluble Cations 615
   18.3.5 Extractable Carbonate and Bicarbonate (Alkalinity) 616
   18.3.6 Extractable Chloride 618
   18.3.7 Extractable Sulphate, Nitrate and Phosphate.............. 620
   18.3.7 Extractable Boron.. 620
   18.3.8 Titration of Extractable Anions by Ionic Chromatography............... 622
   18.3.9 Expression of the Results.. 625
References.. 626

CHAPTER 19 **Exchange Complex**

19.1 Introduction 629
19.2 Origin of Charges.. 630
   19.2.1 Ionic Exchange 630

19.2.2 Exchange Complex 631
19.2.3 Theory 633
References..636
Chronobibliography..637

CHAPTER 20 Isoelectric and Zero Charge Points

20.1 Introduction 645
20.1.1 Charges of Colloids 645
20.1.2 Definitions...647
20.1.3 Conditions for the Measurement of Charge.....................649
20.2 Main Methods 651
20.2.1 Measurement of pH0 (PZSE), Long Equilibrium Time.....................651
20.2.2 Point of Zero Salt Effect (PZSE), Short Equilibrium Time 652
References..655

CHAPTER 21 Permanent and Variable Charges

21.1 Introduction 657
21.2 Main Methods.. 661
21.2.1 Measurement of Variable Charges 661
21.2.2 Determination of Permanent Charges............................. 662
References 664
Bibliography 665

CHAPTER 22 Exchangeable Cations

22.1 Introduction 667
22.1.1 Exchangeable Cations of Soil 667
22.1.2 Extracting Reagents.. 668
22.1.3 Equipment... 669
22.2 Ammonium Acetate Method at pH 7 671
22.2.1 Principle 671
22.2.2 Procedure 671
22.3 Automated Continuous Extraction 674
References 674
Bibliography 676

CHAPTER 23 Exchangeable Acidity

23.1 Introduction 677
23.1.1 Origin of Acidity.. 677
23.1.2 Aims of the Analysis.. 678
23.2 Method... 680
23.2.1 Principle 680
23.2.2 Reagents 680
23.2.3 Procedure 681
23.3 Other Methods 683
References 684
Chronobibliography 685

CHAPTER 24 Lime Requirement

24.1 Introduction 687
   24.1.1 Correction of Soil Acidity.. 687
   24.1.2 Calculation of Correction.. 688
24.2 SMP Buffer Method 690
   24.2.1 Principle 690
   24.2.2 Reagents 691
   24.2.3 Procedure 691
   24.2.4 Remarks 692
References 693
Chronobibliography 693

CHAPTER 25 Exchange Selectivity, Cation Exchange Isotherm

25.1 Introduction 697
25.2 Determination of the Exchange Isotherm............................... 702
   25.2.1 Principle 702
   25.2.2 Reagents 702
   25.2.3 Procedure... 703
   25.2.4 Remarks 704
References.. 705
Chronobibliography.. 706

CHAPTER 26 Cation Exchange Capacity

26.1 Introduction 709
   26.1.1 Theoretical Aspects 709
   26.1.2 Variables that Influence the Determination of CEC.................... 711
26.2 Determination of Effective CEC by Summation (ECEC) 718
   26.2.1 Principle... 718
   26.2.2 Alternative Methods... 718
26.3 CEC Measurement at Soil pH in Not-Buffered Medium 719
   26.3.1 Principle... 719
   26.3.2 Methods Using Not-Buffered Metallic Salts 719
   26.3.3 Procedure Using Not-Buffered Organo Metallic Cations 722
   26.3.4 Not-Buffered Methods Using Organic Cations 728
26.4 CEC Measurement in Buffered Medium 730
   26.4.1 Buffered Methods — General Information 730
   26.4.2 Ammonium Acetate Method at pH 7.0...................................... 732
   26.4.3 Buffered Methods at pH 8.0–8.6... 738
   26.4.4 Buffered Methods at Different pH 743
References.. 745
Bibliography 750
   CEC General Theory.. 750
   Barium Method at soil pH 751
   Buffered Method at pH 7.0 751
   Cobaltihexamine CEC 752
   Silver-Thiourea 753
   CEC with Organic Cations (Coloured Reagents) 753
   Buffered Methods at pH 8.0–8.6... 753
   Barium Chloride-Triethanolamine at pH 8.1 753

CHAPTER 27 **Anion Exchange Capacity**

27.1 Theory 755
27.2 Measurement 758
27.2.1 Principle...758
27.2.2 Method 760
27.3 Simultaneous Measurement of AEC, EC, CEC and net CEC 760
27.3.1 Aim 760
27.3.2 Description 761
References..763

CHAPTER 28 **Inorganic Forms of Nitrogen**

28.1 Introduction 767
28.1.1 Ammonium, Nitrate and Nitrite 767
28.1.3 Sampling Problems 768
28.1.4 Analytical Problems 768
28.2 Usual Methods 769
28.2.1 Extraction of Exchangeable Forms...769
28.2.2 Separation by Micro-Diffusion..770
28.2.3 Colorimetric Titration of Ammonium...773
28.2.4 Colorimetric Titration of Nitrites...775
28.2.5 Colorimetric Titration of Nitrates 778
28.2.6 Extracted Organic Nitrogen..779
28.3 Other Methods 780
28.3.1 Nitrate and Nitrite by Photometric UV Absorption 780
28.3.2 Ammonium Titration Using a Selective Electrode 782
28.3.3 Measurement of Nitrates with an Ion-Selective Electrode.............785
28.3.4 In situ Measurement 788
28.3.5 Non-Exchangeable Ammonium 790
References 791
Bibliography 792

CHAPTER 29 **Phosphorus**

29.1 Introduction 793
29.2 Total Soil Phosphorus 794
29.2.1 Introduction 794
29.2.2 Wet Mineralization for Total Analyses...795
29.2.3 Dry Mineralization 798
29.3 Fractionation of Different Forms of Phosphorus...............................799
29.3.1 Introduction 799
29.3.2 Sequential Methods 800
29.3.3 Selective Extractions – Availability Indices 804
29.3.4 Isotopic Dilution Methods...813
29.3.5 Determination of Organic Phosphorus..814
29.4 Retention of Phosphorus...818
29.4.1 Introduction 818
29.4.2 Determination of P Retention..819

29.5 Titration of P in the Extracts 821
    29.5.1 Introduction 821
    29.5.2 Titration of *Ortho*-phosphoric P by Spectrocolorimetry 823
    29.5.3 P Titration by Atomic Spectrometry 828
    29.5.4 Titration of Different Forms of P by ^{31}P NMR 828
    29.5.5 Separation of P Compounds by Liquid Chromatography 829
29.6 Direct Speciation of P in situ, or on Extracted Particles 830
References 830
Chronobibliography 833

CHAPTER 30 **Sulphur**

30.1 Introduction 835
    30.1.1 Sulphur Compounds 835
    30.1.2 Mineralogical Studies 838
30.2 Total Sulphur and Sulphur Compounds 839
    30.2.1 Characteristics of Fluviomarine Soils 839
    30.2.2 Soil Sampling and Sample Preparation 840
    30.2.3 Testing for Soluble Sulphur Forms 841
    30.2.4 Titration of Total Sulphur 842
    30.2.5 Total S Solubilisation by Alkaline Oxidizing Fusion 843
    30.2.6 Total Solubilisation by Sodium Hypobromite in Alkaline Medium.... 844
    30.2.7 S titration with Methylen Blue Colorimetry 845
    30.2.8 Sulphate Titration by Colorimetry with Methyl Thymol Blue 850
    30.2.9 Total Sulphur by Automated Dry CHN(OS) Ultimate Analysis 853
    30.2.10 Titration of Total SO_4^{2-}-S by Ionic Chromatography 855
    30.2.11 Total S Titration by Plasma Emission Spectrometry 857
    30.2.12 Titration by X-ray Fluorescence 857
    30.2.13 Titration by Atomic Absorption Spectrometry 857
    30.2.14 Analytical Fractionation of Sulphur Compounds 858
    30.2.15 Titration of Organic S bound to C 859
    30.2.16 Titration of Organic S not bound to C 861
    30.2.17 Extraction and Titration of Soluble Sulphides 863
    30.2.18 Titration of Sulphur in Pyrites 865
    30.2.19 Titration of Elementary Sulphur 867
    30.2.20 Titration of Water Soluble Sulphates 869
    30.2.21 Titration of Na_3-EDTA Extractable Sulphates 871
    30.2.22 Titration of Jarosite 873
    30.2.23 Sequential Analysis of S Forms 876
30.3 Sulphur of Gypseous Soils 878
    30.3.1 Gypseous Soils 878
    30.3.2 Preliminary Tests 879
    30.3.3 Extraction and Titration from Multiple Extracts 881
    30.3.4 Gypsum Determination by Acetone Precipitation 882
30.4 Sulphur and Gypsum Requirement of Soil 883
    30.4.1 Introduction 883
    30.4.2 Plant Sulphur Requirement 884
    30.4.3 Gypsum Requirement 886
References 888
Chronobibliography 890

CHAPTER 31 Analysis of Extractable and Total Elements

31.1 Elements of Soils 895
    31.1.1 Major Elements 895
    31.1.2 Trace Elements and Pollutants...897
    31.1.3 Biogenic and Toxic Elements 899
    31.1.4 Analysis of Total Elements 900
    31.1.5 Extractable Elements..901
31.2 Methods using Solubilization..901
    31.2.1 Total Solubilization Methods...901
    31.2.2 Mean Reagents for Complete Dissolutions 903
    31.2.3 Acid Attack in Open Vessel 906
    31.2.4 Acid Attack in Closed Vessel...911
    31.2.5 Microwave Mineralization 913
    31.2.6 Alkaline Fusion 915
    31.2.7 Selective Extractions 920
    31.2.8 Measurement Methods...925
    31.2.9 Spectrocolorimetric Analysis...927
    31.2.10 Analysis by Flame Atomic Emission Spectrometry.........................931
    31.2.11 Analysis by Flame Atomic Absorption Spectrometry 932
    31.2.12 Analysis of Trace Elements by Hydride and Cold Vapour AAS 937
    31.2.13 Analysis of Trace Elements by Electrothermal AAS 940
    31.2.14 Analysis by Inductively Coupled Plasma-AES 941
    31.2.15 Analysis by Inductively Coupled Plasma-Mass Spectrometry 946
31.3 Analysis on Solid Medium 952
    31.3.1 Method 952
    31.3.2 X-ray Fluorescence Analysis...954
    31.3.3 Neutron Activation Analysis 962
References 969

INDEX..975

PERIODIC TABLE OF THE ELEMENTS 993

Part 1

Mineralogical Analysis

Water Content and Loss on Ignition

1.1 Introduction

Schematically, a soil is made up of a solid, mineral and organic phase, a liquid phase and a gas phase. The physical and chemical characteristics of the solid phase result in both marked variability of water contents and a varying degree of resistance to the elimination of moisture.

For all soil analytical studies, the analyst must know the exact quantity of the solid phase in order to transcribe his results in a stable and reproducible form. The liquid phase must be separate, and this operation must not modify the solid matrix significantly (structural water is related to the crystal lattice).

Many definitions exist for the terms "moisture" and "dry soil". The water that is eliminated by moderate heating, or extracted using solvents, represents only one part of total moisture, known as hygroscopic water, which is composed of (1) the water of adsorption retained on the surface of solids by physical absorption (forces of van der Waals), or by chemisorption, (2) the water of capillarity and swelling and (3) the hygrometrical water of the gas fraction of the soil (ratio of the effective pressure of the water vapour to maximum pressure). The limits between these different types of water are not strict.

"Air-dried" soil, which is used as the reference for soil preparation in the laboratory, contains varying amounts of water which depend in particular on the nature of secondary minerals, but also on external forces (temperature, the relative humidity of the air). Some andisols or histosols that are air dried for a period of 6 months can still contain 60% of water in comparison with soils dried at 105°C, and this can lead to unacceptable errors if the analytical results are not compared with a more realistic reference for moisture.[1] Saline soils can also cause problems because of the presence of hygroscopic salts.

It is possible to determine remarkable water contents involving fields of force of retention that are sufficiently reproducible and representative (Table 1.1). These values can be represented in the form of capillary potential (pF), the decimal logarithm of the pressure in millibars needed to bring a sample to a given water content (Table 1.1). It should be noted that because of the forces of van der Waals, there can be differences in state, but not in form, between water likely to evaporate at 20°C and water that does not freeze at –78°C. The analyst defines remarkable points for example:

– *The water holding capacity*, water content where the pressure component of the total potential becomes more significant than the gravitating component; this depends on the texture and the nature of the mineral and approaches *field capacity* which, after suitable drainage, corresponds to a null gravitating flow.

– *The capillary frangible point*, a state of moisture where the continuous water film becomes monomolecular and breaks.

– *The points of temporary and permanent wilting* where the pellicular water retained by the bonding strength balances with osmotic pressure; in this case, except for some halophilous plants, the majority of plants can no longer absorb the water that may still be present in the soil.

– *The hygroscopic water* which cannot be easily eliminated in the natural environment as this requires considerable energy, hygroscopic water evaporates at temperatures above 100°C and does not freeze at –78°C.

– *The water of constitution* and hydration of the mineral molecules can only be eliminated at very high pressures or at high temperatures, with irreversible modification or destruction of the crystal lattice.

These types of water are estimated using different types of measurements to study the water dynamics and the mechanisms related to the mechanical properties of soils in agronomy and agricultural engineering, for example:

– usable reserves (UR), easily usable reserves (EUR), or reserves that are easily available in soil–water–plant relations.

– thresholds of plasticity, adhesiveness, liquidity (limits of Atterberg, etc.).

---

[1] It should be noted that for these types of soil, errors are still amplified by the ponderal expression (because of an apparent density that is able to reach 0.3) this is likely to make the analytical results unsuitable for agronomic studies.

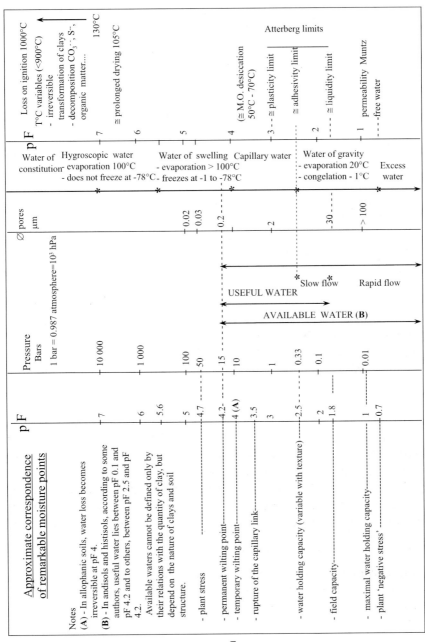

Table 1.1 - Approximate correspondence moistures – pressure – diameter of the pores – types of water and critical points in soils with respect to plant requirements

This brief summary gives an indication of the complexity of the concept of soil moisture and the difficulty for the analyst to find a scientifically defined basis for dry soil where the balance of the solid, liquid and gas phases is constant.

1.2 Water Content at 105°C (H_2O^-)

1.2.1 Principle

By convention, the term "moisture" is considered to be unequivocal. Measurement is carried out by gravimetry after drying at a maximum temperature of 105°C. This increase in temperature maintained for a controlled period of time, is sufficiently high to eliminate "free" forms of water and sufficiently low not to cause a significant loss of organic matter and unstable salts by volatilization. Repeatability and reproducibility are satisfactory in the majority of soils if procedures are rigorously respected.

1.2.2 Materials

– 50 × 30 mm borosilicate glass low form weighing bottle with ground flat top cap.
– Vacuum type Ø 200 mm desiccator made of borosilicate glass with removable porcelain floor, filled with anhydrous magnesium perchlorate [Mg(ClO4)2].
– Thermostatically controlled drying oven with constant speed blower for air circulation and exhausting through a vent in the top of oven – temperature uniformity ± 0.5–1°C.
– Analytical balance: precision 0.1 mg, range 100 g.

1.2.3 Sample

It is essential to measure water content on the same batch of samples prepared at the same time (fine earth with 2 mm particles or ground soil) for subsequent analyses. It should be noted that the moisture content of the prepared soil may change during storage (fluctuations in air moisture and temperature, oxidation of organic matter, loss or fixing of volatile substances, etc.).

This method can be considered "destructive" for certain types of soils and analyses, as the physical and chemical properties can be transformed. Samples dried at 105°C should generally not be used for other measurements.

1.2.4 Procedure

– Dry tared weighing bottles for 2 h at 105°C, let them cool in the desiccator and weigh the tare with the lid placed underneath: m_0
– Place about 5 g of air-dried soil (fine earth sieved through a 2 mm mesh) in the tare box and note the new weight: m_1
– Place the weighing bottles with their flat caps placed underneath in a ventilated drying oven for 4 h at 105°C (the air exit must be open and the drying oven should not be overloaded)
– Cool in the desiccator and weigh (all the lids of the series contained in the desiccator should be closed to avoid moisture input): m_2
– Again place the opened weighing bottles in the drying oven for 1 h at 105°C and weigh under the same conditions; the weight should be constant; if not, continue drying the weighing bottles until their weight is constant

$$\% \text{ water content at } 105°C = 100 \times \frac{m_1 - m_2}{m_1 - m_0}.$$

1.2.5 Remarks

The results can also be expressed in pedological terms of water holding capacity (HC) by the soil: $\text{HC} = 100 \times \dfrac{m_1 - m_2}{m_2 - m_0}$.

The point of measurement at 105°C with constant mass is empirical (Fig. 1.1). A temperature of 130°C makes it possible to release almost all "interstitial water", but this occurs to the detriment of the stability of organic matter. The speed of drying should be a function of the temperature, the surface of diffusion, the division of the solid, ventilation, pressure (vacuum), etc.

Respecting the procedure is thus essential:
– For andisols and histosols, the initial weighing should be systematically carried out after 6 h.
– For saline soils with large quantities of dissolved salts, the sample can be dried directly, soluble salts then being integrated into the "dry soil" or eliminated beforehand by treatment with water.

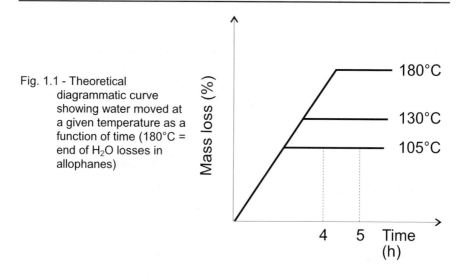

Fig. 1.1 - Theoretical
    diagrammatic curve
    showing water moved at
    a given temperature as a
    function of time (180°C =
    end of H_2O losses in
    allophanes)

1.3 Loss on Ignition at 1,000°C (H_2O^+)

1.3.1 Introduction

As we have just seen, the reference temperature (105°C) selected for the determination of the moisture content of a "dry soil" represents only a totally hypothetical state of the water that is normally referred to as H_2O^-.

When a sample undergoes controlled heating and the uninterrupted ponderal variations are measured, curves of "dehydration" are obtained whose inflections characterize losses in mass at certain critical temperatures (TGA).[1] If one observes the temperature curve compared to a thermically inert substance (Fig. 1.2), it is possible to determine changes in energy between the sample studied and the reference substance, this results in a change in the temperature which can be measured (DTA–DSC).[2]

– If the temperature decreases compared to the reference, an endothermic peak appears that characterizes loss of H_2O (dehydration), of OH^- (dehydroxylation), sublimation, or evaporation, or decomposition of certain substances, etc.

– If the temperature increases compared to the reference, an exothermic peak appears that characterizes transformations of crystalline structures, oxidations ($Fe^{2+} \rightarrow Fe^{3+}$), etc.

---

[2] *TGA* thermogravimetric analysis; *DTA* differential thermal analysis; *DSA* differential scanning calorimetry (cf. Chap. 7).

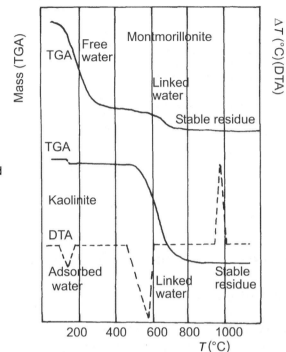

Fig. 1.2 - Schematized
        example of thermal
        analysis curves
        TGA (*solid line*) and
        DTA (*dashed line*)

The simultaneous analysis of the gases or vapours that are emitted and X-ray diffraction (cf. Chap. 4) of the modifications in structure make it possible to validate the inflections of the curves or the different endo- and exothermic peaks.

As can be seen in the highly simplified Table 1.2, the most commonly observed clays are completely dehydroxyled at 1,000°C, oxides at 400°C or 500°C, carbonates, halogens, sulphates, sulphides are broken down or dehydrated between 300°C and 1,000°C, and free or bound organic matter between 300°C and 500°C. The temperature of 1,000°C can thus be retained as a stable reference temperature for loss on ignition, the thermal spectra then being practically flat up to the peaks of fusion which generally only appear at temperatures higher than 1,500°C or even 2,500°C.

1.3.2 Principle

The sample should be gradually heated in oxidizing medium to 1,000°C and maintained at this temperature for 4 h.

Table 1.2 Dehydration and dehydroxylation of some clays, oxides and
          salts as a function of temperature in °C

type	name	dehydration[a]	dehydroxylation[b]
clays 1:1	Kaolinite–halloysite	350	1,000
clays 2:1	smectites – montmorillonite	370	1,000
clays 2:1	Illite – micas	350–370	1,000
clays 2:1	vermiculite	700	1,000
clays 2:1:1	chlorite	600	800
fibrous clays	Sepiolite– palygorskite allophane	300 200	800–900 900–1,000
iron oxides	Hematite α Fe_2O_3	(flat spectrum)	1,000
	goethite α FeO–OH	100	370
	magnetite Fe_2O_3	375	650
Al oxides	gibbsite γ-$Al(OH)_3$	100	350
Ca carbonate	Calcite–aragonite $CaCO_3$	–	950–1,000
Mg carbonate	magnesite $MgCO_3$	–	710
Ca–Mg carbonate	dolomie $CaMg(CO_3)_2$	–	800–940
halogenous compounds	sodium chloride NaCl	–	800 (fusion)
sulphate	gypsum $CaSO_4$, $2H_2O$	–	300
sulphide	pyrite FeS_2	–	615
organic compounds	free or linked organic matter	–	300–500

[a] Dehydration: loss of water adsorbed on outer or inner surfaces, with
or without reversible change in the lattice depending on the types of
clay, water organized in monomolecular film on surface oxygen
atoms or around exchangeable cations.

[b] dehydroxylation (+ decarbonatation and desulphurization reactions),
loss of water linked to lattice (OH^-), irreversible reaction or
destruction of the structure, water present in the cavities, O forming
the base of the tetrahedrons.

Loss on ignition is determined by gravimetry. It includes combined water linked to the crystal lattice plus a little residual non-structural adsorbed water, organic matter, possibly volatile soluble salts (F^-, S^{2-}) and carbonates (CO_3^{2-}, CO_2). The use of an oxidizing atmosphere is essential to ensure combustion of the organic matter and in particular oxidation of reduced forms of iron, this being accompanied by an increase in mass of the soils with minerals rich in Fe^{2+}. A complete analysis generally includes successive measurements of H_2O^- and H_2O^+ on the same sample.

1.3.3 Equipment

– Platinum or Inconel (Ni–Cr–Fe) crucible with cover, diameter 46 mm.
– Analytical balances (id. H_2O^-)
– Desiccator (id. H_2O^-)
– Muffle electric furnace (range 100–1,100°C) with proportional electronic regulation allowing modulation of the impulses with oscillation of about 1°C around the point of instruction; built-in ventilation system for evacuation of smoke and vapour
– Thermal protective gloves
– 300 mm crucible tong

1.3.4 Procedure

– Tare a crucible, heat it to 1,000°C and cool it in the desiccator with its
  lid on: m_0
– Introduce 2–3 g of air-dried soil crushed to 0.1 mm: m_1
– Dry in the drying oven at 105°C for 4 h
– Cool in the desiccator and weigh: m_2
– Adjust the lid of the crucible so it covers approximately 2/3 of the crucible and put it in the electric furnace
– Programme a heating gradient of approximately 6°C per minute with a 20-min stage at 300°C, then a fast rise at full power up to 1,000°C with a 4-h graduation step (the door of the furnace should only be closed after complete combustion of the organic matter)
– Cool the crucible in the desiccator and weigh: m_3

1.3.5 Calculations

$m_1 - m_0 =$ weight of air-dried soil
$m_1 - m_2 =$ moisture at 105°C

$m_2 - m_0 =$ weight of soil dried at 105°C

$m_2 - m_3 =$ loss on ignition

$$H_2O^-\% = 100 \times \frac{m_1 - m_2}{m_1 - m_0}$$

related to air-dried soil

$$H_2O^+\% = 100 \times \frac{m_2 - m_3}{m_2 - m_0}$$

related to soil dried at 105°C

1.3.6 Remarks

Knowing the moisture of the air-dried soil, it is possible to calculate the weight of air-dried soil required to work with a standard weight soil dried at 105°C, thus simplifying calculations during analyses of the samples.

To obtain the equivalent of 1 g of soil dried at 105°C, it is necessary to weigh:

$$\frac{100}{100 - wc}$$ with wc = % water content of air dried soil.

Platinum crucibles are very expensive and are somewhat volatile at 1,000°C, which means they have to be tared before each operation, particularly when operating in reducing conditions.

Combustion of organic matter with insufficient oxygen can lead to the formation of carbide of Pt, sulphides combine with Pt, chlorine attacks Pt, etc.

Bibliography

Campbell GS, Anderson RY (1998) Evaluation of simple transmission line oscillators for soil moisture measurement. *Comput. and Electron. Agric.*, 20, 31–44

Chin Huat Lim, Jackson ML (1982) Dissolution for total elemental analysis. In *Methods of Soil Analysis, Part 2*, Page A.L., Miller R.H., Kenny D.R. ed. Am. Soc. Agronomy, pp. 1–11

Dixon JB (1977) Minerals in soil environments. *Soil Sci. Soc. Am.*

Dubois J, Paindavoine JM (1982) Humidité dans les solides, liquides et gaz. *Techniques de l'ingénieur.*, (P 3760)

Gardner WH (1986) Water content. In *Methods of Soil Analysis, Part 1*, Klute ed. Am. Soc. Agronomy, Soil Sci. Soc. Am., pp. 493–544

Henin S (1977) *Cours de physique du sol: l'eau et le sol tome II.*, Editest, Paris: 1–164

Lane PNJ, Mackenzie DH, Nadler AD (2002) Note of clarification about: Field and laboratory calibration and test of TDR and capacitance techniques for indirect measurement of soil water content. *Aust. J. Soil Res.*, 40, 555–1386

Lane PNJ, Mackenzie DH (2001) Field and laboratory calibration and test of TDR and capacitance techniques for indirect measurement of soil. *Aust. J. Soil Res.*, 39, 1371–1386

NF ISO 11465 (X31-102) (1994) Détermination de la teneur pondérale en matière sèche et en eau. In *Qualité des sols, AFNOR*, 1996, 517–524

Rankin LK, Smajstrla AG (1997) Evaluation of the carbide method for soil moisture measurement in sandy soils. *Soil and Crop Science Society of Florida*, 56, pp. 136–139

Skierucha W (2000) Accuracy of soil moisture measurement by TDR technique. *Int. Agrophys.*, 14, 417–426

Slaughter DC, Pelletier MG, Upadhyaya SK (2001) Sensing soil moisture using NIR spectroscopy. *Appl. Eng. Agric.*, 17, 241–247

Walker JP, Houser PR (2002) Evaluation of the Ohm Mapper instrument for soil moisture measurement. *Soil Sci. Soc. Am. J.*, 66, 728–734

X31-505 (1992) Méthode de détermination du volume, apparent, et du contenu en eau des mottes. In *Qualité des sols, AFNOR*, 1996, 373–384

Yu C, Warrick AW, Conklin MH (1999) Derived functions of time domain reflectometry for soil moisture measurement. *Water Resour. Res.*, 35, 1789–1796

Particle Size Analysis

2.1 Introduction

2.1.1 Particle Size in Soil Science

Determination of grain-size distribution of a sample of soil is an important analysis for various topics in pedology, agronomy, sedimentology, and other fields such as road geotechnics.

Soil texture has an extremely significant influence on the physical and mechanical behaviours of the soil, and on all the properties related to water content and the movement of water, (compactness, plasticity, thrust force, slaking, holding capacity, moisture at different potentials, permeability, capillary movements, etc.).

Particle size analysis of a sample of soil, sometimes called "mechanical analysis", is a concept that has been the subject of much discussion (Hénin 1976). Soil is an organized medium including an assemblage of mineral and organic particles belonging to a continuous dimensional series. The first difficulty is to express the proportion of these different particles according to a standard classification, which is consequently somewhat artificial.

One classification scale was proposed by Atterberg (1912). Today this scale is recognized at different national and international levels and includes two main fractions: fine earth (clay, silts and sands with a grain diameter <2 mm) and coarse elements (gravels, stones with a grain diameter >2 mm). The particle size series (Fig. 2.1) for fine earth is generally expressed after analysis in three size fractions (clay fraction less than 0.002 mm, silt fraction from 0.002 to 0.02 mm, and sand fraction from 0.02 to 2 mm). In some countries, or for the purpose of a particular type of pedological interpretation, a more detailed scale of classes is sometimes used, for example five fractions: fine clays, silts, coarse silts or very fine sands, fine sands, and coarse sands (Fig. 2.1).

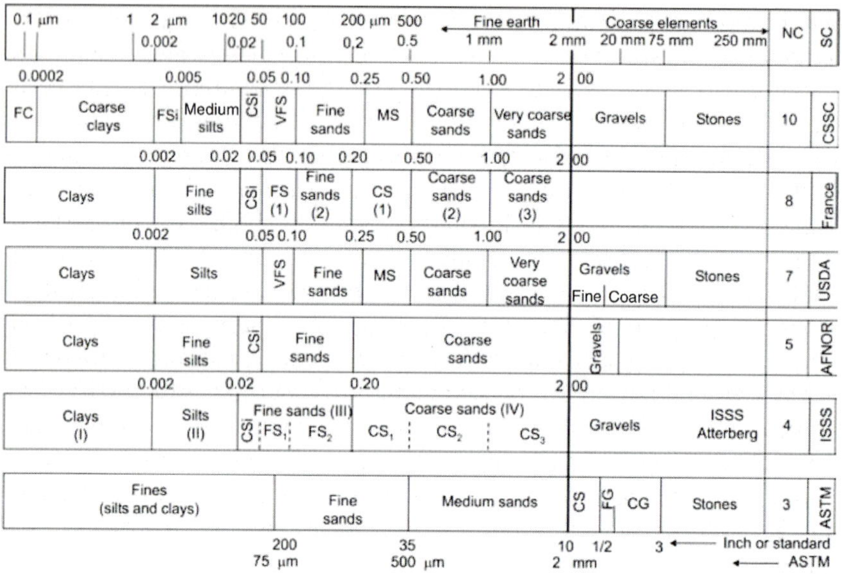

0.1 µm	1	2 µm	1020 50	100	200 µm 500	Fine earth	Coarse elements	NC	SC
		0.002	0.02	0.1	0.2	0.5	1 mm	2 mm 20 mm 75 mm 250 mm		

0.0002	0.005	0.05 0.10	0.25	0.50	1.00	2 00		
FC	Coarse clays	FSi	Medium silts	CSi	VFS	Fine sands	MS	Coarse sands	Very coarse sands	Gravels	Stones	10	CSSC

0.002	0.02 0.05 0.10	0.20	0.50	1.00	2 00
Clays	Fine silts	CSi	FS (1) Fine sands (2)	CS (1)	Coarse sands (2)	Coarse sands (3)	8	France

0.002	0.05 0.10	0.25	0.50	1.00	2 00
Clays	Silts	VFS	Fine sands	MS	Coarse sands	Very coarse sands	Gravels Fine Coarse	Stones	7	USDA

Clays	Fine silts	CSi	Fine sands	Coarse sands	Gravels	5	AFNOR

0.002	0.02	0.20	2 00
Clays (I)	Silts (II)	CSi FS₁ FS₂ Fine sands (III)	CS₁ CS₂ CS₃ Coarse sands (IV)	Gravels	ISSS Atterberg	4	ISSS

Fines (silts and clays)	Fine sands	Medium sands	CS FG CG	Stones	3	ASTM

200 75 µm ; 35 500 µm ; 10 1/2 2 mm ; 3 ← Inch or standard ASTM

Fig. 2.1. Ranges of particle size used for soils (NC number of classes; FSi fine silts, CSi coarse silts; FS, VFS, CS fine, very fine and coarse sands, respectively; FC fine clays; FG, CG fine gravels and coarse gravels), from top to bottom: (CSSC) Canadian Soil Survey Committee (1978): 10 particle size ranges < 2 mm; France (before 1987): 8 ranges; USDA United States Department of Agriculture (1975): 7 ranges; AFNOR Association Française de Normalisation (1987): 5 ranges; ISSS = International Soil Science Society (1966): 4 ranges; ASTM = American Society for Testing Materials (1985): 3 ranges

However, it should be noted that the terminology used does not provide much information about the real nature of the classes; thus clay defined as having a diameter equal to or less than 0.002 mm does not contain only clay corresponding to this mineralogical definition but can also contain sesquioxides, very fine silts, organic matter, carbonates, or compounds without colloidal properties. In the same way, sands, which generally result from fragmentation of the parent rock, can also include pseudo-sands, small ferruginous concretions, small limestone or cemented nodules that are resistant to dispersion treatments. The presence of these pseudo-sands can render the conclusions of particle size analysis illusory.

Another difficulty appears with the fractionation of elementary particles by dissociating them from their original assembly. Here too analytical standards exist, but it should be recognized that in certain cases the rupture of all the forces of cohesion is not complete (the case in hardened cemented soils), or on the contrary the forces are too energetic.

Lastly, particle size analysis accounts for the size but not for the shape of the particles, or their nature. If necessary, these are the subject of specific morphoscopic and mineralogical analyses. The result of particle size analysis is expressed in classes of which the relative proportions can be summed up in the form of a triangular diagram enabling the texture of a sample, a horizon, or a soil to be defined. Depending on the school, there are several different types of triangles that represent textures: GEPPA (*Groupe d'Etude des Problèmes de Pédologie Appliquée*, AFES, Grignon, France) includes 17 textural classes; the USDA's (United States Department of Agriculture) includes 12 classes (Gras 1988); others are simplified to a greater or lesser extent depending on the pedological or agronomic purpose of the study. Starting from these results, different interpretations are usually made in terms of pedogenesis (comparison of the vertical sand percents to check the homogeneity of a given material in a given soil profile, calculation of different indices of leaching, clay transport, etc.); others are more practical (definition of the relation of texture to hydric characteristics for the initial calculation of the amounts and frequencies of irrigation, or for the choice of machinery for cultivation.

2.1.2 Principle

Particle size analysis is a laboratory process, which initially causes dissociation of the material into elementary particles; this implies the destruction of the aggregates by eliminating the action of cements. But this action should not be too violent to avoid the creation of particles that would not naturally exist; the procedure of dispersion must thus be sufficiently effective to break down the aggregates into individual components, but not strong enough to create neo-particles.

Measurements (Table 2.1, Fig. 2.2) then will link the size of the particles to physical characteristics of the suspension of soil after dispersion (cf. Sect. 2.1.3). These measurements may be distorted by the presence of some compounds in the soil: organic matter, soluble salts, sesquioxides, carbonates, or gypsum. The latter compound can be particularly awkward because it can result in two opposing actions (Vieillefon 1979): flocculation due to soluble calcium ions (relative reduction in clay content), and low density of gypsum compared to other minerals (increase in clay content). Particle size analysis thus generally starts with a pre-treatment of the sample that varies with the type of soil; the characteristics of different soils are given in Table 2.3.

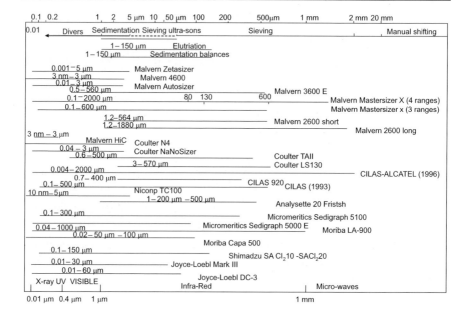

Fig. 2.2. Particle size ranges of some automated particle-measurement instruments

2.1.3 Law of Sedimentation

After possible pretreatment (cf. Sect. 2.2.1), the sample is suspended in aqueous medium in the presence of a dispersant (cf. Sect. 2.2.2). During sedimentation, the particles are then subjected to two essential forces: a force of gravity that attracts them to the bottom, and a force of viscous resistance of the medium in the opposite direction to their displacement. By comparing the particles to spheres of radius r, the force of gravity F_g (dynes) is expressed by:

$$F_g = \frac{4}{3} \pi r^3 \left(\rho_s - \rho_f \right) g$$

r = equivalent radius of the spherical particle in cm;
g = gravity constant, 981 cm s^{-2};
ρ_s = density of the particles in g cm^{-3} (between 2.4 and 2.8 for soils);
ρ_f = density of the liquid of dispersion in g cm^{-3};
The force of resistance of the medium F_r (dynes) is expressed by:

$$F_r = 6\pi\, r\, \eta\, V,$$

$V =$ falling speed in cm s^{-1};
$\eta =$ viscosity of the medium in Poises (g cm^{-1} s^{-1}), at temperature $\theta\,°C$ (Table 2.2).

When the particles reach equilibrium, the forces F_r and F_r are equal, from which their drop speed can be estimated according to the law originally established by Stokes (1851):

$$V = \frac{2\left(\rho_s - \rho_f\right)g\, r^2}{9\,\eta}. \tag{2.1}$$

For calculations, the average density of the solid particles in dispersions of soils is often selected with $\rho_S = 2.65$ or 2.60 g cm^{-3}. Empirical relationships have been established for the calculation of ρ_F and η in aqueous solutions of hexametaphosphate generally used for particle-size distribution of soils (Gee and Bauder 1986):

$$\rho_t = \rho_0\,(1 + 0.630\, C_{HMP}), \tag{2.2}$$

$$\eta = \eta_0\,(1 + 4.25\, C_{HMP}), \tag{2.2'}$$

$\rho_0 =$ density of water (g cm^{-3} at the working temperature (Table 2.2);
$\eta_0 =$ viscosity of water (poise) at the working temperature (Table 2.2);
$C_{HMP} =$ hexametaphosphate concentration in g cm^{-3}.
The constant of Stokes for the medium can thus be defined by:

$$C = 2\,(\rho_s - \rho_f)\, g/9\,\eta.$$

Equation (2.1) shows that the falling speed is proportional to the square of the particle radius and remains constant throughout sedimentation if certain conditions are strictly respected (cf. Sect. 2.1.4). The speed can also be defined by $V = h/t$ where T is the time (s) spent by the particle of radius r(cm) to fall a height H(cm). Either the depth of its sedimentation over a given period, or the time needed for sedimentation to a given depth is determined by:

$$t = \frac{9\, h\, \eta}{2\left(\rho_s - \rho_f\right)g\, r^2} = h\, C^{-1}\, r^{-2}. \tag{2.3}$$

Table 2.1. Systems of particulate characterization for particle size distribution of soils

individualization of particles	– destruction of organic matter (H_2O_2, Na hypochlorite), hypobromite...					
	– destruction of cements (Al, Fe, Si): — acid or basic media — reducer or complexing media					
	– in water					
	chemical — desaturation (elimination cations $^{2+}$) acid medium (some andosols) basic medium: NaOH, NH_4OH, pyrophosphate, hexametaphosphate					

suspension (dispersion)	– preliminary treatments					
	chemical — choice of pH					
	physical — various surfactants, ultrasounds					
	mechanical agitation (disintegration: 40 reversals/min)					
	– choice of concentration — limiting concentrations, wall-attachment effects					

	separation – techniques used – measurements	size range	phase recovery	principle	advantages	drawbacks	1990 firms
measurement of particles	1. sieving	dry	2 mm —		measurement by separation on sieve with vibration with or without ultrasonic waves weighing of the fractions (discontinuous)	simple	fragility of sieves, mesh defects, mesh obtrusions, etc. when dry, fine powders stick to coarse ones	Saulas Tamisor, etc
		wet	0.050 (5 µm)	yes				
	2. surface measurement (for memorandum)	≤ 2 µm	no	measurement of weight of a molecular film (nitrogen, EGME...) retained at the surface of the particles (preliminary separation of phases)	internal and external surface	difficult to measure	micromeritics

	Size range	Wet	Description	Remarks	Effect	Equipment
density soils = 2.65						
3. elutriation — dry			separation measurement inverse of sedimentation: breakdown of gravity force by a gaseous or liquid flow Per Ascensum (discontinuous)	very slow used for sediment studies		
wet	1 – 150 µm	yes				
dry or wet samples						
radioactivity (for memorandum)			for labelled elements			
by fluctuation of conductivity (or photometrics)		no	calibrated hole, distribution of given particles by proportional changes in displaced electrolyte or proportional extinction	hole calibration, obturation	elimination of density effect	Coulter
4. counting	0.5 – 500 µm	no				
by microscopic measurement: optical, MEB, MET... and image analysis		no	counting on image analyzer or manual counting	equipment is expensive	shape, *habitus*	Quantimat 720 Micro-Videomat (Zeiss) Integramat (Leitz)
sedimentation balances	1 – 150 µm	no	gravimetric determination by cumulating vs. time	very slow analysis		Mettler, Becker, Cahn, Sartorius, Prolabo

separation techniques used – measurement	size range	phase recovery	principle	advantages	drawbacks	1990 firms
pipette methods (Robinson, Andreasen) reference method AFNOR standardization simple gravity	1 – 150 µm	yes	volumetric sampling of fine particles. sieving for silts and sands	sedimentation at fixed level vs. time. Critical concentration per unit of volume		
photo-sedimentation (turbidimetry) diffusion diffraction laser.	1 – 20 – 50 µm	no	optical method: absorption, diffusion or dispersion of light (white or monochromatic light or laser)	laser: high intensity lighting of small volume low concentration	influence of shape of colour of particles on extinction coefficient, influence of wavelength diffraction effect for small particles	Stanton Malvern... Cilas
5. sedimentation						
X-ray soft γ attenuation neutron scattering	0.1 – 100 µm	no	measurement by electromagnetic radiation – X-ray or γ	good detection	concentration higher than photometry	Micromeretics 5100...
density variable depth	1 – 50 µm		bouyoucos: measurement of densimeter depth	densimeter (Casagrande, ASTM...)	influence of density, temperature, viscosity, verticality of cylinders	
only one						
method cannot be used for						

	Method	Range		Description			Instruments
	hydrometer constant depth				De Leenher: densimeter with chain	surface evaporation	
all	continuous centrifugation	0,02 – 500 µm	No	increase in gravity force by centrifugation force. Change of concentration at a given depth, photo detection			Shimadzu Capa 500 Horiba 300 Horiba 700 Beckman
classes of	5'. centrifugation						
	discontinuous centrifugation			– weighing of cumulated deposits or measurement of height of deposits – possible approximate separation of phases – pipette centrifuge analyser			
particles	Stokes law: speed of solid fractionation: one static liquid phase – one solid mobile phase, no deformation, no reaction with liquid phase, homogeneously dispersed. Effect of temperature (viscosity, convection flows), effect of density, particle diameter. Repulsive electrostatic effect of particles	0,02 – 2 µm	= yes				Sharples Simcar …
	6) M Brownian movement Zeta potential	0.003 – 2 µm		the frequency of displacements is inversely proportional to particle size	mobility of particles, effective surface charge	fine particles only	Malvern

Particle size analysis by sedimentation consists in determining the content of particles below or equal to a given threshold. Known volumes of solution (pipette method) are generally used for the depth and time of sedimentation chosen as the threshold for a cut point. After drying the pipette sample, weighing and correcting the volume, the content of particles that are smaller than the selected threshold can be determined. In the example in Table 2.2, a pipette sample at a temperature of 20°C, a depth of 10 cm and 8 h 08 min of sedimentation will give the content of the clay fraction (diameter of particle < 2 µm).

In the densimetry method, the relation between the size of the particles (radius r) and the time of sedimentation t can be expressed by:

$$r = S\,t^{-1/2}, \tag{2.4}$$

where S is the parameter of sedimentation. Taking into account (2.3), it can be expressed by:

$$S = C^{-1/2}\,H_r^{1/2}, \tag{2.4'}$$

where H_r is the depth of balance of the densimeter (hydrometer) which represents the effective measurement depth of the particles of radius r.

2.1.4 Conditions for Application of Stokes Law

The formula of Stokes is theoretically only valid for particles with a diameter of less than 0.1 mm, but according to Mériaux (1954), it can be used up to 0.2 mm or even 0.05 mm. Above this value, it is advisable to apply the formula of Oseen; however, particles more than 0.1 mm in diameter can be more precisely sorted by sieving.

For particle size analysis, sedimentation cylinders are used whose walls slow down the falling speed of the particles by friction. Thus, for 0.05 mm quartz spheres, the falling speed at a distance of 0.1 mm from the walls is reduced by 12%, and disturbance becomes negligible at 1 mm (0.28%). In practice, it may be advantageous to use sedimentation tubes (cylinders) with a rather large diameter, at least 5 cm.

In addition, the constant of Stokes is established for minerals with an average density of 2.60 or 2.65, whereas soil materials can contain illite with a density of 2.1 – 2.7, montmorillonite with a density of 1.7 – 2.6 and so on. But the main difficulty is the fact that the particles are neither spherical, nor smooth, which obliges the analyst to introduce the concept of equivalent radius.

Table 2.2. Densities ρ and viscosities η of water and 5% hexametaphosphate solutions related to temperature θ (°C); corresponding to Stoke C constants and falling time t at 10 cm depth for clay particles ≥ 2 μm ($\rho_s = 2.60$ g cm^{-3}) in hexametaphosphate solution

θ	ρ water	η water Poise	ρ corrected (2.2; $C_{HMP} = 0.05$ g cm^{-3})	η corrected (2.2'; $C_{HMP} = 0.05$ g cm^{-3})	C (eau)	C ($C_{HMP} =$ 0.05 g cm^{-3})	t (2.3) for $h = 10$ cm $r = 0.0001$ cm $C_{HMP} =$ 0.05
(°C) (g cm^{-3})		(g cm^{-1} s^{-1})	(g cm^{-3})	(g cm^{-1} s^{-1})	(cm^{-1} s^{-1})	(cm^{-1} s^{-1})	
15	0.999126	0.01139	1.030598	0.01381	30640	30038	9 h 15 min
16	0.99897	0.01109	1.030438	0.01345	31472	30853	9 h 00 min
17	0.998802	0.01081	1.030264	0.01311	32290	31656	8 h 46 min
18	0.998623	0.01053	1.030080	0.01277	33153	32502	8 h 33 min
19	0.998433	0.01027	1.029884	0.01245	33996	33329	8 h 20 min
20	0.998232	0.01002	1.029676	0.01215	34849	34165	8 h 08 min
21	0.998021	0.009779	1.029459	0.01186	35712	35012	7 h 56 min
22	0.997799	0.009548	1.029230	0.01158	36581	35864	7 h 45 min
23	0.997567	0.009325	1.028990	0.01131	37462	36727	7 h 34 min
24	0.997325	0.009111	1.028741	0.01105	38347	37596	7 h 23 min
25	0.997074	0.008904	1.28482	0.01080	39245	38476	7 h 13 min

Particle size analysis is concerned with sedimentation of particles of different sizes. Some particles sediment more quickly than others and this results in variations in viscosity during the course of the experiment and also variations in the density of the fluid. Thus, in order to not diverge too much from the theoretical conditions established for mono-dispersed systems, a too significant concentration of the soil sample should be avoided (never higher than 1%).

The graph of the sedimentation of a heterogeneous sample corresponds to a poly-dispersed system. This construction (Fig. 2.3) makes it possible to evaluate the percentage of particles with a diameter larger than a value "A" corresponding to a sedimentation time 't_x'.

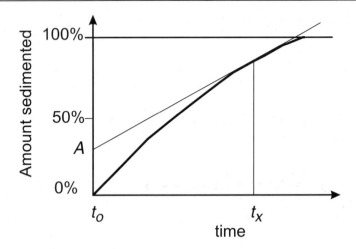

Fig. 2.3. Curve of sedimentation of a complex sample (poly-dispersed system); t_x is time representing the value of the sum of particles X. The intersection of the tangent at point X of the curve with the y-coordinate gives in A the quantity of particles larger than X

2.2. Standard Methods

2.2.1 Pretreatment of the Sample

Adaptation to Soil Type

The sample is dried at room temperature, sieved to 2 mm and carefully partitioned with a manual riffle sampler (Pansu et al. 2001). The weight of the test sample is 10 g; this quantity can be increased to 20 g for soils which are not very rich in clays. The treatments below are defined with respect to the different cases (A – H) listed in Table 2.3.

Carbonated Soils (B)

Reagents

HCl 1 mol L^{-1}

Table 2.3. Characteristic of soils subjected to analysis and preliminary treatments

organo-mineral complex	characterization	treatment
A: complex more or less saturated	few drops of concentrated HCl do not cause any release of CO_2, pH H_2O < 7	treatment with H_2O_2 at 1%, then 30%
B: presence of carbonates	HCl causes release of CO_2 pH H_2O > 7	perform two analyses: one without carbonate destruction, and one with destruction
C: rich in organic matter	OM content > 15% dried <2mm thin earth	suitable treatment with H_2O_2
D: rich in organo-mineral cements and amorphous or individualised sesquioxides	$(SiO_2 + Al_2O_3)$ > 10% of thin earth – ferrallitic, ferruginous tropical soils	– dissolution of mineral cements with HCl and organic cements with H_2O_2 – treatment with Tamm reagent
E: rich in sodic salts, no gypsum	conductivity 1/5 > 0.3 mS cm^{-1}; to 5 mL of aqueous extract, add 5 mL acetone – no precipitate	elimination of salts by washing and decantation–filtration
F: presence of MnO_2	strong reaction with H_2O_2; violet colour of permanganate after oxidation	pretreatment with bisulphite before destruction of organic matter
G: presence of gypsum ≤ 10%	positive reaction to acetone test	elimination of gypsum by washing before agitation
H: presence of gypsum > 10%	estimation of gypsum by heating to 60°, then to 105°C (cf. Sect. 2.2.4)	results difficult to interpret. Special techniques should be used

Procedure

The analytical standard X 31-107 (1983) recommends carrying out this treatment after destruction of organic matter with hydrogen peroxide (H_2O_2). However, oxidation of the organic matter can temporarily produce oxalic acid which results in the neo-formation of calcium oxalate. It is thus preferable to eliminate the limestone at the pretreatment stage.

– Put the sample (equivalent to 10 g soil dried at 105°C for example) weighed at ± 1 mg in a low form 1,000 mL Pyrex beaker.
– Add 100 mL water.
– Agitate and with a burette slowly add the diluted hydrochloric acid (1 mol L^{-1}) until complete destruction of the limestone present.
– The pH should not go below 3.0.
  When all carbon dioxide is eliminated, boil gently for 5 min. Wash by decantation to eliminate calcium and excess acid (chloride test).

Remarks

– Avoid adding too much hydrochloric acid which can destroy the chlorites in certain trioctaedric chlorites.
– Sodium acetate at pH 5 can be used to avoid attacking the lattice of certain clays.
– In the presence of limestone particles involved in the grain-size distribution of the soil, an additional measurement will be required without destroying the $CaCO_3$ (Baize 2000).

Destruction of Organic Matter

Organic matter has a high aggregation capacity. It should thus be destroyed in the majority of soils (A – F in Table 2.3). Generally hydrogen peroxide at 30% (110 volumes) is used or stabilized hydrogen peroxide (Perhydrol or similar) in tropical climates. Some authors propose sodium hypochlorite or bromine in an alkaline medium (2 mol (KOH) L^{-1} solution).

Reagents

– Pure hydrogen peroxide (30% – 110 volumes)
– Ammonia (20%, $d = 0.92$)
– Dispersant, 5% sodium hexametaphosphate solution
– Sodium bisulphite $NaHSO_3$

Case of Soils with Less Than 15% of Organic C

Place the test specimen in a 1,000 mL Pyrex beaker. Add 100 mL of 1%. hydrogen peroxide. Leave in contact in the cold for one hour avoiding excess foaming by agitating, or by using an aerosol to modify the surface charges (alcohol, etc.).

Heat to 60°C and add a little 30% hydrogen peroxide to start the attack again. Add H_2O_2 in small fractions until effervescence stops and there is discolouration of the supernatant. Bring to controlled boiling to destroy surplus H_2O_2 and to reduce the volume without bringing to dry.

Case of Soils Very Rich in Organic Matter (Histosols, Andosols, etc.)

It is important to work on soils preserved in their natural moisture to avoid irreversible changes due to drying as these soils become hydrophobic. A sample equivalent to soil dried at 105°C should be used. The attack must be very gentle at the beginning because as soon as the oxidation reaction starts, it becomes violent; there is a sudden rise in temperature and a risk of overflow of foam.

When sampling wet soil, add distilled water to form slurry. Add 50 mL hydrogen peroxide diluted to 1% and leave in contact in the cold.

Heat each beaker to 60°C to start the reaction. If necessary, adjust the temperature by adding an ice cube made of deionized water.

Add small fractions of hydrogen peroxide until there is no more foam, then bring to the boil. The liquid supernatant should be clear. Wash by decantation and continue the analysis.

Remarks

In certain cases, the organic matter may be "protected" by homogeneous mixture with carbonates and hydrogen peroxide then cannot act. If preliminary destruction of the carbonates (cf. "Carbonated Soils") is not sufficient, the organic matter should be attacked with hypobromite: 3 mL of bromine in 100 mL of frozen 2 mol (KOH) L^{-1} solution.

Mix 50 mL of this mixture with the sample and wait 1 h; boil for 30 min, let cool, add 200 mL distilled water; leave overnight, transfer on a filter and wash (three washings are sufficient) before dispersion.

Presence of MnO₂ (F)

The presence of manganese salts can cause the rapid destruction of hydrogen peroxide. In this case the treatments should be renewed and the colour of the supernatant liquid monitored. Free manganese dioxide is soluble in hydrogen peroxide (Jackson 1969).

Since manganese dioxide causes violent breaking up of hydrogen peroxide, it should first be reduced with sodium bisulphite (Pétard, 1993). Before adding hydrogen peroxide, add 1 g of sodium bisulphite or 10 mL of an aqueous bisulfite solution at 37.5% to the sample. Add 50 mL deionized water and boil for 20 min to reduce the manganese dioxide in Mn^{2+} ion. Then initiate the attack with hydrogen peroxide as described above.

Presence of Amorphous Organo-Mineral Cements (D)

Reagents

- Tamm (1922) buffer: 10.92 g of oxalic acid + 16.11 g of ammonium oxalate for 1,000 mL; adjust to pH 3;
- Hydrochloric acid 2 mol L^{-1} solution: dissolve 166 mL concentrated HCl ($d = 1.18$) in 800 mL water, agitate, cool and complete to 1 L.

Procedure with Tamm Reagent

Add 800 mL of Tamm reagent to a sample weighing 20 g; agitate cold, store in the dark for 4 h, centrifuge, and then filter.

Procedure with HCl/H₂O₂ Reagent

Treat with 300 mL 2 mol (HCl) L^{-1} solution in a sand bath for 1 h at 60°C. Elutriate and wash with deionized water. The acid solution and washing water should be collected and dried at 105°C. Weighing gives the mass M_m of the soluble mineral fraction. If m represents the initial test specimen of soil, the mineral soluble fraction F_m expressed as a percentage is calculated by $F_m = 100\ M_m/m$. This value should be taken into account for the calculation of the balance of particle size fractionation.

After dissolving mineral cements, organic cements should be dissolved as described in above "Destruction of Organic Matter".

Presence of Gypsum (G and H)

Procedure for Rough Estimate of Gypsum

Put a test specimen of 10 g of soil sieved to 2 mm in an aluminium capsule. Place in a ventilated drying oven at 60°C for 24 h to eliminate the water of hydration. Cool in the desiccator and weigh $= P1$; place in a ventilated drying oven regulated at 105°C (for minimum 3 h) to eliminate the water of constitution; cool in the desiccator and weigh $= P2$.

$$\text{Approximate percentage gypsum} = 100\frac{P1 - P2}{10} \times \frac{172}{36} \approx 50(P1 - P2).$$

Procedure in Case of Gypsum ≤ 10% (case G)

At 25°C, gypsum is water soluble at a rate of 2 g L^{-1}. After destruction of organic matter (cf. "Destruction of Organic Matter") and after destruction or not of limestone (cf. "Carbonated Soils"), put the sample (10 g) in a 500 mL beaker with 300 mL distilled water on a magnetic stirrer with agitation. After 1 h, allow it to settle and elutriate the clear part, again add 300 mL distilled water and repeat the operation (usually once again) until the acetone test is negative.

For this test (cf. Chap. 30), use 5 mL aqueous extract, add 5 mL acetone, mix well; in the absence of gypsum, no precipitate will be formed.

Procedure in Case of Gypsum > 10% (case H)

Determination of the exact particle size is difficult and it is advisable to adapt a specific method, for example, that of Vieillefon (1979). Complete dissolution of the gypsum enables the elementary composition of the non-gypseous part of the soil to be determined, but not of the total soil. Instrumental methods are more precise because only a short measurement time is required. Combined with desaturation using ion exchange resins, these methods make it possible to obtain satisfactory results before flocculation occurs.

2.2.2 Particle Suspension and Dispersion

Introduction

Ions that can flocculate clay particles are ranked in descending order:
$$Al^{3+} > Ca^{2+} > NH^{4+} > K^+ > Na^+ > Li^+$$
The replacement of the natural compensation cations with high flocculating capacity is thus necessary to enable dispersion of the soil, i.e. the maintenance of the elementary particles in suspension. The stability of the suspensions is only obtained thanks to interactions between the diffuse layers of the same sign as clays and with control of the forces of attraction of van der Waals.

Coulomb repulsion depends on the concentration of electrolytes and the valence of the ions. If the forces of van der Waals are higher than the force of Coulomb repulsion, the potential energy of the resulting interaction leads to flocculation. The aim is to chemically modify the distribution of charges and pH.

For example, inversion of the edge charges can eliminate edge lattice attractions and produce negative particles with a weak attraction potential. For example hexametaphosphate is fixed by chemisorption on the octahedral cations present on the side faces of crystallites resulting in good dispersion. This dispersant is most often used when analyses are not required on the fractions after measurement of particle size.

The pH should preferably be fixed at a value which is far from the zone of the isoelectric point (cf. Chap. 20) at which flocculation occurs. Generally it should be basic (approximately 10). A too high pH can induce solubilization phenomena.

For oxides like $Fe(OH)_3$, which can exist in a dispersed state with a positive or negative charge, adjustment of the pH to allow dispersion is a function of the isoelectric point. For Andisols, the pH for dispersion will often be acid (around pH 3.5) and always far from the isoelectric point.

These treatments do not avoid lattice associations which are observed in kaolinites with a low negative charge or in micas (illites, muscovite, etc.). In this case it is necessary to use ultrasound for an additional mechanical effect.[1] The optimal amount of dispersant will depend on the effectiveness of the pre-treatments. Optimal effectiveness is obtained with an amount of sodium hexametaphosphate of between 20 and 50 times the CEC. An excess of this reagent should be avoided as it causes flocculation while being adsorbed on colloids. For this reason, and when the fractions are needed for later analysis, it is better to use ion-exchange resins in Na^+ form as dispersants, e.g. Amberlite IR 120 Na (Rouiller et al.1972). These have the advantage of not causing any additional ionic charge of the medium, which is very favourable in the case of horizons with low clay content where a saline medium adds significant weight to the clay content.

Among the dispersants that can be used are ammonia, soda, sodium carbonate, and sodium pyrophosphate. All these agents avoid compression of the double layer of crystallites and avoid raising the Zeta

---

[1] Ultrasounds: (see complementary bibliography for effects on soils). Ultrasonic vibrations are generated by magnetostrictive oscillators. When a bar of a ferromagnetic material is subjected to a magnetic field, it changes length by magnetostriction. When this alternative field is applied in the axis of the bar, this causes an oscillation that is double of the applied field frequency. This vibration is transmitted to the suspended particles by the aqueous medium. The effect of cavitation with a frequency from 20 to 30 kHz makes it possible to break the forces of cohesion of the aggregates without causing significant damage to the elementary particles, as long as the application time is short. The treatment causes a rise in temperature which should be controlled. The apparatus are built so as to avoid the zones of resonance waves which are most destructive. Two types of apparatus are used, either with tanks or with probes with mechanical agitation by blades. Agitation with a bar magnet is not used except to recover magnetic particles if required.

potential, thus maintaining inter-particle forces of repulsion. It should be noted that at a rate of 17 mL per litre, ammonia does not cause an overload for weighing, and that soda dissolves the organic matter and precipitates iron, whereas pyro- and hexametaphosphate maintain it in solution. Aluminium is put in solution in the form of aluminates with soda, but not with ammonia. The responses are thus always slightly different.

As the mixed hexametaphosphate–ammonia dispersant has one component with a higher density than water and one component with a lower density, the resulting density is close to that of water.

Equipment and Reagents

– *Sedimentation cylinders*. graduated 1,000 mL cylinders with ground stoppers (45/40 mm), 400 mm in length and 60 mm in diameter are generally used, but equivalent results can be obtained using transparent PVC tubes with an internal diameter of 71 mm and a length of 30 cm, with a filling mark at 1,000 mL, a square base, and stopped with a rubber stopper for agitation.
– *Dispersing solution*. 15% sodium hexametaphosphate solution (calgon, $(NaPO_3)_6$) in deionized water.
– 20% ammonia ($d = 0.92$) solution.
– Ion exchange resin (Amberlite IR120 Na or similar).

Procedure

Treatment Using the Mixed Dispersant Hexametaphosphate – Ammonia

After subjecting the soil sample to suitable pretreatments, quantitatively place it on an unfolded analytical filter and wash it with deionized water until dispersion begins. Pierce the filter and with jets of water from a washing bottle direct the soil into a cylinder (Fig. 2.4). Add 10 mL of 15% sodium hexametaphosphate solution and 5 mL of 20% ammonia solution. Supplement with approximately 500 mL water, close and place on the rotary agitator for 2 h (4 h for clay soils). In the case of soils of andosol–histosol type, first carry out ultrasonic treatment for 15 min).

After agitation, the sample should be well dispersed and its elementary particles (sands, silts, clays) quite separate from each other. After a few minutes, check there is no flocculation. Bring the volume to 1,000 mL with deionized water and homogenize.

Treatment Using Na Form IR 120 Resin

Before treatment, the resin should be removed from particles smaller than 200 µm by sieving.

Place samples that have been subjected to suitable pretreatment quantitatively on a filter and wash with deionized water until dispersion begins. Pierce the filter and place the soil on a 200-µm mesh sieve in a funnel on a sedimentation cylinder to recover coarse sands. Wash, dry, and filter the recovered sands (cf. "Washing and Measuring Fine and Coarse Sands").

Place the fine particles in the cylinder. Add 50 mL wet Na form resin, then approximately 500 mL deionized water and agitate with the rotary agitator for 4 h (5 h for soils containing < 10% gypsum).

After agitation, recover the resin on a 200 µm mesh sieve placed in a funnel in a 1,000 mL sedimentation cylinder, then wash separately and recover the washing water (the resin can be regenerated for another operation).

The sample can also be brought to 1,000 mL directly with deionized water for sampling of the fine particles, which can be needed for later analyses. It is alsopossible to add 10 mL of 15% sodium hexametaphos-phate solution and 5 mL 20% ammonia, as in the procedure described in "Treatment Using the Mixed dispersant Hexametaphosphate – Ammonia", the densities and viscosities are then similar.

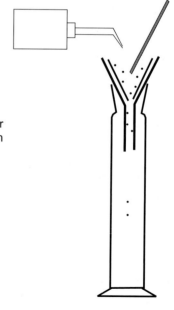

Fig.2.4. Transfer in sedimentation cylinders for dispersion after pretreatment, filtration and washing

2.2.3 Pipette Method after Robinson-Köhn or Andreasen

Principle

The pipette method is based on sedimentation of the particles by gravity according to the law of Stokes (2.1). Recovery of the aliquot at a given depth and a given time makes it possible to identify a specific class of particles when all the particles bigger than the selected diameter have been eliminated.

Equipment

– Sand bath.
– Robinson pipette on moveable frame with toothed rack (Fig. 2.5), aspiration by micropump with flow regulated at 60 mL min^{-1}. The pipette should have undergone preliminary treatment to make it non-wetable (cf. "Hydrophobic Treatment of a Sampling Pipette").
– Fine aluminium capsules with a capacity of 30–40 mL.
– Drying oven with ventilation, regulated at 105°C.
– Thermometer.
– Balances, range: 120 g, sensitivity: 0.1 mg.
– Sets of two sieves with 0.2 and 0.05 mm mesh, with a vibrating sieving machine.
– Rotary agitator able to receive 10 or 20 cylinders, (30 rpm).
– Standard tributylchlorosilane.
– Standard 1-chloronaphtalene.

Preparation of Pipette

Hydrophobic Treatment of a Sampling Pipette

This treatment (Walker method) makes the walls of the pipette non-wetable and eliminates the need for rinsing between sampling.

Prepare the smallest possible quantity of 4% solution of tributylchlorosilane in chloronaphtalene. Clean, carefully degrease the pipette, dry it well then treat the inside of the pipette by aspiration; drain, leave to dry for a minimum of 24 h at room temperature.

Calibration of the Pipette – Overload Reagent

This calibration should be done periodically. The same dispersing liquid used for the analyses is used again but the temperature should be checked as it influences viscosity. Put five fractions of 20 mL in tarred capsules, then weigh (± 1/10 mg). The average weight corresponds to the volume removed. Dry for 5 h at maximum 105°C, weigh the capsules (± 1/10 mg) to determine overload due to the reagent.

Procedure

All operations should be carried out at 20°C in an air-conditioned room, and equipment and reagents should be kept at the same temperature.

Control of Dispersion

After agitation, lay the sedimentation cylinders out in line on the lab table, and open, taking care to include any deposits on the stopper.

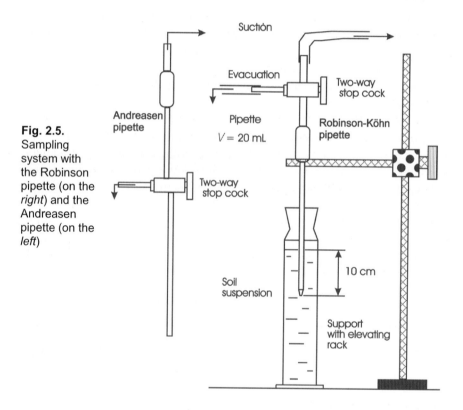

Fig. 2.5. Sampling system with the Robinson pipette (on the *right*) and the Andreasen pipette (on the *left*)

First check the state of the suspension. Carefully check whether flocculation has occurred although this may be only partial and impossible to see. In case of doubt, complete the following steps: measure the temperature of the suspension, calculate (2.1) the falling time at 5 cm and 10 cm (for particles of 0.02 mm), hand shake the cylinder by turning it upside down and back for 1 min; start the chronometer, lower the pipette to 5 cm. Ten seconds before the time is up, remove a 10 mL sample and place it in a capsule. Lower the pipette to 10 cm and remove a sample at the corresponding time under the same conditions. Dry the capsules containing the samples in the drying oven at 105°C for 24 h, then weigh them (± 1 mg); the two weights should be identical, any difference indicates flocculation and its extent. If any doubt remains about possible flocculation, it is better to start the analysis again.

Certain apparatus make it possible to identify the optimal zone of dispersion for certain clays by bringing into play their property of orientation in an electric field.

First Sampling (Clay + Silts)

In the case of big series, a team of two people can be used, who should respect the timing very strictly (Table 2.4). Hand shake the cylinder containing the 1,000 mL suspension by turning it upside down and back to put all the deposits in suspension then place it on the counter top and start the chronometer (remove the stopper after the particles have been removed by agitation).

– Close the three-way stopcock of the pipette; lower the pipette until the tip touches the surface of the suspension. Note the position of the index on the scale. Approximately 30 s before the time is up, (4 min 48 s at 20°C for 10 cm, see Table 2.5), carefully lower the pipette in the first agitated cylinder to the selected depth (here 10 cm).

– Exactly 10 s before the sampling time, begin aspiration of 20 mL (speed intake 1 mL s^{-1}) by slowly opening the stopcock. The distribution around the exact sampling time gives the "average'''". When the liquid rises above the top of the stopcock, turn it off and run the overflow off through the side nozzle.

Table 2.4. Procedure for stirring a series of sedimentation cylinders

stirring first cylinder 1 min		stirring second cylinder 1 min	1 min	etc.
when stirring is finished, start the chronometer: this is the beginning of the timed period	lag time		lag time	

Remove the pipette, quickly wipe the outside of the tube, and empty its contents into a previously tared 50 mL weighing bottle. Evaporate to dry and dry in the drying oven at maximum 105°C for 3 h. Weigh dry residue to precisely 1/10 mg. Correct the weight for overload due to the reagent.

Remarks

Aspiration should not be too fast to limit turbulence and to avoid aspirating particles with a larger diameter than those of the selected sampling range. Aspiration must also be regular.

The pipette does not need to be rinsed between sampling since it has received hydrophobic treatment (cf. "Hydrophobic Treatment of a Sampling Pipette") and any error due to retention is negligible compared with other causes of error.

Blank assays should be made with the dispersant alone (cf. "Calibration of the Pipette – Overload Reagent"). Weigh the sample and the blank after 24 h in the drying oven at 105°C.

Second Sampling: Clay

Table 2.5. *right*: Sampling time of particles (*d* = 2.65) by sedimentometry with a Robinson-Köhn pipette at a depth of 10 cm.
left: Sampling depth of the clay-size fraction at different times

clays ≤ 2 µm				tempe-rature	clays <2 µm	≤ 5 µm	≤ 20 µm	≤ 50 µm
depth of sampling in cm after				*T* (°c)	falling time at 10 cm			
5 h	6 h	7 h	8 h					
6.2	7.5	8.8	10.0	20	8 h 00 min	1 h 16 min 48 s	0 h 04 min 48 s	0 min 47 s
6.4	7.7	9.,0	10.3	21	7 h 48 min	1 h 15 min 00 s	0 h 04 min 41 s	sedimenta-tion
6.5	7.9	9.2	10.5	22	7 h 37 min	1 h 13 min 12 s	0 h 04 min 34 s	method
6.7	8.1	9.4	10.8	23	7 h 26 min	1 h 11 min 30 s	0 h 04 min 28 s	not
6.9	8.3	9.7	11.0	24	7 h 16 min	1 h 09 min 54 s	0 h 04 min 22 s	possible
7.0	8.5	9.9	11.3	25	7 h 06 min	1 h 08 min 18 s	0 h 04 min 15 s	

Proceed as above after 8 h of sedimentation at 20°C (if necessary, a smaller depth can be used to sample clay on the same day: for example, 7 h at 8.8 cm at 20°C – see Table 2.5).

Weigh the residue exactly (± 1/10 mg) and correct the weight for overload due to the reagent (blank).

Intermediate sampling can be performed; remember to take suspensions containing the coarsest phases first and the finest last. For this it is better to use an Andreasen pipette.

Washing and Measuring Fine and Coarse Sands

After the last sampling of clays, siphon off the supernatant liquid to 5 cm from the bottom; decant the deposit in 1,000 mL beakers. Add deionized water with a little hexametaphosphate (approximately 700–800 mL); agitate vigorously to put the deposit in suspension; after the time necessary for 0.02 mm particles to fall below the limit of aspiration of the siphon, siphon off the supernatant liquid (Fig. 2.6).

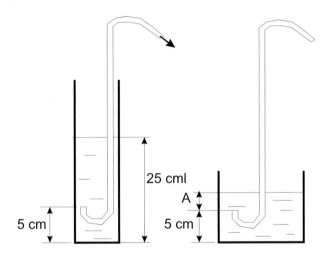

Fig. 2.6. Washing of sands by decantation: *left,* first siphon off, *right,* continue siphoning until supernatant is clear (A = falling height of 0.02 mm particles)

Again add water with a little hexametaphosphate; continue washing until the liquid supernatant is clear; finish with one final washing with distilled water; eliminate the maximum amount of water possible per decantation, quantitatively decant the deposit of sands in a capsule, put to dry in a ventilated drying oven at 105°C; after cooling, weigh total sands; put the sands on the top of two superimposed sieves, one with a 0.2 mm mesh (AFNOR 24), the other with a 0.05 mm mesh (AFNOR 18); sieving with a vibrating apparatus must be complete; check there are no cemented aggregates or plant debris. The mesh of the 0.2 mm sieve represents coarse sands, and the mesh of the 0.05 mm sieve represents fine sands.

The coarse silts or very fine sands are determined by calculating the difference between total sands and the sum of coarse sands and fine sands.

Remark

The washing–decantation operations are long and tiresome, particularly as many samples are required in routine analyses. It is possible and advisable to use an automated system to wash the sands, e.g. the one developed by Susini (1978).

Causes of Error

A strict procedure is required to ensure the temperature remains stable for the duration of sedimentation. This can be achieved by immersing the cylinders in a thermostat bath, but this device is not really suitable for the treatment of the large series required in many laboratories. Consequently the cylinders are simply laid out in line on the lab table. The temperature should be taken in one of the cylinders at the beginning. Since the liquid medium presents good thermal inertia, variation is not very great over a short period, i.e. for the first sampling of about 4 – 5 min. The most favourable temperature is between 15°C and 25°C; above 30°C there is a risk of flocculation; below 15°C the times needed for sedimentation will be too long. For these reasons, in the absence of a thermostat, it is best to work in an air-conditioned room.

But the main causes of error are:

– Too abrupt entry of the pipette in the suspension.

– Error in the depth of sampling.

– Irregular or too rapid aspiration; certain authors recommend a time of 20 s per aspiration for a volume of 10 mL. These requirements exclude aspiration with the mouth.

Optimal working conditions are guaranteed by making sure there is no variation between the way the operators perform the series of operations, i.e. moving the pipette, lowering the pipette into the suspension, exact timing of the beginning of the sampling, very regular sampling, exact volume, careful removal of the pipette, draining of the sample into the capsule, next sampling. The ideal solution is to use a simple automatic unit like that described in Pansu et al. (2001). However, even if the traditional manual system has to be used it is preferable to carry out aspiration with a small electric pump with a fixed flow; peristaltic pumps fulfil this function well.

Calculations

Collected Data

Mass of soil sample (air dried) =	m
Moisture correction coefficient =	
mass sample after drying at 105°C /m =	K
Volume of the sample =	V_p
Mass of blank (reagents without sample) after drying 105°C =	m_B
Mass of first sample (clay + silt) after drying 105°C =	m_1
Mass of second sample (clay) after drying 105°C =	m_2
Mass of total sands after drying 105°C =	m_3
Mass of coarse sands (rejected by 0.2 mm sieve)	
after drying at 105°C =	m_4
Mass of fine sands (rejected by 0.05 mm sieve)	
after drying at 105°C =	m_5

Calculation of the Results in% of Soil Dried at 105°C

Clays = C =	$(m_2 - m_B) \times 1000 \times 100 / (V_p \times m \times K)$
Silts = Si =	$(m_1 - m_2 \times 1000 \times 100 / (V_p \times m \times K)$
Fine sands = FS =	$100 \times m_5 / (m \times K)$
Coarse sands = CS =	$100 \times m_4 / (m \times K)$
Total sands = S =	$100 \times m_3 / (m \times K)$
Coarse silts = CSi	$S - (FS + CS)$

If limestone is present (Table 2.3, B), and particle size analysis was performed without destruction of carbonates, carbonates should be determined on the separated fractions which provides information about the distribution of limestone.

Checking and Correction of the Results

Taking into account the moisture correction factor (cf. "Calculations" under Sect. 2.2.3), the sum: clays + silts + total sands + organic matter + if necessary, carbonates, soluble salts, gypsum, must be between 95 and 102%, preferably between 98 and 102%. Soils rich in organic matter can provide too high balances: in the event of incomplete destruction during pretreatment, organic matter can be counted twice.

A too small sum results from losses during the pretreatments. In the majority of cases, it is impossible to determine the exact proportions of losses in organic matter, soluble salts, carbonates and gypsum. An overall estimate of the losses can be made as follows: using the cylinder in which the samplings were made, add 10 mL of 1 mol ($CaCl_2$) L^{-1} solution and 1 mL of 1 mol (HCl) L^{-1} to flocculate colloids and prevent the formation of calcium carbonate during drying in the drying oven. Allow the particles to deposit, completely remove the clear solution, put the deposit in a tared capsule, dry in the drying oven at 105°C, and then weigh. This gives mass m_r from which losses during the treatments (organic matter, etc.) can be determined and the balances corrected.

2.2.4 Density Method with Variable Depth

Principle

This type of analysis is advantageous because it avoids fractionation of the sediment in dimensional classes and allows the construction of curves of distribution. In the density method proposed by Bouyoucos (1927, 1935, 1962), the heterogeneous suspension is considered to behave in the same way as a homogeneous liquid with the same density. Casagrande (1934) showed that it is then acceptable to use a float densimeter to measure the average density in the suspension column with the float. The plan of average density is located at a distance H_R from the highest level of the suspension. From (9.4) and (9.4') it separates the particles from the radius:

$$r = C^{-1/2} \left(\frac{Hr}{t} \right)^{1/2},$$

(t = sedimentation time), and allows particle size analysis.

The density method can be performed with permanent immersion, which fulfils the conditions of continuous measurement, or by temporary immersion, which resembles discontinuous measurement described in Chap. 1, without the same precision, but for routine measurements it has the advantage of avoiding sampling and weighing. On the other hand, the density method requires a larger number of samples than the pipette method.

Equipment and Reagents

– Cylinders identical to those described in "Equipment" under Sect. 2.2.3, special conical hydrometers to avoid accumulation of the particles on the surface, thermometer, pycnometers, magnifier with long effective focal spot.
– Dispersing reagents of "Equipment and Reagents", isoamylic alcohol.

Checking the Hydrometer

Calculation of Falling Height of the Particles

The relation of Casagrande makes it possible to calculate the value H_r giving the effective depth selected as falling height of the particles. For this calculation, the measurements shown on the hydrometer in Fig. 2.7 are required. The volume of the hydrometer is obtained by liquid displacement.

$$H_r = h_1 + 0.5\,(h - V/S) \tag{2.5}$$

V: volume in cm^3
S: section in cm^2

A graph can be drawn representing depths H_r as a function of the densities. This makes it possible to draw up the table giving the size of the particles as a function of temperature, time, and depth, for an unknown hydrometer.

Checking the Graduations on the Hydrometer

This test is made with pure water and a 2% solution of barium nitrate or chloride. Use a pycnometer to measure the density of water (note the temperature) then the density of the 2% solution (4 significant decimals).

Take the same measurements by submerging the hydrometer in the test-tube successively containing the two liquids; read the densities with the help of a magnifier with a long focal spot (5 or 6 cm).

Note the differences in the measurements obtained with the pycnometer and the hydrometer. If the relative values are the same, the hydrometer is valid even if the indications are not exact, because in the calculations the differences in density are used.

If the differences between the pycnometer and hydrometer measurements are not constant, an abacus of transposition has to be established: values read on the hydrometer/actual values (this is very seldom the case).

This method is similar to that described in Sect. 2.2.3 using 30 g of fine earth (soil air dried and sieved to 2 mm). For dispersion, add 30 mL of 102 g L^{-1} hexametaphosphate solution. Agitate for 4 h by upside down and back rotary shaker, transfer in the cylinders and complete to 1,000 mL.

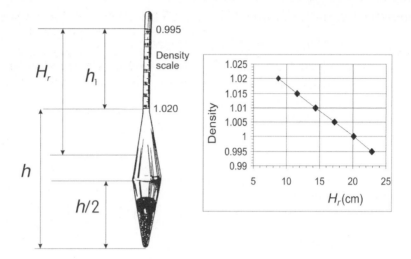

Fig. 2.7. Relation between density and falling height of the particles H_r (2.5) for a hydrometer with the following characteristics: $V = 45$ cm^3, $S = 28.26$ cm^2, $h = 17$ cm, $h_1 = 15.2$ cm).

Procedure

Preparation of the Sample

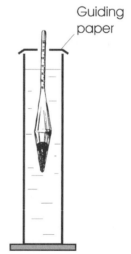

Fig. 2.8. Positioning of hydrometer

Measurement of the Clay + Silt (0.02 mm) Fraction

Table 2.6. Sizes of the particles as a function of temperature, time and the depth: valid for a standard hydrometer (laboratory of sedimentary sequences, IRD Bondy, France, unpublished data)

Particle	t	density→	1.020	1.015	1.010	1.005	1.000
Size	(°C)	(min ↓)	8.7 cm	11.6 cm	14.4 cm	17.2 cm	20.1 cm
		4	21 μm	24.7 μm	27.4 μm	30.1 μm	32.5 μm
	15	6	17.4	20.1	22.4	24.5	26.5
		8	15	17.4	19.4	21	23
		9	14.2	16.4	18.2	20	21.6
20 μm		4	20	23	25.8	28.2	30.3
		6	16.4	19	21	23	24.5
	20	8	14.2	16.3	18.2	19.8	21.4
		9	13.4	15.4	17.2	18.8	20.2
(clays +		3	21.8	25.2	28.1	30.7	33.2
silts)	25	4	19.9	21.8	24.3	26.6	28.7
		6	15.4	17.8	19.8	21.6	23.4
		8	13,4	15,4	17,2	18,8	20,3
particle	t	density→	1.020	1.015	1.010	1.005	1.000
size	(°C)	(hours ↓)					
		6	2.2 μm	2.6 μm	2.9 μm	3.1 μm	3.4 μm
	15	8	1.9	2.2	2.5	2.7	2.9
2 μm		24	1.1	1.3	1.4	1.58	1.7
		6	2.1	2.4	2.7	2.9	3.2
	20	8	1.8	2.1	2.3	2.5	2.7
(clays)		24	1	1.2	1.4	1.5	1.6
		6	2	2.3	2.6	2.8	3
	25	8	1.4	2	2.2	2.4	2.6
		24	1	1.1	1.2	1.4	1.5

If possible measurements should be made in an air-conditioned room at a constant temperature of 20°C. The cylinders containing the suspensions are grouped; check their volume has been completed to 1,000 mL, measure the temperature by referring to a table (such as Table 2.6) giving times of sedimentation for measurements at the selected temperature (for example 4–6–8–9 minutes).

Hand shake the first cylinder by it turning upside down and back for 1 min, add an isoamyl alcohol drop anti-foamer, start timing, introduce the hydrometer very gently so as not to disturb the suspension (this is the most delicate part and a significant cause of error), take care that the hydrometer is maintained in the centre of the suspension, (if need be, make a paper guide see Fig. 2.8), take the readings at the top of the meniscus at 4–6–8 and 9 min. Continue in the same way with the following cylinder.

Take a reading of the blank in a cylinder containing only the dispersant.

Measurement of Clay Fraction (< 0.002 mm)

The time counted starts at the beginning of agitation of the first cylinder during the first reading (clay + silt). To define this time, the average temperature has to be calculated from the beginning of sedimentation until the reading; take readings with the hydrometer at 6–8–24 h carefully respecting the 2 min interval used for the first sampling; transfer the hydrometer very carefully from one cylinder to another in order to avoid disturbances.

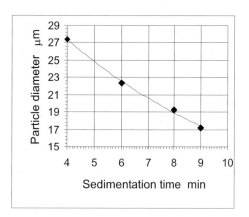

Fig.2.9. Example of abacus: sizes of particles are a function of the time of sedimentation for a given hydrometer and a density close to 1.010.

Remarks

As can be seen in Table 2.6, that selected times do not correspond exactly to the selected particle size; however, in a small space of time, variation in particle size is considered to be continuous; this makes it possible to plot an abacus around a given depth (Fig. 2.9) which then makes it possible to define an exact falling time for a given particle size.

Calculations

The percentage of particles P corresponding to a given density is obtained from the equation:

$$P = \frac{100\ \rho_s}{m\left(\rho_s - \rho_f\right)}\left(\left(\rho \pm \delta_\rho\right) - \rho_f\right) V. \tag{2.6}$$

ρ_s = density of solid = 2.65 for soil;

ρ_f = density of the dispersing solution; in our conditions at $t°C$, one can calculate ρ_f by means of (2.2);

ρ = density read at $t°C$;

δ_ρ = corrections + or – on readings to bring them to 20°C (Table 2.6);

V = volume, 1,000 mL;

m = soil sample, 30 g;

The calculation can be simplified by calculating $K = 100\ \rho_s / m\ (\rho_s - \rho_f)$ which gives $\qquad P\% = K\left[(\rho \pm \delta_\rho) - \rho_f\right] V$
with m = 30 g, at 20°, it gives $K = 5.35$

Determination of Sands

Use the same technique as that described in Sect. 2.2.3.

2.2.5 Density Method with Constant Depth

The density method with variable depth (cf. 2.2.4) has the advantage of greater speed compared to the pipette method as well as allowing uninterrupted measurements if required. However, as the depth of immersion is not constant, the degree of precision is lower and calculations are longer.

The chain hydrometer (de Leenheer system) makes it possible to measure the density of the suspension to a given constant depth of approximately 20 cm, which in turn, makes it possible to approach the principle and the precision of the pipette method while avoiding sampling and weighing (De Leenheer and Macs 1952; De Leenheer et al. 1955; De Leenheer and van Hove 1956; van Ruymbeke and de Leenheer, 1954).

The apparatus (Fig. 2.10) is composed of an immersion body at the end of an arm with (1) a pointer that identifies the level of the liquid and (2) at the top, a support that can receive overload weights in the form of riders, and an equilibrium chain that allows a very fine fit when the pointer locates the surface of the liquid. The depth of sedimentation is represented by the distance from the point of the needle located in the middle of the body of the hydrometer.

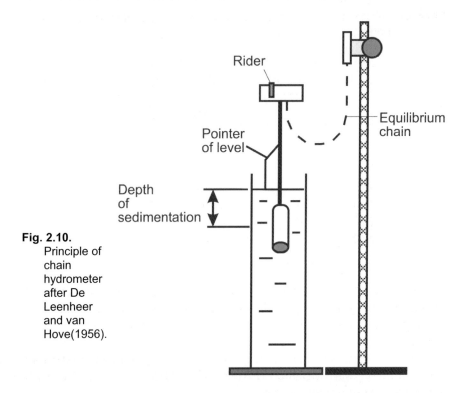

Fig. 2.10.
Principle of
chain
hydrometer
after De
Leenheer
and van
Hove(1956).

One minute before measuring time, carefully introduce the hydrometer into the suspension; add the weights in such way that the reference mark of the needle is 1 – 2 cm above the level of the liquid. At the precise time of the sampling, adjust the needle so that it is in contact with the liquid by quickly adjusting the chain with the screw device. The chain can cause an overload of 100 mg. The reading for total overload gives the weight of the hydrometer. Having determined in advance the volume of the hydrometer (by immersion in distilled water), one thus obtains:

density (ρ) = weight of the hydrometer / hydrometer volume

Continue the calculations in the same way as for the density method with variable depth (2.6).

2.2.6 Particle Size Analysis of Sands Only

Place 100 g of fine earth (standard 2 mm preparation from a perfectly homogenized batch) in a 1,000 mL beaker with 100 mL hydrogen peroxide brought to 30 volumes; leave to act in a cold place overnight, then transfer on a moderately heated hotplate; add hydrogen peroxide in small fractions until complete destruction of the organic matter, then eliminate excess hydrogen peroxide by boiling without going to dry.

Table 2.7. The two sieving columns used successively for particle size analysis of sands

	column 1		column 2
mm	AFNOR standard	mm	AFNOR standard
2	34	0.315	26
1.6	33	0.25	25
1.25	32	0.20	24
1	31	0.16	23
0.8	30	0.125	22
0.63	29	0.100	21
0.50	28	0.08	20
0.40	27	0.063	19
		0.050	18

Transfer the residue in a cylinder and add 500 mL distilled water and 25 mL of 52 g L^{-1} sodium hexametaphosphate solution. Place in a rotating shaker for 4 h in the same way as for complete particle size analysis.

After this operation, transfer the content of the cylinder on a 0.05 mm mesh sieve (French standard AFNOR NF-X-11-504 module°18); wash the residue under running water.

Place the well-washed sands of the 0.05 mm sieve in a 250 mL beaker. Add 100 mL of 6 mol (HCl) L^{-1} solution, cover with a beaker cover, and boil gently for 2 h to dissolve iron.

After cooling, decant and wash by successive decantation until complete elimination of the acid; transfer again on a 0.05 mm sieve, wash, and transfer quantitatively the sands in a capsule; dry for 24 h in drying oven at 105°C. Let cool and weigh total sands.

Sieve dry total sands successively on the two columns of sieves (Table 2.7). Place the columns successively on a vibrating sieve machine (Pansu et al., 2001).

Transfer in column 2 the fraction collected at the bottom of column 1. Sieve 10 min and weigh each fraction (± 0.01 g).

Checking: sum of weighings of each fraction = total sands.

2.3. Automated Equipment

2.3.1 Introduction

The phenomena of slaking of the soils requires precise knowledge of the grain-size distribution of the 2–20 μm fraction; sediment studies require a distribution of the fine phases down to 0.1 μm or even lower. In agronomy, the horizons comprising the formation of clay are studied using ratios for "coarse clay < 2 μm/fine clay < 0.2 μm". Since gravity methods cannot provide all the answers, a range of different techniques is required.

Table 2.1 summarizes the main methods used for measurement of the particle-size distribution of soils. Some methods are well suited for the repetitive measurements needed for studies in the fields of pedology, agronomy, geology or sedimentology; others are more suitable for detailed and in-depth studies. The choice of a method will depend on:

- the degree of precision required, reproducibility and repeatability, and a good correlation with the pipette reference method (cf. 2.2.3) despite its defects;
- the extent of the particle size field and possibility of extending it to sub-micronic or nanometric particles;
- the speed of execution, the time needed to produce a result, the flexibility of use, the possibility to significantly increase the number of analyses;
- the possibility of recovering the particle fractions for later measurements, or of taking other measurements simultaneously (continuous analyses, etc.);
- the cost of equipment and personnel, the importance of the request and available space;
- continuous data acquisition and exploitation (monitoring, calculations, histograms and cumulative frequency curves).

Given the wide granular spectrum of soils, combinations of individual methods that do not cover the complete spectrum are often used. There should be a significant overlap between the methods. The pipette method remains the reference method for all comparisons; analysis by laser diffraction makes it possible to extend the spectrum to the sub-micronic field but still identify silts. The true representativeness of equivalent diameters in a given class can be checked using a microscopic method and image analysis.

2.3.2 Methods Using Sedimentation by Simple Gravity

The majority of apparatus designed to mechanize the pipette method are not widely distributed, as each laboratory tends to develop devices suitable for its own needs. For example, the automatic particle-measurement instrument distributed by "Technology Diffusion France" (Pansu et al., 2001) is based on sedimentation in a thermostated cupboard with an automated pipette.

Analysts, especially those in the industrial sector, need methods that obtain rapid results with good repeatability and the possibility of calibrating the apparatus (using calibrated microball powders). For the main types of automated equipment available and the names of manufacturers see Pansu et al. (2001).

Sedimentation Balances and Automated Sieve Machines for Wet Measurements

These balances (Sartorius, Cahn, Mettler, etc.) make it possible to continuously record the process of sedimentation between approximately 1 and 150 µm (Fig. 2.11), the higher fractions being in the domain of auto-mated wet or dry sieve test machines (Micromeritics, Seishin, etc.).

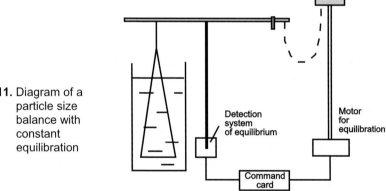

Fig. 2.11. Diagram of a particle size balance with constant equilibration

Sedimentation is carried out after dispersion on samples of reduced weight, i.e. about 1–2 g, in a thermostatic enclosure. Continuous automatic recording of the weight of the sediments deposited makes it possible to create cumulative mass curves as a function of time. Depending on the degree of automation and calculation, frequency charts can also be created. The measurements are reproducible, but require a long time to perform and are thus not suitable for series analysis.

Systems Using Simple Gravity and Measurement by X-ray

The particles are prepared and put in suspension (as described in sections X-ray beam). The particles absorb a quantity of X-ray proportional to their number. The resulting intensity is measured by a scintillation counter.

At the beginning, the resulting intensity of X-rays is at a minimum, then the falling particles cause an increase in the intensity transmitted. To reduce measurement time, the cell containing the suspension gradually moves downwards and the fixed X-ray beam sweeps a portion of the suspension increasingly close to the surface. All these movements are controlled by computer, and the position of the cell is a logarithmic function of time, coupled with the x-axis of the recorder, which makes it possible to determine the diameter that corresponds to the position of the cell. The smallest diameter it is possible to measure is 0.1 µm and the largest is 100 – 300 µm, depending on the model.

Continuous measurements make it possible to express the results in the form of cumulative curves of histograms of weight, or number of surface particles, etc. Computer interfaces make it possible to store the results of the analyses, and a sampler equipped with a carrousel allows uninterrupted treatment of several samples.

It should be noted that X-rays with wavelengths of less than 10 nm are well suited for the measurement of particles which would be impossible to measure in visible light (100 – 800 nm i.e. similar to the diameter of fine clay particles). Repeatability is satisfactory and measurement up to 2 µm takes about 10 min.

This type of equipment has been the subject of comparative studies with the pipette method for the analyses of soils (e.g. Delaune et al., 1991). It is useful for the 50–1 µm fraction, but needs a longer time for finer particles (< 0.2 µm in 50 min). However, undervaluation of coarse silts has been observed when they comprise more than 20% of the soil.

System Using Simple Gravity and Measurement by Light Absorption or Scattering

Methods based on photo-sedimentation (nephelometry, turbidimetry) are subject to many interferences. Their reproducibility and repeatability are low due to the use of white light or monochromatic light in the visible spectrum.

These methods should only be used for rapid comparisons within homogeneous families.

Methods Using Elutriation

In these methods, the falling speed of the particles (the mobile solid phase which is easy to measure) is lower, equal or higher than the speed of the fluid (non-stationary mobile liquid phase).

The liquid phase circulates in the reverse direction to the particles, making it possible to sort them; the finest particles migrate upwards or fall by gravity. The different fractions can be recovered. This system is suitable for certain studies on sediments, but measurements take a long time and are not really suitable for repetitive analysis.

2.3.3 Methods Using Accelerated Sedimentation

Principle

In practice, methods using simple gravity cannot be used for particle sizes <2 μm because of the extremely long time needed for sedimentation of the finest particles. It is difficult to maintain the cylinders of sedimentation without convection currents for long periods and to withdraw the particles from the Brownian movement. However, acceleration of gravity by centrifugation makes it possible to exceed the limits and to mitigate the effect of Brownian movement.

The techniques of separation and the recovery of granulometric phases by this process are discussed in Chap. 3.

Apparatus Using Centrifugal Discs

Some equipment uses successively first simple gravity with the vertical rotor remaining stationary for the largest particles, and second gravity with centrifugation at speeds of 1,800 to 8,000g (Horiba, Shimadzu, Seishin, Union-Giken, Joyce-Loebl-Vickers, etc.).

Analysis is continuous, and recording makes it possible to automatically create curves and histograms. Masses of soil of the order of 1 g can be treated in this way.

Depending on the manufacturer, the measuring cells are intersected either by a filtered incandescent light with measurement of absorption, or – very exceptionally – by laser or X-ray detection (Brook Haven). Particles of 0.01 μm to 100 μm can be identified. Other manufacturers use horizontal discs and samplings at a given distance and at a given time. The fractions are dried, weighed and possibly subjected to other analyses (Fritsch, Simcar, Joyce-Loebl, etc.).

The performances of these apparatus are not always equal for series analysis, and repeatability is not always within the range usually obtained with the pipette method.

For sub-micrometric analysis, one manufacturer offers an ultracentrifuge with a titanium disc at 100,000g in a partial vacuum to avoid heating and noise. A UV scanner (280 nm) makes it possible to analyze soil particles of less than 500 nm (Beckmann Spinco).

Micro-methods using Field flow fractionation (FFF) are still not reliable enough for widespread use in soil studies.

2.3.4 Methods Using Laser Scattering and Diffraction

Laser particle-measurement instruments have undergone spectacular development and can now be used for an increasing range of particle sizes. Certain equipment make it possible to cover ranges from 0.1 to 2,000 µm, but in general, apparatus are particularly powerful for a more limited range. One range is dedicated to sub-micronic, or even nanometric particles, while others with a wider range are particularly useful for the particle size analysis most usually required by soil laboratories.

These measurements are not based on sedimentation and must consequently be calibrated.

A dispersing liquid containing suspended particles circulates in a measuring cell intersected by a monochromatic Laser beam collimated by a condenser on a window of analysis of a defined surface. The light of the Laser is diffracted on the outside of the particles and the angles of diffraction are inversely proportional to the size of the particles. An optical system collects the signals which are analyzed by Fourier transformation and discriminated on a detector engraved with pre-determined angles. The signal is treated to extract the distribution of the particles. The results can be expressed in the form of curves: by average diameter (particle size distribution) expressed as a percentage of total weights, by histograms of weight, surface, number of particles, volume, etc. 32 – 64 classes of sizes can be measured (Malvern, Cilas-Alcatel, Coulter, etc.).

Certain apparatus allow either proportioning on a suspension, or on dry powder, which can be useful for analyzing silts. Serial deflocculation on line is possible by ultrasound. Loading 40 samples with a sample distributor and a using distributor for reagents makes it possible to work without continuous monitoring.

Analytical files enable methods to be pre-determined, including the dispersants. The procedures are simple but vary considerably with the apparatus and it is consequently impossible to give a detailed procedure here.

2.3.5 Methods Using Optical and Electric Properties

Analysis of the distribution of sub-micron particles (3 nm to 3 µm) combines measurements of pH, temperature, conductivity, and relative viscosity making it possible to control the stability of a suspension and the electro-kinetic potential (Zeta potential, potential difference between the dispersed surface layer and the medium of dispersion).

The ionic force is measured in an electrophoresis quartz tank with a Pt–Mo electrode on particles measuring from 1 to 1,000 µm (Malvern, Brookhaven, Coulter, Micromeritics, Mono-Research Lab., Zetameter Inc., Matec Applied Science, etc.).

The effective surface charge of the particles is determined by the measurement of mobility in a liquid–solid system, the permittivity of the liquid being known. This enables the study of the phenomena of flocculation and dispersion.

Other apparatus are designed for the study and optimization of the dispersion of certain clays for industrial use. They make it possible to differentiate flocculated and deflocculated particles. For example, primary Kaolinite particles consist of regular hexagonal discs. The nature of these particles means that in the presence of an electric field a dipole is induced, causing alignment with the field. The neo-aggregates formed by flocculation consist of clusters of randomly arranged primary particles, out of alignment with the electric field. To measure the relative proportions of flocculated and dispersed particles, the suspension is intersected by a Laser beam and the diffused light is analyzed. The result is quantified. Measurements made in different conditions (dispersing concentration, the nature of the dispersant, pH, etc.) enable optimization of the analyses.

2.3.6 Methods Allowing Direct Observation of the Particles

Optical and Electronic Microscopy – Radiation Counter and Image Analyzer

These direct methods are based on the use of optical microscopy, or possibly of electronic microscopy (cf. Chap. 8). Particle fractions isolated by gravity can be used among others. In electronic microscopy, the preparations must be dried and presented on grids or plates (MET-MEB).

Microscopy makes it possible to directly observe the population of particles and their morphological parameters. Shape, length, width, thickness or diameter can be defined on micro-samples, and the fractal properties estimated. Comparison of the particles of the same fraction makes it possible to judge the quality of fractionation (use of tests of bulky diatoms, regularity, influence of density, etc.). Counting can be done by a radiation counter, or by an image and texture analyzer.

In electronic microscopy with an EDX probe it is possible to perform chemical analyses; and in optical microscopy, to use infra-red radiation. This equipment offers a wide range of possibilities (Quantachrome, Zeiss, Leitz, etc.) and makes it possible to establish percentages of cumulated mass, distribution by size of particles, in terms of number, mass and specific surface area (0.1 – 300 μm).

2.3.7 Methods Using Conductivity

While passing through a gauged opening, a particle displaces a volume of electrolyte which modifies electric resistance (differential conductivity). This change in resistance is a function of volume. Counting allows particles to be grouped in classes using an amplitude discriminator.

The results are expressed in 16 counter channels as total percentage weight or the number of particles of a specific dimension; results can be presented in the form of graphs or tables.

The apparatus based on this principle are counters that make it possible to ignore density which can be useful when dealing with soils rich in iron oxides with a high density (4 – 5), i.e. well above the mean of 2.65 used for sedimentation by simple gravity. The shape of the particles is significant for the accuracy of the measurements. Measurements are possible between 1 and 5,000 μm (Coulter), but the optimal field of measurement depends on the choice of a suitable opening. Particles of less than 1 μm are often underestimated. The preparation of the samples is identical to the standard method (cf. Sects. 2.2.1 and 2.2.2).

References

Atterberg A (1912) Die mechanische Bodenanalyse und die klassifikation der mineral böden sechwedens. *Int. Mitt. Bodenk.*, 2, 312–342

Baize D (2000) *Guide des analyses courantes en pédologie.*, INRA, France, 257 p

Bouyoucos GS (1927) The hydrometer as a new method for mechanical analysis of soils. *J. Soil Sci.,* 23, 343

Bouyoucos GS (1935) A hydrometer method for making mechanical analysis of soils. *Bull. Am. Ceram. Soc.,* 14, 259

Bouyoucos GS (1962) Hydrometer method improved for making particle size analysis of soils. *Agron. J.,* 54, 464–465

Casagrande A (1934) Die Aräometer-methode zur Bestimmun der kornverteilung von Boden und anderen materialen. *Springer J.*

De Leenheer L and Van Hove J (1956) Werkwijze voor de mechanische analyse met de kettinghydrometer. *Rijksland Bouwhogeschool (Gand).*, XXI, 249–274

De Leenheer L and Maes L (1952) Analyse granulométrique avec l'hydromètre à chaîne. *Bull. Soc. Belge de Géologie.*, 61, 138–164

De Leenheer L, Van Ruymbeke M and Maes L (1955) L'analyse mécanique au moyen de l'hydromètre à chaîne. *Silicates Industriels.,* Tome XX, n° 6–7, 1–7

Delaune M, Reiffsteck M and Feller C (1991) L'analyse granulométrique de sols et sédiments à l'aide du microgranulomètre sédigraph 5000 et comparaison avec la méthode à la pipette Robinson. *Cahiers ORSTOM sér. Pédol.,* 26, 183–189

Gee GW and Bauder JW (1986) Particle-size analysis. *In Methods of Soil Analysis. Part 1 Physical and Mineralogical Methods.*, Klute A. Ed. Chap. 15. *American Society of Agronomy. Soil Sci. Soc. Am.*, 383–411

Gras R (1988) *Physique du sol pour l'aménagement*, Masson, Paris, 587 p

Hénin S (1976) *Cours de physique du sol*, vol. 1. Orstom-Editest, Bruxelles, 159 p

Jackson (1969) *Soil Chemical Analysis – Advanced Course.,* 2nd ed. University of Wisconsin, Madison, WI

Mériaux S (1954) Contribution à l'étude de l'analyse granulométrique. *Ann. Agro.*, I, 5–53, II, 149–205

Pansu M, Gautheyrou J and Loyer JY (2001) *Soil Analysis – Sampling, Instrumentation and Quality Control*, Balkema publishers, Lisse, Abington, Exton, Tokyo, 512 p

Pétard J (1993) *Les méthodes d'analyse. T1 Analyse de sols.*, Notes techniques laboratoires communs d'analyse, Orstom, Nouméa, Paris

Rouiller J, Burtin G and Souchier B (1972) La dispersion des sols dans l'analyse granulométrique. Méthode utilisant les résines échangeuses d'ions. *Bull. ENSAIA, Nancy, France*, 14, 183–204

Stokes GG (1851) On the effect of the lateral friction of fluids on the motion of pendulums. *Trans. Cambridge Phil. Soc.*, 9, 8–106

Susini J (1978) Realisation d'un ensemble automatique de lavage des sables de l'analyse granulométrique. *Cah. ORSTOM Série Pédol.,* 16, 339–344

Tamm O (1922) Eine Methode zur Bestian on vag der anorganischen komponenten des Gelkomplexes in Boden. *Meddel. Staters Skogsfirsöksanst (Suède)*, 19, 385–404

Van Ruymbeke M and De Leenheer L (1954) Etude comparative d'analyses granulométriques par décantations successives et par l'hydromère à chaîne. *Actes et C. R. du Vème Congrès International de la Science du Sol (Leopoldville)*, II, 322–328

Vieillefon J (1979) Contribution à l'amélioration de l'étude analytique des sols gypseux. *Cah. ORSTOM Sér. Pédol.*, XVII, 195–223

X 31-107 (1983) *Analyse granulométrique par sédimentation. Méthode de la pipette.* In *Qualité des sols 3°ed.*, AFNOR, 357–371

Bibliography

Generality

Barth HG and Shao-Tang Sun (1991) Particle size analysis. *Anal. Chem.*, 63, 1R–10R.

Chamayou H and Legros JP (1989) *Les bases physiques, chimiques et minéralogiques de la Science du sol*, Tech. Vivantes, ACCT Presses Univ. de France, 593 p.

Guillet B and Rouiller J (1979) La granulométrie. In *Pédologie, constituants et propriétés des sols*, Bonneau and Souchier ed., Masson, 317–321.

Johnston, Farina MPW and Lawrence JY (1987) Estimation of soil texture from sample density. *Commun. Soil Sci. Plant Anal.*, 18, 1173–1180.

Jones JL, Kay JJ, Park JJ and Bishop CK (1980) The determination of particle size distribution in soil. A collaborative study. *J. Sci. Food Agric.*, 31, 724–729.

Loveland PJ and Whalley WR (1991) Particle size analysis. In *Soil Analysis: Physical Methods.*, Smith KA, Mullins CEJ ed., Dekker, New York 271–328.

Smith RB and Pratt DN (1984) The variability in soil particle size test results by various sub sampling techniques. *J. Soil Sci.*, 35, 23–26.

Syvitski JPM (1991) Principles, methods and applications of particle size analysis. *Cambridge Univ. Press.*, 366 pages.

Pre-treatment

Organic Matters

Douglas LA and Fiessinger F (1971) Degradation of clay minerals by H_2O_2 treatments to oxidize organic mater. *Clays Clay Miner.*, 19, 67–68

Fisher WR (1984) The oxidation of sol organic matter by KBrO for particle size determination. *Commun. Soil Sci. Plant Anal.*, 15, 1281–1284

Harada Y and Inoko A (1977) The oxidation products formed from soil organic matter by hydrogen peroxide treatment. *Soil Sci. Plant Nutr.*, 23, 513–521

Langeveld AD Van, Gaast SJ Van der and Eisma D (1978) A comparison of the effectiveness of eight methods for the removal of organic matter from clay. *Clays Clay Miner.*, 26, 361–364

Lavkulich LM and Wiens JH (1970) Comparison of organic matter destruction by hydrogen peroxide and sodium hypochlorite and its effects on selected mineral constituents. *Soil Sci. Soc. Am. Proc.*, 34, 755–758

Omueti JAI (1980) Sodium hypochlorite treatment for organic matter destruction in tropical soils of Nigeria. *Soil Sci. Soc. Am. J.*, 44, 878–880

Sequi P and Aringhieri R (1977) Destruction of organic matter by hydrogen peroxide in the presence of pyrophosphate and its effect on soil specific surface area. *Soil Sci. Soc. Am. J.*, 41, 340–342

Visser SA and Caillier M (1988) Observations on the dispersion and aggregation of clays by humic substances. I – Dispersive effects of humic acids. *Geoderma*, 42, 331–337

Vodyannitskii Yu N, Trukhin VT and Bagina OL (1989) The action of perhydral upon iron oxides in soil. *Dokuchzer soil Sci. Inst. (Moscou)*, 1, 20–21

Eliminate Organo-Minerals Compounds

Harward ME, Theisen AA and Evans DD (1962) Effect of iron removal and dispersion methods on clay mineral identification by X-Ray difraction. *Soil Sci. Soc. Am. Proc.*, 26, 535–541

Mehra OP and Jackson ML (1960) Iron oxide removal from soils and clays by a dithiomite-citrate system buffered with sodium bicarbonate. In *Clays and Clay Minerals. Proc. Seventh Conf. Natl Acad. Sci. Natl Res. Counc. Pub.*, 237–317

Eliminate Soluble Salts – Gypsum

Rengasamy P (1983) Clay dispersion in relation to changes in the electrolyte composition of dialysed red–brown earth. *J. Soil Sci.*, 34, 723–732

Rivers ED, Hallmark CT, West LT and Drees LR (1982) A technique for rapid removal of gypsum from soil samples. *Soil Sci. Soc. Am. J.*, 46, 1338–1340

Suspension – Dispersion – Flocculation

Balli P (1965) Critères de la qualité de la suspension en vue de l'analyse granulométrique. *Science du sol*, 1, 15

Bartoli F, Burtin G and Herbillon AJ (1991) Disaggregation and clay dispersion of oxisols: Na Resin, a recommended methodology. *Geoderma*, 49, 301–317

Brewster GR (1980) Effects of chemical pretreatment on X-Ray powder diffraction characteristics of clay minerals derived from volcanic ash. *Clays Clay Miner.*, 28, 303–310

Colmet-Daage F, Gautheyrou J, Gautheyrou M, Kimpe C de (1972) Dispersion et étude des fractions fines des sols à allophane des Antilles et d'Amérique latine. 1ère partie: Techniques de dispersion. *Cah. Orstom, Sér. Pédol.*, Vol. X(2), 169–191

Demolon A and Bastisse E (1935) Sur la dispersion des colloïdes argileux. Applications à leur extraction. *Annales Agronomiques*, 1–15

Dong A, Chesters G and Simsiman GV (1983) Soil dispersibility. *Soil Sci.*, 136, 208–212

Egashira K (1981) Floculation of clay suspensions separated from soils of different soil type. *Soil Sci. Plant Nutr.*, 27, 281–287

Forsyth P, Marcelja S, Mitchell DJ and Ninham BW (1978) Stability of clay dispersions. In *Modidication of Soil Structure.*, Emerson, Bond, Dexter Ed. Wiley, New York. 2, 17–25

Goldberg S and Forster HS (1989) Floculation of reference clays and arid soil clays as affected by electrolyte concentration, exchangeable section percentage, sodium adsorption ratio, pH and clay mineralogy. *Annual Meeting – Clay Minerals Society*, 26, 35

Gupta RK, Bhumbla DK and Abrol IP (1984) Effect of sodicity, pH, organic matter and calcium carbonate on the dispersion behavior of soils. *Soil Sci.*, 137, 245–251

Keren R (1991) Adsorbed sodium fraction's effect on rheology of montmorillinite–kaolinite suspensions. *Soil Sci. Soc. Am. J.*, 55, 376–379

Manfredini T, Pellacani GC, Pozzi P and Corradi AB (1990) Monomeric and oligomeric phosphates as deflocculants of concentrated aqueous clay suspensions. *Appl. Clay Sci.*, 5, 193–201

Miller WP, Frenkel H and Newman KD (1990) FLoculation concentration and sodium/calcium exchange of kaolinitic soil clays. *Soil Sci. Soc. Am. J.*, 54, 346–351

Ohtsubo M and Ibaraki M (1991) Particle-size characterzation of flocs and sedimentation volume in electrolyte clay suspensions. *Appl. Clay Sci.*, 6, 181–194

Oreshkin NG (1979) Device for tating suspension samples for the particle-size analysis of soils. *Soviet Soil Sci.*, 4, 136-138

Reddy SR and Fogler HS (1981) Emulsion stability: determination from turbidity. *J. Colloid Interface Sci.*, 79, 101–104

Reddy SR, Fogler HS (1981) Emulsion stability: delineation of different particle loss mechanisms. *J. Colloid Interface Sci.*, 79, 105–113

Robinson GW (1933) The dispersion of soils in mechanical analysis. *Bur. Soil Sci. Tech. Commun.*, 26, 27–28

Shaviv A, Ravina I and Zaslavsky P (1988) Floculation of clay suspensions by an anionic soil conditioner. *Appl. Clay Sci.*, 3, 193–203

Ultrasonic Dispersion

Arustamyants YEI (1990) Optimizing the ultrasonic preparation of soils for particle-size analysis. *Pochvovedeniye*, 12, 55–68

Busacca AJ, Aniku JR and Singer MJ (1984) Dispersion of soils by an ultrasonic method that eliminates probe contact. *Soil Sci. Soc. Am. J.*, 48, 1125–1129

Edwards AP and Bremner JM (1967) Dispersion of soil particules by sonic vibrations. *J. Soil Sci.*, 18, 1

Feller C, Burtin G and Herbillon A (1991) Utilisation des résines sodiques et des ultra-sons dans le fractionnement granulométrique de la matière organique des sols. Intérêt et limites. *Science du sol*, 29, 77–93

Gregorich EG, Kachandski RG and Voroney RP (1988) Ultrasonic dispersion of aggregates: distribution of organic matter in size fractions. *Can. J. Soil Sci.*, 68, 395–403

Hinds AA and Lowe LE (1980) Dispersion and dissolution effects during ultrasonic dispersion of gleysolic soils in water and in electrolytes. *Can. J. Soil Sci.*, 60, 329–335

Hinds AA and Lowe LE (1980) The use of an ultrasonic probe in soil dispersion and in the bulk isolation of organo-mineral complexes. *Can. J. Soil Sci.*, 60, 389–392

Ilnicki P and Matelska U (1984) Ultrasound application for dispersion of soil samples for particle size analysis. *Roezniki Gleboznaweze*, 35, 15–24

Mikhail EH and Briner GP (1978) Routine particle size analysis of soils using sodium hypochlorite and ultrasonic dispersion. *Aust. J. Soil Res.*, 16, 241–244

Minkin MB, Mulyar IA and Mulyar AI (1985) An ultrasonic method of analysing of water extracts from soils. *Pochvovedeniye*, 3, 136–140

Moen DE and Richardson JL (1984) Ultrasonic dispersion of soil aggregates stabilized by polyvinyl alcohol and T 403-glyoxal polymers. *Soil Sci. Soc. Am. J.*, 48, 628–631

Morra MJ, Blank RR, Freeborn LL and Shafil B (1991) Size fractionation of soil organo-mineral complexes using ultrasonic dispersion. *Soil Sci.*, 4, 294–303

Schulze DG and Dixon JB (1979) High gradient enzymatic separation of iron oxydes and other magnetic minerals from soils clays. *Soil Sci. Soc. Am. J.*, 43, 793–799

Pipette Method

Andreasen AHM and Andersen J (1930) Etude de l'influence de la dilution sur les résultats de l'analyse granulométrique par sédimentation. *Kolloid Z.*, 50, 217

Bloom PR, Meter K and Crum JR (1985) Titration method for determination of clay-sized carbonates. *Soil Sci. Soc. Am. J.*, 49, 1070–1073

Godse NG and Sannigrahi AK (1988) Comparative study on methods of particle-size analysis for vertisols. *J. Indian Soc. Soil Sci.*, 36, 780–783

Indorante SJ, Follmer LR, Hammer RD and Koenig PG (1990) Particle-size analysis by a modified pipette procedure. *Soil Sci. Soc. Am. J.*, 54, 560–563

Krumbein WC (1935) A time chart for mechanical analyses by the pipette method. *J. Sediment. Petrol.*, 5, 93–95

Miller WP and Miller DM (1987) A micro-pipette method for soil mechanical analysis. *Commun. Soil Sci. Plant Anal.*, 18, 1–15

Oreshkin NG (1979) Device for taking suspension samples for the particle-size analysis of soils. *Soviet Soil Sci. (Pochvovedeniye)*, 4, 136–138

Richter M and Svartz H (1984) Analisis granulometrico de suelos en escala reducida. *Ciencia del suelo*, 2, 1–8

Shetron SG and Trettin CC (1984) Influence of mine tailing particle density on pipette procedures. *Soil Sci. Soc. Am. J.*, 48, 418–420

Hydrometer Method

American Society for Testing and Materials (1972) Standard test methode for particle-size analysis of Soils – D 422-463. *Annual Book of ASTM*, 1985

Barthokur NN (1986) Clay fraction determinations with Beta-ray gauge. *Commun. Soil Sci. Plant Anal.*, 17, 533–545

Fontes LEF (1982) A new cylinder for sedimentation of soil suspension in the determination of the clay fraction by the hydrometer method. *Revista brasileira de Ciencia do Solo*, 6, 152–154

Gee GW and Bauder JW (1979) Particle size analysis by hydrometer, a simplified method for routine textural analysis and a sensivity test of measurement parameters. *Soil Sci. Soc. Am. J.*, 43, 1004–1007

Johnson JE, Bowles JA and Knuteson JA (1985) Comparison of pretreatments and dispersants on clay determination by the hydrometer method. *Commun. Soil Sci. Plant Anal.*, 16, 1029–1037

Sur HS and Kvkal SS (1992) A modified hydrometer procedure for particle size analysis. *Soil Sci.*, 153, 1–4

Instrumental Methods

Arustamyants YEI (1992) Instrumental methods for determining the particle-size composition of soils. *Scr. Tech.*, 101–117

Barth, HG (1984) *Modern Methods of Particle Size Analysis.*, Wiley, New York, 209 pages

Cooper LR, Haverland RL, Hendricks DM and Knisel WG (1984) Microtrac particle-size analyzer: an alternative particle-size determination method for sediment and soil. *Soil Sci.*, 132, 138–146

Devyatykh GG, Karpov YU A, Krylov VA and Lazukina OP (1987) Laser-ultra microscopic method of determining suspended particles in high-parity liquids. *Talanta*, 34, 133–139

Hendrix WP and Orr C (1970) Automate sedimentation size analysis instrument. *Particle Size Analysis*, 133–146

Hutton JT (1955) A method of particle size analysis of soils (balance de Plummet). *CSIRO, Report*, 11/55.

Karsten JHM and Kotze WAG (1984) Soil particle analysis with the gamma alternation technique. *Commun. Soil Sci. Plant Anal.*, 15, 731–739

Kirkland JJ and Yau WW (1983) Simultaneaous determination of particle size and density by sedimentation field flow fractionation (FFF). *Anal. Chem.*, 55, 2165–2170

Kirkland JJ, Rementer SW and Yav WW (1981) Time-delayed exponential field-programmed sedimentation field flow fractionation for particle-size distribution analysis. *Anal. Chem.*, 53, 1730–1736

Marshall TI (1956) A Plummett Balance for measuring the size distribution of soil particles. *Aust. J. Appl. Sci.*, 7, 142–147

Mc Connel ML (1981) Particle size determination by quasielastic light scattering. *Anal. Chem.*, 53, 1007–1018

Novich BE and Ring TA (1984) Colloid stability of clays using photron correlation spectroscopy. *Clays Clay Miner.*, 32, 400–406

Oakley DM and Jennings BR (1982) Clay particle sizing by electrically induced birefringence. *Clay Miner.*, 17, 313–325

Pennington KL and Lewis GC (1979) A comparison of electronic and pipet methods for mechanical analysis of soils. *Soil Sci.*, 28, 280–284

Rybina VV (1979) Use of conductimetry for the determination of the particle-size composition of soils. *Pochvovedeniye*, 7, 134–138

Salbu B, Bjornstad HE, Linstrom NS, Lydersen E (1985) Size fractionation techniques in the determination of elements associated with particulate or colloidal material in natural fresh waters. *Talanta*, 32, 907–913

Svarovsky L and Allen T (1970) Performance of a new X-Ray sedimentometer. *Particle Size Analysis*, 147–157

Yang KC and Hogg R (1979) Estimation of particle size distributions from turbidimetric measurements. *Anal. Chem.*, 51, 758–763

Yonker CR, Jones HK and Robertson DM (1987) Non aqueous sedimentation field flow fractionation. *Anal. Chem.*, 59, 2574–2579

Fractionation of the Colloidal Systems

3.1 Introduction

The identification and the quantification of the finest soil fractions are essential to explain the transformation of minerals, as these fractions are directly related to pedogenesis and, in agronomy, to potential fertility.

The nature and properties of these particles are of interest to agronomists (soil chemistry and physics: textural class, fertility, pore system, water storage, cohesion, slaking, etc.), soil scientists (pedogenesis, characterization and functioning of soils, lithological nature, products of alteration, etc.), geologists of the quartz period (sedimentology: origin of wind, marine, or lake deposits, typology of volcanic ash and heavy minerals, etc.), mineralogists and geochemists (assessments of alterations, mineral stocks liable to alteration, origin and nature of materials, etc.).

The majority of the instrumental methods used for the determination of the texture of the soils (cf. Chap. 2) do not enable isolation of the fractions measured, but discontinuous methods based on sedimentation do enable re-use of the sand, silt and clay fractions, as long no contaminating dispersants are used. In practice, the limit of simple gravity methods is fractionation up to approximately 1 μm. Under certain conditions, ultra-centrifugation makes it possible to reach the nanometric domain.

Fractions below 0.5 μm contain practically no more quartz or primary minerals. Fractions below 0.2 μm enable better characterization of argillization horizons. This threshold, proposed around 1931, was at that time regarded as representative of the limit of "the colloidal state" because after elimination of oxides and hydroxides, the fraction presented homogeneous chemical composition comparable to a mono-dispersed system, i.e. the same exchange capacity, the same structural composition of the 0.2 μm, 0.1 μm, and 0.05 μm particles.

When the final purpose of fractionation of the particles is physical or chemical determination, the different treatments that are carried out to put the very fine fractions in suspension can differ considerably from the methods used for textural analysis because secondary products cannot be significantly modified, in particular clays and oxides. In certain cases, it is possible to simply put fine fractions in suspension by ultrasound and to use ion exchange resin for desaturation. Dispersants of the hexametaphosphate or pyrophosphate type (cf. Chap. 2) should not be used.

The criteria of Stokes law are suitable for centrifugation and the same problems will occur with particles whose speed is changing. By quantitatively isolating all the fractions, chemical and physical determination can be refined, and more detailed distribution curves established for the particle continuum.

3.2 Fractionation by Continuous Centrifugation

3.2.1 Principle

After the treatments needed to isolate the primary particles (cf. Chap. 2), the sample is put in suspension for later analyses using a non-contaminating dispersant. The fine fractions (less than 2 μm) are first separated from the coarse fractions by several siphoning operations, which take the falling time of the silts into account. Five to six siphonings are sufficient for a quantitative recovery.

Because of the volumes being dealt with, fractionation of the fine phases is carried out in a centrifuge with continuous inputs per ascensum made up of a vertical tube able to rotate at 52,000g (Fig. 3.1a). A transfer paper placed inside the tube makes it possible to collect the particles that sediment on the wall (Fig. 3.1b). The effluents are collected at the top of the bowl by a single or double chute (depending on the model).

The suspension does not completely fill the tube but forms a concentric ring, the centre being a cylinder of air, R_1 (Fig. 3.1b). The thickness of the film of suspension is $R_2 - R_1$. The particles gradually sediment on the walls of the bowl as a function of their density and of their diameter. They follow a parabolic trajectory starting from the point of deposit of the effluents.

The radial application of the centrifugal force is accompanied by a vertical force. A particle of a given diameter and density will deposit according to the resulting force vector. Viscosity can be modified in the course of centrifugation by variations in temperature, the influence of the pressures created at high speeds and possibly by the presence of thixotropic materials. With soils containing allophanes, it is sometimes possible to observe flocculation if the dispersing medium is not homogeneous throughout the iterative extractions, or due to loss of part of the swelling water. It should be noted that fibres of imogolite, mica plates, tests of diatoms, etc. do not follow Stokes' law and are separated in a random way.

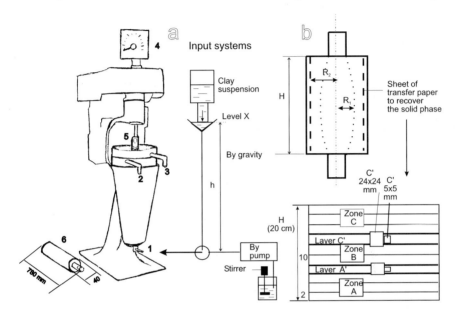

Fig. 3.1. (a) Uninterrupted ultracentrifuge system using compressed air – 45,000*g* (1 input nozzle for injection; 2, 3 exit chutes for effluents; 4 rev counter; 5 connecting with bowl; 6 centrifugation bowl). **(b)** Centrifugation bowl with transfer paper for recovery (division of the delivery points according to procedure in "Fractionation in Four Phases").

The component perpendicular to the axis can be easily calculated starting from Stokes law (cf. Sect. 3.2.2), however, it should be noted that with centrifugation, the deposit rate of the particles is not constant due to variations in the intensity of the field of centrifugation which depend on the diameter of the rotor. The vertical component must be calculated as a function of the flow, which itself depends on the input, on the diameter of the injector channel, and on the diameter of the ring outfall.

In practice, the formulas for computation of the standard Sharples centrifuge cannot be rigorously applied at the bottom and the top of the bowl because of turbulence at these levels (injector channel and deflector at the bottom, ring outfall at the top). Too much deposit can also modify the radius at the bottom of the bowl. However, the height of the deposit can be determined with sufficient accuracy by following a strict procedure. It may be advantageous to collect a relatively small quantity of sediments (not exceeding 10 g) at each treatment.

Under certain operating conditions (number of revolutions, flow, etc.), the finest particles can pass across the bowl without sedimentation because the time of passage is insufficient for the centrifugal force to transfer them to the wall. However, if one of the variables is modified, for example, the flow is slowed down by changing the input tube; these particles can also be collected. With a low flow, separation is differentiated more satisfactorily than with a high flow. For satisfactory separation, it is better to use tubes with a small diameter and a not too high charge. For simple separation (for purification by enrichment) a 2 mm tube and a higher charge (75 cm for example) can be used. The drain may still contain fine particles depending on the number of revolutions applied. The system makes it possible to use the drain again with a lower flow rate and to collect the solid fraction on a new transfer paper placed in the bowl.

Table 3.1. Deposit of particles of various minerals by continuous ultracentrifugation (flow 730 mL min^{-1} speed 20,000g, viscosity 1)

mineral	density	diameter of particles which sediment at a height of 10 cm in the bowl (in μm)
opal	2.10	360
gibbsite	2.40	320
quartz	2.65 (average used for the soils)	280
hematite	5.26	115

It is important to choose a speed and a flow which allow non-uniform deposit to obtain satisfactory classification of the particles. It is difficult to include all the variables in the calculation, and the forecast will be uncertain if the average density of 2.65 used for the soils is not regular. Indeed, if a mixture of minerals of different densities is used whose micro-particles are individualized in the suspension, very different particles with the same diameter will be found at any level (Table 3.1).

At one time, it seemed that graphic methods would be both adequate and fast. Saunders (1948) studied a nomographical representation applicable to continuous ultracentrifugation (1936–1940), and was able to determine that certain factors in the equation of Hauser and Lynn (cf. Sect. 3.2.2) remained constant for a given procedure thus allowing simplification and a move to a nomographical representation with five variables that could be extended to six variables using the method of Davis (1943).

It thus became possible to rapidly determine the height of deposit of elementary particles with different densities but the same diameter.

3.2.2 Theory

The method of Hauser and Lynn (1940) to calculate the size of the particles is one of the most powerful for use with an ultracentrifuge with continuous input. The equation makes it possible to express the vertical distance (Y in cm) from the deposit of a particle of a given size, measured starting from the bottom of the bowl of the centrifugal machine by

$$Y = C \frac{18 \, K_1 Q \, \eta}{\pi (R_2^2 - R_1^2) D^2 \omega^2 \delta\rho} \tag{3.1}$$

where

$$C = \frac{R_2^2}{2} \ln \frac{R_2}{X_0} - \frac{R_1^2}{2} \left(\ln \frac{R_2}{X_0} \right)^2 + \frac{X_0^2 - R_2^2}{4} \tag{3.1'}$$

R_2 = distance from the axis of rotation to the side of the bowl (cm);
R_1 = distance from the axis of rotation on the surface of the liquid in the bowl (cm);
X_0 = distance from the axis of rotation at which a given particle must start to deposit on the side of the bowl (cm);
K_1 = function of the construction of the bowl (cm^{-2})

$$= \frac{R_2^2 - R_1^2}{(3/4)R_1^4 + (1/4)R_2^4 - R_1^2 R_2^2 - R_1^4 \ln(R_1 / R_2)} \tag{3.2}$$

Q = throughput speed (flow of the suspension mL s^{-1});
η = viscosity of the dispersion medium (poise);
D = sphere equivalent diameter of the particles which sediment at Y cm;
ω = angular speed of rotation (radian per second);

$\delta\rho$ = difference in density between the dispersed particles (Table 3.2) and the medium of dispersion (g mL^{-1}).

Under standard conditions (flow and range of the particles), the equation of Hauser and Lynn is related to X_0 and D. For particles of a given diameter, the equation is a function of only X_0, which makes it possible to plot the curve of C vs Y. On this basis, Saunders (1948) established a system of monograms which allows the equivalent diameter of the particles settling in the bowl to be calculated with satisfactory precision.

By defining the constant $A = \dfrac{18\,K_1}{\pi\left(R_2^2 - R_1^2\right)}$, (3.1) becomes:

$$\frac{Y}{C} = \frac{A}{D^2}\frac{\eta}{\omega^2}\frac{Q}{\delta\rho} \tag{3.3}$$

Table 3.2. Specific density of some minerals (average density used for the soils = 2.65)

	minerals	density		minerals	density
Al	boehmite ALO(OH)	3.07	Fe	akaganeite $Fe^{3+}O(OH, Cl)$	3.55
	diaspore AlO(OH)	3.40		goethite FeO(OH)	4.0–4.4
	bayerite Al(OH)$_3$	2.53		lepidocrocite FeO(OH)	3.85
	gibbsite Al(OH)$_3$	2.40		hematite Fe$_2$O$_3$	5.26
	nordstrandite Al(OH)$_3$	2.43		maghemite Fe$_2$O$_3$	5.10
	corundum Al$_2$O$_3$	4.10		magnetite Fe$_3$O$_4$ $(Fe^{2+}Fe_2^{3+}O_4)$	5.17
	akdalaite 4Al$_2$O$_3$, H$_2$O	3.68		ilmenite FeO–TiO$_2$	4.44–4.90
	bauxite Al$_2$O$_3$, 2H$_2$O	2.55		pyrite FeS$_2$	5.02
Mn	manganosite MnO	5.36	clays	kaolinite	2.60
	pyrolusite MnO$_2$	5.06		halloysite	2.10
	ramsdelite MnO$_2$	4.50		dickite	2.60
	manganite MnO(OH)	4.33		montmorillonite	2–3.00
	feitknechtite MnO(OH)	3.80		nontronite	2–3.00
	groutite MnO(OH)	4.15		beidellite	2–3.00

	pyrochlorite $Mn(OH)_2$	3.25	micas:	biotite	3.00
	nsutite $Mn^{+2}Mn^{+4}O_2(OH)_2$	4.50		phlogopite	2.80
	hausmanite $Mn^{+2}Mn_2^{+3}O_4$	4.84		glauconite	2.60
				muscovite	2.80
				illite	2.6–2.9
Si	coesite SiO_2	2.93		feldspar white feldspar Na_2O, Al_2O_3, $6SiO_2$	2.61–2.64
	cristobalite SiO_2	2.33		andesine $(CaO, Na_2O$ Al_2O_3, $4SiO_2)$	2.65–2.69
	quartz SiO_2	2.65		oligoclase $NaAlSi_3O_8 +$ $CaAl_2Si_2O_8$	2.62–2.67
	tridymite SiO_2	2.26		orthoclase $KAlSi_3O_8$	2.56
	silhydrite $3SiO_2$, H_2O	2.14			
	opal SiO_2, nH_2O	2.10			
Ca	calcite $CaCO_3$	2.7–2.9			
	aragonite $CaCO_3$	2.9		gypsum $CaSO_4$, $2H_2O$	2.3

This equation can be treated using the "nomographical method" according to Davis (1943) and gives a value of Y/C to each value of Y. If η is expressed in centipoises, Q in mL min^{-1}, D in nm, ω in rotations min^{-1}, $\delta\rho$ in g mL^{-1} Y in cm and C in cm^2 the equation is written:

$$\frac{Y}{C} = 1.52 \times 10^{12} \frac{A \eta Q}{D^2 \omega^2 \delta\rho} \qquad (3.3')$$

This equation can be reduced to four equations with three variables and three parameters α, β and γ:

$$\log \alpha = \log \eta - \log Y/C$$
$$\log \beta = \log \delta\rho - 2 \log \omega$$
$$\log \gamma = \log \alpha + \log \beta$$
$$2 \log D = \log \gamma + \log Q$$

The nomographical method of Davis (1943) provides a solution by tracing four lines which represent the solution of one of these equations (Fig. 3.2). Constant A is included starting from a scale representing a numerical solution of (3.3'). For example, for a centrifugation tube where $R_1 = 2.175$ cm and $R_2 = 0.735$ cm, constant A is equal to 2.44×10^{12}. The final formula for direct calculation will be:

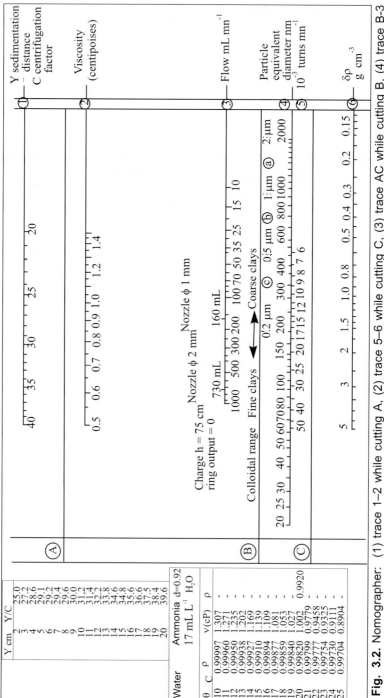

Fig. 3.2. Nomographer: (1) trace 1–2 while cutting A, (2) trace 5–6 while cutting C, (3) trace AC while cutting B, (4) trace B-3 while cutting 4, the equivalent diameter is obtained in nanometres of the particles deposited at the height selected (Y) in the centrifugation bowl

$$D = 2.44 \times 10^{12} \frac{\eta Q}{\left(\omega^2 \delta \rho Y/C\right)^{1/2}}$$

with value Y/C for the height Y and the units of (3.3').

3.2.3 Equipment and reagents

Equipment

– Standard Sharples T1 ultracentrifuge with continuous circulation and a turbine equipped with an 8RY stainless steel bowl with a diameter of 44 mm
– 6 L Pyrex bottle with broad neck with stopper
– Stopper pierced with a glass tube with an interior diameter of 10 mm cut in bevel (for input of suspension)
– 12 cm Conical forceps with jaw punts (to retrieve the transfer paper)
– Small plastic spatula
– Stylet (to lift the transfer paper for removal with the grip)

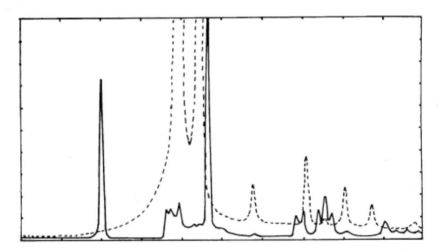

Fig. 3.3. Spectra of X-ray diffraction:
.... dashed line = Tymek support alone,
———— solid line = kaolinite on Tymek support (sufficiently thick to avoid contamination).

– Plastic transfer papers with frosted interior (Integraph, Invar 75 μm, Kodatrace, Chronaflex or Tymek Dupont de Nemours) 204×150 mm sheets; the thickness of this support must be homogeneous, it must have a constant weight per surface unit, be resistant to water, have a flat DRX spectrum or well-defined peaks outside the zones of measurement of the sample (Fig. 3.3)

– 1/10 mg balances

– Set of suitable pillboxes and micro-bottles (plastic, single use, Fig. 3.4)

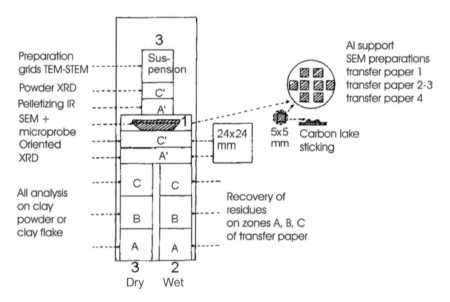

Fig. 3.4. Example of system for processing the fine fractions separated on transfer paper (Fig. 3.1), 1 = regrouping on MEB support, 2 = only andisols– histosols, 3 = pillbox, micro-bottles

– Aluminium supports for scanning electron microscopy

Reagents

Cf. Chap. 2

3.2.4 Procedure

Standard Continuous Ultracentrifugation

– Choose the diameter of the injector channel, the diameter of the ring outfall, and the height h of level X (Fig. 3.1).
–Place in the bowl of the centrifuge a tared transfer paper with the selected cutting plan drawn on the back (the weight of the transfer paper P_0 makes it possible to calculate the weights P_{01}, P_{02}, P_{03}, corresponding to the respective surfaces of zones A, B, C in Fig. 3.1).
– Suspend the bowl on the rotor and place the container for the recovery of the effluents under the chute.
– Fill the funnel to a constant level X with the same dispersant as the samples, taking care not to trap air in the adduction tube.
– Homogenize the bottle containing the clay suspension.
– Remove an aliquot of 2 mL (for grid TEM).
– Rock the bottle on the funnel; switch on the centrifugal machine at the selected speed.
– Place the injector channel under the bowl and open the input cock.

When all the liquid has gone, add 200 mL of the dispersion liquid to drive out all the suspension remaining in the bowl (approximately 150 mL). Adjust to a maximum speed of 52,000g for 2–3 min to stabilize the deposit.

Disconnect the input tube and stop the centrifuge (collect the liquid remaining in the tube in a crystallizer and discard it if it is clear).

Remove the transfer paper carefully by holding the bowl obliquely to not contaminate the top of the bowl with coarse particles. Spread the paper out flat. Recover any trace of deposit on the deflector and add it to the bottom of the transfer paper.

Leave to dry at room temperature (if necessary recover wet clay with a spatula and place it on the appropriate zone of the transfer paper before drying).

Weigh the transfer paper and dried clay: P_1. Deposited clay corresponds to $P_1 - P_0$

Cut the transfer paper following the plan on the back. This makes it possible to weigh zones A, B, C (Fig. 3.1), i.e. P_{11}, P_{12}, P_{13}.

Continuous Fractionation of the Colloidal Particles

The complex and time-consuming method of Hauser and Lynn (1940) enables isolation of the fine fractions from a suspension (Fig. 3.5) and the establishment of cumulative curves of distribution of the particles which can nowadays be accomplished continuously with an automatic apparatus for the measurement of particle size (cf. Chap. 2). This type of apparatus has two centrifugation speeds and seven different flows, i.e. 11 passages in the centrifuge to classify particles between 1 μm and 24 nm with a Sharples continuous centrifuge with a turbine.

This method cannot be used for routine tasks because of the length of the operations, or for fragile samples that are difficult to maintain in suspension like soils with allophane.

The method is nevertheless useful in metallogeny to identify the enriched fractions (release mesh). The suspensions must be diluted to accomplish fractionation without an awkward piston effect.

Fractionation in Four Phases

The method of Gautheyrou and Gautheyrou (1967) is based on the equations of Hauser and Lynn and the nomographical system of Saunders (cf. Sect. 3.2.2). The transfer paper shown in Fig. 3.1b is an example of one layout suited to the needs of mineralogical analysis, but other alternatives are possible considering that the particles deposited in a horizontal plane are similar and that the solid phase varies upwards.

Zones A, B, C (Figs. 3.1 and 3.4) allow separation of the particle size phases whose significance depends on the procedure used (these fractions are used for chemical and physical analyses). Zones A' and C' (Figs. 3.1 and 3.4) enable fractions to be isolated for X-ray diffraction either after crushing for powder diagrams, or pretreatments, or directly for oriented diagrams on the 24×24 mm^2 (cf. Chap. 4). After sticking the 5×5 mm^2 on a suitable support with carbon lacquer (cf. Chap. 8) they can be used for electronic scan microscopy with EDX microanalysis.

After dilution and preparation of the grids, a 1 mL sample of each suspension enables observation by transmission electronic microscopy (cf. Chap. 8).

Adjustments

Charge h: 75 cm (Fig. 3.1); temperature: 20°C; tube: 2 mm diameter; flow: 730 mL min^{-1}; time of passage in the bowl: 15 s; average density: 2.65; ring outfall: 0.

Charge, flow, temperature remain constant; only the speed is modified at each centrifugation: 6,000, 10,000, 25,000, 50,000g (at 50,000g, if the sample contains very fine particles, it may be necessary to use a 1 mm tube corresponding to a flow of 160 mL per minute to fix all the very fine phase).

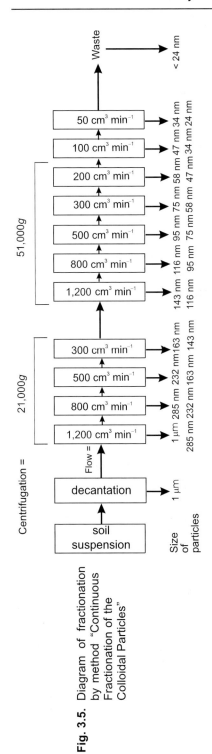

Fig. 3.5. Diagram of fractionation by method "Continuous Fractionation of the Colloidal Particles"

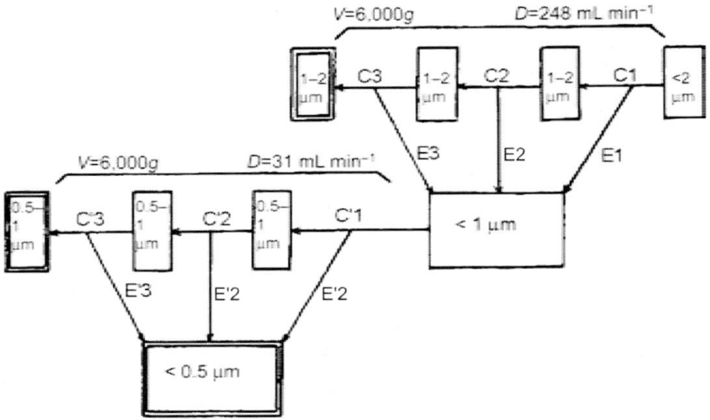

Fig. 3.6. Diagram of fractionation by method "Fractionation with Different Flows"

Fraction 2–1 µm

This fraction is separated at a centrifugation speed 6,000g and recovered on the first transfer paper (TP): weight TP alone: P_{01}, TP + deposit: P_{11}, weight clay: 2–1 µm: $P_{11}-P_{01}$: Pc_1 Express in % compared to the initial weight of soil.

Fraction 1–0.5 µm

Recovered on the second TP at 10,000g: Pc_2

Fraction 0.5–0.2 µm

On the third TP at 25,000g: Pc_3

Fraction 0.2–0.05 µm

On the fourth TP at 50,000g and lower flow of 160 mL min^{-1}, 1 mm tube: Pc_4

Clay < 0.05 µm

This very fine clay is contained in the last draining water and can be recovered by flocculation. This fraction is generally a clear extract that can be discarded because it contains the majority of the residual impurities of the reagents used for the initial preparation of clay. Electronic microscopy can also be used, but concentration by evaporation can result in risks of hydrolysis and neo-formation.

Remarks

If the deposit is too thick, irregular cracking can occur in clays with a high shrinkage coefficient, which makes it impossible to cut the 5×5 mm^2 for oriented XRD. In this case, the squares are not used but instead a sliver of clay is stuck down with carbon lacquer.

In certain soil samples the finest fractions are practically non-existent. In this case it is possible to stop at the second or the third centrifugation.

If major variations are observed between the coarsest phase and the finest phase, preparation and analyses of sub-samples should be performed progressively.

Certain studies may require conservation of part of fresh clay without drying. In this case, the transfer paper should have an additional vertical separation. Fresh clay should be recovered immediately at the outlet of the bowl with a plastic spatula and quickly stored in a pillbox. Quantification can be checked on the fraction which is dried but there is a risk of error due to transformations during drying.

The same method can also be used to:
- Separate and enrich two phases; for example two phases with the same mineral density but different particle size (micro-micas and coarser crystallized kaolinite).
- Separate two products of the same particle size but different density, for example aluminous products with a density <3.0 and ferrous or ferric products with a density of 4–5.
- Collect the particles of a given diameter and density on a narrow zone (metallogeny – separation meshes), etc.

Chlorite, vermiculite, or kaolinite enrichment is often observed in the coarse fractions. Well-crystallized kaolinite is generally present in fractions >0.5 μm. Quartz and muscovite are almost eliminated in the fractions <0.5 μm, which makes it possible "to clean" the spectra.

Gibbsite is mostly retained in the coarse fractions and is only present in very small amounts in the very fine phases.

Halloysite enrichment can be also observed, as well as enrichments in substances with short distance crystalline arrangement in fractions <0.5 μm or 0.2 μm, whereas well-crystallized kaolinite disappears.

Deferrization increases the smoothness of the particles revealing the incorporating effect of iron.

Studying the different fractions by X-ray diffraction enables observation of possible crystallochemical heterogeneity of the colloidal fraction and identification of mineral filiations which occurred during evolution and weathering. Minerals whose spectral signature is readable only above 5% (for example Sepiolite) can also be detected.

Fractionation with Different Flows

In this technique (Biological Centre of Pedology, Nancy, France), the clay suspension >2 μm at a concentration not exceeding 1%, is subjected to an initial series of centrifugation at fixed speed and flows (Fig. 3.6).

A second series of centrifugation with a much lower flow (31 mL min^{-1}) makes it possible to separate the finer fractions. Thanks to repeated centrifugation and the weak concentration of the medium, the separation of the fractions is considered quantitative.

3.3. Pretreatment of the extracted phases

Mineralogical analyses performed directly on total soil samples provide information on all the most abundant components, but do not allow detection of the presence of low concentration phases because of the lack of sensitivity of the instrumental techniques and the occurrence of much interference. These low-concentration phases (<5 %), which can be highly significant in explaining certain processes of soil genesis, are masked by background noise even when they are above their threshold of detection.

It is thus necessary to eliminate interference and to concentrate the "mineralogical clay" phase.

Using a suitable fractionation method, clays are purified and concentrated and appear in a homoionic form: NH_4^+, Ca^{2+}, or H^+ depending on the case. As mineral cements and the organomineral links have been destroyed, it is possible to obtain satisfactory separation of the particles.

The use of ultrasound enables good separation of elementary particles, and complementary pretreatments can be performed on clays to allow the use of specific instrumental techniques.

Selective dissolution makes it possible to eliminate the iron oxides which can obstruct XRD (cf. Chap. 4), fluorescence with a copper tube) and DTA–TGA (cf. Chap. 7), oxidation Fe^{2+}). Different pretreatments make it possible to carry out analyses using NMR, ESR, Mossbauer, etc.

Gels and substances that are amorphous to X-ray and have crystal lattices with short distance arrangement can be dissolved, enabling their quantification and the production of differential spectra (DXRD) to identify them.

Any calcium carbonate that is still present can be eliminated by complexing Ca^{2+} ions with a solution of normal EDTA.

Pretreatments also help improve the orientation of clays (which is disturbed by iron, for example in coatings), the intensity of the spectra of diffraction and the ratio of diffraction to background noise.

Clays often have to be studied after homoionic saturation by a cation (such as Mg^{2+} which regulates the adsorption of water by clays with an expansible interfoliaceous space, or K^+ which limits the adsorption of water and thus the swelling of the layers).

Other treatments, like solvation by polar solvents, or the creation of complexes of intercalation, make it possible to identify certain clays. Heat treatments are also used specifically to cause the collapse of the lattices or to modify surface properties. These methods are described in detail in Chaps. 4–7.

References

Davis DS (1943) Empirical Equations and Nomography. Mc Graw Hill, New York, 1, 104–114

Gautheyrou J and Gautheyrou M (1967) *Mode opératoire pour l'extraction et la purification de la fraction argileuse < 2 μm*. Notes de laboratoire, Orstom-Guadeloupe, mars 1968, 1–9, Orstom

Hauser EA and Lynn JE (1940) Separation and fractionation of colloidal systems. *Ind. Eng. Chem.*, 32, 659–662

Saunders E (1948) Nomograph for particle size determination with the Sharples supercentrifuge. *Anal. Chem.*, 20, 379–381

Bibliography

Atterberg A (1912) Die mechanische bodenanalyse und die klassification der mineralböden schwedens. *Intern. Mitt. Bodenk*, 2, 312–342

Coca Prados J and Bueno de las Heras J (1977) Dinamica de particulas en suspensions solido–liquido. I – Sedimentacion de particulas. *Ingeniera quimica*, 153–162

Colmet-Daage F, Gautheyrou J, Gautheyrou M, Kimpe de C, Fusil G and Sieffermann G (1972) Dispersion et étude des fractions fines de sols à allophane des Antilles et d'Amérique latine. IIème partie : Modifications de la nature et de la composition de la fraction inférieure à 2 microns selon la taille des particules. *Cahiers Orstom, série. Pédol.*, X, 219–241

Davis JM (1986) General retention theory for sedimentation Field-Flow-Fractionation. *Anal. Chem.*, 58, 161–164

Essigton ME, Mattigod SV and Ervin JO (1985) Particles sedimentation rates in the linear density gradient. *Soil Sci. Soc. Am. J.*, 49, 767–771

Gautheyrou J and Gautheyrou M (1982) Fractionnement des systèmes colloïdaux argileux par centrifugation continue. Notes laboratoire Orstom Bondy, 1–38

Hauser EA and Reed CE (1936) Studies in thixotropy. I – Development of a new method for measuring particle-size distribution in colloidal systems. *J. Phys. Chem.*, 40, 1169–1182

Horrocks M (2005) A combined procedure for recovering phytoliths and starch residues from soils, sedimentary deposits and similar materials. *J. Archaeological Sci.*, 32, 1169–1175

Jackson ML, Whittig LD and Pennington RP (1949) Segregation procedure for the mineralogical analysis of soils. *Soil Sci. Soc. Am. Proc.*, 14, 77–81

Jacobsen AE and Sullivan WF (1946) Centrifugal sedimentation method for particle size distribution. *Ind. Eng. Chem.*, 18, 360–364

Jaymes WF and Bigham JM (1986) Concentration of iron oxides from soil clays by density gradient centrifugation. *Soil Sci. Soc. Am. J.*, 50, 1633–1639

Johnson L (1956) Particle size analysis and centrifugal sedimentation. *Trans. Bull. Ceram Soc.*, 55, 267–285

Kamack HJ (1951) Particle size determination by centrifugal pipet sedimentation. *Anal. Chem.*, 23, 844–850

Kittrick JA and Hure EW (1963) A procedure for the particle-size separation of soils for X-Ray diffraction analysis. *Soil Sci.*, 96, 5, 319–325

Koch T and Giddings JC (1986) High-speed separation of large (> 1 µm) particles by steric Field-Flow-Fractionation. *Anal. Chem.,* 58, 994–997

Levitz PE (2005) Confined dynamics, forms and transitions in colloidal systems: from clay to DNA. *Magn. Reson. Imaging*, 23, 147–152

Marshal CE (1931) Studies in the degree of dispersion of the clays, I – Notes on the technique and accuracy of mechanical analysis using the centrifuge. *J. Soc. Chem. Ind.*, SDT, 444–450

Muog E, Taylor JR, Pearson RW, Weeks AE and Simonson RW (1936) Procedure for special type of mechanical and mineralogical soil analysis. *Soil Sci. Soc. Am. Proc.*, 101–112

Rouiller J, Brethes A, Burtin G and Guillet B (1984) Fractionnement des argiles par ultra-centrifugation en continu : évolution des illites en milieu podzolique. *Sci. Géol. Bull.*, 37, 319–331

Schachman HK (1948) Determination of sedimentation constants in the Sharples supercentrifuge. *J. Phys. Colloid. Chem.,* 52, 1034–1045

Tan KH (1996) *Soil Sampling, Preparation and Analysis.* Dekker, New York, 278–361

Tanner CB and Jackson ML (1947) Nomographs of sedimentation times for soil particles under gravity or centrifugal acceleration. *Soil Sci. Soc. Am. Proc.*, 12, 60–65

Tran-Vinh-Ann and Ndejuru E (1972) Analyse granulométrique de la fraction argileuse par centrifugation en flux continu. Mise au point d'une méthode et application à quelques sols tropicaux. *Pédologie*, XXII, 366–382

Truo E, Taylor JR, Simonson RW and Week ME (1936) Mechanical and mineralogical subdivision of the clay separate of soils. *Soil Sci. Soc. Proc.*, 175–179

Tu Y, O'Carroll JB, Kotlyar LS, Sparks BD, Ng S, Chung KH and Cuddy G (2005) Recovery of bitumen from oilsands: gelation of ultra-fine clay in the primary separation vessel. *Fuel*, 84, 653–660

Whittig LD and Allardice WR (1986) X-Ray diffraction techniques – separation of particle – size fraction. In Klute A (ed.), *Method of Soil Analysis Part Physical and Mineralogical Methods*, second edition, American Society or Agronomy, 340–342

Mineralogical Characterization by X-Ray Diffractometry

4.1 Introduction

4.1.1 X-Ray Diffraction and Mineralogy

Methods using optical microscopy in petrography are not suitable for the identification of mineralogical clays with small particles whose crystal lattices vary with water content and with their ionic environment and whose chemical composition is often unclear (Tables 4.1 and 4.2). Among other available methods, X-ray diffraction (XRD) is one of the most efficient. Coherent scattering of the incidental radiation in XRD makes it possible to clearly identify both the parameters of the crystal lattice and the geometrical distribution of the atoms in the crystal mesh.

XRD can be combined with or supplemented by geochemical and isotopic analyses (AAS, ICP, ICP-MS, EXAFS, etc.), thermal analyses (DTA-TGA, DSC, EGD, EGA, etc.), analyses that enable evaluation of interatomic or intermolecular binding energies and order–disorder relations (e.g. FTIR, Raman spectrometry, Mossbauer spectrometry, NMR), high resolution transmission electronic microscopy (+ electron micro-diffraction) and electronic scan microscopy. EDX or WDX probes make it possible to link in situ chemical composition with the shapes of the particles to be observed. Total chemical composition is determined by total analyses after mineralization in mediums that enable solubilization of all the components; selective dissolution makes it possible to sub-divide the sample into fractions of different chemical resistance; these sub-divisions are essential both for quantification and for purification of the samples before analysis by instrumental methods (e.g. XRD, IR or NMR spectroscopy).

Table 4.1. Classification of clays proposed by the international association for the study of clays (AIPEA[1])

type	group (x = charge by unit formula)	sub-group (n = number of cations of octahedral layers)	species
1:1	kaolinite – serpentine ($x = 0$)	kaolinite ($n = 2$) serpentine ($n = 3$)	kaolinite, halloysite, chrysotile, lizardite, antigorite
2:1	pyrophyllite – Talc ($x = 0$) smectites montmorillonite saponite ($x = 0.25$–0.6)	pyrophillite ($n = 2$) talc ($n = 3$) dioctahedral smectites or montmorillonites ($n = 3$) trioctahedral smectites or saponite ($n = 3$)	pyrophillite talc montmorillonite, beidellite, nontronite saponite, hectorite, sauconite
	vermiculite ($x = 0.6$–0.9)	dioctahedral vermiculites ($n = 2$) trioctahedral vermiculites ($n = 3$)	dioctahedral vermiculite trioctahedral vermiculite
	micas[2] ($x = 1$)	dioctahedral micas ($n = 2$)	muscovite, paragonite
	breakable micas ($x = 2$)	trioctahedral micas ($n = 3$) dioctahedral breakable micas ($n = 2$) trioctahedral breakable micas ($n = 3$)	biotite, phlogopite margarite clintonite
2:1:1	chlorite (x variable)	dioctahedral chlorites ($4<n<5$) di-trioctahedral chlorites trioctahedral chlorites ($5 < n < 6$)	donbassite cookeite, sudoïte penninite, clinochlore, prochlorite

Inter-analytical tests can be performed at different levels: on the structure of clays (geochemical relations, pedological differentiation

[1] AIPEA *Association Internationale pour l'Etude des Argiles*, GPO Box 2434, Brisbane, Qld 4001 Australia

[2] Illites (or hydromica), Sericite, etc., many materials labelled illites can be inter-stratified.

within a profile and spatial differentiation), hydrous properties (porosity, permeability, functional waterlogging generated by the nature and the proportion of clays), adsorbing complexes (charge distribution, CEC, etc.).

For a detailed quantitative study, in addition to the clay particle fraction, it is generally necessary to analyse the fine silt fraction which can contain interstratified minerals, particularly in the case of micas and well crystallized kaolinite. A balance takes into account clay and associated phases, oxides, hydroxides, etc. making it possible to explain apparently unmatched results (excessive Si^{4+} content due to diatoms, very fine quartz, high percentages of K^+ originating from potassic feldspars, micas, etc.).

Table. 4.2. Structural lexicon (AIPEA, 1972)

English	French
(atomic) plane	plan (atomique)
(tetrahedral or octahedral) sheet (plane combination)	couche (tétraédrique ou octaédrique,combinaison de plans)
1:1 or 2:1 layer (sheet combination)	feuillet 1:1 ou 2:1 (combinaison de couches)
interlayer space	espace interfoliaire
unit structure = combination of layers + interlayer materials	assemblage de feuillets + matériel inter-foliaire = unité Structurale
lattice	Réseau

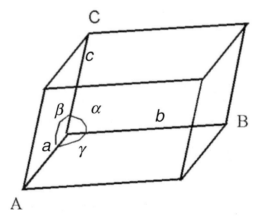

Fig. 4.1. The crystal mesh

4.1.2 Principle

A crystal is defined as a solid made up of atoms assembled in a three-dimensional periodic model. Lengths a, b, c and angles α, β, γ between the planes define the mesh parameters of the basic unit (Fig. 4.1).

When monochromatic X-ray beams of suitable wavelength strike a crystalline plane, the X-rays are reflected by the atoms of the crystal. The signal is reinforced in a particular direction if the rays reflected by the different planes (Fig. 4.2) are in phase. This phenomenon corresponds to Bragg's law

$$2\,d\,\sin\vartheta = n\lambda \tag{4.1}$$

where d is the space between atomic planes or the inter-reticular distance in the crystal ($d(hkl)$); λ is wavelength and θ is angle between beam and atomic plane and n is the order of diffraction (integer number).

All the planes of a crystal diffract the X-ray when the crystal is tilted at certain angles θ of the incidental beam of wavelength λ in accordance with the law (4.1).

The angles θ are linked to wavelength λ and distance d, which are expressed in Angstroms or nanometres ($1\ \text{Å} = 0.1\ \text{nm} = 10^{-10}\ \text{m}$). If the wavelength is known, measuring the angle of reflection makes it possible to determine the inter-reticular spaces.

Remarks

Certain minerals can be "amorphous" to X-ray either because they do not have a specific crystalline arrangement (true of glasses) or because they have short-range organization that is too small to be detected at a wavelength of 1–2 Å.

XRD is not the best technique for the study of non-crystalline solids such as allophanes which are made up of clusters of Si atoms presenting structural elements with interlayer distances corresponding to 1 or 2 neighbouring atoms.

Atoms of silicon in a tetrahedral position and atoms of aluminium in octahedral coordination but with no regular symmetry, cannot give well defined peaks, but only broad and badly defined peaks that appear around 0.33 and 0.22 nm.

4.1.3 XRD Instrumentation

X-rays were discovered in 1895 by Roentgen, but the phenomenon of crystal diffraction was discovered only in 1912.

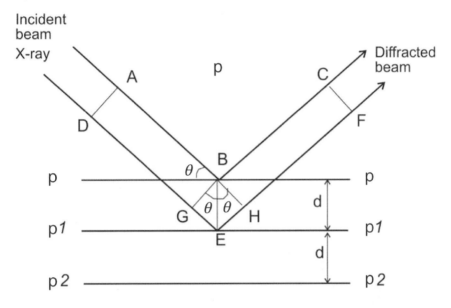

Fig. 4.2 Diffraction of an incidental beam by crystalline reticular planes. Lines p, p1, p2 represent the parallel and equidistant reticular planes separated by space d. An X-ray beam striking the higher plane p will be reflected in the incidental angle θ. To obtain a measurable reflection, all the rays reflected by planes p, p1, p2, etc, must be in phase. To achieve this, GE + EH, the path difference between radiations ABC and DEF must be equal to a whole number of the wavelength. As GE = EH = $d \sin \theta$, the condition is thus the law of Bragg (1).

X-rays are located between UV and gamma radiation wavelengths, i.e. approximately 10 to 10^{-2} nm. In XRD, "hard" radiation is used with wavelengths from 1.5 to 1.9 Å depending on the anti-cathode used (1 Å = 0.1 nm). Radiation X-ray is propagated in a straight line. It is necessary to ensure the radiation is as monochromatic as possible by using a set of filters, slits and a monochromator. The apparatus comprises:
– *a generator* with stabilized high voltage and micro-intensity which supplies the X-ray tube and the counter
– *a sealed* X-ray *tube,* including a source of electrons maintained from 20 to 50 kV by means of a high negative potential and an anode or anti-cathode (Table 4.3) made of thick metal, cooled by a water circuit;

high speed bombardment of the electrons causes transfer of energy to the atoms of the anode-target bringing them to a higher energy level, thus creating orbital vacancies of electrons; the quantum of energy produced is characteristic of the atoms of the anode; X-ray photons leave the tube by 300 μm thick beryllium windows that are transparent to the X-ray (the spot must be as small as possible to concentrate the energy of the electrons on a limited zone of the anode and to ensure a high intensity X-ray source); the power of the tube is limited by the quantity of heat likely to be dissipated by the anode and is expressed by the maximum acceptable value in mA for a given voltage (1–3 kV or more in the case of a rotating anode); characteristic radiations are obtained only starting from a given critical voltage of excitation, thus strict regulation of the voltage and intensity is required to avoid modifying the wavelength

– *a goniometer,* which makes it possible to rotate the sample and the counter under the conditions fixed by the Bragg equation; this provides a support both for the sample whose plane is adjusted very precisely and for the focused detector which turns around the same axis in the same direction at a suitable speed ratio

– a linear beam is obtained by means of the Soller slits and the degree of divergence which limits the opening of the beam; variable slits are now used with openings linked to the angle making it possible to irradiate a constant surface, which is particularly useful with small angles because the effects of the direct beam are limited

– a reception slit limits the width of the beam in the focal plane; the narrower the slit, the higher the resolution, though there is a loss in intensity; a graphite back monochromator limits fluorescence radiation, incoherent radiations and the Compton effect; the perfect alignment of all the different elements determines the quality of the measurements

– *a detection system* (counter) makes it possible to measure the intensity of the X-ray transmitted; the number of pulsations per unit of time is proportional to the quantity of X-ray transmitted; the counter can be linear or proportional, or detection can be by scintillation, or occasionally by semiconductor (semiconductor counter must be kept in liquid nitrogen at −196°C).

Safety

X-ray radiation is dangerous and can cause burns, genetic modifications, cancers, etc. The risks associated with high voltage must be also taken into account.

Careful prevention is essential and strict regulations apply to all apparatuses, which must be equipped with safety devices:

- the sealed tube must be protected by thick walls to eliminate risk of radiation
- the goniometer must be insulated with lead glass or lead plastic to protect the whole apparatus; it should only be opened when the tube is switched off
- the operator must wear a monitoring badge with a sensitive film (dosimeter) that accounts for possible whole-body irradiation (which must be checked regularly), as well as a ring to measure irradiation of the hands
- operators must have regular medical check-ups to detect changes in the blood count (white blood cell count, etc.)
- a Geiger counter must be used to check for radiation leaks: fluorescent screens should be placed on supports made of zinc doped with nickel to identify the zones struck by the beam while alignment is being adjusted.

Table 4.3. Characteristics of some anti-cathodes

anti-cathode	K_α wavelength Å	K_β filter	induced fluorescence	excitation potential (KV)	operating potential (KV)	remarks
Cu	1.542	Ni	Co–Fe	9.0	25–45	penetration and average dispersion, not much affected by air
Co	1.791	Fe	Mn–Cr	7.8	25–35	weak penetration capacity, great dispersion, not much affected by air
Fe	1.947	Mn	Cr–V	7.1	25–35	Weak penetration capacity, great dispersion

4.2. Qualitative diffractometry

4.2.1 Overview of Preparation of the Samples

See Fig. 4.3.

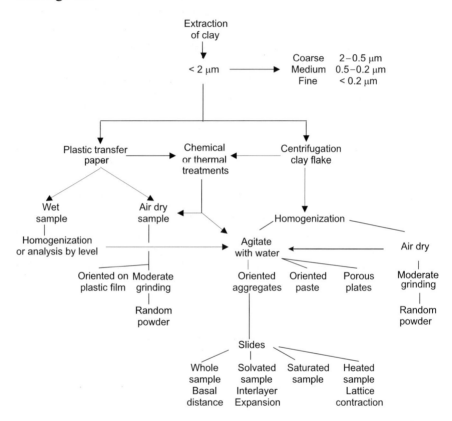

Fig. 4.3. Preparation of samples for X-ray diffractometry

4.2.2. Preparation for Powder Diagrams

Objective

This method is a general way to identify mineral species without preferential orientations. It enables quantitative analysis as the relative intensity of maxima diffractions is approximately proportional to the number of crystals present if the level of anisotropy is low.

Principle

In the method based on the "spectrum of random powder" (Thomson et al., 1972; Peterson et al., 1986; Decarreau, 1990), the crystal is examined in the form of a fine isotropic powder under a monochromatic X-ray beam. Random orientation must statistically represent all possible orientations of the different particles and provide a complete spectrum of minerals likely to diffract the X-ray (clays, oxides, hydroxides, oxyhydroxides, non-weathered primary minerals, various salts, etc.).

Each particle is considered to be a micro-crystal or an assembly of micro-crystals and the powder mass can be compared with a single crystal turning not in only one axis but in all possible axes. The powder spectrum makes it possible to fix the relative intensities of the peaks indexed by JCPDS[3] and for this reason it should always be carried out before any other operation.

After compression in the support at the semi-microscale, the "powder" sample includes micro-aggregates of fractal dimensions with a piled-up structure with open porosity – the grains being only very slightly connected – and its characteristics depend on the crushing, compression and homogeneity of the medium. The total average orientation at this scale is very weak.

On the other hand, at the sub-microscale (a few tens or hundreds of nanometers), the primary morphological units are mixed stacks of clayey crystallites and can consequently present an orientation with a varying degree of disorder depending on the types of clay present. The use of a revolving support improves the level of randomization, but requires a relatively large quantity of powder, i.e. approximately 400 mg.

Procedure

A powder diagram can be performed on whole soil or on soil fractions (cf. Chap. 3). Clay obtained by centrifugation (centrifugation pellet or plastic transfer paper) is air dried and then crushed in an agate mortar to obtain a homogeneous powder:
– With a spatula place in a hollow support (Fig. 4.4) the quantity of powder needed to almost fill the cavity.

---

[3]JCPDS – ICDD = Joint Commitee on Powder Diffraction Standards – International Center for Diffraction Data, Newtown Square Corporate Campus, 12 Campus Bdv, Newtown Square Pennsylvania 19073-3273 (USA).

– With a ground glass slide, gently flatten the powder
– Gradually add powder to fill the remaining cavity and pack gently to
  bring the surface of the powder up to the reference plane

Observations

Randomization

The powder must be sufficiently compact to provide cohesion without
using a binding agent or needing to smooth the surface. Too much
pressure can cause orientation. It is thus necessary to exploit the degree of
"randomization–orientation" by preparing the powders as regularly as
possible. Indeed, as the clay layers are planes, they tend to be oriented,
which is likely to give irregular results.

   This effect can be limited by using a binding agent that is inactive both
with respect to the X-ray and the sample (acetone, lake gum + alcohol,
collodion + acetate of butyl or amyl, gum tragacanthe, etc.). These
treatments make the powders more stable. However, the use of a vertical
goniometer prevents separation of the powder when it is placed in the
beam which makes this kind of preparation unnecessary in the majority of
the cases.

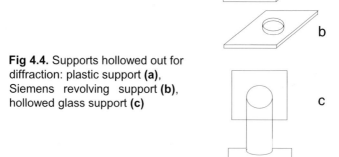

Fig 4.4. Supports hollowed out for
diffraction: plastic support **(a)**,
Siemens revolving support **(b)**,
hollowed glass support **(c)**

   When only a small quantity of sample is available, double-sided
adhesive Scotch tape can be used; this is powdered with the sample (the
surplus can be removed by light tapping) or better still, by placing the
sample on a silicon support.

   Freeze-drying makes it possible to obtain less oriented samples
(although there is a risk of a few packages of layers displaying residual
orientation). Rotating the sample enables maximum possible reflection,

which decreases the risk of error by improving randomization and by limiting fluctuations in intensity due to an insufficient number of particles. The rotating support requires larger quantities of powder.

Granulometry – Focusing

The use of a sample plane is required for satisfactory focusing of the beam. The roughness of the surface has a marked effect on the relative intensities of the lines. If the surface is rough, as is true in the case of a coarse powder, the absorption coefficient will be high and the intensities at small angles will consequently be exceptionally low. The powder must be fine (a particle size of about 10 µm) to avoid such fluctuations in absorption, but not too finely ground to avoid an artificial increase in amorphous minerals:
– at 10 µm, fluctuations will not exceed 2%
– at 50 µm, fluctuations can reach 20%.

On the other hand, with a particle size lower than 0.02 µm, diffractions are diffuse and the intensity decreases.

The width of the diffraction curve increases with a decrease in the thickness of the crystal. The structure of "amorphous" substances is characterized by the absence of periodicity or by short-range organization. In the latter case, they show only one statistical preference for an inter-atomic distance and XRD cannot give satisfactory results but only broad and badly defined peaks (Fig. 4.5).

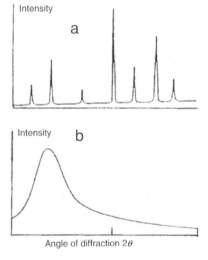

Fig. 4.5. Diffraction diagrams typical of **(a)** a well crystallized substance and **(b)** an amorphous substance with short-range organization

Particular uses of Powder Diagrams

A powder diagram can be used to identify non-transformed primary minerals (quartz, calcite, etc.) or oxides and hydroxides of iron and aluminium, etc, as the degree of crystallinity in the case of kaolinites and the "fire-clays" will be distinguished more clearly: since the mode of stacking of the layers is different, certain peaks of kaolinite do not exist in "fire-clays", which may consequently not be seen on a oriented diagram.

The di- or tri-octahedral nature of the layers can be highlighted by using ray 060 [filling of octahedral cavities by bivalent (1.54 Å) or trivalent (1.49 Å) cations].

Polymorphous illites can provide data that are characteristic of the mode of formation.

4.2.3 Preparation for Oriented Diagrams

Oriented Diagrams on Glass Slides

Objective

The objective is to identify certain clayey minerals capable of being oriented and to observe basal variations by means of heat or chemical treatments. The number of treatments needed depends on the mixture of minerals in the sample.

Principle

In diagrams of oriented aggregates, special weight is given to the crystalline planes parallel to the surface of the layers. The preferential orientation of silicates causes an increase in the maximum of basal differentiation $d(001)$, which makes it possible to detect small quantities of crystalline species present in the mixture.

With this method better diffraction is obtained of the species and fluctuations that are theoretically lower than with randomized powders since the particles do not exceed 2 μm. On the other hand, preferential orientation decreases the number of planes (hkl) in a position of diffraction.

Procedure

(a) Starting from a well-homogenized clay paste obtained by centrifugation, remove a small aliquot (approximately 400 mg) with the spatula and place it in a tube with 5 mL water; agitate to suspend particles.

(b) Starting from a powder (for example recovery of the clay used in Chap. 9), weigh approximately 200 mg of clay, place it in a plastic tube with 5 mL water and a 8 mm glass ball and agitate for 2–3 min to disperse the clay.

(c) Starting from a or b, pipette approximately 1 mL of suspension and spread it evenly on a 24 × 24 mm glass slide. The deposit must be spread evenly over the whole surface of the slide with no areas of extra thickness. If the deposit is too thin, there may be an effect of the support, if it is too thick, diffraction will occur only on the finest clay and the clay film may reticulate itself. Allow to dry at room temperature, then dry in the desiccator. Prepare three slides:

– the first for examination of the rough sample without treatment
– the second for examination of the sample after glycerol or glycol treatment
– the third for heating the sample in the oven at 490°C (depending on requirements, this slide can be used for several thermal treatments at increasing temperatures).

Observations

After the suspension has been spread on the glass slide, micro-fractionation will occur as a function of the size of the clay particles since coarse clay sediments faster than fine clay. However, if drying is rapid, this segregation will not disturb qualitative interpretation.

In contrast to powder techniques (cf. Sect. 4.2.2) that have to be sufficiently thick to limit the effects of orientation, oriented slides must be sufficiently thin so that the maximum number of basic units are suitably oriented. Plotting a black line on the support before use is a good way to judge the quality of the preparation: it should remain very slightly visible through the almost transparent clay film.

In comparative semi-quantitative analysis, the suspended deposit of each sample should contain about the same quantity of clay. This is easy starting from dry clay which can be weighed before suspension. The removal of an aliquot of the sample during agitation results in slides with almost the same quantity of mineral material spread over the same area. From a suspension after agitation and homogenization, quickly remove an aliquot of the same volume and dry and weigh one of the samples to determine the concentration.

For suspensions of wet materials, recover clay on a film of a given surface area and weigh an identical aliquot after drying.

Amorphous minerals can mask part of the diagram. It is often necessary to eliminate them before recording the diffraction diagram.

Diagram on Oriented Paste

Principle

This method is particularly suitable for minerals of the 2:1 type and halloysite–$4H_2O$, the wet sample should be dried at room temperature and maintained at a relative humidity of approximately 80%.

Procedure

After insulation of clay to the required dimension by centrifugation (cf. Chap. 3), recover the wet centrifugation pellet, homogenize with a small stainless steel spatula, deposit it on a hollowed support (Fig. 4a), spread it out in the cavity, then smooth it with a glass slide to a perfect plane suitably located on the reference plane. Allow to dry slowly at ambient temperature taking care to avoid excessive desiccation.

Observations

On coarse 2 µm clays, the clay paste needs to be homogenized after centrifugation, as the part near the surface is able to concentrate fibrous clays which do not respect Stokes law. Smectites deposit preferentially at the surface whereas chlorites and illites sediment more quickly at depth and accumulate more extensively at the base of the centrifugation pellet. The same is true for iron oxides (density 4.5–5) which are heavier than aluminium oxides (density approximately 3).

During drying, clays with a high coefficient of retraction can fissure and detach. A binding agent can be added, though there is a risk of introducing a variable that is not easy to control (disturbed orientation, flocculation, binding agent not amorphous for X-ray, etc).

Specific Uses

In certain cases, it is possible to work on the wet sample. With 2:1 clays, saturating the wet paste with Na^+ or Li^+ makes it possible to observe the phenomenon of unlimited swelling $d(001) > 30$Å. During air drying, clay again reaches values of $d(001) = 18, 15, 14$ Å.

Aggregates Oriented on Porous Ceramic Plate

Objective

To allow retention of minerals that do not adhere on glass slides and/or, to allow successive treatments on the same sample: original sample, cation treatment, polyalcohol treatment, followed by successive heat treatments. This preparation enables satisfactory orientation of clays, and is particularly useful if the spectra are to be exploited for quantitative analysis.

Principle

The clay is fixed on a porous plate by suction using a vacuum pump or by centrifugation using a Poretics ceramic porous disc and a Hettich support.

Procedure

Transfer the clay suspension on a 24×24 mm porous plate placed on a Büchner with a diameter of 40 mm whose bottom of sintered glass has been modified to create a 22 × 22 mm window, which is the only permeable part (Fig. 4.6). Tip the homogenized liquid onto the plate and apply a vacuum using a standard pallet pump. After formation of a thin continuous layer of clay, dry the sample and analyse by X-ray diffraction.

Observations

This medium and procedure gives well-oriented deposits with a reduced fractal dimension of the surface which is preserved after drying and is thus of excellent quality for XRD measurement. The thickness of the deposit must be homogeneous all over the plate and sufficiently thick to avoid the effects of the support, but thin enough to preserve a certain degree of elasticity and to avoid cracking caused by the rheological properties of the medium.

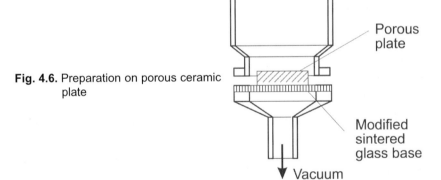

Fig. 4.6. Preparation on porous ceramic plate

Porous plate

Modified sintered glass base

Vacuum

Measurements on porous plate make it possible to avoid excess solvation liquid and also to carry out the treatments required: chemical saturation by Mg^{2+} or K^+ treatment, heating, etc. 0.20 μm millipore filters on glass plates can also be used for measurements (collection of suspended materials in water, airborne dust, etc).

The cleaning of the porous plate is delicate and should be done after washing by slight abrasion of the surface that has been in contact with the clay. It is important to preserve the perfect flatness of the plate and to make sure contamination has not occurred.

Oriented Aggregates Deposited by Ultracentrifugation On Semi-Flexible Film

Objective

The aim of this method is to obtain samples of the same thickness, the same mineralogical composition and the same apparent particle size.

Principle

Particles are deposited by means of a Sharples super-centrifugal machine equipped with a cylinder with a semi-rigid internal plastic film (cf. Chap. 3). The speed is regulated to collect particles of a known average diameter (coarse to fine clay). If necessary, the film can be analyzed at eight successive levels of 24 mm, which makes it possible to monitor modifications in the nature of clays as a function of particle size and density. To ensure the film is not too thick, the proportion of coarse, medium or fine clay must be known, and only the zones that correspond to an optimal density used (test of the black line on the film, cf. section "Oriented Diagrams on Glass Slides).

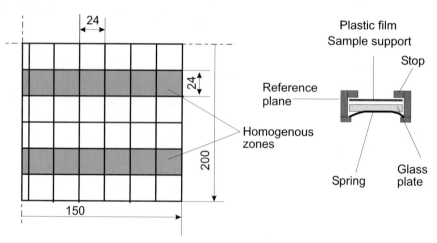

Fig. 4.7. Diagram showing how to cut up a plastic film after continuous flow ultra-centrifuge and how to set it up for XRD.

Procedure

Remove the plastic film from the cylindrical bowl and dry flat for approximately 1 h. When it is still slightly wet and not yet rigid, cut it into sections following the 24 × 24 mm pattern drawn on the back of the film (Fig. 4.7). Each level should be labelled. Assemble the 24 × 24 mm semi-rigid film on a glass plate and place it on a support against a stop corresponding to the reference plane.

Observations

XRD can be performed directly on the oriented sample or after treatments (cf. Sect. 4.2.4) with polyalcohol; heating treatment at 110°C is also possible depending on the nature of the plastic used. The surface of the plastic support must be unpolished naturally without additives as these could cause background noise that is incompatible with the smoothness of measurements.

4.2.4 Pretreatment of Clays

Effect of the Pretreatments

Different types of pretreatments can be used to facilitate the identification of clayey minerals by causing selective changes in the inter-reticular distances of the clayey layers. These treatments and their effects are summarized in Table 4.4. Table 4.5 shows the maximum inter-reticular distances observable in the clayey minerals of soils.

Saturation by Cations

Principle

Saturation by a cation makes it possible to fill the existing cation vacancies and, by displacement of the exchangeable cations, to obtain homoionic samples that present uniform expansion of the layers of the expansible phyllosilicates (the quantities of interlayer water depend on the exchangeable cations). The divalent cations, e.g. Mg^{2+}, Ca^{2+}, Sr^{2+}, give hydrates with two layers that are relatively stable in a broad range of relative humidity and are not very sensitive to the influence of hydronium ions during washing with water.

Mg^{2+} *saturation* gives a stable complex with two layers of inter-layer water which brings the expansible phyllosilicates to $d001 \geq 14$. Expansion of the layers allows differentiation of the non-expansible varieties of clays whose interlayer space is approximately 10 Å (Table 4.5).

K^+ *saturation* restricts interlayer adsorption of water and allows differentiation of 2:1:1 clays of the chlorite type, and of 2:1 clays of the vermiculite type. Non-expansible chlorites are not modified by this treatment, whereas vermiculites break down at 10 Å. The same sample can be also used for smectites after heating to 550°C.

Li⁺ saturation followed by dehydration to approximately 300°C, followed by solvation with glycerol, makes it possible to differentiate montmorillonite from beidellite using the Greene–Kelly test based on the Hofmann–Klemen effect. When a smectite saturated with Li is dehydrated at 300°C, the Li interlayer migrates towards the octahedral layers which have a deficit of positive charges resulting from substitutions. The structure becomes non-expansible and there is no further inflation of the sample with glycerol treatment (9.5Å). A beidellite (or a saponite) whose charges comes from tetraedric substitutions is not affected by such treatments and inflates with glycerol (17.7 Å).

Procedure for Mg²⁺ saturation

– Take an aliquot of 125–250 mg of clay
– put in suspension and acidify with diluted hydrochloric acid to bring it to pH 3.5–4.0 to avoid precipitation of magnesium hydroxide (particularly if initial dispersion was carried out in an alkaline medium)
– add 5 mol L^{-1} magnesium acetate solution to obtain a suspension of approximately 0.5 mol (Mg) L^{-1}
– leave in contact for 30 min
– centrifuge for 5 min at approximately 3,000g and discard the supernatant
– wash the centrifugation pellet twice with 0.5 mol $(Mg(OAc)_2)$ L^{-1} solution to eliminate H^+ from the acid suspension then twice with 0.5 mol $(MgCl_2)$ L^{-1} solution(approximately 10 mL)
– centrifuge and wash with 50% methanol (approximately 10 mL) then with 98% methanol (approximately 10 mL); then with 85% acetone. The silver nitrate test for Cl^- must be negative
– dry at room temperature for the powder spectrum, or prepare the plates for oriented spectrum immediately by adding a little water.

Procedure for K⁺ saturation

– Take an aliquot of 100–250 mg of clays
– put in suspension and add 1 mol (KCl) L^{-1} solution
– centrifuge the flocculated clay after 30 min of contact
– discard the supernatant
– wash the centrifugation pellet with KCl 1 M

Table 4.4. Influence of the treatments on the inter-reticular distance between layers of principal clays: air dried samples, saturated with Mg^{2+} (M = metahalloysite or halloysite,$2H_2O$ (7 Å), H: hydrated halloysite, $4H_2O$ (10 Å). Intergrades of chlorite–vermiculite and chlorite–smectite are also separated by these treatments

	kaolinite	serpentine	M halloysite / H	talc pyrophrylite	micas (illite)	sepiolite palygorskite	smectites	vermiculites	chlorites
group	1:1 (Te – Oc)			2:1 (Te – Oc – Te)					2:1:1 (Te – Oc– Te – Oc)
d (Å)	7		7–10	9.4	10	10–12	14–15		
Stability (inter-layer)	–		H_2O	–	cation	fibrous	water cations		octahedral
Family	kaolinite	serpentine	M halloysite H	talc pyrophrylite	micas (illite)	sepiolite palygorskite	smectites	vermiculites	chlorites
Charges x	0			0	1–2		0.2–0.6	0.6–0.9	variable
Glycerol solvation	nil 7.1 Å	nil 7.3 Å	nil M 7.2 Å H 10.8 Å	nil	nil 10.1 Å	nil S 12.1 Å P 10,48 Å	expansion 17.7 Å	nil 14 - 15 Å	nil except swelling of chlorites 14 Å
K⁺ saturation	nil 7.1 Å	nil 7.3 Å	nil M 7.2 Å H 10 Å	nil	nil 10.1 Å	nil S 12.1 Å P 10,48 Å	contraction 12.4 Å 12.8 Å	contraction 10 Å (avec 14 Å) 14 Å	nil 14 Å
Heating 550°C	collapse	nil 7.3 Å	M collapse H collapse	nil	nil 10 Å	10,4–8,2 Å 9.2 Å 4.7 Å	contraction 10 Å	contraction	nil 14 Å
Formamide intercalation	nil 7.1 Å < 4 h	nil 7.3 Å	expansion M 10.48 Å						
DMSO	expansion 11.18 Å	nil 7.3 Å	M expansion						
Green–Kelly test, 250°C glycerol							montmorillonite 9.5 Å beidellite 17.7 Å		

Table 4.5. Maximum inter-reticular distance of soil minerals saturated with Mg^{2+} and K^+ or solvated by glycerol treatment.

mineral	d (Å)	*hkl* plane
(a) Samples saturated by Mg^{2+}		
chlorite	13.6 – 14.7	001
vermiculite	14.0 – 15.0	002
montmorillonite	14.0 – 15.0	001
mica (Illite)	9.9 – 10.1	001
talc	9.2 – 9.4	002
halloysite	10.1	001
metahalloysite	7.2 – 7.5	001
kaolinite	7.1 – 7.2	001
lepidoscrocite	6.27	020
boehmite	6.11	020
gibbsite	4.85	002
silicates	4.4 – 4.6	110
gypsum	4.27	121
göethite	4.18	110
cristobalite	4.04	101
Illmenite	3.73	102
quartz	3.34	101
feldspar	3.1 – 3.25	
calcite	3.03	100
hematite	2.69	104
magnetite	2.53	311
trioctaedric silicates	1.54	060
dioctaedric silicates	1.49	
(b) Samples saturated by Mg^{2+} and solvated by glycerol		
montmorillonite	17.7	001
vermiculite	14.4	002
chlorite	13.6 – 14.7	001
halloysite	10.1 – 10.7	001
montmorillonite (2nd order)	9.5	001
chlorite – Vermiculite (2nd order)	7.15	002
minerals giving inter-layer spaces similar to 'a'		

(c) Samples saturated by K^+ and air dried

chlorite	13.6 – 14.7	001
montmorillonite	11.0 – 13.0	001
vermiculite	10.0 – 11.0	002
metahalloysite	7.2 – 7.5	001
chlorite (2nd order)	7.15	002

Minerals giving inter-layer spaces similar to 'a'

d) Samples saturated by K^+ and heated at 550°C for 2-3 h

chlorite	13.6 – 14.7	001
montmorillonite	9.9 – 10.1	001
vermiculite	9.9 – 10.1	002
mica (Illite)	9.9 – 10.1	001
chlorite (2nd order)	7.15	002

– then wash with 50% and 95% methanol and finally with 95% acetone until there are no Cl^- ions in the washing solution (no precipitate with addition of $AgNO_3$)
– allow to dry at room temperature or immediately prepare slides for oriented spectrum by adding distilled water.

Procedure for Li^+ saturation

– Take an aliquot of 110 – 250 mg of clay
– put in suspension and add 3 mol (LiCl) L^{-1} solution
– leave in contact for 30 min
– centrifuge and discard the supernatant
– rapidly wash the centrifugation pellet with 1 mol (LiCl) L^{-1} solution then with a little water
– make an oriented slide and dry at 250°C overnight
– carry out the glycerol treatment (1 night) and perform the diffraction spectrum.

Remarks

– This test is not completely selective
– mounting on an ordinary glass slide can cause errors during heating as the Na^+ in glass can exchange with the Li^+ in the clay, which causes incomplete neutralization of the octahedral charges
– the glycerol treatment must be carried out hot for a period of several hours to allow complete expansion of the layers
– an irrational basal sequence indicates inter-stratification.

Removal of Iron

Principle

Iron often has to be removed first to mitigate its action on the process of measurement by XRD using a Cu tube (X-ray fluorescence increases background noise) and second to avoid dilution through a reduction in the intensity of diffraction.

Different methods can be used to eliminate the different forms of iron. These methods vary in vigour and should not transform the phyllo-silicates present, but make it possible to complex and reduce amorphous and crystallized iron in a slightly acid medium with the minimum possible degree of aggressiveness. These methods are similar to those used in Chaps 2 and 6, but the solubilization of iron compounds is generally not controlled (because it is the final residue of the sample will be analyzed by XRD).

It should be noted that the amorphous silicon–iron complexes present in certain sediments will be dissociated in an acid medium giving soluble iron and precipitated amorphous silica.

Hematite and goethite oxides are only slightly affected by an acid oxalate treatment at pH 3. A reducing treatment with complexation of the products of dissolution (oxalate acid + dithionite) is the best way to eliminate most iron while sparing the clay. Oxalate dissolves amorphous iron and dithionite dissolves oxide forms of iron. A slightly acid medium allows extraction of "free iron" but at the same time extracts part of the iron of the lattice of certain clays, for example vermiculites. With dithionite, the presence of sulphur precipitated after reduction does not pose a problem for XRD, except for a dilution effect on the sample. Sulphur should be eliminated from the extraction pellet after centrifugation and drying.

Procedure

The main methods are based on dissolution in an acid or base sequestering medium and/or reducing medium (cf. Chap. 6):

– The DCB method (dithionite, citrate, bicarbonate) extracts iron from the majority of its amorphous and crystalline compounds by reduction and sequestration without significant modification of aluminosilicates or lithogenic hematite
– the method based on acid oxalate at pH 3.0 (in darkness, or with UV photolysis) extracts noncrystalline forms
– the sodium pyrophosphate method at pH 9–10, EDTA at pH 9–10, acetyl acetone extracts organometallic forms

– the tetraborate method at pH 8–9 extracts Fe from monomeric complexes.

The elimination of iron is accompanied by the dissolution of aluminous products, silica, etc. which can be controlled by chemical titration of the extracts.

Solvation Treatments

Principle

Solvation by polar molecules, such as mono or polyhydric alcohols, ethers, amines, results in the formation of interlayer organic complexes. The resulting structure is more stable than the structure of dehydrated 2:1 clay. Swelling is all the easier since the charge of the layers is weaker, or is limited to the octahedral layer. The nature of the interlayer cations modifies the limits of stability of the organic complex. The basal distance of the smectites reaches 17.7 Å with a double interlayer layer of glycerol, and 17.1 Å with ethylene glycol. The rate of hydration can vary considerably. Montmorillonites inflate more easily than the majority of clays.

Impregnation can be accomplished in the liquid or vapour phase by heating to 60°C. In certain cases, the treatment has to be continued for 24 hours to take the slowness of interlayer expansion into account. Condensation of the vapour does not cause any mechanical disturbance and gives more intense lines of diffraction.

Procedure for Glycerol Treatment

This procedure is based on that of Modre and Dixon (1970):
– Prepare a 1:10 mixture of glycerol and water
– on a previously air-dried oriented plate, apply a film of glycerol in a very fine spray, taking care not to create an excess of reagent
– allow to dry for at least 1 or 2 h and then perform XRD.

Caution. The complex loses its effectiveness over time, so it is advisable not to wait more than 20 h. Using ceramic plate for this treatment makes it possible to eliminate excess glycerol.

Procedure for Ethylene Glycol Treatment

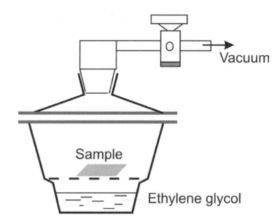

Fig. 4.8. Treatment of the samples with ethylene glycol

This procedure is based on that of Eltantawy and Arnold (1974) and Chassin (1974):

- place the sample (generally for spectrum-oriented aggregates) in a desiccator containing the ethylene glycol (Fig. 4.8)
- create a partial vacuum with the vacuum pump and leave the samples in contact with the vapour phase for at least one night
- remove the sample and perform XRD as soon as possible.

Caution. The complex loses its effectiveness over time, so it is advisable not to wait more than 10 h.

Safety. Ethylene glycol or 1,2 ethanediol: $HOCH_2-CH_2OH$, has a boiling point of 196°C; it is hygroscopic, toxic by ingestion, and can affect the kidneys, lungs and the heart.

Intercalation Complexes

Principle

Intercalation complexes are very useful particularly to separate 1:1 clays and to distinguish well-crystallized forms, disordered forms and halloysites. Since the forms of these species are similar, it is impossible to separate them with precision (kaolinite and halloysite can be found in flat, tubular or glomerular forms). One common procedure is first to form the intercalation complex, then after obtaining the spectrum, to move the complex with water and perform solvation with ethylene glycol or glycerol. The stability of the intercalation complexes is variable and XRD spectra should be performed without delay.

Treatment with *hydrazine hydrate* (Wada and Yamada, 1968; Range et al. 1969; Calvert, 1984) allows the inter-layers of the well-ordered kaolinite to be changed from 7.15 to 10.48Å without modifying the chlorite. The presence of interstratified minerals can be awkward.

In the treatment using *dimethylsulfoxide* (Gonzalez Garcia and Sanchez Camazano 1968 Olejnik et al., 1968 Anton and Rouxhet, 1977; Calvert 1984): (i) kaolinite forms an intercalation complex that increases the interlayer distance from 7.15 to 11.18 Å, which remains stable after heating to 300°C, (ii) halloysite and dickite display identical behaviour, except that heating to 300°C does not result in further expansion, (iii) vermiculites and smectites increase from 18 to 19 Å and (iv) chlorite undergoes no change.

Metahalloysite forms an intercalation complex with formamide. The line rapidly reaches 10.4 Å and whereas for kaolinite there is no reaction even after 4 h of contact (Churchman et al., 1984).

Procedure for Hydrazine Hydrate Treatment

- Place the clay sample on a glass slide or on porous ceramic in a saturator containing the hydrazine hydrate
- create a partial vacuum with the vacuum pump and leave the sample in contact with the vapour phase at 65°C for at least one night
- remove the sample and perform XRD without delay.

Remarks

It should be noted that the complex loses effectiveness over time; so it is advisable not to wait more than 1 h before XRD.

Sequential treatment with hydrazine + water + glycerol makes it possible to increase the basal interlayer distance of halloysite to 11.1 Å, whereas that of kaolinite remains at 7.15 Å.

Safety

- Hydrazine hydrate: H_2NR-NH_2,H_2O, boiling point 119°C
- miscible with water and ethanol
- strong base, very corrosive, attacks glass and the skin
- highly toxic, causes irritation of the eyes, may be carcinogenic.

Procedure for Dimethylsulfoxide Treatment

- Put an aliquot of clay weighing from 100 to 250 mg in suspension in 5 mL of dimethylsulfoxide
- leave in contact for 8 h in a water bath at approximately 40°C
- agitate from time to time
- centrifuge and prepare slide, allow to dry
- rapidly perform XRD after drying.

Table 4.6. Effect of the thermal treatment on the diffraction of clays (TDA = characteristic temperature of change in thermal differential analysis, cf. Chap. 7).

mineral		temp. (°C) 4 H at	TDA	heat effect
1:1 clays	Well crystallized Kaolinite	500	575–625	absence of diffraction
	Disordered kaolinite	500	550–562	absence of diffraction
	Dickite	500	665–700	absence of diffraction
	Nacrite	500	625–680	absence of diffraction
	Halloysite, $4H_2O$	110	125–160	elimination of water
		500	560–605	absence of diffraction
	Metahalloysite, $2H_2O$	110	125–150	elimination of water
		500	560–590	absence of diffraction
Short-range order alumino-silicates	Allophane	110	140–180	elimination of water, no XRD spectrum
	Imogolite	350		difficult identification by XRD →18Å
		500	500	disappearance of 18Å peak, destruction of the mesh
Micas and 2:1 clays	Crystallized micas (muscovite)	490	700	mica spectrum up to 1,000°C
	Illite–micaceous clays	350	125–250	loss of water
		500	350–550	mica spectrum
		500	700	mica spectrum (001)
	Glauconite	500	530–650	loss of water–mica structure
	Celadonite	500	500–600	mica structure
	Biotite	500	700	mica spectrum until 700–1,000°C
	Vermiculite	300	300	Progressive loss of H_2O the initial basal space (001) is a function of moisture: 14–13, 8–11, 6–9Å changes
	Montmorillonite	300	300	Disappearance 15 → 9Å

	Chlorite	500	680–800	no change if structure is well ordered
2:1:1 Clays	Chlorite–Mg	500	650	intensification of line 14 Å – line 3.54 Å not affected (octahedral layer 820°C intercalated layer 640°C)
	Chlorite–Fe	500	500	Attenuation of line 14Å which becomes broad and diffuse. octahedral layer 530°C, Fe^{2+} intercalated layer 430°C, Fe^{2+} intercalated layer 250°C Fe^{3+}
	Chlorite–Al Inter-stratified	500	500 < 600	(octahedral layer 750°C intercalated 900°C layer) effects vary with the mineral species present
Fibrous	Sepiolite	350	<200 >200 350 800	dehydration space 12 Å becomes weak and diffuse → 9.8 Å, space 7.6 Å more intense recrystallization
Clays	Palygorskite	300 500	<400 440 800	dehydration without change in structure, 10.5 Å peak becomes broad and diffuse, destruction of structure

Safety
– Dimethylsulfoxide: C_2H_6OS, boiling point: 189°C
– hygroscopic, irritation of the skin (urticant), keep away from the eyes.

Procedure for Formamide Treatment

– Place the clay sample on a glass slide or preferably on porous ceramic, allow to dry
– vaporize formamide and note the time of application; when the formamide excess has been eliminated (approximately 20 min), perform XRD (repeat with the same sample at the end of the day and compare the two spectra).

Safety

Formamide ($H–CO–NH_2$) is an ionizing solvent which can release a slight odour of ammonia. It dissolves lignin. No known risk to health.

Thermal Pretreatments

Principle

The hydrated minerals undergo modifications due to the effect of the rise in temperature. These modifications occur at certain characteristic temperature stages. The length of time at a given temperature is also significant. The transformations take place with varying rapidity depending on the nature and the degree of crystallinity of the thermally sensitive minerals. In general, 2–4 h are required

Table 4.7 Effect of thermal treatments on oxides and hydroxides of aluminium and iron (TDA: characteristic temperature of change in thermal differential analysis, cf. Chap. 7)

mineral	temperature (°C)		heating effect
	4 H	TDA	
		iron series	
Goethite	300	230–280	spectrum of disordered hematite
	900	900	spectrum of well-crystallized hematite
Goethite	350	240–350	spectrum of disordered hematite
alumineuse		900	spectrum of well-crystallized hematite
Lepidocrocite	300	230–280	γFe_2O_3 broad peak
		400–500	→ hematite spectrum
Maghemite	350	350–450	→ hematite spectrum
Magnetite	500	600–800	→ hematite spectrum
			At 300°, the akaganeite spectrum weakens
Akaganeite	300	200–400	gradually
		420–500	→ hematite spectrum
δFeOOH	300	140–260	→ hematite spectrum with intermediary
			goethite
Feroxyhyte			unstable in air at ambient temperature→
δFeOOH			goethite spectrum after air drying
Ferrihydrite	350	350–400	→ hematite spectrum
(without Si)			

Ferrihydrite (with Si)	500	550–600	→ hematite spectrum
		Aluminium series	
Gibbsite	200	150–200	→ boehmite and γAl_2O_3 spectrum/a?
Bayerite	200	150–200	→ boehmite and γAl_2O_3 spectrum/a?
Nordstrandite	200	150–200	→ bayerite spectrum → boehmite
Boehmite	500	450–500	→ γAl_2O_3 spectrum
Diaspore	500	470–500	→ spectrum of disordered corundum towards spectrum of crystallized corundum

Procedure

Place the samples assembled on glass slides in a cold furnace; bring the furnace to the desired temperature (110, 350, 490, 530°C, etc.) and maintain the temperature for at least 4 h. Heating must be progressive to avoid breaking the glass slides and possible reticulation of the clay film. The furnace should then be allowed to cool gradually, opening the door to accelerate the process if necessary. If they have not undergone irreversible transformations, the slides can be stored in the desiccator until XRD. Table 4.6 shows the influence of heat treatments on the diffraction of clays. Table 4.7 shows the influence of heat on the diffraction of aluminium oxides and iron hydroxides.

Observations

– Loss of interlayer water results in contraction of the mesh and displacement of the basic diffraction lines
– heating to high temperatures can lead to collapse of the lattice and dispersal of the characteristic X-ray spectrum.

Example

Dissociation of kaolinite by heating (Fig. 4.9) to around 490°C can be visualised by the four following reactions:

(1) at 500°C: $Al_2O_3,2SiO_2,2H_2O \rightarrow Al_2O_3,2SiO_2$ (metakaolinite) + 2 H_2O

(2) at 925°C: $Al_2O_3,2SiO_2,2H_2O \rightarrow Al_2O_3,SiO_2$ (sillimanite) + SiO_2 (ß quartz) + 2 H_2O

(3) at 1 100°C: $Al_2O_3,2SiO_2,2H_2O \rightarrow \alpha Al_2O_3 + 2SiO_2$ (ß quartz) + 2H_2O

(4) at 1 400°C: $Al_2O_3,2SiO_2,2H_2O \rightarrow 1/3\ (3Al_2O_3,2SiO_2) + 4/3\ SiO_2$ (ß quartz) + 2H_2O

All these reactions are possible starting from 800 K (approximately 527°C). There is no obstacle to the transition of kaolinite → metakaolinite → sillimanite → mullites → oxides, the most stable system, which depends on the temperature. Thermodynamically reaction (1) occurs first (Fig. 4.9).

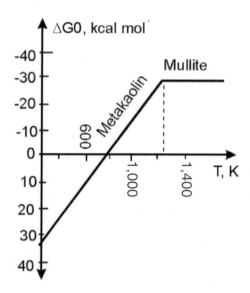

Fig. 4.9. Transformation of kaolinite by heating

Preparation of Iron Oxides for XRD

Principle

The use of XRD to study iron oxides in the soil requires a sufficient concentration of the different iron phases. Consequently the products have to be concentrated and purified without modifying either their crystallinity or the level of substitution by aluminium, and without causing chemical conversions of the phases. The following methods can be used to this end:
– separation methods (concretions, separation by density gradient, magnetic separation, etc
– in situ XRD determination on an uncovered thin slide, or extracted micro-samples with high iron content.

Chemical methods only enable the concentration of iron, which can exist in the form of coating, in amorphous forms (ferrihydrite, etc.), or involve varying degrees of crystallization (goethite, hematite, lepidocrocite, etc.). Clay minerals are dissolved by 5 mol (NaOH) L^{-1} solution under boiling. Kaolinites, halloysite, gibbsite, amorphous aluminosilicates, etc. are destroyed and solubilized, but 2:1 clays are more resistant and are thus only partially attacked. In addition to iron, smectites, illite, quartz, anatase, and rutile are also found in the residue. If the amount of silica present is not sufficient, during heating with 5 mol (NaOH) L^{-1} solution, the ferrihydrites are likely to be transformed into hematite or goethite. If the sample is attacked using 5 mol (NaOH) L^{-1} + 0.2 mol (silica) L^{-1} solution, the rate of aluminium substitution is not significantly modified.

Procedure

– Weigh in PTFE beakers 2–5 g of soil, or granulometric clay <2 μm depending on the total iron content
– attack with 20 mL 5 mol (NaOH) L^{-1} + 0.2 mol (silica) L^{-1} solution, cover the beaker with a PTFE plate and boil for one hour
– allow to cool and decant
– dilute the medium with deionised water, then wash on filter with water until the pH is neutral
– perform XRD

Note: a powder diagram is better than an oriented diagram for these products.

Remarks

– If the soil or clay contains many 2:1 phyllosilicates, the concentration may be too low; in this case it is useful to perform two differential spectra (DXRD), one with the original product, the other with the chemically concentrated product, or with the spectrum obtained after dissolution of iron by the citrate–bicarbonate–dithionite mixture (CBD, cf. Chap. 6)
– a cobalt X-ray tube should be used to avoid fluorescence of iron which occurs with a copper tube
– the PTFE beakers can be used up to a maximum temperature of 250°C;
– in certain cases, destruction of the matrix silicates can be achieved through an HF attack in a PTFE beaker
– heating to 600°C gives anhydrous oxides → hematite.

4.2.5 Qualitative Diffractometry

The sample of whole soil crushed to 0.1 mm and "clay < 2 μm" fractions (or 0.5 or 0.2 μm sub-fractions,) prepared for randomized or oriented powder spectrum are analyzed by XRD.

Each group of clay has its own layered structure which gives basal reflections whose position, intensity and shape enable either immediate identification or after specific treatments. This section describes the interpretation of standard situations that make it possible to evaluate clayey minerals at the scale of the group and the sub-group, and very occasionally at the scale of the species.

Fine Adjustment of Experimental Conditions

The experimental conditions must be precisely determined in advance, i.e. the type of tube (Cu, Co, etc.), the intensity applied to the filament, the opening of the slits, the speed of rotation of the goniometer, tension meter, amplification, adjustment of the constants of time–inertia, sensitivity, signal/background ratio, angular zone, scanning speed, etc.

A cobalt tube X-ray should be used for samples that are rich in iron because it does not generate fluorescence with this ion. Generally, with suitable geometry, an international standard Cu tube give a satisfactory performance, and JCPDS tables and software (see note 1 in Sect. 4.2.2) cited here are based on this standard.

The rotation speed of the goniometer and the selection of the angular zone of scanning determine the time needed for analysis. The choice of the scanning rate of the sample influences the relative precision of the diffractograms. Too high a speed can lead to insufficient discrimination. For the determination standards, a displacement speed of 1 to 2 $°min^{-1}$ (2θ angle) may be sufficiently rapid but does not allow adequate separation of fine doublets such as those of kaolinite (002) and chlorite (004) for which a slower rate is necessary ($<0.5°$ 2θ min^{-1}). For rapid characterization of clay (group and sub-group) the angular zone of scanning can be limited to a 2θ zone of approximately $2 - 40$ degrees, if determination of the $d(060)$ diffraction is not required as this takes much longer. The strong reflection at $2\theta = 60°$ makes it possible to estimate parameter "b" and thus to differentiate dioctahedral minerals (1.48–1.50 Å) from trioctahedral minerals (1.53 – 1.55 Å) and sometimes to provide more evidence for approximate values by bringing these values closer to the intensities of $d(001)$ diffractions, for example in the identification of certain micas. Powder samples are performed by rotating the sample-support in the reference plane, which requires high precision equipment. The oriented sample method makes it possible to reinforce the reflections (001) by directing the particles according to the development plane of clay minerals. All the slides (or any other form of support) for each sample should be made simultaneously and as homogeneously as possible

(same suspension, same quantity of clay per slide, etc.). Three sub-samples are usually essential:
– a reference oriented sub-sample without treatment, dried and observed with a known quantity of relative moisture
– an oriented sub-sample solvated for hydrated 2:1 clays
– an oriented sub-sample for heat treatment (500°C for 4 h).

The samples should be analysed one after another, and the equipment should be regulated in exactly the same way for each sample to enable better comparison of the spectra. In more complex cases, it may be necessary to prepare homoionically saturated samples (K^+, Mg^{2+}) with suitable treatment and intercalation sequences. These should be performed under the same conditions taking into account the relative humidity of the air, relative stability of the solvations and complexes of intercalation, reaction times (in the case of formamide treatment whose action is rapid on halloysite, whereas on kaolinite this treatment can take 4 or 5 h and should thus be performed at the head of the series). If the sample is very small, it may be possible to perform treatments and measurements sequentially on the same sample. In this case porous ceramics should be used (or 0.20 μm Millipore filters if heat treatments are not envisaged). However, as measurements must then be made over a period of several days it is more difficult to maintain constant conditions.

Examination of the Diagrams

Background Noise

The background noise is due to non-specific signals that are inherent to the material, to the process, to minerals with short-range organization, and possibly to fluorescence phenomena resulting from the emission of secondary X-rays. The latter phenomenon can be eliminated by the back monochromator and amplitude discrimination. The background noise can be also smoothed electronically with suitable software. In the zone of the small angles (2θ between 0 and 10° approximately), depending on the adjustment of the slits, the counter may receive part of the direct beam or of reflections from the edges of the support. The use of variable slits generally prevents these phenomena.

The presence of amorphous substances (aluminosilicates, different oxides, etc.) is indicated by broad and diffuse bands. The interpretation software makes it possible to eliminate these zones selectively and to stabilize the base line.

Geometry of the Peaks

The geometry of the peaks enables determination of the degree of crystallinity, particularly for well-crystallized minerals where crystal size is suited to the X-ray wavelength and presents regular inter-reticular variations giving clear diffractions and many harmonics (Fig. 4.5a). Badly crystallized minerals that are not well ordered and whose size is not suitable to X-ray often give broad biconvex peaks whose surfaces are not usable for quantitative analysis (e.g. smectite, Goethite, see Fig. 4.5b). Too many particles such as diatoms, quartz or feldspars, can limit the orientation of clays and render interpretation of the spectra difficult. Superposition of peaks resulting from the cumulative presence of several minerals results in a widening of the signals and an abnormal rise in relative intensities, for example Chlorite (001)–Vermiculite or Kaolinite (001)–Chlorite (002). These samples require different pretreatments to reduce uncertainty and to reveal the masked peaks (cf. Sect. 4.2.4).

Peaks may display low intensity and widening even in the case of minerals that are usually well distinguished such as quartz, calcite or ordered kaolinite (001 or 002) if the sample is not thick enough. Goethites and smectites which have more diffused peaks may be masked. At certain angles, lines that come from the support are also likely to appear.

Particles of approximately 0.5 μm are used for comparative studies on different clayey fractions and for quantitative analysis, when separation was done by ultracentrifugation. Widening at half-height of the peaks of other coarser or finer fractions must be controlled. Indeed, if the crystallites are too fine, the reflections widen; if they are too big, absorption phenomena can disturb the intensity. It should be noted that smectites are concentrated in the finest fractions; kaolinites, illites, chlorites, iron oxides in the 0.2–0.5 μm fractions; detrital micas, chlorites, quartz, feldspars in the 0.5–2 μm fractions. A well-crystallized but incompletely delaminated kaolinite can be found in the fine silt phase.

Location of the Angular Distances

The angular location of the top of the peaks of diffraction must be transformed into interreticular distance "d" in Å, in accordance with the Bragg equation (1) (see table or software depending on the type of anti-cathode used). Each peak should numbered chronologically and its reticular distance given in Angströms or nanometers (international standard), along with its relative intensity. Computer equipment allows on-screen comparisons with reference spectra and an automatic search of the JCPDS database (note 1 of Sect. 4.2.2).

The powder spectrum of *the whole soil* provides an overview of all the minerals present and of the relative intensities of the different components. The spectrum may not be easy to interpret if this is not done by comparing it with other samples of the same sequence but at least makes it possible to select appropriate samples for a more thorough examination. The *clay fractions* of the spectrum powders, which are purified and concentrated by dispersion and particle-size separation treatments, provide more precise information on the clays and on associated minerals. It is possible to determine predominant peaks with strong intensity, and assemblies of characteristic peaks at the level of the reticular distances from 7–, 10–, 12–, 14–15 Å, as well as the peaks of quartz, calcite, etc., and possibly the peaks at 4.40–4.50 Å that are identifiable in the majority of clays. The same limitations apply to complex mixtures. The peaks are often broad, and the profiles asymmetrical; smectites only display a reproducible interlayer space if their state of hydration and ionic saturation are controlled.

The presence of interstratified minerals can cause problems that are difficult to solve, especially for the di- and tri-octahedral sub-groups because of obstruction of the zone (060) around 1.50Å. Depending on the objectives, a spectrum helps determine the strategy to be used e.g. adjustments of the experimental conditions, or of the number of oriented plates with given treatments, and possibly the need for other complementary techniques such as thermal analysis, IR spectrometry, electronic microscopy, selective dissolutions, chemical purifications, and so on.

On oriented spectra that have undergone suitable treatments basal reflections, relative intensities, regrouping of the diagnostic reflections using JCPDS-ICDD interpretation tables (note 1 in Sect. 4.2.2), can be performed rapidly on-screen using suitable software. The table designed by Brindley and Brown (1980) can also be used, it takes into account the most intense lines characteristic of clay and associated minerals in soils, classified in descending order of the values of "d". The "Hanawalt Mineral Search Index" arbitrarily divides the field of the reticular distances from 999.99– to 1.00 Å into 40 groups. The first entry corresponds to the line of maximum intensity. The value "d" of the second line corresponds to the second strongest intensity and determines the sub-group. The entries are then classified within each sub-group by decreasing values of intensity resulting in six additional lines. Since the degree of intensity is difficult to determine, multiple entries make it possible to integrate experimental variations: if the diffraction of a mineral includes 2 or 3 high-density peaks, there can be 2 or 3 entries (with intensities ranging from 100 to 75). The record of the location of the eight peaks should be followed by the name of the mineral and the number of complete JCPDS cards concerning this mineral. The behaviour of minerals under different chemical and thermal treatments facilitates the identification of clay minerals (see Tables 4.4 – 4.7).

4.3. Quantitative mineralogical analysis

4.3.1 Interest

Quantitative mineralogical analysis is used to identify factors that influence or determine current or previous pedogenesis and physical and chemical properties of soils. This type of analysis is the logical continuation of qualitative analysis but many problems are involved and the precision will be influenced by the chemical and structural complexity of the substrate. For a simple substrate with two main mineralogical species, depending on the methods used, the risk of error may be around 3%, but may reach 5–10% with three species and about 30% for mixtures with n species. The presence of substances with short-range order further increases the degree of inaccuracy and can even prevent determination with certain methods, if this is the predominant mineral form. The methods use either:
– a single instrumental technique, XRD being the most widely used
– a group of techniques that make it possible to identify the centesimal composition of the sample more satisfactorily, although with increased complexity and at a higher cost.

4.3.2 Quantitative Mineralogical Analysis by XRD

Principle

The advantage of these analytical methods is their relative simplicity and especially the fact that a single instrumental technique is involved. X-ray intensities obtained for each component of a mixture are directly correlated with the proportion of the component according to the equation:

$$I_p = \frac{k_p W_p}{\bar{\mu}},$$
(4.2)

where W_p is the weight of compound P in the sample; I_p is the intensity of the diffraction of the pure compound P; k is the constant depending on the compound P and the experimental conditions and μ is the attenuation coefficient of mass of the mixture.

When the substances are well crystallized and present a definite chemical composition, resulting in intense specific XRD reflections with no superposition, quantification is easy and the degree of precision is acceptable, particularly with a standard giving the same chemical characteristics. Unfortunately, the imperfection of soil minerals (structural order and disorder), the size of crystallites, chemical variability due to substitutions, and preferential orientations result in modifications in the intensity of peaks for the same mineral and even in angular displacement (which makes the selection of reference minerals for the calibration of measurements difficult). In this case the resulting measurements are very precise. When possible, the reference minerals should come from the same geological formation and have undergone the same type of pedological deterioration in order to reproduce a matrix with a similar degree of disorder and chemical composition (clays under transformation processes).

The samples for quantitative analysis have to be prepared with particular care to limit widening of the lines (over-grinding can result in an increase in structural disorder as well as in an increase in the amorphous phase), the effects of extinction and micro-absorption (crystallites and particles are too coarse), and phenomena of orientation due to the interrelationships between particles (preferential orientation). Measurements are taken on:

– powder samples that account for all the reflections; as the relative intensity of the basal reflections is low, a concentration of approximately 10% may be necessary to quantify a given compound in the mixture;

– an oriented sample which increases the basal reflections of clays, however, this involves the risk of certain components obstructing the regularity of the orientation; this technique is more sensitive and pushes back the limits of detection, but instead of preparing the sample on glass slide, the sample should be prepared on porous ceramic to eliminate the effects of sedimentation (cf. Sect. "Aggregates Oriented on Porous Ceramic Plate").

Sample preparation can include Mg^{2+} saturation, solvation with glycerol and finally, mixing an internal standard and a matrix suppressor. The homogenization of the sample and the internal standard should be carried out in a mixer with an agate ball. When clay samples are separated by ultracentrifugation, a check should be made to make sure there are no variations in composition (the relative proportion of each clay in the mixture may be different and cause bias). Three types of quantitative XRD methods can be used: direct analyses without standard, analyses with an external standard, analyses with an internal standard (addition of standard, matrix suppressor, etc.).

In *direct analysis with no standard* the mineral of reference is taken directly in the sample matrix. Interesting relative values will be obtained for the comparison of samples from the same sequence.

Analysis with an external standard does not require long preparation, but the choice of standard substances for the calculation of the intensities is difficult as is also the case with the other methods. The degree of precision is thus sometimes doubtful except for compounds that give clear reflections in a relatively pure medium with only few major components, for example well-crystallized kaolinite and quartz.

Analysis with an internal standard: these analyses are carried out in the presence of a standard substance presenting (i) a low attenuation coefficient, (ii) a strong XRD reflection that is narrow and is not superimposed on reflections of the minerals to be determined, and, if possible, is low in harmonics and (iii) a density that is close to the minerals in the mixture enabling better homogenization.

The αAl_2O_3 corundum was adopted in 1976 by JCPDS (see note 1 in Sect. 4.2.2) as the standard of reference for the quantitative study of minerals (high-purity synthetic corundum, 1 μm particle size, Linde, by Union Carbide or similar). The basal reflection at 2.085 Å ($I = 100$ for the 1,1,3 plane) is clear. Crystallinity can be increased by heating at 800°C for 1 h. There is no preferential orientation. The 2.106 Å line of MgO, and the 6.11 Å line of Boehmite $\gamma AlOOH$ can also be used.

Several procedures and modes of calculation can be used, e.g. standard additions or matrix suppression. The standard additions method is time consuming and requires the construction of curves of calibration. The technique of Chung (1974 a,b) with matrix suppression is faster and if required, makes it possible to identify the presence of amorphous minerals with short-range organization in the differential balance[4]. However it is necessary to obtain spectra whose principal reflections do not include diffuse bands or zones of superposition as the treatment of these signals is too complex. This method enables elimination of the

---

[4] If the soil sample contains undestroyed organic matter or substances that are transparent to X-ray, these substances can be found in the differential balance.

matrix effects from the intensity – concentration, and all the intensities are obtained with only one scan, which reduces possible instrumental errors.

Procedure

A spectrum is performed on powder samples, on the pure corundum and on the sample mixture + corundum:
– weigh a known weight of corundum (c) and a known weight of sample (A); the proportion of the mixture should be 1:1
– homogenize in a horizontal mixer with a bowl and an agate ball for 20 min
– pour the powder into a support and pack slightly; level with a razor blade to obtain a smooth but not oriented surface; the reference plane must be perfect[5].
– place on a diffractometer under standard conditions using a Cu tube, a variable slit and a graphite monochromator with a time constant enabling accumulation of at least 20,000 counts per peak (minus background noise) and a 2θ scanning rate of $0.5°$ min^{-1} (or even $0.25°$ 2θ min^{-1}); only scan the zone containing significant peaks
– locate the position of the most intense diffracted peaks that are representative of each component, determine their intensity and compare with the internal standard – what does this dash imply? matrix suppressor.

Calculations

Based on the nature of monochromatic X-ray radiation of a defined wavelength, the nature of the matrix effects (absorption) and the basic equation of Klug and Alexander (1959), Chung mathematically extracted the effects of attenuation of mass:

$$I_i = \frac{k_i X_i / Q_i}{\sum \mu_i X_i} = \frac{k_i X_i / Q_i}{\mu_i} \qquad (4.3)$$

where
I_i is the intensity of the X-ray diffracted by a selected plane of component i (unknown);

---

[5] Certain authors prefer to prepare the samples by pelletization although there is a risk of causing a certain orientation of the powder due to the very strong pressure applied. However, there will be fewer errors connected with surface quality or the density of sites likely to diffract.

k_i is the constant which depends on the geometry of the diffractometer and the nature of component i;

X_i is the weight of the fraction of component i;

Q_i is the density of component i;

μ_i is the coefficient of mass absorption (or attenuation coefficient of mass) of the pure component i;

μ_t is the coefficient of absorption of the total sample including component i, the internal standard and possibly a reference material.

The last two terms characterize the effect of adsorption which is often difficult to measure with other methods. The introduction of a definite weight of a matrix suppressor (corundum resembling an internal standard) makes it possible to introduce: X_f is the weight of the matrix suppressor (f, flushing agent) and X_o is the weight of the sample, and the

equation: $$X_f + X_o = X_f + \sum_{i=1}^{n} X_i = 1$$

n being the number of components of the sample, and

$$\left(I_i/I_f\right)\left(I_f^0/I_i^0\right) = \left(X_i/X_f\right)\left(\mu_i/\mu_f\right),$$

where I_f^0 and I_i^0 represent the intensities of the X-ray diffracted by a selected plane of each pure component. By introducing the ratio of intensity of reference $K_i = I_i/I_c$, and other substitutions, one arrives at the equation:

$$X_i = X_f \left(k_f/k_i\right)\left(I_i/I_f\right), \qquad (4.4)$$

which gives the relation between intensity and concentration from which the effect of matrix is eliminated and which is used for quantitative multi-component analysis. With corundum as matrix suppressor the final simple equation ($k_f = k_c = 1$) is:

$$X_i = \left(X_c/k_i\right)\left(I_i/I_c\right), \qquad (4.5)$$

where

X_i is the weight of the sample fraction;

X_c is the weight of corundum;

I_i is the diffracted intensity of sample;

I_c is the diffracted intensity of corundum;

$k_i = I_i/I_c$ = intensity ratio of reference (Table 4.8).

Remarks

Using computerized equipment, it is possible to take into account the height of the reflection and the width at mid-height[6] or the surface of the $d(001)$ reflections which the software calculates automatically taking stabilized background noise into account.

Complementary measurements may be necessary on oriented samples: Mg^{2+} saturated or solvated samples, and the use of multiplicative coefficients accounting for the structure of the minerals (fibrous clays with pseudo-layers that do not give very intense reflections, etc.).

It is possible to combine the results of the average of two reflections as this can provide information on crystallinity, etc. The choice will depend on the shape of the diffractogram, the nature of the components, and the degree of precision desired.

Table 4.8. Recommended values of I_i/I_c ratios (Eq. 5) from Bayliss (1986)

Mineral	I/I_c	d (Å)	Mineral	I/I_c	d (Å)
allophane	0.1	3.3	illite-montmorillonite	0.4	12
biotite	9.0	10.0	kaolinite 1Md	1.1	7.1
boehmite	1.0	6.11	kaolinite 1T	2.1	7.1
calcite	3.7	3.03	muscovite	2.2	10
corundum	1.0	2.09	quartz	4.3	3.35
dickite	2.9	7.2	smectite	3.0	15
gibbsite	1.6	4.85	talc	1.5	9.3
goethite	1.4	4.18			
gypsum	2.2	2.87			
hematite	0.9	2.70			
illite	0.7	10			

For the same mineral species, values of k_i may vary with the geological origin and the nature of pedological alteration and measurements must must thus be carried out under the same conditions. The choice of minerals is made after chemical analysis and XRD.

---

[6] If it is necessary to compare samples by measuring intensity, it should be noted that the ratio of the heights of the peaks is only valid if the widths at mid - height are identical for the two samples.

The I_i/I_c ratio is affected by crystallinity, it approaches 0 if the mineral is not crystalline (allophane – materials with short-range organization) and can reach 8–9 if the size of crystallites and crystallinity is optimum. Chemical substitutions (e.g. heavy Fe^{2+} minerals replacing light Mg^{2+} minerals) cause variations in the I_i/I_c ratio.

4.3.3 Multi-Instrumental Quantitative Mineralogical Analysis

Quantitative methods based on XRD have limited precision particularly when dealing with complex assemblies that give diffuse reflections or reflections that are more or less masked by superposition, or when there is a significant quantity of substances amorphous to X-rays. Multi-instrumental methods combine measurements based on XRD and other chemical and physical measurements making it possible to characterize the different elements. Measurements are generally made on clay fractions, but these measurements can be supplemented by others, for example organic matter destroyed by hydrogen peroxide, carbonates, soluble salts, iron oxides, etc. eliminated during extraction of the <2 µm clay fraction, and finally by analysis of sands and silts separated by sieving.

These methods can only be used in specialized laboratories that have a wide range of instrumental methods such as XRD, IR, TEM, DTA-TGA, AA, ICP, etc., at their disposal. Each component of a mixture has its own chemical and physical characteristics that can be measured. First XRD spectra are qualitatively interpreted to identify clayey minerals (cf. Sect. 4.2.4 and 4.2.5).

Roberts (1974) and Robert et al. (1991) quantified the different elements using their specific properties. The organization, size, and shape of the particles make it possible the right choices and to enhance identification by methods like TEM-HR, STEM, EDX (see Chap. 8) of minerals that only present in small quantities and cannot be detected by XRD. Thermal analysis may be essential for the quantification of kaolinite, oxyhydroxides and chlorite. Losses between 110–300, 300–600, 600–950°C are used. Corrections for the oxidation of iron at high temperatures are required.

Total chemical analysis of clay by a HF–HCl attack (cf. Chap. 31) makes it possible to determine the proportions of the different elements present, which is essential for the identification of the structure of the different mineral phases. Total K enables estimation of micas on the basis of 7.5% of K for illites compared to 8.3 – 10% of K for the other micas. Analysis by "selective" dissolution (cf. Chap. 6) using suitable procedures enables certain phases to be preferentially dissolved without the other elements in the matter undergoing a significant attack. For example, the attack of a sample (heated at 110°C for 4 h) by a 0.5 mol (NaOH) L^{-1} solution followed by boiling for 2 min 30 makes it possible to extract allophane (42.7% SiO_2–36.3% Al_2O_3) and noncrystalline compounds such as colloidal silica (a little montmorillonite and vermiculite is dissolved). Fusion with pyrosulphate or possibly a tri-acid attack (H_2SO_4–HNO_3–HCl) enables isolation of quartz and feldspars in the residue from the attack. This residue is then weighed. The weight should be increased by 3% to compensate for the slight dissolution of quartz and feldspars. The residue is then analyzed by XRD to detect the presence of feldspar then can be analyzed chemically after dissolution. Dissolution with Tamm reagent (in darkness or with UV photolysis) enables isolation of noncrystalline forms of iron and the CBD method (see Chap. 6) enables isolation of crystalline iron hydroxides.

Analyses that identify the activity of clays can enable separation of certain types of 2:1 clay based on their cation exchange capacity using several different treatments: Na^+ saturation and displacement by Mg^{++}, Mg^{2+} saturation and displacement by ammonium acetate, etc. The total specific surface (external and/or internal) can be determined using the (EGME) method, by absorption of methylene blue, or by the BET method.

Table 4.9. Some properties of minerals used for the adjustment of the results

	CEC (cmol kg^{-1})	Specific surface ($m^2 g^{-1}$)	Water loss 540–900°C (%)
mica	25	175	0.50
quartz	2	25	0
feldspars	2	25	0
allophane	100	800 – 1,000	0
kaolinite	5 – 10	45	0
colloidal SiO2	20	200	2
montmorillonite	80 – 100	800	0.88
vermiculite	175 – 200	440	1.83
chlorite	25	175	12.30

All this quantitative information is imported into the software making it possible to specify the proportion of each component in the mixture, to assign the limits of the properties for the various compounds, and to select options for calculations.

References

Anton O and Rouxhet PG (1977) Note on the intercalation of kaolinite, dickitte and halloysite by dimethyl-sulfoxide. *Clays Clay Minerals*, 25, 259–263

Bayliss P (1986) Quantitative analysis of sedimentary minerals by powder X-Ray diffraction. *Powder diffraction*, 1, 37–39

Brindley GW and Brown G (1980) Crystal structure of clay minerals and their X-Ray identification. *Mineralo. Soc.*, 415–438

Calvert CS (1984) Simplified, complete CsCl–hydrazine–dimethylsulfoxide intercalation of kaolinite. *Clays Clay Miner.*, 32, 125-130

Chassin P (1974) Influence de la stéréochimie des diols sur la formation des complexes interfoliaires de la montmorillonite calcique. *Clay Miner.*, 11, 23–30

Chung FH (1974a) Quantitative interpretation of X-Ray diffraction pattern of mixtures. I- matrix flushing method for quantitative multi-component analysis. *J. Appl. Crystallog.*, 7, 519–525

Chung FH (1974b) Quantitative interpretation of X-Ray diffraction patterns of mixtures. II – Adiabatic principle of X-Ray diffraction analysis of mixtures. *J. Appl. Crystallog.*, 7, 526–531

Churchman GJ, Whitton JS, Claridge GGC and Theng BKG (1984) Intercalation method using formamide for differentiating halloysite from kaolinite. *Clays Clay Miner.*, 32, 241–248

Decarreau A (1990) Les poudres : techniques expérimentales et interprétation des diagrammes – Facteurs déterminant le mode d'empilement. In *Structure, propriétés et applications. Société Française de Minéralogie et cristallographie*, Groupe Français des Argiles, 209–236

Eltantawy IM and Arnold PM (1974) Ethylene glycol sorption by homoionic montmorillonites. *J. Soil Sci.*, 25, 99–110

Gonzalez Garcia S. and Sanchez Camazano M. (1968) Differenciation of kaolinite from chlorite by treatment with dimethylsulfoxyde. *Clay Miner. Bull.*, 7, 447–450

Klug HP and Alexander LE (1974) *X-Ray diffraction procedures*. Wiley 2nd edition

Modre DZ and Dixon JB (1970) Glycerol vapor adsorption on clay minerals and montmorilllonite soil clays. *Soil Sci. Soc. Am. Proc.*, 34, 816–822

Olejnik S, Aylmore LAG, Posner AM and Quirk JP (1968) Infra-red spectra of kaolin mineral-dimethyl sulfoxide complexes. *J. Phys. Chem.*, 72, 241–249

Paterson E, Bunch JL and Duthie DML (1986) Preparation of randomly oriented samples for X.Ray diffractometry. *Clay Miner.*, 21, 101-106

Range KJ, Range A and Weiss A (1969) Fireclay type kaolinite or fire-clay mineral? Experimental classification of kaolinite – halloysite minerals. *Proceedings of the International Clays Conference* (Tokyo). Israel Universities Press, 3–13

Roberts JM Jr (1974) *X-Ray diffraction and chemical techniques for quantitative soil clay mineral analysis.* Engineering Thesis, Pennsylvania State University, 78 pages

Robert M, Hardy M and Elsass F (1991) Crystallochemistry, properties and organization of soil clays derived from major sedimentary rocks in France. *Clay Miner.*, 26: 409–420

Thomson A, Duthie DM, Wilson MT (1972) Randomly oriented powders for quantitative determination of clay minerals. *Clay Miner.*, 9, 345–348

Wada K and Yamada H (1968) Hydrazine intercalation, intercalation for differentiation of kaolin mineral, from chlorites. *Am. Miner.*, 53, 334–339

Bibliography

General

Alekseeva TV, Alekseev AO, Sokolovska Z, Khainos M, Sokolowska Z and Hajnos M (1999) Relationship between mineralogical composition and physical properties of soils. *Pochvovedenie.*, 5, 604–613

Brindley GW and Brown E (1980) *Crystal structure of clay minerals and their X-Ray identification.*, Mineralogical Society, 495 p

Caillère S, Hénin S and Rautureau M (1982) *Minéralogie des argiles, 1,* Masson, 184 p

Caillère S, Hénin S and Rautureau M (1982) *Minéralogie des argiles, 2,* Masson, 189 p

Charley H (1989) *Clay Sedimentology.*, Springer Belin Heidelberg New York, 623 p

Dixon JB and Weed SB (1989) *Minerals in soil environments.*, Soil Science Society of America (USA), 2e édition, 1244 pp.

Gautheyrou J and Gautheyrou M (1979) *Etude des argiles par diffraction X. Synthèse bibliographique pour l'identification des argiles.*, Guide pratique. ORSTOM-Antilles, notes de laboratoires, ORSTOM (26 pages + 2 annexes).

ICDD (JCPDS-ASTM)) *Mineral powder diffraction File – PDF-1 DATA BASE* (powder diagramms, interlayer spaces, relative intensity, chemical name, mineralogical formula) - PDF-2 DATA BASE (powder diagramm, inter-layer spaces, relative intensity, chemical name, mineralogical name, Miller's indice, unit cell, physical properties, references) – Shorten ICDD ref: eliminate – version papier (SET 1 à 36, SET 1 à 8 révisés, SETS 37, 38, 39, 40, 41) – version disque compact (CD-ROM DISC SETS 1-41 inorganique – organique pour IBM PC, VAX, McIntosh) – SEARCH MANUAL Alphabetical index – inorganic phases. Hanawalt index – inorganic phases (remise à jour annuelle), ICDD Newton Square PA 19073-3273 (USA)

Inigo AC, Tessier D, Pernes M (2000) Use of X-ray transmission diffractometry for the study of clay-particle orientation at different water contents. *Clays Clay Miner.*, 48, 682–692

Kovda IV, Morgun EG, Tessier D, Pernes M (2000) Particle orientation in clayey soils according to transmission diffractometry data, 8, 989–1003

Manhães RST, Auler LT, Sthel MS, Alexandre J, Massunaga MSO, Carrió JG, dos Santos DR, da Silva EC, Garcia-Quiroz A and Vargas H (2002) Soil characterisation using X-ray diffraction, photoacoustic spectroscopy and electron paramagnetic resonance. *Appl. Clay Sci.,* 21, 303–311.

Martins E de S, de S Martins E (2000) Integrated method of mineralogical characterization of deeply weathered soils. *Comunicado Tecnico Embrapa Cerrados.*, Brazil, 37, 5 pp.

Millot G (1964) *Géologie des argiles.* Masson, Paris, 499 pp.

Newman AC (1987) *Chemistry of clays and clay minerals.*, Mineralogical society, monograph no 6, 480 p

Chen PY (1977) *Table of key lines in X-Ray powder diffraction patterns of minerals in clays and associated rocks. Dept. of Natural resources,* (Indiana, USA). Geological Survey occasional paper no 21, 67 p

Robert M (1975) Principes de détermination quantitative des minéraux argileux à l'aide des rayons X. Problèmes particuliers posés pour les minéraux argileux les plus fréquents dans les sols des régions tempérées. *Ann. Agron.,* 26, 363–399

Stucki JW (Goodman BA and Schwertmann U (1985) *Iron in soils and clay minerals.*, D. Reidel, 893 p.

Teissier D (1984) *Etude expérimentale de l'organisation des matériaux argileux. Hydratation, gonflement et structuration au cours de la dessiccation et de la réhumectation.*, INRA, Thèse doc. Etat, 361 pp.

Thorez (1975) *Phyllosilicates and clay minerals. A laboratory handbook for their X-Ray diffraction analysis.*, Lelotte Ed., 579 p

Wilson MJ (1987) *A handbook of determinative methods in clay mineralogy.*, Blackie – Chapman and Hall, 308 p.

Preparation of Oriented Aggregates on Porous Ceramic Plate

Kinter EB and Diamond S (1956) A new method for preparation and treatment of oriented-aggregat specimens of soil clays for X-Ray diffraction analysis. *Soil Sci.,* 81, 111–120

La Manna JM and Bowers FH (1985) A suction apparatus for orienting clay minerals into porous ceramic tile. *Soil Sci. Soc. Am. J.,* 49, 1318–1319

Rich CI (1969) Suction apparatus for mounting clay specimens on ceramic tile for X-Ray diffraction. *Soil Sci. Soc. Am. Proc.,* 33, 815–816

Shaw HF (1972) The preparation of oriented clay mineral specimens for X-Ray diffraction analysis by a suction unto ceramic tile method. *Clay Miner.,* 9, 349–350

Saturation of Clays by Cations

Brindley GW and Ertem G (1971) Preparation and solvation properties of some variable charge montmorillonite. *Clays Clay Miner.*, 19, 399–404

Bühmann C, Fey MV and De Villiers JM (1985) Aspects of the X-Ray identification of swelling clay minerals in soils and sediments. *S. Afri. J. Sci.*, 81, 505–509

Calvet R and Prost R (1971) Cation migration into empty octahedral sites and surface properties of clays. *Clays Clay Miner.*, 19, 175–186

Hofmann U and Klemen R (1980) Verlust der Austanschfahigeit von lithiumionen an bentonit darch erhitzung (perte d'échangeabilité des ions lithium dans les bentonites après chauffage). *Zeit. Anorganisc Chem.*, 262, 95–99

Lim CH and Jackson ML (1986) Expandable phyllosilicate reactions with lithium on heating. *Clays Clay Miner.*, 34, 346–352

Saturation, Solvation, Intercalation Complexe, Dissolution

Barnhisel RI and Bertsch PM (1989) Chlorites and hydroxy-interlayered vermiculite and smectite. In *Minerals in soil environments* Dixon JB and Weed SB ed., Soil Sci. Soc. of Am., 729–740

Barnhisel RI (1977) Chlorites and hydroxy interlayered vermiculite and smectite, 331-356. In *Minerals in soil environments*, Dixon JB and Weed SB ed., Soil Sci. Soc. Am., Monogr., 331–356

Brindley GW (1966) Ethylene glycol and glycerol complexes of smectites and vermiculites. *Clay Miner.*, 6, 237–260

Brindley GW and Ertem G (1971) Preparation and solvation properties of some variable charge montmorillonites. *Clays clay Miner.*, 19, 399–404

Churchman GJ (1990) Relevance of different intercalation tests for distinguishing halloysite from kaolinite in soils. *Clays and clay Minerals*, 38, 591–599

Follet EAC, McHardy WJ, Mitchell BD and Smith BFL (1965) Chemical dissolution techniques in the study of clays. Part 1. *Clay Miner.*, 6, 23–24

Novich BE and Martin RT (1983) Solvation methods for expandable layers. *Clays Clay Miner.*, 31, 235–238

Suquet H, Iiyama JT, Kodama H and Pezerat N (1977) Synthesis and swelling properties of saponites with increasing layer charge. *Clay Miner.*, 25, 231–242

Suquet M, Calle de la C and Pezerat H (1975) Swelling and structural organization of saponite. *Clays Clay Miner.*, 23, 1–9

Theng BKG, Churchman GJ, Whitton JS and Claridge CGC (1984) Comparison of intercalation methods for differentiating halloysite from kaolinite. *Clays Clay miner.*, 32, 249–258

Walker GF (1958) Reactions of expanding-lattice clay minerals with glycerol and ethylene glycol. *Clay Miner. Bull.*, 302–313

White JL and Jackson ML (1947) Glycerol solvation of soil clays for X-Ray diffraction analysis. *Soil Sci. Soc. Am. Proc.*, 11, 150–154

Preparation of Iron Oxides

Brown G and Wood IG (1985) Estimation of iron oxides in soil clays by profile refinement combined with differential X-Ray diffraction. *Clay Minerals*, 20, 15–27

Campbell AS and Schwertmann U (1985) Evaluation of selected dissolution extractants in soil chemistry and mineralogy by differential X-Ray diffraction. *Clay Miner.*, 20, 515–519

Meunier A and Velde B (1982) X-Ray difffraction of oriented clays in small quantities (0,1 mg). *Clay Miner.*, 17, 259–262

Paterson E, Bunch SL and Duthie DML (1986) Preparation of randomly oriented samples for X-Ray diffractometry. *Clay Miner.*, 21, 101–106

Schwertmann U and Taylor RM (1989) Iron oxides. In *Minerals in Soil environments*, Dixon JB and Weed SB ed. Soil Sci. Soc. Am., 379–438

Schwertmann U, Murad E and Schulze DG (1982) Is there Holocene reddening (hematite formation) in soils of a xeric temperate area. *Geoderma*, 27, 209–223

Torrent J, Schwertmann U and Schulze DG (1980) Iron oxyde mineralogy of some soils of two river terrace sequences in Spain. *Geoderma*, 23, 191–208

Quantitative XRD

Austin GS and Leininger RK (1976) Effect of heat-treating mixed-layer illite-smectite as related to quantitative clay mineral determinations. *J. Sedim. Petrol.*, 46, 206–215.

Brime C (1985) The accuracy of X-Ray diffraction methods for determining mineral mixtures. *Miner. Mag.*, 49, 531–538

Carter RJ, Hatcher MT and Di Carlo L (1987) Quantitative analysis of quartz and cristobalite in bentonite clay based products by X-ray diffraction. *Anal. Chem.*, 59, 513-519

Cody RD and Thomson GL (1976) Quantitative X-ray powder diffraction analysis of clays using an oriented internal standard and pressed discs of bulk shale. *Clays Clay Miners*, 24, 224–231

Davis BL (1980) Standardless X-Ray diffraction quantitative analysis. *Atmosph. Environ.*, 14, 217–220

Decleer J (1985) Comparaison between mounting techniques for clay minerals as a function of quantitative estimations by X-ray diffraction. *Bull. Soc. Belge Géol.*, 94, 275–281

Gavish E and Friedman GF (1973) Quantitative analysis of calcite and Mg–calcite by X-ray diffraction effect of grinding on peak height and peak area. *Sediment.*, 20, 437–444

Goehner RP (1982) X-Ray diffraction quantitative analysis using intensity ratios and external-standards. *Adv. in X-Ray Analy.*, 25, 309–313

Heath GR and Pissas NG (1979) A method for the quantitative estimation of clay minerals in North Pacific deep sea sediments. *Clays Clay Miner.*, 27, 175–184

Hogson M. and Dudgney ANL (1984) Estimation of clay proportions in mixtures by X-Ray. Diffraction and computerized chemical mass balance. *Clays and Clay Miner.*, 32, 19–28

Hooton DH and Giorgetta NE (1977) Quantitative X-Ray diffraction analysis by a direct calculation method. *X-Ray Spectrom.*, 6, 2–5

Hubbard CR and Smith DK (1977) Experimental and calculated standards for quantitative analysis by powder diffraction. *Adv. X-Ray Anal.*, 20, 27–39

Hubbard CR, Evans EH and Smith DK (1976) The reference intensity ratio I/I_c for computer simulated powder patterns. *J. Appl. Cryst.*, 9, 169–174

Johnson LJ, Chu CH and Hussey GA (1985) Quantitative clay mineral analysis simultaneous linear equations. *Clays and Clay Miner.*, 33, 107–117.

Kahle M, Kleber M and Reinhold J (2002) Review of XRD-based quantitative analyses of clay minerals in soils: the suitability of mineral intensity factors. *Geoderma*, 109, 191–205

Norrish K and Taylor RM (1962) Quantitative analysis by X-Ray diffraction. *Clay Miner. Bull.*, 5: 98–109

Ouhadi VR and Yong RN (2003) Impact of clay microstructure and mass absorption coefficient on the quantitative mineral identification by XRD analysis. *Appl. Clay Sci.*, 23, 141–148

Parrot JF, Verdoni PA and Delaune-Mayere (1985) Analyse modale semi-quantitative d'après l'étude des Rayons X. *Analusis*, 13, 373–378

Pawloski GA (1985) Quantitative determination of mineral content of geological samples by X-Ray diffraction. *Am. Mineral.*, 70, 663–667

Persoz (1969) Fidélité de l'analyse quantitative des poudres de roches par diffration X. Bull. *Centre Rech. Pau (SNPA)*, 3, 324–331

Renault J (1987) Quantitative phase analysis by linear regression of chemistry on X-Ray diffraction intensity. *Powder Diffract.*, 2, 96–98

Ruffell A. and Wiltshire P. (2004) Conjunctive use of quantitative and qualitative X-ray diffraction analysis of soils and rocks for forensic analysis. *Forensic Science International*, 145, 13–23

Taylor RM and Norrish K (1972) The measurement of orientation distribution and its application to quantitative determination of clay minerals. *Clay Miner.*, 9, 345–348

Tomita K and Takahashi H (1985) Curves for the quantification of mica/smectite and chlorite/smectite interstratifications by X-Ray powder diffraction. *Clays Clay Miner.*, 33, 379–390.

Mineralogical Analysis by Infra-Red Spectrometry

5.1 Introduction

5.1.1 Principle

The interaction of matter with infra-red (IR) radiation makes it possible to characterize energies of vibration of the molecules on several components (Fig. 5.1): along the axis of the chemical bonds (vibrations of valence or stretching, which, apart from diatomic molecules, are seldom pure) and deformations that are perpendicular to the bond axis (rotation, torsion, shearing, swinging, librations, bending). IR radiations correspond to these energy levels. IR absorption occurs when the frequency of the radiation is equal to that of the vibrations.

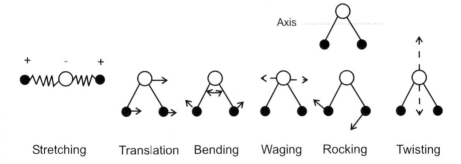

| Stretching | Translation | Bending | Waging | Rocking | Twisting |

Fig. 5.1. Examples of vibration of a simple polyatomic molecule

IR adsorption spectroscopy uses radiations ranging between the visible waves and microwaves. This field is usually divided into three energy zones: near-IR, medium IR and far IR (Fig. 5.2). In these zones, different molecular vibrations correspond to the energy of IR radiations.

– Near infra-red (NIR), as well as visible and UV, account for the high-energy electronic spectra related to fundamental orbitals, for example the change from a link orbital to an empty orbital of higher energy; NIR spectrometry is currently being developed for the study of soil organic matter (cf. Sect. 5.3.1 and Part 2 of this book).

– Medium IR, ranging between 300 and 5,000 cm^{-1} makes it possible to observe vibrations involving protons, (vibrations that correlate well with structure and whose transitions correspond to slight modifications in stretching or deformation of the bond angles in the molecule). Unit cells of clays (crystallographic units) contain polyatomic ions or molecules whose internal modes of vibrations occur between 4,000 and approximately 400 cm^{-1}. These vibratory states have been the subject of detailed studies in mineralogy. Absorption bands make it possible to characterize active molecular groupings satisfactorily.

– Other modes of vibrations which come from the lattice can occur after displacement of a polyatomic group within a unit cell in far IR at very low frequencies between 200 and 10 cm^{-1}. This field, which has not been extensively explored to date, is now accessible thanks to the development of IR spectrometers. Bands of rotational transitions that are not widely spaced enable quantification of the number of revolutions around an axis without stretching or notable modification of the bound angles that are characteristic of the geometry of the crystal.

IR spectrometry is thus used as a complement for X-ray diffraction and chemical and thermal analysis. XRD (cf. Chap. 4) expresses long-distance periodicity satisfactorily, but is not effective in the case of substances that are amorphous to X-ray or minerals with short-range arrangement that appear during sequences of alteration.

With IR, a spectral signature can be identified, along with the nature and the direction of the bonds, and our understanding improved of atomic structures, as well as of the degree of isomorphic substitution in the tetrahedral (Si–Al) and octahedral (Al–Mg) layers. These data are needed to identify certain minerals, to quantify molecular water and constitutive hydroxyls and to detect the presence of crystalline or non-crystalline impurities, which influence the regularity of the lattice structure.

In clays and clay minerals only some molecular groups are likely to vibrate and the spectra are often less complex than for certain organic substances.

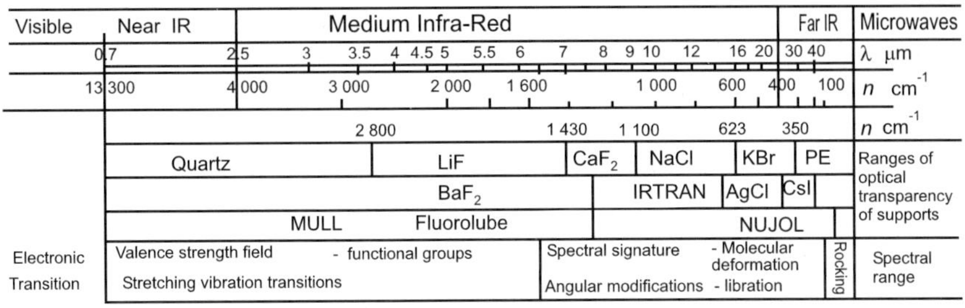

Visible	Near IR	Medium Infra-Red				Far IR	Microwaves
	0.7 2.5	3 3.5 4 4.5 5 5.5 6	7 8 9 10 12	16 20	30 40		λ μm
	13 300 4 000	3 000 2 000 1 600	1 000	600 400	100		n cm^{-1}
		2 800	1 430 1 100	623	350		n cm^{-1}
	Quartz	LiF	CaF$_2$	NaCl	KBr	PE	Ranges of optical transparency of supports
		BaF$_2$		IRTRAN	AgCl	CsI	
	MULL	Fluorolube			NUJOL		
Electronic Transition	Valence strength field - functional groups		Spectral signature - Molecular deformation			Rocking	Spectral range
	Stretching vibration transitions		Angular modifications - libration				

Fig. 5.2. Field of infra-red molecular spectrometry and transparency of the optical elements. The position of the bands in x-coordinate is expressed either in wavelength λ in nm or μm, or often in wavenumber v $(cm^{-1}) = \dfrac{1}{\lambda(cm)} = \dfrac{10^4}{\lambda(\mu m)}$. In ordinate, transmittance expresses percent of radiation that crossed the sample (PE = polyethylene, Mylar)

5.1.2 IR Instrumentation

A spectrometer includes an IR source, optical elements, a detector and a rack of computerized measurements. It is difficult to choose optical equipment that covers the whole spectrum from near IR to far IR (Fig. 5.2).

The source must emit intense polychromatic radiation covering the whole of the IR spectrum. A filter eliminates UV and visible radiations that are emitted simultaneously.

– Sources with filaments of tungsten cover only the field of near IR;
– nickel-chromium filaments make it possible to reach 600 cm^{-1};
– mercury vapour lamps make it possible to reach far IR between 300 and 10 cm^{-1};
– globars (carborundum rods with refractory oxides), which are often used with water cooling to stabilize the temperature of the source at around 1,500°C, emit up to approximately 200 cm^{-1};
– silicon carbide sources emit between approximately 6,500 and 50 cm^{-1}.

Optical equipment (e.g. lenses, windows, dispersive systems) should be selected for their transmittance properties (Fig. 5.2) and resistance to water or solvents. The lenses should preferably be replaced by mirrors (Figs. 5.3 and 5.8).

Filtering of the visible spectrum is generally accomplished by surface treatments with germanium, or black polyethylene films of varying thickness.

The choice of the detector is also limiting and its surface area, the spectral field covered, the sensitivity and the response time of the apparatus, the frequencies to be detected, maintenance needs (operation under liquid nitrogen or helium) should all be taken into account. The detector can be:

– non-selective e.g. a thermocouple or thermopile (several couples connected in series), a bolometer with doped germanium for far IR that operates in liquid helium (2 K), MCT detectors (Mercury, Cadmium, Tellurium), DTGS detectors (Deuterium enriched Triglycine Sulphates) thermostated for medium IR, detectors of Golay with a gas chamber for far IR; these detectors are very sensitive, but very fragile;

– selective (photon–electron transformation as a function of the wavelength), e.g. lead sulphide, lead selenide, or indium antimonide detectors that function in liquid nitrogen.

The optical system can be based on *a dispersive mode* or managed by *interferometry* in a mono or double beam system.

In dispersive mode radiation crosses the sample from where it partially arises (transmission-absorption) to strike a dispersive lattice or a monochromator which divides the beam as a function of wavelength (Fig. 5.3a). Energy is recorded point by point by rotation of the lattice. It is first necessary to determine the zero point of the instrument, and then to determine the basic spectrum without a sample to take into account in particular the CO_2 and H_2O in the air. Transmittance is calculated at each wavelength by the ratio of the two signal-to-noise values. The resolution is often insufficient and energy decreases with an increase in wavelength, which makes it necessary to gradually open the slit of the monochromator and modify the background noise. These operations can be automated, and the degree of precision can be increased by the use of a double beam and measurements on sample and blank taken alternately at each wavelength with the help of a modulator. In this way the energy of the beam is maintained constant. The study of far IR is not possible because of the nature of the apparatuses and insufficient energy. Ratiometric apparatuses are slow and top-of-the-range models are very expensive, as several high resolution lattices are necessary for satisfactory linear dispersion.

Better performances can be obtained by using *an interferometric system* linked with data processing by Fourier transform (Fig. 5.3b). Interferometry is based on rapid movements of a mirror. Each wavelength is modulated at a characteristic frequency determined by the speed of the mirror. The recording of the complex data gives an interferogram that is treated in real time by the Fourier transform. This makes it possible to obtain a spectrum where the amplitude of the signal is recorded as a function of the frequency.

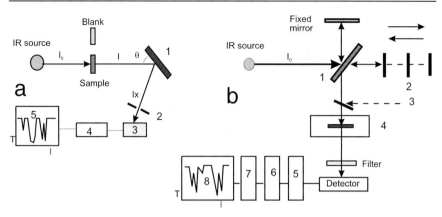

Fig. 5.3. Types of Infra-red spectrometers: **(a)** Dispersive 1: dispersive system: prisms, lattices, monochromator, continuous high resolution interferential wedge, 2: exit slit for precise selection of the field of frequency, 3, 4, 5: detection, amplification and acquisition, I_0 I, I_x : total incidental and transmitted intensities at the selected wavelength x, T: transmittance I/I_0 corresponding to the absorbance $A = -\log T$ **(b)** With interferometer and Fourier transform 1: separation made of KBr with germanium film (400–4,000 cm^{-1}) or made of MYLAR (0–700 cm^{-1}); 2: mobile mirror, spectral composition is a function of the position of the mirror, function resolution of the amplitude of displacement, 3: He–Ne laser for measuring movements of the mobile mirror and indexing mirror direction, 4: sample compartment under vacuum or controlled atmosphere, 5: intensity/position of mirror, 6: interferogram, 7, 8: real-time data acquisition system

In the Michelson interferometer, the polychromatic radiation of the source is divided into two beams by a separation made of KBr or Mylar (covered with a germanium film to filter radiations of the visible spectrum). One of the two beams is sent to a fixed mirror, the other to a mobile mirror that is moved at a known speed by to a linear motor. The two beams are than recombined by the beam splitter. The resolution depends on the maximum stroke of the mobile mirror. Alignment must be maintained during the movement of the mobile mirror with no vibrations or slope likely to deform the spectra and to give erroneous transmittance values. An in–out movement of the mirror allows simultaneous analysis of all the wavelengths of IR radiation.

The changes in the signal reflect variations in modulation of the interferogram. The results are recorded at the different positions of the mirror, which requires knowing its exact position by laser radiation. Each individual signal is located by multiplexing and decoding. The whole spectrum is scanned sequentially as a function of time in less than one second.

To limit the influence of moisture and atmospheric CO_2, the optical circuits function in a sealed enclosure, except for the sample compartment which can be purged with dry nitrogen.

The resolution is generally about 2–4 cm^{-1} but can reach 0.1 cm^{-1} at the price of additional memory which otherwise requires a powerful information processing system.

FTIR apparatuses are generally mono-beam and more rarely, in top-of-the-range models, double-beam which enables the signal-to-noise ratio to be maintained uninterrupted. Suitable software makes it possible to control the spectrometer, collect the results and process the data in real time to restore the spectrum. If necessary, a database search makes it possible to compare the spectra with IR bases for identification, calibration, subtraction of spectra, etc. Calibration is carried out with polystyrene blades that have narrow intense bands distributed between 699 and 3104 cm^{-1}.

In practice, the choice of an apparatus is based primarily on the scientific objectives which determine the main requirements: the wavelength field to be scanned, the nature of materials to be analysed (solid, liquid, gas), the required sensitivity, resolution, data-processing capacity and quality of the software, possible extensions of the basic module (coupled with e.g. liquid or gas chromatography, EGA thermal analysis, Raman spectroscopy, IR or Raman microscopy). As far as price is concerned, instead of purchasing a very expensive top-of-the-range "universal" apparatus, two dedicated complementary apparatuses can be adapted for repetitive laboratory tasks.

For routine soil analysis, an apparatus that covers medium IR up to 220–250 cm^{-1} with an optical system in KBr or better still in CsI and a resolution of about 2 cm^{-1} is sufficient, but for a more specialized laboratory, access to the field of far IR is now necessary.

5.2 IR spectrometry in Mineralogy

5.2.1 Equipment and Products

– Ultra-microbalance, 10^{-6} g sensitivity, range 2–5 g
– IR or FTIR spectrometer suitable for the required ranges of wave-lengths

– IR microscope
– binocular magnifier ($\times$100)
– pellet press (10 tons cm^{-2})
– centrifuge with centrifugation chambers (cf. Chap. 4)
– cooled moisture-proof vibrating grinder with agate ball for crushing in liquid medium
– drying oven (105°C) with precise electronic regulation
– Pyrex glass desiccator
– lab glassware
– quality IR products: KBr, CsI, polyethylene, Nujol (paraffin oil), AgCl, CaF$_2$, IR TRAN 4, solvents, hexachlorobutadiene (Voltalef oil), Fluorolube (fluorinated hydrocarbon oil), various mineral standards.

5.2.2 Preparation of the Samples

Types of Preparation

The preparation of the sample for analysis by IR spectrometry is of prime importance: it conditions the spectral field of analysis and its limits, and indirectly, the sensitivity and the selectivity of measurements.

Determination must be performed on elementary particles that do not exceed 5 μm and even 1 or 2 μm if the MULL technique is used or if quantitative analyses are required.

Clay fractions with a particle size <2 μm in H$^+$, NH$_4^+$ or X$^+$ form, or better fractions <0.5 μm purified with a standard Sharples ultra-centrifuge (cf. Chap. 3) are usually used for analysis. Because of the size of their unit cell, clays display only one negligible distortion of the absorption bands. Crush the samples and homogenize with the agate mortar in the presence of a volatile organic liquid that is inert to IR (Ethanol, acetone, etc.); avoid modifying or destroying the crystalline structure. Too large particles could cause spectral distortion, dispersion of incidental radiation and widening of the absorption bands (Christiansen effect).

Destruction of the organic matter is often necessary first to limit organic absorbance, which is likely to overload the spectrum, and second to avoid excessive retention of adsorbed water, which can mask some absorbance of minerals. However, in some cases this treatment can lead to neogenesis of minerals.

For measurements on solid samples
- In transmission–absorption, clays can be analysed in three main forms:
  a. thin films that are self-supporting or placed on suitable supports,
  b. discs made with binding agents that are transparent to IR,
  c. in a mixture with liquid mulls.
- In NIR or Raman diffuse reflectance, the sample is simply packed in a sample holder taking care to limit preferential orientations.
- In multiple specular reflectance or attenuated total reflectance (ATR), the problems of interface with the soils are often not reproducible and these techniques can generally only be used on thin blades.
- In IR microscopy samples can be analysed on film or as microsamples without preparation.

Pretreatments can cause changes in the properties of the samples: these can be used in comparisons with chemically untreated rough samples preserved in their original conditions (amorphous phases, etc.).

For measurements on liquid samples separated from the soil by chemical means, it is possible to perform the measurements either (i) in solvents that are transparent to IR and do not react with the minerals, or (ii) NIRS measurements on freeze-dried extracts.

For measurements on gas samples resulting from controlled pyrolysis or decomposition of mineral fractions during thermal analyses (EGA and TGA-DTA, see Chap. 7), sample "powders" are used that are identical to those used for standard thermal analyses.

To improve sensitivity, special cells are used to lengthen the path of the beam in the gaseous medium, absorption being proportional to length. Preliminary purging of the air in the sample compartment is required to eliminate any H_2O and CO_2 present.

Preparation of Self-Supporting Films

Technique
This preparation is only possible with certain types of clay, e.g. montmorillonites, vermiculites and fibrous clays, that can be prepared as thin but stable films.

The method of Farmer and Palmieri (1975) has been slightly modified to allow quantification of the measurements. This technique has the advantage of not subjecting the sample to a strong pressure and of avoiding exchange reactions between the sample and the binding agent added in the pelletizing method. The main difficulties are the critical thickness of the film (maximum 4–8 µm), its capacity to transmit a sufficient intensity, its mechanical resistance and the frequent difficultly involved in its removal, which requires great technical skill. Silicated minerals often deposit with preferential orientation, which makes it possible to identify the vibrations caused by the oscillation of the dipoles which should be perpendicular to the plan of the lattice. It is also possible to study polychroism related to the plane using a goniometer.

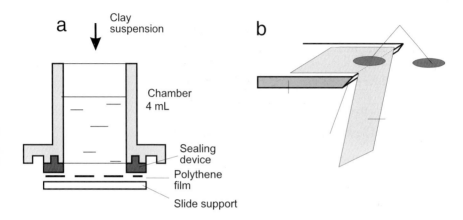

Fig. 5.4. Preparation of self-supporting mineral films: **(a)** centrifugation at 2,500 g in Cyto Hettich chamber, **(b)** removal of self-supporting film

Procedure
– Crush a clayey extract of known weight with an agate mortar with a little water to produce a fluid paste, and then put in suspension in a known volume of distilled water
– transfer the complete suspension on a slide covered with a flexible polythene film in a Cyto Hettich chamber (Fig. 5.4); centrifuge at moderate speed (approximately 2,500 g)
the selected volume of the chamber is 4 mL, making it possible to obtain a film 12.4 mm in diameter, that is to say a surface area of 120 mm^2; in this way it is possible to determine the quantity deposited per unit area (the density must be approximately 1–2 mg per cm^2)
– remove the clear supernatant solution with a pipette and air dry the film containing the deposit
– remove the film by passing the flexible support across the edge of a bevel-edged blade and transfer it onto a support for IR measurement; the deposit can also be transferred onto a thin filter support with rigid

polymeric mesh, which avoids migration thanks to its continuous structure
- store the deposit for 48 h in a desiccator on P_2O_5 before analysis.

Preparation of Film on a Support Transparent to IR

Principle
This system makes it possible to obtain thin films either for oriented deposit by simple gravity or by centrifugation as above.

The following factors have to be taken into account: the thickness of the clay deposit, the choice of a suitable solvent to avoid dissolution of the support, the spectral field useable with this type of support, the reactivity of the clay–solvent-support. In general, KBr slides are used because they are cheap and easy to use, and enable medium-IR scanning up to approximately 400 cm^{-1}, or CsI up to 220 cm^{-1}. Polythene is used for far IR. The sample is put in suspension in a solvent without dissolution. The surface can be impregnated by microvaporization with Nujol to limit reflectance phenomena at the air–clay interface.

Procedure
Depending on the IR domain, select a pellet 13 mm thick obtained by pressure (10 tons cm^{-2} AgCl, CaF$_2$ IRTRAN 2, IRTRAN 4, Ge, Si, KBr, CsI, polythene, etc.).

The sample in suspension in a suitable organic solvent is deposited in the same way as in the preceding procedure by gravity or centrifugation. After drying, carefully heat the disc covered with film in a drying oven at 100°C for 5 h to eliminate all traces of water, then store in a desiccator until analysis.

Preparation of Discs (Solid Solution)

Principle
The solid sample is completely pulverized with an agate mortar in the presence of an organic liquid (for example ethanol) then dried under vacuum in the desiccator with phosphoric anhydride. It is then mixed with a matrix that enables to form self-sustaining discs at high pressure; these disks can be used with quite a wide range of IR radiation.

For swelling smectites, it is preferable to grind a known weight of sample with a little water to form a thick paste, then add the binding agent and grind the wet sample again. After complete drying, homogenize the diluted sample with a microball grinder.

This system is easy to use and is the most widely used, but it has certain disadvantages:

– all materials used as binding agents for the discs have limited transmission in IR so it is impossible to observe the absorbance of a clay on the whole range from near IR to far IR on only one pellet
– the reactivity of the support may result in exchange reactions with clay.

For example potassium bromide (KBr), which is transparent up to 400 cm^{-1} (Fig. 5.2), produces excellent pellets that allow good spectra in a wide range of IR. But with 2:1 clays, such as smectites which contract with K$^+$, exchange phenomena can cause deformation of the absorption spectra (Nyquist and Kagel, 1971). These discs are thus not suitable for studies concerning adsorbed water as K reduces water retention, or for the study of surface cations.

As KBr is hygroscopic, the pellets have to be stored in a desiccator under vacuum with phosphoric anhydride to limit the phenomena of adsorption of water and resulting uncertainties in interpretation between the bands of hydroxyls and those of water adsorbed by minerals and the support. For far IR, polyethylene, polytetrafluoroethylene (Teflon), or paraffin should be used.

Pressure can cause inappropriate transformations by amplifying the effect of the chemical reactivity, but can be used for *in situ* study of the effects of very high pressures obtained with of a diamond-cell anvil making it possible to analyse by IR the induced transformations (Weir et al., 1959; Liu and Mernagh, 1992).

Procedure (Qualitative Analysis)
– Choose the matrix and the diameter of the pellets
– dry the sample in a desiccator for 48 h to eliminate non-structural water whose 3,440 cm^{-1} band can mask that of structural OH; this method of drying is not suitable for all minerals (cf. Chap. 1)
– dry the finely crushed IR-quality binding agent in the drying oven under vacuum at 100°C for one night if its thermal stability permits
– for a disc of approximately 1 mm thickness and a diameter of 13 mm, weigh 0.5–3 mg of clay sample at 0.01 mg precision.
– add 300 mg of KBr (can be changed)
– homogenize with a microhomogenizer with a plastic or agate ball for 2 min, or grind with the agate mortar once more for a perfect mix
– transfer in a stainless steel mould 13 mm in diameter (A in Fig. 5.5b).
– apply light pressure and degas under vacuum for 5 min

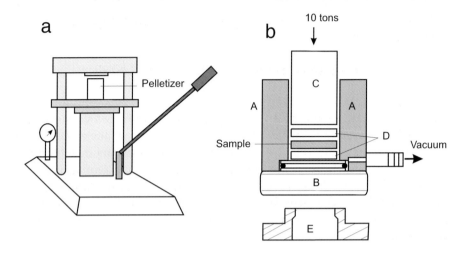

Fig. 5.5. Preparation of the samples in solid solution **(a)**:12 ton manual hydraulic press, **(b)**: detail of a pelletizer: A body, B: removable base, C 13 mm ϕ plunger, D: 13mm ϕ polished cylinders, E: release ring from the mould, *filled circle* represents sealing ring.

– Press (Fig. 5.5a) at 10 tons cm^{-2} for 10 minutes (KBr becomes plastic at this pressure)
– extract the disk from the mould using the release ring (E in Fig. 5.5); it should look homogeneous, smooth and transparent; do not touch it with the hands
– desiccate at 100°C for 2 h and store in a desiccator on P_2O_5 until needed.

  In practice, it is advantageous to make two of even three pellets using the same binding agent at two different concentrations:
– a pellet made with 3 mg of sample for 300 mg of KBr to reach total absorption in the zones around 1,000 cm^{-1} and 500 cm^{-1} (silicates)
– a pellet made with 0.25–0.5 mg of clay sample to obtain details of the spectrum in the areas of intense absorption of silicates
– a third pellet made with a binding agent transparent to far IR will also be needed if spectra below 200 cm^{-1} are required
– perform the spectra under the instrumental conditions selected.

  The time of passage in the spectrometer will depend on the type of material (dispersive or interferometer), the scanning zone with dispersive apparatuses, or the resolution required. After measurement, the pellets can be stored in the desiccator on P_2O_5.

To avoid corrosion, the pelletizer must be cleaned immediately after use without abrasion.

Preparation of the Clay Samples in the Form of Mull

Principle

When interactions are possible between the binding agent and the sample, when it is impossible to make self-supporting films or when pressure is not desirable, the Mull technique can be used with a non-volatile inert oil. Nujol (paraffin oil), hexachlorobutadiene (Voltalef oil) or Fluorolube (fluorinated hydrocarbon oil) is mixed with the sample to form a fluid paste which is pressed between two windows. The method is rapid but only qualitative; the sample is oriented. It is not possible to desiccate the mixture in the drying oven.

Procedure

– Place 10 mg of dried clay sample in a 50 mm agate mortar; add a known quantity of Mull to moisten the powder using a micropipette or a spatula
– crush to obtain a thick paste in which the sample is uniformly dispersed (concentration will be about 0.3–0.5%)
– spread out the mixture with a spatula on a window transparent to IR, then cover with another window to obtain a regular thickness taking care not to trap air inside
– place in the spectrometer and record the spectrum.

The spectral limits of the windows and the zones of absorption specific to the Mull matrix can be taken into account in interpretation. For example, Nujol strongly absorbs between 3,000 and 2,800 cm^{-1} (CH), 1,460 cm^{-1}, 1,375 cm^{-1}, Fluorolube does not absorb between 4,000 and 1,400 cm^{-1}. Both mulls are complementary and two mulls should be made to check that the absorption bands do not mask the bands specific to the sample. The homogeneity of the suspension is difficult to obtain and maintain: prepared samples should thus always be stored horizontally.

Preparation for Specular or Diffuse Reflectance, Attenuated Total Reflectance (ATR)

As the intensity of absorption depends on the angle of incidence, the surface should present weak granulation, and isogranulometric grinding to 0.2 mm is thus necessary. Compression should be carried out as for XRD powders (cf. Chap. 4) avoiding excessive orientation.

The thickness of the powder (approximately 1 mm) is not critical, since the radiation only penetrates a few microns. In certain cases, it is possible to use compressed pellets with or without the addition of binding agents, but in this case the orientation is rather strong. It should be noted that since the refraction index is significant in measurements by reflectance, significant differences will be observed between the spectra obtained by transmission and by reflectance at high wavelengths.

Deuterization

In specialized laboratories, deuterization is an ideal method to study water in clays. In heavy water, deuterium replaces hydrogen. When H_2O is replaced by D_2O, the OH of the interstitial water is deuterated, but not the OH of the lattice (Wada, 1966). The interatomic distances do not change, the mass is doubled and the vibration frequencies drop. It is thus possible to separate the reticular OH or adsorbed water, and eliminate the ambiguity of the measurements in studies of mineral gels (Nail et al., 1976).

Remarks

During preparation, atmospheric contamination of the rough samples must be avoided, for example:
– ammonium can produce absorption around 3,250 and 1,400 cm^{-1} (stretching and deformation)
– in the presence of calcium, attacking organic matter with hydrogen peroxide can lead to the formation of insoluble calcium oxalate which produces absorption near 1,400 cm^{-1}, the destruction of organic matter with sodium hypochlorite does not give oxalate and is consequently more suitable in this particular case
– note that oxidation of organic matter is accompanied by oxidation of mineral compounds like those of Fe^{2+}
– decarbonation and deferrification in an acid medium can destroy minerals like amorphous silicates with precipitation of silica and elimination of Fe et al. (Fröhlich, 1980).

5.2.3 Brief guide to interpretation of the spectra

General Principles

In IR, transitions between the different energy levels are subject to rules of selection as absorption is linked to variation in the dipole moment of the molecules. In the case of polyatomic molecules, all predictable frequencies cannot be observed because energy levels are degenerated for example by symmetry in the molecule. It is thus, very difficult to accurately predict the frequencies of fundamental vibrations in complex structures like those of clays, though recent computer programs have enabled progress to be made.

Tetrahedrons of silica and octahedral aluminium or magnesium form the basic units of clay minerals: a tetrahedral structure can produce four modes of vibrations, and an octahedral structure six, but these are not all active and can be modified by isomorphic substitutions or by the nature of the structural cations.

The interpretation of a clay spectrum can be carried out after comparison with the spectrum of a "pure" substance of comparable nature in order to eliminate uncertainties caused by chemical variations in the composition and order–disorder state. The need for known standard spectra of reference implies each laboratory should record all results of studies on soil minerals to be used as references in addition to consulting available data bases.

Qualitatively, it is first necessary to locate the intensity of the diagnostic absorption bands of minerals and to assign them to molecular groups and possibly to types of precise vibrations. The degree of sensitivity is satisfactory in the case of certain minerals that have intense bands (e.g. kaolinite, quartz, gibbsite, calcite). Quantities of the order of 1% can be detected.

For example, pure hydroxides and oxyhydroxides have a protonic environment that results in net vibrations of specific stretching; on the other hand, in the case of 2:1 and 2:1:1 minerals where chemical variations and isomorphic substitutions are frequent, displacement of the bands can occur; in this case it is useful to simultaneously use XRD analysis (cf. Chap. 4) and chemical analysis by selective dissolution (cf. Chap. 6) for secondary compounds of the soil, making it possible to draw up $\dfrac{\text{(silica of tetrahedrons)}}{\text{(alumina of octahedrons)}}$ ratios that satisfactorily reflect the environment of hydroxyls.

1:1 kaolinite has a SiO_2-to-Al_2O_3 ratio of 2 and presents surface hydroxyls that produce four frequencies of characteristic IR absorptions (Table 5.1).

Smectites and micas have a ratio of approximately 3. As hydroxyls in internal positions are associated with different octahedral cations, the absorption bands are not uniform in the $3,600$ cm^{-1} area and displacement of the frequencies of hydroxyl stretching may be observed. The level of occupation of the octahedral sites (di- and tri-octahedral) can be determined by XRD analysis at line 060, but IR analysis can provide additional information.

In the case of tri-octahedral minerals, the three sites are occupied and the axis of the OH bond of internal hydroxyl is perpendicular to the 001 reticular plane of clays, whereas in di-octahedral minerals only two sites are occupied; the proton of internal hydroxyl is pushed back towards the empty octahedral sites and the spectrum is consequently deformed.

Procedure

The unknown spectra are manually broken up into fields and the bands of maximum intensity are selected along with the wavenumbers of the maxima to compare with reference data. This search can be automated with computerized data bases but in practice also requires the use of laboratory reference data and continuous consultation of the literature.

In solid minerals, interpretation is mainly based on the frequencies of the external molecular group, as the detection of vibrations of the internal crystal is only significant in far IR. IR spectrometry accounts satisfactorily for the molecular groups in which the atoms are in a specific environment. Molecular structures with characteristic bands can be isolated.

IR Absorption Bands in Phyllosilicates

The apparent simplicity of soil minerals masks the complexity of absorption bands of the fundamental modes of vibration (Fig. 5.6). The bands are displaced as a function of the crystalline environment, of substitutions, etc. The frequency and assignment of the bands require very precise spectra to separate slight variations from phases that are often about 2 cm^{-1}. For example, distinction of amorphous silica, opal, biogenic silica by means of the Si–O, Si–O–Si, Si–OH vibrations are of this order of magnitude.

| In the 3,700–3,400 cm^{-1} and 950–600 cm^{-1} zones | – protons in hydroxyls groups, even if there is no long-distance molecular structure, which is useful in the case of "amorphous" substances |
| | – the active modes of tetrahedrons and octahedrons: OH oscillation, dichroism of OH sites in di-octahedral minerals |

	– displacement of the absorption bands as a function of the nature of the octahedral cations, effect of exchange (e.g. interaction of structural OH with interlayer cations)
	– separation of the stretching vibrations of non-bound water allows better distinction of the halloysites disturbed by interfoliaceous water molecules
In the 1,100–500 cm^{-1} zone	– vibrations of the silicate anion that are considered as the spectral print of clays, slightly coupled with vibrations of other structures (silica-oxygen bonds), Si–O stretching towards 1,000 cm^{-1}, Si–O deformation towards 500 cm^{-1};
	– isomorphic substitutions of tetra and octahedral minerals can cause bands in far IR
In the <400 cm^{-1} zone	– Al^{3+} of octahedrons and oxygen bonds of adjacent layers
	– vibrations of exchangeable cations balancing the charges in interfoliaceous spaces of clays and substitution of exchangeable cations

Taking the example of the adsorption bands of a common clay, 1:1 kaolinite (Table 5.1), it is possible to observe:
- a similar configuration of the bands of proton vibration (stretching of external and internal hydroxyls) with respect to crystallinity;
- a level of disorder that is detectable by the coalescence of the 3,669-3,653 cm^{-1} doublet;
- hydration water that is easily differentiated by deuteration and the appearance of a HOH band towards 1,630 cm^{-1}

 − 1,110, 1,036 and 1,010 bands corresponding to stretching vibrations
   characteristic of SiO.

   In the case of Halloysites, widening of the bands can be observed
between 3,700 and 3,600 (OH stretching) because of the structural
distortion caused by variable hydration. Bands 795 and 758 cm^{-1} are of
about the same intensity in kaolinite whereas in halloysites band 795 cm^{-1}
is very weak.

Table 5.1. IR absorption bands of well-crystallized kaolinite
Al$_2$O$_3$,2SiO$_2$,2H$_2$O, <2µm KBr pellet

band (s cm^{-1})	Vibrations		band (s cm^{-1})	Vibrations	
3,695		external OH	690	-	Mg/Al
3,669		external OH	538	deformation	SiO
3,653	stretching	external OH	470	+	+
3,619		internal OH	430		
3,410–3,450^a		OH hydration	364	vibrations	Al/Mg octahedrons
1,630^a	deformation	HOH hydration	345	miscellaneous	
1,106–1,112	stretching	out layer SiO	275		
1,036		SiO...	195		
1,010		SiO...			
938	Deformation	external OH			
912		internal OH			

^{a} water of hydration (towards 3,450 cm^{-1}) can be distinguished from the OH of
  structural hydroxyls by the presence of a HOH band towards 1,630 cm^{-1}

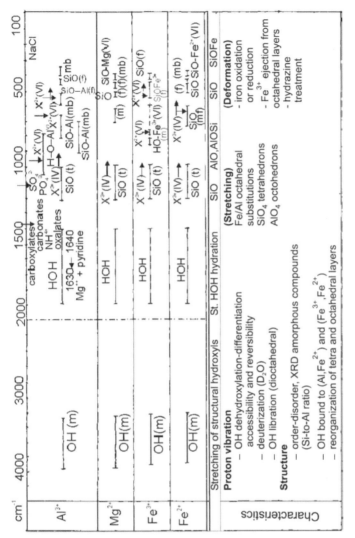

Fig. 5.6. Zones of assignment of the IR absorption bands in phyllosilicates (according to Stubican and Roy, 1961). Bands intensities: (t) very strong, (m) medium, (f) strong, (b) low ↓ changes in intensity → modification of frequencies by substitutions (X^{3+} or X^{2+}) in tetrahedral sites (IV) and octahedral sites (VI)

5.2.4 Quantitative Analysis

Definition

In mineralogy, improvements in quantitative analysis using IR have accompanied improvements in FTIR equipment, and quantitative analysis is an important tool for the study like pedogenic chronosequences, flows and sedimentary series (e.g. paleohydrology, paleoclimatology) or watershed functioning. It is always interesting to observe a mineral in its original state without pretreatment, with the exception of grinding in a non-aggressive liquid medium to reduce granulometry to 1–2 μm, then drying.

The relations between the intensity of absorption of IR radiations and the concentration of mineral species are controlled by the law of Beer–Lambert which is applicable to solid media (Keller and Picket, 1949, or; Duyckaerts, 1959). However, this law is not always applicable to soil minerals for which the characteristic bands are not quite separate and often insufficiently homogeneous. The order–disorder states affect the band widths, and grain sizes influence band intensity. In this case, the limitations are obvious and the photometric response is seldom linear: the absorbance of a band is then no longer proportional to the concentration, and quantification cannot be correctly carried out as it can for gas or organic liquids.

Since standard minerals (with structure, crystallinity, chemical composition and particle size similar to that of the samples) do not exist, only relative quantification can be obtained using this method, nevertheless it is possible to measure variations in the composition of minerals in a profile or toposequences with acceptable precision.

For certain minerals with a relatively characteristic spectrum and a well defined base line such as some quartz, kaolinite, carbonates, the levels of detection will be about 1–2%. Purification by sedimentation allows concentration and simplification of the spectra. The state of crystalline order can cause significant variations, for example in kaolinites when structural OH between 3,700 and 3,600 cm^{-1} are used.

The preparation of the sample is particularly important for quantitative analysis. Maximum absorption (without saturation) and minimum dispersion are required. The isogranulometric size of the particles must be less than 2 μm. The homogeneity of the discs must be perfect, the components should be dried at each stage of preparation or storage, and the thickness of the sample must be constant at less than 1 mm.

Rigorous standardization of the procedures makes it possible to optimize measurements of soil mineral components without depending completely on the degree of crystallinity of powders as in XRD (cf. Chap. 4). Some minerals with short-range organization that are "amorphous" to X-rays, for example some aluminosilicates, crypto crystalline compounds (e.g. allophane, imogolite), and some forms of silica and of iron (e.g. ferrihydrites) can be quantified in this way.

Procedure

Overview

The procedures for qualitative analysis (cf. Sect. 5.2.1 and 5.2.2) are applicable here, and particular care should be taken to:

- desiccate the samples and binders at 105°C for one hour before weighing precisely (10^{-6} g); a temperature of 40°C can be used for heat-sensitive substances
- grind the clay samples to less than 1–2 μm with an agate mortar or preferably with a tightly adjusted cooled vibratory grinder with agate balls in wet medium (in the presence of ethanol or of acetone); after drying, all the particles should pass through a 0.1 mm sieve; fractions that are quantitatively isolated by ultracentrifugation (cf. Chap. 3) can also be used
- weigh a quantity of clay allowing transmittance ranging between approximately 20% and 70% for the whole band range of the spectrum (qualitative tests make it possible to fix the exact proportions between 2 and 5 mg of sample for 1 g of binding agent); mix with the appropriate binding agent (often KBr) and homogenize with a vibratory mixer with agate balls for 5 min
- using 1 g of the above mixture, make three discs with a diameter of 13 mm each by weighing the same quantity of mixture (300–330 mg) to obtain a constant optical pathway of one mm or less; transfer to the pelletizer under vacuum (Fig. 5.5) and apply a pressure of 10 tons cm^{-2} for 2–3 min; the discs should be transparent, smooth, show no surface defects, be of constant thickness and present regular dispersion of the clay particles in the binding agent (this should be checked under the microscope); they should be handled using a forceps and stored in a desiccator with phosphoric anhydride; prepare the calibration discs in the same way
- measure the absorbance of the discs made of binding agent (for the blank assay), sample disks and pure or complex calibration discs made

according to the laboratory reference, which enable calibrations with variable proportions of minerals.

Sediments

Fröhlich (1980, 1989) recommended grinding with an agate ball to less than 2 μm in a cooled inert liquid medium. The fineness of grinding should be checked under the microscope. Optimal dilution is around 0.25%.
– Prepare 1 g of mixture: 2.5 mg of sediment (precision 10^{-5} to 10^{-5} g) and 997.5 mg of KBr
– homogenize carefully with a vibrating grinder with an agate ball;
– press 300 mg of the mixture for 2 min in a 13-mm diameter mould under vacuum.

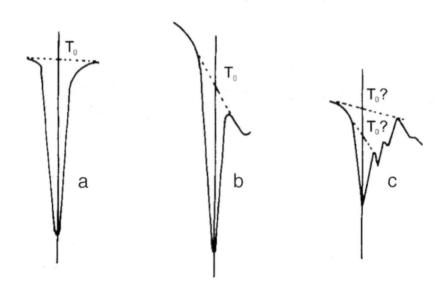

Fig. 5.7. Determination of T_0 :good base line **(a, b)**, approximation **(c)**.

The thickness of the KBr[1] disc should be 0.83 mm and represent the constant optical pathway in all measurements. The disc should be smooth and transparent and should contain 0.75 mg of sample.

Calculations

Any absorbance due to the thinner (KBr) must be subtracted from total absorbance (KBr+sample). The transmission (and by conversion absorbance A) of the substance is measured on the spectrum starting from the base line. This line is often difficult to define for complex mixtures (Fig. 5.7) and requires approximations (effect of matrix, interference between bands, etc.). The relative error is often about 5%, and can be improved for certain minerals.[2] Calibration using "pure" minerals or mineral mixtures with a composition close to that of the samples makes it possible to plot curves of absorbance $= f$ (mass of mineral).

One gram of mixture makes it possible to estimate repeatability on three discs weighing 300 mg.

Remarks

Strong orientation of minerals in the disc can generate errors. In 2:1 clays, variations in intensity of the stretching bands of hydroxyls can result from tri-octahedral components. With micas oriented perpendicular to the beam, only modes of vibration parallel to plane b will appear (Phlogopite). Conversely, in kaolinite, the intensity of the 3,619 cm^{-1} band is independent of the orientation (internal hydroxyl directed towards the vacant octahedral position).

If titrations are carried out with a traditional dispersive apparatus, the resolution can be improved by finer slits but the energy will be weaker. As the width of the slits is not constant throughout the spectrum, care should be taken that the slits are not too wide, because the signals could be deformed and the law of Beer–Lambert would then not apply.

---

[1] Density of KBr: 2.75

[2] In spite of the use of reference minerals, the great variability of the absorption bands as a function of the chemical structure often results in insurmountable difficulties in calibration of 2:1 and 2:1:1 minerals. In this case, it is possible to obtain only semi-quantitative measurements that allow identification of changes in a profile, the mineral tracer being used as standard of comparison at a given level.

5.3. Other IR techniques

5.3.1 Near-infrared spectrometry (NIRS)

Principle

Vibrations of light atoms that have strong molecular bonds with protons (N, C or O) are used to analyse organo-mineral compounds or organic matter. When the bonds are weak and the atoms are heavy, it can be difficult to detect and quantify the vibration phenomena.

Wide bands are reproducible but are influenced by penetration of the radiation, and thus sensitive to the size of the particles and to moisture. Fine grinding is usually required to obtain particles of the same size and to reduce the background noise as much as possible. But acceptable results can be obtained with materials that are not finely ground (D. Brunet, IRD Montpellier, France, personal communication). Bond vibrations cause a response that depends on the number of molecules present and on their environment, this response then enables quantification

The bands in the near-infrared field are more widely spaced than in medium and far IR, which limits the phenomena of overlapping. The first derivative of the signal can be used to improve precision.

Measurements are made either by transmission–absorption, or by diffuse emission–reflectance (NIRA-DRIFT)[3] on powders using wavelengths ranging from 1,000 to 2,500 nm (wavenumbers from 10,000 to 4,000 cm^{-1}) in certain cases such as soil litter (water, protein content, total nitrogen, sugars, etc.), or on liquids using immersed optical fibres.

Material

Measuring equipment with diffuse reflectance IR is somewhat different from IR spectrometry using the transmission–absorption mode (cf. diagram in Fig. 5.8). The optical elements are made of quartz. They allow the complete near-IR spectrum to be acquired in a few seconds.

---

[3] NIRS = near-infrared reflectance spectrometry
NIRA = near-infrared analysis
DRIFT = diffuse reflectance IR with fourier transform

Method

This non-destructive method requires fine grinding, but does not require a reagent, or weighing or measurement of volume. Measurements are rapid ($\cong$30 s) and the unit cost of the measurement is low.

Measurements depend on the physical factors that affect reflectance, i.e. particle size (reflectance, refraction, diffraction), their distribution (heterogeneity) and the distribution of the vacuums (compaction and induced orientations).

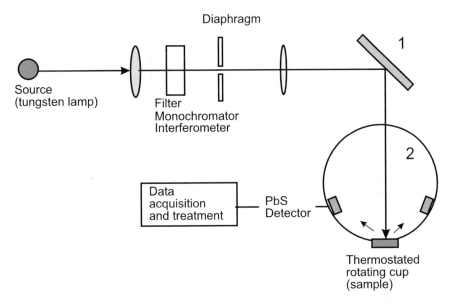

Fig. 5.8. Diagram of a near-infrared spectrometer (NIRS) 1: oscillating mirror allowing adjustment of the incidental beam on the sample and improving reflectance on the walls of the integration sphere. All possible angles must be represented starting from the normal. The total flow from the source that excites the sample is concentrated by quartz lenses. 2: Integration sphere allowing the effect of variations in particle size to be decreased with collection of the most intense radiation but rejection of specular components

Current NIRS systems have been greatly improved by progress in chemometric software which enables calculations that were previously impossible. Quantitative analysis is based on multivariate calibration using all the spectral information, not only absorbance at a given wavelengths but absorbance at all wavelengths of the spectrum. These calibrations use a wide range of methods of calculation, especially principal component analysis (PCA), regression on principal components (RPC), partial least square (PLS) regression and multiple linear regression (MLR). The software includes help in choosing the best method of calibration, even if the choice is still not always easy (Dardenne et al., 2000).

This method is suitable for organic analysis but was extended to many different measurements on soils. Chang et al. (2001) used RPC calibration for FTIR determination of moisture content, total C, total N, CEC, sand content, silt content, clay content, macro-aggregation, potentially mineralisable N, C biomass, total respiration rate and basal respiration rate of soils. The only condition is the need to compile a database of soil references for calibration. For a given variable, calibration consists of (1) obtaining a measurement value by a reference method for all soil references (preferably including a wide range of concentrations of the given variable), (2) obtaining NIR spectra on the same soil references, (3) calculating and plotting the straight line of multivariate calibration with the value measured using the standard method in the x-coordinate and predicted value by NIRS in the y-coordinate. After calibration, the measurement of an unknown sample is very rapid: its real concentration in the x-coordinate can be deduced from its spectral data in the y-coordinate. But the apparently universal application of the method is not quite true. Calibration is always possible but not always significant (e.g. variability of the calibration curves obtained by Chang et al., 2001). Which soils to choose for the soil references (all soil types, or a given soil type)? What type of soil preparation? The complementary bibliography at the end of this chapter lists a few additional applications of NIRS in soil and litter studies.

5.3.2 Coupling Thermal Measurements and FTIR Spectrometry of Volatile Products

Measurements are taken during TGA-DTA[4] and enable determination of the nature of the gas products that appear during heat decomposition of the sample (EGD or EGA)[5] The analyses are carried out by Fourier transform infra-red spectrometry (FTIR) by transmission or absorption in time of flight, as a function of the temperature and heating time.

This dynamic technique enables real-time monitoring of the chemical or physicochemical conversions that take place during the rapid heating

---

[4] DTA = Differential thermal Analyse, TGA = Thermo Gravimetric analyzes, cf. Chap. 7.

[5] EGD = Evolved Gas Detection, EGA = Evolved Gas Analysis.

of the sample (controlled thermolyses or pyrolyses of organic or inorganic material is possible). A rise in temperature at moderate speed makes it possible to detect unstable radicals and molecular fragmentations by linking them to variations in mass and temperature (fusion, exo- and endothermic reactions, decomposition of mineral-carbonates, N, C, S, H compounds, oxidation, reduction, transfers of protons etc.).

Pressure is a variable that affects sublimation and evaporation. Pressure can be modified by too rapid decomposition of an unstable product, but, depending on the temperature, can also cause molecular synthesis. Under low pressure, the most reactive gases diffuse quickly, avoiding possible recombination. Working under argon atmosphere at low pressure is generally recommended. But working under controlled atmosphere can highlight redox phenomena or, on the contrary, avoid them.

Additional information can be collected by selecting a heating rate between 20 and 400°C min^{-1} depending on the speed of evacuation of the gas produced and on its detection or rapid titration before further gaseous reactions occur.

5.3.3 Infrared Microscopy

FTIR analysis is possible on microsamples measuring from 20 to 500 μm. The IR microscope (cf. Chap. 8) consists of lenses with a Cassegrain mirror coupled with a high sensitivity MCT[6] detector cooled with liquid nitrogen. It is possible to work with either transmission or reflectance. The resolution is approximately 8 cm^{-1} depending on the quality of the materials and the number of accumulations of spectra.

It is also possible to use Raman spectrometry where the source of excitation is a monochromatic laser emitting in the red band to avoid the effects of fluorescence which occurs in the presence of certain organic materials. Quantities of the order of a pico and even of a femtogramme can be detected in this way.

5.3.4 Raman scattering spectroscopy

Interest

Raman spectroscopy has not been widely used in earth science because dispersive equipment is very expensive and the performance is often

---

[6] MCT = mercury, cadmium, tellurium.

insufficient due to the difficulty of obtaining a selection of wavelengths with high resolution.

Progress in electronics has made it possible to design very sensitive detectors, very selective monochromators, and powerful monochromatic lasers, and to use FTIR spectrometers thus making this technique accessible and complementary to other IR spectrometries. Data processing enables very rapid treatment of the spectra.

This technique makes it possible to supplement the information obtained in transmission–absorption IR spectrometry, as certain vibrations are only active in one of the two techniques, or their intensity differs because of the rules of selection. The symmetrical vibration bands are stronger in Raman spectroscopy and the asymmetrical vibrations are stronger in IR spectroscopy.

The study of certain molecular structures that are difficult to differentiate such as rutiles, anatases and brookites is possible on microsamples. The nature of the chemical bonds and the orientation of OH groups can be determined without obstruction by any interstitial water that may be present. The method is not destructive and does not require complex preparation. It is possible to work on powder, even wet powder, which is impossible with other IR techniques.

Principle

Raman spectroscopy is based on the inelastic scattering of IR[7] radiation with IR secondary emission at beat frequencies. The spectra are composed of fine lines which require a high resolution apparatus:

– phenomena of fluorescence induced by the electronic transitions can disturb the spectra and mask the Raman signal if an excitation laser that emits in the visible spectrum (488 nm) is used; excitation by Nd:YAG laser emitting at 1,064 nm, the frequency corresponding to a zone of little occupied electronic transition, generally does not generate fluorescence, and coupling with a good-quality FTIR spectrometer eliminates difficulties due to insufficient resolution;

– when a monochromatic radiation beam strikes a sample, a weak fraction of the re-emitted radiation displays modified frequencies that reflect the vibration frequencies of the sample. This fraction is measured in Raman spectrometry; the unchanged radiation fraction (Rayleigh elastic scattering) has to be removed by filtering.

---

[7] Raman spectroscopy in visible or UV radiation can cause photodecomposition of the sample as well as thermal damage.

Apparatus

The basic apparatus is a FTIR spectrometer equipped with an interferometer coupled with data acquisition and processing software. It should have an external window to attach a Nd-YAG laser irradiation, a chamber for sample powders allowing irradiation modes of 90° and 180°, a spectral filtration module and if necessary a specific detector. A Raman-FT microscope and accessories for Raman studies under very high pressure (diamond anvils) can be added to the FTIR spectrometer.

The laser for excitation of the atoms and molecules must be monochromatic or adjustable in wavelength (for better selectivity). It must provide strong intensity (sensitivity of measurements), coherent radiation (spatial and temporal quality), and finally, if the beam is transported by optical fibre, low divergence.

IR and Raman spectroscopy can be supplemented with other techniques for the study of structure (e.g. NMR, EXAFS). In spite of the development of these techniques, the IR and Raman methods remain competitive (ease of handling, reasonable cost of equipment) and allow a sufficiently detailed approach of the structure (including vacancies and substitutions, nature of the bonds in molecules) and of its consequences for rheology, for example, or for the study of pedogenesis phenomena that occur during weathering (e.g. coverings, interactions with the surface, adsorption of molecules). However, the quantification of the phases is often delicate if not impossible, because of the problems of orientation of clays and incomplete spectrum.

References

Chang C.-W., Laird DA, Mausbach M. et Hurburgh CRJr (2001) Near-Infrared Reflectance Spectroscopy-Principal Components regression analysis of soil properties. *Soil Sci. Soc. Am. J.*, 65, 480–490

Dardenne P, Sinnaev G et Baeten V (2000) Multivariate calibration and chemometrics for near infrared spectroscopy: which method. *Journal of Near Infrared Spectroscopy,* 8, 229–237

Duyckaerts G (1959) The infra red analysis of solid substances. *Analyst*, 84, 201–214

Farmer VC et Palmieri F (1975) The characterization of soil minerals by Infrared spectroscopy. In: *Soil components – 2 – Inorganic components,* Gieseking JE ed., Springer, 573–670

Fröhlich F (1980) Néoformation de silicates ferrifères amorphes dans la sédimentation pélagique récente. *Bull. Minéral.*, 103, 596–599

Fröhlich F (1989) Les silicates dans l'environnement pélagique de l'océan indien du cénozoïque. Mémoire Muséum National d'Histoire Naturelle, Paris, XLVI, 206p

Keller WD et Pickett FE (1949) Absorption of IR radiation by powdered silice minerals. *Am. Miner.*, 34, 855–868

Liu LG et Mernagh TP (1992) Phase transitions and Raman spectra of anatase and rutile at high pressures and room temperature. Eur. J. Mineral, 4, 45–22

Nail SL, White JL et Hem SL (1976) IR studies of development of order in aluminium hydroxide gels. *J. Pharm. Sci.*, 65, 231–234

Nyquist RA et Kagel O (1971) *Infrared spectra of inorganic compounds.*, Academic Press, New York

Stubican V et Roy R (1961) Infrared spectra of layer silicates. *J. Am. Ceram. Soc.*, 44, 625

Wada K (1966) Deuterium exchange of hydroxyl groups in allophane. Soil Sci. *Plant Nutr.*, 12, 176–182

Weir CE Lippincott ER Van Valkenburg A et Bunting EN (1959) Infra-red studies in the 1 and 15 microns region to 30 000 atmospheres. *J. Res. Natl. Bur. Stud.*, 63A, 55

Chronobibliography

Tuddenham WM et Lyon R.P (1960) Infrared techniques in the identification and measurement of minerals. *Anal. Chem.*, 32, 1630–1634

Mitchell BD Farmer VC et Mc Hardy WJ (1964) Amorphous inorganic materials in soils. *Academic Press. Adv. Agron.*, 16, 327–383

Hayashi H et Oinuma K (1965) Relationship between infrared absorption spectra in the region of 450–900 cm^{-1} and chemical composition of chlorite. *Am. Miner.*, 50, 476–483

Hayashi H et Oinuma K (1967) Si–O absorption band near 1000 cm^{-1} OH absorption bands of chlorite. *Am. Miner.*, 52, 1206–1210

Russell JD, McHardy WJ et Fraser A.R (1969) Imogolite: a unique alumino-silicate. *Clay Miner.*, 8, 87–99

Wada K et Greenland DJ (1970) Selective dissolution and differential infrared spectroscopy for characterization of amorphous constituents in soil clays. *Clay Miner.*, 8, 241–254

Conley RT (1972) *Infra-red spectroscopy.* Allyn-Bacon, 2nd. Edition

Fieldes M, Furkert R.J et Wells N (1972) Rapid determination of constituants of whole soils using IR absorption. *N. Z. J. Sci.*, 15, 615–627

Miller RGT et Stace BC (1972) *Laboratory methods in Infrared spectroscopy.*, Heyden and Son

Farmer VC (1974) *The Infrared spectra of minerals.* Minerals Sci. (London).

Stepanov IS (1974) Interpretation of the IR spectra of soils. *Pochvovedenie*, 6, 76–88

Gadsden JA (1975) *Infrared spectra of minerals and related inorganic compounds.*, Butterworth

Griffiths PR (1975) *Chemical infrared fourier transform spectroscopy.*, Wiley, New York Chemical Analysis, 43

Brame EG, Grasselli JG (1976) *Infrared and Raman spectroscopy.*, Marcel Dekker, 1A

White JL, Nail SL et Hem SL (1976) Infrared technique for distinguishing between amorphous and crystalline aluminium hydroxide phase. *Proceedings. 7th Conference. clay Mineral Petrology* (Czechoslovakia), 51–59

Marel HW, Van der et Beutelspacher H (1976) *Atlas of infrared spectroscopy of clay minerals and their mixtures.*, Elsevier Amsterdam

Proshina NV (1976) Use of infrared spectroscopy for identification of soil samples. *Nauch. dokl. Vsshei Shk.*, Biol. Naudi, 3, 114–118

Brame EG, Grasselli JG (1977) *Infrared and Raman spectroscopy.*, Marcel Dekker, 1B, 1C

Hlavay J, Jonas K, Elek S et Inczedy J (1977) Characterization of the particle size and the cristallinity of certain minerals by infrared spectrophotometry and instrumental methods. I – Investigations on clay minerals. *Clays Clay Miner.*, 25, 451–456

Hlavay J, Jonas K, Elek S et Inczedy J (1978) Characterization of the particle size and the crystallinity of certain minerals by infrared spectrophotometry and other instrumental methods. II-Investigation on quartz and feldspar. *Clays Clay Miner.*, 26, 139–143

Ferraro JR et Basile LJ (1978) *Fourier transform infrared spectroscopy. Applications to chemical systems.*, Academic, New York, vol. 1

Slonimskaya MV, Besson G, Dainyak LG, Tchoubar C et Drits VA (1978) Interpretation of the IR spectra of celadonites and glaucomites in the region of OH-streching frequencies. *Clay Miner.*, 21, 377–388

Smith AL (1979) *Applied infrared spectroscopy: fundamentals, techniques and analytical problem-solving.*, Wiley, New York, vol. 54 (chemical analysis).

Farmer VC (1979) The role of infrared spectroscopy in a soil research institute: characterization of inorganic materials. *Eur. Spectrosc. News*, 25, 25–27

Ferraro JR et Basile LJ (1979) *Fourier transform infrared spectroscopy. Applications to chemical systems.*, Academic, vol. 2

Hlavay J et Inczedy J (1979) Sources of error of quantitative determination of the solid crystalline minerals by inrared spectroscopy. *Acta Chim.*, (Budapest), 102, 11–18

Olphen H Van et Fripiat JJ (1979) *Data handbook for clay materials and other non-metallic minerals.*, Pergamon

Martin AE (1980) Infrared interferometric spectrometers. In *Vibrational spectra and structure*, Durig J.R. ed., Elsevier, Amsterdam, vol. 8

Pouchert CJ (1981) *The Aldrich library of infrared spectra.*, Aldrich Chemical Co, 1850 p

Shika A, Osipova NN et Sokolova TA (1982) Feasibility of characterizing the mineralogical composition of soils by infrared spectrophotometry. *Moscow Univer. Soil Sci. Bull.*, 37, 34–40

Theng BKG, Russel M, Churchman GJ et Parfitt RL (1982) Surface properties of allophane, halloysite and imogolite. *Clays Clay miner.*, 30, 143–149

Ferraro JR et Basile LJ (1983) *Fourier transform infrared spectroscopy. Applications to chemical systems.*, Academic, New York , vol. 3

Fysh SA et Fredericks PM (1983) Fourier transform infrared studies of aluminous goethites and hematites. *Clays clay Miner.*, 31, 377–382

Velde B (1983) Infra-red OH-stretch bands in potassic micas, talcs and saponites: influence of electronic configuration and site of charge compensation. *Am. miner.*, 68, 1169–1173

Gillette PC et Koenig JL (1984) Objective criteria for absorbance subtraction. *Appl. Spectrosc.*, 38, 334–337

Kosmas CS, Curi N, Bryant RB et Franzmeier DP (1984) Charactrization of iron oxide minerals by second-derivative visible spectroscopy. *Soil Sci. Soc. Am. J.*, 48, 401–405

Prost R (1984) Etude par spectroscopie infra-rouge à basse température de groupes OH de structure de la kaolinite, de la dickite et de la nacrite. *Agronomie*, 4, 403–406

Kodama H (1985) Infrared spectra of minerals. Reference guide to identification and characterization of minerals for the study of soils. *Res. Branch, Agric. Can. Tech. Bull.*, 1E

Mulla DJ, Low PF et Roth CB (1985) Measurement of the specific surface area of clays by internal reflectance spectroscopy. *Clays Clay Miner.*, 33, 391–396

Keller RJ (1986) *The Sigma library of FT-IR spectra.*, Sigma chemical Co, vols. 1–2, 2894 p

Griffiths et Haseth PR (1986) *Fourier transform infrared spectrometry.*, Chemical Analysis Series, Vol. 83, Wiley New York, 672 p

Russel JD (1987) Infrared spectroscopy of inorganic compounds. In *Laboratory methods in infra-red spectroscopy,* Willis H.ed., Wiley, New York

Johannsen PG, Krobok MP et Holzapfel WB (1988) *High-pressure FT-IR spectrometry.*, Bruker report, 39–43

Pouchert CJ (1989) *The Aldrich library of FT-IR Spectra.*, Aldrich Chemical Co, vols. 1-3, 4800 p

Mottana A et Burragato F (1990) *Absorption spectroscopy in mineralogy.*, Elsevier, Amsterdam, Oxford, New York, Tokyo, 294 p

Delvigne JE (1998) Atlas of Micromorphology of mineral alteration and weathering. The Canadian Mineralogist, special publication 3, Ottawa et IRD (ex-Orstom), Paris

Silverstein RM et Webster FX (1998) Spectrometric Identification of organic compounds. Wiley New York, 482 p

McHale JL (1999) *Molecular spectroscopy.*, Prentice-Hall, London, Sydney, Toronto, 463 p

Gillon D, Joffre R et Ibrahima A. (1999) Can litter decomposability be predicted by near infrared reflectance spectroscopy. *Ecology*, 80, 175–186

Confalonieri M, Fornasier F, Ursino A, Boccardi F, Pintus B et Odoardi M (2001) The potential of near infrared reflectance spectroscopy as a tool for the chemical characterisation of agricultural soils. *J. Near Infrared Spectrosc.*, 9, 123–131

Joffre R, Ågren GI, Gillon D et Bosatta E (2001) Organic matter quality in ecological studies: theory meets experiment. *Oikos*, 93, 451–458

Fearn T (2001) Standardisation and calibration transfer for near infrared instruments: a review. *J. Near Infrared Spectrosc.*, 9, 229–244

Ludwig B et Khanna PK (2001) Use of near infrared spectroscopy to determine inorganic and organic carbon fractions in soil and litter. In *Assessment methods for soil carbon*, Lal R, Kimble JM, Follet RF et Stewart BA ed., Lewis, UK

Ozaki Y, Sasic S et Jiang JH (2001) How can we unravel complicated near infrared spectra? – Recent progress in spectral analysis methods for resolution enhancement and band assignments in the near infrared region. *J. Near Infrared Spectrosc.*, 9, 63–95

Reeves J B et McCarty G W (2001) Quantitative analysis of agricultural soils using near infrared reflectance spectroscopy and a fibre-optic probe. *J. Near Infrared Spectrosc.*, 9, 1, 25–34

Tso, Ritchie GE, Gehrlein L et Ciurczak EW (2001) A general test method for the development, validation and routine use of disposable near infrared spectroscopic libraries. *J. Near Infrared Spectrosc.*, 9, 165–184

Fidencio PH, Poppi RJ et de Andrade JC (2002) Determination of organic matter in soils using radial basis function networks and near infrared spectroscopy. *Anal. Chem. Acta.*, 453, 125–134

Coûteaux MM, Berg B and Rovira P (2003) Near infrared reflectance spectroscopy for determination of organic matter fractions including microbial biomass in coniferous forest soils. *Soil Biol. Biochem.*, 35, 1587–1600

Brown DJ, Shepherd KD, Walsh MG, Dewayne Mays M and Reinsch TG (2005). Global soil characterization with VNIR diffuse reflectance spectroscopy. *Geoderma*, doi:10.1016/j.geoderma.2005.04.025

Mineralogical Separation by Selective Dissolution

6.1 Introduction

6.1.1 Crystallinity of Clay Minerals

Mineralogical characterization of cryptocrystalline minerals or minerals with short-range atomic arrangement (Fe, Al, Si, Mn, Ti, P) is essential to understand the geochemical and pedochemical phenomena that occur during the weathering of primary minerals, as well as to explain the evolution and the relative stability of the systems and the kinetics of chemical soil processes. These substances can represent the transition stage between the crystalline parent rock and secondary minerals, and are often regarded as tracers of evolution. The soil is an open system, i.e. it is able to exchange energy and matter with the outside. Most reactions occur under non-equilibrium conditions, and transitory states depend on aqueous or gas flows (chemical reactions at the solid–liquid and liquid–liquid interface), on relaxation times (particle diffusion, transfer of matter, etc.), and of course, on microbial activity.

The individual accumulation of these substances, or their deposit in a fine layer of coating, modifies the activity of the structural sites of crystalline materials, and can inhibit the movement of ions, neutralize charges, or cause substitutions in the lattices. Gels, oxides and oxyhydroxydes, and aluminosilicates can develop charges (some of which are amphoteric). The high level of reactivity induced by their state of division allows adsorption of cations and anions. They can be neutralized by organic substances. These reactions confer greater resistance to weathering and to microbial action. Thus, the ultimate purpose of analysis of non-crystalline products may be soil genesis, and also:

– Soil taxonomy (through processes of podzolisation, andosolisation, laterisation, etc.)
– Soil mineralogy, mineralogical balances, purification before using other techniques (in particular methods that require the elimination of paramagnetic elements) e.g. ESR, EXAFS, Mossbauer, XRD, FTIR, SEM, EDX, WDX, TEM-HR, STEM[1]
– The study of the physical and chemical properties of the soil, studies of soil fertility (Fe deficiencies, P fixing, Al^{3+} toxicity, transport of heavy metals, destruction of the interparticle cements, aggregation factors, etc.)

Identification of non-crystalline substances requires more than one method: XRD is not very useful with gels because if the quantity of gel is significant, or the early stages of development of a long-range crystalline structure are concerned, only broad bands will be obtained. Chemical dissolution methods are not sufficiently selective in mineralogy, as their action is based on acid, base, reducing, or complexing reagents, and consists for example in:

– Breaking electrostatic (e.g. exchange reactions, Al^{3+} bridges) or coordination bonds (e.g. Fe^{3+} bridges)
– Causing ionization of functional groups (organic matter)

Dissolution must not only enable extraction of the different phases that are amorphous to X-ray but also:
– Minimize chemical modifications (relative instability of the products to be extracted compared to the soil matrix, and avoid attacks of the clay lattices and primary minerals)
– Limit hydrolysis of the extracted products
– Avoid molecular rearrangements in the liquid phase (nucleation)
– Maintain the extracted products in solution
– Prevent the creation of chemical barriers (insoluble precipitate under the influence of the reagents) and the neo-formation of solid products

---

[1] ESR electron spin resonance; EXAFS extended X-ray adsorption fine structure; XRD X-ray diffraction; FTIR Fourier transform infra-red; SEM scanning electron microscopy; EDX energy dispersive X-ray; WDX wavelength dispersive X-ray; STEM scanning transmission electron microscopy.

All the extractions (e.g. single reagent or multiple reagents, single or sequential extractions) depend on thermodynamic constraints:
– Ion activity, pH, concentration of the reagents, soil/reagent ratio, order of application of the reagents
– Time factors, kinetics of extraction, stirring velocity, duration of contact, ageing of the gel
– Temperature
– Photolytic energy (UV catalyses of the chemical reactions)

Initially the rate of mineralogical extraction is often significant, but subsequently levels off; it is also linked to the size of crystallites and perfection of crystallinity (defects, degree of disorder), or to the nature and the concentration of the elements in the liquid phase. Agreement with other studies, reproducibility and reliability will thus depend on the extraction procedures used. Unless justified by the need to adapt to specific problems, any modification in the procedure (proportion or concentration of reagents, time of contact, etc.) can cause serious errors in evaluation. The required degree of selectivity of mineral extraction can be obtained only by comparing different extractions that have been carefully purified by ultracentrifugation, and by chemical measurement (1) on the liquid phase containing the extracted products (congruent and incongruent reactions) and (2) on the solid phase (e.g. differential XRD, SEM, and EDX). Automatic calculation and interpretation can be performed with a limited number of reliable methods and this makes it possible to quantify each phase and to establish precise and reproducible geochemical balances.

6.1.2 Instrumental and Chemical Methods

Measurement by X-ray diffraction works well for atomic lattices with long-range organization, but for substances with short-range arrangement without ordered superstructure, XRD gives flat, unusable spectra (Fig. 6.1). This is why substances presenting this type of flat X-ray spectrum are referred to as amorphous substances.

Progress in instrumental methods has now made it possible to specify the nature of the phases and to determine their arrangement more precisely. The crystalline state is characterized by the periodic repetition of an atomic structure along three non-coplanar directions of space (Maziere 1978). The use of "non-crystalline" or crypto-crystalline substances, rather than paracristalline, is now allowed (amorphous, without structure; crypto, masked structure; para, almost a structure). It applies to the solids whose structure does not present a repetitive nature at long distance (molecular area at least 3 nm in diameter), but which presents a degree of order at short distance that confers specific properties. The short-range arrangement takes into account the mutual arrangement with the closest neighbouring atoms at the scale of interatomic distance. These substances do not have a clear spectral signature in X-ray diffraction. With another medium or at the long-distance scale, different types of non-crystallinity can also be observed:

– Zones that present substitution disorders or structural dislocation: this is the case of amorphous substances in a well-arranged periodic structure (structure with defects); high-resolution phase contrast transmission microscopy and scanning transmission electron microscopy (STEM) in micro diffraction mode allow this type of arrangement to be detected and localised.

– Extended zones without periodicity composed of clusters of randomly distributed particles with a short-distance arrangement; this is the case of gels of alumina, iron, silica, and some aluminosilicates (opaline, allophane-like, proto-allophane, allophane, proto-imogolite, gel-like, glass-like, vitric silica etc.).

Some substances display the beginning of medium-distance organization (Fig. 6.1) which results in broad lines in XRD[2] (e.g. imogolite, ferrihydrite, feroxihyte). Spectroscopic techniques can be used to study these minerals (see Fig. 6.2):

– EXAF[2] techniques provide accurate information on the interatomic distances of the closest neighbours and on the organization of the first layer of coordinance, but little information on relations between the polyhedrons (medium-distance coordination).

– XANES[2] techniques enable analysis of the sphere surrounding an atom, but a good knowledge of the structure is a precondition for success.

– NMR[2] spectrometry is selective for chemical structures but not very sensitive; the study of the hyperfine magnetic field of iron oxides makes it possible to measure the degree of crystallinity; in silica gels, the ^{29}Si nucleus enables the different states of SiO_4 bonds to be distinguished. Different forms of ^{31}P can also be studied.

– ESR[2] and ENDOR[2] spectrometry enable analysis of the hyperfine and super-hyper-fine structures by electron spin resonance at the atomic scale.

---

[2] See abbreviations p. 168. ENDOR Electron nuclear double resonance.

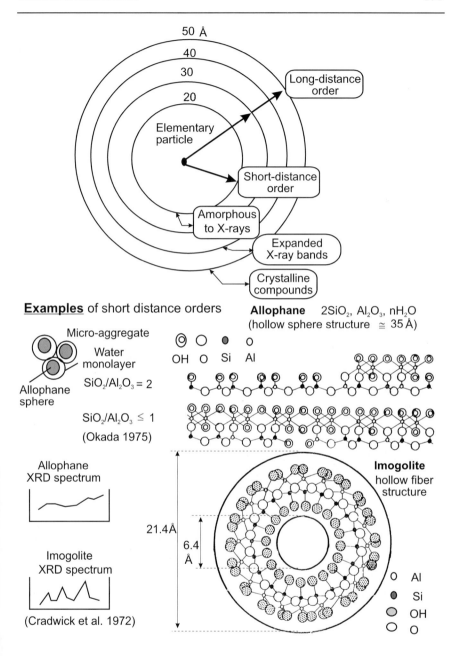

Fig. 6.1. Crystalline and amorphous to X-ray compounds

All these instrumental methods use radiations that correspond to ranges of distance suitable for the sub-micronic scales needed for the study of the structure of soil materials. The range of radiation extends from radio frequencies to X-rays and gamma radiations. Their high purchase price, the degree of specialization of the equipment and their use in very specialised analytical fields limits these types of studies to highly specialised laboratories.

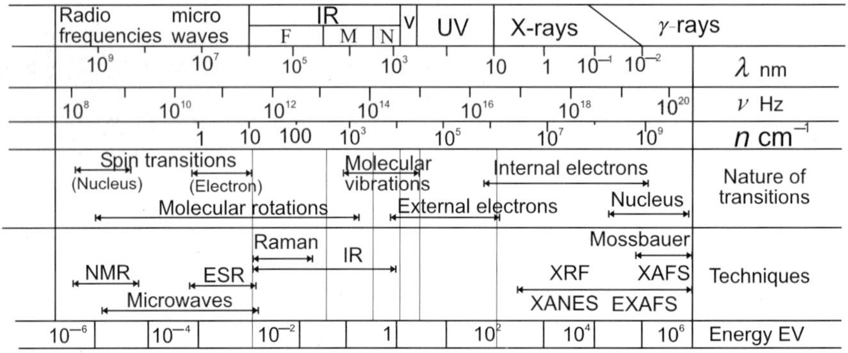

Radio frequencies	micro waves	IR F	M	N	V	UV	X-rays		γ-rays	
10^9	10^7	10^5		10^3		10	1	10^{-1} 10^{-2}		λ nm
10^8	10^{10}	10^{12}		10^{14}		10^{16}	10^{18}	10^{20}		ν Hz
	1	10 100	10^3		10^5		10^7	10^9		n cm^{-1}
Spin transitions (Nucleus) (Electron)	Molecular rotations		Molecular vibrations		Internal electrons External electrons			Nucleus	Nature of transitions	
		Raman	IR					Mossbauer		
NMR	ESR							XRF XAFS	Techniques	
	Microwaves							XANES EXAFS		
10^{-6}	10^{-4}	10^{-2}		1		10^2	10^4	10^6	Energy EV	

Fig. 6.2. Analyses of molecular structures using spectroscopic techniques (electromagnetic spectra and environmental probes; λ, wavelength; ν, frequency; n, wavenumber; radiations: F, far IR; M, medium IR; N, near IR, V, visible; UV, ultraviolet); NMR, nuclear magnetic resonance; ESR, electron spin resonance; XRF, X-ray fluorescence; XAFS, X-ray absorption fine-structure spectroscopy; XANES, X-ray absorption near edge structure; EXAFS, extended X-ray absorption fine structure

Instrumental methods allow observations at the sub-micronic scale, but chemical analysis enables analysis of entities that represent the average activity of certain particles because of their surface and their charge. Thus the continuum produced during weathering can be split in a satisfactory way by a series of extractions that make it possible to isolate compounds of increasing crystallinity that correspond, or not, to different chemical species.

6.1.3 Selective Dissolution Methods

The range of "selective dissolution methods" is obviously limited because of the diversity of soil minerals (Table 6.1) and the difficulty involved in dissolving a well-defined single phase (Table 6.2).

Dissolution depends on different factors:
- The size of the "crystal" and the level of atomic disorder
- Defects in stoechiometry or the blocking of active sites
- The properties of the crystallographic faces (anisotropy)
- The porosity of the systems, the density of surface defects, etc.

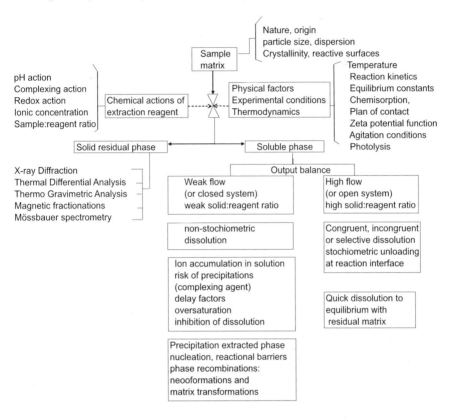

Fig. 6.3. Diagram of factors that control selective dissolution

The reagents used and possible pretreatments should not cause precipitation. They should ensure the maintenance in solution of the extracted products and if possible, limit recombinations in the liquid phase (Figs. 6.3 and 6.4).

Oxides, hydroxides, and oxyhydroxydes cause dependent charges in the soil and their structures, bonds, surfaces, and reactivities vary with their degree of crystallinity and the degree of disorder of their lattices (Table 6.1).

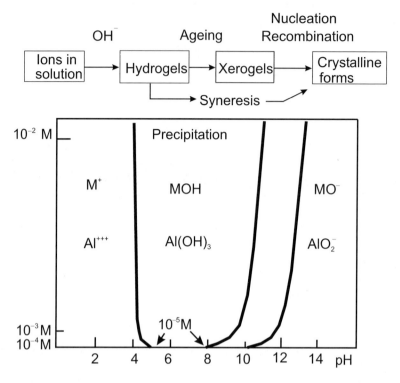

Fig. 6.4. Solubility of hydroxides as a function of pH and concentration (*lower parts*) and transformation of hydroxide gels (*upper part*)

6.1.4 Reagents and Synthetic Standards

The complexity of iron forms and of non-crystalline products often requires the use of pure synthetic models of minerals with a crystallinity or a short-distance atomic arrangement that closely resembles the substances found in the soil.

The precipitates should be prepared starting from products with a high degree of purity, as hydroxides tend to adsorb impurities because of their very great specific surface. Flocculation is achieved by adding H^+ or OH^- ions. Boiling causes transformation by dehydration and ensures the growth of the gel (nucleation). The time factor allows ageing of the gel, i.e. progressive slow crystallization (Fig. 6.4), transformation from a short-distance organization to an organization of a higher nature. For example, with aluminium in a ionic state, first precipitation of a monomer will be observed and then hydroxide:

$$Al^{3+} + 3\ OH^- \rightarrow Al(OH)_3$$

in different steps:

$$Al(OH)^{2+} \rightarrow Al(OH)_2^+ \rightarrow Al_2(OH)_2^{4+}\ etc.$$

dehydratation is accompanied by loss of H^+ during precipitation. With amphoteric aluminium compounds, the precipitates can be redissolved in alkaline medium forming soluble aluminates. All procedures must be strictly respected in order to obtain precipitation products that correspond to reproducible stages of formation.

These procedures were defined by Henry (1958), Towe and Bradley (1967), Atkinson et al. (1968), Schwertmann and Taylor (1972; 1977), Murphy et al. (1976), Jeanroy (1983), Farmer and Fraser (1978), Pollard (1992), Lewis and Schwertmann (1979).

Preparation of Iron Compounds

Goethite
– Dissolve 8.08 g of ferric nitrate ($Fe(NO_3)_3,9H_2O$) in 80 mL water in a 250 mL Erlenmeyer flask.
– Bring the pH to 7.5 by adding approximately 20 mL of 3 mol (KOH) L^{-1} solution drop by drop (while on a magnetic stirrer).
– Leave for 3 h to form a deposit, siphon the supernatant and wash the precipitate four times with water to eliminate any soluble potassium nitrate that has formed.
– Suspend in 100 mL water, then add 3 mol (KOH) L^{-1} solution to bring to a 0.3 mol (OH^-) L^{-1} solution.
– Store the solution in a polypropylene bottle at 20°C with occasional agitation for 2–5 years depending on the degree of nucleation desired.
– Wash until elimination of KOH.
– Dry in a ventilated drying oven at 50°C.

Akaganeite
– Grind a sample of pure $FeCl_2,4H_2O$ in an agate mortar to pass through a 0.5 mm sieve.
– Spread in a thin layer and allow hydrolysis to occur in contact with humid air for 6 months (the product will turn brown over time).
– Wash with H_2O to eliminate remaining Fe^{2+}, then dry at 50°C.

Table 6.1. Main crystalline and non-crystalline oxides and oxyhydroxides in soil (Si, Fe, Al, Mn, Ti, mixed)

Fe	Al	Mn	Ti	Si	mixed gels (with charge)
$Fe^{3+} + e^- \leftrightarrow Fe^{2+}$	Al^{3+}	$Mn^{IV+} + 2e^- \leftrightarrow Mn^{2+}$	$Ti^{4+} + 2e \leftrightarrow Ti^{2+}$	Si^{+IV}	Si, Al, Fe, Mn, P
hematite α-Fe_2O_3	corundum αAl_2O_3 [(1)]	hollandite αMnO_2	rutile TiO_2	α quartz (low) SiO_2	allophane Al_2O_3–$2SiO_2,nH_2O$
maghemite γFe_2O_3	gibbsite $\gamma Al(OH)_3$	cryptomelane αMnO_2	anatase TiO_2	β quartz (high) SiO_2	Imogolite
magnetite Fe_3O_4 ($Fe^{2+}Fe^{3+}O_4$)	bayerite $\alpha Al(OH)_3$ [(1)]	pyrolusite βMnO_2	brookite TiO_2	α tridymite SiO_2	hisingerite Fe_2O_3–$2SiO_2,nH_2O$
goethite α-$FeOOH$	diaspore α-$AlOOH$	birnessite δMnO_2	ilmenite $FeTiO_3$	α cristobalite SiO_2	penwithita SiO_2–Mn
*lepidocrocite $\gamma FeOOH$	boehmite γ-$AlOOH$	manganite $\gamma MnOOH$	(leucoxene see ilmenite)	coesite SiO_2	evansite $Al_3PO_4(OH)_6,7H_2O$
ferrihydrite $Fe_2O_3,2FeOOH$	nordstrandite $Al(OH)_3$	groutite $\alpha MnOOH$		stishovite SiO_2	azovskite $Fe_3PO_4(OH)_6,7H_2O$

*feroxyhite δFeOOH | *(kliachite Al_2O_3,nH_2O) | hausmanite Mn_3O_4 (Mn^{2+} Mn^{3+} O_4) | | *opal SiO_2

akaganeite βFeOOH | | todorokite | | * gel silica $SiO_2(nH_2O)$

*stilpnosidérite (gel) Fe_2O_3,nH_2O | | * vernadite $\delta MnO_2,nH_2O$ | *gel titanium TiO_2,nH_2O | chalcedony (fibrous) SiO_2

(limonite Fe_2O_3,nH_2O see goethite) | | lithiophorite (Al, Li) Mn O_2 (OH)$_2$ | | biogene silica (SiO_2)

[3] pH 7.5 $Fe^{3+}/2Fe^{2+}$ | pH 4.0 + redisolve pH 9.0 | pH 8.5–8.8 | pH 1–3

1   not very frequent or non pedogenic (primary minerals).
2   $\leftrightarrow$ isostructure.
3   theoretical mean pH of precipitation in aqueous medium.
*   gel, short-distance arrangement.
( ) obsolete terminology.

Lepidocrocite
- Dissolve 0.6 g of $FeCl_2,4H_2O$ in 150 mL of a 0.2 mol (NaCl) L^{-1} solution saturated with nitrogen by bubbling using a peristaltic pump regulated at a flow rate of 15 mL min^{-1}.
- Agitate under nitrogen and adjust pH to 6.0 by adding NaOH 1 mol L^{-1} drop by drop.
- Allow the pH to stabilize, then replace nitrogen bubbling by air; maintain the pH during oxidation (2 h 30 min).
- Wash with water, then dry at 50°C.

Poorly ordered Ferrihydrite
- Dissolve 2.02 g of $Fe(NO_3)_3,9H_2O$ in 500 mL distilled water and bring the pH to 7.5 by adding 15 mL of 1 mol (NaOH) L^{-1} solution drop by drop.
- Store for 18 h at pH 7.5.
- Wash with water and dry at 50°C.

Hematite
- Prepare a solution M of ferric chloride ($FeCl_3,6H_2O$).
- Precipitate with NH_4OH at 60°C.
- Filter on rapid filter.
- Wash until the Cl^- test is negative ($AgNO_3$ test).
- Calcinate for 1 h at 500°C.

Maghemite
- Weigh 5 g of ferrous oxalate ($FeC_2O_4,2H_2O$) and place it in a quartz crucible with a lid.
- Heat gradually in an electric furnace at 410–420°C and maintain at this temperature for 1 h to eliminate water of constitution.
The resulting product is close to maghemite.

Organic amorphous iron
- Extract the organic matter (OM) of a 20 g sample of podzolic soil with high humus content with 900 mL of 0.2 mol (NaOH) L^{-1} solution.
- Centrifuge the extract, then filter (calculate the OM content expressed as C content).
- Prepare a ferric nitrate solution ($Fe(NO_3)_3,9H_2O$) containing 108 g L^{-1}.
- In 225 mL of this solution (3.35 g of iron) add the desired proportion of OM extract.
- Agitate while checking the pH with a pH meter; the final pH should be 5.0; a brown–red gel will precipitate.
- Wash with distilled water until complete elimination of sodium.
- Preserve the gel in water and check the iron content (mg mL^{-1}).

Table 6.2. Estimation of extracted phases by differential selective dissolution (*Tamm*, ammonium oxalate reagent; *DCB*, Dithionite Citrate Bicarbonate reagent; *Pyro*, pyrophosphate reagent)

method, extraction reagent	Tamm in darkness	DCB	tetra-borate	Pyro	Na_2CO_3	$NaOH$ 0.5 mol L^{-1}	sequential	alcaline Tiron	NaF or KF
pH of extracted phase	3.0	7.2	9.7	10.0	9.8	>12.0	pH 1–14		
Al non-crystalline hydrated oxides	+++	+++		+	+++	+++	+++	+++	+++
organic complexes	+++	+++	+++	+++	+++	+++	+++	+++	−
crystalline compounds	0	+	+	0	+	+++	+	+	+
Si opaline-gels	0	0		0	+	+++	++	−	+++
crystalline compounds	0	0		0	0	+	+	−	0
Fe non-crystalline hydrated oxides ferrihydrite, feroxyhite	+++	+++	+++	+	0	0	+++	+++	+++
organic complexes	+++	+++	+++	+++	0	0	+++	+++	−
crystalline compounds	0+	+++		0	0	0	+++	+	+
Mn non-crystalline oxides									
crystalline compounds									
allophane	+++	+		+	+	+++	+++	+	+++
imogolite	++	+		+	+	+++	+++	+	+++
allophane-like comp.	+++	+++		+	++	+++	+++	+++	+++
(1)phyllosilicates	0+	0+		0	0	+	+(++)	+	+
									strong pH increase with allophanes

+++ strong to total dissolution, ++ medium or partial dissolution
+ weak dissolution
0 no significant dissolution

Preparation of Al³⁺ Compounds

Boehmite
- Prepare a 0.1 M solution of AlCl₃.
- Neutralize to pH 6 with 0.4 mol (NaHCO₃) L⁻¹ solution.
- Leave in contact for one hour.
- Bring to pH 8 by slowly adding 0.15 mol (NaOH) L⁻¹ solution.
- Store in a closed plastic (PTFE) bottle for 60 h at 160°C.
- Cool, wash until elimination of bicarbonate and remove surplus sodium hydroxyde by centrifugation.
- Store in suspension in closed polythene bottle.

Preparation of mixed compounds

Imogolite
- Place 30 mmol of aluminium perchlorate in 2.5 L of deionised water.
- Add 15 mmol of tetraethyl silicate, this corresponds to approximately 3.3 mL of commercial solution.
- Homogenize, then bring the pH to 4.5 with soda.
- The mixture will become opalescent; leave to stand overnight and the liquid will become clear.
- Boil gently at reflux boiling point for 5 days.
- Leave to cool, then add ammonia to gradually reach pH 9.0; the gel will precipitate.
- Wash until elimination of sodium; store in water and measure the Al and Si concentrations.

6.2 Main Selective Dissolution Methods

6.2.1 Acid Oxalate Method Under Darkness (AOD)

Principle

This dissolution reagent is also called Tamm reagent. The method allows allophane and gels, iron, and aluminium organic complexes, hydrated oxides of iron, and aluminium (ferrihydrite, feroxyhite) to be dissolved. Imogolite is not completely dissolved in only one treatment. Phyllosilicates are only very slightly attacked, except if their level of disorder is significant. Lepidocrocite is sensitive to oxalate reagent. If several treatments (2–3) are performed; some Al and Fe crystalline compounds can be solubilized to a considerable extent.

The ammonium oxalate-oxalic acid buffer induces processes of protonation, complexation, and reduction. In this way it can cause the transfer of protons, electrons and ions (Stum 1985; Furrer 1985–1987; Cornell and Schindler 1987; Schwertmann 1991).

The oxalate ion forms three complexes with ferric iron:

$$Fe^{3+} + C_2O_4^{2-} \Leftrightarrow Fe\, C_2O_4^{+} \tag{6.1}$$

$$Fe^{3+} + 2C_2O_4^{2-} \Leftrightarrow Fe\,(C_2O_4)^{2} \tag{6.2}$$

$$Fe^{3+} + 3C_2O_4^{2-} \Leftrightarrow Fe\,(C_2O_4)_3^{3-} \tag{6.3}$$

(ferrous iron also gives complexes with other constants of stability and solubility).

An excess of oxalate buffer is required to bring the equilibrium reactions to stage (6.3); if not the $C_2O_4^{2-}$ acceptors H^+ and Fe^{3+} can induce competitive reactions, particularly if raising the pH decreases the constants of solubility.

With Al $^{3+}$ a complexation of the following type occurs:

Below a pH of 3.5, the surfaces of the oxides are saturated with protons. The pH 3.0 zone is thus favourable because it controls charges below the point of zero charge (cf. Chap. 20). With respect to the reactional stages, protonation should be the first stage of dissolution of the compound, as this reaction allows better adsorption of the complexes and sumultaneous synergic action.

In the case of non-crystalline compounds of iron and manganese, reduction is preponderant:

$$Fe^{3+} + e^{-} \Leftrightarrow Fe^{2+}$$

The complexing reagent has two effects:
– Ferric ions become less oxidizing as the ferrous ions are more reducing; the $Fe^{3+}:Fe^{2+}$ ratio decreases, solubility increases; the reaction is autocatalytic
– It affects pH (and maintains it at 3.0 with the buffer system) and thus influences the dissolution and stability of complexes; it prevents variations in the oxydoreduction potential which would otherwise be caused by the variations in pH.

Changes in the Method

Tamm (1922, 1931, 1934a,b) recommended an ammonium oxalate-oxalic acid buffer reagent to dissolve the inorganic gels including iron oxides, free silica, and alumina. This author suggested a pH of 3.25.

A rapid examination of the composition of the reagents used since 1922 in the Tamm method highlights the many different procedures used (e.g. variations in the concentration of the reagents, in pH, in the soil/reagent ratio, contact time, agitation, temperature, photolysis, see Fig. 6.5).

Some changes were made to adapt the method to the nature of the sample and its components. Comparisons with old data are often difficult because of complexity of the soil matrix and interactions, and especially because the exact operating conditions are unknown.

Jung (1934) stated that the method was appropriate for light soils, but not for calcareous soils, and that it did not give repeatable results with heavy soils because of the attack of clays. Many studies have been published on different soil types using varying concentrations of reagents and a pH ranging from 3 to 6, or using other organic acids (tartric, citric, salicylic, benzoic, phtalic, malonic acid, etc.) combined or not with reduction with H_2S, nascent hydrogen, or dithionite (Duchaufour and Souchier 1966).

A significant stage in the development of the Tamm method was the discovery of photosensitivity during dissolution (Schoefield 1959) and of the effects of photosensitization (De Endredy 1963, this method being known as Tamm-UV), and especially the establishment of a reference procedure by Schwertmann (1964) also called Tamm reagent in darkness. This method is now used as an international standard.

The time factor has a random influence on the reactions, the dissolution process generally being rapid at the beginning but tending to slow down considerably after 4 or 5 h. The influence of time is generally only critical if it is less than 2 h. Schwertmann fixed the average time at 2 h on the basis of a profile of traditional dissolution indicating the preferential dissolution of certain fractions (ferrihydrite, substances with

short-distance arrangement, etc.). Mc Keague and Day (1966) showed
that in their conditions, dissolution was better when the contact time was
increased to 4 h (in darkness). Although a sequence of treatment of this
duration can have a kinetic effect, only one extraction is the basis of this
method.

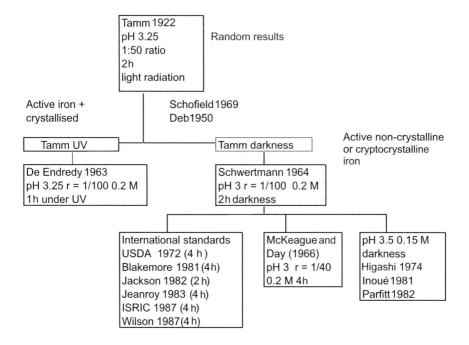

Fig. 6.5. Changes of the Tamm method using ammonium oxalate-oxalic acid
reagent (basic procedures)

The soil/solution ratio generally has a limited influence on the results.
Parfitt (1989) showed that extraction using the 0.15 M reagent at pH 3.0
with a soil/solution ratio of 1:100, agitation for 4 h at 20°C (in darkness)
was satisfactory for many soils, but cannot be used if Al or extractable Fe
exceeds 5%. In this case it is necessary to use a 0.20 M reagent and a
ratio of 1:200.

Extraction with 0.15 M oxalate or 0.20 M reagents at pH 3.0 gives
equivalent results for allophane if the concentration of allophane does not
introduce a limiting factor.

The pH of extraction is critical. It controls the kinetics of dissolution of
the crystalline and non-crystalline compounds. Maximum dissolution is
reached at a pH of between 2.6 and 3.0, the protonation being synergistic
with the reducing and chelating action of the oxalate reagent. If the pH

rises above 4.0, the effectiveness of the buffer decreases drastically, the extracted quantities of iron decrease and selectivity is modified. The pH should thus be fixed at 3.0, to prevent possible variations. Temperature accelerates the reaction and modifies selectivity. The standard temperature is around 20°C.

Preparation of the Reagents

All the reagents should be prepared with reference products, bi-distilled water, or water deionised on a resin column that can fix Si.

Acid ammonium oxalate: 0.2 M oxalate-pH 3.0 Tamm reagent
- Dissolve 16.15 g of ammonium oxalate $(COONH_4)_2,H_2O^3$ and 10.90 g of oxalic acid $(COOH)_2,2H_2O^4$ in approximately 900 mL of water; complete to 1000 mL.
- Check the pH and bring it to pH 3.0 by adding ammonia or 0.2 M oxalic acid.
- Prepare each week and store in a brown bottle protected from the light.
- 0.2% superfloc (flocculation agent) in water (Cyanamid Corp.).
- Matrix corrector for dilutions before atomic spectrometry: for 10,000 ppm K
  weigh 19 g of KCl,
  dissolve in approximately 900 mL of water,
  when the temperature of the solution reaches ambient temperature,
  complete to 1,000 mL.

Procedure

- Measure soil moisture on a separate sub-sample to determine the moisture correction factor (cf. Chap. 1).
- On the laboratory balance, weigh 1 g of air-dried soil sieved with a 0.2 mm mesh (avoid over-grinding).
- Put in a 100 mL bottle.
- Add 50 mL of acid oxalate reagent; for soils with high extractable-oxalate compounds (extracted Al or Fe compounds >2%) add 100 mL oxalate reagent and use a 250 mL bottle.

---

[3] $(NH_4)_2C_2O_4,H_2O$, *mw*: 142.12; can be awkward for certain clays (and can be replaced by sodium oxalate $Na_2C_2O_4$); safety: a classified poison, do not ingest.

[4] COOH–COOH, $2H_2O$, *mw*: 126.07 decomposed by UV radiation; drying at 100°C involves losses by sublimation, decomposition at 160°C; safety: a classified poison – caustic – do not ingest).

– Agitate 4 h in darkness.
– Decant part of the supernatant in a 50 mL centrifugation tube.
– Centrifuge for 10 min at 10,000 g; if the liquid is not perfectly limpid, resuspend, add 3 drops of superfloc and centrifuge again (two reactive blanks should be integrated into each series in addition to a soil standard of reference and two replicates on a sample of the series).

After adequate dilution, analyses are carried out on this extract:
– Si: ICP or AAS spectrometry at 251.6 nm, N_2O/C_2H_2 flame
– Fe: ICP or AAS spectrometry at 248.3 nm, air/C_2H_2 flame
– Al: ICP or AAS at 309.3 nm, N_2O/C_2H_2 flame
– Mn: ICP or AAS at 279.5 nm, air/C_2H_2 flame
and if necessary, Ti and P.

If absorption spectrophotometry is required:
– Destroy the oxalate matrix by boiling with concentrated nitric acid
– Bring to dry and dissolve in 5 M hydrochloric acid
– Evaporate to almost dry and dissolve in water, then complete to the required volume

Calculations

Data collected
– P_1, weight of wet or air-dried soil sample for measurement of moisture.
– P_2, weight of the soil sample dried at 105°C.
– P, weight in mg of soil sample for extraction.
– $A, B,$ contents in the extract and the blank respectively (mg L^{-1}).
– D, dilution of the extract.
– V_R, mL of the oxalate reagent used for extraction.

Moisture correction factor
This measurement is essential to bring back the results to soils dried at 105°C, especially for all soils rich in non-crystalline substances like allophanic soils:

$$H = 100 \ \frac{P_1 - P_2}{P_1} \ (\%)$$

Moisture correction factor $= f = 100/H$

Calculation of contents of elements (Fe, Al, Si, Mn, Ti, P, etc.):

% element $= 0.1 \ (D \ V_R f \ (A{-}B))/P$

Conversion factor of the content of an element to oxide content:

% Fe_2O_3 = % Fe × 1.43   % MnO_2 = % Mn × 1.58
% Al_2O_3 = % Al × 1.89   % SiO_2 = % Si × 2.14

Remarks

The extraction is reliable enough for most soils. Identification of certain phases may sometimes be difficult when clays are disordered. Even when extracts are protected from the light, they can still undergo change. They should thus be analysed rapidly to avoid precipitations due to the instability of the reagent.

The addition of superfloc is generally not necessary given the strong ionic force of the reagent and the resulting complexes. The supernatant liquid can be filtered by siphoning with a syringe equipped with a 0.45 nm filter (after decantation).

Oxalate extraction is used in a number of different fields.
- Pedology and pedogenesis, geochemistry (differential dissolutions and identification of the non-crystalline or little ordered phases, transitions between crystalline phases, chemical and methodological studies, effect on the soil structure, etc.) preferably using data from the dissolved phases.
- Mineralogy uses the solubilized phases and the residual solid phases simultaneously for:
    - The study of substitutions, order–disorder states, compounds with short-range atomic arrangement;
    - For the preparation of samples (dissolution of cements between the particles, elimination of oxides to improve the intensity of diffraction of the crystalline compounds), to carry out differential XRD analyses (DXRD) and to enable analysis after elimination of paramagnetic compounds (Mössbauer, ESR, EXAFS spectrometries), to observe spatial distribution on thin sections of the soluble oxalate phases (Arocena 1988), and finally to model deterioration processes (resulting compounds, etc.).
- Microbiology and agronomy to analyse biophysical and biochemical activity (effect on water retention, plasticity, availability for plants of active iron linked to oxalic acid contents generated in the soil (oxalic acid of biochemical origin causes the disruption of iron oxides).
- In the case of calcareous soils, ammonium oxalate precipitates Ca^{++} cations in the form of calcium oxalate with solubility lower than 0.006 g per litre of water or acetic acid; the carbonate must thus be destroyed with the minimum quantity of acetic acid necessary before extracting ammonium oxalate and complementary measurements of the elements solubilized with acetic acid.
- In reducing conditions (e.g. hydromorphic soils, histosols, andosols under permanent wet climate), the oxalate method cannot provide

information on the initial state of oxidation of iron and manganese in the soil before extraction.
- In andic soils and andosols–andisols the oxalate method can extract as much as the DCB method (cf. Sect. 6.2.2); the organic complexes of iron are dissolved; allophane, which is extracted after 2–4 h agitation with oxalate, can be estimated using the values for extracted silicon based on the hypothesis of the prevalence of Si–O–Al bonds; ferrihydrite can be estimated starting from extracted iron.

6.2.2 Dithionite-Citrate-Bicarbonate Method (DCB)

Principle

This method (Mehra-Jackson 1959–60) makes it possible to solubilize pedogenic oxides and hydroxides:
- crystalline iron oxides (hematite, goethite), non-crystalline iron oxides and iron and aluminium organic complexes, as well as exchangeable iron and manganese oxides, some non-crystalline compounds with a $SiO_2:Al_2O_3$ ratio of less than 0.5;
- magnetite and ilmenite are only slightly attacked, as are gibbsite and allophane-imogolite aluminosilicates; however, magnetite can be significantly solubilized in certain cases (magnetite is strongly oxidized into maghemite in very oxygenated medium);
- clays are not affected, but any iron present in the lattice of vermiculites and non-tronite can be significantly solubilized, particularly if the extraction pH is lowered;

Reduction is the predominant process of this method, dithionite being a very active reducer (Deb 1950) below pH 9–10. Biologically reducible elements like iron or manganese are reduced and maintained in solution by complexation with the citric acid in the system buffered at pH 7.3 with sodium bicarbonate.

The optimum pH for reduction is 7–8. Below pH 6.5, colloidal sulphur can precipitate resulting in a suspension in the extracts that prevents measurement by absorption spectrometry. The use of buffered medium limits this phenomenon. As the dithionite solution rapidly loses its reduction properties, complexation avoids reoxidation as well as the precipitation of iron sulphide and allows maintenance in solution of the extracted phases as long as the extraction time does not exceed 15 min.

Initially, only one addition of dithionite was performed on the first extract. Subsequently, as a result of international influences and on the recommendation of the initiator of the method, two additions of dithionite were recommended.

If required, two or three successive extractions can be performed to include crystallized iron compounds of relatively significant size. In this case, the extracts can either be mixed before analysis or analysed individually to measure a kinetic evolution of the solubility, summation is only carried out after each measurement.

The temperature should be set at 75°C to accelerate the reaction and to limit the appearance of colloidal sulphur and iron sulphide, but also to minimize dithionite decomposition. This temperature should not be exceeded, and localised overheating should be avoided by using a water-bath.

The iron contents should not exceed 0.5 g Fe_2O_3 in order to obtain an excess of reducer and complexant. The reaction of iron reduction in a slightly basic medium can be written:

$$S_2O_4^{2-} + 4\ OH^- \rightarrow 2\ SO_3^{2-} + 2\ H_2O + 2\ e^-$$
$$2\ Fe^{3+} + 2\ e^- \rightarrow 2\ Fe^{2+}$$

and in citric complexing solution

$$S_2O_4^{2-} + Fe_2O_3 + 2\ HOC(COO)_3^{3-} + 2\ H^+ \rightarrow 2\ SO_3^{2-} + 2\ Fe^{II}-HOC(COO)_3^- + H_2O$$

The weight of the sample must be between 1 and 5 g without modifying the composition of the reagent (if iron cannot be complexed due to insufficient citrate, precipitation of black iron sulphide may occur).

A buffered medium is used to avoid a change in pH resulting in variations in the Redox potential, each Fe^{3+} requiring two OH^- during reduction.

Certain authors tested reduction methods using dithionite in citrate with variable pH (Homgren 1967; Avery and Bascom 1982) or Tamm reagent (Duchaufour and Souchier 1966; Hétier and Jeanroy 1973; Loveland and Bullock 1976) or in other buffered and complexing mediums such as sodium tartrate-acetate (Deb 1950) or in a medium with a basic pH such as pyrophosphate (Franzmeier et al. 1965).

Complexes with citric acid (a tridentate sequestering agent) are similar to those formed with oxalic acid and give very stable iron and aluminium compounds. Aluminium citric acid complexes have a stability constant, $\log K1 = 7.37$.

In the natural environment, the presence of citrate prevents, or delays, the precipitation of aluminium, as the sites of coordination are occupied by citrate, its hydrolysis is slowed down:

Replacement of the water molecules and blocking of the sites of coordination occurs in the DCB extraction medium, which has a high concentration of citric acid. Hydrolysis thus becomes impossible (Kwong and Huang 1979). Some minerals, for example pseudo-boehmite, present a particular affinity (Cambier and Sposito 1991).

Two other reagents (hydroxylamine hydrochloride and acidified hydrogen peroxide) were found more efficient than DCB method for selective dissolution of manganese oxides (Neaman et al. 2004a,b).

The DCB treatment can cause structural disorders which can be observed by XRD or electron micro-diffraction. The adsorption of citric groups on certain clays can considerably slow down the departure of interfolayer water. This should be taken into account in the analysis of the residue containing the forms known as "free". It should be noted that under these conditions, proto-imogolite cannot be transformed into the better structured imogolite.

Preparation of the Reagents

All the reagents should be reference products for analysis, water should be bidistilled or possibly deionized on resins suitable for the elimination of silica.

– Sodium dithionite in powder form depending on the number of analyses, only small bottles of the product should be used in order to always have fresh product available.

– Citrate-bicarbonate buffer: dissolve in distilled water before use 79.40 g of trisodium citrate ($C_6H_5Na_3O_7,2H_2O$), 9.24 grams of sodium bi-carbonate ($NaHCO_3$), check the pH which should be 7.3 approximately, bring to 1 L.

– Flocculation use either 400 g saturated sodium chloride, NaCl in 1 L of water, or 375 g saturated potassium chloride, KCl in 1 L of water, if further measurements by atomic absorption or ICP spectrometry are required, potassium chloride should be used in order to avoid stronger sodium concentrations, acetone.

Procedure

- In a flat-bottomed 100 mL centrifugation tube made of polypropylene or PTFE, place from 1 to 5 g of soil (0.2 mm particle size) depending on the estimated concentration of ferric oxide (carbonates, organic matter and soluble salts must be removed from the sample beforehand).
- Add a bar magnet and 45 mL of buffered citrate-bicarbonate reagent by means of a fraction distributor equipped with a PTFE syringe.
- Place on a immersed magnetic stirrer in a water bath regulated at 75°C; when the sample reaches the temperature of the bath, using a measure, add 1 g of dithionite powder and continue to agitate at moderate speed for 5 min.
- Add another gram of dithionite and agitate for 10 min.
- After 15 min digestion, centrifuge for 5 min at 2,500 g to obtain a limpid solution (if the liquid is still cloudy, suspend and add a saturated solution of sodium or potassium chloride to cause flocculation then centrifuge again at 2,500 g; this treatment will make the centrifugation pellet more compact and thus complicate resuspension for a 2nd treatment; for soils originating from volcanic ash, it is often necessary to add 10 mL acetone before centrifugation to achieve satisfactory flocculation).
- Decant the clear supernatant liquid in a 250 mL volumetric flask.
- If the residue displays intense brown, black, or red colour, add 45 mL of buffered reagent and treat as above with two additions of dithionite and heat for 15 min at 75°C, re-suspend the compact centrifugation pellet to allow a homogeneous attack.
- Centrifuge and decant in the same 250 mL flask (or analyze the second extract separately).
- Wash the residue two or three times with 10 mL of buffered reagent, flocculate, centrifuge the rinsing products and add them to the previous extract.
- Add 250 mL distilled water and homogenize.

In each series, introduce two blanks (reagents only) and a reference sample. After adequate dilution (2–10 times) the filtrate containing free oxides and hydroxides should be analysed by atomic absorption spectrometry:

  - Al at 309.3 nm with an acetylene–nitrogen protoxide flame.
  - Fe at 248.3 nm with an acetylene–nitrogen protoxide flame.
  - Si at 251.6 nm with an acetylene–nitrogen protoxide flame.
  - Mn with 279.5 nm with an acetylene–air flame.
  - Ti, P, K, Mg can be also analysed if necessary.

If colorimetry is used, certain methods make it possible to operate directly on the extracts, but it is preferable to destroy the buffered, chelating and reducing matrix by boiling with nitric or sulphuric acid and perhydrol. Iron is measured using 1–10 orthophenantrolin or ferron, aluminium using eryochrome cyanin, silica using molybdate taking phosphorous into account (cf. Chap. 31).

Weigh the purified residue. The residue can be analysed using XRD, an instrumental method; the intensity of the lines is improved by DCB treatment (cf. Chap. 4); IR, ESR, NMR, EXAFS spectrometry (cf. Chap. 12); thermal analysis, DTA-TGA (cf. Chap. 7); or chemical analysis (total analysis, cf. Chap. 31); CEC (cf. Chap. 26); dissolution of aluminosilicates, etc.).

Calculations

Data collected
 – *A, B*: respective contents in the sample and blank extractions in mg L^{-1}.
 – D: dilution factor.
 – f: moisture correction factor (cf. "Calculations" under "Acid oxalate Method under Darkness").
 – *P*: weight of air-dried sample in mg.

Calculations
Oxide percentages should be calculated for all the elements: Fe_2O_3, Al_2O_3, SiO_2, etc. The "weight of the initial sample" minus the "weight of residue" enables total free oxides and hydroxides to be calculated:
Al, Fe, Si... % = 25 (*A–B*) *D f/P*
See "Calculations" under Sect. 6.2.1 for the conversion factors of elements into oxides.

Remarks

This method gives reasonably reproducible results if the crystalline iron forms are sufficiently fine to offer enough surface area to allow a significant attack. Many different procedures have been proposed, but the current standard method is identical for the reagent concentration to that initially suggested by Mehra and Jackson (1959): 0.42 g of sodium bicarbonate and 3.52 g of sodium citrate, $2H_2O$ in 45 mL of water. The main modifications one of the authors made of the method are: double reduction of dithionite on the same extract and the preparation of a single buffer-complexing reagent, which simplifies handling.

The colour of the residue gives a good indication of the effectiveness of the treatment, but the presence of magnetite or ilmenite, which are not attacked by the DCB treatment, can colour the residue black or gray. The DCB method can be used to facilitate dispersion of clay whose suspension may be obstructed by pedogenic oxide and hydroxide coatings.

The method of Holmgren (1967), whose reagent is composed of a rather unstable mixture of 17% sodium citrate and 1.7% sodium dithionite, is now sometimes used instead of the DCB method. It is considered to be equivalent to the Mehra–Jackson method, but simpler to implement and thus more suitable for repetitive analysis.

Grinding to 0.2 mm allows a better attack of the iron forms present in concretions for example. Grinding is consequently generally performed to enable comparisons to be made, and in particular to compare the weight of the residues after treatment.

Heating to temperatures above 80°C (or local overheatings) can cause the precipitation of black iron sulphide. In this case it is better to start the analysis again than to eliminate the precipitate with acetone and carbon tetrachloride.

Dithionite treatment modifies the $Fe^{3+}:Fe^{2+}$ ratio.

Ryan and Gschwend (1991) suggested replacing dithionite with titanium III in the citric-bicarbonate + ethylene diamine tetraacetic acid (EDTA) solution. This reduction method, with the very complexing reagent at a temperature of 80°C, should theoretically enable more complete dissolution of the amorphous ferric oxides and goethite. But hematite is less solubilized. Extraction is more easily achieved with the Ti (III) method than with the DCB method, which gives the Ti (III) method a more selective spectrum of dissolution. The behaviour of the aluminium compounds is different. The use of the cold Ti (III) method increases the degree of selectivity, but the titanium content of the soil must be low.

6.2.3 EDTA method

Principle

The EDTA (salt of Na) method according to Borggaard (1976), enables extraction of iron in an amorphous or very little ordered state as a result of biological deterioration (inorganic and organic non-crystalline iron) the ferrihydrite is dissolved. Both the water-extractable iron and the exchangeable iron must be in solution.

This reagent is not suitable for the extraction of the amorphous and organic forms of aluminium because of the high pH of the extraction solution. The silicates and crystalline forms of iron and aluminium are not dissolved.

The repeatability and selectivity of iron extraction are good. The method is reliable, but has one major disadvantage: the slowness of the extraction, the balance being achieved only after approximately three months of extraction. The most widely used process is hydrolysis and complexation in basic medium at ambient temperature (20°C).

EDTA is an aminopolycarboxylic acid with six atoms suitable for the formation of chelates (from the Greek Khélé = crab grip) to which a metal cation is linked by coordination with the organic radical (e.g. two atoms of nitrogen and four carboxyl groups, see Fig. 6.6). The six positions around the metal (Fe^{2+}) give a high complexing capacity and low selectivity, as most of the di- and trivalent elements are able to enter this type of complex. The constants of stability, log K at 20°C, are 13.8 for Mn^{2+}, 14.3 for Fe^{2+}, 16.1 for Al^{3+}, 25.1 for Fe^{3+}).

In an alkaline solution (pH 10), 1:1 complexes are formed with pedogenic elements. An excess of complexing reagent is needed for satisfactory control of the dissolution rate .

Depending on the pH, it may be possible to obtain H_4Y, H_3Y^-, H_2Y^{2-}, HY^{3-} forms (Y^{4-} being the EDTA anion, see Fig. 6.6).

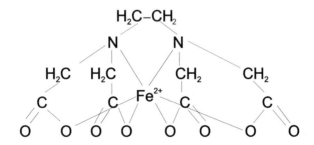

Fig. 6.6. Molecule of EDTA IV (*top*) and coordination complex with iron (*bottom*)

In the extraction continuum, the extractable forms of iron with EDTA appear to be linked with the most active forms in pedogenesis, i.e. with the "free" least crystalline compounds with extensive surface contact and thus great reactivity. Both exchangeable iron and organic chelated forms are solubilized because the pH of the reagent is high and the EDTA complexes are stable.

In agronomy, the availability of iron for plants (nutritional factor or possible chlorosis) is often checked using also two other complexing reagents (Lindsay-Norvell 1976): diethylene triaminopentaacetic acid (DTPA) or ethylene diamine di(o-hydroxyphenylacetic acid (EDDHA).

The correlation between EDTA- and oxalate-extractable iron is good: the ferrihydrite is dissolved by EDTA or by oxalate, but soils containing hydroxyferric complexes can react differently with these reagents (Jeanroy 1983). The time factor is significant. The extraction profile is slow and dissolution is continuous up to around 90 days, when it stabilizes.

The temperature is critical and attempts carried out to accelerate the reactions by raising the temperature to 75°C, as in the DCB method, resulted in unacceptable displacement of selectivity, some crystalline products becoming attackable and solubilizable.

The effect of pH was tested by Borggaard (1976). It cannot be below 7.5. A pH of 10, similar to that used in the pyrophosphate and tetraborate methods, makes it possible to compare the organic phases extracted using the above methods and eliminates the effect of pH. But selectivity is random for aluminium, which, at a pH of 8–9, gives soluble aluminates.

In EDTA, the concentration factor appears to have little influence on extraction, the kinetics of the reaction being controlled by hydrolysis. Intermittent agitation makes it possible to renew the reagent at the liquid–solid interfaces, thus avoiding the phenomena of local saturation. Clarification of the extracts is generally problem free.

Preparation of the Reagents

The initial procedure of Borggaard (1976) is a dynamic method. This author tested the effects of a concentration of the complexing reagent of between 0.01 and 0.1 M and a pH of between 7.5 and 10.5. This method is thus extremely long and cannot be adapted in its original form for repetitive analyses.

A concentration of 0.1 M of EDTA at a pH of 10 is used as standard. This enables comparisons with the reagents which extract organomineral complexes at the same pH, i.e. pyrophosphate at pH 9.6–10 and tetraborate at pH 9.7. Commercially available EDTA is often in the form of sodium salt and is sold under different names: Versenate, Sequestrene,

Titriplex II, Trilon B, etc. The empirical formula $C_{10}H_{16}N_2O_8$ corresponds to a molar mass of 292.25 g.
Solution A: weigh approximately 29.225 g EDTA in 500 mL water.
Soution B: dissolve 20 g NaOH in 250 mL water.
Gradually mix B in A to bring the pH to 10.
Complete to 1 L with distilled water.

Procedure

- On an analytical balance weigh precisely 2 g of soil ground to 0.2 mm in a 100 mL polypropylene or PTFE centrifuge tube.
- Add 50 mL of 0.1 M EDTA reagent.
- Stop the tube and agitate with the Vortex vibrator for 1 min.
- Place the samples on mobile plates that can be used on an oscillating agitator and store the series protected from the light for 90 days with daily agitation for 5 min.
- After 90 days of contact, centrifuge at 5,000 g for 5 min and filter.

The extracted elements (mostly Fe, Al, Si, and P) are analysed by plasma emission or atomic absorption spectrometry. When absorption spectrocolorimetry is used, the EDTA matrix has to be destroyed (cf. "Procedure" under "Acid Oxalate Method Under Darkness"). In each series, introduce two blanks with only reagents and a reference sample.

Calculations

Data collected:
A, B, D, f, P of the same type as in the preceding methods (cf. "Calculations" under section 6.2.1 and "Calculations" under "Dithionite - Citrate - Bicarbonate Method (DCB)" in this chapter).
Contents Fe, Al, Mn, Si, P (%) = 5 (A–B) D f/P
These contents are expressed as per cent of oxides (cf. "Calculations" under section 6.2.1).

Remarks

This method is one of the most reproducible and selective for amorphous iron and can also extract organometallic complexes if the pH exceeds nine. The extracted iron must be compared to the iron extracted by the oxalate reagent taking into account the fact that aluminous products dissolved at high pH can release iron for example resulting from isomorphic substitutions.

It is useful to compare the results with the extraction of active iron available to plants (using DTPA or EDDHA reagents) to link the results to the phenomenon of chlorosis and to proceed from pedogenic observations to the identification of agronomic properties of the soil–plant–climate relationships. From an agronomic point of view, the extraction of phosphorous by EDTA is also useful to identify the proportions of P linked to Fe or Al which form part of the pool of "available P".

6.2.4 Pyrophosphate Method

Principle

This method is used to analyze the forms of iron and aluminium complexed with the soil organic matter, in particular to differentiate the spodic and podzolic horizons where displacement of these complexes can be observed.

Generally a good correlation can be obtained between extracted Al, Fe, and organic C. Well-crystallized iron oxides like goethite and hematite are not attacked and slightly ordered iron oxides are only slightly solubilized.

The original procedure recommended by Alexandrova (1960), and given permanent form by McKeague (1967), cannot be applied as it stands but has to be modified with regard to the clarification of the extracts.

The pyrophosphate anion $P_2O_7^{4-}$ has chelating properties and can react with polyvalent cations to give insoluble compounds and soluble complexes with organic matter, for example:

$$R(COO)_4Ca_2 + Na_4P_2O_7 \rightarrow R(COONa)_4 \text{ soluble} + Ca_2P_2O_7\downarrow$$

But the complete mechanism of pyrophosphate action is not as clear as in the methods described earlier. The action of pyrophosphate has been questioned with regard to the organic forms of iron and aluminium: on one hand concerning the procedures and the reliability of the measurements, and on the other hand with regard to the mechanisms of extraction and the nature of the extracted products. Klamt (1985) mentioned "the denunciation of pyrophosphate extraction of Fe from soils (highly unreliable)", indicating that an international consensus had not been not reached.

With regard to the procedures

The time factor of 16 h is regarded as critical, particularly when the results of this method are compared with those obtained by EDTA extraction after a contact time of 90 days.

The pH, which was tested at different levels, is here fixed at 10.0 to enable comparison with the other extraction methods in basic solutions.

Pyrophosphate has chelating properties. Originally the choice between the use of sodium or potassium pyrophosphate was more or less random. K pyrophosphate extracts slightly more than Na pyrophosphate and makes spectrometric measurements easier by avoiding strong Na^+ concentrations, which are always awkward. But with certain clays, potassium has serious disadvantages[5]. Na pyrophosphate is consequently considered to give the best reproducible extraction and it is now used at a concentration of 0.1 M (Loveland and Digby 1984).

At pH 10, pyrophosphate has peptizing properties which make the extracts very difficult to purify. Suspended particles are mainly responsible for the low rate of reproducibility and the lack of precision of the method, as the material in suspension is not chemically extractable by pyrophosphate. The efficiency of its centrifugation (speed and time of centrifugation) has been tested up to 100,000 g and compared to ultra-fitration. A flocculating agent must be added before centrifugation, usually sodium sulphate at concentrations ranging between 0.25 and 1 M (Schuppli et al. 1983) or superfloc cyanamid N-100 (or Floerger Kemflock F 20 H). In this case the concentration is critical (Ballantyne et al. 1980). It is fixed at 0.2 mL superfloc for 50 mL of extract. Centrifugation at 20,000 g for 15 min results in clear extracts. Ultra filtration with 0.02 μm millipore filters can be used to eliminate any colloidal particles that may still be in suspension. In this case reproducibility is about 10–15%.

With regard to the mechanisms of solubilization

In the reaction between sodium pyrophosphate and soil, complexation cannot be the main mechanism, as iron linked to complex organic forms cannot be dissolved without solubilization of the amorphous forms of iron which are very reactive, as in the case of EDTA solubilization.

---

[5] For example the K^+ ion is specifically adsorbed by vermiculite or deteriored micas because its diameter is compatible with the size of the adsorption sites. The selectivity of K^+ with respect to Ca^{2+} or Mg^{2+} is increased by the hydroxy aluminous polymer deposits on the interfoliaceous surfaces. In the presence of a strong concentration of P, and in certain conditions, K and aluminous oxides together can result in the formation of taranakite.

Compared to amorphous iron oxides, the iron pyrophosphate complex is not considered to be very stable at pH 10.

Bruckert (1979) considered that sodium pyrophosphate shifts the organic matter of its complexes of coordination with the metallic sites of clays (ferric bridges) and is adsorbed instead of the humic compounds which are solubilized at an alkaline pH. Metallic compounds with a high charge, such as amorphous hydroxides, can behave in a similar way. All the complexes extracted by pyrophosphate comprise the "immovable complexes".

Micro-aggregates are destroyed and clayey and colloidal cements are dispersed. Fulvic acid-amorphous iron hydroxides complexes are extracted along with the organic molecules in the coatings on clays.

Jeanroy (1981,1983) considered that dissolution induces a mechanism of peptization and solubilization. Adsorption of pyrophosphate on the soil particles increases the negative charges and increases their solublity in water. In contrast to EDTA, which has a flocculating effect, pyrophosphate puts ferruginous particles into suspension and these subsequently disperse in the extracts.

Separation on millipore filter shows that in EDTA extracts iron is linked to small molecules and thus passes through the membrane. On the other hand, the pyrophosphate extracts contain compounds of greater molecular size that do not pass through the membrane, as only a small proportion of the chelated fraction is able to do so. Similarly ultracentrifugation of the EDTA extract does not separate the phases, clearly demonstrating that iron is in soluble chelate form, whereas pyrophosphate results in a significant colloidal centrifugation pellet.

To summarize: with its peptizing action, pyrophosphate puts into suspension fine ferruginous particles, probably of ferric hydroxides, whose smoothness and small degree of atomic order are explained by the presence of organic matter which inhibits the crystallization of iron oxides. Bruckert's "immovable complexes" appear to be mainly hydroxyferric complexes that reveal the preponderance of the mineral.

From a practical point of view, pyrophosphate is effective only if the soil is under the influence of organic matter. In the opinion of Schuppli et al. (1983), the precipitation of iron in the pyrophosphate extracts could be due to the ageing of the extracts. Another dissolution mechanism could be the release by sodium pyrophosphate of small quantities of iron in the organic complexes, leaving these complexes negatively charged. They then become water soluble. The organic matter makes it possible to maintain quantities of iron in solution, but if the ratio reaches a certain level, precipitation will occur (Petersen 1976).

If this description of the solubilization mechanism is accurate, pyrophosphate extraction could be a selective dissolution technique, especially if uncertainties concerning the purification of the extracts are overcome. From a practical point of view, pyrophosphate extraction enables the behaviour of certain soils to be differentiated for the purpose of classification, though without identifying the precise origin of the extracted iron; however organic forms are considered to be the most probable.

Preparation of the Reagents

Extraction

0.1 M sodium pyrophosphate: dissolve 44.6 g of $Na_4P_2O_7,10H_2O$ in distilled water and bring to 1 L; check the pH which must be 10.0.

Clarification

Superfloc cyanamid N-100 (cyanamid Corp. Gosport, Hampshire, UK): dissolve 0.2 g of superfloc in 100 mL of water and agitate in darkness for 16 h with a PTFE magnetic bar stirrer, protect from the light in a brown bottle; a fresh solution should be made each week.

Procedure

With a laboratory precision balance, weigh one gram of soil (0.2 mm particle size) in a 250 mL polyethylene tube (with screw stopper). Add 100 mL of 0.1 M sodium pyrophosphate reagent and agitate for 16 h at ambient temperature (20°C).

Add 0.2 mL of superfloc and homogenize on a rotary shaker for 10 min, then centrifuge at 20,000 g. With a millipore filter syringe remove from the quantities of supernatant needed to analyze the required elements (mostly Fe, Al, Si, and C). Add two blanks (with only reagents) and two reference samples in each series,.

Measure the concentrations of Al, Fe, Si by plasma emission or atomic absorption spectrometry (cf. Chap. 31) with standards diluted in the extraction matrix. For measurements by absorption spectrocolorimetry, destroy the pyrophosphate matrix before measurement (cf. "Procedure" under "Acid Oxalate Method under Darkness").

Calculations

Data collected:

A, B, D, P, f as in other methods (cf. "Calculations" under Sect. 6.2.1).

% contents (Fe, Al, Si) = 10 (*A–B*) *D f /P*

The results can be expressed in oxides (cf. "Calculations" under Sect. 6.2.1).

Remarks

The method is well suited for differentiation of podzolic B horizons. The conditions governing centrifugation and clarification must be as homogeneous as possible, and the speed and time of centrifugation should be rigorously respected. If the series has to be stored before measurement by spectrography, store protected from the light in the refrigerator at 6–8°C.

The percentages of extracted organic carbon are often measured on automated CHN apparatuses (cf. Chap. 10) at the same time as Fe, Al and Si are measured using spectrographic techniques (cf. Chap. 31). Series of extractions whose action is due to a gradual increase in the pH of the medium are often used. These differential extractions make it possible to characterize increasingly resistant forms:

– A preliminary extraction using 0.1 M sodium tetraborate buffered at pH 9.7[6] enables the electrostatic linkages to be broken by simple exchange. The adsorbed organic molecules of low molecular weight are extracted. They contain complexed iron and aluminium that comprise the recently insolubilised "mobilizable complexes". The soil aggregates are not destroyed (Bruckert 1970, 1974, 1979).

– The 0.1 M pyrophosphate method at pH 10 then makes it possible to break the coordination linkages with the hydroxides and oxides in the coating on clays.

– Lastly, the 0.1 M sodium hydroxide method at pH ≥ 12 (cf. Sect. 6.2.5) enables the organo-mineral linkages to be destroyed, even those of the allophane-humic acid complexes.

---

[6] Preparation of reagent: 0.1 N sodium tetraborate pH = 9.7: dissolve 21 g of $Na_2B_4O_7,10H_2O$ in approximately 900 mL of water; add 1.8 g of sodium hydroxide pellets; homogenize; check the pH which must be 9.7; bring to 1 L with deionised water.
Extraction: 1 g of soil ground to 0.2 mm + 100 mL of 0.1 N sodium tetraborate solution; stir for 1 h; centrifuge at 20,000 g and continue as for pyrophosphate extracts (Al, Si, Fe, C, etc.).

6.2.5 Extraction in strongly alkaline mediums

Principle

Methods using soda and sodium carbonate reagents are based on:
– Dissolution in strongly alkaline medium of some silicon, aluminium, and aluminosilicate compounds; these can form soluble silicates and aluminates according to the simplified reaction:
$Al + NaOH + H_2O \rightarrow NaAlO_2 + 3/2\ H_2$.
– concentration in the residue of insoluble compounds, and especially of iron and manganese.

An attack using boiling 0.5 M sodium hydroxide solution for 2 min 30 s solubilizes organic forms of aluminium and silicon, hydrated non-crystalline and crystalline (gibbsite) aluminium oxides, opaline silica and diatoms, and finally amorphous or crypto-crystalline aluminosilicates like allophane and imogolite ($SiO_2:Al_2O_3$ ratio = 1.5–2.3). Some 1:1 silicates are attacked and partially dissolved. Iron compounds are not extracted.

An attack using 0.5 M sodium carbonate for 16 h at 20°C (Follet et al. 1965) has a more mitigated action and makes it possible to solubilize the organic and non-crystalline aluminium compounds as well as a certain proportion of gibbsite. Very finely divided siliceous compounds and opaline silica can be partially dissolved, amorphous aluminosilicates are solubilized, but allophane and imogolite are not completely solubilized. Phyllosilicates and iron compounds are not attacked.

The iron compounds untouched by these two treatments can be studied in this enriched residue. But a more vigorous method with 5 M NaOH solutions and boiling for 2 h makes it possible to dissolve the majority of 1:1 clays and clay minerals present and thus ensure a higher concentration. Despite this treatment, some minerals such as quartz, anatase, rutile, cristobalite, and some 2:1 clays may still be present in the residue.

The action of the reagents mainly depends on the dispersion of the particles, the state of division of the silicon and aluminium substances, the crystallinity and reactivity of the surfaces of ordered or X-ray amorphous compounds.

Extraction in a 0.5 M NaOH medium with a limited period of boiling enables differential solubilization of aluminium and silicon compounds as well as of organic matter with high reactive surface, whereas well-crystallized compounds are spared as their solubilization requires a much longer period of boiling.

The solubility of aluminium hydroxides is amplified by an initial hydrolysis mechanism of the monomeric forms of aluminium (at low concentrations): $AlOH^{2+}$, $Al(OH)_2^+$, $Al(OH)_3$, $Al(OH)_4^-$, the latter existing only in an alkaline medium according to the reaction:

$$Al^{3+} + 4\,H_2O \rightarrow Al(OH)_4^- + 4\,H^+$$

Aluminium is in tetrahedral coordination. At higher concentrations, the polymeric forms gradually take the form of $[Al_6(OH)_{12},(H_2O)_{12}]^{6+}$ units.

In addition, all the acid groups of organic macromolecules (humic and fulvic acids) are dissociated, and the polar and anion sites are easily solvated. Under these operating conditions, most of the organomineral bonds are broken, even the very resistant ones between allophanic-Al and humic acid of Andosols. The poorly ordered aluminium and silicon compounds or their organic and inorganic derivatives pass in solution in aluminate or silicate form.

Dissolution in sodium hydroxide solution can result in an oxidative medium by breaking down some humic acid forms in the presence of oxygen, which modifies the $Fe^{2+}{:}Fe^{3+}$ ratios in the residues. Operating in nitrogen atmosphere can mitigate this phenomenon and also minimize the carbonation of sodium hydroxide by atmospheric CO_2.

Finally, in addition to the above processes, the strongly dispersing action of sodium hydroxide on the phyllosilicates also has to be considered. The elementary components of the stable micro-aggregates maintained in place by Fe, Al, Si oxide coating are first released by the dissolution process and then dispersed thereby increasing the action of the reagent at the solid–liquid interfaces. The alkaline character of the surfaces of the oxide decreases according to the series:

	Amorphous hydrated Al oxides	> γ- AlO(OH) boehmite	> α- $Al(OH)_3$ bayerite	> γ- $Al(OH)_3$ gibbsite	> γ- Al_2O_3
pH at isoelectric point	9.45	9.40	9.20		8.00

In addition to sodium hydroxide and carbonate, and sodium or potassium pyrophosphate, other reagents that have been used to extract the organic matter and organomineral complexes are: ethylene diamine (EDA), NN-dimethylformamide, sulfolane, pyridine, dimethyl sulfoxide, etc.

Reagents

The three mostly widely used reagents are described here as they correlate well with other selective extraction methods and characterize the resistance to the dissolution of the aluminous or siliceous products satisfactorily. Many alternatives have been proposed whose relative effectiveness (but not the degree of selectivity) is roughly classified in Table 3. Potassium hydroxide solutions are sometimes used instead of sodium hydroxide.

Table 6.3. Strongly alkaline reagents classified in order of decreasing efficiency

5 mol $(NaOH) L^{-1}$ $pH \geq 14$	> 0.5 mol $(NaOH) L^{-1}$ $pH > 12$	≥ 1.25 mol $(NaOH) L^{-1}$	> 0.5 mol $(Na_2CO_3) L^{-1}$ pH 10.7	> 0.5 mol $(Na_2CO_3)L^{-1}$ pH 10.7	> 0.1 mol $(NaOH) L^{-1}$
boiling	boiling	80°C	boiling	20°C	20°C
2 h	2.5 min	20 min (or shorter)	1 h (or variable times)	16 h	
iron enrichment	selective extraction of free oxides allophane imogolite	eliminates gibbsite and free oxides	eliminates inter-particle cements, solubilizes 1:1 minerals	selective extraction of allophane imogolite	clay dispersion
Norrish and Taylor (1961)	Hashimoto and Jackson (1960)			Follet et al. (1965)	

Preparation

– 5 mol $(NaOH) L^{-1}$ solution: carefully dissolve 200 g of analytical grade sodium hydroxide pellets in 1 L of distilled water previously boiled to eliminate carbon dioxide Leave to cool with no contact with air and store in a polythene bottle. Prepare fresh solution every week.

– 0.5 mol (NaOH) L^{-1} solution: dissolve 20 g of sodium hydroxide pellets in 1 L of previously boiled distilled water. Store in a polythene bottle. This reagent should be freshly prepared every day.

– 0.5 mol (Na_2CO_3) L^{-1} solution: dissolve 53 g of anhydrous Na_2CO_3 in 1 L of distilled water and store in a polythene bottle.

– 0.5 mol (HCl) L^{-1}: take 42 mL of HCl $d = 1.19$ and bring to 1 L.

Procedures

Selective dissolution with 0.5 M Na$_2$CO$_3$ at 20°C

(Follet et al. 1965):

– Weigh 100 mg of soil sample ground to 0.2 mm and place in a 100 mL centrifuge tube.

– Add 80 mL of 0.5 M Na_2CO_3 solution; close the tube and shake for 16 h with a rotary shaker.

– Centrifuge at 5,000 g for 10 min.

– Transfer the supernatant in a 200 mL volumetric flask.

– Wash the centrifugation pellet with distilled water and recentrifuge.

– Add to the previous extract and bring to 200 mL with deionised water.

– Carry out spectrometric measurements on the extract without delay using atomic absorption or inductively coupled plasma emission (Si and Al).

Selective dissolution with boiling 0.5 M NaOH

(Hashimoto and Jackson 1960):

– Weigh 100 mg of soil sample ground to 0.2 mm (or use the residue of a DCB extraction) in a 250 mL nickel or PTFE crucible.

– Add 100 mL of 0.5 M NaOH boiling solution and homogenize.

– Maintain boiling for 2 min 30 s.

– Rapidly cool and transfer in a 250 mL polythene centrifuge tube and centrifuge for 10 min at 5,000 g

– Transfer the supernatant in a 500 mL volumetric flask.

– Wash the centrifugation pellet with distilled water, recentrifuge, and add the rinsing solution in the volumetric flask.

– Adjust to volume with distilled water and measure Si and Al without delay using atomic absorption spectrometry or plasma emission spectrometry.

Dissolution with boiling 5 M NaOH (2 h)
(Norris and Taylor 1961):
– Weigh 100 mg of sample ground to 0.2 mm (or use the residue of other
  selective extractions) in a stainless steel or PTFE beaker.
– Add 100 mL of 5 mol (NaOH) L^{-1} solution.
– Boil for 2 h.
– Cool and centrifuge at 5,000 g for 10 min.
– Decant the supernatant (which can be discarded or analysed).
– Wash the centrifugation pellets with a little water, then wash three
  times with 0.5 mol (HCl) L^{-1} solution to dissolve the resulting sodalite
  and to eliminate sodium chloride, then wash again with water until
  negative reaction of chlorides.
  Dry the sample ready for the analysis of manganese and iron oxides.
check the absence of kaolinite and sodalite by XRD.

Calculations

All the results are expressed in oxides (cf. "Calculations" under Sect.
6.2.1).

Remarks

The NaOH:Al ratio influences the development of aluminium hydroxides
(Hsu 1977). It is thus important to standardize the procedures during the
Al precipitation. Studies of ^{27}Al by nuclear magnetic resonance show
that, for a given concentration and pH, the nature of the gel gradually
changes with ageing (Hsu 1984). These modifications, which occur in the
natural environment, also occur in the synthetic mediums though at a
different scale (Stol et al. 1976). NMR spectrometry is a particularly
powerful tool to differentiate suspended or dissolved polynuclear species.
Sometimes the modifications observed can explain such apparently
induced variations by separation techniques such as centrifugation,
ultrafiltration, or dialysis. Consequently it is better to carry out
spectrometric measurements on products that have been recently
extracted by different methods.
  For the 5 mol (NaOH) L^{-1} reagent, Kampf and Schwertmann (1982)
recommend the boiling extraction method and in the presence of gibbsite
to modify the reagent which must contain 0.2 mol (silica) L^{-1} in order to
minimize phase changes and a possible increase in crystallinity, and to
inhibit dissolution and recrystallization of substituted aluminium in
goethites. Ferrihydrite, which can be converted into hematite and/or
goethite, remains almost intact. However, the increase in the silica
content results in more abundant precipitation of sodium and aluminium

silicate (sodalite) which must be eliminated from the residue by several washings with 0.5 mol (HCl) L^{-1} solution.

The method of concentration with 5 mol (NaOH) L^{-1} makes it possible to identify manganese oxides in the residue more clearly. These oxides are generally found at low concentrations and display weak crystallinity in soils. Birnessite and lithiophorite are found with iron oxides. Birnessite can be dissolved in hydroxylamine chloride as goethite and lithiophorite are not affected by this treatment. A final attack using the DCB method makes it possible to dissolve the goethite (Shuman 1982; Tokashiki et al. 1986).

In the method based on boiling soda for 2 min 30 (cf. "Selective dissolution with boiling 0.5 M NaOH"), time is critical and must be carefully respected to avoid excessive solubilization of kaolinite and halloysite which can gradually pass in solution. The chlorites and montmorillonites, which were previously heated to 500°C, are not much affected. Spectrometric measurements should be made rapidly after extraction to avoid ageing of the extracts and precipitation of aluminosilicate.

A large volume of solution compared to the weight of soil sample should be used to avoid the saturation of the extracts by aluminium and silicium. To avoid contamination, only PTFE, stainless steel, or nickel laboratory equipment is recommended. Pyrex glass can cause pollution by Si, Al, Fe.

Dissolution of the gibbsite can be corrected if it is measured by DTA (cf. Chap. 7).

Dissolution with 0.5 mol (NaOH) L^{-1} solution at boiling point does not enable very fine differentiation between amorphous and crystalline products because of the sensitivity of poorly ordered 1:1 clays and gibbsite. However, correlation with the oxalate method is generally good.

6.3 Other Methods, Improvements and Choices

6.3.1 Differential Sequential Methods

Principle

Many methods have been developed. When used in sequence, the methods described in Sect. 6.2 earlier can be considered as sequential multi-reagent methods.

The Ségalen (1968) method uses an alternating process of hydrolysis and protonation in cold acid medium (without complexation or reduction) to solubilize some iron and aluminium compounds, then a treatment in hot alkaline medium (80°C) to solubilize the aluminium and silica compounds (cf. Sect. 6.2.5 earlier). These treatments are alternated several times to establish cumulative curves of quantity *vs* time (Fig. 6.7).

Fractionation expresses the differences in the solubility of compounds in these mediums[7]. Solubilization kinetics and hydrolysis constants depend on (1) the type, nature and concentration of the reagents, the soil/solution ratio and temperature and (2) nature and size of the sample, its elementary particle content, the degree of crystallinity and the extent of specific surface of clay minerals, the molecular arrangements and the degree of substitutions.

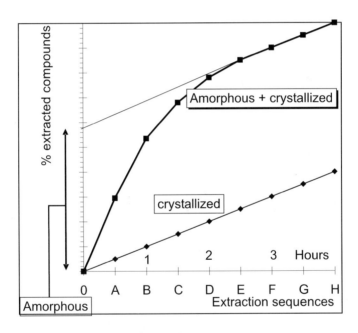

Fig. 6.7. Cumulative curve of extraction

The cumulative curve of the extracted compounds integrates these parameters (1) the lower part of the curve shows a parabolic segment that rises to a greater or lesser extent depending on the soil types which correspond mainly to the rapid dissolution of non-crystalline products

---

[7] For example the dissolution kinetics of the iron forms in 0.5 mol (HCl) L^{-1} solution at 25°C (Shidhu et al. 1981) follows the series: (ferrihydrite, feroxyhite > lepidocrocite > magnetite > akaganeite > maghemite > hematite > goethite).

with a very high specific surface area (Fig. 6.7); the kinetics of dissolution shows that a fraction of very fine crystalline products can also pass in solution in the same time interval; (2) the rectilinear upper segment has a weak slope indicating the weak dissolution of the well-crystallized and chemically not very reactive products.

A gradual change in the slope may indicate the end of dissolution of the very fine crystalline particles, or on the contrary, the appearance of practically non-ordered zones of preferential dissolution. Extrapolation of the upper segment at the intersection with the y-coordinate provides an estimate of the percent of amorphous substances.

Reagents

The reagents recommended by Ségalen (1968) for the acid attack are 2, 4, and 8 mol (HCl) L^{-1} hydrochloric acid solutions (the last concentration was finally retained) and for the alkaline treatment, boiling for 5 min with 0.5 mol (NaOH) L^{-1} solution. The extraction sequence comprises 8 alternating acid-alkaline treatments:
- 8 mol (HCl) L^{-1}: in a 1 L volumetric flask, add 830 mL of reagent grade hydrochloric acid to about 100 mL distilled water, agitate, leave to cool and bring to 1 L; alternatively if 6, 4, 2, or 0.5 mol (HCl) L^{-1} solutions are used, add respectively, 623, 415, 208, or 52 mL hydrochloric acid in the 1 L flask.
- 0.5 mol (NaOH) L^{-1}: add 20 g of NaOH pellets in a 1 L volumetric flask, dissolve in distilled water and bring to 1 L.

The proposed modifications of this method concern the temperature (from ambient to boiling), the duration of contact and finally the use of only one reagent (2 mol (HCl) L^{-1}) without alternating with NaOH.

Procedure

(Ségalen 1968):
- Weigh 500 mg of soil (ground to 0.2 mm) in a 100 mL polyethylene centrifuge tube.
- Add 50 mL of 8 mol (HCl) L^{-1} solution, homogenize and leave in contact for 30 min at room temperature.
- Centrifuge at 5,000 g for 10 min.
- Transfer the supernatant in a 100 mL volumetric flask.
- Add 45 mL of deionised water, resuspend the centrifugation pellet by Vortex agitation.
- Centrifuge at 5,000 g and add the washing water in the volumetric flask.

– Complete to 100 mL; this is extract A (acid) for the measurement of iron, aluminium, and silicon.
– Add 50 mL of NaOH 0.5 mol L^{-1} solution in the centrifuge tube and resuspend.
– Place in the boiling water bath for 5 min.
– Centrifuge at 5,000 g for 10 min.
– Collect the supernatant in a 100 mL volumetric flask.
– Wash the residue with 45 mL distilled water and add the washing water to the extract; complete to 100 mL; this is extract B (alkaline) for the measurement of alumina and silica.
Repeat the double extraction process eight times.

Calculations

All the results obtained by atomic absorption or inductively-coupled plama emission spectrometry are expressed in per cent of oxides (cf. "Calculation" in Sect. 6.2.1).

For alumina and silica, the results obtained on extracts A and B must be added. For iron, the acid solution is used alone. Cumulative curves of iron, alumina, and silica are established (Fig. 6.7); the tangent to the right of the curve gives the percentage of amorphous compounds.

Remarks

The procedure using the above concentrations (alternating 8 mol (HCl) L^{-1} and 0.5 mol (NaOH) L^{-1} with 5 min boiling), was found to be too energetic and insufficiently selective for many pedological situations and many minerals as the amorphous substances were often over-estimated. This method thus needs to be adapted to the type of soil being analysed. The original unmodified method dissolves amorphous iron and complexed iron, but if the use of very aggressive reagents results in the rapid dissolution of the amorphous substances, it also solubilizes crystallized products: 1:1 clays, mica, chlorite, biotite, hornblende, nontronite, gibbsite, etc. (Colmet-Daage et al. 1973; Quantin and Lamouroux 1974; Quantin et al. 1975; Yong et al. 1979; Bentley et al. 1978, 1980; Quigley et al. 1980, 1985; Torrance et al. 1986).

The degree of selectivity may be insufficient for certain soils and amorphous substances will be considerably over-estimated. On their own, the kinetics curves do not show which forms are truly solubilized.

The kinetics of dissolution is significantly correlated with the concentration of the reagents, and to time and temperature. Modifying these parameters can significantly change the dissolution kinetics and selectivity. The results always have to be linked with a precise procedure.

As is true for all the other methods, an excess of reagent is necessary to avoid the effects of saturation. This method is not really suitable for repetitive analysis without robotization because of the length of the successive extractions. Six double extractions can be carried out each day on a small series.

The study of goethite dissolution (Cornell et al. 1974, 1975, 1976; Schwertmann et al. 1985) in 0.5 mol (HCl) L^{-1} at 20 and 60°C using transmission electron microscopy (TEM) shows that preferential zones of dissolution create new surfaces that can give sigmoid curves of dissolution *vs* time. This mechanism of dissolution is related to the structure of the molecular configurations. The kinetics of dissolution of goethite is slowed down by a strong Al^{3+} substitution. These studies highlight the changes in the concepts of dissolution and of "amorphous" substances as well as the need to check the size and the state of surfaces of minerals using SEM and XPS microscopy.

6.3.2 Selective Methods for Amorphous Products

Many other methods are used for the description of amorphous substances, in particular the release of hydroxyls by fluorides and trimethylsilylation.

Release of Hydroxyls by Fluorides

This method is based on the general reaction:

$$(\text{mineral-OH}) + F^- \rightarrow (\text{mineral-F}) + OH^-$$

which satisfactorily accounts for the reactivity of the crypto-crystalline components, aluminosilicates like allophane or imogolite, or amorphous aluminium forms, the reactions being very rapid.

$$Al(OH)_3 + 6NaF \rightarrow Na_3AlF_6 + 3NaOH$$

The above reaction made it possible to develop a NaF field test for andosols. The total released OH^- correlates well with the amorphous forms of Al and Si, with a weak influence of Fe. Quantification is performed by titration at constant pH:
– Put 25 mg of soil ground to 0.2 mm in contact with 0.85 mol (NaF) L^{-1} solution solution at pH 6.8 and at 25°C;

– Using a titrimeter, maintain the pH at 6.8 for 30 min by adding a titrated acid solution. The quantity of acid required for neutralization provides an estimate of the non-crystalline substances.

The reaction can be performed stoechiometrically only in the absence of organic matter and carbonates. The crystalline substances are not sufficiently reactive to react significantly in such a short period of time.

Trimethylsilylation

This method is specifically used for silica compounds; it is derived from organic chemistry and is based on the reaction of the silicic acid with organo-silicic compounds which produce stable and volatile organosilyl derivatives that can be separated and identified by gas chromatography. The basic reaction can be written briefly:

| Monomeric phase with o-silicon bonds | Silicic acid | Trimethylsilyl derivatives |

This reaction makes it possible to determine the degree of polymerization of silica and to link it to different types of deterioration. Inorganic gels that are rich in aluminium are particularly reactive. Crystalline substances are not very active.

Place 50 mg of soil sample in contact with 9 mL of hexamethyl disiloxane (HMDS)[8] at 4°C in 0.2 mL of water and an internal standard (n-Eicosane, $CH_3(CH_2)_{18}CH_3$). After homogenisation, add 2 mL trimethylchlorosilane (TMCS)[8] at 4°C. The hydrolysis releases hydrochloric acid which reacts with the soil amorphous silicates by exchange of cations and protonation. Leave in contact for 16 h at 4°C. The silicic acid forms trimethylsilyl derivatives.

---

[8] TMCS, Trimethylchlorosilane $(CH_3)_3SiCl$; HMDS, Hexamethyldisiloxane $(CH_3)_3Si–O–Si(CH_3)_3$.

Table 6.4. Approximate balance of soil mineral phases from different extractions

Fe forms	symbol	description	Al, Si, Mn, and others
total iron	Fe(T)	– analysis essential for the establishment of geochemical and mineralogical balances and characteristic ratios – the method of attack by boiling HCl is insufficient for satisfactory quantification. An alkaline fusion should be carried out. Minerals such as pyrites, marcasite, and magnetite are difficult to mineralize. <u>ratios</u> Fe(T)/Clays Fe(CBD)/Fe(T) are indices of weathering of the horizons. Degree of evolution of hydromorphic soils.	
free iron crystaline free iron	Fe(f) = Fe(DCB)	iron extractable by DCB reagent (cf. Sect. 6.2.2): iron mobilizable in pedogenetic processes. This iron is of pedological interest since it is not linked with the structure of the silicate lattices (clays, primary minerals) that presents different hydroxylated and hydrated forms with a varying degree of crystallinity. <u>ratios</u> Fe(f)/Clays, Fe(oxda)/Fe(DCB) indicate the degree of weathering and crystallinity of free oxides and concretions. Fe(DCB)/Fe(T) is the index of deterioration and mobility of iron in a profile. Fe(DCB)–Fe(oxda)	total free Al (exchange acidity, exchangeable Al^{3+}, ECEC, etc.), marker of deterioration (acidolyse, complexolyse) free Mn
iron in silicates	Fe(sil)	Fe(T)–Fe(DCB) the iron in silicates originating from primary minerals and the lattices of phyllitic minerals; a reduction indicates progression in deterioration (cambic horizon)	

not well-crystallized iron oxides	Fe(OA)	Fe(oxda)–Fe(EDTA)	
well-crystallized iron oxides	Fe(OC)	Fe(DCB)–Fe(oxda) the well-crystallized iron oxides are identifiable using instrumental techniques (XRD, DTA, etc.). These oxides are inherited or newly formed. The presence of lepidocrocite and magnetite which are sensitive to the oxalate treatment may affect the results. Magnetite is inherited and is not formed during pedogenesis.	
iron in amorphous forms and organic complexes	Fe(pyro)	immovable complex	Al(tetra)/Al(Pyro) decreases with ageing of the gel (soluble aluminates in alkaline medium)
complexed iron	Fe(tetra)	mobile or mobilizable complex. Method used in sequence with reagents of increasing efficiency: Tetraborate pH 9.7<pyrophosphate pH 9.8 < NaOH pH 12 – Fe(tetra):Fe(pyro) characterizes the degree of evolution of complex Fe-organic matter, if Fe(tetra) decreases and Fe(pyro) increases there is pedogenesis with strong biological deterioration.	
	Fe(oxda)	iron extracted by oxalate in darkness (cf. Sect. 6.2.1 above), if Fe(oxob), Fe(EDTA), Fe(pyro) are weak there is weak deterioration	

Add 2 mL H_2O to hydrolize the excess of TMCS. Centrifuge to separate solid and liquid phases and transfer the organic solution on 1 g cation exchange resin (Amberlite 15). After 5 h of contact and filtration, separate the extract and quantify the trimethylsilyl derivatives by gas chromatography with nitrogen as carrier gas.

6.3.3 Brief overview of the use of the differential methods

There are many publications concerning each method of extraction making it possible to find examples of the use of all the methods, either alone or in comparison with other methods, e.g. Aomine and Jackson (1959), Bruckert (1979), Jeanroy (1983), Baize (1988), Krasnodebska-Ostrega et al. (2001).

The final objective may simply be the elimination of substances (e.g. cementing agents) that obstruct dispersion or instrumental observation (e.g. XRD or IR spectra). In this case, it is not essential to identify the soluble products; on the contrary, to understand the mechanisms of mineralogical and pedogenic evolution both the soluble phases and the solid phases have to be taken into account. Comparisons should be made of results expressed in per cent of oxides; this is a practical way to homogeneously quantify the mineralogical phases but does not correspond to the chemical forms actually present in the soil.

The combination of several methods makes it possible to establish an approximate balance of the different aluminium and iron forms in the soil (Table 6.4). Isolated entities are often not sufficiently specific and results are somewhat empirical, but give a precise enough view of the weathering phenomena. In general, variations in extracted contents of a given element (initially iron, then aluminium, silica, and manganese) are compared on the same sample first by total analysis and then by selective analyses (free forms, amorphous forms, etc.). Next, variations between horizons of a soil profile and finally variations between profiles can be compared. Correlations with size and behaviour of components can be highlighted. Iron is the main element used as a tracer of deterioration. It is insoluble in the ferric oxidation state and a loss generally indicates a pedogenic process of reduction, also indicated by the colour of the soil. The processes of biochemical humification result in the formation of iron–organic complexes.

In andosols, Al and Si, components of allophane and imogolite (Fig. 6.1), are measured first. In these soils, allophanic materials can sometimes be estimated indirectly, for example by the measurement of the cation exchange capacity on a sample from which the organic matter has previously been eliminated; one part of the sample is treated with a sodium carbonate solution for 60 min, and another part with a boiling sodium acetate solution for 15 min, and the result will be a difference in cation exchange capacity that correlates well with allophane content (Aomine and Jackson 1959).

An instrumental technique, differential diffractometry, makes it possible to evaluate the action of the dissolution reagents and the behaviour of soil materials. Several diffraction spectra of a sample are made before and after treatment by selective dissolution. An appropriate computer program can be used to calculate the difference between the spectrum of the treated sample and the spectrum of the untreated sample. Quartz or α-alumina is used as an internal standard to calculate the scale factor for the subtraction of the spectra. This enables the spectrum of the dissolved substances to be reconstructed during selective treatment (Campbell and Schwertmann 1985).

References

Alexsandrova LN (1960) The use or pyrophosphate for isolating free humic substances and their organic-mineral compounds from the soil. *Soviet Soil Sci.*, 190–197

Aomine S and Jackson ML (1959) Allophane determination in ando soils by cation exchange delta value. *Soil Sci. Soc. Am. Proc.*, 23, 210–214

Atkinson RR, Posner AM and Quirk J (1968) Crystal nucleation in Fe (III) solutions and hydroxyde gels. *J. Inorg. Nucl. Chem.*, 30, 2371–2381

Avery BW and Bascomb CL (1982) *Soil Survey Laboratory Methods.*, Soil Survey of England-Wales (Harpenden), 6

Baize D (1988) *Guide Des Analyses Courantes En Pédologie: Choix - Expression - Présentation - Interprétation.*, INRA, 172 pages

Ballantyne AKD, Anderson DW and Stonehouse HB (1980) Problems associated with extracting Fe and Al from saskatchewan soils by pyrophosphate and low speed centrifugation. *Can. J. Soil Sci.*, 60, 141–143

Bentley SP, Clark NJ and Smalley IJ (1980) Mineralogy of a Norwegian postglacial clay and some geotechnical implications. *Can. Miner.*, 18, 535–547

Borggaard OK (1976) Selective extraction of amorphous iron oxide by EDTA from a mixture of amorphous iron oxide, goethite and hematite. *J. Soil Sci.*, 27, 478–486

Bruckert S (1979) Analyse des complexes organo-minéraux des sols. In *Pédologie 2, constituants et propriétés du sol*, Bonneau M. and Souchier B. ed. Mason, IX, 187–209

Cambier P and Sposito G (1991) Adsorption of citric acid by synthetic pseudoboehmite. *Clays Clay Miner.*, 39, 369–374

Campbell AS and Schwertmann U (1985) Evaluation of selective dissolution extractants in soil chemistry and mineralogy by diferential X-Ray diffraction. *Clay Miner.*, 20, 515–519

Colmet-Daage F, Gautheyrou J, Gautheyrou M and De Kimpe C (1973) Etude des sols à allophane dérivés de matériaux volcaniques des Antilles et d'Amérique latine à l'aide de techniques de dissolution différentielle. Ière partie. Etude des produits solubilisés. *Cah. ORSTOM série Pédol.*, XI, 97–120

Cornell RA, Posner AM and Quirck J.P (1976) Kinetics and mechanisms of the acid dissolution of goethite (α-Fe OOH). *J. Inorg. Nucl. Chem.*, 38, 563–567

Cornell RM and Schindler PW (1987) Photochemical dissolution of goethite in acid/oxalate solution. *Clays and clay Miner.*, 35, 347–352

Cornell RM, Posner AM and Quirck J.P (1974) Crystal morphology and the dissolution of goethite. *J. Inorg. Nucl. Chem.*, 36, 1937–1946

Cornell R.M., Posner A.M and Quirk JP (1975) The complete dissolution of goethite. *J. Appl. Chem. Biotechnol.*, 25, 701–706

De Endredy AS (1963) Estimation of free iron oxides in soils and clays by a photolytic method. *Clay Miner. Bull.*, 29, 209–217

Deb BC (1950) The estimation of free iron oxides in soils and clays and their removal. *J. Soil Sci.*, 1, 212–220

Duchaufour Ph and Souchier B (1966) Note sur une méthode d'extraction combinée de l'Aluminium et du fer libres dans les sols. *Sci. du Sol*, 1, 17–29

Farmer VC and Fraser AR (1978) Synthetic imogolite, a tubular hydroxy-aluminium silicate. In *International Clay Conference.*, Elsevier, Amsterdam, 547–553

Farmer VC, Fraser AR and Tait JM (1979) Characterization of the chemical structures of natural and synthetic aluminosilicate gels and soils by infrared spectroscopy. *Geochim. Cosmochim. Acta*, 43, 1417–1420

Follett EAC, McHardy WJ, Mitchell BD and Smith BFL (1965) Chemical dissolution techniques in the study of soil clays. *Clay Miner.*, 6, 23–43

Franzmeier DP, Hajek BF and Simonson C.H (1965) Use of amorphous material to identifiy spodic horizons. *Soil Sci. Soc. Am.Proc.*, 29, 737–743

Hashimoto I and Jackson ML (1960) Rapid dissolution of allophane and kaolinite and halloysite after dehydratation. *Clays clay Miner.*, 7, 102–113

Henry S (1958) Synthèse de quelques oxydes de fer au laboratoire. *C.R. du XXXI Congrès intern. de Chimie Industrielle (Liège).*, Mercurius, 1–3

Hetier JM and Jeanroy E (1973) Solubilisation différentielle du fer, de la silice et de l'alumine par le réactif oxalate-dithionite et la soude diluée. *Pédologie*, 23, 85–99

Holmgren GGS (1967) A rapid citrate-dithionite extractable procedure. *Soil Sci. Soc. Am. Proc.*, 31, 210–211

Hsu PH (1977) Aluminium hydroxydes and oxyhydroxyde. In *Minerals in Soil Environments*, Dixon JB Weed SB and ed., *Soil Sci. Sc. Am.*, 99–143

Hsu PH (1984) Aluminium hydroxides and oxyhydroxides in soils: recent developents. *Annu. Meeting and Am. Soc. Agron*

Jeanroy E and Guillet B (1981) The occurence of suspended ferruginous particles in pyrophosphate extracts of some soil horizons. *Geoderma*, 26, 95–105

Jeanroy E (1983) *Diagnostic des formes du fer dans les pédogénèses tempérées. Evaluation par les réactifs chimiques d'extraction et apports de la spectrométrie Mossbauer. (études des formes organiques du fer amorphe dans les sols).*,Thèse Doctorat, Nancy, 109–129

Kampf N and Schwertmann U (1982) The 5M-NaOH concentration treatment for iron oxides in soils. *Clays clay Miner.*, 30, 401–408

Klamt E (1985) Reports of meetings. Iron in soil and clay minerals. Bad Windesheim, West germany, July 1–13 1985. *Bull. Soc. Int. Sci. du Sol*, 2, 9

Krasnodebska-Ostrega B, Emons H and Golimowski J (2001) Selective leaching of elements associated with Mn-Fe oxides in forest soil, and comparison of two sequential extraction methods. *Fresenius J. Anal. Chem.*, 371, 385–390

Kwong KF and Huang PM (1979) The relative influence of low-molecular-weight complexing organic acids on the hydrolysis and precipitation of Aluminium. *Soil Sci.*, 128, 337–342

Lewis DG and Schwertmann U (1979) The influence of Al on iron oxides. Part III - Preparation of Al goethites in M KOH. *Clay Miner.*, 14, 115–126

Lewis DG and Schwertmann U (1979) The influence of Al on the formation of iron oxides. Part IV: The influence of [Al], [OH] and temperature. *Clays clay Miner.*, 27, 195–200

Loveland PJ and Bullock P (1976) Chemical and mineralogical properties of brown podzolic soils in comparison with soils of other groups. *J. Soil Sci.*, 27, 523–540

Loveland PJ and Digby P (1984) The extraction of Fe and Al by 0,1 M pyrophosphate solutions: a comparison of some techniques. *J. Soil Sci.,* 35, 243–250

Mc Keague JA and Day JH (1966) Dithionite and oxalate-extractable Fe and Ag as aids in differentiating various classes of soils. *Canad. J. Soil Sci.*, 46, 13–22

Mc Keague JA (1967) An evaluation of 0,1 M pyrophosphate and pyrophosphate-dithionite in comparison with oxalate as extractants of the accumulation products in podzols and some other soils. *Can. J. Soil Sci.*, 47, 95–99

Neaman A, Mouélé F, Trolard F, Bourrié G (2004a) Improved methods for selective dissolution of Mn oxides : applications for studying trace element associations. *Appl. Geochem.*, 19, 973–979

Neaman A, Waller B, Mouélé F, Trolard F, Bourrié G (2004b) Improved methods for selective dissolution of manganese oxides from soils and rocks. *Eur. J. Soil Sci.*, 55, 47–54

Norrish K and Taylor RM (1961) The isomorphous replacement of iron by aluminium in soil goethites. *J. Soil Sci.*, 12, 294–306

Petersen L (1976) *Podzols and podzolization.*, Thesis Copenhagen (Danmark)

Pollard RJ, Cardile CM, Lewis DG and Brown LJ (1992) Characterization of FeOOH polymorphs and ferrihydrite using low-temperature applied-field, Mösshauer spectroscopy. *Clay Miner.*, 27, 57–71

Quantin P et Lamouroux M (1974) Adaptation de la méthode cinétique de Ségalen à la détermination des constituants minéraux de sols variés. *Cah. ORSTOM, sér. Pédol.*, XII, 1, 13–46

Quigley RM, Haynes JE, Bohdanowicz A and Gwyn QHJ (1985) *Geology, geotechnique, mineralogy and geochemistry of Leda clay from deep Boreholes*, Hawkesbury Area. Ontario Geol. Surv., study 29, 128 pages

Ryan JN and Gschwend PM (1991) Extraction of iron oxides from sediments using reductive dissolution by titanium (III). *Clays and clay Miner.*, 39, 509–518

Schuppli PA, Ross GJ and McKeague JA (1983) The effective removal of suspended materials from pyrophosphate extracts of soil from tropical and temporate regions. *Soil Sci. Soc. Am. J.*, 47, 1026–1032

Schwertmann U (1964) Differenzierung der Eisenoxide des Bodens durch photochemische extraktion mit saurer Ammoniumoxalate-losung. *Z. Pflanzenernähr. Dueng. Bodenk.*, 105, 194–202

Schwertmann U (1991) Solubility and dissolution of iron oxides. *Plant and Soil*, 130, 1–25

Ségalen P (1968) Note sur une méthode de détermination des produits amorphes dans certains sols à hydroxydes tropicaux. *Cahiers ORSTOM Série Pédol.*, 6, 106–126

Shuman LM (1982) Separating soil iron and manganese oxyde fractions for microelement analysis. *Soil Sci. Soc. Amer. J.*, 46, 1099–1102

Stol RJ, Van Helden AD and De Bruyn PL (1976) Hydrolysis-precipitation studies of aluminium solution. II - A kinetic study and a model. *J. Colloïd Interface Sci.*, 57, 115–131

Stumm W (1985) The effects of complex-forming ligands on the dissolution of oxides and alumino silicates. *In The chemistry of weathering.*, Reideil D Drever J ed., 55–74

Tamm O (1922) Eine methode zur Bestimmungder anorqanischen komporentem des Gelkomplexes im Boden. *Meddal. Statens sSkogförsöksanst*, 19, 385–404

Tamm O (1931) *Monthly letter.*, Imperial bureau of soil science, 1 October

Tamm O (1934a) *Monthly letter.*, Imperial bureau of Soil Science, 34, August

Tamm O (1934b) Über die oxalat-methode in der chemischen Boden analyse. *Medd. Skogförsökamsanst*, 27 , 1–20

Tokashiki Y, Dixon JB and Golden DC (1986) Manganese oxide analysis in soils by combined X-Ray diffraction and selective dissolution methods. *Soil Sci. Soc. Amer. J.*, 50, 1079–1084

Torrance JK, Hedges SW and Bowen LH (1986) Mössbauer spectroscopic study of the iron mineralogy of post-glacial marine clays. *Clays clay Miner.*, 34, 314–322

Yong R, Sethi AJ and La Rochelle P (1979) Significance of amorphous material relative to sensivity in some champlain clays. *Canad. Geotechn. J.*, 16, 511–520

Thermal Analysis

7.1 Introduction

7.1.1 Definition

Many different analyses of phase transformations involve the use of temperature. This is true in the case of simple gravimetric measurements after drying at a given temperature (cf. Chap. 1), or after chemical precipitation and drying to constant weight. The generic term "thermal analysis" generally only applies to methods carried out according to a dynamically controlled thermal programme making it possible to reveal and quantify different physicochemical transitions. The most common methods used in soil analysis record transformations by means of the temperature either of mass, energy, or the mechanical properties of the samples (Fig. 7.1).

Measurements of Mass Variations
The abbreviations TGA or TG stand for thermogravimetric analysis and DTG stands for differential thermogravimetry. Losses occur in the form of gases that are simple to detect by (evolved gas detection EGD) and to analyze by (evolved gas analysis EGA).

Measurements of Variations in Energy
These measurements mainly use DTA, differential thermal analysis and DSC, differential scanning calorimetry. They enable quantification of exothermic or endothermic energy changes at each temperature without inevitably modifying weight.

Measurements of Dimensional or Physical Variations

These include TMA, thermo mechanical analysis (dilatometry) and DMA, dynamic mechanical analysis (viscoelasticity). Though these techniques are used especially in the field of ceramics and plastics, they are also suitable for the study of physical soil properties and specifically for the shrinkage and swelling linked to aggregation and water storage properties (Braudeau 1987, 1988; Braudeau et al. 1999, 2004).

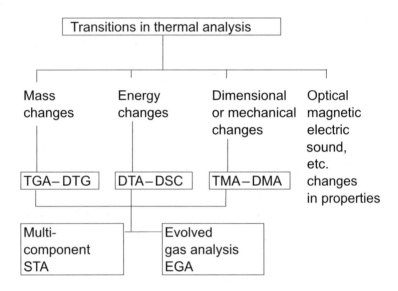

Fig. 7.1. Table summarizing the principal methods of thermal analysis: TGA, thermogravimetric analysis; DTG, differential thermogravimetry; DTA, differential thermal analysis; DSC, differential scanning calorimetry; TMA, thermomechanical analysis; DMA, dynamic mechanical analysis; STA, simultaneous thermal analysis; EGA, evolved gas analysis. The International Confederation for Thermal Analysis (ICTA) uses the term "derivation" for data resulting from mathematical transformations (derivative calculations on initially measured data) and "differential" for experimental measurements of changes in the delay step concerned

Variations in properties (optical, magnetic, electric, or sound) also occur and can be measured analytically (for example, thermo-luminescence is widely used for dating), the loss of magnetic property is represented by the point of Curie, etc.

The equipment used for these analyses has reached a high degree of sophistication thanks to its industrial use in the fields of ceramics, glass, cement, plaster, explosives, radioisotopes, pharmaceutics, and polymers where it is widely used for research and quality control. The simplest equipment is not very expensive, but top-of-the-range apparatuses (multiparametric, high temperature, high pressure, etc.) with their associated peripherals and data processing software, can be very costly.

7.1.2 Interest

Used in combination with XRD (cf. Chap. 4), IR (cf. Chap. 5) and other chemical analyses, thermal analysis techniques are invaluable tools in mineralogy, geology, pedology, soil chemistry, and physics. They allow the qualitative identification and quantitative analysis of clays (Table 7.1) and many minerals, and also the identification of the different forms of water in soils, oxidation of all forms of organic matter and inorganic materials, phase transitions, etc.

The sensitivity of the DTA–DSC methods makes it possible to detect the presence of minerals at the limit of detection of XRD (e.g. goethite, gibbsite at concentration less than 0.25%, substances with short distance atomic arrangement) in clays and soils.

All the techniques used enable the balance of the mineral transformations to be established as a function of different geochemical processes both in a weathering profile and in a topographic sequence.

Reasonably precise quantitative analysis is possible of hydroxides and oxyhydroxides of iron and aluminium, as well as of clays and particularly of 1:1 kaolinite and halloysite. Continental sediments containing organic complexes can be studied by controlled oxidizing or non-oxidizing pyrolysis, and the evolved gases are analyzed by Fourier transform infrared spectrometry (FTIR). DSC can quantify enthalpy changes during dehydration, dehydroxylation and other forms of structural decomposition in a thermal field extending from -150 to $+725°C$. The analysis of evolved gases by FTIR or mass spectrometry during temperature scanning makes it possible to calculate the exact chemical transformations undergone by the sample.

Thermal analysis is particularly useful for the study of soil genesis, the study of soils rich in *para*-crystalline compounds (e.g. andosols, histosols) and characterization of the evolution of compounds with short-distance atomic arrangement that cannot be directly analyzed by XRD.

In certain cases it is possible to use the thermogravimetric method in a range of temperatures from ambient to 200°C to indirectly measure the specific surfaces of clays (internal and external surfaces) by impregnation of the sample with a monomolecular layer of an organic material (e.g. the EGME method) or of a gas (e.g. the BET method).

Table 7.1. Transformation of clays up to 1,200 °C (adsorbed water and bound water)

K	°C						
1,373	1,100-	mullite ↑		γAl_2O_3 leucite corundum cristobalite ↑			eustatite....
		metakaolin end of dehydroxylation					
1,273	1,000-						
1,073	800-	water bound to the crystalline lattice	water bound to the crystalline lattice	bound water	bound water	water bound to the crystalline lattice	bound water
973	700-	≈ 16.0%	≈ 16.0%	≈ 5.3%	≈ 4.7%	≈ 5.1% (700°C) ≈ 5.0% (700°C)	≈ 14.8% (700°C)
873	600-					≈ 4.8% water in cavities ≈ 3.1%	≈ 4.8% water in cavities ≈ 4.7%
673	400-	(350°C) adsorbed water	(350°C) adsorbed water	(350°C) adsorbed water	370°C adsorbed water	adsorbed water in cavities	adsorbed water

Temperature	kaolinite	halloysite 4H₂O	pyrophyllite	muscovite (Illites)	montmorillonite Ca²⁺	montmorillonite Na⁺	Ca²⁺	Na⁺	clinochlore
573 — 300				in cavities ≈ 0.5% (250°C)	≈ 3.4% (250°C)		(250°C)		(250°C) a
473 — 200	adsorbed water < 1.0% (250°C)	adsorbed water ≈ 13.2%	adsorbed water ≈ 0.5–1.5%	adsorbed water ≈ 1.0%	adsorbed interlayer water ≈ 20.1%	adsorbed interlayer water ≈ 14.0% (150°C)	adsorbed interlayer water ≈ 20.0%	water ‾ < 0.5% (150°C)	
373 — 100							adsorbed water ≈ 20.0%	adsorbed water ≈ 10.1%	

1:1 CLAYS		2:1 CLAYS				VERMICULITES	2:1:1 CLAYS
		micas		SMECTITES			
kaolinite	halloysite	pyrophyllite	muscovite (Illites)	montmorillonite Ca²⁺	montmorillonite Na⁺	Ca²⁺ Na⁺	clinochlore

Instrumental thermal dilatometric methods developed by ceramists can be used instead of manual measurements of contraction–dilation (coefficient of linear extension).

7.2 Classical Methods

7.2.1 Thermogravimetric Analysis

Principle

Variations in the mass of the sample (losses or increases) are recorded as a function of temperature or time. For soil studies, a temperature range between ambient temperature and 1,100 or 1,200°C is generally satisfactory, but it may be necessary to study reactions up to temperatures of more than 2,000°C, in particular to determine melting points.

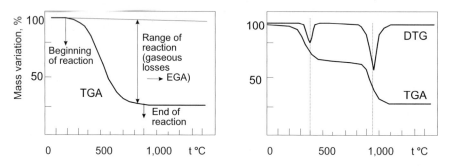

Fig. 7.2. Principle of thermogravimetric analysis $m = f(t)$ (*on the left*) and comparison with differential thermogravimetry $dm/dt = f(t)$ (*on the right*)

In dynamic analysis, the mass of the sample (m) is heated at a constant rate according to a linear programme based on temperature or time (Fig. 7.2). The extent of the reaction interval, the shape of the curve and the nature of the gases released provide information on the nature of the soil sample and its thermal stability.

In TGA by derivation, the first derivative of the variations of mass is recorded as a function of time or of temperature. Two "static" methods can also be used in certain cases, but take a very long time to implement:

– The isothermal method where the sample is subjected to a constant temperature and the sample weight is recorded over time until their equilibrium value is reached;

– The isobar method where the sample is maintained at a constant pressure and the weight recorded as a function of temperature; the pressure can exceed 500 atm. for certain materials.

Clay minerals contain molecules of water and hydroxides bound to the crystal lattice at different energies. During the rise in temperature, this water is gradually moved and eliminated in the form of gas.

In the soil, interstitial water of hydration or adsorption that is not bound is generally released first by dehydration. Dehydration does not cause the destruction of the lattice but can cause a modification in the arrangement of the continuous poly- or monomolecular layers (internal and external surfaces of 2:1 clays and interlayer exchangeable ions) along with a contraction of the interlayer space. This phenomenon is reversible. Water in cavities at the base of the tetrahedrons will be more vigorously bound. On the other hand, the phenomenon may be irreversible in soils with allophane, and rehydration will not be able to reach more than around 10% of the initial moisture content. This is also true of hydrated halloysite, $4H_2O$, which gives metahalloysite, $2H_2O$.

The hydroxyl OH^- ions bound to oxygen atoms at the top of the tetrahedral or octahedral units, or present in the external continuous layers of 1:1 clays, or in the internal or external layers of 2:1 clays (or hydrated 1:1 halloysite) are then moved. Their elimination is irreversible and is accompanied by the destruction of the structure (dehydroxylation). The appearance of new forms at a higher temperature can then be recorded, for example kaolinite giving metakaolinite then mullite. But certain transformations that occur without weight loss are not detectable by TGA. In this case the DTA or DSC spectra have to be recorded.

It should be noted that the transition between free H_2O and OH^- of hydroxyls is not always clear as the water bound to the lattice can start to leave before the interstitial water is completely eliminated. In this case thermal analysis at controlled speed of transformation can be used (Rouquerol 1970, 1989; Rouquerol et al. 1985, 1988)[1].

---

[1] The method of analysis at controlled speed of transformation makes it possible to measure the initial state of water with more precision. In conventional analysis, the programme of temperature increase varies in a linear way over time. With controlled speed of transformation, the pressure caused by the departure of the gas determines the programme for the increase in temperature by means of a captor. Coupling with a quadripolar mass spectrometer enables analysis of evolved gas. When the adsorbed water with weak activation energy is desorbed, the rise in temperature stops until the initial pressure is restored to the pre-determined point. Then heating continues. This makes it easier to study

Implementation

Reagents

– Reagents described in Chaps. 2 and 3 for destruction of organic matter or carbonates, homoionic saturation, etc.
– Clays purified for standardization (samples for the reference system of the laboratory and/or international standards).
– Saturated solution of magnesium nitrate ($Mg(NO_3)_2$, $6H_2O$, 1,250 g L^{-1} at 20°C) (to equilibrate the moisture of clays – 56% of relative moisture at 20°C).
– Drying agents of varying degrees of effectiveness:
  (a) Magnesium perchlorate (dehydrite), $Mg(ClO_4)_2$, molar weight *mw*: 223.23;
  (b) Aluminium oxide Al_2O_3, *mw*: 101.94;
  (c) Silicon dioxide (Silicagel), SiO_2, *mw*: 60.08;
  (d) Anhydrous calcium chloride, $CaCl_2$, *mw*; 110.99;
  (e) Anhydrous calcium sulphate (anhydrite/drierite), $CaSO_4$, *mw*: 136.04;
  (f) Phosphorus pentoxide (phosphoric anhydride), P_2O_5, *mw*: 141.96.

Equipment

– Platinum micro-crucibles;
– Desiccator with saturated solution of magnesium nitrate;
– Desiccators with different drying agents;
– Thermal balance (Fig. 7.3).
    Briefly, a thermal balance is composed of a furnace, a balance and different devices for regulation and data acquisition. Weighing is carried out continuously throughout the thermal cycle. There are two types of equipment:
    – Balances placed above the mobile furnace;
    – Balances placed below the mobile furnace.

In the first, the sample nacelle is suspended on a wire; in the second, a vertical rod equipped with a support holds the sample. Each system has certain disadvantages that must be minimized to optimize measurements.

The balance must allow all losses or increases in mass to be recorded as a function of the temperature and time under all experimental

---

the mechanisms of hydration and possibly the short- or long-distance atomic structure.

conditions. The temperature of the furnace can reach 2,400°C and radiative and magnetic phenomena may occur. The quality of measurements must be the same as with any other analytical microbalance (Pansu et al. 2001). The capacity can vary considerably depending on the use envisaged. For soils, a choice has to be made between (a) relatively big samples, i.e. 100 mg to 1 g with a sensitivity of 10^{-5}–10^{-6} g and (b) micro-samples, i.e. from 1 to 50 mg (e.g. piezo-electric balances with a sensitivity of 10^{-8}–10^{-12} g).

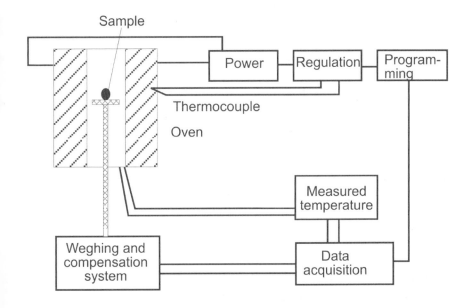

Fig. 7.3. Example of a system for thermogravimetric analysis

Different types of balances are available: deflection balances (e.g. with torsion, beam balance, cantilever, with a beryllium bronze spring) but electronic systems without a beam are rarely used because of the disturbances that can be caused by radiative phenomena.

The furnace is designed as a function of the temperature. It can be the high frequency induction type or more generally the resistance type (Table 7.2). Kanthal resistances enable measurements at 1,200°C, rhodium resistances at 1,800°C and tungsten resistances at 2,500°C.

The furnace is an assembly of metal and ceramic components (high density alumina) which allow resistances to be insulated to ensure homogeneous temperatures in the test zone, and also to allow sealing in the case of controlled atmosphere. The furnace has a sophisticated regulation system. The speed of heating must result in a uniform temperature in the test zone and be monitored by thermocouples appropriate for the work temperature (Table 7.3). The programming of the heating cycle must be highly reproducible. The sample must be located in a precise spot in the furnace. The data acquisition system must enable variations in weight and temperature to be recorded simultaneously, and also to carry out a certain number of mathematical operations (e.g. first derivative, surface of the peaks), to control the temperature programme, and finally to store and print the data.

Table 7.2. Type of resistances – thermal ranges

material	temperature used (°C)	melting point (°C)	material	temperature used (°C)	melting point (°C)
constantan	750	1,200	rhodium (Rh)	1,800	
nichrome	1,000	1,500	molybdenum[a]	2,200	2,500
chromel – alumel	1,100		tantale	–	2,850
kanthal	1,350		tungsten[b]	2,800	3,400
platinum (Pt)	1,400	1,755			
Pt–Rh 10%	1,500				
Pt–Rh 13%	1,700		[a] Hydrogen atmosphere		
super kanthal	1,600		[b] Mechanical resistance up to 1,650°C		

Procedure

The methods have to be standardised if the data obtained in different series is to be compared. The technical characteristics of the thermal balance determine certain obligatory parameters. The nature of the materials to be studied determines the selection of other diagnostic parameters. The samples must be crushed without heating as this could disturb subsequent thermal analysis.

Table 7.3. Types of thermocouples at different temperatures

material	temperature (°C)	material	temp. (°C)
copper–constantan[a]	400 (standard)	tungsten – rhenium	2,200
iron–constantan	800 (standard)	tungsten – 20% rhenium tungsten	2,400
chromel–constantan	1,000 (standard)	tantalum carbide – graphite[b]	3,000
chromel – alumel	1,000 (standard)	[a] Alloy 55% copper + 45% nickel	
nickel chromium – nickel	1,370	[b] Argon atmosphere	
platinum–platinum rhodium (10% or 13% Rh)[c]	1,750	[c] The thermopiles allow the output signal to be increased without amplification	

Initially rough samples (from which organic matter has been eliminated) are reduced by moderate wet crushing. The sample must have a regular particle size and, after air drying, pass through a 0.1 mm sieve. Samples of clays that have been purified and saturated using the methods described in Chap. 3 can also be used. It should be noted that too fine dry grinding can distort the results.[2]

Adjust the moisture of the sample by placing it in a desiccator containing saturated magnesium nitrate for 48 h (relative moisture should be 56% at 20°C at normal pressure). This treatment homogenizes the hydration layers of any interlayer cations that may be present.

Weigh a given weight of sample (5–20 mg) suitable for the range and sensitivity of the balance. Pack the sample in a platinum crucible as

---

[2]Dry grinding can modify the nature of the basal faces and consequently their physical properties. For example, the exchange capacity and some thermal properties of kaolinite can be changed (collapse of the peaks) by too fine grinding which can result in fractures perpendicular to the basal faces and subsequent breakdown of layers.

regularly as possible to limit differences in thermal diffusity. Place the sample in the thermal balance. Adjust the position of the sample to that of the measurement thermocouple in the furnace.

Programme the instrumental variables with the management software, i.e. the linear speed of heating (e.g. $10°C$ min^{-1}), atmosphere of the furnace, final temperature, etc.

Observations

For clay the best quantitative measurements are obtained on homoionically saturated samples (Na^+, K^+, Ca^{2+} or Mg^{2+}), after elimination of organic matter, soluble salts, ferrous iron, etc. Homoionic saturation of clay enables:
– with Na^+ ions, improved differentiation between adsorbed water and water bound to the lattice;
– with Mg^{2+} ions improved separation of 2:1 clays from 1:1 clays on the basis of adsorbed water.

The presence of organic matter (OM) modifies weight loss of mineral origin. The loss of $H_2O + CO_2$ of the OM must be measured. An inert atmosphere can be used to mitigate this phenomenon if it is not too serious, or losses can be estimated by analyzing emitted gas (e.g. by coupled EGA-FTIR).

Ferrous iron will oxidize during heating and increase in weight according to the following equations:

$$Fe^{2+} \rightarrow Fe^{3+} + e^-$$

or $\quad$ $$Fe(OH)_2 \rightarrow FeO + H_2O\uparrow$$

$$2\,FeO + O \rightarrow Fe_2O_3$$

As oxidation of ferrous iron does not result in easily measurable variations in mass, it may be preferable to eliminate it. The same is true for manganese and cobalt. An inert atmosphere can also be used. The elimination of soluble salts avoids secondary recombination.

The choice of the nature of the crucible and its geometry can modify the results. The crucible should not react with the sample, with the selected atmosphere or the evolved gas. Certain metals have a catalytic action. Crucibles made of alumina are relatively porous, silver can be used for medium temperatures, platinum can be used for a temperature of $1,500°C$. The walls of the crucibles must be as thin as possible (approximately 0.5 mm) to minimize variations in temperature. In the same way, the sample layer should be as thin as possible to ensure that the temperature in the centre is the same as at the edges. As certain minerals are expansible or likely to generate projections, deeper crucibles are sometimes necessary or semi-permeable lids have to be used which, however, can modify the gas flow of the losses.

The speed of the increase in temperature influences the decomposition of the sample. For a given temperature interval, slow decomposition is more realistic, than too rapid decomposition which can cause displacement of the characteristic temperatures, a steeper decomposition slope, etc. For exemple, Kotra et al. (1982) showed that a siderite ($FeCO_3$) heated at 1°C min^{-1} had a range of decomposition positioned between 400 and 500°C. At a speed of 20°C min^{-1} this range moved to between 480 and 610°C. However, a micro sample displays fewer variations than a sample of greater mass. Low speed also enables detection of compounds that only display weak inflection at higher speeds.

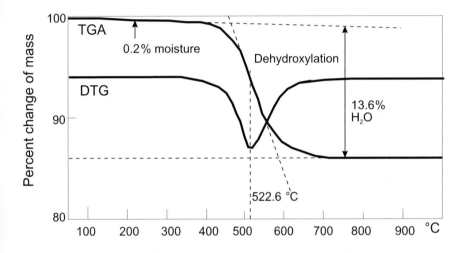

Fig. 7.4. Example of TGA and DTG curves for kaolinite (Mâcon, France). Mass of sample: 25 mg; speed of heating: 10°C min^{-1}; atmosphere: nitrogen 30 mL min^{-1}; and platinum crucible.

The atmosphere of the furnace can greatly influence the results with respect to the nature of the decomposition products and types of reactions. Vacuum, inert or reactive atmosphere induce very different thermal spectra. It may be useful to analyze evolved gases.

Differential thermogravimetric analysis (DTG)

In this type of analysis, peaks are obtained whose surface is directly proportional to changes in the mass of the sample (Figs. 7.2 and 7.4), which facilitates quantitative analysis. When the variations in weight are null one obtains a return to the base line for which $dm/dt = 0$. The curves give an inflection point in the zone where the variation in mass reaches its maximum. The separation of overlapping phenomena is facilitated.

Discussion

The water contents of a clay can be measured on a sample in equilibrium with an atmosphere at approximately 56% relative moisture (obtained by a mixture of nitrate of magnesium saturated in water). In this way an initial point of reference can be obtained that takes into account complex assemblies of minerals and organominerals, and allows better reproducibility.

It is possible to measure water that depends on the exchangeable cations. The water content can be very high for 2:1 clays of the montmorillonite type[3] and weak for 1:1 clays of the kaolinite type. However, it is not possible to measure the energy of activation necessary to release water with TGA or DTG. For this purpose DTA must be used giving the quantity of calories that generates the endothermic peak, the quantity of released water being identified by TGA under the same conditions. Existing equipment allows TGA–DTG and DTA to be used simultaneously in the same treatment cycle up to temperatures of 1,750°C or more on the same micro sample.

Direct quantification is possible if only one reaction occurs at a given temperature. By insulating the components, quantification becomes possible for organic matter in an oxidizing medium, for carbonates (e.g. dolomite, aragonite, calcite, siderite), sulphides (e.g. pyrites) with very low contents. Here combining quantification with analysis of evolved gas is essential.

---

[3] The layers of 2:1 clays adsorb at least two layers of water molecules. They are disorientated with respect to one another with a tendency to form association of layers (turbostratic assemblies with 5 or 6 layers).

7.2.2 Differential Thermal Analysis and Differential Scanning Calorimetry

Principle of DTA

In DTA, the difference in temperature between a soil or clay sample and an inert reference material is recorded as a function of time or temperature with the two substances controlled by the same temperature control programme, at constant linear speed:

$$\Delta T = T_{sample} - T_{reference}.$$

This kind of analysis enables identification of the relations of proportionality that exist between the surface of a peak and the released or absorbed heat during the course of the heating programme. This heat is proportional to the enthalpy of reaction and thus can be used for thermodynamic quantification if the mass of the sample is taken into account. However, in DTA, the simple direct conversion of the peaks into unit of energy is not possible starting only from ΔT as a function of time. Indeed, ΔT depends on the variation in enthalpy, the calorific capacity and the total thermal resistance of the heat flow (R) at a given time. R depends on the nature and the mass of the sample, its preparation (compression, etc.), and the thermal surface of contact between the crucible and the support. These variables are temperature dependent and consequently have to be controlled.

For soils, most analysis is carried out between ambient temperature and 1,200°C. When a reaction occurs during an increase in temperature, a difference in temperature is observed between the sample and the reference (Fig. 7.5):

– If the temperature is lower than that of the inert reference material, an endothermic peak appears (ΔT is negative), this is the case in reactions of dehydration, dehydroxylation, fusion, evaporation, sublimation, etc.

– If, on the contrary, the temperature of the sample exceeds that of the reference, an exothermic peak appears (ΔT is positive), this is the case for oxidation phenomena (combustion of OM, oxidation of sulphides, oxidation of ferrous iron, certain nucleations or decomposition with neoformation.

The recorded differences in temperature are related to the change in enthalpy, but this does not exclude the possibility of two exothermic and endothermic reactions occurring simultaneously. When this is the case, the absence or depression of the DTA peak does not imply the absence of a reaction.

Contrary to TGA, DTA can produce peaks even if there is no loss or increase in weight, e.g. in reversible second-order transformations: variation in specific heat, magnetic susceptibility, Curie point or α/β allotropic transformation of quartz. TGA and DTA are complementary techniques.

The shape, size and temperature of the peaks are influenced by instrumental factors such as the speed of heating, the nature of the sample support and of the thermocouples.

Small samples give a better resolution of the peaks and allow faster heating. Slower speed can increase sensitivity, but to the detriment of temperature, precision, and resolution. A dynamic atmosphere is preferable to a self-generated static atmosphere. This allows continuous evacuation of evolved gas, thus reducing the risks of artefact reactions at higher temperatures. These gases can then be analyzed enabling identification of the molecular structure of the compounds that caused the gaseous emission.

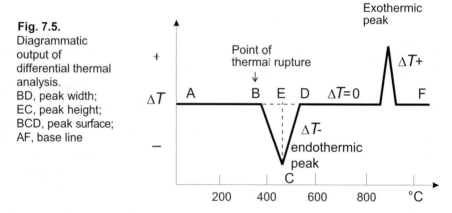

Fig. 7.5.
Diagrammatic output of differential thermal analysis.
BD, peak width;
EC, peak height;
BCD, peak surface;
AF, base line

The range of different types of equipment sold by different manufacturers means complex mathematical demonstrations are not required to validate the different parameters taken into account, see for example Duval (1963), Watson et al. (1964), Garrels and Christ (1965), Allen (1966), Gray (1968), Mackenzie (1970), Brennan (1971), Miller et al. (1973), and McNaughton and Mortimer (1975).

Principle of Differential Scanning Calorimetry

Other techniques to measure energy are grouped under the name of DSC. DSC techniques are often badly defined because patents use the same term for different concepts.

The term DSC applies to apparatuses able to measure specific heat, or the heat capacity of a sample, and to quantify the energy of the reactions during the heat treatment. In DSC with power compensation, the sample and reference are continuously maintained at the same temperature by individual resistances. The parameter that is recorded is the quantity of power consumed by the compensation resistances, that is to say $d(\Delta Q)/dt$ or dH/dt in millicalories per second as a function of the temperature (controlled linear increase).

When a reaction occurs in the sample, thermal energy is added or removed. The quantity of energy added or removed is equivalent to the quantity emitted or absorbed by a given transition. The recording of this balance of energy is a calorimetric measurement of enthalpy.

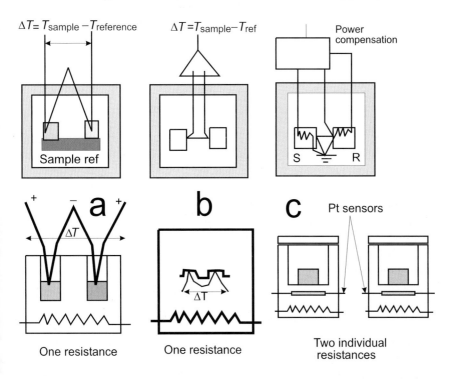

Fig. 7.6. Thermal systems using measurements of energy: a, classical DTA; b, Boersma DTA with heat flow or conventional indirect DSC; and c, DSC with compensation of power

In the Boersma technique, also known as DSC or DTA with heat flow, $\Delta T = T_{sample} - T_{reference}$ are measured like in DTA. The sensors are placed below the crucibles to reduce the effects of variations in the thermal resistance of the sample. This way of assembling the components is similar to other DSC heat flow equipment that records $d\Delta q/dt$ type data or, with thermopiles, $dQ_{sample}/dt - dQ_{reference}/dt = d(\Delta Q)/dt$ enabling the quantitative measurement of enthalpy.

In modulated DSC, the sample is subjected to a linear increase in heating (for example $10°C$ min^{-1}) on which a sinusoidal modulation of temperature (of 30 s and amplitude of $1°C$) is superimposed resulting in a cyclic heating profile. There is thus a speed of constant subjacent heating and instantaneous measurements at sinusoidal speed. The deconvolution of the flow profile resulting from the heating profile provides the total heat flow as in conventional DSC, but also separates flow into two components: reversible specific heat and non-reversible kinetic heat. This technique enables improvement of resolution and sensitivity, because low speed favours good resolution and high heating speed favours good sensitivity.

The functioning temperature of the DSC apparatuses with power compensation is generally limited to $750°C$, which is too low to study certain reactions in the soil. Classical DSC makes it possible to reach temperatures similar to those of DTA or TGA.

Materials

These must be reference products and be ground to 0.1 mm in an agate mortar.
– Products of known melting points to calibrate temperature (Table 7.4).
– Inert reference: alumina (Al_2O_3) calcined to $1,200°C$, and ground to 0.1 mm in an agate mortar does not show any effect of heating except possibly a few irregularities in the base line.
– Purified clays belonging to the laboratory reference set homoionically saturated by Mg^{2+}, Ca^{2+}, or Na^{+}. Clay samples from industrially exploited sedimentary deposits should be distinguished from those coming from soils.
– Pure minerals from the laboratory reference set and industrial reference products for analysis.
– 1,250 g ($Mg(NO_3)_2,6H_2O$) L^{-1} of magnesium nitrate saturated aqueous solution at $20°C$.

Equipment

– DTA micro crucibles made of platinum (or possibly alumina, quartz, tungsten, zirconium oxide, nickel, or aluminium).
– Desiccator with $Mg(NO_3)_2$, $6H_2O$ saturated solution.
– Desiccator with desiccating agents.

– Analytical balance (10^{-6}–10^{-8} g) with a weighing range of 1–100 mg for quantitative analysis.
– Apparatuses: industrial DTA–DSC instruments are designed and built according to different concepts, and this can make comparison of data difficult. It is advisable to use a laboratory reference set to ensure the precision and relevance of the results. The equipment generally comprises different components (Figs. 7.6 and 7.7):

Table 7.4. Calibration products for thermal analysis

product	formula		melting point (°C)	mw (g mol^{-1})
naphthalene	$C_{10}H_8$		80.2	128.16
phenanthrene	$C_{14}H_{10}$		99.3	178.22
benzoic acid	$C_7H_6O_2$	— COOH	122.3 (sublimation)	122.12
barium chloride	$BaCl_2,2H_2O$		130.0 (–2 H_2O)	244.31
[a]calcium sulphate	$CaSO_4,2H_2O$		180.0 (–2 H_2O)	172.18
tin	Sn		231.97	118.70
cadmium carbonate	$CdCO_3$		350.00	172.42
zinc	Zn		419.4 (ignition at air contact)	65.38
lithium bromide	$LiBr,H_2O$ (deliquescent)		553	104.87
quartz	SiO_2		573	60.06
aluminium	Al		660.2	26.98
[a]calcium carbonate (468 cal g^{-1})	$CaCO_3$		850 (CO_2 + CaO)	100.09
silver	Ag		960.8	107.88

[a] Standard material used to measure heat of reaction.

– A furnace equipped with a device to programme temperature, to control atmosphere and to accelerate cooling (between 20 and 40 min before a new cycle starts);
– A support for the sample equipped with differential temperature detectors;
– A management station for analytical programmes and recording of measurements.

Temperatures exceeding 2,000°C are required for ceramics. For soils, a temperature of 1,200°C is generally sufficient but 1,600°C may be needed.

The position of the sample support and the inert reference can vary considerably (Fig. 7.7). The thermocouples can be placed in or outside the crucibles (or to even welded into a cavity in the crucible). Metal crucibles give smaller peaks than ceramics with a faster heat transfer thus limiting the risks of deformation of the peaks. For studies up to approximately 1,000°C, chromel–alumel thermocouples generate a significant electromotive force (EMF = 45.16 mV at 1,100°C) but relatively low chemical resistance. On the other hand, platinum–rhodium or platinum thermocouples generate EMF = 10.74 mV which requires amplification, but can reach temperatures of 1,500°C and are chemically much more resistant.

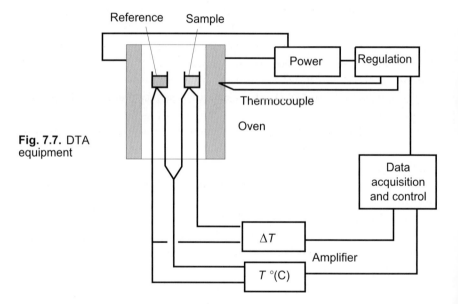

Fig. 7.7. DTA equipment

The position of the thermocouples in the sample and in the reference must be perfectly symmetrical to avoid any variation in the shape of the peaks or displacement of the base line. The measurement station should include a micro computer and associated peripherals and ensure:
– Complete piloting of the temperature cycles (speed of heating, 1–50°C min^{-1} with stabilized voltage, temperature control by means of thermocouples, carrying out instructions, etc.;
– Control of the atmosphere (purging circuits, admission of carrier gas, admission of inert or reactive gases, EGA output, regulation of flows and pressure);

– Simultaneous acquisition of data on temperature and heat transfers with very weak inertia, thermodynamic calculations and print-outs of the results.

As is true for TGA, standardization of the procedures is essential.

Sample

Use a sample of whole soil ground to 0.1 mm (should not be over-ground). Organic matter in humic soils produces a strong exothermic reaction culminating at 300°C (573 K) which obstructs the endothermic peaks of dehydration towards 250–400°C if analysis is carried out in air or in an oxidizing atmosphere. It is consequently better to destroy OM using the procedures described in Chaps. 2 and 3 (or to extract it and use DTA). On whole soil, the peaks are generally of low intensity. Quartz can obstruct, but its peak at 573°C can be used as a marker.

To improve sensitivity, it may be better to use isolated purified and enriched fractions of a given particle size, homoionically saturated in the case of clays and, after air drying, stored in a solution saturated with $Mg(NO_3)_2,6H_2O$ to maintain constant relative moisture (the size and crystallinity of the particles influence the temperature, size, and shape of the peaks).

In sandy fractions (2.0–0.05 mm) primary minerals and concretions rich in iron and manganese can be measured. The endothermic peak of quartz is generally observed at 573°C.

Silt fractions (0.05–0.005 mm) often represent a more complex medium: they contain both primary minerals and deteriorated forms and possibly forms of clay minerals > 2 µm.

Coarse or fine clays (< 2 µm) often give much more intense and quantifiable peaks than whole soils. Substances with short-distance arrangement (e.g. allophane, ferrihydrites) are found in this fraction. Homoionic saturation by a cation (Na^+, K^+, Ca^{2+}, Mg^{2+}, Al^{3+}) enables certain properties such as levels of hydration to be revealed. The first endothermic reaction of volatilization of the adsorbed water varies with the number of water molecules associated with the cation. The cations affect the size and the shape of the peaks, generally without significantly modifying the temperature at which they appear.

It is possible to mix the clay fraction with alumina to avoid caking, retraction, and cracking of the sample, but this has a diluting effect.

Two clay samples from the same profile can be compared under the same experimental conditions. The reference sample will be then one of the samples. If they are identical, ΔT will be equal to 0 and there will be a base line with no peak, as the two samples will cause the same phenomenon to occur at the same time.

Reference Material

The standard must be thermically inert in the temperature range to be used. It must have a thermal conductivity or a thermodiffusivity close to that of the sample. The particle size should be that of soil (ground to 0.1 mm) which allows close contact with the crucibles as well as a favourable bulk density (same proportion of pores near the ground soil).

Generally alumina is used (Al_2O_3 calcined at 1,200°C for 1 h). This reference can be used for several measurements, but slight hygroscopicity of the product may be observed after 4 or 5 measurements.

A clay burnt at 1,200°C and then ground can also be used, but problems often occur with respect to the base line. For example between rough kaolinite and kaolinite calcined to mullite at 1,200°C, thermal conductivity will vary by a factor of two and certain reversible reactions may occur. Quartz, magnesia, or aluminium sheets are sometimes used as reference materials.

Procedure

The procedure is similar to classical qualitative or quantitative DTA–DSC analysis, and takes into account the factors mentioned earlier.
- Weigh on the laboratory balance ($\pm$ 1/100 mg) a given mass of sample (1–100 mg), suited to the characteristics of the apparatus and an identical quantity of inert reference; for DSC with power compensation, an empty crucible similar to that used for the sample can be used as inert reference.
- Pack as homogeneously as possible in platinum crucibles.
- Find the optimal position for the crucibles (in suitable supports) with respect to the thermocouples and the most homogeneous zone of the furnace.

– Cover the crucibles with a lid if required (the displacement of evolved gas will be modified).
– Regulate the speed of linear increase in temperature; higher speed can increase some peak temperatures, but can also improve sensitivity (peak height); generally the range is between 5 and 20°C min^{-1} but certain materials allow speeds of 0.1–200°C min^{-1} (it is also possible to use the reverse technique with recording during cooling).
– Adjust the atmosphere of the furnace taking into account possible analysis of the gaseous phase by interfacing with EGA.

Software packages can monitor and control operating conditions including calculations and printing out the results, in this case all the parameters are optimized.

Interpretation of the Results

Table 7.5. Main thermal effects on the clays of soils

range of temperature (°C)	signals
50–250	endothermic peaks loss of absorbed water, interlayer water (e.g. allophanes, halloysite, smectite)
400–700	exothermic and endothermic peaks crystallisation reactions (e.g. gels of iron or aluminium oxides) diagnostic peaks of the crystalline forms reactions of dehydroxylation
900–1050	exothermic peaks reaction of nucleation or recrystallization (e.g. kaolinite-chlorites)

The same procedure is used for rough samples and extracted fractions of different degrees of purification under inert or reactive atmosphere depending on the nature of the sample studied.

"Pure" standard minerals or minerals in known mixtures (90:10, 80:20%, etc.) can be treated to trace the calibration lines with the same criteria thus enabling quantification of the samples (a reference set of laboratory minerals is necessary).

A distinction must be made between clay minerals from sedimentary deposits whose peaks are generally well defined and minerals from different soils after purification and concentration.

First, well-defined peaks are identified (e.g. the endothermic peak at 500°C and the exothermic peak towards 900°C for kaolinite). The shape of the peaks is an indicator of the thermal process: fusion results in a narrow endothermic peak, decomposition often produce a broad endothermic peak which is often asymmetrical, a second-order transition results in only a slight inflection. Certain minerals give well-defined peaks that are used as markers of characteristic transitions in the thermal programme.

The slope of the base line and the magnitude of the peaks should be taken into account. The main thermal transitions observed in clays are listed in Table 7.5. The "low temperature" zone provides information on adsorbed water and on the presence of certain clays and amorphous substances. The medium temperature zone shows peaks resulting from the predominant influence of crystallinity. Finally the high temperature zone shows phenomena such as nucleation or recrystallization of clays.

Certain standards are used in quantitative analysis like $CaSO_4,2H_2O$ to enable calculation in millicalories per unit of area (calibration between a peak surface and a known emitted or absorbed heat).

Each type of structure can be identified by a characteristic thermal curve (Fig. 7.8). For clays, purification is necessary to limit the artifacts caused by impurities which are likely to be superimposed in the same temperature zone.

Clays with a tetrahedral layer and an octahedral layer will display phenomena related to the decomposition of the octahedral layer. The exothermic volatilization of hygroscopic water may be accompanied by a recombination of the elements of the tetrahedral and octahedral layers.

Quantitative DTA is possible for clays presenting endothermic peaks associated with loss of water bound to the crystal. This is the case of 1:1 clays like kaolinite, but 2:1 clays like montmorillonite, vermiculite, or illite are difficult to quantify with this method.

Deferrification reinforces the exothermic peaks of kaolinite, and iron inhibits exothermic phenomena. The presence of carbonate, organic matter, and alkaline ions must be taken into account. Hydroxides initially present loss of water, and then contraction linked to decomposition of the lattice.

The heights of peaks are faster to use than the surfaces of peaks and can thus be used for approximations. Thermodynamic calculations use all the spectral information as well as the quantities of evolved water measured in TGA.

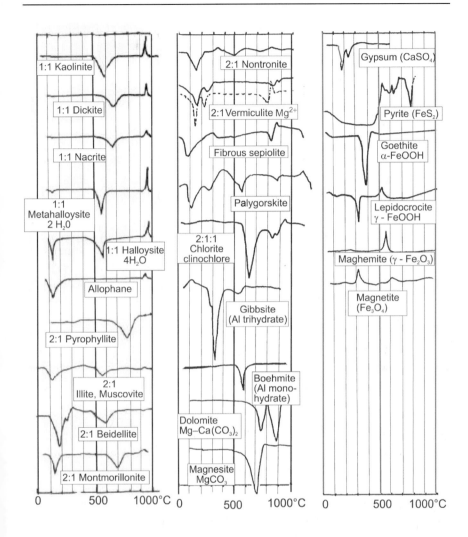

Fig. 7.8. Examples of DTA thermal diagrams on soil minerals (J Gautheyrou, set of reference standards from IRD Bondy, France, unpublished data)

In DSC, the curves are proportional to the enthalpy:

peak surface = $m \, \Delta H / k$

ΔH; heat of transition; m; reactive mass; k; coefficient of calibration (independent of the temperature measured by DSC with power compensation).

7.3 Multi-component Apparatuses for Thermal Analysis

7.3.1 Concepts

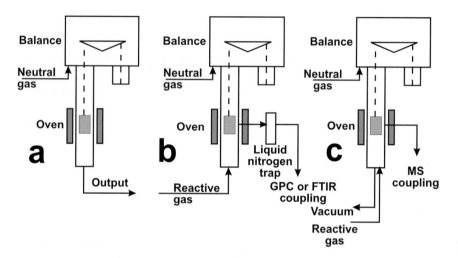

Fig. 7.9. Example of gas sweeping devices for TGA or TGA–DTA. (**a**) Simple displacement by a neutral carrier gas crossing the balance and protecting it from corrosion; (**b**) system with two gases – one neutral and one reactive – with horizontal sweeping of the sample; and (**c**) system with purging by vacuum and later sweeping by neutral gas or neutral gas + reactive gas

The development of new apparatuses was based on several different concepts. In multi-component equipment, several dedicated apparatuses are run by a management station and measurement is computerized. This type of multi-function equipment enables multiple measurements on the same sample subjected to a thermal profile with controlled atmosphere and pressure. Suitable sensors can measure TGA, DTG, DTA and DSC simultaneously thus reducing the time required for analysis, increasing precision and allowing more thorough characterization.

Automated introduction of the samples in the furnace is useful in the case of equipment with a cooling cycle of less than 30 min (return to ambient temperature after heating to 1,700°C).

Certain dedicated measurement peripherals can also detect or quantify evolved gas. This quantification is essential to complete certain DTA spectra (e.g. simultaneous exothermic and endothermic reactions).

The methods selected can be programmed and used in sequence, providing a powerful reference frame, e.g. for the identification of clays and the study of transformations in structure, recrystallization, forms of water, thermal stability or thermal oxidation.

7.3.2 Coupling Thermal Analysis and Evolved Gas Analysis

The analysis of emitted or emanating gas may require coupling of equipment of varying degrees of complexity. A small furnace with an open configuration should be used that is able to ensure rapid evacuation of decomposition gases (Fig. 7.9). The circulation of a carrier gas and the possible presence of reactive gases causes changes in pressure and convection phenomena linked to pressure and local temperatures (as well as thermomolecular forces able to create heterogeneous temperatures inside the furnace) that are controlled by a system of screens. Below is an overview of the most widely used systems.

Simple detection of evolved gas (EGD): a neutral carrier gas draws evolved gas into a catharometer detector; the output signal is proportional to the concentration of evolved gas in the carrier gas. The nature of the evolved gases is not identified. It is possible to trap the heavy products in liquid nitrogen, and then to subject these products to further analysis, for example controlled pyrolisis by thermal analysis.

Analysis of evolved gas (EGA) can be performed by coupling equipment of varying complexity. Gas chromatography, coupled with simultaneous TGA-DTA equipment, makes it possible to characterize evolved gas by automatic discontinuous injections (it is also possible to trap the fractions that are not analyzed in liquid nitrogen). Integration of the peaks makes it possible to quantify evolved and separated gas as a function of their retention times.

Coupling a Fourier transform infra-red spectrometer (FTIR) enables analysis of time of flight thanks to the speed of acquisition and the sensitivity of FTIR. A flow of nitrogen automatically transfers the evolved gases towards the spectrometer. Resolution is about 4 cm^{-1}. Each temperature point is stored in a numerical file corresponding to the number of the selected wavelength at this point. Water is identified in the 3,600 and 1,600 cm^{-1} zones, CO and CO_2 in the 2,000 to 2,400 cm^{-1} zones.

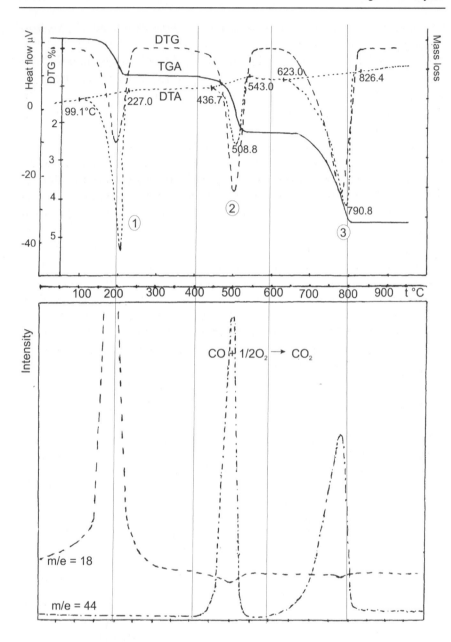

Fig. 7.10. Decomposition of the standard calcium oxalate (CaC_2O_4, H_2O) studied by coupling TGA, DTG and DTA (*at the top*) and mass spectrometry (*at the bottom*) atmosphere, air; speed of heating, 5°C min^{-1}, sample mass, 50 mg.

1. $CaC_2O_4,H_2O \rightarrow CaC_2O_4 + H_2O\uparrow$ (12.2% H_2O)
2. $CaC_2O_4 \rightarrow CaCO_3 + CO\uparrow$ (19.1% CO)
3. $CaCO_3 \rightarrow CaO + CO_2\uparrow$ (30.1% CO_2)

Coupling with a mass spectrometer is very powerful, but difficult to implement, as the mass spectrometer operates under a vacuum of about 10^{-5}–10^{-6} mbar. Interfacing with the thermal analyzer is achieved by means of double stage separators. A quadripole mass spectrometer enables rapid scanning in the mass range of evolved gas up to approximately 100, including ^{12}C, $^{16}CH_4$, ^{28}CO, $^{44}CO_2$, ^{18}HOH, ^{16}O, $^{32}O_2$, $^{34}H_2S$, $^{64}SO_2$, $^{80}SO_3$. This range is not sufficient for the observation of organic materials resulting from controlled pyrolysis (cf. Chap. 12) as the molecular weights are distributed over a larger range, up to 500 or more.

Figure 7.10 shows analysis of the thermal decomposition of oxalate of calcium, which can be used as a standard for calibration. With a combined mass spectrometer with a relatively low speed of acquisition and air atmosphere, decomposition reaction 2, which gives calcium carbonate and carbon monoxide, gives only one peak at mass 44 (CO_2). With nitrogen atmosphere, formation of a CO–CO_2 mixture is observed, showing the beginning of decomposition of the newly formed carbonate. Simultaneous detection of CO and CO_2 can also be achieved by coupling the thermal analyzer with a Fourier transform infra-red spectrometer.

The analysis of radioactive gases emanating from rocks in their solid state at different temperatures can be performed by coupling thermal analysis with a detector of α-particles.

References

Allen JA (1966) *Energy Changes in Chemistry.*, Allyn-Bacon Newton, MA

Braudeau E (1987) Mesure automatique de la rétraction d'échantillons de sol non remaniés. *Science du Sol*, 25, 85–93

Braudeau E (1988) Equation généralisée des courbes de retrait d'échantillons de sols structurés. *Comptes rendus acad. Sci. Fr.*, série 2, 307, 1731–1734

Braudeau E, Costantini JM, Bellier G and Colleuille H (1999) New device and method for soil shrinkage curve measurement and characterization. *Soil Sci. Soc. Am. J.*, 63, 525–535

Braudeau E, Frangi JP and Mothar RH (2004) Characterizing non-rigid dual porosity structured soil medium using its characteristic shrinkage curve. *Soil Sci. Soc. Am. J.*, 68, 359–370

Duval C (1963) *Inorganic Thermogravimetric Analysis.*, Elsevier. Amsterdam. 2ème édition

Garrels RM and Christ CL (1965) *Solutions, Minerals and Equilibra.*, Harper-Row New York

Gray AP (1968) *Symposium Analytical Chlorimetry*, Porter R.S. and Johnson JF ed., Proc. Am. Chem. Soc., Plenum New York, 209

Kotra RK, Gibson EK and Urbancic MA (1982) *Icarus.*, 51, 593

Mackensie RC (1970) *Differential Thermal Analysis.* Academic London. Vol. 1.

McNaughton JL and Mortimer CT (1975) La calorimétrie differentielle à balayage. *Butterworth, Physical Chemistry.*, Série 2, 10. 43 pages

Miller B, Giuham JM, Brennan WP, Nentzer C and Whitwell JC (1973) *Thermochim. Acta*, 5, 257

Pansu M, Gautheyrou J and Loyer JY (2001) – *Soil analysis – sampling, Instrumentation and Quality Control*, Balkema Amsterdam, Lisse, Abington, Exton, Tokyo, 512 p

Rouquerol J (1970) L'analyse thermique de décomposition construite. *J. Therm. Anal.*, 2, 123–140

Rouquerol J (1989) Reciprocal thermal analysis. The hidden face of the thermal analysis. *Thermodyn. Acta*

Rouquerol F, Rouquerol J, Thevand G and Triaca M. (1985) Desorption of chemisorbed species: its study by controlled rate thermal analysis. *Surf. Sci.*, 239–244

Rouquerol J, Rouquerol F, Grillet Y and Ward RJ (1988) A critical assessment of quasi equilibrium as adsorption techniques in volumetry gravimetry, calorimetry. In *Characterization of Porous Solid,* Kunger KK ed., Elsevier Amsterdam, 67–75

Watson ES, O'neill MJ, Justin J and Brenner N (1964) DSC. *Anal. Chem.*, 36, 1233

Bibliography

Bang DV and Atanasov I (1984) Thermal characteristics of the clay fraction of soils overlying zeolites. *Pochvoznanie i Agrokhimiya*, 19, 58–65

Barshad I (1965) Thermal analysis techniques for mineral identification and mineralogical composition. In *Methods of Soil Analysis*, Part 1., Black C.A. ed., A.S.A., S.S.S.A., 9, 699–742

Bishop JL, Banin A, Mancinelli R and Klovstad MR (2002) Detection of soluble and fixed NH_4^+ in clay minerals by DTA and IR reflectance spectroscopy: a potential tool for planetary surface exploration. *Planetary Space Sci.*, 50, 11–19

Brennan WP (1974) Application of differential scanning calorimetry for the study of phase transitions. In *Analytical Calorimetry,* Porter RS and Johnson JF ed., Plenum New York

Caillere S and Henin S (1963) *Mineralogie des argiles.*, Masson Paris

Daniels T (1973) *Thermal Analysis.*, Kogan Page

Dunn JG (1980) L'analyse thermique, une technique de centrale de qualité dans les industries de l'argile, des céramiques et des verres. *Silicates Industriels*, 10, 203

Duval C (1953) *Inorganic Thermogravimetric Analysis.*, Elsevier Amsterdam. 1st edition

Earnest CM (1983) Thermal analysis of Hectorite. Part II. Differential thermal analysis. *Thermochim. Acta.*, 63, 291–306

Emmerich WD and Kaisers Berger E (1979) Simultaneous TG-DTA mass-spectrometry to 1550°C. *J. Therm. Anal.*, 17, 197–212

Ferenc Paulik (1995) *Special Trends in Thermal Analysis.*, Wiley New York, 478 p

Fordham CJ and Smalley IJ (1983) High resolution derivative thermogravimetry of sensitive clays. *Clay Sci.*, 6, 73–79

Gallagher PK (Ed.) (1998) *Handbook of Thermal Analysis and Calorimetry.*, Elsevier

Garn PD (1965) *Thermo Analytical Methods of Investigation.*, Academic London

Giovannini G and Lucchesi S (1984) Differential thermal analysis and infra-red investigations on soil hydrophobic substances. *Soil Sci.*, 137, 457–463

Hatakeyama T and Zhenhai Lui (Ed.), (1998) *Handbook of Thermal Analysis.*, Wiley New York

Keyser de WL (1953) Differential thermobalance: a new research tool. *Nature*, 172, 364

Khanafer K and Vafai K (2002) Thermal analysis of buried land mines over a diurnal cycle. *IEEE Trans. Geosci. Remote Sensing*, 40, 461–473

Lombardi G (1984) Thermal analysis in the investigation of zeolitized and alterad volcanics of Latium, Italy. *Clay Miner.*, 19, 789–801

Mackenzie RC (1963) SCIFAX, *Differential Thermal Analysis Data Index.*, Cleaver-Hume Press

Mackenzie RC, Keattoh CJ, Dollimore D, Forester JA, Hodgson AA and Redfern JP (1972) Nomenclature in thermal analysis II. *Talanta*, 19, 1079–1081

Mackenzie RC and Caillere S (1975) The thermal characteristics of soil minerals and the use of these characteristics in the qualitative and quantitative determination of clay minerals in soils. In *Inorganic componants*, Gieseking E. ed. vol. 2, Springer Berlin 529–571

Madkensie RC and Robertson HS (1961) The quantitative determination of halloysite, goethite and gibbsite. *Acta Univ. Caral. Geol. Suppl.*, 1, 139

Maizenberg MC, Karpachevski LO, Markovich MN and Kurakof VN (1991) The use of differential scanning calorimetry in soil studies. *Moscow Univ. Soil Sci. Bull.*, 46, 31–34

Muller F, Drits V, Plancon A and Robert JLL (2000) Structural transformation of 2:1 dioctahedral layer silicates during dehydroxylation–rehydroxylation reactions. *Clays Clay Miner.*, 48, 572–585

Murphy CB (1962) Differential thermal analysis. A review of fundamental developments in analysis. *Anal. Chem.*, 298–301

Paulik F, Paulik J and Arnold M (1984) Simultaneous TG, DTG, DTA and EGA technique for the determination of carbonate, sulphate, pyrite and organic materials in minerals, soils and rocks. II – Operation of the thermo-gaz-titrimetric device (TGT) and examination procedure. *J. Therm. Anal.*, 29, 333–344

Poerschmann J, Görecki T and Parsi Z (2005) Analytical non-discriminating pyrolysis in soil analysis. *LabPlus Int.*, 19, 8–14

Sarikaya Y, Onal M, Baran B and Alemdaroglu T (2000) The effect of thermal treatment on some of the physicochemical properties of a bentonite. *Clays Clay Miner.*, 48, 557–562

Schnitzer M and Kodama H (1972) Differential thermal analysis of metal-fulvic acid salts and complexes. *Geoderma*, 7, 93–103

Schomburg J (1991) Thermal reactions of clay minerals: their significance as "erchaeological thermometers" in ancient potteries. *Appl. Clay Sci.*, 6, 215–220

Schultze D (1969) *Differential Thermo-Analysis.*, Verlag

Smothers WJ and Chiang YZO (1966) *Handbook of Differential Thermal Analysis.*, Chem. Publ. Co.

Smykatz-Kloss W and Heide K (1988) Progress of thermal analysis in earth Sciences. *J. Therm. Anal.*, (GBR) 33, 1253–1257

Taichev T, Konishev P and Donov D (1984) Application of thermal analysis in studies on the structural evolution of humic substances. *Pochvoznanie i Agrokhimiya*, 19, 82–87

Tan KH and Clark FE (1969) Polysaccharide constituents in fulvic and humic acids extracted from soil. *Geoderma*, 2, 245–255

Tan KH, Hajek BF and Barshad I (1986) Thermal analysis techniques. In *Methods of soil analysis*, Klute A. ed., A. S..A., S.S.S.A., 9, 151–183

Trofimov SA, Tolpeshta II, Sokolova TA (1999) A study of plant material and organic soil horizons using thermal analysis techniques. *Pochvovedenie*, 54, 3–9

Van Olphen H and Fripiat JJ (1979) *Data Handbook for Clay Minerals and Other Non-Metallic Minerals.*, Pergamon New York, 350 pages

Wendlandt WW (1974) *Thermal Methods of Analysis*, Part 1. Wiley New York

Microscopic Analysis

8.1 Introduction

The study of the processes of genesis and weathering of the soils and the characterization of minerals require observations at different spatial and temporal scales. Pedon, horizon, macro- and micro-samples are used as a basis for a range of examinations in which microscopy techniques enable observation of the interfaces of the different phases and even of the ultimate stages of molecular assemblies. Complementary analytical probes enable in particular determination of the chemical nature (e.g. energy dispersive X-ray, EDX or wavelength dispersive X-ray, WDX analysis) and the structural organization (electron micro-diffraction) of these phases.

Whereas classical wet chemical analyses provide information on overall evolution, microscope analyses enable identification of hyperfine chemical heterogeneity and facilitate understanding of transformation mechanisms. Qualitative and quantitative information is obtained on the texture of individual particles, e.g. shape, the presence of cements, inclusions, pores.

Detailed morphological analysis (spatial relations of the different phases, preferential orientation, etc.) is performed by coupling a microscope to an image or texture analyser, and analysing thin sections to reveal the cartography of chemical segregation, micro-profiles, and to improve our knowledge of pedogenesis.

The crystalline structure can be identified by changing scale: i.e. by studying the elementary mesh of clays, regular sequences of silicates in layers, modifications of the basal interlayer, the appearance of aperiodisms, defects, micro-cleavages, growth steps, gels with short-distance atomic arrangements near source crystals which bring about the transformation of one mineral into another at the nano-structural scale. Electron micro-diffraction, which is available on the majority of electron microscopes, enables identification of crystalline structures. All these options make microscopy an extremely powerful tool.

Optic and electronic microscopy and the accompanying peripherals used to determine chemical distribution within the sample are widely used in pedology, mineralogy, crystallography, petrography, metallography, and clay geology, and provide precise information on the mechanical properties, localization of surface charges and exchange properties of the soils.

However, it is extremely important to think about the validity of the observations and to adapt the scale of measurement to the exact requirements of the sample. Sampling conditions and the different stages of sample preparation should always be specified. The season should also be taken into account (samples taken in a wet or dry season present very different pore spaces in soils rich in 2:1 clay). Not only pedogenesis and geostatistics but also geomorphology must be used (the samples may require complementary sampling of the evolution of a profile, or sampling at a larger scale to account for the homogeneity of a zone). When the observations are made, it is important to be aware of the physical and chemical processes that can modify a sample and lead to erroneous results (e.g. contamination, oxidation, neoformation). It is also important to explore the full potential of the equipment, as the full capacity of apparatuses is frequently underexploited.

Electron beams can damage the surface of materials. The depth of penetration of radiation may be limited to near the surface: i.e. approximately 1–3 nm, or on the contrary, may gradually erode the surface resulting in a concentration of profiles (e.g. in plasma bombardment, secondary ion mass spectrometry).

As is true for all methods, the calibration of measurements is essential and requires a reference set of sample observations that will allow comparison with known and clearly identified situations.

8.2 Preparation of the Samples

8.2.1 Interest

Visual examination, followed by examination with a magnifying glass is not enough as it only enables a rough estimate of modes of assembly and physical properties. This type of examination is consequently always supplemented by tactile examinations and other sensorial and chemical tests (described in Pansu et al. 2001).

Observations can be made under an optical or electron microscope on soil samples that have undergone treatments such as:
– purification, concentration, quantitative separation into classes of particle size
– separation in heavy liquids of increasing densities, up to $d = 4.28$ at 20°C (e.g. bromoforme, tetrabromomethane, di-iodomethane, Clerici solution)
– magnetic separation in a Frantz magnetic separator (or similar).

In this case, individual particles are measured (shape, nature, relative proportions of minerals, effects and nature of weathering). To obtain precise information on assemblies, thin sections have to be prepared on glass slides making it possible to study soil transformation and to link this information with field observations.

28×48 mm petrographic slides are the most widely used, but 110×76 mm or even 200×180 mm Mammoth slides are also useful for micro-pedological and micro-morphological studies (however, these are very delicate operations).

8.2.2 Coating and Impregnation, Thin Sections

Principle

The term coating is generally used in the case of massive compact samples with simple geometry, such as pieces of hard stone which can be embedded in a resin that hardens rapidly and facilitates preparation for analysis.

The purpose of impregnation with resin is to consolidate soft porous rocks, products of rock deterioration and soils (Delvigne 1998) for which cohesion is required. Wet soils must be dried in a way that avoids modifying the structure of the sample by contraction or the appearance of cracks due to shrinkage. One way to limit this phenomenon in soils rich in 2:1 clays with low porosity is to saturate the sample with sodium chloride before desiccation by freeze-drying.

For soils rich in allophanes with a water storage capacity reaching 250% of dry soil, water can gradually be replaced by acetone, or dioxane. This technique is also applicable on clay soils, but in this case, samples treated with acetone are more fragile than those treated with dioxane (Tessier 1985). Acetone and dioxane are compatible with certain resins used for impregnation.

Freeze-drying generally preserves the features of the sample better than oven or air drying. For small samples (approximately 30 cm^3) the use of a dehydration apparatus at CO_2 critical point gives excellent results. For bulky wet samples, the use of epoxy resins that are soluble in water is one possible solution (Moran et al. 1989).

Preparing the thin section slides manually is very time consuming and considerable technical skill is needed to obtain thin sections of quality with the required degree of transparency and a uniform thickness of between 20 and 30 μm. Automation of coating and impregnation, slicing, and polishing is possible, but requires a high initial investment which can only be amortized by at least 60 coatings or 40 impregnations per week, i.e. approximately 2,000 slides of format 28 × 48 mm per year. Some computer-controlled modular systems enable automated production of super-thin sections 10 μm thick, with 0.25 μm polishing if required. Standard slides are 30 μm thick with approximately 1 μm polishing. (Fig. 8.1)

It is often preferable to have the thin section slides made in specially equipped laboratories because of the need for explosion-proof electric circuits, vapour evacuation circuits with solvent traps, plus the cost of maintenance of the equipment and the instability of the resins.

Equipment

- Laboratory equipped with a fume hood (with non-deflagrating electric apparatuses)
- combined system for grinding and polishing with a disc 250 mm in diameter
- cutting saw with a diamond grinding stone 350 mm in diameter
- equipment for cold impregnation and coating under vacuum: desiccator 300 mm in diameter with a vacuum stopcock and a device for admission of the mixture of resin + catalyst
- vacuum pump with pressure gauge (0–750 mm Hg)
- ultrasound tank
- drying oven with ventilation (up to 100°C)
- stylograver with a tungsten carbide point
- petrographic glass slides, size 28 × 48 mm, 1.2 mm thickness
- glass sheets 0.13 mm thick for use as slide covers
- boxes for thin section slides
- ultramicrotome with thermally regulated system of displacement
- freeze dryer
- vacuum desiccators with drying products such as silica gel
- binocular microscope
- small equipment such as glass slab, aluminium sheet, grips
- refrigerator (to store resins)

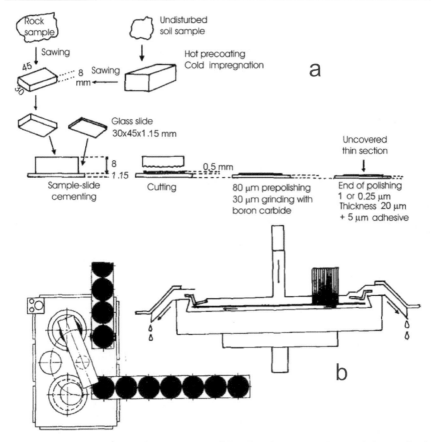

Fig. 8.1. (a) Preparation of thin section slides (equipment and materials required: resins, press, coating, UV polymerization apparatus, grinding stone cutting saw, grinding polishing machine) (b) Computer controlled station for automated modular preparation (Struers)

Materials and Reagents

– Silicon carbide sheets (Carborundum–SiC) MOHS hardness: 9
– boron carbide sheets (B_4C) MOHS hardness: 9
– corundum sheets (Alumina – Al_2O_3) MOHS hardness: 9
– diamond sheets (range of particle sizes)
– polishing cloth
– diamond water–ethanol soluble pastes and sprays: 3, 1, 0.25 µm
– cold epoxy resins + hardener + catalyst + thinner
– acrylic resins with low shrinkage rate
– cold polyester resins
– dyestuff for resin

– canada balsam (+xylene)
– lubricants and solvents: glycerol $HOCH_2$–$CH(OH)CH_2OH$, oil, ethanol, O–xylene $C_6H_4(CH_3)_2$, styrene $C_6H_5CH=CH_2$, 1–4 dioxane, acetone, 99% diethylene triamine H_2N–CH_2CH_2NH–$CH_2CH_2NH_2$
– silicone grease for grinding
   The choice of a resin will depend on its:
   – refraction index (near 1.54)
   – solubility in an organic solvent or water
   – low level of contraction and low viscosity
   – polymerization conditions
   – hardness and strength at the required temperature particularly for observations and quantifications by electronic microscopy of the SEM and EDX type.

Procedure

Compact Hard Samples (Rocks)

Petrographic techniques are described in detail by Hartshorne and Stuart (1970).

The sample is suitably oriented and sawn on one face, then gradually polished and finally stuck on a petrographic slide of format 28 × 48 mm (1 in. × 2 in.). After sawing off a section 2–3 mm thick parallel to the stuck face, thin to 30 µm. Polish the thin section to 1 µm. The thin section slide can be protected from abrasion and oxidation by being stuck onto a thin glass sheet with Canada balsam. The slide should not be covered if subsequent tests require specific dyes, chemistry (elimination of carbonates) or samples are required for SEM-EDX measurements.

Frangible, Porous or Fissured Samples

Samples removed in the field with their natural moisture using cylinder or monolith methods of soil analysis (Pansu et al. 2001) are often oriented vertically in the profile or possibly oriented according to the field slope (Fig. 8.2), these should be stored in airtight boxes then used to produce the 28 × 48 mm standard or Mammoth slides.

Whenever the block is being cut during preparation, the direction of the field micro-section should be taken into account (Fig. 8.2). The sample is dried by freeze-drying or by replacing the water with acetone or dioxane. Slight contraction will allow the sample to be released from the mould unless the system of sampling with two half-cylinders is used.

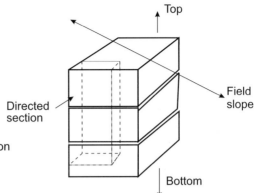

Fig. 8.2. Pedological micro-section

The block should be cut into a rough square with a cutter to reduce its thickness and, depending on the chosen orientation, deposited in a semi-flexible plastic mould (in practice, the bottom of the mould corresponds to the bottom of the profile).

Impregnation

Place the block of soil with its mould in a vacuum desiccator with a ground lid lubricated with silicone grease. Put the desiccator under vacuum at approximately 60 cm Hg (or more) depending on the boiling point of the solvent and the resins. The soil should be degassed for 30 min.

In a flexible plastic container, quickly mix the resin with the hardener (in the proportions recommended by the manufacturer) and the same volume of solvent to fluidify the mixture. Pour the resin mixture into the funnel at the top of the desiccator. Introduce the mixture gradually while monitoring vacuum, input flow and the rise in the level of the impregnation liquid until the sample is completely covered (plus one cm to allow for subsequent retraction of the resin). The mixture must also flow around the sample, and impregnation should take place upwards by capillarity. Depending on the porosity and size of the sample, 5–8 hours are often needed for 48 × 28 mm slides.

Break the vacuum with care and transfer the sample under a fume hood. The thinner will take approximately one week to evaporate. The product becomes increasingly viscous, and then starts to harden (this will take about a month depending on the resin and dilution). Put it in a ventilated drying oven at 45°C for 2 or 3 days until the sample is no longer sticky. Unmould it respecting the orientation.

Cutting

Place the block on a bed of coloured resin (approximately 2 mm thick) that hardens rapidly in order to be able to identify the bottom of the soil profile. Saw the hardened impregnated block according to the preferential orientation (a slight notch can be cut in the side of the block to identify the direction of the field slope).

The circular saw should be lubricated with a solvent that cannot dissolve soluble salts and should be compatible with the resin and with any chemical analyses to be performed later on. When impregnation appears to be complete, cut the block into parallel sections 5–6 mm thick. Each section should match the format of the petrographic slides. Rapidly check the quality of the surface for impregnation defects like cracks or flatness. The surface may need to be impregnated again after cleaning with alcohol and compressed air. Using a spatula, coat the section with a mixture of resin plus catalyst and place it on a flat glass block; cover it with a thin aluminium film pressing to exclude any air bubbles. After solidification, uncover the sample, trim it with a scalpel and leave it to harden in a ventilated drying oven at 45°C. The section is then ready for polishing.

Using a silicon carbide abrasive disc with a rather coarse particle size, polish until almost complete abrasion of the re-impregnation layer, then, after cleaning with a blast of compressed air, continue polishing with a sequence of diamond abrasive paste of increasing smoothness (6, 3 and 1 μm). The surface must be perfectly smooth with no abrasions and no residues of the re-impregnation film. The material will look dull on the polished resin.

Sticking the Sample on a 48 × 28 mm Petrographic Slide
Clean the slide with solvent and dry. Write the slide number with India ink. Mix the resin used to fix the sample with hardener (at 60°C or cold depending on the nature of the sample and of the resin). With a spatula apply the resin to one surface of the holder slide and to the polished section of sample, and then rotate the two faces slowly one against the other moving them very gently to push out any excess adhesive and eliminate air bubbles. Allow to harden and trim the edges. After 48 hours, smooth the external face of the sample by sawing it to approximately 300 μm thickness, then by polishing it with set of diamond powders of decreasing particle size until reaching 30 μm (the usual thickness of thin slides for optical observation gives an orange birefringence in quartz). Each time the particle size of the diamond paste is changed, carefully clean the slide to eliminate all coarse particles which could scratch it. If minerals that are rich in iron are abundant, 30 μm is not thin enough to enable observation and it is necessary to reduce the section to approximately 20 μm to make it sufficiently transparent.

For scanning electron microscopy or EDX probes, the final polishing should be done with a 0.25 μm diamond paste. For high resolution transmission electron microscope observations, the glass support should be removed and the thickness of the micro-zones (diameter 3 mm) reduced, these should be separated and cut with a scalpel. An argon gun is used for thinning. For observation of minerals oriented in the same plane as the slide, a microtome can also be used for cutting. Micro-diffraction will provide some information, but interpretation is often difficult on very thin samples.

Separation on slides of micro-particles of about 50–100 μm is possible with an ultrasound probe equipped with a carbon needle on a micro-manipulator; the slide is observed on a reversed optical microscope. Micro-particles are placed on a silicon plate and are analysed by XRD with slow scanning. The resulting spectra are compatible with angular spaces and standard intensities.

8.2.3 Grids and Replicas for Transmission Electron Microscopy

Principle

The samples can only be observed in transmission electron microscopy if they are less than 1 μm thick and if they are assembled on very thin conducting films. The object subjected to electron bombardment must be crossed by the electron beam. The acceptable thickness depends on the energy of this beam i.e. approximately 0.2 μm penetration at 50 kV, and 3–4 times higher at 100 kV.

The beam–matter interaction heats the sample-target which can cause volatilization of the pore water; the morphology of halloysites is then seriously damaged and there will be contamination of the gun of the microscope. With elements of higher atomic number, heating can be very intense (fusion, phase shift, sublimation, destruction of supporting film).

The supporting film should be transparent to the electrons, sufficiently solid to support the sample, resistant to heat and to electrostatic charges; it should be no thicker than about 100 Å.

Reagents

– Polyvinyl formal (FORMVAR, n_D^{20}: 1.50)
– dichloroethane, $Cl–CH_2–CH_2–Cl$
– 0.15% FORMVAR in dichloroethane solution;
– COLLODION (nitrate of cellulose or pyroxylene $C_{12}H_{16}N_4O_{18}$)
– amyl acetate ($CH_3–CO_2–C_5H_{11}$) or butyl acetate ($CH_3CO_2(CH_2)_3CH_3$)
– 1% collodion solution in amyl acetate
– 1% fluorhydric acid in water.

Equipment

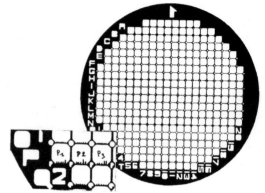

Fig. 8.3. Grid of transmission
   electron microscopy φ 3
   mm   (322   meshes)
   numbers: location of
   x - coordinate
   letters: location   of
   y- ordinate

– Lab glassware
– Cu (or Ni) grids 3.05 mm in diameter (Fig. 8.3); these are also available
  covered with an FORMVAR–carbon film or with a perforated
  FORMVAR–carbon–gold film enabling direct observation of micro-
  particles
– 110 mm non-magnetic stainless grips with ultra-fine points
– plastic film for replicas 0.034 mm thick
– micro-drying oven to melt the replicas at 45°C
– sampling loop.

Procedure

Grids

– Place the required number of 3 mm grids on a glass slide previously
  moistened with water. Place the slide in a cupel and very gradually
  submerge it; the grids should not float
– add a drop of FORMVAR–dichloroethane solution to the surface of the
  water; the drop should form a very thin film (<100 Å) without folds or
  holes which will solidify in the air after evaporation of the solvent (the
  film will be thinner if the water temperature is close to 0°C); eliminate
  the liquid slowly to bring the film into contact with the slide and the
  grids it covers; let dry then cover the grids with flash carbon which
  reinforces the film and makes it conducting; when the grids are grey,
  they are ready to use; check their quality under a binocular microscope

– dilute a drop of sample suspension in water to obtain an almost clear liquid; treat with ultrasound to separate the particles; remove one micro-drop and place it in the centre of the grid[1] the grid should not be turned over during the operation; let dry at air temperature and dehydrate in a critical point apparatus if necessary.

Replicas

Samples which change shape during desiccation are too fragile or too dense to transmit the electrons but can be studied using a one or two-stage replica technique that results in a slight decrease in resolution.

First the sample should be rapidly subjected to directional shading with gold or platinum, then the surface covered with a vertically applied carbon film that is both conducting and resistant.

In this case, cover the sample with a special 0.034 mm thick thermo-fusible film that softens at 45°C and preserves a replica of the surface of the mineral. Dissolve the clay sample with its cover in a diluted hydrofluoric acid solution. The replica remains in the hollows of the sample and can be subjected to gold or carbon treatment (if this has not already been done). Then dissolve the polystyrene film in ethylene chloride. Assemble the carbon replica on a grid and observe using TEM. All these procedures should be carried out with extreme care.

8.2.4   Mounting the Samples for Scanning Electron Microscopy

Principle

The samples may be massive and rough. Depending on the characteristics of the sample vacuum chamber, discs 20 cm in diameter and 4 cm in thickness (8 in. wafers) can be used, but the degasification of large samples is only possible in the case of compact rocks with a limited number of fissures. In practice, it is preferable to use smaller samples. The surface for observation must be a clean break in the sample to enable the study e.g. the plan of cleavage, crystal orientations, defects in the crystal lattice, the presence of occluded impurities.

Surfaces are rendered conducting with flash-carbon or by metallization if micro-probe analysis is not required. Otherwise, if the SEM is

---

[1] The grids should be handled with forceps with ultra-fine points. 0.1 mL micro-syringes of the Hamilton type. Flame-drawn hydrophobic glass tubes treated with PROSYL 28 can also be used.

equipped with an EDX or WDX micro-probe, flat, perfectly polished surfaces (0.25 μm) are required.

Equipment

– Special SEM supports
– storage boxes
– 5 × 5 mm calibration grids with 2 μm squares
– 3 mm carbon slides to mount on SEM supports
– pencil marker for SEM (conducting ink)
– double-face self-adhesive ribbon with low content of volatile elements.

Products

– Silver lacquer
– conducting carbon lacquer
– a set of reference minerals for quantification.

Procedure

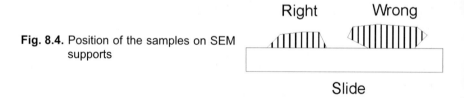

Fig. 8.4. Position of the samples on SEM supports

Small samples can be assembled on aluminium supports by sticking them together with silver or carbon lacquer. In certain cases, carbon supports can be used, or plates of 3 mm thickness stuck on aluminium supports. Carbon lacquer is generally preferable for EDX micro-probe analysis. It is essential to locate the samples precisely (e.g. by squaring, marking, or marking the right direction on the support); it is also important to avoid creating a vacuum under the sample (Fig. 8.4) because this causes discontinuity, and elimination of the charges can be disturbed resulting in scratches on the images which renders the photographs unusable. The lacquer should not cover the sample or fill the cracks. After prolonged drying to eliminate solvents, cover the samples with flash carbon using a metal sprayer with ionic bombardment, or shadow with a metal deposit from an evaporator.

8.2.5   Surface Treatments (Shadowing, Flash-carbon, Metallization)

Vacuum Evaporator

Flash carbon is often used to reinforce the FORMVAR film which supports the samples; it also makes the film conducting. Flash carbon should be applied vertically and uniformly. The micro-samples are sometimes only slightly absorbent and are not very visible in TEM. In this case the sample can be covered with a directional deposit of carbon whose grain is not very apparent, or be metallized with platinum or gold, under a tangential entry. Each space protected by a relief will appear shadowed. Knowing the angle of incidence, it is possible to measure the length of the shadow and deduce the height of the corresponding relief (Fig. 8.5).

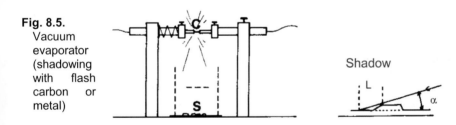

Fig. 8.5.
  Vacuum
  evaporator
  (shadowing
  with   flash
  carbon   or
  metal)

Shadow

Sputtering Metallization

The apparatus consists of an anticathode made of gold shaped in a ring whose internal diameter is longer than the length of the sample support. At the centre, a cylindrical magnet is connected to a magnetic field which forms the other pole and surrounds the anticathode (Fig. 8.6). The electrons, which would otherwise overheat the sample, are deviated by the magnetic field.

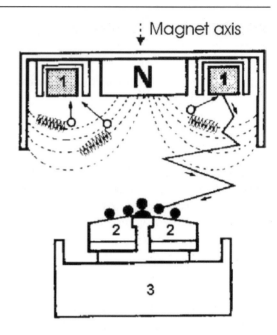

Fig. 8.6. Sputtering metallization apparatus (Bio-Rad –
olaron) for SEM samples. N
magnet, 1 Au anticathode,
2 sample support, 3 cooling
block, filled circle neutral
atoms, *open circle* positive
ions. When the sample
advances in the magnetic
field, all sides are bombarded

The sample support is cooled to 4°C by a Peltier thermoelectric system. Heating is thus reduced and it is consequently possible to treat organic samples.

The treatments are carried out under 10^{-1} Torr vacuum for 30–180 s. The applied voltage can reach 3 kV. Sweeping with a dry neutral gas (argon) enables elimination of residual traces of water, carbon dioxide, oxygen and possible oil contamination from the vacuum pumps. It is sometimes necessary to degas porous samples for several hours. In this way contamination is limited, but it is nevertheless often preferable to dehydrate on the apparatus at critical point before continuing degasification in the metal sprayer and then metallization.

Cryo-fixing is often useful for organic matter and very frangible samples.

This treatment gives excellent surface conductivity and accentuation of the relief of the rough samples by shadowing in SEM.

8.3. Microscope Studies

8.3.1 Optical Microscopy

Description

Optical microscopes allow observation of objects that are too small to be observed with the human eye or with a magnifying glass. Direct observations are carried out under IR to UV radiation including visible radiation, and can be accompanied by photography on film (black and white or colour) or digitalized video images.

The magnifying power of a magnifying glass ranges from 2 to 60 times and of the most powerful microscopes up to 1,500 times. The object can be massive or very thin (a thin slide that is covered or not) to determine properties of soils or soil materials using absorption-transmission. Covering slides protects the surface from oxidation. Covered slides can be used for optical observation in immersion but the slides cannot subsequently be used for electronic microscopy.

Briefly, an optical microscope is composed of a stand which supports a mechanical mount ensuring vertical displacement of an objective, and an eyepiece over an object slide.

The magnifying power and the diameter of the field characterize the relations between the image and the object. Lightness refers to the luminosity of the optics used. The depth of field and the focusing range, as well as the limit of resolution determine the zones where the object can be observed under optimal conditions for a given material. A system of lighting allows observation by reflection or transmission. The lighting can be directed for massive objects (low-voltage lamps, optical fibres). For very thin objects, the lighting can be concentrated into a point by condensers with respect to different backgrounds: pale background, dark background, polarized light, phase contrasts, UV (slides covered or not).

IR microscopes use optical systems with mirrors to avoid adsorption of IR by the materials generally used in the manufacture of lenses.

Polarizing Microscope

In soil sciences, polarizing microscopes are primary tools for the observation of crystals and the characterization of their optical properties. Interference microscopes or phase contrast microscopes (invisible transparent objects against a pale background) are rarely used. Variations in transmission factors can reveal structures that are invisible in natural light and make it possible to identify phenomena of pleochroism, isotropy and anisotropy of structure and mineral associations (as in forms, facies, cleavages, macles) using cross or slightly uncrossed polarizers. These microscopes (Fig. 8.7) enable observation of variations in transmission compared to the direction of polarization of the incidental light. A calibrated compensator placed in front of the analyser allows observations to be quantified. The choice of the objective is important (magnifying power, immersion or not) for the quality of soil observations.

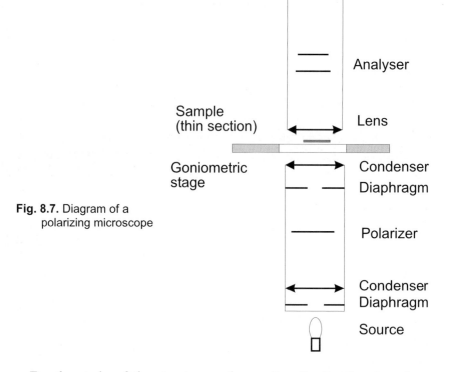

Fig. 8.7. Diagram of a polarizing microscope

For the study of the structure and porosity of soils, the size, shape, associations of individual grains, and distribution of the different phases are determined either on extracted phases, or on thin sections (Jongerius et al. 1972; Bullock and Murphy, 1980).

Procedure

A rotating support, graduated in degrees, makes it possible to measure the extinction angle and to identify primary minerals that are still present as well as to specify the scale and type of weathering. Interpretation requires considerable experience meaning only specialists in petrography are usually able to do it. Orthoscopic methods are time consuming but generally more precise than conoscopic methods (Wahlstom 1969, Hartshorne and Stuart 1970).

This type of analysis is qualitative, but can be quantified by counting the mineral particles originating from the parent rock and minerals liable to weathering in the fractions previously separated by fractionation using particle size, density, hardness, magnetic properties, etc. The shape of the particles (rounded edges, sphericization of softer minerals), surface appearance (such as flatness of the particles, cleavages, cracks, different coverings) are indicators of the form of deterioration, erosion and transport (chemical weathering, micro-corrosion, waterice- or wind-erosion).

The nature of minerals can be deduced from their colour, opacity, and especially from their refractive index and observable modifications in polarized light (e.g. pleochroism). Certain minerals have a more or less clear birefringence. The extinction angle can be reached with varying degrees of rapidity, and may be partial or complete. The shape of certain crystals is characteristic.

These observations can be supplemented by scanning electronic microscopy after rapid mounting of the materials on double face sticking supports made conducting with flash-carbon (cf. Sect. 8.2.5).

Using thin sections allows observation without disturbance of the in situ arrangement of the sample, orientations and associations of minerals, discontinuity of the mineralogical composition of a profile (decrease in or disappearance of certain minerals, ratio of minerals resistant to weathering:minerals liable to weathering giving index of deterioration).

The development of concretions, nodules, the appearance of cementing, the presence of organic matter at different stages of decomposition can be observed and quantified by subsequent measurements using SEM combined with EDX (certain artifacts of preparation, like the filling of neocracks, or holes made by polishing by alumina are easily revealed).

The units of organization (skeleton, plasma, vacuums) can be studied in detail at different scales using extracted fractions or/and thin sections: the skeletal components correspond to particles that are not reorganized, plasma corresponds to fine elements that can move and reorganize (such as clays and oxides), vacuums are related to porosity (circulation of air and solutions in soil). For the specific study of pore spaces, fluorescent colours can be mixed with the impregnation resin during the preparation of thin sections (cf. Sect. 8.2.2).

8.3.2 Electron Microscopy, General Information

All electron microscopes are based on the interaction of electrons with matter. The energy of an electron accelerated by a voltage V is equal to $E = m\,v^2/2 = e\,V$ (with m, v, e = mass, speed and charge of the electron, respectively). High energy radiation (fast electrons) can affect the level of the deep electronic layers of the atoms. Weak energy radiation (slow electrons) only affects the external electronic layers which reflect the chemical state of the atoms. The total effect of the electron beam is related to the electronic cloud of the Z electrons (e^-) of the electronic orbitals around the nucleus of atoms.

The following factors should be taken into account when considering how to change the way radiation affects matter:
– intensity: transmitted or reflected intensity is lower than incidental intensity, absorption occurs
– direction: there is scattering with loss of energy (inelastic scattering modifying internal structure), or without loss of energy (coherent elastic scattering allowing diffraction)
– energy: as some energy is lost, reflected, transmitted or scattered energy is lower than initial energy.

Losses in intensity and energy may be accompanied by modification of the matter due to the effect of the radiation:
– in the case of electron microscopes with very high energy (3,000 kV), the sample can gradually be destroyed
– in the case of microscopes with energy lower than 400 kV, there is transfer of energy by excitation of the electrons, thermal vibrations, particle ejection, and emission of secondary radiations usable for quantification. The heating effect produces phonons. Some chemical effects are reducing (e^- gain). Chemical bonds can be ruptured.

When the transfer of energy is higher than the threshold of displacement (between 15 and 30 eV), the effects of irradiation can cause atomic displacements. With electronic corpuscular incidental radiation of sufficiently high energy, an orbital electron in the deep atomic layers can be ejected with a kinetic energy corresponding to the difference in the energy lost by the incidental radiation and the electron's own energy (secondary electrons). As the excited state is unstable, the atom subsequently returns to a fundamental state; there is release of X-photons or Auger electrons (relaxation phenomena).

With electromagnetic radiation such as incidental or re-emitted X-rays photoelectrons are obtained (IR- to UV-photons, cathodo-luminescence). Electron microscopes can be classified at two levels depending on the geometry of the sample:

– massive samples which, as they are very thick, can be analysed only by the signals that come from their surface by reflection

– samples with a critical thickness that allows radiation to cross them (micro-crystals, thin films, etc.), in which case measurements can be made by transmission.

However, progress in instrumentation has led to changes in this dichotomy with the appearance of hybrid apparatuses allowing measurements on thin samples that use both processes. The following types of equipment are available:

– traditional transmission electron microscopes TEM (possibly with additional functions in transmission scanning mode)

– scanning transmission electron microscopes (STEM)

– microscopes with scanning by reflection (conventional scanning electronic microscopes: SEM)

– microscopes with scanning by reflection with differential vacuum where the observation chamber is under partial vacuum (environmental scanning electronic microscopes: ESEM).

Each type of apparatus allows complementary measurements. The apparatuses are suitable for either very high resolution, or, with multiple configurations, for a range of different chemical and physico-chemical approaches. The signals obtained are complementary in the energy fields.

8.3.3 Transmission Electron Microscopy, Micro-diffraction

Principle

Transmission electron microscopes use an incidental electron beam which, while crossing a very thin sample, provides information on the shape and structural distribution of elementary soil particles. The interaction of the electron beam with the matter results in images and micro-diffraction spectra (and enables selection of elementary chemical analyses as complements to the different electronic micro-probes in STEM).

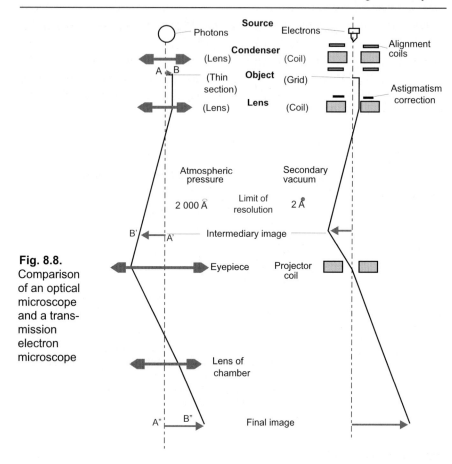

Fig. 8.8. Comparison of an optical microscope and a transmission electron microscope

The geometry of an electron microscope can be compared to that of an optical microscope (Fig. 8.8). A source of electrons (high voltage electron gun) replaces the source of photons. A system of illumination with electromagnetic condensers concentrates the electron beam on the object; an electronic objective forms an intermediary image which is captured by projection lenses to form the final image on a fluorescent screen or a photographic device.

Not all the radiations generated by the incidental electronic beam (Fig. 8.9) are used, since the apparatuses generally have only 1–2 sensors.[2] X-photonic radiation (1, Fig. 8.9) can be collected by an EDX) detector (with Si–Li detection, or diodes without windows for analysis of light elements such as nitrogen and carbon), or WDX (with crystal monochromator).

---

[2] At their maximum configuration, some top-of-the-range commercial analyzers include up to five sensors.

IR–UV–visible photonic radiation (2, Fig. 8.9) can be detected by cathodoluminescence. The scattered electrons (5) can be analysed by electron energy loss spectrometry (EELS) and enables analysis of light elements in STEM. Back-scattered electrons (6), secondary electrons (7), and Auger electrons are used for SEM images and transmitted electrons (12) for TEM and STEM.

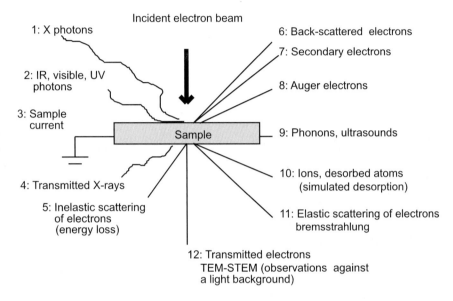

Fig. 8.9. Types of radiations emitted during the bombardment of a sample by an electron beam

The choice of a transmission electron microscope depends on the nature of the observations required (magnifying power, high resolution, the need for high voltage for excitation or penetration, possible chemical quantification) and the cost, but also the versatility and the possibility to up-grade the equipment, its ability to cover the whole range of magnifying power including weak magnifying power, the degree of automation and ease of use, the quality and the cleanliness of the vacuum, contrast and performance against a dark background, possible coupling with systems for chemical analyses and image analysers, etc. The annual cost of maintenance contracts and consumables should also be taken into consideration, as these can represent 3–6% of the initial purchase price.

Emission of electrons

An electron gun is the source of electronic radiation. Generally, radiation is caused by the thermoelectronic emission of a filament of tungsten heated to 2,500°C (or of a tip of lanthanum hexaboride heated to 1,600°C) which forms the cathode (Fig. 8.10).

Fig. 8.10. Thermal-emission electron gun by: (1) tungsten (on the *left* or LaB$_6$ (on the *right*) filament, (2) focusing electrode polarized negatively with respect to the filament (Wehnelt), (3) anode, (4) cross-over (10 to 50 µm). Wehnelt is carried to a negative potential of a few volts to push the emitted electrons out of the axis and to concentrate them in a narrow beam

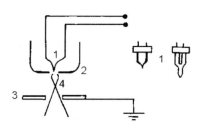

The tungsten filament has a diameter of approximately 0.1 mm, is V shaped and pointed at the end to focus the emission. The filament is heated to a high temperature under vacuum and is subjected to a work voltage of 4.5 eV. The conduction electrons can then cross the barrier of potential and an electronic cloud is formed. These electrons are accelerated by a potential V_0. An electron beam is obtained whose energy is $E_0 = eV_0$. The emitted electrons move into the column at constant speed thanks to the high electric potential between the filament and the anode (supply voltage of the anode).

A cathode made of lanthanum hexaboride (LaB$_6$) with a work voltage of 2.7 eV, i.e. weaker than that of tungsten, can be used at a lower temperature (approximately 1,600°C); brightness is then considerably improved. However, the vacuum must be changed to 10^{-7} Torr, and the reactivity of LaB$_6$ with certain metals can be awkward. Electron guns with field emission are also available whose brightness is much greater than that of thermoelectronic guns and whose energy dispersion is reduced.

The incidental beam of electrons emitted by the electron gun (<1 mm of the cross-over) crosses the column of the microscope following the optical axis. Electromagnetic lenses are solenoid and consequently generate a magnetic field that focuses the electrons. An external shield prevents the dispersion of this magnetic field. The usual acceleration voltage varies from 50 to 1,250 kV, but can reach 3,000 kV. In practice, microscopes are available with (1) voltage of less than 100 kV, (2) medium voltage of between 200 and 500 kV, (3) high and very high voltage electronic microscopes (HVEM), 1,250 kV and above. Those in group (3) are very expensive, very voluminous and require special safety equipment.

Observations

In TEM mode, high resolution electronic microscopes (HREM–HRTEM) (200–300 kV) can be equipped with 15 Å probes which enable the study of the morphology of the samples at different scales, direct observation of the atomic structure of a crystal and of the stacking of atoms (1.5 Å at 400 kV) on micro-samples where XRD is not efficient. These microscopes are thus useful to study problems of fundamental crystallography, phenomena of deterioration (germination and crystal growths, transformation of the phase that is amorphous to X-ray into crypto-crystalline and crystalline phases in the repetitive structures of clays). For example, interstratifications of mica–chlorite and minerals of 7–14 Å were studied by Amouric (1987, 1990) and Amouric et al. (1988), mica–kaolinite associations by Ahn and Peacor (1987).[3]

Using these techniques, it is possible to detect the planar defects, relic layers, and pale fringes of the interlayer levels. Care should be taken with high resolution to ensure that the high electron energies do not cause irradiation damage due to powerful vibrations of electron matter.

Micro-diffraction

In mineralogy, micro-diffraction of electrons is generally carried out simultaneously with the observation of images of normal incidence. The objects are prepared on micro-grids at sufficiently low density to insulate the elementary particles in the same way as for imagery.

Micro-diffraction can be performed with the majority of the TEMs simply by adjusting the diaphragm. The fast electron beam at low wavelength and high energy (20–60 keV or more) strikes the extremely thin micro-crystal (<100 Å); when the angle of incidence on the reticular levels is in agreement with Bragg's law (cf. Chap. 4) spots of diffraction are observed (Fig. 8.11). On submicro-samples, the spectra obtained are characteristic of single-crystal structures. Such a detailed view of crystal arrangements and defects cannot be obtained with traditional XRD (cf. Chap. 4).

---

[3] For these very fine studies, the zones of interest are selected on thin slides with SEM at magnifying powers of about 10,000–20,000. These zones are separated on sections thinned with an ultra-microtome and an argon gun to ensure they are sufficiently transparent for the electrons in HRTEM.

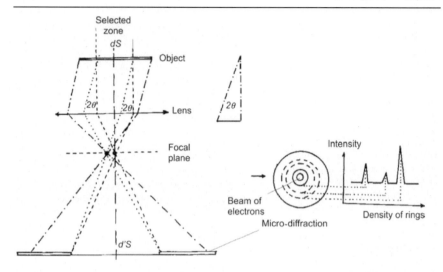

Fig. 8.11. Micro-diffraction by adjustment of the diaphragm

Micro-diffraction by adjustment of the diaphragm uses a diaphragm placed in the image plane which defines a reduced active surface of approximately 1 μm^2. This method enables readable spectra of oriented micro-crystals to be obtained, but the very small wavelength of the electrons induces weak angles of diffraction and associated intensities that are different from the methods of traditional X-ray diffraction described in Chap. 4.

As the sample is very thin, the diffraction spots obtained are characteristic of single-crystal structures. This method is often used as a complement to traditional XRD. On polycrystalline materials like clays, annular spectra can be obtained in about a minute.

Special TEM Techniques

Visualization of Charges with Colloidal Gold

Principle

As colloidal gold is opaque to electrons, it is used as a tracer to reveal edge charges or structural defects in crystalline structures (Photo 8.1 left).

Equipment and reagents

– TEM grids 3.05 mm in diameter covered with an FORMVAR film and carbon
– 5 nm particle size colloidal gold solution (store in the refrigerator protected from light).

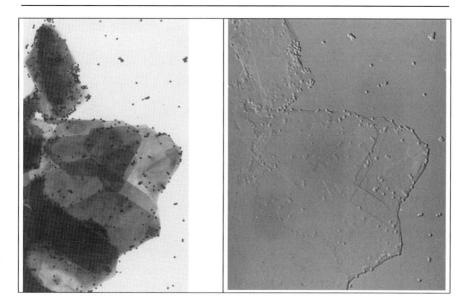

Photo 8.1. Special transmission electron microscopy techniques. On the left, highlighting of edge charges in kaolinite by colloidal gold (see procedure in text of this section), on the right view in paraglyph (see procedure in below), photographs (x 90,000), Gautheyrou J., IRD mineralogical reference set, Bondy, France, unpublished data

– Suspend the colloidal gold solution by agitation
– take 0.5 mL of gold suspension and mix in a glass tube with 0.5 mL of sample of low density in order to obtain well separated minerals; leave in contact for a few minutes; agitate and put a micro-drop on a 3 mm grid.,

Allow to dry in the air and view under a TEM with a magnifying power of about 60,000. Gold preferentially migrates towards the rupture or crystallization zones and reveals the modes of assembly and the active sites of certain clays.

Development in Paraglyph

Principle
The aim is to obtain a pseudo relief by superposition, with a tiny shift of negative and positive transparencies of the same image (Photo 8.1 right).

Equipment and products

– Negative film with strong contrast, format at least 6.5 × 9 cm
– transparent positive film
– photographic development products (developer – fixer).

Procedure

– Choose a clear negative of the image
– by contact trace the image on a positive transparency of similar density
– superimpose the negative and positive and find the optimal shift needed to obtain an effect of relief
– draw by tracing or by enlargement. This type of image makes it possible to see coverings of particles more clearly and the effect of relief can be spectacular.

Opacification of Samples that are "Transparent" to Electrons

Minerals rich in iron are very opaque to electrons and can cause problems if they are too thick as the resulting images are very strongly contrasted and no details are visible.

On the other hand, certain very fine minerals like allophanes are practically transparent to electrons if they are present in low concentrations. These preparations can be opacified with a lead salt ($PbCl_2$ at 1% in water).

The sample is left in contact with lead solution for one hour, then washed, suspended again and diluted to prepare a TEM grid.

Scanning Transmission Electron Microscopy

The electron gun and the condenser system used to produce the electron beam are based on a principle that is similar to traditional TEM, but in TEM the signal is transmitted to the image plane observable on a fluorescent screen via a system of electronic lenses, whereas in scanning transmission electron microscopes (STEM), the signal is directly collected by electron or X-ray detectors, and transmitted on-screen (Fig. 8.12).

In true STEM, an electron gun with field emission, whose cross-over is about 5 nm and whose brightness is more than 1,000 times higher than that of a traditional tungsten source, provides an electron beam which crosses a condenser giving a reduced image of the source (micro-probe).

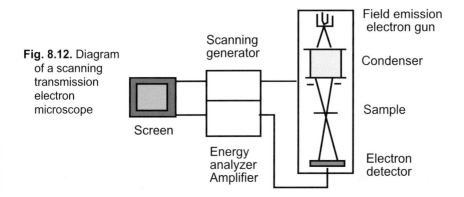

Fig. 8.12. Diagram of a scanning transmission electron microscope

This probe scans the surface of the sample by means of a deflecting coil. The electrons transmitted or diffracted by the sample are collected on a detector with a response that is proportional to their intensity. After amplification, an image is created on the screen stage-by-stage in synchronization with the scanning generator.

Electron guns with field emission are very sensitive to contamination. They require an ultrahigh "dry" vacuum (10^{-10} Torr), which proscribes the use of oil diffusion pumps for the secondary vacuum. In spite of the use of cryoscopic traps, the gun can still break down because of traces of oil.

Very high spatial resolution can be achieved. This equipment can also be equipped with energy analysers such as electron energy loss spectrometers (EELS). They can carry out analyses on surfaces of the order of one nanometer on all the elements of the periodic table (^{3}Li to ^{92}U) on submicroscopic samples.

Dedicated STEM are not the most widely used, many manufacturers prefer to sell hybrid TEM equipped with complementary STEM which perform excellently for a price that is 2 at 3 times lower.

8.3.4 Scanning Electron Microscopy

Scanning Microscopes by Reflection, Microprobes

The concept of the scanning electron microscope (SEM) and that of electronic micro-probes (EM) are complementary, EM comprising probes of less than 1 μm optimized for X-ray analysis.

The thermionic electron gun is subjected to a negative voltage of 10–50 kV. The sample is placed on a goniometric precision support (a binocular magnifying glass enables visual location of the point of impact on the microprobe).

Electromagnetic condensers form the image of the probe which is projected on the sample. The probe is moved by deflection of the beam. A massive sample can be 2–4 cm thick and have a diameter of 20 cm (8 inches wafer). A large-capacity sample chamber requires a clean vacuum system with a strong flow (turbomolecular pump). The magnifying power is the ratio of the amplitude of the scanning of the image (fixed) to the amplitude of the scanning of the object (variable).

Electron–matter interactions (secondary and back-scattered electrons, X-ray, Auger electrons, photoluminescence, transmitted electrons) can be used for analytical measurements.

The image is created stage-by-stage (pixel by pixel) and allows digitalization and treatments using an associated data processing system. The creation of the images is based on two modes:

– in *secondary electrons mode* the incidental primary radiation of the electrons loses energy in contact with the matter; part of the energy is restored in the form of secondary electrons which cross the grid of the collector and are then accelerated in the field of the scintillator; an exploitable signal is obtained which is mixed with the back-scattered electrons which are able to cross the diaphragm of the detector

– in *back-scattered electrons mode* the electrons are collected by the collector of a scintillation detector; the signal is rather weak but detection is improved by using a semiconductor detector in the shape of disc that is perforated in the centre which is placed above the sample; a device installed in two or four different sectors makes it possible to create a topographic contrast.

The chemical composition of the sample sometimes varies in a random way because the rate of penetration is very low. The shade of grey is related to the atomic numbers of the elements observed.

The resolution is about 20–100 Å depending on the element observed. The intensity of the electron beam and of the scanning conditions is chosen to ensure maximum resolution and an optimal signal-to-noise ratio for a given magnifying power. Even in the best conditions strong incidental energy (approximately 30 keV) prevents very fine details from being observed, but generally reasonably good results are obtained. On the other hand, if the material is slightly conducting and cannot be sprayed with metal, it may be better to reduce the charge by using energy below 5 keV.

The diaphragm should be selected to obtain a suitable depth of field, as well as to allow adjustment of the work distance if the relief of the sample is significant.

Environmental Scanning Electron Microscopy

These microscopes enable high resolution images to be obtained by reflection on samples preserved in their natural moisture, without degassing or surface conducting treatment. Some environmental investigations can be made without deformation or transformation of the sample. Two systems are used:
– low vacuum scanning electron microscopes (LV-SEM) are relatively simple and can be used in conventional SEM; they enable a partial vacuum of about 2–4 Torr to be created in the sample chamber; they are generally equipped with a detector of back-scattered electrons
– environmental scanning electron microscopes (ESEM) are dedicated microscopes which enable a high vacuum to be created in the electron gun (10^{-7} Torr) and simultaneously a reduced vacuum of near atmospheric pressure to be created in the observation chamber. This difference in vacuum is obtained in stages with progressive reduction in pressure.

The distance between the sample and the output of the electron beam under high vacuum must be as small as possible in order to avoid a reduction in performance. In conventional SEM, more than 95% of the electrons do not undergo dispersion. In environmental SEM with the sample at a short distance from the beam output under a pressure of 1 Torr, the proportion of non-dispersed electrons can reach 90%, but decreases with the number of gas molecules in the trajectory of the beam.

A specific gaseous secondary electron detector (GSED) enables the quality of the image to be improved by discriminating the back- scattered electrons and the secondary electrons resulting from the interactions of the electrons of the beam and the atoms of the sample. There is no artefact of charge as in conventional SEM (e.g. ionization of gas, production of free electrons, or creation of positive ions compensating for the negative charges). This detector is not sensitive to light or to temperature.

The atmosphere in the sample chamber can be controlled at the same time as the pressure and the temperature and enables observations in a gaseous medium of almost constant composition. Interpretation of the images requires adaptation to phenomena such as condensation on the minerals (for example rounding of the angles), the presence of interstitial water or pollutants and the determination of gas balances. Quantitative measurements by EDX (cf. Sect. 8.3.5) are possible. Many applications in soil science, especially in studies of organic matter, clayey materials, and micro-organisms are now possible using ESEM (Mathieu 1998, Leroux and Morin 1999), for example:

– physical problems involved with expansible minerals, allophane soils with high water retention, structure, texture, porosity, aggregates, transfers between the soil and the environment, dehydration and hydration processes, soil shrinkage, compression, adhesiveness
– effect of heat or chemical treatments, fusion, sublimation, growth of crystals, stabilization of structure, tests under constraint
– dynamics of the degradation of organic matter, micro-fauna.

8.3.5 Ultimate Micro-analysis by X-Ray Spectrometry

Energy Dispersive X-Ray Spectrometry

Micro-determinations are usually carried out by X-ray fluorescence spectrometry (cf. Sect. 31.3.2, Chap. 31) by means of an EDX spectrometer. This system (Fig. 8.13) enables plotting of charts of elementary qualitative distribution at the surface layer and on approximately 1 μm thickness. It is better to use almost flat surfaces; for accurate quantitative analysis, surfaces have to be polished to 0.25 μm to limit possible topographical effects.

A fixed probe can be used if less precise quantitative micro-analyses is needed than that obtained with dedicated analytical probes, but ZAF matrix-correction software (Z: atomic number, A: absorption, F: fluorescence) enable improvement of the results. These analyses can only be performed on elements heavier than ^{11}Na. Light elements require the emission of Auger electrons; but the ultra-high vacuum of 10^{-10} Torr required in Auger spectroscopy cannot be obtained with normal scanning microscopes. A SAM[4] microscope is required where the vacuum is obtained with an ionic pump.

Wavelength Dispersive X-Ray Spectrometry

The source of X-rays emitted at the electron beam–matter interface is placed on a focusing circle called "Rowland circle" (Fig. 8.13). Detection

---

[4] SAM = Scanning Auger Microscope.

is carried out by moving the crystal analyser and the entry slit of the detector (counter with proportional action) along the circle. The detector must be at the effective focal spot (2θ compared to the incidental beam).

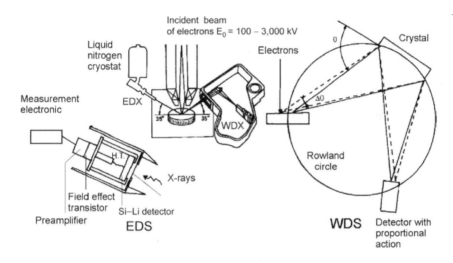

Fig. 8.13. Microprobes with dispersion of energy and wavelength: EDS, EDX: energy dispersive X-ray spectrometry, WDS, WDX: wavelength dispersive X-ray spectrometry (Rowland circle, effect of the defocusing of the electron beam, θ = Bragg angle, $\Delta\theta$ = deviation of the Bragg angle caused by defocusing)

To carry out quantitative analysis, the direction of measurement and the opening must be constant. In practice, the angle of reflection cannot exceed the 5–70° range. It may thus be necessary to use four crystal analysers (Microspec-USA system) at different reticular distances (Bragg's law) to cover the range of wavelengths accessible with this approach (lithium fluoride, LiF, Pentaerythritol, PET, rubidium acid phthalate, RAP, lead stearate, STE). The WDX system is tending to be replaced by the faster EDX system.

References

Ahn JH and Peacor DR (1987) Kaolinization of biotite : TEM data and implications for an alteration mechanism. *Am. Miner.*, 72, 353

Amouric M (1987) Growth and deformation defects in phylllosilicates as seen by HRTEM. *Acta Cryst.*, R43, 57

Amouric M (1990) Etude de l'interstratification mica-chlorite par microscopie électronique. In *Matériaux argileux, structure, propriétés et applications*,

Decarreau A ed., Soc. Fr. de Minéralogie et Cristallographie, Groupe Français des Argiles, 283–287

Amouric M, Bianetto T and Proust D (1988) 7.1 and 14 Å mixed layer phyllosilicates structurally studied by TEM in pelitic rocks. *Bull. Miner.*, 111, 29

Bullock P and Murphy CP (1980) Towards the quantification of soil structure. *Microscopy*, 120, 317–328

Delvigne JE (1998) *Atlas of micromorphology of mineral alteration and weathering*, The Canadian Mineralogist, special publication 3, Ottawa, IRD, Paris

Hartshorne NM and Stuart A (1970) *Crystals and the polarizing microscope.*, Arnold, 219–251

Jongerius A, Schoonderbeeek D, Jager A and Kowalinski S (1972) Electro-optical soil porosity by means of Quantimet B equipment. *Geoderma*, 7, 177–198

Leroux A and Morin P (1999) Evolution de la microscopie à balayage – un progrès pour les applications géo-environnementales. *Bull. Lab. Ponts et Chaussées*, 222, 85–89

Mathieu C (1998) Effects of electron-beam/gas interaction on X-ray microanalysis in the variable pressure *SEM, Microchim. Acta.*, 15, 295–300

Moran C., McBratney AB and Koppi AJ (1989) A rapid analysis method for soil macropore structure. I. Specimen preparation and digital binary image production. *Soil Sci. Soc. Am. J.*, 53, 921–928

Pansu M, Gautheyrou J and Loyer JY (2001) – *Soil analysis – sampling, instrumentation and quality control*, Balkema Publishers, Lisse, Abington, Exton, Tokyo, 512 p.

Tessier D (1985) Validité des techniques de déshydratation pour l'étude de la micro-organisation des sols. In *Soil Micromorphology*, Fedoroff N., Bresson LM and Courty MA ed., AFES

Wahlstrom EE (1969) *Optical crystallography.*, Wiley New York

Chronobibliography

Deer WA, Howie RA and Zussman J (1962, 1963, 1966) *Rock-forming minerals.*, vols. 1–6, Longmans-Green London

Beutelspacher H and van den Marel HW (1968) *Atlas of electron microscopy of clay minerals and their admixtures.*, Elsevier Amsterdam

Reid WP (1969) Mineral staining tests. *Mineral Ind. Bull.*, 12, 1–20

Spry A (1969) *Metamorphic textures.*, Pergamon, Oxford

Hartshorne NH and Stuart A (1970) *Crystals and the polarising microscope.*, Arnold

Gard JA (1971) *Electron-optical investigation of clays.*, Mineral Society

Hutchison CS (1974) *Laboratory handbook of petrographic techniques.*, Wiley New York

Wells OC (1974) *Scanning electron microscopy.*, McGraw-Hill New York

Brewer R (1976) *Fabric and mineral analysis of soils.*, Krieger USA

Goldstein JI and Yakowitz H (1976) *Practical scanning electron microscopy.*, Plenum New York

Zussman JB (1977) *Physical methods in determinative mineralogy.*, Academic New York

Tessier D and Berrier J (1979) Utilisation de la microscopie électronique à balayage dans l'étude des sols. Observation des sols humides soumis à différents pF. *Sci. du Sol.*, 1, 67–82

Jogerius A and Bisdum EBA (1981) Porosity measurements using the quantimet 720 on backscattered electron, scanning images of thin sections of soils. In *Submicroscopy oth soils and weathered rocks.*, Centre Agr. Pub. and Doc., Wageningen, Pays-Bas

Smart T and Tovey NK (1981) *Electron microscopy of soils and sediments*, t1 et t2. Clarendon Oxford

Fleischer M, Wilcox RE and Matzko JJ (1984) Microscopic determination of opaque minerals. *US Geol. Survey Bull.*, 1627

Low AJ, Low EJ and Douglas LA (1984) A motorized grinder for making soil thin sections. *Geoderma*, 32, 335–337

Bullock P, Fedoroff N, Jongerius A, Stoops G, Tursina T (1985) Handbook for Soil Thin Section Description, Waine Research. Publication. Wolverhampton, England

Goldstein JI, Newbury DE, Echlin P, Joy DC, Fiori C and Lifshin E (1985) *Scanning electron microscopy and X-ray microanalysis.*, Plenum New York

Maurice F, Keny L and Tixier R (1985) *Microanalyse et microscopie électronique à balayage.*, Les éditions de Physique

Murphy CP (1985) Fasten methods of liquid-phase acetone replacement of water from soils and sediments prior to resin impregnation. *Geoderma*, 35, 39–45

Willaime C (1987) *Initiation à la microscopie électronique par transmission en minéralogie, science des matériaux.*, Soc. Fr. de Minéralogie et de Cristallographie

Blackburn M, Caillier M, Bourbeau GA and Richard G (1988) Utilisation d'une solution de chlorure de sodium pour le remplacement de l'eau dans les échantillons d'argile lourde avant l'imprégnation. *Geoderma*, 41, 369–373

Takeda H (1988) A rapid method for preparing thin sections of soil organic layers. *Geoderma*, 42, 159–164

Chartres CJ, Ringrose-Noase AJ and Raupach M (1989) A comparison between acetone and dioxane and explanation of their role in water replacement in indisturbed soil samples. *J. Soil Sci.*, 40, 849–863

Wright D, Stanley D, Chen HC, Shultz AW and Fang JM (1990) A frame based expert system to identify minerals in thin section. *Microcomputer applications in geology* II. Pergamon Oxford, 289–299

Zhurov AV (1990) Preparation of polished sections for the study of soil pores and their differentiation by size. *Pochvovedenize*, 8, 144–147

Sludzian G and Galle P (1992) Cartographie de matériaux et d'échantillons biologiques par microscopie ionique à balayage. *La vie des sciences, Compte rendu série générale*, 9, 157–177

Gribble CD and Hall AJ (1993) *Optical mineralogy : principles and practice.*, Chapman and Hall London

Fitzpatrick EA (1993) *Soil microscopy and micromorphology.*, Wiley

Ringrose-Voase AJ and Humphreys GS (1994) *Soil micromorphology, studies in management and genesis ; Proceedings of the IX international working on soil micromorphology.*, Elevier Science Ltd

Lavoie DM, Little BJ, Ray RI, Bennett RH, Lambert MW, Asper V and Baerwald (1994) Environmental scanning electron microscopy of marine aggregates. *J. Microscopy*, 178, 101–106

Vempati RL, Hess TR and Cocke DL (1996) X-ray photoelectron spectroscopy. In *Methods of soil analysis*, Sparks DL ed., SSAA book series No 5

Jonhson RA (1996) Environmental Scanning electron microscopy – An introduction of ESEM, *Philips Electron Opt.,-FEI*, 55p

Mathieu C (1996) Principle and application of the variable pressure SEM, *Microscopy and analysis*, 43, 13

Pichler H, Schmitt-Riegraf C and Hoke L (1997) *Rock-forming minerals in thin section.*, Chapman, London

Hitachi, (2000) Low temperature microscopy using a cooling stage. *Hitachi technical data*, 62

Astley OM, Chanliaud E, Donald AM and Gidley MJ (2001) Structure of Acetobacter cellulose composites in the hydrated state. *Int. J. Biol. Macromole*, 29, 193–202

Slowko W (2001) Secondary electron detector with a micro-porous plate for environmental SEM, *Vacuum*, 63, 457–461

Tai SSW and Tang XM (2001) Manipulating biological samples for environmental scanning electron microscopy observation. *Scanning*, 23, 267–272

Part 2

Organic Analysis

Physical Fractionation of Organic Matter

9.1 Principle and Limitations

9.1.1 Forms of Organic Matter in Soil

Many different organic fragments can be distinguished in soils, most of which are of plant origin (living or dead roots, fragments of wood fibre, fragments of stems and dead leaves) and others of animal origin (e.g. cadavers, faecal pellets, earthworm casts) from macro-fauna such as insects, arachnida, myriapodes, crustacea, gasteropods or earthworms.

Increasing the scale of observation, smaller organic fragments e.g. filamentous roots, partially decomposed animal debris, nematodes, fungi, and algae can be identified with a magnifying glass.

The observation of other micro-organisms (e.g. bacteria, actinomyces, protozoa) and debris of animal or plant origin that are increasingly incorporated in organomineral colloids requires a higher power of magnification.

Initially soil organic matter (SOM) thus appears to be a continuum of increasingly fine fragments that can be physical fractionated.

9.1.2 Principle

The methods of fractionation described in this chapter include both manual or mechanical sorting, and the use of physical techniques for density fractionation, particle-size fractionation by sieving, and analysis of sedimentation. The methods used resemble those used in fractionation of mineral particles (cf. Chap. 2).

Manual sorting is used especially for studies on live roots in the soils. Sorting is facilitated by floating using – for example – water elutriators (cf. Sect. 9.2.2).

Density fractionation is based on the difference in density between matter of plant origin (close to 1) and of mineral origin (around 2.65 for primary minerals). Theoretically, it is thus an ideal technique for the separation of fragments of plant origin that are not decomposed in the soil. This type of measurement is now widely used in studies on the dynamics of carbon in soils. Some compartment models were established with data obtained by densimetric separation (Pansu and Sidi 1987, Arrouays 1994). These techniques are described in Sect. 9.2.4. However, depending on the type of soil, the density fractionation method may be hindered by the close associations between mineral and organic particles. The technique can be improved by combining it with particle size fractionation (Sallih and Pansu, 1993) and with a range of dispersion techniques described in Sect. 9.2.3 of this chapter.

The aim of particle-size fractionation is complete separation of the organic components of the soil. Ideally, coarse fractions of more than 50 µm would contain intact plant debris, silt fractions of 50–2 µm (or 20–2 µm) would contain cells and microbial fragments, coarse clays of 2–0.2 µm would contain organic matter of the organomineral complex, and finally fine clays of 0–0.2 µm would contain recently formed metabolites. Some approaches, such as dating (Anderson and Paul, 1984) or isotopic ^{14}C measurements (Hassink and Dalenberg 1996) or δ^{13}C (Puget et al. 1995) appeared to partially confirm this theory. Other studies showed that micro-organisms and organic materials are closely associated with mineral colloids, and consequently "clean" fractionation of the biological components of soils is impossible (Ahmed and Oades, 1984). Certain review studies (e.g. Christensen 1992, Feller 1994) did, however, identify three main classes of organic matter:

– a plant debris compartment (>20 µm) that is not closely associated with mineral sands with a relatively high C:N ratio (15–25) or with a high xylose to mannose ratio, indicating that this organic matter is of plant origin

– an organic silt complex including a mixture of soil organic matter (SOM) of plant and fungal origin, mineral silts and very stable organo-mineral micro-aggregates; C:N and xylose:mannose ratios are lower than in the previous compartment; the origin of this organic matter is not as clear as that of coarser matter

– an organic-clay compartment (<2 µm) rich in amorphous SOM; this compartment is humified and closely associated with the mineral particles; C:N (8–11) and xylose:mannose ratios are lower, suggesting that the origin of this organic matter is probably microbial.

9.1.3 Difficulties

Particle-size fractionation uses sieving techniques (generally wet sieving) to separate particles until 50 or 20 µm. The separation of the finest particles requires sedimentation techniques similar to those described in Chap. 2 for mineral fractionation. However, an additional difficulty to take into consideration is particle density with respect to the Stokes law of sedimentation (cf. Chap. 2). The average density of 2.65 used for mineral particles is not appropriate for organic fragments (Elliott and Cambardella 1991). However, at this particle-size, organic matter is often closely associated with mineral particles. As SOM content is relatively low compared to mineral particle content, one can consider that the densities of the mineral fractions are not significantly modified.

The main difficulty in physical fractionation by density or particle size separation lies in the close association between minerals and organic matter resulting in different types of aggregates (Fig. 9.1). These aggregates have to be broken down and the organic components released without destroying them. Sect. 9.2.2 of this chapter discusses various techniques of dispersion at some length, and describes their limits and comparative interest.

Preparation and especially rewetting of the sample involves a risk of modifying the organic constituents. The samples are generally dried before storage at the laboratory. Drying, together with other preparation techniques (Pansu et al. 2001), stops the organic functioning of the soil resulting in deactivation or death of micro-organisms. The treatment is brutal and it is preferable to slow down microbial activity by cold storage or even better by freezing the fresh soil.

Whatever the technique of conservation used, stopping the biological activity is necessary to preserve the soil organic state at sampling, as the kinetics of evolution of certain organic components are higher than that of the main inorganic components.

However, rewetting the soil starts biological activity again. Rapid growth of the populations of micro-organisms supplied with the plant debris which are released from their clay protection during the preparation of the samples (effect of grinding) and become available for micro-organisms, as well as by consumption of the microbial biomass killed during these operations. Part of this carbonaceous source is then mineralized or transformed.

There is thus a risk of changing the organic contents of the soil by rewetting of the samples which is required by most of the physical fractionation techniques described later. However, this risk is limited in the presence of a great excess of water, since most active food chains are essentially aerobic. The risk can be also limited by the use of reagents that are unfavourable to the growth of micro-organisms and by performing fractionation as rapidly as possible after moistening.

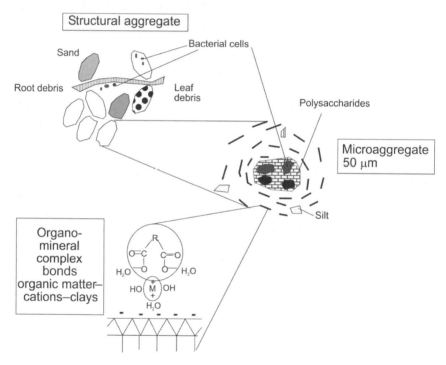

Fig. 9.1. Formation of organomineral complexes, micro-aggregates and structural aggregates (after Bruckert 1994)

9.2 Methods

9.2.1 Classification

Methods for physical fractionation of organic components can be classified in three main groups:
– separation of the plant roots;
– separation by density;
– fractionation in particle-size ranges.

When using these methods, the structure of the soil material should be kept in mind i.e. humified fine organic matter associated with inorganic matter forming *organomineral complexes*. These complexes involve bonds between solid particles resulting in the formation of different types of *aggregates* in the soil. Some of the components that have to be separated are imprisoned in these aggregates (Fig. 9.1). The difficulty in fractionation thus consists in splitting up these aggregates without destroying the components that have to be measured. The principal techniques for aggregate dispersion are described and commented in Sect. 9.2.3.

9.2.2 Extraction of Plant Roots

Objective and Principle

This type of extraction is useful to measure root production in the soil. Indeed the production and turnover of roots is one of the most significant inputs of carbon in the soil, the other inputs being root exudation and above-ground necromass production by the plant. The study of the carbon balance in the soil and in the atmosphere has been the object of intensive research and methodological compilations e.g. Anderson and Ingram (1989) that describe methods to estimate organic inputs in the soil.

Root extractions are also useful for observations of plant physiology such as classification of roots, estimation of their weight and length, chemical analyses, biological associations with fungi and bacteria.

Separation is generally carried out manually but several types of elutriation apparatuses are available.

Procedures

Extraction is performed on intact samples from blocks or cylinders of soil. The samples must be stored in polyethylene bags at low temperatures or even better frozen. If a freezer is not available they can be dried and rewetted before washing, but the best approach consists in washing the roots immediately after returning to the laboratory from the field.

In addition to organic matter content, the texture of the soil, compaction, and structure affect the difficulty of the extraction to a varying extent. The simplest method consists of gently washing the wetted samples with water on a sieve whose mesh size differs with the author: 2 mm for Abo (1984), 0.5 mm for Anderson and Ingram (1989);

The material remaining on the sieve can be washed with water and separated by decantation. To remove all the fragments, the residue often has to be sorted manually under water in flat containers. This work may require a binocular magnifying glass and very fine forceps. The difficulty of the work also depends on the type of soil and roots.

Many machines have been described that wash roots; most separate roots from soil by elutriation, i.e. washing the debris accompanied by their separation by flotation on a 0.5 mm sieve located far from the heavy particles. Fig. 9.2 shows a diagram of the apparatus designed by Smucker et al. (1982) which is based on the principle of hydropneumatic elutriation.

The apparatus built by Bonzon and Picard (1969) is suitable for the separation of roots from intact soil sampled in the form of cylinders or monoliths. It is composed of a set of 4 double sieves made of wood with a brass screen with a rectangular section (50×60 cm) and a cylindrical bottom. The top sieve has a mesh of 1.18 mm, and the bottom sieve of 1.4 mm. The sieves are set in a wooden frame that is moved backwards and forwards at 12.5 oscillations min^{-1} by an engine with a crank-connecting rod system. Samples of a volume of around 2 L are placed on the top sieve and jet water is directed onto the sample. Slurry is evacuated over the top of the raised edge of the top sieve. Once washing is complete, the contents of the sieves are transferred to a funnel equipped with a sieve with a very fine mesh.

This funnel contains the organic fragments but also stones and gravels with a diameter of over 1.4 mm. If there is a lot of gravel, the organic fragments should be separated using a strong jet of water directed at the base of the funnel and transferred onto a sieve placed below.

After mechanical fractionation of soil and roots, it may be necessary to manually sort the roots from the other organic debris and this operation can take several hours. Consequently there is no "ideal" machine that eliminates all manual operations.

All separation methods result in losses of fine roots and washing water and residues should be checked periodically to quantify these losses.

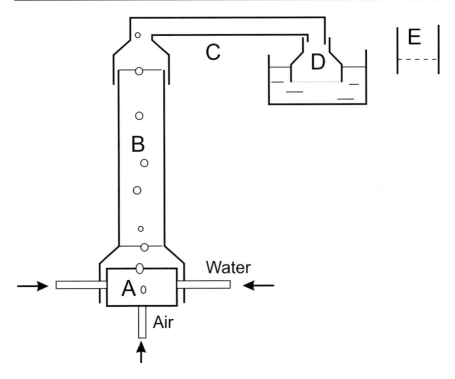

Fig. 9.2. Diagram of an apparatus for the separation of the plant roots from soil by hydropneumatic elutriation (after Smucker et al. 1982). **A:** high energy water washing chamber, **B:** elutriation chamber, **C:** transfer tube, **D:** first sieve with weak kinetic energy (840 μm), **E:** second sieve (420 μm). Tube **C** is separated from **B** for cleaning and to introduce a new sample. The roots are transferred from the weak energy sieve **(D)** by reversal and washing onto the fine sieve **(E)**

Soaking for one night in an aqueous sodium hexametaphosphate solution accelerates the process of washing roots in clay soils, but the chemical action may discolour the roots and break down certain plant tissues thereby rendering subsequent identification of live roots impossible. This type of pretreatment can also interfere with chemical analysis of the roots. In addition, all these treatments can damage the contents of tissues and it is consequently preferable to separate a sub-sample of roots by hand and to wash the roots carefully with a minimum of water to enable accurate chemical analysis.

The washed roots can be stored in the refrigerator in sealed polyethylene bags but freezing is preferable. A small quantity of bactericide such as thymol can also be added.

Dry matter weight and organic carbon and nitrogen content (cf. Chap. 10) can be measured after drying at 70°C for 48 h. Bonzon and Picard (1969) also measured the specific surface of the roots in addition to dry weight. Progressive calcination up to 550°C with successive temperature steps enables determination of the ash weight of the roots and quantification of the inorganic elements after dissolution of the residues in acid solution.

9.2.3 Dispersion of the Particles

Structure of the Soil and Organic Components

As mentioned in the introductory section to this chapter, soil always contains varying proportions of coarse materials of inorganic (coarse sands, gravels) or organic origin (plant fragments), in addition to structural aggregates whose form and stability vary with the type of soil.

In active medium (*mull*), humification processes result in relatively large quantities of transformed organic matter: microbial metabolites with a rapid turnover (e.g. many polysaccharides), and very stable phenolic products, both of which are accounted for by SOM decomposition models (Pansu et al. 2004). Both types of materials can bond to mineral matter to form organomineral complexes such as the cements contained in soil micro-aggregates. These micro-aggregates also comprise the building materials of larger aggregates containing organic particles, organic debris and microbial species (Fig. 9.1).

In soils with a low level of activity (*moder, mor*), the formation of a strongly differentiated profile with a resistant organic matter horizon (*moder, mor*) is likely, along with a horizon in which redistributed organic matter accumulates resulting in the organomineral complexes of the structures of precipitation (Bruckert, 1994).

Fractionation thus depends on the different forces of cohesion of the soil structure. In certain cases, simple moistening is enough to break down the macro-aggregates and disperse the fine particles (slaking). In other cases, more energetic dispersion techniques are needed to release the micro-aggregates and the organic fragments embedded in the structural aggregates.

Dispersion Techniques

Dispersion consists in breaking certain organomineral binding forces without fragmenting plant debris, and if possible avoiding damaging microbial cells or the structure of the micro-aggregates. It should be kept in mind that the aim of granulometric fractionation of organic matters is very different from particle-size analysis of soil (cf. Chap. 2). In particle-size analysis, very energetic methods are used to destroy clay-humic "cements" e.g. destroying organic matter with hydrogen peroxide, destroying organomineral bonds with reagents that are highly complexing for iron and aluminium such as sodium tetraborate or sodium pyrophosphate.

Such techniques are not appropriate here since the organic components need to be recovered without them being damaged or dissolved. The most useful methods can be classified in three groups:
– dispersion with water and possibly with mechanical agitation of varying strength
– sonic and ultrasonic dispersion
– chemical dispersion with dispersing reagents that are not too aggressive for organic matter.

Mechanical Dispersion with Water

Bruckert (1994) recommended this type of dispersion technique rather than techniques using ultrasounds whose action varies considerably with the type of organomineral cement of the aggregates and is considered to be too destructive for some soil compounds as ultrasounds break fragile minerals and damage certain organic matter, but especially "cause the breakdown of the microbial cells from which the protoplasmic contents come to be adsorbed on clays (Mc Gill et al. 1975)".

The technique of Bruckert et al. (1978) is a low-impact mechanical treatment by controlled agitation in the presence of agate balls (35 g of dry soil sample from the fine earth prepared at 2 mm, 200 mL water is placed in a rotary shaker with five agate balls and agitated at 50 rpm for 15 h). Feller (1979) developed a similar technique on tropical sandy soils with low humus content. In this case the recommended mechanical action is even more moderate: 100 g soil agitated for one hour with three glass balls in 300 mL distilled water.

Andreux et al. (1980) studied a standard steppe soil of the *chernozem* type with a very stable clay–humus complex. The dry soil was sieved to 2 mm, shaken by slow rotation (40 rpm) in water (35 g of soil for 200 mL water) for one night at 20°C with different numbers of agate balls. The rates of the fine clay–silt fraction (0–50 μm) obtained by these authors increased from 57% of the soil weight with agitation without agate balls to 90% of the soil weight when mechanical fragmentation was used. Beyond two, the number of balls had a limited influence on the rate of the fine fraction (Fig. 9.3). On the other hand, up to 15 h of agitation the rate increased without reaching the next stage, revealing that destruction of all aggregates bigger than 50 µm is progressive. However, beyond a certain degree of mechanical action (more than three balls for 15 h of agitation or five balls for more than 8 h of agitation), the treatments appear to solubilize part of the carbon, so very aggressive mechanical action is not recommended.

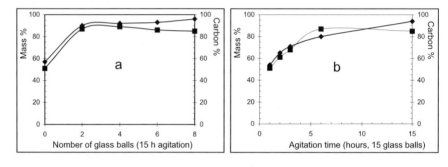

Fig. 9.3. Influence of the number of 10 mm agate balls **(a)**, and length of agitation **(b)** on the fragmentation of the aggregates >50 µm (after Andreux et al. 1980) *filled diamond* mass percent of the 0-50 µm fraction, *filled square* carbon content of the 0–50 µm fraction as a percentage of total C

Sidi (1987) also used fragmentation by agitation with glass balls on a Tunisian carbonated soil. Fig. 9.4a shows the influence of the length of agitation on particle size distribution with or without the presence of three glass balls (15 g of soil, 100 mL water, back and forth agitation with one back and forth movement per second. The main effect of the mechanical treatment was the destruction of the biggest macro-aggregates (200–2000 µm) whereas the percentage of aggregates of intermediate size (50–200 µm) remained almost identical with or without the balls. The shape of the curves also suggested that the process of fragmentation occurs in stages (1) division of the biggest aggregates (>200 µm) into intermediate aggregates (50–200 µm) during the first 30 min of agitation, followed by (2) division of the 50–200 µm aggregates into micro-aggregates of the size of clays and silts (0–50 µm). In contrast to the situation illustrated in Fig. 9.3, one hour of agitation with three glass balls was enough to reach a dispersion plateau for this type of soil.

Monnier et al. (1962) recommended performing dispersion pro-cedures before densimetric fractionations (cf. Sect. 9.2.4): either by dry sieving to 500 μm, or boiling in water followed by one rinse in alcohol and one period in the drying oven.

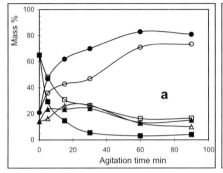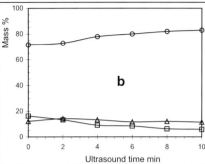

Fig. 9.4. Dispersion of a Mediterranean soil with water (according to Sidi 1987, 15 g soil/150 mL water, back and forth shaking apparatus, 1 backwards-forwards movement per second) **a:** influence of length of agitation with and without three glass balls *filled square, open square* 200–2,000 μm with and without balls, respectively, *filled triangle, open triangle* 50–200 μm with and without balls, *filled circle, open circle* 0–50 μm with and without balls; **b:** influence of ultrasounds (80 W–80 kHz) on agitation for 1 h without balls

Sonic and Ultrasonic Dispersion

Although occasionally severely criticized for being too destructive for certain organic matter (Bruckert 1994), sonic and ultrasonic dispersion techniques are generally recommended for the physical fractionation of soil organic matter.

Edwards and Bremner (1967) subjected an aqueous suspension of the soil sample (10 g soil for 25 mL water) to sonic vibration (9 kHz, 50 W) with a Raytheon S-102A vibrator (Raytheon Co., Norwood, MA USA). For 14 soils of very different texture, dispersion in fine particles of the size of clays (<2 μm s) by sonic vibration for 30 min was evaluated by the pipette particle-size fractionation method (cf. Chap. 9). Fig. 9.5 shows that dispersion was always much higher than by simple agitation in water. Dispersion was comparable with that obtained with the two chemical dispersants tested: calgon peroxide and sodium resin.

The rate of dispersion obtained on the suspensions with an ultrasonic probe MSE Cabinet Model 60 Ultrasonic disintegrator (Measuring and Scientific Equipment Ltd, London) delivering a frequency of 18–20 kHz and a power of 60 W, is very similar to that obtained by sonic vibration (Fig. 9.6). Beyond 30 min (the period recommended by the authors) the duration of sonification had only a slight influence on the percentage of clay obtained (Fig. 9.7), Fig. 9.4b shows a comparison of the influence of the period of sonification observed by Sidi (1987) with a slightly more powerful high frequency ultrasound probe (80 kHz, 80 W); in this case a plateau was reached earlier (at 8–10 min) for the dispersion of the particles the size of silt (0–50 μm).

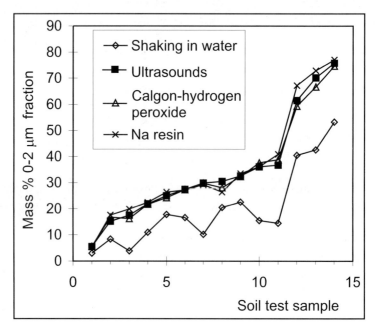

Fig. 9.5. Rates of clayey fractions obtained by ultrasonification and three other dispersion techniques on 14 soils (after Edwards and Bremner 1967)

After a detailed analysis by Watson (1971) of the ultrasonic vibration method applied to the dispersion of soils, Genrich and Bremner (1972) re-evaluated the technique following some criticism of its use. They used 28 soils covering a very varied field of pH (3.6–8.2), carbonate content (0–34% $CaCO_3$, texture (2–59% of sand, 7–72% of clay) and organic content (0.14–9.4% organic C). They tested two types of instruments (Heat Systems Ultrasonics Inc, Plainview, NY USA) (i) a standard Branson W-185C model with probe (20 kHz, 80W) and (ii) a Branson 220 ultrasonic cleaner with stainless steel tank (40 kHz, 100W). Different procedures were used with the tank model (soil:water ratios of the suspensions, sonification in an Erlenmeyer flask or directly in the tank). With the probe model, the end of the probe (diameter 1.27 cm) was immersed to 2 cm below the surface of the suspension (10 g of soil in 25 mL water) in tubes of steel cooled on the outside to less than 20°C.

Fig. 9.6. Comparison of clay rates obtained on five soils by sonic (9 kHz, 50 W) and ultrasonic (18–20 kHz, 60 W) dispersion for 30 min on suspensions of 10 g of sample in 25 mL water (after Edwards and Bremner 1967).

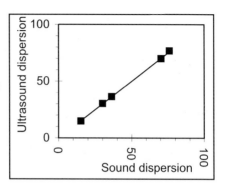

In all cases, more complete dispersion was obtained with the probe model than with the tank model. However, the dispersion provided by the probe depended to a great extent on the quality of its surface: with a pitted probe, the authors observed that the length of time needed for dispersion was two to four times longer than with a probe in good condition. It is consequently important to gently polish the end of the probe with a fine abrasive paper after each 30-min period of use. According to Genrich and Bremner, the imperfect condition of the probes could explain the failures noted by other authors before their trials.

They also showed that with a 15-min period of sonification with the probe, under the conditions described above, the clay rates obtained on their 28 soils were always equal to or higher than those obtained with the sodium peroxide and polyphosphate method of Kilmer and Alexander (1949) which at that time, was the standard method of dispersion (Soil Survey, 1960). This study clearly demonstrated the dispersion power of ultrasonic probes. However, the authors' conclusion was cautious saying that no method of dispersion can be described as universally applicable for all soils.

Anderson et al. (1981) studied the distribution of organic matter in the particle fractions of two soils of the *chernozem* type. They carried out the dispersion of these soils by ultrasonic vibrations for 8 min with more power than previously (300 W, apparatus Bransonic 1510) but applied to more diluted suspensions (soil:water ratio of 1:10). Tiessen and Stewart (1983) studied the effect of cultivation on the organic composition of the particle fractions using a procedure similar to that of Anderson et al. (1981).

On a soil of the *chernozem* type, Shaymukhametov et al. (1984), like Anderson et al. (1981), observed a stage of fragmentation of micro-aggregates (<50 μm) after sonification for 30 min, whereas in one minute, 96.4% of the larger aggregates were destroyed. Their experiment highlighted the very great difference in stability between micro-aggregates and structural aggregates (Fig. 9.1). It should also be noted (Fig. 9.7) that the degree of stability of the three sizes of micro-aggregates between 1 and 50 μm, is very similar, the probable explanation being that ultrasounds cause the progressive release of fine clayey particles from the three classes of the silt-size micro-aggregates with no distinction between the classes. This is different from the behaviour of structural aggregates where there is a clear difference in stability between the 50–200 μm and 0–50 μm fractions (Fig. 9.4).

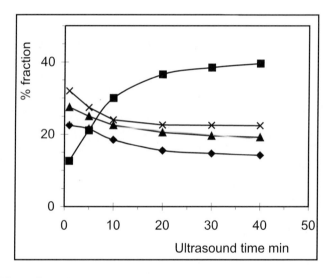

Fig. 9.7. Effect of the duration of ultrasound treatment on fragmentation of micro-aggregates <50 μm (after Shaymukhametov et al. 1984): *filled square* <1 μm, *filled diamond* 1–5μm, *filled triangle* 5–10 μm, *times* 10–50 μm

In order to study the organic matter of an *aquoll,* Catroux and Schnitzer (1987) performed ultrasonic dispersion on soil in water suspensions at a ratio of 1:5 (between the ratios used by Genrich and Bremner, 1972, and by Anderson et al. 1981). 100 g of soil in 500 mL distilled water were agitated on a magnetic stirrer and treated by ultrasound with a Blackstone SS2 generator. Power was applied at 400 W for 15 min, (which is a more energetic treatment than that applied by the preceding authors) and the end of the probe was immersed to 2–3 cm below the surface of the liquid in order to decrease the swirling action.

Gregorich et al. (1988) tried to define and quantify the action of ultrasounds more precisely. Ultrasonic vibrations cause cavitation due to the formation of microscopic bubbles resulting from local reductions in pressure and the subsequent bursting of these bubbles. When the bubbles burst in the suspension, they produced waves of pressure of sufficient mechanical energy to break the aggregation bonds. These authors used a 20 kHz Branson probe whose power could be adjusted from 0 to 150 W. The probe head (diameter 12 mm) was immersed to between 5 and 10 mm below the surface of the suspensions (15 g of 1–2 mm aggregates in 75 mL water). The output power of the probe was gauged by measuring the rise in temperature of a known water mass over a given period. Gregorich et al. considered that the most significant parameter is the quantity of energy applied per mL of suspension:

$$J = P\,t\,V^{-1}$$

where J is the applied energy in J mL^{-1}, P is the output power of the probe in W, t is the time in s, V is the volume of suspension in mL.

Figure 9.8 shows the results obtained by these authors on a melanic humus gley horizon of a cultivated brunisol. This type of material has very resistant silt particles. None of the ultrasonic treatments enabled their fractionation as thoroughly as treatment by agitation in the presence of hydrogen peroxide. The principal bond between these particles thus appears to be primarily organic. These authors also observed stronger bonds between macro-aggregates (or pseudo-sands) than in the majority of studies quoted above, energy ranging between 300 and 500 J mL^{-1} being required to disperse these aggregates which are relatively rich in organic matter. As is true for silt particles, organic matter thus seems to act as cement, particularly in macro-aggregates. One possible explanation is that their organic functioning is a little different (partly anaerobic) in this type of soil from the examples above.

Balesdent et al. (1991) studied the effect of ultrasounds on the granulometric distribution of the organic matter contained in 17 soils (Ap horizons of cultivated soils), type brown soils, or not very processed alluvial soils. The procedure they used combined mechanical and ultrasonic dispersion techniques. The first mechanical dispersion used rotary shaking of the aqueous suspensions with glass balls similar to the techniques described above (Andreux et al. 1980). Sonification was then applied to the fraction below 50 or 25 µm in order to split it into three particle sizes: 0–0.2, 0.2–2, 2–50 μm (or 2–25 μm). The ultrasound apparatus used was the same type as the one used above (Branson cell disintegrator, 20 kHz, 150 kW, probe with a flat head 13 mm in diameter).

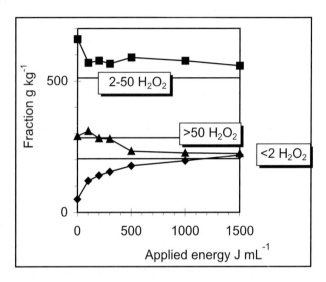

Fig. 9.8. Ultrasonic dispersion of a melanic humus gley horizon of a cultivated brunisol (after Gregorich et al. 1988): *filled triangle* >50 μm fraction, *filled square* 2–50 μm fraction, *filled diamond* <2 μm fraction; horizontal lines represent dispersions obtained after H_2O_2 treatment of destruction of organic matter

A kinetic study of the action of ultrasounds on silt-size micro-aggregates was performed by Balesdent et al. (1991). Sonification was applied to suspensions of 100 mL with a soil:water ratio of 1:3, the probe was immersed to 3 cm below the surface and the apparatus regulated at 70% of its power (corresponding to 0.5 W mL^{-1} from the manufacturer). Figure 9.9 shows changes in 0–0.2 and 0.2–2 μm fractions and their sum (0–2 μm) compared to the reference method (hydrogen peroxide treatment and pyrophosphate dispersion).

Compared to the results of Gregorich et al. (Fig. 9.8), the dispersion of soils studied by Balesdent et al. appears to be easier as it has a stable production of 0–2 μm clay fraction from 300 to 1,800 J mL^{-1} (Fig. 9.9). In comparison, the clay fraction in Fig. 9.8 there is a continuous increase with an increase in the energy applied. However, Fig. 9.8 shows a clean break in the slope of the surve of the clay fraction for an energy of approximately 300 J mL^{-1}, i.e. about the energy needed to reach the stage shown in Fig. 9.9. In a clay latosol, Roscoe et al. (2000) found that energies of 260–275 J mL^{-1} were sufficient to break down unstable aggregates (2,000–100 μm) and to leave stable aggregates (100–2 μm) unchanged.

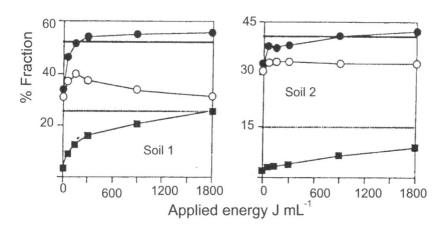

Fig. 9.9. Effect of the energy of the ultrasonic treatment on fragmentation of micro-aggregates the size of clays in an alluvial soil (1) and a weathered brown soil (2); horizontal lines represent dispersions obtained by chemical treatment with H_2O_2 then Na_3PO_4 (Balesdent et al. 1991): *filled square* 0–0.2 μm fraction, *open circle* 0.2–2 μm fraction, *closed circle* 0–2 μm fraction

It is difficult to compare the data of Balesdent et al. (Fig. 9.9) with that of Shaymukhametov et al. (Fig. 9.7) where the cutting threshold of the fine fractions was at 1 μm. However, in both cases, the length of sonification needed to reach the 0–2 μm and 0–1 μm stages was quite similar. The more detailed study by Balesdent et al. of the fractionation of the fine 0–2 μm fraction provided interesting additional information on two aspects:

– even with the highest energy of sonification, a stable stage is not reached for the fine fraction below 0.2 μm, and the dispersion of this fraction is always lower than that obtained with the chemical method of reference;

– on one of the soils, the intermediate fraction (0.2–2 μm) reached maximum after around 5 min of sonification (150 J mL^{-1}). This suggests an initial stage in the fragmentation represented by the division of the aggregates of silt size (2–25 μm) into smaller units (0.2–2 μm) rather than the fragmentation of the 0.2–2 μm fraction. The behaviour of associations within the clay-size fraction is apparently different from that observed within the silt-size fraction where the three particle-size ranges studied (Fig. 9.7) displayed the same stability. Instead it resembles that observed for macro-aggregates (Fig. 9.4): the large structural aggregates (>200 μm) are less stable than the intermediate macro-aggregates (50–200 μm).

Finally, for the soils they studied, Balesdent et al. recommended a sonification period of 10 min (600 J mL^{-1}) in the conditions described above. Dispersion of the silt micro-aggregates (to 2 μm) can then be considered complete, whereas the coarse clay fraction (0.2–2 μm) must be considered as micro-aggregated.

Balesdent et al. also studied the effect of ultrasounds on the coarse organic debris separated in water after the action of glass balls. The study was on an alluvial soil containing 27% clay, and 0.9% organic carbon with a pH of 7. Corn and maize had been grown on the soil for 17 years so the coarse fragments mainly came from these plants. The ultrasound treatment was applied at different energies to aqueous suspensions at a ratio of 1:200 of each of the three light fractions: 200–2,000 μm, 50–200 μm and 25–50 μm. The suspensions were then sieved at 25 μm and if necessary at 50 and 200 μm. The 0–25 μm suspension was separated by sedimentation into fractions of 0–5 μm and 5–25 μm.

The results showed a very destructive effect of ultrasounds on the organic debris. After 10 min (the recommended time for fractionation of clayey particles), more than 60% of the carbon of the initial coarse organic fraction was split into the lower particle-size ranges, and this was the case for each of the particle-size ranges studied. These authors showed that part of this fractionation results from the separation of clay fractions associated with plant fragments; but cleaning of the plant fragments is insufficient to explain the quantities of organic matter transferred to the finer fractions.

The use of ultrasounds under the conditions required for dispersion of clays produces marked fractionation of the coarse plant fragments. This significant observation led the authors to propose a procedure for particle size fractionation that uses only ultrasounds for the suspension of particles of less than 50 μm (cf. Sect. 9.2.4).

Chemical Dispersion

Chemical dispersion techniques are less widely used for organic fractionation than for classical soil particle size analysis (cf. Chap. 2).

As mentioned in Sect. 9.2.2, sequestering reagents such as sodium tetraborate or hexametaphosphate can only be used to disperse clay soils when the aim is to recover roots or coarse plant fragments (Anderson and Ingram, 1989). But even in this case, there is a risk of discolouration that subsequently makes it difficult to identify living roots, and of modification of the organic contents.

Dispersing reagents that are highly destructive for organomineral bonds are not recommended for the study of particle-size distribution of organic matter. Their too high extracting power, in particular of humic and fulvic acids (cf. Chap. 11), is likely to distort the results of such studies. Less aggressive extracting reagents should be used such as monovalent neutral salts which cause the dispersion of clays by exchange with the di- or trivalent cations of the exchange complex and the consecutive rupture of certain organomineral links.

Ladd et al. (1977), Oudinot (1985), Sallih and Pansu (1993) used a sodium bicarbonate solution as a complement to the mechanical action of agitation for the initial dispersion of the soils.

Sodic resins have also been used for the dispersion of soils (Edwards and Bremner 1967, Rouiller et al. 1972). Adapted from studies by Edwards and Bremner, Fig. 5 shows that using the resin technique, dispersion is slightly higher than using the two other methods tested for most of the 14 soils in this experiment.

Feller et al. (1991) compared different dispersion techniques, including an IRN77 amberlite resin in a sodic state. The resin was tested alone (R) or combined with ultrasonic fractionation on the fraction below 50 μm (R/US). The resin technique was compared with five other dispersion methods which were all combined with the same ultrasonic fractionation of the fractions below 50 μm: a B/US method similar to that of Balesdent et al. (1991) described below, an NaCl/US method replacing the water in the suspensions by M sodium chloride solution, an M sodium hydroxide method bringing the suspension to pH10 (pH10/ US) and a 3.3 g L^{-1} sodium hexametaphosphate method (HMP/US).

Figure 9.10 shows the comparative effectiveness of the different methods on a ferrallitic soil from Martinique. Up to the level of fine silts, the most effective dispersion was obtained using the R/US technique (resin on the total soil then ultrasounds on the fraction below 50 μm). On average, solubilization of organic matter was less than 4% of total carbon in the 19 soils studied. Based on the results of this experiment, the R/US technique appears to be preferable to the technique using glass balls plus ultrasounds (B/US) described above (Balesdent et al. 1991). However, the two methods were not tested on the same types of soils. In addition, the authors mentioned practical constraints in the use of the resins: the time needed for resin regeneration and preparation is rather long and there is a risk of contamination of the soil by very fine resin (<50 μm).

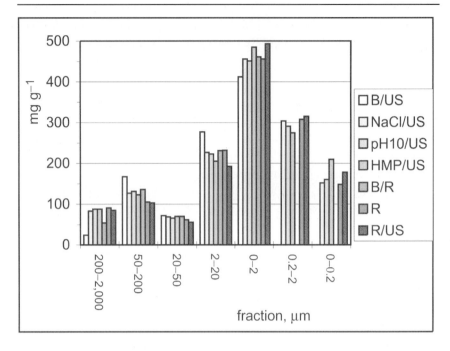

Fig. 9.10. Effect of different dispersion methods on particle size fractionation of a ferrallitic soil from Martinique (according to Feller et al. 1991): **US:** ultrasonification of the 0–50 μm fraction, **B:** stirring with balls, NaCl: NaCl solution, pH10: NaOH solution, HMP: sodium hexametaphosphate solution, **R:** stirring with sodic resin

The sodic resin technique was also shown to be the most effective of the five dispersion techniques for stable oxisols with high gibbsite content (Bartoli et al. 1991). These authors also studied the influence of the soil:sodic resin ratio on dispersion, pH of the suspensions, and carbon solubilization. Volumes of 0, 10, 50, 100, 200, 300, 400 mL Amberlite IR-120 (500 μm) sodic resin in nylon bags with a 50 μm mesh were added to samples of 2.5 g soil in 200 mL distilled water. The suspensions were agitated for 16 h on a rotary shaker at 40 rotations per minute. The results in Fig. 9.11 show a stable stage of aggregate breakdown for volumes of resin ranging between 50 and 200 mL, this corresponds to the volume (100 mL) used by Feller et al. (1991). There was a rise of between one and two units in the pH of the suspensions; in all cases the final pH remained lower than that of the main extracting reagents of the humic acids (cf. Chap. 11). In the deeper horizon, dissolution of organic carbon only became perceptible with volumes of resin above 200 mL; on the other hand, in the cultivated surface horizon, the authors noted dissolution of organic carbon at all doses of resin independently of the added volumes; this horizon probably contains more recently formed organic matter which is not very humified, and is water soluble.

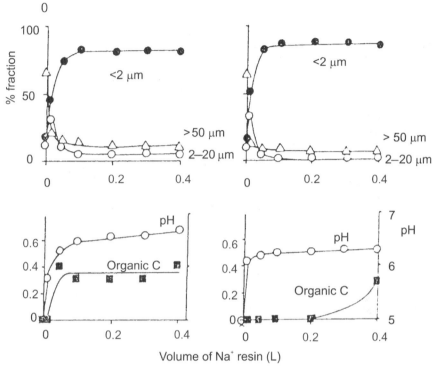

Fig. 9.11. Influence of the volume of sodic resin (2.5 g for 200 mL distilled water) on dispersion of the aggregates, the pH of the soil suspension, and solubilization of organic carbon in a surface horizon (on the left) and a deep horizon (on the *right*) of a Nigerian oxisol (Bartoli et al. 1991)

9.2.4 Separation by Density

The Techniques

The first methods used to separate the organic fragments in the soil were usually based on an obvious physical property: the density of free organic matter, which is close to 1, is lower than that of the organomineral complex. However, the first density techniques were used for the separation of primary minerals (Pearson and Truog, 1937). Starting from the work of Lein (1940), Hénin and Turc (1949) adapted a densimetric separation technique for free organic matter in soils. Fractionation was performed in beakers containing a mixture of bromoforme and benzene.

The technique was improved by Jeanson-Luusinang (1960) by the use of special decantation funnels, and then further improved by Monnier et al. (1962) who adapted an earlier technique of Lein (1940) for density separation by centrifugation.

The centrifugation technique improved the use of differences in density, but neither of these two techniques extracts all the light organic matter. Monnier et al. (1962) carried out tests with synthetic mixtures of mineral soil and oat straw. For fragmentation of straw in particles of less than 0.2 mm, the recovery rate was 73% of the added straw with the technique of Monnier et al. and 44% of the added straw with the technique of Jeanson–Luusinang. The method of Monnier et al. was used to model the evolution of carbon stocks by Arrouays (1994).

Greenland and Ford (1964) used ultrasounds to disperse the aggregates before density separations (cf. sect. 9.2.3). The technique was improved by Ford et al. (1969) with the use of surfactant and of dibromochloro-propane (DBCP density = 2.06) instead of bromoforme for density separations. At that time authors were not concerned with the possible toxicity of these products, which today is widely acknowledged.

Turchenek and Oades (1979) studied methods of density fractionation of organic matter by combining them with preliminary particle-size fractionations. They carried out from 4 to 7 density fractionations with mixtures using decalin (decahydro naphthalene d = 0.88), dibromochloropropane (DBCP d = 2.06) and bromoforme (d = 2.88) on most of the seven standard particle ranges (coarse sands, fine sands, coarse silts, fine silts, coarse clays, medium clays, fine clays).

Their observations showed that more than 50% of the light fraction ($d < 2.06$) with a particle size of coarse and fine sands is made up of organic matter. The fraction comprising coarser particles is mainly made up of recognizable plant fragments with high C:N ratios and low solubility. The fraction made up of finer particles (fine sands to coarse clays) contains a higher proportion of identifiable microbial cellular debris and soluble aromatic humic compounds.

The light clay fractions are also rich in organic materials. Forms of oxidized iron, aluminium and silicon are present to a significant degree in all the fractions, indicating a wide range of different interactions between inorganic and organic matter.

Nowadays none of the density methods using chlorinated heavy solvents are used because of the toxicity of this type of solvent and of the safety requirements in laboratories.

Dabin (1976) proposed a method for the fractionation of organic materials (cf. Chap. 11). The first part of this method comprised density fractionation on phosphoric acid 2 M ($d = 1.2$). In addition to its low toxicity compared to density liquors, this type of acid treatment has the advantage of destroying carbonates in calcareous soils releasing a certain proportion of sequestered plant material. Sidi (1987) used this technique to separate light fractions from mixtures of soils and wheat straw incubated in controlled laboratory conditions. The method was used to propose a descriptive model of carbon dynamics with three compartments (Pansu and Sidi 1987).

The Ladd et al. (1977) method includes a series of particle-size and density fractionations that are also suitable for calcareous soils. A modification of this method allowed, in its first stage, fractionation of the light materials from in vitro incubation experiments of mixtures of soils and ^{14}C labelled wheat straw (Cortez 1989, Sallih and Pansu 1993). The suggested modification concerned the use of an aqueous saturated zinc sulphate solution ($d = 1.4$) as heavy liquid, whereas Ladd et al. had used carbon tetrachloride ($d = 1.59$). Among the different high-density saturated saline solutions possible, zinc sulphate and ferrous sulphate (density = 1.6) appeared to be particularly promising. A zinc sulphate solution was selected to avoid the sequestering of iron on the organomineral complexes. However, it is probable that the zinc element also results in the formation of certain complexes. Other mineral density liquors have also been used including zinc chloride solutions (Besnard et al. 1996), sodium metatungstate (Elliott et al. 1991), sodium polytungstate (Cambardella and Elliott 1993, Golchin et al. 1994, Six et al. 1999), Ludox, aqueous suspension of silica colloidal particles (Meijboom et al. 1995).

Anderson and Ingram (1989) recommended methods of fractionation of light materials with water that are rather similar to those described for the extraction of roots. The light fraction is defined as the fraction (1) which floats when it is dispersed in water, (2) which passes through a sieve of 2 mm but not through a sieve of 0.25 mm. However these authors pointed out that elutriation and sieving methods separate significantly less free organic matter than density methods. The methods of separation in water are nevertheless worthwhile because less organic matter is solubilized in water than in dense liquors, which are often rather corrosive (Beare et al. 1994, Puget et al. 1996).

Procedures

Only procedures for the methods of Monnier et al. (1962), Dabin (1976) and density liquor ZnSO₄ are described here (cf. Sect. 2.4.1 "The Techniques" for modifications).

Method Using Organic Heavy Liquid

The density liquid should be adjusted to the density selected by mixing bromoforme with a lighter solvent, preferably alcohol (Monnier et al. 1962). The density recommended by the authors who worked on silt soils in the area of Versailles (France) is 2. These authors pointed out that more complete separation could be achieved by the successive use liquids of density 1.75, 2 and 2.25.

The soil sample should be air dried and crushed to 2 mm particle size. Weigh 5–10 g of soil depending on the free organic matter content. The weight of the sample can be also adjusted as a function of the techniques to be used for quantification after fractionation (e.g. carbon determination on the whole light fraction). Place the sample in the 100 mL tube of a centrifuge, and fill the tube with the density liquid. After stirring with a glass rod, centrifuge for 5 min with an acceleration of about 1,000g in the centre of the tube. Collect the supernatant on a flat filter and repeat the operation again by suspending the centrifugation pellet in the heavy liquid.

It is possible to destroy aggregates to release embedded light organic matters before fractionation either by boiling in water then washing with alcohol and drying in the drying oven, or by sieving the dry sample at 500 μm.

In the case of soils with high free organic matter content, the risk of sequestration of dense particles within light organic materials is high and it is thus recommended to centrifuge the light materials again after washing in a different tube with the heavy liquid.

Density Method with Phosphoric Acid

The method of Dabin (1976) applies to soil sieved to 0.5 mm. The weight of the sample can vary from 5 g to 40 g depending on the organic content. Agitate for 30 min on a back and forth shaker (1 backwards–forwards movement per second) with 200 mL of a 2 M phosphoric acid aqueous solution (136 mL L⁻¹). Centrifuge for 20 min at 3,000g then transfer the supernatant on a filter. Repeat this operation twice. Dry and weigh the plant matter recovered on the filter. The total carbon of this material can be measured by combustion and determination of released carbon dioxide; nitrogen can be measured simultaneously with a CHN analyser, or separately using the Kjeldhal method (cf. Chap. 10).

Method by Sieving and Inorganic Heavy Liquid

Figure 9.12 summarizes the procedure for extraction of free organic matter (FOM). Sieve a 80 g soil sample on a 5 mm sieve and put in suspension in 300 mL of 0.2 mol (NaHCO$_3$) L^{-1} aqueous solution. After 1 h of moderate agitation on a rotary shaker, centrifuge at 12,000g for 30 min. Collect the light fraction by filtering the supernatant. The extraction can be repeated twice.

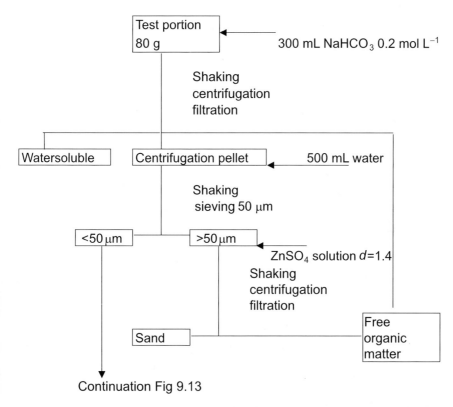

Continuation Fig 9.13

Fig. 9.12. Diagram of the separation of free organic matter by density and sieving

Suspend the centrifugation pellet in 500 mL water. For dispersion, place on a rotary stirrer for 2 min at maximum speed. Sieve on a 50 μm sieve in water. Suspend the coarse fraction (greater than 50 μm) in a heavy aqueous solution saturated in zinc sulphate (density 1.4). After 30 min of agitation at mean velocity, centrifuge at 3,000g, then filtrate the supernatant on a 3 μm Millipore membrane. Wash the light fraction recovered on this filter carefully four times with water, add to the previous light fraction; dry in the drying oven at 30°C.

If the sands do not have to be separated from FOM, the method can be simplified by leaving out density separation on the coarse fraction. In this case FOM is estimated by carbon determination on the fraction: "light matter separated on $NaHCO_3$ + fraction greater than 50 μm". Certain types of soils studies with ^{14}C tracers have shown that this simplified estimate is significantly more exhaustive than the preceding one (Sallih and Bottner, Cefe-CNRS Montpellier, France, unpublished data).

9.2.5 Particle Size Fractionations

Limits of Density Methods

The use of the density method on its own for the study of organic components has sometimes been criticized, but not when density fractionation was coupled with particle-size fractionation. One of the reasons mentioned above is the toxicity of heavy organic liquids. This obstacle can be overcome by using heavy aqueous solutions saturated with mineral salts. According to Bruckert (1994), using density as the only criterion can also be challenged for several reasons:
– the ideal density to use varies with the type of soils. Thus, with a density of 1.8, 90% of the organic matter of andosols can be separated in the light fraction whereas in brown soils the percentage is only 20%
– the density of the plant debris increases during decomposition by incorporation of mineral matter which can be determined by ash quantification
– in the case of organic heavy liquids, organic compounds can fix on clays and perturb subsequent studies. As mentioned earlier, inorganic heavy liquids do not have this disadvantage, but they can modify organomineral complexes.

Procedures for Particle-Size Fractionation

Given the remarks quoted in Sect. 9.2.3 about aggregate dispersion, it is difficult to describe a single procedure for particle size fractionation for all soil types. However four procedures appear to be appropriate for different soil types:
– the continuation of Section "Methods by Sieving and Inorganic Heavy Liquid" adapted from Ladd et al. (1977) on calcareous soils
– Agitation with Glass Balls and Ultrasonification (Balesdent et al. 1991) used on different cultivated soils of France

– "Resin H$^+$ and Ultrasounds" (Feller et al. 1991) used on tropical soils of various origins, with a simplified alternative for sedimentation (Gavinelli et al. 1995)
– a special procedure for use on sandy soils (Feller 1979; Feller et al. 1991).

Continuation of the Procedure Described in "Method by Sieving and Inorganic Heavy Liquid" (cf. Sect. 9.2.4)

In addition to separation of the "free organic matter" fraction described in "Method by Sieving and Inorganic Heavy Liquid" (Fig. 9.12), this method provides:
– a water-soluble organomineral fraction
– a fraction of more than 50 μm (primarily inorganic, density >1.4)
– an organomineral fraction with particles of less than 50 μm.

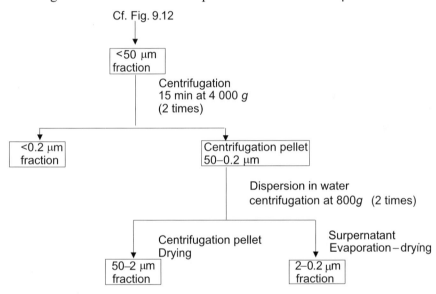

Fig. 9.13. Fractionation by centrifugation of the clay–silt fraction (complement of Fig. 9.12, after Ladd et al.1977)

The complete method includes the separation of this last fraction into particles the size of silts (2–50 μm), coarse clays (0.2–2 μm) and fine clays (0–0.2 μm). The separation procedure described by Ladd et al. (1977) shown in schematic form in Fig. 13 should be used: (1) centrifugation for 15 min at 4,000g in a 250 mL tube makes it possible to separate the fine fraction (less than 0.2 μm) in the supernatant; (2) the centrifugation pellet is then suspended again with water and centrifuged for 5 min at a low speed (800g); repeated twice, this operation makes it possible to isolate a centrifugation pellet of silt size (50–2 μm) and (3) a supernatant of coarse clay size (0.2–2 μm).

The two clay fractions and the water-soluble fraction are concentrated in a vacuum rotary evaporator at 40°C. The method (Figs. 9.12 and 9.13) thus provides six fractions: a water-soluble 0–0.2 μm fraction, a 0.2–2 μm fraction, a 2–50 μm fraction, a heavy coarse fraction (size > 50 μm and density > 1.4), and a light coarse fraction (size > 50 μm and density < 1.4).

Dry each fraction in a Petri dish at a low temperature, depending on subsequent measurements either at room temperature (light matter) or in a drying oven or sand bath.

Agitation with Glass Balls and Ultrasonification

Figure 9.14 is synoptic diagram of fractionation after Balesdent et al. (1991). Dry the soils in air and sieve to 2 mm using a grinding–sieving machine with rollers (Pansu et al. 2001). Put a 50 g sample in a 250 mL plastic bottle with 180 mL of water and ten glass balls 5 mm in diameter. Agitate the bottle on a rotary shaker at 40 rpm for 16 h.

Filter the suspension underwater on a sieve with a 200–μm square mesh. Put the nib in suspension in a beaker. The organic fragments are separated during their transfer to a 200–μm sieve by decantation. Repeat this operation several times until the sands no longer contain any visible organic fragments. Perform the same operation on the fraction of less than 200 μm with a 50–μm sieve to obtain F200–2000, M200–2000, F50–200, M50–200 fractions (F being the organic fragments, M the organomineral part).

Centrifuge the suspension with particles <50 μm to separate the particles of less than 0.2 μm (cf. Continuation of the Procedure Described in); reserve the supernatant. Suspend the centrifugation pellet at a solid:water weight ratio of approximately 1:3. Subject the suspension to ultrasound treatment for 10 min under the conditions described in above i.e. at an applied energy of approximately 300 J mL^{-1}. In samples containing limestone, it is recommended to eliminate carbonates in the suspension after ultrasound treatment by adding HCl solution to a pH of 3.5 on the pH-meter, and to wash the solid residue before subsequent separations.

The 2–50 μm, 0.2–2 μm and 0–0.2 μm fractions are separated by centrifugation techniques similar to those described earlier. The conditions chosen here are only slightly different from those of the previous authors: 25 min at 2,900g to separate the fine fraction <0.2 μm by decantation and 3 min at 800g for the 0.2–2 μm fraction. These conditions must be recomputed each time based on Stokes law as a function of the operating conditions (cf. Chap. 2).

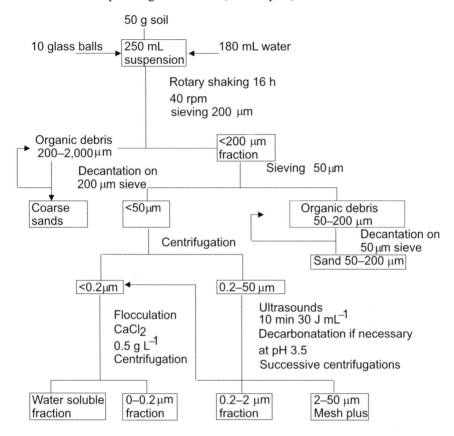

Fig. 9.14. Particle size and centrifuge fractionation after dispersion of the total soil by agitation with glass balls and dispersion of the fraction <50 μm with ultrasounds (Balesdent et al.1991)

The above conditions were calculated by Balesdent et al. (1991) for Stokes diameters of 0.2 or 2 μm, a particle density of 2.5 g cm^{-3} and the data specific to their equipment. The density used corresponds more to mineral than to organic particles. Thus the fractions indicated do not strictly correspond to the size of organic particles, but it is difficult to separate inorganic and organic matters that are associated in the fractions of clay size. After each decantation of the 0–0.2 or 0.2–2 μm supernatant, suspend the centrifugation pellet in water, agitate for 30 min and centrifuge again. These authors advised four sedimentations at 0–0.2 μm then four at 0.2–2 μm. Centrifuge the 0.2–2 μm suspension for 25 min at 2,900g and recover the centrifugation pellet. Mix the supernatant with the previously obtained 0–0.2 μm fractions. Flocculate the suspension by adding a 0.5 g $(CaCl_2)$ L^{-1} solution; store overnight and centrifuge. The centrifugation pellet is the 0–0.2 μm fraction and the supernatant is the final organic water-soluble fraction.

Fractionation of the clay size particles can be performed more easily by continuous flow ultra-centrifugation (cf. Chap. 2).

The fractions over 50 μm should be dried at 60°C, those below 50 μm should be homogenized, frozen and freeze-dried. They are weighed and then crushed to 50 μm for chemical analyses, especially measurement of their C and N content (cf. Chap. 10).

Fractionation using Resin H⁺ and ultrasounds

Decantation method. In this procedure described by Feller et al. (1991), the initial dispersion of the soil is carried out with a cation exchange resin (Amberlite IRN77 in Na^+ form) carefully sieved to 500 μm. The sieving operation must be renewed before each fractionation. Split the resin 100-mL portions and place them in polyamide bags (Nytrel TI45) with a mesh size of 45 μm. Place these bags in 60-μm mesh bags (Nytrel TI60). Close the bags with a rubber band. The double bag protects the soil against contamination in the event the bag should break.

Dispersion is then carried out by agitation of 20 g air dried soil for 16 h with 300 mL distilled water in a 1 L bottle containing one resin bag. Remove the bag from the suspension, wash abundantly with water and reserve for measurement of the small quantities of 20–50 μm soil fraction that may be trapped in the bag (weigh the fraction remaining on a 20-μm sieve after recovery and wash the resin on a 50-μm sieve).

The remaining operations can be performed following the procedure described in "Agitation with Glass Balls and Ultrasonification". However, the procedure of Feller et al. although very similar to the previous section, includes slight differences in ultrasonic energy, and in the clay fractionation method. Sieve the soil–water suspension to 200 and 50 μm. Wash the material remaining on the mesh of the sieves and subject the 0–50 μm suspension obtained in fractions of 1 L to ultrasounds. The apparatus (250 TH, US Annemasse) uses a frequency of 20 kHz, variable electric output (0 to 300 W), and is equipped with a probe with a flat head 9 mm diameter. This sounding head is located 2.5 cm from the bottom of the suspension, ultrasound is applied continuously for 7 min at 75% of maximum capacity, i.e. 0.23 W mL^{-1} suspension, approximately 100 J mL^{-1}.

Sieve the 0–50 μm suspension, wash the material remaining on the mesh, then transfer the 0–20 μm suspension in two sedimentation cylinders and bring to 1 L with distilled water. Shake the cylinders by turning them upside down and back (30 reversals) and place them on the lab table during sedimentation of the 0–2 µm fraction (cf. Chap. 2) for subsequent pipette sampling of this fraction. Repeat this operation until exhaustion (minimum five times). The sediment remaining at the bottom of the cylinder is the 2–20 µm fraction. Centrifuge the sampled 0–2 µm suspensions for 1 h at 2,500g to separate the centrifugation pellet (0.2–2 µm) and the 0–0.2 µm supernatant. Repeat this operation twice. Flocculate all the collected supernatants by additions of 2 mL L^{-1} of saturated SrCl$_2$. Separate the clear supernatant from the centrifugation pellet (0–0.2 µm fraction) by centrifugation.

The following fractions are obtained:
– by wet sieving, the 200–2000, 50–200 and 20–50 µm fractions
– by sedimentation, the 2–20, 0.2–2 and 0–0.2 µm fractions
– a water-soluble organic fraction.

Depending on the type of soil, or when too energetic dispersion is not desired, the same technique can be used on the 0–50 µm suspension without the ultrasound treatment.

Method with sampling of aliquots. This method was described by Gavinelli et al. (1995) and is faster than the preceding one for measurement of the silt and clay fractions. Using a Robinson pipette, remove aliquots from sedimentation cylinders (cf. Chap. 2).

Special Procedure for Sandy Soils

The procedure of Feller (1979) was developed on sandy soils. It includes low energy mechanical dispersion by agitation of the soil–water suspensions (100 g soil–300 mL water) for 1 h with three glass balls. Sieving with water followed by separation of the fractions as in "Resin H$^+$ and Ultrasounds" enables recovery of the M2000, F2000, M200, F200, M50, F50, OM, W fractions (M: organomineral fraction, F: organic fragments, number: lower limit of particle size of the fraction, OM: organomineral fraction below 50 µm separated by centrifugation, W: water-soluble fraction).

The procedure described in "Resin H$^+$ and Ultrasounds" also includes one modification for use with sandy to clayey–sandy soils. The length of agitation of the soil–water–resin suspensions in the bags is reduced to avoid too much deterioration of the plant debris by sands. The procedure is as follows:

Place 40 g of air-dried soil in a 1 L bottle with 300 mL distilled water and a 100 mL bag containing "Amberlite IRN77" cation exchange resin in Na$^+$ form (cf. "Resin H$^+$ and Ultrasounds"). Agitate the bottles on a back and forth shaker for 2 h at moderate speed. Separate the fractions above 50 μm by sieving. Agitate the 0–50 μm suspension for 14 h with the resin. The remaining operations are identical to the procedure described in "Resin H$^+$ and Ultrasounds" of this chapter.

9.2.6 *Precision of the Fractionation Methods*

The precision of the techniques for physical fractionation of organic matters varies considerably with the type of soil and especially with the stage of development of the organic matter. In general, the smaller the quantity of the fraction, the greater the variability. Repeatability increases with the particle size of the fraction. Relative error resulting from fractionation varies in the same way for percentages by weight or the percentage of the carbon of the fraction compared to total carbon.

Because of its weak relative weight, the error on the determination of the coarse and light organic fraction is often the most significant. This error also appears to be linked to the method since Monnier et al. (1962) found for four types of soil, variations ranging from +30 to +60% when comparing the funnel method of Jeanson–Luusinang (1960) with the centrifugation method. Oudinot (1985) found for the fraction with a density lower than 1.4, a relative standard deviation of 28% in the case of a calcareous brown soil and 62% in the case of a fersiallitic soil. Feller (1979) also found a coefficient of variation of 63% calculated on 60 replicates of measurements of a coarse organic F2000 fraction separated by sieving at 2 mm and floating in water. Monnier et al. (1962) obtained for two replicates on four types of soil a pooled relative standard deviation of about 2%.

Table 9.1. Error in the precision of the particle size fractionation of a sandy soil from Senegal (Feller 1979; F: organic fragments, M: organomineral fraction, number: lower particle size threshold, OM: organomineral fraction <50 μm, W: water soluble organic fraction), *m*: carbon percent of the carbon of the sum of the fractions, RSD: relative standard deviation in percent of measurement for ten replicates

fraction	*m*	RSD(%)
F2000	3.0	63
F200	21.6	11
M200	1.2	42
F50	8.8	25
M50	5.8	28
OM	57.6	6
W	2.0	25

Table 9.2. Repeatability of the particle size fractionation of a ferrallitic soil and a vertic soil (Feller et al. 1991). RSD% *m* and RSD% Ct = relative standard deviation of the mass fraction and the carbon fraction (total carbon of fraction/total carbon) for four replicates

soil type	fraction (µm)	RSD% *m*	RSD% Ct
Ferrallitic	0–2	10	23
	2–20	25	48
	20–2000	8	48
Vertic	0–2	4	8
	2–20	4	14
	20–2000	10	30

Feller (1979) also measured the error in the percentages of carbon for each fraction (compared with total soil) obtained by wet sieving and decantation (cf. Special procedure for sandy soils). The results (Table 9.1) underline the significance of the error in precision with respect to quantitative studies of soil organic matter and how error varies with the size of the fraction.

The study of Feller et al. (1991) also included an evaluation of precision related both to the mass of the fractions and their carbon contents compared to total soil carbon (Table 9.2). The error was shown to depend on the type of soil. The error was lower in the case of a vertic soil than in a ferrallitic soil.

9.3. Conclusion and Outlook

Physical fractionation techniques are often used before other studies on soil organic matter. Indeed, they themselves comprise one of the methods of the study of organic matter.

No method enables perfect separation of each component of the soil (plant roots, plant fragments, animal fragments, micro-organisms and metabolites of organomineral complexes). The methods described in this chapter seem to be the most suitable for further development. They have been classified under three main functions: extraction of plant roots; extraction of "free organic matter" corresponding to organic fragments that have not completed deteriorated; fractionation of organic matter in particle-size ranges.

Apparatuses for root-soil separation are based on the principles of elutriation and underwater sieving. Their complexity and the fact that the operations of separation they perform are not exhaustive, led some authors to prefer manual techniques.

Density techniques are relatively simple to use. Coupling density with particle size fractionation of the coarse particles and the use of not very aggressive methods of dispersion of the structural aggregates increases reliability.

The techniques of particle size fractionation enable more extended classification of organic matter, in particular of the three main organic and organomineral compartments mentioned by Feller (1994).

Along with a description of the techniques of physical fractionation, this chapter describes the main types of soil on which the techniques were tested. Adaptations are probably necessary for other soils or to fulfil certain specific research objectives. These adaptations should be also helped by observations of Christensen (2001), Six et al. (2002), Rovira and Vallejo (2003) or Xu et al. (2003). The observations in this chapter should be taken into account, especially precautions related to the use of ultrasounds and dispersing agents; the aim being to obtain better separation of organic fragments and organomineral complexes with less destruction of organic entities.

References

Abo F (1984) *Influence du bore et du manganèse sur la nutrition, le développement et la production de blé sur sols de régions tempérée et aride.*, Thèse d'état, université Paris VII, 390 p

Ahmed M and Oades JM (1984) Distribution of organic matter and adenosine triphosphate after fractionation of soils by physical procedures. *Soil Biol. Biochem.*, 16, 465–470

Anderson DW and Paul EA (1984) Organo-mineral complexes and their study by radiocarbon dating. *Soil Sci. Soc. Am. J.*, 48, 298–301

Anderson DW, Saggar S, Bettany JR and Stewart JWB (1981) Particle size fractions and their use in studies of soil organic matter : I. The nature and distribution of forms of carbon, nitrogen and sulfur. *Soil Sci. Soc. Am. J.*, 45, 767–772

Anderson JM and Ingram JSI (1989) *Tropical soil biology and fertility (TSBF) : a handbook of methods.*, C.A.B. International, 171 p

Andreux F, Bruckert S, Correa A and Souchier B (1980) Sur une méthode de fractionnement physique et chimique des agrégats des sols : origines possibles de la matière organique des fractions obtenues. *C.R. Acad. Sci. Paris*, 291, 381–384

Arrouays D (1994) Intérêt du fractionnement densimétrique des matières organiques en vue de la construction d'un modèle bi-compartimental d'évolution des stocks de carbone du sol. Exemple après défrichement et monoculture de maïs grain des sols de "touyas". *C.R. Acad. Sci. Paris*, 318, II, 787–793

Balesdent J, Pétraud JP and Feller C (1991) Effets des ultrasons sur la distribution granulométrique des matières organiques des sols. *Sci. du Sol.*, 29, 95–106

Bartoli F, Burtin G and Herbillon AJ (1991) Disaggregation and clay dispersion of oxisols : Na resin, a recommended methodology. *Geoderma*, 49, 301–317

Beare MH, Hendrix PF and Coleman D.C (1994) Water-stable aggregates and organic matter fractions in conventional-and no-tillage soils. *Soil Sci. Soc. Am. J.*, 58, 777–786

Besnard E, Chenu C, Balesdent J, Puget P and Arrouays D (1996) Fate of particulate organic matter in soil aggregates during cultivation. *European Journal of Soil Science*, 47, 495–503

Bonzon B and Picard D (1969) Matériel et méthodes pour l'étude de la croissance et du développement en pleine terre des systèmes racinaires. *Cah. ORSTOM sér. Biol.*, 9, 3–9

Bruckert S, Andreux F, Correa A, Ambouta KJM and Souchier B (1978) In *Proc. 11ᵉ Congrès A.I.S.S.*, Edmonton, Canada

Bruckert S (1994) Analyse des complexes organo-minéraux des sols. In – *Pédologie 2. Constituants et propriétés du sol,* Bonneau and Souchier ed., 2nd ed., Masson, Paris, 275–295

Cambardella CA, Elliott ET (1993) Carbon and nitrogen distribution in aggregates from cultivated and native grassland soils. *Soil Sci. Soc. Am. J.*, 57, 1071–1076

Catroux G and Schnitzer M (1987) Chemical, Spectroscopic and Biological Characteristics of the organic matter in particle size fractions separated from an aquoll. *Soil Sci. Soc. Am. J.*, 51, 1200–1207

Christensen BT (1992) Physical fractionation of soil and organic matter in primary particle size and density separates. In *Advances in soil science,* No. 20, Springer Berlin Heidelberg New York Inc, 1–90

Christensen BT (2001) Physical fractionation of soil and structural and functional complexity in organic matter turnover. *Eur. J. Soil Sci.*, 52, 345–353

Dabin B (1976) Méthode d'extraction et de fractionnement des matières humiques du sol. Application à quelques études pédologiques et agronomiques dans les sols tropicaux. *Cah. Orstom, Sér. Pédol.*, XIV, 287–297

Edwards AP and Bremner JM (1967) Dispersion of soil particles by sonic vibration. *J. Soil Sci.*, 18, 47–63

Elliott ET and Cambardella C.A (1991) Physical separation of soil organic matter. *Agriculture, ecosystems and environment.* Elsevier Science Amsterdam, 34, 407–419

Elliott ET, Palm CA, Reuss DE and Monz CA (1991) Organic matter contained in soil aggregates from a tropical chronosequence : correction for sand and light fraction. *Agriculture, Ecosystems and Environment,* 34, 443–451

Feller C (1979) Une méthode de fractionnement granulométrique de la matière organique du sol. *Cah. ORSTOM sér. Pédol.,* XVII, 339–346

Feller C (1994) *La matière organique dans les sols tropicaux à argile 1:1. Recherche de compartiments organiques fonctionnels. Une approche granulométrique.,* IRD-Orstom, Paris, thèses et documents microfichés

Feller C, Burtin G, Gérard B and Balesdent J (1991) Utilisation des résines sodiques et des ultrasons dans le fractionnement granulométrique de la matière organique des sols. Intérêt et limites. *Sci. du Sol.,* 29, 77–93

Ford GW, Greenland DJ and Oades JM (1969) Separation of the light fraction from soils by ultrasonic dispersion in halogenated hydrocarbons containing a surfactant. *J. Soil Sci.,* 20, 291–296

Gavinelli E, Feller C, Larré-Larrouy MC, Bacyé B, Djegui N and Nzila JdD (1995) A routine method to study soil organic matter by particle-size fractionation, examples for tropical soils. *Commun. Soil Sci. Plant Anal.,* 26, 1749–1760

Genrich DA and Bremner JM (1972) A reevaluation of the ultrasonic vibration method of dispersing soils. *Soil Sci. Soc. Amer. Proc.,* 36, 944–947

Golchin A, Oades JM, Skjemstad JO and Clarke P (1994) Study of free and occluded particulate organic matter in soils by solid state 13C CP/MAS NMR spectroscopy and scanning electron microscopy. *Austral. J. Soil Res.,* 32, 285–309

Greenland DJ and Ford GW (1964) Separation of partially humified organic materials from soils by ultrasonic dispersion. *Trans. 8th Int. Congr. Soil Sci.,* 3, 137–148

Gregorich EG, Kachanoski RG and Voroney RP (1988) Ultrasonic dispersion of aggregates : distribution of organic matter in size fractions. *Can. J. Soil. Sci.,* 68, 395–403

Hassink J and Dalenberg JW (1996) Decomposition and transfer of plant residue 14C between size and density fractions in soil. *Plant Soil,* 179, 159–169

Hénin S and Turc L (1949) Essai de fractionnement des matières organiques du sol. *C.R. Acad. Sci.,* Paris, 35, 41–43

Jeanson Luusinang C (1960) Fractionnement par densité de la matière organique des sols. *Ann. Agron.,* 11, 481–496

Kilmer VJ and Alexander LT (1949) Methods of making mechanical analyses of soils. *Soil Sci.,* 68, 15–24

Ladd JN, Parsons JW and Amato M (1977) Studies of nitrogen immobilization and mineralization in calcareous soils – I, Distribution of immobilized nitrogen amongst soil fractions of different particle size and density. *Soil Biol. Biochem.,* 9, 309–318

Lein ZJ (1940) Les formes de liaison de l'humus avec la partie minérale des sols. *Pochvovedeniye*

Mc Gill W.B., Shields J.A. and Paul E.A (1975) Relation between carbon and nitrogen turnover in soil organic fraction of microbial origin. *Soil Biol. Biochem.*, 16, 465–470

Meijboom FW, Hassink J and van Noordwijk M (1995) Density fractionation of soil macroorganic matter using silica suspensions. *Soil Biol. Biochem.*, 27, 1109–1111

Monnier G, Turc L and Jeanson–Luusinang C (1962) Une méthode de fractionnement densimétrique par centrifugation des matières organiques du sol. *Ann. Agron*, 13, 55–63

Oudinot S (1985) *Fractionnement physique de la matière organique. Distribution du carbone natif et marqué entre les fractions granulométriques de deux sols méditerranéens incubés avec du matériel végétal marqué au [14]C.*, DEA, ENSAIA-INP de Lorraine, France, 30 p

Pansu M and Sidi H (1987) Cinétique d'humification et de minéralisation des mélanges sols-résidus végétaux. *Sci. du sol*, 25, 247–265

Pansu M, Bottner P, Sarmiento L and Metsellaar, K (2004) Comparison of five soil organic matter decomposition models using data from a ^{14}C and ^{15}N labeling field experiment. *Global Biogeochem. Cycles*, 18, GB4022, doi: 10.1029/2004GB002230

Pansu M, Gautheyrou J and Loyer JY (2001) *Soil Analysis – Sampling, Instrumentation and Quality control.*, Balkema, Lisse, Abington, Exton, Tokyo, 489 pp

Pearson RW and Truog E (1937) Procedure for the mineralogical subdivision of soil separates by means of heavy liquid specific gravity separations. *Soil Sci. Soc. Am. Proc.*, 2, 109–114

Puget P, Besnard E and Chenu C (1996) Une méthode de fractionnement des matières organiques particulaires des sols en fonction de leur localisation dans les agrégats. *Comptes Rendus de l'Académie des Sciences,* Paris, 322, 965–972

Puget P, Chenu C and Balesdent J (1995) Total and young organic matter distributions in aggregates of silty cultivated soils. *Eur. J. Soil Sci.*, 46, 449–459

Roscoe R, Buurman P and Velthorst EJ (2000) Disruption of soil aggregates by varied amounts of ultrasonic energy in fractionation of organic matter of a clay latosol: carbon, nitrogen and $\delta^{13}C$ distribution in particle-size fractions. *Eur. J. Soil Sci.*, 51, 445–454

Rouiller J, Burtin G and Souchier B (1972) La dispersion des sols dans l'analyse granulométrique. Méthode utilisant les résines échangeuses d'ions. *Bull. ENSAIA Nancy, France*, XIV, 193–205

Rovira P and Vallejo VR (2003) Physical protection and biochemical quality of organic matter in Mediterranean calcareous forest soils: A density fractionation approach. *Soil Biol. Biochem.*, 35, 245–261

Sallih Z and Pansu M (1993) Modelling of soil carbon forms after organic amendment under controlled conditions. *Soil Biol. Biochem.*, 25, 1755–1762

Shaymukhametov MS, Titova NA, Travnikova LS and Labenets YM (1984) Use of physisical fractionation methods to characterize soil organic matter. Translated from : *Pochvovedeniye*, 8, 131–141

Sidi H (1987) *Effet de l'apport de matière organique et de gypse sur la stabilité structurale de sols de région méditerranéenne.*, Thèse Docteur ingénieur, INA Paris Grignon

Six J,. Callewaert P, Lenders S, De Gryze S, Morris SJ, Gregorich EG, Paul EA and Paustian K (2002) Measuring and Understanding Carbon Storage in Afforested Soils by Physical Fractionation. *Soil Sci. Soc. Am. J.*, 66, 1981–1987

Six J, Schultz PA, Jastrow JD and Merckx R (1999) Recycling of sodium polytungstate used in soil organic matter studies. *Soil Biol. Biochem.*, 31, 1193–1196

Smucker AJM, McBurney S and Srivastava AK (1982) Separation of roots from compacted soil profiles by the hydropneumatic elutriation system. *Agron. J.*, 74, 500–503

Soil Survey Staff (1960) *Soil classification – A comprehensive system*, 7th Approximation. USDA, SCS, 265 p

Tiessen H and Stewart JWB (1983) Particle-size fractions and their use in studies of soil organic matter: II. Cultivation effects on organic matter composition in soil fractions. *Soil Sci. Soc. Am. J.*, 47, 509–514

Turchenek LW and Oades JM (1979) Fractionnation of organo-mineral complexes by sedimentation and density techniques. *Geoderma*, 21, 311–343

Watson JR (1971) Ultrasonic vibration as a method of soil dispersion, *Soils and Fertilizers*, 34, 127–134

Xu YC, Shen QR and Ran W (2003) Content and distribution of organic N in soil and particle size fractions after long-term fertilization. *Chemosphere*, 50, 739–745

Organic and Total C, N (H, O, S) Analysis

10.1 Introduction

10.1.1 Soil Organic Matter

Organic matter plays a determining role in pedogenesis and can drastically modify the physical, chemical, and biological properties of soil (structure, plasticity, colour, water retention, CEC, and AEC).

The fundamental processes of evolution include phenomena of mineralization and immobilization and, in particular, of carbon and nitrogen. Mineralization allows the transformation of organic residues into inorganic compounds in the soil, the atmosphere, and the hydrosphere, these are then usable by flora and by micro-organisms. Immobilization is the transformation of organic matter into more stable organic and organo-mineral compounds with high molecular weights that are fixed in the interlayer spaces of clays. These processes are summarized by the following diagram:

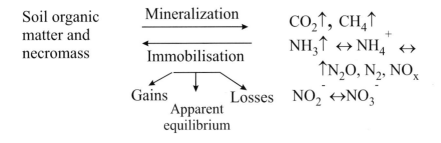

This cycle includes phases of mineralization, humification, ammonification, immobilization, nitrification, and volatilization under the action of specific micro-organisms (Pansu et al. 1998) and is influenced by a number of factors, of which the most significant are:
– climate (temperature and moisture and their effects on microbial activity, micro-fauna and micro-flora)
– topography
– types of vegetation and litters
– the nature of the parental material (mainly texture, mineralogy and pH)
– time (age of the soil and state of equilibrium)
    and, in addition, for cultivated soils
– the effects of farming practices such as ploughing, irrigation, burning, addition of manure, fertilizer, pesticides
– types of crops, exports by crops and use of crop residues.

Soil C and N contents can vary considerably, e.g. a tropical oxisol can contain less than 2% of total C while in andosols and histisols, total C can exceed 30%.

The dynamics of the transformation of C and N are very complex and difficult to model accurately. In addition to the measurement of total C and N, a simple index is needed to clarify the dynamics and allow samples from different climatic zones to be compared, as well as to identify the evolution of the organic matter in a soil profile, or the presence of a buried organic A horizon.

The first in situ observations of humified litters (A_{00}) of the organic A_0 horizon (which are of varying thickness) and of the eluvial or illuvial horizons provide very important information. The evolution of the organic matter is then analysed by studying its chemical structure and physicochemical properties. The different forms of matter can be separated into characteristic entities of varying degrees of polymerization and quantified by physical separation (cf. Chap. 9) by their resistance to hydrolysis (in acid and basic media) and their solubility in specific solvents and reagents (cf Chaps. 11 and 12). Laboratory techniques such as gel permeation chromatography allow determination of the molecular weights of the humified substances after purification. UV, visible, or IR absorption and other spectrographic methods allow identification of the molecular structures and of rates of polymerization. Both active functional groups and the formation of the clay–humus complexes can be studied (cf. Chap. 12). The elementary analysis described in this chapter enables the total chemical composition of the organic matters to be established.

The different factors that control humification, especially climate, parental material, and biomass, result in physicochemical constraints that, in turn, result in a given type of humus e.g. Mor, Moder, forest and calcic Mulls, Anmoor or peats. Microscopic observation (cf. Chap. 8) of the morphology of the systems at different scales allows characterization of the interfaces of organic and inorganic matter and of the mechanisms of humification. Kinetic methods can also be used to analyse the biogeochemical dynamics of the organic residues:

- By measuring, for example, the CO_2 released per unit of time by means of portable chromatographs or IR captors installed in situ (respirometry, biological evolution).
- By using ^{14}C, ^{13}C, and ^{15}N isotopic tracers to monitor the transformation of organic substances added to the soil (turnover rate of soil organic matter).
- By studying the differentiation of stable isotopes such as ^{13}C, ^{14}C, or ^{15}N and and isotopic ratios for studies of paleoclimatology and geochronology.

Table 10.1. Typical C:N ratios of a few main types of humus

type		C:N	pH range
calcic eutrophic Mull		$\cong 10$	7.0–8.4
forest Mull		12–15	5.5–6.5
moder		15–25	4.0–5.0
mor		> 20	< 4.0
	calcic eutrophic peats	< 30	–
hydromorphy	acid oligotrophic peats	$\cong 40$	–
	anmoor	variable	–

The majority of these methods require a high degree of specificity and highly sensitive sensors because of the scales of measurement needed to measure extremely weak variations. They are time consuming and expensive and are not sufficiently universal for use in serial analysis. On the other hand, total-C and -N can be measured using simple methods that are accessible to all laboratories. Improvement in equipment for dry analysis (e.g. CHN(OS)) now makes it possible to standardize analyses and combine precision, speed, and automation. Some of this equipment can handle representative samples of more than 100 mg.

The C:N ratio of the soil in the surface horizons can be determined only using information on total C and N (Table 10.1). This information can then be used as an index that provides relatively reliable information on the biological activity and equilibrium of the two elements that have been subjected to the antagonistic processes of mineralization and immobilization. In regions with a temperate climate, the C:N ratio is about 10–12 for uncultivated soils and generally decreases with an increase in soil depth. In certain soils N can be significantly occluded in clays, especially in deep horizons. In forest soils, peat horizons, or podzols, C:N ratios can reach 20–30 or even higher because of the formation of only slightly biodegradable complexes which are low in nitrogen (e.g. Spodic horizons). At C:N ratios below a threshold near 20, positive N net mineralization is generally observed. In cultivated soils, farming residues recycled in the field have C:N ratios ranging between 15 and 60 due to the presence of lignin-cellulose compounds with a slow rate of degradation. Under forest with acidifying litter, the C:N ratios can reach 150 or even higher.

10.1.2 Sampling, Preparation of the Samples, Analytical Significance

Equipment

– strainer with 2 mm round holes, AFNOR NF34.
– cutting grinder equipped with a 125 µm mesh sieve (AFNOR NF22) and a watertight collector (for litter).
– grinder with retractable hammer equipped with an AFNOR NF22 sieve and a watertight collector (mineral or organo-mineral horizons).
– agate mortar and pestle.
– analytical balances (±0.1 mg or ±0.01 mg depending on test specimens).
– drying oven regulated at 105°C.

Procedures and Precautions

As the heterogeneity of the soil surface horizons near the litters is very high, sampling is difficult and must be carried out with great care. The way samples are collected will subsequently affect the validity of the results. Drying should be carried out in contact with air in a well-ventilated room.

At the laboratory, samples should be crushed to 2 mm to separate non-decayed or only slightly decayed plant debris. Care should be taken to avoid breaking up the organic fragments that have retained their original texture as this could overload the sample significantly. This stage affects the significance of the analytical result as does the weight of the test specimens during analysis (Pansu et al. 2001).

Drying increases the fixing of ammonium particularly if the parental matrix contains 2:1 clays such as montmorillonite or vermiculites. The action of the micro-organisms may not have stopped during storage depending on soil respiration, lignin content, or on residual moisture in the air-dried sample (in andosols and histisols, the moisture rate of air-dried soil can still be 60% after 6 months).

Grinding a whole 2-mm particle-size sub-sample to 125 μm particle size (AFNOR NF22 sieve) can modify the moisture and equilibrium of the reactive surfaces. Moisture content is used to correct the analytical results and must be measured at the same time as analytical sampling is performed. If drying at 105°C does not exceed 3 or 4 h, there is generally no significant loss of C and N in gaseous form; but drying can slightly increase fixing of N in the clay lattice. In the case of instrumental analysis (CHN(OS)), drying the samples at 105°C can avoid the need to correct the results and can limit clogging of the water traps.

Careful grinding into fine particles that are homogenous in size is necessary to improve the reproducibility of the results, soil powder sampling can vary between 5 and 500 mg depending on the instrument used for dry analyses (CHN(OS)). In the case of wet analyses, grinding ensures a more regular and complete attack by considerably increasing the solid–liquid interfaces.

Expression of the Results

If the analytical results are to be used for agronomic purposes, it is advisable to take the soil density into account, particularly in the case of peats, andosols, and histisols where apparent density can approach 0.30. In this case, the concentration expressed per mass unit may be far from the inorganic contents actually available for the plants per unit volume and it is thus essential to correct for density.

In the case of soils with high contents of gravels, stones, rocks, or non-decayed plant debris that display a significant rejection rate during preparation of 2 mm soil samples, it is also better to correct the rough results of analysis to obtain a value approaching the quality of the soil per unit of volume.

Preliminary Tests

A good knowledge of the formation processes and agricultural use of the soils concerned makes it possible to limit the number of tests required.

The number of tests also depends on the analytical method to be used (Table 10.2).

It should be noted that by convention, the "total organic matter of the soil" corresponds to the transformed organic forms and excludes intact plant and animal residues. In practice, since the separation of light or non-decayed fragments of organic matter (cf. Chap. 9) is difficult in repetitive analysis, particles of a size lower than 2 mm are considered to be an essential part of the sample. Living micro-organisms are integrated. A range of different types of tests can be carried out to obtain more detailed knowledge on the analytical substrate to be in a position to choose the appropriate analytical procedures.

Examination with a magnifying glass enables confirmation of presence of seashells, limestone amendments, coals, etc. (soils under crops, coastal soils, calcareous soils, etc.).

HCl Tests: below pH 7.4–7.0, indicates the presence of carbonates and bicarbonates only in the form of isolated particles.

Table 10.2. Analytical methods

method	type	source of interference
dry methods	combustion < 360°C	gypsum, losses of water above 150°C various forms of water (hydration) carbonate decomposition $CO_2\uparrow$
	combustion > 360°C	Na_2CO_3 melting (clogging) various forms of water (bound water)
wet methods	classical N Kjeldahl method	NO_3^-, NO_2^- random recovery (not quantified if not previously reduced) NH_4^+ fixed in the crystal lattice of 2:1 clays (random recovery)
	cold C oxidation	results are too low (multiplicative factor) presence of chloride, oxidative and reducing agents
	hot C oxidation	presence of chloride, oxidative and reducing agents

NO_3^-, NO_2^- test: a rapid test using a soil analytical kit is useful in intensively cultivated and waterlogged soils.

Fixed NH_4 test: only used in soils containing 2:1 clays to check ammonium concentration with two different methods and possibly by destruction of the crystal lattice (cf. Sect. 28.3.5 of Chap. 28).

Preliminary Destruction of Carbonates and Bicarbonates (Dry Combustion Methods)

The samples should be treated at room temperature with a 0.1 mol (HCl) L^{-1} solution until the end of the reaction. If the presence of dolomite, siderite, or biogenic calcite is suspected, contact time should be increased to 2 or 3 h.

$$CaCO_3 + 2H^+ \rightarrow Ca^{2+} + CO_2\uparrow + H_2O$$

Samples containing siderite can be treated using the hot H_3PO_4 or CH_3COOH 0.3 mol $(H^+)L^{-1}$ for 5 h. Destruction is difficult and often incomplete. Dry carefully.

$$\text{Total C} - \text{inorganic C} = \text{organic C} \qquad (10.1)$$

Care should be taken to not lose soluble organic C in the acids (e.g. from amino-acids or phospholipids). Formation of hygroscopic salt can disturb weighing. The presence of manganese dioxide in the soil can cause the release of Cl_2 starting from HCl.

In arid or semi-arid regions, soluble salts that may be present (e.g. carbonates, chlorides, or sulphur compounds) can slow down the organic oxidation of C because of their low melting points (e.g. sodium carbonate) and consequently disturb measurements by dry combustion.

10.2 Wet Methods

10.2.1 Total Carbon: General Information

Strictly speaking the "total carbon" of the soil comes from two principal sources (10.1):
- Organic carbon (only slightly processed organic residues of plant and animal origin, humus, charcoal, fossil organic matter, micro-organisms).
- Inorganic carbon possibly present in the form of carbonates and bicarbonates.

In the majority of methods, the gas phases present in the atmosphere of the soil (CO_2 linked with biological activity, CH_4) are not taken into account.

Some ambiguity persists in the terminology and methods used. Measurements carried out on non-processed soil samples (without preliminary elimination of carbonates) using dry combustion methods in

CHN(OS) apparatuses give organic and inorganic forms of "total carbon". Measurements by oxydo-reduction using wet oxidation give only "organic carbon" corresponding to humified forms and organic matter of debris that are still rich in non-transformed cellulose, but does not include charcoal or fossil organic matter. Although wet methods at room temperature do not allow complete attack of the humus (a correction index will be needed), they are nevertheless used for the determination of "total organic carbon".

"Total inorganic carbon" can be measured using the methods described in Chap. 17 but with varying precision due to the slow chemical decomposition of magnesium carbonate ($MgCO_3$) and especially of siderite ($FeCO_3$).

The term "total organic matter" is often used. Empirically it expresses "total organic carbon" determined by oxidation–reduction but corrected by a coefficient based on the assumption that organic matter contains mainly humic acids at approximately 58% of carbon ($100/58 = 1.724$ van Bemmelen factor). In fact this rate is far from constant even for the horizons near the soil surface. The coefficient is thus not very realistic, particularly for soils containing not very humified Mor or Moder, forest soils, and peats. In these cases a coefficient of up to 2 or even 2.5 will be required. The term "total organic matter" is thus an estimation and cannot be used as an index.

In practice, the term "total carbon" is incorrectly used by some authors to indicate "total organic carbon" as well as to establish balances in total analysis, C:N ratios, or to compare the total C contents of the different horizons of a soil profile and the organic distribution of C as a function of depth.

The term total organic carbon should cover all the organic substances resulting from the humification of C in the soil (microbial residues, humic substances) under the influence of biochemical and chemical reactions. Additionally it represents light organic matter still not completely decomposed that could not be separated on a sieve during the preparation of the samples (litters, coarse organic plant or animal fragments under 2 mm in size). Fossil organic matter (coal, naphthas, resins, etc.) and charcoals in regions exposed to forest fires or in regions with slash and burn agriculture are not subject to this type of dynamics, which means they do not have to be taken into account when wet redox methods are used. However they are always included when dry combustion methods are used and this can lead to difficulties when the results obtained by the two methods have to be compared.

Thus the study of the total organic carbon stock may need to be refined:

- By micro-morphologic observations at different scales to determine the relative proportions of the contents of unprocessed and humified organic matter together with selective extractions in different mediums.
- By the determination of the origin, the nature and the rates of mineralization of the different forms as a function of the pH, the nature of the clays and clay–humus complex, and of soil management practices.

Wet methods require only relatively inexpensive equipment, which means they can be used in all laboratories. These methods make it possible to work with big samples which are more representative of the natural environment. On the other hand, they are time consuming, require the handling of very corrosive products and the elimination of polluting products (Cr^{3+}, H_2SO_4), which can pose problems for the environment.

10.2.2 Organic Carbon by Wet Oxidation at the Temperature of Reaction

Introduction

The determination of total organic carbon by oxidation with potassium dichromate in a strong acid open medium, was proposed first by Schollenberger (1927) then by Walkley and Black (1934) from which it takes its name. After a stage of oxidation/mineralization at the temperature of reaction for a given length of time, the non-reduced dichromate in excess is back titrated by ferrous iron.

Many authors have studied the factors that affect C mineralization: acid concentration (H_2SO_4, H_3PO_4), potassium dichromate concentration, oxidation temperature (from the temperature of reaction to +210°C), the time of contact, the need to condense the vapour to avoid too high concentration of the medium, and to limit destruction of the oxidant by avoiding overheating of the walls. The choice of the temperature resulted in two different types of methods:
- At the temperature of reaction ≅ 120°C (Walkley and Black 1934).
- At standardized boiling ≅ 150°C (Anne 1945; Mebius 1960).

Different procedures were proposed for back titration of dichromate excess such as soil/solution separation by centrifugation and filtration, but direct volumetric titration in the soil suspension was the most widely adopted. Redox indicators (diphenylamine, barium diphenylamine sulphonate, N-phenyl anthranilic acid, ferrous O-phenanthroline) can be absorbed on clays. Additives (e.g. NaF, H_3PO_4) allow better reading by sequestering the coloured products that are formed or dissolved (e.g. Fe^{3+}) and which can mask the reaction.

Principle

Mineralization

Organic forms of C are oxidized in the presence of excess dichromate. The reaction in a concentrated acid medium is exothermic ($\cong 120°C$). It develops at a fast kinetics under the following conditions:

$$3C + 2Cr_2O_7^{2-} + 16H^+ \xrightarrow{120°C} 4Cr^{3+} + 8H_2O + 3CO_2$$

The amount of reduced dichromate is considered to be quantitatively linked to the organic C content of the sample. The likelihood of reduction is assumed to be identical for different forms of organic C and the reducing power is assumed to be constant during mineralization. In practice, at the temperature of reaction without heating, a factor of correction will be required because only the most active forms are oxidized, i.e. 60%–80% of organic matter. This factor was fixed at 1.30 (100/76) to take the variable reactivity of the organic forms into account, but can vary between 1.10 and 1.45 depending on the soils and on the types of vegetation.

The inorganic forms (carbonates, bicarbonates) are destroyed and do not play any role except in the consumption of acid and the production of foam. The precipitation of calcium sulphate can be problematic during final titration if a spectro-colorimetric method is used.

$$CaCO_3 + H_2SO_4 \rightarrow CaSO_4\downarrow + H_2O + CO_2\uparrow$$

Titration

Volumetric back titration of the Cr^{+VI} dichromate not consumed by organic C is carried out by reduction (ferrous sulphate or Mohr's salt) in the presence of an indicator.

$$Cr_2O_7^{2-} + 6Fe^{2+} + 14H^+ \rightarrow 2Cr^{3+} + 6Fe^{3+} + 7H_2O$$

Sodium fluoride or phosphoric acid (H_3PO_4) can be added to fix the ferric iron that is formed or dissolved, and to improve the detection of the equilibrium point of titration:

$$Fe_2O_3 + 3H_2SO_4 \rightarrow Fe_2(SO_4)_3 + 3H_2O$$
$$Fe^{3+} + 6F^- \rightarrow FeF_6^{3-} \text{ (uncoloured)}$$

Nevertheless, the addition of fluoride can result in the formation of hydrofluoric acid which attacks glass and silicates:

$$2NaF + H_2SO_4 \rightarrow Na_2SO_4 + 2HF$$
$$SiO_2 + 6HF \rightarrow H_2SiF_6 + 2H_2O$$

It is thus necessary to clean the lab glassware immediately after titration and to reserve this glassware for the determination of C using this redox method.

Interferences

In saline soils, chlorides cause a positive error by forming chromyl chloride:

$$K_2Cr_2O_7 + 6H_2SO_4 + 4KCl \rightarrow 2CrO_2Cl_2 + 6KHSO_4 + 3H_2O$$

Ferrous iron that may be present is oxidized by dichromate and thus modifies the quantity of ferrous sulphate necessary for back titration. Corrections will be necessary in waterlogged soils in which Fe^{2+} is sometimes abundant.

The method cannot be used in acid sulphated soils that are rich in pyrite (FeS_2):

$$5Cr^{+VI} + FeS_2 \rightarrow Fe^{3+} + 2S^{+VI} + 5Cr^{3+}$$

A high level of Mn^{2+} can also interfere, as can iron metal that can results from wear of the grinding equipment.

Equipment

– Analytical balance ($\pm 1/10$ mg) and a top-loading balance with a capacity of 500 g (± 1 mg).
– 500 mL wide-neck Pyrex Erlenmeyer flasks.
– Insulating plates.
– Teflon flask dispenser.
– Burette for titration.
– Magnetic stirrer with Teflon bars.

Reagents

All the reagents should be of analytical reference grade:
– Distilled or bi-distilled water (avoid water that has been deionised by ion exchange as it can contain fine particles of ion-exchange resins).
– 1 mol (e^-) L^{-1} potassium dichromate (standard): in a 1 L volumetric flask, dissolve 49.040 g of $K_2Cr_2O_7$ (dried under vacuum or on P_2O_5 in a desiccator) in 800 mL of bi-distilled water, then adjust to 1,000 mL.
– Concentrated sulphuric acid, H_2SO_4 $d = 1.84$.
– 0.5 mol (H^+) L^{-1} sulphuric acid solution: in a 1,000 mL Pyrex volumetric cylinder, add 800 mL distilled water, then slowly add 13.9 mL of concentrated sulphuric acid, homogenize. Allow to cool and bring to 1 L with distilled water.

- 0.5 mol (e⁻) L⁻¹ iron and ammonium sulphate (Mohr's salt): in a 1,000 mL volumetric flask, dissolve 196.05 g of $Fe(NH_4)_2SO_4,6H_2O$ (dried on P_2O_5 in a desiccator) in approximately 800 mL of 0.5 mol (H⁺) L⁻¹ H_2SO_4 solution. Adjust to 1,000 mL with the 0.5 mol (H⁺) L⁻¹ H_2SO_4 solution. The liquid should be clear and pale green in colour.
- Concentrated phosphoric acid H_3PO_4 $d = 1.71$ (85%).
- Sodium fluoride NaF in powder form.

- Diphenylamine solution: dissolve 0.5 g diphenylamine in 100 mL of concentrated H_2SO_4. Pour into 20 mL water and store in a brown glass bottle with a ground stopper with dropping pipette.
  Other indicators can be used:

- o-Phenanthroline (1–10 phenanthroline) which forms a ferroine complex with Fe^{2+}: dissolve 14.85 g o-phenanthroline monohydrate and 6.95 g ferrous sulphate ($FeSO_4$, $7H_2O$) in 800 mL distilled water. Bring to 1,000 mL in a volumetric flask and store in a brown glass bottle.
- Barium diphenylamine sulphonate $Ba(C_6H_5–NH–C_6H_4–SO_3)_2$. Dissolve in distilled water.

- N phenyl anthranilic acid .

Procedure

If total N was analysed beforehand, determine the approximate weight of soil required to obtain a sample specimen containing between 10 and 25 mg C (Table 10.3).

Weigh this sample specimen (± 0.1 mg), transfer it in a wide-neck 500 mL Erlenmeyer flask and add exactly 10 mL of the potassium dichromate 1 mol (e⁻) L⁻¹ solution. Homogenize carefully to avoid making the suspension go up the walls of the flask. Quickly add 20 mL of concentrated sulphuric acid with a Teflon dispenser. Agitate by rotation for one minute to homogenize (the temperature of reaction is approximately 120°C). Place on an insulating plate and let oxidation take continue for 30 min.

Add 200 mL distilled water, then 10 mL of phosphoric acid (or approximately 5 g of sodium fluoride with a suitable spatula). Homogenize. Add three drops of diphenylamine.

Titrate the excess dichromate with the 0.5 mol (e⁻) L⁻¹ ferrous iron solution (this reagent should be freshly titrated each day). The end of titration is indicated by the change in colour from purplish blue to a rather luminous greenish blue. Determination of the end point is facilitated by adding 1–2 drops of indicator as soon as the colour begins to change.

Note: the solution should still be orange after the attack of the organic matter indicating an excess of dichromate. If the solution is green, start again using a smaller sample of soil.

Table 10.3. Recommended size of test specimen (P g of soil sample) as a function of nitrogen content (on the basis of a C:N ratio of 10).

N g kg⁻¹	sample P g	mg C sample (theoretical)	N g kg⁻¹	sample P g	mg C sample (theoretical)
0.1–0.2	10	10–20	1–2	1	10–20
0.3–0.4	5	15–20	3–4	0.5	15–20
0.5–0.9	2.5	12.5–22.5	5–10	0.2	10–20

Expression of the Result

It is an accepted fact that the oxygen consumed is proportional to the carbon titrated on the theoretical basis of 1 mL of 1 mol (e⁻) L⁻¹ dichromate solution oxidizing 3 mg C, i.e. corrected by the attack coefficient (1.3 = 100/76) = 3.9 mg C. This attack coefficient can be modulated as a function of the form of C and by comparison with measurements made by dry combustion:

– Total organic C g kg⁻¹ of 105°C dried soil $= \dfrac{3.9(10-0.5\,V)}{P}$

where P is the sample mass in g, V is the volume (mL) of Fe^{2+} solution at a concentration of 0.5 mol L⁻¹ (replace 0.5 by the exact concentration if it is not exactly 0.5) and the quantity of dichromate solution added is 10 mL.

– Total organic matter g kg⁻¹ = total organic C × 1.724

Control

Each day, make two measurements with 10 mL 1 mol (e⁻) L⁻¹ dichromate solution to check the exact concentration of the Fe^{2+} solution.

In each series, carry out two blank titrations with quartz prefired at 1,100°C, and two titration controls on samples of a reference soil of the same type as the soils being analyzed.

10.2.3 Organic Carbon by Wet Oxidation at Controlled Temperature

Introduction and Principle

When measurements are made using wet oxidation at the temperature of reaction, the mineralization/oxidation of active organic carbon is always incomplete. The use of a "standardized" corrective factor of 1.3 introduces a variable that is not easily controllable because in practice, this coefficient ranges from 1.10 to 1.40.

To mitigate this problem, Anne (1945) then Mebius (1960) proposed carrying out total mineralization by maintaining the sample at a constant temperature throughout the process of mineralization without causing thermal decomposition of the dichromate. Effectiveness and reproducibility were tested between 130 and 210°C with different times of oxidation and different acid/dichromate ratios. Above 150°C the dichromate tends to decompose more and more quickly, thus necessitating relatively short attack times. Strict respect of the procedure and precise control of the attack times and the temperature enable an acceptable level of accuracy. In principles this type of measurement and possible interferences are the same as for the method described in Sect. 10.2.2 earlier.

Equipment

– A mineralization block (with from 20 to 40 places regulated thermostatically at 150°C (Tecator, Skalar, Technicon, etc.); mechanization is possible in laboratories that carry out many repetitive analyses; in the Skalar system, for example, a sample holder is capped by a device with 20 reflux condensers. After introducing the samples and reagents, place the unit in the programmed heating block; after the period of mineralization, remove the unit and cool, separate the rack condensers; the sample holder advances on rails towards the dilution stage and possibly towards the titration system.
– Analytical balance (±1/10 mg).
– Digestion tubes with ground joint for the condenser.
– Titration burette.

- Precision volume dispenser ($\pm 1/10$ mL) with Pyrex glass syringe and Teflon piston.
- Magnetic stirrer with 15 mm Teflon bars.

Reagents

- cf. "Reagents" under Sect. 10.2.2.
- 0.2 mol (Fe^{2+}) L^{-1} solution: weigh 78.5 g of Mohr salt (dried in P_2O_5 desiccator), dissolve in 800 mL of 0.5 mol (H^+) L^{-1} sulphuric acid solution. Bring to 1,000 mL with the sulphuric acid solution.

Procedure

Weigh (± 0.1 mg) between 200 mg and 2 g of soil (ground to 125 μm particle size and dried on P_2O_5) to have a sample containing approximately 15 mg C (Table 10.3).

In a Pyrex tube (with ground joint for the condenser), add 10 mL of 1 mol (e^-) L^{-1} potassium dichromate solution and 15 mL of concentrated sulphuric acid. Homogenize. Place the tube in a heating block regulated at 150°C and adjust the condenser. The attack should be maintained for 30 min at the same temperature.

Leave to cool in the air then transfer in a 250 mL wide-necked Erlenmeyer flask and bring to approximately 100 mL with washing water. Titrate with the 0.2 mol (Fe^{2+}) L^{-1} solution (or 0.5 mol L^{-1}) in the presence of the indicator and a sequestering agent (cf. "Procedure" under Sect. 10.2.2). The dark purple colour will change to luminous green at the titration point.

Controls and Calculation

- Titration of the Fe^{2+} solution (two replicates).
- Blank titration of prefired quartz by heating under the same conditions to correct the thermal destruction of the reagent and to establish the effective dichromate concentration (two replicates).
- Analyse a standard carbohydrate under the same conditions to check that oxidation is complete and that a correction coefficient will not be needed.

Without a correction coefficient, total organic C g kg^{-1} of 105°C dried soil $= 3(10.65 \quad V)/P$

See "Expression of the Result" under Sect. 10.2.2 for explanation of symbols and numbers.

10.2.4 Organic Carbon by Wet Oxidation and Spectrocolorimetry

The French standard NF X31-109 (1993) was published for the determination of organic carbon by sulfochromic oxidation allowing the calculation of the organic matter by means of a multiplying coefficient for use in agronomic studies.

Oxidation is conducted at 135°C in a thermostated heating block. The oxidation of a carbon atom requires the transfer of four electrons. Glucose is used as the standard substance and the final determination is by absorption spectrometry at 585 nm on aliquots centrifuged for 10 min at 2,000 g and filtered to eliminate the suspended particles.

The method cannot be used in the presence of mineral reducing materials (e.g. Cl^-, Fe^{2+}) or of pollution by organic compounds. This standard NF X31-109 (1993) is referred to in the detailed procedure.
Notes:
– After centrifugation, titration of organic C in the medium can be carried out at 590 or 625 nm (depending on the author with a standard sucrose).
– To avoid transfers, a probe spectrometer with optical fibre can be used directly in the clarified medium (Baker 1976).

10.2.5 Total Nitrogen by Wet Method: Introduction

After carbon, hydrogen, and oxygen, nitrogen is the most abundant element in living tissue. It plays a major role in agriculture, nitrogen being an essential element for plant growth. In the soil, the organic forms can reach approximately 90% of total nitrogen.

Quantitatively speaking, the total nitrogen value expresses not only the N compounds of the organic matter of the soil and biomass (cf. Chap. 14), but also inorganic nitrogen compounds (cf. Chap. 28). All these compounds represent both short- and long-term reserves, i.e. nitrogen that is directly or potentially available for plants enabling an improvement in yield.

On the other hand, total nitrogen cannot quantify the values of transfer of the different forms of nitrogen between living organisms and inorganic materials. Thus total N cannot qualitatively express the diversity of the forms of nitrogen that vary considerably in soils subjected to specific climatic constraints, environmental conditions such as types of vegetation, or different farming systems, nor can it express the complex interactions between micro organizations which control the nitrogen cycle. The components of proteins, carbohydrates, hemicelluloses, cellulose, and lignin from living organisms are degraded in the soil, lignin being the most stable fraction.

The phases of N immobilization occur in the form of organic and fixed N, and occluded or exchangeable forms of $N-NH_4^+$. The phases of nitrification/denitrification produce NO_2^-, NO_3^-, N_2, nitrogen oxides (with uptake by plant roots and losses through drainage). N processes in the soil can be modified by symbiotic associations between plants (e.g. leguminous plants) and bacteria (rhizobia, actinomycetes) which involve the formation of nodules that enable nitrogen to be fixed from the atmosphere.

The analysis of "Total N" using a wet method derives from that proposed by Kjeldahl (1883). Without time-consuming complementary treatments that method does not allow all the forms of N pools to be recovered entirely. The organic and inorganic nitrogen compounds include (in varying proportions):

– Inorganic forms, (1) NH_4^+-N, which is exchangeable or fixed in the mineral or organomineral lattices, (2) NO_3^-N, which is abundant under intensive cultivation on heavily fertilized soils, (3) NO_2^-N, which is generally negligible except in waterlogged soils or when it results from polluting wastes; NO_3^--N and NO_2^--N are very soluble and are consequently easily leached by water infiltration and run-off.

– Entities whose chemical, physical, and biochemical behaviours are well enough defined to enable them to be grouped in selective pools: plant fractions in different stages of decay, active microbial biomass, biological forms (amino acids, amino sugars, proteins of bacterial cells), N subjected to hydrolysis in an acid medium, N of doubtful composition not subjected to hydrolysis. Part of N is also included in complex humified compounds of varying degrees of stability: relatively instable fulvic acids, humic acids with varying degrees of polycondens-ation, humins (bound on clays and cementing Fe–Al agents) especially protein forms that are weakly attacked by proteases.

The evolution of soil organic nitrogen is linked to the molecular forms of humic compounds. The processes of condensation of humic molecules and of formation of organo-mineral compounds modify the stability of the different pools. These pools can be ranked on the basis of increasing stability as follows: fulvic acids < organo-aluminous compounds < organo-ferric compounds < humic acids < various organo-mineral compounds < humins fixed on clays. The production of ammonium is an indication of instability.

At the physical level, the organic layers adsorbed superficially on the mineral or organomineral matrices react more easily than those fixed in the lattices. At the chemical level, the short nitrogen chains are hydrolysed more rapidly than the long chains or the N compounds fixed in clays.

The addition of water before analysis releases a varying proportion of fixed N by causing swelling of the lattices of certain 2:1 clays. This fixed or occluded N can play a role in plant nutrition (Mengel and Scherer 1981; Keerrthisinghe et al. 1984). Classical Kjeldahl analysis makes it possible to quantify only one part of it; so to control this variable, the mineral matrix must first be destroyed by a mixture of HF–HCl (cf. Sect. 10.3.5 in Chap.10).

The question of whether it is possible to fully describe the relative availability of N compounds in the soil by means of models of the chemical and physical compartment that distinguish all the active and passive forms has not yet been answered. But whether the answer is yes or no, the analysis of total organic and inorganic N is an essential component of mathematical models based on a dynamic simulation of the forms of N in the soil – plant – climate systems.

10.2.6 Total Nitrogen by Kjeldahl Method and Titrimetry

Principle

Mineralization

The aim is to transform organic N forms into ammonium-N form using a wet method in a concentrated sulphuric acid medium in the presence of catalysts.

$$(R_3)N + H_2SO_4 \xrightarrow{\text{catalyst}} (NH_4)_2SO_4 + H_2O + CO_2$$
$$2NH_4^+ + H_2SO_4 \rightarrow (NH_4)_2SO_4 + 2H^+$$

All nitrogen in amide, imide, nitro N–N, nitroso N–O, or other forms is transformed into the ammonium salt form. The thermal stability and the rise in temperature of the reaction medium are ensured by the addition of K_2SO_4. Nitrates and nitrites are probably not accounted for, even with a mercury catalyst:

$$2HNO_3 + 6Hg + 3H_2SO_4 \rightarrow 3Hg_2SO_4 + 4H_2O + 2NO\uparrow$$

Nitrates and nitrites can be reduced by salicylic acid

COOH
OH

and sodium hyposulfite $Na_2S_2O_3$.

NH_4^+ titration

The NH_4^+–N produced is transferred to a basic medium by steam distillation, and then titrated volumetrically in the presence of an indicator.

$$2NH_4OH + H_2SO_4 \rightarrow (NH_4)_2SO_4 + 2H_2O$$
$$(NH_4)_2SO_4 + 2NaOH \rightarrow Na_2SO_4 + 2NH_3\uparrow + 2H_2O$$

After transfer the NH_3 is collected in boric acid (Winkler 1913) and titrated by acidimetry:

$$4H_3BO_3 + 2NH_4OH \rightarrow (NH_4)_2B_4O_7 + 7H_2O$$
$$(NH_4)_2B_4O_7 + 3H_2O \Leftrightarrow 2H_3BO_3 + 2NH_4BO_2$$
$$2NH_4BO_2 + 4H_2O \Leftrightarrow 2H_3BO_3 + 2NH_4OH$$

It is also possible to delay titration, and first to complete distillation, and then to perform titration.

Equipment

- Analytical balance (± 0.1 mg).
- Rack for attacks with gas heating or thermostatic heating blocks regulated at 360°C.
- 350 mL Pyrex Kjeldahl flasks, or Pyrex cylinders for heating blocks.
- Dosing spatula for catalysts ($\cong$ 500 mg, 1 g, 2 g).
- Glass balls of 6 mm dia.
- Teflon flask dispenser.
- Pyrex ball jacks (Fig 10.1a).
- Fume hood with outlets for heavy vapours.
- Distillation or steam distillation apparatus.
- 250 mL Pyrex Erlenmeyer flasks.
- 50 mL burette ($\pm 1/10$ mL).
- Magnetic stirrer with Teflon magnetic stirring bars.
- 5,000 g centrifuge and 100 mL Pyrex centrifugation tubes.
- Spectrocolorimeter.

Reagents

– Sulphuric acid, H_2SO_4 $d = 1.83$.
– Sulphuric acid containing 50 g L^{-1} salicylic acid.
– Catalyst: grind and sieve (Afnor NF22) 100 g of potassium sulphate (K_2SO_4), 20 g of copper sulphate ($Cu(SO_4),5H_2O$), 2 g of grey selenium powder (Se); homogenize and store in a wide-necked bottle.
– 2% boric acid (H_3BO_3) solution in distilled water.
– Taschiro indicator (Ma Zuazaga 1942): mix one part of 0.1% methyl red ethanol solution with three parts of 0.1% bromocresol green ethanol solution; store in a brown bottle with dropper.
– Sodium hydroxide (NaOH) solution $\cong 10$ mol L^{-1}: weigh 2.5 kg of NaOH pellets and carefully dissolve in 6 L of distilled water; let cool in a closed Pyrex bottle (CO_2 is eliminated by precipitation of Na_2CO_3); decant Pyrex bottle then discard the bottom part; store in an airtight bottle.
– 1% phenolphtaleine solution in 30% ethanol solution.
– Standard solutions of 0.1 and 0.05 mol (H+) L^{-1} sulphuric acid.
– Standard ammonium sulphate solution: weigh 4.714 g of $(NH_4)_2SO_4$ dried on P_2O_5; dissolve in deionised water and complete to 1 L; 1mL solution = 1 mg N.

Procedure (Macro-Method)

Mineralization

Weigh 2 g (± 0.1 mg) of soil (ground to 125 μm particle size) on non-gummed cigarette paper (without nitrogen). Close carefully by twisting the paper.

Transfer the sample to a 350 mL glass Pyrex flask. Wet the soil with a jet of distilled water from a wash bottle. Agitate gently until complete homogenisation of the soils. Leave in contact overnight.

Carefully (especially with calcareous soils) add 20 mL of concentrated sulphuric acid. With a dosing spatula, add 2 g of catalyst. Add 3 glass balls (diameter 6 mm), place a ball jack in the neck of the flask and place the flask on the rack (Fig. 10.1a). Adjust the gas flame to low and check for the formation of foam. The flask should be tilted at an angle of 45–60°C to limit the risk of projections and to allow better recovery of condensation on the lower walls (Fig. 10.1a). When the soil organic matter is broken up, the colour of the sample will have faded; raise the heat and boil for 2–3 h without going to dry.

Distillation and titration by acidimetry

Leave to cool. Rinse the jack and the flask walls with about 10 mL distilled water. Fit the flask in the distillation apparatus (Fig. 10.1b). Add 100 mL of 10 mol L^{-1} sodium hydroxide solution. Turn off the tap to begin steam distillation.

Collect the distillate in the Pyrex Erlenmeyer flask containing 20 mL of 2% boric acid solution and 3 drops of Taschiro indicator; take care that the end of the exit tube is below the surface of the liquid in the Erlenmeyer flask. Approximately 80 mL of the distillate are needed for quantitative recovery.

Titrate by volumetry with the 0.1 or 0.05 mol (H$^+$) L^{-1} sulphuric acid solution depending on the estimated quantity of the contents. The end point is indicated by a change in colour from green to greyish purple.

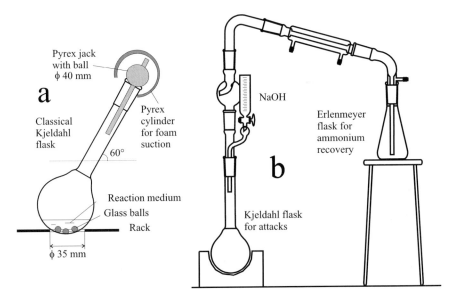

Fig. 10.1. Minimal equipment needed for Kjeldahl titration of total-N, (**a**) acid mineralization with device to limit acid loss, (**b**) distillation of resulting ammonia by addition of soda; for a more powerful apparatus for steam distillation, see Fig. 10.3 in Chap. 14

Expression of the Results

The results T_N are expressed in mg of nitrogen N per kg of soil dried at 105°C:

1 mL H$_2$SO$_4$ 0.1 mol(H+)L^{-1} ⇔ 0.1 mmol NH$_3$ is 1.4 mg N.

If V_A is the volume (mL) of the 0.1 mol (H^+) L^{-1} H_2SO_4 solution and P the mass (g) of the test specimen of soil dried at 105°C, the N content of the soil is expressed in mg (N) g^{-1} (soil) by: $T_N = 1.4 \; V_A/P$.

Controls

Controls are made by distilling an ammonium sulphate solution of known concentration (1) one distillation after attack under the same conditions as the samples in the presence of 1,000°C fired quartz (blank assay), (2) one direct distillation of the ammonium sulphate solution. The value of the blank assay is calculated by the difference between the two. Two reference samples and two replicates of samples chosen randomly in the series should be analysed each day.

Notes

First the experimental standard X 31111 (1983) and then the international standard NF ISO 11261 (1995) were published for the determination of soil total nitrogen by distillation after Kjeldahl mineralization.

Discolouration is not a sign of the end of mineralization, but an indicator of the end of the oxidation of the humified coloured organic matter signalling the end of the production of foam. The conversion of the N organic products into ammonium obeys other criteria such as temperature, catalyst, time, and nature of the N compounds.

The addition of potassium sulphate enables the boiling point of the sulphuric acid to be increased and the attack time to be reduced. To avoid losses, use dose less than 0.5 g K_2SO_4 per millilitre of sulphuric acid with selenium as catalyst. The boiling point of H_2SO_4, normally 330°C, increases to 364°C after addition of 1 g of K_2SO_4 per mL of sulphuric acid.

Catalysts (1) mercuric oxide is very effective but pollute the environment; mercuric oxide can form amino complexes which are not released during distillation unless the sample is not treated with thiosulfate, (2) selenium allows quantitative recovery of N; the temperature should not be too high (<367°C) and attacks should be limited in time (maximum 3 h) to avoid the risk of losses, (3) the NF ISO 11261 standard (1995) recommends replacing Se by anatase TiO_2 which is less polluting for the environment (catalytic mixture 200 g K_2SO_4, 6 g $CuSO_4,5H_2O$, 6 g TiO_2).

Grinding the samples to 125 µm enables micro-methods to be used without a serious reduction in precision (Parnas and Wagner, 1921; Markham 1942), thereby reducing the cost price, pollution, and the extent of work surface required.

The use of heating blocks decreases the turbulence of the attacks as heating is more regularly distributed. Programming the stages of heating makes it possible to accomplish the mineralization cycle without monitoring.

10.2.7 Kjeldahl N, Titration by Spectrocolorimetry

Principle

After digestion in a sulphuric acid medium catalysed by selenium (without copper or titanium) the reaction (Berthelot 1859; Bolleter et al. 1961) is continued in basic medium (sodium hydroxide buffer and dibasic sodium phosphate).

The NH_4^+ ion reacts with the sodium hypochlorite and the sodium phenolate (or the sodium salicylate) to give a blue–green complex. The reaction is catalysed by the sodium nitroprussiate.

Equipment

– cf. "Equipment" under Sect. 10.2.6
– Centrifuge
– Automated segmented continuous-flow analysis with NH_4^+ manifold

Reagents

All the reagents should be of reference analytical grade:
– Mineralization products: see "Reagents" under Sect. 10.2.6.
– Brij 35 detergent: polyoxyethylene lauryl ether $C_{12}H_{25}(OCH_2CH_2)OH$ (to limit contamination of the analytical manifold).
– 20% sodium hydroxide (NaOH) stock solution.
– Sodium phosphate, $Na_2HPO_4,2H_2O$.

- 20% sodium potassium tartrate, $NaKC_4H_4O_6,4H_2O$ (Seignette salt) stock solution.
- Stock buffer solution: dissolve 89 g $Na_2HPO_4,2H_2O$ in 800 mL deionised water; cool and add 50 mL of 20% NaOH solution; homogenize and complete to 1,000 mL.
- Buffer solution: mix 200 mL of buffer stock solution, 250 mL of stock solution and 20% of sodium potassium tartrate; add 60 mL of 20% NaOH stock solution and about 300 mL water; homogenize and cool; add 1 mL of Brij 35; bring to 1 L and homogenize.
- Sodium salicylate: dissolve 150 g of sodium salicylate and 300 mg of sodium nitroprussiate in 800 mL water; bring to 1 L; filter on a Büchner funnel with a blue filter without NH_4 and add 1 mL of Brij 35; store in a brown bottle protected from the light.
- Sodium nitroprussiate, $Na_2Fe(CN)_5NO,2H_2O$.
- Sodium hypochlorite, NaClO: add 5 mL NaClO in 80 mL distilled water, bring to 100 mL; add 2 drops of Brij 35; prepare a fresh solution each day.
- Ammonium sulphate, $(NH_4)_2SO_4$.
- Hydrochloric acid, HCl 37%.
- Standard NH_4: pour 80 mL HCl 37% in 800 mL water; cool and bring to 1,000 mL with water; prepare a stock solution of ammonium sulphate at 100 mg NH_4^+–N mL^{-1}; store in the refrigerator; solutions should be freshly prepared each day starting from the stock solution to provide ranges from 0 to 50 $\mu g\ mL^{-1}$.

Procedure

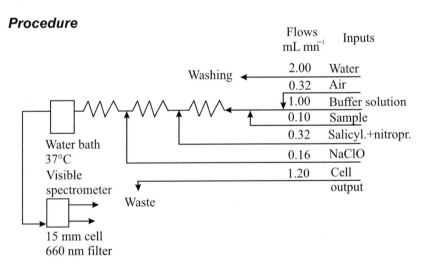

Fig. 10.2. Titration of total nitrogen by segmented continuous-flow analysis after mineralization (Buurmans et al. 1996)

Mineralization is carried out as in "Mineralization" in "Procedure (Macro-Method)" under Sect. 10.2.6, but with no copper sulphate in the catalyst mixture. At the end of the attack, cool the sample, and after complete cooling, dilute and pour into a 250 mL volumetric flask.

After adjusting the volume and homogenisation, centrifuge each aliquot at 3,000 g for 15 min to obtain a clear solution. Remove the test samples for analysis from the supernatant and dilute if necessary in suitable stages of dilution (for example five times) when introducing the sample in the N–NH$_4$ manifold. Titration is by absorption at 660 nm in a 15 mm colorimetric cell. The manifold proposed by Buurmans et al. (1996) is shown in Fig. 10.2 without the dilution stage. In the case of highly calcareous soils, it is sometimes necessary to add EDTA in addition to K and Na tartrate to avoid side effects due to the calcium which is precipitated in the sulphuric acid medium and can give a colloidal precipitate that is not easily visible to the naked eye (Gautheyrou and Gautheyrou 1965).

10.2.8 Kjeldahl N, Titration by a Selective Electrode

Principle

The principle is similar to that described in Sect. 10.3.2 of Chap. 28 for the titration of ammonium nitrogen. Only the conditions of use are a little different. Here the gas diffusion electrode enables the results to be read directly on the calibration curve. The response is linear in the 0.5–500 mg L^{-1} zone of concentration of nitrogen with a lower degree of precision for high concentrations because of the logarithmic response. A range of concentrations of from 0.5 to 10 mg L^{-1} is recommended.

This method has the advantage of being extremely simple and a wide range of concentrations can be analysed. Daily calibration is not necessary if the working temperature is always the same. Under normal working conditions, no interference occurs.

Equipment

– Mineralization equipment: cf. "Equipment" under Sect. 10.2.6.
– Orion model 95–100 gas electrode.
– Ionometer (pHmeter, mVmeter) with a resolution of 0.1 mV.
– Thermostated bath regulated at 25°C.
– Magnetic stirrer.

Reagents

- Mineralization acid: cf. "Reagents" under Sect. 10.2.6.
- Ten mole (NaOH) L^{-1} soda solution.
- Standard solution: dissolve 1.179 g of ammonium sulphate $((NH_4)_2SO_4$, mw = 132.12) in distilled water and bring to 250 mL; this solution contains 1 mg (N) mL^{-1}; dilute 10 times to obtain the initial reference solution 0.1 mg (N) mL^{-1}.
- Ammonium chloride solution to fill and maintain the electrode: 0.1 mol (NH_4Cl) L^{-1}.

Procedure

Mineralization is carried out as in "Mineralization" in "Procedure (Macro-Method)" under Sect. 10.2.6. At the end of the attack, cool the sample and transfer it to a 200 mL volumetric flask. After complete cooling, bring the volume to 200 mL.

Construction of the standard curve: in 50 mL beakers add the volumes of the 0.1 mg (N) mL^{-1} reference solution listed in Table 10.4; complete to 20 mL with additional volumes of the blank attack solution (cf. Sect. 10.2.).

Bring the temperature of the beakers and the blank to 25°C, immerse the electrode in the blank avoiding the presence of air under the membrane; add 2 mL of the 10 mol (NaOH) L^{-1} soda solution; start gentle agitation to limit the Vortex effect; after 5 min, adjust the zero of the ionometer.

Table 10.4. Range of titration of total nitrogen by ionometry; the content of the soil is given for a test sample of 2 g, volume of solution after attack (cf. "Mineralization" in "Procedure (Macro-Method)" under Sect. 10.2.6): 200 mL, aliquot for titration: 20 mL

mL of standard solution 0.1 mg (N) mL^{-1}	mL of attack solution for 20 mL	mL NaOH 10 mol L^{-1}	solution concentration mg (N) L^{-1}	soil concentration mg (N) g^{-1}
1	19	2	5	0.5
2	18	2	10	1
4	16	2	20	2
6	14	2	30	3
8	12	2	40	4
10	10	2	50	5

Proceed in the same way for the different points of the calibration range. Record the signal in mV and plot the calibration curve with the logarithms of nitrogen concentrations on the x-coordinate and mV on the y-coordinate.

The measurements should be carried out on 20 mL aliquots of each attack solution using the same technique as for the calibrations. It is essential to carry out titrations immediately after the addition of soda to avoid loss of ammonia.

Remarks

Before starting analysis, it is important to check the pH of the measurement solutions which must be from 11 to 13 after the addition of soda (Table 10.4). In the case of a lower pH, slightly increase the volume of the 10 mol (NaOH) L^{-1} soda solution.

After use, the electrode should be stored carefully following the manufacturer's instructions. The filling solution should be renewed periodically.

10.2.9 Mechanization and Automation of the Kjeldahl Method

The Kjeldahl method has the advantage of requiring only simple equipment and of being the reference method. However, manual methods are time consuming. They require large laboratory work surfaces and fume hoods to evacuate the heavy vapours. The technique can be improved by automation which makes it possible to avoid direct handling of dangerous reagents such as boiling sulphuric acid or concentrated soda.

The use of programmable heating blocks (e.g. Technicon, Skalar, Tecator) enables the temperatures of mineralization to be regulated and sudden starts and foaming during the attacks to be limited.

Partially automated equipment exists comprising management stations for mineralization, distillation, and titration at the macro and micro scale (e.g. Bicasa, Bucchi, Gerhart, Skalar, Foss-Tecator, Velp). Prolabo, Cem, Questron enable accelerated mineralization by microwave heating; the attack containers are processed automatically.

Complete automation was provided by manufacturers *such as* Tecator, Foss, Perstop, or Gerhart. Mineralization is automated, and final titration is carried out by titrimetry with potentiometric detection of the end point of titration, or by spectrocolorimetry. The job of the analyst is limited to filling up the reagents, regulating the heating programmes and recovering the results at the end of the day. Monitoring is simplified because an alarm goes off in the case of accident.

10.2.10 Modified Procedures for NO_3^-, NO_2^-, and Fixed N

These methods are seldom used in repetitive analyses because of the uncertainty of the results, the length of time required for the procedures, and the fact that the contents are often not very significant.

Nitrate and Nitrite

The determination of total N using wet methods does not take nitrate into account, but as it is generally not present in large quantities in natural environments, there will be no effect on results obtained on dried samples. However, in the case of cultivated soils dressed with manure with a high N content, it is preferable to rapidly check for the presence of nitrate using commercial tests, because nitrate and nitrite can introduce a random error.

Nitrate and nitrite can be included in Total-N by means of redox sequences before Kjeldahl mineralization (1) by $KMnO_4/Fe^{2+}$ where the nitrite is oxidized into nitrate by a potassium permanganate solution, the nitrate then being reduced in ammonium by ferrous iron before the mineralization sequence in the traditional method (cf. "Procedure (Macro-Method)" under Sect. 10.2.6); (2) by a system using salicylic acid/ammonium thiosulfate in which nitration by salicylic acid can occur quantitatively only in absence of water (Fuson 1962); the nitrated compounds are then reduced by ammonium thiosulfate before Kjeldahl mineralization as in "Procedure (Macro-Method)" under Sect. 10.2.6 (Nelson and Sommers 1980; Du Preez and Bate 1989). The international NF ISO 11261 standard (1995) recommends (1) action of 4 mL of a salicylic/sulphuric acid mixture (25 g salicylic acid in 1 L concentrated H_2SO_4) for a few hours or overnight, (2) the addition of 0.5 g of sodium thiosulfate with moderate heating until the foam disappears, (3) cooling the flask and the addition of a catalyst (dioxide of titanium instead of selenium) and sulphuric acid for Kjeldahl mineralization. Nitrate and nitrite can also be titrated separately using the methods described in Chap. 28.

Fixed or Occluded N

The determination of fixed or occluded N is very delicate. Indeed, some authors have raised questions both with respect to its nature (inorganic NH_4^+–N only, or organic and inorganic N) and to its modes of fixing N. Fixed N is not titrated quantitatively by the traditional method particularly in soils containing 2:1 clays. To titrate fixed N, a polyethylene bottle is used, and the clay lattice is destroyed by a mixture HF-KCl or concentrated KOH (cf. Sect. 28.3.5 of Chap. 28). The organic digestion of N is then carried out in traditional Kjeldahl flasks (cf. Sect. 10.2.6).

Remarks

As the glass of the Kjeldahl flasks is seriously affected, their quality deteriorates rapidly and they need to be regularly replaced. The fixing of N–NH$_4$ in the mineral lattices is more important in the deep horizons which are rich in clay and low in N compounds; the increase in N-fixing power as a function of the nature of clays can be expressed by: vermiculites > illites > montmorillonites > kaolinites.

In certain cases the expansion of the lattices, which is obtained by the addition of water, can lead to higher values for total-N (Bal 1925). Conversely, the rate of recovery of NO$_3$-N may be lower (Bremner and Mulvaney 1982).

10.3 Dry Methods

10.3.1 Total Carbon by Simple Volatilization

These methods are based on oxidation of the soil organic matter and on destruction of carbonates by heating of the samples to relatively high temperatures for a given length of time. Measurement of the loss in mass (cf. Chap. 1) allows estimation of gaseous losses that are mainly in the form of CO$_2$ and H$_2$O. Resistance or induction furnaces can function at temperatures of 1,000–1,500°C.

In the simplest case, an open air circuit is used, possibly with oxygen enrichment (low temperature ashing, LTA), or in closed systems with controlled temperature and time. Traps can be used to block some compounds, and catalysts can accelerate the reactions. Gas separation systems of varying degrees of sophistication are used in sequential analyses of evolved gas. To sum up, a temperature range lower than 500°C enables collection of the CO$_2$ released by the organic matter and temperatures higher than 500°C, of CO$_2$ produced from carbonates.

Although calcination methods using an open circuit for the determination of Total-C are very simple to implement, they cannot be regarded as quantitative and generally have be supplemented by thermal analysis techniques (cf. Chap. 7). In an oxidizing atmosphere, gravimetric measurements will represent:
– Organic C transformed into CO$_2$.
– Inorganic C starting from approximately 400°C.

– Different forms of water (hygroscopic, interstitial, water of crystallization, hydroxyl groups) which are moved throughout the thermal cycle.

– Volatile forms of N, S, certain metals, and metalloids (Cl⁻).

These displacements vary with the temperature used and with the times of application. Still other transformations can disturb measurements.

In an oxidizing atmosphere, some compounds of the soil that are sensitive to redox reactions will increase in weight while passing to a higher valence, for example $Fe^{2+} \rightarrow Fe^{3+}$. Sulphur compounds can, by recombination, show simultaneous losses and increases in mass as a function of the medium: $H_2S \rightarrow SO_2 \rightarrow SO_3 \rightarrow SO_4^{2-}$.

The results are thus random, and are related to the atmosphere used (oxidizing, neutral, reducing) and to effects of the matrix. The thermostable residue of the soil can be considered reached between 1,100 and 1,600°C. In most cases, total organic and inorganic C with C obtained by the simple measurement of the losses on ignition cannot be directly assimilated. Below 500°C, C losses at lower temperatures can easily characterize oxidizing C, but it is difficult to quantify this variable.

However, certain soils enable results with a reduced margin of error, in particular sandy soils with low 1:1 clay content, but not calcareous soils, or soils rich in organic matter. The decarboxylation of the organic matter starts around 180°C, and at 250°C, it is estimated that 70% of organic C is oxidized, and 90% around 500°C. Temperatures between 800 and 950°C are needed to obtain 99% of oxidation of organic C.

In the case of carbonates, decomposition starts at around 400°C: calcium and magnesium carbonates (e.g. calcite-aragonite, magnesite, dolomites) generally display the same type of thermal behaviour, but biogenic calcite (shells, skeletons, calcareous debris), iron carbonate (siderite), fossil coals, and resins can respond differently, as can sodium carbonates with a low melting point (851°C).

10.3.2 Simultaneous Instrumental Analysis by Dry Combustion: CHN(OS)

Principle

Thanks to improved equipment, the purchase of entirely automated CHN(OS) apparatuses (Pansu et al. 2001) is very tempting. These apparatuses are very profitable in laboratories that do many repetitive analyses, as they can do simultaneous analysis of C, N, and H and, under adequate operating conditions, of O and S in addition. To ensure the uninterrupted performance of the apparatuses, the operators need to be specially trained. The apparatuses also have to be regularly checked and maintained, and the exact conditions of use clearly defined. In this type of set-up, each element in the chain is linked to the others (furnace, CuO, catalysts, and different traps) and the weakest link in the chain determines the final quality of the analyses. The method is the subject of the international standard NF ISO 10694 (1995) for the analysis of organic carbon and total carbon of soils.

Seal a given mass representative of the sample in a tin (or silver) micro-capsule and place it in a furnace at 1,100°C in a controlled atmosphere in the presence of oxygen and copper oxide. The different forms of organic and inorganic C and N oxidize or break down rapidly according to the principle of the Liebig reaction (1830)

$$C + 2CuO \xrightarrow{\ O_2,\,1,\,800°C\ } CO_2\uparrow + 2Cu$$

The temperature of 1,800°C is reached by flash combustion of the tin capsules. The carbonates and bicarbonates are broken up simultaneously. For titration of organic C, carbonates, and bicarbonates must be eliminated chemically before the sample is placed in the furnace

$$CaCO_3 \xrightarrow{\ 1,000°C\ } CO_2\uparrow + CaO \qquad \text{(thermal destruction)}$$
$$CaCO_3 + 2H^+ \rightarrow CO_2\uparrow + H_2O + Ca^{2+} \quad \text{(chemical destruction)}$$

If methane is present and has to be titrated, Cr_2O_3 should be used to ensure perfect oxidation. The organic nitrogen that is oxidized during combustion gives nitrogen oxides which must be reduced with copper to transform all nitrogen oxides into the N_2 form by the Dumas (1831) method. Inorganic N compounds (NH_4^+, NO_3^-, NO_2^-) are subtracted to obtain total organic N. Different catalysts can be used to accelerate the reactions or to make them quantitative.

Finally, the gas products are identified in suitable detectors; the gaseous compounds can be separated on temporary specific traps or by gas chromatography, depending on the system used. In soils that do not contain carbonates or bicarbonates, or have not received calcareous amendments or lime:
– Inorganic C = 0.
– Total C = total organic C.

Equipment

- Elementary Analyzer CHN(OS), preferably able to handle samples of approximately 100 mg or more to compensate for the heterogeneity of carbon in soil (Pansu et al. 2001)[1].
- Micro analytical balance.
- Needle-nosed pliers to close the capsules.
- Micro pipette adjustable 0.1–0.5 mL.
- Ceramic plate for treatment of calcareous samples.
- Controlled temperature hotplate.

Products

All consumables should be suitable for the procedure and type of analytical materials used (analytical grade reference products):
- Combustive gases, carrier gas purity: 99.98%
- Copper oxide, (CuO)
- Copper in the form of wire or chips (Cu)
- Magnesium perchlorate ($Mg(ClO_4)_2$, ascarite (NaOH-asbestos), MnO_2, etc. for traps
- Tin or silver micro capsules, capacity 100 mg
- A range of catalysts
- Standard substances for calibration and control such as acetanilide (C_8H_9ON, 71.09% C, 6.71% H, 10.36% N, 11.84% O), atropine ($C_{17}H_{25}NO_3$), sulphanilamide $H_2NC_6H_4SO_2NH_2$, picric acid (2,4,6 trinitrophenol $(NO_2)_3C_6H_2OH$), thiourea (H_2NCSNH_2), etc.

Procedure

Non-calcareous soils

All weighing should be done on analytical balances (± 0.1 or ± 0.01 mg)

Calibration: weigh 5 sample specimens of increasing mass of a standard in the range of concentration accepted by the CHN apparatus concerned. The precision of the equipment should be tested by comparing the theoretical contents with the contents obtained.

---

[1] A higher mass of sample specimen increases the representativeness of the sample but produces more ashes in the combustion furnace. The current trend is to reduce the mass of sample specimen to about 10 mg and to increase the homogeneity of the sample by very fine grinding to a particle-size of less than 100 micrometers.

Samples: grind the samples to 125 μm (Sieve AFNOR NF22) and dry for 48 h in a P_2O_5 desiccator to limit saturation of the traps. In tin or silver capsules, carefully weigh from 50 to 100 mg of sample (depending on the estimated contents of C and N) dried on P_2O_5, and seal the capsule. Place the capsules in the sample distributor of the CHN apparatus.

At the same time, weigh 1 g of the same sample to measure residual moisture by drying at 105°C in order to be able to correct the results (cf. Chap. 1). Direct drying of the samples at 105°C before CHN analysis may increase ammonium fixation in the lattice of 2:1 clays, but in most case this is acceptable.

Note

Andosols and histisols pose two problems (1) the residual moisture of air-dried soil is very high, up to 50–60% after 6 months; (2) low bulk density can reach 0.30–0.25. In this case it is not possible to weigh 100 mg in the capsules.

Carbon in calcareous soils

In the case of calcareous samples or soils that have been limed, if there is no siderite (not easily decomposable $FeCO_3$), treatment with 10% hydrochloric acid solution is sufficient to destroy the carbonates and bicarbonates in the sample:
– Weigh 100 mg of sample in a silver capsule.
– Place the open capsule on a ceramic plate.
– With a micro pipette, slowly add 0.1–0.2 mL of 10% HCl depending on the estimated quantities of carbonate and bicarbonate.
– Leave in contact for 2 h then add 0.1 mL of the 10% HCl solution. Check that gaseous emission is complete.
– Place the ceramic plate on a hotplate at 60°C and bring to dry. Leave to cool and seal the capsule. Place the capsule on the CHN sampler to measure total organic C. A second sample can be weighed without destroying carbonates to measure total C. Total inorganic C can be calculated by difference.

On certain apparatuses it is preferable to use phosphoric acid rather than hydrochloric acid to limit the effects of chloride on the catalysts and on the traps.

Calculations

The results are calculated directly and printed by the CHN analyser after measurement of the surface of the C and N peaks. These calculations take the weight of the sample into account.

To determine total organic nitrogen, the results obtained for total inorganic nitrogen have to be taken into account (cf. Chap. 28).

Total N (CHN) = inorganic Nitrogen + organic Nitrogen

Titration of Hydrogen, Oxygen and Sulphur

Hydrogen is titrated together with carbon and nitrogen using the procedure described in "Procedure" under Sect. 10.3.2 by measuring the water formed during combustion. However this measurement is difficult to interpret in most soils because hydrogen resulting from combustion of the organic molecules and hydrogen coming from the different forms of water (e.g. adsorption, hydration, and hydroxylation) is not separated in the H_2O signal. In soils that are not very clayey and when using carefully dried samples, the H_2O signal can represent only H coming from combustion of the organic molecules. The C:H ratios then reveal the stages of evolution of the soil organic matter.

The titration of oxygen and sulphur is generally carried out with standard CHN equipment by simply modifying the instrumental parameters. For sulphur, controlled oxidation is used, generally in the presence of tungstic anhydride. For oxygen, pyrolysis is used instead of combustion (the oxygen supply is cut off) on a sample specimen reserved for this measurement.

Total organic oxygen: the sample is subjected to pyrolysis at 1,100°C in the presence of a catalyst such as a mixture of carbon and nickel. Carbon monoxide (CO) is formed, then isolated by a separation system (generally with a trap or by chromatography) and quantified by a system of detection (e.g. a catharometer). Oxygen is determined by comparison with standards of known O content in the same way as for C and N described in "Procedure" under Sect. 10.3.2: one molecule of CO represents one O atom in the sample.

Total organic oxygen corresponds to only a small fraction of total oxygen of the soil. *Inorganic oxygen,* which is more abundant, is generally estimated starting from the total analysis of the major elements (cf. Chap. 31), by calculating the difference between the sum of the contents expressed in oxides and the sum of the contents expressed in elements.

Total sulphur: the sample is oxidized at 1,100°C in the presence of tungstic anhydride WO_3 or a mixture of tungstic and vanadic oxides.

Oxides of sulphur (e.g. sulphur trioxide SO_3, sulphur dioxide SO_2) are formed. A stage of reduction on a copper column transforms all oxides into the SO_2 form. This gas is then isolated and titrated using a system that will depend on the type of equipment used (traps, chromatography) and the type of detector (catharometer, IR detector): one molecule of SO_2 corresponds to one atom of S in the sample. Depending on the type of equipment used, titration of sulphur may or may not be carried out simultaneously with that of carbon and nitrogen.

Instrumental CHNS methods give a value for the sulphur content that can generally be regarded as the total sulphur content of the soil: oxidation of organic sulphur and sulphides, decomposition of most of the sulphates (Laurent 1990). However, care should be taken given the diversity of natural forms of sulphur. For a more detailed analysis of this element, see Chap. 30.

Remarks

Alkaline salts (e.g. sodium carbonate, chlorides, phosphates) melt to a varying degree and delay the oxidation of C into CO_2 by coating the organic particles and disturbing the cycle of analysis.

Salts that are volatile at 700°C or more (e.g. some chlorides, bromides, or iodides) can contaminate (or corrode) the circuits, traps, and catalysts.

Magnesium perchlorate $Mg(ClO_4)_2$, sold under the name of anhydrone or dehydrite, is used to trap water. It is a relatively unstable product that, after use, must be eliminated in the same way as other dangerous waste by the laboratory.

Residues of calcination in the furnace have to be removed frequently, particularly in the case of carbonated saline soils. Changing the protective nacelles makes it possible (1) to preserve the quality of the filters for elimination of the fine particles likely to be present in the gas phase and (2) to limit the retention of volatile products of combustion. Traps, compounds, catalysts, and filters must be changed regularly, respecting the change-by deadlines. Most breakdowns and doubtful results are due to inadequate maintenance.

The use of synthetic standards can result in errors, as their physical and chemical behaviour may differ from that of soil organic matter. However, the temperature of 1,800°C reached during the flash combustion of the capsules makes it possible to release all the organic compounds. Soil standards with certified organic-C contents are also available for calibration. Elementary CHN(OS) analysers generally give accurate results but these may be higher than wet oxidation.

10.3.3 CHNOS by Thermal Analysis

In detailed studies it is important not to overlook the possibilities offered by instrumental methods such as differential thermal analysis (DTA) and thermogravimetric analysis (TGA), coupled or not with measurements of evolved gas analysis (EGA) (cf. Chap. 7).

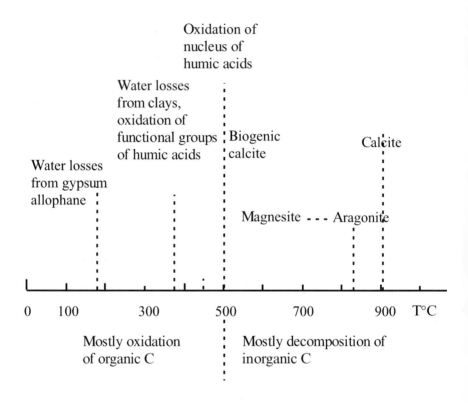

Fig. 10.3. Oxidation of organic C and decomposition of inorganic C as a function of temperature

Controlled pyrolysis (with suitable temperature/time programmes) enables oxidation of the organic matter and the decomposition of the inorganic compounds to be monitored. It is possible to identify and quantify the nature of the gases (e.g. CO_2, CO, CH_4, H_2O, NH_3, H_2S, SO_2) that correspond to the DTA and TGA peaks as a function of temperature, to monitor the decomposition or the transformation of products containing C and N, and to separate exothermic and endothermic peaks of H_2O and CO_2, etc.

For more complete studies, trapping of certain phases at $-180°C$, then their separation by gas chromatography, or by coupling with, for example, infra-red or mass spectrometers detectors, enables detailed characterization of soil organic matter.

The sum of the different carbon phases gives total C; and it is possible to roughly separate total organic C and total inorganic C (Fig. 10.3). In studies of organic geochemistry, the molecular mass of the fragments of pyrolysis is measured in a mass spectrometer with discontinuous injections. The structure of complex substances with high molecular weights can be characterized.

10.3.4 C and N Non-Destructive Instrumental Analysis

Analysis by diffuse reflectance near infra-red spectrometry (NIRS, cf. Chap. 5) is carried out directly on the soil sieved on an AFNOR NF22 sieve (125 μm mesh).

Take a sample weighing approximately 1 g after drying in the drying oven and carefully pack it in a special cup and place the cup in the measuring chamber. The surface of the sample must be perfectly flat. Each component of the organic complexes of the soil has a specific absorption point between 700 and 2,500 nm in the NIR spectrum, due to the vibrations of stretching and deformation of the inter-elements bonds (cf. Sect. 10.3.1 in Chap. 5).

For C and N measurement, information provided by the NIRS spectra must be calibrated to data from other methods of measurement. Then the calibration curve is used to quantify C and N in unknown samples. Good calibration has been obtained with the methods described in Sects. 10.3.1–10.3.3 above (Krishnan et al. 1980; Dalal and Henry 1986; Morra et al. 1991; Fidêncio et al. 2002). The method is non-destructive and the samples can be used for other measurements. As each apparatus has its own particular characteristics with regard to selection and optimization, the manufacturer's recommendations should be followed (e.g. Bran-Luebbe, Bruker, Foss, Leco, Nicolet, Perkin-Elmer, and Perstorp).

Rapid methods to estimate soil C in the field are currently the object of serious investigation in research programmes dedicated to C sequestration in soils as part of the effort to decrease emissions of greenhouse gases in the atmosphere. Though they are less precise than laboratory techniques using a wet method or dry combustion, these methods have the advantage of rapidly providing a very large number of measurements at a lower cost. NIRS methods for the processing of analytical signals have been developed thanks to spectacular progress in software. This software can provides quantitative data based on spectra that chemists previously found very difficult to interpret.

In addition to the NIRS method, the laser induced breakdown spectroscopy method (LIBS) has been proposed for soil carbon (Cremers et al. 1996). The detection limit is approximately 300 mg kg^{-1}, precision 4–5%, accuracy 3–14%, and the speed of analysis is more than one sample per minute (Cremers et al. 2001).

10.3.5 Simultaneous Analysis of the Different C and N Isotopes

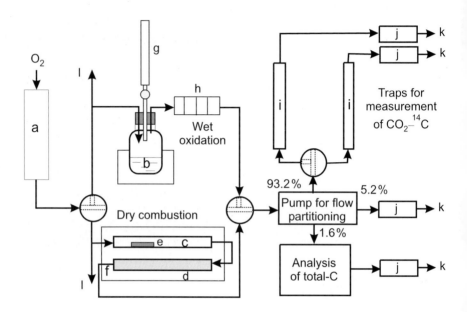

Fig. 10.4. Simultaneous determination of total- and ^{14}C-carbon (diagram by P. Bottner, CEFE-CNRS Montpellier, France, personal communication), (**a**) soda lime for O_2 purification, (**b**) boiling liquid sample + $K_2Cr_2O_7$, (**c**) combustion tube, (**d**) post combustion tube (CuO), (**e**) solid sample, (**f**) 900°C combustion furnace, (**g**) automated burette containing H_2SO_4 + H_3PO_4, (**h**) purification traps (water condensation, chromic and acid foams), (**i**) columns with glass balls impregnated with ethylene glycol mono-ethyl ether + mono-ethanolamine to trap CO_2, (**j**) soda lime traps for security, (**k**) ventilated external output, (**l**) output of excess O_2

Dry combustion analysers – CHN(OS) – can be coupled with mass spectrometers enabling the study of the different isotopes of the elements, particularly ^{14}C, ^{13}C, ^{15}N (Pansu et al. 2001). Often ^{15}N nitrogen is also measured starting from the Kjeldahl distillates in the form of ammonium. The carbon dioxide of the effluent combustion gas can also be trapped for later determination of the isotopes. The Bottner and Warembourg equipment (1976), shown in schematic form in Fig. 10.4, was used for more than 20 years for simultaneous titration of total-C (carmhograph 12A) and ^{14}C-carbon (liquid scintillation) starting from solid (soils, plants) or liquid (water of the soil) samples and proved to be reliable.

References

Anne P (1945) Sur le dosage du carbone organique des sols *Ann. Agron.*, 15, 161–172.

Baker KF (1976) The determination of organic carbon in soil using a probe colorimeter. *Lab. Practice,* 25, 82–83.

Bal DV (1925) The determination of nitrogen in heavy clay soils. *J. Agric. Sci.,* 15, 454–459.

Berthelot MP (1859) Violet d'amiline. *Répertoire chim. Appl.*, 1, 284.

Bolleter WT, Bushman, CJ and Tidwell PW (1961) Spectrophotometric determination of ammonia as indophénol. *Anal. Chem.,* 33, 542–594.

Bottner P and Warembourg F (1976) Method for simultaneous measurement of total and radioactive carbon in soils, soil extracts and plant materials, *Plant Soil*, 45, 273–277.

Bremner JM and Mulvaney CS (1982) Nitrogen total. In *Methods of soil analysis-* part 2. Chemical and microbiological properties. ASA-SSSA, 9, 595–624.

Buurmans P, van Lager B and Velthorst FJ (1996) *Manual for soil and water analysis.*, Backhuis Publishers, Leiden, 17–21.

Cremers DA, Ferris MJ and Davies (1996) Transportable Induced Laser Breakdown Spectroscopy (LIBS) instrument for field-based soil analysis. *Proc. Soc. Photo Opt. Inst. Eng.*, 2835, 190–200.

Cremers DA, Ebinger MH, Breashears DD, Uukefer PJ, Kammerdiener SA, Ferris MJ, Catlett KM and Brown JR (2001) Measuring Total Soil Carbon with Laser-Induced Breakdown Spectroscopy (LIBS). *J. Env. Qual.*, 30, 2202–2206.

Dalal RC and Henry RJ (1986) Simultaneons determination of moisture, organic carbon and total nitrogen by near infrared reflectance spectrometry. *Soil Sci. Soc. Am. J.*, 50, 120–123.

Du Preez DR and Bate GC (1989) A simple method for the quantitative recovery of nitrate N during Kjeldahl analysis of dry soil and plant samples. *Commun. Soil Sci. Plant Anal.,* 20, 345–357.

Fidêncio PH, Poppi RJ and de Andrade JC (2002) Determination of Organic Matter in Soils using function networks and near infrared spectroscopy. *Anal. Chim. Acta.*, 453, 125–134.

Fuson RC (1962) Reactions of organic compounds - A text book for the advanced student. Wiley, Bristol 1962.

Gautheyrou J and Gautheyrou M (1965) Dosage simultané de l'azote ammoniacal et nitrique dans le sols. Contribution à l'étude de la dynamique de l'azote. *Cah. Orstom Sér.Pédol.*, III, 367–391.

Keerrthisinghe GK, Mengel K and De Datta SK (1984) The release of non-exchangeable ammonium (15N Labelled) in wetland rice soils. *Soil Sci. Soc. Am. J.*, 48, 291–294.

Kjeldahl J (1883) Neue méthode zur bestimmung des stickstoffs in organischen körpern. *Z. Anal. Chem.*, 22, 366–382.

Krishnan P, Alexander JD, Butler BJ and Hummel JW (1980) Reflectance techniques for predicting soil organic matter. *Soil Sci. Soc. Am. J.*, 44, 1282–1285.

Laurent JY (1990) Analyse élémentaire d'échantillons de sol et solutions: application de la microanalyse au dosage simultané de l'azote, du carbone et du soufre. In *Actes Journées laboratoire*, Orstom, Bondy, France.

Ma TS and Zuazaga G (1942) Micro - Kjeldahl determination of nitrogen. A new indicator and an improved rapid method. *Ind. Eng. Chem. Anal.*, 14, 280–282.

Markham R (1942) A steam distillation apparatus suitable for micro - Kjeldahl analysis. *Biochem. J.*, 36, 790–791.

Mebius LJ (1960) A rapid method for the determination of organic carbon in soil. *Anal. Chem. Acta.*, 22, 120–124.

Mengel K and Scherer HW (1981) Release of non exchangeable (fixed) soil ammonium under field condition during the growing season. *Soil Sci.*, 131, 226–232.

Morra MJ, Hall MH and Free Born LL (1991) Carbon and nitrogen analysis of soil fraction using near infrared reflectance spectroscopy. *Soil. Sci. Soc. Am. J.*, 55, 281–291.

NF X31-109 (1993) Détermination du carbone organique par oxydation sulfochromique. In *Qualité des sols,* 1996, AFNOR, Paris, 67–73.

NF ISO 10694 (1995) Dosage du carbone organique et du carbone total après combustion sèche (analyse élémentaire). In *Qualité des sols,* 1996, AFNOR, Paris, 189–199.

NF ISO 11261 (1995) Dosage de l'azote total - Méthode de Kjeldahl modifiée. In *Qualité des sols*, 1996, AFNOR, Paris, 257–260.

X 31-111 (1983) Détermination de l'azote total - Méthode par distillation après minéralisation (Kjeldahl). In *Qualité des sols*, 1994, AFNOR, Paris, 69–72.

Pansu M, Sallih Z and Bottner P (1998) A process-based model for carbon and nitrogen transfers in soil organic matter. In *Actes 16e congrès mondial de science du sol*, 20–26 april, Montpellier, France

Pansu M, Gautheyrou J and Loyer JY (2001) Soil Analysis - Sampling, Instrumentation and Quality control. Balkema, Lisse, Abington, Exton, Tokyo, 489.

Parnas JK and Wagner R (1921) Über dieausfuhrung von bestmmungen kleiner stickstoffmengen nach Kjeldahl. *Biochem. Z.*, 125, 253–256.

Schollenberger CJ (1927) A rapid approximate method for determining soil organic matter. *Soil Sci.*, 24, 65–68.

Walkley A and Black A (1934) An examination of the Degtjareff method for determining soil organic matter and a proposed modification of the chromic acid titration method. *Soil Sci.*, 37, 29–38.

Winkler LW (1913) Beitrag zur titrimetrishen bestimmung des ammoniaks. *Z Angew. Chem.*, 26, 231–232.

Bibliography

Allison LE, Bollen WB and Moodie CD (1965) Total carbon. In Black C. A. et A.L. Method of soil an Analysis part 2. Agronomy Monograph n°9. *Am. Soc. Agron.*, 1346–1366.

Alves BJR, Boddey RM and Urquiaga SS (1993) A rapid and sensitive flow injection technique for the analysis of ammonium in soil extracts. *Commun. Soil Sci. Plant Anal.*, 24, 277–284.

Association of Official Analytical Chemists. AOAC (1975) *Official methods of analysis*, 924–925.

Bernoux M and Cerri CEP (2005) Soil organic components. In *Encyclopedia of Analytical Science*, 2nd Edition, Vol. 4, Elsevier, Amsterdam.

Bowman RA, Guenzin WD and Savory DJ (1991) Spectroscopic method for estimation of soil organic carbon. *Soil Sci. Soc. Am. J.*, 55, 563–566.

Bremner JM and Tabatabai M.A (1972) Use of an ammonia electrode for determination of ammonium in Kjeldahl analysis of soils. *Commun. Soil Sci. Plant Anal.*, 3, 159–165.

Burton DL, Gower DA, Rutherford PM and McGill WB (1989) Amino acid interference with ammonium determination in soil extracts using the automated indophenol method. *Commun. In Soil Sci. Plant Anal.*, 20, 555–565.

Carr CE (1973) Gravimetric determination of soil carbon using the Leco induction furnace. *J. Sci. Food Agric.*, 24, 1091–1095.

Cheng HH and Kimble J (2000) Methods of Analysis for Soil Carbon: An Overview. In *Global Climate Change and Tropical Ecosystems.*, CRC, Boca Raton, 333–339.

Chichester FW and Chaison RF (1992) Analysis of carbon in calcareous soil using a two temperature dry combustion infra-red instrumental procedure. *Soil Sci.*, 153, 237–241.

De Bolt DC (1974) A high sample volume procedure for the colorimetric determination of soil organic matter. *Commun. Soil Sci. Plant Anal.*, 5, 131–137.

Decreider and Meaux R (1973) Utilisation d'une electrode ionique spécifique pour le dosage de l'azote par la méthode Kjeldahl. *Analusis*, 2, 442–445.

Diaz-Zorita M (1999) Soil organic carbon recovery by the Walkley-Black method in a typic Hapludoll. *Commun. Soil Sci. Plant Anal.*, 30, 739–745.

Donkin MJ (1991) Loss - on - ignition as an estimator of soil organic carbon in A horizon forestry soils. *Commun. Soil Sci. Plant Anal.*, 22, 233–241.

Froelich PN (1980) Analysis of organic carbon in marine sediments. *Limnol. Oceanogr.*, 25, 564–572.

Gallaher RN, Weldon CO and Bowell FC (1976) A semi-automated procedure for total nitrogen in plant and soil samplers. *Soil. Sci. Soc. Am. J.*, 40, 887–889.

Genty CE and Willis RB (1988) Improved method for automated determination of ammonium in soil extracts. *Commun. In Soil Sci. Plant Anal.*, 19, 721–737.

Graham ER (1948) Determination of soil organic matter by means of a photoelectric colorimeter. *Soil Sci.*, 65, 181–183.

Guillet B (1979) Etude du renouvellement des matières organiques des sols par les radio isotopes ^{14}C. In *Pedologie - constituants et propriétés du sol*, Bonneau M and Souchier B ed. Masson, Paris, 210–226.

Heanes DL (1984) Determination of total organic C in soils by an improved chromic acid digestion and spectrophotometric procedure. *Commun. Soil Sci. Plant Anal.*, 15, 1191–1213.

Henzell EF, Wallis I and Lindquist JE (1968) Automatic colorimetric methods for the determination of nitrogen in digests and extracts of soils. Int. *Cong. Soil Sci. Trans.*, 9th(Adelaïde), 3, 513–520.

Howard PJ A and Howard DM (1990) Use of organic carbon and loss on ignition to estimate soil organic matter in different soil types and horizons. *Biol. Fert. Soils.*, 9, 306–310.

Kalembasa SI and Jenkinson DS (1973) A comparative study of titrimetric and gravimeric methods for determination of organic carbon in soils. *J. Sci. Food Agric.*, 24, 1085–1090.

Kalisz PJ and Sainju UM (1991) Determination of carbon in coal " blooms ". *Commun. Soil Sci. Plant Anal.*, 22, 393–398.

Kempers AJ and Kok CJ (1989) Re-examination of the determination of ammonium as the indophenol blue complex using salicylate. *Anal. Chim. Acta.*, 221, 147–155.

Lal R, Kimble JM, Follet RF and Stewart BA, (2001) *Assessment Methods for Soil Carbon*, Lewis CRC, London/Boca Raton, 676.

Lowther JR, Smethurst PJ, Carlyle JC and Nambiar EKS (1990) Methods for determining organic carbon in podzolic sands. *Commun. Soil Sci. Plant Anal.*, 21, 457–470.

Mc Geehan SL and Naylor DV (1988) Automated instrumental analysis of carbon and nitrogen in plant and soil samples. *Commun. Soil Sci. Plant Anal.*, 19, 493–505.

Merry RH and Spouncer LR (1988) The measurement of carbon in soils using a micro processor - controlled resistance furnace. *Commun. Soil Sci. Plant Anal.*, 19, 707–720.

Nelson DW and Sommers LE (1975) A rapid and accurate procedure for estimation of organic carbon in soil. *Proc. Indiana Acad. Sci.*, 84, 456–462.

Nelson DW and Sommers LE (1982) Total carbon, organic carbon and organic matter. In *Methods of soil analysis part 2*. Page AL, Miller RH and Keeney DR ed. *Agron. Monogr.*, 9, ASA - SSSA Madison., 539–579.

Nelson DW and Sommers LE (1996) Total carbon, organic carbon and organic matter. In *Methods of soil analysis, part 3, chemical methods,* Sparks DL ed. SSSA Book series no 5, 961–1010.

Nelson DW (1983) Determination of ammonium in KCl extracts of soils by the salicylate method. Commun. *Soil Sci. Plant Anal.,* 14, 1051–1062.

Nommik H (1971) A modified procedure for determination of organic carbon in soils by wet combustion. *Soil Sci.,* 111, 330–336.

Patton JC and Crouch SR (1977) Spectrophotometric and kinetics investigation of the Berthelot reaction for the determination of ammonia. *Anal. Chem.,* 3, 464–469.

Pella E (1990) *Elemental organic analysis.* Part 1, historical development, 116–125; part 2, state of the art, 28–32, *Ann. Lab.*

Perrier ER and Kellog M (1960) Colorimetric determination of soil organic matter. *Soil Sci.,* 90, 104–106.

Puttanna K and Prakasa Rao EVS (1993) Determination of nitrate in soil by second derivative ultraviolet spectrometry. *Commun. Soil Sci. Plant Anal.,* 24, 737–743.

Qiu Xing-Chu and Zhu Ying-Quan (1987) Sensitive spectrophotometric determination of ammoniacal nitrogen analysis. *Analusis*, 15, 254–258.

Quinn JG and Salomon M (1964) Chloride interference in the dichromate oxidation of soil hydrolyzates. *Soil Sci. Soc. Am. Proc.,* 28, 456.

Rowland AP (1983) An automated method for the determination of ammonium-N in ecological materials. *Commun. Soil Sci. Plant Anal.,* 14, 49–63.

Schepers JS, Francis DD and Thompson MT (1989) Simultaneous determination of total C, total N, and ^{15}N in soil and plant materiel. *Commun. Soil Sci. Plant Anal.,* 20, 949–959.

Schulte EE, Kaufman C and Peter JB (1991) The influence of sample size and heating time on soil weight loss - on - ignition. *Commun. Soil Sci. Plant Anal.,* 22, 159–168.

Schuman GE, Stanley MA and Knudsen D (1973) Automated total nitrogen analysis of soil and plant samples. *Soil Sci. Soc. Am. Proc.,* 37, 480–481.

Sheldrick BH (1986) Test of the Leco CHN 600 determination for soil carbon and nitrogen analysis. *Canadian J. of Soil Sci.,* 66, 543–545.

Sims JJ and Haby VA (1971) Simplified colorimetric determination of soil organic matter *Soil Sci.,* 112, 137–141.

Skjemstad JO, Reeve R (1976) The determination of nitrogen in soils by rapid high temperature Kjeldahl digestion and auto analysis. *Commun. Soil. Sci. Plant Anal.,* 7, 229–239.

Soon YK and Aboud S (1991) A comparison of some methods for soil organic carbon determination. *Commun. Soil Sci. Plant Anal.,* 22, 943–954.

Stewart RA and Porter LK (1963) Inability of Kjeldahl methods to fully measure indogeneous fixed ammonium in some soil. *Soil Sci. Soc. Am. Proc.,* 27, 41–43.

Szekely E (1991) A rapid colorimetric method for analysis of nitrate nitrogen by reduction to nitrite. *Commun. Soil Sci. Plant Anal.*, 22, 1295–1302.

Tabatabai MA and Bremner JM (1991) Automated instruments for determination of total carbon, nitrogen and sulphur in soils by combustion techniques. In *Soil analysis - Modern instrumental techniques*, Smith KA ed. Marcel Dekker, NY, USA 261–286.

Takesako H (1991) Double-plunger pump system flow injection spectrophotometric determination of inorganic nitrogen in soil extracts, part 1, flow injection analysis of ammonium nitrogen in soil extracts, part 2, flow injection analysis of nitrate nitrogen in soil extracts, *Jpn J Soil Sci. Plant Nut.*, 62, 128–134, 135–140

Tel DA and Jansen J (1992) Determination of total nitrogen in soil digest using a Traacs 800 Autoanalyser. *Commun. Soil Sci. Plant Anal.*, 23, 2729–2736.

Tisley J (1950) Determination of organic carbon in soils by dichromate mixtures in *Trans. 4 th Int. Cong. Soil. Sci.*, 1, 161–169. Hoitsemo Brothers, Groningen.

Verardo DJ, Froelich PN and Mcintyre A (1990) Determination of organic carbon and nitrogen in marine sediments using the Carlo Erba Na. 1500 analyser. *Deep Sea Res.*, 37, 157–165.

Volonteri HJ (1983) Modificacion de un metodo colorimetrico para la determinacion del nitrogeno total en suelos y pastos. *Ciencia del suelo*, 1, 98–99.

Walinga J, Kithome M, Novozamsky I, Houba VJG and Vanderlee JJ (1992) Spectrometric determination of organic carbon in soils. *Commun. Soil Sci. Plant Anal.*, 23, 1935–1944.

Winter JP, Gregorich EG, Voroney RP and Kachanoski RG (1990) Comparison of two samples oxidation methods for quantitative measurement of ^{12}C and ^{14}C in plant and soil. *Canad. J. Soil Sci.*, 70, 525–529.

Yeumans JC and Bremner JM (1991) Carbon and nitrogen analysis of soils by automated combustion techniques. *Commun. Soil Sci. Plant Anal.*, 22, 843–850.

Quantification of Humic Compounds

11.1 Humus in Soils

11.1.1 Definition

Humus plays a fundamental role in ecological processes as a source of carbon for the atmosphere, a sink of carbon for the biosphere, a sink and source of fertilizers for plants, and a factor that influences soil properties, and important reviews are regularly devoted to it (Kononova 1966; Flaig et al. 1975; Schnitzer 1978; Stevenson 1982; 1994; Aiken et al. 1985; Tate 1992; Carter and Stewart 1995; Piccolo 1996; Magdoff et al. 1996; Hessen and Tranvik 1998).

Stevenson (1982) defined the term "humus" (or humified matter) as the sum of organic compounds in the soil with the exclusion of living organisms in the biomass and non-decomposed or partially decomposed organic debris of plant or animal origin (cf. Chap. 9). The use of the term "soil organic matter" is less clear: the term is sometimes used with the same meaning as humus but in fact should refer to the sum of soil organic materials.

Humified matter represents more than half soil total organic carbon and can be classified in two main types, humic and non-humic substances (Schnitzer 1978). The physical and chemical characteristics of non-humic substances e.g. carbohydrates, proteins, peptides, amino acids, lipids, waxes and organic acids of low molecular weight are easily recognizable.

Humic substances on the other hand, do not show such marked physicochemical characteristics. They are more or less dark in colour, their molecular weight varies from a few hundred to several hundred thousand daltons, and they display a complex chemical structure, a hydrophilic character and acid properties.

However, the distinction between the two types of substances is not completely clear since humic substances always contain non-humic substances, which can be released by chemical treatments like acid hydrolysis.

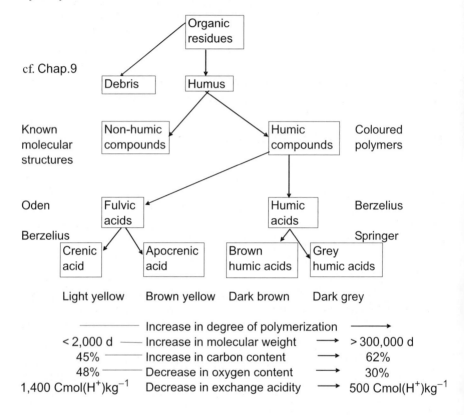

Fig. 11.1. Classification and chemical properties of groups of humic substances (after Stevenson and Elliott 1989)

Humic substances are generally classified into three main groups according to their solubility:

– Humic acids are soluble in diluted bases and insoluble in acid medium; they result from precipitation by acidification of the alkaline extracts of soil.

– Fulvic acids are soluble in both alkaline and acid mediums, the compounds remain in solution after precipitation of humic acids by acidification of the alkaline extracts of soil.

– Humin is the humus fraction that cannot be extracted by acids or diluted bases.

Other names have been given to certain humic substances as a function of their solubility in a range of different solvents. The best known characterize hymatomelanic acids as the fraction of humic acids which are soluble in ethanol. Among fulvic acids, an obsolete distinction is sometimes used to differentiate crenic and apocrenic acids. Some authors, for example Chamayou and Legros (1989), advise against the use of either term. Brown and grey humic acids can be distinguished. These two groups were first identified by Springer (1938) based on their flocculation or dissolution properties in a medium including different degrees of salts. Figure 11.1 shows some of the properties of these compounds.

11.1.2 Role in the Soil and Environment

Humic compounds account for 60–70% of soil carbon, which itself represents the biggest reservoir of organic carbon on the earth's surface. Humic compounds play a significant role as an atmospheric source of CO_2 and as a carbon reservoir which is likely to react to the influence of different external factors (Schnitzer 1978).

Stevenson (1982) quoted nine properties of humus with respect to their effect on the soil:
– Its dark colour, which facilitates absorption of solar radiation and consequently warms the soil.
– Its water-retention capacity; organic matter can to hold up to 20 times its own weight in water, thereby significantly improving the hydrous properties of some soils and particularly of sandy soils.
– Its ability to combine with clay minerals resulting in the cementing of soil particles into structural units called aggregates thereby facilitating gaseous exchange and increasing permeability.
– Chelation which forms stable complexes with many polyvalent cations and influences the availability of nutriments for plants.
– Its solubility in water which is very reduced and the bonds with clays and certain polyvalent cations which minimize organic losses by leaching.
– Its buffer effect, this effect appears at slightly acid, neutral and alkaline pH.
– Its cation exchange capacity, 20–70% of the cation exchange capacity of many soils is due to the presence of organic matter.
– Its mineralization which releases CO_2, NH_4^+, NO_3^-, PO_4^{3-}, SO_4^{2-} and represents a very significant source of nutrients for plant growth.
– Its combination with other organic molecules which affects bioactivity, persistence and biodegradability of pesticides.

This chapter provides details of procedures for the main types of extraction and quantification of soil humic matter. The reference section at the end of the chapter lists a wider range of methods for use in this context.

Extraction methods are described for whole soil samples prepared using standard techniques. However, it is often better to apply these methods to selected fractions after physical fractionation of the organic matter (cf. Chap. 9), in particular for the finest fractions.

11.1.3 Extraction

Organic materials bond with polyvalent cations, hydroxides and clays to form organomineral complexes. The stability of these complexes varies considerably depending on the type of bond.

Organic materials can be released by extractions that break down at least some of the organomineral bonds. Bruckert (1979) distinguished three types of extraction solutions:

– Salt solutions can break electrostatic bonds by simple exchange of ions and help solubilize the organic molecules by ionizing the acid and phenolic functional groups; Bruckert proposed a sodium tetraborate solution at pH 9.7; the extracted organomineral substances of relatively weak molecular weight were referred to as mobile or easily available recently formed complexes (Duchaufour 1977); they are characterized by relatively low metal contents; tetraborate has no effect on calcium complexes.

– Complex-forming solutions able to break the coordination bonds; the best known is sodium pyrophosphate solution which is generally used at pH 9.8; it breaks the bonds of complexes with metal sites on clays; it can also solubilize complexes with high metal contents (amorphous hydroxides), and dissolve calcium humates by forming a complex with calcium, but is as ineffective as tetraborate on allophanic complexes; all the extracted complexes are known as immovable.

– Soda at pH 12 is in fact the most effective extractant as it is able to destroy most organomineral bonds and particularly those of the humic allophone–acid complexes of andosols.

The standard techniques described in Sect. 11.2.1 concern:

– Simple extraction using an alkaline solution, with or without a preceding acid attack.

– Double extraction using a pyrophosphate solution followed by a soda solution (this method is used in the IRD laboratories, France).

Section 11.2 evaluates the respective utility and precision of these methods and describes the main methods for the purification of extracted organic materials.

Some alternatives to these extraction methods, including a technique for fractionation of the humin centrifugation pellet, are presented in Sect. 11.3. Techniques for the fractionation and characterization of humic compounds are described in Chap. 12.

11.2. Main Techniques

11.2.1 Extraction

Principle

As mentioned in Sect. 11.1.3, diluted soda solutions are the most powerful extracting reagents for humified matter. However, the use of these extraction solutions has been criticized for three main reasons (Bruckert 1979):
- Neo-formation of soluble substances from non-humified plant materials.
- Breakdown of humic substances by hydrolysis, oxidation or artificial polymerization.
- *Lysis of microbial organisms.* Sodium hydroxide can destroy bacteria and empty them of their cytoplasmic contents, their cell walls then form a non-extractable residue.

However, Schnitzer (1982) did not consider that extraction using diluted bases in a nitrogen atmosphere and at room temperature significantly modified the structure and characteristics of the extracted organic matter. Lévesque and Schnitzer (1966) showed that 0.1 mol L^{-1} soda solutions extract more organic matter than concentrated solutions. They also showed that 0.5 mol L^{-1} soda solutions extract organic matter with lower ash content.

"Method Schnitzer (1982)" and "Method IHSS" were chosen to maximize extraction of humic compounds and to minimize their degradation. Extraction (one extraction only) is carried out (1) under nitrogen atmosphere, with a 0.1 mol (NaOH) L^{-1} soda solution described in "Method IHSS" (2) with the same reagent or 0.5 mol (NaOH) L^{-1} soda solution or pyrophosphate solution described in "Method Schnitzer (1982)". "Method of Dabin (1976)" separates two types of extracted compounds: organic materials extractable with a pyrophosphate solution at pH 9.8 and organic materials extractable later on with a 0.1 mol (NaOH) L^{-1} soda solution. Nègre et al. (1976) observed qualitative differences between the two extracts particularly in amino acid content; Thomann (1963) observed that pyrophosphate dissolves calcic humates by forming complexes with metal cations; an increase in pH acts more particularly on aggregate dispersion, and pH 9.8 corresponds to a stable stage in the curve of humus extraction as a function of pH.

An alternative approach is acid pretreatment of the soil; this type of pretreatment facilitates the later extraction of humified matter by destroying carbonates and by solubilizing iron and aluminium hydroxides; however, the quantitative effect of the pretreatment is especially visible in calcareous soils. "Method IHSS" recommends systematic acid pretreatment with 1 mol (HCl) L^{-1} hydrochloric acid solution. "Method Schnitzer (1982)" recommends pretreatment with 0.05 mol (H^+) L^{-1} hydrochloric or sulphuric acid solution only in the case of calcareous soils. "Method of Dabin (1976)" recommends systematic pretreatment with 2 mol L^{-1} phosphoric acid. This acid has two advantages (1) higher density (approximately 1.2) which is more favourable for the separation of light organic fragments (cf. Chap. 9), (2) it does not disturb wet carbon titration and thus enables quantification of the organic matter extracted by the acid itself (unbound fulvic acid).

Equipment

– Glass, polypropylene or polyvinyl extraction and centrifugation flasks (volume: 200 mL, and 300–500 mL) with screw caps, for use as centrifugation cylinders, capable of withstanding 10,000g.
– Centrifuge (10,000g) equipped with rotor suitable for use with the centrifugation flasks.

Products

– *Degassed inorganic water.* Most commercial water is appropriate. It should first be checked for the absence of organic matter (blank assay corresponding to the type of characterization required). However, to eliminate organic matter from water, either (1) boil water for 2 h in the presence of 1% $KMnO_4$ and H_2SO_4 then distil or (2) use deionized water purified on activated carbon (e.g. Millipore filter), then degas the water to eliminate dissolved oxygen in order to avoid oxidation of organic matter during extraction. Proceed either by boiling or by bubbling with nitrogen for 10 min.

- *0.1 mol (NaOH) L^{-1} solution*. Dissolve 8 g of soda pellets in a 2 L volumetric flask in degassed inorganic water, complete to 2 L, agitate and store in a carefully stopped bottle.
- *0.5 mol (NaOH) L^{-1} solution*. Same as above with 40 g soda for 2 L.
- *10 mol (NaOH) L^{-1}*. Same as above with 400 g soda for 1 L.
- *0.1 mol ($Na_4P_2O_7$) L^{-1} solution*. Dissolve 89.2 g of $Na_4P_2O_7,10H_2O$ in degassed inorganic water, complete to 2 L and store in a carefully stopped bottle.
- *0.1 mol ($Na_4P_2O_7$,NaOH) L^{-1} solution*. Dissolve 89.2 g of $Na_4P_2O_7,10H_2O$ and 8 g of soda pellets in degassed inorganic water, complete to 2 L and store in a carefully stopped bottle.
- *2 mol (HCl) L^{-1} solution*. dilute 166.7 mL of concentrated HCl (d=1.19) in degassed inorganic water; complete to 1 L.
- *6 mol (HCl) L^{-1} solution*. Dilute 500 mL of concentrated hydrochloric acid in 1 L degassed inorganic water.
- *1 mol (HCl) L^{-1} solution*. Dilute 166.7 mL HCl in 2 L degassed inorganic water.
- *0.5 mol (HCl) L^{-1} solution*. Dilute 83.3 mL HCl in 2 L degassed inorganic water.
- *0.05 mol ($1/2H_2SO_4$) L^{-1} solution*. Dilute 27.8 mL of concentrated H_2SO_4 (d=1.81) in degassed inorganic water; cool and complete to 2 L.
- *2 mol (H_3PO_4) L^{-1} solution*. Dilute 136 mL of concentrated phosphoric acid (d=1.71) in degassed inorganic water and complete to 1 L.

Procedures

Method Schnitzer (1982)

If the soil contains carbonates (reaction to diluted hydrochloric acid), leave it in contact with a 0.05 mol (H^+) L^{-1} hydrochloric or sulphuric acid solution at room temperature until the end of gaseous emission. Rinse the excess acid with inorganic water and leave the soil to dry on a plate at room temperature.

Weigh 10 g of air-dried soil in a 200 mL polypropylene flask. Add 100 mL of selected extraction solution (0.1 or 0.5 mol (NaOH) L^{-1}, 0.1 mol ($Na_4P_2O_7$) L^{-1} or mix 0.1 mol ($Na_4P_2O_7$,NaOH) L^{-1}. Purge the air out of the flask with a stream of nitrogen. Close carefully and agitate for 24 h at room temperature. Separate the dark supernatant solution from the solid phase by centrifugation (preferably for 10 min at 10,000g), suspend the residue in 50 mL degassed inorganic water, separate by centrifugation again and add the flushing water to the previous solution.

Acidify the alkaline extract to pH 2 with 2 mol (HCl) L^{-1} hydrochloric acid. Leave to stand for 24 h at room temperature then separate the soluble matter (fulvic acid) from the coagulated matter (humic acid) by centrifugation. The two fractions can be brought to dry by freeze-drying or by evaporation in a rotary evaporator at 40°C.

Method IHSS[1]

Mix 20 g of air-dried soil with 1 mol (HCl) L^{-1} hydrochloric acid. Adjust to a pH of between 1 and 2 (15–20 mL soda 10 mol L^{-1}) in such a way that the final volume of liquid is 200 mL (liquid/soil ratio = 10 mL per 1 g). Agitate for 1 h and separate the supernatant liquid by centrifugation.

Neutralize the centrifugation pellet to pH 7 with 1 mol (NaOH) L^{-1} soda solution and add 0.1 mol (NaOH) L^{-1} solution under nitrogen atmosphere until a solution:soil ratio of 10:1 is obtained.

Agitate for at least 4 h under nitrogen atmosphere. Leave to stand overnight and centrifuge.

Acidify the centrifugation liquid to pH 1 with 6 mol (HCl) L^{-1} hydrochloric acid under agitation. Leave to stand for 12–16 h and centrifuge to separate the fulvic acids in solution from the coagulated humic acids.

Method of Dabin (1976)

Put 40 g of air-dried soil crushed and sieved on a 0.5 mm mesh sieve in a 300–500 mL centrifugation bottle. Add 200 mL of 2 mol (H_3PO_4) L^{-1} solution, agitate for 30 min with the back and forth shaker and centrifuge for 5 min at 1,500g. Filter the supernatant liquid on a flat filter in a 1 L glass bottle. Repeat the extraction two or three times in the same centrifugation bottle, filtering on the same filter and collecting the acid extracts in the same bottle. The filter contains light organic matter (LOM) from non-humified plant and animal residues (cf. Chap. 9); the acid solution contains a small fraction of organic materials called "free fulvic acids" (FFA) by Dabin (1976). Wash the centrifugation pellet two or three times with 200 mL inorganic water in the same bottle by agitating for 15 min; centrifuge and filter the washing water on the previously used filter to collect the light material still present in the washing water, discard the filtrate.

---

[1] IHSS = International Humic Substance Society, Univ. of California, Los Angeles, CA 90024; Federal Center, mall stop 407, Box 25046, Denver, CO 80225.

Add 200 mL of 0.1 mol $(Na_4P_2O_7)$ L^{-1} solution at pH 9.8. Agitate for 4 h on the back and forth shaker or leave in contact overnight agitating several times. Separate the supernatant liquid by centrifugation for 30 min at 3,000g and transfer it through a filter into a 1 L volumetric flask. Perform a second extraction in the same conditions and combine the extracts. If the second extract is dark in colour, perform a third extraction.

Repeat a similar extraction sequence on the centrifugation pellet, with 0.1 mol (NaOH) L^{-1} soda solution instead of the pH 9.8 pyrophosphate solution.

Humic acids of the pyrophosphate and soda extracts are separated from fulvic acid by acidification at pH 1 with the 2 mol (HCl) L^{-1} solution as described in "Method Schnitzer (1982)". Ultimately, the following fractions are obtained: LOM, FFA, pyrophosphate fulvic acids (PFA), pyrophosphate humic acids (PHA), soda fulvic acids (SFA), soda humic acids (SHA), extraction residue or humin.

Note

In certain soils, the pyrophosphate and soda extracts can contain a high percentage of fine mineralogical clays (smaller than 0.2 µm). It is possible to separate these clays by flocculation with the addition of a little potassium sulphate, but there is a risk of simultaneously flocculating certain grey humic acids (cf. Sect. 11.2.4 and Chap. 12). After centrifugation, the flocculation pellet should either be titrated individually or combined with the previous humin pellet for carbon determination.

11.2.2 Quantification of the Extracts

Principle

Quantification is by carbon titration of each extract (cf. Sect. 11.2.1 above). The techniques used for carbon titration of whole soil can be used on the humin pellet (cf. Chap. 10). For LOM, it is preferable to use a combustion technique. The extracts can also be titrated by combustion on the residue after dry evaporation of an aliquot. Nitrogen can be measured in addition to carbon, hydrogen and possibly sulphur and oxygen by using an analyser of the CHN type. However, wet processes such as dichromate oxidation (described later) are often preferred for titration of the extracts. Another technique calls for a titration apparatus with dissolved carbon. Many of these apparatus are based on titration of the carbon dioxide (generally by infra-red absorption) produced by oxidation of the solution with a powerful oxidant. The titration apparatus of dissolved carbon are rather expensive and reserved to precise environmental studies; the manufacturer's instructions should be respected.

In acid medium, dichromate oxidizes the carbon of the organic matter in CO_2 according to the redox reaction:

$$Cr_2O_7^{2-} + 6\ e^- + 14\ H^+ \rightarrow 2\ Cr^{3+} + 7\ H_2O$$
$$C + 2\ H_2O \rightarrow CO_2 + 4e^- + 4\ H^+$$

With automated apparatuses, the quantity of CO_2 released can be measured directly. With a traditional manual redox technique a dichromate excess is used, which is then back titrated by a ferrous iron solution:

$$Fe^{2+} \rightarrow Fe^{3+} + e^-$$

A mole of ferrous iron corresponds to 1/6 mol of $K_2Cr_2O_7$ is 1/4 atom C or 3 g of carbon.

Equipment

– 50 and 100 mL Pyrex Beakers.
– Precision burette (25 or 50 mL).
– If necessary, a titration apparatus using carbon and dry combustion, but preferably a wet process.

Reagents

– 0.1 mol $(Na_4P_2O_7)$ L^{-1} and 0.1 mol (NaOH) L^{-1} solutions: see preparation in "Products" under Sect. 11.2.1.
– Concentrated sulphuric acid (d=1.81).
– 2 mol ($\frac{1}{2}H_2SO_4$) L^{-1} sulphuric acid: dissolve 56 mL of concentrated sulphuric acid (d=1.81) in 1 L inorganic water.
– 0.1 mol ($\frac{1}{2}H_2SO_4$) L^{-1} sulphuric acid: 2.8 mL of concentrated sulphuric acid (d=1.81) in 1 L inorganic water.
– 2% potassium dichromate solution: dissolve 20g of $K_2Cr_2O_7$ in approximately 400 mL inorganic water, slowly add 500 mL of concentrated sulphuric acid, agitate, let cool and complete to 1 L with inorganic water.
– 0.5 mol ($\frac{1}{6}K_2Cr_2O_7$) L^{-1} solution: gradually dissolve 24.52 g of potassium dichromate in inorganic water then complete to 1 L (solution for the titration of the Mohr salt).

– 0.2 mol $(FeSO_4)$ L^{-1} Mohr salt solution: dissolve 78.4 g of Mohr salt $(FeSO_4,(NH_4)_2SO_4,6H_2O)$ in 500 mL water, add 20 mL of concentrated sulphuric acid, complete to 1 L.
– Sodium fluoride in powder form.
– Sulphuric diphenylamine solution: dissolve 0.5 g of diphenylamine powder in 100 mL of concentrated H_2SO_4, pour into 20 mL water, agitate and store in a brown bottle.

Procedure

Test samples

Total organic materials of the soda and pyrophosphate extracts. In a 100–200 mL shallow beaker, put the exact volume of the extraction solution corresponding to 5–8 mg C. Calculate the volume of the aliquot on the basis of the total C analysis of the sample (cf. Chap. 10). The carbon of the total alkaline extracts is around 40% of total C; C extracted by pyrophosphate is about 25% of total C, and C extracted by soda (after pyrophosphate extraction) is about 15% of total C. Before titration, bring the sample to dry in a drying oven at 70°C.

Humic acids. Take a sample of the extraction solution of more than 50% of the titration sample for total organic materials. Precipitate the humic acids at approximately pH 1 by adding 1 mol (H_2SO_4) L^{-1} (approximately 4–5 mL for 10 mL of total extract, 3 mL for 10 mL of pyrophosphate extract, 1.5 mL for 10 mL of soda extract); leave to flocculate for at least 4 h and centrifuge for at least 5 min at 3,500g; separate the supernatant liquid (fulvic acids) and wash with 0.1 mol $(\frac{1}{2}H_2SO_4)$ L^{-1} solution. Dissolve the centrifugation pellet in 0.1 mol $(NaOH)$ L^{-1} solution, place in a beaker and bring to dry at 70°C before analysis.

Phosphoric acid extract. Take an exact aliquot of 100 mL; concentrate in the drying oven until approximately 10 mL remains (H_3PO_4 cannot go dry) and carry out titration on this concentrated solution.

Fulvic acids. These can be titrated as total organic material after elimination of humic acids but are generally estimated by the difference between total organic materials and humic acids.

Redox Titration

After drying the sample specimens in the beakers, add 10 mL of the 2% potassium dichromate solution in sulphuric acid medium. At the same time, carry out a blank measurement with 10 mL of the same dichromate solution in a beaker. Protect each beaker with a beaker cover and bring to a very gentle boil on a hotplate regulated at 215–220°C; Boil for 5 min but control boiling to avoid overheating or too much evaporation.

Leave to cool, rinse the beaker cover and add in the beaker: 100 mL of inorganic water, 1.5 g of NaF (or 2.5 mL H_3PO_4) and three drops of diphenylamine solution.

With a burette titrate with Mohr salt solution until the colour turns from purple to pale green. V and V' volumes in mL of ferrous solutions are necessary for the respective titration of the blank and of the sample.

If T is the concentration of the Mohr salt solution in mol $(FeSO_4)$ L^{-1}, the quantity of Fe^{2+} equivalent to oxidant mobilized for the titration of the carbon of the sample is: $T(V-V')$ mmol(Fe^{2+}), which according to the redox equations (cf. "Principle" under Sect. 11.2.2), corresponds to $3T(V-V')$ mg of carbon in the beaker. With respect to the whole soil sample, the carbon content in mg (C) g^{-1} (soil) of the fraction is

$$C = 3T(V-V')\ V_t/(A\ m_t) \qquad\qquad (11.1)$$

where:
V_t: total volume of the humic extract in mL,
A: aliquot of the humic extract used for titration in mL,
m_t: soil sample mass used for the extraction in g,
T has to be determined by titration.

Titration of the Mohr Salt Solution

Put in a 250 mL beaker:
– exactly 10 mL of the 0.5 mol (1/6 $K_2Cr_2O_7$) L^{-1} solution
– 100 mL of inorganic water
– 15 mL of concentrated H_2SO_4
Let cool and add
– 3.75 g NaF;
– three drops of diphenylamine indicator

Using the burette, titrate with the Mohr salt solution; if V_f is the volume in mL of the Mohr salt solution, the T of this solution will be $T = 5/V_f$ mol (Fe^{2+}) L^{-1}. The carbon content in (11.1) can thus be expressed in mg (C) g^{-1} (soil) by:

$$C = 15\ (V-V')\ V_t/(A\ m_t\ V_f) \qquad\qquad (11.1')$$

Remarks

Ten millilitres of 2% dichromate solution corresponds to 20.4 mL of the 0.2 mol (Fe^{2+}) L^{-1} Mohr salt solution. The volume of Mohr salt solution used for titration of the sample should be between 7 and 15 mL; below this range, start the analysis again with a weaker sample; above this range start again with a stronger sample.

The quantity of carbon in the phosphoric acid solution is usually low. In this case, oxidize with only 5 mL of 2% dichromate solution adding five drops of concentrated H_2SO_4 before boiling.

Pyrex beakers are attacked by alkaline solutions and NaF in acid medium. They should be rinsed immediately after titration and reserved solely for this purpose.

11.2.3 Precision and Correspondence of the Extraction Methods

Inter-Laboratory Study

An inter-laboratory study by GEMOS[2] (Dabin et al. 1983) involved the quantitative comparison of the quantities of organic materials extracted on seven samples from soils from different areas of France:
1. A silt soil from the plates of Boigneville
2. A humocalcic soil from Pontarlier
3. A A1 horizon of a podzol from the forest of Villers Cotterets
4. A Bh horizon of the same podzol 3
5. A fersiallitic soil from near Montpellier
6. A gley soil with hydromull from Bonneveaux
7. A rendzina on chalk from Chalons sur Marne

Each soil was analysed by four French laboratories:
– the CIRAD[3] laboratory of Montpellier
– the pedology laboratory of the university of Poitiers
– the IRD[4] laboratory of Bondy
– the pedology laboratory of the university of Besancon.

---

[2] GEMOS = *Groupe d'Etude des Matières Organiques des Sols*, sub-group of the *Association Française d'Etude des Sols* (AFES), INRA, 78850 Thiverval-Grignon, France.
[3] CIRAD = *Centre International de Recherche Agronomique pour le Développement*, Avenue d'Agropolis, BP 5035, 34032 Montpellier Cedex, France.
[4] IRD = Institute of Research for the Development (ex-Orstom), 32 Avenue Varagnat, 93143 Bondy, France.

The method of reference chosen for the comparisons was described in "Method IHSS". In addition, the IRD laboratory in Bondy tested the method described in "Method of Dabin (1976)" on the same samples.

Quantities Extracted by the IHSS Method

The results of the inter-laboratory study are summarized in Fig. 11.2. Figure 11.2a shows the carbon value in g for 100 g of dry soil obtained by the sum of the three fractions: acid extract + alkaline extract + non-extracted residue, compared to total carbon measured on whole soil. The fact that the results are located close to the bisecting line shows the absence of bias between the two methods.

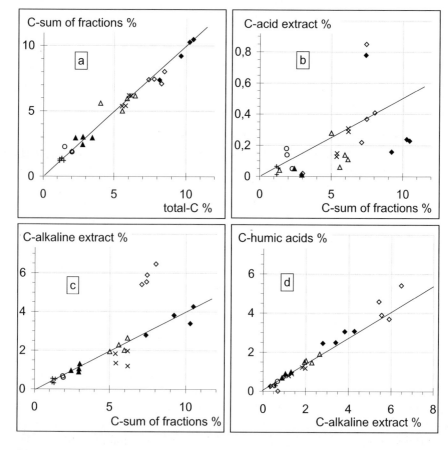

Fig. 11.2. Results of an inter-laboratory comparison using the extraction method described in "Method IHSS" (unpublished data). Results from four laboratories for the seven types of soils described in the text: (*plus*) soil 1, (*open triangle*) soil 2, (*open square*) soil 3, (*open diamond*) soil 4, (*cross*) soil 5, (*filled diamond*) soil 6, (*open circle*) soil 7

Figure 11.2b shows the amount of carbon extracted with the hydrochloric acid solution compared to the total quantity extracted. The quantity of acid extracted was low, below or equal to 5% of total carbon. The two exceptions where the value was 10% are probably due to the presence of additional fragments of light non-humified organic matter. The values measured were very variable and there was no correlation with total carbon.

Figure 11.2c shows the carbon of the alkaline extract compared to total carbon. Two remarks can be made:
– in six of the seven soils, the soda solution extracted 20–40% of total carbon. The values are more grouped than that of the acid extract. Their distribution revealed a maximum threshold of extraction for six samples located at approximately 40% of total carbon (line). The values located under this threshold are probably errors in measurement due to insufficient extraction.
– there was an abnormally high value for soil 4; this can be explained by the fact the soil was from the deep Bh organic horizon of a podzol; the organic matter which was leached to this depth was much more soluble in the soda solution than in the six other soils; in this case, the reagent extracted more than 3/4 of the carbon of the sample.

Figure 11.2d shows the quantity of carbon in humic acid forms compared to the carbon of the total alkaline extract. Whatever the type of soil, the carbon of humic acids accounted for approximately the 2/3 of the carbon of the alkaline extracts, and thus approximately 27% of total carbon. The deviation of the results around this value was limited.

Precision of the IHSS Method

Table 11.1 shows the results of an analysis of variance carried out on the data obtained with the IHSS method: are the measured values on each soil equal or significantly different compared to experimental error.

The *F* test is the ratio of variance between soils (seven soils i.e. six degrees of freedom dof) to within inter-laboratory variance (27 measurements or 20 dof) represented by s_r^2. The pooled estimation of the standard error associated with a measurement from a given laboratory on an unspecified soil is indicated by "*s*" in g (C) 100 g^{-1} (dry soil) in absolute values and by RSD (relative standard deviation) in relative values. These values representing the precision of an inter-laboratory reproducibility test are upper limits of error. Repeatability would be better within one laboratory with well-trained staff.

Carbon measurement was tested in the hydrochloric acid extract, in the soda extract, in the humin residue, in the sum of these three fractions and finally in humic acids and fulvic acids.

Table 11.1 shows that:

– It is impossible to control the quantities extracted by hydrochloric acid, the errors observed in this case being more significant than the variations between the soils; this confirms the distribution in Fig. 11.2b.
– In all the other cases, the differences observed between the soils were significant compared to the residual error representing inter-laboratory variability.

Table 11.1. Precision of measurements in a comparative inter-laboratory test on seven soils using the IHSS method (F: test of significance of the soil values compared to the residual variance s_r^2 between the four laboratories (∗∗∗, significant difference between laboratory data at risk <1%, NS, no significant difference). s and RSD: expected absolute (g (C) 100 g^{-1}dry soil) and relative (%) standard deviations in case of a measurement (no replicate) from any laboratory)

Determination	$F(6,21)$	s_r^2	s	RSD%
C- acid extract	4.2 (NS)	0.026	0.16	83
C- alcaline extract	107 ∗∗∗	0.141	0.38	17
C- humin residue	37 ∗∗∗	0.317	0.56	22
C- sum of fractions	83 ∗∗∗	0.410	0.64	13
C- total soil	100 ∗∗∗	0.403	0.63	13
C- humic acids	67 ∗∗∗	0.131	0.36	22
C- fulvic acids	16 ∗∗∗	0.036	0.19	35

– In the alkaline extracts, the precision of the measurement of humic acids is better than that in the fulvic acids; this is probably due to the greater abundance of humic acids.
– The precision of the measurement of soil total carbon obtained by the sum of the first three measurements is of the same order of magnitude as that obtained by the direct measurement of carbon on the whole soil; moreover, the value obtained is in agreement with the rule of propagation of errors (Pansu et al. 2001); indeed, C-sum is obtained by:

C-sum = C-acid extract + C-alkaline extract + C-humin residue

In the case of normal laws:

$$_sC\text{-sum} = (s^2C\text{-acid extract} + s^2C\text{-alcaline extract} + s^2C\text{-humin})^{1/2}$$

then:

$$_sC\text{-sum} = (0.026 + 0.141 + 0.317)^{1/2}$$

$_sC\text{-sum} = 0.69$ is very close to the values 0.64 and 0.63 found for the synthetic variable and the measurement of total carbon, respectively.

Comparison of the Methods Described in "Method IHSS" and "Method of Dabin (1976)"

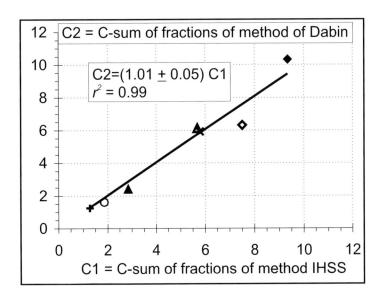

Fig. 11.3. Comparison of the carbon rates found with the two methods of extraction tested. Averages of the results of four laboratories for the seven types of soils described in the text: (*plus*) soil 1, (*open triangle*) soil 2, (*open square*) soil 3, (*open diamond*) soil 4, (*cross*) soil 5, (*filled diamond*) soil 6, (*open circle*) soil 7

Figure 11.3 shows that the total quantities of carbon (acid extract + alkaline extract + humin residue) found with the two methods are very close. However, more detailed comparison of the data in Fig. 11.4 reveals analogies and differences between the methods:

– Extraction of phosphoric acid described in "Method of Dabin (1976)" solubilizes between 1.2 and 4 times more (average 2 times more) organic matter than extraction with hydrochloric acid described in "Method IHSS" (Fig. 11.4a); the closest results for the two techniques were for the deep Bh horizon of the podzol.

– Alkaline extraction gave quantitatively comparable results with the two methods (Fig. 11.4b) when the sum of the extracts pyrophosphate and soda described in "Method of Dabin (1976)" are taken into account; the results are also comparable for humin carbon, although very slightly weaker in the method described in "Method of Dabin (1976)", (Fig. 11.4d).

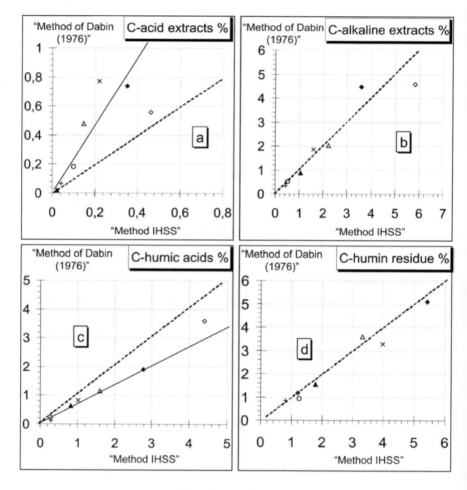

Fig. 11.4. Comparison of the fractions extracted with the two extraction methods in the comparative study. Averages of the results of four laboratories for the seven types of soils described in the text: (*plus*) soil 1, (*open triangle*) soil 2, (*filled triangle*) soil 3, (*open diamond*) soil 4, (*cross*) soil 5, (*filled diamond*) soil 6, (*open circle*) soil 7.

– On the other hand, there was a clear difference between the two methods with respect to the quality of the extracted organic matter since "Method of Dabin (1976)" provided significantly less humic acids; in Fig. 11.4c the C- "Method of Dabin (1976)"/C- "Method IHSS" ratio is approximately 2:3 and the behaviour of sample 4 (deep Bh horizon of the podzol) is a little different; the difference may be due to the effect of the extracting reagent on the extracted molecules i.e. polymerization in "Method IHSS", macromolecular breakdown in "Method of Dabin (1976)" (cf. remarks in the introduction to this chapter).

11.2.4 Purification of humic Materials

Introduction

It is difficult to choose a precise procedure for purification, as many alternatives are possible. According to Schnitzer (1982), the prime objective of purification is to minimize the weight of ash, while the second objective consists in separating the organic molecules of lower molecular weight from the humic materials. However, these definitions may be insufficient because the modes of the bonds between humic, non-humic and inorganic extracted materials are very complex and it is possible that many methods of purification have an influence on the structure of the final compounds isolated.

Nègre et al. (1976) recommend dialysis (Viskins dialysis bags with 24 Å pores) to purify humic materials extracted by pyrophosphate. Like other authors before them, these authors noted some transformation of the fulvic acids into humic polymers of higher molecular weight. It is as if "during the dialysis, which is accompanied by a progressive return of the medium towards neutrality, the molecules that were depolymerized during the alkaline extraction could polymerize again by simple re-establishment of the CO–NH bonds, similar to the peptide bonds leading to the formation of the nucleic acids" (Nègre et al. 1976).

Other simple purification methods enable elimination of certain minerals from the extracted solution by simple coagulation with the addition of a little sodium sulphate and centrifugation (Kumada et al. 1967) or ultracentrifugation (Jacquin et al. 1970).

Humic acids can also be purified by dissolving them in soda medium then precipitating them again in acid medium (Lowe 1980) or by a second process of extraction–fractionation on extracts that have pre-viously been freeze-dried (Schnitzer 1982), or by prolonged freezing of humic solutions which can fractionate the different phases (Bachelier 1983).

The most effective procedure for purification – though only of humic acids – is to chemically attack the minerals with a diluted solution of the HCl–HF mixture to reduce the weight of ashes. Schnitzer (1982) noted that HCl-HF treatment can reduce the ash contents to less than 1%.

Jacquin et al. (1970) obtained less than 3% of ashes on three extracts purified with HCl–HF. Among the four purification methods tested by these authors, infra-red absorption spectra of purified humic materials showed that only the HCl–HF treatment almost completely eliminates the intense absorption bands of the phyllosilicates at 470, 520 and 1,030 cm^{-1} (Fig. 11.5). However, according to these authors, the hydrofluoric treatment leads to transformation of the chemical structure of the molecules, in particular a significant reduction in carboxylic acidity.

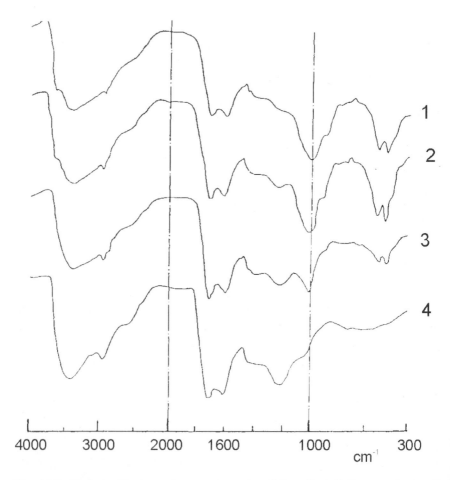

Fig. 11.5. Study by IR absorption spectrometry of the effect of three methods of purification on humic acids extracted from a deep Bh horizon of podzol (Jacquin et al. 1970): 1, non-purified humic acids; 2, humic acids purified by percolation on OH$^-$ and H$^+$ resins; 3, humic acids purified by ultra-centrifugation; 4, humic acids purified by HCl–HF treatment

Fulvic acids can be purified in acid medium by adsorption on non-ionic standard polyacrylic resins of the amberlite XAD-7 type (Aiken et al. 1979). After rinsing the resin in slightly acid medium to eliminate mineral salts, more than 98% of the fulvic acids can be recovered by elution at pH 6.5 (Gregor and Powell 1986). A simpler solution consists in eliminating the metal cations by repeated exchanges on a cation exchange resin in H^+ form (Schnitzer 1982).

Equipment

– 150 mL Teflon or polypropylene bottles
– Glass columns for chromatography with a diameter of 1 or 2 cm and a Teflon stopcock
– *Optional.* Freeze dryer and freezer at −18°C

Products

– Dialysis bags with 24 Å pores
– Non-ionic polyacrylic resin (Amberlite XAD-7 or similar)
– Cation exchange resin Amberlite IR 120, or Dowex 50, in H^+ form
– *HCl–HF mixture.* Dilute 5 mL of concentrated HCl and 5 mL of 52% hydrofluoric acid in 990 mL inorganic water
– *Extracting reagents.* see Sect. 11.2.1

Procedures

Only the techniques for the purification of fulvic acids by cation exchange resins and techniques of purification of humic acids by HCl–HF attack are described here. However, as mentioned in "Introduction", it is important to be very careful when choosing a purification method, which should take into account observations that need to be carried out on the purified products later on. For other methods of purification, see references in the last paragraph of "Introduction" under Sect. 11.2.4.

Agitate a mixture of 1 g of humic acids and 100 mL of HCl–HF solution in a stopped polypropylene flask for 24 h at room temperature. Filter and suspend the filtrate again with 100 mL of HCl-HF solution. Repeat this treatment three or four times, carefully rinse the residue with inorganic water, then dry or freeze-dry.

Purify the fulvic acid solution three or four times on cation ex-change resin in H^+ form, then freeze-dry.

11.3. Further Alternatives and Complementary Methods

11.3.1. Alternative Methods of Extraction

Though the methods described above using diluted soda and sodium pyrophosphate are the most widely used, alternative methods of extraction have been proposed. For example, Kumada et al. (1967) developed a method used at the University of Nagoya (Japan); Lowe (1980) used yet another technique at the University of British Columbia (Canada); and the two techniques were the subject of a comparative test by Lowe and Kumada (1984).

Gregor and Powell (1986) developed a method for the extraction of fulvic acids with pyrophosphate in acid medium; this technique could avoids two potential problems: oxidation of the phenolic compounds in alkaline medium, and oxidation by the Fe^{3+} ions during acidification for precipitation of humic acids.

Several comparative studies of extractions should also be mentioned. For example, Thomann (1963) compared 3% ammonium oxalate, 1% soda, 1% sodium fluoride and sodium pyrophosphate; Jacquin et al. (1970) compared soda, sodium pyrophosphate and ion exchange resins; Hayes et al. (1975) compared saline solutions, organic chelating agents, dipolar aprotic solvents, pyridine, ethylene diamine and soda in solution. They concluded that soda is the best of the reagents they tested for isolation of representative extracts of a broad range of humic substances.

11.3.2 Fractionation of the Humin Residue

Principle

Given that between 40 and 80% of total carbon cannot be extracted with alkaline solvents, Perraud (1971) and Perraud et al. (1971) proposed a technique for the fractionation of the non-extractable humin residue. They performed successively:
– An alkaline extraction after two attacks with hot H_2SO_4: this extract was called "humin bound to iron" (Perraud et al. 1971); the sulphuric attack probably also releases sugars during the destruction of non-extractable polysaccharide like cellulose (cf. Chap. 13).
– An alkaline extraction after six attacks with hot HF–HCl provided organic material bound to clays.

However, these authors showed that the non-extractable fraction was still very high (37–52% of total carbon in their test) in spite of the total destruction of clays which was confirmed by X-ray. From 8 to 23% of this non-extractable fraction solubilized in CH_3COBr probably corresponded to fresh or only slightly transformed organic matter that was not previously trapped in a mineral gangue. The fraction that remained insoluble in CH_3COBr probably corresponded to either (1) organic matter very near to lignin but sufficiently transformed to be insoluble in acetyl bromide or (2) highly polymerized compounds in which the reduction of the functional groups probably resulted in their becoming insoluble in alkaline reagents.

A procedure for fractionation of the humin residue developed from the method of Perraud et al. (1971) and used in IRD laboratories (Bondy, France) is described below.

Procedure

– Weigh 10 g of the extraction residue of Sect. 11.2.1 above that has been dried, crushed and sieved to 0.2 mm.
– Add 50 mL of 1 mol ($\frac{1}{2}H_2SO_4$) L^{-1} sulphuric acid and heat at 70°C for 3 h.
– Centrifuge at 3,000g for 15 min.
– Wash twice with hot water and recover the centrifugation pellet.
– Extract the centrifugation pellet with 50 mL 0.1 mol (NaOH) L^{-1} soda solution for 4 h with agitation and leave to stand overnight.
– Centrifuge at 3,000g for 15 min. The supernatant liquid contains *humin bound to hydroxides* (HH); reserve for titration of fulvic and humic acids as described in Sect. 11.2.2; depending on soil type, the extract can be purified by flocculation of clays with a salt like sodium sulphate; add the flocculate to the centrifugation pellet.
– Take an aliquot of the centrifugation pellet for intermediate titration of carbon and possibly of nitrogen; this titration enables identification of the fraction that is solubilized in the acid (e.g. polysaccharides) by calculating the difference.
– On the other fraction of the centrifugation pellet (the larger fraction), destroy the clay particles by:
(a) four successive attacks with 50 mL of the 1 mol (HCl–HF) L^{-1} mixture at 70°C for 3 h then centrifuge for 15 min at 3,000g
(b) Attack with 50 mL of the 1 mol (HF) L^{-1} solution for 3 h at 70°C, centrifuge at 3,000g for 15 min, wash the centrifugation pellet with hot water and centrifuge again.

– Extract the centrifugation pellet with 50 mL of 0.1 mol (NaOH) L^{-1} solution agitate for 4 h and leave to stand overnight.
– Centrifuge at 3,000g for 15 min. Recover the humic compounds of *humin bound to the silicates* (HS) from the solution; on these compounds measure the carbon of the fulvic and humic acids (cf. Sect. 11.2.2).
– *Inherited humin(IH)*, which is made up of small organic fragments resembling charcoal, can be recovered on the centrifugation pellet:
(a) Add 50 mL H$_3$PO$_4$ $d = 1.4$; subject to ultrasound for 10 min, agitate mechanically for 30 min;
(b) Centrifuge at 1,500g for 10 min, then filter the supernatant on a small funnel stopped with a glass wool plug.

The carbon fragments recovered on this plug are the insoluble IH. As the liquids of previous acid attacks can also include suspended particles, after each centrifugation it is advised to filter the supernatants on the same glass wool plugs. After careful rinsing with inorganic water, dry the funnel at 50°C, crush the inherited humin and glass wool plug with an agate mortar and analyse carbon and nitrogen with a CHN analyser.

The last centrifugation pellet is the final residue of *nonextractable residual humin* (RH), rinse twice with inorganic water to eliminate the phosphoric acid, dry, crush and analyse carbon and nitrogen with a CHN analyser.

Calculations

Data Collected

Weight of soil sample at the beginning: $P0$
Weight of humin (centrifugation pellet cf. "Procedures"
under Sect. 11.2.1): $P1$
Weight of the $P1$ sampling for sulphuric attack: $P2$
Weight of the intermediate pellet (after HH extract): $P3$
Weight of the $P3$ sampling for HF–HCl attack: $P4$
Possible weight of other $P3$ sampling for C titration: $P'4$
(generally, $P4 + P4' = P3$)
Weight of non-extractable RH: $P5$

Concentrations of the Extracts

Humin (initial centrifugation pellet cf. "Procedures"
under Sect. 11.2.1) Ch
Humin bound to hydroxides (mg C on initial humin) Chh
Intermediate centrifugation pellet (after HH extract) mg C g^{-1} Ci

Humin bound to silicates (mg C on the whole extracted)	*Chs*
Carbon from the mixture of the glass wool	
and inherited humin (mg)	*Cih*
Residual humin (mg C g^{-1})	*Crh*

Calculations

Calculated on the initial soil sample, the carbon concentrations, (mg C g^{-1} dry soil) of humin before fractionation (H), humin bound to the hydroxides (HH), intermediate residue (I), humin bound to silicates (HS), inherited humin (IH), residual humin (RH) are expressed by:

$$H = Ch\ P1/P0$$
$$HH = Chh\ P1\ (P2\ P0)^{-1}$$
$$I = Ci\ P3\ P1\ (P4'\ P0)^{-1}$$
$$HS = Chs\ P3\ P1\ (P4\ P2\ P0)^{-1}$$
$$IH = Cih\ P3\ P1\ (P4\ P2\ P0)^{-1}$$
$$RH = Crh\ P5\ P3\ P1\ (P4\ P2\ P0)^{-1}$$

The H–(I+HH) value provides an estimate of the carbon dissolved in the hot sulphuric acid (polysaccharides of humin). The I–(HS+IH+RH) value provides an estimate of the carbon dissolved by the HF–HCl mixture.

References

Humic materials

Aiken GR McKnight DM Wershaw RL and MacCarthy P eds (1985) Humic substances in soil, sediment and water. I. *Geochemistry, Isolation and Characterization*. Wiley, New York, NY, 692 p

Bruckert S (1979) Analyse des complexes organo-minéraux des sols. *In :* *Pédologie 2.Constituants et propriétés du sol*, Bonneau M and Souchier B ed., Masson, Paris, 187–209

Carter MR and Stewart BA eds. (1995) *Structure and Organic Matter Storage in Agricultural Soils* (Advances in Soil Science), Lewis Publishers, Inc., Boca Raton, FL

Chamayou H and Legros JP (1989) *Les bases physiques, chimiques et minéralogiques de la science du sol*. Presses Universitaire de France (Techniques vivantes), 608 p

Duchaufour Ph (1977) *Pédologie.1. Pédogénèse et classification*. Masson, Paris, 477 p

Flaig W, Beutelspacher H and Rietz E (1975) Chemical composition and physical properties of humic substances. In *Soil Components, Vol.1 : Organic Components*, Gieseking JE ed., 1–211

Hessen DO and Tranvik LJ eds. (1998) *Aquatic Humic Substances : Ecology and Biogeochemistry* (Ecological Studies, Vol .133). Springer, Berlin, Heidelberg, New York

Kononova MM (1966) *Soil Organic Matter – Its Nature, Its Role in Soil Formation and in Soil Fertility* (translated from the Russian by Nowakowski PhD and Newman ACD), Pergamon Press, New York

Magdoff F, Tabatabai MA and Hanlon E (1996) Soil Organic Matter: Analysis and Interpretation (*Sssa Special Publication*, No 46), American Society of Agronomy

Piccolo A Ed. (1996) *Humic Substances in Terrestrial Ecosystems*. Elsevier, Amsterdam

Schnitzer M and Kahn SU (1972) *Humic Substances in the Environment*. Dekker, New York, 327 p

Schnitzer M (1978) Humic substances : chemistry and reactions. *In : Soil Organic Matter*, Schnitzer M and Kahn SU ed., Elsevier, Amsterdam, 1, 58

Springer U (1938) Der Heutige stand der Humusuntersuchungsmethodik mit besonderer Berücksichtigung der Trennung, Bestimmung und Charakterisierung der Huminsäùretypen und ihre Anwendung auf Charakteristische Humusformen. *Zeitsc.f.Pflanzen*, 6, 312–373

Stevenson FJ and Elliott ET (1989) Methodologies for assessing the quantity and quality of soil organic matter. *In : Dynamics of Soil Organic Matter in Tropical Ecosystems*, Coleman DC, Oades JM, Uehara G ed. University of Hawaii Press, Honolulu Hawaii 96822, 173–199

Stevenson FJ (1982) *Humus Chemistry*, Wiley, New York, 443 p

Stevenson FJ (1994) *Humus Chemistry : Genesis, Composition, Reactions*, 2nd edition. Wiley, New York, 496 pages

Tate RL (1992) *Soil Organic Matter. Biological and Ecological Effects*. Krieger, Melbourne FL, 304 p

Extraction, titration, purification and fractionation of humic materials

Aiken GR, Thurman EM and Malcolm RL (1979) Comparison of XAD macroporous resins for the concentration of fulvic acid from aqueous solution. *Anal. Chem.*, 51, 1799–1803

Bachelier, G (1983) Variations périodiques dans le degré de condensation des acides humiques: mise en évidence par spectrofluorimétrie, corrélation avec la stabilité structurale des sols. Cahiers ORSTOM. Série Pédologie (FRA), 20(3): 247-254.

Dabin B, Gavinelli E and Pelloux P (1983) Résultats de l'enquête analytique sur l'extraction et le dosage des matières humiques des sols-Réunion GEMOS Montpellier, Mai 1983. Document Orstom-Gemos, 16 p. multigr

Dabin (1976) Méthode d'extraction et de fractionnement des matières humiques du sol, application à quelques études pédologiques et agronomiques dans les sols tropicaux. *Cah.ORSTOM ser.Pédol.*, XIV, 287–297

Gregor JE and Powell HKJ (1986) Acid pyrophosphate extraction of soil fulvic acids. *J. Soil Sci.*, 37, 577–585

Hayes MHB, Swift RS, Wardle RE and Brown JK (1975) Humic materials from an organic soil : A comparison of extractants and of properties of extracts. *Geoderma*, 13, 231–245

Jacquin F, Calvez C, Dormaar JF and Metche M (1970) Contribution à l'étude des processus d'extraction et de caractérisation des composés humiques. *Bull.Ass.Fr.Etude du Sol*, 4, 27–38

Kumada K, Sato O, Ohsumi Y and Ohta S (1967) Humus composition of mountain soils in central Japan with special reference to the distribution of P type humic acid. *Soil. Sci. Plant Nutr.*, 13, 151–158

Lévesque and Schnitzer (1966) Effects of NaOH concentration on the extraction of organic matter and of major inorganic constituents from a soil. *Can. J. Soil Sci.,* 46, 7–12

Lowe LE and Kumada K (1984) A comparison of two methods for routine characterization of humus in pedological studies. *Soil Sci. Plant Nutr.,* 30, 321–331

Lowe LE (1980) Humus fraction ratios as a means of discriminating between horizon types. *Can. J. Soil Sci.*, 60, 219–229

Nègre R, Ghiglione Cl, Pugnet T and Giraud M (1976) Influence des méthodes d'extraction et de purification sur la nature des acides humiques de la cédraie du Petit Lubéron. *Cah.ORSTOM ser.Pédol.*, XIV, 337–350

Pansu M, Gautheyrou J and Loyer JY (2001) Soil Analysis – Sampling, Instrumentation and Quality control. Balkema, Lisse, Abington, Exton, Tokyo, 489 pp

Perraud A (1971) *La matière organique des sols forestiers de la Côte d'Ivoire.*, Thèse Docteur ès-sciences naturelles, Univ. Nancy I, 87 p. + annexes.

Perraud A, Nguyen Kha, Jacquin F (1971) Essai de caractérisation des formes de l'humine dans plusieurs types de sols. *C. R. Acad. Sci. Paris*, série D, 272, 1594–1596

Schnitzer M (1982) Organic Matter Characterization. *In : Methods of Soil Analysis, Part 2 Chemical and Microbiological Properties, 2nd edition*, Page AL, Miller RH and Keeney DR ed. Agronomy monograph N°9, Am. Soc. of Agronomy, Madison, Wisconsin USA, 581–593

Thomann Ch (1963) Quelques observations sur l'extraction de l'humus dans les sols : méthode au pyrophosphate de sodium. *Cah. ORSTOM ser. Pédol.*, 3, 43–72

Characterization of Humic Compounds

12.1 Introduction

12.1.1 Mechanisms of Formation

The synthesis of humic substances has been the object of speculation for many years. Andreux (1994) distinguished lytic mechanisms (lysis of the cellular walls, proteolysis, ligninolysis, transformation of polyphenols and other organic components), the mechanisms of tanning and melanisation which include incorporation of nitrogen and oxygen (Maillard's reaction: condensation of carbohydrates in the presence of amino nitrogen, condensation of polyphenol and amino acids in oxidizing medium) and the incorporation of inherited compounds.

Schnitzer (1978) reported the following four hypotheses about the formation of humic substances:

– *Deterioration of plant material.* Certain fractions of plant tissues, particularly woody materials, are only superficially decomposed in the soil to form humic substances; the nature of this "inherited humus" is thus strongly influenced by the nature of the original plant material; the first stage of humification provides the heaviest humic substances which can then be broken down into lighter substances and ultimately into CO_2 and H_2O.

– *Chemical polymerization.* The plant materials break down into small molecules which are used as a source of energy and carbon by micro-organisms; these micro-organisms then synthesize phenols and amino acids which are polymerized into humic substances; in this case the nature of original material has no effect on the type of substance formed.

– *Cellular autolysis.* The fragments resulting from autolysis of microbial and plant cells (amino sugars, acids, phenols and others aromatic compounds) condense and polymerize via free radicals.

– *Microbial synthesis.* Microbes use plant tissue as a source of carbon and energy to synthesize intercellular organic materials of high molecular weight; at microbial death, these substances are released in the soil; they represent the first stage of humification and can then undergo extracellular microbial degradation into lighter molecules.

12.1.2 Molecular Structure

Based on their solubility properties, humic substances are generally classified in the three following categories: *humic acids, fulvic acids, humins* (cf. Chap. 11).

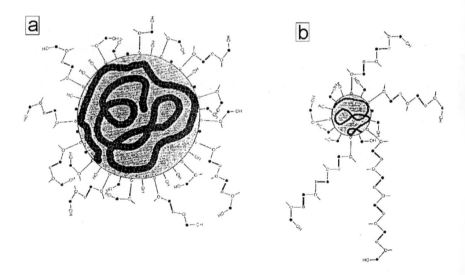

Fig. 12.1. Structure of two humic macromolecules; only the *nuclei* are represented at a scale of molecular weight (mw) for **(a)** mw >50,000, and **(b)** mw <5,000. *filled circle* C=O, *open circle* CH, *open square* NH, — peptide bond, ●— OH carboxyl (Andreux, 1994)

In a review of the literature, Schnitzer and Kahn (1972) showed that these three humic fractions are structurally rather similar. The structure of the humic molecule can be described schematically as a *nucleus* rich in hydroxy-quinonic units linked by C–C or C–O–C bonds (Andreux 1994). The frequency of distribution of the proteic and polypeptide chains fixed on this nucleus varies with the type of soil and the precursors. The molecular size of these structures (Fig. 12.1) depends both on the dimension of the nucleus and on the nature of the phenolic precursors. Their affinity for aqueous solvents thus depends on the number and the length of the peripheral hydrophilic chains carrying the free –COOH groups of polypeptides, however, with significant acidity of the matrix (Andreux 1994).

The properties of the three humic fractions differ especially with respect to their molecular weight, their ultimate analysis, and the number of functional groups. Fulvic acids have the lowest molecular weight, contain more oxygen but less carbon and nitrogen than the other two. The functional groups containing oxygen (CO_2H, OH, C=O) have a rate per unit of weight that is higher in fulvic acids than in humic acids and humin (Stevenson 1982).

Humic acids are also extractable from charcoal (Lawson and Stewart 1989) and research using ^{13}C nuclear magnetic resonance spectroscopy (cf. Sect. 12.3.4) has shown that the stable carbon of Australian soils is mainly charcoal (Skjemstad et al. 1996). Although structural models of humic molecules have been proposed (e.g. Schulten 1995, Schulten and Schnitzer 1997, Schulten and Leinweber 2000, Schulten 2002, Lodygin and Beznosikov 2003), most of the concepts concerning molecular structure are not applicable to humic acids (McCarthy 2001). Further research is needed to obtain precise information about these molecules, their bonds with inorganic (Schulten and Leinweber 2000) and xenobiotic (Piccolo et al. 1999) molecules and their distribution in different soil types, which, in turn, will improve understanding of their role in the environment. All modern instrumental methods are needed for these researches (Hatcher et al. 2001, Piccolo and Conte 2003).

12.2 Classical Techniques

12.2.1 Fractionation of Humic Compounds

Principle

For many years humic acids were characterized according to the degree they bonded with clays (Springer 1938, Tiurin 1951, Duchaufour 1954, 1956).

Brown or free humic acids were considered to be only slightly bonded to clays, to have the lowest molecular weight and to be relatively insensitive to the flocculating action of electrolytes; they were said to derive from the oxidation of lignin under the action of the polyphenoloxidase and to characterize acid soils in particular, e.g. forest soils in a wet climate (Duchaufour 1956).

Grey humic acids are darker in colour, form closer bonds with mineral colloids, have more condensed molecules, flocculate easily in the presence of electrolytes; this type of humus is characteristic of black soils, but is also relatively abundant in all soils that are rich in calcium.

Early methods of fractionation of humic acids were thus based on the properties of the two main types of compounds: extraction in the presence of a flocculating agent in the case of brown humic acids followed by washing the residue in water in the case of grey humic acids (Duchaufour 1956), direct soda extraction of brown humic acids then extraction of two fractions of grey humic acids as a function of their bonds with calcium or iron and aluminium (Duchaufour 1957).

To simplify the procedure, Duchaufour and Jacquin (1966) proposed a method with electrophoretic fractionation of humic acids on pyrophosphate extracts (cf. "Method of Dabin (1976)" Chap. 11). This method was compared with that of Tiurin (1951) by Dabin and Thomann (1970); it was widely used in France, in particular in IRD[1] laboratories (Ratsimbazafy 1973, Dabin 1980). This is the first fractionation method described later. The technique of fractionation of humic acids by exclusion chromatography (Bailly and Margulis 1968, Bailly and Tittonel 1972) is also described later, along with a fractionation procedure for fulvic acids. Other complex techniques for fractionation of humic compounds are described more briefly in Sect. 12.3.1.

Equipment

– Plastic electrophoresis tank with three compartments (Fig. 12.2)
– stabilized supply of direct current adjustable between 0 and 600 V
– photoelectric densitometer to read the electrophoresis diagrams
– columns for liquid chromatography, diameter: 2.5 cm, length: 80 cm
– UV–visible detector equipped with a recorder or a system for data acquisition
– fraction collector (optional)
– peristaltic pump with flow of 50 mL h^{-1} (optional).

---

[1] IRD = Institute of Research for Development (ex-Orstom), Bondy, France.

Products

- Filter paper tapes (Arch 302 or Whatman no. 1 or 2), 5 cm in width and 35 cm in length, cut perpendicular to the direction the filter is filled (when a square sheet of paper is held by one side, the direction perpendicular to filling is where the paper curves most under its own weight)
- extraction solutions (see Sect. 11.2.1 in Chap. 11)
- buffer solution for electrophoresis: in a 2 L volumetric flask add 13.6 g of monobasic potassium phosphate, 2.5 g of soda pellets and approximately 1.5 L of inorganic water (cf. Sect. 11.2.1 of Chap. 11), adjust pH to 7.4 with soda if necessary, agitate well and complete to 2 L
- standard dextrane gel Sephadex G25 for molecular weights ≤5,000
- standard dextrane gel Sephadex G75 for molecular weights ≤50,000
- standard dextrane gel Sephadex G200 for molecular weights ≤200,000
- polyvinylpyrrolidone

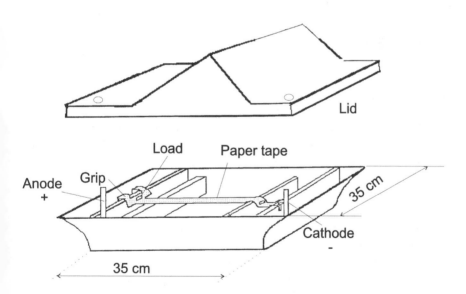

Fig. 12.2. duan tank for paper electrophoresis of humic acids

- TRIS buffer (pH 9, ionic force 0.5): mix 414 mL of M 2-amino-2 hydroxymethyl-propane-1, 3-diol, 50 mL of 1 mol (HCl) L^{-1} solution and complete to 1 L inorganic water
- Borax buffer (pH = 9.1, ionic strength = 0.075): 0.025 mol ($Na_2B_4O_7$) L^{-1}.

Procedure for Electrophoresis Fractionation of Humic Acids

– Take a quantity of humic extract solution (pyrophosphate or soda) corresponding to 25 to 50 mg carbon (cf. titration in Sect. 11.2.2 of Chap. 11).

– Precipitate the humic acids at pH 1 with sulphuric acid, centrifuge and wash the centrifugation pellet several times with a 1 mol ($\frac{1}{2}H_2SO_4$) L^{-1} solution.

– Dissolve the humic acids in approximately 1 mL of normal soda solution so as to obtain a rather thick solution but without solids (cf. purification in Sect. 11.2.4 of Chap. 11) and with a homogenous concentration of carbon; store in a well-stopped hemolysis tube.

– Fill the two external compartments of the electrolysis tank to the same level with electrophoresis buffer solution; wet the paper strip in the buffer solution, dry it between two sheets of filter paper and place it in the electrophoresis tank, pull it tight between the two external compartments as shown in Fig. 12.2.

– With a 100 mm^3 micropipette deposit approximately 40 mm^3 of humic solution at a distance of 5 cm from the cathode following a straight line down the centre of the strip of paper and leaving 1 cm free on each side of the paper; in the case of very concentrated solutions, the deposit can be reduced to 20 mm^3.

– Place the lid on the tank and start the electrical current; regulate the current at 10 V per cm of paper, or approximately 200 V; the intensity of the current depends on the number of paper strips for simultaneous electrophoresis and on the conductivity of the electrolyte (approximately 15 mA with four strips). The negatively charged humic molecules migrate towards the anode; the smaller the molecules, the faster they migrate (e.g. brown humic acids, BHA). Migration is rapid at the beginning then slows down. The time needed for standard electrophoresis is 3 h which corresponds to 10–12 cm displacement by brown humic acids.

– Shut off the current and rapidly remove the paper strips, place them on a flat surface and dry them under IR radiation or in the drying oven at 60°C. Record the radiation transmission of each strip of paper with a photoelectric densitometer.

– An electrophoresis diagram (Fig. 12.3) is obtained in which:

(1) *grey humic acids (GHA)* often display a distinct narrow peak up to 1 cm from the starting line; in the case of the chernozems, Duchaufour and Jacquin (1963) reported a second peak which could migrate up to 2 cm from the starting line; in tropical soils, GHA are frequently spread

out over 3 or even 4 cm with either a single peak, or two or more peaks; it is sometimes rather difficult to detect the limit of GHA and their peak limit has consequently been arbitrarily fixed at 1/3 of the overall length of the diagram, i.e. 3–4 cm for a length of 9–12 cm

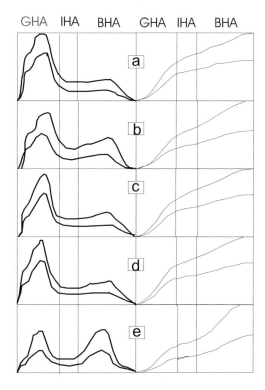

Fig. 12.3. Examples of electrophoresis diagrams of humic acids extracted with a pH 9.8 pyrophosphate solution in a range of tropical soils (Dabin 1980). On the *left*: direct readings with the optical densitometer at wavelengths of 512 nm (*top curve*) and 625 nm. On the *right*: corresponding *integral curves* giving in the *y*-coordinate surfaces corresponding to grey humic acids (GHA: from 0 to 1/3 of the graph), intermediate humic acids (IHA: between 1/3 and 1/2), brown humic acids (BHA: more than ½ of the graph). **a:** tropical podzol (histic tropaquod), A horizon, **b:** tropical podzol (histic tropaquod), B horizon, **c:** humiferous ferrallitic soil (umbriorthox), surface horizon, **d:** humiferous ferrallitic soil (umbriorthox), subsurface horizon, **e:** weathered tropical soil (oxictropudalf).

(2) the humic compounds located between 1/3 and 1/2 of the length of the diagram are called *intermediary humic acids (IHA)*

(3) the *brown humic acids (BHA)* are spread out between the middle and the other end of the diagram.

– The surface area of each fraction is determined; *SG* is the surface of the *GHA, SI* that of the *IHA, SB* that of the *BHA, ST* is the total surface area and % *qt* is the total quantity of humic acids; the total quantity of each fraction is expressed by:

$$GHA \% = qt \ SG/ST$$
$$IHA \% = qt \ SI/ST$$
$$BHA \% = qt \ SB/ST$$

Figure 12.3 shows some examples of electrophoresis diagrams obtained with this method.

Remarks

Any liquid circulating on the paper strips can also cause migration of humic acids. This should be avoided by making sure that the liquid is at the same level at the anode and cathode (otherwise there is a risk of siphoning by the paper), and by avoiding evaporation on the paper. Evaporation can cause the liquid to move by aspiration on both sides of the paper strip. Thus, even without electrical current, certain humic acids may migrate and be found in the centre of the strip. With electrical current, migration will stop when the speed of migration due to the electric potential is equal to the speed of the liquid circulating in the opposite direction. It is thus imperative to use a lid to limit evaporation; the lid should be shaped like a roof to prevent drops of condensation falling onto the paper strips.

The passage of the current enriches the cathodic compartment in the soda and raises its pH; in the case of several electrophoresis series this phenomenon can be compensated for by reversing the direction of the current and thus of the deposit.

Procedure for Humic Acid Fractionation on Dextrane Gels

Fractionations can be carried out in a simple way with elution using inorganic distilled water (Bailly and Margulis 1968, Bailly and Tittonel 1972):

– prepare a concentrated solution of humic acids in the same way as for electrophoresis but with a sample specimen corresponding to 2–10 mg carbon, diluted in 3–10 mL of 1 mol (NaOH) L^{-1} solution
– fill the columns with the Sephadex gel: 50 cm for G25 and G75, 70 cm approximately for G200, these heights are likely to vary with the type of humus (Bailly and Tittonel 1972)

– deposit the test specimen on the G25 column and elute with inorganic water either by gravity (descending chromatography), or with a peristaltic pump at a flow of approximately 30 mL h^{-1} (ascending chromatography)

– carry the effluent in a UV photometer detector regulated at 253.7 nm; record the chromatogram and collect the fractions corresponding to the main peaks (Fig. 12.4);

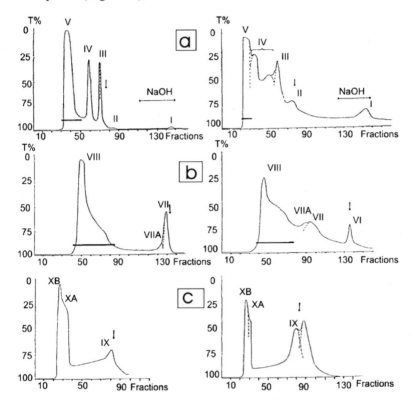

Fig. 12.4. Examples of separation by exclusion chromatography on dextrane gel (Bailly and Tittonel 1972). On the left, grassland podzolic soil, A1 horizon, 0–6 cm depth; on the right, forest grey soil, A2 horizon, depth 16–29 cm. **a:** fractionation of the humic acid extract on Sephadex G25 F, test specimen corresponding to 4.7 mg C, **b:** fractionation on Sephadex G75 of peak V obtained in **a**, **c:** fractionation on Sephadex G200 of peak VIII obtained in **b**.

– the first eluted peak corresponds to the largest molecules that were not separated by gel exclusion; collect this fraction and subject it to exclusion chromatography in a similar way but on column G75; fractionate the new first peak eluted on this column again on column

G200; Fig. 12.8 presents two series of examples of chromatograms obtained successively on the three types of columns with two soils.

This type of fractionation by gel permeation can also be performed in buffered solutions to avoid interactions between the gel and the solution, e.g. Tris and Borax buffers prepared in the same way as in "Products" in Sect. 12.2.1 (Cameron et al. 1972a).

Fractionation of Fulvic Acids

The method of Lowe (1975) is a very simple way to separate fulvic acids into two fractions: a coloured polyphenolic fraction and an almost colourless fraction with a prevalence of polysaccharide. Since C_h, C_f, C_a are carbons in humic acids, fulvic acids and their polyphenolic coloured fraction respectively, the $C_h:C_f$ and $C_a:C_f$ ratios were linked to the types of horizons used in the Canadian soil classification system which facilitate the distinction between some of these types (Lowe 1980):
– treat a fraction of the fulvic acid extract using 1 g polyvinylpyrrolidone for 100 mL of solution
– agitate intermittently for 30 min and filter
– titrate carbon on the filtrate (cf. Sect. 11.2.2 of Chap. 11) to quantify the *Ca* fraction; the fulvic acid sample must be sufficient in volume to allow titration with acceptable precision.

12.2.2 Titration of the Main Functional Groups

Principle

The procedures described here are based on the measurement of total acidity and of carboxylic acidity of Wright and Schnitzer (1959) and of Schnitzer and Gupta (1965).

For measurement of total acidity, the sample is treated with a barium hydroxide solution under N_2 for 24 h. The $Ba(OH)_2$ remaining in the solution after the reaction is then back titrated with a standard acid solution.

For the titration of carboxylic groups, the humic materials are agitated for 24 h with calcium acetate solution in excess which causes the release of acetic acid according to a reaction of the type:

$$2 \, RCOOH + (CH_3COO)_2Ca \rightarrow (RCOO)_2Ca + 2 \, CH_3COOH$$

The acetic acid released is then titrated with a standard soda solution.

The proportion of phenolic groups is calculated by the difference between total acidity and the acidity of the carboxylic groups.

Other measurement techniques for functional groups (phenolic, alcoholic, ketonic, quinoid) are described briefly in Sect. 12.3.

Equipment

– 125 mL Erlenmeyer flasks with screw caps
– titrimeter equipped with a combined electrode for the measurement of pH.

Products

– 0.2 mol (1/2 Ba(OH)$_2$) L^{-1} barium hydroxide solution: weigh 31.548 g of Ba(OH)$_2$,8H$_2$O (quality containing the minimum of carbonate), dissolve in inorganic CO$_2$–free water, complete to 1 L and protect from atmospheric CO$_2$ with a trap containing soda lime
– 0.5 mol (HCl) L^{-1} hydrochloric acid solution: prepare using standard commercial dose; dilute with inorganic CO$_2$–free water.
– 1 mol (1/2Ca(CH$_3$COO) $_2$) L^{-1} calcium acetate solution: dry the pure product at 105°C and weigh 79.085 g under anhydrous atmosphere, dissolve in inorganic water and complete to 1 L.
– 0.1 mol (NaOH) L^{-1} soda solution: prepare using standard commercial dose; dilute with inorganic water, complete to 1 L and protect with a trap containing soda lime during storage.

Procedure

Total Acidity

To obtain the maximum number of exchangeable sites in acid-active form, it is advisable to work with carefully purified humic materials in order to reduce their ash rate (cf. Sect. 11.2.4 of Chap. 11).

Place an exact weight of between 50 and 100 mg of freeze-dried humic material in a 125 mL Erlenmeyer flask with a screw cap and add exactly 20 mL of 0.2 mol (Ba(OH)$_2$) L^{-1} solution. Perform a blank assay containing only the 0.2 mol (Ba(OH)$_2$ L^{-1} solution without the sample. Put the flasks under nitrogen atmosphere, stop well and agitate for 24 h at room temperature. Filter the suspension, wash the residue well with distilled CO$_2$–free water, add the washing waters to the filtrate and carry out potentiometric titration of the resulting extraction solution with 0.5

mol (HCl) L^{-1} solution up to pH 8.4. V_b and V are the volumes of standard acid solution for titration of the blank assay and of the sample, respectively, N_a is the acid normality and P the weight of the sample (mg); total acidity A_t in milliequivalents per gram of humic material is expressed by:

$$A_t = 1,000(V_b - V_s) N_a/P$$

Carboxyl Groups

Place in a 125 mL Erlenmeyer flask with a screw cap an exact weight of between 50 and 100 mg of humic material; add 10 mL of 1 mol ½ $Ca(CH_3COO)_2$ L^{-1} solution and 40 mL of inorganic CO_2–free water. At the same time, perform a blank assay containing the reagents without the humic sample. After 24 h of shaking at room temperature, filter the suspension, rinse the residue with distilled CO_2–free water, combine the filtrate and washing water and perform potentiometric titration with the 0.1 mol (NaOH) L^{-1} solution up to pH 9.8. If V_s and V_b are the volume of titrating solution for the sample and blank assay, respectively (mL), N_b is the normality of the standard soda solution (mol L^{-1}), P the sample weight (mg); the carboxylic acidity A_c in mol $(COOH)\,g^{-1}$ humic material, is expressed by

$$A_c = 1,000(V_s - V_b) N_b/P.$$

Phenolic Acidity

This A_p acidity can be expressed in mol (phenolicOH) g^{-1} humic material by

$$A_p = A_t - A_c.$$

12.2.3 UV–Visible Spectrometry

Principle

Among other molecular spectrometry techniques, UV spectrometry records electronic energy transitions in the molecules whereas lower-energy infra-red radiation records variations in molecular kinetic energy.

Although absorption in the ultraviolet and visible field of the electromagnetic spectrum does not give a band that is very characteristic of humic compounds (Schnitzer and Kahn 1972, Schnitzer 1978), the E4:E6 ratio of absorbance at 465 (E4) and 665 nm (E6) is often used to characterize humus. Ratios lower than 5 are characteristic of humic acids while fulvic acids have higher ratios; this ratio is independent of the concentration of humic materials but is not the same for humic materials extracted from different types of soils.

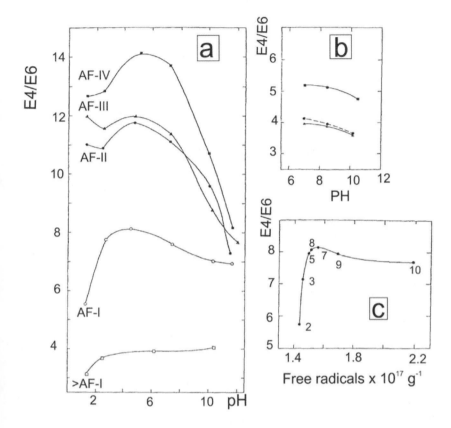

Fig.12.5. Effect of certain factors on the value of the E4:E6 ratio (Chen et al., 1977): **(a)** effect of the pH in different fractions of a fulvic acid (Bh horizon of a Canadian podzol) separated on Sephadex gel; the molecular weights measured by osmometry (Hansen and Schnitzer, 1969) were: 883 for AF-IV, 1181 for AF-III, 1815 for AF-II, 2110 for AF-I and >2110 for >AF-I, **(b)** effect of pH in some humic acids of Ah horizons of Canadian soils from the area round Alberta: Black Chernozem, Solod, Solonetz, **(c)** effect of the concentration of free radicals measured by electron spin resonance (cf. Sect. 12.3.6) for the fulvic acid used in **a,** (the numbers on the curve are pH values).

Kononova (1966) believed that the E4:E6 ratio was related to the degree of condensation of the aromatic carbon lattice, a weak ratio indicating a high degree of condensation of the aromatic humic components, a strong ratio indicating the presence of a higher proportion of aliphatic structures.

Chen et al. (1977) made a thorough study of the information provided by the E4:E6 ratio. Their study showed that the E4:E6 ratio:

– is mainly governed by molecular size (or molecular or particle weight; Fig. 12.5a, b)
– is highly affected by the pH (Fig. 12.5a, b)
– is correlated with the concentration of free radicals (Fig. 12.5c), and with O, C, CO_2H contents and total acidity (these measurements are also correlated with the size of the particles)
– does not present a direct correlation with the concentration of condensed aromatic nuclei, which would invalidate the assumption of Kononova (1966)
– is independent of the concentration of humic or fulvic acid, at least in the field of 100–500 ppm, which confirms the other assumption of Kononova.

In agreement with Kononova (1966), these authors finally showed that the most favorable range of pH to measure E4:E6 ratios is between 7 and 8. This can be obtained by dissolving humic material in a 0.1 mol $(NaHCO_3)$ L^{-1} solution at a concentration of between 200 and 400 mg kg^{-1}.

Ghosh and Schnitzer (1979) proposed a mechanism linking the macromolecular characteristics of humic substances and UV–visible absorption: optical density decrease with an increase in the concentration of neutral electrolyte, indicating a reduction in the size of the particles probably due to a rolling up of the macromolecule.

Equipment

– UV–visible spectrograph with an adjustable double beam and fixed wavelength (465 and 665 nm) or preferably with variable wavelength between 200 and 700 nm
– quartz tanks for UV spectrometry.

Reagents

– 0.05 mol $(NaHCO_3)$ L^{-1} solution: in a 1 L volumetric flask dissolve 4.200 g of $NaHCO_3$ (quality suitable for spectrography) in inorganic distilled water, complete to 1 L and stop the flask well before storage.

Procedure

Dissolve 2–4mg of humic material in 10 mL of the 0.05 mol ($NaHCO_3$) L^{-1} solution. Check the pH after dissolution, it should be close to 8 (the pH of a 0.05 mol ($NaHCO_3$) L^{-1} aqueous solution is 8.3). Fill the quartz measurement tank to mid-height with this solution and fill the reference tank with a pure 0.05 mol ($NaHCO_3$) L^{-1} solution. Measure the absorbance at 465 and 665 nm. The ratio of these two absorbencies is the E4:E6 ratio.

If more detailed studies are required, the optical density (OD) spectrum can be recorded in the 200–350 nm UV range (Ghosh and Schnitzer 1979) or in the 400–700 nm range; in the latter case, the straight lines Log(OD) $= f$(Log k) can be plotted and, according to Chen et al. (1977), its slope should be equal to -6.435 Log(E4:E6)

12.2.4 Infra-Red Spectrography

Principle

The infra-red spectrum between 1 and 100 μm wavelength makes it possible to observe the vibrations of stretching and deformation of the molecules (as the spectrum of molecular rotation corresponds to less energetic radiations of wavelengths higher than 100 μm). In practice, the most useful spectral field for organic chemistry is in medium IR between the two wavelengths λ of 2.5 and 15 μm corresponding to wavenumbers $1/\lambda$ between 4,000 and 660 cm^{-1} (cf. Sect. 5.1.1 of Chap. 5). The near IR zone can also be widely explored with the help of chemometrical software (cf. Sect. 5.3.1 of Chap. 5).

In humic substances, the IR spectrum mainly reflects oxygenated functional groups such as $-CO_2H$, $-OH$ and C–O. Some IR bands are particularly well defined (Schnitzer 1971) at wavenumbers 3,400 cm^{-1} (H bound to OH), 2,900 cm^{-1} (aliphatic CH bonds), 1,725 cm^{-1} (C–O of CO_2H, C–O elongation of ketonic carbonyls), 1,630 cm^{-1} (aromatic C–C, H linked to C–O of carbonyls, COO^{-}), 1,450 cm^{-1} (aliphatic CH), 1,400 cm^{-1} (COO^{-}, aliphatic CH), 1,200 cm^{-1} (CO stretching, OH deformations of CO_2H), 1,050 cm^{-1} (Si–O of the silicated impurities).

The IR spectrum does not provide much information on the chemical structure of the core of humic substances. However, it is very useful for preliminary characterization of humic materials of different origin (Fig. 12.6) to determine the effect of different extractions or chemical purification agents (cf. Sect. 11.2.4 of Chap. 11), and to study the reaction of derivatisation such as silylation, methylation, and acetylation.

The IR spectrum also makes it possible to detect changes in the structure of humic materials following oxidation, pyrolysis or other treatments. Lastly, it is a practical method to characterize the formation of metal–humate and clay–humate complexes or to detect interactions between humic materials and other organic molecules such as pesticides.

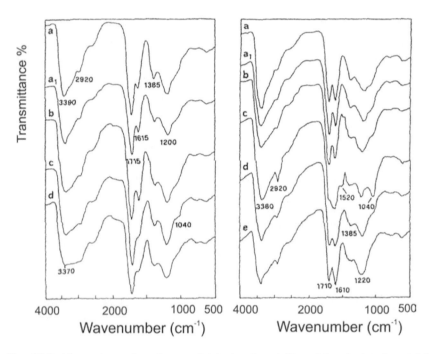

Fig. 12.6. hfra-red spectra of some fulvic (on the *left*) and humic (on the *right*) acids of standard and reference samples of IHSS (Senesi et al. 1989): **(a)** Suwannee River Standard, code IHSS 1S101F (AF) and 1S101H (AH), **(a1)** Suwannee River Reference, code IHSS 1R101F (AF) and 1R101H (AH), **(b)** Nordic aquatic, code 1R105F and 1R105H, **(c)** Soil St, code 1S102Fand 1R102H, **(d)** Peat, code 1R103F and 1R103H, **(e)** Leonardite, code 1R 104 H.

Great care should be taken in interpreting the spectra and particularly to avoid confusing the organic or mineral origin of the absorption bands (Russel and Anderson 1977).

Equipment

– Double beam IR absorption spectrograph with a field frequency between 300 and 4,000 cm^{-1}

– manual hydraulic press for the preparation of pellets for IR spectrography (e.g. standard 12 ton Spex-Carver)
– polished stainless steel vacuum pelletizer, diameter 13 mm.

NB: it is also possible to work without a pelletizer or a hydraulic press; spectra can be obtained in suspensions that are maintained between two IR-transparent blades; spectra can also be obtained in solutions with a solvent that is transparent to IR. The technique described below is not the cheapest but has been shown to be particularly suitable for IR spectrometry.

Product

– Potassium bromide in powder form for IR spectrometry.

Procedure

With the agate mortar, prepare a KBr pellet by mixing 1 mg of humic material with 400 mg of dry KBr. Place the powder in the pelletizer, put it under vacuum and press with a pressure of 7,600 kg cm^{-2} for 20 min (cf. "Preparation of Discs (Solid Solution)" in Chap. 5). Unmould the pellet, which should be vitrified, and place it in the measuring cell of the IR spectrometer, put a pellet of pure KBr in the reference cell and record the spectrum between 300 and 4,000 cm^{-1}.

12.3 Complementary Techniques

12.3.1 Improvements in Fractionation Technologies

The techniques described later are the result of improvements in electrophoresis and gel exclusion chromatography (cf. Sect. 12.2.1).

Electrophoresis – Electrofocusing Method

Cacco et al. (1974) proposed an improvement of the electrophoresis of humic compounds by using the electrofocusing method described by Righetti and Drysdale (1971). In this technique, humic compounds migrate from anode to cathode in a polyacrilamide gel in the presence of ampholines which cause a pH gradient. The migration stops when each compound reaches its isoelectric point. Figure 12.7 shows the results of isoelectrophoretic characterisation (Cacco and Maggioni 1976) of fulvic and humic acids extracted with pyrophosphate at pH 7 from an alpine podzol. Rusina et al. (1983) suggested a system of calculation of molecular parameters by electrophoretic mobility in the polyacrylamide gel. Electrophoresis techniques are generally used for the study of molecular size but also of the electrical charge of humic substances (Duxbury 1989).

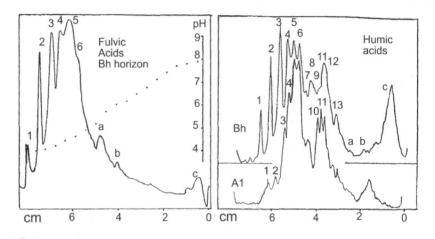

Fig. 12.7. Isoelectrophoretic characterization of fulvic (deep Bh horizon) and humic (surface A1 and deep Bh horizons) acids extracted from an alpine podzol (Cacco and Maggioni 1976)

Gel Exclusion Chromatography

The gel can be calibrated with the molecular weights of humic acids measured jointly using other techniques. Figure 12.8 shows the calibration curves obtained by Cameron et al. (1972a) with four types of gel; the molecular weights (on the x-coordinate) were measured by a sedimentation technique using ultracentrifugation (Cameron et al. 1972b). In such studies, the gel is characterized by the K_{av} parameter suggested by Laurent and Killander (1964):

$$K_{av} = (V_R - V_o)/(V_t - V_o),$$

Where is the V_R: volume of retention, V_O: volume of pores and V_t: volume of total column.

The median values of K_{av} are adjusted to the median molecular weights M (Fig. 12.8) by means of two constants k_1 and k_2 according to law:
$$K_{av} = k_1 \ln M + k_2.$$

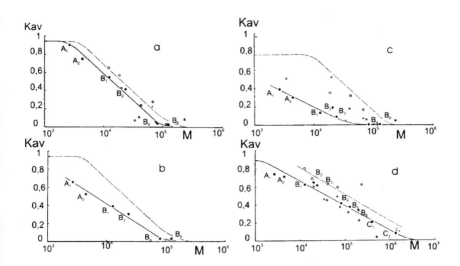

Fig. 12.8. Calibration of four types of gel (Cameron et al. 1972a) for the fractionation of humic acids in comparison with other macromolecular compounds (*solid lines* and *solid circles*: humic acids, *dotted lines* and *open circles*: data from the protein fractionation, sucrose is used to determine the stationary liquid volume V_t See text for K_{av} and M: **(a)** Sephadex G100 in tris buffer (cf. Sect. 12.2.1 for preparation), **(b)** Sephadex G100 in borax buffer (cf. Sect. 12.2.1 for preparation), **(c)** Biogel P-150 in tris buffer and **(d)** Sepharose 6B in tris buffer.

Nowadays, fractionation by gel permeation can be carried out by high pressure liquid chromatograph (HPLC) and in addition, new gels are more powerful than the older Sephadex gels. For example the "Zorbax PSM 1000" silica gel used by Morizur et al. (1984) allowed better recovery of all the organic matter with approximately 1/100 the ion exchange capacity of Sephadex gel.

Beckett et al. (1987) used a *flow field-flow fractionation (flow FFF)* technique for fulvic and humic acid fractionation, which appears to be a powerful tool to obtain information on molecular weights.

12.3.2 Titration of Functional Groups

Section 12.2.2 described titration techniques for the main functional groups of humic compounds, carboxylic and phenolic groups, the latter being obtained by calculating the difference between total acidity and carboxylic acidity.

Chemical titration can be used for other functional groups. The main groups that have been the subject of such investigations are:

– *Total OH groups* can be determined by acetylation of humic substances with acetic anhydride in pyridine (Schnitzer and Skinner, 1965):

$$2\ ROH + (CH_3CO)_2O \rightarrow CH_3COOR + CH_3COOH$$

The acetylated humic substances are then carefully isolated from the reactional medium. Hydrolysis in alkaline medium releases acetates from the acetyl groups; distillation in strong acid medium enables recovery of acetic acid which is titrated by acidimetry. The number of moles of acetic acid collected corresponds to the number of total OH groups of the humic substance.

– *Alcoholic OH groups* can be estimated by "total OH groups" minus "phenolic OH groups". However, as the phenolic OH groups are themselves calculated by difference (cf. Sect. 12.2.2), it is advisable to take the laws of propagation of errors into account.

– *Total C–O Groups* can be quantified by the reaction of humic substances with hydroxylamine chlorhydrate in 2-dimethylaminoethanol medium:

$$R_1R_2C–O + NH_2OH\cdot HCl \rightarrow R_1R_2C–NOH + H_2O + HCl$$

Excess hydroxylamine hydrochlorate is back titrated with a standard $HClO_4$ solution (Fritz et al. 1959).

– *Quinonic C–O groups* can be titrated by reduction in OH^- phenolic groups by ferrous iron in triethanolamine; the excess ferrous iron is back titrated by amperometry with a dichromate solution (Glebko et al. 1970).

– *Ketonic C–O groups* can be estimated by the difference between total C–O groups and quinonic C–O groups.

In addition, Schnitzer (1978) cited several attempts to characterize acid groups by direct potentiometric titration. It was difficult to clearly distinguish the two main types of acidity (OH and CO_2H functional groups) using this method even in a non-aqueous medium. Certain authors did succeed including Rosell et al. (1972), who simultaneously measured three types of acidity by potentiometric titration in 80% *N*-methyl acetamid aqueous solution.

De Nobili et al. (1990) presented an alternative to the technique described in Sect. 12.2.2 for the determination of carboxylic groups: the precipitation of humic substances with cethyltrimethylammonium cation detergent.

12.3.3 Characterization by Fragmentation

One of the ways to study heavy humic macromolecules consists in splitting them up and identifying the fragments. These methods can be classified in four main groups: oxidative fragmentation, reducing frag- mentation, other chemical degradation techniques and thermal fragmenta- tion by pyrolysis.

Oxidative Fragmentation

This group of techniques can be divided into two subgroups. (i) oxidation with permanganate and (ii) other oxidative techniques.

Oxidation with permanganate was widely used on humic materials from different types of soils: e.g. Ah horizons of Solonetz, Solod and Chernozem (Kahn and Schnitzer, 1971a; Kahn and Schnitzer, 1972b), forest grey soil under different farming systems (Kahn and Schnitzer, 1972b), tropical volcanic soils (Griffith and Schnitzer, 1975), mediterranean soils (Chen et al. 1978a), non-hydrolysable humic residues (Ogner, 1973) and fulvic acid fractions (Khan and Schnitzer, 1971b).

The analytical procedure varies with the author. The humic materials can first be fractionated or subjected to a derivatisation reaction (methylation) before oxidation. Kahn and Schnitzer (1971b) oxidated 1 g of humic material by boiling at reflux for 8h with 250 mL of 4% $KMnO_4$ aqueous solution. The excess of permanganate must be destroyed by controlled addition of small volumes of methanol and the solution removed from insoluble MnO_2 by filtration and rinsing. The acidified filtrate is then extracted with ethyl acetate in a liquid-liquid extractor for 48h. The extract is brought to dry in the rotary evaporator, dissolved in a small volume of methanol and methylated with a diazomethane solution in ether. The end products are then split by chromatography and identified with the usual range of spectrographic methods used for molecular characterization (UV, IR, mass and NMR spectrometry), the most widely used method being gas chromatography coupled with mass spectrometry (GC–MS).

Other oxidative reagents have been used for studies of the degradation of organic matter. Neyroud and Schnitzer (1974) then Griffith and Schnitzer (1976) studied the products of alkaline oxidation of humic and fulvic acids by cupric oxide. Oxidation is performed in an autoclave at 170°C on 1g of humic product mixed with 100 mL of NaOH 2 mol L^{-1} solution and 5g CuO; the end of the procedure is almost the same as for permanganate oxidation (see earlier part in this section).

Other methods included nitrobenzene alkaline oxidation (Morrison 1963), nitric acid oxidation (Hansen and Schnitzer, 1967), hypohalogenite oxidation (Chakrabartty et al. 1974) and peracetic acid oxidation (Schnitzer and Skinner, 1974). Griffith and Schnitzer (1989) reviewed oxidative degradation techniques, one of the analytical tools for the study of humic substances (Hatcher et al. 2001).

Reductive Fragmentation

The most commonly used reagent was sodium amalgam (Mendez and Stevenson 1966; Stevenson and Mendez 1967; Piper and Posner 1972) but other reducers were also tested such as zinc powder (Hansen and Schnitzer 1969). Stevenson (1989) reviewed reductive fragmentation techniques.

Other Degradative Chemical Methods

Boiling humic acids in water releases polysaccharides and small quantities of phenolic acids and aldehydes, polypeptides, alkanes and fatty acids (Neyroud and Schnitzer 1975).

Acid hydrolysis at reflux boiling enables between 1/3 and 1/2 of organic matter to be dissolved in most soils (Schnitzer, 1978) but this technique was mostly widely used for the study of the organic forms of nitrogen (cf. Sect. 14.2.1 of Chap. 14); Anderson et al. (1978) studied ether-soluble products of acid hydrolysis of fulvic and humic acids.

Alkaline hydrolysis was also used as a degradation method for the study of humic molecules. Neyroud and Schnitzer (1975) subjected humic materials to four successive series of hydrolysis with a–NaOH 2N solution in an autoclave at 170°C for 3 h. The recovery and identification of the hydrolysed products was accomplished using techniques similar to those of the other degradation methods (cf "Oxidative Fragmentation"). Parsons (1989) analysed the main fragmentation mechanisms in the acid and alkaline hydrolysis of organic materials.

A method developed for depolymerization of coals (Ouchi and Brooks 1967) was applied to degradation of humic acids (Jackson et al. 1972):

reaction with phenol in the presence of *p*-toluenesulfonic acid as catalyst. A review of degradation techniques by phenol and sodium sulphide was published by Hayes and O'Callaghan (1989). Cheshire et al. (1968) studied the effect on humic acids of alkaline fusion after acid boiling.

Thermal Degradation

Thermogravimetry (TG), differential thermogravimetry (DTG), differential thermal analysis (DTA) and isothermal heating were used to explore the mechanism of thermal decomposition of humic materials (Schnitzer 1978). Schnitzer and Hoffmann (1964) studied the chemical evolution of humic and fulvic acids under the action of temperatures up to 540°C; Fig. 12.9 shows the curves of *differential thermogravimetry* these authors observed on their samples.

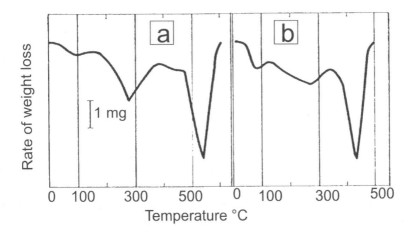

Fig. 12.9. Curves of differential thermogravimetry (Schnitzer and Hoffman 1964) of organic materials of a podzol: **a**: surface O2 horizon, **b**: deep Bh horizon

Kodama and Schnitzer (1970) used *differential thermal analysis* in a study of the mechanism of thermal decomposition of fulvic acids. Chen et al. (1978b) also used this technique to compare the physicochemical characteristics of humic and fulvic acids of Mediterranean soils (Fig. 12.10).

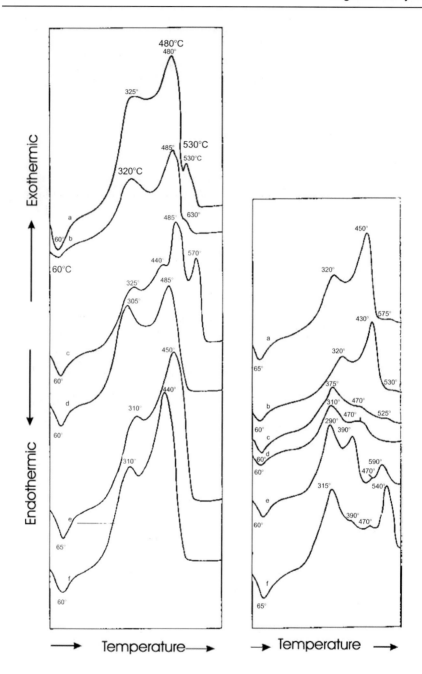

Fig. 12.10. Differential Thermal Analysis applied to humic (on the *left*) and fulvic (on the *right*) acids extracted from Mediterranean soils (Chen et al. 1978): **(a)** clayey brown soil, **(b)** sandy brown soil, **(c)** clayey silty sandy red soil, **(d)** sandy silty red soil, **(e)** silty sandy red soil, **(f)** sandy silty brown soil

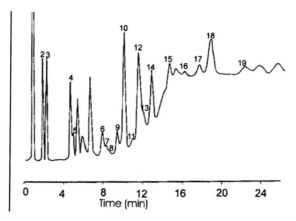

Fig. 12.11.
Chromatogram of pyrolysis products of a fulvic acid extracted with soda in a deep Bh horizon of a podzol (Martin, 1976)

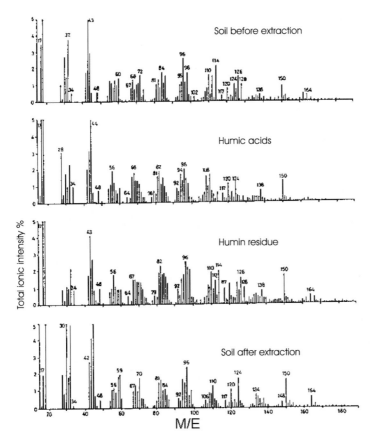

Fig. 12.12. Mass spectra of pyrolysis obtained by Saiz-Jimenez et al. (1979) on a sample of brown soil on granite rock (typical xerochrept); the humin residue fraction was the result of alkaline extraction of the soil following humic acid extraction and complete destruction of silicates by the HF–HCl mixture

Pyrolysis–gas chromatography was developed by Kimber and Searle (1970) for the study of soil organic matter. Figure 12.11 shows one of the chromatograms of pyrolysis obtained by Martin (1976) on fulvic acids of a deep Bh horizon of podzol.

The *pyrolysis mass–spectrometry* described by Meuzelaar et al. (1973) was applied to humic compounds by several authors (e.g. Meuzelaar et al. 1977 Saiz-Jimenez et al. 1979). The humic sample was dispersed in a soda solution or in methanol, covered and placed on a ferromagnetic coil and pyrolyzed at 510°C. An example of the mass spectrum of the pyrolysis products is shown in Fig. 12.12. Reviews by Bracewell et al. (1989) and Schulten (1996) give more data on the thermal degradation products of humic materials.

12.3.4 Nuclear Magnetic Resonance (NMR)

Principle

The majority of atomic nuclei turn around their axis and thus have an angular moment expressed by the formula $[h/2\pi][I(I+1)]^{1/2}$ where h is the Planck constant and I the spin number. The spin number values can be 0, 1/2, 1, 3/2, 2, etc., depending on the nature of the nucleus: for ^1H and ^{13}C, $I = 1/2$, but for ^{12}C, $I=0$. Because of the electric charge, the rotation of the nucleus creates a magnetic field. Conversely, if a nucleus is placed in a magnetic field H_o it can orient itself in one of the $(2I+1)$ directions linked to the direction of the field. Each direction corresponds to an energy state and it is possible to induce a resonance between the energy states by using electromagnetic radiation of a frequency v such as:

$$v = \gamma H_o /2\pi, \tag{12.1}$$

where the gyromagnetic ratio γ is a constant that depends on the type of nucleus.

Table 12.1 Relative detectability (RD) of a nucleus in soil organic matter by NMR (Wilson 1981)

Nucleus	RD
^1H[a]	10^2
^{27}Al	10^1
^{23}Na	10^0

$^1H^b$	10^0
^{55}Mn	10^{-1}
^{29}Si	10^{-1}
^{13}C	10^{-3}
^{14}N	10^{-3}
^{39}K	10^{-3}
^{17}O	10^{-3}
^{25}Mg	10^{-3}
^{67}Zn	10^{-3}
^{31}P	10^{-4}
^{43}Ca	10^{-4}
^{57}Fe	10^{-5}
^{15}N	10^{-6}

[a]: very variable, depends on the water contents and the pH

[b]: H of soil organic matter only

The atom of hydrogen ($I = 1/2$) gives $(2I + 1) = 2$ possible orientations of the nucleus and it is possible to detect its resonance. On the other hand, most nuclei are not detectable: for ^{12}C, $(2I + 1) = 1$ thus there is only one possible orientation of the nucleus in the magnetic field and it is not possible to induce a resonance. Only the ^{13}C isotope of carbon can be studied but is much less abundant than the ^{12}C isotope in the natural state.

Finally, the most important factors in measuring the detectability of an element in soil or in soil extracts are the spin number I, and the gyro-magnetic ratio γ but also the abundance of the element (n) and the relative abundance of the isotope under study (N). Table 12.1 presents the detectability of atomic nuclei in soil as a function of a calculation by Wilson (1981) with the formula: $\gamma^3 NI(I+1)n$. This table does not give the detectability of an element itself but its detectability in the soil or in a soil organic matter medium. Thus, an element that is sensitive to NMR such as ^{31}P will be detected with difficulty because of its low concentration.

The traditional NMR approach consists in subjecting the sample to a radio frequency scan (continuous wave NMR), with a fixed magnetic field (or vice versa) and recording resonance when the irradiation frequency matches the frequency of nuclear transition given by (12.1). The Fourier Transform NMR often enables high quality spectra to be obtained more rapidly. In FTNMR, the nucleus is subjected to short and intense pulsation of radiation and its behaviour is observed. All the nuclei resound simultaneously and the resulting spectrum of the signal as a function of time (free induction decay, FID) is not very useful for the chemist. Signal processing by Fourier transformation should be used to obtain more easily interpretable spectra of the continuous wave NMR type. To increase sensitivity, a large number of "FID" has first to be collected on the computer and then an average used to calculate the Fourier transform.

The NMR technique would provide little useful information for structural chemistry if only the spin transition(s) of the nucleus were measured at frequencies corresponding to (12.1). In fact, the electronic environment of the nucleus protects it from the applied magnetic field (H_0) and the real magnetic field at constant frequency (or the frequency at constant field) necessary for nuclear resonance depends on how effectively the nucleus is protected. In organic molecules, the functional groups have different electronic distributions and the frequencies of resonance of each of their nuclei shift slightly depending on the nature of the functional group. It is then possible to identify these groups. In practice, the shift in frequency is identified by comparing it to a standard, usually tetramethylsilane (TMS), in terms of chemical shift (δ) calculated by the ratio of the "chemical shift of frequency" compared to the "frequency of the standard". As the chemical shifts are weak, δ are generally noted in parts per million: δ(ppm).

Another significant parameter is *relaxation*. After the excitation of a nucleus, some time passes before it returns in its fundamental energy state. In theory, this return occurs in two ways: by interaction with the molecular lattice or by spin energy exchange with "brother" nuclei. The time constants corresponding to these two processes are named spin-lattice relaxation time and spin–spin relaxation time (T1 and T2, respectively). This phenomenon is significant for the soil chemist. In ^{13}C NMR studies, it can affect the quantitative measurement of the carbon of the functional groups.

Following the development of this technique NMR was used for the study of soil organic matter. Originally extracts were analysed in solution by studying ^{1}H proton NMR then ^{13}C NMR, first qualitatively, and then while trying to quantify the observations. The material had to be soluble in a solvent which did not give resonance to the element under study (e.g. for studies of ^{1}H, D_2O was used instead of H_2O), but this is no longer indispensable (Wilson, 1981). More recent studies use NMR on the solid phase. Wilson (1981, 1987) reviewed these methods and their use for the study of soil organic matter. Steelink et al. (1989) provided complementary information in the field of ^{1}H and ^{13}C NMR of humic substances in solution. Wilson (1989) and Tate (1998) provided additional theoretical information in the field of solid state NMR and its use for humic substances. Simpson (2004) applied coupling NMR and separation techniques. ^{15}N NMR was applied to the study of the nitrogen cycle (Thorn and Mikita 2000).

Study of Humic Materials by ^{1}H NMR

Schnitzer and Barton (1963) were the first to observe NMR spectra of organic extracts of soil. They used spectrometry with continuous wave scanning applied to fractions of methylated fulvic acids which provided relatively poor structural information. Subsequently, a relatively large number of authors used the same wave scanning technique ^{1}H NMR. Lentz et al. (1977) obtained spectra of better quality with the Fourier transform technique. Wilson et al. (1978) used the techniques with Fourier transform in a high magnetic field at a very high frequency thereby further increasing the information provided by ^{1}H NMR spectra (Fig. 12.13).

Study of Humic Materials in Solution by ^{13}C NMR

^{13}C NMR has several advantages over ^{1}H NMR for the structural analysis of molecules: it provides direct information on the structural skeleton, which enables observation of functional groups without protons like ketones. The carbon nucleus provides more significant chemical shifts enabling detection of finer differences in molecular structures. The signals can also include narrower peaks, and this reduces the risk of one peak concealing another. On the other hand, the disadvantage of ^{13}C NMR lies in the small proportion of ^{13}C isotopes (only 1.1% of carbon) leading to difficulty in detecting the signals (Wilson 1981).

For satisfactory detection, the conditions required to obtain the ^{13}C spectra always have to be optimized. These spectra are almost always obtained under conditions of decoupling with protons (Proton Decoupled ^{13}C NMR) which induces exaltation of ^{13}C resonance (Nuclear Overhauser Enhancement NOE). The NOE and dipolar ^{13}C–^{1}H relaxation theory in the proton decoupled ^{13}C NMR spectra of the macromolecules was studied by Doddrell et al. (1971).

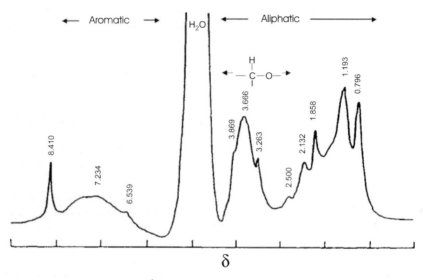

Fig. 12.13. Fourier transform ^{1}H NMR spectrum obtained at 270 MHz by Wilson et al. (1978) on humic materials extracted by a 0.1 mol (NaOH) L^{-1} solution on a silty potter's clay from Wakanui. A pulsation of 10 µs with an inclination angle of 85° was used to visualize a spectral window of 3.6 kHz in 8 ko of data points.

The use of these techniques for soil organic materials was initially unsuccessful (Schnitzer and Neyroud 1974). Subsequently several authors tried to improve the technique, and Newman et al. (1980) achieved noticeable improvement in the quality of the spectra (Fig. 12.14) by optimizing the operating conditions, particularly the spacing between the radiation pulsations. The optimum interval of 0.2 s also corresponded to the acquisition time of the relaxation signals coming from $2\ 10^{5}\ 90°$ impulses of 23 µS. The spectra were obtained on an Varian FT-80A apparatus operating at 20 MHz for ^{13}C with proton decoupling at 80 MHz. Acquisition required collection of 4,000 (coal samples) to 136,000 (soil humic acid samples) free induction decay spectra then multiplication by a filter with a 20 ms time constant, before the Fourier transform. The samples were prepared for analysis by suspension of 300 mg of humic acid in 2 cm^3 of 0.5 mol (NaOH) L^{-1} solution for 1 day at 20°C followed by ultracentrifugation (84,500 g at 4°C). After dilution to 50% with D$_2$O, RM^{-13}C was measured in tubes with a diameter of 10 mm.

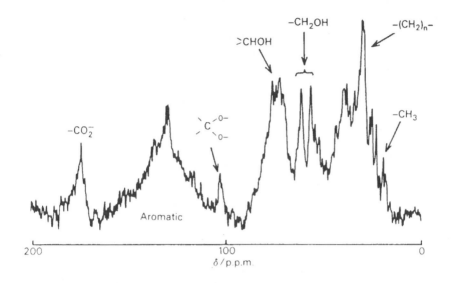

Fig. 12.14. Proton decoupled ^{13}C NMR spectrum of a humic acid in solution obtained by Newman et al. (1980) with optimized acquisition parameters (see conditions described in the text)

Newman and Tate (1984) used very similar conditions to those described above to characterize the humic substances of alkaline extracts of soils, the total time needed for spectral acquisition ranged from 10 to 50 h.

Preston and Schnitzer (1984) studied the effect of the type of extraction (acid or alkaline extraction) and of chemical modifications in the extracted material (methylation, hydrolysis using 6 mol (HCl) L^{-1} followed or not by methylation) on ^{13}C NMR spectra of humic materials from four types of soils. The materials were dissolved in deuterated solvents (CDCl$_3$ for methylated materials, 0.5 mol (NaOD) L^{-1} (D$_2$O) solution for non-methylated materials). The chemical shifts were measured compared to the sodium 3-trimethylsilylpropionate (TSP) for the heavy water (D$_2$O) solutions and with tetramethylsilane (TMS) for the deuterated chloroform (CDCl$_3$) solutions. The spectra were obtained on a Bruker WM 250 spectrometer on 10 mm sample tubes with an interruption technique of ^{1}H decoupling except during the acquisition time (inverse-gated decoupling of Freeman et al. 1972). Some of spectra were comparable with those shown in Figure 12.14.

Study by Solid State ^{13}C NMR

The extraction of organic matter (cf. Sect. 11.2.1 and 11.3.1 of Chap. 11) can result in molecular modifications, particularly if strong bases are used as extraction reagents. Moreover, most materials remain in a non-extractable state in the humin residue. The in situ study of organic matter allows these disadvantages to be overcome.

However, conventional NMR spectroscopy applied to whole soil resulted in only broad and diffuse signals: many dipole–dipole interactions produced signals comprising information on the chemical shifts that was not clear, and moreover, the spin–lattice relaxation times (T1) needed too long to accumulate the free induction decay signals required to obtain quantitative information. The theoretical advance in NMR technique (Pines et al. 1973) subsequently made it possible to overcome the problem and envisage new developments. In the cross polarization or CP-^{13}C NMR technique, the protons are uncoupled from the ^{13}C nucleus and used to increase the relaxation kinetics of the ^{13}C nucleus. The signal peak widths can be reduced to a degree where the functional groups can be partially identified.

However, the detection of the carbon forms in the whole soil using the CP-^{13}C NMR method required very organic soils (6% of C according to Wilson 1981). This limit has gradually been reduced thanks to improvements in the quality of the instruments and also the preliminary use of physical fractionation methods such as those described in Chap. 9, spectral analysis being limited to the most organic fractions (Barron et al. 1980).

The magic angle spinning (MAS) NMR technique, which was originally described by Lowe (1959) and subsequently applied to polymers by Schaefer and Stejskal (1976), can also help get round problems like spectral resolution, and obtain spectra directly on the soils; in this technique, the sample is put in fast rotation at an axial slope of 54°44′, which means anisotropic effects can be reduced and isotropic shifts can be selected. This technique is often used together with cross polarization, and is then known as the CPMAS–^{13}C NMR method.

For soil studies, most authors preferred to apply NMR techniques to previously concentrated humic materials, usually humic or fulvic acids. A study by Newman et al. (1980) clearly showed the difference in resolution that still existed between the ^{13}C NMR techniques in solution and CP ^{13}C NMR on the solid phase (Fig. 12.15a).

Thanks to improvements in this technique, the spectra of CPMAS–^{13}C NMR obtained by Gerasimowicz and Byler (1985) on humic substances showed a better resolution (Fig. 12.15b) than that of Newman et al. (1980). Fründ and Lüdemann (1989) performed instructive comparisons between the technique in solution and CPMAS–^{13}C NMR which showed that the degree of detail provided by the second technique was similar to that of the first; in addition, the spectra obtained on a rendzina soil (4.6% of carbon) and on its humic extracts and humin residue were compared under satisfactory conditions (Fig. 12.15c). The two techniques (liquid phase NMR and solid phase CPMAS–^{13}C NMR) were recommended by Conte et al. (1997a) for the study of organic materials of the soils. State-of-the-art CPMAS–^{13}C NMR allows observation of organic materials in their environment (without fractionation) when the soils are not too low in carbon, as attempted by Kinchesh et al. (1995) on Rothamsted soils (UK). Other studies such as that of Conte et al. (1997b) on volcanic soils used CPMAS–^{13} C NMR on extracted humic substances.

3.4.5 Quantification of Observations by NMR

Different techniques exist for the quantification of the information provided by the NMR signals of humic substances. The oldest derive from the study of coal and coal-like materials.

The method of Brown and Ladner (1960) enables estimation of the aromaticity of these carbonaceous materials using the ^{1}H NMR spectrum. Wilson (1981) proposed an adaptation of this method for use on humic materials.

The rate of aromaticity f_a was most often studied by quantification of ^{13}C NMR signals. However, techniques for the direct quantification of the different peaks of the spectra should be used with caution. The ^{13}C atoms of the different functional groups have different nuclei relaxation times, the nuclei with the shortest times making a weaker contribution to the total spectrum than those with the longest time. In addition, due to proton decoupling, NOE results in an increase in the signal that differs with the nature of the nucleus (Wilson 1981). However, these two factors were sometimes shown to have no significant influence on the direct measurement of the rate of aromaticity (Newman et al. 1980).

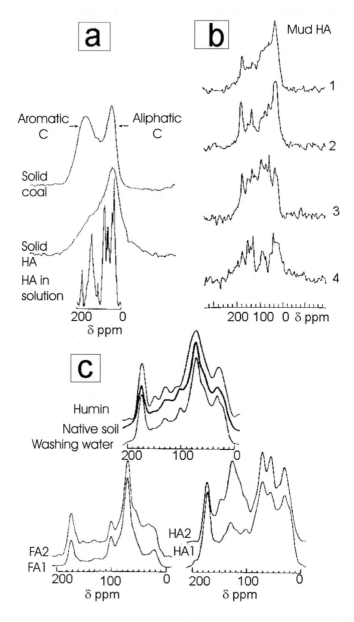

Fig. 12.15 Improvements in solid phase ^{13}C NMR techniques: **(a)** CP ^{13}C NMR spectra obtained by Newman et al. (1980) on solid coal, a solid humic acid (HA), and a solution of HA, **(b)** CP MAS-^{13}C NMR spectra obtained by Gerasimowicz and Byler(1985) on HA from muds at different stages of composting treatments **(C)** CPMAS-^{13}C NMR spectra obtained by Fräd and Lüdem ann (1989) on a rendzina soil, on its fulvic (FA) and humic (HA) extracts and on the humin residue

Fründ and Lüdeman (1989) improved quantitative analysis of humic materials. Their method enabled simultaneous measurements of carboxylic-, aromatic-, carbohydrate- and aliphatic-C rates. Smernik and Oades (2000a) highlighted the effect of paramagnetic impurities and of purifications by HF treatment (Smernik and Oades, 2000b). Smernik and Oades (2003) then Moser and Lefebvre (2004) explored new ways to improve ^{13}C NMR quantification on soil organic matter. Conte et al. (2004) reviewed state-of-the-art CPMAS C-13-NMR spectroscopy applied to natural organic matter.

12.3.5 Fluorescence Spectroscopy

Although less widely used than the visible UV (cf. Sect. 12.2.3) or infra-red (cf Sect. 12.2.4) absorption spectrometry, fluorescence spectrometry has been tested by several authors as a complementary technique to characterize humic substances.

Lévesque (1972) used this technique on Fe and P humic complexes. The emission spectrum of a fulvic acid has a main peak with a not very variable wavelength that moves from 500 to 520 nm when the excitation wavelength moves from 400 to 468 nm. As emission spectra generally provide little information, excitation spectra were used instead. The emission wavelength was then fixed at around 500–520 nm and excitation varied in a continuous way between 250 and 500 nm.

Ghosh and Schnitzer (1980a) observed on their humic substances two quite distinct excitation bands, at 465 and 360 nm, and a decrease in intensity of the fluorescence with an increase in the ionic force and a reduction in the pH; their data were subsequently used to calculate the constant of dissociation of humic acids (Goldberg et al. 1987).

Bachelier (1981) refined these observations with a precise description of the excitation spectra on a larger number of soils; he noted the presence of seven peaks (including two rare ones) corresponding to slope changes on the large 465 nm peak and of two peaks (including one rare one) on the large 360 nm peak.

Bachelier also studied the fluorescence of several types of humic acids split on G25 Sephadex gel (1) humic acids of high molecular weight which are eluted at the head of the column (coarse humic acid cHA) give a weak fluorescent signal; (2) the following band of less condensed brown-yellow humic acids gives bright yellow fluorescence under UV radiation (fluorescent humic acids fHA); (3) lower fluorescence compounds called higher humic acids (hHA) are sometimes found after this band and (4) intermediate humic acids (iHA) are sometimes found between the two cHA and fHA bands. Figure 12.16 shows some excitation spectra obtained on different humic products. Bachelier's observations confirm those of Lévesque on the low fluorescence of the humic complexes with high molecular weight.

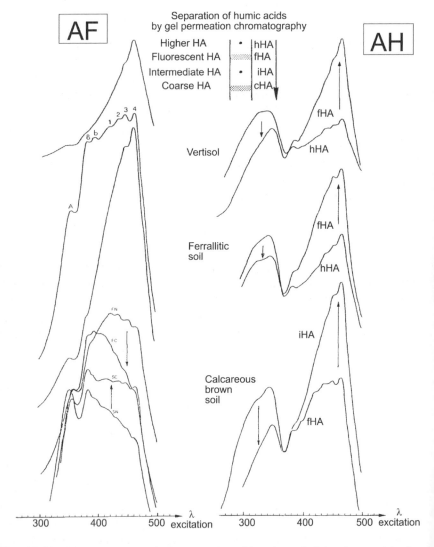

Fig. 12.16. Fluorescence excitation spectra of humic materials observed in the 509–515 nm emission band (Bachelier, 1981): (FA) fulvic acid of various samples of soils, (HA) different fractions of humic acids separated by gel chromatography (see fractionation diagram above the graph)

Bachelier (1984) used fluorescence spectrometry to distinguish the degrees of condensation of humic acids. Nayak et al. (1985) studied the fluorescence of humic acids in different solvents. The fluorescence polarization technique enabled further information to be obtained on the aggregation and conformation of humic molecules and was used to this end in a study of fulvic acid by Lapen and Seitz (1982).

12.3.6 Electron Spin Resonance (ESR) Spectroscopy

When molecules containing unpaired electrons are placed in a magnetic field, interaction occurs between the magnetic moment of these electrons and the applied field which results in decoupling into two discrete states of energy of each unpaired electron. This is electron spin resonance (ESR) sometimes still called electron paramagnetic resonance (EPR). ESR spectroscopy uses electromagnetic excitation radiation located in the spectral field of microwaves; it is used for the study of compounds containing unpaired electrons, primarily free radicals.

The energy of an unpaired electron in a magnetic field is given by
$$E = -g\,\beta\,M_z\,H_O,$$
where G represents the spectroscopic split factor which has a value of 2.0023 for a free electron, β the magneton of Bohr, M_z the component of the angular spin moment in the direction of the z-axis of the applied magnetic field which can take the discrete values $+1/2$ and $-1/2$, H_O the force of the magnetic field. For a given value of H_O the difference in energy ΔE between two states of discrete spin of the electron is
$$\Delta E = g\,\beta\,H_O$$
the phenomenon of resonance occurs when this energy is equal to that of the applied field:
$$\Delta E = h\nu$$
and H being Planck's constant and ν the frequency.

In his pioneer work, Rex (1960) used ESR spectroscopy to highlight the radical nature of humic molecules. MacCarthy and Rice (1985) listed several works reporting the use of ESR spectroscopy for humic substances. The spectra of humic substances are generally simple signals identified by their position and width (Fig. 12.17). The hyperfine lines that can be identified in some molecules are not usually present in humic spectra.

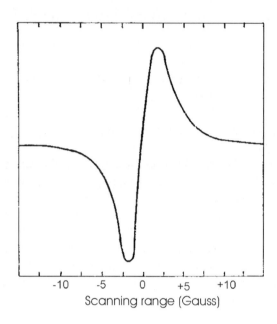

Fig. 12.17 Electron spin resonance spectrum of a fulic acid (Schnitzer and
Skinner, 1969)

Schnitzer and Skinner (1969) showed on ten humic materials that the
most variable parameter deduced from these spectra is the spin
concentration. This is determined by comparison with a standard of
calibration, the number of radicals being proportional to the signal
surface. In humic substances, the concentration is found around 10^{18} spins
g^{-1}. Schnitzer and Skinner also tested the influence of several factors on
the spin concentrations of humic substances (chemical modifications,
heating) as well as the relation between other parameters and the spin
concentration (molecular weight, E4:E6 ratio, number of molecules of a
given weight per free radical). Riffaldi and Schnitzer (1972) studied the
effect of the experimental conditions on the ESR spectra of humic
substances to highlight mistakes due to too rapid interpretation of these
spectra. MacCarty and Rice (1985) also commented on the relative
poverty of the information from ESR spectrometry for the study from the
humic substance. However, subsequent technological developments
changed this situation. For example, Senesi et al. (1989) provided more
detailed spectra than previous authors and Senesi (1990) reviewed state-
of-the-art and potential development of ESR technique in its application
to soil chemistry. Saab and Martin-Neto (2004) studied semiquinone free
radicals of humic substances by ESR.

12.3.7 Measurements of molecular weight and molecular size

Principles

Measurement of molecular weight is a traditional procedure in structural chemistry. As a complement to ultimate analysis, the molecular weight provides an empirical formula for the compound concerned before the determination of the structural formula (functional groups) using spectroscopic and chemical methods. The measurement of molecular weight and size has been attempted many times on humic substances and several reviews have been devoted to the subject (e.g. Orlov et al. 1975; Stevenson 1982; Wershaw and Aiken 1985; Buurman 2001). It has also been used to measure the humic substances of water (Yu-Ping Chin et al. 1994, Yamada et al. 2000) or atmosphere (Samburova et al. 2005) However, the results differed considerably firstly depending on the technique used, and secondly because, as emphasised by the authors of these reviews, humic substances are not discrete chemical entities but complex mixtures of polydisperse organic substances with a wide range of molecular size.

The problem with measuring the molecular weight of mixtures nevertheless was studied during many years. In 1935 Lansing and Kraemer pointed out that the most commonly used methods resulted in *average molecular weights* and that, depending on the method of measurement used, these average weights could not always be compared. Three types of average molecular weights corresponding to three types of measurement are now used:

Number-Average Molecular Weight M_n

This is obtained using methods that measure the number of molecules (generally in a diluted solution) irrespective of their size. It is expressed by:

$$M_n = \Sigma n_i M_i / \Sigma n_i,$$

where n_i is the number of molecules of molecular weight M_i M_n is determined by all measurements corresponding to a thermodynamic property connected to a number of molecules in solution (colligative property): lowering of vapour pressure, lowering of the freezing point, rise in the boiling point (Raoult laws), osmotic pressure.

Weight-Average Molecular Weight M_w

Weight-average molecular weight is measured by methods concerned with the masses of different materials, like light scattering and ultra-centrifuge sedimentation; it is expressed by:

$M_w = \Sigma\ w_i\ M_i\ /\ \Sigma\ w_i = \Sigma\ n_i\ M_i^2 / \Sigma\ n_i\ M_i,$

where w_i represents the mass fraction of each species;

The z-Average Molecular Weight M_z

This can also be calculated with the ultracentrifugation data obtained and is expressed by:

$M_z = \Sigma\ w_i\ M_i^2\ /\ \Sigma\ w_i\ M_i = \Sigma\ n_i\ M_i^3 / \Sigma\ n_i\ M_i^2.$

In a monodisperse system $M_n = M_w = M_z$ but this is not the case in polydisperse systems; the number-average molecular weight then tends to represent the lowest molecular weights whereas M_w tends to represent the heaviest particles of the mixture (Wershaw and Aiken, 1985). Orlov et al. (1975) expected M_w to be better correlated with the known properties of humic substances. In heterogeneous systems, $M_z > M_w > M_n$, the $M_w:M_n$ ratio can generally be used to calculate the degree of polydispersity (Stevenson 1982).

In addition to methods for the measurement of the average molecular weight, another group of methods measures the size of the molecules, e.g. gel filtration, ultrafiltration and small angle X-ray scattering. In these methods, model compounds of known molecular weight and composition are used to determine the molecular weight of humic substances, but problems can occur if these compounds are too different from the humic molecules (Wershaw and Aiken 1985).

Methods for the Measurement of Molecular Size

Gel Exclusion Chromatography

The methods of gel exclusion (or gel permeation) chromatography are described in Sect. 12.2.1 and 12.3.1. It should be noted that Reuter and Perdue (1981) found a very big difference between the expected molecular weights on humic fractions of Sephadex gel and the number-average molecular weights actually measured. Plechanov (1983) used the

Sephadex LH60/dimethylformamide/acetic acid system for the measurement of the molecular weight of humic substances. Nobili et al. (1989) reviewed the use of gel chromatography for the measurement of the molecular size of humic substances.

Ultrafiltration

Ultrafiltration by pressure filtration through a membrane is also used for the separation of macromolecules as a function of their molecular size. This technique is similar to reverse osmosis, except with respect to the size of the particles that can be split: reverse osmosis separates the particles of molecular size near to those of the solvent whereas ultrafiltration separates particles approximately 10 times the size of the solvent i.e. up to 0.5 μm (Wershaw and Aiken 1985). A large number of different types of membranes exist which are classified by their manufacturers according to their threshold of cut expressed in molecular weight. Nevertheless ultrafiltration is not a technique for separation by weight but by molecular size. A review by Wershaw and Aiken (1985) provided a lot of useful information about this technique.

Scattering of Electromagnetic Radiation

The principle of this technique for light scattering was described by Kerker and Milton (1968) and by Guinier and Fournet (1955) for small angle X-ray scattering. The reader is advised to consult these publications for a comprehensive explanation of the phenomenon and to refer to Wershaw and Aiken (1985) and Wershaw (1989) for the use of this technique for humic substances.

Methods of Measurement of Molecular Weight

Determination of the Number-Average Molecular Weight by Measurement of Colligative Properties

By definition, a colligative property is a thermodynamic property which depends on the number of particles in a solution independent of their nature. At the infinite dilution limit, each one of these properties is proportional to the number of molecules of solute present in the solution. The classical theory of each colligative property is described found in all chemistry and physics handbooks. The most widely used techniques for the measurement of molecular weight of humic substances are cryoscopy and vapour pressure osmometry. Cryoscopy records the drop in the temperature during solidification of the solvent in the presence of the solute to be studied. Vapour pressure osmometry measures the change in osmotic pressure resulting from the passage of a solvent through a membrane from a diluted solution to more concentrated one. For a description of these methods and their use for humic substances, see Stevenson (1982), Wershaw and Aiken (1985) and Aiken and Gillam (1989).

Ultracentrifugation

There are two distinct groups of ultracentrifugation techniques, those concerned with sedimentation kinetics, and those concerned with ultracentrifugation equilibrium. The first group was the most commonly used on humic substances (Wershaw and Aiken 1985) sometimes as a complement to other fractionation methods (Cameron et al. 1972b), although the centrifugation equilibrium provides a wealth of information since M_n, M_w and M_z can be determined at the same time (Posner and Creeth 1972). The theory and implementation of the first technique is detailed in Cameron et al. (1972b), the second by Posner and Creeth (1972), and a review by Swift (1989) gives a detailed description of all ultracentrifugation techniques.

Viscosimetry

Measurements of viscosity can provide significant information concerning the size and the shape of the molecules. The well-known Oswald viscometer records the times of passage of the solution and solvent between two reference points marked on the apparatus. The molecular weight can be estimated from measurements of viscosity using the Staudinger equation: $[\eta] = kM^{\alpha}$, in which intrinsic viscosity η is linked to molecular weight M by two adjustable parameters (Ghosh and Schnitzer, 1980b). Techniques based on measurement of viscosity were reviewed by Clapp et al. (1989).

Flow FFF (cf. Sect. 12.3.1) was also once considered to be promising for the measurement of molecular weight of humic substances (Beckett et al. 1987).

12.3.8 Microscopic Observations

Several studies report observations of humic materials using optical microscopy, transmission electron microscopy and scanning electron microscopy. The first difficulty is linked with the different ways the sample can be modified depending on the preparation techniques (e.g. the degree of separation of inorganic materials, molecular modifications with respect to the ionic force and pH), and the second difficulty is the conditions of the observation itself (heating of the sample). Bachelier (1983) carried out observations on nine different types of soil using three techniques: frozen humic acid solutions under a binocular magnifying glass, desiccated humic acid solutions under a transmission electron microscope, humic acid solutions freeze-dried on gilt aluminium film under a scanning electron microscope. The latter requires metallization of the non-conducting substances before observation.

Chen and Schnitzer (1976) studied the influence of pH on the appearance of humic acids by scanning electron microscopy while Stevenson and Schnitzer (1982) studied the same effect by transmission electron microscopy. Chen and Schnitzer (1976) used transmission electron microscopy for the study of metallic complexes of fulvic acids.

Scanning electron microscopy was used by Chen et al. (1978) for the comparison of humic acids from Mediterranean soils. Tan (1985) provided detailed methodological information particularly concerning the preparation of the samples.

12.3.9 Other Techniques

The main techniques used for structural characterization are described in this chapter. However other techniques can also be used to improve our knowledge of the structures of humic compounds and their linkage with mineral materials.

X-ray techniques are not limited to small angle X-ray scattering described in "Scattering of Electromagnetic Radiation" in Sect. 12.3.7; X-ray diffraction was also used by Schnitzer (1978), and can provide useful information in spite of the non-crystalline character of humic substances.

As far as electrochemical methods are concerned, a study of humic acid characterization by polarography was described by Shinozuka and Hayano (1987).

The use of FTIR spectroscopy makes it possible to increase the resolution and to decrease the background noise of the IR spectra. However, these advantages may not be apparent in the study of humic substances because of their molecular nature (MacCarthy and Rice, 1985).

More recent techniques like X-ray photoelectron spectroscopy (XPS) and Mössbauer spectroscopy have not been widely used for the study of humic substances. XPS, also called electron spectroscopy for chemical analysis (ESCA), can only be used with solid materials because it requires a high vacuum; it is based on the analysis of the electrons emitted by the internal electron-shells atoms when they are subjected to X-ray bombardment of sufficient energy; Defosse and Rouxhet (1980) introduced this technique in soil analysis.

Mössbauer spectroscopy is not directly useable for the study of the structure of metal compounds, but can be used for the study of organometallic bonds, and particularly for the study of complexes of iron–humic compounds (Goodman and Cheshire, 1979).

It will be interesting to see whether future progress results from new technologies or from synthetic studies on molecular models as was the case for the identification of the double helix of ADN by Watson and Creek.

References

Molecular Models

Hatcher PG, Dria KJ, Sunghwan Kim, Frazier SW (2001) Modern analytical studies of humic substances. *Soil Science*, 166, 770–794

Lawson GJ and Stewart D (1989) Coal Humic Acids. In *Humic substances II, search of structure*, Hayes HB., MacCarthy P, Malcolm RL and Swift RS ed., Wiley, 641–686

Lodygin ED and Beznosikov VA (2003) The ^{13}C NMR study of the molecular structure of humus acids from podzolic and bog-podzolic soils. *Pochvovedenie*, 9, 1085–1094

Piccolo A and Conte P (2003) Comments on "Modern analytical studies of humic substances" by Hatcher et al. *Soil Sci.*, 168, 73–74

Schulten HR (1995) The three-dimensional structure of humic substances and soil organic matter studied by computational analytical chemistry. *Fresenius J. Anal. Chem.*, 351, 62–73

Schulten HR and Leinweber P (2000) New insights into organic-mineral particles: composition, properties and models of molecular structure. *Biol. Fertil. Soils*, 30, 399–432

Schulten HR and Schnitzer M (1997) Chemical model structures for soil organic matter and soils. *Soil Sci.*, 162, 115–129

Skjemstad JO, Clarke P, Taylor JA, Oades JM and McClure SG (1996) The chemistry and nature of protected carbon in soil. *Aust. J. Soil Res.*, 34, 251–271

Schulten HR (2002) New approaches to the molecular structure and properties of soil organic matter: humic-, xenobiotic-, biological-, and mineral-bonds. In 3rd Symposium on Soil Mineral–Organic Matter–Microorganism Interactions and Ecosystem Health, Naples-Capri, Italy, 22–26 May 2000, Violante A, Huang PM, Bollag JM and Gianfreda L. ed. *Developments in soil science*, volume 28A, 351–381

McCarthy P (2001) The principles of humic substances. *Soil Sci.,* 166, 738–751

Piccolo A, Celano G, Conte P, Zena A and Spacini R (1999) Adsorption of atrazine on humic substances of different molecular structure and their hydrolysed products as modified by pH. In *Human and environmental exposure to xenobiotics* Del Re AAM, Brown CD, Capri E, Evans SP and Trevisan M, ed., *Proceedings of the XI Symposium of Pesticide Chemistry, Cremona, Italy,* September 12–15 1999, 425–431

Fractionation, Determination of Molecular Weights and Molecular Sizes

Aiken GR and Gillam AH (1989) Determination of molecular weights of humic substances by colligative property measurements. *In : Humic substances II.,* Hayes MHB., MacCarthy P, Malcolm RL and Swift RS ed. Wiley New York, 515–544

Bailly JR and Margulis H (1968) Etude de quelques acides humiques sur gel de dextrane. *Plant and soil,* XXIX, 343–361

Bailly JR and Tittonel E (1972) Etude de quelques acides humiques sur gel de dextrane (II). *Plant Soil,* 37, 57–80

Beckett R, Zhang Jue and Giddings JC (1987) Determination of molecular weight distributions of fulvic and humic acids using flow field-flow fractionation. *Environ. Sci. Technol.,* 21, 289–295

Buurman P (2001) Understanding humic substances: advanced methods, properties and applications. *Soil Sci.,* 166, 950–951

Cacco G and Maggioni A (1976) Isoelectrophoretic characterization of humic and fulvic acids extracted from an alpine podzol. *Agrochimica,* 20, 20–28

Cacco G, Maggioni A and Ferrari G (1974) Electrofocusing : a new method for characterization of soil humic matter. *Soil Biol.Biochem.,* 6, 145–148

Cameron RS, Swift RS, Thornton BK and Posner AM (1972a) Calibration of gel permeation chromatography materials for use with humic acid. *J. Soil Sci.,* 23, 343–349

Cameron RS, Thornton BK, Swift RS and Posner AM (1972b) Molecular weight and shape of humic acid from sedimentation and diffusion measurements on fractionated extracts. *J. Soil Sci.,* 23, –342

Clapp CE, Emerson WW and Olness AE (1989) Sizes and shapes of humic substances by viscosity measurements. *In : Humic substances II.,* Hayes MHB, MacCarthy P, Malcolm RL and Swift RS ed. Wiley New York, 497–514

Dabin B (1980) Les matières organiques dans les sols tropicaux normalement drainés. *Cah.ORSTOM sér.Pédol.,* 18, 197–215

Dabin B and Thomann Ch (1970) Etude comparative de deux méthodes de fractionnement des composés humiques (méthode Tiurin et méthode électrophorétique). *ORSTOM ser. Initiation-documentation technique No.16,* 66 p

Duchaufour Ph and Jacquin F (1963) Recherches d'une méthode d'extraction et de fractionnement des composés humiques contrôlés par électrophorèse. *Ann. Agron.*, 19, 6

Duchaufour Ph and Jacquin F (1966) Nouvelles recherches sur l'extraction et le fractionnement des composés humiques. *Bull. ENSAN*, VIII, 1, 3–24

Duchaufour Ph (1954) Propriétés des complexes humiques dans différents types de sols. *Ecole Nationale eaux et forêts*, Nancy, 29 p

Duchaufour Ph (1956) Pédologie: Applications forestières et agricoles. *Ecole Nationale eaux et forêts*, Nancy, 310 p

Duchaufour Ph (1957) Pédologie: tableaux descriptifs et analytiques des sols. *Ecole Nationale eaux et forêts*, Nancy, 87 p

Duxbury JM (1989) Studies of the molecular size and charge of humic substances by electrophoresis. *In : Humic substances II.*, Hayes MHB, MacCarthy P, Malcolm RL and Swift RS ed. Wiley New York, 593–620

Ghosh K and Schnitzer M (1980b) Macromolecular structures of humic substances. *Soil Sci.*, 129, 266–276

Guinier A and Fournet G (1955) *Small angle X-ray scattering.*, Wiley New York, 268 p

Kerker and Milton (1968) Light scattering. *Ind. Eng.Chem.*, 60, 31–46

Lansing WD and Kraemer EO (1935) Molecular weight analysis of mixtures by sedimentation equilibrium in the Svedberg ultracentrifuge. *J. Am. Chem. Soc.*, 57, 1369–1377

Laurent TC and Killander J (1964) A theory of gel filtration and its experimental verification. *J. Chromatog.*, 14, 317–330

Morizur JP, Monegier du Sorbier B, Silly L and Desbene PL (1984) Etude par chromatographie sur gel avec détection spectrométrique de l'évolution de la conformation des acides humiques en fonction de la force ionique et du pH. *C. R. Acad. Sc. Paris*, 299, 1269–1272

Nobili Maria De, Gjessing E and Sequi P (1989) Sizes and shapes of humic substances by gel chromatography. *In : Humic substances II.*, Hayes MHB, MacCarthy P, Malcolm RL and Swift RS ed. Wiley New York, 561–591

Orlov DS, Ammosova YaM, Glebova GI (1975) Molecular parameters of humic acids. *Geoderma*, 13, 211–229

Plechanov N (1983) Studies of molecular weight distributions of fulvic and humic acids by gel permeation chromatography. Examination of the solute molecular composition using RI, UV, Fluorescence and weight measurement as detection techniques. *Org. Geochem.*, 5, 143–149

Posner AM and Creeth JM (1972) A study of humic acids by equilibrium ultracentrifugation. *J. Soil Sci.*, 23, 333–341

Ratsimbazafy CA (1973) Protocole de fractionnement et d'étude de la matière organique des sols hydromorphes de Madagascar. *Cah. ORSTOM sér. Pédol.*, XI, 227–236

Reuter JH and Perdue EM (1981) Calculation of molecular weights of humic substances from colligative data: application to aquatic humus and its molecular size fractions. *Geochim. Cosmochim. Acta*, 45, 2017–2022

Righetti PG and Drysdale JW (1971) Isoelectric focusing in polyacrilamide gels. *Biochem. Biophys. Acta.*, 236, 17–28

Rusina TV, Kasparov SV and Zharikov AV (1983) Method of electrophoretic research of humus substances and proteins in soil solutions (texte Russe, résumé Anglais). *Pocvovedenie*, 1, 38–46

Samburova V, Zenobi R and Kalberer M (2005) Characterization of high molecular weight compounds in urban atmospheric particles. *Atmos. Chem. Phys.*, 5, 2163–2170

Stevenson FJ (1982) Colloidal properties of humic substances. *In : Humus chemistry*, Stevenson FJ ed. Wiley and Sons, 285–308

Swift RS (1989) Molecular weight, shape, and size of humic substances by ultracentrifugation. *In : Humic substances II.*, Hayes MHB, MacCarthy P, Malcolm RL and Swift RS ed. Wiley New York, 467–495

Tiurin (1951) Vers une méthode d'analyse par l'étude comparative des constituants de l'humus du sol. *Trav. Inst. des Sols Dokutchaev*, 38, 32 p

Yamada E, Doi K, Okano K and Fuse Y (2000) Simultaneous determinations of the concentration and molecular weight of humic substances in environmental water by gel chromatography with a fluorescence detector. *Analytical Sci.*, 16, 125–132

Yu-Ping Chin, Alken G, and O'Loughlin E (1994) Molecular weight, polydispersity, and spectroscopic properties of aquatic humic substances. *Environ. Sci. Technol.*, 28, 1853–1858

Wershaw RL and Aiken GR (1985) Molecular size and weight measurements of humic substances. *In : Humic substances in soil, sediment and water.*, Aiken GR, McKnight DM, Wershaw RL and MacCarthy P ed. Wiley New York, 477–492

Wershaw RL (1989) Sizes and shapes of humic substances by scattering techniques. *In : Humic substances II.*, Hayes MHB, MacCarthy P, Malcolm RL and Swift RS ed. Wiley New York, 545–559

Functional Group of Humic Compounds

De Nobili M, Contin M and Leita L (1990) Alternative method for carboxyl group determination in humic substances. *Can. J. Soil Sci.*, 70, 531–536

Fritz JS, Yamamura SS and Bradford EC (1959) Determination of carbonyl compounds. *Anal. Chem.*, 31, 260–263

Glebko LI, Ulkina JU and Maximov OB (1970) A semi-micro method for the determination of quinoid groups in humic acids. *Microchim. Acta.*, 1247–1254

Rosell RA, Allan AL, Agullo E and Gelos B (1972) Estudio potentiometrico del humus. II. Determinacion de varios tipos de acidez (o grupo funcionales) de acidos humicos de suelos de la provincia de Buenos Aires, Argentina. *Turrialba*, 22, 327–332

Schnitzer M and Gupta UC (1965) Determination of acidity in soil organic matter. *Soil Sci. Soc. Am. Proc.*, 29, 274–277

Schnitzer M and Skinner SIM (1965) Organo-metallic interactions in soils : 4.Carboxyl and hydroxyl groups in organic matter and metal retention. *Soil Sci.*, 99, 278–284

Wright JR and Schnitzer M (1959) Oxygen-containing functional groups in the organic matter of a Podzol soil. *Nature, London*, 184, 1462–1463

Spectrometric Characterizations

UV–Visible, IR, Fluorescence, ESR Spectrometries

Lapen AJ and Seitz WR (1982) Fluorescence polarization studies of the conformation of soil fulvic acid. *Anal. Chim. Acta.*, 134, 31–38

Bachelier G (1981) Etude spectrographique de la fluorescence des acides humiques et des acides fulviques de divers sols. *Cah. ORSTOM sér. Pédol.*, 18, 129–145

Chen Y, Senesi N and Schnitzer M (1977) Information provided on humic substances by E4:E6 ratios. *Soil Sci. Soc. Am. J.*, 41, 352–358

Ghosh K and Schnitzer M (1979) UV and visible absorption spectroscopic investigations in relation to macromolecular characteristics of humic substances. *J. Soil Sci.*, 30, 735–745

Ghosh K and Schnitzer M (1980a) Fluorescence excitation spectra of humic substances. *Can J. Soil Sci.*, 60, 373–379

Goldberg MC, Cunningham KM and Weiner ER (1987) The use of isosbestic points in the fluorescence excitation spectrum of humic acid to calculate the dissociation constant. *Can. J. Soil Sci.*, 67, 715–717

Kononova MM (1966) *Soil organic matter, its nature, its role in soil formation and in soil fertility*, 2nd English ed. *Pergamon Oxford*, 544 p

Lévesque M (1972) Fluorescence and gel filtration of humic compounds. *Soil Sci.*, 113, 346–353

MacCarthy Pet Rice JA (1985) Spectroscopic methods (other than NMR) for determining the functionality in humic substances. *In: Humic substances in soil, sediment and water.*, Aiken GR, McKnight DM, Wershaw RL and MacCarthy P ed. Wiley New York, 527–559

Nayak DC, Barman AK, Varadachari C, Ghosh K (1985) Fluorescence excitation spectra of humic acids. *J. Indian Soc. Soil Sci.*, 33, 785–787

Rex RW (1960) Electron paramagnetic resonance studies on stable free radicals in lignins and humic acids. *Nature*, 188, 1185–1186

Riffaldi R and Schnitzer M (1972) Effects of divers experimental conditions on ESR spectra of humic substances. *Geoderma*, 8, 1–10

Russel JD and Anderson HA (1977) Comment on "spectroscopie infra-rouge de quelques fractions d'acides humiques obtenues sur Sephadex" *Plant Soil*, 48, 547–548

Schnitzer M and Skinner SIM (1969) Free radicals in soil humic compounds. *Soil Sci.*, 108, 383–390

Saab SC and Martin–Neto L (2004) Studies of Semiquinone Free Radicals by ESR in the Whole Soil, HA, FA and humin substances. *J. Braz. Chem. Soc.*, 15, 34–37

Senesi N (1990) Application of ESR spectroscopy in soil chemistry. *Adv. in Soil Sci.*, 14, 77–129

Nuclear Magnetic Resonance

Barron PF, Wilson MA, Stephens JF, Cornell BA and Tate KR (1980) Cross-polarization ^{13}C NMR spectroscopy of whole soils. *Nature*, 286, 585–587

Brown JK and Ladner WR (1960) A study of the hydrogen distribution in coal-like materials by high resolution NMR spectroscopy (II). *Fuel*, 39, 87–96

Conte P, Piccolo A, van Lagen B, Buurman P and de Jager PA (1997a) Quantitative differences by liquid- and solid-state ^{13}C NMR spectroscopy. *Geoderma*, 80, 339–352

Conte P, Piccolo A, van Lagen B, Buurman P and de Jager PA (1997b) Quantitative aspects of solid-state ^{13}C NMR spectra of humic substances from soils of volcanic systems. *Geoderma*, 80, 327–338

Conte P, Spaccini R and Piccolo A (2004) State of the art of CPMAS C-13-NMR spectroscopy applied to natural organic matter. *Progress in Nuclear Magnetic Resonance Spectroscopy*, 44, 215–223

Doddrell D, Glushko V and Allerhand A (1972) Theory of the Nuclear Overhauser Enhancement and ^{13}C ^{1}H dipolar relaxation in proton-decoupled carbon-13 NMR spectra of macromolecules. *J. Chem. Physics*, 56, 3683–3689

Freeman R, Hill HDW, Kaptein R (1972) Proton-decoupled NMR spectra of carbon-13 with the nuclear Overhauser effect suppressed. *J. Magn. Res.*, 7, 327–329

Fründ R. and Lüdemann HD (1989) The quantitative analysis of solution and CPMAS-C13 NMR Spectra of humic material. *Sci. Total Environ.*, 81/82, 157–168

Gerasimowicz WV and Byler DM (1985) Carbon-13 CPMAS NMR and FTIR spectroscopic studies of humic acids. *Soil Sci.*, 139, 270–278

Kinchesh P, Powlson DS and Randall EW (1995) ^{13}C NMR studies of organic matter in whole : a case study of some Rothamsted soils. *Eur. J. Soil Sci.*, 46, 139–146

Lentz H, Ludemann HD and Ziechmann W (1977) Proton resonance spectra of humic acids from the solum of a podzol. *Geoderma*, 18, 325–328

Lowe IJ (1959) Free induction decay of rotating solids. *Phys. Rev. Lett.*, 2, 285–287

Moser A, Lefebvre B (2004) Identifying Residues in Natural Organic Matter through Spectral Prediction and Pattern Matching of 2-D NMR datasets. *Magn. Resonance Chem.*, 42, 14–22

Newman RH and Tate KR (1984) Use of alkaline soil extracts for ^{13}C NMR characterization of humic substances. *J. Soil Sci.*, 35, 47–54

Newman RH, Tate KR, Barron PF and Wilson MA (1980) Towards a direct, non-destructive method of characterising soil humic substances using ^{13}C-NMR. *J. Soil Sci.*, 31, 623–631

Pines A, Gibby MG and Waugh JS (1973) Proton enhanced NMR of dilute spins in solids. *J. Chem. Phys.*, 59, 569–590

Preston CM and Schnitzer M (1984) Effects of chemical modifications and extractants on the ^{13}C NMR spectra of humic materials. *Soil Sci. Soc. Am. J.*, 48, 305–311

Schaefer J and Stejskal EO (1976) C-13 NMR of polymers spinning at the magic angle, *J. Am. Chem. Soc.*, 98, 1031–1032

Schnitzer M and Barton DHR (1963) A new approach to the humic acid problem. *Nature*, London 198, 217–219

Schnitzer M and Neyroud JA (1974) The chemistry of high molecular weight fulvic acid fractions. *Can. J. Chem.*, 52, 4123–4132

Simpson AJ, Kingery WL, Williams A, Golotvin S, Kvasha M, Kelleher BK, Simpson AJ, Tseng L, Spraul M, Brauman U, Kingery WL, Kelleher B, Simpson MJ (2004) The application of LC-NMR and LC-SPE-NMR for the separation of Natural Organic Matter. *The Analyst*, 129:1216–1222

Smernik RJ and Oades MJ (2000) The use of spin counting for determining quantitation in solid state ^{13}C NMR spectra of natural organic matter. 1. Model systems and the effects of paramagnetic impurities. *Geoderma*, 96, 101–129

Smernik RJ and Oades MJ (2000) The use of spin counting for determining quantitation in solid state ^{13}C NMR spectra of natural organic matter. 1. HF-treated soil fractions. *Geoderma*, 96, 159–171

Smernik RJ and Oades MJ (2003) Spin accounting and RESTORE, two new methods to improve quantitation in solid-state ^{13}C NMR analysis of soil organic matter, *Eur. J. Soil. Sci.*, 54, doi:10.1046/j.1365–2389.2003.00497.x

Steelink C, Wershaw RL, Thorn KA and Wilson MA (1989) Application of liquid-state NMR spectroscopy to humic substances. *In : Humic substances II*, Hayes MHB, MacCarthy P, Malcolm RL and Swift RS ed. Wiley New York, 281–338

Tate RL (1998) Humic substances and organic matter in soil and water environments: characterization, transformations and interactions. *Soil Sci.*, 163, 675–676

Thorn KA and Mikita MA (2000) Nitrite fixation by humic substances: nitrogen-15 nuclear magnetic resonance. Evidence for potential intermediates in chemodenitrification. *Soil Sci. Soc. Am. J.*, 64, 568–582

Wilson MA (1981) Applications of nuclear magnetic resonance spectroscopy to the study of the structure of soil organic matter *J. Soil Sci.*, 32, 167–186

Wilson MA (1987) *Techniques and applications of NMR spectroscopy in geochemistry and soil science.*, Pergamon, Oxford

Wilson MA (1989) Solid-state NMR spectroscopy of humic substances, basic concepts and techniques. *In : Humic substances II*, Hayes MHB, MacCarthy P, Malcolm RL and Swift RS ed. Wiley and Sons, 309–338

Wilson MA, Jones AJ and Williamson B (1978) NMR spectroscopy of humic materials. *Nature, London*, 276, 487–489

Methods of Characterization by Fragmentation

Anderson HA, Hepburn A and Sim A (1978) Ether-soluble hydrolysis products in humic and fulvic acids. *J Soil Sci.*, 29, 84–87

Bracewell JM, Haider K, Larter SR and Schulten HR (1989) Thermal degradation relevant to structural studies of humic substances. *In : Humic substances II*, Hayes MHB., MacCarthy P, Malcolm RL and Swift RS ed., Wiley New York, 181–222

Chakrabartty SK, Kretschmer HO and Cherwonka S (1974) Hypohalite oxidation of humic acids. *Soil Sci.*, 117, 6

Chen Y, Senesi N and Schnitzer M (1978a) Chemical degradation of humic and fulvic acids extracted from mediterranean soils. *J. Soil Sci.*, 29, 350–359

Chen Y, Senesi N and Schnitzer M (1978b) Chemical and physical characteristics of humic and fulvic acids extracted from soils of the mediterranean region. *Geoderma*, 20, 87–104

Cheshire MV, Cranwell PA and Haworth RD (1968) Humic acid – III. *Tetrahedron*, 24, 5155–5167, Pergamon UK

Griffith SM and Schnitzer M (1989) Oxidative degradation of soil humic substances. *In : Humic substances II*, Hayes MHB, MacCarthy P, Malcolm RL and Swift RS ed., Wiley New York, 69–98

Griffith SM and Schnitzer M (1975) Oxidative degradation of humic and fulvic acids extracted from tropical volcanic soils. *Can. J. Soil Sci.*, 55, 251–267

Griffith SM and Schnitzer M (1976) The alkaline cupric oxide oxidation of humic and fulvic acids extracted from tropical volcanic soils, *Soil Sci.*, 122, 191–201

Hansen EH and Schnitzer M (1967) Nitric acid oxidation of Danish illuvial organic matter. *Soil Sci. Soc. Am. Proc.*, 31, 79–85

Hansen EH and Schnitzer M (1969) Zn–dust distillation and fusion of a soil Humic and fulvic acid. *Soil Sci. Soc. Am. Proceed.*, 33, 29

Hatcher PG, Dria KJ, Kim S., Frazier, SW (2001) Modern Analytical Studies of Humic substances. *Soil Sci.*, 166, 770–794

Hayes MHB and O'Callaghan MR (1989. Degradations with sodium sulfide and with phenol. *In : Humic substances II*, Hayes MHB, MacCarthy P, Malcolm RL and Swift RS ed., Wiley New York, 143–180

Jackson MP, Swift RS, Posner AM, Knox JR (1972) Phenolic degradation of humic acid. *Soil Sci.*, 114, 75–78

Kahn SU and Schnitzer M (1971a) The permanganate oxidation of methylated and unmethylated humic acids extracted from Solonetz, Solod and Chernozem Ah horizons. *Israel J. Chem.*, 9, 667–677

Khan SU and Schnitzer M (1971b) Further investigations on the chemistry of fulvic acid, a soil humic fraction. *Can. J. Chem.*, 49, 2302–2309

Kahn SU and Schnitzer M (1972a) Permanganate oxidation of humic acids, fulvic acids, and humins extracted from Ah horizons of a black chernozem, a black solod and a black solonetz soil. *Can. J. Soil Sci.*, 52, 43–51

Kahn SU and Schnitzer M (1972b) Permanganate oxidation of humic acids extracted from a GrayGrey wooded soil under different cropping systems and fertilizer treatments. *Geoderma*, 7, 113–120

Kimber RWL and Searle PL (1970) Pyrolysis gas chromatography of soil organic matter.1.Introduction and methodology, *Geoderma*, 4, 47–55

Kodama H and Schnitzer M (1970) Kinetics and mechanism of the thermal decomposition of fulvic acid. *Soil Sci.*, 109, 265–271

Martin F (1976) Effects of extractants on analytical characteristics and pyrolysis gas chromatography of podzol fulvic acids. *Geoderma*, 15, 253–265

Mendez J and Stevenson FJ (1966) Reductive cleavage of humic acids with sodium amalgam. *Soil Sci.*, 102, 85

Meuzelaar HLC, Haider K, Nagar BR and Martin JP (1977) Comparative studies of pyrolysis mass spectra from melanins of soil fungi, model phenolic polymers and humic acids from soil, peat and composted straw. *Geoderma*, 17, 239–252

Meuzelaar HLC, Posthumus MA, Kistemaker PG and Kistemaker J (1973) Curie point pyrolysis in direct combination with low voltage electron impact ionization spectrometry. *Anal.Chem.*, 45, 1546–1549

Morrison RI (1963) Products of the alkaline nitrobenzene oxidation of soil organic matter. *J. Soil Sci.*, 14, 2

Neyroud JA and Schnitzer M (1974) The exhaustive alkaline cupric oxide oxidation of humic and fulvic acid, *Soil Sci. Soc. Am. Proc.*, 38, 907–913

Neyroud JA and Schnitzer M (1975) The alkaline hydrolysis of humic substances. *Geoderma*, 13, 171–188

Ogner G (1975) Oxidation of nonhydrolyzable humic residue and its relation to lignin, *Soil Sci.*, 116, 93–100

Ouchi K and Brooks JD (1967) The isolation of certain compounds from depolymerized brown coal. *Fuel*, 46, 367–377

Parsons JW (1989) Hydrolytic degradations of humic substances. *In : Humic substances II*, Hayes MHB, MacCarthy P., Malcolm R.L. and Swift RS ed., Wiley New York, 99–120

Piper TJ and Posner AM (1972) Sodium amalgam reduction of humic acid (I and II). *Soil Biol. Biochem.*, 4, 513–531

Saiz-Jimenez C, Haider K and Meuzelaar HLC (1979) Comparisons of soil organic matter and its fractions by pyrolysis mass-spectrometry. *Geoderma*, 22, 25–37

Schnitzer M and Hoffmann I (1964) Pyrolysis of soil organic matter. *Soil Sci.Soc.Proced.*, 520–525

Schnitzer M and Skinner SIM (1974) The peracetic acid oxidation of humic substances, *Soil Sci.*, 118, 322–331

Schulten HR (1996) Direct pyrolysis–mass spectrometry of soils: a novel tool in agriculture, ecology, forestry and soil science. In *Mass spectrometry of soils*, Boutton TW and Yamasaki S-i ed., Marcel Dekker New York

Stevenson FJ and Mendez J (1967) Reductive cleavage products of soil humic acids. *Soil Sci.*, 103, 383

Stevenson FJ (1989) Reductive cleavage of humic substances. *In : Humic substances II, in search of structure*, Hayes MHB, MacCarthy P, Malcolm RL and Swift RS ed., Wiley New York, 122–142

Other methods (microscopy, X-ray, electrochemistry, etc.)

Bachelier G (1983) Figures de dessication des acides humiques, *Rapport multig. ORSTOM*, 14 p

Chen Y and Schnitzer M (1976) Scanning electron microscopy of a humic acid and of a fulvic acid and its metal and clay complexes. *Soil Sci. Soc. Am. J.*, 40, 682–686

Chen Y, Senesi N and Schnitzer M (1976) Chemical and physical characteristics of humic and fulvic acids extracted from soils of the mediterranean region. *Geoderma*, 20, 87–104

Shinozuka N and Hayano S (1987) Polarographic characterization of humic acid. *Soil Sci.*, 143, 157–161

Stevenson FJ and Schnitzer M (1982) Transmission electron microscopy of extracted humic and fulvic acids, *Soil Sci.*, 133, 334–345

Tan KH (1985) Scanning electron microscopy of humic matter as influenced by methods of preparation. *Soil Sci. Soc. Am. J.*, 49, 1185–1191

Defosse C and Rouxhet PG (1980) Introduction to X-ray photoelectron spectroscopy. *In: Advanced chemical methods of soil and clay mineral research.*, J.W Stucky and W.L. Banwart ed., Reidel, Dordrecht, 165–204

Goodman BA and Cheshire MV (1979) A Mössbauer spectroscopic study of the effect of pH on the reaction between iron and humic acid in aqueous media. *J. Soil Sci.*, 30, 85–91

Measurement of Non-Humic Molecules

13.1 Introduction

13.1.1 Non-Humic Molecules

Soil organic matter probably contains the majority of biochemical compounds synthesized by living organisms (Stevenson 1982). In addition to humic molecules, whose quantification (described in Chap. 11) is technically simpler than the structural characterization of molecules (cf. Chap. 12), a large number of other molecules of known structure are also present in soils. The most abundant can be classified in three main groups:

1. Nitrogenous molecules, which are often studied by their fragmentation products during acid hydrolysis.
2. Polysaccharides, mostly not nitrogenous molecules, which are also often studied by their fragmentation products.
3. The lipid fraction, which are sometimes called soil bitumens and contain a range of molecules extractable with the solvents used for fats; this fraction also contains many of the organic pollutants and xenobiotic residues that can contaminate the soil.

Titration techniques for (1) nitrogenous molecules are described in Chap. 14. This chapter describes the main titration techniques for the second and third types of molecules.

13.1.2 Soil Carbohydrates

Total Composition

Sugars (also improperly called carbohydrates because of an empirical formula corresponding to $C_n(H_2O)_n$) account for 5–25% of soil organic matter. Aside from traces of free sugars which can be extracted from the soil by water, soil carbohydrates are components of polysaccharides. It is practically impossible to isolate soluble fractions of polysaccharides for identification (Cheshire 1979). Consequently it is difficult to know if sugars come from a heterogeneous mixture of polysaccharides or from a single particularly complex polysaccharide.

Eight neutral carbohydrates can be identified by hydrolysis of soils. These can be classified in three main groups: hexose, deoxyhexose and pentose sugars. Two acid sugars (uronic acids) and two basic sugars (hexosamines) can also be identified.

Ranked in descending order, hexose sugars account for from 12–4% of organic matter and include glucose, galactose and mannose. Uronic acids account for 1–5% of soil organic matter and contain roughly equal parts of galacturonic and glucoronic acids. Pentose sugars are present in smaller quantities and contain mainly arabinose and xylose as well as traces of ribose. Fucose and rhamnose deoxyhexoses are found in similar concentrations to pentose sugars.

Amino sugars (cf. Chap. 14) are present still in lower concentrations in the soil; their chief components are hexosamines in the form of galactosamine and glucosamine.

Traces of other sugars can also be found in the soil: four methyl sugars, two alcohol sugars (inositol and manitol), two hexose sugars (fructose and sorbose), a pentose sugar (deoxyribose) and a hexosamine sugar (*N*-acetyl glucosamine).

Sugars and Types of Soils

Many authors have tried to characterize soils by quantification of the sugars that result from acid hydrolysis of polysaccharides. Folsom et al. (1974) found an almost linear relationship between total carbohydrate content and soil organic carbon content; however a curvature appeared for the range of very organic horizons which contained a lower proportion of sugars. These authors reported that grassland soils contained more pentoses and less hexoses than forest soils and also that the proportion of mannose increased with soil depth, indicating greater stability of this sugar.

Singhal and Sharma (1985) reported that total carbohydrates and organic carbon contents of forest soils varied in the same way whatever the tree cover. They observed no difference in the relative proportions of these sugars. MacGrath (1973) also found a very constant value for the relative composition of sugars in 38 Irish grassland soils.

Cheshire and Anderson (1975) observed a higher quantity of total sugar in cultivated soils than in uncultivated soils but the relative proportions were the same.

Distribution and Origin

Another aspect of the problem is linked to the distribution of polysaccharides in the fractions of soil organic matter. Diluted alkaline solutions are the best reagent for polysaccharide extraction although the majority of the polysaccharides remain associated with humin residues. Acidification of alkaline extracts precipitates humic acids and the majority of the polysaccharides remain in the acid soluble fraction of fulvic acid (Cheshire 1979; Barriuso et al. 1985). Bagautdinov et al. (1984) separated one fraction from a fulvic acid solution which contained mainly polysaccharides with a molecular weight of 27,000–28,000.

Many authors have tried to determine whether soil sugars are of microbial or plant origin. This is not a simple task since none of the main sugars can be classified exclusively as being of plant or microbial origin (Cheshire 1979). There are more similarities than differences in sugars between humic acids and fungi melanins (Coelho et al. 1988).

Incubation experiments using labelled glucose led to labelling of all sugars and, to a lesser extent, of amino acids. Deoxyhexoses have been identified as the most stable synthesized sugars (Cheshire 1979). With an increase in incubation time, an increasingly large proportion of labelled carbon was found in humin (Guckert et al. 1971). Hexose sugars are the main sugars synthesized by soil micro-organisms (Oades 1974).

François (1988) and Murayama (1983, 1984, 1988) reported that they had been unable to identify a specific origin for glucose, galactose and ribose but that xylose and arabinose are primarily of plant origin, while rhamnose, mannose and fucose are very often synthesized by micro-organisms but are also present in root exudates of various plants.

François (1988) showed that total sugars are primarily concentrated in fresh roots and in the 5–25 µm soil particle fraction. A marked relative reduction in xylose content and an increase in mannose and rhamnose contents were measured in the finer fractions. Feller (1991) used the xylose:mannose ratio as an indicator of the microbial or plant origin of the organic matter. This ratio had the lowest value (0.5–2) in the organic matter of the clay-organic compartment <2 µm; its value ranged between 1 and 3 in the 2–20 µm fraction and between 5 and 10 in the >20 µm fraction (cf. Chap. 9).

Principle of Titration

Free sugars can be titrated on aqueous extracts of soils. Polysaccharide titration has three main stages:
– Acid hydrolysis of polysaccharides;
– Possible purification of the hydrolysate; and
– Titration of the hydrolysate.
  Titration of free or hydrolysed sugars uses two types of techniques:
– Global colorimetric methods for reducing sugars and
– Chromatographic methods allowing the measurement of each individual sugar.

13.1.3 Soil Lipids

Soil lipids are rather complex mixtures of compounds one of whose common characteristics is solubility in a range of organic solvents or mixtures of solvents. This fraction includes groups such as free fatty acids, hydrocarbons, polar or non-polar lipids, steroids, waxes and resins.

The majority of lipids can be classified in three main groups: fats, waxes and resins. The resins are the most polar compounds and are thus most soluble in methanol and ethanol, and this property can be used to separate them.

Lipids are present in the soil in smaller quantities than nitrogenous compounds and polysaccharides. According to Stevenson (1982) they account for 2–6% of organic matter) and according to Jambu et al. (1978) up to 20% in certain soils. Lipids are generally present in higher concentrations in acid soils. The most fertile soils are generally poor in lipids. The presence of lipids may even be related to the old concept of soil sickness (Stevenson 1966) and depend on humus content, soil aeration and texture (Jambu et al. 1978).

The extraction of soil lipids may be complicated by the fact they bond to a varying extent with other organic or inorganic compounds in the soil. Most pesticides and other organic pollutants of the soils are also extracted with the lipid fraction.

13.1.4 Pesticides and Pollutants

Most of the products used in food and agricultural chemistry can be found in soils.

Organic pollutants that result from the breakdown of products in the environment can be extremely varied, although the majority belong to the following main groups:

- Polychlorinated biphenyls (PCBs) are families of chlorinated pollutants including about 30 compounds; traces of PCB can be detected in a very large number of substrates;
- Polynuclear aromatic hydrocarbons (PAH) include 15–20 compounds (e.g. naphthalene, phenantrene, anthracene or pyrene) that are resistant to degradation; and
- Dioxins are also residues of degradation but are present in more limited quantities.

Pesticides are generally not very stable molecules used in agriculture in a wide range of products like insecticides, acaricides, nematocides, repellents, fungicides, herbicides and poisons. They comprise a very large number of compounds. Although there is a general trend towards molecules that are less and less toxic for humans, and more and more degradable, there is also an increase in the total amount used as a result of gene mutations and of the development of resistance in living organisms. Calvet et al. (2005) summarized current knowledge about pesticides and their agronomic and environmental consequences for soils.

More than one thousand compounds are sold as pesticides and these are difficult to classify. Some of the main families are:

- Organochlorinated products including the first historically sold synthetic molecules such as DDT, dieldrin or lindane; these products are less used today because of their toxicity and low rate of degradability; however, they are still found in the environment since they accumulated in the lipids of living organisms; nowadays new halogenated molecules are used;
- Organophosphorous products were often used to replace the first organochlorinated products;
- Triazine herbicides;
- Acid herbicides like chlorophenoxyacetic acids, picloram or dicamba;
- Carbamates and thiocarbamates, which are often used as systemic insecticides; and
- Pyrethrinoids, which are synthetic molecules derived from natural pyrethrins and are commonly used as insecticides because they are not exchanged in the blood of human beings or warm-blooded animals.

13.2 Classical Techniques

13.2.1 Acid Hydrolysis of Polysaccharides

Principle of the Technique and Main Difficulties

Hot diluted acids are capable of completely hydrolyzing polysaccharides but in most soils they only hydrolyze about 75%.

To achieve complete hydrolysis of polysaccharides, e.g. cellulose or soil polysaccharides, a preliminary treatment with a more concentrated acid is required (Cheshire 1979). During hydrolysis with diluted acids, release of hexose sugars increases with an increase in the concentration of the acid. Alone, diluted acids are generally not appropriate for quantitative titration of hexose sugars.

Pentose sugars are more easily released than hexose sugars but they are also more easily destroyed during acid hydrolysis and, depending on the soil, they may be more efficiently titrated by hydrolysis in more diluted medium.

Ivarson and Sowden (1962) were the first to recommend cold pretreatment with 12 mol L^{-1} sulphuric acid (72%) followed by dilution of the acid to 0.5 mol L^{-1} and heating at reflux. In samples of litter, this attack released almost three times more hexoses than hydrolysis without pretreatment, but the release of pentoses was reduced by approximately 20% in the case of conifer litter.

Gupta and Sowden (1965) confirmed on four soils a very positive effect of pretreatments for the titration of hexoses and pentoses, except in some cases where deoxyhexoses were partly destroyed.

Cheshire and Mundie (1966) optimized the time of cold pretreatment with 12 mol L^{-1} sulphuric acid. The sugars measured by orcinol colorimetry reached maximum towards 16 h then decreased, whereas those measured by anthrone colorimetry (hexoses) continued to increase up to 40 h. The length of pretreatment thus influenced the time of attack at reflux with the 0.5 mol L^{-1} sulphuric acid solution necessary for the maximum release of sugar. After 16 h cold pretreatment, 5 h of hot attack were sufficient to reach maximum, whereas after 2 h pretreatment, nearly 20 h of attack were necessary. Finally, these authors concluded that there is no perfect method of hydrolysis enabling the complete release of glucose without partially destroying pentoses or deoxyhexoses. The 16 h treatment with 12 mol (H_2SO_4) L^{-1} at 20°C followed by heating for 5 h at reflux with 0.5 mol (H_2SO_4) L^{-1} was recommended because in several cases it resulted in the highest rate of release of glucose. This reason is not very convincing in the case of studies on the origin of sugars in the soil where glucose is not representative of a sugar of plant or microbial origin (cf. Sect. 13.1.1).

Oades et al. (1970) focussed on hydrolysis conditions for chromatographic titration of sugars. For a soil with no plant fragments, they found the best extracted sugar contents by direct attack at reflux for 1 h with a 5 mol ($\frac{1}{2}H_2SO_4$) L^{-1} solution. However, this attack released less glucose than another technique similar to that of Cheshire and Mundie (16 h in 13 mol (H_2SO_4) L^{-1} cold reagent followed by heating at reflux for 2 h in 0.5 mol (H_2SO_4) L^{-1}). But Oades' technique released a higher quantity of other sugars, particularly xylose, rhamnose and fucose. However in a sandy silt soil, there is a risk in significant breakdown of sugars when the duration of hydrolysis exceeds 20 min for xylose, 40 min for arabinose and about 1 h for other sugars (not the same risk in the method with pretreatment).

In fact for total sugar contents, the results of the method with heating at reflux for 20 min in 5 mol ($\frac{1}{2}H_2SO_4$) L^{-1} were not very different from those obtained using cold pretreatment, except for samples rich in materials where method with pretreatment is recommended. The Oades' method provided more pentoses and deoxyhexoses but much less glucose. To release glucose, a longer attack with 5 mol ($\frac{1}{2}H_2SO_4$) L^{-1} was necessary but with the risk of destroying pentose and deoxyhexose sugars. To obtain maximum rates for glucose and other sugars simultaneously Oades et al. recommended heating at reflux for 20 min with 5 mol ($\frac{1}{2}H_2SO_4$) L^{-1} reagent then filtration followed by 16 h of cold maceration in 26 mol ($\frac{1}{2}H_2SO_4$) L^{-1} reagent and heating at reflux for 5 h in 1 mol ($\frac{1}{2}H_2SO_4$) L^{-1} reagent. Initial heating at reflux with 5 mol ($\frac{1}{2}H_2SO_4$) L^{-1} reagent for only 20 min may be sufficient for not very organic soils but there is a risk of underestimating glucose.

The majority of more recent studies did not continue to optimize hydrolysis conditions; Coelho et al. (1988), Murayama (1987), Cheshire and Griffiths (1989) used the method of Oades et al. (1970) with hydrolysis in two stages. They sometimes distinguished sugars released by heating at reflux for 20 min with 5 M H_2SO_4, called non-cellulose sugars, from sugars released by later hydrolysis (heating at reflux for 5 h with 1 N H_2SO_4 preceded by maceration in 26 N H_2SO_4), called cellulose sugars.

Arschad and Schnitzer (1987) and Baldock et al. (1987) used the method developed by Spiteller (1980) which is similar to that of Cheshire and Mundie (1966) with respect to the conditions of hydrolysis: maceration for 16 h with 26 N H_2SO_4 followed by boiling at reflux for 5 h with NH_2SO_4. Singhal and Sharma (1985) used the method of Gupta (1967): 2 h of extraction at low temperature with 72% H_2SO_4 then heating at reflux for 16 h after dilution. Benzing-Purdie and Nikiforuk (1989) used a simpler technique for hydrolysis at 105°C for 18 h in 2 N H_2SO_4 and compared it with the method of Cheshire and Mundie (1966). Guckert (1973) also used a similar technique with hydrolysis with 3 mol ($\frac{1}{2}H_2SO_4$) L^{-1} acid at 80°C for 24 h after extraction.

Without cold pretreatment, with 4.5 h hydrolysis, titration of sugars by both anthrone and ferricyanide colorimetry reached maximum with a 5 N acid concentration and a temperature of 100°C (in closed flasks) and displayed a much less significant influence of the acid concentration than of temperature (Pansu 1992). Cold pretreatment increased the quantities of sugars released and the optimum temperature for the subsequent attack moved to between 70 and 90°C with a weaker acid (1 mol ($\frac{1}{2}H_2SO_4$) L^{-1}, in agreement with the results of Cheshire and Mundie (1966).

Pansu (1992) also showed good resistance to the degradation of known quantities of monosaccharides added in the attack solutions. Commercial crystallized cellulose showed good resistance to concentrated acids at 105°C whatever the concentration of the sulphuric acid, and even to hydrochloric acid. Cellulose hydrolysis only became significant (88%) with the method including a cold pretreatment with the 26 mol ($\frac{1}{2}H_2SO_4$) L^{-1} reagent. Hydrolysis of commercial cellulose released not only glucose (66–86% of the total), but also galactose (10–30%), mannose (1–2%), xylose (approximately 1%) and ribose (approximately 1%).

Equipment and Reagents

- Inorganic purified water: demineralized water purified on activated carbon (standard Millipore) or water distilled after reflux attack in the presence of a little potassium permanganate and sulphuric acid.
- Six round bottom boiling flasks (100 mL) with ground stopper or six flasks with PTFE joint screw stopper (100 mL).
- Set of six condensors (only for the method with reflux heating).
- Büchner funnels with standard GF/A glass fibre filters ϕ 4 cm (Whatman No. 1820 042, or similar).
- 13 mol L^{-1} concentrated sulphuric acid solution: add 278 mL inorganic water in a 1 L volumetric flask; carefully add while agitating and cooling in a cold water bath, 722 mL of concentrated reference grade sulphuric acid; complete to 1 L.
- 2.5 mol (H_2SO_4) L^{-1} (5 N) sulphuric acid solution: proceed as given earlier but with 139 mL of acid and complete to 1 L with inorganic water.

Procedure

Section 13.2.1 earlier mentions that our current state of knowledge makes it difficult to recommend a precise standardized attack that is valid for all soils. The conditions of hydrolysis need to be adjusted to the type of study required. Based on the review of the literature in Sect. 13.2.1, the three alternative procedures listed later can all be used.

Attack Favouring the Measurement of Pentoses

Put 5 g of soil and 40 mL of 2.5 mol L^{-1} sulphuric acid in a 100 mL round bottom boiling flask. Connect to the condensor and heat at reflux for 20 min (alternatively heat in a flask with a screw cap at 100°C for 20 min).

Leave to cool and filter on a Büchner funnel on glass fiber filter or centrifuge.

Total Attack

Add the residue of the previous attack (with glass fibre filter) and 2 mL of 13 mol (H_2SO_4) L^{-1} solution in the same 100 mL round bottom flasks used earlier.

Stop the flasks and leave at ambient temperature for 16 h (overnight).

Carefully add 50 mL inorganic water while cooling.

Connect the flasks to the condensors and heat at reflux for 5 h (alternatively, heat at 90°C in a closed bottle).

Filter as mentioned earlier on glass wool.

For the analysis of total sugars, the filtrates described in "Attack Favouring the Measurement of Pentoses" earlier and in "Total Attack" can be mixed. The analysis of each hydrolysate releases (a) sugars that are easily hydrolysable (mainly pentoses) in the hydrolysate described in "Attack Favouring the Measurement of Pentoses", (b) sugars like cellulose that are difficult to hydrolyse in the hydrolysates described in "Total Attack".

Simplified Total Attack

In a 100 mL round bottom flask place 5 g of soil sample and 2 mL of 13 mol (H_2SO_4) L^{-1} solution.

Stop the flask and leave at the ambient temperature for 16 h (overnight).

Carefully add 50 mL inorganic water while cooling.

Connect the boiling flasks to the condensors and heat at reflux for 5 h (alternatively, heat at 90°C in a closed bottle).

Filter as mentioned earlier on glass wool or centrifuge.

13.2.2 Purification of Acid Hydrolysates

Principle of the Technique and Main Difficulties

Particularly for chromatographic titration, the hydrolysates must be purified to remove a significant amount of inorganic compounds especially sulphate ions but also inorganic dissolved solids (particularly iron and aluminium) by the acid attack of the soil. Neutralization of the extracts involves the precipitation of aluminium and iron hydroxides. If neutralization is carried out with a carbonate or hydroxide belonging to the alkaline earths (Ca, Sr or Ba) sulphates can also be precipitated. The risk of error lies in the possible adsorption of neutral sugars by the precipitates. With barium hydroxide or carbonate, neutral sugars and barium salts of uronic acids can be recovered by filtration and by washing the precipitates with water, sometimes by washing with hot water or by ethanol extraction with a Sohxlet apparatus (Cheshire and Mundie 1966). Sodium bicarbonate has also been used for neutralization of the acid extracts with methanol extraction of the sodium sulphate after desiccation (Oades 1967).

Calcium carbonate enables neutralization by eliminating sulphates together with most coloured organic matter (Brink et al. 1960). Oades et al. (1970) preferred strontium carbonate to bring the hydrolysates towards pH 7. When the solutions were left to stand, these authors observed co-precipitation of brown organic matter and iron complexes. After filtration and dry evaporation of the filtrate in a rotary evaporator, sugars were dissolved in 4–5 fractions of 2–4 mL methanol with filtration.

The extracts can be also purified by successive passage on cation and anion resin which also separates neutral sugars and uronic acids. Alternatively, columns filled with a mixture of coal and celite enable sugars to be eluated with 50% ethanol in water after the salts are rinsed in water (Cheshire 1979).

Tests were carried out at IRD[1] (unpublished data) to compare seven methods of purification:
- Water elution on MB1 amberlite resin,
- Methanol elution on MB1 amberlite resin,
- Neutralization with strontium carbonate,
- Neutralization with sodium bicarbonate,
- Neutralization with barium carbonate,

---

[1] IRD, Institute of Research for Development (ex-Orstom), BP 64501, 911 Avenue of Agropolis, 34394 Montpellier Cedex 5, France.

– Neutralization with barite and
– Neutralization with soda.

The method which provided the best recovery of sugars was neutralization with strontium carbonate; this result is in agreement with that of Oades et al. (1970).

Corrective Factors

Studies using synthetic solutions enabled the effect of neutralization with strontium carbonate on the recovery of sugars to be identified (Pansu 1992). In three tests, the internal standard (myoinositol) was added before neutralization, and in three other tests, myoinositol was added before the borohydride reduction of the purified concentrated solutions. Each final solution was injected twice into the chromatograph. Calculations of the absolute contents showed:

– The error due to the method of preparation of the samples was no higher than the error in the chromatographic measurement (F test). For most sugars, this error was about 1%.

– A higher rate of adsorption of the internal standard on the precipitate than adsorption of the other sugars. Thus it is better to introduce the internal standard after purification of the extracts but before derivatization of sugars.

– An average percentage of recovery of sugars of 85%, ranging from 71% for ribose to 91% for rhamnose. Ribose was always recovered in the smallest quantities. Based on these recovery percentages, we propose the following corrective factors: multiply the results of absolute contents of each sugar by 1.21 for rhamnose, 1.08 for fucose, 1.41 for ribose, 1.10 for arabinose and xylose, 1.25 for mannose, 1.21 for galactose and 1.15 for glucose. These factors take into account the response coefficients of each sugar compared to the internal standard.

Equipment and Reagents

– Six 100 mL beakers;
– Magnetic stirrers;
– Six 250 mL round bottom flasks for the rotary evaporator and
– Strontium carbonate, $M = 147.63$ g.

2.2.4 Procedure

Transfer the filtrates or centrifugation solutions described in Sect. 13.2.1 in 100 mL beakers, agitate on a magnetic stirrer. Add the quantity of strontium carbonate in powder form calculated according to the quantity of sulphuric acid to be neutralized plus 10%, i.e.:

   – Hydrolysis A: $1.1 \times 40 \times 2.5 \times 147.63/1000 = 16.2$ g
   – Hydrolysis C: $1.1 \times 2 \times 13 \times 147.63/1000 = 4.2$ g
   – Hydrolysis B: the same as hydrolysis c + 2 mL of 2.5 mol L^{-1}

acid solution which impregnates the a residue, i.e. a total of 4.9 g.

$SrCO_3$ should be added to the solution slowly under agitation to avoid foam overflow.

Leave in contact for at least 1 h under agitation. Check the pH is neutral or slightly basic (add a soda pellet if necessary). Check for precipitation of iron hydroxides which colour the precipitate and discolour the solution.

Centrifuge and collect the supernatant in a round bottom boiling flask for later titration by gas chromatography (GPC) if required (cf. Sect. 13.2.4), and in a 100 mL volumetric flask if not. Rinse the residue with 25 mL methanol while stirring with a glass rod. Centrifuge again and add the supernatant to the previous solution. Repeat this operation once more.

13.2.3 Colorimetric Titration of Sugars

Techniques

Most colorimetric methods are based on one of the two following properties of sugars: their reducing power or, in strong acids, the formation of furfural-type compounds that react easily giving coloured derivatives.

The methods can be classified in different categories corresponding to the measurement of total sugars, hexoses or pentoses.

Colorimetry of Total Sugars

Two titration techniques based on the reducing power of carbohydrates were tested (a) reduction of alkaline cupric salt solutions (Fehling's liquor) resulting in Cu^+ cooper complexes or (b) reduction of yellow ferricyanide solutions resulting in colourless ferrocyanides. The latter was considered preferable for the measurement of soil sugar and was automated by Cheshire and Mundie (1966).

Three techniques use the other property based on furfural derivatives: total sugars with anthrone, phenol or orcinol. Anthrone produces a beautiful green–blue colour when it comes in contact with the furfural derivatives in the concentrated sulphuric acid. This reagent provides the best absorbance of complexes with deoxyhexose and hexose sugars (except for mannose). However the response to pentose sugars is weaker and becomes undetectable when the anthrone content is above 0.05%. This method is also suspected of interfering with other organic matter as well as with iron and nitrates (Cheshire 1979).

Phenol reacts with the furfural derivatives and results in a yellow colouration (Dubois et al. 1956). The similarity of this colour to that of soil hydrolysates could result in overestimation of total sugars with this reagent (McGrath 1973). Overestimated data were observed with direct phenol colorimetric analysis without purification of hydrolysates (Pansu 1992). However, Doutre et al. (1978) considered this method more satisfactory than the anthrone method.

Orcinol or 3,5-dihydroxytoluene also reacts with the furfural derivatives, in this case with the advantage of providing enough similar responses for each sugar. It was used for soil hydrolysates by Bachelier (1966).

Colorimetry of Hexose Sugars

Although originally proposed for total sugars, anthrone is more commonly used to measure hexoses and deoxyhexoses of soil hydro-hydrolysates.

Ivarson and Sowden (1962) also proposed chromotropic acid for the measurement of hexoses. This reagent is not very susceptible to interference with pentose sugars and uronic acids and responded more strongly than anthrone on four samples of soil and litters.

Colorimetry of Pentose Sugars

Cheshire and Mundie (1966) used the orcinol-$FeCl_3$ reagent described by Thomas and Lynch (1961) to measure the maximal release of pentose sugars during hydrolysis. In acetic acid, aniline also reacts with pentose sugars at ambient temperature resulting in a red colouration, with only slight interference by hexose sugars and uronic acids (Ivarson and Sowden 1962; Tracey 1950).

Colorimetry of Deoxyhexose Sugars

The yellow colour formed by heating the carbohydrate extract with cysteine in sulphuric acid medium is quoted as specific to deoxyhexose sugars; this reagent was used for soil hydrolysates by Cheshire and Mundie (1966).

See Chap. 14 for titration of uronic acids and amino sugars.

Equipment and Reagents

– Calibrated 150×25 mm glass test tubes;
– Water bath;

– Visible spectrophotometer;
– Plastic colorimetric cells, length 1 cm;
– Crushed ice;
– Concentrated sulphuric acid 18 mol (H_2SO_4) L^{-1} (d = 1.84);
– 5% phenol solution in water;
– 0.2% solution of anthrone in concentrated H_2SO_4;
– Standard solutions for the phenol method: 0, 5, 10, 25, 50 and 100 mg (glucose) L^{-1} and
– Standard solutions for the anthrone method: 0, 5, 10, 15, 20 and 25 mg (glucose) L^{-1}.

Procedure for the Phenol Method

Put in the test tubes 2 mL of soil hydrolysate (cf. Sect. 13.2.1) or purified soil hydrolysate (cf. Sect. 13.2.2) that has been previously completed to 100 mL in a volumetric flask (a preliminary test of standard additions can be used to check the need for purification).

Add 1 mL phenol solution and then rapidly add 5 mL of concentrated sulphuric acid without allowing it to run along the wall of the flask (taking care not to splash).

Leave to stand for 10 min, agitate the tubes and place them in the water bath at 25–30°C for 20 min, then cool under running water.

Read absorbance at 485 nm (490 nm for hexose sugars, 480 nm for pentose sugars and uronic acids). The colour remains stable for several hours. It is sometimes necessary to homogenize the solutions just before colorimetric reading.

Proceed in the same way for each point of the calibration range.

Procedure for the anthrone method

Bring the hydrolyzed solution (cf. Sects. 13.2.1 or 13.2.2) to 100 mL and homogenize well.

Introduce 5 mL of this solution in a calibrated test tube placed in ice. Proceed in the same way for each calibration point.

Slowly add in each tube 10 mL of anthrone solution letting it run down the side of the tube; swirl the tube to mix.

Seal with a piece of parafilm and immediately place in a 85°C water bath for 35 min.

Cool in an ice-tray and place in a colorimetric cell and read absorbance at at 625 nm. Disposable plastic colorimetric cells (1 cm in length) should be used to limit the number of transfers and washings of the concentrated sulphuric acid solutions.

13.2.4 Titration of Sugars by Gas Chromatography

Principle

The titration of sugars by gas chromatography is rather difficult to implement for two reasons:
– Sugars are too polar to be satisfactorily separated directly on the gas chromatographic columns; it is thus necessary to form derivatives which transform the hydroxyl functional groups into less polar forms;
– Gas chromatography is more selective than liquid chromatography; separation of the carbohydrate can result in many peaks representing the isomers of the different molecular configurations and the chromatograms may then be difficult to interpret.

Most authors used techniques similar to the one described by Oades et al. (1970). Sodium borohydride was added to the neutralized and purified acid extracts, and this transformed the isomers of sugars into their alditol form. After elimination of the boric acid formed by successive evaporations in acetic acid medium, acetylation of the alditols was performed with acetic anhydride.

Alditol acetates were dissolved in methylene chloride for injection into the chromatograph. Oades et al. (1970) used a 2 m column with an interior diameter of 3.5 mm filled with 100–120 mesh GAS Chrom Q impregnated with 5% ECNSS-M. In this way eight major soil sugars were separated in 70 min though with rather poor distinction between rhamnose and fucose.

Spiteller (1980) improved this technique. He separated alditol acetates on a non-polar OV1 25 m capillary column in 25 min by detecting traces of glucosamine and galactosamine. Cheshire et al. (1983) separated alditol acetates with a capillary column of 50 m × 0.3 mm impregnated with SILAR 10 CP with a 90 min temperature programme. Dormaar (1984) obtained separation with a duration similar to that used by Spiteller (1980) with a glass capillary tube impregnated with SP2330. Baldock et al. (1987) used the procedure of Spiteller, as did Arshad and Schnitzer (1987), the latter authors with a capillary tube and a stationary phase with trifluoropropyl-methyl which increased the total duration of the analysis. Coelho et al. (1988) used a filled column, and the length of the separation phase was similar to that of Oades et al. (1970). Like Cheshire and Griffiths (1989) and Murayama (1988) used chromatographic separation of alditol acetates but did not specify the column used.

The reduction and acetylation operations which follow the purification of the hydrolysates are rather long and this means many samples cannot be compared. Blakeney et al. (1983) recommended a method allowing the preparation time to be reduced, but a test performed at the IRD laboratory with this aim in view was unsuccessful (unpublished data).

On the other hand, the chromatographic time (Fig. 13.1) was reduced to 12.5 min using a capillary column impregnated with a SP2330 phase similar to that of Dormaar (1984), but made of silica glass instead of borosilicate glass (Pansu 1992).

Equipment and Reagents

- 5 mL conical cylinder flasks with PTFE joint screw caps (Fig. 13.2);
- Pasteur pipettes with 3 mL squeeze bulbs;
- Thermostated aluminium heating block (Fig. 13.2);
- Nitrogen sweeping for evaporation (Fig. 13.2);
- Gas phase chromatograph equipped with a flame ionization detector;
- SP2330 silica capillary column (Supelco) 15 m in length and 0.25 mm ID;
- Standard carbohydrate solution in 85% methyl alcohol containing 1 mg mL^{-1} of each carbohydrate: rhamnose, fucose, ribose, arabinose, xylose, mannose, galactose and glucose;
- Standard solution containing 1 mg mL^{-1} myoinositol in 50% methyl alcohol;
- Methyl alcohol;
- Strontium carbonate;
- Sodium borohydride;
- Glacial acetic acid;
- Anhydrous solution of 10% acetic acid in methanol (dry on anhydrous Na_2SO_4);
- Acetic anhydride and
- Chloroform.

Preparation of Alditol Acetates

(a) In each boiling flask containing the purified hydrolysates, add an exact volume of the myoinositol internal standard solution appropriate for the estimated quantity of sugars (0.5–2 mL).

(b) Evaporate to just dry with a rotary evaporator; rinse the boiling flask with 3–4 small fractions of methanol using a Pasteur pipette and transfer the washing solutions to a 5 mL flask with screw cap.

(c) Add approximately 10 mg of sodium borohydride and leave to act overnight.

(d) Add 0.1 mL of glacial acetic acid, evaporate to dry at 70°C under a nitrogen flow (Fig. 13.2), add 1 mL of anhydrous 10% acetic acid in the ethyl alcohol solution and evaporate in the same way, repeat this operation five times.

(e) Add 1 mL acetic anhydride, stop the flasks and heat at 135°C for 2 h.

(f) Cool to 70°C and evaporate to dry under a nitrogen flow.

(g) Cool and dissolve in an exact volume of from 0.5 to 2 mL of chloroform depending on the estimated sugar content.

The solutions can be stored or injected directly into the chromatograph.

Preparation of Standards for Alditol Acetates

Add 1 mL standard solution of sugars and 1 mL of internal standard solution in a 5 mL flask with a screw cap and continue as mentioned earlier starting at stage c.

Chromatographic Conditions

– Silica glass Supelco SP2330 capillary column (or similar) length: 15 m, interior diameter: 0.25 mm.
– Carrier gas: 0.7 bar helium.
– Splitter injector, leak-flow: 100 mL min^{-1}.
– Injection: 1 μL.
– Flame ionization detector.
– Temperatures:
    column programmed from 210 to 250°C at 3°C min^{-1},
    injector: 300°C,
    detector: 250°C.

Figure 13.1 shows an example of chromatograms obtained on sugars in a standard solution and in a ferrallitic soil from Congo.

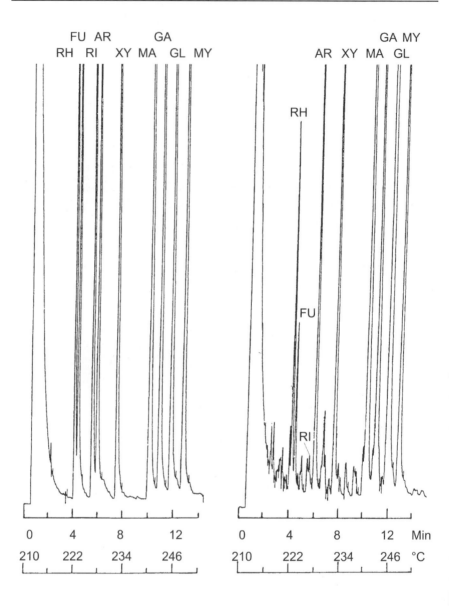

Fig. 13.1. Chromatograms of alditol acetates (conditions described in "Chromatographic conditions", RH, rhamnose; FU, fucose; RI, ribose; AR,
arabinose; XY, xylose; MA, mannose; GA, galactose; GL, glucose;
MY, myoinositol internal standard). *On the left*: standard mixture
corresponding to the injection of 0.2 µg of each sugar. *On the right*:
sugars of a strongly desaturated ferrallitic soil of the Niari valley
(Congo). Hydrolysis according to the procedure described in "Attack
Favouring the Measurement of Pentoses" earlier.

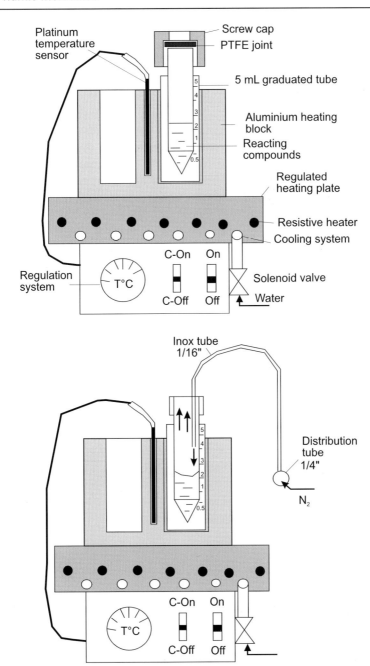

Fig. 13.2 Recommended system for derivatization reactions for GPC. *Top,* reactions in closed micro-flasks at controlled temperature, *bottom,* evaporation of excess solvents and reagents under surface nitrogen flow

13.2.5 Quantification of Total Lipids

Principle

Total lipids are measured gravimetrically after extraction with organic solvents in a Soxhlet extractor. Most lipidic compounds of soils are not very polar, but some are slightly more so (Amblès et al. 1990). The choice of the polarity of the extraction solvent is thus significant, and preliminary tests should be performed. Fahd-Rachid (1993) used chloroform. A mixture of petroleum ether and ethyl acetate (3:1, v:v) is also often recommended and its toxicity is lower than chlorinated solvents. However, this mixture was considered to be less effective than chloroform for the extraction of complex lipids (Jambu et al. 1987).

Solvents do not extract all the lipids since some are associated with humic compounds, clays and various minerals. An acid treatment enables release of the bound lipids which then become accessible for a second Soxhlet extraction. Hydrochloric acid can be used for the acid pre-treatment but according to a technique recommended by Wang et al. (1969), it is better to use a mixture of hydrochloric acid and hydrofluoric acid. Hydrochloric acid enables release of lipids bound to cations, and hydrofluoric acid enables release of lipids bound to the organomineral matrix (Fahd-Rachid 1993).

Equipment and Reagents

– 200 mL Soxhlet extractor with condenser and a 500 mL borosilicate glass round bottom boiling flask with conical ground joints;
– Hemispherical electric heating mantle with temperature regulation for use with a 500 mL boiling flask;
– Soxhlet extraction cartridges 38 mm in diameter and 150 mm in height;
– Vacuum rotary evaporator;
– Pasteur pipettes;
– 25 mL half cylindrical half conical flasks of the volumetric type (graduation is not necessary) with PTFE joint screw cap;
– Glass funnels ϕ 3 cm;
– 250 mL plastic beakers;
– Plastic funnels ϕ approx. 8 cm;
– Filter papers for plastic funnels;
– HCL–HF aqueous solution at 2.5% HF and 2.5% HCl and
– Petroleum ether:ethyl acetate extraction solution (3:1 v:v): mix 750 mL petroleum ether and 250 mL ethyl acetate.

Procedure

Free Lipids

- Put an exact weight P (100–150 g) of air-dried soil sieved to 2 mm in the extraction cartridge and put the cartridge in the Soxhlet extractor.
- Put 200 mL extraction solution and two pumice grains in the 500 mL boiling flask; connect the boiling flask to the Sohxlet extractor.
- Connect the condensor to the top of the extractor.
- Start heating the boiling flask and regulate the heat of the hemispherical mantle so as to obtain good condensation of the solvent from the condenser to the extractor.
- Continue the extraction for 48 h.
- Let cool then connect the boiling flask to the rotary evaporator and evaporate until the volume is reduced to a few mL.
- At the same time, tare a stopped 25 mL half cylindrical half conical flask (after drying in the drying oven and cooling).
- Open the flask and position it under a small funnel stopped with a glass wool plug and half filled with anhydrous sodium sulphate.
- Using a Pasteur pipette, decant the residue of evaporation into the small funnel and collect the dried extract in the 25 mL flask.
- Rinse the evaporation flask and the funnel several times with a few Pasteur pipettes of the extraction mixture to fill approximately 20 mL of the 25 mL flask.
- Evaporate the solvent from the flask under gaseous nitrogen flow (see Fig. 13.2) or under vacuum in the rotary evaporator by means of a ground/screwed connection.
- Stop the flask, let cool and weigh, by deduction of the tare one obtains the weight of free lipids P_1.
- Rate of free lipid $= 100\ P_1/P$.

Bound Lipids

- Place the residue of extraction of the free lipids in a 250 mL plastic beaker and add the HCL–HF solution at a rate of 150 mL for a test sample of 100 g soil.
- Leave in contact for 48 h agitating from time to time.
- Filter on filter paper in plastic funnels.
- Wash the residue with water until pH 5; decant it to a shallow cup or glass beaker cover and leave to dry on the lab table or in a desiccator.
- Extract the lipids using same procedure as for free lipids (cf. "Free Lipids" earlier).

Total Lipids

It is possible to extract the total lipids directly by an attack of the initial sample with the HCL–HF mixture followed by extraction in the Sohxlet. Fahd-Rachid (1993) found excellent agreement between the total extracted lipids and those calculated by the sum "free lipids + bound lipids".

13.2.6 Quantification of the Water-Soluble Organics

Table 13.1.1. Cold water soluble (CWS) and hot water soluble (HWS) compounds obtained on cultivated soils of Boigneville, France (Pansu, unpublished data, see extraction conditions in the text)

No.	weight % of CWS	C % in CWS	CWS C:N ratio	% CWS-C/total soil C	weight % of HWS	C % in HWS	HWS C:N ratio	% HWS-C/total soil C
A	0.026	28.8	2.1	0.75	0.85	8.3		7.1
B	0.033	33.8	2.5	1.12	0.48	22.3		10.7
D	0.004	75.0	2.1	0.30	0.26	21.5		5.6
E	0.021	27.1	1.4	0.57	0.24	25.1	5.5	6.0
F	0.025	30.1	1.8	0.75	0.38	22.4		8.5

For the study of the spatial and temporal dynamics of organic matter, the water-soluble organic fractions of the soil have to be taken into account. These fractions comprise organic acids, simple sugars or light polysaccharides and nitrogenous compounds. These different compounds can have a significant influence on the structural stability and fertility of the soils. Two types of compounds can be distinguished:

– Compounds that are soluble in cold water: these are obtained by agitating the soil with water using different procedures, for example, shake 10 g of soil in 200 mL water or 2 h on a rotary shaker, leave in contact overnight, sake again for 2 h and centrifuge at 14,000 g.

– Compounds that are soluble in hot water: several procedures can be used, for example, boil 4 g of soil at reflux for 16 h with 200 mL water in the presence of three glass balls, cool and centrifuge at 14,000 g. Kouakoua et al. (1997) showed that the extraction of water-soluble compounds of ferrallitic soils from Congo increased continuously with the length of extraction both in a drying oven and in an autoclave. According to Leinweber et al. (1995), this fraction is mainly made up of nitrogenous and carbohydrate compounds.

Table 13.1 lists proportions of these fractions expressed in mass, carbon and nitrogen contents for five cultivated soils in temperate zones.

In waterlogged or poorly aerated soils, the aqueous extracts contain organic acids of low molecular weight (e.g. lactic, pyruvic or acetic acid) under anaerobiosis conditions (Küsel and Drake 1999) which can be titrated in aqueous mediums by gas–solid chromatography (standard column of Porapak or chromosorb 101, or similar) or by ionic chromatography. The aqueous extracts contains also inorganic water soluble compounds (cf. Chap. 18).

13.3 Complementary Techniques

13.3.1 Determination of soil Carbohydrates by Gas Chromatography

If the alditol acetate technique (cf. Sect. 13.2.4) was the most widely used for the measurement of soil carbohydrates, other techniques have also been proposed: Morgenlie (1975) described separation of neutral sugars in the form of their *O*-isopropylidene derivatives. Preparation of the derivatives was performed with 1% sulphuric acid in acetone reagent, and separation required 35–40 min on columns of the XE60 or OV225 type. Traitler et al. (1984) separated trimethylsilyl derivatives of sugars on short apolar columns. Cowie and Hedges (1984) also separated trimethyl-silyl derivatives from sugars from hydrolysates in plankton, sediment and wood. As a preliminary treatment, these authors brought free sugars to their mutarotation equilibrium in the presence of lithium perchlorate to get round the problem of multiple peaks. Larre-Larrouy and Feller (1997) and Larre-Larrouy et al. (2003) analyzed neutral sugars in soil at the same time as uronic acids and hexosamines in the form of their tri-methylsilyl derivatives, each sugar being calculated by the sum of the surfaces of its different isomer forms.

13.3.2 Carbohydrates by Liquid Chromatography

The techniques used for the titration of sugars with liquid chromato-graphy were unsatisfactory for many years. Cheshire et al. (1969) separated eight neutral sugars by ion exchange chromatography with a pH gradient, but separation took 14 h. At the column exit, sugars were analyzed by colorimetry after reaction with the orcinol in the sulphuric acid reagent. Hydrazide of *p*-hydroxybenzoic acid is a better reagent for alkaline eluates; without acidification it gives an yellow colour with carbohydrates.

Hamada and Ono (1984) analyzed sugars on soils of volcanic ash by high performance liquid chromatography (HPLC) with an anion column and detection by fluorescence spectroscopy after reaction with ethanolamine. Separation required 70 min but arabinose, fructose and fucose were eluted under the same peak, as were rhamnose and ribose. Pluijmen (1987) analyzed sugars of different plants by HPLC on a SUGAR PAK TM column (Waters Associates) with a water (or acetonitrile–water) mobile phase, refractometric detection and an anion and cation precolumn. But this author was especially concerned with glucose and fructose and did not provide chromatograms.

Reim and Van Effen (1986) used a technique that appeared to be more promising. They proposed a new detector that was more sensitive than the refractometer and which, in addition, did not require preliminary derivatization reactions as do spectrometric methods. Using an ion exchange column, they simultaneously separated simple sugars and low molecular weight oligomers, but they did not provide a chromatogram of the eight main soil sugars.

Angers et al. (1988) separated sugars from hydrolysates of soils on an aminex HPX-87P column (BIO-RAD labs); but they titrated only five sugars and the detection limit was rather poor.

Martens and Frankenberger (1990) separated ten soil sugars by anion exchange chromatography using the HPAC-PAD system (Dionex, Sunnyvale, CA, USA) with the following chromatographic conditions (Fig.13.3):
– 200 μL injection loops;
– CarboPac PA guard column (25×3 mm);
– Chromatographic column (250×4 mm) filled with a pellicular anion exchange resin: CarboPac PA1;
– Flow of eluent: 0.8 mL min^{-1}, ambient temperature;
  eluent a: purified inorganic water (18 Mohm),
  eluent b: 50 mmol (NaOH) L^{-1} + 1.5 mmol (CH_3COONa) L^{-1} aqueous solution,
  93% eluent a and 7% eluent b for 15 min, gradient up to 100% b in 25 min,
  idem the mobile phase has to be degassed to prevent absorption of CO_2 and the production of carbonates which can move ions and reduce the retention time;
– Detection by pulsed amperometry three times with a gold electrode:
  $E1$:0.1 V, $t1$: 300 ms, oxidation of CHOH groups,
  $E2$: 0.6 V, $t2$: 120 ms, displacement of the reaction products,
  $E3$:–0.8 V, $t3$: 300 ms, cleaning of the electrode at negative potential,
  response time: 1.

The study of Martens and Frankenberger (1990) showed that the HPAC-PAD system had several advantages over another classical HPLC system with detection by refractive index: it produced more precise results, was twice as sensitive (pmole) and had better resolution. The preparation of the soil samples was also simpler in the HPAC-PAD system. After acid attack (cf. Sect. 13.2.1), the samples were treated with 1 mL 0.1 mol (EDTA) L^{-1} solution then brought to pH 4 by adding 5 mol (NaOH) L^{-1} solution and centrifuged at 10,000 g. The coloured materials were then removed by filtration on a solid phase extraction column (SPE) (Supelco^{TM} Bellefonte, Pa, USA) comprising 3 mL of strong cation exchange resin (three propylsulfonic acid, H^+ form) and 3 mL of strong anion exchange resin (quaternary propylammonium 3, Cl-form). The extracts were also filtered on 0.22 μm GS filters (Millipore, Bedford, MA, USA).

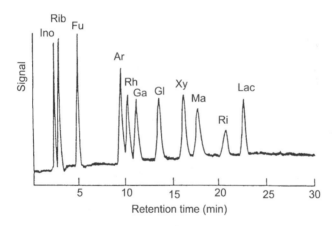

Fig. 13.3. Standard sugar separation by high performance anion exchange chromatography (Martens and Frankenberger 1990); Ino, inositol; Rib, ribitol; Fu, fucose; Rh, rhamnose; Ga, galactose; Gl, glucose; Xy, xylose; Ma, mannose; Ri, ribose; Lac, lactose

Bernal et al. (1996) proposed a chromatographic technique similar to that of Martens and Frankenberger (1990) for sugar titration in coffee and wine.

13.3.3 Fractionation and Study of the Soil Lipid Fraction

Lipid Fractionation

There are many lipid fractionation techniques and the reader is advised to consult relevant handbooks that describe biochemical lipidology techniques, e.g. Kates (1975).

Fractionation can be divided into two stages:
- Separation of the different classes of lipids and
- Measurement of the individual components of each class or of the total fraction.

The exact procedure to apply depends on the lipid concerned. Most lipids of microbial and animal origin contain from 60 to 85% of phosphatides and glycolipids, the remainder being neutral or not polar lipids (glycerides, sterols, hydrocarbons, pigments). Lipids of plant origin contain a larger proportion of neutral lipids and a smaller proportion of phosphatides.

Two main types of techniques are used to separate the classes of lipids:
- Fractionation by solvents and
- Liquid phase chromatography on column, on paper or on thin layer.

The characterization and quantification of lipid components require the chemical breakdown of complex lipids followed by separation techniques such as gas chromatography, generally with a flame ionization detector, possibly coupled with a mass spectrometer for the identification of the molecules.

Fractionation by Solvents

Precipitation by acetone is the simplest method for separating phosphatides and neutral lipids. It is based on the insolubility in cold acetone (0°C) of most phosphatides (particularly of acid phosphatides in salt forms), whereas neutral lipids are soluble. This procedure is well suited for lipids of animal and microbial origin, but is less effective in the presence of high proportions of neutral lipids like most lipids of plant origin (Kates 1975).

The techniques for separation of nonmiscible pairs of solvents (polar and non-polar) are also useful, especially for lipids rich in glycerides. As the first stage of the soil lipid fractionation, Stevenson (1982) recommended the separation of chloroform and an aqueous soda solution. The aqueous phase was then acidified and extracted with ether to recover the free fatty acids. The chloroform phase contains the other lipids which were then separated by chromatography.

Fractionations by Liquid Phase Chromatography

Many methods have been proposed. For preliminary fraction-ation of the total lipidic extract of the soil, Jambu et al. (1991, 1993) and Amblès et al. (1989, 1990) used the technique recommended by McCarthy and

Duthie (1962). Lipids were separated on columns of potassic silica (silicic acid treated with potash in isopropanol) in three fractions: neutral (the first elution with ethyl ether), acid (elution with 2% formic acid in ether solution) and polar. Zelles and Bai (1993) used a similar technique with SPE.

It was then possible to separate the neutral fraction of lipids on silica columns (Kiesselgel 60, Merck, Jambu et al. 1993) or Florisil treated or not with acid (Kates 1975). Elution was carried out initially by hexane or petroleum ether to separate hydrocarbons then by mixtures of increasing polarity to split the other classes of lipids. Mixtures with an increasing proportion of ethyl ether in petroleum ether were used most frequently enabling successive separation of esters (sterilic, methyl esters), ketones, triglycerides, diglycerides, monoglycerides, free alcohols and sterols.

Gas–Liquid Chromatography Techniques

These techniques are often used for fractionation, characterization and quantification of lipid components. They can be applied directly to certain fractions like hydrocarbons or after breakdown of the heavy lipidic compounds into fatty acids and unsaponifiable products (cf. "Fractionation of Fatty Acids and Unsaponifiables").

Fractionation of Fatty Acids and Unsaponifiables

Principle

A saponification reaction enables breakdown of heavy lipidic substances to obtain fatty acids, and other saponification products (like glycerol and sterols) with unsaponifiable compounds. The fatty acids are then methylated, separated, and quantified by Gas–Liquid Chromatography (GLC), the unsaponifiables are also titrated by GLC after silylation of the hydroxyl groups. The technique can be used for total lipidic extracts or for lipid groups that have already been separated as described in "Lipid Fractination" earlier.

Equipment and Reagents

– F1 flasks: 25 mL half cylindrical half conical borosilicate glass flasks, (volumetric flasks without graduation, cf. "Equipment and Reagents" earlier under Sect.13.2.5 and Fig. 13.4) with PTFE screw cap.
– F2 flasks: 25 mL half cylindrical half conical flasks with PTFE screw cap.
– F3 flasks: 10 mL half cylindrical half conical borosilicate glass flasks, (volumetric flask without graduation) with PTFE screw cap.

– F4: half cylindrical half conical borosilicate glass volumetric tubes with PTFE screw caps.
– Funnels with a diameter of 3 cm.
– Pasteur pipettes.
– 0.1 mg precision balance.
– Gas phase chromatograph with splitter or "split-splitless" injector for capillary column and detection by flame ionization detector.
– Anhydrous petroleum ether.
– Anhydrous methanol (stored on anhydrous sodium sulphate).
– 0.3 mol (NaOH) L^{-1} solution in methanol: dissolve 1.2 g of soda in 100 mL anhydrous methanol.
– 3% H_2SO_4 methanolic solution: add 3 mL of concentrated sulphuric acid in a 100 mL volumetric flask containing 70 mL anhydrous methanol, agitate and cool, adjust to 100 mL and stop well.
– 60% methanol in water.
– Anhydrous sodium sulphate.

Procedure

Saponification
– Add 4 mL of petroleum ether and 2 mL methanol in the 25 mL F1 flasks containing the free or bound lipidic extracts (cf. "Procedure" under Sect. 13.2.5), agitate for 1 h.
– Add 8 mL of 0.3 mol (NaOH) L^{-1} solution in methanol.
– Stop the flasks hermetically and heat at 100°C for 2h30 in a thermo-stated aluminium heating block (Fig. 13.2).
– Cool, open the flasks and add 60% methanol in such a way that the petroleum ether phase is in the upper cylindrical part of the flask.
– Using a Pasteur pipette, take the upper phase and decant it in a tared 25 mL conical F2 flask through a small funnel stopped with a glass wool plug and filled with a spatula of anhydrous sodium sulphate (Fig. 13.4).
– Add 3 mL of petroleum ether to the first F1 flask; stop and agitate well then remove the upper phase in the same way and add it to the previous phase through the same device; repeat this procedure four times. This phase contains unsaponifiables and saponification products other than fatty acids (F2).
– Acidify the first flask with 1 mL of concentrated hydrochloric acid diluted two times, then extract again with petroleum ether as previously described. Decant and collect the upper phase in a tared 10 mL F3 flask; this phase contains the fatty acids.

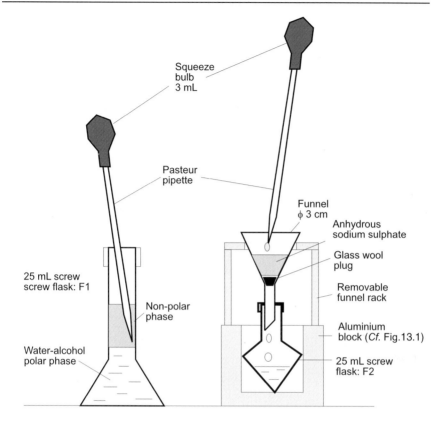

Fig. 13.4. Separation by decantation (*on the left*) and drying of the recovered products (*on the right*)

Non Fatty Acid Compounds
– Evaporate the contents of the F2 flask to dry under nitrogen flow or with a rotary evaporator.
– Stop and weigh the flask to obtain the total quantity.
– Add 100 µL of trimethylchlorosilane (TMCS), 300 µL of hexamethyl-disilane (HMDS) and 600 µL pyridine, stop and heat at 70°C for 5 h (Fig. 13.2).
– Inject 2 µL in the gas phase chromatograph under the following conditions:
    (a) CPWAX capillary column (or similar) length: 25 m, interior diameter: 0.3 mm, temperature 230°C,
    (b) carrier gas He 0.5 B,
    (c) split injector, leak flow 50 mL min^{-1}.

Fatty Acids

– Bring the contents of the 10 mL F3 flasks to dry and weigh to obtain total fatty acids.

–Add 3 mL of anhydrous 3% sulphuric acid in the methanol reagent; stop the flasks and heat at 70°C for 5 h (Fig. 13.2).

– Let cool and add 2 mL petroleum ether and approximately 3 mL water to recover the ether phase in the cylindrical part of the flask (Fig. 13.4).

– Recover the fatty acid methyl esters in 10 mL F4 tubes using the same procedure as for the non-fatty acid lipidic fraction, complete to 10 mL and inject 2 μL in GPC under the following conditions (short acids ≤ C20, Fig. 13.5):

(a) 25 m × 0.3 mm silica glass capillary column impregnated with CPWAX phase (or similar),

(b) He carrier gas, input pressure 0.6 B,

(c) Split injector 180°C, leak-flow 60 mL min^{-1},

(d) Temperature programme 180°C $\xrightarrow{\text{2°C min}^{-1}}$ 240°C,

(e) Flame ionisation detector, 240°C.

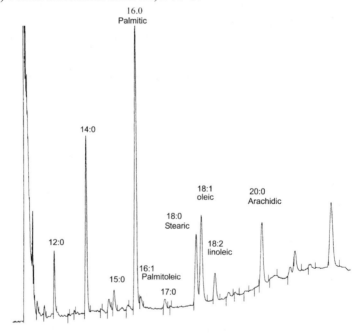

Fig. 13.5. Fractionation of methyl esters of short fatty acids of a tropical ferruginous soil from Burkina–Faso by gas chromatography (conditions described in the text; M Pansu, unpublished data)

Notes

- Some reagents are much faster than MeOH–H₂SO₄ making it possible to obtain fatty acid methyl esters instantaneously at room temperature (e.g. BF₃–CH₃OH or diazomethane); the reagent described in "Procedure" under Sect. 13.3.3 earlier was used because it is not expensive and the heating system is suitable for derivatization.
- For soils poor in fatty acids, the 10 mL volumetric half cylindrical half conical F4 tubes are very useful for the concentration of the mixture by solvent evaporation under nitrogen flow.
- The chromatographic column used to obtain separation of Fig. 13.5 is not suitable for the fractionation of long chain fatty acids of soil (C20–C34); for this purpose a shorter column or a different impregnation phase is required.
- The procedure described in "Equipments and Products" later can be simplified for the determination of fatty acids alone; use direct transmethylation on the lipidic fraction with the H₂SO₄–methanol reagent; extract the fatty acid methyl esters by decantation in petroleum ether after adding water (Fig. 13.4); however, this technique may complicate the reading of the chromatograms due to a risk of peaks of fatty acid methyl esters overlapping peaks of unsaponifiable compounds.

13.3.4 Measurement of Pesticide Residues and Pollutants

Principle

Like lipids, pesticides and pollutants are soluble in organic solvents. They can be extracted using similar techniques (cf. Sect. 13.2.5), although extraction with the Soxhlet apparatus is not recommended for pesticides. Indeed, the molecules are often degradable and prolonged boiling of the mixture of solvent and extracted products could lead to underestimation of the contents of residues.

Due to problems of degradability, the most commonly used methods use cold extraction in solvents, specially micro-methods (Steinwandter 1992) and methods using supercritical fluids (Richter 1992; Table 13.2). If the soil samples have to be stored before extraction, they should be frozen or freeze-dried.

After the extraction phase, if lipid content is high, purification may be necessary. Two techniques are available (a) separation using solvents of different polarities and (b) liquid chromatography on a Florisil or alumina column.

It is usually necessary to concentrate the soil extracts as much as possible to improve the limit of detection. It is useful to carry out the final concentration phase using a gaseous nitrogen flow on the surface of the extract in half cylindrical half conical volumetric tubes (cf. Sect. 13.3.3).

Table 13.2. Some supercritical fluid techniques used for the extraction of soil pesticide residues (Richter 1992)

pesticide	extraction conditions
permethrin, atrazine, deltamethrin, dieldrin, carbofuran, diuron, 2,4 D, methylparathion	Methanol 250 °C, 150 bars, 1 mL min^{-1}, 2 h
DDT	CO_2, 40 °C, 100 bars, 0.7 g s^{-1}, 10 min
DDT	CO_2 + 5% methanol or toluene, 40 or 100°C, 0.7 g s^{-1}, 5 min
lindane, aldrin, DDT	CO_2, 138 bars, 15 min
linuron, diuron	CO_2 + methanol, ethanol or acetonitrile, 75 to 120°C, 100–400 bars, 2.5–8.5 mL min^{-1}, 15–180 min
sulfonylurea	CO_2 + 2% methanol, 40°C, 223 bars, 6 mL min^{-1}, 2–15 min
simazine, atrazine, propazine, terbutylazin, cyanazine	CO_2 to 48°C, 230 bars, 1.7 mL min^{-1}, 30 min
organochlorides, organophosphorus	CO_2 100% and CO_2 + 10% methanol, 50–70°C, 150 or 300 bars, 25–60 min
DDT, DDE, DDD, lindane, aldrin	CO_2 + 5% acetone, 75°C, 400 bars, 60 min

The recommended choice for the analysis of the extract is gas chromatography because of (a) its good selectivity, particularly with capillary columns and (b) the large number of selective and very sensitive detectors that are available. The recommended injector for most non-volatile pesticides is a glass-needle injector which ensures the maximum possible concentration of the solutes during injection. Alternately split-splitless injector can be used. Other techniques are based on HPLC, generally with UV detection.

The diversity of the pesticides and pollutants present in the soil (cf. Sect. 13.1.4 later) has resulted in the development of a very large number of specific analytical procedures which cannot be exhaustively described here. Based on the literature and laboratory practice, a choice of procedures for the extraction, purification and chromatographic analysis of the main families of products is provided later. In the future, these procedures will change as a result of further advances in analytical chemistry and some of the recommendations later will need to be updated. For example, Gennaro et al. (1996) presented the simultaneous separation of phenoxyacetic acid, triazins and phenylureas herbicide residues in soils by HPLC. Celi et al. (1993) proposed a way of measuring fenoxatrop and ethyl fenoxatrop in a range of soils. Anon (1993) proposed a method for the simultaneous measurements of 27 herbicides in the soil using HPLC. Kiang and Grob (1986) proposed a method for simultaneous measurement of 49 soil pollutants by capillary gas chromatography.

Equipment and Products

– Back and forth shaker.
– Decanting funnels in borosilicate glass with ground Teflon stoppers: 50, 125, 250 mL.
– Columns for liquid chromatography, diameter: 1 cm, length: 50 cm, with a PTFE stopcock and a solvent tank.
– 10 mL half cylindrical half conical volumetric tubes.
– Rotary evaporator with 50, 125, 250 mL boiling flasks.
– Regulated aluminium heating block and system of evaporation under flow of nitrogen (Fig. 13.2). Alternatively, a centrifugal evaporator under vacuum, type: speed-vac, can be used.
– Gas phase chromatograph with several selective detectors (e.g. electron capture detector for halogenated compounds, thermoionic detector for organophosphorous compounds) and non-selective (e.g. flame ionization or mass spectrometry). The use of a glass needle injector is recommended, or failing that a split-splitless or on column injector (Pansu et al. 2001).
– HPLC with UV detector if required;
– Certified solvents, free from pesticides and pollutants. Each solvent should be tested by injection in the chromatograph after concentration by evaporation in the rotary evaporator (approximately 200 mL giving 1 mL). The most commonly used solvents are acetone, petroleum ether, hexane, ethyl ether, methanol, acetonitrile, dichloromethane, ethyl acetate.
– Different standard pesticides.
– Activated florisil (60–80 mesh particle size, 3% of water).
– Anhydrous sodium sulphate.
– Sodium chloride.

Extractions

Acid Herbicides

Jensen and Glass (1990) tested several techniques before recommending cold extraction with ethyl ether in acid medium. When well agitated for a rather long period, this technique is effective even for residues that have been incorporated in the soil for a year. A sufficient volume of water and acid have to be added to reduce the viscosity of the soil sample and ensure good contact with the ether phase. The authors advised three successive extractions with ether and one hour agitation each time.

Triazine Herbicides

Several different solvents can be used. For extractions in aqueous medium, a mixture of ethyl ether and petroleum ether (v/v) may be appropriate. For soils, we prefer a 1/5 mixture of methylene chloride and ethyl acetate. We recommend three successive extractions with a back and forth shaker on 20 g of sample with respectively, 100, 50 and 50 mL of solvent mixture.

Organochlorides

Wheeler and Thompson (1990) reviewed the large number of techniques used for the extraction of this type of compound. Methods used for soils are often based on those used in food analysis. A simple way is to agitate the soil sample (50 g) with acetone (100 mL) or an acetone-petroleum ether mixture on a back and forth shaker. With a wet sample, add anhydrous sodium sulphate as desiccant.

Organophosphorous

Freeze-drying is usually advised for the conservation of soil samples. Several solvents or mixtures of solvents have been used for standard extraction of organophosphorous compounds in the soil: acetone, acetone–water, dichloromethane, ethyl acetate, acetone–hexane, acetone–dichloromethane, methanol–water (Barcelo and Lawrence, 1992). These compounds can be extracted jointly with organochlorides (acetone, acetone–hexane), pyrethrinoids (acetone–hexane), and carbamates (acetone–dichloromethane).

Carbamates

Carbamates can be titrated with a rather complex technique of multi-residue analysis (Seiber 1990). The following method was tested by Pansu et al. (1981a) with an average extraction yield of 72 ± 8%. Prepare the soil samples by freeze-drying, sieve to 2 mm particle size and divide into sample specimens of 10 g each. Shake the sample specimen with 50 mL methanol and 50 mL water for 6 h on a back-and-forth shaker, add

100 µL of 1 mol (HCl) L^{-1} solution and filter under vacuum. Wash the residue with the extraction solution and add the washing solutions to the filtrate. Extract the filtrate three times in a 200 mL decanting funnel with respectively, 30, 20 and 20 mL chloroform.

Pyrethrinoids

In biological substrates, pyrethrinoids are extracted satisfactorily by two successive extractions with hexane in the presence of anhydrous sodium sulphate (Pansu et al. 1981b). For soils, a mixture of hexane with 3% acetone is more efficient.

Preparation of the Extracts for Chromatography

Principle

Most extracts have to be purified before chromatography to eliminate interference with other lipidic compounds in the soil. The use of detectors that are selective for the main families of products (such as organochlorides or organo-phosphorus) makes it possible to limit the number of purifications. However, some of these detectors (electron capture for example) are very sensitive to pollution and the extracts need to be purified so as not to perturb the sensitivity of the detector.

The extracts should be concentrated as much as possible to improve detection of ultra-trace residues. Extracts are usually concentrated in vacuum rotary evaporators during the first stage by micro-techniques such as gaseous nitrogen flow (Fig. 13.2) or a speed-vac centrifugal evaporator in the final stage. If too polar solvents are used for extraction (not easily eluted from chromatographic columns) or if they are incompatible with the detection system, the extract may have to be transferred into another solvent before injection. For example, if an electron capture detector is being used, chlorinated solvents have to be completely eliminated before injection. Except for volatile pesticides, this is accomplished by drying the extract several times, each time with dissolution in a non-halogenous solvent.

Finally, some polar compounds require derivatization reactions before injection into the chromatograph.

Acid Herbicides

Purification can be achieved by separation into solvents (Jensen and Glass 1990). The ether extracts (see "Acid Herbicides" in "Extractions" under Sect.13.3.4) are agitated with a sodium bicarbonate aqueous solution. In the aqueous solution, acid herbicides are transformed into salts, while the majority of the coloured organic compounds remain in the organic phase. This phase is eliminated, and the acid herbicides are re-extracted with ether after acidification of the aqueous phase and saturation by sodium chloride.

If gas chromatography is used for analysis, the extracts usually need to be methylated before injection, as acid herbicides are too polar. Several different reagents can be used in techniques similar to fatty acid methylation (cf. "Procedure" under Sect. 13.3.3 earlier). Diazomethane is a particularly effective methylation agent.

Triazines

The main lipids can be eliminated by acetonitrile-hexane partition. Concentrate the methylene chloride-ethyl acetate extracts to 2 mL (cf. "Triozine Herbicides"). Add 20 mL acetonitrile saturated with petroleum ether (AN). Add 10 mL petroleum ether saturated with acetonitrile (PE) and agitate. Recover the AN phase. Re-extract PE with 10 mL AN. Discard PE. Add all the AN phases in the decanting funnel, add 120 mL water and 10 mL of a NaCl saturated aqueous solution. Extract triazines twice with 50 mL of the ethyl ether/petroleum–ether v/v mixture. Mix the ether phases, dry on sodium sulphate and concentrate to the exact volume desired (2 mL for example) before injection.

Organochlorides

First the acetone extract must be transferred in a hexane phase. Put the acetone extract in a decanting funnel (cf. "Organochlorides" earlier in "Extractions" under Sect. 13.3.4) with four times its volume of water and 25 mL hexane. Swirl gently and decant the organic phase. Extract the aqueous phase again with 25 mL hexane, mix the hexanic extracts, dry on anhydrous sodium sulphate and concentrate to 5 or 10 mL.

Purify the extracts on a column filled with activated Florisil (3% water). Weigh 5 g of Florisil and place it in a column with a diameter of 1 cm stopped with a glass wool plug and partially filled with petroleum ether. Add 2–3 cm of anhydrous sodium sulphate, rinse with 50 mL hexane until the liquid comes to the top the sodium sulphate phase.

Deposit the hexanic extract on the column with a Pasteur pipette. Regulate the flow to approximately 15–20 drops per minute with the PTFE stopcock. When the level of the liquid comes to the top of the sodium sulphate phase, add a little hexane while rinsing with the pipette; repeat this procedure once. Elute with exactly the volume of hexane needed to obtain PCB, i.e. approximately 20–30 mL. This E1 eluate may also contain hexachlorobenzene (HCB) and dichlorodiphenylethane (DDE), one of the breakdown products of DDT. The exact quantity of solvent for the E1 eluate must first be determined under the same conditions with standard mixtures. For PCB, these standards are made of sets of products providing typical chromatograms (e.g. dp5 and dp6 mixtures).

After collection of the E1 eluate, elution should be continued with the 10% of dichloromethane in the petroleum ether (or hexane) mixture until a sufficient volume has been obtained for collection of the other organo-chlorinated compounds (E2 eluate). The exact volume of E2 should first be determined with one or more standard compounds, dieldrin for example.

The E2 eluate has to be removed from the dichloromethane. Bring just to dry in a rotary evaporator. Add a little petroleum ether and bring just to dry again. Repeat this operation four or five times. Bring the E1 and E2 eluates to the exact volume of hexane chosen for chromatographic titration.

Organophosphorous

First the acetone extract has to be transferred in a hexanic phase. Place the extract in a decanting funnel (cf. "Organophosphorous" earlier in "Extractions" under Sec. 13.3.4) with four times its volume of water and 25 mL methylene chloride. Swirl gently and decant the organic phase. Extract again with 25 mL methylene chloride, mix the extracts, dry them on anhydrous sodium sulphate and evaporate just to dry in a rotary evaporator. Add a little petroleum ether and bring just to dry again. Repeat this procedure three times. Rinse several times with 10 mL total volume of hexane at 10% of acetone, mix the rinsing solutions, stop and store for chromatographic determination.

Carbamates

Chloroformic extracts (cf. "Carbamates" earlier in "Extractions" under Sect. 13.3.4) can be purified in the following way. Evaporate to dry, recover in 10 mL methanol + 10 mL 0.1 mol (HCl) L^{-1} solution, cool 15 min, filter the suspended matter and wash the filter with a v/v mixture of water and 0.1 mol (HCl) L^{-1} solution. Extract the filtrate three times with 25 mL chloroform, dry the extracts on anhydrous sodium sulphate and transfer in a 100 mL round bottom boiling flask. To eliminate the chloroform, evaporate just to dry on the rotary evaporator, add a little methanol and again evaporate just to dry, repeat this procedure three times. Finally transfer in exactly 10 mL methanol in half cylindrical half conical volumetric tubes with screw caps, washing several times the boiling flask with a few mL of methanol. If the injection in the chromatograph cannot be carried out immediately, store at −20°C. To improve the detection limit the extract can be concentrated in the tubes under nitrogen flow at 40°C (Fig. 13.2).

Note: Some carbamates can also be transformed into glycosides by plants. During extraction (See "Carbamates" in "Extractions" under Sect. 13.3.4) these forms are not found in the chloroformic fraction, but remain in the hydro-alcoholic fraction. To identify them, it is necessary to break the glycoside bonds by reflux boiling saponification and to re-extract with chloroform (Pansu et al. 1981a).

Pyrethrinoids

The extracts of "Pyrethrinoids" in "Extractions" under Sec. 13.3.4 should be purified before being injected in a chromatograph equipped with an electron capture detector. Purification is carried out on chromatographic columns (diameter 1 cm) filled with 5 g Florisil at 3% of water and 2 g of anhydrous sodium sulphate.

Two different procedures are used for extracts that contain fat substances and extracts that do not (Pansu et al. 1981b). In the absence of lipids, pyrethrinoids are recovered by elution with 70 mL of a mixture of 10% ethyl ether in petroleum ether. In the presence of lipids, preliminary elution with approximately 110 mL hexane enables elimination of the lipids before pyrethrinoid elution as previously described. The exact volumes of the eluting solutions must first be determined by tests with standard pyrethrinoids (decamethrin) and by gravimetry of the eluted fat substances. Bring the eluate containing the pyrethrinoids just to dry and dissolve again in exactly 10 mL hexane in a half cylindrical half conical volumetric tube with a PTFE screw cap for chromatographic determination. To improve detection, the extracts can subsequently be concentrated in the tubes.

Chromatographic Determination

A large range of columns and chromatographic conditions are suitable for the determination of pesticides and pollutants, among which the techniques later are worth mentioning.

Acid Herbicides

The measurement of acid herbicides by GPC requires prelimin-ary methylation of the acid functions (cf. "Fractionation of Fatty Acids and Unsaponifiable" earlier). For the separation of methylated esters of 2,4D and 2,4,5T, use a column 1.5 m in length with an interior diameter of 4 mm filled with a 5% OV225 phase on a chromosorbW support of 100–120 mesh particle size at an isothermal temperature of 220°C, with a electron capture detector. Acid herbicides can also be measured by liquid chromatography.

Triazines

Atrazine and simazine can be measured by GPC under similar conditions to those described earlier for acid herbicides but using a thermionic detector. For simultaneous measurement of all nitrogenized herbicides, it is preferable to use a capillary column such as PTE5 30 m × 0.25 mm ID (Supelco), with a temperature programme of 40°C (5 min) to 100 °C (30°C min^{-1}) then to 275°C (5°C min^{-1}).

Organochlorides

For measurement of the residues, the best sensitivity is obtained with GPC on an electron capture detector. Different types of impregnation phases can be used for the columns, e.g. SE30, OV1, or OV225.

For fractionation of the many PCB peaks, a silica glass capillary column of the SPB-octyl type (Supelco) is recommended, 60 or 30 m in length depending on the temperature programme, with an interior diameter of 0.25 mm and with a 0.25 μm SPB-octyl film.

For chlorinated pesticides, use a capillary column of the SPB-5 type, length: 15 m, interior diameter: 0.20 mm, with a 0.20 μm Supelco film and a temperature programme of 120–290°C.

Organophosphorous Pesticides

Organophosphorous pesticides are usually measured by GPC with a thermionic detector or possibly by mass spectrometry. Different columns have been recommended for organochlorinated compounds. A capillary column of the PTE-5 type, length: 30 m, interior diameter: 0.25 mm, with a 0.25 μm Supelco film is recommended for the fractionation of a mixture of nine organophosphorus pesticides, with a temperature programme of 50–300°C.

Carbamates and Urea Derived Pesticides

Carbamates and urea derived pesticides can be fractionated by high pressure liquid chromatography with a Supelcosil LC-8 column, length: 15 cm, interior diameter: 4.6 mm, particles of 5 μm (Supelco) with an acetonitrile water gradient of 18–65% in 9 min, flow 2 mL min^{-1}, temperature 40°C and UV detection at 240 nm.

Another technique enables measurement of all N-methyl carbamates by GPC in only one peak (Pansu et al. 1981a). The injected mixture is transmethylated in situ at the top of the chromatographic column and the peak of the resulting O-methyl N-methyl carbamates is quantified at the exit of the column. The conditions are as follows: a thermionic detector, a Pyrex column, length: 1.4 m, interior diameter: 2 mm, filled with chromosorb 101 (80–100 mesh) on 1.3 m and with Volaspher A2 (80–100 Mesh, transmethylation catalyst) on the last 10 cm near the injector, carrier gas N$_2$ at 30 mL min^{-1}. Inject 2 μL of the mixture: 950 μL of the methanolic extract (see Carbamates) + 50 μL of a 0.2 mol (NaOH) L^{-1} methanol solution prepared just before injection.

Pyrethrinoids

These rather heavy and unstable products can nevertheless be measured by electron capture GLC using short columns and strong carrier gas flows to minimize decomposition (Pansu et al. 1981b). For the simultaneous titration of permethrine and decamethrine, use a column 80 cm in length with an interior diameter of 4 mm filled with 3% SE30 on a chromosorb W, 80–100 Mesh, with a column temperature of 215°C, using nitrogen as carrier gas at a flow of 85 mL min^{-1}.

References

Soil carbohydrates

Angers DA, Nadeau P and Mehuys GR (1988) Determination of carbohydrate composition of soil hydrolysates by high-performance liquid chromatography. *J. Chromatogr.*, 454, 444–449

Arshad and Schnitzer (1987) Characteristics of the organic matter in a slightly and in a severely crusted soil. *Pflanzenernahr Bodenk.*, 150, 412–416

Bachelier G (1966) Les sucres dans les sols et leur dosage global. *Cah. ORSTOM Ser. Pedol.*, 4, 9–22

Bagautdinov FY, Khaziyev FK and Shcherbukhin VD (1984) Polysaccharide fraction of humic substances from a typical chernozem and a gray forest soil. *Soviet Soil Sci.*, 16, 37–42

Baldock JA, Kay BD and Schnitzer M (1987) Influence of cropping treatments on the monosaccharide content of the hydrolysates of a soil and its aggregate fractions. *Can. J. Soil Sci.*, 67, 489–499

Barriuso E, Andreux F and Portal JM (1985) Etude de la répartition des glucides associés aux constituants humiques dans un sol humifère de montagne. *C.R. Acad. Sci. Paris*, 300, II, 16, 827–830

Benzing-Purdie LM and Nikiforuk JH (1989) Carbohydrate composition of hay and maize soils and their possible importance in soil structure. *J. Soil Sci.*, 40, 125–130

Bernal JL, Del Nozal MJ, Toribio L and Del Alamo M (1996) HPLC analysis of carbohydrates in wines and instant coffees using anion exchange chromatography coupled to pulsed amperometric detection. *J. Agric. Food Chem.*, 44, 507–511

Blakeney AB, Harris PJ, Henry RJ and Stone BA (1983) A simple and rapid preparation of alditol acetates monosaccharide analysis. *Carbohydrate Res.*, 113, 291–299

Brink RH, Dubach P and Lynch DL (1960) Measurement of carbohydrates in soil hydrolysates with anthrone. *Soil Sci.*, 89, 157–166

Cheshire MV and Anderson G (1975) Soil polysaccharides and carbohydrate phosphates. *Soil Sci.*, 119, 356–362

Cheshire MV and Griffiths BS (1989) The influence of earthworms and cranely larvae on the decomposition of uniformly ^{14}C labelled plant material in soil. *J. Soil Sci.*, 40, 117–124

Cheshire, M.V., C.M. Mundie, and H. Shepherd. 1969. Transformation of ^{14}C glucose and starch in soil. Soil Biol. Biochem. 1:117–130.

Cheshire MV and Mundie CM (1966) The hydrolytic extraction of carbohydrates from soil by sulfuric acid. *J. Soil Sci.*, 17, 372–381

Cheshire, M.V., C.M. Mundie, J.M. Bracewell, G.W. Robertson, J.D. Russell, and A.R. Fraser. 1983. The extraction and characterization of soil polysaccharide by whole soil methylation. J. Soil Sci., 34:539–554.

Cheshire MV (1979) *Nature and origin of carbohydrates in soils.*, Academic London, 216 p

Coelho RRR, Linhares LF and Martin JP (1988) Sugars in hydrolysates of fungal melanins and soil humic acids. *Plant Soils*, 106, 127–133

Cowie GL and Hedges JI (1984) Determination of neutral sugars in plankton, sediments and wood by capillary gas chromatography of equilibrated isomeric mixtures. *Anal. Chem.*, 56, 497–504

Dormaar JF (1984) Monosaccharides in hydrolysates of water-stable aggregates after 67 years of cropping to spring wheat as determined by capillary gas chromatography. *Can. J. Soil Sci.*, 64, 647–656

Doutre DA, Hay GW, Hood A and van Loon GW (1978) Spectrophotometric methods to determine carbohydrates in soil. *Soil Biol. Biochem.*, 10, 457–462

Dubois, M., K.A. Gilles, J.K. Hamilton, P.A. Rebers, and F. Smith. 1956. Colorimetric Method for Determination of Sugars and Related Substances. Analytical Chemistry 28:350–356.

Folsom BL, Wagner GH and Scrivner CL (1974) Comparison of soil carbohydrate in several prairie and forest soils by gas–liquid chromatography. *Soil Sci. Soc. Amer. Proc.*, 38, 305–309

Feller, C., C. François, G. Villemin, J.M. Portal, F. Toutain, and J.L. Morel. 1991. Nature des matières organiques associées aux fractions argileuses d'un sol ferrallitique. C.R. Acad. Sci. Paris 312:1491–1497.

François C (1988) Les sucres neutres in "*Devenir à court terme de différentes formes de l'azote dans un ferrisol*"., Doctorat de l'université de Nancy I, 67–75

Guckert A, Cure B and Jacquin F (1971) Comparative evolution of the polysaccharides of the humin after incubation of glucose ^{14}C and straw [14]C. *Trans. Intern. Symposium "humus et plante V"*-Prague, 155–160

Guckert (1973) *Contribution à l'étude des polysaccharides dans les sols et de leur rôle dans les mécanismes d'agrégation.*, Thèse doct. d'état, Univ. Nancy I, 124 p.

Gupta UC and Sowden FJ (1965) Studies on methods for the determination of sugars and uronic acids in soils. *Can. J. Soil Sci.*, 45, 237–240

Gupta UC (1967) Carbohydrates. In *Soil Biochemistry* McLaren et Peterson ed., Marcel Dekker, New York, 91–118

Hamada R and Ono A (1984) Determination of carbohydrates in hydrolysates of volcanic ash soil by liquid chromatography with fluorescence spectroscopy, *Soil Sci. Plant Nutr.*, 30, 145–150

Ivarson KC and Sowden FJ (1962) Methods for the analysis of carbohydrate material in soil, *Soil Sci.*, 94, 245–250

Larre-Larrouy MC and Feller C (1997) Determination of carbohydrates in two ferrallitic soils: analysis by capillary gas chromatography after derivatization by silylation. *Soil Biol. Biochem.*, 29, 1585–1589

Larré-Larrouy, M.C., A. Albrecht, E. Blanchart, T. Chevallier, and C. Feller. 2003. Carbon and monosaccharides of a tropical Vertisol under pasture and market-gardening: distribution in primary organomineral separates. Geoderma 117, 63–79.

Martens DA and Frankenberger WT (1990) Determination of saccharides by high performance anion exchange chromatography with pulsed amperometric detection. *Chromatographia*, 29, 7–12

McGrath D (1973) Sugars and uronic acids in irish soils. *Geoderma*, 10, 227–235

Morgenlie S (1975) Analysis of mixtures of the common aldoses by gas chromatography-mass spectrometry of their O-isopropylidene derivatives. Carbohydrate Research, 41, 285–289

Murayama S (1983) Changes in the monosaccharide composition during the decomposition of straws under field conditions. *Soil Sci. Plant Nutr.*, 30, 367–381

Murayama S (1984) Decomposition kinetics of straw saccharides and synthesis of microbial saccharides under field conditions. *J. Soil Sci.*, 35, 231–242

Murayama S (1988) Microbial synthesis of saccharides in soils incubated with ^{13}C labelled glucose. *Soil Biol. Biochem.*, 20, 193–199

Oades JM (1967) Gas-liquid chromatography of alditol acetates and its application to the analysis of sugars in complex hydrolysates. *J. Chromatogr.*, 28, 246–252

Oades JM (1974) Synthesis of polysaccharides in soil by microorganisms. *Trans. Intern. Congr. Soil Sci. 10th- Moscow*, 93–100

Oades JM, Kirkman MA and Wagner GH (1970) The use of gas-liquid chromatography for the determination of sugars extracted from soils by sulfuric acid. *Soil Sci. Soc. Am. Proc.*, 34, 230–235

Pansu, M (1992) Les sucres neutres dans les sols : opportunité et tentatives d'amélioration. de leur détermination. Document IRD (ex-Orstom) Montpellier, 24 p.

Pluijmen MHM (1987) Sugar analysis with the Shaffer-Somogyi micro-analysis, High Performance Liquid Chromatography and enzymatic analysis in crop samples. *Commun. Soil Sci. Plant Anal.*, 18, 1049–1059

Reim RE and van Effen RM (1986) Determination of carbohydrates by liquid chromatography with oxidation at a nickel(III) oxide electrode. *Anal. Chem.*, 58, 3203–3207

Singhal and Sharma (1985) Status of carbohydrates in the acid hydrolysates of soils and humic acids of Dehra dun forests (Uttar Pradesh). *Proc. Indian ntn. Sci. Acad.*, B51, 3, 348–352

Spiteller M (1980) Kapillargaschromatographische bestimmung von zuckern unterschiedlicher boden. *Z. Pflanzenernaehr. Bodenkd.*, 143, 720–729

Stevenson FJ (1982) Soil carbohydrates. In *Humus chemistry*, Wiley New York, 147–171

Thomas and Lynch, (1961) A method for the quantitative estimation of pentoses in soil. *Soil Sci.*, (1961), 91, 312–316

Tracey MV (1950) A colorimetric method for the determination of pentoses in the presence of hexoses and uronic acids. *Biochem. J.*, 47, 433–436

Traitler H, Del Vedovo S and Schweizer TF (1984) Gas chromatographic separation of sugars by on-column injection on glass capillary columns. *J. High Resol. Chromatog. Chromatogr. Commun.*, 7, 558–562

Soil lipids

Wang TSC, Yu-Cheng Liang and Wey-Chiang Shen (1969) Method of extraction and analysis of higher fatty acids and triglycerides in soils. *Soil Sci.*, 107, 181–187

Fahd-Rachid A (1993) *Effet à long terme d'apports continus de déchets urbains sur les caractéristiques du sol. Conséquences sur les propriétés de la matière organique en relation avec sa teneur en lipides.*, Thèse Doctorat Sciences agronomiques, INRA-Bordeaux, 151 p

Ambles A, Jambu P and Ntsikoussalabongui B (1989) Evolution des lipides naturels d'un podzol forestier induite par l'apport d'engrais minéraux : hydrocarbures, cétones, alcools. *Science du Sol.*, 27, 201–214

Ambles A, Jambu P and Ntsikoussalabongui B (1990) Evolution des acides gras d'un podzol forestier induite par l'apport d'engrais minéraux. *Science du Sol.*, 28, 27–42

Jambu P, Fustec E and Jacquesy R (1978) Les lipides des sols : nature, origine, évolution, propriétés. *Science du Sol.*, 4, 229–240

Jambu P, Bilong P, Ambles A, Ntsikoussalabongui B and Fustec E (1987) Influence d'apports minéraux sur l'évolution des lipides naturels des sols acides. *Science du sol.*, 25, 161–172

Jambu, P., A. Amblés, H. Dinel, and B. Secouet. 1991. Incorporation of natural hydrocarbons from plant residues into an hydromorphic humic podzol following afforestation and fertilization. *Journal of Soil Science* 42:629–636

Jambu, P., A. Amblés, J.C. Jacquesy, B. Secouet, and E. Parlanti. 1993. Incorporation of natural alcohols from plant residues into a hydromorphic forest-podzol. *Journal of Soil Science* 44:135–146

McCarthy RD and Duthie AH (1962) A rapid quantitative method for the separation of free fatty acids from other lipids. *J. Lipid Res.*, 3, 117–119

Stevenson FJ (1966) Lipids in soils. *J. Am. Oil Chemists Soc.*, 43, 203–210

Stevenson FJ (1982) Soil lipids. In *Humus Chemistry.*, Wiley, 172–194

Kates M (1975) Techniques of lipidology. In *Laboratory Techniques in Biochemistry and Molecular Biology*, Work TS and Work E ed. Elsevier Amsterdam, 269–610

Zelles, L., and Q.Y. Bai. 1993. Fractionation of fatty acids derived from soil lipids by solid phase extraction and their quantitative analysis by GC-MS. *Soil Biology Biochemistry* 25:495–507

Aqueous extract

Leinweber P, Schulten HR and Körschens M (1995) Hot water extracted organic matter : chemical composition and temporal variations in a long-term field experiment. *Biol. Fertil. Soils*, 20, 17–23

Kouakoua E, Sala GH, Barthès B, Larre-Larrouy MC, Albrecht A and Feller C (1997) La matière organique soluble à l'eau chaude et la stabilité de l'agrégation. Aspects méthodologiques et application à des sols ferrallitiques du Congo. *Eur. J. Soil Sci.*, 48, 239–247

Küsel K and Drake HL (1999) Microbial turnover of low molecular weight organic acids during leaf litter decomposition. *Soil Biol. Biochem.*, 31, 107–118

Pesticides and pollutants

Anon (1993) Determination of herbicides in soils by HPLC with UV-Detection. *Agrobiological Res.*, 46, 155–174

Barcelo D and Lawrence JF (1992) Residue analysis of organophosphorus pesticides. In *Emerging strategies for pesticide analysis*, Cairns T and Sherma J ed. CRC, 127–149

Calvet R, Barriuso E, Bedos C, Benoit P, Charnay MP and Coquet Y (2005) Les pesticides dans le sol – Conséquences agronomiques et environnementales. Edition France Agricole, Paris, 637 p

Celi L, Nègre M and Gennari M (1993) HPLC determination of fenoxatrop and fenoxatrop-ethy in different soils. *Pestic. Sci.*, 38, 43–47

Gennaro MC, Giacosa D, Baglieto C, Gennari M and Negre M (1996) Simultaneous separation of phenylurea-, triazine-, and phenoxyacid herbicides by reverse phase ion-interaction HPLC. Application to soil analysis. *J. Liq. Chrom. Rel. Technol.*, 196, 911–924

Jensen DJ and Glass RD (1990) Analysis for residues of acidic herbicides. In *Analysis of Pesticide Residues*, Moye HA ed. Krieger, 223–261

Kiang PH and Grob RL (1986) Developpement of a screening method for the determination of 49 priority pollutants in soil. *J. Environ. Sci. Health*, A21, 15–53

Pansu M, Gautheyrou J and Loyer JY (2001) *Soil Analysis – Sampling, Instrumentation and Quality Control.*, Balkema, Lisse, Abington, Exton, Tokyo, 489 pp

Pansu M, Al Salti MN, Aubert H and Gry J (1981a) Contribution à l'étude de l'activité systémique du carbofuran au moyen de la chromatographie en phase gazeuse. *Phytiatrie-Phytopharmacie*, 30, 203–214

Pansu M, Dhouibi MH and Pinta M (1981b) Détermination des traces de pyréthrinoïdes (bioperméthrine et décaméthrine) dans les substrats biologiques par chromatographie en phase gazeuse. *Analusis*, 9, 55–59

Richter BE (1992) Supercritical fluid extraction methods. In *Emerging Strategies for Pesticide Analysis*, Cairns T and Sherma J ed. CRC, 51–68

Seiber JN (1990) Carbamate insecticide residue analysis by gas–liquid chromatography. In *Analysis of Pesticide Residues*, Moye HA ed. Krieger, 333–378

Steinwandter H (1992) Development of microextraction methods in residue analysis. In *Emerging Strategies for Pesticide Analysis*, Cairns T and Sherma J ed. CRC, 3–38

Wheeler WB and Thompson NP (1990) Analysis of chlorinated hydrocarbons. In *Analysis of Pesticide Residues*, Moye HA ed. Krieger, 199–222

Organic Forms of Nitrogen, Mineralizable Nitrogen (and Carbon)

14.1 Introduction

14.1.1 The Nitrogen Cycle

Following his own studies and those of Cavendish on "mephitic air" or atmospheric "mofette", Lavoisier (1789) discovered gaseous nitrogen and gave it the French name "azote", meaning lifeless. Based on the relative chemical stability of the N_2 molecule, this name is still plausible from a geochemical point of view (Table 14.1), as the nitrogen of the biosphere represents a very small quantity compared to atmospheric nitrogen and a negligible quantity compared to the total nitrogen of the planet.

Table 14.1. Geochemical distribution of nitrogen according to Stevenson (1982c)

Localization	weight N (tons)
Lithosphere	$1{,}636 \times 10^{14}$
Atmosphere	38.6×10^{14}
Biosphere	0.0028×10^{14}
soil organic matter	0.0022×10^{14}
NH_4^+-N of clays	0.0002×10^{14}

However, for the physiologist or the agronomist, nitrogen is one of the main sources of life along with carbon, hydrogen and oxygen; life appeared on earth with the synthesis of the first amino acids.

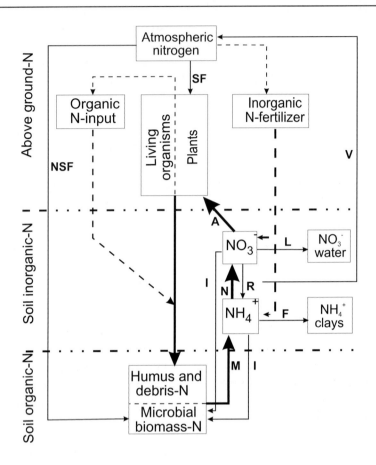

Fig. 14.1. Scheme of the nitrogen cycle: - - dotted lines enthropogenic incidence; solid lines = natural cycle; — bold lines main natural cycle in well-aerated media. A, assimilation by plants; M, mineralization of soil organic matter in ammonium; N, nitrification of ammonium; R, reduction of nitrates; I, microbial immobilization of inorganic nitrogen; V, volatization during nitrification and denitrification processes; F, ammonium fixation in the clay layers; L, leaching of nitrates; SF, symbiotic plant fixation of atmospheric nitrogen; NSF, nonsymbiotic fixation by soil microbial biomass

At the beginning of the cycle, nitrogen in living organisms originates mainly from the assimilation of N-inorganic forms by plant roots (cf. Chap. 28), primarily $N-NO_3$, in well-aerated soil. Given that nitrates represent only a very small nitrogen fraction, and that more than 90% of soil nitrogen is in organic forms (Stevenson 1982b), the interest of studying the nitrogen cycle is obvious. Figure 14.1 shows the origin of nitrates: some contributions come from outside sources, but most is soil organic N. Irrespective of whether it is made up of (1) unbroken organic fragments (cf. Chap. 9), (2) humified molecules (cf. Chaps. 11 and 12) or (3) living soil organisms, part of this nitrogen is mineralized into ammonium. Ammonium is then immobilized by micro-organisms or transformed into nitrites under the action of other micro-organisms, oxidized to nitrates, or lost as N_2O or other gaseous forms.

A precise knowledge of the soil organic nitrogen reserves is thus very useful to study ammonium and nitrate availability and plant growth. Measurements of total organic nitrogen (cf. Chap. 10) or of the supply of inorganic nitrogen during cultivation (cf. Chap. 28) are used by agronomists to estimate the quantity of fertilizer required (Dahnke and Johnson 1990). However, these two indices are not really representative of the real nitrogen cycle but are only rough approximations:
– At a given time, the quantity of nitrate or ammonium present in a soil does not include inorganic N forms, which can be produced by mineralization or be consumed by reorganization, reduction, denitrification.
– There are very great differences in stability between the substances that comprise available organic nitrogen (Schulten and Schnitzer 1998; Schipper et al., 2004); the processes of mineralization effects only a small fraction of this supply which thus has to be determined.
– Most humification processes require the consumption of inorganic nitrogen, which thus becomes temporarily unavailable for plants.
– The economic and ecological risks resulting from unreasonable use of nitrogen amendments (and resulting in leaching of nitrates and water pollution, N volatilization and possible in an increase in greenhouse gases, and in the fixation of ammonium in clays) are convincing arguments in favour of analyses that enable a better knowledge of the nitrogen cycle and particularly of the forms of organic nitrogen that represent the biggest potential reserve in the soils for plant uptake (Matsumoto et al. 2002).

14.1.2 Types of Methods

The problems listed above have generated many studies on soil organic nitrogen and these can be classified in two main groups:
– Studies of the forms of organic nitrogen: e.g. Bremner (1965), Jocteur Monrozier and Andreux (1981), Jocteur Monrozier (1984), Kelley and Stevenson (1995), Stevenson (1982a, b, c, 1996).

– Studies with the more immediate agronomic objective of understanding nitrogen supplied by the soil i.e. potentially available nitrogen (e.g. Keeney and Bremner 1966; Cornforth and Walmsley 1971; Juma and Paul 1984; Gianello and Bremner 1986, Catroux et al. 1987, Giroux and Sen Tran 1987; Cabrera and Kissel 1988) and the kinetics of C and N mineralization.

The first group of studies usually analyses the forms of nitrogen in solution after hydrolysis has broken down the large organic molecules. The most recent analyses of these forms of nitrogen are presented in this chapter along with analysis of urea, a specific form of nitrogen.

The second group of studies uses two types of approach to determine soil nitrogen availability indices:

– A biological approach to estimate inorganic nitrogen produced by incubation in controlled conditions.

– Techniques for chemical extraction.

The techniques described in this chapter include extraction by electro-ultrafiltration (EUF) and techniques for the characterization of the forms of nitrogen in acid hydrolysates. Isotopic techniques using ^{15}N tracer are also powerful tools for the study of nitrogen transfer between organic and inorganic compartments (Guiraud 1984; Chotte 1986; Pansu et al., 1998). The methods described later can be combined with measurement of ^{15}N nitrogen.

14.2. Classical Methods

14.2.1 Forms of Organic Nitrogen Released by Acid Hydrolysis

Principle

The method of reference comes from Bremner (1965) and was further recommended by Stevenson (1982a, 1996). It results from adaptations of much older techniques for the characterization of protein by hydrolysis (Van Slyke, 1911–1912).

According to Bremner, 60–80% of total nitrogen from the soil surface is solubilized by the treatment used for acid hydrolysis of proteins. Stevenson (1982b) stated that between 25 and 35% of nitrogen is not solubilized by acid attack. According to Stevenson, this nitrogen does not result from the known artefact of condensation between amino acids and reducing sugars, but is a structural component of humic substances. An additional fraction can be extracted by diluted bases then solubilized by acid hydrolysis (Griffith et al. 1976). Pretreatments with hydrofluoric acid (cf. Sect. 14.3.1) also improve solubilization of nitrogen.

The proteinic character of soil organic nitrogen is in agreement with the fact that most hydrolyzed nitrogen is found in the form of amino acids: 20–40% according to Bremner (1965), 30–45% according to Stevenson (1982b).

This method of attack also provides 20–35% of total soil nitrogen (Stevenson, 1982b) in ammoniacal form (in a quantity similar to amino acids). This ammonia comes from different sources: degradation of amid forms of proteins, total or partial destruction of certain amino acids (such as tryptophan, serine, threonine), partial destruction of hexosamines, and release of ammonium fixed by clays.

The nitrogen in amino sugars represents between 5 and 10% of soil nitrogen. Lastly, 10–20% of soil nitrogen is in unknown form, i.e. is not included in the forms quoted above (Stevenson 1982b).

The hydrolysis conditions recommended below are those adopted by Bremner (1965) and subsequently by Stevenson (1982a). Other possible alternatives are discussed in Sect. 14.3.1.

The method developed by Bremner to estimate the different forms of nitrogen in hydrolysates includes fractionation by steam distillation of the free ammonium, hexosamines, and amino acids (Table 14.2). Although perhaps less precise and less selective than spectrometric and chromato-graphic methods (cf. Sect. 14.3.2), the steam distillation technique has the advantage of simplicity. The same distillation equipment (Fig. 14.3) can be used to measure all the fractions. The same equipment can also be used for the analysis of total nitrogen (cf. Chap. 10) and of the inorganic forms of nitrogen in the case of sufficiently nitrogen-rich soils (cf. Chap. 28). In addition, this technique has the advantage of providing each fraction in the form of an ammoniacal distillate, which is ideal for all studies using ^{15}N labelled nitrogen since the measurement of this isotope can be performed on molecular gas nitrogen obtained by oxidation of an ammoniacal form of nitrogen.

The determination of the (NH$_3$+amino sugars)-N fraction in hydro-lysates is based on the fact that (1) glucosamine and galactosamine are quickly broken down in alkaline medium giving ammonium and (2) hexosamines can be estimated from the ammonium released when hexosamines are steam distilled with a phosphate–borate buffer at pH 11.2 (Tracey, 1952).

Table 14.2. Methods of steam distillation to measure the different forms of nitrogen in soil hydrolysates and the percentage of each form as a function of total soil nitrogen (after Bremner 1965, Keeney and Bremner 1967 and Stevenson 1982a,b)

N form	Method	% soil-N
ammonia-N	steam distillation with MgO	20–35
Amino sugar-N	steam distillation with phosphate–borate buffer at pH 11.2 and deduction of ammonia-N	5–10
Amino acid-N	steam distillation with phosphate–borate buffer after treatment with NaOH at 100°C to decompose hexosamines and eliminate ammonium then with ninhydrin (pH 2.5; 100°C) to convert α-amino-N to NH_3-N	30–45
(serine+threonine)-N	steam distillation with phosphate–borate buffer after removal of (ammonium+hexosamine)-N forms by steam distillation with the same buffer and treatments with periodate to convert (serine+threonine)-N to NH_3-N and with *meta*-arsenite to Reduce the excess of periodate	
(ammonia+amino sugar+amino acid)-N	steam distillation with buffer phosphate–borate after treatment with ninhydrin (pH 2.5 ; 100°C) to convert α-amino-N to NH_3-N	
(total hydrolyzable)-N	steam distillation with NaOH after Kjeldahl digestion with the mixture H_2SO_4–K_2SO_4-catalyst	65–80
unknown hydrolysable-N	total hydrolysable-N (NH_3-N + amino-N) Sugars+αamino acids-N+(serine+ threonine)-N	10–20

The measurement of ammoniacal NH_3-N forms is based on the observation of Bremner (1960): the interference of hexosamines and other not very stable forms in the measurement of ammonium by distillation in alkaline medium can be eliminated if steam distillation is performed with a small quantity of MgO and a very short distillation time.

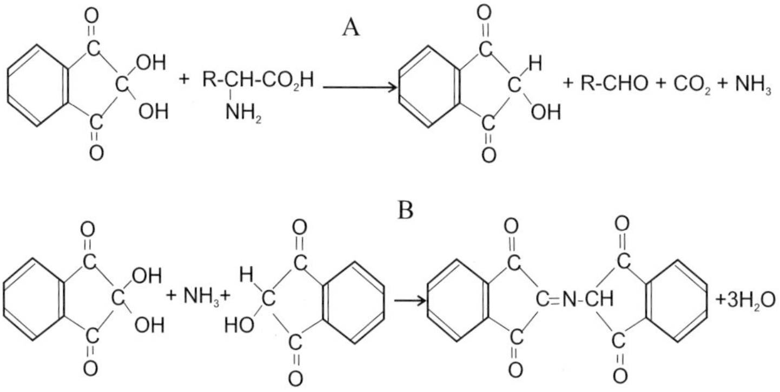

Fig. 14.2. Reaction of α-amino acids with ninhydrin. At pH 2.5, NH_3 is a stable reaction product (reaction A); when the reaction is brought to pH 5, the ammonium released by reaction A combines with the reduced and oxidized forms of ninhydrin (reaction B) to give a blue coloured compound (Bremner 1965; Stevenson 1982a)

The method for the measurement of α-amino acid forms is based on that of ammonia released by oxidation with ninhydrin (Fig. 14.2). It was developed after the discovery (Bremner 1960) that the reaction of condensation B (Fig. 14.2) leading to the trapping of released ammonia (reaction A) in a coloured compound does not occur at pH 2.5. Titration of α-amino acids can thus be carried out by a ninhydrin treatment at pH 2.5 followed by steam distillation of the reaction products in the presence of the phosphate–borate buffer at pH 11.2.

The specific method for nitrogen of serine and threonine is based on the property of compounds containing amino and hydroxyl groups on adjacent atoms to be oxidized by the periodate, resulting in ammonia:

$$R_1\text{–CH(OH)–CH(NH}_2\text{)–R}_2 + NaIO_4 \rightarrow R_1CHO + R_2CHO + NH_3 + NaIO_3$$

Interference with the (ammonium+hexosamine)-N forms can be eliminated by preliminary distillation with phosphate–borate buffer at pH 11.2. The ammonium released by oxidation with periodate is then determined by steam distillation after addition of *meta*-arsenite to eliminate excess periodate (Keeney and Bremner 1967):

$$NaAsO_2 + NaIO_4 \rightarrow NaAsO_3 + NaIO_3$$

Equipment

– Micro-Kjeldahl digestion unit.
– Steam distillation apparatus (Fig. 14.3) which can be also used for the titration of inorganic nitrogen in the case of N-rich soils (cf. Chap. 28) and for the titration of total nitrogen (cf. Chap. 10) instead of an automated distiller.
– 50 and 100 mL Pyrex Kjeldahl distillation flasks, with standard 29/32 ground glass joints and hooks to attach springs.
– 5 mL graduated microburette with 0.01 mL intervals or automated titrimeter with double electrode for pH measurement and an automated 5 mL burette.

Reagents

1. *6 mol L^{-1} hydrochloric acid.* Add 513 mL of concentrated HCl (d = 1.19) to approximately 500 mL water, cool and complete to 1 L in a volumetric flask.
2. *n-octylic alcohol.*
3. Potassium sulphate-catalyst mixture for Kjeldahl digestion: see preparation in "Reagents" under Sect. 10.2.6 of Chap. 10.
4. *10 mol (NaOH) L^{-1} soda solution.* See preparation in "Reagents" under Sect. 10.2.6 of Chap. 10.
5. *5 mol (NaOH) L^{-1} soda solution.* Dilute 500 mL of 10 mol L^{-1} soda to 1 L and store in a well-stopped bottle.
6. *0.5 mol (NaOH) L^{-1} soda solution.* Dilute 50 mL of 10 mol L^{-1} soda to 1 L and store in a stopped bottle.
7. *Boric acid-indicator solution.* Dissolve 100 g of boric acid in 4 L of deionized water, add 100 mL of mixed indicator (0.495 g of bromo-cresol green and 0.33 g of methyl red in 500 mL ethanol), adjust the pH to 4.8–5.0 (reddish purple colour) by the addition of a little diluted soda or hydrochloric acid and bring the volume to 5 L.
8. 0.005 mol ($\frac{1}{2}H_2SO_4$) L^{-1} sulphuric acid solution: use standard commercial solution.
9. *Anhydrous magnesium oxide.* If necessary, calcinate in the muffle furnace at 600–700°C for 2 h.
10. *Ninhydrin.* $C_9H_4O_3,H_2O$, tested as amino-acid reagents.

11. *phosphate–borate buffer at pH 11.2.* Put 100 g of sodium phosphate ($Na_3PO_4,12H_2O$), 25 g of borax ($Na_2B_4O_7,10H_2O$) and approximately 900 mL water into a 1 L volumetric flask; agitate until dissolution, complete to 1 L and store in a well-stopped flask.
12. citric acid ($C_6H_8O_7,H_2O$);
13. *citrate buffer pH 2.6.* Mix 2.06 g of dihydrate sodium citrate ($Na_3C_6H_5O_7,2H_2O$) and 19.15 g of citric acid ($C_6H_8O_7,H_2O$), crush well in a mortar and store in a small stopped bottle.

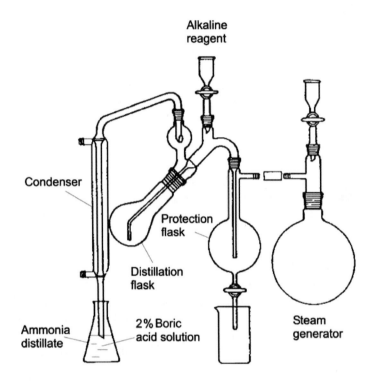

Fig. 14.3. Steam distillation apparatus

14. *0.2 mol L^{-1} periodic acid solution.* Dissolve 4.6 g of $HIO_4,2H_2O$ in 100 mL water and store in a glass bottle with ground stopper.
15. *1 mol L^{-1} sodium metaarsenite solution.* Dissolve 13 g of $NaAsO_2$ in 100 mL water and store in well-stopped flask.
16. *Standard solution A (NH_4^+ + amino sugar + amino acid).* Dissolve 0.189 g of $(NH_4)_2SO_4$, 0.308 g of glucosamine HCl and 0.254 g of alanine in water; dilute to 2 L in a volumetric flask while agitating vigorously; this solution contains 20 µg of NH_4-N + 10 µg of amino sugar-N and 20 µg of α-amino acid-N by mL; store in the refrigerator at 4°C;

17. *Standard solution B (serine + threonine)-N.* Dissolve 150 mg of serine and 170 mg of threonine in water, dilute the solution to a volume of 2 L in a volumetric flask and agitate vigorously; prepared with pure dry products this solution contains 10 µg of serine-N and 10 µg of threonine-N by mL; store in the refrigerator at 4°C.

Procedure

Acid Hydrolysis

Weigh an air-dried and finely crushed (<100 mesh) soil sample containing approximately 10 mg of total nitrogen (cf. Chap. 10) and place it in a 125 mL Pyrex round bottom boiling flask with a standard ground stopper.

Add two drops of octylic alcohol and 20 mL of 6 mol (HCl) L^{-1} solution. Agitate well then connect the boiling flask to a Liebig condenser and boil at reflux for 12 h.

Cool and filter under vacuum on a Büchner funnel with a standard Whatman N°50 type filter paper. Rinse the residue in small fractions until 50 mL total filtrate have been collected. Cool the filtrate in crushed ice and neutralize to pH 6.5 ± 0.1 by adding soda while measuring the pH with a pH-meter. Gently add the soda under agitation (the solution must not become alkaline), first using the 5 mol L^{-1} solution until approximately pH 5 then the 0.5 mol L^{-1} solution until neutralization. Transfer in a volumetric flask, bring back to ambient temperature and complete to 100 mL by carefully rinsing the used glass flasks and the pH electrodes with distilled water; stop carefully and agitate well.

Separations by Distillation – Precautions

In each of the following techniques for the determination of nitrogen, put 5 or 10 mL of the hydrolysate (see "Acid Hydrolysis" under Sect. 14.2.1) into a 50 or 100 mL distillation flask. After suitable treatment, connect the flask to the steam distillation apparatus. The required form of nitrogen corresponds to the quantity of ammonia distilled in 2–4 min.

The apparatus should be run before each use to eliminate all traces of ammonia. The speed of distillation should be adjusted to collect 7–8 mL of distillate per minute. The flow of the condenser should be adjusted so that the temperature of the distillate at this distillation speed does not exceed 22°C.

To obtain a representative sub-sample of the hydrolysate, it is essential to agitate the contents of the volumetric flask well before each sub-sampling. The ends of the pipettes should not be too small to enable rapid transfer of the sample into the distillation flask. Pipettes with very small openings can cause sampling errors because some of materials in suspension in the sample can be retained and, in addition, the openings are easily blocked. If titration does not have to be performed rapidly by steam distillation, it is preferable to store the hydrolysate in an acid medium and to neutralize it immediately before titration.

Determination of Total Nitrogen of the Hydrolysate

Put 5 mL of neutralized hydrolysate into a 50 mL distillation flask; add 0.5 g of K_2SO_4-catalyst mixture and 2 mL of concentrated sulphuric acid. Carefully heat on a micro-Kjeldahl attack unit until the water has been eliminated and there is no more white smoke. Increase the heat until the mixture clarifies and then completes digestion by boiling gently for 1 h.

Let cool and carefully add 10 mL of distilled water while agitating. Cool under water and in crushed ice. Add 5 mL of boric acid-indicator solution in a 50 mL Erlenmeyer flask with a volume mark at 35 mL, and place the flask under the condenser of the distillation apparatus (Fig. 14.3). Connect the attack flask to the apparatus, place 10 mL of 10 mol $(NaOH)$ L^{-1} solution in the funnel and add slowly to the flask. When the soda is almost completely added, rinse the funnel with approximately 5 mL water, and then add approximately 3 mL water before turning off the tap. Begin distillation by turning off the steam by-pass tap and stop distillation by opening the same tap when the distillate reaches the 35 mL mark (approximately 4 min of distillation). Rinse the end of the condenser and measure the NH_3-N corresponding to total-N of the hydrolysate by titration with the 5 mmol $(\frac{1}{2}H_2SO_4\ L^{-1})$ solution. At titration point, the colour will change from green to pink.

If $V1$ is the volume of titrating solution in mL, the quantity of nitrogen in the sub-sample is 70 $V1$ μg. If P is the weight of the soil sample (grams), the quantity of hydrolyzed nitrogen will be 70 $V1$ 100/(5P) μg g^{-1} soil, i.e. 1.4 $V1$ P^{-1} mg g^{-1} soil.

Determination of (NH_3+Amino sugars)-N

Put exactly 10 mL of hydrolysate in a 100 mL distillation flask, add 10 mL of phosphate–borate buffer and continue as above until a volume of 35 mL distillate is reached (approximately 4 min). Titrate the released ammonium as above. If $V2$ is the volume of the 5 mmol $(\frac{1}{2}H_2SO_4)$ L^{-1} solution, the quantity of (NH_3+amino sugars)-N is 0.7 $V2$ P^{-1} mg g^{-1} soil.

Determination of NH_4^+-N

Put 10 mL of hydrolysate into a 50 or 100 mL distillation flask, add 0.07 ± 0.01 g MgO and continue as above until a volume of 20 mL distillate is reached (approximately 2 min of distillation). Titrate the distillate as above. If $V3$ is the volume of 5 mmol ($\frac{1}{2}H_2SO_4$) L^{-1} solution used, the quantity of NH_4^+-N resulting from the soil hydrolysis is 0.7 $V3$ P^{-1} mg g^{-1} soil. The quantity of amino sugars-N is estimated residually: 0.7 ($V2$ - $V3$) P^{-1} mg g^{-1} soil.

Determination of (NH_4^+ + Amino sugars + α-amino acid)-N

Put 5 mL of hydrolysate into a 50 mL distillation flask, add 100 mg of citrate buffer and 100 mg of ninhydrin, place the flask in a boiling water bath for 10 min; after 1 min, agitate. Cool the flask, add 10 mL of phosphate-borate buffer, distil until a volume of 35 mL distillate has been obtained (approximately 4 min) and titrate the distillate as above. If $V4$ is the volume of the 5 mmol ($\frac{1}{2}H_2SO_4$) L^{-1} solution at the titration point, (NH_4^+ + amino sugars + α-amino acid)-N is 1.4 $V4$ P^{-1} mg g^{-1} soil. α-amino-N can be estimated residually: 0.7($2V4$–$V2$) P^{-1} mg g^{-1} soil. It is also possible to control the α-amino acid-N content by first eliminating (NH_4^+ + amino sugars)-N forms as described below.

Determination of α-amino acid-N

Put 5 mL of hydrolysate in a 50 mL distillation flask, add 1 mL of the 0.5 mol L^{-1} NaOH solution and heat the flask in a boiling water bath until the volume is reduced to about 2–3 mL (approximately 20 min). Let cool, add 500 mg of citric acid and 100 mg of ninhydrin, place the flask in a boiling water bath for 10 min; after 1 min, agitate. Cool the flask; add 10 mL of phosphate–borate buffer and 1 mL of 5 mol L^{-1} NaOH solution. Distil until a volume of 35 mL of distillate is obtained (approximately 4 min) and titrate the distillate as above. If $V5$ is the volume of 5 mmol ($\frac{1}{2}H_2SO_4$) L^{-1} solution, α-amino acid-N is 1.4 $V5$ P^{-1} mg g^{-1} soil.

Determination of (Serine + Threonine)-N

Proceed up to the determination of (NH_4^+ + amino sugars)-N as described in "Determination of (NH_4 + amino sugars)-N. Then remove the distillation flask, rinse the input vapour tube and cool under the cold tap. Add 2 mL of the periodic acid solution. After agitating the flask for approximately 30 s add 2 mL of sodium arsenite solution. Connect to the distillation apparatus and run until approximately 35 mL of distillate is collected (4 min). Titrate the distillate as above. If $V6$ is the volume of 5 mmol ($\frac{1}{2}H_2SO_4$) L^{-1} solution, (serine+threonine)-N is 0.7 $V6$ P^{-1} mg g^{-1} soil.

Calibration of the Method

These distillation procedures can be tested using the standard solutions A and B, the recommended aliquot volumes being 5 mL of A solution for NH_4^+-N, amino acid-N or (ammonium + hexosamines + amino acids)-N, 10 mL of A solution for N-(amino sugars) and 10 mL of B solution for N-(threonine+serine). If they are stored in the refrigerator, the two standard solutions will remain stable for several months. For details of other precautions concerning this technique, please refer to the original publication (Bremner 1965).

14.2.2 Organic Forms of Nitrogen: Simplified Method

Principle

With respect to the acid attack, the technique is similar to the one described in Sect. 14.1.1. The distillation procedure is simplified, only two fractions are determined on the hydrolysate.

 – dhN: fraction distillable in alkaline medium which thus primarily includes the NH_4-N + and amino sugar-N forms, but also some amid and amino phenol forms (Egouminides et al. 1987).

 – ndhN: non-distillable fraction which contains mainly amino acids and unidentified nitrogen. This fraction is obtained by the difference between hN, total hydrolysable nitrogen (obtained by Kjeldahl digestion) and dhN, distillable hydrolysable nitrogen.

Non-hydrolysable nhN can be obtained as previously either by the difference between the Kjeldahl total nitrogen and the total hydrolysable nitrogen, or by Kjeldahl mineralization of the residue of hydrolysis (cf. Sect. 14.2.1). This simplified method was developed and used by Egouminides et al. (1987) to measure the potential fertility of tropical soils, which are generally much poorer in nitrogen than soils in temperate climates.

Equipment and Reagents

 – The same equipment as listed in "Equipment" under Sect. 14.2.1.
 – reagents N° 1, 3, 4, 7 and standard solutions 16, 17 in "Reagents" under Sect. 14.2.1.
 – 0.02 mol ($\frac{1}{2}H_2SO_4$ L^{-1}) sulphuric acid solution: prepare with a standard commercial dose.

Procedure

Acid Hydrolysis

The test specimen should be adjusted as described in Sect. 14.2.1 with respect to the nitrogen content of the samples. In practice, possible weights of air dried soils are 5 g for an andosol, 10–20 g for a ferrallitic soil, 20–50 g for a tropical ferruginous soil.

Put the sample in a 250 mL round bottom boiling flask with a standard ground stopper and add 100 mL of 6 mol (HCl) L^{-1} hydrochloric acid. Connect the boiling flask to a Liebig condenser and boil at reflux for 16 h (i.e. from 5 p.m. to 9 a.m. the following day).

Stop heating, let cool, and transfer in 250 mL centrifugation flasks, rinsing the condenser and boiling flask with distilled water. Centrifuge at 4,000g for 15 min and collect the supernatant in a 200, 250 or 500 mL volumetric flask, the size depending on the number of washings. Wash the centrifugation pellet two or three times with 20–40 mL distilled water centrifuging each time in the same conditions and adding the washing water to the volumetric flask. Complete to the exact volume required while shaking well. The hydrolysate in acid medium can be stored in the volumetric flask before analysis. Recover the centrifugation pellet, dry at 40°C and weigh with precision.

Determination of Distillable Hydrolysable Nitrogen dhN

Put an aliquot of the hydrolysate in a 100 mL distillation flask. Place a 100 mL Erlenmeyer flask containing 10 mL of boric acid-indicator solution under the condenser of the steam distillation apparatus (Fig. 14.3). Connect the distillation flask to the apparatus and add via the funnel (Fig. 14.3) a volume of 10 mol L^{-1} soda corresponding to neutralization plus a slight excess (for a hydrolysate containing 3 mol L^{-1}, add 1/3 of the volume of aliquot in the form of 10 mol (NaOH) L^{-1} solution). Allow the vapour to distil until a volume of 50–80 mL of distillate has been obtained. Titrate the contents of the Erlenmeyer flask with the 0.02 mol L^{-1} sulphuric acid solution. If P, V_0, V_{01} and V_1 are the weight of the soil test specimen (g), the total hydrolyzed volume, the sub-sampling volume of hydrolysate, and the volume of titrating solution (mL), respectively: dhN = 0.28 V_0 V_1 (V_{01} P^{-1}) mg of distillable hydrolysable nitrogen per gram of soil.

Determination of Total Hydrolysable Nitrogen hN

Make Kjeldahl mineralization on an aliquot of hydrolysate (cf. Sect. 14.2.1): if V_{02} is the sub-sampling volume of hydrolysate (mL) and V_2 the volume of titrating solution (mL), hN = 0.28 V_0 V_2 $(V_{02}$ $P)^{-1}$. The non-distillable nitrogen hydrolyzable is estimated residually: ndhN = hN − dhN.

Determination of Not Hydrolysable Nitrogen nhN

This value is determined by Kjeldahl mineralization on the hydrolysis residue dried at 40°C (cf. Sect. 11.2.1). If the weight of the residue is lower than 10 g, use the whole residue, if not, weigh a precise aliquot of the residue. If P_0, P_{01}, V_3 are the weight of the residue, the weight of aliquot, and the volume of titrating solution, respectively, nhN = 0.28 P_0 V_3 $(P_{01}$ $P)^{-1}$.

14.2.3 Urea titration

Principle

Urea is used as nitrogenized fertilizer on cultivated soils all over the world (Beaton 1978). Consequently reliable methods are needed to determine the residue of urea in the soil. Two main types of titration techniques can be distinguished:

– Colorimetric methods based on the colour reaction of urea with diacetyl monoxime (DAM) (Fearon 1939) or with *p*-dimethyl-amino-benzaldehyde (Watt and Crisp 1954) in acid medium.

– Enzymatic methods which enable the ammonium produced during urease hydrolysis of urea to be measured; after incubation, this procedure uses steam distillation with the same equipment described above (Fig. 14.3 and Sects. 14.2.1 and 14.2.2).

The reaction of urea with DAM produces a yellow compound. In the presence of thiosemicarbazide (TSC), a red compound is formed. Douglas and Bremner (1970) developed a technique using the latter reaction which allows precise measurement for the analysis of soil solutions containing less than 20 mg (urea) L^{-1}. The soil urea is extracted by a KCl solution in the presence of a urease inhibitor. The extracts are then titrated using the spectro-colorimetric technique. The initial method of Douglas and Bremner was slightly modified by Mulvaney and Bremner (1979). The latter technique is described below. The extraction solutions can also be titrated on an automatic colorimeter (Douglas et al. 1977). For more details on methods of measuring urea, see Bremner (1982).

Reagents

- *Phenyl-mercury acetate (PMA) solution.* Dissolve 50 mg of PMA in 1 L of purified water.
- Potassium chloride and PMA solution (2M KCl-PMA): dissolve 1,500g of KCl in 9 L of water and add 1 L of PMA solution.
- *DAM solution.* Dissolve 2.5 g of DAM in 100 mL water.
- *TSC solution.* Dissolve 0.25 g of TSC in 100 mL water.
- *Acid reagent.* Add 40 mL of concentrated sulphuric acid to 1 L of phosphoric acid solution (85% in weight), dilute the mixture to 2 L with water (add the acid to the water) under agitation.
- *Colouring reagent.* Mix 50 mL of DAM solution with 30 mL of TSC solution and dilute the mixture to 1 L with the acid reagent; this reagent cannot be stored and should be prepared just before use.
- *Standard urea-N solution.* Dissolve 0.4288 g of pure dry urea in the KCl-PMA solution, complete to 2 L with the same solution and agitate well. This solution contains 100 µg of urea-N by mL. Store in the refrigerator.

Procedure

Place 5 g of soil in a 100 mL bottle and add 50 mL of 2 M KCl-PMA solution. Stop the bottle, agitate for 1 h on a mechanical agitator and filter (Whatman n°42 filter paper).

Remove a precise aliquot of the extract (1–10 mL) containing between 10 and 100 µg of urea-N and place it in a 50 mL volumetric flask. Complete to 10 mL with the 2 M KCl-PMA solution and add 30 mL of colouring reagent. Agitate the flask quickly to mix and leave it in a thermostatic bath at $85 \pm 0.5°C$ for 30 min. Cool for 10 min with cold water (12–15°C), complete to 50 mL with water and agitate well. Measure the red colour absorption with the colorimeter at 527 nm. If the colorimeter is not equipped with a monochromator, a green filter can be used instead. Calculate the concentration using a calibration curve with 0, 10, 50, 100 µg of urea-N.

To prepare the calibration curve, dilute 20 mL of standard urea-N solution in a 200 mL volumetric flask with the 2 M KCl-PMA solution and agitate well. Pipette 0, 1, 5, 10 mL aliquots of the solution in 50 mL volumetric flasks. Complete to 10 mL with the 2 M KCl-PMA solution and continue in the same way as for the soil extracts. Make a calibration curve for each series of analyses.

14.2.4 Potentially Available Nitrogen – Biological Methods

Principle

These methods analyse the capacity of a soil to provide inorganic nitrogen to plants. Different names are used for the methods such as nitrogen availability indices, potentially mineralizable nitrogen, net mineralization, mineralization potential.

The biological methods tend to simulate in vitro the evolution of the soil in natural conditions. They measure inorganic nitrogen produced in a soil sample after a given incubation time in controlled conditions.

The implementation of these methods thus appears to be simple, but in practice, it is very difficult to choose the appropriate procedure because so many alternatives are available. Keeney (1982) listed 29 incubation procedures that were tested with respect to measurements of nitrogen consumption by various types of plants. Fahd-Rachid (1990) listed 11 methods, three of which were not mentioned by Keeney.

The most frequently quoted of these methods was originally proposed by Stanford and Smith (1972). It is based on the concept of decomposition of a pool of available nitrogen according to first-order kinetics (Fig. 14.4). During a time interval dt the variation in the organic nitrogen content d[No] can be expressed according to the kinetic constant of mineralization k by the expression:

$$d[No]/dt = -k\,[No] \qquad (14.1)$$

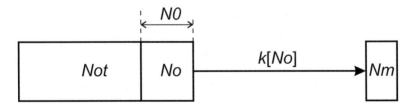

Fig. 14.4. Diagrammatic representation of nitrogen mineralization according to Stanford and Smith (1972): *Not*, total organic nitrogen of the soil; *No*, mineralizable soil organic nitrogen; *N0*, potentially mineralizable organic nitrogen; *Nm*, mineralized nitrogen ($NH_4^+ + NO_3^- + NO_2^-$); *k*, kinetic constant = fraction of organic nitrogen mineralized during the time interval *dt*

By integration, $N0$ being the quantity of mineralizable organic nitrogen at time 0 (potentially mineralizable nitrogen), (14.1) gives

$$[No] = N0 \, e^{-kt} \tag{14.2}$$

In addition, if pre-existing inorganic nitrogen in the soil is calculated, the balance of nitrogen is written

$$[No] + [Nm] = N0 \tag{14.3}$$

According to the (14.2) and (14.3) the evolution Nm of inorganic nitrogen is thus written

$$[Nm] = N0 \, (1 - e^{-kt}) \tag{14.4}$$

This technique consists in measuring inorganic nitrogen produced at a range of incubation times and plotting the cumulated values as a function of time. By adjusting the data in (14.4), an estimate of potentially mineralizable nitrogen $N0$ and the kinetic constant of mineralization k can be obtained simultaneously. A range of adjustments was proposed. Stanford and Smith (1972) initially observed linear adjustments of cumulated inorganic nitrogen according to the square root of the incubation time. For the calculation of potentially mineralizable nitrogen and speed of mineralization, they used a calculation of linear regression. After logarithmic transformation, (14.4) can be written:

$$\mathrm{Log}(N0 - Nm) = \mathrm{Log} \, N0 - kt \tag{14.5}$$

By fixing a value of $N0$ in the left part of the equation, a linear adjustment between the variables $\log(N0 - Nm)$ and t, makes it possible to estimate k. The curves obtained on semi-logarithmic paper for different values chosen for $N0$ are convex for estimated $N0$ value < true $N0$ value, concave for estimated $N0$ > true $N0$ and linear for estimated $N0$ = true $N0$. An iterative procedure enabled estimation of the optimal $N0$ value. Using this technique, Stanford and Smith observed values for $N0$ ranging between 5 and 40% of total nitrogen on 39 very different soils. On the other hand, constant speed k did not differ significantly between the soils and the authors estimated it at 0.054 ± 0.009 week^{-1}. This method of adjustment was then criticized, especially because the logarithmic transformation of the data involves the concomitant transformation of the experimental error (Campbell 1978; Smith et al. 1980; Reynolds and Beauchamp 1984). The technique favoured the points far from the origin and this smoothing effect could explain the low variability observed for k by Stanford and Smith (Mary and Rémy 1979). Most authors now prefer nonlinear adjustment techniques. Benedetti and Sebastiani (1996) compared three estimation techniques: maximum likelihood, linear adjustment according to (14.5) and nonlinear adjustment. Based on their results, the last technique appears to be preferable to the two others. Figure 14.5 shows two examples of nonlinear fittings obtained by Fahd-Rachid (1990) according to the Marquardt (1963) algorithm.

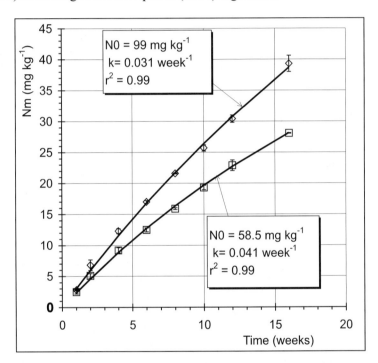

Fig. 14.5. Observed and adjusted values (Fahd-Rachid 1990) of accumulated inorganic nitrogen vs time of incubation, according to the technique of Stanford and Smith (1972) with nonlinear adjustment of (14.4). c, neutral colluvial soil; a, alluvial calcareous soil, cold preserved samples 50 days before incubation

Alternatives

One disadvantage of this technique is the number of measurements it requires and the duration of the experiment, even if the authors proposed to reduce the 210 days variable (aerobic incubation of Stanford and Smith 1972) to 26 days (Stanford et al. 1974).

Although they are less precise, faster biological techniques have been proposed. Gianello and Bremner (1986) compared different biological and chemical alternatives by carrying out tests on 30 types of soils with a broad range of organic contents (0.3–9% of carbon).

The following biological procedures were compared:

- m13 method of Waring and Bremner (1964) modified by Keeney and Bremner (1966), used determination of ammonium produced by anaerobic incubation in water saturated medium of 5 g of soil at 40°C for 7 days.
- m14 method of Keeney and Bremner (1967) used determination of $(NH_4^+ + NO_3^- + NO_2^-)$-N produced by aerobic incubation of 10 g soil mixed with 30 g of quartz sand (30–60 mesh particle size) and 6 mL distilled water at 30°C for 14 days.
- m15 method of Stanford and Smith (cf. "Procedure" under Sect. 11.2.4) for incubation times of 2, 4, 6, 8 and 12 weeks, the result cumulated at 12 weeks.
- m16 result of m15 for 2 weeks.
- m17: calculation of $N0$ of Stanford and Smith (14.5) using all the m15 data.

Figure 14.6 shows the results published by these authors according to each soil number ranked in ascending order of carbon content (Fig. 14.6a, c), on one hand to compare the values of $N0$ with those of total nitrogen of the soil, on the other hand to compare methods m14, m15, m16 with the $N0$ (m17) method.

The comparison with total nitrogen shows similar variations illustrating the correlation observed by Gianello and Bremner ($r = 0.86$, $P < 0.1\%$). However, in some cases, the significant relation of proportionality calculated between $N0$ and N-total can lead to significant errors: Figure 14.6b shows differences between adjusted values and actual values which can reach 100 mg kg^{-1}; this represents approximately 300 kg of inorganic-N ha^{-1} and is a big difference which prevents accurate estimation of N fertilization in the field. The calculated proportionality coefficient gives an average estimate of potentially mineralizable nitrogen at approximately 6.5% of total nitrogen of the soil.

The comparison of $N0$ and the other tests using biological techniques (Fig. 14.6c) illustrates the correlations (significant at $P < 0.1\%$) between the data of Gianello and Bremner: $r = 0.96$ between $N0$ and m13 or m15, $r = 0.90$ between $N0$ and m16; $r = 0.81$ between $N0$ and m14. The proportionality factors in Fig. 14.6d can be used to compare methods with less uncertainty than the previous comparison with total nitrogen (Fig. 14.6b). Thus, it is possible to estimate $N0$ with simpler experiments than those of Stanford and Smith (1972):

– anaerobic incubation of the M13 type allows estimation near

$$N0 = NH_4^+\text{-}N/0.44.$$

– aerobic incubation of M14 and M16 types allows estimation near

$$N0 = (NH_4^+ + NO_3^- + NO_2^-)\text{-}N/0.27.$$

The two M14 and M16 techniques using 2-week aerobic incubation provide the same proportionality factor. However, the variations observed between adjusted and real values (Fig. 14.6d) are more significant than with the two other methods. The anaerobic M13 method of 1-week incubation appears to be the most reliable, at least in comparison with $N0$. The comparison with the M15 method is of little interest since $N0$ is calculated from M15.

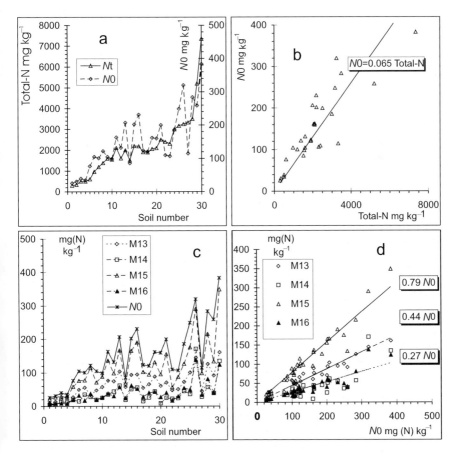

Fig. 14.6. Comparisons of measurements on 30 soil samples of different types (according to Gianello and Bremner, 1986). (**a**) and (**b**) potential of mineralization ($N0$ of Stanford and Smith, 1972) and total nitrogen (total-N), (**c**) and (**d**) $N0$ and four other biological measurements of potentially available nitrogen

Because of the large number of incubation techniques proposed, the only method described here is an adaptation of the Stanford and Smith (1972) method used at the IRD[1] centre of Montpellier (J.C. Talineau, personal communication; Fahd-Rachid 1990).

Equipment

- 10–30 polypropylene Büchner funnels (depending on the size of the sample series) with a 5.5 or 7 cm diameter for tropical soils low in nitrogen
- Standard glass fibre filters type Whatman GF/A corresponding to the size of the Büchner funnels
- Film permeable to air and impermeable to water such as parafilm (Rhône-Poulenc, France) to cover the beakers
- Drying oven (for incubation) precisely adjustable between 20 and 50°C (proportional regulation)
- 10–30 150 mL beakers
- 10–30 250 mL filter flasks
- A pressure gauge in the 0–1 atmosphere range
- A microcomputer equipped with statistical software allowing adjustment of linear and nonlinear regression, or semi-logarithmic graph paper

Products

- Pure sand, free from organic matter, sieved to between 0.5 and 2 mm.
- *0.01 mol (CaCl$_2$) L^{-1} solution.* Dissolve 7.35 g of CaCl$_2$,2H$_2$0 in distilled water, complete to 5 L and agitate well.
- Ion saturation solution without nitrogen 0.002 mol (CaSO$_4$) L^{-1}, 0.002 mol (MgSO$_4$) L^{-1}, 0.005 mol (CaHPO$_4$) L^{-1}, 0.0025 mol (K$_2$SO$_4$) L^{-1}: dissolve 0.689 g of CaSO$_4$,2H$_2$O, 0.482 g of MgSO$_4$, 1.720 g of CaHPO$_4$,2H$_2$O, 0.871 g of K$_2$SO$_4$ in distilled water, complete to 2 L and agitate well.

---

[1]IRD = Institute of Research for the Development (ex-Orstom), P.O. Box 64501, 911 Avenue d'Agropolis, 34 394 Montpellier Cedex, France.

Procedure

(a) For non-sandy soils, mix 30 g of air-dried soil sieved to 5 mm particle
    size with 10 g of sieved coarse sand, place it in a Büchner funnel
    (diameter 55 mm, capacity 80 mL) equipped with a fibre glass filter.
    For low-N sandy soils, place 50 g of soil (without the addition of sand)
    in funnels with a diameter of 70 mm. Some studies advise starting with
    fresh soil to minimize the initial flush of mineralization after water is
    added to a dried sample (Fahd-Rachid 1990). Stop the funnels with a
    plug of glass wool to protect the surface quality of the materials when
    moistening.

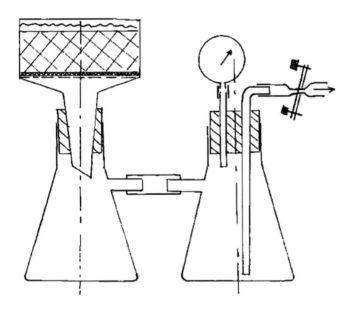

Fig. 14.7. Device used to adjust the moisture of the sample and ion equilibrium
before incubation

(b) Carry out percolation by simple gravity with 100 mL of 0.01 mol
    $(CaCl_2)$ L^{-1} solution then with 25 mL of the ion saturation solution by
    collecting the whole of the leachate in the 150 mL beakers.
(c) Regulate the moisture of the samples by causing a depression of 0.03
    MPa compared to normal atmospheric pressure (corresponding absolute
    pressure: 0.0713 Mpa). According to several authors, this depression
    corresponds to the optimal mineralization moisture for many soils
    (Talineau JC, IRD Montpellier, personal communication). The
    equipment shown in Fig. 14.7 enables this operation to be carried out

very simply using a glass filter pump and a tubing clamp. The solution collected in the filter flask is added to the previous percolation solution and can be temporarily cold stored before analysis.

(d) Cover the funnels with parafilm and incubate in an incubator at 28°C. Place a flat water container in the incubator to maintain a moist atmosphere. It is possible to make a very simple rack to hold the Büchner funnels using an expanded polyurethane plate approximately 5 cm thick by drilling small holes to hold the funnel stems.

(e) Remove the funnels from the incubator and start again from (b) for the periods of incubation chosen, e.g. 2, 4, 6, 8, 10, 12, 16 weeks (Fahd-Rachid 1990, Fig. 14.5).

(f) Using the percolation solutions, identify the different forms of inorganic nitrogen: ammonium, nitrites, or nitrates, either by distillation of ammonia in the presence of a reducing agent (Dewarda alloy, Iron), using a steam distillation apparatus (Fig. 14.3) or any other method suitable for inorganic nitrogen (cf. Chap. 28). The percolation solutions at time 0 can be discarded or used to determine initial soil inorganic nitrogen. These initial results are not taken into account to determine potentially mineralizable nitrogen.

(g) Write on a graph the cumulated values of inorganic nitrogen as a function of the incubation time (Fig. 14.5) and estimate the parameters of the adjustment (cf. "Principle" under Sect. 14.2.4).

Discussion

The results depend to a large extent on the state of conservation and on the preparation of the soil samples. These operations always induce additional mineralization at the beginning of incubation partly by releasing organic matter sequestered in soil aggregates but especially by killing part of the microbial biomass. Dead biomass and released materials are consumed more rapidly at the beginning of incubation and this can result in overestimated results of mineralizable nitrogen. However, by comparing results obtained on an air-dried sample and on the same sample preserved fresh at cold temperature, Fahd-Rachid (1990) made two interesting observations:

– The differences between the sub-samples affected in particular the k value, which was approximately four times lower in fresh soil than in air-dried soil; the $N0$ values were modified by only approximately 20%.

– In the case of the dry soil, by subtracting the two first values of cumulated inorganic nitrogen (1 and 2 weeks of incubation) from the other values, one obtains a curve and parameters close to those observed in fresh soil.

The model of Stanford and Smith corresponding to (14.5) is not the only one that has been tested but is the simplest. Mary and Rémy (1979) proposed using the product $kN0$ to estimate the rough mineralization potential of soil nitrogen. Several authors tested models of evolution that are a little more complex: $Nm=N0(1-e^{-k_1t}) + k_2t$ (Chaussod et al. 1986; Seyfried and Rao 1988), $Nt=N01(1-e^{-k_1t}) + N02(1-e^{-k_2t})$ (Nuske and Richter 1981; Deans et al. 1986) and even a model made up of n pools of nitrogen with n mineralization kinetics (Richter et al. 1982). The use of these different models does not change the operational incubation procedure described earlier.

It is often possible to estimate mineralized nitrogen simply by the titration of nitrates, NH_4^+ and NO_2^- being transition forms present in smaller quantities in a well-aerated medium.

The standard procedure of Stanford and Smith is only a rather rough simulation of the processes that occur in natural conditions. It can be criticised for two main reasons:

– It does not simulate the nitrogen cycle (Fig. 14.1) since the regular leaching of inorganic nitrogen favours mineralization and nitrification processes rather than immobilization and reduction processes. It is useful for the estimation of potentially mineralizable nitrogen (which may be overestimated) but does not enable estimation of the inorganic nitrogen that is really available for the plant at a given time.

– Leaching by the 0.01 mol $(CaCl_2)$ L^{-1} solution eliminates soluble organic nitrogen which could mineralize later (Robertson et al. 1988) resulting in underestimation of mineralizable nitrogen.

Moreover, if the simulation of the dynamic aspect of the formation of inorganic nitrogen has the undeniable advantage of reliability, the duration of the experiments may be an obstacle to their implementation. Consequently, many techniques have been proposed for faster determination of potentially available nitrogen (1) using faster biological methods (cf. "Alternatives") and (2) using chemical extraction methods (cf. Sect. 11.2.5).

14.2.5 Potentially Mineralizable Nitrogen: Chemical Methods

Principle

As potentially mineralizable nitrogen represents only a fraction ranging between 5 and 10% of total nitrogen (an average of 6.5% according to the comparison in Fig. 14.6b), the energetic techniques of acid attack used in the determination of nitrogen forms (cf. Sects. 14.2.1 and 14.2.2) cannot be used here.

Many authors developed methods using less aggressive extracting reagents that were often tested with respect to plant needs in specific situations. These methods use the action of solutions such as (1) neutral salts (KCl, $CaCl_2$) in cold solutions but more often in hot solutions and (2) more or less alkaline salts in hot or slightly oxidizing solutions. The ammonium nitrogen extracted by these solutions is then measured.

Velly et al. (1980) observed a very good correlation between plant N-needs and total nitrogen extracted using the technique of Giraud and Fardeau (1977) on cold KCl extracts. The methods using hot KCl extracts were the subject of most investigations (e.g. Фien and Selmer-Olsen 1980; Whitehead 1981; Gianello and Bremner 1986). Whitehead (1981) noted that his home-made extraction method i.e. boiling for 1 h with 1 mol (KCl) L^{-1} solution, gave a good estimate of the quantities of nitrogen taken up by pastures. Fox and Piekielek (1978) tested extractions with $NaHCO_3$ 0.01 N solutions according to the method of Mac Lean (1964) followed by UV absorption measurements of nitrates and nitrites at 205 nm. Keeney (1982) recommended the use of a $CaCl_2$ solution in an autoclave. Gianello and Bremner (1986, 1988) re-commended measuring ammonium by distillation in the presence of a solution of phosphate–borate buffer at pH 11.2. Stanford and Smith (1978) proposed titration of the ammonium released by attack with a $KMnO_4$ solution in acid medium. Stanford (1978) proposed extraction with a permanganate solution in alkaline medium.

The study by Gianello and Bremner (1986) on 30 soils with very different organic contents enables the relative effectiveness of different techniques to be compared.

Figure 14.8 groups all their results with the samples ranked according to their increasing organic contents. As in Fig. 14.6, the $N0$ value of Stanford and Smith (cf. Sect. 14.2.4) is used for comparison. The methods compared were classified in four graphs representing different levels of extracted nitrogen.

–The M3, M4, M5 graph groups three alternative methods of extraction with 2 mol (KCl) L^{-1} hot solutions in a closed bottle (M3: heating at 100°C for 4 h, M4: heating at 95°C for 16 h, M5 (Фien and Selmer-Olsen 1980): heating at 80°C for 20 h. The average extracted quantities account for 8–20% of $N0$, the M4 method giving the higher extraction. The respective correlation coefficients with $N0$ are all highly significant: 0.95 for M3, 0.96 for M4, 0.93 for M5.

–The M6, M7 graph groups two other alternative extractions with hot 1 mol (KCl) L^{-1} solutions: M6 (Whitehead 1981): boiling 1 h in a digestion tube, M7: heating 1 h at 100°C in a stopped tube. The two methods give very comparable results, but the quantities extracted are the lowest of all the methods, lower than 5% of $N0$ (Fig. 14.9).

Moreover, these two methods are the least correlated with $N0$ ($r = 0.81$ and 0.83, respectively).

– The M8, M9 graph compares the two methods "distillation with phosphate–borate buffer" (M8, Gianello and Bremner 1986, 1988) and "$CaCl_2$ – autoclave" (M9, Keeney 1982). The quantity of extracted nitrogen is a lot higher than in all the KCl tests with an average of 27% of $N0$ for M8 and 50% of $N0$ for M9. The M8 method with the phosphate–borate buffer thus extracts almost half less nitrogen than the M9 autoclave method. However, it provides results that are better correlated with $N0$ ($r = 0.95$ for M8 and 0.92 for M9; Fig. 14.9c).

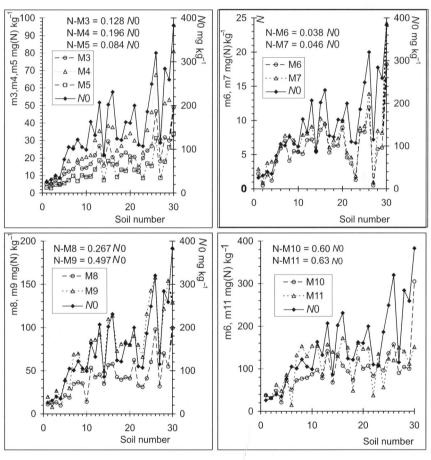

Fig. 14.8. Comparison of measurements of potentially mineralizable nitrogen using chemical methods with the potential of mineralization $N0$ of Stanford and Smith (1972); the 30 soils tested correspond to those in Fig. 14.6; they are ranked in order of increasing organic carbon content (according to Gianello and Bremner 1986); the average fractions extracted by each method compared to $N0$ are given for the 30 soils

– The M10, M11 graph compares the methods using controlled oxidation with permanganate in acid medium (M10, Stanford and Smith 1978) and in alkaline medium (M11, Stanford 1978). These two methods extract the most nitrogen. The average extracted values in the two methods are very close, 60–65% of $N0$. However, there is very little correlation between the two types of results and their correlations with $N0$ are the least significant of the methods compared, particularly for alkaline oxidation ($r = 0.85$ for M10; $r = 0.48$ for M11).

Only the procedure M8 for the method by distillation of ammonium in the presence of phosphate–borate buffer of Gianello and Bremner (1988) is described below. This procedure has the best correlation with the $N0$ of Stanford and Smith (Fig. 14.8). Its implementation is relatively simple and uses the same type of steam distillation equipment as for the determination of forms of nitrogen (cf. Fig. 14.3, Sects. 14.2.1 and 14.2.2). According to Gianello and Bremner, the samples showed practically no effect of drying and storage.

Nevertheless, this procedure has seldom been tested with respect to the real nitrogen needs of plants, so the other procedures for extraction using neutral salts should not to be rejected (Campbell et al. 1997). In addition, a method such as permanganate oxidation in acid medium may provide results that are closer to $N0$ in absolute value. For details on the other procedures, please refer to the original publications cited earlier. The coefficients in Fig. 14.8 enable estimation of the approximate correspondence between the different results.

Equipment and Reagents

Equipment

– Steam distillation apparatus (cf. Fig. 14.3 and Sects. 14.2.1 and 14.2.2).
– 200 mL Kjeldahl distillation flasks with standard 29/32 ground joints with hooks to attach springs.
– titrimeter equipped for acidimetry or a 5 mL precision manual burette graduated at 0.01 mL intervals.

Reagents

- Phosphate–borate buffer pH 11.2 (cf. solution 11 in "Reagents" under Sect. 28.2.1): put 200 g $Na_3PO_4,12H_2O$, 50 g of $Na_2B_4O_7,10H_2O$ and approximately 1,800 mL water in a 2 L volumetric flask. Agitate until complete dissolution. Adjust the pH solution to 11.2 by adding H_3PO_4 then complete the volume to 2 L. Store in a well-stopped bottle.
- Boric acid indicator solution: cf. solution 5 in "Reagents" under Sect. 28.2.1.
- Solution 0.005 mol ($\frac{1}{2}H_2SO_4$) L^{-1}: cf. solution 6 in "Reagents" under Sect. 28.2.1.
- MgO powder: Cf. product 9 in "Reagents" under section 28.2.1.
- Solution 2 mol (KCl) L^{-1}: dissolve 149.1 g of KCl in distilled water. Complete to 1 L, homogenize and preserve in well-stopped bottle.

Procedure

- Put 5 mL of the boric acid-indicator solution in a 100 mL Erlenmeyer flask with a mark indicating 50 mL volume and place under the condenser of the steam distillation apparatus (Fig. 14.3).
- Put 4 g soil sieved to 2 mm in a 200 mL distillation flask. Add 40 mL of phosphate–borate buffer solution at pH 11.2 and connect to the distillation apparatus.
- Begin distillation immediately by opening the vapour tap and stop when the distillate reaches the 50 mL mark.
- Titrate the ammonium by manual or automatic titration with the 0.005 mol ($\frac{1}{2}H_2SO_4$) L^{-1} solution. If $V1$ mL is the volume of titrating solution, the content of total ammonium (initial + mineralized) of the sample is $tNH_3\text{-}N = 17.5\ V1\ \mu g\ g^{-1}$ soil.
- If the exchangeable ammonium NH_3-N of the sample was determined beforehand (cf. Chap. 28), the mineralizable nitrogen can be calculated by the difference between tNH_3-N and NH_3-N. If not, initial NH_3-N can be determined using the same steam distillation equipment and the method of Keeney and Bremner (1966): distillation for 3.3 min on a 4 g sample in the presence of 20 mL of a 2 mol (KCl) L^{-1} solution and 0.2 mg MgO. If $V2$ is the volume of the 0.005 mol ($\frac{1}{2}H_2SO_4$) L^{-1} solution necessary for the titration of distilled ammonia, the mineralized NH_3-N from organic nitrogen is: $17.5\ (V1 - V2)\ \mu g\ g^{-1}$ of soil.

14.2.6 Kinetics of Mineralization

Principle

Methods for the determination of potentially mineralizable nitrogen (Sects. 14.2.4 and 14.2.5) measure the maximum potential of nitrogen fertility, but are far from the real nitrogen cycle which is closely linked to the carbon cycle (Pansu et al. 1998). Kinetic studies consist in simultaneously measuring the mineralization and transformation of carbon and nitrogen (1) in natural conditions using labelled ^{14}C or ^{13}C and ^{15}N (Bottner et al. 2000) or unlabelled materials or (2) in controlled laboratory conditions: measurements of CO_2, NH_4^+ and NO_3^- produced by soils and labelled or unlabelled soil-input mixtures. The laboratory method adapted and used at IRD, Montpellier (Thuriès et al. 2000) is described below. The procedure varies particularly with respect to the length of incubation. To understand the kinetics of evolution of the unstable compartments, experiments lasting only 1 month or even less are often performed. To understand the evolution of more stable compartments, the incubation period must be longer than 100 days (Blet-Charaudeau et al. 1990). A 6-month period is often used. The extra work caused by experiments of long duration is not a major handicap because sampling is programmed logarithmically vs incubation time. Thus many samples are needed in the early stages but only a few in the last stages of incubation.

Equipment

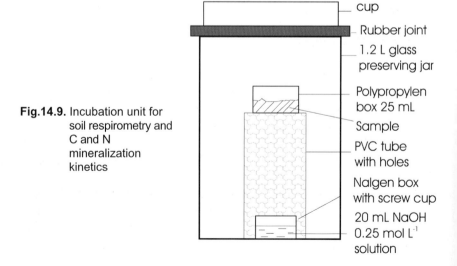

Fig.14.9. Incubation unit for soil respirometry and C and N mineralization kinetics

Airtight cup

Rubber joint

1.2 L glass preserving jar

Polypropylen box 25 mL

Sample

PVC tube with holes

Nalgen box with screw cup

20 mL NaOH 0.25 mol L^{-1} solution

- A large bacteriological incubator adjustable to the chosen temperature ± 0.3°C, here 28°C.
- 1.2 L glass preserving jars with rubber seal.
- Sample holder made out of a PVC tube Ø 8 cm, height 12 cm, with holes drilled in it and with two crossed wires at the end to hold the sample boxes (Fig. 9).
- Cylindrical 50 mL polypropylene boxes, Ø 5 cm.
- 60 mL Nalgene boxes with screw lid.
- Desiccator filled with lime or baryta (CO_2 adsorption).
- Titrimeter equipped with a titration cell under nitrogen flow.
- Precise volume distributor (for 20 mL standard soda solution) protected by a CO_2 trap (NaOH pellets) at the top of the bottle.
- Products for titration of inorganic nitrogen (cf. Chap. 28).

2.6.3 Reagents

- Commercial standard 0.25 mol (NaOH) L^{-1} solution: quantitatively transfer the content of a plastic cartridge of commercial standard 0.5 mol (NaOH) L^{-1} solution in a 2 L volumetric flask, complete to volume and homogenize. Store in a volume distributor bottle with a trap filled with soda pellets fixed to the stopper.
- Commercial standard 0.25 mol (HCl) L^{-1} solution: dilute the required amount of commercial standard 0.5 mol (HCl) L^{-1} solution in a 2 L volumetric flask, complete to volume and homogenize.
- 20% barium chloride solution: dissolve 200 g $BaCl_2$ in 800 mL water, agitate and complete to 1 L, if the solution is turbid, filter on fine filter paper.
- Products for extraction (molar KCl or K_2SO_4 solution) and titration of inorganic forms of nitrogen (cf. Chap. 28).

Incubation Procedure

Determine the maximum water holding capacity (whc in g kg^{-1}) and the actual water content (wc in g kg^{-1}) of the soil concerned.

Calculate the weight of the water (ww) to be added to the test specimen of soil weight sw (in g, here 25 g):
ww = 0.75 (whc–wc) sw/1000.

Choose the sampling design (Table 14.3) for C and N mineralization as a function of time t (days).

Weigh in the polypropylene boxes the required number of 25 g soil samples, bearing in mind that measurements on nitrogen are destructive but that measurements on carbon are not destructive for the sample. Programme 3 replicates.

In aluminium squares, weigh the test specimens of organic matter (added organic matter, AOM) that are added to the samples in case of experiment of kinetics of AOM mineralization. AOM is dried and prepared at the selected particle size, weight calculated according to the C:N ratio of AOM (Table 14.4). Fold these samples carefully in the aluminium squares, write their number with a felt pen and store in the refrigerator. For the experiments of kinetics of AOM mineralization, always include soil samples without addition (blanks). For the experiments of soil respirometry, include blanks without soil samples.

The day the test is started, moisten the soil samples on the balance with a weight of water $<ww$, add the AOM, homogenize carefully with a spatula and finish moistening on the balance with the exact ww weight of water. Note total weight tw of the moistened sample. Complete homogenisation.

Put the samples in the bacteriological incubator regulated at the temperature selected (28°C at IRD Montpellier). Most of the boxes samples should be placed in plastic tanks covered with a plastic film perforated by piercing with a pin (permeable to the air but retaining the moisture in the sample). Only the samples intended for sampling $t = 1$ (Table 14.3) should be placed in the incubation jars (Fig. 14.9). Place in each jar a Nalgene box containing exactly 20 mL of 0.25 mol (NaOH) L^{-1} aqueous solution. Stop carefully and leave in the incubator.

Table 14.3. Sampling design vs incubation time (t in day) for C and N mineralization kinetics (× = sampling occasion)

T	0	1	2	3	5	7	10	14	21	28	41	61	90	100	120	130	152	180
C	×	×	×	×	×	×	×	×	×	×	×	×	×	×	×	×	×	×
N	×	×	×		×		×		×		×		×					×

Table 14.4. Recommended specimen test for studies of mineralization kinetics of added organic matter (AOM) in the soil

AOM	C:N ratio of AOM	weight of AOM
Organic–inorganic fertilizer, organic fertilizer	< 3	75–125 mg
organic fertilizer	3–15	250 mg
organic amendments, poor-N residue from fallow system or crop	> 15	500 mg or more

At time $t = 1$, open the glass jar, remove the polypropylene box containing the sample and store in the freezer for titration of inorganic nitrogen, remove the Nalgene box containing soda, close and preserve in the desiccator on lime or barite. Refill each jar with the following sample and a new Nalgene box containing 20 mL of 0.25 mol (NaOH) L^{-1}

aqueous solution and repeat the same operation at each N sampling (Table 14.2). On days when only C is sampled, only change the soda solution and put back to incubate with the same sample.

Every 5 days, on the balance readjust the moisture of each sample to the weight previously noted tw.

Titrations

For mineralized nitrogen, extraction is performed with molar KCl or K_2SO_4 aqueous solutions and titration following the instructions given in Chap. 28.

For mineralized carbon:
- Adjust the titrimeter by means of buffer solutions at pH 4 and 7; select the titration programme "with no initial addition, detection at a fixed final pH of 8.6, low speed of addition".
- Quickly transfer the contents from the Nalgene box containing the soda-sample into the titration cell containing a small bar magnet while rinsing with a jet of water from the wash bottle, add 5 mL of $BaCl_2$ solution.
- Start moderate bubbling of nitrogen in the solution; introduce the pH electrode and the input tube of the acid titrating solution.
- Start titration, continue until it stops automatically and read the added volume of acid titrating solution in mL: sV for the sample, cV for the control (soil alone for AOM mineralization kinetics), and bV for the blank (without a sample of soil for soil respirometry).

Calculations

Microbial respiration in the incubation pots causes carbonation of soda according to the reaction:
$$2\ NaOH + CO_2 \rightarrow Na_2CO_3 + H_2O$$
The carbonate formed is precipitated by barium chloride according to the reaction:
$$Na_2CO_3 + BaCl_2 \rightarrow BaCO_3{\downarrow} + 2\ NaCl$$
Excess soda is neutralized by hydrochloric acid:
$$NaOH + HCl \rightarrow NaCl + H_2O$$
If at the beginning there are n moles of soda which are then carbonated by x moles of CO_2, $n - 2x$ moles of soda will remain in the sample. The titration of the blank (soil respirometry) or control (AOM kinetics) relates to n moles of soda, consequently the respired CO_2 is obtained by: $n - (n -$

2 x) = 2 x and if aT is the acid titer (mol L^{-1}), CO_2-C from the sample is
expressed in millimoles by:

$$x = \frac{bV - cV}{2} aT \quad \text{for soil respiration,}$$

$$x = \frac{cV - sV}{2} aT \quad \text{for AOM kinetics.}$$

Please refer to Thuriès et al. (2001, 2002), Pansu and Thuriès (2003)
and Pansu et al. (2003) for a more complete expression of these results
and for details on modelling of the kinetics of mineralization.

Remarks

- For AOM kinetics, the difference between inorganic nitrogen of the
  sample and inorganic nitrogen of the control can be positive (net
  mineralization) or negative (immobilization of the pre-existing
  inorganic nitrogen). Net mineralization occurs with relatively N-rich
  AOM and immobilization with low-N AOM. Recous et al. (1995) and
  Henriksen and Breland (1999) observed that when the nitrogen (from
  soil + AOM) is lower than 0.012 × (dry matter AOM), the growth of
  microbial biomass, and mineralization of C are all significantly
  reduced.
- The procedure described above remains valid for ^{13}C, ^{14}C and ^{15}N
  isotopic studies on measured inorganic forms of C and N: on soda
  solutions for C isotopes, and on KCl or K_2SO_4 extracts for N isotopes.
- In addition to titrimetry, other techniques can be used for the titration of
  CO_2 directly in the atmosphere of the incubation jars: by gas
  chromatography (gas–solid chromatography, catharometer detector) or
  by infra-red spectrometry.
- Calculations of the initial weight of soil test samples must take into
  account the risk of anoxia in the incubation jars. To avoid slowing
  down microbial respiration by the atmosphere, the oxygen content of
  the atmosphere in the jar should not drop by more than one-third of its
  initial value.
- The arrangement in the incubation jars (Fig. 14.9) is due to the fact that
  CO_2 is heavier than air. It is thus more logical to place the sample box
  above the soda box.

14.3. Complementary Methods

14.3.1 Alternative Procedures for Acid Hydrolysis

Discontinuous Acid Hydrolysis

Janel et al. (1979) criticized the use of hydrolysis methods for protein studies of complex mediums like soils (cf. Sects. 14.2.1 and 14.2.2 above). This technique is likely to give rise to "secondary reactions between nitrogen compounds and other breakdown products, sugars and other reducing compounds which involve insolubilizations and desaminations".

These authors compared two hydrolysis techniques by reflux boiling with 3 mol (HCl) L^{-1} solutions applied to beech tree litter. Hydrolysis was conducted in parallel for 40 h (1) uninterrupted hydrolysis and (2) discontinuous hydrolysis by decanting the hydrolysate at selected times and replacing it with a fresh attack solution. Changes in total-, amino- and ammonia-nitrogen were monitored in each solution series.

There were similarities between the results of the two hydrolysis techniques, but the changes in the different forms were much more regular in the case of discontinuous hydrolysis: the growth of amino nitrogen followed the growth of hydrolysable total nitrogen, the NH_3-N rate was weaker and almost constant and the rate of non-hydrolyzable nitrogen was under 10%, i.e. much lower than that reported by Bremner (1965) and Stevenson (1982a,b) (Table 14.4). On the other hand, the fraction called combined-N representing unknown hydrolyzed nitrogen remained almost constant at approximately 35% of nitrogen at each hydrolysis time in both methods. This probably represents unstable products that are easily transformed right from the beginning of hydrolysis.

The discontinuous technique thus appeared to be more reliable and was recommended to replace the methods listed earlier in Sects. 14.2.1 and 14.2.2. However, it does not use the same concentration of acid, and has not been tested on a large number of samples. In addition it is considerably more complex to implement. The debate is still open on the type of hydrolysis to use. For example, Egoumenides et al. (1987) used the continuous classical technique, whereas Barriuso et al. (1990) chose to adapt the technique of Janel et al. (1979).

Acid Hydrolysis with Hydrofluoric Pre-Attack

Some observations showed a weak recovery of the amino acids in clay sediments poor in nitrogen. For this reason, a hydrofluoric acid pretreatment was sometimes recommended in hydrolysis procedures (e.g. Cheng et al. 1975; Stevenson and Cheng 1970). The pre-treatment was also recommended by Stevenson (1982a) in the case of further colorimetric titration of amino acids (cf. Sect. 14.3.2):

– Place 50–125 mg of finely crushed soil in a 50 mL polypropylene centrifuge tube, add 2.5 mL of a 5 mol (HF)–0.1 mol (HCl) L^{-1} solution and agitate for 24 h on a back and forth shaker (for calcareous samples, acidify with HCl 6 mol L^{-1} before adding the HCl–HF solution).
– Add 5 mL of distilled water and freeze-dry to eliminate the hydrofluoric acid.
– Add 10 mL of 6 mol (HCl) L^{-1} solution and heat in an oil bath at 110°C with a cooling finger inside the tube to avoid evaporation.
– Let cool and filter on Whatman n°42 filter paper; wash the residue with 10–15 mL of distilled water.

14.3.2 Determination of Amino Acids

Principle

The distillation method in the presence of ninhydrin described in Section 14.2.1 above is well suited for the analysis of soils and sediments containing relatively large quantities of amino acids. For N-poor substrates, it is essential to use more sensitive techniques e.g. colorimetric or chromatographic methods.

For a complete and relatively rapid measurement, the most widely used colorimetric method (e.g. Moore and Stein 1948; Stevenson 1965, 1982a,b,c) measures absorbance of the blue complex produced with ninhydrin at pH 5 (Fig. 14.2). Interference with the metal cations of the hydrolysates can be avoided by conducting the reaction in the presence of a chelating agent. Ammonium and the other nitrogen compounds that are unstable in basic medium (amino sugars) are eliminated by an alkaline pretreatment before the ninhydrin reaction.

Chromatographic methods are more difficult to implement. However, they are more reliable and less subject to interference than colorimetric methods. They also deliver approximately 20 times more information with the individual titration of each amino acid. Nevertheless, the information is difficult to interpret in complex mediums like soils and there are not many studies on this subject.

The free amino acids of the soil solutions can be separated using thin layer chromatography (TLC) with two dimensions (Monreal and McGill 1985). However, the most reliable techniques use liquid ion exchange chromatography and specific apparatuses are available for the measurement of amino acids which function by double ionic exchange. Reverse phase high performance liquid chromatography (HPLC) with precolumn derivatisation with *o*-phtalaldehyde has also been successfully used in soil chemistry (e.g. Warman and Bishop 1985, 1987). Gas chromatography has also been used (e.g. Jocteur Monrozier 1984; Barriuso et al. 1990; Pansu, unpublished data). These techniques have the disadvantage of requiring double derivatization to block the acid and amine functions before injection into the chromatograph, but they have the advantage of good resolution and high sensitivity.

Colorimetry with Ninhydrin

This procedure was proposed by Stevenson (1965, 1982a,b,c).
- Perform the 6 mol (HCl) L^{-1} hydrolysis with a hydrofluoric acid pre-attack (cf. Sect. 14.3.1).
- Collect the filtrate and washing water of the hydrolysis in a second 50 mL polypropylene centrifugation tube and freeze-dry to eliminate HCl.
- To eliminate ammonium and amino sugars: dissolve the residue in 5 mL of distilled water, add two or three drops of phenolphthalein (0.1% ethanolic solution) and titrate with the 5 mol (NaOH) L^{-1} solution until it turns pink (at approximately pH 11). Put the tube in an oil bath at 100°C; after 10 min, evaporate by sweeping the surface with a small air flow to reduce the volume to approximately 2 mL.
- Add the 6 mol (HCl) L^{-1} solution drop by drop until dissolution of the metal hydroxides (solution turns pale yellow) and complete the volume with ammonium-free water.
- *Colorimetry.* Put 0.5 mL of solution in a test tube and add 0.5 mL of a 0.2 mol L^{-1} sodium citrate solution (177.6 mg of dehydrated sodium citrate in 1 L of water). Shake well then add 2 mL of solution prepared as follows: 25 mL of pH 5 sodium acetate buffer solution (500 g $CH_3COONa,3H_2O$ + 100 mL CH_3COOH in 1 L aqueous solution), 50 mL of ninhydrin reagent (4% solution in methyl cellosolve, Kodak) stored in the dark under nitrogen in the presence of Dowex-50 resin in H form, 25 mL water and 80 mg of $SnCl_2,2H_2O$. Cover with an aluminium capsule and place the tube in a boiling water bath at 100°C for 30 min. Cool with cold water, add 5 mL of 50% ethanol solution and measure colour absorbance at 570 nm. Dilute the over-concentrated samples with more 50% ethanol. Compare with a standard range prepared starting from a standard leucine solution containing 28 mg (amino-N) L^{-1}: 0.262 g of leucine + 100 mL 0.1 mol (HCl) L^{-1} solution in 1 L water.

Gas–liquid Chromatography

Principle

A procedure developed for the analysis of the amino acids of proteins by Zanetta and Vincendon (1973) was adapted for soil analysis. Gas–liquid chromatography is performed on the N(O)-heptafluoro-butyrate derivatives of the isoamyl esters of amino acids. The technique is thus rather similar to a previously described technique for the separation of N-trifluoroacetates of butylic esters of amino acids (Gehrke et al. 1971), and used in soil analysis (Jocteur Monrozier 1984; Barriuso et al. 1990). According to Zanetta and Vincendon, the N(O)-heptafluorobutyrate technique may have two advantages over the N-trifluoroacetate technique (1) all the amino acids are more easily separated on commonly used columns and (2) the derivatives are less volatile and the acylation products can be eliminated before injection without risk of loss. The separation obtained by Zanetta and Vincendon was improved at IRD laboratories by the use of a capillary column (Fig. 14.10).

Preparation of samples

– Place 5 mL of soil extract or soil hydrolysate and 100 μL of a 10 μmol mL^{-1} pipecolic acid solution (internal standard) in a cylindrical conical Pyrex flask with a PTFE screw cap.
– Bring to dry by freeze-drying, add 400 μL of anhydrous 1.25 mol (HCl) L^{-1} methanolic solution (prepared by dissolution in anhydrous methanol) of HCl vapour produced by action of H_2SO_4 on NaCl and dried by bubbling in pure H_2SO_4). Let cool for 30 min to 1 h then bring to dry by sweeping the surface with a nitrogen flow at 50°C.
– Add 400 μL of the 1.25 mol (HCl) L^{-1} isoamyl alcohol solution (prepared in the same way as the methanol–HCl solution) and heat the hermetically stopped reaction flasks at 110°C for 2 h 30 min. Cool and bring to dry under a nitrogen flow at 80°C as previously described.
– Dissolve the isoamyl esters in 400 μL of acetonitrile and add 60 μL of heptafluorobutyric anhydride. Heat the hermetically stopped reaction flasks at 150°C for 10 min. Cool and bring just to dry under a nitrogen flow as previously described.
– Dissolve the N(O)-heptafluorobutyrate derivatives of the isoamyl esters of amino acids in 0.5 mL ethyl acetate and inject into the chromatograph or store in the refrigerator until injection.
– At the same time and in the same way, prepare a standard mixture with (1) 1 mL of a solution containing 1 μmol mL^{-1} of each amino acid (commercial standard) and (2) 100 μL of a 10 μmol (pipecolic acid) mL^{-1} solution (internal standard). This solution is used to determine the

response coefficients of each amino acid compared to the pipecolic acid.

Note

If the solutions are rich in inorganic matter, it is advisable to separate these materials before amino acid titration. The simplest way consists in filtering the mixture either immediately before injection, or at the first stage (methanol–HCl) using a syringe filter. Preliminary fractionation by ion exchange is also possible (Gehrke et al. 1971).

Chromatographic Conditions

– Capillary column with no-polar phase e.g. SE30, interior diameter 0.3 mm and length 50 m
– Carrier gas helium, input pressure 1.1 bar
– Programming of furnace: 70–270°C at 4°C min^{-1}
– Flame ionization detector, 250°C
– Splitter-injector, leak flow 50 mL min^{-1}
    Figure 14.10 shows a chromatogram obtained under these conditions.

Note

Although the detection limit is often satisfactory for soils, it can still be considerably improved (1) by using an injector with elimination of solvents (glass needle or split–splitless injector) and (2) by using an electron capture detector (sensitive to the fluorinated derivatives), the latter enables detection of ultratraces of amino acids.

14.3.3 Determination of Amino Sugars

Colorimetric Determination

The colorimetric procedures used for determination of amino sugar in the soil are based on the method described by Elson and Morgan (1933). In alkaline medium, amino sugars react with acetylacetone to give a pyrrole derivative. In acid medium, this derivative produces red condensation with the Ehrlich reagent (*p*-dimethylamino-benzaldehyde in an ethanol–HCl mixture).

    The problem with this technique is its relative lack of selectivity; many substances like iron, amino sugar–acid mixtures, and brown humified products are able to interfere with colouration. In addition, this method suggested by Stevenson (1982a) is rather complex. Before colorimetry, double purification of the extracts has to be performed, first on anion resin, then on cation resin.

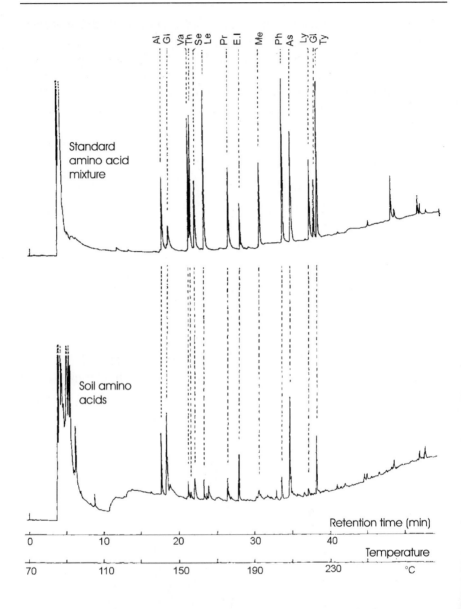

Fig.14.10. Separation by gas chromatography on a standard mixture of amino acids and on a soil extract (Pansu, unpublished data) in the chromatographic conditions described in text. *Al* Alanine, *Gl* Glycine, *Va* Valine, *Th* Threonine, *Se* Serine, *Le* Leucine, *E.I.* pipecolic acid internal standard, *Me* Methionine, *Ph* Phenylalanine, *As* Asparagine, *Ly* Lysine, *Gl* Glutamic acid, *Ty* Tyrosine

More recently, Scheidt and Zech (1990) developed a simplified method for soils inspired by the work of Butseva et al. (1985). This technique, which is still based on that of Elson and Morgan (1933), does not require preliminary purification. After colorimetry, the typical amino sugar chromophore is separated by alkalization and extracted in ethyl ether for colorimetric measurement. This technique appeared to be promising but was not often tested.

Chromatography

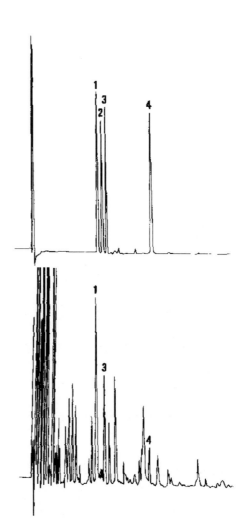

Fig. 14.11. Separation by gas chromatography of amino sugars from a standard solution and a soil hydrolysate (Kögel and Bochter 1985); 1 glucosamine, 2 mannosamine, 3 galactosamine, 4 *p*-amino-phenol–HCl internal standard)

Although like for amino acids, the most widely used techniques are based on ion exchange liquid chromatography, a gas chromatography method was specially developed for the determination of amino sugars in soils (Benzing-Purdie 1981; 1984; Kögel and Bochter 1985). After elimination of the hydrochloric acid of hydrolysis, amino sugar forms are reduced with a solution of sodium borohydride ($NaBH_4$) then the trifluoro-acetate derivatives are synthesized by the action of trifluoroacetic anhydride. These derivatives are separated on a capillary column, then identified and quantified by a detector that selects nitrogen compounds, using p-amino-phenol as internal standard (Fig. 14.11).

14.3.4 Proteins and Glycoproteins (glomalin)

The proteins and glycoproteins in soils originate from decomposition products or are synthesized in situ by micro-organisms. The latter is true of glomalin, a glycoprotein identified by immunofluorescence on hyphae of arbuscular mycorrhizal fungi during active colonization of roots (Wright et al. 1996). Wright and Upadhyaya (1996) observed abundant concentrations of glomalin, ranging from 4 to 15 mg (protein) g^{-1} (soil) on 12 American soils they tested. Glomalin was studied for its role in the structural stability of soils (Wright et al. 1999; Franzluebbers et al. 2000). It is difficult to solubilize, Wright and Upadhyaya (1998) distinguished:
– An "easily" extractable glomalin fraction: 0.25 g soil + 2 mL 20 mM sodium citrate extracting reagent at pH 7 and at 121°C for 30 min.
– *Total glomalin*. The same as above with 50 mM citrate at pH 8 and at 121°C for 90 min or more (sequential extractions).

After centrifuging for 5 min at 5,000g, the protein of the supernatant is measured on a perforated micro titration plate by means of a colouring test for the analysis of proteins using steer serum albumin as standard of calibration.

14.3.5 Potentially Mineralizable Nitrogen by EUF

The technique of EUF was sometimes used to try to separate cations and anions in soluble or more or less exchangeable forms from the organomineral complex in the soil. Figure 14.12 illustrates the principle of this method. A continuous electric field is applied to the water–soil suspension between two filtration membranes. The cations and anions which cross the membranes are collected in the cathodic and anodic compartments, respectively. This method appears to be appropriate but has two disadvantages (1) the accumulation of clays on the anodic filter membrane which slows down the anion exchange processes (nitrates) and

(2) a rise in the pH of the cation cell which is likely to result in loss of ammonium by volatilization (Németh et al. 1988). The second problem can be avoided by adding a hydrochloric acid solution in the cathode compartment.

This method was also proposed for the study of the different forms of nitrogen (Németh et al. 1979; Németh 1985) using two extractions:
– 0–35 min at 20°C and 200 V; this corresponds to the extraction of the actual inorganic nitrogen (ammonium and nitrate).
– 35–40 min at 80°C and 400 V; this characterizes mineralizable organic nitrogen available for plants during their periods of growth.

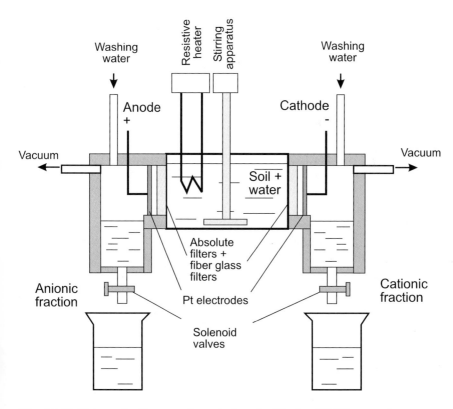

Fig. 14.12. Schematic diagram of an electro-ultrafiltration (EUF) apparatus

EUF techniques have been the object of sometimes contradictory criticism: reproducibility was considered acceptable (Sheehan 1985) but sometimes less so than the reproducibility of more common extraction techniques that are also easier to implement (Houba et al. 1986). Fahd-Rachid (1990) found reproducibility to be generally acceptable for extractable nitric nitrogen but generally unacceptable for EUF mineralizable organic nitrogen. Mengel (1996) used EUF to study the turnover of soil organic nitrogen and its availability for crops, Diez and Vallejo (2004) compared EUF and other methods to determine potentially available organic-N.

References[2]

Organic Nitrogen Forms: General Articles

Chotte JL (1986) Evolution d'une biomasse racinaire doublement marquée (^{14}C, ^{15}N) dans un système sol-plante : étude sur un cycle annuel d'une culture de maïs. Thèse Doctor. Univ. Nancy I, 116 p.+annexes

Guiraud G (1984) *Contribution du marquage isotopique à l'évaluation des transferts d'azote entre les compartiments organiques et minéraux dans les systèmes sol-plante.*, Thèse Doct. es Sciences, Paris 6, 335 p

Jocteur Monrozier L and Andreux F (1981) L'azote organique des sols, exemples de quantification des formes protéiques et des combinaisons complexes. *Science du sol.*, 3, 219–242

Jocteur Monrozier L (1984) *Nature et évolution de l'azote organique dans les sols et les sédiments marins récents.*, Thèse Doct. Etat, Univ. Nancy1, 176 p

Kelley KR and Stevenson FJ (1995) Forms and nature of organic N in soil. *Fert. Res.*, 42, 1–11

Lavoisier AL (1789) Traité élémentaire de chimie, Paris

Matsumoto S, Yamagata M, Koga N and Ae N (2001) Identification of organic forms of nitrogen in soils and possible direct uptake by plants. *Dev. Plant Soil Sci.*, 92, 208–209

Schipper LA, Percival HJ and Sparling G.P. (2004) An approach for estimating when soils will reach maximum nitrogen storage. *Soil Use Manage.*, 20, 281–286

Schulten HR and Schnitzer M (1998) The chemistry of soil organic nitrogen : a review. *Biol. Fertil. Soils*, 26, 1–15

Stevenson FJ (1982a) Nitrogen-organic forms. In *Methods of Soil Analysis*, Page AL, Miller RH and Keeney DR ed. ASA-SSSA N°9 part 2, 2nd edition, 625–641

Stevenson FJ (1982b) Organic forms of soil nitrogen. In *Humus Chemistry*, Wiley, New York, 55–119

Stevenson FJ (1982c) Origin and distribution of nitrogen in soil. In *Nitrogen in Agricultural Soils*, Stevenson FJ ed. American Society of Agronomy, 1–42

Stevenson FJ (1996) Nitrogen-organic forms. In *Methods of Soil Analysis*, Bigham JM and Bartels JM ed. ASA-SSSA N°5 part 3, 3rd edition, 1185–1200

---

[2] The authors quoted several times in the text are indicated in only heading where their contribution was considered to be the most significant.

Nitrogen Forms by Acid Hydrolysis and Distillation

Bremner (1960) Forms of nitrogen in soils and plants. *Rothamsted Exp. Stat. Rep.*, for 1959, p 59

Bremner (1965) Organic forms of soil nitrogen. In *Methods of Soil Analysis*, Black CA et al. ed. American Society of Agronomy, USA 9, part 2, 1238–1255

Egoumenides C, Risterucci A and Melebou KE (1987) Appréciation de la fertilité azotée des sols tropicaux : étude des fractions organiques de l'azote. *L'agronomie tropicale*, 42, 85–93

Keeney DR and Bemner JM (1967) A simple steam distillation method of estimating β-hydroxy-α-amino acids. *Anal. Biochem.*, 18, 274–285

Tracey MV (1952) The determination of glucosamine by alkaline decomposition. *Biochem. J.*, 52, 265–267

Van Slyke (1911–1912) The analysis of proteins by determination of the chemical groups characteristic of the different amino-acids. *J. Biol. Chem.*, 10, 15–55

Improvement of Acid Hydrolysis

Barriuso E, Andreux F and Portal JM (1990) Caractérisation par hydrolyse acide de l'azote des fractions organiques et organo-minérales d'un sol humifère. *Science du sol.*, 1990, 28, 223–236

Cheng CN, Shufeldt RC and Stevenson FJ (1975) Amino acid analysis of soils and sediments : extraction and desalting. *Soil Biol. Biochem.*, 7, 143–151

Griffith SM, Sowden FJ and Schnitzer M (1976) The alkaline hydrolysis of acid-resistant soil and humic acid residues. *Soil Biol. Biochem.*, 8, 529

Janel Ph, Jocteur Monrozier L and Toutain F (1979) Caractérisation de l'azote des litières et des sols par hydrolyse acide, *Soil Biol. Biochem.*, 11, 141–146

Determination of Amino Acids

Gehrke CW, Zumwalt RW and Kuo K (1971) Quantitative amino acid analysis by gas-liquid chromatography. *J. Agric. Food Chem.*, 19, 605–618

Monreal CM and McGill WB (1985) Centrifugal extraction and determination of free amino acids in soil solutions by TLC using tritiated 1-fluoro-2,4-dinitrobenzène. *Soil Biol. Biochem.*, 17, 533–539

Moore S and Stein WH (1948) Photometric ninhydrin method for use in the chromatography of amino acids. *J. Biol. Chem.*, 176, 367–388

Stevenson FJ and Cheng CN (1970) Amino acids in sediments : recovery by acid hydrolysis and quantitative estimation by a colorimetric procedure. *Geochim. Cosmochim. Acta.*, 34, 77–88

Stevenson (1965) Amino acids. In *Methods of Soil Analysis*, Black C.A. et al. ed. American Society of Agronomy 9, part 2, 1437–1451

Warman PR and Bishop C (1985) The use of reverse-phase HPLC for soil amino-N analysis, *J. Liquid Chromat.*, 8, 2595–2606

Warman PR and Bishop C (1987) Free and HF–HCl-extractable amino acids determined by high performance liquid chromatography in a loamy sand soil. *Biol Fertil. Soils*, 5, 215–218

Zanetta JP and Vincendon G (1973) Gas–liquid chromatography of the N(O)-heptafluorobutyrates of the isoamyl esters of amino acids. I. Separation and quantitative determination of the constituent amino acids of proteins. *J. Chromat.*, 76, 91–99

Determination of Amino Sugars

Benzing-Purdie L (1981) Glucosamine and galactosamine distribution in a soil as determined by gas-liquid chromatography on soil hydrolysates : effect of acid strength and cations. *Soil Sci. Soc. Am. J.*, 45, 66–70

Benzing-Purdie L (1984) Amino sugar distribution in four soils as determined by high resolution gas chromatography. *Soil Sci. Soc. Am. J.*, 48, 219–222

Burtseva TI, Cherkasova SA and Ovodov YuS (1985) Quantitative determination of amino sugars in bacterial lipopolysaccharides. *Khimiya Prirodnykh Soedinenii*, 6, 739–743

Elson LA and Morgan WTJ (1933) A colorimetric method for the determination of glucosamine and chondrosamine. *Biochem. J.*, 27, 1824–1828

Kögel I and Bochter R (1985) Amino sugar determination in organic soils by capillary gas chromatography using a nitrogen-selective detector. *Z. Pflanzenernaehr. Bodenk.*, 148, 260–267

Scheidt M and Zech W (1990) A simplified procedure for the photometric determination of amino sugars in soil. *Z. Pflanzenernähr. Bodenk.*, 153, 207–208

Glomalin

Franzluebbers AJ, Wright SF and Stuedemann JA (2000) Soil aggregation and glomalin under pastures in the southern piedmont USA. *Soil Sci. Soc. Am. J.*, 64, 1018–1026

Wright SF, Franke-Snyder M, Morton JB and Upadhyaya A (1996) Time-course study and partial characterization of a protein on hyphae of arbuscular mycorrhizal fungi during active colonization of roots. *Plant Soil*, 181, 193–203

Wright SF and Upadhyaya A (1996) Extraction of an abundant and unusual protein from soil and comparison with hyphal protein of arbuscular mycorrhizal fungi. *Soil Sci.*, 161, 575–586

Wright SF and Upadhyaya A (1998) A survey of soils for aggregate stability and glomalin, a glycoprotein produced by hyphae of arbuscular mycorrhizal fungi. *Plant Soil*, 198, 97–107

Wright SF, Starr JL and Paltineanu IC (1999) Changes in aggregate stability and concentration of Glomalin during tillage management transition. *Soil Sci. Soc. Am. J.*, 63, 1825–1829

Urea Titration

Beaton JD (1978) Urea– its popularity grows as a dry source of nitrogen. *Crops Soils*, 30, 11–14

Bremner JM (1982) Nitrogen-Urea. In *Methods of Soil Analysis, Part 2*, Page AL et al. ed. ASA-SSSA N°9 part 2, 2rd edition, 699–709

Douglas LA and Bremner JM (1970) Extraction and colorimetric determination of urea in soils. *Soil Sci. Soc. Am. Proc.*, 34, 859–862

Douglas LA, Sochtig H, and Flaig W (1977) Colorimetric determination of urea in soil extracts using an automated system. *Soil Sci. Soc. Am. J.*, 42, 291–292

Fearon WR (1939) The carbamido diacetyl reaction : a test for citrullin. *Biochem. J.*, 33, 902–907

Mulvaney RL and Bremner JM (1979) A modified diacetyl monoxime method for colorimetric determination of urea in soil extracts. *Commun. Soil Sci. Plant Anal.*, 10, 1163–1170

Watt GW and Chrisp JD (1954) Spectrophotometric method for determination of urea. *Anal. Chem.*, 26, 452–453

Potentially Mineralizable Nitrogen : General Papers

Catroux G, Chaussod R and Nicolardot B (1987) Appréciation de la fourniture d'azote par le sol. *C. R. Acad. Agric. Fr.*, 73, 71–79

Cornforth IS and Walmsley D (1971) Methods of measuring available nutrients in west indian soils.1.Nitrogen. *Plant Soil*, 35, 389–399

Dahnke WC and Johnson GV (1990) Testing soils for available nitrogen. In *soil Testing and Plant Analysis*, 3rd. ed. SSSA book series, n°3, 127–139

Fahd-Rachid (1990) *Mise au point méthodologique sur l'estimation de l'azote organique potentiellement minéralisable dans le sol.*, DEA INP-ENSAT Toulouse, Document ORSTOM-Montpellier N°1, 60 p. multig.

Gianello C and Bremner JM (1986) Comparison of chemical methods of assessing potentially available organic nitrogen in soil, *Commun. Soil Sci. Plant Anal.*, 17, 215–236

Giroux M and Sen Tran T (1987) Comparaison de différentes méthodes d'analyse de l'azote du sol en relation avec sa disponibilité pour les plantes. *Can. J. Soil Sci.*, 67, 521–531

Juma NG and Paul EA (1984) Mineralizable soil nitrogen : Amounts and extractability ratios, *Soil Sci. Soc. Am. J.*, 48, 76–80

Keeney DR and Bremner JM (1966) Comparison and evaluation of laboratory methods of obtaining an index of soil nitrogen availability. *Agron. J.*, 58, 498–503

Keeney DR (1982) Nitrogen-Availability indices. In *Methods of Soil Analysis, Part 2*, Page AL et al. ed. ASA-SSSA N°9 part 2, 2nd edition, 711–733

Potentially Mineralizable Nitrogen : Biological Methods

Benedetti, A., Sebastiani, G. 1996. Determination of potentially mineralizable nitrogen in agricultural soils. Biology and Fertility of Soils 21, 114–120

Cabrera ML and Kissel DE (1988) Evaluation of a method to predict nitrogen mineralized from soil organic matter under field conditions. Soil Sci. Soc. Am. J., 52, 1027–1031

Campbell CA (1978) Soil organic carbon, Nitrogen and fertility. In Soil Organic Matter, Schnitzer and Khan ed. Elsevier, Amsterdam, 224–225 and 254

Chaussod R, Nicolardot B, Soulas G and Joannes H (1986) Mesure de la biomasse microbienne dans les sols cultivés. II-Cinétique de minéralisation de matière organique microbienne marquée au C^{14}. Rev. Ecol. Biol. Sol., 23, 183–196

Deans JR, Molina JAE and Clapp CE (1986) Models for predicting potentially mineralizable nitrogen and decomposition rate constants. Soil Sci. Soc. Am. J., 50, 323–326

Keeney DR and Bremner JM (1967) Determination and isotope ratio analysis of different forms of nitrogen in soil : 6. mineralizable nitrogen. Soil Sci. Soc. Am. Proc., 31, 34

Marquardt DW (1963) An algorithm for least-squares estimations of nonlinear parameters. J. Soc. Ind. Appl. Math., 11, 431–441

Mary B and Rémy JC (1979) Essai d'appréciation de la capacité de minéralisation de l'azote des sols de grande culture. I. Signification des cinétiques de minéralisation de la matière organique humifiée. Ann. Agron., 30, 513–527

Nuske A and Richter J (1981) N-mineralization in löss-parabrownearthes : incubation experiments. Plant Soil, 59, 237–247

Reynolds WD and Beauchamp EG (1984) Comments on " Potential errors in the first-order model for estimating soil nitrogen mineralization potentials ", Soil Sci. Soc. Am. J., 48, 698

Richter J, Nuske A, Habenicht and W Bauer J (1982) Optimized N-mineralization parameters of loess soils from incubation experiment. Plant Soil, 68, 379–388

Robertson K, Schnürer J, Clarholm M, Bonde TA and Rosswall T (1988) Microbial biomass in relation to C and N mineralization during laboratory incubations. Soil Biol. Biochem., 20, 281–286

Seyfried MS and Rao PSC (1988) Kinetic of nitrogen mineralization in Costa Rican soils: model evaluation and pretreatment effects. Plant Soil, 106, 159–169

Smith JL, Schnabel RR, McNeal BL and Campbell GS (1980) Potential errors in the first-order model for estimating soil nitrogen mineralization potentials. Soil Sci. Soc. Am. J., 44, 996–1000

Stanford G and Smith SJ (1972) Nitrogen mineralization potentials of soils. Soil Sci. Soc. Am. Proc., 36, 465–472

Stanford G, Carter JN, and Smith SJ (1974) Estimates of potentially mineralizable soil nitrogen based on short-term incubations. *Soil Sci. Soc. Am. Proc.*, 38, 99–102

Waring SA and Bremner JM (1964) Ammonium production in soil under waterlogged conditions as an index of nitrogen availability. *Nature (London)*, 201, 951

Potentially Mineralizable Nitrogen: Chemical Methods

Campbell CA, Jame YW, Jalil A and Schoenau J (1997) Use of hot KCl-NH4-N to estimate fertilizer N requirements. *Can. J. Soil Sci.*, 77,161–166

Fox RH and Piekielek WP (1978) A rapid method for estimating the nitrogen-supplying capability of a soil. *Soil Sci. Soc. Am. J.*, 42, 751–753

Gianello C and Bremner JM, (1988) A rapid steam distillation method of assessing potentially available organic nitrogen in soil, *Commun. Soil Sci. Plant Anal.*, 19, 1551-1568

Guiraud G and Fardeau JC (1977) Dosage par la méthode Kjeldahl des nitrates contenus dans les sols et les végétaux. *Ann. Agron.*, 28, 329–333

Mac Lean OA (1964) Measurement of nitrogen supplying power of soils by extraction with sodium bicarbonate. *Nature*, 203, 1307–1308

Фien A and Selmer-Olsen AR (1980) A laboratory method for evaluation of available nitrogen in soil. *Acta Agric. Scand.*, 30, 149

Stanford G and Smith SJ (1978) Oxidative release of potentially mineralizable soil nitrogen by acid permanganate extraction, *Soil Sci.*, 126, 210

Stanford G (1978) Evaluation of ammonium release by alcaline permanganate extraction as an index of soil nitrogen availability. *Soil Sci.*, 126, 244

Velly J, Egoumenides C, Pichot J and Marger JL (1980) L'azote extractible par une solution de KCl et la fourniture d'azote à la plante dans 40 sols tropicaux. *Agronomie tropicale*, 35, 374–380

Whitehead DC (1981) An improved chemical extraction method for predicting the supply of available soil nitrogen. *J. Sci. Food Agric.*, 32, 359–365

Potentially Mineralizable Nitrogen by EUF

Diez JA and Vallejo A (2004) Comparison of two methods for nitrogen extraction of irrigated Spanish soils and related nitrogen balance calibrations. *Commun. in Soil Sci. Plant Anal.*, 35, 2227–2242

Houba VJG, Novozamsky I, Huybregts AWM and Van der Lee JJ (1986) Comparison of soil extractions by 0.01M $CaCl_2$, by EUF and by some conventional extraction procedures. *Plant Soil*, 96, 433–437

Mengel K (1996) Turnover of organic nitrogen in soils and its availability to crops. *Plant soil*, 181, 83–93

Nemeth K (1985) Recent advances in EUF research (1980-1983). *Plant and Soil*, 83, 1–19

Nemeth K, Bartels H, Vogel H and Mengel K (1988) Organic nitrogen compounds extracted from arable and forest soils by EUF and recovery rats of amino acids. *Biol. Fertil. Soils*, 5, 271–275

Nemeth K, Makhdum IQ, Koch K and Beringer H (1979) Determination of categories of soil nitrogen by electro-ultrafiltration (EUF). *Plant Soil*, 53, 445–453

Sheehan MP (1985) Experiments on the reproducibility of results from EUF soil extracts with possible improvements resulting from these experiments. *Plant Soil*, 83, 85–92

Mineralization Kinetics

Blet-Charaudeau, C, Muller, J and Laudelout, H (1990) Kinetics of carbon dioxide evolution in relation to microbial biomass and temperature. *Soil Sci. Soc. of Am. J.,* 54, 1324–1328

Bottner P, Coûteaux MM, Anderson JM, Berg B, Billès G, Bolger T, Casabianca H, Romanya J and Rovira P (2000) Decomposition of ^{13}C labelled plant material in a European 65-40° latitudinal transect of coniferous forest soils: simulation of climate change by translocation of soils. *Soil Biol. & Biochem.*, 32, 527–543

Henriksen, TM and Breland, TA (1999) Nitrogen availability effects on carbon mineralization, fungal and bacterial growth, and enzyme activities during decomposition of wheat straw in soil. *Soil Biol. & Biochem.,* 31, 1121–1134

Pansu M, Sallih Z and Bottner P (1998) Modelling of soil nitrogen forms after organic amendments under controlled conditions. *Soil Biol. & Biochem.*, 30, 19–29

Pansu M and Thuriès L (2003). Kinetics of C and N mineralization, N immobilization and N volatilization of organic inputs in soil. *Soil Biol. & Biochem.*, 35, 37–48

Pansu M, Thuriès L, Larré-Larrouy MC and Bottner P (2003) Predicting N transformations from organic inputs in soil in relation to incubation time and biochemical composition. *Soil Biol. & Biochem.*, 35, 353–363

Recous, S, Robin, D, Darwis, D and Mary, B (1995) Soil inorganic N availability: effect on maize residue decomposition. *Soil Biol. & Biochem.*, 27, 1529–1538

Thuriès L, Larré-Larrouy MC and Pansu M (2000) Evaluation of three incubation designs for mineralization kinetics of organic materials in soil. *Commun. Soil Sci. Plant Analy.*, 31, 289–304

Thuriès L, Pansu M, Feller C, Hermann P, and Rémy JC (2001) Kinetics of added organic matter decomposition in a mediterranean sandy soil. *Soil Biol. & Biochem.*, 33, 997–1010

Thuriès L, Pansu M, Larre-Larrouy MC and Feller C (2002) Biochemical composition and mineralization kinetics of organic inputs in a sandy soil. *Soil Biol. & Biochem.*, 34, 239–250

Part 3

Inorganic Analysis

Exchangable and Total Elements

pH Measurement

15.1 Introduction

15.1.1 Soil pH

In the range of measurements available to characterize a soil at a given time, the measurement of pH (potential of the H^+ ion) is undoubtedly one of the most widely used. Its simplicity and speed of implementation make measuring soil pH a routine laboratory operation.

In soil science, for practical purposes, the pH range is reduced from 0–14 to 1–12. Soils with an extreme pH are strongly influenced by salts, resulting in very acid sulphated soils to highly alkaline carbonated soils. The aim of pH measurement depends on the user as described later.

In the laboratory, preliminary measurement of pH enables suitable methods of extraction and measurement to be chosen that are appropriate for acid, neutral or basic soils as a function of the pH of the soil concerned (e.g. measurement of exchangeable cation or available elements like phosphorus). However, it should be kept in mind that "soil pH" represents only the pH of a solution in equilibrium with the soil.

From a soil scientist's point of view, measurement of the pH of a soil sample is a global assessment. The French pedological reference base (INRA, 1995) gives the following classification for the pH spectrum:

pH lower than 3.5	hyper-acid
between 3.5 and 5.0	very acid
between 5.0 and 6.5	acid
between 6.5 and 7.5	neutral
between 7.5 and 8.7	basic
greater than 8.7	very basic.

The pH characterizes the physicochemical environment of a soil at a given site, this being the result of instantaneous equilibriums controlled by different components of the medium, for example:

– Mixed sulphated salts with hyper-acid reaction resulting from sulphide oxidation of the mangrove (acid sulphated soils).
– A range of organic or inorganic acids and elements such as aluminium or iron which are likely to acidify the soil solution after acid hydrolysis starting from minerals or from the exchange complex.
– Neutral salts of strong acids and strong bases, or soils with a saturated exchange complex but with low calcium carbonate which have a pH close to neutral.
– In the presence of calcium carbonate in an open system at partial pressure of atmospheric CO_2, equilibrium is established around pH 8.4 in soil suspensions; CO_2 pressure can reach higher values, especially in deep soil horizons, and can significantly affect the equilibrium pH.
– In certain soils, magnesium carbonate results in high pH values i.e. around pH 9. Sodic carbonated salts result in the highest values which can exceed pH 10.

This review of the pH spectrum of soils emphasizes *from a static point of view* the influence of two types of factors on this complex equilibrium:

– At the extremes of the range, the influence of large quantities of very soluble acid or basic salts; and, to a lesser extent, the influence of organic or inorganic acids and of all compounds that can cause acid hydrolysis.
– In soils, the system is generally more dependent on CO_2 pressure and on elements involved in the exchange complex (H^+ ions, metal ions) which buffer possible variations in pH through permanent exchanges between the soil and the soil solution.

However, it is essential to consider pH measurement *from a dynamic point of view* because of the many different types of equilibrium likely to be established at different times which oscillate under the influence of different internal and external factors. Waterlogging of the soil undoubtedly has the most influence on the physicochemical environment. Seasonal variations in moisture and especially the rhythm of these variations can significantly modify the concentration of the soil solution by hydrolysis and by the release of protons or cations, dissolution and leaching, or on the contrary, by concentration and precipitation. These general remarks about environmental aspects emphasize several different concepts concerning the pH of the soil:

– Actual acidity or alkalinity expressed by the concentration of dissociated protons in the soil solution.
– Exchange acidity resulting from protons fixed on the exchangeable complex and likely to move after exchange with neutral salts (KCl).

– Potential acidity expressed by the acidity (measured in saturation conditions) of sulphides (acid sulphated soils) or more generally after displacement of all the acid functions of the soil by hydrolysis.
– Buffering capacity which limits variations in pH by continuous exchange between the soil and soil solution, the most important determining factors being the degree of dilution and the quality of the exchange complex (clay type and saturation rate).

From an agronomic point of view the pH is initially an indicator of the state of soil fertility. It provides information about possible chemical degradation of the soil due to desaturation, the possible presence of certain toxic salts, and about microbial activity, as well as the degree of assimilability of elements by plants, the best range of solubility being between pH 5.5 and pH 6.5. Below pH 5.5, certain elements can be toxic (e.g. free aluminium, manganese), other elements may not be in available forms (e.g. phosphorus) or may sometimes be fixed in the solid phase. Above 6.5, other elements cannot be available (e.g. trace elements).

Knowledge of soil pH also makes it possible to choose to grow crops e.g. acidophilic plants like tea or coffee, or plants with neutrophilic cells. Finally it provides useful information enabling the right choice of corrective action (1) fertilizer with an acidifying (e.g. ammonia salts), neutralizing or alkalizing (e.g. saltpetre, ammonia) action and (2) fertilizer or amendment to increase or decrease the pH and to improve the fertility of cultivated soils (e.g. liming). However, knowledge of the pH alone is not sufficient to evaluate, for example, the precise lime requirements (cf. Chap. 24) or exchange acidity and aluminium toxicity (cf. Chap. 23).

15.1.2 Difficulties

Measuring pH is simple, but this simplicity can be misleading as the pH measurement can be wrong if careful attention is not paid to details (such as the state of junction of the electrodes and electric stability). A precise measurement procedure should be used and the technical choices should be appropriate. Several other aspects should also be considered when interpreting results:
– pH measurements are most often carried out in standardized conditions, on disturbed samples and soil suspensions, and this means they do not reflect the real conditions.
– The problem of the spatial variability of measurement linked to the heterogeneous condition of the soil horizons, of aggregates and of organized microsites.
– Natural or induced temporal variations due to the influence of external factors like moisture or the cultivation system.

All these points argue in favour of in situ pH measurement. If *carried out continuously* under perfect technical conditions, the results of in situ pH measurement (cf. Sect. 15.3) will be the closest possible to the real conditions in the field and thus the most likely to provide information on the complex equilibria between the soil and its solution, as well as on the many external factors that influence them. Despite these facts, standardized laboratory measurements remain the most widely used because they are simple to implement.

15.1.3 Theoretical Aspects

According to Brönsted, acids release protons by dissociation during the reaction:

$$\text{Acid} \Leftrightarrow \text{base} + H^+ \cdot \qquad\qquad (15.1)$$

This reaction takes place in the presence of an acceptor of protons. A strong acid is an acid which can release protons more easily. Two solutions of equal molecular concentration, one of hydrochloric acid, the other of acetic acid, both require the same quantity of soda to be neutralized. But a rise in temperature during neutralization has a stronger effect on hydrochloric acid: it can thus be said that hydrochloric acid is "stronger" than acetic acid. It is this concept of "strength" – which for a long time remained unclear – which is quantified by the measurement of pH. In the case of a strong acid, the equilibrium of reaction (15.1) is strongly moved to the right. It is possible to quantify the strength of an acid by determining the quantity of H^+ ions the acid can dissociate.

The dissociation of an acid (HA) in a solvent (S) can be written:

$$HA + S \Leftrightarrow A^- + SH^+$$

Most often the acid is in aqueous solution. The water solvent can play the role of either an acid:

$$H_2O \Leftrightarrow OH^- + H^+$$

or a base :

$$H_2O + H^+ \Leftrightarrow H_3O^+$$

Applying the mass action law:

$$|OH^-| \, |H_3O^+| \, /(H_2O)^2 = K$$

K is a dissociation constant determined at a given temperature. As the dissociated part remains extremely weak compared to the total number of water molecules, the denominator can be regarded as constant, thus:

$$|H_3O^+| \, |OH^-| = K_{H_2O} \qquad\qquad (15.2)$$

with $K_{H_2O} = 10^{-14}$ at 25°C. As in pure water, ionized H_3O^+ and OH^- forms are equal: $|H_3O^+| = |OH^-| = 10^{-7}$. Thus in aqueous solution, the addition of an acid will increase the quantity of H_3O^+ hydronium ions giving $H_3O^+ > 10^{-7}$. In neutral medium $H_3O^+ = 10^{-7}$ and in alkaline medium $H_3O^+ < 10^{-7}$. The Sorensen representation (1909), called pH, was adopted because of its convenience:

$$pH = - \log |H_3O^+| \qquad (15.3)$$

pH expresses the activity of the hydronium ion. In the case of an aqueous solution of strong acid, this activity is comparable with the concentration of the acid. In the case of a strong base, it can be calculated with formula (15.2). pH ranges between pH 0 (very acid) and pH 14 (very basic). Ten-fold dilution modifies the pH by one unit (in the case of strong acids or bases). In practice, if the concentration of the H^+ ions is multiplied by two, the pH decreases by approximately 0.3. According to (15.1) and the law of mass action:

$$|Base|\,|H_3O^+|\,/\,|acid| = K_A. \qquad (15.4)$$

K_A defines the acidity constant of the acid/base couple (in activities). It is more convenient to use:

$$pK_A = - \log K_A. \qquad (15.5)$$

An acid is stronger since its pK_A is low. Equations (15.3–15.5) enable the creation of a general formula of pH of an acid solution in equilibrium with its combined base:

$$pH = pK_A + \log (|Base|\,/\,|Acid|). \qquad (15.6)$$

Equation (15.6) shows that the fluctuations in the pH of a solution decrease with variations in concentration when the acid form is in balance with a similar quantity of the corresponding basic form. The pH then approaches pK_A. Such a solution has a stable pH, and is not very sensitive to the addition of an acid or base. This stabilizing effect is called *buffer effect*. It is obtained by mixing an acid and corresponding base or an acid and one of its ionized salts. Buffer solutions are used as reference pH or to maintain a fixed pH in certain reactions. The exchange complex of soils has also a buffering effect on the soil solution in equilibrium while fixing or releasing protons.

Equation (15.6) is not valid in the case of acids or bases alone in solution (pH would then tend to $-\infty$ or $+\infty$, respectively). However it is always easy to calculate the pH using formulas (15.2–15.5) with the following approximations:

In the case of an aqueous solution of weak acid the equilibrium reaction of dissolution $AH + H_2O \Leftrightarrow H_3O^+ + A^-$ shows that the concentration of the A^- basic form is similar to the concentration of the H_3O^+ ions induced by dissolution. In addition, if C_A is the total concentration of the acid, the concentration of the AH acid form becomes $C_A - |H_3O^+|$. In the case of a weak acid, the concentration of the hydronium ions can be considered as weak compared to C_A. Equation

(15.4) thus becomes $K_A = |H_3O^+|^2 / C_A$ which, applying equations (15.3) and (15.5) with C_A expressed in normality, gives:

$$pH = (pK_A - \log C_A)/2. \quad\quad (15.7)$$

In the case of a weak basic aqueous solution the equilibrium reaction is written: $B + H_2O \Leftrightarrow BH + OH^-$. The concentration of the acid form BH is similar to that of OH^- ions induced by dissolution. If C_B is the total concentration of the base, the concentration of the basic form B is written: $C_B - |OH^-|$. In the case of a weak base, the concentration of OH^- ions remains weak compared to C_B and (15.4) relating to the equilibrium of BH acid can be written: $K_A = C_B |H_3O^+| / |OH^-|$
which, applying (15.2), (15.3) and (15.5), gives:

$$pH = 7 + 1/2 \, (pK_A + \log C_B). \quad\quad (15.8)$$

Lewis applied the acid–base concept of Bronsted to non-protonic systems suitable for all solvents, an acid being a substance that can accept electrons and a base being a substance that can produce electrons. The pooling of an electronic doublet of the base with the free orbital of the acid results in neutralization. Clay minerals with sites that can produce electrons can be regarded as Lewis bases, whereas hydroxyl and carboxyl groups of soil organic matter that can accept electrons correspond to Lewis acids.

15.2 Classical Measurements

15.2.1 Methods

As described in Sect. 15.1.3, pH defines the activity of the hydronium ion. This ion activity is only comparable with the ion concentration in the case of sufficiently diluted solutions. The concentration of an acid is its titration acidity (total acidity). The activity defines the quantity of "free" (i.e. dissociated) H^+ ions taken into account in the pH measurement. Two methods are used (1) the colorimetric method, which is inexpensive and fast but not very precise especially in turbid or coloured mediums and (2) the electrometric method which is more commonly used.

Table 15.1. Main coloured indicators available in the range of pH of soils

common name	chemical name	acid form	pH transition	basic form
thymol blue	thymol sulphone phthalein	red	1.9 orange	yellow
dinitrophenol	2,6 ou 2,4 dinitrophenol	colourless	3.1	yellow
methyl orange	dimethyl amino azo benzene sodium sulphonate	red	3.7 yellow	orange
bromo phenol blue	tetra bromo phenol sulphone phthalein	yellow	4.0 purple	violet
bromo cresol green	tetra bromo m-cresol sulphone phthalein	yellow	4.6 green	blue
chloro phenol red	dichloro phenol sulphone phthalein	yellow	5.6 pink orange	purple
p-nitrophenol	p nitro phenol	colourless	5.2	yellow
methyl red	dimethyl amino azo benzene o-carboxylic acid	red	5.7 orange	yellow
bromo cresol purple	dibromo o-cresol sulphone phthalein	yellow	6.2 purple	violet
bromo thymol blue	dibromo thymol sulphone phthalein	yellow	6.9 green	blue
phenol red	phenol sulphone phthalein	yellow	7.3 red orange	violet
m-cresol purple	m-cresol sulphone phthalein	yellow	8.3 orange	red
phenolphthalein	phenolphthalein	colourless	8.3 pink	pink
thymol blue	thymol sulphone phthalein	yellow	8.9 purple	blue violet
alizarine yellow	nitrobenzene azo salicylic acid	yellow	10.3 orange	red

15.2.2 Colorimetric Method

Principle

This is a cheap fast method which can be used for a rapid investigation of the soil. The main difficulty is making a visual comparison with a coloured standard, and comparison can be particularly difficult in the case of coloured or turbid solutions. An apparatus for photoelectric comparison can be used to avoid errors resulting from observations made with the naked eye.

It was known for many years that coloured substances were likely to change colour as a function of the acid or basic nature of a solution (Table 15.1). How the colour indicators functioned finally became clear in the light of the theory of electrolytic dissociation. Coloured indicators can be regarded as weak electrolytes in which one of the ions is coloured, whereas the condensed form is colourless or of another colour, according to a dissociation equilibrium of type:

indicator–H (colourless) $\Leftrightarrow$ indicator (coloured) $+ H^+$

pH indicators also frequently use impregnation of paper strips that can be put in direct contact with most soils. This method is very rapid but not very precise (disturbance by the ionic micellar mediums, salts, time of equilibrium, etc.). It is used for preliminary tests in the field or laboratory (Pansu et al. 2001).

Measurements

Variation in colour is only perceptible within the transition zone, which for the majority of indicators represents a change of one pH unit. The existing indicators cover a range from pH 1 to pH 12 (Tables 15.1 and 15.2). Measurement consists in comparing the colour of an indicator in a buffer solution of given pH (Table 15.3) with the colour obtained by adding the indicator to the unknown solution. Using chrysoidine, Qiu and Zhu (1986) simultaneously determined the pH, the buffer power and the lime requirement of soils.

The unknown solution is put in a tube of the same shape as the tube containing the standard buffers; and a predetermined number of drops of indicator are added to the solution. As mentioned earlier, visual comparison is often difficult because the unknown solutions may themselves be slightly coloured or turbid. Comparison can be improved by using a standard comparator (Fig. 15.1).

Table 15.2. Preparation of indicators for soils with a pH range from 2.8 to 11

indicator	pH transition	colour transition	concentration of solutions	pK at 18°C
α dinitrophenol	2.4–4.4	colourless to yellow	0.1 g in 200 mL water	4.06
γ dinitrophenol	4–5.4	colourless to yellow	0.1 g in 440 mL water	5.15
p-nitrophenol	5.2–7.6	colourless to yellow	0.1 g in 100 mL water	7.18
m-nitrophenol	6.6–8.8	colourless to yellow	0.3 g in 100 mL water	8.33
phenolphthalein	8.5–10.5	colourless to red	0.04 g in 100 mL alcohol at 30%	9.73
alizarine yellow	10–12	colourless to yellow	0.05 g in 100 mL alcohol at 50%	11.16

Table 15.3. Preparation of pH reference solutions with Britton and Robinson's universal buffer

V: volume in mL of solution 2 to add to 100 mL of solution 1 to obtain the corresponding pH

Solution 1	Phosphoric acid	H_3PO_4 mw = 98, d = 1.70 (85%)	2.71 mL
	Acetic acid	CH_3COOH, mw = 60, d = 1.05 (100%)	2.28 mL
	Boric acid	H_3BO_3, mw = 61.8, 99%	2.5 g
	Dissolve and bring to 1,000 mL		
Solution 2	Aqueous solution NaOH M/5 (carbonate free)		

α dinitrophenol		γ dinitrophenol		p-nitrophenol		m-nitrophenol		phenolphthalein	
V	pH	V	pH	V	pH	V	pH	V	pH
17.5	2.87	25	4.10	37.5	5.3	50	6.8	65	8.69
20	3.29	27.5	4.35	40	5.72	52.5	7	67.5	8.95
22.5	3.78	30	4.56	42.5	6.09	55	7.24	70	9.15
25	4.10	32.5	4.78	45	6.37	57.5	7.54	72.5	9.37
27.5	4.35	35	5.02	47.5	6.59	60	7.96	75	9.62
		37.5	5.33	50	6.80	62.5	8.36	77.5	9.91
				52.5	7	65	8.69	80	10.38

Procedure

To make scales of comparison, add 6 mL of buffer solution (Table 15.3) in a graduated test tube suitable for use with the Walpole standard comparator (Fig. 15.1). Add 1 mL of the indicator solution that is appropriate for the pH concerned (Table 15.2). Treat the soil solution in the same way.

The aim is to obtain the same colours in (1) the tube containing the unknown solution (position 2 in Fig 15.1) as in (2) the standard tubes representing gradual variations in pH (and thus in colour) in positions 1 and 3. Places 6 and 4 are occupied by the unknown solution with no indicator to eliminate the effect of the original colour of this solution. These measurements are rapid and have an accuracy of only 0.2 pH units. If the solution is turbid, preliminary standard filtration on a Millipore filter is recommended.

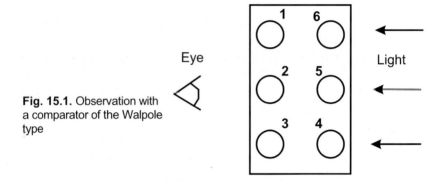

Fig. 15.1. Observation with a comparator of the Walpole type

15.2.3 Electrometric Method

Principle

The electrometric method is the most frequently used method for soil analysis as it is more precise than the colorimetric method. It enables both turbid and coloured mediums to be analysed and continuous measurements to be made.

To measure true pH values a thin layer of hydrogen can be obtained by saturating of nascent hydrogen a platinum electrode covered with platinum black. Plunging this electrode into a solution measures the potential difference E (volts) as a function of the concentration in H^+ ions which can be estimated by the relation of Nernst (in standard conditions for partial pressure of hydrogen):

$$E = (RT \, \text{Ln} \, |H^+|) / nF = 0.0001983 \, T \log (H^+)$$
$$= 0.058 \log (H^+) \qquad \text{(at 20°C)}, \qquad (15.9)$$

where R is the gas constant, T is the absolute temperature, n is the ion charge and F is the Faraday (96,500°C).

The hydrogen electrode is not easy to use. Other reference electrodes of known potential compared to hydrogen electrode are used instead. The pH value is deduced from the electromotive force (EMF) measured between the reference electrode and a measurement electrode.

pH Meters

Electronic equipment used for pH measurement can be classified in two groups (1) potentiometric systems and (2) systems with direct, analogical or numerical readings. The potentiometric method with measurements at null current is the most accurate but has the disadvantage of being time consuming and is consequently no longer used for routine tasks. Direct reading models are the most commonly used particularly numerical models. The choice of a pH meter will depend on the quality of measurement required:

– for routine tasks, the apparatus should have an input impedance of approximately 10^{10} Ω to allow measurement at a precision of 0.1 pH unit, manual correction of temperature, a potentiometer for scale fitting and a potentiometer for slope fitting.
– for more precise work, the input impedance should be at least 10^{12} Ω, the resolution $\pm$ 0.002 pH corresponding to 0.1 mV, with auto-correction of scale, slope and temperature. Output in millivolts means the apparatus can be used with an impedance adapter and also be connected to a recorder or a computerized acquisition system.

For use with several specific types of electrodes, a model whose adjustments and calibrations are programmed by microprocessor is advisable (cf. Sect. 15.3 below).

Measurement Electrode

The measurement electrode is sensitive to the H^+ ions and for measurements to be valid it must be combined with a reference electrode.

The glass electrode is the most widespread pH electrode. Nernst appears to be the first to have explained its principle, but the idea of using a glass electrode originated with Haber and Klemsiewicz in 1909. If two solutions of different acidity are separated by a very thin glass membrane (a few microns thick), a difference in potential will be established between them that depends on the difference in H^+ concentration.

In practical terms, the electrode consists of a bulb of blown glass at the end of a tube. Not all types of glass can be used for the manufacture of electrodes. A "soft" glass, rich in sodium (type Corning 015) is generally used. The electrode is then filled with an HCl solution or a buffer solution containing an Ag/AgCl electrode. Two values are used for the internal solution, one giving at pH 7 an EMF equal to zero compared to the calomel/saturated KCl reference electrode, the other giving for pH = 0 EMF = 0. The former system is the most commonly used.

The response time of a glass electrode to a change in pH is very short. It is insensitive to oxidizing or reducing media. The potential developed is stable at around 58 mV per unit of pH at 25°C, the scale of differences in the potential measured extending to $\pm$ 500 mV. The range of internal resistance is very big (100–1,000 MΩ) requiring a measuring apparatus with a very *high input resistance* i.e. at least 10^{10} Ω.

There may be slight differences in response from one electrode to another. This shift is due to an asymmetry potential created by slight differences in manufacture. The glass electrode is especially sensitive to dehydration. It should be always stored in distilled water. Before using the electrode for the first time, it should be steeped in distilled water for 24 h.

Glass electrodes are often sold in a combined form including a measurement and a reference electrode. This model is not recommended for measurements on soil suspensions as the porous sintered glass of the reference contact easily becomes blocked in the presence of clayey minerals and this can result in a very unstable signal over time. However, combined electrodes have in the meantime been somewhat improved and are safer than models made of porous sintered glass (Hach-one type).[1]

Electrodes made of glass membrane on a plane surface have also been recommended for the measurement of soil pH, particularly in the case of low water contents (cf. Sect. 15.3, in situ measurements). With these electrodes, Breltembeck and Bremner (1984) found pH values that were stable, reproducible and correlated with other classical measurements on 15 soils with a water potential of from −15 to −0.3 bars.

Because it is robust and easy to use in mediums that are difficult to access, the antimony electrode has also been used for the measurement of the pH of soils, muds or slurries even though it is less precise than glass electrodes. A stick of antimony acquires a potential that varies linearly with pH in the range of pH 1–pH 10. Conkling and Blanchar (1988) presented data on soil pH measured with a glass electrode that correlated well with data from an antimony electrode, although some values were a little higher with the latter.

From the historical point of view the platinum/quinhydrone electrode should also be mentioned. It was initially used to simulate the hydrogen electrode, as quinhydrone dissociates in solution by producing nascent hydrogen. It was recommended at the Second International Congress of Soil Science in 1927 but has not been used in soil chemistry for many years now.

Reference Electrodes

Reference electrodes comprise half the element of known electrical potential (which should be as stable as possible) required for comparison with the measurement electrode. The most often used and the best studied is the calomel electrode, but other models are available which may be

---

[1] Hach Europe SA, LP 51, Namur, Belgium.

suitable in certain cases, in particular the silver/silver chloride electrode, or the thallium amalgam electrode that enables measurements at temperatures up to 135°C.

Calomel Electrode

The calomel electrode consists of a mercury base covered with a layer of calomel (mercurous chloride) in a potassium chloride solution. Its assembly is described in Appendix 1 at the end of this chapter. Though current pH meters take measurements at null current, in fact a low negative or positive electric flow does not affect the potential of the electrode. The potential depends on the KCl concentration of the filling solution. Three types of KCl concentrations are used: 0.1 mol L^{-1}, 1 mol L^{-1} and saturated. The 0.1 mol L^{-1} solution is recommended for precise measurements; it is not very sensitive to temperature but difficult to preserve. Usually a saturated electrode is used which is easy to maintain, but its temperature coefficient is high (see Appendix 1). At 25°C its potential is +245.8 mV with respect to that of the hydrogen reference electrode. One potential problem involved in the use of a reference electrode is electrical contact between the KCl filling solution and the measured solution. A porous sintered glass tube with a leak-flow of around 0.2 mL h^{-1} is generally used. For precise measurements, a device with ground joints can be used; the degree of leak equals the desired sealing defect. Gel electrolyte can also be used to solve the problem of contact without risk of diffusion, but it can only be stored for a limited time.

It is important to emphasize the problems that can arise from the use of porous junctions in the case of measurements on soil suspensions. Junctions are easily blocked which implies that measurements are not reproducible. They must always be cleaned well by brushing and aspiration. Most of the difficulties involved in measurements come from the reference electrode particularly in turbid mediums like soil extracts. Devices for contact with the potassium chloride solution rapidly become clogged and measurements are then incorrect. A solid reference electrode (TBI – Recomat SA) has been recommended. It is made of wooden rings that are well-impregnated with the potassium chloride saturated solution and behaves remarkably well in very polluting mediums like those found at water purification stations.

If the presence of chloride or potassium ions is undesirable for measurement, an intermediate bridge with a double junction should be used. In this case calibration should be performed with "TRIS" buffer solutions (cf. Appendix 3).

Silver/silver chloride electrode

This electrode is more rarely used but its robustness may make it worth using. Its simplicity also makes it useful for miniaturized assemblies. It is most often used in combination with a glass electrode or with ion selective electrodes.

This electrode makes it possible to work at temperatures ranging from -30 to $+135°C$. At $25°C$, when filled with saturated potassium chloride, its potential is $+200$ mV compared to a standard hydrogen electrode (see appendix 1). Its potential is -45 mV compared to the calomel electrode at $25°C$. It is advisable to monitor the stability of this electrode, as measurement currents can cause the transformation of silver by micro-electrolysis; it can be improved by a thin coating of Teflon film.

15.2.4 Electrometric Checking and Calibration

The pH meter has to be calibrated before measurements are made. The apparatus chosen must be able to correct slope and temperature. In most cases, a precision of ± 0.1 pH unit is sufficient as other causes of errors are greater (e.g. heterogeneity of the sample). For measurements on suspensions, it is preferable to choose a device with a separate reference electrode as the risk of errors caused by clogging of the porous junction is reduced and it is easier to access when problems occur.

The apparatus should be switched on some time before beginning the measurements (there is often a waiting position which maintains the circuits in equilibrium), and then the electrodes are immersed in the appropriate buffer. It is advisable to begin with buffer T4AC (cf. Appendix 3, at the end of this chapter), which is particularly stable with respect to temperature. Adjust the pH meter to the appropriate value, then move on to the second buffer, which should be very close to the values to be measured. The apparatus should then display the value for the new buffer (corrected for temperature, see Appendix 3). Compensate for any slight variation while correcting slope. If correction is not possible, the coupling of the electrodes may not be satisfactory, particularly due to the glass electrode which does not display a strictly linear response between the two pH values selected. If this is the case, choose a narrower range of pH: for example, instead of pH 4 and 9, choose 7 and 9 or 6 and 8. The closer the value of the standard buffer to the value to be measured, the better the measurement. Agitation is not advised during measurement. In the case of problems of linearity, carefully clean the porous junction of the electrode by brushing it with a hard brush. It can also be cleaned by suction using a filter pump.

Measurements of soil pH can be classified in four main types:
1. On aqueous suspensions of soils
2. On saturated pastes
3. On extracts of saturation
4. "In situ" measurements

15.2.5 Measurement on Aqueous Soil Suspensions

Specifications vary with the soil:solution ratio due to the diversity of soil materials. In France, the experimental AFNOR standard NF X-31-103 (1998) recommends a 1:2.5 soil:water ratio. The International standard NF ISO 10390 (1994) recommends a ratio of 1:5.

Procedure

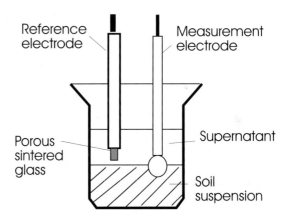

Fig. 15.2. Recommended position of the electrodes

– Weigh 10 g of soil dried at room temperature and sieved to 2 mm (a test specimen of at least 5 mL being the ISO standard), add 25 mL (or five times the volume of the test specimen, ISO standard) of boiled distilled water (CO_2 removed); shake for 1 h on an oscillating table (energetic agitation for 5 min, ISO standard).
– let decant for 30 min (at least 2 h but not more than 24 h, ISO standard), immerse the electrodes taking care that the porous part of the reference electrode is submerged in the clear part of the suspension (Fig. 15.2). Read the pH value after stabilization of the measurement. Note the temperature, and check correction for temperature on the pH meter.

Remarks

As the value of the pH drops with a rise in temperature, it is usual to bring back all the values to 25°C. For precise measurements, a thermostatic bath should be used; as soil suspensions often have a buffering effect that it is impossible to correct by calculation.

Measurements should be made without agitation. For certain soils, the indications provided by the pH meter may not be stable, giving a permanent drift. In such cases, it is advisable to read the pH after a specific time interval, for example, 3 min, and to use the same time interval for the other measurements, not forgetting to mention the fact when noting the results.

Measurements on soil suspensions and more importantly on saturated pastes induce a phenomenon called "paste effect" or "suspension effect" which can modify the results by ± 1 pH unit (Fig. 15.3). This effect is especially significant when the electrodes – and particularly the reference electrode – are in contact with the sediment. This effect could be due to the difference in mobility of the K^+ and Cl^- ions of the diffusion solution of the reference electrode when colloids (charged particles, strong cation exchange capacity) are present. Grewling and Peech (1960) reported that this phenomenon could be minimized by taking measurements with a 0.01 molar solution of $CaCl_2$ (pH_{Ca}).

Although the soil:solution ratio influences the results of measurement of pH in water, it has very little effect in saline solutions such as $CaCl_2$ 0.01 mol L^{-1} (Conyers and Davey 1988). Nilsson et al. (1995) recommended water: soil ratios higher than 10 (v:w or 2 in v:v) to obtain reliable measurements of pH_{water} on organic soils.

The time of contact between water and soil also influences the pH. According to Conyers and Davey (1988) agitation times of more than a few hours are not advisable because they generate variations and make it impossible to obtain a stable value. Qiu and Zhu (1986) reported stabilization of their measurements after 30 min (and up to 1 h) of agitation.

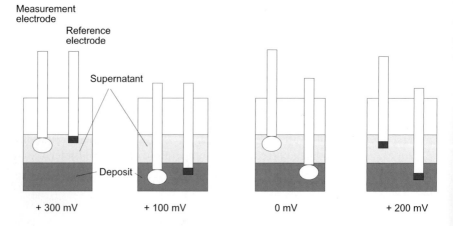

Fig. 15.3. Possible errors due to the effect of suspension for a soil in distilled water (Bates 1973)

15.2.6 Determination of the pH-K and pH-Ca

When measured in water, the pH value does not take total acidity into account, particularly the protons and the aluminium forms fixed on the exchange complex which represent potential acidity. In addition to the first measurement in water, it is consequently necessary to carry out a measurement in 1 mol (KCl) L^{-1} aqueous solution with the same soil: solution ratio (1:2.5 for the procedure described in "Procedure" under Sect. 15.2.5) and using the same technique. This gives pH_K.

pH_K measurements usually give lower pH values[2] than pH_{H2O} measurements. The difference (ΔpH) can be as much as one pH unit. A value of $\Delta pH > 0$ indicates that the cation exchange capacity is higher than the anion exchange capacity. There is a significant correlation between a positive ΔpH and exchange acidity. However, although this is true in the case of one family of soils, it is not true of a general comparison.

This measurement was the subject of an experimental an AFNOR standard NF-X31-104 (1988) and became part of the international NF ISO 10390 standard (1994).

Measurements in 0.01 mol ($CaCl_2$) L^{-1} aqueous solution are also used because Ca ions cause flocculation of the solution and minimize the paste and dilution effect. pH expression is thus less random and comparison is easier between different soils and particularly saline soils. pH_{Ca} measurements induce lower ΔpH than pH_K measurement The study of Conyers and Davey (1988) showed that pH_{water}, pH_K, and pH_{Ca} are closely correlated on soils with a broad range of pH. For non-saline soils with a negative net charge, they found the relation:

$$pH_{Ca} = 1.05\ pH_{eau} - 0.9$$

The procedure described in "Procedure" under Sect. 15.2.5 is valid in all cases, whether in water or saline solution.

15.2.7 Measurement on "Saturated Pastes"

pH measurement on saturated paste aims to reproduce the conditions of the natural environment as closely as possible. This technique is very delicate to implement. It is necessary to start by preparing a "saturated paste":

---

[2] In some Andosols rich in allophane, pH_{KCl} can be higher than pH_{H2O} (amphoteric medium).

– Weigh 200 g of air-dried soil sieved to 2 mm, put it in a cylindrical container of approximately 500 mL with a wide neck and a tightly fitting lid.
– Add 50–70 mL of boiled distilled water depending on the texture of the soil, i.e. whether it is more or less clayey; enough water should be added to just moisten the soil.
– Note the volume of water added in mL.
– cover and let stand for 30 min.
– Using a laboratory burette, while stirring add distilled water in small fractions to obtain a homogeneous paste. The main problem is to know when to stop adding water, i.e. when the paste is water saturated. Note the total volume of water added, cover and let stand for 30 min.

At saturation the paste should be glossy and sufficiently fluid to slip off the spatula. If a hole is made in the middle of the paste, water should not collect at the bottom of the hole unless there is excess water. If water does appear, a little more soil should be added and the total weight of the soil taken into account in the final calculation. In spite of the subjective judgement, in practice replicates on the same sample produce very similar results. For the least clayey soils, only a very small quantity of water should be added. The soil paste is characterized by its percentage of saturation:

Saturation% = weight of added water × 100 / soil weight.

The electrode should be inserted with extreme care. The reference electrode can have a double junction to avoid obstruction of the porous junction. It is preferable to use an electrode filled with saturated KCl or a gel solution with agar-agar to reduce the diffusion of liquid. As far as the measurement electrode is concerned, some models are designed for penetration and are less fragile than models with a bulb, though also less sensitive.

The pH meter should be read after stabilization of the measurement, which can take a few minutes. More than for the other techniques, these measurements are influenced by a phenomenon called paste effect which can modify real measurements of pH by 1 unit. The measure ments obtained will be higher than for 1:2.5 soil:water suspension (cf. "Procedure under Sect. 15.2.5), but comparable with those on the saturation extract described below.

15.2.8 Measurement on the Saturation Extract

Faced with the difficulty of rendering an aqueous extract as representative as possible of the real in situ soil solution at water holding capacity of the soil, Richards (1954) proposed the saturation extract as an intermediate method between field and laboratory measurement.

To characterize the degree of salinization of a soil, the most common procedure uses a saturation extract on which the pH can be measured, respecting the precautions and techniques described in Sect. 15.2.5.

First make a saturated paste (cf. Sect. 15.2.7). Store it for 24 h, while protecting it from desiccation. Then transfer it on a filter paper on a Büchner funnel under vacuum. Collect the filtrate during filtration which can take quite a long time, sometimes more than 2 h. If the extract is still turbid, filter it again. Measure the pH. If the measurement cannot be made immediately after extraction, store the solution in a well-stopped bottle in the refrigerator. The solution can also be used for other measurements such as conductivity and titration of cations and anions (cf. Chap. 18).

15.2.9 Measurement of the pH-NaF

Principle

This measurement complements the in situ NaF test on a filter (Pansu et al. 2001). It is used to identify the presence of substances with short-range organization in the soils, particularly aluminium in active $Al(OH)_3$ form. The principle of this measurement is a consequence of the reaction:

$Al(OH)_3 + 6\ NaF \rightarrow Na_3AlF_6 + 3\ NaOH$

The release of OH^- ions causes an increase in the pH which indicates quite large quantities of substances with short-range organization. The disadvantage of this technique is that the presence of fluoride soon damages the glass electrode, so it is advisable to reserve one electrode for this particular use.

Procedure

– Prepare 1 L of a sodium-fluoride-saturated solution by weighing 45 g of NaF. Mix well in a polyethylene bottle and complete to 1,000 mL with distilled water. Let stand for 2 days shaking the bottle from time to time. If partial crystallization of NaF occurs, only use the clear part of the supernatant.

– Weigh 1 g of fine soil sieved to 2 mm, air-dried or preferably with its initial moisture content. Measure the moisture content on another test specimen in order to later bring back calculations to values for soil dried at 110°C. Put the sample in a 100 mL polyethylene beaker. Add 50 mL NaF solution, agitate and introduce the electrodes. Note the initial value at time $t = 0$ then at $t = 2$ min, 10 min and finally 30 min. Note the results on a graph $pH = f(t)$.

15.3 In situ Measurements

Field measurements in natural conditions provide the most accurate information for the study of soil processes. This is particularly true for pH measurements considering how many physicochemical reactions can affect the pH.

In addition to the measurement of pH, other electrochemical sensors (Pansu et al. 2001) are used to measure conductance, redox potential and ionometry using electrodes that are sensitive to ions other than H^+, like Na^+, K^+, Ca^{2+} and NH_4^+ ions (cf. Chaps. 16 and 18). Moreover, use of a measurement station means data time series can be acquired which characterize changes in processes over time these being more instructive than a one-off characterization at a given time. Electrometric measurements can also provide information about activities of the ionic forms which are more useful for thermodynamic calculations than concentrations alone (Le Brusq et al. 1987). This kind of data is invaluable for the study of transfer mechanisms in the soil.

15.3.1 Equipment

The pH meter must have an input impedance of at least $10^9\ \Omega$ or better $10^{11}\ \Omega$, and the ability to correct origin, slope and temperature. Correction must be automatic if measurements have to be made over a long period of time. It must be possible to regularly check calibration by programming these operations on a microprocessor, which also ensures good reproducibility.

Sensitivity of 0.1 pH unit is sufficient given the heterogeneity of the medium. The apparatus should be able to function independently (battery). The output should be in mV, and preferably a magnetic system of data acquisition for later reprocessing.

The pH-meter should enable shield assembly with connections to a triaxial cable thereby eliminating disturbances caused by the length of the connecting cables to the sensors. A simpler solution consists in using electrodes with their own built-in amplifier. This enables problems to be avoided both due to the length of the cable (up to 200 m) and to moisture through faulty insulation. A model with separate measurement electrodes and reference electrodes is preferable (Fig. 15.4). To monitor several electrodes, the switching box should generally include five stations, with potentiometric adjustment possible for each station enabling correction of the slight differences between the points of origin of the electrodes.

15.3.2 Installation in the Field

Manual Measurements

After the site has been chosen, initial characterization of the soil has to be performed. Sampling should be carried out at the depth at which the electrodes will be placed. The minimum measurements required are moisture, conductivity, ionic balance and exchangeable cations. A meteorological station should be installed with at least a rain gauge and a temperature gauge. A temperature probe should be placed in the soil near the other electrodes. The measurement electrode should be inserted with great care in a hole previously dug with a soil core sampler. The hole around the electrode should be filled with some of the soil that was removed. Care should be taken to ensure the quality of the contact with the bulb of the electrode. Flat glass membrane electrodes can also be used (Breltenbeck and Bremner 1984). The electric cord of approximately a metre with a coaxial plug at the end should end in a plastic box with a lid to protect the connection between measurement periods (Fig. 15.4). The junction for the reference electrode is made of a glass tube 3–4 mm in diameter and 30 cm in length, with a 50 mL tank with a lid at one end. The bottom section of the buried part is made of porous sintered glass (Fig. 15.4). Fill the tube to 3 or 4 cm above the porous section with a 3.5 mol (KCl) L^{-1} aqueous solution gelled by 4% agar containing one thymol crystal to protect it against mould. Continue filling with the 3.5 mol (KCl) L^{-1} solution until the tank is half full. The gel above the porous section prevents over-diffusion of the KCl solution. The junctions are placed at intervals of 10-50-100 cm from the measurement electrode (Fig. 15.4a); this makes it possible to detect electrode malfunction caused by insufficient soil water content (Kolsi and Susini 1984).

In the case of sufficient moisture (this varies with the soil, but is generally 10% or higher), measurements compared using reference 1–2–3 (Fig. 15.4) should give almost the same values. If measurements 1 and 2 diverge, insufficient moisture is probably the cause. If 3 is different, this is a warning signal and a sample should be taken to check the moisture content. If the differences between reference electrodes are big, these measurements should not be used. Generally, measurements are taken using reference 1 after an initial check of the other positions.

All the measuring equipment including a switching box with four entries connected to a pH meter with an autonomous power supply should be conveniently packed in a case to allow easy transport in the field.

The switching box should be regulated in a buffer for each electrode, in order to be able to bring all the shift potentials back to the same value (mark the values on the potentiometers).

Measurements

Open the lids protecting the sensors and place a calomel-saturated KCl electrode in junction tube 1. Connect the measurement electrode and the reference electrode to the switching box. Read the pH value, place the mobile reference in junction tube 2 and read the new value. Proceed in the same way in junction tube 3, repeating the procedure if there are several measurement electrodes, using the switching box. For correction, the temperature gauge must of course be connected to the pH meter (Fig. 15.4b).

15.3.3 Measurements on Soil Monoliths

As they closely resemble in situ measurements, soil monoliths provide a wealth of useful information. Even if the measurements are not identical to those made in the field, they are easier to record and give data from controlled climatic conditions.

The monolith used by Susini and Loyer (1967) comprised a soil core enclosed in an PVC parallelepiped three sides of which were opaque, and the fourth transparent, with a square cross-sectional shape of 30 cm and a height of 1 m. The soil monolith was cut in the field with the same dimensions as the box except for a few centimetres left at the bottom for a gravel bed to allow drainage. The whole object was sealed with Rubson cement. 3×3 holes were cut in the transparent side at three different levels for the pH, the reference, and when necessary, for a platinum electrode for the measurement of Eh (cf. Chap. 16). Three holes 40 mm in diameter were cut in the left side to enable sampling, and closed with rubber stoppers. On the other side, one hole was cut at each level to allow insertion of Bouyoucos moisture sensors. Only one reference electrode was used for all three levels with flexible tubes to transport the potassium chloride solution.

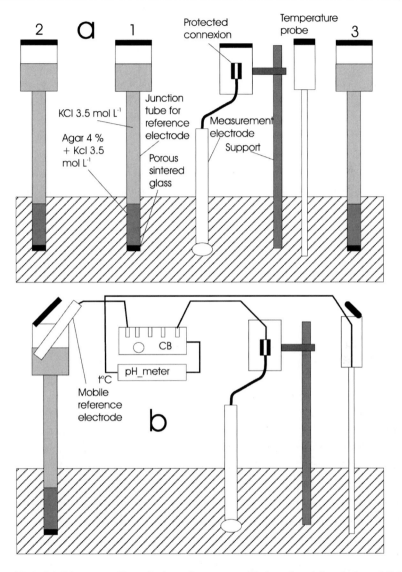

Fig. 15.4. (a) Diagram of installation of sensors with junction tubes1, 2 and 3 for the electrode of reference;
(b) = phase of acquisition (CB = connecting box for several electrodes)

References

Bates R (1973) *Détermination du pH*, Wiley, New York

Breltenbeck CA and Bremner JM (1984) Use of a flat-surface combination pH electrode for measurement of soil pH. *Commun. Soil Sci. Plant Anal.*, 15, 87–98

Conkling BL and Blanchar RW (1988) A comparison of pH measurements using the antimony microelectrode and glass electrode. *Agron. J.*, 80, 275–278

Conyers MK and Davey BG (1988) Observation on some routine methods for soil pH determination. *Soil Sci.*, 145, 29–36

Grewling, T and Peech (1960) Chemical soil tests. *Cornell Univ. Agric. Exp. Sta. Bull.*, 960 p

INRA (1995) Référentiel pédologique. Association Française d'étude des sols, INRA, 332 p

Kolsi and Susini J (1984) Publications ES 209 – Direction des Sols, ORSTOM, Tunis

Le Brusq JY, Zante P and Peraudeau M (1987) La mesure *in situ* des paramètres physico-chimiques (pH et Eh) dans un sol sulfaté acide de Casamance (Sénégal). *Cah. Orstom Ser. Pédol.*, XXIII, 55–66

NF ISO-10390 (1994) Détermination du pH. In *Qualité des sols*, AFNOR, 1996

NF X31-103 (1988) Détermination du pH dans l'eau - Méthode électrométrique. In *Qualité des sols*, AFNOR, 1994

NF X31-104 (1988) Détermination du pH dans une solution de KCl – Méthode électrométrique. In *Qualité des sols*, AFNOR, 1994

Nilsson T, Kranz-Eliasson B and Bjurman M (1995) Measurement of pH in soil samples from a cutover peatland in Sweden: the effect of electrolyte and solution/soil ratio. *Commun. Soil Sci. Plant Anal.*, 26, 371–374

Pansu M, Gautheyrou J and Loyer JY (2001) *Soil Analysis – Sampling, Instrumentation and Quality Control.*, Balkema, Lisse, Abington, Exton, Tokyo, 489 p

Qiu Xing-Chu and Zhu Ying-Quan (1986) Spectrophotometric determinations of pH value, Buffer capacity and rate of lime need in acidic soil, using chrysoidine as a chromogenic agent. *Soil Sci.*, 142, 275–278

Richards LA (1954) Saline and alkali soil – United States Agriculture – Handbook no. 60: 84

Susini J and Loyer JY (1967) *Utilisation d'un ensemble automatique pour la mesure en continu du pH.*, DRES-ORSTOM-Tunis

Bibliography

Beaumann EW (1973) Détermination du pH dans les solutions salines concentrées. *Anal. Chim. Acta.*, 64, 284–288

Billmann E (1927) L'électrode à quinhydrone et ses applications. *Bull. Soc. Chem. Fr.*, 213, 41–42

Bower (1961) Studies on the suspension effect with a sodium electrode. *Soil Sci. Amer. Proc.*, 25, 18–21

Cheng KI (1989) pH glass electrode and its mechanisms. In *Am. Chem. Soc. Symp. Ser.*, Stock JT and Orna MV ed., 390, 286–302

Clark JS (1964) An examination of the pH of calcareous soils. *Soil Sci.*, 9, 145–151

Clark J.S (1996) The pH values of soils suspended in dilute salt solutions. *Soil. Sci. Soc. Am. Proc.*, 30, 11–14

Colin C, Collings K, Drummond P, and Lund E. (2004) *A Mobile Sensor Platform for Measurement of Soil pH and Buffering.*, American Society of Agricultural and Biological Engineers, St. Joseph, Michigan, USA

Peech M, Olsen RA and Bolt GH (1953) The significance of potentiometric measurements involving liquid junction in clay and soil suspensions. *Soil Sci. Soc. Proc.*, 214–218

Perley, GA (1939) Sur l'électrode antimoine. *Ind. Eng. Chem. Anal.*, 11, 316–319

Peverill KI, Sparrow LA and Reuter DJ (2001) *Soil Analysis – An interpretation manual*, CSIRO Publishing, Australia

Raupach (1954) The essor involved in pH determinations in soils. *J. Agric. Res.*, 5, 716–729

Schofield RK and Taylor AN (1955) The measurement of soil pH. *Soil Sci. Soc. Am. Proc.*, 19, 164–167

Sistverson DL and Wurfelt BE (1984) Methods for reliable pH measurements of precipitation samples. *Inter. J. Environ. Anal. Chem.*, 18, 143–160

Soil and Plant Analysis Council Inc (1999) *Soil Analysis – Handbook of reference methods*, CRC, Boca Raton

Stevens G, Dunn D and Phipps B (2001) How to diagnose soil acidity and alkalinity problems in crops: A comparison of soil pH test kits. *J. Extension*, 39, 4

Thomas GW (1996) Soil pH and soil acidity. In *Methods of Soil Analysis*, Part 3, Chemical Methods, Bigham JM and Bartels JM ed., ASA-SSSA, Madison, Etats-Unis, 475–490

Thunjai T., Boyd C.E., Dube K (2001) Pond soil pH measurement. *J. World Aquacult. Soc.*, 32, 141–152

Yang SX, Cheng KL, Kurtz LT and Peck TR (1989) Suspension effects in potentiometry. *Part. Sci. Technol.*, 7, 131–152

Appendices

15.1. Table of electrode potentials
15.2. Constants of dissociation of certain equilibriums
15.3. Buffer solutions
15.4. Indicators

Appendix 15.1: Table of Electrode Potentials

Table 15.4. Potential of three types of calomel electrode from 15 to 30°C in mV compared to the hydrogen electrode

temperature (°C)	electrode solution		
	KCl 0.1 mol L^{-1}	KCl 1 mol L^{-1}	saturated KCl
15	338.1	285.2	252.5
16	337.9	284.9	251.7
17	337.8	284.5	250.9
18	337.7	284.2	250.3
19	337.6	283.8	249.5
20	337.5	283.5	248.8
21	337.4	283.2	248.2
22	337.3	282.9	247.5
23	337.2	282.6	246.8
24	337.0	282.2	246.3
25	336.9	281.9	245.8
26	336.8	281.6	245.3
27	336.7	281.2	244.8
28	336.6	281.9	244.3
29	336.5	280.5	243.8
30	336.4	280.2	243.4

Table 15.5. Potential of silver/silver chloride electrode from 0 to 95°C in millivolts compared to the hydrogen electrode

T (°C)	mV	t (°C)	mV
0	236.5	40	212.0
5	234.1	45	208.3
10	231.4	50	204.4
15	228.5	55	200.5
20	225.5	60	196.4
25	222.3	70	187.8
30	219.0	80	178.7
35	215.6	90	169.5
		95	165.1

Appendix 2: Constants of Dissociation of Certain Equilibriums

compound		formula	K at 18°C in water		pK at 18°C
acetic acid		CH_3COOH	1.8	10^{-5}	4.75
ammonium		NH_4^+	3.2	10^{-10}	9.5
boric acid		H_3BO_3	5.25	10^{-10}	9.26
orthophosphoric acid	1	H_3PO_4	7.6	10^{-3}	2.12
orthophosphoric acid	2	$H_2PO_4^-$	7.5	10^{-8}	7.12
orthophosphoric acid	3	HPO_4^{2-}	3.5	10^{-13}	12.45
citric acid	1	$CH_2C(OH)-(CO_2H)_3$	8.4	10^{-4}	3.08
citric acid	2	$CH_2-C(OH)-(CO_2H)_2CO_2^-$	1.77	10^{-5}	4.75
citric acid	3	$CH_2-C(OH)-CO_2H(CO_2)_2^{2-}$	3.9	10^{-6}	5.41
acid sulphate ion		HSO_4^-	1.27	10^{-3}	2.89

Appendix 3: Buffer Solutions

A buffer solution is a chemical system which tends to maintain the concentration in H^+ ions constant and consequently also the pH in spite of dilution or the addition of limited quantities of certain acids or bases. Generally the buffer solutions are mixtures of an acid and one of its ionized salts. The buffer value β is defined starting from the equation $\beta = \Delta b/\Delta pH$ or $\Delta a/\Delta pH$ which expresses the pH variation induced by addition of an acid (Δa) or a base (Δb). The pH of a buffer solution (Table 15.6) is given by:

$$pH \text{ buffer} = pK + \log (\text{salt C} / \text{acid C})$$

Table 15.6. pH values and characteristics of few commercial buffer solutions *I*, ionic strength; ΔpH1/2, variation in pH when the buffer solution is diluted with an equal volume of distilled water; β, buffering power $\Delta b/\Delta pH$, Δb increase in strong base or acid concentration of the buffer solution giving a pH change ΔpH

Ref. T (°C)	T1	T2	T3	T4HP	T4AC	T6	T7	T8	T9a	T9b	T10	T12
0	1.10	1.666		4.003		6.984	7.534		8.464	9.46	10.317	13.423
5	1.10	1.666		3.999		6.951	7.500		8.395	9.39	10.245	13.207
10	1.10	1.670		3.999	4.65	6.923	7.472	8.40	8.332	9.33	10.179	13.003
15	1.10	1.672		3.999		6.900	7.448	8.28	8.276	9.27	10.118	12.810
20	1.10	1.675	3.560	4.002	4.65	6.881	7.429	8.14	8.225	9.22	10.082	12.627
25	1.10	1.679	3.557	4.008	4.65	6.865	7.413	8.00	8.180	9.18	10.012	12.454
30	1.10	1.683	3.552	4.015		6.853	7.400	7.87	8.139	9.14	9.966	12.289
35	1.10	1.688	3.549	4.024		6.844	7.839	7.75	8.102	9.10	9.325	12.133
40	1.10	1.694	3.547	4.035	4.65	6.838	7.380	7.62	8.058	9.07	9.889	11.984
45	1.10	1.700	3.547	4.047		6.834	7.373	7.50	8.038	9.04	9.856	11.841
50	1.10	1.707	3.549	4.060		6.833	7.367	7.38	8.011	9.01	9.828	11.705
55	1.11	1.715	3.554	4.075		6.834			8.985	8.98		11.574
60	1.11	1.723	3.560	4.091		6.836			8.962	8.95		11.449
70	1.11	1.743	3.580	4.126		6.845			8.921	8.92		
80	1.11	1.766	3.609	4.164		6.859			8.885	8.89		
90	1.12	1.792	3.650	4.205		6.877			8.850	8.87		
95	1.12	1.806	3.674	4.227		6.886			8.833	8.87		
I				0.1	0.1	0.1	0.03					
ΔpH1/2	+0.28	+0.186	+0.049	0.052	+0.016	+0.08	+0.07	−0.02	+0.01	−0.0	+0.079	−0.26
ß	0.12	0.07	0.027	0.016	0.1	0.029	0.016	0.029	0.02	0.05	0.029	0.09

T1 = HCl 0.1 mol L^{-1},
T2 = potassium tetraoxalate $KH_3C_4O_8$ 0.05 mol L^{-1},
T3 = saturated potassium hydrogentartrate $KH_3C_4O_8$,
T4HP = potassium hydrogenphtalate 0.05 mol ($KH_3C_4O_8$) L^{-1},
T4AC = 0.1 mol (CH_3COOH) L^{-1} + 0.1 mol (CH_3COONa) L^{-1} (particularly recommended for its pH stability with temperature),
T6 = 0.025 mol (KH_2PO_4) L^{-1} + 0.025 mol (Na_2HPO_4) L^{-1},
T7 = 0.087 mol (KH_2PO_4) L^{-1} + 0.0304 mol (Na_2HPO_4) L^{-1},
T8 = Tris(hydroxymethyl) aminomethane 0.05 mol L^{-1} + 0.0292 mol (HCl) L^{-1} (particularly recommended in biology and ionometry),
T9a = 0.01 mol ($Na_2B_4O_7,10H_2O$) L^{-1},
T9b = (0.05 mol $Na_2B_4O_7,10H_2O$) L^{-1},
T10 = 0.025 mol ($NaHCO_3$) L^{-1} + 0.025 mol (Na_2CO_3) L^{-1},
T12 = $Ca(OH)_2$ sat

Appendix 4: Coloured Indicators

composition of A and B solutions	A:B ratio v:v	colour acid form	basic form	transition pH	remark
A: methyl orange (0.1% in water) B: indigo carmine (0.25% in water)	1:1	violet	green	4.1	very useful for titrating under artificial light
A: bromocresol blue (0.2% in alcohol) B: methyl red (0.2% in alcohol)	3:1	red	green	5.1	quick change of colour at transition point
A: neutral red (0.1% in water) B: methylene blue (0.1% in water)	1:1	blue-violet	green	7.0	store in dark flask
A: phenolphthalein (0.1% in 50% alcohol) B: naphtolphtaleine (0.1% in 50% alcohol)	3:1	light pink	violet	8.9	light green at pH 8.6
A: thymol blue (0.1% in 30% alcohol) B: phenolphtaleine (0.1% in 50% alcohol)	1:3	yellow	violet	9.0	green at pH 9.0

Redox Potential

16.1 Definitions and Principle

The measurements described in this chapter enable characterization of variables especially linked with the diffusion of air in the soil:

Eh = oxydoreduction potential

ODR = oxygen diffusion rate.

First a reminder of certain definitions: oxidation is characterized by a loss of electrons, reduction is characterized by a gain of electrons. Thus, in a redox reaction, the oxidant is reduced and the reducing agent oxidized with an exchange of n electrons (e^-):

oxidant + n e^- ⇔ reducing agent

Measurement of the redox potential Eh allows quantitative appraisal of the force and tendency of the system. It can be measured by the difference between the potential of the hydrogen electrode (or more easily, of the calomel electrode) and the potential of a platinum electrode immersed in the medium (Fig. 16.1). It is expressed by:

$$Eh = E_0 + \frac{0.058}{n} \log \frac{[Ox]^a}{[Red]^b} .$$

[Ox] and [Red] are the activities of, respectively, the oxidative and reducing agents. a and b are the numbers of respective equivalents in the reaction and n the number of electrons exchanged. E_0 is the standard potential that characterizes the redox couple and is a characteristic of this couple (for example, for $Fe^{3+} + e^- \Leftrightarrow Fe^{2+}$, $E_0 = 770$ mV).

In soils, Eh varies between 900 and −300 mV. The potential can change under the influence of pH or in the presence of complexing ions. The apparently normal potential must thus be defined. It is useful to monitor variations in Eh with pH ($E_0 = f(pH)$). It should be noted that when Eh decreases by approximately 100 mV, pH increases by one unit.

Other factors like moisture, and organic or inorganic matter also have an effect so it is only possible to define a qualitative value representative of a soil state. For this reason, it is often more instructive to consider *variations in* Eh that indicate the direction of an evolving process. Table 16.1 summarizes the main biochemical processes for different water-logged soils in temperate zones.

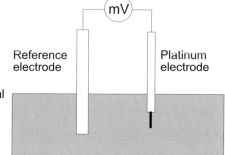

Fig. 16.1. Measurement of Eh potential

Table 16.1. Some of the main biogeochemical processes at different Eh values

phase	process	Eh in mV	microbial metabolism	soluble organic matter
phase I	disappearance of O_2	600 to 300	aerobiosis	biological breakdown
	disappearance of NO_3^-	500 to 300		
phase II	Mn^{4+} reduction	400 to 200	facultative anaerobiosis	temporary accumulation
	Fe^{3+} reduction	300 to 100		
phase III	SO_4^{2-} reduction	0 to −150	strict anaerobiosis	strong accumulation biological breakdown by anaerobiosis
	H_2 and CH_4 production	−150 to −220		

In addition to redox potential, it is useful to measure the oxygen diffusion rate (ODR). This represents the potential oxygen supply and combines diffusion in the gas phase, and dissolution and transfer in the liquid phase. Plant growth depends on oxygen in this dissolved form. Growth is satisfactory at an ODR value of more than 20 and is optimum towards 40. The ODR can decrease to 5 in waterlogged soil, and to 0 in reducing groundwater.

The notation rH = – log pH$_2$ is also used (pH$_2$ being pressure of molecular hydrogen). This value, which is less often quoted than Eh, links measurements of Eh with those of pH:

$$rH = \frac{Eh + 0.06 \ pH}{0.03}.$$

On the rH scale, oxydoreduction is neutral at value rH = 27.7 at 20°C and pH 7. Lower values correspond to reducing solutions. Higher values (from 27 to 40) correspond to oxidizing solutions.

16.2 Equipment and Reagents

16.2.1 Electrodes

Fig. 16.2. Platinum electrode. (1) platinum wire in the shape of a corkscrew; (2) resin, e.g. araldite; (3) connection immersed in mercury ensuring the contact; (4) glass or PVC tube; (5) electric wire

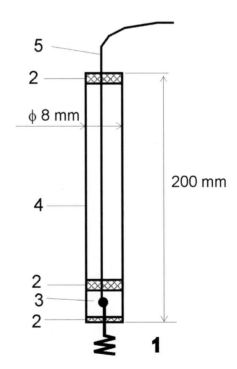

The platinum electrode is made of a 1 mm diameter platinum wire the bottom 2 cm of which is, shaped like a corkscrew. This shape means it can be screwed into the soil thereby ensuring good contact (Fig. 16.2).

The body of the electrode comprises a glass or PVC tube 8 mm in diameter and 20 cm in length.

The reference electrode should be of the calomel-saturated KCl type (cf. Chap. 15).

16.2.2 Salt Bridge for Connection

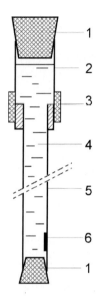

Fig. 16.3. Salt bridge for connection (1) stoppers; (2) PVC electrode holder; (3) resin connection made of Araldite; (4) conducting gel; (5) PVC tube 15 mm in diameter and of varying length; (6) filter paper window

The salt bridge is made of an opaque PVC tube 15 mm in diameter whose length depends on the depth chosen. It provides permanent contact with the soil. A window (Fig. 16.3) of a few mm near the bottom of the tube ensures the electric connection with the soil. It is sealed with a piece of filter paper. The top end sticks out of the soil and is slightly bigger to hold the reference electrode during measurement. This assembly is filled with a heated (to fluidify) mixture of 350 g (KCl) + 3% gelose L^{-1} and few grains of phenol for conservation, then stopped until the gel solidifies. The salt bridge described here resembles that proposed by Veneman and Pickering (1983).

16.2.3 System of Measurement

Either a pH meter (cf. Chap. 15) with a mV scale with the zero value at the centre (enabling negative measurements) or more simply, a millivoltmeter can be used. But one characteristic is crucial: the input resistance must be high in order to maintain a very weak measurement current to avoid the phenomenon of polarization of the platinum electrode which can result in erroneous measurements. An impedance adapter mounted on an operational amplifier in potential mode can be also linked to the controller input.

16.2.4 Calibration Solutions

– Zobell's solution, mix:

potassium ferrocyanide	1.26 g,
potassium ferricyanide	0.99 g,
potassium chloride	7.50 g;

dissolve and bring to 1,000 mL;
At a temperature of 25°C, the Eh of this solution = 429 ± 2.4 mV compared to the hydrogen electrode

– Solution of Light (1972), mix:

ammonium ferrous sulphate ($6H_2O$)	39.21 g,
ammonium ferric sulphate ($12H_2O$)	48.22 g,
sulphuric acid ($d = 1.84$)	56 mL;

bring to 1,000 mL;
At 25°C, the Eh of this solution is 675 mV compared to the hydrogen electrode.

For measurements taken with a reference electrode other than the hydrogen electrode, the following relation is used:

Eh (H_2) = measured EM + Er of the reference,
with Er values at 25°C:

calomel/saturated KCl reference	244.4 mV
mercury/mercury sulphate reference	636.0 mV
Ag/AgCl reference	198.7 mV

16.3 Procedure

16.3.1 Pretreatment of the Electrode

Before being used for measurements, the surface of the platinum electrode has to be treated to erase all traces of previous memory:
– Soak in perhydrol for 15 min.
– Rinse in distilled water.
– Soak in pure nitric acid ($d = 1.37$) for 15 min.
– Rinse in pure hydrochloric acid ($d = 1.19$) 15 min.
– Wash under running water for 2 h

16.3.2 Measurement on Soil Sample

This type of measurement is used relatively rarely. The information it provides is influenced by the concentration of reduced or oxidized substances, but does not give the degree of soil aeration, which depends on moisture and porosity. However, if care is taken, measurements can be made on saturated paste. The pastes are prepared using the same technique as for the extraction of soluble salts (cf. Sect. 16.2.2), with certain precautions: the distilled water must be completely degassed by vacuum boiling; the assembly, (Fig. 16.4) should allow measurements to be made in a vacuum. The measurement should only be recorded if the difference between two readings does not exceed 2 mV.

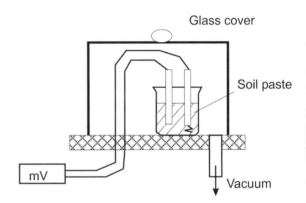

Fig. 16.4. Device for measurement of Eh on soil suspension or saturated paste

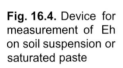

    Liu and Yu (1984) proposed an improvement of this measurement by preliminary polarization of the platinum electrode followed by plotting depolarization curves as a function of time. The intersection of the two curves obtained after anodic and cathodic polarization provides a value of Eh.

16.3.3 Measurement on Soil Monolith

Measurement in controlled laboratory conditions provides an alternative to in situ measurement. A soil column is placed in a opaque PVC tube with a diameter ranging from 30 to 40 cm for a length of 1 m (0.12–0.15 m^3). The salt bridge is identical to that described in Sect. 16.2.2, with a window for electrical contact at the level of each platinum electrode located at a different height.

    When sampling soil in the field requires extreme care should be taken to exactly reproduce the field soil profile in the monolith. Access windows for measurements should have stoppers and enable small samples to be taken when necessary, to monitor soil moisture for example.

16.3.4 In situ Measurements

This type of measurement provides the most relevant data. Once the site is chosen, start by drilling a hole with approximately the same diameter as the electrode (8 mm) using an auger so as to disturb the structure of the walls as little as possible. Insert the electrode and screw the platinum wire into the soil. This ensures good electrical contact between the soil and the platinum.

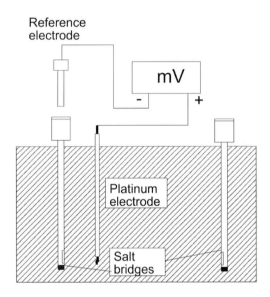

Fig. 16.5. In situ Measurement

Firm the soil around the electrode to avoid infiltration as the electrode remains in place between measurements and the electrical contacts needs to be protected. Place the salt bridge approximately 6 cm from the electrode (Fig. 16.5). The opening at the top should be stopped between measurements. It is advisable to place a second bridge 20 cm from the first which can be used to check the measurements are correct. To do this, a measurement should be taken immediately after connecting the first bridge. The two values will be identical if soil conditions have not changed (in particular moisture). Bad measurements are often due to faulty electrical contacts. It is thus preferable to maintain permanent contacts using a box with multiple connections controlled by a rotary switch.

16.3.5 Measurement of the Oxygen Diffusion Rate

This measurement is based on the principle of polarographic measurement. In oxygenated medium, when the potential of the polarizable electrode reaches –200 mV, oxygen reduction begins and an electrical current is set up. Oxygen reduction increases with the potential. In the zone where the current intensity is independent of the voltage, the concentration of dissolved oxygen and its rate of diffusion towards the cathode are the only limiting factors. This technique was proposed by Lemon and Erickson (1955) to measure the diffusion of oxygen towards plant roots. The root resembles a cylinder surrounded by a mostly liquid contact zone which varies with the degree of saturation of the medium. Atmospheric oxygen dissolves and diffuses from the liquid phase towards the root. The device for Eh and ODR measurement should be assembled as shown in Fig. 16.6.

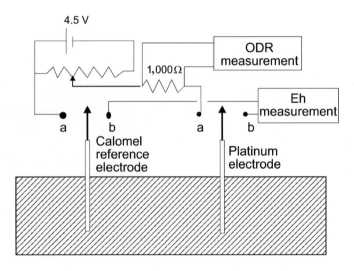

Fig. 16.6. Combined measurement device **(a)** oxygen diffusion rate (ODR) and **(b)** Eh (after Vilain and Ruelle 1974)

A salt bridge (Fig. 16.3) is inserted in the soil to a depth of approximately 15 cm to connect the calomel-saturated KCl reference electrode. The measurement electrode (platinum wire 1 mm in diameter and 6.5 mm in length, cf. Sect. 16.2.1) is checked using the calibration solutions (cf. Sect. 16.2.4) and then positioned at the same depth (15 cm)

Measurement of Eh precedes measurement of ODR. The measurement of ODR requires polarization of the platinum electrode using the recommended potential of –650 mV compared to the reference. Read the equilibrium current 3 min after switching on the polarization circuit.

Integration of the equation of diffusion shows that the ODR is roughly proportional to the equilibrium current according to the expression:

$$ODR = (0.5 / A) \, I.$$

ODR: oxygen diffusion rate (10^{-8} g cm^{-2} min^{-1}),
A: surface of the platinum electrode (cm^2),
I: current intensity (μA).

Though the influence of temperature is negligible in the measurement of Eh, the same is not true for the measurement of ODR. Vilain and Ruelle Druelle (1974) recommended an average corrective factor of 2% per°C. The repeatability of measurements may be about 10% after 2–3 months of installation in the field.

16.3.6 Colorimetric Test of Eh

Table 16.2. Coloured indicators of oxyreduction, colourless in reducing medium, values at pH 7 and 20°C (according to Voiret and Froquet 1950)

Coloured indicator	Eh mV	rH
neutral red	– 340	10
safranine T	– 290	
indigo potassium disulphonate	– 125	
methylene blue	+ 11	23
quinhydrone	+ 50	24.4
pure water	+ 145	27.7
indophenol	+ 248	31.2
potassium ferricyanide	+ 430	37.5

Redox potential can be determined using coloured indicators.

The method consists in observing the transition from the coloured to the colourless form which occurs at the Eh value characteristic of the reagent concerned (Table 16.2). This technique entails many difficulties in soil analysis, but is nevertheless useful as a preliminary test.

References

Lemon ER and Erickson AE (1955) Principe of the platinum micro electrode as a method of characterizing soil aeration. *Soil Sci.*, 79, 383–392

Liu ZG and Yu TR (1984) Depolarisation of platinum electrode in soil its utilisation for the measurement of redox potential. *J. Soil Sci.*, 35, 469–479

Veneman PLM and Pickering W (1983) Salt bridge for field redox potential measurements. *Commun. Soil Sci. Plant Anal.*, 14, 669–677

Vilain M and Ruelle JP (1974) Appréciation d'un état d'aération par l'utilisation de techniques électrochimiques, principes et observations. *Ann. Agron.*, 25, 1–23

Voiret EG and Froquet L (1950) Le rH : la pratique de sa mesure. *Applications. Chimie et industrie*, 64 , 439

Bibliography

Bohn HL (1968) Electromotive force of inert electrodes in soil suspensions. *Soil Science Society American Proceedings*, 32, 211–215

Eshel G and Banin A (2002) Feasibility study of long-term continuous field measurement of soil redox potential. *Communications in Soil Science and Plant Analysis*, 33, 695–709

Fisterer UP and Gribbohm S (1989) Constructing platinum electrodes for redox measuring. *Zeitschrift fur Pflanzenernahrung und Bodenkund*, 152, 455–456

Gao S, Tanji KK, Scardaci SC and Chow AT (2002) Comparison of redox indicators in a paddy soil during rice-growing season. *Soil Science Society of America Journal*, 66, 805–817

Grundl TJ and Macalady DL (1989) Electrode measurement of redox potential in anaerobic ferric/ferrous chloride systems. *Journal of Contaminant Hydrology*, 5, 97–117

Holm TR and Curtiss CD (1989) A comparison of oxidation–reduction potentials calculated from the As(V)/As(III) and Fe(III)/Fe(II) couples with measured platinum-electrode potentials in groundwater. *Journal of Contaminant Hydrology*, 5, 67–81

Hunter JD, Scoggins DK, Hawk RM and Sims RA (1986) Development of a microcomputer controlled multi-probe instrument for automated time-dependent measurement of redox potential and oxygen diffusion rate. *Analytical Instrumentation*, 15, 51–62

ISO 11271 (2002) A field method for the determination of soil redox potential (Eh). International Organization for Standardization

Komada M (1990) Redox potential measurements in a flooded paddy field using a compact computer system. In *Transactions 14th International Congress of Soil Science*, Kyoto, Japan, 44–49

Kukec A, Berovic M, Celan S and Wondra M (2002) The role of on-line redox potential measurement in Sauvignon blanc fermentation. *Food Technology and Biotechnology*, 40, 49–55

Le Brusq JY, Zante P and Péraudeau M (1987) La mesure in situ de paramètres physico-chimiques (pH-Eh) dans les sols sulfatés de Casamance. *Cah. ORSTOM Sér. Pédol.*, XXIII, 55–66

Mueller SC, Stolzy LH and Fick GW (1985) Constructing and screening platinum microelectrodes for measuring soil redox potential. *Soil Science*, 139, 558–560

Patrick WH, Gambrell RP and Faulkner SP (1996) Redox measurements of soils. In *Methods of Soil Analysis, Part 3 Chemical Methods*, Bigham JM and Bartels JM ed. SSSA-ASA, Madison, Wisconsin, Etats-Unis

Susini J and Loyer JY (1977) *Réalisation d'un ensemble automatique pour la mesure en continu et in situ du pH, du Eh, du pNa du sol.*, ORSTOM-DRES, Tunis, 17 p

van Bochove E, Beauchemin S and Thériault G (2002) Continuous multiple measurement of soil redox potential using platinum microelectrodes. *Soil Science Society of America Journal,* 66, 1813–1820

Vizier JF (1971) Etude de l'état d'oxydo-réduction du sol et ses conséquences sur la dynamique du fer dans les sols hydromorphes. *Cah. ORSTOM Sér. Pédol.*, IX, 376–380

Vizier JF (1989) Etude du fonctionnement des milieux saturés d'eau. *Cah. ORSTOM sér. Pédol.*, XXV, 431–442

Carbonates

17.1 Introduction

Carbonates are abundant in the terrestrial biosphere and comprise a group of minerals with more than 130 species, mainly forms of:

- Ca^{2+} ($CaCO_3$, calcite and some rarer polymorphic forms, aragonite, vaterite, ikaite)
- Mg^{2+} ($MgCO_3$, magnesite, lansfordite and substituted $CaMg(CO_3)_2$ forms, dolomite, huntite)
- Na^+ (Na_2CO_3, e.g. natron, thermonatrite)
- Fe^{2+} ($FeCO_3$, e.g. siderite and substituted forms as ankerite (Fe–Ca–Mg–Mn)

Many groups have intermediate species with two or three metallic elements and different substitutions. Carbonates were formed during geological times under the action of physical, chemical and biochemical factors (Chamayou and Legros 1990) particularly during the transgression of the Jurassic and of the Cretaceous according to reactions giving the simplified balance:

$$Ca^{2+} + 2HCO_3^- \xrightarrow{t°C, \text{ pressure}, CO_2} \underset{\downarrow}{CaCO_3} + H_2O + CO_2^{\uparrow}$$

Carbonates were deposited by sedimentation in marine or lake environments and may originate from precipitation products that differ in their relative solubility (Garrels and Christ 1967): approximately 0.014 g L^{-1} for calcite, 0.106 g L^{-1} for magnesite, 71 g L^{-1} for natron 0.067 g L^{-1} for siderite (a reducing medium is necessary to obtain bivalent iron of siderite).

Carbonates can also originate within organic materials resulting from living organisms (biogenic limestones from polypiers, algae, various foraminifera, shells, etc.) or detrital products resulting from the degradation of limestone rocks through erosion.

Pedogenic and biogeochemical processes are responsible for another type of differentiation: calcium and magnesium carbonates that are not very soluble give rise to different calcimagnesic soils which vary with climatic conditions, topography, origin of the parent rock, pH, type of vegetation and level of biochemical activity. Magnesium is more soluble and is generally more easily moved.

In arid and semi-arid climates, illuvial hardened horizons can be observed with high calcium contents (petrocalcic horizon) and possibly precipitation of gypsum.

The very soluble sodium carbonate is generally very quickly eliminated but in arid climates it can accumulate and result in sodic alkaline soils. Its geochemical formation gives rise to three fundamental reactions:

$$CaX + 2NaCl \rightarrow Na_2X + CaCl_2 \text{ (leaching)}$$
$$Na_2X + 2H_2O \rightarrow H_2X + 2NaOH \text{ (hydrolysis)}$$
$$2NaOH + CO_2 \rightarrow Na_2CO_3 + H_2O \text{ (carbonation)}$$

This carbonate is measured with soluble salts (cf. Chap. 18). The disaggregation of the carbonated parent rock leads to the progressive elimination of Ca^{2+} but also results in highly differentiated particles that vary with the process of formation of carbonates in soils: forms of sands, silts, nodules, oolites, crusts, pellicular coverings or interparticle cements.

Calcareous chalks and marls, which are highly porous and have pores about one micron in size, result in enrichment in fine sands and silts in contact with CO_2 charged water. Less porous, more compact limestones give mostly coarser particles such as gravels and sands.

Disaggregation by plants and micro-organisms can also cause simultaneous mechanical and biochemical processes under the combined action of roots and organic acids. Concentrations and precipitations of calcite can be observed in the vicinity of the roots and even within the roots in not very wet climates (Jaillard 1984). When calcium carbonate is abundant, especially in the form of very fine particles, its reactive surface is extensive inducing particularly high reactivity. Calcium carbonate can combine with the organic phase and modify deterioration processes. Soils resulting from calcareous chalks or marls in particular, can cause the saturation of the soil solution in Ca^{2+} ions according to the reaction:

$$CaCO_3 + CO_2 + H_2O \underset{pH}{\overset{\text{pression } CO_2}{\rightleftarrows}} Ca(HCO_3)_2 \quad \text{soluble}[1]$$

---

[1] Detailed equations in Garrel and Christ (1967), Chamayou and Legros (1990).

In this case, analysis of total carbonates is of no use to agronomists. Two soils with the same concentration of total carbonates can have a different capacity to induce plant chlorosis.

Studies based on the analysis of active calcium carbonate were undertaken to identify the thresholds that induce calcic and ferric chlorosis.

The analysis of "total carbonates" enables the creation of gradients of the distribution of carbonates in a profile, the contribution of the parent rock (inherited carbonates), of amendments, of colluvial deposition etc. But this analysis cannot distinguish pedogenic Ca from inherited Ca. The total carbonate contents can vary from 2 to 50%, or even more.

The analysis of "active carbonates", the significance of which was underlined by Callot and Dupuis (1980), is linked with the content of calcareous silts and the rate of extractable iron (Juste and Pouget 1972). It may be possible to establish a correlation between active carbonates and total carbonates using fractions below 20 μm.

17.2 Measurement of Total Carbonates

17.2.1 Introduction

In situ pH measurements between approximately 7.5 and 8.5 indicate the presence of carbonates. A higher pH (towards 10) can indicate the presence of sodium carbonate.

A rapid test with a 10% hydrochloric acid solution produces effervescence. The degree of effervescence observed provides information about the carbonate content but does not explain the origin of the carbonate (Ca, Mg, Na, Fe, etc.). Ca^{2+} and Na^+ carbonates react instantaneously with hydrochloric acid, while Mg^{2+} and Fe^{2+} carbonates release CO_2 slowly. The distribution of carbonates can vary greatly with the soil particles and one way of distinguishing the differences is in the location of the effervescence around the small insulated particles such as nodules or oolites.

It is important to identify the nature of mineral components in order to choose the best procedure to use i.e. XRD (Chap. 4), observation by SEM + EDX or FTIR microscope (Chap. 8), or thermal analysis (Chap. 7).

Methods for the measurement of total carbonates are generally based on the release of carbon dioxide by acid attack. Alternative methods measure:

1. The volume of CO_2 produced under well-controlled analytical conditions particularly temperature and pressure
2. Released CO_2 by infrared absorption spectrometry
3. Released CO_2 by gas chromatography after separation from other gases
4. Thermogravimetric evolution coupled with evolved gas analysis (EGA, cf. Chap. 7)
5. Breakdown of carbonates by an acid solution and back-titration of the remaining acid in the solution

None of these methods is perfect. Method (1) allows representative sampling by modulating the weight of the samples and by iso-granulometric crushing into fine particles which regulates the time of attack. This method is simple and fast and has proved satisfactory for repetitive analysis if pressure and temperature conditions are respected. It is used for soils with carbonate contents higher than 2–5%. Methods (2), (3), (4) can only be used for microsamples, the results are not really representative, and they require relatively sophisticated equipment that is not accessible for all laboratories. Because of the heterogeneity of the soil, these methods are used for detailed mineralogical studies, for example to differentiate calcite and magnesite, or siderite. Method (5) is simple to implement but is often not precise enough in the case of low contents.

17.2.2 Volumetric Measurements by Calcimetry

Principle

The carbonates are destroyed by hydrochloric acid and the volume of released carbon dioxide is measured at controlled temperature and pressure.

$$CaCO_3 + 2HCl \rightarrow CaCl_2 + H_2O + CO_2 \quad \text{(fast reaction)}$$
$$\text{or } MgCO_3 + 2HCl \rightarrow MgCl_2 + H_2O + CO_2 \quad \text{(slow reaction)}$$

This method is part of the international standard (NF ISO 10693 1995). Balázs Horvátha et al. (2005) propose an improvement of this method using the pressure calcimeter. The pressure change caused by the reaction between HCl and the soil sample is measured with a digital plunge-in manometer through a silicone–rubber septum placed on a screw-capped tube.

Equipment

– Analytical balance (± 0.1 mg)
– Bernard calcimeter with two-way stopcock and 250 mL Erlenmeyer flask fitted with finger (Fig. 17.1)
– Large wooden grip
– Barometer

Products

– Deionized boiled water
– Calcium carbonate ($CaCO_3$) in powder form, dried in a desiccator
– 18 mol (HCl) L^{-1} hydrochloric acid: mix one volume of deionized boiled water with one volume of concentrated hydrochloric acid ($d = 1.19$)
– Filling solution for the calcimeter: saturated sodium chloride containing a colour reagent

Procedure

– Work in an air-conditioned room at 20°C on a soil sample crushed to 0.1 mm particle size and dried in the desiccator.
– Weigh from 1 to 10 g of soil to obtain a volume of CO_2 of about 60–80 mL.
– Pour the soil onto a non-gummed cigarette paper and wrap carefully without losing any of the sample.
– Use a 10 mL pipette to introduce the hydrochloric acid into the finger of the Erlenmeyer flask without allowing any of the acid solution to reach the bottom of the flask (Fig. 17.1).
– Add the soil sample.
– Moisten with 2 mL of deionized water to release the soil from the cigarette paper.
– Avoid heating the elements of the calcimeter with your hands, open tap a and stop the Erlenmeyer flask.
– Use the mobile tank c to adjust to level 0 in the graduated cylinder, then turn off the tap a.
– Using the wooden grip, rock the flask to bring the acid and the soil into contact.

- Agitate and gradually lower the tank (c in Fig. 17.1) monitoring the decrease in the level of the liquid in the graduated cylinder.
- When the level has stabilized, bring the level of the liquid in the tank to the level of the liquid in the graduated column and make the reading, V mL CO_2.
- Note the temperature and the atmospheric pressure.

Calibration of the apparatus

Weigh 0.3 g of calcium carbonate dried in the desiccator and place it in a non-gummed cigarette paper. Continue as above and note the volume obtained. Repeat this procedure with 0.2 g and 0.1 g of calcium carbonate.

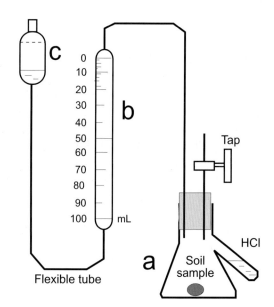

Fig. 17.1. Calcimeter of the Bernard type with 100 mL graduated tube

Calculation

The result is generally expressed as a percentage of limestone:

$$\mathrm{CaCO_3\%} = \frac{V \times M \times 2.28 \times 100}{1{,}000 \times P}$$

V: volume of evolved CO_2 per sample (mL), M: mass in g of 1 L of CO_2 in titration pressure and temperature conditions (Table 17.1), P: weight of sample (g), $2.28 = \dfrac{\mathrm{CaCO_3}}{\mathrm{CO_2}} = \dfrac{100.09}{44.01}$

Table 17.1. Mass in grams of 1 L of dry CO_2 at different temperatures and pressures

	millibars	986.66	1,000.00	1,013.33	1,026.6
$t°C$	mm Hg	740	750	760	770
20°		1.7423	1.7665	1.7906	1.8147
21°		1.7338	1.7530	1.7818	1.8059
22°		1.7251	1.7443	1.7730	1.7970
23°		1.7164	1.7355	1.7641	1.7880
24°		1.7075	1.7265	1.7551	1.7789

Remarks

- The column is filled with a coloured saturated sodium chloride solution to limit dissolution of carbon dioxide and to facilitate reading.
- The temperature measured is ambient temperature; as the HCl + $CaCO_3$ reaction is exothermic, the real temperature may be slightly higher; wait one minute for the temperature to stabilize before reading.
- The calcimeter can be calibrated by preparing corresponding ranges from 5 to 50% of $CaCO_3$.
- The measurement may be distorted by excess if sulphides are present; at the end of analysis, check the odour of hydrogen sulphide in the evolved carbon dioxide.
- Siderite is not completely attacked which results in underestimation of carbonate content.
- In the presence of dolomite [$CaMg(CO_3)_2$], two readings should be made, the first after 1 min, the second after 3 min, as dolomite reacts more slowly than limestone.

17.2.3 Acidimetry

Principle

This rapid method is based on neutralization of the sample by a titrated acid. Back-titration by a base makes it possible to determine equivalent calcium carbonate. As the dissolution of calcite is not selective, magnesite, dolomite and part of the siderite will also be dissolved.

Equipment

– Laboratory glassware
– Centrifuge with 250 mL centrifugation tubes with screw caps
– Agitator

Reagents

– Boiled deionized water.
– Hydrochloric acid, $d = 1.19$.
– 1 mol L^{-1} hydrochloric acid solution: add 42.5 mL of concentrated hydrochloric acid in approximately 400 mL deionized water while homogenizing by agitation; let cool and complete to 500 mL.
– Standard commercial dose 0.5 mol L^{-1} hydrochloric acid.
– 0.5 mol L^{-1} sodium hydroxide solution: dissolve 20 g of soda pellets in a 1 L boiling flask containing 1,000 mL deionized boiled water; let cool protected from the air; homogenize and immediately titrate with the 0.5 mol (HCl) L^{-1} solution. This solution does not keep and should be prepared every two days and titrated before each use.
– 0.1% phenolphthalein indicator in ethanol solution.

Procedure

– Weigh 5 g of soil crushed to 0.1 mm (or 2.5 g for soils with high limestone content).
– Add 100 mL of 1 mol (HCl) L^{-1} solution and agitate in a 250 mL centrifugation tube.
– Leave in contact overnight.
– Close the tube and agitate for 2 h.
– Centrifuge at 2,000 g and pipette 10 mL of the supernatant liquid into a 100 mL Erlenmeyer flask.
– Add 25 mL water, two drops of phenolphthalein and titrate using 0.5 mol (NaOH) L^{-1} solution.
– Under the same conditions, treat two blanks and a control specimen of 500 mg of calcium carbonate.

Calculations

The result is generally expressed as a percentage of limestone ($M_{1/2CaCO_3} = 50$ g):

$$CaCO_3\% = 50\ N\ \frac{a - b}{S}$$

(correct by moisture measured after drying at 105°C on a separated sample)

a: mL NaOH used for blank titrations;
b: mL NaOH used for titration of the soil sample;
S: weight of sample dried in the desiccator (g);
N: concentration of the soda solution (mol L^{-1}).

Remarks

– Equivalent $CaCO_3$ may be overestimated if HCl reacts with non-carbonated substances in the soil.
– Dolomite and magnesite are completely dissolved, but only part of siderite.
– Analysing Ca and Mg in the solution makes it possible to distinguish $CaCO_3$ and $MgCO_3$.

17.3 Titration of Active Carbonate

Also called the Drouineau and Galet method, titration of active carbonate is standardized in the international NF X31-106 standard (1982) and was proposed by Loeppert and Suarez (1996).

17.3.1 Principle

The soil sample is put in contact with ammonium oxalate under standard time conditions for attack and agitation. Ammonium oxalate having not reacted with carbonates, is then back titrated by manganimetry:

$$CaCO_3 + (NH_4)_2 C_2O_4 \rightarrow \underset{\downarrow}{CaC_2O_4} + (NH_4)_2 CO_3$$

$$5(NH_4)_2C_2O_4 + 2KMnO_4 + 8H_2SO_4 \rightarrow 2MnSO_4 + K_2SO_4 + 5(NH_4)_2SO_4 + 8H_2O + 10CO_2$$

The method should not be used for very organic or gypseous soils. The presence of reducing substances should be avoided.

17.3.2 Implementation

Equipment

– Analytical balance.
– Reverse agitator.
– A range of lab glassware.

Reagents

– Deionized boiled water.
– Distilled water for the oxidizing solutions.
– Ammonium oxalate $(NH_4)_2C_2O_4$, H_2O mw $= 142.11$ g.
– 0.2 mol $(\frac{1}{2}NH_4)_2C_2O_4)$ L^{-1} extraction solution:
    (a) Weigh 14.2110 g of ammonium oxalate (dried in the desiccator for 48 h)
    (b) Dissolve in deionized water at 80°C and complete to 1 L after cooling
    (c) Titrate with a 0.1 mol $(1/5KMnO_4)$ L^{-1} standard potassium permanganate solution.
– Sulphuric acid, $d = 1.84$.
– Diluted solution of sulphuric acid: slowly pour 50 mL H_2SO_4 into 200 mL deionized water; let cool.
– Potassium permanganate, $KMnO_4$, mw $= 158.03$ g.
– 0.1 mol $(1/5KMnO_4)$ L^{-1} standard solution: use commercial standard dose or weigh 3.1606 g of potassium permanganate, dissolve in 800 mL distilled water in a 1 L volumetric flask; agitate until potassium permanganate is completely dissolved, complete to 1,000 mL (check purity with oxalic acid 0.1 mol $(\frac{1}{2}H_2C_2O_4)$ L^{-1} standard solution.

Procedure

Samples: crush a specimen of 2 mm air-dried soil to 1 mm. Measure the residual moisture of the 1 mm crushed soil to correct the results which will be expressed on the basis of the soil dried at 105°C.
– Weigh 2.5 g of soil and place in a 500 mL Erlenmeyer flask.
– Add 250 mL ammonium oxalate 0.2 mol $(\frac{1}{2}NH_4)_2C_2O_4)$ L^{-1} and agitate for 2 h in a rotary agitator.
– Filter on blue analytical filter; discard the first fractions if they are turbid.
– Take 10 mL of clear filtrate and pour into a 250 mL Erlenmeyer flask.
– Add approximately 75 mL of distilled water.
– Add 25 mL of diluted sulphuric acid.
– Heat at 60°C on the heating turntable of a magnetic stirrer and titrate with the potassium permanganate 0.1 mol $(1/5KMnO_4)$ L^{-1} solution until a stable pale pink colour is obtained: X mL. Titrate 10 mL of the oxalate solution in the same way: Y mL. The difference between the two titrations corresponds to the quantity of calcium carbonate that has reacted with ammonium oxalate.

Calculation

The percentage of active limestone of the sample is expressed by: Active

$$\text{CaCO}_3\% = 50 \times 0.1 \ (Y - X) \ \frac{250}{10} \ \frac{100}{2500} \ \frac{c}{0.1} = 50 \ c \ (Y\!-\!X),$$

where Y and X are volumes (mL) of manganic solution for respective titrations of the blank and of the sample, and c is the real content of this solution in equivalents per litre.

Remarks

The organic matter can be slightly solubilized and consume a little permanganate. It should be noted that many other methods have been developed in reducing medium at pH 4.8 (for extractable Fe, Al, Si), or complexants with the EDTA, DTPA, CDTA or EDDHA[2] (cf. Chap. 31).

17.3.3 Index of Chlorosis Potential

In the presence of an excessive concentration of active calcium carbonate, the development of calcifuge plants can be inhibited and the plants will display pathological symptoms. Active calcium carbonate is also antagonistic to iron and can cause ferric chlorosis. Iron, which is essential to chlorophyllian plants, is immobilized and results in deficient plant growth. Thorne and Wallace (1944) recommended the determination of "free" iron extractable with 0.5% oxalic acid solution to determine the levels of iron deficiency. Juste and Pouget (1972) defined an "index of chlorosis potential" (CP) which binds active calcium carbonate and extractable iron titrated in the same ammonium oxalate medium (Fe can be determined by atomic absorption spectrometry at 243.3 nm with air-acetylene flame).

$$\text{CP} = \frac{\text{active calcium carbonate \%}}{\text{extractable iron (ppm)}} 10^4$$

The method was proposed as FD X31-146 standard (1996), but the reproducibility of an inter-laboratory test was not very satisfactory.

---

[2] *EDTA*, ethylene diamine tetra-acetic acid; *DTPA*, diethylene triamine penta-acetic Acid; *CDTA trans*-1,2 diamino cyclohexane N, N, N', N' Tetra-acetic Acid; *EDDHA*, ethylene diamine di (*O*-Hydroxyphenyl acetic Acid).

References

Balázs H, Opara-Nadib O and Beesea F (2005) A simple method for measuring the carbonate content of soil. *Soil Sci. Soc. Am. J.*, 69, 1066–1068, DOI: 10.2136/sssaj2004.0010

Callot G and Dupuis M (1980) Le calcaire actif des sols et sa signification. *Sci. du Sol.*, 1, 17–26

Chamayou H and Legros JP (1990) Les bases physiques, chimiques et minéralogiques de la science du sol. *Presses Univ. France*, 593 pages

FD X31-146 (1996) Détermination de l'indice de pouvoir chlorosant (IPC) selon Juste et Pouget. In *Qualité des sols*, AFNOR, 117–125

Garrels MA and Christ GL (1967) Equilibre des minéraux et de leurs solutions aqueuses. Gauthier-Villard, Paris, France

ISO 10693 (1995) Soil quality - Determination of carbonate content - Volumetric method. International Organisation for Standardization

Jaillard B (1984) Mise en évidence de la néogenèse des sables calcaires sous l'influence des racines: incidence de la granulométrie du sol. *Agronomie.*, 4, 91–100

Juste C and Pouget R (1972) Appréciation du pouvoir chlorosant des sols par un nouvel indice faisant intervenir le calcaire actif et le fer facilement extractible. *C.R. Acad. Agric. de Fr.*, 58, 352–357

Loeppert RH and Suarez DL (1996) Carbonate and gypsum. In *Methods of Soil Analysis*, Part 3, Chemical Methods, Bigham JM and Bartels JM ed. SSSA, ASA, Madison, Wisconsin, Etats-Unis, 437–474

NF ISO 10693 (1995) Détermination de la teneur en carbonate - Méthode volumétrique. In *Qualité des sols*, AFNOR, 177–186

NF X31-106 (1982) Détermination du calcaire actif. In *Qualité des sols*, AFNOR, 55–58

Thorne DW and Wallace A (1944) Some factors affecting chlorosis on high-line soils. I - Ferrous and Ferric iron. *Soil Sci.*, 57, 299–312

Soluble Salts

18.1 Introduction

The term "soluble salts" covers a range of anions and cations present in the soil in either crystallized solid form (e.g. efflorescence, crusts, microcrystalline clusters), or in dissolved form in the soil solution – other than soluble organic matter (cf. Chap. 13). Soluble salts are different from the cations of the soil exchange complex (cf. Chap. 19) adsorbed on the surface of clays (cf. Chap. 22) with which they are in equilibrium.

Soil soluble salts are often compared to a combination of major elements including the Na^+, K^+, Ca^{2+} and Mg^{2+} cations and the Cl^-, HCO_3^-, CO_3^{2-}, SO_4^{2-} anions. When present in sufficient quantities in the soil, these salt systems belong to the group of saline soils named *Halomorphes, Solontchaks, Salisols* or *Salic* soils depending on the system of classification used (INRA 1995; FAO 1998). These soils are common in all dry regions in the world and near the sea (primary salinity). Land under irrigation also frequently displays saline characteristics (secondary or anthropic salinity) induced by the poor quality of the water used, by fertilization or by bad agricultural practices, particularly the absence of drainage (Bouteyre and Loyer 1995; Qadir et al. 2001).

These salts can originate from very diverse marine, petrographic or eruptive sources. In sedimentary mediums, they are mainly in the form of chlorides and sulphates, whereas carbonates and bicarbonates dominate in crystalline mediums. As well as these major anions, nitrates, borates or even arsenic salts are also found in certain systems, sometimes in quite high proportions.

The most soluble and most frequently recognized salts in soils are halite or sodium chloride (NaCl), sylvinite or potassium chloride (KCl), sodium sulphates (thenardite and mirabilite), potassium and magnesium sulphates (epsomite, and hexahydrite), sodium and magnesium sulphates (bloedite), many mixed aluminium sulphates (of the alum type), sodium carbonate (natron). High solubility in water, higher than the gypsum (2.6 g L^{-1}), is the major characteristic that allows differentiation of saline soils from, for example, purely gypseous soils (Loyer 1991). Solubility generally increases with temperature; the solubility of gypsum increases up to 2.653 g L^{-1} at 40°C then decreases up to 2.049 g L^{-1} at 100°C. Table 18.1 lists the solubility of a few soluble salts at 20°C.

Table 18.1. Solubility of a few salts frequently present in soils (K = solubility product)

salt	mineral	g L^{-1} at 20°C	log K
NaCl	halite	360	+ 1.55
Na$_2$SO$_4$	thenardite	209	− 0.86
Na$_2$CO$_3$,H$_2$O	thermonatrite	215	+ 0.1
NaNO$_3$	nitratite	880	
KCl	sylvinite	350	+ 0.80
K$_2$SO$_4$	arcanite	109	
MgCl$_2$	chloromagnesite	543	+ 22
CaCl$_2$	hydrophilite	427	+ 11.5

Among the factors which influence the solubility of each salt, the presence of other salts should not be neglected. For example, gypsum solubility increases considerably in the presence of sodium chloride, but decreases in the presence of sodium sulphate due to the effect of common ions (Pouget 1968; Harvie and Weare 1980; Harvie et al. 1984).

Laboratory measurement of the soluble salts in the soil involves three stages:
– Extraction by water at different soil/solution ratios (saturation extracts, aqueous extracts 1:1, 1:5, 1:10).
– Measurement of the total salt concentration of the extract (electric conductivity, dissolved solid matter).
– Titration of the different anions and cations contained in the extract

18.2 Extraction

18.2.1 Soil/Solution Ratio

The choice of the soil/solution ratio used for the extraction of soluble salts depends on several different criteria and in particular on the purpose and the execution speed. The time-consuming method of extraction of saturated paste is used with the aim of reproducing as closely as possible the real in situ soil solution from which the plants take up nutrients. Methods using diluted extracts are faster and allow monitoring of vertical and spatial variations in salinity and of changes over time due to the external or internal factors that influence salinity. The relations that bind the different extracts are not the same everywhere (cf. Sect. 18.23) but depend on the type of salts in the geographical area concerned (Le Brusq and Loyer 1982).

18.2.2 Extraction of Saturated Paste

Principle

This is the international reference method recommended by Riverside Salinity Laboratory, USA (Richards 1954). Given the difficulty in obtaining an extract that is representative of the soil solution which lies between water content at field capacity and water content at wilting point at a given time, this standardized method consists in bringing the sample to saturation, i.e. close to its liquidity limit (Servant 1975; Baize 1988).

Procedure

- In a capsule with a lid, weigh between 250 and 500 g of soil sieved to 2 mm, air dried and of known moisture content.
- Prepare the paste by adding a known quantity of distilled water while mixing with a spatula until saturation. From time to time consolidate the mixture by striking the container on the laboratory table.
- With the exception of very clayey soils, when saturated, the soil paste will shine in the light, run slightly when the capsule is tilted, and slide easily along the spatula.
- Cover the capsule and let stand for 1 h or more before checking saturation. Correct if necessary by adding either water or soil in known quantities.
- Weigh the capsule and calculate the percentage of water at saturation (cf. "Water Content of Saturated Paste" under Sect. 18.2.2) with respect to the quantity of water added and to the initial moisture of the soil (or after drying part of the saturated paste at 105°C).
- Filter on a Büchner funnel and collect the solution in a filter-flask, avoid using Pyrex glass if boron titration is required.

– If the filtrate is turbid, filter again on membrane or centrifuge. If analysis of carbonates and bicarbonates is required, adding a drop of 0.1% sodium hexametaphosphate solution (0.1 g of sodium hexametaphosphate diluted in 100 mL of deionized water) for 25 mL of extract, prevents the precipitation of $CaCO_3$. Preserve the extract in a closed bottle for later measurements and titrations.

Remark

For rapid measurement of soil salinity, filtration can be performed a few minutes after preparation of the paste. In other cases it is preferable to wait a few hours. If the soil is gypseous, let the paste stand for several hours (4–16 h) before extracting the solution.

Water Content of Saturated Paste

If W_s is the weight of the test specimen of soil dried at 105°C, and W_w is the weight of added water (including water initially present in the soil sample), the percentage of water at saturation SW is obtained by:

$$SW = 100 \ \frac{W_w}{W_S} \tag{18.1}$$

18.2.3 Diluted Extracts

Comparative Interest

In this more rapid technique, a given weight of soil W_s must be put in contact with a variable weight of water W_w so that a ratio $W_w{:}W_s = n$ is obtained (instead of SW:100 in (1)). One of the consequences of dilution is that the total ionic concentration of the more or less diluted aqueous extracts (C_n) is theoretically lower than that measured on the saturated extract (C_{se}) from the sole effect of dilution:

$$C_n = \frac{C_{se} \ SW}{100 \ n} . \tag{18.2}$$

If the electrical conductivity EC and the corresponding concentration of the aqueous extract are proportional, one can write:

$$EC_n = \frac{EC_{se} \ SW}{100 \ n} . \tag{18.3}$$

Initially it could be expected that the multiplicative factor necessary to pass from one to another measurement is inversely proportional to dilution. However, the conductivity measured on the diluted extracts is often higher than the conductivity calculated starting from (3) (Le Brusq and Loyer 1982). In fact, certain extracts, especially the 1:10 extract, result in significant supplementary dissolution of salts compared to the saturated extract. This proves that the relation between the conductivities of the different extracts is not only directly proportional to the water volume but in practice varies with different factors such as soil texture, salinity and the ionic composition of the dissolved compounds.

Diluted extracts are especially useful in the case of low saline concentrations with a relatively low proportion of gypsum. From a practical point of view in the case of serial analyses of numerous samples, the conductivity of the 1:2 extracts should be measured first. Those which give by calculation values for $C_{se} > 10$ dS m^{-1} can then be started again using (1) a saturated paste, and (2) a very diluted extract for total gypsum. For the samples where $C_{se} < 10$ dS m^{-1}, the 1:2 extract is sufficient. In the 1:2 extracts the anion: cation balance is only slightly modified or not modified at all. In the 1:5 and 1:10 extracts, the phenomena of hydrolysis of sodium and exchange with calcium in the extraction solution have to be taken into consideration as they can lead to modifications in the balance between salts.

Procedure

- Weigh a sample of air-dried soil sieved to 2 mm and place it in a bottle suitable for the volume of the extract required; add the quantity of distilled water necessary to obtain the desired ratio of soil to solution (1:1, 1:2, 1:5, 1:10).
- Correct for the initial moisture of the soil especially when using low soil/solution ratios (for example for the 1:1 extract, with 2% of initial moisture, add 98 mL of water to 102 g of soil), or if a high degree of accuracy is required.
- Agitate mechanically for 1 h (or shake vigorously by hand 4 times at 30 min intervals) and filter.
- Add one drop of 0.1% sodium hexametaphosphate solution for 25 mL of extract and close the container tightly before titration.

18.2.4 In Situ Sampling of Soil Water

When soil water is measured in situ a more accurate account is obtained of thermodynamic equilibriums of ions in contact with the plant roots. Different types of soil water can be distinguished (e.g. interstitial water, bound water, see Chap. 1) corresponding to different techniques of water sampling (Pansu et al. 2001), particularly that of the porous plugs analyzed by Cheverry (1983) and described by Rhoades and Oster (1986) for the study of saline soils.

18.2.5 Extracts with Hot Water

Hot water enables a much larger quantity of materials to be solubilized than cold water (from 10 to more than 50 times on *Luvisol* soils cf. Chap. 13). Extraction with hot water can thus be an indicator of potentially extractable elements and compounds and is recommended for boron quantification (NF X31-122 1993). The procedures are rather difficult to standardize because on certain soils dissolution does not seem to be complete for a given length of attack (Kouakoua et al. 1997). The attack necessary to the selective extraction of boron (cf. Sect. 31.2.7 of Chap. 31) is not very aggressive. The attack used to quantify water-soluble organic origin (reflux 16 h, cf. Sect. 13.2.6 of Chap. 13) is more aggressive. This attack extracts a considerable quantity of anions in addition to those extracted by cold water (see Fig. 18.2).

18.3 Measurement and Titration

18.3.1 Electrical Conductivity of the Extracts

Benefits

In contrast to perfectly pure water, saline solutions have the conduction property of electric current. The electric conductivity (EC) measured is proportional to the quantity and nature of salts dissolved in the solutions. Thus a good general relationship of proportionality exists between electrical conductivity (in deciSiemens per metre) and total concentration (tC) of anions or cations (in meq L^{-1} or mg L^{-1}):

$$- \text{ in meq } L^{-1}, tC = (10 \text{ to } 12) \times EC \qquad (18.4)$$

$$- \text{ in mg } L^{-1}, tC = (600 \text{ to } 650) \times EC. \qquad (18.4')$$

However, the variability of the proportionality factor shows that this relation is not universal. It depends on the ionic composition of the soil solutions (Job 1985), and is thus not necessarily transferable from one geographical region to another. It is advisable to establish the relation

$EC = f(tC)$ applicable to the specific saline context concerned rather than use the average line obtained by Richards (1954) on soils in the west of the United States.

Measurement of electrical conductivity is the most widely used soil salinity test (Rhoades and Miyamoto 1990; Shirokova et al. 2000). It is usually carried out on the saturated or diluted extract, but sometimes directly on the saturated paste itself. This measurement is highly dependent on the temperature (increase of almost 2% per degree), and must consequently be adjusted to a reference temperature of 25°C after measurement of the temperature of the solution. When measured at the same time as pH, measurement of conductivity is a good indicator of soil quality (Smith and Doran 1996). Measurement of the specific conductivity of the 1:5 extract is the subject of the international standard NF ISO 11265 standard (1995).

Principle

Measurement of EC is based on the measurement of electrical resistance between two parallel electrodes immersed in the aqueous extract obtained as in Sect. 18.2.

The traditional conductivimeter is based on the principle of the Wheastone bridge. It includes a cell made of two platinum electrodes of defined surface area and spacing, usually covered with platinum black to decrease the resistance of the interface electrode-solution. Alternating frequency high voltage is applied between the electrodes to measure resistance. Specific resistance sR of a solution is defined by the resistance of a cube with sides measuring 1 cm (surface of electrode 1 cm^2, distance between electrodes 1 cm). In practice, the inter-electrode volume is not exactly 1 cm^3 and consequently resistance R (measured in Ohms) is not exactly the same as specific resistance. A cell constant should thus be defined:

$K = R/sR$.

The reverse of R expresses the conductance in mhos or Siemens, which, with this type of electrode, gives a specific electric conductivity EC:

$$EC = 1/sR = K/R. \qquad (18.5)$$

Expressed in the international system (IS units) in Siemens per m, or sub-units according to the calibration selected (1 S m^{-1} = 10 dS m^{-1} = 10 mS cm^{-1} = 10 mmhos cm^{-1} = 1,000 mS m^{-1} = 10,000 µS cm^{-1}).

The cell constant, generally provided by the manufacturer, should be checked against standard solutions of potassium chloride whose conductivity (Table 18.2) is in the expected range of measurements to be made.

Most conductivimeters have a logarithmic reading scale and are equipped with a switch of extended range allowing the use of scale multiplicative factors using powers of 10.

Table 18.2. EC of a few aqueous KCl solutions at 25°C

mol (KCl) L^{-1}	0.001	0.01	0.02	0.05	0.1	0.2	0.5	1
EC dS m^{-1}	0.147	1.413	2.767	6.668	12.900	24.820	58.640	111.900

Reagents

– 0.05 mol (KCl) L^{-1} stock solution: dissolve 3.728 g of dry KCl in 1 L of deionised water at 25°C.
– 0.01 mol (KCl) L^{-1}: 50 mL of stock solution in 250 mL of deionized water.
– 0.005 mol (KCl) L^{-1}: 25 mL of stock solution in 250 mL of deionized water.
– Cleaning solution for the electrode: mix equal volumes of isopropanol, ethyl ether and hydrochloric acid.
– Solution for platinum coating: dissolve 1 g of chloroplatinic acid ($H_2PtCl_6,6H_2O$) and 12 mg of lead acetate in 100 mL of pure water.

Preparation of the Platinum Electrodes

In the event of measurements that are not very stable or are too far from the theoretical values of the standard solutions, (cf. "Checking the Cell Constant" by below), the electrodes can be prepared or regenerated as described later.

Clean the electrodes with the sulphochromic mixture, immerse in the platinum solution and connect the two electrode plugs to the negative pole of a 1.5 V electric cell. Connect the positive pole to a platinum wire placed in the solution and electrolyse at a weak current (to avoid gaseous emissions) until the electrodes are coated with black platinum. Rinse the electrode carefully and store in distilled water.

Checking the Cell Constant

Rinse the cell 3 or 4 times with the appropriate standard solution of KCl (in general 0.01 mol L^{-1}) before measuring conductivity and temperature (or only conductivity if you are working in a thermostated medium at 25°C). Check the stability of measurement on a new aliquot of standard solution. EC_t is the theoretical conductivity of the standard solution at 25°C (Table 18.2), EC_m is the measured conductance, ϑ the temperature (°C) and f a possible multiplicative factor of the conductance scale. The cell constant K is obtained by:

$$K = \frac{EC_t}{f \ EC_m \ (1+0.019 \ (25-\vartheta))} . \qquad (18.6)$$

Conductivity of the Sample

Take the measurement as in "Checking the Cell Constant" under Sect. 18.3.1 but replace the standard solution by the sample solution. With reference to the symbols defined above in "Checking the Cell Constant" under Sect. 18.3.1, conductivity at 25°C (EC_{25} in dS m^{-1} is obtained by:

$$EC_{25} = K \ EC_m \ (1+ 0,019 \ (25-\vartheta)) . \qquad (18.7)$$

18.3.2 In situ Conductivity

Although less precise than the methods described in Sect. 18.3.1, direct measurement of soil conductivity is useful for rapid mapping of the field distribution of salts or checking salinity dynamics (Simon and Garcia 1999). Several techniques can be used. Porous matrix sensors containing platinum electrodes are inserted in the soil to measure the conductivity of the soil solution (with additional measurement of temperature). Other more sophisticated instrumental techniques can also be used e.g. quadripole probes, electromagnetic conductivimetry (Boivin et al. 1989; Job et al. 1997) or time-domain reflectometry sensors. Descriptions of the use of these techniques can be found in Rhoades and Oster (1986) or Corwin and Lesch (2004), to cite two examples.

An alternative solution to in situ measurements consists in measuring the electric conductivity of the soil solution after sampling in the field (cf. Sect. 18.2.4).

Another technique consists in measuring the electric conductivity of the saturated paste obtained directly in the field in appropriate cups (Rhoades 1996).

18.3.3 Total Dissolved Solid Material

Principle

The quantity of total dissolved solids (TDS) in the aqueous extracts (dry residue of the extract) is determined by weighing the evaporation residue of the extract previously filtered on a 0.45 μm membrane. This measurement is normally closely linked with that of electric conductivity (4) and the summation of measurements of extractable cations and anions (cf. Sects. 18.3.4 and 18.3.5), and possibly of the extractable organic matter (cf. Chap. 13). It is thus not necessary to carry out TDS measurements systematically if reliable measurements of electric conductivity are available. Measurement of TDS is useful for precise calibration of (4') enabling a site to be surveyed by measurement of conductivity.

Equipment

– System of filtration on 0.45 μm membrane (Pansu et al. 2001).
– Pyrex glass Petri dishes for evaporation, approximate capacity 200 mL.
– Ventilated drying oven that can run at 180°C.

Procedure

– Dry the Petri dishes in the drying oven at 180°C for 2 h, let cool in the desiccator and tare to 1/10 mg: *P0*.
– Choose a sufficient volume *V* of aqueous extract (cf. Sect. 18.2) to obtain a 50–100 mg residue, filter at 0.45 μm and place the filtrate (all or part) in the Petri dishes for evaporation.
– Evaporate in the ventilated drying oven at 105°C, if necessary adding the remainder of the filtrate after the volume is reduced.
– Heat the dry residue at 180°C for 1 h to eliminate the water retained in the micropores, let cool in the desiccator and weigh: *P1*

The TDS content is expressed in mg L^{-1} by:

$$TDS = 1,000 \ (P1 - P0)/V \qquad (18.8)$$

18.3.4 Soluble Cations

Methods

The preferred methods in the laboratory are flame emission or atomic absorption spectrometry. Inductively coupled plasma emission can also be used. These methods generally provide a good estimate of the total contents of the elements in solution by destroying some forms linked to organic matter as well as some mineral forms that are able to precipitate in the extraction water (e.g. carbonates). The implementation of these techniques is described in Chap. 31 The only adaptation to be envisaged is in the range of calibration. Matrix interferences are generally reduced compared to that of the total analyses (cf. Chap. 31) because the extraction solutions are less concentrated.

The ionic forms of the elements can also be estimated using electrochemical methods, particularly ionometry with selective electrodes. This method is also recommended for monitoring in situ changes in elements in the soil solution, as a complement to monitoring changes in total salinity electrochemically or by conductimetry, or other measurements (Pansu et al. 2001). For example, the sodium electrode developed for the study of saline soils by Susini et al. (1972) was integrated in a set of in situ data acquisition of pH, pNa and Eh (Loyer and Susini 1978).

Ionic chromatography is also a useful alternative to cation titration but less justified than for anion titrations given the satisfactory performance of spectrometric methods for cation titrations.

Sodic Character of the Aqueous Extracts

This parameter is widely used and is based on the analysis of the major cations Ca, Mg and Na (in mmol L^{-1}) of the aqueous extracts and defined by the sodium adsorption ratio (SAR, Richards et al. 1954):

$$SAR = \frac{Na}{\sqrt{(Ca+Mg)/2}} \qquad (18.9)$$

This parameter must be suitable for the specific type of aqueous extract used. It varies with the quantity of water used for extraction particularly due to possible dissolution of minerals containing calcium, such as calcite and gypsum.

18.3.5 Extractable Carbonate and Bicarbonate (Alkalinity)

Principle

Carbonate anions define the alkalinity of the extracts, although other ions such as hydroxides, borates, phosphates and silicates may also play a minor role. Bicarbonates are an expected component of the aqueous extracts of saline soils whereas carbonates, which are less frequent, are often present in continental alkaline soils (Cheverry 1974). These anions cannot be measured by ionic chromatography using the technique described in Sect. 18.3.6, because they are involved in the composition of the eluent. The recommended methods described below are based on titration by diluted acids, either by automatic titrimetry (Rhoades 1982) or alternatively using the two-indicator technique (Bower and Wilcox 1965). Other automated techniques are also available (Sá et al. 2002).

Apparatus and Reagents

– Automatic Titrimeter with a glass electrode for pH measurement and a reference electrode (or combined electrode) or failing this, a 10 mL titration burette.
– 0.01 or 0.02 mol (H^+) L^{-1} sulphuric or hydrochloric acid solution (precisely titrated).
– Standard buffer solutions at pH 4 and pH 7.
– Phenolphthalein indicator: dissolve 0.25 g in 100 mL 50% alcohol in water.
– Methyl orange indicator: dissolve 0.1 g in 100 mL water.

Procedure

Automatic Titrimetry

– Calibrate the titrimeter with the buffer solutions at pH 4 and 7; carefully rinse the pH electrodes and place them in the aliquot of solution to be titrated (1–20 mL). Agitate on the magnetic stirrer. Note the initial pH value which characterizes the soil sample (cf. Chap. 15).
– Start titration by recording the curve. Note the volume of acid *V1* needed to reach the first titration point of CO_3^{2-} at pH 8.3. Note the total volume of acid V_t needed to reach the second titration point which

is accompanied by the release of CO_2 due to destruction of bicarbonates at pH 4.5.

Two Coloured Indicators

– Pipette the aliquot of solution to be titrated into the titration beaker.
– Add two drops of phenolphthalein indicator. If the solution remains colourless, it does not contain carbonate. If this is not the case, titrate carbonates until discolouration ($V1$ volume).
– Add two drops of methyl orange indicator. Titrate bicarbonates until the colour changes. Note the volume: V_t.

Calculations

If $V0$ (mL) represents the volume of aliquot and T the acid concentration in mol (H^+) L^{-1}:

– The carbonates are expressed in mmol $(CO_3)^{2-}$ L^{-1} by $\dfrac{1,000}{V0} \times V1 \times T$.

– The bicarbonates are expressed in mmol (HCO_3^-) L^{-1} by

$$\dfrac{1,000}{V0} \times (V_t - V1) \times T.$$

Remarks

Certain aqueous extracts of alkaline soils can be very dark in colour which makes the method described in "Two Coloured Indicators" in "Procedure" under Sect. 18.3.5 difficult. In this case the titrimetric method described in "Automatic Titrimetry" in "Procedure" under Sect. 18.3.5 should be used.

If possible alkalinity (CO_3^{2-} and HCO_3^-) should be measured immediately after extraction to avoid possible modifications (precipitations, exchange with atmospheric carbon dioxide), although these changes can be slowed down by the addition of hexametaphosphate. When several measurements have to be made, alkalinity should be the first measurement to be made on the extracts.

18.3.6 Extractable Chloride

Aim

Chloride is often the major anion of saline soils and Mg, Ca, Na and K chlorides are all very soluble (Table 18.1). Chloride is a very conservative ion which is used as tracer to monitor changes in the concentration of the aqueous solutions. Measuring chloride content is also important because of the toxicity of this anion for certain plants.

Methods

Because of its specific chemical properties, the chloride anion can be titrated relatively easily and precisely using many different methods. Several volumetric, titrimetric and colorimetric methods use the property of the chloride anion to quantitatively precipitate the silver cation. These methods can be used directly on the initial extract or after the titration of carbonates and bicarbonates (cf. Sect. 18.3.5) on the same aliquot after increasing the pH to between 4.2 and 8.3 by adding a small quantity of sodium bicarbonate.

Volumetry: titration with a standard solution of 0.025 mol L^{-1} silver nitrate with detection of the end of the reaction with K_2CrO_4 (red brown precipitate of silver chromate).

Titrimetry: automatic titration (cf. "Automatic Titrimetry" in "Procedure" under Sect. 18.3.5) according to the same principle as volumetry with detection of the end of the reaction with a silver electrode (abrupt change of potential at the end of precipitation of the ions Ag^+).

Coulometry: production of Ag^+ ions by electrolysis from a silver electrode, precipitation of silver chloride before the appearance of free Ag^+ ions is used to detect the end of the reaction by amperometry using two other indicating electrodes. The chloride rate is calculated directly from the quantity of electricity used for the production of Ag^+ ions. This coulometric technique is very practical because it does not require any reagent and the apparatus is easy to transport.

Selective electrodes are also a low-cost method allowing in situ monitoring of the activity of the chloride ion in the soil solution at the same time as other electrochemical measurements if required (Susini and Nedhir 1980).

The *colorimetric method* with mercuric thiocyanate (cf. "Titration of Chloride by Colorimetry" under Sect. 18.3.6) was very often used because of its great sensitivity and good precision.

Titration of Chloride by Colorimetry

Principle

Chloride ions react with mercuric thiocyanate giving mercuric chloride and thiocyanate ions. In the presence of iron alum, the thiocyanate ions form an orange red complex: ferric thiocyanate. The intensity of colour can be measured at 480 nm.

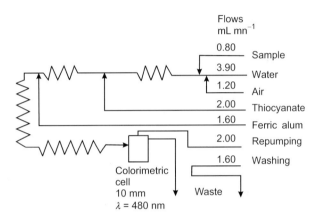

Fig. 18.1.4. Titration of chlorides by automatic colorimetry with segmented continuous flow analysis. For low contents (range 0–0.5 mg L^{-1}) inverse sample and water tubes

Equipment and Reagents

– Colorimeter with quartz or plastic cells or automatic colorimetry by segmented continuous flow analysis.
– Ferric alum $FeNH_4(SO_4)_2,12H_2O$: 60 g in 1 L of 6 mol (HNO_3) L^{-1} nitric acid solution.
– Mercuric thiocyanate: 3.5 g in 1 L of water.
– 50 mmol (Cl^-) L^{-1} stock solution: weigh 3.728 g of dry KCl, bring to 1L with ultrapure water.
– Calibration standard: 0–5 mg L^{-1} by dilution of the stock solution, 0–0.5 mg L^{-1} for low contents.

Procedure

Figure 18.1 shows a manifold for chloride titration by automatic coulorimetry adapted by Paycheng (1980). For manual coulorimetry, use proportions of reagents similar to the flows indicated.

18.3.7 Extractable Sulphate, Nitrate and Phosphate

Uses

Besides carbonate, bicarbonate and chloride, sulphate is a major anion of saline soils. Nitrates are a serious contaminant because of their great solubility. Nitrate content should be checked particularly in irrigated or polluted zones (Cheverry 1998). Sulphate content can be roughly estimated in milli-equivalents by the difference between the sum of cations (Na, K, Ca, Mg) and the sum of anions CO_3^{2-}, HCO_3^-, Cl^-, NO_3^-. Phosphates are not characteristic of saline soils but are often present in aqueous extracts of cultivated soils.

Titration

The methods described in Chap. 28 can be used for *titration of nitrate*. The most recommended method to use for surveys of saline soils is the nitrate selective electrode in the response range 0–0.01–0.1–1–10–100 mmol (NO_3^-) L^{-1} either on water extracts, or in situ measurements on soil solutions.

Titration of sulphate is described in Chap. 30. Two methods are generally used for aqueous extracts of saline soils. In concentrated samples, turbidity caused by precipitation of barium sulphate can be measured. In more diluted samples ($<$ 5 mmol $(\frac{1}{2}SO_4)^{2-}$ L^{-1}) sulphate should be titrated by automatic titrimetry with a 0.002 mmol L^{-1} lead perchlorate solution and potentiometric detection with a Pb^{2+} specific electrode (Rhoades 1982).

Titration of phosphates is described in Chap. 29.

18.3.7 Extractable Boron

Aim

Although boron is present in much smaller quantities than the main elements of the aqueous extracts (cf. Sects. 18.3.4–18.3.6), in saline soils it tends to accumulate with other salts. Its study is sometimes necessary, especially because of the influence this element has on plant growth. Its threshold of deficiency is very close to its threshold of toxicity.

Methods

Boron can be measured in aqueous extracts by inductively coupled plasma emission spectrometry (cf. Chap. 31) at the wavelength of 249.773 nm, with a limit of detection of about 10 µg L^{-1}. Iron can interfere at the 249.782 nm line and its concentration in the extracts should not be too high, i.e. less than 1,000 times that of boron (Pansu et al. 2001).

The boron in the extracts can also be measured by a selective electrode for BF_4^- ions. This method requires a rather long conversion into tetrafluoroborate ions (Keren 1996) and the electrodes cannot be used in situ.

A number of colorimetric methods have also been proposed to titrate boron using carmine, curcumin and azomethine-H. The latter was chosen by Rhoades (1982) for saline soils and for the standard NF X31-122 (1993).

Colorimetry with Azomethine-H

Reagents

– Buffer solution to mask interferences: 400 mL deionized water, 250 g ammonium acetate, 125 mL glacial acid acetic, 15 g ethylene diamine tetraacetic acid (EDTA).
– Azomethine-H colour reagent: 0.5 g azomethine-H, 1g L-ascorbic acid in 100 mL deionized water (prepare before each analysis).
– Standard stock solution 100 mg (B) L^{-1}: 0.572 g of boric acid in 1,000 mL water.
– Standard range of calibration between 0 and 4 mg (B) L^{-1}: by dilution of the stock solution.

Procedure

– In a plastic test tube add:
   1 mL of aqueous extract or standard solution or water (blank assay)
   2 mL of buffer solution (for masking); mix well
   2 mL of azomethine reagent
– Agitate well, let stand for 1h in the refrigerator and measure absorbance at 420 nm.

Note

Because of the risk of contamination, glass should not be used for the titration of boron. Polypropylene is recommended instead.

18.3.8 Titration of Extractable Anions by Ionic Chromatography

Principle

Ionic chromatography is the most efficient method for titration of aqueous extracts. Depending on the column and operating conditions, it can be used either for the simultaneous analysis of cations, or for that of anions. It is useful for cations when atomic spectrometry is not available. In aqueous extracts, the simultaneous analysis of anions is less time-consuming than sequential methods of titration of each anion (cf. Sects. 18.3.5–18.3.7). However, the most widely used techniques do not allow simultaneous titration of carbonates and bicarbonates with other anions because carbonate and bicarbonate are involved in the composition of the eluent. It is possible to adapt the method, but instead we recommend the acidimetric technique for titration of alkalinity described in Sect. 18.3.5. Another problem can appear due to masking of certain peaks by too high concentrations of one element, e.g. chlorides in certain saline soils. One possible solution is to use the operating conditions described below which give a chloride peak that is clearly separated from the others (Fig. 18.2).

Minimum Equipment

– Ionic chromatograph with constant flow, without gradient programming, work pressure 150 bars, equipped with:
  (a) Injection loop of 10, 25 or 50 μL
  (b) Guard column, OmniPac PAX-100 (Dionex, Sunnyvale CA, USA), or similar
  (c) Analytical column, OmniPac PAX-100 (Dionex), or similar
  (d) Anion membrane suppressor
  (e) Conductimetric detector
– 0.2 μm filtration system suitable for large volumes (eluent) and a 1mL syring equipped within-line microfiltration with a filtration membrane of 0.2 μm (Pansu et al. 2001)
– Microbubble input of ultrapure helium

Reagents

– Ultrapure Water (resistivity >18 Mohms) filtered at 0.2 μm and degassed under helium.
– Eluent: 3.9 mmol ($NaHCO_3$) L^{-1}, 3.1 mmol (Na_2CO_3) L^{-1}, 5% CH_3OH: in a 5 L volumetric flask, mix 1.638 g of pure dry $NaHCO_3$ and 1.643 g of pure dry Na_2CO_3, add 250 mL pure methanol, dissolve and complete to 5 L with ultrapure water.
– Regenerating 12.5 mmol L^{-1} sulphuric acid solution: in a 5 L volumetric flask add 1 L of ultrapure water, 3.472 mL of ultrapure 18 mol (H_2SO_4) L^{-1} sulphuric acid, agitate and complete to 5 L with ultrapure water.
– Standards for multi-anion calibrations of type:

Cl^-	0.1–15 mg L^{-1},
NO_3^-	0.02–1 mg L^{-1},
SO_4^{2-}	0.05–10 mg L^{-1},
PO_4^{3-}	0.1–5 mg L^{-1},
F^-	0.1–5 mg L^{-1}.

Procedure

– Connect or check the connections of the chromatography circuit: injection loop, guard column, column, suppressor, conductimetric detector.
– Check the connection of the regenerating circuit on the suppressor.
– Degas eluent by bubbling with helium.
– Start the pump at high pressure, regulate the eluent flow at 1 mL min^{-1} (input pressure 100–130 bars).
– Regulate the flow of regenerating solution at 7 mL min^{-1} under pressure of nitrogen.
– Start the detector and let the system stabilize. The base line of the chromatogram must be stable with a conductivity of background noise of approximately 20 μS.
– Inject a standard mixture using a 1 mL syringe with in-line microfiltration. Wait approximately 10 min until the output of the chromatogram is complete before injecting the following solution for calibration or measurement.

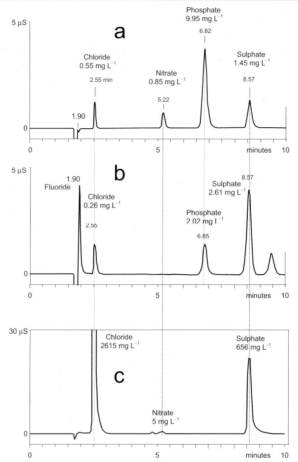

Fig. 18.2. Analysis of soluble anions of soils by ionic chromatography (Doulbeau and Rochette, IRD Montpellier, France, unpublished data). **(a)** cold water extract (10 g 200 mL^{-1}, agitate for 4 h) of a *Luvisol (Hapludalf)* developed on loess, cultivated at Boigneville (France), injection without dilution **(b)** hot water extract of the *a-Luvisol* previously extracted with cold water (reflux boiling for 16 h), injection without dilution **(c)** 1:5 extract at 20°C of a surface horizon of a chloruro-sulphated *Salisol* *(Maison de la Nature*, Latte, France), 1:50 dilution of the extract before injection. The contents are those of the undiluted extract.

Using a syringe with in-line filtration, filter the sample solutions and if necessary dilute them before injection. In case of doubt about the concentrations, start with diluted solutions (1/200, 1/50, etc.).

Figure 18.2 shows an example of chromatograms obtained under these conditions on extracts with cold water "a" and hot water "b" of *L uvisol (Hapludalf)* developed on loess cultivated in an experimental station (ITCF, Boigneville, Essonne, France) as well as a cold water extract "c" of a chloruro-sulphated *Salisol* from a Mediterranean sedimentary lagoon. Extract "c" had to be diluted 50 times and the sensitivity reduced by a factor of 6 compared to the "a" and "b" extracts injected without dilution. These conditions did not prevent titration of nitrates of extract "c" in spite of the fact the nitrate content was 8 times lower (dilution 1:50) than that of extract "a" and in the presence of a chloride content that was 5,000 times higher. This method can be used in a very broad range of concentrations for different types of soils and studies.

18.3.9 Expression of the Results

Table 18.3. Example of ion balance (Fig. 18.2c), 1:5 extract of a Mediterranean chloruro-sulphated *Salisol* (Szwarc, CIRAD, Montpellier, France, unpublished data)

pH	EC dS m^{-1}	cations mmol (+) L^{-1} (extract)					anions mmol (−) L^{-1} (extract)			
		Ca	Mg	K	Na	NH$_4$	Cl	SO$_4$	NO$_3$	HCO$_3$
7.63	8.18	9.80	19.18	1.04	60.30	0.06	73.66	13.66	0.08	1.48
(4)		Σ+ = 90.38 = 11.05 EC					Σ− = 88.88 = 10.89 EC			
		cations mg L^{-1} (extract)					anions mg L^{-1} (extract)			
		196	233	41	1,387	1	2,615	656	5	90
(4′)		total dissolved materials = 5,224 mg L^{-1} = 639 EC								
		cations mmol (+) kg^{-1} (soil)					anions mmol (−) kg^{-1} (soil)			
		49.0	95.9	5.2	301.5	0.3	368.3	68.3	0.4	7.4
		cations mg kg^{-1} (soil)					anions mg kg^{-1} (soil)			
		980	1,165	205	6,935	5	13,075	3,280	25	450

The expression of the data in milli-equivalents per litre of extract enables immediate verification of the coherence of the results, especially when different methods of measurement are used (Ludwig et al. 1999). The sum of the cations (Σ+) must be equal to the sum of the anions (Σ−) and (18.4) must be checked, that is to say the double equality:

$$(\Sigma+) = (\Sigma-) = (10\text{--}12)\ EC \qquad (18.10)$$

The results can also be expressed based on the soil. n is the ratio of the volume of water of the extract (mL) to the weight of the soil test specimen in grams (cf. "Comparative Interest" under Sect. 18.2.3). The soil contents (Ts in mmol (+) kg^{-1} or mmol (−) kg^{-1}) are expressed compared to those of the extract (Te in mmol (+) L^{-1} or mmol (–) L^{-1} by the simple relation:

$$Ts = n\, Te \qquad (18.11)$$

M being the equivalent molar mass of each ion, the results can also be expressed in mg L^{-1} (extract) by the relation Te (mg L^{-1}) = M Te (mmol (+ or –) L^{-1}). Thus the balance with the TDS and (18.4') must be checked if TDS are measured (cf. Sect. 18.3.3). Equation 18.11 remains valid to calculate the extractable masses of the soil, with Ts in mg kg^{-1} and Te in mg L^{-1}.

The results corresponding to the example (Fig. 18.2c) of an ion balance on 1:5 extracts of a chloruro-sulphated soil from Latte (France), are shown in Table 18.3.

References

Baize D (1988) Guide des analyses courantes en Pédologie. INRA, Paris, 172 p.

Boivin P, Hachicha M, Job JO and Loyer JY (1989) Une méthode de cartographie de la salinité des sols : conductivité électromagnétique et interpolation par krigeage. *Sci. du sol.*, 27, 69–72

Bouteyre G and Loyer JY (1995) Sodisols et Salsodisols. In *Encyclopaedia Universalis*, 235–236

Bower CA and Wilcox LV (1965) Soluble salts. In *Methods of Soil Analysis, Part 2, Chemical and Microbiological Properties*, Black CA ed. ASA, SSSA, Madison, USA

Cheverry C (1974) *Contribution à l'étude pédologique des polders du lac Tchad. Dynamique des sels en milieu continental sub-aride dans des sédiments argileux et organiques.*, These University Strasbourg, France, 275 p

Cheverry C (1983) L'extraction de la solution du sol par le biais de bougies poreuses : synthèse bibliographique des problèmes méthodologiques posés par ces dispositifs. *Bull. Groupe Français d'Humidimétrie Neutronique*, 14, 47–71

Cheverry C (1998) Agriculture intensive et qualité des eaux. *INRA, Paris*, 297p

Corwin DL and Lesch SM (2004) Characterizing soil spatial variability with apparent electrical conductivity. *Computers and Electronics in Agriculture*, doi:10.1016/j.compag.2004.11.002

FAO, ISSS, ISRIC (1998) World Reference Base for Soil Resources. *World Soil Resources Reports*, FAO, Rome no 84, 88 p

Harvie CE and Weare JH (1980) The prediction of mineral solubilities in natural waters : the Na-K-Mg-Ca-Cl-SO_4-H_2O system from zero to high concentration at 25°C. *Geochim. Cosmochim. Acta.*, 44, 981–997

Harvie CE, Moller NE and Weare JH (1984) The prediction in mineral solubilities in natural waters : the Na-K-Mg-Ca-H-Cl-SO$_4$-OH-HCO$_3$-CO$_3$-CO$_2$-H$_2$O system to high ionic strengths at 25°C, *Geochim. Cosmochim. Acta.*, 48, 723–751

INRA-AFES, (1995) *Référentiel Pédologique.*, INRA, Paris, 332 p

Job JO (1985) *Essais de corrélation entre la conductivité électrique et la composition ionique des solutions du sol.*, ENSAM-USTL, Montpellier, France, 86 p.

Job JO Gonzalez Barrios JL and Rivera Gonzalez M (1997) Détermination précise de la salinité des sols par conductivimétrie électromagnétique. In *Géophysique des sols et des formations superficielles.*, Orstom, Paris, 143–145

Keren R (1996) Boron. In *Methods of Soil Analysis, Part 3, Chemical Methods.*, SSSA book series 5, 603–626

Kouakoua E , Sala GH , Barthès B , Larre-Larrouy MC , Albrecht A and Feller C (1997) La matière organique soluble à l'eau chaude et la stabilité de l'agrégation. Aspects méthodologiques et application à des sols ferrallitiques du Congo, *Eur. J. Soil Sci.*, 48, 239–247

Le Brusq JY and Loyer JY (1982) Relations entre les mesures de conductivités sur des extraits de sols de rapports *sol/solution* variables, dans la vallée du fleuve Sénégal. *Cah. Orstom, sér. Pédol.*, 3, 293–301

Loyer JY and Susini J (1978) Réalisation et utilisation d'un ensemble automatique pour la mesure en continu et in situ du pH, du Eh et du pNa du sol. *Cah. ORSTOM.Sér. Pédologie*, 16, 425–437

Loyer JY (1991) Classification des sols salés : les sols *Salic. Cah. Orstom Ser. Pédol.*, XXVI, 51–61

Ludwig B, Meiwes KJ, Gehlen R, Fortmann H, Hildebrand EE and Khanna P (1999) Comparison of different laboratory methods with lysimetry for soil solution composition - experimental and model results. *Zeitschrift für Pflanzenernahrung und Bodenkunde*, 162, 343–351

NF X 31-122, (1993) Extraction du bore soluble à l'eau bouillante. In *Qualité des sols, 3e ed.*, AFNOR, Paris, 91–95

NF ISO 11265, (1995) Détermination de la conductivité électrique spécifique. In *Qualité des sols, 3e ed.*, AFNOR, Paris, 279–282

Pansu M, Gautheyrou J and Loyer JY (2001) Soil Analysis - Sampling, Instrumentation and Quality control. Balkema, Lisse, Abington, Exton, Tokyo, 489 p

Paycheng C (1980) *Méthodes d'analyses utilisées au laboratoire commun de Dakar*, IRD-Orstom, Dakar, Paris, 104 p

Pouget M (1968) Contribution à l'étude des croûtes et encroûtements gypseux de nappe dans le Sud Tunisien. *Cah. Orstom, sér. pédol.*, 3–4, 309–366

Qadir M, Schubert S and Ghafoor Aet Murtaza G (2001) Amelioration strategies for sodic soils: A review. *Land degradation and development*, 12, 357–386

Rhoades JD and Miyamoto S (1990) Testing soils for salinity and sodicity. In *Soil Testing and Plant Analysis, 3rd ed.*, SSSA book series 3, 299–336

Rhoades JD and Oster JD (1986) Solute content. In *Methods of soil analysis, part 1, Physical and Mineralogical Methods, 3rd ed.*, ASA-SSSA, Agronomy monograph 9, 985–1005

Rhoades JD (1982) Soluble salts. In *Methods of soil analysis, Part 2, Chemical and Microbiological Properties, 2nd ed.*, ASA-SSSA, Agronomy monograph 9, 167–179

Rhoades JD (1996) Salinity : electrical conductivity and total dissolved solids. In *Methods of Soil Analysis, Part 3, Chemical Methods.*, SSSA book series 5, 417–433

Richards LA ed (1954) *Diagnosis and Improvement of Saline and Alkali Soils*, US Salinity Laboratory Staff. Agricultural Department, Handbook no 60

Sá SMO, Sartini RP, Oliveira CC and Zagatto EAG (2002) A flow-injection system with a quartz crystal microbalance for the determination of dissolved inorganic carbon in mineral waters. *J. Flow Injection Anal.*, 19, 25–28

Servant J (1975) *Contribution à l'Etude des Terrains Halomorphes.*, Inra, Ensa Montpellier, 194 p. et annexes

Shirokova Y, Forkutsa I and Sharafutdinova N (2000) Use of electrical conductivity instead of soluble salts for soil salinity monitoring in Central Asia. *Irrigation-and-Drainage-Systems*, 14, 199–205

Simon M and Garcia I (1999) Physico-chemical properties of the soil-saturation extracts: estimation from electrical conductivity *Geoderma*, 90. 99–109

Smith JL and Doran JW (1996) Measurement and use of pH and electrical conductivity for soil quality analysis. In *Methods for Assessing Soil Quality*, SSSA special publication. 49, 169–185

Susini J and Nedhir M (1980) *Utilisation d'électrodes sensibles aux ions pour la mesure en continu, avec enregistrement du pH, pNa, pCl, pCa + Mg dans l'étude des eaux d'irrigation et de drainage et essais dans les sols : 1ère partie. Réalisation et description de l'ensemble de mesure.*, DRES, Orstom, Tunis (TN), 17 p

Susini J, Rouault, M and Kerkeb A (1972) Essais d'utilisation en analyse des sols salés d'une électrode sensible aux ions sodium, *Cah. ORSTOM. Sér. Pédologie*, 10, 309–318

Exchange Complex

19.1 Introduction

Soil is a dynamic complex of solid, liquid and gas phases. During its evolution under the influence of geological, biological, climatic and hydrological constraints, the soil acquires electric and electromagnetic charges which confer specific physicochemical and thermodynamic properties. These charges are of different origin and different scales i.e. colloidal, molecular and atomic. Some occur during the deterioration and formation of secondary substances like clays, aluminosilicates, oxides and humified organic matter (pedogenesis).

The soil thus appears in the form of a *continuum* that is heterogeneous at a given scale. It is an open medium in a state of precarious and evolutionary equilibrium subject to cycles of immobilization and release of ionic species that vary with the climatic constraints. Its properties can be more or less arbitrarily gathered in analytical pools because of the similarity of the *mutatis–mutandis* phenomena in the biosphere. Among these phenomena, the entity represented by the exchange complex (or adsorbing complex) is of primary importance because of its direct influence on intrinsic soil fertility and soil chemical processes. In a wet tropical medium, the intense biochemical activity, which is sometimes coupled with intensive agriculture, considerably accelerates the weathering processes.

For the chemist, the vast analytical field represented by interactions between charges includes measurements of cation and anion exchange capacities, exchangeable cations, exchange isotherms, exchange acidity and its agronomic correction, (lime amendments), exchangeable sodium and sodium adsorption ratio (SAR), exchange of anions like phosphates, the measurement of isoelectric point or zero point charge (ZPC), permanent and variable charges, entropies and free enthalpies, dispersion, flocculation, electrophoretic mobility, Zeta potential, Brownian movement, as well as interrelationships with pH and Eh.

19.2 Origin of Charges

19.2.1 Ionic Exchange

The discovery of ion exchange dates back to 1848–1850. Thomson (1850) observed that leaching a soil column with an ammon-ium sulphate solution led to the appearance of calcium sulphate in the filtrate. Way (1850–1852), a chemist who belonged to the Royal Company of English Agriculture, published the first work on cation exchange:

$$Ca^{2+} \text{ (soil)} + 2\,NH_4^+ \text{ (liquid phase)} \leftrightarrow NH_4^+ \text{ (soil)} + Ca^{2+} \text{ (liquid phase)}$$

Theoretical studies continued to appear, those particularly worth mentioning are: Bolt (1982), Gabis and Lagache (1982), Sparks (1986), Sposito (1981–1984–1989), Chamayou and Legros (1989), Fenton and Helyar (2000).

During weathering processes some primary or secondary components pass into the soil solution resulting in the creation of site vacancies and/or the creation of new surfaces resulting in the disruption of local equilibriums. Reactions between components of the liquid phase and liquid phase–solid phase are not always instantaneous but depend on the nature of chemical functions, free surface energy, critical surface tension, etc.

Various phenomena can be observed in this ionic reservoir such as adsorption–desorption, chelation with organic and inorganic ligands, dissolution or precipitation at the solid–liquid interfaces.

The combination of atoms and plans of atoms results in the creation of atomic lattices and structural units such as those of the phyllosilicates whose charge is well defined (Table 19.1). However, as the reactions are not rigorously stoechiometric, defects appear and substitutions occur in the internal structure of minerals, modifying the distribution of charges and the nature of the components. In addition, the surfaces of minerals and organic functional groups can ionize and generate new charges. For example, unhydrated micas, whose cation exchange capacity (CEC) is theoretically null, can open during the weathering process (Fig. 19.1) to give first hydrated forms of increasing CEC and second vermiculites with a high exchange capacity according to the models presented by Dawson et al. (1974) and Jackson and Juo (1986).

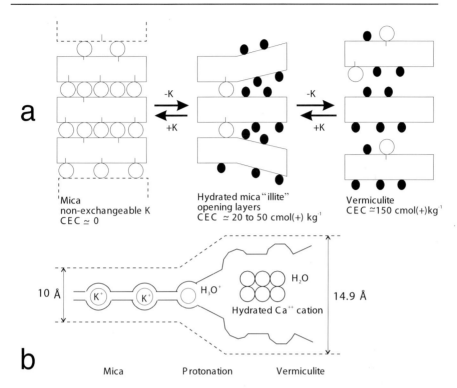

Fig. 19.1. Models of deterioration of micas: **a**: Dawson et al. (1984), **b**: Jackson and Juo (1986)

19.2.2 Exchange Complex

All solid, liquid or gas material is made of atoms comprising elementary particles which, for the chemist, can be limited to protons, neutrons and electrons. The unit is electrically neutral but if an electron leaves an atom (transfer of electron of the external layer), it causes an electric imbalance, the nucleus then taking the charge ^+e and becoming a positively charged ion (cation). Conversely, an electron fixed on the atom (complement of the external layer) brings an additional negative charge that characterizes the charge of the unit (anion).

As atoms are bound by electrostatic forces, they join together to form ionic assemblies, which are easily identifiable thanks to their crystal properties or to their short-range organization, and are the result of atomic bonds corresponding to equilibrium between attracting and repelling forces (Fig. 19.2). The interpenetration of the electron shells, with pooling of electrons, gives covalent atomic bonds that are limited to the number of available electrons in the external layer.

Table 19.1. Classification of clays linked to their theoretical negative charges by layer (*Agence internationale pour l'étude des argiles AIPEA*)

clay		octahedral layer	negative charges
1 :1	kaolinite	dioctahedral	0
	serpentines	trioctahedral	0
2 :1	pyrophyllite	dioctahedral	0
	talc	trioctahedral	0
	hydrated micas	dioctahedral	2
		trioctahedral	2
	smectites	dioctahedral	0.5–1.2
		trioctahedral	0.5–1.2
	vermiculites	dioctahedral	1.2–1.9
		trioctahedral	1.2–1.9
2 :1 :1	chlorites	dioctahedral	variable
		di-trioctahedral	variable
		trioctahedral	variable
	fibrous clays		variable
	allophane–Imogolite		variable

Weathering processes in the soil induce changes from ionic states to colloidal mesomorphic states (which have not all been clearly defined to date), then into states that are invisible to X-ray where the compounds acquire a short-range organization and then again start to acquire a long-organization and finally a crystalline state. The scale of time of each one of these states depends on climatic, geological and biological variables and can vary from a few days to a few millennia.

Electrically charged surfaces of materials present either an excess or a deficit of electrons. Whatever the origin of the surface charges, their neutralization necessitates the introduction of an equal quantity of positive and negative charges in the liquid phase, i.e. the soil solution.

Exchange theory cannot cover every possible case. Several different equations are needed because of the complexity and diversity of the exchange phenomena. For modelling purposes, the most influential parameters are retained after successive approximations. The thermodynamic approach can be used to integrate mass action laws, selectivity of equilibrium constants or to choose to retain some mechanisms of adsorption at the solid–liquid interfaces, quantification of ion transfers, anion interactions, etc.

It is important to take into account the reference works that first established current theories. These theories are concerned with the solid exchange matrix, the soil solution or the mobile phase (extracting reagents: surface charges, colloidal stability, rheological properties, ionic properties, selectivity, concentration, valence, pH and their interrelation-ships).

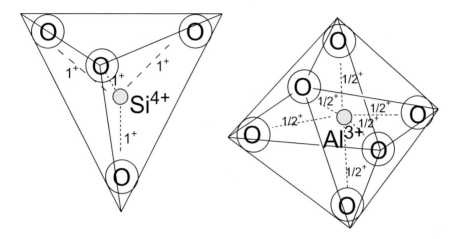

Fig. 19.2. Fundamental units of clays

Pioneer scientists like Helmotz (1835), de Quincke (1861), Gibbs (1906), Gouy (1910), Chapman (1913), Freundlich (1916), Stern (1924), Mattson (1926), Jenny (1926), Pauling (1927), Kerr (1928), Vageler (1932), Vanselow (1932), Gapon (1933), Langmuir (1938) gave their name to the reference equations cited in the following chapters.

Exchange phenomenon represents a transfer of ions between a solid exchanger and an index ion in liquid phase or a chemical phenomenon related to the application of the law of mass action.

19.2.3 Theory

Despite certain imperfections, the theory of the double layer (Fig. 19.3) of Gouy (1910), Chapman (1913) and Stern (1924), seems to correspond more satisfactorily to the reality of soil charges than the Donnan equilibrium.

The theory of the double layer applies to ion exchanges and links the soil cationic charge, the electrolyte concentration and the electric potential. The applied forces are exerted within a lattice of short-range organization, without a very clear definition of the atomic distances in spite of conceptual advances which have modified the original theory published by Gouy (1910). In the Gouy and Chapman model, the charges σ are considered to be uniformly distributed on the exchanger surface which constitutes an infinite plan. In clay, this plan is charged negatively and the law of electric neutrality implies the attraction of the same quantity of positively charged cations.

The cluster of ions brought by the liquid mobile phase cancels the electric force field. However, the diffusion forces tend to redistribute the ions: the cationic contents decrease exponentially starting at the surface, and consequently there is a deficit of anions near this surface. The charged surface and the redistribution phenomenon make up the double layer theory. Its quantitative application is of doubtful validity in the case of soils with variable charge, the ions being regarded as concentrated charges, without taking the counter ions into account. The theory gives too high predictions.

The theory of Stern (1924) corrects these excesses by supposing that, given their volume, the ions likely to come into contact with a surface can do so only at the distance of a few angstroms (Fig. 19.3).

The ions adsorbed on the surface form a compact layer of the same thickness as the ionic diameter, and the diffuse layer of Gouy and Chapman comes after the compact layer. This model enables differentiation of high affinities of specific adsorption which refer to a chemisorption phenomenon (coordination) and low affinities of adsorption which refer to the Stern layer. The approach is generally sufficient for soils with permanent charges.

In the case of soils with a variable charge, the model of triple layers with four plans (Bowden et al. 1977, 1980, Sposito 1984) enables calculations to be refined and extended to reactions of surface complexation (Fig. 19.3):
– protons and hydroxyls form inner-sphere surface complexes; these complexes are bound by ionic or/and covalent bonds; there are no solvent molecules between the surface of the functional group and the adjacent molecule
– the other organic and inorganic cations and anions form less stable outer-sphere complexes, bonded by electrostatic bonds, with a solvent molecule between the functional group and the bonded molecule.

The knowledge of sorption phenomena is essential in pedology and agronomy in order to understand short and medium term evolution of soil under given climatic conditions and possibly to correct some forms of degradation.

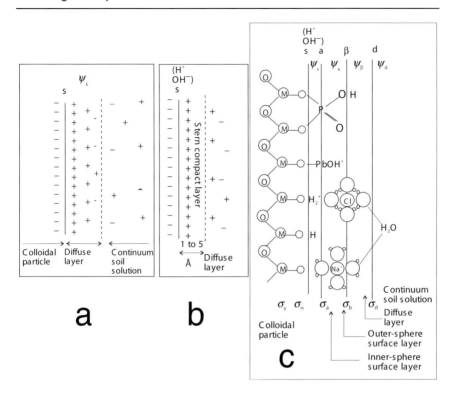

Fig. 19.3. Theoretical models of exchange sites

a: the model of Gouy and Chapman (1910–1913) defines the sites as a simple plan with a decrease in the electric potential linked the distance of the colloid surface:

$$\Psi = \sigma \frac{F}{C}$$ where σ is the surface charge in mole cm^{-2}, C is the capacitance in Farad m^{-2} and F is the Faraday constant. The size of the counter ion is not taken into account.

b: the model of Stern (1924) is defined as a simple plan taking into account the complexes of surface formed with the hydrated ions (specific and nonspecific adsorptions), total charge $\sigma_T = \sigma_1 + \sigma_2$

c: model with three layers and four plans according to Sposito (1984), Bowden et al. (1977–1980). This model satisfactorily describes the selective adsorption of anions (phosphate, seleniate, citrate, sulphate, fluoride, silicate) or of cations (e.g. Cu, Pb, Zn) as well as effects like electrolyte concentration or electrophoretic mobility.

References

Bolt GH and Bruggenwert MGM (1982) *Soil chemistry A – Basic elements.*, Elsevier developments in soil science, 5A

Bowden JW, Posner AM and Quirk JP (1977) Ionic adsorption on variable charge mineral surfaces theoretical charge development and titration curves. *Austr. J. Soil Res.*, 15, 121–136

Bowden JW, Nagarajah S, Barow NJ, Posner AM and Quirck JP (1980) Describing the adsorption of phosphate, citrate and selemite on a variable-charge mineral surface. *Austr. J. Soil Res.*, 18, 49–60

Chamayou M and Legros JR (1989) *Les bases physiques, chimiques et minéralogiques de la science du sol.*, Presses Universitaires de France.

Chapman DL (1913) A contribution to the theory of electrocapillarity. *Philos. Mag.*, 6, 475–481

Dawson M, Foth MD, Page AL and McLean EO (1974) *Cation exchange properties of soils. A slide show.* Div. S-2. *Soil Chemistry.*, Soil Science. Society of America, 8 p + 45 diapositives couleur

Fenton G and Helyar KR (2000) Soil acidification, in PEV Charman and BW Murphy (eds), *Soils: Their Properties and Management,* Oxford University Press, Melbourne

Freundlich H (1926) *Colloid and capillary chemistry.*, Metwuen London.

Gabis V. and Lagache M (1982) Les surfaces des solides minéraux ; adsorption: 109-179 ; l'échange d'ions. 297–353. *Soc. Fr. de Minéralogie et cristallographie*, 1–2

Gouy G (1910) Sur la constitution de la charge électrique à la surface d'un électrolyte. *J. Ann. Phys.*, 457, 457–468

Jackson M.L. and Juo J.X (1986) Potassium-release mechanism on drying soils: iron exchangeable to exchangeable potassium by protonation of micas. *Soil Sci.*, 141, 225–229

Sparks D.L (1986) *Soil physical chemistry.* CRC Boca Raton, FL 308 p

Sposito G (1981) *The thermodynamics of soils solutions.*, Clarendon Oxford, 223 pages

Sposito G (1984) *The surface chemistry of soils.*, Clarendon Oxford, 234 p

Sposito G (1989) *The chemistry of soils.* Oxford University. Press, Oxford 277 p

Stern O (1924) Zur theorie der elektrischen doppelschischt. *Z. Elektrochem*, 30, 508–516

Thomson HS (1850) On the absorbent power of soils. *J. Royal Agric. Soc. Engl.*, 11, 68–74

Way JT (1850) On the power of soils to absorb manure. *J. Royal Agric. Soc. Eng.*, 11, 311–379

Way JT (1852) On the power of soils to absorb manure. *J. Royal Agric. Soc. Eng.*, 13, 123–143

Chronobibliography

Johnson SW (1859) On some points of agricultural science. *Am. J. Sci. Arts*, 2, 71–85

Freundlich H (1926) *Colloïd and capillary chemistry.*, Methuen, London.

Page JB and Bauer LB (1940) Ionic size in relation to fixation of cations by coloidal clay. *Soil Sci. Soc. Am. Proc.*, 4, 150–155

Hendricks SB., Nelson RA and Alexander LI (1940) Hydratation mechanism of the clay mineral montmorillonite saturated with various cations. *J. Am. Chem. Soc.*, 62, 1457–1464

Barshad I (1948) Vermiculite and its relation to biotite as revearled by base exchange reaction, X-Ray analysis, differential thermal curses and water content. *Am. Miner.*, 33, 655–678

Mehrlich A (1948) Determination of cation and anion-exchange properties of soils. *Soil Sci.*, 66, 429–445

Standford G (1948) Fixation of potassium in soils under moist conditions and on claying in relation to type of clay mineral. *Soil Sci. Soc. Am. Proc.*, 12, 167–171

Schofield RK (1949) Effect of pH on electric charges carried by clay particles. *J. Soil Sci.*, 1, 1–8

Wear JL and White JL (1951) Potassium fixation in clay minerals as related to crystal structure. *Soil Sci.*, 71, 1–14

Bolt GH (1952) *The significance of the measurement of the zeta potential and the membrane potential in soil and clay suspensions.*, Master thesis Cornell University

Overbeek J Th (1952) Electrochemistry of the double-layer. *Colloid Sci.*, 1, 115

Pratt PF and Holowaychuck NA (1954) A comparison of ammonium acetate, barium acetate and buffered barium chloride methods of determining cation-exchange capacity. *Soil Sci. Soc. Am. Proc.*, 18, 365–368

Schofield RK and Samson HR (1954) Floculation of kaolinite due to the attraction of oppositely-charged crystal faces. *Disc. Faraday Soc.*, 18, 138–145

Bolt GH (1955) Analysis of the validity of the Gouy–Chapman theory of the electric double layer. *J. Colloid Sci.*, 10, 206–218

Schuffellen AC and Van der Marel HW (1955) Potassium fixation in soils. *Potass. Symp.*, 2, 157 (180 references)

Diamond S and Kinter EB (1956) Surface areas of clay minerals as derived from measurements of glycerol retention. *Clays Clay Miner.*, 5, 334

De Mumbrum LE and Jackson ML (1957) Formation of basic cations of copper, zinc, iron and aluminium. *Soil Sci. Soc. Am. Proc.*, 21, 662

White ML (1957) The occurence of zinc in soil. *Econ. Geol.*, 52, 645

Garrett WG and Walker GF (1959) The cation exchange capacity of hydrated halloysite and the formation of halloysite-salt complexes. *Clay Miner. Bull.*, 4, 75–80

Johansen RT and Dunning HN (1959) Water-vapor adsorption on clay. *Clays Clay Miner.*, 6, 249

Van der Marel HW (1959) Potassium fixation, a beneficial soil characteristic for crop production. *Z. Pflanzenerährung dungung, Bodenkunde*, 84, 51–62

Giles CH, Maewan TH, Nakhwa SN and Smith D (1960) Studies in adsorption XI. A study of classification of solution adsorption isotherms and its use in diagnosis of adsorption mechanisms and in measurement of specific surface area of solids. *J. Chem. Soc.*, 3973

Hsu PH and Rich CI (1960) Aluminium fixation in a synthetic cation exchanger. *Soil Sci. Soc. Am. Proc.*, 24, 21–25

Rich CI (1960) Aluminium in interlayers of vermiculite. *Soil Sci. Soc. Am. Proc.*, 24, 26–32

Toujan S (1960) Essai de distribution analytique entre sels solubles et cations échangeables en sols alcalins salés. *Cah. ORSTOM Sér. Pédol.*, X, 25

Pratt PF (1961) Effect on pH on the cation exchange capacity of surface soils. *Soil Sci. Soc. Am. Proc.*, 21, 96

Dixon JR and Jackson ML (1962) Properties of intergradient chlorite-expansible layer silicates of soils. *Soil Sci. Soc. Am. Proc.*, 26, 358–362

Shen MJ and Rich CI (1962) Aluminium fixation in montmorillonite. *Soil Sci. Soc. Am. Proc.*, 86, 33–36

Babcok KL (1963) Theory of the chemical properties of soil colloidal systems at equilibrium. *Hilgardia*, V, 11

Bower CA (1963) Adsorption of o. phenanthroline by clay minerals and soils. *Soil Sci.*, 95, 192

Coleman NT, Craig D and Lewis RJ (1963) Ion exchange reactions of cesium. *Soil Sci. Soc. Am. Proc.*, 27, 287–289

Coleman NT, Lewis RJ and Craig D (1963) Sorption of cesium by soils and its displacement by salt solution. *Soil Sci. Soc. Am. Proc.*, 27, 290–294

Bear FE (1984) *Chemistry of the soil*, Reinhold

Bingham FT, Page AL and Sims JK (1964) Retention of Cu an Zn by H-Montmorillonite. *Soil Sci. Soc. Am. Proc.*, 28, 351–354

Coleman NT and Thomas GW (1964) Buffer curves of acid clays as affected by the presence of ferric iron and aluminum. *Soil Sci. Soc. Am. Proc.*, 28, 187–190

Greenland DJ and Quirk JP (1964) Determination of total specific surface areas of soils by absorption of cetyl pyridinium bromide. *J. Soil Sci.*, 15, 178

Helling CJ, Chesters G and Corey RB (1964) Contribution of organic matter and clay to soil cation exchange capacity as affected by the pH of the saturating solution. *Soil Sci. Soc. Am. Proc.*, 28, 517

Marshall CE (1964) *The physical chemistry and mineralogy of soils.*, Wiley New York

McLean EO, Hourigan WR, Shoemaker HE and Bhumbla DR (1964) Aluminum in soils: V Form of aluminum as a cause of soil acidity and a complication in its measurements. *Soil Sci.*, 97, 119–126

Sawhney BL (1964) Sorption and fixation of micro-quantities of Cs by clay minerals. Effect of saturating cations. *Soil Sci. Soc. Am. Proc.*, 28, 183–186

Schnitzer M and Gupta VC (1964) Chemical characteristics of the organic matters extracted from the O and B$_2$ horizons of a gray wooded soil. *Soil Sci. Soc. Am. Proc.*, 28, 374

Bhumbla DR and McLean EQ (1965) Aluminium in soils. VI – Changes in pH dependent acidity, cation ion exchange capacity and extractable aluminium with addition of lime to surface soils. *Soil Sci. Soc. Am. Proc.*, 29, 370

Bolt GH and Page AL (1965) Ion-exchange equations based on double layer theory. *Soil Science*, 99, 357–361

Carter DL, Heilman MD and Gonzalez CL (1965) Ethylene glycol monoethyl ether for determining surface area of silicate minerals. *Soil Sci.*, 100, 356

Follet EAC (1965) The retention of amorphous colloidal "ferric hydroxide" by kaolinites. *J. Soil Sci.*, 16, 334–341

Fripiat J.J., Cloos P and Poncelet A (1965) Comparaison entre les propriétés d'échange de la montmorillonite et d'une résine vis-à-vis des cations alcalins et alcalino-terreux. I – Reversibilité des processus. *Bull. Soc. Chim. de France*, 208–214

Marshall CE and McDowell LL (1965) The surface reactivity of micas. *Soil Sci.*, 99, 115–131

Parks GA (1965) The isoelectric points of solids oxides, solid hydroxides and aqueous hydroxo complex systems. *Chem. Rev.*, 65, 177–193

Kittrick JA (1966) Forces involved in ion fixation by vermiculite. *Soil Sci. Soc. Am. Proc.*, 30, 801–803

Shainberg I and Kemper WD (1966) Hydration status of adsorbed cations. *Soil Sci. Soc. Am. Proc.*, 30, 707–713

Stanton DA and Burger R de T (1966) Zinc in orange free state soils. I – An assessment of the zinc status of suface soils. *S. Afr. J. Agr. Sci.*, 601

Stanton DA and Burger R de T (1966) Zinc in orange free state soils. II - Distribution of zinc in selected soils profiles and in particle size fractions. *S. Afr. J. Agr. Sci.*, 809

De Villiers JM and Jackson ML (1967) Cation exchange capacity variations with pH in soil clay. *Soil Sci. Soc. Am. Proc.*, 31, 473

Parks GA (1967) Aqueous surface chemistry of oxides and couplage oxide minerals in Stumm, W. : Equilibrium concepts in natural water systems. *Adv. Chem. Series*, 67, 121–160

Parks GM (1967) Isoelectric point and zero point charge. *Adv. in Chem.*, 67, 121–160

Ruellan A and Deletang J (1967) *Les phénomènes d'échange de cations et d'anions dans les sols*. IRD (ex-Orstom), Doc. Techno., no. 5, Paris

Grim RE (1968) *Clay Mineralogy*. McGraw-Hill, New York 185–233

Murray DJ, Healy TW and Fuersteneau DW (1968) The adsorption of aqueous metal and colloidal hydrous manganese oxide. *Adv. Chem. Ser.*, 79, 74–81

Rich CI (1968) Mineralogy of soil potassium. In Kilmer VJ, Younts S.E., Brady NC. *The role of potassium in agriculture*. Am. Soc. Agron., US, 79–108

Flegman AW, Goodwin JW and Ottewill RA (1969) Rheological studies on kaolinite suspensions. *Proc. Brit. Ceram. Soc.*, 13, 31–45

Gautheyrou J and Gautheyrou M (1969) Index bibliographique "Echange" 1960–1967. ORSTOM-Antilles, Notes de laboratoire, no. 10, 56 p

Kalb GW and Curry RB (1969) Determination of surface area by surfactant adsorption in aqueous suspension. I – Dodecylamine hydrochloride. *Clays Clay Miner.*, 17, 47

Hingston FJ (1970) *Specific adsorption of anions on goethite and gibbsite.*, Ph. D diss., University Western Australia Perth

Sawhney BL, Frinck CR and Hill DE (1970) Components of pH dependent cation exchange capacity. *Soil Sci.*, 109, 272

Sawhney BL (1972) Selective sorption and fixation of cations by clay minerals: a review. *Clays clay Miner.*, 20, 93–100

Van Raij B and Peech M (1972) Electro chemical properties of some oxisols and alfisols of the tropics. *Soil Sci. Soc. Am. Proc.*, 36, 587–593

Brace R and Matijevic E (1973) Aluminum hydrous oxide sols. I – Spherical particles of narrow size distribution. *J. Inorg. Nucl. Chem.*, 35, 3691–3705

McLaren RG and Crawford DV (1973) Soil copper. I – fractionnation of copper in soils. *J. Soil Sci.*, 24, 172

McBride MB and Mortland MM (1974) Copper (II) interactions with montmorillonite: evidence from physical methods. *Soil Sci. Soc. Am. Proc.*, 38, 408–415

Espinoza W, Gast RG and Adams RS Jr (1975) Charge characteristics and nitrate by two andepts from south-central Chile. *Soil Sci. Soc. Am. Proc.*, 39, 842–846

Ferris AP and Jepson WB (1975) The exchange capacities of kaolinite and the proportion of homo-ionic clays. *J. Colloid Interface Sci.*, 51, 245–259

Gupta SK and Chen KY (1975) Partitioning of trace metals in selective chemical fractions of nearshore sediments. *Environ. Lett.*, 10, 129

Baes CF and Mesmer RE (1976) *The hydrolysis of cations.* Wiley, New York

Bolland MDA, Posner AM and Quirk JP (1976) Surface charge on kaolinites in aqueous suspensions. *Aust. J. Soil Res.*, 14, 197–216

Bolt GHM, Bruggenwert GM and Kamphorst A (1976) Adsorption of cations by soil. In *Soil chemistry A - Basic elements.*, Elsevier Amsterdam, 54–95

Gallez A, Juo ASR and Herbillon AJ (1976) Surface and charge characterisitcs of selected soils in the tropics. *Soil Sci. Soc. Am. Proc.*, 40, 601–608

Gillman GP and Bell LC (1976) Surface charge characteristics of six weathered soils from tropical N. Queensland. *Austr. J. Soil Res.*, 14, 351–360

Herbillon AJ, Mestadgh MM, Vielvoye L and Derouane EG (1976) Iron in kaolinite with special reference to kaolinite from tropical soils. *Clay Miner.*, 11, 201–220

Gast RC (1977) Surface and colloid chemistry. In Dixon JB, Weed SB, Kittrick JA, Milford MM, White JL. *Minerals in soils environment.*, Soil Science Society of America: 27–73

Laverdière MM and Weaver RM (1977) Charge characteristics of spodic horizons. *Soil Sci. Soc. Am. J.*, 41, 505–510

Sposito G and Mattigod SV (1977) On the chemical foundation of the sodium adsorption ratio. *Soil Sci. Soc. Am. J.*, 41, 323–329

Thomas GW (1977) Historical developments in soil chemistry: ion exchange. *Soil Sci. Soc. Am. J.*, 41, 230–238

Carr RM, Chaikum N and Paterson N (1978) Intercalation of salts in halloysite. *Clays Clay Miner.*, 26, 144–152

Gessa C, Melis P, Bellu G and Testin C (1978) Inactivation of clay pH-dependent charge in organo-mineral complexes. *J. Soil Sci.*, 28, 58

Gillman GP and Bell LC (1978) Soil solution studies on weathered soils from tropical North Queensland. *Austr. J. Soil Res.*, 16, 66–77

Hendershot WH (1978) Measurement technique effects of the value of zero point of charge and its displacement from zero point of titration. *Can. J. Sol Sci.*, 58, 439

McBride MB (1978) Copper (II) interactions with kaolinite factors controlling adsorption. *Clays Clay Miner.*, 26, 101–106

Parfitt RL (1978) Anion adsorption by soils and soil materials. *Adv. Agronomy*, 30, 1–80

Wann SS and Uehara G (1978) Surface charge manipulation in constant surface potential soil colloids. I – Relation to adsorbed phosphorus. *Soil Sci. Soc. Am. J.*, 42, 565–570

Wann SS and Uehara G (1978) II – Effect on solute transport. *Soil Sci. Soc. Am. J.*, 42, 886–888

Keng JCW (1979) *Surface chemistry of some constant potential soil colloids.*, Thesis University Hawaii

Lindsay WL (1979) *Chemical equilibrium in soils.*, Wiley New York

Shuman LM (1979) Zinc, manganese and copper in soil fractions. *Soil Sci.*, 127, 10

Yoon RH, Salman T and Donnay G (1979) Predicting points of zero charge of oxides and hydroxides. *J. Colloid Interface Sci.*, 70, 483

Bowden JW, Posner AM, Quirk JP (1980) Adsorption and charging phenomena in variable charge soils. In Theng BKG soils with variable charge. *NZ Soc. Soil Sci.*, 147

Bowden JW, Nagarajah S, Barrow NJ, Posner AM and Quirk JP (1980) Describing the adsorption of phosphate, citrate and selenite on a variable-charge mineral surface. *Austr. J. Soil Research*, 18, 49–60

Gillman GP and Uehara G (1980) Charge characteristics of soils with variable and permanent charge minerals. II - experimental. *Soil Sci. Soc. Am. J.*, 44, 252–255

Lim CH, Jackson ML, Koons RD and Helmke PA (1980) kaolins: sources of differences in cation exchange capacities and cesium retention. *Clays Clay Miner.*, 28, 223–229

Ninham BW (1980) Long-range vs short-range forces. The present state of play. *J. Phys. Chem.*, 84, 1423–1430

Sposito G (1980) Cation exchange in soils: an historical and theorical perspective. In: Baker DE *Chemistry in the soil environment.*, ASA, 40, 13

Stoops W (1980) Ion adsorption mechanisms in oxidic soils: implications for ZPC determinations. *Geod.*, 23, 303–314

Uehara G and Gillman GP (1980) Charge characteristics of soils with variable and permanent charge minerals. I – Theory. *Soil Sci. Soc. Am. J.*, 44, 250–252

Westhall J and Hohl H (1980) A comparison of electrostatic models for the oxide/solution interface. *Adv. in colloid and interface science*, 12, 265–290

Maksimovic Z, White JL and Logar M (1981) Chromium-bearing dickite and chromium-bearing kaolinite from Teslic (Yougoslavia). *Clays clay mineral*, 29, 213–218

Morel FMM, Westall JC and Yeasted JG (1981) Adsorption models: a mathematical analysis in the frame work of general equilibrium calculations. In: Anderson MA, Rubin AJ.: *Adsorption of inorganics at solid–liquid interfaces.*, Ann. Arbor. Sci. Pub.

Tazaki K (1981) Analytical electron microscopic studies of halloysite formation processus-morphology and composition of halloysite. *Proc. Int. Clay Conf.* Elsevier, Amsterdam 573–584

El-Swaify SA (1982) *Soil physical chemistry.*, Hawai Univ., booklet n° 640

Wada SI and Mizota C (1982) Ironrich halloysite (10 Å) with crumpled lamellar morphology from Hokkaido – Japan. *Clays Clay Miner.*, 30, 315–317

Gillman GP, Bruce RC, Davey BG, Kimble JM, Searle PL and Skjemstad JO (1983) A comprarison of methods used for determination of cation exchange capacity. *Commun. Soil Sci. Plant Anal.*, 14, 1005–1014

Hodges SC and Zelazny (1983) Interactions of dilute hydrolysed aluminum solutions with clays, peat and resin. *Soil Sci. Soc. Am. J.*, 47, 206–212

Kleijn WB and Oster JD (1983) Effects of permanent charge on the electrical double-layer properties of clays and oxides. *Soil Sci. Soc. Am. J.*, 47, 821–827

Bleam W and McBride MB (1984) Cluster formation versus isolated-site adsorption. A study of Mn(II) and Mg(II) adsorption on boehmite and goethite. *J. Colloid Interface Sci.*, 103: 124–132

Barrow NJ (1985) Reactions of anions and cations with variable-charge soils. *Adr. Agron.*, 38, 183–230

Fallavier P (1985) Densité de charge variable et point de charge nulle dans les sols tropicaux. Définition, mesure et utilisation. *Agronomie tropicale*, 40, 239–245

Gillman GP (1987) Modification of the compulsive exchange method for cation exchange capacity determination. *Soil Sci. Soc. Am. J.*, 51, 840–841

Lambert K (1987) *Cation exchange in Indonesian peat soils.*, Thesis Gent Univ., 68 p

Matjue N and Wada K (1987) Comments on "modification of the compulsive exchange method for cation exchange capacity determination". *Soil Sci. Soc. Am. J.*, 51, 841

Marcano-Martinez E and McBride MB (1989) Comparaison of titration and ion adsorption methods for surface charge measurement in oxisol. *Soil Sci. Soc. Am. J.*, 53, 1040–1045

Bolt GH, De Boodt MF, Hayes MHB and McBride MB (1991) *Interactions at the soil colloid-soil solution interface.* Kluwer Academic Publishers – Nato Asi Series. Series E: Applied Sciences, vol. 190, 603 p

Song KC and Ishiguro M (1992) Effects of solution pH on ion transport in allophanic andisol. *Soil Sci. Plant Nutr.*, 38, 477–484

Sposito G (1994) *Chemical Equilibria and Kinetics in Soils.*, Oxford University Press, Oxford

Sposito G (ed)itor (1996) *The environmental chemistry of aluminum.*, Lewis UK 464 p

Comans RNJ, Hilton J, Voitsekhovitch O, Laptev G, Popov V, Madruga MJ, Bulgakov A, Smith JT, Movchan Net Konoplev A (1998) A comparative study of radiocesium mobility measurements in soils and sediments from the catchment of a small upland oligotrophic lake (Devoke Water, U.K.). *Water Res. Oxford*, 32, 2846–2855

Vogeler I (2001) Copper and calcium transport through an unsaturated soil column. *Journal of environmental quality*, 30, 927–933

Cervini-Silva Jet Sposito G (2002) Steady-state dissolution kinetics of aluminium–goethite in the presence of deferrioxamine-B and oxalate ligands. *Environ. Sci. Technol.*, 36, 337–342

Isoelectric and Zero Charge Points

20.1 Introduction

20.1.1 Charges of Colloids

Table 20.1. Explanation of abbreviations

abbreviation	Explanation
PZC or ZPC	point of zero charge or zero point charge
PZNC or ZPNC	point of zero net charge or zero point of net charge
PZNPC	point of zero net proton charge
PZSE	point of zero salt effect
ZPT	zero point titration
PPZC	pristine point of zero charge (case where PZC = IEP)
IEP	isoelectric point
pH0	determines the sign of the net charge of surface

In the last 50 years, the points of zero charge (Parks and de Bruyn 1962) have enabled a conceptual approach to soil charge phenomena in particular in tropical soils whose physicochemical characteristics are closely linked to the presence of variable charges. The terminology used, which is still changing (Table 20.1), sometimes leads to confusion and the significance of measurements of parameters may be erroneous.

Zero point charge (ZPC) defines pH values associated with specific conditions applied to one or more densities of surface charge, or more precisely, values of pH for which one or more of the surface charges cancel each other (Sposito 1984). The ZPC can vary depending on the layers taken into account in defining the solid surface (cf. Chap. 19).

Studies by Uehara and Gillman (1981), Sposito (1981, 1984, 1989), Sparks (1986), Barrow (1987), Gangaiya and Morrison (1987), Cruz-Huerta and Kientz (2000), Gustafsson (2001) showed that in practice it is possible to use simpler operational definitions obtained from analytical results (like pH0 or PZNC, cf. Sect. 20.1.2). The possible discrepancy between characteristic pH values highlights the heterogeneity of the molecular environment of the interfaces, the complexity of the soil system and associated concepts. Since the soil simultaneously contains components that have permanent and variable charges, all the charges σ_T of a system are broken down as follows:

σ_p: permanent structural charges originating from the silicate lattices and isomorphic substitutions by ions of different valence. In most cases, σ_p is negative. These charges are significant in 2:1 clays, but generally weak in 1:1 clays and hydrated oxides.

σ_v (or σ_H): variable charges or net proton charges originating from iron and aluminium oxides, aluminosilicates, organic matter, edge charges and charges of surface functional groups. They are dominant in strongly weathered soils, rich in hydroxyl groups. These charges can be null, positive or negative. The protons of the diffuse layer are not accounted for: $\sigma_v = qH - qOH$.

σ_A (or σ_{is}): charges due to complexes able to form very stable covalent or ionic bonds (other than H^+ and OH^-), whose origin is not electrostatic, with no water molecule between the surface of the functional groups and the ion complexes (inner-sphere surface complex, Sposito, 1981). The charges can be null, positive or negative and can be regarded as specific adsorptions.

σ_β (or σ_{os}): charges of electrostatic origin coming from outer-sphere complex ions (other than H^+ and OH^-) which are regarded as nonspecific. There is a water molecule between the functional group and the bound ion. These ions are slightly adsorbed.

σ_d: ion charges of the diffuse layer which enable a balance between total vacant charges and ensure neutrality. The ions of this layer are maintained by weak electrostatic forces, but can diffuse in the soil solution.

These charges, or density of charge, can be expressed in moles m^{-2} or Coulomb m^{-2} and in moles (charge) kg^{-1}. Electric neutrality implies use of the following equation:

$$\sigma_T = \sigma_p + \sigma_v + \sigma_a + \sigma_\beta + \sigma_d = 0$$

The term of surface charge σ_S of a particle must be defined (double layer model) as well as the different layers which are involved in this phenomenon. For example if:

$$\sigma_S = \sigma_p + \sigma_v + \sigma_a + \sigma_\beta$$

ZPC in this case, is the point where $\sigma_S = 0$

or $$\sigma_S = -(\sigma_d).$$

If surface charge is considered as: $\sigma_S = \sigma_p + \sigma_v + \sigma_a,$

ZPC is the point where $$\sigma_S = 0,$$

$$\sigma_S = -(\sigma_\beta + \sigma_d).$$

By potentiometric titration, the surface charge can be titrated as a function of pH and of the concentration of electrolytes, and the pH0 value deduced. The intersection of the titration curves occurs at the point where the surface charge is not influenced by the concentration of indifferent electrolytes.

If the pH = pH0, pH does not change with a change in the electrolyte concentration, only in this case:

$$\sigma_v = 0$$

and $$\sigma_S = \sigma_p + \sigma_a,$$

however, ZPC requires $\sigma_S = \sigma_p + \sigma_v + \sigma_a = 0.$
With this type of analysis, if there is no significant permanent charge, ZPC and pH0 will be confused. However, it is necessary to take into account the fact that pH0 can vary slightly if there is adsorption presenting a specific affinity and resulting in the creation of a more negative or more positive surface.

20.1.2 Definitions

Zero Point Charge (ZPC)

This is the value of pH for which the total net charge σ_T is cancelled ($\sigma_T = 0$). Since the inter-particle forces are inactivated, the particles flocculate and do not move when an electric field is applied (electrophoretic mobility is null). This property is significant for the formation of soil aggregates and the retention of ions. By raising the soil pH above the ZPC value, the charge σ becomes negative and the cation exchange capacity is increased. Conversely, by decreasing the pH below ZPC a positive charge appears creating an anion exchange capacity.

Estimation of ZPC enables prediction of the soil response to modifications in environmental conditions (e.g. cultivation, use of fertilizers). For a soil in balance in an electrolyte solution with cations and anions forming only external sphere complexes (cf. Chap. 19): ZPC = PZNC = PZSE.

Point of Zero Net Proton Charge (PZNPC)

This is the pH value for which the variable charge σ_v is cancelled ($\sigma_v = 0$). In general, this point drops with a rise in pH. If there is no permanent charge in the lattice and no other ions determining the potential (H^+ and OH^-): PZNPC = ZPC = PIE (isoelectric point, cf. Sect. 20.1.1).

Point of Zero Net Charge (PZNC)

This is the pH value for which the net charge of adsorbed ion, other than σ_v i.e. $\sigma_a + \sigma_\beta + \sigma_d$, is cancelled (Parker et al. 1979; Sposito 1984). This value depends on the concentration of electrolytes and can also vary slightly with the ion index used though in a not very significant way with indifferent electrolytes (Na^+, Li^+, Cl^-, NO_3^-). Measurements are made in a saturated solution, NaCl for example, as a function of the pH at a constant ionic force.

This value is useful to understand the phenomena of ion retention in the soil. At this point, equal quantities of cations and anions are adsorbed with an indifferent electrolyte and the cation exchange capacity (CEC) is equal to the anion exchange capacity (AEC), that is to say CEC – AEC = 0.

If the system contains notable quantities of permanent and variable charges, pH0 (cf. below) and PZNC do not result in the same pH value.

If pH (PZNC) < pH0 → indication of negative permanent charge.

If pH (PZNC) > pH0 → indication of positive permanent charges.

PZNC = ZPC if the surface net charge of the complexes is cancelled.

Point of Zero Salt Effect (PZSE)

σ_v is often measured by titration in an indifferent electrolyte at different ionic forces. The pH at which the curves intersect is the point of zero salt effect (PZSE), this being a particular case in which σ_v is invariable. At this point, the salt concentration no longer has any effect on the pH, but it is not necessarily equal to ZPC (Parker et al. 1979), except if the densities of charges of σ_a and σ_β do not vary with the ionic force of the electrolyte. If there is no permanent charge and if specific adsorption does not vary with the ionic force of the solution (indifferent electrolytes): PZSE = PZNC.

Zero Point Titration (ZPT)

This is the point used during analysis that corresponds to the pH equilibrium before addition of any acid (H^+) or base (OH^-). It does not characterize the charges themselves, but the starting pH point of titration in a given medium of definite ionic force.

Isoelectric Point (IEP)

The isoelectric point is the pH at which the zeta potential is null or, when referring to the diffuse double layer theory, the pH at which the charge of the plan separating the Stern layer and the Gouy diffuse layer is null (Breeuwsma, 1973, Sparks 1986): $\sigma_v = 0$ and $\sigma_p = \sigma_a = \sigma_\beta = 0$. With an indifferent electrolyte that does not cause any specific adsorption in the Stern layer, IEP is nearly equal to pH0 in a system dominated by variable charges. The term IEP is used for measurements of electrophoretic mobility.

pH0 Point

This is the point at which the net variable charge σ_v is equal to zero (Uehara-Gillman, 1981). At pH0, H^+ and OH^- adsorptions are equal. The point can refer to ZPC and IEP, but can be different from ZPC and may be somewhat inaccurate as the ion exchange between protons added by titration and cations adsorbed on the sites of permanent charges is able to consume protons without affecting the variable charge. Sparks (1986) provided the following definition: pH0 is the pH value of a hydroxylated surface which presents a net surface charge equal to zero. It is a significant parameter in soils with variable charges because it determines whether the net charge of the surface is positive or negative.

For tropical soils with variable charges where the permanent charges are weak, the values of ZPC, PZNPC, PZSE, PZNC are close, which avoids the need to use very precise time-consuming methods that require considerable quantities of soil.

20.1.3 Conditions for the Measurement of Charge

Whole soils or clay fractions can be used, possibly after pretreatments which modify the variable charge distributions as a function of the pH and of the ionic force of the solutions. The elimination of organic matter masks total-C-to-ZPC correlations, KCl treatment enables extraction of exchangeable Al^{3+}, acid oxalate and DCB methods (cf. Chap. 6) enable elimination of oxide and hydroxide layer and reveal negative permanent charges. These measurements are also influenced by other factors such as:

– The Z valence of the counter-ion

– the dielectric constant ε (the use of nonaqueous solvents like ethanol to eliminate excess reagents can deteriorate the surface charges and introduce serious errors)

– the absolute temperature T

– the concentration of electrolytes.

The addition of an electrolyte to a soil with variable charge decreases the surface potential, but increases the surface charge. The lowering of the surface potential is indicated by a change in the pH of the solution. For a negative surface charge, the pH decreases with the concentration of electrolyte, and inversely, the pH increases with a positive surface charge. If there is no change in pH, the net surface charge is considered to be null.

As soil pH determines the magnitude of the net charge, the variable charges can be roughly estimated during measurement of pH_{H_2O} and pH_{KCl} by calculating $\Delta pH = pH_{H_2O} - pH_{KCl}$ (cf. Chap. 15). If ΔpH is between -0.5 and $+0.5$, the soils are dominated by components with variable charges and pH0 can be estimated (Uehara and Gillman, 1981) by the sum $pH_{KCl} + \Delta pH$ or

$$pH0 = 2\,(pH_{KCl}) - (pH_{H_2O}).$$

These measurements should be regarded as a preliminary test before analysis. As pH_{H_2O} is affected by the concentration of electrolytes in the soil solution, it is difficult to decide whether observed differences are due to the concentration of electrolytes or to the nature of the surface charges. Measuring pH_{KCl} is more reliable as the effects of the presence of electrolyte in the solution are masked and the relationship with Al^{3+} extraction is improved. Schematically, the analytical operations required for the measurement of charge are simple, but their implementation can be long and delicate and must be carried out under rigorous operating conditions including:

– Contact between the soil and solutions of fixed composition and concentration, with controlled pressure and temperature and for a defined time to establish the reaction equilibriums; this contact can be made in a suspension or on a column under controlled atmosphere if the phases are unstable in air (redox phenomena, CO_2 equilibrium)

– possible separation of phases by gravity, filtration, or centrifugation

– chemical and physicochemical measurements on the residual soil or on the liquid phase after extraction

– calculations and graphical interpretation.

Computer programs make it possible to describe and model the reactions of the ions with the soil (e.g. Barrow 1987) considerably simplifying the processing of data. Repetitive analyses can be carried out to monitor the changes in clay charges in order to reach the equilibrium state.

20.2. Main Methods

20.2.1 Measurement of pH0 (PZSE), long equilibrium time

Simplified method of Uehara and Gillman (1981).

Reagents

– sodium chloride	NaCl	mw =58.44	0.1 mol L^{-1}
– calcium chloride	CaCl$_2$	mw =110.99 (dried on P$_2$O$_5$)	
			0.1 mol L^{-1}
– sodium chloride			2 mol L^{-1}
– calcium chloride			2 mol L^{-1}
– hydrochloric acid	HCl		0.1 mol L^{-1}
– sodium hydroxide	NaOH		0.1 mol L^{-1}.

The residual moisture of the samples has to be measured beforehand in order to bring back weights of wet soil to standard weights of soil dried at 105°C. In this way all the results are all expressed on the basis of the soil dried at 105°C and have the same relative surface during analysis whatever the moisture content.

Procedure

– Weigh 4 g of soil sieved at 0.5 mm (or equivalent weight dried at 105°C) in 15 replicates and place in 50 mL beakers numbered from 1 to 15 (Table 20.2).

– add 0.5 mL of indifferent electrolyte 0.1 mol (+) L^{-1} solution (NaCl for soils with mostly monovalent elements in exchangeable cations or CaCl$_2$ for soils with mostly bivalent elements (Ca^{2+}, Mg^{2+})

– to beakers 1 – 7 add increasing quantities of 0.1 mol (HCl) L^{-1} solution and to beakers 9 – 15 add increasing quantities of 0.1 mol (NaOH) L^{-1} solution.

– bring the volume to 20 mL with distilled water

– let it stand for 4 days agitating occasionally

– measure the pH → pH 0.002 M

– add 0.5 mL of electrolyte solution 2 mol L^{-1} and agitate for 3 h.

– measure the pH → pH 0.05 M

– for each beaker, calculate ΔpH = [pH 0.05 M – pH 0.002 M] and on a
graph, note the values ΔpH versus pH 0.002 M to determine the point
where ΔpH = 0 which corresponds to pH0, i.e. the value of the pH that
is independent of the salt concentration.

20.2.2 Point of Zero Salt Effect (PZSE), Short Equilibrium Time

Principle

The method (Block and de Bruyn 1970, Hendershot and Laukulich 1979,
1983) is based on the indirect measurement of PZSE by potentiometric
titration of the net adsorption of H^+ and OH^- at different pH and different
ionic forces.

Because of the amphoteric character of certain colloids, the curves
intersect at a given pH where the adsorption of protons is independent of
the ionic force. This is the point of zero salt effect (Parker et al. 1979).

Reagents

– Indifferent electrolyte:
   NaCl   0.001; 0.01; 0.05; 0.2 mol L^{-1}
   Preparation starting from commercial standard doses
– HCl 0.1 mol L^{-1}
– NaOH 0.1 mol L^{-1}.

Procedure

Reduce the sample that has been air dried for more than two months (for
Andosols) to 2 mm (fine earth), then crush it to 0.5 mm (sieve AFNOR
NF X11-501, module 28) in order to allow regular exchange and to
minimize dispersion of the results.

Eight sample specimens (of 2 – 4 g) are needed for titration using four
concentrations of the HCl and NaOH mediums (three concentrations are
often sufficient if the intersection of the curves is correct):
– Weigh 2 g of soil
– add 40 mL of 0.001 mol L^{-1} indifferent electrolyte
– agitate with a bar magnet for 5 min without stopping, then measure the
   initial pH which corresponds to ZPT

Table 20.2. Experimental procedure for pH0 (PZSE)

4 g soil	1	2	3	4	5	6	7	8	9	10	11	12	13	14	15
mL water	10	10	10	10	10	10	10	10	10	10	10	10	10	10	10
mL electrolyte 0.1 mol L^{-1}	0.5	0.5	0.5	0.5	0.5	0.5	0.5	0.5	0.5	0.5	0.5	0.5	0.5	0.5	0.5
		0.1 mol (HCl) L^{-1}							Control (water)		0.1 mol (NaOH) L^{-1}				
mL HCl or NaOH	0.25	0.50	1.0	1.5	2.0	2.5	3.0	/	0.25	0.50	1.0	1.5	2.0	2.5	3.0
mL water	9.25	9.00	8.5	8.0	7.5	7.0	6.5	9.5	9.25	9.00	8.5	8.0	7.5	7.0	6.5
mL total	20	20	20	20	20	20	20	20	20	20	20	20	20	20	20

– using an automatic titrimeter connected to a combined electrode, begin titration with 0.1 mol (HCl) L^{-1} solution by regulating the additions to one drop every 2 min (Fig. 20.1)
– continue titration until pH 3.0. This will take approximately 2 h.

On another test specimen of 2 g soil:
– add 40 mL of 0.001 mol L^{-1} indifferent electrolyte
– agitate with a bar magnet for 5 min and measure the pH which corresponds to ZPT
– carry out titration with 0.1 mol (NaOH) L^{-1} solution and titrate at a speed of one drop every 2 min until pH 9.5 – 10.0 (because of the risk of carbonation, it is preferable to work in a controlled nitrogen atmosphere which enables all contact with atmospheric CO_2 to be avoided).
  Complete the remaining titrations with additions of indifferent electrolyte 0.01, 0.05 and 0.2 mol L^{-1} idem under the same conditions, plus a blank (reagents without soil) to correct the results if necessary.

Calculations

The results are calculated in mmol kg^{-1} of adsorbed acid or base; the value of the ZPC-PZSE and charges σ_i are given on the recording tape at constant run (Fig. 1).

Remarks

The pH0 value corresponds to a point of maximum chemical stability. This measurement can be made on rough untreated soil as well as on samples that have been subjected to pretreatment. For example:
– saturation by 1 mol(NaCl) L^{-1} solution (Hendershot, Lavkulich, 1979; Gautheyrou et al. 1981)
– destruction of organic matter by sodium hypochlorite;
– elimination of oxides and hydroxides (methods DCB, acid ammonium oxalate, pyrophosphate, Segalen et al. 1983)

On untreated soil:
– if the pH measured in water is higher than that measured in KCl (pH_{H_2O} > pH_{CaCl_2} > pH_{KCl}), the ZPC is located below ZPT and σ_i is negative;
– if the pH measured in water is lower than the pH_{KCl} (pH_{H_2O} < pH_{CaCl_2} < pH_{KCl}) the ZPC is above ZPT and σ_i is positive.
The higher the rate of oxide–hydroxides, the higher the ZPC.
On soil saturated by NaCl, the variations in ZPC and in values of σ_i reflect the balance between the quantities of cations (Al^{3+}) and anions (PO_4^{3-}) exchanged by Na^+ and Cl^-. If the clay content is relatively low, variations will be weak.

Comparison of the samples saturated in Na$^+$ and those which have undergone more or less complete elimination of organic matter by hypochlorite shows the depressor effect of organic matter on the ZPC.

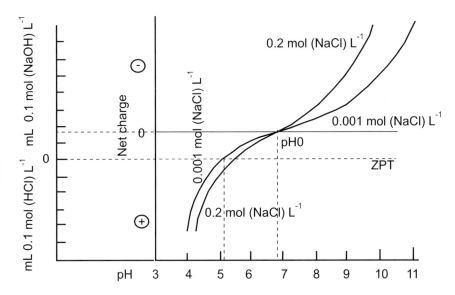

Fig. 20.1 Determination of point of zero salt effect by titration

Iron and aluminium oxides have relatively high values of between pH 7 and pH 9 depending on their nature and their crystallinity.

The presence of silica and organic matter results in relatively low pH0 values which increase the CEC of the andosols and allow the retention of cations.

References

Barrow NJ (1987) Reactions with variable-charge soils. In Martinus Nijhoff – Developments in plant and soil science, eiden 31, 191 p

Blok L and de Bruyn PL (1970) The ionic double layer et ZnO/solution surface. I – The experimental point of zero charge. *J. Colloid Interface Sci.*, 32, 518–525

Breeuwsma A (1973) *Adsorption of ion on hematite* (αFe_2O_3). Ph.D. diss. Wageningen (Hollande)

Cruz-Huerta L and Kientz DG (2000) Electric charge of andosols of 'Cofre de Perote', Veracruz, Mexico. *Terra*, 18, 115–124

Gangaiya P and Morrison RJ (1987) A review of the problems associated with applying the terms surface and zero point of charge to soils. *Commun. in Soil Science Plant Analysis*, 18, 1431–1451

Gautheyrou J and Gautheyrou M (1981) Comparison of electric charges in soils formed in a tropical climate. *Fourth Intern. Soil classification workshop Rwanda*, 7 p

Gautheyrou J and Gautheyrou M (1981) *Point de charge zéro des sols à allophane, à imogolite, vertisols et oxisols de Guadeloupe et Martinique (Antilles françaises)*. ORSTOM-Antilles, notes laboratoire, 29 p

Gustafsson JP (2001) The surface chemistry of imogolite. *Clays and Clay Minerals*, 49, 73–80

Hendershot WH and Lavkulich LM (1979) The effect of sodium chloride saturation and organic matter removal on the value of zero point of charge. *Soil Sci.*, 128, 136–141

Hendershot WH and Lavkulich LM (1983) Effect of sesquioxyde coatings on surface charge of standard mineral and soil samples. *Soil Sci. Soc. Am. J.*, 47, 1252–1260

Parker JG, Zelazny LW, Sampath S and Harris WG (1979) A critical evaluation of the extension of zero point of charge (ZPC) theory to soil systems. *Soil Sci. Soc. Am. J.*, 43: 668–673

Parks GA and De Bruyn PL (1962) The zero point of charge of oxides. *J. Phys. Chem.*, 66, 967–973

Segalen P, Gautheyrou M, Guenin H, Caracho E, Bosch D and Cardenas A (1983) Etude d'un sol dérivé de péridotite dans l'ouest de Cuba. Aspects physiques et chimiques (1). *Cahiers ORSTOM, série Pédologie*, XX, 239–245

Sparks DL (1986) *Soil physical chemistry.*, CRC, Boca Raton, 308 p

Sposito G (1981) The operational definition of the zero point charge in soils. *Soil Sci. Soc. Am. J.*, 45, 292–297

Sposito G (1984) *The surface chemistry of soils.*, Clarendon Oxford, 234 p

Sposito G (1989) *The chemistry of soils.*, Oxford University Press, 277 p

Uehara G and Gillman G (1981) *The mineralogy, chemistry and physics of tropical soils with variable charge clays.*, Westview Tropical Agriculture Series, 4, 170 p

Permanent and Variable Charges

21.1 Introduction

This terminology was introduced by Coleman et al. (1959) to characterize the charges linked to three main groups of soil components: clays, oxyhydroxides, and organic matter. Since then, advances in research no longer allow such a strict definition of the nature and origin of these charges. For example, clays are able to display both types of charges simultaneously. In certain types of tropical soil such as andisols varying charges are predominant whereas in soils in temperate regions permanent charges are predominant.

Well crystallized clays display a null or negative theoretical charge which occurs in the lattice structure and a variable charge which comes from the groups along the edge. The negative charge depends on the nature of the clay and the level of substitution of cations in the tetrahedral and octahedral layers. For example, Al^{3+} can replace Si^{4+} in the tetrahedral layer (e.g. Beidellite, Nontronite, Saponite), or Mg^{2+} can replace Al^{3+} in the octahedral layer (e.g. Montmorillonite, Illite). These isomorphic substitutions give rise to a deficit of positive charges and thus to an excess of negative charges which will be compensated for by external or interlayer cations. These charges are directly related to the permanent charges and do not depend on the pH or the ionic force.

In 1:1 clays of the Kaolinite type, which have a tetrahedral layer and a slightly deformed octahedral layer, the structure is electrically neutral. Isomorphic substitutions of Al^{3+} by Fe^{3+} in the octahedral layer are rare. Kaolinites thus present a weak permanent charge which means that if there are no structural disorders, measurements of cation exchange capacity (CEC) will not be much disturbed by variations in pH.

The rupture of the atom lattice reveals discontinuities that are not compensated for in hydroxylated surfaces, and are likely to ionize (Fig. 21.1). These edge charges depend on pH and the specific surface area.

Al_3^+ atoms in VI coordination and Si–OH groups can dissociate at around pH 7.0.

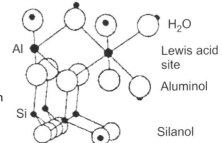

Fig. 21.1. Aluminol and silanol groups in kaolinite (Sposito 1984)

In halloysite-$4H_2O$, which has layers of interfoliaceous water, the CEC is higher and can be modified by cations with low hydration energy.

In 2:1 clays some phyllosilicates like pyrophyllite or talc are formed by an octahedral layer (Al^{3+} or Mg^{2+}) enclosed between two tetrahedral layers Si_4^+ which form an electrically neutral unit. Smectites on the other hand, which derive from this type of formation after substitution of ion Mg^{2+} with ions Al^{3+} in the octahedral layer, present a deficit of positive charges (or excess negative charges) which must be compensated for by interlayer cations. The plan of the atoms of oxygen on the surface of 2:1 clays, called "siloxane", is characterized by deformed hexagonal symmetry. This cavity of approximately 2.6 Å is bordered by the six orbitals of the hexagonal ring and its reactivity is linked to the charges distributed in the structure of the layers. If there are no isomorphic substitutions, and thus no deficit of positive charges, the siloxane cavity is a donor of electrons which can form unstable complexes. If, on the contrary, there is isomorphic substitution of Al^{3+} by Mg^{2+} or Fe^{2+} in the octahedral layer, the excess charge is close to surface oxygen atoms and the complexes are stable.

Vermiculites derived from trioctahedral Mg talc are replaced by Al^{3+} in the Si_4^+ tetrahedral layer, creating negative structural charges which are compensated for by interfoliaceous cations, etc.

All these faults appear within the structural unit and no balance of charges can be considered to be a natural law. The concentration of electrolytes, the valence of the counter-ion and the potential of the double layer do not modify the surface charge. In practice, this permanent charge can be linked to the exchange capacity measured at soil pH in soils in temperate regions, as the variable charges are generally weak.

Permanent charges ρ_p and variable charges ρ_v make up the inherent surface charge which is a reflection of the degree of soil weathering and of the presence of organic matter and oxide.

$\sigma_p + \sigma_v$ = inherent surface charge of the soil.

The oxides, hydroxides and oxyhydroxides that are free or cover the crystal lattices, as well as aluminosilicates with short-range organization, have a hydroxylated surface which is able to adsorb H^+ protons or OH^- hydroxides. An acid medium causes excess adsorption of H^+ ions and an alkaline medium excess OH^- (Fig. 21.2). These ions are also referred to as "ion determining potential (IDP)".

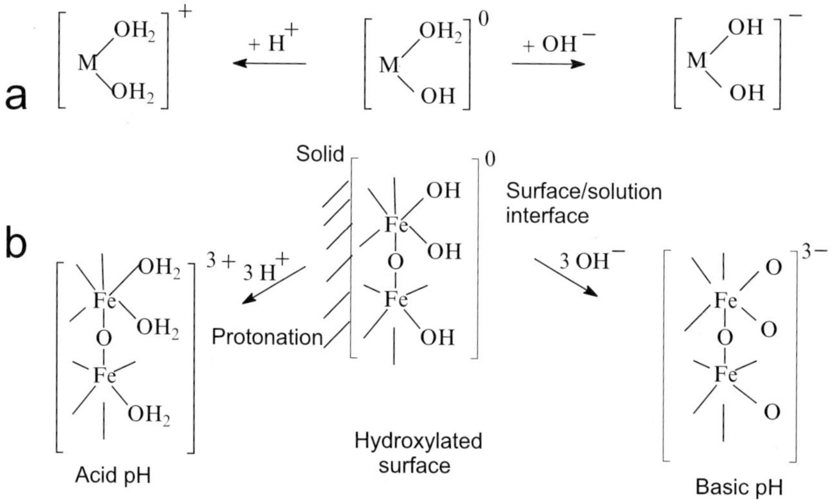

Fig. 21.2. Surface charge of hydroxylated materials
(a) diagram of Parks and de Bruyn (1962); (b) hematite, iron oxide (Uehara and Gillman 1981)

For a given pH, the surface potential is fixed, but the surface charge depends on many factors such as (1) the pH of the solution, (2) the nature of the electrolyte, its valence and concentration, (3) the permittivity of the medium, (4) the temperature and the conditions of measurement compared to natural conditions. The point of null net charge is at the pH where the density of the positive charges is equal to the density of the negative charges.

The variable charge generally develops strongly at a pH equal to or higher than 7.0, but this pH value is empirical. Variable charges are a surface phenomenon and are thus related to the surface of colloids rather than to their absolute concentration. During weathering, variable charges can develop during the noncongruent dissolution of a crystal or on the contrary, at the time of transition from an amorphous state to a crystalline state.

In aluminosilicates of the allophane type, cation exchange capacities that are able to reach very high values can develop in basic medium. The permanent charge is linked to Al(IV), while the variable charge originates from the hexacoordinate Al (Fieldes 1962; Fripia 1964).

The positive charges decrease with an increase in pH and can be measured using the results of CBD analysis (cf. Sect. 6.2.2 in Chap. 6) and possibly differentiated using the Fe:Ti and Fe:Mn ratios, if the positive charges originate from isomorphic substitutions of Ti_4^+ or Mn_4^+ in the Fe_3^+ oxide structures.

In organic matters the presence of ionisable functional groups can confer strong negative net charges on these groups. The HOOC– carboxylic and HO– phenolic groups, which are the most active, give variable negative charges and the cation exchange capacity can reach $4 \text{ mol } (+) \text{ kg}^{-1}$. Organic matter thus plays a major role in the surface horizons, and is involved in the soil buffering effect (regulation of the pH and of the concentration of exchangeable cations of the soil solution).

$$\text{Humus}\begin{matrix} H^+ \\ H^- \end{matrix} + \text{soil solution-}Ca^{2+} \rightarrow \text{humus-}Ca^{2+} + 2H^+ \text{ (soil solution)}$$

The nonionic organic structures can also react by the means of Van der Waals forces of attraction which induce only weak bonds, for example through molecules present at very short distances (about one Angström).

However, the very large humic, nonpolar polymer molecules cannot attract water molecules which explains the phenomenon of hydrophobicity of organic matter. Thus, in certain soils, it is necessary to use samples preserved in their natural moisture. The humified organic matter reacts with the soil minerals and forms aggregates.

$$(B^+) + (M^+\underline{=}) \rightarrow B^+\underline{=} + M^+$$

(B^+)	organic molecular unit in aqueous solution.
$(M^+\underline{=})$	exchangeable monovalent cation bound to soil colloids.
$(B^+\underline{=})$	organic molecular unit bound to clay.
(M^+)	monovalent cation in aqueous solution.

The organic molecular units that are involved in the exchange of cations and protons contain functional groups like carboxylate, carbonyls, and amino, aromatic, or N-heterocyclic groups. Exchange of anions is also possible with the carboxylate groups, as is formation of stronger bonds of the ligand type.

21.2 Main Methods

21.2.1 Measurement of Variable Charges

Principle

At pH0, i.e. the intersection point of the titration curves in an electrolyte with variable concentration, the cation exchange capacity equivalent to the variable charges is measured on a graph enabling the increase in the density of negative charges between the soil pH and pH0 (Uehara and Gillman 1981) to be displayed (Fig. 21.3).

Reagents

Hydrochloric acid HCl	0.1 mol L^{-1}
Sodium hydroxide NaOH	0.1 mol L^{-1}
Potassium chloride (mw $= 74.56$ g)	2 mol L^{-1}

Procedure

– Add 4 g of soil (equivalent to soil dried at 105°C) sieved at 0.5 mm in each of 11 centrifugation tubes of 50 mL (Table 21.1).
– Add 10 mL of distilled water and homogenize.
– Add increasing quantities of 0.1 mol (HCl) L^{-1} solution in tubes 1–5, (Table 21.1) and same quantities of 0.1 mol (NaOH) L^{-1} solution in tubes 7–11.
– Tube 6 is the control.
– Complete to 20 mL with water.
– Close the tubes and let stand for 4 days agitating periodically.
– Measure the pH in each tube: pH1 (water).
– Add 1 mL of 2 mol (KCl) L^{-1} in each tube.
– Agitate for 3 h and measure the pH in each tube: pH2 (KCl).
– Plot the titration curves of pH1 and pH2 correcting with the blank values if necessary.

The intersection of the two curves gives pH0. The variable exchange capacity is given by the density of charges between pH0 and the pH$_{water}$ of the soil (Fig. 21.3).

Table 21.1. Experimental procedure for determination of variable charge

blanks		tube number										
B1	B2	1	2	3	4	5	6 control	7	8	9	10	11
mL water	10	10	10	10	10	10	10	10	10	10	10	10
		0.1 mol (HCl) L^{-1}						0.1 mol (NaOH) L^{-1}				
mL HCl or NaOH	0.5	1.0	2.0	3.0	4.0			0.5	1.0	2.0	3.0	4.0
mL water	9.5	9.0	8.0	7.0	6.0	10		9.5	9.0	8.0	7.0	6.0
	Final volume 20 mL											

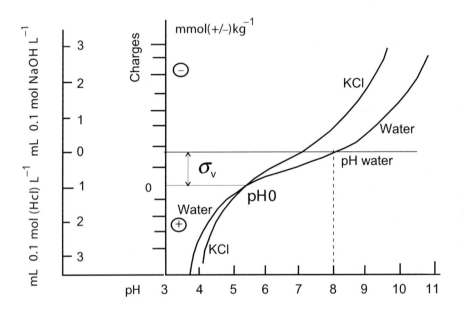

Fig. 21.3. Determination of variable charges σ_v

21.2.2 Determination of Permanent Charges

Principle

The measurement of the permanent charge σ_p in a soil with permanent and variable charges is based on the adsorption of ions at pH0. At this point, there is equal adsorption of cations and anions on surfaces with variable charges, the density of the charge being null (Uehara and Gillman 1981).

Any excess adsorption of cations or anions at pH0 constitutes a measure of the permanent negative charge and permanent positive charge, respectively. A pretreatment is carried out to eliminate the specifically adsorbed ions and render the medium homoionic.

Reagents

– 1 mol (KCl) L^{-1} potassium chloride solution (KCl, mw = 74.56)
– 0.2 mol L^{-1} potassium chloride solution
– 0.01 mol L^{-1} potassium chloride solution
– 0.002 mol L^{-1} potassium chloride solution
– 0.1 mol (HCl) L^{-1} hydrochloric acid solution from
– 0.1 mol (KOH) L^{-1} potassium hydroxide solution
– 0.1 mol (NaOH) L^{-1} sodium hydroxide solution
– 0.5 mol (NH$_4$NO$_3$) L^{-1} ammonium nitrate solution (NH$_4$NO$_3$, mw = 80.04)

Procedure

Preliminary Treatment of Soil

This treatment enables elimination of specifically adsorbed ions such as SO_4^{2-}.
– Weigh 100 g of air-dried soil (equivalent to soil dried at 105°C) sieved to 0.5 mm.
– Put in contact with 500 mL of 1 mol (KCl) L^{-1} solution and adjust the pH to 7.5 with 0.1 mol (KOH) L^{-1} solution. Let stand for 1 h and discard the supernatant.
– Again put in contact with 500 mL of 1 mol (KCl) L^{-1} and repeat the previous treatment twice.
– Wash with distilled water until the conductivity of the liquid phase is equal to that of a of 0.002 mol (KCl) L^{-1} standard solution.
– Dry in the air and sieve on a 0.5 mm mesh sieve.

Measurement of σ_p

– Weigh 4 g fractions of previously treated soil (equivalent to soil dried at 105°C) and place in 50 mL beakers.
– Measure the pH0 in the same way as for variable charges (cf. Sect. 21.2.1), saturation of K^+ and elimination of the specifically adsorbed ions can modify the pH0 value.
– Recover the soil residue. Use the tube with the pH closest to pH0 for the determination of the permanent charges.

– Wash the residue with 20 mL of 0.2 mol (KCl) L^{-1} solution and transfer in a 50 mL centrifugation tube.
– Agitate for 1 h, centrifuge and discard the supernatant.
– Add 20 mL of 0.01 mol (KCl) L^{-1} solution and using HCl or NaOH 0.1 mol L^{-1}, adjust the pH to the value found for pH0.
– Leave in contact for 1 h.
– Centrifuge and recover the supernatant, titrate K^+ and Cl^-, is K^{+1} and Cl^{-1} mmol mL^{-1}.
– Weigh the tube containing the centrifugation pellet to determine the volume of 0.01 mol (KCl) L^{-1} solution retained (VmL).
– Move the K^+ and Cl^- adsorbed ions on the centrifugation pellet by washing it five times with 20 mL of 0.5 mol (NH_4NO_3) L^{-1} solution.
– Mix the five filtrates and titrate the moved K^+ and Cl^- (K^+_2 and Cl^-_2 mmol mL^{-1}).

Calculation

Adsorbed K^+ (mmol(+)kg^{-1}) = 25 (100 $K^+_2 - K^+_1$ V)
Adsorbed Cl^- (mmol(–)kg^{-1}) = 25 (100 $Cl^-_2 - Cl^-_1$ V)
Permanent charge = adsorbed K^+ – adsorbed Cl^-

Remarks

– K^+ and Cl^- are generally titrated by, respectively, flame emission spectrometry and adsorption colorimetry (Pansu et al. 2001).
– The sum of the permanent and variable charges roughly corresponds to the cation exchange capacity measured by ammonium acetate buffered at pH 7.0 (cf. Chap. 22).

References

Coleman NT, Weed SB and McCracken RJ (1959) Cation exchange capacity and exchangeable cations in Piedmont soils of North Carolina. *Soil Sci. Soc. Am. Proc.*, 23, 146–149

Fripia JJ (1964) Surface properties of Alumino-silicates. *Clays Clay Miner.*, 12, 327

Pansu M Gautheyrou J and Loyer JY (2001) Soil Analysis - Sampling, Instrumentation and Quality control. Balkema, Lisse, Abington, Exton, Tokyo, 489 pp

Parks GA and De Bruyn PL (1962) The zero point of charge of oxides. *J. Phys. Chem.*, 66, 967–973

Sposito G (1984) *The surface chemistry of soils.*, Oxford-Clarendon Press, Oxford, 274 p

Uehara G and Gillman G (1981) The mineralogy, chemistry and physics of tropical soils with variable charges clays. *West view trop. Agric. Ser.*, 4, 170 p

Bibliography

Bortoluzzi EC, Tessier D, Rheinheimer DS and Julien JL (2005) The cation exchange capacity of a sandy soil in southern Brazil: an estimation of permanent and pH-dependent charges. *Eur. J. Soil Sci.,* doi:10.1111/j.1365-2389..00746.x

Coleman NT, Weed SB and McCracken RJ (1959) Cation exchange capacity and exchangeable cations in Piedmont soils of North Carolina. *Soil Sci. Soc. Am. Proc.*, 23, 146–149

Conyers MK, Helyar KR and Poile GJ (2000) pH buffering: the chemical response of acidic soils to added alkali. *Soil Sci.*, 165, 560–566

Zelazny LW, Liming He and An Vanwormhoudt (1996) – Charge analysis of soils and anion exchange. In *Methods of soil analysis, part 3, Chemical methods*, Bigham JM and Bartels JM ed. SSSA-ASA, Madison, WI Etats-Unis, 1231–1253

Julien JL and Turpin A (1999) Reactive surfaces and the reasoning of a few chemical characteristics of acid soils. *Comptes-Rendus-de-l'Academie-d'Agriculture-de-France*, 85, 25–35

Van-Ranst E, Utami SR and Shamsuddin J (2002) Andisols on volcanic ash from Java Island, Indonesia: Physico-chemical properties and classification. *Soil Sci.*, 167, 68–79

22

Exchangeable Cations

22.1 Introduction

22.1.1 Exchangeable Cations of Soil

This measurement is also widely known by its former name "exchangeable bases" which was the after-effect of analytical formulae expressed in oxide form (basic oxides such as K_2O, Na_2O; in 1929, Bray and Willhite performed soil lixiviation with neutral ammonium acetate followed by calcination to volatilize the acetate and to transform the elements into carbonate and oxides), and possibly to contrast it with exchangeable acidity. The older name may now seem obsolete, but it is still widely used.

Adsorption of exchangeable cations during deterioration processes represents the net accumulation of materials at the interface of the solid phase and the soil solution, but does not imply the development of a three–dimensional molecular structure as is in the case with precipitation. These ions can be moved by an electrolyte solution of known composition at a given pH.

In agronomy, the adsorption of exchangeable cations and the CEC[1] are very important for the determination of intrinsic soil fertility, fertilizer retention capacity, plant nutrition and so on. The adsorbed cations are available for plants which generate H^+ ions at the level of their small roots in contact with the soil solution.

Fertilizers but also environmental pollutants (like pesticides and toxic cations) are retained by the charges of the colloidal surfaces which prevent lixiviation. The adsorbing complex thus acts as an element of storage and of regulation for ions (inorganic and organic cations or anions). The measurement of exchangeable cations naturally present in

---

[1]CEC = Cation Exchange Capacity.

the soil gives their sum S ($\leq$CEC). Combined with the CEC (T), the $S{:}T$ ratio of saturation of the soil in fertilizing elements can be estimated at a given time, generally at the end of the farming cycle in cultivated zones. S measurement is affected by many factors: Ca^{2+}, Mg^{2+}, K^+, Na^+ contents can vary rapidly under the influence of fertilizers, amendments and plant cover, irrigation can cause transformations such as sodification.

Other ions that are removable by more active reagents (e.g. H^+, Al^{3+}) and exchangeable trace elements (e.g. Mn, Zn, Cu, Ni, Co, Ti, U, Cs, Sr, Pb, V) are not taken into account in the majority of studies, with the exception of studies on fertilization, toxicity or environmental pollution (for example the elimination of toxic or radioactive residues, ethrophication of groundwater and rivers).

Measurement of exchangeable calcium serves no purpose in limestone or gypseous soils because of saturation of the exchange complex and errors introduced by the solubility of calcium carbonate and gypsum. However, the Ca:Mg and Ca:Na ratios and the measurement of "active" calcium are useful (cf. Chap. 17).

In saline soils, the exchange complex is saturated by sodium ions and the presence of soluble salts makes measurement of exchangeable cations impossible, meaning other criteria have to be used (such as SAR, PAR, cf. Chap. 18). In soils characterized by ion supersaturation, the sum of the extracted cations (S) tends to exceed CEC (T).

The analysis of exchangeable cations retained by the negative charges of clays is important in evaluating the transfer rate of the ionic compounds through soil profiles (leaching) and enables the kinetics of exchange vs. time and space to be identified. For routine analysis, the exchange times are short (a few minutes), but to allow rehydration of inflating clays (like in montmorillonite) and also to take into account slower interfoliaceous exchanges (like in vermiculite), the sample is often left in contact with the reagent overnight before percolation.

In the case of illites, K^+ is easily trapped in the hexagonal cavities of the tetrahedral layers and is then difficult to extract. The exchange is no longer quantitative.

22.1.2 Extracting Reagents

The displacement of the exchangeable cations depends on the nature of the cations used to move them. Multivalent ions are theoretically more effective than monovalent ions. The reagent should move the exchangeable cations as selectively as possible without being too aggressive and without dissolving products that are not involved in adsorption–desorption.

In practice, the sum of the main exchangeable cations (Ca^{2+}, Mg^{2+}, K^+, Na^+) extracted by normal ammonium acetate at pH 7.0 is still used in most laboratories as a reference for classification systems and for cartography. The interest of NH_4^+ is that it is not usually present to a significant degree in the exchange complex. This method is part of the standard NF X31-108 (1992). The extraction of exchangeable cations can also be combined with other techniques available for CEC (cf. Chap. 26) as in the international standard NF X31-130 (1993).

In oxidic soils in which divalent cations are predominant, the use of a cation like Ba^{2+} makes extraction more complete. Extraction is difficult due to adsorption in the Stern layer and it is necessary to know if when this charge of exchangeable cations is used, there will be a correlation with their availability for plants. For measurement of the effective CEC (NF ISO 11260, 1994) titration of exchangeable cations can be carried out on the 0.1 mol $(BaCl_2)$ L^{-1} extraction solutions at the soil pH or, for the measurement of the potential CEC (NF ISO 13536, 1995), on the 1 mol $(BaCl_2)$ L^{-1} solutions buffered at pH 8.1.

Many authors, including Okazaki et al. (1962) and Gillman et al. (1982) have compared different extraction methods for exchangeable cations. In most soils, even those with variable charges, the values are basically independent of the method used provided the extraction pH does not exceed 7.0. However, it should be noted that exchangeable K^+ may appear to be slightly lower if the Ba^{2+} counter-ion is used instead of NH_4^+ (this is not the case for CEC, cf. Chap. 26).

22.1.3 Equipment

Manual or semi-automatic laboratory systems can be used for the extraction of exchangeable cations (Fig. 22.1):
– simple agitation with all the extraction reagents followed by separation (decantation, centrifugation, filtration) and titration of the cations in the liquid phase
– a system of contact with iterative additions and separation of the reagents, which allows the reagent to be continually renewed
– by percolation on a column with inert filtration additives

– by simple gravity with a constant level reagent delivery system, of the "Mariotte flask" type
– a bottom up system (per ascensum) enabling elimination of the air bubbles likely to disturb the solid–liquid contact
– a partial vacuum system using apparatuses equipped with multiple syringes that allow automatically programmed regular percolation.

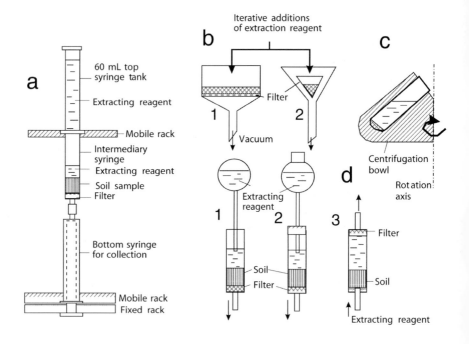

Fig. 22.1. Devices for putting in contact and separating the solid and liquid phases. **a**: automated extraction according to Kalra and Maynard (1991), **b**: percolation on filter, 1: Büchner funnel under vacuum, 2: simple gravity system, **c**: contact and separation by centrifugation, **d**:percolation on column, 1: closed flask, 2: open flask, 3: *per ascensum*

When using systems on columns, variable local speeds (preferential or laminar currents) and a radial gradient of permeability have to be avoided. The quality of filling can be critical and the quantity of the soil sample should consequently be limited to ensure satisfactory permeability, but also to avoid excessive concentration of the percolation front.

22.2 Ammonium Acetate Method at pH 7

22.2.1 Principle

The soil is saturated by the NH_4^+ cation in a buffered (or not buffered) medium at pH 7.0. The exchangeable cations are moved and pass into the liquid phase where they are titrated by atomic absorption or inductively coupled plasma spectrometry.

$$\text{Clay}\begin{pmatrix} Ca^{2+} \\ Mg^{2+} \\ K^+ \\ Na^+ \end{pmatrix} + NH_4^+ \longrightarrow \text{Clay}\begin{pmatrix} NH_4^+ \end{pmatrix} + \begin{pmatrix} Ca^{2+} \\ Mg^{2+} \\ K^+ \\ Na^+ \end{pmatrix} \text{Solution}$$

This method is reliable for most soils except in the presence of high rates of limestone, gypsum, soluble salts (solubilization) and hydrated vermiculite or micas (retrogradation).

The method in not buffered medium extracts the exchangeable cations at a pH near to that of the soil. It is used for effective cation exchange capacity (cf. Sect. 26.2 of Chap. 26). In soils with mainly variable charges, the method in buffered medium at pH 7.0 gives higher results than not buffered medium. Exchangeable manganese can be titrated in this medium to check manganese toxicity.

In soils able to fix potassium, NH_4^+ can partially replace fixed K^+, giving too high results for exchangeable K^+.

22.2.2 Procedure

Reagents

Ammonium Acetate 1 mol L^{-1} Buffered at pH 7
– Dissolve 77.08 g of RP CH_3COONH_4 in about 950 mL of deionized water
– bring the pH to 7.0 by adding diluted ammonia or acetic acid
– complete to 1,000 mL with deionized water.
        Or:
– Add 58 mL of glacial acetic acid (CH_3COOH)
– add about 300 mL of deionized water, then 71 mL of RP ammonia density = 0.90
– let cool

– adjust the pH to 7.0 by adding ammonia or acetic acid
– bring the volume to 1,000 mL with deionized water.

Ammonium Chloride 1 mol L^{-1}
– Dissolve 53.5 g of RP NH_4 Cl in deionized water and bring to 1,000 mL (the pH is about 4.5–5.0).

Manual Method – Usual Procedure

– Weigh 10 g (equivalent to soil dried at 105°C) of soil sample sieved to 2 mm
– put in contact with 25 mL of extracting reagent (ammonium acetate chloride) in a 100 mL beaker
– homogenize and leave in contact overnight
– agitate and let decant, then filter; repeat this procedure three times leaving in contact for 15 min between each extraction; mix the extracted portions and bring to 100 mL; homogenize
– titrate Ca^{2+}, Mg^{2+}, K^+, Na^+ in this filtrate by flame emission or atomic absorption spectrometry or by inductively coupled plasma spectrometry (Pansu et al. 2001). Titrate the same elements in the blank essay (extractant only) and deduce the values from the previous ones.

The results are expressed in Cmol (+) kg^{-1} of soil dried at 105°C.

Two controls should be performed per series: a standard control for reproducibility over time, and a randomly chosen soil replicate for reproducibility within the series.

Remarks

The international standard NF X 31-108 (1992) recommends only one agitation and 1 h for the test specimens and volumes listed in Table 22.1.

Table 22.1. Sample specimens and volumes recommended in standard NF X 31-108 (1992)

sample specimen (g)	volume of extracting solution (mL)	vessel volume (mL)
5	100	125–150
10	200	250–300

In the case of saline soils, if conductivity exceeds 0.5 mS, the soil should be washed to eliminate soluble salts before measuring exchangeable cations. As the exchange complex is Na^+ saturated, the elimination of soluble salts modifies the distribution of the exchangeable cations.

In the case of calcareous and/or gypseous soils, ammonium acetate can cause solubilization of calcium and magnesium carbonates or sulphates.

If the limestone content is high, the exchange complex can be considered to be Ca^{2+} saturated. The pH 8.1 extraction method can limit the effects of carbonate dissolution.

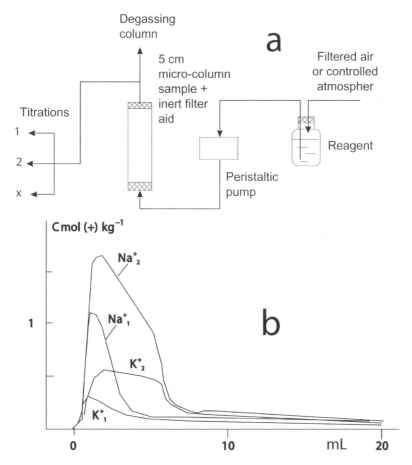

Fig. 22.2. Example of the dynamics of column extraction (**a**) automated system with continuous titration (**b**) example of cation exchange at pH 7 with the 1 mol (CH_3COONH_4) L^{-1} solution. 1: without previous contact, 2: with 24 h contact Gautheyrou et al., 1967)

Another possible approach uses double percolation: the first includes exchangeable plus solubilized elements, the second, solubilized elements. The exchangeable elements are obtained by calculating the difference between the two.

The procedure using normal ammonium acetate at pH 7 can be combined with the measurement of CEC with NH_4 (cf. Chap. 26) of which it represents the initial phase of saturation.

22.3. Automated Continuous Extraction

The use of dynamic displacement techniques makes it possible to analyse adsorption and desorption phenomena by means of soil columns percolated per ascensum by a mobile liquid phase of suitable concentration (Fig. 22.2). The flow is controlled and maintained constant by peristaltic pumps and the titration of the effluents is uninterrupted (Gautheyrou et al. 1967–1981). Continuous flow should be selected to reach the exchange equilibrium in a short time.

Data analysis allows the equilibrium laws of the exchangeable cations to be studied. Column methods were used to control exchange kinetics with respect to – for example (1) the mineralogical nature of clays and the lixiviation phenomena, (2) potassium fixing capacity, (3) chemical transport of cations and anions (e.g. Sparks et al. 1980, Sparks and Jardine 1981, Schweich et al. 1983, van Genuchten and Parker 1984, Carski and Sparks 1985, Shaviv et al. 1986, Jardine et al. 1988, Kool et al. 1989, Moog et al. 1998, Communar et al. 2004).

References

Carski TH and Sparks DL (1985) A modified miscible displacement technique for investigating adsorption–desorption kinetics in soils. *Soil Sci. Soc. Am. J.*, 49, 114–116

Communar G, Keren R and FaHu Li (2004) Deriving boron adsorption isotherms from soil column displacement experiments. *Soil Sci. Soc. Am. J.*, 68:481–488

Gautheyrou J and Gautheyrou M (1981) *Contribution à l'étude de la capacité d'échange des sols à allophane. Aspects analytiques de la CEC et ses conséquences sur l'interprétation pédo-agronomique.*, ORSTOM-Antilles, notes de laboratoire. Tome I: 276 p Tome II: 129 p Tome III: profils (200 p)

Gautheyrou J and Gautheyrou M (1967) *Dosage des cations échangeables du sol.*, ORSTOM-Antilles, notes de laboratoire, 27 p

Gillman GP, Skjemstad JO and Bruce RC (1982) A comparison of methods used in Queensland for determining cation exchange properties. *CSIRO Aust. Div. Soils Tech. Pap.*, 44, 1–18

Jardine PM, Wilson GV and Luxmoore RJ (1988) Modeling the transport of inorganic ions through undisturbed soil columns from two contrasting watersheds. *Soil Sci. Soc. Am. J.*, 52 : 1252–1259

Kalra YP and Maynard DG (1991) *Methods manual for forest soil and plant analysis.*, Forestry Canada, Northern Forestry Center, Information report NORX-319, 15, 84–94

Kool JB, Parker JC and Zelazny LW (1989) On the estimation of cation exchange parameters from column displacement experiments. *Soil Sci. Soc. Am. J.*, 53, 1347–1355

Moog HC, Streck T, Cammenga HK (1998) Modeling Ca/K exchange kinetics by montmorillonite and vermiculite. *Soil Sci.*, 163, 382–39

NF X 31-108 (1992) Détermnation des cations Ca, Mg, K, Na extractibles par l'acétate d'ammonium. In *Qualité des sols*, AFNOR, Paris, 1996, 59–65

NF X 31-130 (1993) Détermination de la capacité d'échange cationique et des cations extractibles. In *Qualité des sols*, AFNOR, Paris, 1996, 103–116

NF ISO 11260 (1994) Détermination de la capacité d'échange cationique effective et du taux de saturation en bases échangeables à l'aide d'une solution de chlorure de baryum. In *Qualité des sols*, AFNOR, Paris, 1996, 243–256

NF ISO 13536 (1995) Détermination de la capacité d'échange cationique potentielle et de la teneur en cations échangeables en utilisant une solution tampon de chlorure de baryum à pH = 8.1. In *Qualité des sols*, AFNOR, Paris, 1996, 293–303

Okazaki R, Smith HW and Moodie CD (1962) Development of a cation-exchange capacity procedure with few inherent errors. *Soil Sci.*, 93, 343–349

Pansu M, Gautheyrou J and Loyer JY (2001) Soil Analysis – Sampling, Instrumentation and Quality control. Balkema, Lisse, Abington, Exton, Tokyo, 489 p

Schweich D, Sardin N and Gaudet JP (1983) Measurement of a cation exchange isotherm from elution curves obtained in a soil column: preliminary results. *Soil Sci. Soc. Am. J.*, 47, 32–37

Shaviv A, Jury WA and Pratt PF (1986) Exchange, fixation and precipitation of cations during leaching of soils amended with manure: 1/ column experiments. *Soil Sci.*, 141, 237–243

Sparks DL, Zelazny LW and Martens DC (1980) Kinetics of potassium desorption in soil using miscible displacement. *Soil Sci. Soc. Am. J.*, 44, 1205–1208

Sparks DL and Jardine PM (1981) Thermodynamics of potassium exchange in soil using a kinetics approach. *Soil Sci. Soc. Am. J.*, 45, 1094–1099

Van Genuchten MTh and Parker JC (1984) Boundary conditions for displacement experiments through short laboratory columns. *Soil Sci. Soc. Am. J.*, 48, 703–708

Bibliography

Hao XY and Chang C (2002) Effect of 25 annual cattle manure applications on soluble and exchangeable cations in soil. *Soil Sci.*, 167, 126–134

Holmgren GGS, Juve RL and Geschwender RC (1977) A mechanically controlled variable rate leaching device. *Soil Sci. Soc. Am. J.*, 41, 1207–1208

Kukier U, Sumner ME and Miller WP (2001) Distribution of exchangeable cations and trace elements in the profiles of soils amended with coal combustion. *Soil Sci.*, 166, 585–597

Liu CL, Wang MK and Yang CC (2001) Determination of cation exchange capacity by one-step soil leaching column method. *Communications in Soil Science and Plant Analysis*, 32, 2359–2372

Luer B and Bohmer A (2000) Comparison between percolation and extraction with 1M NH₄Cl solution to determine the effective cation exchange capacity (CECeff) of soils. *J. Plant Nutr. Soil Sci.*, 163, 555–557

Ogwada RA and Sparks DL (1986) Kinetics of ion exchange on clay minerals and soil : evaluation of methods. *Soil Sci. Soc. Am. J.*, 50, 1158–1162 and 1162–1166

Van Reuwijk LP (1987) *Procedures for soil analysis.*, ISRIC, 9–1 à 9–11.

Exchangeable Acidity

23.1 Introduction

23.1.1 Origin of Acidity

Exchangeable acidity, which appears during soil genesis processes (e.g. podzolization), can be regarded as a deterioration of the exchange surfaces (Pedro 1987). Clay can undergo hydrolysis (acidolysis, acidocomplexolysis) which causes destabilization of the 2:1 lattices, resulting in some of the Al^{3+} cations of the octahedral layer passing into exchangeable positions. So the surface exchangeable cations decrease and gradually aluminium dominates the negative charges, the pH of the soil drops towards 4.0 and phenomena of non-congruent dissolution can occur.

Acid rains that accompany fossil fuel emissions, and repeated application of acidifying fertilizers during crop cycles can accelerate soil deterioration. For example, with ammonium fertilizers, protons are produced during nitrification:

$$NH_4^+ + 3/2\ O_2 \rightarrow NO_2^- + H_2O + 2\ H^+$$
$$NO_2^- + 1/2\ O_2 \rightarrow NO_3^-$$

Is on the whole:

$$NH_4^+ + 2\ O_2 \rightarrow NO_3^- + H_2O + 2\ H^+$$

If the sample is treated with a not buffered electrolyte solution e.g. a potassium chloride solution, Al^{3+} ions are exchanged and transferred into solution where they can be hydrolyzed with release of protons. These reactions are complex. According to the Lewis theory, the Al^{3+} ion is an acceptor of electrons, able to hydrate itself:

$$Al^{3+} + 6\ (:OH_2) \Leftrightarrow [Al(:OH_2)_6]^{3+}$$

There is then a sequence of dissociation in aqueous medium.

$$[Al(H_2O)_6]^{3+} + H_2O \Leftrightarrow H_3O^+ + [Al(H_2O)_5OH]^{2+}$$
$$[Al(H_2O)_5OH]^{2+} + H_2O \Leftrightarrow H_3O^+ + [Al(H_2O)_4OH_2]^+$$

In addition, Al^{3+} can react with the anions as a function of the pH.

$$Al^{3+} + 3\ OH^- \Leftrightarrow Al(OH)_3$$
$$Al(OH)_3 + OH^- \Leftrightarrow [Al(OH)_4]^-$$
$$[Al(OH)_4]^- + OH^- \Leftrightarrow [Al(OH)_5]^{2-}$$
$$[Al(OH)_5]^{2-} + OH^- \Leftrightarrow [Al(OH)_6]^{3-}$$

Monomeric forms are the most abundant at low pH, i.e. towards pH 4.0, whereas polymeric forms gradually become predominant towards pH 4.5‾ 4.7.

Organic compounds can release protons, and, in acid soils containing reduced forms of sulphur (mangroves, organic soils subjected to waterlogging), acidity can result from oxidation reactions in contact with the air. With pyrite, for example:

$$FeS_2 + 7/2\ O_2 + H_2O \Leftrightarrow Fe_2^+ + 2\ SO_4^{2-} + 2H^+$$
$$Fe^{2+} + 1/4\ O_2 + 5/2\ H_2O \Leftrightarrow Fe(OH)_3 + 2H^+$$

Below pH 4.5 the microbial activity of *Thiobacillus ferroxidans* is strong and acidification increases according to the reaction:

$$FeS_2 + 14\ Fe^{3+} + 8H_2O \Leftrightarrow 15\ Fe^{2+} + 2\ SO_4^{2-} + 16H^+$$

In reducing medium below pH 5.5, the Mn^{2+} ion can present phytotoxicity which is added to that of Al^{3+}.

Exchangeable acidity is distinguished from free acidity that results from the concentration of H^+ ions in the soil solution. Exchangeable acidity forms part of potential acidity which includes more or less ionized acid functions, weak organic acids and easily exchangeable cations.

Potential acidity can be measured volumetrically by neutralizing the charges with a strong base. Potential acidity is one of the main components of the soil buffering effect. Acidity known as "extractable" is measured at pH 8.2 with a $BaCl_2$–triethanolamine reagent, and its measurement can be combined with that of charges that depend on the pH.

23.1.2 Aims of the Analysis

For soil taxonomy, the 1 mol (KCl) L^{-1} extract is considered to include only exchangeable forms Al^{3+}, $AlOH^{2+}$, $Al(OH)_2^+$ and H^+, possibly neglecting non-exchangeable solubilized products (e.g. amorphous gel, hydroxypolymers, gibbsite, aluminium phosphate, Fe^{2+} iron, Mn^{2+}).

The actual acidity of a soil is measured in moles of protons which can be titrated per unit mass (this exchangeable acidity is sometimes called acidity displaced by salts). In practice, above pH 5.2, no significant quantities of exchangeable aluminium are found as the Al ion is precipitated at this pH.

It is possible to separate exchangeable from non-exchangeable aluminium in an unambiguous way by leaching with strong electrolytes and plotting curves of cumulated solubility values (Skeen and Sumner 1965). As the dissolved quantities of non-exchangeable aluminium during extraction are constant, the sum of these contributions is then subtracted.

KCl exchangeable acidity is used for the measurement of effective cation exchange capacity by summation with the exchangeable cations extracted at soil pH (Ca^{2+}, Mg^{2+}, K^+, Na^+). A relatively high concentration of the extraction solution at 1 mol L^{-1} is necessary to account for the effect of the diffuse layer.

Measurement of exchangeable acidity is useful in agronomy to determine aluminic phytotoxicity which is closely correlated with the rate of exchangeable aluminium. However, this measurement does not constitute an index of toxicity: indeed, forms of mono- or polymeric aluminium and the ionic force of soil solution influence aluminium bio-activity, as does the presence of phosphorous and calcium in the root environment. The plant genotype must also be taken into account as some plants are more tolerant than others. In some tropical soils, Al^{3+} extractable by KCl is not always correlated with pH_{water}. Certain soils with a pH close to 4 can contain less exchangeable aluminium than soils with a pH near 5. The correlation with pH_{KCl} is more satisfactory. The $\Delta pH = pH_{KCl} - pH_{water}$ can be an indicator of mineralogical instability if it is significant (on the other hand if it is very weak, the soil pH is close to pH_0, (cf. Chap. 20).

The exchangeable Al:CEC ratio (with CEC measured at the soil pH) allows estimation of the risk of Al-phytotoxicity or Al tolerance for a given crop. Espiau and Peyronnel (1976, 1977) suggested the use of the rate of exchange acidity:

$$A\% = 100 \, \frac{A}{\text{effective} T}$$

Where A = exchangeable acidity extracted by 1 mol (KCl) L^{-1} solution = $Al^{3+} + H^+$ cmol (+) kg^{-1} and effective T = effective CEC = ECEC = A + $\Sigma(K^+, Na^+, Ca^{2+}, Mg^{2+})$ in cmol (+) kg^{-1}.

The desaturation percent is expressed by: $100\dfrac{T-S}{T}$ (T being the cation exchange capacity and S the sum of exchangeable cations). In many cases measurement of T–S at soil pH is sufficient.

23.2 Method

23.2.1 Principle

The sample is percolated with a not buffered 1 mol (KCl) L^{-1} solution which enables extraction of exchangeable acidity (H^+ and Al^{3+}). Titration is carried out by volumetry. Aluminium is measured either by volumetry or by atomic absorption spectrometry.

23.2.2 Reagents

– 1 mol L^{-1} potassium chloride: weigh 74.56 g of KCl; dissolve in about 950 mL of deionized water; let the temperature stabilize and complete to 1,000 mL
– 0.025 mol L^{-1} sodium hydroxide: dissolve 4 g of NaOH pellets in deionized water and after cooling, bring to 1,000 mL; titrate with the standard HCl solution; store in plastic bottles protected from air CO_2; the solution should be freshly prepared at least once a week; titrated commercial solutions can be used but their concentration must be checked by titration
– 0.025 mol L^{-1} hydrochloric acid: starting from a titrated commercial solution, prepare 0.1 mol L^{-1} commercial solution
– Phenolphthalein: dissolve 100 mg phenolphthalein in 100 mL of 15% ethanol solution
– 1 mol L^{-1} potassium fluoride (or possibly less soluble 40 g L^{-1} sodium fluoride): dissolve 58.10 g KF in about 950 mL water, then bring to 1,000 mL.

23.2.3 Procedure

The moisture content of the air-dried soil should be measured on a separate sample to correct the results to soil dried at 105°C.

Extraction

- Place 10 g of soil sieved to 2 mm in a 100 mL beaker
- add 20 mL of 1 mol (KCl) L^{-1} solution and leave in contact for 15 min agitating from time to time
- filter on thin analytical filter (blue filter)
- collect the filtrate in a 100 mL volumetric flask
- add fractions of approximately 10 mL of the KCl solution, leave in contact for 15 min after each addition
- after adding the last fraction, complete to 100 mL and homogenize
- the total duration of the extraction should be standardized at 120 – 150 min

Measurement of Exchangeable Acidity

$$[H^+ + OH^- \rightarrow H_2O]$$
$$[Al^{3+} + 3\ OH^- \rightarrow Al(OH)_3]$$

- pour an aliquot of 25 mL of extract described in section 2.3.1 into a 250 mL Erlenmeyer flask; add three drops of phenolphthalein solution
- titrate with 0.025 mol (NaOH) L^{-1} solution until the mixture turns pale pink
- add one drop of phenolphthalein and wait 1 min; the colour should remain stable; do not titrate to dark pink to limit the precipitation of aluminium hydroxide
- make two blank assays. Preserve the extracts to measure aluminium by titrimetry

Calculation

$$\text{Exchange acidity cmol (H+) kg}^{-1} \text{ (soil)} = \frac{100\ (x - y)\ MAf}{w}$$

w is the weight of air dried soil, x is the mL NaOH used for titration, y is the mL NaOH used for blank assay, M is the molarity of NaOH, A is the aliquot factor (= 4), f is the correction factor to express results as soil dried at 105°C.

Note

This result can be used for effective cation exchange capacity (ECEC cf. Chap. 26)

ECEC = exchangeable acidity cmol (+) kg^{-1} + exchangeable cations $(Ca^{2+}, Mg^{2+}, K^+, Na^+)$.

Measurement of Exchangeable Aluminium

Depending on the laboratory equipment available, exchangeable aluminium can be measured by atomic absorption or inductively coupled plasma spectrometry, or possibly by titrimetry or automated colorimetry with continuous-flow analysis (Pansu et al. 2001).

Atomic Absorption Spectrometry

– Prepare calibration ranges of 0, 10, 20, 30, 40, 50 mg (Al) L^{-1} in 1 mol (KCl) L^{-1} medium starting from a 500 mg (Al) L^{-1} stock solution
– take absorption measurements at 309.3 nm in a C_2H_2 / N_2O flame directly on the extraction, calibration and blank solutions
– express the results in cmol (+) kg^{-1} of aluminium and subtract from the exchangeable acidity to obtain exchangeable H^+:
   exchangeable acidity = $H^+ + Al^{3+}$ in cmol (+) kg^{-1}

This result can be used for the calculation of ECEC (cf. Chap. 26) by differentiating Al^{3+} and H^+.

Titrimetry

– To the 25 mL of solution used to measure exchangeable acidity (cf. "Measurement of Exchangeable Acidity"), add a micro-drop of 0.025 mol (HCl) L^{-1} solution to return to just before the end point and to destroy the pale pink colour.
– add 10 mL of potassium fluoride 1 mo l(KF) L^{-1} to complex aluminium. If aluminium is present, the solution will again turn pink after the alkalizing reaction:
   $Al (OH)_3 + 6 KF \rightarrow K_3Al F_6 + 3 KOH.$
   (If the solution does not turn pink, it is not necessary to continue, and exchangeable aluminium can be considered to be absent)
– titrate with 0.025 mol (HCl) L^{-1} solution until discolouration occurs. Wait 1–2 minutes and add one drop of phenolphthalein to check discolouration is permanent. The quantity of acid added corresponds to the quantity of exchangeable aluminium. Treat the blanks in the same way. They should not consume HCl. The difference between exchangeable acidity and exchangeable aluminium gives exchangeable protons.

Calculation

Exchangeable aluminium cmol $(1/3Al^{3+})$ kg^{-1} sol $= \dfrac{100\, V\; MA\, f}{w}$

Where w is the weight of air dried soil, V is the mL HCl used for titration, M is the HCl molarity, A is the aliquot factor $(= 4)$, f is the correction factor to express results as soil dried at 105°C.

Exchangeable H$^+$ (cmol kg^{-1}) = exchangeable acidity (cmol kg^{-1}) exchangeable Al (cmol $(1/3Al^{3+})$ kg^{-1}).

Observations

– The expression of results on the basis of soil dried at 105°C is particularly necessary for soils containing high rates of oxides and hydroxides, or aluminosilicates of the allophane type, because of the very variable but nevertheless high residual moisture content of air-dried soils. This form of expression enables comparison with other analytical results

– the presence of iron oxide can cause errors: if the extract is coloured by iron, it may be necessary to carry out iron titrations at the same time as aluminium titration by spectrometry

– the presence of soluble organic matter can obstruct volumetric titration.

23.3 Other Methods

The charge deficit can vary with the extraction medium (nature and concentration of the electrolyte, pH, etc.). The best extraction would be at the same pH as soil pH in the field with a liquid phase identical to the soil solution.

Many saline mediums have been tested to determine exchangeable aluminium selectively: either not buffered mediums at different concentrations which react at a pH near the soil pH, or buffered mediums at different pH.

Not buffered salts include: KCl (Yuan 1959), NaCl and BaCl$_2$ (McLean et al. 1959), NH$_4$Cl, MgCl$_2$, CaCl$_2$ (Skeen and Sumner 1967), LaCl$_3$ (Bloom, 1979), CuCl$_2$ (Juo and Kamprath 1979). Buffered salts include: acetates of K, Na, La, Cu at concentrations of from 0.2 to 1 or 2 mol L^{-1}.

All these reagents allow extraction of different forms of Al^{3+} which have been named, for example, exchangeable Al, organic matter associated Al, interfoliaceous Al or non-exchangeable polymeric hydroxy-Al.

The KCl method described in section 2 above is simple to use and seems to give the best performance, but the barium method is useful for more diversified studies (Pratt and Bair 1961, Skeen and Sumner 1965, Vermeulen et al. 1975, Espiau and Peyronnel 1976, Gillman 1979, Espiau and Pedro 1980). Thus, exchangeable acidity in an extract with barium chloride was the object of a proposal for the international NF ISO 14254 (1997) standard, as the extraction also allows the measurement of the effective cation exchange capacity and exchangeable cations (NF ISO 11260 1994).

References

Bloom PR (1979) Titration behavior of aluminum organic matter. *Soil Sci. Soc. Am. J.*, 43, 815–817

Espiau P and Pedro G (1980) Caractérisation du complexe d'échange des sols acides. Le taux d'acidité d'échange et sa signification pédogénétique sous climat tempéré. *Ann. Agron.*, 31, 363–383

Espiau P and Peyronel A (1976) L'acidité d'échange dans les sols. Méthode de détermination de l'aluminium échangeable et des protons échangeables. *Sci. du Sol.*, 3, 161–175

Gillman GP (1979) A proposed method for the measurement of exchange properties of highly weathered soils. *Austr. J. Soil Res.*, 17, 129–139

Juo ASR and Kamprat EJ (1979) Copper chloride as an extractant for estimating the potentially reactive Al pool in acid soils. *Soil Sci. Soc. Am. J.*, 43, 35–38

NF ISO 14254 (1997) Détermination de l'acidité échangeable dans un extrait au chlorure de baryum, AFNOR, Paris, X31–422

NF ISO 11260 (1994) Détermination de la capacité d'échange cationique effective et du taux de saturation en bases échangeables à l'aide d'une solution de chlorure de baryum. In *Qualité des sols*, AFNOR, Paris, 1996

Pansu M, Gautheyrou J and Loyer JY (2001) *Soil analysis – sampling, instrumentation and quality control.* Balkema, Lisse, Abingdon, Exton, Tokyo, 489 p

Pédro G (1987) Géochimie, mineralogie et organisation des sols. Aspects coordonnés des problèmes pédogénétiques. *Cah. ORSTOM Ser. Pédol.*, XXIII, 169–186

Pratt PR and Bair FL (1961) A comparison of three reagents aluminium for the extraction of Aluminium. *Soil Sci.*, 91, 355–357

Skeen JB and Sumner ME (1965) Measurement of exchangeable Aluminium in acid soils. *Nature*, 208, 712

Chronobibliography

Hissink DJ (1925) Base exchange in soils. *Trans. Far. Soc.*, 551–617

Jackson ML (1963) Aluminium bonding in soils: a unifying principle in soil science. *Soil Sci. Soc. Am. Proc.*, 27, 1–10

Little I (1964) The determination of exchangeable aluminium in soils. *Austr. J. Soil Res.*, 2, 76–82

Rich CI (1970) Conductometric and potentiometric titration of exchangeable aluminium. *Soil Sci. Soc. Am. Proc.*, 34, 31–38

Sivasubramaniam S and Talibudeen O (1972) Potassium–aluminium exchange in acid soils. I – Kinetics. *J. Soil Sci.*, 23, 163–176

Herbillon AJ (1974) Modifications des propriétés de charge provoquées par l'altération chimique. *Pédol.*, 24, 100–118

Rouiller J, Guillet B and Bruckert S (1980) Cations acides échangeables et acidités de surface. Approche analytique et incidences pédogénétiques. *Sci. du Sol.*, 2, 161–175

Herbillon AJ (1981) Degree of weathering and surface properties of clays. In *Characterisation of soils in relation to their classification and mangement*, Greenland DJ ed. Oxford University Press, 5, 80–97

Aleksandova AM, Krupskiy NK and Daragan YuV (1983) The nature of soil acidity. *Pochvovedeniye*, 3, 34–43

Gillman GP and Sumpter EA (1985) KCl-extractable aluminium in highly weathered soils. Is it exchangeable? *Commun. Soil Sci. Plant Anal.*, 16, 561–568

Logan Kab, Floate MJS and Ironside AD (1985) Determination of exchangeable acidity and exchangeable aluminium in hill soils. Part I – Exchangeable acidity. *Soil Sci. Plant Anal.*, 16, 301–308

Wagatsuma T and Ezoe Y (1985) Effect of pH on ionic species of aluminium in medium and on aluminum toxicity under solution culture. *Soil Sci. Plant Nutr.*, 31, 547–561

Manrique LA (1986) Ther relationship of soil pH to aluminum saturation and exchangeable aluminum in ultisols and oxisols. *Commun. Soil Sci. Plant Anal.*, 17, 439–455

Willoughby EJ (1986) A comparison of methods for measuring aluminium in KCl extracts of soils. Commun. *Soil Sci. Plant Anal.*, 17, 667–677

Wagatsuma T and Kaneko M (1987) High toxicity of hydroxy-aluminum polymer ions to plant roots. *Soil Sci. Plant Nutr.*, 33, 57–67

Pansu M, Gavinelli R and Espiau P (1990) Etude de précision des mesures de l'acidité d'échange par KCl N dans les sols. In *Actes Journées laboratoires,* IRD (ex-Orstom*)*, Paris, 114–126

Bertsch PM and Bloom PR (1996) Aluminium. In *Methods of soil analysis, part 3 Chemical methods*, Bigham JM and Bartels JM ed., SSSA, ASA, Madison WI, Etats-Unis, 517–550

Coscione AR, Andrade JC de, Raij B van (1998) Revisiting titration procedures for the determination of exchangeable acidity and exchangeable aluminum in soils. *Communications-in-Soil-Science-and-Plant-Analysis*, 29, 1973–1982

Derome J, Lindroos AJ (1998) Effects of heavy metal contamination on macronutrient availability and acidification parameters in forest soil in the vicinity of the Harjavalta Cu–Ni smelter, SW Finland, Environmental-Pollution., 99, 225–232

Filep G and Filep T (1999) Characterization of forms of potential soil acidity. A potencialis talajsavanyusag formainak jellemzese, *Agrok. Talajtan.*, 48, 33–48

Dai KH and Richter DD (2000) A re-examination of exchangeable acidity as extracted by potassium chloride and potassium fluoride. *Commun. Soil. Sci. Plant Anal.*, 31, 115–139

Lime Requirement

24.1 Introduction

24.1.1 Correction of Soil Acidity

The English physicist Davy was the first to explain the effect of liming by the "neutralization of soil acidity" in 1813. The measurement of "lime requirement" (which is essential for land use of very acid soils) can be defined as the part of the charges that depend on pH between the natural soil pH and the pH required for a given crop. When total soil acidity is more than about 15% of cation exchange capacity, problems of phytotoxicity can appear depending on:

– Acidity itself for certain plants and micro-organisms
– Aluminic (and manganic) toxicity, by inhibition of root growth
– Induced deficiencies in major elements (e.g. Ca or Mg lixiviation) or in trace elements

This phenomenon can be very serious in soils with permanent charges of the 2:1 clay type. It can be corrected by amendments which decrease acidity and increase the pH to a level that enables better land use.

On the one hand, the increase in pH increases mineralization kinetics and on the other hand, decreases the value of soluble and exchangeable Al^{3+} which forms hydroxyaluminum polymers (cf. Chap. 23). These polymers improve the availability of phosphorus for plants.

Depending on the crop, the optimal pH will take into account (1) the economic constraints (minimum inputs and thus minimum cost for the best possible output), (2) plant tolerance to Al–Mn acidity and toxicity, (3) the mineralogical nature of clays and different colloids, (4) the quantity of organic matter, (5) climatic constraints and seasonal variations in pH, (6) irrigation, (7) lixiviation and proton inputs during application of acidifying fertilizers.

The precipitation of Al^{3+}, $Al(OH)_3$ or $Al(OH)SO_4,5H_2O$ (jurbanite) can be induced by addition of calcium carbonate (limestone) or calcium sulphate (gypsum). Clay is then gradually saturated by Ca^{2+} ions which means fertilization must be balanced, or as an old French proverb puts it "liming without manuring brings unforeseen ruin"[1].

In soils with variable charges in which the minerals are stable at relatively acid pH, the buffering effect is weak at pH0 (cf. Chap. 20), but becomes strong on each side of pH0. During liming, the increase in pH in these soils is slow and the study of the range between pH 4 and pH 6 – which is useful for agronomy – will suffice, as well as reaching the critical pH for $Al(OH)_3$ precipitation, i.e. 5.2–5.5. Many large-scale farms have improved their output by raising the soil pH to this level, as the assimilation of N, P, K, Ca, Mg, S, B and Mo is then facilitated. On the other hand, increasing pH to more than 7.5 can result in deficiencies in P, B, Zn, Fe, but can reduce Mn toxicity.

Increasing pH initially causes the neutralization of H^+ sites then stops the genesis of exchangeable aluminium, and finally induces formation of $Al(OH)^{2+}$ and $Al(OH)_2{}^+$ polymers covering active surfaces of colloids and decreasing exchangeable acidity. In addition, the adsorbing complex becomes saturated with Ca^{2+} ions:

$$2CaCO_3 + 2H_2O \rightarrow Ca(OH)_2 + Ca(HCO3)_2$$
$$Clay(H)_4 + Ca(OH)_2 + Ca(HCO3)_2 \rightarrow Clay(Ca^{2+})_2 + 2H_2O + 2H_2CO_3$$
$$2H_2CO_3 \rightarrow 2CO_2 + 2H_2O$$

If the pH drops at the level of the plant roots (acid exudation), the exchangeable Ca^{2+} cations again pass in solution. In soils containing 2:1 clays where acidity is aluminic, phosphorus is precipitated in the form of aluminum phosphate; by eliminating soluble Al^{3+}, liming modifies the fixing of P.

If exchangeable Al is neutralized (polymeric Al, organo-Al compounds), sites are created that are accessible for cation exchange and CEC increases slightly.

24.1.2 Calculation of Correction

In the laboratory, lime requirement is expressed in milli-equivalents of $CaCO_3$ per kg of soil and in agronomy in tons of $CaCO_3$ per hectare.

---

[1] In French: *"Qui chaule sans fumer, se ruine sans y penser"*.

Initially, due to their lack of knowledge on the complexity of exchange in different soils, when trying to correct soil pH agronomists systematically aimed for neutrality. The lime requirement could then be estimated from $T - S$ (T being total cation exchange capacity in buffered solution at pH 7, S being the sum of exchangeable cations).

Mehlich (1939) located the lime requirement between the exchangeable acidity extracted by a not buffered saline solution and the total acidity neutralized by a buffer solution adjusted to pH 8.1. An estimate of the exchangeable acidity per $T - S$ with T measured at soil pH also enables calculation of the quantity of calcium needed for the correction of acidity (Duchaufour and Souchier 1980).

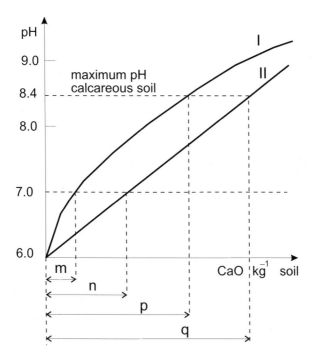

Fig. 24.1. Chaminade method (1933). I, pH values measured at To; II, pH values measured at T48 h

$$x = n \frac{q}{p - m + n} = CaO\% \text{ soil necessary for neutralization at pH 7.0}$$

$(CaCO_3/CaO) = (100/56) = 1.786$

Lime requirements can also be evaluated by titration using techniques similar to those used for the measurement of exchange acidity (cf. Chap. 23) or with pH0 and measurement of charge (cf. Chaps. 20 and 21). However, equilibrium takes a long time to establish in the soils and most acidity is not detectable by instantaneous reaction with a base. The analytical determination is influenced by the degree of weathering, the content of clay and organic matter, the forms of acidity and the initial soil pH. Thus the amount of crushed limestone measured in the laboratory in soils from Congo would not cause exactly the expected increase of pH in natural conditions (Djondo 1995). In practice, the three following types of approach are used:

– Analysis by incubation with limestone; this is a time-consuming method in which laboratory conditions closely resemble field conditions (moisture, temperature, microbial activity).
– Incubation with progressively increasing quantities of calcium hydroxide (lime water) and titration after contact of a few hours.
– Soil–buffer equilibration enabling acidity to be neutralized without subjecting the soil to a pH higher than that desired, taking into account the soil matrix and the crops to be cultivated.

Lime water methods (of which the stability is random since it is closely linked with the composition of the surrounding atmosphere) combined with measurements of pH at times T0 and T48 h (Fig. 24.1) were formerly used to correct soil acidity (Chaminade 1933). These methods have been more or less abandoned because of the temporary excessive rise in pH they cause. The procedure described in Sect. 24.2 below concerns an equilibration technique with buffer solutions.

24.2 SMP Buffer Method

24.2.1 Principle

This method was proposed by Shoemaker, McLean and Pratt (1962) which explains its name 'SMP'. A complex buffer is used with a pH close to neutral, that of carbonate–bicarbonate–CO_2 equilibrium of the soil atmosphere at normal pressure. It enables neutralization of both bases and acids and avoids variations in pH in a soil system that itself possesses buffering power. In this way, the soil is not subjected to localized increases in pH that are too high.

The pH of a solution expresses the energy level of protons, the pH of a buffer measures potential acidity. The change in pH of the buffer enables quantification of the lime requirement of soils whose initial pH water is lower than 6.0 and whose aluminic toxicity is high.

The method described here is that of the double buffer (McLean 1982; Sims 1996) partly based on the procedure of the initial SMP method

(Shoemaker, McLean and Pratt 1962) of equilibration in a buffer solution and partly on a supplement to this procedure (McLean et al. 1977, 1978).

24.2.2 Reagents

SMP buffer solution at pH 7.5
- Weigh 3.24 g of p-nitrophenol $C_6 H_5 NO_3$ (mw = 139.11).
- Weigh 5.40 g of potassium chromate $K_2 CrO_4$ (mw = 194.20).
- Weigh 95.58 g of calcium chloride dihydrate $CaCl_2 , 2H_2O$ (mw = 147.03)
  Place these in a 2 L Pyrex bottle (with a graduation mark at 1,800 mL) with approximately 900 mL water. Agitate by turning the bottle upside down and back for 5 min to avoid caking → solution A.
- Weigh 3.60 g of calcium acetate $Ca(CH_3 COO)_2 , H_2 O$, mw = 176.18 and dissolve in 500 mL of deionized water → solution B.
- Mix solution A and solution B → solution C; shake for 3 h on a rotary shaker.
- Add 4.5 mL of triethanolamine $N(CH_2 - CH_2 OH)3$ mw = 149.19 and shake for 8 h on a rotary shaker → solution D.
- Bring to 1,800 mL and adjust to pH 7.5 with a 0.2 mol (NaOH) L^{-1} solution with pH meter.
- Filter and preserve from free atmospheric carbon dioxide with a trap made from a tube filled with ascarite (asbestos impregnated with soda) between two tubes filled with drierite or anhydrite (anhydrous calcium sulphate); use rapidly.

24.2.3 Procedure

In a 50 mL centrifugation tube that can be closed hermetically:
- Weigh 5 g (equivalent weight of soil dried at 105°C) of air-dried soil sieved to 0.5 mm.
- Add 5 mL water.
- Mix and leave in contact for 1h.
- With a pH meter previously standardized between pH 7.0 and 4.0, measure the pH of the soil suspension while agitating the electrode in the fluid paste until a stable reading is reached (cf. Chap. 15) →pH water.
- Add 10 mL of SMP buffer solution to this suspension and agitate for 15 min; let stand for 15 min, agitate until stabilization and measure the pH

of the suspension → pH_1 soil–buffer; this is the pH of the suspension before addition of any acid.
- Add to the suspension an aliquot of HCl at the quantity required to bring 10 mL of buffer solution from pH 7.5 to pH 6.0 (1 mL of HCl 0.206 mol $L^{-1} = 0.206$ mmol L^{-1}.
- Agitate for 10 min – let stand for 30 min and read the pH of the suspension while agitating → pH_2 soil–buffer; this is the final pH of the soil–buffer suspension after addition of HCl acid.

The acidity "A" measured in mmol (H+) for 5 g of soil is written:

$$A = \Delta pH_2 \frac{\Delta d^o_2}{\Delta pH^0_2} + \left[\left(\Delta pH_1 \frac{\Delta d^o_1}{\Delta pH^o_1} - \Delta pH_2 \frac{\Delta d^o_2}{\Delta pH^0_2} \right) \left(\frac{6 \cdot 5 - pH_2}{pH_1 - pH_2} \right) \right],$$

where ΔpH_1 is $7.5 - pH_1$, ΔpH_2 is $6.0 - pH_2$, $\Delta d^0_1 \big/ \Delta pH^0_1$ is

change in acidity per unit change in pH of 10 mL of pH 7.5 buffer obtained by titration with standard HCl, i.e. approximately 0.137 mmol per unit of pH,

$$\Delta d^0_2 \big/ \Delta pH^0_2 = \text{change in acidity per unit change in pH of}$$

10 mL of pH 6 buffer, i.e. approximately 0.129 mmol per unit of pH,
6.5 is the desired pH of the soil after liming (another pH can be selected).

The lime requirement (LR) is expressed in the laboratory by:
LR in cmol (+) $kg^{-1} = 1.69 (20\ A) - 0.86 = 33.8\ A - 0.86$
and in field units at a depth of 20 cm:
LR in ton $ha^{-1} = 45.5\ A - 1.16$.

24.2.4 Remarks

This method takes total H^+, and soluble and exchangeable aluminum into account. It is suitable for soils which require lime correction of more than 1 ton per hectare (soil depth of 20 cm) whose pH is lower than 5.8–6.0.

The content of organic matter should not exceed about 15%. It is not usually necessary to make this measurement on soils with a pH of more than 6.0, as in this case the soil does not require liming, but possibly calcic fertilizer. Very organic soils are only significantly improved by liming if their pH is lower than 5.3.

The method of Adams and Evans (1962) is also a rapid technique for equilibration in buffer solution (pH 8.0), it is often used in sandy soils or soils with low organic matter contents.

References

Adams F and Evans CE (1962) A rapid method for measuring lime requirement of red-yellow podzolic soils. *Soil Sci. Soc. Am. Proc.*, 26, 355–357.

Chaminade R (1933) Mode d'action de la chaux sur les sols et correction de leur activité. *Ann. Agron.*, 453–477.

Davy H (1813) *Elements of agricultural chemistry.*, Longman éd.

Djondo MY (1995) *Propriétés d'échange ionique des sols ferrallitiques argileux de la vallée du Niari et sableux du plateau Mbe-Bateke au Congo - application à la correction de leur acidité.*, Thèse, Document IRD (ex-Orstom) Montpellier, France, 5.

Mclean EO, Trieweiler JF and Eckert DJ (1977) Improved SMP buffer method for determining lime requirement in acid soils. *Commun. Soil Sc. Plant Anal.*, 8, 667–675.

McLean EO, Eckert DJ, Reddy GY and Trierweiler JF (1978) An improved SMP soil lime requirement method incorporating double-buffer and quick-test features. *Soil Sci. Soc. Am. J.*, 42, 311–316.

McLean EO (1982) Soil pH and lime requirement. In *Methods of soil analysis. Part 2. Chemical and microbiological properties* 2nd edition), Page AL ed., *Am. Soc. Agronomy., Soil Sci. Soc. Am.*, 199–224.

Shoemaker HE, McLean, EO and Pratt PF (1962) Buffer methods for determination of lime requirement of soils with appreciable amount of exchangeable aluminium. *Soil Sci. Soc. Am. Proc.*, 25, 274–277.

Sims JT (1996) Lime requirement. In *Methods of soil analysis. Part 3. Chemical methods*, Bigham JM and Bartels JM, *Soil Sci. Soc. Am., Am. Soc. Agronomy*, Madison, WI, 491–515.

Mehlich A (1939) Use of triethanolanine acetate-baryum hydroxide buffer for the determination of some base-exchange properties and lime requirement of soil. *Soil Sci. Soc. Am. Proc.*, 3, 162–166.

Chronobibliography

Davy H (1813) *Elements of agricultural chemistry.*, Longman, éd.

Clark JS and Nichol WE (1966) The lime potential, percent base saturation relations of acid surface horizons of mineral and organic soils. *Can. J. Soil Sci.*, 46, 281–315.

Collins JB, Whiteside EP and Cress CE (1970) Seasonal variability of pH and lime requirements in several southern Michigan soils when measured in different ways. *Soil Sci. Soc. Am. Proc.*, 34, 56–61.

Kamprath EJ (1970) Exchangeable aluminium as a criterion for liming leached mineral soils. *Soil Sci. Soc. Am. Proc.*, 34, 252–254.

McLean EO (1970) Lime requirements of soils. In active toxic substances or favorable pH range ? *Soil Sci. Soc. Am. Proc.*, 34, 363–364.

CAB (1971) Annotated bibliography no 1529. *Liming of tropical soils*, 1971–1959. CAB : 25 pages, 101 references.

Yuan TL (1974) A double buffer method for the determination of lime requirement of acid soils. *Soil Sci. Soc. Am. J.*, 38, 437–440.

Almeida de AM and Bornemisza E (1977) Efecto del encalado sobre las carqas electricas y otros propriedades quimicas de tres inceptisoles de Costa-Rica. *Turrialba*, 27, 333–342.

McLean EO (1978) Principles underlying the practice of determining lime requirements of acid soils by use of buffer methods. *Commun. Soil Sci. Plant Anal.*, 9, 699–715.

Cochrane TT, Salinas JG and Sanchez RA (1980) An equation for liming acid mineral soils to compensate crop aluminium tolerance. *Trop. Agric.*, 57, 133–139.

Duchaufour P and Souchier B (1980) pH et besoins en chaux. *C. R. Acad. Agric. (Fr.)*, 66, 391–399.

Totev TP, Palaveyev TD and Kolarov V (1982) Advantages of a KCl extracts for determining soil acidity and liming requirements. *Pochvovedeniye*, 3, 117–120.

Nômmik H (1983) A modified procedure for rapid determination of titrable acidity and lime requirement in soils. *Acta Agric. Scand.*, 33, 337–348.

Oates KM and Kamprath EJ (1983) Soil acidity and liming. I : effect of the extracting solution cation and pH on the removal of aluminium from acid soils. *Soil Sci. Soc. Am. J.*, 47, 686–689.

Oates KM and Kamprath EJ (1983) Soil acidity and liming. II - Evaluation of using aluminum extracted by various chloride salts for determining lime requirements. *Soil Sci. Soc. Am. J.*, 47, 690–692.

Pavan MA, Bingham FT and Pratt PF (1984) Redistribution of exchangeable calcium, magnesium, and aluminum following lime or gypsum applications to a brazilian oxisol. *Soil Sci. Soc. Am. J.*, 48, 33–38.

Haile A, Pieri C and Egoumenides C (1985) Effet des amendements minéraux sur les propriétés d'échange de sols acides tropicaux. *Agron. Trop.*, 40, 98–106.

Alva AK, Edwards DG, Asher CJ and Blamey FPC (1986) Effects of phosphorus/aluminum molar ratio and calcium concentration on plant response to aluminum toxicity. *Soil Sci. Soc. Am. J.*, 50, 113–137.

Harvey KC and Dollhoph D (1986) *Acid mine-soil reclamation advancements in the Northen plains.*, Montana State Univ. Res. Publ. (01).

Meng Ci-Fu, Luu Yong-Jin, Kong Fan-Gen and Shui jian-Guo (1986) Effects of limestone on soil acidity and cropyields on a red earth. *Soil Science Society of China. Current progress in soil research in people's republic of China*, 377–383.

Borges AL, Braga JM, Defelipo BV, Ribeiro AC and Thiebaut JTL (1987) Evaluation of analytical methods for estimating soil liming requirement. *Revista Cérés*, 34, 17–32.

Nobrega de MT (1988) *Contribuiçao ao estudo da estabilizaçao de solos tropicais com adiçao de cal para fins rodoviarios. Aspectos mineralogicos e morfologicos de alguns solos das regioes sul e sudeste do Brasil.*, Dissertaçao de maetrado University Sao Paulo, 189 p.

Bailey JS, Stevens RJ and Kilpatrick DJ (1989) A rapid method for predicting the lime requirement of acidic temperate soils with widely varying organic matter contents : I - development of the lime requirement model. *J. Soil Sci.*, 40, 807–820.

Naidu R, Syers JK, Tillman RW and Kirkman JH (1990) Effect of liming and added phosphate on charge characteristics of acid soils. *J. Soil Sci.*, 41, 157–164.

Rossi PL, Ildefonse P, Nobrega de AT and Chauvel A (1990) Transformations mineralogiques et structurales d'argiles latéritiques brésiliennes provoquées par l'addition de chaux. In *ORSTOM Séminaire «Organisation et fonctionnement des altérites et des sols.*, (5 fév.) Thème 5 (multigraphié).

Aitken RL, Moody PW, Dickson T, Date RA (ed.), Grundon NJ (ed.); Rayment G.E. (ed.), Probert ME (1995). In *Plant–soil interactions at low pH: principles and management. Proceedings of the Third International Symposium, Brisbane.*, Kluwer; Dordrecht, 479–484.

Tsakelidou R (1995) Comparison of lime requirement methods on acid soils of northern Greece. *Commun. Soil Sci. Plant Anal.*, 26, 541–551.

Owusu-Bennoah E, Acquaye DK, Mahamah T (1995) Comparative study of selected lime requirement methods for some acid Ghanaian soils. *Commun. Soil Sci. Plant Anal.*, 26, 937–950.

Coutinho J (1997) Calibration of the single- and double- buffer SMP lime requirement methods by root elongation biossay, *Commun. Soil Sci. Plant Anal.*, 28, 1127–1139.

Pottker D and Ben JR (1998) Lime for a crop rotation under direct planting. Calagem para uma rotacao de culturas no sistema plantio direto. *Revista Brasileira de Ciencia do Solo*, 22, 675–684.

Quigley MN, Wallace A (ed.) and Terry RE (1998) Testing soils for lime requirement. In *Handbook of soil conditioners: substances that enhance the physical properties of soil*, Dekker, New York, 293–308.

Rossel RAV and McBraney AB (1998) A response-surface calibration model for rapid and versatile site-specific lime-requirement predictions in south-eastern Australia, *Aust. J. Soil Res.*, 2001, 39, 185–201.

Gustafsson K and Stafford JV (1999) Models for precision application of lime. In *Precision agriculture, Papers-presented at the 2nd European*

Conference on Precision Agriculture, Odense, Denmark, 11–15 July 1999, Sheffield Academic, Sheffield, UK.

Pintro JC and Tescaro MD (1999) Correction of an acid soil using the base saturation method and influence on chemical parameters. *Acta Scientiarum*, 21, 479–482.

Rajkhowa KM and Talukdar MC (1999) Lime requirement of soils as influenced by soil test methods, *J. Agri. Sci. Soc. North East India*, 12, 9–12.

Rossel RAV, McBratney AB and Stafford JV (1999) Calibration of a lime requirement buffer for site-specific lime applications in South-Eastern Australia. In *Precision agriculture, Papers-presented at the 2nd European Conference on Precision Agriculture*, Odense, Denmark, 11–15 July 1999, Sheffield Academic, Sheffield, UK.

Martins E de S, Linhares NW, Giustina C and de S Martins E (2000) Rock analysis reference method for correcting soil acidity. Metodo de referencia para caracterizacao de rochas utilizadas como corretivos de acidez do solo. Comunicado-Tecnico -Embrapa-Cerrados., No.38, 3 p.

Gilmour JT and Anderson P (2001) A new approach to lime recommendations in Arkansas. *Res. Ser. Arkansas Agri. Exp. Station*, 480, 39–41.

Ozenc DB and Mehlenbacher SA (2001) Methods of determining lime requirements of soils in the Eastern Black Sea hazelnut growing region. *Acta Horticulturae*, 556, 335–341.

Exchange Selectivity, Cation Exchange Isotherm

25.1 Introduction

The study of the adsorption-desorption properties of the exchange complex by measurement of exchangeable cations (cf. Chap. 22) can be supplemented by the measurement of exchange selectivity which enables a better understanding of the exchange processes during soil weathering.

When a soil is subjected to cycles of leaching–retention, the state of the exchange complex can be measured by evaluating the retention of exchangeable cations. This measurement only indirectly reflects the possible selectivity of a system for a given element. Indeed, if the exchange properties of the soils were only under the influence of the concentration and the charge of the cations, the ratios between cations fixed on the complex would be identical to the ratios of the same cations in solution. The soluble elements of the parent rock would then be fixed at their respective concentrations. Other factors occur that modify the retention properties of two cations (or anions) A and B whose charge is identical:

$$\frac{A \quad solution}{B \quad solution} = K \frac{A \quad adsorbed}{B \quad adsorbed}$$

where K is the selectivity coefficient. It expresses the inequality of the activity ratios of A and B ions in solution and adsorbed.

By measuring the changes in composition of the adsorbed phase and of the liquid phase containing ions added in given proportions, an exchange isotherm can be built. The term isotherm, which refers to thermodynamics, should not mask other significant variables of the system such as ion valences and concentrations, the degree of hydration, the density of charges of colloids. An isotherm is a partition diagram which results in a graph of the balance of ion concentrations between an ionic liquid phase and a solid exchange matrix at constant ionic strength. The ionic strength of the liquid phase or the temperature can also be changed to determine thermodynamic parameters.

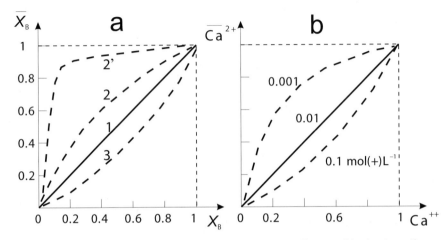

Fig. 25.1. (a) Exchange isotherm at constant concentrations and ionic strength:

$\bar{X}_B = f(X_B)$, where $\bar{X}_B$ equivalent fraction of the B ion retained by the exchanger and X_B equivalent fraction of the B ion in solution. 1, linear isotherm - no selectivity, same affinity for ions A and B. 2, selectivity for A. 2', strong selectivity for A. 3, selectivity for B (Sometimes S-curves can be observed with inversion of selectivity starting from a certain concentration. The curve then crosses 1 at the inversion point), **(b)** isotherm variable with concentration and ionic force (dilution effect) ex: Na^+ homoionic system and displacement Na^+-Ca^{2+}. The variability of the selectivity coefficient with the ionic strength of the solution poses a problem for the portion of the equations concerning the liquid phase

As shown in Fig. 25.1a and b, only graphs plotted under the same conditions of temperature, concentration and ionic force should be compared in order to avoid erroneous interpretation. Measurement of the ion moved during adsorption in a homoionic system enables the constancy of the cation exchange capacity to be verified.

The soil components form an inorganic and organic complex exchange matrix including reactions that are often very different. This analysis can be performed either on the whole soil or on fractions selected by granulometry and/or chemical treatments.

All exchange selectivity equations take the ratios of the ion activities in solution into account. The law of the exchange ratios of Schofield (1967) specifies the conditions of selectivity of the mono-, di- and trivalent ions.

Since studies by Kerr (1928), many empirical equations have been established, improved or simplified to make them suitable for different soil situations and to attempt to replicate field conditions under a variety of mineralogical and climatic constraints.

The Kerr equation (1928)

$$K_{\text{Kerr}} = \frac{\left[M^{y+}_{\text{adsorbed}} \right]^x \left[M^{x+}_{\text{solution}} \right]^y}{\left[M^{x+}_{\text{adsorbed}} \right]^y \left[M^{y+}_{\text{solution}} \right]^x}$$

is for a heterovalent system (M^+ is the monovalent cation and M^{2+} is the divalent cation)

$$K_{\text{Kerr}} = \frac{\left[M^{+}_{\text{adsorbed}} \right]^2 \left[M^{2+}_{\text{solution}} \right]}{\left[M^{2+}_{\text{adsorbed}} \right] \left[M^{+}_{\text{solution}} \right]^2}.$$

In the processes of heterovalent exchange, modification of the Kerr equation by Vanselow (1932) allows the cumulated activities of the ions to be taken into account:

$$K_{\text{Vanselow}} = \frac{\left[M^{y+}_{\text{adsorbed}} \right]^x \left[M^{x+}_{\text{solution}} \right]^y}{\left[M^{x+}_{\text{adsorbed}} \right]^y \left[M^{y+}_{\text{solution}} \right]^x} \left[M^{y+}_{\text{adsorbed}} + M^{x+}_{\text{adsorbed}} \right]^{y-x}$$

for example in a Ca^{2+}–NH_4^+ system:

$$K_v = \frac{\left[NH_{4\ \text{adsorbed}}^{+} \right]^2 \left[Ca^{2+}_{\text{solution}} \right]}{\left[Ca^{2+}_{\text{adsorbed}} \right] \left[NH_{4\ \text{solution}}^{+} \right]^2} \cdot \frac{1}{\left[Ca^{2+}_{\text{adsorbed}} + NH_{4\ \text{adsorbed}}^{+} \right]}.$$

Following statistical studies, this equation was again modified by Krishnamoorthy and Overstreet (1949) by assigning variable coefficients to the ions according to valence, which gave the general equation:

$$K_{\text{K-O}} = \frac{\left[M^{y+}_{\text{adsorbed}} \right]^x \left[M^{x+}_{\text{solution}} \right]^y}{\left[M^{x+}_{\text{adsorbed}} \right]^y \left[M^{y+}_{\text{solution}} \right]^x} \left[a\ M^{x+}_{\text{adsorbed}} + a\ M^{y+}_{\text{adsorbed}} \right]^{y-x},$$

where $a = 1$ for the monovalent cations, 1.5 for the divalent cations, and 2.0 for the trivalent cations. In a system of di- and monovalent ions:

$$K_{\text{K-O}} = \frac{\left[M^{2+}_{\text{solution}} \right] \left[M^{+}_{\text{adsorbed}} \right]^2}{\left[M^{+}_{\text{solution}} \right]^2 \left[M^{2+}_{\text{adsorbed}} \right]} \cdot \frac{1}{\left[M^{+}_{\text{adsorbed}} + 1,5\ M^{2+}_{\text{adsorbed}} \right]}.$$

To correct the solvent effects in the Kerr formula, Gaines and Thomas (1983) introduced a factor that took into account the fraction of the sites occupied by a cation A and molar quantities of adsorbed cations.

$$K_{G-T} = \frac{\left[M^{y+}_{adsorbed}\right]^x \left[M^{x+}_{solution}\right]^y}{\left[M^{x+}_{adsorbed}\right]^y \left[M^{y+}_{solution}\right]^x} \quad \frac{x}{y} \quad \left[x\, M^{x+}_{adsorbed} + y\, M^{y+}_{adsorbed}\right]^{y-x}$$

$$= \frac{x}{y}\, K_{Kerr} \left[x\, M^{x+}_{adsorbed} + y\, M^{y+}_{adsorbed}\right]^{y-x}$$

in a binary heterovalent system:

$$K_{G-T} = \frac{\left[M^{2+}_{solution}\right]\left[M^{+}_{adsorbed}\right]^2}{\left[M^{+}_{solution}\right]^2 \left[M^{2+}_{adsorbed}\right]} \quad \frac{1}{2 \left[M^{+}_{adsorbed} + 2\, M^{2+}_{adsorbed}\right]}.$$

All these equations are based on molar expression. The coefficient of Gapon (1933) was also widely used, but was subject to criticism (Sposito, 1977) because it was based on an expression in equivalents:

$$K_{Gapon} = \frac{\left[M^{y+}_{adsorbed}\right]}{\left[M^{x+}_{adsorbed}\right]} \frac{\left(M^{x+}\right)^{1/x}}{\left(M^{y+}\right)^{1/y}}$$

is in a 1–2 system:

$$K_{Gapon} = \frac{\left[M^{+}_{adsorbed}\right]}{\left[M^{2+}_{1/2\ adsorbed}\right]} \frac{\left(M^{2+}_{solution}\right)^{1/2}}{\left(M^{+}_{solution}\right)}.$$

Selectivity equations were established for certain soils with specific problems, for example saline soils (sodic–salic) with Na^+, Ca^{2+}, Mg^{2+} systems (Richards, 1954; cf. Chap. 18). An equation for sodium adsorption ratio (SAR) is used:

$$SAR_{(mmoles\ L^{-1})} = \frac{\left[Na^+\right]}{\left(\left[Mg^{2+}\right]+\left[Ca^{2+}\right]\right)^{1/2}}.$$

Generally, SAR is given simultaneously with the exchangeable sodium ratio (ESR).

$$ESR_{(cmol\ Kg^{-1})} = \frac{Na_{ech}}{CEC - Na_{ech}}$$

In K^+, Ca^{2+}, Mg^{2+} systems a nonreversible exchange or a nonlinear exchange is often observed, often with low rates of K^+ compared to Ca^{2+} and Mg^{2+}. The potassium adsorption ratio (KAR or PAR) can enable interpretation of the effects of liming (cf. Chap. 24) on the activity ratios and K^+ release. Affinity order, often called lyotropic series, can be modified by the mineral matrix, for example 2:1 smectites preferentially adsorb the least hydrated cations likely to be fixed in the interfoliaceous cavities.

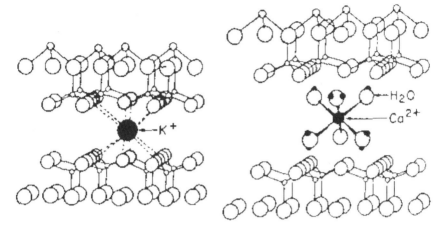

Fig. 25.2. Adsorption of K^+ and Ca^{2+} (Sposito 1984): inner-sphere surface complex of potassium in vermiculite *(left)*, outer-sphere surface complex of calcium in montmorillonite *(right)*.

In practice, the exchange complex of anthropic soils can be modified by selectively adsorbed anions (e.g. phosphate-enriched fertilizers), elimination of organic matter by burning or deforestation, changes in oxide contents, etc. This can lead to different relative equilibration rates which have to be measured in agronomical and soil genesis studies. Modifications in the relative concentrations of cations in the soil solution also modify the trophic capacity per unit of time. This selectivity is due to reactions governed by chemical thermodynamics.

For example with monovalent ions and 2:1 smectites there is no selectivity if the adsorption mechanisms only use outer-sphere surface complexes (for example calcium hexahydrated ion in montmorillonite, Fig. 25.2). On the other hand, if inner-sphere complexes are formed (inclusion of potassium ion in vermiculite for example), there is necessarily exchange between water molecules of cation solvation and the hydroxyl ions of surface functional groups.

The complexes with inner-sphere surface, which are more stable, form a Lewis base with the monovalent cations, which are rather weak acids because of their solvation by water molecules. The ionization energy and the ionic radius of the monovalent cations give the sequence: $Cs^+ > Rb^+ > K^+ \cong NH_4^+ > Na^+ > Li^+$ for the stability of the complexes with inner-sphere surface formed in the siloxane cavities.

For di- or plurivalent cations, the problem is more complex, cations can present different valences depending on redox conditions of the medium, and a complex of the ligand type can be neo-formed in the soluble phase (congruent and incongruent isotherms). Ca^{2+} and Mg^{2+} can produce $CaCl^+$ and $MgCl^+$ complexes presenting higher affinities than the free Ca^{2+} and Mg^{2+} cations. The selectivity of Ca on Mg could be explained by the better thermodynamic stability of $CaCl^+$ (Sposito et al. 1983).

25.2 Determination of the Exchange Isotherm

25.2.1 Principle

The different points of the isotherm are plotted by means of a not buffered ionic binary liquid phase whose total equivalent concentration is constant (Sondag et al. 1990). In this binary mixture, each ion can react alone or in relation to the other ions. For each point, the proportion of the two cations is variable. After saturation of the sample, allow it to reach equilibrium (at the end of cation adsorption), then desorb the two cations with a counter-ion. Titrate the two cations by atomic absorption or inductively coupled plasma spectrometry and plot the isotherm, using the model with two sites (Duffey and Delvaux 1989) which enables a realistic approach to the functioning of the soil when it is subjected to variable hydrous and chemical constraints.

25.2.2 Reagents

First solution of equilibration–saturation (K^+–Ca^{2+} equilibrium). From potassium chloride (mw = 74.56), prepare a 1 mol (KCl) L^{-1} solution and from anhydrous calcium chloride (mw = 110.99) a 1 mol $(CaCl_2)$ L^{-1} solution. Prepare K–Ca stock solutions 1 mol (+) L^{-1} corresponding to the $\frac{K}{\sqrt{Ca}}$ ratios in Table 25.1.

Second K–Ca equilibration solutions. Prepare as above but with 0.01 mol (+) L^{-1} solutions (Table 25.1).

Desorption solution 1 mol L^{-1} ammonium chloride prepared from NH_4Cl (mw = 53.49)

Standard solution: ranges
  K^+ 0–6 mg L^{-1},
  Ca^{2+} 0–6 mg L^{-1},
  Al^{3+} 0–1 mg L^{-1}.

Table 25.1. Composition of equilibration solutions (total normality = 0.01 (+) L^{-1}; N_K and N_{Ca} = K and Ca normalities)

$K/\sqrt{Ca}$ (mol $L^{-1})^{1/2}$	K(mmol L^{-1})	Ca(mmol L^{-1})	N_K (Meq (+) L^{-1})	N_{Ca} (meq (+) L^{-1})
0.2	0.44	4.78	0.44	9.56
0.4	0.86	4.57	0.86	9.14
0.8	1.64	4.18	1.64	8.36
1.6	2.99	3.50	2.99	7.01
2.4	4.12	2.94	4.12	5.88
3.2	5.04	2.48	5.04	4.96
6.6	7.45	1.27	7.45	2.55
29.6	9.78	0.11	9.78	0.22

22.2.3 Procedure

– Tare a series of eight 50 mL centrifugation tubes
– weigh 3 g of air-dried soil in each tube.

First Equilibration

– In each tube, add 25 mL of K + Ca 1 mol (+) L^{-1} solution with a $K/\sqrt{Ca}$ ratio corresponding to the isotherm to be determined
– shake for 1 h, centrifuge and decant the supernatant
– wash quickly with deionised water to put the centrifugation pellet in suspension
– centrifuge; repeat this treatment twice.

Isotherm Measurement

– Carry out six successive equilibrations with 25 mL of 0.01 mol (+) L^{-1} K–Ca solution with a $K/\sqrt{Ca}$ ratio corresponding to that of the isotherm to be determined (with no intermediate washing with water)
– for each equilibration, maintain contact for 30 min
– centrifuge at 5,000g
– after the sixth equilibration, titrate K and/or Ca and continue equilibrations if the value is different from that of the corresponding exchange solution (a simple check of equality of spectrometric absorbance is sufficient)
– when equilibrium is reached, determine the exact K and Ca concentration (which is always a little different from the initial concentration) and measure aluminium in order to check that it is not involved in the exchange (concentration $< 10^{-5}$–10^{-7} mol L^{-1}).

Desorption

– After the last centrifugation, weigh the centrifugation tube in order to determine the quantity of solution trapped in the centrifugation pellet
– add 20 mL of 1 mol (NH_4Cl) L^{-1} solution; agitate for 2 h
– centrifuge and decant the supernatant in a 100 mL volumetric flask
– repeat desorption twice each time leaving the suspension in contact for 1 h
– complete the total extract to 100 mL with deionised water

Titration

– Titrate K, Ca and Al and subtract the concentration of the trapped solution to determine the K/K + Ca point of the isotherm.
– K and Ca should be titrated ten times by atomic absorption spectrometry using a diluted range from 0 to 6 mg L^{-1} with addition of lanthanum; Al is titrated by inductively coupled plasma spectrometry or spectro-colorimetry (Pansu et al. 2001).

25.2.4 Remarks

The soil exchange complex is a composite unit which does not be considered to present uniform surfaces with homogeneous densities of charge.

The influence of organic matter on the surface properties can be studied on samples before and after destruction of organic matter. Each granulometric phase (sands, silts, coarse clays, clays <0.2 µm) can present very different selectivity (Sondag et al. 1990).

The economic importance of the calcium–potassium exchanges led to many studies that attempted to explain the adsorption of K in the presence of Ca more satisfactorily (Beckett and Nafady 1967, Goulding and Talibudeen 1980, Escudey and Galindo 1988, Rhue and Mansell 1988, Dufey and Delvaux 1989, Sondag et al. 1990).

Simultaneous estimation of the cation exchange capacity and the coefficients of exchange selectivity starting from disturbed or undisturbed soil columns was attempted using different mono- and divalent binary systems (e.g. Scheich et al. 1983, Parker et al. 1984, Kool et al. 1989).

The development of data-processing models now enables the study of the transfer of ionic species in soil–ion exchanges. These methods can be used for ions that are usually taken into account in the determination of exchangeable cations and cation exchange capacity: the simplest model with two cations is then sufficient (Duffey and Delvaux, 1989). In environmental studies, more sophisticated multi-species models may be necessary to measure – for example – the migration of heavy metals in field soil conditions, as these can pollute the groundwater (Mansell et al. 1986).

References

Beckett PHT and Nafady MHM (1967) Potassium-calcium exchange equilibria in soils : the location of non specific gapon and specific exchange sites. *J. Soil Sci.*, 18, 263–281

Delvaux B (1988) *Constituants et propriétés de surface des sols dérivés de pyroclastes basaltiques du Cameroun occidental. Approche génétique de leur fertilité.*, Thèse UCL Fac. Sc. Agron., 335 p

Duffey JE and Delvaux B (1989) Modeling potassium–calcium exchange isotherms in soils. *Soil Sci. Soc. A. J.*, 53, 1297–1299

Escudey M and Galindo G (1988) Potassium–calcium exchange on inorganic clay fractions of Chilean andepts. *Géoderma*, 41, 275–285

Gapon EN (1933) Theory of exchange adsorption in soils. *J. Gen. Chem.*, USSR, 3, 144

Goulding KWT and Talibudeen O (1980) Heterogeneicity of cation exchange sites for Ca–Mg exchange in alumino-silicates. *J. Colloid Interface Sci.*, 78, 15–24

Kerr HW (1928) The identification and composition of the soil aluminosilicate active in base exchange and soil acidity. *Soil Sci.*, 26, 385

Kool JB, Parker JC and Zelazny LW (1989) On the estimation of cation exchange parameters from column displacement experiments. *Soil Sci. Soc. Am. J.*, 53, 1347–1355

Krishna Moorthy C and Overstreet R (1949) Theory of ion-exchange relation ships. *Soil Sci.*, 68, 307

Mansell RS, Bloom SA, Rhue RD and Selim HM (1986) Multispecies cation leaching during continuous displacement of electrolyte solutions through soil columns. *Geoderma,* 38, 61–75

Pansu M, Gautheyrou J and Loyer JY (2001) *Soil analysis – sampling, instrumentation and quality control.*, Balkema, Lisse, Abington, Exton, Tokyo, 489 pp.

Parker JC and Genuchten MTh van (1984) Determining transport parameters from laboratory and field tracer experiments. *Virg. Univ. Agric. Exp. Station*, 84, 3

Rhue RD and Mansell RS (1988) The effect of pH on sodium-calcium and potassium–calcium exchange selectivity for Cecil soil. *Soil Sci. Soc. Am. J.*, 52, 641–647

Richards LA (1954) *Diagnosis and improvement of saline and alkali soils.*, USDA, Agriculture Handbook, 60, 160 p

Schweich D, Sardin M and Gaudet JP (1983) Measurement of a cation exchange isotherme from solution curves obtained in a soil column – preliminary results. *Soil Sci. Soc. Am. J.,* 47, 32–37

Sondag F, Feller C and Delcambre L (1990) Etude de la sélectivité d'échange K-Ca dans divers sols tropicaux. Effet de la matière organique. In *ORSTOM – Journées Laboratoires (Bondy, France)*, 127–138

Sposito G (1977) The Gapon and Vanselow selectivity coefficients. *Soil Sci. Soc. Am. J.*, 41, 1205

Sposito G, Hotzclaw KM, Jouany C and Charlet L (1983) Cation selectivity of sodium–calcium, sodium–magnesium and calcium–magnesium exchange on Wyoming bentonite at 298 K. *Soil Sci. Soc. Am. J.*, 47, 917–921

Sposito G (1984) *The surface chemistry of soils.* Oxford University Press, 234 p

Vanselow AP (1932) Equilibria of the base-exchange reactions of bentonites, permutites, soil colloids and zolites. *Soil Sci.*, 33, 95

Chronobibliography

Schofield RK (1947) A ratio law governing the equilibrium of cations in the soil solution. *Proc. 11th Int. Congr. Pure Appl. Chem.*, 3, 257

Gaines GL Jr and Thomas HC (1953) Adsorption studies on clay minerals. II, A formulation of the thermodynamics of exchange adsorption. *J. Chem. Phys.*, 21, 714

Assa A (1976) Phénomène de sélectivité d'échange cationique dans certains minéraux argileux. I – La sélectivité du potassium dans un système potassium–calcium. *Cahiers ORSTOM – Sér. Pédol.*, XIV, 219–226

Delvaux B (1988) *Constituants et propriétés de surface des sols dérivés de pyroclastes basaltiques du Cameroun occidental. Approche génétique de leur fertilité.* Thèse Un. Cat. Louvain Fac. Sc. Agron., 335 p

Fontaine S, Delvaux B, Dufey JE and Herbillon AJ (1989) Potassium exchange behaviour in Carribean volcanic ash soil under banana cultivation. *Plant Soil*, 120, 283–290

Bond WJ and Phillips JR (1990) Cation exchange isotherms obtained with batch and miscible displacement techniques. *Soil Sci. Soc. Am. J.*, 54, 722–728

Phillips IR and Black AS (1991) Predicting exchangeable cation distributions in soil by using exchange coefficients and solution activity ratios. *Austr. J. Soil Res.*, 29, 403–414

Ishiguro M (1992) Ion transport in soil with ion exchange reaction: effect of distribution ratio. *Soil Sci. Soc. of Am. J.*, 56, 1738–1743

Wada SI, Matsuura T and Seki H (1993) Prediction of cation exchange isotherms at different total cationic concentrations. *Soil Sci. and Plant Nutri.*, 39, 183–187

Baruah TC, Raj Pal, Poonia SR and Siyag RS (1995) Calcium-potassium, ammonium-potassium and calcium-ammonium exchange equilibria in soils of semi-arid region of Haryana and humid region of Assam. *J. of Potass. Res.*, 11, 277–290

Bond WJ (1995) On the Rothmund-Kornfeld description of cation exchange. *Soil Sci. Soc. Am. J.*, 59, 436–443

Siantar DP and Fripiat JJ (1995) Lead retention and complexation in a magnesium smectite (hectorite). *J. Colloid Interface Sci.*, 169, 400–407

Borah N, Baruah TC, Patgiri DK and Thakur AC (1996) Exchange equilibria of calcium versus aluminium, potassium and ammonium in Alfisols of Assam. In *Proceedings of the Seminar on Problems and Prospects of Agricultural Research and Development in North-East India.*, Assam Agricultural University, Jorhat, India, 27–28 November 1995, 204–212

Butcher B, Hinz C, Gfeller M and Fluhler H (1996) Cadmium transport in an unsaturated stony subsoil monolith. *Soil Sci. Soc. Am. J.*, 60, 716–721

Mukhopadhyay SS (1996) Calcium-potassium exchange and thermodynamics in micaceous soils. *J. Potassium Res.*, 12, 1–13

Sumner ME and Miller WP (1996) Cation exchange capacity and exchange coefficients. In *Methods of soil analysis, part 3, chemical methods*, Bigham JM and Bartels JM ed., SSSA-ASA, Madison, WI Etats-Unis, 1201–1229

Shen SiYan, Tu Shu I and Kemper WD (1997) Equilibrium and kinetic study of ammonium adsorption and fixation in sodium-treated vermiculite. *Soil Sci. Soc. Am. J.*, 61, 1611–1618

Moog HC, Streck T and Cammenga HK (1998) Modeling Ca/K exchange kinetics on montmorillonite and vermiculite. *Soil Sci.*, 163, 382–393

Endo T, Yamamoto S, Honna T, Eneji AE (2002) Sodium–calcium exchange selectivity as influenced by clay minerals and composition. *Soil Science*, 167, 117–125

Saeki, K, Wada SI, Shibata M (2004) $Ca^{2+}-Fe^{2+}$ and $Ca^{2+}-Mn^{2+}$ exchange selectivity of kaolinite, montmorillonite and illite. *Soil Science*, 169, 125–132

Cation Exchange Capacity

26.1 Introduction

26.1.1 Theoretical Aspects

Like pH measurement or analysis of exchangeable cations (cf. Chap. 22), cation exchange capacity (CEC) is an essential measurement in agronomy and soil science to estimate the physicochemical state of a soil. It enables distinctions to be made in the classification of certain soils like oxisols, alfisols or ultisols.

In precisely defined conditions (particularly pH) it expresses the potential quantity of cations likely to neutralize the negative charges of a soil. Converted into cmol (+) kg^{-1}, these results allow comparison of the agronomic value of soils and exchange complexes that developed under different climates and inorganic or organic matrices.

As the colloidal fraction of the soil has a very large electrically charged surface, it can retain varying quantities of cations and anions, which enables some groundwater and air pollution to be avoided and also represents a source of nutrients for plants. The complex interactions of permanent and variable surface charges limit variations in the soil pH under the influence of chemical and biological factors that result in a buffering power. When the concentration of the soil solution stored in the micropores decreases, the exchange complex releases ions to equilibrate the system. The equations concerning the exchange phenomena have in common a constant relationship between adsorbed cations and free cations in solution (law of mass action, Gapon theory, Donnan equilibrium, etc.).

Soil negative charges are the result of isomorphic substitutions in phyllosilicate structures, non-compensated bonds at the edges of reticular plans, or dissociation of functional organic groups (cf. Chap. 19). These charges can be schematically divided into (a) permanent or fixed charges, which are independent of the pH, valence and nature of the counter-ion, soil-to-solution ratio and (b) variable charges, which depend closely on the pH and on all the parameters that characterize the liquid and solid mediums and the interface of the two phases:

– Concentration, nature, valence, ionic strength, dissociation constant of the reagent, nature of the anion associated with the index ion, temperature, contact time, exchange kinetics, soil-to-solution ratio, and the polymers and complexes that can be formed;

– Dielectric constant of the medium, preliminary drying of the sample, crushing, surface potential of the adsorbent, nature of the surfaces and charges, preferential or selective adsorptions.

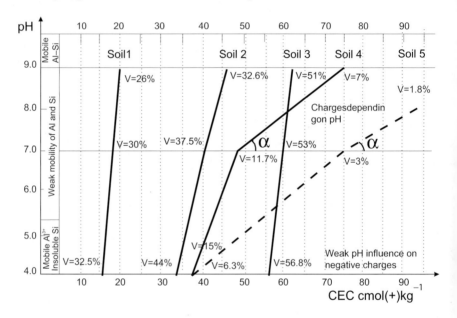

Fig. 26.1. Effect of pH on CEC measurement and on calculation of the saturation percent V (26.1) for some tropical soils of different texture (Gautheyrou and Gautheyrou 1981): soil 1, ferrallitic soil with kaolinite from Guadeloupe; soil 2, eutrophic soil with halloysite from Martinique; soil 3, vertisol with acid montmorillonite from Martinique; soils 4 and 5, andosols from Costa Rica α, strong predominance of Allophane

Methods for measuring CEC thus depend on measuring conditions, and the constraints are more obvious than for the measurement of exchangeable cations. For publication in abstract bulletins, the method used should be justified, and the reference state of the exchange matrix specified, i.e. total untreated soil, pretreated sample (e.g. drying, crushing, destruction of organic matter, elimination of soluble salts, iron removal, homoionic treatment for clay saturation). Results without these precise details are only of limited value.

In the past, it was common practice to characterize the adsorbing complex and to evaluate potential fertility by the saturation rate "V" obtained by the ratio of the exchangeable cations S (sum of Ca^{2+}, Mg^{2+}, K^+ Na^+) and the CEC T:

$$V = 100\frac{S}{T} \qquad (26.1)$$

with S and T in cmol (+) kg^{-1} (soil).

This rate of saturation is unfortunately very variable and is also subject to errors in the estimation of CEC generated by the choice of pH for extraction, the initial soil pH, the nature of the exchange complex and charges. Figure 26.1 shows that the rate of saturation can vary greatly in soils with predominantly variable charges.

26.1.2 Variables that Influence the Determination of CEC

Influence of pH

The choice of pH for extraction gave rise to controversy that was not necessarily always justified, but subsequently, thanks to the study of the nature of charges of the exchange complex (cf. Chap. 19), these arguments became more reasonable. The concept of chemical equili-bration enables quantification of the parameters that determine the lattice bonds. The methods used can be grouped in three main categories:
1. Measurement of CEC at the soil pH → effective CEC;
2. Measurement of CEC at a given buffered pH;
3. Measurement of CEC at the pH for which the charge is zero (zero point charge (ZPC) or pH 0 (cf. Chap. 20).

Measurement of CEC at the Soil pH

This measurement enables the existing CEC to be identified and the phenomenon to be observed under conditions that are close to real conditions. Both the evolution of soils subjected to entropic constraints (influence of anion fixation of phosphorus or of calcium silicate causing a decrease in pH 0 and a rise in CEC, the influence of liming which increases the net charge, etc.) and the nutritional aspect of the exchange complex can be studied. This method enables calculation of the effective CEC by summation which is a good indicator of the real negative charges under field conditions.

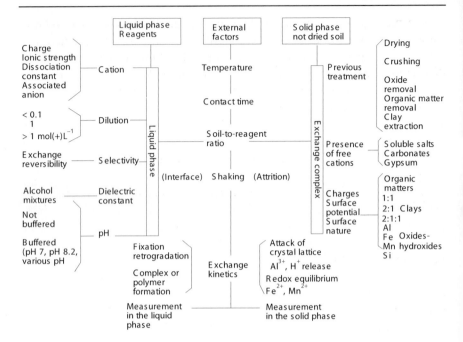

Fig. 26.2. Factors influencing measurement of CEC (Gautheyrou and Gautheyrou 1981)

Not-buffered reagents are used (e.g. KCl, NH4Cl, organo-metallic cations) to quantify firstly exchangeable cations (Ca^{2+}, Mg^{2+}, K^+, Na^+), and secondly the cations involved in exchangeable acidity (like H^+, Al^{3+}, Fe^{2+}, Mn^{2+}).

This method is suitable for acid soils with variable charges and with large quantities of interlayer aluminium hydroxyl-polymers which partially neutralize negative charges.

Measurements in Buffered Medium

Buffered solutions are used to eliminate the influence of variations in pH on the measurement and to express all the results on the same basis, i.e. the chosen pH. These methods are standardized and the two most frequently used pH values are 7.0 and 8.1–8.2.

The methods at pH 7.0 were selected by international decision to try and homogenize the results used for the soil classification. pH 7.0 corresponds to neutrality. It is close to the pH equilibrium of the soil-HCO_3^-–CO_2 buffer system at normal atmospheric pressure.

The method using molar ammonium acetate at pH 7 belongs to this category. It has been used for nearly 60 years as an international reference because it is easy to implement, titration ends with a simple distillation and titrimetry, and it can be performed in the field. In addition, as ammonium is used to move the exchangeable cations in the saturation phase of the exchange complex, two methods can be combined and the saturation coefficient can be measured on the same extract. The ammonium acetate CEC method was considered to be precise, at least at the agronomic scale, which explains why this method has continued to be used.

However, this does not mean that it has never been subject to criticism, especially in the presence of illites, smectites and vermiculites where phenomena of selective adsorption of NH_4^+ can be observed. Many other salts have been used to try to mitigate these problems or to adapt the method to specific cases.

These methods are appropriate for soils with predominant permanent charges or for soils presenting pH values close to neutral. The CEC of acid soils is often overestimated, especially for soils with significant variable charges, their saturation rate then appears to be lower.

The methods at pH 8.1–8.2 were designed for soils with an exchange complex in which divalent cations predominate and with a high pH. At 25°C, pH 8.2–8.4 corresponds to the CO_2 equilibrium at normal pressure of a system where bicarbonate is transformed into carbonate (upper titration point), and is also close to the complete neutralization of hydroxy-aluminium compounds. The charges measured are close to those that are actually observed in calcareous soils.

These methods include total exchangeable acidity, the CEC of variable charges; furthermore, using a well-buffered medium at this pH means measurements are "independent" of the initial soil pH. A cation like divalent barium is generally chosen as counter-ion because (a) it is practically non-existent in most soils and (b) its valence is the same as calcium and magnesium which are predominant in the adsorbing complex. However, this method is not suitable for soil genesis studies in acid medium.

CEC extractions and titration at several buffered pH enable estimation of changes in the charge at a given pH (Fig. 26.1). Below pH 5.2, the influence of Al^{3+}, Fe^{2+}, Fe^{3+} is more and more marked thereby weakening the CEC.

Between pH 5.2 and 8.5–9.0, Al and Fe are precipitated but as they are practically electrically neutral, they no longer significantly influence the results. Above pH 9.0, $Al(OH)_3$ is transformed into AlO_2^- aluminate which is added to the clay negative charge, increasing the CEC and edge Al ions, Al–OH aluminols are transformed into anion form. Thus values between pH 4.0 and pH 9.0 are used to avoid the zones where significant dissolution of ions could disturb the exchange processes to be observed.

Measurements at pH Corresponding to ZPC-pH 0

These measurements are used for detailed studies but are not suitable for repetitive analysis because of the length and cost of the procedure which is difficult to robotize.

At the ZPC value (cf. Chap. 20) the soil has equal capacities for cation (CEC) and anion (ECA) exchange. If the pH of extraction is higher than the ZPC, the charge Σ_v is negative and the CEC is overestimated.

If the pH is lower than the ZPC, the positive charges increase and the anion exchange capacity (AEC) are overestimated. These methods enable studies on the nature of the ionic environments and the energy levels of the equilibriums during hydrogeochemical cycles.

Influence of the Nature and Concentration of Cations

Monovalent and divalent ions are the most widely used. Hydrated ions, which are completely dissociated in diluted aqueous medium, are generally easily exchangeable and follow the lyotropic series shown in Table 26.1 for a concentration lower than $0.1 \text{ mol } (+) \text{ L}^{-1}$.

Table 26.1. Exchangeable monovalent or divalent cations

monovalent	Cs^+	Rb^+	$K^+ NH_4^+$	Na^+	Li^+
ionic radius (Å)	1.67	1.52	1.38	1.02	0.76
Divalent		Ba^{2+}	Sr^{2+}	Ca^{2+}	Mg^{2+}
ionic radius (Å)		1.35	1.18	1.0	0.72

Except in case of selective adsorption, the exchange capacity is in the same as the order of valence:
$$M^+ < M^{2+} < M^{3+}$$
then $Na^+ < K^+ < Mg^{2+} < Ca^{2+} < Al^{3+}$.

However, above a concentration of $0.1 \text{ mol } (+) \text{ L}^{-1}$, some monovalent cations can have an exchange capacity with different selectivity.

In smectites, the least hydrated ions reach the interfoliaceous cavities (K^+, NH_4^+) more easily, but because of the contraction of 2:1 clays, these ions can be trapped and become non-exchangeable (fixed or retrogressed ions). The basal space can be as small as 9.8–10.8 Å (cf. Chap. 4).

Conversely, with ions like Ca^{2+}, and Mg^{2+} with strong hydration energy and which are completely solvated, interfoliaceous expansion of up to 15–20 Å occurs which makes the cations more mobile and the exchange reversible, without marked exchange selectivity (cf. Chap. 25).

This phenomenon can be observed in micas and illites, vermiculites and minerals with a strong interlayer charge. The cations are sometimes replaced by organomineral compounds. These large molecules (for example the cobaltihexamine ion which has a ionic radius of 7 Å) can display steric impossibilities to reach some exchange positions. In certain clays, abnormally low exchange capacities are then observed with a significant interfoliaceous surface, or zeolites which play the role of molecular sieves.

Influence of Contact Times, Agitation and Equilibration

These methods use very different contact times which can influence the resulting values:
– A short contact time of less than 1 h may be necessary if the kinetics of dissolution of the exchange matrix is high, involving an increase in background noise (double percolation can be used to correct the results); in this case, diffusion of the liquid within the structure of clays and colloids has to be rapid to enable the exchange phenomena to reach a stable value as soon as possible; gentle agitation by ultrasound often enables satisfactory exchange: dissolution ratio to be obtained;
– A contact time of less than 24 h is usually used with reagents that enable complete reagents-matrix exchange equilibriums without significant dissolution and
– A time of contact of more than 24 h requires reagents with limited dissolving capacity.

It is necessary to check for matrix solubilization, possible neo-formation in the crystalline or amorphous phase, and the stoichiometry of the exchanges.

Influence of the Modes of Extraction: Soil-to-Solution Ratio

The CEC is measured in a system with two phases, each of which is analyzed (Fig. 26.2):
– a stationary solid phase represented by the soil exchange matrix and
– a mobile liquid phase containing a counter-ion (index ion).

Equilibration between these two phases defines the exchange (adsorption–sorption relations) and the total charge of the solid. The exchange is more complete if the ratio of the liquid to the solid phase is high (weak concentration in the liquid phase).

The ionic force of the counter-ion must be sufficient to move the ions fixed on the exchange matrix but not to solubilize other materials. The analytical conditions of measurement are far from real conditions. The CEC can be measured in the liquid phase which is enriched in elements released by the soil matrix and in which counter-ions are reduced. Excess counter-ions are measured before and after the exchange and the CEC is given by the difference between the two.

CEC can also be measured on the solid phase made homoionic after saturation by the counter-ion and by the elimination of excess counter-ions. This ion is thus exchanged and analyzed directly from the solid phase, provided this phase does not release other ions of similar nature (for example, direct distillation of the soil to titrate fixed NH_4^+). The CEC is then equal to the total charge of the fixed ions.

CEC can also be measured by a method combining saturation by a counter-ion, elimination of the excess, then displacement of the counter-ion by another counter-ion, assuming a stoichiometric exchange in both cases.

The excess counter-ion solution is eliminated by a highly diluted solution of the same ion to avoid dispersion or excessive hydrolysis, then by weighing to measure the quantity of solution retained in order to correct the results. Elimination can also be achieved with miscible solvents (methanol, ethanol, isopropanol) which modify the permittivity of the medium. ISRIC[1] (1987) recommended washing with an ethanol–water mixture (80% ethanol).

Influence of Free Ions, Soluble Salts, Limestone, Gypsum

The presence of these substances in the soil disturbs measurements and causes an immediately detectable anomaly between the sum of extracted cations (S) and the exchangeable capacity (T): $S > T$ whereas in most other cases $S < T$ or at the most $S = T$. The CEC value is thus erroneous as are values for the exchangeable cations. The exchange complex is saturated with Ca^{2+}, Mg^{2+}, or Na^+ depending on the case.

---

[1] ISRIC, International Soil Research Information Center, P.O. Box 353, 6700 AJ Wageningen, the Netherlands. Tel. +31 - 317 – 471711; Fax: +31 - 317 –471700. E-mail:soil.isric@wur.nl

Influence of Soil Pretreatments

Drying

In andosols with permanent moisture, drying results in a very significant reduction in the CEC. Measurements must thus be made on samples stored with their field moisture, and the water contained in the samples must be taken into account in calculations. A specific volume of soil corresponding to an equivalent weight of soil dried at 105°C is used in order to obtain results corresponding to the same exchange surface whatever the initial moisture of the samples (between 10 and 300%). The results are expressed in cmol (+) kg^{-1} of soil dried at 105°C.

Crushing

In clays with a weak charge like 1:1 clays, the effect of edge charges increases with over grinding because of the discontinuities of structure caused by the treatment. During weathering, the presence of badly crystallized forms can have the same effect (silanol–aluminol groups, cf. Chap. 21).

In 2:1 clays, whose charge is high, the edge charge can be negligible in proportion to the total charge. The effect of moderate crushing will consequently be less serious than in 1:1 clays.

Amorphous substances and gels with very high charges are practically unchanged by crushing, whereas the apparent CEC can increase in crystalline forms with weak charges.

Chemical Pretreatments

The CEC can be drastically modified by preliminary saturation of an andosol sample by reagents containing anions that can be fixed selectively. Among these anions, the following series is particularly active: $F^- > PO_4^{3-} > SO_4^{2-}$.

The CEC of allophane soils can be increased three or four times by the simple addition of phosphate.

Sometimes oxalate can be observed during destruction of organic matter by perhydrol and this can disturb measurements. The addition of concentrated ammonia to destroy the excess of perhydrol can saturate the complex with the NH_4^+ ion and cause errors in 2:1 clays.

The elimination of amorphous substances using the CBD method involves reduction of ferric iron to ferrous iron. In 2:1 minerals, if this action occurs at the level of the octahedral layers, the negative surface charge increases. During soil washings, ferro-iron can precipitate again as ferri-iron and be adsorbed with silicon and aluminium ions on the matrix thereby blocking exchange sites and giving incorrect CEC values

(Stucki et al. 1984). In this case it is necessary to estimate the possible effects of this treatment in minerals containing iron in their structure, like nontronite.

26.2 Determination of Effective CEC by Summation (ECEC)

26.2.1 Principle

Exchangeable cations (Ca^{2+}, Mg^{2+}, K^+, Na^+, cf. Chap. 22) are added to the cations extracted with the exchangeable acidity method (H^+, Al^{3+}, Fe^{2+}, Fe^{3+}, Mn^{2+}), cf. Chap. 23; Yuan 1959):

ECEC (cmol (+) kg^{-1}) = $[Ca^{2+} + Mg^{2+} + K^+ + Na^+] + [H^+ + Al^{3+} + (Fe^{2+} + Fe^{3+} + Mn^{2+})]$

This measurement (Coleman and Thomas 1967; Kamprath 1970) is considered to be representative of the CEC measured at the soil pH under conditions of surface charges identical to natural conditions (Juo et al. 1976). It applies to acid or neutral soils. However, the ionic strength of the extraction solution is higher than that of the soil solution. This has the advantage of allowing the results of two different analyses to be used:

– exchangeable cations, which estimates the proportion and nature of the available elements in soil;
– exchangeable acidity, which specifies the nature of soil acidity (e.g. H^+, Al^{3+}).

The rate of saturation V obtained by these two analyses is close to field conditions but appears to be more representative of acid soils with variable charge.

26.2.2 Alternative Methods

Either the method using 0.1 mol L^{-1} ammonium acetate at pH 7 or a method using a not-buffered solution of 1 mol L^{-1} ammonium chloride can be used to extract the exchangeable cations.

The determination of exchangeable aluminium with multiple mono- and polymeric forms can result in values that are too low, as not all the forms are exchangeable.

Other methods have been proposed for the ECEC. They all use not-buffered reagents that are likely to exchange either the exchangeable cations, or cations representing the exchange acidity: Ag–thiourea (Pleysier and Juo 1980), $SrCl_2$ (Edmeades et al. 1981), NH_4–NO_3 (Stuanes et al. 1984), $BaCl_2$ (Hendershot and Duquette 1986), NH_4Cl (Gangaiya and Morrison 1987).

26.3 CEC Measurement at Soil pH in Not-Buffered Medium

26.3.1 Principle

The soil is saturated with a counter-cation in not-buffered medium. The exchange is carried out at a pH near the soil pH. After elimination of excess counter-cation with a diluted solution of the same ion, this cation is moved by another counter-cation. The titration of the moved cation enables determination of the CEC.

Diluted solutions of ionic force near to that found in the soil solution at a moisture rate of approximately pF 2 (cf. Table 1.1 of Chap. 1) should be used to avoid serious deterioration of the surface of colloids (Gillman 1979; Gillman et al. 1983; Rhoades 1982). These methods are only suitable for acid soils with variable charges, as the measurement of CEC at pH 7.0 gives highly over-estimated values. The acid or neutral soils should not contain soluble salts or gypsum. The organic matter can also be dissolved resulting in a too low CEC.

26.3.2 Methods Using Not-Buffered Metallic Salts

Barium Chloride and Magnesium Sulphate–Procedure

Principle

In this well-described technique (Gillman 1979; Rhoades 1982; NF ISO 11260 1994), the exchangeable cations are extracted with a not-buffered 0.1 mol $(BaCl_2)$ L^{-1} solution. The exchangeable cations (like Ca^{2+}, Mg^{2+}, K^+ Na^+) can be titrated in the extract. The soil residue is put in contact with a 0.02 mol $(MgSO_4)$ L^{-1} solution. The Mg^{2+} ions move the exchanged Ba^{2+} ions and $BaSO_4$ precipitates in the medium maintained at an ionic strength near that of the soil solution. The difference between the added Mg^{2+} and the Mg^{2+} which remains in solution gives the CEC. Magnesium is titrated by atomic absorption spectrometry (AAS).

Reagents

– *Saturation solution* of 0.1 mol L^{-1} barium chloride: dissolve 24.43 g of $BaCl_2$, $2H_2O$ (mw = 244.3) and bring to 1 L with deionised water.

– *Equilibration solution* of 0.0025 mol L^{-1} barium chloride: take 25 mL of 0.1 mol $(BaCl_2)$ L^{-1} solution and bring to 1 L with deionized water.
– *Counter-ion solution* of 0.02 mol L^{-1} magnesium sulphate: dissolve 4.9296 g of $MgSO_4$, $7H_2O$ (mw = 246.50) in 1 L of deionized water.
– *Reagents for titration by atomic absorption and emission spectrometry:*
 (a) *Lanthanum nitrate:* weigh 15.7 g of $La(NO_3)_3,6H_2O$ (mw = 433.02); add 42 mL of concentrated HCl and bring to 500 mL with deionized water;
 (b) *Caesium chloride:* weigh 10 g of CsCl (mw 168.36); add 83 mL of concentrated HCl and bring to 1 L with deionized water;
 (c) *Mg standards:* range 0, 0.01, 0.02, 0.03, 0.04 and 0.05 mmol L^{-1} (CEC);
 (d) *Na standards:* range 0, 4, 8, 12, 16, 20 mg L^{-1} (EC);
 (e) *K standards:* range 0, 10, 20, 30, 40, 50 mg L^{-1} (EC);
 (f) *Ca and Mg standards:* mixed range (EC) containing:
   Mg: 0, 0.1, 0.2, 0.3, 0.4, 0.5 mg L^{-1},
   Ca: 0, 1, 2, 3, 4, 5 mg L^{-1}.

Procedure

Displacements

Measure the soil moisture on another sample specimen to correct the results on the basis of soil dried at 105°C if necessary (cf. Chap. 1).
– Put 2.5 g of soil < 2 mm in a 50 mL centrifugation tube, and weigh tube + soil + screw cap: m_1
– Add 30 mL of 0.1 mol $(BaCl_2)$ L^{-1} solution and agitate for 1 h.
– Centrifuge at 5,000g and transfer the supernatant in a 100 mL volumetric flask.
– Repeat saturation twice and mix the extracts in a 100 mL flask.
– Complete to 100 mL; this solution contains the exchangeable cations: S1 solution.
– Add 30 mL of 0.0025 mol $(BaCl2)$ L^{-1} to the centrifugation pellet and shake overnight.
– Centrifuge, discard the supernatant and weigh the tube + centrifugation pellet + retained 0.0025 mol $(BaCl_2)$ L^{-1} solution: m_2.
– Add 30 mL of 0.02 mol $(MgSO_2)$ L^{-1} solution and agitate for 2 h.
– Centrifuge and filter the supernatant for CEC quantification: S2 solution.

Measurement of CEC

- Place 0.2 mL of the S2 filtrate in a 100 mL volumetric flask.
- Place 0.2 mL of the counter-ion solution ($MgSO_4$) in another 100 mL flask.
- Add 10 mL of the 10 g (La) L^{-1} solution to each flask and complete to 100 mL.
- Measure the Mg concentrations by AAS at 285.2 nm:

     C_0 is the concentration of the diluted counter-ion solution,

     C_1 is the concentration of the diluted S2 solution.

Calculation of CEC

Correct the C_1 concentration for the effect of the volume of liquid retained in the sample after treatment:

$$C_2 = \frac{C_1 \left(30 + m_2 - m_1\right)}{30}$$

C_2:   corrected Mg concentration mmol L^{-1}

C_1:   Mg concentration from AAS measurement mmol L^{-1}

m_1:   weight tube + soil

m_2:   weight tube + soil + retained liquid

$$CEC = \frac{3{,}000 \left(C_2 - C_0\right)}{m} \qquad \text{(in cmol (+) kg}^{-1}\text{)}$$

m: sample weight in g (2.5 g)

C_0:   concentration of the diluted counter-ion solution.

   If CEC exceeds 40 cmol (+) kg^{-1}, repeat the analysis with a lower weight of soil.

Measurement of the Exchangeable Cations

- In 10 mL volumetric flasks, pipette 2 mL of the S1 solution, add 1 mL of CsCl and bring the volume to 10 mL with deionised water.
- Measure Na and K by flame emission.
- Again pipette 1 mL of the S1 extracts in 10 mL volumetric flasks, add 1 mL of lanthanum nitrate solution and bring to 10 mL with deionised water.
- Measure Ca and Mg by AAS.

Calculation of the Exchangeable Cations

$$Cech = \frac{c - c_b}{m} \times \frac{10\, v}{M}$$

   $Cech$, concentration of the exchangeable Na, K, Ca or Mg cation in cmol (+) kg^{-1}, C and C_b, concentrations in the extracts and blank, respectively, in mg L^{-1}; m, weight of soil in g; v, charge of the cation (1 for Na and K, 2 for Ca and Mg); M, atomic mass of the cation in g.

Remarks

This method is relatively simple and enables measurement of the permanent and variable charges of strongly weathered tropical soils, as well as of exchangeable cations and possibly of exchangeable acidity (NF ISO 14254 1997).

The use of $MgSO_4$ is questionable for andosols because of the selective fixing of sulphate ion in these soils in which the presence of allophane and substances with short distance organization are predominant. Matsue and Wada (1985) proposed the use of 0.01 mol $(SrCl_2)L^{-1}$ for saturation of the complex, then desorption of exchanged Sr with a 0.5 mol (HCl) L^{-1} solution.

Another approach was recommended by Hendershot and Duquette (1986) in which $MgSO_4$ is replaced by $MgCl_2$ as Cl^- is not selectively retained by soils containing allophane. A similar method was used for peats: $BaCl_2 - MgCl_2$ (Lambert et al. 1988).

Ba^{2+}, Sr^{2+}, Mg^{2+} do not cause contraction of any 2:1 clays that may be present.

When it is possible to compare Sr^{2+} and Ba^{2+} in not-buffered medium and with a moderate ionic force ($C = 0.01-0.1$ mol L^{-1}) the results will be similar to those obtained with the ammonium method (not-buffered medium).

It is also possible to measure aluminium, manganese and iron in the extracts; these elements may be present in large quantities in spodosols.

26.3.3 Procedure Using Not-Buffered Organometallic Cations

Cobalti-Hexamine Chloride System

Principle

The steric obstruction of certain organometallic cations makes it possible to avoid their penetration in the clay layers. Measuring the CEC with cobalti-hexamine chloride (Esquevin 1954; Morel 1957; Amavis 1959) gives values that are generally low but well suited to repetitive measurements of acid soils with variable charges.

The soil is saturated by the cobalti-hexamine cation $Co(NH_3)_6^{3+}$ in excess (3–7 times the expected CEC according to Rémy and Orsini 1976). Ca, Mg, K, Na, Al cations are titrated directly in this solution.

The CEC is calculated by the difference between the quantity added and the quantity remaining in solution. The calculated adsorbed Co^{3+} corresponds to the soil CEC in not-buffered medium at a pH near the soil pH. The analysis can be performed on the whole soil or on clay fractions, and macro or micro methods can be used.

Reagent

Cobalti-hexamine chloride $(Co(NH_3)_6Cl_3$ mw $= 267.50)$ $1/60$ mol L^{-1} $(0.05$ mol $(+)$ $L^{-1})$ solution: weigh 4.4583 of $Co(NH_3)_6Cl_3$ and dissolve in 1 L of water (1 mL $= 0.05$ milliequivalents CEC); prepare fresh each week and store in a brown lightproof bottle.

Procedure

– Weigh 4 g of soil in a 150 mL centrifugation tube.
– Add 100 mL of N/20 cobalti-hexamine chloride solution.

The concentration should be adjusted as a function of the CEC and be suitable for a minimum of two to a maximum of seven times the theoretical value of the CEC. Alternatively the weight of the sample of soil or clay can be changed. For example, at a concentration of 0.05 mol $(+)$ L^{-1}, 100 mL of reagent representing 5 mmol $(+)$ CEC, it is possible to measure the CEC of a sample of 2 g montmorillonite with a CEC of approximately 100 cmol $(+)$ kg^{-1} with adequate precision.

– Mix and shake on a rotary agitator for 2 h.
– Centrifuge at 5,000 g for 5 min and recover the supernatant.
– Titrate $\qquad$ Ca^{2+}, Mg^{2+}, K^+, Na^+ (exchangeable cations),
$\qquad$ Al^{3+} (exchangeable acidity),
$\qquad$ Co^{3+} (CEC),

by atomic absorption or inductively coupled plasma emission spectrometry (Pansu et al. 2001). Alternatively, the CEC can be titrated by ammonium distillation directly on the extract, the cobalti-hexamine chloride being broken up above pH 10 in the presence of soda according to the reaction:

$Co(NH_3)_6Cl_3 + 3$ NaOH $\rightarrow 6$ $NH_3 + Co(OH)_3$ (precipitate) $+ 3$ NaCl.

Ammonia is then titrated by acidimetry, which makes this method usable even under uncertain analytical conditions (Esquevin 1954; Gautheyrou and Gautheyrou 1958). Orsini and Rémy (1976) proposed ammonium titration by automated spectrocolorimetry.

The results are expressed in cmol $(+)$ kg^{-1} knowing that $1/3$ mole Co^{13+} $\longleftrightarrow 2$ NH_3.

Remarks

Cobalti-hexamine chloride dissolves only a very low fraction of carbonates, which allows quantification of exchangeable calcium in not too calcareous soils.

Under certain conditions, the cobalti-hexamine chloride may be broken down giving an overestimation of the CEC (Cornell and Aksoyoglu 1991).

The works of Mantin and Glaeser (1960) Johanson (1961) Fripiat and Helsen (1966) Oliver (1984) Fallavier et al. (1985) and Keita and Van Der Pol (1987) studied these reactions in detail and compared methods.

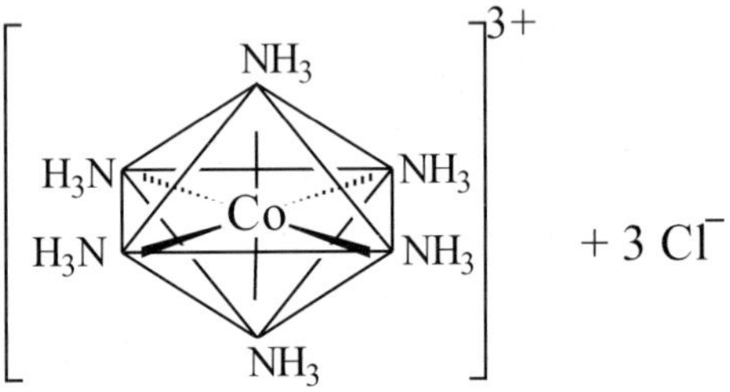

Fig. 26.3. Cobalti-hexamine chloride

Cobalti-hexamine chloride or hexamino-cobalt chloride is a large organometallic cation obtained by oxidation of an ammoniacal solution of cobalt chloride containing ammonium chloride in the presence of activated carbon as catalyst:

$$2\ CoCl_2 + 2\ NH_4Cl + 10\ NH_3 + H_2O_2 \Leftrightarrow 2\ Co(NH_3)_6Cl_3 + 2\ H_2O.$$

The cobalt atom is hexacoordinate (Fig. 26.3), each NH_3-nitrogen being located at the apical ends of a regular octahedron. The radius of the cobalti-hexamine is approximately 3.25 Å, which may explain the phenomena of steric limitation on interfoliaceous surface of clays and the weak ionic force.

Ag–Thiourea System

Principle

The soil is saturated by a monovalent organometallic cation (silver–thiourea), which displays strong affinity for the negative charges of colloids.

The exchangeable cations pass in solution where they can be titrated. The titration of Ag^+ ion remaining in solution enables quantification of the fixed Ag^+ by difference and thereby determination of the CEC. The medium is not buffered and extraction is performed at the soil pH (Pleyssier and Juo 1980; Searle 1986; ISRIC 1987).

The ionic strength of the reagent solution is lower than that of the 1 mol (KCl) L^{-1} solution ($I \approx 0.01$).

Reagents

– *Silver nitrate 0.02 mol L^{-1}*: dissolve 3.4 g of $AgNO_3$ (mw = 169.89) in 500 mL of water and store in a brown lightproof bottle.
– *0.2 mol (thiourea) L^{-1} solution*: dissolve 15.25 g of thiourea (H_2N–CS–NH_2 mw = 76.12) in 900 mL water and bring to 1,000 mL. Let stand overnight and filter if there is a deposit.
  Toxicity: thiourea is slightly toxic by inhalation or by contact.
– *Solution to determine the CEC at the soil pH:* just before use, mix in the following order: 1 L of 0.2 mol (thiourea) L^{-1} solution, 500 mL of deionised water and homogenize; slowly add 500 mL of 0.02 mol L^{-1} silver nitrate solution while agitating; silver forms a stable complex with thiourea (Bolt 1982).
– *Standards for silver titration by AAS*: put 50 mL of a 1,000 mg (Ag^+) L^{-1} stock solution in a 200 mL volumetric flask and complete to 200 mL with deionised water: solution A (250 mg L^{-1} solution). Put 2.5 mL of 0.2 mol (thiourea) L^{-1} solution and 5 mL of 1 mol (HNO_3) L^{-1} solution into six 250 mL volumetric flasks. Take exact volumes of 0-5-10-15-20-25 mL of solution A and add them in each flask while agitating. Bring to volume with deionised water and homogenize, giving a standard range of 0-5-10-15-20-25 mg (Ag) L^{-1}.

Procedure (ISRIC 1987)

Extraction

– Weigh 1 g of soil (0.5 mm particle size) in a centrifugation tube;
– add 40 mL of silver–thiourea solution and close the tube;
– shake for 4 h, centrifuge at 5,000g and recover the supernatant.

Exchangeable Cations

– Titrate Ca^{2+}, Mg^{2+}, K^+, Na^+ and Ag by AAS with standards containing the same thiourea matrix;
– titrate two blanks (the same reagents without the soil sample), a reference sample and a randomly chosen control sample in the series.

CEC

Take 2 mL of the extract, add 5 mL 1 mol (HNO_3) L^{-1} solution and bring to volume with 100 mL water. Homogenize and measure Ag^+ by AAS at 328.1 nm using the 0–25 mg L^{-1} standard range.

Calculation

$$Ag^+ = 107.87$$

$$CEC \ (\text{cmol}\,(+)\ kg^{-1}) = \frac{(b-a) \times 50 \times 100 \ f}{25 \times 107.87 \ w} = \frac{1.85 \ (b-a) \ f}{w}$$

a: mg (Ag^+) L^{-1} in the extract diluted 50 times;
b: mg (Ag^+) L^{-1} in the blank diluted 50 times;
w: weight of air-dried soil sample;
f: moisture correction factor.

Remarks

The method is rapid and only one extraction is needed to titrate the exchangeable cations (Ca, Mg, K, Na) and CEC (Pleysier and Cremer 1975; Chabra et al. 1976). It enables measurement of the CEC up to 20 cmol (+) kg^{-1} (soil). If the CEC exceeds this value, the sample can be extracted with 80 mL of silver–thiourea reagent or a smaller soil sample can be used; these modifications then need to be taken into account in the calculations.

The silver–thiourea solution can damage the electrodes of pH-meters. The electrodes should not be left in contact with the solution for too long and should be rinsed immediately after use with diluted nitric acid and then soaked in deionised water (Siegried et al. 1986). A concentration of 1 mol (HNO_3) L^{-1} should not be exceeded in order to avoid the precipitation of an insoluble thiouronium nitrate compound.

It is possible to use this method at fixed pH by incorporating 0.1 mg L^{-1} ammonium acetate or sodium acetate buffer.

The method can be used up to pH 9.0 for calcareous or gypseous soils, (Van Rosmalen 1980), saline soils and possibly soils containing organic matter and with variable charges, like histosols, podzols or andisols (Pleyser and Juo 1980; Bolt 1982; Searle 1986). The stability of the reagent is modified in alkaline medium at pH > 8.0. The decomposition of the silver–thiourea complex results in deterioration of the extraction solution.

The exchange affinity is high for clay minerals like montmorillonite, illite, kaolinite and even vermiculite, where the silver–thiourea complex seems to penetrate the interlayer space (Pleysier and Cremer 1973, 1975). Selectivity is slightly different from that observed for ammonium acetate extraction at pH 7. Extracted K^+ is often higher in the silver–thiourea method. On the other hand, extracted Ca^{2+} and Mg^{2+} are generally lower depending on the organic matter content and the soil pH (Pleysier et al. 1986). However, calcite can be slightly dissolved resulting in overestimation of the exchangeable cations.

Effective CEC (cf. Sect. 26.2 earlier) can be measured using this method. The results are a little lower than with the ammonium acetate or potassium chloride methods. However, extraction of manganese by the silver–thiourea complex can be higher than by potassium chloride (Searle 1986). The effect on iron extraction should be checked as thiourea is a neutral ligand with reducing properties.

Not-Buffered Ethylene Diamine + Inorganic Cations

Clay is saturated by a cation (e.g. Co, Cu) giving homoionic clay. Ethylene diamine is added in excess and, through contact with the added cation, is fixed quantitatively. If there is formation of a soluble complex of the cation with ethylenediamine, there will be saturation of the exchangeable positions (Fripiat and Helsen 1996; Mantin 1969). These complexes are strongly stabilized within clay (Peigneur 1976; Mas et al. 1978). The CEC corresponds to the concentration of the complex fixed by the matrix, resulting in a reduction in the concentration of ethylene diamine (Cornell and Aksoyoglu 1991).

These methods have the same disadvantage as a method by difference. It should be noted that the reagent can irritate the skin and mucous membranes and cause allergic dermatoses and asthma; these risks can be avoided by working under a fume hood.

Researchers studying soil genesis and weathering processes also use the exchange of the alkylammonium ion which makes it possible to measure the density of interlayer cations if the molecular weight of the basic exchanger unit is known. Only purified fractions should be used. In 2:1 clays, depending on the degree of crystallinity of the clay, the total CEC generally includes approximately 80% of interlayer CEC for approximately 20% of edge CEC. For example, the transformation processes of micas (of illite into smectites) or the transformation of bentonite into smectites can be monitored (Lagaly 1981).

Complexes of ethylene diamine ($NH_2-CH_2-CH_2-NH_2$) with cations like Al, Co, Cu, Fe, Mn, Ni, Zn have also been used; however these methods are used more especially for detailed studies on clays.

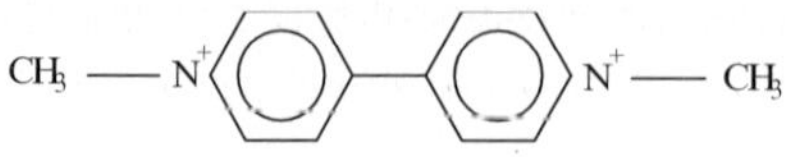

Paraquat

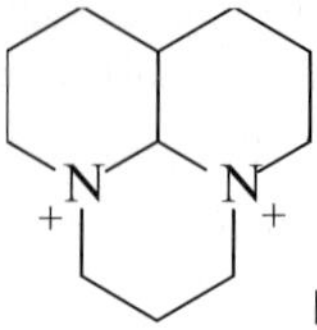

Diquat

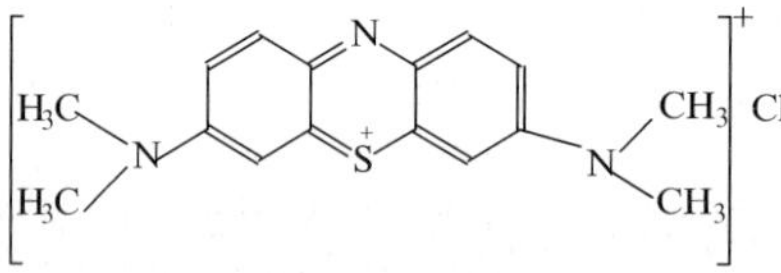

Methylene blue
(3,7 bis(dimethylamino phenazathionum chloride; mw = 973.9)

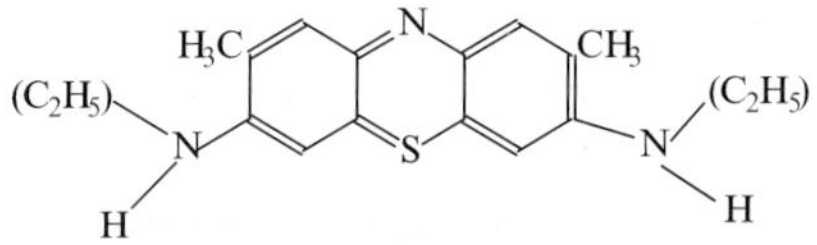

Methylene blue II

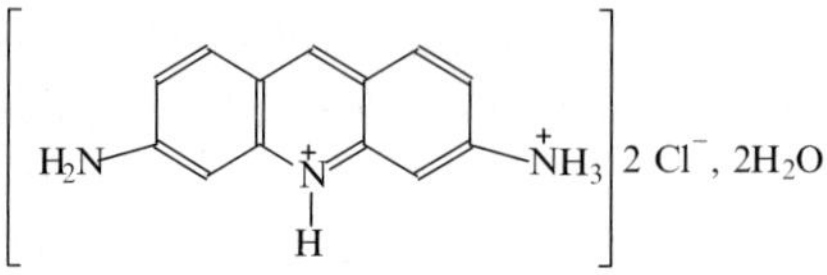

Proflavine (mw = 318.2)

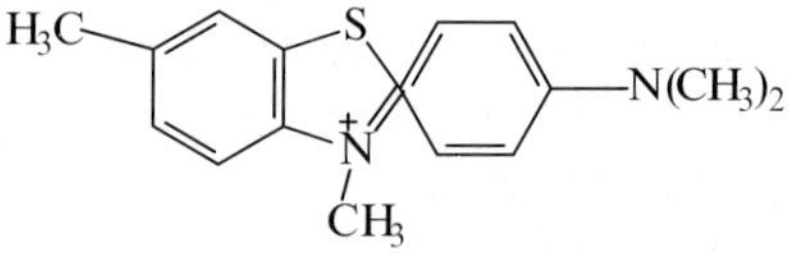

Thioflavine T

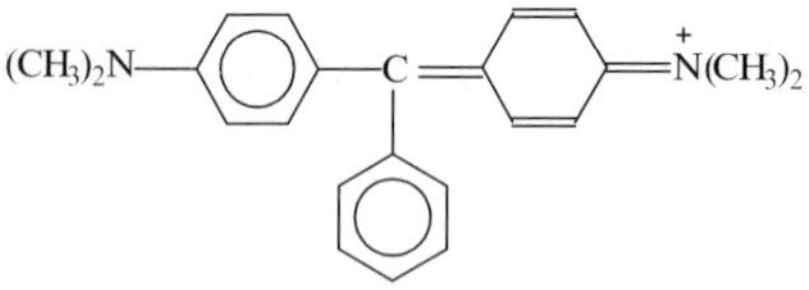

Malachite green (mw = 364.9)

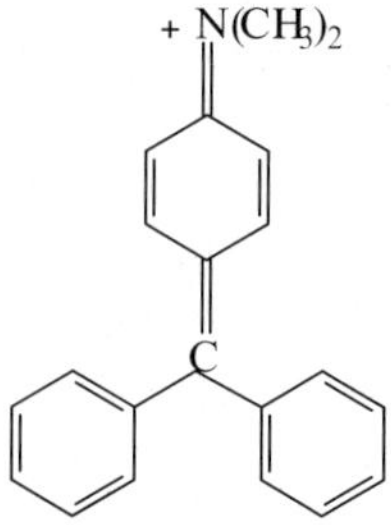

Crystal violet

Fig. 26.4. Organic molecules used for measurement of cation exchange capacity

26.3.4 Not-Buffered Methods Using Organic Cations

Interest in these methods increased with the commercial availability of large organic molecules (Fig. 26.4) used as pesticides and with knowledge of the environmental impact of such molecules (e.g. saturation of the adsorbing complex, biodegradation, pollution of ground water by Paraquat and Diquat).

If possible, these methods should be combined with methods for the determination of clay specific surfaces and macro-methods for the determination of the CEC.

The study of the fixation mechanisms requires knowledge of the modes of action of monovalent or divalent organo-cations in order to avoid confusion between exchange and physical adsorption.

The quantities of inorganic cations exchanged by the organo-cation should be proportional or equal to the quantities of adsorbed exchanger. The size of the organic ions means methods of centrifugation at high speed which would be likely to separate molecules of the exchanger should not be used. Exchange capacities are determined starting from the plates of the exchange isotherms (Margulies et al. 1988). The main colorants used are methylene blue, flavins, malachite green, and crystal violet (Fig. 26.4).

The methods used are based on incubation of Na^+ homoionic clay with the colouring exchangers for a period of from 1 to 15 days depending on the clay.

A 20 mL sample clay in 0.5% solution is sufficient.

After percolation and filtration on Millipore 0.45 µm filter, absorption is measured:

  – at 662 nm for methylene blue;
  – at 588 nm for crystal violet.

The displaced inorganic cations are titrated by inductively coupled plasma spectrometry (Rytwo et al. 1991). Saturation by Na^+ is best with methylene blue (Hoffman and Dammler 1969). Potassium delays the sorption of this colouring reagent.

The dimerisation of methylene blue can result in errors by modifying the concentration curves. The concentration of the aqueous solution must be carefully controlled. The absorption bands of monomer species decrease and, at low wavelengths, the bands of dimer and trimer species become more intense (metachromatism). The monomer methylene blue absorbs at 673 and 653 nm, the dimer at 600 nm, and the trimer at 570 nm (Cenens and Schoonheydt 1990; Bergmann and O'konski 1963).

26.4 CEC Measurement in Buffered Medium

26.4.1 Buffered Methods — General Information

The determination of charges of the soil exchange complex at constant pH is used with mono- or divalent cations at different pH (cf. "Influence of pH" in section 26.1.2). In a well-buffered medium, variations due to the soil pH are eliminated, but if the buffered pH is higher than the soil pH, they are likely to create negative charges on clay minerals and organic matter by dissociation of weak organic acids. The results are then overestimated, particularly in acid soils with variable charge.

For *monovalent cations* the most widely used buffering systems are:
– Ammonium acetate (CH_3COONH_4, mw = 77.08) at pH 4.0, 7.0 or 9.0;
– Sodium acetate ($CH_3COONa,3H_2O$, mw = 136.09) at pH 4.0, 8.0 or 8.2;
– Potassium acetate (CH_3COOK, mw = 98.14) at pH 7.0 or 8.3;
– Lithium acetate ($CH_3COOLi,2H_2O$, mw = 102.02) at pH 8.2;

and for divalent cations:
– Calcium acetate ($CH_3–COO)_2Ca,H_2O$, mw = 176.18) at pH 4.8, 7.0 or 8.2;
– Calcium chloride ($CaCl_2$, mw = 110.99) + triethanolamine (TEA, $N(CH_2CH_2OH)_3$, mw = 149.19) at pH 7.0;
– Barium acetate ($CH_3–COO)_2Ba,H_2O$, mw = 273.47) at pH 7.0;
– Barium chloride ($BaCl_2,2H_2O$, mw = 244.31) + triethanolamine at pH 8.1–8.2;
– Magnesium acetate ($Mg(CH_3COO)_2,4H_2O$, mw = 214.47);
– Strontium acetate ($Sr(CH_3COO)_2,1/2H_2O$, mw = 214.73).

Counting the combinations of different salts used for saturation of the exchange complex (counter-cation), concentrations, contact times, soil-to-solution ratios, pH, processes of elimination of the excess of counter-cation and its displacement and the methods of characterization, more than 200 different or alternative methods were proposed between 1960 and 1980 alone (Gautheyrou and Gautheyrou 1981). However in practice, only a few methods are used regularly at the international scale:
– the 1 mol L^{-1} ammonium acetate method at pH 7.0 which is regarded as the reference method for soil cartography and taxonomy;
– the barium method at pH 8.1 or 8.2 buffered by triethanolamine;

– Some methods are suitable for soils whose CEC is particularly difficult to measure, like that of soils that evolved in an arid climate which are generally rich in limestone, gypsum or soluble salts.

Andisols and soils with variable charge are usually analyzed by not-buffered methods.

Methods using a cation that does not exist in the soil make it possible to measure exchangeable cations (Ca, Mg, K, Na) in the saturation phase.

The choice of a method is often determined by the laboratory equipment available, the simplicity of the procedures and the ability to conduct serial analyses at an acceptable cost. For example, *in fine* the ammonium ion can be distilled and titrated by volumetry, the titration of the potassium ion is more sensitive than sodium titration by flame photometry using air-propane flame (calcium and barium ions are not measurable), the dispersion of clays is more frequent with sodium salts which make separation difficult without ultracentrifugation, and the high sodium contents are awkward during titration by emission spectrometry, etc.

Some studies focus on the requirements of agronomy and soil science such as the risk of potassium and ammonium fixation for example in illites and vermiculites, the predominant presence of divalent calcium and magnesium cations in the majority of non-acid soils, the questionable efficiency of the ammonium ion to displace protons and aluminium ions in 1:1 clays, the use of sodium as counter-ion in saline soils to limit the displacement of charges, the choice of a high pH to approach the pH of equilibration of certain soils with pH > 7.0 and to limit the phenomena of solubilization.

For repetitive analyses the quality: price ratio is obviously important and the methods used must be able to deal with large sample numbers (cartography, agronomic controls). Methods based on knowledge acquired through research have been available for many years. The statistical exploitation of the results may enable models to be developed or farming advisory systems to be set up (for example, the DRIS[2] and the PARADES[3] system in California, which covers nearly 60 crops and many different climatic conditions with or without irrigation).

---

[2] DRIS, Diagnosis and Recommendation Integrated System (interactive system of research and extension).
[3] PARADES, Plant Analysis Recommendations and Diagnosis System.

26.4.2 Ammonium Acetate Method at pH 7.0

Principle

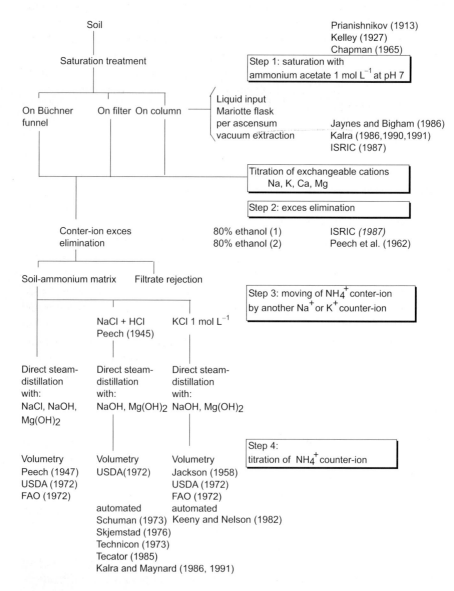

Fig. 26.5. Basic methods using ammonium acetate buffered solution

The soil is saturated by the ammonium counter-ion in a buffered medium at pH 7.0. Ammonium is adsorbed and an equivalent quantity of cation is moved. The exchangeable cations are titrated in the percolation solution by flame photometry, atomic absorption or ICP spectrometry (Pansu et al. 2001). The excess counter-ion is eliminated by a solvent (e.g. 80% ethanol) thereby limiting hydrolysis. The counter-ion is moved by the potassium ion of a standard not-buffered potassium chloride solution (or by sodium acetate at pH 7.0, or by sodium chloride). To measure the CEC (total quantity of counter-cation that a soil can retain), ammonium can be titrated by distillation and volumetric analysis or automated spectrocolorimetry (Fig. 26.5). Note that the possible fixing of ammonium by clays is not significant in the determination of exchangeable cations, but can lower the CEC.

Improvements in the Method

Determination of the CEC with buffered ammonium acetate is a multi-form method that has undergone considerable modification (Fig. 26.5). Originally used for the titration of exchangeable potassium (Prianishnikov 1913), then for the soil reaction (Schollenberger 1927) and finally for determination of the CEC (Schollenberger and Simons 1945; Kelley 1948; Peech et al. 1947), in the last 50 years the method has become an international reference.

The combination of the initial saturation treatment with treatments for the elimination of the excess ammonium ion, the nature of the counter-cation needed to displace ammonium and the final titration techniques led to very different procedures that generate significantly different results. Figure 26.5 lists some modifications made to the method that are still applied.

Reagents

– *1 mol L^{-1} ammonium acetate at pH 7.0*: weigh 770.08 g of CH_3COONH_4 (mw = 77.08) or dilute 600 mL of glacial acetic acid (CH_3–COOH, mw = 60.05) in approximately 9 L of deionised water and gradually add 750 mL of ammonia (NH_4OH, d = 0.90); let cool and check the pH; adjust to pH 7.0 with ammonia or acetic acid and complete to 10 L with deionised water.
– *Ethanol*: 80% ethanol 96° + 20% deionised water.
– *1 mol L^{-1} potassium chloride*: dissolve 745 g of KCl (mw = 74.5) in approximately 9 L of deionised water; after temperature equilibration, complete to 10 L with deionised water.
– *Nessler reagent* (test): (a) weigh 45.5 g of mercuric iodide (HgI_2, mw = 454.45) and 35.0 g of potassium iodide (KI, mw = 166.02); dissolve in a little water; (b) weigh 112 g of potassium hydroxide (KOH mw =

56.10) and dissolve in 500 mL of deionised water (from which CO_2 has been eliminated by boiling for 1 h and the water was stored safe from the air while cooling); mix a and b and bring to 1 L; store in a brown lightproof bottle protected from the air; prepare fresh each week; in the presence of ammonium ion the reagent gives a yellow–brown colouring (or brown flocculation if the ammonium contents are very high).

– *Taschiro reagent:* mix one part of 0.1% methyl red in ethanol and three parts of 0.1% bromocresol green in ethanol.
– *Calcined heavy magnesia:* $(Mg(OH)_2$, mw = 58.34).
– *2% boric acid* $(H_3BO_3$ mw = 61.84) in water.
– *1/40 mol L^{-1} (N/20) standard sulphuric acid solution.*
– *1% phenolphthalein in ethanol.*

Procedure Using Steam Distillation

Exchange with the Ammonium Ion

– Measure the moisture of the samples to correct the results on the basis of soil dried at 105°C.
– Weigh 2 g (or 5 g if the CEC is weak) of air-dried soil sieved to 0.5 mm.
– Put the soil in a 100 mL centrifugation tube with a screw cap and add 30 mL of 1 mol L^{-1} ammonium acetate solution at pH 7.0.
– Homogenize on the vortex mixer for 2 min.
– Leave in contact overnight.
– Agitate again on the vortex mixer for 2 min and centrifuge at 5,000g for 5–10 min (depending on the physical properties of the soil).
– Decant the supernatant which must be limpid, without soil loss.
– Suspend again in 30 mL of ammonium acetate on the vortex mixer and leave in contact for 15 min.
– Centrifuge and decant the supernatant, add to the former.
– Repeat this treatment a third time, mixing all the supernatants.
– Titrate the exchangeable cations (Ca, Mg, K, Na) in the supernatant solution.

Washing the Excess of Ammonium Ion

– Add 30 mL of 80% ethanol.
– Homogenize on the vortex mixer.
– Centrifuge and discard supernatant alcohol.
– Repeat this treatment taking care to avoid soil loss.
– Using Nessler reagent, check the absence of ammonium in the third alcohol supernatant.

Displacement of the Ammonium Ion

– Add 30 mL of 1 mol (KCl) L^{-1} solution.
– Shake on the vortex mixer and leave in contact for 30 min.
– Centrifuge and recover the supernatant taking care to avoid soil loss.
– Repeat this treatment twice; mix all the supernatants.
– Rinse the extraction solution carefully in a 600 mL Kjeldahl distillation flask (the solution can also be kept for ammonium titration by automated colorimetry).

Titration of the Ammonium Ion by Steam Distillation

– Immediately proceed to steam distillation (cf. section 14.2.1 in Chap. 14) after adding 5 g of calcined magnesia and one drop of phenol phthalein in the Kjeldahl flask (if a pink colour does not appear, add more magnesia to obtain an alkaline medium).
– Collect the distillate (approximately 100 mL) in 20 mL of 2% boric acid containing 3 drops of Taschiro indicator.
– Titrate with 1/40 mol (H_2SO_4) L^{-1} solution until the colour turns greyish pink.

Calculations

One millilitre of H_2SO_4 1/40 mol L^{-1} titrates 0.05 milliequivalents of CEC. For V mL of sulphuric acid solution, the CEC T is expressed in cmol (+) kg^{-1} of air-dried soil:

$T = V \times 0.05 \times 100$.

The result can be corrected to take soil moisture into account. For soils with variable charge analyzed without preliminary drying, T is expressed compared to soil dried at 105°C by

$T = V \times 0.05 \times 100 \times f$

where f is moisture correction factor.

Alternative Procedure Using Automated Colorimetry

Principle

This alternative concerns only the final titration of the ammonium ion, while the other extraction and displacement procedures remain unchanged (cf. Sect. "Titration of the Ammonium Ion by Steam Distillation" earlier). The indophenol blue reaction in automated continuous-flow analysis was recommended for soil CEC by Nelson (1982) and Kalra and Maynard (1986, 1991). In alkaline medium and in the presence of sodium hypochlorite, ammonium ion results in a blue colouring catalysed by sodium nitroprusside. The intensity of the colour is proportional to the quantity of ammonium ion and thus to the CEC.

Reagents

– *Ammonium stock solution*: dissolve 0.4717 g of ammonium sulphate $((NH_4)_2SO_4$, mw = 132.14) in distilled water and dilute to 1 L; the solution contains 100 µg (NH_4^+-N) mL^{-1}; store in a brown lightproof bottle in the refrigerator.

– *2 µg (NH_4^+-N) mL^{-1} ammonium solution*: dilute 4 mL of stock solution to 200 mL.

– *Standard range for ammonium*: in 25 mL volumetric flasks, put 0, 2, 4, 6, 8, 10, 12 µg of NH_4^+-N (0–6 mL of 2 µg $(NH_4^+$-N) mL^{-1} ammonium solution) and add 15 mL of the NaCl or KCl reagent used for the displacement of the ammonium ion (or the same quantity as the volume actually used, cf. "Displacement of the Ammonium Ion" later); complete to 25 mL with deionised water.

– *Sodium nitroprusside reagent* ($Na_2Fe(CN)_5NO$, $2H_2O$, mw = 297.95): dissolve 68 mg in 100 mL deionised water; homogenize and store in a brown lightproof bottle in the refrigerator.

– *Phenol reagent* (mw = 94.11): dissolve 7 g of phenol in 100 mL deionised water; store in a brown lightproof bottle in the refrigerator.

– *Hypochlorite buffered reagent*: dissolve 1.480 g of sodium hydroxide (NaOH) in approximately 70 mL deionised water; add 4.98 g of anhydrous disodic phosphate (Na_2HPO_4, mw = 141.98); homogenize and after complete dissolution add 20 mL of a recently prepared 5% solution of sodium hypochlorite (NaClO); the pH should be between 11.4 and 12; bring to 100 mL with deionised water.

– *Disodic EDTA*: dissolve 6 g of ethylene diamine tetra-acetic sodium salt ($C_{10}H_{14}O_8K_2Na_2$, $2H_2O$, mw = 336.24) in approximately 80 mL deionised water; when dissolution is complete, adjust the pH to 7.0 with sodium hydroxide and complete to 100 mL.

Procedure

– Take a filtered aliquot of the final KCl solution of the CEC (from 3 to 5 mL depending on the concentration).
– Add in a 25 mL volumetric flask:
      1 mL of EDTA reagent,
      2 mL of phenol reagent,
      2 mL of nitroprusside reagent,
      4 mL of buffered hypochlorite reagent
      homogenize after each addition

- Bring to 25 mL with deionised water.
- Place in the water bath at 40 °C for 30 min, then cool for 15 min and measure absorbance at 636 nm.
- Measure two blanks (reagents without soil sample) and read all results from the curve of the standard range obtained in the same conditions.

This method can also be performed automatically by segmented continuous-flow analysis using the manifold shown in Fig. 26.6.

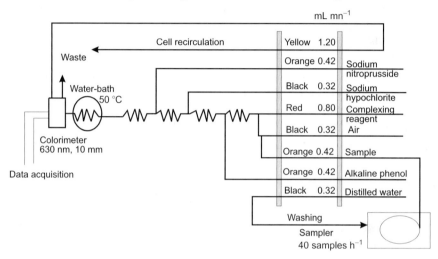

Fig. 26.6. Titration of ammonium ions in the NaCl extracts for measurement of the soil CEC by colorimetry with automated segmented continuous-flow analysis (Kalra and Maynard 1986, 1991).

Remarks

The ammonium acetate method at pH 7 is appropriate for not-calcareous soils with a moderate pH of between 5.5 and 7.5 and permanent charges, but it is not recommended for organic soils, composts, and peats because of the solubility of organic matter in ammonium acetate and ethanol.

Calcium and magnesium carbonates, as well as soluble gypsum and salts, are more or less soluble in ammonium acetate and interfere in the exchange. In soils with variable acid charges, the CEC is then overestimated.

In the case of 1:1 minerals like kaolinite and halloysite, the ammonium ion cannot completely move the Al^{3+} and H^+ ions. In 2:1 minerals like vermiculite and micas-illite, ammonium can be fixed and become non-exchangeable. For this reason, sodium and barium ions are sometimes preferred as nowadays they are more completely exchanged and easily titrated.

The type of ammonium acetate (cf. "Reagents") depends on financial and practical considerations. Commercial salt is more expensive than its ammonia and acetic acid components and tends to harden in the bottle during prolonged storage.

The successive cation exchanges and stages of rinsing are potential sources of error, for example due to soil loss by dispersion or incomplete exchanges. Some authors prefer to use Büchner funnels equipped with a double filter. The 80% ethanol should be neutral but does not have to be neutralized by ammonia in the presence of an indicator. Ethanol can be distilled on calcium hydroxide. The 80% ethanol: 20% water mixture enables excessive dehydration to be avoided (ISRIC 1987).

Checking the elimination of surplus ammonium in the ethanol filtrates is based on the Nessler reaction:

$$2 \, HgI_4^- + 2 \, NH_3 \rightarrow 2 \, NH_3HgI_2 + 4 \, I^-$$
$$2 \, NH_3HgI_2 \rightarrow NH_2HgI_3 \text{ (brown–orange precipitate)} + I^- + NH_4^+$$

Direct distillation of the soil enables errors to be avoided by removing three sub-stages of saturation by the counter-ion with the risk of losses. But distillation can result in a positive error by releasing ammonium from organic matter, particularly if soda is used instead of magnesia.

26.4.3 Buffered method at pH 8.0–8.6

Principle

These methods were usually developed for soils resulting from weathering processes which, in arid regions, involves the release of alkaline and alkaline-earth salts. The exchange complex may be saturated with Na^+, Ca^{2+}, Mg^{2+} ions in calcareous ($CaCO_3$, $MgCO_3$), gypseous ($CaSO_4$), salic and sodic (containing soluble salts giving Na^+, Cl^{-1} SO_4^{2-}, CO_3^{2-} ions) soils. Some humic or peat acid soils are also analyzed by buffered methods at pH $\geq$ 8.0. The main methods are based on:
– Buffered solutions at pH 8.0–8.6 close to the soil pH with low chemical dissolution of the alkaline-earth carbonates which could compete with the counter-cation; the use of anion exchange resins enables elimination of the dissolved carbonates and sulphate (Bergseth and Abdel-Aal 1975);
– the use of divalent ions that do not exist in the soil, and an exchange capacity close to calcium and magnesium ions which predominate in

the main types of soils or possibly the use of sodium ions for saline soils, in order to limit modifications in charges;
– the use of solvents like ethanol or methanol which are less polar than water and limit solubilization and hydrolysis phenomena.

However, a modification in the degree of solvation of the exchangeable cations can affect some properties, in particular in the presence of zeolites (steric obstruction, molecular sieve). There is no universal method for the determination of the CEC on all soils in temperate and tropical climates, aridic or aquic systems.

The methods are more complex and less precise when the CEC has to be determined in a medium that contains soluble limestone, gypsum and salts at the same time.

Many studies have been undertaken to try and obtain satisfactory results for complex soil genesis, to simplify procedures and improve the precision and specificity while eliminating stages that can generate errors.

Monovalent cations like sodium or lithium (linked to anions like acetate, formate or chloride), or divalent cations like barium, calcium or magnesium (chloride, nitrate, sulphate), have been used in combination with triethanolamine (TEA) to buffer the medium.

All these methods originated in the works of Mehlich (1938, 1942, 1953), Bower et al. (1952), Yaalon et al. (1962), Bascomb (1964), Bergseth and Abdel-Aal (1975), Polemio and Rhoades (1977), Sayeh et al. (1978), Gillman (1979), Rhoades (1982), Misopolinos and Kavovoulos (1984); Gupta et al. (1985), Tucker (1985), Frenkel et al. (1986), Begheyn (1987), Drechsel (1987), and Sharma and Dubey (1988).

Sodium Acetate Buffered at pH 8.2

Principle

This method includes two stages (Rhoades 1982):
– The cationic sites of the exchange complex are saturated by sodium ions in the form of acetate or chloride as markers in a solution containing 60% of 95° ethanol to limit solubilization of the non-exchangeable forms;
– Sodium counter-ion is extracted with a magnesium cation in nitrate solution.

Sodium and chloride are titrated in the final extract (excess soluble sodium in the extraction solution can be deduced from total measured sodium giving exchangeable sodium equivalent to the CEC).

This method is suitable for soils containing carbonates, gypsum and zeolites and can also be used on salic and sodic soils. However, Gupta et al. (1985) mentioned some difficulties in saline soils with a higher pH and suggest the pH of the saturation solution should be adjusted to that of the soil in aqueous medium and include a second stage with a magnesium nitrate solution at pH 8.6.

Reagents

- *Saturation solution* of 0.4 mol L^{-1} sodium acetate and 0.1 mol L^{-1} sodium chloride in 60% ethanol: weigh 54.4320 g of sodium acetate ($CH_3COONa,3H_2O$, mw = 136.09) and 5.8450 g of sodium chloride (NaCl, mw = 58.45); dissolve in approximately 300 mL of deionised water; add 600 mL of pure 95° ethanol and adjust the pH to 8.2 with 6 mol L^{-1} soda; complete to 1 L with deionised water; titrate sodium and chloride ions and determine the Na^+:Cl^- ratio of the solution.
- *Extraction solution* of 0.25 mol L^{-1} magnesium nitrate: weigh 6.411 g of magnesium nitrate ($Mg(NO_3)_2$, $6H_2O$, mw = 256.43) and dissolve in approximately 900 mL of deionised water; complete to 1 L.

Procedure

- Determine the moisture of the samples to bring back the results to soils dried at 105°C.
- Weigh 5 g of air dried soil sieved to 0.5 mm in a 100 mL centrifugation tube with a screw cap.

Saturation

- Add 33 mL of saturation solution (if the electric conductivity of the salt content is higher than 4 mmhos cm^{-1} first carry out a preliminary extraction with 33 mL of deionised water).
- Centrifuge at 2,500g for 5 min and decant the supernatant taking care to avoid soil loss.
- Add 33 mL of saturation solution and shake the tube on the vortex mixer to remove the centrifugation pellet, then in an ultrasound tank for 30 s to disperse the sample.
- Agitate for 5 min, centrifuge and decant the supernatant.
- Repeat this treatment twice and discard the liquid fractions.

Displacement of the Sodium Counter-Ion

- Add 33 mL of magnesium nitrate extraction solution to the centrifugation pellet.
- Stir on the vortex mixer and shake for 5 min.
- Centrifuge and decant the supernatant in a 100 mL volumetric flask.
- Again add 33 mL of extraction solution and repeat the extraction twice.
- Mix the three supernatants, complete to 100 mL with the extraction solution and homogenize.

Titration of the Displaced Sodium Counter-Ion

– Determine total sodium $[Na^+T]$ by flame photometry and total chloride $[Cl^-T]$ by coulometry–amperometry (cf. Sect. 18.3.6 of Chap. 18), in cmol L^{-1} in the extracts, using calibration ranges prepared in the magnesium nitrate extraction solution.

Calculations

$$CEC = (Na^+T \text{ - soluble } Na^+) \text{ in cmol } (+) \text{ kg}^{-1} \text{ (soil)}$$

$$CEC = \frac{10}{w}([Na^+_T] Df_{Na^+} - [Cl^-_T] Df_{Cl^-})$$

w, sample weight; Df, dilution factor, i.e. ratio of the final volume to volume of the aliquot.

Barium Chloride–Triethanolamine (TEA) at pH 8.1

Principle

The soil is saturated by barium ion in medium buffered by triethanolamine (TEA) at pH 8.1.

The barium counter-cation is moved by the magnesium divalent cation. Titration of the displaced barium is carried out by emission spectrometry at 489 nm or by atomic absorption spectrometry and gives the potential CEC at this pH; this is considered to be representative of the basic quantity adsorbed by a soil in the presence of limestone in equilibrium with air CO_2 at normal pressure.

This method is used for acid, organic, calcareous or 1:1 clay soils. It overestimates the CEC values of soils whose pH is lower than 8.2.

It also enables measurement of total potential acidity to determine liming requirements (cf. Chap. 24).

Reagents

– *Barium chloride–triethanolamine buffered solution:* weigh 61.077 g of $BaCl_2, 2H_2O$ (mw = 244.31); dissolve in about 900 mL of boiled deionised CO_2-free water, add 29.84 g of triethanolamine ($N(CH_2-CH_2OH)_3$, mw = 169.19); homogenize and bring to pH 8.1 with HCl; complete to 1 L; protect the reagent from contact with atmospheric CO_2 by storing it in a bottle closed by a air intake tube filled with soda lime.
– *Replacement solution:* weigh 61.077 g of $BaCl_2,2H_2O$, dissolve in approximately 900 mL boiled deionised CO_2-free water, add 0.4 mL of the above buffered solution; complete to 1 L and protect from atmspheric CO_2 in the same way as the buffered solution.

– *Final exchange solution*: weigh 123.21 g of magnesium nitrate ($Mg(NO_3)_2$, $6H_2O$ (mw = 256.43) well dried in a desiccator; dissolve in about 900 mL of deionised water; bring to 1 L.
– *Bromocresol green indicator* (3,3′, 5,5′ tetrabromo m cresol sulfone phthalein): make a 0.1% solution in water.
– *Mixed indicator*: weigh 1.250 g of methyl red (*p*-dimethylamino azobenzene *O*-carboxylic acid; mw = 269.29); weigh 0.825 g of methylene blue (3,7 bis dimethylamino phenazathionium chloride, mw = 373.90); dissolve in 1 L of neutral 90° ethanol.

Procedure

– Measure the soil moisture in order to correct the results to soil dried at 105°C.
– Weigh 5 g of soil, add 25 mL of buffer solution and homogenize.
– Leave in contact for 1 h avoiding contact with atmospheric CO_2.
– Transfer on a small Büchner funnel with a diameter of 50 mm equipped with a fine filter for quantitative analysis and filter slowly.
– Percolate with 75 mL buffer solution, added in small fractions at regular intervals.
– Place the percolate in a 200 mL volumetric flask.
– Add 100 mL of replacement $BaCl_2$ solution in small fractions and mix the percolate in the 200 mL flask.
– Complete volume to 200 mL with the replacement solution (EA solution); store the wet soil in the Büchner funnel while waiting to continue CEC titration.
– Prepare a blank with 100 mL of buffer-TEA solution and 100 mL of replacement solution.
– Wash the soil with approximately 100 mL methanol until chloride is eliminated ($AgNO_3$ test).
– Remove excess methanol by washing with 0.0005 mol L^{-1} (0.001 N) barium chloride solution.
– Pack the soil flat in the Büchner to eliminate 0.001 N $BaCl_2$ (the error due to the presence of residual 0.001 N $BaCl_2$ is negligible, but can be corrected by weighing Büchner + filter + soil).
– Add 250 mL of $Mg(NO_3)_2$ exchange solution in small fractions leaving the Büchner under weak vacuum to obtain a total contact time of approximately 16 h.
– Complete the volume of the exchange solution to 250 mL (CEC solution).
– Titrate the barium ion by atomic emission (489 nm) or absorption or ICP spectrometry (Pansu et al. 2001), using a standard range prepared in the $Mg(NO)_3)_2$ exchange solution.

Measurement of exchangeable acidity in EA solution: add two drops of bromocresol green indicator and few drops of mixed indicator; titrate with a 0.1 mol (HCl) L^{-1} solution until the colour turns greyish violet.

Calculations

The exchange acidity *EA* is expressed in cmol (H$^+$) kg^{-1} (soil) by:

$$EA = \frac{100\,(V_b - V_s)\,N}{w},$$

where V_b, V_s are volumes of 0.1 mol (HCl) L^{-1} solution necessary for the back-titration of the blank and the sample, respectively (EA percolate), w is the weight of the sample with correction of moisture content to that of soil dried at 105°C.

The CEC is expressed in cmol (+) kg^{-1} by:

$$CEC = 25\,\frac{T_{Ba}}{w}\,Df,$$

where T_{Ba} is the barium title of the CEC solution in mmol (1/2Ba^{++}) L^{-1} given on the calibration curve, Df is the dilution factor.

Remarks

This method involves the neutralization of several types of acidity (cf. Chap. 23):

– Acidity generated by exchangeable protons;
– Acidity resulting from hydrolysis phenomena in soils with a pH < 5.2,

$$Al^{3+} + 3\,OH^- \rightarrow Al\,(OH)_3$$
$$Al^x(OH)_3^{x-y} + y\,OH^- \rightarrow Al^x(OH)_3^{x}$$

– Acidity resulting from organic matter (acid functional groups) especially at pH < 5.5 (Thomas 1982).

26.4.4 Buffered Method at Different pH

These methods are very useful for the study of soils with variable charges. They enable standardization of repetitive procedures using CEC techniques in buffered medium with a simple change of extraction reagent. Charges developed at different pH can be checked using two or three measurements at acid, neutral and basic pH depending on the soil type. This gives an acceptable approximation of the CEC at the soil pH and helps sort out samples on which more complete charge analyses have to be performed (e.g. ZPC, cf. Chap. 20).

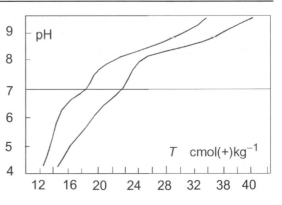

Fig. 26.7. Relation between pH and cation exchange capacity (measured with 1 mol L^{-1} ammonium acetate solution on air-dried samples) on allophanic soils from Guadeloupe (Gautheyrou and Gautheyrou 1981)

The exchange properties of allophanic soils have been characterized by measurements of the ΔCEC = CEC measured at pH 3.5 minus CEC measured at pH 10.5. But the dissolution phenomena of mineral and organic fractions which appear at extreme pH in these types of soil sometimes make this measurement uncertain (Aomine and Jackson 1959; Yoshinaga and Aomine 1962; Alexiades and Paxinos 1965; Espinoza 1969).

The method of Fey and Leroux (1976) using 0.05 mol ($\frac{1}{2}$CaCl$_2$) L^{-1} was used

– at pH 3, 5 and 7 to measure the surface charges that depend on pH (CEC–AEC; Hendershot and Lavkulich 1983);

– at pH 3, 4, 5, 6, 7, 8 with a Ca(NO$_3$)$_2$–NH$_4$Cl system (Duquette and Hendershot 1987).

The 1 mol L^{-1} ammonium acetate method was used from pH 4–9 for allophanic soils (Gautheyrou and Gautheyrou 1981), the stability constants of the ammonium acetate buffer enabling this pH zone to be covered without the use of other systems (Fig. 26.7).

In andosols, allophanic substances that are invisible to X-ray are easily detected by the sodium fluoride test, but the significant variations in the CEC values at pH 7 and especially at pH 9 are characteristic of soils with variable charges. This method makes it possible to measure (for a single pH) changes in the charges of a soil both preserved in its original moisture and after prolonged air drying. The effect of pretreatments can also be examined, for example the saturation of the AEC by a PO$_4^{3-}$ reagent. Indeed, addition of PO$_4^{3-}$ causes packing of the negative surface charges in the hydrandepts resulting in the lowering of the pH 0 value (El Swaify and Sayegh 1975).

$$M\text{–}OH_2 + H_2PO_2^- \xrightarrow[\ pH \leq 5,5\ ]{} M\text{–}H_2PO_4^- + H_2O$$

creation of negative charges (M = Fe, Al, Si, Ti).

In soils with strong aluminic acidity, the opposite effect can be observed with aluminium (Uehara and Keng 1975). Table 26.2 shows the effect of the phosphate ion on the CEC of different soils (Gautheyrou and Gautheyrou 1981).

Table 26.2. Variations in the CEC as a function of pretreatments of anionic saturation with phosphate ions (Gautheyrou and Gautheyrou 1981; soils in their natural moisture, not air-dried, results brought back to soils dried at 105°C)

soil	ref.	moisture %	$T(NH_4)$ pH 7.0 $cmol(+)kg^{-1}$ 1	2	total P cg kg^{-1} 1	2
cryandept	Ecuador E 264 a	35.31	10.50	13.50	100.00	234
hydrandept	AntillesB 570 c	189.43	22.25	38.00	177.50	1,450
imogolitic	Antilles B 570 f	116.68	19.50	44.00	67.25	1,700
ferrallitic	Antilles L 415 a	4.59	14.00	15.00	42.50	244
ferrallitic	Antilles L 415 b	4.23	11.50	11.50	25.00	310
halloysite	Antilles L 21 b	8.58	16.50	20.00	37.50	275

1, without preliminary treatment;
2, with saturation by dipotassic phosphate.

References

Alexiades CA and Paxinos SA (1965) A method for determination of allophane in soil clays. *Agric. Anals. Aristotelian Univ. (Thessaloniki)*, 275–301

Amavis (1959) Comparaison des méthodes de mesure de la capacité d'échange d'ions d'un sol. Mise au point d'une méthode rapide. *Science du Sol*, AFES, 8, 317-325

Aomine S and Jackson ML (1959) Allophane determination in ando soils by cation-exchange capacity delta value. *Soil Sci. Soc. Am. Proc.*, 23, 210–213

Bascomb CL (1964) A rapid method for the determination of cation exchange capacity of calcareous and non calcareous soils. *J. Sci. Food. Agric.*, 15, 821–823

Begheyn L Th (1987) A rapid method to determine cation exchange capacity and exchangeable bases in calcareous, gypsiferons, saline and sodic soils. *Commun. Soil Sci. Plant Anal.*, 18, 911–932

Bergmann K and O'Konski CT (1963) A spectroscopic study of methylene blue monomer, dimer and complexes with montmorillonite. *J. Phys. Chem.*, 67, 2169–2177

Bergseth H and Abdel-Aal ShI (1975) Ion exchange removal of calcium carbonate and gypsum from mineral material prior to determination of cation exchange capacity using 89 Sr^{2+}. *Colloïd Polym. Sci.*, 253, 322–324

Bolt GM (1982) Soil Chemistry – B – physico-chemical models. ELSEVIER, Developments in soil science 5B, 226–229

Cenens J and Schoonheydt RA (1990) Quantitative absorption spectroscopy of cationic dyes on clays. Proc. 9th Intern. Clay Conference, Strasbourg. In *Pub. Sci. Geol. Mem.*, Farmer VC and Tardy Y ed. 85, 15–23

Chabra R, Pleysier J and Cremers A (1976) The measurement of the cation exchange capacity and exchangeable cations in soils : a new method. *Proc. Int. Clay Conf.*, 1, 439–449

Coleman NT and Thomas GW (1967) The basic chemistry of soil acidity. In *Soil Acidity and Liming*, Pearson RN et Adams F ed. Am. Soc. Agr.

Cornell RM and Aksoyoglu ES (1991) Simultaneaous determination of the cation exchange capacity and the exchangeable cations on marl. *Clay Miner.*, 26, 567–570

Cornell RM and Aksoyoglu ES (1991) Simultaneous determination of the cation exchange capacity and the exchangeable cations on marl. *Clay Miner.*, 26, 567–570

Drechsel P (1987) Determining cation exchange capacity and exchangeable cations in saline, calcareous and gypserous soils. *Z. Pflanzenernähr. Bodenk.*, 150, 357

Duquette M and Hendershot WH (1987) Contribution of exchangeable aluminium to cation exchange capacity at low pH. *Canad. J. Soil Sci.*, 67, 175–185

Edmeades DC and Clinton OE (1981) A simple rapid method for the measurement of exchangeable cations and effective cation exchange capacity. *Commun. Soil Sci. Plant Anal.*, 12, 683–695

El Swaify SA and Sayegh AW (1975) Charge characteristics of an oxisol and an inceptisol from Hawaï. *Soil Sci.*, 120, 49

Espinoza WG (1969) Determinacion de alofan en suelos de Nuble mediante el valor delta de la capacidad total de intercambio cationico. *Agricultura Tecnica (Chili)*, 29, 127–132

Esquevin J (1954) *Mesure de la CEC des argiles par le chlorure de cobalti-hexamine*. Museum Histoire Naturelle, Paris

Fallavier P, Babre D and Breysse M (1985) Détermination de la capacité d'échange cationique des sols tropicaux acides. *Agronomie Tropicale*, 40, 298–308

Fey MV and Leroux J (1976) Electric charges on sesquioxidic soils clays. *Soil Sci. Soc. Am. J.*, 40, 359–364

Frenkel H, Gerstl Z and Van de Veen JR (1986) Determination of gypsum and cation exchange capacity in arid soils by a resin method. *Geoderma*, 39, 67–77

Fripiat JJ and Helsen J (1966) Use of cobalt hexamine in the cation exchange capacity determination of clays. *Clays Clay Miner.*, 14, 163–169

Gangaiya P and Morrison RJ (1987) A simple non-atomic absorption procedure for determining the effective cation exchange capacity of tropical soils. *Soil Sci. Plant Anal.*, 18, 1421–1430

Gautheyrou J and Gautheyrou M (1981) *Contribution à l'étude de la capacité d'échange des sols à allophane : aspect analytique de la CEC et ses conséquences sur l'interprétation pédo-agronomique.*, Notes laboratoires, Vol. 1, 274 pp., vol. 2, 123 pp. + annexe, 154 profils, IRD (ex-Orstom), Antilles, Paris

Gillman GP (1979) A proposed method for the measurement of exchange properties of highly weathered soils. *Austr. J. Soil Res.*, 17, 129–139

Gupta RK, Singh CP and Abrol IP (1985) Determining cation-exchange capacity and exchangeable sodium in alkali soils. *Soil Sci.*, 139, 326–332

Hendershot WH and Lavkulich LM (1983) Effect of sesquioxide coatings on surface charge of standard mineral and soil samples. *Soil Sci. Soc. Am. J.*, 47, 1252–1260

Hoffman U and Dammler J (1969) Die methylenblauadsorption on montmorilonite. *Chimia*, 23, 476–480

ISRIC (1987) *Procedures for Soil Analysis*, 9-5/9-7. International soil reference and information center, 2e edition

Johanson A (1961) Cobalt – an expedient agent in soil testing for T, S and exchangeable Ca, Mg and Mn. *Soil Sci.*, 364–368

Johnson CE Jr (1957) Méthylène blue adsorption and surface area measurements. *131st National Meeting Am. Chem. Soc.*, 7–12

Juo ASR, Ayanjala SA and Ogunwale JA (1976) An evaluation of cation exchange capacity measurements of soils in the tropics. *Commun. Soil Sci. Plant Anal.*, 1, 751–761

Kamprath EJ (1970) Exchangeable Al as a criterium for liming leached mineral soils. *Soil Sci. Soc. Am. Proc.*, 34, 252–254

Keita MK and Van Der Pol F (1987) Comparison of exchangeable bases and CEC by the cobalti-hexamine method and the standard ammonium acetate method on some malinese soils. *ISRIC*, 87–98

Kelley WP (1948) *Cation exchange in soils.*, Reinhold. ACS Monograph no. 109, 144 pages

Lagaly G (1981) Characterization of clays by organic compounds. *Clay Minerals*, 16, 1–21

Mantin I and Glaeser R (1960) Fixation des ions cobalti–hexamine par les montmorillonites acides. *Bull. Groupe Fr. Argiles*, 12, 83–88

Mantin I (1969) Mesure de la capacité d'échange des minéraux argileux par l'éthylène diamine et les ions complexes et l'éthylène-diamine. *C.R. Acad. Sc. Paris*, 269, 815–818

Mas A, Peigneur P and Cremers A (1978) Stability of metal (uncharged) ligand complexes in ion exchanges. Part 2 : The copper–ethylene–diamine complex in montmorillonite and sulphonic acid resin. *J. Chem. Soc. Faraday Trans.*, 1 (74), 182–189

Mehlich A (1938) Use for triethanolamine acetate–barium hydroxyde buffer for determination of some base exchange properties and lime requirements of soil. *Soil Sci. Soc. Am. Proc.*, 3, 165–166

Mehlich A (1942) Rapid estimation of base-exchange properties of soils. *Soil Sci.*, 53, 1–14

Mehlich A (1953) Rapid determination of cation and anion exchange properties and pH of soils. *J. Assoc. Agr. Chem.*, 36, 445–457

Misopolinos ND and Kalovoulos JM (1984) Determination of CEC and exchangeable Ca and Mg in non-saline calcareous soils. *Soil Sci.*, 35, 93–98

Morel R (1957) Etude expérimentale des phénomènes d'échange sur différents minéraux argileux. *Ann. Agron.*, 6, 5–90

Nevins MJ and Weintritt DJ (1967) Determination of cation exchange capacity by methylene blue adsorption. *Am. Ceram. Soc. Bull.*, 46, 587–592

NF ISO 11260 (1994) Détermination de la capacité d'échange cationique effective et du taux de saturation en bases échangeables à l'aide d'une solution de chlorure de Baryum. In *Qualité des sols*, 1999, AFNOR, Paris, 415–428

NF ISO 14254 (1997) *Détermination de l'acidité échangeable dans un extrait au chlorure de baryum.*, AFNOR, Paris

Oliver R (1984) Etude comparative de deux méthodes d'extraction et de dosage des bases et de la capacité d'échange sur les sols du Sénégal. *Agronomie Tropicale*, 39, 14–21

Orsini, L. & Remy, J.C. 1976. Utilisation du chlorure de cobaltihexammine pour la détermination simultanée de la capacité d'échange et des bases échangeables des sols. Science du Sol, 4, 269–275.

Pansu M, Gautheyrou J and Loyer JY (2001) *Soil Analysis – Sampling, Instrumentation and Quality Control.*, Balkema, Lisse, Abington, Exton, Tokyo, 489 pp

Peech M, Alexander LT, Dean LA and Ree JF (1947) *Methods of Soil Analysis for Soil Fertility Investigations.*, US Dept. Agr., 757, 25 p

Peigneur P (1976) *Stability and Adsorption Affinity of Some Transition Metalamine Complexes in Alumino-Silicates.*, Thèse Univ. Louvain

Phelps GW and Harris DL (1967) Specific surface and dry strength by methylene blue adsorption. *Am. Ceram. Soc. Bull.*, 47, 1146–1150

CEC with organic cations

Pleysier J and Cremers A (1973) Adsorption of silver thiourea complexe in montmorillonite. *J. Nat.*, 243, 86–87

Pleysier J and Cremers A (1975) Stability of silver–thiourea complexes in montmorillonite clay. *Chem. J. Soc. Faraday Trans.*, I (71), 256–264

Pleysier JL and Juo ASR (1980) A simple extraction method using silver. Thiourea for measuring exchangeable cations and effective CEC in soils with variable charges. *Soil Sci.*, 129, 205–211

Polemio M and Rhoades JD (1977) Determining cation exchange capacity : a new procedure for calcareous and gypserous soil. *Soil Sci. Soc. Am. J.*, 41, 524–528

Prianishnikov D (1913) Quantitative bestimmung der in boden vorhanden absorptiv gebunden basen. *Landw. Vers. Stat*, (79/80), 667–680

Rhoades JD (1982) Cation exchange capacity. In *Methods of Soil Analysis*, part 2, Page AL, Miller RH and Keeney DR ed. Am. Soc. Agronomy, 2, 154–157

Rytwo G, Serban C, Nir S and Margulies L (1991) Use of methylene blue aid crystal violet for determination of exchangeable cations in montmorillonite. *Clays Clay Miner.*, 39, 551–555

Sayeh AH, Khan NA, Khan P and Ryan J (1978) Factors affecting gypsum and cation exchange capacity determinations in gypsiferous soils. *Soil Sci.*, 125, 294–300

Schollenberger CJ and Simons RH (1945) Determination of exchange capacity and exchangeable bases in soils. *Soil Sci.*, 59, 13–24

Schollenberger CJ (1927) Exchangeable hydrogen and soil reaction. *Science*, 65, 552–553

Searle PL (1986) The measurement of soil cation exchange properties using the single extraction, silver thiourea method : an evaluation using a range of New Zealand soils. *Austr. J. Soil Res.*, 2, 193–200

Sharma OP and Dubey DD (1988) Evaluation of suitable method for estimating CEC of sodic black soils. *J. Indian Soc. Soil Sci.*, 36, 546–549

Siegried CH, Weinert W and Strelow FWE (1986) The influence of thiourea on the cation-exchange behaviour of various elements in dilute nitric and hydrochloric acids. *Talanta*, 33, 481–487

Stuanes PO, Ognes G and Opem M (1984) Ammonium nitrate as extractant for soil exchangeable cations, exchangeable acidity and aluminum commun. *Soil Sci. Plant Anal.*, 15, 773–778

Stucki JW, Golden DC Roth CB, (1984) Effects of reduction and reoxydation of structural iron on the surface charge and dissolution of diodahedral smectites. *Clays Clay Miner.*, 32, 350–356

Thomas GW (1982) Exchangeable cations. In *Methods of Soil Analysis*, part 2, Page AL, Miller RH and Keeney DR ed. Am. Soc. Agronomy, 2e edition, 9 (2), 159–165

Tucker BM (1985) A proposed New Reagent for the measurement of cation exchange properties of carbonate soils. *Aust. J. Soil Res.*, 23, 633–642

Uehara G and Keng J (1975) Management implications of soil mineralogy in Latin America. In *Soil Management in Tropical America*, Bornemisza E et Alvarado A ed. North-Carolina Univ. Press, 351

Van Rosmalen HA (1980) *Evolution and Modification of the Determination of Exchangeable Bases and Cation Exchange Capacity of Calcareous and Gysiferous Soils by Using Silver–Thiourea.*, Royal Tropical Inst. Dept. Agric. Res. Project AOBO39 (Amsterdam), Report BO, 80–83

Yaalon DH, Van Schuylenborgh J and Slager S (1962) The determination of cation exchange characteristics of saline and calcareous soils. *Nether. J. Agr. Sci.*, 10, 218–222

Yoshinaga N and Aomine S (1962) Imogolite in some ando soils. *Soil Sci. Plant Nutr.*, 8, 22–29

Yuan TL (1959) Determination of exchangeable hydrogen in soils by a titration method. *Soil Sci.*, 88, 164–167

Bibliography

CEC general theory

Chu CH and Johnson LJ (1979) Cation-exchange behavior of clays and synthetic aluminosilica gels. *Clays Clay Miner.*, 27, 87–90

Dyer A, Shaheen T and Newton GWA (1995) Speciation observed by cation exchange. *Sci. Total Environ.*, 173–174, 301–311

Effron D, Jimenez MP, Horra AM de la (2000) Cation exchange capacity at the soil pH level to be applied to acid soils: methods and determination. Capacidad de intercambio cationica al pH del suelo, para suelos acidos: metodo de determinacion. *Agrochimica.*, 44, 61–68

Erp PJ van, Houba VJG and Beusichem ML van (2001) Actual cation exchange capacity of agricultural soils and its relationship with pH and content of organic carbon, *Communications-in-Soil-Science-and-Plant-Analysis*, 32, 19–31

Fauziah CI, Jamilah I and Omar SRS (1997) An evaluation of cation exchange capacity methods for acid tropical soils, *Pertanika J. Tropical Agric. Sci.*, 20, 113–119

Kalra YP and Maynard DG (1994) A comparison of extractants for the determination of cation exchange capacity and extractable cations by a mechanical vacuum extractor. *Commun. Soil Sci. Plant Anal.*, 25, 1505–1515

Khan NA (1994) Comparison of CEC values with and without pretreatment of gypsiferous soils. *Sarhad Journal of Agriculture*, 10, 713–720

Liu CL, Wang MK and Yang CC (2001) Determination of cation exchange capacity by one-step soil leaching column method. *Commun. Soil Sci. Plant Anal.*, 32, 2359–2372

Pleysier JL, Jansens J and Cremers A (1986a) A clay suspension stability and point titration method for measuring cation exchange capacity of soils. *Soil Sci. Soc. Am. J.*, 50, 887–891

Pleysier JL, Jansens J and Cremers A (1986b) Extraction of cations from some kaolinitic soils of the tropics. ISRIC – *Proceedings of International Workshop on Laboratory Methods and Data Exchange Programme*, 51–65

Ralchev T and Toncheva R (1997) Kinetics of the desorption of cations. I. A mathematical model testing. *Pochvoznanie, Agrokhimiya y Ekologiya.*, 32, 34–36

Stucki JN, Golden DC and Roth CB (1984) Effects of reduction and reoxydation of structural iron on the surface charge and dissolution of dioctahedral smectites. *Clays Clay Miner.*, 32, 350–356

Sumner ME and Miller WP (1996) Cation exchange capacity and exchange coefficients, (1996). In *Methods of Soil Analysis, part 3, Chemical Methods*, Bigham JM and Bartels JM ed. SSSA–ASA, Madison, WI Etats-Unis, 1201–1229

Zhao BJ, Lam MT, Back MH, Gamble DS and Wang C (1997) Soil cation exchange capacity measurements using ultrafiltration techniques: comparison of different metal ions as substitutes. *Commun. Soil Sci. Plant Anal.*, 28, 161–171

Zhi ZL, Rios A and Valcarel M (1994) Direct determination of the cation-exchange capacity of soils with automatic sample pretreatment in a flow system. *Anal. Chim. Acta.*, 298, 387–392

Barium Method at soil pH

Gillman GP, Bruce RC, Davey BG, Kimble JM, Searle PL and Skjemstad JO (1983) A comparison of methods used for the determination of cation exchange capacity. *Commun. Soil Sci. Plant Anal.*, 14, 1005–1014

Hendershot WH and Duquette M (1986) A simple Barium chloride method for determining cation exchange capacity and exchangeable cations. *Soil Sci. Soc. Am. J.*, 50, 605–608

Lambert K, Vanderdeelen J and Baert L (1988) An improved method for cation exchange capacity determination of peat soils. *Pédologie*, XXXVIII(1), 5–14

Matsue N and Wada K (1985) A new equilibrium method for cation exchange capacity measurement. *Soil Sci. Soc. Am. J.*, 49, 574–578

Buffered Method at pH 7.0

Arbelo CD and Hernandez-Moreno JM (1992) Cation exchange capacity of Andosols as determined by the ammonium acetate (pH7) method. Capacidad de cambio en Andosoles pro los metodos del acetato amonico (pH7) y cloruro de basio no tamponado. *Agrochimica*, 36: 1–2, 53–62

Chapman HD (1965) Cation-exchange capacity. In *Methods of Soil Analysis. Part 2. Chemical and Microbiological Properties,* Black C.A. et al. ed. American Society of Agronomy, 9, 891–901

FAO (1972) *Physical and Chemical Methods of Soil and Water Analysis.*, FAO Soils Bulletin no. 10

Jackson ML (1958) *Soil Chemical Analysis.*, Prentice-Hall, New York

Jaynes WF and Bigham JM (1986) Multiple cation-exchange capacity measurements on standard clays using a commercial mechanical extractor. *Clays Clay Miner.*, 1, 93–98

Kalra YP and Maynard DG (1986) An evaluation of automated and manual methods for NH_4–N analysis in the determination of cation exchange capacity of soils. In *Proceedings of International Workshop on the Laboratory Methods and Data Exchange Programme (Wageningen),* Pleijsier LK ed. 67–76

Kalra YP and Maynard DG (1990) An evaluation of a mechanical vacuum extractor for the determination of cation exchange capacity and extractable cations in calcareous soils. *Trans. 14th Int. Cong. Soil. Sci.,* Kyoto II, 451–452

Kalra YP and Maynard DG (1991) Methods manual for forest soil and plant analysis. *Forêts Canada – Information Report NOR-X-319,* 84–94

Kelley WP (1927) A general discussion of the chemical and physical properties of alkali soils. *1st Int. Congr. Soil Sci. Proc.,* 483–489

Metson AT (1956) *Methods of Chemical Analysis for Soil Survey Samples.,* USDA – Soil Bureau, Bull. 12

Peech M (1945) Determination of exchangeable cations and exchange capacity of soils. Rapid micromethods utilizing centrifuge and spectro photometer. *Soil Sci.,* 59, 25–38

Schuman GE, Stanley MA and Knudsen D (1973) Automated total nitrogen analysis of soil and plant samples. *Soil Sci. Soc. Am. Proc.,* 37, 480–481

Skjemstad JO and Reeve R (1976) The determination of nitrogen in soils by rapid high-temperature kjeldahl digestion and autoanalysis. *Commun. Soil Sci. Plant Anal.,* 7, 229–239

TECHNICON (1973) *Method for NH_4N 154-71 W (colorimetry).,* Technicon Instrument Corporation Industrial Methods

USDA (1972) *Soil Survey Laboratory Methods and Procedures for Collecting Soil Samples.,* USDA – Soil survey investigations, report no. 1

Cobaltihexamine CEC

Gautheyrou J and Gautheyrou M (1958) *Détermination des cations échangeables et de la CEC des sols à allophane dévelopés sur cendres volcaniques récentes (soufrière de Guadeloupe) avec le chlorure de cobalti-hexamine.*, IRD (ex-Orstom), Guadeloupe, Paris, rapport multigraphié, 1–4

Maes A, Tits J, Mermans G and Dierckx A (1992) Measurement of the potentially available charge and the dissociation behaviour of humic acid from cobalti-hexamine adsorption. *J. Soil Sci.*, 43, 669–677

Ciesielski H and Sterckeman T (1997) Determination of cation exchange capacity and exchangeable cations in soils by means of cobalt hexamine trichloride. Effects of experimental conditions. Agronomie, 17: 1, 1–7

Silver–Thiourea

Pleysier J (1976) *Silver uncharged ligand complexes in aluminosilicates: adsorption and stability.*, These Univ. Louvain

Van Reeuwijk LP (1987) Procedures for soil analysis cation exchange capacity and exchangeable bases (silver-thiourea method). ISRIC, *International Soil Reference and Information Center, 2e edition*, 10-1 à 10-6

CEC with organic cations (coloured reagents)

Brindley GW and Thompson TD (1970) Methylene blue adsorption by montmorillonite. Determination of surface areas and exchange capacities with different initial cation saturations. *Isr. J. Chem.*, 8, 409–415

Cenens J and Schoonheydt RA (1988) Visible spectroscopy of methylene blue on hectorite, laponite B and barasym in aqueous suspension. *Clays Clay Miner.*, 36, 214–224

Hang PT and Brindley GW (1970) Methylene blue absorption by clay minerals. Determination of surface areas and cation-exchange capacities (clay-organic studies XVII). *Clays Clay Miner.*, 18, 203–212

Marguliers L, Rozen H and Nir S (1988) Model for competitive adsorption of organic cations on clays. *Clays Clay Miner.*, 36, 270–276

Phelps GW and Harris DL (1967) Specific surface and dry strength by methylene blue adsorption. *Am. Ceram. Soc. Bull.*, 47, 1146–1150

Santoni S, Bonifacio E and Zanini E (2001) Indophenol blue colorimetric method for measuring cation exchange capacity in sandy soils. *Commun. Soil Sci. Plant Anal.*, 32, 2519–2530

Buffered methods pH 8.0–8.6

Bower CA, ReiteMeier PF and Fireman M (1952) Exchangeable cation analysis of saline and alkali soils. *Soil Sci.*, 73, 251–261

Barium chloride–Triethanolamine at pH 8.1

Bradfields R and Allison WH (1933) Criteria of base saturation in soils. *Trans. 2d Comm. Int. Soil Sci.*, A, 63–79

Mehlich A (1938) Use of triethanolamine acetate–barium hydroxyde buffer for determination of some base exchange properties and lime requirement of soil. *Soil Sci. Soc. Am. Proc.*, 3, 162–166

Mehlich A (1953) Rapid determination of cation and anions exchange properties and pH_0 of soils. *J. Assoc. Agric. Chem.*, 36, 445–457

Peech M (1965) Exchange acidity. In *Methods of Soil Analysis* Black C.A. et al. part 2. *Am. Soc. Agronomy*, 9, 905–913

USDA (1972) *Soil Survey Laboratory Methods and Procedures for Collecting Soil Samples.*, USDA. Soil survey investigations report no. 1, p. 23

Anion Exchange Capacity

27.1 Theory

Positive charges in the soil originate either from rupture of planes of the structural units and the resulting edge charges or of iron and aluminium oxides that cover some crystalline clays or occupy an interlayer position in lattice layers. These charges induce adsorption of anions (Zelazny et al. 1996).

Before 1975 anion exchange capacity (AEC) was rarely studied mainly because in the main soils in temperate zones the influence of anions is weaker than cations which link with negatively charged surfaces. This is particularly true for 2:1 clays whose zero point charge (ZPC, cf. Chap. 20) is badly defined, as the permanent negative charge is too great to be balanced by the less significant positive charges (Fig. 27.1) which appear at the edge of the rupture zones of the structural units, giving very high ratios of CEC to CEA (Bingham et al. 1965).

As the CEC is relatively low in 1:1 clays, the effects of the edge charges give low ratios of CEC to CEA, and the influence of AEC is consequently more significant, especially if the particles are small and display a significant level of disorder. These phenomena are significant in certain acid tropical soils including metallic oxides and organic anions (Theng 1979; Tate and Theng 1980; Eick et al. 1999). In spodosols, ultisols, oxisols and andosols, the values can vary from 1 to 10 mmol kg^{-1} with ratios of CEC to CEA ≤ 1. In andosols, allophane-imogolite and organic matter content can drastically modify exchange properties. The development of positive charges at the soil pH is high in these soils which have a ratio of silica to alumina of near one (Wada and Okamura 1977, 1980; Okamura and Wada 1978; Cruz Huerta and Kientz 2000).

On the other hand, if these soils contain aluminium–humus complexes, the positive charges are weak, and this makes it possible to differentiate Al–OH complexes in humus and in the mineral fraction (organic matter has a low pH0 which lowers the soil pH0 when it fixes large organic anions).

There is significant adsorption of phosphorous in andosols that involves exchange mechanisms as well as structural displacements (Rajan 1975; Parfitt and Henmi 1980).

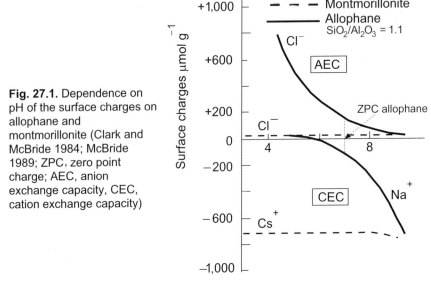

Fig. 27.1. Dependence on pH of the surface charges on allophane and montmorillonite (Clark and McBride 1984; McBride 1989; ZPC, zero point charge; AEC, anion exchange capacity, CEC, cation exchange capacity)

The polymers of iron oxides and aluminium hydroxides induce a strong AEC (Schwertmann and Taylor 1989).

In strongly weathered soils, the AEC values can be higher than the CEC values; for example when the method of Gillmann (1979) is used, acrohumox can have a CEC of 0.6 cmol (+) kg^{-1} and an AEC of 3.7 cmol (−) kg^{-1}.

The AEC was long considered to be a less important measurement than the CEC because the different anions involved in these exchanges are seldom retained by simple electrostatic bonds, but only by more complex strengths. Without selective fixation, only the exchange of Cl$^-$, NO$_3^-$ and ClO$_4^-$ anions is possible; the exchange of one anion with another anion of similar ionic force does not modify the electrophoretic mobility of the particles. There is no change in specificity related to the size of the anion and probably not to phenomena of steric impossibility (Schwertmann and Taylor 1989).

Other anions can be more strongly retained on the oxide surfaces by coordination bonds or chemisorption (e.g. different silicates, molybdates, arsenates, selenates, organic anions). Acetate is adsorbed by coulombic interaction, whereas citrate, which forms ligands with aluminium, is strongly retained. The behaviour of the anions can be defined by the adsorption model of Bowden et al. (1980).

In the case of polyanions, whose economic repercussions in agronomy are considerable (e.g. PO_4^{3-}, SO_4^{2-}), the AEC cannot account for exchangeable forms. Indeed, in addition to the exchange phenomena, other phenomena like precipitation of insoluble salts with iron, aluminium or alkaline-earth elements also have to be considered. Phosphate retention can be empirically divided into two fractions:

– A labile fraction which is extractable in different acid or basic reagents using many different methods. This labile fraction is often wrongly named "plant available phosphorus" or "easily available phosphorus" or "extractable phosphorus" (cf. Chap. 29).
– A fraction which is fixed by different mechanisms, in particular by precipitation or inclusion in complexes and can be quantified by differential analysis in a saturating medium containing an excess of phosphorus using retention methods (cf. Sect. 29.4 in Chap. 29).

Soils with variable charges that are rich in aluminium and iron oxides, and have a soil pH < pH 0(i.e. more acid than the equilibrium pH where positive and negative charges are in equal quantities, cf. Chap. 20), have a positively charged surface. As iron and aluminium hydroxides have high pH0 values of around pH 7–8, the soils in which these hydroxides are predominant have a strong AEC.

The specific fixation of anions such as fluoride can also result in considerable release of OH^- which makes it possible to test the soils containing active aluminium forms (allophanic soils, soils containing organometallic aluminium–humus complexes) using the NaF test (Kawaguchi et al. 1954; Fieldes and Perrott 1966; USDA 1975; Shoji and Ono 1978; Parfitt and Henmi 1980; Pansu et al. 2001).

Saturation of the positive charges of the exchange complex by PO_4^{3-} ions can have an indirect effect by increasing the CEC of allophanic soils as reported by many authors (Mekarus and Uehara 1972; Schalscha et al. 1972, 1974; Juo and Madukar 1972; Sawhney 1974; Rajan 1976; Ryden and Syrs 1975, 1976; Parfitt and Atkinson 1976; Galindo and Bingham 1977; Garcia-Miragaya 1984). The replacement of the water molecule bound to a metal by phosphate leads to a reduction in the positive charge and thus to an increase in the net negative charge. Additional negative charges can be created in anthropic mediums by addition of phosphate-enriched fertilizers. In the field, the reactions are slow and continuous, and phosphorous mobility is low (Fig. 27.2). The structure of the bonds at the colloid surfaces is not yet well known, in particular for aluminium, iron or manganese oxides and amorphous substances. Mono or binuclear complexes can be formed with iron (Fig. 27.3; Schwertmann and Taylor 1989). The exchange capacity can be modified at the water–colloid interface (Charlet and Schlegel 1999), in particular under the effect of waterlogging (Triana et al. 1995).

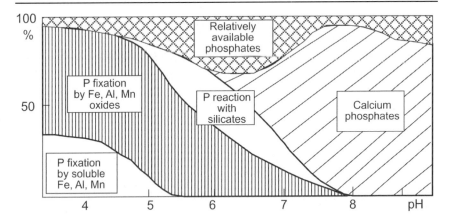

Fig. 27.2. Soil fixation and phosphate availability for plants as a function of the soil pH (after Brady 1974)

Fig. 27.3. Mono and binuclear iron–phosphorous complexes

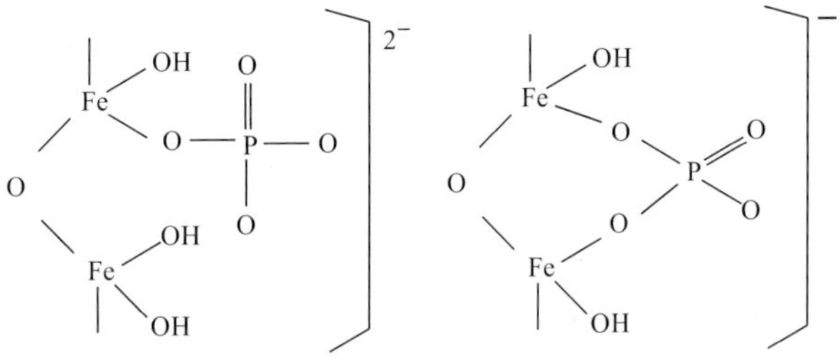

When there is no precipitation of insoluble salts, the lyotropic series of the most current anions in agronomy is (Bolt and De Hann 1982):

$$SiO_4^{4-} > \quad PO_4^{3-} > \quad SO_4^{2-} > \quad NO_3^- > Cl^-$$
$$38\ Å \qquad 36\ Å \qquad 27\ Å$$

Figure 27.4 shows adsorption of the fluoride, silicate and phosphate anions on goethite as a function of pH.

27.2 Measurement

27.2.1 Principle

Methods for the measurement of the AEC are based on the same principles as the CEC and are subject to the same constraints. Only the valence signs have to be reversed. If the surface is positively charged, any anion excess maintained by electrostatic links in the double layer is exchangeable. The AEC is the maximum quantity of anion likely to be linked per unit of soil weight.

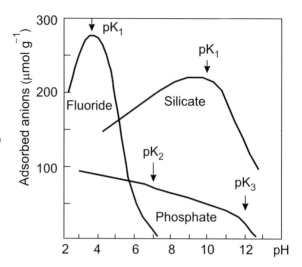

Fig. 27.4. Sorption of the phosphate, silicate and fluoride anions on goethite (after Hingston et al. 1972)

The anion exchange complex is saturated by a counter-anion that is not specifically fixed under suitable conditions of pH and ionic strength (generally chloride or nitrate anions, as nitrate cannot be used in the presence of marked redox phenomena). The anion excess is then eliminated, the fixed counter-anion is moved by another counter-anion and measured in moles of adsorbed anion per mass unit.

Similar rules to those for the determination of the CEC must be respected: the ratio of the pH concentration of solutions to sorbed quantities, the need for iterative additions to lower the buffering capacity and to move the equilibriums, the influence of contact times and of temperature which affects reaction kinetics towards equilibrium.

As the AEC is concerned with ions that can be easily moved, polyvalent anions like sulphate and phosphate cannot be used because of their specific adsorption (coordination) and because of precipitation of insoluble salts with the exchangeable cations of the medium. The AEC generally accounts for 1–5% of the CEC (Bolt and de Haan, 1982).

The method described below was proposed by Wada and Okamura (1977).

27.2.2 Method

Reagents

– 1 mol L^{-1} ammonium chloride solution (NH_4Cl, mw = 53.50).
– 0.1 mol L^{-1} ammonium chloride solution.
– 1 mol L^{-1} potassium nitrate solution (KNO_3, mw = 101.10).

Procedure

– Measure the moisture content of the sample to bring back the results to soil dried at 105°C.
– Weigh 0.5 g of soil ground to 0.5 mm in a previously tared centrifugation tube.
– Add 10 mL of the 1 mol (NH_4Cl) L^{-1} saturation solution (the pH of this solution should be around 6.0).
– Shake for 30 min; centrifuge at 5,000g and discard the supernatant.
– Suspend the centrifugation pellet five times in 10 mL of the 0.1 mol (NH_4Cl) L^{-1} solution centrifuging between each treatment.
– Weigh the tube containing the centrifugation pellet of Cl^- saturated soil in order to quantify the quantity of 0.1 mol (NH_4Cl) L^{-1} solution retained: rC in cmol (−) kg^{-1} (soil).
– Move the Cl^- ion by five additions of 10 mL of 1 mol (KNO_3) L^{-1} solution centrifuging between each treatment; mix the extracts and bring to 50 mL, this is total Cl^-.
– Titrate Cl^- in the extract by spectrophotometry; tC is expressed in cmol (−) kg^{-1} (soil).

The AEC is expressed in cmol (−) kg^{-1} (soil) by tC− rC.

27.3 Simultaneous Measurement of AEC, EC, CEC and net CEC

27.3.1 Aim

Many analytical methods have been tested with the aim of simultaneously characterizing the potential and charge of the soil which are the cause of the exchange phenomena in strongly weathered soils. Not-buffered and very dilute mediums were used to try to approach field conditions (pH and ionic strength of the soil solution).

The use of Ba^{2+} barium cation and its salts was included in many methods (e.g. Bascomb 1964; Gillman 1979; Gillman and Bakker 1979; Uehara and Gillman 1981; Gillman and Sumpter 1986).

Unfortunately Ba^{2+} cannot be used with anions like sulphate which is often present in allophanic soils or is used to correct soil deficiencies and the effects of aluminic acidity in strongly weathered soils (e.g. super-phosphate fertilizer or calcium sulphate amendments). Other anions like chloride and nitrate were consequently tested as they are not very abundant in the exchange complex and not likely to be bonded by selective adsorption. The simplicity of the titrations and their low cost means they can be used for routine analysis with a satisfactory degree of reproducibility.

27.3.2 Description

Principle

The method described here (Cochrane and De Souza 1985) concerns strongly weathered soils with variable charges. The soil sample is equilibrated with a diluted saturation solution of a counter-cation and a counter-anion with an ionic strength close to that of the soil solution. The fixed cation and anion are then moved by other counter-ions and titrated for the calculation of CEC and AEC with correction for weight. The net CEC is obtained by difference.

Reagents

– *Ionic saturation.* 0.5 $mol\,L^{-1}$ ammonium nitrate solution (NH_4NO_3, mw = 80.05): weigh 40.02 g of NH_4NO_3 and dissolve in about 900 mL of deionized water, complete to 1 L.

– *Ionic strength equilibration.* 0.0215 $mol\,L^{-1}$ ammonium nitrate solution: weigh 1.721 g of NH_4NO_3 and dissolve in 1 L of deionized water.

– *Displacement of the counter-ion.* 0.02 $mol\,L^{-1}$ potassium chloride solution (KCl, mw = 74.55): weigh 1.491 g of KCl and dissolve in about 900 mL of deionized water; complete to 1,000 mL after equilibration of the temperature.

Procedure

Extractions

- Weigh 3 g of soil sieved to 0.5 mm and put in a previously tared 50 mL centrifugation tube with a screw cap.
- Add 30 mL of 0.5 mol (NH_4NO_3) L^{-1} solution.
- Shake for 2 h and centrifuge at 6,000g.
- Decant the supernatant: this is solution A.
- Suspend the soil residue in 30 mL of 0.0215 mol (NH_4NO_3) L^{-1} solution which roughly represents the value of the osmotic potential of the soil solution (this concentration can be adjusted to fit a particular case).
- Shake for 60 min.
- Centrifuge at 6,000g.
- Discard the supernatant; repeat this equilibration twice.
- Weigh the tube + the soil centrifugation pellet to calculate the quantity of 0.0215 mol (NH_4NO_3) L^{-1} solution retained, rA is the ammonium (or nitrate) retained expressed in cmol kg^{-1} (soil).
- Add 30 mL of the 0.02 mol (KCl) L^{-1} displacement solution (which has an osmotic potential similar to the 0.0215 mol (NH_4NO_3) L^{-1} solution).
- Suspend and shake for 60 min.
- Centrifuge at 6,000g.
- Reserve the supernatant containing exchanged ammonium and nitrate ions.
- Repeat this treatment twice and mix the three extracts.
- Bring to 100 mL with 0.02 mol (KCl) L^{-1} solution: this is solution B.

Determination of the CEC and the AEC

- On solution B, titrate total ammonium (cf. Chap. 28 or use the method of Bremner and Keeney 1966) which includes exchangeable ammonium and ammonium resulting from the 0.0215 mol (NH_4NO_3) L^{-1} solution (titration is generally carried out by automated colorimetry or micro distillation and volumetry): this is tA.
  Calculate the CEC by the exchanged ammonium (cf. Chap. 26) express the results in cmol (+) kg^{-1} (soil):
  CEC = tA − rA.
- Titrate total nitrate (cf. Chap. 28) which includes exchangeable nitrate and nitrate resulting from the 0.0215 mol (NH_4NO_3) L^{-1} solution: this is tN.
  Calculate the AEC by exchanged nitrates, the results are expressed in cmol (−) kg^{-1} by:
  AEC = tN − rA;

– The net CEC is obtained by:

Net CEC = CEC – AEC

If titration cannot be performed the same day as extraction, add two drops of toluene to prevent biochemical evolution and store the extracts in the refrigerator protected from the light.

Determination of Exchangeable Cations

On solution A, measure the pH and titrate Ca, Mg, K, Na, Fe, Mn, Al by atomic absorption or inductively coupled plasma spectrometry, measure sulphate and chloride by absorption spectrometry (cf. Chap. 31 or Pansu et al. 2001):

Ca + Mg + K + Na = EC (exchangeable cations)

Al + Fe + Mn ≅ EA (exchangeable acidity)

EC + EA = effective CEC by summation.

Excess of chloride or sulphate indicates that the soil contains probably soluble salts or gypsum.

References

Bascomb CL (1964) Rapid method for the determination of cation-exchange capacity of calcareous and non-calcareous soils. *J. Sci. Food Agric.*, 15, 821–823

Bingham FT, Sims JR and Page AL (1965) Retention of acetate by montmorillonite. *Soil Sci. Soc. Am. J.*, 29, 670–672

Bolt GH and De Haan FAM (1982) Anion exclusion in soil. In *Soil Chemistry, B – Physico Chemical Models*, Bolt GH ed. Elsevier Amsterdam, Development in Soil Sciences, 5 B, 233–257

Bowden JW, Nagarajah S, Barrow NJ, Posner A and Quirk JP (1980) Describing the adsorption of phosphate, citrate and selenite on a variable charge mineral surface. *Aust. J. Soil Res.*, 18, 49–60

Brady NC (1974) *The Nature and Properties of Soils.*, MacMillan New York, 8th edition

Bremner JM and Keeney DR (1966) Determination and isotope ratio analysis of different forms of nitrogen in soils : 3-exchangeable ammonium, nitrate and nitrite by extraction-distillation methods. *Soil Sci. Soc. Am. Proc.*, 30, 577–583

Charlet L and Schlegel ML (1999) La capacite d'echange des sols. Structures et charges a l'interface eau/particule. *Comptes-Rendus-de-l'Academie-d'Agriculture-de-France*, 85, 7–24

Clark CJ and McBride MB (1984) Cation and anion retention by natural and synthetic allophane and imogolite. *Clays Clay Miner.*, 32, 291–299

Cochrane TT and Desouza GDM (1985) Measuring suface charge characteristics in oxisols and ultisols. *Soil Sci.*, 140, 223–229

Fieldes M and Perrott KW (1966) The nature of allophane in soils. Part 3, Rapid field and laboratory test for allophane. *N. Z. J. Sci.*, 9, 623–629

Galindo GG and Bingham FT (1977) Homovalent and heterovalent cation exchange equilibria in soils with variable surface charge. *Soil Sci. Soc. Am. J.*, 41, 883–886

Garcia-Miragaya J (1984) Effect of phosphate sorption of the cation exchange capacity of two Savannah ultisols from Venezuela. *Commun. Soil Sci. Plant Anal.*, 15, 935–943

Cruz Huerta L and Kientz DG (2000) Electric charge of andosols of 'Cofre de Perote', Veracruz, Mexico Carga electrica de los andosoles del Cofre de Perote, Veracruz, Mexico. *Terra*, 18, 115–124

Eick MJ, Brady WD and Lynch CK (1999) Charge properties and nitrate adsorption of some acid southeastern soils. *J. of Environ. Quality*, 28, 138–144

Gillman GP and Bakker P (1979) *The Compulsive Exchange Method for Measuring Surface Charge Characteristics of Soil.*, CSIRO-Division of Soils, Report 40

Gillman GP and Sumpter EA (1986) Modifications to the compulsive exchange method for measuring exchange characteristics of soils. *Aust. J. Soil Res.*, 24, 61–66

Gillman GP (1979) A proposed method for the measurement of exchange properties of highly weathered soils. *Aust. J. Soil Res.*, 17, 129–139

Hingston FJ, Posner AM and Quirk JM (1972) Anion adsorption by goethite and gibbsite. 1) The role of the proton in determining adsorption envelopes. *J. Soil Sci.*, 23, 177–192

Juo ASR and Madukar HP (1974) Phosphate sorption of some nigerian soils and its effect on cation exchange capacity. *Commun. Soil Sci. Plant Anal.*, 5, 479–497

Kawaguchi KH, Fukutani H, Murakami H and Hattori T (1954) Ascension of pH valves of ventral NaF extracts of allitic soils and semi quantitative determination of active alumina by the titration method. *Bull. Res. Inst. Food Sci.*, (Kyoto University, Japan), 14, 82–91

McBride MB (1989) Surface chemistry of soil minerals. In *Minerals in Soil Environments,* Dixon JB and Weed SB ed. Soil Science Society of America, 2, 35–88

Mekarus T and Uehara G (1972) Anion adsorption in ferruginous tropical soils. *Soil Sci. Soc. Am. Proc.*, 36, 296–300

Okamura Y and Wada K (1978) Charge characteristics of Kuroboku soils : effect of pH and ion concentration. *Soil Sci. Soil Manure* (Japan), 24, 32

Pansu M, Gautheyrou J and Loyer JY (2001) *Soil Analysis – Sampling, Instrumentation and Quality Control.*, Balkema, Lisse, Abington, Exton, Tokyo, 489 p

Parfitt RL and Atkinson RJ (1976) Phosphate adsorption of goethite (α.FeOOH). *Nature*, 264, 740–742

Parfitt RL and Henmi T (1980) Structure of some allophanes from New Zealand. *Clays Clay Miner.*, 28, 285–294

Rajan SSS (1975) Mechanism of phosphate adsorption by allophanic clays. *N. Z. J. Sci.*, 18, 93–101

Rajan SSS (1976) Changes in net surface charge of hydrous alumina with phosphate adsorption. *Nature*, 262, 45–46

Ryden JC and Syers JK (1975) Charge relationships of phosphate sorption. *Nature*, 255, 51–53

Ryden JC and Syers JK (1976) Calcium retention in response to phosphate sorption by soils. *Soil Sci. Soc. Am. J.*, 40, 845–846

Sawhney BL (1974) Charge characteristics of soils as affected by phosphate sorption. *Soil Sci. Soc. Am. Proc.*, 38, 159–160

Schalscha EB, Pratt PF and Soto D (1974) Effect of phosphate adsorption on the cation-exchange capacity of volcanic ash soils. *Soil Sci. Soc. Am. Proc.*, 38, 539–540

Schalscha EB, Pratt PF, Kinjo T and Amar JA (1972) Effect of phosphate salts as saturation solutions in cation-exchange capacity determinations. *Soil Sci. Soc. Am. Proc.*, 39, 912–914

Schwertmann U and Taylor RM (1989) Iron hydroxydes. In *Minerals in Soil Environments*, Dixon JB and Weed SB ed. Soil Science Society of America, 8, 379–438

Shoji S and Ono T (1978) Physical and chemical properties and clay mineralogy of andosols from Kitakami (Japan). *Japan Soil Sci.*, 126, 297–312

Tate KR and Theng BKG (1980) In *Soils with Variable Charge. Organic Matter and its Interactions with Inorganic Soil Constituents*, Theng BKG ed. New Zealand Society of Soil Science, 225–249

Theng BKG (1979) *Formation and Properties of Clay–Polymer Complexes.*, Elsevier Amsterdam, 362 pages

Triana A, Lefroy RDB, Blair GJ, Date RA ed. Grundon NJ ed. Rayment GE ed. and Probert ME (1995) The effect of flooding on S sorption capacity and AEC of variable charge soils. In *Proceedings of the Third International Symposium, Brisbane, Queensland, Australia, 12–16 September 1993*, Kluwer Dordrecht, 135–139

Uehara G and Gillman G (1981) *The Mineralogy Chemistry and Physics of Tropical Soils with Variable Charge Clays.*, Westview Tropical Agriculture Series, 4, 170 pages

USDA (1975) *Soil Survey Staff., A Basic System for Making and Interpreting Soil Surveys.*, USDA Handbook, 436 p

Wada K and Okamura Y (1977) Measurements of exchange capacities and hydrolysis as means of characterizing cation and anion retention by soils. Proceedings of the International Seminar on Soil Environment and Fertility Management in Intensive Agriculture. *Soc. Sci. Soil Manure* (Japan), 811–815

Wada K and Okamura Y (1980) Electric charge characteristics of ando A_1 and buried A_1 horizon soils. *J. Soil Sci.*, 31, 307–314

Zelazny LW, Liming HE and An Vanwormhoudt M (1996) Charge analysis of soils
    and anion exchange. In *Methods of Soil Analysis, Part 3, Chemical
    Methods*, Bigham JM and Bartels JM ed. SSSA-ASA, Madison, WI
    Etats-Unis, 1231–1253

Inorganic forms of nitrogen

28.1 Introduction

28.1.1 Ammonium, Nitrate and Nitrite

The degradation of nitrogenous organic matter results in ammonia salts, which oxidize into nitrites and nitrates under the influence of nitrifying bacteria. Nitrate anion is found in drainage water, spring waters and rivers after leaching by irrigation or rainwater. In tropical areas where thunderstorms are frequent, rainwater can contribute some nitrates which result from direct synthesis starting from atmospheric nitrogen.

In the soil, ammonia salts are partly adsorbed on the exchange complex and are not directly extractable with water, in contrast to nitrates which are very soluble. Extraction of exchangeable ammonium thus requires displacement by exchange with another cation of a saline solution. Moreover, part of ammonium can be fixed in the clay layers thereby becoming inaccessible for exchange.

Nitrate anion is considered to be a health risk at a concentration of 80 mg L^{-1} in water. WHO[1] standards recommend maximum values of 44 mg L^{-1} for adults and 20 mg L^{-1} for children. The massive presence of nitrates is often a sign of pollution. In lakes, they contribute to eutrophication phenomena. Nitrates can be reduced to nitrites by denitrifying germs.

Nitrite anion is not stable in natural water. When its presence is observed in water, it is a sign of pollution and the water probably has a nitrite content of more than 0.1 mg L^{-1}. The sterilization of water by chloramines generates ammonia transformed into nitrite by bacteria.

---

[1]WHO: World Health Organization.

28.1.2 Sampling Problems

The distribution of ammonia, nitrate and nitrite varies considerably in the soil. Differences of up to 40% have been found between samples taken from an area of only 2 ha. Sampling should thus be undertaken with great care for this type of analysis.

For the results to be accurate, it is essential to use a strict procedure for both field sampling and for the preparation of the samples, and all operations should be perfectly standardized. It is better to use the sampling device designed by Guiot (1975) than a helical auger. The Guiot probe resembles a semi-cylindrical auger and allows samples to be taken at a precise soil depth and, in addition, the soil samples are less disturbed than with the other devices.

The samples should be prepared immediately in their wet state and stored at less than 10°C for not more than 3 days. Alternatively, extraction can be performed in the field and the solutions brought back to the laboratory. In addition, one aliquot of each sample should be dried in the drying oven at 105°C to identify the corrective coefficient factor for the results. Soil sampling and sample storage for the determination of inorganic nitrogen on fresh soil are the subject of the standard XP X31-115 (1995). If possible, measurements should be taken in situ.

28.1.3 Analytical Problems

The extracts can be unstable but can be stabilized by adding 1 mL of a saturated solution of mercurous chloride per 100 mL, particularly if nitrite titration is required.

The extraction medium inevitably contains many awkward ions at unknown concentrations and may also be coloured or turbid. These phenomena can make precise colorimetric titration difficult, if not impossible.

The classical method of titration of ammonia salts by distillation in alkaline medium involves the risk of neo-formation of ammonia starting from soluble nitrogenous organic matter, even when working under vacuum.

Consequently is often preferable to first separate the inorganic nitrogen form to be titrated. Separation by micro-diffusion of ammonium (cf. Sect. 28.2.2) is suitable for trace titration and is easy to implement. After separation, ammonium can be titrated without interference.

28.2. Usual Methods

28.2.1 Extraction of Exchangeable Forms

Simple extraction with water is theoretically appropriate for nitrates that are very soluble, but in this case the extraction of other forms of inorganic N is not complete, particularly ammonium adsorbed on the exchange complex. Consequently, salt solutions should be used for extraction. The most widely used is 1 mol L^{-1} potassium chloride solution. However, in soils containing gypsum, the solubility of calcium sulphate can cause errors during titration particularly by colorimetry. The use of a 0.5 mol L^{-1} potassium sulphate solution enables solubility of calcium sulphate to be reduced with the same efficiency as potassium chloride for the extraction of the ammonium ion.

Equipment and Reagents

– 500 mL bottles with stopper
– Rotary agitator, 30 rotations min^{-1}
– *Extraction solution.* 0.5 mol (K$_2$SO$_4$) L^{-1} potassium sulphate solution

Procedure

– Place 50 g of soil, (see preparation in Sect. 28.1.2) in the 500 mL bottles with 100 mL of extraction solution.
– Shake the stopped bottles for 1 h on the rotary agitator; decant until a clear supernatant solution is obtained; if the solution is not clear, filter or centrifuge.
– The filtrate is used for the titration of exchangeable ammonium, nitrite and nitrate. If titration cannot be performed immediately, store the solutions at 4°C protected from the light.

Note

Fifty grams is the recommended weight of a sample specimen of soil for soils low in nitrogen (tropical soils). For richer soils, the sample weight can be lower. Keeney and Nelson (1982) and Mulvaney (1996) proposed 10 g of soil for the same 100 mL volume of extraction solution.

28.2.2 Separation by Micro-diffusion

Principle

This method was discovered and used by Schloesing in 1851 and by Fresenius in 1889, and was codified by Conway in 1962. It is recommended for soil analysis because of its simplicity and precision particularly on coloured and turbid extracts (Mulvaney 1996; Mulvaney et al. 1997; Mulvaney and Khan 1999; Khan et al. 2000).

It has been demonstrated that at room temperature, a slightly alkaline solution containing ammonium ions with a large surface area and a low thickness, can lose all its ammonium as gaseous ammonia. The method consists in selectively moving the molecules concerned from a solution where their vapour pressure is high to a solution where their vapour pressure is nil.

The inorganic forms of nitrogen have to be transformed into the removable volatile form of ammonia. For ammonium ions, simple alkalization of the medium is sufficient. Nitrates and nitrites must first be transformed into ammonium ions by reduction with Dewarda mixture.

The displaced ammonia can be collected in a boric acid solution containing an indicator and titrated with a 0.01 mol L^{-1} sulphuric acid solution in a technique similar to the titration of total nitrogen (cf. "Procedure (Macro-Method)" in Chap. 10) and of organic forms of nitrogen (cf. Sect. 14.2.1 in Chap. 14). But as the rate of inorganic forms of N is often low, it is better to use the technique described below based on highly sensitive colorimetric titration.

Equipment

The equipment required is simple; it was inspired by the Conway technique and adapted for soil analysis by Blachère and Ferry (1957). The device described below enables serial analyses (Susini and Gandjui 1964).

Wide mouth 500 mL Erlenmeyer flasks are used; they should have rubber stopper intersected by a glass tube with a diameter of 10 mm ending in a hollow glass bulb approximately 20 mm in diameter. When the stopper is in place, the glass bulb should be suspended half way from the bottom of the flask (see Fig. 28.1).

Reagents

– *Normal solution of sulphuric acid.* Put 2.7 mL of concentrated sulphuric acid in 100 mL of distilled water; this solution is used to impregnate the glass bulbs.

– Saturated solution of potassium carbonate (approximately 112 g for 100 mL at 20°C).
– *Conway solution.* One part of 40% caustic soda solution and three parts of saturated potassium carbonate solution.
– Dewarda mixture in powder form (50% aluminium powder, 45% copper powder and 5% zinc powder), 1 g of this mixture can release approximately 50 mL of nascent hydrogen.
– *Sulphamic acid (NH$_2$SO$_3$H).* Put 2 g in 100 mL water; store in the refrigerator and prepare just before each analysis series to limit hydrolysis.

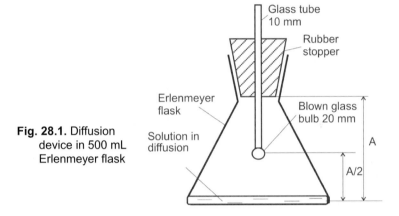

Fig. 28.1. Diffusion device in 500 mL Erlenmeyer flask

Procedure (Ammonium, Nitrate + Nitrite)

Put exactly 20 mL of the extract obtained in "Procedure" under Sect. 28.2.1 into a 500 mL Erlenmeyer flask (Fig. 28.1). It is a good idea to prepare series of ten flasks at a time. Start by soaking the glass bulb in the N sulphuric acid solution. Wet carefully with the liquid, withdraw and drain off excess. Put 1.5 mL of saturated potassium carbonate solution into each flask; insert the stopper with the glass bulb. Make sure the flask is well stopped. Let stand at room temperature for 48 h.

After this period, carefully open the flask taking care not to touch the walls with the glass bulb and not to lose a drop of liquid impregnating the ball. Hold the glass bulb over the funnel (cf. Fig. 28.2) and rinse the bulb with a little distilled water, allowing the rinsing water to collect in a 20 mL volumetric flask. Complete to 20 mL with distilled water, stop and leave to stand until titration. Add 40–50 mg of Dewarda mixture in powder form to the Erlenmeyer flask containing the extraction residue.

As before, soak the glass bulb in the sulphuric acid solution. Add 4.5 mL of Conway mixture in the Erlenmeyer flask; stop the flask immediately and continue as before. This time the displaced ammonium corresponds to nitrates and nitrites reduced by the Dewarda mixture.

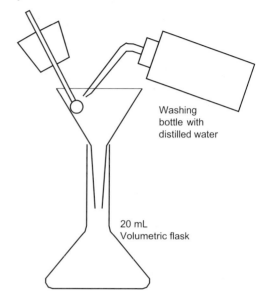

Fig. 28.2. Recovery of the displaced ammonium (Fig. 1)

Note

The Dewarda mixture can result in the release of hydrogen creating a slight overpressure which may eject the stopper; care should be taken to ensure the stopper is really secure or weighed down.

Destruction and Estimation of Nitrites

The term "nitrates" is often used for the sum of nitrates + nitrites; both react to treatment with Dewarda mixture in the same way. As nitrites are particularly unstable, they may be thought to make a negligible concentration in comparison to nitrates, but this is not always the case and it may be necessary to titrate the nitrites separately.

It is also possible to destroy the nitrite before titration of nitrate. Acidification of the extract at pH 1 plus contact with the air for 1 h is sufficient to destroy nitrite. Another technique is to add 0.2 mL of sulphamic acid solution, agitate and wait 5 min before starting micro-diffusion. The combination of the procedures with and without nitrite destruction makes it possible to estimate nitrite by difference.

28.2.3 Colorimetric Titration of Ammonium

Principle

This colorimetric method is suitable for micro-determination. In alkaline medium and in the presence of hypochlorite and with phenol, ammonia gives a blue colour due to the formation of indophenol. This titration is a reference method. If it is carried out on ammonia separated by micro-diffusion (cf. Sect. 28.2.2), no interference will occur. This method enables measurement of:

– Ammonium on the extract of the first micro-diffusion
– the sum of nitrites + nitrates on the second micro-diffusion in the presence of Dewarda mixture
– nitrates alone if nitrites have been eliminated beforehand (cf. "Destruction and Estimation of Nitrites")

Ammonium can also be titrated directly on the extraction solution (cf. Sect. 28.2.1) in a concentration range of 0.005–20 mg L^{-1} (Keeney and Nelson 1982) but with the risk of additional error due to interference by calcium and magnesium. These interferences can be reduced by using a very diluted medium and by adding EDTA.

Colorimetric titration of ammonium can also be automated as described in Chap. 10 ("Procedure" under Sect. 10.2.7) and Chap. 26 ("Procedure" under Sect. 26.4.2).

Equipment and Reagents

Colorimetry is carried out in monochromatic radiation. Choose the wavelength that gives the strongest absorption (636 nm according to Keeney and Nelson 1982) in the 590–650 nm zone (orange). A colorimetric cell of 20 mm optical course provides good sensitivity. Values from 0.05 to 0.3 mg (N) L^{-1} display a linear response.

Reagents for the Colorimetric Reaction

– *Sodium phenolate solution.* Dissolve 2.5 g of caustic soda in approximately 40–50 mL of distilled water; let cool, add 5 g of very pure phenol, dissolve and bring to 100 mL; this solution must be perfectly colourless.
– *0.2 mol (Na$_2$HPO$_4$) L^{-1} disodic phosphate solution.* Add 71.65 g of Na$_2$HPO$_4$,12H$_2$O in 1 L of deionized water.
– 0.05% sodium nitroprussiate solution prepared just before use, starting from a 1% stock solution.

– Sodium hypochlorite solution at four chlorometric degrees, starting from a commercial solution at 20–22°. The exact titre of commercial solutions should be checked in the following way: take 1 mL of commercial solution, add 50 mL of distilled water, a few potassium iodide crystals and 5 mL of pure acetic acid; shake the mixture and titrate (until disappearance of the yellow colour due to the released iodine) with a sodium hyposulphite solution containing 24.8 g of $Na_2S_2O_3,5H_2O$ per litre (0.1 N). The titre of the solution is expressed by:

Chlorometric degree = mL hyposulphite solution × 1.12.

– *EDTA solution*. Dissolve 6 g of disodic salt of ethylene diamine tetraacetic acid in 80 mL deionized water, adjust the pH to 7, bring the volume to 100 mL and shake well.

Standard Range

A- *Stock solution of ammonium chloride*. Weigh 0.191 g of pure NH_4Cl; bring to 500 mL with distilled water. One mL of solution A contains 0.1 mg of N.

B- Make diluted ammonium chloride solution by diluting solution A 1:100. One mL of solution B contains 0.001 mg of N.

Note.

Solution B cannot be kept for more than a few hours. A significant difference between the results and data from previous series means that all the standard solutions need to be freshly made.

Procedure

Calibration

Put the volumes of ammonium chloride solution B shown in Table 28.1 in 20 mL volumetric flasks, and then add in the following order, agitating after each addition:

– 2 mL of sodium phenolate

– 2 mL of 0.2 mol L^{-1} disodic phosphate solution

– 0.5 mL of 0.05% nitroprussiate solution

– 2 mL of sodium hypochlorite solution at 4 chlorometric degrees

Complete to 20 mL with distilled water. Shake, let the colour develop for at least 30 min in the dark. Then take the colorimetric measurement at the optimal wavelength in the 590–650 nm zone (cf. "Equipment and reagents" under Sect. 28.2.3). The Beer-Lambert law applies in the concentration range given in Table 28.1. The adjustment "Optical density $=f$(concentration)" is linear, and the colour remains stable for more than 24 h.

Table 28.1. Preparation of the colorimetric range of titration by dilution of 1 μg N mL^{-1} B solution

mL of B solution for 20 mL	mg (N) L^{-1} (solution)	μg (N) g^{-1} (soil)	μg (NH$_4$) g^{-1} (soil)	μg (NO$_3$) g^{-1} (soil)
1	0.05	0.1	0.13	0.44
2	0.1	0.2	0.26	0.89
4	0.2	0.4	0.51	1.77
6	0.3	0.6	0.77	2.66
10	0.5	1	1.29	4.43

(Corresponding soil concentrations for inorganic N extracted from 50 g of soil in 100 mL)

Titrations

Add exactly the same quantities of reagents as for the standard curve (see "Calibration" above in this Sect. 28.2.3) to the 20 mL volumetric flasks containing the rinsing solution collected after rinsing the glass bulbs. Let the colour develop and read absorptions in the same way as for the standard calibration.

Depending on the micro-diffusion technique used (cf. Sect. 28.2.2), the results express either ammonium, or the sum of nitrites + nitrates, or nitrates alone.

Solutions that are too deeply coloured can be diluted. The control should be diluted to exactly the same degree.

It is also possible to increase sensitivity by concentrating the colour using an extraction of the coloured complex in isobutanol and reading the absorption at 655 nm.

Note

If the micro-diffusion technique (cf. Sect. 28.2.2) is not being used, place an aliquot of exactly 5 mL of the extract described in Sect. 28.2.1 above in the 20 mL volumetric flasks. Add 1 mL of 5 g (EDTA) L^{-1} solution, shake and wait 1 min then continue as in "Titrations" above. In this case, the calibration range ("Calibration") should be prepared using the extraction solution (cf. Sect. 28.2.1).

28.2.4 Colorimetric Titration of Nitrites

Principle

This technique (Rodier 1984; Charlot 1974) uses diazotization of nitrites with sulfanilic acid at pH 2.5, and then reaction of the compound formed with α-naphthylamine (Griess reagent). A red azo dye is obtained and the colorimetric absorption is measured at 520 nm. Sensitivity can be increased by concentrating the coloured complex by extraction with chloroform at pH 9.5–10.

Reagents

For the preparation of reagents and solutions, nitrite-free water should be used that has been purified by ion exchange on a mixed resin (1 volume of cationic resin+ 2 volumes of anionic resin).
– *Sulfanilic acid solution.* Add 1.2 g of pure sulfanilic acid in approximately 140 mL of hot purified water, cool, add 40 mL of pure hydrochloric acid, complete to 200 mL with deionized water.
– *α-Naphthylamine solution.* Add 1.2 g of pure α-naphthylamine, 2 mL of pure hydrochloric acid, complete to 200 mL with deionized water.
– *Sodium acetate buffer solution.* Weigh 54.4 g $CH_3COONa,3H_2O$ (or 32.8 g of anhydrous salt), dissolve and complete to 200 mL with deionized water.
– *5 g (EDTA) L^{-1} solution.* Used to complex iron and heavy metals which can cause interference.

Standard Solution of Nitrite

Preparation

This solution is prepared starting from sodium nitrite ($NaNO_2$), a hygroscopic and very water soluble salt with a melting point of 271°C which is very easily oxidized in contact with air or moisture. It is thus advisable to check the quality of the product before use. The solutions can be preserved by adding a little chloroform. Weigh exactly 150 mg of sodium nitrite, dissolve and complete to 100 mL with deionized water. One mL of this solution contains 0.1 mg of nitrite.

As nitrites are extremely unstable, the concentration of the standard solution should be checked.

Checking

Principle
Check the solution by volumetric analysis using the following oxidation technique with an excess of potassium permanganate:
$$2\ MnO_4^- + 5\ NO_2^- + 6\ H^+ \rightarrow 2\ Mn^{2+} + 5\ NO_3^- + 3\ H_2O$$
The excess of oxidant is titrated by iodometry.

Procedure

- Add exactly 10 mL of 0.01 N permanganate solution, and 2 mL of ½ sulphuric acid to a sample volume SV (20 mL) of the nitrite solution to be titrated.
- Shake and add 5 mL of 10% potassium iodide solution.
- Titrate iodine with the sodium hyposulphite solution ($C = 0.01$ N), this gives volume V of hyposulphite solution.
- Repeat the titration using 20 mL of distilled water instead of the nitrite solution, this gives V_0 the new volume of hyposulphite solution.

$$NO_2^- \text{ in mg L}^{-1} = C \frac{V_0 - V}{SV} 23{,}000$$

Starting from this solution, prepare a stock solution containing 1 mg (NO^-_2) L^{-1}

Range of Calibration

Prepare the calibration range shown in Table 28.2 starting from the stock solution containing 1 mg (NO^-_2) L^{-1}.

Table 28.2. Calibration range for the colorimetric titration of nitrites

volume of the 1 mg (NO_2^-) L^{-1} solution (mL)	Corresponding concentration of the 50 mL solution (mg L^{-1})
1	0.02
2	0.04
4	0.08
6	0.12
8	0.16
10	0.20

Procedure

- Take a sample specimen of the soil extract (cf. "Procedure" under Sect. 28.2.1) within the calibration range (i.e. 50 mL or less); complete to 50 mL with deionized water.
- Add 1 mL of EDTA solution; shake.
- Add 1 mL of sulfanilic acid solution; shake and wait 10 min.
- Add 1 mL of α-naphthylamine solution, 1 mL of buffer solution, shake, wait 30 min, perform colorimetric measurement at maximum absorbance (520–540 nm); the total volume of the solution measured is 54 mL; the absorbance curve is linear in the range concerned.

If C_S and C_L express the soil concentration in µg (NO_2-N) g^{-1} and the extract concentration in µg (NO_2-N) mL^{-1} respectively, and if f is the corrective moisture factor:

$$C_s = 2\ C_L f.$$

Note

If the soil extraction solution (cf. Sect. 28.2.1) is coloured or turbid, it can be purified before measurement as follows:
- To 100 mL of extract, add 5 mL of the 120 g L^{-1} aluminium sulphate solution, then gradually add alkalizing solution (100 g of $Na_2CO_3,10H_2O$ + 50 g of NaOH in a total volume of 300 mL) until alkaline reaction.
- Separate the precipitate by filtration.
- Recover the clear solution of the filtrate for titration.

28.2.5 Colorimetric Titration of Nitrates

Principle

Nitrates can be titrated by selective micro-diffusion (Sect. 28.2.2) on the soil extracts (Sect. 28.2.1), reduction and colorimetric titration of ammonium (Sect. 28.2.3). Several other colorimetric techniques are available for nitrates. One of the most sensitive and accurate consists in reducing nitrate into nitrite then titrating nitrite by colorimetry as described in Sect. 28.2.4. Nitrates are reduced by passing the soil extract solutions (Sect. 28.2.1) on columns of copper cadmium

Equipment and Reagents

- *Copper cadmium for reduction*. Put 50 g of cadmium in coarse powder or granule form (1 × 2 mm) in a 400 mL Erlenmeyer flask; attack for 1 min with 250 mL of 6 mol (HCl) L^{-1} chlorhydric acid; decant the acid and rinse well with deionized water; treat twice with 250 mL of 2% cupric sulphate solution (w/v of $CuSO_4,5H_2O$); decant and rinse several times with deionized water.
- *20% ammonium chloride solution*. Dissolve 100 g of NH_4Cl in deionized water and complete to 500 mL.
- *Diluted NH_4Cl solution*. Take 50 mL of 20% NH_4Cl solution and complete to 2 L with deionized water.
- *Other reagents*. See "Reagents" under Sect. 28.2.4.

Procedure

Reduction can be carried out manually on Pyrex columns with a diameter of 1 cm filled to 20 cm with the copper cadmium and eluted with approximately 75 mL diluted solution of NH_4Cl. But this operation is time consuming and it is better to automate the method using continuous flow equipment. A well-designed manifold enables titration of nitrates and nitrites with or without a passage on the reduction column.

28.2.6 Extracted Organic Nitrogen

Principle

The extracting reagent used in Sect. 28.2.1 (0.5 mol (K_2SO_4) L^{-1} potassium sulphate solution) can solubilize a little organic nitrogen. The alkaline reagent used for ammonia displacement starting from ammonium salts during micro-diffusion (cf. Sect. 28.2.2) can act on the N organic matter of the extract. A little supplementary ammonia may be formed that does not come from the soil ammonium ion. It has been shown that more alkaline is the displacement reagent, more the dissolved organic matter is transformed to ammonia. With caustic potash, the transformation can reach 50% (Blachère and Fery 1957), whereas it is only 20% with the Conway reagent and 6% with saturated potassium carbonate. It is recommended to use this property to quantify possible changes in N organic matter (with respect to its state of complexity).

Procedure

The extracted solution (cf. Sect. 28.2.1) is subjected to double diffusion (cf. Sect. 2.2):
- The first sample specimen is subjected to diffusion using saturated potassium carbonate.
- The second sample specimen is subjected to diffusion using the Conway reagent.

Ammonia is titrated on the two displaced solutions. The comparison of the results and calculation of the ratio of the two titrations indicates the stability of organic matter and enables its transformation to be monitored.

28.3. Other Methods

28.3.1 Nitrate and Nitrite by UV Photometric Absorption

Principle

Solutions containing nitrate and nitrite strongly absorb ultraviolet radiation, particularly at 210 nm. At this wavelength, the law of Beer-Lambert is applicable up to approximately 10 mg (N) L^{-1}.

The sum of nitrate + nitrite is estimated by measurement of UV absorption at 210 nm before and after elimination of these anions by treatment with Raney catalyst (Ni–Al). Nitrite is estimated before and after its elimination with sulphamic acid.

This technique is satisfactory for the analysis of soil extracts (Norman and Stucki 1981; Norman et al. 1985). Its main advantage is simplicity as it does not require a colouring reagent.

However, it does require a UV spectrophotometer, which is more expensive than a simple visible spectrometer. Moreover, the limit of detection is higher than in the colorimetric method described in Sect. 28.2.5.

Reagents

– 20% sulphuric acid solution, made from concentrated H_2SO_4, $d = 1.84$.
– 2% sulphamic acid solution from H_3NO_3S should be stored in the refrigerator.
– Raney catalyst (approximately 50% Ni and 50% Al).
– *Standard solutions of nitrate.* For the stock solution, weigh 3.606 g of pure KNO_3, dissolve in deionized water, complete to 1,000 mL, 1 mL contains 0.5 mg of N or 2.214 mg of NO_3^-, 1:50 diluted solution of stock solution, 1 mL contains 0.01 mg of N or 0.044 mg of NO_3^-.
– 0.1 mg (NO_2) mL^{-1} standard solution of nitrite (see "Standard Solution of Nitrite").
– *Extraction solution.* 0.5 mol L^{-1} potassium sulphate (see "Equipment and Reagents" under Sect. 28.2.1).
– *Discolouration solution.* 120 g L^{-1} aluminium sulphate.
– *Alkalizing solution.* 100 g Na_2CO_3 + 50 g NaOH in 300 mL of deionized water.

Procedure

Preparation of the Soil Solution

Put 10 g of soil (see preparation in Sect. 28.1.2) then 30 mL of extraction solution in 100 mL bottles, stop, agitate on a rotary shaker for 10 min, decant and filter the clear part. If the solution is coloured, add 1 mL aluminium sulphate solution, alkalize by progressive addition of alkalizing solution until formation of hydroxide and then filter.

Preparation of Ranges of Calibration Standards

Prepare two series of solutions for nitrate and nitrite using the range of standard solutions listed in Table 28.3. Bring to a volume of 30 mL with the extraction solution. Measure absorption compared to a blank containing the extraction reagent alone in the following spectrometric conditions: wavelength 210 nm, narrow slit of approximately 0.8 mm, quartz measuring cell with a path length of 1 cm. Plot two calibration curves, one for nitrate and the other for nitrite.

Table 28.3. Range of calibration standards for titration of nitrate and nitrite by UV spectrometry

	mL of the 0.044 mg (NO_3^-) mL^{-1} solution for 30 mL	$\mu g\ (NO_3^-)\ g^{-1}$ (soil) for 10 g soil in 30 mL
	0.5	2.2
	1	4.4
NO_3^-	2	8.8
	4	17.6
	8	35.2
	10	44
	mL of the 0.1 mg (NO_2^-) mL^{-1} solution for 30 mL	$\mu g\ (NO_2^-)\ g^{-1}$ (soil) for 10 g soil in 30 mL
	0.1	1
	0.2	2
NO_2^-	0.4	4
	1	10
	2	20
	4	10

Titration of Nitrate

– To 25 mL of the extracted solution, add 1 mL of the 2% sulphamic acid solution; shake for 1 min to obtain a solution free from nitrite. Measure its absorption at 210 nm; compare it with a 25 mL blank containing 1 mL of sulphamic acid solution in the extraction solution; this value is "A".

– To 5 mL of the nitrite-free solution, add successively: approximately 0.3 g of catalyst, 0.5 mL of 20% sulphuric solution; mix well, place the tube in a drying oven regulated at 60°C for about 40 min; let cool; this solution is free from nitrate and nitrite. Measure its absorption at 210 nm, compare it with a blank containing 5 mL of extraction solution plus 1 mL of sulphamic acid solution plus 0.3 g of catalyst, plus 0.5 mL of 20% sulphuric acid solution, dry in the oven like the sample; this adsorption value is "B".

The absorption value originating from the nitrate is:

$(1.04\ A) - (1.1\ B)$.

To obtain the result in $\mu g\,(NO_3^-)\ g^{-1}$ (soil), the absorption values should be plotted on the calibration curve for nitrate. The coefficients 1.04 and 1.1 correct the influence of the slight dilutions caused by the sulphamic acid and sulphuric acid.

Titration of Nitrite

Put 5 mL of the soil extract solution in a test tube, measure its absorption at 210 nm; compare it with a blank containing 5 mL of extraction solution, this value is "D".

Add 5 mL of the sulphamic acid solution to the 5 mL of soil extract and shake for 1 min; read absorption at 210 nm; compare it with a blank containing 5 mL of the extraction solution plus 5 mL of sulphamic acid solution, this value is "E".

The absorption value of nitrites is: $D - (2E)$.

(Coefficient 2 corrects for dilution in the second measurement).

Calculation of the Results

The values are obtained by reading the calibration curves, for the operating conditions described earlier. Each value obtained should be corrected by the moisture coefficient of the soil sample.

28.3.2 Ammonium Titration Using a Selective Electrode

The Measurement Electrode

The electrode is of the gas diffusion type (Fig. 28.3) and consists of a gas-permeable hydrophobic membrane. Ammonium contained in the sample has to be moved by an alkaline solution. The ammonium diffuses through the electrode membrane until equilibrium is reached between the partial pressures on each side. The gas dissolves in the internal solution giving hydroxyl ions.

$$NH_3 + H_2O \Leftrightarrow NH_4^+ + OH^-$$

The equilibrium constant is expressed by:

$$K = [NH_4^+][OH^-]/[NH_3]$$

The internal ammonium ion concentration (0.22 mol (NH_4 Cl) L^{-1}) can be considered as constant, thus: $[OH^-] = K'[NH_3]$

The electrode (like a pH electrode) is sensitive to hydroxyl ions. The potential of the electrode is thus linked with the ammonia concentration of the sample.

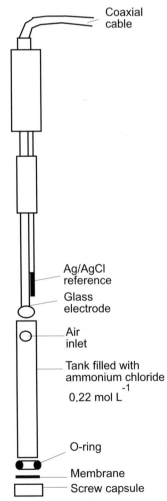

Fig. 28.3. Schematic diagram of a gas diffusion electrode for titration of the ammonium ion

Coaxial cable

Ag/AgCl reference

Glass electrode

Air inlet

Tank filled with ammonium chloride 0.22 mol L^{-1}

O-ring

Membrane

Screw capsule

Equipment and Reagents

Reagents

– *0.22 mol L^{-1} ammonium chloride solution (to fill the electrode).* Weigh 1.17 g of pure NH_4Cl, dissolve and complete to 100 mL with distilled water.

– *0.5 mg (N) mL^{-1} standard stock solution of ammonium chloride (A).* Weigh 0.955 g of pure NH_4Cl, dissolve and complete to 500 mL with distilled water.

– *0.01 mg (N) L^{-1} solution of ammonium chloride (B).* Dilute solution A 1/50.

– *Calibration range.* Prepare the calibration solutions in 20 mL volumetric flasks using the quantities of standard solutions listed in Table 4.

Table 28.4. Range of calibration for titration of exchangeable ammonium and nitrates using the ammonium electrode, the extraction procedures of Sect. 28.2.1 and micro-diffusion procedures in Sect. 28.2.2 (50 g soil sample, 100 mL extracting reagents, 20 mL sample specimen for diffusion, calibration points completed to 20 mL)

mL of NH_4Cl solutions for 20 mL				
solution A 0.5 mg (N) mL^{-1}	solution B 0.01 mg (N) mL^{-1}	mg (N) L^{-1}	µg (N) g^{-1} (soil)	µg (NO_3) g^{-1} (soil)
	0.5	0.25	0.5	2.21
	1	0.5	1	4.42
	2	1	2	8.84
	4	2	4	17.7
	10	5	10	44.2
	20	10	20	88.7
0.8		20	40	176.6
2		50	100	442

Preparation of the Electrode

Depending on the make, all the electrodes may not look the same, but the components are always similar.

– Unscrew the cap and remove the glass electrode (Fig. 28.3).

– Put the glass bulb of the electrode to soak in a 0.1 mol L^{-1} hydrochloric acid solution. The acid solution must not reach the reference part of the electrode which consists of a silver wire covered with silver chloride.

– After 24 h of contact, rinse abundantly with distilled water and then leave in distilled water until use.

– Place a very fine membrane of Teflon at the bottom of the electrode tank (Fig. 28.3) and then screw the cap tight.

- Lower the glass electrode until the membrane bulges slightly, showing that the glass bulb is in contact with the membrane.
- Fill the tank electrode with the reference liquid, in this case 1 mL of a 0.22 mol L^{-1} ammonium chloride solution.

The electrode is now ready for use. It can be stored in a 0.1 mol L^{-1} ammonium chloride solution. When it is not going to be used for more than 2 weeks, tank and electrodes should be separated and the glass electrode stored in distilled water.

Procedure

Calibration of the Electrode, Value of the Slope "S"

- Before using the electrode, the slope value of the response curve should be established; this is expressed in mV (generally ranging between 45 and 60 mV for a variation of concentration of a factor 10).
- In 20 mL volumetric flasks, prepare five points: 0.5, 1, 5, 10, 50 mg (N) L^{-1} for the volumes of solution listed in Table 28.4. Complete to 20 mL with distilled water; all these solutions will be brought to a temperature of 25°C for measurement.
- Put 20 mL of distilled water (25°C) in a beaker, immerse the electrode prepared as described in "Equipment and Reagents" under Sect. 28.3.2; add 2 mL of 40% soda and shake; after 5 min, read the potential in mV. If adjustment of potential is possible, adjust to zero value; if not, note the E_0 value
- Measure the first point of the calibration range, 0.5 mg L^{-1} by transvasing the 20 mL flask containing this solution in a beaker. Immerse the electrode, add 2 mL soda, and agitate. After 5 min, read the potential E_1. Repeat the operation up to point E_5 and plot the calibration curve mV $= f(N)$ to determine the slope of the electrode.

Measurements

Measurements are carried out on the 20 mL of soil extract as previously described (cf. Sect. 28.2.2). Use direct measurements from the slope or the standard addition method.

If C_e is the content of nitrogen in mg L^{-1} found in the extract and f the moisture corrective factor, the ammonium-N content C_S in μg (N) g^{-1} (soil) is expressed by:

$$C_S = 2 \, C_l f.$$

Expressed in μg (NH_4^+) g^{-1} and μg (NO_3^-) g^{-1} (previous reduction by Raney catalyst, see section 3.1), the contents are:

$$C_S^{NH4} = 2.56 \, C_l f,$$
$$C_S^{NO3} = 8.84 \, C_l f.$$

28.3.3 Measurement of Nitrates with an Ion-Selective Electrode

Combined Measurement-Reference Electrode

The response to the nitrate ions of a compact combined electrode with an active plastic membrane (Ingold) is approximately 56 mV when concentration is multiplied or divided by 10. It is linear for nitrate contents ranging from 1 g L^{-1} to 5 mg L^{-1}. Beyond the limit of the linearity domain, the electrode is still usable down to 1 mg L^{-1}.

Among anions found in soil extracts, the most serious interferences come from NO_2^-, Cl$^-$, HCO_3^- ions and to a lesser extent from SO_4^{2-} ions. A nitrate-to-nitrite ratio equal to one induces 20% error. The Cl$^-$-to-NO_3^- ratio must be lower than one, the HCO_3^--to-NO_3^- ratio must be lower than 25, the SO_4^{2-}-to-NO_3^- ratio must be lower than 100.

It is possible to work in a broad range of pH (between 2 and 12).

A reference electrode of the mercurous sulphate/potassium sulphate type should be used to avoid pollution of the medium by the chloride ion. At 22°C, this electrode develops an electromotive force of +402 mV more than the calomel electrode in saturated potassium chloride. It can be used in a temperature range of from 0 to 60°C, with a thermal coefficient of +0.13 mV K^{-1}.

Equipment and Reagents

– pH/mV meter allowing a resolution of ± 0.5 mV for a measurement range of ± 1 V.
– Ingold nitrate electrode (or similar).
– Reference mercurous sulphate electrode (or similar).
– *Calibration solutions.* 0.5 mg(NO_3-N) mL^{-1} and 0.01 mg (NO_3-N) mL^{-1}, see "Reagents" under Sect. 28.3.1.
– *Extraction solution.* 0.005 mol L^{-1} potassium sulphate.
– 2% sulphamic acid solution $NH_2 SO_3 H$.

Calibration

Put the test specimens listed in Table 28.5 in 50 mL beakers, complete to 20 mL with the extraction solution. Add 0.5 mL of sulphamic acid solution, shake for 1 min and let stand for 10 min. Note the temperature which should be close to 25°C. Immerse the electrodes and take measurements without agitating. Read the potential in mV after stabilization of the measurement (2 min) and plot the calibration curve.

Make a blank with 20 mL of extraction solution treated with sulphamic acid in the same way as for the samples.

Titration

- Carry out the soil extraction as described in Sect. 28.2.1, but using the diluted solution of potassium sulphate.
- Put 20 mL of the soil extract solution in 50 mL beakers.
- Add 0.5 mL of sulphamic acid solution in each beaker; shake for 1 min and let stand for 10 min to remove nitrites.

Table 28.5. Preparation of the calibration range for nitrate titration by ionometry

calibration points mg (NO_3-N) L^{-1}	mL of the 0.01 mg (NO_3-N) mL^{-1} solution	Volume needed to complete to 20 mL	mL of the 0.5 mg (NO_3-N) mL^{-1} solution	volume needed to complete to 20 mL
2	4	16		
3	6	14		
5	10	10		
10			0.4	19.6
50			2	18
100			4	16

Complete to 20 mL with the 0.005 mol (K_2SO_4) L^{-1} extraction solution

- Note the temperature which should be close to the calibration temperature.
- Immerse the electrodes in the blank and check that the zero point set for calibration has not changed.
- Immerse in the sample solutions. After allowing the measurement to stabilize for approximately 2 min read the potential in mV without agitating. Note the corresponding concentrations C_l expressed in mg (NO_3-N) L^{-1} on the calibration curve.

Using the procedure described in Sect. 28.2.1 above (50 g soil, 100 mL extraction solution), the concentration C_S is expressed in µg (NO_3^-) g^{-1} (soil):

$$C_s = \frac{4.428 \times 1.02 \times 100 \times 20}{1,000} \, C_l f = 9.032 \, C_l f,$$

(f is the moisture correction factor, 4.428 is the NO_3:N ratio, 1.02 = 20.5/20 is the sulphamic acid correction factor). If the concentration is too high, dilute the test specimen. If the concentration is too low, increase the soil sample.

28.3.4 In situ Measurement

Principle

Forms of mineral nitrogen can change rapidly and the turnover can be high. Consequently in situ measurement can be particularly useful for optimizing cultivation techniques or controlling pollution. A Tensionic (SDEC[2]) consists of a porous plug tensiometer adapted for measurements on the soil solution. Djurhuus and Jacobsen (1995) compared the method using porous ceramic plugs and extraction with potassium chloride for nitrate titration. Exchange is by simple ionic diffusion between the soil solution and the internal water of the plug; the apparatus gives the tensiometric value at the same time.

Description

The Probe

The probe is a porous plug (Fig. 28.4) for the measurement of high-flow soil moisture.[3] It is tightly stopped with a PVC stopper, and three fine Nylon capillary tubes go down to the bottom of the plug. One tube is used for tensiometric measurement, and another is used for extraction of the solution contained in the plug. The third tube emerges at the top of the plug and allows the circuit to be purged at the beginning and can also be used to put the solution back after analysis. The whole unit is contained in an opaque PVC rod whose length depends on the aim of the study (often 50 cm or 1 m).

The Measuring Apparatus

The probe is supplied with a battery and a peristaltic pump which works in two directions and is connected to the exit of the collection and purging tubes, and emerges in a watertight tank with an ionic electrode connected to a milli-voltmeter for measurement. A three-way stopcock on the pump circuit enables aliquots to be removed for other analyses.

---

[2] - SDEC, BP 4233, 37 000 Tours, France.
[3] - Soil Moisture, P.O. Box 30025, Santa Barbara, CA 93105, USA.

Procedure

During purging the plug device should be filled with distilled water to avoid creation of a vacuum. After purging, close the purging and collection tubes with clamps. Dig a cylindrical cavity in the soil that is slightly broader than the plug; remove soil in sections as a function of depth. Mix the soil from the bottom with distilled water, and inject the resulting paste back into the bottom of the hole. Insert the plug and push it down to the bottom of the paste; fill the remainder of the hole with the soil corresponding to the depth at which it was removed; pack the soil down slightly. Place a protective ring on the surface of the soil to prevent infiltration around the plug.

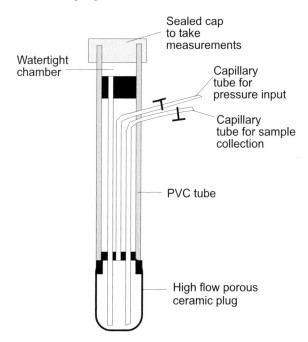

Fig. 28.4. Schematic diagram of the Tensionic apparatus (SDEC)

Measurements can be taken after equilibration of the soil solution, which requires 8–10 days. Start the pump to transfer the solution from the plug into the watertight tank containing the electrodes. The technique described in Sect. 28.3.3 can be used for nitrate titration without the addition of sulphamic acid to destroy nitrites, which are titrated with nitrates.

28.3.5 Non-Exchangeable Ammonium

Principle

Some soil ammonium may be fixed in the clay layers and are not exchangeable in saline solutions and thus practically inaccessible to plants and micro-organisms. Three methods have been proposed for the estimation of non-exchangeable soil ammonium (1) Kjeldhal distillation at 400°C after elimination of organic nitrogen and exchangeable ammonium, (2) estimation by the difference between ammonium distilled in the presence of soda and ammonium distilled with potash and (3) estimation of the ammonium released by hydrofluoric acid treatment for destruction of the clay layers. The method described here, which is based on that of Keeney and Nelson (1982), belongs to the last category. Before the HF treatment, the organic matter and exchangeable ammonium are destroyed using a mixture of potash and potassium hypobromite which is known to be not too destructive for non-exchangeable ammonium.

Equipment and Reagents

– *Potassium hypobromite solution (KBrO)*. Slowly add 6 mL of bromine to 200 mL of stirred, ice-cold 2 mol L^{-1} potash solution; this solution should be prepared immediately before use.
– *0.5 mol (KCl) L^{-1} solution*. Dissolve 186 g of KCl in 5 L of water.
– *5 mol (HF)–1 mol (HCl) L^{-1} solution*. Use a polyethylene flask with a graduation mark at 2 L. Fill with about 1.5 L of water, then while stirring, add 167 mL of concentrated hydrochloric acid (HCl, d=1.19) and 325 mL of 52% hydrofluoric acid (31 mol L^{-1}). Complete to 2 L with deionized water and swirl the contents of the flask carefully.

Procedure

Place 1 g of finely crushed soil sample in a 200 mL tall form beaker and add 20 mL of potassium hypobromite solution. Stir and cover the beaker with a beaker cover; let stand for 2 h. Add 60 mL of water and boil for 5 min. Let stand overnight and decant the clear supernatant. Transfer the residue in a 100 mL polyethylene centrifugation tube using a washing bottle filled with the 0.5 mol (KCl) L^{-1} solution. Fill the tube to around 80 mL with the 0.5 mol (KCl) L^{-1} solution (equilibrate the weight between samples), stop, shake manually for a few seconds and centrifuge at 1,100g for 10 min. Decant the supernatant and repeat the extraction operation with the 0.5 mol (KCl) L^{-1} solution.

Add 20 mL of HF–HCl solution to the centrifugation pellet using a polyethylene volumetric tube. Close the centrifugation tube and shake for 24 h on a mechanical shaker.

Released ammonium can be titrated directly by distillation (cf. Chaps. 10 and 14) or by micro-diffusion as described in Sect. 28.2.2 above. In each case care should be taken to avoid contact between the solution containing hydrofluoric acid and the glass walls of the equipment: Use long-stemmed polyethylene funnels to transfer the contents of the centrifugation tube in alkaline medium, use plastic Erlenmeyer flasks for micro-diffusion.

References

Blachère H and Ferry P (1957) Dosage de l'azote minéral dans les sols par micro-diffusion. *Ann. Agr.*, 8, 111–118, 495–498

Charlot G (1974) *Chimie analytique quantitative.* Masson. T II, 347

Conway EJ (1962) *Micro-diffusion analysis and volumétric error.*, Crosby lockwood, London, 5ème édit

Djurhuus J and Jacobsen OH (1995) Comparison of ceramic suction cups and KCl extraction for the determination of nitrate in soil. *Eur. J. Soil Sci.*, 46, 387–395

Guiot J (1975) Estimation des réserves azotées du sol par détermination de l'azote minéral. *Revue de l'Agriculture*, 5, 1117–1132

Guito J, Goffart JP and Destain JP (1992) Le dosage des nitrates dans le sol. *Bull. Rech. Agron.*, Gembloux, 27, 61–74

Keeney DR and Nelson DW (1982) Nitrogen – inorganic forms. In *Methods of Soil Analysis*, Page AL, Miller RH and Keeney DR ed. ASA-SSSA, Agron. Monograph No 9,2nd ed. Madison, WI Etats-Unis, 643–698

Khan SA, Mulvaney RL and Hoeft RG (2000) Direct-diffusion methods for inorganic-nitrogen analysis of soil. *Soil Sci. Soc. Am. J.*, 64, 1083–1089

Mulvaney RL and Khan SA (1999) Use of diffusion to determine inorganic nitrogen in a complex organic matrix. *Soil Sci. Soc. Am. J.*, 63, 240–246

Mulvaney RL (1996) Nitrogen – Inorganic forme. In *Methods of Soil Analysis, Part 3, Chemical Methods*, Bigham JM and Bartels JM ed. SSSA-ASA, Madison, WI Etats-Unis, 1123–1184

Mulvaney RL, Khan SA, Stevens WB and Mulvaney CS (1997) Improved diffusion methods for determination of inorganic nitrogen in soil extracts and water. *Biol. Fertil. Soils*, 24, 413–420

Norman RJ and Stucki JW (1981) The determination of nitrates and nitrites in soil extracts by UV spectrophotometry, *Soil Sci. Soc. Am. J.*, 45, 347–353

Norman RJ, Edberg JC and Stucki JW (1985) Determination of nitrates in soil extracts by dual-wavelengths UV spectrophotometry, *Soil Sci. Soc. Am. J.*, 49, 1182–1185

Rodier J (1984) *Analyse chimique et physico-chimique de l'eau*. Dunod (Paris

Susini J and N'Gandjui C (1964) Dosage de l'azote minéral. *Cah. ORSTOM Sér. Pédol.*, 2, 57–71

XP X31-115 (1995) Qualité des sols. Prélèvement et conservation des échantillons de sol en vue de la détermination de l'azote minéral sur sol frais, *AFNOR*, 8 p

Bibliography

Boltz DF and Howell JA (1978) *Colorimetric Determination of Non Metals.*, Wiley, New York

Bremmer JM (1987) Laboratory techniques for determination of different forms of nitrogen cycling in agriculture ecosystems. *Proc. Symp. Adv. Nitrogen*, Brisbane, Australia : 11–15 mai 1987

Cheverry C (1983) L'extraction de la "Solution du Sol" par le biais de bougies poreuses. *Bulletin du groupe français d'humidimétrie neutronique (GFHN)*, 14, 47–71

Gautheyrou J and Gautheyrou M (1965) Dosage simultané de l'azote ammoniacal et nitrique dans les sols – Contribution à l'étude de la dynamique de l'azote. *Cah. Orstom Ser. Pédol.*, 4, 367–391

Morie GP and Ledeford CJ (1972) Determination of nitrate and nitrite in mixtures with a nitrate ion electrode. *Anal. Chim. Acta.*, 60, 397–403

Moutonnet P, Guiraud G and Marol C (1989) Le tensiomètre et la teneur en nitrates de la solution du sol. *Bulletin du groupe français d'humidimétrie neutronique (GFHN)*, 26, 11–28

prNF ISO 14256-2 (2002) *Qualité du sol* – Dosage des nitrates, des nitrites et de l'ammonium dans des sols bruts par extraction avec une solution de chlorure de potassium. AFNOR, X 31-423-2

Taras MJ (1971) Standard methods for the examination of water of wastewater. *13e edit. American Public health association*, Washington, DC 20036

Phosphorus

29.1 Introduction

Although phosphorus (P) is not very abundant[1] in soils, it is nevertheless a major element and plays a fundamental role in agronomy and biogeochemical cycles. P exists in all the living organisms. It is able to form innumerable covalent organo-phosphorous compounds and to bind to C, N, O, Al, Fe, Ca. It is involved in the fundamental transfer processes from radiant electromagnetic energy to chemical energy (photosynthesis) and sustains the development of the radicular systems of the plants.

The characterization and speciation of the different forms of P in the soil are thus indispensable for the quantification of plant needs and the implementation of land management methods likely to satisfy them. This nutritional aspect is closely linked with pedogenic transformations and to the risk of environmental pollution.

More than 220 minerals containing P have been identified that are stable at the geological time scale. In addition, manufactured products such as fertilizers, pesticides, detergents and compounds like water-softeners, fire retardants, fuel additives, and plastics contain a very wide range of phosphorous compounds. These compounds are widespread in the human environment and play an important role in ecology. They represent new problems for the analyst, one example being the impact of anthropization of arable lands and certain farming techniques. For example slash and burn agriculture generates pyrophosphates, applying sewage sludge adds polyphosphates and organic forms of P that do not exist in the natural environment. It is generally accepted that plants can

---

[1] P is quantitatively ranked ninth of the elements composing the earth's crust. It is particularly common in the orthophosphate state bound to calcium (apatites) with average contents estimated at about 0.1%.

only assimilate phosphorus directly in the form of orthophosphates in the soil solution.

The main organic forms of P (50–75%) are used as reserves and are in continual transformation, the cycle of immobilization and mineralization of organic–inorganic-P in soil being influenced by pH, redox and biochemical phenomena (phosphatases) such as climatic conditions. In soils with a pH of between 3.5 and 10, the orthophosphate forms are primarily $H_2PO_4^-$ in acid medium and HPO_4^{2-} in basic medium. The activity of the two ions is about equal at pH 7.2, the H_3PO_4 form becomes predominant below pH 3.5 and the PO_4^{3-} form is predominant above pH 11–12.

The purpose of the different methods is to evaluate total P, especially the forms that are available to varying degrees in the short and medium term (White and Beckett 1964, Dalal and Hallsworth 1976, Roche et al. 1978, Pierzynski 2000):
– quantity (Q) of different forms of P: extractable, occluded, total P
– intensity (I), chemical potential of the PO_4^{3-} ions in the soil solution that enable normal plant growth throughout the vegetative cycle
– capacity of maintenance of the P concentration in the soil solution expressed by the fixing power of P, adsorption isotherms ($\Delta Q/\Delta I$)
– kinetics of desorption over time
– diffusibility, extent of the zone likely to provide the soil solution.

Thus the chemical and biochemical changes which occur during the dynamic process of the phosphorus cycle can be measured, and possibly controlled and directed.

Unlike the C, H, N, O, S cycles, in the P cycle, no losses occur due to volatilization (except possibly H_3P whose existence in the natural state has not yet been demonstrated, even in very reducing medium). This specificity can increase the risk of water eutrophication by pollution, as the action of P continues over a period of many years, even after the sources of pollution have been removed.

29.2 Total Soil Phosphorus

29.2.1 Introduction

The term total phosphorus covers all forms of P in the soil, i.e. organic, inorganic, occluded and available P. It is the total flow of P at a given time. The soil P content depends on the nature of the parent rock, climatic factors and the deterioration that results (degree of weathering, biotic activity, erosion, leaching). P contents are very varied. Soils on calcareous mediums that are rich in apatite can contain high percentages of total P in not very wet climates. On the other hand, acid soils that developed on granitic rocks with low P contents, also present low P contents in their natural state.

Chemical analysis first has to destroy the matrix (inorganic and organic) in order to solubilize the fixed or occluded forms which are mainly insoluble (like some calcium, iron or aluminium phosphates) and which correspond to medium and long-term soil reserves.

Mineralization can be accomplished (i) using a wet process e.g. an acid attack in oxidizing medium to avoid loss of forms of phosphorus which could appear in the reducing medium, (ii) using dry methods e.g. alkaline fusion in oxygenated furnace followed by an acid attack of the products of fusion.

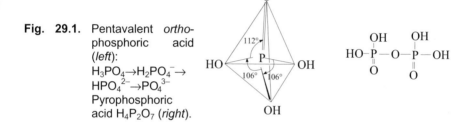

Fig. 29.1. Pentavalent *ortho*-phosphoric acid (*left*): $H_3PO_4 \to H_2PO_4^- \to HPO_4^{2-} \to PO_4^{3-}$ Pyrophosphoric acid $H_4P_2O_7$ (*right*).

Phosphorus has five valence electrons and forms almost only covalent bonds. In the fundamental state there are three p orbitals, each filled by only one electron. This corresponds to an electronic distribution of spherical symmetry and a great energy of ionization. Phosphorus often forms covalent compounds. Free enthalpies of the different oxidation states in solution at pH0 show that the molecules are relatively unstable and can be transformed. Hydrolysis results in maximum oxidation giving *ortho*-phosphoric acid, the pentavalent form of phosphorus with maximum thermodynamic stability. It thus provides the basis for the majority of chemical titrations (Fig. 29.1).

29.2.2 Wet Mineralization for Total Analyses

Principle

Wet mineralization procedures for total analysis (cf. Sect. 31.2 of Chap. 31) can be used for analysis of total P. However, if the only analysis required is total phosphorus, the procedures can be simplified. The soil is subjected to an oxidizing acid attack i.e. prolonged boiling with nitric or perchloric acid. The different forms of P are all brought to the *ortho* state. The organic matter is destroyed and the P compounds on which it was bound are released. Apatites are dissolved along with phosphates of iron and aluminium, phosphites (HPO_3^{2-}), tripolyphosphates ($Na_5P_3O_{10}$), metaphosphates and pyrophosphates.

However, the soil residue may still contain primary minerals with unattacked P inclusions that can only be destroyed with hydrofluoric acid (cf. Sects. 31.2.3 and 31.2.4 of Chap. 31).

Equipment

– Analytical balance (1/10 mg)
– electric sand bath or hotplate
– 150 mL Pyrex boiling Kjeldahl flasks
– rack for filtration and funnels
– hardened analytical filters
– lab glassware.

Reagents

– Nitric acid (HNO_3 *d*: 1.4, (boiling point 120°C)
– 60% perchloric acid for analysis (can be deflagrating)
– deionized water.

Procedure with Nitric Acid

– Weigh aliquots of 5 g of soil dried at 105°C and crushed to 0.2 or 0.1 mm and put them in 150 mL Pyrex boiling Kjeldahl flasks
– add 30 mL of concentrated nitric acid
– cover with long-stemmed micro-funnels; place in the sand bath and boil for 3 h (do not allow to go dry)
– cool and dilute carefully with deionized water
– filter on hardened analytical filters in long stem funnels
– wash the filter with deionized boiling water and collect all filtrates in a 250 mL Pyrex beaker
– evaporate to almost dry
– dissolve with 1 mL of perchloric acid (or sulphuric acid)
– dilute with deionized water to 50 or 100 mL (depending on the soil type and supposed contents); homogenize.

Titration is carried out on aliquots by spectrocolorimetry or other spectographic methods (cf. Sect. 29.5 below or Chap. 31). The results are expressed on the basis of soil dried at 105°C.

Remarks

Nitric attack does not mineralize the entire soil matrix and leaves a relatively large residue.

In organic (e.g. histosols) or humus-bearing soils, the organic matter is unlikely to be completely destroyed. In this case, bring to almost dry and add perhydrol until complete discolouration, then attack again with 1 mL of nitric acid

The attack solution contains silica. If it is dried, silica can become sintered and not easily resolubilized but can be partly eliminated by filtration.

The nitric method may have certain disadvantages, but involves fewer risks than mineralization with perchloric acid (cf. the following section).

Procedure with Perchloric Acid

– Weigh 2–5 g of soil dried at 105°C and crushed to 0.2 or 0.1 mm
– put it in a 150 mL Pyrex boiling Kjeldahl flask and add 30 mL of 60% perchloric acid
– continue as described in 2.2.4 above boiling gently for approximately 30 min until white smoke appears and discolouration occurs
– without boiling, reduce the volume until almost white sands are obtained
– filter and complete the volume to 250 mL, homogenize.
Titrate on an aliquot (cf. Sect. 29.5 or Chap. 31).

Remarks

As the perchlorates are unstable, they must not be allowed to go dry.

Boiling should be gentle particularly at the beginning of mineralization when organic matter is still abundant (for very organic soils, the destruction of organic matter can be incomplete and require addition of nitric acid then concentration to almost dry and an attack with 1 mL of perchloric acid).

29.2.3 Dry Mineralization

Principle

Alkaline fusion can destroy the structural matrix resulting in amorphous solid solutions that are easily attacked in acid medium. The attack is generally very complete and is suitable for total analyses, including refractory elements. Thus in addition to the method described in this section, the methods described in Sect. 31.2.6 of Chap. 31 can also be used for the analysis of total P.

Soil is mixed with sodium carbonate in a platinum crucible and melted in open oxidizing medium. The different forms of P are transformed into orthophosphate form, and then solubilized by an acid attack. Too-prolonged heating after fusion should be avoided because of the risk of the appearance of monoperphosphoric (H_3PO_5) and perphosphoric ($H_4P_2O_3$) acids.

Equipment

– 50 mL platinum crucibles
– electric furnace able to function while open (oxidizing atmosphere)
– crucible tongs
– lab glassware.

Reagents

– Anhydrous sodium carbonate (Na_2CO_3, melting point = 851°C);
– deionized water
– 5 mol (HNO_3) L^{-1} nitric acid
– 5 mol ($\frac{1}{2}H_2SO_4$) L^{-1} sulphuric acid.

Procedure

– Weigh 1 g of soil dried at 105°C and crushed to 0.2 or 0.1 mm
– place the soil in a platinum crucible and mix with 5 g of sodium carbonate
– heat the sample gradually and move it around in the furnace until the beginning of fusion (850°C approximately) taking care to avoid projections

– half cover the crucible with the lid to preserve an oxidizing atmosphere and maintain the temperature of the furnace for 20 min
– holding the crucible with the tongs, swirl the contents around to distribute the product in fusion on the walls; let cool
– put the crucible and its lid in a 250 mL Pyrex beaker, gradually and carefully add 30 mL of 5 mol ($\frac{1}{2}H_2SO_4\,L^{-1}$) acid taking care not to cause projections (avoid HCl which can attack the platinum crucibles)
– boil until complete dissolution
– if necessary add 5mL of 1 mol ($\frac{1}{2}H_2SO_4\,L^{-1}$) L^{-1} sulphuric acid solution
– filter on analytical hardened filter
– complete to 250 mL with deionized water and homogenize
– remove one aliquot for P titration (cf. Sect. 29.5)
– calculate the results on the basis of soil dried at 105°C.

Remark

Total P is directly linked with the content of the parent rock and the processes involved in the evolution of the soil; it provides no information about the availability of P for plants. Total P accounts for the total phosphorous balance of a natural soil and the evolution of a cultivated soil undergoing regular fertilization. It enables monitoring of P enrichment or of exports by different processes such as harvesting, erosion or leaching.

29.3 Fractionation of Different Forms of Phosphorus

29.3.1 Introduction

Analysis of total P sheds no light on the complex chemical and microbiological mechanisms that modify the forms of P. The organic fraction can vary between 20% and 80%. The different forms of P are usually present in too small quantities and are too finely differentiated to be easily detected with instrumental methods like XRD, IR spectrometry (cf. Chap. 4 and 5) or differential thermal analysis (cf. Chap. 7). Direct methods using electronic microscopy and EDX probes (cf. Chap. 8) are useful for detailed studies of mineralogical evolution but are not a reliable test of potential fertility.

Indirect methods use extraction reagents following a precise procedure which enables titration of solubilized forms of P. Some sequential methods make it possible to isolate different representative pools. Reagents modify the chemical equilibriums of the soil. Buffered or not-buffered mediums can be used. The selectivity of these methods varies with the type of soil and with farming practices, making it possible to define the general tendency of the P reactions as a function of climate and of biogeochemical processes. Farming experimentation is the method of choice to identify correlations between plant yields and extracted forms of P and to define the assimilability of P in a given area. Most plants are known to assimilate P in the $H_2PO_4^-$ and/or HPO_4^{2-} forms contained in the soil solution but this depends on the pH. Organic P has sometimes been considered to be a direct source for plants, but this issue is very controversial. The complex process of plant assimilation involves enzymes (e.g. phosphatases) in contact with the rootlets that are able to release *ortho*-P. In the rhizosphere, exchanges between pools are rather rapid at least until equilibrium of the soil solution has been reached.

29.3.2 Sequential Methods

Principle

These methods allow some petrologic, mineralogical, biogeochemical or agronomic mechanisms to be revealed by measuring the differences in solubility of inorganic- or organic-P in "selective" reagents. Many attempts have been made (particularly the Chang and Jackson method, 1957) to measure the inorganic forms of P and the transformation of P added in the form of amendments or fertilizer. The reagents used enable separation of P fractions assumed to be bound to aluminium, iron or calcium and two fractions of P occluded in iron-aluminium complexes. But some reagents are not specific enough. In particular, the use of ammonium fluoride in calcareous soils often causes the precipitation of calcium fluoride from calcium carbonate and leaching of P which is then found in another form.

The methods of Williams et al. (1967) and Syers et al. (1972) improved specificity by modifying the nature and concentration of some reagents. Unfortunately, these methods are very time consuming and do not account for organic P which predominates in the soil and plays a major role in the P cycle.

A more complex method was developed by Hedley et al. (1982) that makes it possible to split soil P into six pools including organic and inorganic forms. Treatment with chloroform causes lysis of microbial cells, providing an additional biochemical dimension. The technique can be used to identify the equilibriums of the forms of soil P in long fallow systems and long-term experiments, but also in short-term incubation tests or crop trials in the greenhouse. In this way short-term dynamics can be quantified then extended to try and explain long-term transformations.

Equipment

- 0.1 mm mesh sieve
- small mesh nylon bags (for the resin)
- centrifuge and 50 mL centrifugation tubes with screw caps
- shaker
- ultrasonic tank
- micro-wave furnace for mineralization with 50 mL Teflon bottle
- lab glassware.

Products

- Deionized water
- Dowex 1 8X50 anionic resin in bicarbonate form (or similar)
- 0.5 mol ($NaHCO_3$) L^{-1}, sodium hydrogen carbonate
- chloroform, $CHCl_3$
- analytical filters
- 0.1 mol (NaOH) L^{-1}, sodium hydroxide
- 1 mol (HCl) L^{-1}, hydrochloric acid
- perhydrol
- concentrated sulphuric acid.

Sample

Organic phosphorus can be modified by air drying and prolonged crushing. It is recommended to use soil samples that have been stored in their natural moisture at –40°C before analysis. The samples should then be rapidly dried in a thin layer in the air and then crushed to 2 mm. One aliquot should be crushed to 0.1 mm.

Residual moisture should be measured on another sample specimen to calculate all the results on the basis of soil dried at 105°C.

Procedure

– Weigh two 0.5 g soil samples crushed to 0.1 mm (cf. "Products" in Sect. 29.3.2) and put the two samples (A and B) in 100 mL centrifugation tubes with screw caps
– add a nylon bag containing 0.4 g of anion exchange resin
– add 30 mL of water; shake for 16 h at 24°C
– remove the nylon bag and rinse it to recover all the soil
– centrifuge the water/sample mixture and discard the supernatant
– phosphorus fixed on the resin is the most biologically available inorganic P, similar to P in the soil solution. The resin can either be (i) destroyed by attack with a strong acid (perchloric acid) or (ii) extracted by exchange with 10 mL of a 10% NaCl solution at 80°C (cf. "Procedure" in Sect. 29.3.2); complete the extraction or attack solution to 50 mL with deionized water This is compartment 1, "resin extractable P".

The soil residue is used for subsequent extraction. It can be stored wet for 24 h at 24°C without closing the tubes to ensure incubation in sufficiently oxygenated medium.

Sample A

– To residue A from the resin extraction, add 30 mL of the 0.5 mol $(NaHCO_3)$ L^{-1} solution and shake for 16 h at 24°C
– centrifuge and filter the supernatant which contains labile inorganic and organic P with a little P of microbial origin. Discard the soil residue
– bring the liquid to 50 mL by neutralizing with 5 mL of 4 mol L^{-1} sulphuric or perchloric acid. This is compartment 2A, "bicarbonate extractable P".

Sample B

– To residue B from the resin extraction, add 1 mL of chloroform
– close the tube and agitate for 1 h
– evaporate chloroform overnight
– add 30 mL of the 0.5 mol $(NaHCO_3)$ L^{-1} solution
– shake for 16 h at 24°C
– centrifuge and filter the supernatant
– bring to 50 mL by neutralizing with 5 mL of 4 mol L^{-1} sulphuric or perchloric acid. This is compartment 2B, "Chloroform–bicarbonate extractable P"
– calculate the P resulting from microbial lysis by difference:
[compartment 2B-P] – [compartment 2A-P].

Perform the following sequential extraction on soil residue B:
– Add 30 mL of the 0.1 mol (NaOH) L^{-1} solution; shake for 16 h at 24°C
– centrifuge and filter the supernatant which contains inorganic and organic P retained by chemisorption of iron and aluminium compounds at the surface of the particles; bring to 50 mL while neutralizing as previously. This is compartment 3, "diluted soda extractable P".

Again place the soil residue in contact with 20 mL of the 0.1 mol (NaOH) L^{-1} solution and subject it to ultrasound for 2 min in a tank containing melting ice. Complete the volume to 30 mL with the 0.1 mol (NaOH) L^{-1} solution and shake for 16 h at 24°C. Centrifuge and filter the supernatant which contains inorganic and organic P retained on the internal surfaces of the soil aggregates. Bring to 50 mL while neutralizing. This is compartment 4, "ultrasound-assisted diluted soda extractable P".

Put the soil residue in contact with 30 mL of the 1 mol (HCl) L^{-1} solution. Shake for 16 h, centrifuge and filter the supernatant which contains apatitic minerals and also some inorganic and organic P occluded in the weathered soils. Bring to 50 mL with deionized water. This is compartment 5, "hydrochloric acid extractable P".

Subject the residual soil to oxidizing acid mineralization using a mixture of sulphuric acid and perhydrol (or perchloric acid, cf. Sect. 29.2.2) for 3 h. This enables solubilization of stable forms of organic P and not easily soluble forms of inorganic P. Cool, filter and bring the filtrate to 50 mL with deionized water. This is compartment 6, "Residual P".

For analysis of each extract, take:
– one aliquot at the concentration suitable for P titration by spectrocolorimetry (cf. Sect. 29.5.2); this method should be used to titrate only the *ortho*-P form;
– one aliquot which will be mineralized by sulphuric acid plus perhydrol before titration in order to obtain total P (organic + inorganic; mineralization need not be performed in the case of inductively coupled plasma spectrographic titration of organic plus inorganic-P). In this way organic P can be distinguished by difference. Titration should be carried out without delay to limit hydrolysis.

In compartment 1 "Resin extractable-P" and in the final soil residue, it is difficult to separate the organic and inorganic forms which comprise medium and long-term reserves.

Remarks

This method is time consuming and cannot be used for routine agronomic tests, but may be useful for research programs that include plant tests or soil incubation.

A correction factor of microbial P suitable for the soil type is often used to estimate total bacterial and fungic microbial flora.

The spectrocolorimetric method used is that of Murphy and Riley (1962) or with later improvements. This method is specific to *ortho*-phosphates and allows inorganic and organics forms of P to be distinguished. Separation is satisfactory in spite of the risk of hydrolysis of the organic forms.

Direct determination of soil total P (cf. Sect. 29.2) makes it possible to check summation of the extracted forms.

The forms of organic P present in the bicarbonate, soda and soda-ultrasound extracts have molecular weights <30,000. In the "residual soil" compartment, organic P is included in molecules of weights ranging between 30,000 and 70,000 which may correspond to the humin fractions (cf. Chap. 11).

29.3.3 Selective Extractions – Availability Indices

Presentation of the Methods

These methods are based on a single extraction of inorganic *ortho*-P with a reagent carefully chosen to dissolve specific available form of P. These methods are only suitable for mediums with acid or basic pH, either for soil chemistry studies or for simple fertility tests.

The soil may come from uncultivated land or intensively cultivated land ploughed regular, and include the reuse or not of plant residues, inputs of more or less soluble fertilizer (for rectification, maintenance, correction of deficiencies) which seriously disturb the dynamics of P turnover and influence the agricultural management of soils. The terminology used for the evaluation of the different extracted forms varies considerably reflecting the complexity of the phenomena of distribution and exchanges of P in the soil, and the intensity of the inter-compartmental flows that determine the dynamics of the system.

These methods enable quantification of two categories of P forms:
- mobile P forms from weak chemical bonds, called active, easily removable, available, exchangeable, extractable, easily hydrolyzed, unstable, soluble or usable P forms, depending on the author;
- not easily removable and/or strongly adsorbed P forms from chelation bonds, calcium or iron P inclusion, occluded organic and inorganic P, biomass P, P fixed to the lattice.

Table 29.1. Some reagents used for P extraction in soil

Type	method, extracting reagent	author(s)
miscellaneous	water, anionic resin, ^{32}P or ^{33}P isotopic dilution, electrodialysis, electro-ultrafiltration	
extraction with complexing agents	EDTA, NH_4HCO_3, + DTPA pH 7.6	Soltanpour
extractions at basic pH	NaOH, KOH, NH_4OH, Na_2CO_3, $NaHCO_3$ pH 8.5 K_2CO_3, $(NH_4)_2CO_3$	Olsen Michigin
extraction with organic acids and their salts	acetic acid – ammonium or sodium acetate at pH 2.5 and pH 4.8 citric acid – ammonium citrate	Morgan Dyer (1894) Demolon (1932) NF X31-160 (1993)
	lactic acid – ammonium or calcium lactate oxalic acid – ammonium oxalate	Joret and Hébert (1955) NF X31-161 (1993)
	thioglycolic acid + NH_4F acetic acid + ammonium lactate	Egner-Riehm
extraction with strong inorganic acids and their salts	HCl + H_2SO_4 HCl + NH_4F H_2SO_4 0.001 mol L^{-1} pH 3.0 0.01 mol L^{-1} pH 2.0 0.005 mol L^{-1} 0.2 mol L^{-1} $CaSO_4$ 0.005 mol L^{-1} $CaCl_2$ 0.005 mol L^{-1}	Mehlich (no. 1) (1953) Bray and Kurtz (1) (1945) Truog Peech Keer Stieglitz

Many methods are available to evaluate the capacity of fixation and exchange, potential, retention, retrogradation or adsorbing capacity of phosphorus in soils.

If some terms express the mobile character of P (like exchangeable P), not all the procedures result in a selective form. In theory, a direct relationship exists between available P and the normal needs of the plant which can increase plant growth and yield (response to fertilization). However, unless a correlation has been established between the plant, the soil type and extracted P, the use of the term 'available P' is completely arbitrary.

There are many methods that use acid, basic or complexing reagents which act in different ways such as simple dissolution, iron reduction, complexation or precipitation of aluminium, iron or calcium. The most widely used reagents are buffered or not buffered strong or weak inorganic or organic acids, and a range of inorganic and organic bases and the salts of these acids and bases (Table 29.1). Each method has an index value. The pH of the reagents is generally buffered in zones where $H_2PO_4^-$ and HPO_4^{2-} exist, i.e. between pH 2.0 and 6.0 for acid soils and at pH 8.5 for alkaline soils. In other cases, the soil pH determines the method of extraction (e.g. water extraction, electrodialysis, electro ultra-filtration, resin extraction).

For a given reagent, a number of experimental variables can influence the dissolution process: pH, concentration, soil-to-solution ratio, contact time, temperature, particle size, agitation (ultrasounds). When results have to be compared, it is essential to ensure procedures are rigorously respected.

Water extraction gives the P concentration in the soil solution. Basic reagents enable extraction of organic and inorganic labile forms and a little microbial P at around pH 8.5. The insoluble forms bound to calcium are not really attacked by the reagent at this pH. At higher pH, P forms bound to humus are solubilized and the compounds retained by chemisorption are extracted.

Humic, fulvic acids and some humin are extracted with a hot 5 mol $(NaOH)$ L^{-1} solution with intense colouring of the extracts.

Weak organic acids or their salts can be used to make well-buffered mediums. The extraction pH varies between 2 and 8 depending on the method. Oxalic acid-ammonium oxalate reagent can complex aluminium and iron and active calcium if precipitated. Citric acid–ammonium citrate reagent can attack the crystal lattice of silicates, precipitate calcium, attack iron compounds towards pH 5.0 and aluminium compounds from pH 3–8.

A mixture of tartaric acid and tartarates can complex iron and aluminium (pH 3.2–7.5). A mixture of lactic acid and lactates preferentially extracts P bound to calcium, and only a little P bound to iron or aluminium (pH 3.5–3.7). Mixtures of boric acid and borates and of acetic acid and acetates at pH 2.5 or 4.8 extract only a little P.

Diluted strong inorganic acids can solubilize P bound to calcium, and varying quantities of P bound to iron and aluminium. The pH generally ranges from 1 to 3 (apatite P, occluded P, weathered soils). The effectiveness of the extraction (which is not linked with farming practices) depends on the type of acid in the lyotropic series H_2SO_4 > HCl > HNO_3. For example, HCl facilitates the separation of P from organic colloids (rupture of the bonds of polyvalent salts). Strong acids cause hydrolysis of organic P which is not easy to control. Hydrofluoric acid can solubilize organic and inorganic P by attacking the silicate lattices. Ammonium fluoride and fluorhydric acid can complex aluminium and iron in acid soils, but cannot be used in a calcareous medium because of the random precipitation of calcium fluoride (Syers et al. 1972):

$$CaCO_3 + 2\ NH_4F \rightarrow CaF_2\!\downarrow + (NH_4)_2CO_3$$

The calcium fluoride that is formed results in underestimation of the P not occluded in iron and P bound to aluminium, and overestimation of P occluded with iron oxides and iron hydroxides, and of P bound to calcium.

Sequestering agents like EDTA or DTPA, enable solubilization of P bound to oxides and hydroxides of aluminium and iron, and to different forms of calcium. The reaction is generally slow, except in the labile forms.

Equipment

Except for a few minor details (like size of the centrifugation tubes), similar equipment is required for all methods of section 29.3.3 explained later:
– analytical balances (±1/10 mg)
– 100 and 250 mL centrifugation tubes with screw caps
– shaker
– centrifuge
– long-stemmed Pyrex funnels for filtration
– 20 mL syringe for filtration
– lab glassware
– stainless steel sieve Ø 50, 0.25 mm mesh standard AFNOR NF 25 (cf. recovery of resin in the following "Procedure").

Water Soluble P

Principle

The method of extraction in water (or in 0.01 mol L^{-1} solution of calcium chloride or calcium sulphate) enables evaluation of a P concentration close to that in the soil solution and of possible thresholds of deficiency.

The permanent turnover of P in the soil solution is very important for plant nutrition throughout the vegetative cycle. It is ensured by the action of micro-organisms and enzymes like phosphatases. If the kinetics of P input in the soil solution is lower than the transfer to the plant of the quantity of P required for normal growth (deficiency threshold), there will be a reduction in plant activity (e.g. dwarfism).

Equipment and Reagents

– Deionized water
– disc-filters or 0.22 μm membrane for syringe
– very fine analytical filters
– 0.01 mol L^{-1} calcium chloride solution
– 0.01 mol L^{-1} calcium sulphate solution (solubility 2.09 g L^{-1}).

Procedure

– Weigh 5 g of air-dried soil (2 mm particle size) in a centrifugation tube with a screw cap; add 50 mL of deionized water and shake for 5 min
– centrifuge for 15 min at 10,000g until the liquid is clear; filter on very fine analytical filter (blue) or on a 0.22 μm filter placed in the 20 mL syringe; remove an aliquot containing approximately 10 μm of P to analyse water soluble P (cf. Sect. 29.5).

Remarks. If the soil solution is obtained in situ using low-pressure microporous tubes, the concentration will be very close to that of the solution in contact with the plant roots; however, this requires the installation of equipment at field stations, which limits its use. Climatic conditions make sampling impossible at certain periods of the year in particular in arid areas, when the equilibrium between "soil solution P" and "labile inorganic P" is modified or non-existent as is the activity of micro-organisms.

Sodium Bicarbonate Extractable P at pH 8.5 (Olsen)

Principle

When extracted with this method, P corresponds to the most biologically available forms of P, i.e. labile organic and inorganic forms and includes a fraction of microbial P.

This method can be used for basic, neutral or acid soils. The extracting agent decreases the concentration of the calcium in solution by precipitating insoluble calcium carbonate. The solubility of calcium phosphates increases with a decrease in calcium activity (effect of liming on P availability). The reagent extracts part of labile organic P and of inorganic P bound to calcium. In acid soils, phosphates of iron and aluminium (strengite–variscite) become more soluble with an increase in pH, with an optimum towards pH 6–7 where levels of $H_2PO_4^-$ and HPO_4^{2-} forms are the same. In the Olsen method, which was modified by Dabin (1967), ammonium fluoride is added. This reagent enables iron and aluminium to be complexed and thus a greater quantity of P to be solubilized. In certain tropical soils with low calcium content, extracted P is better correlated with plant yields.

Reagents

– 0.5 mol L^{-1} solution of sodium bicarbonate ($NaHCO_3$ mw = 84.01): adjust to pH 8.5 with a 1 mol (NaOH) L^{-1} solution; the solutions should be freshly made and stored in hermetically sealed bottles.
– P-free activated carbon (DARCO 60, or similar), if necessary for controls purify with a 2 mol (HCl) L^{-1} solution then with $NaHCO_3$ reagent and rinse with deionized water.

Procedure

– Weigh 5 g of air-dried soil (2 mm particle size); put in a 250 mL centrifugation tube.
– add 100 mL of sodium bicarbonate reagent; shake for 30 min.
– centrifuge for 5 min at 10,000 g and filter (adding P-free activated carbon enables a clear and colourless filtrate to be obtained for colorimetric analysis, however this addition should not be systematic but should be reserved for samples where the extraction solution is still turbid after filtration); remove one aliquot for titration after neutralisation (cf. Sect. 29.5).

Anion Exchange Resin Extractable P

Principle

Resins enable extraction of most biologically available forms of inorganic P. Varying the contact time can also provide information on the kinetics of P extraction. An anion exchange resin with a particle size greater than 0.5 mm should be used.

Reagents

– Anion exchange resin (e.g. Dowex 1X8-50) in bicarbonate form
– anion exchange resin (Dowex 2) in chloride form
– resin fractions should have a particle size equal to or higher than 0.5 mm, check by sieving wet. Discard the finest particles
– 10% sodium chloride solution.

Procedure

– Weigh 5 g of air-dried soil crushed to 0.1 mm in a 100 mL centrifugation bottle
– add 5 g of sieved resin
– add 50 mL of deionized water; shake for 16 h
– separate the resin on a sieve with a 0.250 mm mesh (AFNOR NF 25); wash with water and recover the resin on the sieve
– with a jet of water from a washing bottle, transfer the resin in a 50 mL beaker; eliminate water by decantation and add 25 mL of the 10% NaCl solution; heat in a water bath at 80°C for 45 min
– cool and decant the solution in a 50 mL volumetric flask; rinse the resin with 10% NaCl solution and bring to 50 mL; homogenize and remove one aliquot to titrate exchanged P.

Note. With this method P can be extracted without deteriorating the sample or modifying the soil pH and the method also enables root action to be simulated. By leaving the sample in contact for varying periods of time, precise information can be obtained on the quantity, capacity and kinetics of P. In this case the method requires prolonged contact of from 48 h to three weeks or more.

Ammonium Oxalate Extractable P

Principle

This method (Jorret and Hébert 1955) is the subject of the AFNOR NF X31-161 (1993) standard. It can be used for all types of soil except those very rich in organic matter.

Reagents

– Deionized water
– ammonium oxalate, $(NH_4)_2C_2O_4,H_2O$
– 0.1 mol (NH_4OH) L^{-1} ammonia solution
– extraction solution (should be freshly made each day): dissolve 14.21 g of ammonium oxalate in 900 mL of deionized water agitating the solution with a magnetic stirrer with a Teflon bar; adjust the pH to 7.0 with the ammonia solution; transfer the solution in a 1 L volumetric flask; rinse the beaker with water and bring to 1,000 mL; homogenize.

Procedure

– Weigh 5 g of air-dried soil (particle size 2 mm) and put in a 250 mL centrifugation tube with a screw cap; add 100 mL of ammonium oxalate solution at 20°C; shake for 2 h
– filter the extract which should be clear and titrate P on an aliquot fraction (in the presence of As^{5-}, arsenic interference can be eliminated by reducing As^{5-} to As^{3-} by adding sodium hyposulphite, and formol to clarify the solution).

Double Acid Extractable P (HCl–H₂SO₄)

Principle

This method was developed by Mehlich (1953) for acid soils (North Carolina, USA) that fix P vigorously and have low organic matter content. It is used as a basic method for testing soil in fertilization studies like the methods of Bray (1945) and Olsen (calcareous soils).

It uses a mixture of hydrochloric and sulphuric acid which is considered to be more effective than hydrochloric acid alone for extraction of P linked with the response of plants cultivated on soils rich in iron phosphate. The method is simple, fast and reproducible, but cannot be used in calcareous soils because of random neutralization of the extraction solution.

Reagents

– Deionized water
– concentrated sulphuric acid, H_2SO_4 d: 1.84
– concentrated hydrochloric acid, HCl d: 1.19
– extraction solution: mix 6 mL of concentrated sulphuric acid and 36 mL of concentrated hydrochloric acid in approximately 7.5 L of deionized water; bring the volume to 9 L (the extraction solution is 0.05 mol (HCl) L^{-1} and 0.025 mol $(1/2H_2SO_4)$ L^{-1}
– activated carbon (DARCO G6 or similar) (free from P)
– analytical filters.

Procedure

– Weigh 5 g of air-dried soil (2 mm particle size) in a 50 mL centrifugation tube; add 200 mg of activated carbon, then 20 mL of extraction solution
– shake for 5 min and filter on analytical blue filter or with a syringe equipped with a 0.45 or 0.20 μm filter-membrane; remove one aliquot for P titration.

Ammonium Fluoride Hydrochloric Acid Extractable P

Principle

The first method proposed by Bray (1945) was based on solubilization of P compound in acid and on the action of fluoride anion to reduce the activity of the Al^{+++} cation and of Fe^{+++} and Ca^{++} cations by forming complexes.

It is used for neutral and acid soils, but cannot be used in calcareous soils (random neutralization of the reagent, dissolution of calcium carbonate and precipitation of calcium fluoride). Repeatability depends on how rigorously the procedure is respected.

Reagents

– Deionized water
– 0.5 mol (HCl) L^{-1} hydrochloric acid solution: add 20.3 mL HCl in 500 mL of deionized water
– ammonium fluoride NH_4F
– 1 mol (NH_4F) L^{-1} solution: dissolve 37 g of ammonium fluoride in 400 mL of deionized water in a plastic beaker; dilute and bring to 1,000 mL; homogenize and store in a polyethylene bottle
– extraction solution: mix 30 mL of the 1 mol (NH_4F) L^{-1} solution and 50 mL of the 0.5 mol (HCl) L^{-1} solution. Bring to 1,000 mL with deionized water. The solution contains 0.025 mol (HCl) L^{-1} and 0.03

mol (NH_4F) L^{-1}, the pH is 2.6; the reagent is stable if stored in a polyethylene bottle.

Procedure

– Weigh 2 g of air-dried soil (particle size 2 mm) in a 50 mL centrifugation tube
– add 20 mL of extraction solution at pH 2.6 and shake for 5 min on an oscillating shaker (regulated at 180 oscillations per minute)
– immediately filter on fine analytical paper (blue) or with a syringe equipped with a 0.45 or 0.20 μm filter membrane. Titrate P on one aliquot of this solution.

Remarks. The action of ammonium fluoride enables aluminium and ferric phosphates to be dissolved with the formation of aluminium and iron complexes, the forms bound to calcium should be extracted by the action of acid.

A number of modifications aimed at obtaining a better correlation of P extracts with plant yields, either by increasing the volume of extracting reagent, or by increasing the extraction time from 1 to 5 min. Reproducibility is difficult to ensure with contact times under 5 min, and the procedure is difficult to implement without automation, for example agitation on site with filtration by aspiration on 0.20 μm micro-membrane.

29.3.4 Isotopic Dilution Methods

Methods for the study of fertilization based on ^{32}P isotopic dilution appeared in the 1950s (Dean et al. 1947).

Different techniques were developed to estimate the quantity of P isotope exchange by means of a plant test (L value, Larsen 1952) or to measure the flow of phosphate ions per unit of time in a soil-solution system (E value, Gunnarson-Frederickson 1952).

This method gives a good estimation of the bioavailability of P in the soil and the sediments. Bioavailable phosphorus was defined (Fardeau 1997) as "all phosphorus that can move into the soil solution in the form of phosphate ions in a time that is compatible with the requirements of the growing plant".

The method of kinetics of ^{32}P exchange with stationary systems enables factors of intensity (concentration of P in the soil solution), quantity and capacity to be identified by measuring the ions transferred from the solid phase to the liquid phase in 1 min, one day, three months, one year or even longer, however, without providing precise details on the mineralization of the organic matter.

These methods require special laboratory management for the handling of labelled substances. To obtain a high degree of accuracy, it is necessary to eliminate fine particles in suspension, which means centrifugation at more than 100,000g or filtering on 0.01 µm membranes. Measurements are taken without modifying the state of the system making it possible to quantify labile forms.

These methods also require special equipment like a liquid scintillation counter or a 120,000g ultracentrifuge. Tracer techniques should be implemented away from other activities in which isotopic tracers are naturally abundant to avoid possible contamination. P tracer procedures are described in detail in Fardeau (1988–1993) and Gachon (1988).

29.3.5 Determination of Organic Phosphorus

Introduction

The study of organic P is extremely complex due to the diversity of the organic forms, but also because permanent transformation occurs under the influence of micro-organisms. Biological turnover results in biochemical and chemical reactions between the plant and the soil. Mineralization and immobilization reactions occur with respect to clays and oxides, and during the course of soil genesis these differentiate the compartments where P exists in forms of varying degrees of availability.

Depending on the type of soil, climatic conditions and the activity of micro-organisms, organic phosphorus can represent from 20% to 80% of total P. Specific compounds can be found inside this P compartment; the most common forms being inositol phosphate, which can represent more than half organic P, phospholipides (approximately 5%) and nucleic acids (approximately 2%).

All these forms are difficult to analyse because they hydrolyze with varying degrees of difficulty. Methods like nuclear magnetic resonance (^{31}P-NMR) make it possible to identify the molecular structure of some simple products if they are sufficiently abundant. But NMR is not very sensitive (10^{-5} g approximately), is expensive and consequently not suitable for repetitive analysis. Other methods have been developed which can be classified in two main groups: overall estimation of organic P by calcination, in which the organic matter is destroyed (cf. "Measurement of Organic P by Thermal Destruction") or solubilization and extraction in acid and base solutions (cf. "Extraction of Organic P in Acid and Base Reagents").

Measurement of Organic P by Thermal Destruction

Principle

Organic P is converted into inorganic P by calcination and estimated by difference:

organic P = inorganic P of burnt soil - inorganic P of untreated soil.

This method is simple and fast, but its precision is low due to (i) hydrolysis of organic P during extraction in untreated soil and (ii) the error transmitted during calculation by difference (Pansu et al. 2001).

Equipment

– Muffle furnace
– porcelain or quartz crucibles 45 mm in diameter
– 100 mL polyethylene centrifugation tubes with screw caps
– centrifuge
– filtration rack
– analytical hardened filters
– lab glassware.

Reagent

– 0.5 mol (H_2SO_4) L^{-1} sulphuric acid solution.

Procedure

(1) Calcination extract

– Weigh 1 g of soil crushed to 0.1 mm in a porcelain or quartz crucible
– place in a cold furnace and gradually raise the temperature to 550°C in oxygenated medium; maintain this temperature for 2 h
– let the crucible cool, transfer the soil residue in a 100 mL centrifugation tube (A); add 50 mL of the 0.5 mol (H_2SO_4) L^{-1} solution.

(2) Direct extract

– Weigh 1 g of soil crushed to 0.1 mm in a 100 mL centrifugation tube (B)
– add 50 mL of the 0.5 mol (H_2SO_4) L^{-1} solution.

(3) Extraction

– Close the A and B tubes and shake for 16 h
– centrifuge at 5 000 g for 10 min
– filter on hardened filter and store a suitable aliquot in a plastic bottle for P titration. Organic P is calculated by difference: P of burnt soil minus P of the unheated sample (these results are compared to total P to estimate inorganic P).

Remarks. Soil should be calcinated in a well-oxygenated furnace to avoid losses by reduction which can occur above 400°C (H3P).

The final temperature and calcination time must be respected to avoid modifying the relative solubility of the products obtained at this temperature as this would cause random estimates of organic P.

Extraction of Organic P in Acid and Basic Reagents

Principle

These methods (Mehta et al. 1954) extract the organic and inorganic P forms chemically (sequential treatments with strong acid and strong base).

Pretreatment with strong acids enables the polyvalent bonds to be broken and the bound cations to be extracted (mostly Fe, Al and Ca) which makes inorganic P insoluble, with the hydrolysis of organic compounds as a side effect. The alkaline treatment that makes it possible to solubilize the organic matter also causes hydrolysis of organic P.

Mineralization is performed on one aliquot of the extract; organic phosphorus is transformed into *ortho*-phosphates and estimated by difference:

organic P = inorganic P after mineralization – inorganic P in the initial extract.

Equipment

– Aluminium mineralization block or rack for the attack
– 100 mL polyethylene centrifugation tube with a screw cap
– Water bath heated to 70–90°C
– vortex stirrer
– ventilated drying oven heated to 100°C.

Reagents

– Concentrated hydrochloric acid
– 0.5 mol (NaOH) L^{-1} aqueous solution
– deionized water.

Procedure

Extraction:

– Weigh 1 g of air-dried soil (0.1 mm particle size) in a 100 mL centrifugation tube
– add 10 mL of concentrated hydrochloric acid; homogenize and heat in a water bath for 10 min at 70°C
– add another 10 mL of concentrated hydrochloric acid and leave in contact for 1h at ambient temperature; add 50 mL of water; homogenize and centrifuge at 5,000 g for 5 min
– decant the supernatant in a 250 mL volumetric flask; wash the centrifugation pellet with a little water and centrifuge for 5 min; decant in the same 250 mL volumetric flask
– treat the soil residue with 30 mL of 0.5 mol (NaOH) L^{-1}; suspend by shaking energetically with the vortex stirrer and leave in contact for 1 h at ambient temperature
– centrifuge and decant the supernatant in the volumetric flask containing the hydrochloric extract (decant very gradually while homogenizing)
– add another 60 mL of the 0.5 mol (NaOH) L^{-1} solution to the residue, suspend by shaking energetically with the vortex stirrer and maintain at 90°C for 8 h in the water bath or in a ventilated drying oven
– centrifuge; after complete cooling transfer the supernatant in the 250 mL volumetric flask containing the other extracts; complete the volume with deionized water and homogenize; this is solution (A).

Mineralization of total extracted P:

– Shake solution A to put the precipitated materials in suspension and quickly remove a 5 mL aliquot in a Pyrex tube that fits in the mineralization block (or use a tall form beaker)
– add 2 drops of concentrated sulphuric acid and 1 mL of 72% perchloric acid
– homogenize, cover with a watch glass and mineralize until white smoke appears; leave to digest for 30 min at 200°C
– cool and transfer in a 50 mL volumetric flask while rinsing with deionized water, complete to 50 mL.

If the soil has a high P content, take a suitable aliquot for titration; for low P content use a volumetric flask for P analysis.

Inorganic and organic P analysis:

– Let solution A decant; take an aliquot of supernatant, filtrate and titrate inorganic P as above
– organic P is calculated by the difference between total P titrated in the mineralized extract and inorganic P titrated in extract A (spectrocolorimetry, cf. Sect. 29.5.2).

Remarks:

– The extracts of soils with high humus content may be coloured. They should then be treated with activated carbon (Darco 60 free from P)
– hydrochloric acid treatment can cause hydrolysis of phosphorous esters, e.g. glycerophosphates
– about 80% of P is extracted by this method (to be compared to total P extracted by perchloric acid attack)
– the 16 h extraction can be replaced by a shorter treatment using ultrasound
– organic P is underestimated as a consequence of hydrolysis, and the results obtained by difference are not very precise
– the percentage of total organic P can be linked to soil microbial biomass and to the activity of micro-organisms, and can reveal transport of P by plants with a vertical distribution of P that is modified by the deposit of organic residues at the surface of the soil.

29.4 Retention of Phosphorus

29.4.1 Introduction

Soil cultivation results in exports of phosphorous from the soil to harvested crops and in the relatively long term, a deficiency in fertilizing elements. This decrease in available elements is partly due to acceleration of carbon mineralization which accompanies farming practices, and the organic matter content is significantly reduced.

Fertilization enables a satisfactory level of available P to be maintained for plant growth and the flows of phosphorus to be regulated. To maintain the equilibrium of inputs in phosphate-enriched fertilizers, it is necessary to estimate exports, and also to determine the capacity of a soil to retain and restore P.

Anions can be bound on exchange sites and play a role in the anion exchange capacity (AEC, cf. Chap. 27). Generally the AEC is much lower than the CEC (cf. Chap. 26), and depends on the soil pH, electrolyte level and type of clay. The lyotropic series: $SiO_4^{4-} > PO_4^{3-} >> SO_4^{2-} > NO_3^- \cong Cl^-$ shows that SiO_4^{4-} and PO_4^{3-} are strongly adsorbed in acid soils as a consequence of the PO_4^{3-} bonds with octahedral aluminium. Phosphates remain insoluble and not easily usable for plants. This is the phenomena of (i) "P retention" which can be measured by extraction in a highly diluted acid or (ii) "fixing of P" which represents forms of P that cannot be extracted using diluted acids.

The lower the pH, the higher the concentration of polyvalent cations (Al, Fe, Mn) and the greater the rate of P retention. The acidification process can lead to formation of insoluble P forms: variscite ($AlPO_4,2H_2O$) and strengite ($FePO_4,2H_2O$) in the soil. Silicates, arsenites, selenites, and fluorides can replace phosphate forms. In alkaline conditions, phosphates can react with different forms of calcium (especially carbonates) giving insoluble calcium phosphates which pose serious problems for the cultivation of arid carbonated soils.

Certain soils like andosols can adsorb large quantities of P. Failure to respond to fertilization and changes in the CEC (CEC can be multiplied by two or three) will be observed in these soils when they are cultivated. It is thus necessary to measure the level of P retention of the soil, to determine adsorption indices, and to establish isotherms of adsorption according to Lang-Muir or Freundlich's equation. The soils can then be classified according to their adsorption characteristics and links established between the quantities of adsorbed P in g per m^2 and the concentration of the soil solution at equilibrium.

29.4.2 Determination of P Retention

Principle

The method proposed by Blakemore et al. (1981) uses equilibration of a soil sample with a solution containing soluble P, and measurement of phosphate remaining in solution. At pH 4.6, retention of P is close to maximum.

Equipment

– Centrifuge
– shaker.

Reagents

– Deionized water
– solution for P retention (1,000 ppm P): dissolve 8.79 g of potassium dihydrogen phosphate and 32.8 g of anhydrous sodium acetate in about 1 L of water; add 23 mL of glacial acetic acid; complete to 2 L in a volumetric flask with deionized water.

Procedure

– Weigh 5 g of air-dried soil (particle size 2 mm) and put in a 50 mL centrifugation tube with a screw cap; add 25 mL of P retention solution
– shake for 24 h at 20°C
– centrifuge at 5,000g for 15 min
– filter, homogenize and remove one aliquot for titration of P remaining in the solution, and an identical aliquot of the reagent (blank) to calculate P retention by difference. Titrate the two solutions by spectrocolorimetry.

Calculation. –Calculate P retention by difference: P in the blank minus P in the equilibration solution, and express the result as a percentage.

Remarks. In oxisols and lateritic soils, P is very strongly fixed at pH < 4.0 (P–Fe and P–Al bonds) and results in severe deficiencies. Iron and aluminium oxides are positively charged below the zero point charge. In allophanic soils P fixes on the surface of oxides to form P-organic matter complexes and inorganic aluminium bridges.

29.5. Titration of P in the Extracts

29.5.1 Introduction

Methods

Many methods have been developed for the titration of P. Their sensitivity is not the same and some are suitable for extracts with high P contents and other for extracts containing only traces of P.

Gravimetric methods, which are rarely used today, are based on precipitation of ammoniaco-magnesian phosphate or ammonium phosphomolybdate. Titrimetric methods may use this precipitate for dissolution in soda and back titration by acidimetry, or the precipitate can be titrated by techniques like complexometry or manganimetry. The most common spectrocolorimetric absorption methods use a molybdo-vanadophosphoric complex which absorbs at 430 nm, or molybdenum blue which absorbs between 650 and 890 nm, depending on its composition. Sometimes these measurements are automated or even robotized.

Other physicochemical methods such as atomic absorption, amperometry, potentiometry, conductimetry, coulometry, and polarography, use indirect determination, for example via molybdenum after formation of phos-phomolybdate complex. Flame or inductively coupled plasma emission can titrate the organic and inorganic forms simultaneously, but cannot titrate them separately. These measurements are not very sensitive to P (cf. Chap. 31).

Clarification of the Extracts

Whatever the method of titration, the extracts must contain only soluble forms and no mineral or organic particles in suspension.

Filtration on a very fine blue cellulose filter (or hardened filters for very acid extracts) is often insufficient, but can be improved by recycling the first filtered fractions to partly clog the filter. Membranes with pores of about 0.45–0.20 μm mounted on syringe filters of the Luer type are suitable. These membranes have a very low flow and quickly become clogged, but when they are equipped with a pre-filter, the membranes rapidly provide 1–2 mL of extract, which is sufficient for routine analyses and ensures satisfactory precision. For difficult cases, for example in the case of proteins, simultaneous ultracentrifugation at about 50,000–100,000g may be necessary.

Electrodialysis (or electro-ultrafiltration) is sometimes used, the breaking threshold being at about 0.02 μm. But there is a risk of a change in pH near the electrodes inducing a risk of precipitation and excessive dilution of the sample. For very detailed research, certain authors count the residual contents of suspended particles with Laser radiation counters (Nanosizer) and check the nature of the particles with an electron microscope.

Types of Titration

After the extract has been purified, the optimal zones of titration, the range of concentration, maximum sensitivity and possible interferences should be taken into account when choosing the appropriate measurement method.

Generally direct titration on the extraction solution is chosen. But it is sometimes necessary to choose the minimal volume of extract that can be measured with precision in order to limit interactions between very fine elements in suspension or in solution.

Narrow measurement cells are preferable for spectrocolorimetric methods if they are sufficiently sensitive. The use of 50 or 100 mm cells amplifies the effects of micro-particles in suspension making careful preliminary ultrafiltration necessary. The reactions can take place cold or hot in mediums of varying degrees of acidity or alkalinity. To limit hydrolysis of organic P, cold titration in mediums with a weak concentration at controlled pH should be used. But phytins cannot be titrated cold and some phytins are titrated at 60°C by spectrocolorimetry. The same goes for inorganic P in the pyrophosphate state or in other forms.

If possible, intermediate stages should be avoided as some separation treatments have random effects on results (e.g. changes in pH, contamination, resin purification of extracts, extraction of coloured compounds, additives for filtration, activated carbon which is seldom P-free).

The selectivity of the titration is important:
- spectrocolorimetric titrations (manual, flow injection analysis, segmented flow) are only selective for *ortho*-phosphate forms and organic forms are not titrated in the extracts
- atomic spectrometry (inductively coupled plasma or flame spectrometry) measures all forms of P; the results can be two to three times higher than with colorimetry
- [31]P nuclear magnetic resonance (^{31}P-NMR) differentiates the different P forms; *ortho- pyro-* and organic-P can be estimated simultaneously without destroying the sample.

29.5.2 Titration of *Ortho*-phosphoric P by Spectrocolorimetry

Spectrocolorimetry Using Molybdenum Blue

Principle

A thorough knowledge of the chemical reactions and of possible interferences is very important for quality control. Controlled experimental conditions enable measurement of the intensity of the spectra at the optimal wavelength on a compound with a perfectly defined chemical composition (Gautheyrou and Gautheyrou 1989).

The molybdenum blue reaction must be carried out under well-defined conditions of pH, acid concentration, redox potential, temperature and reaction time to move equilibrium towards the most condensed forms, as a maximum of 12 atoms of molybdenum can surround the P atom. With this composition optical density remains constant. Only high rates of silica, arsenic and germanium interfere.

The reaction consists in combining molybdic acid with *ortho* forms of phosphorus. This condensation can only be carried out in acid medium with a high ionic force. A reducing compound catalysed by the antimonyl tartrate leads to the formation of the highly coloured blue complex of the phosphomolybdic anion.

$$HPO_4^{2-} + 12\ MoO_4^{2-} + 23\ H^{+-} \rightarrow [PO_4(MoO_3)_{12}]^{3-} + 12\ H_2O$$
$$\text{Blue reduced form}$$

Remarks. The redox potential depends on the pH. It is thus necessary to standardize the procedures to ensure that the quantity of acid and reducer is as constant as possible and that the temperature remains the same. The kinetics of formation of phosphomolybdate is proportional to the concentration of P.

Many mineral and organic reducing compounds have been used.[2] Ascorbic acid combined with potassium antimonyl tartrate (Murphy and Riley 1962) has a strong catalytic power in cold acid medium. It enables an intense blue complex to be obtained that is stable for 24 h. A 1:1 Sb-to-P ratio is required to obtain maximal intensity, and this ratio should not be exceeded to avoid precipitation.[3] Absorbance is maximal at the limit of the visible and near infrared spectra: 880–890 nm.

Sensitivity is lower in hydrochloric acid than in sulphuric acid medium. The stability of the compounds is excellent in a perchloric acid medium. A sulphuric acid concentration of from 0.15 to 0.25 mol L^{-1} makes it possible to work at a pH below one.

Interferences. In the structure of a P polyanion, either oxygen atoms or the central atom can replace an element with a similar ionic radius and structural properties like Si, Ge, As, Ti. Compounds like $(SiMo_{12}O_{40})^{4-}$ or $(AsMo_{12}O_{40})^{3-}$ can be formed. The optimal conditions for formation of P, As or Si compounds are not identical: for P and As, the stable molybdic compound is formed specifically between pH 0.8 and 1.4. Si and Ge complexes are formed only between pH 1.8 and 2.5. It is thus necessary to carry out the reaction in sufficiently acid medium to limit interference by silicium. Arsenic is generally relatively problem free. Interferences can also be caused by:

– elements that can replace molybdenum, for example tungsten which has an ionic radius of 0.60 Å close to that of molybdenum (0.59 Å), or vanadium (0.58 Å)
– elements that catalyze the reaction (Sn, Sb, Bi) whose action is synergistic during reduction (as the contents of these elements in the soil are low, this type of interference is not very significant)
– elements with coloured salts: the presence of Cr^{3+}, Ni^{2+}, Ni^{4+}, Cu^{2+}, Mn^{2+}, Mn^{4+}, Fe^{3+} is tolerable up to approximately 1,000 mg L^{-1} (although organic matter absorbs at another wavelength, it can cause interference by reducing radiation transmission and should consequently be destroyed)
– elements that are likely to precipitate in the medium resulting in insoluble compounds
– oxidizing elements that interfere with the reduction reaction

---

[2] For example 1 amino 2 naphthol 4 sulphonic acid, ascorbic acid, $SnCl_2$, diaminophenol, hydrazine, hydroquinone, thiourea

[3] Solubility is improved by heating, but there is a risk of hydrolysis of organic P compounds.

– organic acids are able to complex molybdenum (e.g. oxalic acid and oxalates, tartaric acid and tartrates, citric acid and citrates); if the pool extracted by these reagents has to be analyzed, the matrix should be destroyed to avoid obstruct the phosphomolybdic reaction
– alcohols in which potassium antimonyl tartrate is not very soluble
– proteins which can precipitate slightly.

Equipment

– Spectrocolorimeter usable in the 800–900 nm zone
– 10–100 mm measuring cells.

Reagents

– 2.5 mol (H_2SO_4) L^{-1} sulphuric acid: carefully add 140 mL of concentrated sulphuric acid in 900 mL of deionized water; let cool and complete to 1,000 mL
– ammonium molybdate solution: weigh 20 g of $(NH_4)_6Mo_7O_{24}$ and dissolve in 500 mL of deionized water (prepare fresh each week)
– hemihydrate potassium antimonyl tartrate solution $KSbOC_4H_4O_6,0.5H_2O$

(mw 333.93): weigh 1.375 g and dissolve in 500 mL of water (prepare fresh each week)
– ascorbic acid solution

: dissolve 8.75 g of ascorbic acid in 500 mL of deionized water (prepare fresh each day)
– mixed reagent: mix in the order below, agitating and homogenizing between each addition: 165 mL of 2.5 mol (H_2SO_4) L^{-1} solution, 50 mL of ammonium molybdate solution, 100 mL of ascorbic acid solution, 16 mL of potassium antimonyl tartrate solution, complete to 100 mL with deionized water (prepare fresh each day).

Phosphate Standards. For each type of extract, it is better to prepare the calibration range in the same medium as the samples to be analyzed and to systematically (i) make a blank just with reagents subjected to the same treatments as the samples, (ii) regularly reconstruct the calibration range and compare it with the previous range to detect any temporal drift, or possibly modifications which could reduce precision.

– 100 µg (P) mL^{-1} stock solution: dissolve 0.4393 g of dihydrogen potassium phosphate (KH$_2$PO$_4$) in deionized water and complete to 1,000 mL; 1 mL contains 100 µg of P; store in the refrigerator protected from the light
– intermediate solution (A) 10 µg (P) mL^{-1} (can be stored in the refrigerator for one week): dilute 100 mL of stock solution in 1,000 mL of deionized water.
– intermediate solution (B) 1 µg (P) mL^{-1}: dilute 100 mL of intermediate solution (A) and complete to 1,000 mL (prepare before each series) with deionized water.
– calibration ranges suitable for each method: each day prepare the volume required for the analytical apparatus to be used, 50 or 100 mL. 0.0 (blank), 0.1, 0.2, 0.4, 0.6, 0.8, 1.0, 2.0 µg (P) mL^{-1}

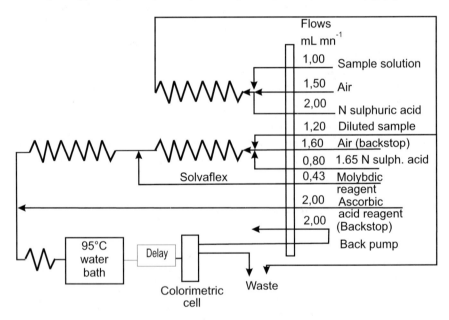

Fig. 29.2. Titration of total *ortho*-phosphorus by automatic colorimetry at 625 nm (Gautheyrou and Gautheyrou 1978)

Procedure

- Take exactly V0 mL of the extraction solution containing between 10 and 20 μg of P, i.e. an aliquot of from 1 to 15 mL maximum (for water, resin or isotopic extraction of ^{32}P, the volume of the aliquot is the biggest; for extraction methods of mobile forms in acid or basic medium, the volume of the aliquot is smaller; for total P, intermediate dilution rates are used)
- put the aliquot in a 25 mL volumetric flask; add 5 mL of mixed reagent and complete to 25 mL with deionized water; homogenize; wait 30 min for titration (colour will remain stable for around 24 h).
- read absorbance at 890 nm on the spectrocolorimeter using a 10 mm colorimetric cell (or a larger cell depending on the intensity of the colour, possibly a 100 mm cell for water extracts). Continue in the same way for each point of the calibration range
- plot a graph with P concentration on the X-coordinate and absorbance on the Y-coordinate. Read the P concentration of the sample solution: x μg mL^{-1}. If V is the volume (mL) of the extraction solution, P the weight of soil sample (g) and f the possible moisture correction factor, the results are expressed on the basis of soil dried at 105°C, and the soil content is expressed by:

$$C = f x\ V/P$$
in mg (P) kg^{-1} (soil)
or $C = 2.29\ f x\ V/P$
in mg (P$_2$O$_5$) kg^{-1} (soil)

Alternatively, the process can be automated, for example in a system with segmented continuous flow analysis (see manifold for total phosphorus in Fig. 29.2).

P Titration by Spectrocolorimetry of the Phosphomolybdic Yellow Complex

This method is less sensitive than the method described in "Spectrocolorimetry Using Molybdenum Blue" and is often used for P titration in extracts of total-, total organic- or retention-P with high P contents. *Ortho*-phosphate forms are titrated spectrometrically according to the reaction of the formation of a yellow complex absorbing at 420–466 nm:

$$H_3PO_4 + 12\ (NH_4)_2MoO_4 + 21\ HNO_3 \xrightarrow{80°C} (NH_4)_3PMo_{12}O_{40}$$
$$+21\ NH_4NO_3 + 12\ H_2O$$

Arsenates can produce $(NH_4)_3AsMo_{12}O_{40}$ which interferes with the measurement of colour. Iron can obstruct and must be eliminated if it colours the extracts (Salvage and Dixon 1965, Ruf 1966).

29.5.3 P Titration by Atomic Spectrometry

P titration by inductively coupled plasma atomic absorption spectrometry (cf. Sect. 31.2.14 in Chap. 31) accounts for all P forms in an extract but cannot differentiate between them (between organic and inorganic P, for example). The sensitivity of the method is low enough for direct titration of P. Lines 213.62 and 214.91 nm are generally used. Copper, chromium, iron, vanadium, and titanium interfere. Inter-element corrections reduce precision.

The separation of the PMo_{12} complex (cf. Sects. 29.5.1 and 29.5.2) and molybdenum titration is sensitive and precise using the UV lines 177.50, 178.77 nm and especially 178.29 nm. Vanadium, titanium, nickel copper manganese and chromium do not interfere up to 200 mg L^{-1}. Iron, aluminium, calcium, silicium do not interfere up to around 1,000 mg L^{-1}.

In flame emission spectrometry, the initial state of P does not influence the results to any great extent and the intensity of emission reflects the concentration of total P. The emission spectra are complex. Bands 5249, 5597 or 5097 Å (H–PO) and bands 2478, 2464, 2540 Å (PO) can be used. The limit of detection is around 1 mg L^{-1} depending on the source of excitation used.

29.5.4 Titration of Different Forms of P by ^{31}P NMR

The NMR technique (cf. Sect. 12.3.4 of Chap. 12) produces different signals for *ortho-* and pyrophosphate forms and for the more or less complex organic forms of P.

The ^{31}P nucleus presents a spin magnetic moment. When it is placed in a magnetic field and excited by radiometric waves, transition energy is produced. The resulting spectrum provides information on the immediate chemical environment of the P atom without destroying the sample (Fig. 29.3). High resolution NMR applied to the liquid phase is currently the most commonly used for soil P studies; solid phase NMR is used less frequently. Sensitivity is lower than the proton NMR spectrum, i.e. about 10^{-5} g.

Forms of inorganic phosphates produce clearly differentiated peaks for the short linear chains (*ortho*-P, pyro-P, tripolyphosphates). Molar ratios are obtained by measuring the surfaces of the peaks. Mono- and di-esters of P are easy to measure. Inorganic phosphates with long chains and condensed organic phosphates can have complex spectra. Correct interpretation may require the simultaneous use of ^{31}P- and proton-NMR spectra.

This method is very specific and can be used for different P extracts of soil (Gautheyrou et al. 1990).

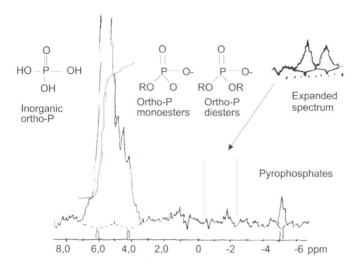

Fig. 29.3. ^{31}P NMR Spectrum of P forms in a 0,5 mol (NaOH) L^{-1} extract of soil (Gautheyrou et al. 1990)

29.5.5 Separation of P Compounds by Liquid Chromatography

The extracts are injected and entrained by a mobile phase (for example phtalic acid 0.5 mmol L^{-1} at pH 2.7) in a column filled with an anion exchange resin (Karlson and Frankenberger 1987). The technique is used particularly for the determination of organo-phosphorous pesticides (cf. Sect. 13.3.4 of Chap. 13), but also to separate anionic forms of P. Phospholipids can be also studied by chromatography (cf. lipid studies in Sects. 13.2.5 and 13.3.3 of Chap. 13) after extraction with solvents.

29.6. Direct Speciation of P in situ, or on Extracted Particles

Determining P on thin sections (cf. Sect. 2.2 of Chap. 8) or on minerals separated by particle size fractionation (cf. Chap. 3) is extremely complex. Indeed, more than 220 natural minerals containing P are known to exist with numerous atom substitutions. Although forms bound to calcium, aluminium and iron predominate, the soil particles are difficult to identify.

The P minerals are generally concentrated in the clay and oxide fractions (e.g. apatites, alumino-phosphates, variscite, vivianite). The magnetic fraction extracted from certain tropical soils contains more iron oxide forms with short range organization than crystalline. This explains the mechanisms of P sorption on iron oxide and hydroxides surfaces e.g. on goethite, hematite, lepidocracite or amorphous gels (Schwertmann, 1964).

The addition of phosphate-enriched fertilizers can result in very high local concentrations of P and redistribution in the soil based on displacement of organic P. The product of this reaction can be estimated chemically using physicochemical techniques like micro-diffraction (Belle and Black 1970). Needles of calcium sulphate formed on apatite micro-crystals can be observed under an optical microscope or a scanning electron microscope with an EDX microprobe on uncovered thin blades treated with diluted sulphuric acid. Distribution charts of calcium and phosphorus can be drawn up if local concentrations are sufficient (Subrarao and Ellis 1975). In scanning transmission electron microscopy and scanning electron microscopy with energy dispersive X-ray microprobes, the bombardment of electrons generates X-rays which enable observation of P concentrations around particles and identification of the chemical composition of a zone of about 1 μm^2. By micro-diffraction, the structure of mineralogical associations allows forms of P minerals to be identified. The thermodynamic properties of these compounds can be transformed into solubility values enabling relations with P of the soil solution to be established. The P/Al, P/Fe, P/Ca ratios can be calculated, but the organic forms require a more complex approach. Such methods are required for a detailed study of mineralogical and petrographic mechanisms, in particular during the fixing of fertilizers by the soil (El Zahaby and Chien 1982, Freeman and Rowell 1981, Henstra et al. 1981).

References

Bell BC and Black CA (1970) Comparison of methods for identifying crystalline phosphate produced by interaction of orthophosphate fertilizers with soils. *Soil Sci. Soc. Am. Proc.*, 34, 579–582

Blackemore LC, Searle PL and Daly BK (1981) *Methods for chemical analysis of soils.*, N.Z. Soil Bur. Sci., Rep. 10A

Bray RH and Kurtz LT (1945) Determination of total, organic and available forms of phosphorus in soils. *Soil Sci.*, 59, 39–45

Chang SC and Jackson ML (1957) Fractionation of soil phosphorus. *Soil Sci.*, 84, 133–144

Dabin B (1967) Application des dosages automatiques à l'analyse des sols (3° partie) – 3. Analyse du phosphore assimilable dans les sols tropicaux. *Cah. Orstom Ser. Pédol.*, V, 278–286

Dalal RC and Hallsworth EG (1976) Evaluation of the parameters of soil phosphorus availability factors in predicting yield response and phosphorus uptake. *Soil Sci. Soc. Amer. J.*, 40, 541–546

Dean L.A (1947) Application of radioactive tracer technique to studies of phosphatic fertilizer utilization by crops. I – Greenhouse experiments. *Soil Sci. Soc. Am. Proc.*, 12, 107–112

Demolon A (1932) *La dynamique du sol.* Dunod, 262

Dyer B (1894) On the analytical determination of probably available " mineral " plant food in soils. *J. Chem. Soc.*, 65, 115–167

El Zahaby EM and Chien SH (1982) Effect of small amounts of pyrophosphate sorption by calcium carbonate and calcareous soil. *Soil Sci. Soc. Am. P*, 46, 38–46

Fardeau JC and Jappe J (1988) Valeurs caractéristiques des cinétiques de dilution isotopique des ions phosphate dans les systèmes sols-solution. In *Phosphore et Potassium dans les relations sol-plante, conséquence sur la fertilisation*, Gachon L. ed. Lavoisier-INRA, 79–99

Fardeau JC (1993) Le phosphore assimilable des sols : sa représentation par un modèle fonctionnel à plusieurs compartiments. *Agronomie*, 13, 317–331

Fardeau JC (1997) Biodisponibilité du phosphore dans les sols, les déchets et les sédiments : des approches isotopiques. In *Le phosphore dans les sols, les déchets et les eaux, AFES, Journées thématiques* de Mars

Freeman JS and Rowell DL (1981) The adsorption and precipitation of phosphate on calcite. *J. Soil Sci.*, 32, 75–84

Gachon L (1988) *Phosphore et Potassium dans les relations sol-plante, conséquence sur la fertilisation.*, Lavoisier-INRA, 79–99

Gautheyrou J and Gautheyrou M (1978) *Méthodologies mécanisées – Introduction à l'automatisation des opérations analytiques dans les sols, les végétaux et les eaux d'irrigation.*, IRD (ex-Orstom), Guadeloupe, Paris, Notes laboratoire, 113 p

Gautheyrou J and Gautheyrou M (1989) Dosage du phosphore ortho. la réaction céruléo molybdique. In Compte-rendu *Journées laboratoires IRD*, Bondy, France, 134–154

Gautheyrou M, Gautheyrou J and Quantin P (1990) La spectroscopie RMN haute résolution de 31P – Etude des formes de phosphore d'un Andosol soumis à l'écobuage. Actes *Congrès Int. Sci. du Sol*, Kyoto, Japan

Gunnarson O and Frederickson L (1951) A Method for determining plant available phosphorous in soil by means of ^{32}P. *Proc. isotope technical conf.*, Oxford, 1, 427–431

Hedley MJ, Stewart WB and Chauhan BS (1982) changes in inorganic and organic soil phosphorous fractions induced by cultivation practices and by laboratory incubations. *Soil Sci. Soc. Am. J.*, 46, 970–976

Henstra SD, Eijk van der, Boekestein A, Thiel F and Plas van L (1981) Compositional change in triple superphosphate fertilizer granule. *Scanning Electron Microscopy*, 1, 439–446

Joret G and Hebert J (1955) Contribution à la détermination du besoin des sols en acide phosphorique. *Ann. Agron.*, 2, 233–299

Karlson U and Frankenberger Jr.WT (1987) Single column ion chromatography. III – Determination of orthophosphate in soils. *Soil Sci. Soc. Am. J.*, 51, 72–74

Larsen S (1952) The use of ^{32}P in studies on the uptake of phosphorous by plants. *Plant and Soil*, 4, 1–10

Mehlich A (1953) *Determination of P, Ca, Mg, K, Na, NH$_4$*. North Carolina Soil Test Division, Rapport multigraphié

Mehta NC, Legg JD, Goring CAI and Black CA (1954) Determination of organic phosphorous in soil. 1. Extraction method. *Soil Sci. Soc. Am. Proc.*, 18, 443–449

Murphy J and Riley JP (1962) A modified simple solution method for the determination of phosphates in natural waters. *Anal. Chim. Acta.*, 27, 31–36

NF X31-160 (1993) Détermination du phosphore soluble dans une solution à 20 g L^{-1} d'acide citrique monohydraté. In *Qualité des sols*, 3rd ed. 1996, AFNOR, 147–154

NF X31–161 (1993) Détermination du phosphore soluble dans une solution d'oxalate d'ammonium à 0.1 mol L^{-1}. In *Qualité des sols*, 3rd ed. 1996, AFNOR, 157–165

Pansu M, Gautheyrou J and Loyer JY (2001) *Soil Analysis – Sampling, Instrumentation and Quality control*, Balkema, Lisse, Abington, Exton, Tokyo, 489 p

Pierzynski GM ed. (2000) *Methods of Phosphorus Analysis for Soils, Sediments, Residuals, and Waters*, South. Coop. Ser. Bull. 396, Dep. of Agronomy, 2004 Throckmorton Plant Sciences Ctr., Kansas USA, http://www.soil.ncsu.edu/sera17/publications/sera17-2/pm_cover.htm

Roche P, Grière L, Babre D, Calba H and Fallavier P (1978) La carence en phosphore des sols intertropicaux et ses méthodes d'appréciation. *Science du sol.*, 4, 251–268

Ruf F (1966) The conditions for spectrophotometric determination of orthophosphate with molybdovanado phosphate. *C.R. Geol. Com. Nat. Malgache Geol.*, 70, 4

Salvage T and Dixon JP (1965) The colorimetric determination of phosphorus in organic compounds on the microgram scale. *Analyst.*, 90, 24–28

Schwertmann U (1964) The differentiation of iron oxide in soils by a photochemical extraction with acid ammonium oxalate. *Z. Planzenenahr. Dueng Bodenkd*, 105, 194–292

Subbarao YV and Ellis R (1975) Reaction products of polyphosphates and orthophosphates with soils and influence of uptake of phosphates by plants. *Soil Sci. Soc. Am. Proc.*, 39, 1085–1088

Syers JK, Smillie GW and Williams JDH (1972) Calcium fluoride formation during extraction of calcareous soils with fluoride. I – Implications to inorganic P fractionation schemes. *Soil Sci. Soc. Am. Proc.*, 36, 20–25

White RE and Beckett PT (1964) Studies on phosphate potentials of soils. 1 – The measurement of phosphate potential. *Plant and Soil*, 20, 1–16

Williams JDH, Syers JK and Walker TN (1967) Fractionation of soil inorganic phosphate by a modification of Chang and Jackson's procedure. *Soil Sci. Soc. Amer. Proc.*, 31, 736

Chronobibliography

Kurtz LT (1942) Elimination of fluoride interference in molybdenum blue reaction. *Ind. Eng. Chem. Anal.*, 14, 855

Palache C, Berman M and Frondel C (1951) *The systems of mineralogy.*, Wiley Chapman, New York/London

Olsen SR (1952) Measurement of surface phosphate on hydroxylapatite and phosphate rock with radiophosphorus. *J. Phys. Chem.*, 56, 630–632

Nelson WL, Mehlich A and Winters E (1953) The development, evaluation and use of soil tests for phosphorus availability. In *Soil and fertilizer phosphorus*, Pierre W.H. and Norman A.G. ed., A.S.A. No. 4

Watanabe FJ and Olsen SR (1965) Test of an ascorbic acid method for determining phosphorus in water and $NaHCO_3$ extracts from soils. *Soil Sci. Soc. Am. Proc.*, 29, 677

Lehr JR, Brown EH, Frazier AW, Smith JP and Thrasher RD (1967) Crystallographic properties of fertilizer compounds. *Chem. Eng. Bull.*, (Alabama, Etats-Unis) No. 6

Fox RL and Kamprath EJ (1970) Phosphate sorption isotherms for evaluating the phosphate requirements of soils. *Soil Sci. Soc. Am. Proc.*, 34, 902–907

Povarennykh AS (1972) *Crystal chemical classification of minerals.*, Plennum New York, Vols. I and II

Franzen DW and Peck TR (1995) Spatial variability of plant analysis phosphorus levels. *Commun. in Soil Sci. Plant Anal.*, 26, 2929–2940

Frossard E, Brossard M, Hedley MJ and Metherel A (1995) Reactions controling the cycling of P in soils. In *Phosphorus in the global environment.*, Wiley New York 107–137

Fardeau JC, Guiraud DG and Morel C (1996) The role of isotopic techniques on the evaluation of effectiveness of P fertilizers. *Fert. Res.*, 45, 101–109

Kuo S (1996) Phosphorus. In *Methods of soil analysis, part 3, chemical methods*, Bigham J.M. and Bartels J.M. ed., SSSA-ASA, Madison, WI Etats-Unis, 869–919

Cade-Menun BJ and Preston CM (1996) A comparaison of soil extraction procedures for ^{31}P NMR spectroscopy. *Soil Science*, 161, 770–785

Condron HJ and Frossard LME (1997) Isotopes techniques to study phosphorus cycling in agricultural and forest soils : a review. *Fert. Res.*, 24, 1–12

Robinson JS and Johnston CT (1998) Combined chemical and 31P-NMR spectroscopic analysis of phosphorus in wetland organic soils. *Soil Sci.*, 163, 705–713

Isik Y and Ekiz H (2000) The phosphorus demand of durum wheat grown in Konya and the calibration of Olsen phosphorus analysis. Konya yoresinde yetistirilen makarnalik bugdayin fosforlu gubre istegi ve Olsen fosfor analiz metodunun kalibrasyonu. Ministry of Agriculture and Rural Affairs, Bahri Dagdas International Winter Cereals Research Center; Konya; Turkey 230–239

Steegen A, Govers G, Beuselinck L, Oost K van, Quine TA, Rombaut A, Stone M (2000) The use of phosphorus as a tracer in erosion/sedimentation studies. In *The role of erosion and sediment transport in nutrient and contaminant transfer. Proceedings of a symposium held at Waterloo*, Ontario, Canada in July 2000, IAHS Wallingford, UK

Elrashidi MA (2001) Testing methods for phosporus and organic matter. http://soils.usda.gov/technical/methods

Boruvka L, Rechcigl JE (2003) Phosphorus retention by the AP horiszon of a spodosol as inflenced by calcium amendments. *Soil Sci.*, 168, 699–706

Escudey M, Galindo G and Briceno M (2004) Influence of particle size on ^{31}P NMR analysis of extracts from volcanic ash-derived soils in Chile. *J. Chil. Chem. Soc.*, 49, 5–9

Sulphur

30.1 Introduction

30.1.1 Sulphur Compounds

Sulphur is not a very abundant element in most soils and can come from various origins: volcanic emission of sulphur products, deterioration of eruptive rocks, metamorphic or sedimentary transformations, the action of surface water, ground water, or sea water, the biological contribution of different animals and plants. Agricultural, industrial and domestic activities also contribute to soil enrichment in sulphur compounds, in particular the use of amendments, fertilizer, compost and pesticides. The use of fossil fuels also contaminates the atmosphere and has consequences for soils through rainfall. Except in certain specific soils such as acid sulphated soils, swampy histosols or gypseous soils, the sulphur content of most soils is usually low (a few tens of mg kg^{-1}).

Qualitatively speaking, sulphur exists in both organic and mineral forms. The variety of simple or complex, amorphous or crystalline molecular structures of sulphur compounds in soils is a characteristic of this element. The existence and stability of the different sulphur derivatives depends to a large extent on the physicochemical conditions of the medium (in particular on redox potential and soil pH). The different forms of sulphur can also be determined by analysing the micro-biological reactions generated by sulfato-reducing or sulfo-oxidizing bacteria. Apart from some relatively stable, not very soluble sulphated forms such as gypsum or jarosite, most sulphur compounds are subject to transformations that are part of the sulphur cycle in soils and in living organisms.

Table 30.1. Main sulphur minerals present in sedimentary deposits (evaporites*), efflorescences, crusts and soils

oxidation state	link	mineral	chemical formula	inter-reticular distance (Å)			solubility g L^{-1} water		
							0°C	30°C	100°C
sulphates	Ca^{2+}	gypsum	$CaSO_4,2H_2O$	7.56	3.05	4.27	2.41	2.6	2.22
		hemihydrate	$CaSO_4,0.5H_2O$	3.00	6.01	2.80		3.0	
		bassanite	$CaSO_4,0.5H_2O$	3.00	6.01	2.80			
		*anhydrite	$CaSO_4$	3.49	2.85	2.32		2.09	1.62
	Mg^{2+}	epsomite	$MgCaSO_4,7H_2O$	4.21	5.35	2.68		710.0	910.0 (40°C)
		hexahydrite	$MgCaSO_4,6H_2O$	4.43	4.04	2.94			
		*kieserite	$MgCaSO_4,H_2O$	3.41	4.84	3.33			684.0
	Na^+	thenardite	Na_2SO_4	2.78	4.66	3.18	47.6		427.0
		mirabilite	$Na_2SO_4,10H_2O$	5.48	3.28	3.26	110.0	927.0	
oxidized forms	Mixte	bloedite	$Na_2Mg(SO_4)_2,4H_2O$	3.25	4.56	3.29			
		*loeweite	$Na_2Mg(SO_4)_2,5/2H_2O$	3.17	4.29	4.04			
		*vanthoffite	$Na_2Mg(SO_4)_2,5/2H_2O$	2.91	3.44	3.43			
		natrojarosite	$NaFe_3(OH)_6(SO_4)_2$	5.04	3.05	3.12			
		*langbeinite	$K_2Mg_2(SO_4)_3$	3.14	2.65	4.05			
		*picromerite	$K_2Mg(SO_4)_2,6H_2O$	3.70	3.04	2.38			
		*polykalite	$K_2MgCa_2(SO_4)_4,2H_2O$	2.90	3.18	2.85			

		jarosite	$KFe_3(OH)_6(SO_4)_2$	3.11	3.08	5.09	
		coquimbite	$Fe_2(SO_4)_3,5$ or $9H_2O$	8.26	2.76	5.45	
		alunite	$KAl_3(SO_4)_2(OH)_6$	2.99	2.89	2.29	
		natro alunite	$NaAl_3(SO_4)_2(OH)_6$	2.96	4.90	2.97	
		basaluminite	$Al_4(SO_4)(OH)_{10},5H_2O$	9.40	4.68	3.68	
		jurbanite	$Al(SO_4)(OH),5H_2O$	—	—	—	
S element		sulphur S^0		3.29	6.65	3.74	
	H	hydrogen sulphide	H_2S	—	—	—	
sulphides (reduced forms)	Fe	mackinawite	FeS	5.03	2.97	2.31	0.0062
	Fe	pyrite	FeS_2	1.63	2.70	2.42	0.0049
	Fe	marcassite	FeS_2	2.71	1.76	3.44	0.0049
	Fe	greigite	$Fe_3S_4(Fe^{2+}Fe^{3+}S_4)$	2.98	2.47	1.74	
	Fe, Ca	chalcopyrite	$CaFeS_2$	3.03	1.85	1.59	

From an agricultural point of view, as sulphur is an essential element for plant growth, it can cause a crop to fail. Failures can be due to sulphur either deficiency or toxicity in the soil environment, with thresholds that vary depending on the sensitivity of the species.

Two types of soils that are particularly rich in sulphur require specific analyses (1) acid sulphated fluviomarine soils (e.g. mangroves or polders) and (2) gypseous soils. Some analytical techniques described in this chapter are designed specifically for one or the other of these two soil types. Most of the techniques can be used with other soils that are less rich in sulphur compounds.

30.1.2 Mineralogical Studies

Two hundred mineral sulphates and 228 sulphide species have been indexed in the natural environment. Sulphur exists in countless natural and industrial organic forms. The most common inorganic forms in soils are listed in Table 30.1. In soils under arid or semi-arid climates, surface crystallizations are frequently preserved in their natural state. Oxidized forms are stable and no particular problems are involved in their storage.

On the other hand, samples comprising reduced forms (e.g. iron sulphides) should be stored in closed bottles protected from the light, and crushed immediately before analysis.

Mineralogical observations can be carried out under the optical microscope or the scanning electron microscope coupled to an EDX microprobe (cf. Chap. 8). In the latter case, possible transformations caused by the instrumental technique (e.g. high vacuum or intensity of the electron beam) need to be taken into account.

Widespread Mineral Forms and Soil Classification

Evaporites. Geological deposits – sediments accumulated by drainage and evaporation – hydrothermal action. The most soluble salts accumulate in efflorescence forms due to capillary bottom-up flows and surface evaporation. Very soluble magnesium or sodium sulphates are found on the soil surface only under arid climates.

Thenardite (Na_2SO_4) is more stable than *mirabilite* ($Na_2SO_4,10H_2O$) and other sulphates like *bloedite* ($Na_2Mg(SO_4)_2,4H_2O$), *hexahydrite* ($MgSO_4,6H_2O$), *epsomite* ($MgSO_4,7H_2O$). Temperature should be taken into account since it affects solubility. *Gypsum* ($CaSO_4,2H_2O$) is the least soluble soil sulphate and the most abundant in natural environments. Gypsum deposits often occur simultaneously with calcium carbonate deposits when calcium sulphate solubility is exceeded.

The first field tests made it possible to perform analyses safely. Soils whose main properties depend on the presence of sulphur compounds are indexed in international soil classification systems.

In the French classification system (CPCS 1967), sulphur compounds appear in a subclass (gypseous soils) and group with respect to the individualization of calcium sulphate; in a class (sodic soils) and subclass (saline soils) with respect to soils containing sulfidic materials in a reduced state in hydromorphic–halomorphic environments, or in a oxidized state in aerobic drained environments.

The main FAO units (1968) yermosols and xerosols include gypsic subdivisions, and Gleysols and Fluvisols include thionic subdivisions for mangrove soils.

In the US Soil Taxonomy (USDA 1975), sulphur compounds appear in main groups (*gypsiorthids, natrargids, natriborolls*) and in inorganic and organic reduced soil groups (*sulfaquents, sulfihemists*) or in acid sulphated soil groups (*sulfaguepts, sulfohemists*); and finally, in the group of horizons with predominance of a process involving the passage of time: *gypsic, petrogypsic, sulphuric* soils and even *salic* or *natric* soils in the presence of different soluble salts.

In practice, only a limited number of sufficiently stable minerals can be identified due to the lack of sensitivity of the methods and the difficulty involved in separating the different components without causing structural modifications (particularly in the case of compounds with low sulphur content in saline matrices with very high sulphur contents), but also because of climatic constraints (e.g. the temperature or rainfall regime) or drainage conditions.

30.2 Total Sulphur and Sulphur Compounds

30.2.1 Characteristics of Fluviomarine Soils

This type of soil is particularly rich in sulphur and is found in deltas, estuaries or polders under different climates. Under equatorial or tropical climates in particular, the brackish soils and sediments are colonized by specific mangrove vegetation with a very dense root system that produces abundant organic matter.

In this submerged reducing medium, marine sulphates are reduced by microbial action into sulphides which, by reaction with ferruginous materials, produce pyrites. If the environment remains anaerobic, the accumulation of pyrites in soil materials remains stable. A drop in the level of groundwater due to natural drought or artificial drainage disturbs this equilibrium causing oxidation of pyrite and release of sulphuric acid and iron oxyhydroxides. The soil environment is acidified; under drier tropical conditions, salinization may be also intensified by the concentration of salts. Intense acidification can release aluminium by attacking the crystal lattices of clays (acidolysis). The result of these processes is the formation of a mixture of sulphate of aluminium, iron and magnesium represented by jarosite, natrojarosite and different forms of alums (Vieillefon 1974; Marius 1980; Le Brusq et al. 1987; Montoroi 1994; Génin et al. 2001; Montoroi et al. 2002).

The rapid changes, which affect these soil environments and their components, mean special care has to be taken during sampling and storage, as well as during the extraction and titration of the different forms of sulphur present at a given time in soils (Pansu et al. 2001). The S element is represented by a mixture of different isotopes (^{32}S and ^{34}S). S compounds are found in gaseous forms (e.g. hydrogen sulphide), soluble forms (sulphides, sulphates), not very soluble or insoluble forms (polysulphides, pyrites, elementary sulphur, gypsum, mixed sulphates), and more or less oxidizable organic compounds.

To interpret soil genesis, during analysis a clear distinction must be made between the sulphur forms in a fresh sample which are representative of *in situ* conditions (sulphide forms) from the S forms which can appear after oxidation (sulphate forms) in an air-dried soil (Marius et al. 1976).

30.2.2 Soil Sampling and Sample Preparation

In soils containing oxidized products (e.g. gypsum cf. Sect. 30.3), sampling is standard and the soil samples are prepared in the usual way.

Soils in reducing environments often pose particular sampling problems. Oxidation of sulphur compounds has to be avoided. Hydrogen sulphide is lost very rapidly. The evolution of sulphides (even in their metastable forms) has to be controlled by protecting the samples from contact with the air and by storing them at a low temperature protected from the light.

In mangroves and mud flats, sampling is carried out with a hollow mud scoop (with a diameter of 60–100 mm) that has a sharp edge to cut fibrous materials or roots (Pansu et al. 2001). A succession of extension rods (1 m in length) makes it possible to take progressively deeper samples. Generally 1 m is sufficient for agronomic studies. The mud scoop is inserted vertically in the movable sediments, then rotated slightly to free the base of the soil column and extracted taking care not to disturb the sample. The mud scoop is then laid flat on the ground and the core separated with a blade. Each level of the soil should be noted, the necessary sample specimens removed, and direct measurements made on the soil column (pH and certain field tests).

When deeper samples are required, samplers equipped with a stationary piston in metal or plastic tubes of varying length (1–3 m) enable cores to be removed undisturbed. The ends of the tubes containing the cores should immediately be tightly sealed with plastic. If possible the tubes should be kept in a cold room until they are sawed open lengthwise in the laboratory. The samples taken at different depths are usually separated into four fractions:

– A section of undisturbed sample for examination of soil morphology should be stored in the refrigerator in an airtight box.
– One fraction should be air dried and sieved to 2 mm; part of this fraction should be crushed on an AFNOR NF 21 sieve (100 μm) and used for total analysis, as reduced forms are usually oxidized.
– One fraction should be stored wet for analysis of the reduced forms; after rapid homogenisation on a 4 mm sieve to eliminate roots and stones, the sample specimens can be stored for a short time in airtight lightproof bottles in the refrigerator, or for a long time in the freezer. The water content should be measured.
– One fraction should be freeze-dried to avoid hardening of the sample and reduced metastable forms.

Samples should be stored in lightproof bottles in the refrigerator. The moisture content should be measured at each sampling.

In the field, water should be sampled in the sampling hole for immediate analysis e.g. pH, conductivity, H_2S content; one water sample should put in an airtight bottle to take back to the laboratory. Leaving piezometers in the most representative sampling holes enables subsequent changes in the ground water to be monitored (e.g. level, pH, salt concentration).

30.2.3 Testing for Soluble Sulphur Forms

An in situ search for soluble sulphur forms and particularly sulphides can be made on a sample of water from a waterlogged soil (using a field test e.g. Hach H-5-6 n° 223800, ranges: 0–0.6 or 0–5 mg H_2S).

The presence of hydrogen sulphide is perceptible by its odour even at very low contents (0.025 mg kg^{-1}) and it is water soluble (0.102 mol L^{-1}).

The presence of soluble sulphides is revealed by an acid attack followed by a lead acetate test:
- Attack a few grams of soil with 6 mol (HCl) L^{-1} hydrochloric acid in a test-tube:

$$S^{2-} + 2\ HCl \rightarrow H_2S\uparrow + 2\ Cl^-$$

- Cover the opening with lead acetate paper for 5 s; the appearance of a dark reddish brown colour indicates high levels of hydrogen sulphide according to the reaction:

$$H_2S + PbCl_2 \rightarrow PbS\downarrow + 2\ HCl$$

30.2.4 Titration of Total Sulphur

Many organic- and inorganic-S compounds can result from (1) the many oxidation states of the S element (−2 to +6), (2) possible S bonds (covalence, coordination, ionic) and (3) the different coordination geometries. For total analysis, it is consequently necessary to transform S forms into stable forms:
- By oxidation into the S^{+VI} state (sulphate), which is very stable.
- By reduction into the S^{2-} state (sulphide); because thermodynamically stable sulphides are very easily oxidizable, titration must be performed protected from the air; this technique is used for titration especially after oxidation into sulphate.

Dry or wet oxidation methods can be used. Dry methods include:
- Alkaline fusion in the presence or not of an oxidizing additive: Na_2CO_3, $Na_2CO_3 + NaNO_3$, $Na_2CO_3 + Na_2O_2$;
- Calcination (1) in the presence of $NaHCO_3 + Ag_2O$, (2) in an oxygen flow, (3) in a closed medium in the presence of sodium carbonate and (4) with the Schöniger technique (or similar) in a stream of oxygen in a closed environment.

Wet oxidation can take place in an:
- Acid medium $H_3PO_4 + K_2Cr_2O_7$
                          $HClO_4 + HNO_3$
                          $KMnO_4 + H_3PO_5$ (peroxophosphoric acid)
- Alkaline medium with sodium hypobromite (the risk of loss of H_2S, SO_2, SO_3 is reduced)

Titration of sulphur depends on the quantities present, the forms of S obtained and the composition of the soil matrix. The different methods used include gravimetry, turbidimetry, colorimetry, ionic chromatography(IC), indirect spectrography.

30.2.5 Total S Solubilization by Alkaline Oxidizing Fusion

Principle

The S compounds of soil are transformed into sulphate by fusion at 700°C in the presence of a mixture of sodium carbonate and potassium nitrate (the oxidizing agent potassium nitrate can be replaced by sodium nitrate or by sodium peroxide, Na_2O_2).

Equipment

– Tall form platinum or nickel crucibles with lids (40 mL)
– 1,000°C muffle furnace
– Water bath
– Pyrex lab glassware
– Centrifuge and filtering device
– Laboratory balances (± 1/10 mg)

Reagents

– Sodium carbonate, Na_2CO_3.
– Potassium nitrate, KNO_3.
– *Fusion mixture.* mix 100 g of Na_2CO_3 and 10 g of KNO_3.
– Concentrated hydrochloric acid HCl (37%).
– ≈ *2 mol (HCl) L^{-1} hydrochloric acid solution.* In a Pyrex volumetric test tube, mix 800 mL of deionised water and 160 mL of concentrated hydrochloric acid; cool and complete to 1,000 mL with deionized water while homogenizing.

Procedure

Dry the soil sample in the air or preferably freeze-dry and crush to 0.1 mm.
– Weigh on the precision balance between 200 and 500 mg of soil in a 40 mL tall form platinum crucible.
– Weigh 1 g of the fusion mixture, mix with the sample; add 200 mg of the fusion mixture on the surface.
– Put the closed crucible in the open muffle furnace and gradually heat to 700°C; maintain at 700°C for 40 min.
– Swirl the crucible to distribute the fusion mass on the walls; allow to cool.

– Carefully add 10 mL of 2 mol (HCl) L^{-1} solution; if necessary disaggregate the mass with a Pyrex rod.

After effervescence has ended, place the crucible in a boiling water bath to finish the reaction. Cool and transfer in a centrifugation tube. Centrifuge and filter the supernatant in a 100 mL volumetric flask while rinsing the centrifugation pellet.

Bring to 100 mL with deionized water and homogenize.

This acid solution containing the S compounds in sulphate oxidized form is ready for the analysis of total S.

Remarks

The residue is mainly composed of precipitated white silica.

If the mass is greenish and becomes pink in hydrochloric solution, manganese can be assumed to be present (the platinum crucibles may be slightly attacked by the hydrochloric acid).

If the mass is opaque and strongly coloured, the attack was incomplete.

30.2.6 Total Solubilization by Sodium Hypobromite in Alkaline Medium

Principle

The organic and inorganic forms of sulphur are oxidized in sulphate by sodium hypobromite (Tabatabai and Bremner 1970a).

Equipment

– Lab glassware and special apparatus after Johnson and Nishita (1952)
– Magnetic stirrer with Teflon bar magnets
– 5 mL Teflon micro-pipette
– Sand bath
– Fume hood

Reagents

– Sodium hydroxide, NaOH, in pellet form.
– ≈ *2 mol (NaOH) L^{-1} sodium hydroxide solution.* Dissolve 80 g of sodium hydroxide in 1,000 mL of deionized water and protect from the carbon dioxide of the air during storage.

– Suprapur bromine, Br$_2$.
– *Sodium hypobromite solution, (NaBrO,* prepare just before use under a fume hood) Add 100 mL of the 2 mol L^{-1} soda solution in a 150 mL Erlenmeyer flask. Stir with a magnetic stirrer equipped with a Teflon bar and, using a micropipette, add 3 mL of bromine drop by drop. Cover with a beaker cover and use as soon as possible.
– Formic acid, HCOOH.

Procedure

Use air-dried soil (or preferably freeze-dried soil) crushed to 0.1 mm.
– Weigh 100–200 mg of soil (containing from 20–50 µg of S) and put it into the 50 mL boiling flask (B in Fig. 30.1) of the Johnson and Nishita apparatus; work under a fume hood.
– Add 3 mL of hypobromite solution; swirl the flask for a few seconds and leave in contact for 5 min.
– Swirl again to put the particles into suspension.
– Heat on the sand bath heated to $255 \pm 5°C$ avoiding foam overflow; evaporate to dry; maintain heat for 30 min; cool.
– Add 1 mL of water and heat for a moment to suspend the residue; cool.
    Titrate this solution as soon as possible using the method of Johnson and Nishita (1952) with methylene blue (cf. Sect. 30.2.7).

30.2.7 S Titration with Methylene Blue Colorimetry

Principle

According to the method of Johnson and Nishita (1952), the sulphates obtained by oxidizing mineralization are reduced to hydrogen sulphide with a mixed solution of hydroiodic (HI), phosphinic (hypophosphorous acid, H$_3$PO$_2$[1]) and formic (H-COOH)[2] acid. The hydrogen sulphide released is adsorbed in a zinc acetate and sodium acetate buffer forming sulphides. Treatment with the mixture of *p*-aminodimethylaniline

---

[1] Hypophosphorous acid is a reducing oxoacid whose group is ionizable and a donor of protons.

[2] Formic acid enables acidification of the medium and reduction of the bromine residues according to the reaction: HCOOH + Br$_2 \rightarrow$ CO$_2\uparrow$ + 2HBr. Salts of formic acid play an identical role e.g. HCOONa + Br$_2 \rightarrow$ CO$_2\uparrow$ + HBr + NaBr. In the case of total analysis, where the destroyed organic compounds are not likely to be hydrolyzed, the formic acid prevents interference by nitrates.

sulphate and double ammonium–iron sulphate results in methylene blue (reaction of 2 mol of p-aminodimethylaniline + 1 mol of sulphide).

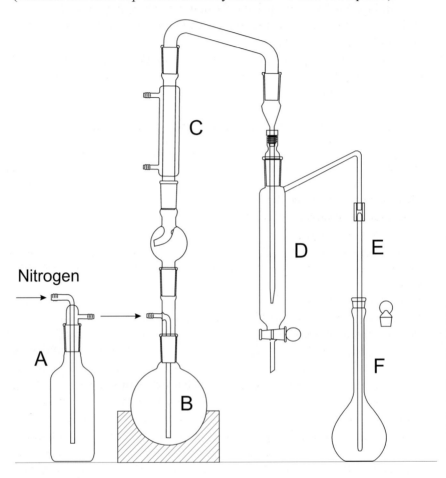

Fig. 30.1. Johnson and Nishita apparatus (1952)

The intensity of the colour is measured at 667–670 nm. The colour remains stable for 24 h if the solutions are stored in the dark protected from the air.

Equipment

Apparatus of Johnson and Nishita (1952) including:
– A nitrogen tank (99.90% N_2) with pressure regulator
– 125 mL washing bottle (A in Fig. 30.1)
– 50 mL Pyrex round bottom boiling flask (for digestion and distillation, B in Fig. 30.1)

– A bubbling device, guard bulb and condenser (C in Fig. 30.1)
– A bubbling device with plug cock (D in Fig. 1) and an outlet tube at the
  top equipped with a removable bubbling tube (E in Fig. 30.1)
– A 100 mL volumetric flask with a ground stopper (F in Fig. 30.1)
– An electric heating flask.

   All ground glass joints should be standardized and used with
Teflon sealing sleeves made to fit by damping with deionized water but
without silicone grease.
– Spectrocolorimeter
– Apparatus for preparation of the reducing reagent (Fig. 30.2)

Reagents

– Deionized water (without S).
– Potassium permanganate, $KMnO_4$.
– Mercuric chloride, $HgCl_2$.
– *Solution for purification of nitrogen.* Mix 100 mL of 2% solution of
  potassium permanganate in deionized water and 10 g of mercuric
  chloride.
– Hydroiodic acid, HI $d = 1.70$.
– Hypophosphorous (or phosphinic) acid, 50% H_3PO_2.
– 90% formic acid, HCOOH.
– *Reducing mixture.* Under a fume hood mix 400 mL of hydroiodic acid,
  100 mL of hypophosphorous acid (phosphinic acid) and 200 mL of
  formic acid in a 1 L three-necked round bottom boiling flask (Fig. 30.2);
  place in a thermostatically controlled heating mantle; connect the
  boiling flask to the nitrogen bubbling tube, the thermometer and a
  splash head; connect the splash head to an Erlenmeyer flask containing
  approximately 150 mL of cold water; open the pressure regulator of the
  nitrogen bottle and regulate the bubbling speed (two bubbles a second)
  in the purifying flask (between the nitrogen bottle and the boiling
  flask); after 2–3 minutes, slowly heat to $116 \pm 1°C$ and maintain for 10
  min at this temperature without exceeding 117°C (release of toxic
  phosphine, H_3P); cool under continuous nitrogen bubbling. Transfer in
  a 1 L bottle and store in the dark.
– 1, 2, 3 benzene triol (pyrogallol).
– Sodium dihydrogen phosphate, NaH_2PO_4, H_2O.
– *Solution for elimination of the oxidizing gas products.* Dissolve 10 g
  of sodium dihydrogen phosphate and 10 g of pyrogallol in 10 mL of
  deionized water; bubble the mixture with nitrogen during dissolution;
  this solution should be freshly made each day.
– Dihydrate zinc acetate, $(CH_3COO)_2Zn, 2H_2O$.
– Sodium acetate trihydrate $CH_3COONa, 3H_2O$.

– *Solution for adsorption of hydrogen sulphide.* Dissolve 50 g of zinc acetate and 12.5 g of sodium acetate in 800 mL of deionized water; complete to 1,000 mL; the mixture should be clear; if not filter on blue analytical filter.

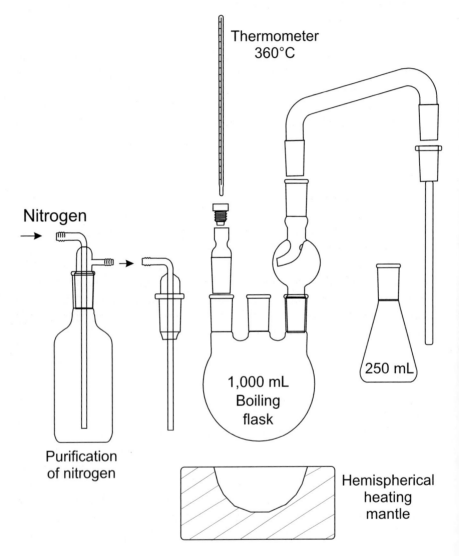

Fig. 30.2. Apparatus for preparation of the reducing reagent

– Sulphuric acid H_2SO_4, $d = 1.80$.
– *p-aminodimethylaniline sulphate solution.* Dissolve 2 g of *p-amino-dimethylaniline sulphate in 1.5 L of deionized water in a 2 L Pyrex boiling flask. Place in cold water with ice and slowly add 400 mL of

concentrated sulphuric acid while agitating with a Pyrex rod. Let cool and bring to 2,000 mL.

– *Double sulphate of ammonium and iron, $Fe_2(SO_4)_3(NH_4)_2SO_4, 24H_2O$*. Dissolve 25 g of double sulphate in a mixture of 195 mL of deionized water and 5 mL of sulphuric acid; let cool; stir on magnetic stirrer until complete dissolution.

– Potassium sulphate, K_2SO_4.

– *Standard stock solution.* Weigh 5.434 g of potassium sulphate and dissolve in 800 mL of S-free deionised water; complete to 1 L. One millilitre contains 1 mg of SO_4^{2-}-S.

– *Calibration range.* Add 1, 2, 3, 4, 5 mL of standard stock solution in 100 mL volumetric flasks and complete to 100 mL with S-free distilled water. One millilitre contains 10, 20, 30, 40, 50 µg of SO_4^{2-}-S.

Procedure

– *Starting the Johnson and Nishita apparatus.* All ground glass joints should be assembled with a Teflon sleeve moistened with deionised water to make it adhere. Pipette 10 mL of pyrogallol–sodium phosphate solution in the bubble trap (D in Fig. 30.1). Add 10 mL of zinc and sodium acetate in the 100 mL volumetric flask (F in Fig. 30.1), add 50 mL of deionised water and homogenize. Submerge the tube (E in Fig. 30.1) until it touches the bottom of the volumetric flask and connect it to the outlet of the bubble trap (D in Fig. 30.1) with a flexible connection made of Tygon. Start the water circulating in the condenser (C in Fig. 30.1).

Analysis

– After preparing the sample using the oxidation method described in Sect. 30.2.6[3] mix the sample with 1 mL of formic acid in the boiling flask B (Fig. 30.1). Homogenize and leave in contact for 30 min agitating by rotation two or three times. Quickly add with a pipette 4 mL of mixed reducing solution (HI + H_3PO_2 + HCOOH) and connect boiling flask B to the apparatus using a Teflon ring that fits the ground glass joint. Regulate the nitrogen flow in the washing bottle A to two bubbles a second, i.e. approximately 200 mL a minute. Nitrogen purges the air and is then used as a neutral vector for hydrogen sulphide. Purge for 5 min.

---

[3] If the fusion-oxidation method (cf. Sect. 30.2.5) is used, take an aliquot of from 1 to 10 mL of the hydrochloric solution containing approximately 50 µg of SO_4^{2-}-S and reduce the volume to approximately 2 mL by boiling gently. In this case formic acid treatment is not necessary.

– Boil gently for 1 h. Disconnect the flexible Tygon connection from the tube (E in Fig. 30.1) and remove the volumetric flask (F). Quickly rinse the tube (E) with a jet from the washing bottle (if the tube contains zinc sulphide deposits, it should be used as an agitator in the following *p*-amino dimethyl aniline treatment and rinsed afterwards).

– With the Teflon precision pipette, add 10 mL of the *p*-amino dimethyl aniline solution in the volumetric flask (F). Close the flask and shake to homogenize. Add 2 mL of the solution of ammonium and iron double sulphate. Close the flask and homogenize. Complete to 100 mL with deionized water and homogenize. Let the reaction develop for 30 min (the colour remains stable for approximately 24 h if the solution is protected from the air and light during storage).

– Treat 1 mL aliquots of solution of from 0 to 50 µg (SO_4^{2-}S) mL^{-1} (calibration range) and the blank with 4 mL of reducing mixture under the same conditions as the samples. Plot the calibration curves for the absorbance/SO_4^{2-}-S concentrations.

Remarks

Maximum absorbance is at 667.8 nm. In the range 1–50 µg mL^{-1}, absorbance follows the Beer-Lambert law and the calibration curve is linear. A higher concentration can be evaluated after dilution in the same medium (*p*-amino dimethyl aniline and double sulphate of iron and ammonium). But if the quantities of *p*-amino dimethyl aniline are insufficient to react with all the sulphides, addition of ferric iron will oxidize the surplus of sulphides making the results more or less erroneous due to dilution. A second analysis using a smaller sample of soil will provide more reliable results.

This method can also be used for the analysis of plants and water.

Some authors prefer to finish titration after hypobromite oxidation by turbidimetry with colloidal bismuth sulphide (Kowalenko and Lowe 1972; Kowalenko 1985; Buurman et al. 1996).

30.2.8 Sulphate Titration by Colorimetry with Methyl Thymol Blue

Principle

These methods quantify the forms of S oxidized in the form of sulphate. Methyl thymol blue (MTB) includes two N.N' groups (dicarboxy methyl) amino methyl bound in positions 3 and 3' (Fig. 30.3), so it can sequester one metal atom on each one of its apical groups.

The reagent is composed of an equimolecular mixture of MTB and barium chloride. In the absence of sulphate, all barium ions are sequestered resulting in a dark blue colour which absorbs at 610 nm in strongly basic medium:

$$Ba^{2+} + MTB^{6-} \xleftarrow{\quad pH\ 12 \quad} ...BaMTB^{4-}$$

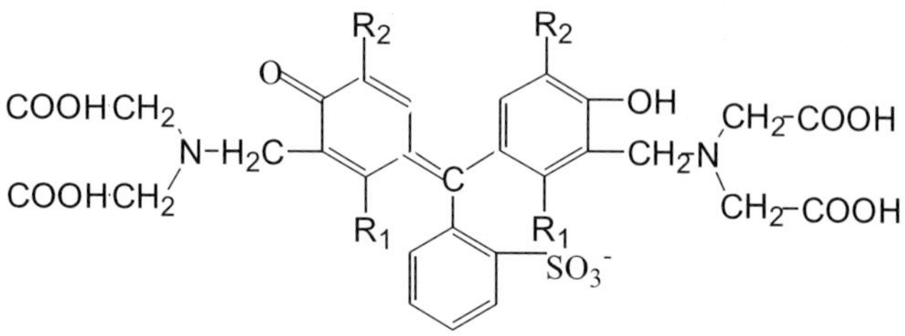

Fig. 30.3. Methyl thymol blue (MTB)

In the presence of SO_4^{2-} ions, the reagent produces barium sulphate with release of MTB^{6-} ions which absorb at 460 nm (grey).

$$BaMTB^{4-}...+ SO_4^{2-} \xleftarrow{\quad pH\ 12 \quad} BaSO_4\downarrow + MTB^{6-}$$

Progressive shades of blue appear whose intensity reveals the presence of unsequestered methyl thymol (grey) linked with the concentration of the sulphate. Measurement of absorbance at 460 nm is not significantly disturbed by the presence of the residual colour as this absorbs at 610 nm.

Calcium ions interfere and should be eliminated on cation resin either directly on the manifold, or beforehand by filtering each sample on a microfilter containing 1.0 g of cation exchange resin (e.g. Dowex 50W-X8).

Equipment

– Segmented continuous-flow analytical chain with manifold and filter for colorimetric measurement at 460 nm (Fig. 30.4).
– Lab glassware.

Reagents

– *Barium chloride solution.* Dissolve 1.526 g of dihydrate barium chloride ($BaCl_2,2H_2O$) in 800 mL of deionized water; homogenize and complete to 1,000 mL; filter on blue analytical filter if necessary.
– Sodium hydroxide in pellet form.

– *0.18 mol (NaOH) L⁻¹ solution.* Dissolve 7.2 g of sodium hydroxide in 1,000 mL of deionized water.
– Methanol, CH_3OH (or ethanol C_2H_5OH).
– Concentrated hydrochloric acid and 1 mol (HCl) L⁻¹ solution.
– *Methyl thymol blue[4] (MTB or 3,3'-Bis[N,N-di(carboxymethyl) amino-methyl] thymolsulfonephthalein, sodium salt).* Dissolve 0.1182 g of MTB in 500 mL of methanol; add 25 mL of barium chloride solution, 4 mL of 1 mol (HCl) L⁻¹ solution, 71 mL of deionized water. Complete to 1,000 mL with methanol. The purity of the MTB should be tested after each new purchase.

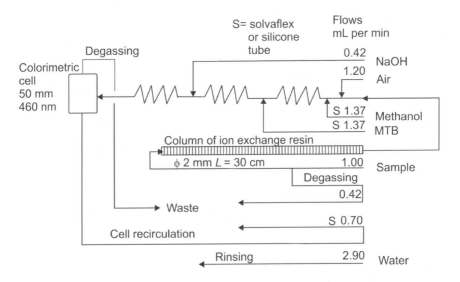

Fig. 30.4. Titration of the sulphate extracts by automatic colorimetry with segmented continuous-flow analysis

– Potassium sulphate, K_2SO_4.
– *Calibration range.* 0–10 µg (SO_4^{2-}) mL⁻¹ depending on the manifold used.

---

[4] Commercial colouring agents like MTB are only 90% or even 80% pure. Their purity should consequently be checked in order to respect the equimolarity of the reagent which determines the linearity of response absorbance vs. sulphate concentration (Colovos et al. 1976). If MTB is not pure, there will be excess Ba^{2+} in the reagent and binuclear complexes will be formed according to the reaction: $Ba_2MTB^{2-} + SO_4^{2-} \Leftrightarrow BaSO_4 + BaMTB^{4-}$.
The absorption of the binuclear complex at 460 nm is lower than that of the expected mononuclear compound and consequently, absorption appears to represent only part of the sulphate ion that reacted.

Procedure

If the organic matrix was destroyed using the Schöniger method, the samples should no longer contain excess perhydrol to avoid decomposition of the organic colouring reagents. The extract containing the sample sulphur in sulphate form is titrated by automated spectrocolorimetry with segmented continuous flow (Fig. 30.4) in comparison with the calibration range of standard sulphates (McSwain et al. 1974; Colovos et al. 1976).

The sensitivity of titration can be increased either by choosing a longer measurement cell for example a 50 mm cell instead of 15 mm cell but with the risk of an increase in background noise, or by changing the input flow of the sample, for example 2.00 mL min^{-1} instead of 1.00 mL min^{-1}.

For the same coding, the flows in R4000 Solvaflex tubes (recommended for solvents) are slightly different from flows in PVC tubes of the Tygon 3603 type. Silicone tubes are more resistant and less subject to deformation than Solvaflex tubes. With the 50 mm measurement cell which is more easily contaminated, faster cell recirculation can limit deposits.

30.2.9 Total Sulphur by Automated Dry CHN(OS) Ultimate Analysis

With suitable catalysts, CHN(OS) apparatus allow analysis of samples containing different forms of S using dry processes (cf. Chap. 10). Automation enables rapid analysis of total S in a sample that is simply crushed to 0.1 mm.

Analysis of ^{34}S and ^{32}S isotopes can also be performed if the apparatus is coupled with a mass spectrometer detector.

Very sensitive and selective electron capture detectors can be used to titrate traces of sulphur, as sulphur dioxide has an affinity for free electrons.

Each manufacturer has their own system of traps and catalysts: tungstic anhydride (WO_3) allows the conversion of S into SO_2, vanadium pentoxide (V_2O_5) is often used for oxidation of SO_2 into SO_3.

Apparatus of the 'Fisons 1108 CHN-OS' type include two furnaces for thermal treatment of the samples. The furnace used for S measurement contains tungstic anhydride. The different forms of S are oxidized in the furnace heated to 1,100°C. The combustion-flash of the tin capsule containing the sample increases the temperature to 1,600°C. A flow of helium carries the combustion gases on a copper column then on a chromatographic column where SO_2-S is separated. Quantification is then carried out on a thermal conductivity detector (catharometer). The NA 1,500 (NCS) apparatus can handle samples up to 100 mg and performs a complete analysis in approximately 10 min.

The 'Perkin Elmer CHNS' uses a water trap for H determination and a catharometer to measure CO_2-C, N_2-N and SO_2-S.

For the determination of total S, the 'LECO-S' analyzer uses combustion accelerators (CrO_3, MoO_3, powder iron) in the presence of oxygen, the temperature of the induction furnace being 1,600°C. The SO_2 released is titrated by iodometry on an automatic titrimeter: $SO_2 + I_2 + 2H_2O \rightarrow H_2SO_4 + 2$ HI. The SC 132 model, which is equipped with a furnace heated to 1,400°C in oxygen atmosphere, uses IR absorption through an IR cell to quantify gaseous SO_2-S.

In the 'Herraeus' apparatus (Foss-UIC) the sample is placed in a furnace heated to 1,150°C containing tungsten oxide. A flow of 90% helium–10% oxygen carries SO_2-S on a magnesium perchlorate column where it is dehydrated. A chromatographic column (e.g. Porapak) separates impurities such as methane. Finally SO_2-S is measured by IR detection.

'Antek' apparatuses use detection by chemi-luminescence for determination of nitrogen and pyro-fluorescence for determination of total S. Soil samples of from 50 mg to 1 g can be used depending on the sulphur content. The sample is oxidized in a furnace heated to 1,000°C with a catalyst to release sulphur dioxide. After drying on the trap, the gas is exposed to UV radiation: $SO_2 + H\nu \rightarrow SO_2 + H\nu'$. A photomultiplier amplifies the fluorescence signal of frequency ν'. This reaction is specific to SO_2-S and the response vs concentration is linear.

Wösthoff proposed a dedicated apparatus called a sulmograph. Total sulphur is titrated by combustion of the sample in a current of oxygen at 1,350°C producing sulphur dioxide. SO_2-S is then absorbed by an oxidizing sulphuric acid aqueous solution in which carbon dioxide is not retained. The sulphur concentration is then determined by the change in conductivity before and after passage of the gas in the cell containing the oxidizing solution. This equipment was not automated, which made it less attractive despite its satisfactory precision (Marius et al. 1976).

These examples show the wide range of dry methods that can be used for S determination. Specific procedures have to be respected in each case. Automated apparatuses with computerized measurement procedures are generally the simplest to use. The sample is reduced to 0.1 mm, dried on phosphoric anhydride or in a drying oven at 105°C, weighed in a silver or tin capsule, then introduced directly into the system by a sampler. The results are printed directly by the software.

However, perfect maintenance and management of the equipment is necessary to ensure satisfactory performance: renewal of catalysts, changing the traps, cleaning the furnaces, filters, O-rings, etc. There is a risk of explosion when samples containing flammable and volatile products are analysed using dry methods.

Apparatuses for thermal analysis (cf. Chap. 7) are also used for the study of sulphur in soils, particularly when they are coupled with apparatuses for the analysis of evolved gases (EGA). Many measurements can be made simultaneously like weight loss, transition and decomposition temperatures and the nature of evolved gas like SO_2, SO_3 or H_2S. For a description of these methods, see Gerzabek and Schaffer (1986), David et al. (1989), Bremner and Tabatabai (1971), Bergheijn and van Schuylenborgh (1971), Tabatabai and Bremner (1970b, 1991).

30.2.10 Titration of Total SO_4^{2-}-S by Ionic Chromatography

IC is a fast, selective and very sensitive method that makes it possible to simultaneously analyse many anions and cations in complex solutions (cf. Sect. 18.3.8 of Chap. 18). In spite of these advantages, IC is not a universal method and its operating range is limited in total analysis. In the natural environment, it is a useful alternative to chemical analysis in not very saline soils, as the detection limits are about 0.2 mg $(SO_4^{2-}S)$ L^{-1} and the titration range lies between 0.5 and 100 mg L^{-1} (cf. Chap. 18).

Equipment and Principle

IC is a high pressure liquid chromatography (HPLC) technique specifically used for ion analysis (Pansu et al. 2001). Schematically, the apparatus consists of an ion exchange column which is the stationary phase (for SO_4^{2-} an anion resin in H–CO_3^- form can be used) subjected to the flow of a mobile phase by means of a constant-displacement pump. The sample to be analysed is injected in the mobile phase. The ions are retained by the stationary phase depending on their affinity; they then leave the column after a reproducible retention time and are quantified on a conductimetric detector.

The direct injection of polyelectrolyte solutions on the exchange column can decrease the life of the column and reduce its performance due to contamination. A precolumn filled with the same analytical resin is recommended to protect the separation column. Alternatively Donnan dialysis can be used to separate the dominant anions of the matrix. In this way the reduction in the performance of the column and its consequences (gradual modification of retention times and decrease in resolution) is limited.

As detection is by conductimetry, the ions of the eluting phase have to be eliminated physicochemically or electronically.

Sulphate anion has a relatively high retention time that varies with pH. A buffered mobile phase at a pH allowing a sufficiently short retention time for sulphate should thus be chosen. For anion determination of sulphate, the mobile phase is generally a carbonate–bicarbonate buffer with an isocratic flow.

Application range

The samples should not contain solid particles so the solutions should be filtered on discs with 0.45 or 0.22 µm pores.

For total S analysis, all the S forms in the soil have to be oxidized to sulphate forms. These operations imply still other difficulties because the oxidation procedures by alkaline fusion (cf. Sect. 30.2.4) or by hypobromite (cf. Sect. 30.2.5) result in significant quantities of salts of strong acids (nitrate, chloride, perchlorate). Even after strong dilution, these solutions are unsuitable for titration by IC, because of the too high ionic charge on the columns and resulting disturbance due to too intense peaks. Oxidation methods using perhydrol should be used instead. All the sulphides and the S forms bound to organic matter are quantitatively solubilized without creating an excess of anion.

The organic matter has to be destroyed to release the organic forms of S but the residual colouring of this organic matter does not interfere with detection of conductivity.

The concentration of the extraction reagents (e.g. Morgan reagent) required for the analysis of some S pools makes determination impossible. On the other hand, analysis of the soil solution by simple filtration and dilution is easy if the total content of soluble salts is not too high (cf. Chap. 18).

If solubilization is not complete, downward biases may be significant, for example in soils containing insoluble barite ($BaSO_4$).

In the natural environment, a high rate of a dominant anion mineral species, for example chloride in sea water, polders, mangroves, natural salinas, can prevent precise measurement. Oxidation is essential in hydrogeothermal mediums as well as in acid sulphated soils with pyrite rich in sulphides.

It should be noted that organic anions have an equivalent conductance lower than that of inorganic anions and give narrower peaks. Acetic acid should be preferred to oxalic acid because of the insoluble salts the latter forms with calcium.

The elution order of anions may vary depending on the operating conditions. In most cases the following series is observed in increasing order of retention time: $F^- < Cl^- < NO_2^- < NO_3^- < PO_4^{3-} < Br^- < SO_4^{2-}$. The SO_3^{2-} peak is not usually separated from the SO_4^{2-} peak. A $S_2O_3^{2-}$ peak seldom appears. More information can be found in the works of Tabatabai and Dick (1979), Tabatabai et al. (1988), Tabatabai and Bremner (1991), Artiola and Ali (1990), Tabatabai and Basta (1991), Kamarkar and Tabatabai (1992), Aswa and Tabatai (1993), Tabatabai and Frankenberger (1996).

30.2.11 Total S Titration by Plasma Emission Spectrometry

Soil samples weighing from 0.5 g to 2 g are used. The soil is air dried and crushed to 0.1 mm and mineralized by alkaline fusion (cf. Sect. 31.2.6 of Chap. 31) or ignition by $NaHCO_3/Ag_2O$ or $NaBrO$. The total sulphur obtained in sulphate form is dissolved in a $1 \text{ mol (HCl) L}^{-1}$ solution, filtered and brought to the required volume.

The emission line at 182.03 nm is used to limit calcium interference in measurement of the background noise at 182.08 nm.

Interference by iron and aluminium must be controlled. Iron presents a weak emission line at 182.04 nm and a broad diffuse emission band at 182.02–182.12 nm. Aluminium presents an emission band from 193 to 181.9 nm.

Salt contents must not be too high to avoid obstruction of the nebulizer (Perrott et al. 1991).

30.2.12 Titration by X-ray Fluorescence

It should be noted that this method can only be used by geo-chemistry laboratories able to justify the cost of semi-heavy equipment. This is the reference method described in Sect. 31.3.2 of Chap. 31. For total S, the procedure involves fusion and pelletizing. If organic matter contents are high (histosols, andosols, peats), weight losses mean the matrix effects will require correction (Tabatabai and Bremner, 1970b).

30.2.13 Titration by Atomic Absorption Spectrometry

In this case titration is indirect. After oxidizing mineralization, the sulphates obtained are precipitated in barium sulphate. After separation of the precipitate, washing and acid dissolution, the barium corresponding to the initial sulphate ions is titrated at 553.5 nm with an acetylene–nitrous oxide flame and correction of background noise.

30.2.14 Analytical Fractionation of Sulphur Compounds

Forms of Sulphur and their Biogeochemical Cycle

In the natural environment, soil is subjected to phases of mineralization and immobilization of S compounds controlled by the activity of micro-organisms, climatic constraints and vegetation. The S biogeochemical cycle is linked to the C and N cycle and the establishment of charac-teristic C:S and N:S ratios enables net losses and increases to be determined.

The weathering of mineral compounds, inputs from irrigation and rainwater of the gaseous form of S from the atmosphere, inputs of fertilizer in agricultural areas enables plants to find the energy they need for growth. They transform sulphate (the most stable and oxidized mineral form) into complex organic compounds linked to C and N. The plant residues are then subjected to complex biotic processes of reduction and oxidation. Organic and inorganic S is transformed and partly incorporated in the microbial and fungic biomass. The intensity of flows from the different S pools varies considerably depending on the type of soil and vegetation. At equilibrium in a given system, organic forms of S can represent up to 90% of total S.

Organic S

The chemical nature of sulphur compounds in soil organic matter is complex and has not yet been clearly defined. Reliable methods to specifically isolate the total organic S pool are not yet available. First, organic S is quantified by the difference between total S (obtained by alkaline fusion, or a wet oxidation process) and inorganic S obtained by extraction using water, diluted acids (HCl), or salts (NaHCO$_3$).

The study of the chemical nature of the S compounds in soil resulted in two groups whose properties and behaviour were recognized to be different, but whose limits were not clearly defined (Tabatabai and Bremner 1970b; Freney et al. 1970).

S organic Compounds Bound to C (S–C)

This group includes compounds containing sulphur amino acids like:

$$
\begin{array}{lllll}
\text{H}_2\text{C—SH} & \text{H}_2\text{C—CH}_2\text{—S—CH}_3 & \text{H}_2\text{C—SO}_3\text{H} & & \text{H}_2\text{C—S—S—CH}_2 \\
\quad | & \quad | & \quad | & \text{H}_2\text{N—CH} & \quad | \\
\text{HC—NH}_2 & \text{HC—NH}_2 & \text{H}_2\text{C—NH}_2 & \quad | & \text{HC—NH}_2 \\
\quad | & \quad | & & \text{COOH} & \quad | \\
\text{COOH} & \text{COOH} & & & \text{COOH} \\
\text{Cysteine} & \text{Methionine} & \text{Taurine} & \multicolumn{2}{c}{\text{Cystine}}
\end{array}
$$

These compounds resist to microbial attacks and are hydrolyzed very slowly to sulphate. They are reduced by Raney alloy (Ni–Al), whereas S combined with humic and fulvic acids are not, or only partially, reduced.

S organic compounds not directly bound to C

These compounds are mostly sulphate esters (e.g. $C–O–SO_3H$, phenolic esters, polysaccharides), for example, choline sulphate. They are hydrolyzed into sulphates by acids and bases. Compounds with high and low molecular weight can be regarded as transitory forms resulting from short-term mineralization. They are reduced by hydroiodic acid (HI) in hydrogen sulphide.

Other compounds may be retained as they are not reduced either by HI, or by Raney alloy. These compounds can be estimated by difference in the balances, and are probably of the C–S bound type, though this has not yet been demonstrated.

30.2.15 Titration of Organic S Bound to C

Principle

These compounds can be estimated by reduction with Raney alloy (nickel – 50% aluminium). In the form of finely divided powder, this alloy reacts quickly in strongly basic medium and enables hydrogenation of the S organic compounds. The reduction is catalyzed by nickel:

$$2\ NaOH + 2\ Al + 2\ H_2O \xrightarrow{\ Ni\ } 2\ NaAlO_2 + 6\ H$$

This method is used to determine S bound to C (SC) but also elementary S and certain rare inorganic forms of S in soils ($S_2O_3^{2-}$ thiosulfate, $S_2O_4^{2-}$ dithionite, $S_4O_6^{2-}$ tetrathionate). For example elementary S is reduced in the reaction:

$$S° + 2\ H \rightarrow H_2S\uparrow$$

H$_2$S released by acidification is titrated by colorimetry using methylene blue (cf. Sect. 30.2.7).

S bound to C can also be estimated by difference between total S and HI reducible S while ignoring unknown products whose presence can distort the results.

Equipment

– The same equipment as listed in Sect. 30.2.7.
– Adapter for the Johnson and Nishita apparatus (Fig. 30.1) to add hydrochloric acid (Fig. 30.5).
– 150 mL boiling flask (B in Fig. 30.1) with a Teflon sleeve.

Reagents

– Sodium hydroxide (NaOH) in pellet form.
– *5% soda solution.* Dissolve 50 g of NaOH in 800 mL water; homogenize, let cool and complete to 1,000 mL with deionized water.
– 20% hydrochloric acid (HCl, $d = 1.17$) solution.
– Activated Raney alloy catalyst in powder form; the Raney alloy gradually loses its reducing power after about 6 months; it is classified "suspected to be carcinogenic".

Procedure

– Dry the soil in the air and crush to 0.1 mm. Measure residual moisture. Weigh 0.2–0.5 g of soil containing from 10 to 50 µg of C bound S in a boiling flask (B in Fig. 30.1) for digestion. Add 100 mg of Raney catalyst, 5 mL of 5% soda solution, and 25 mL of deionized water and homogenize. Fit a Teflon sleeve on the ground glass joint of the boiling flask and attach it to the apparatus. Open the water flow in the condenser; start a nitrogen flow of 200 mL min^{-1} into the reaction mixture. Boil gently for 30 min avoiding the formation of excess foam. Let cool under a stream of nitrogen.
– Put the reagents in the washing column D and reception flask F (Fig. 30.1) of the Johnson and Nishita apparatus as described in "Procedure" under Sect. 30.2.7. Using the adapter shown in Fig. 30.5, add 5 mL of 20% hydrochloric acid solution to the boiling flask (B). Continue bubbling and boil gently for 30 min until complete displacement of hydrogen sulphide. Produce and titrate methylene blue as described in "Procedure" under Sect. 30.2.7. Check there are no traces of precipitated sulphide on the walls of the flask.

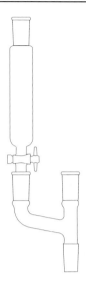

Fig. 30.5. Adapter to add hydrochloric acid for the determination of S bound to C using the Johnson and Nishita apparatus (see Fig. 30.1)

Remark

The result of the analysis can be checked by adding standard compounds of known composition. For example for an amino acid sample (L-methionine), weigh 116.3 mg of L-methionine and dissolve in approximately 300 mL of water. Bring to 500 mL with deionized water. The solution contains 50 mg (S) L^{-1}. Take 600 µL and transfer in the boiling flask (B in Fig. 30.1).

30.2.16 Titration of Organic S not Bound to C

Principle

This method is based on reduction by hydroiodic acid; it enables extraction of the most unstable forms of organic S which can be hydrolyzed into sulphate S in strongly basic and acid mediums. S-organic compounds in the form of sulphate esters (C–O–S– bonds) are reduced as are S-polysaccharides, S-lipids, S-choline. Some components of fulvic and humic acids are also reduced. Soluble inorganic forms of S (in water or 0.1 mol (LiCl) L^{-1} solution) are also reduced, which means the results need to be corrected:

HI-reducible organic S = HI-reducible total S – soluble inorganic S

The main redox reactions between sulphur and iodine compound were reported by pioneer chemists:

$$H_2SO_4 + 6\ HI \leftrightarrow 3I_2 + 4\ H_2O + S \qquad \text{Smith and Mayer (1924)}$$
$$SO_2 + 4\ HI \leftrightarrow 2I_2 + 2\ H_2O + S \qquad \text{Volhard (1887)}$$
$$H_2S + I_2 \leftrightarrow 2\ HI + S \qquad \text{Seil (1926)}$$
$$S + 2\ HI \leftrightarrow H_2S + I_2 \qquad \text{Worris and Cottrell (1896)}$$

Equipment

– Johnson and Nishita apparatus (Fig. 30.1)
– Lab glassware
– Precision balance (±1/10 mg)

Reagents

– cf. "Reagents" under Sect. 30.2.

Procedure

Dry in the air a recently sampled soil sample and crush to 0.1 mm. Measure residual moisture.
– Weigh 0.2–0.5 g of soil containing between 20 and 100 µg of total S and put it in the distillation flask (B in Fig. 30.1) of the Johnson and Nishita apparatus. Add 2 mL of water and 4 mL of reducing mixture ($HI + H_3PO_2 + HCOOH$) and carry out reduction as in Sect. 30.2.15 followed by methylene blue colorimetry (cf. Sect. 30.2.7).
– Correct the results for moisture and the rate of inorganic S extractable by water or 0.1 mol (LiCl) L^{-1} solution (cf. "Principle" under Sect. 30.2.16).

Remarks

– The use of fresh samples stored in the freezer limits the degradation of HI-reducible S compounds.
– In air-dried samples rich in organic matter, light particles can float and may have bad contact with the water; swirl the flask well to homogenize.
– The efficiency of the reducing treatment can be tested on a sample of 4-nitrophenyl sulphate (potassium salt, $O_2NC_6H_4OSO_3K,H_2O$).

30.2.17 Extraction and Titration of Soluble Sulphides

Principle

The hydrogen sulphide is moved in a closed environment by hydrochloric acid and collected in a zinc and cadmium acetate solution. The resulting zinc and cadmium sulphides are titrated by iodometry according to the reactions:

$$(CH_3COO)_2Zn + H_2S \xrightarrow{CH_3COOH} ZnS + 2\ CH_3COOH$$

$$S^{2-} + I_2 \xrightarrow{acid^*} S + 2\ I^- \qquad \text{(Charlot and Bézier 1955)}$$

$$I_2 + 2\ S_2O_3^{2-} \rightarrow S_4O_6^{2-} + 2\ I^- \qquad \text{back titration with thiosulfate}$$

*The redox potential of I is independent of pH up to pH 9, but iodine can be more oxidizing at higher pH values than in other systems whose redox potential decreases with an increase in pH. This is why it is necessary to use an acid medium. In a basic medium, the following reaction can occur:

$$S^{2-} + 4\ I_2 + 4\ H_2O \xrightarrow{OH^-} SO_4^{2-} + 8\ I^- + 8\ H^+$$

Equipment

– Analytical balance (± 0.1 mg)
– Distillation apparatus (Fig. 30.1)
– Washing bottles
– Titration burette (± 1/10 mL)
– Lab glassware

Reagents

– Zinc acetate, $Zn(CH_3COO)_2$.
– Cadmium acetate, $Cd(CH_3COO)_2$.
– Acetic acid, CH_3COOH.
– *Mixed solution.* Weigh 17 g of zinc acetate and 8 g of cadmium acetate; dissolve in a mixture of 200 mL of acetic acid and 600 mL of distilled water; bring to 1,000 mL with distilled water.
– Hydrochloric acid, HCl, $d = 1.16$.
– ≈ 1 *mol (HCl) L^{-1} solution.* Take 100 mL of concentrated hydrochloric acid and bring to 1,000 mL with distilled water.

– Soluble starch powder.

– Mercuric iodide, HgI_2.

– *Starch indicator.* Weigh 10 g of starch powder and dissolve in 50 mL of distilled water. Add 40 mg of mercuric iodide (or 40 mg of hydroxybenzoic acid) as preservative agent. Pour the mixture into 950 mL of boiling distilled water. Boil for 2 min. Let cool and complete to 1,000 mL. Store in a brown bottle stopped with emery. The solution is stable for approximately 6 months. The indicator is blue up to pH 8.0 and colourless above this limit.

– 0.1 N iodine, commercial volumetric solution.

– 0.1 N sodium hyposulfite ($Na_2S_2O_3,5H_2O$), commercial volumetric solution.

– Carbon dioxide, CO_2 in a gas bottle with a pressure reducer and regulator.

Procedure

Using the technique of Gony and Parent (1966), weigh the fresh sample (50 g) and place it in a boiling flask with a ground glass joint (another sample specimen should be used to measure the soil moisture). Add 50 mL of 1 mol (HCl) L^{-1} solution. Switch on the condenser (Fig. 30.1) and set up two consecutive wash-bottles filled with 50 mL of zinc and cadmium solution at the gas outlet. Boil gently for 1 h. While transferring the hydrogen sulphide in a flow of carbon dioxide (3–4 bubbles a second) in the first wash-bottle. The second wash-bottle makes it possible to check if all hydrogen sulphide has been trapped.

Titration

In the first wash-bottle, add 5 mL of the 0.1 N iodine solution (or 10 mL of 0.01 N iodine solution if the sulphide precipitate is weak) then 2 mL of the starch indicator. Titrate the excess iodine with 0.1 N (or 0.01 N) sodium hyposulfite solution.

Calculations

1 mL $Na_2S_2O_3$ 0.1 N = 1.603 mg of S
The results are expressed in g (S) kg^{-1} of soil dried at 105°C.

Remarks

The action of cold hydrochloric acid enables free hydrogen sulphide and H_2S–S of amorphous iron sulphide to be moved. Mackinawite and greigite, which are more stable forms of iron minerals, only react when hot. Micro crystallites of pyrite do not react in this hydrochloric medium.

Other volatile compounds can be identified in a waterlogged natural environment, e.g. a combination of S and C synthesized by micro-organisms:

CS_2 Carbon disulphide (CH_4 methane $+ 4S \rightarrow CS_2 + 2H_2S$),
CH_3–SH methyl mercaptan,
CH_3–S–CH_3 dimethyl sulphide,
CH_3–S–S–CH_3 dimethyl disulphide,
CH_3–CH_2–S–CH_2–CH_3 diethyl sulphide,
C–O–S carbonyl sulphide.

30.2.18 Titration of Sulphur in Pyrites

Introduction

Pyrites, sulphides and polysulphides formed in reducing mediums can be observed in soils in the form of small black concretions. As the density of pyrite is 5.02, it can be isolated by washing and flotation. These compounds deteriorate rapidly in oxidizing medium. In waterlogged soils, proteolytic bacteria are able to release hydrogen sulphide by hydrolysis of sulphur compounds like sulphured amino acids (e.g. cysteine, cystine, methionine). The process can also occur by reduction of sulphate.

Studies of the diagenesis of pyrite compounds led to the identification of complex reaction kinetics where the sulphur reduced to hydrogen sulphide reacts with the amorphous reduced compounds of iron to form a metastable iron sulphide which crystallizes in the form of tetragonal mackinawite (FeS), thermally stable hexagonal pyrrhotite (FeS), greigite Fe_3S_4, orthorhombic marcasite in old sediments, or cubic pyrite in recent marine sediments. This anthigenic pyrite form is thermally stable and must be measured because it is the end product of a process of evolution.

Pyrite is insoluble in hot hydrochloric acid, which means it can be distinguished from other soluble sulphides titrated using the method described in Sect. 30.2.17.

Tests

X-ray diffractometry (XRD) is an excellent way to determine pyrites extracted by flotation. But generally XRD is not sensitive enough to detect the intermediate phases without concentration. Table 1 lists the characteristic XRD peaks of pyrite, marcasite, greigite and mackinavite.

In differential thermal analysis (DTA), pyrite presents endothermic reactions at 354, 443, 551 and 613°C and an exothermic peak at 450°C.

Under the scanning electron microscope (+EDX microprobe), pyrite is easily detected in the form of 1–10 μm grains of characteristic raspberry shape. This enables the pyrites of biogenic origin to be distinguished from the crystalline pyrite clusters found in volcanic environments.

Principle

In the case of reducing soils without sulphate or jarosite, the sample should be used on which the reduced compounds of sulphur (different non-pyrite sulphides) and the ferric and ferrous compounds have already been extracted in hydrochloric acid medium. This sample is then oxidized by hot nitric acid. The solubilized iron is titrated by atomic absorption spectrometry.

If the soils contain both oxidized (sulphate-jarosite) and reduced (pyrites) minerals, the sample should be used on which the Na_3-EDTA soluble forms have already been extracted. Sulphates obtained by oxidation are titrated by turbidimetry or colorimetry (cf. Sect. 30.2.21).

Equipment

– Lab glassware
– Freeze dryer
– Thermostatic water bath
– Atomic absorption spectrometer (AAS)

Reagents

– Nitric acid HNO_3 (70%).
– Hydrochloric acid, HCl, $d = 1.17$.
– *4 mol (HCl) L^{-1} solution.* In a 1 L volumetric flask, put about 500 mL of deionized water and add 320 mL of hydrochloric acid; let cool, complete to 1,000 mL with deionized water and homogenize.
– Commercial standard iron solution for AAS containing 1 mg (Fe) mL^{-1}.
– Sodium chloride, NaCl.

– *Dilution solution for the determination of iron (1% NaCl–0.2 mol (HCl) L^{-1}).* Dissolve 10 g of sodium chloride in about 500 mL of water; add 50 mL of 4 mol (HCl) L^{-1} solution, complete to 1,000 mL and homogenize.

– *Standard stock solution of iron at 100 mg L^{-1}.* Use a precision pipette to put 10 mL of the 1 mg (Fe) mL^{-1} standard iron solution in a 100 mL volumetric flask; complete to volume and homogenize.

– *Standard calibration range.* In 100 mL volumetric flasks put 0, 5, 10, 15, 20, 25 mL of the iron solution containing 100 mg (Fe) L^{-1}; add 2.5 mL of 4 mol (HCl) L^{-1} solution in each flask, complete to 100 mL with deionized water and homogenize. The concentrations of the calibration range are: 0 (blank), 5.0, 10.0, 15.0, 20.0 and 25.0 mg (Fe) L^{-1}.

Procedure

– Wash the sample remaining after sulphide extraction (cf. Sect. 30.2.17) then dehydrate by freeze-drying; if necessary crush with an agate mortar to 0.1 mm.

– Weigh a sample of 250–500 mg and place in a 50 mL Pyrex boiling flask.

– Add 10 mL of 70% nitric acid and put in the boiling water bath.

– Evaporate to dry, and then add 5 mL of 4 mol (HCl) L^{-1} to the residue and heat for 5 min in the water bath.

– Transfer in a centrifugation tube and centrifuge for 10 min at 5,000g.

– Decant the supernatant in a 100 mL volumetric flask.

– Add approximately 40 mL of deionized water in the centrifugation tube and centrifuge again for 10 min at 5,000g.

– Add the supernatant to the first fraction; filter and wash the soil residue; complete to 100 mL and homogenize.

– Titrate iron in this solution; make a v:v mixture with the 1% NaCl + 0.2 mol (HCl) L^{-1} dilution solution and perform the AAS measurement at 248.3 nm in air–acetylene flame.

30.2.19 Titration of Elementary Sulphur

Origin

In certain soil horizons or in the rhizosphere, the rise of water in the soil due to capillary action starting from a groundwater rich in sulphides can cause crystallization of elementary sulphur (plots of straw yellow colour) near the soil surface, or in certain soil horizons, or near the plant roots.

Tests

– Sulphur with a density of 2.07 can be enriched by flotation.
– DTA reveals an enantiotropic change from the orthorhombic into monoclinic form at 113°C under inert atmosphere. Fusion occurs at 124°C, followed by other transformations and boiling at 179°C and 446°C.
– Scanning electron microscopy makes it possible to determine the crystalline system in certain cases (orthorhombic), but stability under the electronic beam is low.

Principle

After removal of hydrogen sulphide with hydrochloric acid (cf. Sect. 10.2.17), elementary sulphur is extracted with acetone.[5] Titration is by turbidimetric analysis of colloidal sulphur in water (it is also possible to perform Soxhlet extraction in presence of metallic copper, then to titrate the resulting copper sulphide by iodometry, for example).

Equipment

– Shaker
– Centrifuge
– Spectrophotometer turbidimeter
– Analytical balance (± 1/10 mg)

Reagents

Do not use rubber caps for any reagents that contain sulphur.

------

[5] – Acetone (2-propanone) is the least dangerous solvent of elementary sulphur, in spite of the fact that it is flammable and can cause irritation when inhaled. S solubility in acetone is 2.65 g for 100 mL at 25°C.
Other solvents are more dangerous and should be avoided:
– Benzene S (solubility 24 g L^{-1} at 30°C) is toxic by inhalation and carcinogenous.
– Trichloromethane (chloroform) $CHCl_3$, S solubility 15 g L^{-1} at 18°C toxic by inhalation, and anaesthetic.
– CH_2I_2 – di-iodomethane (methylene iodide) S solubility 91 g L^{-1} at 10°C viscous, high density).
– Pyridine C_5H_5N toxic by inhalation.

– Acetone, CH_3–CO–CH_3.
– 99.99% (or 99.5%) sulphur S.
– *Calibration range of elementary sulphur.* Weigh 62.5 mg of sulphur in fine powder form and transfer in a 250 mL boiling flask; add 150 mL of acetone and shake until complete dissolution; transfer in a 250 mL volumetric flask, complete to volume with acetone and homogenize; 1 mL contains 0.25 mg of elementary sulphur; put (0) 1, 2, 3, 4, 5 mL of this standard solution in 100 mL volumetric flasks containing 80 mL of water; homogenize acetone contents by adding 5 mL of acetone in flask 0 , 4 mL in flask 1, 3 mL in flask 2, 2 mL in flask 3, 1 mL in flask 4, 0 mL in flask 5; complete to volume with water and homogenize;

The contents of the calibration range are 2.5, 5.0, 7.5, 10.0, 12.5 mg (S) L^{-1}.

Procedure

– Use the solid residue remaining after sulphide extraction (cf. Sect. 30.2.17). Wash the residue, freeze-dry it, and again crush to 0.1 mm if necessary. Weigh 250 mg of the residue in a 20 mL centrifugation tube with a polypropylene screw cap. Add exactly 10 mL of acetone, shake for 30 min and centrifuge for 15 min at 5,000g.
– Put 80 mL of deionized water in a 100 mL volumetric flask. Using a precision pipette, add 5 mL of the acetone extract. Shake and complete to 100 mL with deionized water. Let stand for 3 h with occasional shaking. Measure absorbance at 420 nm.

The absorbance vs concentration response is linear in the calibration range. Organic matter can interfere by co-precipitation or colouring.

30.2.20 Titration of Water Soluble Sulphates

Forms

Sulphated salts are of marine origin but have undergone transformation during soil genesis, i.e. reduction, reoxidation, leaching and precipitation. Sulphates can be found in calcium sulphate form in calcareous-rich soils (cf. Sect. 30.3). Tropical soils, which are generally poor in calcium, are more likely to contain sodium sulphate in deteriorated zones or very soluble mixed sulphates (alums) of aluminium, iron and magnesium (Le Brusq et al. 1987; Montoroi, 1994).

Extraction

Soluble sulphate can be titrated on the 1:10 aqueous extract for the determination of soluble salts (cf. Chap. 20). This extract will quantitatively account for calcium sulphate only in the case of low sulphate contents. The same goes for barium or strontium sulphates co-precipitated with calcium carbonate. Basic sulphates of iron and aluminium, coquinbite ($Fe_2(SO_4)_3,5H_2O$) and jarosite $KFe_3(OH)_6(SO_4)_2$, are not solubilized and are thus not accounted for with soluble sulphates.

For agronomic studies, a range of saline extracts can also be used to characterize exchangeable and soluble sulphate (cf. Sect. 30.4.2).

Equipment

– Lab glassware
– Analytical balance ($\pm$ 1/10 mg)
– Muffle furnace (1,000°C)

Reagents

– 10% Barium chloride ($BaCl_2$) solution
– 10% Hydrochloric acid (HCl) solution
– 1% Silver nitrate ($AgNO_3$) solution

Procedure

Take an aliquot of the 1:10 water extract (cf. Chap. 18) as a function of total soil salinity (20–50 mL). Put in a 250 mL beaker and add 5 mL of the 10% hydrochloric acid solution. Bring to the boil and add the barium chloride solution in the boiling liquid drop by drop. Let cool and leave to stand for 24 h. Filter on blue laboratory filter with a diameter of 20 mm, wash the precipitate until elimination of chloride (silver nitrate test). Put the filter in a tared refractory crucible and heat to 900°C in the muffle furnace in contact with the air. Let cool, weigh and calculate the results in mmol ($\frac{1}{2}SO_4^{2-}$) L^{-1} and mg (S) kg^{-1}.

30.2.21 Titration of Na₃-EDTA Extractable Sulphates

Principle

Gypsum, little soluble sulphate and exchangeable sulphates are extracted by the Na₃–EDTA sequestering reagent. The extracted SO_4^{2-}-S is measured by turbidimetry after precipitation of barium sulphate.

Equipment

– Lab glassware
– Shaker
– Thermostatic water bath
– Spectrophotometer

Reagents

– Trisodic ethylene diamin tetraacetic acid (Na₃-EDTA) monohydrate,

$$\text{NaOOC-CH}_2 \underset{\text{NaOOC-CH}_2}{\overset{}{\diagdown}} \text{N-CH}_2\text{-CH}_2\text{-N} \overset{\text{CH}_2\text{-COONa}}{\underset{\text{H}_2\text{C-COOH}}{\diagup}}$$

  mw = 376.21.
– *0.1 mol L⁻¹ Na₃-EDTA solution.* Dissolve 18.8 g of Na₃-EDTA in about 250 mL of water, bring to 500 mL and homogenize.
– 65% nitric acid, HNO₃.
– 37% hydrochloric acid, HCl.
– *Aqua regia.* Under a fume hood, mix 180 mL of 37% HCl and 60 mL of 65% HNO₃ in a beaker and cover with a beaker cover.
– *25% nitric acid solution.* Add 600 mL of water and 360 mL of nitric acid in a 1 L graduated cylinder; let cool, bring to 1,000 mL with deionized water and homogenize.
– 85% phosphoric acid, H₃PO₄ .
– Glacial acetic acid, CH₃COOH.
– *Acetic acid phosphoric acid solution.* Mix 180 mL of glacial acetic acid and 60 mL of 85% phosphoric acid.
– *Gum arabic and acetic acid.* Weigh 0.5 g of gum arabic and dissolve in 50 mL of deionized water; add 50 mL of glacial acetic acid; mix and filter on hardened acid-resistant laboratory filter.
– Sodium sulphate, Na₂SO₄.
– *0.3% sodium sulphate solution.* Dissolve 0.3 g of sodium sulphate in 100 mL of deionized water.

– Barium chloride, $BaCl_2$, $2H_2O$.
– *Barium chloride solution.* Dissolve 18.0 g of barium chloride in 44 mL of water heated to 80°C; add 1.5 mL of 0.3% sodium sulphate solution; bring to the boil; cool rapidly and add 4 mL of gum arabic-acetic acid solution; prepare before each analysis series.
– Standard calibration range S-SO_4^{2-} (cf. Sects. 30.2.7 and 30.2.8).

Procedure

Extraction

This method is adapted from Buurman et al. 1996. The soil sample is freeze-dried and crushed to 0.1 mm (moisture is measured on another sample specimen).
– Weigh a 250 mg sample and put it in a 20 mL polypropylene centrifugation tube. Add 10 mL of the Na_3–EDTA solution and agitate on a rotary agitator for 3 h. Centrifuge for 15 min at 5,000*g* (after washing, the centrifugation pellet can be kept for jarosite analysis, if required).
– Put 2 mL of the supernatant liquid in a 50 mL Pyrex capsule. Add 2 mL of aqua regia and 1 mL of 85% phosphoric acid. Evaporate in a boiling water bath until nearly dry, then add 2 mL of aqua regia and evaporate. Add 10 mL of deionized water and put in the boiling water bath for a few minutes. Let cool, homogenize and transfer in a 50 mL volumetric flask. Wash, complete to 50 mL with deionized water and homogenize.

Titration

– With a precision pipette, transfer 20 mL of the extraction solution (see "Titration" under Sect. 30.2.21) in a 50 mL volumetric flask with a ground stopper. Add 10 mL of water, 5 mL of 25% nitric acid solution and 3 mL of glacial acetic acid. Homogenize, add 1 mL of barium chloride solution and immediately add 0.5 g of $BaCl_2$,$2H_2O$ in powder form, swirl the flask after each addition.
– After 15 min shake, then again after 5 min. Add 2 mL of gum arabic-acetic acid solution. The reagent addition must be very constant[6]. Bring

---

[6] The kinetics of precipitation of barium sulphate in solutions containing hydrochloric acid (to avoid the precipitation of calcium sulphate and of sulphates of heavy di- and quadrivalent elements which can interfere with titration) must be controlled by respecting a strict procedure. Precipitation is slowed down by hydrochloric acid. Acid concentration, temperature, the solution to $BaCl_2$ ratio, the concentration of $BaCl_2$, addition of saline products and mode of addition can upset the uniformity of charge distribution, and the regularity of nucleation and granulation kinetics.

to 50 mL with deionized water and homogenize. Let stand for 90 min, agitate and take the spectrometric measurement at 438 nm.
– Continue in the same way for the calibration standards: put 0, 1, 2, 3, 4, 5 mL of the 500 mg $(SO_4^{2-}S)$ L^{-1} stock solution in 50 mL volumetric flasks. Dilute to about 30 mL, add 4 mL of a mixture of acetic acid and phosphoric acid. Homogenize, and then continue as for the samples. Plot the absorbance vs concentration curve to calculate the results.

Remark

Organic matter can interfere either by precipitation or colouring of the reaction medium.

30.2.22 Titration of Jarosite

Introduction

In soils containing jarosite resulting from the influence of abiotic and biotic phenomena, the alteration process includes two phases that concern forms of sulphur, iron, potassium or sodium.

The reduction phase where the influence of sulphate-reducing bacteria in hydromorphic (and sometimes halomorphic) medium enables reduction of sulphate and organic sulphur to the hydrosulphide HS^- state. At the same time, ferric iron is reduced into ferrous iron.

$SO_4^{2-} \rightarrow HS^-$ ⟶ Amorphous FeS Jarosite and natrojarosite + H_2SO_4
$Fe^{3+} \rightarrow Fe^{2+}$ ⟶ pyrite FeS_2 $CaSO_4,2H_2O$ gypsum
$CaCO_3 \rightarrow CO_2\uparrow + HCO_3^-$
Reducing medium (*Disulfovibrio*) Oxidizing medium (*Thiobacillus*)
(van Breemen and Harmsen, 1973–1975)

During the oxidation phase resulting from a natural or artificial drop in the groundwater level, S-rich sediments are in an aerobic environment. Pyrites are more or less rapidly oxidized depending on the degree of contraction of the soil with the formation of fissures and an increase in drainage. The soil pH can decrease to pH 3.5, pH 3 or even lower (Le Brusq et al. 1987). If the soil contains calcium carbonate, the decrease in pH is smaller. Carbonate is broken down into carbon dioxide and soluble hydrogenocarbonate which can be eliminated. Gypsum is formed simultaneously.

Jarosite ($KFe_3(OH)_6(SO_4)_2$) appears at the same time as the formation of sulphuric acid, which can make the drained soils very acid (sulphuric horizons, sulfaquept, sulfohemist). Some clay lattice structures can become unstable. Aluminic acidity can appear.

Glauconite alteration is a source of potassium for the production of jarosite in this environment. In marine environments, natrojarosite ($NaFe_3(OH)_6(SO_4)_2$) can be found. The ammonium ion obstructs the formation of these compounds. Jarosite is metastable at pH < 4.5 in soil and can be hydrolyzed into goethite-$FeO(OH)$ which results in the appearance of rust-coloured spots at the top of soil profiles.

Jarosite and natrojarosite produce yellow efflorescence in the soil when drying, or near plant roots. Chamayou and Legros (1989) described a series of chemical reactions concerning pyrite oxidation in these soils. One pyrite mole produces one H^+ mole when all the iron is oxidized into ferric iron:

$$FeS_2 + 15/2\ O_2 + 1/2\ H_2O \Leftrightarrow Fe^{3+} + 2\ SO_4^{2-} + H^+$$

If the medium is not sufficiently oxygenated, iron remains in ferrous form but acidification is high:

$$FeS_2 + 15/2\ O_2 + H_2O \Leftrightarrow Fe^{2+} + 2\ SO_4^{2-} + 2\ H^+$$

Acidification is also high if iron is transformed into ferric hydroxide . The soil pH can reach pH 2 in very wet but well-aerated soil:

$$FeS_2 + 15/2\ O_2 + 7/2\ H_2O \Leftrightarrow Fe(OH)_3 + 2\ SO_4^{2-} + 4\ H^+$$

$$FeS_2 + 15/2\ O_2 + 5/2\ H_2O + 1/3\ K^+ \Leftrightarrow 1/3\ KFe_3(OH)_6(SO_4)_2 + 4/3\ SO_4^{2-} + 3H^+$$
$$\text{Jarosite}$$

Tests

Yellow efflorescences on the surface of the soil or near plant roots can be collected and stored in sealed flasks after rapid drying in the air. Purity is about 80%.

XRD spectra can be obtained after saturation treatments with magnesium or potassium cations, glycerol treatment and heating to 300 and 550°C (cf. Chap. 4). Inter-reticular distances enable identification of:

K jarosite   3.08–3.11–2.29 Å (copper radiation on powder)
Na jarosite   5.06–3.06–3.12 Å (copper radiation on powder)

DTA in nitrogen atmosphere (cf. Chap. 7) gives an exo-thermic peak near 500°C corresponding to a $KFe_3(SO_4)_2(OH)_6$ degradation giving K_2SO_4, $X_2(SO_4)_3$. The second peak near 800°C corresponds to decomposition of $X_2(SO_4)_3$. An endothermic peak is also observed at 416°C.

Scanning electron microscopy (cf. Chap. 8) reveals cubic particles with small octahedral faces. Measurement of the 1:2.5 water pH just after the soil and water is mixed, then 24 h later reveals acidification induced by jarosite hydrolysis.

Principle of Titration

After determination of Na_3–EDTA soluble sulphates, (cf. Sect. 30.2.21). The solid residue of the soil sample is used for titration of jarosite. Jarosite is dissolved in hot hydrochloric acid which does not attack pyrite. The extracted sulphate is titrated by turbidimetry using the barium method.

Equipment

– Lab glassware
– Thermostatic water-bath
– Spectrophotometer
– Centrifuge.

Reagents

– 37% hydrochloric acid, HCl.
– *4 mol (HCl) L^{-1} solution.* Under a fume-hood add about 500 mL of deionised water then 320 mL of 37% hydrochloric acid in a 1 L graduated cylinder. Cool, complete to 1,000 mL with deionized water and homogenize.
– See also reagents for Na_3–EDTA analysis ("Reagents" under Sect. 30.2.21).

Procedure

– After determination of Na_3–EDTA soluble sulphates, wash the residue twice by centrifugation for 10 min at 5,000g with 10 mL of deionized water. Discard the washing water.
– Transfer the residue in a 50 mL beaker and add 10 mL of 4 mol (HCl) L^{-1} solution. Cover with a beaker cover and place in a boiling water-bath for 2 h. Let cool, transfer in a centrifugation tube and centrifuge for 10 min at 5,000g. Decant the supernatant in a 50 mL volumetric flask, bring to volume with deionized water and homogenize. Titrate sulphate in this solution by turbidimetric titration as in "Titration" under Sect. 30.2.21 above. The soil residue can be used for pyrite titration (cf. Sect. 30.2.18).

30.2.23 Sequential Analysis of S Forms

Analytical objectives and environmental conditions determine the choice of the methods described earlier. These analyses can also be performed in sequence depending on the solubility criteria and the order of elimination of titrated S forms. The method in Fig. 30.6 was recommended for acid sulphated soils by the Department of Soil Science and Geology of Wageningen Agricultural University (Buurman et al. 1996).

IC may be suitable for sulphur anions, but the carrier solution can react with some forms. For example, H_2S and $H_2S_2O_3$ are not stable in acid medium; polysulphides produce elementary sulphur or hydrogen sulphide.

An original chemical approach was proposed by Sonne and Dasgupta (1991) for analysis of inorganic S forms in kerogen zones. The simultaneous analysis of sulphide, polysulphides, sulphite, thiosulphate and sulphate is performed by automated continuous-flow injection analysis (FIA) using turbidimetric and colorimetric detection on soil water extracts and saline waters. A complex manifold enables simultaneous measurement of:

– Sulphides and polysulphides by moderate acidification of the medium and displacement of sulphur; turbidimetric measurement of colloidal sulphur enables quantification of polysulphides; colorimetric measurement using pentacyanonitroferrate (II) in alkaline medium enables quantification of the resulting hydrogen sulphide (sulphite does not cause interference).

– Sulphites by displacement of sulphur dioxide and colorimetric measurement specific to S^{IV} valence (discolouring of triphenylmethane in neutral solution).

– Thiosulphates by discolouring of potassium permanganate in weak acid medium after precipitation of sulphide and polysulphide and sequestering of sulphite by hydroxymethylsulphonate.

– Sulphates with turbidimetric measurement after precipitation with barium chloride; the precipitation of polysulphide is compensated for by differential measurement of absorbance before and after the addition of barium chloride.

Fig. 30.6. Sequential analysis of sulphur forms in acid sulphated soils (*gypsum, slightly soluble or extractable sulphates)

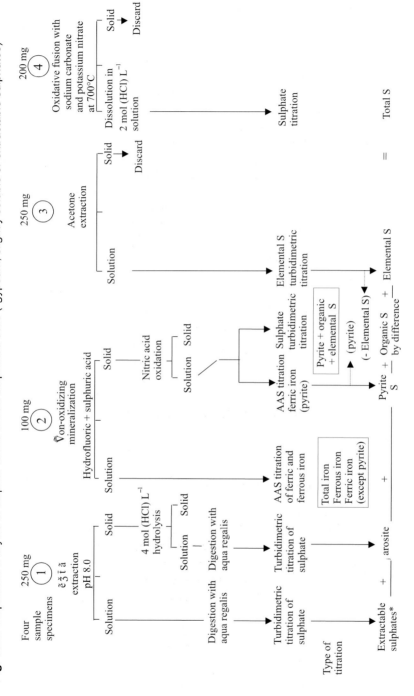

30.3. Sulphur of Gypseous Soils

30.3.1 Gypseous Soils

In mangrove soils, calcium sulphate can originate from original sediments or from transformations undergone by different sulphur compounds during soil genesis in these specific environments. But calcium sulphate contents are generally low and these are titrated at the same time as insoluble sulphates of the jarosite type (cf. Sects. 30.2.20, 30.2.21, 30.2.22).

Real gypseous soils (*gypsosols, gypsisols*) are characteristic of arid and semi-arid zones and are common in North Africa and the Middle East. The main source of gypsum is evaporitic material. Calcium sulphates are also redistributed by water transport in these soils. Newly formed gypsum can also accumulate deep in certain soils in easily flooded environments and is linked to the genesis of hydromorphic or saline soils.

The forms of calcium sulphate observed in these soils belong to three principal chemical components linked to the degree of dehydration of salt:

– Gypsum, $CaSO_4,2H_2O$, which represents the most stable phase
– Bassamite, $CaSO_4,0.5H_2O$, semi-hydrated phase
– Anhydrite, $CaSO_4$ with no water molecule

The solubility of gypsum in pure water is 2.6 g L^{-1} at 25°C, but its solubility is highly influenced by temperature and by the presence of other salts. Salts like sodium sulphate or calcium carbonate decrease the solubility of calcium sulphate, whereas a salt like sodium chloride considerably increases its solubility. These different degrees of solubility due to salt interactions present serious problems for extraction and titration.

From a quantitative point of view, the gypsum contents measured in a soil can be very high (> 50%), even if its accumulation is not clearly visible (e.g. crust, encrusting, desert rose crystals, cluster nodules, pseudo-mycelium). There are many microscopic forms (Pouget 1995) disseminated in the soil mass.

30.3.2 Preliminary Tests

Water of Crystallization

Principle

Soil samples containing gypsum have to subject to specific treatment because of the lower solubility of calcium sulphate compared to other soluble salts extracted with water (cf. Chap. 30). In the absence of visual confirmation of the presence of gypsum, it is recommended to carry out a preliminary detection test in order to select the most appropriate soil-to-water ratio for complete extraction of the sample.

The principle is based on measurement of the weight loss of a gypseous sample by drying in a drying oven until constant weight compared to weight loss under phosphoric anhydride

This test gives a reasonably precise estimate of gypsum content. It is quite rapid and can be used for series analyses. The best results are found in the *gypsic* or *petrogypsic* horizons (which can represent 60–85% of gypsum).

Procedure

- Weigh 5 g of air-dried soil and place it in a desiccator containing phosphoric anhydride or silica gel and leave for 48 h.
- Weigh with the laboratory balance (± 1/10 mg); place the sample in a drying oven at 125°C (or 150°C) for 24 h; transfer in the desiccator, let cool and weigh.

Calculate the weight loss. The second weight gives the soil moisture. The third weight gives the loss of water of crystallization from the gypsum.

Remark

In DTA at low temperatures, a double endothermic peak is observed corresponding to the loss of 1.5 mol H_2O resulting in hemihydrite, and then to the loss of 0.5 mol H_2O resulting in anhydrite:

$$CaSO_4,2H_2O \xrightarrow{\approx 110°C} CaSO_4,0.5H_2O \xrightarrow{\approx 150°C} \gamma\, CaSO_4 \xrightarrow{\approx 600°C} \beta CaSO_4$$

Gypsum	bassanite	anhydrite	anhydrite
	Hemihydrate	soluble	insoluble

$$\xrightarrow{1,100°C} CaO + SO_3\uparrow$$

Interferences are minimal if the temperature is kept under (1) the breakdown point of organic molecular structures and (2) the dehydration points of clays and oxides (e.g. gibbsite). At 150°C the results are a little too high.

XRD Test

– XRD lines at 7.56, 3.059, 4.27 Å

IR test

Figure 30.7 shows the characteristic spectra of gypsum materials.

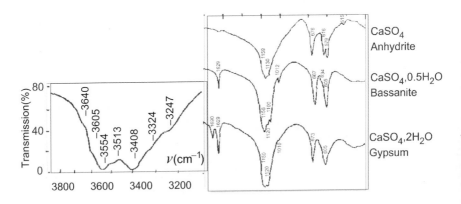

Fig. 30.7. Infra-red spectra of gypseous materials (KBr pelletizing); on the left, stretching vibrations of the OH zone: water molecules are in equivalent positions in the lattice, each one forms two hydrogen bonds with the oxygen atoms of the sulphate ion

Acetone Test

This method is based on the solubility differential. To a given volume of diluted aqueous extract (1:2 or 1:5), the same volume of acetone (CH_3–CO–CH_3) is added. The presence of gypsum is indicated by the immediate formation of varying degrees of off-white precipitate (Richards 1954) depending on the quantity of the dissolved calcium sulphate precipitated in acetone. This test can also be used to titrate gypsum (cf. Sect. 20.3.4).

30.3.3 Extraction and Titration from Multiple Extracts

Principle

All the gypsum in the gypseous sample is not dissolved in a simple saturated extract. Several extractions with more and more diluted aqueous extracts are needed to obtain complete extraction of gypsum. Air-dried samples are generally used rather than oven-dried samples. Loeppert and Suarez (1996) recommend the successive use of three extracts: saturated, 1:4 (soil: water) and 1:40 (gypsum is the least soluble of the sulphated minerals found in significant quantities in soils). The calcium ion is titrated by atomic absorption spectrometry (AAS), and the sulphate anion is titrated gravimetrically using the barium method.

Extraction and Titration

Prepare about 100 g of air-dried soil sample crushed to 200 μm and homogenized. Split into three fractions of 25 g:
– Use the first fraction to prepare the saturated extract (cf. Chap. 18);
– Extract the second 25 g fraction with 100 mL of deionized water;
– Extract the third fraction with 1 L of deionized water.
    Shake the two last soil/water suspensions overnight and then filter. Titrate calcium with AAS at 422.7 nm. Sulphate is titrated by weighing the barium sulphate precipitate obtained with barium chloride.

Calculations

The molar concentration of gypsum is considered to be that of calcium ions and sulphate ions. Excess calcium content may be due to the release of calcium from exchange complexes, so it is better to use the concentration of sulphate. If Vs and $V1$ (mL) are the respective water volumes of the saturated and diluted extracts, and $T_{S\text{-}SO4}$ and $T_{1\text{-}SO4}$ are the corresponding sulphate concentrations of the extracts in mmol mL^{-1}, the extracted gypsum is expressed in mmoles by:

$$n_{gypsum} = T_{1\text{-}SO4} \, V1 - T_{S\text{-}SO4} \, Vs$$
and the soil concentration is expressed in g kg^{-1} by:
$$C_{gypsum} = 0.172 \times n_{gypsum} \times 1,000/25 = 6.88 n_{gypsum}$$

Remarks

If the soil is heated to 105°C the night before crushing, gypsum is transformed into bassanite (Rivera et al. 1982) which is more soluble and more rapidly dissolved than gypsum, resulting in a more complete dissolution reaction.

Slightly soluble sulphates (alkaline earth sulphates) and lead, chromium, iron, mercury and bismuth sulphates do not cause significant interference. These elements can, however, be titrated in the extraction solution by AAS if necessary.

30.3.4 Gypsum Determination by Acetone Precipitation

Principle

A test of the presence of gypsum (cf. "Acetone Test") can be used for quantitative determination (Buurman et al. 1996). Soil gypsum is dissolved in a water extract at varying degrees of dilution depending on the gypsum content of the sample. The gypsum precipitate is separated and then dissolved again in water. The calcium in the final solution is titrated by AAS.

Reagents

– Control sample of pure gypsum, $CaSO_4,2H_2O$.
– 37% Hydrochloric acid, HCl.
– *Barium chloride solution.* Add 60 g of $BaCl_2,H_2O$ in 25 mL of water.
– Acetone, CH_3COCH_3.
– *2% lanthanum oxide solution, La_2O_3.* Mix 100 mL of 5% lanthanum solution, 50 mL of $1 mol (HCl) L^{-1}$ hydrochloric acid solution, and complete to 250 mL with deionized water.
– *Calibration range.* Put exactly 5 mL of a $1,000 mg (Ca) L^{-1}$ standard commercial solution in a 100 mL volumetric flask, complete to 100 mL with deionized water giving a $50 mg (Ca) L^{-1}$ stock solution; put successively 0 (blank assay), 5, 10, 20 mL of stock solution in 50 mL volumetric flasks; add 10 mL of the 5% lanthanum solution and bring to 50 mL to give the calibration range $0, 5, 10, 20 mg (Ca) L^{-1}$.

Procedure

- Weigh 10 g of soil sample (200 μm particle size) in a 250 mL flask. Add 100 mL of deionized water and shake overnight.
- Put 35 mL of the suspension in a 50 mL centrifugation tube made of transparent glass and centrifuge for 15 min at 3,500g (solution A).
- *To check the presence of calcium sulphate.* Take 3 mL of supernatant and add ten drops of 1 mol (HCl) L^{-1} solution and 2 mL of $BaCl_2$ solution. If the solution remains clear, the soil does not contains gypsum, if a precipitate is formed, continue analysis.
- Take 20 mL of the supernatant solution A. Add 20 mL of acetone, homogenize and wait 10 min. Centrifuge for 10 min at 2,500g and discard the supernatant.
- Dry the centrifugation tube in a ventilated drying oven at 50°C. Let cool, and then add 40 mL of deionized water to solubilize the precipitate. Take 5 mL, add 5 mL of the 2% lanthanum solution and homogenize.
- Analyse calcium by AAS at 422.7 nm after diluting with 1% lanthanum solution if necessary.

Calculations

If C and B are the calcium concentrations of the extract and blank respectively, V the volume of water used for extraction (100 mL), D the dilution factor ($D = 4$ in most cases: 20 mL aliquot of aqueous extract in 40 mL of water, 5 mL of sample specimen mixed with 5 mL of lanthanum solution), f the moisture corrective factor and P the soil sample weight, gypsum (G) is expressed in mg g^{-1} (soil) by:

$$G = \frac{(C-B)\,V\,D\,f}{1,000\,P}\,\frac{M_{CaSO_4 \cdot 2H_2O}}{M_{Ca}} \cong 0.172\,(C-B)\,f.$$

Remark

If the gypsum content of the soil is higher than 2%, a more diluted soil:water ratio should be used for extraction.

30.4. Sulphur and Gypsum Requirement of Soil

30.4.1 Introduction

A clear distinction must be made between (1) methods intended to identify requirements and deficiencies in S compounds which is an essential element for plant growth and (2) the gypsum requirements intended to amend saline soils and to allow them to be cultivated.

S plays a very important role in soil fertility. Its deficiency results in serious plant growth disorders like dwarfism, leaf symptoms, reduction in photosynthetic activity and severe disturbances in fructification.

In wet or semi-wet areas, most S is in organic forms. The multiple organic components and their relationships with plant nutrition are still not well understood. The biochemical synthesis of some essential living components like certain proteolysis enzymes, amino acids and proteins, hormones or glycosides can only be accomplished when S is present in the medium.

A high total S soil content does not provide information about the state of each S form and does not always mean there is sufficient S for plant nutrition. Total S contents can be low, e.g. about 0.05% in peat soils and arid soils.

Simple ratios between C, N and S contents can be calculated as characteristics of links of these three elements in the biogeochemical cycle. The C:N ratio (cf. introduction in Chap. 10) is very widely used in soil science. In the same way, the C:S and N:S ratios are useful data. A low N:S ratio indicates a high level of non-proteinic S. Soluble sulphates are considered to be the most representative of the capacity of the soil to satisfy plant nutritional requirements. But the aptitude of soils to generate this form depends on many factors like (1) the nature and properties of the soil matrix (e.g. pH, CEC, clay content), (2) plant compounds and S content of plant residues, (3) the climatic constraints (especially temperature and moisture) that control microbial activity and (4) changes in aerobic or anaerobic conditions.

Sulphur is subjected to an annual cycle which, in contrasted climates, includes strong oscillations, for example little activity below 10°C and serious leaching in rainy periods.

30.4.2 Plant Sulphur Requirement

Soil preparation should not significantly modify the distribution of S forms. But simple air drying can result in an increase in the rate of available sulphate.

Furthermore, variations in S depend on spatial distribution (vertically in a soil profile or horizontally in the surface soil of agricultural land) and time distribution (sampling season, storage and length of exposure to the air). So the interpretation of the results is often difficult.

Microbiological Techniques

These approaches simulate microbiological and biochemical processes (of the Neubauer type) resembling those in the soil in natural conditions. Constant incubation temperatures are generally used to optimize microbial activity depending on the particular mediums and climatic areas.

The soluble sulphate produced is measured after a given incubation time. Estimation of S requirement for a given crop should be linked (1) to observed yields which represent the global response and (2) if possible to plant analysis (leaf diagnosis) which enable deficiencies to be corrected.

Microbiological techniques require care in the choice of:
– Representative soil and plant samples.
– Dates of sampling allowing evaluation of plant requirements at different stages of the vegetative cycle (seeding, root development and plant growth, flowering and fruit production), and of microbial activity (depending on moisture and temperature) linked to S mineralization or immobilization.

Other plant nutriments, particularly nitrogen, should also be taken into account. These analyses enable scales of correlation to be established with simple, rapid and reproducible methods of extraction using chemical reagents.

Chemical Extraction

To solubilize the different forms of S, the extracting reagents need to be selective, but in practice, extracting reagents are rarely selective; depending on the reagent used, variable quantities of adsorbed SO_4^{2-}-S or hydrolyzed organic S can be solubilized. Insoluble sulphates (like barium sulphate or mixed aluminium and iron sulphate) are not titrated. Elementary sulphur has to be displaced.

The simplest test uses water extraction, but often results in soil dispersion.

Extraction in diluted saline reagents (like 0.01 mol $(CaCl_2)$ L^{-1}, $MgCl_2$, 0.15% LiCl) limits dispersion but extracts some adsorbed S. Furthermore, lithium acts as an inhibitor of microbial activity.

Extraction in buffered medium (0.25 mol L^{-1} acetic acid + 0.5 mol L^{-1} ammonium acetate) limits the hydrolysis of organic S compounds.

Extraction with the alkaline Olsen reagent (0.5 mol $(NaHCO_3)$ L^{-1} at pH 8.5) is better suited for soils with a pH > 7 but sodium hydrogen carbonate can solubilize a little organic S and block the pores of the filter making separation of the solid and liquid phase difficult.

In extraction with phosphate solutions (0.01 M KH_2PO_4 or $Ca(H_2PO_4)_2$) the phosphate anion displaces the sulphate anion from the adsorption sites thereby increasing negative surface charges. Some labile S that is available in the short term can be extracted with phosphoric salts thanks to the eluting power of P anions. In decreasing order of eluting power, anions are classified as follows:

hydroxyls > phosphates > sulphates = acetates > nitrates = chlorides

Titration is performed after extraction using the methods described in previous sections: colorimetry (Sects. 30.2.7 and 30.2.8), turbidimetry ("Titration" under Sect. 30.2.21) or AAS (Sect. 30.2.13).

Remark

Soils like andosols with high rates of compounds with short range organization (e.g. allophane) can strongly fix SO_4^{2-}-S by absorption.

30.4.3 Gypsum Requirement

Introduction

Sodic soils (sodisols) whose structure is degraded by an excess of exchangeable sodium (Na/T > 15%) can be restored by gypsum amendments (or directly by sulphuric acid in the case of calcareous soils). Under rainfall or irrigation water, sodium fixed on the exchange complex (cf. Chap. 22) is progressively replaced by the calcium of gypsum and the soil structure and hydrodynamic properties are progressively improved. The sodium sulphate that results is eliminated from the soil profile by leaching:

$$Na_2CO_3 + CaSO_4 \Leftrightarrow CaCO_3 + Na_2SO_4$$
$$2\ Clay\text{-}Na^+ + CaSO_4 \rightarrow (Clay)_2\text{-}Ca^{2+} + Na_2SO_4 \text{ (drain water)}$$

Equipment

– Lab glassware
– Mechanical shaker
– Laboratory balance
– Atomic absorption spectrometer

Reagents

– Calcium sulphate, $CaSO_4,2H_2O$ (gypsum).
– *Saturated solution.* 5 g of $CaSO_4,2H_2O$ in 1 L of deionized water, stir for 1 h, filter on blue analytical filter and measure the exact calcium concentration (mmol ($\frac{1}{2}Ca^{2+}$) L^{-1}) by AAS.

Procedure

– Weigh 5 g of air-dried soil in a 250 mL Pyrex flask.
– Using a precise dispenser of volumic fractions add exactly 100 mL of saturated $CaSO_4$ solution. Shake for 30 min on a rotary shaker.
– Filter on blue analytical filter (without washing).
– Titrate calcium by AAS on a clear aliquot fraction of the filtrate.

Calculation

Gypsum requirement (B_g) in mmol ($\frac{1}{2}Ca^{2+}$) kg^{-1} (soil):

$$B_g = (A - B) \frac{100}{5} \frac{1,000}{1,000} = 20(A - B)$$

A is the concentration of the initial solution and B is the concentration of the filtrate in mmol ($\frac{1}{2}Ca^{2+}$) L^{-1}.
These results can be expressed in tons (gypsum) ha^{-1} as a function of the depth of soil to be transformed. For example, for a depth of 10 cm (1,500 tons (soil) ha^{-1} for soil bulk density $\approx$ 1.5), the gypsum requirement in mol ($\frac{1}{2}Ca^{2+}$) ha^{-1} is:

$$D_g = 1,500 \, B_g$$

i.e. in tons (gypsum) ha^{-1}:

$$P_g = 0.129 B_g$$

Remarks

In practice, the solid-solution contacts are lower since the sodium exchange by calcium in the field is not the same as in the laboratory. The amount of sodium actually exchanged is consequently lower than the amount calculated in the laboratory and the calculated amount of gypsum amendment should be increased by about 25%.

For example, to exchange 10 mmol (Na+) kg^{-1} (soil), it is necessary to add 1,300 kg (gypsum) ha^{-1}. Generally the quantities required to improve saline soils are in the range of 5–10 tons (gypsum) ha^{-1}.

References

Artiola FF and Ali AMS (1990) Determination of total sulphur in soil and plant samples using sodium bicarbonate/silveroxide, dry ashing and ion chromatography. *Commun. Soil Sci. Plant Anal.*, 21, 941–949

Aswa HA and Tabatabai MA (1993) Comparison of some methods for determination of sulfate in soils. *Commun. Soil Sci. Plant Anal.*, 24, 1817–1832

Begheijn L and Van Schuylenborgh J (1971) *Methods for the analysis of soils used in the laboratory of soil genesis of the Department of Regional Science*, Wageningen

Bremner JM and Tabatabai MA (1971) Use of automated combustion techniques for total carbon, total nitrogen and total sulfur in soils. In *Instrumental Methods for Analysis of Soils and Plant Tissue,* Walsh L.M. ed., SSSA, 1–15

Buurman P, Van Lagen B and Velthorst EJ (1996) *Manual for Soil and Water analysis.*, Backhuys, Leiden, The Netherlands, 314 p

Chamayou H and Legros JP (1989) *Les bases physiques et minéralogiques de la Science du Sol.*, Presses Universitaires de France, 485–486

Charlot G and Bezier D (1955) *Analyse quantitative minérale*, Masson, Paris.

Colovos G, Panesar MR and Parry EP (1976) Lime arizing the calibration curve in determination of sulfate by the methylthymol blue method. *Anal. Chem.,* 48, 1693–1696

Commission de pédologie et de cartographie des sols (CPCS), (1967) *Classification des sols.*, Lab. Geol. Pedol., Ecole Nat. Sup. Agron., Grignon, France, 87 p

David MB, Mitchell MJ, Aldcorn D and Harrison RB (1989) Analysis of sulfur in soil, plant and sediment materials. Sample handling and use of an automated analyser. *Soil Biol. Biochem.*, 21, 119–123

FAO, (1968) *Definition of Soil Units for the Soil Map or the World*, no. 33

Freney JR, Melville GE and Williams CH (1970) The determination of carbon bounded sulphur in soils. *Soil Sci.*, 109, 310–318

Génin JMR, Refait P, Bourrié G, Abdelmoula M and Trolard F (2001) Structure and stability of Fe (II) – Fe (III) green rust "fougerite" mineral and its potential for reducing pollutants in soil solutions. *Appl. Geochem.*, 16, 559–570

Gerzabek MH and Schaffer K (1986) Determination of total sulphur in soil. A comparison of methods. *Bodenkultur*, 37, 1–6

Gony J and Parent Ch (1966) Etude géochimique d'une tranche de sédiments fins actuels. *Bull. BRGM*, 5, 28–31

Johnson CM and Nishita H (1952) Microestimation of sulfur in plant materials, soils and irrigation waters. *Anal. Chem.*, 24, 736–742

Karmarkar SV and Tabatabai MA (1992) Eluent composition effect on ion chromatographic determination of oxyanions in solution equilibrated with soils. *Chromatographia*, 34, 643–648

Kowalenko CG and Lowe LE (1972) Observations on the bismuth sulphide colorimetric procedure for sulphate analysis in soil. *Commun. Soil Plant Anal.*, 3, 79–86

Kowalenko CG (1985) A modified apparatus for quick and versatile sulphate sulphur analysis using hydroiodic acid reduction. *Commun. Soil Sci. Plant Anal.*, 16, 289–300

Le Brusq JY, Loyer JY, Mouguenot B and Carn M (1987) Nouvelles paragenèses à sulfates d'aluminium, de fer et de magnésium, et leur distribution dans les sols sulfatés acides du Sénégal. *Sc. du Sol.*, 25, 173–184

Loeppert RH and Suarez DL (1996) Carbonate and Gypsum. In *Methods of Soils Analysis. Part 3, Chemical Methods*, Sparks DL et al. ed., SSSA book series no. 5, 437–474

Marius C (1980) *Les mangroves du Sénégal. Ecologie, pédologie et utilisation.*, IRD (ex. Orstom) éd., Paris

Marius C, Paycheng C and Lopez J (1976) *La détermination du soufre et de ses composés au laboratoire Orstom de Dakar*, Sénégal. Documentation IRD, Dakar, Paris, 16 p

McSwain MR, Watrous RJ and Douglas, JE (1974) Improved methyl thymol blue procedure for automated sulfate determinations. *Anal. Chem.*, 46, 1329–1331

Montoroi JP (1994) *Dynamique de l'eau et géochimie des sels d'un bassin versant aménagé de Basse-Casamance*, Sénégal. Th. Univ. Nancy I, 349 p

Montoroi JP, Grunberger O and Nasri S (2002) Groundwater geochemistry of a small reservoir catchment in central Tunisia. *Appl. Geochem.*, 17, 1047–1060

Pansu M, Gautheyrou J and Loyer JY (2001) *Soil Analysis – Sampling, Instrumentation and Quality control.*, Balkema, Lisse, Abington, Exton, Tokyo, 489 p

Perrott KW, Kerr BE, Kear MJ and Sutton MM (1991) Determination of total sulphur in soil using inductively coupled plasma atomic emission spectrometry. *Commun. Soil Sci. Plant Anal.*, 22, 1477–1487

Pouget M (1995) Gypsosols. In *Référentiel Pédologique*, INRA, France, 161–165

Richards LA (1954) *Diagnosis and Improvement of Saline and Alkali Soils.*, USDA Handbooks, 60, US Gov. Print Office, 160 p

Rivera ED, Hallmark CT, West LT and Drees LR (1982) A technique for rapid removal of gypsum from soil samples. *Soil Sci. Soc. Am. J.*, 46, 1338–1340

Sonne K and Dasgupta PK (1991) Simultaneous photometric flow injection determination of sulfide, polysulfide, sulfite, thiosulfate and sulfate. *Anal. Chem.*, 63, 427–432

Tabatabai MA and Basta NT (1991) Ion chromatography. *In Soil Analysis*, Smith KA ed., Dekker, New York, 229–259

Tabatabai MA and Bremner JM (1970a) An alkaline oxidation method for determination of total sulfur in soils. *Soil Sci. Soc. Am. Proc.*, 34, 62–65

Tabatabai MA and Bremner JM (1970b) Comparison of some methods for determination of total sulfur in soils. *Soil Sci. Soc. Am. Proc.*, 34, 417–420

Tabatabai MA and Dick WA (1979) Ion chromatographic analysis of sulfate and nitrate in soils. In *Ion Chromatographic Analysis of Environmental Pollutants*, Mulik JD and Sawickie ed., Ann. Arbor Sci. Publ., 2, 361–370

Tabatabai MA and Frankenberger WT Jr (1996) Liquid chromatography. In *Methods of Soil Analysis, Part III Chemical Methods*, Sparks DL et al., SSSA Book, 5, 225–245

Tabatabai MA (1996) Sulfur. In *Methods of Soil Analysis, Part 3, Chemical Methods*, Bigham JM and Bartels JM ed., ASA-SSSA Book, Serie no. 5, Madison, WI Etats-Unis, 921–960

Tabatabai MA, Basta NT and Pirela HJ (1988) Determination of total sulphur in soils and plant materials by ion chromatography. *Commun. Soil Sci. Plant Anal.*, 19, 1701–1714

USDA, (1975) *Soil Taxonomy. A Basic System of Soil Classification for Making and Interpreting Soil Surveys.*, USDA, Agriculture Handbook no. 436, 754

van Breemen N and Harmsen K (1975) Translocation of iron in acid sulfate soils. I – Soil morphology and the chemistry and microbiology of iron in a chronosequence of acid sulfate soils. *Soil Sci. Soc. Am. Proc.*, 39, 1140–1148

Vieillefon J (1974) *Les sols de mangroves et de tannes de Basse Casamance, Sénégal.*, IRD (ex. Orstom) ed. Paris

Chronobibliography

Johnson CM and Ulrich A (1959) *Analytical Methods for Use in Plant Analysis.*, California Agric. Exp. Str. Bull., 766

Gustafsson L (1960) Determination of ultra micro amounts of sulphate as methylene blue. 1ère partie : Réaction. *Talanta*, 4, 222–235

Gustafsson L (1960) Determination of ultra micro amounts of sulphate as methylene blue. 2ème partie : Réduction. *Talanta*, 4, 236–243

Kilmer VJ and Nearpass DC (1960) The determination of available sulfur in soils. *Soil Sci. Soc. Proc.*, 337–339

Sherman GD, Schultz F and Alway FJ (1962) Dolomite in soils of the red rivervalley, Minnesota. *Soil Sci.*, 94, 304–313

Steinbergs A, Iismaa O, Freney JR and Barrow NJ (1962) Determination of total sulphur in soil and plant material. *Anal. Chim. Acta.*, 27, 158–164

Bardsley CE and Lancaster JO (1965) Sulfur. In *Methods of Soil Analysis.*, American Society of Agronomy, 1102–1116

Dean GA (1966) A simple colorimetric finish for the Johnson–Nishita micro-distillation of sulphur. *Analyst*, 91, 530–532

Beaton JD, Burns GR and Platou J (1968) *Determination of Sulphur in Soils and Plant Material.*, Sulphur Institute (Washington), Technical Bulletin no. 14

Khan SU and Webster GR (1968) Determination of gypsum in solonetz soils by an XR technique. *Analyst*, 93, 400–402

Lowe LE (1969) Sulfur fraction of selected alberta profiles of the gleysolic order. *Can. J. Soil Sci.*, 49, 375–381

Tabatabai M and Bremner JM (1970) An alkaline oxydation method for determination of total sulphur in soils. *Soil Sci. Soc. Am. Proc.*, 34, 62–65

Wakayama FJ (1971) Calcium complexing and the enhanced solubility of gypsum in concentrated sodium-salt solutions. *Soil Sci. Am. Proc.*, 35, 881–883

Hesse PR (1972) *A Textbook of Soil Chemical Analysis.*, Chemical Publishing Co., 520 p

Darmody RG, Fanning DJ, Drummond WJ Jr and Foss J. (1977) Determination of total sulfur in tidal marsh soils by X-Ray spectroscopy. *Soil Sci. Soc. Am. J.*, 41, 761–765

Nor YM and Tabatabai MA (1977) Oxidation of elemental sulfur in soils. *Soil Sci. Soc. Am. J.*, 41, 736–741

Begheijn LTh, Van Breemen N and Velthorst EJ (1978) Analysis of sulphur compounds in acid sulphate soils and other recent marine soil. *Commun. Soil Sci. Plant Anal.*, 9, 873–882

Nelson RE, Klameth LC and Nettleton WD (1978) Determining soil gypsum content and expressing properties of gypsiferous soils. *Soil Sci. Soc. Am. J.*, 42, 659–661

Cronan CS (1979) Determination of sulfate in organically colored water samples. *Anal. Chem.*, 51, 1333–1335

Siemer DD (1980) Reduction-distillation method for sulfate determination. *Anal. Chem.*, 52, 1271–1274

Rivera ED, Hallmark CT, West LT, Drees LR (1982) A technique for rapide removal of gypsum from soil samples. *Soil Sci. Soc. Am. J.*, 46, 1338–1340

Freney JR, Jacq VA and Baldensberger JF (1982) The significance of the biological sulfur cycle in rice production. *In Microbiology of Tropical Soils and Plant Productivity,* Dommergues YR and Diem AG ed. Martinus Wijhoff, 10, 271–317

Adams TMCM and Lane PW (1984) A comparison of four methods of analysing aqueous soil extracts for sulphate. *J. Sci. Food Agric.*, 35, 740–744

Lebel A and Teh Fu Yen, (1984) Ion chromatography for determination of metabolic pattern of sulfate-reducing bacteria. *Anal. Chem.*, 56, 807–808

Wainwright M (1984) Sulfur oxidation in soils. In *Advances in Agronomy*, Academic, New York, 37, 350–396

Lee R, Blakemore LC, Daly BK, Gibson EJ, Speirt W and Orchard VA (1985) Sulphur supply to ryegrass during a pot trial and correlations with soil biological activity: The influence of two different methods of determining the adsorbed sulphate status of soils. *Commun. Soil Sci. Plant Anal.*, 16, 97–117

Kowalenko CG (1985) A modified apparatus for quick and versatile sulphate sulphur analysis hydroiodic acid reduction. *Commun. Soil Sci. Plant Anal.*, 16, 284–300

Scott NM (1985) Sulphur in soils and plants. In *Soil Organic Matter and Biological Activity,* Vaughan D and Malcolm RE ed., Martinus Njhoff/Junk, 379–401

Gimeno Adelantado JV and Bosch Reig F (1986) Mineralization of some organic sulphur compounds by fusion with molteno alkali. *Talanta*, 33, 757–759

Keller LP, Mc Carthy GF and Richardson JL (1986) Mineralogy and stability of soil evaporites in North-Dakota. *Soil Sci. Soc. Am. J.*, 50, 1069–1071

Krupa SV and Tabatabai MA (1986) Measurement of sulfur in the atmosphere and in natural waters. In *Sulfur in Agriculture*, Tabatabai MA ed. ASA, CSSA, Agron. Monogr. 27, 491–548

Bansal KN and Npal AR (1987) Evaluation of a soil test method and plant analysis for determining the sulphur status of alluvial soil. *Plant and Soil*, 98, 331–336

Vaugh CE, Junes MB and Center DM (1987) Sulfur tests on Northern California sub-clones annual grass pasture surface soils. *Soil Sci.*, 143, 184–191

Bolan NS, Syers JK, Tillman RW and Scotter DR (1988) Effect of liming and phosphate additions on sulphate leaching in soils. *J. Soils Sci.*, 39, 493–504

David MB, Mitchell MJ, Aldcorn D and Harrison RB (1989) Analysis of sulfur in soil, plant and sediment materials: sample handling and use of an automated analyser. *Biol. Biochem.*, 21, 119–123

Sharp GS, Hoque S, Killham K, Sinclair AH and Chapman ST (1989) Comparison of methods to evaluate the sulphur status of soils. *Commun. Soil Sci. Plant Anal.*, 20, 1821–1832

Hue NV, Fox RL and Wolt JD (1990) Sulfur status of volcanic ash-derived soils in Hawaï. *Commun. Soil Sci. Plant Anal.*, 21, 299–310

Hauge S and Maroy K (1991) Detection of sulphate by flamme emission spectrometry. *Anal. Chim. Acta.*, 243, 227–237

Morante C (1991) Determination of plant sulphur and sulphate-sulphur by flow-injection analysis using a two-live manifold. *Anal. Chim. Acta.*, 249, 479–488

Singh RP, Pambid ER and Abbas NM (1991) Determination of sulfate in deen sub surface waters by suppressed ion chromatography. *Anal. Chem.*, 63, 1897–1901

Tabatabai MA and Bremner JM (1991) Automated instruments for determination of total carbon nitrogen and sulfur in soils by combustion technique. In *Soil Analysis*, Smith K.A. ed., Dekker, New York, 261–285

Michel JP and Fairbridge RW (1992) *Dictionnary of Earth-Sciences.*, Wiley, New York, 300 p

Blanc GJ, Lefroy RDB, Chinoim N, Anderson GC and Barrow NJ (1993) Sulfur soil testing. *Plant Soil,* 383–386

Boruah RK and Ghosh P (1993) Quantitative estimation of available sulphur in tea soils *Two and a Bud*, 40, 26–30

Jansson H (1994) Sulphur status of soils – a global study *Norwegian J. Agric. Sci.*, SN 15, 27–30

Tan Z, McLaren RG and Cameron KC (1994) Forms of sulfur extracted from soils after different methods of sample preparation. *Aust. J. Soil Res.*, 32, 823–834

Trivedi BS, Gami RC and Patel KG (1994) Standardization of method for determining available sulphur and its critical limit for lowland paddy. *Gujarat Agric. Univ. Res. J.*, 20, 35–41.

Zhao F and McGrath SP (1994) Extractable sulphate and organic sulphur in soils and their availability to plants. *Plant Soil*, 164, 243–250

Santoso D, Lefroy RDB and Blair GJ (1995) A comparison of sulfur extractants of wealthered acid soils. *Aust. J. Soil Res.*, 33, 125–133

Shaw Xiao-Quan and Chen Bin (1995) Determination of carbon-bonded sulfur in soils by hydroiodic acid reduction and hydrogen penoxide oxidation. *Fresenius J. Anal. Chem.*, 351, 762–767

Simo R and Grimalt JO (1996) Determination of volatile sulphur species in soil samples of interest for prospecting for metal sulphide deposits. *J. Chromatog.*, A, 726, 161–166

Zhao FJ, Loke SY, Crosland AR and McGrath SP (1996) Method to determine elemental sulphur in soils applied to measure sulphur oxidation. *Soil Biol. Biochem.*, 28, 1083–1087

Prochnow LI, Boaretto AE and Vitti GC (1997) Ion-exchange resin to evaluate sulphur availability in soils. Utilizacao da resina trocadora de ions para avaliacao do enxofre disponivel do solo. *Revista Brasileira de Ciencia do Solo*, 21, 335–339

Gowrisankar D and Shukla LM (1999) Evaluation of extractants for predicting availability of sulphur to mustard in Inceptisols. *Communi. Soil Sci. Plant Anal.*, 30, 19–20, 2643–2654; 33 ref

Matula J (1999) Use of multinutrient soil tests for sulphur determination. *Commun. Soil Sci. and Plant Anal.*, 30, 1733–1746

Zbiral J (1999) Comparison of some extraction methods for determination of sulphur in soils of the Czech Republic. Porovnani vybranych extrakcnich postupu pro stanoveni siry v pudach cr. *Rostlinna Vyroba*, 45, 439–444

Prietzel J and Hirsch C (2000) Ammonium fluoride extraction for determining inorganic sulphur in acid forest soils. *Eur. J. Soil Sci.*, 51, 323-333

Crosland AR, Zhao FJ and McGrath SP (2001) Inter-laboratory comparison of sulphur and nitrogen analysis in plants and soils. *Commun. Soil Sci. Plant Anal.*, 32, 685–695

Analysis of Extractable and Total Elements

31.1 Elements of Soils

31.1.1 Major Elements

Soils contain the chemical elements of the lithosphere, i.e. stable elements of the periodic table, with respect to geochemical distribution and soil genesis processes. This chapter deals with the analysis of solid phases only. Oxygen is the most abundant element in soils and rocks, but it is generally not titrated; instead its approximate content is deduced from the rates of other major elements during conversions of elements to oxide concentrations (Table 31.1). The analysis of carbon, which is the main chemical element in organic matters and carbonate minerals is dealt with in Part 2 and in Chap. 17, respectively. Hydrogen, another important element in rocks, water and organic matter is usually analysed in its organic form (plus constitutive water) when an automated CHN analyser is available (cf. Chap. 10), during thermal analysis (cf. Chap. 7), or in proton exchange studies (cf. Chaps. 15 and 23). Nitrogen is another important element in the biosphere and in the atmosphere; nitrogen analysis is discussed in Chaps. 10 (total N), 14 (organic N) and 28 (inorganic N).

Silicated minerals originating from igneous rocks contain mostly oxygen and major elements of the third and fourth period of the periodic table. These metals can produce basic oxides, the most basic of which originate from alkaline metals, sodium and potassium, then from alkaline earth metals: calcium and potassium, and finally from transition metals (iron, titanium and manganese) and aluminium. Silicated minerals also include non-metals (especially silicon and phosphorus) that produce acid oxides. Two types of magmas are classified on the basis of their silica content. One is described as acid and granitic with a high silica content (>60%) and relatively high sodium and potassium contents. The other is basic and basaltic with a silica content lower than 50% and relatively high iron, magnesium and calcium contents. For a more precise classification, see Table 31.1.

Table 31.1. Mean elemental composition of few igneous rocks (from Turekian and Wedepohl 1961)

El.	stable oxide	k	percentage concentration							
			Ultra-basic rocks $SiO_2 <45\%$		Basaltic rocks $45 < SiO_2 <52\%$		Granitic rocks $52 < SiO_2 <68\%$		Acid rocks $SiO_2 > 66\%$	
			El.	Ox.	El.	Ox.	El.	Ox.	El.	Ox.
Si	SiO_2	2.139	20.5	43.9	23.0	49.2	31.4	67.2	34.7	74.3
Al	Al_2O_3	1.889	2.0	3.8	7.8	14.7	8.2	15.5	7.2	13.6
Fe	Fe_2O_3[a]	1.430	9.4	13.4	8.6	12.3	3.0	4.3	1.4	2.0
Ca	CaO	1.399	2.5	3.5	7.6	10.6	2.5	3.5	0.5	0.7
Mg	MgO	1.658	20.4	33.8	4.6	7.6	0.9	1.5	0.2	0.3
Na	Na_2O	1.348	0.4	0.5	2.0	2.7	2.8	3.8	2.6	3.5
K	K_2O	1.205	0.004	0.005	0.8	1.0	2.5	3.0	4.2	5.1
Ti	TiO_2	1.668	0.030	0.050	1.4	2.3	0.34	0.6	0.12	0.2
Mn	MnO	1.291	0.160	0.207	0.15	0.2	0.054	0.1	0.04	0.1
P	P_2O_5	2.291	0.022	0.050	0.11	0.3	0.092	0.2	0.06	0.1
	total%			99.2		101.0		99.6		99.9
O	%			43.8		44.9		47.8		48.9

El. element, Ox. stable oxide, k: multiplicative coefficient = oxide mw-to-element mw ratio
[a] In reducing medium, replace by FeO (k = 1.286)

The composition of the soil (Greenland and Hayes 1983) varies depending on its genesis under different weathering processes and also on human activities. But the major elements of igneous rocks are often found in variable proportions in soils. As shown in Table 31.1, the first way to check the accuracy of the analysis consists in adding the calculated percent of the more stable oxides of the major elements. Taking moisture and organic matter into account, and in some cases other elements present in large quantities, the total should be near 100%.

31.1.2 Trace Elements and Pollutants

As is true for the major elements, the concentrations of trace elements in soils (Baize 1997) are often linked to the concentrations of the subjacent parent rock, though with marked irregularities. The subjacent rock does not always have the most influence, soil materials may also originate from allochton heterogeneous parent rocks or pollution.

Table 31.2 summarizes the range of concentrations reported by Aubert and Pinta (1971) for a few trace elements in soils. The contents of some elements such as chromium, vanadium or zinc, are generally well correlated with parent rock content. Other elements like boron, cobalt or molybdenum depend on the soil type and genesis. Elements like iodine or lead are generally found in much higher concentrations in soils than in subjacent rocks (particularly in sedimentary contributions of marine origin as is the case for iodine). Organic soils can be very rich in certain elements like selenium.

In the case of organic pollution, the pollutant molecules were usually not originally present in the soil and can consequently be identified and titrated (cf. Chap. 13) perhaps with difficulty, but at least with no doubt about their origin. The same is not true for inorganic elements: it is not always easy to distinguish geochemical and anthropogenic origins (Bourrelier and Berthelin 1998).

Depending on his or her knowledge of the soil type and parent rock, the trained geochemist will note concentrations which appear to be too high. This is sometimes obvious for elements like copper whose contents are generally well correlated with soil type and parent rock, but which is found in excess in most vineyard soils.

However, in most cases identifying the origin is more difficult, and the content at the suspected source of pollution and the contents of neighbouring samples of the same type of soil and parent rock have to be statistically compared. The contents are also linked to exchange properties of elements with the soil exchange complex (cf. Chap. 19).

Table 31.2. Concentration of a few trace elements in soil (From Aubert and Pinta 1971), total elements (mg kg^{-1}) and easily extractable elements (% of total elements)

element	minimal concentration (mg kg^{-1})	maximal concentration (mg kg^{-1})	mean concentration (mg kg^{-1})	mean easily extractable fraction (% of total concentration)	
B	1–2 (podzols Belarus)	250–270 (eutrophic peat, Israel)	20–50	0.1–10 or more (sodic soils)	(1)
Cr	traces	3,000–4,000	100–300	0.01–0.4 0.1–1	(2) (3)
Co	0.05 (podzols Russia)	300 (Vertisols Central Aafrica)	10–15	0.5–50	(2)
Cu	traces	200–250 (Vertisols India)	15–40	0.3–21 0.05–5 7–17 18–60	(3) (2) (4) (5)
I	0.1 (hydromorphic, amour daria)	25 (humic gley – Latvia)	1–5		
Mo	traces	24 (forest brown soil, Russia)	1–2	2–20	(3, 2, 6)
Ni	traces	>5,000 (indurate horizons, New Caledonia)		2 7–20	(2) (5)
Pb	traces	1,200 (podzols, Canada)	15–25	1–30	(2)
Se	0.1	1,000 (peat soil, Ireland)	1–7		
V	traces	400	100–200	0.4–0.6	(2)
Zn	traces	900	50–100	0.2–20	(3)
Li	5	200			
Rb	10	500			
Ba	100	3,000	500		
Sr	50	1,000	350		
Ga	2	100	30		

Right column: extracting reagent: (1) hot water, (2) 2.5% CH_3COOH pH 2.5, (3) 1 mol (CH_3COONH_4) L^{-1} at pH 7, (4) EDTA, (5) 1mol (HCl) L^{-1}, (6) buffered oxalic acid–ammonium oxalate solution at pH 3.3 (Grigg's reagent)

31.1.3 Biogenic and Toxic Elements

Some major elements (cf. Sect. 31.1.1) and trace elements (cf. Sect. 31.1.2) are particularly important for life on Earth; in these cases analysis is more often required and the behaviour of these elements in soils must be carefully analysed.

The major elements that make up plant tissues are carbon, oxygen, hydrogen, nitrogen, phosphorous, sulphur, potassium, calcium, magnesium and sometimes sodium in salt-resistant plants or silicon in graminaceae or exceptional accumulation of another element.

Other elements are necessary for plant physiology, mainly copper, iron, manganese, zinc, boron and molybdenum. Though present in cellular tissues at often very low rates (minor or trace elements) from a few mg kg^{-1} to few g kg^{-1}, a deficiency in these elements can inhibit plant growth. Inversely too high availability results in toxicity (Coppenet and Juste 1982, Abo 1984). A good knowledge of the concentration and availability of biogenic and toxic elements is thus required.

In soils, these elements are often found at a trace level (copper, zinc, boron and molybdenum) but they can also be major elements (iron or manganese). Their availability depends not only on their concentration, but also on the physico-chemical equilibrium with the molecular structures of the soil (cf. Mineralogy in Part 1. and Organic materials in Part 2) and is thus linked to soil pH (cf. Chap. 15), redox potential (cf. Chap. 16), the charges of the exchange complex (cf. Chaps. 20 and 21), cation exchange capacity (cf. Chap. 26), and anion exchange capacity (cf. Chap. 27). Other elements like aluminium, which can result in exchange acidity (cf. Chap. 23), may also be toxic for plants in certain environments.

Other elements are also important for living organisms even though they are present at lower trace levels (Aubert and Pinta 1971, Baize 1997). For example, animals need cobalt for the formation of haemoglobin. Bovines and ovines can suffer from anaemia as a result of cobalt deficiency in soils and consequently in forage plants. Iodine is an important element for humans, and plays a role in the composition of thyroid hormone. Its deficiency can cause goitre, which, in the past, was a common disease in regions with iodine deficiency. Molybdenum plays an important role in both plants and animals, for example in the nitrogen cycle, where it facilitates reduction of nitrogen dioxide to nitrogen. Vanadium has a similar function. Selenium can accumulate in plants and become toxic for livestock.

31.1.4 Analysis of Total Elements

Total analysis uses a whole range of chemical and physico-chemical methods (Smith 1991, Tan 1996, He et Xiang 1999, Pansu et al. 2001). These include (i) analyses which require the separation of the elements from the organic and mineral lattices by solubilization, (ii) analyses which can be performed directly on solid mediums.

Analysis by Solubilization

The first methods developed for analysis of natural silicate materials used solubilization. Indeed classical chemical methods of analysis are based on the properties of the elements in solution.

These methods were subsequently extended to atomic spectrographic measurements and are still widely used today because atomic absorption spectrometry (AAS), inductively coupled plasma (ICP) atomic emission spectrometry (ICP-AES) and ICP mass spectrometry (ICP-MS) are performed more easily on liquid mediums than on solid mediums.

Analysis on Solid Medium

For analysis on a solid medium the material is subjected to an appropriate flux of radiation. The aim is to induce transformations in atomic structures at the level of electronic layers or of the atomic nucleus. The measurement of radiation energies during the relaxation processes enables identification and quantification of the elements.

When the energies used are not too high, the corresponding methods are called non-destructive: atoms are brought back to their fundamental state, so the original state of the matter is considered to be unmodified. This is not always the case for transitions occurring at the level of the nucleus, such as neutron activation analysis, or when the matter is subjected to too high thermal energy, as in arc or spark spectrography or ICP emission in solid medium.

Depending on the excitation source and on the analysis of the radiation emitted, many techniques are available to analyse the solid medium.

The most common are X-ray fluorescence using excitation of deep electronic layers in a X-ray flux (cf. Sect. 31.3.2), electronic microprobes which use energy from an electron flux (cf. Chap. 8) and neutron activation analysis in which matter is subjected to a neutron flux (cf. Sect. 31.3.3).

31.1.5 Extractable Elements

Assay of total elements does not always provide sufficient information about the availability for plants of nutritive elements in the soil. Moreover in small laboratories with limited equipment, total analysis of big analytical series can be cumbersome. Reagents are often very aggressive so safety requirements are strict and laboratory equipment is expensive. This is why for many years agronomists have been trying to replace total analysis with simple but sufficiently accurate chemical or biochemical tests to identify thresholds of deficiency and toxicity for plants (Peck and Soltanpour 1990). As the aim of these tests is often to identify fertilizer requirements, they are designed for specific environments and cannot be used in all cropping systems.

The efficiency of the extraction varies with the type of soil. The correlation between the extractability of a given element and the effect of this element on the plant concerned must be known, either in the field or in controlled conditions in the greenhouse. Different degrees of availability can be estimated depending on the extracting power of the reagent used. The elements most commonly studied with respect to their availability are major plant nutriments: inorganic nitrogen (cf. Chap. 28), potentially available nitrogen (cf. Chap. 14), forms of phosphorus (cf. Chap. 29), forms of sulphur (cf. Chap. 30), exchangeable cations (cf. Chap. 22). This chapter deals with complementary procedures for the study of other forms of elements in soils that are available or potentially available.

31.2. Methods Using Solubilization

31.2.1 Total Solubilization Methods

Solubilization methods for ultimate analysis of soils are similar to methods for more general geochemical analyses. Adjustments are sometimes necessary depending on the conditions found in certain soil mediums, for example high organic matter content.

Total analysis requires destruction of both the organic matter structures and of the mineralogical lattice of aluminosilicates. Attacks generally have to be strong, they take a rather long time, and can be dangerous. Thus, the methods to be used should be chosen with care (Kawasaki and Arai 1996). There are three main causes of error in total analysis using solubilization (i) contamination by the reagents and equipment, (ii) incomplete attack of the soil matrix and (iii) interference caused by the attack reagents during measurements.

Contamination can affect the titration of trace elements. Blank assays (with all the reagents and the entire reaction process but no sample) are often needed to be able to subtract the concentration in the blank from the concentration in the sample. During these calculations, the variance of the blank and sample measurements is added. When the concentration in the sample approaches the concentration in the blank, measurement by solubilization becomes impossible, and instead reagents with a higher degree of purity must be used, or analysis must be carried out on directly the solid medium. Ongoing progress in instrumentation and new analytical needs for environmental studies and geosciences results in the identification of new requirements with respect to purity and choice of reagents.

Incomplete attack of the soil matrix is another possible source of error. Certain minerals can be extremely difficult to solubilize completely even if solid residues are no longer visible after the attack. Among the elements that are very difficult to solubilize are chromium, titanium and zirconium. To complete the dissolution of these elements, it is sometime necessary to change the type and proportion of reagents and the attack process (e.g. open or closed vessel, heating on hot plate, microwave heating, etc.).

Several types of *interference* can be caused by reagents depending on the analytical method used. A typical physical interference that can result in serious errors both in atomic absorption spectrometry (AAS) and in flame or plasma emission spectrometry originates from the dissolved solid material from the analytical matrix which can clog the sample input system. One of the main causes of error noted by Burman (1987) in ICP-AES was caused by deposit of solids in the nebulizer, which affected the input flow in the burner. In AAS, reagents can cause several different types of chemical interferences. However, the careful choice of attack reagents can avoid interferences (Jeanroy 1974). In emission spectrometry, possible spectral interference should be taken into account. In ICP-MS, the different polyatomic species that can form between plasma atoms and reagents and possible interference with the titrated element due to their mass should be taken into account.

Solubilization methods can be classified in three groups:
- acid digestion in an open vessel
- acid attack in a closed vessel
- alkaline fusion.

Different acids can be used for digestion of the sample depending on the type of material concerned. The choice of the attack reagent also depends on the technique to be used for subsequent analytical measurements. It is important to examine the properties of the main analytical reagents with respect to their suitability for a given analytical method.

31.2.2 Main Reagents for Complete Dissolution

Hydrochloric Acid

At high temperatures, concentrated hydrochloric acid (36%, 12 mol (HCl) L^{-1}, *d*: 1.18) can attack many silicates, oxides, sulphates and fluoride minerals. It has a weak reducing power and is generally not suitable for the digestion of organic materials, apart from specific uses like protein hydrolysis to separate amino acids (cf. Chap. 14). It has often been used as the final medium in the preparation of solutions for AAS titration because it reduces the impact of some interferences. But it is not suitable for ICP-MS analysis because some polyatomic species like $ArCl^+$, ClO^+ or $ClOH^+$ can cause major interferences in the titration of As, V, Cr, Fe, Ga, Ge, Se, Ti, Zn (Jarvis 1994b). As the boiling point of $HCl-H_2O$ azeotrope is lower than that of azeotrope (HNO_3-H_2O), hydrochloric acid can be eliminated efficiently by successive evaporations with nitric acid.

Nitric Acid

Nitric acid is one of the most frequently used reagents for the preparation of samples. It can liberate trace elements in the nitrate state which are very soluble in a complex matrix. One volume of concentrated HNO_3 (16 mol L^{-1}) mixed with three volumes of concentrated HCl (12 mol L^{-1}) is called "aqua regia", a strong reagent recommended for the solubilization of trace elements in soils (AFNOR standard NF ISO 11,466 1995). Concentrated nitric acid (68%, 16 mol (HNO_3) L^{-1}, *d*: 1.42) is a strong oxidizing reagent that can destroy organic matter in soils with low organic content. However, its oxidizing power is reduced because the boiling point of azeotrope (122°C) limits the temperature of the attack in an open vessel. The complete destruction of the organic matrix often requires reagents with higher oxidizing power like hydrogen peroxide or perchloric acid. To avoid the risk of explosion when dealing with very organic samples, a preliminary attack with nitric acid is recommended before stronger oxidizing reagents are used.

Like hydrochloric acid, nitric acid is a suitable medium for titration solutions for AAS and emission spectrometry despite its weaker corrective effect on some interferences. The nitric medium is especially useful for ICP-MS techniques, as the polyatomic species that can be produced by HNO_3 in the argon plasma at high temperatures are no different from those resulting from the constant presence in plasma of H, N and O elements.

Hydrofluoric Acid

This is the only acid able to dissolve silica-based materials by forming hexafluorosilicate ions which can be transformed into volatile silicium tetrafluoride according to global reactions of the following type:

$$SiO_2 + 6\ HF \rightarrow H_2SiF_6 + 2H_2O$$
$$H_2SiF_6 \rightarrow SiF_4 + 2\ HF$$

Because of the volatility of SiF_4, hydrofluoric acid cannot be used for attacks in open vessels for the quantification of silica. Furthermore, fluorides of other elements like boron, arsenic, antimony and germanium, may also be volatile depending on their degree of oxidation. Attacks are generally performed with mixtures of concentrated hydrofluoric acid (48%, 29 mol (HF) L^{-1}, d: 1.16) and oxidizing acids (like nitric or perchloric acid) which complete dissolution and result in high oxidation states of the elements dissolved in the analytical medium.

If silica does not have to be quantified, eliminating this major element may be an advantage as it reduces the quantity of solids in the analytical solution thereby minimizing often serious error due to clogging of the nebulization systems in emission and absorption spectrometry (Burman 1987). Hydrofluoric acid has a rather high vapour pressure and results in an azeotrope with water with a relatively low boiling point: 112°C. This acid can thus be easily eliminated from the final medium by evaporation.

One disadvantage of hydrofluoric acid is its ability to attack glass and silica even at weak concentrations. This means only plastic containers should be used, preferably PTFE. Furthermore, in plasma emission spectrometry, this acid can attack certain nebulizers and silica ICP-torches and must consequently be completely eliminated from the final mediums. It can be sequestered by adding saturated boric acid, but this has the disadvantage of increasing of the quantity of solids. If titration of silica is not required, silicon and hydrofluoric acid should be eliminated by successive evaporations, though with a risk of losses of other elements.

Safety

Hydrofluoric acid is a highly corrosive and toxic compound and it is extremely dangerous to handle. It can rapidly cause irreversible lesions of the skin and eyes. It is essential that the laboratory be equipped with a fume hood in good working order. Protective clothing is recommended. In the case of contact with the skin, rinse abundantly with water and, if possible, apply a calcium gluconate gel to the skin. In case of contact with the eyes, a doctor or the emergency service of the nearest hospital should be contacted without delay.

Perchloric Acid

Perchloric acid is one of the strongest inorganic acids and is a very strong oxidative reagent. In the concentrated state ($HClO_4$ 72%, $d = 1.67$) and when hot, it can explode in contact with organic material (particularly with fats), but this does not occur when it is used cold or is diluted. Perchloric acid should consequently only be used diluted at least four times in another acid, generally nitric acid. A preliminary attack with nitric acid is also used.

Perchloric acid gives an azeotropic mixture with water at 72% $HClO_4$ with a boiling point of 203°C. Used in combination with hydrofluoric acid, it facilitates the attack of refractory minerals by raising the boiling point. The mixture then has increased power to dissolve minerals and to simultaneously mineralize organic materials. Furthermore, the higher boiling point favours the elimination of HF and SiF_4 during the evaporation stage.

Another advantage of this acid is that it produces soluble salts with the majority of elements, which is not true of all acids, particularly sulphuric acid. One disadvantage of perchloric acid for analysis by ICP-MS is interference in the measurement of small quantities of arsenic and vanadium: $^{40}Ar^{35}Cl^+$ on ^{75}As, $^{35}Cl^{16}O^+$ on ^{51}V (Jarvis 1994b).

Safety Precautions

Perchloric acid is not recommended for the direct attack of very organic samples, particularly if they contain large quantities of fats (certain sewage sludges for example). In this case, a preliminary attack using another technique is required. Oils and greases will not be attacked by the perchloric acid-nitric acid mixture and will explode during evaporation with nitric acid. Many solid pechlorates are explosive.

Safety precautions must be strictly respected when perchloric acid is used. Fume hoods made of inert plastic equipped with a fume cleaning system must be used. The inside surfaces must be cleaned regularly to avoid accumulation of potentially explosive perchlorates. The fume hood should only be used for acid attacks and should in no circumstances contain organic products.

Reagents for Alkaline Fusion

These methods use alkaline reagents able to destroy the silicate lattices at high temperature and to form solid solutions (glasses) during cooling. Dissolution of these solid solutions in diluted acids is then easy. These methods are suitable for attack of geological materials but not of biological materials. Their advantage is that there is usually total dissolution without volatilization enabling quantification of silica, for example. Their main disadvantage is the introduction of a large quantity of dissolved solids in the analytical solutions which often requires high dilution and increases the detection threshold in the analysis of trace elements.

Different melting reagents have been recommended: strontium metaborate ($SrBO_2$), lithium metaborate ($LiBO_2$), lithium tetraborate ($Li_2B_4O_7$), carbonates (Na_2CO_3, K_2CO_3), hydroxides (e.g. NaOH, KOH), peroxides (e.g. Na_2O_2), fluorides (KHF_2). Strontium metaborate was recommended for flame atomic absorption spectrometry (FAAS) (Jeanroy 1974) because strontium facilitates correction of interactions.

These methods are not well adapted to analysis by ICP-MS because of the large number of spectral interferences caused by the atoms of the melting reagent. Lithium metaborate is considered to be the best substrate for ICP-MS (Jarvis 1994a).

31.2.3 Acid Attack in an Open Vessel

Principle

This technique is suitable for titration of many elements including Zn, Cu, Ni, Co, Ti, Mn, Mo, Sc, and rare earths. It cannot be used for titration of silica, or of volatile elements like Pb, Cd, As or Hg. It is suitable for spectrometric titration particularly of trace elements, because it results in reduced quantities of dissolved solids from reagents and lowers the total quantity of dissolved solids by volatilization of silica. Errors due to clogging of the input circuits of nebulizers of the spectrophotometers are then also avoided (cf. Sect. 31.2.1).

Different solutions have been proposed for acid attacks. The AFNOR standard NF X 31-151 (1993) recommends two types of attacks for soils, sediments and sewage sludge (i) a reflux attack with aqua regia, (ii) calcination at 450°C followed by digestion with a mixture of hydrofluoric acid and perchloric acid on a hot plate. Hossner (1996) recommended digestion with a mixture of hydrofluoric, sulphuric and perchloric acid. The French AFNOR standard NF X 31-147 (1996) and the international standard Pr ISO CD 14869-part 1 (1998) suggest only digestion with the hydrofluoric and perchloric acid mixture, possibly with pretreatments in the case of very organic soils.

The technique described below is based on the international standard. Hydrofluoric acid (cf. "Perchloric Acid") enables destruction of silicate lattices in combination with perchloric acid (cf. "Reagents for Alkaline Fusion") which raises the boiling temperature. Perchloric acid is a very strong oxidizing reagent which enables total destruction of organic matter. However, with very organic soils, the reaction may result in some explosive stages and a more moderate attack is thus recommended. The French AFNOR standard NF X 31-147 (1996) recommends three alternative methods depending on the rate of organic carbon (C):

   – C < 20 g kg^{-1}, no pre-treatment
   – 20 < C < 40 g kg^{-1}, preliminary nitric acid digestion
   – C > 40 g kg^{-1}, no calcination before attack.

These ranges show that (i) a pretreatment with nitric acid is generally sufficient for most soils that developed under cold or moderate climates, (ii) attack without pre-treatment can be used with a lot of tropical soils. In all cases, it is better to avoid the use of sulphuric acid in the attack mixture as it results in insoluble salts, is viscous, difficult to eliminate by volatilization and not compatible with ICP-MS measurements (Jarvis 1994a).

Reagents

– Ultra-pure deionized water with conductivity lower than 0.5 µS cm^{-1}
– hydrofluoric acid, HF, *d*: 1.16
– perchloric acid, HClO$_4$, *d*: 1.67
– hydrochloric acid, HCl, *d*: 1.19
– nitric acid, HNO$_3$, *d*: 1.41
– ½HCl solution: mix 500 mL of HCl (*d*: 1.19) with 450 mL of water, shake, let cool, complete the volume to 1 L while homogenizing
– ½HNO$_3$ solution: as above but with 500 mL of HNO$_3$ (*d*: 1.41).

All acids must be of high purity recommended for spectrographic analysis. Blank assays should be performed to check the purity of reagents.

Equipment

- Polytetrafluorethylene (PTFE) crucibles,[1] interior diameter: 5 cm, height: 2 cm, approximate volume: 40 mL; the crucibles should be left filled with diluted nitric acid at least overnight and rinsed with deionized water. The treatment is more efficient if the crucibles are boiled for several hours with 8 mol (HNO_3) L^{-1}, followed by abundant rinsing with deionized water and then drying at 105°C to eliminate any absorbed acid (Jarvis 1994a). Worn crucibles should be replaced as they can more easily adsorb and desorb elements.
- Alternatively use platinum crucibles,[2] interior diameter: 4 cm, height: 2.5 cm, approximate volume: 30 mL.
- Acid-proof hot plate (but in any case, no equipment can survive contact with the mixtures used for very long).
- Efficient, easy to clean, plastic laboratory fume hood (cf. safety precautions in "Perchloric Acid") equipped with a fume cleaning system for acids. For attacks required for the analysis of trace elements, the atmosphere should be dust free. One solution consists in using a laminar flow hood. The fume hood can be also installed in a clean room with an air filtration system. It is imperative to use protective clothing (nylon overalls, plastic goggles and gloves) and to respect safety precautions, particularly for handling hydrofluoric and perchloric acid (cf. "Hydrofluoric Acid" and "Perchloric Acid").
- 50 mL volumetric flasks.
- Muffle furnace with temperature programming up to 500°C.

Procedure

Not very Organic Soils

Soil samples prepared in a standard way by crushing to 0.2 mm (Pansu et al. 2001) are generally used.

- (E1) accurately weigh approximately 0.5 g (±0.1 mg) of sample in a PTFE capsule or platinum crucible
- (E2) add few drops of deionized water to moisten the whole sample
- (E3) add in the following order: approximately 10 mL of concentrated HF and 5 mL of concentrated $HClO_4$
- cover the samples with a PTFE plate (leaving a space between the sample and the lid to avoid condensation) and leave in contact overnight

---

[1] Techniverre, 93 380 Pierrefitte sur Seine, France.
[2] Lyon Alemand Louyot SA, 75 139 Paris Cedex 03, France.

– uncover, heat on a hot plate at 40–50°C until the appearance of white smoke indicating the beginning of evaporation of perchloric acid
– add 5 mL of concentrated hydrofluoric acid. Raise the heat to around 150°C
– dry until there is no more white smoke.

– (R1) Add 10 mL of ½HCl solution to the residue
– bring to dry slowly without additional calcination
– (R2) add 5 mL ½HCl solution
– add boiling deionized water, if necessary heat for a few minutes to facilitate dissolution
– let cool and transfer quantitatively in a 50 mL volumetric flask
– complete to 50 mL with deionized water.

Remarks. This medium (5% hydrochloric acid) is appropriate for molecular and atomic absorption spectrometry and also for flame- or ICP-AES.

Platinum capsules are very expensive but are easier to use than PTFE capsules. They allow the heating time to be reduced and better control of temperature.

Alternative Method for ICP-MS

The following precautions should be respected when using this highly sensitive technique: work in a clean dust-free room, protect your body, hair and shoes, use only ultra-pure reagents.

The final medium should be diluted with nitric acid instead of hydrochloric acid (cf. Sect. 31.2.2). Perchloric acid should be completely eliminated in the titration matrix.

Up to stage R1, the method is identical to that described in "Not Very Organic Soil":
– (R1) Add 10 mL ½HNO₃ to the residue
– bring to dry slowly without additional calcination
– add 10 mL ½HNO₃ and repeat the previous stage
– (R2) add 5 mL ½HNO₃ and continue as in "Not Very Organic Soil".

Five percent nitric acid can also be used as a final medium for other spectrometric methods in spite of its reduced ability to correct certain interferences.

Alternative for Soils with Medium Organic Content

For soils containing less than 40 g (C) kg^{-1}:
– proceed as in "Not Very Organic Soil" for stages E1 and E2, then
– add 10 mL of concentrated nitric acid
– heat on hot plate for about 30 min.

Let cool, add a few drops of deionized water and continue as in "Not Very Organic Soils" starting from stage E3.

Alternative for Very Organic Soils

- (E1) Weigh approximately 0.5 g (±0.1 mg) of sample in a platinum capsule (or failing this a porcelain crucible).
- Place in a muffle furnace and programme a slow increase in temperature up to 450°C in about 1 h (slow increase avoids losses by projection). Maintain the same temperature for 3 h.

Let cool. If you are using a platinum capsule, proceed as in "Not Very Organic Soils" starting from stage E2, possibly dividing the volumes of acids in half (if the capsules are too small). If a platinum capsule is not available, quantitatively transfer the content of the porcelain crucible in a PTFE capsule and then proceed as in "Not Very Organic Soils" starting from stage E2.

Alternative for Refractory Minerals

Refractory minerals like chromite, garnet, magnetite or zirconia are only partially attacked using the procedure described above. During the first recovery of stage R1 described in "Not Very Organic Soils", the possible presence of not attacked solid fragments should be checked. Attack can be completed by bringing to dry again and repeating stage E3. But an incomplete attack does not inevitably result in problems in titration, particularly if elements like Cr, Hf, Mo, Sc, Zr or heavy rare earth Gd to Lu do not have to be analysed (Totland et al. 1992). In this case, the final mediums should be decanted or preferably centrifuged before spectrometric measurements are made to avoid interference by solid residues. The presence of solid residues should also be mentioned in the final analytical report.

Sulphur minerals may not be completely decomposed by the HF–$HClO_4$ mixture. Jarvis (1994a) recommended their elimination with a preliminary attack of 10 mL of aqua regia (1 volume HNO_3 + 3 volumes HCl). Let the sample react at room temperature until the end of effervescence, bring to 60°C and let stand for one hour before dry evaporation at 150°C. Finally complete digestion with the HF-$HClO_4$ mixture as described in "Not Very Organic Soils".

Vernet and Govindaraju (1992) suggested other modifications of the analytical procedure: adding nitric acid to the HF–$HClO_4$ mixture to dissolve certain sulphurized minerals like galena or pyrite, limiting the temperature to 100°C to avoid transformation of phosphorus into phosphates, and using aqua regia for mercury analysis.

31.2.4 Acid Attack in a Closed Vessel

Principle

Attacks in closed vessels are mainly used for quantification at the trace and ultra-trace level of volatile elements like Pb, Cd, As, Sc, B, Hg, Sb, Se or Sn. This type of attack also facilitates the dissolution of refractory phases and shortens the attack time. It allow temperatures to be increased due to the increase in the boiling point of acids and in pressure. Smaller volumes of reagents should be used since they will not evaporate. The smaller quantities of reagents means less contamination and increased protection against dust particles. In addition, the quantity of acid, corrosive and toxic fumes is reduced.

Depending on the temperature to be reached, different types of attack containers or "bombs" are available. The high pressure Parr acid digestion bomb enables temperatures of over 250°C and internal pressures of 12.4 MPa (safety valve at 24 MPa) to be used. The pack includes a 23 mL PTFE beaker with a PTFE cover, and the whole device comes in a steel container with a screw cap ensuring a satisfactory seal between the beaker and cap. These bombs are expensive and not easy to use. If the attacks are to be performed at a lower temperature and pressure, simpler forms of attack containers can be used. In the method described here, the attack containers are entirely made of Tefon, and have a PTFE screw cap.

Different authors have described attacks using different mixtures, for example: HNO_3–$HClO_4$–HF (Totland et al. 1992), HNO_3–HF (Jarvis 1994a), aqua regia-HF (Hossner 1996), HNO_3–HCl–HF below. The attack can be followed by acid elimination (especially hydrofluoric acid), by successive dry evaporations with the addition of diluted nitric or hydrochloric acid. Like the technique described in Sect. 31.2.3, this technique enables the quantity of dissolved solids to be reduced and hydrofluoric acid to be eliminated as these can upset titration. However, it does not allow quantification of silica and includes the risk of loss of certain fluorides by volatilization or insolubilization.

The addition of an excess of boric acid after the attack is another way to avoid evaporation. Boric acid reacts with hydrofluoric acid resulting in fluoboric acid (HBF_4) according to the two-stage exothermic reaction:

$$H_3BO_3 + 3HF \Leftrightarrow HBF_3OH + 2H_2O$$
$$HBF_3OH + HF \Leftrightarrow HBF_4 + H_2O$$

Reactions are strongly moved towards the right in the presence of an excess of boric acid. Hydrofluoric acid is sequestered and does not cause problems for at least two hours (Bernas 1968). According to Lim and

Jackson (1982), the addition of boric acid completes digestion by dissolving insoluble metallic hexafluorides, and the "HBF_4–H_3BO_3–silicate ionic component" medium is suitable for titration using atomic absorption spectrometry.

According to Jarvis (1994a), this technique is less suitable for titration by plasma emission spectrometry. Even when neutralized, hydrofluoric acid can still attack glass, particularly in the fragile atomizers of the Meinhard type. Furthermore, the required quantity of boric acid results in a large quantity of solid residues, more than alkaline fusion techniques, and this can interfere with the detection of many trace elements.

Reagents

All reagents must be of the degree of purity required for the type of spectrographic analysis used. Blank assays should be performed to check the purity of reagents:
– concentrated hydrofluoric acid
– concentrated nitric acid
– concentrated hydrochloric acid
– boric acid
– ultra-pure deionized water of conductivity less than 0.5 $\mu S\ cm^{-1}$.

Equipment

– Attack containers with PTFE screw caps, interior diameter: 45 mm, height: 60 mm (Techniverre, 93,380 Pierrefitte sur Seine, France)
– Thermostatically regulated water bath
– heating plate
– ultra-sonic tank
– 25 mL volumetric flasks
– plastic fume-hood with system for washing fumes.

Procedure

Usual Method

(A) Weigh about 250 mg ($\pm$0.1 mg) of sample (200 μm particle size) and put in a PTFE reactor:
– add a few drops of deionized water to moisten the whole sample
– add 1 mL of concentrated HF, 1 mL of concentrated HNO_3, and 1 mL of concentrated HCl
– close the reactor and leave in contact overnight
– subject to ultra-sonic dispersion for 10 min

– leave in a water bath at 60°C for 24 h
– let cool, open the reactor and check if the attack is complete or if solid residues are still present.
(B) If the attack is complete, evaporate to dry on a hot plate at about 40°C protecting the sample against dust with a PTFE cover placed a few centimetres above the reactor:
– add 1 mL of concentrated nitric acid
– evaporate to dry
– add 1 mL of concentrated nitric acid and hot ultra-pure deionized water
– transfer quantitatively in a 25 mL volumetric flask
– let cool and bring to 25 mL with ultra-pure deionized water.

The final medium contains 4% nitric acid and is suitable for titration of trace elements by atomic absorption spectrometry using the hydride method or electrothermal atomization. It is also suitable for titration by ICP-AES.

Alternative Method for Refractory Materials

If the attack in "Usual Method" is not complete, at the end of stage A:
– add 1 mL of concentrated HF, and 1 mL of concentrated HNO_3
– stop the PTFE reactor and leave in the water-bath at 60°C for 24 h
– continue as in "Usual Method", stage B.

Alternative Method to Prevent Fluoride Volatilization

– After the attack described in "Usual Method" stage A, or "Alternative Method for Refractory Materials", add boric acid to the reactor (2 g H_3BO_3 dissolved in a small volume of water)
– stop, heat at 130°C for 15 min; let cool
– complete the volume to 200 mL with 1 mol (HNO3) L^{-1} nitric acid and, if measurement is not carried out immediately, store in polypropylene bottles
– for ICP-MS analysis, the solutions must be diluted ten times before titration (Jarvis 1994a).

31.2.5 Microwave Mineralization

Compared to the spectacular progress in analytical instrumentation, the preparation of the sample is still a limiting factor in the analytical capacity of a laboratory. A modern spectrometer can provide the analytical results of several elements in only three to four minutes per sample. Acid solubilization of the same sample can require three to four days. Two ways were explored to improve the manual operations required before measurement, and were sometimes combined (1) automation and robotization, (2) improvement in the equipment used for preparation.

The first microwave apparatus for mineralization was produced in 1975 with the aim of reducing the time required for dissolution of the sample. These apparatus are often used with closed containers equipped with safety valves for the attack. The combined effect of the pressure and the energy of the microwave apparatus enables the time needed for solubilization to be reduced considerably. The organic materials are quickly broken up without the need for perchloric acid (Vernet and Govindaraju 1992), which also reduces the evaporation time after attack.

Microwave dissolution systems are also available for use with open vessels. They are more suitable when the procedure is completed automated starting from the input of the reagent up to final dissolution. It is possible to programme complex cycles including many attacks which can be performed without human intervention. In this way, the health hazards linked to the handling of dangerous acids (cf. Sect. 31.2.2) are minimized.

Historically, microwaves were first applied to biological samples. They were later used for geological materials, initially for mining (in 1970), and subsequently for other geochemical applications (Lamothe et al. 1986; Totland et al. 1992, Le Cornec et al. 1994). Comparative studies show that classical attacks in open vessels and microwave attacks give similar results for most of the elements of geological materials. Both techniques have problems of accuracy in the titration of Cr, Hf and Zr on certain samples. Consequently it is better to quantify these elements after alkaline attack by fusion with lithium metaborate (Totland et al. 1992).

According to Le Cornec et al. (1994), it is easier to control the different stages of acid digestion (cf. Sects. 31.2.3 and 31.2.4) in an open system. Moreover, the final evaporation is more difficult to control using microwave systems than the hot plate system. Zischa and Knapp (1997) believe that automated closed systems will be developed for microwave mineralization of solid materials, whereas systems for continuous flow mineralization will continue to be preferred for liquids and sludges.

Given the diversity of microwave systems, it is difficult to recommend a universal procedure for microwave acid digestions. We recommend adapting the classical systems described in Sects. 31.2.3 and 31.2.4 to suit your individual requirements.

31.2.6 Alkaline Fusion

Principle

This technique has three main advantages:
- it is suitable for titration of all major elements since it does not present the risk of elimination of silica;
- it is more rapid than classical acid attacks requiring heating on a hot plate or in a water bath in an open or closed vessel;
- it usually results in complete dissolution of the sample, and is thus the most efficient dissolution method for titration of refractory elements like V, Cr, Zr or Y.

The main disadvantage of the method is the quantity of solid residue that is generated. For spectrometry, greater dilution is needed to avoid clogging the nebulizers which can result in a decrease in sensitivity of titration of trace and ultra-trace elements.

In addition, the degree of heating required to perform the alkaline fusion can result in losses of certain volatile trace elements.

Even though many different reagents have been proposed for alkaline fusion (cf. "Reagents for Alkaline Fusion" in section 31.2.2), lithium metaborate is currently one of the most widely used. It is suitable for several different measurement techniques, especially ICP-MS (Jarvis 1994a). Another older fusion technique using strontium metaborate (Jeanroy 1974) was formerly used for atomic absorption spectrometry (Riandey et al. 1982), but today lithium metaborate is considered to be a better fusion reagent (Le Cornec, IRD Bondy, France, personal communication). The former procedure rules out lithium titration, and the second rules out strontium titration which is useful in soils. Furthermore, both procedures exclude the titration of boron, a trace element that can cause deficiency or toxicity during plant growth. Total boron can be determined by spectrocolorimetry or plasma emission spectrometry (ICP-AES) after solubilization using fusion with soda (Abo 1984).

Reagents

- Ultra-pure deionized water of conductivity lower than 0.5 $\mu S\ cm^{-1}$.
- Fusion reagents and other reagents must be of high purity with certified concentrations with respect to the elements concerned.
- Lithium metaborate ($LiBO_2$), or if not, an equimolar mixture of:
  - lithium oxide Li_2O or lithium carbonate Li_2CO_3
  - boron oxide B_2O_3.

– Strontium metaborate $Sr(BO_2)_2$, or if not, an equimolar mixture of:
> – strontium carbonate $SrCO_3$
> – boron oxide B_2O_3.

– Concentrated nitric or hydrochloric acid.
– 5% HCl or 5% HNO_3: in a 2 L volumetric flask, add 100 mL of concentrated HCl or HNO_3 to approximately 1.8 L of ultra-pure water, shake, let cool and complete the volume to 2 L.
– 2% HCl or 2% HNO_3: in a 2 L volumetric flask, add 20 mL of concentrated HCl or HNO_3 to approximately 1.8 L of water, shake, let cool and complete the volume to 2 L.

Remarks. If $Sr(BO_2)_2$ is not available, the equivalent quantities of $SrCO_3$ plus B_2O_3 can be used (1 mol of each for 1 mol of $Sr(BO_2)_2$). At the temperature of the crucible in the furnace, strontium metaborate is synthesized according to the reaction:

$$SrCO_3 + B_2O_3 \rightarrow Sr(BO_2)_2 + CO_2$$

The same is true for $LiBO_2$ which is equivalent to the equimolar mixture $Li_2O–B_2O_3$ or $Li_2CO_3–B_2O_3$.

Lithium tetraborate ($Li_2B_4O_7$ or a mixture of $Li_2O–2B_2O_3$, with a melting point of 915°C), has been used as fusion reagent instead of metaborate (mp: 845°C) which is more basic. Metaborate is better for attacking more acid siliceous materials , whereas tetraborate is better for more basic materials (aluminous, refractory, carbonaceous, etc.). A mixture of metaborate and tetraborate resulting in an eutectic point at 832°C, was recognized as an almost universal fusion reagent for geological materials (Vernet and Govindaraju 1992). It can be obtained by mixing 73% B_2O_3 and 27% Li_2O.

Equipment

– Round bottom cylindrical crucibles made of graphite[3] height = external diameter: 24 mm, depth and internal diameter: 18 mm
– muffle furnace set at 1,100°C or preferably an induction furnace under nitrogen atmosphere (Fig. 31.1)
– 200 mL beakers, with PTFE bar magnets for stirring
– 200 mL volumetric flasks
– 50 mL volumetric flasks.

---

[3] Sodemi, 95 370 St Ouen l'Aumone, France.

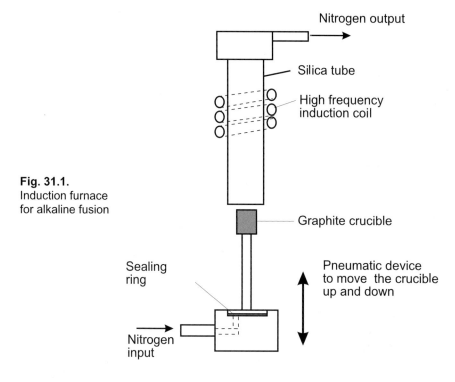

Nitrogen output

Silica tube

High frequency
induction coil

Fig. 31.1.
Induction furnace
for alkaline fusion

Graphite crucible

Sealing
ring

Pneumatic device
to move the crucible
up and down

Nitrogen
input

Remarks. An induction furnace is preferable to a muffle furnace for two reasons: first the heating mode increases the attack and dissolution (less than 5 min instead of 15–30 min), second its design facilitates work in a nitrogen atmosphere and greatly increases the shelf life of graphite crucibles. In a muffle furnace, the damage to crucibles by combustion can be reduced by placing them in graphite boxes.

Graphite crucibles are advantageous first because they are commercially available in very pure forms compatible with titration of trace elements, and second because the surface tension of the bead in fusion on graphite is weak which facilitates its quantitative transfer in the acid reagent for dissolution. Nevertheless, retention problems can occur with certain crucibles and worn crucibles should be replaced.

Some reduction phenomena can result in losses of elements like iron or cobalt during the fusion process. But these phenomena are not common during the fusion of silicate materials, especially when using an induction furnace which reduces the dissolution time.

Crucibles made of platinum–gold or gold–platinum–rhodium, non-dampening alloys, are interesting alternatives which are generally used for fusion with a muffle furnace or a Mecker gas burner. In this case, oxidizing conditions must be maintained, to avoid formation of alloys between the crucible and elements of the sample.

Procedure Using Strontium Metaborate

– In a graphite crucible, accurately weigh approximately 100 mg (±0.1 mg) of soil sample (200 μm particle size or less).
– Add 1 g of strontium metaborate (or equivalent $SrCO_3 + B_2O_3$) and mix thoroughly.
– If the soil is organic (C > 40 g kg^{-1}), put it in a regulated furnace and increase the temperature slowly (over about 1 h) to 450°C. Maintain this temperature for 1 h.
– Bring to 1,100–1,200°C for 5 min in an induction furnace, or for 15 min in a muffle furnace.
– Holding the crucible with a crucible tong, check the homogeneity of the melted bead and transfer it hot in a 200 mL beaker containing about 150 mL of 2% nitric acid.
– Let the crucible cool near the beaker. Then check for the presence of solid fragments and transfer them to the beaker if necessary.
– Put a PTFE bar magnet in the beaker and stir on a magnetic stirrer until total dissolution (about 30 min).
– Quantitatively transfer the content of the beaker to a volumetric flask and bring to 200 mL with the 2% nitric acid solution. The titration matrix is 0.5% $Sr(BO_2)_2$, 2% HNO_3.

Remarks. This solution is suitable for the titration of major elements and some trace elements by atomic absorption spectrometry, e.g.
    – Fe, Mn, Mg, Na, K, Cu, Ni in air–acetylene flame;
    – Si, Al, Ti, Ca in nitrous oxide–acetylene flame;
    – and other trace elements by electrothermal atomization.
Si, Al, Ti and P can also be measured satisfactorily by spectro-colorimetry.

Procedure Using Lithium Metaborate

Major Elements

– Weigh in a graphite crucible approximately 60 mg (±0.1 mg) of soil sample (200 μm particle size or less).

– Add 0.5 g of $LiBO_2$ and mix thoroughly with a spatula.
– If the soil is organic (C > 40 g kg^{-1}), place in a regulated furnace and slowly raise the heat (over about 1 h) to 450°C. Maintain this temperature for 1 h.
– Heat at 1,100°C in the high frequency induction furnace (or in a muffle furnace).
– Transfer the melted bead rapidly in a 250 mL beaker containing a PTFE bar magnet and 100 mL of 2% HCl solution. If necessary, transfer any solid fragments that remain after cooling.
– Stir until complete dissolution (15–20 min).
– Quantitatively transfer in a 200 mL volumetric flask and complete to volume with ultra-pure water. The final titration matrix is 1% HCl, 0.25% $LiBO_2$.

Remarks. This solution enables simultaneous quantification of the major elements: Ti, Fe, K, Na, Mg, Ca, Al, Si and possibly P in the case of high P content (P_2O_5 > 1%) by plasma emission (ICP-AES).

Alternatively, titration by flame emission or AAS can be used as described in "Procedure Using Strontium Metaborate", with the addition of lanthanum to correct interference. Phosphorus and the Si, Al and Ti elements should also be sensitively quantified using spectrocolorimetry.

A 2% nitric acid solution can be used instead of 2% HCl in the final medium.

Alternative Methods for Titration of Trace Elements (e.g. V, Cr, Zr, Y)

Proceed as in "Major Elements", but with a bigger sample specimen of 0.1 g or more. After alkaline fusion, dissolve the bead obtained in 5% HCl solution and bring to a final volume of 50 mL.

Remarks. This solution enables quantification of trace elements by ICP-AES and electrothermal AAS (EAAS). It is mostly useful for trace elements like V, Cr, Zr, Y which are refractory to acid attacks.

As the sample specimen is weaker than for acid attacks, the final medium more diluted, and the quantity of dissolved solids larger, this method is less convenient than acid attacks (cf. Sects. 31.2.3 and 31.2.4) for the other trace elements.

The technique is suitable for ICP-MS titration of ultra-trace elements but the 5% HCl final medium should be replaced by the 5% HNO_3 medium.

31.2.7 Selective Extractions

Extracting Reagents

Many of the chemical extracting reagents used for agronomic tests only provide information on equilibrium values in the soil at a given date. Other methods (e.g. soil incubation) enable quantification of microbial action on the availability of a given element, for example nitrogen (cf. Chap. 14), phosphorus (cf. Chap. 29) or sulphur (cf. Chap. 30) studies. Plant roots have also complex effects on the extraction of nutrients (Callot et al. 1982) which are difficult to simulate accurately with simple tests.

Extraction with water (cf. Chap. 18) only provides information on the actual availability of elements from the soil solution. Boiling water is a more aggressive reagent which can be used to test boron availability for example (see S8 in "Extraction Solutions" or the AFNOR standard NF X 31-122, 1993).

Other reagents, used cold or hot, involve different mechanisms, hydrolysis, ion exchange, change in pH or redox potential, sequestering effect, etc.

Many different reagents are available for *extraction by ion exchange* in buffered or not buffered mediums. Potassium or calcium chloride, and sodium fluoride mediums enable titration of exchangeable protons or hydroxyls (cf. Chap. 15). Ammonium or sodium acetate, and barium chloride are typical reagents for exchangeable cations or analysing exchange capacities (cf. Chap. 22 and Chap. 26). Ammonium or sodium acetate buffered at pH 4.8 or 3 is used for studies of exchangeable iron linked to plant chlorosis, as is ammonium oxalate (standard FD X31-146, 1996). Potassium chloride and ammonium acetate enable quantification of exchangeable aluminium (cf. Chap. 23) and exchangeable manganese (Martens and Lindsay 1990). Reagents that work by ionic exchange are also used in studies of different forms of nitrogen (cf. Chap. 28), phosphorus (cf. Chap. 29) or sulphur (cf. Chap. 30). Ions can also act in solid form using ion exchange resins.

Sequestering reagents are also widely used for selective solubilization (which generally involves rather long equilibrium times) by chelate formation, often in combination with other reagents acting by ion exchange, redox or acid action. The most widely used sequestering reagents are ethylene diamin tetra-acetic acid (EDTA), diethylen triamin penta-acetic acid (DTPA), and triethanolamin (TEA). The standard NF X31-120 (1992) recommends extraction of cooper, manganese (Gambrell and Patrick 1982) and zinc with a mixture of ammonium acetate and EDTA. The standard NF X31-121 (1993) is used for the estimation of the same elements plus iron including DTPA action. This standard uses the reagent DTPA–CaCl$_2$–TEA, which is also recommended for extraction of toxic metals (Risser and Baker 1990).

Reducing or oxidizing reagents enable extraction of different forms of valence of certain elements. For example, specific forms of iron are extracted by 0.5% oxalic acid, 0.2% hydroquinone and ammonium acetate. One form of easily reducible manganese is extracted in the presence of sodium dithionite.

Acid reagents are often used to displace potentially available forms that are not easily extracted. Acetic acid at pH 2.5 enables the "total exchangeable cation" fraction to be solubilized. Boiling concentrated acetic acid solubilizes siderite. Hydrochloric acid is used at different dilutions (0.1, 0.5, 1 mol L^{-1}) to extract some forms of Cu, Ni, Zn, Cd, Cr, Hg or Pb, and the same goes for phosphoric acid (e.g. forms of Mn). Attacking silicated lattices with hydrofluoric acid enables estimation of non-exchangeable ammonium (cf. Chap. 28).

An attack using three concentrated acids (1 vol. HNO$_3$, 2 vol. HCl, 4 vol. H$_2$SO$_4$) has been recommended at various times for the differentiation of practically insoluble primary minerals from more recently formed minerals that are all soluble (Hardy and Follet-Smith 1931, Claisse 1968, Njopwouo and Orliac 1979).

Extraction Solutions

Only standardized solutions and the most widely used extraction solutions are described here as too many possible alternatives exist to be able to describe them all.

– (S1) Standard NF X 31-120 (1992): solution of 1 mol L^{-1} ammonium acetate and 0.01 mol L^{-1} EDTA (extraction of Cu, Mn, Zn). Dissolve 3.723 g of EDTA (C$_{10}$H$_{14}$Na$_2$O$_8$,2H$_2$O) and 77 g of ammonium acetate (CH$_3$COONH$_4$) in a 1 L volumetric flask containing about 400 mL of deionized water. Bring to 800 mL. Measure the pH value and if necessary adjust to pH 7.0 with 1 mol L^{-1} solution of ammonia or acetic acid. Complete to 1 L with deionized water while homogenizing.

- (S2) Lindsay and Norvell (1978), Risser and Baker (1990), standard NF X 31-121 (1993) and NF ISO 14870 (1998): mix 0.1 mol (TEA) L^{-1}, 0.01 mol ($CaCl_2$) L^{-1}, 0.005 mol (DTPA) L^{-1} (extraction of Cu, Mn, Zn, Fe, biogenic trace elements, toxic metals).
  In a 1 L volumetric flask dissolve in deionized water: 14.92 g of TEA, 1.967 g of DTPA and 1.47 g of calcium chloride di-hydrate. Bring to 800 mL with deionized water and adjust to pH 7.3 with ½HCl solution under agitation. Let cool and complete to 1 L with deionized water while homogenizing.
- (S3) Risser and Baker, 1990: diluted hydrochloric acid solution, 0.1 mol (HCl) L^{-1} (Zn, alkalinity, toxic metals).
  Dilute 8.3 mL of concentrated hydrochloric acid in a 1 L volumetric flask containing 800 mL of deionized water. Complete to 1 L while homogenizing.
- (S4) Cox (1968), Risser and Baker (1990): double acid (toxic metals, soils with low pH, low CEC and low organic matter content).
  Dilute 8.3 mL of concentrated hydrochloric acid and 1.4 mL of concentrated sulphuric acid in 2 L of deionized water.
- (S5) Easily reducible manganese (Gambrell and Patrick 1982). Mixture of 1 mol (CH_3COONH_4) L^{-1} ammonium acetate solution at pH 7, and 0.2% hydroquinone (or hydroxylamine).
  Dissolve 77.1 g of ammonium acetate in a 1 L beaker containing 750 mL of deionized water. Add 2 g of hydroxylamine chlorhydrate (NH_2OH, HCl) or hydroquinone. Adjust the pH to 7 with a ½ammonia solution or a ½acetic acid solution. Complete the volume to 1 L.
- (S6) Total absorbed metals (US EPA,[4] 1986): concentrated nitric acid, concentrated hydrochloric acid, 30% hydrogen peroxide.
- (S7) "Free oxide" iron (Deb 1950, Pétard 1993). Sodium acetate and tartrate solution.
  In a 400 mL beaker dissolve 136 g of $CH_3COONa \cdot 3H_2O$ in the minimum volume of deionized water necessary; in a 250 mL beaker dissolve 23 g of $C_4H_4Na_2O_6$, $2H_2O$ in the minimum volume of deionized water necessary; mix the two solutions and complete to 1 L.
- (S8) Boiling water boron (NF X 31-122, 1993), 0.01 mol ($CaCl_2$) L^{-1} solution.
  Use deionized boron-free water (check with a blank titration), dissolve 1.47 g of $CaCl_2$, $2H_2O$ in a 1 L volumetric flask, complete to 1 L with boron-free water while homogenizing.

---

[4] US EPA = US Environment Protection Agency.

Equipment

Only the most commonly used equipment is listed here:
– Top-loading balance (±1 cg) with suitable plastic scoop for powder
– 50, 100, and 200 mL plastic extraction flasks (tubes) with screw caps, if possible that can also be used for centrifugation
– flask for conservation of the extraction solution with suitable volume dispenser
– back and forth shaker or upside down rotation shaker able to load a sufficient number of 50, 100 or 200 mL extraction flasks. The agitation conditions should be regulated to insure they are reproducible at a speed enabling the entire mass of solid sample to be moved, without the speed of agitation being too high. The isothermal conditions of the shaker should be set at 20°C (±1°C)
– Centrifuge (at 5,000g) in tubes corresponding to extraction volumes.
– α-cellulose funnels and filters (Whatman No. 42 or similar) or a filtration device with a 0.45 μm filter membrane
– 250 mL round bottom boiling flasks with ground glass joint and suitable condenser for extraction of boron with boiling water
– 100 mL beakers with suitable beaker covers.

Procedure

General Procedure

Use a soil sample prepared according to the procedure selected, (usually sieved to 2 mm and air dried)
– weigh the required mass (with respect to a specific standard, see below) of sample (±0.01 g) using a plastic powder scoop
– put the sample in an extraction flask of suitable volume (see later)
– add the required volume of extraction reagent
– stop the flask and shake on a preset shaker or shake manually in a thermostated room at a temperature of 20°C for the required time (see later).
– centrifuge or filter (or both) and store the extract until analysis.

Remarks. All operating conditions and particularly the extraction time should be standardized. Attack and equilibration phenomena need a rather long time, particularly sequestering reactions.

Always run a blank assay (reagent without sample using the same procedure).

Prepare the calibration ranges for spectrometric titration with the solution used for the extractions.

For extracts in neutral medium, limit storage of the extract to less than two days before analysis.

Conditions for Extraction Reagent S1

Flask: 100 mL, sample mass: 5 g, volume of extraction reagent; 50 mL, extraction time: 2 hours.

Conditions for Extraction Reagent S2

Flask: 100 mL, sample mass: 10 g, volume of extraction reagent: 20 mL, extraction time: 2 hours.

Conditions for Extraction Reagent S3

Flask (or stopped centrifugation tube): 50 mL, sample mass: 2 g, volume of extraction reagent: 20 mL, extraction time: 5 min, 3 successive extractions, bring the final volume to 100 mL.

Conditions for Extraction Reagent S4

Flask: 50 mL, sample mass: 5 g, volume of extraction reagent: 25 mL, extraction time: 15 min.

Conditions for Extraction Reagent S5

Flask: 200 mL, sample mass: 10 g, volume of extraction reagent: 100 mL, extraction time: 30 min (agitation), contact time: 6 h (intermittent agitation). Easily reducible manganese is obtained by subtracting the content found in this extract from the content of exchangeable manganese extracted with ammonium acetate 1 mol L^{-1} at pH 7 (cf. Chap. 22).

Alternative Method for Total Absorbed Metals S6 (US EPA 1986)

Put 2 g of sample in a 100 mL Pyrex beaker, add 10 mL of concentrated nitric acid, cover with a beaker cover and heat for 25 min on a heating plate at 95°C without boiling. Let cool, add 5 mL of nitric acid and heat again for 30 min. Repeat this operation. Uncover ¼ of the surface of the beaker and evaporate to a final volume of 5 mL without boiling. Cool, carefully add 2 mL of deionized water and 3 mL of 30% hydrogen peroxide. Heat carefully avoiding excess effervescence. Continue to add hydrogen peroxide in fractions of 1 mL until effervescence ends. Add 5 mL of concentrated hydrochloric acid and 10 mL of deionized water. Cover and heat again for 15 min without boiling. Filter on Whatman No. 41 filter paper (or similar) and complete to 50 mL with deionized water.

The final hydrochloric acid medium is not suitable for certain analytical techniques such as EAAS or ICP-MS. In these cases continue to heat the HNO_3–H_2O_2 mixture until the volume is reduced to approximately 5 mL. Filter and complete the volume to 50 mL as previously. This method is not recommended for Hg analysis. It is designed to give concentrations of exchangeable trace elements or trace elements adsorbed by the soil components (e.g. Cd, Ni, Pb, Cr, As, Se), mostly to detect pollutants of industrial origin. It is not suitable for total elements associated with silicates nor is it recommended for total analysis.

Alternative Method for Free Iron Oxide

This is an alternative to the method proposed by Deb (1950) which is used by many laboratories (Pétard 1993).

Put 1 g of sample in a 100 mL centrifugation tube, add 50 mL of S7 acetate–tartrate solution, agitate vigorously with a glass rod, add 2g of sodium hydrosulphite and agitate well. Put in a water bath at 40°C for 40 min while stirring every 5 min. Centrifuge for 3 min at 3,000g and decant the supernatant in a 1 L volumetric flask. Add 50 mL of a 0.05 mol (HCl) L^{-1} solution to the centrifugation pellet, and again place in the water bath for 15 min while stirring at regular intervals. Centrifuge and decant the supernatant in the same volumetric flask. Repeat the extraction sequences (tartrate–acetate + hydrosulphite and washing with diluted hydrochloric acid) twice, adding each extract in the same 1 L volumetric flask. Add 10 mL of concentrated hydrochloric acid to the flask and complete to 1 L with deionized water while homogenizing. Let stand overnight and filter the solution before iron titration by atomic spectrometry or spectrocolorimetry.

Alternative Method for Extractable Boron

Weigh 25 g of sample and put it in a 250 mL boiling flask with a ground stopper. Add 50 mL of 0.01 mol $(CaCl_2)$ L^{-1} solution (S8). Homogenize and boil for 5 min in a reflux condenser. Cool, filter at low filtration speed on ashless filter paper. Titrate boron by ICP-AES or by spectrocolorimetry using azomethine H.

31.2.8 Measurement Methods

Before improvements in atomic spectrometry, analysing even major elements in soils or rocks was a long process. Analysis of only one particular element was often required rather than of all elements. In the same way, the methods of attack for multi-element analysis were not as standardized as the methods described in Sects. 31.2.3–31.2.6, but often only suitable for one particular element. For example, concentrated nitric acid was the reagent used to attack total phosphorus (cf. Sect. 29.2.2 in Chap. 29), limestone was analysed by acid attack and volumetric measurement of carbon dioxide (cf. Chap. 17).

Total silica is often quantified after alkaline fusion (cf. Sect. 31.2.6) to avoid it being volatilized in the presence of hydrofluoric acid. Volatilization can be used for approximate gravimetric estimation of silica, but for more precise results, spectrocolorimetry is used. Silica reacts with ammonium molybdate at acid pH giving a yellow colour due to the production of silicomolybdic acid; oxalic acid is added to avoid interference with phosphorous and the colour can be measured at 420 nm. Silica can be also quantified by AAS using nitrous oxide–acetylene flame, but the detection limit is high. Analysis of silica by ICP-AES is more precise.

Phosphorous is almost unquantifiable by AAS and its analysis by ICP-AES is neither precise nor sensitive. The best method for analysis of phosphorous in solution is spectrocolorimetry: formation of a phosphor-molybdic complex with ammonium molybdate in acid medium. The yellow complex can be either directly measured by spectrophotometry around 420 nm, or reduced resulting in a blue complex form measured at 830 nm (cf. Chap. 30).

Aluminium and titanium can be measured by AAS using nitrous oxide–acetylene flame but the method is not very sensitive as these two elements are refractory. Analysis using ICP-AES is better, but spectrocolorimetry is both a precise and inexpensive alternative for measurement of aluminium and titanium. Aluminium gives a red complex with eriochrome cyanine, titanium gives a yellow-orange complex with hydrogen peroxide in sulphuric acid medium.

Flame emission spectrometry is the recommended method for analysis of alkaline metals, particularly sodium and potassium, even using classical atomic absorption or emission spectrometers, and even using small cheap spectrometers, which, however, should be reserved for the titration of these elements (Pansu et al. 2001). The other major elements can be accurately measured by classical AAS using air–acetylene flame for Fe, Mn, Mg, Ni (or Na or K), and nitrous oxide–acetylene flame for Ca. In most soils, ICP-AES enables simultaneous quantification of all the major elements except phosphorous.

Analysis of trace elements is more problematic, but many methods have been explored over a period of many years (Pinta 1962). These methods were greatly improved by AAS techniques such as the hydride method, the cold vapour method and especially electrothermal atomization. The ICP-AES technique also represented great analytical progress especially for multi-element analysis, but for many trace elements, ICP-AES is less sensitive than improved AAS techniques, for example electrothermal atomization.

A new era in the analysis of trace elements began with the introduction of ICP-MS. This technique enabled almost all elements of the periodic table to be studied, often with a better detection limit than with other techniques. In addition, it enabled access to certain isotopes of great interest for geochronological and ecological studies. But it is an expensive technique and is difficult to implement and is consequently usually reserved for certain specific research programmes.

The methods presented in this chapter concern the analysis:
– of P, Si, Al, Ti by spectrocolorimetry (cf. Sect. 31.2.9);
– of alkaline elements by flame emission spectrometry (cf. Sect. 31.2.10);
– by FAAS (cf. Sect. 31.2.11);
– by AAS, hydride and cold vapour methods (cf. Sect. 31.2.12);
– by EAAS (cf. Sect. 31.2.13);
– by ICP-AES (cf. Sect. 31.2.14);
– by ICP-MS (cf. Sect. 31.2.15).

31.2.9 Spectrocolorimetric Analysis

Phosphorous

When in *ortho*-phosphoric acid form, phosphorous reacts with molybdic acid giving a yellow phosphomolybdic complex. Absorbance can be measured at 420 nm. Reduction gives a blue colour which can be measured at 830 nm. Titration is very sensitive and selective for the *ortho*-phosphoric form. See procedure in Chap. 29.

Silicium

Principle

With ammonium molybdate at pH 1.2 silica results in yellow coloration of silicomolybdic acid. Oxalic acid prevents interference by phosphorous. Analytical solutions resulting from alkaline fusion are recommended (cf. Sect. 13) with a sample specimen weight of 60 mg, an analytical matrix of 1% HCl in a final volume of 200 mL.

Reagents

- 1.5% hydrochloric acid solution
- 10% ammonium molybdate solution: dissolve 50 g in 500 mL of deionized water, shake and filter. The solution is only stable for few days
- 50 g L^{-1} oxalic acid solution
- standard solution: as the silica solution is not stable, a standard solution should be freshly prepared for each analytical series; during alkaline fusion (cf. Sect. 31.2.5), add a graphite crucible containing 60 mg of pure dried silica and subject it to alkaline fusion using the same procedure as for the soil samples.
- The calibration range prepared by dilution of the standard solution with 1% HCl solution is:

mL for 100 mL	0	10	20	50	100
% SiO$_2$ in the solid soil sample	0	10	20	50	100

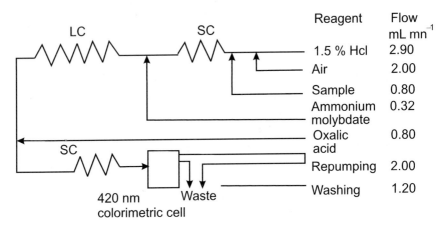

Fig. 31.2. Automation of the spectrocolorimetric titration of silica by segmented continuous-flow analysis (Paycheng 1980): SC: small mixing coil, LC: large coil, wavelength: 420 nm, rinsing with distilled water, speed: 30 samples per hour

Alternately, reference materials with known silica content can be used.

Procedure

– In 50 mL flasks, add:
  – 10 mL of calibration or sample solution
  – 30 mL of 1.5% HCl solution
  – 5 mL of 10% ammonium molybdate solution
  – 5 mL of 5% oxalic acid solution.
– Homogenize, transfer in a colorimetric cell and measure absorbance at 420 nm. The calibration range provides the silica content of the initial solid sample without moisture correction. This titration can be automated by continuous-flow analysis (Fig. 31.2).

Aluminium

Principle

With eriochrome cyanine, aluminium gives a red-violet compound according to a very sensitive reaction which is not very stable. The procedure should be rigorously respected. The pH should be adjusted to 6.3. Interference by Fe^{III} is prevented by reduction into Fe^{II} by ascorbic acid.

Reagents

– *1 g L^{-1} eriochrome cyanine solution.* Dissolve 1 g in 800 mL of deionized water, add 1 mL of concentrated nitric acid and complete to 1 L.
– 0.5% ascorbic acid solution.
– *Buffer solution at pH 6.3.* Dissolve 250 g of sodium acetate (anhydrous form or equivalent crystal form) in 500 mL of deionized water, add 10 mL of acetic acid. If necessary, adjust the pH on a pH-meter and complete the volume to 1 L with deionized water.
– *100 mg (Al_2O_3) L^{-1} stock solution.* Attack 52.9 mg of pure aluminium powder with 10 mL of concentrated hydrochloric acid, complete to 1 L with deionized water, (more precise standard commercial solutions are also available).
– *Calibration range.* Between 0 and 50 mg (Al_2O_3) L^{-1}, dilute the stock solution with 1% hydrochloric acid solution.

Procedure

Solutions resulting from alkaline fusion in 1% HCl medium (cf. Sect. 31.2.6) are recommended.

- In a 50 mL flask, put 5 mL of sample or calibration point, add 15 mL of ascorbic acid solution
- allow to react for a few minutes then add 25 mL of buffer solution and 5 mL of eriochrome cyanine
- perform colorimetric measurement at 535 nm.

Remarks

If the buffer solution is not sufficient to buffer the pH, treat with ammonia to neutralize the pH to a value just before the titration point.

Thioglycolate can be used as a reducing and sequestering agent instead of ascorbic acid.

A blank assay can be run by masking iron and aluminium with EDTA to enable subtraction of background absorbance coming from other elements (Charlot 1984).

Alternatively, eriochrome cyanine can be prepared according to Charlot (1984): in 200 mL of water, add 1 g of eriochrome cyanine, 25 g of sodium chloride, 25 g of ammonium nitrate, 2 mL of nitric acid, dissolve and bring to 1 L with deionized water. This preparation was found to be more efficient on extracts of saline soils than that described above in "Reagents" section (Paycheng 1980).

Titanium

Principle

The orange-yellow colour produced by titanium with hydrogen peroxide in sulphuric medium is measured. The addition of phosphoric acid enables correction of colour interference due to a high ferric iron content. The solution must not contain fluorides.

Other ions can also result in coloured complexes, but their intensity is generally weak (U, Mo, Nb), except in the case of V, which can be very awkward. Vanadium can be measured simultaneously with Ti^{IV} with a colorimetric measurement using two wavelengths: 410 (Ti) and 460 (V) nm. Addition of fluoride masks the titanium complex so that vanadium can be measured.

Reagents

- 3% hydrogen peroxide solution: dilute 30% nitrogen peroxide ten times with deionized water
- sulphuric acid diluted eight times with deionized water
- phosphoric acid diluted three times with deionized water
- 1% hydrochloric acid solution

- 1 g (TiO$_2$) L^{-1} standard stock solution: weigh 600 mg of K$_2$TiF$_6$ in a platinum crucible, add a few drops of deionized water and about three mL of concentrated sulphuric acid, evaporate to dry; repeat this operation, dissolve in 5% H$_2$SO$_4$ solution and complete to 200 mL with deionized water
- Standard range: from 0 to 100 mg (TiO$_2$) L^{-1}, dilute stock solution with 1% HCl solution.

Procedure

For major elements (cf. Sect. 31.2.6), extracts resulting from alkaline fusion in 1% HCl solution are recommended.

In a 50 mL flask, add 20 mL of sample or calibration solution, 10 mL of 1/8 sulphuric acid, 15 mL of 1/3 phosphoric acid, 5 mL of 3% hydrogen peroxide solution. Perform the colorimetric measurement at 410–420 nm.

31.2.10 Analysis by Flame Atomic Emission Spectrometry

Conditions

Although atomic absorption spectrometry is often used instead of flame emission spectrometry (FES), FES is nevertheless useful for titration of alkaline elements, especially sodium and potassium. These elements are the easiest to atomize and ionize. To obtain maximum atomization and minimum ionization, the flame should not be too hot. An air–town gas, air–butane, air–propane or air–acetylene flame can be used. Alkaline elements can also be analyzed by plasma emission spectrometry (cf. Sect. 31.2.14), but sensitivity will be lower due to the high temperature of the plasma.

Table 31.3. Basal emission wavelength of alkaline elements in flame

element	Li	Na	K	Rb	Cs
λ (nm)	670.79	589.00	766.49	780.02	852.11
		589.59	766.90	794.47	894.35

Ray of the shortest wavelengths (*top line*) is generally chosen for spectrometry, as the intensity is almost double that of the other

Emission corresponding to the transition between the fundamental electronic layer and the first excitation layer is the most useful for titration of alkaline elements. It often gives a radiating doublet with approximately double the intensity of radiation at a lower wavelength (Table 31.3). The radiation of these radiating doublets is not always separated by commercial spectrometers, although this does not prevent satisfactory titration when the whole ray is used.

Other operating conditions depend on the type of apparatus. Elements other than alkaline elements can be also titrated by FES but AAS is generally preferred.

Calibration range and calculations

Contents depend on the type of element and substrate. A range from 0 to 100 mg (K_2O) L^{-1} is generally chosen for potassium. A range between 0 and 50 mg (Na_2O) L^{-1} can be used for sodium. Commercial standard solutions can be used as can pure commercial products like K_2CO_3 or Na_2CO_3 using a technique similar to that used for the preparation of standards for AAS (cf. "Calibration Range"). The same standard can be used for AES and AAS techniques.

31.2.11 Analysis by Flame Atomic Absorption Spectrometry

Major Elements by FAAS

Operating Conditions

Table 31.4 lists the main instrumental conditions for titration of the major elements in soil solutions; the elements are classified according to their detection limit. In practice, phosphorous cannot be analysed using this method and Si, Ti and Al elements are less sensitive to this technique than to spectrocolorimetry (cf. Sect. 31.2.9). Trade publications (e.g. Wright and Stuczynski 1996; Pansu et al. 2001) or documentation accompanying commercial apparatuses should be consulted for more details on operating conditions.

Calibration Range

Products
– Commercial calibration solutions (cf. "Multi-Element Calibration for Major Elements") or commercial ultra-pure products can be used to prepare calibration ranges. The latter are classified in Table 31.5
– high-purity lanthanum oxide, La_2O_3
– ultra-pure concentrated hydrochloric acid
– ultra-pure concentrated nitric acid
– lithium metaborate (cf. Sect. 31.2.6)
– strontium metaborate (cf. Sect. 31.2.6).

Table 31.4. Main instrumental conditions for FAAS analysis of major elements of soils classified according to their detection limit (DL) in: (1) pure water (Varian documentation), (2) soil extract by alkaline fusion with mixture 0.5% $Sr(BO_2)_2$ and 2% HNO_3 (Jeanroy 1972)

element	λ (nm)	DL ($\mu g\ L^{-1}$) (1)	DL ($\mu g\ L^{-1}$) (2)	flame
Na	589.0	0.2	1	$Air–C_2H_2$
Mg	285.2	0.3	0.8	$Air–C_2H_2$
Ca	422.7	1	4	$N_2O–C_2H_2$
Mn	279.5	2	5	$Air–C_2H_2$
K	766.5	3	2	$Air–C_2H_2$
Fe	248.3	6	12	$Air–C_2H_2$
Al	309.3	30	140	$N_2O–C_2H_2$
Ti	365.4	50	250	$N_2O–C_2H_2$
	364.3	100		
Si	251.6	300	400	$N_2O–C_2H_2$
P	213.6	40,000		$N_2O–C_2H_2$

- Matrix solution (A) according to the procedure for alkaline fusion described in "Procedure Using Strontium Metaborate" of section 31.2.6: dissolve 25 g of strontium metaborate in 200 mL of deionized water and 100 mL of concentrated nitric acid. Let cool and complete to 1 L. The resulting medium contains 2.5% of metaborate and 10% of nitric acid (five times the content of the attack matrix described in "Procedure Using Strontium Metaborate").
- Matrix solution (A′) according to the procedure for alkaline fusion described in "Procedure Using Lithium Metaborate" of section 31.2.6: dissolve 12.5 g of lithium metaborate in 200 mL of deionized water and 50 mL of concentrated hydrochloric acid. Let cool and complete to 1 L. The resulting medium contains 1.25% of metaborate and 5% of hydro–chloric acid (five times the content of the attack matrix described in "Procedure Using Lithium Metaborate").

– Lanthanum solution (L): dissolve 23.45 g of La_2O_3 in 10 mL of 2% hydrochloric acid (10 mL of water + 2 mL of concentrated hydrochloric acid), complete to 100 mL. This solution contains 20% of lanthanum.

Stock solution – procedure

Table 31.5. Preparation of stock solutions (E or E') for analysis of major elements by atomic absorption spectrometry

element	oxide	maximal % oxide in the sample	solution concentration μg (oxide) mL^{-1}		usable product	weight in mg for 1L	
			attack of section 21.2.6			attack of section 21.2.6	
			E	E'		E	E'
Al	Al_2O_3	50	1,250	750	Al powder	661.7	397.0
Fe	Fe_2O_3	30	750	450	Fe powder	524.8	314.9
Mn	MnO	5	125	75	MnO_2	153.2	91.9
Mg	MgO	30	750	450	MgO	750.0	450.0
Ca	CaO	30	750	450	$CaCO_3$	1,339.3	803.6
Na	Na_2O	20	500	300	Na_2CO_3	854.8	512.9
K	K_2O	30	750	450	K_2CO_3	1,101.1	660.7
Ti	TiO_2	10	250	150	Ti powder	150.0	90.0
Si	SiO_2	100	2,500	1,500	SiO_2	2,500.0	1,500.0

The concentrations of stock solutions (column 4) correspond to five times the maximal concentration of the attack solution (cf. Sect. 21.2.6), i.e.
– for the attack E described in "Procedure Using Strontium Metaborate": 100 mg sample, 200 mL final solution containing 0.5% $Sr(BO_2)_2$ and 2% HNO_3
– for the attack E'described in "Procedure Using Lithium Metaborate": 60 mg sample, 200 mL final solution containing 0.25% $LiBO_2$ and 1% HCl

The calibration solutions are prepared according to Jeanroy (1972) and Riandey et al. (1982). Table 31.5 lists the ingredients for the preparation of stock solutions for calibration ranges for the two types of soil attack by alkaline fusion described in "Procedure Using Strontium Metaborate" (E solution) and "Procedure Using Lithium Metaborate" (E' solution) with a concentration five times higher than the maximal content generally found in soils. Calibration solutions can be prepared either for one element or for several elements in complex calibration solutions. Silica should be avoided in complex solutions as it leads to precipitation of alumino-silicates. The silica solution is prepared alone by alkaline fusion of pure silica, in the same way as for the fusion of the sample (cf. "Silicium"). Calibration solutions must be prepared in the same matrix as the attack matrix. Commercial standard solutions for AAS can be used. Alternatively solutions can be made with high-purity products (metals, oxides, carbonates, sulphates, etc.) as in the example below.

In a 400 mL beaker, put the exact mass of each standard product listed in Table 31.5 that is appropriate for the attack method used. Add a few mL of deionized water, then 20 mL of nitric acid (for the attack described in "Procedure Using Strontium Metaborate") or 10 mL of hydrochloric acid (for the attack described in "Procedure Using Lithium Metaborate"). Cover with a beaker cover and allow the attack to continue until total dissolution, heating slightly if needed. Let cool, transfer in a volumetric flask and complete to 1 L with deionized water.

Table 31.6. Required volumes of stock solution E or E′ (Table 31.5) for 250 mL and corresponding contents in % oxide of soil samples for both attacks described in Section 31.2.6

no	volume of E or E′ (mL) stock solution	Al_2O_3 (%)	Fe_2O_3 (%)	MnO (%)	MgO (%)	CaO (%)	Na_2O (%)	K_2O (%)	TiO_2 (%)	SiO_2 (%)
0	0	0	0	0	0	0	0	0	0	0
1	1	1	0.6	0.1	0.6	0.6	0.4	0.6	0.2	2
2	5	5	3	0.5	3	3	2	3	1	10
3	10	10	6	1	6	6	4	6	2	20
4	25	25	15	2.5	15	15	10	15	5	50
5	50	50	30	5	30	30	20	30	10	100

Calibration Range – Procedure
In 250 mL volumetric flasks, add the volumes of stock solution E or E′ listed in Table 31.6. Add 50 mL of matrix solution A ("Procedure Using Strontium Metaborate") or A′ ("Procedure Using Lithium Metaborate").

For solutions corresponding to the attack described in "Procedure Using Lithium Metaborate" add 1.25 mL of lanthanum solution L (for the attack described in "Procedure Using Strontium Metaborate", strontium is sufficient to correct interference). Complete to 250 mL with deionized water.

Read the soil concentrations directly in % oxide on the calibration curves corresponding to Table 31.6 for the two attack procedures and "Procedure Using Strontium Metaborate" using sample specimens of respectively 100 mg E and 60 mg E' for 200 mL of solution. For other soil sample specimens using P (mg), multiply the final result by $100/P$ (E) and $60/P$ (E'), respectively. Moisture correction may be also necessary.

As an alternative to this external calibration technique (Table 31.6), the stock solutions listed in Table 31.5 can also be used for titration based on the method of standard additions.

Table 31.7. Trace elements measurable by FAAS using air–acetylene and nitrous oxide–acetylene flames

air–C$_2$H$_2$ flame			N$_2$O–C$_2$H$_2$ flame		
element	λ (nm)	DL (μg L^{-1})	Element	λ (nm)	DL (μg L^{-1})
Cu	324.7	3	Mo	313.3	20
Co	240.7	5	Ba	553.6	20
Ni	232.0	10	Be	234.9	1
Cd	228.8	2	Eu	459.4	1.5
Zn	213.9	1	Sr	460.7	2
Ag	328.1	2	Tm	371.8	20
Cr	357.9	6	Yb	398.8	4
Cs	852.1	4			
Pb	217.0	10			
Pd	244.8	10			
Rb	780.0	10			
Rh	343.5	5			
Au	242.8	10			

Detection limits (DL) are for pure water and are thus lower than the DL that can be measured on soil extracts

Trace Elements by FAAS

A large number of trace elements can be determined by FAAS if their concentrations are not too low. Table 31.7 lists the main operating conditions for these elements.

The calibration ranges must be appropriate for the material to be analysed. For elements like Cu, Co, Ni, the usual ranges are between 0 and 2% oxide in soil. Generally the addition of lanthanum (cf. "Major Elements by FAAS" above) is not necessary for trace elements, but complementary assays should be run with and without added lanthanum. The calibration range can be prepared in the same way as for analysis of trace elements by ICP-AES, cf. "Complex Calibration Range for Titration of Trace Elements" in section 31.2.14).

31.2.12 Analysis of Trace Elements by Hydride and Cold-Vapour AAS

Hydride AAS Technique

Principle

Table 31.8. Elements titrated with the hydride method

element	CC $(\mu g\ L^{-1})$	λ (nm)
As	0.2	193.7
Bi	0.2	223.1
Hg	0.4	253.7
Sb	0.15	217.6
Se	0.3	196.0
Sn	0.4	235.5
Te	0.15	214.3

CC: characteristic concentration giving an absorbance signal of 0.0044 (1% absorption of incidental radiation), CC is 5–20 times greater than DL. λ is the recommended wavelength in nm

Some elements (see Table 31.8) can produce hydrides by action of sodium borhydride ($NaBH_4$) in acid medium (HCl or H_2SO_4). For an element E the reaction can be written:

$$NaBH_4 + 3\ H_2O + HCl \rightarrow H_3BO_3 + NaCl + 8\ H$$
$$E^{n+} + m\ H \rightarrow EH_m\uparrow$$

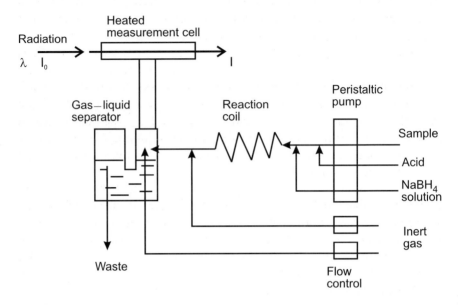

Fig. 31.3. Hydride atomic absorption spectrometry

Hydrides in gaseous form are drawn into an absorption cell formed by a silica tube (Fig. 31.3). Moderate heating of this tube at 800–900°C with an air–acetylene flame enables hydrides to be broken down into atomic forms of the elements. Absorbance of these elements is thus higher than in classical flame atomization (cf. Sect. 31.2.11) and the detection limit is greatly improved.

Most of the elements in Table 31.8 can be volatilized at high temperatures. Their determination in soils requires a suitable method of attack. We recommend acid attack in a closed vessel as described in Sect. 31.2.4.

Reagents

– 0.6% sodium borohydride solution: in 50 mL of ultra-pure water, dissolve 0.5 g of soda then 0.6 g of sodium borohydride and complete to 100 mL with ultra-pure water. Fresh solution should be prepared each day
– ½ hydrochloric acid: add 50 mL of spectrographic grade concentrated hydrochloric acid in 40 mL of ultra-pure water, shake, let cool and complete to 100 mL
– 10% potassium iodide in ultra-pure water.

Standards

Titrations in the 0–100 µg L^{-1} range can be performed for all elements in Table 31.8. Sometimes calibration curves are more linear in the 0–20 µg L^{-1} range. It is easier to start with commercial standard solutions. For example, arsenic titration can start from a commercial solution at 1,000 mg (As) L^{-1} which is diluted to 1 mg (As) L^{-1} (two successive dilutions of 10 mL in 100 mL) to obtain the stock solution used to prepare the calibration range. In four 100 mL volumetric flasks, add 0, 0.5, 1 and 2 mL of the 1 mg (As) L^{-1} stock solution. Complete the volumes to obtain the calibration range 0, 5, 10 and 20 µg (As) L^{-1}. The final medium should be the same as that of the sample solution, (for the attack described in Sect. 31.2.4, add 4 ml of concentrated nitric acid giving a 4% nitric acid medium).

For certain elements like arsenic, it is recommended to perform reduction before analysis so only the As^{+III} form is used. Indeed, the sensitivity of this titration depends on the yield of hydrides formed, which is itself linked to the oxidation state of this element in solution. Mix a sample of the As solution with 5 mL of ½HCl + 5 mL of 10% KI solution. Heat for 20 min in a water bath at 60°C, let cool and complete to 50 mL with ultra-pure water.

Calculation

If X is the content of a given element on the calibration curve in µg L^{-1} and V the volume (mL) of the attack solution, D the possible dilution factor before analysis and P the sample specimen of soil (g), the content T in ng (element) g^{-1} (soil) is expressed by $T = X V D / P$.

Cold-Vapour Technique

Principle

This very sensitive technique is only used for titration of mercury. The apparatus is set up in the same way as for the hydride method shown in Fig. 31.3. The only difference is the measurement tube whose geometry is slightly different, allowing the output vapour to be trapped. A peristaltic pump enables addition of a stannous chloride solution and a hydroxylamine chlorhydrate solution which reduce mercury to the atomic state. The Hg^0 element is then transported in vapour form by the inert gas into the measurement tube where absorbance is measured at 253.7 nm.

Reagents

- 10% stannous chloride solution: dissolve 10 g of stannous chloride in 10 mL of ultra-pure hydrochloric acid, heat until complete dissolution, let cool and complete to 100 mL with ultra-pure water; fresh solution should be prepared each day
- 10% hydroxylamine chlorhydrate solution: dissolve 10 g in 100 mL of ultra-pure water
- ½ hydrochloric acid in ultra-pure water
- calibration range 0, 5, 10, 20 μg (Hg) L^{-1} starting from a 1 mg (Hg) L^{-1} stock solution: in 100 mL volumetric flasks, add 50 mL of ultra-pure water, 4 mL of spectrographic grade concentrated nitric acid and 0, 0.5, 1 and 2 mL of stock solution, respectively. Complete to volume with ultra-pure water
- trap solution for mercury vapours: dissolve 3 g of potassium iodide and 0.25 g of iodine in 100 mL of deionized water.

Calculations are identical to those described in "Calculation".

31.2.13 Analysis of Trace Elements by Electrothermal AAS

EAAS is currently one of the most sensitive techniques for titration of trace elements. For many elements, the detection limit of FAAS is lower by a factor of 100–1,000 with EAAS. The EAAS technique is particularly efficient when coupled with systems to correct non-selective absorption, particularly the Zeeman effect correcting system (Pansu et al. 2001). Furthermore, on liquid medium it is the most appropriate method for microanalysis as it requires only a few μL of solution for each element to be analyzed (usually 20 μL).

Satisfactory implementation of EAAS relies on optimization of instrumental parameters for each element in the titration medium, and very precise optimal atomization and decomposition temperatures. Chemical interferences can be minimized by using matrix corrective solutions added in the capillary tube at injection (for example 1 μL for 10 μL of sample). A matrix modifier that is often recommended is palladium nitrate ($Pd(NO_3)_2$). Other modifiers can be used e.g. $Mg(NO_3)_2$, $Ni(NO_3)_2$ or $NH_4H_2PO_4$ (see e.g. Hoenig and Kersabiec 1990). Table 31.9 lists the main trace elements titrated by EAAS. In addition, major elements can be titrated with much higher sensitivity than with FAAS (cf. "Major Elements by FAAS" in Sect. 31.2.11), however, these titrations generally do not justify the use of EAAS, which is more sophisticated and less repeatable than FAAS. These elements are consequently not included in Table 31.9.

The calibration range varies with the element concerned, and is often similar to the calibration ranges described in Sect. 31.2.12. Calculations are identical to those described in "Calculation" in Sect. 31.2.12.

Table 31.9. Trace elements in soils which can be analyzed by EAAS

ele-ment	λ (nm)	CC ($\mu g\ L^{-1}$)	ele-ment	λ (nm)	CC ($\mu g\ L^{-1}$)	ele-ment	λ (nm)	CC ($\mu g\ L^{-1}$)
Ag	328.1	0.035	As	193.7	0.5	Au	242.8	0.22
Ba	553.6	0.85	Be	234.9	0.025	Bi	223.1	0.45
Cd	228.8	0.01	Co	240.7	0.21	Cr	357.9	0.075
Cs	852.1	0.55	Cu	324.7	0.3			
Ga	294.4	0.23	Ge	265.1	0.45	In	303.9	0.35
Li	670.8	0.2	Mo	313.3	0.35	Ni	232.0	0.24
Pb	217.0	0.28	Pd	244.8	0.43	Pt	265.9	3.5
Rb	780.0	0.05	Rh	343.5	0.4	Ru	349.9	0.75
Sb	217.6	0.5	Se	196.0	0.7	Sn	235.5	0.5
Sr	460.7	0.1						
Tb	432.7	0.18	Te	214.3	0.45	Tl	276.8	0.75
V	318.5	1.1	Yb	398.8	0.15	Zn	213.9	0.0075

CC: characteristic concentration in pure water giving an absorbance signal of 0.0044 (1% absorption of incidental radiation), CC is greater than DL, λ is the recommended wavelength in nm. The major elements in soils are not included in this table

31.2.14 Analysis by Inductively Coupled Plasma–AES

Interest and Limitations

ICP-AES is being increasingly used in geochemistry mainly because it is a multi-element technique. For most elements, its sensitivity is similar to

FAAS (cf. Sect. 31.2.11), but ICP-AES is less sensitive than EAAS (cf. Sect. 31.2.13), hydride or cold-vapour AAS (cf. Sect. 31.2.12), and ICP-MS (cf. Sect. 31.2.15).

Most disturbances that occur are caused by spectral interference due to the number of lines emitted at high temperatures in complex mediums. Mechanical disturbances may also occur due to changes in the input flow of the analytical solution and the resulting clogging of nebulizers in the case of solutions containing too high quantities of dissolved materials.

Another problem concerns the choice of a multi-element calibration strategy. Calibration solutions must have concentration ranges near the ranges of the mediums to be measured. Matrix interference is not common but can result in changes in sensitivity and in the curvature of the calibration curves, which may be different from those of the sample solutions. Two fundamental causes of variation in the emitted signal are (i) change in the temperature of the plasma, (ii) change in the input of analytical solution. Two possible ways to correct these disturbances are based on the use of internal standards. Ramsey and Coles (1992) recommended the use of a correcting programme based on two internal standards: rubidium to correct the change in sample input flow, and mercury to correct the emission temperature. For analysis of major elements (Si, Al, Fe, Mg, Ca and Na), Walsh (1992) proposed the use of gallium, cadmium and lithium as internal standards to reduce relative standard variation to about 0.5%. The elements added as internal standards are not analyzed; their initial amount in the analytical solution should be insignificant.

According to Walsh (1992) the random error resulting from the use of classical ICP-AES technique for analysis of geological materials is about 2%, i.e. of the same order of magnitude as other analytical techniques. In most cases the classical external calibration method can be used. For analytical mediums containing a small quantity of dissolved solid materials, precision is improved if the composition of the multi-element calibration range is as near as possible to that of the analytical medium. In addition, as with other methods, reference materials from inter-laboratory comparisons (Abbey 1992) enable the accuracy of analytical series to be checked.

Multi-Element Calibration for Major Elements

The medium for multi-element calibration range must be as similar as possible to the sample solution. The preparation described here concerns total analysis using the procedure with lithium metaborate described in "Procedure Using Lithium Metaborate". The weight of the sample specimen is 60 mg for a final volume of 200 mL. The final medium is 1% HCl, 0.25% LiBO$_2$.

Table 31.10. Preparation of a multielement calibration range for major elements; contents expressed in % oxide in the soil sample (attack described in "Procedure Using Lithium Metaborate" of section 31.2.6: 60 mg sample specimen, 200 mL final volume), commercial stock solutions at 1 g (element) L^{-1}.

		Al$_2$O$_3$ (%)	Fe$_2$O$_3$ (%)	TiO$_2$ (%)	CaO (%)	MgO (%)	Na$_2$O (%)	K$_2$O (%)	MnO (%)
	oxide solution								
mL of	0	0	0	0	0	0	0	0	0
1 g (el.) L^{-1}	I	12.5	15	2.5	15	12.5	10	20	2.5
solution	II	25	30	5	30	25	20	40	5
	III	50	60	10	60	50	40	80	10
content of	0	0	0	0	0	0	0	0	0
solution (1 L)	I	23.62	21.45	4.17	20.99	20.73	13.48	24.09	3.23
mg (ox) L^{-1}	II	47.24	42.89	8.34	41.98	41.45	26.96	48.18	6.46
	III	94.47	85.78	16.68	83.95	82.90	53.92	96.37	12.91
% oxide	0	0	0	0	0	0	0	0	0
in soil	I	7.87	7.15	1.67	7.00	6.91	4.49	8.03	1.08
sample	II	15.75	14.30	2.78	13.99	13.81	8.99	16.06	2.15
	III	31.49	28.59	5.56	27.98	27.63	17.97	32.12	4.30

The calibration range in Table 31.10 corresponds to the elements Al, Fe, Ti, Ca, Mg, Na, K and Mn, the elements Si and P being quantified separately. For each element, prepare a blank assay (0) and 3 calibration points (I, II, III in Table 31.10) corresponding to possible oxide contents in soils and rocks.

Place the appropriate volume of each 1 g L^{-1} stock solution in a 1 L volumetric flask (see Table 31.10), add 200 ml of a 12.5 g (LiBO$_2$) L^{-1} in 5% HCl solution. Complete to 1 L with deionized water to obtain the final medium of the sample solutions after attack (cf. "Procedure Using Lithium Metaborate"), i.e. 0.25% LiBO$_2$, 1% HCl. This multi-element calibration range enables the results to be obtained directly as the percentage of oxide in the soil sample for a test specimen of 60 mg

(Table 31.10) and a final extraction volume of 200 ml. For a test specimen of M mg, the result has to be multiplied by $60/M$.

Titration of phosphorus is not very precise nor very sensitive with ICP-AES. Nevertheless, the P content can be measured if it is not too low. A calibration range can be prepared starting from a 1 g (P) L^{-1} stock solution, giving P contents of 0, 10, 25, 50, 75 μg mL^{-1}, corresponding to P_2O_5 contents of 0, 22.90, 57.26, 114.52 and 171.77 μg mL^{-1} in the solution and 0% 7.63% 19.09% 38.17% 57.25% in the initial sample.

Solutions containing silicon are not very stable. To measure silica, a standard reference material should be used (e.g. Geostandard, CRPG-CNRS 54 501 Vandœuvre les Nancy, France) and attacked in the same way as the samples. Alternatively, a known weight of pure commercial silica can be used. These solutions do not keep and silica should be titrated within two days after the attack.

Complex Calibration Range for Titration of Trace Elements

The ICP-AES technique makes it possible to titrate 70 elements of the periodic table. In the same way as for the major elements (cf. "Multi-Element Calibration for Major Elements"), the standard solutions for the multi-element calibration range of trace elements should be prepared in the preparation medium. The sample calibration range in Table 31.11 corresponds to the eight trace elements that are most often titrated in soils and rocks. It is prepared in the same medium as for total attack in an open vessel (cf. "Procedure" in Sect. 31.2.3) and consequently does not include elements that can be lost by volatilization during the attack, e.g. Pb, Cd, As or Se. The Cr value may be underestimated in the event of incomplete attack of certain refractory minerals. As in "Multi-Element Calibration for Major Elements", the calibration range should be established starting from commercial stock solutions.

Prepare the solutions in 1 L volumetric flasks by adding the volumes of stock solutions listed in Table 31.11. Add 500 mL of ultra-pure deionized water, then 50 mL of concentrated hydrochloric acid and complete to 1 L with ultra-pure water at 20°C. Solution 0 (blank) can be prepared in the same way, but without addition of stock standard solution.

Calculation

For a sample specimen of P g (0.5 g) in a final volume V (mL) of solution (50 mL), the concentration C_s (μg g^{-1}) for each element of the sample results from that found on the corresponding calibration curve C_l (μg mL^{-1}) by: $C_s = C_l V/P$.

Table 31.11. Example of multi-element calibration range for trace elements

element	mL of stock solution at 1 g L^{-1} for 1 L of solution III	solution III (mg L^{-1})	solution II (mg L^{-1})	solution I (mg L^{-1})
Ba	15	15	7.50	3.75
Be	1	1	0.50	0.25
Co	5	5	2.50	1.25
Cr	5	5	2.50	1.25
Cu	2.5	2.5	1.25	0.62
Ni	5	5	2.50	1.25
Sr	15	15	7.50	3.75
Zn	5	5	2.50	1.25

Calibration Range for Titration of Rare Earth

Prepare the calibration range in the same way as for the other trace elements (cf. above "Complex Calibration Range for Titration of Trace Elements") in a 5% hydrochloric acid medium corresponding to total attack in an open vessel (cf. "Procedure" in Sect. 31.2.3). Commercial stock solutions can be used. Quantities for the most concentrated solution III are listed in Table 31.12 (Le Cornec, IRD, Bondy, France, personal communication). The standard solutions are all in 5% hydrochloric acid medium.

Operating Conditions for ICP-AES Equipment

As each type of apparatus requires specific adjustments, the reader is advised to consult specialized publications and to respect the manufacturer's instructions. Table 31.13 gives some wavelengths that can be used for the emission lines of soil elements by plasma emission spectrometry. For other measurements, the reader should refer to more complete publications (e.g. Boumans 1981; Winge et al. 1982).

Table 31.12. Preparation of a multi-element calibration range for titration of rare earth (+ Yttrium)

element	stock solution $(g\,L^{-1})$	mL stock solution for 1 L solution III	solution III $(mg\,L^{-1})$	solution II $(mg\,L^{-1})$	solution I $(mg\,L^{-1})$
Ce	1.0	2.0	2.00	1.000	0.500
Dy	0.1	5.0	0.50	0.250	0.125
Eu	0.1	2.5	0.25	0.125	0.062
Er	0.1	5.0	0.50	0.250	0.125
La	1.0	1.0	1.00	0.500	0.250
Nd	1.0	1.0	1.00	0.500	0.250
Sm	0.1	5.0	0.50	0.250	0.125
Yb	0.1	5.0	0.50	0.250	0.125
Y	1.0	2.0	2.00	1.000	0.500

31.2.15 Analysis by Inductively Coupled Plasma-Mass Spectrometry

Interest and Dfialties

ICP-MS is analysis by mass spectrometry of ions emitted in a plasma into which the sample solution is injected (Fig. 31.4). In theory, all the elements of the periodic table and their isotopes can be measured by mass spectrometry, and, in addition, this type of detection is extremely sensitive.

However, in practice its implementation is rather delicate and requires an experienced operator. The equipment is expensive and is time-consuming to install. All analyses and attacks should be performed in a dust-free room. Protective clothing must be worn, the lab glassware must be very carefully cleaned and all the reagents must be of high purity. These requirements are similar to those of other techniques for analysis of trace element such as EAAS (cf. Sect. 31.2.13) but in this case it is even more important to respect them.

Table 31.13. Some wavelengths (λ in nm) of emission lines usable in soil analysis by ICP-AES and corresponding detection limits (DL)

ele-ment	λ (nm)	DL ($\mu g\ L^{-1}$)	ele-ment	λ (nm)	DL ($\mu g\ L^{-1}$)	ele-ment	λ (nm)	DL ($\mu g\ L^{-1}$)
Al	396.152 167.081	4 1.5	Ti	337.280 334.941	1 0.6	Si	288.158 251.611	18 5
Fe	259.940	1.5	Mn	257.610	0.3			
Ca	317.933 393.366	6 0.03	Na	588.995	1	P	213.618 177.499	19 18
Mg	285.213 279.553	0.9 0.1	K	769.896 766.490	20 10			
Sr	421.552 407.771	0.06 0.02	Cu	324.754	2	Co	228.616	5
Ni	231.604	5.5	Ba	455.403	0.07	Cr	267.716	4
Zn	213.856	0.9						
Y	371.030	0.2	La	408.672 379.478	0.02 0.02	Ce	413.380 418.660	9 7.5
Nd	430.358 401.225	2.5 2	Dy	353.603 353.170	0.3	Sm	359.262 442.434	8 7
Yb	328.937	0.3	Eu	381.967	0.3			

Remarks: DL ($\mu g\ L^{-1}$) is measured in pure water matrix, for soil extracts the DL can be higher
– lines of Al at 167.081 nm and P at 177.499 nm require purging of the optical channel and monochromator (vacuum, Ar, N_2) to avoid absorbance of O_2
– line Ca at 393.366 nm may be too sensitive if the concentration is high
– line K at 766.490 nm can be obstructed by Mg
– line La at 379.478 nm is obstructed by V and Fe
– line Sm at 442.434 nm, the spectral background is disturbed by an argon line located nearby

Another important question is the choice of the isotopes or isotopic combinations to take into account for the analysis of a given element. The mass spectra record the response of the detector (per unit of time) according to the *m/z* ratio characteristic of each ionized form of mass *m* and charge *z*. Because of the high temperature of the argon plasma (>5,000 K), normally all the chemical species are atomized and ionized.

However the temperature decreases very rapidly at the plasma output and at the input of the spectrometer, and recombination of ions can occur particularly in the most abundant species: argon, oxygen, nitrogen, ions coming from the acid medium, and major matrix ions. It is thus important to consider all the atomic and molecular species that can exist in the spectrometer, even in a very transitory way. This phenomenon could cause isobaric interferences (the same m/z for two species) which then have to be located.

Many authors proposed solutions for problems of interference. A lot of elements have several isotopes of known natural abundance that can be used to avoid analytical interferences. It is more difficult to find solutions for naturally monoisotopic elements (natural abundance is 100%, Table 31.14).

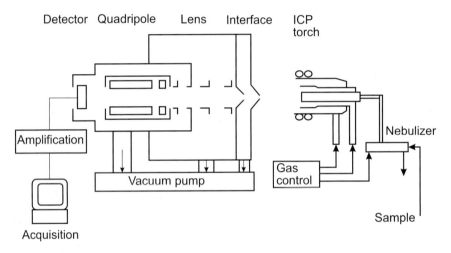

Fig. 31.4. Inductively Coupled Plasma - Mass Spectrometer

Table 31.14 lists the most commonly used isotopes and certain inter-ferences, but other choices are possible depending on the type of study. For example, for paleoclimatology, Le Cornec and Corrège (1997) titrated U, Ca and Sr simultaneously in corals. There are marked differences in concentration between the ultra-traces of uranium and the major elements Ca and Sr. For uranium, the most abundant isotope ^{238}U is used. The isotope ^{40}Ca cannot be used due to interference with ^{40}Ar. Because of the strong calcium concentration, the ^{44}Ca (natural abundance na: 2.086% of total calcium) and ^{42}Ca (na: 0.647%) isotopes are not usable as they saturate the detector. The ^{43}Ca (na: 0.135%) and

^{48}Ca (na: 0.187%) isotopes are used instead, but interference ^{43}Ca –^{43}Ca with ^{86}Sr should be checked.

Another problem with the ICP-MS technique is the instability of measurements when analytical solutions are used that have large quantities of dissolved solids or particulate solid residues. The diagram in Fig. 31.4 shows the difficulty involved in setting up and running the apparatus. The torch provides an argon plasma at atmospheric pressure at more than 5,000 K, whereas the mass spectrometer functions cold and under vacuum. The vacuum pumps must have a strong flow. The interface between the torch and the spectrometer is formed by two cones each with a small opening through which gas species from the plasma penetrate at supersonic speed. Variations in flow at the interface can cause serious instability. The cones should be cleaned regularly. Methods such as internal calibration and isotopic dilution are recommended to control instability during the course of measurement. The time lag and number of rinses between each injection should be sufficient to avoid effects of memory from one sample to another. With matrix solutions with a small quantity of solid residues, stability is comparable to plasma atomic emission spectrometry and sensitivity is around 1,000 times better.

In spite of the above-mentioned difficulties, plasma-mass spectrometry is a very promising method thanks to its great sensitivity and especially to the availability of a great number of isotopes of natural elements. Exploration of the range of possibilities offered by this method for geochemistry (Falkner et al. 1995), cosmochemistry (Shinotsuka and Ebihara 1997), pedology (Soltanpour et al. 1996), sciences of the environment (Trolard et al. 2002), sedimentology, etc. is only beginning. There is no doubt that it represents progress in the entire range of soil sciences.

Implementation

The preparation of the sample solutions for ICP-MS has to be particularly thorough to avoid isobaric interference with the matrix solution. Diluted nitric acid is recommended as final medium (cf. Sect. 31.2.2) starting from acid digestions (cf. Sects. 31.2.3 and 31.2.4) after careful elimination of other acids. Lithium metaborate is also recommended as reagent for alkaline fusion (cf. Sect. 31.2.6). The preparation of multi-element calibration ranges is similar to plasma emission spectrometry (cf. Sect. 31.2.14). Microwave digestion is also possible (Das et al. 2001).

Table 31.14. Frequently used isotopes for ICP-MS analysis (from Jarvis 1994b, Navez 1997)

element	m/z	abundance	Interference	Element	m/z	abundance	interference
Li	7	92.5		Be	9	100	
B	11	80		Na	23	100	
Mg	24	79		Al	27	100	
Si	29	4.7	NH	P	31	100	NO, NOH
S	33	0.75	O_2H	Cl	35	75.8	little sensitive
K	39	93.3		Ca	44	2.08	N_2O
Sc	45	100	CaH	Ti	47/49	7.3/5.5	SOH, CaH
V	51	99.7	ClO	Cr	52/53	83.8/9.5	ClOH
Mn	55	100		Fe	56/57	91.7/2.2	ArO, ArOH
Co	59	100		Ni	60	26.1	
Cu	63/65	69.2/30.8		Zn	66/68	27.9/18.8	S_2
Ga	71	39.9		Ge	72/73	27.4/7.8	FeO, FeOH
As	75	100	ArCl	Se	77	7.6	ArCl
Br	79/81	50.7/49.3		Rb	85	72.2	
Sr	88	82.6		Y	89	100	
Zr	90	51.4		Nb	93	100	
Mo	95	15.9[2]		Ru	99/101	12.7/17.0	
Rh	103	100		Pd	105	22.3	
Ag	107/109	51.8/48.2		Cd	111	12.8	
In	115	95.7	Sn	Sn	118	24.2	
Sb	121	57.3		Te	125	7.1	
I	127	100		Cs	133	100	
Ba	137	11.2		La	139	99.9	
Ce	140	88.5		Pr	141	100	
Nd	143/145/146	44.4		Sm	147/149/152	28.8/26.7	BaOH, CeO
Eu	151/153	47.8/52.2	BaO	Gd	157	15.7	PrO, CeOH
Tb	159	100		Dy	163	24.9	NdOH, SmO
Ho	165	100	SmO	Er	166/167	33.4/56.3	SmO, NdO

Tm	169	100	GdOH	Yb	172/173	21.8/38.1	GdO
Lu	175	97.4	GdOH	Hf	178	27.2	DyO
Ta	181	99.9		W	182	26.3	
Re	185	37.4		Os	189	16.1	
Ir	193	62.7		Pt	194/195	32.9/33.8	
Au	197	100		Hg	202	29.8	
Tl	205	70.5		Pb	206/207/208	98.6	sum of isotopes
Bi	209	100		Th	232	100	
U	238	99.3					

According to Falkner et al. (1995), *external calibration* methods ensure acceptable precision (3–8% coefficient of variation) for measurements far from the detection limits (DL) when similar mediums are used for calibration solutions and sample solutions. Measurements must be sufficiently spaced and rinsing must be sufficient to avoid possible effects of memory. At the IRD laboratory of Bondy (France), the degree of precision of the external calibration method is generally lower than 3% for concentrations above the DL, and 5–10% for concentrations close to DL (Le Cornec, IRD Bondy, France, personal communication). The method of *standard additions* can also improve the results in the case of complex and variable matrices. The *internal standard* method enables precision to be improved to 2–5% in both the external calibration method and the standard additions method. The internal standard must be close to the analyte in mass and ionization potential. This makes it possible to correct the measured signal by using its relationship with that of the internal standard as well as the standards or the samples. The *isotopic dilution* method uses one of the isotopes of the measured element as internal standard, thereby minimising the error of the internal standard method resulting from the proximity of the two isotopes in mass and ionization potential. Known volumes, concentrations and enrichment of the desired isotope (spike) have to be added to known volumes of titrated solutions. The concentration of the titrated element can then be calculated with a high degree of precision (0.1–1%).

The ICP-MS technique can be used to determine isotopic ratios, though generally with lower precision than that of thermal ionization-mass spectrometry (TIMS).

31.3. Analysis on Solid Medium

31.3.1 Methods

It has always been more difficult to chemically analyse solids than solutions. The atomic organization of solids is very elaborate, electrons of the external layers of atoms are mobilized in the conduction and valence bands, and are thus not directly accessible for chemical analysis. Formerly, it was necessary to destroy the lattice to break down the atomic entities, after which the usual range of chemical reactions could be used.

However, the situation changed completely after major discoveries concerning atomic structure, quantum chemistry and the interactions between radiation and matter. These fundamental discoveries led to an increase in the number of techniques available making it possible to observe the different energy levels of matter (Pansu et al. 2001).

The study of the organization of solid structures or mineralogy is concerned with lower energetic levels (cf. Part 1). Optical and electronic microscopy use photons or electrons transmitted or reflected by the surface layers for imaging techniques. X-rays or electronic radiations from deeper crystalline plans make it possible to characterize crystalline structures. The vibrations caused by infra-red radiations enable characterization of certain molecular bonds.

Higher energy levels of excitation are necessary for the physico-chemical analysis of solid materials. In conducting materials, a high-intensity flow of electrons allows atomization of the matter into a gas state and excitation of the outer electron layers of the atoms. The radiation emitted during the relaxation processes makes it possible to characterize and quantify these atoms. This is arc or spark spectrometry which resembles techniques with other energy sources of atomization such as flame or plasma emission spectrometry described in Sect. 31.2.

Excitation can also concern internal electronic layers of atoms with more complex processes of relaxation. Depending on the source of excitation and radiation from the target material, a wide range of spectroscopic methods are available, particularly methods using X-ray fluorescence. Microprobe techniques provide an accurate map of the chemical composition of solid materials at a microscopic scale. Lastly, excitation can affect the atomic nucleus itself, generally under the effect of a neutron bombardment, and analysis of the radiation emission from relaxation of the nucleus. This is neutron activation analysis.

Most of the spectrometric techniques described in Sect. 31.2 can theoretically also be used for solid materials. And some of them, for example EAAS using the Zeeman effect, have in fact been used. However, their use for solid materials is often limited by methodological problems. The main difficulty in flame or plasma emission spectrometry, in AAS and in plasma mass spectrometry is the reproducible introduction of a solid sample into the atomization source. This problem has already been the subject of many tests and proposals. It was partly solved by introducing the solid sample in the form of a suspension (slurry) into a liquid. Nevertheless, analysis of solid samples has never been particularly successful. Consequently most analysts preferred the methods using solubilization described in Sect. 31.2 of this chapter as they are well tested and much more reproducible. This preference was often reinforced by the difficulty of obtaining standards with a solid matrix close to that of the samples. Today this argument is less justified thanks to the availability of reference materials.

Arc and spark spectrometry requires conducting samples and thus cannot be directly used for the main soil materials. The sample generally has to be prepared by mixing it with graphite powder to make it conducting. This is undoubtedly the reason these methods have been more commonly used in metallurgy than in geology and soil sciences, where they have often remained at the qualitative or semi-quantitative stage in spite of promising beginnings (Voïnovitch 1988).

The main methods of quantitative analysis that are currently used for solid geological materials are: (i) microprobe techniques (at a microscopic scale, cf. Chap. 8), (ii) at a macroscopic scale X-ray fluorescence (cf. Sect. 31.3.2) and neutron activation analysis (cf. Sect. 31.3.3).

31.3.2 X-ray Fluorescence Analysis

Principle

When a sample is bombarded with high-energy X-ray radiation, a secondary X-ray is emitted at different wavelengths characteristic of each element of the sample. The same type of emission spectrum can be observed when other excitation sources are used, for example a flow of electrons in electronic microprobe of Castaing (1961). This X-ray emission spectrum results from excitation of the electrons of the internal atomic layers which change temporarily to higher quantum levels of energy: K to L layer, K to M layer, L to M layer, etc. While returning to its initial state, the excited electron emits an energy E (eV) related to the wavelength λ (nm) according to the Planck relation: $E = \dfrac{1240}{\lambda}$.

The X-ray range extends from the 0.01 to 20 nm, between UV and γ radiations, but the range used in X-ray fluorescence is limited to from 0.02 to 2 nm. The lightest elements, H and He, do not have a spectrum of X-ray fluorescence. The number of possible transitions increases greatly with the atomic number, but the transitions used in analysis are generally simple. They are often those of the deep layers, particularly the K layer. These lines are also referred by the Siegbahn terminology, i.e. for an element of symbol Sy: SyKα1, SyKβ2, SyLα, etc. This terminology shows the position of the electronic vacancy (e.g. layer K, L), the transition (α: vacancy layer to next layer, β: vacancy layer to following layer, etc.) and relative intensity of the transition (1 more intense than 2, etc.). Lines Kβ are approximately six times less intense than the corresponding Kα lines.

Equipment

A diagram of X-ray fluorescence equipment can be seen in Fig. 31.5. The excitation source is an X-ray tube whose principle is well-known. Electrons emitted by a filament heated to a high temperature are accelerated in an electric field (the potential can reach 50 kV) towards an metallic anode (anticathode). The electrons are slowed down in contact with the anode with emission of an X-ray spectrum made of a continuous band, and lines of metal with high atomic numbers comprise the anode (e.g. rhodium, tungsten). The lowest wavelength of the spectrum can be calculated according to the relation of Planck (cf. "Principle" in Sect. 31.3.2).

The main difference between the apparatuses is the identification mode of secondary X rays emitted by the sample: one-channel system with filter, wavelength dispersion, energy dispersion. Apparatuses with *wavelength dispersion* are the most widely used in earth science. They function according to the Bragg law (cf. Chap. 4), connecting the wavelength λ, the incidence angle of the beam θ and the reticular distance d: $\lambda = 2d \sin \theta$. With a crystal of known d, the wavelength is directly related to the angle of incidence on the rotating crystal. Several materials can be used for this crystal (Jones 1991). The choice of a suitable apparatus depends on the wavelengths analysed, the ideal being that the *2d* spacing of the reticular plans is similar to that of the wavelengths. Systems with a curved crystal aim to optimize focusing on the detector. The collimator is replaced by a slit, crystal and detectors are located on the same circle of focus or Rowland circle. *Energy dispersion* systems have been improved since the 1960s as a result of progress in electronics. A semi-conductor makes it possible to recognize each photon according to its energy and to count it in a measurement channel (multi-channel detectors).

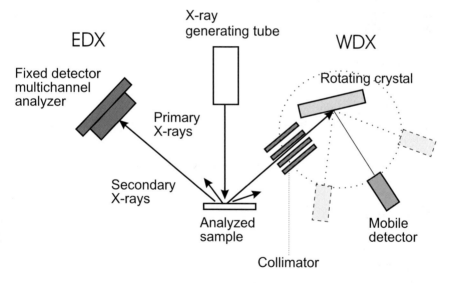

Fig. 31.5. Diagram of X-ray fluorescence equipment showing two possible types of detection: wavelength dispersive X-ray using flat or curved crystal (WDX on the *right*) and, energy dispersive X-ray (EDX on the *left*)

Interest and Limits

Another interesting aspect is that it is not destructive for the sample as during the relaxation process, the atoms return to their initial state.

X-ray fluorescence is a rapid analytical method that has a double advantage (i) multi-element analysis and (ii) direct analysis on solid materials. It enables detection of more than 80 elements with atomic numbers higher than eight (starting from fluorine). The method was used even for the analysis of lighter elements: carbon, nitrogen and oxygen in soils (Jones 1991). Certain elements like Br, S and P can be sensitively analyzed by X-ray fluorescence whereas their analysis using other techniques can be problematic.

X-ray fluorescence makes analysis of trace elements possible. However its sensitivity is often lower than the more powerful techniques of atomic absorption (cf. Sects. 31.2.12 and 31.2.13), plasma emission (cf. Sects. 31.2.14 and 31.2.15) or neutron activation (cf. Sect. 31.3.3). Jones (1991) provided an approximate guide to the minimum detectable concentrations which vary greatly with the atomic number of the element concerned. Thus from sodium ($Z = 11$) to calcium ($Z = 20$) the detectable minima decrease exponentially with the atomic number from 1,000 µg g^{-1} for Na to approximately 2 µg g^{-1} for Ca. The most sensitive elements are transition metals Cr to Zn with a detection limit near 1 µg g^{-1}. This threshold then increases with the atomic number, and the detection limit for Ba ($Z = 56$) is approximately 10 µg g^{-1}.

The main difficulty in analysis by X-ray fluorescence concerns the matrix effects; this often resulted in the method only being used for qualitative or semi-quantitative analysis. Some disturbances are physical and concern homogeneity, particle size, surface quality and thickness of the sample. Other disturbances are chemical (i) spectral interferences between elements, (ii) inter-element effects of absorption or exaltation of the re-emitted radiation. Background noise from the matrix is a serious source of potential error. Indeed, contents are calculated by difference between a peak and the background noise on both sides of this peak.

Solid samples must be carefully prepared by very fine crushing, the sample must have a very smooth surface, and not be too thick to reduce background noise but thick enough to avoid reducing fluorescence. The composition of the calibration standards must be close to that of the sample.

For analysis of major elements, the best way to prepare a sample is to make a solid solution or glass with an alkaline borate in a similar way as for attack by alkaline fusion (cf. Sect. 31.2.6). In this way samples and standards are transformed into homogeneous thin flat discs. The works of Norrish and Hutton (1969) provided a reference for geological materials on this subject. The same authors also proposed a method of calculation allowing correction of the matrix effects, thereby making X-ray fluorescence an appropriate method for quantitative analysis.

Alkaline solid solutions result in dilution of the sample and are consequently not suitable for analysis of trace elements, or even for analysis of not very sensitive major elements like sodium (and even magnesium in certain samples). Instead compressed disks are recommended for these elements in which great pressure is applied to the finely crushed sample and a thin flat disc is obtained.

Analysis of Major Elements

The method described here was originally proposed by Norrish and Hutton (1969), then by Jones (1982) and by Karathanasis and Hajek (1996).

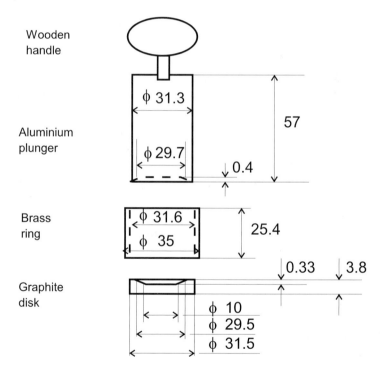

Fig. 31.6. Mould for preparation of disc-shaped samples of solid solution of borated glass for analysis of the major elements by X-ray fluorescence (according to Norrish and Hutton 1969; dimensions in mm)

Equipment

– 15 mL crucibles made of 95% Pt and 5% Au alloy
– tongs with platinum tips for handling hot crucibles or a ring made of platinum wire for stirring the molten mixtures
– mould for the discs (Fig. 31.6)
– Meker burner or muffle furnace (1,000°C)
– heating plate regulated at 200°C.

Products

– Fusion mixture: use a commercial mixture or prepare a synthesis mixture as follows: for 100 g, mix 46.53 g of lithium tetraborate ($Li_2B_4O_7$), 36.24 g of lithium carbonate (Li_2CO_3), 16.17 g of lanthanum oxide (LaO), and 1.07 g of lithium nitrate ($LiNO_3$)
– sodium carbonate and diluted hydrochloric acid for cleaning the crucibles
– pure silica and other major oxides of soils for disks for the blank assay and standards of calibration.

Procedure

– Use samples crushed to less than 200 µm and dried at 110°C.
– Heat the mould (Fig. 31.6) on a heating plate set at 220°C.
– Introduce exactly 340 mg of sample and 1.8 g of melting mixture in a previously tared Pt/Au crucible. Mix carefully with a spatula, then bring slowly to melting with a Mecker burner or in a muffle furnace at 1,000°C. Stir the liquid in fusion with the platinum wire or swirl the crucible with a tong to mix well and to eliminate bubbles.
– Place the brass ring around the graphite disc (Fig. 31.6). Decant the melted mixture in the centre of the disk and immediately level it with the aluminium plunger. Withdraw the plunger and ring and transfer the disc sample between two heat insulators placed on the heating plate. At the end of the procedure, cool the heating plate slowly then put the disc-shaped samples into small numbered envelopes and store in a desiccator until analysis.
– In the same way as the samples prepare (i) a disc made of pure silica which is used as a blank for measurement of background noise, (ii) standard calibration discs starting from oxides mixed with pure silica. Reference samples can also be used as standards.
– For quantitative analysis, measure the weight loss of a sample separately by heating it to 1,000°C under the same conditions.

The measurement procedure for counting X-ray fluorescence radiations depends on the equipment used. As a source of excitation applied to the disc-samples, a chromium X-ray tube under 40–50 kV is appropriate for all the major elements except Mn for which a tungsten tube is recommended.

Calculations

For a given element, N_p is the measured counting rate of the sample peak or the standard peak (corrected for dead time of the equipment), and N_b is the peak of the background noise or blank assay.

Calculate the counting rate of the peak sample (N_e) or standard (N_s) by the respective differences peak minus blank ($N_p - N_b$) or peak minus background noise ($N_p - (N_{b+} + N_{b-})/2$ where N_{b+} and N_{b-} is the background noise measured on both sides of the peak).

C_s being the percent concentration of the standard (in oxide percentage), the initial estimation of concentration C_e of the sample is expressed by

$$C_e = C_s \frac{N_e}{N_s}.$$

The sum of percents of major elements and weight loss during fusion should be close to 100%. For more precise measurements, the calculation of matrix correction developed by Norrish and Hutton (1969) can be applied

$$C_e^1 = C_e \left(M + \sum_i p_i m_i + p_p m_p \right),$$

where C_e^1 is the corrected concentration of oxide as a percentage of element e,

p_i is the mass fraction of each oxide ($p_i = C_i/100$),
p_p is the mass fraction of loss by volatilization during preparation,
M is the correction coefficient of the matrix (borated glass) for element e,
m_i and m_p are the correction coefficients for element e of each oxide i of the sample and for loss by volatilization, respectively.

The correction coefficients M, m_i and m_p were determined by Norrish and Hutton (1969) and by Jones (1982). For example, application of the formula to calculate the corrected percent of Fe_2O_3 for an approximate concentration $C_e = 8.4\%$ with a weight loss of 9.5% gives

$$C_{Fe_2O_3}^1 = 8.4\,[1.046 + (0.084\times(-0.027)) - 0.031 p_{MnO} + 0.146 p_{TiO_2} +$$
$$0.134 p_{CaO} + 0.126 p_{K_2O} - 0.06 p_{SO_3} - 0.06 p_{P_2O_5} - 0.065 p_{SiO_2}$$
$$- 0.074 p_{Al_2O_3} - 0.09 p_{MgO} - 0.110 p_{Na_2O} + (0.095\times(-0.163))]$$

The formula is applied in a similar way for all the oxides in the sample. Starting from the corrected percentages C_e^1, the new mass fractions are deduced and the correction formula is again applied to obtain the new estimated percentage C_e^2. The correction process is continued until the difference between one and the following estimate is negligible. In the best possible case, the sum of corrected values and weight loss should be $100 \pm 0.1\%$. Manual calculations of correction coefficients are rather time-consuming, but can be done very rapidly with a computer thereby avoiding the risk of introducing errors in the coefficients.

Analysis of Minor and Trace Elements

There are many alternative methods for the analysis of minor and trace elements using X-ray fluorescence. The method described below was inspired by Norrish and Chappell (1977), Jones (1982) and Karathanasis and Hajek (1996). The goal is to obtain a pelletized sample with a homogeneous surface that is as flat and as smooth as possible for analysis. This is not possible with all soils and alternative solutions will be required, e.g. additives for crushing and pelletising or using film as a support.

Equipment and Reagents

– Non-polluting grinder to reduce the samples to a very fine particle-size i.e. under 50 μm. Several alternatives are possible, see Tan, 1996; Pansu et al. 2001
– 25 ton hydraulic press
– pressing mould of the type shown in Fig. 31.7.
– boric acid or cellulose or other type of coating to maintain the shape of the pellets.

Procedure

Assemble the cylinder and the polished steel base plate of the mould (Fig. 31.7). Insert the filler tube in the aluminium cylinder. Add approximately 2 g of sample or standard in fine powder form with a particle size below 50 μm. Flatten by pressing and rotating the filling piston. Withdraw the piston and filling cylinder so as to leave a vacuum between the compression cylinder and the sample. Cautiously add the coating powder around and above the sample.

Insert the polished steel piston in the cylinder and using the hydraulic press, apply enough pressure to obtain a satisfactory pellet (generally 5–10 ton for 1–2 min).

Replace the moulding base plate with the unmoulding plate (Fig. 31.7) and unmould the pellet with the press. Store the pellet samples and standards in small individual numbered envelopes in a desiccator until analysis.

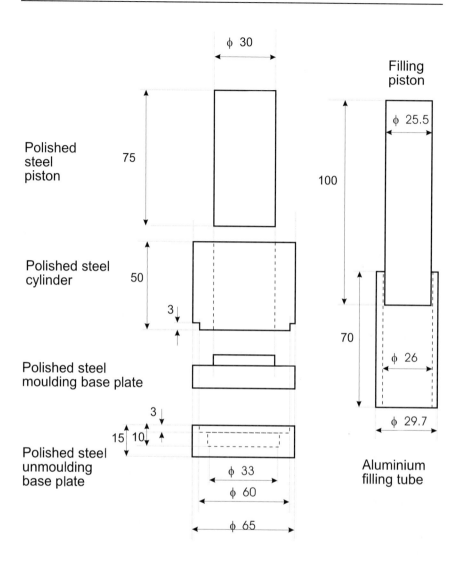

Fig. 31.7. Example of pelletising mould for analysis of minor and trace elements by X-ray fluorescence

Calculations

For the samples and standards, calculate the number of net impulsions measured during counting (cf. "Calculations" in "Analysis of major elements" above). Trace the calibration lines of the impulses vs. concentration for each element of the calibration standards and estimate the content of the samples starting from these lines. Matrix corrections may also be necessary. They should be estimated for each type of sample and element and are less standardized than in "Calculations" in Analysis of major elements.

31.3.3 Neutron Activation Analysis

Interest and Limits

Whereas the main spectroscopic methods use transitions originating from electrons of the external (cf. Sect. 31.2) or internal (cf. Sect. 31.3.2) electronic layers of the atoms, neutron activation analysis (NAA) is concerned with transitions originating from the atomic nucleus. In this case, the results are not affected by variations in the state of the chemical bonds between elements.

NAA is a very sensitive and precise method which enables the determination of more than 70 elements of the periodic table. It was often used as reference for comparison with other techniques to test their precision. Contrary to many spectroscopic methods which require dissolutions (cf. Sect. 31.2), NAA is particularly well suited for the analysis of solid materials like soils and rocks. A possible source of error originating from dissolution is thus eliminated. Liquid materials can also be analysed by NAA, but these analyses are not recommended because of the dangers linked with the expansion of these mediums during irradiation.

The method was first proposed in 1936 only four years after the discovery of neutrons. At the beginning, these analyses used not very selective detectors and chemical separation was thus required; many different procedures were proposed by pioneers like Albert (1964). The primary interest of these separation methods was that they were applied after labelling of the sample by neutron activation. No pollution was introduced by unlabelled reagents as only labelled elements were measured. On the contrary, addition of the unlabelled form of the element to be quantified enabled the separation of the labelled form in a much more effective way than in a traditional chemical separation. This was the technique of isotopic carriers.

Today progress in electronics and detection systems enables quantification of many elements without chemical separation even at trace levels. Instrumental neutron activation (INAA) enables routine analysis of around 30 elements in soils, and this is consequently the only technique described here. But separation is required in a few cases to quantify ultra-traces of elements: the detection limit of the method can be lowered more than 1,000 times when using post-irradiation chemical separation. So the separation methods with isotopic carriers are still useful for certain geochemical or environmental studies.

One drawback of the method is the aptitude of the elements to form radioactive isotopes with measurable radiation. The main technical difficulty is obtaining access to a nuclear reactor for neutron activation. The number of safety measures to be respected when handling the radioisotopes is also a serious constraint.

Principle

General Description

Neutron activation analysis initially consists of exposing the material to a flow of radiation able to cause transformation of the atomic nuclei and produce artificial radioisotopes. The study of the radiations emitted by these synthetic radioisotopes then enables identification and quantification of the elements contained in the sample. Artificial radioisotopes of all the elements can be obtained using different types of projectiles: neutrons, protons, α particles ($_2^4He^{2+}$), deutons ($_2^1H^+$) or photons γ. However, neutron activation is the most widely used. The most common capture of a neutron by an element E of atomic mass m and atomic number Z is written:

$$_Z^m E + {}_0^1 n \rightarrow {}_Z^{m+1} E^* + \gamma$$

To simplify, specialists often describe this reaction by $^m E(n, \gamma)^{m+1}E$, e.g., for potassium: $^{41}K(n, \gamma)^{42}K$.

The radioactive relaxation of activated atoms can take place in five different ways: ejection of an electron (β^-) from the nucleus, ejection of a positron (β^+), ejection of 2 protons and 2 neutrons ($_4^2He$, α), electron capture and fission. The most common way a decrease occurs in the isotopes produced by neutron activation is β^- emission which tends to compensate for the increase in the neutron/proton ratio of the nuclei by neutron activation. The radioactive decrease is accompanied by emission of γ radiations of different energies resulting from relaxation of the activated nuclear forms according to a specific relaxation scheme for each element. For an activated element E, the reaction is written:

$$_Z^{m+1} E^* \rightarrow {}_{Z+1}^{m+1}E^* + \beta^- + \gamma$$

γ-ray spectrometry is the most widely used approach in neutron activation because detection of γ radiations is the easiest. Each activated element provides a spectrum of radioactive decrease that is well indexed in reference works and publications such as Lederer and Shirley (1978), Erdtmann and Soyka (1975a, 1975b), Lis et al. (1975a, 1975b). The choice of a γ line for analysis requires taking into account the half-life of the isotope, the intensity and the energy of the line and possible spectral interferences with other radioisotopes. Compilations like those of Koons and Helmke (1978), Helmke (1982) or Helmke (1996) provide useful information for the main soils.

Quantitative Analysis

After irradiation, the decrease rate of a $^{m+1}_{\quad z}E*$ atom is proportional to N the number of this atom in the sample and λ the kinetic constant of decrease, i.e. $dN/dt = -\lambda N$. By integration, N_0 being the number of atoms at time origin t_0, the decrease law is expressed by:

$$N = N_0 \; e^{-\lambda t}$$

The kinetic constant is often replaced by the half-life of the radioelement: $T_{1/2}$ when $N = N_0/2$ and thus $T_{1/2} = \dfrac{\ln 2}{\lambda}$.

If all the atoms of the element to be titrated were systematically transformed into measured radioisotopes, the decrease law would enable their concentration to be determined immediately using the initial number of atoms N_0. In practice, the number of radioactive atoms produced by irradiation of an element is proportional to its capture cross section and to the flow of neutrons. NAA is performed by comparison of the radiation counted on the sample and on a standard of calibration. As counting is not performed simultaneously on the sample and the standard, the exact time and date of counting of each one should be carefully recorded. All measurements are then brought back to the same reference time t_0 by means of the above equation before calculation of the concentration.

Apparatus and Measurements

Neutron Activation

Although small neutron generators exist, the best sources of radiation for NAA of geochemical materials are the nuclear reactors used for research. They enable sensitive analysis because they provide big homogeneous flows of thermal neutrons of from 10^{13} to 10^{15} neutrons $cm^{-2} s^{-1}$.

Samples and standards are encapsulated in containers made of materials with a weak and homogeneous neutron capture section. These containers are transported automatically (usually pneumatically) into the flow of neutrons in the middle of the reactor. The length of irradiation depends on the analysis to be carried out. A duration of several times the half-life of the element to be analyzed may be required to obtain the maximum level of induced activity. Compromise and optimization is required in the case of multi-element titration. In practice, the irradiation times of geological materials vary from a few seconds for short-lived elements to 4–12 h for long-lived elements.

Irradiation is generally carried out by thermal neutrons, as most reactors, (e.g. Osiris, Saclay, France) provide an energy distribution of neutrons in the 0.01 eV zone. Depending on analytical requirements, it is possible to modify the relative activities of the activated elements. Indeed, the cross-sections of the elements vary with the energy of the neutrons. Thus, thermal neutrons can be eliminated from the radiation flux by surrounding the sample with cadmium leaf. In this case, only the epithermal neutrons with energy higher than 0.5 eV take part in activation (the length of irradiation is then generally increased, i.e. up to 25 h). Under these conditions the activity of certain elements like ^{46}Sc, which produce high background noise, is considerably reduced and as a result, the titration of other elements, like Nd, Zr and Ni, is much more precise (Chayla et al. 1973).

γ-Ray Spectrometry

The function of the detector is to convert radiation into an electric signal whose amplitude is proportional to its energy. For γ-ray spectrometry, old scintillation detectors like NaI crystal doped with Tl, were replaced by modern detectors using semiconductors. Among the latter, the Ge(Li) detector (germanium doped with lithium) was used for many years. This detector performed well, but had the disadvantage of being very fragile due to the mobility of lithium at room temperature. The crystal had to be permanently cooled with liquid nitrogen and, in the absence of liquid nitrogen, detection properties could be destroyed in a few minutes. This is why Ge(Li) detectors have now been replaced by the *ultra-pure germanium detector*, also called intrinsic detector. This detector has a very good energy-discriminating capacity. But even though it is not destroyed at ambient temperature, it still needs to be cooled with liquid nitrogen during measurements.

The resolution of a γ-ray spectrometer varies with energetic level of the line concerned which is usually defined in terms of "full width at half the maximum height (FWHM)" of a peak. A resolution of 1.6 or 1.9 keV at 1,330 keV (^{60}Co) is useful to distinguish very close peaks of several major elements in soils (e.g. Sc and Zn, Br, As and Sb). The yield of a detector increases with its size, especially for high energy γ-rays. The cost also increases with size, so it is often necessary to find a compromise. The detector should be assembled on a cryostat containing about 30 L of liquid nitrogen. It should be set up far from any source of radiation and be protected from cosmic and terrestrial radiations with lead leaf.

Multi-channel analysers are needed to enable discrimination of the pulsation heights and count them in each channel connected to the incidental energy of radiation. They must have a minimum of 2,048 channels but 4,096 channels or more are preferable in INA. Both analog and digital systems are available. The time required for signal acquisition (counting time) varies from a few minutes to one to ten hours depending on the element analysed, the irradiation used and the delay between irradiation and acquisition. The geometry and positioning of the samples and standards on the detector must be perfectly reproducible.

After acquisition, the signal is treated by computer (manual treatment is also possible but time consuming) to locate the peaks and to identify them via the energy channel, to separate badly identified peaks by signal deconvolution, and to measure surfaces while subtracting_background noise. Mass and time are then corrected on the samples and standards before the concentrations are calculated.

Procedure

Miscellaneous

Many alternative procedures can be used depending on the aims of the analysis. The optimum length of irradiation depends on the element concerned (cf. "Neutron Activation"). The same is true of the time lag between irradiation and measurement. Salmon and Cawse (1991) demonstrated the importance of this time lag depending on the elements to be measured. A few minutes after irradiation, medium and long-lived elements are masked by considerable background noise, while very short-lived elements like Al, Mg or V are available. As the radioactivity of the sample decreases, the background noise decreases and other elements are detected and become measurable: Ca at 30 min, Mn and Na at 3 h, Br, La, Sc, K at 3–4 days, Tb, Th, Cr, Eu, Fe, Co after ten days, etc. The procedure described below is used at the Pierre Sue laboratory, Saclay, France, for titration of rare earth and medium and long-lived trace elements in rocks and soils.

Equipment and Reagents

– Standard amples of soil and rocks provided by national or international organizations for quality control and standardization (Pansu et al. 2001)
– aluminium or plastic irradiation shuttles 10 cm length and 2 cm in diameter tightly sealed by crimping the edges
– ultra-pure aluminium paper
– nuclear reactor or neutron source
– automated system of transport between the laboratory and the neutron source with a special hood equipped with remote arm manipulators for the reception of irradiated samples
– glove box with sealed Plexiglas airlock
– 1 cm^3 cylindro-conical plastic container with tight stoppers
– lead bricks for protection
– ultra-pure germanium γ-ray detector (or Ge(Li) detector) with a resolution of less than 2 keV at 1,333 keV and a yield of 15–25%
– complementary cooling equipment containing about 30 L of liquid nitrogen
– lead leaf for radiation protection
– multi-channel analyser using 4,096 energy channels
– micro-computer with suitable software for the acquisition and treatment of signals.

Sample Preparation and Irradiation

It is advisable to use two standards per irradiation shuttle: the first (E) for calculation of concentration by calibration, the second (C) for control of accuracy. Samples and standards must be dried in the same way (in the air or in a drying oven) and finely crushed to a particle-size of less than 100 μm. Some crushing materials, such as tungsten carbide, should not be used because of pollution by trace elements. Agate crushers are recommended because of their high purity.

With scissors cut squares of aluminium paper with sides of approximately 3 cm. Fold the squares in half and write the reference of the sample or standard in felt pen. Unfold and accurately weigh approximately (depending on the contents) 100 mg (±0.1 mg) of the sample or standard in the square. Using fine laboratory forceps, carefully crimp the three edges of the square to seal the powder inside.

Pile up samples and standards in the shuttle (10–20) with one E standard at each end and one in the middle, and a C standard in the middle. For irradiation with epithermal neutrons, wrap all the samples in a cadmium leaf. Close the shuttle by crimping.

Send the shuttle into the flow of neutrons (2×10^{14} n cm^{-2} s^{-1} at the Osiris reactor in Saclay, France) for the selected irradiation time: about 6 h under total flux for determination of rare earth and some transition elements, 12–25 h with epithermal neutrons.

Measurements

Recover the irradiated shuttle and let it stand behind lead bricks in the recovery hood for ten days. Unseal the shuttle and transfer it in a glove box with a sealed airlock behind two lead bricks.

Using fine laboratory forceps, cautiously open the aluminium paper of each sample or standard and quantitatively transfer the sample powder in a 1 cm^3 cylindro-conical plastic container marked with the same reference number as the corresponding aluminium paper. This should be carried out close to a moist filter paper to recover volatile radioactive dust.

Carefully stop the plastic containers. Recover the shuttle and used aluminium papers, the wet filter paper and the cleaning paper and put them in a small airtight bag in the radioactive waste bin. Check the radioactivity of the glove box with the Geiger counter and clean again with a wet filter paper if necessary.

Each plastic container to be counted should be successively placed in exactly the same position in the detector (the distance should be adjusted at the beginning as a function of signal amplitude), and the exact time and date of counting recorded. Let count for approximately 50 minutes using the same counting time for each sample or standard (note the time).

Again allow the activity of the samples to decrease behind lead bricks for approximately one month. Count in the same way as previously, but this time for ten hours. This counting is performed 40 days after irradiation and provides more complete and precise results on long-lived elements than the first counting 10 days after irradiation.

Calculations

Locate and identify the element corresponding to each peak depending on the γ-ray energy of the measurement channel. Measure the peak surface by numerical integration of the counting rates "peak minus background noise". It is necessary to take all peak overlapping into account as this could distort measurements. A range of methods make it possible to avoid the overlap error: e.g. peak location by the null first derivative (top of peak) or null second derivatives (inflexion points), adjustment using the Gaussian law (or similar) and deconvolution, Fourrier transformation. Moreover, the γ-ray spectrum of each element is well known and the possible spectral interferences clearly identified. Each element can be calculated several times using the different peaks of its γ-ray spectrum. The relative intensities between these peaks being known, spectrum libraries can be used to deconvoluate the whole signal.

For a given element, if S_i is the counting rate found for the sample i of mass m_i, whose counting was carried out at time t_i. S_e, m_e and t_e are the corresponding values for the standard e, of concentration C_e. If λ is the kinetic constant for decrease in the activity of the titrated element, the activities have to be corrected by means of the decrease formula (cf. "Quantitative Analysis" in Sect. 31.3.3) and the mass of the sample specimen. This results in Sc_i the corrected activity of the sample i and Sc_e the corrected activity of standard e. By choosing an arbitrary time t_0 as decrease origin (date and time of the first sample counting for example):

$$Sc_i = \frac{S_i \, e^{\lambda (t_i - t_0)}}{m_i},$$

$$Sc_e = \frac{S_e \, e^{\lambda (t_e - t_0)}}{m_e},$$

The Sc_e is calculated for each repetition of the standard E (cf. "Sample Preparation and Irradiation" in Sect. 31.3.3). The average value or the average after elimination of a doubtful measurement must then be used. The result found for the standard of control C can help to make the choice. Finally, the concentration C_i of the sample is found by:

$$C_i = \frac{Sc_i}{Sc_e} C_e$$

The same calculation can be carried out for several peaks of the same element. The average value or that which appears to be the most reliable (most intense peak, value of the C standard, etc.) should be retained. The relative titration error is lower than 1%.

References

Abbey S (1992) Evaluation and application of reference materials for the analysis of rocks and minerals. *Chem. Geol.*, 95, 123–130

Abo F (1984) *Influence du bore et du manganèse sur la production et le développement du blé sur sols de régions tempérée et aride.*, Thèse doctorat ès-sciences, Université Paris VII, 89–90

Albert P (1964) L'analyse par radioactivation. In *Applications des sciences nucléaires*, Lefort M. ed. A de Visscher, Gauthier-Villars, Paris

Aubert H and Pinta M (1971) Les éléments traces dans les sols. ORSTOM, Paris

Baize D (1997) *Teneur totale en éléments traces dans les sols.*, INRA, Versailles, France

Bernas B (1968) A new method for decomposition and comprehensive analysis of silicates by atomic absorption spectrometry. *Anal. Chem.*, 40, 1682–1686

Boumans PWJM (1981) Conversion of «Tables of Spectral-Line Intensities» for NBS copper arc into tables for inductively coupled argon plasmas. *Spectrochim. Acta.*, 36B, 169–203

Bourrelier PH and Berthelin J ed. (1998) *Contamination des sols par les éléments en traces: les risques et leur gestion.*, Académie des sciences, France, rapport No 42, Lavoisier (Technique et documentation), Paris

Burman JO (1987) Applications: geological. In *Inductively Coupled Plasma Emission Spectroscopy*, Part 2, Boumans PWJM ed. Wiley, 27–47

Callot G, Chamayou H, Maertens C and Salsac L (1982) *Mieux comprendre les interactions sol-racine.*, INRA, Paris

Castaing R (1961) The fundamentals of quantitative electron probe microanalysis. *Adv. X-Ray Anal.*, 4, 351–369

Charlot G (1984) *Chimie analytique quantitative, tome II.*, Masson, Paris

Chayla B, Jaffrezic H and Joron JL (1973) Analyse par activation dans les neutrons épithermiques. Application à la détermination d'éléments en trace dans les roches. *C.R. Acad. Sci. Paris*, 277, D, 273–275

Claisse G (1968) Etude expérimentale de l'analyse aux trois acides – comportement du quartz pur à l'attaque triacide. *Cah. Orstom sér. Pédol.*, VI, 129–149

Coppenet M and Juste C (1982) Trace elements essential to the growth of plants and toxicity phenomena. In *Constituents and properties of soils*, Bonneau M and Souchier B ed. Masson, Paris, 458–466

Cox (1968) Development of a yield response prediction and manganese soil test interpretation for soybeans. *Agron. J.*, 60, 521–524

Das AK, Chakraborty R, Guardia M de la, Cervera ML and Goswami D (2001) multielement determination in fly ash after microwave-assisted digestion of samples. Talanta., 54, 975–981

Deb BC (1950) The estimation of free oxides in soils and clays and their removal. *J. Soil Sci.*, 1, 212–220

Erdtmann G and Soyka W (1975a) The gamma-ray lines of radionuclides, ordered by atomic and mass number, part 1. *J. Radioanal. Chem.*, 26, 375–495

Erdtmann G and Soyka W (1975b) The gamma-ray lines of radionuclides, ordered by atomic and mass number, part 2. *J. Radioanal. Chem.*, 27, 137–286

Falkner KK, Klinkhammer GP, Ungerer CA and Christie DM (1995) Inductively coupled plasma mass spectrometry in geochemistry. *Annu. Rev. Earth Planet. Sci.*, 23, 409–449

FD X31-146, (1996) Détermination de l'indice de pouvoir chlorosant (IPC) selon Juste and Pouget. In *Qualité des sols*, AFNOR, 117–125

Gambrell RP and Patrick WH (1982) Manganèse. In *Methods of soil analysis, part 2 – chemical and microbiological properties 2nd ed.*, Page AL, Miller RH and Keeney DR ed. ASA–SSSA

Greenland DJ and Hayes MHB (1983) Soils and soil chemistry. In *The chemistry of soil constituents*, Greenland DJ and Hayes MHB ed. Wiley, 1–27

Hardy F and Follet-Smith RR (1931) Studies in tropical soils. – II. Some characteristic igneous rocks soil profiles in British Guiana, South america. *J. Agric. Sci.*, 739p

Helmke PA (1982) Neutron Activation Analysis. In *Methods of soil analysis, part 2 – chemical and microbiological properties*, ASA–SSSA

He LiYuan and Xiang YaLing (1999) Soil sampling error in agricultural environment. *Chinese J. Appl. Ecol.*, 10, 353–356

Helmke PA (1996) Neutron Activation Analysis. In *Methods of soil analysis, part 3 – chemical Methods*, Bigham JM and Bartels JM ed. SSSA-ASA, Madison, WI Etats-Unis,SSSA, 141–159

Hoenig M and Kersabiec AM de (1990) *L'atomisation électrothermique en spectrométrie d'absorption atomique.*, Masson, Paris

Hossner LR (1996) Dissolution for total elemental analysis. In *Methods of Soil Analysis, Part 3, Chemical methods*, Bigham JM and Bartels JM ed. SSSA-ASA, Madison, WI Etats-Unis, 49–64

Jarvis I (1994a) Sample preparation for *ICP–MS*. In *Handbook of inductively coupled plasma mass spectrometry,* Jarvis KE, Gray AL and Houk RS ed. Blackie academic & professional, 172–224

Jarvis I (1994b) Elemental analysis of solutions and applications. In *Handbook of Inductively Coupled Plasma Mass Spectrometry,* Jarvis KE, Gray AL and Houk RS ed. Blackie Academic and Professional, 225–264

Jeanroy E (1972) Analyse totale des silicates naturels par spectrométrie d'absorption atomique. Application au sol et à ses constituants. *Chim. Anal.*, 54, 159–166

Jeanroy E (1974) Analyse totale par spectrométrie d'absorption atomique, des roches, sols, minerais, ciments après fusion au métaborate de strontium. *Analusis*, 2, 703–712

Jones AA (1982) X-ray Fluorescence Spectrometry. In *Methods of Soil Analysis – part 2*, Page AL, Miller RH and Keeney DR ed. ASA-SSSA, 85–121

Jones AA (1991) X-Ray Fluorescence Analysis. In *Soil analysis – modern instrumental techniques*, 2nd ed. Smith K.A. ed. Dekker

Karathanasis AD and Hajek BF (1996) Elemental Analysis by X-ray Fluorescence Spectroscopy. In *Methods of soil analysis, part 3*, Bigham JM and Bartels JM ed. SSSA-ASA, Madison, WI Etats-Unis, 161–223

Kawasaki A and Arai S (1996) Evaluation of digestion methods for multi-elemental analysis of organic wastes by inductively coupled plasma mass spectrometry. *Soil Sci. Plant Nutr.*, 42, 251–260

Koons RD and Helmke PA (1978) Neutron Activation Analysis of Standard Soils. *Soil Sci. Soc. Am. J.*, 42, 237–240

Lamothe PJ, Fries TL and Consul JJ (1986) Evaluation of a microwave oven system for the dissolution of geological samples. *Anal. Chem.*, 58, 1881–1886

Le Cornec F and Corrège T (1997) Determination of uranium to calcium and strontium to calcium ratios in corals by Inductively Coupled Plasma Mass Spectrometry. *J. Anal. Atom. Spectrom.*, 12, 969–973

Le Cornec F, Riandey C and Richard ML (1994) Minéralisation par micro-ondes de matériaux géologiques (roches et sols) et comparaison avec les méthodes classiques de mise en solution. In *L'échantillonnage, du prélèvement à l'analyse*, Rambaud D ed. Orstom, Paris

Lederer CM and Shirley VS (1978) *Table of isotopes*, 7th ed. Wiley, New York

Lim CH and Jackson ML (1982) Dissolution for total elemental analysis. In *Methods of soil analysis, part 2*, Page AL, Miller RH and Keeney DR ed. ASA-SSSA

Lindsay WL and Norvell WA (1978) Development of a DTPA test for zinc, iron, manganese and copper. *Soil Sci. Soc. Am. J.*, 42, 421–428

Lis SA, Hopke PK and Fasching JL (1975a) Gamma-ray tables for neutron, fast-neutron and photon activation analysis – 1 – List of all the nuclides with their associated gamma-rays in order of increasing atomic number and mass. *J. Radioanal. Chem.*, 24, 125–247

Lis SA, Hopke PK and Fasching JL (1975b) Gamma-ray tables for neutron, fast-neutron and photon activation analysis – 2 – list of all the nuclides with their associated gamma-rays in order of increasing atomic number and mass. *J. Radioanal. Chem.*, 25, 303–428

Martens DC and Lindsay WL (1990) Testing soils for copper, iron, manganese an zinc. In *Soil testing and plant analysis 3nd ed.*, Westerman RL ed. SSSA book series 3, 231–260

NF ISO 11466 (1995) Eléments en traces solubles dans l'eau régale. In *Qualité des sols*, AFNOR, 283–292

NF ISO 14870 (X 31-427), 1998) *Extraction des oligo-éléments par une solution tamponnée de DTPA*, AFNOR, à l'étude

NF X 31-147 (1996) Sols, sédiments – Mise en solution totale par attaque acide. In *Qualité des sols*, AFNOR, 127–138

NF X 31-151 (1993) Sols, sédiments, boues de stations d'épuration – Mise en solution d'éléments métalliques en traces (Cd, Co, Cr, Cu, Mn, Ni, Pb, Zn) par attaques acides. In *Qualité des sols*, AFNOR, 139–145

NF X 31-120 (1992) Détermination du cuivre, du manganèse et du zinc – Extraction par l'acétate d'ammonium en présence d'EDTA. In *Qualité des sols*, AFNOR, 75–81

NF X 31-121 (1993) Détermination du cuivre, du manganèse, du zinc et du fer – Extraction en présence de DTPA. In *Qualité des sols*, AFNOR, 83–89

NF X 31-122 (1993) Extraction du bore soluble à l'eau bouillante. In *Qualité des sols.*, AFNOR, 91–95

Njopwouo D and Orliac M (1979) Note sur le comportement de certains minéraux à l'attaque triacide. *Cah. Orstom sér. Pédol.*, XVII, 283–328

Norrish K and Chappell BW (1977) X-ray fluorescence spectrometry. In *Physical methods in determinative mineralogy*, 2nd ed. Zussman J ed. Academic Press Inc., 201–272

Norrish K and Hutton JT (1969) An accurate X-ray spectrographic method for the analysis of a wide range of geological samples. *Geochim. Cosmochim. Acta.*, 33, 431–453

Pansu M, Gautheyrou J and Loyer JY (2001) *Soil analysis – sampling, instrumentation and quality control*, 489 p, Balkema, Lisse, Abington, Exton, Tokyo

Paycheng C (1980) *Méthodes d'analyse utilisées au laboratoire commun de Dakar.*, Document Orstom – Dakar – Paris, 103 p

Peck TR and Soltanpour PN (1990) The principles of soil testing. In *Soil testing and plant analysis 3nd ed.*, Westerman RL ed. SSSA book series 3, 3–9

Pétard J (1993) *Les méthodes d'analyse. Tome 1: analyses de sols.*, Notes techniques No. 5, Orstom, Nouméa, Paris

Pinta M (1962) *Recherche et dosage des éléments traces.*, Dunod, Paris, 726 p

Pr ISO CD 14869 (1998) *Soil quality – determination of total trace elements content – part 1: digestion with hydrofluoric and perchloric acids for the determination of total contents – part 2: solubilisation by allkaline fusion.*, AFNOR, Paris

Ramsey MH and Coles BJ (1992) Strategies of multielement calibration for maximising the accuracy of geochemical analysis by inductively coupled plasma-atomic emission spectrometry. *Chemi. Geol.*, 95, 99–112

Riandey C, Alphonse P, Gavinelli R and Pinta M (1982) Détermination des éléments majeurs des sols et des roches par spectrométrie d'émission de plasma et spectrométrie d'absorption atomique. *Analusis*, 10, 323–332

Risser JA and Baker DE (1990) Testing soils for toxic metals. In *Soil testing and plant analysis 3nd ed.*, Westerman RL ed. SSSA book series 3, 275–298

Shinotsuka K and Ebihara M (1997) Precise determination of rare earth elements, thorium and uranium in chondritic meteorites by inductively coupled plasma mass spectrometry – a comparative study with radiochemical neutron activation analysis. *Anal. Chim. Acta.*, *338*, 237–246

Smith KA ed. (1991) *Soil analysis – modern instrumental techniques*, 2nd ed. Dekker

Soltanpour PN, Johnson GW, Workman SM, Jones JB and Miller RO (1996) Inductively coupled plasma emission spectrometry and inductively coupled plasma mass spectrometry. In *Methods of soil analysis, part 3, chemical methods*, Bigham JM and Bartels JM ed. SSSA-ASA, Madison, WI Etats-Unis, 91–139

Tan KH (1996) *Soil sampling, preparation and analysis*, Dekker

Totland M, Jarvis I and Jarvis K (1992) An assessment of dissolution techniques for the analysis of geological samples by plasma spectrometry. *In Plasma spectrometry in the earth sciences*, Jarvis I and Jarvis K ed. *Chemical geology*, special issue, 35–62

Trolard F, Bourrié G, Jaffrezic A (2002) Distribution spatiale et mobilité des ETM dans les sols en région d'élevage intensif en Bretagne. In: Les éléments traces métalliques dans les sols – approches fonctionnelles et spatiales, (coord. M. Tercé & D. Baize), pp. 183–199. INRA, Collection un point sur..., Paris

Turekian KK and Wedepohl KH (1961) Distribution of the elements in some major units of the earth's crust. *Geol. Soc. Am. Bull*, 72, 175–191

US Environmental Protection Agency, 1986) Acid digestion of sediment, sludge and soils. *In Test methods for evaluating solid waste*, SW-846. USEPA, Cincinnati

Vernet M and Govindaraju K (1992) *Mise en solution des matériaux avant analyse.*, Techniques de l'ingénieur, P 222, 1–16

Voïnovitch IA (1988) *Analyses des sols, roches et ciments – méthodes choisies.*, Masson, Paris

Walsh JN (1992) Use of multiple internal standards for high-precision, routine analysis of geological samples by inductively coupled plasma-atomic emission spectrometry. *Chem. Geol.*, 95, 113–121

Winge RK, Fassel VA, Peterson VJ, Floyd MA (1982) ICP emission spectrometry: on the selection of analytical lines, line coincidence tables, and wavelength tables. *Appl. Spectrosc.*, 36, 210–221

Wright RJ and Stuczynski T (1996) Atomic absorption and flame emission spectrometry. In *Methods of soil analysis, part 3, chemical methods*, Bigham JM and Bartels JM ed. SSSA-ASA, Madison, WI Etats-Unis, 65–90

Zischa M and Knapp G (1997) Microwave-assisted sample decomposition progress and challenges. *Analysis Europa*, Novembre, 18–23

Index

(α amino acid)-N analysis, 508
(NH$_3$+amino sugars)-N analysis, 508
(NH$_4^+$)-N analysis, 508, 767, 773, 782
γ-ray spectrometry, 962, 963
(serine + threonine)-N analysis, 509
^{13}C, 290, 325, 326, 329, 363, 401, 432, 447, 448, 526, 530, 546
^{13}C-NMR, 427, 432, 433
^{14}C, 290, 314, 325, 329, 363, 367, 370, 526, 530, 540
^{15}N, 329, 363, 365, 369, 500, 502, 526, 530, 540
^{1}H-NMR, 427
2,4 D, 484
^{31}P-NMR, 815
^{32}P isotopic dilution, 805, 813

AAS, 83, 185, 683, 704, 721, 726, 733, 743, 763, 900, 902, 926, 935-941, 945
acetone precipitation, 882
acid attack in closed vessel, 911
acid attack in open vessel, 906
acid digestions in open vessel, 902
acid dissociation, 554
acid herbicides, 457, 485, 488, 491
acid hydrolysis of polysaccharides, 458
acid hydrolysis, 372, 500
acid reagents, 168, 806, 921
acid sulphated soils, 337, 552, 553, 835, 836, 857, 876, 877, 889
acidity constant, 555
acidity, 212, 390, 401, 408, 409, 410, 411, 417, 418, 553, 557, 561, 567, 629, 667, 677-684, 685, 687, 688, 689, 691, 692,

693, 712, 713, 718, 719, 722, 723, 738, 741, 743, 745, 748, 761, 763, 822, 874, 899
actinomycete, 289, 343
active carbonate titration, 601
active carbonates, 595, 602-604
adsorbing complex, 629
adsorption water, 3
AEC, 327, 648, 714, 755, 756, 757, 759, 760, 761, 763, 819
aggregates, 17, 32, 39, 54, 91, 94, 106, 128, 198, 200, 282, 291-323, 326, 373, 521, 554, 647, 660, 803
akaganeite, 110, 175
akdalaite, 71
Al^{3+} toxicity, 168
aldrin, 484
algae, 289, 593
alkaline fusion, 915
alkaline hydrolysis, 420
alkalinity, 553, 616, 617, 622, 822, 922
allophane, 123, 125, 176, 179, 203, 215, 632, 710, 746
aluminic toxicity, 553, 687, 691, 874
aluminium phytotoxicity, 679
aluminium, 111, 202, 216, 217, 239, 638, 639, 682, 684, 685, 928
aluminosilicates, 104, 113, 115, 167, 170, 187, 200, 201, 206, 210, 646, 659, 683, 706, 749
alunite, 839
amid forms of proteins, 501
amino acids, 371, 376, 399, 455, 501, 505, 510, 532-536, 537, 538, 541, 866, 884, 903
amino sugars, 466, 501, 533, 537, 538, 542

amino-sugars by gas chromatography, 537
ammonium acetate (pH 7.0), 732
ammonium, 767, 769, 772, 773-775, 778, 782-791, 792, 807, 811, 812, 813, 825, 832, 833, 847, 849, 850, 920-927, 971
analysis after solubilization, 900
analysis of trace elements, 935, 939
analysis on solid medium, 950
anatase, 176
andesine, 71
andosol, 20, 29, 33, 186, 210, 215, 223, 315, 328, 331, 359, 374, 655, 656, 710, 717, 722, 744, 755, 756, 764, 765, 819, 858, 886
anhydrite, 838
anion exchange capacity, 755, 757, 819
anions by ionic chromatography, 624
ankerite, 593
Anne method, 335, 340, 364
anticathode, 87, 89
antigorite, 84
antimony electrode, 562
arachnids, 289
aragonite, 10, 71, 234, 356, 593
arcanite, 606
artificial radioisotopes, 961
atomic absorption analysis, 858
atomic absorption spectrometry, hydride and cold vapour, 927
atomic absorption, 190, 195, 199, 603, 672, 680, 682, 720, 722, 723, 725, 726, 741, 821, 867, 881, 882, 883, 887, 900, 903, 904, 912, 913, 915, 918, 919, 926, 931, 933, 934, 937, 940, 951, 954, 969, 970, 972
atomic plan, 85
atomic spectrometry, 615, 622, 925

atrazine, 484, 491
attack using three concentrated acids, 921
attenuated total reflectance, 146
attenuated total reflection, 140
Atterberg's limits, 6
Auger electrons, 271, 280, 283
automated extraction, 670
availability index, 804
azovskite, 177

back-scattered electrons, 273, 280
bacteria, 289, 343, 375, 767, 768, 835, 866, 874
basaluminite, 839
bassanite, 838
bauxite, 71
bayerite, 111
beidellite, 71, 84, 101, 657
Bernard calcimeter, 598
bicarbonate extractable P, 809
bioavailability of P, 814
biochemical processes function of Eh, 582
biogenic and toxic elements, 899
biogenic carbonates, 593
biogenic silica, 177
biological methods, 513, 522, 544
biological P, 809
biotite, 71, 84, 123
birnessite, 176
bloedite, 838
boehmite, 70, 102, 111, 120, 123, 176
bound lipids, 473
Bouyoucos, 22, 42, 56, 573
Bronsted acid-base concept, 556
brookite, 176
brown humic acids, 373, 401, 402, 404, 405
tanning mechanisms, 399
buffered methods at different pH, 743

buffering effect, 373, 555, 660, 678
buffering power, 553, 555, 559, 566, 577, 578, 688, 690, 709

C, N (H, O, S), 327
C:N ratio, 290, 329
cadavers, 289
calcareous nodules, 17
chalcedony, 177
calcimeter determination, 596
calcination at low temperature, 355
calcite, 71, 103, 123, 356
calibration in thermal analysis, 239
calibration range, 621, 623, 774, 849, 928, 929, 930, 931, 939
calomel electrode, 563
capillary water, 3
carbamates, 457, 487, 490, 491, 492
carbofuran, 484, 496
carbonate analysis, 689
carbonates, 593, 616
Casagrande relation, 42
cation exchange capacity, 125, 373, 566, 567, 658, 679, 709, 711, 747, 748
cation saturation, 99
CEC and AEC determination, 762
CEC at soil pH, 711, 719, 725, 744
CEC function of pretreatments, 745
CEC in buffered medium, 730
CEC, 32, 85, 125, 190, 215, 327, 631, 648, 655, 657, 658, 660, 661, 664, 667, 668, 669, 673, 674, 679, 680, 687, 688, 698, 705, 710-753, 755, 756, 757, 759, 760, 761, 762, 763, 819, 885, 922
celadonite, 108
cell constant, 612, 613
cellular autolysis, 399
chain hydrometer, 46
chalcopyrite, 839

characterization by fragmentation, 419
charge distribution, 31, 85, 631, 649, 873
chelation, 373, 630, 806
chemical dispersion, 297
chemical methods, 112, 168, 172, 522, 545, 900
chemical polymerisation, 399
chemisorption, 3, 31, 636, 756, 803, 806
chloride by colorimetry, 619
chlorite, 84, 102, 103, 116, 125
chlorites, 28, 96, 99, 101, 116, 127, 206, 243
chloromagnesite, 606
CHN(OS), 329-363, 853
chromatogram of alditol acetates, 471
chromatographic methods, 419, 456, 535
chrysotile, 84
clarification of extracts, 821
clay classification, 632
clay minerals, 84, 94, 99, 113, 114, 117, 124, 128, 147, 223, 227, 243, 373, 556, 707, 727, 730, 748
clay transformations, 224
clay-organic compartment, 291, 456
clinochlore, 84
clintonite, 84
coarse particles, 15
coarse sands, 16, 34, 39, 41, 296, 310, 311
coarse silts, 16, 39, 51, 310
coating and impregnation, 255
coesite, 71
cohesion, 17, 32, 65, 92, 255, 297, 303
cold water soluble, 474
colligative properties, 440
colloidal particles, 75, 197, 312

colloidal systems, 65, 81
colloids, 32, 41, 59, 289, 401, 566,
    630, 645, 652, 659, 660, 688,
    697, 715, 719, 725, 758, 807,
    899
colorimetric determination of
    ammonium, 773
colorimetric determination of
    nitrate, 778
colorimetric determination of nitrite,
    775
colorimetric methods, 456, 558,
    464, 511, 533, 621
colorimetric titration of Si, 928
colorimetry of deoxyhexose sugars,
    465
colorimetry of hexose sugars, 465
colorimetry of pentose sugars, 465
colorimetry of total sugars, 464
colorimetry with azomethine-H, 621
colorimetry with methyl thymol
    blue, 851
colorimetry with methylene blue,
    846, 860, 863
colorimetry with ninhydrin, 533
column percolation, 669, 670
compactness, 15
comparison of measurements, 517
complex with outer sphere, 701
complex with inner sphere, 646, 701
complex calibration range for trace
    elements, 943
complex calibration range, 941, 943,
    944
complexing reagents, 307, 920
conductance, 612, 613, 857
conductivity *in situ*, 613
conductivity meter, 611
constitution water, 4, 30, 178, 895
continuous extraction, 673
cookeite, 84
coquinbite, 839
corundum, 71, 123

coulometry, 618
CPMAS-^{13}C NMR, 431
cristobalite, 71, 102
cryptocrystalline substances, 167
crystalline mesh, 85
cyanazine, 484

dating, 222, 290
DDD, 484
DDE, 484, 489
DDT, 457, 484, 489
dehydration, 8, 10, 99, 174, 223,
    227, 235, 256, 282, 284, 562,
    738, 879
dehydroxylation, 8, 10
deltamethrin, 484
densimetric method, 42
density separation, 293
deoxyhexoses, 456, 457, 467, 468
derivatives for GPC, 470
detection limits, 119, 828, 856, 936,
    949, 961
deuteration, 146, 150
dextran gel, 403, 406, 443
diaspore, 71, 111, 176
diatoms, 55, 67, 85, 116, 201
dickite, 71, 108, 123
dieldrin, 457, 484, 489
differential conductivity, 55
differential enthalpy analysis, 221
differential scanning calorimetry,
    222, 235, 236
differential sequential methods, 206
differential thermal analysis, 221
differential thermogravimetry, 221
diffraction spectra, 72
diffractograms, 113, 114
diffuse reflectance, 138, 140, 156,
    362
diffusion of electromagnetic
    radiations, 439
digestion in closed vessel, 911

dilatometry, 222
diluted extracts, 607, 609, 882
dioctahedral minerals, 114, 148, 149
dioctahedral silicates, 103
dioctahedral vermiculite, 84
dioxins, 457
direct P speciation, 830
discontinuous acid hydrolysis, 531
dispersing reagent, 18, 28, 31-37, 45, 46, 53, 55, 66, 67, 75, 202
dispersion in water, 297
dispersion, 17, 18, 19, 20, 22, 23, 29-36, 44, 46, 51, 54, 57, 58, 59, 60, 61, 69, 70, 75, 82, 89, 100, 111, 117, 136, 140, 153, 191, 201, 214, 281, 282, 283, 297-309, 313-326, 376, 385, 589, 630, 652, 716, 731, 738, 886, 953, 954
dissociation constant, 433, 555, 710
dissolved solid matters, 614, 625
distillable fraction, 509
dithionite-citrate-bicarbonate method, 187
diuron, 484
dolomite, 593, 599, 600
donbassite, 84
Donnan's equilibrium, 634, 709
DSC, 8, 83, 221-223, 227, 236, 237, 238, 239, 242, 245, 246, 250
DTA, 8, 9, 80, 83, 108, 110, 124, 140, 158, 190, 213, 221-248, 361, 362, 421
DTG, 221, 222, 230, 233, 234, 248, 421
dynamic mechanical analysis, 222
dynamics of extraction, 673

E4:E6 ratio, 410-412, 437
EAAS, 919, 924, 939, 951
earth's gravity, 19, 21

EC, 236, 609, 611, 612, 625, 720, 760, 763
ECEC, 212, 671, 681, 682, 712, 718, 719, 727
EDTA method, 192
EDX probes, 83
EDX, 55, 76, 124, 168, 169, 253, 258, 261, 264, 265, 270, 273, 282-284, 596, 800, 830, 836, 866
EELS, 273, 279
effect of attenuation of mass, 121
effective CEC by summation, 718, 763
EGA, 83, 140, 158, 222, 232, 240, 251, 361, 596, 855
EGD, 83, 158, 221, 247
Eh colorimetric determination, 589
Eh, 573, 574, 581-591, 615, 627, 630
elastic scattering, 273
electrical conductivity, 610
electro spin resonance, 411, 435, 436
electrofocusing, 415
electromagnetic lens, 275
electrometric measurement, 564
electrometric method, 560, 574
electron energy loss spectrometry, 279
electron gun, 274, 280, 281
electron microdiffraction, 83, 210
electron microprobe, 258, 280, 901, 952
electronic microscopy, 55, 74, 76, 78, 83, 117, 261-264, 267, 269-285, 441, 799
electrophoresis, 402, 415
electrothermal atomic absorption spectrometry, 927, 939
electrothermal AAS, 939, 941, 945
electro-ultrafiltration, 500, 538, 539
elemental sulphur titration, 868

elements quantified by hydrid method, 937

elutriation, 52, 293, 294, 295, 312, 322

elutriator, 290

emanating radioactive gas analysis, 221, 249

emission lines of alkaline elements, 931

ENDOR, 170

energies of vibration, 133

environmental scanning electron microscopy, 281

environmental SEM, 271, 281

EPR, 80, 168, 170, 186, 190, 435

epsomite, 838

ESEM, 271, 281, 286

ESR, 435, 436, 437, 446

ETA, 221

ethylene glycol treatment, 105

evansite, 176

evolved gas analysis, 221

evolved gas detection, 221

EXAFS, 83, 160, 168, 170, 186, 190

exchange acidity determination, 677

exchange acidity, 553, 567, 629, 667, 677-679, 682-685, 712, 718, 719, 723, 743, 763

exchange isotherm, 629, 697, 729

exchange selectivity, 697-707

exchangeable acidity, 680, 681, 682, 683, 684, 688, 748

exchangeable Al, 679, 682, 683, 688

exchangeable aluminium, 681, 682, 683, 684, 920

exchangeable bases, 549, 571, 667-675, 684, 748, 749

exchangeable cations analysis, 667, 721, 753, 763

exchangeable cations, 10, 99, 149, 234, 638, 651, 660, 667-675, 677, 679, 680, 683, 689, 697, 705, 709, 711, 712, 713, 717,
718, 719, 720, 721, 722, 723, 725, 726, 727, 731, 732, 734, 739, 760, 763, 901, 920, 921

exchangeable complex, 631

exchangeable sodium ratio, 700

extractable boron, 620

extractable carbonates and bicarbonates, 616

extractable cations, 615

extractable chloride, 618

extractable elements, 901

extractable P by ammonium oxalate method, 811

extractable P by anionic resin, 810

extractable P by double acid method, 811

extractable P by $HCl + NH_4F$ method, 812

extracted phases by selective dissolutions, 179

extraction by chemical way, 886

extraction of plant-roots, 293

extraction solutions, 921

extraction with Soxhlet apparatus, 472

faecal pellets, 289

fall height, 39, 42, 43

far infrared, 172

fatty acids, 420, 456, 478, 479-483, 488, 495

feitknechtite, 71

feldspath, 71, 103

FeOOH, 110, 176, 177, 218, 764

feroxyhite, 177, 179

ferrihydrite, 110, 177, 178, 179

ferruginous concretions, 17

fertility, 65, 168, 474, 510, 526, 541, 553, 629, 667, 705, 707, 711, 800, 804, 884

field capacity, 4, 607

filter percolation, 670

fine earth, 6, 7, 15, 27, 570, 652,
672
fine fractions, 59, 66, 74, 75, 81,
305
fine gravels, 16
fine sands, 16, 38, 39, 41, 46, 310,
311
fine silts, 16, 85, 116, 308, 310, 594
fixed or occluded N, 354
flam atomic absorption
spectrometry, 906, 927, 932,
935, 936, 939, 941
flam emission spectrometry, 902,
919, 926, 927, 930, 951
flash-carbon, 264, 265, 269
flocculation, 18, 31, 32, 33, 36, 40,
54, 78, 96, 174, 184, 190, 319,
373, 379, 393, 567, 630
flocculating power, 31
fluorescence spectroscopy, 433
forms of soil water, 223
Fourier transform, 136, 426, 427,
428
fractionation by solvents, 478
fractionation of fatty acid methyl
esters, 482
fractionation of humin residue, 392
fragments of fibres, 289
free acidity, 678
free fatty acids, 456, 478
free iron oxides, 924
free lipids, 473
free organic matters, 9, 10, 310,
313, 314, 315, 322
free sugars, 454, 456, 475
freeze dryer, 257, 391, 867
FTIR, 138, 168
FTIR, 83
fulvic acid fractionation, 407
fulvic acids, 198, 343, 372-446, 455
fundamental units of clays, 633
fungi, 289, 885

gamma-rays, 87
Gapon coefficient, 700
gas phase, 3, 247, 357, 362, 419,
421, 467, 468, 478, 480, 481,
482, 485, 488, 490, 496, 531,
535, 582
gas-liquid chromatography, 479,
534
gastropod, 289
Ge(Li) detector, 964
gel exclusion chromatography,
416
gel permeation, 407
gels, 80, 146, 162, 167, 168, 170,
174, 179, 180, 182, 205, 211,
213, 215, 216, 243, 253, 328,
389, 406, 407, 415, 416, 417,
439, 445, 678, 717, 746, 830
geochemical distribution of
nitrogen, 497
gibbsite, 69, 71, 102, 111, 123, 176
glass electrode, 561, 562, 564, 616,
784
glauconite, 71
glomalin, 538, 539, 542
glycerides, 478
glycerol treatment, 105
glycolipids, 478
goethite, 102
goniometer, 88, 89, 92, 114, 141
groutite, 71
gravels, 15, 294, 296, 331, 573, 594
greigite, 839, 866
grey humic acids, 379, 401, 402,
404, 405
grid of transmission electron
microscopy, 262
gypseous soils, 57, 738, 835, 836,
837, 878
gypsum requirement, 884
gypsum, 71, 102, 123, 332, 838,
880

half-life of radioelement, 962
halite, 606
halloysite, 71, 84, 102, 103, 127, 152, 225, 262, 745
Hauser and Lynn method, 69
hausmanite, 71, 177
heavy metal transport, 168
heavy mineral liquor, 313
hectorite, 69, 71, 84, 103, 123, 178, 251
hemihydrate, 838
Hettich cyto chamber, 141
hexahydrite, 838
hexametaphosphate, 19, 25, 28, 31, 32, 33, 34, 39, 45, 48, 295, 307, 308, 608, 610, 617
hexosamins, 454, 475, 501-503, 509
hexose sugars, 454, 455, 458, 464-466, 495
hisingerite, 176
histosols, 3, 7, 29, 33, 74, 186, 223, 726, 797, 835, 858
homoionic form, 80
homoionic saturation, 228, 232, 241
hot water extracts, 610
hot water soluble, 474
humic acid fractionation, 402, 403, 406
humic acids, 200, 202, 307, 309, 334, 343, 372-450, 455, 806, 860, 862
humic compounds, 197, 311, 343, 371-445, 472
humified matters, 371, 375, 376
humin residue, 375, 379, 385, 388, 392-395, 431
humin, 343, 372, 400, 804, 806
humus typology, 329
humus, 298, 325, 329, 333, 334, 371-373, 376, 397, 399, 402, 406, 445, 453, 456, 493, 660, 756, 757, 806

huntite, 593
hydride and cold vapour AAS, 935
hydrocarbons, 456, 457, 478, 479, 495
hydrofluoric acid attack, 532, 533
hydrogen determination, 360
hydrogen sulphide, 839
hydrophilite, 606
hydroxy-aluminium polymers, 687
hygrometric water, 3
hygroscopic water, 4, 244
hymatomelanic acids, 373

ICP, 83, 124, 185, 189, 209, 671, 682, 702, 704, 729, 733, 743, 763, 821, 823, 828, 900-909, 914, 916, 919, 920, 924, 925, 926, 935, 940-950, 969, 972
ICP-AES, 900, 902, 909, 916, 919, 925, 926, 935, 940-944, 946
ICP-MS, 83, 900, 902, 903, 904, 905, 906, 907, 909, 914, 920, 924, 926, 941, 945-950
IEP, 645
ikaïte, 593
illite, 71, 123, 657
ilmenite, 71
imogolite, 108, 162, 176, 179, 180, 203, 632, 750
in situ measurement, 570, 586, 587, 788
in situ sampling of soil water, 610
INA, 961, 964
INAA, 961
index of chlorosis, 603
indicators in the 2.8 to 11 pH range, 558
induction furnace, 917
inductively coupled plasma emission spectrometry, 913, 92?
inductively coupled plasma mass spectrometry, 927

indurated soils, 4, 8, 17, 337, 567, 605, 606, 610, 615, 618, 620, 621, 622, 627, 628, 668, 672, 700, 731, 739, 898, 929
inelastic scattering, 273
infrared microscopy, 158
infrared spectra of gypseous materials, 881
infrared spectrography, 413
infrared spectrometry, 133, 134
inorganic carbon, 333, 334
inorganic oxygen, 360
insects, 289
installation of sensors, 572
instrumental conditions of titration, by flame AAS, 932
Instrumental Neutron Activation Analysis, 961
instrumental neutron activation, 961
intercalation complex, 80, 106, 115
inter-laboratory calibration, 385
interlayer space, 80, 99, 117, 227
interlayer water, 99, 111, 189, 243, 658
inter-reticular distance of minerals, 102
ion exchange extracting reagents, 920
ion exchange resins, 32, 920
ion selective electrode, 786
ionic balance, 571, 625-626
ionic chromatography, 475, 615, 616, 622, 843, 856, 857, 876
ionic probe, 254
ionometry, 352, 570, 578, 615, 787
IR absorption bands in phyllosilicates, 149, 151
IR microscope, 139
IR spectrometry, 139, 160
IR, 32, 33, 117, 133, 134-161, 164, 172, 210, 214, 223, 252, 267, 271, 273, 309, 360, 391, 414, 415, 419, 442, 446, 799, 824

iron deficiency, 168
iron removal, 104
isoelectric point, 31, 32, 415, 630, 648, 649
isoelectric point, 640, 645
isotopes often used, 948
isotopic studies, 290, 530

jarosite analysis, 873
jarosite, 838, 874, 875
Johnson and Nishita apparatus, 845, 861
jurbanite, 839
kaolinite, 54, 71, 84, 102, 116, 123, 125, 225, 632, 657
KBr pellet, 154
Kerr's equation, 699
kieserite, 838
Kjeldahl method, 344, 353, 367, 545
Kjeldahl, 332, 343-348, 351-354, 363, 365, 366, 367, 369, 502, 504, 507, 510, 511, 525
kliachite, 177

labelled elements, 21, 329, 961
langbeinite, 838
lansfordite, 593
Laser particle size analyser, 53
law of mass action, 555, 709
law of Stokes, 24, 34, 66, 67, 96, 318
lepidocrocite, 71, 110, 175
leucoxene, 176
lime requirement, 553, 629, 687, 689-694
lime water methods, 689
liming effect, 687
limonite, 177
lindane, 457, 484
linuron, 484
lipid classes, 478, 479

lipids, 333, 371, 453, 456, 457,
    472-474, 477-483, 484, 488,
    490, 495, 862
liquid chromatography, 138, 402,
    467, 475, 484, 485, 491, 533,
    538, 830, 856
liquid phase chromatography, 478,
    479
liquid phase, 3, 23, 52, 105, 168,
    169, 173, 582, 588, 630, 633,
    634, 651, 663, 669, 671, 674,
    683, 697, 698, 716, 761, 814
lithiophorite, 177
lizardite, 84
loeweite, 838
lyotropic series, 701, 758, 807, 819
lytic mechanisms, 399

mackinawite, 839
macro-aggregate fractionation, 297
macrofauna, 289
maghemite, 110
magnesite, 593
magnetite, 103, 110
Maillard's reaction, 399
major elements by X-ray
    fluorescence, 956
major elements, 895, 919, 932
manganite, 71, 176
manganosite, 71
marcassite, 839
margarite, 84
mass spectrometers, 249, 362, 363
maximal water holding capacity,
    528
mean elemental composition, 896
measurement at soil pH, 711
measurement of molecular size, 439
measurement on buffered medium,
    712
measurement on soil monolith, 573

measurement on soil suspensions,
    565
medium infrared, 134, 363
metahalloysite, 102, 103
metallization, 264, 265, 267, 441
method precision, 320
methods using solubilization, 901
methylparathion, 484
mica (illite), 102, 103
mica weathering, 631, 727
micas, 71, 84, 108, 225, 632
Michelson's interferometer, 137
micro-aggregate fragmentation, 302,
    305
microbial respiration, 530
microbial synthesis, 400
microbiological techniques, 885
microdiffraction, 272, 275, 276
microscopic analysis, 253
microscopic observations, 441
microwave mineralization, 914, 970
mineralizable nitrogen (and carbon),
    497
mineralization kinetics, 526, 546
mineralization potential de, 513,
    517, 521, 523
mineralization rack, 340
mineralization, 83, 325, 327, 328,
    330-340, 343, 347, 348, 349,
    350, 351, 352, 353, 354, 366,
    373, 498, 499, 500, 510, 511,
    513, 514, 519, 521, 526-530,
    540, 544, 687, 794-797, 801,
    803, 814, 817-819, 846,
    858-860, 885, 905, 915
mineralogical analysis, 79
mineralogical extraction, 169
mineralogical separations, 167
minor and trace elements by X-ray
    fluorescence, 958, 959
mirabilite, 838
MnO_2, 29, 71, 358, 934

model with three layers and four plans, 635
moisture adjustment, 520
moisture storage, 65
moisture, 3-8, 11, 12, 15, 29, 40, 41, 95, 99, 108, 115, 138, 184, 191, 227, 228, 231, 234, 241, 259, 281, 328, 331, 359, 519, 528, 529, 552, 554, 570, 571, 572, 573, 600, 602, 607, 608, 610, 651, 660, 680, 683, 717, 719, 720, 734, 740, 742, 743, 744, 745, 760, 782, 801, 802, 841, 861, 863, 865, 872, 880, 884, 885, 935
molecular weight determination, 437-440
montmorillonite, 71, 84, 101, 102, 103, 123, 125, 639, 657
morphoscopic analysis, 17
Mössbauer spectroscopy, 442
Mössbauer, 80, 83, 168, 172, 217
mould for pelletizing, 959
multichannel analyzers, 964
multi-element analysis of rare earth elements, 945
multi-element calibration solution, 942, 944
multiple specular reflection, 138, 140
muscovite, 71, 84, 123, 225
myriapodes, 289

Na₃-EDTA extractable sulphates, 871
nacrite, 108
natroalunite, 839
natrojarosite, 838
natron, 593
near infrared, 134, 156
nematodes, 289

net charge of surface, 645, 648, 649, 650
neutral lipids, 478
neutron activation analysis, 960
neutron activation, 900, 901, 951, 952, 954, 960, 961, 962
neutron generators, 963
NIRS, 156, 157, 362, 363
nitrate analysis, 521, 620, 773, 787, 788, 791
nitrates and nitrites, 344, 354, 780
nitratite, 606
nitrogen cycle, 498, 499, 521
NMR, 80, 83, 160, 170, 190, 205, 325, 419, 424-433, 442, 446, 447, 448, 815, 823, 829, 832
nomographic method, 71
non distillable fraction, 510
non disturbed samples, 294
non humic molecules, 453
non-exchangeable ammonium, 790, 921
non-hydrolysable nitrogen, 510, 511, 531
nontronite, 71, 84, 657
nordstrandite, 71, 111
nsutite, 71
nuclear magnetic resonance, 170, 424, 829
number-average molecular weight, 438, 440

octahedral layer, 632
ODR, 581, 582, 587, 588, 589
Oligochaetes, 289
oligoclase, 71
opal, 69, 71
optical microscopy, 55, 83, 441, 951
organic carbon, 200, 306, 309, 333, 334, 335, 340, 342, 357, 364, 366, 371, 454, 523, 907

organic forms of nitrogen, 497, 500, 509
organic P, 794, 795, 800-804, 807, 809, 814-818, 822-824, 828, 830
organic phosphorous analysis, 814
organic pollutants, 453, 456, 457
organic S bound to C, 860
organic S not bound to C, 862
organic S, 842, 859, 860, 862, 886
organochlorines, 457, 491
organo-mineral bonds, 80, 200, 307, 374
organo-mineral colloids, 289
organophosphorous, 457, 484, 491, 793
oriented diagrams, 94
orthoclase, 71
orthophosphates, 793, 794, 798, 817, 833
orthophosphoric acid, 795
oxidative alkaline fusion, 843
oxidative fragmentation, 419
oxidative or reducing reagents, 921
oxygen and sulphur determination, 360
oxyhydroxides, 91, 124, 148, 167, 172, 173, 176, 223, 659, 840

P extraction, 195, 804, 805, 810
P fixation, 168
P form study by ^{31}P-NMR, 828
P forms, 793, 795, 796, 798, 799-810, 823, 828, 830
P titration, 821
paragonite, 84
particle dispersion, 296
particle size analysers, 18, 53, 75
particle size analysis, 15-59, 61, 297, 307, 326
particle size composition, 15, 28, 49
particle size distribution, 152, 304, 323

particle size fractionation, 15, 293, 290, 291, 310, 311, 314, 320
PCBs, 457, 491
penetrating ability, 15
penninite, 84
pentose sugars, 454, 458, 459, 461, 464, 465, 466, 495
penwithita, 176
permanent charges, 630, 646, 648, 649, 650, 657, 662, 710, 713, 737
permeability, 15, 85, 373, 670
permethrin, 484
pesticide residues, 453, 483, 484
pesticides, 328, 374, 414, 456-458, 483-492, 496, 667, 729, 793, 830, 835
P-Fe complex, 758
pH 7 methods, 712
pH 8.1-8.2 methods, 713
pH determination, 549, 553, 689
pH measurement, 549, 569
pH reference solutions, 558
pH0, 645
pH-K and pH-Ca determination, 56
phlogopite, 71, 84
pH-meter, 318, 506, 561-573, 584, 726, 738, 929
pH-NaF measurement, 569
phosphate analysis, 620
phosphate availability, 758
phosphatides, 478
phosphomolybdic complex, 828
phosphorous retention, 819
phosphorous, 793, 831, 832, 927
photoelectron spectroscopy, 442
phyllosilicates, 99, 103, 113, 180, 201, 202, 284, 390, 631, 658, 710
physical fractionation of organic matters, 289
picromerite, 838
pigments, 478

pKA, 555
plant debris compartment, 290
plant residue weathering, 399
plant roots, 289, 290, 293-296, 307,
      312, 322, 455, 499, 594, 604,
      610, 679, 687, 688, 808, 810,
      841, 874, 875, 920
plasma emission spectrometry, 913,
      927, 931, 940, 944, 949, 972
plasma mass spectrometry, 915,
      926, 927, 944, 949, 951
plasticity, 6, 15, 186, 327
platinum quinhydron electrode, 562
point of zero charge, 181, 643, 645,
      711, 756
point of zero net charge, 645, 648
point of zero net proton charge, 645,
      648
point of zero salt effect, 645, 648,
      655
polar lipids, 456
polarization microscopes, 268
pollutants, 282, 335, 453, 456-457,
      483-490, 496, 667, 897
polychlorobiphenyls, 457
polyhalite, 836
polynuclear aromatic hydrocarbons,
      457
polyphosphates, 793, 833
polysaccharides, 296, 392, 393, 395,
      408, 420, 453-458, 493, 494,
      860, 862
poral system, 65
pore spaces, 172, 254, 270
positive charges in soil, 755
potential acidity, 553, 567, 678, 691,
      741
potential of H^+ ion, 549
potentially mineralizable nitrogen,
      500, 513-526
potentiometric method, 561
potentiometric titration, 647, 652
powder diagrams, 76, 90, 93

PPZC, 645
pretreatment of clays, 99
pretreatment of the electrode, 585
preparation mould, 956
preparation of alditol acetates, 469
preparation of platinum electrode,
      612
Pristine point of zero charge, 645
prochlorite, 84
propazine, 484
protozoaires, 289
pseudo-sands, 17, 303
Pt electrode, 583
purification methods, 375, 389, 390,
      391, 463
purification of fulvic acids, 391
purification of humic matters, 389
pyrethrinoids, 457, 487, 490, 496
pyrite, 71, 839
pyrochlorite, 71
pyrolusite, 71
pyrolysis products, 362, 423, 424
pyrophillite, 84
pyrophosphate method, 196
PZC, 642, 645, 755, 756
PZNC, 645-649
PZNPC, 645, 648, 649
PZSE, 645, 648, 649-654

quantitative infrared analysis, 152
quartz, 69, 71, 103, 123, 125, 239,
      242
ramsdelite, 71
random error, 321, 322
rare earth elements, 944
rate of oxygen diffusion, 582, 587,
      588
rate of saturation, 553, 675, 684,
      710, 711, 719, 748
rate of water saturation, 608
reagents for total dissolutions, 903
redox potential measurement, 581

redox potential, 581, 824
reducing fragmentation, 420
reflux heating acid hydrolysis, 420
relaxation time, 167, 427, 430, 433
resins, 32, 57, 60, 184, 189, 256,
    257, 258, 259, 307, 308, 323,
    324, 326, 334, 337, 356, 390,
    391, 392, 456, 738, 776, 806,
    810, 823, 920
respirometry, 329, 527, 528, 530
reticular plans, 87, 276, 953
rH, 583, 589, 590
Robinson-Köhn pipette, 34, 38
rotating stage, 269
rutile, 176

salt bridge of connection, 584
SANS, 170, 171
saponification, 479, 480, 481, 482,
    490
saponite, 84, 657
saturated paste extract, 607
sauconite, 84
SAXS, 170, 171
scale of magnifying power, 267
scanning electron microscopy, 74,
    76, 83, 264, 269, 285, 441
reflection scanning microscopes,
    280
scanning transmission electron
    microscopes, 279
scattering, 273, 281
scintillation detector, 964
secondary electrons, 271, 273, 280,
    281
sedimentation cylinder, 24, 37, 320
sedimentometry, 38, 290
selective dissolution, 148, 167, 173,
    180, 198, 215
selective electrode, 620, 621, 615,
    618, 782
selective extractions, 804, 920

selectivity coefficient, 697, 698
selectivity equations, 699, 700
selectivity, 139, 160, 169, 183, 192,
    193, 194, 197, 203, 209, 485,
    633, 697-707, 715, 727, 800,
    806, 823
SEM, 21, 55, 74, 168, 169, 210,
    258, 264-267, 269-273, 275,
    280-282, 596, 830
separation by centrifugation, 670
separation by distillation, 506
sepiolite, 79
sequential analysis of sulphur forms,
    877
sesquioxides, 16, 18, 27
shellfishes, 289
short range organization, 80, 93,
    115, 120, 124, 134, 153, 167,
    169, 170, 172, 174, 177, 186,
    223, 632, 634, 659, 830, 886
siderite, 233, 234, 332, 333, 334,
    359, 593, 596, 599, 600
sieving, 24, 33, 39, 48, 124, 290,
    299, 312, 313, 314, 319, 320,
    321, 322, 328, 330, 487, 568,
    810
silhydrite, 71
silica gel, 177
silicates, 56, 102, 103, 108, 251
silicium, 258, 927
silt-organic complex, 291
silver/silver chloride electrode, 564
simazine, 484
SIMS, 254
slaking, 15, 49, 65, 297
SMP buffer method, 690
sodium adsorption ratio, 59, 616,
    641, 700
soil lipids, 456, 495
sol sugars, 453, 492
solid phase, 3, 52, 76, 169, 477, 47
    630, 667, 716, 814, 895
solid-state ^{13}C-NMR, 430

solubility of hydroxides, 174
soluble salts, 8, 10, 18, 41, 59, 124, 189, 232, 260, 333, 586, 594, 605-638, 668, 671, 672, 700, 711, 717, 719, 731, 737, 738, 739, 763, 837, 870, 879
soluble sulphates, 870, 871, 875, 876, 884
soluble sulphides, 842, 863, 866, 870
soluble sulphured forms, 842
solution of Light, 585
solution of Zobell, 585
solvation, 80, 97, 99, 104, 106, 120, 129, 702, 739
sonic and ultrasonic dispersion, 297
sorption of anions, 759
specific electrical conductivity, 612, 627
spectra of differential thermal analysis, 245
spectrocolorimetric method, 804
spectrocolorimetric methods, 824
spectrocolorimetry, 195, 199, 336, 341, 348, 353, 704, 724, 733, 797, 818, 822, 823, 828, 853, 916-919, 925-927, 932
spectrum ^{31}P-NMR, 829
spin number, 424, 425
sputtering metallization apparatus, 266
standard stock solutions, 934
steam distillation, 504, 505, 512, 525
STEM, 124, 168, 170, 271-273, 279, 830
Stern theory, 635
steroids, 456
sterols, 478, 479
stilpnosiderite, 177
stishovite, 177
stones, 15, 16, 294, 331, 841
stretching vibrations, 149, 150

structural models of humic molecules, 401
structural unit, 85, 658
structure of humic molecule, 400
submicrometric analysis, 53
substances with short range organization, 79, 118, 182, 241, 569, 722
sudoite, 84
sugars by liquid chromatography, 475
sulfonylurea, 484
sulphate analysis, 620, 878
sulphate colorimetric titration, 852
sulphates, 9, 360, 462, 605, 606, 620, 672, 836, 840, 846, 851, 853, 860, 862, 866, 867, 870-878, 882, 884, 886, 889, 903, 933
sulphides, 9, 12, 234, 235, 360, 552, 553, 599, 836, 840-842, 847, 850, 857, 863, 865, 866, 868, 870, 874, 878
sulphur amino acids, 859
sulphur compounds, 835, 836, 837, 841, 858, 859, 878, 885
sulphur forms, 858
sulphur in pyrites, 865
sulphur of gypseous soils, 878
sulphur requirement of soil, 884
sulphur, 360, 835, 837, 839, 853, 869
surface charge, 645, 647, 650, 659, 744
surface charges of hydroxylated materials, 659
swelling water, 67
sylvinite, 606

talc, 84, 101, 102, 123, 632
Tamm, 30, 57, 179, 182, 184, 188, 218

Tamm's reagent, 27, 30, 125, 180
technique of cold vapour, 938
technique of hydrides in AAS, 935
technique of sodic resins, 308
techniques of dispersion, 290, 291,
    293, 297, 299, 300, 304, 307,
    308
techniques of sieving, 291
TEM-HR, 124, 168
Tensionic apparatus, 789
terbutylazine, 484
textural classes, 17, 65
texture triangles, 17
TG, 221, 251, 421, 884
TGA, 8, 9, 80, 83, 124, 140, 158,
    190, 221-248, 361
thenardite, 606, 838
theory of double layer, 634, 649
theory of Gouy and Chapman, 635
thermal analysis, 8, 9, 83, 117, 124,
    138, 140, 158, 190, 221-251,
    355, 361, 421, 596, 799, 855,
    866, 868, 875, 880
thermal degradation, 421
thermal effects on soil minerals, 243
thermal treatment, 108, 115, 237
thermo mechanical analysis, 222
thermobalance, 228, 231, 232, 250
thermocouples, 231
thermogravimetric analysis, 158,
    221, 222, 226, 229, 361
thermonatrite, 606
thin section, 112, 253, 267, 269, 830
thin sections, 140, 186, 255-261,
    269, 270, 275, 830
thiocarbamates, 457
titanium gel, 177
titanium, 930
titration of carboxyl groups, 408
titration of functional groups, 417
titrimeter, 616
titrimetry, 344, 353, 531, 616, 617,
    618, 620, 682, 770

TMA, 222
todorokite, 177
total absorbed metals, 924
total acidity determination, 408
total analysis, 970
total carbonate analysis, 595
total carbonates, 334, 595, 596, 925
total elements, 900
total lipids, 471, 473
total nitrogen of hydrolysat, 507
total organic matters, 332, 334
total organic oxygen, 360
total SO_4^{2-}-S by ionic
    chromatography, 855
total solubilization by hypobromite,
    844
total solubilization, 901
total sulphur analysis, 842
total sulphur ultimate analysis, 853
total sulphur, 360, 837, 853
trace elements, 897, 935, 936, 940
transmission electron microscopy,
    261, 277
transmittance, 135, 136, 137, 138,
    153
triazins, 457, 485, 488
tridymite, 71
trimethylsilyl derivatives, 475
trimethylsilylation, 211
trioctahedral minerals, 114, 148
trioctahedral silicates, 103
trioctahedral vermiculite, 84
turbomolecular pumps, 280
types of radiation, 273

ultimate analysis, 327, 365
ultimate microanalysis, 282
ultracentrifugation, 65, 68, 69, 97,
    116, 120, 139, 153, 429, 440,
    445, 731, 822
ultracentrifuge, 53, 67, 69, 72, 98,
    416, 814

ultrafiltration, 438, 439, 545, 751, 822
ultramicrobalance, 139
ultrapure germanium detector, 964
ultrasonic probe, 300
ultrasonics, 20, 32, 33, 54, 60, 299, 394, 912
unsaponifiable products, 479
urea analysis, 511, 543
uronic acids, 454, 462, 465, 466, 475
useful water storage, 6
UV-visible spectrometry, 410, 446

valence vibrations, 133
Van der Waals forces, 3, 4, 31
vanthoffite, 838
variable charges, 645, 646, 649, 650, 657, 659, 661, 662, 663, 669, 671, 688, 710, 711, 712, 713, 723, 726, 744, 757, 761
vaterite, 593
vermiculite, 84, 102, 103, 116, 125, 637
vernadite, 177
very fine sands, 16, 39
viscoelasticity, 222
viscosimetry, 440
viscosity, 19, 22, 23, 25, 35, 54, 66, 69, 258, 440, 486
volumetry, 618

Walkley and Black, 335
Walpole comparator, 559, 560
water extractions, 920
water holding capacity, 4, 7, 15, 569
water soluble organic, 474
water soluble P, 808

waxes, 371, 456
WDX, 83, 168, 253, 264, 273, 283
weak acid aqueous solution, 556
weak base aqueous solution, 556
weight-average molecular weight, 438
wet mineralization, 796
wilting point, 4
worm pile, 289

XANES, 170
X-ray diffraction, 83
X-ray diffractometry, 83, 90, 866
X-ray fluorescence analysis, 858, 952
X-ray fluorescence apparatus, 954
X-ray fluorescence, 102, 900, 952, 953, 954, 955, 957
X-ray tube, 87, 88, 114, 953, 957
X-ray, 9, 22, 51, 53, 72, 76, 79, 80, 86-130, 153, 172, 271, 275, 276, 279, 282, 284, 393, 438, 439, 442, 450, 632, 830, 901, 952
X-rays, 86, 124, 128, 172, 442, 951, 952, 953
XRD, 74, 78, 80, 83-130, 134, 146, 148, 153, 168, 169, 170, 189, 190, 205, 210, 213, 214, 223, 261, 275, 276, 595, 799, 866, 875, 880
zero point charge, 630, 645
zero point of net charge, 645
zero point titration, 645, 649
zeta potential, 32, 54
ZPC, 630, 645, 647-649, 654-656, 711, 714, 744, 765
ZPNC, 645
ZPT, 645, 649, 654, 655

Periodic table of the elements[*]

Period | | | | | | | | | Group

	IA	IIA	IIIB	IVB	VB	VIB	VIIB		VIII
	1	2	3	4	5	6	7	8	9

Legend box:

Atomic number 14 28.0855 **Atomic mass**
Oxidation degree[°]
+2,± 4
Symbol **Si**
(Ne)3s^{2}3p^2 Electronic
Name Silicon configuration

Period 1

1 1.00794
1,-1
H
1s^1
Hydrogen

Period 2

3 6.941 / +1 / **Li** / 1s^{2}2s^1 / Lithium
4 9.01218 / +2 / **Be** / 1s^{2}2s^2 / Beryllium

Period 3

11 22.9898 / +1 / **Na** / (Ne)3s^1 / Sodium
12 24.305 / +2 / **Mg** / (Ne)3s^2 / Magnesium

Period 4

19 39.0983 / +1 / **K** / (Ar)4s^1 / Potassium
20 40.078 / +2 / **Ca** / (Ar)4s^2 / Calcium
21 44.95591 / +3 / **Sc** / (Ar)3d^{1}4s^2 / Scandium
22 47.867 / +4,3,2 / **Ti** / (Ar)3d^{2}4s^2 / Titanium
23 50.9415 / +5,4,3,2 / **V** / (Ar)3d^{3}4s^2 / Vanadium
24 51.9961 / +6,3,2 / **Cr** / (Ar)3d^{5}4s^1 / Chromium
25 54.93805 / +7,4,3,2 / **Mn** / (Ar)3d^{5}4s^2 / Manganese
26 55.845 / +2,3 / **Fe** / (Ar)3d^{6}4s^2 / Iron
27 58.9332 / +2,3 / **Co** / (Ar)3d^{7}4s^2 / Cobalt

Period 5

37 85.4678 / +1 / **Rb** / (Kr)5s^1 / Rubidium
38 87.62 / +2 / **Sr** / (Kr)5s^2 / Strontium
39 88.90585 / +3 / **Y** / (Kr)4d^{1}5s^2 / Yttrium
40 91.224 / +4 / **Zr** / (Kr)4d^{2}5s^2 / Zirconium
41 92.9064 / +5,3 / **Nb** / (Kr)4d^{4}5s^1 / Niobium
42 95.94 / +6,4 / **Mo** / (Kr)4d^{5}5s^1 / Molybdenum
43 97.9072 / +7,6,4 / **Tc** / (Kr)4d^{6}5s^1 / Technetium
44 101.07 / +2,3,4 / **Ru** / (Kr)4d^{7}5s^1 / Ruthenium
45 102.905 / +1,3 / **Rh** / (Kr)4d^{8}5s^1 / Rhodium

Period 6

55 132.905 / +1 / **Cs** / (Xe)6s^1 / Caesium
56 137.327 / +2 / **Ba** / (Xe)6s^2 / Barium
57 138.905 / +3 / **La** / (Xe)5d^{1}6s^2 / Lanthanum
72 178.49 / +4 / **Hf** / 4f^{14}5d^{2}6s^2 / Hafnium
73 180.948 / +5 / **Ta** / 4f^{14}5d^{3}6s^2 / Tantalum
74 183.84 / +6,4 / **W** / 4f^{14}5d^{4}6s^2 / Tungsten
75 186.207 / +7,6,4 / **Re** / 4f^{14}5d^{5}6s^2 / Rhenium
76 190.23 / +3,4,6 / **Os** / 4f^{14}5d^{6}6s^2 / Osmium
77 192.217 / +3,4 / **Ir** / 4f^{14}5d^{7}6s^2 / Iridium

Period 7

87 223.020 / +1 / **Fr** / (Rn)7s^1 / Francium
88 226.025 / +2 / **Ra** / (Rn)7s^2 / Radium
89 227.028 / +3 / **Ac** / (Rn)6d^{1}7s^2 / Actinium
104 261.11 / +4 / **Unq** / 5f^{14}6d^{2}7s^2 / Unnilquad.
105 262.1 / **Unp** / 5f^{14}6d^{3}7s^2 / Unnilpent.
106 263.12 / **Unh** / 5f^{14}6d^{4}7s^2 / Unnilhex.
107 262.12 / **Uns** / 5f^{14}6d^{5}7s^2 / Unnilsept.
108 (265) / **Uno** / 5f^{14}6d^{6}7s^2 / Unniloctium
109 (267) / **Une** / 5f^{14}6d^{7}7s^2 / Unnilen.

Alkaline | **Alkaline earth**

Rare earth - Lanthanides

Period 6

58 140.115 / +3,4 / **Ce** / 4f^{2}5d^{0}6s^2 / Cerium
59 140.908 / +3 / **Pr** / 4f^{3}5d^{0}6s^2 / Praseodymium
60 144.24 / +3 / **Nd** / 4f^{4}5d^{0}6s^2 / Neodymium
61 146.915 / +3 / **Pm** / 4f^{5}5d^{0}6s^2 / Promethium
62 150.36 / +3,2 / **Sm** / 4f^{6}5d^{0}6s^2 / Samarium
63 151.965 / +3,2 / **Eu** / 4f^{7}5d^{0}6s^2 / Europium
64 157.25 / +3 / **Gd** / 4f^{7}5d^{1}6s^2 / Gadolinium

Rare earth - Actinides

Period 7

90 232.038 / +4 / **Th** / (Rn)6d^{2}7s^2 / Thorium
91 231.036 / +5,4 / **Pa** / 5f^{2}6d^{1}7s^2 / Protactinium
92 238.029 / +6,5,4,3 / **U** / 5f^{3}6d^{1}7s^2 / Uranium
93 237.048 / +6,5,4,3 / **Np** / 5f^{4}6d^{1}7s^2 / Neptunium
94 244.064 / +6,5,4,3 / **Pu** / 5f^{6}6d^{0}7s^2 / Plutonium
95 243.061 / +6,5,4,3 / **Am** / 5f^{7}6d^{0}7s^2 / Americium
96 247.070 / +3 / **Cm** / 5f^{7}6d^{1}7s^2 / Curium

[°]Only the oxidation degrees most commonly found in natural conditions are included
[*]IUPAC base (International Union of Pure and Applied Chemistry, 1996-2001)
[°]systematic IUPAC name (not discovered)

Group   **Atomic layer**

10	IB 11	IIB 12	IIIA 13	IVA 14	VA 15	VIA 16	VIIA 17	0 18	
								2 4.002602 0 **He** $1s^2$ Helium	K
			5 10.811 +3 **B** $1s^22s^22p^1$ Boron	**6** 12.011 ± 4,+2 **C** $1s^22s^22p^2$ Carbon	**7** 14.0067 ± 3,2,1,+4,5 **N** $1s^22s^22p^3$ Nitrogen	**8** 15.9994 -2 **O** $1s^22s^22p^4$ Oxygen	**9** 18.9984 -1 **F** $1s^22s^22p^5$ Fluorine	**10** 20.180 0 **Ne** $1s^22s^22p^6$ Neon	K L
			13 26.9815 +3 **Al** $(Ne)3s^23p^1$ Aluminium	**14** 28.0855 ± 4,+2 **Si** $(Ne)3s^23p^2$ Silicon	**15** 30.9738 ± 3,+5 **P** $(Ne)3s^23p^3$ Phosphorus	**16** 32.066 ± 2,+4,6 **S** $(Ne)3s^23p^4$ Sulphur	**17** 35.4527 ± 1,+3,5,7 **Cl** $(Ne)3s^23p^5$ Chlorine	**18** 39.948 0 **Ar** $(Ne)3s^23p^6$ Argon	K L M
28 58.693 +2,3 **Ni** $(Ar)3d^84s^2$ Nickel	**29** 63.546 +2,1 **Cu** $(Ar)3d^{10}4s^1$ Copper	**30** 65.39 +2 **Zn** $(Ar)3d^{10}4s^2$ Zinc	**31** 69.723 +3 **Ga** $3d^{10}4s^24p^1$ Gallium	**32** 72.61 +4,+2 **Ge** $3d^{10}4s^24p^2$ Germanium	**33** 74.9216 ± 3,+5 **As** $3d^{10}4s^24p^3$ Arsenic	**34** 78.96 -2,+4,6 **Se** $3d^{10}4s^24p^4$ Selenium	**35** 79.904 ± 1,+3,5 **Br** $3d^{10}4s^24p^5$ Bromine	**36** 83.80 0 **Kr** $3d^{10}4s^24p^6$ Krypton	L M N
46 106.42 +2,4 **Pd** $(Kr)4d^{10}$ Palladium	**47** 107.868 +1 **Ag** $(Kr)4d^{10}5s^1$ Silver	**48** 112.411 +2 **Cd** $(Kr)4d^{10}5s^2$ Cadmium	**49** 114.818 +3 **In** $4d^{10}5s^25p^1$ Indium	**50** 118.710 ± 4,+2 **Sn** $4d^{10}5s^25p^2$ Tin	**51** 121.760 ± 3,+5 **Sb** $4d^{10}5s^25p^3$ Antimony	**52** 127.60 ± 2,+ 4,6 **Te** $4d^{10}5s^25p^4$ Tellurium	**53** 126.9045 ± 1,+3,5,7 **I** $4d^{10}5s^25p^5$ iodine	**54** 131.29 0 **Xe** $4d^{10}5s^25p^6$ Xenon	M N O
78 195.08 + 2,4 **Pt** $4f^{14}5d^96s^1$ Platinum	**79** 196.967 + 3,1 **Au** $4f^{14}5d^{10}6s^1$ Gold	**80** 200.59 + 2,1 **Hg** $4f^{14}5d^{10}6s^2$ Mercury	**81** 204.383 + 3,1 **Tl** $5d^{10}6s^26p^1$ Thallium	**82** 207.2 + 4,2 **Pb** $5d^{10}6s^26p^2$ Lead	**83** 208.980 +3,5 **Bi** $5d^{10}6s^26p^3$ Bismuth	**84** (209) ± 2,+4 **Po** $5d^{10}6s^26p^4$ Polonium	**85** (210) ± 1,+5,7 **At** $5d^{10}6s^26p^5$ Astatine	**86** 222.02 0 **Rn** $5d^{10}6s^26p^6$ Radon	N O P
110 **Uun** Ununnili.	**111** **Uuu** Unununi.	**112** **Uub**° Ununbium	**113** **Uut**° Ununtrium	**114** **Uuq**° Ununquad.	**115** **Uup**° Ununpent.	**116** **Uuh**° Ununhex.	**117** **Uus**° Ununsept.	**118** **Uuo**° Ununoct.	O P Q

Noble gases

65 158.925 + 3 **Tb** $4f\,^95d^06s^2$ Terbium	**66** 162.50 + 3 **Dy** $4f\,^{10}5d^06s^2$ Dysprosium	**67** 164.930 + 3 **Ho** $4f\,^{11}5d^06s^2$ Holmium	**68** 167.26 + 3 **Er** $4f\,^{12}5d^06s^2$ Erbium	**69** 168.934 + 3 **Tm** $4f\,^{13}5d^06s^2$ Thulium	**70** 173.04 + 3,2 **Yb** $4f\,^{14}5d^06s^2$ Ytterbium	**71** 174.967 + 3 **Lu** $4f\,^{14}5d^16s^2$ Lutetium	N O P

97 247.07 + 4,3 **Bk** $5f\,^96d^07s^2$ Berkelium	**98** 251.08 + 3 **Cf** $5f\,^{10}6d^07s^2$ Californium	**99** 252.08 +3 **Es** $5f\,^{11}6d^07s^2$ Einsteinium	**100** 257.10 +3 **Fm** $5f\,^{12}6d^07s^2$ Fermium	**101** 258.098 +2,3 **Md** $5f\,^{13}6d^07s^2$ Mendelevium	**102** 259.10 +2,3 **No** $5f\,^{14}6d^07s^2$ Nobelium	**103** 262.11 +3 **Lr** $5f\,^{14}6d^17s^2$ Lawrencium	O P Q

Printing: Krips bv, Meppel
Binding: Stürtz, Würzburg